The only Official Guide to QUALITY

BED AND BREAKFAST

GUEST ACCOMMODATION

England

Sturford Mead, Warminster

Welcome to this new and fully up-dated edition of Where to Stay

VisitBritain

VisitBritain is a new organisation created on 1 April 2003 to market Britain to the rest of the world and England to the British. Formed by the merger of the British Tourist Authority and the English Tourism Council, its mission is to build the value of tourism by creating world class destination brands and marketing campaigns. It will also build partnerships with – and provide insights to – other organisations which have a stake in British and English tourism.

1

The **only** official guide to quality accommodation in England

- This guide contains the widest choice of quality assured accommodation to suit all budgets and tastes.
- It includes an EXCLUSIVE listing of ALL Guest Accommodation in VisitBritain's National Quality Assurance Standard.

Looking for accommodation in a particular area?

- The guide's divided into the 9 English Regional Tourist Board areas and accommodation is listed alphabetically by place name.
- Use the regional maps which show every place with accommodation in the regional sections.
- Look in the town index at the back of the guide. It also includes tourism areas such as the New Forest or Cotswolds.
- A handy reference to counties is also at the back.

More information as well as places to stay

Each regional section is packed with information:

Visitor Attractions

A selection of places to visit highlighting those receiving our quality assurance marque.

Tourist Information Centres

Phone numbers are shown in the blue bands next to place names in accommodation entries.

Guides and maps

As well as contact details, we list regional tourist board free and saleable tourism publications.

Travel details

Directions for travel by road and rail to each region.

Town descriptions

At the end of each section is a brief description of the main places where accommodation is listed.

PICTURES
1. Omnia Somnia, Ashbourne
2. Jeake's House, Rye

KEY TO SYMBOLS:
A key to symbols can be found on the inside back cover.
Keep it open for easy reference.

Contents

Accommodation, Places to Visit and Information:

Everything you need to know for a great **English break**

Whether you're looking for country style, seaside splendour or city chic, you'll find nearly 10,000 places to stay here, all Diamond rated and with a range of prices for all pockets. Detailed entries and pictures help you make the right choice.

There's also advice on making a booking and an explanation of accommodation ratings and awards, handy location maps plus ideas on what to do and see in each region.

A fantastic selection of **quality** bed & breakfasts to suit all budgets and **tastes**

You'll find nearly **10,000** places to stay, all **quality** assessed

PICTURES

1. The Knoll, Henley-on-Thames
2. The Victoria, Broadstairs
3. Burr Bank, Pickering
4. Ing Hill Lodge, Kirkby Stephen
5. Sturford Mead, Warminster
6. Woodstock Hotel, Croydon

Ratings and awards – your reliable guide to quality

Reliable, rigorous, easy to use – VisitBritain's ratings and awards system will help you choose with confidence.

All the accommodation in this guide has been inspected and rated for quality by VisitBritain, so you can be sure that the accommodation you choose will meet your expectations. Visitor attractions can also receive a special quality marque. These are the ratings and awards to look for:

Diamond ratings

Establishments are awarded a rating of One to Five Diamonds for quality. VisitBritain has over 50 trained assessors who visit establishments every year, staying overnight as an anonymous guest. They award ratings based on the overall experience of their stay, from how their telephone booking was dealt with to heating and comfort, and expect high standards of housekeeping.

There are strict guidelines to ensure every property is assessed to the same criteria.

Gold and Silver Awards

These awards are given to establishments offering high levels of quality in all areas, and particularly in service and hospitality, in addition to the overall quality of their Diamond rating. VisitBritain's assessor will make recommendations during an assessment visit, and this can result in an establishment receiving a Gold or Silver Award for high quality customer service and bedroom/bathroom accommodation above that expected of the overall Diamond rating.

National Accessible Scheme

Establishments with a National Accessible rating provide access and facilities for guests with visual, hearing and mobility impairment.

Excellence in England Awards

The 'Oscars' of the tourist industry, these awards are run by VisitBritain in association with England's 9 regional tourist boards. There are 12 categories including Bed & Breakfast of the Year, and winners will be announced in Spring 2004.

Visitor Attraction Quality Assurance

To receive this award, attractions must achieve high standards in all aspects of the visitor experience, from initial telephone enquiries to departure, customer services to catering, as well as all facilities and activities. All participating attractions are visited every year by trained assessors.

Welcome to Excellence

VisitBritain's special 'Welcome to Excellence' award is given to accommodation and other tourism organisations that show a commitment to improving customer service through staff training.

PICTURES
1. The Bunk Inn, Curridge
2. Bolebroke Castle, Hartfield
3. Bidewell Farm & Haybarton, Honiton

When you're looking for a place to stay, you need a rating system you can trust. VisitBritain's ratings give a clear guide to what to expect, in an easy-to-understand form. Properties are visited annually by trained, impartial assessors, so you can have the confidence that your accommodation has been thoroughly checked and rated for quality before you make your booking.

Diamond Ratings

Ratings are awarded from One to Five Diamonds. The more Diamonds, the higher the quality and the greater the range of facilities and level of service provided. The brief explanations of the Diamond ratings outlined here show what is included at each rating level (note that each rating also includes what is provided at a lower Diamond rating).

◆ An acceptable overall level of quality and helpful service. Accommodation offering, as a minimum, a full cooked or continental breakfast. Other meals, if provided, will be freshly prepared. Towels are provided and heating and hot water will be available at reasonable times.

◆◆ A good overall level of quality and comfort, with greater emphasis on guest care in all areas.

◆◆◆ A very good overall level of quality in areas such as comfortable bedrooms, well maintained, practical decor, a good choice of quality items at breakfast, customer care and all-round comfort. Where other meals are provided these will be freshly cooked from good quality ingredients.

◆◆◆◆ An excellent level of quality in all areas. Customer care showing very good attention to your needs.

◆◆◆◆◆ An exceptional overall level of quality - for example, ample space with a degree of luxury, a high quality bed and furniture, excellent interior design and customer care which anticipates your needs. Breakfast offering a wide choice of high quality fresh ingredients. Where other meals are provided these will feature fresh, seasonal, and often local ingredients.

Guest Accommodation 2004
Gold and Silver Awards

VisitBritain's unique Gold and Silver Awards are given in recognition of exceptional quality in guest accommodation.

VisitBritain's assessors make recommendations for Gold and Silver awards during assessments in recognition of the highest levels of quality. While Diamond ratings are based on overall quality, Gold and Silver Awards recognise comfort and service in areas identified by guests as being particularly important to them. These include quality of bedrooms and bathrooms – facilities, comfort and ease of use – and the service received and its efficiency. There are no specific guidelines or checklists for accommodation providers looking to achieve a Gold or Silver Award.

On these pages we feature guest accommodation with a Gold Award and for which Standard or Enhanced entries are included in the regional pages. Use the town index to find their page numbers.

Gold Award B&Bs

Alden Cottage, Stonyhurst, Lancashire
Annes Cottage, Farnham, Surrey
Athole Guest House, Bath, Bath And North East Somerset
Ayrlington, Bath, Bath And North East Somerset
Blounts Court Farm, Devizes, Wiltshire
Bracken House Country, Bratton Fleming, Devon
Briantcroft, Milford-On-Sea, Hampshire
Bromley Court B&B, Ludlow, Shropshire
Brookfield House, Bovey Tracey, Devon
Burhill Farm, Broadway, Worcestershire
Burr Bank, Pickering, North Yorkshire
Canfield Moat, Little Canfield, Essex
Coniston Lodge, Coniston, Cumbria
The Cottage, Bishop's Stortford, Hertfordshire
Cotteswold House, Bibury, Gloucestershire
Earsham Park Farm, Bungay, Suffolk
Field House, Hindringham, Norfolk
Forest Edge, Ross-On-Wye, Herefordshire
Greenwood Lodge City Guest, Nottingham, Nottinghamshire
Grendon Guesthouse, Buxton, Derbyshire
The Grey Cottage, Stonehouse, Gloucestershire
Hazel Bank Country House, Borrowdale, Cumbria
Helm, Askrigg, North Yorkshire
Hill Farm House, Worcester, Worcestershire
Hill House Farm, Ely, Cambridgeshire
Hill View House, Dartmouth, Devon
Holly Lodge, Fakenham, Norfolk
Katerina's Guest House, Rothbury, Northumbria
Leathermill Grange, Nuneaton, Warwickshire
Magnolia House, Canterbury, Kent
Manor Farm Oast, Rye, East Sussex
The Manor House, Wellingborough, Northamptonshire
Monkshill, Bath, Bath And North East Somerset
Nineveh Farm, Chipping Campden, Gloucestershire
The Nurse's Cottage, Sway, Hampshire
The Old Coach House, Blackpool, Lancashire
The Old Rectory, Whitwell, Isle Of Wight
Peacock House, Beetley, Norfolk
Ravencroft B&B, Ripon, North Yorkshire
Rookhurst Country House, Hawes, North Yorkshire
St Ervan Manor & Country Cottages, Padstow, Cornwall
Southcroft, Bridport, Dorset
Spence Farm, Charmouth, Dorset
The Three Lions, Fordingbridge, Hampshire
Tower House, Hastings, East Sussex
Villa Magdala, Bath, Bath And North East Somerset
Websters, Salisbury, Wiltshire
West Vale Country House & Restaurant, Sawrey, Cumbria

PICTURES
1. Alden Cottage, Stonyhurst
2. Canfield Moat, Little Canfield
3. Ayrlington Hotel, Bath
4. Hazel Bank Country House, Borrowdale
5. Nineveh Farm, Chipping Campden
6. Forest Edge, Ross-on-Wye
7. Leathermill Grange, Nuneaton

2

3

4

5

6

7

National Accessible **Scheme**

VisitBritain's National Accessible Scheme for accommodation includes standards for hearing and visually impaired guests in addition to standards for guests with mobility impairment.

Accommodation taking part in the National Accessible Scheme, include in their guide entry appropriate symbols as shown opposite.

There is a complete list of all guest accommodation participating in the National Accessible Scheme at the back of this guide.

VisitBritian has a variety of accessible accommodation in its scheme, and the different accessible ratings will help you choose the one that best suits your needs.

When you see one of the following symbols, you can be sure that the accommodation has been thoroughly assessed against demanding criteria. If you have additional needs or special requirements we strongly recommend that you make sure these can be met by your chosen establishment before you confirm your booking. The criteria VisitBritain and National and Regional Tourist Boards have adopted do not necessarily conform to British Standards or to Building Regulations. They reflect what the Boards understand to be acceptable to meet the practical needs of guests with mobility or sensory impairments.

Acccommodation is **assessed** against **demanding criteria**

PICTURES

1. Bracken House Country Hotel, Bratton Fleming
2. Smallicombe Farm, Colyton
3. Moorlands Country Guesthouse, Weston-Super-Mare
4. Websters, Salisbury
5. Rudstone Walk Country Accommodation, Beverley

The National Accessible Scheme forms part of the Tourism for All Campaign that is being promoted by VisitBritain and National and Regional Tourist Boards. Additional help and guidance on finding suitable holiday accommodation for those with special needs can be obtained from:

Holiday Care/Tourism for All Holidays Ltd
7th Floor - Sunley House,
4 Bedford Park
CROYDON CR0 2AP

Telephone: Admin/consultancy 0845 124 9974
Information helpline 0845 124 9971
(9-5 Mon, Tues and 9-1pm Wed-Fri)
Reservation/Friends 0845 124 9973
Fax: 0845 124 9972
Minicom: 0845 124 9976

Email: info@holidaycare.org
Web: www.holidaycare.org

HOLIDAY CARE

Access Symbols

Mobility

LEVEL 1 – Typically suitable for a person with sufficient mobility to climb a flight of steps but who would benefit from points of fixtures and fittings to aid balance.

LEVEL 2 – Typically suitable for a person with restricted walking ability and for those that may need to use a wheelchair some of the time.

LEVEL 3 – Typically suitable for a person who depends on the use of a wheelchair and transfers unaided to and from the wheelchair in a seated position.

LEVEL 4 – Typically suitable for a person who depends on the use of a wheelchair in a seated position. They can require personal/mechanical assistance to aid transfer (eg carer, hoist).

Hearing Impairment

LEVEL 1 – Minimum entry requirements to meet the National Accessible Standards for guests with hearing impairment, from mild hearing loss to profoundly deaf.

LEVEL 2 – Recommended (Best Practice) additional requirements to meet the National Accessible Standards for guests with hearing impairment, from mild hearing loss to profoundly deaf.

Visual Impairment

LEVEL 1 – Minimum entry requirements to meet the National Accessible Standards for visually impaired guests.

LEVEL 2 – Recommended (Best Practice) additional requirements to meet the National Accessible Standards for visually impaired guests.

How do we arrive at a Diamond Rating

VisitBritain has more than 50 trained assessors throughout England who visit properties annually, generally staying overnight as an anonymous guest.

They award ratings based on the overall experience of their stay, and there are strict guidelines to ensure every property is assessed to the same criteria.

High standards of housekeeping are a major requirement; heating, lighting, comfort and convenience are also part of the assessment.

The assessor's role - guest, assessor and advisor

Assessors book their accommodation as a 'normal' guest. They will take into account all aspects of the visiting experience, from how the telephone enquiry is dealt with to the quality of the service on offer.

During their stay assessors try to experience as many things as possible including the quality of food, the knowledge of staff and services. They will even check under the bed!

After paying the bill assessors reveal who they are and ask to look round the rest of the establishment. They will then advise the proprietor of the Diamond rating that has been awarded, discussing the reasons why, as well as suggesting areas for improvement.

So you can see it's a very thorough process to ensure that when you book accommodation with a particular Diamond rating you can be confident it will meet your expectations. After all, meeting customer expectations is what makes happy guests.

50 **trained assessors** visit properties annually

PICTURES
1. Ing Hill Lodge, Kirkby Stephen
2. Ramsees Hotel, London
3. Esplanade House, Watchet

Accommodation
entries explained

Each accommodation entry contains detailed information to help you decide if it is right for you.

This information has been provided by the proprietors themselves, and our aim has been to ensure that it is as objective and factual as possible.

To the left of the establishment name you will find the Diamond rating and quality award, if appropriate.

At-a-glance symbols at the end of each entry give you additional information on services and facilities - a key can be found on the back cover flap. Keep this open to refer to as you read.

Campus Accommodation

For details of the Campus accommodation ratings and accommodation available, see pages 446 to 448.

Sample enhanced entry

1. Listing under town or village with map reference
2. VisitBritain Diamond rating plus Gold and Silver Awards where applicable
3. Accessible rating where applicable
4. Colour picture for enhanced entries
5. Description
6. At-a-glance facility symbols
7. Establishment name, address, telephone and fax numbers, e-mail and web site address
8. Prices for bed and breakfast (B&B) and half board (HB) accommodation
9. Shows establishment is open all year
10. Accommodation details including credit cards accepted
11. Special promotions and themed breaks

Inspiring ideas for a

Short Break

At any time of year, a short break is a great way to revive and refresh yourself. Whether you're looking for romance and luxury or thrills and excitement, or you want to learn new skills and meet new people, this guide is full of ideas. Look out for the special offers and promotions, highlighted in red.

Winter warmers

Beat the winter blues with a few days away, for Christmas shopping, a New Year holiday or just to brighten up a dull February. **The Eight Bells, Chipping Camden**, a 14th century Cotswold stone house, offers 3 night breaks with welcoming log fires and a la carte dinners served in the oak beamed dining room. For a traditional, relaxed Christmas with a 5 course lunch, stay at **St Georges Country Hotel, Perranporth. Georgian Severn Lodge, Ironbridge**, has glorious views down the gorge and is just two minutes from the famous bridge and beautiful winter walks.

Out of the ordinary

Make it a break to remember with a new experience. Take a hot air balloon ride or helicopter sightseeing trip over Wiltshire's ancient sites and crop circles from the private airstrip of **Manor Farm B&B, Collingbourne Kingston**. Go back in time to 1528 with the Henry VIII Experience at **Bolebroke Castle, Hartfield**, a 16th century hunting lodge where the King courted Anne Boleyn.

Relax and unwind. Go on! You owe it to **yourself**

3

A glorious selection of **gourmet** breaks to suit all **tastes**

Learn something new on a residential course at **The Hill House, Ross-on-Wye**, which hosts special themed weekends from Druidism and poetry to canoeing and poker school, or the **Ring of Bells Inn**, in the picturesque village of **North Bovey, Dartmoor**, with courses on yoga, bookbinding, digital photography and watercolour painting.

Something to celebrate

For a very special occasion, choose a break with a romantic setting - and the little luxuries that really make a difference. Enjoy chocolates and champagne at **Hidelow House, Malvern**, a secluded country retreat with log fires and lovely views, while at **Grendon Guest House, Buxton**, a carved mahogany bed and elegant, antique filled rooms ensure a weekend of pleasure and indulgence.

The individually themed rooms at **Ivydene Guest House, Cheltenham**, will make every stay different – try the African room for an exotically romantic feel. **Helm in Askrigg** has new gourmet breaks, with fine food and wine served with gleaming glassware and the best bone china in the candlelit dining room.

House party heaven

For family gatherings, celebrations and get togethers of all shapes and sizes, why not hire a house and have the whole place to yourselves. **West Vale Country House, Sawrey**, in the Lake District, hosts groups for golfing and fishing, racing and shopping, while guests at **Rudstone Walk Country Accommodation, Beverley**, can hold country house style dinner parties in the old farmhouse dining room. **Clarence Gardens Hotel, York**, has a luxurious dormitory sleeping 20 people with full en suite facilities, great for hen and stag parties. Residential watercolour painting courses for groups of up to six people are held at **Trevinhurst Lodge, Eastbourne**, so whether you're a novice or experienced, you'll have plenty of individual advice from the professional artist tutor.

PICTURES
1. Balloon - Manor Farm B&B, Collingbourne Kingston
2. Hidelow House, Malvern
3. Ivydene Guest House, Cheltenham
4. Bolebrook Castle, Hartfield
5. West Vale Country House and Restaurant, Sawrey

4

5

The Excellence in England awards 2004

The Excellence in England Awards are all about blowing English tourism's trumpet and telling the world what a fantastic place England is to visit, whether it's for a day trip, a weekend break or a fortnight's holiday.

The Awards, now in their 15th year, are run by VisitBritain in association with England's regional tourist boards. This year there are 12 categories including B&B of the Year, Hotel of the Year and Visitor Attraction of the Year and an award for the best tourism website.

Winners of the 2004 awards will receive their trophies at an event to be held on Thursday 22nd April 2004 followed by a media event to be held on St George's Day (23 April) in London. The day will celebrate excellence in tourism in England.

The winners of the 2003 Excellence in England Bed and Breakfast of the Year Award are:

Gold winner

The Old Bakery, Blockley, Moreton-in-Marsh, Gloucestershire

Silver winners:

Bracken House, Bratton Flemming, Barnstaple, Devon

The Moorlands Country House, Levisham, Pickering, North Yorkshire

For more information about the Excellence in England Awards visit

www.visitengland.com

VisitBritain Gold and Silver Awards

Our unique Gold and Silver Awards recognise exceptional quality in serviced accommodation. Our assessors make recommendations for Gold and Silver awards during assessments in recognition of levels of quality over and above that expected at a particular rating.

Look for the Gold and Silver Awards in the regional sections or you can find an index to accommodation with a Gold and Silver Award at the back of this guide.

Visitor Attraction Quality Assurance

VisitBritain operates a Visitor Attraction Quality Assurance Standard. Participating attractions are visited annually by trained, impartial assessors who look at all aspects of the visit, from initial telephone enquiries to departure, customer services to catering, as well as facilities and activities. Only those attractions which have been assessed by VisitBritain and meet the standard receive the quality marque, your sign of a 'Quality Assured Visitor Attraction'.

Look out for the quality marque and visit with confidence.

A

B

1

Location Maps

Every place name featured in the regional accommodation sections of this Where to Stay guide has a map reference to help you locate it on the maps which follow. For example, to find Colchester, Essex, which has 'Map ref 3B2', turn to Map 3 and refer to grid square B2.

All place names appearing in the regional sections are shown in black type on the maps. This enables you to find other places in your chosen area which may have suitable accommodation - the Town Index (at the back of this guide) gives page numbers.

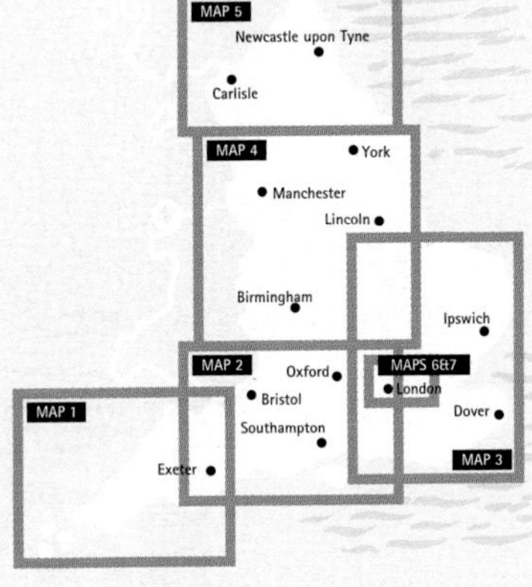

2

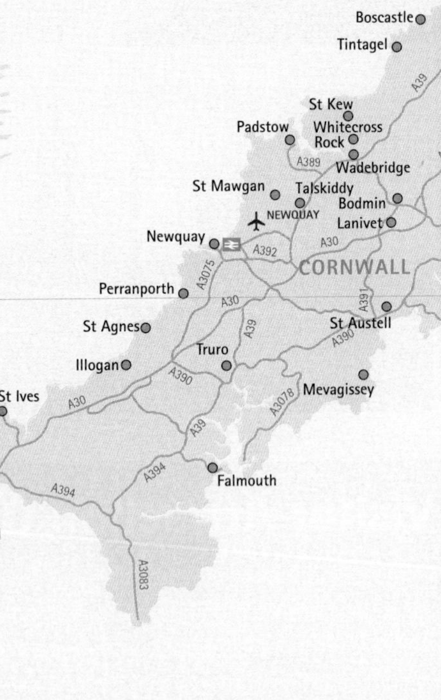

3

ISLES OF SCILLY

Isles of Scilly (St Mary's)

St Mary's

Key to regions: South West

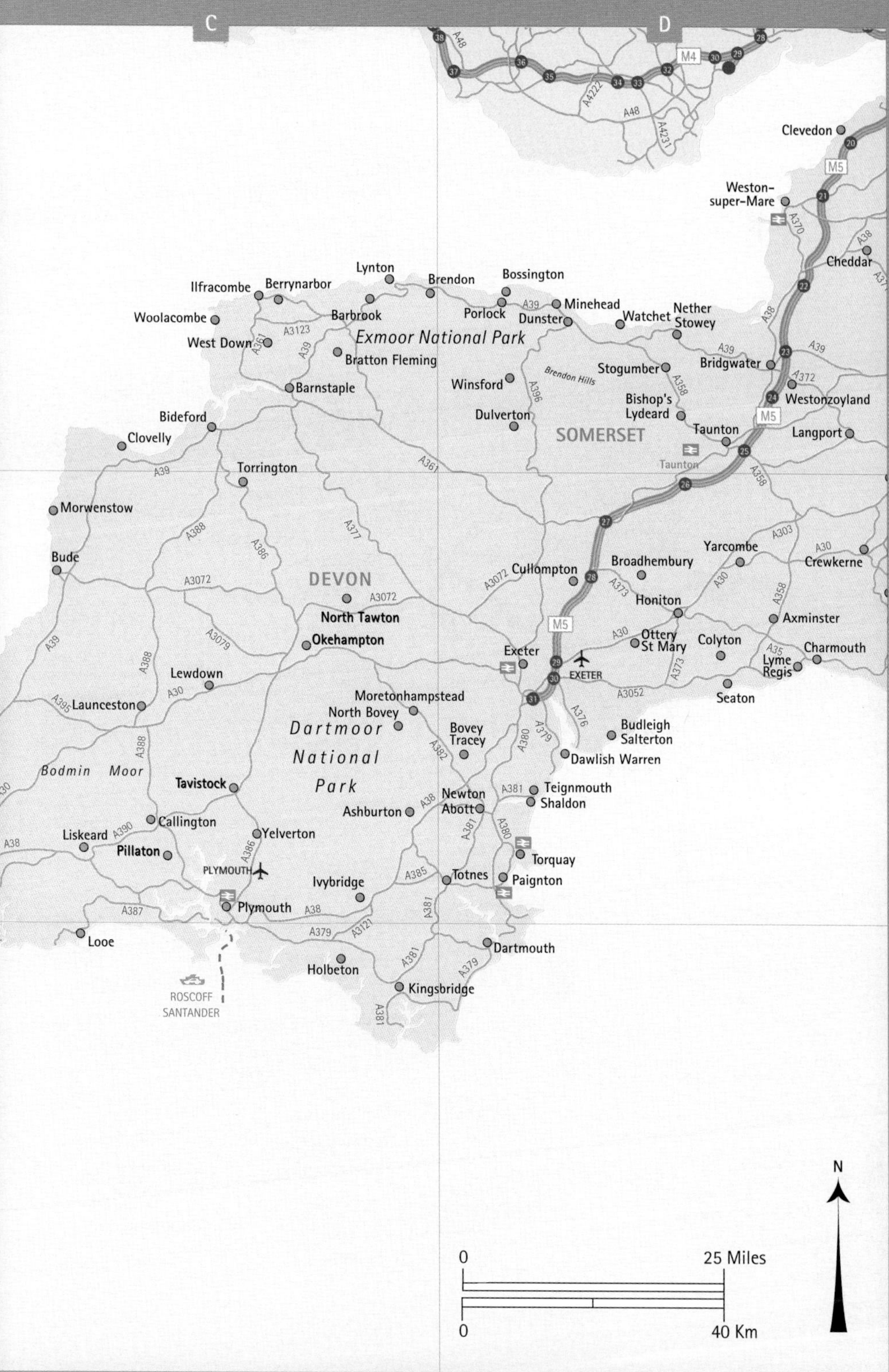

All place names in black offer accommodation in this guide.

MAP 2

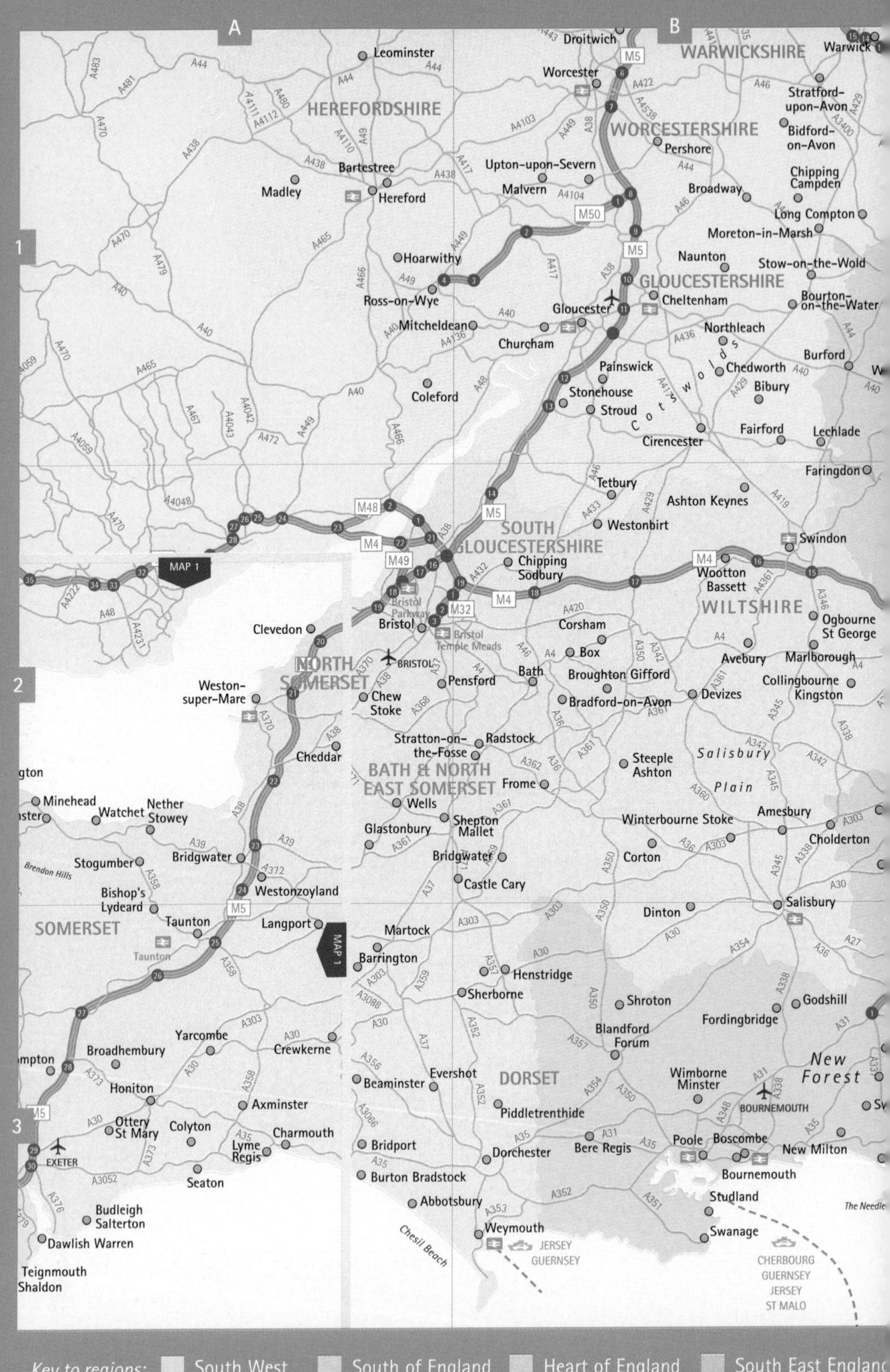

Key to regions: South West South of England Heart of England South East England

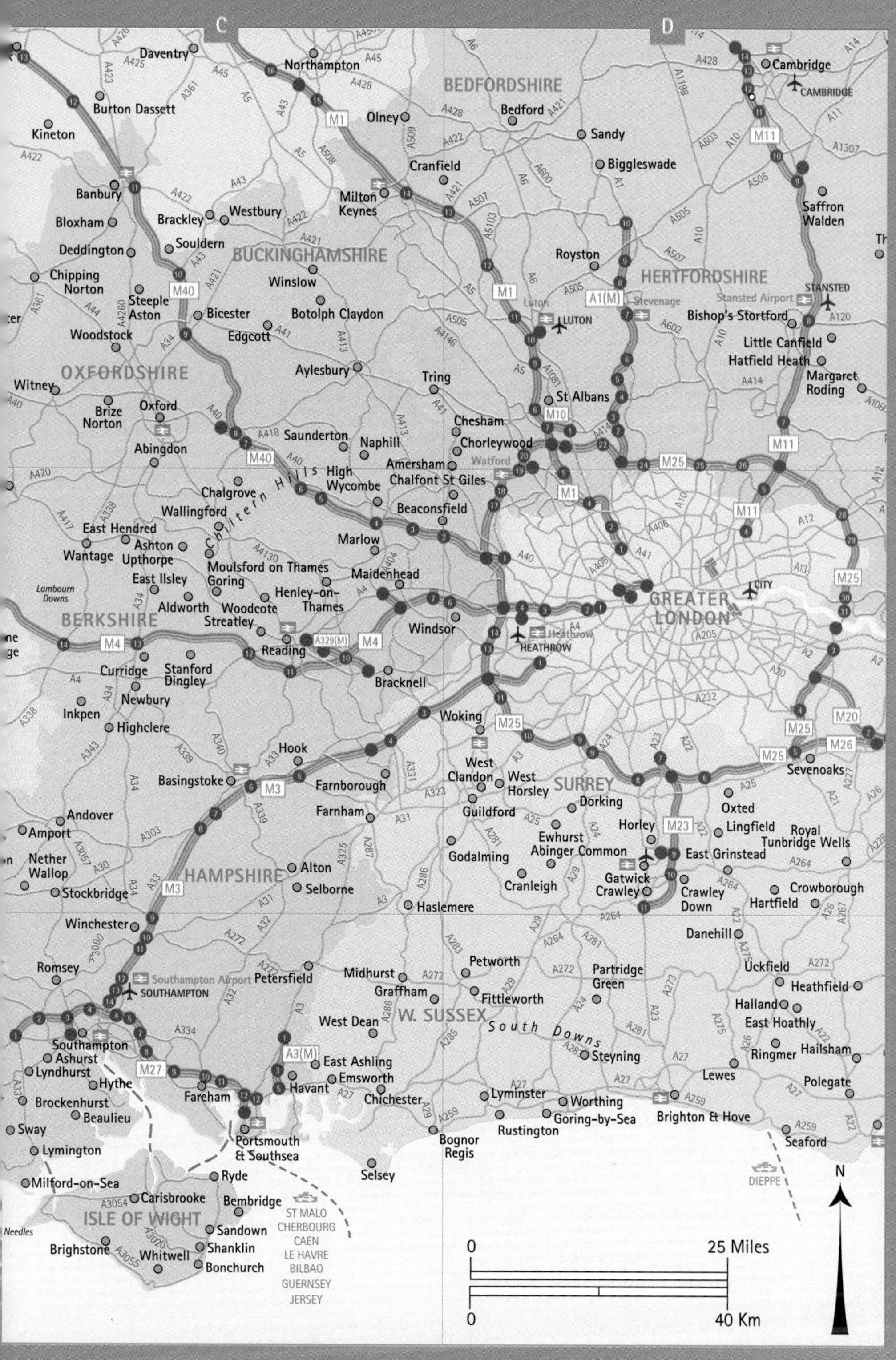

East of England

All place names in black offer accommodation in this guide.

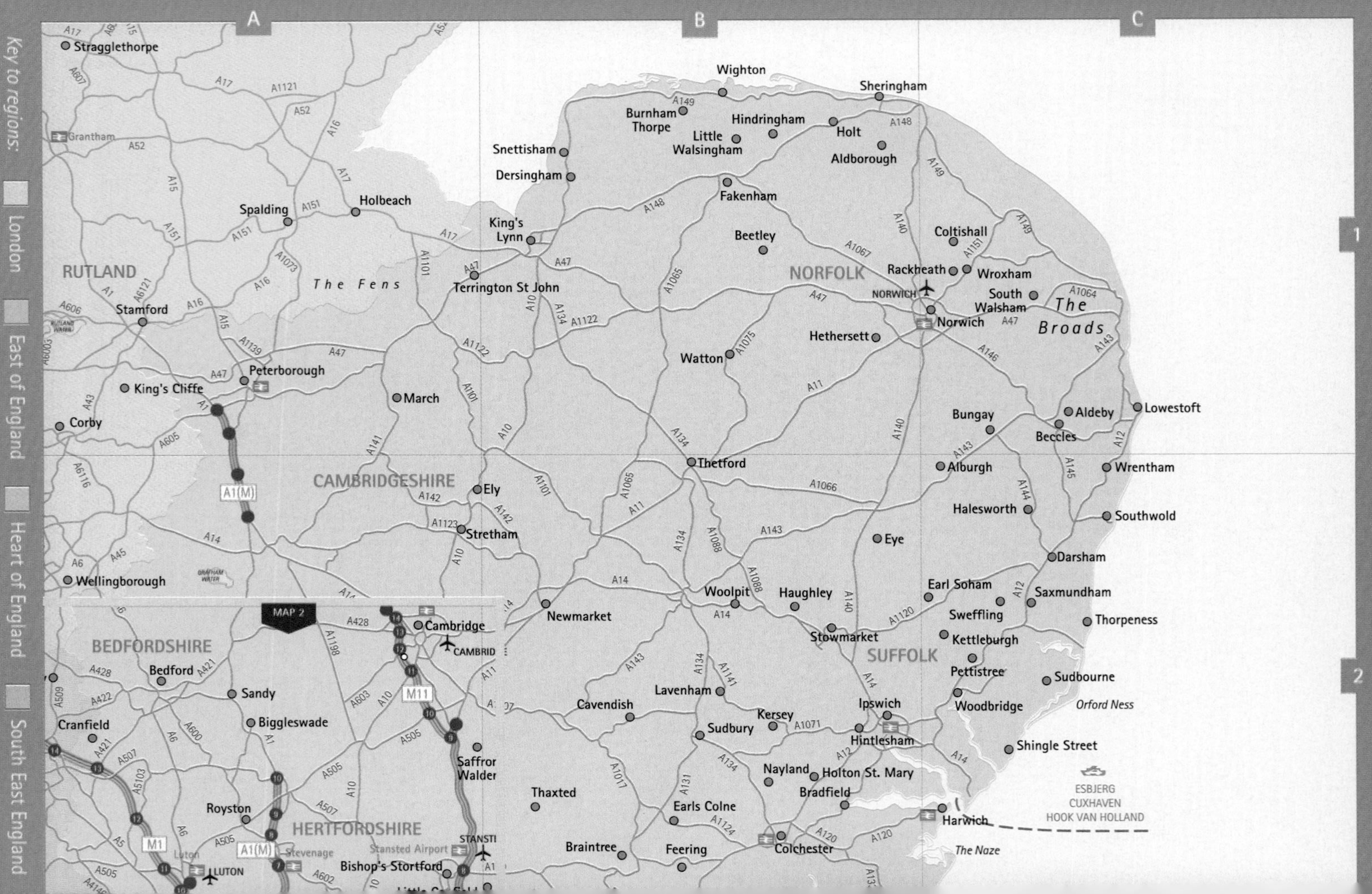

Key to regions: London East of England Heart of England South East England

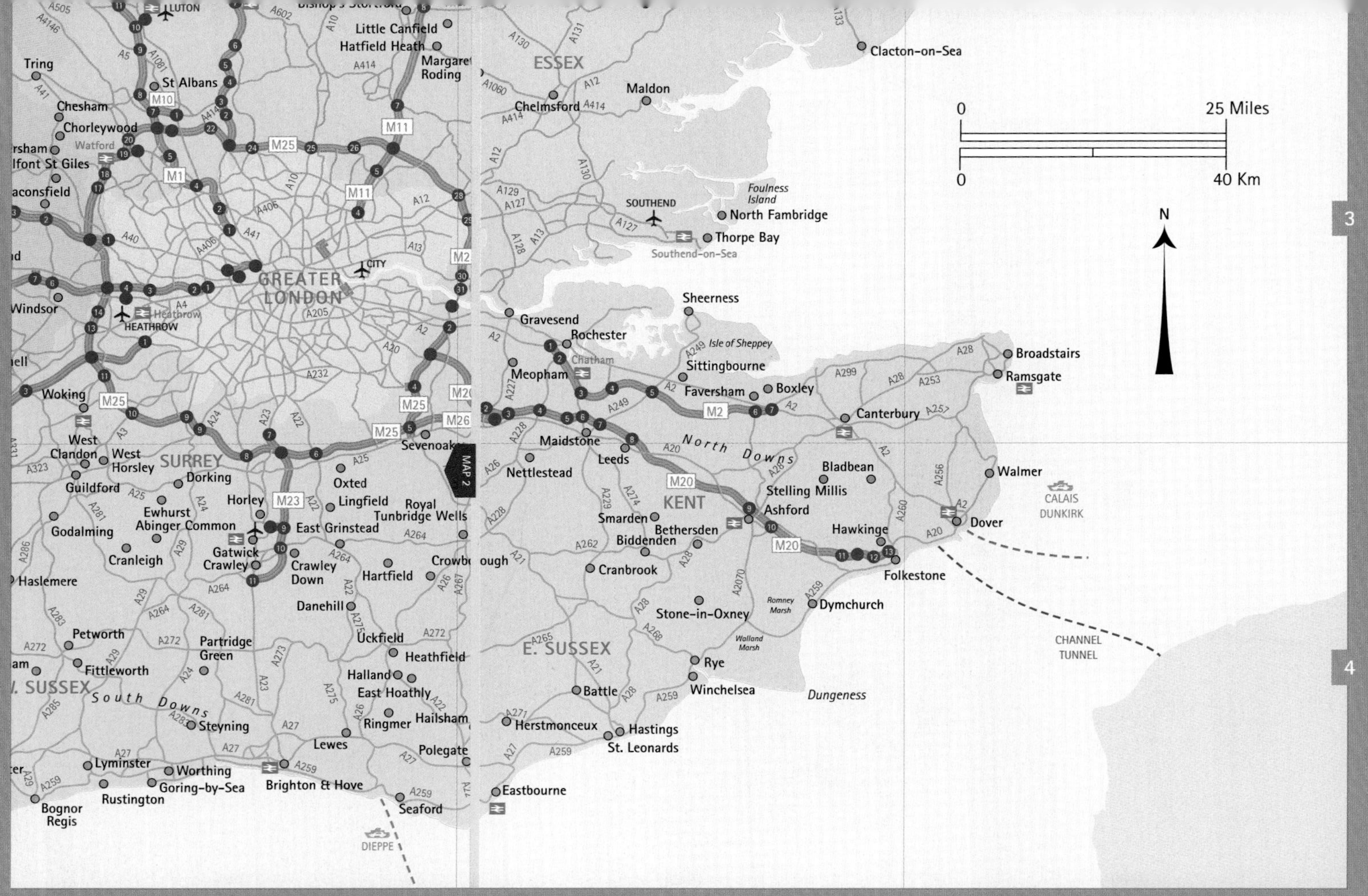

All place names in black offer accommodation in this guide.

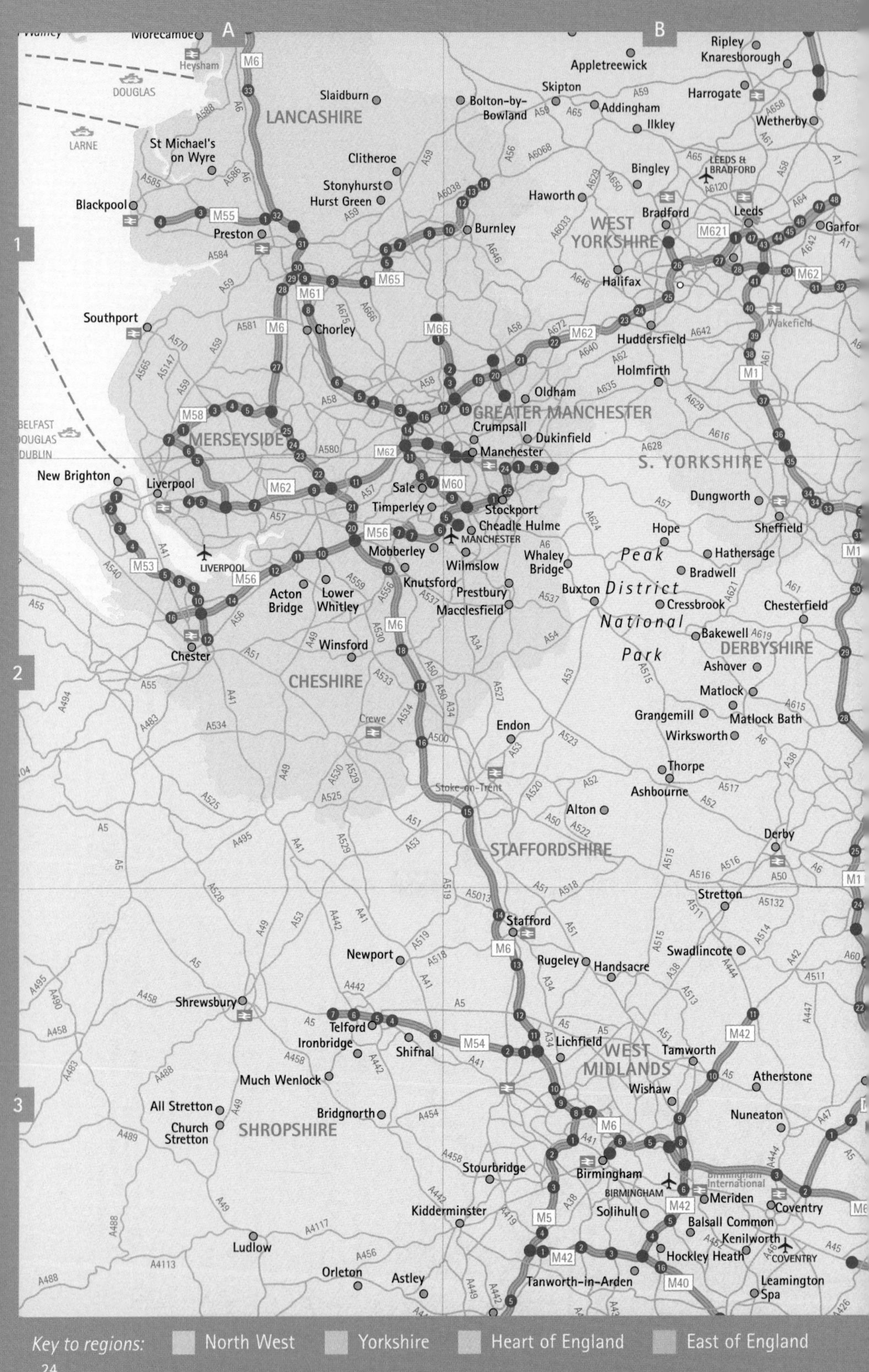

Key to regions: North West Yorkshire Heart of England East of England

All place names in black offer accommodation in this guide.

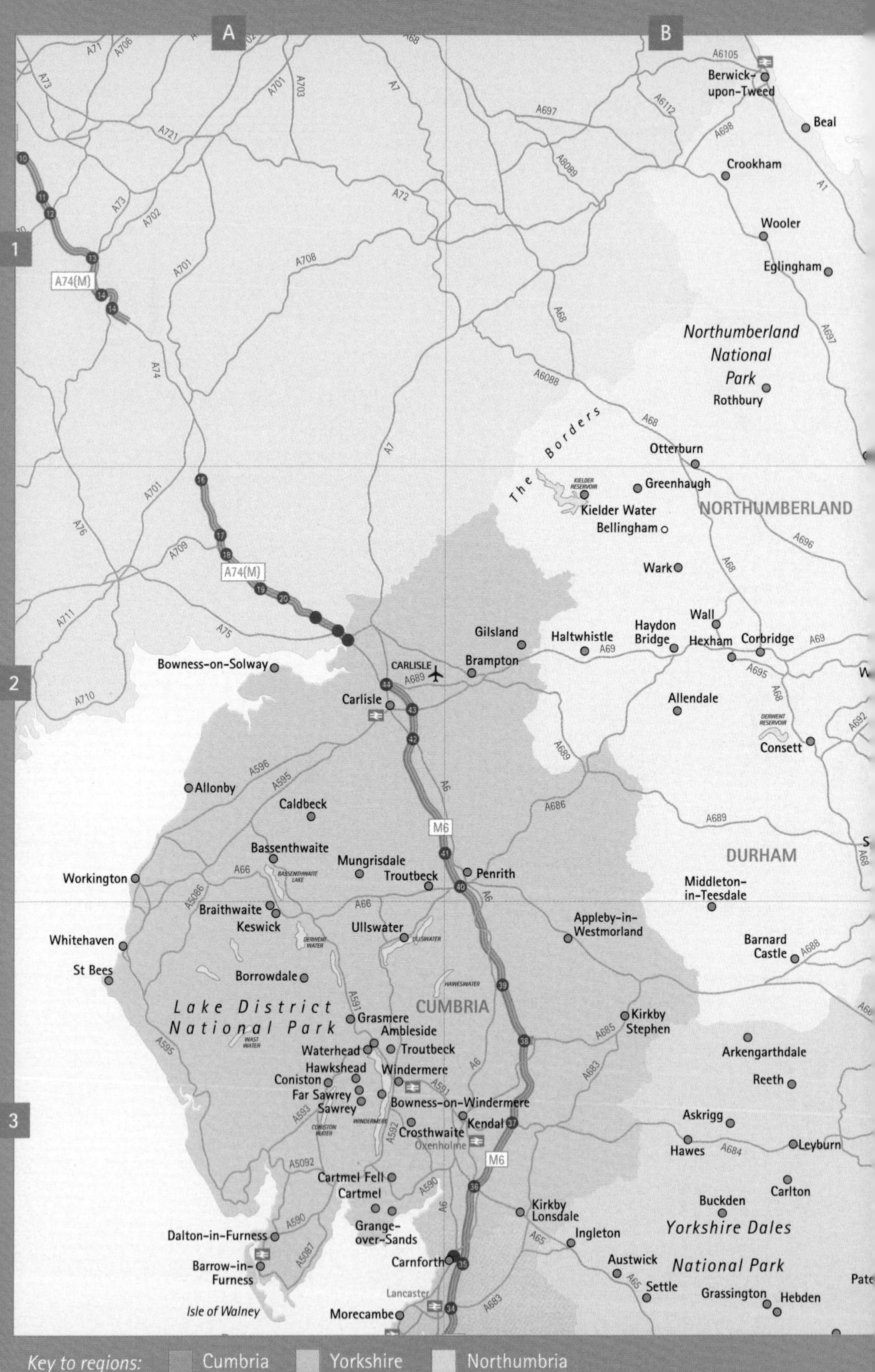

Key to regions: Cumbria Yorkshire Northumbria

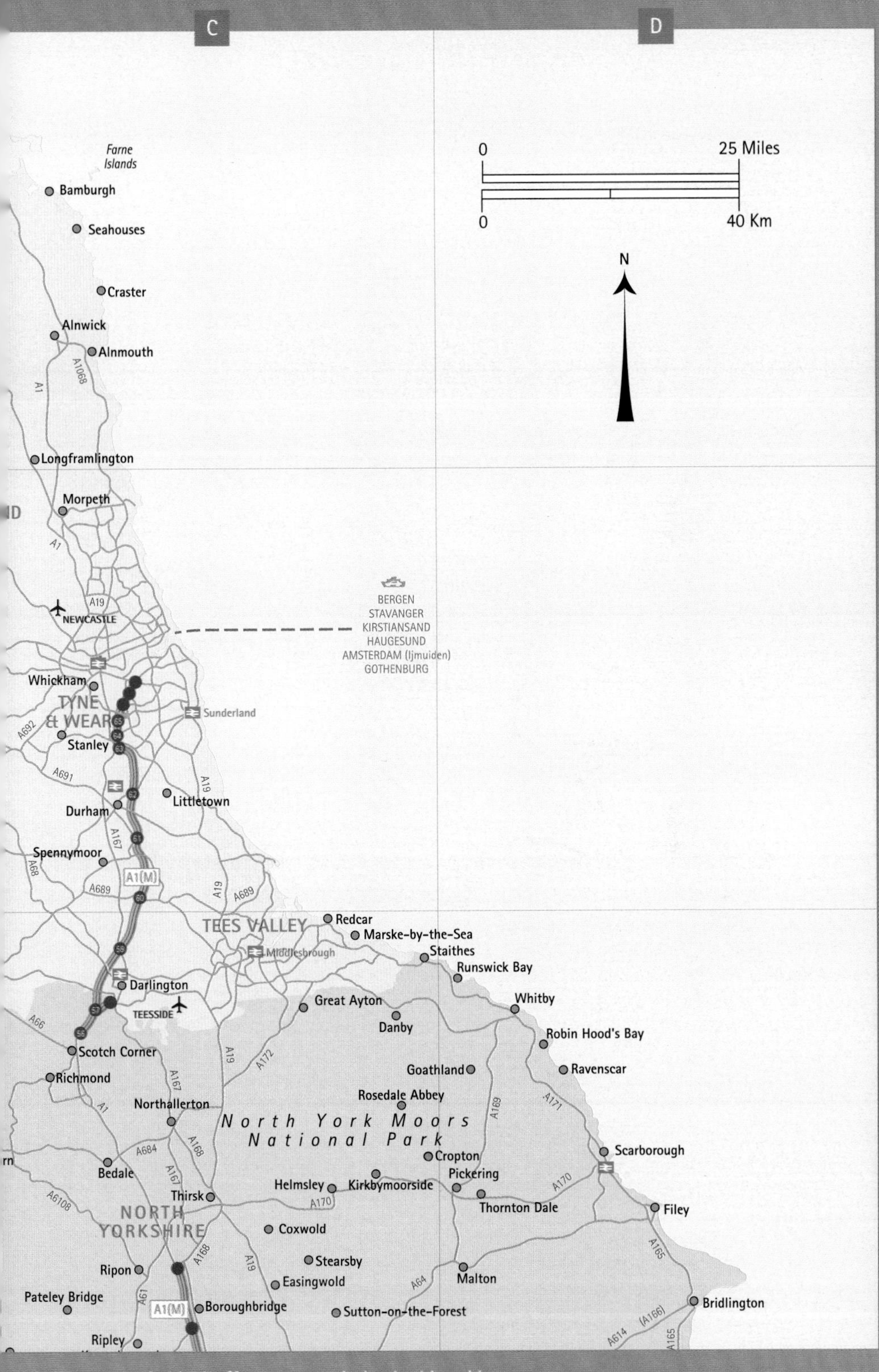

All place names in black offer accommodation in this guide.

M25
A1(M)
M1
M40
M4
M3
BARNET
HARROW
BRENT
CAMDEN
HARINGEY
ISLINGTON
HILLINGDON
EALING
HAMMERSMITH & FULHAM
KENSINGTON & CHELSEA
WESTMINSTER
HOUNSLOW
RICHMOND UPON THAMES
WANDSWORTH
MERTON
SUTTON
KINGSTON UPON THAMES
See map 7
London Heathrow Airport
NORTH CIRCULAR
A40(M)

M11
A414
M25
25
26
A113
A12
NFIELD
M25
A218
A129
WALTHAM
FOREST
28
A218
A12
A127
A127
29
REDBRIDGE
HAVERING
HACKNEY
M25
A102(M)
TOWER
HAMLETS
NEWHAM
BARKING &
DAGENHAM
A13
A1306
ITY
SOUTHWARK
30
31
GREENWICH
BEXLEY
A2
1A
A2226
1B
2
LEWISHAM
SOUTH CIRCULAR
M25
A20
M20
BROMLEY
M25
4
CROYDON
2
2
3
M2
2A
M26
5
A25
M25
S
A25
6
© Arka Cartographics Ltd. 1999

Central London

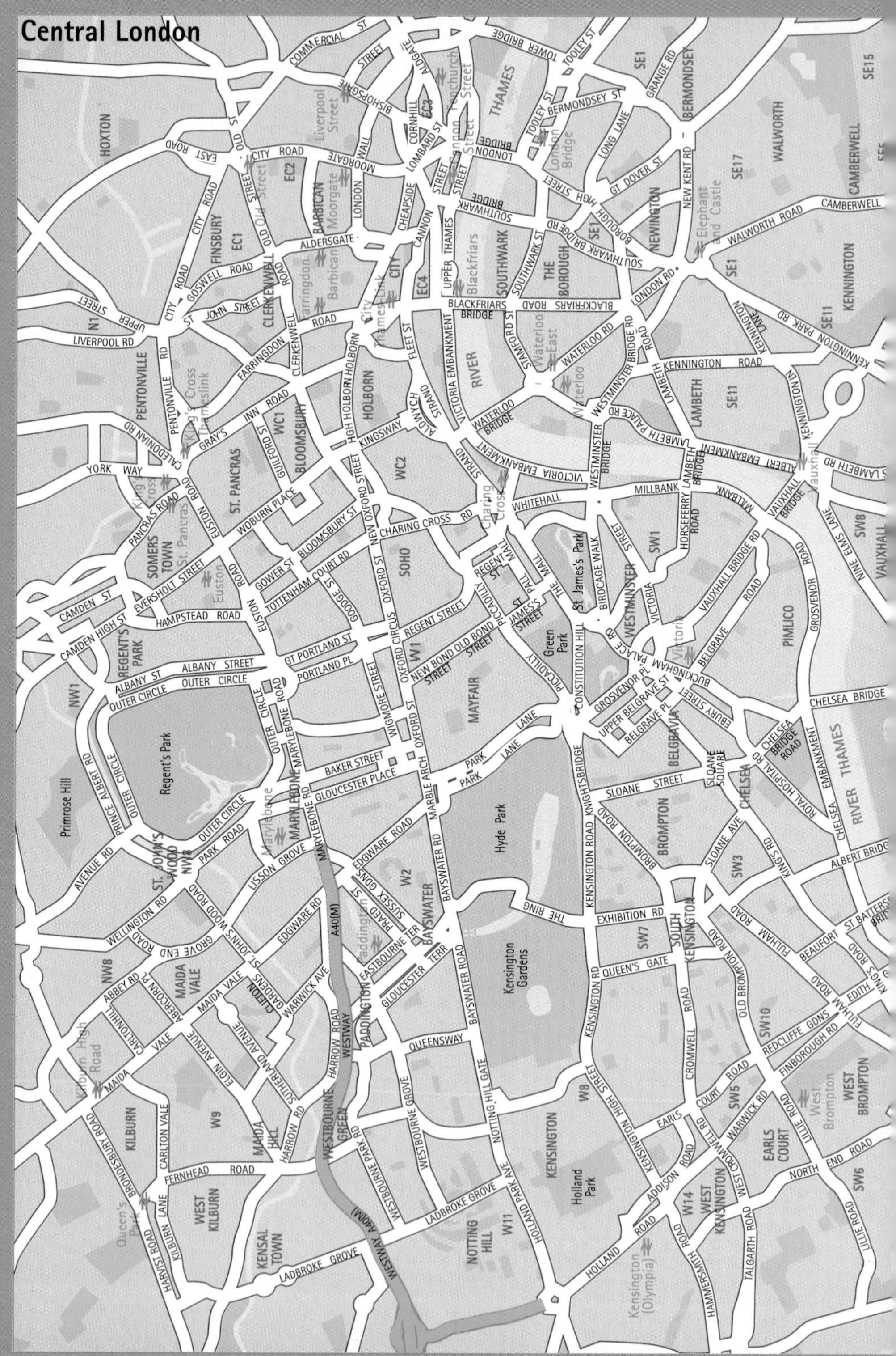

London

A dynamic mix of history and heritage, cool and contemporary. Great museums, stunning art collections, royal palaces, hip nightlife and stylish shopping, from ritzy Bond Street to cutting-edge Hoxton.

Classic sights
St Paul's Cathedral – Wren's famous church
Tower of London – 900 years of British history
London Eye – spectacular views from the world's highest 'big wheel'

Arts for all
National Gallery – Botticelli, Rembrandt, Turner and more
Tate Modern – 20thC art in a former power station
Victoria & Albert Museum – decorative arts

City lights
Theatre: Musicals – West End;
drama – Royal Court and National Theatre;
Music: Classical – Wigmore Hall and Royal Festival Hall;
jazz – Ronnie Scott's;
Ballet & Opera – Royal Opera House

Insider London
Dennis Severs's House, E1 – candlelit tours of this authentically 18thC house

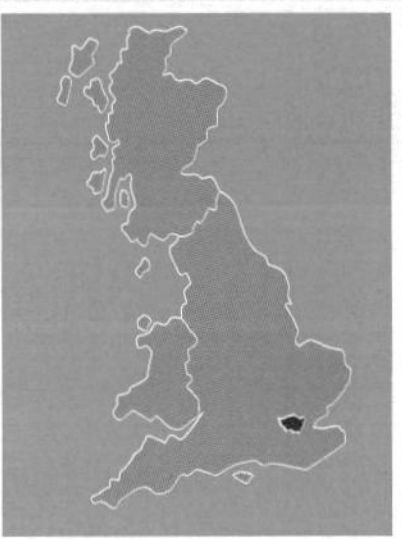

Greater London, comprising the 32 London Boroughs

For more information contact:
Visit London
1 Warwick Row,
London SW1E 5ER

www.visitlondon.com

Telephone enquiries -
see London Line on page 36

1. Piccadilly Circus
2. Millennium Bridge across River Thames and St Paul's

You will find hundreds of interesting places to visit during your stay, just some of which are listed in these pages. Contact any Tourist Information Centre in and around London for more ideas on days out.

Awarded VisitBritain's 'Quality Assured Visitor Attraction' marque.

British Airways London Eye
Jubilee Gardens, South Bank, SE1 7PB
Tel: 0870 5000600 www.ba-londoneye.com
The British Airways London eye is the world's largest observation wheel. Take in over 55 of London's most famous landmarks in just 30 minutes!

British Museum
Great Russell Street, WC1B 3DG
Tel: (020) 7323 8000
www.thebritishmuseum.ac.uk
One of the great museums of the world, showing the works of man from prehistoric to modern times with collections drawn from the whole world.

Cabinet War Rooms
Clive Steps, King Charles Street, SW1A 2AQ
Tel: (020) 7930 6961 www.iwm.org.uk
The underground headquarters used by Winston Churchill and the British Government during World War II. Includes Cabinet Room, Transatlantic Telephone Room and Map Room.

Chessington World of Adventures
Leatherhead Road, Chessington, KT9 2NE
Tel: (01372) 729560 www.chessington.com
Fun family adventures include the 'fang-tastic' New Vampire ride, Tomb Blaster, an action packed adventure ride, and a mischievous new attraction in Beanoland.

Design Museum
28 Shad Thames, SE1 2YD
Tel: (020) 7403 6933 www.designmuseum.org
The world's leading museum of industrial design, fashion and architecture. Its exhibition programme captures the excitement and ingenuity of design's evolution.

Hampton Court Palace
Hampton Court, East Molesey, KT8 9AU
Tel: (020) 8781 9500 www.hrp.org.uk
The oldest Tudor palace in England with many attractions including the Tudor kitchens, tennis courts, maze and State Apartments and King's Apartments.

HMS Belfast
Morgan's Lane, Tooley Street, SE1 2JH
Tel: (020) 7940 6300 www.iwm.org.uk
World War II cruiser weighing 11,500 tonnes, now a floating naval museum, with 9 decks to explore, from the Captain's Bridge to the Boiler and Engine rooms.

Imperial War Museum
Lambeth Road, SE1 6HZ
Tel: (020) 7416 5320 www.iwm.org.uk
Museum tells the story of 20thC war from Flanders to Bosnia. Special features include the Blitz Experience, the Trench Experience and the world of Espionage.

Kensington Palace State Apartments
Kensington Gardens, W8 4PX
Tel: 0870 7515180 www.hrp.org.uk
Furniture and ceiling paintings from Stuart-Hanoverian periods, rooms from Victorian era and works of art from the Royal Collection. Also Royal Ceremonial Dress Collection.

Kew Gardens (Royal Botanic Gardens)
Richmond, TW9 3AB
Tel: (020) 8332 5655 www.kew.org
300 acres (120ha) containing living collections of over 40,000 varieties of plants. Seven spectacular glasshouses, 2 art galleries, Japanese and rock garden.

London Aquarium
County Hall, Riverside Building, SE1 7PB
Tel: (020) 7967 8000
www.londonaquarium.co.uk
Dive down deep beneath the Thames and submerge yourself in one of Europe's largest displays of aquatic life from sharks and piranhas to seahorses and starfish.

London Planetarium
Marylebone Road, NW1 5LR
Tel: 0870 4003000
www.london-planetarium.com
Visitors can experience a virtual reality trip through space and find out about Black Holes and extra terrestrials in the interactive Space Zones before the show.

London Transport Museum
Covent Garden Piazza, WC2E 7BB
Tel: (020) 7379 6344 www.ltmuseum.co.uk
The history of transport for everyone, from spectacular vehicles, special exhibitions, actors and guided tours to film shows, gallery talks and children's craft workshops.

London Zoo
Regent's Park, NW1 4RY
Tel: (020) 7722 3333 www.londonzoo.co.uk
Escape the stress of city life and visit the amazing animals at the world famous London Zoo. See Asian lions, Sloth bears and the incredible 'Animals in Action'.

Museum of London
150 London Wall, EC2Y 5HN
Tel: (020) 7600 3699
www.museumoflondon.org.uk
Discover over 2000 years of the capital's history, from prehistoric to modern times. Regular temporary exhibitions and lunchtime lecture programmes.

National Gallery
Trafalgar Square, WC2N 5DN
Tel: (020) 7747 2885
www.nationalgallery.org.uk
Gallery displaying Western European painting from about 1250-1900. Includes work by Botticelli, Leonardo da Vinci, Rembrandt, Gainsborough, Turner, Renoir, Cezanne.

National Maritime Museum
Romney Road, SE10 9NF
Tel: (020) 8858 4422 www.nmm.ac.uk
This national museum explains Britain's worldwide influence through its explorers, traders, migrants and naval power. Features on ship models, costume, and ecology of the sea.

National Portrait Gallery
St Martin's Place, WC2H 0HE
Tel: (020) 7306 0055 www.npg.org.uk
Permanent collection of portraits of famous men and women from the Middle Ages to the present day. Free, but charge for some exhibitions.

Natural History Museum
Cromwell Road, SW7 5BD
Tel: (020) 7942 5000 www.nhm.ac.uk
Home of the wonders of the natural world with hundreds of exciting, interactive exhibits. Don't miss 'Dinosaurs', 'Creepy-Crawlies' and the new Darwin Centre.

Royal Mews
Buckingham Palace, SW1A 1AA
Tel: (020) 7321 2233 www.royal.gov.uk
One of the finest working stables in existence, the Royal Mews is responsible for all road travel arrangements for the Queen and Royal Family.

2

3

1. The London Eye
2. Buckingham Palace
3. Notting Hill Carnival

Royal Observatory Greenwich
Greenwich Park, SE10 9NF
Tel: (020) 8858 4422 www.nmm.ac.uk
Museum of time and space and site of the Greenwich Meridian. Working telescopes and planetarium, timeball, Wren's Octagon Room and intricate clocks and computer simulations.

St Paul's Cathedral
St Paul's Churchyard, EC4M 8AD
Tel: (020) 7236 4128 www.stpauls.co.uk
Wren's famous cathedral church of the diocese of London incorporating the Crypt, Ambulatory and Whispering Gallery.

Science Museum
Exhibition Road, SW7 2DD
Tel: 0870 8704868
www.sciencemuseum.org.uk
See, touch and experience the major scientific advances of the last 300 years at the largest Museum of its kind in the world.

Shakespeare's Globe Exhibition and Tour
Bankside, SE1 9DT
Tel: (020) 7902 1500
www.shakespeares-globe.org
Against the historical background of Elizabethan Bankside, the City of London's playground in Shakespeare's time, the exhibition focuses on actors, architecture and audiences.

Tate Britain
Millbank, SW1P 4RG
Tel: (020) 7887 8008 www.tate.org.uk
The world's greatest collection of British art including work by Constable, Gainsborough, Hockney, Rossetti and Turner, presented in a dynamic series of new displays and exhibitions.

Tate Modern
Bankside, SE1 9TG
Tel: (020) 7887 8008 www.tate.org.uk
Houses the Tate Collection of international modern art from 1900 to the present day, including major works by Matisse and Picasso plus contemporary work by Sarah Lucas and Rachel Whiteread.

Theatre Museum
Russell Street, WC2E 7PA
Tel: (020) 7943 4700 www.theatremuseum.org
Exhibitions, events based on the world's most exciting performing arts collections, and galleries brought to life by tour guides, all celebrate performance in Britain.

Tower Bridge Experience
Tower Bridge, SE1 2UP
Tel: (020) 7403 3761
www.towerbridge.org.uk
Exhibition explaining the history of the bridge and how it operates. Enjoy the panoramic views from the Walkway 150ft (45m) above the Thames and visit the original Engines.

Tower of London
Tower Hill, EC3N 4AB
Tel: 0870 7567070
www.hrp.org.uk
Home of the 'Beefeaters' and ravens, the building spans 900 years of British history. On display are the nation's Crown Jewels, regalia and armoury robes.

1

Victoria and Albert Museum
Cromwell Road, SW7 2RL
Tel: (020) 7942 2000 www.vam.ac.uk
Large and varied collections of decorative arts from 3000BC to the present day. The new British Galleries explore British art and design from Tudor times to the Victorian era.

Vinopolis - London's Wine Tasting Visitor Attraction
1 Bank End, SE1 9BU
Tel: 0870 2414040 www.vinopolis.co.uk
Vinopolis is London's Wine Tasting Visitor Attraction. For anyone who enjoys a glass of wine it is one of the few attractions where guests grow merrier as they walk through!

Westminster Abbey
Parliament Square, SW1P 3PA
Tel: (020) 7222 5152
www.westminster-abbey.org
One of Britain's finest Gothic buildings. Scene of the coronation, marriage and burial of British monarchs. Nave and cloisters, Royal Chapels and Undercroft Museum.

2

Visit London

1 Warwick Row, London SW1E 5ER
www.visitlondon.com

1. Tower Bridge
2. Houses of Paliament
3. Queens Guard

Tourist Information Centres

INNER LONDON

- **Britain and London Visitor Centre,** 1 Regent Street, Piccadilly Circus, SW1Y 4XT. Open: Mon 0930-1830,Tue-Fri 0900-1830, Sat & Sun 1000-1600; Jun-Oct, Sat 0900-1700.
- **Greenwich TIC,** Pepys House, 2 Cutty Sark Gardens, Greenwich SE10 9LW. Tel: 0870 608 2000; Fax: 020 8853 4607. Open: Daily 1000-1700.
- **Lewisham TIC,** Lewisham Library, 199-201 Lewisham High Street, SE13 6LG. Tel: 020 8297 8317; Fax: 020 8297 9241. Open: Mon 1000-1700, Tue-Fri 0900-1700, Sat 1000-1600.
- **London Visitors Centre,** Arrivals Hall, Waterloo International Terminal, SE1 7LT. Open: Daily 0830-2230.

OUTER LONDON

- **Bexley Hall Place TIC,** Bourne Road, Bexley, Kent, DA5 1PQ. Tel: 01322 558676; Fax 01322 522921. Open: Mon-Sat 1000-1630, Sun 1400-1730.
- **Croydon TIC, Katharine Street,** Croydon, CR9 1ET. Tel: 020 8253 1009; Fax: 020 8253 1008. Open: Mon-Wed & Fri 0900-1800, Thu 0930-1800, Sat 0900-1700, Sun 1400-1700.
- **Harrow TIC,** Civic Centre, Station Road, Harrow, HA1 2XF. Tel: 020 8424 1103; Fax: 020 8424 1134. Open: Mon-Fri 0900-1700.
- **Hillingdon TIC,** Central Library, 14-15 High Street, Uxbridge, UB8 1HD. Tel: 01895 250706; Fax: 01895 239794. Open: Mon, Tue & Thu 0930-2000, Wed 0930-1730, Fri 1000-1730, Sat 0930-1600.
- **Hounslow TIC,** The Treaty Centre, High Street, Hounslow, TW3 1ES. Tel: 0845 4562929; Fax: 0845 4562904 Open: Mon, Tues & Thurs 0930-2000; Wed, Fri & Sat 0930-1730; Sun 1130-1600.
- **Kingston TIC,** Market House, Market Place, Kingston upon Thames, KT1 1JS. Tel: 020 8547 5592; Fax: 020 8547 5594. Open: Mon-Sat 1000-1700.
- **Richmond TIC,** Old Town Hall, Whittaker Avenue; Richmond, TW9 1TP. Tel: 020 8940 6899; Fax: 020 8940 6899. Open: Mon-Sat 1000-1700; May-Sep, Sun 1030-1330.
- **Swanley TIC,** London Road, BR8 7AE. Tel: 01322 614660; Fax: 01322 666154. Open: Mon-Thu 0930-1730, Fri 0930-1800, Sat 0900-1600.
- **Twickenham TIC,** The Atrium, Civic Centre, York Street, Twickenham, Middlesex, TW1 3BZ. Tel: 020 8891 7272; Fax: 020 8891 7738. Open: Mon-Thu 0900-1715, Fri 0900-1700.

INFORMATION PACK

For a London information pack call 0870 240 4326. Calls are charged at national rate.

LONDON LINE

Visit London's recorded telephone information service provides information on museums, galleries, attractions, riverboat trips, sightseeing tours, accommodation, theatre, what's on, changing the Guard, children's London, shopping, eating out and gay and lesbian London.

Available 24 hours a day. Calls cost 60p per minute as at July 2003. Call 09068 663344.

ARTSLINE

London's information and advice service for disabled people on arts and entertainment. Call (020) 7388 2227.

HOTEL ACCOMMODATION SERVICE

Accommodation reservations can be made throughout London. Call Visit London's Telephone Accommodation Service on (020) 7932 2020 with your requirements and MasterCard/Visa/Switch details or email your request on book@visitlondon.com

WHICH PART OF LONDON

The majority of tourist accommodation is situated in the central parts of London and is therefore very convenient for most of the city's attractions and nightlife.

However, there are many hotels in outer London which provide other advantages, such as easier parking. In the 'Where to Stay' pages which follow, you will find accommodation listed under INNER LONDON (covering the E1 to W14 London Postal Area) and OUTER LONDON (covering the remainder of Greater London). Colour maps 6 and 7 at the front of the guide show place names and London Postal Area codes and will help you to locate accommodation in your chosen area of London.

1

Getting to London

BY ROAD: Major trunk roads into London include: A1, M1, A5, A10, A11, M11, A13, A2, M2, A23, A3, M3, A4, M4, A40, M40, A41, M25 (London orbital). London Transport is responsible for running London's bus services and the underground rail network. (020) 7222 1234 (24 hour telephone service; calls answered in rotation).

BY RAIL: Main rail termini: Victoria/Waterloo/Charing Cross - serving the South/South East; King's Cross - serving the North East; Euston - serving the North West/Midlands; Liverpool Street - serving the East; Paddington - serving the Thames Valley/West.

1. London Underground Station
2. The Mall

2

LONDON INDEX

If you are looking for accommodation in a particular establishment in London and you know its name, this index will give you the page number of the full entry in the guide.

Where to stay in

London

Entries in this region are listed under Inner London (postcode areas E1 to W14) and Outer London (the remainder of Greater London).

All place names in the blue bands under which accommodation is listed, are shown on the maps at the front of this guide.

Symbols give useful information about services and facilities. Inside the back cover flap there's a key to these symbols which you can keep open for easy reference.

A complete listing of all the VisitBritain assessed accommodation covered by this guide appears at the back of this guide.

INNER LONDON

LONDON E4

RIDGEWAY HOTEL
115-117 The Ridgeway,
North Chingford, London E4 6QU
T: (020) 8529 1964
F: (020) 8542 9130

Bedrooms: 11 double, 8 single, 1 family
Bathrooms: 8 en suite

CC: Amex, Delta, Mastercard, Switch, Visa

Family-run hotel situated five minutes from Epping Forest and 20 minutes from central London. Easy access to the M25.

B&B per person per night:
S £52.00
D £32.50

OPEN All Year

LONDON E7

FOREST VIEW HOTEL
227 Romford Road, Forest Gate,
London E7 9HL
T: (020) 8534 4844
F: (020) 8534 8959
E: forestviewhotel@hotmail.com
I: www.forestviewhotel.net

Bedrooms: 15 double, 8 single, 5 family
Bathrooms: 16 private

Evening meal available
CC: Delta, Mastercard, Switch, Visa

Catering for business and tourist clientele. En suite rooms with tea/coffee-making facilities, direct-dial telephone and TV. Full English breakfast. Warm and friendly atmosphere.

B&B per person per night:
S £36.00
D £26.50–£35.25

HB per person per night:
DY £45.30–£50.00

OPEN All Year

IMPORTANT NOTE Information on accommodation listed in this guide has been supplied by the proprietors. As changes may occur you are advised to check details at the time of booking.

LONDON N1

KANDARA GUEST HOUSE

68 Ockendon Road, Islington, London N1 3NW
T: (020) 7226 5721
F: (020) 7226 3379
E: admin@kandara.co.uk
I: www.kandara.co.uk

A family-run guesthouse near the Angel, Islington. Quietly situated in a conservation area. All bedrooms and bathrooms have recently been decorated and fitted to a high standard. Nine bus routes and two underground stations provide excellent public transport services.

Bedrooms: 3 double, 4 single, 4 family

CC: Delta, Mastercard, Visa

Book for 3 nights or more and save 10%.

B&B per person per night:
S £43.00–£49.00
D £27.00–£31.00

OPEN All Year

LONDON N7

EUROPA HOTEL

60-62 Anson Road, London N7 0AA
T: (020) 7607 5935
F: (020) 7607 5909
E: info@europahotellondon.co.uk
I: www.europahotellondon.co.uk

Bedrooms: 12 double, 7 single, 9 family
Bathrooms: 28 en suite

CC: Delta, Diners, Mastercard, Switch, Visa

Georgian properties, all rooms en suite. Free zone parking. Nearest station Tufnell Park. Convenient for West End, London Zoo, Highgate. Two miles from Kings Cross.

B&B per person per night:
S £30.00–£35.00
D £22.50–£24.50

OPEN All Year

LONDON N8

WHITE LODGE HOTEL

1 Church Lane, Hornsey, London N8 7BU
T: (020) 8348 9765
F: (020) 8340 7851

Bedrooms: 6 double, 7 single, 3 family
Bathrooms: 8 en suite

Evening meal available
CC: Mastercard, Visa

Small, friendly, family hotel offering personal service. Easy access to all transport, for sightseeing and business trips.

B&B per person per night:
S £32.00–£36.00
D £21.00–£25.00

OPEN All Year

LONDON N10

THE MUSWELL HILL HOTEL

73 Muswell Hill Road, Muswell Hill, London N10 3HT
T: (020) 8883 6447
F: (020) 8883 5158
E: reception@muswellhillhotel.co.uk
I: www.muswellhillhotel.co.uk

Bedrooms: 7 double, 4 single, 3 family
Bathrooms: 10 en suite

CC: Mastercard, Switch, Visa

A comfortable three-storey Edwardian corner property, close to Muswell Hill and Alexandra Palace, offering a warm, friendly service.

B&B per person per night:
S Min £40.00
D Min £27.50

OPEN All Year

LONDON N22

PANE RESIDENCE

154 Boundary Road, Wood Green, London N22 6AE
T: (020) 8889 3735

Bedrooms: 2 double, 1 single

In a pleasant location six minutes' walk from Turnpike Lane underground station and near Alexandra Palace. Kitchen facilities available.

B&B per person per night:
S £22.00–£24.00
D £17.00–£19.00

OPEN All Year

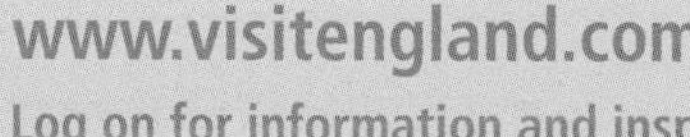

LONDON NW3

DILLONS HOTEL

21 Belsize Park, Hampstead, London
NW3 4DU
T: (020) 7794 3360
F: (020) 7431 7900
E: desk@dillonshotel.com
I: www.dillonshotel.com

Located just six minutes' walk from either Swiss Cottage or Belsize Park underground stations, close to the Royal Free Hospital and convenient for Camden Market and central London. Dillons Hotel provides comfortable, reasonably priced bed and breakfast accommodation. All rooms have colour TV and many have private shower/wc.

Bedrooms: 8 double, 1 single, 4 family
Bathrooms: 8 en suite

CC: Delta, Mastercard, Switch, Visa

Discounts available for stays of 7 or more nights. Ask at the time of booking.

B&B per person per night:
S £32.00–£46.00
D £25.00–£32.00

OPEN All Year

LONDON NW6

◆◆◆◆

CAVENDISH GUEST HOUSE

24 Cavendish Road, London
NW6 7XP
T: (020) 8451 3249
F: (020) 8451 3249

Bedrooms: 2 double, 5 single, 1 family
Bathrooms: 2 en suite

In a quiet residential street, five minutes' walk from Kilburn underground station, 15 minutes' travelling time to the West End. Easy access to Wembley Stadium, Heathrow, Gatwick.

B&B per person per night:
S £36.00–£51.00
D £27.50–£30.50

OPEN All Year

LONDON SE3

59A LEE ROAD

Blackheath, London SE3 9EN
T: (020) 8318 7244
E: angecall@blackheath318.freeserve.co.uk

Bedrooms: 1 double

Charming accommodation in leafy location. Minutes from amenities of Blackheath village. Extremely convenient for historic Greenwich, central London and Docklands Light Railway.

B&B per person per night:
S £35.00–£40.00
D £25.00–£27.50

OPEN All Year

NUMBER NINE BLACKHEATH

9 Charlton Road, Blackheath, London
SE3 7EU
T: (020) 8858 4175
F: (020) 8858 4175
E: derek@numbernineblackheath.com
I: www.numbernineblackheath.com

A family-run Victorian guesthouse, recently refurbished. Blackheath and Greenwich within 15 minutes' walk. Central London 25 minutes by public transport. Bathrobes and security boxes in all rooms. Quad/triple family rooms, all en suite. Full English breakfast. Sky TV/video in all rooms. Guests' garden. All major credit cards accepted.

Bedrooms: 4 double, 2 family
Bathrooms: 2 en suite

CC: Amex, Delta, Mastercard, Switch, Visa

Weekend bookings are reduced by 10%. Children under 6 free in same room. Argos cots supplied.

B&B per person per night:
S £58.75–£65.00
D £37.50–£42.50

OPEN All Year

3 TILBROOK ROAD

Kidbrooke, London SE3 9QD
T: (020) 8319 8843
E: m.hutson@ntlworld.com

Bedrooms: 3 double

Semi-detached house, eight minutes from Eltham Street station by bus and 20 minutes to Greenwich. Central London is 20 minutes by train. Easy access to major roads.

B&B per person per night:
S Min £25.00
D £22.50–£30.00

OPEN All Year

LONDON SE6

♦♦♦

THE HEATHERS

71 Verdant Lane, Catford, London SE6 1JD
T: (020) 8698 8340
F: (020) 8461 3980
E: berylheath@yahoo.co.uk
I: www.theheathersbb.com

Bedrooms: 2 double

B&B per person per night:
S £30.00–£35.00
D £22.50–£25.00

OPEN All Year

A comfortable, family-run 'home from home'. Beryl and Ron will do their best to ensure you really enjoy your visit.

♦♦♦

TULIP TREE HOUSE

41 Minard Road, Catford, London SE6 1NP
T: (020) 8697 2596
F: (020) 8698 2020

Bedrooms: 2 double, 1 single

Evening meal available

B&B per person per night:
S £25.00
D £23.00–£25.00

OPEN All Year

English home in quiet residential area off A205 South Circular Road. 10 minutes' walk to Hither Green station for 20-minute journey to central London.

LONDON SE9

BENVENUTI

217 Court Road, Eltham, London SE9 4TG
T: (020) 8857 4855
F: (020) 8265 5635
E: val-alan@benvenuti-guesthouse.co.uk
I: www.benvenuti-guesthouse.co.uk

B&B per person per night:
S £30.00–£40.00
D £45.00–£60.00

OPEN All Year

Friendly, family-run B&B within the London Borough of Greenwich, four minutes' walk from train station. Central London 20 minutes by train. Very convenient for the M25, M20, A20, A2 and M2. No-smoking establishment.

Bedrooms: 2 double, 1 family

LONDON SE13

♦♦♦

MANNA HOUSE

320 Hither Green Lane, Lewisham, London SE13 6TS
T: (020) 8461 5984
F: (020) 8695 5316
E: mannahouse@aol.com
I: www.members.aol.com/mannahouse

Bedrooms: 2 double, 1 single

CC: Delta, Mastercard, Switch, Visa

B&B per person per night:
S £25.00–£35.00
D £25.00–£30.00

OPEN All Year

Mrs Lynne Rawlins welcomes you to her family home – a Victorian terraced house near historic Greenwich. Twenty minutes by train to central London. Free off-street parking.

LONDON SE20

♦♦♦♦

MELROSE HOUSE

89 Lennard Road, London SE20 7LY
T: (020) 8776 8884
F: (020) 8325 7636
E: melrose.hotel@virgin.net
I: www.guesthouseaccommodation.co.uk

Bedrooms: 3 double, 1 single
Bathrooms: 1 private

CC: Delta, Mastercard, Switch, Visa

B&B per person per night:
S £35.00–£50.00
D £27.50–£35.00

OPEN All Year

Superb, friendly accommodation in Victorian house with spacious, en suite bedrooms. Easy access to West End. Quiet, respectable and welcoming. Disabled facilities.

CONFIRM YOUR BOOKING

You are advised to confirm your booking in writing.

LONDON SW1

◆◆

CARLTON HOTEL

90 Belgrave Road, Victoria, London SW1V 2BJ
T: (020) 7976 6634
F: (020) 7821 8020
E: info@cityhotelcarlton.co.uk
I: www.cityhotelcarlton.co.uk

Bedrooms: 6 double, 4 single, 7 family
Bathrooms: 17 en suite

CC: Amex, Delta, Diners, Mastercard, Switch, Visa

B&B per person per night:
S £49.00–£59.00
D £29.50–£34.50

OPEN All Year

Small, friendly B&B near Victoria station and within walking distance of famous landmarks such as Buckingham Palace, Trafalgar Square, Piccadilly Circus. A lot to offer at a moderate, all-inclusive rate.

P

◆◆◆

COLLIN HOUSE

104 Ebury Street, London SW1W 9QD
T: (020) 7730 8031
F: (020) 7730 8031
E: booking@collinhouse.co.uk
I: www.collinhouse.co.uk

Bedrooms: 4 double, 3 single, 1 family
Bathrooms: 5 en suite

CC: Delta, Mastercard, Switch, Visa

B&B per person per night:
S £55.00
D £34.00–£41.00

OPEN All Year

A well maintained B&B offering good value accommodation, close to Victoria rail, underground and coach stations. Ideal for visiting London's places of interest.

P €

◆◆

DOVER HOTEL

44 Belgrave Road, London SW1V 1RG
T: (020) 7821 9085
F: (020) 7834 6425
E: reception@dover-hotel.co.uk
I: www.dover-hotel.co.uk

Bedrooms: 20 double, 4 single, 9 family
Bathrooms: 29 en suite

CC: Amex, Delta, Diners, Mastercard, Switch, Visa

B&B per person per night:
S £30.00–£55.00
D £20.00–£32.50

OPEN All Year

Friendly bed and breakfast hotel within minutes of Victoria station and Gatwick Express. Most rooms with satellite TV, shower/wc, telephone, hairdryer. Very competitive prices.

P €

◆◆◆◆

KNIGHTSBRIDGE GREEN HOTEL

159 Knightsbridge, London SW1X 7PD
T: (020) 7584 6274
F: (020) 7225 1635
E: thekghotel@aol.com
I: www.thekghotel.co.uk

Bedrooms: 9 double, 7 single, 12 family
Bathrooms: 28 en suite

CC: Amex, Diners, Mastercard, Visa

B&B per person per night:
S £103.50–£120.50
D £76.00–£95.50

OPEN All Year

Small, family-owned hotel close to Harrods, offering spacious accommodation at competitive rates. Finalist in 1997 and 1998 London Tourism Awards.

◆◆◆

MELITA HOUSE HOTEL

35 Charlwood Street, Victoria, London SW1V 2DU
T: (020) 7828 0471
F: (020) 7932 0988
E: reserve@melitahotel.com
I: www.melitahotel.com

Bedrooms: 9 double, 2 single, 8 family
Bathrooms: 19 en suite

CC: Amex, Delta, Diners, Mastercard, Switch, Visa

B&B per person per night:
S £50.00–£80.00
D £35.00–£50.00

OPEN All Year

Elegant, family-run hotel in excellent location close to Victoria station. Rooms have extensive modern facilities. Warm, friendly welcome, full English breakfast included.

P €

AT-A-GLANCE SYMBOLS

Symbols at the end of each accommodation entry give useful information about services and facilities. A key to symbols can be found inside the back cover flap. Keep this open for easy reference.

LONDON SW1 continued

◆◆

STANLEY HOUSE HOTEL

19-21 Belgrave Road, Victoria, London SW1V 1RB
T: (020) 7834 5042
F: (020) 7834 8439
E: cmahotel@aol.com
I: www.londonbudgethotels.co.uk

In elegant Belgravia, only a few minutes' walk from Victoria station and with easy access to West End. All rooms en suite, with colour TV, direct-dial telephone, hairdryer. Friendly, relaxing atmosphere at affordable rates.

Bedrooms: 30 double, 4 single, 10 family
Bathrooms: 44 en suite

CC: Amex, Delta, Diners, Mastercard, Switch, Visa

B&B per person per night:
S £30.00–£40.00
D £20.00–£25.00

OPEN All Year

LONDON SW5

◆◆

LORD JIM HOTEL

23-25 Penywern Road, London SW5 9TT
T: (020) 7370 6071
F: (020) 7373 8919
E: ljh@lgh-hotels.com
I: www.lgh-hotels.com

A good-quality hotel for both business travellers and tourists. Bedrooms are modern and mostly en suite, with colour TV, telephone and hairdryer. Two minutes' walk from Earls Court station which is directly linked to Heathrow and Gatwick Airports (via Victoria). Earls Court and Olympia exhibition halls within walking distance.

Bedrooms: 19 double, 10 single, 14 family
Bathrooms: 31 en suite

CC: Amex, Delta, Diners, Mastercard, Switch, Visa

Special discounts available in low seasons.

B&B per person per night:
S £35.00–£55.00
D £22.50–£32.50

OPEN All Year

◆◆◆

LORD KENSINGTON HOTEL

38 Trebovir Road, Earls Court, London SW5 9NJ
T: (020) 7373 7331
F: (020) 7460 3524
E: lkh@lgh-hotels.com
I: www.lgh-hotels.com

A hotel in the heart of Kensington, having recently undergone extensive refurbishment. All en suite rooms with colour TV, direct-dial telephone, PC modem, tea and coffee. Only two minutes from Earls Court station. Earls Court and Olympia exhibition halls within walking distance.

Bedrooms: 7 double, 2 single, 14 family
Bathrooms: 18 en suite

CC: Amex, Delta, Diners, Mastercard, Switch, Visa

B&B per person per night:
S £45.00–£75.00
D £25.00–£47.50

OPEN All Year

CREDIT CARD BOOKINGS If you book by telephone and are asked for your credit card number it is advisable to check the proprietor's policy should you cancel your reservation.

LONDON SW5 continued

◆◆

MERLYN COURT HOTEL

2 Barkston Gardens, London SW5 0EN
T: (020) 7370 1640
F: (020) 7370 4986
E: london@merlyncourthotel.com
I: www.merlyncourthotel.com

B&B per person per night:
S £30.00–£50.00
D £30.00–£40.00

OPEN All Year

Quiet, non-smoking, family-run, good-value hotel in quiet Edwardian square with bright, airy rooms. Family rooms available. Close to Earls Court and Olympia. Direct underground link to Heathrow, the West End and rail stations. Easy access to motorways and airports. Car park nearby.

Bedrooms: 10 double, 7 single, 3 family
Bathrooms: 13 en suite

CC: Delta, Mastercard, Switch, Visa

Nov-Mar: 2/3-night stays at reduced rates on application.

◆◆◆

OLIVER PLAZA HOTEL
33 Trebovir Road, Earls Court, London SW5 9NF
T: (020) 7373 7183
F: (020) 7244 6021
E: oliverplaza@capricornhotels.co.uk
I: www.capricornhotels.co.uk

Bedrooms: 27 double, 3 single, 8 family
Bathrooms: 38 en suite

CC: Amex, Delta, Diners, Mastercard, Switch, Visa

B&B per person per night:
S £35.00–£45.00
D £27.50–£37.50

OPEN All Year

Friendly hotel with emphasis on efficiency of service and comfort for guests. Fully refurbished in 1999. Good access to public transport and shopping facilities.

P

RATING All accommodation in this guide has been rated, or is awaiting a rating, by a trained VisitBritain assessor.

USE YOUR *i*s

There are more than 550 Tourist Information Centres throughout England offering friendly help with accommodation and holiday ideas as well as suggestions of places to visit and things to do. You'll find TIC addresses in the local Phone Book.

LONDON SW5 continued

◆◆

RAMSEES HOTEL

32-36 Hogarth Road, Earl's Court, London SW5 0PU
T: (020) 7370 1445
F: (020) 7244 6835
E: ramsees@rasool.demon.co.uk
I: www.ramseeshotel.com

B&B per person per night:
S £30.00–£42.00
D £22.50–£27.50

OPEN All Year

Our friendly staff are here to make your stay comfortable. Ideally located in fashionable Kensington, close to the heart of the city. One minute's walk Earl's Court station, making major shopping areas of Knightsbridge, Oxford Street and tourist attractions of Buckingham Palace, Tower of London and museums within easy reach.

Bedrooms: 39 double, 15 single, 13 family
Bathrooms: 57 en suite

CC: Amex, Delta, Diners, Mastercard, Switch, Visa

◆◆

RASOOL COURT HOTEL

19-21 Penywern Road, Earl's Court, London SW5 9TT
T: (020) 7373 8900
F: (020) 7244 6835
E: rasool@rasool.demon.co.uk
I: www.rasoolcourthotel.com

B&B per person per night:
S £30.00–£42.00
D £45.00–£55.00

OPEN All Year

Family-run hotel ideally located in fashionable Kensington within one minute's walk of Earl's Court station, making the shopping areas of Knightsbridge and Oxford Street and the tourist attractions of Buckingham Palace, the Tower of London and museums within easy reach. The immediate area has a variety of restaurants and shops for your convenience.

Bedrooms: 25 double, 35 single, 7 family
Bathrooms: 44 en suite

CC: Amex, Delta, Diners, Mastercard, Switch, Visa

◆◆◆

SWISS HOUSE HOTEL

171 Old Brompton Road, London SW5 0AN
T: (020) 7373 2769
F: (020) 7373 4983
E: recep@swiss-hh.demon.co.uk
I: www.swiss-hh.demon.co.uk

B&B per person per night:
S £56.00–£78.00
D £49.00–£57.00

OPEN All Year

The Swiss House Hotel is located in the heart of South Kensington, one of London's smartest and most fashionable districts, and is close to most of London's main attractions. Whether your visit is for business or pleasure, the Swiss House extends a warm welcome and ensures a comfortable stay.

Bedrooms: 7 double, 4 single, 4 family
Bathrooms: 14 en suite

CC: Amex, Delta, Diners, Mastercard, Switch, Visa

Children under 4 stay for free. 5% discount for more than 5-day stay during winter time.

ACCESSIBILITY

Look for the symbols which indicate National Accessible Scheme standards for hearing and visually impaired guests in addition to standards for guests with mobility impairment. You can find an index of all scheme participants at the back of this guide.

LONDON SW7

FIVE SUMNER PLACE HOTEL

5 Sumner Place, London SW7 3EE
T: (020) 7584 7586
F: (020) 7823 9962
E: reservations@sumnerplace.com
I: www.sumnerplace.com

Awarded 'best small hotel'. In South Kensington, one of the most stylish and sought-after locations in London, the hotel brings the charm and elegance of a former age to the 21st century. Ideally placed for visiting the sights. This family-owned and run hotel offers excellent service and personal attention.

Bedrooms: 10 double, 3 single
Bathrooms: 13 en suite

CC: Amex, Delta, Diners, Mastercard, Switch, Visa

Special offers available Nov-Feb.

B&B per person per night:
S £75.00–£100.00
D £57.50–£76.50

OPEN All Year

LONDON SW8

COMFORT INN

87 South Lambeth Road, London SW8 1RN
T: (020) 7735 9494
F: (020) 7735 1001
E: stay@comfortinnvx.co.uk
I: www.comfortinnvx.co.uk

This recently built, modern, award-winning hotel offers en suite and well-equipped rooms, located in the heart of London close to major tourist attractions, famous shopping areas and public transport access. Offers excellent value for money. Theatres, restaurants and wine bars are all within easy reach of the hotel.

Bedrooms: 78 double, 16 family
Bathrooms: 94 en suite

CC: Amex, Delta, Diners, Mastercard, Switch, Visa

Special and promotional rates available for online bookings only on www.comfortinnvx.co.uk.

B&B per person per night:
S £69.00–£130.00
D £34.50–£65.00

OPEN All Year

LONDON SW14

THE PLOUGH INN

42 Christchurch Road, East Sheen, London SW14 7AF
T: (020) 8876 7833
F: (020) 8392 8801
E: ploughthe@hotmail.com
I: www.theplough.org

Bedrooms: 6 double, 1 single, 1 family
Bathrooms: 8 en suite

CC: Amex, Delta, Mastercard, Switch, Visa

Delightful old pub, part 16thC, next to Richmond Park. En suite accommodation, traditional ales, home-cooked food.

P €

B&B per person per night:
S Min £65.00
D £43.00–£45.00

HB per person per night:
DY £53.00–£58.00

OPEN All Year

LONDON W1

BLANDFORD HOTEL

80 Chiltern Street, London W1U 5AF
T: (020) 7486 3103
F: (020) 7487 2786
E: blandfordhotel@dial.pipex.com
I: www.capricornhotels.co.uk

Bedrooms: 14 double, 8 single, 11 family
Bathrooms: 33 en suite

CC: Amex, Delta, Mastercard, Switch, Visa

Centrally located hotel, close to Baker Street underground station and Madame Tussaud's. Oxford Street and other attractions in the West End are within walking distance.

P

B&B per person per night:
S £40.00–£65.00
D £30.00–£45.00

OPEN All Year

VISTBRITAIN'S WHERE TO STAY
Please mention this guide when making your booking.

LONDON W1 continued

◆◆◆

HALLAM HOTEL

12 Hallam Street, Portland Place, London W1W 6JF
T: (020) 7580 1166
F: (020) 7323 4527
E: hallam_hotel@hotmail.com
I: www.hallamhotel.com

Ideally placed in the heart of London's West End. Situated five minutes from Oxford Circus, West End shopping and theatreland.

Bedrooms: 10 double, 15 single
Bathrooms: 25 en suite

CC: Amex, Delta, Diners, Mastercard, Switch, Visa

B&B per person per night:
S £39.00–£69.00
D £29.00–£39.00

OPEN All Year

◆◆

LINCOLN HOUSE HOTEL – CENTRAL LONDON

33 Gloucester Place, Marble Arch, London W1U 8HY
T: (020) 7486 7630
F: (020) 7486 0166
E: reservations@lincoln-house-hotel.co.uk
I: www.lincoln-house-hotel.co.uk

Built in the days of King George III, this hotel offers Georgian townhouse charm and character with en suite rooms and modern comforts. Ideally located in the heart of London's West End, next to Oxford Street shopping. Within easy reach of most theatres, museums and exhibitions. Suitable for business and leisure.

Bedrooms: 10 double, 9 single, 4 family
Bathrooms: 29 en suite

CC: Amex, Delta, Diners, Mastercard, Switch, Visa

Long-stay discounts on request. Most Sundays discounted. For latest long-stay and other special offers visit our website.

€

B&B per person per night:
S £59.00–£69.00
D £34.50–£39.50

OPEN All Year

◆◆

MARBLE ARCH INN
49-50 Upper Berkeley Street, Marble Arch, London W1H 5QR
T: (020) 7723 7888
F: (020) 7723 6060
E: sales@marblearch-inn.co.uk
I: www.marblearch-inn.co.uk

Bedrooms: 18 double, 2 single, 9 family
Bathrooms: 25 en suite

CC: Amex, Delta, Diners, Mastercard, Switch, Visa

B&B per person per night:
S £30.00–£60.00
D £20.00–£35.00

OPEN All Year

Friendly bed and breakfast hotel within minutes of Hyde Park, Oxford Street, Heathrow Express. Most rooms with satellite TV, shower/wc, telephone, hairdryer. Very competitive prices.

P €

LONDON W2

◆◆

ALBRO HOUSE HOTEL
155 Sussex Gardens, Hyde Park, London W2 2RY
T: (020) 7724 2931
F: (020) 7262 2278
E: joe@albrohotel.freeserve.co.uk
I: www.albrohousehotel.co.uk

Bedrooms: 12 double, 2 single, 4 family
Bathrooms: 17 en suite

CC: Mastercard, Visa

B&B per person per night:
S £38.00–£52.00
D £27.00–£34.00

OPEN All Year

Ideally located in pleasant, central area near public transport. Nice, comfortable rooms, all en suite. English breakfast. Languages spoken. Friendly and safe. Some parking available.

P €

QUALITY ASSURANCE SCHEME

Diamond ratings and awards were correct at the time of going to press but are subject to change. Please check at the time of booking.

LONDON W2 continued

◆◆◆

ASHLEY HOTEL

13-17 Norfolk Square, London W2 1RU
T: (020) 7723 3375
F: (020) 7723 0173
E: ashhot@btinternet.com
I: www.ashleyhotels.com

Bedrooms: 21 double, 20 single, 12 family
Bathrooms: 43 en suite, 2 private

CC: Delta, Mastercard, Switch, Visa

B&B per person per night:
S £36.50–£49.00
D £36.50–£38.50

OPEN All Year

Victorian townhouse hotel located in a quiet garden square in the heart of London, owned and managed by the same family for over 35 years.

◆◆◆

BARRY HOUSE HOTEL

12 Sussex Place, London W2 2TP
T: (020) 7723 7340
F: (020) 7723 9775
E: hotel@barryhouse.co.uk
I: www.barryhouse.co.uk

B&B per person per night:
S £39.00–£45.00
D £38.00–£45.00

OPEN All Year

We believe in family-like care. Comfortable, en suite rooms with TV, telephone and hospitality tray. Located close to Hyde Park, the West End, Paddington station and many tourist attractions. We offer tourist information, sightseeing and tours arranged, theatre tickets and taxis booked.

Bedrooms: 11 double, 1 single, 4 family
Bathrooms: 16 en suite

CC: Amex, Delta, Diners, Mastercard, Switch, Visa

◆◆

HYDE PARK ROOMS HOTEL

137 Sussex Gardens, Hyde Park, London W2 2RX
T: (020) 7723 0225
I: www.hydeparkroomshotel.com

Bedrooms: 7 double, 5 single, 2 family
Bathrooms: 6 en suite

CC: Amex, Diners, Mastercard, Visa

B&B per person per night:
S £30.00–£45.00
D £22.50–£30.00

OPEN All Year

Small, centrally located, private hotel with personal service. Clean, comfortable and friendly. Within walking distance of Hyde Park and Kensington Gardens. Car parking available.

◆

MANOR COURT HOTEL

7 Clanricarde Gardens, London W2 4JJ
T: (020) 7727 5407
F: (020) 7229 2875

Bedrooms: 11 double, 5 single, 4 family
Bathrooms: 15 en suite

CC: Amex, Delta, Diners, Mastercard, Switch, Visa

B&B per person per night:
S £30.00–£45.00
D £22.50–£27.50

OPEN All Year

Bed and breakfast hotel within walking distance of Hyde Park and Kensington Gardens. Near Notting Hill Gate underground and Airbus stop. All rooms have colour TV and telephone.

◆◆◆

ROSE COURT HOTEL

1-3 Talbot Square, London W2 1TR
T: (020) 7723 5128
F: (020) 7723 1855
E: rosehotel@aol.com
I: www.rosecourthotel.com

Bedrooms: 25 double, 7 single, 11 family
Bathrooms: 41 en suite

CC: Amex, Delta, Diners, Mastercard, Switch, Visa

B&B per person per night:
S £40.00–£60.00
D £25.00–£37.50

OPEN All Year

Privately run Victorian townhouse in a quiet garden square. Close to Paddington and the West End.

LONDON W4

◆◆

FOUBERT'S HOTEL

162-166 Chiswick High Road, London W4 1PR
T: (020) 8994 5202

Bedrooms: 13 double, 15 single, 3 family
Bathrooms: 31 en suite

Evening meal available
CC: Mastercard, Visa

B&B per person per night:
S £45.00–£50.00
D £32.50–£35.00

OPEN All Year

Family-run hotel, close to central London and Heathrow Airport. Fully licensed cafe/restaurant open daily 0800-2300. Children welcome. Outside seating for 60 persons.

LONDON W5

ABBEY LODGE HOTEL

51 Grange Park, Ealing, London W5 3PR
T: (020) 8567 7914
F: (020) 8579 5350
E: enquiries@londonlodgehotels.com
I: www.londonlodgehotels.com

Bedrooms: 3 double, 10 single, 3 family
Bathrooms: 16 en suite

CC: Delta, Diners, Mastercard, Switch, Visa

B&B per person per night:
S £43.00–£49.00
D £53.00–£59.00

OPEN All Year

All rooms en suite, with colour TV, tea/coffee-making facilities and radio-alarm clock. Very close to three underground lines. Midway central London and Heathrow.

€

GRANGE LODGE HOTEL

48-50 Grange Road, Ealing, London W5 5BX
T: (020) 8567 1049
F: (020) 8579 5350
E: enquiries@londonlodgehotels.com
I: www.londonlodgehotels.com

Bedrooms: 4 double, 7 single, 3 family
Bathrooms: 9 en suite

CC: Amex, Delta, Diners, Mastercard, Switch, Visa

B&B per person per night:
S £33.00–£47.00
D £24.00–£29.50

OPEN All Year

Quiet, comfortable hotel, close to three underground stations. Midway central London and Heathrow. Colour TV, tea/coffee-making facilities, radio/alarm, most rooms en suite.

P €

LONDON W6

HOTEL ORLANDO

83 Shepherds Bush Road, Hammersmith, London W6 7LR
T: (020) 7603 4890
F: (020) 7603 4890
E: hotelorlando@btconnect.com
I: www.hotelorlando.co.uk

Bedrooms: 6 double, 4 single, 4 family
Bathrooms: 14 en suite

CC: Amex, Delta, Mastercard, Switch, Visa

B&B per person per night:
S £40.00–£48.00
D £26.00–£30.00

OPEN All Year

Italian family-run business for the last 22 years. Situated near Hammersmith tube station, ideal for easy connection to central London. Recently decorated.

€

LONDON WC1

CRESCENT HOTEL

49-50 Cartwright Gardens, Bloomsbury, London WC1H 9EL
T: (020) 7387 1515
F: (020) 7383 2054
E: General.Enquiries@CrescentHotelofLondon.com
I: www.CrescentHotelofLondon.com

Comfortable, elegant, family-run hotel in quiet Georgian crescent, with private garden square and tennis courts. All rooms have colour TV, tea/coffee tray and direct-dial telephone, most en suite. The individually prepared English breakfast will sustain you for the best part of the day.

Bedrooms: 5 double, 12 single, 10 family
Bathrooms: 18 en suite

CC: Delta, Mastercard, Switch, Visa

10% discount on stays of 3 nights, to include Sun and Mon (excl Christmas and New Year).

B&B per person per night:
S £45.00–£75.00
D £43.50–£45.00

OPEN All Year

GOWER HOUSE HOTEL

57 Gower Street, London WC1E 6HJ
T: (020) 7636 4685
F: (020) 7636 4685
E: info@gowerhousehotel.co.uk
I: www.gowerhousehotel.co.uk

Bedrooms: 7 double, 2 single, 4 family
Bathrooms: 6 en suite

CC: Mastercard, Switch, Visa

B&B per person per night:
S £40.00–£45.00
D £25.00–£35.00

OPEN All Year

Friendly bed and breakfast hotel within easy walking distance of the British Museum, shops, theatres and restaurants. Near Goodge Street underground station and Euston station.

LONDON WC1 continued

◆ **ST ATHANS HOTEL**

20 Tavistock Place, Russell Square, London WC1H 9RE
T: (020) 7837 9140
F: (020) 7833 8352
E: stathans@ukonline.co.uk
I: www.stathanshotel.com

Bedrooms: 28 double, 14 single, 6 family
Bathrooms: 8 en suite

CC: Amex, Diners, Mastercard, Visa

B&B per person per night:
S £38.00–£55.00
D £24.00–£32.50

OPEN All Year

Simple, small, clean, family-run hotel offering bed and breakfast.

OUTER LONDON
CROYDON *Tourist Information Centre Tel: (020) 8253 1009*

◆◆◆ **CROYDON FRIENDLY GUESTHOUSE**

16 St Peter's Road, Croydon CR0 1HD
T: (020) 8680 4428
E: admin@croydonhotel.com
I: www.croydonhotel.com

Bedrooms: 2 double, 5 single, 3 family
Bathrooms: 4 en suite

B&B per person per night:
S £30.00–£40.00
D £25.00–£30.00

OPEN All Year

Detached house with comfortable, well-appointed rooms, all with private facilities. Friendly, family atmosphere with ample, off-road parking. Perfect base for London or Croydon.

◆◆◆ **CROYDON HOTEL**

112 Lower Addiscombe Road, Croydon CR0 6AD
T: (020) 8656 7233
F: (020) 8655 0211
I: www.croydonhotel.co.uk

Bedrooms: 5 double, 1 single, 2 family
Bathrooms: 7 en suite

CC: Delta, Mastercard, Visa

B&B per person per night:
S £35.00–£50.00
D £27.50–£30.00

OPEN All Year

Close to central Croydon (route A222) and 10 minutes' walk from East Croydon station. Opposite shops and restaurants. Frequent direct trains to Victoria and Gatwick Airport.

QUALITY ASSURANCE SCHEME

For an explanation of the quality and facilities represented by the Diamonds please refer to the front of this guide. A more detailed explanation can be found in the information pages at the back.

CROYDON continued

WOODSTOCK HOTEL

30 Woodstock Road, Croydon CR0 1JR
T: (020) 8680 1489
F: (020) 8667 1229
E: woodstockhotel@croydon-surrey.fsworld.co.uk
I: www.woodstockhotel.co.uk

B&B per person per night:
S £40.80–£45.90
D £35.70

OPEN All Year

Located in a quiet residential area with well-appointed, good-sized rooms. Five minutes' walk to the town centre, public amenities, transport and East Croydon railway station. Frequent trains run into central London within 12 minutes and Gatwick Airport within 20 minutes.

Bedrooms: 2 double, 4 single, 2 family
Bathrooms: 2 en suite

CC: Amex, Delta, Mastercard, Switch, Visa

P €

HAMPTON

♦♦♦

RIVERINE

Taggs Island, Hampton Court Road, Hampton TW12 2HA
T: (020) 8979 2266
E: malcolm@feedtheducks.com
I: www.feedtheducks.com

Bedrooms: 3 double

B&B per person per night:
S £40.00–£60.00
D £25.00–£35.00

OPEN All Year

A Thames houseboat moored on Taggs Island which is just upstream from Hampton Court Palace. Easy access and private parking. Delightfully different.

P

HARROW

CRESCENT HOTEL

58-62 Welldon Crescent, Harrow HA1 1QR
T: (020) 8863 5491
F: (020) 8427 5965
E: jivraj@crsnthtl.demon.co.uk
I: www.crsnthtl.demon.co.uk

B&B per person per night:
S £35.00–£45.00
D £25.00–£30.00

OPEN All Year

Friendly, family-run hotel in the heart of Harrow. Convenient for Business Parks of Wembley, Heathrow and central London. Reasonable rates and personal service second to none. We will be happy to welcome you to your home away from home, allowing you to concentrate on the purpose of your travel, albeit business or pleasure.

Bedrooms: 12 double, 5 single, 10 family
Bathrooms: 18 en suite

CC: Amex, Delta, Diners, Mastercard, Switch, Visa

P €

HEATHROW AIRPORT

See under Hounslow

USE YOUR *i*s

There are more than 550 Tourist Information Centres throughout England offering friendly help with accommodation and holiday ideas as well as suggestions of places to visit and things to do. You'll find TIC addresses in the local Phone Book.

HOUNSLOW *Tourist Information Centre Tel: 0845 456 2929*

SHALIMAR HOTEL

215-221 Staines Road, Hounslow TW3 3JJ
T: (020) 8577 7070
F: (020) 8569 6789
E: shalimarhotel@aol.com
I: www.shalimarhotel.co.uk

B&B per person per night:
S Max £55.00
D £30.00–£32.50

OPEN All Year

Located in centre of Hounslow, close to underground, M4, M25, M3 and three miles from Heathrow. Fantastic shopping centre within walking distance. En suite rooms, colour TV, tea/coffee bar. Beautiful, illuminated large lawn and garden. TV lounge and bar.

Bedrooms: 15 double, 12 single, 6 family
Bathrooms: 33 en suite

CC: Amex, Delta, Diners, Mastercard, Switch, Visa

KINGSTON UPON THAMES *Tourist Information Centre Tel: (020) 8547 5592*

8 ST ALBANS ROAD

Kingston upon Thames KT2 5HQ
T: (020) 8549 5910

Bedrooms: 2 single
Bathrooms: 1 en suite, 1 private

B&B per person per night:
S Min £35.00

OPEN All Year

Near River Thames, gardens, town, station and Richmond Park. City 25 minutes. No smoking.

MORDEN

28 MONKLEIGH ROAD

Morden SM4 4EW
T: (020) 8542 5595

Bedrooms: 1 double, 1 single

B&B per person per night:
S £18.50–£19.00
D £18.50–£19.00

OPEN All Year

Clean and comfortable, family-run bed and breakfast. With easy access to main London attractions and Wimbledon tennis. Approximately 45 minutes to Heathrow or Gatwick.

RICHMOND *Tourist Information Centre Tel: (020) 8940 9125*

HOBART HALL HOTEL

43-47 Petersham Road, Richmond
TW10 6UL
T: (020) 8940 0435
F: (020) 8332 2996
E: hobarthall@aol.com
I: www.smoothhound.co.uk/hotels/hobarthall.html

B&B per person per night:
S £45.00–£65.00
D £45.00–£75.00

OPEN All Year

Built c1690. Past tenants include the Earl of Buckinghamshire and the Duke of Clarence (King William IV). Situated on the banks of the River Thames, but also in the historic town of Richmond, guests have the best of both worlds. Richmond has tubes and trains and is 15 minutes from Heathrow.

Bedrooms: 12 double, 10 single, 6 family
Bathrooms: 18 en suite, 3 private

CC: Amex, Delta, Diners, Mastercard, Switch, Visa

Subject to availability, weekend special deals recommended at great prices. Play golf, watch rugby, watch history unfold before your eyes.

GOLD & SILVER AWARDS

These exclusive VisitBritain awards are given to establishments achieving the highest levels of quality and service. Further information can be found at the front of the guide. An index to all accommodation achieving these awards are at the back of this guide.

RICHMOND continued

◆◆◆

IVY COTTAGE

Upper Ham Road, Ham Common, Richmond TW10 5LA
T: (020) 8940 8601
F: (020) 8940 3865
E: taylor@dbta.freeserve.co.uk
I: www.dbta.freeserve.co.uk

Bedrooms: 2 double, 1 single, 1 family
Bathrooms: 2 private

Evening meal available

B&B per person per night:
S £30.00–£40.00
D £23.00–£30.00

OPEN All Year

Charming, wisteria-clad Georgian home offering exceptional views over Ham Common. Period features dating from 1760. Large garden. Self-catering an option. Good bus route and parking.

◆◆◆

THE RED COW

59 Sheen Road, Richmond TW9 1YJ
T: (020) 8940 2511
F: (020) 8940 2581
E: tom@redcowpub.com
I: www.redcowpub.com

Bedrooms: 4 double
Bathrooms: 4 en suite

Evening meal available
CC: Delta, Mastercard, Switch, Visa

B&B per person per night:
S £60.00–£75.00
D £35.00–£45.00

OPEN All Year

Traditional Victorian inn retaining some lovely original features. Just a short walk from Richmond town centre, river, Royal parks and rail links to London.

P

TWICKENHAM *Tourist Information Centre Tel: (020) 8891 7272*

39 GRANGE AVENUE

Twickenham TW2 5TW
T: (020) 8894 1055
F: (020) 8893 3346
E: carole@fanfoliage.fsbusiness.co.uk

Bedrooms: 1 double
Bathrooms: 1 en suite

B&B per person per night:
S Min £50.00
D Min £25.00

OPEN All Year except Christmas

En suite, double room opening onto sunny patio. Situated in a quiet cul-de-sac with parking. Station three minutes' walk. Central London 30 minutes. Easy access to Kew, Hampton Court.

P €

WORCESTER PARK

THE GRAYE HOUSE

24 The Glebe, Worcester Park KT4 7PF
T: (020) 8330 1277
F: (020) 8255 7850
E: graye.house@virgin.net
I: www.s-h-systems.co.uk

Bedrooms: 4 double, 2 family
Bathrooms: 4 en suite

B&B per person per night:
S £35.00–£45.00
D £25.00–£27.50

OPEN All Year

A modern, comfortable townhouse which serves as a family home. Rooms are en suite. Close to stations and amenities. Annexe with four larger rooms also available.

P

AT-A-GLANCE SYMBOLS

Symbols at the end of each accommodation entry give useful information about services and facilities. A key to symbols can be found inside the back cover flap. Keep this open for easy reference.

2004 Where to Stay

The official and best selling guides,
offering the reassurance of quality assured accommodation

Hotels, Townhouses and Travel Accommodation in England 2004

£10.99

Guesthouses, Bed & Breakfast, Farmhouses, Inns and Campus Accommodation in England 2004

£11.99

Self-Catering Holiday Homes in England 2004

£10.99

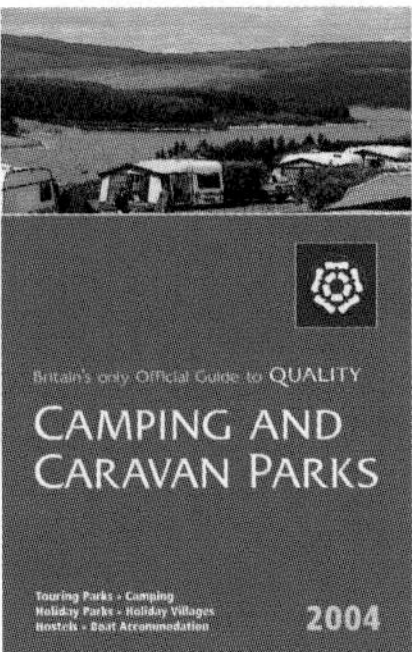

Camping & Caravan Parks, Hostels, Holiday Villages and Boat Accommodation in Britain 2004

£6.99

Somewhere Special in England 2004

£8.99

Look out also for:
SOMEWHERE SPECIAL IN ENGLAND 2004

Accommodation achieving the highest standards in facilities and quality of service - the perfect guide for the discerning traveller.

NOW ALSO FEATURING SELF-CATERING ACCOMMODATION

The guides include

• Accommodation entries packed with information • Full colour maps • Places to visit • Tourist Information Centres

INFORMATIVE • EASY TO USE • GREAT VALUE FOR MONEY

**From all good bookshops or by mail order from the:
VisitBritain Fulfilment Centre,
C/o Westex Ltd, 7 St Andrews Way, Devons Road, Bromley-by-Bow, London E3 3PA
Tel: 0870 606 7204 Fax: 020 8563 3289 Email: fulfilment@visitbritain.org**

Cumbria

Cumbria's dynamic and breathtaking landscapes, from the famous Lakes to the rugged mountains and fells, have inspired poets and artists for hundreds of years.

Classic sights
Hadrian's Wall – a reminder of Roman occupation
Lake Windermere – largest lake in England

Coast & country
Scafell Pike – England's highest mountain
Whitehaven – historic port

Literary links
William Wordsworth – the poet's homes: Wordsworth House, Dove Cottage and Rydal Mount
Beatrix Potter – her home, Hill Top; The Beatrix Potter Gallery; The World of Beatrix Potter attraction.

Distinctively different
The Gondola – sail Coniston Water aboard the opulent 1859 steam yacht Gondola
Cars of the Stars Museum – cars from TV and Film, including Chitty Chitty Bang Bang and the Batmobile

The County of Cumbria

For more information contact:
Cumbria Tourist Board
Ashleigh, Holly Road,
Windermere, Cumbria
LA23 2AQ

E: info@golakes.co.uk
www.golakes.co.uk
www.lakedistrictoutdoors.co.uk
www.lastminutelakedistrict.co.uk

Telephone enquiries -
T: (015394) 44444
F: (015394) 44041

1. Jetty on Derwent Water
2. Snowboarder, near Alston
3. Bluebells at Brantwood

Places to **Visit**

You will find hundreds of interesting places to visit during your stay, just some of which are listed in these pages. Contact any Tourist Information Centre in the region for more ideas on days out.

Awarded VisitBritain's 'Quality Assured Visitor Attraction' marque.

The Beacon
West Strand, Whitehaven
Tel: (01946) 592302
www.copelandbc.gov.uk
Award-winning attraction and museum superbly situated overlooking the Georgian harbour of Whitehaven, one of England's 'gem towns'.

Brantwood, Home of John Ruskin
Standish Street, Coniston
Tel: (015394) 41396 www.brantwood.org.uk
The most beautifully situated house in the Lake District, home of John Ruskin from 1872 until 1900. Discover the wealth of things to do at Brantwood.

Cars of the Stars Motor Museum
Keswick
Tel: (017687) 73757 www.carsofthestars.com
Features TV and film vehicles including the Batmobile, Chitty Chitty Bang Bang, the James Bond Aston Martin, Herbie, FAB 1 plus many other famous cars and motorcycles.

The Dock Museum
North Road, Barrow-in-Furness
Tel: (01229) 894444 www.dockmuseum.org.uk
Spectacular modern museum built over an original Victorian graving dock. Galleries include multi-media interactives, and impressive ship models.

Dove Cottage and Wordsworth Museum
Town End, Grasmere, Ambleside
Tel: (015394) 35544 www.wordsworth.org.uk
Wordsworth's home 1799-1808. Museum with manuscripts, farmhouse reconstruction, paintings and drawings. Special events throughout the year.

Furness Abbey (English Heritage)
Barrow-in-Furness
Tel: (01229) 823420
www.english heritage.org.uk
Ruins of 12thC Cistercian abbey, the 2nd wealthiest in England. Extensive remains include transepts, choir and west tower of church, canopied seats, arches, church.

Gleaston Water Mill
Gleaston, Ulverston
Tel: (01229) 869244 www.watermill.co.uk
A truly rural experience abounding with all things country - a water cornmill, artefacts, traditions, folklore and cooking and of course the acclaimed Pig's Whisper Store.

Heron Glass Ltd
The Lakes Glass Centre, Ulverston
Tel: (01229) 581121
www.herongiftware.com
Heron Glass Ltd and Cumbria Crystal, displays of making handblown glass giftware and lead crystal. Lighthouse cafe and restaurant.
A Gateway to Furness Exhibition.

Hill Top (National Trust)
Near Sawrey, Ambleside
Tel: (015394) 36269 www.nationaltrust.org.uk
Beatrix Potter wrote many of her popular Peter Rabbit stories and other books in this charming little house which still contains her own china and furniture.

Holker Hall and Gardens

Cark in Cartmel, Grange-over-Sands
Tel: (015395) 58328
www.holker-hall.co.uk
Including Victorian new wing, formal and woodland garden, deer park, motor museum, adventure playground, cafe and gift shop.

Jennings Brothers plc
The Castle Brewery, Cockermouth
Tel: 0845 1297185
www.jenningsbrewery.co.uk
Guided tours of Jennings traditional brewery and sampling of the ales in the Old Cooperage Bar.

K Village Outlet Centre
Lound Road, Kendal,
Tel: (01539) 732363 www.kvillage.co.uk
Famous named brands such as K-shoes, Van Heusen, Denby, National Trust Shop, Tog24 and Ponden Mill all at discounts. Open 7 days per week with full disabled access.

The Lake District Coast Aquarium Maryport
South Quay, Maryport,
Tel: (01900) 817760
www.lakedistrict-coastaquarium.co.uk
Purpose-built independent aquarium with over 35 displays. Largest collection of native marine species in Cumbria. Cafe and gift shop.

The Lake District Visitor Centre Brockhole
Windermere
Tel: (015394) 46601
www.lake-district.gov.uk
Brockhole is an Edwardian house on the shores of Windermere with extensive landscaped gardens, superb views, lake cruises, adventure playground, walks, events & activities.

Lakeland Sheep and Wool Centre
Egremont Road, Cockermouth
Tel: (01900) 822673
www.sheep-woolcentre.co.uk
Live farm show including cows, sheep, dogs and ducks, all displaying their working qualities. Large gift shop and licensed cafe/restaurant. All weather attraction.

Levens Hall
Levens, Kendal
Tel: (015395) 60321
www.levenshall.co.uk
Elizabethan home of the Bagot family incorporating 13thC pele tower, world-famous topiary gardens, Bellingham Buttery, Potting Shed gift shop, plant centre and play area.

Muncaster Castle, Gardens, Owl Centre and Meadow Vole Maze
Ravenglass
Tel: (01229) 717614 www.muncaster.co.uk
Muncaster Castle with the most beautifully situated Owl Centre in the world. See the birds fly, picnic in the gardens, visit the Pennington family home.

Ravenglass and Eskdale Railway
Ravenglass
Tel: (01229) 717171
www.ravenglass-railway.co.uk
England's oldest narrow-gauge railway runs for 7 miles (12km) through glorious scenery to the foot of England's highest hills. Most trains are steam hauled.

Rheged - The Village in the Hill
Redhills, Penrith
Tel: (01768) 868000 www.rheged.com
Award-winning Rheged is home to giant cinema screen showing 3 movies daily, the National Mountaineering Exhibition, speciality shops, indoor play area and restaurant.

The Rum Story
27 Lowther Street, Whitehaven
Tel: (01946) 592933 www.rumstory.co.uk
'The Rum Story' - the world's first exhibition depicting the unique story of the UK rum trade in the original Jefferson's wine merchant premises.

1. Lake Windermere
2. Esk River, Eskdale
3. Thirlmere Valley

Rydal Mount and Gardens
Rydal, Ambleside
Tel: (015394) 33002
www.wordsworthlakes.co.uk
Nestling between the majestic fells, Lake Windermere and Rydal Water, lies the 'most beloved' home of William Wordsworth from 1813-1850.

Senhouse Roman Museum
The Battery, Sea Brows, Maryport
Tel: (01900) 816168
www.senhousemuseum.co.uk
Once the headquarters of Hadrian's Coastal Defence system. UK's largest group of Roman altar stones and inscriptions on one site.

Sizergh Castle (National Trust)
Kendal
Tel: (015395) 60070 www.nationaltrust.org.uk
Strickland family home for 750 years, now National Trust owned, with 14thC pele tower, 15thC great hall, 16thC wings and Stuart connections. Rock garden, rose garden, daffodils.

South Lakes Wild Animal Park Ltd
Crossgates, Dalton-in-Furness
Tel: (01229) 466086
www.wildanimalpark.co.uk
Wild zoo park in over 17 acres (7ha) of grounds. Giraffe, rhino, tiger, lions, toilets, car/coach park. Miniature railway. Over 120 species of animals from all around the world.

South Tynedale Railway
Railway Station, Alston
Tel: (01434) 381696 www.strps.org.uk
Narrow gauge railway along part of the route of the former Alston to Haltwhistle branch line through South Tynedale with preserved steam and diesel engines.

Steam Yacht Gondola (National Trust)
Pier Cottage, Coniston
Tel: (015394) 41288
www.nationaltrust.org.uk/gondola
Victorian steam-powered vessel now National Trust owned and completely renovated with an opulently-upholstered saloon. Superb way to appreciate the beauty of Coniston Water.

Theatre by the Lake
Lakeside, Keswick
Tel: (017687) 74411
www.theatrebythelake.com
Offering a summer season of plays, a Christmas show and an Easter production. The theatre also hosts visiting drams, music, dance, talks and comedy.

Tullie House Museum and Art Gallery

Castle Street, Carlisle
Tel: (01228) 534781
www.tulliehouse.co.uk
Visit our Georgian Mansion housing our magnificent pre-Raphaelite collection, Victorian childhood gallery, 1689 fireplace and Jacobean oak staircase.

Ullswater 'Steamers'
The Pier House, Glenridding
Tel: (017684) 82229
www.ullswater-steamers.co.uk
Relax and enjoy a beautiful Ullswater cruise with walks and picnic areas. Boat services operating all year round.

Windermere Lake Cruises
Ambleside, Bowness-on-Windermere
Tel: (015395) 31188
www.windermere-lakecruises.co.uk
Steamers and launches sail daily throughout the year between Ambleside, Lakeside and Bowness. Seasonal sailings to Brockhole, L&H Steam Railway and Aquarium of the Lakes.

Windermere Steamboats & Museum
Rayrigg Road, Bowness-on-Windermere
Tel: (015394) 45565
www.steamboat.co.uk
A wealth of interest and information about life on bygone Windermere. Regular steam launch trips, vintage vessels and classic motorboats. Model boat pond, lakeside picnic area.

The World Famous Old Blacksmith's Shop Centre
Gretna Green
Tel: (01461) 338441 www.gretnagreen.com
The original Blacksmith's Shop museum and a shopping centre selling, cashmere and woollen knitwear, crystal and china. Taste local produce in the Old Smithy Restaurant.

Cumbria Tourist Board

Ashleigh, Holly Road, Windermere,
Cumbria L23 2AQ
T: (015394) 44444 F: (015394) 44041
E: info@golakes.co.uk
www.golakes.co.uk
www.lakedistrictoutdoors.co.uk
www.lastminutelakedistrict.co.uk

THE FOLLOWING PUBLICATIONS ARE AVAILABLE FROM THE CUMBRIA TOURIST BOARD

Cumbria – the Lake District Holidays & Breaks Guide (free) T: 08705 133059

The Flora and Fauna of Cumbria - the Lake District (free)

The Caravan and Camping Guide of Cumbria – the Lake District (free)

The Taste District (free) Food & drink guide
Events Listing (free)

Getting to Cumbria

BY ROAD: The M1/M6/M25/M40 provide a link with London and the South East and the M5/M6 provide access from the South West. The M6 links the Midlands and North West and the M62/M6 links the East of England and Yorkshire. Approximate journey time from London is 5 hours, from Manchester 1 hour 30 minutes.

BY RAIL: From London (Euston) to Oxenholme (Kendal) takes approximately 3 hours 30 minutes. From Oxenholme (connecting station for all main line trains) to Windermere takes approximately 20 minutes. From Carlisle to Barrow-in-Furness via the coastal route, with stops at many of the towns in between, takes approximately 2 hours. Trains from Edinburgh to Carlisle take approximately 2 hours 15 minutes. The historic Settle-Carlisle line also runs through the county bringing passengers from Yorkshire via the Eden Valley.

www.golakes.co.uk/transport.html

1. The village of Kikoswald, Eden Valley
2. Wordsworth House, Cockermouth

Where to stay in

Cumbria

All place names in the blue bands under which accommodation is listed, are shown on the maps at the front of this guide.

Symbols give useful information about services and facilities. Inside the back cover flap there's a key to these symbols which you can keep open for easy reference.

A complete listing of all the VisitBritain assessed accommodation covered by this guide appears at the back of this guide.

ALLONBY, Cumbria Map ref 5A2

SHIP HOTEL

Main Street, Allonby, Maryport
CA15 6QF
T: (01900) 881017
F: (01900) 881017
E: theshipallonby@aol.com

Bedrooms: 4 double, 3 twin, 1 single, 2 family, 1 suite
Bathrooms: 8 en suite, 1 private

Evening meal available
CC: Amex, Delta, Mastercard, Switch, Visa

B&B per person per night:
S £22.50–£27.50
D £27.50–£37.50

OPEN All Year

A 17thC Grade II Listed coaching inn where Charles Dickens and Wilkie Collins stayed in 1857. Situated on the Solway coastline, close to Lake District.

AMBLESIDE, Cumbria Map ref 5A3 *Tourist Information Centre Tel: (015394) 32582*

BROADVIEW

Low Fold, Lake Road, Ambleside
LA22 0DN
T: (015394) 32431
E: enquiries@broadviewguesthouse.co.uk
I: www.broadviewguesthouse.co.uk

Bedrooms: 3 double, 1 twin, 2 family
Bathrooms: 4 en suite, 1 private

CC: Amex, Delta, Mastercard, Switch, Visa

B&B per person per night:
S £20.00–£60.00
D £20.00–£30.00

OPEN All Year

Quality, friendly Victorian guesthouse near lake and village. Some rooms en suite with lovely views. Great breakfasts and a warm welcome. Non-smoking establishment.

IMPORTANT NOTE Information on accommodation listed in this guide has been supplied by the proprietors. As changes may occur you are advised to check details at the time of booking.

AMBLESIDE continued

◆◆◆◆

THE DOWER HOUSE
Wray Castle, Ambleside LA22 0JA
T: (015394) 33211
F: (015394) 33211

Bedrooms: 2 double, 1 twin
Bathrooms: 3 en suite

Evening meal available

The house overlooks Lake Windermere, three miles from Ambleside. Situated through the main gates of Wray Castle and up the drive. A bird-watcher's paradise.

5 P

B&B per person per night:
S £28.00–£29.00
D £27.00–£28.00

HB per person per night:
DY £40.50–£41.50

OPEN All Year except Christmas

◆◆◆◆

ELDER GROVE
Lake Road, Ambleside LA22 0DB
T: (015394) 32504
F: (015394) 32251
E: info@eldergrove.co.uk
I: www.eldergrove.co.uk

Bedrooms: 6 double, 1 twin, 2 single, 1 family
Bathrooms: 10 en suite

CC: Delta, Mastercard, Switch, Visa

Enjoy quality accommodation and service in our Victorian house. Pretty bedrooms with private bathrooms, relaxing bar and lounge, hearty Cumbrian breakfast, car park. Non-smoking.

P

B&B per person per night:
S £25.00–£33.00
D £25.00–£35.00

OPEN All Year except Christmas

◆◆◆

FERN COTTAGE
6 Waterhead Terrace, Ambleside LA22 0HA
T: (015394) 33007

Bedrooms: 2 double, 1 twin

Homely Lakeland-stone cottage on edge of village. Two minutes to head of Lake Windermere and steamer pier. Friendly atmosphere, hearty breakfast. Non-smoking.

4

B&B per person per night:
S £20.00–£24.00
D £17.00–£19.00

OPEN All Year except Christmas

◆◆◆

FERNDALE LODGE
Lake Road, Ambleside LA22 0DB
T: (015394) 32207
E: info@ferndalehotel.com
I: www.ferndalehotel.com

Bedrooms: 8 double, 1 twin, 1 single
Bathrooms: 10 en suite

CC: Amex, Delta, Mastercard, Switch, Visa

Small, family-run guesthouse in the heart of the Lakes, offering comfortable accommodation and traditional English fare. En suite bedrooms, some with views of the surrounding mountains and fells.

P

B&B per person per night:
S £28.00
D £26.00–£28.00

OPEN All Year except Christmas

◆◆◆◆

HOLMESHEAD FARM
Skelwith Fold, Ambleside LA22 0HU
T: (015394) 33048
E: info@holmesheadfarm.co.uk
I: www.amblesideonline.co.uk/adverts/holmeshead/main.html

Bedrooms: 1 double, 1 twin, 1 family
Bathrooms: 3 en suite

Evening meal available

300-acre livestock farm. Comfortable farmhouse nestling between Ambleside/Hawkshead in the hamlet of Skelwith Fold at the foot of the famous Langdale Valley.

P

B&B per person per night:
D £25.00–£30.00

OPEN All Year

◆◆◆◆
Silver Award

KENT HOUSE
Lake Road, Ambleside LA22 0AD
T: (015394) 33279
F: (015394) 33279
E: mail@kent-house.com
I: www.kent-house.com

Bedrooms: 3 double, 2 family
Bathrooms: 4 en suite, 1 private

CC: Delta, Mastercard, Switch, Visa

A Lakeland townhouse in the heart of Ambleside offering comfortable accommodation. In top 100 of the 'Best of the Best B&B'.

B&B per person per night:
S £40.00–£50.00
D £25.00–£35.00

OPEN All Year except Christmas

AMBLESIDE continued

◆◆◆

LYNDALE GUESTHOUSE
Low Fold, Lake Road, Ambleside LA22 0DN
T: (015394) 34244
E: alison@lyndale-guesthouse.co.uk
I: www.lyndale-guesthouse.co.uk

Bedrooms: 2 double, 2 single, 2 family
Bathrooms: 2 en suite

CC: Delta, Mastercard, Switch, Visa

B&B per person per night:
S £20.00–£25.00
D £23.00–£27.00

OPEN All Year

Victorian guesthouse providing spacious, comfortable accommodation. Hearty breakfasts and excellent services. Located midway between Lake Windermere and Ambleside. Great for touring and walking. Great value for money.

◆◆◆

LYNDHURST HOTEL
Wansfell Road, Ambleside LA22 0EG
T: (015394) 32421
F: (015394) 32421
E: lyndhurst@amblesidehotels.co.uk
I: www.amblesidehotels.co.uk

Bedrooms: 8 double
Bathrooms: 8 en suite

B&B per person per night:
S £30.00–£35.00
D £20.00–£30.50

OPEN All Year except Christmas

Small, attractive, Lakeland-stone hotel with private car park. Quietly situated for town and lake. Pretty rooms, delicious food – a delightful experience.

P

◆◆◆◆

THE OLD VICARAGE

Vicarage Road, Ambleside LA22 9DH
T: (015394) 33364
F: (015394) 34734
E: the.old.vicarage@kencomp.net
I: www.oldvicarageambleside.co.uk

B&B per person per night:
D £35.00–£50.00

OPEN All Year

Quietly situated in own grounds in heart of village. Car park. Pets welcome. Heated indoor swimming pool, sauna and hot tub. Quality accommodation with TV, video player, cd, clock-radio, hairdryer, mini fridge, controllable central heating, en suite bath/shower and wc. Some 4-posters, spa baths and some rooms on ground floor.

Bedrooms: 8 double, 2 family
Bathrooms: 10 en suite

CC: Delta, Mastercard, Switch, Visa

P

◆◆◆◆

RIVERSIDE HOTEL

Under Loughrigg, Rothay Bridge, Ambleside LA22 9LJ
T: (015394) 32395
F: (015394) 32440
E: info@riverside-at-ambleside.co.uk
I: www.riverside-at-ambleside.co.uk

B&B per person per night:
S £29.00–£40.00
D £29.00–£40.00

OPEN All Year except Christmas

Riverside is a beautiful and stylish Victorian country house and gardens, situated on the River Rothay on a quiet lane within 10 minutes' walk of the village. Riverside provides high-quality bed and breakfast and is ideally situated for easy access to all Lake District attractions.

Bedrooms: 3 double, 1 twin, 1 family
Bathrooms: 5 en suite

CC: Delta, Mastercard, Visa

Up to 10% discount for stays of 3 nights or more.

5 P

CREDIT CARD BOOKINGS If you book by telephone and are asked for your credit card number it is advisable to check the proprietor's policy should you cancel your reservation.

AMBLESIDE continued

TOCK HOW FARM
High Wray, Ambleside LA22 0JF
T: (015394) 36106
F: (015394) 36294
E: info@tock-how-farm.com
I: www.tock-how-farm.com

Bedrooms: 1 double, 1 twin, 1 family
Bathrooms: 3 en suite

CC: Amex, Mastercard, Switch, Visa

Traditional working farm set in a stunning location overlooking Lake Windermere and surrounding fells. All rooms en suite. Separate dining room and lounge with log fire.

B&B per person per night:
S £30.00–£40.00
D £23.00–£26.00

OPEN All Year except Christmas

WANSLEA GUEST HOUSE

Low Fold, Lake Road, Ambleside LA22 0DN
T: (015394) 33884
E: wanslea.guesthouse@virgin.net
I: www.wansleaguesthouse.co.uk

Just a short stroll from the centre of Ambleside and Lake Windermere, Wanslea is the ideal base for walking, cycling or a more relaxing break. We offer spacious, comfortable rooms (we plan to add more in November 2003), a good Cumbrian breakfast and friendly service. Families welcome. Pets by arrangement.

Bedrooms: 2 double, 1 single, 4 family
Bathrooms: 4 en suite

CC: Delta, Mastercard, Switch, Visa

4 nights for 3 Oct-Mar (excl school holidays, Christmas and New Year). Ring for other current promotions.

B&B per person per night:
S £25.00–£35.00
D £25.00–£32.00

APPLEBY-IN-WESTMORLAND, Cumbria Map ref 5B3 *Tourist Information Centre Tel: (017683) 51177*

BROOM HOUSE
Long Marton, Appleby-in-Westmorland CA16 6JP
T: (017683) 61318
F: (017683) 61318
E: sandra@bland01.freeserve.co.uk
I: www.broomhouseappleby.co.uk

Bedrooms: 1 double, 1 family
Bathrooms: 1 en suite

Former farmhouse set in open countryside in the beautiful Eden Valley, with views of the Pennines, easy access to A66 and M6, good home cooking, en suite facilities.

B&B per person per night:
S £21.00–£27.50
D £21.00–£27.50

HB per person per night:
DY £34.00–£45.00

BARROW-IN-FURNESS, Cumbria Map ref 5A3 *Tourist Information Centre Tel: (01229) 894784*

KING ALFRED HOTEL
Ocean Road, Walney Island, Barrow-in-Furness LA14 3DU
T: (01229) 474717
F: (01229) 476181
E: kingalfred@walney4.fsnet.co.uk
I: www.thekingalfred.co.uk

Bedrooms: 4 twin, 1 single, 1 family
Bathrooms: 6 en suite

Evening meal available
CC: Amex, Delta, Mastercard, Switch, Visa

Public house with sea views. Ample parking. Good food and drink served all day. Children welcome.

B&B per person per night:
S £30.00–£35.00
D £30.00–£35.00

OPEN All Year

BASSENTHWAITE, Cumbria Map ref 5A2

Silver Award

HIGH SIDE FARMHOUSE
Embleton, Cockermouth CA13 9TN
T: (017687) 76893
F: (017687) 76893
E: enquiries@highsidefarmhouse.co.uk
I: www.highsidefarmhouse.co.uk

Bedrooms: 1 double, 1 twin
Bathrooms: 2 en suite

17thC farmhouse in peaceful location with glorious views. Ideal base for touring. Sitting room with log fire. Home-cooked food. Relaxed and friendly atmosphere.

B&B per person per night:
S £30.00–£32.00
D £25.00–£27.00

OPEN All Year

HALF BOARD PRICES Half board prices are given per person, but in some cases these may be based on double/twin occupancy.

BASSENTHWAITE continued

LINK HOUSE

Bassenthwaite Lake, Cockermouth
CA13 9YD
T: (017687) 76291
F: (017687) 76670
E: info@link-house.co.uk
I: www.link-house.co.uk

B&B per person per night:
S £26.00–£32.50
D £28.00–£30.00

HB per person per night:
DY £41.00–£43.00

OPEN All Year

An interesting, inviting, late-Victorian house enjoying lovely views, set in rural location near Keswick and Cockermouth. This well-maintained house offers spotlessly clean and comfortable accommodation. Bedrooms of varying sizes are equipped with en suite showers or baths. A homely atmosphere is maintained by friendly, helpful hosts.

Bedrooms: 3 double, 2 twin, 3 single, 1 family
Bathrooms: 8 en suite, 1 private

Evening meal available
CC: Delta, Mastercard, Switch, Visa

Winter breaks – 3 nights' B&B, £75pp (excl Christmas, New Year and Public Holidays), from 1 Nov-1 Mar only. Bargain breaks – 2 nights' DB&B, £75pp (subject to availabilty).

BASSENTHWAITE LAKE, Cumbria Map ref 5A2

♦♦♦♦
Silver Award

LAKESIDE GUESTHOUSE

Dubwath, Bassenthwaite Lake CA13 9YD
T: (017687) 76358
E: info@lakesidebassenthwaite.co.uk
I: www.lakesidebassenthwaite.co.uk

B&B per person per night:
S £35.00–£40.00
D £29.00–£35.00

HB per person per night:
DY £46.00–£52.00

OPEN All Year except Christmas

Elegant, Edwardian house with private parking, superbly situated overlooking Bassenthwaite Lake and mountains. Oak-panelled entrance and immaculate (no-smoking), en suite accommodation, some with lake views. The accent is on fine cuisine at affordable prices, caringly prepared by experienced and qualified owner/chef. Enjoy our hospitality in tranquil surroundings.

Bedrooms: 5 double, 2 twin, 1 family
Bathrooms: 7 en suite, 1 private

Evening meal available
CC: Amex, Delta, Mastercard, Switch, Visa

Discounts for 4-night stays or longer. Mid-week winter breaks available.

BORROWDALE, Cumbria Map ref 5A3

HAZEL BANK COUNTRY HOUSE

Rosthwaite, Borrowdale, Keswick CA12 5XB
T: (017687) 77248
F: (017687) 77373
E: enquiries@hazelbankhotel.co.uk
I: www.hazelbankhotel.co.uk

HB per person per night:
DY £56.00–£79.50

OPEN All Year except Christmas

Award-winning, Victorian country house set in four-acre grounds. Peaceful location, superb views of central Lakeland Fells. Bedrooms all en suite. Rosette-standard cuisine using local produce. Puddings and sauces a speciality, vegetarians welcome. Ideal base for walking. No smokers. No pets. Self-catering cottage for two. Best in Cumbria 2001 and 2002. Finalist Best in England 2003.

Bedrooms: 6 double, 2 twin
Bathrooms: 8 en suite

Evening meal available
CC: Delta, Mastercard, Switch, Visa

Discounts available when bookings are made more than 3 months in advance of arrival.

BOWNESS-ON-SOLWAY, Cumbria Map ref 5A2

WALLSEND HOUSE

The Old Rectory, Church Lane, Bowness-on-Solway, Carlisle CA7 5AF
T: (016973) 51055
E: wallsend@btinternet.com
I: www.wallsend.net

B&B per person per night:
S £25.00–£28.00
D £22.00–£25.00

OPEN All Year except Christmas

Peaceful old rectory located in own wooded grounds at end of Hadrian's Wall on Solway coast, Area of Outstanding Natural Beauty. All rooms en suite. Picturesque village with local pub/restaurant 150 yards. Easy access to historic city of Carlisle, North Lakes and Scotland. Ideal for walkers and cyclists. Warm welcome, relaxing atmosphere.

Bedrooms: 2 double, 2 single, 1 family
Bathrooms: 5 en suite

Reductions for 3 nights or more.

4 P €

BRAITHWAITE, Cumbria Map ref 5A3

COLEDALE INN
Braithwaite, Keswick CA12 5TN
T: (017687) 78272
F: (017687) 78416
E: info@coledale-inn.com
I: www.coledale-inn.co.uk

Bedrooms: 6 double, 1 twin, 1 single, 4 family
Bathrooms: 12 en suite

Evening meal available
CC: Delta, Mastercard, Switch, Visa

B&B per person per night:
S £27.00–£32.00
D £27.00–£32.00

OPEN All Year

Victorian country-house hotel and Georgian inn, in a peaceful hillside position away from traffic, with superb mountain views. Families and pets welcome.

P

♦♦♦

MIDDLE RUDDINGS HOTEL
Braithwaite, Keswick CA12 5RY
T: (017687) 78436
F: (017687) 78438
E: info@middle-ruddings.com
I: www.middle-ruddings.co.uk

Bedrooms: 7 double, 3 twin, 2 single, 2 family
Bathrooms: 13 en suite

Evening meal available
CC: Delta, Mastercard, Switch, Visa

B&B per person per night:
S £27.00–£33.00
D £25.00–£32.00

OPEN All Year

Lakeland country hotel in two acres facing Skiddaw, with magnificent views all round. Pets and families most welcome.

P €

BRAMPTON, Cumbria Map ref 5B2

BLACKSMITHS ARMS HOTEL
Talkin, Brampton CA8 1LE
T: (01697) 73452
F: (01697) 73396
E: blacksmithsarmstalkin@yahoo.co.uk
I: www.blacksmithsarmstalkin.co.uk

Bedrooms: 3 double, 2 twin
Bathrooms: 5 en suite

Evening meal available
CC: Amex, Delta, Mastercard, Switch, Visa

B&B per person per night:
S £35.00
D £25.00

OPEN All Year

Country inn in scenic countryside 0.5 miles from Talkin Tarn. Walking, golf, pony-trekking, sailing, windsurfing, fishing, Hadrian's Wall and Lake District within easy reach.

P €

QUALITY ASSURANCE SCHEME

For an explanation of the quality and facilities represented by the Diamonds please refer to the front of this guide. A more detailed explanation can be found in the information pages at the back.

BRAMPTON continued

VALLUM BARN

Irthington, Carlisle CA6 4NN
T: (01697) 742478
E: vallumbarn@tinyworld.co.uk
I: www.vallumbarn.co.uk

B&B per person per night:
S £25.00–£27.00
D £20.00–£22.00

OPEN All Year except Christmas

Relax and unwind in our spacious converted barn, easily accessible from M6 and only five minutes' walk from country pub serving evening meals. Comfortable guest lounge with open fire, ground floor bedroom suitable for disabled guests, hospitality tray with homemade biscuits. Enjoy a good, hearty breakfast using local produce before exploring this lovely area.

Bedrooms: 2 family
Bathrooms: 2 en suite

Evening meal available

Discount for 3 nights or more.

P

CALDBECK, Cumbria Map ref 5A2

♦♦♦

THE BRIARS

Friar Row, Caldbeck, Wigton
CA7 8DS
T: (01697) 478633

Bedrooms: 1 double, 1 twin, 1 single
Bathrooms: 1 en suite

B&B per person per night:
S £25.00–£27.00
D £21.00–£22.00

OPEN All Year except Christmas

140-acre mixed farm. In lovely village of Caldbeck overlooking Caldbeck Fells. Ideal for touring Lakes and Scottish Borders. Right on Cumbria Way route.

P

♦♦♦♦
Silver Award

SWALEDALE WATCH

Whelpo, Caldbeck, Wigton CA7 8HQ
T: (01697) 478409
F: (01697) 478409
E: nan.savage@talk21.com
I: www.swaledale-watch.co.uk

B&B per person per night:
S £21.00–£25.00
D £19.00–£22.00

OPEN All Year except Christmas

A working farm outside picturesque Caldbeck. Enjoy great comfort, excellent food and a warm welcome amidst peaceful, unspoilt countryside. Central for touring, walking or discovering the rolling northern fells. A memorable walk into Caldbeck is through 'The Howk', a limestone gorge. Relax 'at home' with open fires – your happiness is our priority.

Bedrooms: 2 double, 1 twin, 1 family
Bathrooms: 4 en suite

Evening meal available

Honeymoon extras. Special nature walks. Badger-watching evenings.

P

CARLISLE, Cumbria Map ref 5A2 *Tourist Information Centre Tel: (01228) 625600*

♦♦♦♦

ABBERLEY HOUSE

33 Victoria Place, Carlisle CA1 1HP
T: (01228) 521645
E: stay@abberleyhouse.co.uk
I: www.abberleyhouse.co.uk

Bedrooms: 2 double, 2 twin, 3 single, 1 family
Bathrooms: 8 en suite

B&B per person per night:
S £25.00–£30.00
D £20.00–£25.00

OPEN All Year except Christmas

Family-run guesthouse in residential area of Carlisle, close to the city centre, River Eden and the golf course.

P

CORNERWAYS GUEST HOUSE

107 Warwick Road, Carlisle
CA1 1EA
T: (01228) 521733

Bedrooms: 1 double, 3 twin, 4 single, 2 family
Bathrooms: 4 en suite

B&B per person per night:
S £16.00–£18.00
D £16.00–£18.00

OPEN All Year except Christmas

Five minutes to rail and bus stations and city centre. M6 exit 43. Colour TV, central heating in all bedrooms. Tea and coffee facilities. Lounge, payphone.

P

CARTMEL, Cumbria Map ref 5A3

PRIOR'S YEAT

Aynsome Road, Cartmel, Grange-over-Sands LA11 6PR
T: (015395) 35178
E: priorsyeat@hotmail.com

B&B per person per night:
D £24.00–£28.00

OPEN All Year except Christmas

Edwardian house in historic village betwixt lakes and sea. Elegantly furnished with luxury, en suite bedrooms. Peaceful, relaxed and friendly.

Bedrooms: 2 double, 1 twin
Bathrooms: 2 en suite, 1 private

Short-break and weekly rates available.

10 P

CARTMEL FELL, Cumbria Map ref 5A3

♦♦♦♦

LIGHTWOOD COUNTRY GUESTHOUSE

Cartmel Fell, Grange-over-Sands LA11 6NP
T: (015395) 31454
F: (015395) 31454
E: enquiries@lightwoodguesthouse.com
I: www.lightwoodguesthouse.com

B&B per person per night:
S £35.00–£40.00
D £25.00–£32.00

HB per person per night:
DY £45.50–£50.00

OPEN All Year except Christmas

Built in 1656, Lightwood maintains original features and charm whilst offering modern home comforts. Warm hospitality and excellent home cooking with Italian inspiration. All diets catered for. Set in two acres of beautiful gardens. Great local walks, 2.5 miles from Lake Windermere. On-site, complementary therapies. A recipe for wellbeing and relaxation.

Bedrooms: 2 double, 2 twin, 2 family
Bathrooms: 6 en suite

Evening meal available
CC: Delta, Mastercard, Switch, Visa

Weekly rate from £25pp. 3-night break from £26pp. Mid-week Wellbeing breaks. Introduction to Aromatherapy courses. Italian evenings.

P

CONISTON, Cumbria Map ref 5A3

♦♦♦♦♦
Gold Award

CONISTON LODGE

Station Road, Coniston LA21 8HH
T: (015394) 41201
F: (015394) 41201
E: info@coniston-lodge.com
I: www.coniston-lodge.com

Bedrooms: 3 double, 3 twin
Bathrooms: 6 en suite

Evening meal available
CC: Amex, Delta, Mastercard, Switch, Visa

B&B per person per night:
S £41.00–£55.00
D £41.00–£49.50

OPEN All Year except Christmas

Small, family-run hotel in beautiful surroundings, offering superior accommodation and good home cooking. Non-smoking.

10 P

♦♦♦♦

OAKLANDS

Yewdale Road, Coniston LA21 8DX
T: (015394) 41245
F: (015394) 41245
E: judithzeke@oaklandsguesthouse.fsnet.co.uk
I: www.geocities.com/oaklandsguesthouse

Bedrooms: 3 double, 1 twin, 1 single
Bathrooms: 3 en suite, 1 private

B&B per person per night:
S £23.00–£25.00
D £23.00–£25.00

OPEN All Year except Christmas

Spacious 100-year-old Lakeland house, village location, mountain views. Quality breakfast, special diets, owner's personal attention. Parking. Non-smoking.

10 P €

ACCESSIBILITY

Look for the symbols which indicate National Accessible Scheme standards for hearing and visually impaired guests in addition to standards for guests with mobility impairment. You can find an index of all scheme participants at the back of this guide.

CONISTON continued

SUNNY BRAE COTTAGE

Haws Bank, Coniston LA21 8AR
T: (015394) 41654
F: (015394) 41532
E: sunnybraecottage@aol.com
I: www.sunnybraecottage.co.uk

B&B per person per night:
S £22.50–£35.00
D £20.00–£35.00

OPEN All Year

A traditional, whitewashed, 16thC cottage on the edge of Coniston Village with views of Coniston Old Man and fells. On the Cumbrian Way and close to Coniston Water. A friendly, family-run B&B. We serve traditional and vegetarian breakfasts. Well-behaved dogs are welcome.

Bedrooms: 2 double, 2 twin, 1 single
Bathrooms: 5 en suite

Evening meal available

3-night, mid-week breaks £20-£22.50pppn. 1 week's break £20-£22.50pppn.

♦♦♦♦♦

WHEELGATE COUNTRY GUESTHOUSE

Little Arrow, Coniston LA21 8AU
T: (015394) 41418
F: (015394) 41114
E: wheelgate@conistoncottages.co.uk
I: www.wheelgate.co.uk

B&B per person per night:
S £30.00–£35.00
D £26.00–£35.00

OPEN All Year except Christmas

A delightful, 17thC former farmhouse with a warm, relaxed atmosphere in a peaceful, rural location, close to the heart of Lakeland. Set in delightful, award-winning gardens, the house features attractive, individually designed bedrooms, cosy bar, oak-beamed lounge with log fire. Super breakfasts. Complimentary leisure club. The perfect Lakeland retreat.

Bedrooms: 3 double, 2 single
Bathrooms: 5 en suite

CC: Delta, Mastercard, Switch, Visa

Special mid-week and weekly rates available.

♦♦♦

WILSON ARMS

Torver, Coniston LA21 8BB
T: (015394) 41237
F: (015394) 41590

B&B per person per night:
S £30.00–£40.00
D £27.00–£30.00

OPEN All Year except Christmas

In the small village of Torver, 2.5 miles from Coniston. Ideal walking area. Well-stocked bar, log fire on cooler days. Good central location for touring the lakes. Meals prepared with local fresh produce. Surrounded by beautiful fells.

Bedrooms: 5 double, 1 single, 2 family
Bathrooms: 7 en suite, 1 private

Evening meal available
CC: Amex, Delta, Diners, Mastercard, Switch, Visa

Mid-week breaks of 2 or more nights from £25pp.

CROSTHWAITE, Cumbria Map ref 5A3

CROSTHWAITE HOUSE

Crosthwaite, Kendal LA8 8BP
T: (01539) 568264
F: (01539) 568264
E: bookings@crosthwaitehouse.co.uk
I: www.crosthwaitehouse.co.uk

Bedrooms: 5 double, 1 single
Bathrooms: 6 en suite

Evening meal available

B&B per person per night:
S £22.00–£25.00
D £22.00–£25.00

HB per person per night:
DY £37.00–£40.00

Mid-18thC building with unspoilt views of the Lyth and Winster valleys, five miles from Bowness and Kendal. Family atmosphere and home cooking. Self-catering cottages also available.

CROSTHWAITE continued

THE PUNCH BOWL INN

Crosthwaite, Kendal LA8 8HR
T: (015395) 68237
F: (015395) 68875
E: enquiries@punchbowl.fsnet.co.uk
I: www.punchbowl.fsnet.co.uk

Bedrooms: 3 double, 1 single
Bathrooms: 3 en suite

Evening meal available
CC: Delta, Mastercard, Switch, Visa

Coaching inn with three double bedrooms, all with private facilities. Adjacent to Crosthwaite Church in the Lyth Valley, five miles from Windermere and Kendal.

B&B per person per night:
S Max £37.50
D Max £30.00

HB per person per night:
DY £52.50–£60.00

OPEN All Year

DALTON-IN-FURNESS, Cumbria Map ref 5A3

BLACK DOG INN

Holmes Green, Broughton Road, Dalton-in-Furness LA15 8JP
T: (01229) 462561
F: (01229) 468036
E: jack@blackdoginn.freeserve.co.uk
I: www.blackdoginn.freeserve.co.uk

Bedrooms: 2 double
Bathrooms: 2 en suite

Evening meal available
CC: Mastercard, Switch, Visa

Old coaching inn, situated in rural surroundings, with log fires, cask ales and home-cooked food. No music, no games machines, no pool.

B&B per person per night:
S £17.50–£25.00
D £20.00–£30.00

HB per person per night:
DY £27.50–£37.50

OPEN All Year

♦♦♦♦
Silver Award

PARK COTTAGE

Dalton-in-Furness LA15 8JZ
T: (01229) 462850
E: nicholson.parkcottage@quista.net
I: www.parkcottagedalton.co.uk

Surrounded by woodland, farmland and overlooking Burlington Trout Lake, this 17thC country house is an idyllic retreat. 4 acres of grounds (woodland, lawns and garden) with prolific birdlife. Relax to sounds of bird-song in this award-winning guesthouse – comfortable accommodation in tranquil surroundings. Good home cooking.

Bedrooms: 2 double, 1 family
Bathrooms: 3 en suite

Evening meal available

20% reduction on 3 or more nights, Nov-mid-March.

B&B per person per night:
S £24.00–£28.00
D £18.50–£23.00

HB per person per night:
DY £28.50–£33.00

OPEN All Year

GILSLAND, Cumbria Map ref 5B2

THE HILL

Gilsland, Brampton CA8 7DA
T: (016977) 47214
F: (016977) 47214
E: info@hadrians-wallbedandbreakfast.com
I: www.hadrians-wallbedandbreakfast.com

A 16thC farmhouse in one acre of gardens with outstanding views over the Irthing Valley and Hadrian's Wall at Birdoswald Roman fort. Spacious guest bedrooms/lounge. A splendid situation in the greatest of comfort. Delicious home cooking. Ideal centre for walking/touring/stopover for Scotland. Ample parking.

Bedrooms: 1 double, 2 twin
Bathrooms: 2 en suite, 1 private

Evening meal available

Off-season discounts apply – please call for details.

B&B per person per night:
S £35.00–£37.50
D £25.00–£27.50

HB per person per night:
DY £40.00–£42.50

OPEN All Year

VISITOR ATTRACTIONS For ideas on places to visit refer to the introduction at the beginning of this section. Look out too for the VisitBritain Quality Assured Visitor Attraction signs.

GRANGE-OVER-SANDS, Cumbria Map ref 5A3 *Tourist Information Centre Tel: (015395) 34026*

ELTON HOTEL

Windermere Road, Grange-over-Sands
LA11 6EQ
T: (015395) 32838
F: (015395) 32838
E: chris.crane@btclick.com

B&B per person per night:
S £27.00–£30.00
D £20.00–£25.00

HB per person per night:
DY £32.00–£37.00

Our superior rooms have all the little extras to make them 'home from home', with the emphasis on clean and comfortable. Good home cooking a speciality. Two minutes on level to all amenities. Ground floor rooms. Ideal location for touring Lakes. Come and enjoy a warm welcome from Ian and Christine.

Bedrooms: 4 double, 2 twin, 1 family
Bathrooms: 5 en suite

Evening meal available

Silver Award

GREENACRES COUNTRY GUESTHOUSE

Lindale, Grange-over-Sands LA11 6LP
T: (015395) 34578
F: (015395) 34578
I: www.smoothhound.co.uk/hotels/greenacres.html

B&B per person per night:
S £30.00–£35.00
D £26.00–£30.00

OPEN All Year except Christmas

The very best of friendly hospitality, food and accommodation awaits you in our attractive guesthouse for non-smokers. Well-equipped bedrooms with spacious, en suite bathrooms, comfortable lounge with log fire, and conservatory too. An ideal base for Lakeland attractions, Morecambe Bay and the Yorkshire Dales.

Bedrooms: 2 double, 1 twin, 1 family
Bathrooms: 4 en suite

CC: Delta, Mastercard, Switch, Visa

GRASMERE, Cumbria Map ref 5A3 *Tourist Information Centre Tel: (015394) 35245*

♦♦♦

THE HARWOOD

Red Lion Square, Grasmere, Ambleside LA22 9SP
T: (015394) 35248
F: (015394) 35545
E: harwoodian@aol.com
I: www.harwoodhotel.co.uk

Bedrooms: 4 double, 1 twin, 2 single
Bathrooms: 3 en suite, 4 private

CC: Delta, Mastercard, Switch, Visa

B&B per person per night:
S £24.50–£35.50
D £24.50–£35.50

OPEN All Year except Christmas

Traditional Lakeland-stone Victorian hotel in the heart of Grasmere. Comfortable rooms all with private facilities and TV. Friendly and welcoming, speciality Cumbrian breakfasts.

♦♦♦

HOW FOOT LODGE

Town End, Grasmere, Ambleside LA22 9SQ
T: (015394) 35366
F: (015394) 35268
E: enquiries@howfoot.co.uk
I: www.howfoot.co.uk

Bedrooms: 4 double, 2 twin
Bathrooms: 6 en suite

CC: Delta, Mastercard, Switch, Visa

B&B per person per night:
D £28.00–£30.00

Beautiful Victorian house in peaceful surroundings. Spacious rooms with lovely views. Ideal base for walking and exploring the Lake District.

QUALITY ASSURANCE SCHEME

Diamond ratings and awards were correct at the time of going to press but are subject to change. Please check at the time of booking.

GRASMERE continued

♦♦♦♦ Silver Award

RIVERSDALE

White Bridge, Grasmere, Ambleside
LA22 9RQ
T: (015394) 35619
E: riversdalegrasmere@nascr.net
I: www.riversdalegrasmere.co.uk

B&B per person per night:
S £35.00–£50.00
D £25.00–£35.00

HB per person per night:
DY £40.00–£55.00

OPEN All Year

Quietly situated on the edge of the village, with the river in front and the fells behind, our comfortable house will give you the chance to relax and unwind. Catering exclusively for non-smokers we provide our guests with a warm welcome, well-equipped bedrooms and an extensive choice at breakfast.

Bedrooms: 2 double, 1 twin
Bathrooms: 3 en suite

Evening meal available

Please see our website or phone for details of special promotions, including Christmas and New Year breaks.

P

♦♦♦♦

SILVER LEA GUEST HOUSE

Easedale Road, Grasmere,
Ambleside LA22 9QE
T: (015394) 35657
F: (015394) 35657
I: www.silverlea.com

Bedrooms: 1 double, 1 twin, 2 suites
Bathrooms: 2 en suite

Evening meal available

B&B per person per night:
D £34.00–£40.00

HB per person per night:
DY £42.50–£48.50

Cosy, comfortable Lakeland-stone house close to village centre. Home cooking and a warm, welcoming atmosphere. Special breaks February to 1st April.

11 P

♦♦♦

TRAVELLERS REST

Grasmere, Ambleside LA22 9RR
T: (015394) 35604
F: (017687) 72309
E: stay@lakedistrictinns.co.uk
I: www.lakedistrictinns.co.uk

B&B per person per night:
S £25.00–£45.00
D £25.00–£45.00

OPEN All Year

Located on the outskirts of Grasmere village, this 16thC coaching inn is renowned for its food and hospitality. Cosy and welcoming, with real fires and real ales. Comfortable, en suite bedrooms offer wonderful views of the surrounding fells. An ideal base for exploring the area.

Bedrooms: 5 double
Bathrooms: 4 en suite, 1 private

Evening meal available
CC: Delta, Mastercard, Switch, Visa

Special mid-week winter breaks from £20pppn B&B. Christmas and New Year packages also available.

P

♦♦♦♦ Silver Award

WOODLAND CRAG COUNTRY HOUSE

How Head Lane, Grasmere, Ambleside
LA22 9SG
T: (015394) 35351
F: (015394) 35351
E: woodlandcrag@aol.com
I: www.woodlandcrag.com

B&B per person per night:
D £22.50–£35.00

OPEN All Year except Christmas

Traditional Lakeland-stone Victorian country house in quiet, secluded location, a short walk from village centre. Dove Cottage (William Wordsworth) 200 metres. Lovely lake and fell views. One acre woodland garden. Tastefully decorated rooms. Drying room. Enclosed parking. Vegetarians catered for. Ideal for touring. Many walks radiate from here.

Bedrooms: 3 double, 1 twin
Bathrooms: 4 en suite

CC: Delta, Mastercard, Switch, Visa

10% discount for 3 nights or more. 3 nights for the price of 2, 1 Nov-28 Feb.

12 P €

HAWKSHEAD, Cumbria Map ref 5A3

♦♦♦♦ Silver Award

BORWICK LODGE

Outgate, Ambleside LA22 0PU
T: (015394) 36332
F: (015394) 36332
E: borwicklodge@talk21.com
I: www.borwicklodge.com

A leafy driveway entices you to a rather special 17thC country house with panoramic lake and mountain views, quietly secluded in the heart of the Lakes. Beautiful en suite bedrooms include special occasions and romantic breaks with king-size 4-poster beds. Margaret and Malcolm MacFarlane welcome you to this most beautiful corner of England. Totally non-smoking.

Bedrooms: 5 double, 1 single
Bathrooms: 6 en suite

8 P €

B&B per person per night:
S Min £39.00
D £30.00–£39.00

OPEN All Year

♦♦♦♦

WALKER GROUND MANOR

Vicarage Lane, Hawkshead, Ambleside LA22 0PD
T: (015394) 36219
E: info@walkerground.co.uk
I: www.walkerground.co.uk

A 16thC traditional Lakeland house with extensive landscaped gardens. Full of charm and character, with many original features, it combines a high standard of accommodation with a relaxed and friendly family atmosphere. Walker Ground offers a quiet and relaxing experience. An ideal base for visiting the whole of South Lakeland.

Bedrooms: 1 double, 2 twin
Bathrooms: 3 en suite

Evening meal available

Autumn, Winter, Spring breaks available including long weekends – £75pppn. Mid-week breaks – £69pppn – both minimum of 3 nights.

V P

B&B per person per night:
D £25.00–£30.00

HB per person per night:
DY £40.00–£48.00

OPEN All Year except Christmas

KENDAL, Cumbria Map ref 5B3 *Tourist Information Centre Tel: (01539) 725758*

♦♦♦♦

BURROW HALL
Plantation Bridge, Kendal LA8 9JR
T: (01539) 821711
F: (01539) 821711
E: info@burrowhall.fsnet.co.uk
I: www.burrowhall.co.uk

Bedrooms: 2 double, 1 twin
Bathrooms: 3 en suite

CC: Mastercard, Visa

Tastefully furnished, 17thC Lakeland house enjoying modern-day comforts. Sits peacefully in idyllic South Lakeland countryside between Kendal and Windermere, on A591.

12 P

B&B per person per night:
S £25.00–£30.00
D £25.00–£50.00

OPEN All Year except Christmas

USE YOUR *i*s

There are more than 550 Tourist Information Centres throughout England offering friendly help with accommodation and holiday ideas as well as suggestions of places to visit and things to do. You'll find TIC addresses in the local Phone Book.

KENDAL continued

LAKELAND NATURAL VEGETARIAN GUESTHOUSE

Low Slack, Queens Road, Kendal LA9 4PH
T: (01539) 733011
F: (01539) 733011
E: relax@lakelandnatural.co.uk
I: www.lakelandnatural.co.uk

Unwind in our spacious Victorian home, with stunning views overlooking Kendal and the surrounding fells. Adjacent woodland walks and golf course. Only five minutes' walk from the town centre. Non-smoking. Safe, off-street parking. Children and dogs welcome. Brilliant breakfasts and imaginative evening meals using largely organic produce. Licensed.

Bedrooms: 1 double, 1 twin, 1 single, 1 family
Bathrooms: 4 en suite

Evening meal available
CC: Delta, Mastercard, Switch, Visa

B&B per person per night:
S £38.50–£39.50
D £32.75–£33.75

HB per person per night:
DY £49.35–£56.50

OPEN All Year

♦♦♦

UNION TAVERN

159 Stricklandgate, Kendal LA9 4RF
T: (01539) 724004
E: uniontavern@edirectory.co.uk
I: www.edirectory.co.uk/uniontavern

Bedrooms: 8 double, 2 family
Bathrooms: 10 en suite

Evening meal available
CC: Amex, Delta, Mastercard, Switch, Visa

B&B per person per night:
S Max £30.00
D Max £22.50

OPEN All Year

Newly refurbished family hotel on main Windermere A5284 road, close to market-town centre. Evening restaurant, live entertainment at weekends. Close to pay-and-play golf.

KESWICK, Cumbria Map ref 5A3 *Tourist Information Centre Tel: (017687) 72645*

Silver Award

ABACOURT HOUSE

26 Stanger Street, Keswick CA12 5JU
T: (017687) 72967
E: abacourt@btinternet.com
I: www.abacourt.co.uk

Bedrooms: 5 double
Bathrooms: 5 en suite

B&B per person per night:
D £24.00

OPEN All Year except Christmas

Victorian townhouse, lovingly restored to the highest of standards. Beautifully furnished, fully double glazed. Superior en suites in all bedrooms. Central, quiet, cosy and friendly. Brochure available.

♦♦♦♦

THE ANCHORAGE

14 Ambleside Road, Keswick CA12 4DL
T: (017687) 72813
E: anchorage.keswick@btopenworld.com
I: www.anchorage-keswick.co.uk

Bedrooms: 3 double, 1 single, 2 family
Bathrooms: 6 en suite

Evening meal available

B&B per person per night:
S £22.00–£26.00
D £22.00–£26.00

OPEN All Year except Christmas

Small guesthouse with friendly owners. All rooms en suite with tea/coffee-making facilities. Five minutes' walk to town centre, close to lake and parks. Private parking.

TOWN INDEX

This can be found at the back of the guide. If you know where you want to stay, the index will give you the page number listing accommodation in your chosen town, city or village.

KESWICK continued

AVONDALE GUEST HOUSE

20 Southey Street, Keswick CA12 4EF
T: (017687) 72735
F: (017687) 75431
E: enquiries@avondaleguesthouse.com
I: www.avondaleguesthouse.com

High-quality Victorian guesthouse with well-appointed en suite rooms. Close to town centre, theatre, lake and parks. Excellent English and vegetarian breakfasts. In our comfortable guest lounge you can just relax and chat to fellow guests or read from the choice of books and magazines. Non-smokers only please.

Bedrooms: 4 double, 1 twin, 1 single
Bathrooms: 6 en suite

CC: Delta, Mastercard, Switch, Visa

Weekly B&B rate £159.

B&B per person per night:
S £24.00–£27.00
D £24.00–£25.50

OPEN All Year except Christmas

BADGERS WOOD

30 Stanger Street, Keswick CA12 5JU
T: (017687) 72621
E: enquiries@badgers-wood.co.uk
I: www.badgers-wood.co.uk

Spacious, friendly guesthouse with high standards of housekeeping. Comfortable, attractive rooms, with views of our local hills and fells. All are en suite, with soft towels and white cotton sheets. Ideally situated for walking and sightseeing. Our Welcome Host and Heartbeat Awards assure you of our ongoing commitment to your holiday comfort and enjoyment.

Bedrooms: 3 double, 1 twin, 1 single
Bathrooms: 5 en suite

B&B per person per night:
S £26.00
D £25.00

BIRKRIGG FARM

Newlands, Keswick CA12 5TS
T: (017687) 78278

Bedrooms: 2 double, 1 single, 1 family

100-acre mixed farm. Pleasantly and peacefully located in the lovely Newlands Valley, amongst beautiful mountain scenery. Five miles from Keswick, between Braithwaite and Buttermere.

B&B per person per night:
S £18.00–£22.00
D £18.00–£22.00

GLENCOE GUEST HOUSE

21 Helvellyn Street, Keswick CA12 4EN
T: (017687) 71016
E: enquiries@glencoeguesthouse.co.uk
I: www.glencoeguesthouse.co.uk

Bedrooms: 3 double, 1 twin, 1 single, 1 family
Bathrooms: 4 en suite

Evening meal available

Victorian townhouse decorated to high standards, spacious rooms. Quiet, yet conveniently situated for town and all amenities. Friendly, warm welcome. Excellent breakfasts and service guaranteed.

B&B per person per night:
S £19.00–£25.00
D £19.00–£25.00

OPEN All Year

GOLD & SILVER AWARDS

These exclusive VisitBritain awards are given to establishments achieving the highest levels of quality and service. Further information can be found at the front of the guide. An index to all accommodation achieving these awards are at the back of this guide.

KESWICK continued

GREYSTONES HOTEL

Ambleside Road, Keswick CA12 4DP
T: (017687) 73108
E: greystones@keslakes.freeserve.co.uk
I: www.greystones.tv

B&B per person per night:
S £23.00–£28.00
D £23.00–£28.00

OPEN All Year except Christmas

Greystones enjoys an enviable, tranquil location with splendid mountain views, yet the hotel is only a short walk from Lake Derwentwater and the historic Market Square with its restaurants, traditional pubs and craft shops. The accommodation is stylish and comfortable. Private car park.

Bedrooms: 5 double, 2 twin, 1 single
Bathrooms: 7 en suite, 1 private

CC: Mastercard, Visa

Mid-week special rates available.

10 **P**

♦♦♦♦

HAZELDENE HOTEL

The Heads, Keswick CA12 5ER
T: (017687) 72106
F: (017687) 75435
E: info@hazeldene-hotel.co.uk
I: www.hazeldene-hotel.co.uk

B&B per person per night:
S £25.00–£40.00
D £25.00–£50.00

At Hazeldene Hotel our aim is simple: to provide our guests with exceptional quality and value accommodation in an outstanding location. Large and well-furnished en suite bedrooms, excellent food and a peaceful, relaxed atmosphere combine to make Hazeldene Hotel a perfect haven for your visit to the Lake District.

Bedrooms: 10 double, 3 twin, 1 single, 3 family
Bathrooms: 17 en suite

CC: Delta, Mastercard, Switch, Visa

P

♦♦♦♦

HUNTERS WAY GUEST HOUSE

4 Eskin Street, Keswick CA12 4DH
T: (017687) 72324
F: (017687) 75459

Bedrooms: 2 double, 1 twin, 2 single, 1 family
Bathrooms: 4 en suite

Evening meal available
CC: Delta, Mastercard, Switch, Visa

Victorian guesthouse, warm and friendly welcome. Five minutes' walk from town centre, ten minutes' walk from Derwentwater and theatre. Non-smoking.

B&B per person per night:
S £19.00–£20.00
D £23.00–£24.00

HB per person per night:
DY £28.00–£35.00

OPEN All Year

♦♦♦♦

LATRIGG HOUSE

St Herbert Street, Keswick CA12 4DF
T: (017687) 73068
F: (017687) 72801
E: info@latrigghouse.com
I: www.latrigghouse.com

B&B per person per night:
S £25.00–£28.00
D £25.00–£28.00

OPEN All Year except Christmas

Annie and Ian promise you a warm and friendly welcome when you stay at our very comfortable, quiet guesthouse. Relax, make yourself at home and enjoy an excellent fresh breakfast to set you up for the day.

Bedrooms: 3 double, 1 twin, 2 single
Bathrooms: 6 en suite

CC: Amex, Delta, Mastercard, Switch, Visa

P €

SYMBOLS The symbols in each entry give information about services and facilities. A key to these symbols appears at the back of this guide.

KESWICK continued

LINCOLN GUEST HOUSE

23 Stanger Street, Keswick
CA12 5JX
T: (017687) 72597
F: (017687) 73014
E: joan@lincoln-guesthouse.fsnet.co.uk
I: www.lincoln-guesthouse.fsnet.co.uk

Bedrooms: 3 double, 2 single, 2 family
Bathrooms: 2 en suite

B&B per person per night:
S £19.00
D £19.00–£25.00

OPEN All Year

Situated in a quiet cul-de-sac near town centre and bus station. Private parking. Excellent breakfast, homemade Cumberland sausage. Magnificent views from bedrooms.

P

LITTLETOWN FARM

Newlands, Keswick CA12 5TU
T: (017687) 78353
F: (017687) 78437
I: www.littletownfarm.co.uk

Bedrooms: 6 double, 1 single, 2 family
Bathrooms: 6 en suite

Evening meal available
CC: Mastercard, Visa

B&B per person per night:
S £30.00–£35.00
D £30.00–£35.00

HB per person per night:
DY £43.00–£47.00

150-acre mixed farm in the beautiful, unspoilt Newlands Valley. Comfortable residents' lounge, dining room and cosy bar. Traditional 4-course dinner six nights a week.

P

LYNWOOD HOUSE

35 Helvellyn Street, Keswick CA12 4EP
T: (017687) 72398
E: info@lynwoodhouse.net
I: www.lynwoodhouse.net

B&B per person per night:
S £31.00–£33.00
D £21.00–£23.00

OPEN All Year except Christmas

Situated in a quiet, residential area, our family-run Victorian guesthouse is a 5-minute stroll from Keswick town centre. En suite double room includes a single futon bed. Standard double room has exclusive use of a private bathroom. Breakfast menu includes traditional, vegetarian and organic options. Welcome Host holder.

Bedrooms: 2 double
Bathrooms: 1 en suite, 1 private

3

SANDON GUESTHOUSE

13 Southey Street, Keswick
CA12 4EG
T: (017687) 73648
E: enquiries@sandonguesthouse.com
I: www.sandonguesthouse.com

Bedrooms: 2 double, 1 twin, 2 single, 1 family
Bathrooms: 4 en suite

Evening meal available

B&B per person per night:
S £23.00–£24.00
D £23.00–£24.00

OPEN All Year except Christmas

Charming Lakeland-stone Victorian guesthouse, conveniently situated for town, theatre or lake. Friendly, comfortable accommodation. Ideal base for walking or cycling holidays. Superb English breakfast.

4

CHECK THE MAPS

The colour maps at the front of this guide show all the cities, towns and villages for which you will find accommodation entries. Refer to the town index to find the page on which they are listed.

KESWICK continued

SEYMOUR HOUSE

36 Lake Road, Keswick CA12 5DQ
T: (017687) 72764
F: (017687) 71289
E: andy042195@aol.com
I: www.seymour-house.com

B&B per person per night:
S £25.00–£55.00
D £25.00–£30.00

HB per person per night:
DY £35.00–£45.00

OPEN All Year

This is the place to stay. A warm welcome is assured every visit, breakfast is great, the rooms comfortable and the location hard to beat – quiet, yet in the heart of the town, close to Derwentwater, 'queen of the Lakes'. Talk Andy into cooking dinner and you're in for a treat.

Bedrooms: 3 double, 1 single, 6 family
Bathrooms: 4 en suite

CC: Delta, Diners, Mastercard, Switch, Visa

6 nights' room only £99, Sun-Fri, Feb-Jun. See website for other promotions.

◆◆◆◆

SUNNYSIDE GUEST HOUSE

25 Southey Street, Keswick CA12 4EF
T: (017687) 72446
E: enquiries@sunnysideguesthouse.com
I: www.sunnysideguesthouse.com

Bedrooms: 4 double, 1 twin, 1 single, 1 family
Bathrooms: 5 en suite, 2 private

CC: Amex, Delta, Mastercard, Switch, Visa

B&B per person per night:
S £27.00
D £23.00–£27.00

OPEN All Year

A comfortable Victorian house providing well-equipped and tastefully furnished rooms, most being en suite. Relaxing guest lounge. Central location. Parking for 8 cars. Non-smoking throughout.

◆◆◆◆

WATENDLATH GUEST HOUSE

15 Acorn Street, Keswick CA12 4EA
T: (017687) 74165
F: (017687) 74165
E: linda@watendlathguesthouse.co.uk
I: www.watendlathguesthouse.co.uk

Bedrooms: 2 double, 2 family
Bathrooms: 4 en suite

B&B per person per night:
D £20.00–£25.00

Within easy walking distance of the lake, hills and town centre. We offer a warm and friendly welcome and traditional English breakfast.

KIRKBY LONSDALE, Cumbria Map ref 5B3 *Tourist Information Centre Tel: (015242) 71437*

◆◆

THE COPPER KETTLE

3-5 Market Street, Kirkby Lonsdale, Carnforth LA6 2AU
T: (015242) 71714
F: (015242) 71714

Bedrooms: 4 double, 1 twin
Bathrooms: 4 en suite

Evening meal available
CC: Amex, Delta, Diners, Mastercard, Switch, Visa

B&B per person per night:
S £18.00–£23.50
D £18.00–£21.50

HB per person per night:
DY £25.00–£30.00

OPEN All Year

Part of an old manor house, built in 1610, on the border between the Yorkshire Dales and the Lakes.

◆◆◆

TOSSBECK FARM

Middleton, Kirkby Lonsdale, Carnforth LA6 2LZ
T: (015242) 76214
E: postmaster@tossbeck.f9.co.uk
I: www.tossbeck.co.uk

Bedrooms: 1 double, 1 family
Bathrooms: 1 en suite, 1 private

B&B per person per night:
S £20.00–£25.00
D £19.00–£22.00

OPEN All Year except Christmas

A warm welcome awaits you at Tossbeck, a working farm situated in the quiet, unspoilt Lune Valley. An ideal touring base for Lakes and Dales.

PRICES
Please check prices and other details at the time of booking.

KIRKBY STEPHEN, Cumbria Map ref 5B3 *Tourist Information Centre Tel: (017683) 71199*

ING HILL LODGE

Mallerstang, Kirkby Stephen CA17 4JT
T: (017683) 71153
F: (017683) 72710
E: inghill@fsbdial.co.uk
I: www.ing-hill-lodge.co.uk

Unwind in peace and comfort at this small Georgian house in Mallerstang, a little-known Dale on the fringe of the National Park. Superb views, peace and quiet. Comfortable en suite bedrooms with TV. Lounge with books, maps and open fire. Central heating throughout for your comfort.

Bedrooms: 3 double
Bathrooms: 3 en suite

B&B per person per night:
S £25.00–£30.00
D £20.00–£25.00

◆◆◆◆

RIDDLESAY FARM

Soulby, Kirkby Stephen CA17 4PX
T: (017683) 71474
F: (017683) 71483
E: mrarmstrong@btinternet.com

Bedrooms: 1 double, 1 twin
Bathrooms: 2 en suite

Evening meal available

Warm and friendly farmhouse in the Eden Valley, one mile north of Kirkby Stephen (A66) on the A685. Double and twin room, both en suite, TV, tea/coffee-making facilities, hairdryer, radio, decorated to high standard. Enjoy a hearty breakfast to start your day. Dog-friendly kennels. Ideal for Pennines and The Lake District.

B&B per person per night:
S £22.00–£25.00
D £20.00–£22.00

HB per person per night:
DY Min £34.00

OPEN All Year except Christmas

WEST VIEW

Ravenstonedale, Kirkby Stephen CA17 4NG
T: (015396) 23415
E: enquiries@westview-cumbria.co.uk
I: www.enquiries@westview-cumbria.co.uk

Westview is a 16thC farmhouse overlooking the village green in the unspoiled village of Ravenstonedale. There are two pubs, three churches and a small golf course all within minutes of Westview, also an excellent walking area. Westview is an ideal base for touring the Lakes, Eden Valley and Yorkshire Dales. Ample parking.

Bedrooms: 2 double, 1 twin
Bathrooms: 2 en suite, 1 private

Evening meal available

B&B per person per night:
S £27.00–£30.00
D £22.00–£25.00

HB per person per night:
DY £32.00–£35.00

OPEN All Year except Christmas

MUNGRISDALE, Cumbria Map ref 5A2

NEAR HOWE HOTEL

Mungrisdale, Penrith CA11 0SH
T: (017687) 79678
F: (017687) 79462
E: nearhowe@btopenworld.com
I: www.nearhowe.co.uk

Farmhouse in quiet surroundings within easy reach of all lakes. Good walking. Homely hotel offering good home-cooked food and bar. Ideal stop-over for trips to Scotland.

Bedrooms: 3 double, 1 twin, 3 family
Bathrooms: 5 en suite

Evening meal available

B&B per person per night:
S £25.00–£30.00
D £20.00–£25.00

HB per person per night:
DY £30.00–£35.00

PENRITH, Cumbria Map ref 5B2 *Tourist Information Centre Tel: (01768) 867466*

♦♦♦♦

GLENDALE GUEST HOUSE

4 Portland Place, Penrith CA11 7QN
T: (01768) 862579
F: (01768) 867934
E: glendale@lineone.net
I: www.glendaleguesthouse.net

Julie, Mike and Gabriella invite you to enjoy a relaxing break in this family-run guesthouse set in a Victorian townhouse overlooking pleasant gardens. Built in the 1860s, it is a property of considerable charm which we hope provides a homely atmosphere. Children and pets are especially welcome.

Bedrooms: 2 double, 1 single, 4 family
Bathrooms: 6 en suite, 1 private

CC: Delta, Mastercard, Switch, Visa

B&B per person per night:
S £30.00–£36.00
D £20.00–£25.00

OPEN All Year except Christmas

♦♦♦♦

HORNBY HALL COUNTRY GUEST HOUSE

Brougham, Penrith CA10 2AR
T: (01768) 891114
F: (01768) 891114
E: enquire@hornbyhall.co.uk
I: www.hornbyhall.co.uk

You will receive a warm welcome to this 16thC farmhouse. It is situated in open farmland yet only four miles from the M6. Fresh flowers, log fires in winter and full of antiques. Home-cooked local produce, generous breakfast. Easy reach of Lakes and Yorkshire. Private fishing available on River Eamont.

Bedrooms: 2 double, 4 twin, 1 family
Bathrooms: 4 en suite, 2 private

Evening meal available
CC: Amex, Delta, Mastercard, Switch, Visa

B&B per person per night:
S £25.00–£37.00
D £25.00–£40.00

HB per person per night:
DY £44.00–£61.00

OPEN All Year

♦♦♦

LITTLE BLENCOWE FARM
Blencow, Penrith CA11 0DG
T: (017684) 83338
F: (017684) 83054
E: bart.fawcett@ukgateway.net

Bedrooms: 2 double
Bathrooms: 2 private

Evening meal available

Friendly, comfortable accommodation in 18thC, Grade III Listed house. All bedrooms have TV and hostess tray. Situated on a farm with pedigree Ayrshire cows and sheep.

B&B per person per night:
S £20.00–£25.00
D £18.00–£22.00

OPEN All Year except Christmas

♦♦♦♦♦
Silver Award

THE OLD SCHOOL

Newbiggin, Stainton, Penrith CA11 0HT
T: (017684) 83709
F: (017684) 83709
E: info@theold-school.com
I: www.theold-school.com

A refurbished Victorian school house built in 1866. Now offers en suite rooms, some with baths, queen- and king-sized beds, and furnished to a very high standard. We serve a hearty and extensive breakfast menu with homemade bread and home-grown tomatoes when in season.

Bedrooms: 1 double, 1 twin, 1 single
Bathrooms: 3 en suite

Evening meal available
CC: Delta, Mastercard, Switch, Visa

B&B per person per night:
S £35.00–£41.00
D £27.50–£30.00

HB per person per night:
DY £45.50–£58.00

PENRITH continued

ROUNDTHORN COUNTRY HOUSE

Beacon Edge, Penrith CA11 8SJ
T: (01768) 863952
F: (01768) 864100
E: enquiries@roundthorn.co.uk
I: www.roundthorn.co.uk

Grade II Listed Georgian mansion, set in landscaped grounds, from which there are panoramic views of the Eden Valley, Pennines and Lakeland fells. All rooms are en suite and have TV and tea/coffee-making facilities. The house is fully licensed and rates include a hearty Cumbrian breakfast.

Bedrooms: 7 double, 3 family
Bathrooms: 10 en suite

Evening meal available
CC: Amex, Delta, Diners, Mastercard, Switch, Visa

B&B per person per night:
S £47.00–£52.00
D £31.50–£36.00

OPEN All Year except Christmas

ST BEES, Cumbria Map ref 5A3

Silver Award

FLEATHAM HOUSE

High House Road, St Bees CA27 0BX
T: (019468) 22341
F: (019468) 20862
E: fleathamhouse@aol.com
I: www.fleathamhouse.com

Victorian country house set in seven acres of secluded garden overlooking St Bees Head and Solway Firth. An ideal base for exploring the Western Lakes. Fleatham House offers a very personal service in a peaceful setting. All rooms are spacious and en suite.

Bedrooms: 2 double, 1 twin, 3 single
Bathrooms: 6 en suite

Evening meal available
CC: Amex, Mastercard, Switch, Visa

Weekend rates available.

B&B per person per night:
S £35.00–£49.50
D £35.00–£65.00

HB per person per night:
DY £55.00–£85.00

OPEN All Year

♦♦♦

STONE HOUSE FARM

133 Main Street, St Bees CA27 0DE
T: (019468) 22224
F: (019468) 24933
E: csmith.stonehouse@btopenworld.com
I: www.stonehousefarm.net

Bedrooms: 3 double, 1 single, 3 family
Bathrooms: 7 en suite

50-acre livestock farm. Modernised, Georgian, Listed farmhouse, conveniently and attractively situated next to station, shops and hotels. Start of Coast-to-Coast Walk. Golf course, long-stay car park.

B&B per person per night:
S £22.00–£27.00
D £22.00

OPEN All Year except Christmas

SAWREY, Cumbria Map ref 5A3

BUCKLE YEAT GUEST HOUSE

Sawrey, Ambleside LA22 0LF
T: (015394) 36446
E: info@buckle-yeat.co.uk
I: www.buckle-yeat.co.uk

Bedrooms: 3 double, 2 twin, 1 single, 1 family
Bathrooms: 6 en suite, 1 private

CC: Amex, Delta, Mastercard, Switch, Visa

17thC oak-beamed cottage, famous for its connections with Beatrix Potter, provides a warm, friendly and centrally located base, and excellent value for money.

B&B per person per night:
S £30.00–£32.50
D £30.00–£32.50

OPEN All Year except Christmas

TOWER BANK ARMS

Near Sawrey, Ambleside LA22 0LF
T: (015394) 36334
F: (015394) 36448
E: sales@towerbankarms.fsnet.co.uk

Bedrooms: 3 double
Bathrooms: 3 en suite

Evening meal available
CC: Amex, Delta, Mastercard, Switch, Visa

Next door to Hill Top, the former home of Beatrix Potter. It features in the tale of Jemima Puddleduck.

B&B per person per night:
S £38.00–£40.00
D £27.50–£29.00

OPEN All Year except Christmas

SAWREY continued

◆◆◆◆◆ Gold Award

WEST VALE COUNTRY HOUSE AND RESTAURANT

Far Sawrey, Hawkshead, Ambleside LA22 0LQ
T: (015394) 42817
F: (015394) 45302
E: enquiries@westvalecountryhouse.co.uk
I: www.westvalecountryhouse.co.uk

An elegant, Victorian, stone-built house, renovated to a high standard and complemented by fine antique furnishings and prints. This, together with superb fell views from all the spacious en suite bedrooms and excellent food and wine, makes West Vale an ideal base to relax or explore the Lake District.

Bedrooms: 7 double, 1 twin
Bathrooms: 6 en suite, 2 private

Evening meal available
CC: Amex, Delta, Mastercard, Switch, Visa

Take advantage of our free fishing weekend. Hire a small country house for the weekend. Winter-warmer weekends.

12 P

B&B per person per night:
S £50.00–£62.00
D £39.00–£49.00

HB per person per night:
DY £64.00–£74.00

OPEN All Year except Christmas

TROUTBECK, Cumbria Map ref 5A2

◆◆◆

GILL HEAD FARM

Troutbeck, Penrith CA11 0ST
T: (017687) 79652
F: (017687) 79130
E: enquiries@gillheadfarm.co.uk
I: www.gillheadfarm.co.uk

Stay in our lovely 17thC farmhouse set against the dramatic backdrop of the northern fells, where a warm welcome and traditional hospitality is assured. Relax in the comfort of our attractive, en suite rooms, log fires in our cosy oak-beamed sitting room and, of course, lots of delicious home cooking!

Bedrooms: 3 double, 2 twin
Bathrooms: 5 en suite

Evening meal available

Discounts for group bookings. Seasonal short breaks.

P

B&B per person per night:
S £22.00
D £22.00

TROUTBECK, Cumbria Map ref 5A3

◆◆◆◆

HIGH FOLD FARM

Troutbeck, Windermere LA23 1PG
T: (015394) 32200
E: enquiries@highfoldfarm.co.uk
I: www.highfoldfarm.co.uk

Bedrooms: 3 double, 2 family
Bathrooms: 4 en suite, 1 private

Unbeatable views over the Troutbeck Valley. Well-furnished, comfortable accommodation of the highest standard. Excellent breakfasts. An ideal centre for walkers and for touring Lakeland.

P €

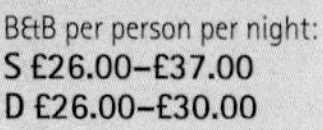

B&B per person per night:
S £26.00–£37.00
D £26.00–£30.00

OPEN All Year except Christmas

COUNTRY CODE Always follow the Country Code · Enjoy the countryside and respect its life and work · Guard against all risk of fire · Fasten all gates · Keep your dogs under close control · Keep to public paths across farmland · Use gates and stiles to cross fences, hedges and walls · Leave livestock, crops and machinery alone · Take your litter home · Help to keep all water clean · Protect wildlife, plants and trees · Take special care on country roads · Make no unnecessary noise

TROUTBECK continued

♦♦♦♦

HIGH GREEN LODGE

High Green, Troutbeck, Windermere
LA23 1PN
T: (015394) 33005

B&B per person per night:
S £40.00–£60.00
D £30.00–£60.00

OPEN All Year except Christmas

Here all mornings are magical. En suite, king-size rooms in peaceful lodge with fantastic views down to Valley Lake/Garbon Pass. Also 'Hill Top Studios', state-of-the-art with 4-poster/French sleigh beds, steam showers, jacuzzi baths, DVDs and TVs, water fountains, drink coolers etc. Truly fabulous!

Bedrooms: 3 double
Bathrooms: 3 en suite

CC: Delta, Mastercard, Switch, Visa

P

ULLSWATER, Cumbria Map ref 5A3

♦♦♦♦
Silver Award

BANK HOUSE FARM

Matterdale End, Penrith CA11 0LF
T: (017684) 82040
E: tjnhargreaves@aol.com
I: www.bankhousefarm.net

B&B per person per night:
S £32.50
D £30.00–£32.50

OPEN All Year except Christmas

Set above the small Lakeland hamlet of Matterdale End with magnificent views of the Ullswater Fells, this delightful farmhouse offers a peaceful, tranquil base from which to explore the National Park. Comfortable surroundings, Aga-cooked breakfasts and seven acres to relax in make this the perfect holiday location.

Bedrooms: 2 double, 1 twin
Bathrooms: 3 en suite

Evening meal available

Short breaks of 3 or more nights available at special rates.

P

♦♦♦

LAND ENDS COUNTRY LODGE

Watermillock, Ullswater, Penrith CA11 0NB
T: (017684) 86438
F: (017684) 86959
E: infolandends@btinternet.com
I: www.landends.co.uk

B&B per person per night:
S £34.00–£35.00
D £28.50–£35.00

A haven of peace and quiet, set in 25 acres with two pretty lakes, ducks, red squirrels and wonderful birdlife, our traditional farmhouse has been tastefully restored providing en suite bedrooms, one with 4-poster. Light snacks available evenings. Cosy lounge and bar. Close to lake, Ullswater and high fells.

Bedrooms: 5 double, 1 twin, 2 single
Bathrooms: 8 en suite

Evening meal available

3 nights for 2 on specific dates.

P

CHECK THE MAPS

The colour maps at the front of this guide show all the cities, towns and villages for which you will find accommodation entries.
Refer to the town index to find the page on which they are listed.

ULLSWATER continued

♦♦♦

MOSS CRAG

Eagle Road, Glenridding, Penrith CA11 0PA
T: (017684) 82500
F: (017684) 82500
E: info@mosscrag.co.uk
I: www.mosscrag.co.uk

B&B per person per night:
S £30.00–£35.00
D £24.00–£32.00

HB per person per night:
DY £40.50–£48.50

Small, friendly, family-run guesthouse overlooking Glenridding Beck, and close to Ullswater shore. Individually, tastefully decorated rooms await your arrival. All rooms have TV, hospitality tray etc. A good wholesome breakfast will start your day, whether walking, climbing, fishing, sailing or just touring the area.

Bedrooms: 6 double
Bathrooms: 4 en suite

Evening meal available
CC: Delta, Mastercard, Switch, Visa

B&B weekly breaks from £139-£189. DB&B from £240-£290. B&B 3-day breaks from £60-£81 (excl Bank Holidays).

5 P

♦♦♦♦

TYMPARON HALL

Newbiggin, Stainton, Penrith CA11 0HS
T: (01768) 483236
F: (01768) 483236
E: margaret@tymparon.freeserve.co.uk
I: www.tymparon.freeserve.co.uk

B&B per person per night:
S £20.00–£30.00
D £23.00–£26.00

HB per person per night:
DY £32.00–£38.00

OPEN All Year except Christmas

Spacious and very comfortable 18thC manor house situated on fringe of quiet village, a 10-minute drive to Lake Ullswater and close to M6 jct 40. En suite rooms available and excellent home cooking. Cosy residents' lounge with log fire. Ample private parking.

Bedrooms: 3 double
Bathrooms: 2 en suite, 1 private

Evening meal available

Reductions for 3-night, mid-week breaks.

P

WATERHEAD, Cumbria Map ref 5A3

♦♦♦

WATERHEAD COUNTRY GUEST HOUSE

Waterhead, Coniston LA21 8AJ
T: (015394) 41442
F: (015394) 41476
E: waterheadsteve@aol.com
I: www.waterheadguesthouse.co.uk

B&B per person per night:
S £30.00–£35.00
D £30.00–£35.00

OPEN All Year except Christmas

In its own grounds with superb views of the fells, relaxing residents' lounge/licenced bar, first floor, self-catering flat available, all within 100 yards of the lake and 0.5 miles from the centre of Coniston. All guest rooms are on the ground floor. Ample off-road parking provided.

Bedrooms: 3 double, 1 twin, 1 single
Bathrooms: 4 en suite

CC: Delta, Mastercard, Switch, Visa

Last night's accommodation is free for 3-night bookings (or more), mid-week Nov-Jan (excl Christmas and New Year).

P

SPECIAL BREAKS

Many establishments offer special promotions and themed breaks. These are highlighted in red. (All such offers are subject to availability.)

WHITEHAVEN, Cumbria Map ref 5A3 *Tourist Information Centre Tel: (01946) 852939*

Silver Award

MORESBY HALL

Moresby, Whitehaven CA28 6PJ
T: (01946) 696317
F: (01946) 694385
E: etc@moresbyhall.co.uk
I: www.moresbyhall.co.uk

B&B per person per night:
S £55.00–£75.00
D £35.00–£45.00

HB per person per night:
DY £55.00–£85.00

OPEN All Year

Moresby Hall is a historical, 16thC, Grade I Listed building, one of the oldest residences in Cumbria. Semi-rural, walled gardens, good parking. Near Whitehaven, a Georgian harbour town. Delightful, well-equipped, spacious rooms. Renowned for our delicious breakfasts and imaginative dinners. Fully licensed. Lakes, fells, golf, cultural and tourist locations close by.

Bedrooms: 3 double, 1 twin
Bathrooms: 4 en suite

Evening meal available
CC: Amex, Delta, Diners, Mastercard, Switch, Visa

10 P €

WINDERMERE, Cumbria Map ref 5A3 *Tourist Information Centre Tel: (015394) 46499*

APHRODITES LODGE

Longtail Hill, Bowness-on-Windermere, Windermere LA23 3JD
T: (015394) 45052
F: (015394) 46702
E: enquiries@aphroditeslodge.co.uk
I: www.aphroditeslodge.co.uk

B&B per person per night:
S £35.00–£80.00
D £30.00–£80.00

HB per person per night:
DY £45.00–£100.00

OPEN All Year

The highest-quality rooms, all themed, with suites, huge spa baths, fabulous garden views and glimpses of the lake, some with private patios. Outstanding gardens, outdoor heated swimming pool. Near restaurants and village centre. Clients have free use of nearby private leisure club.

Bedrooms: 6 double
Bathrooms: 6 en suite

CC: Delta, Mastercard, Switch, Visa

Half-price, mid-week breaks, low season.

P

APPLEGARTH HOTEL

College Road, Windermere LA23 1BU
T: (015394) 43206
F: (015394) 46636
E: info@lakesapplegarth.co.uk
I: www.lakesapplegarth.co.uk

B&B per person per night:
S £35.00–£40.00
D £30.00–£42.50

HB per person per night:
DY £50.00–£62.50

OPEN All Year

Detached, elegant Victorian mansion house in quiet area of central Windermere close to bus/train terminals. Comfortable lounge bar with conservatory/restaurant serving table d'hote and light snacks. The building, which is rich with historical interest, has been lovingly refurbished to provide high-quality accommodation. Many rooms have stunning lake and fell views.

Bedrooms: 11 double, 4 single, 3 family
Bathrooms: 18 en suite

Evening meal available
CC: Delta, Mastercard, Switch, Visa

3 nights mid-week from £85pp.

P

MAP REFERENCES

Map references apply to the colour maps at the front of this guide.

WINDERMERE continued

APPLETHWAITE HOUSE

1 Upper Oak Street, Windermere LA23 2LB
T: (015394) 44689
E: info@applethwaitehouse.co.uk
I: www.applethwaitehouse.co.uk

We offer you a warm welcome and a hearty breakfast in our family-run guesthouse. Clean, comfortable rooms with colour TV and complimentary hot drinks. Situated in a quiet cul-de-sac just minutes from the village centre. Garage for cycle storage. Families, vegetarians and pets all most welcome.

Bedrooms: 1 double, 3 family
Bathrooms: 3 en suite, 1 private

CC: Delta, Diners, Mastercard, Switch, Visa

10% discount on mid-week bookings of 2 or more nights (excl Jun-Sep).

B&B per person per night:
S £19.00–£38.00
D £19.00–£28.00

OPEN All Year

◆◆◆◆

THE ARCHWAY

13 College Road, Windermere LA23 1BU
T: (015394) 45613
F: (015394) 45613
E: archway@btinternet.com
I: www.communiken.com/archway

The Archway is a small, comfortable, non-smoking Victorian guesthouse situated in a quiet street close to the village centre. Fully centrally heated and tastefully furnished throughout. All rooms have en suite facilities, colour TV, clock-radio, hairdryer, and a well-stocked beverage tray. The front rooms also have fine mountain views.

Bedrooms: 2 double, 2 twin
Bathrooms: 4 en suite

CC: Delta, Mastercard, Switch, Visa

Please see our website for current offers.

B&B per person per night:
S £25.00–£45.00
D £20.00–£30.00

OPEN All Year

◆◆◆

AUTUMN LEAVES GUEST HOUSE

29 Broad Street, Windermere
LA23 2AB
T: (015394) 48410
E: autumnleaves@nascr.net
I: www.autumnleaves.gbr.cc

Bedrooms: 3 double, 1 twin, 1 single, 1 family
Bathrooms: 3 en suite

CC: Delta, Mastercard, Switch, Visa

A comfortable Victorian guesthouse located in the heart of Windermere, providing an excellent quality of service and friendly atmosphere. Five minutes' walk from train/bus station.

B&B per person per night:
S £17.00–£22.00
D £18.00–£24.50

OPEN All Year

BECKSIDE COTTAGE

4 Park Road, Windermere
LA23 2AW
T: (015394) 42069
E: becksidecottage@hotmail.com

Bedrooms: 2 double, 1 single, 1 family
Bathrooms: 4 en suite

Comfortable cottage. En suite bedrooms with full central heating, colour TV, tea/coffee and clock-radio. Full English breakfast served. Ideally situated, close to Windermere village.

B&B per person per night:
S £20.00–£25.00
D £18.00–£25.00

OPEN All Year

QUALITY ASSURANCE SCHEME

Diamond ratings and awards were correct at the time of going to press but are subject to change. Please check at the time of booking.

WINDERMERE continued

BELSFIELD HOUSE

4 Belsfield Terrace, Bowness-on-Windermere, Windermere LA23 3EQ
T: (015394) 45823
F: (015394) 45913
E: enquiries@BelsfieldHouse.co.uk
I: www.belsfieldhouse.co.uk

An exceptionally well-appointed guesthouse offering a high degree of comfort, value for money and, most important of all, a warm, friendly atmosphere. Guests have free access to Burnside Leisure Complex – an excellent way to unwind after a busy day exploring the nooks and crannies of the Lake District.

Bedrooms: 3 double, 2 single, 4 family
Bathrooms: 9 en suite

CC: Delta, Diners, Mastercard, Switch, Visa

10% discount to all guests dining in the Nissi Restaurant, Bowness.

B&B per person per night:
S £25.00–£35.00
D £25.00–£35.00

OPEN All Year except Christmas

♦♦♦

BOWFELL COTTAGE

Middle Entrance Drive, Storrs Park, Bowness-on-Windermere, Windermere LA23 3JY
T: (015394) 44835
F: (015394) 44835

Bedrooms: 1 double, 1 twin, 1 family
Bathrooms: 1 en suite

Evening meal available

Cottage in a delightful setting, about one mile south of Bowness just off the A5074, offering traditional Lakeland hospitality. Secluded parking in own grounds.

B&B per person per night:
S £22.00–£25.00
D £21.00–£24.00

HB per person per night:
DY £33.00–£36.00

OPEN All Year

♦♦♦

BROOK HOUSE

30 Ellerthwaite Road, Windermere LA23 2AH
T: (015394) 44932
E: brookhouse@nascr.net

Bedrooms: 4 double, 1 twin, 1 single
Bathrooms: 3 en suite

CC: Amex, Delta, Diners, Mastercard, Switch, Visa

This immaculately kept guesthouse, in a quiet part of Windermere, offers en suite facilities, tea/coffee making, private car park, good food, warm personal welcome.

B&B per person per night:
S £20.00–£24.00
D £18.50–£27.00

OPEN All Year

Silver Award

CEDAR MANOR COUNTRY LODGE

Ambleside Road, Windermere LA23 1AX
T: (015394) 43192
F: (015394) 45970
E: cedarmanor@fsbdial.co.uk
I: www.cedarmanor.co.uk

A charming gentleman's residence, close to the village and Lake Windermere. Central for exploring Lakeland. The lodge has 11, individually furnished bedrooms, some with king-sized beds and spa bath. Breakfast is a very special occasion, with an emphasis on local produce, freshly baked breads and homemade jams. We offer complimentary afternoon tea with home-baked cakes and biscuits. Superior bed and breakfast accommodation with all the comforts of a quality hotel.

Bedrooms: 6 double, 2 twin, 2 family, 1 suite
Bathrooms: 10 en suite

CC: Mastercard, Visa

B&B per person per night:
S £33.50–£65.00
D £33.50–£70.00

OPEN All Year except Christmas

QUALITY ASSURANCE SCHEME

Diamond ratings and awards are explained at the back of this guide.

WINDERMERE continued

COLLEGE HOUSE

15 College Road, Windermere LA23 1BU
T: (015394) 45767
E: clghse@aol.com
I: www.college-house.com

B&B per person per night:
S £19.00–£30.00
D £19.00–£30.00

OPEN All Year

Quiet, comfortable Victorian family house offering a warm and friendly welcome. Close to village centre and bus/railway station. Front rooms have superb mountain views, all are en suite and have colour TV, tea/coffee-making facilities and full central heating. Delicious breakfast choice. Colourful, sunny garden. Non-smoking. Private parking.

Bedrooms: 2 double, 1 twin
Bathrooms: 3 en suite

♦♦♦

DENE CREST

Woodland Road, Windermere LA23 2AE
T: (015394) 44979
E: denecrest@btinternet.com
I: www.denecrest.com

B&B per person per night:
S £20.00–£35.00
D £17.00–£24.00

OPEN All Year

Small guesthouse, 100 years old, built in local stone. Quiet but close to town centre. Excellent breakfast and warm welcome guaranteed.

Bedrooms: 3 double, 1 family
Bathrooms: 4 en suite

CC: Amex, Delta, Diners, Mastercard, Switch, Visa

♦♦♦♦

EASTBOURNE

Biskey Howe Road, Bowness-on-Windermere, Windermere LA23 2JR
T: (015394) 43525
F: (015394) 43525
E: mail@eastbourne-guesthouse.co.uk
I: www.eastbourne-guesthouse.co.uk

Bedrooms: 5 double, 2 family
Bathrooms: 7 en suite

CC: Delta, Mastercard, Switch, Visa

B&B per person per night:
D £22.00–£32.00

OPEN All Year

Small family-run hotel offering private facilities and a friendly welcome. Located in a quiet position close to Lake Windermere, an ideal central touring base.

♦♦♦♦
Silver Award

FAIR RIGG

Ferry View, Bowness-on-Windermere, Windermere LA23 3JB
T: (015394) 43941
E: rtodd51257@aol.com
I: www.fairrigg.co.uk

B&B per person per night:
S £34.00–£60.00
D £28.00–£37.00

OPEN All Year

In a superb rural setting just a few minutes' walk from Bowness centre and the lakeshore, this Victorian gentleman's residence has been lovingly refurbished to provide high-quality, well-proportioned guesthouse accommodation. Comfort and relaxation are assured, with personal service and fine views up Lake Windermere to the Cumbrian Fells.

Bedrooms: 5 double, 1 twin
Bathrooms: 6 en suite

Reductions are often available for breaks of 3 nights or more.

WINDERMERE continued

THE FAIRFIELD GARDEN GUEST HOUSE

Brantfell Road, Bowness-on-Windermere, Windermere LA23 3AE
T: (015394) 46565
F: (015394) 46565
E: info@the-fairfield.co.uk
I: www.the-fairfield.co.uk

Small, friendly, family-run, 200-year-old Lakeland, non-smoking guesthouse. Set in a peaceful garden environment, close to Bowness village and lakeshore. Well-appointed and tastefully furnished bedrooms all with TV, hairdryer, welcome tray etc. Breakfasts are a speciality. Genuine hospitality and a warm welcome. Private parking. Open year round.

Bedrooms: 6 double, 1 twin, 1 single, 1 family, 1 suite
Bathrooms: 8 en suite, 1 private

Evening meal available
CC: Amex, Delta, Mastercard, Switch, Visa

Reduced prices for 2, 3 or more nights during weekdays, or extended weekends in low season.

B&B per person per night:
S £27.00–£49.00
D £27.00–£40.00

HB per person per night:
DY £44.50–£57.50

OPEN All Year except Christmas

FIRGARTH

Ambleside Road, Windermere
LA23 1EU
T: (015394) 46974
F: (015394) 42384
E: thefirgarth@KTDinternet.com

Bedrooms: 3 double, 1 single, 4 family
Bathrooms: 8 en suite

CC: Delta, Mastercard, Switch, Visa

Elegant Victorian country house. Good breakfasts, friendly atmosphere, private parking and close to a lake view-point. Ideally situated for touring all areas of Lakeland.

P €

B&B per person per night:
S £21.00–£29.00
D £19.00–£26.00

OPEN All Year except Christmas

◆◆◆◆
Silver Award

HIGH VIEW

Sun Hill Lane, Troutbeck Bridge, Windermere LA23 1HJ
T: (015394) 44618
F: (015394) 42731
E: info@accommodationlakedistrict.com
I: www.accommodationlakedistrict.com

Bedrooms: 1 double, 1 family
Bathrooms: 2 en suite

A delightful bungalow in an elevated position overlooking Lake Windermere. Within walking distance of Troutbeck, Windermere and Bowness. Breakfast a real speciality.

P

B&B per person per night:
S £22.00–£27.00
D £22.00–£27.00

OPEN All Year

HOLLY LODGE

6 College Road, Windermere
LA23 1BX
T: (015394) 43873
F: (015394) 43873
E: anneandbarry@hollylodge6.fsnet.co.uk
I: www.hollylodge20.fsnet.co.uk

Bedrooms: 6 double, 4 family
Bathrooms: 8 en suite

CC: Delta, Mastercard, Switch, Visa

Traditional Lakeland, family-run guesthouse in a quiet location close to shops, restaurants, buses and trains. Friendly atmosphere. Hearty English breakfast. Each bedroom individually furnished.

P

B&B per person per night:
S £20.00–£35.00
D £20.00–£30.00

OPEN All Year

IMPORTANT NOTE Information on accommodation listed in this guide has been supplied by the proprietors. As changes may occur you are advised to check details at the time of booking.

WINDERMERE continued

HOLLY-WOOD

Holly Road, Windermere LA23 2AF
T: (015394) 42219
F: (015394) 42219
I: www.hollywoodguesthouse.co.uk

B&B per person per night:
S £20.00–£29.00
D £18.50–£27.00

Comfortable Victorian house in a quiet position, a three-minute walk from village centre. En suite and budget rooms available, all with TV, hairdryer, clock-radio and tea/coffee-maker. Central heating and cosy residents' lounge. Off-street parking, free bus/rail station transfer (please ask when booking).

Bedrooms: 4 double, 1 twin, 1 family
Bathrooms: 4 en suite

CC: Amex, Mastercard, Switch, Visa

Reduced rates for 3-day breaks and longer stays (excl Bank Holidays).

3 P

◆◆◆

HOLMLEA
Kendal Road, Bowness-on-Windermere, Windermere
LA23 3EW
T: (015394) 42597

Bedrooms: 4 double, 2 single, 1 family
Bathrooms: 5 en suite

B&B per person per night:
S £23.00–£25.00
D £25.00–£28.00

OPEN All Year except Christmas

Friendly, comfortable guesthouse in quiet location three minutes' walk from lake and amenities. Car park, generous breakfast, warm welcome assured.

P

◆◆◆

KENILWORTH GUEST HOUSE

Holly Road, Windermere LA23 2AF
T: (015394) 44004
E: busby@kenilworth-lake-district.co.uk

B&B per person per night:
S £18.00–£26.00
D £18.00–£28.00

OPEN All Year except Christmas

Grand Victorian house in secluded, yet central location. Hearty breakfast with vegetarian alternatives. Private parking. Free station transfer (Windermere). Non-smoking throughout.

Bedrooms: 2 double, 2 twin, 1 single, 1 family
Bathrooms: 3 en suite

CC: Amex, Delta, Mastercard, Switch, Visa

5 P €

◆◆◆◆

21 THE LAKES

Lake Road, Windermere LA23 2EQ
T: (015394) 45052
F: (015394) 46702
E: enquiries@21thelakes.co.uk
I: www.21thelakes.co.uk

B&B per person per night:
S £30.00–£80.00
D £30.00–£80.00

HB per person per night:
DY £45.00–£100.00

OPEN All Year

21 The Lakes Hotel is a new, boutique-style hotel offering high-quality suites with a variety of king-size beds, both contemporary and traditional. All bathrooms are luxurious with large spa-bath tubs. The suites have large TV, DVD, CD and satellite channels.

Bedrooms: 13 double, 1 family
Bathrooms: 14 en suite

Evening meal available
CC: Mastercard, Switch, Visa

Mid-week, low season, half-price special breaks.

P

COLOUR MAPS Colour maps at the front of this guide pinpoint all places under which you will find accommodation listed.

WINDERMERE continued

♦♦♦♦

LAUREL COTTAGE

St. Martin's Square, Bowness-on-Windermere, Windermere LA23 3EF
T: (015394) 45594
F: (015394) 45594
E: enquiries@laurelcottage-bnb.co.uk
I: www.laurelcottage-bnb.co.uk

B&B per person per night:
S £21.00–£28.00
D £22.00–£36.00

OPEN All Year

Charming, early-17thC cottage (1613), originally the village grammar school, located one minute's stroll from the lake at Bowness Bay. Ideally situated for all local attractions and amenities. Whilst the cottage retains many original features we continue to give all our guests the comforts of the present. Free membership of local leisure club.

Bedrooms: 7 double, 2 twin, 2 single, 2 family
Bathrooms: 11 en suite

CC: Delta, Mastercard, Switch, Visa

Low season: any 2 consecutive nights (excl weekends) deduct £2. High season: any 3 consecutive nights (excl weekends) deduct £2.

P

♦♦♦

LINDISFARNE HOUSE

Sunny Bank Road, Windermere LA23 2EN
T: (015394) 46295
E: enquiries@lindisfarne-house.co.uk
I: www.lindisfarne-house.co.uk

B&B per person per night:
D £23.00–£30.00

OPEN All Year

Traditional, detached Lakeland house in quiet location conveniently situated between Windermere and Bowness, close to lake, shops and scenic walks. Comfortable, friendly atmosphere, good, healthy home-cooked English breakfasts. Off-road parking. Non-smoking.

Bedrooms: 1 double, 1 twin, 2 family
Bathrooms: 2 en suite, 2 private

Reductions available for breaks of 3 nights or more (excl Bank Holiday periods).

8 P

♦♦♦♦

LINGWOOD

Birkett Hill, Bowness-on-Windermere, Windermere LA23 3EZ
T: (015394) 44680
F: (015394) 48154
E: enquiries@lingwood-guesthouse.co.uk
I: www.lingwood-guesthouse.co.uk

B&B per person per night:
S £25.00–£40.00
D £20.00–£30.00

OPEN All Year

Small, friendly, family-run guesthouse set in own gardens but within 400 yards of lake shore, shops and restaurants. Hearty breakfast provided. With ample private car parking and safe storage for bicycles, Lingwood is ideally placed for exploring both the Lake District and surrounding areas.

Bedrooms: 3 double, 3 family
Bathrooms: 4 en suite, 2 private

CC: Delta, Mastercard, Switch, Visa

Mid-week breaks available (excl Bank Holidays).

P

◆◆◆◆◆

OAKBANK HOUSE HOTEL

Helm Road, Bowness-on-Windermere, Windermere LA23 3BU
T: (015394) 43386
F: (015394) 47965
E: enquiries@oakbankhousehotel.co.uk
I: www.oakbankhousehotel.co.uk

The only ETB 5-diamond-rated guesthouse in Bowness, panoramic views of Lake Windermere and the Langdale Heights. Quality, spacious, en suite accommodation with TV/video and complimentary video library. Parking and free guest membership to private leisure club. Renowned for our exceptional breakfasts and friendly service.

Bedrooms: 10 double, 1 twin, 1 family
Bathrooms: 11 en suite, 1 private

CC: Amex, Delta, Mastercard, Switch, Visa

Long weekend: stay Fri, Sat, Sun for £32. Nov-Jun, Sun-Thu: 3 nights £25. Low-season rates available on request.

P €

B&B per person per night:
S £40.00–£70.00
D £25.00–£50.00

OPEN All Year except Christmas

◆◆◆◆

OLDFIELD HOUSE

Oldfield Road, Windermere LA23 2BY
T: (015394) 88445
E: ben.want@kencomp.net
I: www.oldfieldhouse.co.uk

Style, comfort and hospitality in a 19thC residence located in a quiet area of Windermere. All of our rooms are en suite. They include premier and standard doubles, twin, singles and a family room. Outstanding breakfast menu, use of leisure club, packed lunches, car park, photographic portrait sessions.

Bedrooms: 4 double, 1 twin, 2 single, 1 family
Bathrooms: 8 en suite

CC: Mastercard, Switch, Visa

Celebration pack of flowers, chocolates, 1/2 bottle champagne, champagne flutes, from £45.00. Mid-week specials: 2 nights' B&B plus 1 night's dinner from £155 for 2.

2 P

B&B per person per night:
S £26.00–£32.00
D £24.00–£35.00

OPEN All Year except Christmas

◆◆◆◆

1 PARK ROAD

Windermere LA23 2AW
T: (015394) 42107
F: (015394) 48997
E: enquiries@1parkroad.com
I: www.1parkroad.com

Bedrooms: 3 double, 3 family
Bathrooms: 6 en suite

Evening meal available
CC: Amex, Delta, Mastercard, Switch, Visa

Beautiful, contemporary, renovated Victorian property with spacious en suite rooms. Five minutes from the pubs, shops, rail/coach stations. Licensed bar, car parking, great candlelit dinners.

P €

B&B per person per night:
S £40.00–£50.00
D £30.00–£35.00

HB per person per night:
DY £45.00–£50.00

OPEN All Year

AT-A-GLANCE SYMBOLS

Symbols at the end of each accommodation entry give useful information about services and facilities. A key to symbols can be found inside the back cover flap. Keep this open for easy reference.

WINDERMERE continued

ST JOHN'S LODGE

Lake Road, Windermere LA23 2EQ
T: (015394) 43078
F: (015394) 88054
E: mail@st-johns-lodge.co.uk
I: www.st-johns-lodge.co.uk

B&B per person per night:
S £22.00–£40.00
D £20.00–£34.00

OPEN All Year except Christmas

Pretty Lakeland guesthouse between Windermere village and lake. Close to all amenities. Comfortable, spotlessly clean, en suite bedrooms. Choose from over 15 freshly cooked breakfast dishes. Offering a relaxed atmosphere, good service, a little bit of humor and excellent value for money. Free use of nearby leisure club. Free internet access.

Bedrooms: 9 double, 2 single, 3 family
Bathrooms: 12 en suite, 2 private

CC: Delta, Mastercard, Switch, Visa

3-day breaks (price per person): low season from £57, mid-season from £69, high season from £78.

4 P €

♦♦♦♦

TARN RIGG

Thornbarrow Road, Windermere LA23 2DG
T: (015394) 88777
E: stay@tarnrigg-guesthouse.co.uk
I: www.tarnrigg-guesthouse.co.uk

B&B per person per night:
S £35.00–£50.00
D £22.50–£32.50

OPEN All Year

Welcome to the Lake District. Built in 1903, Tarn Rigg is situated in an ideal position midway between Windermere and Bowness. Panoramic Langdale Pike views. Quiet, convenient location, ample parking, beautiful 0.75-acre grounds. Spacious, en suite rooms with excellent modern facilities. Rooms with lake views available.

Bedrooms: 3 double, 2 family
Bathrooms: 5 en suite

CC: Delta, Mastercard, Switch, Visa

Special off-peak offer: 3 nights for £99. Discount from high-season prices available all year for 3-night stays.

P €

WORKINGTON, Cumbria Map ref 5A2 *Tourist Information Centre Tel: (01900) 606699*

♦♦♦

MORVEN GUEST HOUSE
Siddick Road, Siddick, Workington CA14 1LE
T: (01900) 602118
F: (01900) 602118
E: cnelsonmorven@aol.com
I: www.smoothhound.co.uk/hotels/morvenguesthouse.html

Bedrooms: 1 double, 4 twin, 1 single
Bathrooms: 6 en suite

Evening meal available

B&B per person per night:
S £25.00–£28.00
D £22.00–£23.00

OPEN All Year

Detached house north-west of town. Ideal base for western Lakes and coast. Start of coast-to-coast cycleway. Car park, cycle storage.

P

QUALITY ASSURANCE SCHEME

For an explanation of the quality and facilities represented by the Diamonds please refer to the front of this guide. A more detailed explanation can be found in the information pages at the back.

WORKINGTON continued

THE OLD GINN HOUSE

Great Clifton, Workington CA14 1TS
T: (01900) 64616
F: (01900) 873384
E: enquiries@oldginnhouse.co.uk
I: www.oldginnhouse.co.uk

The Old Ginn House has been sucessfully converted from a 17thC farm into a charming village inn, full of character and modern facilities, built around an attractive courtyard. The inn offers quality accomodation, great food and a warm welcome for those looking to explore the Western Lake District and Solway coast.

Bedrooms: 13 double, 2 family
Bathrooms: 15 en suite

Evening meal available
CC: Amex, Delta, Mastercard, Switch, Visa

Weekend breaks from £150 for 2 people for 3 nights – Fri, Sat, Sun (offer subject to availabilty).

B&B per person per night:
S £45.00–£55.00
D £30.00–£35.00

OPEN All Year except Christmas

USE YOUR *i*s

There are more than 550 Tourist Information Centres throughout England offering friendly help with accommodation and holiday ideas as well as suggestions of places to visit and things to do. You'll find TIC addresses in the local Phone Book.

A brief guide to the main Towns and Villages offering accommodation in **Cumbria**

A ALLONBY, CUMBRIA - Small village on Solway Firth with good sandy beaches, once famous for its herring fishing and as a fashionable resort of Victorian gentry. Good views across the Firth to Criffel and the Galloway mountains.

AMBLESIDE, CUMBRIA - Market town situated at the head of Lake Windermere and surrounded by fells. The historic town centre is now a conservation area and the country around Ambleside is rich in historic and literary associations. Good centre for touring, walking and climbing.

APPLEBY-IN-WESTMORLAND, CUMBRIA - Former county town of Westmorland, at the foot of the Pennines in the Eden Valley. The castle was rebuilt in the 17th C, except for its Norman keep, ditches and ramparts. It now houses a Rare Breeds Survival Trust Centre. Good centre for exploring the Eden Valley.

B BARROW-IN-FURNESS, CUMBRIA - On the Furness Peninsula in Morecambe Bay, an industrial and commercial centre with sandy beaches and nature reserves on Walney Island. Ruins of 12th C Cistercian Furness Abbey. The Dock Museum tells the story of the area and Forum 28 houses a modern theatre and arts centre.

BASSENTHWAITE LAKE, CUMBRIA - The northernmost and only true "lake" in the Lake District. Visited annually by many species of migratory birds.

BORROWDALE, CUMBRIA - Stretching south of Derwentwater to Seathwaite in the heart of the Lake District, the valley is walled by high fellsides. It can justly claim to be the most scenically impressive valley in the Lake District. Excellent centre for walking and climbing.

BOWNESS-ON-SOLWAY, CUMBRIA - Coastal village near the site of the Roman fort Maia at the western end of Hadrian's Wall.

BOWNESS-ON-WINDERMERE, CUMBRIA - Bowness is the older of the two towns of Bowness and Windermere and dates from the 11th C. It is a busy tourist resort set on the shores of Lake Windermere, England's largest lake. Good location for touring, walking, boating and fishing.

BRAITHWAITE, CUMBRIA - Braithwaite nestles at the foot of the Whinlatter Pass and has a magnificent backdrop of the mountains forming the Coledale Horseshoe.

BRAMPTON, CUMBRIA - Excellent centre for exploring Hadrian's Wall. Wednesday is market day around the Moot Hall in this delightful sandstone-built town. Wall plaque marks the site of Bonnie Prince Charlie and his Jacobite army's headquarters whilst they laid siege to Carlisle Castle in 1745.

C CALDBECK, CUMBRIA - Quaint limestone village lying on the northern fringe of the Lake District National Park. John Peel, the famous huntsman who is immortalised in song, is buried in the churchyard. The fells surrounding Caldbeck were once heavily mined, being rich in lead, copper and barytes.

CARLISLE, CUMBRIA - Cumbria's only city is rich in history. Attractions include the small red sandstone cathedral and 900-year-old castle with magnificent views from the keep. Award-winning Tullie House Museum and Art Gallery brings 2,000 years of Border history dramatically to life. Excellent centre for shopping.

CARTMEL, CUMBRIA - Picturesque conserved village based on a 12th C priory with a well-preserved church and gatehouse. Just half a mile outside the Lake District National Park, this is a peaceful base for walking and touring, with historic houses and beautiful scenery.

CONISTON, CUMBRIA - The 803m fell Coniston Old Man dominates the skyline to the east of this village at the northern end of Coniston Water. Arthur Ransome set his "Swallows and Amazons" stories here. Coniston's most famous resident was John Ruskin, whose home, Brantwood, is open to the public. Good centre for walking.

CROSTHWAITE, CUMBRIA - Small village in the picturesque Lyth Valley off the A5074.

D DALTON-IN-FURNESS, CUMBRIA - Conveniently located between Ulverston and Barrow. There exists the remains of a 14th C tower in the main street of the village.

G GRANGE-OVER-SANDS, CUMBRIA - Set on the beautiful Cartmel Peninsula, this tranquil resort, known as Lakeland's Riviera, overlooks Morecambe Bay. Pleasant seafront walks and beautiful gardens. The bay attracts many species of wading birds.

GRASMERE, CUMBRIA - Described by William Wordsworth as "the loveliest spot that man hath ever found", this village, famous for its gingerbread, is in a beautiful setting overlooked by Helm Grag. Wordsworth lived at Dove Cottage. The cottage and museum are open to the public.

H HAWKSHEAD, CUMBRIA - Lying near Esthwaite Water, this village has great charm and character. Its small squares are linked by flagged or cobbled alleys and the main square is dominated by the market house, or Shambles, where the butchers had their stalls in days gone by.

K KENDAL, CUMBRIA - The "Auld Grey Town" lies in the valley of the River Kent with a backcloth of limestone fells. Situated just outside the Lake District National Park, it is a good centre for touring the Lakes and surrounding country. Ruined castle, reputed birthplace of Catherine Parr.

KESWICK, CUMBRIA - Beautifully positioned town beside Derwentwater and below the mountains of Skiddaw and Blencathra. Excellent base for walking, climbing, watersports and touring. Motor-launches operate on Derwentwater and motor boats, rowing boats and canoes can be hired.

KIRKBY LONSDALE, CUMBRIA - Charming old town of narrow streets and Georgian buildings, set in the superb scenery of the Lune Valley. The Devil's Bridge over the River Lune is probably 13th C.

KIRKBY STEPHEN, CUMBRIA - Old market town close to the River Eden, with many fine Georgian buildings and an attractive market square. St Stephen's Church is known as the "Cathedral of the Dales". Good base for exploring the Eden Valley and the Dales.

M MUNGRISDALE, CUMBRIA - Set in an unspoilt valley, this hamlet has a simple, white church with a 3-decker pulpit and box pews.

P PENRITH, CUMBRIA - Ancient and historic market town, the northern gateway to the Lake District. Penrith Castle was built as a defence against the Scots. Its ruins, open to the public, stand in the public park. High above the town is the Penrith Beacon, made famous by William Wordsworth.

S SAWREY, CUMBRIA - Far Sawrey and Near Sawrey lie near Esthwaite Water. Both villages are small but Near Sawrey is famous for Hill Top Farm, home of Beatrix Potter, now owned by the National Trust and open to the public.

ST BEES, CUMBRIA - Small seaside village with fine Norman church and a public school founded in the 16th C. Dramatic red sandstone cliffs make up impressive St Bees Head, parts of which are RSPB reserves and homes to puffins and black guillemot. Start or finishing point of Wainwright's Coast to Coast walk.

T TROUTBECK, CUMBRIA - Most of the houses in this picturesque village are 17th C, some retain their spinning galleries and oak-mullioned windows. At the south end of the village is Townend, owned by the National Trust and open to the public, an excellently preserved example of a yeoman farmer's or statesman's house.

U ULLSWATER, CUMBRIA - This beautiful lake, which is over 7 miles long, runs from Glenridding to Pooley Bridge. Lofty peaks ranging around the lake make an impressive background. A steamer service operates along the lake between Pooley Bridge, Howtown and Glenridding in the summer.

W WHITEHAVEN, CUMBRIA - Historic Georgian port on the west coast. The town was developed in the 17th C and many fine buildings have been preserved. The Beacon Heritage Centre includes a Meteorological Office Weather Gallery. Start or finishing point of Coast to Coast, Whitehaven to Sunderland, cycleway.

WINDERMERE, CUMBRIA - Once a tiny hamlet before the introduction of the railway in 1847, now adjoins Bowness which is on the lakeside. Centre for sailing and boating. A good way to see the lake is a trip on a passenger steamer. Steamboat Museum has a fine collection of old boats.

WORKINGTON, CUMBRIA - A deep-water port on the west Cumbrian coast. There are the ruins of the 14th C Workington Hall, where Mary Queen of Scots stayed in 1568.

COUNTRY CODE Always follow the Country Code • Enjoy the countryside and respect its life and work • Guard against all risk of fire • Fasten all gates • Keep your dogs under close control • Keep to public paths across farmland • Use gates and stiles to cross fences, hedges and walls • Leave livestock, crops and machinery alone • Take your litter home • Help to keep all water clean • Protect wildlife, plants and trees • Take special care on country roads • Make no unnecessary noise

VisitBritain Gold and Silver Awards

Our unique Gold and Silver Awards recognise exceptional quality in serviced accommodation. Our assessors make recommendations for Gold and Silver awards during assessments in recognition of levels of quality over and above that expected at a particular rating.

Look for the Gold and Silver Awards in the regional sections or you can find an index to accommodation with a Gold and Silver Award at the back of this guide.

Visitor Attraction Quality Assurance

VisitBritain operates a Visitor Attraction Quality Assurance Standard. Participating attractions are visited annually by trained, impartial assessors who look at all aspects of the visit, from initial telephone enquiries to departure, customer services to catering, as well as facilities and activities. Only those attractions which have been assessed by VisitBritain and meet the standard receive the quality marque, your sign of a 'Quality Assured Visitor Attraction'.

Look out for the quality marque and visit with confidence.

Northumbria

Romans, sailors and industrial pioneers have all left their mark here. Northunbria's exciting cities, castle-studded countyside and white-sanded coastline make it an undiscovered gem.

Classic sights
Lindisfarne Castle – on Holy Island
Housesteads Roman Fort – the most impressive Roman fort on Hadrian's Wall
Durham Cathedral & Hadrian's Wall – 2 World Heritage Sites

Coast & country
Kielder Water and Forest Park – perfect for walking, cycling and watersports
Saltburn – beach of broad sands
Seahouses – picturesque fishing village

Maritime history
HMS Trincomalee – magnificent 1817 British warship
Captain Cook – birthplace museum and replica of his ship, *Endeavour*
Grace Darling – museum commemorating her rescue of shipwreck survivors in 1838

Arts for all
Angel of the North – awe-inspiring sculpture by Antony Gormley
BALTIC – The Centre for Contemporary Art in Gateshead

Distinctively different
St Mary's Lighthouse – great views from the top

The Counties of Durham, Northumberland, Tees Valley and Tyne & Wear

For more information contact:
Northumbria Tourist Board
Aykley Heads,
Durham DH1 5UX

www.visitnorthumbria.com

Telephone enquiries -
T: (0191) 375 3049
F: (0191) 386 0899

1. The Angel of the North, Gateshead
2. Town Crier, Alnwick Fair
3. Walkers on the Northumbrian Coast

Places to Visit

You will find hundreds of interesting places to visit during your stay, just some of which are listed in these pages. Contact any Tourist Information Centre in the region for more ideas on days out.

Awarded VisitBritain's 'Quality Assured Visitor Attraction' marque.

Alnwick Castle
Alnwick
Tel: (01665) 510777 www.alnwickcastle.com
Home of the Percy's, Dukes of Northumberland, since 1309, this imposing medieval fortress has magnificent 19thC interiors in the Italian Renaissance style.

Alnwick Garden
Alnwick
Tel: (01665) 511350 www.alnwickgarden.com
New 12-acre (5ha) garden with fabulous water feature, rose garden, ornamental garden, woodland walk and viewpoint.

BALTIC The Centre for Contemporary Art
Quayside, Gateshead
Tel: (0191) 478 1810 www.balticmill.com
A major international centre for contemporary art in a converted warehouse, with a constantly changing programme of exhibitions and events.

Bamburgh Castle
Bamburgh
Tel: (01668) 214515
www.bamburghcastle.com
Magnificent coastal castle completely restored in 1900. Collections of china, porcelain, furniture, paintings, arms and armour.

Beamish The North of England Open Air Museum
Beamish
Tel: (0191) 370 4000
www.beamish.org.uk
Visit the town, colliery village, working farm, Pockerley Manor and 1825 railway, recreating life in the North East in the early 1800s and 1900s.

Bede's World

Church Bank, Jarrow
Tel: (0191) 489 2106
www.bedesworld.co.uk
Discover the exciting world of the Venerable Bede, early medieval Europe's greatest scholar. Church, monastic site, museum with exhibitions and recreated Anglo-Saxon farm.

Belsay Hall, Castle and Gardens (English Heritage)
Belsay, Newcastle upon Tyne
Tel: (01661) 881636
www.english-heritage.org.uk
Home of the Middleton family for 600 years. 14thC castle, ruined 17thC manor house and neo-classical hall, set in 30 acres (12ha) of landscaped gardens and winter garden.

Blue Reef Aquarium
Grand Parade, Tynemouth
Tel: (0191) 258 1031
www.bluereefaquarium.co.uk
More than 30 living displays exploring the drama of the North Sea and the dazzling beauty of a spectacular coral reef with its own underwater tunnel.

Bowes Museum
Barnard Castle
Tel: (01833) 690606
www.bowesmuseum.org.uk
French-style chateau, housing art collections of national importance and archaeology of south west Durham.

Captain Cook Birthplace Museum
Stewart Park, Middlesborough
Tel: (01642) 311211
Early life and voyages of Captain Cook and the countries he visited. Temporary exhibitions. One person free with every group of 10 visiting.

Centre For Life
Times Square, Newcastle upon Tyne
Tel: (0191) 243 8210 www.centre-for-life.co.uk
Meet your 4 billion year old family, explore what makes us all different, test your brain power and enjoy the thrill of the crazy motion ride.

Cherryburn: Thomas Bewick Birthplace Museum (National Trust)
Station Bank, Stocksfield
Tel: (01661) 843276 www.nationaltrust.org.uk
Birthplace cottage (1700) and farmyard. Printing house using original printing blocks. Introductory exhibition of the life, work and countryside.

Chesters Roman Fort (Cilurnum), Hadrian's Wall
Chollerford, Humshaugh, Hexham
Tel: (01434) 681379
Fort built for 500 cavalrymen. Remains include 5 gateways, barrack blocks, commandant's house and headquarters. Finest military bath house in Britain.

Chillingham Castle
Chillingham, Wooler
Tel: (01668) 215359
www.chillingham-castle.com
Medieval fortress with Tudor additions, torture chamber, shop, dungeon, tearoom, woodland walks, furnished rooms and topiary garden.

Cragside House, Gardens and Estate (National Trust)
Rothbury, Morpeth
Tel: (01669) 620333 www.nationaltrust.org.uk
Built in 1864-84 for Tyneside industrialist Lord Armstrong, Cragside was the first house to be lit by electricity generated by water power.

Discovery Museum
Blandford Square, Newcastle upon Tyne
Tel: (0191) 232 6789 www.twmuseums.org.uk
Discovery Museum offers a wide variety of experiences for all the family to enjoy. Explore the Newcastle Story, Live Wires, Science Maze and Fashion Works.

Dunstanburgh Castle (English Heritage)
Craster, Alnwick
Tel: (01665) 576231
www.english-heritage.org.uk
Romantic ruins of extensive 14thC castle in dramatic coastal situation on 100ft (30.5km) cliffs. Built by Thomas, Earl of Lancaster. Remains include gatehouse and curtain wall.

Durham Castle
Palace Green, Durham
Tel: (0191) 374 3863 www.durhamcastle.com
Castle founded in 1072, Norman chapel dating from 1080. Kitchens and great hall dated 1499 and 1284 respectively. Fine example of motte-and-bailey castle.

Durham Cathedral
The College, Durham
Tel: (0191) 386 4266
www.durhamcathedral.co.uk
Durham Cathedral is thought by many to be the finest example of Norman church architecture in England. Contains the tombs of St Cuthbert and The Venerable Bede.

2

3

1. Lindisfarne Castle, Holy Island
2. Hadrian's Wall
3. Bridges over the Tyne, Newcastle

Hall Hill Farm
Lanchester, Durham
Tel: (01388) 730300 www.hallhillfarm.co.uk
Family fun set in attractive countryside with an opportunity to see and touch the animals at close quarters. Farm trailer ride, riverside walk, teashop and play area.

Hartlepool Historic Quay
Maritime Avenue, Hartlepool
Tel: (01429) 860006
www.destinationhartlepool.com
Hartlepool Historic Quay is an exciting reconstruction of a seaport of the 1800s with buildings and lively quayside, authentically reconstructed.

Housesteads Roman Fort (Vercovicium), Hadrian's Wall (National Trust)
Haydon Bridge, Hexham
Tel: (01434) 344363 www.nationaltrust.org.uk
Best preserved and most impressive of the Roman forts. Vercovicium was a 5-acre (2ha) fort for an extensive 800 civil settlement. Only example of a Roman hospital.

Killhope, The North of England Lead Mining Museum
Cowshill, Bishop Auckland
Tel: (01388) 537505
www.durham.gov.uk/killhope
Most complete lead mining site in Great Britain. Mine tours available, 34-ft- (10m-) diameter waterwheel, reconstruction of Victorian machinery, miners lodging and woodland walks.

Lindisfarne Castle (National Trust)
Holy Island, Berwick-upon-Tweed
Tel: (01289) 389244 www.nationaltrust.org.uk
The castle was built in 1550 and restored and converted into a private home for Edward Hudson by the architect Sir Edwin Lutyens in 1903.

National Glass Centre

Liberty Way, Sunderland
Tel: (0191) 515 5555
www.nationalglasscentre.com
A unique visitor attraction presenting the best in contemporary glass. Master craftspeople will demonstrate glass-making techniques. Classes and workshops available.

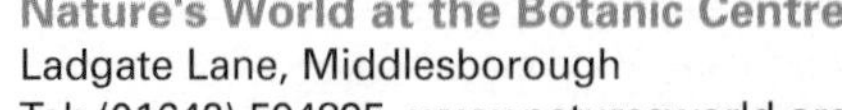

Nature's World at the Botanic Centre
Ladgate Lane, Middlesborough
Tel: (01642) 594895 www.naturesworld.org.uk
Demonstration gardens, wildlife pond, white garden, environmental exhibition hall, shop, tearoom and River Tees model. Hydroponicum and Eco centre now open.

Otter Trust's North Pennines Reserve
Bowes, Barnard Castle
Tel: (01833) 628339
A branch of the famous Otter Trust. Visitors can see Asian and British otters, red and fallow deer and several rare breeds of farm animals in this 230-acre (93ha) wildlife reserve.

Raby Castle
Staindrop, Darlington
Tel: (01833) 660202 www.rabycastle.com
The medieval castle, home of Lord Barnard's family since 1626, includes a 200-acre (80ha) deer park, walled gardens, carriage collection, adventure playground, shop and tearoom.

St Nicholas Cathedral
St Nicholas Street, Newcastle upon Tyne
Tel: (0191) 232 1939
www.newcastle-ang-cathedralstnicholas.org.uk
13thC and 14thC church, added to in 18thC-20thC. Famous lantern tower, pre-reformation font and font cover, 15thC stained glass roundel in the side chapel.

Wallington House, Walled Garden and Grounds (National Trust)
Wallington, Morpeth
Tel: (01670) 773600 www.nationaltrust.org.uk
Escape to the beautiful walled garden and its conservatory or enjoy a walk in the woods or along by the river. Bring the family to one of the many events at Wallington.

Washington Old Hall (National Trust)
The Avenue, Washington
Tel: (0191) 416 6879 www.nationaltrust.org.uk
From 1183 to 1399 the home of George Washington's direct ancestors, remaining in the family until 1613. The manor, from which the family took its name, was restored in 1936.

Wildfowl and Wetlands Trust Washington
District 15, Washington
Tel: (0191) 416 5454 www.wwt.org.uk
Collection of 1,000 wildfowl of 85 varieties. Viewing gallery, picnic areas, hides and winter wild bird-feeding station, flamingos and wild grey heron. Waterside cafe.

Northumbria Tourist Board

Aykley Heads, Durham DH1 5UX.
Tel: (0191) 375 3049 Fax: (0191) 386 0899
www.visitnorthumbria.com

THE FOLLOWING PUBLICATIONS ARE AVAILABLE FROM NORTHUMBRIA TOURIST BOARD UNLESS OTHERWISE STATED:

Northumbria 2004 –
information on the region, including hotels, bed and breakfast and self-catering accommodation, caravan and camping parks, attractions, shopping, eating and drinking

Group Travel & Education Directory –
guide contains information on group accommodation providers, places to visit, suggested itineraries, coaching information and events. Also provides information to help plan educational visits within the region. Uncover a wide variety of places to visit with unique learning opportunities

Discover Northumbria on two wheels –
information on cycling in the region including an order form allowing the reader to order maps/leaflets from a central ordering point

Discover Northumbria on two feet –
information on walking in the region including an order form allowing the reader to order maps/leaflets from a central ordering point

Getting to Northumbria

BY ROAD: The north/south routes on the A1 and A19 thread the region as does the A68. East/west routes like the A66 and A69 easily link with the western side of the country. Within Northumbria you will find fast, modern interconnecting roads between all the main centres, a vast network of scenic, traffic-free country roads to make motoring a pleasure and frequent local bus services operating to all towns and villages.

BY RAIL: London to Edinburgh InterCity service stops at Darlington, Durham, Newcastle and Berwick upon Tweed. 26 trains daily make the journey between London and Newcastle in just under 3 hours. The London to Middlesbrough journey (changing at Darlington) takes 3 hours. Birmingham to Darlington 3 hours 15 minutes. Bristol to Durham 5 hours and Sheffield to Newcastle just over 2 hours. Direct services operate to Newcastle from Liverpool, Manchester, Glasgow, Stranraer and Carlisle. Regional services to areas of scenic beauty operate frequently, allowing the traveller easy access. The Tyne & Wear Metro makes it possible to travel to many destinations within the Tyneside area, such as Gateshead, South Shields, Whitley Bay and Newcastle International Airport, in minutes.

1. Dunstanburgh Castle

Where to stay in

Northumbria

All place names in the blue bands under which accommodation is listed, are shown on the maps at the front of this guide.

Symbols give useful information about services and facilities. Inside the back cover flap there's a key to these symbols which you can keep open for easy reference.

A complete listing of all the VisitBritain assessed accommodation covered by this guide appears at the back of this guide.

ALLENDALE, Northumberland Map ref 5B2

STRUTHERS FARM
Catton, Allendale, Hexham
NE47 9LP
T: (01434) 683580

Bedrooms: 1 double, 1 twin
Bathrooms: 2 en suite

Evening meal available

Working farm in beautiful countryside near Hadrian's Wall. Well-appointed, en suite rooms, double/twin optional. Evening meal. Nine miles from Hexham. Good parking.

B&B per person per night:
S £22.00–£25.00
D £22.00–£25.00

OPEN All Year

ALNMOUTH, Northumberland Map ref 5C1

BEECH LODGE
8 Alnwood, Alnmouth, Alnwick
NE66 3NN
T: (01665) 830709
I: www.alnmouth.com

Bedrooms: 1 double, 1 twin
Bathrooms: 1 en suite

A warm welcome and quality decoration and furnishings reflect the high standard of accommodation in our spacious, modern, detached bungalow in a woodland setting in village.

B&B per person per night:
D £25.00–£28.00

ALNWICK, Northumberland Map ref 5C1 *Tourist Information Centre Tel: (01665) 510665*

BONDGATE HOUSE
20 Bondgate Without, Alnwick
NE66 1PN
T: (01665) 602025
E: aclarvin@aol.com
I: www.bondgatehouse.ntb.org.uk

Bedrooms: 3 double, 2 twin, 1 single, 2 family
Bathrooms: 7 en suite

Family-run Georgian townhouse, abutting the Alnwick Garden, near the medieval town gateway and interesting local shops. Well placed for touring. En suite rooms.

B&B per person per night:
S £27.50–£35.00
D £16.25–£30.00

OPEN All Year except Christmas

ALNWICK continued

CHARLTON HOUSE

2 Aydon Gardens, South Road, Alnwick NE66 2NT
T: (01665) 605185
I: www.s-h-systems.co.uk/hotels/charlt2.html

B&B per person per night:
S £24.00–£26.00
D £24.00–£26.00

OPEN All Year except Christmas

Victorian townhouse on the edge of historic Alnwick where a warm welcome awaits. Ideally situated to walk to Alnwick Castle and spectacular gardens, plus easy driving to the beautiful coast and countryside of Northumberland. Beautiful en suite bedrooms, TV, alarm clock/radio, hairdryer, hospitality tray. Breakfasts to suit all tastes.

Bedrooms: 3 double, 1 twin, 1 single
Bathrooms: 5 en suite

BAMBURGH, Northumberland Map ref 5C1

♦♦♦♦

GLENANDER BED & BREAKFAST

27 Lucker Road, Bamburgh NE69 7BS
T: (01668) 214336
F: (01668) 214695
E: johntoland@tiscali.co.uk
I: www.glenander.com

B&B per person per night:
S £25.00–£35.00
D £25.00–£30.00

OPEN All Year

Glenander has comfortable double/twin rooms which are available throughout the year. Each bedroom is individually and tastefully furnished in modern design. Amenities include hospitality tray, hairdryer, colour TV and en suite facilities. There is a spacious ground floor guest lounge complete with TV and video.

Bedrooms: 3 double
Bathrooms: 3 en suite

BARNARD CASTLE, Durham Map ref 5B3 *Tourist Information Centre Tel: (01833) 690909*

♦♦♦

MOORCOCK INN

Hill Top, Gordon Bank, Eggleston, Barnard Castle DL12 0AU
T: (01833) 650395
F: (01833) 650052
E: zach1@talk21.com
I: www.moorcock-Inn.co.uk

B&B per person per night:
S £20.00–£25.00
D £16.00–£18.50

OPEN All Year

Country inn with scenic views over Teesdale. Ideal walking country. Cosy en suite bedrooms, open log fire in lounge bar. Over 50 malt whiskies and a selection of real ales. Excellent home-cooked food using local produce. Our speciality is Teesdale lamb and locally produced beef and pork. Also, extensive fish menu.

Bedrooms: 5 double, 2 single
Bathrooms: 4 en suite, 1 private

Evening meal available
CC: Delta, Mastercard, Switch, Visa

CREDIT CARD BOOKINGS If you book by telephone and are asked for your credit card number it is advisable to check the proprietor's policy should you cancel your reservation.

BEAL, Northumberland Map ref 5B1

◆◆◆

BROCK MILL FARMHOUSE

Brock Mill, Beal, Berwick-upon-Tweed TD15 2PB
T: (01289) 381283
F: (01289) 381283
E: brockmillfarmhouse@btopenworld.com

220-acre mixed farm. Peaceful, idyllic surroundings, ideal as a base for touring North Northumberland and Scottish Borders. Quality accommodation with spacious, well-furnished rooms. Residents' lounge. Enjoy our superb English breakfasts or our tasty vegetarian alternatives. Golf and fishing nearby. A warm, friendly welcome awaits.

Bedrooms: 1 double, 1 single, 1 family

CC: Amex, Delta, Mastercard, Switch, Visa

Mid-week deals – prices on request.

B&B per person per night:
S £25.00–£30.00
D £22.50–£25.00

OPEN All Year except Christmas

BELLINGHAM, Northumberland Map ref 5B2 *Tourist Information Centre Tel: (01434) 220616*

◆◆◆◆

LYNDALE GUEST HOUSE

Bellingham, Hexham NE48 2AW
T: (01434) 220361
F: (01434) 220361
E: ken&joy@lyndalegh.fsnet.co.uk
I: www.SmoothHound.co.uk/hotels/lyndale.html

Bedrooms: 2 double, 1 twin
Bathrooms: 2 en suite, 1 private

Evening meal available
CC: Delta, Mastercard, Visa

Country lovers – after a great day out you might like: tea/coffee in the garden, a jacuzzi bath, dinner in our sun lounge – overlooking the famous Pennine Way.

B&B per person per night:
S £25.00–£28.00
D £25.00–£28.00

HB per person per night:
DY £39.50–£42.50

OPEN All Year except Christmas

BERWICK-UPON-TWEED, Northumberland Map ref 5B1 *Tourist Information Centre Tel: (01289) 330733*

◆◆◆

COBBLED YARD HOTEL

40 Walkergate, Berwick-upon-Tweed TD15 1DJ
T: (01289) 308407
F: (01289) 330623
E: cobbledyardhotel@berwick35.fsnet.co.uk
I: www.cobbledyardhotel.com

Bedrooms: 2 double, 3 family
Bathrooms: 5 en suite

Evening meal available
CC: Delta, Diners, Mastercard, Switch, Visa

Two minutes from town centre, within town walls, close to beach, golf course and railway station. Family-run hotel, good food. Car park.

B&B per person per night:
S £35.00–£55.00
D £27.50

OPEN All Year

◆◆◆◆

LADYTHORNE HOUSE

Cheswick, Berwick-upon-Tweed TD15 2RW
T: (01289) 387382
F: (01289) 387073
E: valparker@ladythorneguesthouse.freeserve.co.uk
I: www.ladythorneguesthouse.freeserve.co.uk

Bedrooms: 1 double, 2 twin, 1 single, 2 family

Grade II Listed Georgian house dated 1721. Magnificent views of the countryside, close to unspoilt beaches. Large garden, families welcome. Meals available within five minutes' drive.

B&B per person per night:
S £18.00–£20.00
D £18.00–£25.00

OPEN All Year

ACCESSIBILITY

Look for the symbols which indicate National Accessible Scheme standards for hearing and visually impaired guests in addition to standards for guests with mobility impairment. You can find an index of all scheme participants at the back of this guide.

BERWICK-UPON-TWEED continued

ROB ROY

Dock Road, Tweedmouth, Berwick-upon-Tweed TD15 2BE
T: (01289) 306428
F: (01289) 303629
E: therobroy@btinternet.com
I: www.therobroy.co.uk

Stone-built pub with cosy bar and log fire. One mile to Berwick centre from our riverside location. Our restaurant and bar menus offer choice local seafood, lobster, oysters, scallops. Visit Northumbria's beautiful coastline and castles, walk the Cheviots or the beautiful Tweed Valley. Or just enjoy Rob Roy hospitality.

Bedrooms: 1 double, 1 twin
Bathrooms: 2 en suite

Evening meal available
CC: Amex, Delta, Diners, Mastercard, Switch, Visa

Reduced out of season offers. Nov-May deals on website.

B&B per person per night:
S £30.00–£34.00
D £23.00–£27.00

OPEN All Year except Christmas

CONSETT, Durham Map ref 5B2

BEE COTTAGE FARMHOUSE

Castleside, Consett DH8 9HW
T: (01207) 508224
E: welcome@beecottagefarmhouse.freeserve.co.uk
I: www.smoothhound.co.uk/hotels/beecottage.html

Situated on the edge of the Durham Dales with stunning views. A wonderful place to relax. Peaceful walking and cycling (next to C2C). Ideal base for Beamish, Durham, Newcastle, Hadrian's Wall. Newly refurbished farmhouse rooms. Some ground floor rooms, all en suite. Dinner available. Licensed. Non-smoking. You will be most welcome.

Bedrooms: 2 double, 2 twin, 3 family, 1 suite
Bathrooms: 7 en suite

Evening meal available
CC: Amex, Mastercard, Switch, Visa

B&B per person per night:
S £30.00–£35.00
D £28.00–£35.00

HB per person per night:
DY £43.50–£50.50

OPEN All Year except Christmas

WHARNLEY BURN FARM

Castleside, Consett DH8 9AY
T: (01207) 508374
F: (01207) 503420

14thC farmhouse on A68 Durham/Northumberland border. Beamed ceilings, low doorways, log fires. Guest lounge, conservatory and cottage garden. En suite, TV, tea/coffee facilities. Ideal touring base or travel to/from England/Scotland, in picturesque surroundings. Once home to local highwayman. We keep horses, goats, geese, ducks etc.

Bedrooms: 1 double
Bathrooms: 1 en suite

B&B per person per night:
S £30.00
D £25.00

OPEN All Year except Christmas

QUALITY ASSURANCE SCHEME

Diamond ratings and awards were correct at the time of going to press but are subject to change. Please check at the time of booking.

CORBRIDGE, Northumberland Map ref 5B2

♦♦♦♦

FELLCROFT

Station Road, Corbridge NE45 5AY
T: (01434) 632384
F: (01434) 633918
E: tove.brown@ukonline.co.uk

Bedrooms: 1 double, 1 twin
Bathrooms: 1 en suite, 1 private

Evening meal available

Well-appointed, stone-built, Edwardian house with full, private facilities. Quiet road in country setting, 0.5 miles south of market square. Non-smokers only, please.

B&B per person per night:
S £21.00–£23.00
D £17.50–£19.00

OPEN All Year except Christmas

♦♦♦♦

LOW FOTHERLEY FARMHOUSE BED AND BREAKFAST

Riding Mill NE44 6BB
T: (01434) 682277
F: (01434) 682277
E: hugh@lowfotherley.fsnet.co.uk
I: www.westfarm.freeserve.co.uk

Built in the 19thC, Low Fotherley is an impressive Victorian farmhouse full of character and history situated close to the A68 with outstanding views. Spacious, comfortable house with full central heating. Quality bedrooms with TV and hospitality tray. Close to Hexham, Hadrian's Wall and Durham. Aga breakfast, homemade bread and preserves.

Bedrooms: 2 double
Bathrooms: 1 en suite, 1 private

B&B per person per night:
S £25.00–£30.00
D £22.50–£25.00

OPEN All Year except Christmas

CRASTER, Northumberland Map ref 5C1 *Tourist Information Centre Tel: (01665) 576007*

♦♦♦

HOWICK SCAR FARMHOUSE

Craster, Alnwick NE66 3SU
T: (01665) 576665
F: (01665) 576665
E: howick.scar@virgin.net
I: www.howickscar.co.uk

Bedrooms: 2 double

250-acre mixed farm. Comfortable farmhouse with television lounge. Seven miles from Alnwick between Craster and Howick on the coast. Lovely scenery and walks.

B&B per person per night:
D £20.00–£22.00

CROOKHAM, Northumberland Map ref 5B1

♦♦♦♦

THE COACH HOUSE AT CROOKHAM

Crookham, Cornhill-on-Tweed TD12 4TD
T: (01890) 820293
F: (01890) 820284
E: stay@coachhousecrookham.com
I: www.coachhousecrookham.com

Bedrooms: 4 double, 5 twin
Bathrooms: 7 en suite

Evening meal available
CC: Mastercard, Visa

Spacious rooms, arranged around a courtyard, in rolling country near the Scottish border. Home-cooked, quality fresh food. Rooms specially equipped for disabled guests.

B&B per person per night:
S £25.00–£47.00
D £25.00–£47.00

HB per person per night:
DY £44.50–£66.50

DARLINGTON, Tees Valley Map ref 5C3 *Tourist Information Centre Tel: (01325) 388666*

♦♦♦

BOOT & SHOE

Church Row, Darlington DL1 5QD
T: (01325) 287501
F: (01325) 287501
E: enquiries@bootandshoe.com
I: www.bootandshoe.com

Bedrooms: 9 double
Bathrooms: 7 en suite, 2 private

CC: Delta, Mastercard, Switch, Visa

A Grade II Listed building situated on Darlington's busy market place, fully refurbished in 2000. Only minutes away from train and bus station and A1.

B&B per person per night:
S £25.00–£35.00
D £25.00

OPEN All Year

CONFIRM YOUR BOOKING

You are advised to confirm your booking in writing.

DURHAM, Durham Map ref 5C2 *Tourist Information Centre Tel: (0191) 384 3720*

◆◆◆◆

CASTLE VIEW GUEST HOUSE

4 Crossgate, Durham DH1 4PS
T: (0191) 3868852
F: (0191) 3868852
E: castle_view@hotmail.com

Bedrooms: 5 double, 1 single
Bathrooms: 6 en suite

CC: Delta, Mastercard, Switch, Visa

B&B per person per night:
S £45.00–£50.00
D £30.00–£35.00

OPEN All Year except Christmas

Two-hundred-and-fifty-year-old, Listed building in the heart of the old city, with woodland and riverside walks and a magnificent view of the cathedral and castle.

◆◆◆

CASTLEDENE

37 Nevilledale Terrace, Durham DH1 4QG
T: (0191) 3848386
F: (0191) 3848386

Bedrooms: 2 twin

B&B per person per night:
S Max £25.00
D Max £20.00

Edwardian, end-of-terrace house 0.5 miles west of the market place. Within walking distance of the riverside, cathedral and castle.

ST AIDAN'S COLLEGE

University of Durham, Windmill Hill, Durham DH1 3LJ
T: (0191) 3345769
F: (0191) 3345770
E: aidans.conf@durham.ac.uk
I: www.st-aidans.org.uk

B&B per person per night:
S £21.00–£34.00
D £27.50–£32.00

Set in landscaped gardens, overlooking the magnificent cathedral, which has proved to be Britain's best-loved visitor attraction. Single/twin en suite bedrooms and a spacious, airy dining room. We are an ideal venue for anyone wishing to visit the many and varied museums/castles to be found in the area.

Bedrooms: 24 twin, 72 single
Bathrooms: 96 en suite

Evening meal available
CC: Delta, Mastercard, Switch, Visa

EGLINGHAM, Northumberland Map ref 5B1

◆◆◆◆

ASH TREE HOUSE

The Terrace, Eglingham, Alnwick NE66 2UA
T: (01665) 578533
E: prudence@ukpc.net
I: www.ashtreehouse.com

B&B per person per night:
S £28.00
D £23.00–£30.00

HB per person per night:
DY £38.00–£43.00

OPEN All Year

A warm Northumbrian welcome with excellent home cooking awaits you in our lovely stone-built home set in the glorious North Northumbrian countryside, seven miles from Alnwick. Eglingham is a conservation village between the Cheviot Hills and the Heritage Coast within easy reach of Lindisfarne and the Farne Islands.

Bedrooms: 1 double, 1 twin
Bathrooms: 1 en suite

Evening meal available

GREENHAUGH, Northumberland Map ref 5B2

Rating Applied For

HOLLYBUSH INN

Greenhaugh, Hexham NE48 1PW
T: (01434) 240391
E: timmorris.hollybush@virgin.net
I: www.vizual4U.co.uk/hollybush.htm

Bedrooms: 3 double
Bathrooms: 3 en suite

Evening meal available
CC: Amex, Delta, Mastercard, Switch, Visa

B&B per person per night:
S £30.00–£40.00
D £25.00–£35.00

OPEN All Year except Christmas

A 200-year-old inn, with original beamed ceilings, open log fire and cosy atmosphere. Convenient for Kielder Water, Hadrian's Wall and the Borders.

HALTWHISTLE, Northumberland Map ref 5B2 *Tourist Information Centre Tel: (01434) 322002*

HALL MEADOWS

Main Street, Haltwhistle NE49 0AZ
T: (01434) 321021
F: (01434) 321021

Bedrooms: 3 double
Bathrooms: 2 en suite, 1 private

B&B per person per night:
S £20.00–£30.00
D £20.00–£25.00

OPEN All Year except Christmas

Built in 1888, a large family house with pleasant garden in the centre of town. Ideally placed for Hadrian's Wall and close to bus and rail connections.

HAMSTERLEY FOREST

See under Barnard Castle

HAYDON BRIDGE, Northumberland Map ref 5B2

HADRIAN LODGE

Hindshield Moss, North Road, Haydon Bridge, Hexham NE47 6NF
T: (01434) 684867
F: (01434) 684867
E: hadrianlodge@hadrianswall.co.uk
I: www.hadrianswall.co.uk

Bedrooms: 5 double, 1 single, 1 twin, 3 family
Bathrooms: 9 en suite, 1 private

Evening meal available
CC: Amex, Mastercard, Switch, Visa

B&B per person per night:
S £32.50–£39.50
D £27.50–£29.75

HB per person per night:
DY £39.50–£45.00

OPEN All Year

Idyllic rural location, overlooking lakes (fishing available), near Housesteads Roman Fort and Hadrian's Wall. Cosy residents' bar, delicious home-cooked meals. Warm welcome. Write/ring for brochure.

HEXHAM, Northumberland Map ref 5B2 *Tourist Information Centre Tel: (01434) 652220*

Silver Award

BLACK HALL

Black Hall, Juniper, Hexham NE47 0LD
T: (01434) 673218
F: (01434) 673218
E: nblackhall@lineone.net
I: www.blackhall-hexham.co.uk

B&B per person per night:
S £35.00–£37.00
D £25.00–£27.00

HB per person per night:
DY £45.00–£57.00

OPEN All Year except Christmas

Black Hall is a peaceful Grade II Listed country house set in its own parkland. Spacious, warm, south-facing rooms with open views over our fields and woods. We are five miles south of Hexham within easy reach of Hadrian's Wall and the many attractions of Northumberland.

Bedrooms: 1 double, 1 twin
Bathrooms: 2 private

Evening meal available
CC: Delta, Mastercard, Switch, Visa

KIELDER FOREST

See under Bellingham, Wark

TOWN INDEX

This can be found at the back of the guide. If you know where you want to stay, the index will give you the page number listing accommodation in your chosen town, city or village.

KIELDER WATER, Northumberland Map ref 5B2

THE PHEASANT INN (BY KIELDER WATER)

Stannersburn, Falstone, Hexham NE48 1DD
T: (01434) 240382
F: (01434) 240382
E: thepheasantinn@kielderwater.demon.co.uk
I: www.thepheasantinn.com

Charming 16thC inn, retaining its character while providing comfortable, modern, en suite accommodation. Features include stone walls and low-beamed ceilings in the bars, antique artefacts and open fires. Emphasis on traditional home cooking, using fresh vegetables, served in bar or dining room. Sunday roasts are renowned for their quality. Double/twins with en suite. One family room with en suite.

Bedrooms: 4 double, 3 twin, 1 family
Bathrooms: 8 en suite

Evening meal available
CC: Delta, Mastercard, Switch, Visa

Reduced rates Oct-May, DB&B £48pppn.

B&B per person per night:
S £40.00–£45.00
D £32.50–£35.00

HB per person per night:
DY £48.00–£50.00

OPEN All Year except Christmas

LITTLETOWN, Durham Map ref 5C2

LITTLETOWN LODGE

Front Street, Littletown, Durham DH6 1PZ
T: (0191) 3723712
E: littletownlodge@aol.com
I: www.littletownlodge.co.uk

A warm welcome awaits you in this traditional country guesthouse situated in a tranquil rural setting only minutes from Durham City centre. Beautiful 4-poster rooms are available for that extra-special break. It is an ideal base for walking, cycling or touring, with collection and delivery service available.

Bedrooms: 3 double, 2 family
Bathrooms: 5 en suite

Evening meal available
CC: Mastercard, Visa

Romantic weekend (2 nights) in one of our 4-poster room suites available from £120 per room, including complimentary bottle of champagne.

B&B per person per night:
S Min £30.00
D Min £22.50

OPEN All Year

LONGFRAMLINGTON, Northumberland Map ref 5C1

COQUET BED & BREAKFAST

Elyhaugh Farm, Longframlington, Morpeth NE65 8BE
T: (01665) 570305
F: (01665) 570305
E: coquetbb@fsmail.net

Ground floor bedrooms situated in a Listed building conversion next to the farmhouse. Original features have been retained to create the perfect ambience for a relaxing break. The River Coquet flows in front of the farmhouse, where private fishing is available. A central location for many attractions.

Bedrooms: 2 double, 1 twin
Bathrooms: 3 en suite

B&B per person per night:
S £30.00–£35.00
D £22.50–£25.00

OPEN All Year except Christmas

RATING All accommodation in this guide has been rated, or is awaiting a rating, by a trained VisitBritain assessor.

MARSKE-BY-THE-SEA, Tees Valley Map ref 5C3

SHIP INN

High Street, Marske-by-the-Sea TS11 7LL
T: (01642) 482640
F: (01642) 482640
E: shipmates@supanet.com

B&B per person per night:
S £31.50–£41.50
D £20.75–£22.50

OPEN All Year

The Ship has a warm, friendly atmosphere. Close to beach (300 yards). Grade II Listed with impressive exterior. Good, home-cooked food, ales and wines.

Bedrooms: 4 double, 1 family
Bathrooms: 2 en suite, 1 private

Evening meal available
CC: Amex, Delta, Mastercard, Switch, Visa

P €

MIDDLETON-IN-TEESDALE, Durham Map ref 5B3 *Tourist Information Centre Tel: (01833) 641001*

BELVEDERE HOUSE

54 Market Place, Middleton-in-Teesdale, Barnard Castle DL12 0QH
T: (01833) 640884
E: belvedere@thecoachhouse.net
I: www.thecoachhouse.net

Bedrooms: 3 double
Bathrooms: 3 en suite

B&B per person per night:
S £21.00
D £19.00

OPEN All Year except Christmas

18thC house, centrally situated in Dales village. Enjoy a warm welcome and great breakfast. Explore Teesdale's beautiful countryside and places of historic interest. Magnificent waterfalls.

P

MORPETH, Northumberland Map ref 5C2 *Tourist Information Centre Tel: (01670) 500700*

♦♦♦

COTTAGE VIEW GUEST HOUSE

6 Staithes Lane, Morpeth NE61 1TD
T: (01670) 518550
F: (01670) 510840
E: cottageview.morpeth@virgin.net
I: www.cottageview.co.uk

B&B per person per night:
S £27.50–£32.50
D £19.25–£21.75

OPEN All Year

Centrally situated, family-run guesthouse. Private car parking, reception bar, two lounges (one private), e-mail and fax facilities (small charge made). Night porter available for late arrivals/early departures. We can accommodate over 50 people – ideal for wedding guests. So don't delay, book today!

Bedrooms: 13 double, 4 twin, 4 single, 4 family
Bathrooms: 16 en suite

CC: Amex, Delta, Diners, Mastercard, Switch, Visa

Child discounts available.

P

OTTERBURN, Northumberland Map ref 5B1 *Tourist Information Centre Tel: (01830) 520093*

♦♦♦♦

BUTTERCHURN GUEST HOUSE

Main Street, Otterburn NE19 1NP
T: (01830) 520585
E: keith@butterchurnguesthouse.co.uk
I: www.butterchurnguesthouse.co.uk

B&B per person per night:
S £25.00–£30.00
D £24.00–£30.00

OPEN All Year

Excellent family-run guesthouse in quiet village location renowned for its welcome, quality of service and ambience. Situated in Northumberland National Park, on the scenic route to Scotland. Central for Hadrian's Wall, Kielder Water, coast and castles. Everyone welcome in the county known as the 'Land of Far Horizons'.

Bedrooms: 4 double, 3 family
Bathrooms: 7 en suite

CC: Delta, Mastercard, Visa

P €

OTTERBURN continued

REDESDALE ARMS HOTEL

Rochester, Otterburn,
Newcastle upon Tyne NE19 1TA
T: (01830) 520668
F: (01830) 520063
E: redesdalehotel@hotmail.com
I: www.redesdale-hotel.co.uk

Bedrooms: 7 double, 3 family
Bathrooms: 10 en suite

Evening meal available
CC: Amex, Delta, Mastercard, Switch, Visa

B&B per person per night:
S £43.00–£48.00
D £35.00–£45.00

OPEN All Year except Christmas

Family-run old coaching inn with log fires and fine food. Central for Hadrian's Wall and the Kielder Forest. Beautiful en suite country bedrooms.

REDCAR, Tees Valley Map ref 5C3 *Tourist Information Centre Tel: (01642) 471921*

FALCON HOTEL

13 Station Road, Redcar TS10 1AH
T: (01642) 484300

Bedrooms: 2 double, 5 twin, 9 single, 3 family
Bathrooms: 12 en suite

Evening meal available

B&B per person per night:
S £17.00–£26.00
D £15.00–£38.00

OPEN All Year

Licensed hotel in centre of town with recent extension of en suite twins and singles. Within easy reach of the Cleveland Hills.

ROTHBURY, Northumberland Map ref 5B1 *Tourist Information Centre Tel: (01669) 620887*

Gold Award

KATERINA'S GUEST HOUSE

Sun Buildings, High Street,
Rothbury, Morpeth NE65 7TQ
T: (01669) 620691
F: (01669) 620691
E: cath@katerinasguesthouse.co.uk
I: www.katerinasguesthouse.co.uk

Bedrooms: 3 double
Bathrooms: 3 en suite

Evening meal available

B&B per person per night:
S £36.00–£50.00
D £23.00–£25.00

HB per person per night:
DY £58.00–£62.00

OPEN All Year

Situated in beautiful country village. All rooms en suite, 4-poster beds, TV. Ideal centre for exploring Northumberland hills, beaches, Scottish Borders. Evening meals by arrangement.

THE QUEENS HEAD

Townfoot, Rothbury, Morpeth
NE65 7SR
T: (01669) 620470
E: enqs@queensheadrothbury.com
I: www.queensheadrothbury.com

Bedrooms: 3 double, 3 twin, 1 family
Bathrooms: 7 en suite

Evening meal available
CC: Delta, Mastercard, Switch, Visa

B&B per person per night:
S £30.00–£35.00
D £25.00–£30.00

HB per person per night:
DY £40.00–£50.00

OPEN All Year

Traditional friendly pub in the lovely village of Rotherby in the heart of the Coquet Valley. Excellent food, comfortable rooms and great service.

SEAHOUSES, Northumberland Map ref 5C1

WESTFIELD FARMHOUSE

North Sunderland, Seahouses
NE68 7UR
T: (01665) 720161
F: (01665) 720713
E: info@westfieldfarmhouse.co.uk
I: www.westfieldfarmhouse.co.uk

Bedrooms: 1 double, 1 twin
Bathrooms: 2 en suite

CC: Amex, Delta, Mastercard, Switch, Visa

B&B per person per night:
S £35.00
D £27.50–£32.50

Traditional stone farmhouse, luxury en suites (bath/shower). Aga-cooked Northumbrian breakfast. Walled garden. Ideal location for coastline, castles and countryside.

CHECK THE MAPS

The colour maps at the front of this guide show all the cities, towns and villages for which you will find accommodation entries. Refer to the town index to find the page on which they are listed.

SPENNYMOOR, Durham Map ref 5C2

HIGHVIEW COUNTRY HOUSE

Kirkmerrington, Spennymoor DL16 7JT
T: (01388) 811006
F: (01388) 811006
E: highviewhouse@genie.co.uk
I: www.highviewcountryhouse.co.uk

B&B per person per night:
S £28.50–£35.50
D £24.50–£27.50

OPEN All Year except Christmas

Country house in one acre of gardens surrounded by rolling countryside. Peace and tranquillity awaits. Safe and secure parking. Situated on the edge of delightful village. Good pubs, Saxon church. Only 10 minutes from motorway/Durham. Brochure available.

Bedrooms: 5 double, 1 single, 1 family
Bathrooms: 7 en suite

Evening meal available

Contact us for weekly rates.

P

STANLEY, Durham Map ref 5C2

♦♦♦

BUSHBLADES FARM

Harperley, Stanley DH9 9UA
T: (01207) 232722

B&B per person per night:
S £25.00–£30.00
D £19.50–£22.50

OPEN All Year except Christmas

60-acre livestock farm. Georgian house with large garden in rural setting. All rooms are spacious with colour TV, tea/coffee facilities and comfortable chairs. Ideal base or stopover. A1M 10 minutes. Easy reach of Durham City, Beamish Museum, Hadrian's Wall and the Northumberland Coast. Ample parking.

Bedrooms: 3 double
Bathrooms: 1 en suite

12 P

WALL, Northumberland Map ref 5B2

THE HADRIAN HOTEL

Wall, Hexham NE46 4EE
T: (01434) 681232
E: david.lindsay13@btinternet.com
I: www.hadrianhotel.com

Bedrooms: 2 double, 4 twin
Bathrooms: 4 en suite

Evening meal available
CC: Delta, Mastercard, Switch, Visa

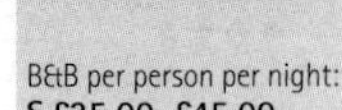
B&B per person per night:
S £35.00–£45.00
D £20.00–£27.50

OPEN All Year

Attractive 18thC former coaching inn. Excellent bar meals, real ales, open fires and tranquil gardens. Situated close to Hadrian's Wall and near Hexham.

P €

COUNTRY CODE Always follow the Country Code · Enjoy the countryside and respect its life and work · Guard against all risk of fire · Fasten all gates · Keep your dogs under close control · Keep to public paths across farmland · Use gates and stiles to cross fences, hedges and walls · Leave livestock, crops and machinery alone · Take your litter home · Help to keep all water clean · Protect wildlife, plants and trees · Take special care on country roads · Make no unnecessary noise

WARK, Northumberland Map ref 5B2

◆◆◆

BATTLESTEADS HOTEL

Wark, Hexham NE48 3LS
T: (01434) 230209
F: (01434) 230730
E: info@battlesteads-hotel.co.uk
I: www.Battlesteads-Hotel.co.uk

18thC inn, formerly a farmhouse, in the heart of rural Northumberland, close to the Roman Wall and Kielder Water. An ideal centre for exploring Border country and for relaxing, walking, cycling or horse-riding. Collection and delivery service operated for walkers and cyclists. Ground floor bedrooms also available.

Bedrooms: 4 double, 7 twin, 1 single, 2 family
Bathrooms: 14 en suite

Evening meal available
CC: Amex, Delta, Mastercard, Switch, Visa

Nov-Mar: 2 nights' B&B – 20% off, 3 nights' B&B – 30% off. Please see website.

B&B per person per night:
S £45.00
D £40.00

HB per person per night:
DY £54.95–£59.95

OPEN All Year

WHICKHAM, Tyne and Wear Map ref 5C2

◆◆◆◆
Silver Award

EAST BYERMOOR GUEST HOUSE

Fellside Road, Whickham,
Newcastle upon Tyne NE16 5BD
T: (01207) 272687
F: (01207) 272145
E: eastbyermoor-gh.arbon@virgin.net
I: www.eastbyermoor.co.uk

Bedrooms: 4 double, 2 twin
Bathrooms: 5 en suite, 1 private

Evening meal available
CC: Delta, Mastercard, Switch, Visa

B&B per person per night:
S £23.00–£25.00
D £23.00–£25.00

OPEN All Year

Large, stone, former farmhouse in open countryside, convenient for Gateshead MetroCentre, Newcastle, Durham and Sunderland. Comfortable guests' lounge, quiet reading room, landscaped garden. Christian proprietors.

WOOLER, Northumberland Map ref 5B1 *Tourist Information Centre Tel: (01668) 282123*

◆◆◆

RYECROFT HOTEL

28 Ryecroft Way, Wooler NE71 6AB
T: (01668) 281459
F: (01668) 282214
E: ryecroftthtl@aol.com
I: www.ryecroft-hotel.com

Bedrooms: 6 double, 2 single, 2 family
Bathrooms: 10 en suite

Evening meal available
CC: Amex, Delta, Mastercard, Switch, Visa

B&B per person per night:
S £25.00–£30.00
D £25.00–£30.00

OPEN All Year

Small, family-run hotel renowned for its home-cooked food and fine ales. A great base for exploring Northumberland and the Scottish Borders.

AT-A-GLANCE SYMBOLS

Symbols at the end of each accommodation entry give useful information about services and facilities. A key to symbols can be found inside the back cover flap. Keep this open for easy reference.

A brief guide to the main Towns and Villages offering accommodation in **Northumbria**

A ALLENDALE, NORTHUMBERLAND - Attractive small town set amongst moors, 10 miles south-west of Hexham and claimed to be the geographical centre of Britain. Surrounded by unspoilt walking country, with many well-signposted walks along the East and West Allen Rivers. Traditional Baal ceremony at New Year.

ALNMOUTH, NORTHUMBERLAND - Quiet village with pleasant old buildings, at the mouth of the River Aln where extensive dunes and sands stretch along Alnmouth Bay. 18th C granaries, some converted to dwellings, still stand.

ALNWICK, NORTHUMBERLAND - Ancient and historic market town, entered through the Hotspur Tower, an original gate in the town walls. The medieval castle, the second biggest in England and still the seat of the Dukes of Northumberland, was restored from ruin in the 18th C.

B BAMBURGH, NORTHUMBERLAND - Village with a spectacular red sandstone castle standing 150 ft above the sea. On the village green the magnificent Norman church stands opposite a museum containing mementoes of the heroine Grace Darling.

BARNARD CASTLE, DURHAM - High over the Tees, a thriving market town with a busy market square. Bernard Baliol's 12th C castle (now ruins) stands nearby. The Bowes Museum, housed in a grand 19th C French chateau, holds fine paintings and furniture. Nearby are some magnificent buildings.

BEAL, NORTHUMBERLAND - Tiny hamlet with an inn at the junction of the A1 which leads on to the causeway to Holy Island. Some farmhouses and buildings are dated 1674.

BELLINGHAM, NORTHUMBERLAND - Set in the beautiful valley of the North Tyne close to the Kielder Forest, Kielder Water and lonely moorland below the Cheviots. The church has an ancient stone wagon roof fortified in the 18th C with buttresses.

BERWICK-UPON-TWEED, NORTHUMBERLAND - Guarding the mouth of the Tweed, England's northernmost town with the best 16th C city walls in Europe. The handsome Guildhall and barracks date from the 18th C. Three bridges cross to Tweedmouth, the oldest built in 1634.

C CONSETT, DURHAM - Former steel town on the edge of rolling moors. Modern development includes the shopping centre and a handsome Roman Catholic church, designed by a local architect. To the west, the Derwent Reservoir provides water sports and pleasant walks.

CORBRIDGE, NORTHUMBERLAND - Small town on the River Tyne. Close by are extensive remains of the Roman military town Corstopitum, with a museum housing important discoveries from excavations. The town itself is attractive with shady trees, a 17th C bridge and interesting old buildings, notably a 14th C vicarage.

D DARLINGTON, DURHAM - Largest town in County Durham, standing on the River Skerne and home of the earliest passenger railway which first ran to Stockton in 1825. Now the home of a railway museum. Originally a prosperous market town occupying the site of an Anglo-Saxon settlement, it still holds an open market.

DURHAM, DURHAM - Ancient city with its Norman castle and cathedral, now a World Heritage site, set on a bluff high over the Wear. A market and university town and regional centre, spreading beyond the market-place on both banks of the river.

H HALTWHISTLE, NORTHUMBERLAND - Small market town with interesting 12th C church, old inns and blacksmith's smithy. North of the town are several important sites and interpretation centres of Hadrian's Wall. Ideal centre for archaeology, outdoor activity or touring holidays.

HAYDON BRIDGE, NORTHUMBERLAND - Small town on the banks of the South Tyne with an ancient church, built of stone from sites along the Roman Wall just north. Ideally situated for exploring Hadrian's Wall and also the Border country.

HEXHAM, NORTHUMBERLAND - Old coaching and market town near Hadrian's Wall. Since pre-Norman times a weekly market has been held in the centre with its market-place and abbey park, and the richly furnished 12th C abbey church has a superb Anglo-Saxon crypt.

K KIELDER WATER, NORTHUMBERLAND - A magnificent man-made lake, the largest in Northern Europe, with over 27 miles of shoreline. On the edge of the Northumberland National Park and near the Scottish border, Kielder can be explored by car, on foot or by ferry.

L LONGFRAMLINGTON, NORTHUMBERLAND - Pleasant village with an interesting church of the Transitional style. On Hall Hill are the remains of a camp with triple entrenchment. Brinkburn Priory is to be found nearby.

M MARSKE-BY-THE-SEA, TEES VALLEY - Residential town and resort 2 miles west of Saltburn.

MIDDLETON-IN-TEESDALE, DURHAM - Small stone town of hillside terraces overlooking the river, developed by the London Lead Company in the 18th C. Five miles up-river is the spectacular 70-ft waterfall, High Force.

MORPETH, NORTHUMBERLAND - Market town on the River Wansbeck. There are charming gardens and parks, among them Carlisle Park which lies close to the ancient remains of Morpeth Castle. The chantry building houses the Northumbrian Craft Centre and the bagpipe museum.

O **OTTERBURN, NORTHUMBERLAND -** Small village set at the meeting of the River Rede with Otter Burn, the site of the Battle of Otterburn in 1388. A peaceful tradition continues in the sale of Otterburn tweeds in this beautiful region, which is ideal for exploring the Border country and the Cheviots.

R **ROTHBURY, NORTHUMBERLAND -** Old market town on the River Coquet near the Simonside Hills. It makes an ideal centre for walking and fishing or for exploring this beautiful area from the coast to the Cheviots. Cragside House and Gardens (National Trust) are open to the public.

S **SEAHOUSES, NORTHUMBERLAND** -Small modern resort developed around a 19th C herring port. Just offshore, and reached by boat from here, are the rocky Farne Islands (National Trust) where there is an important bird reserve. The bird observatory occupies a medieval pele tower.

SPENNYMOOR, DURHAM - Booming coal and iron town from the 18th C until early in the 20th century when traditional industry gave way to lighter manufacturing and trading estates were built. On the moors south of the town there are fine views of the Wear Valley.

W **WOOLER, NORTHUMBERLAND -** Old grey-stone town, market-place for foresters and hill farmers, set at the edge of the north-east Cheviots. This makes a good base for excursions to Northumberland's loveliest coastline, or for angling and walking in the Borderlands.

USE YOUR *i*s

There are more than 550 Tourist Information Centres throughout England offering friendly help with accommodation and holiday ideas as well as suggestions of places to visit and things to do. There may well be a centre in your home town which can help you before you set out. You'll find addresses in the local Phone Book.

Finding **accommodation** is as easy as 1 2 3

Where to Stay makes it quick and easy to find a place to stay. There are several ways to use this guide.

1 TOWN INDEX

The town index at the back, lists all the places with accommodation featured in the regional sections. The index gives a page number where you can find full accommodation and contact details.

2 COLOUR MAPS

All the place names in black on the colour maps at the front have an entry in the regional sections. Refer to the town index for the page number where you will find one or more establishments offering accommodation in your chosen town or village.

3 ACCOMMODATION LISTING

Contact details for **all** VisitBritain assessed accommodation throughout England, together with their national Diamond rating are given in the listing section of this guide. Establishments with a full entry in the regional sections are shown in blue. Look in the town index for the page number on which their full entry appears.

North West

Home of pop stars, world-famous football teams, Blackpool Tower and Coronation Street, the great North West has vibrant cities, idyllic countryside and world-class art collections too.

Classic sights
Blackpool Tower & Pleasure Beach – unashamed razzamatazz
Football – museums and tours at Manchester United and Liverpool football clubs
The Beatles – The Beatles Story, Magical Mystery Tour Bus and Macca's former home

Coast & country
The Ribble Valley – unchanged rolling landscapes
Formby – a glorious beach of sand dunes and pine woods
Wildfowl & Wetlands Trust, near Ormskirk – 120 types of birds including flamingos

Arts for all
The Tate Liverpool – modern art
The Lowry – the world's largest collection of LS Lowry paintings

The Counties of Chesire, Greater Manchester, Lancashire, Merseyside and the High Peak District of Derbyshire

For more information contact:
North West Tourist Board
Swan House,
Swan Meadow Road,
Wigan Pier, Wigan WN3 5BB

www.visitnorthwest.com

Telephone enquiries -
T: (01942) 821222
F: (01942) 820002

1. Blackpool Tower
2. Walkers on Kinder Scout, Derbyshire

Places to Visit

You will find hundreds of interesting places to visit during your stay, just some of which are listed in these pages. Contact any Tourist Information Centre in the region for more ideas on days out.

Awarded VisitBritain's 'Quality Assured Visitor Attraction' marque.

Arley Hall and Gardens

Arley, Northwich
Tel: (01565) 777353
www.arleyestate.zuunet.co.uk

Early Victorian building set in 12 acres (5ha) of magnificent gardens, with a 15thC tithe barn. Plant nursery, gift shop and restaurant. A plantsman's paradise!

Astley Hall Museum and Art Gallery

Astley Park, Chorley
Tel: (01257) 515555 www.astleyhall.co.uk

Astley Hall dates from 1580 with subsequent additions. Unique collections of furniture including a fine Elizabethan bed and the famous Shovel Board Table.

The Beatles Story

Albert Dock, Liverpool
Tel: (0151) 709 1963 www.beatlesstory.com

Liverpool's award-winning visitor attraction with a replica of the original Cavern Club. Available for private parties.

Blackpool Pleasure Beach

Ocean Boulevard, Blackpool
Tel: 0870 4445566
www.blackpoolpleasurebeach.co.uk

Europe's greatest show and amusement park. Blackpool Pleasure Beach offers over 145 rides and attractions, plus spectacular shows.

Blackpool Tower and Circus

The Promenade, Blackpool
Tel: (01253) 292029
www.theblackpooltower.co.uk

Inside Blackpool Tower you will find the UK's best circus, world famous Tower Ballroom, children's entertainment plus Jungle Jim's Playground, Tower Top Ride and Undersea World.

Boat Museum

South Pier Road, Ellesmere Port
Tel: (0151) 355 5017
www.boatmuseum.org.uk

Home to the UK's largest collection of inland waterway craft. Working forge, Power Hall, Pump House, 7 exhibitions of industrial heritage. Gift shop and cafeteria.

Botany Bay Villages and Puddletown Pirates

Canal Mill, Chorley
Tel: (01257) 261220 www.botanybay.co.uk

A shopping, leisure and heritage experience including Puddletown Pirates, the North West's largest indoor adventure play centre.

Bridgemere Garden World

Bridgemere, Nantwich
Tel: (01270) 520381 www.bridgemere.co.uk

Bridgemere Garden World, 25 fascinating acres (10ha) of plants, gardens, greenhouses and shop. Coffee shop, restaurant and over 20 different display gardens in the Garden Kingdom.

Camelot Theme Park

Charnock Richard, Chorley
Tel: (01257) 453044
www.camelotthemepark.co.uk

The Magical Kingdom of Camelot voted Lancashire's Family Attraction of the Year 2002 is a world of thrilling rides, fantastic entertainment and family fun.

CATALYST: Science Discovery Centre

Mersey Road, Widnes
Tel: (0151) 420 1121 www.catalyst.org.uk

Catalyst is the award-winning family day out where science and technology fuse with fun.

Chester Zoo

Upton-by-Chester, Chester
Tel: (01244) 380280
www.chesterzoo.org.uk
Chester Zoo is one of Europe's leading conservation zoos, with over 7,000 animals in spacious and natural enclosures. Now featuring the 'Tsavo' African Black Rhino Experience.

Croxteth Hall and Country Park
Croxteth Hall Lane, Liverpool
Tel: (0151) 228 5311
www.croxteth.co.uk
An Edwardian stately home set in 500 acres (200ha) of countryside (woodlands and pasture), featuring a Victorian walled garden and animal collection.

Dunham Massey Hall Park and Garden (National Trust)
Altrincham
Tel: (0161) 941 1025
www.thenationaltrust.org.uk
An 18thC mansion in a 250-acre (100-ha) wooded deer park with furniture, paintings and silver. A 25-acre (10-ha) informal garden with mature trees and waterside plantings.

East Lancashire Railway
Bolton Street, Bury
Tel: (0161) 764 7790
www.east-lancs-rly.co.uk
Eight miles of preserved railway, operated principally by steam. Traction Transport Museum close by.

Jodrell Bank Science Centre, Planetarium and Arboretum
Lower Withington, Macclesfield
Tel: (01477) 571339 www.jb.man.ac.uk/scicen
Exhibition and interactive exhibits on astronomy, space, energy and the environment. Planetarium, 3D theatre and the world-famous Lovell telescope, plus a 35-acre (14-ha) arboretum.

Knowsley Safari Park
Prescot
Tel: (0151) 430 9009
www.knowsley.com
A 5-mile safari through 500 acres (200ha) of rolling countryside and the world's wildest animals roaming free - that's the wonderful world of freedom you'll find at the park.

Lady Lever Art Gallery
Port Sunlight Village, Wirral
Tel: (0151) 478 4136
www.ladyleverartgallery.org.uk
The 1st Lord Leverhulme's magnificent collection of British paintings dated 1750-1900, British furniture, Wedgewood pottery and oriental porcelain.

Lancaster Castle
Castle Parade, Lancaster
Tel: (01524) 64998 www.lancastercastle.com
Shire Hall has a collection of coats of arms, a crown court, a grand jury room, a 'drop room' and dungeons. Also external tour of castle.

Lyme Park (National Trust)
Disley, Stockport
Tel: (01663) 762023 www.nationaltrust.org.uk
Lyme Park is a National Trust country estate set in 1,377 acres (557ha) of moorland, woodland and park. This magnificent house has 17 acres (7ha) of historic gardens.

1. Rochdale Canal
2. Imperial War Museum North, Salford Quays, Manchester
3. Blackpool Pleasure Beach

Macclesfield Silk Museum
Roe Street, Macclesfield
Tel: (01625) 613210 www.silk-macclesfield.org
A silk museum is situated in the Heritage Centre, a Grade II Listed former Sunday school.

Merseyside Maritime Museum
Albert Dock, Liverpool
Tel: (0151) 478 4499
www.merseysidemaritimemuseum.org.uk

Liverpool's seafaring heritage brought to life in the historic Albert Dock.

The Museum of Science & Industry in Manchester
Castlefield, Manchester
Tel: (0161) 832 2244 www.msim.org.uk
Based in the world's oldest passenger railway station, this museum has galleries that amaze, amuse and entertain, full of working exhibits including industrial machines and historic planes.

The National Football Museum
Deepdale Stadium, Preston
Tel: (01772) 908442
www.nationalfootballmuseum.com
The National Football Museum exists to explain how and why football has become the people's game.

Norton Priory Museum and Gardens
Manor Park, Runcorn
Tel: (01928) 569895
www.nortonpriory.org
Medieval priory remains, purpose-built museum, St Christopher's statue, sculpture trail and award-winning walled garden, all set in 38 acres (15ha) of beautiful gardens.

Pleasureland Theme Park
Marine Drive, Southport
Tel: 0870 2200204 www.pleasureland.uk.com
Over 100 rides and attractions, including the TRAUMAtizer and the Lucozade Space Shot.

Rufford Old Hall (National Trust)
Rufford, Ormskirk
Tel: (01704) 821254 www.nationaltrust.org.uk
One of the finest 16thC buildings in Lancashire, with a magnificent hall, particularly noted for its immense moveable screen.

Sandcastle Tropical Waterworld
South Promenade, Blackpool
Tel: (01253) 343602
www.blackpool-sandcastle.co.uk
Wave pool, fun pools, giant water flumes, sauna, white-knuckle water slides, kiddies safe harbour, play area, catering, bar shops and amusements.

Southport Zoo and Conservation Trust
Princes Park, Southport
Tel: (01704) 538102 www.southportzoo.co.uk
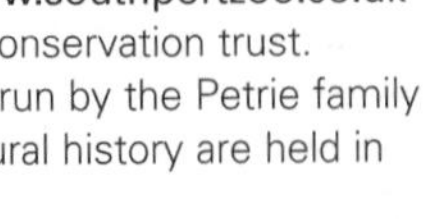
Zoological gardens and conservation trust. Southport Zoo has been run by the Petrie family since 1964. Talks on natural history are held in the schoolroom.

Tate Liverpool

Albert Dock, Liverpool
Tel: (0151) 702 7400
www.tate.org.uk/liverpool/
The Tate Liverpool in historic Albert Dock has 4 floors of art and houses the National Collection of Modern Art.

Tatton Park (National Trust)
Knutsford
Tel: (01625) 534400
www.tattonpark.org.uk
Historic mansion with a 50-acre (20-ha) garden, traditional working farm, Tudor manor-house and a 1,000-acre (400-ha) deer park and children's adventure playground.

Wigan Pier

Trencherfield Mill, Wigan
Tel: (01942) 323666
www.wiganmbc.gov.uk
Wigan Pier combines interaction with displays and reconstructions and the Wigan Pier Theatre Company. Facilities include shops and a cafe.

Wildfowl and Wetland Trust Martin Mere
Burscough, Ormskirk
Tel: (01704) 895181 www.wwt.org.uk
Martin Mere Wildfowl and Wetland Centre is home to over 1,600 ducks, geese and swans.

North West Tourist Board

Swan House, Swan Meadow Road,
Wigan Pier, Wigan WN3 5BB
T: (01942) 821222 F: (01942) 820002
www.visitnorthwest.com

THE FOLLOWING PUBLICATIONS ARE AVAILABLE FROM NORTH WEST TOURIST BOARD:

Discover England's North West –
a guide to information on the region

Great Days Out in England's North West –
a non-accommodation guide, A1 (folded to A4) map including list of visitor attractions, what to see and where to go

Freedom –
forming part of a family of publications about camping and caravan parks in the north of England

Stay on a Farm –
a guide to farm accommodation in the north of England

Group Travel Planner –
a guide to choosing the right accommodation, attraction or venue for group organisers

Getting to the North West

BY ROAD: Motorways intersect within the region which has the best road network in the country. Travelling north or south use the M6, and east or west the M62.

BY RAIL: Most North West coastal resorts are connected to InterCity routes with trains from many parts of the country, and there are through trains to major cities and towns.

1. The Lowry, Salford Quays, Manchester
2. Chester Clock

Where to stay in the
North West

All place names in the blue bands under which accommodation is listed, are shown on the maps at the front of this guide.

Symbols give useful information about services and facilities. Inside the back cover flap there's a key to these symbols which you can keep open for easy reference.

A complete listing of all the VisitBritain assessed accommodation covered by this guide appears at the back of this guide.

ACTON BRIDGE, Cheshire Map ref 4A2

MANOR FARM

Cliff Road, Acton Bridge, Northwich
CW8 3QP
T: (01606) 853181
F: (01606) 853181
E: terri.mac.manorfarm@care4free.net

B&B per person per night:
S Min £25.00
D £25.00–£33.00

OPEN All Year except Christmas and New Year

Peaceful, elegantly furnished country house. Open views from all rooms. Situated down long, private drive, above wooded banks of the River Weaver. Large garden provides access to private path through woodland into the picturesque valley. In central Cheshire, ideal location for business or pleasure, convenient for Chester, Merseyside and motorways.

Bedrooms: 1 double, 1 twin, 1 single
Bathrooms: 1 en suite
Babies 0-3 free, children 3-5 £5.00, 5-12 half price. Long distance or circular walks on Delamere Way and sandstone trail.

P €

GOLD & SILVER AWARDS
These exclusive VisitBritain awards are given to establishments achieving the highest levels of quality and service. Further information can be found at the front of the guide. An index to all accommodation achieving these awards are at the back of this guide.

BLACKPOOL, Lancashire Map ref 4A1 *Tourist Information Centre Tel: (01253) 478222*

◆◆◆

BEACHCOMBER HOTEL

78 Reads Avenue, Blackpool FY1 4DE
T: (01253) 621622
F: (01253) 299254
E: info@beachcomberhotel.net
I: www.beachcomberhotel.net

Bedrooms: 4 double, 1 single, 5 family
Bathrooms: 10 en suite

Evening meal available
CC: Delta, Diners, Mastercard, Switch, Visa

Comfortable hotel having en suite rooms with TV, tea/coffee facilities and central heating. Choice of menu, table licence – no noisy bar. Car park.

P

B&B per person per night:
S £19.00–£25.00
D £19.00–£25.00

HB per person per night:
DY £24.00–£32.00

OPEN All Year

◆◆◆

BOLTONIA HOTEL

124-126 Albert Road, Blackpool FY1 4PN
T: (01253) 620248
F: (01253) 299064
E: info@boltoniahotel.co.uk
I: www.boltoniahotel.co.uk

Family-run and -owned establishment. Ideal for holiday or mini-breaks and illuminations. Close to conference centre, dance festival venues, theatres and shops. All bedrooms are en suite with colour TV, complimentary tea/coffee facilities, hairdryer and shaver point. This small, licensed hotel also benefits from its own private car park.

2 P

Bedrooms: 8 double, 4 twin, 6 single, 3 family
Bathrooms: 21 en suite

Evening meal available
CC: Amex, Delta, Diners, Mastercard, Switch, Visa

Any 4 nights' B&B plus evening dinner £95, any 4 nights' B&B £84, from 3 Nov 2003 to 2 Sep 2004 (excl Christmas, New Year and Bank Holidays).

B&B per person per night:
S £22.00–£32.00
D £22.00–£32.00

HB per person per night:
DY £27.00–£37.00

OPEN All Year

◆◆◆

BONA VISTA HOTEL

104-106 Queens Promenade, Blackpool FY2 9NX
T: (01253) 351396
F: (01253) 594985
E: bona.vista@talk21.com
I: www.bonavistahotel.com

Bedrooms: 10 double, 3 twin, 2 single
Bathrooms: 14 en suite

Evening meal available
CC: Amex, Delta, Diners, Mastercard, Switch, Visa

Detached seafront hotel on North Shore overlooking sea and cliff walks. Furnished to high standard with large car park. Choice of dinner menu. Full English breakfast.

P

B&B per person per night:
S £23.00–£29.50
D £23.00–£29.50

HB per person per night:
DY £31.50–£38.00

OPEN All Year

◆◆

CLIFF HEAD HOTEL

174 Queens Promenade, Bispham, Blackpool FY2 9JN
T: (01253) 591086
F: (01253) 590952

Bedrooms: 4 double, 2 twin, 2 single, 1 family
Bathrooms: 9 en suite

Evening meal available

Promenade hotel, adjacent to tram and bus stops, close to shops and amenities. A nicer, and more relaxing part of Blackpool.

P

B&B per person per night:
S £19.50–£25.50
D £19.50–£25.50

HB per person per night:
DY £27.00–£32.00

OPEN All Year

◆◆◆

ELGIN HOTEL

36-42 Queens Promenade, Blackpool FY2 9RW
T: (01253) 351433
F: (01253) 353535
E: info@elginhotel.com
I: www.elginhotel.com

Bedrooms: 21 double, 30 twin, 7 single, 34 family
Bathrooms: 90 en suite

Evening meal available
CC: Delta, Mastercard, Switch, Visa

Friendly, family-run hotel offering fun, food and service in beautiful surroundings. A real home from home atmosphere.

P

B&B per person per night:
S £37.00–£51.00
D £32.00–£46.00

HB per person per night:
DY £39.00–£51.00

OPEN All Year

BLACKPOOL continued

♦♦♦

GLENEAGLES HOTEL
75 Albert Road, Blackpool FY1 4PW
T: (01253) 295266

Bedrooms: 9 double, 3 single, 3 family
Bathrooms: 15 en suite

Evening meal available

B&B per person per night:
S £22.00–£33.00
D £19.00–£30.00

HB per person per night:
DY £29.00–£40.00

OPEN All Year

Ideally situated close to the Tower, Winter Gardens, theatres, beach, municipal car park and main shopping area. All rooms en suite.

♦♦♦

LLANRYAN GUEST HOUSE
37 Reads Avenue, Blackpool
FY1 4DD
T: (01253) 628446
E: keith@llanryanguesthouse.co.uk
I: www.llanryanguesthouse.co.uk

Bedrooms: 3 double, 2 single, 3 family
Bathrooms: 6 en suite

Evening meal available
CC: Delta, Mastercard, Switch, Visa

B&B per person per night:
S £14.00–£18.00
D £16.50–£20.50

HB per person per night:
DY £18.50–£25.00

OPEN All Year

Convenient for the many attractions of Blackppol. Just a few minutes' walk from the town centre, Tower, Winter Gardens, theatres and working men's clubs.

♦♦

MANOR GROVE HOTEL
24 Leopold Grove, Blackpool
FY1 4LD
T: (01253) 625577
F: (01253) 625577
E: lyndon@evans2000.freeserve.co.uk
I: www.manorgrovehotel.co.uk

Bedrooms: 2 double, 8 single, 2 family
Bathrooms: 12 en suite

Evening meal available
CC: Amex, Delta, Diners, Mastercard, Switch, Visa

B&B per person per night:
S £20.00–£24.99
D £20.00–£49.98

OPEN All Year

Lovely, bright, clean, modern rooms. Family-run guesthouse, central location behind the Winter Gardens. All rooms en suite, TV, direct-dial telephone and hairdryer.

P €

MAY-DENE LICENSED HOTEL
10 Dean Street, Blackpool FY4 1AU
T: (01253) 343464
F: (01253) 401424
E: may_dene_hotel@hotmail.com

Bedrooms: 6 double, 1 twin, 4 family
Bathrooms: 8 en suite

Evening meal available
CC: Amex, Delta, Diners, Mastercard, Switch, Visa

B&B per person per night:
S £25.00–£60.00
D £21.00–£35.00

HB per person per night:
DY £28.00–£45.00

OPEN All Year

In a sun trap area close to South Promenade, Sandcastle, Pleasure Beach, markets and pier. Clean and friendly. Good food prepared by C&G-qualified cooks.

P

♦♦♦♦♦
Gold Award

THE OLD COACH HOUSE
50 Dean Street, Blackpool FY4 1BP
T: (01253) 349195
F: (01253) 344330
E: blackpool@theoldcoachhouse.freeserve.co.uk
I: www.theoldcoachhouse.freeserve.co.uk

Bedrooms: 11 double
Bathrooms: 11 en suite

Evening meal available
CC: Delta, Diners, Mastercard, Switch, Visa

B&B per person per night:
S £50.00–£65.00
D £35.00–£45.00

HB per person per night:
DY £55.00–£65.00

OPEN All Year

A large detached house set in beautiful gardens. Situated near the promenade and the South Pier. Superior rooms with 4-poster beds and baths also available.

P

♦♦♦

ROCKCLIFFE HOTEL
248 North Promenade, Blackpool
FY1 1RZ
T: (01253) 623476
F: (01253) 473825
I: www.rockcliffehotel.co.uk

Bedrooms: 11 double, 4 single, 1 family
Bathrooms: 16 en suite

Evening meal available
CC: Amex, Delta, Diners, Mastercard, Switch, Visa

B&B per person per night:
S £20.00–£40.00
D £20.00–£40.00

HB per person per night:
DY £27.00–£46.00

OPEN All Year

Situated on the seafront in a desirable part of Blackpool. Close to the North Station, theatres, shops and all major nightlife.

P

HALF BOARD PRICES Half board prices are given per person, but in some cases these may be based on double/twin occupancy.

BLACKPOOL continued

SUNNYSIDE HOTEL

36 King Edward Avenue, North Shore, Blackpool FY2 9TA
T: (01253) 352031
F: (01253) 354255
E: stuart@sunnysidehotel.com
I: www.sunnysidehotel.com

Small hotel, BIG welcome, situated adjacent to promenade in a select, quiet area of North Shore yet near the town centre attractions. South-facing sun lounge, bar lounge, spacious dining area with varied menu to suit your needs. All bedrooms are en suite. Unrestricted street parking, and private parking by arrangement.

Bedrooms: 3 double, 3 twin, 1 single, 3 family
Bathrooms: 10 en suite
Evening meal available

Early-season savers (excl Bank Holidays), Feb-Jun. Weekly B&B from £120, 4 nights' B&B from £70, 3 nights' B&B from £57.

B&B per person per night:
S £19.00–£26.50
D £16.50–£24.00

HB per person per night:
DY £24.00–£32.00

OPEN All Year

P

BOLTON-BY-BOWLAND, Lancashire Map ref 4B1

♦♦♦

THE COACH AND HORSES

20 Main Street, Bolton-by-Bowland, Clitheroe BB7 4NW
T: (01200) 447202
F: (01200) 447202

Bedrooms: 2 double, 1 family
Bathrooms: 3 en suite

Evening meal available
CC: Delta, Mastercard, Switch, Visa

B&B per person per night:
S Min £35.00
D Min £25.00

OPEN All Year

Old coaching inn overlooking village green, situated in the picturesque Forest of Bowland. Intimate dining room with open fire. Well-appointed, spacious and comfortable bedrooms.

P

BURNLEY, Lancashire Map ref 4B1 *Tourist Information Centre Tel: (01282) 664421*

ORMEROD HOTEL

121-123 Ormerod Road, Burnley BB11 3QW
T: (01282) 423255

Bedrooms: 4 double, 4 single, 2 family
Bathrooms: 10 en suite

B&B per person per night:
S £26.00–£29.00
D £22.50

OPEN All Year

Small bed and breakfast hotel in quiet, pleasant surroundings facing local parks. Recently refurbished, all en suite facilities. Five minutes from town centre.

P

CARNFORTH, Lancashire Map ref 5B3

LONGLANDS HOTEL

Tewitfield, Carnforth LA6 1JH
T: (01524) 781256
F: (01524) 781004
E: info@thelonglandshotel.co.uk
I: www.thelonglandshotel.co.uk

B&B per person per night:
S £25.00–£37.50
D £25.00

OPEN All Year

Ideally situated for the Lakes, Yorkshire Dales, the seaside resort of Morecambe and historic Lancaster. Located 0.5 miles from M6 exit 35A on the A6070. Regular live entertainment. Functions catered for. Bar snacks and a la carte restaurant. All bedrooms en suite. A warm welcome guaranteed.

Bedrooms: 5 double, 4 twin, 2 single, 1 family
Bathrooms: 12 en suite

Evening meal available
CC: Delta, Mastercard, Switch, Visa

P

CHEADLE HULME, Greater Manchester Map ref 4B2

SPRING COTTAGE GUEST HOUSE

60 Hulme Hall Road, Cheadle Hulme, Cheadle SK8 6JZ
T: (0161) 485 1037
F: (0161) 486 1037

Bedrooms: 1 double, 3 twin, 1 single, 2 family
Bathrooms: 3 en suite

B&B per person per night:
S £26.00–£32.00
D £20.50–£22.50

OPEN All Year

Beautifully furnished Victorian house, in historic part of Cheadle Hulme. Convenient for airport, rail station and variety of local restaurants.

P

CHESTER, Cheshire Map ref 4A2 *Tourist Information Centre Tel: (01244) 402111*

◆◆◆

THE COMMERCIAL HOTEL
St Peters Churchyard, Chester
CH1 2HG
T: (01244) 320749
F: (01244) 348318
I: www.stayhereuk.com

Bedrooms: 4 double, 2 family
Bathrooms: 6 en suite

CC: Mastercard, Visa

B&B per person per night:
S Min £38.00
D Min £26.00

OPEN All Year

A Georgian inn having six en suite rooms. Set in the heart of the city. Hand-pulled ales, freshly cooked food. Relaxed atmosphere.

CHORLEY, Lancashire Map ref 4A1

◆◆◆◆

PARR HALL FARM
Parr Lane, Eccleston, Chorley PR7 5SL
T: (01257) 451917
F: (01257) 453749
E: parrhall@talk21.com

B&B per person per night:
S £30.00–£40.00
D £25.00–£30.00

OPEN All Year

Georgian farmhouse built in 1721 and tastefully restored. Quiet, rural location within easy walking distance of good public houses, restaurants and village amenities. Conveniently situated for Lancashire coast and countryside, Lake District and Yorkshire Dales. Manchester Airport 45 minutes, M6 jct 27 five miles north on B5250.

Bedrooms: 3 double, 1 single
Bathrooms: 4 en suite

CC: Delta, Mastercard, Switch, Visa

CLITHEROE, Lancashire Map ref 4A1 *Tourist Information Centre Tel: (01200) 425566*

RAKEFOOT FARM
Thornley Road, Chaigley,
Near Clitheroe BB7 3LY
T: (01995) 61332
F: (01995) 61296
E: info@rakefootfarm.co.uk
I: www.rakefootfarm.co.uk

Bedrooms: 4 double, 2 twin, 1 single, 3 family, 1 suite
Bathrooms: 9 en suite

Evening meal available

B&B per person per night:
S £17.50–£30.00
D £17.50–£25.00

OPEN All Year

Family farm, 17thC farmhouse and traditional stone barn, original features. En suite, ground floor available. Panoramic views. Forest of Bowland between Clitheroe and Chipping. Home cooking. Also self-catering.

CRUMPSALL, Greater Manchester Map ref 4B1

WILTON GRANGE HOTEL
2 Crumpsall Lane, Crumpsall, Manchester
M8 5FB
T: 0800 0563 468
F: (0161) 795 4354
E: robfiddaman@fsmail.net
I: www.wiltongrange.com

B&B per person per night:
S Max £35.00
D Max £23.75

OPEN All Year

Warm, family-owned hotel, recently refurbished, with spacious, en suite rooms and secure car parking. Situated close to the motorway networks and Metrolink station to explore the real Manchester.

Bedrooms: 3 double, 2 twin, 5 single, 4 family
Bathrooms: 14 en suite

Evening meal available

CHECK THE MAPS

The colour maps at the front of this guide show all the cities, towns and villages for which you will find accommodation entries.
Refer to the town index to find the page on which they are listed.

DUKINFIELD, Greater Manchester Map ref 4B1

◆◆◆

BARTON VILLA GUEST HOUSE

Crescent Road, Dukinfield SK16 4EY
T: (0161) 330 3952
F: (0161) 285 8488
E: enquiries@bartonvilla.co.uk
I: www.bartonvilla.co.uk

Bedrooms: 6 double, 1 twin, 7 single, 3 family
Bathrooms: 14 en suite

Evening meal available
CC: Amex, Delta, Mastercard, Switch, Visa

B&B per person per night:
S £30.00–£40.00
D £20.00–£25.00

OPEN All Year

Large detached house in own grounds with car park and separate annexe. Within easy reach of town centre.

P

HURST GREEN, Lancashire Map ref 4A1

◆◆◆◆

THE FOLD

15 Smith Row, Hurst Green, Clitheroe BB7 9QA
T: (01254) 826252
E: derek.harwood1@virgin.net

Bedrooms: 1 double, 1 family
Bathrooms: 2 en suite

B&B per person per night:
D £25.00–£28.50

OPEN All Year

A warm, friendly bed and breakfast offering quality accommodation, set in picturesque village of Hurst Green, close to Stonyhurst College, two minutes from nearest pub/ restaurant.

P

KNUTSFORD, Cheshire Map ref 4A2 *Tourist Information Centre Tel: (01565) 632611*

◆◆◆

MOAT HALL HOTEL

Chelford Road, Marthall, Knutsford WA16 8SU
T: (01625) 860367
F: (01625) 861136
E: val@moathall.fsnet.co.uk
I: www.moat-hall-motel.co.uk

Bedrooms: 2 double, 1 twin, 2 single, 1 family
Bathrooms: 6 en suite

CC: Mastercard, Switch, Visa

B&B per person per night:
S £30.00–£40.00
D £20.00–£30.00

OPEN All Year

Modern accommodation on Cheshire farm, six miles from Manchester Airport. Knutsford three miles (M6 jct 19). All rooms en suite with TV, microwave and fridge. Suitable for business and touring guests.

P

LIVERPOOL, Merseyside Map ref 4A2 *Tourist Information Centre Tel: 0906 680 6886 (Premium rate number)*

◆◆◆

DOLBY HOTEL

36-42 Chaloner Street, Queen's Dock, Liverpool L3 4DE
T: (0151) 708 7272
F: (0151) 708 7266
E: liverpool@dolbyhotels.co.uk
I: www.dolbyhotels.co.uk

Bedrooms: 2 double, 63 family
Bathrooms: 65 en suite

Evening meal available
CC: Delta, Mastercard, Switch, Visa

B&B per person per night:
S £41.45–£47.95

OPEN All Year

On the famous Liverpool waterfront, 10 minutes from city centre. Free parking. All rooms en suite with tea/coffee-making facilities and TV. Reception 24 hours.

P

◆◆◆

SOMERSBY

100 Green Lane, Calderstones, Liverpool L18 2ER
T: (0151) 722 7549
F: (0151) 722 7549

B&B per person per night:
S £25.00
D £25.00

OPEN All Year

Somersby was built in 1925 and, as was customary for the period, provides generously proportioned, airy rooms. Situated in a leafy residential area 4.5 miles from the city centre. Easy access to M62, airport and universities. Extensive parkland and an excellent selection of restaurants and wine bars within easy walking distance.

Bedrooms: 2 double, 1 single, 1 family
Bathrooms: 1 en suite

Evening meal available

P

VISITOR ATTRACTIONS For ideas on places to visit refer to the introduction at the beginning of this section. Look out too for the VisitBritain Quality Assured Visitor Attraction signs.

LOWER WHITLEY, Cheshire Map ref 4A2

TALL TREES LODGE

Tarporley Road, Lower Whitley, Warrington WA4 4EZ
T: (01928) 790824
F: (01928) 791330
E: bookings@talltreeslodge.co.uk
I: www.talltreeslodge.co.uk

Bedrooms: 14 double, 6 family
Bathrooms: 20 en suite

CC: Amex, Delta, Mastercard, Switch, Visa

B&B per person per night:
D £19.00–£24.00

OPEN All Year

Two and a half miles south of jct 10, off the M56. Take A49 towards Whitchurch. Little Chef and Texaco garage on site. A warm welcome awaits you.

P

MACCLESFIELD, Cheshire Map ref 4B2 *Tourist Information Centre Tel: (01625) 504114*

SANDPIT FARM

Messuage Lane, Marton, Macclesfield SK11 9HS
T: (01260) 224254

Bedrooms: 1 double, 2 twin
Bathrooms: 2 en suite

Evening meal available

B&B per person per night:
S £23.00–£25.00
D £23.00–£25.00

OPEN All Year

A friendly welcome to our 300-year-old, oak-beamed farmhouse. Excellent touring centre for Peak District, Potteries, Chester, stately homes. Manchester Airport 14 miles.

P

MANCHESTER, Greater Manchester Map ref 4B1 *Tourist Information Centre Tel: (0161) 234 3157*

DOLBY HOTEL-MANCHESTER

55 Blackfriars Road, Manchester M3 7DB
T: (0161) 907 2277
F: (0161) 907 2266
E: info@dolbyhotel.com
I: www.dolbyhotel.com

Modern, purpose-built hotel offering excellent value for money. Free car parking, city-centre location, close to railway station. Five minutes' walk from the MEN Arena, and further five minutes from GMEX and MICC. Residents' bar open until 0100. Breakfast from £1.95 to £5.95 for a full English.

Bedrooms: 25 double, 12 twin, 28 family
Bathrooms: 65 en suite

Evening meal available

B&B per person per night:
S £23.50–£28.50
D £23.50–£28.50

OPEN All Year

P

LUTHER KING HOUSE

Brighton Grove, Wilmslow Road, Manchester M14 5JP
T: (0161) 224 6404
F: (0161) 248 9201
E: reception@lkh.co.uk
I: www.lkh.co.uk

Located in a tree-lined suburb just a short way from the city centre in a private 2-acre site, Luther King House provides a full range of bed and breakfast and conference/meeting facilities. Noted for its peaceful location and very friendly atmosphere, it is the perfect choice for quality, inexpensive accommodation.

Bedrooms: 7 double, 9 twin, 27 single
Bathrooms: 25 en suite

Evening meal available
CC: Delta, Mastercard, Switch, Visa

B&B per person per night:
S £24.00–£34.00
D £17.50–£21.00

HB per person per night:
DY £34.00–£39.00

OPEN All Year except Christmas

P €

MANCHESTER AIRPORT

See under Cheadle Hulme, Knutsford, Manchester, Mobberley, Sale, Stockport, Wilmslow

SYMBOLS The symbols in each entry give information about services and facilities. A key to these symbols appears at the back of this guide.

MOBBERLEY, Cheshire Map ref 4A2

Silver Award

THE HINTON

Town Lane, Mobberley, Knutsford
WA16 7HH
T: (01565) 873484
F: (01565) 873484
I: www.hinton.co.uk

Award-winning bed and breakfast for both business and private guests. Within easy reach of M6, M56, Manchester Airport and InterCity rail network. Ideal touring base, on the B5085 between Knutsford and Wilmslow. Beautifully appointed rooms with many extras. All good home cooking.

Bedrooms: 2 double, 2 single, 1 family
Bathrooms: 5 en suite

Evening meal available
CC: Amex, Diners, Mastercard, Visa

B&B per person per night:
S £39.00–£44.00
D £25.00–£29.00

OPEN All Year

MORECAMBE, Lancashire Map ref 5A3 *Tourist Information Centre Tel: (01524) 582808*

BELLE VUE HOTEL

330 Marine Road, Morecambe
LA4 5AA
T: (01524) 411375
F: (01524) 411375

Bedrooms: 5 double, 20 twin, 12 single, 3 family
Bathrooms: 40 en suite

Evening meal available
CC: Visa

Situated on central promenade. Panoramic sea views. Convenient base for touring Lake District and Yorkshire Dales.

B&B per person per night:
S £28.00
D £26.00–£28.00

HB per person per night:
DY £35.00–£37.00

NEW BRIGHTON, Merseyside Map ref 4A2

SHERWOOD GUEST HOUSE

55 Wellington Road, New Brighton, Wirral CH45 2ND
T: (0151) 639 5198
F: (0151) 639 9079
E: sheila@sherwood-guest-house.co.uk

Bedrooms: 1 single, 3 twin, 2 family
Bathrooms: 3 en suite

Evening meal available

Family guesthouse facing promenade and Irish Sea. Close to station and M53. Ideal centre for Chester, North Wales, Lakes and Liverpool (15 minutes).

B&B per person per night:
S £18.00–£20.00

OPEN All Year

OLDHAM, Greater Manchester Map ref 4B1 *Tourist Information Centre Tel: (0161) 627 1024*

GLOBE FARM GUEST HOUSE

Huddersfield Road, Standedge, Delph, Oldham OL3 5LU
T: (01457) 873040
F: (01457) 873040
E: bookings@globe-farm.com
I: www.globefarm.co.uk

Bedrooms: 5 double, 4 twin, 3 single, 1 family
Bathrooms: 13 en suite

CC: Delta, Mastercard, Switch, Visa

17-acre farm, 0.25 miles from the Pennine Way and high walking country. En suite bedrooms and small campsite. Large car park.

B&B per person per night:
S £25.00
D Min £22.50

OPEN All Year

PRESTBURY, Cheshire Map ref 4B2

ARTIZANA SUITE

The Village, Prestbury, Macclesfield
SK10 4DG
T: (01625) 827582
F: (01625) 827582
E: suite@artizana.co.uk
I: www.artizana.co.uk/suite

Bedrooms: 1 double
Bathrooms: 1 en suite

CC: Amex, Delta, Diners, Mastercard, Switch, Visa

A new concept in accommodation for discerning visitors. Lavishly furnished and fully serviced apartment. A B&B with a difference combining privacy, convenience and elegance. Ideal for executives and businessmen.

B&B per person per night:
S £89.50–£99.50
D £50.00–£60.00

OPEN All Year

PRESTON, Lancashire Map ref 4A1 *Tourist Information Centre Tel: (01772) 253731*

◆◆◆

ASHWOOD HOTEL
11-13 Fishergate Hill, Preston
PR1 8JB
T: (01772) 203302
F: (01772) 203302

Bedrooms: 4 double, 2 twin, 7 single, 2 family
Bathrooms: 10 en suite

CC: Delta, Mastercard, Switch, Visa

B&B per person per night:
S £25.00–£30.00
D £23.00–£24.00

OPEN All Year except Christmas

Warm and comfortable family-run hotel. En suite facilities. Five minutes' walk from town centre, railway station and university. Tea/coffee facilities and colour TV in all bedrooms.

RIBBLE VALLEY

See under Clitheroe, Hurst Green, Slaidburn

ST MICHAEL'S ON WYRE, Lancashire Map ref 4A1

COMPTON HOUSE
Garstang Road,
St Michael's on Wyre, Preston
PR3 0TE
T: (01995) 679378
F: (01995) 679378
E: dave@compton-hs.co.uk
I: www.compton-hs.co.uk

Bedrooms: 3 double
Bathrooms: 3 en suite

B&B per person per night:
S £25.00
D £20.00

OPEN All Year

Well-furnished country house in own grounds in a picturesque village, near M6 and 40 minutes from Lake District. Fishing in the Wyre. 'Best-Kept Guesthouse' award 1995, 1996 and 2001.

SALE, Greater Manchester Map ref 4A2

BELFORTE HOUSE HOTEL
7-9 Broad Road, Sale M33 2AE
T: (0161) 973 8779
F: (0161) 973 8779
E: belfortehotel@aol.com

Bedrooms: 3 double, 3 twin, 14 single, 1 family
Bathrooms: 17 en suite

Evening meal available
CC: Amex, Delta, Diners, Mastercard, Switch, Visa

B&B per person per night:
S £32.00–£42.50
D £22.50–£25.00

HB per person per night:
DY £35.00–£55.00

OPEN All Year except Christmas

Privately owned hotel with a personal, friendly approach. Ideally located for Manchester Airport, the Metrolink and the city centre. Situated directly opposite Sale Leisure Centre.

SLAIDBURN, Lancashire Map ref 4A1

◆◆◆

HARK TO BOUNTY INN
Slaidburn, Clitheroe BB7 3EP
T: (01200) 446246
F: (01200) 446361
E: isobel@hark-to-bounty.co.uk
I: www.hark-to-bounty.co.uk

Bedrooms: 3 double, 2 twin, 2 single, 1 family
Bathrooms: 8 en suite

Evening meal available
CC: Delta, Mastercard, Switch, Visa

B&B per person per night:
S £29.50–£34.50
D £27.25–£34.75

OPEN All Year

Family-run country inn at the heart of the Forest of Bowland. Ideally placed for walkers and cyclists to explore the area.

SOUTHPORT, Merseyside Map ref 4A1 *Tourist Information Centre Tel: (01704) 533333*

LEICESTER HOTEL
24 Leicester Street, Southport
PR9 0EZ
T: (01704) 530049
F: (01704) 545561
E: leicester.hotel@mail.cybase.co.uk
I: www.leicesterhotelsouthport.co.uk

Bedrooms: 2 double, 3 twin, 3 single
Bathrooms: 5 en suite

Evening meal available
CC: Amex, Mastercard, Switch, Visa

B&B per person per night:
S £20.00–£25.00
D £20.00–£25.00

HB per person per night:
DY £27.50–£32.50

OPEN All Year except Christmas

Family-run hotel with personal attention, clean and comfortable, close to all amenities. Car park. Licensed bar. TV in all rooms. En suite available.

SPECIAL BREAKS

Many establishments offer special promotions and themed breaks. These are highlighted in red. (All such offers are subject to availability.)

SOUTHPORT continued

◆◆◆

SANDY BROOK FARM

52 Wyke Cop Road, Scarisbrick, Southport PR8 5LR
T: (01704) 880337
F: (01704) 880337
E: sandybrookfarm@lycos.co.uk

Bedrooms: 3 double, 1 single, 2 family
Bathrooms: 6 en suite

27-acre arable farm. Comfortable accommodation in converted farm buildings in rural area of Scarisbrick, 3.5 miles from Southport. Special facilities for disabled guests.

B&B per person per night:
S £24.00
D £19.00

OPEN All Year except Christmas

STOCKPORT, Greater Manchester Map ref 4B2 *Tourist Information Centre Tel: (0161) 474 4444*

◆◆◆

NEEDHAMS FARM

Uplands Road, Werneth Low, Gee Cross, Hyde SK14 3AG
T: (0161) 368 4610
F: (0161) 367 9106
E: charlotte@needhamsfarm.co.uk
I: www.needhamsfarm.co.uk

Bedrooms: 4 double, 1 twin, 1 single, 1 family
Bathrooms: 6 en suite, 1 private

Evening meal available

30-acre, non-working farm. Five-hundred-year-old farmhouse with exposed beams and open fire in bar/dining room. Excellent views. Well placed for Manchester city and airport.

B&B per person per night:
S £22.00–£24.00
D £18.00–£19.00

HB per person per night:
DY £30.00–£32.00

OPEN All Year

STONYHURST, Lancashire Map ref 4A1

◆◆◆◆
Gold Award

ALDEN COTTAGE

Kemple End, Birdy Brow, Stonyhurst, Clitheroe BB7 9QY
T: (01254) 826468
F: (01254) 826468
E: carpenter@aldencottage.f9.co.uk
I: http://fp.aldencottage.f9.co.uk

Quality accommodation in idyllic country cottage, situated in an Area of Outstanding Natural Beauty overlooking the Ribble and Hodder Valleys. Charmingly furnished rooms with all modern comforts, fresh flowers etc. Private facilities include jacuzzi bath. Ribble Valley Design and Conservation Award winner.

Bedrooms: 2 double, 1 twin
Bathrooms: 3 en suite

5% discount for 3 or more nights, 10% discount for 6 or more nights (based on 2 people sharing).

B&B per person per night:
S Max £33.00
D Max £28.00

OPEN All Year

TIMPERLEY, Greater Manchester Map ref 4A2

◆◆◆

ACORN OF OAKMERE

6 Wingate Drive, Timperley, Altrincham WA15 7PX
T: (0161) 980 8391
F: (0161) 980 8391
E: oakmere@handbag.com

Bedrooms: 1 twin, 1 single

Comfortable, quiet accommodation with sunken spa bath and separate dining room. Private, walled garden. Two minutes' walk from golf course. Close to the airport and motorways.

B&B per person per night:
S £27.50–£30.00
D £27.50–£30.00

OPEN All Year

WILMSLOW, Cheshire Map ref 4B2 *Tourist Information Centre Tel: (01625) 522275*

KING WILLIAM HOTEL

35 Manchester Road, Wilmslow SK9 1BQ
T: (01625) 524022
I: www.kingwilliam.20m.com

Bedrooms: 4 double, 2 single
Bathrooms: 6 en suite

CC: Amex, Delta, Diners, Mastercard, Switch, Visa

Old coaching house offering excellent food, en suite rooms and friendly atmosphere. Two minutes to train and bus stations, 10 minutes to airport. Catering for meetings and events.

B&B per person per night:
S £29.00
D £22.50

OPEN All Year

PRICES
Please check prices and other details at the time of booking.

WILMSLOW continued

◆◆◆◆

MARIGOLD HOUSE
132 Knutsford Road, Wilmslow
SK9 6JH
T: (01625) 584414

Bedrooms: 1 double,
2 twin
Bathrooms: 3 en suite

18thC period house with oak beams, flagged floors and antique furnishings. Log fires in winter. Private sitting room and dining room. Courtesy car to airport.

B&B per person per night:
S £35.00
D £22.50

OPEN All Year except Christmas

WINSFORD, Cheshire Map ref 4A2

◆◆◆

ELM COTTAGE
Chester Lane, Winsford CW7 2QJ
T: (01829) 760544
F: (01829) 760544
E: chris@elmcottagecp.co.uk
I: www.elmcottagecp.co.uk

Bedrooms: 2 double,
1 family
Bathrooms: 1 en suite

Character cottage accommodation. Close to Oulton Park racing circuit and the historic city of Chester. Ideal base for exploring the beautiful Cheshire countryside.

B&B per person per night:
S £30.00–£35.00
D £20.00–£25.00

OPEN All Year except Christmas

WIRRAL

See under New Brighton

QUALITY ASSURANCE SCHEME

For an explanation of the quality and facilities represented by the Diamonds please refer to the front of this guide. A more detailed explanation can be found in the information pages at the back.

A brief guide to the main Towns and Villages offering accommodation in the **North West**

A ACTON BRIDGE, CHESHIRE - Village with old farmsteads and cottages on a picturesque section of the River Weaver. Riverside walks pass the great Dutton Viaduct on the former Grand Junction Railway and shipping locks on the Weaver Navigation Canal.

B BLACKPOOL, LANCASHIRE - Britain's largest fun resort, with Blackpool Pleasure Beach, 3 piers and the famous Tower. Host to the spectacular autumn illuminations.

BOLTON-BY-BOWLAND, LANCASHIRE - Village near the Ribble Valley with 2 greens, one with stump of 13th C market cross and stocks. Whitewashed and greystone cottages.

BURNLEY, LANCASHIRE - A town amidst the Pennines. Towneley Hall has fine period rooms and is home to Burnley's art gallery and museum. The Kay-Shuttleworth collection of lace and embroidery can be seen at Gawthorpe Hall (National Trust). Burnley Mechanics Arts Centre is a well-known jazz and blues venue.

C CARNFORTH, LANCASHIRE - Carnforth station was the setting for the film "Brief Encounter". Nearby are Borwick Hall, an Elizabethan manor house, and Leighton Hall which has good paintings and Gillow furniture and is open to the public.

CHEADLE HULME, GREATER MANCHESTER - Residential area near Manchester with some older buildings dating from the 19th C once occupied by merchants and industrialists from surrounding towns. Several fine timber-framed houses, shopping centre and easy access to Manchester Airport.

CHESTER, CHESHIRE - Roman and medieval walled city rich in treasures. Black and white buildings are a hallmark, including 'The Rows' - two-tier shopping galleries. 900-year-old cathedral and the famous Chester Zoo.

CHORLEY, LANCASHIRE - Set between the Pennine moors and the Lancashire Plain, Chorley has been an important town since medieval times, with its covered markets. The rich heritage includes Astley Hall and Park, Hoghton Tower, Rivington Country Park and the Leeds-Liverpool Canal.

CLITHEROE, LANCASHIRE - Ancient market town with a 800-year-old castle keep and a wide range of award-winning shops. Good base for touring Ribble Valley, Trough of Bowland and Pennine moorland. Country market on Tuesdays and Saturdays.

K KNUTSFORD, CHESHIRE - Delightful town with many buildings of architectural and historic interest. The setting of Elizabeth Gaskell's "Cranford". Annual May Day celebration and decorative "sanding" of the pavements are unique to the town. Popular Heritage Centre.

L LIVERPOOL, MERSEYSIDE - Vibrant city which became prominent in the 18th C as a result of its sugar, spice and tobacco trade with the Americas. Today the historic waterfront is a major attraction. Home to the Beatles, the Grand National, two 20th C cathedrals and many museums and galleries.

M MACCLESFIELD, CHESHIRE - Cobbled streets and quaint old buildings stand side by side with modern shops and three markets. Centuries of association with the silk industry; museums feature working exhibits and social history. Stunning views of the Peak District National Park.

MANCHESTER, GREATER MANCHESTER - The Gateway to the North, offering one of Britain's largest selections of arts venues and theatre productions, a wide range of chain stores and specialist shops, a legendary, lively nightlife, spectacular architecture and a plethora of eating and drinking places.

N NEW BRIGHTON, MERSEYSIDE - This resort on the Mersey Estuary has 7 miles of coastline, with fishing off the sea wall and pleasant walks along the promenade. Attractions include New Palace Amusements, Floral Pavilion Theatre, ten pin bowling and good sports facilities.

O OLDHAM, GREATER MANCHESTER - The magnificent mill buildings which made Oldham one of the world's leading cotton-spinning towns still dominate the landscape. Ideally situated on the edge of the Peak District, it is now a centre of culture, sport and shopping. Good art gallery.

P PRESTON, LANCASHIRE - Scene of decisive Royalist defeat by Cromwell in the Civil War and later of riots in the Industrial Revolution. Local history exhibited in Harris museum. Famous for its Guild and the celebration that takes place every 20 years.

S SALE, GREATER MANCHESTER - Located between Manchester and Altrincham, Sale owes its name to the 12th C landowner Thomas de Sale. It is now home to Trafford Water Sports Centre and Park, which offers the best in aquatic leisure and countryside activities.

SOUTHPORT, MERSEYSIDE - Delightful Victorian resort noted for gardens, sandy beaches and 6 golf-courses, particularly Royal Birkdale. Attractions include the Atkinson Art Gallery, Southport Railway Centre, Pleasureland and the annual Southport Flower Show. Excellent shopping, particularly in Lord Street's elegant boulevard.

ST MICHAEL'S ON WYRE, LANCASHIRE - Lancashire Village near Blackpool with interesting 13th C church of St Michael containing medieval stained glass window depicting sheep shearing, and clock tower bell made in 1548.

STOCKPORT, GREATER MANCHESTER - Once an important cotton-spinning and manufacturing centre, Stockport has an impressive railway viaduct, a shopping precinct built over the River Mersey and a new leisure complex. Lyme Hall and Vernon Park Museum nearby.

T TIMPERLEY, GREATER MANCHESTER - Located between the towns of Sale and Altrincham, Timperley retains its village atmosphere with spacious tree-lined roads, excellent shopping facilities, restaurants and hostelries offering traditional ales, hearty meals and local speciality dishes.

W WILMSLOW, CHESHIRE - Nestling in the valleys of the Rivers Bollin and Dane, Wilmslow retains an intimate village atmosphere. Easy to reach attractions include Quarry Bank Mill at Style. Lindow Man was discovered on a nearby common. Romany's caravan sits in a memorial garden.

COUNTRY CODE

Always follow the Country Code · Enjoy the countryside and respect its life and work · Guard against all risk of fire · Fasten all gates · Keep your dogs under close control · Keep to public paths across farmland · Use gates and stiles to cross fences, hedges and walls · Leave livestock, crops and machinery alone · Take your litter home · Help to keep all water clean · Protect wildlife, plants and trees · Take special care on country roads · Make no unnecessary noise

Yorkshire

Yorkshire combines wild and brooding moors with historic cities, elegant spa towns and a varied coastline of traditional resorts and working fishing ports.

Classic sights
Fountains Abbey & Studley Royal – 12thC Cistercian abbey and Georgian water garden
Nostell Priory – 18thC house with outstanding art collection
York Minster – largest medieval Gothic cathedral north of the Alps

Coast & country
The Pennines – dramatic moors and rocks
Whitby – unspoilt fishing port, famous for jet (black stone)

Literary links
Bronte parsonage, Haworth – home of the Bronte sisters; inspiration for 'Wuthering Heights' and 'Jane Eyre'

Arts for all
National Museum of Photography, Film and Television, Bradford – hi-tech and hands-on

Distinctively different
The Original Ghost Walk of York – spooky tours every night

The Counties of North, South, East and West Yorkshire, and Northern Lincolnshire

For more information contact:
Yorkshire Tourist Board
312 Tadcaster Road,
York YO24 1GS

E: info@ytb.org.uk
www.yorkshirevisitor.com

Telephone enquiries -
T: (01904) 707070
(24-hr Brochure Line)
F: (01904) 701414

1. Yorkshire Dales
2. Castle Howard, North Yorkshire
3. Flamborough, East Riding of Yorkshire

Places to Visit

You will find hundreds of interesting places to visit during your stay, just some of which are listed in these pages. Contact any Tourist Information Centre in the region for more ideas on days out.

Awarded VisitBritain's 'Quality Assured Visitor Attraction' marque.

Beningbrough Hall & Gardens (National Trust)
Beningborough, York
Tel: (01904) 470666 www.nationaltrust.org.uk
Handsome Baroque house, built in 1716. With 100 pictures from the National Portrait Gallery, Victorian laundry, potting shed and restored walled garden.

Bolton Abbey Estate
Skipton
Tel: (01756) 718009 www.boltonabbey.com
Ruins of 12thC priory in a parkland setting by the River Wharfe. Tearooms, catering, nature trails, fishing, fell-walking and picturesque countryside.

Cusworth Hall Museum of South Yorkshire Life
Cusworth Lane, Doncaster
Tel: (01302) 782342
www.museum@doncaster.gov.uk
Georgian mansion in landscaped park containing Museum of South Yorkshire Life, with displays of costumes, childhood and transport. Special educational facilities.

The Deep
Hull
Tel: (01482) 381000 www.thedeep.co.uk
Find out all about the world's oceans in entertaining and informative displays. The Deep also has a learning centre and research facility.

Eden Camp Modern History Theme Museum
Malton
Tel: (01653) 697777 www.edencamp.co.uk
This museum transports you back to wartime Britain in a series of expertly-recreated scenes covering all aspects of World War II.

Eureka! The Museum for Children
Discovery Road, Halifax
Tel: (01422) 330069 www.eureka.org.uk
Eureka! is the first museum of its kind designed especially for children up to the age of 12 with over 400 hands-on exhibits.

Fountains Abbey and Studley Royal (National Trust)

Studley Park, Ripon
Tel: (01765) 608888
www.fountainsabbey.org.uk
Largest monastic ruin in Britain, founded by Cistercian monks in 1132. Landscaped garden laid between 1720-40 with lake, formal water garden, temples and deer park.

Freeport Hornsea Outlet Village
Rolston Road, Hornsea
Tel: (01964) 534211 www.freeportplc.com
Set in 25 acres (10ha) of landscaped gardens with over 40 quality high-street names all selling stock with discounts of up to 50%, licensed restaurant. Leisure attractions.

Helmsley Castle (English Heritage)
Helmsley, York
Tel: (01439) 770442
www.english-heritage.org.uk
Great ruined keep dominates the town. Other remains include a 16thC domestic range with original panelling and plasterwork. Spectacular earthwork defences.

JORVIK – The Viking City
Coppergate, York
Tel: (01904) 543403
www.vikingjorvik.com
Journey back to York in AD975 and experience the sights, sounds and even smells of the Viking Age. Special exhibitions complete the experience.

Last of the Summer Wine Exhibition (Compo's House)

30 Huddersfield Road, Holmfirth
Tel: (01484) 681408
Collection of photographs and memorabilia connected with the television series 'Last of the Summer Wine'.

Leeds City Art Gallery

The Headrow, Leeds
Tel: (0113) 247 8248
www.leeds.gov.uk/tourinfo/attract/museums/artgall.html
Interesting collections of British paintings, sculptures, prints and drawings of the 19th/20thC. Henry Moore gallery with permanent collection of 20thC sculpture.

Lightwater Valley Theme Park and Country Shopping Village

North Stainley, Ripon
Tel: 0870 4580060 www.lightwatervalley.net
Set in 175 acres (70ha) of parkland, Lightwater Valley features a number of white-knuckle rides and attractions for all the family, shopping, a restaurant and picnic areas.

Magna

Quality Assured Visitor Attraction

Sheffield Road, Rotherham
Tel: (01709) 720002
www.magnatrust.org.uk
Magna is the UK's 1st Science Adventure Centre set in the vast Templeborough steelworks in Rotherham. Fun is unavoidable here with giant interactive displays.

National Centre for Early Music

St Margarets Church, York
Tel: (01904) 645738 www.yorkearlymusic.org
The National Centre for Early Music is a unique combination of music, heritage and new technology and offers a perfect venue for musicmaking, drama, recordings and conferences.

National Fishing Heritage Centre

Alexandra Dock, Grimsby
Tel: (01472) 323345
www.welcome.to/NFHCentre/
A journey of discovery, experience the reality of life on a deep-sea trawler. Interactive games and displays. Children's area.

National Museum of Photography, Film & Television

Bradford
Tel: (01274) 202030 www.nmpft.org.uk
Experience the past, present and future of photography, film and television with amazing interactive displays and spectacular 3D IMAX cinema. Museum admission is free.

National Railway Museum

Quality Assured Visitor Attraction

Leeman Road, York
Tel: (01904) 621261 www.nrm.org.uk
Discover the story of the train in a great day out for all the family. The National Railway Museum mixes fascination and education with hours of fun. And best of all, it's free.

Newby Hall & Gardens

Quality Assured Visitor Attraction

Ripon
Tel: (01423) 322583
www.newbyhall.com
Late 17thC house with additions, interior by Robert Adam, classical sculpture, Gobelins tapestries, 25 acres (10ha) of gardens, miniature railway, children's adventure garden.

2

3

1. Worsbrough Mill Museum, South Yorkshire
2. Staithes, North Yorkshire
3. North Yorkshire Moors, Railway Steam Train

North Yorkshire Moors Railway

Pickering Station, Pickering
Tel: (01751) 472508
www.nymr.demon.co.uk
Britain's most popular heritage railway travelling through the beautiful North York Moors National Park.

Nunnington Hall (National Trust)
Nunnington, York
Tel: (01439) 748283 www.nationaltrust.org.uk
Large 17thC manor-house situated on banks of River Rye. With hall, bedrooms, nursery, maid's room (haunted), Carlisle collection of miniature rooms. National Trust shop.

Pleasure Island Family Theme Park
Kings Road, Cleethorpes
Tel: (01472) 211511 www.pleasure-island.co.uk
The East Coast's biggest fun day out, with over 50 rides and attractions. Whatever the weather, fun is guaranteed with lots of undercover attractions. Shows from around the world.

Ripley Castle
Ripley, Harrogate
Tel: (01423) 770152
www.ripleycastle.co.uk
Ripley Castle, home to the Ingilby family for over 26 generations is set in the heart of a delightful estate with Victorian walled gardens, deer park and pleasure grounds.

Royal Armouries Museum
Armouries Drive, Leeds
Tel: (0113) 220 1916 www.armouries.org.uk
Experience more than 3,000 years of history covered by over 8,000 spectacular exhibits and stunning surroundings. Arms and armour.

Ryedale Folk Museum
Hutton-le-Hole, York
Tel: (01751) 417367
www.ryedalefolkmuseum.co.uk
Reconstructed local buildings including cruck-framed long-houses Elizabethan manor-house, furnished cottages, craftsmen's tools, household/agricultural implements.

Sea Life and Marine Sanctuary
Scalby Mills, Scarborough
Tel: (01723) 376125 www.sealife.co.uk
At the Sea Life Centre you have the opportunity to meet creatures that live in and around the oceans of the British Isles, ranging from starfish and crabs to rays and seals.

Sheffield Botanical Gardens
Clarkehouse Road, Sheffield
Tel: (0114) 267 6496 www.sbg.org.uk
Extensive gardens with over 5,500 species of plants, Grade II Listed garden pavilion (now closed).

Skipton Castle

Skipton
Tel: (01756) 792442
www.skiptoncastle.co.uk
Fully-roofed Skipton Castle is in excellent condition. One of the most complete and well-preserved medieval castles in England.

Wensleydale Cheese Visitor Centre
Gayle Lane, Hawes
Tel: (01969) 667664 www.wensleydale.co.uk
Viewing gallery, see real Wensleydale cheese being made by hand. Interpretation area, including rolling video, display and photographic boards. Museum, shop and cafe.

Wigfield Farm
Worsbrough Bridge, Barnsley
Tel: (01226) 733702
http://sites.barnsley.ac.uk/wigfield
Open working farm with rare and commercial breeds of farm animals including pigs, cattle, sheep, goats, donkeys, ponies and small pet animals.

York Castle Museum
The Eye of York, York
Tel: (01904) 653611 www.york.gov.uk
England's most popular museum of everyday life including reconstructed streets and period rooms.

York Minster
Deangate, York
Tel: (01904) 557200 www.yorkminster.org
York Minster is the largest medieval Gothic cathedral north of the alps. Museum of Roman/Norman remains. Chapter house.

Yorkshire Tourist Board

312 Tadcaster Road, York YO24 1GS.
T: (01904) 707070 (24-hour brochure line)
F: (01904) 701414
E: info@ytb.org.uk
www.yorkshirevisitor.com

THE FOLLOWING PUBLICATIONS ARE AVAILABLE FROM YORKSHIRE TOURIST BOARD:

Yorkshire Visitor Guide 2004 –
information on Yorkshire and Northern Lincolnshire, including hotels, self-catering, camping and caravan parks. Also attractions, shops, restaurants and major events

Walk Yorkshire –
a walking pack tailored to meet the individual's needs according to the area they are interested in

Hidden Yorkshire –
a guide to Yorkshire's less well known haunts

Yorkshire on Screen –
a guide to Yorkshire's TV, Movie, and Literary heritage

Eating out Guide –
information on eateries in Yorkshire

Getting to Yorkshire

BY ROAD: Motorways: M1, M62, M606, M621, M18, M180, M181, A1(M). Trunk roads: A1, A19, A57, A58, A59, A61, A62, A63, A64, A65, A66.

BY RAIL: InterCity services to Bradford, Doncaster, Harrogate, Kingston upon Hull, Leeds, Sheffield, Wakefield and York. Frequent regional railway services city centre to city centre including Manchester Airport service to Scarborough, York and Leeds.

1. The Humber Bridge
2. Whitby, North Yorkshire

Where to stay in

Yorkshire

All place names in the blue bands under which accommodation is listed, are shown on the maps at the front of this guide.

Symbols give useful information about services and facilities. Inside the back cover flap there's a key to these symbols which you can keep open for easy reference.

A complete listing of all the VisitBritain assessed accommodation covered by this guide appears at the back of this guide.

ADDINGHAM, West Yorkshire Map ref 4B1

THE CROWN INN
Main Street, Addingham, Ilkley
LS29 0NS
T: (01943) 830278
F: (01943) 831715
E: mariawells350@aol.com

Bedrooms: 2 double
Bathrooms: 2 en suite

CC: Amex, Delta, Mastercard, Switch, Visa

B&B per person per night:
D £30.00–£50.00

OPEN All Year

17thC coaching inn. Ideal base for walking the Yorkshire Dales. Excellent facilities, newly refurbished rooms, en suite bathrooms.

APPLETREEWICK, North Yorkshire Map ref 4B1

Silver Award

KNOWLES LODGE
Appletreewick, Skipton BD23 6DQ
T: (01756) 720228
F: (01756) 720381
E: pam@knowleslodge.com
I: www.knowleslodge.com

Bedrooms: 2 double, 1 twin
Bathrooms: 3 en suite

Evening meal available
CC: Amex, Delta, Mastercard, Switch, Visa

B&B per person per night:
S £35.00
D £30.00

HB per person per night:
DY £48.00–£53.00

In a spectacular setting of garden, meadow and woodland, Knowles Lodge overlooks River Wharfe. Accommodation comprises 3 stylishly appointed bedrooms, each with en suite bathroom.

MAP REFERENCES The map references refer to the colour maps at the front of this guide. The first figure is the map number; the letter and figure which follow indicate the grid reference on the map.

ARKENGARTHDALE, North Yorkshire Map ref 5B3

♦♦♦♦
Silver Award

THE CHARLES BATHURST INN

Arkengarthdale, Richmond DL11 6EN
T: (01748) 884567
F: (01748) 884599
E: info@cbinn.co.uk
I: www.cbinn.co.uk

B&B per person per night:
S £55.00–£60.00
D £35.00–£42.50

HB per person per night:
DY £55.00–£60.00

OPEN All Year

An 18thC inn steeped in local history offering outstanding fresh food in a warm and friendly atmosphere. Open fires and antique pine furnish the bar and restaurant. Each of the en suite rooms has been individually designed and decorated and commands marvellous views of the Stang and Arkengarthdale.

Bedrooms: 12 double, 6 twin
Bathrooms: 18 en suite

Evening meal available
CC: Delta, Mastercard, Switch, Visa

Special offers posted on our website throughout the year.

ASKRIGG, North Yorkshire Map ref 5B3

♦♦♦♦♦
Gold Award

HELM

Askrigg, Leyburn DL8 3JF
T: (01969) 650443
F: (01969) 650443
E: holiday@helmyorkshire.com
I: www.helmyorkshire.com

B&B per person per night:
S £51.00–£60.00
D £33.50–£42.50

HB per person per night:
DY £53.50–£62.50

OPEN All Year except Christmas

Award-winning, luxury accommodation with 'the finest view in Wensleydale'. Delightful Dales hillside, 17thC farmhouse with perfect combination of character and comfort. All rooms en suite. Superb food and wines. Open fires and warm, relaxed atmosphere. Visiting the website is a must!

Bedrooms: 2 double, 1 twin
Bathrooms: 3 en suite

Evening meal available
CC: Delta, Mastercard, Switch, Visa

Special 3-night (Fri-Sun) gourmet breaks.

10 P

♦♦♦

HOME FARM

Stalling Busk, Askrigg, Leyburn DL8 3DH
T: (01969) 650360

B&B per person per night:
D £19.00

HB per person per night:
DY £30.00

OPEN All Year

Situated amidst breathtaking scenery overlooking Semerwater Lake in Wensleydale. The 17thC beamed farmhouse with log fires is beautifully furnished with antiques, brass beds, patchwork quilts etc. Bed and breakfast with optional evening meal. Traditional cooking and homemade bread are the order of the day. Licensed.

Bedrooms: 3 single

Evening meal available

8 P

NB

IMPORTANT NOTE Information on accommodation listed in this guide has been supplied by the proprietors. As changes may occur you are advised to check details at the time of booking.

AUSTWICK, North Yorkshire Map ref 5B3

◆◆◆◆

WOOD VIEW
The Green, Austwick, Lancaster
LA2 8BB
T: (015242) 51268
F: (015242) 51268
E: jennifersuri@msn.com
I: www.yorkshiredales.com

Bedrooms: 4 double, 1 twin, 2 family
Bathrooms: 7 en suite

CC: Delta, Mastercard, Switch, Visa

B&B per person per night:
S £35.00–£40.00
D £28.00–£35.00

OPEN All Year

One of the oldest (c1700) farmhouses in Austwick, an elegant, Grade II Listed building on The Green. All rooms en suite. Packed lunch available. Welcome drink on arrival.

BARNETBY, South Humberside Map ref 4C1

◆◆◆◆

REGINALD HOUSE
27 Queens Road, Barnetby
DN38 6JH
T: (01652) 688566
F: (01652) 688510

Bedrooms: 2 double, 1 single
Bathrooms: 3 en suite

Evening meal available

B&B per person per night:
S Max £25.00

OPEN All Year

Quiet, family-run guesthouse in Barnetby village. Five minutes from M180 and railway station, three miles from Humberside Airport. Near to Grimsby, Scunthorpe and Hull.

BEDALE, North Yorkshire Map ref 5C3

THE CASTLE ARMS INN

Snape, Bedale DL8 2TB
T: (01677) 470270
F: (01677) 470837
E: castlearms@aol.com

B&B per person per night:
S £47.50
D £31.25

HB per person per night:
DY £39.00–£50.00

OPEN All Year

A family-run 14thC inn which has been completely refurbished. Nine en suite twin/double bedrooms have been added, all furnished to an exceptional standard and including TV and tea/coffee-making facilities. A warm welcome awaits you, with open fires, traditional ales and real home cooking.

Bedrooms: 9 double
Bathrooms: 9 en suite

Evening meal available
CC: Delta, Mastercard, Switch, Visa

Special seasonal rates available Oct-Mar.

◆◆◆◆◆

ELMFIELD COUNTRY HOUSE
Arrathorne, Bedale DL8 1NE
T: (01677) 450558
F: (01677) 450557
E: stay@elmfieldhouse.freeserve.co.uk
I: www.elmfieldhouse.co.uk

Bedrooms: 5 double, 2 twin, 2 family
Bathrooms: 9 en suite

Evening meal available
CC: Delta, Mastercard, Switch, Visa

B&B per person per night:
S £39.00–£43.00
D £29.00–£35.00

HB per person per night:
DY £44.00–£54.00

OPEN All Year

Country house in own grounds with special emphasis on standards and home cooking. All rooms en suite. Bar, games room, solarium. Ample secure parking.

USE YOUR *i*s

There are more than 550 Tourist Information Centres throughout England offering friendly help with accommodation and holiday ideas as well as suggestions of places to visit and things to do. You'll find TIC addresses in the local Phone Book.

BEDALE continued

♦♦♦♦♦ Silver Award

MILL CLOSE FARM

Patrick Brompton, Bedale DL8 1JY
T: (01677) 450257
F: (01677) 450585
E: millclosefarm@btopenworld.com
I: www.smoothhound.co.uk/hotels/millclosefarm.html

B&B per person per night:
D £27.50–£35.00

Peace and tranquillity in beautiful, rural setting. Luxurious, en suite bedrooms, two with spa baths. Large (6ft), comfortable beds, televideos, tea trays, guest fridges with complimentary fruit, mineral water and homemade chocolates. Walled garden with pond and summer-house. Delicious traditional and speciality breakfasts. Excellent local inns. Colour leaflet.

Bedrooms: 2 double, 1 twin
Bathrooms: 3 en suite

BEVERLEY, East Riding of Yorkshire Map ref 4C1 *Tourist Information Centre Tel: (01482) 867430*

♦♦♦

EASTGATE GUEST HOUSE

7 Eastgate, Beverley HU17 0DR
T: (01482) 868464
F: (01482) 871899

B&B per person per night:
S £18.00–£40.00
D £15.00–£26.00

OPEN All Year

Family-run Victorian guesthouse, established and run by the same proprietor for 31 years. Close to town centre, Beverley Minster, Museum of Army Transport and railway station. 15 minutes to Hull city centre and The Deep. Excellent central location for exploring the surrounding Wolds.

Bedrooms: 8 double, 5 single, 3 family
Bathrooms: 7 en suite

♦♦♦♦

RUDSTONE WALK COUNTRY ACCOMMODATION

South Cave, Near Beverley, Brough HU15 2AH
T: (01430) 422230
F: (01430) 424552
E: office@rudstone-walk.co.uk
I: www.rudstone-walk.co.uk

B&B per person per night:
S £44.00–£48.00
D £27.50–£30.00

HB per person per night:
DY £46.00–£66.50

OPEN All Year

Nestled in the Yorkshire Wolds with magnificent views, Rudstone Walk provides a relaxing retreat with luxury, en suite accommodation. Fully licensed. Superb home-cooked food is served in the beautiful 400-year-old farmhouse. Ideal for Beverley, York, coast and moors. 3-day and weekend special rates available. Colour brochure on request.

Bedrooms: 7 double, 7 single
Bathrooms: 14 en suite

Evening meal available
CC: Amex, Delta, Diners, Mastercard, Switch, Visa

Exclusive use of 14 B&B rooms and dinner for clubs, annual reunions, family gatherings and weekend meetings. Details on request.

MAP REFERENCES

Map references apply to the colour maps at the front of this guide.

BINGLEY, West Yorkshire Map ref 4B1

Silver Award

FIVE RISE LOCKS HOTEL & RESTAURANT

Beck Lane, Bingley BD16 4DD
T: (01274) 565296
F: (01274) 568828
E: info@five-rise-locks.co.uk
I: www.five-rise-locks.co.uk

Bedrooms: 8 double, 1 single
Bathrooms: 9 en suite

Evening meal available
CC: Delta, Mastercard, Switch, Visa

Victorian residence in tranquil rural setting of the canal conservation area. Relaxed atmosphere. Elegantly designed, en suite bedrooms. Award-winning restaurant.

B&B per person per night:
S £45.00–£60.00
D £32.50–£37.50

OPEN All Year

BOLTON PERCY, North Yorkshire Map ref 4C1

◆◆◆◆

GLEBE FARM

Bolton Percy, York YO23 7AL
T: (01904) 744228

Bedrooms: 1 double
Bathrooms: 1 en suite

225-acre mixed farm. Excellent accommodation in self-contained, en suite annexe on family-run farm. Conservatory, garden, ample parking.

B&B per person per night:
S £25.00–£28.00
D £24.00–£28.00

BOROUGHBRIDGE, North Yorkshire Map ref 5C3

◆◆◆

BURTON GRANGE

Helperby, York YO61 2RY
T: (01423) 360825
E: burton_grange@hotmail.com

Bedrooms: 1 double, 1 twin

18thC farmhouse in the beautiful Vale of York. Working farm offering a peaceful and comfortable stay. Close to A1 at Boroughbridge.

B&B per person per night:
S Min £25.00
D Min £22.00

OPEN All Year except Christmas

BRADFORD, West Yorkshire Map ref 4B1 *Tourist Information Centre Tel: (01274) 433678*

◆◆

IVY GUEST HOUSE

3 Melbourne Place, Bradford BD5 0HZ
T: (01274) 727060
F: (01274) 306347
E: nickbaggio@aol.com

Bedrooms: 4 double, 3 twin, 2 single, 1 family

CC: Amex, Delta, Diners, Mastercard, Switch, Visa

Large, detached, Listed, Yorkshire-stone house. Close to city centre, National Museum of Photography, Film and Television, Alhambra Theatre and the University of Bradford.

B&B per person per night:
S £22.00
D £18.00

OPEN All Year

BRIDLINGTON, East Riding of Yorkshire Map ref 5D3 *Tourist Information Centre Tel: (01262) 673474*

◆◆◆

THE GRANTLEA GUEST HOUSE

2 South Street, Bridlington YO15 3BY
T: (01262) 400190

Bedrooms: 3 double, 2 twin, 1 single
Bathrooms: 4 en suite, 2 private

Situated on the south side, one minute from the beach, spa, theatre and harbour. Within easy walking distance of the town centre and coach/rail stations.

B&B per person per night:
S £20.00
D £20.00

OPEN All Year except Christmas

◆◆◆◆

MARYLAND BED & BREAKFAST

66 Wellington Road, Bridlington YO15 2AZ
T: (01262) 671088
E: mills@marylandbandb.fsbusiness.co.uk

Bedrooms: 1 double, 1 single, 1 family

Great holidays start here at our Victorian home, only 10 minutes from beach and all the attractions. A friendly welcome awaits you in this caring, family-run B&B.

B&B per person per night:
S £20.00
D £20.00

◆◆◆

WAVERLEY HOTEL

105 Cardigan Road, Bridlington YO15 3LP
T: (01262) 671040

Bedrooms: 1 twin, 4 family
Bathrooms: 4 en suite, 1 private

Small, friendly, family-run hotel in a quiet residential area close to the South Beach and golf course. Ample parking.

B&B per person per night:
S £21.00–£22.00
D £21.00–£22.00

OPEN All Year except Christmas

BRIDLINGTON continued

THE WHITE ROSE

123 Cardigan Road, Bridlington
YO15 3LP
T: (01262) 673245
F: (01262) 401362
E: c.a.young@tesco.net
I: www.smoothhound.co.uk/hotels/thewhiterose

Bedrooms: 2 double, 2 twin, 1 family
Bathrooms: 4 en suite, 1 private

Evening meal available
CC: Mastercard, Visa

Personal attention with warm, friendly hospitality and emphasis on food. No hidden extras. Near the South Beach, spa and harbour. Special pensioners' weeks at discount prices.

B&B per person per night:
S £30.00
D £23.00–£25.00

HB per person per night:
DY £30.50–£32.50

OPEN All Year

BUCKDEN, North Yorkshire Map ref 5B3

THE WHITE LION INN

Cray, Buckden, Skipton BD23 5JB
T: (01756) 760262
F: (01756) 761024
E: admin.whitelion@btinternet.com
I: www.whitelioncray.com

Located in Upper Wharfedale, you are assured a warm welcome to our traditional 17thC Dales inn. Relax in the friendly atmosphere and enjoy the country charm of stone-flagged floors, roaring log fire, quality home-prepared foods and real ales. Idyllic location with excellent walks direct from our door!

Bedrooms: 6 double, 1 twin, 1 family
Bathrooms: 8 en suite

Evening meal available
CC: Delta, Mastercard, Switch, Visa

3 nights for the price of 2, subject to eating from the full evening menu every night (one main course per person).

B&B per person per night:
S Min £37.50
D £27.50–£32.50

OPEN All Year

CARLTON, North Yorkshire Map ref 5B3

MIDDLEHAM HOUSE

Carlton, Leyburn DL8 4BB
T: (01969) 640645
E: info@middlehamhouse.co.uk
I: www.middlehamhouse.co.uk

Bedrooms: 2 double, 1 twin
Bathrooms: 2 en suite

Traditional stone-built Dales house. Warm welcome guaranteed. Attractive bedrooms with outstanding views over Coverdale and village. Ideally situated for walking, cycling, touring. Pub nearby.

B&B per person per night:
S £25.00–£29.00
D £20.00–£24.00

OPEN All Year except Christmas

COXWOLD, North Yorkshire Map ref 5C3

NEWBURGH HOUSE

Coxwold, York YO61 4AS
T: (01347) 868177
F: (01347) 868177
E: info@newburghhouse.com
I: www.newburghhouse.com

Bedrooms: 2 double, 1 twin
Bathrooms: 3 en suite

Evening meal available

Spacious period country house adjacent to Newburgh Lake. Luxury bedrooms, large residents' sitting room with ample books, videos and games. Log fires/home cooking. Special breaks.

B&B per person per night:
S £35.00–£45.00
D £30.00–£40.00

HB per person per night:
DY £48.50–£58.50

OPEN All Year except Christmas

TOWN INDEX

This can be found at the back of the guide. If you know where you want to stay, the index will give you the page number listing accommodation in your chosen town, city or village.

CROPTON, North Yorkshire Map ref 5C3

Silver Award

HIGH FARM

Cropton, Pickering YO18 8HL
T: (01751) 417461
F: (01751) 417807
E: highfarmcropton@aol.com
I: www.hhml.com/bb/highfarmcropton.htm

B&B per person per night:
S £29.00
D £24.00

OPEN All Year

Relax in the friendly atmosphere of this elegant Victorian farmhouse surrounded by beautiful gardens, on the edge of quiet, unspoilt village and overlooking North York Moors National Park. Peaceful base for walkers, nature/garden lovers. Steam railway and Castle Howard nearby. Village inn has own brewery. A warm welcome awaits.

Bedrooms: 3 double
Bathrooms: 3 en suite

CC: Delta, Mastercard, Switch, Visa

10 P

♦♦♦

NEW INN AND CROPTON BREWERY

Cropton, Pickering YO18 8HH
T: (01751) 417330
F: (01751) 417582
E: info@croptonbrewery.co.uk
I: www.croptonbrewery.co.uk

B&B per person per night:
S £33.00–£39.00
D £27.00–£33.00

HB per person per night:
DY £43.50–£49.50

OPEN All Year

Traditional, family-run country inn and micro-brewery on the edge of the North York National Park. Convenient for the Moors and coast. Offering excellent home-cooked meals, comfortable en suite accommodation and award-winning real ales from own brewery in an informal, friendly atmosphere. Brewery tours are available.

Bedrooms: 7 double, 2 family, 1 suite
Bathrooms: 9 en suite

Evening meal available
CC: Amex, Delta, Mastercard, Switch, Visa

P €

DANBY, North Yorkshire Map ref 5C3

THE FOX & HOUNDS INN

45 Brook Lane, Ainthorpe, Danby, Whitby YO21 2LD
T: (01287) 660218
F: (01287) 660030
E: ajbfox@globalnet.co.uk
I: www.foxandhounds-ainthorpe.com

Bedrooms: 6 double, 1 family
Bathrooms: 7 en suite

Evening meal available
CC: Amex, Delta, Diners, Mastercard, Switch, Visa

B&B per person per night:
S £35.00–£40.00
D £30.00–£35.00

OPEN All Year

16thC former coaching inn, now a high-quality residential country inn and restaurant. Set amidst the beautiful North York Moors National Park.

P €

DRIFFIELD, East Riding of Yorkshire Map ref 4C1

KELLEYTHORPE FARM

Driffield YO25 9DW
T: (01377) 252297
E: jhopper@kelleythorpe.fsbusiness.co.uk

Bedrooms: 1 double, 1 family
Bathrooms: 1 en suite, 1 private

Evening meal available

B&B per person per night:
S Min £25.00
D £20.00–£22.00

HB per person per night:
DY £32.00–£34.00

OPEN All Year except Christmas

200-acre livestock farm. Comfortable Georgian farmhouse overlooking a trout lake, woods and paddocks. Aberdeen Angus cattle, pigs and peacocks on the farm. Central for York and the coast.

P

QUALITY ASSURANCE SCHEME

Diamond ratings and awards are explained at the back of this guide.

DUNGWORTH, South Yorkshire Map ref 4B2

THE ROYAL HOTEL

Main Road, Dungworth, Bradfield, Sheffield S6 6HF
T: (0114) 2851213
F: (0114) 2851723
E: reception@royalhotel-dungworth.co.uk
I: www.royalhotel-dungworth.co.uk

The Royal Hotel is a 19thC, family-run public house on the edge of the Peak Park yet only six miles from the centre of Sheffield and Meadowhall/M1. Located on the hillside overlooking the Vale of Bradfield in idyllic countryside for walking, with fishing and golfing close by.

Bedrooms: 3 double
Bathrooms: 3 en suite

Evening meal available
CC: Mastercard, Switch, Visa

B&B per person per night:
S £35.00
D £25.00

OPEN All Year

EASINGWOLD, North Yorkshire Map ref 5C3

YEOMAN'S COURSE HOUSE

Thornton Hill, Easingwold, York
YO61 3PY
T: (01347) 868126
F: (01347) 868129
E: chris@yeomanscourse.fsnet.co.uk
I: www.yeomanscourse.co.uk

Bedrooms: 2 double, 1 twin

Built c1800 as part of Newburgh Priory Estate. Set in the Howardian Hills overlooking the Vale of York and beyond. Open Easter to end September.

12

B&B per person per night:
S £21.00–£24.00
D £20.00–£24.00

FILEY, North Yorkshire Map ref 5D3

SEAFIELD HOTEL

9-11 Rutland Street, Filey YO14 9JA
T: (01723) 513715

Bedrooms: 4 double, 2 single, 9 family
Bathrooms: 14 en suite

Evening meal available
CC: Delta, Mastercard, Visa

Small, friendly and comfortable hotel in the centre of Filey, close to the beach and all amenities. Car park. Family rooms.

B&B per person per night:
S £19.00–£21.00
D £19.00–£21.00

HB per person per night:
DY £25.00–£27.00

OPEN All Year except Christmas

GARFORTH, West Yorkshire Map ref 4B1

MYRTLE HOUSE

31 Wakefield Road, Garforth, Leeds
LS25 1AN
T: (0113) 2866445

Bedrooms: 2 double, 1 single, 3 family

Spacious Victorian terraced house between M62 and A1 (M1, jct 47). All rooms have tea and coffee-making facilities, TV, vanity basin and central heating.

B&B per person per night:
S £19.00–£22.00
D £19.00–£22.00

OPEN All Year except Christmas

CHECK THE MAPS

The colour maps at the front of this guide show all the cities, towns and villages for which you will find accommodation entries. Refer to the town index to find the page on which they are listed.

GOATHLAND, North Yorkshire Map ref 5D3

Silver Award

PRUDOM GUEST HOUSE

Goathland, Whitby YO22 5AN
T: (01947) 896368
F: (01947) 896030
E: info@prudomhouse.co.uk
I: www.prudomhouse.co.uk

B&B per person per night:
S £35.00
D £35.00

OPEN All Year except Christmas and New Year

A warm welcome awaits you at our cosy, family-owned, 18thC farmhouse in the village of Goathland. Situated opposite the church and surrounded by magnificent moorland views. Perfect for walking and touring. Quality accommodation, log fires, pretty cottage gardens and excellent food using local produce.

Bedrooms: 3 double, 2 twin, 1 single
Bathrooms: 6 en suite

CC: Delta, Mastercard, Switch, Visa

GOOLE, East Riding of Yorkshire Map ref 4C1

♦♦♦

THE BRIARCROFT HOTEL

49-51 Clifton Gardens, Goole
DN14 6AR
T: (01405) 763024
F: (01405) 767317
E: briarcofthotel@aol.com
I: hometown.aol.co.uk/briarcrofthotel/brochure.html

Bedrooms: 9 double, 5 single, 1 family
Bathrooms: 8 en suite

CC: Delta, Mastercard, Switch, Visa

B&B per person per night:
S £26.00–£44.00
D £20.00–£27.00

OPEN All Year

Friendly hotel with a range of rooms from standard to en suite and prices to suit most budgets. Ideally situated for touring or business in East Yorkshire.

GRASSINGTON, North Yorkshire Map ref 5B3 *Tourist Information Centre Tel: (01756) 752774*

♦♦♦

FORESTERS ARMS HOTEL

20 Main Street, Grassington, Skipton BD23 5AA
T: (01756) 752349
F: (01756) 753633
E: theforesters@totalise.co.uk

Bedrooms: 5 double, 2 family
Bathrooms: 7 en suite

Evening meal available
CC: Delta, Mastercard, Switch, Visa

B&B per person per night:
S £25.00–£35.00
D £25.00–£35.00

OPEN All Year except Christmas

Formerly an old coaching inn, situated in picturesque village, serving lunch and evening meals. Hand-pulled ales and en suite accommodation.

NEW LAITHE HOUSE

Wood Lane, Grassington, Skipton
BD23 5LU
T: (01756) 752764
E: enquiries@newlaithehouse.co.uk
I: www.newlaithehouse.co.uk

B&B per person per night:
D £26.00–£30.00

Family-run guesthouse with spacious rooms. Situated in a quiet location in Grassington with lovely views over open countryside. Ideal base for walking, fishing and visiting the many historic towns in North and West Yorkshire. Large garden with private parking.

Bedrooms: 5 double, 1 family
Bathrooms: 4 en suite, 1 private

www.visitengland.com

Log on for information and inspiration. The latest information on places to visit, events and quality assessed accommodation.

GREAT AYTON, North Yorkshire Map ref 5C3

◆◆◆

ROYAL OAK HOTEL

High Green, Great Ayton, Middlesbrough TS9 6BW
T: (01642) 722361
F: (01642) 724047

Bedrooms: 3 double, 1 twin, 1 single
Bathrooms: 3 en suite, 1 private

Evening meal available
CC: Amex, Delta, Diners, Mastercard, Switch, Visa

18thC coaching inn offering bar and extensive and varied restaurant menus.

B&B per person per night:
S £30.00–£40.00
D £30.00

OPEN All Year

◆◆◆◆

SUSIE D'S B & B

Crossways, 116 Newton Road, Great Ayton, Middlesbrough TS9 6DL
T: (01642) 724351
E: susieD's@crossways26.fsnet.co.uk

Bedrooms: 1 double, 2 single

Superb accommodation in large, detatched house with extensive gardens. Ideally situated for North York Moors, Cleveland Way and Captain Cook Trail.

P

B&B per person per night:
S Min £22.00
D £22.50–£27.50

OPEN All Year

HALIFAX, West Yorkshire Map ref 4B1 *Tourist Information Centre Tel: (01422) 368725*

Silver Award

ROSE COTTAGE

Shibden Fold, Halifax HX3 6XP
T: (01422) 365437
E: reservations@shibden-fold.co.uk
I: www.shibden-fold.co.uk

Spacious, comfortable accommodation in a lovely private home. Built in the 16thC in rural surroundings. Beautifully decorated, en suite bedrooms and visitors' study. Excellent walking and sightseeing, Eureka! Children's Museum and Shibden Hall are very close. Enjoy the gardens, streams and 15 acres with good food and personal service.

Bedrooms: 1 double, 1 twin
Bathrooms: 2 en suite

Evening meal available
CC: Mastercard, Visa

P €

B&B per person per night:
S £35.00–£40.00
D £27.50–£30.00

HB per person per night:
DY £45.00–£65.00

OPEN All Year

HARROGATE, North Yorkshire Map ref 4B1 *Tourist Information Centre Tel: (01423) 537300*

◆◆◆◆

ALAMAH GUEST HOUSE

88 Kings Road, Harrogate HG1 5JX
T: (01423) 502187
F: (01423) 566175

Bedrooms: 2 double, 2 twin, 2 single, 1 family
Bathrooms: 6 en suite, 1 private

CC: Delta, Mastercard, Switch, Visa

Comfortable rooms, personal attention, friendly atmosphere and full English breakfast. Three hundred metres from town centre, 150 metres from Exhibition Centre. Garages/parking.

P

B&B per person per night:
S £28.00–£30.00
D £30.00

OPEN All Year except Christmas

◆◆◆◆

THE ALEXANDER

88 Franklin Road, Harrogate HG1 5EN
T: (01423) 503348
F: (01423) 540230
E: thealexander@amserve.net

Bedrooms: 2 double, 2 single, 3 family
Bathrooms: 5 en suite

Friendly, family-run, elegant Victorian guesthouse with some en suite facilities. Ideal for conference centre and Harrogate town. Good touring centre for Dales. Non-smokers only, please.

8

B&B per person per night:
S £28.00–£32.00
D £28.00–£32.00

OPEN All Year except Christmas

COLOUR MAPS Colour maps at the front of this guide pinpoint all places under which you will find accommodation listed.

HARROGATE continued

♦♦♦♦

CAVENDISH HOTEL
3 Valley Drive, Harrogate HG2 0JJ
T: (01423) 509637
F: (01423) 504434

Bedrooms: 4 double, 2 twin, 3 single
Bathrooms: 9 en suite

CC: Delta, Mastercard, Switch, Visa

Overlooking the beautiful Valley Gardens in a quiet location yet close to conference centre and extensive shopping area. Ideal for business or pleasure.

B&B per person per night:
S £35.00–£45.00
D £27.50–£37.50

OPEN All Year

♦♦♦♦ Silver Award

CENTRAL HOUSE FARM
Haverah Park, Harrogate HG3 1SQ
T: (01423) 566050
F: (01423) 709152
E: jayne-ryder@lineone.net
I: www.centralhousefarm.co.uk

Bedrooms: 3 double
Bathrooms: 3 en suite

Traditional farmhouse in picturesque, rural location. Private lounge with open log fire. Close to Harrogate and its amenities. York 30 miles, Leeds 20 miles. All rooms are en suite.

P

B&B per person per night:
S £35.00–£40.00
D £25.00–£27.00

OPEN All Year

♦♦♦♦

GARDEN HOUSE HOTEL
14 Harlow Moor Drive, Harrogate HG2 0JX
T: (01423) 503059
F: (01423) 503059
E: gardenhouse@harrogate.com
I: www.harrogate.com/gardenhouse

Bedrooms: 2 double, 2 twin, 3 single
Bathrooms: 5 en suite

CC: Delta, Mastercard, Switch, Visa

Small, family-run, Victorian hotel overlooking Valley Gardens, in a quiet location with unrestricted parking. Non-smokers only please.

2

B&B per person per night:
S Min £26.00
D Min £27.50

OPEN All Year except Christmas

♦♦♦♦

OAK BECK BUNGALOW
4 Oakdale Glen, Harrogate HG1 2JZ
T: (01423) 507336

Bedrooms: 1 twin, 1 single
Bathrooms: 1 en suite

Evening meal available

Quiet residential area next to Oakdale Golf Club. Home-cooked evening meals including special diets available. Eight-minute walk to conference centre-courtesy car optional.

5 P €

B&B per person per night:
S £25.00–£30.00
D £25.00–£30.00

HB per person per night:
DY £33.00–£35.00

OPEN All Year

♦♦♦

SCOTIA HOUSE HOTEL
66-68 Kings Road, Harrogate HG1 5JR
T: (01423) 504361
F: (01423) 526578
E: info@scotiahotel.harrogate.net
I: www.scotiahotel.harrogate.net

Bedrooms: 8 double, 6 single, 1 family
Bathrooms: 12 en suite

CC: Amex, Delta, Mastercard, Switch, Visa

Award-winning, warm, friendly hotel opposite conference centre and close to town and amenities. Individually styled bedrooms offering colour TV, telephone, beverage tray, modem point etc.

P €

B&B per person per night:
S £25.00–£40.00
D £25.00–£32.00

OPEN All Year

HAWES, North Yorkshire Map ref 5B3 *Tourist Information Centre Tel: (01969) 667450*

♦♦♦

EBOR GUEST HOUSE
Burtersett Road, Hawes DL8 3NT
T: (01969) 667337
F: (01969) 667337
E: gwen@eborhouse.freeserve.co.uk

Bedrooms: 3 double
Bathrooms: 2 en suite

Small, friendly, centrally located and family run. Walkers and cyclists catered for with drying facilities and under-cover bike store, hearty breakfasts and packed lunches.

P

B&B per person per night:
S £25.00–£27.00
D £20.00–£22.00

OPEN All Year except Christmas

CONFIRM YOUR BOOKING
You are advised to confirm your booking in writing.

HAWES continued

HERRIOTS HOTEL & RESTAURANT

Main Street, Hawes DL8 3QW
T: (01969) 667536
F: (01969) 667810
E: herriotshotel@aol.com
I: www.herriotshotel.com

Situated on the original cobbled streets of Hawes, this 18thC hotel offers excellent, en suite accommodation. Our very popular restaurant provides modern English and Mediterranean cuisine using the finest local produce. Joanne and Andy look forward to welcoming you to Herriots and the lovely market town of Hawes.

Bedrooms: 4 double, 1 twin, 1 single, 1 family
Bathrooms: 7 en suite

Evening meal available
CC: Delta, Mastercard, Switch, Visa

Special offers available along with celebration packages. Please call for information or visit www.herriotshotel.com.

B&B per person per night:
S £29.50–£35.00
D £29.50–£31.50

OPEN All Year except Christmas

♦♦♦

LABURNUM HOUSE

The Holme, Hawes DL8 3QR
T: (01969) 667717
F: (01969) 667041
E: info@stayatlaburnumhouse.co.uk
I: www.stayatlaburnumhouse.co.uk

18thC Dales House in Hawes, central for walking and touring. Warm welcome, hearty breakfast.

Bedrooms: 2 double, 1 family
Bathrooms: 3 en suite

B&B per person per night:
D Max £23.00

OPEN All Year

♦♦♦♦♦
Gold Award

ROOKHURST COUNTRY HOUSE HOTEL

West End, Gayle, Hawes DL8 3RT
T: (01969) 667454
F: (01969) 667128
E: rookhurst@lineone.net
I: www.rookhurst.co.uk

Relax, wind down and let us pamper you in our 'no smoking, no children' ambience. Enjoy a glass or two with dinner (food award). The house is part Victorian-Gothic and part 17th/18thC. Dales farmhouse with many original features – oak and pine beams, tiled floor, open fire, carved stone and ironwork.

Bedrooms: 4 double, 1 twin
Bathrooms: 5 en suite

Evening meal available
CC: Delta, Mastercard, Switch, Visa

Mid-week breaks throughout the year – please call for details.

12 P

B&B per person per night:
D £45.00–£60.00

HB per person per night:
DY £65.00–£85.00

OPEN All Year except Christmas

♦♦♦

WHITE HART INN
Main Street, Hawes DL8 3QL
T: (01969) 667259
F: (01969) 667259
E: whitehart@wensleydale.org
I: www.wensleydale.org

Bedrooms: 5 double, 1 single

Evening meal available
CC: Delta, Diners, Mastercard, Switch, Visa

17thC coaching inn with a friendly welcome, offering traditional fare. Open fires, Yorkshire ales. Central for exploring the Dales.

P

B&B per person per night:
S £23.50–£28.00
D £22.50–£25.00

OPEN All Year except Christmas

RATING All accommodation in this guide has been rated, or is awaiting a rating, by a trained VisitBritain assessor.

HAWORTH, West Yorkshire Map ref 4B1 *Tourist Information Centre Tel: (01535) 642329*

◆◆◆

THE APOTHECARY GUEST HOUSE
86 Main Street, Haworth, Keighley
BD22 8DP
T: (01535) 643642
F: (01535) 643642
E: Sisleyd@aol.com
I: theapothecaryguesthouse.co.uk

Bedrooms: 3 double, 2 twin, 1 single, 1 family
Bathrooms: 6 en suite, 1 private

CC: Mastercard, Visa

B&B per person per night:
S £20.00–£25.00
D £20.00–£22.50

OPEN All Year

At the top of Haworth Main Street opposite the famous Bronte church, one minute from the Parsonage and Moors. Ten minutes' walk from steam railway.

◆◆

BRONTE HOTEL
Lees Lane, Haworth, Keighley
BD22 8RA
T: (01535) 644112
F: (01535) 646725
E: Brontehotel@btinternet.com
I: www.bronte-hotel.co.uk

Bedrooms: 5 double, 3 single, 3 family
Bathrooms: 8 en suite

Evening meal available
CC: Amex, Mastercard, Switch, Visa

B&B per person per night:
S £25.00–£35.00
D £22.50–£30.00

OPEN All Year except Christmas

On the edge of the Moors, five minutes' walk from the station and 15 minutes' walk to the Parsonage, the former home of the Brontes.

◆◆◆◆

THE OLD REGISTRY

2-4 Main Street, Haworth, Keighley
BD22 8DA
T: (01535) 646503
F: (01535) 646503
E: oldregistry.haworth@virgin.net
I: www.oldregistry.com

Situated in prime position, on the main cobbled street overlooking the park, this beautiful guesthouse offers the very best in bed and breakfast. Themed rooms, decorated to a high standard, most with 4-poster beds, all en suite. Business or pleasure, you'll be glad it was us you chose.

Bedrooms: 10 double, 2 twin, 1 family
Bathrooms: 13 en suite

CC: Delta, Mastercard, Switch, Visa

Book our very special, mid-week winter package: 2 nights, 2 people, full breakfast, 4-poster bed – £100.

B&B per person per night:
S £45.00–£60.00
D £30.00–£40.00

OPEN All Year

HEBDEN, North Yorkshire Map ref 5B3

◆◆◆

COURT CROFT
Church Lane, Hebden, Skipton
BD23 5DX
T: (01756) 753406

Bedrooms: 2 twin

B&B per person per night:
S £27.50
D £25.00

OPEN All Year

500-acre livestock farm. Farmhouse in village location close to the Dalesway. Ideal for touring the Dales.

HELMSLEY, North Yorkshire Map ref 5C3

◆◆◆◆

THE HAWNBY HOTEL

Hill Top, Hawnby, York YO62 5QS
T: (01439) 798202
F: (01439) 798344
E: info@hawnbyhotel.co.uk
I: www.hawnbyhotel.co.uk

Situated in an unspoilt village in the heart of the North Yorkshire Moors National Park, offering spectacular views from its hilltop location. Six exceptional en suite bedrooms. A peaceful, relaxing break at any time of year. Easy access for hiking, climbing, horse-riding, hang-gliding and stately homes. York 45 miles.

Bedrooms: 6 double, 3 twin
Bathrooms: 9 en suite

Evening meal available
CC: Delta, Mastercard, Switch, Visa

3-night stay: £60 per room per night at any time.

B&B per person per night:
S £45.00–£49.00
D £30.00–£34.50

OPEN All Year

HOLMFIRTH, West Yorkshire Map ref 4B1 *Tourist Information Centre Tel: (01484) 222444*

UPPERGATE FARM

Hepworth, Holmfirth, Huddersfield
HD9 1TG
T: (01484) 681369
F: (01484) 687343
E: stevenal.booth@virgin.net
I: www.uppergatefarm.co.uk

17thC farmhouse set in beautiful countryside on the edge of Hepworth, a lovely Pennine village. En suite bedrooms furnished to highest standards. Spacious, full of character, panelled rooms, oak beams, flag floors and guests' lounge. Extensive parking, gardens and woodland walks. Excellent pub/restaurant within a five-minute walk.

Bedrooms: 1 twin, 1 family
Bathrooms: 2 en suite

Weekend and short breaks available throughout the year. Farm activities for children. Safe play areas.

B&B per person per night:
S £30.00
D £25.00–£28.00

OPEN All Year except Christmas

HOOTON PAGNELL, South Yorkshire Map ref 4C1

♦♦♦

ROCK FARM

Hooton Pagnell, Doncaster DN5 7BT
T: (01977) 642200
F: (01977) 642200
E: info@rock-farm.com
I: www.rock-farm.com

Bedrooms: 1 double, 1 single, 1 family
Bathrooms: 1 en suite

200-acre mixed farm. Grade II Listed farmhouse in an unspoilt, picturesque stone village on the B6422, 6 miles north-west of Doncaster and 1.5 miles west of the A1.

B&B per person per night:
S £20.00–£21.00
D £12.00–£12.50

OPEN All Year except Christmas

HUDDERSFIELD, West Yorkshire Map ref 4B1 *Tourist Information Centre Tel: (01484) 223200*

♦♦♦

CAMBRIDGE LODGE

4 Clare Hill, Huddersfield HD1 5BS
T: (01484) 519892
F: (01484) 534534
E: cambridgelodge@btconnect.com
I: www.cambridgelodge.co.uk

Bedrooms: 12 double, 7 twin, 12 single, 3 family
Bathrooms: 34 en suite

CC: Amex, Delta, Diners, Mastercard, Switch, Visa

All rooms double sized and en suite, with tea/coffee-making facilities, telephone and colour TV. Ample free parking and CCTV coverage.

B&B per person per night:
S £30.00
D £17.50

OPEN All Year

ELM CREST

2 Queens Road, Edgerton, Huddersfield
HD2 2AG
T: (01484) 530990
F: (01484) 516227
E: gmitchell@elmcrest.biz
I: www.elmcrest.biz

You always receive a warm welcome at Elm Crest, a no-smoking, Grade II Listed, Victorian building providing excellent meals and set in attractive grounds. It is ideally located just five minutes from the M62 and Huddersfield town centre, providing an ideal base for people wishing to tour the surrounding countryside.

Bedrooms: 2 double, 3 twin, 2 single
Bathrooms: 5 en suite, 2 private

Evening meal available
CC: Amex, Delta, Mastercard, Switch, Visa

B&B per person per night:
S £29.50–£37.00
D £25.00–£27.50

HB per person per night:
DY £35.00–£39.50

OPEN All Year

CREDIT CARD BOOKINGS If you book by telephone and are asked for your credit card number it is advisable to check the proprietor's policy should you cancel your reservation.

HULL, East Riding of Yorkshire Map ref 4C1 *Tourist Information Centre Tel: (01482) 223559 (Paragon Street)*

♦♦♦♦

ROSEBERRY HOUSE
86 Marlborough Avenue, Hull
HU5 3JT
T: (01482) 445256
F: (01482) 343215
I: www.smoothhound.co.uk/hotels/conway.html

Bedrooms: 2 double, 1 single, 1 family
Bathrooms: 3 en suite

CC: Mastercard, Visa

Comfortable guesthouse in quiet conservation area. Emphasis on good food, cleanliness and service, in a friendly atmosphere.

B&B per person per night:
S £20.00–£30.00
D £19.00–£21.00

OPEN All Year

ILKLEY, West Yorkshire Map ref 4B1

♦♦♦

SUMMERHILL GUEST HOUSE
24 Crossbeck Road, Ilkley LS29 9JN
T: (01943) 607067

Bedrooms: 3 double, 2 single
Bathrooms: 1 en suite

Elegant Victorian villa with beautiful garden opening onto Ilkley Moor. Quiet position, lovely views, private parking. Easy walking distance to town.

B&B per person per night:
S £20.00–£30.00
D £20.00–£24.00

OPEN All Year except Christmas

INGLETON, North Yorkshire Map ref 5B3

♦♦♦♦

INGLEBOROUGH VIEW GUEST HOUSE
Main Street, Ingleton, Carnforth
LA6 3HH
T: (01524) 241523
E: anne@ingleboroughview.co.uk
I: www.ingleboroughview.co.uk

Bedrooms: 3 double, 1 family
Bathrooms: 2 en suite, 2 private

Attractive Victorian house with picturesque riverside location. All rooms have superb views. Highly recommended for food, comfort and hospitality. Ideally situated for local walks/touring Dales.

B&B per person per night:
S £30.00–£35.00
D £22.00–£24.00

OPEN All Year except Christmas

♦♦♦

Detached Victorian villa, large garden with patio down to River Greta. Home-grown vegetables in season, home cooking. Private fishing. Pets welcome. All credit cards are accepted.

SPRINGFIELD COUNTRY HOUSE HOTEL

26 Main Street, Ingleton, Carnforth
LA6 3HJ
T: (01524) 241280
F: (01524) 241280
I: www.destination-england.co.uk.springfield

Bedrooms: 4 double, 1 family
Bathrooms: 5 en suite

Evening meal available
CC: Delta, Diners, Mastercard, Switch, Visa

Special terms for 2 or more days: single £22, double £44. B&B: weekly terms – £147pp. B&B plus evening meal: weekly terms – £234.50pp. Single-room supplement for weekly: £56 per room.

B&B per person per night:
S £30.00–£32.00
D £22.00–£24.00

HB per person per night:
DY £34.50–£36.50

OPEN All Year except Christmas

♦♦♦

STATION INN
Ribblehead, Ingleton, Carnforth
LA6 3AS
T: (01524) 241274
E: enquiries@thestationinn.net
I: www.thestationinn.net

Bedrooms: 3 double, 1 single, 1 family
Bathrooms: 4 en suite, 1 private

Evening meal available
CC: Delta, Mastercard, Switch, Visa

Public house with good beer, food and accommodation and excellent views. Centre of the Yorkshire Three Peaks and next to the impressive Ribblehead viaduct.

B&B per person per night:
S Min £27.00
D £21.50–£23.00

OPEN All Year except Christmas

VISTBRITAIN'S WHERE TO STAY
Please mention this guide when making your booking.

KIRKBYMOORSIDE, North Yorkshire Map ref 5C3

♦♦♦♦ Silver Award

THE CORNMILL

Kirkby Mills, Kirkbymoorside, York
YO62 6NP
T: (01751) 432000
F: (01751) 432300
E: cornmill@kirbymills.demon.co.uk
I: www.kirbymills.demon.co.uk

Converted 18thC watermill and Victorian farmhouse providing well-appointed bed and breakfast accommodation on the River Dove. Bedrooms (some with 4-posters and one for wheelchairs), lounge, bar, woodburning stove and bootroom are in the farmhouse. Sumptuous breakfasts and pre-booked group dinners are served in the mill, with viewing panel in the floor.

Bedrooms: 5 double
Bathrooms: 5 en suite

Evening meal available
CC: Delta, Mastercard, Switch, Visa

B&B per person per night:
S £35.00–£47.50
D £25.00–£40.00

OPEN All Year except Christmas

P

♦♦♦

THE LION INN

Blakey Ridge, Kirkbymoorside, York
YO62 7LQ
T: (01751) 417320
F: (01751) 417717
E: info@lionblakey.co.uk
I: www.lionblakey.co.uk

Family-run, 16thC freehouse at the highest point of the North Yorkshire Moors, spectacular views, excellent location for walking and cycling. Eight real ales, bar meals served all day. Candlelit a la carte restaurant open every evening and for Sunday lunch. Conference facilities. Fortnightly live music nights – ring for details.

Bedrooms: 6 double, 1 twin, 3 family
Bathrooms: 8 en suite

Evening meal available
CC: Delta, Mastercard, Switch, Visa

Oct-Apr: book for more than 1 night and receive 25% discount on subsequent nights (excl Fri and Sat).

B&B per person per night:
S £18.00–£36.50
D £25.00–£32.00

OPEN All Year

P

KNARESBOROUGH, North Yorkshire Map ref 4B1

♦♦♦

BAY HORSE INN

York Road, Green Hammerton, York
YO26 8BN
T: (01423) 330338
F: (01423) 331279
E: thebayhorseinn@aol.com
I: www.thebayhorse.com

Bedrooms: 5 double, 4 twin, 1 family
Bathrooms: 10 en suite

Evening meal available
CC: Delta, Mastercard, Switch, Visa

B&B per person per night:
S £45.00
D £32.50

OPEN All Year

Village inn 10 miles from York and Harrogate on the A59 and three miles off the A1. Restaurant and bar meals. Weekly rates on request.

8 P €

♦♦♦

EBOR MOUNT

18 York Place, Knaresborough
HG5 0AA
T: (01423) 863315
F: (01423) 863315

Bedrooms: 4 double, 1 twin, 1 single, 2 family
Bathrooms: 8 en suite

CC: Delta, Mastercard, Switch, Visa

B&B per person per night:
S £25.00–£45.00
D £22.50–£27.50

Charming 18thC townhouse with private car park, providing bed and breakfast accommodation in a non-smoking environment. Ideal touring centre.

5 P

ACCESSIBILITY

Look for the symbols which indicate National Accessible Scheme standards for hearing and visually impaired guests in addition to standards for guests with mobility impairment. You can find an index of all scheme participants at the back of this guide.

KNARESBOROUGH continued

◆◆◆◆

NEWTON HOUSE
5-7 York Place, Knaresborough
HG5 0AD
T: (01423) 863539
F: (01423) 869748
E: newtonhouse@btinternet.com
I: www.newtonhousehotel.com

Bedrooms: 6 double, 1 twin, 1 single, 3 family
Bathrooms: 10 en suite, 1 private

Evening meal available
CC: Delta, Mastercard, Switch, Visa

B&B per person per night:
S £40.00–£45.00
D £32.50–£37.50

Charming, family-run, 18thC former coaching inn, two minutes' walk from the market square, castle and river. Spacious and comfortable accommodation. Ideal Harrogate, York, Dales.

◆◆◆◆

WATERGATE LODGE

Watergate Haven, Ripley Road,
Knaresborough HG5 9BU
T: (01423) 864627
F: (01423) 861087
E: info@watergatehaven.com
I: www.watergatehaven.com

B&B per person per night:
S £39.50–£54.50
D £27.25–£34.75

OPEN All Year

Comfortable, en suite bedrooms, ideal for business or holidays. Tastefully appointed with many personal touches. Spectacular setting with woodland walks to River Nidd, Knaresborough and the beautiful Nidd Gorge. Good travel links to all areas. Many nearby attractions. Convenient for Harrogate, York and the Yorkshire Dales. Also self-catering apartments.

Bedrooms: 2 double, 1 twin, 1 family
Bathrooms: 4 en suite

CC: Delta, Mastercard, Switch, Visa

Weekend breaks – Sun night free (min 2 persons, 3 nights). Discounts for stays of more than 3 nights.

€

LEEDS, West Yorkshire Map ref 4B1 *Tourist Information Centre Tel: (0113) 242 5242*

◆◆◆

AVALON GUEST HOUSE
132 Woodsley Road, Leeds LS2 9LZ
T: (0113) 2432545
F: (0113) 2420649

Bedrooms: 5 double, 4 single, 1 family
Bathrooms: 5 en suite

CC: Delta, Mastercard, Switch, Visa

B&B per person per night:
S £30.00–£40.00
D £25.00–£30.00

OPEN All Year

Superbly decorated Victorian establishment close to the university, Leeds General Infirmary and less than one mile from the city centre.

◆◆◆

BROOMHURST HOTEL
12 Chapel Lane, Off Cardigan Road,
Headingley, Leeds LS6 3BW
T: (0113) 2786836
F: (0113) 2307099
E: broomhursthotel@hotmail.com
I: www.leeds-headingleyhotels.com

Bedrooms: 4 double, 5 single, 4 family
Bathrooms: 13 en suite

Evening meal available
CC: Delta, Mastercard, Switch, Visa

B&B per person per night:
S £25.00–£37.00
D £19.50–£23.50

HB per person per night:
DY £27.50–£45.00

OPEN All Year

Small, comfortable hotel in a quiet, pleasantly wooded conservation area, 1.5 miles from the city centre. Convenient for Yorkshire County Cricket Ground and university. Warm welcome.

◆◆

GLENGARTH HOTEL
162 Woodsley Road, Leeds LS2 9LZ
T: (0113) 2457940
F: (0113) 2168033

Bedrooms: 2 double, 8 single, 4 family
Bathrooms: 10 en suite

Evening meal available
CC: Delta, Mastercard, Switch, Visa

B&B per person per night:
S £30.00–£40.00
D £25.00–£30.00

OPEN All Year

Attractive, clean, family-run hotel close to city centre, university and city hospital. Twenty minutes from Leeds City Airport. Easy access to M1 and M62. Most of the rooms have en suite facilities and colour TV.

HALF BOARD PRICES Half board prices are given per person, but in some cases may be based on double/twin occupancy.

LEEDS continued

♦♦

MANXDENE PRIVATE HOTEL

154 Woodsley Road, Leeds LS2 9LZ
T: (0113) 2432586
F: (0113) 2432586
E: manxdene@dial.pipex.com

Bedrooms: 3 double, 3 twin, 5 single, 2 family

Evening meal available
CC: Delta, Mastercard, Switch, Visa

A family-run, friendly hotel in a Victorian house. Convenient for city centre, universities, hospitals, football and Yorkshire cricket. A warm, comfortable welcome awaits you.

B&B per person per night:
S £30.00–£40.00
D £20.00–£27.50

OPEN All Year except Christmas

♦♦♦

ST MICHAEL'S TOWER HOTEL

5 St Michael's Villas, Cardigan Road, Headingley, Leeds LS6 3AF
T: (0113) 2755557
F: (0113) 2307491
E: saint_michaels@ntlworld.com
I: www.leeds-headingleyhotels.com

Bedrooms: 14 double, 8 single, 2 family
Bathrooms: 13 en suite

Evening meal available
CC: Delta, Mastercard, Switch, Visa

Comfortable, licensed hotel, 1.5 miles from city centre and close to Headingley Cricket Ground and university. Easy access to Yorkshire countryside. Warm welcome from friendly staff.

B&B per person per night:
S £25.00–£33.00
D £19.50–£21.50

HB per person per night:
DY £26.00–£39.00

OPEN All Year except Christmas

LEEDS/BRADFORD AIRPORT

See under Bingley, Bradford, Leeds

LEYBURN, North Yorkshire Map ref 5B3 *Tourist Information Centre Tel: (01969) 623069*

THE OLD VICARAGE

Main Street, West Witton, Leyburn DL8 4LX
T: (01969) 622108
E: info@dalesbreaks.co.uk
I: www.dalesbreaks.co.uk

B&B per person per night:
S £27.00–£30.00
D £22.00–£25.00

OPEN All Year

En suite rooms and all facilities provided in this charming Grade II Listed former Dales vicarage in two acres of gardens, with wonderful views right across Wensleydale. Spacious private car parking. Centrally placed for visiting the Dales, Lake District, Whitby or York. Friends old and new most welcome.

Bedrooms: 4 double, 1 single
Bathrooms: 4 en suite, 1 private

Stay 4 nights for the price of 3, Sun-Thu, Sep-Mar inclusive (mention 'Where to Stay' guide offer).

PARK GATE HOUSE

Constable Burton, Leyburn DL8 5RG
T: (01677) 450466
E: parkgatehouse@freenet.co.uk
I: www.parkgatehouse.co.uk

B&B per person per night:
S £35.00–£40.00
D £30.00–£35.00

HB per person per night:
DY £40.00–£45.00

OPEN All Year except Christmas

18thC house of character and charm, conveniently situated in Lower Wensleydale. Attractively furnished to a high standard with low oak beams, inglenook fireplace and cottage gardens. Each bedroom is decorated in country style with pretty fabrics and old pine furniture. Private facilities, TV and refreshment tray.

Bedrooms: 3 double, 1 twin
Bathrooms: 3 en suite, 1 private

Evening meal available
CC: Mastercard, Visa

Any 2 nights' DB&B £40pp (excl Bank Holidays), Oct-May inclusive.

12

VISITOR ATTRACTIONS For ideas on places to visit refer to the introduction at the beginning of this section. Look out too for the VisitBritain Quality Assured Visitor Attraction signs.

MALTON, North Yorkshire Map ref 5D3 *Tourist Information Centre Tel: (01653) 600048*

THE WENTWORTH ARMS

111 Town Street, Old Malton, Malton
YO17 7HD
T: (01653) 692618
F: (01653) 600061
E: wentwortharms@btinternet.com

Former coaching inn offering a central base to explore York, the east coast and North York Moors. Excellent food available in our restaurant or bar.

Bedrooms: 3 double, 2 twin
Bathrooms: 4 en suite, 1 private

Evening meal available
CC: Delta, Mastercard, Switch, Visa

8 P

B&B per person per night:
S £24.00–£28.00
D £24.00–£28.00

OPEN All Year

MILLINGTON, East Riding of Yorkshire Map ref 4C1

LABURNUM COTTAGE
Millington, York YO42 1TX
T: (01759) 303055
E: Roger&Maureen@labcott.fslife.co.uk

Bedrooms: 1 double, 1 family
Bathrooms: 2 en suite

Evening meal available

Attractive country cottage. Two bedrooms with private facilities. Guest lounge. Gardeners' garden. Situated in quiet, unspoilt area. Numerous countryside pathways. Near York and east coast.

P

B&B per person per night:
S £23.00–£25.00
D £23.00–£25.00

HB per person per night:
DY £30.00–£32.00

NORTHALLERTON, North Yorkshire Map ref 5C3

Silver Award

ELMSCOTT

10 Hatfield Road, Northallerton DL7 8QX
T: (01609) 760575
E: elmscott@freenet.co.uk
I: www.elmscottbedandbreakfast.co.uk

Elmscott is a charming property set in a delightful, landscaped garden giving seclusion, yet being situated close to the centre of this thriving market town which is located midway between the North York Moors and Yorkshire Dales National Parks. There are two attractive bedrooms, both with en suite bathrooms. Private parking. Non-smoking.

Bedrooms: 1 double, 1 twin
Bathrooms: 2 en suite

Discounts for longer stays.

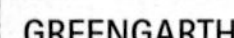

B&B per person per night:
S Min £30.00
D Min £26.00

OPEN All Year except Christmas

PATELEY BRIDGE, North Yorkshire Map ref 5C3

GREENGARTH
Greenwood Road, Pateley Bridge, Harrogate HG3 5LR
T: (01423) 711688
E: greengarth.bb@btopenworld.com
I: www.bedandbreakfastexplorer.co.uk

Bedrooms: 2 double, 1 twin, 1 single
Bathrooms: 2 en suite

Large, detached bungalow, quietly situated within five minutes' walk of all local amenities. All rooms are on the ground floor. Private parking.

5 P

B&B per person per night:
S £20.00–£30.00
D £20.00–£22.00

OPEN All Year except Christmas

QUALITY ASSURANCE SCHEME

Diamond ratings and awards were correct at the time of going to press but are subject to change. Please check at the time of booking.

PICKERING, North Yorkshire Map ref 5D3 *Tourist Information Centre Tel: (01751) 473791*

♦♦♦♦♦ Gold Award

BURR BANK

Cropton, Pickering YO18 8HL
T: (01751) 417777
F: (01751) 417789
E: bandb@burrbank.com
I: www.burrbank.com

Winner of 'Guest Accommodation of the Year'. Comfortable, quiet and spacious with home cooking and personal attention. 2-acre garden, 80-acre grounds. Wonderful views of Moors and forest. Close to York, Moors, dales, coast. Excursions and route plans. Local golf, fishing and riding.

Bedrooms: 1 double, 1 twin
Bathrooms: 2 en suite

Evening meal available

B&B per person per night:
S £29.00
D £29.00

HB per person per night:
DY £47.00

OPEN All Year

♦♦♦

GIVENDALE HEAD FARM

Ebberston, Scarborough YO13 9PU
T: (01723) 859383
F: (01723) 859383
E: sue.gwilliam@talk21.com
I: www.givendaleheadfarm.co.uk

A warm welcome awaits at our family-run, mixed farm on the edge of Dalby Forest. An ideal place to relax, walk, bike or tour the area (Castle Howard, York, Moors, coast etc). Take breakfast in the conservatory and enjoy our outstanding views of the Yorkshire countryside.

Bedrooms: 3 double
Bathrooms: 3 en suite

Evening meal available

B&B per person per night:
S £25.00–£28.00
D £25.00–£28.00

OPEN All Year except Christmas

♦♦♦♦

THE OLD MANSE

Middleton Road, Pickering
YO18 8AL
T: (01751) 476484
F: (01751) 477124
E: the_old_manse@btopenworld.com
I: www.theoldmansepickering.co.uk

Bedrooms: 7 double, 1 single, 2 family
Bathrooms: 10 en suite

Evening meal available
CC: Delta, Mastercard, Switch, Visa

Fine Edwardian house in one acre of garden/orchard. A short walk to steam railway and town centre. All rooms en suite, car parking on site.

B&B per person per night:
S £29.00–£35.00
D £28.00–£31.00

HB per person per night:
DY £44.00–£50.00

OPEN All Year

COUNTRY CODE Always follow the Country Code · Enjoy the countryside and respect its life and work · Guard against all risk of fire · Fasten all gates · Keep your dogs under close control · Keep to public paths across farmland · Use gates and stiles to cross fences, hedges and walls · Leave livestock, crops and machinery alone · Take your litter home · Help to keep all water clean · Protect wildlife, plants and trees · Take special care on country roads · Make no unnecessary noise

PICKERING continued

RECTORY FARM HOUSE

Levisham, Pickering YO18 7NL
T: (01751) 460491
E: rectory@levisham.com
I: www.levisham.com

B&B per person per night:
S £28.00
D £22.00–£28.00

HB per person per night:
DY £32.00–£40.00

OPEN All Year

Warmth and comfort are the key notes of this family home. Log fires on chilly nights, afternoon tea with home baking, luxury, en suite bedrooms, freshly prepared evening meals. Picturesque village four miles from Pickering offering peace and tranquillity. Central for Moors, coast and many of Yorkshire's finest attractions. Superb walking/riding/biking or just relaxing.

Bedrooms: 3 double
Bathrooms: 3 en suite

Evening meal available

Weekly rates from £285 per couple.

V P

♦♦♦♦

TANGALWOOD
Roxby Road, Thornton Dale, Pickering YO18 7SX
T: (01751) 474688
I: www.smoothhound.co.uk/hotels/tangalwood

Bedrooms: 1 double, 1 twin, 1 single
Bathrooms: 2 en suite, 1 private

B&B per person per night:
S £23.00–£25.00
D £21.00–£23.00

Situated in quiet part of this picturesque village. We offer a warm welcome to all guests, a high standard of comfortable accommodation and a good English breakfast.

7 V P

♦♦♦♦
Silver Award

WILDSMITH HOUSE

Marton, Sinnington, Pickering, York YO62 6RD
T: (01751) 432702
E: wildsmithhouse@talk21.com
I: www.pb-design.com/swiftlink/bb/1102.htm

B&B per person per night:
S £29.00–£32.00
D £24.00–£28.00

Charming farmhouse originating from 1720, set on village green in pretty village at the edge of North York Moors. High-quality, en suite rooms with TV, refreshment tray and warm towels. Delicious, home-cooked breakfasts using local produce. Ideally situated for exploring the area with Moors, coast and city of York accessible.

Bedrooms: 2 twin
Bathrooms: 2 en suite

12 V P €

AT-A-GLANCE SYMBOLS

Symbols at the end of each accommodation entry give useful information about services and facilities. A key to symbols can be found inside the back cover flap. Keep this open for easy reference.

RAVENSCAR, North Yorkshire Map ref 5D3

SMUGGLERS ROCK COUNTRY HOUSE

Staintondale Road, Ravenscar, Scarborough YO13 0ER
T: (01723) 870044
E: info@smugglersrock.co.uk
I: www.smugglersrock.co.uk

Georgian country house, reputedly a former smugglers' haunt, with panoramic views over National Park and sea. In open countryside with wonderful walks. Ideal country holiday area – located at southern end of Robin Hood's Bay. Whitby, Scarborough and 'Heartbeat' country within easy reach. Self-catering cottages also available.

Bedrooms: 3 double, 1 twin, 1 single, 3 family
Bathrooms: 8 en suite

CC: Delta, Mastercard, Visa

B&B per person per night:
S £27.00–£29.00
D £25.00–£27.00

OPEN All Year except Christmas

REETH, North Yorkshire Map ref 5B3

♦♦♦

ELDER PEAK

Arkengarthdale Road, Reeth, Richmond DL11 6QX
T: (01748) 884770

Bedrooms: 1 double, 1 twin

Quiet, comfortable family home, within easy walking distance of village centre. Panoramic views across the valley.

5 P

B&B per person per night:
S £18.00–£20.00
D £17.50–£20.00

RICHMOND, North Yorkshire Map ref 5C3 *Tourist Information Centre Tel: (01748) 850252*

♦♦♦

EMMANUEL GUEST HOUSE

41 Maison Dieu, Richmond DL10 7AU
T: (01748) 823584
F: (01748) 821554

Bedrooms: 3 twin, 2 single
Bathrooms: 1 en suite

Small, stone-built, family-run guesthouse offering a warm welcome. Tea or coffee on arrival. Only five minutes' walk from town centre.

P

B&B per person per night:
S £19.00–£20.00
D £20.00–£21.00

OPEN All Year except Christmas

RIPLEY, North Yorkshire Map ref 4B1

♦♦♦

SLATE RIGG FARM

Birthwaite Lane, Ripley, Harrogate HG3 3JQ
T: (01423) 770135

Bedrooms: 1 twin, 1 family

Relaxed and friendly working farm, superbly situated with excellent view of scenic Nidderdale and historic village of Ripley. Only 10 minutes from Harrogate.

P

B&B per person per night:
S £25.00–£35.00
D £22.50–£25.00

OPEN All Year except Christmas

RIPON, North Yorkshire Map ref 5C3

♦♦♦

BISHOPTON GROVE HOUSE

Bishopton, Ripon HG4 2QL
T: (01765) 600888
E: wimpress@bronco.co.uk

Bedrooms: 1 double, 1 twin, 1 family
Bathrooms: 3 en suite

Restored Georgian (pink) house in a lovely rural corner of Ripon, near the River Laver and Fountains Abbey. Ten minutes' walk to town centre.

P

B&B per person per night:
S £20.00–£30.00
D £20.00–£25.00

OPEN All Year

GOLD & SILVER AWARDS

These exclusive VisitBritain awards are given to establishments achieving the highest levels of quality and service. Further information can be found at the front of the guide. An index to all accommodation achieving these awards are at the back of this guide.

RIPON continued

Gold Award

RAVENCROFT B&B

Moorside Avenue, Ripon HG4 1TA
T: (01765) 602543
F: (01765) 606058
E: guestmail@btopenworld.com
I: www.ravencroftbandb.com

B&B per person per night:
S £40.00–£45.00
D £25.00–£30.00

OPEN All Year

Luxury, en suite accommodation and kitchen-dining suite. Hospitable family home in peaceful location. Conservatory lounge during BST. Optional summer al fresco breakfasts on south-facing patio. High-quality, personal service includes complimentary daily newspaper and, usually, transport to city/restaurants. Ripon bypass two minutes. Cathedral one mile. Fountains Abbey 3.5 miles.

Bedrooms: 1 double, 1 family
Bathrooms: 2 en suite

CC: Amex, Delta, Diners, Mastercard, Switch, Visa

ROBIN HOOD'S BAY, North Yorkshire Map ref 5D3

FLASK INN AND FLASK INN TRAVEL LODGE

Robin Hood's Bay, Fylingdales, Whitby YO22 4QH
T: (01947) 880692
F: (01947) 880592
E: flaskinn@aol.com
I: www.flaskinn.com

B&B per person per night:
S £30.00
D £27.50

OPEN All Year except Christmas

Originally a 17thC coaching inn, situated on the A171 Scarborough to Whitby road in the North York Moors National Park. Adjoining the inn is the Travel Lodge. All rooms are on the ground floor. Coffee house serving homemade cakes and snacks.

Bedrooms: 4 double, 4 twin, 1 single, 3 family
Bathrooms: 12 en suite

Evening meal available
CC: Delta, Mastercard, Switch, Visa

ROSEDALE ABBEY, North Yorkshire Map ref 5C3

Silver Award

SEVENFORD HOUSE

Rosedale Abbey, Pickering YO18 8SE
T: (01751) 417283
E: sevenford@aol.com
I: www.sevenford.com

B&B per person per night:
S £35.00–£40.00
D £25.00–£30.00

OPEN All Year except Christmas

In the heart of the North York Moors National Park lies the picturesque village of Rosedale Abbey. Nestling halfway up the valleyside, Sevenford House sits in four acres of grounds overlooking the village and moorland. Expect a warm welcome at this Victorian vicarage which offers beautifully charming, en suite accommodation with outstanding views.

Bedrooms: 2 double, 1 family
Bathrooms: 3 en suite

Winter warmer breaks Nov-Mar.

CHECK THE MAPS

The colour maps at the front of this guide show all the cities, towns and villages for which you will find accommodation entries.
Refer to the town index to find the page on which they are listed.

RUNSWICK BAY, North Yorkshire Map ref 5D3

THE FIRS

26 Hinderwell Lane, Runswick, Runswick Bay, Saltburn-by-the-Sea TS13 5HR
T: (01947) 840433
F: (01947) 841616
E: mandy.shackleton@talk21.com
I: www.the-firs.co.uk

Bedrooms: 6 double, 1 single, 5 family
Bathrooms: 12 en suite

Evening meal available

BεB per person per night:
S £35.00–£40.00
D £27.50–£30.00

HB per person per night:
DY £44.00–£56.50

In a coastal village, eight miles north of Whitby. All rooms en suite with colour TV, tea/coffee facilities. Private parking. Children and dogs welcome.

SCARBOROUGH, North Yorkshire Map ref 5D3 *Tourist Information Centre Tel: (01723) 373333*

◆◆◆◆

GORDON HOTEL

Ryndleside, Scarborough YO12 6AD
T: (01723) 362177
E: sales@gordonhotel.co.uk
I: www.gordonhotel.co.uk

Bedrooms: 6 double, 1 single, 3 family
Bathrooms: 7 en suite

Evening meal available
CC: Amex, Delta, Mastercard, Switch, Visa

BεB per person per night:
S £20.00–£25.00
D £20.00–£25.00

HB per person per night:
DY £27.50–£29.50

OPEN All Year except Christmas

Friendly, family-run, licensed hotel overlooking Peasholme Park. Family rooms are available. Senior Citizen discount. TV, complimentary tray, hairdryer and clock-radio in all rooms.

◆◆◆◆

HOWDALE HOTEL

North Marine Road, 121 Queens Parade, Scarborough YO12 7HU
T: (01723) 372696
F: (01723) 372696
E: mail@howdalehotel.co.uk
I: www.howdalehotel.co.uk

BεB per person per night:
S £20.00–£22.00
D £23.00–£25.00

Beautifully situated overlooking North Bay and Scarborough Castle, yet close to town. We are renowned for cleanliness and the friendly, efficient service we provide in a comfortable atmosphere. Our substantial breakfasts are deservedly famous. Thirteen of our excellent bedrooms are en suite, many have sea views. All have TVs, tea/coffee facilities, hairdryers etc.

Bedrooms: 11 double, 2 twin, 1 single, 1 family
Bathrooms: 13 en suite

CC: Delta, Mastercard, Switch, Visa

Mini-breaks (3 nights minimum) from Feb-Jul and Sep-Nov, £21pppn.

Silver Award

THE WHITELEY HOTEL

99-101 Queens Parade, Scarborough YO12 7HY
T: (01723) 373514
F: (01723) 373007
E: whiteleyhotel@bigfoot.com
I: www.yorkshirecoast.co.uk/whiteley

BεB per person per night:
S £26.50–£28.50
D £21.50–£25.00

Small, family-run, non-smoking, licensed hotel located in an elevated position overlooking the North Bay, close to the town centre and ideally situated for all amenities. The bedrooms are well co-ordinated and equipped with useful extras, many with sea views. Good home cooking is served in the traditional dining room.

Bedrooms: 7 double, 3 family
Bathrooms: 10 en suite

Evening meal available
CC: Delta, Mastercard, Switch, Visa

SYMBOLS The symbols in each entry give information about services and facilities. A key to these symbols appears at the back of this guide.

SCOTCH CORNER, North Yorkshire Map ref 5C3

◆◆◆

VINTAGE HOTEL

Middleton Tyas, Scotch Corner, Richmond DL10 6NP
T: (01748) 824424
F: (01748) 826272
E: thevintagescotchcorner@btopenworld.com
I: www.vintagehotel.co.uk

Bedrooms: 3 double, 2 twin, 3 single
Bathrooms: 5 en suite

Evening meal available
CC: Amex, Delta, Diners, Mastercard, Switch, Visa

Family-run roadside inn with friendly atmosphere, conveniently situated on A66 (Penrith road) only 200 metres from A1 Scotch Corner junction. (Richmond three miles).

B&B per person per night:
S £27.50–£42.50
D £23.50–£29.00

HB per person per night:
DY £41.00–£52.00

OPEN All Year except Christmas

SELBY, North Yorkshire Map ref 4C1 *Tourist Information Centre Tel: (01757) 703263*

◆◆◆

HAZELDENE GUEST HOUSE

34 Brook Street, Doncaster Road, Selby YO8 4AR
T: (01757) 704809
E: selbystay@breathe.com
I: www.hazeldene-selby.co.uk

Bedrooms: 2 double, 3 twin, 2 single
Bathrooms: 5 en suite

CC: Delta, Mastercard, Switch, Visa

Victorian townhouse in a pleasant market town location, 12 miles south of York. On the A19 with easy access to the A1 and M62 motorways.

B&B per person per night:
S £31.00–£33.00
D £22.00–£23.00

OPEN All Year except Christmas

SETTLE, North Yorkshire Map ref 5B3 *Tourist Information Centre Tel: (01729) 825192*

◆◆◆◆

ARBUTUS GUEST HOUSE

Riverside, Clapham, Near Settle LA2 8DS
T: (01524) 251240
F: (01524) 251197
E: info@arbutus.co.uk
I: www.arbutus.co.uk

Bedrooms: 3 double, 1 single, 2 family
Bathrooms: 5 en suite, 1 private

Evening meal available

Situated in the heart of the beautiful village of Clapham. Country guesthouse offering traditional home cooking and a friendly atmosphere. Ideal for touring, walking and relaxing.

B&B per person per night:
S £20.00–£26.00
D £24.50–£26.00

HB per person per night:
DY £35.50–£41.50

OPEN All Year

◆◆◆◆

SCAR CLOSE FARM

Feizor, Austwick, Lancaster LA2 8DF
T: (01729) 823496

High-standard, en suite accommodation and food in a farmhouse in one of the quietest and most picturesque hamlets in the Yorkshire Dales. Popular walking and touring centre. TV and tea-makers in all rooms. Double, twin and family rooms.

Bedrooms: 2 double, 2 family
Bathrooms: 4 en suite

Evening meal available

B&B per person per night:
S £35.00–£36.00
D £25.00–£26.00

HB per person per night:
DY £36.50–£47.50

OPEN All Year except Christmas

QUALITY ASSURANCE SCHEME

For an explanation of the quality and facilities represented by the Diamonds please refer to the front of this guide. A more detailed explanation can be found in the information pages at the back.

SETTLE continued

STATION HOUSE

Station Road, Settle BD24 9AA
T: (01729) 822533
E: stationhouse@btinternet.com
I: www.stationhouse.btinternet.co.uk

B&B per person per night:
S £35.00–£45.00
D £22.50–£25.00

The original stationmaster's house, built in 1875, retains much of the charm and character of those old railway days. The house stands in an elevated position with spectacular views of open countryside. Settle's market square is only a stroll away and yet our garden is a haven of tranquillity.

Bedrooms: 2 double

10% reduction given for more than 3 nights.

◆◆◆

WHITEFRIARS COUNTRY GUEST HOUSE

Church Street, Settle BD24 9JD
T: (01729) 823753
E: info@whitefriars-settle.co.uk
I: www.whitefriars-settle.co.uk

B&B per person per night:
S Min £20.00
D £20.00–£25.50

HB per person per night:
DY Min £34.50

OPEN All Year except Christmas

17thC family home standing in 0.75 acres of secluded gardens, 50 yards from the town's central market place. This delightful guest house offers traditional, pleasantly furnished accommodation. Two lounges together with a beamed dining room, where good home cooking is served. The house is fully non-smoking.

Bedrooms: 4 double, 2 twin, 1 single, 2 family
Bathrooms: 5 en suite, 1 private

Evening meal available

SHEFFIELD, South Yorkshire Map ref 4B2 *Tourist Information Centre Tel: (0114) 221 1900*

◆◆◆

ETRURIA HOUSE HOTEL

91 Crookes Road, Broomhill, Sheffield S10 5BD
T: (0114) 2662241
F: (0114) 2670853
E: etruria@waitrose.com

Bedrooms: 3 double, 2 twin, 4 single, 1 family
Bathrooms: 6 en suite

CC: Mastercard, Visa

B&B per person per night:
S £32.00–£40.00
D £23.00–£27.00

Small, family-run hotel, giving personal service. Five minutes from the city centre/hospitals/universities. Peak District easily accessible.

SKIPTON, North Yorkshire Map ref 4B1 *Tourist Information Centre Tel: (01756) 792809*

◆◆◆

CRAVEN HEIFER INN

Grassington Road, Skipton BD23 3LA
T: (01756) 792521
F: (01756) 794442
E: philandlynn@cravenheifer.co.uk
I: www.cravenheifer.co.uk

B&B per person per night:
S £44.95
D £22.50

HB per person per night:
DY £54.95

OPEN All Year

Traditional country inn, serving cask ale and excellent home-cooked food, all day every day. Bar food or enjoy a meal in our restaurant overlooking the Yorkshire Dales. Excellent car parking. Most rooms ground floor. Non-smoking restaurant. Non-smoking rooms available.

Bedrooms: 15 double, 1 single, 4 family
Bathrooms: 17 en suite

Evening meal available
CC: Delta, Mastercard, Switch, Visa

Winter breaks: 3 nights for the price of 2 Nov/Dec/Jan/Feb.

SKIPTON continued

NAPIER'S RESTAURANT & ACCOMMODATION

Chapel Hill, Skipton BD23 1NL
T: (01756) 799688
F: (01756) 798111
I: www.restaurant-skipton.co.uk

Bedrooms: 5 double, 1 single
Bathrooms: 3 en suite, 1 private

Evening meal available
CC: Amex, Delta, Mastercard, Switch, Visa

Napier's dates back to the 18thC. Originally a large farmhouse, but now offering luxury accommodation in a picturesque corner of the historic centre of Skipton.

B&B per person per night:
S £55.00
D £34.00

HB per person per night:
DY £54.00

OPEN All Year

THE WOOLLY SHEEP

28 Sheep Street, Skipton BD23 1HY
T: (01756) 700966
F: (01756) 794815
I: www.timothytaylor.co.uk

The Woolly Sheep is a traditional English inn situated in Skipton's centre. At the heart is the busy bar and dining area serving home-cooked food. Rooms are en suite and fitted with luxurious pine furnishings, colour TV and tea/coffe-making facilities. Non-smoking rooms and car parking are available.

Bedrooms: 5 double, 1 single, 3 family
Bathrooms: 9 en suite

Evening meal available
CC: Delta, Mastercard, Switch, Visa

B&B per person per night:
S £35.00–£50.00
D £27.50–£30.00

OPEN All Year

STAITHES, North Yorkshire Map ref 5C3

BROOKLYN

Brown's Terrace, Staithes, Saltburn-by-the-Sea TS13 5BG
T: (01947) 841396

Bedrooms: 2 double, 1 twin

Sea Captain's house in picturesque historic fishing village. Comfortable, individually decorated rooms with view of Cowbar cliffs. Pets and children welcome.

B&B per person per night:
S £22.50
D £22.50

OPEN All Year except Christmas

STEARSBY, North Yorkshire Map ref 5C3

Silver Award

THE GRANARY

Stearsby, York YO61 4SA
T: (01347) 888652
F: (01347) 888652
E: robertturl@thegranary.org.uk
I: www.thegranary-stearsby.com

18thC converted granary set in beautiful one acre garden. Surrounded by woodland, yet only 12 miles from York. Ideally located for York, Yorkshire Dales, North Yorkshire Moors and Herriot country. En suite rooms with own sitting rooms in barn annexe, en suite double in main house. Breakfast in south-facing conservatory overlooking the pool.

Bedrooms: 3 double
Bathrooms: 3 en suite

3 nights for price of 2 for mid-week stays (Mon-Thu) Apr-Jun and Sep-Oct.

B&B per person per night:
S £30.00–£35.00
D £25.00–£27.50

SPECIAL BREAKS

Many establishments offer special promotions and themed breaks. These are highlighted in red. (All such offers are subject to availability.)

SUTTON-ON-THE-FOREST, North Yorkshire Map ref 5C3

THE OLD VILLAGE STORES

Main Street, Sutton-on-the-Forest, York YO61 1DP
T: (01347) 811376
E: oldvillagestores@talk21.com
I: www.oldyork.co.uk

Lovely old cottage in one of North Yorkshire's prettiest villages. Eight miles north of York and within easy reach of the Dales and the North York Moors. A truly personal service with homely atmosphere. We make our own bread, jam and yoghurt, and we use local produce.

Bedrooms: 2 double
Bathrooms: 1 en suite
Evening meal available

If you are staying Sat night you can have £10pp off Fri night (subject to availability).

B&B per person per night:
D £25.00–£30.00

OPEN All Year except Christmas

THIRSK, North Yorkshire Map ref 5C3 *Tourist Information Centre Tel: (01845) 522755*

THE POPLARS

Carlton Miniott, Thirsk YO7 4LX
T: (01845) 522712
F: (01845) 522712
I: www.yorkshirebandb.co.uk

Large house in lovely garden close to Thirsk. Warm and friendly welcome. You will have a comfortable room and a breakfast that is just a bit special. Ideal base for touring Moors and Dales, York, Herriot country and Yorkshire's friendly villages and markets.

Bedrooms: 2 double
Bathrooms: 2 en suite
Evening meal available

B&B per person per night:
S £20.00–£25.00
D £23.00–£25.00

HB per person per night:
DY Max £35.00

OPEN All Year

♦♦♦

TOWN PASTURE FARM

Boltby, Thirsk YO7 2DY
T: (01845) 537298

Bedrooms: 1 twin, 1 family
Bathrooms: 2 en suite
Evening meal available

180-acre mixed farm. Farmhouse, with views of the Hambleton Hills, in picturesque Boltby village within the boundary of the North York Moors National Park.

B&B per person per night:
S £24.00–£25.00
D Min £22.00

OPEN All Year except Christmas

THORNTON DALE, North Yorkshire Map ref 5D3

♦♦♦♦

BANAVIE

Roxby Road, Thornton Dale, Pickering YO18 7SX
T: (01751) 474616
E: info@banavie.uk.com
I: www.banavie.uk.com

Bedrooms: 3 double
Bathrooms: 3 en suite

Banavie is in a quiet area with splendid views overlooking this famous village with its meandering stream and thatched cottage. Close to moors and coast. Contact: Mrs Bowes.

B&B per person per night:
D £21.00–£24.00

OPEN All Year except Christmas

♦♦♦

THE BUCK HOTEL

Chestnut Avenue, Thornton Dale, Pickering YO18 7RW
T: (01751) 474212
F: (01751) 474212
E: buckhotel.tld@btopenworld.com

Bedrooms: 2 double, 1 twin, 1 family
Bathrooms: 4 en suite
Evening meal available

In the beautiful village of Thornton Dale, a comfortable, family-run hotel with excellent en suite accommodation. Village inn atmosphere. Quality food. Open all year.

B&B per person per night:
D £23.50

OPEN All Year

WHITBY, North Yorkshire Map ref 5D3 *Tourist Information Centre Tel: (01947) 602674*

ARCHES GUESTHOUSE

8 Havelock Place, Hudson Street, Whitby
YO21 3ER
T: (01947) 601880
E: archeswhitby@freeola.com
I: www.whitbyguesthouses.co.uk

B&B per person per night:
S £20.00–£24.00
D £20.00–£24.00

OPEN All Year

Friendly, family-run guesthouse which prides itself on cleanliness, a warm welcome and large breakfasts. The ideal base for experiencing the old world charms of this historic seaside town, whose tranquil and pleasant atmosphere guarantees rest and relaxation. Pets welcome. Ground floor rooms. Strictly non-smoking.

Bedrooms: 3 double, 1 twin, 2 single, 3 family
Bathrooms: 6 en suite, 1 private

CC: Delta, Mastercard, Switch, Visa

Stay 7 nights for the price of 6 with our compliments.

♦♦♦♦

GLENDALE GUEST HOUSE
16 Crescent Avenue, Whitby
YO21 3ED
T: (01947) 604242

Bedrooms: 4 double, 1 single, 1 family
Bathrooms: 5 en suite

Evening meal available

B&B per person per night:
S £24.00–£25.00
D £24.00–£25.00

HB per person per night:
DY £35.00–£36.00

Family-run Victorian guesthouse. On the West Cliff, offering good food and cleanliness. Rooms are attractively decorated and have excellent facilities. Private parking, pets welcome.

♦♦♦♦

MORNINGSIDE HOTEL

10 North Promenade, West Cliff, Whitby
YO21 3JX
T: (01947) 602643

B&B per person per night:
S £27.00–£54.00
D £27.00–£40.00

HB per person per night:
DY £43.50–£56.50

OPEN All Year except Christmas

Within easy distance of sports ground, indoor swimming pool, Spa Theatre and Pavilion, and 0.5 miles to the 18-hole golf course. Set in quiet location overlooking the sea. All rooms en suite with TV and welcome tray. Table d'hote menu using fresh, local produce. Senior Citizens' reductions. Hospitable staff guarantee a warm welcome. Open all year.

Bedrooms: 11 double, 3 twin, 1 family
Bathrooms: 15 en suite

Evening meal available
CC: Mastercard, Switch, Visa

Mid-week breaks from £69pp for 3 nights, and £92pp for 4 nights (excl Aug and Bank Holidays). Winter breaks now available.

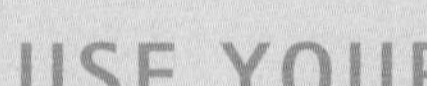

USE YOUR *i*s

There are more than 550 Tourist Information Centres throughout England offering friendly help with accommodation and holiday ideas as well as suggestions of places to visit and things to do. You'll find TIC addresses in the local Phone Book.

WHITBY continued

SANDPIPER GUEST HOUSE

4 Belle Vue Terrace, Whitby YO21 3EY
T: (01947) 600246
F: (01947) 600246
E: enquiries@sandpiperhouse.co.uk
I: www.sandpiperhouse.co.uk

Elegant, charming, welcoming guesthouse, close to beach, promenade, shops, restaurants, cafes. The tastefully decorated rooms are all en suite with colour TV, some with video, hospitality tray, tea/coffee, radio-alarm clock, hairdryer. Excellent, robust, full English breakfast and full vegetarian, served in lovely dining room. Beautiful lounge. Ground floor bedrooms. Fully centrally heated.

Bedrooms: 2 double, 1 twin, 3 single, 2 family
Bathrooms: 8 en suite

B&B per person per night:
S £25.50–£29.50
D £23.50–£25.50

OPEN All Year except Christmas

♦♦♦♦

SEACLIFFE HOTEL

12 North Promenade, West Cliff, Whitby YO21 3JX
T: (01947) 603139
F: (01947) 603139
E: julie@seacliffe.fsnet.co.uk
I: www.seacliffe.co.uk

Whitby's premier family hotel overlooking the sea. All rooms en suite. Wine and dine in our candlelit, a la carte restaurant. Local seafood a speciality. Golf course nearby. Tee-off times may be booked through the hotel.

Bedrooms: 15 double, 2 twin, 1 single, 4 family
Bathrooms: 22 en suite

Evening meal available
CC: Amex, Delta, Diners, Mastercard, Switch, Visa

Yorkshire Rose break: 2 nights' DB&B £99pp.

B&B per person per night:
S £42.50–£49.50
D £34.50–£38.50

HB per person per night:
DY Min £49.50

OPEN All Year

♦♦♦♦

THE WHITE LINEN GUEST HOUSE

24 Bagdale, Whitby YO21 1QS
T: (01947) 600265
F: (01947) 603635
E: mail@whitelinenguesthouse.co.uk
I: www.whitelinenguesthouse.co.uk

Bedrooms: 4 double, 1 single, 4 family
Bathrooms: 9 en suite

CC: Delta, Mastercard, Switch, Visa

Beautifully renovated Georgian townhouse in centre of Whitby. All rooms classically furnished and tastefully decorated with superb, en suite facilities. Limited parking available for residents.

B&B per person per night:
S £35.00–£50.00
D £30.00–£45.00

OPEN All Year except Christmas

TOWN INDEX

This can be found at the back of the guide. If you know where you want to stay, the index will give you the page number listing accommodation in your chosen town, city or village.

YORK, North Yorkshire Map ref 4C1 *Tourist Information Centre Tel: (01904) 621756*

♦♦♦♦ Silver Award

THE ACER HOTEL

52 Scarcroft Hill, York YO24 1DE
T: (01904) 653839
F: (01904) 677017
E: info@acerhotel.co.uk
I: www.acerhotel.co.uk

B&B per person per night:
S £45.00
D £30.00–£40.00

OPEN All Year except Christmas

Elegant, multi-award-winning accommodation. All rooms en suite. Beautiful 4-poster room and family room. Service and housekeeping of the highest standard. Quality breakfasts including special vegetarian. Friendly Yorkshire welcome assured. Celebration packages of champagne, chocolates and flowers available. Convenient for city centre, railway station, racecourse and historic attractions. Non-smoking.

Bedrooms: 2 double, 1 twin, 1 family
Bathrooms: 4 en suite

CC: Amex, Delta, Mastercard, Switch, Visa

Honeymoon, anniversary and birthday stays. Off-peak offers.

€

♦♦♦♦ Silver Award

ASCOT HOUSE

80 East Parade, York YO31 7YH
T: (01904) 426826
F: (01904) 431077
E: j&k@ascot-house-york.demon.co.uk
I: www.ascothouseyork.com

B&B per person per night:
S £26.00–£55.00
D £26.00–£32.00

OPEN All Year except Christmas

A family-run Victorian villa, built in 1869, with en suite rooms of character and many 4-poster or canopy beds. Delicious traditional English breakfasts. Fifteen minutes' walk to city centre, Jorvik Viking Museum or York Minster. Residential licence and residents' lounge, sauna, private enclosed car park.

Bedrooms: 11 double, 1 single, 3 family
Bathrooms: 12 en suite, 1 private

CC: Delta, Diners, Mastercard, Switch, Visa

P

♦♦♦♦ Silver Award

ASHBOURNE HOUSE

139 Fulford Road, York YO10 4HG
T: (01904) 639912
F: (01904) 631332
E: ashbourneh@aol.com
I: www.ashbourne-house.com

B&B per person per night:
S £40.00–£50.00
D £22.50–£30.00

OPEN All Year except Christmas

Charming, family-run Victorian private house on the main route into York from the south. Licensed, with a small bar in a comfortable guest lounge. En suite bedrooms furnished in a contemporary style and fully equipped. Within walking distance of city centre. Close to university and golf course. Car parking.

Bedrooms: 3 double, 2 twin, 2 family
Bathrooms: 6 en suite, 1 private

CC: Amex, Delta, Diners, Mastercard, Switch, Visa

Reductions for stays of 3 nights or more and for mid-week stays of 2 nights out of season.

P

MAP REFERENCES The map references refer to the colour maps at the front of this guide. The first figure is the map number; the letter and figure which follow indicate the grid reference on the map.

YORK continued

AVONDALE GUEST HOUSE

61 Bishopthorpe Road, York
YO23 1NX
T: (01904) 633989
E: kaleda@avondaleguesthouse.freeserve.co.uk
I: www.avondaleguesthouse.co.uk

Bedrooms: 4 double, 1 single, 1 family
Bathrooms: 6 en suite

Small, friendly guesthouse, close to city centre. All rooms en suite with TV and tea/coffee facilities. Extensive selection of breakfasts. Non-smoking.

B&B per person per night:
S Min £32.00
D Min £28.00

OPEN All Year except Christmas

Silver Award

BARBICAN HOUSE

20 Barbican Road, York YO10 5AA
T: (01904) 627617
F: (01904) 647140
E: info@barbicanhouse.com
I: www.barbicanhouse.com

Small, friendly, family-run Victorian residence of charm and character, lovingly restored. Overlooking medieval city walls. Leave your car in our floodlit car park and take a short stroll to most city centre attractions. The Barbican Centre is a two-minute walk away. Yorkshire University is 10 minutes away.

Bedrooms: 4 double, 1 twin
Bathrooms: 5 en suite

CC: Amex, Delta, Mastercard, Switch, Visa

B&B per person per night:
S £50.00–£54.00
D £30.00–£34.00

◆◆◆

BAY TREE GUEST HOUSE

92 Bishopthorpe Road, York
YO23 1JS
T: (01904) 659462
E: info@baytree-york.co.uk
I: www.baytree-york.co.uk

Bedrooms: 2 double, 1 twin, 2 single, 1 family
Bathrooms: 3 en suite

CC: Mastercard, Switch, Visa

Victorian terraced house, seven minutes' walk from the city centre and 0.5 miles from the racecourse. Free parking.

B&B per person per night:
S £25.00–£30.00
D £25.00–£30.00

BEDFORD HOTEL

108-110 Bootham, York YO30 7DG
T: (01904) 624412
F: (01904) 632851
E: info@bedfordhotelyork.co.uk
I: www.bedfordhotelyork.co.uk

Enjoy a relaxing stay in this tastefully converted Victorian house where the resident owners assure you of a warm welcome and comfortable stay. Licensed hotel, all bedrooms en suite and non-smoking. Car park. Five minutes' walk along historic Bootham to the famous York Minster and city centre.

Bedrooms: 10 double, 2 twin, 2 single, 3 family
Bathrooms: 17 en suite

Evening meal available
CC: Amex, Delta, Diners, Mastercard, Switch, Visa

B&B per person per night:
S £41.00–£55.00
D £27.00–£38.00

OPEN All Year except Christmas

◆◆◆

THE BEECH HOUSE HOTEL

6-7 Longfield Terrace, Bootham,
York YO30 7DJ
T: (01904) 634581
E: beechhouse@beeb.net
I: www.beech-house-york.co.uk

Bedrooms: 7 double, 2 twin, 1 single
Bathrooms: 10 en suite

CC: Delta, Mastercard, Switch, Visa

Beech House is centrally situated five minutes' walk from York Minster. Rooms have en suite, colour TV, clock/radio, hairdryer, tea-making facilities and telephone.

B&B per person per night:
S £28.00–£31.00
D £25.00–£28.00

YORK continued

BLAKENEY HOTEL

180 Stockton Lane, York YO31 1ES
T: (01904) 422786
F: (01904) 422786
E: reception@blakeneyhotel-york.co.uk
I: www.blakeneyhotel-york.co.uk

B&B per person per night:
S £40.00–£55.00
D £34.00–£36.00

HB per person per night:
DY £52.50–£67.50

OPEN All Year except Christmas

Friendly, family-run hotel situated within easy reach of city centre. Well-appointed, en suite bedrooms (two ground floor), colour TV and tea/coffee-making facilities. Comfortable lounge and licensed bar. The Derby Restaurant offers full English breakfasts and evening dinner – excellent cuisine/wines, special diets catered for. Private car park.

Bedrooms: 3 double, 1 twin, 3 single, 10 family
Bathrooms: 14 en suite, 1 private

Evening meal available
CC: Amex, Delta, Mastercard, Switch, Visa

10% discount for 7 or more nights. Special rates for 3 nights' DB&B.

1 P €

◆◆◆

BRIAR LEA GUEST HOUSE

8 Longfield Terrace, Bootham, York YO30 7DJ
T: (01904) 635061
F: (01904) 330356
E: briarleahouse@msn.com
I: www.briarlea.co.uk

Bedrooms: 3 double, 2 twin, 1 family
Bathrooms: 6 en suite

CC: Amex, Delta, Diners, Mastercard, Switch, Visa

B&B per person per night:
S £25.00–£35.00
D £25.00–£27.00

OPEN All Year except Christmas

Victorian house with all rooms en suite, 6 minutes' walk from the city centre and railway station. No-smoking establishment.

P €

THE CAVALIER

39 Monkgate, York YO31 7PB
T: (01904) 636615
F: (01904) 636615
E: julia@cavalierhotel.co.uk
I: www.cavalierhotel.co.uk

B&B per person per night:
S £35.00–£65.00
D £27.50–£37.50

OPEN All Year

Georgian, family-run hotel close to the city centre, only yards from the ancient Bar Walls, Minster and many of York's famous historic landmarks. High standards, traditional English breakfast, sauna and private parking ensure the comfort of our guests. Please phone for a map and brochure.

Bedrooms: 1 double, 2 single, 2 family
Bathrooms: 2 en suite

CC: Delta, Mastercard, Switch, Visa

P €

Silver Award

CITY GUEST HOUSE

68 Monkgate, York YO31 7PF
T: (01904) 622483
E: info@cityguesthouse.co.uk
I: www.cityguesthouse.co.uk

Bedrooms: 4 double, 1 twin, 1 single, 1 family
Bathrooms: 6 en suite, 1 private

CC: Amex, Delta, Mastercard, Switch, Visa

B&B per person per night:
S £35.00–£38.00
D £30.00–£33.00

OPEN All Year except Christmas

Small, friendly, family-run guesthouse in attractive Victorian townhouse. Five minutes' walk to York Minster, close to attractions. Private parking. Cosy, en suite rooms. Restaurants nearby. Non-smoking.

12 P

IMPORTANT NOTE Information on accommodation listed in this guide has been supplied by the proprietors. As changes may occur you are advised to check details at the time of booking.

♦♦♦

A warm welcome awaits you in this family-run hotel just 10 minutes' walk to the historic and beautiful city of York. The hotel offers all en suite rooms, licensed bar, restaurant. Large car park with adjacent bowling green and children's park.

CLARENCE GARDENS HOTEL

Haxby Road, York YO31 8JS
T: (01904) 624252
F: (01904) 671293
E: stay@clarencegardenshotel.com
I: www.clarencegardenshotel.com

Bedrooms: 4 double, 9 twin, 1 single, 6 family
Bathrooms: 20 en suite

Evening meal available
CC: Amex, Delta, Mastercard, Switch, Visa

Our luxurious dorm is now available for group bookings – hen/stag parties, shopping trips, sports groups etc.

P

B&B per person per night:
S £37.50–£50.00
D £27.50–£35.00

♦♦♦

COOK'S GUEST HOUSE

120 Bishopthorpe Road, York YO23 1JX
T: (01904) 652519
F: (01904) 652519
E: jslcook@hotmail.com

Bedrooms: 1 double, 1 family
Bathrooms: 2 en suite

CC: Visa

Featured on TV's 'This Morning'. Small, friendly and comfortable guesthouse with unique Walt Disney murals. Ten minutes' walk to city, railway station and racecourse. Suitable for walking disabled.

7 P

B&B per person per night:
S £30.00–£40.00
D £25.00–£30.00

OPEN All Year

♦♦♦

CORNMILL LODGE VEGETARIAN GUEST HOUSE

120 Haxby Road, York YO31 8JP
T: (01904) 620566
F: (01904) 620566
E: cornmillyork@aol.com
I: www.cornmillyork.co.uk

Bedrooms: 2 double, 1 family
Bathrooms: 3 en suite

CC: Delta, Mastercard, Switch, Visa

Well-appointed guesthouse only 12 minutes' walk from York Minster. No smoking. Car park. Launderette nearby. Friendly welcome. En suite rooms. Vegetarian/vegan. Organic/ Fair Trade where possible.

P

B&B per person per night:
S £30.00–£35.00
D £24.00–£30.00

OPEN All Year

♦♦♦

CUMBRIA HOUSE

2 Vyner Street, Haxby Road, York YO31 8HS
T: (01904) 636817
E: candj@cumbriahouse.freeserve.co.uk
I: www.cumbriahouse.com

Bedrooms: 3 double, 1 single, 2 family
Bathrooms: 2 en suite

CC: Delta, Mastercard, Switch, Visa

Family-run guesthouse, warm welcome assured, 12 minutes' walk from York Minster. En suites available. Easily located from ring road. Private car park. Brochure.

P €

B&B per person per night:
S £25.00–£28.00
D £25.00–£30.00

OPEN All Year

CHECK THE MAPS

The colour maps at the front of this guide show all the cities, towns and villages for which you will find accommodation entries. Refer to the town index to find the page on which they are listed.

YORK continued

CURZON LODGE AND STABLE COTTAGES

23 Tadcaster Road, Dringhouses, York YO24 1QG
T: (01904) 703157
F: (01904) 703157
I: www.smoothhound.co.uk/hotels/curzon.html

Charming 17thC Listed house and former stables in a conservation area overlooking York racecourse. Comfortable en suite rooms, some with 4-poster or brass beds. Country antiques, books, prints, fresh flowers and complimentary sherry lend traditional ambience. Delicious breakfasts. Warm, relaxed atmosphere with restaurants a minute's walk. Entirely non-smoking. Parking in grounds.

Bedrooms: 7 double, 1 single, 2 family
Bathrooms: 10 en suite

CC: Delta, Mastercard, Switch, Visa

B&B per person per night:
S £43.50–£52.00
D £29.50–£38.00

OPEN All Year except Christmas

♦♦♦♦

FARTHINGS HOTEL

5 Nunthorpe Avenue, York YO23 1PF
T: (01904) 653545
F: (01904) 628355
E: stay@farthingsyork.co.uk
I: www.farthingsyork.co.uk

Bill and Barbara Dickson extend a warm welcome to their guests. Ideally situated in a quiet cul-de-sac 10 minutes' stroll to city centre. The Farthings is a charming Victorian residence. Selection of quality rooms including en suite, all fully equipped. Breakfast freshly cooked including vegetarian. Unrestricted street parking. Non-smoking throughout.

Bedrooms: 4 double, 2 twin, 1 single, 2 family
Bathrooms: 5 en suite

CC: Delta, Mastercard, Switch, Visa

Winter breaks and mid-week packages available – prices on request (excl Bank Holidays, Christmas and New Year).

B&B per person per night:
S £25.00–£37.50
D £22.50–£27.50

OPEN All Year

♦♦♦

FOSS BANK GUEST HOUSE

16 Huntington Road, York YO31 8RB
T: (01904) 635548
I: www.fossbank.co.uk

At the Foss Bank Guest House you will be assured of a friendly welcome, delicious breakfast and comfortable accommodation. Overlooking the River Foss, just a 10-minute stroll to the city centre. Private car park. Non-smoking.

Bedrooms: 3 double, 1 twin, 1 single
Bathrooms: 2 en suite

Reduction for 3 nights or more, all year round.

B&B per person per night:
S £24.00–£26.00
D £22.00–£27.00

OPEN All Year except Christmas

YORK continued

◆◆◆

FOURPOSTER LODGE HOTEL

68-70 Heslington Road, Barbican Road, York YO10 5AU
T: (01904) 651170
F: (01904) 651170
E: fourposter.lodge@virgin.net
I: www.fourposterlodgehotel.co.uk

Your hosts Shirley and Gary welcome you to their Victorian villa. Enjoy the comfort and luxury of our 4-poster beds. Start the day with the house speciality 'a hearty English breakfast'. 10 minutes' walk to the city centre, close to The Barbican Centre, Fulford Golf Course and York University. Licensed. Car park.

Bedrooms: 8 double, 1 twin, 1 single, 1 family
Bathrooms: 10 en suite, 1 private

Evening meal available
CC: Amex, Delta, Mastercard, Switch, Visa

Reduction for 3 nights or more, all year round.

B&B per person per night:
S £40.00–£55.00
D £27.00–£45.00

HB per person per night:
DY £42.00–£60.00

OPEN All Year

◆◆◆

GOLDSMITHS GUEST HOUSE
18 Longfield Terrace, York YO30 7DJ
T: (01904) 655738
F: (01904) 675577
E: susan@goldsmith18.freeserve
I: www.goldsmithsguesthouse.co.uk

Bedrooms: 3 double, 2 twin, 2 single, 1 family
Bathrooms: 8 en suite

CC: Delta, Mastercard, Switch, Visa

Experience the comforts of Goldsmiths bed and breakfast accommodation. You'll find us tucked away on a quiet street only five minutes' walk from York Minster.

5 P €

B&B per person per night:
S £27.00–£35.00

HB per person per night:
DY £25.00–£28.00

OPEN All Year except Christmas

◆◆◆

GRANGE LODGE
52 Bootham Crescent, Bootham, York YO30 7AH
T: (01904) 621137
E: grangeldg@aol.com
I: grangelodge.co.uk

Bedrooms: 5 double, 1 single, 1 family
Bathrooms: 5 en suite

Evening meal available
CC: Delta, Mastercard, Switch, Visa

Attractive, tastefully furnished Victorian townhouse with a friendly atmosphere. Special emphasis is given to food, cleanliness and hospitality. Lunch and evening meals are available by arrangement.

€

B&B per person per night:
S £22.00–£30.00
D £22.00–£30.00

HB per person per night:
DY £30.00–£38.00

OPEN All Year except Christmas

◆◆◆

GREENSIDE

124 Clifton, York YO30 6BQ
T: (01904) 623631
F: (01904) 623631
E: greenside@amserve.com
I: www.greensideguesthouse.co.uk

Charming, detached, conservation, owner-run guesthouse fronting onto Clifton Green. Ideally situated, 10 minutes' walk from the city walls and all York's attractions. Offers many facilities, including an enclosed, locked car park. All types of ground/first floor bedrooms are available in a warm, homely atmosphere.

Bedrooms: 3 double, 1 single, 4 family
Bathrooms: 2 en suite

Evening meal available

P €

B&B per person per night:
S Min £22.00
D Min £20.00

OPEN All Year

CREDIT CARD BOOKINGS If you book by telephone and are asked for your credit card number it is advisable to check the proprietor's policy should you cancel your reservation.

YORK continued

♦♦♦♦ Silver Award

THE HAZELWOOD

24-25 Portland Street, York YO31 7EH
T: (01904) 626548
F: (01904) 628032
E: Reservations@thehazelwoodyork.com
I: www.thehazelwoodyork.com

B&B per person per night:
S £40.00–£95.00
D £37.50–£50.00

OPEN All Year

Situated in the very heart of York in an extremely quiet residential area only 400 yards from York Minster. Elegant Victorian townhouse with private car park providing high-quality accommodation in individually designed, en suite bedrooms. Wide choice of delicious breakfasts catering for all tastes including vegetarian. Completely non-smoking.

Bedrooms: 8 double, 3 twin, 1 single, 2 family
Bathrooms: 14 en suite

CC: Delta, Mastercard, Switch, Visa

♦♦♦♦

HOLLY LODGE

206 Fulford Road, York YO10 4DD
T: (01904) 646005
I: www.thehollylodge.co.uk

B&B per person per night:
S £58.00–£78.00
D £34.00–£44.00

OPEN All Year except Christmas

Beautifully appointed Georgian Grade II Listed building where you are assured of a warm welcome. 10 minutes' riverside stroll to centre, conveniently located for all York's attractions including Barbican and university. All rooms individually furnished, each overlooking garden or terrace. On-site parking, easy to find. Booking recommended.

Bedrooms: 4 double, 1 family
Bathrooms: 5 en suite

CC: Delta, Mastercard, Visa

♦♦♦

LINDEN LODGE

6 Nunthorpe Avenue, Scarcroft Road, York YO23 1PF
T: (01904) 620107
F: (01904) 620985
E: bookings@lindenlodge.yorks.net
I: www.yorkshirenet.co.uk/stayat/lindenlodge

B&B per person per night:
S £27.00–£29.00
D £27.00–£28.00

OPEN All Year

Linden Lodge is a friendly, licensed hotel, with a warm welcome. All rooms have remote-control colour TV, welcome tray and hairdryer. Choice of singles, twins, doubles and family rooms, en suite or standard. Situated 10 minutes' walk from city centre, railway station and racecourse. Unrestricted parking.

Bedrooms: 9 double, 2 single, 2 family
Bathrooms: 10 en suite

CC: Amex, Delta, Mastercard, Switch, Visa

ACCESSIBILITY

Look for the symbols which indicate National Accessible Scheme standards for hearing and visually impaired guests in addition to standards for guests with mobility impairment. You can find an index of all scheme participants at the back of this guide.

YORK continued

♦♦♦

MIDWAY HOUSE HOTEL

145 Fulford Road, York YO10 4HG
T: (01904) 659272
E: midway.house@virgin.net
I: www.s-h-systems.co.uk/hotels/midway.html

York Tourism Awards 2001 and 2002, Best Guesthouse – runner up. Welcome to our 1897 villa. Totally non-smoking. Cleanliness and care a continuing priority. Close to York centre, via riverside walk, and university. Private car park for all. Residential license and guests' lounge. 4-poster and ground floor available.

Bedrooms: 9 double, 1 single, 2 family
Bathrooms: 10 en suite

CC: Delta, Mastercard, Switch, Visa

Mid-week, off-peak breaks available. Please enquire.

P

B&B per person per night:
S £25.00–£40.00
D £23.00–£35.00

OPEN All Year except Christmas

♦♦♦

MOWBRAY HOUSE

34 Haxby Road, York YO31 8JX
T: (01904) 637710
E: carol@mowbrayhouse.co.uk
I: www.mowbrayhouse.co.uk

Bedrooms: 3 double
Bathrooms: 3 en suite

Family-run, non-smoking guesthouse, 10 minutes' walk from York Minster. Tastefully decorated en suite rooms are on offer along with a full English breakfast.

P

B&B per person per night:
D £25.00–£28.00

OPEN All Year except Christmas

♦♦♦♦

OAKLANDS GUEST HOUSE

351 Strensall Road, Earswick, York YO32 9SW
T: (01904) 768443
E: mavmo@oaklands5.fsnet.co.uk
I: www.holidayguides.com

A very warm welcome awaits you at our attractive and comfortable home set in open countryside, yet only three miles north of the City of York, with easy access to A64, A1 and A1237. Ideally situated for city, coast, Dales and Moors. Discounts available.

Bedrooms: 1 double, 1 twin, 1 single, 1 family
Bathrooms: 2 en suite

P

B&B per person per night:
S £17.00–£31.00
D £17.00–£25.00

OPEN All Year

♦♦♦

PARK VIEW GUEST HOUSE

34 Grosvenor Terrace, Bootham, York YO30 7AG
T: (01904) 620437
F: (01904) 620437
E: theparkviewyork@aol.com

An elegant Victorian townhouse close to the city centre with views of the Minster. 4-poster and ground floor rooms are provided in a totally non-smoking environment. An excellent full English breakfast with vegetarian option can be enjoyed in relaxed surroundings. On-street permit parking is available.

Bedrooms: 3 double, 1 twin, 1 single, 2 family
Bathrooms: 6 en suite, 1 private

12 P

B&B per person per night:
S £29.00–£39.00
D £22.50–£32.50

OPEN All Year except Christmas

YORK continued

THE PRIORY HOTEL

126-128 Fulford Road, York YO10 4BE
T: (01904) 625280
F: (01904) 637330
E: reservations@priory-hotelyork.co.uk
I: www.priory-hotelyork.co.uk

A Victorian-style, family-run guesthouse, only a few minutes' walk to city centre. The university and racecourse are only 1.5 miles, the McArthurGlen Centre and golf course two miles. Ample parking. Please send for brochure.

Bedrooms: 8 double, 1 single, 7 family
Bathrooms: 16 en suite

Evening meal available
CC: Amex, Delta, Diners, Mastercard, Switch, Visa

Enquire about our Special Breaks in York, 3 nights, B&B.

B&B per person per night:
S £40.00–£60.00
D £25.00–£40.00

HB per person per night:
DY £40.00–£50.00

OPEN All Year except Christmas

◆◆◆

ROMLEY GUEST HOUSE

2 Millfield Road, Scarcroft Road, York YO23 1NQ
T: (01904) 652822
E: info@romleyhouse.co.uk
I: www.romleyhouse.co.uk

Family-run guesthouse, few minutes' walk from city centre and all attractions, offers happy atmosphere, hearty breakfast, home comforts. All rooms are well appointed (en suite available) with colour TV, radio-alarm clock, tea/coffee-making facilities. Comfortable residents' lounge with licensed bar.

Bedrooms: 3 double, 1 single, 2 family
Bathrooms: 2 en suite

CC: Delta, Mastercard, Switch, Visa

B&B per person per night:
S £25.00
D £20.00–£27.00

OPEN All Year except Christmas

Silver Award

23 ST MARYS

Bootham, York YO30 7DD
T: (01904) 622738
F: (01904) 628802
E: stmarys23@hotmail.com
I: www.23stmarys.co.uk

Large, Victorian, terraced house peacefully set within five minutes' stroll of city centre. Spacious rooms, antique furnishings, en suite bedrooms of different sizes and character. Extensive breakfast menu in elegant surroundings. Julie and Chris will offer you a warm welcome to their home.

Bedrooms: 7 double, 2 single, 1 family
Bathrooms: 10 en suite

CC: Delta, Mastercard, Switch, Visa

Third night at 50% reduction (excl peak periods).

B&B per person per night:
S £32.00–£40.00
D £56.00–£80.00

OPEN All Year except Christmas

◆◆◆

SAXON HOUSE HOTEL

Fishergate, 71-73 Fulford Road, York YO10 4BD
T: (01904) 622106
F: (01904) 633764
E: saxon@househotel.freeserve.co.uk
I: www.saxonhousehotel.co.uk

Bedrooms: 7 double, 2 single, 5 family
Bathrooms: 14 en suite

CC: Delta, Mastercard, Switch, Visa

Victorian hotel offering a friendly welcome and personal service. Close to all city-centre attractions, golf course, race course, university, Barbican leisure centre and Designer Outlet.

B&B per person per night:
S £30.00–£50.00
D £25.00–£35.00

OPEN All Year except Christmas

YORK continued

◆◆◆

TYBURN HOUSE HOTEL
11 Albemarle Road, The Mount, York YO23 1EN
T: (01904) 655069
F: (01904) 655069
E: york@tyburnhotel.freeserve.co.uk

Bedrooms: 6 double, 2 single, 5 family
Bathrooms: 12 en suite, 1 private

B&B per person per night:
S £35.00–£40.00
D £35.00–£50.00

Family-owned and-run guesthouse overlooking the racecourse. In a quiet and beautiful area, close to the city centre and railway station.

◆◆◆

WARRENS GUEST HOUSE

30-32 Scarcroft Road, York YO23 1NF
T: (01904) 643139
F: (01904) 658297
I: www.warrensgh.co.uk

B&B per person per night:
S £35.00–£50.00
D £22.50–£35.00

OPEN All Year except Christmas

Excellent location in convservation area, 350 yards from City Walls. Park your car in our flood-lit, gated car park and walk into town. All our rooms are en suite with trouser press, complimentary tray, hairdryer, colour TV, some with 4-poster beds. Enjoy a full Yorkshire breakfast in our conservatory (vegetarian option available).

Bedrooms: 2 double, 1 twin, 3 family
Bathrooms: 6 en suite

Reductions for 3 or more days Sun-Thu inclusive (excl Bank Holidays and race days).

P €

◆◆◆

WATERS EDGE

5 Earlsborough Terrace, Marygate, York YO30 7BQ
T: (01904) 644625
F: (01904) 671325
E: julie@watersedgeyork.co.uk
I: www.watersedgeyork.co.uk

B&B per person per night:
S £40.00–£55.00
D £27.50–£32.50

OPEN All Year

Quiet positon on water's edge, five minutes' walk to Minster, short walk to all attractions. 4-poster rooms overlooking river. Free parking.

Bedrooms: 5 double
Bathrooms: 5 en suite

CC: Delta, Mastercard, Switch, Visa

8 P €

◆◆◆◆

YORK HOUSE

62 Heworth Green, York YO31 7TQ
T: (01904) 427070
F: (01904) 427070
E: yorkhouse.bandb@tiscali.co.uk
I: www.yorkhouseyork.com

B&B per person per night:
S £25.00–£30.00
D £25.00–£35.00

OPEN All Year

Located a short stroll from the heart of one of Europe's most historic cities, York House is the perfect base for a visit to beautiful York or the surrounding area. Refurbished Georgian guesthouse with luxury rooms featuring all the modern conveniences you could possibly need for a relaxing, enjoyable stay.

Bedrooms: 6 double, 1 twin, 1 single, 1 family
Bathrooms: 7 en suite, 2 private

CC: Delta, Mastercard, Switch, Visa

Adults: 10% discount for 3 or more consecutive nights – bookings made direct with York House. Senior Citizens – 10% discount.

P €

PRICES
Please check prices and other details at the time of booking.

A brief guide to the main Towns and Villages offering accommodation in **Yorkshire**

A APPLETREEWICK, NORTH YORKSHIRE - Wharfedale village below the craggy summit of "Simon's Seat". Halfway through the village, stands High Hall, former home of the Craven family.

ARKENGARTHDALE, NORTH YORKSHIRE - Picturesque Yorkshire dale, in the valley of Arkle Beck, once an important and prosperous lead-mining valley developed by Charles Bathurst in the 18th C.

ASKRIGG, NORTH YORKSHIRE - The name of this dales village means "ash tree ridge". It is centred on a steep main street of high, narrow 3-storey houses and thrived on cotton and later wool in 18th C. Once famous for its clock making.

AUSTWICK, NORTH YORKSHIRE - Picturesque, peaceful dales village with pleasant cottages, a green, an old cross and an Elizabethan Hall.

B BEDALE, NORTH YORKSHIRE - Ancient church of St Gregory and Georgian Bedale Hall occupy commanding positions over this market town situated in good hunting country. The hall, which contains interesting architectural features including a great ballroom and flying-type staircase, houses a library and museum.

BEVERLEY, NORTH HUMBERSIDE - Beverley's most famous landmark is its beautiful medieval Minster dating from 1220, with Percy family tomb. Many attractive squares and streets, notably Wednesday and Saturday Market and North Bar Gateway. Famous racecourse. Market cross dates from 1714.

BOLTON PERCY, NORTH YORKSHIRE - Secluded village of limestone with red-brick buildings. Exceptional 15th C parish church contains medieval stained glass and monument to Fairfaxes. 15th C half-timbered gatehouses with carved timber-work.

BOROUGHBRIDGE, NORTH YORKSHIRE - On the River Ure, Boroughbridge was once an important coaching centre with 22 inns and in the 18th C a port for Knaresborough's linens. It has fine old houses, many trees and a cobbled square with market cross. Nearby stand 3 megaliths known as the Devil's Arrows.

BRADFORD, WEST YORKSHIRE - City founded on wool, with fine Victorian and modern buildings. Attractions include the cathedral, city hall, Cartwright Hall, Lister Park, Moorside Mills Industrial Museum and National Museum of Photography, Film and Television.

BRIDLINGTON, EAST RIDING OF YORKSHIRE - Lively seaside resort with long sandy beaches, Leisure World and busy harbour with fishing trips in cobles. Priory church of St Mary whose Bayle Gate is now a museum. Mementoes of flying pioneer, Amy Johnson, in Sewerby Hall. Harbour Museum and Aquarium.

C CARLTON, NORTH YORKSHIRE - At the edge of the Yorkshire Dales, Carlton is a good base for exploring Coverdale and visiting the National Park Centre.

CROPTON, NORTH YORKSHIRE - Moorland village at the top of a high ridge with stone houses, some of cruck construction, a Victorian church and the remains of a 12th C moated castle. Cropton Forest and Cropton Brewery nearby.

D DANBY, NORTH YORKSHIRE - Eskdale village 12 miles west of Whitby. Visit the Moors Centre at Danby Lodge, a former shooting lodge in 13 acres of grounds including woodland and riverside meadow. Remains of medieval Danby Castle.

E EASINGWOLD, NORTH YORKSHIRE - Market town of charm and character with a cobbled square and many fine Georgian buildings.

F FILEY, NORTH YORKSHIRE - Resort with elegant Regency buildings along the front and 6 miles of sandy beaches bounded by natural breakwater, Filey Brigg. Starting point of the Cleveland Way. St Oswald's church, overlooking a ravine, belonged to Augustinian canons until the Dissolution.

G GARFORTH, WEST YORKSHIRE - Town 7 miles east of Leeds, between Temple Newsam Estate and Lotherton Hall. Old coal mining district of Leeds.

GOATHLAND, NORTH YORKSHIRE - Spacious village with several large greens grazed by sheep, an ideal centre for walking the North York Moors. Nearby are several waterfalls, among them Mallyan Spout. Plough Monday celebrations held in January. Location for filming of TV's "Heartbeat" series.

GOOLE, EAST RIDING OF YORKSHIRE - Busy port on the River Ouse developed with the opening of the Aire and Calder Canal in 1826 and reminiscent of the Netherlands with its red brick buildings and flat, watery landscape. The Goole Museum houses Garside Local History Collection.

GRASSINGTON, NORTH YORKSHIRE - Tourists visit this former lead-mining village to see its "smiddy", antique and craft shops and Upper Wharfedale Museum of country trades. Popular with fishermen and walkers. Cobbled market square, numerous prehistoric sites. Grassington Feast in October. National Park Centre.

H HALIFAX, WEST YORKSHIRE - Founded on the cloth trade, and famous for its building society, textiles, carpets and toffee. Most notable landmark is Piece Hall where wool merchants traded, now restored to house shops, museums and art gallery. Home also to Eureka! The Museum for Children.

HARROGATE, NORTH YORKSHIRE - Major conference, exhibition and shopping centre, renowned for its spa heritage and award-winning floral displays, spacious parks and gardens. Famous for antiques, toffee, fine shopping and excellent tea shops, also its Royal Pump Rooms and Baths. Annual Great Yorkshire Show in July.

HAWES, NORTH YORKSHIRE - The capital of Upper Wensleydale on the famous Pennine Way, Yorkshire's highest market town and renowned for great cheeses. Popular with walkers. Dales National Park Information Centre and Folk Museum. Nearby is spectacular Hardraw Force waterfall.

HAWORTH, WEST YORKSHIRE - Famous since 1820 as home of the Bronte family. The Parsonage is now a Bronte Museum where furniture and possessions of the family are displayed. Moors and Bronte waterfalls nearby and steam trains on the Keighley and Worth Valley Railway pass through.

HEBDEN, NORTH YORKSHIRE - Situated between Grassington and Pateley Bridge. The present bridge across the ravine was built in 1827, but the old stone bridge can still be seen. Close by is Scala Force. Abundant remains of lead-mining activity.

HELMSLEY, NORTH YORKSHIRE - Delightful small market town with red roofs, warm stone buildings and cobbled market square, on the River Rye at the entrance to Ryedale and the North York Moors. Remains of 12th C castle, several inns and All Saints' Church.

HOLMFIRTH, WEST YORKSHIRE - Village on the edge of the Peak District National Park, famous as the location for the filming of the TV series "Last of the Summer Wine".

HUDDERSFIELD, WEST YORKSHIRE - Founded on wool and cloth, has a famous choral society. Town centre redeveloped, but several good Victorian buildings remain, including railway station, St Peter's Church, Tolson Memorial Museum, art gallery and nearby Colne Valley Museum.

HULL, EAST RIDING OF YORKSHIRE - Busy seaport with a modern city centre and excellent shopping facilities. Maritime traditions in the town, docks museum, and the home of William Wilberforce, the slavery abolitionist, whose house is now a museum. The Humber Bridge is 5 miles west.

I ILKLEY, WEST YORKSHIRE - Former spa with an elegant shopping centre and famous for its ballad. The 16th C manor house, now a museum, displays local prehistoric and Roman relics. Popular walk leads up Heber's Ghyll to Ilkley Moor, with the mysterious Swastika Stone and White Wells, 18th C plunge baths.

K KIRKBYMOORSIDE, NORTH YORKSHIRE - Attractive market town with remains of Norman castle. Good centre for exploring moors. Nearby are the wild daffodils of Farndale.

KNARESBOROUGH, NORTH YORKSHIRE - Picturesque market town on the River Nidd. The 14th C keep is the best-preserved part of John of Gaunt's castle, and the manor house with its chequerboard walls was presented by James I to his son Charles as a fishing lodge. Prophetess Mother Shipton's cave. Boating on river.

L LEEDS, WEST YORKSHIRE - Large city with excellent modern shopping centre and splendid Victorian architecture. Museums and galleries including Temple Newsam House (the Hampton Court of the North), Tetley's Brewery Wharf and the Royal Armouries Museum; also home of Opera North.

LEYBURN, NORTH YORKSHIRE - Attractive dales market town where Mary Queen of Scots was reputedly captured after her escape from Bolton Castle. Fine views over Wensleydale from nearby.

M MALTON, NORTH YORKSHIRE - Thriving farming town on the River Derwent with large livestock market. Famous for racehorse training. The local museum has Roman remains and the Eden Camp Modern History Theme Museum transports visitors back to wartime Britain. Castle Howard within easy reach.

N NORTHALLERTON, NORTH YORKSHIRE - Formerly a staging post on coaching route to the North and later a railway town. Today a lively market town and administrative capital of North Yorkshire. Parish church of All Saints dates from 1200. Dickens stayed at The Fleece.

P PATELEY BRIDGE, NORTH YORKSHIRE - Market town at centre of Upper Nidderdale. Flax and linen industries once flourished in this remote and beautiful setting. Remains of Bronze Age settlements and disused lead mines.

PICKERING, NORTH YORKSHIRE - Market town and tourist centre on edge of North York Moors. Parish church has complete set of 15th C wall paintings depicting lives of saints. Part of 12th C castle still stands. Beck Isle Museum. The North York Moors Railway begins here.

R RAVENSCAR, NORTH YORKSHIRE - Splendidly positioned small coastal resort with magnificent views over Robin Hood's Bay. Its Old Peak is the end of the famous Lyke Wake Walk or "corpse way".

REETH, NORTH YORKSHIRE - Once a market town and lead-mining centre, Reeth today serves holiday-makers in Swaledale with its folk museum and 18th C shops and inns lining the green at High Row.

RICHMOND, NORTH YORKSHIRE - Market town on edge of Swaledale with 11th C castle, Georgian and Victorian buildings surrounding cobbled market-place. Green Howards' Museum is in the former Holy Trinity Church. Attractions include the Georgian Theatre, restored Theatre Royal, Richmondshire Museum and Easby Abbey.

RIPON, NORTH YORKSHIRE - Ancient city with impressive cathedral containing Saxon crypt which houses church treasures from all over Yorkshire. Charter granted in 886 by Alfred the Great. "Setting the Watch" tradition kept nightly by horn-blower in Market Square. Fountains Abbey nearby.

ROBIN HOOD'S BAY, NORTH YORKSHIRE - Picturesque village of red-roofed cottages with main street running from cliff top down ravine to seashore, a magnet for artists. Scene of much smuggling and shipwrecks in 18th C. Robin Hood reputed to have escaped to continent by boat from here.

ROSEDALE ABBEY, NORTH YORKSHIRE -Sturdy hamlet built around Cistercian nunnery in the reign of Henry II, in the middle of Rosedale, largest of the moorland valleys. Remains of 12th C priory. Disused lead mines on the surrounding moors.

RUNSWICK BAY, NORTH YORKSHIRE - Holiday and fishing village on the west side of Runswick Bay.

S SCARBOROUGH, NORTH YORKSHIRE - Large, popular East Coast seaside resort, formerly a spa town. Beautiful gardens and two splendid sandy beaches. Castle ruins date from 1100; fine Georgian and Victorian houses. Scarborough Millennium depicts 1,000 years of town's history. Sea Life Centre.

SCOTCH CORNER, NORTH YORKSHIRE - Famous milestone at the junction of the A1 and A66 near Richmond.

SELBY, NORTH YORKSHIRE - Small market town on the River Ouse, believed to have been birthplace of Henry I, with a magnificent abbey containing much fine Norman and Early English architecture.

SETTLE, NORTH YORKSHIRE - Town of narrow streets and Georgian houses in an area of great limestone hills and crags. Panoramic view from Castleberg Crag which stands 300 ft above town.

SHEFFIELD, SOUTH YORKSHIRE - Local iron ore and coal gave Sheffield its prosperous steel and cutlery industries. The modern city centre has many interesting buildings - cathedral, Cutlers' Hall, Crucible Theatre, Graves and Mappin Art Galleries. Meadowhall Shopping Centre nearby.

SKIPTON, NORTH YORKSHIRE - Pleasant market town at gateway to dales, with farming community atmosphere, a Palladian Town Hall, parish church and fully roofed castle at the top of the High Street. The Clifford family motto, "Desoramis" is sculpted in huge letters on the parapet over the castle gateway.

STAITHES, NORTH YORKSHIRE - Busy fishing village until growth of Whitby, Staithes is a maze of steep, cobbled streets packed with tall houses of red brick and bright paintwork. Smuggling was rife in 18th C. Cotton bonnets worn by fisherwomen can still be seen. Strong associations with Captain Cook.

T THIRSK, NORTH YORKSHIRE - Thriving market town with cobbled square surrounded by old shops and inns. St Mary's Church is probably the best example of Perpendicular work in Yorkshire. House of Thomas Lord - founder of Lord's Cricket Ground - is now a folk museum.

THORNTON DALE, NORTH YORKSHIRE - Picturesque village with Thorntondale Beck, traversed by tiny stone footbridges at the edge of pretty cottage gardens.

W WHITBY, NORTH YORKSHIRE - Holiday town with narrow streets and steep alleys at the mouth of the River Esk. Captain James Cook, the famous navigator, lived in Grape Lane. 199 steps lead to St Mary's Church and St Hilda's Abbey overlooking harbour. Dracula connections. Gothic weekend every April.

Y YORK, NORTH YORKSHIRE - Ancient walled city nearly 2,000 years old, containing many well-preserved medieval buildings. Its Minster has over 100 stained glass windows and is the largest Gothic cathedral in England. Attractions include Castle Museum, National Railway Museum, Jorvik Viking Centre and York Dungeon.

TOWN INDEX

This can be found at the back of the guide. If you know where you want to stay, the index will give you the page number listing accommodation in your chosen town, city or village.

Heart of England

A multi-cultural region with a diverse mix of vibrant cities, picturesque villages and dramatic countryside, the Heart of England has much to enjoy, from its industrial heritage to the famous 'balti' curry.

Classic sights
Chatsworth House – one of the great treasure houses of England
Ironbridge – birthplace of the industrial revolution
Pottery and porcelain – world-famous Royal Crown Derby, Wedgewood and Spode potteries

Coast and country
Herefordshire – peaceful countryside with black and white timber-framed villages
Skegness – seaside fun
Peak District – stunning landscapes in England's first National Park

City lights
Birmingham – world class visual and performing arts, designer labels, jewellery and the famous Balti Quarter
Nottingham, Leicester, Derby – lively, contemporary cities with bags of culture and style

Distinctively different
Ludlow – acclaimed Michelin-starred restaurants
National Space Centre – look into the future
Alton Towers – thrills, spills and white-knuckle rides galore

The Counties of Derbyshire, Gloucestershire, Herefordshire, Leicestershire, Lincolnshire, Northamptonshire, Nottinghamshire, Rutland, Shropshire, Staffordshire, Warrickshire, Worcestershire and West Midlands.

For more information contact:
Visit Heart of England –
The Regional Tourist Board
Larkhill Road, Worcester
WR5 2EZ

www.visitheartofengland.com

Telephone enquiries -
T: (01905) 761100
F: (01905) 763450

1. Chipping Campden
2. Burghley House, Lincolnshire
3. Rutland Water

You will find hundreds of interesting places to visit during your stay, just some of which are listed in these pages. Contact any Tourist Information Centre in the region for more ideas on days out.

Awarded VisitBritain's 'Quality Assured Visitor Attraction' marque.

Acton Scott Historic Working Farm
Wenlock Lodge, Church Stretton
Tel: (01694) 781306
www.actonscotmuseum.co.uk
This historic working farm demonstrates farming and rural life in south Shropshire at the close of the 19th century.

Alton Towers Theme Park
Alton, Stoke-on-Trent
Tel: 0870 5204060 www.altontowers.com
Theme park with over 125 rides and attractions such as Air, Oblivion, Nemesis, Congo River Rapids, Log Flume and many children's attractions including 'Blobmaster' live show.

The American Adventure
Ilkeston
Tel: 0845 3302929
www.americanadventure.co.uk
Action and entertainment for all ages, with The Missile white-knuckle rollercoaster, Europe's tallest skycoaster and the world's wettest log flume.

Belton House, Park and Gardens (National Trust)
Belton, Grantham
Tel: (01476) 566116
www.nationaltrust.org.uk
The crowning achievement of restoration country house architecture, built in 1685-88 for Sir John Brownlow with alterations by James Wyatt in 1777.

Belvoir Castle
Belvoir, Grantham
Tel: (01476) 871002 www.belvoircastle.com
The present castle is the 4th to be built on this site and dates from 1816. Art treasures include works by Poussin, Rubens, Holbein and Reynolds. Queens Royal Lancers display.

Birmingham Botanical Gardens and Glasshouses

Westbourne Road, Edgbaston
Tel: (0121) 454 1860
www.birminghambotanicalgardens.org.uk
15 acres (6ha) of ornamental gardens and glasshouses. Widest range of plants in the Midlands from tropical rainforest to arid desert. Aviaries with exotic birds, child's play area.

Black Country Living Museum
Tipton Road, Dudley
Tel: (0121) 557 9643 www.bclm.co.uk
A warm welcome awaits you at Britain's friendliest open-air museum. Wander around original shops and houses, or ride on fair attractions and take a look down the mine.

Museum of British Road Transport
Hales Street, Coventry
Tel: (024) 7683 2425 www.mbrt.co.uk
Two hundred cars and commercial vehicles from 1896 to date, 200 cycles from 1818 to date, 90 motorcycles from 1920 to date and 'Thrust 2' and 'Thrust SSC' land speed record cars.

Butlins
Roman Bank, Skegness
Tel: (01754) 762311
www.butlinsonline.co.uk
Butlins has a Skyline Pavilion, Toyland, Sub Tropical Waterworld, tenpin bowling and entertainment centre with live shows.

Cadbury World
Bournville, Birmingham
Tel: (0121) 451 4180 www.cadburyworld.co.uk
The story of Cadbury's chocolate includes chocolate-making demonstration and attractions for all ages, with free samples, free parking, shop and restaurant.

Chatsworth House, Garden, Farmyard & Adventure Playground
Chatsworth, Bakewell
Tel: (01246) 582204 www.chatsworth.org
Visitors to Chatsworth see more than 30 richly decorated rooms; the garden with fountains, a cascade and maze and the Farmyard and Adventure Playground.

Cotswold Farm Park
Guiting Power, Cheltenham
Tel: (01451) 850307
www.cotswoldfarmpark.co.uk
Collection of rare breeds of British farm animals. Pet's corner, adventure playground, Tractor School, picnic area, gift shop and cafe and seasonal farming displays.

Crich Tramway Village
Crich, Matlock
Tel: (01773) 852565 www.tramway.co.uk
A collection of over 70 trams from Britain and overseas from 1873-1969 with tram rides on a 1-mile (1.5-km) route, a period street scene, depots, a power station, workshops and exhibitions.

Drayton Manor Family Theme Park
Tamworth
Tel: (01827) 287979 www.draytonmanor.co.uk
A major theme park with over 100 rides and attractions, plus children's rides, Zoo, farm, museums and the new live 'Popeye Show'.

The Elgar Birthplace Museum
Lower Broadheath, Worcester
Tel: (01905) 333224 www.elgar.org
Country cottage birthplace of Sir Edward Elgar and the new Elgar Centre, giving a fascinating insight into his life, music, family, friends and inspirations.

The Galleries of Justice
Shire Hall, Nottingham
Tel: (0115) 952 0555
www.galleriesofjustice.org.uk
An atmospheric experience of justice over the ages located in and around an original 19thC courthouse and county gaol, brought to life by live actors.

The Heights of Abraham Cable Cars, Caverns and Hilltop Park
Matlock Bath, Matlock
Tel: (01629) 582365
www.heights-of-abraham.co.uk
A spectacular cable car ride takes you to the summit where, within the grounds, there are a wide variety of attractions for young and old alike. Gift shop and coffee shop.

Ikon Gallery
1 Oozells Square, Birmingham
Tel: (0121) 248 0708 www.ikon-gallery.co.uk
One of Europe's foremost galleries, presenting the work of national and international artists within an innovative educational framework.

Ironbridge Gorge Museum
Coalbrookdale, Telford
Tel: (01952) 433522
www.ironbridge.org.uk
World's first cast-iron bridge, Museum of the Gorge, Tar Tunnel, Jackfield Tile Museum, Coalport China Museum, Rosehill House, Blists Hill and Iron and Enginuity Museum.

Lincoln Castle
Castle Hill, Lincoln
Tel: (01522) 511068
www.lincolnshire.gov.uk/lccconnect/culturalservices/heritage/LincolnCastle
A medieval castle including towers and ramparts with a Magna Carta exhibition, a prison chapel experience, reconstructed Westgate and popular events throughout the summer.

2

3

1. Quayside Wharf, Birmingham
2. Rolling Hills and rural landscapes in the Heart of England
3. Robin Hood Statue, Nottingham

Midland Railway Centre
Butterley Station, Derby
Tel: (01773) 747674
www.midlandrailwaycentre.co.uk
Over 50 locomotives and over 100 items of historic rolling stock of Midland and LMS origin with a steam-hauled passenger service, a museum site, country and farm park.

National Sea Life Centre
The Water's Edge, Birmingham
Tel: (0121) 633 4700 www.sealife.co.uk
Over 55 fascinating displays. The opportunity to come face-to-face with literally 100's of fascinating sea creatures from sharks to shrimps. Now also includes otters.

Nottingham Industrial Museum
Courtyard Buildings, Nottingham
Tel: (0115) 915 3910
www.nottinghamcity.gov.uk
An 18thC stables presenting the history of Nottingham's industries: printing, pharmacy, hosiery and lace. There is also a Victorian beam engine, a horse gin and transport.

Peak District Mining Museum
The Pavilion, Matlock Bath
Tel: (01629) 583834 www.peakmines.co.uk
A large exhibition on 3500 years of lead mining with displays on geology, mines and miners, tools and engines. The climbing shafts make it suitable for children as well.

Rockingham Castle
Rockingham, Market Harborough
Tel: (01536) 770240
www.rockinghamcastle.com
An Elizabethan house within the walls of a Norman castle with fine pictures, extensive views and gardens with roses and an ancient yew hedge.

Rugby School Museum
10 Little Church Street, Rugby
Tel: (01788) 556109
www.rugbyschool.net/bt/museum_intro.htm
Rugby School Museum tells the story of the school, scene of 'Tom Brown's Schoolday's', and contains the earlier memorabilia of the game invented on the school close.

Severn Valley Railway
The Railway Station, Bewdley
Tel: (01299) 403816 www.svr.co.uk
Preserved standard gauge steam railway running 16 miles (27km) between Kidderminster, Bewdley and Bridgnorth. Collection of locomotives and passenger coaches.

Shakespeare's Birthplace
Henley Street, Stratford-upon-Avon
Tel: (01789) 201822 www.shakespeare.org.uk
The world famous house where William Shakespeare was born in 1564 and where he grew up. See the highly acclaimed Shakespeare Exhibition.

Shugborough Estate (National Trust)
Milford, Stafford
Tel: (01889) 881388
www.staffordshire.gov.uk/shugborough
18thC mansion house with fine collection of furniture. Gardens and park contain beautiful neo-classical monuments.

Skegness Natureland Seal Sanctuary
The Promenade, Skegness
Tel: (01754) 764345
www.skegnessnatureland.co.uk
Collection of performing seals, baby seals, penguins, aquarium, crocodiles, snakes, terrapins, scorpions, tropical birds, butterflies (April-October) and pets.

Snibston Discovery Park
Coalville, Leicester
Tel: (01530) 278444
www.leics.gov.uk/museums
Award-winning science and industrial heritage museum. Over 90 indoor and outdoor hands-on displays, plus exhibits from Leicestershire's industrial past.

Spode Visitor Centre
Church Street, Stoke-on-Trent
Tel: (01782) 744011 www.spode.co.uk
Visitors are shown the various processes in the making of bone china. Visitors can 'have a go' themselves in the craft demonstration area.

The Tales of Robin Hood
30-38 Maid Marian Way, Nottingham
Tel: (0115) 948 3284 www.robinhood.uk.com
Join the world's greatest medieval adventure. Ride through the magical green wood and play the Silver Arrow game, in the search for Robin Hood.

Twycross Zoo

Twycross, Atherstone
Tel: (01827) 880250
www.twycrosszoo.com
A zoo with gorillas, orang-utans, chimpanzees, a modern gibbon complex, elephants, lions, giraffes, a reptile house, pets' corner and rides.

Walsall Arboretum
Lichfield Street, Walsall
Tel: (01922) 653148
www.walsallarboretum.co.uk
Picturesque Victorian park with over 170 acres (70ha) of gardens, lakes and parkland. Home to the famous Walsall Illuminations each Autumn.

Warwick Castle
Warwick
Tel: 0870 4422000 www.warwick-castle.co.uk
Set in 60 acres (24ha) of grounds with state rooms, armoury, dungeon, torture chamber, 'A Royal Weekend Party 1898', 'Kingmaker' and the new Mill and Engine House attraction.

The Wedgwood Story Visitor Centre

Barlaston, Stoke-on-Trent
Tel: (01782) 204218
www.thewedgwoodstory.com
This £4.5 million visitor centre exhibits centuries of craftmanship on a plate. Audio-guided tour includes exhibition and demonstration areas. Shop and restaurants.

The Wildfowl and Wetlands Trust Slimbridge
Slimbridge, Gloucester
Tel: (01453) 890333 www.wwt.org.uk
Tropical house, hides, heated observatory, exhibits, shop, restaurant and children's playground, pond zone.

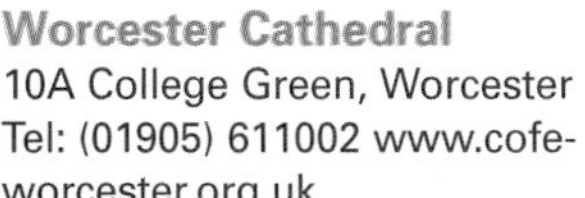

Worcester Cathedral
10A College Green, Worcester
Tel: (01905) 611002 www.cofe-worcester.org.uk
Worcester Cathedral is England's loveliest cathedral. We welcome families, groups and individuals with refreshments, gift shop and disabled access to all facilities and gardens.

1. Food and drink in the Heart of England
2. Stratford

Visit Heart of England – The Regional Tourist Board

Larkhill Road, Worcester WR5 2EZ.
T: (01905) 761100
F: (01905) 763450
www.visitheartofengland.com

THE FOLLOWING PUBLICATIONS ARE AVAILABLE FROM VISIT HEART OF ENGLAND:

Bed & Breakfast Touring Map including Camping and Caravan Parks 2004

Escape to the Heart 2004/5

Great Places to Visit in the Heart of England 2004

Getting to the Heart of England

BY ROAD: Britain's main motorways (M1/M6/M5) meet in the Heart of England; the M40 links with the M42 south of Birmingham while the M4 provides fast access from London to the south of the region. These road links ensure that the Heart of England is more accessible by road than any other region in the UK.

BY RAIL: The Heart of England lies at the centre of the country's rail network.
There are direct trains from London and other major cities to many towns and cities within the region.

1. Shrewsbury Castle
2. Stokesay Castle, Shropshire

Where to stay in the

Heart of England

Accommodation entries in this region are listed in alphabetical order of place name, and then in alphabetical order of establishment. As West Oxfordshire and Cherwell are promoted in both Heart of England and The South East, places in these areas with accommodation are listed in this section. See The South East for full West Oxfordshire and Cherwell entries.

All place names in the blue bands under which accommodation is listed, are shown on the maps at the front of this guide.

Symbols give useful information about services and facilities. Inside the back cover flap there's a key to these symbols which you can keep open for easy reference.

A complete listing of all the VisitBritain assessed accommodation covered by this guide appears at the back of this guide.

ALL STRETTON, Shropshire Map ref 4A3

◆◆◆◆

INWOOD FARM
All Stretton, Church Stretton
SY6 6LA
T: (01694) 724781
E: pauline.traill@btopenworld.com

Bedrooms: 3 double
Bathrooms: 2 en suite, 1 private

Evening meal available

Peaceful, old, comfortable house with large grounds and access to the Long Mynd. Ideal for walkers and riders. Mostly en suite rooms. Children and pets welcome.

P

B&B per person per night:
S £20.00–£25.00
D £20.00–£25.00

HB per person per night:
DY £30.00–£35.00

OPEN All Year

ALTON, Staffordshire Map ref 4B2

◆◆◆◆

BRADLEY ELMS FARM
Alton Road, Threapwood, Cheadle
ST10 4RB
T: (01538) 753135
F: (01538) 750202

Nine tastefully converted farm buildings all with en suite facilities, colour TV and tea/coffee. Residents' lounge, children's play area, excellent car parking. Three miles to Alton Towers. Within easy reach of The Potteries and the Peak District. Ideal for walkers and cyclists. Full English or continental breakfast included.

Bedrooms: 3 double, 3 twin, 3 family
Bathrooms: 9 en suite

P

B&B per person per night:
S Min £32.00
D Min £25.00

OPEN All Year except Christmas

ALTON continued

♦♦♦♦ Silver Award

FIELDS FARM

Chapel Lane, Threapwood, Alton, Stoke-on-Trent ST10 4QZ
T: (01538) 752721
F: (01538) 757404
E: pat.massey@ukonline.co.uk
I: www.fieldsfarmbb.co.uk

Traditional farmhouse hospitality and comfort in the picturesque Churnet Valley, 10 minutes from Alton Towers. Near Peak Park and within easy reach of Potteries and many stately homes. Stabling available. Ideal for walking, cycling, riding and fishing. Dogs by arrangement. Proprietor Pat Massey.

Bedrooms: 2 double, 1 family
Bathrooms: 2 en suite, 1 private

Evening meal available

B&B per person per night:
S £25.00–£32.00
D £17.50–£21.00

HB per person per night:
DY £25.00–£33.00

OPEN All Year except Christmas

♦♦♦

HILLSIDE FARM

Alton Road, Denstone, Uttoxeter ST14 5HG
T: (01889) 590760
F: (01889) 590760
I: www.smoothhound.co.uk/hotels/hillside.html

Bedrooms: 1 double, 3 family
Bathrooms: 1 en suite, 1 private

Victorian farmhouse with extensive views to the Weaver Hills and Churnet Valley. Situated two miles south of Alton Towers on B5032.

B&B per person per night:
S £20.00–£25.00
D £19.00–£22.00

ASHBOURNE, Derbyshire Map ref 4B2 *Tourist Information Centre Tel: (01335) 343666*

♦♦♦

THE BLACK HORSE INN

Main Road, Hulland Ward, Ashbourne DE6 3EE
T: (01335) 370206
F: (01335) 370206

Dating from the 1690s and personally run by owners. 4-poster, en suite accommodation. Home-cooked food, vegetarian options, traditional Sunday carvery. Guest beers, bar games, beer garden. Set in Derbyshire Dales on edge of Peak District National Park, four miles Ashbourne. Ideal for Carsington Water, Alton Towers, Chatsworth and Dovedale.

Bedrooms: 4 double
Bathrooms: 4 en suite

Evening meal available
CC: Delta, Mastercard, Switch, Visa

B&B per person per night:
S £40.00–£45.00
D £30.00–£35.00

OPEN All Year

♦♦♦♦

CROSS FARM

Main Road, Ellastone, Ashbourne DE6 2GZ
T: (01335) 324668
F: (01335) 324039
E: janecliffe@hotmail.com
I: www.cross-farm.co.uk

Bedrooms: 2 double, 1 family
Bathrooms: 3 en suite

19thC stone farmhouse near Alton Towers, Potteries, NT properties. Comfortable accommodation including large family room. Traditional Aga cooking with hearty breakfasts. Pub within walking distance.

B&B per person per night:
S £20.00–£25.00
D £18.00–£22.50

OPEN All Year

CONFIRM YOUR BOOKING
You are advised to confirm your booking in writing.

ASHBOURNE continued

♦♦♦♦

HOLLY MEADOW FARM

Bradley, Ashbourne DE6 1PN
T: (01335) 370261
F: (01335) 370261
I: www.hollymeadowbandb.freeserve.co.uk

Bedrooms: 2 double
Bathrooms: 2 en suite

B&B per person per night:
D £25.00–£28.00

OPEN All Year except Christmas

Quiet en suite B&B on 260-acre mixed farm. Fine views over open countryside. Ideal bird-watching, walking, exploring. Hearty farmhouse breakfasts. A warm welcome awaits you.

P

MONA VILLAS BED AND BREAKFAST

1 Mona Villas, Church Lane, Mayfield, Ashbourne DE6 2JS
T: (01335) 343773
F: (01335) 343773

Bedrooms: 2 double, 1 twin
Bathrooms: 3 en suite

B&B per person per night:
S £22.50–£30.00
D £22.50–£26.00

OPEN All Year except Christmas

A warm, friendly welcome to our Edwardian home with purpose-built, en suite accommodation. Beautiful views over open countryside. Near Alton Towers, Dovedale etc.

P

ASHOVER, Derbyshire Map ref 4B2

TWITCH NOOK

Hardwick Lane, Ashover, Chesterfield S45 0DE
T: (01246) 590153
F: (01246) 591641
E: valerieferrol@twitchnook.demon.co.uk
I: www.twitchnook.co.uk

Bedrooms: 3 double

B&B per person per night:
S £25.00
D £20.00–£22.50

OPEN All Year except Christmas

Spacious country house set in two-acre garden. A truly rural location offering magnificent views over open countryside. Comfortable, newly decorated rooms with colour TV, radio etc. Enjoy a full British breakfast to set you up for the day. Dogs catered for. A real home from home.

P €

ASTLEY, Worcestershire Map ref 4A3

WOODHAMPTON HOUSE

Weather Lane, Astley, Stourport-on-Severn DY13 0SF
T: (01299) 826510
F: (01299) 827059
E: pete-a@sally-a.freeserve.co.uk

Bedrooms: 1 double, 1 family
Bathrooms: 2 en suite

B&B per person per night:
S Min £30.00
D £25.00–£60.00

OPEN All Year except Christmas

Delightful coach house set in rural location, yet close to Stourport and other places of interest. Always a warm and friendly welcome. Excellent breakfast.

5 P

ATHERSTONE, Warwickshire Map ref 4B3

VICKI GARLAND'S BED & BREAKFAST

Mythe Farm, Pinwall Lane, Sheepy Magna, Atherstone CV9 3PF
T: (01827) 712367
F: (01827) 715738
E: bosworth/advertising@connectfree.co.uk

Bedrooms: 4 double, 1 single
Bathrooms: 2 en suite

B&B per person per night:
S £20.00–£35.00
D £17.50–£25.00

OPEN All Year except Christmas

Elegant Regency farmhouse set in attractive countryside in the heart of the Midlands. Beautiful riverside walks on this working farm. A warm welcome guaranteed.

P

IMPORTANT NOTE Information on accommodation listed in this guide has been supplied by the proprietors. As changes may occur you are advised to check details at the time of booking.

BAKEWELL, Derbyshire Map ref 4B2 *Tourist Information Centre Tel: (01629) 813227*

CASTLE CLIFFE

Monsal Head, Bakewell DE45 1NL
T: (01629) 640258
F: (01629) 640258
E: relax@castle-cliffe.com
I: www.castle-cliffe.com

B&B per person per night:
S £35.00–£40.00
D £25.00–£30.00

OPEN All Year except Christmas

Stunning position overlooking the beautiful Monsal Dale. Noted for its friendly atmosphere, hearty breakfasts and exceptional views. Drinks in the garden or around open log fire in winter. Centrally situated for Chatsworth, Haddon Hall and other attractions. Choice of dinner venues within an easy stroll. Walks in all directions.

Bedrooms: 2 double, 2 twin, 2 family
Bathrooms: 6 en suite

CC: Delta, Mastercard, Switch, Visa

3 nights for price of 2: Nov-Mar, Sun-Thu (excl Christmas and New Year).

P

♦♦♦♦

HOUSLEY COTTAGE

Housley, Foolow S32 5QB
T: (01433) 631505
E: kevin@housley-cottage.freeserve.co.uk

B&B per person per night:
S £20.00–£24.00
D £20.00–£24.00

OPEN All Year except Christmas

A 16thC farm cottage set in open countryside but within 10 minutes' walk of the Bulls Head pub in Foolow village. Public footpaths pass our garden gate to Millers Dale, Chatsworth House, Eyam and Castleton. All rooms en suite with views over open countryside. Full English breakfast or vegetarian.

Bedrooms: 2 double, 1 twin, 1 family
Bathrooms: 4 en suite

2 nights: £22pppn. 3 nights mid-week: £20pppn. Family room (Sleeps 4): Children half price.

P €

BALSALL COMMON, West Midlands Map ref 4B3

♦♦

AVONLEA

135 Kenilworth Road,
Balsall Common, Coventry CV7 7EU
T: (01676) 533003
F: (01676) 533003
E: frank.welsh@ntl.com

Bedrooms: 3 double, 1 single

B&B per person per night:
S £25.00–£30.00
D £25.00–£30.00

OPEN All Year

19thC cottage extended to provide spacious and comfortable accommodation, set back from main A425 road. Ample, off-road parking. Near NEC, NAC and motorways.

P €

♦♦♦

BLYTHE PADDOCKS

Barston Lane, Balsall Common,
Coventry CV7 7BT
T: (01676) 533050
F: (01676) 533050

Bedrooms: 2 double, 2 single
Bathrooms: 1 en suite

B&B per person per night:
S £22.00
D £24.00

OPEN All Year except Christmas

Family home standing in five acres. Ten minutes from Birmingham Airport and National Exhibition Centre. NAC Stoneleigh eight miles. Countryside location. Find us in Birmingham A-Z, page 168, square 1D.

P

BANBURY, Oxfordshire

See South East region for entries

BARTESTREE, Herefordshire Map ref 2A1

♦♦♦

PROSPECT COTTAGE BED AND BREAKFAST

Bartestree, Hereford HR1 4BY
T: (01432) 851164
E: christine@prospectorganics.freeserve.co.uk

Bedrooms: 3 double
Bathrooms: 1 en suite

Evening meal available

Charming, part black and white cottage set in large, landscaped gardens. Perfectly situated for exploring the delights of Herefordshire's countryside and cathedral city of Hereford.

B&B per person per night:
S £28.00–£32.00
D £20.00–£22.50

OPEN All Year except Christmas

BIBURY, Gloucestershire Map ref 2B1

Gold Award

COTTESWOLD HOUSE

Arlington, Bibury, Cirencester GL7 5ND
T: (01285) 740609
F: (01285) 740609
E: cotteswold.house@btconnect.com
I: http://home.btconnect.com/cotteswold.house

Situated in this picturesque village, Cotteswold House offers high-quality accommodation in a relaxed, friendly atmosphere. Tastefully furnished bedrooms with en suite facilities, colour TV and tea/coffee. Spacious guest lounge/dining room. Cotteswold House is an ideal centre for touring Cotswolds and surrounding area. No smoking/pets. Private parking.

Bedrooms: 2 double, 1 twin
Bathrooms: 3 en suite

CC: Mastercard, Visa

B&B per person per night:
S Max £40.00
D Max £27.50

OPEN All Year

BICESTER, Oxfordshire

See South East region for entries

BIDFORD-ON-AVON, Warwickshire Map ref 2B1

BROOM HALL INN

Bidford Road, Broom, Alcester B50 4HE
T: (01789) 773757
F: (01789) 778741

Family-owned country inn with carvery restaurant and extensive range of bar meals. Close to Stratford-upon-Avon and Cotswolds. Roaring log fires in the winter and a large garden with rare trees to relax in during the summer months.

Bedrooms: 8 double, 3 single
Bathrooms: 8 en suite, 3 private

Evening meal available
CC: Delta, Mastercard, Visa

B&B per person per night:
S £27.50–£37.50
D £27.50–£30.00

HB per person per night:
DY £34.50

OPEN All Year

BIRMINGHAM, West Midlands Map ref 4B3 *Tourist Information Centre Tel: (0121) 643 2514 (City Arcade)*

♦♦♦

ATHOLL LODGE

16 Elmdon Road, Acocks Green, Birmingham B27 6LH
T: (0121) 7074417
F: (0121) 7074417
E: davey@which.net

Bedrooms: 1 double, 1 twin, 7 single, 1 family
Bathrooms: 5 en suite

Evening meal available
CC: Mastercard, Switch, Visa

Friendly guesthouse in a quiet location on the south side of Birmingham. The National Exhibition Centre, airport and city centre are all within easy reach.

B&B per person per night:
S £25.00–£35.00
D £25.00–£27.50

OPEN All Year except Christmas

VISTBRITAIN'S WHERE TO STAY
Please mention this guide when making your booking.

BIRMINGHAM continued

◆◆◆

ELMDON GUEST HOUSE
2369 Coventry Road, Sheldon, Birmingham B26 3PN
T: (0121) 7421626
F: (0121) 7421626
E: maurice66@blueyonder.co.uk

Bedrooms: 4 double, 2 single, 1 family
Bathrooms: 7 en suite

Evening meal available
CC: Delta, Mastercard, Switch, Visa

Family-run guesthouse with en suite facilities. TV in all rooms, including Sky. On main A45 close to the National Exhibition Centre, airport, railway and city centre.

P

B&B per person per night:
S £34.00–£42.00
D £24.00–£27.50

HB per person per night:
DY £40.50–£55.50

OPEN All Year

◆◆◆

HOMELEA
2399 Coventry Road, Sheldon, Birmingham B26 3PN
T: (0121) 7420017
F: (0121) 6881879

Bedrooms: 1 double, 1 twin, 1 single
Bathrooms: 2 en suite, 1 private

CC: Delta, Mastercard, Switch, Visa

A friendly bed and breakfast close to National Exhibition Centre and airport. Comfortable rooms all with TV. Full English breakfast included. Pubs and restaurants within walking distance.

P

B&B per person per night:
S £22.50–£28.00
D £22.50

OPEN All Year

◆◆◆

Family atmosphere. Full central heating, evening meals, discount for long stay, disabled ground floor rooms. Close to all amenities and motorways.

KENSINGTON GUEST HOUSE HOTEL

785 Pershore Road, Selly Park, Birmingham B29 7LR
T: (0121) 4727086
F: (0121) 4725520
E: mail@kensingtonhotel.co.uk
I: www.kensingtonhotel.co.uk

Bedrooms: 19 double, 4 single, 9 family
Bathrooms: 22 en suite

Evening meal available
CC: Amex, Delta, Diners, Mastercard, Switch, Visa

P

B&B per person per night:
S £40.00–£45.00
D £50.00–£55.00

HB per person per night:
DY £53.00

OPEN All Year

◆◆

ROLLASON WOOD HOTEL
130 Wood End Road, Erdington, Birmingham B24 8BJ
T: (0121) 3731230
F: (0121) 3822578
E: rollwood@globalnet.co.uk

Bedrooms: 14 double, 19 single, 4 family
Bathrooms: 13 en suite

Evening meal available
CC: Amex, Delta, Diners, Mastercard, Switch, Visa

Friendly, family-run hotel, one mile from M6, exit 6. Convenient for city centre, NEC and convention centre. A la carte restaurant and bar.

P

B&B per person per night:
S £19.00–£38.00
D £17.00–£24.75

OPEN All Year except Christmas

BIRMINGHAM AIRPORT

See under Balsall Common, Birmingham, Coventry, Meriden, Solihull

BLOXHAM, Oxfordshire

See South East region for entries

BOURTON-ON-THE-WATER, Gloucestershire Map ref 2B1 *Tourist Information Centre Tel: (01451) 820211*

◆◆◆

KINGSBRIDGE AND CHESTER HOUSE HOTEL
Victoria Street, Bourton-on-the-Water, Cheltenham GL54 2BU
T: (01451) 820286
F: (01451) 820471
E: kingsbridgeinn.bourtononthewater@eldridge.pope.co.uk
I: www.roomathteinn.info

Bedrooms: 22 double
Bathrooms: 22 en suite

CC: Amex, Delta, Mastercard, Switch, Visa

Ideal centre for touring the Cotswolds. All rooms have bathroom, colour TV, radio, central heating, tea/coffee facilities.

P

B&B per person per night:
S £49.00–£59.00
D £29.50–£49.50

OPEN All Year

RATING All accommodation in this guide has been rated, or is awaiting a rating, by a trained VisitBritain assessor.

BOURTON-ON-THE-WATER continued

LANSDOWNE HOUSE

Lansdowne, Bourton-on-the-Water, Cheltenham GL54 2AT
T: (01451) 820812
F: (01451) 822484
E: heart@lansdownehouse.co.uk
I: www.lansdownehouse.co.uk

Large, period, stone, family house. Tastefully furnished, en suite accommodation with a combination of old and antique furniture. All rooms have tea/coffee trays and colour TV. There is parking and a garden for guests' use and a good selection of guide books to help you explore the area.

Bedrooms: 2 double, 1 family
Bathrooms: 3 en suite

B&B per person per night:
D £25.00

OPEN All Year except Christmas

♦♦♦

MOUSETRAP INN

Lansdowne, Bourton-on-the-Water, Cheltenham GL54 2AR
T: (01451) 820579
F: (01451) 822393
E: mtinn@waverider.co.uk
I: www.mousetrap-inn.co.uk

Bedrooms: 6 double, 3 twin, 1 suite
Bathrooms: 9 en suite

Evening meal available
CC: Delta, Mastercard, Switch, Visa

Small homely inn. All rooms en suite with TV and tea/coffee facilities. Excellent food served in relaxed surroundings. Open fire in the winter.

B&B per person per night:
D £22.50–£42.50

HB per person per night:
DY £34.00–£57.50

OPEN All Year

BRACKLEY, Northamptonshire Map ref 2C1 *Tourist Information Centre Tel: (01280) 700111*

HILL FARM

Halse, Brackley NN13 6DY
T: (01280) 703300
F: (01280) 704999
E: jg.robinson@farmline.com

A charming Georgian farmhouse set in beautiful countryside. Antique 4-poster bed. Close to Silverstone, Stowe, Oxford, Blenheim and the Cotswolds.

Bedrooms: 2 double, 1 twin, 1 single
Bathrooms: 1 en suite, 1 private

Evening meal available

B&B per person per night:
S £25.00–£45.00
D £25.00–£50.00

OPEN All Year except Christmas

BRADWELL, Derbyshire Map ref 4B2

Rating Applied For

TRAVELLERS REST

Brough Lane End, Brough, Bradwell, Hope Valley S33 9HG
T: (01433) 620363
F: (01433) 623338
E: elliottstephen@btconnect.com
I: www.travellers-rest.net

Bedrooms: 2 double, 3 twin
Bathrooms: 5 en suite

Evening meal available
CC: Delta, Mastercard, Switch, Visa

Country inn set in the picturesque Hope Valley in the Peak District. Friendly, with great food and beer.

B&B per person per night:
S £30.00–£37.00
D Max £28.50

OPEN All Year

ACCESSIBILITY

Look for the symbols which indicate National Accessible Scheme standards for hearing and visually impaired guests in addition to standards for guests with mobility impairment. You can find an index of all scheme participants at the back of this guide.

BRIDGNORTH, Shropshire Map ref 4A3 *Tourist Information Centre Tel: (01746) 763257*

♦♦♦♦

BULLS HEAD INN

Chelmarsh, Bridgnorth WV16 6BA
T: (01746) 861469
F: (01746) 862646
E: dave@bullshead.fsnet.co.uk
I: www.virtual-shropshire.co.uk/bulls-head-inn

17thC country inn offering excellent accommodation and country fare, approximately four miles from Bridgnorth. All bedrooms are en suite with tea/coffee-making facilities. Three ground floor bedrooms for people with disabilities. Choice of cottages/apartments for self-catering or bed and breakfast. Fishing parties welcome - lock-up store for tackle and bait.

Bedrooms: 3 double, 2 twin, 1 single, 3 family
Bathrooms: 9 en suite

Evening meal available
CC: Delta, Mastercard, Switch, Visa

Short breaks Nov-Feb, minimum 2 nights.

B&B per person per night:
S £36.00–£48.00
D £26.50–£36.50

OPEN All Year except Christmas

BRIZE NORTON, Oxfordshire

See South East region for entries

BROADWAY, Worcestershire Map ref 2B1

♦♦♦♦

THE BELL AT WILLERSEY

The Bell Inn, Willersey, Broadway WR12 7PJ
T: (01386) 858405
F: (01386) 853563
E: reservations@bellatwillersey.fsnet.co.uk
I: www.the-bell-willersey.com

17thC inn overlooking the village green and duck pond. One mile from Broadway, a perfect location for touring. Enjoys a high reputation for home-produced food. Restaurant open lunchtime and evenings. Relax in our brand-new bedrooms situated in our courtyard.

Bedrooms: 2 double, 1 twin, 2 family
Bathrooms: 5 en suite

Evening meal available
CC: Delta, Mastercard, Switch, Visa

B&B per person per night:
S Min £50.00
D £30.00–£35.00

OPEN All Year

♦♦♦♦♦
Gold Award

BURHILL FARM

Buckland, Broadway WR12 7LY
T: (01386) 858171
F: (01386) 858171
E: burhillfarm@yahoo.co.uk
I: www.burhillfarm.co.uk

A warm welcome awaits guests at our mainly grass farm lying in the folds of the Cotswolds, just two miles south of Broadway. Both guest rooms are en suite and have TV and tea/coffee facilities. The Cotswold Way runs through the middle of the farm providing many lovely walks.

Bedrooms: 2 double
Bathrooms: 2 en suite

10 P

B&B per person per night:
D £25.00–£30.00

OPEN All Year except Christmas

QUALITY ASSURANCE SCHEME

Diamond ratings and awards were correct at the time of going to press but are subject to change. Please check at the time of booking.

BROADWAY continued

CROWN AND TRUMPET INN

Church Street, Broadway WR12 7AE
T: (01386) 853202
E: ascott@cotswoldholidays.co.uk
I: www.cotswoldholidays.co.uk

17thC Cotswold-stone inn in picturesque Broadway, gateway to the Cotswolds and an ideal touring base. Extensive menu of seasonal and local dishes, many homemade, and fine selection of traditional beers and seasonal drinks. Oak beams, log fires in winter. Special offers for off-season and extended stays – telephone for details.

Bedrooms: 5 double
Bathrooms: 5 en suite

Evening meal available
CC: Delta, Mastercard, Switch, Visa

3-night stays available Oct-May (excl Christmas, New Year, Easter).

B&B per person per night:
S Min £48.00
D £28.00–£38.00

OPEN All Year

♦♦♦♦
Silver Award

LEASOW HOUSE

Laverton Meadow, Broadway WR12 7NA
T: (01386) 584526
F: (01386) 584596
E: leasow@clara.net
I: www.leasow.co.uk

Set in tranquil countryside close to Broadway. Leasow House is a 16thC farmhouse, ideally based for touring the Cotwolds and Shakespeare country.

Bedrooms: 5 double, 2 family
Bathrooms: 7 en suite

CC: Amex, Mastercard, Visa

B&B per person per night:
S £35.00–£55.00
D £28.00–£35.00

OPEN All Year except Christmas

Silver Award

OLIVE BRANCH GUEST HOUSE

78 High Street, Broadway
WR12 7AJ
T: (01386) 853440
F: (01386) 859070
E: broadway@theolive-branch.co.uk
I: www.theolivebranch-broadway.com

Bedrooms: 5 double, 1 single, 2 family
Bathrooms: 7 en suite, 1 private

Evening meal available
CC: Delta, Mastercard, Switch, Visa

16thC house with modern amenities close to centre of village. Traditional English breakfast served. Reduced rates for three nights or more.

B&B per person per night:
S £38.00–£55.00
D £30.00–£38.00

HB per person per night:
DY £45.00–£56.00

OPEN All Year

Silver Award

SHEEPSCOMBE HOUSE

Snowshill, Broadway WR12 7JU
T: (01386) 853769
F: (01386) 853769
E: reservations@snowshill-broadway.co.uk
I: www.broadway-cotswolds.co.uk

Situated in the heart of the Cotswolds, Sheepscombe House is surrounded by beautiful countryside with spectacular views. Accommodation is warm and very comfortable. Good, fresh breakfast, ample parking, ideal touring base for the Cotswolds and Stratford-upon-Avon. Excellent walking (600 metres to Cotswold Way). Open all year except Christmas.

Bedrooms: 2 double, 1 twin
Bathrooms: 1 en suite

Mid-week breaks: 4 nights for price of 3 for 2 people sharing room (excl Jul, Aug, Sep and Bank Holidays).

B&B per person per night:
D £30.00–£40.00

OPEN All Year except Christmas

BROADWAY continued

♦♦♦♦ Silver Award

SOUTHWOLD GUEST HOUSE

Station Road, Broadway WR12 7DE
T: (01386) 853681
F: (01386) 854610
E: susan.smiles1@btopenworld.com
I: www.broadway-southwold.co.uk

Bedrooms: 4 double, 2 twin, 1 single, 1 family
Bathrooms: 7 en suite, 1 private

CC: Mastercard, Switch, Visa

B&B per person per night:
S £34.00–£37.00
D £27.00–£30.00

OPEN All Year except Christmas

Edwardian house situated in picturesque Cotswolds. High standard of decoration and room amenities. Cosy guest lounge. Four minutes' walk to village centre and Cotswold Way.

P

♦♦♦♦ Silver Award

WINDRUSH HOUSE

Station Road, Broadway WR12 7DE
T: (01386) 853577
F: (01386) 853790
E: richard@broadway-windrush.co.uk
I: www.broadway-windrush.co.uk

Bedrooms: 5 double, 1 family
Bathrooms: 6 en suite

B&B per person per night:
S £40.00–£55.00
D £25.00–£32.50

OPEN All Year

An outstanding example of Edwardian elegance, located a few minutes' walk from the centre of Broadway. Spacious, relaxed and sophisticated surroundings combine with a homely and welcoming atmosphere.

4 P

BROXHOLME, Lincolnshire Map ref 4C2

♦♦♦♦

CARRIER'S FARM

Broxholme, Lincoln LN1 2NG
T: (01522) 702976
E: igilkison@aaugonline.net

Bedrooms: 1 double, 2 single
Bathrooms: 1 en suite, 1 private

B&B per person per night:
S £25.00–£28.00
D £45.00–£48.00

OPEN All Year except Christmas

Hamlet, secluded in six acres, paddocks, woodland, mature gardens. Direct access to River Till, walks, wildlife. Organic free-range produce, vegetarian option. Cotton linen. Ten minutes Lincoln.

P €

BURFORD, Oxfordshire

See South East region for entries

BURTON DASSETT, Warwickshire Map ref 2C1

♦♦♦♦ Silver Award

THE WHITE HOUSE BED AND BREAKFAST

Burton Dassett, Southam CV47 2AB
T: (01295) 770143
F: (01295) 770143
E: lisa@whitehouse10.freeserve.co.uk
I: www.thewhitehousebandb.info

Bedrooms: 2 double, 1 twin
Bathrooms: 3 en suite

B&B per person per night:
S £40.00–£45.00
D £25.00–£27.50

OPEN All Year

Peaceful, rural location at the top of the Burton Dassett Hills, magnificent views, high standard of accommodation, comfort and service. Homely and welcoming. Please telephone for brochure.

P

BUXTON, Derbyshire Map ref 4B2 *Tourist Information Centre Tel: (01298) 25106*

♦♦♦♦♦ Silver Award

BUXTON'S VICTORIAN GUESTHOUSE

3A Broad Walk, Buxton SK17 6JE
T: (01298) 78759
F: (01298) 74732
E: buxvic@tiscali.co.uk
I: www.buxtonvictorian.co.uk

Bedrooms: 6 double, 1 twin, 2 family
Bathrooms: 9 en suite

CC: Delta, Mastercard, Switch, Visa

B&B per person per night:
S £42.00–£68.00
D £29.00–£39.00

OPEN All Year

Built in 1860, an elegant, Grade II Listed townhouse, recently refurbished in classical Victorian style. On a quiet, tree-lined promenade, overlooking 40-acre park and Opera House.

5 P

♦♦♦

DEVONSHIRE ARMS

Peak Forest, Buxton SK17 8EJ
T: (01298) 23875
F: (01298) 23598
E: fiona.clough@virgin.net
I: www.devarms.com

Bedrooms: 4 double, 2 family
Bathrooms: 6 en suite

Evening meal available
CC: Delta, Mastercard, Switch, Visa

B&B per person per night:
S Min £29.50
D Min £23.00

OPEN All Year except Christmas

Traditional Peak District inn. High-standard, en suite rooms with TV and coffee facilities. Excellent food, traditional ales. Dogs and children free. Discounts available – phone for details.

P

BUXTON continued

◆◆◆

FAIRHAVEN
1 Dale Terrace, Buxton SK17 6LU
T: (01298) 24481
F: (01298) 24481
E: paulandcatherine@fairhavenguesthouse.freeserve.co.uk
I: www.fairhavenbedandbreakfast.com

Bedrooms: 4 double, 1 single, 1 family
Bathrooms: 1 private

CC: Delta, Mastercard, Switch, Visa

Within easy reach of the Opera House, Pavilion Gardens, two golf courses and the many and varied attractions of Derbyshire's Peak District.

B&B per person per night:
S £18.50–£23.00
D £16.00–£19.00

OPEN All Year except Christmas

◆◆◆◆◆
Gold Award

GRENDON GUESTHOUSE

Bishops Lane, Buxton SK17 6UN
T: (01298) 78831
F: (01298) 79257
E: parkerh1@talk21.com
I: www.grendonguesthouse.co.uk

Grendon is a beautiful, elegant family home with a stunning rural outlook yet close to Buxton's amenities. No expense spared to offer our guests a memorable visit in deluxe, exceedingly comfortable, spacious and hospitable surroundings. Superb 4-poster suite available.

Bedrooms: 2 double, 1 twin, 1 single
Bathrooms: 3 en suite, 1 private

Evening meal available
CC: Delta, Mastercard, Switch, Visa

Celebratory packages, 4-poster suite: champagne, flowers and chocolates, B&B tariff plus £30.

B&B per person per night:
S £25.00–£30.00
D £25.00–£35.00

HB per person per night:
DY Min £37.00

OPEN All Year

◆◆◆◆

GROSVENOR HOUSE
1 Broad Walk, Buxton SK17 6JE
T: (01298) 72439
F: (01298) 214185
E: grosvenor.buxton@btopenworld.com
I: www.grosvenorbuxton.co.uk

Bedrooms: 6 double, 1 twin, 2 family
Bathrooms: 9 en suite

CC: Amex, Delta, Mastercard, Switch, Visa

Privately run, Victorian residence enjoying splendid views of Pavilion Gardens/theatre. Homely and peaceful atmosphere. Home-cooked traditional English food. Newly refurbished and decorated. Non-smoking.

B&B per person per night:
S £45.00–£50.00
D £25.00–£37.50

OPEN All Year

◆◆◆◆
Silver Award

HAREFIELD

15 Marlborough Road, Buxton SK17 6RD
T: (01298) 24029
F: (01298) 24029
E: hardie@harefield1.freeserve.co.uk
I: www.harefield1.freeserve.co.uk

Elegant Victorian property set in its own grounds overlooking Buxton. Quiet location just a few minutes' walk from the historic town centre and an ideal base for exploring the beautiful Peak District. Spacious and comfortable accommodation with all bedrooms en suite. Friendly atmosphere, delicious food and lovely gardens to enjoy.

Bedrooms: 3 double, 2 twin, 1 single
Bathrooms: 6 en suite

Evening meal available

B&B per person per night:
S £24.00–£26.00
D £24.00–£28.00

HB per person per night:
DY £34.00–£38.00

OPEN All Year except Christmas

BUXTON continued

LAKENHAM GUESTHOUSE

11 Burlington Road, Buxton SK17 9AL
T: (01298) 79209

B&B per person per night:
D £30.00–£35.00

OPEN All Year

Sample Victorian elegance in one of Buxton's finest guesthouses. Lakenham offers all modern facilities yet retains its Victorian character. Period furniture and antiquities. Superb, central location overlooking picturesque Pavilion Gardens. Spacious, tastefully furnished, en suite bedrooms with TV/Satellite, hospitality tray, fridge/mini bar. First-class, personal service in a friendly, relaxed atmosphere.

Bedrooms: 4 double, 2 twin
Bathrooms: 5 en suite, 1 private

P

CHEDWORTH, Gloucestershire Map ref 2B1

♦♦♦

THE VICARAGE

Chedworth, Cheltenham GL54 4AA
T: (01285) 720392

Bedrooms: 1 double, 1 single
Bathrooms: 1 en suite

B&B per person per night:
S £20.00
D £19.00

OPEN All Year

Modern Cotswold-style house with large garden. Open all year. Peacefully situated. Scenic views. Ideal for touring the Cotswolds. Private parking.

P

CHELTENHAM, Gloucestershire Map ref 2B1 *Tourist Information Centre Tel: (01242) 522878*

Rating Applied For

BUTLERS HOTEL

Western Road, Cheltenham GL50 3RN
T: (01242) 570771
F: (01242) 528724
E: info@butlers-hotel.co.uk
I: www.butlers-hotel.co.uk

B&B per person per night:
S £42.00–£65.00
D £32.50–£47.50

OPEN All Year

Originally built in 1837 as a gentleman's residence, our unique Regency home is situated in a central, yet quiet area of Cheltenham and provides the perfect base for working in or visiting the area. A short stroll will take you to the Promenade, town centre and the quaint Montpellier district.

Bedrooms: 3 double, 2 twin, 1 single, 3 family
Bathrooms: 9 en suite

CC: Amex, Delta, Mastercard, Switch, Visa

Self-catering studios within hotel also available for vacation and professional lets.

P

♦♦♦

HOME COTTAGE

1 Priors Road, Cheltenham GL52 5AB
T: (01242) 518144
F: (01242) 518144
E: barrycott@msn.com
I: www.homecottage.co.uk

Bedrooms: 1 double, 1 family
Bathrooms: 2 en suite

Evening meal available

B&B per person per night:
S £30.00–£35.00
D £22.50–£25.00

OPEN All Year

A warm welcome in a small and comfortable late-Victorian cottage, set in an old-fashioned English country garden. Town centre within walking distance. Off-road parking.

5 P

GOLD & SILVER AWARDS

These exclusive VisitBritain awards are given to establishments achieving the highest levels of quality and service. Further information can be found at the front of the guide. An index to all accommodation achieving these awards are at the back of this guide.

CHELTENHAM continued

◆◆◆◆

HOME FARM

Stockwell Lane, Woodmancote, Cheltenham GL52 9QE
T: (01242) 675816
F: (01242) 701319
E: info@homefarmbb.co.uk
I: www.homefarmbb.co.uk

17thC farmhouse nestling in the slopes of Cleeve Hill in an Area of Outstanding Natural Beauty. Very quiet. Two restaurants within walking distance. Racecourse two miles. All bedrooms have original beams, charm and character with a private guest bathroom. Cosy lounge with stunning views. Local country walks.

Bedrooms: 1 double, 1 twin, 1 single

B&B per person per night:
S £28.00–£30.00
D £22.00–£25.00

OPEN All Year

◆◆◆

IVYDENE GUEST HOUSE

145 Hewlett Road, Cheltenham GL52 6TS
T: (01242) 521726
F: (01242) 525694
E: info@ivydenehouse.co.uk
I: www.ivydenehouse.co.uk

Stylish, yet economical, quality accommodation; walking distance to town centre. Popular with tourists and business people alike. Designer-themed rooms, e.g. Greek, African, Old Scandinavian. Artwork display. Also two economy single rooms. Generous breakfasts in grand breakfast room. Close to racecourse and Cheltenham F.C. ground. Car park.

Bedrooms: 3 double, 2 twin, 3 single, 1 family
Bathrooms: 7 en suite

CC: Delta, Mastercard, Switch, Visa

Romantic weekend breaks (minimum 2-night stay) with complimentary bottle of wine and chocolates.

B&B per person per night:
S £30.00–£40.00
D £27.50–£32.50

OPEN All Year except Christmas

◆◆◆

LAWN HOTEL

5 Pittville Lawn, Cheltenham GL52 2BE
T: (01242) 526638
F: (01242) 526638

Bedrooms: 1 double, 1 twin, 4 single, 1 family
Bathrooms: 5 en suite

Regency building along Pittville Park/pumproom. Central to Promenade. Vegetarians welcome. Non-smoking. Artist/designer owner. Art workshops available. Workshop/ conference room.

B&B per person per night:
S Min £25.00
D £25.00–£30.00

OPEN All Year except Christmas

CHESTERFIELD, Derbyshire Map ref 4B2 *Tourist Information Centre Tel: (01246) 345777*

◆◆◆

ABIGAILS

62 Brockwell Lane, Chesterfield S40 4EE
T: (01246) 279391
F: (01246) 854468
E: gail@abigails.fsnet.co.uk
I: www.abigailsguesthouse.co.uk

Bedrooms: 3 double, 2 twin, 2 single
Bathrooms: 7 en suite

Relax taking breakfast in the conservatory overlooking Chesterfield and surrounding moorlands. Garden with pond and waterfall, private car park. Best B&B winners 2000.

B&B per person per night:
S £29.00
D £22.00

OPEN All Year

HALF BOARD PRICES Half board prices are given per person, but in some cases these may be based on double/twin occupancy.

CHESTERFIELD continued

◆◆◆

CLARENDON GUESTHOUSE
32 Clarence Road, West Bars,
Chesterfield S40 1LN
T: (01246) 235004

Bedrooms: 1 double, 2 twin, 2 single
Bathrooms: 4 en suite

Evening meal available

Victorian town residence, near town centre, leisure facilities, theatres and Peak National Park. Special diets catered for. Overnight laundry service always available.

B&B per person per night:
S £17.00–£27.00
D £15.00–£19.00

HB per person per night:
DY £24.00–£28.00

OPEN All Year

CHIPPING CAMPDEN, Gloucestershire Map ref 2B1

◆◆◆

THE EIGHT BELLS

Church Street, Chipping Campden
GL55 6JG
T: (01386) 840371
F: (01386) 841669
E: neilhargreaves@bellinn.fsnet.co.uk
I: www.eightbellsinn.co.uk

An unspoilt 14thC Cotswold inn featuring open fires in winter and candlelit tables all year round. In addition there is a sun-drenched courtyard and terraced beer garden which overlooks the church. All accommodation is en suite, food is of the very highest standard and a friendly but informal welcome awaits you.

Bedrooms: 2 double, 1 twin, 1 family
Bathrooms: 4 en suite

Evening meal available
CC: Delta, Mastercard, Switch, Visa

Oct-Mar: 3 nights for the price of 2 (Sun-Thu). DB&B offers – see website for "winter warmers".

B&B per person per night:
S Min £45.00
D Min £40.00

OPEN All Year

◆◆◆

THE MALINS
21 Station Road, Blockley,
Moreton-in-Marsh GL56 9ED
T: (01386) 700402
F: (01386) 700402
E: johnmalin@btinternet.com
I: www.chippingcampden.co.uk/themalins.htm

Bedrooms: 1 double
Bathrooms: 1 en suite

Beautifully presented Cotswold-stone house on edge of delightful village. Ideal base for touring Cotswolds and Shakespeare country. Tastefully decorated, comfortable, non-smoking accommodation. A warm welcome awaits.

B&B per person per night:
S £35.00
D £22.00

OPEN All Year

◆◆◆◆

MANOR FARM

Weston Subedge, Chipping Campden
GL55 6QH
T: (01386) 840390
F: (08701) 640638
E: lucy@manorfarmbnb.demon.co.uk
I: www.manorfarmbnb.demon.co.uk

Luxury king-size beds, contemporary bathrooms, antique furniture in a Cotswold-stone, oak-beamed farmhouse built in 1624. Sumptuous breakfasts using fresh, local produce when available. Ideal position for exploring the Cotswolds, Stratford, Cheltenham and Oxford from our 800-acre farm with animals and an abundance of wildlife. Village pub serves meals.

Bedrooms: 2 double, 1 twin
Bathrooms: 3 en suite

CC: Delta, Mastercard, Switch, Visa

Reductions for stays of 4 nights or more.

B&B per person per night:
S £35.00–£60.00
D £25.00–£30.00

OPEN All Year

VISITOR ATTRACTIONS For ideas on places to visit refer to the introduction at the beginning of this section. Look out too for the VisitBritain Quality Assured Visitor Attraction signs.

CHIPPING CAMPDEN continued

◆◆◆◆◆ Gold Award

NINEVEH FARM

Campden Road, Mickleton,
Chipping Campden GL55 6PS
T: (01386) 438923
E: stay@ninevehfarm.co.uk
I: www.ninevehfarm.co.uk

18thC farmhouse with oak beams, flagstone floors and a warm welcome. Gardens of 1.5 acres in open countryside just 0.25 miles from village pubs. Ideal for exploring Cotswolds, Stratford-upon-Avon and Warwick. Cream teas and free loan of cycles.

Bedrooms: 3 double, 1 twin, 1 family
Bathrooms: 5 en suite

CC: Delta, Mastercard, Switch, Visa

Details of short breaks on request.

B&B per person per night:
D £27.50–£30.00

OPEN All Year

CHIPPING NORTON, Oxfordshire

See South East region for entries

CHURCH STRETTON, Shropshire Map ref 4A3

◆◆◆◆

BELVEDERE GUEST HOUSE

Burway Road, Church Stretton
SY6 6DP
T: (01694) 722232
F: (01694) 722232
E: belv@bigfoot.com
I: www.belvedereguesthouse.btinternet.co.uk

Bedrooms: 5 double, 3 single, 4 family
Bathrooms: 6 en suite

CC: Delta, Mastercard, Switch, Visa

Quiet detached house set in its own grounds, convenient for Church Stretton town centre and Longmynd Hills. Adequate parking.

B&B per person per night:
S £26.00–£34.00
D £26.00–£29.00

OPEN All Year except Christmas

CHURCHAM, Gloucestershire Map ref 2B1

THE PINETUM LODGE

Pinetum, Churcham, Gloucester GL2 8AD
T: (01452) 750554
F: (01452) 750402
E: carol@igeek.co.uk
I: www.pinetumlodge.ik.com

Intriguing Victorian hunting lodge in magical setting. 13 acres of beautiful woodland garden planted by Thomas Gambier Parry in 1844. Only four miles west of Gloucester. Views across rolling Cotswold hills and Severn Vale. Daffodils, bluebells, nightingales in spring. Easy walks. Haven for wildlife. Heated outdoor pool in the summer.

Bedrooms: 2 double, 1 single
Bathrooms: 2 en suite, 1 private

Evening meal available

Third and fourth night less 10%.

B&B per person per night:
S £30.00–£35.00
D £25.00–£30.00

HB per person per night:
DY £46.50–£51.50

OPEN All Year except Christmas

CIRENCESTER, Gloucestershire Map ref 2B1 *Tourist Information Centre Tel: (01285) 654180*

◆◆◆

THE BLACK HORSE

17 Castle Street, Cirencester
GL7 1QD
T: (01285) 653187
F: (01285) 659772

Bedrooms: 4 double
Bathrooms: 4 en suite

Evening meal available
CC: Amex, Delta, Mastercard, Switch, Visa

Situated in the centre of the historic Roman town of Cirencester. Built of Cotswold stone, it is thought to be around 400 years old.

B&B per person per night:
S £40.00–£45.00
D £25.00–£35.00

OPEN All Year

VISTBRITAIN'S WHERE TO STAY
Please mention this guide when making your booking.

CIRENCESTER continued

♦♦♦

BROOKLANDS FARM
Ewen, Cirencester GL7 6BU
T: (01285) 770487
F: (01285) 770487
I: www.glosfarmhols.co.uk

Bedrooms: 2 double

150-acre mixed farm on the banks of infant River Thames. Cirencester, the Cotswold Water Park and Cirencester Park are all within three miles. Mob: 07790 948931.

B&B per person per night:
S £20.00–£25.00
D £20.00–£25.00

OPEN All Year

♦♦♦♦
Silver
Award

COTSWOLD WILLOW POOL

Oaksey Road, Poole Keynes, Cirencester GL7 6DZ
T: (01285) 861485
E: enquiries@willowpool.com
I: www.willowpool.com

Willow Pool, set in 32 acres, is a nature lover's paradise. All rooms enjoy panoramic views across our peaceful private lakes (free fishing). Quality accommodation in a friendly and relaxed environment. Our outstanding location makes us a popular choice for visitors requiring a base from which to explore the Cotswolds.

Bedrooms: 1 double, 1 family
Bathrooms: 2 private

B&B per person per night:
S £30.00–£35.00
D £25.00–£30.00

OPEN All Year

♦♦♦♦

ELIOT ARMS HOTEL FREE HOUSE
Clarks Hay, South Cerney, Cirencester GL7 5UA
T: (01285) 860215
F: (01285) 861121
E: eliotarms.cirencester@eldridge.pope.co.uk

Bedrooms: 9 double, 1 single, 2 family
Bathrooms: 12 en suite

Evening meal available
CC: Amex, Delta, Mastercard, Switch, Visa

Dating from the 16thC, a comfortable Cotswold freehouse hotel, 2.5 miles from Cirencester, just off the A419. Reputation for fine food and hospitality. Riverside gardens.

B&B per person per night:
S £49.00–£54.00
D £29.50–£39.50

OPEN All Year

♦♦♦♦
Silver
Award

SMERRILL BARNS

Kemble, Cirencester GL7 6BW
T: (01285) 770907
F: (01285) 770706
E: gsopher@smerrillbarns.com
I: www.smerrillbarns.com

Enjoy a friendly welcome at Smerrill Barns, a wonderful old barn dating from the 1700s and sympathetically converted in 1992. The bedrooooms are comfortable and well equipped and there is a light and spacious sitting room in which to relax. Breakfasts are excellent and vegetarians are well catered for.

Bedrooms: 5 double, 1 twin, 1 family
Bathrooms: 7 en suite

CC: Delta, Mastercard, Switch, Visa

B&B per person per night:
S £45.00–£60.00
D £30.00–£40.00

OPEN All Year except Christmas

SPECIAL BREAKS

Many establishments offer special promotions and themed breaks. These are highlighted in red. (All such offers are subject to availability.)

COLEFORD, Gloucestershire Map ref 2A1 *Tourist Information Centre Tel: (01594) 812388*

FOREST HOUSE HOTEL

Cinder Hill, Coleford GL16 8HQ
T: (01594) 832424
F: (01594) 838030
E: suesparkes@tumphouse.fsnet.co.uk
I: www.forest-house-hotel.co.uk

Delightfully restored 18thC Listed former home of steel pioneers. Spacious, comfortable rooms, all en suite. Bluebell Restaurant offers excellent food cooked to order by award-winning chef. This family-run hotel is an excellent base for exploring the stunningly beautiful Royal Forest of Dean and Wye Valley.

Bedrooms: 4 double, 1 twin, 2 family
Bathrooms: 7 en suite

Evening meal available
CC: Amex, Delta, Mastercard, Switch, Visa

3 P

B&B per person per night:
D £30.00–£35.00

OPEN All Year except Christmas

CORBY, Northamptonshire Map ref 3A1 *Tourist Information Centre Tel: (01536) 407507*

MOAT COTTAGE

18 Little Oakley, Little Oakley, Corby NN18 8HA
T: (01536) 745013
F: (01536) 745013
E: enquiries@moat-cottage.fsbusiness.co.uk
I: www.moat-cottage.fsbusiness.co.uk

16thC beamed, thatched cottage in the centre of a quiet conservation village in the heart of rural Northamptonshire, yet only four miles from Rockingham speedway. Two private suites with own seating area in beautiful, south-facing garden. Locally sourced, organic produce used wherever possible, regional British dishes our speciality.

Bedrooms: 2 double
Bathrooms: 2 en suite

Weekly breaks: self-catering in the Lavender Barn, en suite shower, own kitchen/sitting room. £150 low season, £200 high season.

P

B&B per person per night:
S £35.00
D £22.50–£37.50

HB per person per night:
DY £32.50–£45.00

OPEN All Year except Christmas

COTSWOLDS

See under Bibury, Bourton-on-the-Water, Broadway, Chedworth, Cheltenham, Chipping Campden, Cirencester, Fairford, Gloucester, Lechlade, Long Compton, Moreton-in-Marsh, Naunton, Northleach, Painswick, Stonehouse, Stow-on-the-Wold, Stroud, Tetbury

See also Cotswolds in South East region

COVENTRY, West Midlands Map ref 4B3 *Tourist Information Centre Tel: (02476) 227264*

◆◆◆

ABIGAIL GUESTHOUSE

39 St Patrick's Road, Coventry CV1 2LP
T: (024) 76221378
F: (024) 76221378
E: ag002a@netgates.co.uk
I: www.abigailuk.com

Bedrooms: 1 double, 1 twin, 3 single, 1 family

Family-run establishment in centre of city, very clean and friendly. Convenient for station, cathedral and city centre shopping, also NEC and NAC.

P

B&B per person per night:
S £20.00–£25.00
D £20.00–£22.50

OPEN All Year except Christmas

ALBANY GUEST HOUSE

121 Holyhead Road, Coundon, Coventry CV1 3AD
T: (024) 76223601
F: (024) 76223601
I: www.smoothhound.com

Bedrooms: 1 double, 2 twin, 2 single, 1 family

Friendly, family-run guesthouse 10 minutes' walk to city centre. Near to National Exhibition Centre, National Agricultural Centre, Birmingham Airport, and Coventry and Warwick universities.

5

B&B per person per night:
S £18.00–£21.00
D £17.00–£19.00

OPEN All Year except Christmas

COVENTRY continued

♦♦♦

ASHDOWNS GUEST HOUSE

12 Regent Street, Earlsdon, Coventry CV1 3EP
T: (024) 7622 9280

Bedrooms: 3 double, 2 twin, 2 single, 1 family
Bathrooms: 7 en suite

A warm welcome awaits you in this relaxed, non-smoking family home. Convenient for city centre, rail and bus services. Private car park at rear.

B&B per person per night:
S £25.00–£30.00
D £22.50–£25.00

HB per person per night:
DY £45.00–£50.00

OPEN All Year

♦♦♦

ASHLEIGH HOUSE

17 Park Road, Coventry CV1 2LH
T: (024) 76223804
F: (024) 76223804

Bedrooms: 1 twin, 5 single, 4 family
Bathrooms: 10 en suite

Recently renovated guesthouse only 100 yards from the railway station. All city amenities within five minutes' walk. Licensed, evening meals.

B&B per person per night:
S £25.00–£30.00
D £22.00–£25.00

OPEN All Year

CRESSBROOK, Derbyshire Map ref 4B2

CRESSBROOK HALL

Cressbrook, Buxton SK17 8SY
T: (01298) 871289
F: (01298) 871845
E: stay@cressbrookhall.co.uk
I: www.cressbrookhall.co.uk

Bedrooms: 1 double, 1 twin, 1 family
Bathrooms: 3 en suite

Evening meal available
CC: Delta, Mastercard, Switch, Visa

Accommodation with a difference. Enjoy this magnificent family home built in 1835, set in 23 acres, with spectacular views around the compass.

B&B per person per night:
S £55.00–£87.50
D £37.50–£52.50

OPEN All Year except Christmas

DAVENTRY, Northamptonshire Map ref 2C1 *Tourist Information Centre Tel: (01327) 300277*

♦♦♦♦
Silver Award

THE OLD COACH HOUSE

Lower Catesby, Daventry NN11 6LF
T: (01327) 310390
F: (01327) 312220
E: coachhouse@lowercatesby.co.uk
I: www.lowercatesby.co.uk

A Victorian former coach house in open countryside, elegantly converted into a large-roomed family home with superb comfort. Beautiful gardens, a monastic pool and terraces with westerly views make this a special place to stay. All rooms have private or en suite bathrooms. A rural idyll yet within 15/20 minutes of M1/M40.

Bedrooms: 1 double, 1 twin
Bathrooms: 1 en suite, 1 private

B&B per person per night:
S £45.00
D £35.00–£40.00

OPEN All Year except Christmas

DEDDINGTON, Oxfordshire

See South East region for entries

DERBY, Derbyshire Map ref 4B2 *Tourist Information Centre Tel: (01332) 255802*

BONEHILL FARM

Etwall Road, Mickleover, Derby DE3 0DN
T: (01332) 513553
E: bonehillfarm@hotmail.com

A 120-acre mixed farm. Comfortable Georgian farmhouse in rural setting, three miles from Derby. Alton Towers, Peak District, historic houses and The Potteries within easy reach. Peaceful location.

Bedrooms: 2 double, 1 family
Bathrooms: 2 en suite

B&B per person per night:
S £22.00–£25.00
D £22.00–£25.00

OPEN All Year except Christmas

DROITWICH, Worcestershire Map ref 2B1 *Tourist Information Centre Tel: (01905) 774312*

◆◆

RICHMOND GUEST HOUSE
3 Ombersley St. West, Droitwich
WR9 8HZ
T: (01905) 775722
F: (01905) 794642
I: www.infotel.co.uk/hotels/36340.htm

Bedrooms: 2 double, 6 single, 4 family

B&B per person per night:
S £22.00–£23.00
D £18.00–£19.00

OPEN All Year except Christmas

Homely Victorian guesthouse in the town centre, five minutes from the railway station/bus routes. Thirty minutes from the NEC via M5/M42. Full English breakfast.

ELMESTHORPE, Leicestershire Map ref 4C3

◆◆◆◆

BADGERS MOUNT

6 Station Road, Elmesthorpe, Leicester
LE9 7SG
T: (01455) 848161
F: (01455) 848161
E: info@badgersmount.com
I: www.badgersmount.com

B&B per person per night:
S £37.00–£52.00
D £23.50–£34.75

OPEN All Year except Christmas

Set in countryside surroundings between M1 and M69 for easy travel to Leicester, Coventry, Birmingham and many Midlands' tourist attractions. The atmosphere is relaxed and informal. Residential licence, bar room overlooking large patio and spacious gardens. Outdoor heated swimming pool for summer use.

Bedrooms: 10 double, 2 family
Bathrooms: 12 en suite

Evening meal available
CC: Amex, Delta, Mastercard, Switch, Visa

ENDON, Staffordshire Map ref 4B2

◆◆◆

HOLLINHURST FARM
Park Lane, Endon, Stoke-on-Trent
ST9 9JB
T: (01782) 502633
E: hjball@ukf.net

Bedrooms: 2 double, 1 family
Bathrooms: 2 en suite, 1 private

B&B per person per night:
S £18.00–£20.00
D £18.00–£20.00

OPEN All Year

116-acre dairy farm. 17thC farmhouse within easy reach of Potteries, Peak District and Alton Towers. Panoramic views, walking and touring.

FAIRFORD, Gloucestershire Map ref 2B1

◆◆◆

KEMPSFORD MANOR
High Street, Kempsford, Fairford
GL7 4EQ
T: (01285) 810131
F: (01285) 810131
E: ipek@lineone.net
I: members.lycos.co.uk/kempsford_manor

Bedrooms: 2 double
Bathrooms: 1 en suite

Evening meal available

B&B per person per night:
S £30.00–£35.00
D £27.50–£32.50

HB per person per night:
DY £42.50–£45.00

OPEN All Year

17thC manor house set in peaceful gardens. Spacious bedrooms, elegant reception rooms, excellent cuisine with organic, home-grown vegetables.

€

◆◆◆◆

MILTON FARM
Fairford GL7 4HZ
T: (01285) 712205
F: (01285) 711349
E: milton@farmersweekly.net
I: www.milton-farm.co.uk

Bedrooms: 1 double, 1 twin, 1 family
Bathrooms: 3 en suite

CC: Mastercard, Switch, Visa

B&B per person per night:
S £25.00–£35.00
D £20.00–£27.50

OPEN All Year except Christmas

Impressive Georgian farmhouse with spacious and distinctive en suite bedrooms. Working farm, on edge of attractive market town. A welcoming and ideal base for exploring the Cotswolds.

SYMBOLS The symbols in each entry give information about services and facilities. A key to these symbols appears at the back of this guide.

FAIRFORD continued

WAITEN HILL FARM

Fairford GL7 4JG
T: (01285) 712652
F: (01285) 712652

Bedrooms: 3 double
Bathrooms: 2 en suite

B&B per person per night:
S Max £25.00
D Max £20.00

OPEN All Year

350-acre mixed farm. Imposing 19thC farmhouse, overlooking River Coln, old mill and famous church. Short walk to shops, pubs, restaurants. Ideal for touring Cotswolds and water parks.

FOREST OF DEAN

See under Coleford, Mitcheldean

GLOUCESTER, Gloucestershire Map ref 2B1

BROOKTHORPE LODGE

Stroud Road, Brookthorpe, Gloucester
GL4 0UQ
T: (01452) 812645
F: (01452) 812645
E: enq@brookthorpelodge.demon.co.uk
I: www.brookthorpelodge.demon.co.uk

B&B per person per night:
S £23.50–£35.00
D £22.50–£27.50

HB per person per night:
DY £35.00–£46.50

OPEN All Year

Licensed, family-run, spacious and comfortable Georgian detached house on the outskirts of Gloucester (3.5 miles). Set in lovely countryside at the foot of the Cotswold escarpment. Close to ski-slope and golfing facilities. Excellent walking country. Ideal base for visiting the Cotswolds, Cheltenham, Bath and nearby WWT reserve at Slimbridge.

Bedrooms: 2 double, 3 twin, 3 single, 2 family
Bathrooms: 6 en suite

Evening meal available
CC: Delta, Mastercard, Switch, Visa

Special discounts on 3-day weekend and 5-day, mid-week breaks.

◆◆◆◆

KILMORIE SMALL HOLDING

Gloucester Road, Corse, Snigs End, Staunton, Gloucester GL19 3RQ
T: (01452) 840224
F: (01452) 840224
E: sheila-barnfield@supanet.com
I: www.SmoothHound.co.uk/hotels/kilmorie.html

B&B per person per night:
S £22.00–£25.00
D £20.00–£25.00

HB per person per night:
DY £28.00–£33.00

All ground floor quality rural accommodation, within a conservation area. Colour TV, tea tray, radio in all bedrooms. Most are en suite. Grade II Listed Chartist smallholding (c1848) keeping free-range hens which provide excellent eggs for breakfast. Ample parking. Ideally situated for walking countryside or touring Cotswolds, Forest of Dean, Malvern Hills.

Bedrooms: 2 double, 1 twin, 1 single, 1 family
Bathrooms: 3 en suite, 2 private

Evening meal available

Reduced rates on stays of 4 nights, further reduced on stays of 7 nights, reduced rates children 5-12 years.

5

GRANGEMILL, Derbyshire Map ref 4B2

MIDDLE HILLS FARM

Grangemill, Derby DE4 4HY
T: (01629) 650368
F: (01629) 650368
E: l.lomas@btinernet.com
I: www.peakdistrictfarmhols.co.uk

Bedrooms: 1 double, 2 family
Bathrooms: 3 en suite

B&B per person per night:
S Max £30.00
D Max £30.00

OPEN All Year

40-acre mixed farm. This limestone farmhouse, built in 1980 in beautiful countryside, is near to Chatsworth, Dovedale and many other places of interest.

GREAT DALBY, Leicestershire Map ref 4C3

♦♦♦

DAIRY FARM

8 Burrough End, Great Dalby,
Melton Mowbray LE14 2EW
T: (01664) 562783

Bedrooms: 3 double
Bathrooms: 2 en suite,
1 private

Working dairy farm three miles south of Melton Mowbray. Brilliant walks and bridle rides close by – bring your own horse or hire. Good pub food in the village.

B&B per person per night:
S £20.00–£25.00
D £18.00–£20.00

OPEN All Year

HANDSACRE, Staffordshire Map ref 4B3

♦♦♦♦

THE OLDE PECULIAR

The Green, Handsacre, Rugeley
WS15 4DP
T: (01543) 491891
F: (01543) 493733

Bedrooms: 2 twin
Bathrooms: 2 en suite

Evening meal available
CC: Mastercard, Switch, Visa

A traditional village pub serving real ales and homemade food. Situated four miles from Lichfield city centre on the A513.

B&B per person per night:
S £29.50
D £22.00

OPEN All Year

HATHERSAGE, Derbyshire Map ref 4B2

♦♦♦♦
Silver Award

THE PLOUGH INN

Leadmill Bridge, Hathersage,
Hope Valley S32 1BA
T: (01433) 650319
F: (01433) 651049

Bedrooms: 3 double,
2 twin
Bathrooms: 5 en suite

Evening meal available
CC: Delta, Mastercard, Switch, Visa

17thC stone-built inn standing in nine acres of land bounded by River Derwent. Situated in Peak District National Park, ideal base for visiting stately homes. Excellent food, warm atmosphere.

B&B per person per night:
S £49.50–£99.50
D £34.75–£49.75

OPEN All Year except Christmas

HEREFORD, Herefordshire Map ref 2A1 *Tourist Information Centre Tel: (01432) 268430*

♦♦♦♦

HEDLEY LODGE

Belmont Abbey, Abergavenny Road,
Hereford HR2 9RZ
T: (01432) 374747
F: (01432) 277318
E: hedleylodge@aol.com
I: www.hedleylodge.com

Set in lovely grounds of Belmont Abbey (above), this friendly, modern guesthouse offers comfortably appointed bedrooms with en suite facilities, TV and telephone. Our licensed restaurant offers a wide selection of snacks or main meals. Located 2.5 miles from Hereford off A465, an ideal venue for visiting the Wye Valley.

Bedrooms: 6 double,
10 twin, 1 family
Bathrooms: 17 en suite

Evening meal available
CC: Delta, Mastercard, Switch, Visa

B&B per person per night:
S Min £35.00
D Min £27.50

OPEN All Year

HOARWITHY, Herefordshire Map ref 2A1

♦♦♦♦
Silver Award

OLD MILL

Hoarwithy, Hereford HR2 6QH
T: (01432) 840602
F: (01432) 840602
E: carol.probert@virgin.net
I: www.theoldmillhoarwithy.co.uk

Bedrooms: 4 double,
1 twin, 1 single
Bathrooms: 5 en suite,
1 private

Evening meal available

18thC black and white farmhouse offering a homely and friendly atmosphere. Home cooking. Close to the River Wye. Evening meals served.

B&B per person per night:
S £22.00–£24.00
D £22.00–£24.00

OPEN All Year

MAP REFERENCES The map references refer to the colour maps at the front of this guide. The first figure is the map number; the letter and figure which follow indicate the grid reference on the map.

HOLBEACH, Lincolnshire Map ref 3A1

◆◆

THE BULL INN
Old Main Road,
Fleet Hargate, Holbeach, Spalding
PE12 8LH
T: (01406) 426866

Bedrooms: 3 double

Evening meal available
CC: Mastercard, Switch, Visa

Ancient coaching inn on the road round The Wash. Grade II Listed building, site of archaeological interest. Bar, restaurant, rooms, car park and beer garden.

B&B per person per night:
S £20.00
D £17.50

OPEN All Year

HOPE, Derbyshire Map ref 4B2

Silver Award

UNDERLEIGH HOUSE
Off Edale Road, Hope, Hope Valley S33 6RF
T: (01433) 621372
F: (01433) 621324
E: underleigh.house@btinternet.com
I: www.underleighhouse.co.uk

Secluded cottage and barn conversion near the village of Hope with magnificent countryside views. Ideal for walking and exploring the Peak District. Delicious breakfasts featuring local and homemade specialities, served in flagstoned dining hall. Welcoming and relaxing atmosphere with a log fire on chilly evenings in the charming, beamed lounge.

Bedrooms: 4 double, 1 twin, 1 suite
Bathrooms: 5 en suite

CC: Delta, Mastercard, Switch, Visa

12

B&B per person per night:
S £40.00–£49.00
D £32.00–£34.50

OPEN All Year except Christmas

HUSBANDS BOSWORTH, Leicestershire Map ref 4C3

MRS ARMITAGE'S
31-33 High Street,
Husbands Bosworth, Lutterworth
LE17 6LJ
T: (01858) 880066

Bedrooms: 1 twin, 1 single, 1 family

Village-centre home of character on A4304/A427, with wholesome cooking and warm welcome. Good choice of reasonably priced evening meals at local inns.

B&B per person per night:
S £17.00–£19.00
D £17.00–£19.00

OPEN All Year

IRONBRIDGE, Shropshire Map ref 4A3 *Tourist Information Centre Tel: (01952) 432166*

Silver Award

BRIDGE HOUSE
Buildwas, Telford TF8 7BN
T: (01952) 432105
F: (01952) 432105
I: www.smoothhound.co.uk/hotels/bridgehs.html

Charming 17thC country house situated by the River Severn and close to the famous Ironbridge. A house full of character and charm. Beautiful rooms all individually decorated and en suite, with a breakfast to be remembered. In all, the place to stay when visiting the famous Ironbridge Gorge.

Bedrooms: 3 double, 1 family
Bathrooms: 4 en suite

CC: Amex, Delta, Diners, Mastercard, Switch, Visa

B&B per person per night:
S £45.00–£48.00
D £30.00–£32.50

OPEN All Year except Christmas

IMPORTANT NOTE Information on accommodation listed in this guide has been supplied by the proprietors. As changes may occur you are advised to check details at the time of booking.

IRONBRIDGE continued

♦♦♦

BRIDGE VIEW
10 Tontine Hill, Ironbridge, Telford TF8 7AL
T: (01952) 432541
F: (01952) 433405
I: www.ironbridgeview.co.uk

Bedrooms: 3 double, 1 twin, 1 family
Bathrooms: 4 en suite, 1 private

CC: Delta, Mastercard, Switch, Visa

B&B per person per night:
S £35.00–£45.00
D £22.50–£27.50

OPEN All Year

Right in the heart of Ironbridge with breathtaking views of the bridge. All rooms with en suite or private bathroom, colour TV, beverage tray. English breakfast. Private car park.

♦♦♦

THE FIRS GUEST HOUSE
32 Buildwas Road, Ironbridge, Telford TF8 7BJ
T: (01952) 432121
F: (01952) 433010
E: thefirsironbridge@tiscali.co.uk
I: www.ironbridge.ws/search/accomodation/hotels.asp?VID=49

B&B per person per night:
S £30.00–£40.00
D £25.00–£30.00

OPEN All Year

Situated on the banks of the River Severn, a short walk from Ironbridge. Fishing available for guests. Short-break offer: phone or fax for details. Family rooms are available, including one with walk-in bathroom suite.

Bedrooms: 2 double, 1 twin, 1 single, 4 family
Bathrooms: 6 en suite, 1 private

♦♦♦♦

THE GOLDEN BALL INN
Newbridge Road, Ironbridge, Telford TF8 7BA
T: (01952) 432179
F: (01952) 433123
E: matrowland@hotmail.com
I: www.goldenballinn.com

Bedrooms: 2 double, 1 twin
Bathrooms: 3 en suite

Evening meal available
CC: Delta, Mastercard, Switch, Visa

B&B per person per night:
S £45.00–£50.00
D £29.00–£35.00

OPEN All Year

Ironbridge's oldest and finest inn, specialising in guest ale, wine and freshly prepared restaurant and bar meals. Friendly and informal atmosphere. Open every day.

♦♦♦♦

THE MALTHOUSE
The Wharfage, Ironbridge, Telford TF8 7NH
T: (01952) 433712
F: (01952) 433298
E: enquiries@malthousepubs.co.uk
I: malthousepubs.co.uk

Bedrooms: 5 double, 1 twin
Bathrooms: 6 en suite

Evening meal available
CC: Amex, Mastercard, Switch, Visa

B&B per person per night:
D £27.50–£35.00

HB per person per night:
DY £45.00–£55.00

OPEN All Year except Christmas

A country pub, restaurant and bar with six individual en suite rooms. A fresh-food restaurant and bar with live jazz, folk and blues Wednesday to Saturday.

♦♦♦♦♦
Silver Award

SEVERN LODGE
New Road, Ironbridge, Telford TF8 7AU
T: (01952) 432147
F: (01952) 432148
E: julia@severnlodge.com
I: www.severnlodge.com

B&B per person per night:
S £52.00–£56.00
D £33.00–£37.00

Superb Grade II Listed Georgian residence, imposing central position. Exquisite, en suite bedrooms, delightfully and classically styled, with colour TV and hospitality tray. Secure parking within breathtaking walled garden with gorge and townscape views. Superb breakfast using local organic produce. Delightful dining hall, sitting room.

Bedrooms: 2 double, 1 twin
Bathrooms: 3 en suite

Carp-and pleasure-fishing breaks on privately owned, 2 acre lake. NRA rules apply. Nov, Dec, Jan: 4 nights for price of 3.

KENILWORTH, Warwickshire Map ref 4B3

♦♦♦♦

ENDERLEY GUEST HOUSE

20 Queens Road, Kenilworth
CV8 1JQ
T: (01926) 855388
F: (01926) 850450
E: enderleyguesthouse@supanet.com

Bedrooms: 2 double, 1 twin, 1 single, 1 family
Bathrooms: 5 en suite

B&B per person per night:
S £28.00–£35.00
D £23.00–£25.00

OPEN All Year

Family-run guesthouse, quietly situated near town centre and convenient for Warwick, Stratford-upon-Avon, Stoneleigh, Warwick University and National Exhibition Centre.

♦♦♦♦

THE QUINCE HOUSE

29 Moseley Road, Kenilworth
CV8 2AR
T: (01926) 858652
E: georgina.thomas@ntlworld.com
I: www.balldesi.demon.co.uk/b_b.html

Bedrooms: 2 twin
Bathrooms: 2 en suite

B&B per person per night:
S £30.00–£35.00
D £22.50–£27.50

OPEN All Year

Comfortable accommodation in private house on the outskirts of Kenilworth. Near to M40, only 25 minutes from Birmingham Airport and the National Exhibition Centre.

♦♦♦♦

VICTORIA LODGE HOTEL

180 Warwick Road, Kenilworth
CV8 1HU
T: (01926) 512020
F: (01926) 858703
E: info@victorialodgehotel.co.uk
I: www.victorialodgehotel.co.uk

Bedrooms: 7 double, 1 single, 1 family
Bathrooms: 9 en suite

CC: Amex, Delta, Mastercard, Switch, Visa

B&B per person per night:
S £42.00–£60.00
D £32.00–£37.50

OPEN All Year except Christmas

Prestigious, small hotel with a warming ambience. Luxurious bedrooms with individual appeal and character, complemented by traditional hospitality. Non-smoking.

KEXBY, Lincolnshire Map ref 4C2

THE GRANGE

Kexby, Gainsborough DN21 5PJ
T: (01427) 788265

Bedrooms: 1 double, 1 single
Bathrooms: 1 private

Evening meal available

B&B per person per night:
S £18.00–£20.00
D £18.00

OPEN All Year except Christmas

650-acre mixed farm. Victorian farmhouse offering warm welcome. Four miles from Gainsborough. Convenient for Lincoln, Hemswell Antique Centre and Wolds. Double room has private bathroom.

KIDDERMINSTER, Worcestershire Map ref 4B3

THE BROOK HOUSE

Hemming Way, Chaddesley Corbett,
Kidderminster DY10 4SF
T: (01562) 777453
F: (01562) 777453
E: kenbartlett@lineone.net
I: www.thebrookhouse.co.uk

B&B per person per night:
S Min £30.00
D Min £25.00

OPEN All Year

Situated in the picturesque village of Chaddesley Corbett in North Worcestershire. Surrounded by a large garden and overlooking fields. Within walking distance of three village inns. Convenient for M42 and M5. Relax after a busy day in our attractive lounge with sky TV and log fire in winter.

Bedrooms: 1 double, 1 twin
Bathrooms: 2 private

PRICES
Please check prices and other details at the time of booking.

KIDDERMINSTER continued

PARKMORE FARM

Torton Lane, Hartlebury,
Kidderminster DY10 4HX
T: (01299) 251827
E: info@parkmorefarm
I: www.parkmorefarm.co.uk

Bedrooms: 1 double,
1 twin, 1 single
Bathrooms: 1 en suite

Georgian farmhouse set in 16 acres in heart of Worcestershire. NEC and Birmingham Airport 30 minutes' drive.

B&B per person per night:
S £25.00–£30.00
D £25.00–£30.00

OPEN All Year except Christmas

KINETON, Warwickshire Map ref 2C1

THE CASTLE INN

Edgehill, Nr Banbury, Warwick
OX15 6DJ
T: (01295) 670255
F: (01295) 670521
E: castleedgehill@btopenworld.com
I: www.thecastle-edgehill.co.uk

Bedrooms: 2 double,
1 family
Bathrooms: 3 en suite

Evening meal available
CC: Amex, Delta, Diners, Mastercard, Switch, Visa

'Folly' built by Sanderson-Miller. Copy of Guy's Tower at Warwick Castle. Erected to commemorate 100th aniversary of Battle of Edgehill (1642) traditionally where King Charles I stood.

B&B per person per night:
D £28.75–£33.75

OPEN All Year

KING'S CLIFFE, Northamptonshire Map ref 3A1

19 WEST STREET

King's Cliffe, Peterborough PE8 6XB
T: (01780) 470365
F: (01780) 470623
E: kjhl_dixon@hotmail.com
I: www.kingjohnhuntinglodge.com

Grade II Listed, 500-year-old stone house, beautiful walled garden, reputedly one of King John's hunting lodges. Situated in centre of unspoilt stone village near Stamford. Rooms have private bathroom and colour TV. Dinner on request. Central location for many stately homes and a number of other attractions. Secure parking.

Bedrooms: 1 double,
1 twin, 1 single
Bathrooms: 3 private

Evening meal available

B&B per person per night:
S £20.00–£30.00
D £20.00–£25.00

HB per person per night:
DY £30.00–£45.00

OPEN All Year

LEAMINGTON SPA, Warwickshire Map ref 4B3 *Tourist Information Centre Tel: (01926) 742762*

Silver Award

8 CLARENDON CRESCENT

Leamington Spa CV32 5NR
T: (01926) 429840
F: (01926) 424641
E: lawson@lawson71.fsnet.co.uk
I: www.shakespeare-country.co.uk

Grade II Listed Regency house overlooking private dell, in quiet backwater of Leamington Spa with its many shops and restaurants. Elegantly furnished with antiques. Individually designed en suite bedrooms. Five minutes' walk town centre, convenient for Warwick, Stratford, Royal Agricultural Centre and NEC.

Bedrooms: 2 double,
1 twin, 1 single
Bathrooms: 3 en suite,
1 private

B&B per person per night:
S £35.00–£40.00
D £30.00

OPEN All Year except Christmas

LEAMINGTON SPA continued

◆◆◆◆ Silver Award

THE COACH HOUSE

Snowford Hall Farm, Hunningham, Leamington Spa CV33 9ES
T: (01926) 632297
F: (01926) 633599
E: the_coach_house@lineone.net
I: lineone.net/~the_coach_house

Bedrooms: 3 double
Bathrooms: 2 en suite, 1 private

B&B per person per night:
S £32.00–£36.00
D £21.00–£23.00

OPEN All Year except Christmas

200-acre arable farm. Converted barn farmhouse off the Fosse Way, on the edge of Hunningham village. On elevated ground overlooking quiet surrounding countryside.

P

◆◆◆◆

HILL FARM

Lewis Road, Radford Semele, Leamington Spa CV31 1UX
T: (01926) 337571
E: rebecca@hillfarm3000.fsnet.co.uk

Bedrooms: 3 double, 1 twin
Bathrooms: 3 en suite, 1 private

B&B per person per night:
S £30.00
D £25.00

OPEN All Year except Christmas

350-acre mixed farm. Farmhouse set in large attractive garden, two miles from Leamington town centre and close to Warwick Castle and Stratford-upon-Avon.

12 P

◆◆◆◆

VICTORIA PARK HOTEL

12 Adelaide Road, Leamington Spa CV31 3PW
T: (01926) 424195
F: (01926) 421521
E: info@victoriaparkhotelleamingtonspa.co.uk
I: www.victoriaparkhotelleamingtonspa.co.uk

Bedrooms: 7 double, 6 single, 7 family
Bathrooms: 20 en suite

Evening meal available
CC: Amex, Delta, Mastercard, Switch, Visa

B&B per person per night:
S £45.00–£55.00
D £32.50–£40.00

OPEN All Year except Christmas

Victorian house close to bus and railway stations and town centre. Park, Pump Room, gardens, bowls, tennis and river all three minutes' walk away.

P

◆◆◆◆◆ Silver Award

WYMONDLEY LODGE

8 Adelaide Road, Leamington Spa CV31 3PW
T: (01926) 882669
F: (01926) 882669

Bedrooms: 1 double, 1 twin
Bathrooms: 2 en suite

B&B per person per night:
S £35.00–£40.00
D £25.00–£30.00

Elegant Victorian townhouse, few minutes' walk from town centre, shops, restaurants and railway station. Convenient for historic Warwick, Kenilworth, Stratford and the NAC.

5 P

LECHLADE-ON-THAMES, Gloucestershire Map ref 2B1

◆◆◆◆ Silver Award

CAMBRAI LODGE

Oak Street, Lechlade-on-Thames GL7 3AY
T: (01367) 253173

Bedrooms: 3 double, 2 single, 1 family
Bathrooms: 4 en suite

B&B per person per night:
S £30.00–£40.00
D £25.00–£30.00

OPEN All Year

Friendly, family-run guesthouse, recently modernised, close to River Thames. Ideal base for touring the Cotswolds. 4-poster bedroom, garden and ample parking.

P €

◆◆◆

NEW INN HOTEL

Market Square, Lechlade-on-Thames, Lechlade GL7 3AB
T: (01367) 252296
F: (01367) 252315
E: info@newinnhotel.com
I: www.newinnhotel.co.uk

Bedrooms: 12 double, 12 twin, 2 single, 3 family
Bathrooms: 29 en suite

Evening meal available
CC: Amex, Delta, Mastercard, Switch, Visa

B&B per person per night:
S £42.50–£55.00
D £27.50–£32.50

HB per person per night:
DY £55.00

OPEN All Year except Christmas

Situated in a tranquil riverside setting, offering a comfortable blend of traditional hospitality and all modern advantages. Private parking. Restaurant and freehouse with en suite bedrooms.

P €

LEICESTER, Leicestershire Map ref 4C3 *Tourist Information Centre Tel: 0906 294 1113 (Premium rate number)*

◆◆◆

ABINGER GUEST HOUSE
175 Hinckley Road, Leicester
LE3 0TF
T: (0116) 2554674
F: (0116) 2554674
E: bobwel1234@aol.com
I: www.openroads.com

Bedrooms: 3 double, 5 twin, 1 single, 2 family

CC: Amex, Delta, Diners, Mastercard, Switch, Visa

B&B per person per night:
S £24.00–£31.00
D £18.00–£24.00

OPEN All Year except Christmas

Extensively modernised guesthouse situated a mile from Leicester city centre. Friendly staff, great breakfasts and extremely comfortable beds. Freeview TV in every room.

P

◆

GLENFIELD LODGE HOTEL

4 Glenfield Road, Leicester LE3 6AP
T: (0116) 2627554

B&B per person per night:
S £24.00
D £20.00

OPEN All Year except Christmas

Small, friendly hotel with an interesting ornamental courtyard, home-cooked food and cosy, relaxed surroundings. Close to city centre.

Bedrooms: 7 double, 6 single, 2 family

Evening meal available

P

◆◆◆◆

HAYNES HOTEL
185 Uppingham Road, Leicester
LE5 4BQ
T: (0116) 2768973
F: (0116) 2768973
E: hayneshotel@yahoo.co.uk

Bedrooms: 5 double, 1 single, 1 family
Bathrooms: 7 en suite

CC: Amex, Delta, Diners, Mastercard, Switch, Visa

B&B per person per night:
S £35.00–£40.00
D £22.50–£30.00

HB per person per night:
DY £43.00–£55.00

OPEN All Year

Victorian townhouse with many original features, two miles from city centre, on a bus route, and two miles from main line station.

P €

◆◆◆

SPINDLE LODGE HOTEL

2 West Walk, Leicester LE1 7NA
T: (0116) 2338801
F: (0116) 2338804
E: spindlelodgeleicester@orange.net
I: www.smoothhound.co.uk/hotels/spindle.html

B&B per person per night:
S £25.00–£47.50
D £30.00–£32.50

OPEN All Year except Christmas

Located in a tree-lined conservation area and built in 1876, charming Spindle Lodge is in a quiet location, yet centrally positioned. A family-run Victorian house with a friendly atmosphere, within easy walking distance of city centre, railway station, universities, civic and entertainment centres.

Bedrooms: 2 double, 3 twin, 6 single, 2 family
Bathrooms: 8 en suite

Evening meal available
CC: Delta, Mastercard, Switch, Visa

Complimentary tickets for a family of 3 to visit the National Space Centre if you stay 2 nights or more.

P €

LEOMINSTER, Herefordshire Map ref 2A1 *Tourist Information Centre Tel: (01568) 616460*

◆◆◆

ROSSENDALE HOUSE
46 Broad Street, Leominster
HR6 8BS
T: 0845 1668831
F: (01568) 612464
E: enquiries@rossendalehouse.co.uk
I: www.rossendalehouse.co.uk

Bedrooms: 2 double, 2 twin, 6 single
Bathrooms: 1 en suite

B&B per person per night:
S £20.00–£40.00
D £20.00–£40.00

OPEN All Year

A Listed 17thC coaching inn providing bed and breakfast hospitality for business and leisure. Secluded gardens and private car park. All major credit cards.

5 P

LEOMINSTER continued

♦♦♦

TYN-Y-COED

Shobdon, Leominster HR6 9NY
T: (01568) 708277
F: (01568) 708277
E: jandrews@shobdondesign.kc3.co.uk

Bedrooms: 1 double, 1 twin
Bathrooms: 2 en suite

Country house in large garden on Mortimer Trail, close to Croft Castle and Berrington Hall (NT). Convenient for Leominster, Ludlow and Presteigne.

10 P

B&B per person per night:
S £23.00
D £23.00

LICHFIELD, Staffordshire Map ref 4B3 *Tourist Information Centre Tel: (01543) 308209*

♦♦♦

COPPERS END GUEST HOUSE

Walsall Road, Muckley Corner, Lichfield WS14 0BG
T: (01543) 372910
F: (01543) 360423
E: info@coppersendguesthouse.co.uk
I: www.coppersendguesthouse.co.uk

Detached guesthouse of character and charm in its own grounds. Conservatory dining room, large walled garden with patio, guests' own lounge, residential licence. All bedrooms non-smoking. Off-road parking. Easy access to M6, M42 and M1, Lichfield, Walsall and Birmingham. 16 miles to NEC, six miles Whittington Barracks. Motorcyle friendly.

Bedrooms: 6 double
Bathrooms: 4 en suite

CC: Amex, Delta, Diners, Mastercard, Switch, Visa

P

B&B per person per night:
S £32.00–£35.00
D £21.00–£26.00

OPEN All Year except Christmas

THE WHITE HOUSE

Market Lane, Wall, Lichfield WS14 0AS
T: (01543) 480384

Bedrooms: 2 double

CC: Visa

House built on site of Roman Baths. Some old beams in the house. Very peaceful, good garden. Near to Motorway, NEC etc.

P

B&B per person per night:
S Min £20.00
D Min £20.00

OPEN All Year

LINCOLN, Lincolnshire Map ref 4C2

♦♦♦

NEWPORT GUEST HOUSE

26-28 Newport, Lincoln LN1 3DF
T: (01522) 528590
F: (01522) 542868
E: info@newportguesthouse.co.uk
I: www.newportguesthouse.co.uk

Bedrooms: 3 double, 1 twin, 2 single, 2 family
Bathrooms: 8 en suite

CC: Amex, Delta, Diners, Mastercard, Switch, Visa

A Victorian double-fronted property, walking distance from historic centre of Lincoln. Own off-street parking for guests.

8 P €

B&B per person per night:
S £28.00–£50.00
D £20.00–£25.00

OPEN All Year except Christmas

♦♦♦

73 STATION ROAD

Branston, Lincoln LN4 1LG
T: (01522) 828658

Bedrooms: 1 double, 1 twin
Bathrooms: 1 en suite, 1 private

Bed and breakfast three miles from the city of Lincoln. Two bedrooms on ground floor overlooking attractive gardens. Off-street parking.

5 P

B&B per person per night:
S Min £25.00
D Min £25.00

OPEN All Year except Christmas

♦♦♦♦

WELBECK COTTAGE

19 Meadow Lane, South Hykeham, Lincoln LN6 9PF
T: (01522) 692669
F: (01522) 692669
E: mad@wellbeck1.demon.co.uk

Bedrooms: 2 double, 1 twin
Bathrooms: 3 en suite

Evening meal available

Friendly welcome to semi-detached cottage in pleasant rural location. Near historic city of Lincoln. Evening meal available on request.

5 P

B&B per person per night:
S £20.00–£22.00
D £19.00–£20.00

HB per person per night:
DY £26.00–£28.00

OPEN All Year

LONG COMPTON, Warwickshire Map ref 2B1

◆◆◆

BUTLERS ROAD FARM
Long Compton, Shipston-on-Stour
CV36 5JZ
T: (01608) 684262
F: (01608) 684262
E: eileenwhittaker@easicom.com

Bedrooms: 2 double

B&B per person per night:
S £25.00
D £20.00

OPEN All Year

120-acre stock farm. Listed Cotswold-stone farmhouse adjacent to A3400 between Oxford and Stratford-upon-Avon. Home comforts. Local pub nearby.

LOUGHBOROUGH, Leicestershire Map ref 4C3 *Tourist Information Centre Tel: (01509) 218113*

CHARNWOOD LODGE
136 Leicester Road, Loughborough
LE11 2AQ
T: (01509) 211120
F: (01509) 211121
E: charnwoodlodge@charwat.freeserve.co.uk
I: www.morningtonweb.com/charnwood

Elegant Victorian licensed hotel in pretty gardens with private parking. Peaceful yet close to town centre, steam railway and university. Spacious, comfortable interior with very attractive en suite rooms including a 4-poster suite. Seven ground floor rooms, one with disabled facilities. Guests' lounge, bar. Warm, friendly service assured.

Bedrooms: 10 double, 1 single, 3 family
Bathrooms: 14 en suite

Evening meal available
CC: Delta, Diners, Mastercard, Switch, Visa

B&B per person per night:
S £30.00–£45.00
D £23.50–£30.00

HB per person per night:
DY £37.50–£41.50

OPEN All Year except Christmas

DEMONTFORT HOTEL
88 Leicester Road, Loughborough
LE11 2AQ
T: (01509) 216061
F: (01509) 233667
E: thedemontforthotel@amserve.com
I: www.thedemontforthotel.co.uk

Bedrooms: 4 double, 1 twin, 1 single, 3 family
Bathrooms: 7 en suite

Evening meal available
CC: Amex, Delta, Diners, Mastercard, Switch, Visa

B&B per person per night:
S £30.00–£40.00
D £22.50–£25.00

HB per person per night:
DY Min £37.00

OPEN All Year

Family-run hotel in Victorian house, with beautifully decorated rooms and warm, friendly atmosphere. Close to town centre, Steam Trust, Bell Foundry, university.

FOREST RISE HOTEL
55-57 Forest Road, Loughborough
LE11 3NW
T: (01509) 215928
F: (01509) 210506

Family-run establishment, friendly personal service, excellent standards throughout. Short walking distance to the town centre, university. Easy access to M1, M42, airport, Donington Park, Prestwold and Beaumanour Halls. Ample secure car parking, bar, a la carte menu and night porter. En suite bedrooms including executive, bridal, family and 4-poster rooms. All prices include full English breakfast.

Bedrooms: 11 double, 1 twin, 8 single, 3 family
Bathrooms: 19 en suite

Evening meal available
CC: Delta, Diners, Mastercard, Switch, Visa

Stay 7 consecutive nights and you only pay for 6 nights (not including weekend prices).

B&B per person per night:
S £25.00–£60.00
D £17.50–£42.50

HB per person per night:
DY £40.00–£80.00

OPEN All Year except Christmas

MAP REFERENCES
Map references apply to the colour maps at the front of this guide.

LOUGHBOROUGH continued

◆◆◆◆

THE MOUNTSORREL HOTEL
217 Loughborough Road, Mountsorrel, Loughborough LE12 7AR
T: (01509) 412627
F: (01509) 416105
E: info@mountsorrelhotel.co.uk
I: www.mountsorrelhotel.co.uk

Bedrooms: 9 double, 3 single, 2 family
Bathrooms: 14 en suite

Evening meal available
CC: Delta, Mastercard, Switch, Visa

B&B per person per night:
S £35.00–£50.00
D £22.50–£32.50

HB per person per night:
DY £35.00–£50.00

OPEN All Year

A friendly, family-run hotel in secluded grounds midway between Leicester and Loughborough. The Great Central Railway is on the doorstep. Ample car parking in private drive.

P

LUDLOW, Shropshire Map ref 4A3 *Tourist Information Centre Tel: (01584) 875053*

◆◆◆◆◆
Gold Award

BROMLEY COURT B&B
73 Lower Broad Street, Ludlow SY8 1PH
T: 0845 0656 192
E: phil@ross-b-and-b-ludlow.co.uk
I: www.ross-b-and-b-ludlow.co.uk

B&B per person per night:
S £85.00–£105.00
D £45.00–£55.00

OPEN All Year

Tudor cottages of great charm, in old Ludlow town. Each cottage forms a delightful, individually furnished suite – for total privacy & relaxation. Within walking distance of everything that is anything in Ludlow; including the Michelins! Come, therefore, to Ludlow to eat like lords and to Bromley Court to stay like them!

Bedrooms: 3 suites

CC: Delta, Mastercard, Switch, Visa

No special offers – just very reasonable rack rates!

P

◆◆◆

BULL HOTEL
14 The Bull Ring, Ludlow SY8 1AD
T: (01584) 873611
F: (01584) 873666
E: info@bull-ludlow.co.uk
I: www.bull-ludlow.co.uk

Bedrooms: 1 double, 2 twin, 1 family
Bathrooms: 4 en suite

CC: Amex, Delta, Mastercard, Visa

B&B per person per night:
S £32.50–£50.00
D £25.00

OPEN All Year except Christmas

Situated in town centre. Oldest pub in Ludlow, earliest mention c1343. Was known as Peter of Proctor's House and probably dates back to c1199.

P

◆◆◆

CECIL GUEST HOUSE
Sheet Road, Ludlow SY8 1LR
T: (01584) 872442
F: (01584) 872442

Bedrooms: 3 double, 3 twin, 2 single, 1 family
Bathrooms: 7 en suite

Evening meal available
CC: Delta, Mastercard, Visa

B&B per person per night:
S £21.00–£38.00
D £27.00–£30.00

HB per person per night:
DY £38.50–£55.50

OPEN All Year

Attractive guesthouse 15 minutes' walk from town centre and station. Freshly cooked food from local produce. Residents' bar and lounge. Off-street parking.

P

◆◆◆◆

EARNSTREY HILL HOUSE
Abdon, Craven Arms SY7 9HU
T: (01746) 712579
F: (01746) 712631

Bedrooms: 1 double, 2 twin
Bathrooms: 1 en suite

Evening meal available

B&B per person per night:
S £30.00
D £25.00

HB per person per night:
DY £43.50–£48.50

OPEN All Year except Christmas

Comfortable light-stone and brick house built 12 years ago. On site of farm cottage, 1200 feet up Brown Clee Hill. Superb views. Warm welcome.

P

QUALITY ASSURANCE SCHEME
Diamond ratings and awards are explained at the back of this guide.

LUDLOW continued

◆◆◆

ELM LODGE B&B
Fishmore, Ludlow SY8 3DP
T: (01584) 877394
F: (01584) 877397
E: apartments@sjweaver.fsnet.co.uk
I: www.ludlow.org.uk/elmlodge

Bedrooms: 2 double
Bathrooms: 2 en suite

CC: Delta, Mastercard, Switch, Visa

Converted Georgian coach house on outskirts of town. Overlooks own golf course. Views to Ludlow and Welsh Borders. Short breaks available. Self-catering apartments also available.

10

B&B per person per night:
S Max £35.00
D Max £25.00

◆◆◆◆

MULBERRY HOUSE

10 Corve Street, Ludlow SY8 1DA
T: (01584) 876765
F: (01584) 879871
E: bookings@tencorvestreet.co.uk
I: www.tencorvestreet.co.uk

Mulberry House is an elegant, Grade II Listed, Georgian townhouse, dating back to about 1800, which has recently been refurbished. Centrally located and within easy walking distance of all three of Ludlow's Michelin-starred restaurants. We offer three comfortable bedrooms and full English breakfast using fresh, local produce.

Bedrooms: 3 double
Bathrooms: 3 en suite

B&B per person per night:
S £55.00–£60.00
D £40.00

OPEN All Year except Christmas

◆◆◆◆

THE WHEATSHEAF INN
Lower Broad Street, Ludlow
SY8 1PQ
T: (01584) 872980
F: (01584) 877990
E: karen.wheatsheaf@tinyworld.co.uk

Bedrooms: 4 double, 1 twin
Bathrooms: 5 en suite

Evening meal available
CC: Delta, Mastercard, Switch, Visa

Family-run, mid-17thC beamed inn, 100 yards from the town centre, nestling under Ludlow's historic 13thC Broad Gate, the last remaining of seven town gates.

B&B per person per night:
S £30.00–£50.00
D £22.50–£25.00

OPEN All Year

LYDDINGTON, Rutland Map ref 4C3

◆◆◆◆

LYDBROOKE
2 Colley Rise, Lyddington, Oakham
LE15 9LL
T: (01572) 821471
F: (01572) 821471
E: lydbrookebb@hotmail.com

Bedrooms: 1 double, 1 twin, 1 single
Bathrooms: 3 en suite

En suite accommodation and excellent breakfasts offered in the peaceful setting of comfortable, detached home in picturesque, conservation village of Lyddington. Ideal base for touring/sightseeing break.

B&B per person per night:
S Min £27.50
D Min £25.00

OPEN All Year except Christmas

MADLEY, Herefordshire Map ref 2A1

◆◆◆◆

SHENMORE COTTAGE BED AND BREAKFAST
Shenmore Cottage,
Upper Shenmore, Madley, Hereford
HR2 9NX
T: (01981) 250507
E: shenmorecottage@aol.com
I: www.smoothhound.co.uk/hotels/shenmore.html

Bedrooms: 1 double, 1 twin
Bathrooms: 2 en suite

Evening meal available

Country cottage on edge of Golden Valley. Beautiful views, peace and quiet. Good home cooking using local produce. Family home. A warm welcome awaits you.

B&B per person per night:
S £25.00
D £25.00

HB per person per night:
DY Max £40.00

OPEN All Year except Christmas

MALVERN, Worcestershire Map ref 2B1 *Tourist Information Centre Tel: (01684) 892289*

Silver Award

HIDELOW HOUSE

Acton Green, Acton Beauchamp, Malvern WR6 5AH
T: (01886) 884547
F: (01886) 884658
E: stay@hidelow.co.uk
I: www.hidelow.co.uk

Small country house amongst peaceful pastureland, central for many places of historical interest, walking and golf. En suite rooms, magnificent residents' lounge with grand piano and sun-terrace overlooking extensive, landscaped gardens, fish-pool, waterfall and stunning views across unspoilt countryside. Breakfasts and home-cooked evening meals using local produce.

Bedrooms: 2 double, 1 suite
Bathrooms: 2 en suite

Evening meal available
CC: Delta, Mastercard, Switch, Visa

For special occasions – birthdays and anniversaries – champagne and roses and breakfast in bed. 4-poster suite available.

B&B per person per night:
S Min £34.95
D £29.95–£39.95

HB per person per night:
DY £46.90–£56.90

OPEN All Year

MARKET HARBOROUGH, Leicestershire Map ref 4C3 *Tourist Information Centre Tel: (01858) 821270*

◆◆◆◆

HUNTERS LODGE

By Foxton Locks, Gumley, Market Harborough LE16 7RT
T: (0116) 2793744
F: (0116) 2793855
E: info@hunterslodgefoxton.co.uk
I: www.hunterslodgefoxton.co.uk

Bedrooms: 1 double, 1 family
Bathrooms: 2 en suite

CC: Delta, Mastercard, Switch, Visa

Attractive bungalow set in open countryside a short walk from Foxton Locks, convenient for many local attractions. Comfortable en suite rooms, separate dining/sitting room and patio.

B&B per person per night:
S Min £30.00
D Min £24.50

OPEN All Year except Christmas

MATLOCK, Derbyshire Map ref 4B2 *Tourist Information Centre Tel: (01629) 583388*

◆◆◆◆ Silver Award

BANK HOUSE

12 Snitterton Road, Matlock DE4 3LZ
T: (01629) 56101
E: jennyderbydales@hotmail.com

Bedrooms: 1 double, 1 twin
Bathrooms: 1 en suite, 1 private

A warm welcome awaits you at our 17thC beamed cottage. Accommodation includes converted stable. Conveniently located for walking, visitor attractions and public transport links.

B&B per person per night:
S £30.00–£35.00
D £23.00–£30.00

OPEN All Year except Christmas

◆◆◆

HOME FARM

Ible, Grange Mill, Matlock DE4 4HS
T: (01629) 650349

Bedrooms: 1 double, 1 twin
Bathrooms: 2 en suite

Evening meal available

A retired farm, but still a few animals. Plenty of walks and places to visit, and a warm welcome to all.

B&B per person per night:
S £20.00–£25.00
D £18.00–£20.00

HB per person per night:
DY £25.00–£27.00

OPEN All Year except Christmas

CREDIT CARD BOOKINGS If you book by telephone and are asked for your credit card number it is advisable to check the proprietor's policy should you cancel your reservation.

MATLOCK continued

Silver Award

SHERIFF LODGE

51 Dimple Road, Matlock DE4 3JX
T: (01629) 760760
F: (01629) 760860
E: info@sherifflodge.co.uk
I: www.sherifflodge.co.uk

Graceful, stone-built house dating in part from the 17thC, providing quality accommodation with every modern provision for our discerning guests. 'Much more than a bed and breakfast'.

Bedrooms: 2 double, 2 twin
Bathrooms: 4 en suite

CC: Amex, Delta, Mastercard, Switch, Visa

B&B per person per night:
S £38.00–£41.00
D £28.50–£31.00

HB per person per night:
DY £43.50–£46.00

OPEN All Year except Christmas

♦♦♦♦

TOWN HEAD FARMHOUSE

70 High Street, Bonsall, Matlock DE4 2AR
T: (01629) 823762

Bedrooms: 4 double, 2 twin
Bathrooms: 6 en suite

In a lovely setting, Town Head is an 18thC farmhouse, now converted to provide comfortable, friendly accommodation. Eat well, sleep well and enjoy beautiful Derbyshire.

B&B per person per night:
S £26.00–£32.00
D £25.00–£28.00

OPEN All Year

MATLOCK BATH, Derbyshire Map ref 4B2

♦♦♦

ASHDALE

92 North Parade, Matlock Bath, Matlock DE4 3NS
T: (01629) 57826
E: ashdale@matlockbath.fsnet.co.uk
I: www.ashdaleguesthouse.co.uk

Bedrooms: 1 double, 1 twin, 2 family
Bathrooms: 4 en suite

CC: Amex, Delta, Diners, Mastercard, Switch, Visa

A Grade II Listed Georgian villa situated in the centre of Matlock Bath. Large comfortable rooms, level walking to local amenities and station.

B&B per person per night:
S £25.00–£40.00
D £22.50–£25.00

OPEN All Year

MEDBOURNE, Leicestershire Map ref 4C3

Silver Award

HOMESTEAD HOUSE

5 Ashley Road, Medbourne, Market Harborough LE16 8DL
T: (01858) 565724
F: (01858) 565324
E: june@homesteadhouse.co.uk
I: www.homesteadhouse.co.uk

In an elevated position overlooking the Welland Valley on the outskirts of Medbourne, a picturesque village dating back to Roman times. Surrounded by open countryside and within easy reach of many places of interest. Three tastefully decorated bedrooms with rural views. A warm welcome awaits you.

Bedrooms: 3 twin
Bathrooms: 3 en suite

CC: Mastercard, Switch, Visa

B&B per person per night:
S Min £27.00
D Min £22.50

OPEN All Year

MERIDEN, West Midlands Map ref 4B3

BONNIFINGLAS GUEST HOUSE

3 Berkswell Road, Meriden, Coventry CV7 7LB
T: (01676) 523193
F: (01676) 523193

Bedrooms: 1 double, 4 twin, 2 single, 1 family
Bathrooms: 8 en suite

Country house, all rooms en suite with TV. Several pubs and restaurants within walking distance. Fire certificate. Large, off-road car park. Five minutes NEC.

B&B per person per night:
S £30.00
D Max £22.50

OPEN All Year except Christmas

MIDDLETON, Northamptonshire Map ref 4C3

♦♦♦

VALLEY VIEW

3 Camsdale Walk, Middleton,
Market Harborough LE16 8YR
T: (01536) 770874

Bedrooms: 2 double

Elevated, stone-built house with panoramic views of the Welland Valley. Within easy distance of Market Harborough, Corby and Rockingham raceway.

B&B per person per night:
S £20.00–£22.00
D £20.00–£22.00

OPEN All Year

MITCHELDEAN, Gloucestershire Map ref 2B1

Silver Award

GUNN MILL HOUSE

Lower Spout Lane, Mitcheldean GL17 0EA
T: (01594) 827577
F: (01594) 827577
E: info@gunnmillhouse.co.uk
I: www.gunnmillhouse.co.uk

David and Rosie Lucas invite you to share the beautiful setting and tranquillity of their Georgian home in the Royal Forest of Dean. Relax in the luxury of large, en suite bedrooms (including suites and 4-poster) and dine in the gallery by a roaring log fire.

Bedrooms: 3 double, 1 twin, 1 family, 3 suites
Bathrooms: 5 en suite

Evening meal available
CC: Amex, Delta, Mastercard, Switch, Visa

B&B per person per night:
S £30.00–£45.00
D £25.00–£40.00

HB per person per night:
DY £40.75–£69.50

OPEN All Year

MORETON-IN-MARSH, Gloucestershire Map ref 2B1

THE BELL INN

High Street, Moreton-in-Marsh GL56 0AF
T: (01608) 651688
F: (01608) 652195
E: keith.pendry@virgin.net
I: www.bellinncotswold.com

Traditional Cotswold coaching inn with en suite rooms and one large family suite, all converted from original 16thC barn and stables. Quality homemade food, vegetarian and fish menu, much of which is locally sourced. Six 'cask marque' real ales and a delightful mix of local and tourist trade.

Bedrooms: 1 double, 1 twin, 3 family
Bathrooms: 5 en suite

Evening meal available
CC: Amex, Delta, Mastercard, Switch, Visa

Book 3 or 4 nights (Sun-Thu incl) at our special mid-week break tariff – includes 1 evening meal with house wine.

€

B&B per person per night:
S £40.00–£50.00
D £37.50–£45.00

HB per person per night:
DY £50.00–£65.00

OPEN All Year

FOSSEWAY FARM B&B

Stow Road, Moreton-in-Marsh
GL56 0DS
T: (01608) 650503

Bedrooms: 3 double, 1 family
Bathrooms: 4 en suite

CC: Delta, Mastercard, Visa

Fosseway Farm is just a five-minute walk into Moreton-in-Marsh town. All rooms en suite with TV, hairdryer and refreshments. Camping facilities.

14

B&B per person per night:
S £30.00–£35.00
D £22.50–£27.00

OPEN All Year except Christmas

ACCESSIBILITY

Look for the symbols which indicate National Accessible Scheme standards for hearing and visually impaired guests in addition to standards for guests with mobility impairment. You can find an index of all scheme participants at the back of this guide.

MORETON-IN-MARSH continued

NEIGHBROOK MANOR

Near Aston Magna, Moreton-in-Marsh GL56 9QP
T: (01386) 593232
F: (01386) 593500
E: info@neighbrookmanor.com
I: www.neighbrookmanor.com

Neighbrook was originally a church on the site of an extinct medieval village mentioned in the Domesday Book in 1086. It was converted to a manor in 1610 and is set in 37 acres. The gardens are glorious with a trout lake and wonderful views.

Bedrooms: 1 double, 1 twin, 1 single
Bathrooms: 2 en suite, 1 private

CC: Mastercard, Switch, Visa

B&B per person per night:
S Min £48.00
D Min £42.50

OPEN All Year except Christmas

♦♦♦

NEW FARM

Dorn, Moreton-in-Marsh GL56 9NS
T: (01608) 650782
F: (01608) 652704
E: cath.righton@amserve.net
I: www.smoothhound.co.uk/hotels/newfa.html

Guests can enjoy first-class accommodation at very competitive terms in this old farmhouse. Beautiful double 4-poster bed and very pretty twin room. All rooms spacious with colour TV, coffee/tea, private facilities and furnished with antiques. Dining room has large, impressive fireplace. Breakfast served with hot, crispy bread.

Bedrooms: 2 double, 1 twin
Bathrooms: 2 en suite, 1 private

B&B per person per night:
D £21.00–£25.00

OPEN All Year

♦♦♦

OLD FARM

Dorn, Moreton-in-Marsh GL56 9NS
T: (01608) 650394
F: (01608) 651700
E: info@oldfarmdorn.co.uk
I: www.oldfarm.co.uk

Enjoy the delights of a 15thC farmhouse on a 280-acre mixed farm surrounded by beautiful Cotswold countryside. Spacious, en suite double and twin bedrooms including 4-poster. Croquet on lawn. Children welcome (cot/extra beds available). Peaceful setting for relaxing break, ideal base for visiting Cotswolds/Stratford and only one mile from Moreton.

Bedrooms: 1 double, 1 twin, 1 family
Bathrooms: 3 en suite

Evening meal available

Discounts available for stays of 3 nights or more.

B&B per person per night:
S £30.00–£45.00
D £23.00–£28.00

OPEN All Year except Christmas

♦♦♦♦

TREETOPS

London Road, Moreton-in-Marsh GL56 0HE
T: (01608) 651036
F: (01608) 651036
E: treetops1@talk21.com

Bedrooms: 5 double, 1 family
Bathrooms: 6 en suite

CC: Amex, Delta, Mastercard, Switch, Visa

Family guesthouse on the A44, set in 0.5 acres of secluded gardens. Five minutes' walk from the village centre.

B&B per person per night:
S £30.00–£35.00
D £22.50–£25.00

OPEN All Year except Christmas

MUCH WENLOCK, Shropshire Map ref 4A3

THE LONGVILLE ARMS

Longville in the Dale,
Much Wenlock TF13 6DT
T: (01694) 771206
F: (01694) 771742
E: longvillearms@aol.com

Bedrooms: 2 double, 1 single, 2 family
Bathrooms: 5 en suite

Evening meal available
CC: Amex, Delta, Mastercard, Switch, Visa

B&B per person per night:
S £30.00
D £24.00–£30.00

OPEN All Year

The main building dates back to 1726 and inside are all original exposed beams. The bedrooms are converted from an old stable.

P

NAUNTON, Gloucestershire Map ref 2B1

FOX HILL

Old Stow Road, Naunton,
Cheltenham GL54 5RL
T: (01451) 850496
F: (01451) 850602

Bedrooms: 2 double, 1 family
Bathrooms: 3 en suite

B&B per person per night:
S £30.00–£35.00
D £22.50–£25.00

OPEN All Year

This rural idyll in the high Cotswolds offers bed and breakfast in a sympathetically converted 17thC pub. All facilities, pets welcome.

5 P

NETTLEHAM, Lincolnshire Map ref 4C2

THE OLD VICARAGE

East Street, Nettleham, Lincoln LN2 2SL
T: (01522) 750819
F: (01522) 750819
E: susan@oldvic.net

B&B per person per night:
S £30.00
D £25.00

OPEN All Year except Christmas

Welcome to our Listed Georgian farmhouse near the centre of an attractive village with traditional village green and beck. A warm welcome, tastefully furnished rooms and excellent location make us an ideal base when visiting historic Lincoln and surrounding counties.

Bedrooms: 1 double, 1 twin
Bathrooms: 1 en suite, 1 private

15 P

NEWARK, Nottinghamshire Map ref 4C2 *Tourist Information Centre Tel: (01636) 655765*

THE BOOT AND SHOE INN

Main Street, Flintham, Newark NG23 5LA
T: (01636) 525246
E: bootshoe@flintham1234.fsbusiness.co.uk
I: www.bootandshoe.net

B&B per person per night:
S £35.00
D £25.00

OPEN All Year

A 17thC village pub recently renovated to a high standard. All rooms en suite. Situated in an unspoilt conservation area at the edge of the Vale of Belvoir, six miles from Newark. Easy access off A46 to Nottingham, Leicester and Lincoln.

Bedrooms: 2 double, 1 twin, 1 single, 1 family
Bathrooms: 5 en suite

Evening meal available
CC: Delta, Mastercard, Switch, Visa

P

QUALITY ASSURANCE SCHEME

Diamond ratings and awards were correct at the time of going to press but are subject to change. Please check at the time of booking.

NEWPORT, Shropshire Map ref 4A3

♦♦♦♦ Silver Award

LANE END FARM

Chester Road, Chetwynd, Newport
TF10 8BN
T: (01952) 550337
F: (01952) 550337
E: jan.park@bushinternet.com
I: www.virtual-shropshire.co.uk/lef

Bedrooms: 3 double
Bathrooms: 2 en suite, 1 private

Evening meal available

Delightful period farmhouse in lovely countryside, on A41 near Newport. Ideal for business/leisure, with good local walks. Reductions for three nights or more.

P €

B&B per person per night:
S £25.00–£30.00
D £22.50

HB per person per night:
DY £34.50–£42.00

OPEN All Year

NORTH SOMERCOTES, Lincolnshire Map ref 4D2

♦♦

PIGEON COTTAGE BED & BREAKFAST & LLA SUMMER CAMPS

Conisholme Road,
North Somercotes, Louth LN11 7PS
T: (01507) 359063
F: (01507) 359063
E: lla.hill@ukgateway.net
I: www.llalincs.co.uk

Bedrooms: 1 double, 1 twin, 1 single, 2 family
Bathrooms: 5 en suite

Evening meal available

Bed and breakfast establishment with on-site, coarse-fishing lake and craft centre. Also providing child care sessions for over fours.

P

B&B per person per night:
S £22.00
D £20.00

OPEN All Year except Christmas

NORTHAMPTON, Northamptonshire Map ref 2C1 *Tourist Information Centre Tel: (01604) 622677*

♦♦

AARANDALE REGENT HOTEL AND GUESTHOUSE

6-8 Royal Terrace,
Barrack Road (A508), Northampton
NN1 3RF
T: (01604) 631096
F: (01604) 621035
E: info@aarandale.co.uk
I: www.aarandale.co.uk

Bedrooms: 12 double, 3 single, 4 family
Bathrooms: 5 en suite

Evening meal available
CC: Delta, Mastercard, Switch, Visa

Small and cosy, family-run hotel/guesthouse within easy walking distance of town centre, bus and train stations.

P

B&B per person per night:
S £32.00–£40.00
D £31.00–£28.00

HB per person per night:
DY £25.00–£45.00

OPEN All Year except Christmas

♦♦♦♦

HASELBECH HOUSE FARM

Haselbech Hill, Haselbech, Northampton
NN6 9LL
T: (01604) 686266
F: (01604) 686266
E: lesueur@haselbech.freeserve.co.uk
I: www.haselbechhousefarm.co.uk

Comfortable, elegantly decorated, friendly family home surrounded by very beautiful countryside. Ideal for family walking, cycling, riding and peace and quiet. Within 10 minutes of stately homes, gardens and sporting venues. Character villages and pubs abound.

Bedrooms: 1 double, 1 twin

Evening meal available

Weekend breaks: separate self-catering bedsit, £125 for 2 nights. Weekly rates available on request.

8 P €

B&B per person per night:
S Min £40.00
D Min £35.00

OPEN All Year except Christmas

AT-A-GLANCE SYMBOLS

Symbols at the end of each accommodation entry give useful information about services and facilities. A key to symbols can be found inside the back cover flap. Keep this open for easy reference.

NORTHLEACH, Gloucestershire Map ref 2B1

◆◆◆◆ Silver Award

NORTHFIELD BED AND BREAKFAST

Cirencester Road (A429), Northleach, Cheltenham GL54 3JL
T: (01451) 860427
F: (01451) 860427
E: nrthfield0@aol.com
I: www.northfieldbandb.co.uk

Detached family house with large gardens and home-grown produce. Evening meals available. Excellent centre for visiting the Cotswolds. A warm welcome awaits you.

Bedrooms: 2 double, 1 family
Bathrooms: 3 en suite

Evening meal available
CC: Amex, Delta, Mastercard, Switch, Visa

B&B per person per night:
S £35.00–£50.00
D £25.00–£29.00

OPEN All Year except Christmas

NOTTINGHAM, Nottinghamshire Map ref 4C2 *Tourist Information Centre Tel: (0115) 915 5330*

◆◆◆

THE GALLERY HOTEL

8-10 Radcliffe Road, West Bridgford, Nottingham NG2 5FW
T: (0115) 9813651
F: (0115) 9813732
I: www.yell.co.uk/sites/galleryhotel/

Bedrooms: 9 double, 3 single, 4 family
Bathrooms: 13 en suite

CC: Delta, Mastercard, Switch, Visa

B&B per person per night:
S £30.00–£36.00
D £25.00–£24.50

OPEN All Year

This hotel is near to Trent Bridge cricket ground, Nottingham Forest football ground and the city centre. Close to Holme Pierrepont Water Sports Centre.

◆◆◆◆◆ Gold Award

GREENWOOD LODGE CITY GUESTHOUSE

Third Avenue, Sherwood Rise, Nottingham NG7 6JH
T: (0115) 9621206
F: (0115) 9621206
E: pdouglas71@aol.com
I: www.greenwoodlodgecityguesthouse.co.uk

Bedrooms: 4 double, 1 twin, 1 single
Bathrooms: 6 en suite

Evening meal available
CC: Delta, Mastercard, Switch, Visa

B&B per person per night:
S £43.00–£55.00
D £35.00–£45.00

HB per person per night:
DY £50.00–£70.00

OPEN All Year

Warm and welcoming Victorian house, one mile from city centre. All rooms en suite with tea/coffee facilities, trouser press, and TV. Magnificent dining conservatory in elegant gardens.

10

NUNEATON, Warwickshire Map ref 4B3 *Tourist Information Centre Tel: (024) 7634 7006*

◆◆◆◆◆ Gold Award

LEATHERMILL GRANGE

Leathermill Lane, Caldecote, Nuneaton CV10 0RX
T: (01827) 714637
F: (01827) 716422
E: davidcodd@leathermillgrange.co.uk
I: www.leathermillgrange.co.uk

Beautifully refurbished, 19thC, Victorian farmhouse set in five acres of ground with landscaped gardens and lake, surrounded by farmland. Spacious and elegant interior with high-quality decor and furnishing. Bedrooms, including one 4-poster, have en suite shower rooms. Home cooking and attention to detail is our speciality. A non-smoking house.

Bedrooms: 2 double, 1 twin
Bathrooms: 3 en suite

Evening meal available
CC: Delta, Mastercard, Switch, Visa

B&B per person per night:
S £60.00–£70.00
D £40.00–£45.00

OPEN All Year except Christmas

GOLD & SILVER AWARDS

These exclusive VisitBritain awards are given to establishments achieving the highest levels of quality and service. Further information can be found at the front of the guide. An index to all accommodation achieving these awards are at the back of this guide.

NUNEATON continued

LA TAVOLA CALDA
70 Midland Road, Abbey Green, Nuneaton CV11 5DY
T: (024) 76383195
F: (024) 76381816
I: http://tavolacalda.bravepages.com

Bedrooms: 5 twin, 1 single, 2 family
Bathrooms: 8 en suite

Evening meal available
CC: Amex, Delta, Diners, Mastercard, Switch, Visa

B&B per person per night:
S £25.00–£30.00
D £20.00

HB per person per night:
DY £38.00–£60.00

OPEN All Year

Family-run Italian restaurant and hotel.

ORLETON, Herefordshire Map ref 4A3

Silver Award

ROSECROFT

Orleton, Ludlow SY8 4HN
T: (01568) 780565
F: (01568) 780565
E: gailanddavid@rosecroftorleton.freeserve.co.uk
I: www.stmem.com/rosecroft

B&B per person per night:
S £40.00–£45.00
D £30.00–£32.50

OPEN All Year

Rosecroft is an 18thC house in the middle of the picturesque village of Orleton. We offer a relaxed atmosphere and delicious breakfasts. There is a lovely garden to sit in and off-road parking. We are close to several NT and English Heritage properties and many gardens.

Bedrooms: 1 double
Bathrooms: 1 en suite

OXTON, Nottinghamshire Map ref 4C2

FAR BAULKER FARM

Oxton, Southwell NG25 0RQ
T: (01623) 882375
F: (01623) 882375
E: j.esam@virgin.net
I: www.farbaulkerfarm.info

B&B per person per night:
S £20.00–£30.00
D £20.00–£35.00

OPEN All Year

300-acre mixed farm. Attractive farmhouse with pleasant gardens. Situated in peaceful, rural environment in the heart of Sherwood, yet within easy reach of Nottingham, Newark and Mansfield.

Bedrooms: 3 double
Bathrooms: 2 en suite

PAINSWICK, Gloucestershire Map ref 2B1

CARDYNHAM HOUSE
The Cross, Painswick, Stroud GL6 6XX
T: (01452) 814006
F: (01452) 812321
E: info@cardynham.co.uk
I: www.cardynham.co.uk

Bedrooms: 6 double, 3 family
Bathrooms: 8 en suite, 1 private

Evening meal available
CC: Amex, Delta, Mastercard, Switch, Visa

B&B per person per night:
S £47.00–£75.00
D £34.50–£80.00

OPEN All Year

Rooms of great character, each with a different theme and style. All with 4-poster beds and one room with its own heated pool.

PEAK DISTRICT

See under Ashbourne, Bakewell, Buxton, Cressbrook, Grangemill, Hathersage, Hope, Thorpe

CHECK THE MAPS

The colour maps at the front of this guide show all the cities, towns and villages for which you will find accommodation entries.
Refer to the town index to find the page on which they are listed.

PERSHORE, Worcestershire Map ref 2B1

♦♦♦♦ Silver Award

ALDBURY HOUSE

George Lane, Wyre Piddle, Pershore
WR10 2HX
T: (01386) 553754
F: (01386) 553754
E: aldbury@onetel.net.uk

B&B per person per night:
S £30.00–£35.00
D £22.00–£50.00

OPEN All Year

Charming, spacious, quietly situated family home in a small village near Pershore. En suite rooms, guests' lounge, safe, off-road parking. Use of garden, summerhouse and patio. Friendly welcome assured. Nearby riverside inn serves meals. Ideally situated for visits to Stratford-upon-Avon, Worcester, the Malverns and Cotswolds. French spoken.

Bedrooms: 3 double
Bathrooms: 3 en suite

Reduction for stays of 3 nights or more for full occupancy of a double/twin room.

P €

♦♦♦♦ Silver Award

ARBOUR HOUSE

Main Road, Wyre Piddle, Pershore
WR10 2HU
T: (01386) 555833
F: (01386) 555833
E: lizbrownsdon@hotmail.com
I: www.smoothhound.co.uk/arbourhouse.html

B&B per person per night:
S £30.00–£36.00
D £25.00–£28.00

OPEN All Year

A fine Grade II Listed character home with oak beams, overlooking Bredon Hill and close to the River Avon. Comfortable accommodation and generous breakfasts in a relaxed, friendly atmosphere. Excellent riverside pub opposite. No smoking. Private car park. An ideal base for visiting the Cotswolds, Stratford, Worcester and Malvern.

Bedrooms: 1 double, 2 twin
Bathrooms: 3 en suite

10 P

♦♦♦♦

TIBBITTS FARM
Russell Street, Great Comberton,
Pershore WR10 3DT
T: (01386) 710210
F: (01386) 710210
E: pixiefarr@aol.com

Bedrooms: 2 double
Bathrooms: 1 en suite, 1 private

Evening meal available

B&B per person per night:
S £30.00–£36.00
D £24.00–£30.00

OPEN All Year except Christmas

16thC farmhouse in small picturesque village on the slopes of Bredon Hill. Very quiet and beautiful. Self-catering annexe also available. Good walking country.

P

QUALITY ASSURANCE SCHEME

For an explanation of the quality and facilities represented by the Diamonds please refer to the front of this guide. A more detailed explanation can be found in the information pages at the back.

ROSS-ON-WYE, Herefordshire Map ref 2A1 *Tourist Information Centre Tel: (01989) 562768*

♦♦♦♦ Gold Award

FOREST EDGE

4 Noden Drive, Lea, Ross-on-Wye HR9 7NB
T: (01989) 750682
E: don@wood11.freeserve.co.uk
I: www.wood11.freeserve.co.uk

B&B per person per night:
S £27.00–£39.00
D £25.00–£29.00

OPEN All Year except Christmas

A warm, friendly welcome is assured at our modern home which is located in a quiet, rural, Area of Outstanding Natural Beauty with fine views towards the Royal Forest of Dean. Rooms are furnished and equipped to high standards, and a quality breakfast is served. Good pubs and restaurants nearby.

Bedrooms: 1 double, 1 twin
Bathrooms: 2 en suite

All guests will receive complimentary refreshments in the conservatory on arrival. Only £25pppn when staying 5 nights or more.

14 P

♦♦♦

THE HILL HOUSE

Howle Hill, Ross-on-Wye HR9 5ST
T: (01989) 562033
E: thehillhouse2000@hotmail.com
I: www.thehowlinghillhouse.com

B&B per person per night:
S £25.00–£35.00
D £22.00–£25.00

HB per person per night:
DY £29.00–£35.00

OPEN All Year

Something different: secluded, private, woodland setting on Wye Valley walk. Spectacular views, close to Ross and the Forest of Dean. Local organic food, friendly ghosts, sauna. Amazing rooms including 'the Dryad suite' with 7-foot 4-poster bed and sheepskin rugs in front of woodburning stove. Perfect for naughty and good weekends. Relax!

Bedrooms: 2 double, 1 family
Bathrooms: 3 en suite

Evening meal available
CC: Delta, Mastercard, Switch, Visa

Special-interest themed weekends, all-inclusive prices, long list including: witchcraft, painting, poetry, storytelling, canoeing, nature walks, poker school, stress management.

P €

RUGBY, Warwickshire Map ref 4C3 *Tourist Information Centre Tel: (01788) 534970*

♦♦♦♦

CARLTON HOTEL

130 Railway Terrace, Rugby CV21 3HE
T: (01788) 560211
F: (01788) 563939
I: www.thecarltonrugby.co.uk

Bedrooms: 9 double, 8 single
Bathrooms: 17 en suite

Evening meal available
CC: Amex, Delta, Mastercard, Switch, Visa

B&B per person per night:
S £37.00–£49.00
D £23.00–£28.50

HB per person per night:
DY £37.00–£70.00

OPEN All Year

The hotel is family run and has been refurbished to a high standard. It is close to the railway station and the town centre. Home-cooked food, fresh vegetables, homemade sauces and desserts.

P

♦♦♦

WHITE LION INN

Coventry Road, Pailton, Rugby CV23 0QD
T: (01788) 832359
F: (01788) 832359
I: ww.whitelionpailton.co.uk

Bedrooms: 7 twin, 2 family
Bathrooms: 5 en suite

Evening meal available
CC: Delta, Mastercard, Switch, Visa

B&B per person per night:
S £25.00–£35.00
D £22.50–£27.50

HB per person per night:
DY £35.00–£45.00

OPEN All Year

17thC coaching inn, recently refurbished but retaining all old world features. Close to Rugby, Coventry and Stratford. Within four miles of motorways. Home-cooked food served daily.

P

SPECIAL BREAKS

Many establishments offer special promotions and themed breaks. These are highlighted in red. (All such offers are subject to availability.)

RUGELEY, Staffordshire Map ref 4B3

PARK FARM

Hawkesyard, Armitage Lane,
Rugeley WS15 1ED
T: (01889) 583477
F: (01889) 583477

Bedrooms: 2 family
Bathrooms: 2 en suite

40-acre livestock farm. While convenient for towns and attractions in the area, Park Farm is quietly tucked away in scenic hills.

B&B per person per night:
S £20.00–£24.00
D £20.00–£22.50

OPEN All Year except Christmas

SHERWOOD FOREST

See under Newark, Oxton, Southwell

SHIFNAL, Shropshire Map ref 4A3

ODFELLOWS-THE WINE BAR

Market Place, Shifnal TF11 9AU
T: (01952) 461517
F: (01952) 463855
E: odfellows@odley.co.uk

Comfortable, well-appointed bedrooms upstairs, with a lively, fun-filled bar/restaurant downstairs. Modern British food delights, complemented by an intelligently assembled wine list and draught-beer range. Whilst served caddishly late, the cooked breakfast is well worth the wait, whilst the early birds are amply served the continental.

Bedrooms: 7 double
Bathrooms: 7 en suite

Evening meal available
CC: Amex, Delta, Mastercard, Switch, Visa

B&B per person per night:
S £40.00–£50.00
D £26.25–£30.00

HB per person per night:
DY £36.25–£50.00

OPEN All Year except Christmas

SHREWSBURY, Shropshire Map ref 4A3 *Tourist Information Centre Tel: (01743) 281200*

ABBEY COURT HOUSE

134 Abbey Foregate, Shrewsbury SY2 6AU
T: (01743) 364416
F: (01743) 358559
E: info@abbeycourt.org
I: www.abbeycourt.org

Quality accommodation in a Grade II Listed building. Close to town centre and abbey. We have off-road parking, and a regular bus service is available outside the front door. Very comfortable rooms, all with hospitality tray, teletext TV, direct-dial telephone. Ground floor rooms available. Good choice of breakfasts, including vegetarian.

Bedrooms: 6 double, 2 single, 2 family
Bathrooms: 4 en suite

CC: Amex, Delta, Mastercard, Switch, Visa

Discounted rates available for longer stays.

B&B per person per night:
S £30.00–£35.00
D £23.00–£25.00

OPEN All Year except Christmas

USE YOUR *i*s

There are more than 550 Tourist Information Centres throughout England offering friendly help with accommodation and holiday ideas as well as suggestions of places to visit and things to do. You'll find TIC addresses in the local Phone Book.

SHREWSBURY continued

ANTON GUEST HOUSE

1 Canon Street, Monkmoor, Shrewsbury SY2 5HG
T: (01743) 359275
F: (01743) 270168
E: clairealford@hotmail.com
I: www.antonhouse.supanet.com

Graham and Claire welcome you to this imposing, corner-positioned Victorian house within easy walking distance of the town centre and Shrewsbury Abbey. Comfortable, attractive bedrooms and a hearty English breakfast await you.

Bedrooms: 2 double, 1 twin
Bathrooms: 2 en suite, 1 private

Special breaks: 3 days for the price of 2, Oct-Feb.

P

B&B per person per night:
D £22.50–£27.50

OPEN All Year except Christmas

SKEGNESS, Lincolnshire Map ref 4D2 *Tourist Information Centre Tel: (01754) 764821/899887*

Rating Applied For

GROSVENOR HOUSE HOTEL

North Parade, Skegness PE25 2TE
T: (01754) 763376
F: (01754) 764650

Bedrooms: 11 double, 7 single, 12 family
Bathrooms: 24 en suite

Evening meal available
CC: Amex, Delta, Diners, Mastercard, Visa

A family hotel, well renowned for its friendly atmosphere and service. Situated midway along sea front, near all foreshore attractions, Embassy centre and bowling greens.

P

B&B per person per night:
S £28.00–£36.50
D £28.00–£36.50

HB per person per night:
DY £38.50–£47.00

♦♦♦

MERTON HOTEL

14 Firbeck Avenue, Skegness PE25 3JY
T: (01754) 764423
F: (01754) 766627
I: www.skegness-resort.co.uk/merton

A popular, family-run hotel in a quiet residental area yet only a few minutes' walk from the beach, town centre and all attractions. Excellent English cuisine. Service and cleanliness assured.

Bedrooms: 11 double, 5 single
Bathrooms: 11 en suite, 1 private

Evening meal available
CC: Delta, Mastercard, Switch, Visa

Special breaks in low season: 3 nights for price of 2, Oct-Mar (excl Christmas, New Year and Easter).

P

B&B per person per night:
S £23.00–£26.00
D £23.00–£26.00

HB per person per night:
DY £33.00–£36.00

OPEN All Year

SOLIHULL, West Midlands Map ref 4B3 *Tourist Information Centre Tel: (0121) 704 6130*

♦♦♦♦ Silver Award

ACORN GUEST HOUSE

29 Links Drive, Solihull B91 2DJ
T: (0121) 7055241
E: acorn.wood@btinternet.com

Bedrooms: 1 double, 2 twin, 2 single
Bathrooms: 1 en suite

Comfortable, quiet family home with ample private facilities, overlooking golf course. Parking and easy access to NEC, airport, M42 and Solihull centre.

P €

B&B per person per night:
S £22.00–£30.00
D £25.00–£27.50

OPEN All Year except Christmas

♦♦♦♦

CHELSEA LODGE

48 Meriden Road, Hampton in Arden, Solihull B92 0BT
T: (01675) 442408
F: (01675) 442408
E: chelsealodgebnb@aol.com
I: www.chelsealodgebnb.co.uk

Bedrooms: 3 twin
Bathrooms: 2 en suite, 1 private

Comfortable, detached property with delightful gardens. Walking distance to Hampton in Arden station (direct NEC/Birmingham Airport) and village pubs. Village location, three miles NEC/Solihull.

8 P

B&B per person per night:
S Min £30.00
D £25.00–£27.50

OPEN All Year except Christmas

SOULDERN, Oxfordshire

See South East region for entries

SOUTHWELL, Nottinghamshire Map ref 4C2

ASHDENE

Radley Road, Halam, Southwell NG22 8AH
T: (01636) 812335
E: david@herbert.newsurf.net

B&B per person per night:
S £30.00
D £25.00–£30.00

OPEN All Year

Ashdene is a 16thC Yeoman farmhouse set in extensive gardens which are opened regularly each year in Open Garden Scheme. Ample parking. Guest sitting room with open fire. Children welcome. Ideal centre to explore Southwell Minster, the Dukeries and Lincoln. German and Italian spoken.

Bedrooms: 3 double
Bathrooms: 1 en suite, 1 private

Evening meal available

SPALDING, Lincolnshire Map ref 3A1 *Tourist Information Centre Tel: (01775) 725468*

♦♦♦♦

THE ESCAPE
The Cottage, Lutton Bank, Lutton, Spalding PE12 9LL
T: (01406) 363528
E: traceyneil@lineone.net
I: www.escapetothecottage.co.uk

Bedrooms: 1 double, 1 twin

B&B per person per night:
S Min £20.00
D Min £20.00

OPEN All Year except Christmas

Edwardian house in rural setting, 10 minutes from the Wash. Ideally located for bird-watching, cycling and walking. Courtesy taxi service to local pubs/restaurants.

STAFFORD, Staffordshire Map ref 4B3 *Tourist Information Centre Tel: (01785) 619619*

♦♦♦♦

LITTYWOOD HOUSE

Bradley, Stafford ST18 9DW
T: (01785) 780234
E: suebusby@amserve.com
I: www.littywood.co.uk

B&B per person per night:
S £30.00–£35.00
D £22.50–£25.00

OPEN All Year except Christmas

Littywood is a beautiful, double-moated 14thC manor house, set in its own grounds and surrounded by open countryside. Tastefully furnished with antiques and tapestries throughout. We are easily accessible from the M6 motorway, approximately 15 minutes from jct 13. Ideally situated for Alton Towers, Shugborough Hall, Weston Park and The Potteries. Centrally heated.

Bedrooms: 1 double, 1 family
Bathrooms: 1 en suite, 1 private

Discounts for 3 nights or more.

STAMFORD, Lincolnshire Map ref 3A1 *Tourist Information Centre Tel: (01780) 755611*

♦♦

DOLPHIN GUESTHOUSE
12 East Street, Stamford PE9 1QD
T: (01780) 757515
F: (01780) 757515
E: mikdolphin@mikdolphin.demon.co.uk

Bedrooms: 7 double, 1 family
Bathrooms: 6 en suite

CC: Delta, Mastercard, Visa

B&B per person per night:
S £20.00–£35.00
D £20.00–£30.00

OPEN All Year except Christmas

En suite, hotel-style accommodation. Off-road secure car parking and only 100 yards from the town centre.

CONFIRM YOUR BOOKING
You are advised to confirm your booking in writing.

STAMFORD continued

◆◆◆◆◆ Silver Award

ROCK LODGE
1 Empingham Road, Stamford
PE9 2RH
T: (01780) 481758
F: (01780) 481757
E: rocklodge@innpro.co.uk
I: www.rock-lodge.co.uk

Bedrooms: 2 double, 1 twin, 1 family
Bathrooms: 4 en suite

CC: Delta, Mastercard, Switch, Visa

B&B per person per night:
S £58.00–£90.00
D £34.00–£45.00

OPEN All Year

Family-run Edwardian townhouse. Individually decorated en suite rooms with fridges. Set in walled garden with off-street parking. Five minutes' walk to town centre.

5 P

STANTON-ON-THE-WOLDS, Nottinghamshire Map ref 4C2

◆◆◆

LAUREL FARM
Browns Lane, Stanton-on-the-Wolds, Keyworth, Nottingham
NG12 5BL
T: (0115) 9373488
F: (0115) 9376490
E: laurelfarm@yahoo.com
I: www.s-h-systems.co.uk/laurelfa.html

Bedrooms: 3 double
Bathrooms: 2 en suite, 1 private

CC: Delta, Mastercard, Switch, Visa

B&B per person per night:
D £25.00–£30.00

OPEN All Year except Christmas

Old farmhouse in three acres. Lovely en suite/private rooms with many extras. Only fresh local produce used for breakfast. Non-smokers only. Nearest roads M1, A46, A606.

5 P

STEEPLE ASTON, Oxfordshire

See South East region for entries

STONEHOUSE, Gloucestershire Map ref 2B1

◆◆◆◆◆ Gold Award

THE GREY COTTAGE

Bath Road, Leonard Stanley, Stonehouse
GL10 3LU
T: (01453) 822515
F: (01453) 822515
I: www.greycottage.ik.com

B&B per person per night:
S £45.00–£47.00
D £27.50–£33.50

HB per person per night:
DY £68.00–£70.00

OPEN All Year

Early-Victorian, Cotswold-stone cottage featuring tessellated tiling, stonework and open log fires. Bedrooms include many thoughtful extras to enhance your visit. Comfortable sitting and elegant dining rooms. Cosy ambience. Sumptuous breakfasts imaginatively presented. Impressive dinners served using organic produce. Charming flower garden with distinctive Cedar Wellingtonia and yew hedge planted 1841.

Bedrooms: 1 double, 1 twin, 1 single
Bathrooms: 2 en suite, 1 private

Evening meal available

10 P €

◆◆

MERTON LODGE
8 Ebley Road, Stonehouse GL10 2LQ
T: (01453) 822018

Bedrooms: 3 double
Bathrooms: 1 en suite

B&B per person per night:
S £20.00–£23.00
D £20.00–£23.00

OPEN All Year except Christmas

Former gentleman's residence offering a warm welcome. Non-smoking. Three miles from M5 jct 13, over four roundabouts. Along Ebley Road, under footbridge.

P

MAP REFERENCES The map references refer to the colour maps at the front of this guide. The first figure is the map number; the letter and figure which follow indicate the grid reference on the map.

STOURBRIDGE, West Midlands Map ref 4B3

Beautiful country cottage with lovely garden and swimming pool. Interior professionally decorated throughout. Close to all motorway links. Destinations within easy reach – Symphony Hall, Convention Centre in Birmingham, Black Country Museum, Stourbridge crystal factories, Severn Valley railway. Twenty-five minutes from NEC and Birmingham Airport.

ST. ELIZABETH'S COTTAGE

Woodman Lane, Clent, Stourbridge
DY9 9PX
T: (01562) 883883
F: (01562) 885034
E: st_elizabeth_cot@btconnect.com

Bedrooms: 2 double, 1 twin
Bathrooms: 3 en suite

B&B per person per night:
S £30.00–£32.00
D £29.00–£30.00

OPEN All Year

STOW-ON-THE-WOLD, Gloucestershire Map ref 2B1 *Tourist Information Centre Tel: (01451) 831082*

Traditional farmhouse with spectacular views of Cotswold countryside. Peaceful location one mile from Stow-on-the-Wold. Ideally situated for exploring all Cotswold villages, Cheltenham, Stratford-on-Avon, Blenheim and Warwick. All rooms centrally heated with TV, tea tray and hairdryer. Relaxing guest lounge/dining room. Excellent pub food five minutes' walk.

CORSHAM FIELD FARMHOUSE

Bledington Road, Stow-on-the-Wold, Cheltenham GL54 1JH
T: (01451) 831750
F: (01451) 832247
E: farmhouse@corshamfield.co.uk
I: www.corshamfield.co.uk

Bedrooms: 3 double, 2 twin, 3 family
Bathrooms: 6 en suite

B&B per person per night:
S £25.00–£35.00
D £22.50–£25.00

OPEN All Year except Christmas

♦♦♦♦

A friendly, family-run bed and breakfast in a Listed Cotswold-stone farmhouse on the outskirts of Stow-on-the-Wold. Ideally situated for touring, walking or cycling in the Cotswolds. The town square is only 10 minutes' walk away and we have ample parking for guests.

SOUTH HILL FARMHOUSE

Fosseway, Stow-on-the-Wold, Cheltenham
GL54 1JU
T: (01451) 831888
F: (01451) 832255
E: info@southhill.co.uk
I: www.southhill.co.uk

Bedrooms: 3 double, 1 twin, 1 single, 1 family
Bathrooms: 5 en suite, 1 private

CC: Delta, Mastercard, Switch, Visa

B&B per person per night:
S £38.00
D £26.00

OPEN All Year except Christmas

IMPORTANT NOTE Information on accommodation listed in this guide has been supplied by the proprietors. As changes may occur you are advised to check details at the time of booking.

STRAGGLETHORPE, Lincolnshire Map ref 3A1

♦♦♦♦
Silver Award

STRAGGLETHORPE HALL

Stragglethorpe, Lincoln LN5 0QZ
T: (01400) 272308
F: (01400) 273816
E: stragglethorpe@compuserve.com
I: www.stragglethorpe.com

B&B per person per night:
S £40.00–£60.00
D £45.00

Situated just south of Lincoln, Stragglethorpe is a Grade II Listed Tudor manor set in formal gardens and furnished with antiques. Individually furnished en suites, including two 4-poster rooms, have all modern amenities. Ideal for touring the country or simply stopping over between York and Cambridge off the A1.

Bedrooms: 3 double
Bathrooms: 3 en suite

Meals provided for parties of 5 or more.

P €

STRATFORD-UPON-AVON, Warwickshire Map ref 2B1 *Tourist Information Centre Tel: (01789) 293127*

♦♦♦♦

AVONLEA

47 Shipston Road, Stratford-upon-Avon
CV37 7LN
T: (01789) 205940
F: (01789) 209115
E: avonlea-stratford@lineone.net
I: www.avonlea-stratford.co.uk

B&B per person per night:
S £35.00–£48.00
D £25.00–£36.00

OPEN All Year except Christmas

Stylish Victorian townhouse situated only five minutes' walk from the theatre and town centre. All rooms are en suite and furnished to the highest quality. Our guests are assured of a warm welcome and friendly atmosphere.

Bedrooms: 5 double, 1 twin, 1 single, 1 family
Bathrooms: 7 en suite, 1 private

CC: Mastercard, Switch, Visa

3 nights for the price of 2 from Oct-Mar.

P €

♦♦♦♦

BROADLANDS GUEST HOUSE

23 Evesham Place, Stratford-upon-Avon
CV37 6HT
T: (01789) 299181
F: (01789) 551382
E: broadlands.com@virgin.net
I: www.stratford-upon-avon.co.uk/broadlands.htm

B&B per person per night:
S £30.00–£38.00
D £26.00–£32.00

OPEN All Year except Christmas

Located just five minutes' walk from the centre of the beautiful and historic market town of Stratford-upon-Avon, Broadlands offers an exemplary standard of accommodation. The atmosphere is relaxed and friendly and each of our bedrooms has either en suite or private facilities, colour TV and complimentary refreshment tray.

Bedrooms: 4 double, 2 single
Bathrooms: 5 en suite, 1 private

CC: Delta, Mastercard, Switch, Visa

2 nights for the price of 1, Jan-Mar inclusive.

12 P €

STRATFORD-UPON-AVON continued

♦♦♦♦

FAVIERE

127 Shipston Road, Stratford-upon-Avon CV37 7LW
T: (01789) 293764
F: (01789) 269365
E: reservations@faviere.com
I: www.faviere.com

Bedrooms: 3 double, 2 family, 1 suite
Bathrooms: 5 en suite

A warm, friendly welcome awaits you at this comfortable, family-run guesthouse situated close to the river. A 10-minute walk will take you to the theatre and town centre.

P

B&B per person per night:
S £25.00–£40.00
D £20.00–£30.00

OPEN All Year except Christmas

♦♦♦♦

MELITA PRIVATE HOTEL

37 Shipston Road, Stratford-upon-Avon CV37 7LN
T: (01789) 292432
F: (01789) 204867
E: info@melitahotel.co.uk
I: www.melitahotel.co.uk

Once a Victorian home, the Melita is now a warm and friendly hotel managed by caring proprietors. Accommodation and service are of a high standard, and breakfasts are individually prepared to suit guests' requirements. The Melita is only 400 metres from the theatres and town centre and has free, private, on-site car parking.

Bedrooms: 5 double, 2 twin, 3 single, 2 family
Bathrooms: 10 en suite, 2 private

CC: Amex, Delta, Mastercard, Switch, Visa

Discounts available Nov-Mar 2004 (excl Sat and locally important dates).

P

B&B per person per night:
S £37.00–£49.00
D £27.00–£41.00

OPEN All Year except Christmas

♦♦♦

MOONLIGHT BED & BREAKFAST

144 Alcester Road, Stratford-upon-Avon CV37 9DR
T: (01789) 298213

Bedrooms: 2 double, 1 single, 1 family
Bathrooms: 2 en suite

Small family guesthouse near town centre and station, offering comfortable accommodation at reasonable prices. Tea/coffee-making facilities, colour TV. En suite rooms available.

P €

B&B per person per night:
S £18.00–£20.00
D £18.00–£20.00

OPEN All Year except Christmas

♦♦♦

PARKFIELD

3 Broad Walk, Stratford-upon-Avon CV37 6HS
T: (01789) 293313
F: (01789) 293313
E: parkfield@btinternet.com
I: www.parkfieldbandb.co.uk

Bedrooms: 3 double, 2 twin, 1 single, 1 family
Bathrooms: 6 en suite, 1 private

CC: Mastercard, Visa

Delightful Victorian house. Quiet location, five minutes' walk from theatre and town. Most rooms en suite. Colour TV, tea and coffee facilities, parking. Choice of breakfast, including vegetarian. A non-smoking house.

5 P €

B&B per person per night:
S £28.00
D £24.00–£25.00

OPEN All Year

TOWN INDEX

This can be found at the back of the guide. If you know where you want to stay, the index will give you the page number listing accommodation in your chosen town, city or village.

STRATFORD-UPON-AVON continued

RAVENHURST

2 Broad Walk, Stratford-upon-Avon
CV37 6HS
T: (01789) 292515
E: ravaccom@waverider.co.uk
I: www.stratford-ravenhurst.co.uk

B&B per person per night:
S £30.00–£35.00
D £22.00–£26.00

OPEN All Year except Christmas

Victorian townhouse built in 1865, quiet location, a few minutes' walk from town centre, historical buildings and Royal Shakespeare Theatre. Comfortable home. Breakfasts a speciality. Off-street parking available. All bedrooms en suite, non-smoking. Richard Workman and family offer you a warm welcome and a vast amount of local knowledge. Credit cards welcome.

Bedrooms: 4 double, 1 twin
Bathrooms: 5 en suite

CC: Amex, Delta, Mastercard, Switch, Visa

3 nights for price of 2, Sun-Thu inclusive, Nov-Mar inclusive.

Silver Award

THE WHITE HOUSE

Kings Lane, Bishopton, Stratford-upon-Avon CV37 0RD
T: (01789) 294296
F: (01789) 294411
E: enquiries@stratfordwhitehouse.co.uk
I: www.stratfordwhitehouse.co.uk

Bedrooms: 2 double, 1 twin
Bathrooms: 2 en suite, 1 private

B&B per person per night:
S £40.00–£50.00
D £27.50–£30.00

OPEN All Year except Christmas

Country home built early 1900s, retaining many original features. Mellow pine interior, log fires, antique furnishings. Rural location 1.5 miles north of Stratford-upon-Avon.

STRETTON, Staffordshire Map ref 4B3

Silver Award

DOVECLIFF HALL

Dovecliff Road, Stretton, Burton upon Trent DE13 0DJ
T: (01283) 531818
F: (01283) 516546
E: enquiry@dovecliffhallhotel.co.uk
I: www.dovecliffhallhotel.co.uk

Bedrooms: 13 double, 2 twin, 1 single
Bathrooms: 16 en suite

Evening meal available
CC: Amex, Delta, Mastercard, Switch, Visa

B&B per person per night:
S £65.00–£160.00
D £50.00–£80.00

OPEN All Year

Magnificent Georgian house, with breathtaking views, overlooking the River Dove and set in seven acres of landscaped gardens in open countryside. 0.5 miles from A38.

STROUD, Gloucestershire Map ref 2B1

HILLENVALE

The Plain, Whiteshill, Stroud GL6 6AB
T: (01453) 753441
F: (01453) 753441
E: bobsue@hillenvale.co.uk
I: www.hillenvale.co.uk

B&B per person per night:
S £30.00
D £22.50

OPEN All Year

A warm welcome, comfort and high-quality accommodation is guaranteed in this country house between Bath and Cheltenham on the edge of the Cotswold Way. The conservatory/lounge and gardens have stunning panoramic views. With the M5 and M4 a short distance away, we are in an ideal tourist location.

Bedrooms: 1 double, 2 twin
Bathrooms: 3 en suite

CC: Mastercard, Switch, Visa

Introductory offer: Fri night to Mon morning on selected weekends – only £100 per couple. £70 single for B&B.

STROUD continued

◆◆◆◆ Silver Award

PRETORIA VILLA
Wells Road, Eastcombe, Stroud GL6 7EE
T: (01452) 770435
F: (01452) 770435
E: glynis@gsolomon.freeserve.co.uk

Bedrooms: 1 double, 1 twin, 1 single
Bathrooms: 2 en suite, 1 private

Evening meal available

Cotswold-stone double-fronted detached house, built c1900, with private gardens. In quiet village lane with beautiful views.

B&B per person per night:
S £25.00
D £25.00

HB per person per night:
DY £40.00

OPEN All Year except Christmas

SWADLINCOTE, Derbyshire Map ref 4B3

◆◆◆◆

MANOR FARM

Coton in the Elms, Swadlincote DE12 8EP
T: (01283) 760340
F: (01283) 760340

B&B per person per night:
S £25.00–£35.00
D £25.00–£27.50

OPEN All Year except Christmas

Grade II Listed Georgian farmhouse, traditionally furbished interior with comfortable, spacious rooms, all en suite. Situated in small, attractive village in the heart of the National Forest. Village pub meals available. Well situated for M42, A38, A444. A warm welcome awaits. Open all year except Christmas and New Year.

Bedrooms: 3 double
Bathrooms: 2 en suite, 1 private

TAMWORTH, Staffordshire Map ref 4B3 *Tourist Information Centre Tel: (01827) 709581*

◆◆◆◆ Silver Award

THE CHESTNUTS COUNTRY GUEST HOUSE
Watling Street, Grendon, Atherstone CV9 2PZ
T: (01827) 331355
F: (01827) 896951
E: cclLtd@aol.com
I: www.thechestnutshotel.com

Bedrooms: 2 double, 2 single
Bathrooms: 4 en suite

Evening meal available
CC: Amex, Mastercard, Switch, Visa

Beautiful 100-year-old country cottage with beams and inglenook. Home cooking, fine wine, luxuriously comfortable. Ideal business, special occasion, leisure break. Visit website or call.

B&B per person per night:
S £30.00–£42.50
D £27.50–£32.50

OPEN All Year except Christmas

TANWORTH-IN-ARDEN, Warwickshire Map ref 4B3

◆◆◆◆

GRANGE FARM
Forde Hall Lane, Tanworth-in-Arden, Solihull B94 5AX
T: (01564) 742911
I: www.grange-farm.com

Bedrooms: 1 double, 1 twin, 1 family
Bathrooms: 2 en suite

Evening meal available

Peaceful 17thC farmhouse set in 200 acres of beautiful countryside with footpaths and wildlife pools. Very attractive en suite bedrooms. Three miles from M42, jct 3.

B&B per person per night:
S £35.00–£40.00
D £30.00–£35.00

HB per person per night:
DY £40.00–£45.00

OPEN All Year

TELFORD, Shropshire Map ref 4A3 *Tourist Information Centre Tel: (01952) 238008*

◆◆◆

FALCON HOTEL
Holyhead Road, Wellington, Telford TF1 2DD
T: (01952) 255011
E: falconhotel@hotmail.com

Bedrooms: 4 double, 4 twin, 2 single, 1 family
Bathrooms: 7 en suite

Evening meal available
CC: Delta, Mastercard, Visa

Small, family-run, 18thC coaching hotel, 10 miles from Shrewsbury, four miles from Ironbridge, 18 miles from M6 at the end of M54 (exit 7).

B&B per person per night:
S £31.00–£42.00
D £19.50–£25.50

OPEN All Year except Christmas

RATING All accommodation in this guide has been rated, or is awaiting a rating, by a trained VisitBritain assessor.

TELFORD continued

◆◆◆◆

GROVE HOUSE GUESTHOUSE

Stafford Street, St Georges, Telford
TF2 9JW
T: (01952) 616140
F: (01952) 616140

Bedrooms: 4 double,
2 twin, 2 single
Bathrooms: 7 en suite,
1 private

Originally built as a hunting lodge. Close to Telford town centre/exhibition centre/ Ironbridge. Accessed from jct 4, M54. Centrally situated for Shropshire attractions.

B&B per person per night:
S £23.00–£30.00
D £19.00–£20.00

OPEN All Year except Christmas

TETBURY, Gloucestershire Map ref 2B2 *Tourist Information Centre Tel: (01666) 503552*

FOLLY FARM COTTAGES

Long Newnton, Tetbury GL8 8XA
T: (01666) 502475
F: (01666) 502358
E: info@gtb.co.uk
I: www.gtb.co.uk

Bedrooms: 7 double,
7 twin, 2 family
Bathrooms: 16 en suite

CC: Mastercard, Switch, Visa

220-acre farm. Queen Anne farmhouse, just three minutes' walk into Royal Tetbury and close to M4 and M5 motorways. Resident host.

B&B per person per night:
S £45.00–£55.00
D £27.50

OPEN All Year

THORPE, Derbyshire Map ref 4B2

HILLCREST HOUSE

Dovedale, Thorpe, Ashbourne DE6 2AW
T: (01335) 350436
E: hillcresthouse@freenet.co.uk
I: www.ashbourne-town.com/accom/hilcrest/

Former coaching inn leading to Dovedale and the famous Stepping Stones. Leave the car parked safely, walk from the doorstep and enjoy outstanding views. Relax in our warm and friendly atmosphere. Licensed lounge. Family-run 'home from home'. Cook yourselves a meal on our barbecue, or use our dining room for take-aways.

Bedrooms: 5 double,
1 twin, 1 single
Bathrooms: 5 en suite

CC: Delta, Mastercard, Switch, Visa

3 nights: 5% discount, 7 nights: 10% discount.

B&B per person per night:
S Min £25.00
D £25.00–£35.00

OPEN All Year except Christmas

UPPINGHAM, Rutland Map ref 4C3

THE VAULTS

Market Place, Uppingham, Oakham
LE15 9QH
T: (01572) 823259
F: (01572) 820019
I: www.Rutnet.co.uk/vaults

Bedrooms: 3 twin,
1 family
Bathrooms: 4 en suite

Evening meal available
CC: Amex, Delta, Mastercard, Switch, Visa

In the market place of this delightful Rutland town in the heart of the East Midlands. Convenient for Leicester, Corby, Peterborough, Melton Mowbray and Rutland Water.

B&B per person per night:
S Max £35.00
D Max £22.50

OPEN All Year

UPTON-UPON-SEVERN, Worcestershire Map ref 2B1 *Tourist Information Centre Tel: (01684) 594200*

◆◆◆◆

WELLAND COURT

Welland Court Lane, Upton-upon-Severn, Worcester WR8 0ST
T: (01684) 594426
F: (01684) 594426
E: archer@wellandcourt.freeserve.co.uk
I: www.wellandcourt.co.uk

Bedrooms: 2 double,
1 twin
Bathrooms: 3 en suite

Built c1450 and enlarged in the 18thC. Rescued from a dilapidated state and modernised to a high standard. At the foot of the Malvern Hills, an ideal base for touring.

B&B per person per night:
S £40.00–£50.00
D £37.50–£40.00

OPEN All Year except Christmas

VISTBRITAIN'S WHERE TO STAY
Please mention this guide when making your booking.

WARWICK, Warwickshire Map ref 2B1 *Tourist Information Centre Tel: (01926) 492212*

◆◆◆

AUSTIN HOUSE
96 Emscote Road, Warwick
CV34 5QJ
T: (01926) 493583
F: (01926) 493679
E: mike.austinhouse96@ntlworld.com
I: www.austinhousewarwick.co.uk

Bedrooms: 2 double, 2 twin, 1 single, 2 family
Bathrooms: 5 en suite

CC: Delta, Mastercard, Switch, Visa

B&B per person per night:
S Min £25.00
D £20.00–£24.00

OPEN All Year except Christmas

Black and white Victorian house one mile from Warwick town and castle. Three miles from Royal Leamington Spa, eight miles from Stratford-upon-Avon.

◆◆◆◆

AVON GUEST HOUSE
7 Emscote Road, Warwick
CV34 4PH
T: (01926) 491367
E: sue@comphouse.demon.co.uk
I: www.comphouse.demon.co.uk

Bedrooms: 1 double, 2 twin, 1 single, 2 family
Bathrooms: 6 en suite

B&B per person per night:
S Min £25.00
D Min £24.00

OPEN All Year except Christmas

Family-run guesthouse. All rooms en suite with colour TV, tea/coffee facilities and hairdryer. Car park. Five minutes' walk from castle and town centre.

◆◆◆◆

THE CROFT GUESTHOUSE

Haseley Knob, Warwick CV35 7NL
T: (01926) 484447
F: (01926) 484447
E: david@croftguesthouse.co.uk
I: www.croftguesthouse.co.uk

A non-smoking, friendly family guesthouse providing high-quality, clean and comfortable, en suite accommodation at reasonable prices. Centrally located (off A4177) for exploring Warwick, Stratford, Coventry and Kenilworth, or for visiting NEC (15 minutes), National Agricultural Centre (15 minutes). Sky TV, fax and e-mail facilities. More details on our website.

Bedrooms: 3 double, 2 twin, 1 single, 3 family
Bathrooms: 6 en suite, 3 private

CC: Amex, Delta, Mastercard, Switch, Visa

B&B per person per night:
S £35.00–£40.00
D £25.00–£27.50

OPEN All Year except Christmas

◆◆◆◆
Silver Award

FORTH HOUSE
44 High Street, Warwick CV34 4AX
T: (01926) 401512
F: (01926) 490809
E: info@forthhouseuk.co.uk
I: www.forthhouseuk.co.uk

Bedrooms: 1 double, 1 family
Bathrooms: 2 en suite

CC: Delta, Mastercard, Switch, Visa

B&B per person per night:
S £45.00–£52.00
D £34.00–£37.00

OPEN All Year

Ground floor and first floor guest suites with private sitting rooms and bathrooms. At the back of the house, overlooking peaceful garden, in town centre.

CHECK THE MAPS

The colour maps at the front of this guide show all the cities, towns and villages for which you will find accommodation entries. Refer to the town index to find the page on which they are listed.

WARWICK continued

Silver Award

NORTHLEIGH HOUSE

Five Ways Road, Hatton, Warwick
CV35 7HZ
T: (01926) 484203
F: (01926) 484006
E: sylviafen@amserve.com
I: www.northleigh.co.uk

The personal welcome and the individually designed en suite rooms with many thoughtful extras make this the perfect rural retreat. A full English breakfast is freshly cooked to suit each guest. Excellent country pubs nearby, also Stratford-upon-Avon, Warwick and the Exhibition Centres. Please ring Sylvia Fenwick for brochures.

Bedrooms: 5 double, 1 twin, 1 single
Bathrooms: 7 en suite

CC: Delta, Mastercard, Switch, Visa

Weekend discounts: 5% for 2 nights, 7% for 3 nights.

B&B per person per night:
S £38.00–£45.00
D £28.00–£32.50

◆◆◆

PEACOCK LODGE
97 West Street, Warwick CV34 6AH
T: (01926) 419480
F: (01926) 411892

Bedrooms: 4 double
Bathrooms: 4 en suite

CC: Delta, Diners, Mastercard, Switch, Visa

Three-storey, early-Victorian terraced house. Two of the guest rooms are situated in adjoining converted stables, one on the ground floor.

B&B per person per night:
S £40.00–£47.50
D £27.50–£30.00

OPEN All Year

◆◆◆◆
Silver Award

SHREWLEY POOLS FARM

Haseley, Warwick CV35 7HB
T: (01926) 484315
E: cathydodd@hotmail.com
I: www.s-h-systems.co.uk/hotels/shrewley.html

Glorious 17thC traditional family farmhouse with log fires, oak floors, beams etc, set in an acre of outstanding garden featuring herbaceous borders and unusual trees and shrubs. Two spacious, en suite bedrooms and own sitting room with books and games. Perfectly situated for numerous attractions. Surrounded by picturesque farmland. Private fishing.

Bedrooms: 1 double, 1 family
Bathrooms: 2 en suite

Evening meal available

Stay 3 nights (2 people sharing) and get fishing half price.

B&B per person per night:
S £30.00–£45.00
D £22.50–£30.00

HB per person per night:
DY £40.00–£60.00

OPEN All Year except Christmas

WELLINGBOROUGH, Northamptonshire Map ref 3A2 *Tourist Information Centre Tel: (01933) 276412*

Gold Award

THE MANOR HOUSE
1 Orlingbury Road,
Great Harrowden, Wellingborough
NN9 5AF
T: (01933) 678505
E: info@harrowdenmanor.com
I: www.harrowdenmanor.com

Bedrooms: 3 double
Bathrooms: 3 en suite

Evening meal available
CC: Amex, Mastercard, Visa

16thC country manor house. Beautiful en suite bedrooms, large gardens, village location, centrally situated for undiscovered Northamptonshire market towns and stately homes. Major roads easily accessible.

B&B per person per night:
S Min £80.00
D Min £45.00

OPEN All Year except Christmas

HALF BOARD PRICES Half board prices are given per person, but in some cases these may be based on double/twin occupancy.

WESTBURY, Northamptonshire Map ref 2C1

MILL FARM HOUSE

Westbury, Brackley NN13 5JS
T: (01280) 704843
F: (01280) 704843

Bedrooms: 1 double, 1 single, 1 family
Bathrooms: 2 en suite

B&B per person per night:
S £25.00–£30.00
D £22.50–£27.50

1000-acre mixed farm. Grade II Listed farmhouse overlooking a colourful garden including a covered, heated swimming pool. Situated in the centre of Westbury village.

OPEN All Year

WESTONBIRT, Gloucestershire Map ref 2B2

♦♦♦

AVENUE FARM

Knockdown, Westonbirt, Tetbury GL8 8QY
T: (01454) 238207
F: (01454) 238207
E: sonjames@breathemail.net
I: www.glosfarmhols.co.uk

B&B per person per night:
S £30.00
D £25.00

OPEN All Year except Christmas

Our 17thC farmhouse offers home comforts and good home produce. It is adjacent to Westonbirt Arboretum with its fine collection of trees and shrubs and varied summer programme available on request. Close to the ancient borough of Malmesbury and the old wool town of Tetbury; also Bath, Bristol and Gloucester.

Bedrooms: 1 double, 2 twin
Bathrooms: 2 en suite, 1 private

WHALEY BRIDGE, Derbyshire Map ref 4B2

Rating Applied For

SPRINGBANK GUESTHOUSE

Reservoir Road, Whaley Bridge, High Peak SK23 7BL
T: (01663) 732819
E: margot@whaleyspringbank.co.uk
I: www.whaleyspringbank.co.uk

Bedrooms: 2 double, 1 family
Bathrooms: 3 en suite

Evening meal available

B&B per person per night:
S £30.00–£50.00
D £22.50–£32.50

HB per person per night:
DY £42.00–£77.00

Victorian doctors' surgery. Quiet location. One minute's walk to the facilities of this small, friendly town. Evening meals or use of the dining room for take-aways.

OPEN All Year

WIRKSWORTH, Derbyshire Map ref 4B2

RED LION

Market Place, Wirksworth, Derby DE4 4ET
T: (01629) 822214
E: shfarrand@aol.com
I: www.redlionwirksworth.co.uk

Bedrooms: 2 double, 2 twin, 2 family
Bathrooms: 4 en suite

Evening meal available

B&B per person per night:
S £30.00–£35.00
D £25.00–£30.00

HB per person per night:
DY £30.00–£35.00

Quality en suite rooms in this delightful 18thC coaching inn with busy public bar, restaurant and function room. Within historic market town close to the Peak District.

OPEN All Year

WISHAW, Warwickshire Map ref 4B3

ASH HOUSE

The Gravel, Wishaw, Sutton Coldfield B76 9QB
T: (01675) 475782
F: (01675) 475782
E: kate@rectory80.freeserve.co.uk

Bedrooms: 2 double, 1 family
Bathrooms: 2 en suite, 1 private

CC: Delta, Mastercard, Visa

B&B per person per night:
S Max £35.00
D £25.00–£30.00

OPEN All Year except Christmas

Former rectory with lovely views. Few minutes' walk from Belfry Golf and Leisure Hotel. 0.5 miles M42, 10 minutes' drive from Birmingham Airport/NEC. Drayton Manor Park and zoo five miles.

5

WITNEY, Oxfordshire

See South East region for entries

VISITOR ATTRACTIONS For ideas on places to visit refer to the introduction at the beginning of this section. Look out too for the VisitBritain Quality Assured Visitor Attraction signs.

WOODSTOCK, Oxfordshire

See South East region for entries

WORCESTER, Worcestershire Map ref 2B1 *Tourist Information Centre Tel: (01905) 726311*

♦♦♦♦ Gold Award

HILL FARM HOUSE

Dormston Lane, Dormston,
Worcester WR7 4JS
T: (01386) 793159
F: (01386) 793239
E: jim@hillfarmhouse.co.uk
I: www.hillfarmhouse.co.uk

Bedrooms: 2 double,
1 single, 1 family
Bathrooms: 3 en suite

B&B per person per night:
S £30.00–£40.00
D £28.50–£33.50

OPEN All Year except Christmas

A traditional former farmhouse and converted buildings in quiet rural location. King-size, en suite rooms with pastoral views. Ideal for Stratford, Cotswolds, Worcester and the Malverns.

P €

Silver Award

YEW TREE HOUSE

Norchard, Crossway Green, Stourport-on-Severn DY13 9SN
T: (01299) 250921
F: (01299) 253472
E: yewtreehouse1@btopenworld.com
I: www.yewtreeworcester.co.uk

B&B per person per night:
S £35.00–£37.50
D £27.50–£30.00

HB per person per night:
DY £45.00–£57.50

OPEN All Year

Built in 1754, Yew Tree House has a special ambience permeating through a beautifully furnished home. We also have an Elizabethan annexe to the main house called The Cider House. The whole is set peacefully in secluded gardens but within easy reach of the M5 and numerous excellent eating establishments. Freephone: 0800 0935423

Bedrooms: 2 double,
2 twin, 1 family
Bathrooms: 5 en suite

Evening meal available

Discount of 10% for mid-week business use of 2 or more consecutive nights' stay.

P

WYE VALLEY

See under Hereford, Ross-on-Wye

COUNTRY CODE Always follow the Country Code Enjoy the countryside and respect its life and work Guard against all risk of fire Fasten all gates Keep your dogs under close control Keep to public paths across farmland Use gates and stiles to cross fences, hedges and walls Leave livestock, crops and machinery alone Take your litter home Help to keep all water clean Protect wildlife, plants and trees Take special care on country roads Make no unnecessary noise

A brief guide to the main Towns and Villages offering accommodation in the **Heart of England**

A ALTON, STAFFORDSHIRE - Alton Castle, an impressive 19th C building, dominates the village which is set in spectacular scenery. Nearby is Alton Towers, a romantic 19th C ruin with innumerable tourist attractions within one of England's largest theme parks in its 800 acres of magnificent gardens.

ASHBOURNE, DERBYSHIRE - Market town on the edge of the Peak District National Park and an excellent centre for walking. Its impressive church with 212-ft spire stands in an unspoilt old street. Ashbourne is well-known for gingerbread and its Shrovetide football match.

ATHERSTONE, WARWICKSHIRE - Pleasant market town with some 18th C houses and interesting old inns. Every Shrove Tuesday a game of football is played in the streets, a tradition which dates from the 13th C. Twycross Zoo is nearby with an extensive collection of reptiles and butterflies.

B BAKEWELL, DERBYSHIRE - Pleasant market town, famous for its pudding. It is set in beautiful countryside on the River Wye and is an excellent centre for exploring the Derbyshire Dales, the Peak District National Park, Chatsworth and Haddon Hall.

BALSALL COMMON, WEST MIDLANDS - Close to Birmingham NEC and Kenilworth and within easy reach of Coventry.

BIBURY, GLOUCESTERSHIRE - Village on the River Coln with stone houses and the famous 17th C Arlington Row, former weavers' cottages. Arlington Mill is now a folk museum. Trout farm and Barnsley House Gardens nearby are open to the public.

BIDFORD-ON-AVON, WARWICKSHIRE - Attractive village with an ancient 8-arched bridge. Riverside picnic area and a main street with some interesting 15th C houses.

BIRMINGHAM, WEST MIDLANDS - Britain's second city, whose attractions include Centenary Square and the ICC with Symphony Hall, the NEC, the City Art Gallery, Barber Institute of Fine Arts, 17th C Aston Hall, science and railway museums, Jewellery Quarter, Cadbury World, 2 cathedrals and Botanical Gardens.

BOURTON-ON-THE-WATER, GLOUCESTERSHIRE - The River Windrush flows through this famous Cotswold village which has a green, and cottages and houses of Cotswold stone. Its many attractions include a model village, Birdland, a Motor Museum and the Cotswold Perfumery.

BRACKLEY, NORTHAMPTONSHIRE - Historic market town of mellow stone, with many fine buildings lining the wide High Street and Market Place. Sulgrave Manor (George Washington's ancestral home) and Silverstone Circuit are nearby.

BRIDGNORTH, SHROPSHIRE - Red sandstone riverside town in 2 parts - High and Low - linked by a cliff railway. Much of interest including a ruined Norman keep, half-timbered 16th C houses, Midland Motor Museum and Severn Valley Railway.

BROADWAY, WORCESTERSHIRE - Beautiful Cotswold village called the "Show village of England", with 16th C stone houses and cottages. Near the village is Broadway Tower with magnificent views over 12 counties and a country park with nature trails and adventure playground.

BURTON DASSETT, WARWICKSHIRE - The church tower looks out over the site of the Battle of Edgehill and it is said that Cromwell himself climbed the tower to watch the fighting. Nearby is a 16th C beacon tower from which news of the battle was sent.

BUXTON, DERBYSHIRE - The highest market town in England and one of the oldest spas, with an elegant Crescent, Poole's Cavern, Opera House and attractive Pavilion Gardens. An excellent centre for exploring the Peak District.

C CHELTENHAM, GLOUCESTERSHIRE - Cheltenham was developed as a spa town in the 18th C and has some beautiful Regency architecture, in particular the Pittville Pump Room. It holds international music and literature festivals and is also famous for its race meetings and cricket.

CHESTERFIELD, DERBYSHIRE - Famous for the twisted spire of its parish church, Chesterfield has some fine modern buildings and excellent shopping facilities, including a large, traditional open-air market. Hardwick Hall and Bolsover Castle are nearby.

CHIPPING CAMPDEN, GLOUCESTERSHIRE - Outstanding Cotswold wool town with many old stone gabled houses, a splendid church and 17th C almshouses. Nearby are Kiftsgate Court Gardens and Hidcote Manor Gardens (National Trust).

CHURCH STRETTON, SHROPSHIRE - Church Stretton lies under the eastern slope of the Longmynd surrounded by hills. It is ideal for walkers, with marvellous views, golf and gliding. Wenlock Edge is not far away.

CIRENCESTER, GLOUCESTERSHIRE - "Capital of the Cotswolds", Cirencester was Britain's second most important Roman town with many finds housed in the Corinium Museum. It has a very fine Perpendicular church and old houses around the market place.

COLEFORD, GLOUCESTERSHIRE - Small town in the Forest of Dean with the ancient iron mines at Clearwell Caves nearby, where mining equipment and geological samples are displayed. There are several forest trails in the area.

COVENTRY, WEST MIDLANDS - Modern city with a long history. It has many places of interest including the post-war and ruined medieval cathedrals, art gallery and museums, some 16th C almshouses, St Mary's Guildhall, Lunt Roman fort and the Belgrade Theatre.

CRESSBROOK, DERBYSHIRE - Delightful dale with stone hall and pleasant houses, steep wooded slopes and superb views.

D DERBY, DERBYSHIRE - Modern industrial city but with ancient origins. There is a wide range of attractions including several museums (notably Royal Crown Derby), a theatre, a concert hall, and the cathedral with fine ironwork and Bess of Hardwick's tomb.

DROITWICH, WORCESTERSHIRE - Old town with natural brine springs, now incorporated into the Brine Baths Health Centre, developed as a spa at the beginning of the 19th C. Of particular interest is the Church of the Sacred Heart with splendid mosaics. Fine parks and a Heritage Centre.

E ELMESTHORPE, LEICESTERSHIRE - Silhouetted against the horizon, the picturesque church of St Mary has a 17th C tower and 12th or 13th C font and is set in a beautiful churchyard with lovely views.

F FAIRFORD, GLOUCESTERSHIRE - Small town with a 15th C wool church famous for its complete 15th C stained glass windows, interesting carvings and original wall paintings. It is an excellent touring centre and the Cotswolds Wildlife Park is nearby.

G GLOUCESTER, GLOUCESTERSHIRE - A Roman city and inland port, its cathedral is one of the most beautiful in Britain. Gloucester's many attractions include museums and the restored warehouses in the Victorian docks containing the National Waterways Museum, Robert Opie Packaging Collection and other attractions.

H HATHERSAGE, DERBYSHIRE - Hillside village in the Peak District, dominated by the church with many good brasses and monuments to the Eyre family which provide a link with Charlotte Bronte. Little John, friend of Robin Hood, is said to be buried here.

HEREFORD, HEREFORDSHIRE - Agricultural county town, its cathedral containing much Norman work, a large chained library and the world-famous Mappa Mundi exhibition. Among the city's varied attractions are several museums including the Cider Museum and the Old House.

HOLBEACH, LINCOLNSHIRE - Small town, mentioned in the Domesday Book, has splendid 14th C church with a fine tower and spire. The surrounding villages also have interesting churches, and the area is well known for its bulb fields.

HOPE, DERBYSHIRE - Village in the Hope Valley which is an excellent base for walking in the Peak District and for fishing and shooting. There is a well-dressing ceremony each June and its August sheep dog trials are well-known. Castleton Caves are nearby.

HUSBANDS BOSWORTH, LEICESTERSHIRE - This village is situated at the crossroads between Lutterworth and Market Harborough and the A50, Northampton/Leicester. Stanford Hall is within easy reach.

I IRONBRIDGE, SHROPSHIRE - Small town on the Severn where the Industrial Revolution began. It has the world's first iron bridge built in 1779. The Ironbridge Gorge Museum, of exceptional interest, comprises a rebuilt turn-of-the-century town and sites spread over 6 square miles.

K KENILWORTH, WARWICKSHIRE - The main feature of the town is the ruined 12th C castle. It has many royal associations but was damaged by Cromwell. A good base for visiting Coventry, Leamington Spa and Warwick.

KIDDERMINSTER, WORCESTERSHIRE - The town is the centre for carpet manufacturing. It has a medieval church with good monuments and a statue of Sir Rowland Hill, a native of the town and founder of the penny post. West Midlands Safari Park is nearby. Severn Valley Railway station.

KINETON, WARWICKSHIRE - Attractive old village in rolling countryside. 1 mile from site of famous battle of Edgehill. Medieval church of St Peter.

L LEAMINGTON SPA, WARWICKSHIRE - 18th C spa town with many fine Georgian and Regency houses. The refurbished 19th C Pump Rooms with Heritage Centre. The attractive Jephson Gardens are laid out alongside the river.

LECHLADE-ON-THAMES, GLOUCESTERSHIRE -Attractive village on the River Thames and a popular spot for boating. It has a number of fine Georgian houses and a 15th C church. Nearby is Kelmscott Manor, with its William Morris furnishings, and 18th C Buscot House (National Trust).

LEICESTER, LEICESTERSHIRE - Modern industrial city with a wide variety of attractions including Roman remains, ancient churches, Georgian houses and a Victorian clock tower. Excellent shopping precincts, arcades and market, museums, theatres, concert hall and sports and leisure centres.

LEOMINSTER, HEREFORDSHIRE - The town owed its prosperity to wool and has many interesting buildings, notably the timber-framed Grange Court, a former town hall. The impressive Norman priory church has 3 naves and a ducking stool. Berrington Hall (National Trust) is nearby.

LICHFIELD, STAFFORDSHIRE - Lichfield is Dr Samuel Johnson's birthplace and commemorates him with a museum and statue. The 13th C cathedral has 3 spires and the west front is full of statues. Among the attractive town buildings is the Heritage Centre. The Regimental Museum is in Whittington Barracks.

LINCOLN, LINCOLNSHIRE - Ancient city dominated by the magnificent 11th C cathedral with its triple towers. A Roman gateway is still used and there are medieval houses lining narrow, cobbled streets. Other attractions include the Norman castle, several museums and the Usher Gallery.

LOUGHBOROUGH, LEICESTERSHIRE - Industrial town famous for its bell foundry and 47-bell Carillon Tower. The Great Central Railway operates steam railway rides of over 8 miles through the attractive scenery of Charnwood Forest.

LUDLOW, SHROPSHIRE - Outstandingly interesting border town with a magnificent castle high above the River Teme, 2 half-timbered old inns and an impressive 15th C church. The Reader's House, with its 3-storey Jacobean porch, should also be seen.

M **MARKET HARBOROUGH, LEICESTERSHIRE -** There have been markets here since the early 13th C, and the town was also an important coaching centre, with several ancient hostelries. The early 17th C grammar school was once the butter market.

MATLOCK, DERBYSHIRE - The town lies beside the narrow valley of the River Derwent surrounded by steep wooded hills. Good centre for exploring Derbyshire's best scenery.

MATLOCK BATH, DERBYSHIRE - 19th C spa town with many attractions including several caverns to visit, a lead mining museum and a family fun park. There are marvellous views over the surrounding countryside from the Heights of Abraham, to which a cable car gives easy access.

MEDBOURNE, LEICESTERSHIRE - Picturesque village with medieval bridge.

MERIDEN, WEST MIDLANDS - Village halfway between Coventry and Birmingham. Said to be the centre of England, marked by a cross on the green.

MORETON-IN-MARSH, GLOUCESTERSHIRE - Attractive town of Cotswold stone with 17th C houses, an ideal base for touring the Cotswolds. Some of the local attractions include Batsford Park Arboretum, the Jacobean Chastleton House and Sezincote Garden.

MUCH WENLOCK, SHROPSHIRE - Small town close to Wenlock Edge in beautiful scenery and full of interest. In particular there are the remains of an 11th C priory with fine carving and the black and white 16th C Guildhall.

N **NAUNTON, GLOUCESTERSHIRE -** A high place on the Windrush, renowned for its wild flowers and with an attractive dovecote.

NEWARK, NOTTINGHAMSHIRE - The town has many fine old houses and ancient inns near the large, cobbled market-place. Substantial ruins of the 12th C castle, where King John died, dominate the riverside walk and there are several interesting museums. Sherwood Forest is nearby.

NEWPORT, SHROPSHIRE - Small market town on the Shropshire Union Canal has a wide High Street and a church with some interesting monuments. Newport is close to Aqualate Mere which is the largest lake in Staffordshire.

NORTHAMPTON, NORTHAMPTONSHIRE - A bustling town and a shoe manufacturing centre, with excellent shopping facilities, several museums and parks, a theatre and a concert hall. Several old churches include 1 of only 4 round churches in Britain.

NORTHLEACH, GLOUCESTERSHIRE - Village famous for its beautiful 15th C wool church with its lovely porch and interesting interior. There are also some fine houses including a 17th C wool merchant's house containing Keith Harding's World of Mechanical Music. The Cotswold Countryside Collection is in the former prison.

NOTTINGHAM, NOTTINGHAMSHIRE - Attractive modern city with a rich history. Outside its castle, now a museum, is Robin Hood's statue. Attractions include "The Tales of Robin Hood"; the Lace Hall; Wollaton Hall; museums and excellent facilities for shopping, sports and entertainment.

NUNEATON, WARWICKSHIRE - Busy town with an art gallery and museum which has a permanent exhibition of the work of George Eliot. The library also has an interesting collection of material. Arbury Hall, a fine example of Gothic architecture, is nearby.

P **PAINSWICK, GLOUCESTERSHIRE -** Picturesque wool town with inns and houses dating from the 14th C. Painswick Rococo Garden is open to visitors from January to November, and the house is a Palladian mansion. The churchyard is famous for its yew trees.

PERSHORE, WORCESTERSHIRE - Attractive Georgian town on the River Avon close to the Vale of Evesham, with fine houses and old inns. The remains of the beautiful Pershore Abbey form the parish church.

R **ROSS-ON-WYE, HEREFORDSHIRE -** Attractive market town with a 17th C market hall, set above the River Wye. There are lovely views over the surrounding countryside from the Prospect and the town is close to Goodrich Castle and the Welsh border.

RUGBY, WARWICKSHIRE - Town famous for its public school which gave its name to Rugby Union football and which featured in Tom Brown's Schooldays.

RUGELEY, STAFFORDSHIRE - Town close to Cannock Chase which has over 2,000 acres of heath and woodlands with forest trails and picnic sites. Nearby is Shugborough Hall (National Trust) with a fine collection of 18th C furniture and interesting monuments in the grounds.

S **SHREWSBURY, SHROPSHIRE -** Beautiful historic town on the River Severn retaining many fine old timber-framed houses. Its attractions include Rowley's Museum with Roman finds, remains of a castle, Clive House Museum, St Chad's 18th C round church, rowing on the river and the Shrewsbury Flower Show in August.

SKEGNESS, LINCOLNSHIRE - Famous seaside resort with 6 miles of sandy beaches and bracing air. Attractions include swimming pools, bowling greens, gardens, Natureland Marine Zoo, golf-courses and a wide range of entertainment at the Embassy Centre. Nearby is Gibraltar Point Nature Reserve.

SOLIHULL, WEST MIDLANDS - On the outskirts of Birmingham. Some Tudor houses and a 13th C church remain amongst the new public buildings and shopping centre. The 16th C Malvern Hall is now a school and the 15th C Chester House at Knowle is now a library.

SOUTHWELL, NOTTINGHAMSHIRE - Town dominated by the Norman minster which has some beautiful 13th C stone carvings in the Chapter House. Charles I spent his last night of freedom in one of the inns. The original Bramley apple tree can still be seen.

SPALDING, LINCOLNSHIRE - Fenland town famous for its bulbfields. A spectacular Flower Parade takes place at the beginning of May each year and the tulips at Springfields show gardens are followed by displays of roses and bedding plants in summer. Interesting local museum.

STAFFORD, STAFFORDSHIRE - The town has a long history and some half-timbered buildings still remain, notably the 16th C High House. There are several museums in the town and Shugborough Hall and the famous angler Izaak Walton's cottage, now a museum, are nearby.

STAMFORD, LINCOLNSHIRE - Exceptionally beautiful and historic town with many houses of architectural interest, several notable churches and other public buildings all in the local stone. Burghley House, built by William Cecil, is a magnificent Tudor mansion on the edge of the town.

STANTON-ON-THE-WOLDS, NOTTINGHAMSHIRE - Quiet village with golf course, just off the main route between Nottingham and Melton Mowbray, giving easy access to nearby attractions.

STONEHOUSE, GLOUCESTERSHIRE - Village in the Stroud Valley with an Elizabethan Court, later restored and altered by Lutyens.

STOURBRIDGE, WEST MIDLANDS - Town on the River Stour, famous for its glassworks. Several of the factories can be visited and glassware purchased at the factory shops.

STOW-ON-THE-WOLD, GLOUCESTERSHIRE - Attractive Cotswold wool town with a large market-place and some fine houses, especially the old grammar school. There is an interesting church dating from Norman times. Stow-on-the-Wold is surrounded by lovely countryside and Cotswold villages.

STRATFORD-UPON-AVON, WARWICKSHIRE - Famous as Shakespeare's home town, Stratford's many attractions include his birthplace, New Place where he died, the Royal Shakespeare Theatre and Gallery and Hall's Croft (his daughter's house).

STROUD, GLOUCESTERSHIRE - This old town, surrounded by attractive hilly country, has been producing broadcloth for centuries, the local museum has an interesting display on the subject. Many of the mills have been converted into craft centres and for other uses.

T **TELFORD, SHROPSHIRE -** New Town named after Thomas Telford, the famous engineer who designed many of the country's canals, bridges and viaducts. It is close to Ironbridge with its monuments and museums to the Industrial Revolution, including restored 18th C buildings.

TETBURY, GLOUCESTERSHIRE - Small market town with 18th C houses and an attractive 17th C Town Hall. It is a good touring centre with many places of interest nearby including Badminton House and Westonbirt Arboretum.

U **UPPINGHAM, RUTLAND -** Quiet market town dominated by its famous public school which was founded in 1584. It has many stone houses and is surrounded by attractive countryside.

UPTON-UPON-SEVERN, WORCESTERSHIRE - Attractive country town on the banks of the Severn and a good river cruising centre. It has many pleasant old houses and inns, and the pepperpot landmark is now the Heritage Centre.

W **WARWICK, WARWICKSHIRE -** Castle rising above the River Avon, 15th C Beauchamp Chapel attached to St Mary's Church, medieval Lord Leycester's Hospital almshouses and several museums. Nearby is Ashorne Hall Nickelodeon and the National Heritage museum at Gaydon.

WELLINGBOROUGH, NORTHAMPTONSHIRE - Manufacturing town, mentioned in the Domesday Book, with some old buildings and inns, in one of which Cromwell stayed on his way to Naseby. It has attractive gardens in the centre of the town and 2 interesting churches.

WIRKSWORTH, DERBYSHIRE - Small town which was once the centre of the lead-mining industry in Derbyshire. It has many old buildings of interest, including the church of St Mary, narrow streets and alleys, a Heritage Centre and the National Stone Centre. There is a well-dressing ceremony in May.

WISHAW, WARWICKSHIRE - A village with interesting features in the small church, and is now well known as the location of the National Golf Centre within easy reach of jct. 9 of the M42, close to Sutton Coldfield.

WORCESTER, WORCESTERSHIRE - Lovely riverside city dominated by its Norman and Early English cathedral, King John's burial place. Many old buildings including the 15th C Commandery and the 18th C Guildhall. There are several museums and the Royal Worcester porcelain factory.

www.visitengland.com

Log on for information and inspiration. The latest information on places to visit, events and quality assessed accommodation.

East of England

Discover England as you always thought it should be. Gently rolling countryside and unspoilt coastline, excellent for cycling, walking and bird-watching. Explore charming villages, historic market towns, traditional seaside resorts and bustling cities; awesome gothic cathedrals, magnificent stately homes and famous gardens.

Classic sights
Hatfield House – childhood home of Queen Elizabeth I
Blickling Hall – one of England's greatest Jacobean houses
Sutton Hoo – important burial site of Anglo-Saxon kings

Coast and country
The Chilterns – beautiful chalk life flora and fauna at the regions highest point
The Norfolk Broads – miles of reed-fringed waterways, man-made broads and nature reserves
The Fens – unique panorama of rivers and dykes, wide open skies and unforgettable sunsets

Glorious gardens
Anglesey Abbey – outstanding all year round gardens
The Gardens of the Rose – wander amongst 30,000 rose species
RHS Garden: Hyde Hall – rose, water and woodland gardens

Arts for all
Aldeburgh festival – internationally acclaimed festival of music and the arts
Luton Carnival – Britain's biggest one-day carnival

Delightfully different
Stilton – where each May they roll wooden cheeses down the High Street
St. Peters-on-the Wall – oldest Saxon church in England

The Counties of Bedfordshire, Cambridgeshire, Essex, Hertfordshire, Norfolk and Suffolk

For more information contact:
East of England Tourist Board
Toppesfield Hall, Hadleigh,
Suffolk IP7 5DN

E: jbowers@eetb.org.uk
www.eastofenglandtouristboard.com

Telephone enquiries -
T: 0870 225 4800
F: 0870 225 4890

1. Punting on the River Cam, Cambridge
2. Globe Inn, Linslade, Bedfordshire

Places to Visit

You will find hundreds of interesting places to visit during your stay, just some of which are listed in these pages. Contact any Tourist Information Centre in the region for more ideas on days out.

Awarded VisitBritain's 'Quality Assured Visitor Attraction' marque.

Audley End House and Park (English Heritage)

Audley End, Saffron Walden
Tel: (01799) 522399
www.english-heritage.org.uk

A palatial Jacobean house remodelled in the 18th-19thC with a magnificent great hall with 17thC plaster ceilings. Rooms and furniture by Robert Adam and park by 'Capability' Brown.

Banham Zoo

Banham, Norwich
Tel: (01953) 887771
www.banhamzoo.co.uk

Wildlife spectacular which will take you on a journey to experience tigers, leopards and zebra and some of the world's most exotic, rare and endangered animals.

Barleylands Farm

Barleylands Road, Billericay
Tel: (01268) 290229
www.barleylandsfarm.co.uk

Visitor centre with a rural museum, animal centre, craft studios, blacksmith's shop, glass-blowing studio with a viewing gallery, miniature steam railway and a restaurant.

Blickling Hall (National Trust)

Blickling, Norwich
Tel: (01263) 738030 www.nationaltrust.org.uk

A Jacobean redbrick mansion with garden, orangery, parkland and lake. There is also a display of fine tapestries and furniture.

Bressingham Steam Experience and Gardens

Bressingham, Diss
Tel: (01379) 686900 www.bressingham.co.uk

Steam rides through 4 miles (6.5km) of woodland. Six acres (2.5ha) of the Island Beds plant centre. Main line locomotives, the Victorian Gallopers and over 50 steam engines.

Bure Valley Railway

Aylsham Station, Norwich
Tel: (01263) 733858 www.bvrw.co.uk

A 15-inch narrow-gauge steam railway covering 9 miles (14.5km) of track from Wroxham in the heart of the Norfolk Broads to the bustling market town of Aylsham.

Colchester Castle

Castle Park, Colchester
Tel: (01206) 282939
www.colchestermuseums.org.uk

A Norman keep on the foundations of a Roman temple. The archaeological material includes much on Roman Colchester (Camulodunum).

Colchester Zoo

Stanway, Colchester
Tel: (01206) 331292
www.colchester-zoo.co.uk

Zoo with 200 species and some of the best cat and primate collections in the UK, 60 acres (24ha) of gardens and lakes, award-winning animal enclosures and picnic areas.

Ely Cathedral

The College, Ely
Tel: (01353) 667735
www.cathedral.ely.anglican.org.uk

One of England's finest cathedrals with guided tours and tours of the Octagon and West Tower, monastic precincts and also a brass rubbing centre and Stained Glass Museum.

Fritton Lake Country World

Fritton, Great Yarmouth
Tel: (01493) 488208
www.frittonlake.co.uk
A 250-acre (100-ha) centre with a children's assault course, putting, an adventure playground, golf, fishing, boating, wildfowl, heavy horses, cart rides, falconry and flying displays.

The Gardens of the Rose

Chiswell Green, St Albans
Tel: (01727) 850461 www.roses.co.uk
The Royal National Rose Society's Garden with 27 acres (11ha) of garden and trial grounds for new varieties of rose. 30,000 roses of all types and 1,700 different varieties are on display .

Hatfield House, Park and Gardens

Hatfield
Tel: (01707) 287010
www.hatfield-house.co.uk
Magnificent Jacobean house, home of the Marquess of Salisbury. Exquisite gardens, model soldiers and park trails. Childhood home of Queen Elizabeth I.

Hedingham Castle

Castle Hedingham, Halstead
Tel: (01787) 460261
www.hedinghamcastle.co.uk
The finest Norman keep in England, built in 1140 by the deVeres, Earls of Oxford. Visited by Kings Henry VII and VIII and Queen Elizabeth I and besieged by King John.

Holkham Hall

Wells-next-the-Sea
Tel: (01328) 710806
www.holkham.co.uk
A classic 18thC Palladian-style mansion. Part of a great agricultural estate and a living treasure house of artistic and architectural history along with a bygones collection.

Ickworth House, Park and Gardens (National Trust)

Horringer, Bury St Edmunds
Tel: (01284) 735270 www.nationaltrust.org.uk
An extraordinary oval house with flanking wings, begun in 1795. Fine paintings, a beautiful collection of Georgian silver, an Italian garden and stunning parkland.

Imperial War Museum Duxford

Duxford, Cambridge
Tel: (01223) 835000 www.iwm.org.uk
Almost 200 aircraft on display with tanks, vehicles and guns, an adventure playground, shops and a restaurant.

Kentwell Hall

Long Melford, Sudbury
Tel: (01787) 310207 www.kentwell.co.uk
Tudor manor house, still a lived-in family home. Winner of the '2001 Heritage Building of the Year' in the Good Britain Guide.

Knebworth House, Gardens and Park

Knebworth, Stevenage
Tel: (01438) 812661
www.knebworthhouse.com
Tudor manor house, re-fashioned in the 19thC, housing a collection of manuscripts, portraits and Jacobean banquet hall. Formal gardens, parkland and adventure playground.

2

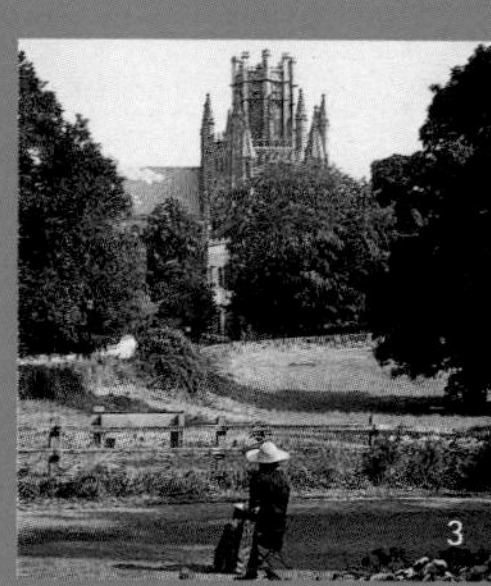
3

1. River Wensum, Norfolk
2. Cambridge
3. Ely Cathedral

Leighton Buzzard Railway
Page's Park Station, Leighton Buzzard
Tel: (01525) 373888 www.buzzrail.co.uk
An authentic narrow-gauge light railway, built in 1919, offering a 65 minute return journey into the Bedfordshire countryside.

Marsh Farm Country Park
South Woodham Ferrers, Chelmsford
Tel: (01245) 321552
www.marshfarmcountrypark.co.uk
A farm centre with sheep, a pig unit, free-range chickens, milking demonstrations, an indoor and outdoor adventure play areas, nature reserve, walks, picnic area and pet's corner.

Melford Hall (National Trust)
Long Melford, Sudbury
Tel: (01787) 880286
www.nationaltrust.org.uk/eastanglia
Turreted brick Tudor mansion with 18thC and Regency interiors. Collection of Chinese porcelain, gardens and a walk in the grounds. Dogs on leads, where permitted.

National Horseracing Museum and Tours
99 High Street, Newmarket
Tel: (01638) 667333 www.nhrm.co.uk
Award-winning display of the people and horses involved in racing's amazing history. Minibus tours to gallops, stables and equine pool. Hands-on gallery with horse simulator.

National Stud

Newmarket
Tel: (01638) 663464 x203
www.nationalstud.co.uk
A conducted tour which includes top thoroughbred stallions, mares and foals, and gives an insight into the day to day running of a modern stud farm.

New Pleasurewood Hills Leisure Park
Corton, Lowestoft
Tel: (01502) 586000
www.pleasurewoodhills.co.uk
Tidal wave watercoaster, log flume, chairlift, 2 railways, pirate ship, parrot/sealion shows, go-karts and rattlesnake coaster. Mega-Drop Tower and new circus theatre shows.

Norfolk Lavender Limited

Heacham, King's Lynn
Tel: (01485) 570384
www.norfolk-lavender.co.uk
Find out how lavender is distilled from the flowers and the oil made into a wide range of gifts. There is a slide show when the distillery is not working.

Norwich Cathedral
62 The Close, Norwich
Tel: (01603) 218321 www.cathedral.org.uk
A Norman cathedral from 1096 with 14thC roof bosses depicting bible scenes from Adam and Eve to the Day of Judgement, cloisters, cathedral close, shop and restaurant.

Oliver Cromwell's House

29 St Marys Street, Ely
Tel: (01353) 662062
www.elyeastcambs.co.uk
The family home of Oliver Cromwell with a 17thC kitchen, parlour, a haunted bedroom, a Tourist Information Centre, souvenirs and gift shop.

Peter Beales Roses
London Road, Attleborough
Tel: (01953) 454707 www.classicroses.co.uk
2.5-acre (1-ha) rose garden displaying most of the company's collection of 1200 varieties of roses, plus the national collection of Rosa species.

Pleasure Beach
South Beach Parade, Great Yarmouth
Tel: (01493) 844585 www.pleasure-beach.co.uk
Rollercoaster, Terminator, log flume, Twister, monorail, galloping horses, caterpillar, ghost train and fun house. Height restrictions are in force on some rides.

The Royal Air Force Air Defence Radar Museum
RAF Neatishead, Norwich
Tel: (01692) 633309
www.neatishead.raf.mod.uk
History of the development and use of radar in the UK and overseas from 1935 to date. Winner of the Regional Visitor Attraction (under 100,000 visitors). National Silver Award.

RSPB Minsmere Nature Reserve
Westleton, Saxmundham
Tel: (01728) 648281 www.rspb.org.uk
RSPB reserve on Suffolk coast with bird-watching hides and trails, year-round events and guided walk and visitor centre with large shop and welcoming tearoom.

Sainsbury Centre for Visual Arts
University of East Anglia, Norwich
Tel: (01603) 593199 www.uea.ac.uk/scva
Housing the Sainsbury Collection of works by artists such as Picasso, Bacon and Henry Moore alongside many objects of pottery and art from across time and cultures.

Sandringham
Sandringham, King's Lynn
Tel: (01553) 612908
www.sandringhamestate.co.uk
The country retreat of HM The Queen. A delightful house and 60 acres (24ha) of grounds and lakes. There is also a museum of royal vehicles and royal memorabilia.

Shuttleworth Collection
Old Warden Aerodrome, Biggleswade
Tel: (01767) 627288 www.shuttleworth.org
A unique historical collection of aircraft from a 1909 Bleriot to a 1942 Spitfire in flying condition and cars dating from an 1898 Panhard in running order.

Somerleyton Hall and Gardens
Somerleyton, Lowestoft
Tel: (01502) 730224
www.somerleyton.co.uk
Early Victorian stately mansion in Anglo-Italian style, with lavish features and fine state rooms. Beautiful 12-acre (5-ha) gardens, with historic Yew hedge maze, gift shop.

Stondon Museum
Henlow
Tel: (01462) 850339
www.transportmuseum.co.uk
A museum with transport exhibits from the early 1900s to the 1980s. The largest private collection in England of bygone vehicles from the beginning of the century.

Thursford Collection
Thursford, Fakenham
Tel: (01328) 878477
A live musical show with 9 mechanical organs and a Wurlitzer show starring Robert Wolfe.

Wimpole Hall and Home Farm (National Trust)
Arrington, Royston
Tel: (01223) 207257 www.wimpole.org
An 18thC house in a landscaped park with a folly, Chinese bridge, plunge bath and yellow drawing room in the house, the work of John Soane. Home Farm has a rare breeds centre.

Woburn Abbey
Woburn, Milton Keynes
Tel: (01525) 290666 www.woburnabbey.co.uk
An 18thC Palladian mansion, altered by Henry Holland, the Prince Regent's architect, containing a collection of English silver, French and English furniture and art.

Woburn Safari Park

Woburn, Milton Keynes
Tel: (01525) 290407
www.woburnsafari.co.uk
Drive through the safari park with 30 species of animals in natural groups just a windscreen's width away plus the action-packed Wild World Leisure Area.

1. Theme Park, Essex

East of England Tourist Board

Toppesfield Hall, Hadleigh, Suffolk IP7 5DN
T: 0870 225 4800 F: 0870 225 4890
E: jbowers@eetb.org.uk
www.eastofenglandtouristboard.com

THE FOLLOWING PUBLICATIONS ARE AVAILABLE FROM THE EAST OF ENGLAND TOURIST BOARD:

Great days out in the East of England 2004 – an information-packed A5 guide featuring all you need to know about places to visit and things to see and do in the East of England. From historic houses to garden centres, from animal collections to craft centres - this guide has it all, including film and TV locations, city, town and village information, events, shopping, car tours plus lots more! (£4.50 excl p&p)

England's Cycling Country – the East of England offers perfect cycling country - from quiet country lanes to ancient trackways. This free publication promotes the many Cycling Discovery Maps that are available to buy (£1.50 excl p&p), as well as providing useful information for anyone planning a cycling tour of the region

1

Getting to the East of England

BY ROAD: The region is easily accessible. From London and the south via the A1(M), M11, M25, A10, M1, A46 and A12. From the north via the A1(M), A15, A5, M1 and A6. From the west via the A14, A47, A421, A428, A418, A41, A422, A17 and A427.

BY RAIL: Regular fast trains run to all major cities and towns in the region. London stations which serve the region are Liverpool Street, Kings Cross, Fenchurch Street, St Pancras, London Marylebone and London Euston. Bedford, Luton and St Albans are on the Thameslink line which runs to Kings Cross and on to London Gatwick Airport. There is also a direct link between London Stansted Airport and Liverpool Street. Through the Channel Tunnel, there are trains direct from Paris and Brussels to Waterloo Station, London. A short journey on the Underground will bring passengers to those stations operating services into the East of England. Further information on rail journeys in the East of England can be obtained on 08457 484 950.

1. Windmill, Norfolk

Where to stay in the

East of England

All place names in the blue bands under which accommodation is listed, are shown on the maps at the front of this guide.

Symbols give useful information about services and facilities. Inside the back cover flap there's a key to these symbols which you can keep open for easy reference.

A complete listing of all the VisitBritain assessed accommodation covered by this guide appears at the back of this guide.

ALBURGH, Norfolk Map ref 3C2

Award-winning chef, Robert, runs a country French restaurant. Ideal for families (family room available) – children in bed whilst the parents enjoy a romantic evening. Ideal touring base with Southwold, Norwich, Beccles and the Broads all within a 15-mile radius and the Heritage Coast an easy drive. German and French spoken.

THE DOVE – A RESTAURANT WITH ROOMS

Holbrook Hill, Alburgh, Harleston IP20 0EP
T: (01986) 788315
F: (01986) 788315
E: thedovenorfolk@freeola.com
I: www.thedovenorfolk.co.uk

Bedrooms: 1 double, 1 twin, 1 family
Bathrooms: 1 en suite, 1 private

Evening meal available
CC: Delta, Diners, Mastercard, Switch, Visa

B&B per person per night:
S Min £26.50
D Min £24.75

HB per person per night:
DY £36.00–£45.00

OPEN All Year

IMPORTANT NOTE Information on accommodation listed in this guide has been supplied by the proprietors. As changes may occur you are advised to check details at the time of booking.

ALDBOROUGH, Norfolk Map ref 3B1

BUTTERFLY COTTAGE

The Green, Aldborough, Norwich
NR11 7AA
T: (01263) 768198
F: (01263) 768198
E: butterflycottage@btopenworld.com
I: www.butterflycottage.com

Bedrooms: 2 family
Bathrooms: 2 en suite

B&B per person per night:
S £25.00–£27.00
D £25.00–£27.00

OPEN All Year

On the Weavers Way. Comfortable cottage-style, well-equipped, friendly atmosphere. Rooms overlook large garden or village green. Each has own entrance. Car parking.

ALDEBY, Norfolk Map ref 3C1

THE OLD VICARAGE

Rectory Road, Aldeby, Beccles
NR34 0BJ
T: (01502) 678229
E: butler@beccles33.freeserve.co.uk

Bedrooms: 2 double, 1 family
Bathrooms: 1 en suite, 2 private

B&B per person per night:
S £22.00–£25.00
D £22.00–£25.00

OPEN All Year except Christmas

Spacious accommodation, quiet rural location. Ground floor suite available. Non-smoking. Convenient for Norfolk Broads boating and bird-watching. Ample off-road parking for cars, bicycles and canoes.

BECCLES, Suffolk Map ref 3C1

CATHERINE HOUSE

2 Ringsfield Road, Beccles
NR34 9PQ
T: (01502) 716428
F: (01502) 716428

Bedrooms: 3 double
Bathrooms: 2 en suite, 1 private

B&B per person per night:
S £30.00–£34.00
D £22.00–£25.00

OPEN All Year

Family home, tastefully decorated to high standard, in quiet position overlooking Waveney Valley. Five minutes' walk to town centre.

BEDFORD, Bedfordshire Map ref 2D1 *Tourist Information Centre Tel: (01234) 215226*

Silver Award

CORNFIELDS RESTAURANT AND HOTEL

Wilden Road, Colmworth, Bedford
MK44 2NJ
T: (01234) 378990
F: (01234) 376370
E: reservations@cornfieldsrestaurant.co.uk
I: www.cornfieldsrestaurant.co.uk

Bedrooms: 5 double
Bathrooms: 5 en suite

Evening meal available
CC: Amex, Delta, Mastercard, Switch, Visa

B&B per person per night:
S £60.00–£70.00
D £43.00–£60.00

OPEN All Year

A fresh-food restaurant with five individually furnished rooms in the heart of the Bedfordshire countryside at Colmworth near Bedford.

BEETLEY, Norfolk Map ref 3B1

♦♦♦♦
Gold Award

PEACOCK HOUSE

Peacock Lane, Beetley, East Dereham
NR20 4DG
T: (01362) 860371
E: PeackH@aol.com
I: www.smoothhound.co.uk/hotels/peacockh.html/

Bedrooms: 1 double, 1 twin, 1 family
Bathrooms: 3 en suite

B&B per person per night:
S £28.00–£30.00
D £23.50–£25.00

OPEN All Year

Beautiful old farmhouse, peacefully situated in lovely garden and grounds. Offering excellent accommodation with all facilities, guests' lounge, open fires, beamed dining room, home cooking and a warm welcome. Centrally situated with Norwich, Sandringham, National Trust houses and the coast all within easy reach, and golf, fishing and swimming all close by.

BIGGLESWADE, Bedfordshire Map ref 2D1

◆◆◆

OLD WARDEN GUESTHOUSE
Shop and Post Office, Old Warden, Biggleswade SG18 9HQ
T: (01767) 627201

Bedrooms: 2 double, 1 twin
Bathrooms: 3 en suite

Listed, 19thC building, adjacent to shop and post office. Between Biggleswade and Bedford. One mile from Shuttleworth Collection. All rooms en suite.

B&B per person per night:
S £27.00–£30.00
D £22.50

OPEN All Year except Christmas

BISHOP'S STORTFORD, Hertfordshire Map ref 2D1 *Tourist Information Centre Tel: (01279) 655831*

Gold Award

THE COTTAGE
71 Birchanger Lane, Birchanger, Bishop's Stortford CM23 5QA
T: (01279) 812349
F: (01279) 815045
E: bookings@thecottagebirchanger.co.uk
I: www.thecottagebirchanger.co.uk

The Cottage is a 17thC Listed house with panelled rooms and woodburning stove. Conservatory-style breakfast room overlooks large, mature garden. Quiet and peaceful village setting yet near M11 jct 8, Stansted Airport and Bishop's Stortford. Guest rooms are furnished in a traditional cottage style, all with colour TV and tea/coffee facilities.

Bedrooms: 7 double, 5 twin, 2 single
Bathrooms: 12 en suite

CC: Delta, Mastercard, Switch, Visa

B&B per person per night:
S £45.00–£56.00
D £36.00–£40.00

OPEN All Year

BRADFIELD, Essex Map ref 3B2

EMSWORTH HOUSE
Ship Hill, Bradfield, Manningtree CO11 2UP
T: (01255) 870860
E: emsworthhouse@hotmail.com
I: www.emsworthhouse.co.uk

Bedrooms: 1 double, 1 twin
Bathrooms: 2 en suite

Evening meal available

Formerly the vicarage. Spacious rooms with stunning views of the countryside and River Stour. Near Colchester and Harwich. On holiday, business or en route to the continent, it's perfect!

B&B per person per night:
S £30.00–£48.00
D £22.00–£29.00

HB per person per night:
DY £40.00–£63.00

OPEN All Year

BRAINTREE, Essex Map ref 3B2 *Tourist Information Centre Tel: (01376) 550066*

70 HIGH GARRETT
Braintree CM7 5NT
T: (01376) 345330

Bedrooms: 1 twin, 1 single, 1 family

Three-bedroom bed and breakfast situated on main road between Braintree and Halstead. Convenient for Colchester, Chelmsford, Constable country. One hour to London. Non-smokers only.

B&B per person per night:
S £25.00
D £25.00

OPEN All Year

AT-A-GLANCE SYMBOLS
Symbols at the end of each accommodation entry give useful information about services and facilities. A key to symbols can be found inside the back cover flap. Keep this open for easy reference.

BUNGAY, Suffolk Map ref 3C1

♦♦♦♦ Gold Award

EARSHAM PARK FARM

Harleston Road, Earsham, Bungay
NR35 2AQ
T: (01986) 892180
F: (01986) 892180
E: etb@earsham-parkfarm.co.uk
I: www.earsham-parkfarm.co.uk

Bedrooms: 2 double, 1 twin
Bathrooms: 3 en suite

Evening meal available
CC: Delta, Mastercard, Switch, Visa

B&B per person per night:
S Min £36.00
D Min £26.00

OPEN All Year

Friendly but elegant and spacious farmhouse in a quiet location with panoramic views. Decorated to a high standard with unique stencilling and paint finishes. Quality and antique furnishings are complemented by extensive facilities. Delicious breakfasts including home produce are a feature of this property. Excellent hospitality.

BURNHAM THORPE, Norfolk Map ref 3B1

♦♦♦♦

WHITEHALL FARM

Burnham Thorpe, King's Lynn
PE31 8HN
T: (01328) 738416
F: (01328) 730937
E: barrysoutherland@aol.com
I: www.whitehallfarm-accommodation.com

Bedrooms: 1 double, 1 twin, 1 family
Bathrooms: 1 en suite, 2 private

CC: Delta, Mastercard, Switch, Visa

B&B per person per night:
D £27.50–£30.00

OPEN All Year

Barry and Valerie welcome you for a quiet, relaxed stay in north Norfolk, two miles from coast. Family rooms with full facilities in 16thC farmhouse.

CAMBRIDGE, Cambridgeshire Map ref 2D1 *Tourist Information Centre Tel: 0906 586 2526 (Premium rate number)*

♦♦♦

ARBURY LODGE GUESTHOUSE

82 Arbury Road, Cambridge
CB4 2JE
T: (01223) 364319
F: (01223) 566988
E: arburylodge@ntlworld.com
I: www.guesthousecambridge.com

Bedrooms: 3 double, 2 twin, 1 single, 1 family
Bathrooms: 4 en suite

CC: Amex, Delta, Mastercard, Switch, Visa

B&B per person per night:
S £28.00–£50.00
D £22.50–£32.50

OPEN All Year except Christmas

Comfortable family-run guesthouse, 1.5 miles north of city centre and colleges. Easy access from A14/M11. Large car park and garden.

♦♦♦

ASHLEY HOTEL

74 Chesterton Road, Cambridge
CB4 1ER
T: (01223) 350059
F: (01223) 350900
E: info@arundelhousehotels.co.uk
I: www.arundelhousehotels.co.uk

Bedrooms: 7 double, 3 twin, 6 family
Bathrooms: 16 en suite

CC: Mastercard, Visa

B&B per person per night:
S £59.50–£69.50
D £34.75–£39.75

OPEN All Year except Christmas

Well-appointed, recently refurbished small hotel with modern facilities close to city centre. Nearby Arundel House Hotel's facilities available to Ashley residents (under same ownership).

CAMBRIDGE continued

AYLESBRAY LODGE GUESTHOUSE

5 Mowbray Road, Cambridge CB1 7SR
T: (01223) 240089
F: (01223) 528678
E: stay@aylesbray.com
I: www.aylesbray.com

All rooms are en suite, tastefully decorated and have complimentary extras. 4-poster rooms, satellite TV, direct-dial telephones, radio-alarm and hairdryer, free car parking. Close to Addenbrookes Hospital and within easy reach of rail station, colleges and historic city centre. Easy access to M11, A14, A10. Convenient for local businesses.

Bedrooms: 1 double, 1 twin, 1 single, 2 family
Bathrooms: 5 en suite

CC: Amex, Delta, Mastercard, Switch, Visa

B&B per person per night:
S £40.00–£50.00
D £32.50–£42.50

OPEN All Year

♦♦♦

DYKELANDS GUESTHOUSE

157 Mowbray Road, Cambridge CB1 7SP
T: (01223) 244300
F: (01223) 566746
E: dykelands@fsbdial.co.uk
I: www.dykelands.com

Highly recommended guesthouse in south of city, only 1.75 miles from historic city centre. Ideally located for city and for touring. We offer modern, spacious accommodation, most en suite. Two bedrooms on ground floor. A non-smoking establishment. Traditional English breakfast or vegetarian alternatives. Car parking on site.

Bedrooms: 5 double, 1 single, 3 family
Bathrooms: 7 en suite

CC: Delta, Mastercard, Switch, Visa

B&B per person per night:
S Min £32.00
D £21.00–£26.00

OPEN All Year

♦♦♦♦

FINCHES
144 Thornton Road, Girton, Cambridge CB3 0ND
T: (01223) 276653
F: (01223) 276653
E: liz.green.b-b@talk21.com
I: www.smoothhound.co.uk/hotels/finches

Bedrooms: 3 double
Bathrooms: 3 en suite

A three-bedroom bed and breakfast establishment situated on the corner of Huntingdon Road, Cambridge. All en suite.

B&B per person per night:
S £45.00–£55.00
D £25.00–£29.00

OPEN All Year except Christmas

♦♦♦

HAMILTON HOTEL

156 Chesterton Road, Cambridge CB4 1DA
T: (01223) 365664
F: (01223) 314866

Recently refurbished hotel less than one mile from centre of city. Easy access from A14 and M11. Most rooms have en suite shower and toilet. All rooms have colour TV, direct-dial telephone and hospitality tray.

Bedrooms: 16 double, 5 single, 4 family
Bathrooms: 20 en suite

Evening meal available
CC: Amex, Delta, Diners, Mastercard, Switch, Visa

B&B per person per night:
S £28.00–£50.00
D £25.00–£35.00

HB per person per night:
DY £37.00–£44.00

OPEN All Year except Christmas

CAMBRIDGE continued

◆◆◆◆

HOME FROM HOME
78B Milton Road, Cambridge
CB4 1LA
T: (01223) 323555
F: (01223) 236078
E: homefromhome@tesco.net
I: www.homefromhomecambridge.co.uk

Bedrooms: 1 double, 1 family
Bathrooms: 1 en suite, 1 private

CC: Amex, Delta, Mastercard, Switch, Visa

B&B per person per night:
S £35.00–£50.00
D £25.00–£32.50

OPEN All Year

Centrally located near river and colleges. Providing home-from-home hospitality.

P

◆◆◆◆

KING'S TITHE
13a Comberton Road, Barton, Cambridge
CB3 7BA
T: (01223) 263610
F: (01223) 263610

B&B per person per night:
S £36.00–£40.00
D £25.00–£30.00

OPEN All Year

A quiet family home in a prime position to which our guests often return. Guests have their own private bathroom (shared between the two bedrooms, bathrobes supplied) with shower and bath and separate toilet. Bedrooms overlook open country. A wide choice of breakfasts and good village pubs. Close to the M11, jct 12.

Bedrooms: 2 twin

8 P

◆◆◆

RAILWAY LODGE GUEST HOUSE
150 Tenison Road, Cambridge
CB1 2DP
T: (01223) 467688
F: (01223) 461934
E: railwaylodge@cambridge-guesthouse-accommodation.co.uk
I: www.cambridge-guesthouse-accommodation.co.uk

Bedrooms: 3 double, 1 single, 2 family
Bathrooms: 6 en suite

Evening meal available
CC: Delta, Mastercard, Switch, Visa

B&B per person per night:
S £30.00–£45.00
D £22.50–£30.00

OPEN All Year

A friendly, famly-run guesthouse within minutes' walk from both the railway station and the city centre. All rooms have en suite facilities.

P €

◆◆◆

SEGOVIA LODGE
2 Barton Road, Newnham,
Cambridge CB3 9JZ
T: (01223) 354105
F: (01223) 323011

Bedrooms: 1 double, 1 twin
Bathrooms: 2 en suite

B&B per person per night:
D £55.00–£60.00

OPEN All Year except Christmas

A modern house situated on the western side of Cambridge close to M11 (jct 12), A10 and A603, walking distance to city centre. Parking. No credit cards. Non-smoking.

P €

◆◆◆

SOUTHAMPTON GUEST HOUSE
7 Elizabeth Way, Cambridge
CB4 1DE
T: (01223) 357780
F: (01223) 314297
E: southamptonhouse@telco4u.net
I: www.southamptonguesthouse.com

Bedrooms: 1 double, 1 single, 3 family
Bathrooms: 5 en suite

B&B per person per night:
S £35.00–£45.00
D £24.00–£29.00

OPEN All Year

Victorian property with friendly atmosphere, only 15 minutes' walk along riverside to city centre, colleges and new shopping mall.

P

CREDIT CARD BOOKINGS If you book by telephone and are asked for your credit card number it is advisable to check the proprietor's policy should you cancel your reservation.

CAMBRIDGE continued

◆◆◆◆

SYCAMORE HOUSE
56 High Street, Great Wilbraham, Cambridge CB1 5JD
T: (01223) 880751
F: (01223) 880751
E: barry@thesycamorehouse.co.uk
I: www.thesycamorehouse.co.uk

Bedrooms: 2 double, 1 single

B&B per person per night:
S £25.00–£35.00
D £25.00–£30.00

OPEN All Year except Christmas

Detatched house in small village with pub and shop, six miles Cambridge/Newmarket. Ideal for touring/racing/golf. English breakfast served in conservatory overlooking large gardens.

◆◆◆◆

TUDOR COTTAGE

292 Histon Road, Cambridge CB4 3HS
T: (01223) 565212
F: (01223) 508656
E: tudor.cottage@ntlworld.com

B&B per person per night:
S £25.00–£38.00
D £22.50–£27.50

OPEN All Year

Comfortable, friendly Tudor-style cottage situated within 30 mintues' walking distance of city centre. En suite or shared facilities, central heating, colour TV, tea/coffee-making facilities. Excellent food and friendly, personal service. Off-street parking. Easy access to A14/M11.

Bedrooms: 2 double, 1 single
Bathrooms: 2 en suite

◆◆◆◆ Silver Award

WORTH HOUSE
152 Chesterton Road, Cambridge CB4 1DA
T: (01223) 316074
F: (01223) 316074
E: enquiry@worth-house.co.uk
I: www.worth-house.co.uk

Bedrooms: 2 double
Bathrooms: 2 en suite

B&B per person per night:
S £35.00–£45.00
D £25.00–£30.00

OPEN All Year

Worth House offers quiet, comfortable and spacious accommodation in this Victorian home. Within easy reach of the city centre. 'Which?' recommended.

8

CAVENDISH, Suffolk Map ref 3B2

◆◆◆◆ Silver Award

EMBLETON HOUSE

Melford Road, Cavendish, Sudbury CO10 8AA
T: (01787) 280447
F: (01787) 282396
E: silverned@aol.com
I: www.smoothhound.co.uk/hotels/embleton

B&B per person per night:
S £35.00–£55.00
D £27.50–£35.00

OPEN All Year

A large, family-run, 1930's house set well back from the road within its own secluded, mature gardens at the eastern edge of Cavendish village. Five spacious, recently appointed en suite bedrooms. Stour Valley views. Suffolk breakfast. Good pub within eight minutes' walk. Ideal base for exploring Long Melford, Clare, Lavenham and beyond.

Bedrooms: 2 double, 3 twin
Bathrooms: 5 en suite

Evening meal available

Special rates for stays of 3 nights or more. 'Stress Busting' break – holistic therapies, heated pool (May-Sep) and tennis court.

8

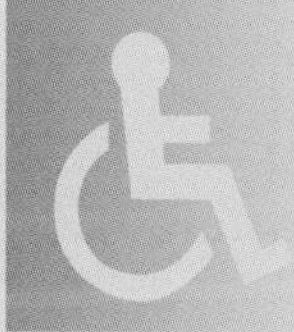

ACCESSIBILITY

Look for the symbols which indicate National Accessible Scheme standards for hearing and visually impaired guests in addition to standards for guests with mobility impairment. You can find an index of all scheme participants at the back of this guide.

CHELMSFORD, Essex Map ref 3B3 *Tourist Information Centre Tel: (01245) 283400*

♦♦♦

BEECHCROFT PRIVATE HOTEL
211 New London Road, Chelmsford
CM2 0AJ
T: (01245) 352462
F: (01245) 347833
E: enquiries@beechcrofthotel.com
I: www.beechcrofthotel.com

Bedrooms: 7 double, 10 single, 2 family
Bathrooms: 13 en suite

CC: Delta, Diners, Mastercard, Switch, Visa

B&B per person per night:
S £36.00–£48.00
D £26.00–£32.50

OPEN All Year

Central hotel offering clean and comfortable accommodation with friendly service. Under family ownership and management. Within walking distance of town centre and Essex cricket ground. Fully refurbished last year.

♦♦♦♦

BOSWELL HOUSE HOTEL
118 Springfield Road, Chelmsford
CM2 6LF
T: (01245) 287587
F: (01245) 287587
E: SteveBoorman@aol.com

Bedrooms: 6 double, 5 single, 2 family
Bathrooms: 13 en suite

Evening meal available
CC: Amex, Delta, Diners, Mastercard, Switch, Visa

B&B per person per night:
S £50.00–£52.00
D £32.50–£35.00

OPEN All Year except Christmas

Victorian townhouse in central location with car park. High-standard accommodation in friendly and informal surroundings. Family atmosphere and home cooking, lounge bar.

CHORLEYWOOD, Hertfordshire Map ref 2D1

♦♦♦♦
Silver Award

ASHBURTON HOUSE
48 Berks Hill, Chorleywood, Rickmansworth WD3 5AH
T: (01923) 285510
F: (01923) 285513
E: vales@onetel.net.uk
I: www.ashburtonhouse.co.uk

B&B per person per night:
S £45.00–£55.00
D £30.00–£40.00

OPEN All Year

Ashburton House is a traditional Tudor-style house, set in beautiful gardens, yet only 30 minutes by underground train into London, a perfect base to explore the capital and historic England. Candlelit breakfast is served in our oak-panelled dining room, and the standard throughout is exceptional.

Bedrooms: 1 double, 2 twin
Bathrooms: 2 en suite

Golfing breaks arranged – fourth night free. Romantic breaks with late check-out: flowers, chocolates etc ordered.

CLACTON-ON-SEA, Essex Map ref 3B3 *Tourist Information Centre Tel: (01255) 423400*

♦♦♦♦

POND HOUSE FARMHOUSE BED & BREAKFAST
Pond House, Earls Hall Farm, Clacton-on-Sea CO16 8BP
T: (01255) 820458
F: (01255) 822370
E: brenda_lord@farming.co.uk
I: www.earlshallfarm.info

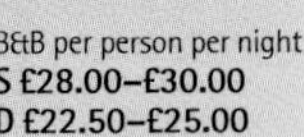

B&B per person per night:
S £28.00–£30.00
D £22.50–£25.00

OPEN All Year

A warm welcome awaits you at our Victorian farmhouse, set in the centre of our working farm. Two miles from the coast and local attractions. Large garden in which to wander and relax, and footpaths around the farm. Home cooking using British, local produce and homemade preserves.

Bedrooms: 1 double
Bathrooms: 1 en suite

QUALITY ASSURANCE SCHEME
Diamond ratings and awards were correct at the time of going to press but are subject to change. Please check at the time of booking.

CLACTON-ON-SEA continued

SANDROCK HOTEL
1 Penfold Road,
Marine Parade West, Clacton-on-Sea CO15 1JN
T: (01255) 428215
F: (01255) 428215

Bedrooms: 7 double, 1 family
Bathrooms: 8 en suite

Evening meal available
CC: Amex, Delta, Diners, Mastercard, Switch, Visa

Private hotel in central position, just off seafront and close to town. Comfortable bedrooms with co-ordinated soft furnishings. Excellent, freshly cooked food. Licensed. Car park.

P €

B&B per person per night:
S £35.00–£40.00
D £27.00–£29.50

HB per person per night:
DY £41.50–£44.00

OPEN All Year

COLCHESTER, Essex Map ref 3B2 *Tourist Information Centre Tel: (01206) 282920*

PEVERIL HOTEL
51 North Hill, Colchester CO1 1PY
T: (01206) 574001
F: (01206) 574001

Bedrooms: 12 double, 5 single
Bathrooms: 6 en suite

Evening meal available
CC: Amex, Delta, Diners, Mastercard, Switch, Visa

Town centre, family-run hotel with excellent bar and restaurant facilities. Five minutes from the castle and town centre.

P €

B&B per person per night:
S £30.00–£50.00
D £21.00–£29.00

HB per person per night:
DY £38.00–£50.00

OPEN All Year except Christmas

♦♦

SCHEREGATE HOTEL
36 Osborne Street,
via St John's Street, Colchester
CO2 7DB
T: (01206) 573034
F: (01206) 541561

Bedrooms: 14 double, 11 single, 2 family
Bathrooms: 10 en suite

CC: Delta, Mastercard, Switch, Visa

Interesting 15thC building, centrally situated, providing accommodation at moderate prices.

P

B&B per person per night:
S £24.00–£35.00
D £20.00–£25.00

OPEN All Year except Christmas

COLTISHALL, Norfolk Map ref 3C1

THE HEDGES GUESTHOUSE

Tunstead Road, Coltishall, Norwich
NR12 7AL
T: (01603) 738361
F: (01603) 738983
E: info@hedgesbandb.co.uk
I: www.hedgesbandb.co.uk

Hear evening owlsong and the dawn chorus at this friendly family-run guesthouse. Set in large, peaceful gardens surrounded by open countryside, yet convenient for local amenities. Ideal base for exploring the Norfolk Broads, Norwich and Norfolk coast. Families welcome, spacious lounge with log fire, licensed, plenty of parking.

Bedrooms: 3 double, 2 family
Bathrooms: 5 en suite

Evening meal available
CC: Delta, Mastercard, Switch, Visa

3 nights for price of 2 Nov-Apr. Quote 342 when booking.

P €

B&B per person per night:
S £23.50–£30.00
D £23.50–£24.50

OPEN All Year except Christmas

TOWN INDEX

This can be found at the back of the guide. If you know where you want to stay, the index will give you the page number listing accommodation in your chosen town, city or village.

COLTISHALL continued

TERRA NOVA LODGE

14 Westbourne Road, Coltishall, Norwich
NR12 7HT
T: (01603) 736264

B&B per person per night:
S Min £40.00
D £23.00–£25.00

OPEN All Year except Christmas

Terranova Lodge offers tranquil accommodation in a lovely Broadland village. Large, tastefully furnished en suite rooms, private entrance for guests, TV and hospitality tray. Full English breakfast served in our conservatory overlooking delightful gardens. Easy access to the coast, the Broads and the fine medieval city of Norwich.

Bedrooms: 1 double, 1 twin
Bathrooms: 2 en suite

P

CRANFIELD, Bedfordshire Map ref 2D1

CROFT END BED & BREAKFAST

10 Hotch Croft, Cranfield, Bedford
MK43 0BN
T: (01234) 750753
E: chambers@xalt.co.uk

B&B per person per night:
S £14.50–£18.00
D £20.00–£25.00

OPEN All Year except Christmas

Family run with countryside views from all windows, situated halfway between central Milton Keynes and Bedford, five miles from M1 jcts 13 and 14 and one hour from London by train. Nearby: Woburn Abbey, safari park and golf course, real-snow ski slope, theatre, art gallery. Greensand Ridge and Bunyon Way walks pass the house.

Bedrooms: 1 double, 3 single, 1 family
Bathrooms: 2 en suite

Evening meal available

Long-stay discounts available.

P

DARSHAM, Suffolk Map ref 3C2

WHITE HOUSE FARM

Main Road, Darsham, Saxmundham
IP17 3PP
T: (01728) 668632
F: (01728) 668169
E: VNewm1@aol.com

Bedrooms: 2 double, 1 twin
Bathrooms: 1 en suite

B&B per person per night:
S £25.00–£35.00
D £20.00–£27.50

OPEN All Year except Christmas

Small, family-run, modernised farmhouse with pleasant gardens, on edge of village. Easy access to Aldeburgh, Southwold, Dunwich, Minsmere. Large gardens. Hearty farmhouse breakfasts.

5 P

USE YOUR *i*s

There are more than 550 Tourist Information Centres throughout England offering friendly help with accommodation and holiday ideas as well as suggestions of places to visit and things to do. You'll find TIC addresses in the local Phone Book.

DERSINGHAM, Norfolk Map ref 3B1

ASHDENE HOUSE

Dersingham, King's Lynn PE31 6HQ
T: (01485) 540395
I: www3.mistral.co.uk/ashdene

An elegant Victorian house in village centre bordering Royal Estate with woodland walks and close to North Norfolk coastal attractions and nature reserves. Ashdene House is set in a pleasant garden with ample car parking facilities. A warm welcome and friendly personal service is guaranteed.

Bedrooms: 2 double, 2 twin, 1 family
Bathrooms: 5 en suite

Evening meal available
CC: Delta, Mastercard, Switch, Visa

3 P

B&B per person per night:
S £20.00–£25.00
D £22.50–£24.00

HB per person per night:
DY £29.00–£31.50

OPEN All Year except Christmas

EARL SOHAM, Suffolk Map ref 3C2

Silver Award

BRIDGE HOUSE

Earl Soham, Framlingham, Woodbridge IP13 7RT
T: (01728) 685473
F: (01728) 685289
E: bridgehouse46@hotmail.com
I: www.jenniferbaker.co.uk

Bedrooms: 2 double, 1 twin
Bathrooms: 3 en suite

Evening meal available

Bridge House is an attractive, 16thC property near Heritage Coast. A warm welcome and excellent food add charm to well-appointed, comfortable accommodation.

10 P

B&B per person per night:
S £30.00–£35.00
D £25.00–£30.00

HB per person per night:
DY £37.00–£49.00

OPEN All Year

EARLS COLNE, Essex Map ref 3B2

RIVERSIDE LODGE

40 Lower Holt Street, Earls Colne, Colchester CO6 2PH
T: (01787) 223487
F: (01787) 223487
E: bandb@riversidelodge-uk.com
I: www.riversidelodge-uk.com

Bedrooms: 2 double, 3 twin
Bathrooms: 5 en suite

CC: Mastercard, Visa

On the A1124 Colchester-Halstead road, single storey, en suite chalets on the banks of the River Colne. Restaurants, pubs and village amenities within walking distance.

P

B&B per person per night:
S £38.50–£40.50
D £23.50–£25.50

ELY, Cambridgeshire Map ref 3A2 *Tourist Information Centre Tel: (01353) 662062*

THE FOUNTAIN

1 Churchgate Street, Soham, Ely CB7 5DS
T: (01353) 720374
F: (01353) 722103
E: enquiries@thefountain.co.uk
I: www.thefountain.co.uk

Bedrooms: 3 twin
Bathrooms: 3 en suite

Evening meal available
CC: Delta, Mastercard, Switch, Visa

Well-appointed accommodation in town centre within easy reach of Ely and Newmarket. Hosting restaurant/bar facilities, offering a wide range of home-cooked meals.

P

B&B per person per night:
S £29.00
D £21.50

OPEN All Year

TOWN INDEX

This can be found at the back of the guide. If you know where you want to stay, the index will give you the page number listing accommodation in your chosen town, city or village.

ELY continued

♦♦♦♦
Gold Award

HILL HOUSE FARM

9 Main Street, Coveney, Ely CB6 2DJ
T: (01353) 778369
F: (01353) 778369
E: hill_house@madasafish.com

B&B per person per night:
S £30.00–£40.00
D £24.00–£27.00

OPEN All Year except Christmas

Fine Victorian farmhouse on arable working farm three miles west of Ely. First-class breakfast served in traditional dining room. Open views of surrounding countryside. No smoking, no pets, children over 12 welcome. Access from A142 or A10. Situated in the centre of quiet village. Convenient for Ely, Cambridge, Newmarket.

Bedrooms: 2 double, 1 twin
Bathrooms: 3 en suite

CC: Delta, Mastercard, Switch, Visa

12 P

♦♦♦♦

SPINNEY ABBEY

Stretham Road, Wicken, Ely CB7 5XQ
T: (01353) 720971
E: spinney.abbey@tesco.net
I: www.spinneyabbey.co.uk

B&B per person per night:
D Min £25.00

OPEN All Year except Christmas

This attractive Georgian Grade II Listed farmhouse, surrounded by pasture fields, stands next to our dairy farm which borders the National Trust Nature Reserve, 'Wicken Fen', on the southern edge of the Fens. Guests are welcome to make full use of spacious garden and all-weather tennis court. All rooms have private facilities.

Bedrooms: 1 double, 1 twin, 1 family
Bathrooms: 2 en suite, 1 private

5 P

EYE, Suffolk Map ref 3B2

♦♦♦♦♦
Silver Award

THE BULL AUBERGE

Ipswich Road, Yaxley, Eye IP23 8BZ
T: (01379) 783604
F: (01379) 788486
E: bullauberge@aol.com

B&B per person per night:
S £50.00–£70.00
D £30.00–£40.00

HB per person per night:
DY £64.00–£74.00

OPEN All Year except Christmas

A family-run concern. Well situated in the heart of East Anglia. Twenty-five miles Norwich, 20 miles Ipswich, 25 miles coast. Menu changed daily. Perfect place for a glass of champagne and a dozen oysters or any kind of fruits de mer (24 hours' notice). Bookings advisable.

Bedrooms: 3 double, 1 twin
Bathrooms: 4 en suite

Evening meal available
CC: Amex, Delta, Diners, Mastercard, Switch, Visa

P €

GOLD & SILVER AWARDS

These exclusive VisitBritain awards are given to establishments achieving the highest levels of quality and service. Further information can be found at the front of the guide. An index to all accommodation achieving these awards are at the back of this guide.

EYE continued

◆◆◆

THE WHITE HORSE INN

Stoke Ash, Eye IP23 7ET
T: (01379) 678222
F: (01379) 678557
E: whitehorse@stokeash.fsbusiness.co.uk
I: www.whitehorseinn.fsnet.co.uk

B&B per person per night:
S £39.95–£42.50
D £27.50

HB per person per night:
DY £37.50

OPEN All Year

Ideally situated and easy to find on the main A140. Modern, comfortable and quiet double- and twin-bedded accommodation with 24-hour access and many extras. Early check in/out available. The main building is heavily timbered with many period features. Hot food served all day, every day.

Bedrooms: 3 double, 3 twin, 1 family
Bathrooms: 7 en suite

Evening meal available
CC: Delta, Mastercard, Switch, Visa

Stay 2 nights, get third night free! (subject to availability) Fri/Sat/Sun. £54.95 per double.

FAKENHAM, Norfolk Map ref 3B1

◆◆◆

ABBOTT FARM

Walsingham Road, Binham, Fakenham NR21 0AW
T: (01328) 830519
F: (01328) 830519
E: abbot.farm@btinternet.com

Bedrooms: 1 double, 2 twin
Bathrooms: 3 en suite

B&B per person per night:
S £20.00–£24.00
D £20.00–£24.00

OPEN All Year except Christmas

126-acre arable farm. Rural views of North Norfolk including the historic Binham Priory. Liz and Alan offer a warm welcome to their guesthouse.

◆◆◆◆◆
Gold Award

HOLLY LODGE

The Street, Thursford Green, Fakenham NR21 0AS
T: (01328) 878465
F: (01328) 878465
E: hollyguestlodge@btopenworld.com
I: www.hollylodgeguesthouse.co.uk

B&B per person per night:
S £50.00–£70.00
D £60.00–£80.00

Warm and welcoming atmosphere at our 18thC house and guest cottages. Picturesque setting, period charm. Stylish, luxurious rooms, all en suite, centrally heated, TV/VCR, tea/coffee facilities, beams, 4-poster, antique furniture. Home-cooked breakfast, car parking. Ideally situated for places of interest, Norfolk coast and countryside. 'Highly commended Guesthouse of the Year'.

Bedrooms: 3 double
Bathrooms: 3 en suite

7 nights for the price of 6.

14

◆◆◆◆

THE OLD BRICK KILNS GUESTHOUSE

Little Barney Lane, Barney, Fakenham NR21 0NL
T: (01328) 878305
F: (01328) 878948
E: enquire@old-brick-kilns.co.uk
I: www.old-brick-kilns.co.uk

Bedrooms: 2 double, 1 single
Bathrooms: 3 en suite

Evening meal available
CC: Delta, Diners, Mastercard, Switch, Visa

B&B per person per night:
S Min £25.00
D Min £25.00

OPEN All Year except Christmas

Private 7-acre park with fishing pond (David Bellamy Gold Conservation Award 1997 and 1998), home cooking with fresh produce (Heartbeat Award). No pets, no smoking.

CHECK THE MAPS

The colour maps at the front of this guide show all the cities, towns and villages for which you will find accommodation entries.
Refer to the town index to find the page on which they are listed.

FEERING, Essex Map ref 3B2

◆◆◆

OLD WILLS FARM

Wittletey Road, Feering, Colchester
CO5 9RP
T: (01376) 570259
F: (01376) 570259
E: janecrayston@btconnect.com

Attractive and comfortable Essex farmhouse on a working arable farm with a large garden. Offering homely surroundings and atmosphere. Ideal relaxing base from which to sample the many and varied visitor attractions in the area, including historic sites, coastal regions and good restaurants.

Bedrooms: 1 double, 1 single, 1 family
Bathrooms: 1 en suite, 1 private

B&B per person per night:
S £27.00–£30.00
D £22.50–£25.00

OPEN All Year except Christmas

HALESWORTH, Suffolk Map ref 3C2

◆◆◆

FEN-WAY GUEST HOUSE

Fen-Way, School Lane, Halesworth
IP19 8BW
T: (01986) 873574

Bedrooms: 2 double, 1 twin
Bathrooms: 1 en suite

Spacious bungalow in seven acres of peaceful meadowland. Pets include sheep and lambs. Five minutes' walk from town centre. Convenient for many places including Southwold (nine miles).

5

B&B per person per night:
S £19.00–£25.00
D £19.00–£23.00

OPEN All Year

HARWICH, Essex Map ref 3C2 *Tourist Information Centre Tel: (01255) 506139*

◆◆

OCEANVIEW

86 Main Road, Dovercourt, Harwich
CO12 3LH
T: (01255) 554078
F: (01255) 554519
E: oceanview@dovercourt.org.uk
I: www.oceanview.fsbusiness.co.uk

Bedrooms: 2 double, 1 single, 2 family
Bathrooms: 2 en suite

Bed and breakfast with en suite, self-catering, family rooms and budget rooms. Vegetarian menu available. Garage parking.

B&B per person per night:
S £20.00–£25.00
D £17.50–£22.50

OPEN All Year except Christmas

◆◆◆

PASTON LODGE

1 Una Road, Parkeston, Harwich
CO12 4PP
T: (01255) 551390

Bedrooms: 1 double, 1 twin, 1 single, 1 family
Bathrooms: 4 en suite

Edwardian house offering comfortable, en suite, bed and breakfast facilities, situated within walking distance of Harwich International port. All rooms are non-smoking.

1 P €

B&B per person per night:
S £25.00–£27.00
D £48.00–£52.00

OPEN All Year except Christmas

◆◆◆◆ Silver Award

WOODVIEW COTTAGE

Wrabness Road, Ramsey, Harwich
CO12 5ND
T: (01255) 886413
E: anne@woodview-cottage.co.uk
I: www.woodview-cottage.co.uk

Bedrooms: 1 double, 1 single
Bathrooms: 2 en suite

Spacious, homely accommodation in pretty, peaceful country cottage adjacent to nature reserve and Stour estuary. Harwich Port four miles. Reductions for two or more nights.

B&B per person per night:
S £35.00
D £24.00

OPEN All Year

HATFIELD

See ad opposite

SPECIAL BREAKS

Many establishments offer special promotions and themed breaks. These are highlighted in red. (All such offers are subject to availability.)

HATFIELD HEATH, Essex Map ref 2D1

◆◆◆◆

FRIARS FARM
Hatfield Heath, Bishop's Stortford
CM22 7AP
T: (01279) 730244
F: (01279) 730244

Bedrooms: 1 double,
1 twin
Bathrooms: 1 en suite,
1 private

B&B per person per night:
S £25.00–£30.00
D £22.50–£30.00

OPEN All Year except Christmas

Ivy-clad 19thC farmhouse in rural location. Friars has been home to the Hockley family for over a century.

HAUGHLEY, Suffolk Map ref 3B2

RED HOUSE FARM
Station Road, Haughley,
Stowmarket IP14 3QP
T: (01449) 673323
F: (01449) 675413
E: mary@noy1.fsnet.co.uk
I: www.farmstayanglia.co.uk

Bedrooms: 1 double,
1 twin, 2 single
Bathrooms: 4 en suite

B&B per person per night:
S £30.00–£35.00
D £25.00–£27.50

OPEN All Year except Christmas

Attractive farmhouse in rural location on small grassland farm. First-class breakfast. Central heating and large garden.

HETHERSETT, Norfolk Map ref 3B1

MAGNOLIA HOUSE
Cromwell Close, Hethersett,
Norwich NR9 3HD
T: (01603) 810749
F: (01603) 810749

Bedrooms: 2 double,
1 twin, 2 single

B&B per person per night:
S £24.00–£28.00
D £22.00–£24.00

OPEN All Year

Family-run B&B. All rooms centrally heated, colour TV, hot water, tea/coffee-making facilities. Laundry, public telephone and fax available. Weekend-break discounts. Private car park.

CONFIRM YOUR BOOKING
You are advised to confirm your booking in writing.

HINDRINGHAM, Norfolk Map ref 3B1

♦♦♦♦♦
Gold Award

FIELD HOUSE

Moorgate Road, Hindringham, Fakenham
NR21 0PT
T: (01328) 878726
F: (01328) 878955
E: stay@fieldhousehindringham.co.uk
I: www.fieldhousehindringham.co.uk

Field House stands in lovely gardens on the edge of the peaceful village, close to the North Norfolk coast, and enjoys fine views of the Norfolk countryside. Luxurious bedrooms with many thoughtful extras. Quality cooking, with dinner being a highlight. Relaxing and friendly hospitality. A great place to unwind.

Bedrooms: 2 double
Bathrooms: 2 en suite

Evening meal available

B&B per person per night:
D £35.00–£45.00

HB per person per night:
DY £60.00–£70.00

OPEN All Year except Christmas

HINTLESHAM, Suffolk Map ref 3B2

♦♦♦♦
Silver Award

COLLEGE FARM

Back Road, Hintlesham, Ipswich
IP8 3NT
T: (01473) 652253
F: (01473) 652253
E: bryce1@agripro.co.uk
I: www.smoothhound.co.uk/hotels/collegefarm

Bedrooms: 2 double, 1 single, 1 family
Bathrooms: 2 en suite

Peaceful, 500-year-old beamed house on 600-acre arable farm near Ipswich. Convenient for Constable country, Sutton Hoo and the coast. Well-appointed, comfortable rooms. Good food locally.

B&B per person per night:
S £22.00–£32.00
D £22.50–£30.00

OPEN All Year except Christmas

HOLT, Norfolk Map ref 3B1

♦♦♦♦

LAWNS HOTEL

Station Road, Holt NR25 6BS
T: (01263) 713390
F: (01263) 710642
E: info@lawnshotel.co.uk
I: www.lawnshotel.co.uk

Situated in North Norfolk's historic town of Holt. Ideal for exploring both the enchanting coastline and scenic countryside, the Lawns is a charming Georgian hotel providing spacious accommodation with tranquil setting and delightful walled gardens. Car park. Much emphasis on hospitality and courteous service. The perfect retreat at any time.

Bedrooms: 6 double, 2 twin, 1 single, 1 family
Bathrooms: 9 en suite, 1 private

CC: Delta, Mastercard, Switch, Visa

Please ask when booking for out-of-season special offers.

B&B per person per night:
S £26.00–£40.00
D £26.00–£37.50

OPEN All Year

HOLTON ST MARY, Suffolk Map ref 3B2

STRATFORD HOUSE

Holton St Mary, Colchester
CO7 6NT
T: (01206) 298246
F: (01206) 298246
E: fjs.stratho@brutus.go-plus.net

Bedrooms: 1 double, 1 twin, 1 single
Bathrooms: 1 en suite

Evening meal available

Quality accommodation in comfortable home in Constable country, one mile from Flatford Mill. Easy access to A12/A14. Good food locally.

B&B per person per night:
S £25.00–£30.00
D £25.00–£30.00

OPEN All Year except Christmas

RATING All accommodation in this guide has been rated, or is awaiting a rating, by a trained VisitBritain assessor.

IPSWICH, Suffolk Map ref 3B2 *Tourist Information Centre Tel: (01473) 258070*

♦♦♦♦ Silver Award

LATTICE LODGE GUEST HOUSE
499 Woodbridge Road, Ipswich
IP4 4EP
T: (01473) 712474
F: (01473) 272239
E: lattice.lodge@btinternet.com
I: www.latticelodge.co.uk

Bedrooms: 5 double, 3 twin, 1 single, 1 family
Bathrooms: 10 en suite

Edwardian, spacious, clean, detached house, good food and modern facilities. Situated on main road a short distance from town centre. Good-size car park.

B&B per person per night:
S £35.25
D £48.00–£56.40

OPEN All Year except Christmas

KERSEY, Suffolk Map ref 3B2

♦♦♦

RED HOUSE FARM
Wickerstreet Green, Kersey, Ipswich
IP7 6EY
T: (01787) 210245

Bedrooms: 1 double, 1 twin, 1 single
Bathrooms: 2 en suite

Evening meal available

Comfortable, Listed farmhouse between Kersey and Boxford, central for Constable country. Rooms have TV and tea-making facilities. Swimming pool.

B&B per person per night:
S £28.00–£30.00
D £22.00–£24.00

HB per person per night:
DY £32.00–£40.00

OPEN All Year except Christmas

KETTLEBURGH, Suffolk Map ref 3C2

♦♦♦

CHURCH FARM
Kettleburgh, Woodbridge IP13 7LF
T: (01728) 723532
E: jbater@suffolkonline.net

Bedrooms: 1 double, 2 twin
Bathrooms: 1 en suite

Evening meal available

Oak-beamed, 350-year-old farmhouse on a working farm. Double bedrooms with lovely views and every comfort. Excellent food from home-grown produce.

B&B per person per night:
S £23.00–£26.00

HB per person per night:
DY £35.00–£38.00

OPEN All Year

KING'S LYNN, Norfolk Map ref 3B1 *Tourist Information Centre Tel: (01553) 763044*

♦♦♦

THE BEECHES GUESTHOUSE
2 Guanock Terrace, King's Lynn
PE30 5QT
T: (01553) 766577
F: (01553) 776664

Bedrooms: 5 double, 1 single, 1 family
Bathrooms: 4 en suite

Evening meal available
CC: Amex, Delta, Mastercard, Switch, Visa

Detached Victorian house, all rooms with TV, tea/coffee facilities and telephone. Most rooms en suite. Full English breakfast and three-course evening meal with coffee.

B&B per person per night:
S £24.00–£32.00
D £21.00–£25.00

HB per person per night:
DY £32.50–£40.00

OPEN All Year except Christmas

♦♦♦

THE VICTORY INN

Main Road, Clenchwarton, King's Lynn
PE34 4AQ
T: (01553) 660682
E: trevorswift8@btopenworld.com

Large car park. Beer garden and barbecue. King's Lynn historical town just one mile. Easy access to main routes for Norfolk Broads and Lincolnshire.

Bedrooms: 2 twin

Evening meal available

B&B per person per night:
S £22.00–£25.00

HB per person per night:
DY £29.00–£31.00

OPEN All Year except Christmas

MAP REFERENCES The map references refer to the colour maps at the front of this guide. The first figure is the map number; the letter and figure which follow indicate the grid reference on the map.

LAVENHAM, Suffolk Map ref 3B2

♦♦♦♦
Silver Award

LAVENHAM GREAT HOUSE HOTEL

Market Place, Lavenham, Sudbury CO10 9QZ
T: (01787) 247431
F: (01787) 248007
E: info@greathouse.co.uk
I: www.greathouse.co.uk

Delightful 16thC house with award-winning restaurant on magnificent Lavenham square. Beautifully decorated, individual bedooms, all furnished with antiques (one 4-poster bedroom). Most have sitting areas and provide every comfort to modern travellers. Daily-changing lunch and dinner (not Saturday) set menus offer excellent value.

Bedrooms: 2 twin, 1 family, 2 suites
Bathrooms: 3 en suite

Evening meal available
CC: Amex, Delta, Mastercard, Switch, Visa

2/3-night stay from £69.95pppn including DB&B and full English breakfast. Available Tue-Thu inclusive.

B&B per person per night:
S £70.00–£99.00
D £40.00–£80.00

HB per person per night:
DY £69.95–£115.00

♦♦♦♦

THE OLD CONVENT

The Street, Kettlebaston, Ipswich IP7 7QA
T: (01449) 741557
E: holidays@kettlebaston.fsnet.co.uk
I: www.kettlebaston.fsnet.co.uk

A warm welcome awaits you in our comfortable 17thC Grade II Listed thatched home. We are committed to providing you with a memorable, comfortable stay. Attractive bedrooms with en suite facilities. Exposed beams, seasonal log fires, hearty, imaginative breakfasts. Ample off-street parking. Guests' TV lounge. Centrally located for touring. Colour brochure available.

Bedrooms: 2 double, 1 twin
Bathrooms: 3 en suite

3-night mid-week stay: £150 double B&B – Jun, Sep, Oct.

B&B per person per night:
S £32.50–£40.00
D £25.00–£32.50

OPEN All Year except Christmas

LITTLE CANFIELD, Essex Map ref 2D1

♦♦♦♦♦
Gold Award

CANFIELD MOAT

High Cross Lane West, Little Canfield, Great Dunmow CM6 1TD
T: (01371) 872565
F: (01371) 876264
E: falk@canfieldmoat.co.uk
I: www.canfieldmoat.co.uk

A Georgian rectory set in eight acres including lawns, paddocks, woodland and a small lake. All rooms are spacious and beautifully furnished. Antique furniture and log fires feature in the public rooms. Breakfast includes eggs from our own chickens. Afternoon tea with homemade cakes often available at no extra cost.

Bedrooms: 1 double, 1 twin
Bathrooms: 2 en suite

B&B per person per night:
S £40.00–£50.00
D £32.50–£35.00

OPEN All Year except Christmas

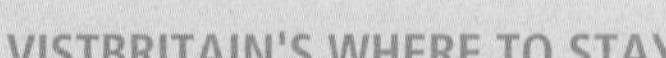

VISTBRITAIN'S WHERE TO STAY
Please mention this guide when making your booking.

LITTLE WALSINGHAM, Norfolk Map ref 3B1

ST DAVID'S HOUSE

Friday Market, Little Walsingham, Walsingham NR22 6BY
T: (01328) 820633
E: stdavidshouse@amserve.net
I: www.stilwell.co.uk

Bedrooms: 3 double, 2 family
Bathrooms: 2 en suite

Evening meal available

16thC brick house in a delightful medieval village. The village is fully signposted from Fakenham (A148). Four miles from the coast.

B&B per person per night:
S £24.00–£27.00
D £24.00–£27.00

HB per person per night:
DY £37.00–£40.00

OPEN All Year

LOWESTOFT, Suffolk Map ref 3C1 *Tourist Information Centre Tel: (01502) 533600*

♦♦♦

HOMELEA GUEST HOUSE

33 Marine Parade, Lowestoft
NR33 0QN
T: (01502) 511640

Bedrooms: 3 double, 2 family
Bathrooms: 4 en suite, 1 private

Evening meal available

Family-run guesthouse on seafront. Homely accommodation for tourists and travellers.

3 P €

B&B per person per night:
S £20.00–£25.00
D £20.00–£22.50

HB per person per night:
DY Min £27.50

OPEN All Year except Christmas

MALDON, Essex Map ref 3B3 *Tourist Information Centre Tel: (01621) 856503*

♦♦♦

LITTLE OWLS

Post Office Road,
Woodham Mortimer, Maldon
CM9 6ST
T: (01245) 224355
F: (01245) 224355
E: the.bushes@virgin.net

Bedrooms: 1 double, 1 twin, 1 family
Bathrooms: 1 en suite

Friendly, family-run establishment, set in rural Essex. Bedrooms are light and spacious with panoramic views over surrounding countryside. Large garden with heated indoor swimming pool.

P

B&B per person per night:
S £25.00–£35.00
D £20.00–£25.00

OPEN All Year except Christmas

MARCH, Cambridgeshire Map ref 3A1

♦♦♦

CAUSEWAY GUEST HOUSE

6 The Causeway, March PE15 9NT
T: (01354) 650823
F: (01354) 661068

Bedrooms: 11 double, 4 single, 1 family
Bathrooms: 16 en suite

CC: Delta, Mastercard, Switch, Visa

This 19thC house offers en suite accommodation, colour TV and tea/coffee facilities in all rooms. Private car park. Situated five minutes' walk from town centre.

P

B&B per person per night:
S Max £24.00
D Max £17.50

OPEN All Year

MARGARET RODING, Essex Map ref 2D1

Silver Award

GARNISH HALL

Margaret Roding CM6 1QL
T: (01245) 231209
F: (01245) 231224

A 15thC manor house, once moated. Graceful curved staircase. Bedrooms with lovely views of the island. On A1060 Chelmsford road, adjacent to a Norman church which boasts perhaps the most attractive doorway in Essex. Black swans, carp. Tennis court, walled garden. Walking distance of Reid Rooms, popular for the Punchbowl Restaurant.

Bedrooms: 3 double
Bathrooms: 1 en suite, 2 private

Evening meal available

Mid-week breaks – 3 nights for the price of 2 (Mon-Thu).

P

B&B per person per night:
S £35.00–£40.00
D £35.00–£40.00

HB per person per night:
DY £60.00–£65.00

OPEN All Year except Christmas

HALF BOARD PRICES Half board prices are given per person, but in some cases these may be based on double/twin occupancy.

MARGARET RODING continued

◆◆◆

GREYS

Ongar Road, Margaret Roding, Great Dunmow CM6 1QR
T: (01245) 231509

Bedrooms: 3 double

B&B in old beamed cottage on family arable farm. A non-smoking house. Tiny village. Turn off A1060 at sign to Berners Roding. 0.5 miles along.

B&B per person per night:
S Min £25.00
D Min £22.50

OPEN All Year except Christmas

NAYLAND, Suffolk Map ref 3B2

◆◆◆◆

GLADWINS FARM

Harpers Hill, Nayland, Colchester CO6 4NU
T: (01206) 262261
F: (01206) 263001
E: gladwinsfarm@aol.com
I: www.gladwinsfarm.co.uk

Bedrooms: 2 double, 1 single
Bathrooms: 2 en suite

CC: Delta, Mastercard, Switch, Visa

22-acre smallholding. Timbered farmhouse in peaceful wooded surroundings in Constable country. Entrance on A134. Fishing, tennis, heated indoor pool and sauna. Home and local produce. Colour brochure.

B&B per person per night:
S £28.00
D £15.00–£16.25

OPEN All Year except Christmas

NEWMARKET, Suffolk Map ref 3B2 *Tourist Information Centre Tel: (01638) 667200*

THE MEADOW HOUSE

2A High Street, Burwell, Cambridge CB5 0HB
T: (01638) 741926
F: (01638) 741861
E: hilary@themeadowhouse.co.uk
I: www.themeadowhouse.co.uk

Large, well-equipped modern house set in grounds of two acres, close to Newmarket Racecourse, Cambridge and Ely. King-size double beds. Family suites available, also coach house available in grounds. Large car park. Generous breakfasts. Two rooms suitable for the moderately disabled. More colour pictures available on our website.

Bedrooms: 3 double, 3 family
Bathrooms: 4 en suite

B&B per person per night:
S £25.00–£27.00
D £23.00–£25.00

OPEN All Year except Christmas

NORFOLK BROADS

See under Beccles, Bungay, Coltishall, Lowestoft, Norwich, Rackheath, South Walsham, Wroxham

NORTH FAMBRIDGE, Essex Map ref 3B3

FERRY BOAT INN

North Fambridge, Chelmsford CM3 6LR
T: (01621) 740208
F: (01621) 740208
E: sylviaferryboat@aol.com
I: www.ferryboatinn.net

A 500-year-old riverside inn bursting with character. Open fires, a wealth of exposed beams and a large garden for the warmer times. The pub serves traditional ales as well as keg lagers and a wide range of bottles beers. A new annexe offers warm, comfortable rooms at affordable prices.

Bedrooms: 3 double, 3 twin
Bathrooms: 6 en suite

Evening meal available
CC: Amex, Delta, Mastercard, Switch, Visa

B&B per person per night:
S £30.00–£35.00
D £20.00–£22.50

OPEN All Year except Christmas

NORWICH, Norfolk Map ref 3C1 *Tourist Information Centre Tel: (01603) 727927*

♦♦♦♦

BECKLANDS

105 Holt Road, Horsford, Norwich NR10 3AB
T: (01603) 898582
F: (01603) 754223
E: becklands@aol.com

Bedrooms: 5 double, 4 single
Bathrooms: 7 en suite, 1 private

CC: Diners, Mastercard, Visa

B&B per person per night:
S £25.00–£30.00
D £22.50–£25.00

OPEN All Year

Quietly located modern house overlooking open countryside five miles north of Norwich. Central for the Broads and coastal areas.

P

♦♦♦♦

CAVELL HOUSE

The Common, Swardeston, Norwich NR14 8DZ
T: (01508) 578195
F: (01508) 578195
E: joljean.harris@virgin.net

Bedrooms: 1 double, 1 twin
Bathrooms: 1 en suite

Evening meal available

B&B per person per night:
S £22.00–£25.00
D £22.00–£45.00

OPEN All Year except Christmas

Birthplace of nurse Edith Cavell. Rural Georgian farmhouse on edge of Swardeston village. Off B1113 south of Norwich, five miles from centre. Near university, new hospital.

P

♦♦♦♦

CHURCH FARM GUESTHOUSE

Church Street, Horsford, Norwich NR10 3DB
T: (01603) 898020
F: (01603) 891649
E: churchfarmguesthouse.@btopenworld.com

Bedrooms: 7 double, 2 twin, 1 single
Bathrooms: 10 en suite

CC: Delta, Diners, Mastercard, Switch, Visa

B&B per person per night:
S £30.00–£35.00
D £22.50–£25.00

HB per person per night:
DY £55.00–£60.00

OPEN All Year

Quiet, modernised, 17thC farmhouse. Separate entrance, lounge and dining room for guests. Approximately four miles north of Norwich. All rooms en suite.

P

♦♦♦

EDMAR LODGE

64 Earlham Road, Norwich NR2 3DF
T: (01603) 615599
F: (01603) 495599
E: mail@edmarlodge.co.uk
I: www.edmarlodge.co.uk

B&B per person per night:
S £30.00–£35.00
D £20.00–£24.00

OPEN All Year

Edmar Lodge is a family-run guesthouse where you will receive a warm welcome from Ray and Sue. We are situated only 10 minutes' walk from the city centre. All rooms have en suite facilities and digital TV. We are well-known for our excellent breakfasts that set you up for the day.

Bedrooms: 4 double, 1 family
Bathrooms: 5 en suite

CC: Amex, Delta, Mastercard, Switch, Visa

Weekend breaks Oct–Mar – special rates including discount on evening meals at local restaurant.

P €

CHECK THE MAPS

The colour maps at the front of this guide show all the cities, towns and villages for which you will find accommodation entries. Refer to the town index to find the page on which they are listed.

NORWICH continued

♦♦♦♦

THE GABLES GUESTHOUSE

527 Earlham Road, Norwich NR4 7HN
T: (01603) 456666
F: (01603) 250320

Friendly, family-run, non-smoking guesthouse with very high-quality, en suite accommodation and relaxing residents' lounge. Excellent full English breakfast served in our delightful conservatory. Illuminated car park at rear within secluded gardens. Situated within easy walking distance of university and close to Research Park, hospital and city centre.

Bedrooms: 6 double, 4 twin, 1 family
Bathrooms: 11 en suite

CC: Delta, Mastercard, Switch, Visa

B&B per person per night:
S £42.00
D £31.00–£33.50

♦♦♦♦

MANOR BARN HOUSE

Back Lane, Rackheath, Norwich NR13 6NN
T: (01603) 783543
E: jane.roger@manorbarnhouse.co.uk
I: www.manorbarnhouse.co.uk

Bedrooms: 3 double, 2 twin
Bathrooms: 4 en suite, 1 private

Traditional Norfolk barn conversion with exposed beams in quiet setting with pleasant gardens. Close to heart of the Broads, five miles Norwich. All rooms en suite.

5 P

B&B per person per night:
S £25.00–£32.00
D £25.00–£27.00

OPEN All Year

♦♦♦

MARLBOROUGH HOUSE HOTEL

22 Stracey Road, Norwich NR1 1EZ
T: (01603) 628005
F: (01603) 628005

Bedrooms: 3 double, 3 twin, 3 single, 2 family
Bathrooms: 11 en suite

Evening meal available

Long-established family hotel, close city centre, new Riverside development, Castle Mall, museum, cathedral. All double, twin and family rooms are en suite. Licensed bar, car park.

P €

B&B per person per night:
S £35.00–£46.00
D £29.00–£31.00

HB per person per night:
DY £50.00–£61.00

OPEN All Year

♦♦♦♦
Silver Award

THE OLD RECTORY

Hall Road, Framingham Earl, Norwich NR14 7SB
T: (01508) 493590
F: (01508) 495110
E: oldrectory@f-earl.fsnet.co.uk
I: www.f-earl.fsnet.co.uk

Bedrooms: 1 double, 1 twin

Beautifully renovated and extended 17thC family house set in two acres of country garden. Wealth of beams in lounge and dining room. Village 4.5 miles south-east of Norwich.

P

B&B per person per night:
S £28.00–£32.00
D £24.00–£29.00

OPEN All Year except Christmas

PETERBOROUGH, Cambridgeshire Map ref 3A1 *Tourist Information Centre Tel: (01733) 452336*

♦♦

PARK ROAD GUESTHOUSE

67 Park Road, Peterborough PE1 2TN
T: (01733) 562220
F: (01733) 344279

Bedrooms: 1 double, 1 twin, 2 single, 1 family
Bathrooms: 4 en suite, 1 private

Comfortable, family-run, five minutes from city centre, close to coach and railway station. Good English breakfast, centrally heated. All rooms en suite, tea/coffee, colour TV and hairdryer.

5 P

B&B per person per night:
S £30.00–£35.00
D £22.50–£25.00

OPEN All Year except Christmas

VISITOR ATTRACTIONS For ideas on places to visit refer to the introduction at the beginning of this section. Look out too for the VisitBritain Quality Assured Visitor Attraction signs.

PETTISTREE, Suffolk Map ref 3C2

THE THREE TUNS COACHING INN

Main Road, Pettistree, Woodbridge
IP13 0HW
T: (01728) 747979
F: (01728) 746244
E: jon@threetuns-coachinginn.co.uk
I: www.threetuns-coachinginn.co.uk

John and Brenda invite you to visit their enchanting coaching inn, ideally situated for visiting the Suffolk Heritage Coast. All rooms are en suite and fully equipped. After experiencing local ales at the bar and fine food in the restaurant, just relax in the comfortable lounge with its open log fires.

Bedrooms: 8 double, 2 twin, 1 single
Bathrooms: 11 en suite

Evening meal available
CC: Amex, Delta, Mastercard, Switch, Visa

Mid-week/weekend breaks on application.

B&B per person per night:
S £45.00–£55.00
D £32.50–£40.00

HB per person per night:
DY £47.50–£55.00

OPEN All Year

RACKHEATH, Norfolk Map ref 3C1

BARN COURT

6 Back Lane, Rackheath, Norwich
NR13 6NN
T: (01603) 782536
F: (01603) 782536
E: barncourtbb@hotmail.com

Bedrooms: 3 double
Bathrooms: 1 en suite, 2 private

Evening meal available

Spacious accommodation in a traditional Norfolk barn conversion, built around a courtyard. Ideal base for exploring Norfolk – three miles Norwich. Friendly atmosphere and good home cooking.

B&B per person per night:
S £20.00–£25.00
D £20.00–£25.00

OPEN All Year except Christmas

ROYSTON, Hertfordshire Map ref 2D1

THE ARIS INN HOTEL

Flint Cross, Newmarket Road, (A505),
Nr Royston SG8 7PN
T: (01763) 208272
F: (01763) 208268
E: arisinn@hotmail.com
I: www.arisinn.co.uk

Budget hotel in a contemporary style, converted from an old flint-stoned coaching inn. Indian and international-cuisine restaurant opening in 2004. In six acres of land, situated close to Cambridge and Royston and convenient for Stanstead. Three miles from Duxford Museum.

Bedrooms: 10 double, 3 twin, 5 single, 2 family
Bathrooms: 20 en suite

Evening meal available
CC: Amex, Delta, Mastercard, Switch, Visa

B&B per person per night:
S £35.00–£46.00
D £25.00–£32.50

HB per person per night:
DY £60.00–£70.00

OPEN All Year

SAFFRON WALDEN, Essex Map ref 2D1 *Tourist Information Centre Tel: (01799) 510444*

Silver Award

THE BONNET

Overhall Lane, Stevington End,
Ashdon, Saffron Walden CB10 2JE
T: (01799) 584955
E: thebonnetuk@yahoo.co.uk
I: www.thebonnett.co.uk

Bedrooms: 3 double
Bathrooms: 2 en suite, 1 private

The Bonnet was built in the 16thC with two acres of gardens. Ideally located for exploring historic North Essex, Cambridge, Suffolk. Convenient for M11, Stansted.

B&B per person per night:
S £50.00–£60.00
D £27.50–£32.50

OPEN All Year except Christmas

SYMBOLS The symbols in each entry give information about services and facilities. A key to these symbols appears at the back of this guide.

SAFFRON WALDEN continued

THE CRICKETERS

Clavering, Saffron Walden CB11 4QT
T: (01799) 550442
F: (01799) 550882
E: cricketers@lineone.net
I: www.thecricketers.co.uk

16thC freehouse near Stansted Airport, with beamed interior, well-established restaurant and bar-meal trade with adjacent accommodation. Jamie Oliver grew up here and cooked here from the age of eight. Although he no longer cooks here, it is still owned and run by his parents, Trevor and Sally Oliver.

Bedrooms: 11 double, 3 twin
Bathrooms: 14 en suite

Evening meal available
CC: Amex, Delta, Mastercard, Switch, Visa

20% reduction for B&B on any Sun or Fri. Please quote 'English Tourism Council'.

B&B per person per night:
S £70.00
D £50.00

HB per person per night:
DY £76.00

OPEN All Year except Christmas

1 GUNTERS COTTAGES

Thaxted Road, Saffron Walden CB10 2UT
T: (01799) 522091

Bedrooms: 1 double
Bathrooms: 1 private

Rebuilt 19thC cottages with views over open farmland. Indoor heated swimming pool. On Thaxted/Saffron Walden road, two miles from Saffron Walden.

B&B per person per night:
S Max £24.50
D Max £20.00

OPEN All Year

ST ALBANS, Hertfordshire Map ref 2D1 *Tourist Information Centre Tel: (01727) 864511*

TRESCO

76 Clarence Road, St Albans AL1 4NG
T: (01727) 864880
F: (01727) 864880
E: pat.leggatt@talk21.com
I: www.twistedsilicon.co.uk/76/index.htm

Bedrooms: 1 twin, 1 single

Spacious Edwardian house with quiet, comfortable rooms and pleasant conservatory. Park nearby. Easy walk to station for fast trains to London (20 minutes).

B&B per person per night:
S £30.00–£35.00
D £26.00–£28.00

OPEN All Year except Christmas

SANDY, Bedfordshire Map ref 2D1 *Tourist Information Centre Tel: (01767) 682728*

Silver Award

HIGHFIELD FARM

Tempsford Road, Great North Road, Sandy SG19 2AQ
T: (01767) 682332
F: (01767) 692503
E: margaret@highfield-farm.co.uk

Beautifully peaceful, welcoming farmhouse plus barn conversion on attractive arable farm. Wonderful location well back from A1. Bedford, Cambridge, Biggleswade, St Neots, Hitchin and Stevenage all within easy reach. All bedrooms en suite. London just 50 minutes by train. Delightful sitting room for guests' use. Hospitality tray in each bedroom. Safe parking. Most guests return.

Bedrooms: 4 double, 4 twin, 2 family
Bathrooms: 9 en suite, 1 private

CC: Delta, Mastercard, Switch, Visa

B&B per person per night:
S £45.00–£55.00
D £30.00–£32.50

OPEN All Year

PRICES
Please check prices and other details at the time of booking.

SAXMUNDHAM, Suffolk Map ref 3C2

♦♦♦♦

MOAT HOUSE FARM

Rendham Road, Carlton,
Saxmundham IP17 2QN
T: (01728) 602228
F: (01728) 602228
E: sally@goodacres.com
I: www.goodacres.com

Bedrooms: 1 double,
1 twin
Bathrooms: 2 en suite

B&B per person per night:
S £30.00–£35.00
D £25.00–£30.00

OPEN All Year

Detached property set in grounds of 3.5 acres with traditional Suffolk barns. We are surrounded by open farmland. Easy access to the A12 trunk road.

SHERINGHAM, Norfolk Map ref 3B1

CAMBERLEY GUESTHOUSE

62 Cliff Road, Sheringham NR26 8BJ
T: (01263) 823101
F: (01263) 821433
E: graham@camberleyguesthouse.co.uk
I: www.camberleyguesthouse.co.uk

Friendly, relaxing and spacious guesthouse in a quiet part of Sheringham. Views overlooking sea, town and countryside. All bedrooms en suite. Car parking in grounds.

Bedrooms: 5 double,
1 single
Bathrooms: 6 en suite

B&B per person per night:
S £27.00–£33.00
D £22.00–£28.00

OPEN All Year except Christmas

SHINGLE STREET, Suffolk Map ref 3C2

♦♦♦♦

LARK COTTAGE

Shingle Street, Woodbridge
IP12 3BE
T: (01394) 411292

Bedrooms: 1 double,
1 single
Bathrooms: 1 private

Evening meal available

B&B per person per night:
S £23.00–£25.00
D £22.50

HB per person per night:
DY £32.50

Beachside bungalow, very quiet location. Interesting sea/land birds, plants of special interest. Sutton Hoo four miles. One double with private shower/wc, one single with shared bathroom.

SNETTISHAM, Norfolk Map ref 3B1

♦♦♦♦

THE ROUND HOUSE

131 Lynn Road, Snettisham,
King's Lynn PE31 7QG
T: (01485) 540580
F: (01485) 543415
E: ziphac@aol.com

Bedrooms: 1 double,
1 twin
Bathrooms: 2 en suite

B&B per person per night:
S £37.50
D £30.00

OPEN All Year

Small Grade II Listed building, recently extensively restored, situated on edge of historic village and bounded by river and paddocks.

SOUTH WALSHAM, Norfolk Map ref 3C1

♦♦♦♦

OLD HALL FARM

Newport Road, South Walsham,
Norwich NR13 6DS
T: (01603) 270271
E: veronica@oldhallfarm.co.uk
I: www.oldhallfarm.co.uk

Bedrooms: 2 double,
1 twin
Bathrooms: 3 en suite

B&B per person per night:
S £25.00–£30.00
D £22.50–£25.00

OPEN All Year

Recently restored 17thC thatched farmhouse. Comfortable rooms, all en suite. Wide range of cooked breakfasts. Ideal centre for Norwich coast and Norfolk Broads. Non-smoking.

IMPORTANT NOTE Information on accommodation listed in this guide has been supplied by the proprietors. As changes may occur you are advised to check details at the time of booking.

SOUTHWOLD, Suffolk Map ref 3C2 *Tourist Information Centre Tel: (01502) 724729*

◆◆◆◆

NORTHCLIFFE GUESTHOUSE
20 North Parade, Southwold
IP18 6LT
T: (01502) 724074
F: (01502) 722218
E: northcliffe.southwold@virgin.net
I: www.northcliffe-southwold.co.uk

Bedrooms: 4 double, 2 twin
Bathrooms: 6 en suite

Select, en suite accommodation. Individually designed rooms of a high standard. Panoramic sea views. In quiet location next to beach, close to town centre. Lounge with log fire. Licensed.

B&B per person per night:
S £50.00–£70.00
D £35.00–£40.00

OPEN All Year

STOWMARKET, Suffolk Map ref 3B2 *Tourist Information Centre Tel: (01449) 676800*

STRICKLANDS

Stricklands Road, Stowmarket IP14 1AP
T: (01449) 612450
F: (01449) 614944
E: poppy@stricklandshouse.fsnet.co.uk

Stricklands is family run, extending a warm welcome. An oasis within the town of Stowmarket. Gardens have a large pond and many mature trees. Ample parking available. Full of character, the house is 14th-19thC. Part with oak beams, part Victorian, graced by spacious rooms with high ceilings.

Bedrooms: 2 double, 3 single, 2 family
Bathrooms: 3 en suite

B&B per person per night:
S £22.50–£27.50
D £22.50–£27.50

HB per person per night:
DY £28.00–£33.00

OPEN All Year except Christmas

STRETHAM, Cambridgeshire Map ref 3A2

THE RED LION

High Street, Stretham, Ely CB6 3JQ
T: (01353) 648132
F: (01353) 648327
E: frank.hayes@gateway.net

A village inn, completely refurbished, with en suite bedrooms, ideally situated for visiting the Fens and other tourist attractions. Four miles from Ely on A10. Cambridge 12 miles, Newmarket 14 miles. Pets welcome. Car park. Non-smoking conservatory restaurant.

Bedrooms: 5 double, 2 twin, 2 single, 3 family
Bathrooms: 12 en suite

Evening meal available
CC: Amex, Delta, Diners, Mastercard, Switch, Visa

B&B per person per night:
S £39.75
D £24.88–£43.75

HB per person per night:
DY £39.00–£59.00

OPEN All Year

SUDBOURNE, Suffolk Map ref 3C2

LONG MEADOWS
Gorse Lane, Sudbourne,
Woodbridge IP12 2BD
T: (01394) 450269

Bedrooms: 2 double, 1 single
Bathrooms: 1 private

Attractive cottage-style bungalow with show garden in rural location within the village. Consideration to guests' comfort and needs paramount.

B&B per person per night:
S £22.00–£24.00
D £23.00–£25.00

OPEN All Year except Christmas

www.visitengland.com

Log on for information and inspiration. The latest information on places to visit, events and quality assessed accommodation.

SUDBURY, Suffolk Map ref 3B2 *Tourist Information Centre Tel: (01787) 881320*

FIDDLESTICKS
Pinkuah Lane, Pentlow Ridge, Pentlow, Sudbury CO10 7JW
T: (01787) 280154
F: (01787) 280154
E: sarah@fiddlesticks.biz
I: www.fiddlesticks.biz

Bedrooms: 1 double, 1 single
Bathrooms: 2 en suite

Evening meal available

Warm hospitality and Aga cooking. Near to Cambridge, Colchester, Ely, Bury St Edmunds, 10 minutes to Long Melford, Clare and Cavendish. Lots to see and do.

B&B per person per night:
S £25.00–£40.00
D Max £30.00

HB per person per night:
DY £40.00–£47.50

OPEN All Year

SWEFFLING, Suffolk Map ref 3C2

SWEFFLING HALL FARM
Sweffling, Saxmundham IP17 2BT
T: (01728) 663644
F: (01728) 663644
E: stephenmann@suffolkonline.net

Bedrooms: 1 double, 1 family
Bathrooms: 2 en suite

Evening meal available

Set well back from main road in quiet location. Own milk and eggs. Wood fires in season. Always a warm welcome.

B&B per person per night:
S £23.00–£28.00
D £15.00–£20.00

OPEN All Year except Christmas

TERRINGTON ST JOHN, Norfolk Map ref 3A1

Silver Award

SOMERVILLE HOUSE

Church Road, Terrington St John, Wisbech PE14 7RY
T: (01945) 880952
F: (01945) 881150
E: somervillemc@hotmail.com
I: www.somervillehouse.co.uk

Period country house in large, mature gardens. Comfortable, spacious accommodation with licensed, fine-dining restaurant. Small, friendly, family-run business.

Bedrooms: 1 double, 1 twin, 1 single
Bathrooms: 2 en suite

Evening meal available
CC: Delta, Mastercard, Switch, Visa

Weekend break: 2 nights' DB&B, complimentary bottle of wine – £85pp.

B&B per person per night:
S £32.50–£35.00
D £27.50

HB per person per night:
DY £42.45–£49.95

OPEN All Year

THAXTED, Essex Map ref 3B2

Silver Award

CROSSWAYS GUESTHOUSE
32 Town Street, Thaxted, Great Dunmow CM6 2LA
T: (01371) 830348

Bedrooms: 2 double
Bathrooms: 2 en suite

Elegant 16thC house with Georgian additions, situated on B184 in centre of Thaxted opposite the 600-year-old Guildhall. Good pubs and restaurants in the town.

B&B per person per night:
S £40.00–£42.00
D £29.00–£30.00

OPEN All Year

COUNTRY CODE Always follow the Country Code · Enjoy the countryside and respect its life and work · Guard against all risk of fire · Fasten all gates · Keep your dogs under close control · Keep to public paths across farmland · Use gates and stiles to cross fences, hedges and walls · Leave livestock, crops and machinery alone · Take your litter home · Help to keep all water clean · Protect wildlife, plants and trees · Take special care on country roads · Make no unnecessary noise

THETFORD, Norfolk Map ref 3B2

THE GLEBE COUNTRY HOUSE BED AND BREAKFAST

34 London Road, Elveden, Thetford IP24 3TL
T: (01842) 890027
F: (01842) 890027
E: deirdre@jrudderham.freeserve.co.uk
I: www.glebecountryhouse.co.uk

Glebe House is a gracious manor house in its own extensive grounds with three absolutely stunning, spacious and elegant guest bedrooms, each of which is tastefully decorated and furnished. Offering exceptionally comfortable accommodation in a relaxed atmosphere, this distinctive country house is just 15 minutes from Newmarket and will delight all visitors.

Bedrooms: 1 double, 2 twin
Bathrooms: 1 en suite

Special discounts for stays of 1 week or more.

P

B&B per person per night:
S £30.00–£38.00
D £24.00–£28.00

OPEN All Year

THORPE BAY, Essex Map ref 3B2

Silver Award

BEACHES
192 Eastern Esplanade, Thorpe Bay, Southend-on-Sea SS1 3AA
T: (01702) 586124
F: (01702) 587793
E: beaches@adriancw.demon.co.uk
I: www.smoothhound.co.uk/hotels/beaches

Bedrooms: 5 double, 1 twin, 1 single
Bathrooms: 7 en suite

CC: Amex, Delta, Mastercard, Switch, Visa

Virtually on the beach with stunning estuary views. All rooms en suite, some with balconies. Ground floor rooms available. Stylish, comfortable and impeccably maintained.

€

B&B per person per night:
S £25.00–£35.00
D £27.50–£37.50

OPEN All Year

THORPENESS, Suffolk Map ref 3C2

THE DOLPHIN INN

Thorpeness, Leiston IP16 4NA
T: (01728) 454994
F: (01728) 453868
E: info@thorpeness.co.uk
I: www.thorpeness.co.uk

Located in the heart of Thorpeness, the Dolphin Inn is a traditional village inn offering good food and award-winning, en suite accommodation. Al fresco dining in the summer, including barbecues. Ideal for families.

Bedrooms: 3 double
Bathrooms: 3 en suite

Evening meal available
CC: Amex, Delta, Diners, Mastercard, Switch, Visa

P

B&B per person per night:
S £55.00–£58.00
D £37.50–£39.50

OPEN All Year

TRING, Hertfordshire Map ref 2C1

LIVINGSTON'S BED & BREAKFAST
Chimanimani, Toms Hill Road, Aldbury, Tring HP23 5SA
T: (01442) 851527

Bedrooms: 1 double, 2 twin
Bathrooms: 2 en suite, 1 private

Country house in idyllic surroundings of outstanding beauty, offering excellent, comfortable accommodation with convenient communications. Friendly and hospitable. Private parking. Two good pubs in village.

12 P €

B&B per person per night:
S £30.00–£33.00
D £28.00–£30.00

OPEN All Year except Christmas

MAP REFERENCES

Map references apply to the colour maps at the front of this guide.

WATTON, Norfolk Map ref 3B1

♦♦♦♦ Silver Award

PARK FARM BED & BREAKFAST

Park Farm, Caston Road, Griston, Thetford IP25 6QD
T: (01953) 483020
F: (01953) 483056
E: parkfarm@eidosnet.co.uk
I: www.parkfarmbreckland.co.uk

A friendly, relaxed atmosphere awaits in a quiet, rural setting. A working arable farm offering ground floor accommodation in converted farm buildings. The rooms are en suite and wheelchair friendly. Separate guest lounge/breakfast room with patio. Central for exploring Breckland, visiting the Broads or surrounding coastline. Easy link A11, A14.

Bedrooms: 1 double, 1 twin
Bathrooms: 2 en suite

Mid-week breaks from £57pp for 2 sharing for 3-night stay during Oct-Mar (excl Christmas and New Year).

B&B per person per night:
S £25.00–£30.00
D £23.00–£25.00

WELLS-NEXT-THE-SEA, Norfolk Map ref 3B1

♦♦♦♦

MEADOW VIEW GUEST HOUSE

53 High Street, Wighton, Wells-next-the-Sea NR23 1PF
T: (01328) 821527
E: bookings@meadowview.net
I: www.meadow-view.net

Beautiful restored guesthouse three miles from the sea, luxurious and peaceful with views of the countryside to enjoy with a happy family atmosphere. Have breakfast in the spacious garden while the cows graze in the meadows beyond.

Bedrooms: 2 double, 2 family
Bathrooms: 2 en suite

Evening meal available
CC: Amex, Delta, Mastercard, Switch, Visa

B&B per person per night:
D £30.00–£35.00

OPEN All Year

WOODBRIDGE, Suffolk Map ref 3C2 *Tourist Information Centre Tel: (01394) 382240*

♦♦♦♦ Silver Award

THE OLD RECTORY

Campsey Ashe, Woodbridge IP13 0PU
T: (01728) 746524
F: (01728) 746524
E: mail@theoldrectorysuffolk.com
I: www.theoldrectorysuffolk.com

Elegant Georgian rectory set in acres of garden. Fabulous, en suite bedrooms with twin, double and 4-poster beds. Superb home coooking using lots of local ingredients. Breakfast includes homemade jams and marmalades and eggs from the family's hens! Great for exploring the Suffolk coastline, visiting Sutton Hoo and Snape Maltings.

Bedrooms: 5 double, 2 twin, 1 single
Bathrooms: 8 en suite

Evening meal available
CC: Delta, Mastercard, Switch, Visa

B&B per person per night:
S £55.00–£70.00
D £37.50–£45.00

OPEN All Year except Christmas

CREDIT CARD BOOKINGS If you book by telephone and are asked for your credit card number it is advisable to check the proprietor's policy should you cancel your reservation.

WOODBRIDGE continued

SANDPIT HOUSE

Loudham, Nr Wickham Market, Woodbridge IP13 0NW
T: (01728) 747435
E: gilbey@sandpithouse@fsnet.co.uk

Bedrooms: 1 double, 1 single
Bathrooms: 1 private

Evening meal available

B&B per person per night:
S £25.00–£28.00
D £22.50–£25.00

HB per person per night:
DY £32.50–£35.00

OPEN All Year except Christmas

17thC house set in four acres of meadows and woodland in a delightful, secluded position, bounded by the River Deben yet only minutes from Woodbridge.

3 P

WOOLPIT, Suffolk Map ref 3B2

THE BULL INN & RESTAURANT

The Street, Woolpit, Bury St Edmunds IP30 9SA
T: (01359) 240393
F: (01359) 240393
E: trevor@howling.fsbusiness.co.uk
I: www.bullinnwoolpit.co.uk

Bedrooms: 2 double, 1 single, 1 family
Bathrooms: 4 en suite

Evening meal available
CC: Amex, Delta, Mastercard, Switch, Visa

B&B per person per night:
S Min £27.50
D £27.50–£30.00

HB per person per night:
DY £32.00–£40.00

OPEN All Year

Public house and restaurant offering good accommodation in centre of pretty village. Large garden, ample parking. Ideal base for touring Suffolk.

2 P

WRENTHAM, Suffolk Map ref 3C2

SOUTHWOLD LODGE

67 Southwold Road, Wrentham, Beccles NR34 7JE
T: (01502) 676148
F: (01986) 784797
E: qhbfield@aol.com
I: www.queensheadbramfield.co.uk/accommodation.htm

Bedrooms: 2 double, 1 twin
Bathrooms: 3 en suite

B&B per person per night:
S £25.00–£35.00
D £20.00–£25.00

OPEN All Year

Modern, tasteful village house with bright rooms. Owned by same family as The Queens Head, Bramfield. The 2001 and 2002 Suffolk Dining Pub of the year.

P

WROXHAM, Norfolk Map ref 3C1

WROXHAM PARK LODGE

142 Norwich Road, Wroxham, Norwich NR12 8SA
T: (01603) 782991
E: prklodge@nascr.net
I: www.smoothhound.co.uk/hotels/wroxhamp.html

Warm welcome in comfortable Victorian house. All rooms en suite and non-smoking, TV, tea/coffee facilities. Situated in Norfolk Broads' 'capital' of Wroxham. Central for visiting North Norfolk and its coast, Norfolk Broads, Norwich and Bure Valley Railway. Large garden, pets by arrangement, car park.

Bedrooms: 2 double, 1 twin
Bathrooms: 3 en suite

B&B per person per night:
S £24.00–£30.00
D £22.00–£25.00

OPEN All Year

P

AT-A-GLANCE SYMBOLS

Symbols at the end of each accommodation entry give useful information about services and facilities. A key to symbols can be found inside the back cover flap. Keep this open for easy reference.

A brief guide to the main Towns and Villages offering accommodation in the **East of England**

A ALDBOROUGH, NORFOLK - Aldborough is a picturesque village with a large green and winner of Best Kept Village 1999. Situated on the "Weaver's Way". The location is ideal for visiting local National Trust properties, Norfolk Broads and the North Norfolk coastal area.

B BECCLES, SUFFOLK - Fire destroyed the town in the 16th C and it was rebuilt in Georgian red brick. The River Waveney, on which the town stands, is popular with boating enthusiasts and has an annual regatta. Home of Beccles and District Museum.

BEETLEY, NORFOLK - Rural village close to Dereham with its picturesque pargeted cottages.

BIGGLESWADE, BEDFORDSHIRE - Busy centre for market gardening set on the River Ivel spanned by a 14th C bridge. Some interesting old buildings in the market-place. Nearby are the Shuttleworth collection of historic aeroplanes and Jordan's Mill.

BISHOP'S STORTFORD, HERTFORDSHIRE - Fine old town on the River Stort with many interesting buildings, particularly Victorian, and an imposing parish church. The vicarage where Cecil Rhodes was born is now a museum.

BRAINTREE, ESSEX - The Heritage Centre in the Town Hall describes Braintree's former international importance in wool, silk and engineering. St Michael's parish church includes some Roman bricks. Braintree market was first chartered in 1199.

BUNGAY, SUFFOLK - Market town and yachting centre on the River Waveney with the remains of a great 12th C castle. In the market-place stands the Butter Cross, rebuilt in 1689 after being largely destroyed by fire. Nearby at Earsham the Otter Trust.

C CAMBRIDGE, CAMBRIDGESHIRE - A most important and beautiful city on the River Cam with 31 colleges forming one of the oldest universities in the world. Numerous museums, good shopping centre, restaurants, theatres, cinema and fine bookshops.

CAVENDISH, SUFFOLK - One of the most picturesque villages in East Anglia, with a number of pretty thatched timber-framed and colour-washed cottages grouped around a large green. Sue Ryder Foundation Museum and coffee room are in the High Street.

CHELMSFORD, ESSEX - The county town of Essex, originally a Roman settlement, Caesaromagus, thought to have been destroyed by Boudicca. Growth of the town's industry can be traced in the excellent museum in Oaklands Park. 15th C parish church has been Chelmsford Cathedral since 1914.

CLACTON-ON-SEA, ESSEX - Developed in the 1870s into a popular holiday resort with pier, pavilion, funfair, theatres and traditional amusements. The Martello Towers on the seafront were built like many others in the early 19th C to defend Britain against Napoleon.

COLCHESTER, ESSEX - Britain's oldest recorded town standing on the River Colne and famous for its oysters. Numerous historic buildings, ancient remains and museums. Plenty of parks and gardens, extensive shopping centre, theatre and zoo.

COLTISHALL, NORFOLK - On the River Bure, with an RAF station nearby. The village is attractive with many pleasant 18th C brick houses and a thatched church.

D DARSHAM, SUFFOLK - Well placed for touring North Suffolk and the coast. The nearby Otter Trust is fascinating to visit.

DERSINGHAM, NORFOLK - Large parish church, mostly of Perpendicular period, with14th C font and Elizabethan barn dated 1672.

E EARL SOHAM, SUFFOLK - A good base for visiting Bury St Edmunds, Ipswich and the east of Suffolk. The church of St Mary is notable for its hammerbeam nave roof decorated with angels and its 17th C pulpit with hour-glasses.

EARLS COLNE, ESSEX - In the Colne Valley. Large village with a fine 14th C church and some old houses with interesting pargeting.

ELY, CAMBRIDGESHIRE - Until the 17th C, when the Fens were drained, Ely was an island. The cathedral, completed in 1189, dominates the surrounding area. One particular feature is the central octagonal tower with a fan-vaulted timber roof and wooden lantern.

EYE, SUFFOLK - "Eye" means island and this town was once surrounded by marsh. The fine church of SS Peter and Paul has a tower over 100ft high and a carving of the Archangel Gabriel can be seen on the 16th C Guildhall.

F FAKENHAM, NORFOLK - Attractive, small market town dates from Saxon times and was a Royal Manor until the 17th C. Its market place has 2 old coaching inns, both showing traces of earlier work behind Georgian facades, and the parish church has a commanding 15th C tower.

H HALESWORTH, SUFFOLK - Small market town which grew firstly with navigation on the Blyth in the 18th C and then with the coming of the railways in the 19th C. Opposite the church in a beautiful 14th C building is the Halesworth Gallery.

HARWICH, ESSEX - Port where the Rivers Orwell and Stour converge and enter the North Sea. The old town still has a medieval atmosphere with its narrow streets. To the south is the seaside resort of Dovercourt with long sandy beaches.

HAUGHLEY, SUFFOLK - In the heart of Suffolk, very well placed for touring.

HETHERSETT, NORFOLK - Conveniently located for Norwich.

I IPSWICH, SUFFOLK - Interesting county town and major port on the River Orwell. Birthplace of Cardinal Wolsey. Christchurch Mansion, set in a fine park, contains a good collection of furniture and pictures, with works by Gainsborough, Constable and Munnings.

K KERSEY, SUFFOLK - A most picturesque village, which was famous for cloth-making, set in a valley with a water-splash. The church of St Mary is an impressive building at the top of the hill.

KING'S LYNN, NORFOLK - A busy town with many outstanding buildings. The Guildhall and Town Hall are both built of flint in a striking chequer design. Behind the Guildhall in the Old Gaol House the sounds and smells of prison life 2 centuries ago are recreated.

L LAVENHAM, SUFFOLK - A former prosperous wool town of timber-framed buildings with the cathedral-like church and its tall tower. The market-place is 13th C and the Guildhall now houses a museum.

LITTLE WALSINGHAM, NORFOLK - Little Walsingham is larger than its neighbour Great Walsingham and more important because of its long history as a religious shrine to which many pilgrimages were made. The village has many picturesque buildings of the 16th C and later.

LOWESTOFT, SUFFOLK - Seaside town with wide sandy beaches. Important fishing port with picturesque fishing quarter. Home of the famous Lowestoft porcelain and birthplace of Benjamin Britten. East Point Pavilion's exhibition describes the Lowestoft story.

M MALDON, ESSEX - The Blackwater Estuary has made Maldon a natural base for yachtsmen. Boat-building is also an important industry. Numerous buildings of interest. The 13th C church of All Saints has the only triangular church tower in Britain. Also a museum and maritime centre.

MARGARET RODING, ESSEX - One of the six Rodings, a group of old villages clustered in the rural Roding Valley. The church features some fine Norman work.

N NEWMARKET, SUFFOLK - Centre of the English horse-racing world and the headquarters of the Jockey Club and National Stud. Racecourse and horse sales. The National Horse Racing Museum traces the history and development of the Sport of Kings.

NORWICH, NORFOLK - Beautiful cathedral city and county town on the River Wensum with many fine museums and medieval churches. Norman castle, Guildhall and interesting medieval streets. Good shopping centre and market.

P PETERBOROUGH, CAMBRIDGESHIRE - Prosperous and rapidly expanding cathedral city on the edge of the Fens on the River Nene. Catherine of Aragon is buried in the cathedral. City Museum and Art Gallery. Ferry Meadows Country Park has numerous leisure facilities.

S SAFFRON WALDEN, ESSEX - Takes its name from the saffron crocus once grown around the town. The church of St Mary has superb carvings, magnificent roofs and brasses. A town maze can be seen on the common. Two miles south-west is Audley End, a magnificent Jacobean mansion owned by English Heritage.

SANDY, BEDFORDSHIRE - Small town on the River Ivel on the site of a Roman settlement. Sandy is mentioned in Domesday.

SAXMUNDHAM, SUFFOLK - The church of St John the Baptist has a hammer-beam roof and contains a number of good monuments.

SHERINGHAM, NORFOLK - Holiday resort with Victorian and Edwardian hotels and a sand and shingle beach where the fishing boats are hauled up. The North Norfolk Railway operates from Sheringham station during the summer. Other attractions include museums, theatre and Splash Fun Pool.

SNETTISHAM, NORFOLK - Village with a superb decorated church. The 17th C Old Hall is a distinguished-looking house with Dutch gables over the 2 bays. Snettisham Pits is a reserve of the Royal Society for the Protection of Birds. Red deer herd and other animals, farm trails and nature walks at Park Farm.

SOUTH WALSHAM, NORFOLK - Village famous for having 2 churches in adjoining churchyards. South Walsham Broad consists of an inner and outer section, the former being private. Alongside, the Fairhaven Garden Trust has woodland and water-gardens open to the public.

SOUTHWOLD, SUFFOLK - Pleasant and attractive seaside town with a triangular market square and spacious greens around which stand flint, brick and colour-washed cottages. The parish church of St Edmund is one of the greatest churches in Suffolk.

ST ALBANS, HERTFORDSHIRE - As Verulamium this was one of the largest towns in Roman Britain and its remains can be seen in the museum. The Norman cathedral was built from Roman materials to commemorate Alban, the first British Christian martyr.

STOWMARKET, SUFFOLK - Small market town where routes converge. There is an open-air museum of rural life at the Museum of East Anglian Life.

STRETHAM, CAMBRIDGESHIRE - On the edge of the Fens, Stretham is noted for its 20-ft-high village cross dating from around 1400.

T **THAXTED, ESSEX -** Small town rich in outstanding buildings and dominated by its hilltop medieval church. The magnificent Guildhall was built by the Cutlers' Guild in the late 14th C. A windmill built in 1804 has been restored and houses a rural museum.

THORPENESS, SUFFOLK - A planned mock-Tudor seaside resort, built in the early 20th C, with a 65-acre artificial lake. The House in the Clouds was built to disguise a water-tower. The windmill contains an exhibition on Suffolk's heritage coast.

W **WELLS-NEXT-THE-SEA, NORFOLK** - Seaside resort and small port on the north coast. The Buttlands is a large tree-lined green surrounded by Georgian houses and from here narrow streets lead to the quay.

WOODBRIDGE, SUFFOLK - Once a busy seaport, the town is now a sailing centre on the River Deben. There are many buildings of architectural merit including the Bell and Angel Inns. The 18th C Tide Mill is now restored and open to the public.

WOOLPIT, SUFFOLK - Village with a number of attractive timber-framed Tudor and Georgian houses. St Mary's Church is one of the most beautiful churches in Suffolk and has a fine porch. The brass eagle lectern is said to have been donated by Elizabeth I.

WROXHAM, NORFOLK - Yachting centre on the River Bure which houses the headquarters of the Norfolk Broads Yacht Club. The church of St Mary has a famous doorway and the manor house nearby dates back to 1623.

COUNTRY CODE

Always follow the Country Code ✤ Enjoy the countryside and respect its life and work ✤ Guard against all risk of fire ✤ Fasten all gates ✤ Keep your dogs under close control ✤ Keep to public paths across farmland ✤ Use gates and stiles to cross fences, hedges and walls ✤ Leave livestock, crops and machinery alone ✤ Take your litter home ✤ Help to keep all water clean ✤ Protect wildlife, plants and trees ✤ Take special care on country roads ✤ Make no unnecessary noise ✤

Ratings **you** can trust

When you're looking for a place to stay, you need a rating system you can trust. VisitBritain's ratings are your clear guide to what to expect, in an easy-to-understand form. Properties are visited annually by our trained, impartial assessors, so you can have confidence that your accommodation has been thoroughly checked and rated for quality before you make a booking.

Using a simple One to five Diamond rating, the system puts great emphasis on quality and is based on research which shows exactly what consumers are looking for when when choosing accommodation.

"Guest Accommodation" covers a wide variety of serviced accommodation for which England is renowned, including guesthouses, bed and breakfasts, inns and farmhouses. Establishments are rated from One to Five Diamonds. Progressively higher levels of quality and customer care must be provided for each of the One to Five Diamond ratings. The rating reflects the unique character of Guest Accommodation, and covers areas such as cleanliness, service and hospitality, bedrooms, bathrooms and food quality.

Look out, too for VisitBritain's Gold and Silver Awards, which are awarded to those establishments which not only achieve the overall quality required for their Diamond rating, but also reach the highest levels of quality in those specific areas which guests identify as being really important for them. They will reflect the quality of comfort and cleanliness you'll find in the bedrooms and bathrooms and the quality of service you'll enjoy throughout your stay.

The ratings are you sign of quality assurance, giving you the confidence to book the accommodation that meets your expectations.

South West

A land of myths and legends – and beautiful beaches. The region has cathedral cities, Georgian Bath and maritme Bristol, mysterios castles, evocative country houses and sub tropical gardens to discover, too.

Classic sights
Eden Project – plant life from around the world
English Riviera – family-friendly beaches
Dartmoor & Exmoor – wild open moorland, rocky tors and woodland

Coast & country
Jurassic Coast – World Heritage Coastline
Runnymede – riverside meadows and woodland
Pegwell Bay & Goodwin Sands – a haven for birds and seals

Glorious gardens
Stourhead – 18thC landscaped garden
Westonbirt Arboretum – Over 3,700 different varieties of tree

Art for all
Tate Gallery St Ives – modern art and the St Ives School
Arnolfini Gallery, Bristol – contemporary arts

Distinctively different
Daphne du Maurier – Cornwall inspired many of her novels
Agatha Christie – follow the trail in Torquay

The Counties of Bath & Bristol, Cornwall & Isles of Scilly, Devon, Dorset (Western), Gloucestershire South, Somerset and Wiltshire

For more information contact:
South West Tourism
Admail 3186,
Exeter EX2 7WH

E: info@westcountryholidays.com
www.visitsouthwest.co.uk

Telephone enquiries -
T: (0870) 442 0880

1. Roman Bath, Bath

You will find hundreds of interesting places to visit during your stay, just some of which are listed in these pages. Contact any Tourist Information Centre in the region for more ideas on days out.

Awarded VisitBritain's 'Quality Assured Visitor Attraction' marque.

At Bristol
Harbourside, Bristol
Tel: 08453 451235 www.at-bristol.org.uk
3 exciting new attractions which will take you on the interactive adventure of a lifetime – Explore, Wildwalk and the IMAX Theatre.

Atwell-Wilson Motor Museum Trust
Stockley Lane, Calne
Tel: (01249) 813119 www.atwell-wilson.org
Motor museum with vintage, post-vintage and classic cars, including American models. Classic motorbikes. A 17thC water meadow walk. Car clubs welcome for rallies. Play area.

Babbacombe Model Village
Babbacombe, Torquay
Tel: (01803) 315315
www.babbacombemodelvillage.co.uk
Over 400 models many with sound and animation with 4 acres (1.6ha) of award-winning gardens. See modern towns, villages and rural areas. Stunning illuminations and Aquaviva.

Bristol City Museum & Art Gallery
Queen's Road, Bristol
Tel: (0117) 922 3571
www.bristol-city.gov.uk/museums
Outstanding collections of applied, oriental and fine art, archaeology, geology, natural history, ethnography and Egyptology.

Bristol Zoo Gardens
Clifton, Bristol
Tel: (0117) 974 7300
www.bristolzoo.org.uk
Enjoy an exciting real life experience and see over 300 species of wildlife in beautiful gardens. Favourites include Gorilla Island, Bug World and Sea and Penguin Coasts with underwater viewing.

Buckland Abbey (National Trust)
Yelverton
Tel: (01822) 853607 www.nationaltrust.org.uk
Originally Cistercian monastery, then home of Sir Francis Drake. Ancient buildings, exhibitions, herb garden, craft workshops and estate walks. Elizabethan garden.

Cheddar Caves and Gorge
Cheddar
Tel: (01934) 742343 www.cheddarcaves.co.uk
Beautiful caves located in Cheddar Gorge. Gough's Cave with its cathedral-like caverns and Cox's Cave with stalagmites and stalactites. Also 'The Crystal Quest' fantasy adventure.

Combe Martin Wildlife and Dinosaur Park
Combe Martin, Ilfracombe
Tel: (01271) 882486 www.dinosaur-uk.com
The land that time forgot. A subtropical paradise with hundreds of birds and animals, and animatronics dinosaurs, so real they're alive!

Crealy Park
Clyst St Mary, Exeter
Tel: (01395) 233200 www.crealy.co.uk
One of Devon's largest animal farms. Milk a cow, feed a lamb and pick up a piglet. Adventure playgrounds. Dragonfly Lake and farm trails.

Dairyland Farm World

Summercourt, Newquay
Tel: (01872) 510246
www.dairylandfarmworld.com
120 cows milked in Clarabelle's 'Spage-age' orbiter, adventure playground, country life museum, nature trail, farm park, pets and daily events.

Eden Project
Bodelva, St Austell
Tel: (01726) 811911 www.edenproject.com
An unforgettable experience in a breathtaking epic location. Eden is a gateway into the fascinating world of plants and people.

Exmoor Falconry & Animal Farm
West Lynch Farm, Minehead
Tel: (01643) 862816
www.exmoorfalconry.co.uk
Historic 15thC farm with hand-tame, rare breed farm animals, pets' corner, birds of prey and owls. Flying displays daily. Short activity breaks.

Flambards Village
Culdrose Manor, Helston
Tel: (01326) 573404 www.flambards.co.uk
Life-size Victorian village with fully stocked shops, carriages and fashions. 'Britain in the Blitz' life-size wartime street, historic aircraft. Science centre and rides.

Heale Garden & Plant Centre
Middle Woodford, Salisbury
Tel: (01722) 782504
Mature traditional garden with shrubs, musk and other roses, and kitchen garden. Authentic Japanese teahouse in water garden. Magnolias. Snowdrops and aconites in winter.

International Animal Rescue
Animal Tracks, South Molton
Tel: (01769) 550277 www.iar.org.uk
A 60-acre (24-ha) animal sanctuary with a wide range of rescued animals from monkeys to chinchillas and from shire horses and ponies to donkeys, goats and pigs. Also rare plant nursery.

Jamaica Inn Museums (Potters Museum of Curiosity)
Bolventor, Launceston
Tel: (01566) 86838
www.pottersjamaicainn.com
Museums contain lifetime work of Walter Potter, a Victorian taxidermist. Exhibits include 'Kittens' Wedding' and 'Death of Cock Robin' and 'The Story of Smuggling'.

Longleat
Longleat, Warminster
Tel: (01985) 844400 www.longleat.co.uk
Elizabethan stately home, safari park plus a wonderland of 10 family attractions. 'World's Longest Hedge Maze', Safari Boats, Pets Corner, Longleat railway and Adventure Castle.

The Lost Gardens of Heligan
Heligan, St Austell
Tel: (01726) 845100 www.heligan.com
Gardeners' World 'The Nation's Favourite Garden' 2002. The world famous, award winning garden restoration is now complemented by a pioneering wildlife conservation project.

Lyme Regis Philpot Museum
Bridge Street, Lyme Regis
Tel: (01297) 443370
www.lymeregismuseum.co.uk
Fossils, geology, local history, literary connections – The story of Lyme in its landscape.

1. Stourhead Gardens, Wiltshire
2. Clifton Suspension Bridge, Bristol
3. Water sports in Torquay

National Marine Aquarium

Rope Walk, Plymouth
Tel: (01752) 600301
www.national-aquarium.co.uk
The United Kingdom's only world-class aquarium, located in the heart of Plymouth. Visitor experiences include a mountain stream and Caribbean reef complete with sharks.

Newquay Zoo

Trenance Park, Newquay
Tel: (01637) 873342
www.newquayzoo.co.uk
A modern award-winning zoo, where you can have fun and learn at the same time. A varied collection of animals, from Antelope to Zebra.

Paignton Zoo Environmental Park

Totnes Road, Paignton
Tel: (01803) 697500
www.paigntonzoo.org.uk
One of England's largest zoos with over 1,200 animals in the beautiful setting of 75 acres (30ha) of botanical gardens. The zoo is one of Devon's most popular family days out.

Plant World

St Marychurch Road, Newton Abbot
Tel: (01803) 872939
Four acres of gardens including the unique 'map of the world' gardens. Cottage garden. Panoramic views. Comprehensive nursery of rare and more unusual plants.

Powderham Castle

Kenton, Exeter
Tel: (01626) 890243 www.powderham.co.uk
Built c1390, restored in 18thC, Georgian interiors, china, furnishings and paintings. Family home of the Courtenays for over 600 years. Fine views across deer park and River Exe.

Railway Village Museum

34 Faringdon Road, Swindon
Tel: (01793) 466553
www.steam-museum.org.uk
Foreman's house in original Great Western Railway village. Furnished to re-create a Victorian working-class home.

Roman Baths

Pump Room, Bath
Tel: (01225) 477785
www.romanbaths.co.uk
2000 years ago, around Britain's hot springs, the Romans built this great temple and spa that still flows with natural hot water.

St Michael's Mount

Marazion, Penzance
Tel: (01736) 710507
www.stmichaelsmount.co.uk
Originally the site of a Benedictine chapel, castle on its rock dates from 12thC. Fine views towards Land's End and the Lizard. Reached by foot, or ferry at high tide in summer.

Smugglers Barn

Abbotsbury, Weymouth
Tel: (01305) 871817
www.abbotsbury-tourism.co.uk
Soft play undercover with a smuggling theme for children under 11 years. Other activities include rabbit and guinea pig cuddling. Pony rides (extra charge).

Steam – Museum of the Great Western Railway

Kemble Drive, Swindon
Tel: (01793) 466646
www.steam-museum.org.uk
Historic Great Western Railway locomotives, wide range of nameplates, models, illustrations, posters and tickets.

Stonehenge

Amesbury, Salisbury
Tel: (01980) 624715
www.stonehengemasterplan.org
World-famous prehistoric monument built as a ceremonial centre. Started 5000 years ago and remodelled several times in next 1500 years.

Stourhead House and Garden (National Trust)

Stourton, Warminster
Tel: (01747) 841152 www.nationaltrust.org.uk
Landscaped garden laid out c1741-80, with lakes, temples, rare trees and plants. House begun in c1721 by Colen Campbell, contains fine paintings and Chippendale furniture.

Tate Gallery St Ives

Porthmeor Beach, St Ives
Tel: (01736) 796226 www.tate.org.uk
Opened in 1993 and offering a unique introduction to modern art. Changing displays focus on the modern movement St Ives is famous for. Major contemporary exhibitions.

Teignmouth Museum
29 French Street, Teignmouth
Tel: (01626) 777041
www.lineone.net/-teignmuseum
Exhibits include 16thC cannon and artefacts from Armada wreck and local history, 1920s pier machines and c1877 cannon.

Tintagel Castle (English Heritage)
Tintagel
Tel: (01840) 770328
www.english-heritage.org.uk
Medieval ruined castle on wild, wind-swept coast. Famous for associations with Arthurian legend. Built largely in 13thC by Richard, Earl of Cornwall.

Totnes Costume Museum – Devonshire Collection of Period Costume
Bogan House, Totnes
Tel: (01803) 863821
New exhibition of costumes and accessories each season, displayed in one of the historic merchant's houses of Totnes, Bogan House, restored by Mitchell Trust.

Woodlands Leisure Park
Blackawton, Totnes
Tel: (01803) 712598
www.woodlandspark.com
All weather fun guaranteed; unique combination indoor and outdoor attractions, 3 water coasters, toboggan run, indoor venture centre with rides. Falconry and animals.

Wookey Hole Caves and Papermill
Wookey Hole, Wells
Tel: (01749) 672243 www.wookey.co.uk
Spectacular caves and legendary home of the Witch of Wookey. Working Victorian paper mill including Old Penny Arcade, Magical Mirror Maze and Cave Diving Museum.

1. Land's End, Cornwall

South West Tourism
Admail 3186,
Exeter EX2 7WH
T: (0870) 442 0880
E: info@westcountryholidays.com
www.visitsouthwest.co.uk

THE FOLLOWING OFFICIAL GUIDES ARE AVAILABLE FREE FROM SOUTH WEST TOURISM:

Quality Bed & Breakfast

Holiday Homes, Cottages & Apartments

Hotels and Guesthouses

Holiday Parks, Camping and Caravan

Attractions and Days Out

Trencherman's Restaurant Guide

South West Walks

Sailing and Watersports

Getting to the South West

BY ROAD: The region is easily accessible from London, the South East, the North and Midlands by the M6/M5 which extends just beyond Exeter, where it links in with the dual carriageways of the A38 to Plymouth, A380 to Torbay and the A30 into Cornwall. The North Devon Link Road A361 joins Junction 37 with the coast of North Devon and the A39, which then becomes the Atlantic Highway into Cornwall.

BY RAIL: The main towns in the South West are served throughout the year by fast, direct and frequent rail services from all over the country. Trains operate from London (Paddington) to Chippenham, Swindon, Bath, Bristol, Weston-super-Mare, Taunton, Exeter, Plymouth and Penzance, and also from Scotland, the North East and the Midlands to the South West. A service runs from London (Waterloo) to Exeter, via Salisbury, Yeovil and Crewkerne. Sleeper services operate between Devon and Cornwall and London as well as between Bristol and Glasgow and Edinburgh. Motorail services operate from strategic points to key South West locations.

1. Salisbury Cathedral, Wiltshire
2. Selworthy, Somerset

Where to stay in the

South West

All place names in the blue bands under which accommodation is listed, are shown on the maps at the front of this guide.

Symbols give useful information about services and facilities. Inside the back cover flap there's a key to these symbols which you can keep open for easy reference.

A complete listing of all the VisitBritain assessed accommodation covered by this guide appears at the back of this guide.

ABBOTSBURY, Dorset Map ref 2A3

SWAN LODGE
Rodden Row, Abbotsbury, Weymouth DT3 4JL
T: (01305) 871249
F: (01305) 871249

Bedrooms: 3 double
Bathrooms: 1 en suite

Evening meal available
CC: Mastercard, Visa

Situated on the B3157 coastal road between Weymouth and Bridport. Swan Inn public house opposite, where food is served all day in season, is under the same ownership.

B&B per person per night:
S £32.00–£42.00
D £24.00–£30.00

OPEN All Year

AMESBURY, Wiltshire Map ref 2B2 *Tourist Information Centre Tel: (01980) 622833*

VALE HOUSE
Figheldean, Salisbury SP4 8JJ
T: (01980) 670713
E: strefford@valehouse.fslife.co.uk

Bedrooms: 1 twin, 1 single, 1 family
Bathrooms: 2 en suite

Secluded house in centre of picturesque village, four miles north of Amesbury on A345, two miles from Stonehenge. Winchester, Bath, Oxford within easy reach.

B&B per person per night:
S £20.00–£25.00
D £20.00–£22.50

OPEN All Year except Christmas

ASHBURTON, Devon Map ref 1C2

Silver Award

GAGES MILL

Ashburton, Newton Abbot TQ13 7JW
T: (01364) 652391
F: (01364) 652391
E: moore@gagesmill.co.uk
I: www.gagesmill.co.uk

B&B per person per night:
S £22.00–£32.00
D £22.00–£32.00

HB per person per night:
DY £37.00–£47.00

14thC former wool mill in over an acre of gardens. A friendly welcome and comfortable accommodation. High standard of cooking. Licensed. One mile from the ancient Stannary town of Ashburton. An ideal base for exploring South Devon, with its many NT properties, pretty villages and, of course, Dartmoor.

Bedrooms: 6 double, 1 twin, 1 single
Bathrooms: 7 en suite

Evening meal available

12 P

ASHTON KEYNES, Wiltshire Map ref 2B2

CORNER COTTAGE

Fore Street, Ashton Keynes, Swindon SN6 6NP
T: (01285) 861454

Bedrooms: 1 double, 1 suite
Bathrooms: 1 en suite

B&B per person per night:
S £30.00–£35.00
D £22.50–£27.50

Homely, 17thC stone cottage in centre of best-kept village within the Cotswold Water Park and on route of Thames Path. Ideal for touring Cotswolds.

OPEN All Year except Christmas

P

AVEBURY, Wiltshire Map ref 2B2 *Tourist Information Centre Tel: (01672) 539425*

♦♦♦

THE NEW INN

Winterbourne Monkton, Swindon SN4 9NW
T: (01672) 539240
F: (01672) 539150
E: the_new_inn@hotmail.com
I: www.thenewinn.net

Bedrooms: 2 double, 2 twin, 1 family
Bathrooms: 5 en suite

Evening meal available
CC: Delta, Mastercard, Switch, Visa

B&B per person per night:
S £25.00–£40.00
D £25.00–£30.00

OPEN All Year

A 200-year-old country pub with beautiful restaurant and friendly, helpful staff, set in outstanding Wiltshire countryside only one mile from Avebury stone circle.

P

AXMINSTER, Devon Map ref 1D2

CHATTAN HALL

Woodbury Lane, Axminster EX13 5TL
T: (01297) 32365
F: (01297) 32365
E: boston@chattanhall.co.uk
I: www.chattanhall.co.uk

B&B per person per night:
S £45.00–£50.00
D £40.00–£45.00

HB per person per night:
DY £55.00–£65.00

OPEN All Year except Christmas

Elegant Victorian country house with splendid big rooms set in two acres. Wonderful gardens with many specimen trees, shrubs and colourful borders...a garden lover's paradise. Only one couple at a time, unless requested. Guests can enjoy conservatory, gardens, drawing room. Own private balcony with spectacular views. Exclusive, private and secluded.

Bedrooms: 1 double
Bathrooms: 1 private

Evening meal available

10% reduction for 3 or more nights.

12 P

CREDIT CARD BOOKINGS If you book by telephone and are asked for your credit card number it is advisable to check the proprietor's policy should you cancel your reservation.

BARBROOK, Devon Map ref 1C1

♦♦♦♦

WEST LYN FARMHOUSE
Barbrook, Lynton EX35 6LD
T: (01598) 753618
F: (01598) 753618
E: info@westlynfarm.co.uk
I: www.westlynfarm.co.uk

Bedrooms: 1 double, 1 family
Bathrooms: 2 en suite

B&B per person per night:
S £18.00–£20.00
D £20.00–£25.00

OPEN All Year except Christmas

Peaceful farmhouse on Exmoor National Park. Comfortable rooms with en suite facilities. Superb views over Lynton and coast. Ideal for walking, or easy drive to beaches.

BARNSTAPLE, Devon Map ref 1C1 *Tourist Information Centre Tel: (01271) 375000*

♦♦♦♦
Silver Award

THE SPINNEY

Shirwell, Barnstaple EX31 4JR
T: (01271) 850282
E: thespinney@shirwell.fsnet.co.uk
I: www.thespinneyshirwell.co.uk

B&B per person per night:
S £20.00–£24.00
D £20.00–£24.00

HB per person per night:
DY £33.00–£37.00

OPEN All Year

Set in over an acre of grounds with views towards Exmoor, a former rectory. Spacious accommodation, en suite available. Centrally heated. Delicious meals cooked by chef/proprietor, served during summer months in our restored Victorian conservatory under the ancient vine. Residential licence. The Spinney is non-smoking.

Bedrooms: 2 double, 1 single, 2 family
Bathrooms: 3 en suite, 1 private

Evening meal available

BARRINGTON, Somerset Map ref 2A3

♦♦♦♦
Silver Award

KENT HOUSE
Barrington, Ilminster TA19 0JP
T: (01460) 52613
E: jrclushington@yahoo.co.uk

Bedrooms: 1 double
Bathrooms: 1 private

B&B per person per night:
S £30.00–£35.00
D £27.50–£30.00

OPEN All Year except Christmas

Delicious West Country breakfasts in an 18thC farmhouse set in three acres of garden, orchard and wild-flower hill.

BATH, Bath and North East Somerset Map ref 2B2 *Tourist Information Centre Tel: 0906 711 2000 (Premium rate number)*

AQUAE SULIS

174/176 Newbridge Road, Bath BA1 3LE
T: (01225) 420061
F: (01225) 446077
E: enquiries@aquaesulishotel.com
I: www.aquaesulishotel.com

B&B per person per night:
S £45.00–£59.00
D £27.50–£44.50

OPEN All Year

Conveniently situated hotel with period charm. Attractive, no-smoking bedrooms, patio and garden with all the extras of a modern hotel. Satellite TV. Bar and smoking/no-smoking lounges. A la carte menu. Large monitored car park. Frequent shuttle or level walk to abbey. Free unlimited golf locally.

Bedrooms: 5 double, 3 single, 5 family
Bathrooms: 11 en suite, 2 private

Evening meal available
CC: Amex, Delta, Diners, Mastercard, Switch, Visa

See website or phone for special weekday offers (Sun-Thu) from £45 (single) and £55 (double) per room.

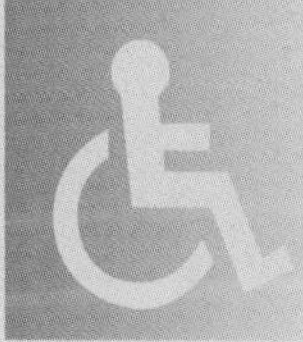

ACCESSIBILITY

Look for the symbols which indicate National Accessible Scheme standards for hearing and visually impaired guests in addition to standards for guests with mobility impairment. You can find an index of all scheme participants at the back of this guide.

BATH continued

♦♦♦♦♦ Gold Award

ATHOLE GUEST HOUSE

33 Upper Oldfield Park, Bath BA2 3JX
T: (01225) 334307
F: (01225) 320009
E: info@atholehouse.co.uk
I: www.atholehouse.co.uk

B&B per person per night:
S £48.00–£58.00
D £34.00–£39.00

OPEN All Year

Large Victorian home restored to give bright, inviting, quiet bedrooms, sleek furniture, sparkling bathrooms, hotel facilities (mini-bar, laptop connection, satellite TV, safe). Hospitality is old-style. Award-winning breakfasts. Relax in our gardens, or let us help you explore the area. Secure parking behind remote-control gates or in garage. Twelve minutes' walk from centre.

Bedrooms: 2 double, 1 family
Bathrooms: 3 en suite

CC: Amex, Delta, Mastercard, Switch, Visa

4 nights (incl 1 night free), all year. 3 nights (incl 1 night free) or 5 nights (incl 2 nights free), Nov-Feb inclusive.

P €

♦♦♦♦♦ Gold Award

AYRLINGTON HOTEL

24/25 Pulteney Road, Bath BA2 4EZ
T: (01225) 425495
F: (01225) 469029
E: mail@ayrlington.com
I: www.ayrlington.com

B&B per person per night:
D £85.00–£160.00

Located within an easy five-minute level walk of Bath city centre, The Ayrlington is a small, tranquil, non-smoking luxury hotel. Its elegantly appointed rooms boast every modern amenity. Some feature 4-poster beds and spa baths. Private parking, walled gardens overlooking Bath Abbey and access to a nearby golf course are among its many facilities.

Bedrooms: 12 double
Bathrooms: 12 en suite

CC: Amex, Delta, Diners, Mastercard, Switch, Visa

We offer short break weekday packages during Dec/Feb winter season. Details available on request.

P

♦♦♦

BAILBROOK LODGE HOTEL

35/37 London Road West, Bath BA1 7HZ
T: (01225) 859090
F: (01225) 852299
E: hotel@bailbrooklodge.co.uk
I: www.bailbrooklodge.co.uk

B&B per person per night:
S £39.00–£95.00
D £35.00–£47.50

OPEN All Year

Welcome to a fine Georgian house. All bedrooms en suite (some 4-posters), with antiques and many original features. The lounge bar and dining room overlook the patio and lawns. Excellently located one mile from Bath's centre and close to A46 for M4 and beautiful surrounding countryside. Ample car parking.

Bedrooms: 6 double, 2 twin, 4 family
Bathrooms: 12 en suite

CC: Amex, Delta, Diners, Mastercard, Switch, Visa

Third night half price (excl Sat); 2 nights for the price of 1, Nov-Feb (excl Sat).

P

QUALITY ASSURANCE SCHEME

Diamond ratings and awards were correct at the time of going to press but are subject to change. Please check at the time of booking.

BATH continued

♦♦♦♦

BAY TREE HOUSE
12 Crescent Gardens, Bath BA1 2NA
T: (01225) 483699
F: (01225) 483699
E: enquires@bay-tree-house.fsnet.co.uk
I: www.wherenow.net/baytree

Bedrooms: 2 double, 1 family

CC: Amex, Delta, Diners, Mastercard, Switch, Visa

Homely, relaxed, stylish, central Victorian home with private parking. All rooms individually and tastefully decorated. Non-smoking. Visit our virtual reality website for a tour.

B&B per person per night:
S £35.00–£48.00
D £23.00–£40.00

OPEN All Year

♦♦♦♦

BROMPTON HOUSE
St John's Road, Bath BA2 6PT
T: (01225) 420972
F: (01225) 420505
E: bromptonhouse@btinternet.com
I: www.bromptonhouse.co.uk

Bedrooms: 14 double, 1 single, 1 family
Bathrooms: 16 en suite

CC: Amex, Delta, Mastercard, Switch, Visa

Charming Georgian rectory in beautiful secluded gardens, five minutes' level walk to city centre. Free, private car park. No smoking, please. All rooms en suite.

15

B&B per person per night:
S Min £48.00
D £30.00–£48.00

OPEN All Year except Christmas

♦♦♦♦

CARFAX HOTEL

Great Pulteney Street, Bath BA2 4BS
T: (01225) 462089
F: (01225) 443257
E: reservations@carfaxhotel.co.uk
I: www.carfaxhotel.co.uk

A trio of Georgian houses overlooking Henrietta Park with a view to the surrounding hills. A stroll to the Pump Rooms, Roman baths, canal and river. Recently restored and refurbished, well-appointed rooms. Lift to all floors. Car park for 13 cars. Senior Citizens' rates all year.

Bedrooms: 20 double, 2 twin, 8 single, 3 family
Bathrooms: 33 en suite

Evening meal available
CC: Amex, Delta, Mastercard, Switch, Visa

4 nights for the price of 3, mid-week booking Sun to Thur inclusive, Quote ETB04.

B&B per person per night:
S £56.00–£69.00
D £40.00–£55.25

HB per person per night:
DY £47.75–£63.00

OPEN All Year

♦♦♦

CHURCH FARM
Monkton Farleigh, Bradford-on-Avon BA15 2QJ
T: (01225) 858583
F: (01225) 852474
E: rebecca@tuckerb.fsnet.co.uk
I: www.tuckerb.fsnet.co.uk

Bedrooms: 2 double, 1 family
Bathrooms: 3 en suite

Converted farmhouse barn with exceptional views in peaceful, idyllic setting. Ten minutes from Bath, ideal base for touring/walking South West England. Families/dogs welcome.

B&B per person per night:
S £35.00
D £25.00

OPEN All Year

CHECK THE MAPS

The colour maps at the front of this guide show all the cities, towns and villages for which you will find accommodation entries. Refer to the town index to find the page on which they are listed.

BATH continued

CRESCENT GUEST HOUSE

21 Crescent Gardens, Upper Bristol Road, Bath BA1 2NA
T: (01225) 425945
E: info@crescentbath.co.uk
I: www.crescentbath.co.uk

Service is our speciality, and this includes a complimentary shoe-shine. Relaxed, cosy atmosphere and breakfast prepared to order from fresh, local ingredients, including vegetarian options. Stylish, welcoming rooms and only five minutes' level walk from Bath's shops and attractions. Public parking at rear. A very special guesthouse experience.

Bedrooms: 3 double, 1 single, 1 family
Bathrooms: 3 en suite, 2 private

Oct-Mar, Sun-Thu: 10% discount, minimum 2 nights.

B&B per person per night:
S £35.00–£42.00
D £24.00–£34.00

OPEN All Year except Christmas

◆◆◆

EDGAR HOTEL
64 Great Pulteney Street, Bath BA2 4DN
T: (01225) 420619
F: (01225) 466916
E: edgar-hotel@pgen.net
I: www.edgar-hotel.co.uk

Bedrooms: 15 double, 2 single, 1 family
Bathrooms: 18 en suite

CC: Delta, Mastercard, Switch, Visa

Georgian townhouse hotel, close to city centre and Roman Baths. Privately run. All rooms with en suite facilities. 4-poster bed available.

B&B per person per night:
S £20.00–£25.00
D £27.50–£42.50

OPEN All Year except Christmas

◆◆◆

FLAXLEY VILLA
9 Newbridge Hill, Bath BA1 3PW
T: (01225) 313237

Bedrooms: 3 double
Bathrooms: 2 en suite

Comfortable Victorian house, just a few minutes by car to city centre and within easy reach of Royal Crescent and main attractions. Also river walks nearby.

B&B per person per night:
S £26.00–£40.00
D £40.00–£65.00

OPEN All Year

◆◆◆

HERMITAGE
Bath Road, Box, Corsham SN13 8DT
T: (01225) 744187
F: (01225) 743447
E: hermitage@telecall.co.uk

Bedrooms: 4 double, 1 family
Bathrooms: 5 en suite

16thC house with heated pool in summer. Dining room with vaulted ceiling. Six miles from Bath on A4 to Chippenham, first drive on left by 30mph sign.

B&B per person per night:
S £35.00–£45.00
D £25.00–£30.00

OPEN All Year except Christmas

◆◆◆◆◆

HIGHFIELDS

207 Bailbrook Lane, Batheaston, Bath BA1 7AB
T: (01225) 859782
F: (01225) 852778
E: acham@supanet.com
I: www.highfieldsbath.co.uk

The perfect place from which to explore Bath and the surrounding area. Peacefully situated with stunning views down the Avon Valley, yet only a few minutes from the city centre. Home from home comforts. A garden with plunge pool to relax in.

Bedrooms: 2 double, 1 single
Bathrooms: 3 private

Discounts on stays of 4 days or more.

B&B per person per night:
S £40.00–£60.00
D £35.00–£40.00

OPEN All Year except Christmas

BATH continued

HIGHWAYS HOUSE

143 Wells Road, Bath BA2 3AL
T: (01225) 421238
F: (01225) 481169
E: stay@highwayshouse.co.uk
I: www.highwayshouse.co.uk

B&B per person per night:
S £40.00–£50.00
D £30.00–£37.50

OPEN All Year

Elegant Victorian home set in mature gardens, only ten minutes' walk from city centre. Off-street parking, non-smoking. Clean, comfortable rooms, excellent beds (some king size). One triple room. Large guest lounge. Full English breakfast, cooked to order. Double glazing and central heating throughout.

Bedrooms: 4 double, 1 twin, 1 single
Bathrooms: 5 en suite, 1 private

CC: Amex, Delta, Mastercard, Switch, Visa

5 P €

♦♦♦♦
Silver Award

THE HOLLIES

Hatfield Road, Bath BA2 2BD
T: (01225) 313366
F: (01225) 313366
E: davcartwright@lineone.net
I: www.visitus.co.uk/bath/hotel.hollies.html

B&B per person per night:
D £32.50–£37.50

OPEN All Year except Christmas

The Hollies was built in 1851 and stands in its own gardens just 15 minutes' walk from Bath centre. Offering peace and quiet, the owners have recently upgraded and redecorated the pretty guest rooms, all with bathrooms. The house is furnished with antiques with your comfort in mind.

Bedrooms: 2 double, 1 twin
Bathrooms: 2 en suite, 1 private

CC: Delta, Mastercard, Switch, Visa

4 nights or more, 10% discount.

P

♦♦♦♦

LAURA PLACE HOTEL

3 Laura Place,
Great Pulteney Street, Bath
BA2 4BH
T: (01225) 463815
F: (01225) 310222

Bedrooms: 1 double, 1 family
Bathrooms: 1 en suite

CC: Amex, Mastercard, Visa

B&B per person per night:
S £60.00–£70.00
D £37.50–£49.00

OPEN All Year

18thC townhouse, centrally located in Georgian square. Two minutes from Roman Baths, Pump Rooms and abbey.

6 P

♦♦♦♦

LINDISFARNE GUEST HOUSE

41a Warminster Road, Bathampton, Bath BA2 6XJ
T: (01225) 466342
E: lindisfarne-bath@talk21.com
I: www.bath.org/hotel/lindisfarne.htm

Bedrooms: 2 double, 1 twin, 1 family
Bathrooms: 4 en suite

CC: Amex, Delta, Diners, Mastercard, Switch, Visa

B&B per person per night:
S £35.00–£39.00
D £25.00–£30.00

OPEN All Year except Christmas

Spacious house with friendly proprietors. Within walking distance of good eating places, about 1.5 miles from Bath city centre. Large car park.

8 P

GOLD & SILVER AWARDS

These exclusive VisitBritain awards are given to establishments achieving the highest levels of quality and service. Further information can be found at the front of the guide. An index to all accommodation achieving these awards are at the back of this guide.

BATH continued

♦♦♦♦♦ Gold Award

MONKSHILL

Shaft Road, Monkton Combe, Bath
BA2 7HL
T: (01225) 833028
F: (01225) 833028
E: monks.hill@virgin.net
I: www.monkshill.com

You are assured of a warm welcome in this secluded and very comfortable country residence surrounded by its own extensive gardens. The emphasis is on luxurious comfort. The individually styled bedrooms are graciously appointed and command excellent views over the garden, with its croquet lawn, the woodland and valley below.

Bedrooms: 2 double, 1 twin
Bathrooms: 2 en suite, 1 private

CC: Amex, Delta, Mastercard, Switch, Visa

B&B per person per night:
S £55.00–£70.00
D £35.00–£42.50

OPEN All Year except Christmas

♦♦♦♦ Silver Award

NUMBER 30 CRESCENT GARDENS

Bath BA1 2NB
T: (01225) 337393
F: (01225) 337393
E: david.greenwood12@btinternet.com
I: www.numberthirty.com

Bedrooms: 4 double, 1 twin, 1 single
Bathrooms: 6 en suite

CC: Delta, Mastercard, Switch, Visa

A small, privately owned Victorian house in the centre of Bath. Outstanding housekeeping. Private car parking. Easy walk to shops and to Roman Baths.

12 P €

B&B per person per night:
S £55.00–£75.00
D £37.00–£55.00

OPEN All Year except Christmas

♦♦♦

PULTENEY HOTEL

14 Pulteney Road, Bath BA2 4HA
T: (01225) 460991
F: (01225) 460991
E: pulteney@tinyworld.co.uk
I: www.pulteneyhotel.co.uk

Large, elegant, Victorian house set in its own picturesque, south-facing gardens with fine views of Bath Abbey. Large, private car park. Located only 5-10 minutes' walk from city centre. An ideal base for exploring Bath and surrounding areas. All rooms (except one) en suite with hairdryer, TV, tea/coffee facilities.

Bedrooms: 8 double, 4 twin, 2 single, 3 family
Bathrooms: 16 en suite, 1 private

CC: Diners, Mastercard, Switch, Visa

Reduced rates for stays of 3 nights or more – each booking assessed individually.

B&B per person per night:
S £40.00–£50.00
D £32.50–£47.50

OPEN All Year

♦♦

ROYAL PARK GUEST HOUSE

16 Crescent Gardens, Bath BA1 2NA
T: (01225) 317651
F: (01225) 483950
E: royal@parkb-b.freeserve.co.uk

Bedrooms: 2 double, 1 single, 1 family
Bathrooms: 3 en suite, 1 private

A small, friendly, family-run Victorian guesthouse within a five-minute walk of Bath city centre.

4 P

B&B per person per night:
S £27.00–£32.00
D £23.00–£26.00

OPEN All Year except Christmas

CHECK THE MAPS

The colour maps at the front of this guide show all the cities, towns and villages for which you will find accommodation entries. Refer to the town index to find the page on which they are listed.

BATH continued

◆◆◆◆◆
Gold Award

VILLA MAGDALA HOTEL

Henrietta Road, Bath BA2 6LX
T: (01225) 466329
F: (01225) 483207
E: office@villamagdala.co.uk
I: www.villamagdala.co.uk

B&B per person per night:
S £70.00–£105.00
D £42.50–£75.00

OPEN All Year except Christmas

Ideally situated, this charming Victorian townhouse hotel enjoys a peaceful location overlooking Henrietta Park, only five minutes' level walk to the city centre and Roman Baths. The spacious rooms, some with 4-poster beds, all have pleasant views. Private parking is available in the hotel grounds. The Villa Magdala is a non-smoking hotel.

Bedrooms: 11 double, 2 single, 5 family
Bathrooms: 18 en suite

CC: Amex, Delta, Mastercard, Switch, Visa

BEAMINSTER, Dorset Map ref 2A3

Silver Award

THE WALNUTS

2 Prout Bridge, Beaminster DT8 3AY
T: (01308) 862211
F: (01308) 862211
E: caroline@thewalnuts.co.uk
I: www.thewalnuts.co.uk

Bedrooms: 3 double
Bathrooms: 2 en suite

B&B per person per night:
S £26.00–£37.00
D £25.00–£31.00

OPEN All Year except Christmas

Tastefully refurbished building with very attractive bedrooms. Friendly, family-run establishment. Very well situated within short walk of local inns and tasteful small shops.

BERRYNARBOR, Devon Map ref 1C1

LANGLEIGH HOUSE

The Village, Berrynarbor, Ilfracombe
EX34 9SG
T: (01271) 883410
F: (01271) 882396
E: langleigh@hotmail.com

B&B per person per night:
S £21.00–£24.50
D £21.00–£24.50

OPEN All Year

Langleigh House is in the centre of the beautiful village of Berrynarbor, winner of Village in Bloom and Best Kept Village. Large garden overlooking hills. One mile from sea between Ilfracombe and Combe Martin. Ideally situated for Exmoor and award-winning beaches.

Bedrooms: 4 double, 1 family
Bathrooms: 5 en suite

CC: Delta, Mastercard, Switch, Visa

USE YOUR *i*s

There are more than 550 Tourist Information Centres throughout England offering friendly help with accommodation and holiday ideas as well as suggestions of places to visit and things to do. You'll find TIC addresses in the local Phone Book.

BIDEFORD, Devon Map ref 1C1 *Tourist Information Centre Tel: (01237) 477676*

BULWORTHY COTTAGE

Stony Cross, Bideford EX39 4PY
T: (01271) 858441
E: bulworthy@aol.com

B&B per person per night:
S £24.00–£28.00
D £24.00–£28.00

HB per person per night:
DY £36.00–£45.50

OPEN All Year except Christmas

18thC miners' cottages, sympathetically renovated whilst retaining many original features. Standing in quiet countryside within easy reach of Moors, Tarka Trail, SW coastal path, Rosemoor and NT properties. Attractive, en suite accommodation. Choice of breakfasts and evening meals, with a wine list to complement the local food.

Bedrooms: 2 double
Bathrooms: 2 en suite

Evening meal available
CC: Amex, Mastercard, Switch, Visa

Nov-Mar: 3 nights' B&B for the price of 2.

10 P

SUNSET HOTEL

Landcross, Bideford EX39 5JA
T: (01237) 472962
F: (01237) 422520
E: hazellamb@hotmail.com

B&B per person per night:
S £50.00–£60.00
D £31.50–£34.00

OPEN All Year

Small country hotel set in beautiful gardens in a quiet, peaceful location, overlooking spectacular scenery, 1.5 miles from town. Beautifully decorated and spotlessly clean. Highly recommended, quality accommodation. All en suites with colour TV and beverages. Licensed. Private parking. Non-smoking establishment.

Bedrooms: 2 double, 1 twin, 1 family
Bathrooms: 4 en suite

CC: Mastercard, Visa

Reduced rates for 3, 5 and 7 days.

P

BISHOP'S LYDEARD, Somerset Map ref 1D1

♦♦♦

THE LETHBRIDGE ARMS

Gore Square, Bishop's Lydeard, Taunton TA4 3BW
T: (01823) 432234
F: (01823) 433982
E: thelethbridge@aol.com

B&B per person per night:
S £30.00–£40.00
D £22.50–£27.50

OPEN All Year

A warm welcome awaits you at this 16thC inn set in lovely grounds with a children's play area. Close by is the West Somerset Railway and Quantock Hills. Bishop's Lydeard is on the main route to Butlins, Minehead. Ten minutes from M5 motorway. Home cooking and real ales are our speciality. Excellent, comfortable accommodation.

Bedrooms: 4 double, 4 family
Bathrooms: 3 en suite

Evening meal available
CC: Delta, Mastercard, Switch, Visa

P

SPECIAL BREAKS

Many establishments offer special promotions and themed breaks. These are highlighted in red. (All such offers are subject to availability.)

BODMIN, Cornwall Map ref 1B2 *Tourist Information Centre Tel: (01208) 76616*

♦♦♦♦♦ Silver Award

BOKIDDICK FARM

Lanivet, Bodmin PL30 5HP
T: (01208) 831481
F: (01208) 831481
E: gillhugo@bokiddickfarm.co.uk
I: www.bokiddickfarm.co.uk

Welcome to our lovely Georgian farmhouse and luxury converted barn. Oak beams, wood panelling, spacious en suite bedrooms with super king-size beds. Peaceful location, magnificent views. Central Cornwall, two miles from A30. Close to Eden and Lanhydrock. Delicious Aga-cooked breakfasts. Relax and enjoy. The perfect place for that special break.

Bedrooms: 5 double
Bathrooms: 5 en suite

CC: Mastercard, Switch, Visa

B&B per person per night:
S £35.00–£42.00
D £27.00–£33.00

OPEN All Year except Christmas

BOSCASTLE, Cornwall Map ref 1B2

♦♦♦♦

THE OLD COACH HOUSE

Tintagel Road, Boscastle PL35 0AS
T: (01840) 250398
F: (01840) 250346
E: parsons@old-coach.co.uk
I: www.old-coach.co.uk

Bedrooms: 5 double, 1 twin, 3 family
Bathrooms: 9 en suite

CC: Delta, Mastercard, Switch, Visa

Relax in beautiful 300-year-old former coach house. All rooms en suite with colour TV, teamaker, hairdryer, etc. Friendly and helpful owners. Good parking.

B&B per person per night:
S £25.00–£44.00
D £22.00–£24.00

OPEN All Year except Christmas

♦♦♦♦

REDDIVALLEN FARMHOUSE

Trevalga, Boscastle PL35 0EE
T: (01840) 250854
F: (01840) 250854
E: cardew@lineone.net
I: www.reddivallenfarm.co.uk

Bedrooms: 2 double
Bathrooms: 2 en suite

Evening meal available
CC: Amex, Delta, Mastercard, Switch, Visa

17thC farmhouse on a working farm just three miles from Boscastle and Tintagel. Offering excellent facilities and the peace and quiet of the countryside.

B&B per person per night:
S £22.00–£30.00
D £22.00–£27.00

HB per person per night:
DY £34.00–£37.00

OPEN All Year

♦♦♦

ST CHRISTOPHER'S HOTEL

High Street, Boscastle PL35 0BD
T: (01840) 250412
F: (01840) 250412
E: stchristophers@hotmail.com
I: www.stchristophershotel.co.uk

A warm, friendly welcome can be found at St Christopher's Hotel, a 17thC former merchant's house set in the older, upper part of Boscastle village. Dramatic views of the North Cornish coast can be seen from some rooms and the garden. All rooms tastefully decorated with en suite facilities.

Bedrooms: 7 double, 2 single
Bathrooms: 9 en suite

CC: Delta, Mastercard, Switch, Visa

B&B per person per night:
S £20.00–£32.50

OPEN All Year

MAP REFERENCES The map references refer to the colour maps at the front of this guide. The first figure is the map number; the letter and figure which follow indicate the grid reference on the map.

BOSSINGTON, Somerset Map ref 1D1

◆◆◆◆

BUCKLEY LODGE

Bossington, Minehead TA24 8HQ
T: (01643) 862521
E: bucklodgeuk@yahoo.co.uk

Bedrooms: 2 family
Bathrooms: 1 en suite, 1 private

House is situated in small, picturesque NT village. 0.5 miles from sea and backed by woods. Ideal walking area.

B&B per person per night:
S £25.00–£27.00
D £18.50–£21.00

BOVEY TRACEY, Devon Map ref 1D2

◆◆◆◆◆
Gold Award

BROOKFIELD HOUSE

Challabrook Lane, Bovey Tracey,
Newton Abbot TQ13 9DF
T: (01626) 836181
F: (01626) 836182
E: brookfieldh@tinyworld.co.uk
I: www.brookfield-house.com

Spacious early Edwardian residence situated on the edge of Bovey Tracey and Dartmoor. Set in two acres with panoramic moor views and bounded by the gently flowing Pottery Leat. Secluded tranquillity yet within easy walking distance of town, local attractions and moorland. Individually decorated bedrooms, all with comfortable seating areas.

Bedrooms: 3 double, 1 twin
Bathrooms: 2 en suite, 2 private

Evening meal available
CC: Mastercard, Switch, Visa

Special rates on application for stays of 4 nights or more, and also weekly terms.

12

B&B per person per night:
S £37.50–£43.00
D £27.50–£33.00

HB per person per night:
DY £49.50–£55.00

BOX, Wiltshire Map ref 2B2

◆◆◆◆

LORNE HOUSE

London Road, Box, Corsham
SN13 8NA
T: (01225) 742597
E: lornehousebandb@aol.com
I: www.lornehouse.net

Bedrooms: 3 double, 1 family
Bathrooms: 4 en suite

CC: Delta, Mastercard, Switch, Visa

Listed in guide books in Germany, Canada and America, this Victorian property boasts excellent service and accommodation to discerning travellers. Situated six miles from Bath.

B&B per person per night:
S £30.00–£35.00
D £22.50–£25.00

OPEN All Year except Christmas

BRADFORD-ON-AVON, Wiltshire Map ref 2B2 *Tourist Information Centre Tel: (01225) 865797*

◆◆◆◆◆

WIDBROOK GRANGE

Trowbridge Road, Widbrook,
Bradford-on-Avon BA15 1UH
T: (01225) 864750
F: (01225) 862890
E: stay@widbrookgrange.com
I: www.widbrookgrange.com

Bedrooms: 16 double, 1 single, 3 family
Bathrooms: 19 en suite, 1 private

Evening meal available
CC: Amex, Delta, Diners, Mastercard, Switch, Visa

19thC Bath-stone house and courtyard rooms in own grounds, on outskirts of Bradford-on-Avon. Riding and boating nearby. Exquisitely furnished and decorated. Beautifully tranquil.

B&B per person per night:
S £60.00–£90.00
D £40.00–£62.50

HB per person per night:
DY £90.00–£120.00

OPEN All Year except Christmas

TOWN INDEX

This can be found at the back of the guide. If you know where you want to stay, the index will give you the page number listing accommodation in your chosen town, city or village.

BRATTON FLEMING, Devon Map ref 1C1

♦♦♦♦♦ Gold Award

BRACKEN HOUSE COUNTRY HOTEL

Bratton Fleming, Barnstaple EX31 4TG
T: (01598) 710320
E: holidays@brackenhousehotel.com
I: www.brackenhousehotel.com

B&B per person per night:
D £30.00–£49.00

HB per person per night:
DY £55.00–£69.00

Charming, small country hotel set in eight peaceful acres of garden, woodland, pond and pasture. Extensive views. Convenient for Rosemoor, Marwood, Arlington, North Devon and Exmoor with its magnificent coastline. En suite bedrooms include two on ground floor. Country-style Aga cooking. Ideal for dogs with well-trained owners.

Bedrooms: 4 double, 4 twin
Bathrooms: 8 en suite

Evening meal available
CC: Delta, Mastercard, Switch, Visa

Reduced tariff for Sun-Sun bookings. Lower prices in Aug. Reductions for late bookings.

BRENDON, Devon Map ref 1C1

♦♦♦♦

BRENDON HOUSE

Brendon, Lynton EX35 6PS
T: (01598) 741206
E: brendonhouse4u@aol.com
I: www.brendonvalley.co.uk/brendon_house.htm

B&B per person per night:
S £27.00–£36.00
D £20.00–£27.00

HB per person per night:
DY £36.00–£43.00

OPEN All Year except Christmas

Licensed, former 18thC farmhouse, nestling in the delightful Lyn Valley. Fully equipped, en suite bedrooms, comfortable residents' lounge and spacious gardens set in stunning Exmoor scenery. Diners can choose from our extensive menu of delicious, fine, country fare, seafood dishes, local game and good wines. Vegetarian dishes also available.

Bedrooms: 2 double, 1 twin, 1 single, 1 family
Bathrooms: 4 en suite, 1 private

Evening meal available

Weekly and off-season discounts.

BRIDGWATER, Somerset Map ref 1D1

♦♦♦

QUANTOCK VIEW GUEST HOUSE

Bridgwater Road, North Petherton, Bridgwater TA6 6PR
T: (01278) 663309
E: irene@quantockview.freeserve.co.uk
I: www.smoothhound.co.uk/hotels/quantock

Bedrooms: 1 double, 1 twin, 1 single, 1 family
Bathrooms: 4 en suite

Evening meal available
CC: Amex, Delta, Mastercard, Switch, Visa

B&B per person per night:
S £25.00–£27.00
D £20.00–£21.00

HB per person per night:
DY £25.00–£32.50

OPEN All Year except Christmas

Comfortable, family-run guesthouse in central Somerset. En suite facilities in all rooms. Close to hills and coast, yet only minutes from M5, jct 24.

CHECK THE MAPS

The colour maps at the front of this guide show all the cities, towns and villages for which you will find accommodation entries. Refer to the town index to find the page on which they are listed.

BRIDPORT, Dorset Map ref 2A3 *Tourist Information Centre Tel: (01308) 424901*

BRITMEAD HOUSE

West Bay Road, Bridport DT6 4EG
T: (01308) 422941
F: (01308) 422516
E: britmead@talk21.com
I: www.britmeadhouse.co.uk

B&B per person per night:
S £30.00–£44.00
D £24.00–£32.00

OPEN All Year

An elegant Edwardian house situated just off the A35 between the historic market town of Bridport and the harbour at West Bay, the ideal location for exploring the beautiful Dorset countryside. Family-run, en suite accommodation with many thoughtful extras. 10 minutes' walk to harbour, beaches, golf course and the coastal path.

Bedrooms: 4 double, 2 twin, 2 family
Bathrooms: 8 en suite

CC: Delta, Mastercard, Switch, Visa

Discounts available on stays of 2 or more nights.

♦♦♦♦
Gold Award

SOUTHCROFT

Park Road, Bridport DT6 5DA
T: (01308) 423335
F: (01308) 423335
E: info@southcroftguesthouse.com
I: www.southcroftguesthouse.com

B&B per person per night:
S £30.00–£40.00
D £24.00–£29.00

OPEN All Year except Christmas

Overlooking the small market town of Bridport, we are located in one of the most beautiful parts of England. The scenery – coastal or country – is stunning; the small villages are picturesque; the harbour at West Bay, with its flotilla of small fishing boats, is fascinating. A really lovely place to visit, to stay and enjoy.

Bedrooms: 1 double, 2 suites
Bathrooms: 1 private

CC: Delta, Mastercard, Switch, Visa

Winter breaks Nov-Mar (excl Christmas, New Year and Easter). Discounts for doubles 2 nights and over, including breakfast.

BRISTOL Map ref 2A2 *Tourist Information Centre Tel: (0117) 926 0767*

THE PADDOCK

Hung Road, Shirehampton, Bristol BS11 9XJ
T: (0117) 9235140

Bedrooms: 4 double, 1 single
Bathrooms: 5 en suite

B&B per person per night:
S Min £30.00
D Min £25.00

OPEN All Year except Christmas

Modern detached house, set in approximately one acre of grounds, offering quality accommodation.

BROADHEMBURY, Devon Map ref 1D2

STAFFORD BARTON FARM

Broadhembury, Honiton EX14 3LU
T: (01404) 841403
E: jeanwalters1@tesco.net

Bedrooms: 1 double, 1 twin
Bathrooms: 2 en suite

B&B per person per night:
S Min £25.00
D Min £25.00

OPEN All Year except Christmas

55-acre mixed farm. Delightful, modern, Scandinavian-style house, on genuine working farm, close to thatched village. Beautiful gardens and views.

IMPORTANT NOTE Information on accommodation listed in this guide has been supplied by the proprietors. As changes may occur you are advised to check details at the time of booking.

BROUGHTON GIFFORD, Wiltshire Map ref 2B2

HONEYSUCKLE COTTAGE

95 The Common, Broughton Gifford, Melksham SN12 8ND
T: (01225) 782463
E: dmehta@globalnet.co.uk
I: www.honeysucklecottage.org.uk

Comfortable country cottage dating back to the 18thC. Tranquil situation facing village common. Ideal base for Bath, Bradford-on-Avon, Lacock and numerous historic locations. Accommodation in double en suite and twin/family with private facilities. Breakfast is freshly prepared using local produce when possible.

Bedrooms: 1 double, 1 twin
Bathrooms: 1 en suite, 1 private

5 P

B&B per person per night:
S £30.00
D £22.50–£27.50

OPEN All Year except Christmas

BUDE, Cornwall Map ref 1C2 *Tourist Information Centre Tel: (01288) 354240*

♦♦♦♦
Silver Award

HAREFIELD COTTAGE

Upton, Bude EX23 0LY
T: (01288) 352350
F: (01288) 352712
E: sales@coast-countryside.co.uk
I: www.coast-countryside.co.uk

Stone-built cottage with outstanding coastal views. Luxurious and spacious, en suite bedrooms, king-size beds and 4-poster available. Home cooking our speciality. All diets catered for. Personal attention assured at all times. Only 250 yards from the coastal footpath. One mile downhill to the national cycle network. Hot tub available.

Bedrooms: 3 double
Bathrooms: 3 en suite

Evening meal available

Special 3-night walking break including DB&B, packed lunch, transport and professional guide – £110pp.

P

B&B per person per night:
S Min £30.00
D Min £46.00

HB per person per night:
DY Min £34.00

OPEN All Year except Christmas

HIGHBRE CREST

Whitstone, Holsworthy EX22 6UF
T: (01288) 341002
E: lindacole@ukonline.co.uk

Do you need a break? Come and relax in our garden or conservatory and savour the breathtaking views. Beautiful sunsets over the sea and scenic views of the moors of Devon and Cornwall. All bedrooms en suite. Full-size snooker table. A splendid house with comfort and food to match. Bude seven miles.

Bedrooms: 2 double, 1 twin
Bathrooms: 3 en suite

Evening meal available

12 P

B&B per person per night:
S £25.00–£30.00
D £25.00–£30.00

HB per person per night:
DY £36.00–£46.00

OPEN All Year except Christmas

BUDE continued

♦♦

INN ON THE GREEN

Crooklets Beach, Bude EX23 8NF
T: (01288) 356013
F: (01288) 356244
E: info@innonthegreen.info
I: www.innonthegreen.info

B&B per person per night:
S £22.00–£37.00
D £22.00–£37.00

HB per person per night:
DY £40.00–£55.00

OPEN All Year

Our family-run Victorian hotel has a reputation for comfort and service. It is situated at Crooklets Beach and faces south with a view over Bude golf course. We serve a varied menu of wholesome, home-produced food.

Bedrooms: 3 double, 7 twin, 4 single, 3 family
Bathrooms: 17 en suite

Evening meal available
CC: Amex, Delta, Mastercard, Switch, Visa

BUDLEIGH SALTERTON, Devon Map ref 1D2 *Tourist Information Centre Tel: (01395) 445275*

♦♦♦♦
Silver Award

LUFFLANDS

Yettington, Budleigh Salterton EX9 7BP
T: (01395) 568422
F: (01395) 568810
E: stay@lufflands.co.uk
I: www.lufflands.co.uk

B&B per person per night:
S £21.00–£24.00
D £21.00–£24.00

OPEN All Year

A warm welcome can be found at Lufflands, a 17thC former farmhouse. All rooms equipped to a high standard, and your breakfast is freshly cooked to order in the guest dining room/lounge with inglenook and bread ovens. Large garden, ample off-street parking. Close to beaches. Excellent walking.

Bedrooms: 1 double, 1 single, 1 family
Bathrooms: 2 en suite, 1 private

CC: Delta, Mastercard, Switch, Visa

Short breaks available: Apr-Oct £22pppn, Nov-Mar £20.50pppn. Minimum 3 nights.

BURTON BRADSTOCK, Dorset Map ref 2A3

♦♦♦♦

PEBBLE BEACH LODGE

Coast Road, Burton Bradstock, Bridport DT6 4RJ
T: (01308) 897428
E: pebblebeachlodge@supanet.com
I: www.burtonbradstock.org.uk/pebblebeachlodge

Bedrooms: 4 double, 1 single, 2 family
Bathrooms: 7 en suite

B&B per person per night:
S £27.50–£30.00
D £27.50–£30.00

OPEN All Year except Christmas

Located on B3157 coast road, affording panoramic views of heritage coastline. Direct access to beach. Spacious and attractive accommodation, large conservatory.

CALLINGTON, Cornwall Map ref 1C2

♦♦♦

GREEN PASTURES

Longhill, Callington PL17 8AU
T: (01579) 382566
E: greenpast@aol.com
I: www.tamarvalleyview.co.uk

Bedrooms: 2 double, 1 twin
Bathrooms: 2 en suite, 1 private

B&B per person per night:
S £22.50–£25.00
D £20.00–£23.00

OPEN All Year

Spacious, detached bungalow set within five acres of pastoral land. Large car park. Extensive views towards Dartmoor, Tamar Valley. Cotehele, Morwellam Quay within easy reach.

CREDIT CARD BOOKINGS If you book by telephone and are asked for your credit card number it is advisable to check the proprietor's policy should you cancel your reservation.

CASTLE CARY, Somerset Map ref 2B2

♦♦♦

THE HORSE POND INN AND MOTEL

The Triangle, Castle Cary BA7 7BD
T: (01963) 350318
F: (01963) 351764
E: horsepondinn@aol.com
I: www.horsepondinn.co.uk

Bedrooms: 2 double, 2 family
Bathrooms: 4 en suite

Evening meal available
CC: Diners, Mastercard, Switch, Visa

Nestling at the foot of Castle Cary, centrally located, an ideal base for travelling around Somerset, West Devon, Dorset and Wiltshire either for business or pleasure.

B&B per person per night:
S £35.00–£40.00
D £27.50–£32.50

HB per person per night:
DY £40.00–£55.00

OPEN All Year

CHARMOUTH, Dorset Map ref 1D2

♦♦♦♦

QUEEN'S ARMES HOTEL

The Street, Charmouth, Bridport DT6 6QF
T: (01297) 560339
F: (01297) 560339
E: peterm@netcomuk.co.uk

Bedrooms: 5 double, 3 twin, 2 single, 1 family
Bathrooms: 10 en suite, 1 private

CC: Delta, Mastercard, Switch, Visa

Built around 1500, this former coaching inn with oak beams and wall panels is situated in centre of village on the Heritage Coastline.

B&B per person per night:
S £30.50–£37.50
D £30.50–£37.50

HB per person per night:
DY £45.50–£52.50

♦♦♦♦♦
Gold Award

SPENCE FARM

Wootton Fitzpaine, Charmouth DT6 6DF
T: (01297) 560814
F: (01297) 560727
E: bookings@spence-farm.com
I: www.spence-farm.com

Dorset-stone, long farmhouse set in 100 acres of rolling countryside with views overlooking Charmouth to Lyme Bay. All bedrooms en suite with full facilities and sea views. Guest lounge and landscaped gardens with stunning woodland walks. Panelled-wood dining room with full English breakfast. Family suite available.

Bedrooms: 3 double, 1 family
Bathrooms: 3 en suite

Evening meal available
CC: Delta, Mastercard, Switch, Visa

Mid-week and 3-night-stay deals.

B&B per person per night:
S £40.00–£44.00
D £65.00–£70.00

HB per person per night:
DY £60.00–£70.00

CHEDDAR, Somerset Map ref 1D1

♦♦♦

BAY ROSE HOUSE

The Bays, Cheddar BS27 3QN
T: (01934) 741377
F: (01934) 741377
E: enquiries@bayrose.co.uk
I: www.bayrose.co.uk

Bedrooms: 3 double
Bathrooms: 2 en suite, 1 private

Evening meal available
CC: Amex, Delta, Mastercard, Switch, Visa

Cottage situated at the foot of Cheddar Gorge, close to caves, ideal base for touring, cycling and walking holidays. Extensive breakfast selection with vegetarian options.

B&B per person per night:
S £25.00–£35.00
D £20.00–£27.50

HB per person per night:
DY £31.50–£46.50

OPEN All Year

CHEW STOKE, Bath and North East Somerset Map ref 2A2

♦♦♦

ORCHARD HOUSE

Bristol Road, Chew Stoke, Bristol BS40 8UB
T: (01275) 333143
F: (01275) 333754
E: orchardhse@ukgateway.net
I: www.orchardhse.ukgateway.net

Bedrooms: 1 double, 2 twin, 1 single, 1 family
Bathrooms: 4 en suite, 1 private

CC: Delta, Mastercard, Switch, Visa

Comfortable accommodation in a carefully modernised Georgian house and coach house annexe. Good eating in local pubs. Convenient access to Bristol and Bath.

B&B per person per night:
S £25.00–£27.00
D £23.50–£25.00

OPEN All Year

COLOUR MAPS Colour maps at the front of this guide pinpoint all places under which you will find accommodation listed.

CHIPPING SODBURY, South Gloucestershire Map ref 2B2

Silver Award

ROUNCEVAL HOUSE HOTEL

Rounceval Street, Chipping Sodbury, Bristol BS37 6AR
T: (01454) 334410
F: (01454) 314944
E: rouncevalhousehotel@tiscali.co.uk
I: www.rouncevalhousehotel.co.uk

Grade II Listed Georgian house refurbished to a very high standard to form a comfortable country-house hotel set within its own grounds in the medieval market town of Chipping Sodbury with its many pubs and restaurants. All rooms have been tastefully modernised to provide superior, en suite accommodation.

Bedrooms: 10 double
Bathrooms: 10 en suite

CC: Amex, Mastercard, Switch, Visa

B&B per person per night:
S £65.00–£90.00
D £45.00–£55.00

OPEN All Year

CLEVEDON, Somerset Map ref 1D1

HIGHCLIFFE HOTEL

Wellington Terrace, Clevedon BS21 7PU
T: (01275) 873250
F: (01275) 873572
E: highcliffehotel@aol.com
I: www.highcliffehotel.com

Bedrooms: 15 double, 2 single, 2 family
Bathrooms: 19 en suite

Evening meal available
CC: Delta, Mastercard, Switch, Visa

Located jct 20, M5. Quiet situation and friendly staff. Spacious, en suite rooms, restaurant, bar, parking, lovely function room. Ideal business or leisure traveller. Phone for special deals.

B&B per person per night:
S £30.00–£50.00
D £25.00–£32.50

HB per person per night:
DY £39.50–£49.50

OPEN All Year except Christmas

CLOVELLY, Devon Map ref 1C1

FUCHSIA COTTAGE

Burscott, Clovelly, Bideford EX39 5RR
T: (01237) 431398
E: curtis@fuchsiacottage.fslife.co.uk
I: www.clovelly-holidays.co.uk

Bedrooms: 2 double, 1 single
Bathrooms: 2 en suite

Evening meal available

Fuchsia Cottage has comfortable, ground and first floor, en suite accommodation. Surrounded by beautiful views of sea and country. Good walking area. Ample parking.

B&B per person per night:
S Max £18.00
D Max £22.00

OPEN All Year except Christmas

COLLINGBOURNE KINGSTON, Wiltshire Map ref 2B2

MANOR FARM B & B

Collingbourne Kingston, Marlborough SN8 3SD
T: (01264) 850859
F: (01264) 850859
E: stay@manorfm.com
I: www.manorfm.com

An attractive Grade II Listed period village farmhouse with comfortable and spacious rooms on a working family farm. Sumptuous traditional, vegetarian, gluten-free and other special-diet breakfasts. Beautiful countryside with superb walking and cycling from the farm. Horses and pets welcome. Exciting "Aerial Adventures" from our private airstrip (see website).

Bedrooms: 1 double, 1 single, 1 family
Bathrooms: 1 en suite

CC: Amex, Delta, Mastercard, Switch, Visa

Pleasure flights from our private airstrip over Wiltshire's ancient places, white horses and crop circles by balloon, aeroplane and helicopter.

B&B per person per night:
S £25.00–£30.00
D £25.00–£30.00

OPEN All Year

COLYTON, Devon Map ref 1D2

Silver Award

SMALLICOMBE FARM

Northleigh, Colyton EX24 6BU
T: (01404) 831310
F: (01404) 831431
E: maggie_todd@yahoo.com
I: www.smallicombe.com

B&B per person per night:
S £35.00–£40.00
D £25.00–£30.00

OPEN All Year

Relax in a really special place, an idyllic rural setting abounding with wildlife yet close to the coast. Scrumptious farmhouse breakfasts including prize-winning Smallicombe sausages from our rare-breed pigs. All rooms en suite, overlooking an unspoilt valley landscape. The Garden Suite of sitting room, bedroom and bathroom is wheelchair accessible.

Bedrooms: 1 double, 1 family
Bathrooms: 2 en suite

Evening meal available
CC: Visa

CORSHAM, Wiltshire Map ref 2B2 *Tourist Information Centre Tel: (01249) 714660*

Silver Award

HEATHERLY COTTAGE

Ladbrook Lane, Gastard, Corsham SN13 9PE
T: (01249) 701402
F: (01249) 701412
E: ladbrook1@aol.com
I: www.smoothhound.co.uk/hotels/heather3.html

B&B per person per night:
S £30.00–£35.00
D £24.00–£27.00

OPEN All Year except Christmas

Delightful 17thC cottage in a quiet lane with two acres and beautiful views across open countryside. Guests have a separate wing of the house with their own entrance. All rooms en suite, one with king-size bed. Colour TV, clock-radio, hospitality tray, hairdryer. Many pubs serving good food nearby. Off-road parking.

Bedrooms: 2 double, 1 twin
Bathrooms: 3 en suite

10 P

CORTON, Wiltshire Map ref 2B2

THE DOVE INN

Corton, Warminster BA12 0SZ
T: (01985) 850109
F: (01985) 851041
E: info@thedove.co.uk
I: www.thedove.co.uk

Bedrooms: 5 double
Bathrooms: 5 en suite

Evening meal available
CC: Delta, Mastercard, Switch, Visa

B&B per person per night:
S Min £49.50
D Min £35.00

OPEN All Year

The Dove is a thriving, traditional village pub offering en suite, double rooms. Carefully chosen beers, ales and wines complement the Dove's delightful food.

CREWKERNE, Somerset Map ref 1D2

THE GEORGE HOTEL & COURTYARD RESTAURANT

Market Square, Crewkerne TA18 7LP
T: (01460) 73650
F: (01460) 72974
E: eddie@thegeorgehotel.sagehost.co.uk
I: www.thegeorgehotel.sagenet.co.uk

Bedrooms: 6 double, 2 twin, 3 single, 2 family
Bathrooms: 8 en suite, 2 private

Evening meal available
CC: Amex, Delta, Diners, Mastercard, Switch, Visa

B&B per person per night:
S £26.00–£50.00
D £27.50–£40.00

OPEN All Year

Recently refurbished, 17thC, Grade II Listed coaching inn in the market square. Ideally located for touring. Fine food, real ales, warm welcome!

P

CREWKERNE continued

HONEYDOWN FARM

Seaborough Hill, Crewkerne
TA18 8PL
T: (01460) 72665
F: (01460) 72665
E: cb@honeydown.freeserve.co.uk
I: www.honeydown.freeserve.co.uk

Bedrooms: 2 double, 1 twin
Bathrooms: 1 en suite

Evening meal available

B&B per person per night:
S £27.00–£30.00
D £25.00–£27.00

OPEN All Year except Christmas

A warm welcome awaits in our modern farmhouse on working dairy farm. Quiet situation 1.5 miles from Crewkerne with panoramic views. Local produce served.

CULLOMPTON, Devon Map ref 1D2

NEWCOURT BARTON

Langford, Cullompton EX15 1SE
T: (01884) 277326
F: (01884) 277326
E: newcourtbarton@btinternet.com
I: www.newcourtbarton-devon.co.uk

B&B per person per night:
S £20.00–£26.00
D £19.00–£23.00

OPEN All Year except Christmas

Convenient overnight stop or restful break. We're ideally placed, being set in peaceful countryside with delightful views yet close to M5 jct 28 for easy access to the Moors, coast, Exeter and NT properties. Plenty to see and do. Play area, coarse fishing, nearby Birds of Prey Centre – courses available.

Bedrooms: 1 double, 1 family
Bathrooms: 2 en suite

Child/weekly reductions.

CC: Visa

DARTMOOR

See under Ashburton, Bovey Tracey, Moretonhampstead, North Bovey, Okehampton, Tavistock, Yelverton

DARTMOUTH, Devon Map ref 1D3 *Tourist Information Centre Tel: (01803) 834224*

Gold Award

HILL VIEW HOUSE

76 Victoria Road, Dartmouth
TQ6 9DZ
T: (01803) 839372
F: (01803) 839372
E: enquiries@hillviewdartmouth.co.uk
I: www.hillviewdartmouth.co.uk

Bedrooms: 3 double, 2 twin
Bathrooms: 5 en suite

CC: Delta, Diners, Mastercard, Switch, Visa

B&B per person per night:
S £38.50–£56.00
D £28.50–£41.00

OPEN All Year

Extensively refurbished period townhouse five minutes' walk from Dartmouth centre and riverfront. Environmentally friendly, all bedding mite free, quality breakfasts, special diets catered for.

DAWLISH WARREN, Devon Map ref 1D2

SHUTTERTON FARM

Shutterton Lane, Dawlish Warren,
Dawlish EX7 0PD
T: (01626) 863766
F: (01626) 863766
E: shuttertonfarm@aol.com
I: www.shuttertonfarm.co.uk

Bedrooms: 1 double
Bathrooms: 1 en suite

B&B per person per night:
S £25.00
D £25.00

OPEN All Year

16thC Listed thatch cottage with accommodation in former dairy. Set in 1.5 acres, surrounded by farmland, 1.5 miles from beach and nature reserve.

ACCESSIBILITY

Look for the symbols which indicate National Accessible Scheme standards for hearing and visually impaired guests in addition to standards for guests with mobility impairment. You can find an index of all scheme participants at the back of this guide.

DEVIZES, Wiltshire Map ref 2B2 *Tourist Information Centre Tel: (01380) 729408*

◆◆◆◆◆ Gold Award

BLOUNTS COURT FARM

Coxhill Lane, Potterne, Devizes SN10 5PH
T: (01380) 727180
E: caroline@blountscourtfarm.co.uk
I: www.blountscourtfarm.co.uk

B&B per person per night:
S £32.00–£38.00
D £26.00–£29.00

OPEN All Year

Situated in a peaceful countryside setting of 150 acres with woodland backdrop. Traditional stone-built farmhouse with ground floor guest accommodation in recently converted stables adjoining house. Tastefully furnished rooms including 4-poster bed. Guests' own sitting room. Warm and homely atmosphere. Ideal base to explore this exciting part of Wiltshire.

Bedrooms: 1 double, 1 twin, 1 single
Bathrooms: 3 en suite

CC: Delta, Mastercard, Switch, Visa

8 P

◆◆◆

EASTCOTT MANOR

Easterton, Devizes SN10 4PH
T: (01380) 813313

B&B per person per night:
S Min £25.00
D Min £28.00

HB per person per night:
DY £42.00–£52.00

*Very comfortable Grade II * Elizabethan manor house on north edge of Salisbury Plain. Wonderful walking, convenient for Kennet and Avon Canal, Bath, Salisbury, Stonehenge, Avebury, NT properties and other beautiful houses. Large garden, set in own 20-acre grounds. Tranquil setting; nearest road B3098.*

Bedrooms: 1 double, 1 twin, 2 single
Bathrooms: 2 en suite, 2 private

Evening meal available

P

◆◆◆◆

LITTLETON LODGE

High Street, Littleton Panell, (A360), West Lavington, Devizes SN10 4ES
T: (01380) 813131
F: (01380) 816969
E: stay@littletonlodge.co.uk
I: www.littletonlodge.co.uk

Bedrooms: 3 double
Bathrooms: 3 en suite

CC: Amex, Mastercard, Visa

B&B per person per night:
S £40.00–£45.00
D £27.50–£32.50

OPEN All Year

Charming Victorian house c1850 in a conservation village. Delightful rural views and large garden overlooking a vineyard. Three good pubs within 5-10 minutes' walk. Private parking.

P

DINTON, Wiltshire Map ref 2B3

◆◆◆

MORRIS' FARM HOUSE

Baverstock, Dinton, Salisbury SP3 5EL
T: (01722) 716874
F: (01722) 716874
E: marriott@waitrose.com
I: www.kgp-publishing.co.uk

Bedrooms: 1 double, 1 twin

B&B per person per night:
S Max £29.00
D Max £23.00

OPEN All Year except Christmas

Small Victorian farmhouse facing south – very light – country view. Attractive garden with patio. Breakfast in south-facing conservatory. Off-road parking.

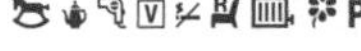

P

CONFIRM YOUR BOOKING

You are advised to confirm your booking in writing.

DORCHESTER, Dorset Map ref 2B3 *Tourist Information Centre Tel: (01305) 267992*

♦♦♦♦

CHURCHVIEW GUEST HOUSE

Winterbourne Abbas, Dorchester DT2 9LS
T: (01305) 889296
F: (01305) 889296
E: stay@churchview.co.uk
I: www.churchview.co.uk

Beautiful 17thC guesthouse set in a small village near Dorchester, offers a warm welcome and delicious home-cooked meals. Character bedrooms with hospitality tray, TV and radio. Two comfortable lounges and licensed bar. Your hosts will give every assistance with information to ensure a memorable stay.

Bedrooms: 4 double, 3 twin, 1 single, 1 family
Bathrooms: 8 en suite, 1 private

Evening meal available
CC: Delta, Mastercard, Switch, Visa

Prices reduced by £2pp daily, for stays of 2 nights or more with evening meals.

5 V P

B&B per person per night:
S £26.00–£37.00
D £26.00–£32.00

HB per person per night:
DY £41.00–£47.00

OPEN All Year except Christmas

♦♦♦♦ Silver Award

THE OLD RECTORY

Winterbourne Steepleton, Dorchester DT2 9LG
T: (01305) 889468
F: (01305) 889737
E: trees@eurobell.co.uk
I: www.trees.eurobell.co.uk

Bedrooms: 4 double
Bathrooms: 4 en suite

Built 1850 on one acre of private ground in a quiet hamlet, surrounded by spectacular walks. Six miles from historic Dorchester, eight miles from Weymouth's sandy beach. We offer a peaceful stay with a memorable breakfast including many homemade, organic products. Excellent local pubs and restaurants. French spoken. Mob: 07818 037183.

V P €

B&B per person per night:
S £50.00
D £27.50–£55.00

OPEN All Year except Christmas

♦♦♦♦ Silver Award

YELLOWHAM FARM

Yellowham Wood, Dorchester
DT2 8RW
T: (01305) 262892
F: (01305) 848155
E: b&b@yellowham.freeserve.co.uk
I: www.yellowham.freeserve.co.uk

Bedrooms: 3 double, 1 twin
Bathrooms: 4 en suite

Evening meal available
CC: Mastercard, Switch, Visa

Situated in the heart of Hardy country on the edge of the idyllic Yellowham Wood in 120 acres of farmland. Peace and tranquillity guaranteed.

4 V P

B&B per person per night:
S £35.00–£52.00
D £28.00–£32.00

HB per person per night:
DY £49.00–£52.00

OPEN All Year

DULVERTON, Somerset Map ref 1D1

♦♦♦♦ Silver Award

TOWN MILLS

High Street, Dulverton TA22 9HB
T: (01398) 323124
E: townmills@onetel.net.uk
I: www.townmillsdulverton.co.uk

Bedrooms: 3 double, 2 twin
Bathrooms: 4 en suite, 1 private

CC: Amex, Delta, Mastercard, Switch, Visa

Our 19thC mill house is secluded but in the centre of Dulverton. We serve you full English breakfast in your spacious room; some have log fires.

V P €

B&B per person per night:
S £32.00–£46.00
D £25.00–£28.00

OPEN All Year

QUALITY ASSURANCE SCHEME

Diamond ratings and awards were correct at the time of going to press but are subject to change. Please check at the time of booking.

DUNSTER, Somerset Map ref 1D1

♦♦♦♦ Silver Award

SPEARS CROSS HOTEL
1 West Street, Dunster TA24 6SN
T: (01643) 821439
E: mjcapel@aol.com
I: www.SmoothHound.co.uk/hotels/spearsx.html

Bedrooms: 1 double, 1 twin, 1 family
Bathrooms: 3 en suite

Evening meal available
CC: Delta, Mastercard, Switch, Visa

B&B per person per night:
S £30.00–£35.00
D £25.50–£28.50

OPEN All Year except Christmas

15thC family-run hotel in medieval village of Dunster. Warm welcome. Excellent breakfasts. Ideal base for exploring coast, Exmoor National Park. Parking, licensed, en suite, terraced gardens.

EVERSHOT, Dorset Map ref 2A3

THE ACORN INN
28 Fore Street, Evershot, Dorchester DT2 0JW
T: (01935) 83228
F: (01935) 83707
E: stay@acorn-inn.co.uk
I: www.acorn-inn.co.uk

B&B per person per night:
S £60.00–£80.00
D £40.00–£65.00

OPEN All Year

Friendly, family-run, quality, 16thC village coaching inn set in breathtaking countryside. Excellent fresh, local produce cooked to perfection, thoughtful wine list and great real ales. Dogs welcome. Mid-week breaks: book two nights, third night free, book three nights, fourth and fifth night free. Pensioners and repeat bookings less 10%.

Bedrooms: 6 double, 3 twin
Bathrooms: 9 en suite

Evening meal available
CC: Amex, Delta, Mastercard, Switch, Visa

EXETER, Devon Map ref 1D2 *Tourist Information Centre Tel: (01392) 265700*

♦♦♦♦

FAIRWINDS VILLAGE HOUSE HOTEL
Kennford, Exeter EX6 7UD
T: (01392) 832911
E: fairwindshotbun@aol.com

Bedrooms: 4 double, 1 twin, 1 family
Bathrooms: 6 en suite

Evening meal available
CC: Delta, Mastercard, Switch, Visa

B&B per person per night:
S £42.00–£44.00
D £29.00–£30.00

HB per person per night:
DY £42.00–£48.00

Friendly little hotel, south of Exeter. Exclusively for non-smokers. Beautiful rural surroundings. Delightful en suite bedrooms (some on ground floor). Delicious homemade food. Bargain breaks available.

♦♦♦♦

THE GRANGE
Stoke Hill, Exeter EX4 7JH
T: (01392) 259723
E: dudleythegrange@aol.com

Bedrooms: 2 double
Bathrooms: 2 en suite

B&B per person per night:
S £30.00–£34.00
D £22.00–£24.00

OPEN All Year except Christmas

Country house set in three acres of woodlands, 1.5 miles from the city centre. Ideal for holidays and off-season breaks. En suite rooms.

COUNTRY CODE Always follow the Country Code • Enjoy the countryside and respect its life and work • Guard against all risk of fire • Fasten all gates • Keep your dogs under close control • Keep to public paths across farmland • Use gates and stiles to cross fences, hedges and walls • Leave livestock, crops and machinery alone • Take your litter home • Help to keep all water clean • Protect wildlife, plants and trees • Take special care on country roads • Make no unnecessary noise

EXETER continued

RYDON FARM

Woodbury, Exeter EX5 1LB
T: (01395) 232341
F: (01395) 232341
E: sallyglanvill@hotmail.com

B&B per person per night:
S £30.00–£37.00
D £26.00–£30.00

OPEN All Year

Guests return time and time again to this delightful, 16thC, Devon longhouse set amidst a 400-acre dairy farm, farmed by the same family for many generations. Exposed beams and inglenook fireplace. Romantic 4-poster. Delicious farmhouse breakfasts using fresh, local produce. Several local pubs and restaurants. Highly recommended.

Bedrooms: 1 double, 1 twin, 1 family
Bathrooms: 2 en suite, 1 private

CC: Delta, Mastercard, Switch, Visa

♦♦♦♦

ST ANDREWS HOTEL

28 Alphington Road, Exeter EX2 8HN
T: (01392) 276784
F: (01392) 250249

B&B per person per night:
S Min £40.00
D Min £27.50

OPEN All Year except Christmas

St Andrews is a long-established family-run hotel offering a high standard of comfort and service in a friendly, relaxing atmosphere. Excellent home cooking. Large car park at rear. Weekend breaks. Brochure on request.

Bedrooms: 8 double, 3 twin, 4 single, 2 family
Bathrooms: 17 en suite

Evening meal available
CC: Amex, Delta, Diners, Mastercard, Switch, Visa

Weekend breaks all year, must include Sat night. Ideally situated for Christmas shopping or summer touring breaks.

EXMOOR

See under Brendon, Dulverton, Dunster, Lynton, Minehead, Porlock, Winsford

FALMOUTH, Cornwall Map ref 1B3 *Tourist Information Centre Tel: (01326) 312300*

APPLE TREE COTTAGE

Laity Moor, Ponsanooth, Truro TR3 7HR
T: (01872) 865047
E: appletreecottage@talk21.com
I: www.cornwall-online.co.uk

B&B per person per night:
S £28.00–£30.00
D £25.00–£28.00

OPEN All Year except Christmas

Set amid countryside between Falmouth and Truro with a river meandering through the gardens. Rooms are furnished in a country style and guests are offered traditional farmhouse fare cooked on the Aga. Close to superb Cornish gardens and beaches. Non-smoking. For brochure contact Mrs A Tremayne.

Bedrooms: 2 double

GOLD & SILVER AWARDS

These exclusive VisitBritain awards are given to establishments achieving the highest levels of quality and service. Further information can be found at the front of the guide. An index to all accommodation achieving these awards are at the back of this guide.

FALMOUTH continued

◆◆◆◆◆ Silver Award

DOLVEAN HOTEL

50 Melvill Road, Falmouth TR11 4DQ
T: (01326) 313658
F: (01326) 313995
E: reservations@dolvean.co.uk
I: www.dolvean.co.uk

B&B per person per night:
S £30.00–£45.00
D £35.00–£45.00

OPEN All Year except Christmas

Experience the elegance and comfort of our Victorian home where carefully chosen antiques, fine china and fascinating books create an ambience where you can relax and feel at home. Each bedroom has its own character with pretty pictures and lots of ribbon and lace, creating an atmosphere that makes every stay a special occasion.

Bedrooms: 8 double, 3 single
Bathrooms: 11 en suite

CC: Amex, Delta, Mastercard, Switch, Visa

3-night special breaks available in winter, spring and autumn. Check our website for more details.

12 P

◆◆◆◆

IVANHOE GUEST HOUSE
7 Melvill Road, Falmouth TR11 4AS
T: (01326) 319083
F: (01326) 319083
E: ivanhoe@enterprise.net
I: www.smoothhound.co.uk/hotels/ivanhoe

Bedrooms: 2 double, 1 twin, 2 single, 1 family
Bathrooms: 4 en suite

B&B per person per night:
S £20.00–£24.00
D £24.00–£27.00

OPEN All Year

A warm and comfortable guesthouse with particularly well-equipped, en suite rooms. Minutes from the beaches, harbour and town. Off-road parking.

5 P

◆◆◆

WICKHAM GUEST HOUSE

21 Gyllyngvase Terrace, Falmouth TR11 4DL
T: (01326) 311140
E: enquiries@wickhamhotel.freeserve.co.uk
I: www.wickham-hotel.co.uk

B&B per person per night:
S £21.00–£23.00
D £23.00–£25.00

OPEN All Year except Christmas

Small, friendly, no-smoking guesthouse. Situated between harbour and beach with views over Falmouth Bay, Wickham is the ideal base for exploring Falmouth and South Cornwall's gardens, castles, harbours, coastal footpath and much more. All rooms have TV and tea/coffee facilities, some have sea views.

Bedrooms: 2 double, 2 single, 2 family
Bathrooms: 3 en suite

CC: Delta, Mastercard, Switch, Visa

P

FROME, Somerset Map ref 2B2 *Tourist Information Centre Tel: (01373) 467271*

◆◆◆◆

THE LODGE
Monkley Lane, Rode, Nr Frome BA11 6QQ
T: (01373) 830071
E: mcdougal@nildram.co.uk

Bedrooms: 2 double, 1 twin
Bathrooms: 1 en suite, 1 private

B&B per person per night:
S £25.00–£40.00
D £25.00–£30.00

OPEN All Year except Christmas

Old stone cottage with beautiful gardens and views. Quiet, rural, yet convenient location. Between Trowbridge and Frome. Bath 11 miles. Lovely rooms and warm welcome.

3 P

CHECK THE MAPS

The colour maps at the front of this guide show all the cities, towns and villages for which you will find accommodation entries.
Refer to the town index to find the page on which they are listed.

GLASTONBURY, Somerset Map ref 2A2 *Tourist Information Centre Tel: (01458) 832954*

MEADOW BARN

Middlewick Holiday Cottages, Wick Lane, Glastonbury BA6 8JW
T: (01458) 832351
F: (01458) 832351
E: info@middlewickholidaycottages.co.uk
I: www.middlewickholidaycottages.co.uk

Meadow Barn is ground floor, en suite accommodation in an old converted barn. It has country-style decor and old world charm, set in beautiful grounds, cottage gardens, meadows and apple orchards. Lovely walks and beautiful views of the Somerset Levels and the Mendip Hills beyond. Indoor heated swimming pool.

Bedrooms: 1 double, 1 twin
Bathrooms: 2 en suite

CC: Mastercard, Visa

B&B per person per night:
S £28.00–£30.00
D £24.00–£25.00

OPEN All Year except Christmas

HENSTRIDGE, Somerset Map ref 2B3

FOUNTAIN INN

High Street, Henstridge, Templecombe BA8 0RA
T: (01963) 362722
I: www.fountaininnmotel.com

Bedrooms: 5 double, 1 twin
Bathrooms: 6 en suite

Evening meal available
CC: Amex, Delta, Mastercard, Switch, Visa

Just off the A30 on the A357 Henstridge to Stalbridge road. Country inn (1700) with modern, en suite, motel-type accommodation.

B&B per person per night:
S £29.50–£32.00
D £22.00–£25.00

OPEN All Year

HOLBETON, Devon Map ref 1C3

Silver Award

BUGLE ROCKS

Battisborough Cross, Holbeton, Plymouth PL8 1JX
T: (01752) 830422
F: (01752) 830558
E: stay@buglerocks.co.uk
I: www.buglerocks.co.uk

Converted coach house and stable block located in an Area of Outstanding Natural Beauty. Formerly part of a gentleman's country residence, in a secluded valley overlooking the sea. Close to the spectacular coastal footpath, five minutes from the famous Mothecombe beach.

Bedrooms: 3 double, 1 single, 1 family
Bathrooms: 3 en suite, 2 private

CC: Delta, Mastercard, Switch, Visa

B&B per person per night:
S Max £32.00
D Max £28.00

AT-A-GLANCE SYMBOLS

Symbols at the end of each accommodation entry give useful information about services and facilities. A key to symbols can be found inside the back cover flap. Keep this open for easy reference.

HONITON, Devon Map ref 1D2 *Tourist Information Centre Tel: (01404) 43716*

BIDWELL FARM AND HAYBARTON ANNEXE

Bidwell Farm, Upottery, Honiton EX14 9PP
T: (01404) 861122
F: (08700) 554960
E: pat@rbwells.demon.co.uk
I: www.bidwellfarm.co.uk

Nestling in the beautiful Blackdown Hills, Bidwell Farm offers quality accommodation and the warmest of welcomes. Explore Dartmoor, Exmoor or Devon's Jurassic coastline. Walk, bird-watch, play golf or fish in our on-stream trout pond. Enjoy our full breakfast menu and stroll to our village inn for dinner.

Bedrooms: 3 double, 1 twin, 1 family
Bathrooms: 3 en suite, 2 private

Discount for children. Free fishing.

P €

B&B per person per night:
S £30.00–£35.00
D £25.00–£30.00

OPEN All Year

ILFRACOMBE, Devon Map ref 1C1 *Tourist Information Centre Tel: (01271) 863001*

LASTON HOUSE HOTEL

Hillsborough Road, Ilfracombe EX34 9NT
T: (01271) 866557
F: (01271) 867754
E: hilary@lastonhouse.com
I: www.lastonhouse.com

Come and enjoy the ambience of a Georgian house with mature gardens, comfortable interior and real fires during the colder months. The house is set in a peaceful area, yet is near to the harbour, shops and other amenities. We are an excellent base to explore Exmoor and North Devon.

Bedrooms: 5 double, 1 single
Bathrooms: 6 en suite

Evening meal available
CC: Delta, Mastercard, Switch, Visa

V P €

B&B per person per night:
S £30.00–£32.50
D £27.50–£30.00

HB per person per night:
DY £42.50–£45.00

OPEN All Year

Silver Award

STRATHMORE HOTEL

57 St Brannocks Road, Ilfracombe EX34 8EQ
T: (01271) 862248
F: (01271) 862243
E: strathmore@ukhotels.com
I: www.strathmore.ukhotels.com

Bedrooms: 3 double, 1 twin, 2 single, 2 family
Bathrooms: 8 en suite

Evening meal available
CC: Mastercard, Switch, Visa

Quality hotel recommended for its superbly prepared home-cooked food, comfort and service. Licensed bar and parking. Close to beautiful beaches and Exmoor. Pets, children welcome.

V P €

B&B per person per night:
S £40.00–£50.00
D £29.00–£44.00

HB per person per night:
DY £53.50–£73.00

OPEN All Year

QUALITY ASSURANCE SCHEME

For an explanation of the quality and facilities represented by the Diamonds please refer to the front of this guide. A more detailed explanation can be found in the information pages at the back.

ILLOGAN, Cornwall Map ref 1B3

AVIARY COURT HOTEL

Mary's Well, Illogan, Redruth TR16 4QZ
T: (01209) 842256
F: (01209) 843744
E: info@aviarycourthotel.co.uk
I: www.aviarycourthotel.co.uk

Charming country house in two acres of secluded, well-kept gardens with tennis court. Family run, personal service, good food. Superior en suite bedrooms with TV, telephone, tea/coffee, fresh fruit. Ideal touring location (coast five minutes). St Ives, Tate, Heligan and Eden Project all within easy reach.

Bedrooms: 4 double, 1 twin, 1 family
Bathrooms: 6 en suite

Evening meal available
CC: Delta, Mastercard, Switch, Visa

B&B per person per night:
S £47.50
D £34.25–£35.75

HB per person per night:
DY £49.75–£51.25

OPEN All Year

ISLES OF SCILLY Map ref 1A3 *Tourist Information Centre Tel: (01720) 422536*

Silver Award

SEAVIEW MOORINGS

Strand, St. Mary's TR21 0PT
T: (01720) 422327
F: (01720) 422211
E: enquiries@islesofscillyholidays.com
I: www.islesofscillyholidays.com

Our four individual suites of rooms have everything provided for your comfort and convenience. All overlook St Mary's harbour. We are 15 yards from the harbour beach and a few minutes' walk from the town amenities. Friendly and comfortable home from home.

Bedrooms: 2 double, 2 twin
Bathrooms: 4 en suite

B&B per person per night:
D £40.00

IVYBRIDGE, Devon Map ref 1C2 *Tourist Information Centre Tel: (01752) 897035*

Silver Award

HILLHEAD FARM

Ugborough, Ivybridge PL21 0HQ
T: (01752) 892674
F: (01752) 690111
I: www.hillhead-farm.co.uk

Antique furniture and light, sunny rooms combine to create a welcoming atmosphere in this peaceful, friendly farmhouse with lovely views over rolling Devon countryside. Turn off A38 at Wrangaton, turn left, take third right, continue over next crossroads, after 0.75 miles, turn left at Hillheadcross, entrance 75 yards on left.

Bedrooms: 2 double, 1 twin
Bathrooms: 2 en suite, 1 private

Evening meal available

B&B per person per night:
S £22.00–£25.00
D £22.00–£25.00

HB per person per night:
DY £37.00–£40.00

SPECIAL BREAKS
Many establishments offer special promotions and themed breaks. These are highlighted in red. (All such offers are subject to availability.)

IVYBRIDGE continued

VENN FARM
Ugborough, Ivybridge PL21 0PE
T: (01364) 73240
F: (01364) 73240
I: www.smoothhound.co.uk/hotels/vennfarm

Bedrooms: 3 family
Bathrooms: 3 en suite

Evening meal available

Only three miles from A38. Large, private gardens, streams, lake, wildlife ponds, gypsy caravan, woodland glade, unlimited parking. You will want to return!

B&B per person per night:
S £25.00–£30.00
D £25.00–£30.00

HB per person per night:
DY £38.00–£43.00

OPEN All Year

KINGSBRIDGE, Devon Map ref 1C3 *Tourist Information Centre Tel: (01548) 853195*

◆◆◆◆

ASHLEIGH HOUSE
Ashleigh Road, Kingsbridge
TQ7 1HB
T: (01548) 852893
F: (01548) 854648
E: reception@ashleigh-house.co.uk
I: www.ashleigh-house.co.uk

Bedrooms: 5 double, 1 twin, 2 family
Bathrooms: 8 en suite

Evening meal available
CC: Delta, Mastercard, Switch, Visa

Comfortable, informal, licensed Victorian guesthouse. Edge of town, easy walk. All rooms en suite, colour TV and beverage tray. Sun lounge, bar. Off-road parking.

B&B per person per night:
S £34.00–£38.00
D £24.00–£28.00

HB per person per night:
DY £39.00–£43.00

LANGPORT, Somerset Map ref 1D1

THE OLD POUND INN
Aller, Langport TA10 0RA
T: (01458) 250469
F: (01458) 250469

Built in 1571 and upgraded to modern standards with en suite bedrooms, 50-seat dining room and function room for 200. Log fires. Bar meals from £1.95. Ideal for country lovers, walking, fishing, bird-watching. 'Best Pub of the Year' 1999 and 2000.

Bedrooms: 4 double, 1 twin, 1 single, 1 family
Bathrooms: 7 en suite

Evening meal available
CC: Amex, Delta, Mastercard, Switch, Visa

B&B per person per night:
S £35.00
D £27.50

OPEN All Year except Christmas

LANIVET, Cornwall Map ref 1B2

TREMEERE MANOR
Lanivet, Bodmin PL30 5BG
T: (01208) 831513
F: (01208) 832417
E: oliver.tremeere.manor@fwi.co.uk

A 17thC Listed manor house on working farm with beautiful countryside views, very peaceful. Ideally situated for touring Cornwall. Close to Eden Project, Lanhydrock House (NT), Heligan Gardens. Easy access to coasts and Moors. Halfway stop-over for Saintsway. Comfortable rooms. Full English breakfast or variations if required. A warm welcome.

Bedrooms: 2 double, 1 twin
Bathrooms: 2 en suite, 1 private

B&B per person per night:
S £25.00–£30.00
D £22.00–£26.00

OPEN All Year except Christmas

RATING All accommodation in this guide has been rated, or is awaiting a rating, by a trained VisitBritain assessor.

LAUNCESTON, Cornwall Map ref 1C2 *Tourist Information Centre Tel: (01566) 772321*

◆◆◆

LYNHER FARM

North Hill, Launceston PL15 7NR
T: (01566) 782273
F: (01566) 782273
E: wegribble@farmersweekly.net
I: users.farmersweekly.net/wegribble

Bedrooms: 2 double, 1 twin
Bathrooms: 1 en suite

B&B per person per night:
S £20.00–£22.00
D £20.00–£22.00

OPEN All Year

Enjoy a special welcome at Lynher Farm! Unique accommodation set close to the tranqil River Lynher in an Area of Outstanding Natural Beauty.

LEWDOWN, Devon Map ref 1C2

◆◆

STOWFORD GRANGE FARM

Lewdown, Okehampton EX20 4BZ
T: (01566) 783298

Bedrooms: 2 double, 1 family

Evening meal available

B&B per person per night:
S Min £17.00
D Min £16.50

220-acre mixed farm. Listed building in quiet village. Home-cooked food, fresh vegetables, poultry. Ten miles from Okehampton, seven miles Launceston. 0.5 miles from old A30, turn by the Old Inn.

LISKEARD, Cornwall Map ref 1C2

TRECORME BARTON

Quethiock, Liskeard PL14 3SH
T: (01579) 342646
F: (01579) 342646
E: renfree@trecormebarton.fsnet.co.uk

Bedrooms: 2 double
Bathrooms: 2 en suite

B&B per person per night:
D £25.00–£27.50

OPEN All Year except Christmas

Lovely, stone-built farmhouse with wonderful views, in rolling countryside. En suite rooms. Near south coast and Moors. Close to Eden, Cotehele and Antony House.

Silver Award

TREGONDALE FARM

Menheniot, Liskeard PL14 3RG
T: (01579) 342407
F: (01579) 342407
E: tregondale@connectfree.co.uk
I: www.tregondalefarm.co.uk

Bedrooms: 2 double, 1 twin
Bathrooms: 3 en suite

Evening meal available
CC: Delta, Diners, Mastercard, Switch, Visa

B&B per person per night:
S £30.00–£35.00
D £25.00–£28.00

HB per person per night:
DY £40.00–£42.00

OPEN All Year

Superior en suite character farmhouse, beautiful countryside, local home produce a speciality. Log fires. Tennis court, woodland farm trail. Near Eden Project, N.E. Menheniot between A38/A390.

LOOE, Cornwall Map ref 1C3

Silver Award

BUCKLAWREN FARM

St Martin-by-Looe, Looe PL13 1NZ
T: (01503) 240738
F: (01503) 240481
E: bucklawren@btopenworld.com
I: www.bucklawren.com

B&B per person per night:
S £27.50–£35.00
D £25.00–£27.50

Delightful farmhouse set in glorious countryside with spectacular sea views. Quiet location, situated one mile from the beach and three miles from the fishing village of Looe. An award-winning farm with all bedrooms en suite. Granary Restaurant close by.

Bedrooms: 4 double, 2 family
Bathrooms: 6 en suite

CC: Mastercard, Visa

MAP REFERENCES The map references refer to the colour maps at the front of this guide. The first figure is the map number; the letter and figure which follow indicate the grid reference on the map.

LOOE continued

♦♦♦♦ Silver Award

LITTLE LARNICK FARM

Pelynt, Looe PL13 2NB
T: (01503) 262837
F: (01503) 262837
E: littlelarnick@btclick.com

B&B per person per night:
D £22.50–£27.50

OPEN All Year except Christmas

200-acre dairy farm situated in the beautiful West Looe River valley. The farmhouse and recently converted barn offer peaceful and relaxing, character, en suite accommodation, including a barn suite and ground floor bedroom. Wonderful walks from the door. Drying room available. Special 'Winter Warmer' breaks.

Bedrooms: 5 double, 1 family
Bathrooms: 6 en suite

CC: Amex, Delta, Diners, Mastercard, Switch, Visa

'Winter Warmer' breaks Nov-Mar.

3 P

♦♦♦♦

THE PANORAMA HOTEL

Hannafore Road, Looe PL13 2DE
T: (01503) 262123
F: (01503) 265654
E: stay@looe.co.uk
I: www.looe.co.uk

Bedrooms: 3 double, 2 single, 4 family
Bathrooms: 9 en suite

CC: Delta, Mastercard, Switch, Visa

B&B per person per night:
S £24.50–£38.50
D £23.00–£38.50

HB per person per night:
DY £39.00–£53.00

OPEN All Year

Family-run hotel, good food, friendly atmosphere. Magnificent setting overlooking harbour, beach and miles of beautiful coastline.

5 P

♦♦♦♦ Silver Award

TALEHAY

Tremaine, Pelynt, Looe PL13 2LT
T: (01503) 220252
F: (01503) 220252
E: paul@talehay.co.uk
I: www.talehay.co.uk

B&B per person per night:
S £35.00–£38.00
D £25.00–£28.00

OPEN All Year except Christmas

Quality, en suite B&B on 17thC, non-working farmstead. Provides a high standard of accommodation and delicious breakfasts making use of local produce, the farm's free-range eggs and homemade marmalade. An ideal base for exploring the many attractions of Cornwall. Eden Project 20 minutes.

Bedrooms: 2 double
Bathrooms: 2 en suite

CC: Amex, Delta, Diners, Mastercard, Switch, Visa

3 nights for price of 2 Nov-Mar (excl Christmas and New Year).

P €

LYME REGIS, Dorset Map ref 1D2 *Tourist Information Centre Tel: (01297) 442138*

♦♦♦♦

CHARNWOOD GUEST HOUSE

21 Woodmead Road, Lyme Regis DT7 3AD
T: (01297) 445281
E: enqetc@lymeregisaccommodation.com
I: www.lymeregisaccommodation.com

B&B per person per night:
S £25.00–£28.00
D £24.00–£28.00

OPEN All Year except Christmas

Quaint Edwardian guesthouse in quiet area, 5-10 minutes' walk from main shops/restaurants and the sea. Off-road car parking. Sea views from three rooms. We serve an English, vegetarian, or fruit and yoghurt breakfast and can cater for most special requirements. Visit fossil walk or beach – enjoy!

Bedrooms: 3 double, 1 single, 1 family
Bathrooms: 5 en suite

CC: Delta, Mastercard, Switch, Visa

Sun to Thu: 5% discount on 3/4 nights, 10% discount on 5 nights, 10% discount on 7 nights or more.

5 P €

LYME REGIS continued

SPRINGFIELD

Woodmead Road, Lyme Regis DT7 3LJ
T: (01297) 443409
F: (01297) 443685
E: springfield@lymeregis.com
I: www.lymeregis.com/springfield

B&B per person per night:
S £28.00–£30.00
D £24.00–£26.00

Elegant Georgian house in partly walled garden with conservatory. Well-proportioned rooms, all with far-reaching views over the sea and Dorset coastline. A short walk to the shops and seafront. Close to major footpaths. Concession at local golf course.

Bedrooms: 2 double, 2 twin, 2 family
Bathrooms: 5 en suite, 1 private

LYNTON, Devon Map ref 1C1 *Tourist Information Centre Tel: (0845) 660 3232*

Silver Award

LONGMEAD HOUSE HOTEL
9 Longmead, Lynton EX35 6DQ
T: (01598) 752523
F: (01598) 752523
E: info@longmeadhouse.co.uk
I: www.longmeadhouse.co.uk

Bedrooms: 3 double, 1 twin, 1 single, 1 family, 1 suite
Bathrooms: 6 en suite

Evening meal available
CC: Delta, Diners, Mastercard, Switch, Visa

B&B per person per night:
S £25.00
D £24.00–£26.00

HB per person per night:
DY £30.00–£40.00

One of Lynton's best-kept secrets! Delightful house and gardens quietly situated towards the Valley of the Rocks. Comfortable, relaxed atmosphere with excellent hospitality and cooking.

MARLBOROUGH, Wiltshire Map ref 2B2 *Tourist Information Centre Tel: (01672) 513989*

FISHERMANS HOUSE

Mildenhall, Marlborough SN8 2LZ
T: (01672) 515390
F: (01672) 519009

B&B per person per night:
S £35.00
D £35.00

OPEN All Year except Christmas

Set in the beautiful valley of the River Kennet is this exquisite Georgian house. Jeremy and Heather serve breakfast in the elegant conservatory which leads into the charming garden with the lawn sloping down to the river – the perfect place to sit and enjoy the wildlife and magnificent view.

Bedrooms: 1 double, 1 single
Bathrooms: 1 en suite, 1 private

There are more than 550 Tourist Information Centres throughout England offering friendly help with accommodation and holiday ideas as well as suggestions of places to visit and things to do. You'll find TIC addresses in the local Phone Book.

MARLBOROUGH continued

MONKS REST LODGE

Salisbury Road, Marlborough SN8 4AE
T: (01672) 512169
F: (01672) 516360
E: andrew@monksrest.co.uk
I: www.monksrest.co.uk

B&B per person per night:
S £50.00–£65.00
D £27.50–£35.00

OPEN All Year except Christmas

New, purpose-built guest lodge set in shady garden of private home. Accommodation comprises three tastefully decorated, en suite bedrooms and lobby, where buffet-style breakfasts and other refreshments are served. Lodge entirely separate from owner's accommodation. Ample, off-road parking. Easy walking distance to town-centre attractions.

Bedrooms: 3 double
Bathrooms: 3 en suite

CC: Amex, Delta, Mastercard, Switch, Visa

Central England Holidays. Have exclusive use of entire lodge. 3 bedrooms. Minimum 3 days. £150-£180 per day B&B.

♦♦♦♦

WESTCOURT BOTTOM

165 Westcourt, Burbage, Marlborough SN8 3BW
T: (01672) 810924
F: (01672) 810924
E: westcourt.b-and-b@virgin.net
I: www.westcourtbottom.co.uk

B&B per person per night:
S £30.00–£35.00
D £25.00–£30.00

OPEN All Year except Christmas

Large 17thC thatched cottage five miles south of Marlborough. The half-timbered bedrooms, sitting room with TV and large garden with swimming pool offer a quiet, relaxed and informal atmosphere. Good local pubs. Ideal base for Ridgeway and Savernake Forest walks, Marlborough, Avebury and Stonehenge. Wonderful free-range breakfasts! Ample parking. Children negotiable.

Bedrooms: 2 double, 1 twin
Bathrooms: 1 en suite, 1 private

Evening meal available

MARTOCK, Somerset Map ref 2A3

THE WHITE HART HOTEL

East Street, Martock TA12 6JQ
T: (01935) 822005
F: (01935) 822056
E: enquiries@whiteharthotelmartock.co.uk
I: www.whiteharthotelmartock.co.uk

Bedrooms: 2 double, 5 family
Bathrooms: 7 en suite

Evening meal available
CC: Delta, Mastercard, Switch, Visa

B&B per person per night:
S Min £37.00
D Min £27.50

OPEN All Year

Pleasant Hamstone, Grade II Listed coaching inn. Centre of Martock, seven miles from Yeovil and two miles off the A303. Top-class, fresh food served.

MEVAGISSEY, Cornwall Map ref 1B3

♦♦♦♦

KERRYANNA COUNTRY HOUSE

Treleaven Farm, Mevagissey, St Austell PL26 6RZ
T: (01726) 843558
F: (01726) 843558
E: linda.hennah@btinternet.com
I: www.kerryanna.co.uk

Bedrooms: 6 double, 2 twin
Bathrooms: 8 en suite

CC: Delta, Mastercard, Switch, Visa

B&B per person per night:
D £30.00–£38.00

Country house overlooking village, surrounded by rambling farmland, wild flowers and wildlife. Outdoor swimming pool, games barn, putting green. Farm cooking. Close to Eden and Heligan.

MINEHEAD, Somerset Map ref 1D1 *Tourist Information Centre Tel: (01643) 702624*

◆◆◆◆

GASCONY HOTEL
The Avenue, Minehead TA24 5BB
T: (01643) 705939
F: (01643) 709926

Bedrooms: 10 double, 3 twin, 3 single, 4 family
Bathrooms: 20 en suite

Evening meal available
CC: Delta, Mastercard, Switch, Visa

Comfortable and well-appointed Victorian house hotel. Ideally positioned on the level, close to seafront. Home cooking. Large secure car park. Short breaks available.

B&B per person per night:
S £30.00–£35.00
D £26.00–£29.00

HB per person per night:
DY £38.00–£44.00

Rating Applied For

KINGSWAY HOTEL
36 Ponsford Road, Minehead
TA24 5DY
T: (01643) 702313
F: (01643) 702313
E: kingswayhotel@msn.com
I: www.kingswayhotelminehead.co.uk

Bedrooms: 4 double, 3 family
Bathrooms: 7 en suite

Evening meal available
CC: Delta, Mastercard, Switch, Visa

A small, family-run hotel with spacious and comfortable rooms. Delicious home cooking. Ideally placed for touring Exmoor.

3

B&B per person per night:
D £25.00–£29.00

HB per person per night:
DY £39.00–£45.00

MORETONHAMPSTEAD, Devon Map ref 1C2

◆◆◆◆

GREAT DOCCOMBE FARM
Doccombe, Moretonhampstead, Newton Abbot TQ13 8SS
T: (01647) 440694
E: david.oakey3@btopenworld.com
I: www.greatdoccombefarm.co.uk

Bedrooms: 1 double, 1 family
Bathrooms: 2 en suite

In pretty Dartmoor hamlet, 300-year-old farmhouse in Dartmoor National Park. En suite rooms, farmhouse cooking. Ideal for exploring Dartmoor's delights.

B&B per person per night:
D £22.00–£24.00

OPEN All Year except Christmas

◆◆◆◆
Silver Award

GREAT SLONCOMBE FARM
Moretonhampstead, Newton Abbot TQ13 8QF
T: (01647) 440595
F: (01647) 440595
E: hmerchant@sloncombe.freeserve.co.uk
I: www.greatsloncombefarm.co.uk

Bedrooms: 2 double, 1 twin
Bathrooms: 3 en suite

Evening meal available

13thC farmhouse in a magical Dartmoor valley. Meadows, woodland, wild flowers, animals. Farmhouse breakfast with freshly baked bread. Everything provided for an enjoyable break.

8

B&B per person per night:
S £25.00–£27.00
D £25.00–£27.00

OPEN All Year

◆◆◆◆
Silver Award

GREAT WOOSTON FARM BED & BREAKFAST
Moretonhampstead, Newton Abbot TQ13 8QA
T: (01647) 440367
F: (01647) 440367
E: info@greatwoostonfarm.com
I: www.greatwoostonfarm.com

Bedrooms: 3 double
Bathrooms: 2 en suite, 1 private

CC: Mastercard, Switch, Visa

Great Wooston is a peaceful haven with views across the moor and walks nearby. Two rooms en suite, one with 4-poster. Excellent breakfast. Quality accommodation.

8

B&B per person per night:
S £25.00–£30.00
D £23.00–£26.00

OPEN All Year

MORWENSTOW, Cornwall Map ref 1C2

◆◆◆

CORNAKEY FARM
Morwenstow, Bude EX23 9SS
T: (01288) 331260

Bedrooms: 3 double
Bathrooms: 1 en suite

Evening meal available

220-acre mixed farm. Convenient coastal walking area with extensive views of sea and cliffs from bedrooms. Home cooking. Reduced rates for children. Good touring centre.

B&B per person per night:
S £20.00
D £20.00

HB per person per night:
DY £30.00–£31.00

NETHER STOWEY, Somerset Map ref 1D1

◆◆◆◆◆ Silver Award

CASTLE OF COMFORT COUNTRY HOUSE

Dodington, Nether Stowey, Bridgwater TA5 1LE
T: (01278) 741264
F: (01278) 741144
E: reception@castle-of-comfort.co.uk
I: www.castle-of-comfort.co.uk

Bedrooms: 4 double, 1 twin, 2 single, 1 family
Bathrooms: 8 en suite

Evening meal available
CC: Delta, Mastercard, Switch, Visa

16thC country-house hotel and restaurant nestling in the Quantock Hills with four acres of grounds. Luxurious accommodation of the highest standard.

B&B per person per night:
S £35.00–£77.00
D £44.00–£59.00

HB per person per night:
DY £68.50–£95.50

OPEN All Year except Christmas

◆◆◆◆

THE OLD CIDER HOUSE

25 Castle Street, Nether Stowey, Bridgwater TA5 1LN
T: (01278) 732228
F: (01278) 732228
E: info@theoldciderhouse.co.uk
I: www.theoldciderhouse.co.uk

Bedrooms: 2 double, 3 twin
Bathrooms: 5 en suite

Evening meal available
CC: Amex, Delta, Mastercard, Switch, Visa

Licensed Edwardian guesthouse in the historic village of Nether Stowey at the foot of the Quantocks. Coleridge's Cottage (NT) nearby. Home cooking. Warm welcome assured.

B&B per person per night:
S £35.00–£40.00
D £25.00–£37.50

HB per person per night:
DY £35.95–£48.45

OPEN All Year

NEWQUAY, Cornwall Map ref 1B2 *Tourist Information Centre Tel: (01637) 854020*

◆

CHICHESTER INTEREST HOLIDAYS AND ACCOMMODATION

14 Bay View Terrace, Newquay TR7 2LR
T: (01637) 874216
F: (01637) 874216
E: sheila.harper@virgin.net
I: http://freespace.virgin.net/sheila.harper

Bedrooms: 3 double, 1 twin, 2 single, 1 family
Bathrooms: 5 en suite

Evening meal available

Comfortable, licensed establishment convenient for shops, beaches and gardens. Showers in most bedrooms, many extras. Walking, mineral collecting, archaeology and Cornish heritage holidays in spring and autumn.

2 P

B&B per person per night:
S £18.00
D £18.00

HB per person per night:
DY £23.00

OPEN All Year except Christmas

◆◆◆◆ Silver Award

DEGEMBRIS FARMHOUSE

St Newlyn East, Newquay TR8 5HY
T: (01872) 510555
F: (01872) 510230
E: kathy@degembris.co.uk
I: www.degembris.co.uk

Degembris inspires imagination of former times, remaining an unspoilt gem of Cornish history. From the car-parking area, a few steps lead up to the pretty front garden which overlooks a beautiful wooded valley. The attractive, individually furnished bedrooms vary in size from small, flowery single to spacious family rooms.

Bedrooms: 2 double, 1 twin, 1 single, 1 family
Bathrooms: 3 en suite

CC: Delta, Mastercard, Switch, Visa

B&B per person per night:
S £25.00
D £25.00–£28.00

OPEN All Year except Christmas

NEWTON ABBOT, Devon Map ref 1D2 *Tourist Information Centre Tel: (01626) 215667*

◆◆◆◆ Silver Award

FAIRWAYS

Shaldon Road, Combeinteignhead, Newton Abbot TQ12 4RR
T: (01626) 871095
I: www.visitwestcountry.com/fairways

Bedrooms: 1 suite

Lovely retreat. Private, peaceful suite. Rural setting overlooking Teign Estuary. Wonderful, leisurely breakfasts using local produce. Own entrance via steepish driveway and steps.

12 P €

B&B per person per night:
S £45.00
D £30.00

NORTH BOVEY, Devon Map ref 1C2

RING OF BELLS INN

The Village, North Bovey, Dartmoor
TQ13 8RB
T: (01647) 440375
F: (01647) 440218
E: info@ringofbellsinn.com
I: www.ringofbellsinn.com

The Ring of Bells is a 13thC thatched inn located in North Bovey, the quintessential Dartmoor village. We offer extremely comfortable, en suite accommodation, 4-posters, great atmosphere, real ales, excellent wines and locally farmed produce prepared to order by our top chefs. Ideally situated for exploring the Moors.

Bedrooms: 3 double, 2 twin, 3 family
Bathrooms: 8 en suite

Evening meal available
CC: Delta, Mastercard, Switch, Visa

We often offer out-of-season, special mid-week and weekend breaks, as well as our Inntuition Program – see www.inntuition.net for details.

B&B per person per night:
S £35.00–£50.00
D £25.00–£40.00

OPEN All Year except Christmas

NORTH TAWTON, Devon Map ref 1C2

OAKLANDS FARM
North Tawton EX20 2BQ
T: (01837) 82340

Bedrooms: 1 family, 1 suite
Bathrooms: 1 en suite

130-acre mixed farm. Centrally situated for north and south Devon coasts and Dartmoor. Very warm welcome. Easy access on level drive. Farmhouse cooking.

B&B per person per night:
S £22.00–£25.00
D £22.00–£25.00

OPEN All Year except Christmas

OGBOURNE ST GEORGE, Wiltshire Map ref 2B2

THE OLD CROWN 'THE INN WITH THE WELL'

Marlborough Road, Ogbourne St George, Marlborough SN8 1SQ
T: (01672) 841445
F: (01672) 841056
E: theinnwiththewell@compuserve.com
I: theinnwiththewell.com

Traditional inn (1658), completely renovated during 2002. Renowned restaurant and gravity-poured real ale. En suite accommodation built in 2001. Same owners since 1991.

Bedrooms: 2 double, 3 twin, 1 family
Bathrooms: 6 en suite

Evening meal available
CC: Amex, Delta, Diners, Mastercard, Switch, Visa

B&B per person per night:
S £25.00–£30.00
D £25.00–£30.00

OPEN All Year

OKEHAMPTON, Devon Map ref 1C2

Silver Award

THE KNOLE FARM

Bridestowe, Okehampton EX20 4HA
T: (01837) 861241
F: (01837) 861241
E: mavis.bickle@btconnect.com
I: knolefarm-dartmoor-holidays.co.uk

Guests return annually for the breathtaking views of Dartmoor, delicious food, a warm welcome and a real countryside holiday. Walking, castles, golfing and pony-trekking are all on the doorstep of this working family farm. En suite rooms. Closed Christmas and New Year.

Bedrooms: 2 double, 3 family
Bathrooms: 5 en suite

Evening meal available
CC: Amex, Mastercard, Switch, Visa

B&B per person per night:
D £22.00–£24.00

HB per person per night:
DY £36.00–£38.00

OKEHAMPTON continued

◆◆◆◆

LOWER TRECOTT FARM

Wellsprings Lane,
Sampford Courtenay, Okehampton
EX20 2TD
T: (01837) 880118
E: craig@trecott.fsnet.co.uk

Bedrooms: 1 double, 1 single, 1 family
Bathrooms: 1 private

B&B per person per night:
S Min £20.00
D £20.00–£24.00

OPEN All Year except Christmas

16thC farmhouse in delightful, peaceful hamlet. Enjoy true hospitality and a cream tea on arrival. Own eggs and honey. Village inn 1.5 miles.

◆◆◆◆

WEEK FARM COUNTRY HOLIDAYS

Bridestowe, Okehampton EX20 4HZ
T: (01837) 861221
F: (01837) 861221
E: accom@weekfarmonline.com
I: www.weekfarmonline.com

B&B per person per night:
S £25.00–£26.00
D £25.00–£26.00

HB per person per night:
DY £37.00–£40.00

OPEN All Year except Christmas

200-acre sheep farm. A warm welcome awaits at this homely 17thC farmhouse, in Devonshire countryside and six miles Okehampton. Three new coarse-fishing lakes. Good home cooking assured and every comfort. Ideal touring base Dartmoor and coasts, walking, cycling, pony trekking, fishing. Outdoor heated swimming pool. Come and spoil yourselves.

Bedrooms: 2 double, 2 family
Bathrooms: 4 en suite

Evening meal available
CC: Amex, Delta, Mastercard, Switch, Visa

Fishing weekend breaks. 3 well-stocked coarse-fishing lakes, something for the whole family.

OTTERY ST MARY, Devon Map ref 1D2

◆◆◆◆

PITT FARM

Fairmile, Ottery St Mary EX11 1NL
T: (01404) 812439
F: (01404) 812439
E: pittfarm@tiscali.co.uk
I: www.pitt-farm-devon.co.uk

Bedrooms: 4 double, 2 family
Bathrooms: 2 en suite, 2 private

CC: Amex, Delta, Diners, Mastercard, Switch, Visa

B&B per person per night:
S £23.00–£25.00
D £23.00–£25.00

OPEN All Year except Christmas

190-acre mixed farm. 16thC thatched farmhouse. En suite rooms available, log fires in season. 0.5 miles off A30 on B3176. M5 six miles.

PADSTOW, Cornwall Map ref 1B2 *Tourist Information Centre Tel: (01841) 533449*

◆◆◆◆◆
Gold Award

ST ERVAN MANOR AND COUNTRY COTTAGES

The Old Rectory, St Ervan, Padstow
PL27 7TA
T: (01841) 540255
F: (01841) 540255
E: mail@stervanmanor.freeserve.co.uk
I: www.stervanmanor.co.uk

B&B per person per night:
S £60.00–£100.00
D £35.00–£65.00

OPEN All Year except Christmas

Elegant, Grade II Listed, Victorian rectory set in beautiful grounds of four acres. Fantastic, peaceful setting yet only four miles from Padstow, three miles from North Cornwall beaches and 30 minutes from Eden Project. Individual, luxurious bedrooms including feature master bedroom, 4-poster and twin.

Bedrooms: 4 double, 1 twin
Bathrooms: 4 en suite, 1 private

CC: Amex, Delta, Mastercard, Switch, Visa

Open 1 Feb-15 Dec. 3 nights for the price of 2, Oct-Mar.

HALF BOARD PRICES Half board prices are given per person, but in some cases these may be based on double/twin occupancy.

PADSTOW continued

SYMPLY PADSTOW

32 Dennis Road, Padstow PL28 8DE
T: (01841) 532814
F: (01841) 533480
E: buttfish@btinternet.com
I: www.symply-padstow.co.uk

An elegant Edwardian house with stunning estuary views. Quiet, yet only a stone's throw from the bustling quayside with its world-famous restaurant and exciting shops. Spacious, comfortable interior with attractive bedrooms, all en suite. Padstow is an ideal base for exploring all the delights of Cornwall, and we guarantee a warm welcome and a relaxing stay.

Bedrooms: 2 double, 1 twin
Bathrooms: 3 en suite

B&B per person per night:
D £28.00–£30.00

OPEN All Year except Christmas

♦♦♦♦

TREVONE BAY HOTEL

Dobbin Close, Trevone, Padstow PL28 8QS
T: (01841) 520243
F: (01841) 521195
E: webb@trevonebay.demon.co.uk
I: www.trevonebay.co.uk

Situated in the quiet village of Trevone, with panoramic sea views. Just a short walk from the beach and approximately two miles from Padstow. A quiet and tranquil place for you to relax and enjoy the fresh Cornish air, yet within easy reach of many of Cornwall's tourist attractions including the Eden Project.

Bedrooms: 5 double, 2 twin, 3 single, 2 family
Bathrooms: 12 en suite

Evening meal available
CC: Delta, Mastercard, Switch, Visa

B&B per person per night:
S £33.00–£42.00
D £31.00–£42.00

HB per person per night:
DY £46.50–£57.50

PAIGNTON, Devon Map ref 1D2 *Tourist Information Centre Tel: 0906 680 1268 (Premium rate number)*

THE SANDS HOTEL

32 Sands Road, Paignton TQ4 6EJ
T: (01803) 551282
E: hotel.sands@virgin.net

Bedrooms: 6 double, 2 twin, 2 single, 2 family
Bathrooms: 10 en suite

Evening meal available
CC: Amex, Delta, Mastercard, Switch, Visa

The hotel is situated on the seafront, close to level walk to harbour, pier, shops and all other amenities. Spectacular bay views.

B&B per person per night:
D £20.00–£26.00

HB per person per night:
DY £32.00–£38.00

OPEN All Year except Christmas

WYNNCROFT HOTEL

2 Elmsleigh Park, Paignton TQ4 5AT
T: (01803) 525728
F: (01803) 526335
E: wynncrofthotel@aol.com
I: www.wynncroft.co.uk

Bedrooms: 6 double, 1 twin, 2 family
Bathrooms: 8 en suite, 1 private

Evening meal available
CC: Amex, Delta, Mastercard, Switch, Visa

Comfort, service and a warm, friendly welcome in our family-run, licensed Victorian hotel. Short level walk from the beach or town. Large free car park.

B&B per person per night:
S £24.00–£30.00
D £24.00–£30.00

HB per person per night:
DY £36.00–£42.00

IMPORTANT NOTE Information on accommodation listed in this guide has been supplied by the proprietors. As changes may occur you are advised to check details at the time of booking.

PENSFORD, Bath and North East Somerset Map ref 2A2

♦♦♦

GREEN ACRES
Stanton Wick, Pensford BS39 4BX
T: (01761) 490397
F: (01761) 490397

Bedrooms: 2 double, 1 twin, 2 single
Bathrooms: 2 en suite

A friendly welcome awaits you in peaceful setting, off A37/A368. Relax and enjoy panoramic views across Chew Valley to Dundry Hills.

P

B&B per person per night:
S £22.00–£27.00
D £22.00–£27.00

OPEN All Year

PENZANCE, Cornwall Map ref 1A3 *Tourist Information Centre Tel: (01736) 362207*

♦♦♦

LYNWOOD GUEST HOUSE
41 Morrab Road, Penzance
TR18 4EX
T: (01736) 365871
F: (01736) 365871
E: lynwoodpz@aol.com
I: www.lynwood-guesthouse.co.uk

Bedrooms: 2 double, 1 twin, 2 single, 2 family
Bathrooms: 5 en suite

CC: Amex, Delta, Diners, Mastercard, Switch, Visa

A well-established, family-run guesthouse offering a warm welcome, cleanliness and good food. Ideal for touring Land's End, Lizard peninsula and St Michael's Mount.

P €

B&B per person per night:
S £17.50–£35.00
D £17.50–£21.50

OPEN All Year

♦♦♦♦

ROSE FARM
Chyanhal, Buryas Bridge, Penzance
TR19 6AN
T: (01736) 731808
F: (01736) 731808
E: lally@rosefarmcornwall.co.uk
I: www.rosefarmcornwall.co.uk

Bedrooms: 2 double, 1 family
Bathrooms: 3 en suite

CC: Mastercard, Switch, Visa

25-acre farm with many animals including livestock and horses. Near beaches and shops. Land's End seven miles, Mousehole two miles. Lovely walks. 4-poster bed available. Cosy and relaxing.

P

B&B per person per night:
S £35.00–£40.00
D £25.00–£30.00

OPEN All Year except Christmas

♦♦♦

WARWICK HOUSE HOTEL

17 Regent Terrace, Penzance TR18 4DW
T: (01736) 363881
F: (01736) 363881
E: jules@warwickhouse.fsworld.co.uk
I: www.warwickhousepenzance.co.uk

Charming Regency guesthouse where our personal service will assure your absolute comfort. Most rooms have stunning views over Mounts Bay, as do the sunny patios. We are an ideal base for exploring West Cornwall. Coastal footpaths, Scilly Isles and Eden Project are all easily reached. Private car parking.

4 P

Bedrooms: 4 double, 3 single, 1 family
Bathrooms: 5 en suite

CC: Delta, Mastercard, Switch, Visa

'3 nights for the price of 2' breaks available low season.

B&B per person per night:
S £23.00–£30.00
D £23.00–£30.00

OPEN All Year

♦♦♦

WOODSTOCK GUEST HOUSE

29 Morrab Road, Penzance TR18 4EZ
T: (01736) 369049
F: (01736) 369049
E: info@woodstockguesthouse.co.uk
I: www.woodstockguesthouse.co.uk

Victorian townhouse offering bed and breakfast. Most rooms en suite, TV, radio, hairdryer and tea-making facilities. Ideal for coastal path or accommodation en route to Isles of Scilly. Open February to December. Children over five and dogs allowed.

5

Bedrooms: 4 double, 1 twin, 3 single, 1 family
Bathrooms: 7 en suite

CC: Delta, Mastercard, Switch, Visa

B&B per person per night:
S £18.00–£26.00
D £18.00–£28.00

OPEN All Year except Christmas

PENZANCE continued

♦♦♦

WYMERING BED AND BREAKFAST

15 Regent Square, Penzance
TR18 4BG
T: (01736) 362126
F: (01736) 362126
E: pam@wymering.com
I: www.wymering.com

Bedrooms: 1 double, 1 twin, 2 family
Bathrooms: 1 en suite, 3 private

CC: Amex, Delta, Mastercard, Switch, Visa

B&B per person per night:
D £16.00–£25.00

OPEN All Year

Small, select guesthouse situated in a peaceful Regency square, just off the beach. Town centre, promenade, bathing pool, bus, coach and train station all nearby.

PERRANPORTH, Cornwall Map ref 1B2

ST GEORGES COUNTRY HOTEL

St Georges Hill, Perranporth TR6 0ED
T: (01872) 572184
F: (01872) 572184
E: nikcn@aol.com
I: www.stgeorgescountryhotel.com

B&B per person per night:
S £30.00–£40.00
D £30.00–£40.00

HB per person per night:
DY £45.00–£55.00

On the coast road between Perranporth and St Agnes, this charming, detached hotel offers a high standard of accommodation with beautiful, panoramic views. A central base for visiting The Eden Project and gardens. Dinner served in Eden's restaurant and the tropical conservatory. A warm welcome awaits you at St Georges Country Hotel.

Bedrooms: 6 double, 1 twin, 1 single, 1 family
Bathrooms: 7 en suite

Evening meal available
CC: Amex, Delta, Mastercard, Switch, Visa

Special 4-night Eden break (incl fast-track Eden tickets) Sep-Jun. Honeymoon and Christmas breaks.

12

PIDDLETRENTHIDE, Dorset Map ref 2B3

THE POACHERS INN

Piddletrenthide, Dorchester DT2 7QX
T: (01300) 348358
F: (01300) 348153
E: thepoachersinn@piddletrenthide.fsbusiness.co.uk
I: www.thepoachersinn.co.uk

B&B per person per night:
S £35.00
D £30.00

HB per person per night:
DY £45.00

OPEN All Year except Christmas

Country inn, with riverside garden and swimming pool, within easy reach of all Dorset's attractions. All rooms en suite, restaurant where half board guests choose from our a la carte menu at no extra cost.

Bedrooms: 14 double, 3 twin, 1 family
Bathrooms: 18 en suite

Evening meal available
CC: Delta, Mastercard, Switch, Visa

Stay 2 nights (£90pp DB&B) and get third night free (DB&B) – Oct 2003-Apr 2004 (excl Bank Holiday weekends).

PILLATON, Cornwall Map ref 1C2

THE WEARY FRIAR INN

Pillaton, Saltash PL12 6QS
T: (01579) 350238
F: (01579) 350238

Bedrooms: 8 double, 2 twin, 1 family
Bathrooms: 11 en suite

Evening meal available
CC: Delta, Mastercard, Switch, Visa

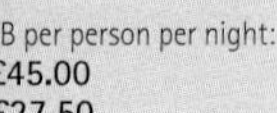

B&B per person per night:
S £45.00
D £27.50

OPEN All Year

Charming 12thC country inn far from the madding crowd. Ideally placed for visiting NT properties, gardens, and exploring inland and coastal areas. Special weekly tariff.

PLYMOUTH, Devon Map ref 1C2 *Tourist Information Centre Tel: (01752) 304849/266030*

♦♦♦♦

ATHENAEUM LODGE

4 Athenaeum Street, The Hoe, Plymouth PL1 2RQ
T: (01752) 665005
F: (01752) 665005
E: us@athenaeumlodge.com

B&B per person per night:
S £27.00–£35.00
D £19.00–£25.00

OPEN All Year except Christmas

Elegant, Grade II Listed guesthouse, ideally situated on The Hoe and near the prestigious Barbican area. The city centre is a five-minute walk away. We are close to the Theatre Royal, Plymouth Pavilions, university, cinemas, Brittany ferries, bus and rail station. Completely non-smoking, private car parking, internet facilities.

Bedrooms: 3 double, 1 single, 5 family
Bathrooms: 7 en suite

CC: Amex, Delta, Diners, Mastercard, Switch, Visa

Special winter breaks Jan-Mar: 5 nights for the price of 4.

5 P

♦♦♦♦♦
Silver Award

BOWLING GREEN HOTEL

9-10 Osborne Place, Lockyer Street, Plymouth PL1 2PU
T: (01752) 209090
F: (01752) 209092
E: dave@bowlinggreenhotel.freeserve.co.uk
I: www.smoothhound.co.uk/hotels/bowling.html

B&B per person per night:
S £40.00–£48.00
D £28.00–£29.00

OPEN All Year except Christmas

Opposite Drake's bowling green, this elegant Victorian hotel has superbly appointed bedrooms offering all modern facilities. Our friendly and efficient staff will make your stay a memorable one. Centrally situated for the Barbican, Theatre Royal, leisure/conference centre, ferry port, National Marine Aquarium, with Dartmoor only a few minutes away.

Bedrooms: 10 double, 1 single, 1 family
Bathrooms: 12 en suite

CC: Amex, Delta, Diners, Mastercard, Switch, Visa

Special weekend breaks Nov-Mar inclusive. Prices on application.

P

♦♦♦

GABBER FARM

Down Thomas, Plymouth PL9 0AW
T: (01752) 862269
F: (01752) 862269
E: gabberfarm@tiscali.co.uk

Bedrooms: 2 double, 1 single, 2 family
Bathrooms: 3 en suite

Evening meal available

B&B per person per night:
S £19.00–£21.00
D £19.00–£21.00

HB per person per night:
DY £29.00–£31.00

OPEN All Year

Courteous welcome at this farm, near coast and Bovisand diving centre. Lovely walks. Special weekly rates, especially for Senior Citizens and children. Directions provided.

P €

♦♦♦

LAMPLIGHTER HOTEL

103 Citadel Road, The Hoe, Plymouth PL1 2RN
T: (01752) 663855
F: (01752) 228139
E: lamplighterhotel@ukonline.co.uk

Bedrooms: 7 double, 2 family
Bathrooms: 7 en suite, 2 private

CC: Amex, Delta, Mastercard, Visa

B&B per person per night:
S £18.00–£32.00
D £14.00–£21.00

OPEN All Year except Christmas

Small friendly hotel on Plymouth Hoe, 5 minutes' walk from the city centre and seafront.

P

CREDIT CARD BOOKINGS If you book by telephone and are asked for your credit card number it is advisable to check the proprietor's policy should you cancel your reservation.

PLYMOUTH continued

♦♦♦

OLD PIER GUEST HOUSE

20 Radford Road, West Hoe, Plymouth PL1 3BY
T: (01752) 268468
E: enquiries@oldpier.co.uk
I: www.oldpier.co.uk

Bedrooms: 2 double, 2 twin, 1 single, 1 family
Bathrooms: 1 en suite

CC: Delta, Mastercard, Switch, Visa

B&B per person per night:
S £16.00–£30.00
D £16.00–£30.00

OPEN All Year except Christmas

South West coastal path, Sustrans cycle route, famous Plymouth seafront 100 metres. Walking distance city centre, theatre, Pavilions, Barbican, Brittany Ferries. Smoking in guest lounge only.

10 €

♦♦♦

WESTWINDS HOTEL

99 Citadel Road, The Hoe, Plymouth PL1 2RN
T: (01752) 601777
F: (01752) 662158
E: paul.colman@btinternet.com
I: business.thisisplymouth.co.uk/westwindshotel

Bedrooms: 8 double, 1 single, 1 family
Bathrooms: 4 en suite

CC: Amex, Delta, Mastercard, Visa

B&B per person per night:
S £18.00–£35.00
D £17.00–£23.00

OPEN All Year except Christmas

A family-owned hotel which takes pride in looking after our guests in a professional, friendly and homely environment.

PORLOCK, Somerset Map ref 1D1

♦♦♦

MYRTLE COTTAGE

High Street, Porlock, Minehead TA24 8PU
T: (01643) 862978
F: (01243) 862978
E: bob.steer@talk21.com
I: www.smoothhound.co.uk/hotels/myrtle.html

Bedrooms: 5 double, 3 twin, 5 single, 3 family
Bathrooms: 10 en suite, 6 private

CC: Delta, Mastercard, Switch, Visa

B&B per person per night:
S Min £30.00
D £23.50–£25.00

OPEN All Year

Charming 16thC thatched cottage situated in the centre of this picturesque village. Ideal base for walking and exploring Exmoor.

P

RADSTOCK, Bath and North East Somerset Map ref 2B2

♦♦♦

RADSTOCK HOTEL & BAR

Market Place, Radstock BA3 3AD
T: (01761) 420776
F: (01761) 420520
I: www.chapmansgroup.com

Bedrooms: 4 double, 2 single
Bathrooms: 6 en suite

Evening meal available
CC: Delta, Mastercard, Switch, Visa

B&B per person per night:
S £34.95–£44.95
D £24.95–£39.95

HB per person per night:
DY £34.95–£49.95

OPEN All Year

Dating from Cromwellian times, the Radstock has been recently renovated and now boasts beautiful new bedrooms, an inviting bar and restaurant area and large beer garden.

P

THE ROOKERY

Wells Road, Radstock BA3 3RS
T: (01761) 432626
F: (01761) 432626
E: brandons@therookeryguesthouse.co.uk
I: www.therookeryguesthouse.co.uk

B&B per person per night:
S £42.00–£45.00
D £31.00–£35.00

HB per person per night:
DY £42.00–£60.00

OPEN All Year except Christmas

A 200-year-old, family-run property centrally situated for Bath, Wells and the Mendips. We have a relaxing lounge, residents' bar and restaurant and offer the best in service, coupled with an easy-going atmosphere. En suite rooms with hot-beverage facilities, TV, telephone and hairdryer. Large car park.

Bedrooms: 6 double, 2 twin, 1 single, 3 family
Bathrooms: 12 en suite

Evening meal available
CC: Delta, Mastercard, Switch, Visa

For £40pppn, get away and relax in a warm and friendly atmosphere: afternoon tea, DB&B, newspaper and welcome drink.

P

VISITOR ATTRACTIONS For ideas on places to visit refer to the introduction at the beginning of this section. Look out too for the VisitBritain Quality Assured Visitor Attraction signs.

ROCK, Cornwall Map ref 1B2

♦♦♦

SILVERMEAD
Rock, Wadebridge PL27 6LB
T: (01208) 862425
F: (01208) 862919

Bedrooms: 3 double, 1 twin, 2 single, 2 family
Bathrooms: 6 en suite

B&B per person per night:
S £30.00–£50.00
D £30.00

OPEN All Year except Christmas

Family-run licensed guesthouse overlooking the Camel estuary on the North Cornwall coast. Spacious accommodation, most en suite with colour television. Watersports centre nearby.

P

ST AGNES, Cornwall Map ref 1B3

♦♦

PENKERRIS

Penwinnick Road, St Agnes TR5 0PA
T: (01872) 552262
F: (01872) 552262
E: info@penkerris.co.uk
I: www.penkerris.co.uk

B&B per person per night:
S £20.00–£35.00
D £17.50–£25.00

HB per person per night:
DY £30.00–£37.50

OPEN All Year

This creeper-clad, Edwardian residence, with a lawned garden and parking, is a home from home offering real food, comfortable bedrooms with all usual facilities (three en suite) and a cosy lounge with piano, TV, video and log fire in winter. Dinner usually available on order. Licensed. Dramatic cliff walks and beaches nearby.

Bedrooms: 4 double, 2 single, 2 family
Bathrooms: 3 en suite

Evening meal available
CC: Amex, Delta, Mastercard, Switch, Visa

P €

ST AUSTELL, Cornwall Map ref 1B3 *Tourist Information Centre Tel: (01726) 879500*

♦♦♦♦

THE ELMS

14 Penwinnick Road, St Austell PL25 5DW
T: (01726) 74981
F: (01726) 74981
E: sue@edenbb.co.uk
I: www.edenbb.co.uk

B&B per person per night:
S £35.00–£60.00
D £25.00–£35.00

OPEN All Year

Small family-run guesthouse within walking distance of town centre. The Eden Project and the Lost Gardens of Heligan approximately 10-15 minutes' drive. The historic port of Charlestown and fishing village of Mevagissey easily reached as are many sandy beaches.

Bedrooms: 3 double
Bathrooms: 3 en suite

Evening meal available
CC: Delta, Mastercard, Switch, Visa

Special offers available through winter months – check website for details.

10 P

ST IVES, Cornwall Map ref 1B3 *Tourist Information Centre Tel: (01736) 796297*

♦♦♦♦

THE ANCHORAGE GUEST HOUSE
5 Bunkers Hill, St Ives TR26 1LJ
T: (01736) 797135
F: (01736) 797135
E: james@theanchoragebb.fsnet.co.uk
I: www.theanchoragebb.fsnet.co.uk

Bedrooms: 3 double, 1 twin, 1 single, 1 family
Bathrooms: 5 en suite

CC: Amex, Mastercard, Visa

B&B per person per night:
S £25.00
D £25.00–£28.00

OPEN All Year

18thC fisherman's cottage, 30 yards from harbour front and beaches, full of old world charm. Two minutes from Tate Gallery. Open all year.

ACCESSIBILITY

Look for the symbols which indicate National Accessible Scheme standards for hearing and visually impaired guests in addition to standards for guests with mobility impairment. You can find an index of all scheme participants at the back of this guide.

ST IVES continued

CHY AN GWEDHEN

St Ives Road, Treloyan, St Ives TR26 2JN
T: (01736) 798684
F: (01736) 798684
E: info@chyangwedhen.com
I: www.chyangwedhen.com

B&B per person per night:
S £30.00–£45.00
D £25.00–£33.00

OPEN All Year except Christmas

Mary and Les welcome you to Chy An Gwedhen, a haven for non-smokers. Award-winning B&B, comfortable, en suite rooms, delicious choice of breakfast. Private car park, adjacent to coastal footpath leading to Carbis Bay and St Ives' gorgeous beaches. Tate, Barbara Hepworth, wonderful restaurants all within walking distance. A relaxing holiday destination.

Bedrooms: 4 double, 1 family
Bathrooms: 5 en suite

CC: Amex, Delta, Mastercard, Switch, Visa

P

ST JUST-IN-PENWITH, Cornwall Map ref 1A3

◆◆◆

BOSAVERN HOUSE

Bosavern, St Just-in-Penwith TR19 7RD
T: (01736) 788301
F: (01736) 788301
E: info@bosavern.com
I: www.bosavern.com

B&B per person per night:
S £23.00–£32.00
D £23.00–£32.00

OPEN All Year except Christmas

A charming 17thC country house offering the very best in good taste and comfort at an affordable price. All rooms offer en suite facilities, TV, hairdryer and refreshment tray. Relax in our extensive gardens, walk the coastal footpath to an isolated sandy cove or explore West Cornwall. The choice is yours.

Bedrooms: 3 double, 2 twin, 1 single, 2 family
Bathrooms: 5 en suite, 3 private

CC: Delta, Mastercard, Switch, Visa

P €

QUALITY ASSURANCE SCHEME

Diamond ratings and awards were correct at the time of going to press but are subject to change. Please check at the time of booking.

ST JUST-IN-PENWITH continued

◆◆◆

THE OLD SUNDAY SCHOOL

Cape Cornwall Street, St Just-in-Penwith TR19 7JZ
T: (01736) 788444
F: (01736) 788444
E: info@oldsundayschool.co.uk
I: www.oldsundayschool.co.uk

Bedrooms: 2 double, 2 family
Bathrooms: 4 en suite

CC: Amex, Delta, Diners, Mastercard, Switch, Visa

B&B per person per night:
S £30.00–£40.00
D £25.00–£35.00

OPEN All Year

Unique guest house and gallery in beautiful, converted chapel. Close to cafes, shops and the spectacular coastline of West Penwith.

ST KEW, Cornwall Map ref 1B2

TREGELLIST FARM

Tregellist, St Kew, Bodmin PL30 3HG
T: (01208) 880537
F: (01208) 881017
E: jillcleave@tregellist.fsbusiness.co.uk
I: www.tregellistfarm.co.uk

B&B per person per night:
S Min £30.00
D Min £26.00

HB per person per night:
DY Min £42.00

OPEN All Year except Christmas

Delightful farmhouse set in pleasant countryside on a 130-acre sheep farm. Delicious home cooking. All bedrooms are en suite with colour TVs and tea/coffee facilities. Some ground floor bedrooms are disabled-friendly. Close to North Cornwall beaches and moors. Camel trail. Within easy reach of Eden Project and Lost Gardens of Heligan. Credit cards accepted.

Bedrooms: 4 double, 1 twin, 1 family
Bathrooms: 6 en suite

Evening meal available
CC: Delta, Diners, Mastercard, Switch, Visa

ST MARY'S, Isles of Scilly Map ref 1A3 *Tourist Information Centre Tel: (01720) 422536*

◆◆◆

THE BYLET

Church Road, St Mary's, Isles of Scilly TR21 0NA
T: (01720) 422479
F: (01720) 422479
E: thebylet@bushinternet.com
I: www.byletholidays.com

Bedrooms: 3 double, 1 single, 2 family
Bathrooms: 6 en suite

B&B per person per night:
S £33.00–£34.00
D £30.00–£32.00

Family-run guesthouse, five minutes to beaches and other amenities. Convenient for boat trips to other islands. Advice on travel and mainland parking.

ST MAWGAN, Cornwall Map ref 1B2

THE FALCON INN

St Mawgan, Newquay TR8 4EP
T: (01637) 860225
F: (01637) 860884
E: enquiries@falconinn.net
I: www.falconinn.net

B&B per person per night:
S £26.00–£42.00
D £26.00–£37.00

OPEN All Year

16thC, wisteria-covered inn with beautiful gardens in the Vale of Lanherne. Unspoilt, peaceful situation. Quality accommodation and excellent food. Only 20 minutes from Eden Project and the closest inn to Newquay Airport. Log fires, malt whisky and a good wine list enhance the experience.

Bedrooms: 2 double, 1 twin, 1 single
Bathrooms: 2 en suite

Evening meal available
CC: Delta, Diners, Mastercard, Switch, Visa

10% off stays of 3 nights or more.

SYMBOLS The symbols in each entry give information about services and facilities. A key to these symbols appears at the back of this guide.

SALISBURY, Wiltshire Map ref 2B3 *Tourist Information Centre Tel: (01722) 334956*

◆◆◆

ALABARE HOUSE
15 Tollgate Road, Salisbury SP1 2JA
T: (01722) 340206
F: (01722) 501586
E: alabarehouse@fsmail.net
I: www.alabare.org

Bedrooms: 5 double, 2 single, 1 family
Bathrooms: 4 en suite, 1 private

Evening meal available
CC: Amex, Diners, Mastercard, Switch, Visa

B&B per person per night:
S £26.00–£35.00
D £25.00–£35.00

OPEN All Year except Christmas

In a secluded location and within easy walking distance of the cathedral and the town's market square and nightlife. A warm welcome awaits you.

◆◆◆◆

BURCOMBE MANOR
Burcombe, Salisbury SP2 0E3
T: (01722) 744288
E: nick@burcombemanor.fsnet.co.uk
I: www.burcombemanor.com

B&B per person per night:
S £35.00–£50.00
D £25.00

OPEN All Year except Christmas

Burcombe Manor is set in the Nidder Valley four miles west of Salisbury. The house, built in 1865, has large, oak-floor hall, oak banisters, centrally heated bedrooms, most en suite. Guests have their own sitting room to plan their day. Local base to explore Wilton, Salisbury and the surrounding area.

Bedrooms: 3 double
Bathrooms: 2 en suite

Evening meal available
CC: Mastercard, Switch, Visa

◆◆◆

BYWAYS HOUSE
31 Fowlers Road, Salisbury SP1 2QP
T: (01722) 328364
F: (01722) 322146
E: byways@bed-breakfast-salisbury.co.uk
I: www.bed-breakfast-salisbury.co.uk

B&B per person per night:
S £39.00–£60.00
D £30.00–£42.50

OPEN All Year except Christmas

Attractive, family-run Victorian house close to cathedral in quiet area of city centre. Large car park. Bedrooms with private bathroom and colour satellite TV, 4-poster beds. Traditional English and vegetarian breakfasts. From Byways you can walk all around Salisbury. Ideal for Stonehenge and Wilton House.

Bedrooms: 10 double, 4 single, 9 family
Bathrooms: 20 en suite

CC: Delta, Mastercard, Switch, Visa

◆◆◆

LEENA'S GUEST HOUSE
50 Castle Road, Salisbury SP1 3RL
T: (01722) 335419
F: (01722) 335419

Bedrooms: 2 double, 2 twin, 1 single, 1 family
Bathrooms: 5 en suite

B&B per person per night:
S £26.00–£30.00
D £24.00–£29.00

OPEN All Year

Friendly, family-run guesthouse with pretty bedrooms and delightful public areas. Close to riverside walk to city centre and cathedral.

GOLD & SILVER AWARDS
These exclusive VisitBritain awards are given to establishments achieving the highest levels of quality and service. Further information can be found at the front of the guide. An index to all accommodation achieving these awards are at the back of this guide.

SALISBURY continued

MANOR FARM

Burcombe Lane, Burcombe, Salisbury
SP2 0EJ
T: (01722) 742177
F: (01722) 744600
E: sacombes@talk21.com

B&B per person per night:
D £23.00–£24.00

Comfortable farmhouse, warm and attractively furnished, on 1400-acre mixed farm in a quiet, pretty village 0.25 miles off A30, west of Salisbury. Ideal base for touring this lovely area. Nearby attractions include Wilton House, Salisbury and Stonehenge. Wonderful walks, good riding. Pub with good food nearby. No smoking.

Bedrooms: 1 double, 1 twin
Bathrooms: 2 en suite

CC: Amex, Delta, Diners, Mastercard, Switch, Visa

Reduction for stays of 3 nights or more.

P €

♦♦♦♦♦
Silver Award

NEWTON FARM HOUSE

Southampton Road, Whiteparish, Salisbury
SP5 2QL
T: (01794) 884416
F: (01794) 884416
E: enquiries@newtonfarmhouse.co.uk
I: www.newtonfarmhouse.co.uk

B&B per person per night:
S £40.00–£50.00
D £27.50–£37.50

HB per person per night:
DY £62.50–£65.00

OPEN All Year

Historic 16thC farmhouse, once part of the Trafalgar Estate. Delightfully decorated en suite bedrooms, five with genuine 4-posters (see our website). Beamed dining room with flagstones, bread oven and Nelson memorabilia. Superb breakfasts include fresh fruits, homemade bread and preserves and free-range eggs. Extensive grounds with swimming pool.

Bedrooms: 5 double, 3 family
Bathrooms: 8 en suite

Evening meal available

P €

♦♦♦♦

THE OLD RECTORY BED & BREAKFAST

75 Belle Vue Road, Salisbury
SP1 3YE
T: (01722) 502702
F: (01722) 501135
E: stay@theoldrectory-bb.co.uk
I: www.theoldrectory-bb.co.uk

Bedrooms: 2 double, 1 twin
Bathrooms: 2 en suite, 1 private

B&B per person per night:
S £35.00–£60.00
D £25.00–£35.00

OPEN All Year

Victorian rectory in quiet street, a short walk from the heart of Salisbury and convenient for all attractions. Warm, welcoming atmosphere. Visit our website.

10 P

TOWN INDEX

This can be found at the back of the guide. If you know where you want to stay, the index will give you the page number listing accommodation in your chosen town, city or village.

SALISBURY continued

♦♦♦♦
Silver Award

THE ROKEBY GUEST HOUSE

3 Wain-a-Long Road, Salisbury SP1 1LJ
T: (01722) 329800
F: (01722) 329800
I: www.rokebyguesthouse.co.uk

B&B per person per night:
S £38.00–£45.00
D £22.50–£27.50

OPEN All Year

Beautiful, nostalgic, Victorian guesthouse, quietly situated, 10 minutes' stroll city centre/cathedral. Large landscaped gardens, summerhouse, elegant 2-storey conservatory, licensed restaurant, gymnasium. Brochure available. Our guests say 'thoroughly enjoyable stay', 'wonderful house – wonderful hosts', 'absolutely excellent'. Come and see for yourself.

Bedrooms: 2 double, 3 twin, 3 family
Bathrooms: 6 en suite, 2 private

Evening meal available

Organised tandem parachute descents with qualified British Parachute Association instructors – ideal for sponsored charity fundraising.

♦♦♦♦
Gold Award

WEBSTERS

11 Hartington Road, Salisbury SP2 7LG
T: (01722) 339779
F: (01722) 421903
E: enquiries@websters-bed-breakfast
I: www.websters-bed-breakfast.com

B&B per person per night:
S £35.00–£38.00
D £22.50–£24.00

OPEN All Year except Christmas

Our guests can tell you why Websters is a regional Excellence in England award winner: 'wonderful B&B', 'the best', 'comfortable', 'friendly', 'helpful', 'fantastic', 'thank you, we've been thoroughly spoilt'. Come and experience excellent hospitality delivered with good humour and find out why so many of our guests return again and again.

Bedrooms: 1 double, 2 twin, 2 single
Bathrooms: 5 en suite

CC: Delta, Mastercard, Switch, Visa

12

SALISBURY PLAIN

See under Amesbury, Salisbury, Winterbourne Stoke

SEATON, Devon Map ref 1D2 *Tourist Information Centre Tel: (01297) 21660*

BEAUMONT

Castle Hill, Seaton EX12 2QW
T: (01297) 20832
F: (0870) 0554708
E: tony@lymebay.demon.co.uk
I: www.smoothhound.co.uk/hotels/beaumon1.html

B&B per person per night:
D £25.00–£28.00

HB per person per night:
DY £40.00–£45.00

OPEN All Year except Christmas

Select Victorian seafront family guesthouse on World Heritage Coast. Two minutes' walk from town. Excellent walks, country parks, attractions and sporting facilities. Unrivalled views over Lyme Bay. Limited parking.

Bedrooms: 3 double, 2 twin
Bathrooms: 5 en suite

Evening meal available

CHECK THE MAPS

The colour maps at the front of this guide show all the cities, towns and villages for which you will find accommodation entries. Refer to the town index to find the page on which they are listed.

SHALDON, Devon Map ref 1D2

POTTERS MOORING

30 The Green, Shaldon, Teignmouth
TQ14 0DN
T: (01626) 873225
F: (01626) 872909
E: mail@pottersmooring.co.uk
I: www.pottersmooring.co.uk

B&B per person per night:
S £35.00–£45.00
D £37.50–£45.00

Potters Mooring was formerly a sea captain's residence and dates from 1625 when Shaldon was a small fishing community. Overlooking the bowling green at the front and the beautiful River Teign at the rear, all rooms, and the family cottage suite, are en suite and furnished to the highest standards.

Bedrooms: 5 double, 2 family
Bathrooms: 6 en suite, 1 private

CC: Delta, Mastercard, Switch, Visa

Stay 3 nights or more and enjoy the last night free – Oct–Mar (excl Christmas and New Year).

SHEPTON MALLET, Somerset Map ref 2A2 *Tourist Information Centre Tel: (01749) 345258*

♦♦

PECKING MILL INN AND HOTEL

A371 Evercreech, Shepton Mallet
BA4 6PG
T: (01749) 830336
F: (01749) 831316
E: peckingmill@peckingmill.freeserve.co.uk

Bedrooms: 5 double, 1 single
Bathrooms: 6 en suite

Evening meal available
CC: Amex, Delta, Diners, Mastercard, Switch, Visa

B&B per person per night:
S £35.00–£45.00
D £27.50–£30.00

OPEN All Year except Christmas

16thC inn with oak-beamed restaurant and open log fire. Old world atmosphere with all modern amenities. Family room now open. Patio by running stream.

SHERBORNE, Dorset Map ref 2B3 *Tourist Information Centre Tel: (01935) 815341*

♦♦♦♦

CUMBERLAND HOUSE

Green Hill, Sherborne DT9 4EP
T: (01935) 817554
F: (01935) 817398
E: cumberlandbandb@aol.com

Bedrooms: 2 double
Bathrooms: 1 en suite, 1 private

Evening meal available

B&B per person per night:
D Min £34.00

OPEN All Year

A comfortable, Listed townhouse, centrally situated, with a warm and friendly atmosphere. Shopping, railway station and golf course are all nearby.

♦♦♦♦♦

THE OLD VICARAGE HOTEL

Sherborne Road, Milborne Port, Sherborne
DT9 5AT
T: (01963) 251117
F: (01963) 251515
E: theoldvicarage@milborneport.freeserve.co.uk
I: www.milborneport.freeserve.co.uk

B&B per person per night:
S £47.00–£77.00
D £30.00–£53.00

HB per person per night:
DY £61.00–£70.00

Listed Victorian Gothic building, elegantly furnished with antiques, set in 3.5 acres of beautiful grounds. The spacious lounge and the dining room afford magnificent views of open country. On Fridays and Saturdays one of the partners, a highly acclaimed chef, prepares dinner. On other nights food can be provided by a pub restaurant 200 yards away.

Bedrooms: 3 double, 3 family
Bathrooms: 6 en suite

Evening meal available
CC: Amex, Delta, Mastercard, Switch, Visa

DB&B for 2 Fri and Sat from £206 (2 nights).

SPECIAL BREAKS

Many establishments offer special promotions and themed breaks. These are highlighted in red. (All such offers are subject to availability.)

STEEPLE ASHTON, Wiltshire Map ref 2B2

♦♦♦

LONGS ARMS INN

High Street, Steeple Ashton, Trowbridge BA14 6EU
T: (01380) 870245
F: (01380) 870245
E: chantal@stayatthepub.freeserve.co.uk
I: www.stayatthepub.freeserve.co.uk

Bedrooms: 1 family
Bathrooms: 1 en suite

Evening meal available
CC: Delta, Mastercard, Switch, Visa

B&B per person per night:
S £25.00–£35.00
D £25.00–£35.00

OPEN All Year

Stone cottage adjoining 16thC village pub with two bedrooms, lounge and dining room. Excellent food, ale available. Weekend deals with dinner a must.

P €

STOGUMBER, Somerset Map ref 1D1

♦♦♦♦

Silver Award

NORTHAM MILL

Water Lane, Stogumber, Taunton TA4 3TT
T: (01984) 656916
F: (01984) 656144
E: bmsspicer@aol.com
I: www.northam-mill.co.uk

B&B per person per night:
S £30.00
D £27.50–£40.00

HB per person per night:
DY £55.00–£65.00

Hidden for 300 years. Nestling between the Quantock and Brendon Hills, in five acres of picturesque gardens with trout stream. Welcoming and comfortable, log fires and original beams. All rooms en suite including luxury garden suite. Superior, home-cooked food from daily-changing menu. Walking, shooting, fishing and archery. House-party weekends.

Bedrooms: 3 double, 1 twin, 1 single, 1 suite
Bathrooms: 3 en suite, 1 private

Evening meal available
CC: Amex, Delta, Diners, Mastercard, Switch, Visa

P €

STRATTON-ON-THE-FOSSE, Somerset Map ref 2B2

♦♦♦

OVAL HOUSE

Fosse Road, Stratton-on-the-Fosse, Nr Bath BA3 4RB
T: (01761) 232183
F: (01761) 232183
E: mellotte@clara.co.uk
I: www.mellotte.clara.co.uk

Bedrooms: 1 twin, 1 single

CC: Amex, Mastercard, Visa

B&B per person per night:
S £20.00–£22.00
D £20.00–£22.00

OPEN All Year

Charming 17thC home on ancient Roman Fosseway, 20 minutes from Bath, providing warm welcome. Ideal centre for visiting Bath, Wells, Glastonbury, Cheddar. Excellent pubs nearby.

P €

SWINDON, Wiltshire Map ref 2B2 *Tourist Information Centre Tel: (01793) 530328*

♦♦♦♦

COURTLEIGH HOUSE

40 Draycott Road, Chiseldon, Swindon SN4 0LS
T: (01793) 740246

Bedrooms: 2 twin, 1 single
Bathrooms: 2 en suite, 1 private

B&B per person per night:
S £25.00–£30.00
D £28.00–£30.00

OPEN All Year except Christmas

Large, detached village house with downland views, ample parking, tennis court and gardens. Comfortable, relaxing rooms. Easy access to Marlborough, Swindon, M4 and Cotswolds.

P

♦♦♦♦

THE ROYSTON HOTEL

34 Victoria Road, Oldtown, Swindon SN1 3AS
T: (01793) 522990
F: (01793) 522991
E: info@roystonhotel.co.uk
I: www.roystonhotel.co.uk

Bedrooms: 7 double, 6 single, 1 family
Bathrooms: 10 en suite

CC: Amex, Delta, Diners, Mastercard, Switch, Visa

B&B per person per night:
S £26.50–£45.00
D £22.50–£32.50

OPEN All Year

An ivy-clad Victorian townhouse with all the amenities offered by our four-diamond rating, including a lounge, bar, satellite TV and complimentary car parking.

P

TALSKIDDY, Cornwall Map ref 1B2

♦♦♦♦ Silver Award

PENNATILLIE FARM

Talskiddy, St Columb TR9 6EF
T: (01637) 880280
F: (01637) 880280
E: angela@pennatillie.fsnet.co.uk
I: www.cornish-riviera.co.uk/pennatilliefarm.htm

Family dairy farm set in 450 acres of beautiful countryside. Three spacious en suite guest bedrooms, including a stunning 4-poster (super king-size) bedroom. All bedrooms well equipped. Eden, the Lost Gardens of Heligan and NT properties are all nearby. Aga-cooked breakfasts with good choice of menu. Warm welcome guaranteed.

Bedrooms: 2 double, 1 twin
Bathrooms: 3 en suite

Evening meal available
CC: Amex, Mastercard, Switch, Visa

B&B per person per night:
S £30.00–£35.00
D £27.00–£32.00

HB per person per night:
DY £42.00–£47.00

OPEN All Year

TAUNTON, Somerset Map ref 1D1 *Tourist Information Centre Tel: (01823) 336344*

♦♦♦♦

RYDON FARM

West Newton, Taunton TA7 0BZ
T: (01278) 663472
F: (01278) 663472
E: rydon@onet.co.uk
I: www.rydonfarm.com

Bedrooms: 2 double, 1 twin
Bathrooms: 1 en suite

16thC beamed farmhouse set in beautiful landscaped gardens. Situated midway between Taunton and Bridgwater. Spacious rooms are tastefully furnished and include many period features.

B&B per person per night:
S £28.00–£35.00
D £25.00–£30.00

OPEN All Year except Christmas

TAVISTOCK, Devon Map ref 1C2 *Tourist Information Centre Tel: (01822) 612938*

♦♦♦♦

HARRABEER COUNTRY HOUSE HOTEL

Harrowbeer Lane, Yelverton PL20 6EA
T: (01822) 853302
E: reception@harrabeer.co.uk
I: www.harrabeer.co.uk

Delightful country-house hotel close to the ever-amazing surroundings of Dartmoor. Small, quiet, friendly and family-run, the hotel was a top-20 finalist for a prestigious Landlady of the Year 2002 award. Specialising in food, comfort and service with a smile! Small conferences by arrangement.

Bedrooms: 4 double, 2 twin
Bathrooms: 4 en suite, 2 private

Evening meal available
CC: Amex, Mastercard, Switch, Visa

Special offers for weekly and out-of-season breaks. Visit our website for up-to-date information.

B&B per person per night:
S £44.95–£51.95
D £30.00–£51.00

HB per person per night:
DY £46.50–£57.50

CHECK THE MAPS

The colour maps at the front of this guide show all the cities, towns and villages for which you will find accommodation entries. Refer to the town index to find the page on which they are listed.

TEIGNMOUTH, Devon Map ref 1D2 *Tourist Information Centre Tel: (01626) 215666*

Silver Award

BRITANNIA HOUSE B&B

26 Teign Street, Teignmouth TQ14 8EG
T: (01626) 770051
F: (01626) 776302
E: gillettbritannia@aol.com
I: www.britanniahouse.org

B&B per person per night:
S £45.00–£55.00
D £27.50–£35.00

This 17thC Listed house is situated in a conservation area of old Teignmouth. Recently refurbished to a high standard, bedrooms are luxuriously equipped, en suite and have high-pressure, thermostatically controlled showers. A sumptuous breakfast can be taken in the beautiful dining room or peaceful, walled garden.

Bedrooms: 3 double
Bathrooms: 3 en suite

CC: Amex, Delta, Mastercard, Switch, Visa

Prices reduce by £5 per night up to 4 nights for a double room.

TINTAGEL, Cornwall Map ref 1B2

Rating Applied For

BOSAYNE GUEST HOUSE

Atlantic Road, Tintagel PL34 0DE
T: (01840) 770514
E: clark@clarky100.freeserve.co.uk
I: www.bosayne.co.uk

Bedrooms: 2 double, 1 twin, 3 single, 1 family, 1 suite
Bathrooms: 3 en suite, 1 private

B&B per person per night:
S £22.00–£26.00
D £22.50–£28.00

OPEN All Year except Christmas

Comfortable, friendly, family-run guesthouse situated in a historical beauty spot, offering a warm welcome and personal service, with great cooking. A home away from home.

◆◆

THE TREWARMETT INN

Trewarmett, Tintagel PL34 0ET
T: (01840) 770460
F: (01840) 779011
E: edwina@trewarmettlodge.co.uk
I: www.trewarmettinn.co.uk

Bedrooms: 1 double

Evening meal available
CC: Delta, Mastercard, Switch, Visa

B&B per person per night:
S £20.00–£25.00
D £20.00–£22.50

OPEN All Year

Traditional Cornish inn. Comfortable en suite accommodation. Good, home-cooked food. Featured in CAMRA Good Beer Guide 2003. Sea views. Live folk music every Wednesday and Saturday.

TORQUAY, Devon Map ref 1D2 *Tourist Information Centre Tel: 0906 680 1268 (Premium rate number)*

◆◆◆

AVENUE PARK GUEST HOUSE

3 Avenue Road, Torquay TQ2 5LA
T: (01803) 293902
F: (01803) 293902
E: avenuepark@bushinternet.com
I: www.torbay.gov.uk/tourism/t-hotels/avepark.htm

Bedrooms: 3 double, 1 single, 4 family
Bathrooms: 8 en suite

B&B per person per night:
S £18.00–£23.00
D £18.00–£20.00

OPEN All Year except Christmas

Friendly, family-run guesthouse overlooking parkland. Seafront 350 yards, close to town, Riviera Centre, Abbey Gardens. Railway station nearby. Cleanliness and comfort assured.

COUNTRY CODE Always follow the Country Code ✿ Enjoy the countryside and respect its life and work ✿ Guard against all risk of fire ✿ Fasten all gates ✿ Keep your dogs under close control ✿ Keep to public paths across farmland ✿ Use gates and stiles to cross fences, hedges and walls ✿ Leave livestock, crops and machinery alone ✿ Take your litter home ✿ Help to keep all water clean ✿ Protect wildlife, plants and trees ✿ Take special care on country roads ✿ Make no unnecessary noise

TORQUAY continued

THE DAYLESFORD HOTEL

60 Bampfylde Road, Torquay TQ2 5AY
T: (01803) 294435
F: (01803) 292635
E: info@daylesfordhotel.com
I: www.daylesfordhotel.com

Simon and Dianne Lever invite you to the Daylesford Hotel in glorious Devon, with its beautiful countryside, coastline and historic attractions. Our mission is to make your stay enjoyable and relaxing. We are close to the station, conference centre, bowling greens, Torre Abbey Gardens, promenade, Princess Theatre and Cockington Village.

Bedrooms: 5 double, 1 twin, 2 single, 1 suite
Bathrooms: 8 en suite

Evening meal available
CC: Amex, Mastercard, Switch, Visa

Theatre breaks in co-operation with the Princess Theatre. 'Walking Westward' organises tours and gentle walks with expert guide. Includes transport.

P €

B&B per person per night:
S £20.00–£21.00
D £24.00–£30.00

HB per person per night:
DY £33.00–£43.00

OPEN All Year except Christmas

◆◆◆

GLENROY HOTEL
10 Bampfylde Road, Torquay TQ2 5AR
T: (01803) 299255
F: (01803) 299255
E: glenroyhotel@aol.com
I: www.glenroy-hotel.co.uk

Bedrooms: 2 double, 5 single, 3 family
Bathrooms: 4 en suite, 1 private

Evening meal available
CC: Amex, Delta, Diners, Mastercard, Switch, Visa

Family-run hotel close to all amenities. Friendly and comfortable atmosphere.

3 P

B&B per person per night:
S £17.00–£20.00
D £18.00–£25.00

HB per person per night:
DY £32.50–£37.50

OPEN All Year

◆◆◆◆

HEATHCLIFF HOUSE HOTEL

16 Newton Road, Torquay TQ2 5BZ
T: (01803) 211580
E: heathcliffhouse@aol.com

A former vicarage, now a quality, family-run hotel equipped for today yet retaining its Victorian charm. All rooms en suite, full English breakfast included, own parking space. Conveniently located with seafront and harbour, theatre, restaurants and high-street shops nearby. We have regular guests returning time after time.

Bedrooms: 8 double, 2 family
Bathrooms: 10 en suite

Evening meal available
CC: Delta, Mastercard, Switch, Visa

Reduced rates from Nov-Feb, minimum 2-night stay on double-occupancy basis (excl Christmas and New Year).

3 P

B&B per person per night:
S £20.00–£35.00
D £18.00–£25.00

OPEN All Year

◆◆◆◆

MAPLE LODGE GUEST HOUSE
36 Ash Hill Road, Torquay TQ1 3JD
T: (01803) 297391
E: TheMapleLodge@aol.com
I: www.themaplelodge.co.uk

Bedrooms: 3 double, 1 twin, 1 single, 2 family
Bathrooms: 6 en suite, 1 private

Evening meal available
CC: Delta, Mastercard, Switch, Visa

Licensed, detached guesthouse with beautiful sea views. Excellent food and hospitality. All rooms en suite. Centrally situated for town and beaches. Open all year.

2 P

B&B per person per night:
S £20.00–£25.00
D £20.00–£25.00

HB per person per night:
DY £27.50–£32.50

OPEN All Year

MAP REFERENCES The map references refer to the colour maps at the front of this guide. The first figure is the map number; the letter and figure which follow indicate the grid reference on the map.

TORQUAY continued

♦♦♦♦

ROBIN HILL INTERNATIONAL HOTEL

74 Braddons Hill Road East, Torquay
TQ1 1HF
T: (01803) 214518
F: (01803) 291410
E: jo@robinhillhotel.co.uk
I: www.robinhillhotel.co.uk

'Our priorities are simple, they're yours'. David and Joanna's 35 years' experience in hotels ensures first-class service at this award-winning hotel. Four years' recipient of the prestigious 'Commitment to Quality Award'. Upgraded yearly. Imposingly situated in pretty, south-facing, terraced gardens. Only 450 metres from harbour, shop and restaurants.

Bedrooms: 12 double, 3 single, 2 family
Bathrooms: 17 en suite

Evening meal available
CC: Delta, Mastercard, Switch, Visa

B&B per person per night:
S £26.00–£35.00
D £26.00–£35.00

♦♦♦

TRELAWNEY HOTEL
48 Belgrave Road, Torquay TQ2 5HS
T: (01803) 296049
F: (01803) 296049
E: trelawneyhotel@hotmail.com
I: www.trelawneyhotel.net

Bedrooms: 9 double, 2 twin, 1 family
Bathrooms: 12 en suite

Evening meal available
CC: Amex, Delta, Mastercard, Switch, Visa

Friendly, family-run, licensed hotel. Close to main shops, beaches, theatres, conference/leisure centre. A warm welcome always guaranteed. Highly recommended. Non-smoking.

B&B per person per night:
D £20.00–£30.00

HB per person per night:
DY £32.00–£42.00

OPEN All Year except Christmas

TORRINGTON, Devon Map ref 1C2 *Tourist Information Centre Tel: (01805) 626140*

♦♦♦♦

BEAFORD HOUSE HOTEL
Beaford, Winkleigh EX19 8AB
T: (01805) 603305
F: (01805) 603305
E: katie_squire@hotmail.com
I: www.beafordhousehotel.co.uk

Bedrooms: 2 double, 1 single, 6 family
Bathrooms: 6 en suite, 2 private

Evening meal available
CC: Amex, Mastercard, Switch, Visa

Elegant country hotel overlooking River Torridge, five miles south-east of Torrington, Tarka Trail. Excellent cuisine, heated pool, tennis, golf and riding. Near Rosemoor Gardens.

B&B per person per night:
S Min £50.00
D Min £40.00

HB per person per night:
DY £56.00–£66.00

TOTNES, Devon Map ref 1D2 *Tourist Information Centre Tel: (01803) 863168*

♦♦♦♦

FOUR SEASONS GUEST HOUSE
13 Bridgetown, Totnes TQ9 5AB
T: (01803) 862146
F: (01803) 867779
E: fourseasonsdevon@btopenworld.com
I: www.fourseasonsdevon.com

Bedrooms: 3 double, 2 twin, 1 single, 1 family
Bathrooms: 7 en suite

Evening meal available

Close to River Dart and town centre. Ideal base for local attractions. All rooms beverage tray, TV, trouser-press, hairdryer, security safe. Evening meals by arrangement.

B&B per person per night:
S Min £25.00
D Min £23.00

HB per person per night:
DY Min £35.00

OPEN All Year

AT-A-GLANCE SYMBOLS

Symbols at the end of each accommodation entry give useful information about services and facilities. A key to symbols can be found inside the back cover flap. Keep this open for easy reference.

TOTNES continued

♦♦♦♦
Silver Award

THE OLD FORGE AT TOTNES

Seymour Place, Totnes TQ9 5AY
T: (01803) 862174
F: (01803) 865385
E: enq@oldforgetotnes.com
I: www.oldforgetotnes.com

B&B per person per night:
S £44.00–£64.00
D £27.00–£37.00

HB per person per night:
DY £39.00–£94.00

OPEN All Year except Christmas

A warm welcome assured at this delightful 600-year-old stone building with walled garden and car parking. Whirlpool spa. Evening meals by prior arrangement. Extensive breakfast menu. Quiet yet close to town and river. Coast and Dartmoor nearby, Eden Project 1.5 hours. Two-bedroomed cottage suite and family room with roof terrace.

Bedrooms: 8 double, 2 family
Bathrooms: 9 en suite, 1 private

Evening meal available
CC: Amex, Delta, Mastercard, Switch, Visa

3-day breaks (Nov-Mar): £4 off price of room per night.

P

TRURO, Cornwall Map ref 1B3 *Tourist Information Centre Tel: (01872) 274555*

♦♦♦♦♦
Silver Award

BISSICK OLD MILL

Ladock, Truro TR2 4PG
T: (01726) 882557
F: (01726) 884057
E: sonia.v@bissickoldmill.ndo.co.uk

B&B per person per night:
D £32.50–£40.00

17thC water mill sympathetically converted to provide well-appointed accommodation with exceptional standards throughout and a relaxing, friendly atmosphere. All bedrooms en suite and well equipped. Candlelit dinners prepared with fresh, quality ingredients and served in a beamed dining room. Ideal base for visiting the Eden Project and Cornwall's beautiful gardens.

Bedrooms: 2 double, 2 twin, 2 suites
Bathrooms: 4 en suite

Evening meal available
CC: Delta, Mastercard, Switch, Visa

10 P

♦♦♦

NANSAVALLAN FARM
Killiow, Truro TR3 6AD
T: (01872) 272350
F: (01872) 272350

Bedrooms: 2 double, 1 family
Bathrooms: 2 en suite

B&B per person per night:
S £25.00
D £22.00–£25.00

OPEN All Year

Set in the heart of the countryside yet only 0.5 miles from Truro. A warm welcome awaits you. Twenty minutes' drive to the north- or south-coast beaches.

P

QUALITY ASSURANCE SCHEME

For an explanation of the quality and facilities represented by the Diamonds please refer to the front of this guide. A more detailed explanation can be found in the information pages at the back.

WADEBRIDGE, Cornwall Map ref 1B2 *Tourist Information Centre Tel: (01208) 813725*

Silver Award

BROOKFIELDS B & B

Hendra Lane, St Kew Highway, Wadebridge PL30 3EQ
T: (01208) 841698
F: (01208) 841174
E: robbie.caswell@btinternet.com
I: www.brookfields-stkew.co.uk

Quality, en suite accommodation in modern country house, set in our own grounds amidst beautiful countryside. Warm and friendly hospitality, clean, fresh rooms including superb family room, good breakfasts, own door keys, Fire Safety certificate, easy parking. Centrally located for towns, coast, beaches, Moors, attractions, walking, cycling and the Eden Project. Brochure available.

Bedrooms: 2 double, 1 family
Bathrooms: 3 en suite

B&B per person per night:
S £32.00–£35.00
D £25.00–£30.00

OPEN All Year except Christmas

WATCHET, Somerset Map ref 1D1

ESPLANADE HOUSE

The Esplanade, Watchet TA23 0AJ
T: (01984) 633444

Esplanade House is a Listed Georgian former farmhouse, situated within a beautiful walled garden, on Watchet's historic harbour/marina front. Well situated for steam railway enthusiasts, sea fishing. Lovely walks on Quantocks/Exmoor, loan of maps, guidebooks etc. En suite rooms. Dogs welcome by arrangement.

Bedrooms: 2 double, 1 twin
Bathrooms: 2 en suite, 1 private

B&B per person per night:
S £25.00–£30.00
D £22.50–£25.00

OPEN All Year except Christmas

WELLS, Somerset Map ref 2A2 *Tourist Information Centre Tel: (01749) 672552*

BURCOTT MILL HISTORIC WATERMILL AND GUESTHOUSE

Wookey Road, Wookey, Wells BA5 1NJ
T: (01749) 673118
F: (01749) 677376
E: theburts@burcottmill.com
I: www.burcottmill.com

Authentically restored Victorian watermill dating from Domesday, still stonegrinding flour daily. Enjoy a personal tour with the miller. Families especially welcome: playground, birds, small animals, tearoom. Opposite country pub for evening meals. Ideal for Cheddar, Wells, Glastonbury. Flexible accommodation. Wheelchair-friendly suite. You won't be disappointed!

Bedrooms: 1 double, 1 single, 4 family
Bathrooms: 5 en suite, 1 private

CC: Mastercard, Switch, Visa

10% discount for 2-to 6-night stays. 20% discount for week-long stays. Further reductions for children up to 15.

B&B per person per night:
S £24.00
D £21.00–£32.00

OPEN All Year except Christmas

WELLS continued

◆◆◆

FRANKLYNS FARM

Chewton Mendip, Bath BA3 4NB
T: (01761) 241372

Bedrooms: 3 double
Bathrooms: 2 en suite, 1 private

Cosy farmhouse in heart of Mendip. Superb views, peaceful setting. Large garden with tennis court. Offering genuine hospitality and delicious breakfast. Ideal touring Bath, Wells, Cheddar.

B&B per person per night:
S £20.00–£22.00
D £20.00–£22.00

OPEN All Year

LITTLEWELL FARM GUEST HOUSE

Coxley, Wells BA5 1QP
T: (01749) 677914

B&B per person per night:
S £26.00–£30.00
D £25.00–£27.00

HB per person per night:
DY £47.00–£50.00

OPEN All Year

Delightful 18thC farmhouse on non-working farm, set in pretty garden and enjoying extensive views over beautiful countryside. Charming en suite bedrooms with antique furniture offer comfort and high standards coupled with personal and thoughtful touches. Our candlelit dinner is skilfully prepared and beautifully presented, using only the best of local produce. One mile south-west of Wells.

Bedrooms: 4 double, 1 single
Bathrooms: 4 en suite, 1 private

Evening meal available

◆◆◆

THE POUND INN

Burcott Lane, Coxley, Wells BA5 1QZ
T: (01749) 672785
E: poundinnwells@aol.com

Bedrooms: 1 double, 1 family
Bathrooms: 2 en suite

Evening meal available
CC: Delta, Mastercard, Switch, Visa

B&B per person per night:
D Min £44.00

OPEN All Year except Christmas

A traditional 17thC village inn 1.5 miles from Wells on A39 to Glastonbury. Varied menu using fresh, local produce. Convenient base for local tourist attractions.

WEST DOWN, Devon Map ref 1C1

THE LONG HOUSE

The Square, West Down, Ilfracombe EX34 8NF
T: (01271) 863242

Bedrooms: 2 double, 2 twin
Bathrooms: 4 en suite

B&B per person per night:
D £26.00

18thC cottage guesthouse near North Devon Blue Flag beaches and Exmoor. Cosy yet spacious en suite, centrally heated bedrooms in a village setting.

WESTON-SUPER-MARE, Somerset Map ref 1D1 *Tourist Information Centre Tel: (01934) 888800*

BRAESIDE HOTEL

2 Victoria Park, Weston-super-Mare BS23 2HZ
T: (01934) 626642
F: (01934) 626642
E: braeside@tesco.net
I: www.braesidehotel.co.uk

B&B per person per night:
S £27.00
D £27.00

OPEN All Year except Christmas

Fabulous views over Weston Bay; two minutes' walk from sandy beach. Quiet location with unrestricted on-street parking. Single rooms always available. Directions: with sea on left, take first right after Winter Gardens, then first left into Lower Church Road. Victoria Park is on the right after the left-hand bend.

Bedrooms: 5 double, 1 twin, 2 single, 1 family
Bathrooms: 9 en suite

Stay 2 nights and have a third night free, 1 Nov-end Apr (excl Easter).

WESTON-SUPER-MARE continued

MOORLANDS COUNTRY GUESTHOUSE

Hutton, Weston-super-Mare BS24 9QH
T: (01934) 812283
F: (01934) 812283
E: margaret_holt@email.com
I: www.guestaccom.co.uk/35.htm

Family-run 18thC house in mature landscaped grounds. The Holts have been at Moorlands for the past 35 years. Hutton is a pretty village with a pub serving meals. Close to hill and country walks and many places of interest easily reached by car. Riding can be arranged for children.

Bedrooms: 3 double, 3 family
Bathrooms: 5 en suite

CC: Amex, Delta, Diners, Mastercard, Switch, Visa

B&B per person per night:
S £22.00–£32.00
D £22.00–£27.00

OPEN All Year

WESTONZOYLAND, Somerset Map ref 1D1

Silver Award

STADDLESTONES GUEST HOUSE

3 Standards Road, Westonzoyland, Bridgwater TA7 0EL
T: (01278) 691179
F: (01278) 691333
E: staddlestones@euphony.net
I: www.staddlestonesguesthouse.co.uk

Bedrooms: 2 double, 1 twin
Bathrooms: 2 en suite, 1 private

Evening meal available
CC: Delta, Mastercard, Switch, Visa

Elegant, Georgian, converted 17thC farmhouse in centre of village. Comfortable rooms with private facilities. Guest lounge, large garden, parking.

B&B per person per night:
S £32.00–£36.00
D £27.00–£32.00

HB per person per night:
DY £42.00–£50.00

OPEN All Year except Christmas

WEYMOUTH, Dorset Map ref 2B3 *Tourist Information Centre Tel: (01305) 785747*

♦♦♦♦

THE BAY GUEST HOUSE

10 Waterloo Place, Weymouth DT4 7PE
T: (01305) 786289

Bedrooms: 1 double, 1 single

CC: Delta, Diners, Mastercard, Switch, Visa

The Bay has all the facilities you would expect from a four-diamond-graded building. Situated just across the road from the beach. Private, off-road parking.

B&B per person per night:
S £25.00–£47.00
D £22.00–£32.00

OPEN All Year

♦♦♦

BRUNSWICK GUEST HOUSE

9 Brunswick Terrace, Weymouth DT4 7RW
T: (01305) 785408
F: (01305) 785408

Enjoy our seafront cul-de-sac position in a picturesque Georgian terrace, with panoramic views of the bay. You are assured of a warm welcome and hearty breakfasts. Walk along the esplanade to the many amenities and attractions. Rail, bus, coach approximately five minutes' walk. Full central heating, ideal for out of season breaks.

Bedrooms: 3 double, 1 twin, 1 single, 2 family
Bathrooms: 6 en suite, 1 private

CC: Delta, Mastercard, Switch, Visa

B&B per person per night:
S £22.00–£28.00
D £44.00–£56.00

OPEN All Year except Christmas

NB

IMPORTANT NOTE Information on accommodation listed in this guide has been supplied by the proprietors. As changes may occur you are advised to check details at the time of booking.

WEYMOUTH continued

Silver Award

HEATHWICK HOUSE

Chickerell, Weymouth DT3 4EA
T: (01305) 777272
E: enquiries@heathwickhouse.com
I: www.heathwickhouse.com

B&B per person per night:
S £30.00–£55.00
D £25.00–£40.00

HB per person per night:
DY £40.00–£75.00

Quality, en suite accommodation with beautiful views over Dorset's rolling countryside. Weymouth is nearby, also the World Heritage Coastline. Walks within 200 yards lead to coastal footpaths and Chesil Beach. Weymouth town, marina, seafront and beach are three miles away, from where you can catch the Condor Ferry to the Channel Islands.

Bedrooms: 3 double, 2 twin
Bathrooms: 5 en suite

CC: Delta, Mastercard, Switch, Visa

Book Honeymoon Suite for 3 nights, enjoy complimentary chocolates, flowers and bubbly. Special diets, including coeliac, and early business breakfasts.

P €

♦♦♦

WEYSIDE GUEST HOUSE
1a Abbotsbury Road, Weymouth DT4 0AD
T: (01305) 772685
E: weysideguesthouse@btinternet.com
I: www.weysideguesthouse.btinternet.co.uk

Bedrooms: 2 double, 2 family
Bathrooms: 4 en suite

B&B per person per night:
S £24.00
D £24.00

A well-established guesthouse within walking distance of all attractions. All rooms en suite with television and radio. Catering for families and couples. Limited parking.

P

WHITECROSS, Cornwall Map ref 1B2

HYCROFT
Whitecross, Wadebridge PL27 7JD
T: (01208) 816568
E: vipcurr@freeuk.com

Bedrooms: 1 double, 1 twin, 1 single
Bathrooms: 1 private

B&B per person per night:
S £18.00–£20.00
D £18.00–£20.00

OPEN All Year except Christmas

Country-style bungalow opposite Royal Cornwall Showground. Parking for four cars. Close to shops, pub and restaurants. Wadebridge one mile. Padstow six miles.

P

WINSFORD, Somerset Map ref 1D1

LARCOMBE FOOT

Winsford, Minehead TA24 7HS
T: (01643) 851306

B&B per person per night:
S Max £24.00
D Max £24.00

HB per person per night:
DY Max £38.00

Attractive period house in beautiful, tranquil Exe Valley. Guests' comfort within a warm, happy atmosphere is paramount. Footpath access to the moor and surrounding wildlife make Larcombe Foot an idyllic rural retreat. Dogs welcome.

Bedrooms: 2 double, 1 single
Bathrooms: 1 en suite, 1 private

Evening meal available

6 P €

WINTERBOURNE STOKE, Wiltshire Map ref 2B2

SCOTLAND LODGE FARM

Winterbourne Stoke, Salisbury SP3 4TF
T: (01980) 621199
F: (01980) 621188
E: william.lockwood@bigwig.net
I: www.smoothhound.co.uk/hotels/scotlandl.html

Warm welcome at family-run competition yard set in 46 acres of grassland. Lovely views and walks, Stonehenge/Salisbury nearby. Dogs, children and horses welcomed – stabling available on shavings. Conservatory for guests' use. French, German, Italian spoken. Easy access off A303 with entry through automatic gate. Excellent local pubs.

Bedrooms: 2 double, 1 twin
Bathrooms: 1 en suite, 2 private

CC: Delta, Mastercard, Switch, Visa

Discounts for more than 3 nights.

B&B per person per night:
S £30.00
D £24.00–£25.00

OPEN All Year

WOOLACOMBE, Devon Map ref 1C1 *Tourist Information Centre Tel: (01271) 870553*

♦♦♦♦

SANDUNES GUEST HOUSE

Beach Road, Woolacombe EX34 7BT
T: (01271) 870661
E: beaconhts@u.genie.co.uk
I: www.sandwool.fsnet.co.uk

Small, friendly guesthouse overlooking NT land and three miles of golden beach. An ideal base for exploring the beautiful area of North Devon. Balcony rooms available to sit and enjoy the spectacular scenery. All rooms tastefully decorated and furnished to a high standard. Local, organic produce used wherever possible.

Bedrooms: 4 double
Bathrooms: 4 en suite

Nov-Easter: 2-night breaks £45pp (based on 2 people sharing a double room).

B&B per person per night:
D £23.00–£32.00

OPEN All Year except Christmas

WOOTTON BASSETT, Wiltshire Map ref 2B2

♦♦♦

THE HOLLIES
Greenhill, Wootton Bassett, Swindon SN4 8EH
T: (01793) 770795
F: (01793) 770795

Bedrooms: 2 double, 2 single
Bathrooms: 1 en suite

Evening meal available

In beautiful countryside looking across the valley to the Cotswolds. Large garden, ample parking, non-smoking. One room en suite. Four miles west of Swindon, eight miles Cotswold Water Park.

12 P

B&B per person per night:
S £22.00–£28.00
D £19.00–£22.50

HB per person per night:
DY £28.00–£34.00

OPEN All Year except Christmas

YARCOMBE, Devon Map ref 1D2

STOCKHOUSE COTTAGE
Yarcombe, Honiton EX14 9AT
T: (01404) 861306
E: stockhouse.yarcombe@virgin.net

Bedrooms: 2 double, 1 family
Bathrooms: 1 en suite

Evening meal available

Charming character cottage peacefully situated in delightful gardens with magnificent views over Yarty Valley. Easy for touring three counties and coast. Good local pubs and restaurants.

B&B per person per night:
S £25.00–£38.00
D £22.50–£24.50

OPEN All Year except Christmas

PRICES
Please check prices and other details at the time of booking.

YELVERTON, Devon Map ref 1C2

◆◆◆◆◆ Silver Award

BROOK HOUSE

Horrabridge, Yelverton PL20 7QT
T: (01822) 859225
F: (01822) 859225
E: info@brook-house.com
I: www.brook-house.com

B&B per person per night:
S £35.00–£53.00
D £25.00–£38.00

OPEN All Year except Christmas

Lovely Victorian home in five acres of gardens on the edge of Dartmoor with stunning views across the Walkham Valley. Brook House offers a warm, friendly welcome with spacious, sunny bedrooms and delicious Aga-cooked breakfasts using fresh, local produce. Excellent location for exploring Dartmoor, the South Hams and Cornwall.

Bedrooms: 2 double, 1 twin
Bathrooms: 3 en suite

CC: Mastercard, Switch, Visa

Winter breaks: 3 nights for the price of 2 (excl public holidays).

P

◆◆◆◆

TORRFIELDS
Sheepstor, Yelverton PL20 6PF
T: (01822) 852161

Bedrooms: 2 double, 1 twin
Bathrooms: 3 en suite

Evening meal available

B&B per person per night:
S £18.50
D £18.50

HB per person per night:
DY £26.00–£30.00

OPEN All Year except Christmas

Detached property in own grounds, with good views and direct access on to moorland. Super setting in Dartmoor National Park – ideal for walkers. Value for money.

P

A brief guide to the main Towns and Villages offering accommodation in the **South West**

A **ABBOTSBURY, DORSET** - Beautiful village near Chesil Beach, with a long main street of mellow stone and thatched cottages and the ruins of a Benedictine monastery. High above the village on a hill is a prominent 15th C chapel. Abbotsbury's famous swannery and sub-tropical gardens lie just outside the village.

AMESBURY, WILTSHIRE - Standing on the banks of the River Avon, this is the nearest town to Stonehenge on Salisbury Plain. The area is rich in prehistoric sites.

ASHBURTON, DEVON - Formerly a thriving wool centre and important as one of Dartmoor's 4 stannary towns. Today's busy market town has many period buildings. Ancient tradition is maintained in the annual ale-tasting and bread-weighing ceremony. Good centre for exploring Dartmoor or the South Devon coast.

AVEBURY, WILTSHIRE - Set in a landscape of earthworks and megalithic standing stones, Avebury has a fine church and an Elizabethan manor. Remains from excavations may be seen in the museum. The area abounds in important prehistoric sites, among them Silbury Hill. Stonehenge stands about 20 miles due south.

AXMINSTER, DEVON - This tree-shaded market town on the banks of the River Axe was one of Devon's earliest West Saxon settlements, but is better known for its carpet making. Based on Turkish methods, the industry began in 1755, declined in the 1830s and was revived in 1937.

B **BARNSTAPLE, DEVON** - At the head of the Taw Estuary, once a ship-building and textile town, now an agricultural centre with attractive period buildings, a modern civic centre and leisure centre. Attractions include Queen Anne's Walk, a charming colonnaded arcade, and Pannier Market.

BATH, BATH AND NORTH EAST SOMERSET - Georgian spa city beside the River Avon. Important Roman site with impressive reconstructed baths, uncovered in the 19th C. Bath Abbey built on the site of the monastery where the first king of England was crowned (AD 973). Fine architecture in mellow local stone. Pump Room and museums.

BEAMINSTER, DORSET - Old country town of mellow local stone set amid hills and rural vales. Mainly Georgian buildings; attractive almshouses date from 1603. The 17th C church with its ornate, pinnacled tower was restored inside by the Victorians. Parnham, a Tudor manor house, lies 1 mile south.

BERRYNARBOR, DEVON - Picturesque, old-world village, winner of best-kept village awards, adjoining the lovely, wooded Sterridge Valley. On scenic route between Ilfracombe and Combe Martin.

BIDEFORD, DEVON - The home port of Sir Richard Grenville, the town, with its 17th C merchants' houses, flourished as a shipbuilding and cloth town. The bridge of 24 arches was built about 1460. Charles Kingsley stayed here while writing Westward Ho!

BISHOP'S LYDEARD, SOMERSET - Village 5 miles north-west of Taunton, the county town. Terminus for the West Somerset steam railway.

BODMIN, CORNWALL - County town south-west of Bodmin Moor with a ruined priory and church dedicated to St Petroc. Nearby are Lanhydrock House and Pencarrow House.

BOSCASTLE, CORNWALL - Small, unspoilt village in Valency Valley. Active as a port until onset of railway era, its natural harbour affords rare shelter on this wild coast. Attractions include spectacular blow-hole, Celtic field strips, part-Norman church. Nearby St Juliot Church was restored by Thomas Hardy.

BOVEY TRACEY, DEVON - Standing by the river just east of Dartmoor National Park, this old town has good moorland views. Its church, with a 14th C tower, holds one of Devon's finest medieval rood screens.

BOX, WILTSHIRE - Village in an Area of Outstanding Natural Beauty, 7 miles south-west of Chippenham. It is famed for Box ground stone, used for centuries on buildings of national importance.

BRADFORD-ON-AVON, WILTSHIRE - Huddled beside the river, the buildings of this former cloth-weaving town reflect continuing prosperity from the Middle Ages. There is a tiny Anglo-Saxon church, part of a monastery. The part-14th C bridge carries a medieval chapel, later used as a gaol.

BRIDGWATER, SOMERSET - Former medieval port on the River Parrett, now a small industrial town with mostly 19th C or modern architecture. Georgian Castle Street leads to West Quay and site of 13th C castle razed to the ground by Cromwell. Birthplace of Cromwellian Admiral Robert Blake is now a museum. Arts centre.

RATING All accommodation in this guide has been rated, or is awaiting a rating, by a trained VisitBritain assessor.

BRIDPORT, DORSET - Market town and chief producer of nets and ropes just inland of dramatic Dorset coast. Old, broad streets built for drying and twisting and long gardens for rope-walks. Grand arcaded Town Hall and Georgian buildings. Local history museum has Roman relics.

BRISTOL - Famous for maritime links, historic harbour, Georgian terraces and Brunel's Clifton suspension bridge. Many attractions including SS Great Britain, Bristol Zoo, museums and art galleries and top-name entertainments. Events include Balloon Fiesta and Regatta.

BROADHEMBURY, DEVON - Thatch-and-cob village with 14th/15th C church built largely of local Beer stone. South-east of the village, 884ft above sea level, is the Iron Age Hembury Fort.

BUDE, CORNWALL - Resort on dramatic Atlantic coast. High cliffs give spectacular sea and inland views. Golf course, cricket pitch, folly, surfing, coarse-fishing and boating. Mother-town Stratton was base of Royalist Sir Bevil Grenville.

BUDLEIGH SALTERTON, DEVON - Small resort with pebble beach on coast of red cliffs, setting for famous Victorian painting "The Boyhood of Raleigh". Sir Walter Raleigh was born at Hayes Barton. A salt-panning village in medieval times, today's resort has some Georgian houses.

C **CALLINGTON, CORNWALL -** A quiet market town standing on high ground above the River Lynher. The 15th C church of St Mary's has an alabaster monument to Lord Willoughby de Broke, Henry VII's marshal. A 15th C chapel, 1 mile east, houses Dupath Well, one of the Cornish Holy Wells.

CASTLE CARY, SOMERSET - One of south Somerset's most attractive market towns, with a picturesque winding high street of golden stone and thatch, market-house and famous round 18th C lock-up.

CHARMOUTH, DORSET - Set back from the fossil-rich cliffs, a small coastal town where Charles II came to the Queen's Armes when seeking escape to France. Just south at low tide, the sandy beach rewards fossil-hunters; at Black Ven an ichthyosaurus (now in London's Natural History Museum) was found.

CHEDDAR, SOMERSET - Large village at foot of Mendips just south of the spectacular Cheddar Gorge. Close by are Roman and Saxon sites and famous show caves. Traditional Cheddar cheese is still made here.

CHEW STOKE, BATH AND NORTH EAST SOMERSET - Attractive village in the Mendip Hills with an interesting Tudor rectory and the remains of a Roman villa. To the south is the Chew Valley reservoir with its extensive leisure facilities.

CHIPPING SODBURY, SOUTH GLOUCESTERSHIRE - Old market town, its buildings a mixture of Cotswold stone and mellowed brickwork. The 15th C church and the market cross are of interest. Horton Court (National Trust) stands 4 miles north-east and preserves a very rare Norman hall.

CLOVELLY, DEVON - Clinging to wooded cliffs, fishing village with steep cobbled street zigzagging, or cut in steps, to harbour. Carrying sledges stand beside whitewashed, flower-decked cottages. Charles Kingsley's father was rector of the church set high up near the Hamlyn family's Clovelly Court.

COLYTON, DEVON - Surrounded by fertile farmland, this small riverside town was an early Saxon settlement. Medieval prosperity from the wool trade built the grand church tower with its octagonal lantern and the church's fine west window.

CORSHAM, WILTSHIRE - Growing town with old centre showing Flemish influence, legacy of former prosperity from weaving. The church, restored last century, retains Norman features. The Elizabethan Corsham Court, with additions by Capability Brown, has fine furniture.

CREWKERNE, SOMERSET - This charming little market town on the Dorset border nestles in undulating farmland and orchards in a conservation area. Built of local sandstone with Roman and Saxon origins. The magnificent St Bartholomew's Church dates from 15th C; St Bartholomew's Fair is held in September.

D **DARTMOUTH, DEVON -** Ancient port at mouth of Dart. Has fine period buildings, notably town houses near Quay and Butterwalk of 1635. Harbour castle ruin. In 12th C Crusader fleets assembled here. Royal Naval College dominates from hill. Carnival, June; Regatta, August.

DAWLISH WARREN, DEVON - Popular with campers and caravanners, a sandy spit of land at the mouth of the River Exe. The sand dunes, with their golf links, are rich in plant and bird life. Brunel's atmospheric railway once ran along the dramatic line between jagged red cliffs and sandy shore.

DEVIZES, WILTSHIRE - Old market town standing on the Kennet and Avon Canal. Rebuilt Norman castle, good 18th C buildings. St John's church has 12th C work and Norman tower. Museum of Wiltshire's archaeology and natural history reflects wealth of prehistoric sites in the county.

DORCHESTER, DORSET - Busy medieval county town destroyed by fires in 17th and 18th C. Cromwellian stronghold and scene of Judge Jeffreys' Bloody Assize after Monmouth Rebellion of 1685. Tolpuddle Martyrs were tried in Shire Hall. Museum has Roman and earlier exhibits and Hardy relics.

DULVERTON, SOMERSET - Set among woods and hills of south-west Exmoor, a busy riverside town with a 13th C church. The Rivers Barle and Exe are rich in salmon and trout. The information centre at the Exmoor National Park Headquarters at Dulverton is open throughout the year.

DUNSTER, SOMERSET - Ancient town with views of Exmoor. The hilltop castle has been continuously occupied since 1070. Medieval prosperity from cloth built 16th C octagonal Yarn Market and the church. A riverside mill, packhorse bridge and 18th C hilltop folly occupy other interesting corners in the town.

E **EXETER, DEVON** - University city rebuilt after the 1940s around its cathedral. Attractions include 13th C cathedral with fine west front; notable waterfront buildings; Guildhall; Royal Albert Memorial Museum; underground passages; Northcott Theatre.

F **FALMOUTH, CORNWALL** - Busy port and fishing harbour, a popular resort on the balmy Cornish Riviera. Henry VIII's Pendennis Castle faces St Mawes Castle across the broad natural harbour and yacht basin Carrick Roads, which receives 7 rivers.

FROME, SOMERSET - Old market town with modern light industry, its medieval centre watered by the River Frome. Above Cheap Street, with its flagstones and watercourse, is the church showing work of varying periods. Interesting buildings include 18th C wool merchants' houses.

G **GLASTONBURY, SOMERSET** - Market town associated with Joseph of Arimathea and the birth of English Christianity. Built around its 7th C abbey, said to be the site of King Arthur's burial. Glastonbury Tor, with its ancient tower, gives panoramic views over flat country and the Mendip Hills.

H **HONITON, DEVON** - Old coaching town in undulating farmland. Formerly famous for lace-making, it is now an antiques trade centre and market town. Small museum.

I **ILFRACOMBE, DEVON** - Resort of Victorian grandeur set on hillside between cliffs with sandy coves. At the mouth of the harbour stands an 18th C lighthouse, built over a medieval chapel. There are fine formal gardens and a museum. Chambercombe Manor, an interesting old house, is nearby.

ILLOGAN, CORNWALL - Former mining village 2 miles north-west of Redruth and close to the coast. The Victorian engineer and benefactor, Sir Richard Tangye, was born here in 1833.

ISLES OF SCILLY - Picturesque group of islands and granitic rocks south-west of Land's End. Peaceful and unspoilt, they are noted for natural beauty, romantic maritime history, silver sands, early flowers and sub-tropical gardens on Tresco. Main island is St Mary's.

IVYBRIDGE, DEVON - Town set in delightful woodlands on the River Erme. Brunel designed the local railway viaduct. South Dartmoor Leisure Centre.

K **KINGSBRIDGE, DEVON** - Formerly important as a port, now a market town overlooking head of beautiful wooded estuary winding deep into rural countryside. Summer art exhibitions; Cookworthy Museum.

L **LANGPORT, SOMERSET** - Small market town with Anglo-Saxon origins, sloping to River Parrett. Well known for glove-making and, formerly, for eels. Interesting old buildings include some fine local churches.

LAUNCESTON, CORNWALL - Medieval "Gateway to Cornwall", county town until 1838, founded by the Normans under their hilltop castle near the original monastic settlement. This market town, overlooked by its castle ruin, has a square with Georgian houses and an elaborately carved granite church.

LEWDOWN, DEVON - Small village on the very edge of Dartmoor. Lydford Castle is 4 miles to the east.

LISKEARD, CORNWALL - Former stannary town with a livestock market and light industry, at the head of a valley running to the coast. Handsome Georgian and Victorian residences and a Victorian Guildhall reflect the prosperity of the mining boom. The large church has an early 20th C tower and a Norman font.

LOOE, CORNWALL - Small resort developed around former fishing and smuggling ports occupying the deep estuary of the East and West Looe Rivers. Narrow, winding streets with old inns; museum and art gallery are housed in interesting old buildings. Shark-fishing centre, boat trips; busy harbour.

LYNTON, DEVON - Hilltop resort on Exmoor coast linked to its seaside twin, Lynmouth, by a water-operated cliff railway which descends from the town hall. Spectacular surroundings of moorland cliffs with steep chasms of conifer and rocks through which rivers cascade.

M **MARTOCK, SOMERSET** - Large village with many handsome buildings of hamstone and a beautiful old church with tie-beam roof. Medieval treasurer's house where a 10' x 6' medieval mural has recently been discovered during National Trust restoration work. Georgian market house, 17th C manor.

MEVAGISSEY, CORNWALL - Small fishing town, a favourite with holidaymakers. Earlier prosperity came from pilchard fisheries, boat-building and smuggling. By the harbour are fish cellars, some converted, and a local history museum is housed in an old boat-building shed. Handsome Methodist chapel; shark fishing, sailing.

MINEHEAD, SOMERSET - Victorian resort with spreading sands developed around old fishing port on the coast below Exmoor. Former fishermen's cottages stand beside the 17th C harbour; cobbled streets climb the hill in steps to the church. Boat trips, steam railway. Hobby Horse festival 1 May.

MORETONHAMPSTEAD, DEVON - Small market town with a row of 17th C almshouses standing on the Exeter road. Surrounding moorland is scattered with ancient farmhouses. Prehistoric sites.

N **NETHER STOWEY, SOMERSET** - Winding village below east slopes of Quantocks with attractive old cottages of varying periods. A Victorian clock tower stands at its centre, where a village road climbs the hill beside a small stream. Cottage owned by Coleridge is open to the public.

NEWQUAY, CORNWALL - Popular resort spread over dramatic cliffs around its old fishing port. Many beaches with abundant sands, caves and rock pools; excellent surf. Pilots' gigs are still raced from the harbour, and on the headland stands the stone Huer's House from the pilchard-fishing days.

NEWTON ABBOT, DEVON - Lively market town at the head of the Teign Estuary. A former railway town, well placed for moorland or seaside excursions. Interesting old houses nearby include Bradley Manor, dating from the 15th C, and Forde House, visited by Charles I and William of Orange.

O **OKEHAMPTON, DEVON** - Busy market town near the high tors of northern Dartmoor. The Victorian church, with William Morris windows and a 15th C tower, stands on the site of a Saxon church. A Norman castle ruin overlooks the river to the west of the town. Museum of Dartmoor Life in a restored mill.

P **PADSTOW, CORNWALL** - Old town encircling its harbour on the Camel Estuary. The 15th C church has notable bench-ends. There are fine houses on North Quay and Raleigh's Court House on South Quay. Tall cliffs and golden sands along the coast, and ferry to Rock. Famous 'Obby 'Oss Festival on 1 May.

PAIGNTON, DEVON - Lively seaside resort with a pretty harbour on Torbay. Bronze Age and Saxon sites are occupied by the 15th C church, which has a Norman door and font. The beautiful Chantry Chapel was built by local landowners,the Kirkhams.

PENSFORD, BATH AND NORTH EAST SOMERSET - Village 6 miles south of Bristol and within easy reach of the City of Bath. Chew Valley and Blagdon Lakes close by.

PENZANCE, CORNWALL - Resort and fishing port on Mount's Bay with mainly Victorian promenade and some fine Regency terraces. Former prosperity came from tin trade and pilchard fishing. Grand Georgian-style church by harbour. Georgian Egyptian building at head of Chapel Street and Morrab Gardens.

PERRANPORTH, CORNWALL - Small seaside resort developed around a former mining village. Today's attractions include exciting surf, rocks, caves and extensive sand dunes.

PIDDLETRENTHIDE, DORSET - Situated on the River Piddle, north of Puddletown and Dorchester. Norman church with 15th C towers.

PILLATON, CORNWALL - Peaceful village on the slopes of the River Lynher in steeply wooded country near the Devon border. Within easy reach of the coast and rugged walking country on Bodmin Moor.

PLYMOUTH, DEVON - Devon's largest city, major port and naval base. Old houses on the Barbican and ambitious architecture in modern centre, with new National Marine Aquarium, museum and art gallery, the Dome - a heritage centre on the Hoe. Superb coastal views over Plymouth Sound from the Hoe.

PORLOCK, SOMERSET - Village set between steep Exmoor hills and the sea at the head of beautiful Porlock Vale. The narrow high street shows a medley of building styles. South-westward is Porlock Weir with its old houses and tiny harbour, and further along the shore at Culbone is England's smallest church.

R **RADSTOCK, BATH AND NORTH EAST SOMERSET** - Thriving small town ideally situated for touring the Mendip Hills.

ROCK, CORNWALL - Small resort and boating centre beside the abundant sands of the Camel Estuary. A fine golf course stretches northward along the shore to Brea Hill, thought to be the site of a Roman settlement. Passenger ferry service from Padstow.

S **SALISBURY, WILTSHIRE** - Beautiful city and ancient regional capital set amid water meadows. Buildings of all periods are dominated by the cathedral whose spire is the tallest in England. Built between 1220 and 1258, it is one of the purest examples of Early English architecture.

SEATON, DEVON - Small resort lying near the mouth of the River Axe. A mile-long beach extends to the dramatic cliffs of Beer Head. Annual art exhibition in July.

SHALDON, DEVON - Pretty resort facing Teignmouth from the south bank of the Teign Estuary. Regency houses harmonise with others of later periods; there are old cottages and narrow lanes. On the Ness, a sandstone promontory nearby, a tunnel, built in the 19th C, leads to a beach revealed at low tide.

SHEPTON MALLET, SOMERSET - Historic town in the Mendip foothills, important in Roman times and site of many significant archaeological finds. The cloth industry reached its peak in the 17th C, and many fine examples of cloth merchants' houses remain. Beautiful parish church, market cross, local history museum, Collett Park.

ST AGNES, CORNWALL - Small town in a once-rich mining area on the north coast. Terraced cottages and granite houses slope to the church. Some old mine workings remain, but the attraction must be the magnificent coastal scenery and superb walks. St Agnes Beacon offers one of Cornwall's most extensive views.

ST AUSTELL, CORNWALL - Leading market town, the meeting point of old and new Cornwall. One mile from St Austell Bay with its sandy beaches, old fishing villages and attractive countryside. Ancient narrow streets, pedestrian shopping precincts. Fine church of Pentewan stone and Italianate Town Hall.

ST IVES, CORNWALL - Old fishing port, artists' colony and holiday town with good surfing beach. Fishermen's cottages, granite fish cellars, a sandy harbour and magnificent headlands typify a charm that has survived since the 19th C pilchard boom. Tate Gallery opened in 1993.

ST JUST-IN-PENWITH, CORNWALL - Coastal parish of craggy moorland scattered with engine houses and chimney stacks of disused mines. The old mining town of St Just has handsome 19th C granite buildings. North of the town are the dramatic ruined tin mines at Botallack.

ST KEW, CORNWALL - Old village sheltered by trees standing beside a stream. The church is noted for its medieval glass showing the Passion and the remains of a scene of the Tree of Jesse.

ST MAWGAN, CORNWALL - Pretty village of great historic interest, on wooded slopes in the Vale of Lanherne. At its centre, an old stone bridge over the River Menahyl is overlooked by the church with its lofty, buttressed tower. Among ancient stone crosses in the churchyard is a 15th C lantern cross with carved figures.

STEEPLE ASHTON, WILTSHIRE - Old village dominated by its magnificent Perpendicular church, built at a time of prosperity from the medieval wool trade.

SWINDON, WILTSHIRE - Wiltshire's industrial and commercial centre, an important railway town in the 19th C, situated just north of the Marlborough Downs. The railway village, created in the mid-19th C, has been preserved. Railway museum, art gallery, theatre and leisure centre. Designer shopping village.

TAVISTOCK, DEVON - Old market town beside the River Tavy on the western edge of Dartmoor. Developed around its 10th C abbey, of which some fragments remain, it became a stannary town in 1305 when tin-streaming thrived on the moors. Tavistock Goose Fair, October.

TINTAGEL, CORNWALL - Coastal village near the legendary home of King Arthur. There is a lofty headland with the ruin of a Norman castle, and traces of a Celtic monastery are still visible in the turf.

TORQUAY, DEVON - Devon's grandest resort, developed from a fishing village. Smart apartments and terraces rise from the seafront, and Marine Drive along the headland gives views of beaches and colourful cliffs.

TORRINGTON, DEVON - Perched high above the River Torridge, with a charming market square, Georgian Town Hall and a museum. The famous Dartington Crystal Factory, Rosemoor Gardens and Plough Arts Centre are all located in the town.

TOTNES, DEVON - Old market town steeply built near the head of the Dart Estuary. Remains of motte and bailey castle, medieval gateways, a noble church, 16th C Guildhall and medley of period houses recall former wealth from cloth and shipping, continued in rural and water industries.

TRURO, CORNWALL - Cornwall's administrative centre and cathedral city, set at the head of Truro River on the Fal Estuary. A medieval stannary town, it handled mineral ore from west Cornwall; fine Georgian buildings recall its heyday as a society haunt in the second mining boom.

WADEBRIDGE, CORNWALL - Old market town with Cornwall's finest medieval bridge, spanning the Camel at its highest navigable point. Twice widened, the bridge is said to have been built on woolpacks sunk in the unstable sands of the river bed.

WATCHET, SOMERSET - Small port on Bridgwater Bay, sheltered by the Quantocks and the Brendon Hills. A thriving paper industry keeps the harbour busy; in the 19th C it handled iron from the Brendon Hills. Cleeve Abbey, a ruined Cistercian monastery, is 3 miles to the south-west.

WELLS, SOMERSET - Small city set beneath the southern slopes of the Mendips. Built between 1180 and 1424, the magnificent cathedral is preserved in much of its original glory and, with its ancient precincts, forms one of our loveliest and most unified groups of medieval buildings.

WESTON-SUPER-MARE, NORTH SOMERSET - Large, friendly resort developed in the 19th C. Traditional seaside attractions include theatres and a dance hall. The museum has a Victorian seaside gallery and Iron Age finds from a hill fort on Worlebury Hill in Weston Woods.

WEYMOUTH, DORSET - Ancient port and one of the south's earliest resorts. Curving beside a long, sandy beach, the elegant Georgian esplanade is graced with a statue of George III and a cheerful Victorian Jubilee clock tower. Museum, Sea Life Centre.

WINSFORD, SOMERSET - Small village in Exmoor National Park, on the River Exe in splendid walking country under Winsford Hill. On the other side of the hill is a Celtic standing stone, the Caractacus Stone, and nearby across the River Barle stretches an ancient packhorse bridge, Tarr Steps.

WOOLACOMBE, DEVON - Between Morte Point and Baggy Point, Woolacombe and Mortehoe offer 3 miles of the finest sand and surf on this outstanding coastline. Much of the area is owned by the National Trust.

WOOTTON BASSETT, WILTSHIRE - Small hillside town with attractive old buildings and a 13th C church. The church and the half-timbered town hall were both restored in the 19th C and the stocks and ducking pool are preserved.

YELVERTON, DEVON - Village on the edge of Dartmoor, where ponies wander over the flat common. Buckland Abbey is 2 miles south-west, while Burrator Reservoir is 2 miles to the east.

VISITOR ATTRACTIONS For ideas on places to visit refer to the introduction at the beginning of this section. Look out too for the VisitBritain Quality Assured Visitor Attraction signs.

South East

From Kent, the 'Garden of England', to the breathtaking Dorset Coast and from the magical Isle of Wight to the mellow Oxfordshire Cotswolds, the South East provides the perfect holiday mix – quaint villages, rolling countryside, dramatic coastline, seaside chic and cool heritage cities.

Classic sights
Stonehenge – ancient and mysterious standing stones
Battle Abbey – the site that marked the end of the Battle of Hastings in 1066
Blenheim Palace – birthplace of Sir Winston Churchill

Coast and country
Runnymede Meadow – the Magna Carta was signed here by King John in 1215
Chiltern Hills – tranquil country walks
The Needles – chalk pillars extending out into the Solent
New Forest – 900 year old historic wood and heathland

Glorious gardens
Leonardslee Lakes and Gardens – rhododendrons and azaleas ablaze with colour in May
Mottisfont Abbey – the perfect English rose garden designed by Graham Stuart Thomas
Savill Garden – woodland garden with royal connections
Sheffield Park Gardens – great 18thC, Capability Brown-designed landscaped gardens

Literary links
Jane Austen – her home in Chawton is now a museum and she is buried in Winchester Cathedral
Charles Dickens – Rochester; his home, Gad's Hill Place

The Counties of Berkshire, Buckinghamshire, Dorset (Eastern), East Sussex, Hampshire, Isle of Wight, Kent, Oxfordshire, Surrey, and West Sussex.

For more information contact:
Tourism South East
The Old Brew House
Warwick Park, Tunbridge Wells,
Kent TN2 5TU

Telephone enquiries -
T: (01892) 540766
F: (01892) 511008

Tourism South East
40 Chamberlayne Road
Eastleigh,
Hampshire SO50 5JH

Telephone enquiries -
T: (023) 8062 5505
F: (023) 8062 0010

E: enquiries@tourismse.com
www.gosouth.co.uk

1. Stonehenge, Wiltshire
2. Oast House, Kent

Places to Visit

You will find hundreds of interesting places to visit during your stay, just some of which are listed in these pages. Contact any Tourist Information Centre in the region for more ideas on days out.

Awarded VisitBritain's 'Quality Assured Visitor Attraction' marque.

A Day at the Wells
The Pantiles, Royal Tunbridge Wells
Tel: (01892) 546545
www.heritageattractions.co.uk
With commentary on personal stereos visitors experience the sights and sounds of 18thC Tunbridge Wells in its heyday as a spa town, escorted by Beau Nash, renowned dandy and MC.

Amberley Working Museum
Amberley, Arundel
Tel: (01798) 831370
www.amberleymuseum.co.uk
Open-air industrial history centre in chalk quarry. Working craftsmen, narrow-gauge railway, early buses, working machines and other exhibits. Nature trail and visitor centre.

Arundel Castle
Arundel
Tel: (01903) 883136 www.arundelcastle.org
An impressive Norman stronghold in extensive grounds, much restored 18/19thC, 11thC keep, 13thC barbican. Barons' hall, armoury, chapel. Van Dyck and Gainsborough paintings.

Battle Abbey and Battlefield
High Street, Battle
Tel: (01424) 773792
www.english-heritage.org.uk
Abbey founded by William the Conqueror on the site of the Battle of Hastings. The church altar is on the spot where King Harold was killed. Battlefield views and exhibition.

Bekonscot Model Village
Warwick Road, Beaconsfield
Tel: (01494) 672919 www.bekonscot.org.uk
The oldest model village in the world, Bekonscot depicts rural England in the 1930s, where time has stood still for 70 years. Narrow gauge ride-on railway.

Bentley Wildfowl and Motor Museum
QUALITY ASSURED VISITOR ATTRACTION
Halland, Lewes
Tel: (01825) 840573 www.bentley.org.uk
Over 1,000 wildfowl in parkland with lakes. Motor museum with vintage cars, house, children's play facilities and woodland walk.

Blenheim Palace
Woodstock
Tel: (01993) 811325 www.blenheimpalace.com
Home of the 11th Duke of Marlborough. Birthplace of Sir Winston Churchill. Designed by Vanbrugh in the English baroque style. Landscaped by 'Capability' Brown.

Breamore House
Breamore, Fordingbridge
Tel: (01725) 512233
Elizabethan manor house of 1583, with fine collection of works of art. Furniture, tapestries, needlework, paintings mainly Dutch School 17th and 18thC.

Brooklands Museum
Brooklands Road, Weybridge
Tel: (01932) 857381
www.brooklandsmuseum.com
Original 1907 motor racing circuit. Features the most historic and steepest section of the old banked track and 1-in-4 test hill. Motoring village and Grand Prix exhibition.

The Canterbury Tales

St Margaret's Street, Canterbury
Tel: (01227) 479227
www.canterburytales.org.uk
An audiovisual recreation of life in medieval England. Join Chaucer's pilgrims on their journey from the Tabard Inn in London to St. Thomas Becket's shrine at Canterbury.

QUALITY ASSURED VISITOR ATTRACTION

Chatley Heath Semaphore Tower

Pointers Road, Cobham
Tel: (01372) 458822
A restored historic semaphore tower displaying the history of overland naval communications in early 19thC set in woodland. Working semaphore mast and models.

Compton Acres

Canford Cliffs, Poole
Tel: (01202) 700778 www.comptonacres.co.uk
11 distinct gardens of the world. The gardens include Italian, Japanese, Spanish water garden. Deer sanctuary with treetop lookout. Restaurant and a craft centre.

Dapdune Wharf (National Trust)

Wharf Road, Guildford
Tel: (01483) 561389
www.nationaltrust.org.uk/southern
Dapdune Wharf is the home of 'Reliance', a restored Wey barge, as well as an interactive exhibition which tells the story of the waterway and those who lived and worked on it.

Didcot Railway Centre

Great Western Society, Didcot
Tel: (01235) 817200
www.didcotrailwaycentre.org.uk
Living museum recreating the golden age of the Great Western Railway. Steam locomotives and trains, engine shed and small relics museum.

Dover Castle and Secret Wartime Tunnels (English Heritage)

Dover
Tel: (01304) 211067
www.english-heritage.org.uk
One of the most powerful medieval fortresses in Western Europe. St Mary-in-Castro Saxon church. Roman lighthouse, secret wartime tunnels, Henry II Great Keep.

Eagle Heights

Hulberry Farm, Eynsford, Dartford
Tel: (01322) 866466 www.eagleheights.co.uk
Bird of prey centre housed undercover where visitors can see eagles, hawks, falcons, owls and vultures from all over the world. Reptile centre, play area and sandpit.

Gilbert White's House and The Oates Museum

Selbourne, Alton
Tel: (01420) 511275
Historic house and garden, home of Gilbert White, author of `The Natural History of Selborne'. Exhibition on Frank Oates, explorer and Captain Lawrence Oates of Antarctic fame.

Hastings Castle and 1066 Story

West Hill, Hastings
Tel: (01424) 781112
www.smugglersadventure.co.uk
Fragmentary remains of Norman Castle built on West Hill after William the Conqueror's victory at the Battle of Hastings. 1066 Story interpretation centre in siege tent.

1. The Stade, Hastings
2. The Needles, Isle of Wight
3. Shefield Park Gardens, East Sussex

The Hawk Conservancy and Country Park
Andover
Tel: (01264) 772252
www.hawk-conservancy.org
Unique to Great Britain – 'Valley of the Eagles' held here daily at 1400, plus 250 birds of prey and 22 acres (9ha) of woodland gardens.

High Beeches Gardens
Handcross, Haywards Heath
Tel: (01444) 400589
www.highbeeches.com
25 acres (10ha) of peaceful, landscaped woodland and water gardens with many rare plants, wildflower meadow, spring bulbs and glorious autumn colour.

QUALITY ASSURED VISITOR ATTRACTION

Kent & East Sussex Railway
Tenterden Town Station, Tenterden
Tel: (01580) 765155 www.kesr.org.uk
Full-size steam railway with restored Edwardian stations at Tenterden and Northiam, 14 steam engines, Victorian coaches and Pullman carriages. Museum and children's play area.

QUALITY ASSURED VISITOR ATTRACTION

Kingston Lacy (National Trust)
Wimborne Minster
Tel: (01202) 883402
www.kingstonlacy@ntrust.org.uk
A 17thC house designed for Sir Ralph Bankes by Sir Roger Pratt altered by Sir Charles Barry in 19thC. Collection of paintings, 250-acre (101-ha) wooded park, herd of Devon cattle.

QUALITY ASSURED VISITOR ATTRACTION

LEGOLAND Windsor
Winkfield Road, Windsor
Tel: 0870 5040404 www.legoland.co.uk
A family park with hands-on activities, rides, themed playscapes and more LEGO bricks than you ever dreamed possible.

The Living Rainforest
Thatcham, Newbury
Tel: (01635) 202444 www.livingrainforest.org
Two tropical rainforests, all under cover, approximately 20,000 sq ft (1,858sq m). Collection of rare and exotic tropical plants together with small representation of wildlife in rainforest.

Manor Farm (Farm and Museum)
Botley, Southampton
Tel: (01489) 787055
www.hants.gov.uk/countryside/manorfarm
Traditional Hampshire farmstead with a range of buildings, farm animals, machinery and equipment. Pre-1950's farmhouse and 13thC church set for 1900 living history site.

National Motor Museum
Beaulieu, Brockenhurst
Tel: (01590) 612345 www.beaulieu.co.uk
Motor museum with over 250 exhibits showing history of motoring from 1896. Also Palace House, Wheels Experience, Beaulieu Abbey ruins and a display of monastic life.

Newport Roman Villa
Cypress Road, Newport
Tel: (01983) 529720
Underfloor heated bath system; tesselated floors displayed in reconstructed rooms; corn-drying kiln, small site museum of objects recovered.

Oceanarium
West Beach, Bournemouth
Tel: (01202) 311993 www.oceanarium.co.uk
Situated in the heart of Bournemouth, next to the pier, the Oceanarium will take you on a fascinating voyage on the undersea world from elegant seahorses to sinister sharks.

Osborne House (English Heritage)
Yorke Avenue, East Cowes
Tel: (01983) 200022
www.english-heritage.org.uk
Queen Victoria and Prince Albert's seaside holiday home. Swiss Cottage where royal children learnt cooking and gardening. Victorian carriage rides.

The Oxford Story
6 Broad Street, Oxford
Tel: (01865) 728822 www.oxfordstory.co.uk
Take your seat on our amazing 'dark' ride and journey through scenes from 900 years of university's history, complete with sights, sounds and smells!

Port Lympne Wild Animal Park, Mansion and Gardens
Lympe, Hythe
Tel: (01303) 264647 www.howletts.net
Set in 400 acres (160 ha) with historic mansion and gardens, black rhino, tigers, elephants, small cats, monkeys, Barbary lions, red pandas, tapirs and 'Palace of the Apes'.

Portsmouth Historic Dockyard
1/7 College Road, HM Naval Base, Portsmouth
Tel: (023) 9286 1533
www.historicdockyard.co.uk
A fascinating day out – Action Stations, Mary Rose, HMS Victory, HMS Warrior 1860, Royal Naval Museum, 'Warships by water' harbour tours, Dockyard Apprentice exhibition.

St Mary's House and Gardens
Bramber, Steyning
Tel: (01903) 816205
A medieval timber-framed Grade I house with rare 16thC wall-leather, fine panelled rooms and a unique painted room. Topiary gardens.

The Sir Harold Hillier Gardens and Arboretum
Ampfield, Romsey
Tel: (01794) 368787 www.hillier.hants.gov.uk/
Established in 1953, The Sir Harold Hillier Gardens and Arboretum comprises the greatest collection of wild and cultivated woody plants in the world.

South of England Rare Breeds Centre
Highlands Farm, Woodchurch
Tel: (01233) 861493 www.rarebreeds.org.uk
Large collection of rare farm breeds on a working farm with children's play activities. Home to the 'Tamworth Two'. Woodland walks.

Swanage Railway
Station House, Swanage
Tel: (01929) 425800
www.swanagerailway.co.uk
Enjoy a nostalgic steam-train ride on the Purbeck line. Steam trains run every weekend throughout the year with daily running April to October.

The Tank Museum
Bovington, Wareham
Tel: (01929) 405096 www.tankmuseum.co.uk
The world's finest display of armoured fighting vehicles. Experimental vehicles, interactive displays, disabled access and facilities.

The Vyne (National Trust)
Sherborne St John, Basingstoke
Tel: (01256) 881337
www.nationaltrust.org.uk/places/thevyne
Original house dating back to Henry VIII's time. Extensively altered in mid 17thC. Tudor chapel, beautiful gardens and lake.

Waterperry Gardens Limited
Waterperry, Oxford
Tel: (01844) 339254
www.waterperrygardens.co.uk
Ornamental gardens covering 6 acres (2.4ha) of the 83-acre (33.5-ha) 18thC Waterperry House estate. A Saxon village church, garden shop teashop, art and craft gallery are found within the grounds.

Weald and Downland Open Air Museum
Singleton, Chichester
Tel: (01243) 811348 www.wealddown.co.uk
Over 40 rescued historic buildings from South East England, reconstructed on a downland country park site. Homes and workplaces of the past include a medieval farmstead.

West Dean Gardens

West Dean, Chichester
Tel: (01243) 818210
www.westdean.org.uk
Extensive downland garden with specimen trees, 300-ft (91-m) pergola, rustic summerhouses and restored walled kitchen garden. Walk in parkland and 45-acre (18-ha) arboretum.

Whitchurch Silk Mill
28 Winchester Street, Whitchurch
Tel: (01256) 892065
www.whitchurchsilkmill.org.uk
Unique Georgian silk-weaving watermill, now a working museum producing fine silk fabrics on Victorian machinery. Riverside garden, tearoom for light meals, silk gift shop.

Wilderness Wood
Hadlow Down, Uckfield
Tel: (01825) 830509
www.wildernesswood.co.uk
A family-run working woodland of 60 acres (24ha), beautiful in all seasons. There are trails, a bluebell walk, a play area, workshop and a timber barn with exhibition.

Winchester Cathedral
The Close, Winchester
Tel: (01962) 857225
www.winchester-cathedral.org.uk
Magnificent medieval cathedral, soaring gothic nave converted from original Norman. 12thC illuminated Winchester Bible, Jane Austen's tomb, library, gallery, crypt, chapels.

Winkworth Arboretum (National Trust)

Hascombe, Godalming
Tel: (01483) 208477
www.nationaltrust.org.uk/winkwortharboretum
100 acres (40ha) of hillside planted with rare trees and shrubs. Good views, lakes, newly-restored boathouse, azaleas, bluebells, wild spring flowers and autumn colours.

Tourism South East

The Old Brew House,
Warwick Park, Tunbridge Wells,
Kent TN2 5TU
T: (01892) 540766
F: (01892) 511008

40 Chamberlayne Road,
Eastleigh,
Hampshire, SO50 5JH
T: (023) 8062 5505
F: (023) 8062 0010

E: enquiries@tourismse.com
www.gosouth.co.uk

THE FOLLOWING PUBLICATIONS ARE AVAILABLE FROM TOURISM SOUTH EAST:

South East Breaks
Southern England
Days Out in Southern England
Days Out in Thames & Chilterns Country
Favourite Gardens & Garden Stays in South East England
Glorious Gardens & Historic Houses in Southern England
Walk South East England
Escape into the Countryside

Getting to the South East

BY ROAD: From the north east – M1 & M25; the north west – M6, M40 & M25; the west and Wales – M4 & M25; the east – M25; the south west – M5, M4 & M25; London – M25, M2, M20, M23, M3, M4 or M40.

BY RAIL: Regular services from London's Charing Cross, Victoria, Waterloo and Waterloo East stations to all parts of the South East. Further information on rail journeys in the South East can be obtained on 08457 484950.

1. Savill Garden
2. Dreaming Spires, Oxford

Where to stay in the

South East

All place names in the blue bands under which accommodation is listed, are shown on the maps at the front of this guide.

Symbols give useful information about services and facilities. Inside the back cover flap there's a key to these symbols which you can keep open for easy reference.

A complete listing of all the VisitBritain assessed accommodation covered by this guide appears at the back of this guide.

ABINGDON, Oxfordshire Map ref 2C1 *Tourist Information Centre Tel: (01235) 522711*

♦♦♦♦

BARROWS END

3 The Copse, Barrows End,
Abingdon OX14 3YW
T: (01235) 523541
F: (01235) 523541
E: dsharm@tesco.net

Bedrooms: 3 twin
Bathrooms: 1 en suite, 2 private

B&B per person per night:
S £28.00–£32.00
D £24.00–£26.00

OPEN All Year

Modern, architecturally designed chalet bungalow in a peaceful setting backing on to a nature reserve. Easy walking distance to Abingdon. Near bus stops to Oxford/Abingdon.

P

♦♦♦

75 NORTHCOURT ROAD

Abingdon OX14 1NN
T: (01235) 521195

B&B per person per night:
S £27.00
D £25.00

OPEN All Year except Christmas

We welcome you to our home with its comfortable, en suite accommodation. The rooms are double bedded and are also available for single occupancy. Conveniently situated, we are only a short walk from Abingdon town centre and within easy reach of Oxford by car/bus. Special diets catered for. Ample, off-street parking.

Bedrooms: 2 double
Bathrooms: 2 en suite

P

ABINGER COMMON, Surrey Map ref 2D2

LEYLANDS FARM

Leylands Lane, Abinger Common, Dorking RH5 6JU
T: (01306) 730115
F: (01306) 731675
E: annieblf@btopenworld.com

B&B per person per night:
S £40.00
D £27.50

OPEN All Year

Attractively furnished, self-contained annexe of period farmhouse. Double bedroom, en suite bathroom, lounge, own television and tea-making facilities. Central heating. Log fire. Set in lovely seven-acre gardens amidst woodland. Easy access to airports and motorways. Mob: 07818 422881

Bedrooms: 1 double, 1 family
Bathrooms: 1 en suite

P

ALDWORTH, West Berkshire Map ref 2C2

FIELDVIEW COTTAGE

Bell Lane, Aldworth, Reading RG8 9SB
T: (01635) 578964
E: hunt@fieldview.freeserve.co.uk

B&B per person per night:
S £25.00–£30.00
D £25.00–£30.00

Fieldview is a pretty cottage in the centre of Aldworth, situated high on the Downs and adjoining the Ridgeway, an ideal base for walking, cycling and horse riding. M4/A34 jct 12/13, Oxford, Bath, Windsor and Heathrow within easy reach. Only 2.5 miles from main railway line – Paddington 45 minutes.

Bedrooms: 2 double
Bathrooms: 2 private

P

ALTON, Hampshire Map ref 2C2 *Tourist Information Centre Tel: (01420) 88448*

Silver Award

BOUNDARY HOUSE B & B

Gosport Road, Lower Farringdon, Alton GU34 3DH
T: (01420) 587076
F: (01420) 587047
E: BoundaryS@messages.co.uk
I: www.boundaryhouse.co.uk

B&B per person per night:
S £27.50–£30.00
D £27.50

Situated on the edge of the Meon Valley and on the boundary of the village of Lower Farringdon. Guests are assured of a warm welcome with comfortable accommodation in a relaxed atmosphere. Lovely garden, excellent breakfast. Ideal touring/ walking base. Many places of interest and good pubs/restaurants nearby. Parking.

Bedrooms: 1 double, 1 twin, 1 single
Bathrooms: 3 private

CC: Delta, Mastercard, Switch, Visa

P €

CREDIT CARD BOOKINGS If you book by telephone and are asked for your credit card number it is advisable to check the proprietor's policy should you cancel your reservation.

ALTON continued

ST MARY'S HALL

18 Albert Road, Alton GU34 1LP
T: (01420) 82235

B&B per person per night:
S £30.00–£35.00
D £25.00–£27.50

OPEN All Year except Christmas

Beautifully converted church with lots of old world charm. A warm welcome from Tom and Jackie. Visitors' reception hall, lovely garden. Walking distance of sports centre, Jane Austen's house, good pub and railway station for main line and steam trains. Full English breakfast served in vaulted/galleried lounge. Lift from station available. Contact telephone: 07762 701221.

Bedrooms: 2 twin, 1 single
Bathrooms: 1 en suite

The lower rates are for long-term, uninterrupted stays.

10 P

AMERSHAM, Buckinghamshire Map ref 2D1

Silver Award

39 QUARRENDON ROAD

Amersham HP7 9EF
T: (01494) 727959

Bedrooms: 1 double, 1 single

B&B per person per night:
S £27.50–£32.50
D £25.00–£27.50

OPEN All Year

Detached house, comfortable, with friendly atmosphere. Residents' lounge, private parking, pleasant garden. One mile to London Underground station, easy reach of M25, M40 and A40.

12 P

AMPORT, Hampshire Map ref 2C2

BROADWATER

Amport, Andover SP11 8AY
T: (01264) 772240
F: (01264) 772240
E: broadwater@dmac.co.uk
I: www.dmac.co.uk/carolyn

B&B per person per night:
S Min £35.00
D Min £30.00

OPEN All Year except Christmas

Listed thatched cottage in delightful secluded garden, providing relaxed and cosy atmosphere in peaceful village setting. Large bedrooms with en suite facilities. Sitting room with open log fire in winter. Excellent stop-over for West Country and airport travellers (A303 0.5 miles). Stonehenge only 15 minutes' drive, Salisbury and Winchester 30 minutes.

Bedrooms: 3 double
Bathrooms: 3 en suite

CC: Delta, Mastercard, Switch, Visa

P

ANDOVER, Hampshire Map ref 2C2 *Tourist Information Centre Tel: (01264) 324320*

AMBERLEY HOTEL

70 Weyhill Road, Andover
SP10 3NP
T: (01264) 352224
F: (01264) 392555
E: amberleyand@fsbdial.co.uk

Bedrooms: 5 double, 4 twin, 3 single, 3 family
Bathrooms: 15 en suite

Evening meal available
CC: Amex, Diners, Mastercard, Switch, Visa

B&B per person per night:
S £45.00–£60.00
D Min £30.00

HB per person per night:
DY Min £40.00

OPEN All Year except Christmas

Compact 15-bedroom hotel, all en suite. Attractive a la carte and table d'hote restaurant and bar lounge. Private meetings and wedding receptions can be booked in Wightman room.

P

MAP REFERENCES

Map references apply to the colour maps at the front of this guide.

ANDOVER continued

◆◆◆

AMPORT INN

Amport, Andover SP11 8AE
T: (01264) 710371
F: (01264) 710112

Bedrooms: 7 double, 1 single, 1 family
Bathrooms: 8 en suite, 1 private

Evening meal available
CC: Mastercard, Switch, Visa

B&B per person per night:
D £29.00–£30.50

OPEN All Year

Friendly inn in attractive Hampshire village, with racecourses, riding and fishing nearby. Business people welcome weekdays. Breakaway weekends available. Good food.

P

◆◆◆◆ Silver Award

MAY COTTAGE

Thruxton, Andover SP11 8LZ
T: (01264) 771241
F: (01264) 771770
E: info@maycottage-thruxton.co.uk
I: www.maycottage-thruxton.co.uk

B&B per person per night:
S £40.00–£50.00
D £30.00–£40.00

OPEN All Year

May Cottage dates back to 1740 and is situated in the heart of this picturesque, tranquil village with two old inns serving food. All rooms have en suite/private bathroom, TV, radio, beverage tray. Guests' own sitting/dining room. Pretty, secluded garden with stream. Many NT and stately homes/gardens within easy reach. Private parking. Non-smoking establishment.

Bedrooms: 2 double, 1 twin
Bathrooms: 2 en suite, 1 private

4 P

ASHDOWN FOREST

See under Hartfield

ASHFORD, Kent Map ref 3B4 *Tourist Information Centre Tel: (01233) 629165*

◆◆◆

DEAN COURT FARM

Challock Lane, Westwell, Ashford TN25 4NH
T: (01233) 712924

Bedrooms: 1 double, 1 twin, 1 family
Bathrooms: 1 en suite

Evening meal available

B&B per person per night:
S £30.00
D £25.00

OPEN All Year except Christmas

Period farmhouse on working farm with modern amenities. Magnificent views in quiet valley. Comfortable accommodation with separate sitting room for guests.

 P

ASHURST, Hampshire Map ref 2C3

◆◆◆◆

FOREST GATE LODGE

161 Lyndhurst Road, Ashurst, Southampton SO40 7AW
T: (023) 8029 3026
F: (023) 8029 3026
I: www.ukworld.net/forestgatelodge

B&B per person per night:
D £25.00–£30.00

OPEN All Year

Large Victorian house with direct access to New Forest and its attractions – walks, riding, cycling. Pubs and restaurants nearby, Lyndhurst – 'capital of the New Forest' – five minutes' drive. Full English breakfast or vegetarian by prior arrangement.

Bedrooms: 4 double, 1 family
Bathrooms: 5 en suite

Special rates: 3 nights for price of 2, weekdays, Oct-Apr inclusive.

2 P

ACCESSIBILITY

Look for the symbols which indicate National Accessible Scheme standards for hearing and visually impaired guests in addition to standards for guests with mobility impairment. You can find an index of all scheme participants at the back of this guide.

ASTON UPTHORPE, Oxfordshire Map ref 2C2

MIDDLE FELL
Moreton Road, Aston Upthorpe,
Didcot OX11 9ER
T: (01235) 850207
F: (01235) 850207
E: middlefell@ic24.net

Bedrooms: 1 double, 1 single, 1 family
Bathrooms: 3 en suite

B&B per person per night:
S £35.00–£45.00
D £22.50–£27.50

OPEN All Year except Christmas

Georgian detached house offering tasteful accommodation, in a studio and cottage with large gardens bordering Aston Stud. Good village pub. Reduction for continental breakfast.

10 P

AYLESBURY, Buckinghamshire Map ref 2C1 *Tourist Information Centre Tel: (01296) 330559*

THE OLD FORGE BARN
Ridings Way, Cublington,
Leighton Buzzard LU7 0LW
T: (01296) 681194
F: (01296) 681194
E: waples@ukonline.co.uk

Bedrooms: 1 twin
Bathrooms: 1 private

B&B per person per night:
S Max £25.00
D Max £20.00

OPEN All Year except Christmas

Converted barn in village location, close to Aylesbury, Leighton Buzzard, Milton Keynes. Restaurants and pubs serving meals nearby. Friendly welcome.

V P

Silver Award

TANAMERA

37 Bishopstone Village, Aylesbury
HP17 8SH
T: (01296) 748551
E: tanamera@macunlimited.net

B&B per person per night:
S £39.50
D £27.50

A warm welcome with owner's personal attention. Quality English breakfast, excellent accommodation, large, attractive, en suite, twin or kingsize double, TV/video, tea/coffe, central heating. Central location, good train service, interesting area, historic houses (Waddesdon Manor, Chequers), Quainton working-steam museum. Country pub in village, private parking, non-smoking.

Bedrooms: 1 double, 1 twin
Bathrooms: 2 en suite

V P €

BANBURY, Oxfordshire Map ref 2C1 *Tourist Information Centre Tel: (01295) 259855*

AVONLEA GUEST HOUSE
41 Southam Road, Banbury
OX16 2EP
T: (01295) 267837
F: (01295) 271946
E: whitforddebbie@hotmail.com

Bedrooms: 1 double, 1 twin, 1 single, 1 family
Bathrooms: 4 en suite

CC: Delta, Mastercard, Switch, Visa

B&B per person per night:
S £30.00–£35.00
D Min £22.50

A friendly, family-run guesthouse, recently refurbished. Five minutes' walk to town centre. All rooms en suite. Off-road parking.

V P

TOWN INDEX

This can be found at the back of the guide. If you know where you want to stay, the index will give you the page number listing accommodation in your chosen town, city or village.

BANBURY continued

♦♦♦

EASINGTON HOUSE

50 Oxford Road, Banbury OX16 9AN
T: (01295) 270181
F: (01295) 269527
E: enquiries@easingtonhouse.co.uk
I: www.easingtonhouse.co.uk

14thC farmhouse in pretty gardens close to town centre. Convenient for Stratford, Oxford, Cotswolds. All rooms en suite with TV, telephone, complimentary tray, toiletries. Enjoy full English breakfast including free-range eggs, British bacon and sausages, local produce used where possible, selection of cereals, juices, yoghurts. Vegetarians catered for. Private parking.

Bedrooms: 6 double, 2 twin, 3 single, 1 family, 1 suite
Bathrooms: 12 en suite

CC: Delta, Mastercard, Switch, Visa

Stay 3 nights and get a reduced price. Example: double room: £65 per night, special promotion: £60 per night.

10 P €

B&B per person per night:
S £55.00–£65.00
D £32.50–£37.50

OPEN All Year except Christmas

♦♦♦♦

THE LODGE

Main Road, Middleton Cheney, Banbury OX17 2PP
T: (01295) 710355

A charming period gatehouse recently extended to provide a comfortable and gracious haven of peace for discerning guests. We welcome you warmly and invite you to relax with all the freedom of home and the enjoyment of our delightful garden. Situated in lovely countryside one mile from M40 jct 11.

Bedrooms: 1 double, 1 twin
Bathrooms: 2 en suite

3 P

B&B per person per night:
S £35.00
D £30.00

OPEN All Year except Christmas

♦♦♦

PROSPECT HOUSE GUEST HOUSE

70 Oxford Road, Banbury OX16 9AN
T: (01295) 268749
F: (01295) 268749

Detached house standing in lovely gardens, situated on the A4260 only a few minutes' walk from Banbury Cross and Oxfordshire's newest regional shopping centre (Castle Quay). Modern en suite rooms, TV, tea and coffee, on-site parking. Conveniently situated for Blenheim Palace, Warwick Castle and Stratford-upon-Avon.

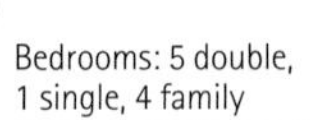

Bedrooms: 5 double, 1 single, 4 family
Bathrooms: 10 en suite

CC: Amex, Delta, Mastercard, Switch, Visa

Special weekend rates Jan-May.

P

B&B per person per night:
S £32.00–£39.50
D £20.00–£24.75

OPEN All Year except Christmas

QUALITY ASSURANCE SCHEME

Diamond ratings and awards were correct at the time of going to press but are subject to change. Please check at the time of booking.

BANBURY continued

ST MARTINS HOUSE

Warkworth, Banbury OX17 2AG
T: (01295) 712684
F: (01295) 712838

600-year-old Listed converted barn with galleried dining room. Comfortable en suite rooms with TV. Safe parking, evening meals by arrangement, French and English country cooking.

Bedrooms: 2 double
Bathrooms: 1 en suite, 1 private

Evening meal available

B&B per person per night:
S £27.50–£30.00
D £27.50–£30.00

HB per person per night:
DY £45.50–£48.00

OPEN All Year

BASINGSTOKE, Hampshire Map ref 2C2 *Tourist Information Centre Tel: (01256) 817618*

♦♦♦♦

FERNBANK HOTEL

4 Fairfields Road, Basingstoke
RG21 3DR
T: (01256) 321191
F: (01256) 461476
E: availability@fernbankhotel.co.uk
I: www.fernbankhotel.co.uk

Bedrooms: 8 double, 8 single
Bathrooms: 16 en suite

CC: Amex, Delta, Mastercard, Switch, Visa

B&B per person per night:
S £55.00–£85.00
D £33.00–£48.00

OPEN All Year except Christmas

Well-appointed bijou hotel specialising in business people. Private parking. Quiet area, five minutes to centre.

BATTLE, East Sussex Map ref 3B4 *Tourist Information Centre Tel: (01424) 773721*

♦♦♦

MOONS HILL FARM

The Green, Ninfield, Battle
TN33 9LH
T: (01424) 892645
F: (01424) 892645
E: june@ive13.fsnet.co.uk

Bedrooms: 3 double
Bathrooms: 3 en suite

B&B per person per night:
S £20.00–£25.00
D £20.00–£25.00

10-acre mixed farm. Modernised farmhouse in Ninfield village centre, in the heart of '1066' country. A warm welcome and Sussex home cooking. Pub opposite. Large car park.

BEACONSFIELD, Buckinghamshire Map ref 2C2

HIGHCLERE FARM

Newbarn Lane, Seer Green, Beaconsfield
HP9 2QZ
T: (01494) 875665
F: (01494) 875238

Comfortable, family-run annexed farm accommodation with all rooms en suite. Two family rooms available. Quiet location, yet within easy reach of Windsor (12 miles) and London.

Bedrooms: 6 double, 1 single, 2 family
Bathrooms: 9 en suite

CC: Amex, Delta, Diners, Mastercard, Switch, Visa

B&B per person per night:
S £45.00–£48.00
D £32.50–£35.00

GOLD & SILVER AWARDS

These exclusive VisitBritain awards are given to establishments achieving the highest levels of quality and service. Further information can be found at the front of the guide. An index to all accommodation achieving these awards are at the back of this guide.

BEAULIEU, Hampshire Map ref 2C3

DALE FARM HOUSE

Manor Road, Applemore Hill, Dibden, Southampton SO45 5TJ
T: (023) 8084 9632
F: (023) 8084 0285
E: info@dalefarmhouse.co.uk
I: www.dalefarmhouse.co.uk

B&B per person per night:
S £27.00–£32.00
D £21.00–£28.00

OPEN All Year

Beautiful 18thC converted farmhouse in secluded wooded setting with direct access for walks or cycling. Peaceful garden in which to unwind and a bird-watcher's paradise. Excellent food to satisfy your appetite. Barbecues on request. Spoil yourself at this BBC holiday programme-featured bed and breakfast.

Bedrooms: 2 double, 1 twin, 1 single, 1 family
Bathrooms: 4 en suite

Evening meal available

10% discount for Christmas breaks on a room-only basis. 3 for 2 weekend breaks Oct-Mar (excl Bank Holidays).

BEMBRIDGE, Isle of Wight Map ref 2C3

Silver Award

SEA CHANGE

22 Beachfield Road, Bembridge PO35 5TN
T: (01983) 875558
F: (01983) 875667
E: seachangewight@aol.com
I: www.wightonline.co.uk/accommodation/bandb/seachange.html

B&B per person per night:
S £28.00–£32.00
D £24.00–£28.00

Superbly located home in quiet, private road 100 metres from beautiful unspoilt beach, pub/restaurant and beach cafe. All rooms en suite with tea and coffee, TV, fridge and hairdryer. 15-20 minutes' walk to harbour, windmill, village centre shops, pubs and restaurants. Lovely walks and ideal touring base for all island attractions.

Bedrooms: 2 double, 1 twin
Bathrooms: 3 en suite

BERE REGIS, Dorset Map ref 2B3

Rating Applied For

THE ROYAL OAK

West Street, Bere Regis, Wareham BH20 7HQ
T: (01929) 471203
F: (01929) 471203
E: lizjayne@saintives82.fsnet.co.uk
I: www.theroyaloakhotel.co.uk

B&B per person per night:
S £40.00–£90.00
D £40.00–£90.00

OPEN All Year

16thC hotel, where Thomas Hardy once stayed. Pretty location at the edge of historic village. Beautifully appointed, en suite rooms with colour TV, tea/coffee facilities and hairdryer. Spacious dining room offering wide variety of home-cooked specialities. Attractive, walled garden and child-safe garden. Relaxed atmosphere, friendly service.

Bedrooms: 2 double, 1 twin, 1 single, 1 family
Bathrooms: 5 en suite

Evening meal available
CC: Amex, Delta, Mastercard, Switch, Visa

CHECK THE MAPS

The colour maps at the front of this guide show all the cities, towns and villages for which you will find accommodation entries. Refer to the town index to find the page on which they are listed.

BETHERSDEN, Kent Map ref 3B4

◆◆◆

THE COACH HOUSE

Oakmead Farm, Bethersden,
Ashford TN26 3DU
T: (01233) 820583
F: (01233) 820583

Bedrooms: 3 double
Bathrooms: 2 en suite,
1 private

Comfortable family home in five acres of garden and paddocks. One mile from village. Central for ferries, Channel Tunnel, Eurostar, Canterbury, Leeds Castle, Sissinghurst.

P

B&B per person per night:
S £25.00
D £20.00

OPEN All Year except Christmas

BICESTER, Oxfordshire Map ref 2C1 *Tourist Information Centre Tel: (01869) 369055*

HOME FARM

Mansmore Lane,
Charlton on Otmoor, Kidlington
OX5 2US
T: (01865) 331267
F: (01865) 331267
E: triciahomefarm@aol.com

Bedrooms: 1 twin,
1 single

Modern farmhouse on sheep and arable farm. In quiet location 0.5 miles from village. Pets welcome. Stabling available. Central for Bicester, Woodstock, Oxford and Thame.

P

B&B per person per night:
S £20.00–£30.00
D £20.00–£30.00

OPEN All Year

BIDDENDEN, Kent Map ref 3B4

HERON COTTAGE

Biddenden, Ashford TN27 8HH
T: (01580) 291358

Bedrooms: 3 double,
2 twin, 1 family
Bathrooms: 5 en suite

Evening meal available

Peacefully set in unspoilt countryside. Walled garden with pond for fishing and animals to visit. Situated between the historic village of Biddenden and Sissinghurst Castle.

P

B&B per person per night:
S £30.00–£40.00
D £25.00–£27.50

HB per person per night:
DY £45.00–£55.00

BLADBEAN, Kent Map ref 3B4

MOLEHILLS

Bladbean, Canterbury CT4 6LU
T: (01303) 840051
E: molehills84@hotmail.com

The house, in large gardens, is situated in a peaceful hamlet within the beautiful Elham Valley. We are within easy reach of Canterbury and the Channel terminals. We produce home-grown vegetables and excellent home cooking. Our comfortable accommodation includes ground floor bedrooms, sitting room with woodburning stove and conservatory.

Bedrooms: 1 double,
1 twin
Bathrooms: 2 en suite

Evening meal available

3 P €

B&B per person per night:
S £25.00–£30.00
D £22.50–£25.00

HB per person per night:
DY £28.50–£42.00

OPEN All Year except Christmas

QUALITY ASSURANCE SCHEME

For an explanation of the quality and facilities represented by the Diamonds please refer to the front of this guide. A more detailed explanation can be found in the information pages at the back.

BLANDFORD FORUM, Dorset Map ref 2B3 *Tourist Information Centre Tel: (01258) 454770*

◆◆◆◆◆ Silver Award

FARNHAM FARM HOUSE

Farnham, Blandford Forum DT11 8DG
T: (01725) 516254
F: (01725) 516306
E: info@farnhamfarmhouse.co.uk
I: www.farnhamfarmhouse.co.uk

A private drive leads to this picturesque 19thC farmhouse nestling in the secluded, rolling slopes of the Cranborne Chase, having flagstone floors, open fires and an acre of tranquil garden. A comfortable and relaxing base, enhanced by the addition of the Sarpenela Treatment Room offering therapeutic massage and holistic therapies.

Bedrooms: 2 double, 1 twin
Bathrooms: 3 en suite

B&B per person per night:
S £40.00–£50.00
D £25.00–£30.00

OPEN All Year except Christmas

◆◆◆◆ Silver Award

MEADOW HOUSE
Tarrant Hinton, Blandford Forum DT11 8JG
T: (01258) 830498
F: (01258) 830498

Bedrooms: 1 double, 1 single, 1 family

A 17th-18thC brick and flint farmhouse set in 4.5 acres. A warm welcome in peaceful, comfortable, family home. Ideal base for touring.

B&B per person per night:
S £22.50–£25.00
D £22.50–£25.00

OPEN All Year except Christmas

BLOXHAM, Oxfordshire Map ref 2C1

◆◆◆◆

ROWAN COURT
Milton Road, Bloxham, Banbury OX15 4HD
T: (01295) 722566
F: (01295) 722566
E: enquiries@rowancourt.co.uk
I: www.rowancourt.com

Bedrooms: 2 double
Bathrooms: 1 en suite, 1 private

A friendly welcome to a traditional family home in a village setting. Comfortable rooms in classic English cottage style. Conservatory and beautiful gardens.

P €

B&B per person per night:
S £25.00
D £25.00

HB per person per night:
DY £25.00

OPEN All Year except Christmas

BOGNOR REGIS, West Sussex Map ref 2C3 *Tourist Information Centre Tel: (01243) 823140*

◆◆◆◆

ALDERWASLEY COTTAGE

Off West Street, Bognor Regis PO21 1XH
T: (01243) 821339
E: alderwasley@btinternet.com

Lovely old cottage set in a pretty, walled garden on a private road close to the beach. Adjacent, off-road parking. All our comfortable rooms overlook the sea. Book-lined sitting room for guests, warmed by a log fire on chilly evenings. Ideal base for exploring beautiful West Sussex and Hampshire.

Bedrooms: 1 double, 1 twin
Bathrooms: 1 en suite, 1 private

B&B per person per night:
S £30.00–£40.00
D £25.00–£30.00

OPEN All Year

SPECIAL BREAKS

Many establishments offer special promotions and themed breaks. These are highlighted in red. (All such offers are subject to availability.)

BOGNOR REGIS continued

♦♦♦

JUBILEE GUEST HOUSE
5 Gloucester Road, Bognor Regis
PO21 1NU
T: (01243) 863016
F: (01243) 868017
E: jubileeguesthouse@breathemail.net
I: www.jubileeguesthouse.com

Bedrooms: 1 double, 2 single, 3 family
Bathrooms: 2 en suite

CC: Delta, Mastercard, Switch, Visa

B&B per person per night:
S £25.00–£40.00
D £25.00–£40.00

OPEN All Year except Christmas

Family-run business, 75 yards from seafront and beach. Ideal for visiting 'Butlin's family entertainment resort', Chichester, Goodwood, Fontwell, Arundel, Portsmouth and IOW.

P €

♦♦♦

REGIS LODGE
3 Gloucester Road, Bognor Regis
PO21 1NU
T: (01243) 827110
F: (01243) 827110
E: frank@regislodge.fsbusiness.co.uk
I: www.regislodge.co.uk

Bedrooms: 2 double, 2 twin, 1 single, 6 family
Bathrooms: 11 en suite

B&B per person per night:
S £30.00–£40.00
D £25.00–£30.00

OPEN All Year

Our guesthouse offers comfortable rooms with private facilities. Close to town centre and its amenities, yet only 40 metres from beach, opposite Southcoast World.

5 P €

BONCHURCH, Isle of Wight Map ref 2C3

THE LAKE HOTEL

Shore Road, Bonchurch, Ventnor PO38 1RF
T: (01983) 852613
F: (01983) 852613
E: enquiries@lakehotel.co.uk
I: www.lakehotel.co.uk

B&B per person per night:
S £33.00–£63.00
D £28.00–£35.00

HB per person per night:
DY £38.00–£45.00

OPEN All Year except Christmas

Charming country-house hotel in two acres of beautiful gardens. Located on the seaward side of Bonchurch pond in the old world village of Bonchurch. Run by the same family for over 35 years. We are confident of offering you the best-value accommodation and food on our beautiful island.

Bedrooms: 7 double, 5 twin, 1 single, 7 family
Bathrooms: 20 en suite

Evening meal available

4-night special break including breakfast, dinner and car ferry from any port £160 inclusive.

3 P €

BOSCOMBE, Dorset Map ref 2B3

AU-LEVANT HOTEL
15 Westby Road, Boscombe, Bournemouth BH5 1HA
T: (01202) 394884

Bedrooms: 3 double, 2 twin, 3 single, 1 family
Bathrooms: 4 en suite

Evening meal available

B&B per person per night:
S £16.00–£36.00
D £17.50–£22.50

OPEN All Year except Christmas

Family run, home cooking, licensed bar, tea/coffee-making facilities, en suite rooms. Near sea, shops, local transport. Bournemouth Airport three miles.

3 P

BOTOLPH CLAYDON, Buckinghamshire Map ref 2C1

BOTOLPH FARMHOUSE
Botyl Road, Botolph Claydon, Buckingham MK18 2LR
T: (01296) 712640
F: (01296) 714806
E: clive@tcsgroup.co.uk
I: www.botolphfarm.co.uk

Bedrooms: 1 double, 1 single
Bathrooms: 1 en suite

B&B per person per night:
S £25.00
D £23.00–£28.00

OPEN All Year except Christmas

Listed Georgian farmhouse offering self-contained accommodation. Own door to sitting/dining room. TV, underfloor heating. Provisions for self-catering breakfast. Cooked breakfast on request.

5 P

QUALITY ASSURANCE SCHEME
Diamond ratings and awards are explained at the back of this guide.

BOURNEMOUTH, Dorset Map ref 2B3

◆◆◆◆ Silver Award

ALEXANDER LODGE HOTEL

21 Southern Road, Southbourne, Bournemouth BH6 3SR
T: (01202) 421662
F: (01202) 421662
E: alexanderlodge@yahoo.com
I: www.s-h-systems.co.uk/a28852.html

Delightful small hotel offering a friendly welcome, in quiet Bournemouth suburb, 200 yards from Blue Flag sandy beach, cliff-top and lift. Excellent home-cooked meals, comfortable en suite rooms, licensed bar, parking. Low-season specials! Ideal for holidays, short breaks and stop-overs. Perfect for visiting Christchurch, New Forest, Bournemouth and Dorset.

Bedrooms: 3 double, 1 twin, 2 family
Bathrooms: 6 en suite

Evening meal available
CC: Delta, Mastercard, Switch, Visa

3-night specials available from Sep-Jun. Prices from £62pp B&B, £90pp DB&B.

B&B per person per night:
D £21.00–£29.00

HB per person per night:
DY £31.00–£41.00

OPEN All Year except Christmas

◆◆◆

CHELSEA HOTEL
32 St Swithuns Road, East Cliff, Bournemouth BH1 3RH
T: (01202) 290111
F: (01202) 290111
E: info@thechelseahotel.co.uk
I: www.thechelseahotel.co.uk

Bedrooms: 2 double, 2 twin, 1 single, 5 family
Bathrooms: 7 en suite

CC: Amex, Delta, Mastercard, Switch, Visa

Small, friendly, family-run hotel three minutes from train, coach and bus stations. Ten minutes from town centre and all other amenities. Group bookings taken.

B&B per person per night:
S £18.00–£35.00
D £18.00–£35.00

OPEN All Year

◆◆◆

DENEWOOD HOTEL
1 Percy Road, Boscombe, Bournemouth BH5 1JE
T: (01202) 394493
F: (01202) 391155
E: peteer@denewood.co.uk
I: www.denewood.co.uk

Bedrooms: 3 double, 2 twin, 2 single, 3 family, 1 suite
Bathrooms: 10 en suite

CC: Amex, Delta, Diners, Mastercard, Switch, Visa

Friendly family hotel ideally situated to take advantage of the famous Bournemouth beaches. On-site parking, varied breakfasts served, health and beauty centre.

B&B per person per night:
S £22.50–£28.00
D £22.50–£28.00

OPEN All Year except Christmas

◆◆◆◆

FAIRMOUNT HOTEL

15 Priory Road, West Cliff, Bournemouth BH2 5DF
T: (01202) 551105
F: (01202) 553210
E: stay@fairmounthotel.co.uk
I: www.fairmounthotel.co.uk

Clean, comfortable, family-run hotel within three minutes of beach, pier, conference centre, main shopping centre and leisure facilities. All rooms with private facilities. Large, secure car/boat park. Renowned hospitality.

Bedrooms: 9 double, 4 single, 7 family
Bathrooms: 19 en suite, 1 private

Evening meal available
CC: Amex, Delta, Mastercard, Switch, Visa

Discounts available at many local tourist attractions. 3 nights for the price of 2, Oct-Mar (excl Christmas and New Year).

B&B per person per night:
S £27.50–£39.00
D £27.50–£40.00

HB per person per night:
DY £38.00–£50.00

OPEN All Year except Christmas

MAP REFERENCES The map references refer to the colour maps at the front of this guide. The first figure is the map number; the letter and figure which follow indicate the grid reference on the map.

BOURNEMOUTH continued

♦♦♦♦

INVERNESS HOTEL

26 Tregonwell Road, West Cliff, Bournemouth BH2 5NS
T: (01202) 554968
F: (01202) 294197
E: inverness.hotel@btinternet.com
I: www.invernesshotel.net

Located on the West Cliff, a short walk from the shops, restaurants, beaches and Bournemouth International Centre. Stylish, en suite rooms. We pride ourselves in offering good food and service. Half board available during high season and by arrangement at other times. Car park. Contact Avril & Paul Holdaway for colour brochure.

Bedrooms: 6 double, 1 twin, 1 single, 2 family
Bathrooms: 9 en suite, 1 private

Evening meal available
CC: Delta, Mastercard, Switch, Visa

Nov-Mar: Bargain weekends - 3 nights for price of 2. 10% off mid-week breaks of 3 nights or more - quote WTSG.

B&B per person per night:
S £24.00–£36.00
D £24.00–£36.00

HB per person per night:
DY £36.00–£48.00

OPEN All Year except Christmas

♦♦♦♦ Silver Award

MAYFIELD GUEST HOUSE

46 Frances Road, Knyveton Gardens, Bournemouth BH1 3SA
T: (01202) 551839
F: (01202) 551839
E: accom@mayfieldguesthouse.com
I: www.mayfieldguesthouse.com

Bedrooms: 4 double, 2 twin, 1 single, 1 family
Bathrooms: 7 en suite, 1 private

Evening meal available

B&B per person per night:
S £23.00–£26.00
D £23.00–£26.00

HB per person per night:
DY £30.00–£33.00

Ideally situated for all amenities, opposite Knyveton Gardens with bowling greens, sensory garden, tennis courts. Handy for rail/coach stations, sea, shops and BIC.

6 P

♦♦♦♦

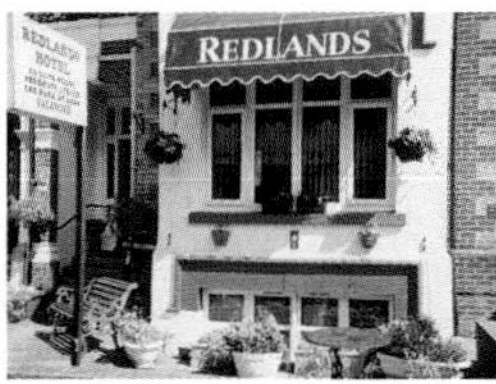

REDLANDS HOTEL

79 St Michaels Road, West Cliff, Bournemouth BH2 5DR
T: (01202) 553714
E: enquiries@redlandshotel.co.uk
I: www.redlandshotel.co.uk

A charming Victorian guesthouse in Bournemouth town centre, close to the sea, shops and theatres. All rooms are to a high standard, mostly en suite. Tea/coffee tray provided. Car parking at rear for guests. Ideal for families, couples, reps and delegates.

Bedrooms: 5 double, 2 twin, 1 single, 3 family
Bathrooms: 11 en suite

CC: Amex, Delta, Mastercard, Switch, Visa

4-night stays: £22-£30.

B&B per person per night:
S £24.00–£32.00
D £24.00–£32.00

OPEN All Year

P

♦♦♦

SOUTHERNHAY HOTEL

42 Alum Chine Road, Westbourne, Bournemouth BH4 8DX
T: (01202) 761251
F: (01202) 761251
E: enquiries@southernhayhotel.co.uk
I: www.southernhayhotel.co.uk

Bedrooms: 3 double, 1 single, 2 family
Bathrooms: 4 en suite

B&B per person per night:
S £18.00–£25.00
D £20.00–£25.00

OPEN All Year

High-standard accommodation, near beach, restaurants and shops. Full English breakfast, rooms with colour TV, radio-alarm, hairdryer and tea/coffee facilities. Large car park.

P €

VISITOR ATTRACTIONS For ideas on places to visit refer to the introduction at the beginning of this section. Look out too for the VisitBritain Quality Assured Visitor Attraction signs.

BOURNEMOUTH continued

♦♦♦♦

THE VENTURA HOTEL
1 Herbert Road, Bournemouth
BH4 8HD
T: (01202) 761265
F: (01202) 757673
E: enquiries@venturahotel.co.uk
I: www.venturahotel.co.uk

Bedrooms: 6 double, 2 family
Bathrooms: 8 en suite

CC: Delta, Mastercard, Switch, Visa

B&B per person per night:
S £35.00–£39.00
D £25.00–£29.00

OPEN All Year except Christmas

Small, luxury bed and breakfast hotel in Alum Chine, 10 minutes' walk from beach. Stylish, en suite rooms. Delicious breakfasts served with homemade bread and preserves.

5 P

THE WOODLANDS HOTEL

28 Percy Road, Boscombe Manor,
Bournemouth BH5 1JG
T: (01202) 396499
F: (01202) 396499
E: thewoodlandshotel@tinyworld.co.uk
I: www.the-woodlands-hotel.co.uk

The Woodlands is a non-smoking, family-run, licensed hotel, very close to Blue Flag-awarded beaches and town centre. We offer a high standard of rooms, food and service. All rooms have colour TV, tea and coffee facilities. Off-road parking. Open all year. Terry and Sandra offer you a warm welcome. 4-Poster rooms.

Bedrooms: 4 double, 1 twin, 3 single, 2 family
Bathrooms: 4 en suite, 1 private

Evening meal available

Golfing breaks: 2 for 1.

B&B per person per night:
S £20.00–£26.00
D £23.00–£30.00

HB per person per night:
DY £29.00–£36.00

OPEN All Year except Christmas

P €

BOXLEY, Kent Map ref 3B3

BARN COTTAGE
Harbourland, Boxley, Maidstone
ME14 3DN
T: (01622) 675891
F: (01622) 675891

Bedrooms: 2 double
Bathrooms: 2 en suite

Evening meal available

B&B per person per night:
S Min £25.00
D Min £25.00

OPEN All Year except Christmas

16thC converted barn in lovely location in Boxley Valley overlooking North Downs. Close to M20, M2, Rochester, Leeds Castle. Friendly and comfortable.

5 P

BRACKNELL, Berkshire Map ref 2C2

ELIZABETH HOUSE HOTEL LTD

Rounds Hill, Wokingham Road, Bracknell
RG42 1PB
T: (01344) 868480
F: (01344) 648453
E: rooms@elizabeth-house.freeserve.co.uk
I: www.elizabeth-house.freeserve.co.uk

We pride ourselves on our standards of care, hygiene and comfort. You are always sure of a warm welcome as well as a comfortable stay. Our breakfast is a real treat and very popular among guests' comments.

Bedrooms: 5 double, 2 single, 1 family
Bathrooms: 8 en suite

CC: Amex, Delta, Mastercard, Switch, Visa

Weekend rates for Fri/Sat/Sun nights – please enquire by telephone. Weddings, group rates available.

B&B per person per night:
S £50.00–£75.00
D £27.50–£40.00

OPEN All Year except Christmas

10 P €

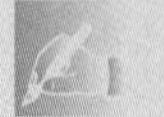

CONFIRM YOUR BOOKING
You are advised to confirm your booking in writing.

BRIGHSTONE, Isle of Wight Map ref 2C3

CHILTON FARM

Chilton Lane, Brighstone, Newport
PO30 4DS
T: (01983) 740338
F: (01983) 741370
E: info@chiltonfarm.co.uk
I: www.chiltonfarm.co.uk

Bedrooms: 1 double
Bathrooms: 1 en suite

3-night stay from Feb-Jun and Sep-Dec: £165 for 2 including car crossing from Southampton.

A warm welcome assured on our 800-acre working farm. All rooms en suite in separate accommodation in courtyard behind the main farmhouse (pictured). Breakfast in farmhouse, in lovely old brew-house dining room. Two tennis courts, large garden, close to sea.

B&B per person per night:
S £30.00–£35.00
D £25.00

BRIGHTON & HOVE, East Sussex Map ref 2D3

♦♦♦♦

AINSLEY HOUSE HOTEL

28 New Steine, Brighton BN2 1PD
T: (01273) 605310
F: (01273) 688604
E: ahhotel@fastnet.co.uk
I: www.ainsleyhotel.co.uk

Bedrooms: 7 double, 3 single
Bathrooms: 8 en suite

CC: Amex, Delta, Diners, Mastercard, Switch, Visa

Charming, comfortable, family-run, non-smoking hotel. Situated on a pretty garden square overlooking the sea. Close to all amenities. Extensive breakfast menu, warm welcome guaranteed.

B&B per person per night:
S £28.00–£38.00
D £27.50–£45.00

OPEN All Year except Christmas

♦♦♦♦

AMBASSADOR HOTEL

22 New Steine, Marine Parade, Brighton
BN2 1PD
T: (01273) 676869
F: (01273) 689988
E: ambassadorhoteluk@hotmail.com
I: www.ambassadorhotelbrighton.com

Bedrooms: 7 double, 7 single, 9 family
Bathrooms: 23 en suite

CC: Amex, Delta, Diners, Mastercard, Switch, Visa

Family-run, licensed hotel in a seafront garden square, overlooking the sea and Palace Pier. Close to Royal Pavilion, shops, conference halls and entertainments. All rooms en suite with colour TV, direct-dial telephone, radio, hospitality tray. Ground floor and no-smoking rooms available.

B&B per person per night:
S £35.00–£45.00
D £34.00–£45.00

OPEN All Year except Christmas

♦♦♦

ATLANTIC HOTEL

16 Marine Parade, Brighton
BN2 1TL
T: (01273) 695944
F: (01273) 694944

Bedrooms: 6 double, 1 single, 3 family
Bathrooms: 10 en suite

Evening meal available
CC: Amex, Diners, Mastercard, Switch, Visa

Attractive family-run hotel facing seafront. Sea Life Centre, Palace Pier, historic Royal Pavilion and famous Lanes are just down the road. Brighton Centre nearby.

B&B per person per night:
S £25.00–£30.00
D £25.00–£30.00

OPEN All Year

♦♦♦♦

BRIGHTSIDE

4 Shirley Road, Hove, Brighton
BN3 6NN
T: (01273) 552557
F: (01273) 552557
E: mary.nimmo1@btopenworld.com

Bedrooms: 1 double, 1 single

A warm welcome awaits at this small B&B. Easy, free parking. Light, comfortable, pretty English-style bedrooms overlooking garden. Delicious English breakfast. Quiet location.

B&B per person per night:
S £30.00–£35.00
D £30.00–£35.00

OPEN All Year except Christmas

BRIGHTON & HOVE continued

♦♦♦♦

FYFIELD HOUSE

26 New Steine, Brighton BN2 1PD
T: (01273) 602770
F: (01273) 602770
E: fyfield@aol.com
I: www.fyfieldhotelbrighton.com

Bedrooms: 5 double, 2 twin, 2 single, 1 family
Bathrooms: 8 en suite

CC: Delta, Diners, Mastercard, Switch, Visa

B&B per person per night:
S £25.00–£50.00
D £32.50–£60.00

OPEN All Year

Excellent, clean, private hotel, central to all attractions in and out of town. All rooms tastefully decorated, some luxury theme rooms. Superb breakfast menu, including vegetarian.

♦♦♦

RUSSELL GUEST HOUSE

19 Russell Square, Brighton
BN1 2EE
T: (01273) 327969
F: (01273) 821535
E: russell.brighton@btinternet.com
I: www.smoothhound.co.uk/hotels/russellgh

Bedrooms: 3 double, 2 twin, 3 family
Bathrooms: 8 en suite

CC: Amex, Delta, Mastercard, Switch, Visa

B&B per person per night:
S £40.00–£45.00
D £30.00–£35.00

OPEN All Year except Christmas

Five-storey town-centre guesthouse in pleasant garden square. Close to the Brighton Centre, seafront and main shopping area. Unrestricted access. Theatres, cinemas and nightclubs all nearby.

♦♦

SANDPIPER GUEST HOUSE

11 Russell Square, Brighton
BN1 2EE
T: (01273) 328202
F: (01273) 329974
E: sandpiper@brighton.co.uk

Bedrooms: 2 double, 3 single, 1 family

CC: Amex, Delta, Mastercard, Switch, Visa

B&B per person per night:
S £18.00–£32.00
D £18.00–£32.00

OPEN All Year

Newly refurbished guesthouse, two minutes from conference centre, shopping area, leisure centres and seafront. All rooms have central heating, colour TV, tea/coffee. Unrestricted access.

BRIZE NORTON, Oxfordshire Map ref 2C1

THE PRIORY MANOR FARM

Manor Road, Brize Norton OX18 3NA
T: (01993) 843062
F: (01993) 843062
E: mail@thepriorymanor.co.uk
I: www.thepriorymanor.co.uk

Beautiful character house in natural stone. Set in 0.75 acres of beautiful gardens with ample parking. Comfortable rooms with tea/coffee-making facilities and colour TV. Close to many Cotswold attractions, Burford, Blenheim Palace, Oxford and golf. Ground floor and family, twin or single accommodation available.

Bedrooms: 3 double
Bathrooms: 2 en suite, 1 private

Evening meal by arrangement. Prices for longer-stay B&B negotiable. Open all year round.

B&B per person per night:
S £30.00–£35.00
D £30.00–£35.00

HB per person per night:
DY £30.00–£35.00

OPEN All Year except Christmas

COUNTRY CODE Always follow the Country Code · Enjoy the countryside and respect its life and work · Guard against all risk of fire · Fasten all gates · Keep your dogs under close control · Keep to public paths across farmland · Use gates and stiles to cross fences, hedges and walls · Leave livestock, crops and machinery alone · Take your litter home · Help to keep all water clean · Protect wildlife, plants and trees · Take special care on country roads · Make no unnecessary noise

BROADSTAIRS, Kent Map ref 3C3 *Tourist Information Centre Tel: (01843) 583333/583334*

BAY TREE HOTEL

12 Eastern Esplanade, Broadstairs
CT10 1DR
T: (01843) 862502
F: (01843) 860589

B&B per person per night:
S £32.00–£36.00
D £32.00–£36.00

HB per person per night:
DY £49.00–£53.00

OPEN All Year except Christmas

Situated on the lovely Eastern Esplanade overlooking Stone Bay, the hotel enjoys panoramic sea views across the English Channel. Minutes from the town centre and sandy beaches. A warm welcome awaits you at this family-run hotel.

Bedrooms: 9 double, 1 single
Bathrooms: 10 en suite

Evening meal available
CC: Delta, Mastercard, Switch, Visa

10 V P

◆◆◆◆◆
Silver Award

THE VICTORIA

23 Victoria Parade, Broadstairs CT10 1QL
T: (01843) 871010
F: (01843) 860888
E: mullin@thevictoriabroadstairs.co.uk
I: www.thevictoriabroadstairs.co.uk

B&B per person per night:
S £30.00–£80.00
D £35.00–£50.00

OPEN All Year

A late-Victorian house lovingly restored to retain its original elegance. Rooms are individually decorated, featuring original fireplaces, quality furnishings and sparkling, en suite bathrooms. Sea-facing rooms have panoramic views of Broadstairs harbour. Situated in the heart of this charming Dickensian town, The Victoria is a memorable place to stay.

Bedrooms: 6 double
Bathrooms: 6 en suite

CC: Mastercard, Visa

Off-peak offers. Sun specials: £50 per room (2 sharing).

12 V P €

BROCKENHURST, Hampshire Map ref 2C3

GOLDENHAYES

9 Chestnut Road, Brockenhurst
SO42 7RF
T: (01590) 623743

Bedrooms: 1 double

B&B per person per night:
S £18.00–£24.00
D £15.00–£20.00

OPEN All Year

Single-storey, owner-occupied home, in central but quiet situation. Close to village, station and open forest. Large garden.

V P €

BURFORD, Oxfordshire Map ref 2B1 *Tourist Information Centre Tel: (01993) 823558*

Silver Award

BARLEY PARK

Shilton Road, Burford, Oxford
OX18 4PD
T: (01993) 823573
F: (01993) 824220
E: barley_park@hotmail.com
I: www.burford-bed-and-breakfast.co.uk

Bedrooms: 1 double
Bathrooms: 1 en suite

B&B per person per night:
S £36.00–£40.00
D £27.00–£30.00

OPEN All Year except Christmas

Immaculate, self-contained annexe with king-size bed, bathroom, fully-equipped dining kitchen and living room. Excellent breakfast provided with local and/or organic produce.

V P €

IMPORTANT NOTE Information on accommodation listed in this guide has been supplied by the proprietors. As changes may occur you are advised to check details at the time of booking.

BURFORD continued

♦♦♦

THE HIGHWAY

117 High Street, Burford, Oxford OX18 4RG
T: (01993) 822136
F: (01993) 824740
E: rbx20@dial.pipex.com
I: www.oxlink.co.uk/burford

B&B per person per night:
S £36.00–£55.00
D £27.50–£35.00

OPEN All Year

Built circa 1520, The Highway was old when Elizabeth I was on the throne. Today this beamed, medieval, Cotswold guesthouse offers en suite bedrooms with TV, telephone, hairdryer etc. Perfect base for touring the Cotswolds. Also incorporating the highly acclaimed needlecraft centre.

Bedrooms: 9 double, 2 family
Bathrooms: 9 en suite

CC: Amex, Delta, Diners, Mastercard, Switch, Visa

♦♦♦

ST WINNOW
160 The Hill, Burford, Oxford
OX18 4QY
T: (01993) 823843
E: b&b@stwinnow.com
I: www.stwinnow.com

Bedrooms: 2 double, 1 twin
Bathrooms: 1 en suite

B&B per person per night:
S £30.00–£40.00
D £25.00–£30.00

OPEN All Year

Grade II Listed, 16thC, Cotswold house above the historic high street. Close to restaurants and shops. Garden and parking at rear. Organic/special diets provided.

P

CANTERBURY, Kent Map ref 3B3 *Tourist Information Centre Tel: (01227) 378100*

♦♦♦

ALICANTE GUEST HOUSE

4 Roper Road, Canterbury CT2 7EH
T: (01227) 766277
F: (01227) 766277

B&B per person per night:
S £30.00–£35.00
D £25.00–£27.50

OPEN All Year

A warm welcome awaits at our attractive Victorian guesthouse situated near West Station. The cathedral, Marlow Theatre and a good selection of restaurants and bars close by. Free parking vouchers.

Bedrooms: 5 double, 1 single, 1 family
Bathrooms: 6 en suite, 1 private

€

♦♦♦

CATHEDRAL GATE HOTEL

36 Burgate, Canterbury CT1 2HA
T: (01227) 464381
F: (01227) 462800
E: cgate@cgate.demon.co.uk
I: www.cathgate.co.uk

B&B per person per night:
S £25.00–£60.00
D £24.00–£45.00

OPEN All Year

Pilgrims slept here! This 1438 building, with massive beams, sloping floors and low doorways, offers modern comfort and is centrally situated at the main cathedral gateway. Our rooms have telephone, TV, welcome tray. Quiet lounge, bar and home-cooked meals in our bow-window dining room. Continental breakfast included, cooked breakfast extra.

Bedrooms: 9 double, 7 twin, 6 single, 5 family
Bathrooms: 12 en suite

Evening meal available
CC: Amex, Delta, Diners, Mastercard, Switch, Visa

Special DB&B breaks (full English breakfast), minimum 2 nights.

CHAUCER LODGE

62 New Dover Road, Canterbury CT1 3DT
T: (01227) 459141
F: (01227) 459141
E: wchaucerldg@aol.com
I: www.thechaucerlodge.co.uk

B&B per person per night:
S £25.00–£30.00
D £21.00–£26.00

OPEN All Year

Alistair and Maria Wilson extend a very warm welcome to their family-run guesthouse. The highest standards of cleanliness and service are provided in a friendly and relaxed atmosphere. Large, well-appointed, quiet, elegantly decorated en suite bedrooms. Ideally situated close to city centre, cathedral, bus, coach and railway station.

Bedrooms: 3 double, 2 twin, 2 single, 2 family
Bathrooms: 9 en suite

Evening meal available
CC: Delta, Mastercard, Visa

Discounts for 3 nights Nov-Mar (excl Christmas and New Year).

P €

♦♦♦♦
Silver Award

CLARE-ELLEN GUEST HOUSE

9 Victoria Road, Wincheap, Canterbury CT1 3SG
T: (01227) 760205
F: (01227) 784482
E: loraine.williams@clareellenguesthouse.co.uk
I: www.clareellenguesthouse.co.uk

B&B per person per night:
S £29.00–£32.00
D £25.00–£30.00

OPEN All Year

A warm welcome and bed and breakfast in style. Large, quiet, elegant, en suite rooms all with colour TV, clock-radio, hairdryer and tea/coffee-making facilities. Full English breakfast. Vegetarian and special diets on request. Six minutes' walk to city centre, five minutes to Canterbury East train station. Car park/garage available.

Bedrooms: 2 double, 1 single, 2 family
Bathrooms: 5 en suite

CC: Delta, Mastercard, Switch, Visa

Discounts for 2/3-night stay Nov-Mar (excl Christmas and New Year).

P

♦♦♦♦

HORNBEAMS

Jesses Hill, Kingston, Canterbury CT4 6JD
T: (01227) 830119
F: (01227) 830119
E: b&b@hornbeams.co.uk
I: www.hornbeams.co.uk

B&B per person per night:
S £35.00–£45.00
D £30.00–£35.00

OPEN All Year except Christmas

Rolling hills and woodland, long views over luscious Kent, and a lovely garden. Hornbeams is an idylic place to stay, the ultimate escapism, yet near to local town and historical landmarks. Canterbury seven miles, Dover 10 miles, Channel Tunnel 20 minutes. Good private parking.

Bedrooms: 1 double, 1 twin
Bathrooms: 1 en suite, 1 private

Evening meal available

P

CANTERBURY continued

♦♦♦♦♦
Gold Award

MAGNOLIA HOUSE

36 St Dunstans Terrace, Canterbury CT2 8AX
T: (01227) 765121
F: (01227) 765121
E: magnolia_house_canterbury@yahoo.com
I: http://freespace.virgin.net/magnolia.canterbury

B&B per person per night:
S £48.00–£65.00
D £42.50–£62.50

OPEN All Year

Charming, late-Georgian house in quiet residential street, a 10-minute stroll from the city centre. Bedrooms, individually co-ordinated, have every facility for an enjoyable stay. Varied breakfasts are served overlooking the attractive walled garden, where you are welcome to relax after a busy day's sightseeing. Evening meals available November to February by prior arrangement.

Bedrooms: 5 double, 1 single, 1 suite
Bathrooms: 6 en suite

Evening meal available
CC: Amex, Delta, Diners, Mastercard, Switch, Visa

12 P

♦♦♦♦

THE WHITE HOUSE

6 St Peters Lane, Canterbury CT1 2BP
T: (01227) 761836
E: whwelcome@aol.com
I: www.smoothhound.co.uk/hotels/thewhitehouse/html

B&B per person per night:
S £35.00–£40.00
D £27.50–£30.00

OPEN All Year

Regency house situated in quiet location within city walls by the Marlowe Theatre. Superior family-run accommodation, all rooms en suite. Two minutes' walk to a charming mix of shops, restaurants, pretty parks and rivers. Cathedral and other major attractions also close by. Excellent English or vegetarian breakfast.

Bedrooms: 5 double, 1 twin, 1 single, 2 family
Bathrooms: 9 en suite

3 nights for the price of 2 (excl Christmas and New Year) Nov-Mar.

P

♦♦♦♦
Silver Award

YORKE LODGE HOTEL

50 London Road, Canterbury CT2 8LF
T: (01227) 451243
F: (01227) 462006
E: enquiries@yorkelodge.com
I: www.yorkelodge.com

B&B per person per night:
S £35.00–£45.00
D £30.00–£45.00

OPEN All Year

Special Victorian bed and breakfast hotel, 10 minutes' walk to city centre and cathedral. Spacious, en suite accommodation including family rooms and, for a special occasion, our new 4-poster rooms. Lounge bar and large garden with sun terrace. Private car park. Close university. Thirty minutes' drive Channel ports and Eurotunnel.

Bedrooms: 4 double, 2 twin, 1 single, 1 family
Bathrooms: 8 en suite

CC: Amex, Delta, Diners, Mastercard, Switch, Visa

P

CARISBROOKE, Isle of Wight Map ref 2C3

♦♦♦

ALVINGTON MANOR FARM
Carisbrooke, Newport PO30 5SP
T: (01983) 523463
F: (01983) 523463

Bedrooms: 2 double, 3 twin, 1 family
Bathrooms: 6 en suite

B&B per person per night:
S £20.00–£22.50
D £20.00–£22.50

OPEN All Year

17thC farmhouse, gardens and parking, three en suite double/twin rooms. Ideal base in centre of island for walking, cycling etc.

P

CHALFONT ST GILES, Buckinghamshire Map ref 2D2

GORELANDS CORNER
Gorelands Lane, Chalfont St Giles
HP8 4HQ
T: (01494) 872689
F: (01494) 872689
E: bickfordcsg@onetel.net.uk

Bedrooms: 1 double, 1 family
Bathrooms: 1 en suite

Family home, set in large garden, close to picturesque village. Easy access to M25, M40, M4, London underground and London Heathrow Airport.

B&B per person per night:
S £25.00–£30.00
D £25.00–£30.00

OPEN All Year

CHALGROVE, Oxfordshire Map ref 2C2

CORNERSTONES
1 Cromwell Close, Chalgrove,
Oxford OX44 7SE
T: (01865) 890298
E: corner.stones@virgin.net

Bedrooms: 2 twin

Bungalow in pretty village with thatched cottages. The Red Lion (0.5 miles away) serves good and reasonably priced food.

B&B per person per night:
S £25.00
D £20.00

OPEN All Year except Christmas

CHESHAM, Buckinghamshire Map ref 2D1

Silver Award

BRAZIERS WELL

Oak Lane, Braziers End, Chesham HP5 2UL
T: (01494) 758956
E: info@brazierswell.co.uk
I: www.brazierswell.co.uk

B&B per person per night:
S £40.00
D £27.50

OPEN All Year except Christmas

Set in peaceful countryside, a friendly welcome awaits you. The ground floor, double-room accommodation is comfortable and spacious and looks out onto the pretty walled garden. Reasonably close to the Ridgeway Path, we are conveniently situated for Wendover, Halton and Berkhamsted with easy access to London via mainline and underground trains.

Bedrooms: 1 double
Bathrooms: 1 en suite

CHICHESTER, West Sussex Map ref 2C3 *Tourist Information Centre Tel: (01243) 775888*

DRAYMANS

112 St Pancras, Chichester PO19 7LH
T: (01243) 789872
F: (01243) 785474
E: liz@jaegerl.freeserve.co.uk
I: www.jaegerl.freeserve.co.uk

B&B per person per night:
S £23.00–£25.00
D £23.00–£27.50

OPEN All Year

A warm welcome to Draymans, a Georgian house centrally situated with unrestricted street parking and within easy walking distance of railway and bus stations. Three centrally heated bedrooms: double with en suite bathroom, double and single sharing bathroom with shower. Breakfast is served in a sunny room overlooking a courtyard garden.

Bedrooms: 2 double, 1 single
Bathrooms: 1 en suite

RATING All accommodation in this guide has been rated, or is awaiting a rating, by a trained VisitBritain assessor.

CHICHESTER continued

◆◆◆

KIA-ORA NURSERY

Main Road, Nutbourne, Chichester
PO18 8RT
T: (01243) 572858
F: (01243) 572858
E: ruthiefp@aol.com

Bedrooms: 1 double
Bathrooms: 1 en suite

B&B per person per night:
S £25.00
D £20.00–£25.00

OPEN All Year except Christmas

Views to Chichester harbour. Warm welcome in comfortable family house. Large garden. Restaurants and country pubs within walking distance.

THE OLD STORE GUEST HOUSE

Stane Street, Halnaker, Chichester
PO18 0QL
T: (01243) 531977
E: theoldstore4@aol.com
I: www.smoothhound.co.uk/hotels/store.html

Bedrooms: 2 double, 3 twin, 1 single, 1 family
Bathrooms: 7 en suite

CC: Delta, Mastercard, Switch, Visa

B&B per person per night:
S £30.00–£34.00
D £30.00–£32.50

OPEN All Year except Christmas

Lovely 18thC Grade II Listed home. Seven comfortable rooms, all en suite. Adjoins Goodwood Estate. Close to Chichester, convenient for Petworth, Arundel and the coast.

Silver Award

WHITE BARN

Crede Lane, Bosham, Chichester
PO18 8NX
T: (01243) 573113
F: (01243) 573113
E: chrissie@whitebarn.biz
I: www.whitebarn.biz

Bedrooms: 2 double, 1 twin
Bathrooms: 3 en suite

Evening meal available
CC: Delta, Mastercard, Switch, Visa

B&B per person per night:
S £40.00–£60.00
D £30.00–£40.00

OPEN All Year

Contemporary barn in a quiet corner of this beautiful Saxon harbour village. Convenient for Goodwood, Chichester and Portsmouth. Home comforts and a warm welcome.

WOODSTOCK HOUSE HOTEL

Charlton, Chichester PO18 0HU
T: (01243) 811666
F: (01243) 811666
E: info@woodstockhousehotel.co.uk
I: www.woodstockhousehotel.co.uk

Converted from an old farmhouse, our licensed bed and breakfast hotel is set in the heart of the magnificent South Downs. All bedrooms are en suite with full modern amenities. Area rich in spectacular walks with Goodwood's many attractions, The Weald and Downland museum and many National Trust properties.

Bedrooms: 6 double, 4 twin, 2 single
Bathrooms: 12 en suite

CC: Amex, Delta, Mastercard, Switch, Visa

3 nights for price of 2 Sun-Thu (excl Jul and Aug).

B&B per person per night:
S £48.00–£53.00
D £34.50–£48.00

OPEN All Year except Christmas

CHIPPING NORTON, Oxfordshire Map ref 2C1 *Tourist Information Centre Tel: (01608) 644379*

Rating Applied For

THE BELL INN

56 West Street, Chipping Norton OX7 5ER
T: (01608) 642521
F: (01608) 646145

Traditional, friendly public house with recently refurbished bedrooms. Standard accommodation is available in a single and twin room, and superior in twin and double rooms with their own facilities. There is a large car park at the rear.

Bedrooms: 3 double, 1 single
Bathrooms: 2 en suite

Evening meal available
CC: Delta, Mastercard, Switch, Visa

B&B per person per night:
S £25.00–£35.00
D £22.50–£27.50

HB per person per night:
DY £33.50–£38.50

OPEN All Year

CHOLDERTON, Hampshire Map ref 2B2

PARKHOUSE MOTEL
Cholderton, Salisbury SP4 0EG
T: (01980) 629256
F: (01980) 629256

Bedrooms: 24 double, 6 single, 3 family
Bathrooms: 23 en suite

Evening meal available
CC: Delta, Mastercard, Switch, Visa

Attractive, family-run, 17thC former coaching inn, five miles east of Stonehenge, 10 miles north of Salisbury and seven miles west of Andover.

B&B per person per night:
S £34.00–£48.50
D £27.50–£31.00

HB per person per night:
DY £46.50–£62.50

OPEN All Year

COTSWOLDS

See under Brize Norton, Burford, Chipping Norton, Witney, Woodstock

See also Cotswolds in Heart of England region

CRANBROOK, Kent Map ref 3B4

SWATTENDEN RIDGE
Swattenden Lane, Cranbrook
TN17 3PR
T: (01580) 712327
F: (01580) 712327
I: www.swattendenridge.co.uk

Bedrooms: 2 double
Bathrooms: 1 en suite, 1 private

Evening meal available

Modern, quiet farmhouse. Wonderful views and ancient woodlands. Close to Benenden, Sissinghurst and many castles and gardens. Outdoor pool for summer use. Evening meals by arrangement.

B&B per person per night:
S £40.00
D £25.00

HB per person per night:
DY £40.00–£42.00

CRANLEIGH, Surrey Map ref 2D2

LONG COPSE
Pitch Hill, Ewhurst, Cranleigh
GU6 7NN
T: (01483) 277458
F: (01483) 268195

Bedrooms: 1 double, 1 twin

Long Copse offers a warm welcome, a beautiful Arts and Crafts house, magnificent views, miles of footpaths and easy access to many places of interest.

B&B per person per night:
S Max £30.00
D Max £55.00

OPEN All Year except Christmas

CRAWLEY, West Sussex Map ref 2D2

LITTLE FOXES HOTEL
Charlwood Road, Ifield Wood, Crawley
RH11 0JY
T: (01293) 529206
F: (01293) 551434
E: info@littlefoxeshotel.co.uk
I: www.littlefoxeshotel.co.uk

Little Foxes Hotel is a small, family-run establishment in peaceful setting four miles from Gatwick, offering quality accommodation and secure holiday parking. All rooms en suite with TV, tea/coffee-making facilities, telephones etc. Prices include full English breakfast (or continental for early leavers).

Bedrooms: 3 double, 2 twin, 2 single, 4 family
Bathrooms: 11 en suite

CC: Delta, Mastercard, Switch, Visa

B&B per person per night:
S £35.00–£45.00
D £27.50–£30.00

OPEN All Year except Christmas

AT-A-GLANCE SYMBOLS

Symbols at the end of each accommodation entry give useful information about services and facilities. A key to symbols can be found inside the back cover flap. Keep this open for easy reference.

CRAWLEY DOWN, West Sussex Map ref 2D2

Silver Award

TILTWOOD HOUSE

Hophurst Lane, Crawley Down, Crawley
RH10 4LL
T: (01342) 712942
E: vjohnstiltwood@aol.com

The centre part of an elegant Victorian country house. Luxurious, spacious, en suite bedrooms, high ceilings with beautiful moulding and cornices, king-size beds, TV/video, tea/coffee facilities. Within easy reach of Hickstead, South of England Showground, Lingfield racecourse, Brighton, London. Ideal for honeymooners, being seven miles from Gatwick.

Bedrooms: 2 double
Bathrooms: 2 en suite

B&B per person per night:
S £45.00–£55.00
D £32.50–£43.50

OPEN All Year except Christmas

CROWBOROUGH, East Sussex Map ref 2D2

♦♦♦♦

ARTHUR FAMILY BED & BREAKFAST

2 The Grove, Southview Road,
Crowborough TN6 1NY
T: (01892) 653328
F: (01892) 653328
E: arthur.family@virgin.net

Bedrooms: 1 twin, 1 family
Bathrooms: 2 en suite

Evening meal available

Friendly, family home welcomes non-smokers. Quiet location near town-centre shops/ pubs, near bus routes. Fax/email facilities. French, German, Russian spoken. Euros accepted.

B&B per person per night:
S £23.00–£27.00
D £23.00–£25.00

HB per person per night:
DY £30.00–£34.00

OPEN All Year except Christmas

♦♦♦♦

Silver Award

BRAEMORE

Eridge Road, Steel Cross,
Crowborough TN6 2SS
T: (01892) 665700

Bedrooms: 2 double
Bathrooms: 1 en suite, 1 private

Detached family house in semi-rural position. One mile from Crowborough town centre, six miles from major town of Tunbridge Wells.

B&B per person per night:
S £25.00–£30.00
D £22.50–£25.00

OPEN All Year except Christmas

CURRIDGE, West Berkshire Map ref 2C2

THE BUNK INN

Curridge Village, Curridge, Thatcham
RG18 9DS
T: (01635) 200400
F: (01635) 200336
I: www.thebunkinn.co.uk

Set in rural Berkshire, yet only five minutes from jct 13 of the M4, this delightful restaurant with rooms is quite unique. Owned and run by the Liquorish family for 12 years, their latest addition of six exceptionally comfortable bedrooms, all en suite, are proving very popular. Booking advised.

Bedrooms: 6 double
Bathrooms: 6 en suite

CC: Amex, Delta, Diners, Mastercard, Switch, Visa

Weekend rates apply Fri/Sat/Sun night.

B&B per person per night:
S £60.00–£95.00
D £37.50–£55.00

OPEN All Year

CREDIT CARD BOOKINGS If you book by telephone and are asked for your credit card number it is advisable to check the proprietor's policy should you cancel your reservation.

DANEHILL, East Sussex Map ref 2D3

♦♦♦♦

NEW GLENMORE
Sliders Lane, Furners Green,
Uckfield TN22 3RU
T: (01825) 790783
E: alan.robinson@bigfoot.com

Bedrooms: 1 twin,
1 family
Bathrooms: 1 en suite,
1 private

Spacious bungalow set in six acres of grounds. Rural location close to Bluebell Steam Railway and Sheffield Park. Breakfast includes our own eggs, honey and home-baked bread.

B&B per person per night:
S £20.00–£30.00
D £20.00–£30.00

OPEN All Year except Christmas

DEDDINGTON, Oxfordshire Map ref 2C1

♦♦

STONECROP GUEST HOUSE
Hempton Road, Deddington,
Banbury OX15 0QH
T: (01869) 338335
F: (01869) 338505
E: info@stonecropguesthouse.co.uk
I: www.stonecropguesthouse.co.uk

Bedrooms: 2 double,
1 single, 1 family

Modern, detached accommodation, close to major roads, shops and places of interest.

B&B per person per night:
S £20.00–£25.00
D £20.00–£25.00

OPEN All Year except Christmas

DORKING, Surrey Map ref 2D2

DENBIES FARMHOUSE B&B

Denbies Wine Estate, London Road,
Dorking RH5 6AA
T: (01306) 876777
F: (01306) 888930
E: info@denbiesvineyard.co.uk
I: www.denbiesvineyard.co.uk

Denbies Farmhouse B&B is located in the heart of England's largest vineyard on the beautiful North Downs of Surrey. Tastefully converted from the original farmhouse it offers double en suite bedrooms, all with TV, tea/coffee facilities and trouser press. Spectacular scenery makes it a favourite with walkers, wine lovers and artists.

Bedrooms: 5 double,
1 family
Bathrooms: 6 en suite

CC: Mastercard, Visa

B&B per person per night:
S Min £60.00
D Min £35.00

OPEN All Year

♦♦♦

FAIRDENE GUEST HOUSE
Moores Road, Dorking RH4 2BG
T: (01306) 888337
E: zoe.richardson@ntlworld.com

Bedrooms: 2 double,
2 twin, 3 family
Bathrooms: 4 en suite

Late-Victorian house in convenient location, close to town centre, Gatwick Airport and North Downs Way. Friendly and homely atmosphere. Off-street parking.

B&B per person per night:
S £40.00–£45.00
D £27.50–£30.00

OPEN All Year

QUALITY ASSURANCE SCHEME

For an explanation of the quality and facilities represented by the Diamonds please refer to the front of this guide. A more detailed explanation can be found in the information pages at the back.

DOVER, Kent Map ref 3C4 *Tourist Information Centre Tel: (01304) 205108*

CASTLE GUEST HOUSE

10 Castle Hill Road, Dover CT16 1QW
T: (01304) 201656
F: (01304) 210197
E: dimechr@aol.com
I: www.castle-guesthouse.co.uk

B&B per person per night:
S £28.00–£35.00
D £21.00–£26.00

OPEN All Year except Christmas

Ideally located in a conservation area below Dover Castle, close to the town centre, seafront and port. An excellent breakfast is available from 0600 for those with an early start. All bedrooms are en suite and are individually and tastefully furnished. Ample, off-street parking.

Bedrooms: 3 double, 1 single, 1 family
Bathrooms: 5 en suite

CC: Amex, Delta, Diners, Mastercard, Switch, Visa

◆◆◆◆

COLRET HOUSE

The Green, Coldred, Dover CT15 5AP
T: (01304) 830388
F: (01304) 830388
E: jackie.colret@evnet.co.uk
I: www.colrethouse.co.uk

B&B per person per night:
S £25.00–£30.00
D £25.00–£30.00

OPEN All Year

An early-Edwardian property with modern, purpose-built, en suite garden rooms, standing in extensive, well-maintained grounds. Situated beside the village green in a conservation area on downs above Dover. Ideally situated for overnight stays when travelling by ferries or shuttle. Close to Canterbury and Sandwich. Ample secure parking.

Bedrooms: 2 double
Bathrooms: 2 en suite

◆◆◆◆

LODDINGTON HOUSE HOTEL

14 East Cliff,
(Seafront - Marine Parade), Dover
CT16 1LX
T: (01304) 201947
F: (01304) 201947
E: sscupper@aol.com

Bedrooms: 5 double, 1 single
Bathrooms: 4 en suite, 2 private

Evening meal available
CC: Amex, Delta, Mastercard, Switch, Visa

B&B per person per night:
S £35.00–£45.00
D £27.00–£35.00

OPEN All Year except Christmas

Well-positioned small hotel in Georgian terrace overlooking harbour. Quality food and wine – prices on request. Yards from east ferry terminal.

◆◆◆◆
Silver Award

OWLER LODGE

Alkham Valley Road, Alkham, Dover
CT15 7DF
T: (01304) 826375
F: (01304) 829372
E: owlerlodge@aol.com
I: www.owlerlodge.co.uk

Bedrooms: 2 double, 1 family
Bathrooms: 3 en suite

Evening meal available

B&B per person per night:
S £33.00–£39.00
D £24.00–£27.00

OPEN All Year except Christmas

Small guesthouse situated in the beautiful Alkham Valley between Dover and Folkestone, three miles from Channel Tunnel. Beautiful garden with Koi ponds. Off-street parking. Non-smoking residence.

ACCESSIBILITY

Look for the  symbols which indicate National Accessible Scheme standards for hearing and visually impaired guests in addition to standards for guests with mobility impairment. You can find an index of all scheme participants at the back of this guide.

DOVER continued

♦♦♦♦
Silver Award

THE PARK INN

1-2 Park Place, Ladywell, Dover CT16 1DQ
T: (01304) 203300
F: (01304) 203324
E: theparkinn@aol.com
I: www.theparkinnatdover.co.uk

B&B per person per night:
S £35.00–£45.00
D £27.00–£37.00

OPEN All Year

The feel of Victorian England immediately embraces guests on arrival at the Park Inn. An extremely high standard of finish in decor, furnishings and fittings prevails in our en suite rooms which complement our successful inn and restaurant. All our rooms are cosy and comfortable and contain many facilities.

Bedrooms: 1 double, 2 twin, 1 single, 1 family
Bathrooms: 5 en suite

Evening meal available
CC: Amex, Delta, Diners, Mastercard, Switch, Visa

DYMCHURCH, Kent Map ref 3B4

♦♦♦♦

WATERSIDE GUEST HOUSE

15 Hythe Road, Dymchurch, Romney Marsh TN29 0LN
T: (01303) 872253
F: (01303) 872253
E: info@watersideguesthouse.co.uk
I: www.watersideguesthouse.co.uk

B&B per person per night:
S £30.00–£50.00
D £20.00–£25.00

HB per person per night:
DY £28.00–£58.00

OPEN All Year

Cottage-style house offering comfortable rooms and attractive gardens, ideally situated for Channel crossings and touring historic Romney Marsh countryside by foot or transport. Experience the RH&D railway, visit Port Lympne Wild Animal Park or stroll along nearby sandy beaches, finally enjoying a drink or meal from our varied menu.

Bedrooms: 2 double, 2 twin, 1 family
Bathrooms: 5 en suite

Evening meal available
CC: Delta, Mastercard, Switch, Visa

2-, 3-or 4-day short breaks (DB&B). Also Christmas specials – contact for details.

EAST ASHLING, West Sussex Map ref 2C3

HORSE & GROOM

East Ashling, Chichester PO18 9AX
T: (01243) 575339
F: (01243) 575560
E: horseandgroomea@aol.com
I: www.horseandgroom.sageweb.co.uk

B&B per person per night:
S Min £40.00
D £35.00–£55.00

OPEN All Year

A traditional 17thC inn with en suite accommodation. Friendly country-style inn with fine cuisine, real ales and cast-iron range. Plenty of parking. Close to Goodwood.

Bedrooms: 11 double
Bathrooms: 11 en suite

Evening meal available
CC: Amex, Delta, Mastercard, Switch, Visa

QUALITY ASSURANCE SCHEME

Diamond ratings and awards were correct at the time of going to press but are subject to change. Please check at the time of booking.

EAST GRINSTEAD, West Sussex Map ref 2D2

◆◆◆

CRANSTON HOUSE

Cranston Road, East Grinstead
RH19 3HW
T: (01342) 323609
F: (01342) 323609
E: stay@cranstonhouse.screaming.net
I: www.cranstonehouse.co.uk

Bedrooms: 2 double, 4 twin, 1 family
Bathrooms: 6 en suite, 1 private

CC: Delta, Mastercard, Switch, Visa

B&B per person per night:
S £28.00–£35.00
D £20.00–£25.00

OPEN All Year

Attractive detached house in quiet location near town centre and station, 15 minutes' drive from Gatwick. Spacious, high-quality, en suite accommodation. Ample off-road parking.

◆◆

TOWN HOUSE

6 De la Warr Road, East Grinstead
RH19 3BN
T: (01342) 300310
F: (01342) 324200

Bedrooms: 3 double

B&B per person per night:
S £25.00–£30.00
D £20.00–£22.50

OPEN All Year

Cosy, friendly, quiet, very clean, en suite rooms. Five minutes from train, town centre, near shops and resturants, 15 minutes from Gatwick. English breakfast.

EAST HENDRED, Oxfordshire Map ref 2C2

◆◆◆

A MONKS COURT

Newbury Road, East Hendred,
Wantage OX12 8LG
T: (01235) 833797
F: (01235) 862554
E: udsl@udg.org.uk

Bedrooms: 1 double, 1 twin
Bathrooms: 1 en suite, 1 private

B&B per person per night:
S £25.00–£35.00
D £25.00–£30.00

OPEN All Year

Comfortable family house on edge of beautiful medieval village. Convenient for all commercial and leisure activities including The Ridgeway, Lains Barn and Ardington House.

EAST HOATHLY, East Sussex Map ref 2D3

◆◆◆◆

ABERDEEN HOUSE BED & BREAKFAST

5 High Street, East Hoathly, Lewes
BN8 6DR
T: (01825) 840219

Bedrooms: 2 double, 1 single
Bathrooms: 1 en suite

B&B per person per night:
D £45.00–£55.00

OPEN All Year

18thC Grade II Listed house in quiet village conservation area with beautiful walled garden. On A22 close to historic Lewes and Glyndebourne.

EAST ILSLEY, Berkshire Map ref 2C2

THE STAR INN

High Street, East Ilsley, Newbury RG20 7LE
T: (01635) 281215
E: kimrichstar@aol.com
I: www.starinnhotel.co.uk

B&B per person per night:
S Min £50.00
D £30.00–£60.00

OPEN All Year except Christmas

Traditional 15thC country village inn, in the heart of the rolling Berkshire Downs. Ideal for walkers, close to Oxford, very popular with local horse-racing fraternity. Well-appointed, en suite bedrooms full of character and charm. Traditional English pub food, real ales, open fire, patio, beer garden, warm welcome guaranteed.

Bedrooms: 4 double, 1 twin, 3 single, 1 family
Bathrooms: 9 en suite

Evening meal available
CC: Delta, Mastercard, Switch, Visa

Special rates for guests staying Newbury Races weekends. Double room £50pn.

VISTBRITAIN'S WHERE TO STAY
Please mention this guide when making your booking.

EASTBOURNE, East Sussex Map ref 3B4 *Tourist Information Centre Tel: (01323) 411400*

◆◆◆

BIRLING GAP HOTEL

Birling Gap, Seven Sisters Cliffs, East Dean, Eastbourne BN20 0AB
T: (01323) 423197
F: (01323) 423030
E: info@birlinggaphotel.co.uk
I: www.birlinggaphotel.co.uk

Magnificent Seven Sisters cliff-top position, with views of country, sea, beach. Superb downland and beach walks. Old world 'Thatched Bar' and 'Oak Room Restaurant'. Coffee shop and games room, function and conference suite. Off A259 coast road at East Dean, 1.5 miles west of Beachy Head.

Bedrooms: 5 double, 1 single, 3 family
Bathrooms: 9 en suite

Evening meal available
CC: Amex, Delta, Diners, Mastercard, Switch, Visa

3 nights for the price of 2, Oct-Mar (excl Christmas and New Year). Pre-booked only.

P €

B&B per person per night:
S £25.00–£40.00
D £25.00–£35.00

OPEN All Year

◆◆◆◆
Silver Award

BRAYSCROFT HOTEL

13 South Cliff Avenue, Eastbourne BN20 7AH
T: (01323) 647005
F: (01323) 720705
E: brayscroft@hotmail.com
I: www.brayscrofthotel.co.uk

Elegant, award-winning, small hotel, one of only a handful in Eastbourne with coveted ETC 4 Diamonds – Silver Award for 'outstanding accommodation and hospitality'. Superb position less than a minute from seafront in fashionable Meads district and ideally situated for South Downs, theatres, restaurants and town centre. Totally non-smoking.

Bedrooms: 2 double, 2 twin, 1 single
Bathrooms: 5 en suite

Evening meal available
CC: Amex, Delta, Mastercard, Switch, Visa

Upgrade from single room to double/twin at no extra cost except at peak holiday times. 4-night and weekly breaks.

14 V P

B&B per person per night:
S £29.00–£32.00
D £29.00–£32.00

HB per person per night:
DY £41.00–£44.00

OPEN All Year

◆◆◆◆

LITTLE FOXES

24 Wannock Road, Eastbourne BN22 7JU
T: (01323) 640670
F: (01323) 640670
E: chris@foxholes55.freeserve.co.uk

Bedrooms: 1 twin, 1 single
Bathrooms: 2 en suite

Personally run B&B. Close to beach and one kilometre town centre. En suite facilities. Guests' lounge with Sky TV. All ages welcome. No smoking.

V €

B&B per person per night:
S £20.00–£25.00
D £20.00–£25.00

OPEN All Year

◆◆◆

SHERWOOD HOTEL

7 Lascelles Terrace, Eastbourne BN21 4BJ
T: (01323) 724002
F: (01323) 439989
E: sherwood-hotel@supanet.com
I: www.sherwoodhotel.com

Bedrooms: 3 double, 3 twin, 5 single, 3 family
Bathrooms: 13 en suite, 1 private

Evening meal available
CC: Amex, Delta, Diners, Mastercard, Switch, Visa

Cosy hotel. All rooms en suite with TV and tea-making facilities. Ideally located for seafront, theatres and town. Friendly, courteous service. Value for money.

V

B&B per person per night:
S £22.00–£35.00
D £22.00–£35.00

OPEN All Year except Christmas

GOLD & SILVER AWARDS

These exclusive VisitBritain awards are given to establishments achieving the highest levels of quality and service. Further information can be found at the front of the guide. An index to all accommodation achieving these awards are at the back of this guide.

EASTBOURNE continued

Silver Award

TREVINHURST LODGE

10 Baslow Road, Meads, Eastbourne
BN20 7UJ
T: (01323) 410023
F: (01323) 643238
E: enquiries@trevinhurstlodge.com
I: www.trevinhurstlodge.com

A warm welcome awaits those looking for a discerning break in a non-smoking, relaxed, informal atmosphere. With attractive, spacious bedrooms we can guarantee the individual attention you would expect. Fine food offered in our elegant dining room completes the picture. Speciality watercolour courses are also available.

Bedrooms: 3 double
Bathrooms: 2 en suite, 1 private

Evening meal available

Proprietor Brian Smith, a professional artist, offers weekend or mid-week residential watercolour courses for small groups.

B&B per person per night:
S £48.00–£56.00
D £34.00–£47.00

HB per person per night:
DY £56.00–£78.00

OPEN All Year

EDGCOTT, Buckinghamshire Map ref 2C1

◆◆

PERRY MANOR FARM

Buckingham Road, Edgcott,
Aylesbury HP18 0TR
T: (01296) 770257

Bedrooms: 2 double,
1 single

200-acre working sheep farm, offering peaceful and comfortable accommodation, with en suite toilet and basin. Extensive views over Aylesbury Vale. Walkers welcome. Non-smokers only, please.

B&B per person per night:
S £23.00
D £19.00

OPEN All Year

EMSWORTH, Hampshire Map ref 2C3

QUACKERS COTTAGE

40 Bath Road, Emsworth PO10 7ER
T: (01243) 377177
F: (01243) 377177
E: quackerscottage@talk21.com

Bedrooms: 1 double
Bathrooms: 1 en suite

We are a small, friendly, family-run bed and breakfast overlooking the millpond, close to pubs and restaurants. Near to Chichester, Portsmouth and Goodwood.

B&B per person per night:
S Max £30.00
D Max £30.00

OPEN All Year except Christmas

EWHURST, Surrey Map ref 2D2

SIXPENNY BUCKLE

Gransden Close, Ewhurst, Cranleigh
GU6 7RL
T: (01483) 273988
E: dandpmort@tiscali.co.uk

Bedrooms: 2 twin

Spacious bungalow amid Surrey hills with beautiful garden and pool. Wonderful walks and local village pubs. Quiet location, central village.

B&B per person per night:
S £25.00–£30.00
D £25.00

OPEN All Year

FAREHAM, Hampshire Map ref 2C3 *Tourist Information Centre Tel: (01329) 221342*

AVENUE HOUSE HOTEL

22 The Avenue, Fareham PO14 1NS
T: (01329) 232175
F: (01329) 232196
I: www.travelrest.co.uk

Bedrooms: 14 double,
2 single, 3 family
Bathrooms: 19 en suite

Evening meal available
CC: Amex, Delta, Mastercard, Switch, Visa

Comfortable, small hotel with charm and character, set in landscaped gardens. Five minutes' walk to town centre, railway station and restaurants. Ideal location between Southampton and Portsmouth.

B&B per person per night:
S £55.00
D £30.00–£35.00

OPEN All Year

CHECK THE MAPS

The colour maps at the front of this guide show all the cities, towns and villages for which you will find accommodation entries.
Refer to the town index to find the page on which they are listed.

FAREHAM continued

BRIDGE HOUSE

1 Waterside Gardens, Wallington, Fareham PO16 8SD
T: (01329) 287775
F: (01329) 287775
E: maryhb@fish.co.uk

Bedrooms: 2 double
Bathrooms: 1 en suite, 1 private

Comfortable Georgian family home, all facilities, Japanese garden. Full English or continental breakfast. Ample parking. Easy access to M27, jct 11 and town centre.

B&B per person per night:
S £35.00–£39.00
D £30.00–£37.50

OPEN All Year except Christmas

FARINGDON, Oxfordshire Map ref 2B2 *Tourist Information Centre Tel: (01367) 242191*

PORTWELL HOUSE HOTEL

Market Place, Faringdon SN7 7HU
T: (01367) 240197
F: (01367) 244330
E: enquiries@portwellhouse.com
I: www.portwellhouse.com

Small, friendly, family-run hotel, situated in the market place of historic Faringdon, close to Oxford, Thames, Uffington White Horse Hill and Ridgeway, and Cotswolds. Non-smoking throughout, Portwell offers good-sized rooms, all with en suite bathroom, colour TV, tea and coffee, and direct-dial telephone. Freshly cooked evening meals available on request.

Bedrooms: 4 double, 2 twin, 1 single, 1 family
Bathrooms: 8 en suite

Evening meal available
CC: Delta, Mastercard, Switch, Visa

B&B per person per night:
S £45.00–£55.00
D £30.00–£39.50

OPEN All Year

FARNBOROUGH, Hampshire Map ref 2C2

THE OAK TREE GUEST HOUSE

112 Farnborough Road, Farnborough GU14 6TN
T: (01252) 545491
F: (01252) 545491
E: joanne.dickinson21@ntlworld.com
I: www.theoaktreeguesthouse.com

Family-run guesthouse with a home from home atmosphere. All rooms are non-smoking with colour TV, mini-fridge and dining table and chairs. Cost includes continental breakfast. East access to M3, A3, airport, mainline station and business parks. Car parking available. Business guests and families welcome.

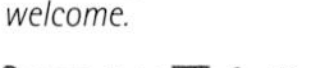

Bedrooms: 3 double, 1 single, 2 family
Bathrooms: 3 en suite

CC: Amex, Delta, Mastercard, Switch, Visa

Close to Chessington World of Adventures, Thorpe Park, Legoland and Windsor.

B&B per person per night:
S £30.00–£50.00
D £25.00–£32.50

OPEN All Year except Christmas

FARNHAM, Surrey Map ref 2C2 *Tourist Information Centre Tel: (01252) 715109*

Gold Award

ANNE'S COTTAGE

Green Cross Lane, Churt, Farnham
GU10 2ND
T: (01428) 714181

B&B per person per night:
S £30.00–£35.00
D Max £27.50

OPEN All Year

Pre-dating 1447, when Fareham's manorial role records the rent unpaid due possibly to 'The Black Death', this cosy, low-beamed cottage is a quiet haven. Furnishings are traditional, the plumbing modern. Local produce and homemade preserves are used and the welcome is warm, ensuring every comfort and care.

Bedrooms: 2 double, 1 single
Bathrooms: 1 en suite, 1 private

Evening meal available

Honeymoon and anniversary weekends (2 nights minimum).

FAVERSHAM, Kent Map ref 3B3 *Tourist Information Centre Tel: (01795) 534542*

♦♦♦

BARNSFIELD

Fostall, Hernhill, Faversham
ME13 9JH
T: (01227) 750973
F: (01227) 273098
E: barnsfield@yahoo.com
I: www.barnsfield.co.uk

Bedrooms: 2 double, 1 twin, 1 family
Bathrooms: 3 en suite

Evening meal available

B&B per person per night:
S £25.00–£35.00
D £16.00–£29.00

OPEN All Year except Christmas

Grade II Listed country cottage accommodation, just off A299, set in three acres of orchards, six miles from Canterbury. Convenient for ports and touring.

Silver Award

PRESTON LEA

Canterbury Road, Faversham ME13 8XA
T: (01795) 535266
F: (01795) 533388
E: preston.lea@which.net
I: homepages.which.net/~alan.turner10

B&B per person per night:
S £35.00–£40.00
D £27.50–£30.00

OPEN All Year

A unique and elegant Victorian Gothic house with turrets set in large, secluded gardens. Spacious, sunny bedrooms with garden views and antique furniture. Beautiful guest drawing room, panelled dining room and delicious breakfasts. Only 15 minutes from Canterbury, 35 minutes from ports, Eurotunnel, 70 minutes by train to London.

Bedrooms: 1 double, 1 twin, 1 single
Bathrooms: 2 en suite, 1 private

CC: Amex, Delta, Mastercard, Switch, Visa

TOWN INDEX

This can be found at the back of the guide. If you know where you want to stay, the index will give you the page number listing accommodation in your chosen town, city or village.

FITTLEWORTH, West Sussex Map ref 2D3

♦♦♦♦ Silver Award

SWAN INN

Lower Street, Fittleworth, Pulborough RH20 1EN
T: (01798) 865429
F: (01798) 865721
E: hotel@swaninn.com
I: www.swaninn.com

Listed 14thC coaching inn, well placed for visiting many of the historic houses and places of interest in the area. Public bar with welcoming log fires in the winter. Large garden. Cosy oak-beamed restaurant serving homemade food with a fine selection of fresh fish, meat and poultry dishes.

Bedrooms: 8 double, 4 twin, 3 single
Bathrooms: 15 en suite

Evening meal available
CC: Amex, Delta, Mastercard, Switch, Visa

Special DB&B breaks available, minimum 2 nights.

B&B per person per night:
S £35.00–£45.00
D £30.00–£62.50

HB per person per night:
DY £44.50–£81.00

OPEN All Year

FOLKESTONE, Kent Map ref 3B4 *Tourist Information Centre Tel: (01303) 258594*

♦♦♦

BEACHBOROUGH PARK

Newington, Folkestone CT18 8BW
T: (01303) 275432
F: (01843) 845131
I: www.kentaccess.org.uk

Bedrooms: 6 double, 2 family
Bathrooms: 8 en suite

CC: Mastercard, Switch, Visa

Beautiful setting, ideal for sightseeing and very convenient for tunnel and ferries. Very comfortable for both active people and those just seeking peace and quiet.

B&B per person per night:
S £25.00–£30.00
D £22.50–£25.00

OPEN All Year

FORDINGBRIDGE, Hampshire Map ref 2B3

♦♦♦♦♦ Gold Award

THE THREE LIONS

Stuckton, Fordingbridge SP6 2HF
T: (01425) 652489
F: (01425) 656144
E: the3lions@btinternet.com
I: www.thethreelionsrestaurant.co.uk

Bedrooms: 3 double, 1 family
Bathrooms: 4 en suite

Evening meal available
CC: Amex, Delta, Mastercard, Switch, Visa

Quiet restaurant with rooms, all individually decorated and overlooking gardens. Wheelchair access. Whirlpool jacuzzi and sauna. English/French cuisine. Rosettes awarded for food.

B&B per person per night:
S £59.00–£75.00
D £32.50–£42.50

OPEN All Year

GATWICK, West Sussex Map ref 2D2

♦♦♦

COLLENDEAN BARN

Collendean Lane, Norwood Hill, Horley RH6 0HP
T: (01293) 862433
F: (01293) 863102
E: collendean.barn@amserve.net

Bedrooms: 1 double, 1 single, 1 family
Bathrooms: 3 en suite

CC: Mastercard, Switch, Visa

Bed and breakfast in a self-contained, converted barn with en suite, on a 16thC farm in lovely countryside, three miles from Gatwick and trains. Outdoor spa bath.

B&B per person per night:
S £30.00–£35.00
D £25.00

OPEN All Year

♦♦♦

GAINSBOROUGH LODGE

39 Massetts Road, Horley RH6 7DT
T: (01293) 783982
F: (01293) 785365
E: enquiries@gainsborough-lodge.co.uk
I: www.gainsborough-lodge.co.uk

Bedrooms: 15 double, 7 single, 4 family
Bathrooms: 24 en suite

CC: Diners, Mastercard, Switch, Visa

Family-run house set in attractive garden. Gatwick five minutes in courtesy bus (every 30 minutes), long-term parking. Central London 35 minutes by train.

B&B per person per night:
S Min £42.00
D Min £28.00

OPEN All Year

HALF BOARD PRICES Half board prices are given per person, but in some cases these may be based on double/twin occupancy.

GATWICK continued

THE MANOR HOUSE

Bonnetts Lane, Ifield, Crawley
RH11 0NY
T: (01293) 512298
F: (01293) 518046
E: info@manorhouse-gatwick.co.uk
I: www.manorhouse-gatwick.co.uk

Bedrooms: 3 double, 1 single, 2 family
Bathrooms: 4 en suite

CC: Amex, Delta, Mastercard, Visa

B&B per person per night:
S £30.00–£37.00
D £22.50–£25.00

OPEN All Year except Christmas

One-hundred-year-old manor house in pleasant rural surroundings on Gatwick's doorstep. Family-run establishment offering comfortable and spacious accommodation. Off-road parking, courtesy car.

P

SOUTHBOURNE GUEST HOUSE GATWICK

34 Massetts Road, Horley RH6 7DS
T: (01293) 771991
F: (01293) 820112
E: reservations@southbournegatwick.com
I: www.southbournegatwick.com

A warm welcome awaits you in our family-run guesthouse. Ideally located for Gatwick Airport, and exploring Surrey, Sussex and London. Five minutes' walk from Horley train station, restaurants, shops and pubs and 30 minutes by train from London. Five minutes' drive from Gatwick with free courtesy transport from 0930-2130.

Bedrooms: 2 double, 3 twin, 2 single, 2 family
Bathrooms: 2 en suite

CC: Delta, Mastercard, Switch, Visa

B&B per person per night:
S £30.00–£40.00
D £22.50–£27.50

OPEN All Year except Christmas

P

GATWICK AIRPORT

See under Crawley, East Grinstead, Horley

GODALMING, Surrey Map ref 2D2

HEATH HALL FARM

Bowlhead Green, Godalming GU8 6NW
T: (01428) 682808
F: (01428) 684025
E: heathhallfarm@btinternet.com
I: www.heathhallfarm.co.uk

Secluded farmhouse, converted stable courtyard, surrounded by own land. Free range fowl. Tennis court. Relaxed atmosphere. Ground floor accommodation. Ample parking. Single pet welcome by arrangement. Wonderful walking. Green Sand Way and National Nature Reserve. Easy access to A3. Simple supper available.

Bedrooms: 1 double, 1 twin, 1 single, 1 family
Bathrooms: 2 en suite, 1 private

Evening meal available

B&B per person per night:
S £27.50–£30.00
D £27.50

HB per person per night:
DY £37.50–£42.00

OPEN All Year except Christmas

P €

SPECIAL BREAKS

Many establishments offer special promotions and themed breaks. These are highlighted in red. (All such offers are subject to availability.)

GODSHILL, Hampshire Map ref 2C3

THE FIGHTING COCKS

Godshill, Fordingbridge SP6 2LL
T: (01425) 652462
F: (01425) 625462

B&B per person per night:
S £40.00–£70.00
D £35.00–£40.00

OPEN All Year except Christmas

A traditional, friendly pub nestled on the edge of the New Forest, ideal for walking or cycling. Spacious bedrooms all with a king-size bed and en suite shower room. Family suites available. Food is served from 1200-2200 with homemade specialities, steaks, fresh fish, forest fayre and light snacks.

Bedrooms: 1 double, 2 family
Bathrooms: 3 en suite

Evening meal available
CC: Delta, Switch, Visa

GORING, Oxfordshire Map ref 2C2

◆◆◆

MILLER OF MANSFIELD

High Street, Goring, Reading
RG8 9AW
T: (01491) 872829
F: (01491) 874200
I: www.millerofmansfield.co.uk

Bedrooms: 4 double, 4 twin, 2 single
Bathrooms: 10 en suite

Evening meal available
CC: Delta, Mastercard, Switch, Visa

B&B per person per night:
S £49.50–£54.50
D £32.50–£37.50

OPEN All Year except Christmas

Ivy-covered inn with Tudor-style exterior. Interior has original beams, open fires and comfortable bedrooms. Excellent bar and restaurant serving quality food, wines and beers.

GRAFFHAM, West Sussex Map ref 2C3

◆◆◆◆◆
Silver Award

BROOK BARN

Selham Road, Graffham, Petworth
GU28 0PU
T: (01798) 867356

Bedrooms: 1 double
Bathrooms: 1 en suite

B&B per person per night:
S £40.00–£50.00
D £30.00–£37.00

OPEN All Year except Christmas

Large double bedroom with en suite bathroom and its own conservatory, which leads to beautiful, secluded two-acre garden. From the garden is direct access to woodland walks.

GRAVESEND, Kent Map ref 3B3 *Tourist Information Centre Tel: (01474) 337600*

◆◆◆

DOT'S B & B

23 St James's Road, Gravesend
DA11 0HF
T: (01474) 332193
E: dotriley@agassiz.worldonline.co.uk

Bedrooms: 1 double, 1 twin

Evening meal available

B&B per person per night:
S £20.00–£22.00
D £20.00–£22.00

OPEN All Year

Comfortable Victorian house in conservation area with pretty garden; close to town centre and station, with frequent trains to London. A warm welcome is assured.

GUILDFORD, Surrey Map ref 2D2 *Tourist Information Centre Tel: (01483) 444333*

◆◆◆

BLUEBELLS

21 Coltsfoot Drive, Burpham, Guildford GU1 1YH
T: (01483) 826124
E: hughes.a@ntlworld.com

Bedrooms: 1 double, 1 single
Bathrooms: 2 en suite

B&B per person per night:
S £31.00–£33.00
D £24.00–£26.00

OPEN All Year except Christmas

Quietly situated, detached bungalow, close to Guildford and convenient for A3 and M25. High-quality, comfortable accommodation with attentive and friendly service. Bedrooms: one double, one single (both en suite).

MAP REFERENCES The map references refer to the colour maps at the front of this guide. The first figure is the map number; the letter and figure which follow indicate the grid reference on the map.

GUILDFORD continued

CHALKLANDS
Beech Avenue, Effingham, Leatherhead KT24 5PJ
T: (01372) 454936
F: (01372) 459569
E: rreilly@onetel.net.uk

Bedrooms: 2 double
Bathrooms: 1 en suite, 1 private

Evening meal available

B&B per person per night:
S £30.00–£35.00
D £25.00–£27.50

OPEN All Year except Christmas

Detached house backing onto Effingham golf course. Thirty minutes from Heathrow/Gatwick Airports, 35 minutes from London Waterloo station. Excellent pub food nearby.

HIGH EDSER
Shere Road, Ewhurst, Cranleigh GU6 7PQ
T: (01483) 278214
F: (01483) 278200
E: franklinadams@highedser.demon.co.uk

Bedrooms: 3 double

B&B per person per night:
S £25.00–£35.00
D £27.50–£30.00

OPEN All Year except Christmas

Early 16thC family home in Area of Outstanding Natural Beauty. Ten miles from Guildford and Dorking, easy reach airports and many tourist attractions. Non-smokers only, please.

PLAEGAN HOUSE
96 Wodeland Avenue, Guildford GU2 4LD
T: (01483) 822181
E: roxanephillips@onetel.net.uk

Bedrooms: 1 twin
Bathrooms: 1 en suite

B&B per person per night:
S £45.00
D £30.00

OPEN All Year except Christmas

Large room in friendly, accommodating house with lovely views directly on to the North Downs. Tastefully refurbished property within walking distance of town centre and university. Mob: 07961 919430.

HAILSHAM, East Sussex Map ref 2D3

WINDESWORTH
Carters Corner, Hailsham BN27 4HT
T: (01323) 847178
F: (01323) 440696
E: windesworth.bed&breakfast@virgin.net

Bedrooms: 2 double, 1 single
Bathrooms: 1 en suite, 1 private

B&B per person per night:
S £24.00–£25.00
D £20.00–£22.00

OPEN All Year except Christmas

Family home in quiet, rural location with views towards the Pevensey Levels and South Downs. Coast and 1066 country within easy reach.

HALLAND, East Sussex Map ref 2D3

Silver Award

TAMBERRY HALL

Eastbourne Road, Halland, Lewes BN8 6PS
T: (01825) 880090
F: (01825) 880090
E: bedandbreakfast@tamberryhall.fsbusiness.co.uk
I: www.tamberryhall.co.uk

Bedrooms: 2 double, 1 family
Bathrooms: 3 en suite

B&B per person per night:
D £27.50–£32.50

OPEN All Year except Christmas

Delightful country house in three acres. Comfortable, friendly atmosphere, exposed beams and inglenook fireplace in guests' lounge. Central for touring this Area of Outstanding Natural Beauty, the coast, gardens, National Trust properties. Glyndebourne and golf nearby, restaurant and pub within walking distance. Self-catering annexe. Vegetarian cooking a speciality. Mid-week special breaks.

Mid-week breaks: Double en suite – 3 nights £135, 4 nights £170. 'Weekend Plus': double en suite – 3 nights £165, 4 nights £210. All prices per room.

10

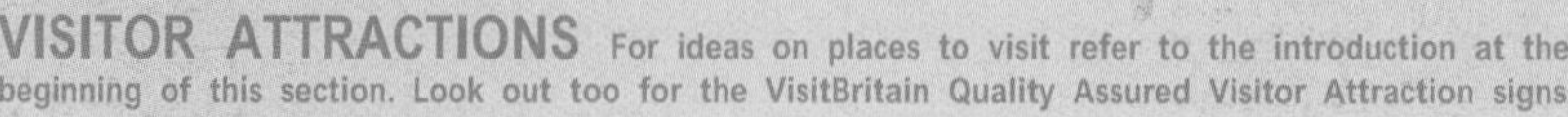

HARTFIELD, East Sussex Map ref 2D2

BOLEBROKE CASTLE

Edenbridge Road, Hartfield TN7 4JJ
T: (01892) 770061
F: (01892) 771041
E: bolebroke@btclick.com
I: www.bolebrokecastle.co.uk

B&B per person per night:
S £35.00–£49.00
D £27.50–£39.50

OPEN All Year

Henry VIII's hunting lodge set in a stunningly beautiful location on 30-acre estate away from main roads and noise. Two lakes, woodlands, views to Ashdown Forest, original beamed ceilings, second-largest fireplace in England, 4-poster suite, TV, tea/coffee. Tunbridge Wells five miles, Brighton 30 miles.

Bedrooms: 6 double
Bathrooms: 5 en suite, 1 private

CC: Amex, Delta, Mastercard, Switch, Visa

Regular medieval banquets with entertainment provided by minstrels. Henry VIII experience exhibition.

HASLEMERE, Surrey Map ref 2C2

SHEPS HOLLOW

Henley Common, Haslemere GU27 3HB
T: (01428) 653120

Bedrooms: 2 double, 2 single
Bathrooms: 2 en suite

Evening meal available

B&B per person per night:
S £30.00–£35.00

HB per person per night:
DY £40.00–£45.00

OPEN All Year

Charming 500-year-old cottage in a rural setting. TV with Sky and video channels in all rooms. Small barn for holiday lets.

HASTINGS, East Sussex Map ref 3B4 *Tourist Information Centre Tel: (01424) 781111*

♦♦♦♦

EAGLE HOUSE HOTEL

12 Pevensey Road, St Leonards-on-Sea, Hastings TN38 0JZ
T: (01424) 430535
F: (01424) 437771
E: info@eaglehousehotel.com
I: www.eaglehousehotel.com

Bedrooms: 16 double, 2 family
Bathrooms: 18 en suite

Evening meal available
CC: Amex, Delta, Diners, Mastercard, Switch, Visa

B&B per person per night:
S £38.00–£41.00
D £28.50–£29.50

HB per person per night:
DY £62.95–£65.95

OPEN All Year

You are assured of a warm welcome at the Eagle House Hotel, situated a few minutes' walk from Warrior Square railway station. Spacious, Victorian reception rooms.

♦♦♦♦

HOTEL LINDUM

1A Carlisle Parade, Hastings TN34 1JG
T: (01424) 434070
F: (01424) 718833
E: Hotellindum@aol.com
I: www.hotellindum.co.uk

Bedrooms: 7 double, 2 twin, 3 single
Bathrooms: 12 en suite

CC: Amex, Delta, Mastercard, Switch, Visa

B&B per person per night:
S £20.00–£45.00
D £20.00–£40.00

OPEN All Year

Situated in a prime location on Hastings seafront. All rooms en suite with 20" TV, tea/coffee facilities, hairdryer. Complimentary continental breakfast on request.

Gold Award

TOWER HOUSE

26-28 Tower Road West, St Leonards, Hastings TN38 0RG
T: (01424) 427217
F: (01424) 430165
E: reservations@towerhousehotel.com
I: www.towerhousehotel.com

Bedrooms: 8 double, 1 single, 1 family
Bathrooms: 9 en suite

Evening meal available
CC: Amex, Delta, Mastercard, Switch, Visa

B&B per person per night:
S £45.00–£55.00
D £30.00–£35.00

HB per person per night:
DY £62.50–£65.00

OPEN All Year except Christmas

Elegant Victorian house situated 0.5 miles from seafront. Pleasant gardens. Separate, licensed bar leading to garden patio. Freshly cooked meals. Ample parking.

SYMBOLS The symbols in each entry give information about services and facilities. A key to these symbols appears at the back of this guide.

HAVANT, Hampshire Map ref 2C3 *Tourist Information Centre Tel: (023) 9248 0024*

♦♦♦

HIGH TOWERS

14 Portsdown Hill Road,
Bedhampton, Havant PO9 3JY
T: (023) 92471748
F: (023) 92452770
E: hightowers14@aol.com
I: www.hightowers.co.uk

Bedrooms: 1 double, 1 twin, 1 single, 1 family
Bathrooms: 3 en suite, 1 private

On Wayfarers Walk, near Palmerston's Forts and A3M/M27. Superb views over Portsmouth, countryside and sea. Portsmouth centre/ferries 15 minutes, Havant five minutes. Non-smokers only.

5 P

B&B per person per night:
S £25.00–£30.00
D £22.00–£25.00

OPEN All Year except Christmas

HAWKINGE, Kent Map ref 3B4

BRAEHEID BED & BREAKFAST

2 Westland Way, Hawkinge,
Folkestone CT18 7PW
T: (01303) 893928
E: bill@forrest68.fsnet.co.uk

Bedrooms: 1 double, 1 twin
Bathrooms: 2 en suite

New property in quiet cul-de-sac. Near Channel Tunnel and Dover ferries. Westland Way is on the Downs, an Area of Outstanding Natural Beauty.

14 P

B&B per person per night:
D £19.00–£21.00

OPEN All Year except Christmas

HEATHFIELD, East Sussex Map ref 2D3

Silver Award

IWOOD B & B

Mutton Hall Lane, Heathfield TN21 8NR
T: (01435) 863918
F: (01435) 868575
E: iwoodbb@aol.com
I: www.iwoodbb.co.uk

Secluded house in lovely gardens with distant views of South Downs and sea. Situated within coastal towns including 1066 attractions around Hastings and historic towns of Battle, Rye, Lewes and Tunbridge Wells. Excellent standards maintained to ensure a comfortable stay. Be prepared for an excellent breakfast! Suitable for partially disabled.

Bedrooms: 1 twin, 1 single, 1 family
Bathrooms: 2 en suite, 1 private

Concessionary rates in excess 7 nights' stay.

P

B&B per person per night:
S £25.00–£35.00
D £23.00–£30.00

OPEN All Year except Christmas

♦♦♦♦

SPICERS BED & BREAKFAST

21 Spicers Cottages, Cade Street,
Heathfield TN21 9BS
T: (01435) 866363
F: (01435) 866363
E: beds@spicersbb.co.uk
I: www.spicersbb.co.uk

Bedrooms: 1 double, 1 twin, 1 single
Bathrooms: 1 en suite, 2 private

Evening meal available
CC: Delta, Mastercard, Switch, Visa

Beamed cottage in hamlet of Cade Street near Heathfield on the High Weald, between Eastbourne and Tunbridge Wells. Convenient for many places of interest.

P

B&B per person per night:
S £23.00–£30.00
D £22.00–£28.00

HB per person per night:
DY £38.00–£45.00

OPEN All Year

HENLEY-ON-THAMES, Oxfordshire Map ref 2C2 *Tourist Information Centre Tel: (01491) 578034*

ABBOTTSLEIGH

107 St Marks Road, Henley-on-Thames RG9 1LP
T: (01491) 572982
F: (01491) 572982
E: abbottsleigh@hotmail.com

Bedrooms: 1 double, 1 single, 1 family
Bathrooms: 2 en suite, 1 private

A mature, detatched home. Quiet location. Good parking. Comfortable rooms. Walking distance to town centre, river and station. Warm welcome. Good for London, Windsor, Oxford.

8 P

B&B per person per night:
S £36.00–£48.00
D £28.00–£32.50

OPEN All Year

HENLEY-ON-THAMES continued

♦♦♦♦

ALFTRUDIS
8 Norman Avenue, Henley-on-Thames RG9 1SG
T: (01491) 573099
F: (01491) 411747
E: sue@alftrudis.co.uk
I: www.alftrudis.co.uk

Bedrooms: 2 double, 1 twin
Bathrooms: 2 en suite, 1 private

Grade II Listed Victorian home in peaceful, tree-lined cul-de-sac a few minutes' level walk from the town centre, station and river.

8 P

B&B per person per night:
S £45.00–£55.00
D £27.50–£32.50

OPEN All Year except Christmas

COLDHARBOUR HOUSE

3 Coldharbour Close, Henley-on-Thames RG9 1QF
T: (01491) 575229
F: (01491) 575229
E: coldharbourhouse@aol.com

Pretty farmhouse-style home in a quiet close, 15 minutes' walk from the town and river. It has character features and is surrounded by a lovely walled garden. Breakfast is served in the dining room overlooking the garden, and there is a sun lounge for relaxation. Off-street parking.

Bedrooms: 1 double, 1 twin
Bathrooms: 1 en suite, 1 private

P

B&B per person per night:
S £40.00–£50.00
D £27.50–£35.00

OPEN All Year except Christmas

HOLMWOOD

Shiplake Row, Binfield Heath, Henley-on-Thames RG9 4DP
T: (0118) 9478747
F: (0118) 9478637
E: wendy.cook@freenet.co.uk

Large, elegant, peaceful Georgian country house with very beautiful gardens and views over the Thames Valley. All bedrooms are large and en suite and furnished with period and antique furnishings. Holmwood is in Binfield Heath, which is signposted off the A4155, equidistant from Henley-on-Thames and Reading.

Bedrooms: 2 double, 2 twin, 1 single
Bathrooms: 5 en suite

CC: Delta, Mastercard, Switch, Visa

12 P

B&B per person per night:
S £45.00
D £32.50

OPEN All Year except Christmas

Silver Award

THE KNOLL

Crowsley Road, Shiplake, Henley-on-Thames RG9 3JT
T: (01189) 402705
F: (01189) 402705
E: theknollhenley@aol.com
I: www.theknollhenley.co.uk

Beautifully restored home with every modern convenience, riverside walks and landscaped garden. Good base for Cotswolds, Oxford, Windsor, London and Heathrow. Free internet access and local calls. Winner of the Bed & Breakfast of the Year Award Southern England. Nominated Best British Breakfast.

Bedrooms: 1 double, 1 family
Bathrooms: 2 en suite

P €

B&B per person per night:
S £49.00
D £30.00

OPEN All Year

HENLEY-ON-THAMES continued

LENWADE

3 Western Road, Henley-on-Thames
RG9 1JL
T: (01491) 573468
F: (01491) 411664
E: lenwadeuk@aol.com
I: www.w3b-ink.com/lenwade

This beautiful Victorian home is in a quiet residential road within walking distance of town, river and station. Ample parking. Superb, individually cooked breakfasts. Convenient base for Oxford, Heathrow, Windsor. All rooms are en suite or with private bathrooms. All have telephone with modem connection.

Bedrooms: 2 double, 1 twin
Bathrooms: 2 en suite, 1 private

B&B per person per night:
S £45.00–£50.00
D £30.00–£32.50

OPEN All Year except Christmas

◆◆◆◆◆
Silver Award

THAMESMEAD HOUSE HOTEL

Remenham Lane, Remenham, Henley-on-Thames RG9 2LR
T: (01491) 574745
F: (01491) 579944
E: thamesmead@supanet.com
I: www.thamesmeadhousehotel.co.uk

Small, family-owned and managed hotel in a quiet location close to the town and river with the famous regatta course. The rooms are bright, stylish and contemporary. The art and decor is interesting, the ambience chic, and the atmosphere...totally relaxed.

Bedrooms: 4 double, 1 twin, 1 single
Bathrooms: 6 en suite

CC: Amex, Delta, Mastercard, Switch, Visa

Autumn and winter weekend breaks, stay Sat night and get Sun night half-price.

B&B per person per night:
S £105.00–£120.00
D £62.50–£67.50

OPEN All Year except Christmas

HERSTMONCEUX, East Sussex Map ref 3B4

◆◆◆◆

SANDHURST
Church Road, Herstmonceux, Hailsham BN27 1RG
T: (01323) 833088
F: (01323) 833088
E: junealanruss@aol.com

Bedrooms: 1 double, 2 family
Bathrooms: 3 en suite

Large bungalow with plenty of off-road parking. Within walking distance of Herstmonceux village and close to Herstmonceux Castle. Twenty minutes' drive to sea. No smoking.

B&B per person per night:
S £40.00–£50.00
D £25.00–£30.00

OPEN All Year except Christmas

HIGH WYCOMBE, Buckinghamshire Map ref 2C2 *Tourist Information Centre Tel: (01494) 421892*

AYAM MANOR

Hammersley Lane, High Wycombe
HP10 8HF
T: (01494) 816932
F: (01494) 816338
E: jeansenior@ayammanor.freeserve.co.uk
I: www.ayammanorguesthouse.co.uk

Very large Georgian house, decorated to a high standard, with spacious bedrooms, games room, swimming pool and sitting room. Secure off-road parking. A warm, friendly welcome awaits guests.

Bedrooms: 2 double, 2 single
Bathrooms: 4 en suite

Evening meal available
CC: Amex, Delta, Diners, Mastercard, Switch, Visa

Book 7 nights pay for 5.

B&B per person per night:
S £30.00–£60.00
D £30.00–£42.50

HB per person per night:
DY £40.00–£70.00

OPEN All Year except Christmas

HIGHCLERE, Hampshire Map ref 2C2

♦♦♦

HIGHCLERE FARM
Highclere, Newbury RG20 9PY
T: (01635) 255013
E: walshhighclere@newburyweb.net

Bedrooms: 1 double
Bathrooms: 1 en suite

An extremely comfortable converted coach house close to Highclere Castle in an Area of Outstanding Natural Beauty.

B&B per person per night:
S £35.00–£40.00
D £22.50–£25.00

OPEN All Year

HOOK, Hampshire Map ref 2C2

♦♦♦

OAKLEA GUEST HOUSE
London Road, Hook RG27 9LA
T: (01256) 762673
F: (01256) 762150
E: oakleaguesthouse@amserve.net

Bedrooms: 5 double, 2 twin, 2 single, 2 family
Bathrooms: 11 en suite

Evening meal available
CC: Delta, Mastercard, Switch, Visa

We have single, double and family rooms, all en suite, with colour TV, tea/coffee etc, also home-cooked evening meals. Ample car parking.

B&B per person per night:
S £35.00–£42.00
D £22.50–£27.50

HB per person per night:
DY £45.00–£65.00

OPEN All Year

HORLEY, Surrey Map ref 2D2

Silver Award

THE LAWN GUEST HOUSE

30 Massetts Road, Gatwick, Horley RH6 7DF
T: (01293) 775751
F: (01293) 821803
E: info@lawnguesthouse.co.uk
I: www.lawnguesthouse.co.uk

Imposing Victorian house in pretty gardens. Five minutes Gatwick. Two minutes' walk Horley. Station 300 yards. London 40 minutes. Bedrooms all en suite. Full English breakfast and continental for early departures. Guests' ice machine. On-line residents' computer for emails. Overnight/long-term parking. Airport transfers by arrangement.

Bedrooms: 3 double, 3 twin, 6 family
Bathrooms: 12 en suite

CC: Amex, Delta, Mastercard, Switch, Visa

B&B per person per night:
S £40.00–£45.00
D £27.50–£30.00

OPEN All Year

HOVE

See under Brighton & Hove

HYTHE, Hampshire Map ref 2C3

CHANGRI-LA
12 Ashleigh Close, Hythe, Southampton SO45 3QP
T: (023) 80846664

Bedrooms: 1 double, 1 twin
Bathrooms: 1 en suite, 1 private

Comfortable home on the edge of the New Forest close to Beaulieu, Bucklers Hard, Exbury Gardens, Calshot for sailing, windsurfing etc, and many more places of interest.

B&B per person per night:
S Min £25.00
D Min £23.00

OPEN All Year except Christmas

CHECK THE MAPS

The colour maps at the front of this guide show all the cities, towns and villages for which you will find accommodation entries. Refer to the town index to find the page on which they are listed.

INKPEN, Berkshire Map ref 2C2

THE SWAN INN

Inkpen, Hungerford RG17 9DX
T: (01488) 668326
F: (01488) 668306
E: enquiries@theswaninn-organics.co.uk
I: www.theswaninn-organics.co.uk

B&B per person per night:
S £40.00–£65.00
D £37.50–£45.00

OPEN All Year except Christmas

17thC inn located in an Area of Outstanding Natural Beauty, one mile from Coombe Gibbet, the highest point in Southern England (965ft). En suite bedrooms. Owned by local organic beef farmers, the bar food and restaurant use the best fresh organic ingredients. West Berkshire CAMRA 'Pub of the Year' 2000.

Bedrooms: 3 double, 4 twin, 1 single, 2 family
Bathrooms: 10 en suite

Evening meal available
CC: Delta, Mastercard, Switch, Visa

ISLE OF WIGHT

See under Bembridge, Bonchurch, Brighstone, Carisbrooke, Godshill, Ryde, Sandown, Shanklin, Whitwell

LEEDS, Kent Map ref 3B4

FURTHER FIELDS

Caring Lane, Leeds, Maidstone ME17 1TJ
T: (01622) 861288
E: furtherfields@aol.com

Bedrooms: 1 twin, 1 single

Evening meal available

B&B per person per night:
S £23.00
D Min £22.50

HB per person per night:
DY Min £31.50

OPEN All Year

A warm welcome in comfortable bungalow. Spectacular views of the Downs. Quiet countryside location, yet minutes from M20. Traditional home cooking using home-grown produce.

1 P

LEWES, East Sussex Map ref 2D3 *Tourist Information Centre Tel: (01273) 483448*

THE CROWN INN

High Street, Lewes BN7 2NA
T: (01273) 480670
F: (01273) 480679
E: sales@crowninn-lewes.co.uk
I: www.crowninn-lewes.co.uk

Bedrooms: 5 double, 2 single, 1 family
Bathrooms: 6 en suite

CC: Amex, Delta, Mastercard, Switch, Visa

B&B per person per night:
S £40.00–£55.00
D £30.00–£40.00

OPEN All Year

Family-run inn at the centre of historic town offering traditional food. Licensed bar open all day. Most rooms en suite. Meeting room available.

P €

13 HILL ROAD

Lewes BN7 1DB
T: (01273) 477723
F: (01273) 477723
E: kmyles@btclick.com

Bedrooms: 1 double
Bathrooms: 1 en suite

B&B per person per night:
S £30.00

OPEN All Year

House with self-contained flat which is the only part to be let. Property positioned on a hill with far-reaching views.

P

LINGFIELD, Surrey Map ref 2D2

LONG ACRES FARM

Newchapel Road, Lingfield RH7 6LE
T: (01342) 833205
F: (01622) 735038

Bedrooms: 2 family
Bathrooms: 2 en suite

B&B per person per night:
S Min £23.00
D Min £20.50

OPEN All Year

Modern bungalow. Off-road parking. Convenient base to visit London by train. Also Surrey, Kent and Sussex. Many local attractions. Six miles south M25 jct 6.

P

PRICES

Please check prices and other details at the time of booking.

LYMINGTON, Hampshire Map ref 2C3

♦♦♦

DURLSTON HOUSE
Gosport Street, Lymington
SO41 9EG
T: (01590) 677364
F: (01590) 689077
E: durlstonhouse@aol.com

Bedrooms: 4 double, 2 family
Bathrooms: 6 en suite

Evening meal available

B&B per person per night:
S £25.00–£40.00
D £25.00–£30.00

OPEN All Year

Detached house, all en suite bedrooms. Car park. Close to town centre, railway and IOW ferry. Warm, friendly welcome in comfortable surroundings.

P

LYMINSTER, West Sussex Map ref 2D3

SANDFIELD HOUSE
Lyminster Road, Wick,
Littlehampton BN17 7PG
T: (01903) 724129
F: (01903) 715041
E: thefbs@aol.com

Bedrooms: 1 double, 1 twin

B&B per person per night:
S £25.00–£40.00
D £20.00–£25.00

OPEN All Year

Spacious country-style family house in two acres. Between Arundel and sea, near Area of Outstanding Natural Beauty. Tourist Board Blue Badge Guide available.

P €

LYNDHURST, Hampshire Map ref 2C3

Silver Award

BURWOOD LODGE
27 Romsey Road, Lyndhurst SO43 7AA
T: (023) 80282445
F: (023) 80284104
E: burwood.1@ukonline.co.uk
I: www.burwoodlodge.co.uk

B&B per person per night:
S £30.00–£35.00
D £23.00–£30.00

OPEN All Year except Christmas

Lovely Edwardian house in 0.5-acre grounds, located just three minutes' walk to village high street, five minutes from open forest. Guest lounge and separate dining room overlook the gardens, promoting a relaxing environment. Bedrooms tastefully decorated: family, twin, single and a 4-poster room for those special, romantic occasions.

Bedrooms: 4 double, 1 single, 1 family
Bathrooms: 6 en suite

3 P €

♦♦♦♦

LITTLE HAYES
43 Romsey Road, Lyndhurst SO43 7AR
T: (023) 80283816
E: info@little-hayes.co.uk
I: www.little-hayes.co.uk

B&B per person per night:
S £25.00–£40.00
D £22.50–£32.50

OPEN All Year except Christmas

Delightful Victorian house set in beautiful, landscaped gardens. Superb location close to village and open forest. Ideal base for cycling and walking etc. Luxurious 4-poster, en suite bedrooms offering outstanding accommodation at affordable prices. Excellent food and exceptional service ensure a memorable stay. Little Hayes – a little bit special!

Bedrooms: 3 double, 1 twin, 1 family
Bathrooms: 4 en suite, 1 private

CC: Amex, Delta, Mastercard, Switch, Visa

Extended stay and out-of-season special rates available. Romantic breaks our speciality – call us to discuss your personal requirements.

6 P

MAP REFERENCES
Map references apply to the colour maps at the front of this guide.

LYNDHURST continued

THE PENNY FARTHING HOTEL

Romsey Road, Lyndhurst SO43 7AA
T: (023) 80284422
F: (023) 80284488
E: stay@pennyfarthinghotel.co.uk
I: www.pennyfarthinghotel.co.uk

Welcome to our cheerful hotel, conveniently situated a moment's walk from the village centre. Our cosy, centrally heated bedrooms have en suite shower or bath and wc, colour TV, clock, radio and tea/coffee-making facilities. We also provide a residents' bar/lounge, lock-up bicycle store and large, private car park.

Bedrooms: 13 double, 2 twin, 4 single, 3 family
Bathrooms: 22 en suite

CC: Amex, Delta, Diners, Mastercard, Switch, Visa

B&B per person per night:
S £35.00–£49.50
D £29.50–£49.50

OPEN All Year except Christmas

♦♦♦

ROSEDALE BED & BREAKFAST
24 Shaggs Meadow, Lyndhurst SO43 7BN
T: (023) 80283793
E: jenny@theangels.freeserve.co.uk

Bedrooms: 1 double, 1 twin, 1 family
Bathrooms: 2 en suite

Evening meal available

Family-run bed and breakfast in the centre of Lyndhurst. We cater for families. Colour TV, tea/coffee facilities. Breakfast served at your convenience. Evening meals by arrangement.

B&B per person per night:
S £25.00–£27.50
D £25.00–£27.50

HB per person per night:
DY £33.00–£39.50

OPEN All Year

MAIDENHEAD, Berkshire Map ref 2C2

♦♦

CARTLANDS COTTAGE
Kings Lane, Cookham Dean, Cookham, Maidenhead SL6 9AY
T: (01628) 482196

Bedrooms: 1 family
Bathrooms: 1 en suite

Family room in self-contained garden studio. Meals in delightful, timbered, character cottage with exposed beams. Traditional cottage garden. NT common land. Very quiet.

B&B per person per night:
S £27.50–£37.50
D £22.50–£30.00

OPEN All Year

Silver Award

MOOR FARM

Ascot Road, Holyport, Maidenhead SL6 2HY
T: (01628) 633761
F: (01628) 636167
E: moorfm@aol.com
I: www.windsor.gov.uk/moorfarm

Guests staying at Moor Farm enjoy exclusive use of a wing of this ancient manor house, dating from the early 13thC. Although convenient to jct 8/9 of the M4, Moor Farm enjoys a rural location on the edge of the conservation village of Holyport. Windsor four miles, Maidenhead one mile, Heathrow 12 miles. Self-catering also available.

Bedrooms: 2 double
Bathrooms: 1 en suite, 1 private

B&B per person per night:
S £45.00–£50.00
D £25.00–£30.00

OPEN All Year

MAIDSTONE, Kent Map ref 3B3 *Tourist Information Centre Tel: (01622) 602169*

♦♦♦

ROCK HOUSE HOTEL
102 Tonbridge Road, Maidstone ME16 8SL
T: (01622) 751616
F: (01622) 756119

Bedrooms: 7 double, 3 single, 4 family
Bathrooms: 8 en suite

CC: Delta, Mastercard, Switch, Visa

Family-run guesthouse close to town centre and M20, 30 minutes from the Channel Tunnel. Centrally situated for London, Gatwick and channel ports. French and German spoken.

B&B per person per night:
S £33.00–£41.00
D £23.50–£25.50

OPEN All Year except Christmas

MARLOW, Buckinghamshire Map ref 2C2 *Tourist Information Centre Tel: (01628) 483597*

◆◆◆

ACHA PANI

Bovingdon Green, Marlow SL7 2JL
T: (01628) 483435
F: (01628) 483435
E: mary@achapani.freeserve.co.uk

Bedrooms: 1 double, 1 twin, 1 single
Bathrooms: 1 en suite

Evening meal available

Modern house with large garden, in quiet location one mile north of Marlow. Easy access London, Windsor, Oxford Chilterns and Thames path.

10 P €

B&B per person per night:
S £20.00–£25.00
D £20.00–£24.00

OPEN All Year

◆◆◆

ACORN LODGE

79 Marlow Bottom Road, Marlow Bottom, Marlow SL7 3NA
T: (01628) 472197
F: (01628) 472197
E: acornlodge@btconnect.com
I: www.acornlodgemarlow.co.uk

Comfortable, peaceful accommodation with well-appointed, spacious rooms backing onto woodland. We offer a warm welcome and a good night's sleep in home-from-home surroundings. Minutes from motorway access. Perfect for a restful night and a good breakfast. Peggy, David and their happy little dog look forward to welcoming you to their home.

Bedrooms: 1 double, 2 suites
Bathrooms: 1 private

CC: Amex, Delta, Mastercard, Switch, Visa

For the business person requiring a longer or regular let, serviced, self-catering suites available – rates on request.

10 P

B&B per person per night:
S £39.00–£55.00
D £27.50–£37.50

OPEN All Year except Christmas

◆◆◆◆

HOLLY TREE HOUSE

Burford Close, Marlow Bottom, Marlow SL7 3NE
T: (01628) 891110
F: (01628) 481278
E: hollytreeaccommodation@yahoo.co.uk

Bedrooms: 6 double, 1 twin, 3 single, 2 family
Bathrooms: 12 en suite

CC: Delta, Diners, Mastercard, Switch, Visa

Detached property set in large gardens with fine views over the valley. Quiet yet convenient location. All rooms fully en suite. Outdoor heated swimming pool.

P

B&B per person per night:
S £74.50
D £44.75

OPEN All Year except Christmas

MEOPHAM, Kent Map ref 3B3

◆◆

NURSTEAD COURT

Nurstead Church Lane, Meopham, Gravesend DA13 9AD
T: (01474) 812121
F: (01474) 815133
E: info@nursteadcourt.co.uk
I: www.nursteadcourt.co.uk

Bedrooms: 2 double, 1 single, 1 family
Bathrooms: 2 en suite

Built in 1320, Nurstead Court is Grade I Listed historically, comfortable and in the country. Forty minutes from London, 15 minutes from Medway towns.

P

B&B per person per night:
S £25.00–£30.00
D £25.00–£37.50

OPEN All Year

MIDHURST, West Sussex Map ref 2C3 *Tourist Information Centre Tel: (01730) 817322*

◆◆◆◆

10 ASHFIELD CLOSE

Midhurst GU29 9RP
T: (01730) 814858
E: jennifer_morley@lineone.net

Bedrooms: 1 double, 1 twin
Bathrooms: 2 private

Located in the heart of Midhurst, quiet cul-de-sac. Choice of twin or double bedroom with private bathroom including power shower. Warm, friendly welcome.

P

B&B per person per night:
S £30.00–£40.00
D £25.00

OPEN All Year except Christmas

NB

IMPORTANT NOTE Information on accommodation listed in this guide has been supplied by the proprietors. As changes may occur you are advised to check details at the time of booking.

MILFORD-ON-SEA, Hampshire Map ref 2C3

♦♦♦♦

ALMA MATER

4 Knowland Drive, Milford-on-Sea, Lymington SO41 0RH
T: (01590) 642811
F: (01590) 642811
E: bandbalmamater@aol.com
I: www.almamater.org.uk

Bedrooms: 2 double, 1 twin
Bathrooms: 3 en suite

Evening meal available

Detached, quiet, spacious, non-smoking chalet bunglow with en suite bedrooms overlooking lovely garden. Close to village, beaches, New Forest and IOW. Evening meals by request.

B&B per person per night:
S £35.00–£40.00
D £27.00–£30.00

HB per person per night:
DY £44.00–£47.00

OPEN All Year

♦♦♦♦♦ Gold Award

BRIANTCROFT

George Road, Milford-on-Sea, Lymington SO41 0RS
T: (01590) 644355
F: (01590) 644185
E: florence.iles@lineone.net
I: www.briantcroft.co.uk

Elegant Edwardian house with spacious and luxurious rooms. Leafy lane and peaceful surroundings at the edge of the New Forest. Ten minutes' walk to the beach. Bedrooms have a 3-seater sofa, refreshment tray, colour TV, hairdryer etc. Breakfasts are a gourmet experience with traditional and tempting options using fresh and local produce.

Bedrooms: 2 double, 1 family
Bathrooms: 2 en suite, 1 private

Try our mid-week stress-buster in spring and winter – 4 nights (Mon-Thu) for the price of 3!

B&B per person per night:
S £40.00–£50.00
D £30.00–£37.50

OPEN All Year except Christmas

♦♦♦♦♦ Silver Award

HA'PENNY HOUSE

16 Whitby Road, Milford-on-Sea, Lymington SO41 0ND
T: (01590) 641210
F: (01590) 641227
E: info@hapennyhouse.co.uk
I: www.hapennyhouse.co.uk

A delightful character house with a warm, friendly atmosphere, set in a quiet area near the sea and village. The New Forest, Lymington and Isle of Wight are close by. The beautifully decorated bedrooms are all en suite with TV and tea/coffee facilities. Excellent breakfasts with many choices. Guest lounge. Ample private parking.

Bedrooms: 3 double, 1 twin
Bathrooms: 4 en suite

CC: Amex, Delta, Mastercard, Switch, Visa

B&B per person per night:
S £32.00–£38.00
D £24.00–£28.00

OPEN All Year

MILTON KEYNES, Buckinghamshire Map ref 2C1

♦♦♦

CHANTRY FARM

Pindon End, Hanslope, Milton Keynes MK19 7HL
T: (01908) 510269
F: (01908) 510269
E: chuff.wake@tiscali.co.uk

Bedrooms: 1 double, 2 twin
Bathrooms: 2 en suite

500-acre farm. Stone farmhouse, 1650, with inglenook. Surrounded by beautiful countryside. Swimming pool, trout lake, table tennis, croquet, clay-pigeon shooting. Fifteen minutes from centre.

B&B per person per night:
S £20.00–£30.00
D £20.00–£30.00

HB per person per night:
DY £25.00–£30.00

OPEN All Year except Christmas

QUALITY ASSURANCE SCHEME

Diamond ratings and awards are explained at the back of this guide.

MILTON KEYNES continued

♦♦♦

KINGFISHERS

9 Rylstone Close, Heelands,
Milton Keynes MK13 7QT
T: (01908) 310231
F: (01908) 318601
E: kanjass@yahoo.com
I: www.kingfishersmk.co.uk

Bedrooms: 1 double, 1 twin, 1 single, 1 family
Bathrooms: 2 en suite, 2 private

Large, private home in 0.25 acres of grounds, convenient for city centre, shopping, theatre and railway station. Very comfortable, a warm welcome assured. Mob: 07866 424 417.

B&B per person per night:
S £20.00–£30.00
D £30.00–£40.00

HB per person per night:
DY £30.00–£40.00

OPEN All Year

MOULSFORD ON THAMES, Oxfordshire Map ref 2C2

♦♦♦♦ Silver Award

WHITE HOUSE

Moulsford on Thames, Wallingford
OX10 9JD
T: (01491) 651397
F: (01491) 652560
E: mwatsham@hotmail.com

Bedrooms: 1 double, 1 twin, 1 single
Bathrooms: 1 en suite

Evening meal available

Beautifully appointed ground floor accommodation in a detached family home surrounded by large garden. Picturesque Thames-side village, convenient for Oxford, Henley and Reading.

B&B per person per night:
S £35.00
D Min £30.00

HB per person per night:
DY £45.00–£55.00

NAPHILL, Buckinghamshire Map ref 2C1

♦♦♦

WOODPECKERS

244 Main Road, Naphill, High Wycombe
HP14 4RX
T: (01494) 563728
E: angela.brand@virgin.net
I: www.woodpeckersbedandbreakfast.co.uk

Situated in Chiltern Hills. Accommodation in modernised annexe with garden which can also be rented as a separate holiday cottage. Rooms en suite. Easily accessible for London, Oxford, Windsor, Henley, Heathrow Airport. Beautiful walks, pub food and places of interest minutes away. Warm welcome guaranteed.

Bedrooms: 2 double, 1 single
Bathrooms: 2 en suite, 1 private

Evening meal available

B&B per person per night:
S £24.00–£30.00
D £23.00–£25.00

OPEN All Year

NETHER WALLOP, Hampshire Map ref 2C2

♦♦♦

HALCYON

Church Hill, Nether Wallop,
Stockbridge SO20 8EY
T: (01264) 781348

Bedrooms: 1 double, 1 single, 1 family
Bathrooms: 1 en suite

Large, modern bungalow, situated in peaceful surroundings in country lane above church. Ten minutes' walking distance from Five Bells pub which provides very good evening meals.

B&B per person per night:
S £26.00–£30.00
D £23.00–£25.00

OPEN All Year

♦♦♦♦

YORK LODGE

Five Bells Lane, Nether Wallop,
Stockbridge SO20 8HE
T: (01264) 781313
F: (01264) 781313
E: bradley@yorklodge.fslife.co.uk
I: www.york-lodge.co.uk

Bedrooms: 2 twin
Bathrooms: 2 en suite

Evening meal available

Comfortable, self-contained wing of charming modern house in peaceful, secluded garden on edge of picturesque village. Pub nearby. Easy reach of Stonehenge, Salisbury and Winchester.

B&B per person per night:
S £30.00–£35.00
D £25.00–£35.00

HB per person per night:
DY £45.00–£55.00

OPEN All Year

COLOUR MAPS Colour maps at the front of this guide pinpoint all places under which you will find accommodation listed.

NETTLESTEAD, Kent Map ref 3B4

ROCK FARM HOUSE

Gibbs Hill, Nettlestead, Maidstone
ME18 5HT
T: (01622) 812244
F: (01622) 812244
I: www.rockfarmhousebandb.co.uk

B&B per person per night:
S £35.00
D £30.00

OPEN All Year except Christmas

Delightful 18thC Kentish farmhouse situated in a quiet and idyllic position on a farm with extensive views and surrounded by two acres of beautiful garden developed by Sue Corfe, a professional horticulturalist, and opened to the public through the National Gardens Scheme and Good Garden Guide. Well-furnished, spacious, light and airy rooms with en suite or sole-use facilities.

Bedrooms: 1 double, 2 twin
Bathrooms: 2 en suite, 1 private

NEW FOREST

See under Ashurst, Beaulieu, Brockenhurst, Fordingbridge, Godshill, Hythe, Lymington, Lyndhurst, Milford-on-Sea, New Milton, Sway

NEW MILTON, Hampshire Map ref 2B3

TAVERNERS COTTAGE

Bashley Cross Road, Bashley,
New Milton BH25 5SZ
T: (01425) 615403
F: (01425) 632177
E: jbaines@supanet.com
I: www.taverners.cottage.bandb.baines.com

Bedrooms: 1 double, 1 family
Bathrooms: 2 en suite

B&B per person per night:
S £26.00–£36.00
D £24.00–£26.00

OPEN All Year except Christmas

Pretty white-painted cob cottage, dating back some 300 years, overlooking open farmland. Warm welcome in quality accommodation. Close to both sea and forest.

♦♦♦

WILLY'S WELL

Bashley Common Road, Wootton,
New Milton BH25 5SF
T: (01425) 616834
E: moyramac2@hotmail.com

B&B per person per night:
S £30.00
D £25.00

OPEN All Year

A warm welcome awaits you at our mid-1700s Listed thatched cottage standing in one acre of mature gardens also available for your enjoyment. We have direct forest access through six acres of pasture and are three miles from the sea. Ideal for walking, cycling, horse-riding.

Bedrooms: 2 double
Bathrooms: 1 en suite, 1 private

Mid-week reduced breaks: 4 nights for the price of 3.

NEWBURY, Berkshire Map ref 2C2 *Tourist Information Centre Tel: (01635) 30267*

Silver Award

MANOR FARM HOUSE

Church Street, Hampstead Norreys, Thatcham RG18 0TD
T: (01635) 201276
F: (01635) 201035
E: bettsbedandbreakfast@hotmail.com
I: www.bettsbedandbreakfast.co.uk

Spacious and comfortable, Grade II Listed farmhouse. Arable and beef farm in centre of attractive village of Hampstead Norreys, just seven miles north of Newbury. Ideal base for touring in the Thames Valley and Oxford area. Well positioned for journeys to the West Country and Heathrow Airport (50 minutes).

Bedrooms: 1 double, 1 family, 1 suite
Bathrooms: 2 en suite

Weekend breaks (2 nights) from £50pp

B&B per person per night:
S £35.00–£40.00
D £25.00–£27.50

OPEN All Year except Christmas

♦♦♦♦
Silver Award

THE OLD FARMHOUSE

Downend Lane, Chieveley, Newbury RG20 8TN
T: (01635) 248361
E: palletts@aol.com
I: www.smoothhound.co.uk/hotels/oldfarmhouse

Period farmhouse on edge of village within two miles of M4/A34 (jct13), five miles north of Newbury. Accommodation in ground floor annexe comprising hall, kitchenette, sitting room (with bed settee), double bedroom, bathroom. Large gardens overlooking countryside. Oxford, Bath, Windsor and Heathrow Airport within easy reach. London approximately one hour.

Bedrooms: 1 double
Bathrooms: 1 en suite

B&B per person per night:
S £38.00–£42.00
D £29.00–£31.00

OPEN All Year

OLNEY, Buckinghamshire Map ref 2C1

♦♦♦♦

THE LINDENS

30A High Street, Olney MK46 4BB
T: (01234) 712891
E: thelindens@amserve.net
I: www.thelindens.com

Bedrooms: 1 double, 2 twin, 1 family
Bathrooms: 2 en suite

Late-Victorian townhouse with large garden, situated on high street of historic market town. Good-quality restaurants nearby.

B&B per person per night:
S £25.00–£35.00
D £20.00–£25.00

OPEN All Year

TILE BARN

11 Spring Lane, Olney MK46 5HT
T: (01234) 713723
E: trevorcooper820@msn.com

Bedrooms: 1 double
Bathrooms: 1 en suite

Luxury, non-smoking, self-contained. Double-bedded room, integral lounge/kitchenette, en suite shower/toilet. Patio doors to decking and garden. Close to town centre.

B&B per person per night:
S £35.00
D £30.00

OPEN All Year except Christmas

OXFORD, Oxfordshire Map ref 2C1 *Tourist Information Centre Tel: (01865) 726871*

♦

BECKET HOUSE

5 Becket Street, Oxford OX1 7PP
T: (01865) 724675
F: (01865) 724675

Bedrooms: 3 double, 2 twin, 2 single
Bathrooms: 4 en suite, 1 private

CC: Delta, Mastercard, Switch, Visa

Friendly guesthouse convenient for rail and bus station, within walking distance of city centre and colleges. Good, clean accommodation, en suite rooms.

B&B per person per night:
S £30.00–£45.00
D £24.00–£34.00

OPEN All Year except Christmas

OXFORD continued

◆◆◆

THE BUNGALOW
Mill Lane, Old Marston, Oxford
OX3 0QF
T: (01865) 557171

Bedrooms: 2 double,
1 twin
Bathrooms: 2 en suite

B&B per person per night:
S £25.00–£35.00
D £25.00–£55.00

Modern bungalow set in five acres, in quiet location with views over open countryside, three miles from city centre. No smoking. No bus route – car essential.

6 P

◆◆◆◆◆
Silver Award

COTSWOLD HOUSE
363 Banbury Road, Oxford OX2 7PL
T: (01865) 310558
F: (01865) 310558
E: d.r.walker@talk21.com
I: www.house363.freeserve.co.uk

Bedrooms: 3 double,
2 single, 2 family
Bathrooms: 7 en suite

CC: Delta, Mastercard,
Switch, Visa

B&B per person per night:
S £50.00–£60.00
D £37.50–£45.00

OPEN All Year

A well situated and elegant property, offering good accommodation and service. Cotswold House is in a most desirable part of Oxford.

6 P

◆◆◆

DIAL HOUSE
25 London Road, Headington,
Oxford OX3 7RE
T: (01865) 425100
F: (01865) 427388
E: dialhouse@ntlworld.com
I: www.dialhouseoxford.co.uk

Bedrooms: 5 double,
2 twin, 1 family
Bathrooms: 8 en suite

CC: Amex, Delta,
Mastercard, Switch, Visa

B&B per person per night:
S £48.00–£60.00
D £29.50–£35.00

OPEN All Year

Internet-accessible guesthouse built in a Tudor style. Close to city centre, walking distance to hospitals, on main bus route to London Heathrow Airport.

P €

◆◆◆◆

HEYFORD HILL GARDENS
Heyford Hill Lane, Littlemore,
Oxford OX4 4YH
T: (01865) 777403
F: (01865) 395334
E: heyfordhillgdns@aol.com
I: www.guestaccom.co.uk/879.htm

Bedrooms: 1 double,
1 twin
Bathrooms: 2 en suite

Evening meal available

B&B per person per night:
S £40.00–£45.00
D £30.00–£35.00

OPEN All Year

One-hundred-and-fifty-year-old stone farmhouse in 15 acres. Three miles from Oxford. Ground floor guest rooms in converted barn with breakfast served in large conservatory.

10 P €

◆◆◆

HIGHFIELD WEST
188 Cumnor Hill, Oxford OX2 9PJ
T: (01865) 863007
E: highfieldwest@msn.com
I: www.oxfordcity.co.uk/accom/
highfield-west

Bedrooms: 1 double,
1 twin, 2 single, 1 family
Bathrooms: 3 en suite

B&B per person per night:
S £30.00–£33.00
D £27.50–£32.50

OPEN All Year except
Christmas

Comfortable accommodation with good access to city centre and ring road. Large outdoor, heated swimming pool (summer season only). Vegetarian cooked breakfast. Non-smoking.

P

◆◆◆◆
Silver Award

HOME FARM HOUSE
Holton, Nr Wheatley, Oxford
OX33 1QA
T: (01865) 872334
F: (01865) 876220
E: sonja.barter@tiscali.co.uk

Bedrooms: 1 double,
1 twin
Bathrooms: 1 en suite,
1 private

B&B per person per night:
D £30.00

OPEN All Year except
Christmas

Private country home, large garden set in 15 acres of historic parkland with lake. A quiet, peaceful location close to all amenities and main roads.

P

◆◆

ISIS GUEST HOUSE
45-53 Iffley Road, Oxford OX4 1ED
T: (01865) 248894
F: (01865) 243492
E: isis@herald.ox.ac.uk

Bedrooms: 22 double,
1 twin, 12 single,
2 family
Bathrooms: 14 en suite

CC: Mastercard, Switch,
Visa

B&B per person per night:
S £28.00–£32.00
D £28.00–£30.00

HB per person per night:
DY £28.00–£32.00

Modernised, Victorian, city centre guesthouse within walking distance of colleges and shops. Easy access to ring road.

P

OXFORD continued

◆◆◆◆

THE LODGE
Horton Hill, Horton cum Studley, Oxford OX33 1AY
T: (01865) 351235
F: (01865) 351721
E: res@studleylodge.com
I: www.studleylodge.com

Bedrooms: 14 double, 1 single, 1 family
Bathrooms: 16 en suite

Evening meal available
CC: Amex, Delta, Diners, Mastercard, Switch, Visa

B&B per person per night:
S £55.00–£75.00
D £35.00–£50.00

OPEN All Year

Charming hotel with a unique atmosphere, in a village close to Oxford. Easy access to M40. Excellent restaurant. Themed bedrooms, some with balcony or patio.

◆◆◆◆

MARLBOROUGH HOUSE HOTEL

321 Woodstock Road, Oxford OX2 7NY
T: (01865) 311321
F: (01865) 515329
E: marlboroughhouse@btconnect.com
I: www.oxfordcity.co.uk/hotels/marlborough

B&B per person per night:
S £75.00
D £41.50

OPEN All Year

Immaculate, spacious, privately owned hotel located in attractive leafy area of Victorian houses, 1.5 miles city centre. Bedrooms equipped with a kitchenette containing fridge, microwave, tea/coffee-making facilities, telephone and TV, comfortable chairs, dining table and desk. Restaurants and shops are located within 10 minutes' walk.

Bedrooms: 11 double, 1 twin, 2 single, 2 family
Bathrooms: 16 en suite

CC: Amex, Delta, Diners, Mastercard, Switch, Visa

◆◆◆

MILKA'S GUEST HOUSE
379 Iffley Road, Oxford OX4 4DP
T: (01865) 778458
F: (01865) 776477
E: reservations@milkas.co.uk
I: www.milkas.co.uk

Bedrooms: 3 double
Bathrooms: 1 en suite

CC: Amex, Delta, Mastercard, Switch, Visa

B&B per person per night:
S £35.00–£55.00
D £30.00–£35.00

OPEN All Year

A pleasant, family-run guesthouse on main road, only one mile from city centre.

CREDIT CARD BOOKINGS If you book by telephone and are asked for your credit card number it is advisable to check the proprietor's policy should you cancel your reservation.

OXFORD continued

◆◆◆

NEWTON HOUSE
82-84 Abingdon Road, Oxford
OX1 4PL
T: (01865) 240561
F: (01865) 244647
E: newton.house@btinternet.com
I: www.oxfordcity.co.uk/accom/newton

Bedrooms: 6 double, 7 family
Bathrooms: 11 en suite

CC: Amex, Delta, Mastercard, Switch, Visa

B&B per person per night:
S £38.00–£48.00
D £24.00–£33.50

OPEN All Year

Handsome Victorian townhouses linked to form a sizeable guesthouse. Many original features and period furniture. Located close to restaurants, pubs and shops. Vegetarian and special diets catered for.

P

◆◆◆

PARK HOUSE
7 St Bernard's Road, Oxford
OX2 6EH
T: (01865) 310824

Bedrooms: 1 double, 1 single

B&B per person per night:
S £30.00–£35.00
D £30.00

HB per person per night:
DY Min £30.00

OPEN All Year

Traditional, Victorian, terraced house in north Oxford, five minutes' walk from city centre and within easy reach of all amenities.

P

◆◆◆◆

PICKWICKS GUEST HOUSE
15-17 London Road, Headington,
Oxford OX3 7SP
T: (01865) 750487
F: (01865) 742208
E: pickwicks@tiscali.co.uk
I: www.oxfordcity.co.uk/accom/pickwicks/

Bedrooms: 7 double, 4 single, 4 family
Bathrooms: 13 en suite

CC: Amex, Delta, Diners, Mastercard, Switch, Visa

B&B per person per night:
S £30.00–£45.00
D £30.00–£40.00

OPEN All Year except Christmas

Comfortable guesthouse within five minutes' drive of Oxford ring road and M40 motorway. Nearby coach stop for 24-hour service to central London, Heathrow and Gatwick airports.

P

◆◆◆

RED MULLIONS
23 London Road, Headington,
Oxford OX3 7RE
T: (01865) 742741
F: (01865) 769944
E: redmullion@aol.com
I: www.oxfordcity.co.uk/accom/redmullions

Bedrooms: 8 double, 4 family
Bathrooms: 11 en suite, 1 private

CC: Amex, Delta, Mastercard, Switch, Visa

B&B per person per night:
S £50.00–£60.00
D £30.00–£35.00

OPEN All Year

Large, detached house close to shops, hospitals and ring road. Bus stops outside for city centre and London.

P €

◆◆◆

RIVER HOTEL
17 Botley Road, Oxford OX2 0AA
T: (01865) 243475
F: (01865) 724306
E: reception@riverhotel.co.uk
I: www.riverhotel.co.uk

B&B per person per night:
S £32.50–£35.00
D £35.00–£45.00

OPEN All Year except Christmas

Excellent, picturesque location beside Osney bridge on River Thames Walk. Originally a master builder's home built c1870s, run many years as an independent small hotel by proprietor and staff. Like so much of Oxford the property is owned by an Oxford College. Twenty, well-equipped bedrooms, all own bathroom. Car park on site.

Bedrooms: 9 double, 2 twin, 2 single, 5 family
Bathrooms: 17 en suite, 1 private

CC: Mastercard, Visa

5 P

OXFORD continued

SPORTSVIEW GUEST HOUSE

106-110 Abingdon Road, Oxford OX1 4PX
T: (01865) 200089
F: (01865) 249270
E: stay@sportsview.guest-house.freeserve.co.uk
I: www.smoothhound.co.uk/hotels/sportsvi.html

Friendly, family-run Victorian guesthouse overlooking Queens College sports ground, 0.5 miles from city centre. Close to open-air swimming pool. See the colleges and other famous landmarks such as the Sheldonian theatre and Botanical Gardens. Frequent and direct bus services to London and Blenheim Palace.

Bedrooms: 9 double, 6 single, 5 family
Bathrooms: 16 en suite

CC: Delta, Mastercard, Switch, Visa

B&B per person per night:
S £30.00–£50.00
D £23.00–£34.00

◆◆◆◆

THE TOWER HOUSE HOTEL
15 Ship Street, Oxford OX1 3DA
T: (01865) 246828
F: (01865) 247508
E: thetowerhouse@btconnect.com
I: www.towerhouseoxford.co.uk

Bedrooms: 7 double
Bathrooms: 4 en suite

CC: Amex, Delta, Mastercard, Switch, Visa

17thC guesthouse in university city centre, renowned for its warm hospitality and good, hearty breakfasts. Recently awarded 4 diamonds. This establishment is also of historical interest.

B&B per person per night:
S £65.00–£85.00
D £37.50–£55.00

OPEN All Year except Christmas

OXTED, Surrey Map ref 2D2

◆◆◆

ARAWA
58 Granville Road, Oxted RH8 0BZ
T: (01883) 714104
F: (01883) 714104
E: david@davidgibbs.co.uk

Bedrooms: 1 twin, 1 family
Bathrooms: 1 en suite, 1 private

Family home near North Downs Way, Chartwell and Hever. Near rail service to London and 30 minutes to Gatwick by car. Friendly and comfortable. Enjoy your stay!

B&B per person per night:
S £25.00–£45.00
D £25.00–£35.00

OPEN All Year

◆◆◆

THE NEW BUNGALOW
Old Hall Farm, Tandridge Lane, Oxted RH8 9NS
T: (01342) 892508
F: (01342) 892508
E: don.nunn@tesco.net

Bedrooms: 2 double, 1 twin
Bathrooms: 1 en suite

Spacious, modern bungalow set in green fields and reached by a private drive. 5 minutes' drive from M25. London easily accessible by train.

B&B per person per night:
S £25.00–£32.00
D £20.00–£22.50

OPEN All Year except Christmas

PARTRIDGE GREEN, West Sussex Map ref 2D3

◆◆◆

POUND COTTAGE BED & BREAKFAST
Mill Lane, Littleworth, Partridge Green, Horsham RH13 8JU
T: (01403) 710218
F: (01403) 711337
E: poundcottagebb@amserve.net
I: www.horsham.co.uk/poundcottage.html

Bedrooms: 1 double, 1 twin, 1 single
Bathrooms: 1 en suite

Pleasant country house in quiet surroundings, 8 miles from Horsham, 25 minutes from Gatwick. Just off the B2135 West Grinstead to Steyning road.

B&B per person per night:
S £22.00–£24.00
D £22.00–£24.00

OPEN All Year

CONFIRM YOUR BOOKING
You are advised to confirm your booking in writing.

PETERSFIELD, Hampshire Map ref 2C3 *Tourist Information Centre Tel: (01730) 268829*

◆◆◆

HEATH FARMHOUSE

Heath Road East, Petersfield
GU31 4HU
T: (01730) 264709
E: info@heathfarmhouse.co.uk
I: www.heathfarmhouse.co.uk

Bedrooms: 1 double, 1 twin, 1 family
Bathrooms: 2 en suite, 1 private

Georgian farmhouse with lovely views and large garden. Surrounded by quiet farmland only 0.75 miles from town centre. Within easy reach of Portsmouth, Chichester, Winchester.

B&B per person per night:
S £25.00–£35.00
D £22.00–£25.00

OPEN All Year except Christmas

◆◆◆◆

1 THE SPAIN

Sheep Street, Petersfield GU32 3JZ
T: (01730) 263261
F: (01730) 261084
E: allantarva@cw.com.net

Bedrooms: 2 double, 1 twin
Bathrooms: 2 en suite, 1 private

18thC house with charming walled garden, in conservation area of Petersfield. Good eating places nearby, lovely walks, plenty to see and do.

B&B per person per night:
S £23.00–£30.00
D £21.00–£23.00

OPEN All Year

PETWORTH, West Sussex Map ref 2D3

◆◆◆◆

EEDES COTTAGE

Bignor Park Road, Bury Gate,
Pulborough RH20 1EZ
T: (01798) 831438
F: (01798) 831942
E: eedes.bandb.hare@amserve.com
I: www.visitsussex.org/eedescottage

Bedrooms: 1 double, 2 twin
Bathrooms: 1 ensuite

Quiet country house surrounded by farmland. Convenient main roads to Arundel, Chichester and Brighton. Dogs, horses accommodated. TV in all rooms.

B&B per person per night:
S Min £30.00
D £25.00–£27.50

OPEN All Year

POLEGATE, East Sussex Map ref 2D3

◆◆◆◆

THE COTTAGE

Dittons Road, Polegate BN26 6HS
T: (01323) 482011
F: (01323) 482011
E: Dream@tinyworld.co.uk

Bedrooms: 3 double
Bathrooms: 2 private

The Cottage is situated on the rural outskirts of Polegate. Ample, well-lit parking available and easy access to the A27.

B&B per person per night:
S £25.00–£35.00
D £20.00–£25.00

OPEN All Year except Christmas

POOLE, Dorset Map ref 2B3 *Tourist Information Centre Tel: (01202) 253253*

◆◆◆◆

THE SHAH OF PERSIA

173 Longfleet Road, Poole
BH15 2HS
T: (01202) 676587
F: (01202) 679327

Bedrooms: 9 double, 4 single, 2 family
Bathrooms: 15 en suite

Evening meal available
CC: Amex, Delta, Mastercard, Switch, Visa

The Shah is a landmark building in the heart of Poole.

B&B per person per night:
S £49.00–£54.00
D £29.50–£39.50

OPEN All Year

PORTSMOUTH & SOUTHSEA, Hampshire Map ref 2C3

◆◆◆

BEMBELL COURT HOTEL

69 Festing Road, Southsea PO4 0NQ
T: (023) 92735915
F: (023) 92756497
E: keith@bembell.co.uk
I: www.bembell.co.uk

Bedrooms: 4 double, 3 twin, 1 single, 3 family
Bathrooms: 11 en suite

CC: Amex, Delta, Diners, Mastercard, Switch, Visa

Friendly, family-run hotel ideally situated in Portsmouth's prime holiday area. A short stroll from shops, restaurants, pubs, boating lake and rose gardens. Close to ferries.

B&B per person per night:
S £43.00–£46.00
D £28.00–£29.50

OPEN All Year

RATING All accommodation in this guide has been rated, or is awaiting a rating, by a trained VisitBritain assessor.

PORTSMOUTH & SOUTHSEA continued

◆◆◆◆

HAMILTON HOUSE

95 Victoria Road North, Portsmouth
PO5 1PS
T: (023) 92823502
F: (023) 92823502
E: sandra@hamiltonhouse.co.uk
I: www.hamiltonhouse.co.uk

Bedrooms: 5 double, 2 twin, 2 family
Bathrooms: 6 en suite

CC: Delta, Mastercard, Switch, Visa

B&B per person per night:
S £30.00–£50.00
D £23.00–£27.00

OPEN All Year

Delightful Victorian townhouse, many original features. Five minutes to continental/IOW ferry ports, stations, university, historic ships/museums. Ideal touring base. Breakfast served from 0615.

P €

◆◆◆◆ Silver Award

131 THE HIGH STREET

Old Portsmouth, Portsmouth
PO1 2HW
T: (023) 92730903

Bedrooms: 2 double
Bathrooms: 1 en suite, 1 private

B&B per person per night:
D £29.00–£31.00

18thC Georgian house near seafront, historic dockyard, station, ferries and restaurants. Offers luxurious bedrooms, breakfast in bed, parking, warm welcome. Non-smokers only.

P €

◆◆◆◆ Silver Award

THE ROWANS GUEST HOUSE

43 Festing Grove, Southsea
PO4 9QB
T: (023) 92736614
F: (023) 92823711
E: mikejsmart@yahoo.com

Bedrooms: 3 double
Bathrooms: 2 en suite

B&B per person per night:
S £28.00–£38.00
D £25.00–£56.00

OPEN All Year

Elegant Victorian guesthouse in quiet residential area. Close to seafront and all amenities. Convenient for ferry ports. Early breakfasts available. Off- and on-street parking.

P

RAMSGATE, Kent Map ref 3C3 *Tourist Information Centre Tel: (01843) 583333/583334*

◆◆◆◆

GLENDEVON GUEST HOUSE

8 Truro Road, Ramsgate CT11 8DB
T: (01843) 570909
F: (01843) 570909
E: adrian.everix@btopenworld.com

Bedrooms: 2 double, 2 twin, 2 family
Bathrooms: 6 en suite

CC: Amex, Delta, Mastercard, Switch, Visa

B&B per person per night:
S £24.00
D £18.00–£24.00

OPEN All Year

Delightful converted Victorian house near beach, harbour and town. Very comfortable rooms, all en suite and each containing attractive feature of modern kitchen/dining area.

5

READING, Berkshire Map ref 2C2 *Tourist Information Centre Tel: (0118) 956 6226*

◆◆◆

DITTISHAM GUEST HOUSE

63 Tilehurst Road, Reading
RG30 2JL
T: (0118) 9569483
E: dittishamgh@aol.com

Bedrooms: 1 double, 4 single
Bathrooms: 3 en suite

CC: Delta, Mastercard, Switch, Visa

B&B per person per night:
S £27.50–£35.00
D £18.75–£27.50

OPEN All Year

Renovated Edwardian property with garden, in a quiet but central location. Good value and quality. On bus routes for centre of town. Car park.

P €

RINGMER, East Sussex Map ref 2D3

◆◆◆◆

BRYN-CLAI

Uckfield Road, Ringmer, Lewes
BN8 5RU
T: (01273) 814042
I: www.brynclai.co.uk

Bedrooms: 1 double, 1 twin, 1 family
Bathrooms: 1 en suite, 1 private

B&B per person per night:
S £25.00–£35.00
D £45.00–£55.00

OPEN All Year

Modern house set in seven acres. All rooms have TV and tea-making facilities. Second night at reduced rates. Good parking. Close to Glyndebourne.

P

ACCESSIBILITY

Look for the symbols which indicate National Accessible Scheme standards for hearing and visually impaired guests in addition to standards for guests with mobility impairment. You can find an index of all scheme participants at the back of this guide.

ROCHESTER, Kent Map ref 3B3 *Tourist Information Centre Tel: (01634) 843666*

KING CHARLES HOTEL

Brompton Road, Gillingham ME7 5QT
T: (01634) 830303
F: (01634) 829430
E: enquiries@kingcharleshotel.co.uk
I: www.kingcharleshotel.co.uk

B&B per person per night:
S £37.00–£39.00
D £22.00–£23.00

OPEN All Year

A privately owned, modern hotel with a cosy restaurant and first-class conference and banqueting facilities. All bedrooms have en suite bathroom, tea/coffee-making facilities, hairdryer, telephone and TV. We are ideal as a base for exploring South East England and London, and we offer extremely competitive group rates.

Bedrooms: 30 double, 30 twin, 5 single, 31 family, 2 suites
Bathrooms: 96 en suite

Evening meal available
CC: Amex, Delta, Diners, Mastercard, Switch, Visa

P €

♦♦♦

ST MARTIN

104 Borstal Road, Rochester
ME1 3BD
T: (01634) 848192
E: icolvin@stmartin.freeserve.co.uk

Bedrooms: 3 double

Evening meal available

B&B per person per night:
S £18.00
D £18.00

Victorian family home overlooking the River Medway, close to city centre. Ideal for North Downs Way.

€

ROMSEY, Hampshire Map ref 2C3 *Tourist Information Centre Tel: (01794) 512987*

♦♦♦♦

RANVILLES FARM HOUSE

Ower, Romsey SO51 6AA
T: (023) 80814481
F: (023) 80814481
E: info@ranvilles.com
I: www.ranvilles.com

Bedrooms: 1 double, 1 single, 1 family
Bathrooms: 3 en suite

B&B per person per night:
S £30.00–£35.00
D £25.00–£30.00

OPEN All Year except Christmas

A historic farmhouse near Winchester, Salisbury, the New Forest, and one mile from Romsey. Peaceful situation, set in five acres of gardens and paddocks. Extra-large beds.

P

♦♦♦♦

ROSELEA

Hamdown Crescent, East Wellow, Romsey SO51 6BJ
T: (01794) 323262
F: (01794) 323262
E: beds@roselea.info
I: www.roselea.info

Bedrooms: 2 double, 1 single
Bathrooms: 2 en suite

B&B per person per night:
S £18.00–£25.00
D £20.00–£22.50

OPEN All Year except Christmas

Quiet, ground floor accommodation on the edge of the New Forest. Honey from our own bees, together with home-produced or local food served for breakfast.

8 P

COUNTRY CODE Always follow the Country Code ❦ Enjoy the countryside and respect its life and work ❦ Guard against all risk of fire ❦ Fasten all gates ❦ Keep your dogs under close control ❦ Keep to public paths across farmland ❦ Use gates and stiles to cross fences, hedges and walls ❦ Leave livestock, crops and machinery alone ❦ Take your litter home ❦ Help to keep all water clean ❦ Protect wildlife, plants and trees ❦ Take special care on country roads ❦ Make no unnecessary noise

ROYAL TUNBRIDGE WELLS, Kent Map ref 2D2 *Tourist Information Centre Tel: (01892) 515675*

BURRSWOOD CHAPEL HOUSE

Burrswood, Bird in Hand Lane, Groombridge, Royal Tunbridge Wells TN3 9PY
T: (01892) 863637
F: (01892) 862597
E: admin@burrswood.org.uk
I: www.burrswood.org.uk

Chapel House is a country guesthouse in the beautiful High Weald of Kent. Set in the landscaped grounds adjacent to Burrswood Hospital, it offers magnificent views, tranquil walks, good food and comfortable, en suite rooms. Guests enjoy the gardens, lovely Italianate church, bookshop, gift shop and welcoming tea room.

Bedrooms: 5 double, 6 single
Bathrooms: 11 en suite

Evening meal available
CC: Delta, Mastercard, Switch, Visa

B&B per person per night:
S £41.50–£46.50
D £35.00–£46.50

HB per person per night:
DY £42.00–£53.50

OPEN All Year

♦♦♦♦

CHEVIOTS

Cousley Wood, Wadhurst TN5 6HD
T: (01892) 782952
E: b&b@cheviots99.freeserve.co.uk
I: www.cheviots.info

Cheviots is a large country house set in a beautiful six-acre garden in the heart of the Weald countryside. There is a guests' lounge and games room. We serve full English breakfast with local produce. Good base for walking, cycling. Many NT properties nearby including Sissinghurst and Chartwell. Close Bewl Water.

Bedrooms: 1 double, 1 twin, 1 single
Bathrooms: 2 en suite

Evening meal available
CC: Delta, Mastercard, Switch, Visa

4 nights for the price of 3.

B&B per person per night:
S £25.00–£35.00
D £25.00–£30.00

OPEN All Year

♦♦♦

MANOR COURT FARM

Ashurst, Royal Tunbridge Wells TN3 9TB
T: (01892) 740279
F: (01892) 740919
E: jsoyke@jsoyke.freeserve.co.uk
I: www.manorcourtfarm.co.uk

Georgian farmhouse with friendly atmosphere, spacious rooms and lovely views of Medway Valley. 350-acre mixed farm, many animals. Good base for walking. Penshurst Place, Hever Castle, Chartwell, Sissinghurst etc all within easy reach by car. London 50 minutes by train from Tonbridge. Guest lounge. Excellent camping facilities. On A264 0.5 miles east of Ashurst village.

Bedrooms: 1 double, 2 twin

Reductions for longer stays. Reductions for children.

B&B per person per night:
S £24.00–£30.00
D £24.00–£30.00

OPEN All Year

QUALITY ASSURANCE SCHEME

Diamond ratings and awards were correct at the time of going to press but are subject to change. Please check at the time of booking.

ROYAL TUNBRIDGE WELLS continued

VALE ROYAL HOTEL

54-57 London Road, Royal Tunbridge Wells TN1 1DS
T: (01892) 525580
F: (01892) 526022
E: reservations@valeroyalhotel.co.uk
I: www.valeroyalhotel.co.uk

Family hotel overlooking the common, set in beautiful, secluded shrub garden. All rooms have telephone, TV, tea/coffee-making facilities. Victorian conservatory leading on to the patio.

Bedrooms: 7 double, 6 single, 3 family
Bathrooms: 3 en suite

Evening meal available
CC: Delta, Diners, Mastercard, Switch, Visa

B&B per person per night:
S £42.00–£64.60
D £32.03–£43.05

HB per person per night:
DY £42.23–£74.80

OPEN All Year

RUSTINGTON, West Sussex Map ref 2D3

♦♦♦♦
Silver Award

KENMORE

Claigmar Road, Rustington, Littlehampton BN16 2NL
T: (01903) 784634
F: (01903) 784634
E: kenmoreguesthouse@amserve.net
I: www.kenmoreguesthouse.co.uk

Secluded Edwardian house in a garden setting in the heart of the village and close to sea. Attractive en suite rooms, individually decorated and comfortably furnished. Private parking. Ideal for touring historic towns, castles, cathedrals and stately homes. Sylvia and Ray Dobbs offer a warm and friendly welcome.

Bedrooms: 2 double, 1 single, 4 family
Bathrooms: 7 en suite

CC: Amex, Mastercard, Visa

B&B per person per night:
S £26.00–£38.50
D Min £26.00

OPEN All Year except Christmas

RYDE, Isle of Wight Map ref 2C3 *Tourist Information Centre Tel: (01983) 813818*

CLAVERTON

12 The Strand, Ryde PO33 1JE
T: (01983) 613015
F: (01983) 613015
E: clavertonhouse@aol.com

Bedrooms: 1 double, 1 family
Bathrooms: 2 en suite

Family-run bed and breakfast in a Victorian house providing panoramic views across the Solent. Landscaped garden with pond. Convenient for the town centre and beaches.

B&B per person per night:
D £20.00–£25.00

OPEN All Year except Christmas

RYE, East Sussex Map ref 3B4 *Tourist Information Centre Tel: (01797) 226696*

♦♦♦

AT WISTERIA CORNER

47 Ferry Road (Sloane Terrace), Rye TN31 7DJ
T: (01797) 225011
E: mmpartridge@line.net
I: www.rye-tourism.co.uk/wisteria

Bedrooms: 2 double

Our small B&B is only two minutes' walk from the ancient town centre of Rye. Sandy beach and scenic countryside walks are within easy reach.

B&B per person per night:
S £24.00–£25.00
D £18.00–£20.00

OPEN All Year except Christmas

♦♦♦

AVIEMORE GUEST HOUSE

28-30 Fishmarket Road, Rye TN31 7LP
T: (01797) 223052
F: (01797) 223052
E: aviemore@lineone.net
I: www.SmoothHound.co.uk/hotels/aviemore.html

Bedrooms: 4 double, 4 twin
Bathrooms: 4 en suite

CC: Amex, Mastercard, Switch, Visa

Owner-operated, imposing Victorian guesthouse overlooking green expanse of the Salts. Five minutes' walk town centre. En suite and standard rooms, breakfast room, guests' lounge and bar.

B&B per person per night:
S £25.00
D £21.00–£25.00

OPEN All Year except Christmas

RYE continued

♦♦♦♦♦
Silver Award

DURRANT HOUSE HOTEL

2 Market Street, Rye TN31 7LA
T: (01797) 223182
F: (01797) 226940
E: kingslands@compuserve.com
I: www.durranthouse.com

B&B per person per night:
S £45.00–£68.00
D £30.00–£45.00

A charming Listed building located in the centre of ancient Rye. Comfortable and individually decorated bedrooms, including 4-poster and triple rooms, all en suite and equipped to a high standard. The hotel offers an informal and friendly atmosphere, wholesome food and is the perfect location for a relaxing break.

Bedrooms: 5 double, 1 family
Bathrooms: 6 en suite

Evening meal available
CC: Delta, Mastercard, Switch, Visa

Dec-Easter: Sun-Fri mini-breaks – 2 nights 10% discount, 3 nights or more 15% discount, based on 2 people sharing a room.

♦♦♦♦♦
Silver Award

JEAKE'S HOUSE

Mermaid Street, Rye TN31 7ET
T: (01797) 222828
F: (01797) 222623
E: jeakeshouse@btinternet.com
I: www.jeakeshouse.com

B&B per person per night:
S £37.00–£77.00
D £42.00–£58.00

OPEN All Year

Ideally located historic house on winding, cobbled street in the heart of ancient medieval town. Individually restored rooms provide traditional luxury combined with all modern facilities. A book-lined bar and cosy parlours. Extensive breakfast menu to suit all tastes. Easy walking distance to restaurants and shops. Private car park.

Bedrooms: 8 double, 1 single, 3 family
Bathrooms: 9 en suite, 1 private

CC: Delta, Mastercard, Switch, Visa

Reductions for a stay of 4 or more nights. Mid-week winter breaks.

12 P

♦♦♦♦♦
Gold Award

MANOR FARM OAST

Main Road, Icklesham, Winchelsea TN36 4AJ
T: (01424) 813787
F: (01424) 813787
E: manor.farm.oast@lineone.net
I: www.manorfarmoast.com

B&B per person per night:
S £42.00–£47.00
D £34.00–£39.50

HB per person per night:
DY £56.50–£62.00

OPEN All Year

Three-roundel oast house in the heart of 1066 country. Quiet and secluded in orchards, close to Rye, Battle and Hastings. Beautiful walled garden for romantic breaks, wedding license and receptions. All rooms are tastefully furnished, the original round room particularly restful. Home-cooked dinners exceptionally good using local produce.

Bedrooms: 3 double
Bathrooms: 2 en suite, 1 private

Evening meal available
CC: Delta, Mastercard, Switch, Visa

Group Murder Mystery dinners. Honeymoon breaks. Romantic dinners. Bed & Breakfast of the Year 2000 for South East.

12 P €

GOLD & SILVER AWARDS

These exclusive VisitBritain awards are given to establishments achieving the highest levels of quality and service. Further information can be found at the front of the guide. An index to all accommodation achieving these awards are at the back of this guide.

RYE continued

◆◆◆

THE OLD VICARAGE

Rye Harbour Road, Rye TN31 7TT
T: (01797) 222088
F: (01797) 229620
E: jonathan@oldvicarageryeharbour.fsnet.co.uk

Bedrooms: 1 twin, 1 single
Bathrooms: 1 en suite

B&B per person per night:
S £25.00–£50.00
D £39.00–£59.00

OPEN All Year except Christmas

Imposing Victorian former vicarage, quietly situated close to sea and nature reserve. Antique furniture and open fires. Magnificent English breakfast. Classic excellence and old-fashioned hospitality.

P €

◆◆◆◆ Silver Award

THE STRAND HOUSE

Tanyard's Lane, Winchelsea TN36 4JT
T: (01797) 226276
F: (01797) 224806
E: strandhouse@winchelsea98.fsnet.co.uk
I: www.s-h-systems.co.uk/hotels/strand.html

B&B per person per night:
S £38.00–£42.00
D £28.00–£42.00

OPEN All Year except Christmas

A warm welcome awaits in the 15thC old world charm of Winchelsea's old workhouse. Now Grade II Listed with many original beams and inglenooks. Well-furnished rooms. Overlooking NT pastureland. 4-poster bedroom. Residents' bar. Traditional breakfasts utilising local produce served in the heavily beamed dining room. Log fires. Pretty gardens.

Bedrooms: 6 double, 1 twin, 1 single, 2 family
Bathrooms: 9 en suite, 1 private

CC: Delta, Mastercard, Switch, Visa

Winter weekend breaks (2 nights min). Special rates off-season mid-week (3 nights min).

5 P

ST LEONARDS, East Sussex Map ref 3B4

◆◆◆

SHERWOOD GUEST HOUSE

15 Grosvenor Crescent, St Leonards, Hastings TN38 0AA
T: (01424) 433331
F: (01424) 433331
E: wendy@sherwoodhastings.co.uk
I: www.sherwoodhastings.co.uk

Bedrooms: 3 double, 1 twin, 2 single, 3 family
Bathrooms: 5 en suite, 2 private

CC: Delta, Mastercard, Switch, Visa

B&B per person per night:
S £22.00–£25.00
D £25.00–£27.50

OPEN All Year except Christmas

Seafront hotel facing putting green. Attractive gardens, easy parking. Main feature of hotel is attractive Victorian staircase and antiques in keeping with the building.

5

SANDOWN, Isle of Wight Map ref 2C3 *Tourist Information Centre Tel: (01983) 813818*

◆◆◆

THE MONTPELIER

Pier Street, Sandown PO36 8JR
T: (01983) 403964
F: (07092) 212734
E: enquiries@themontpelier.co.uk
I: www.themontpelier.co.uk

Bedrooms: 3 double, 1 single, 2 family
Bathrooms: 5 en suite, 1 private

CC: Delta, Mastercard, Switch, Visa

B&B per person per night:
S £20.00–£26.00
D £20.00–£26.00

OPEN All Year

The Montpelier is situated opposite the pier and beaches with the high street just around the corner.

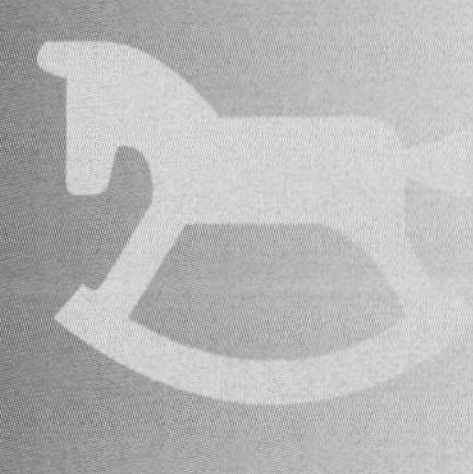

AT-A-GLANCE SYMBOLS

Symbols at the end of each accommodation entry give useful information about services and facilities. A key to symbols can be found inside the back cover flap. Keep this open for easy reference.

SAUNDERTON, Buckinghamshire Map ref 2C1

♦♦♦

HUNTERS GATE

Deanfield, Saunderton, High Wycombe
HP14 4JR
T: (01494) 481718
E: dadykes@attglobal.net
I: www.huntersgatebandb.co.uk

A quiet smallholding beside the bridle path in the heart of the Chilterns. 0.5 miles from mainline station to London (45 mins) with easy access to Oxford, Windsor and Henley. Only six miles from the M40 motorway and one mile from The Ridgeway long-distance path.

Bedrooms: 2 double
Bathrooms: 1 en suite, 1 private

B&B per person per night:
D £20.00–£30.00

OPEN All Year

SEAFORD, East Sussex Map ref 2D3 *Tourist Information Centre Tel: (01323) 897426*

♦♦♦♦

THE SILVERDALE

21 Sutton Park Road, Seaford BN25 1RH
T: (01323) 491849
F: (01323) 891131
E: silverdale@mistral.co.uk
I: www.mistral.co.uk/silverdale/silver.htm

Small, expertly run house-hotel in the centre of peaceful Edwardian seaside town. Beautifully prepared food and a host of English wines. Over 120 single-malt whiskies. Only a few minutes' walk from the seaside, the antique shops and the friendly local pubs. We'd love to meet you!

Bedrooms: 5 double, 1 single, 2 family
Bathrooms: 6 en suite

Evening meal available
CC: Amex, Delta, Diners, Mastercard, Switch, Visa

Special winter deals – contact us for more details.

B&B per person per night:
S £25.00–£40.00
D £25.00–£65.00

OPEN All Year

SELBORNE, Hampshire Map ref 2C2

♦♦♦♦

8 GOSLINGS CROFT

Selborne, Alton GU34 3HZ
T: (01420) 511285
F: (01420) 587451
E: timothyrouse@hotmail.com

Bedrooms: 1 twin
Bathrooms: 1 en suite

Family home, set on edge of historic village, adjacent to NT land. Ideal base for walking and touring. Non-smokers only, please.

B&B per person per night:
S £25.00
D £25.00

OPEN All Year

♦♦♦♦

IVANHOE

Oakhanger, Selborne, Alton
GU35 9JG
T: (01420) 473464

Bedrooms: 1 double, 1 twin

Warm welcome in comfortable, homely accommodation with views to open countryside. Ideal touring centre. NT properties and walks within easy reach. Good pub nearby.

B&B per person per night:
S Min £27.50
D Min £22.50

OPEN All Year except Christmas

CHECK THE MAPS

The colour maps at the front of this guide show all the cities, towns and villages for which you will find accommodation entries.
Refer to the town index to find the page on which they are listed.

SELSEY, West Sussex Map ref 2C3

ST ANDREWS LODGE

Chichester Road, Selsey, Chichester
PO20 0LX
T: (01243) 606899
F: (01243) 607826
E: info@standrewslodge.co.uk
I: www.standrewslodge.co.uk

Friendly, family-run hotel with a reputation for an excellent, hearty breakfast. Situated on the Manhood peninsular south of Chichester close to unspoilt beaches and countryside. All bedrooms en suite, some on ground floor, licensed bar, spacious lounge with log fire, large garden and sun-trap patio. Ample private parking.

Bedrooms: 3 double, 2 twin, 1 single, 4 family
Bathrooms: 10 en suite

Evening meal available
CC: Delta, Diners, Mastercard, Switch, Visa

Special winter offers available Nov-Feb – please telephone for details.

B&B per person per night:
S £30.00–£45.00
D £30.00–£40.00

OPEN All Year except Christmas

SEVENOAKS, Kent Map ref 2D2 *Tourist Information Centre Tel: (01732) 450305*

♦♦♦

THE MOORINGS HOTEL

97 Hitchen Hatch Lane, Sevenoaks
TN13 3BE
T: (01732) 452589
F: (01732) 456462
E: moorings-hotel@btconnect.com
I: www.mooringshotel.co.uk

Bedrooms: 16 double, 5 single, 2 family
Bathrooms: 23 en suite

Evening meal available
CC: Amex, Delta, Diners, Mastercard, Switch, Visa

Friendly family hotel offering high-standard accommodation for tourists and business travellers. Thirty minutes from London. Close to station.

B&B per person per night:
S £44.00–£56.00
D £33.50–£56.00

HB per person per night:
DY £54.00–£66.00

OPEN All Year

SHANKLIN, Isle of Wight Map ref 2C3 *Tourist Information Centre Tel: (01983) 813818*

♦♦♦

HAZELWOOD HOTEL

14 Clarence Road, Shanklin
PO37 7BH
T: (01983) 862824
F: (01983) 862824
E: barbara.tubbs@thehazelwood.free-online.co.uk
I: www.thehazelwood.free-online.co.uk

Bedrooms: 5 double, 1 single, 2 suites
Bathrooms: 6 en suite

Evening meal available
CC: Diners, Mastercard, Switch, Visa

Detached, friendly, comfortable hotel in a quiet, tree-lined road, close to all amenities. Daily bookings taken. Parking available. All rooms en suite, family suites available.

B&B per person per night:
S £20.00–£22.00
D £20.00–£22.00

HB per person per night:
DY £28.00–£30.00

OPEN All Year except Christmas

SHEERNESS, Kent Map ref 3B3

♦

SHEPPEY GUEST HOUSE

214 Queenborough Road, Minster-on-Sea, Sheerness ME12 3DF
T: (01795) 665950
F: (01795) 661200
E: sophie@allen3877.fsbusiness.co.uk

Bedrooms: 3 double, 1 single, 5 family
Bathrooms: 9 en suite

Evening meal available

Family-run establishment in a semi-rural location. Large parking area, indoor swimming pool. All rooms en suite, Sky TV. Table licence. Large gardens.

B&B per person per night:
S Min £20.00
D Min £15.00

HB per person per night:
DY £22.95–£28.00

OPEN All Year

SHROTON, Dorset Map ref 2B3

♦♦♦♦♦
Silver Award

THE CRICKETERS

Main Street, Shroton, Blandford Forum DT11 8QD
T: (01258) 860421
F: (01258) 861800
E: the_cricketers@hotmail.com

Bedrooms: 1 double
Bathrooms: 1 en suite

Evening meal available
CC: Mastercard, Switch, Visa

In a pretty Dorset village, our accommodation is a separate, delightful garden room with bay window overlooking clematis-strewn pergola and secluded garden, and is alongside pub.

B&B per person per night:
S Min £39.99
D £30.00–£35.00

OPEN All Year

SMARDEN, Kent Map ref 3B4

CHEQUERS INN

The Street, Smarden, Ashford TN27 8QA
T: (01233) 770217
F: (01233) 770623
I: www.thechequerssmarden.activehotels.co.uk

B&B per person per night:
S Min £40.00
D Min £35.00

OPEN All Year

Listed 14thC inn, in heart of the Weald. Wealth of oak beams, beautifully landscaped gardens with duck pond. All rooms individually decorated. Ideal for touring and visiting many places of historic interest, including Leeds Castle and Sissinghurst Gardens. Many interesting walks, five golf courses nearby. Good food always available.

Bedrooms: 2 double, 1 twin, 1 family
Bathrooms: 4 en suite

Evening meal available
CC: Amex, Delta, Mastercard, Switch, Visa

SOULDERN, Oxfordshire Map ref 2C1

♦♦♦

TOWER FIELDS

Tusmore Road, Souldern, Bicester OX27 7HY
T: (01869) 346554
F: (01869) 345157
E: hgould@strayduck.com
I: www.towerfields.com

Bedrooms: 1 double, 1 twin, 1 single, 1 family
Bathrooms: 4 en suite

B&B per person per night:
S £35.00
D £27.50–£30.00

OPEN All Year

Converted 18thC cottages and 14-acre smallholding with rare breeds of poultry, sheep and cattle. Small collection of vintage cars.

SOUTHAMPTON, Hampshire Map ref 2C3

♦♦♦

BANISTER HOUSE HOTEL

Banister Road, Southampton SO15 2JJ
T: (023) 80221279
F: (023) 80226551
E: banisterhotel@btconnect.com
I: www.banisterhotel.co.uk

Bedrooms: 8 double, 12 single, 2 family
Bathrooms: 12 en suite

CC: Delta, Mastercard, Switch, Visa

B&B per person per night:
S £28.00–£34.00
D £24.00–£26.00

OPEN All Year except Christmas

Friendly, warm welcome in this family-run hotel which is central and in a residential area. Off A33 (The Avenue) into Southampton.

♦♦♦

BRUNSWICK LODGE

100-104 Anglesea Road, Shirley, Southampton SO15 5QS
T: (02380) 774777
I: www.brunswicklodge.co.uk

Bedrooms: 7 twin, 4 single
Bathrooms: 5 en suite

CC: Delta, Mastercard, Switch, Visa

B&B per person per night:
S £25.00–£35.00
D £22.50–£27.50

OPEN All Year except Christmas

Substantial 1832 property under new family ownership. Completely non-smoking. Close M3, M27 and airport. Fifteen minutes' walk to Southampton General Hospital. Large car park.

QUALITY ASSURANCE SCHEME

For an explanation of the quality and facilities represented by the Diamonds please refer to the front of this guide. A more detailed explanation can be found in the information pages at the back.

SOUTHAMPTON continued

♦♦♦♦

DORMY HOUSE HOTEL

21 Barnes Lane, Sarisbury Green, Southampton SO31 7DA
T: (01489) 572626
F: (01489) 573370
E: dormyhousehotel@warsash.globalnet.co.uk
I: www.dormyhousehotel.net

A tranquil Victorian house set in an attractive garden, featuring en suite bedrooms, one of which is a superior, queen-bedded room. All with tea/coffee-making facilities, direct-dial telephone, hairdryer and remote-control TV. Close to River Hamble, Portsmouth and local business parks. Eight miles from Southampton.

Bedrooms: 7 double, 3 single, 2 family
Bathrooms: 12 en suite

CC: Mastercard, Switch, Visa

B&B per person per night:
S £48.00–£53.00
D £29.00–£39.00

OPEN All Year except Christmas

♦♦♦

EATON COURT HOTEL
32 Hill Lane, Southampton SO15 5AY
T: (023) 80223081
F: (023) 80322006
E: ecourthot@aol.com
I: www.eatoncourtsouthampton.co.uk

Bedrooms: 4 double, 3 twin, 8 single
Bathrooms: 7 en suite, 1 private

Evening meal available
CC: Amex, Delta, Diners, Mastercard, Switch, Visa

B&B per person per night:
S £30.00–£39.00
D £22.00–£25.00

OPEN All Year except Christmas

Comfortable, small, owner-run hotel for business or leisure stays. Bedrooms have all amenities and a generous traditional breakfast is served.

♦♦♦

MAYVIEW GUEST HOUSE
30 The Polygon, Southampton SO15 2BN
T: (023) 80220907
F: (07977) 017921
E: mayview@yahoo.co.uk

Bedrooms: 2 double, 5 single, 2 family
Bathrooms: 1 en suite

CC: Delta, Mastercard, Switch, Visa

B&B per person per night:
S £20.00–£24.50
D £17.50–£26.00

OPEN All Year except Christmas

Small, family-run guesthouse in the city centre, providing a comfortable stay in clean and friendly surroundings.

10

SOUTHSEA

See under Portsmouth & Southsea

STANFORD DINGLEY, West Berkshire Map ref 2C2

♦♦♦♦

THE BULL COUNTRY INN
Stanford Dingley, Stanford Dingley, Reading RG7 6LS
T: (0118) 9744409
F: (0118) 9745249
E: admin@thebullatstanforddingley.co.uk
I: www.thebullatstanforddingley.co.uk

Bedrooms: 5 double, 1 family
Bathrooms: 6 en suite

Evening meal available
CC: Amex, Delta, Mastercard, Switch, Visa

B&B per person per night:
S £55.00–£65.00
D £35.00–£40.00

OPEN All Year

15thC, family-owned, traditional inn. Two bars, dining room, large garden. Located between Reading and Newbury, five miles from M4 jct 12. Families welcome.

SPECIAL BREAKS

Many establishments offer special promotions and themed breaks. These are highlighted in red. (All such offers are subject to availability.)

STEEPLE ASTON, Oxfordshire Map ref 2C1

WESTFIELD FARM MOTEL

Fenway, Steeple Aston, Oxford
OX25 4SS
T: (01869) 340591
F: (01869) 347594
E: info@westfieldmotel.u-net.com
I: www.oxlink.co.uk/accom/westfield-farm/

Bedrooms: 6 double, 3 family
Bathrooms: 9 en suite

Evening meal available
CC: Amex, Delta, Diners, Mastercard, Switch, Visa

B&B per person per night:
S £50.00–£60.00
D £32.50–£40.00

OPEN All Year

Converted stable block with comfortable bedroom units. Combined lounge, dining room and bar. Good touring centre. Fringe of Cotswolds, off A4260, nine miles Banbury, five miles Woodstock.

P

STELLING MILLIS, West Sussex Map ref 3B4

Silver Award

BOWER FARM HOUSE

Bossingham Road, Stelling Minnis,
Canterbury CT4 6BB
T: (01227) 709430
E: anne@bowerbb.freeserve.co.uk
I: www.bowerfarmhouse.co.uk

Bedrooms: 1 double, 1 twin
Bathrooms: 1 en suite, 1 private

B&B per person per night:
S £25.00–£30.00
D £22.50–£25.00

OPEN All Year except Christmas

Delightful, heavily beamed, 17thC farmhouse between the villages of Stelling Minnis and Bossingham. Canterbury and Hythe are approximately seven miles away.

P

STEYNING, West Sussex Map ref 2D3

CHEQUER INN

41 High Street, Steyning BN44 3RE
T: (01903) 814437
F: (01903) 879707
E: chequerinn@btinternet.com

B&B per person per night:
S Min £35.00
D Min £22.50

OPEN All Year

A fine historic hostelry in the heart of picturesque Steyning. The Chequer Inn is over 500 years old with open fires and many original features. En suite rooms are comfortably appointed and the inn offers fine food and an excellent cellar. A perfect base to explore the beauty of Sussex.

Bedrooms: 3 double
Bathrooms: 3 en suite

Evening meal available
CC: Amex, Delta, Mastercard, Switch, Visa

P

STOCKBRIDGE, Hampshire Map ref 2C2

CARBERY GUEST HOUSE

Salisbury Hill, Stockbridge SO20 6EZ
T: (01264) 810771
F: (01264) 811022

B&B per person per night:
S £32.00–£40.00
D £27.00–£29.00

HB per person per night:
DY £47.00–£55.00

OPEN All Year except Christmas

Fine old Georgian house in an acre of landscaped gardens and lawns, overlooking the River Test. Games and swimming facilities, riding and fishing can be arranged. Ideal for touring the south coast and the New Forest.

Bedrooms: 4 double, 3 twin, 4 single, 1 family
Bathrooms: 9 en suite

Evening meal available
CC: Delta, Mastercard, Switch, Visa

P

MAP REFERENCES The map references refer to the colour maps at the front of this guide. The first figure is the map number; the letter and figure which follow indicate the grid reference on the map.

STONE-IN-OXNEY, Kent Map ref 3B4

TIGHE FARMHOUSE

Stone-in-Oxney, Tenterden TN30 7JU
T: (01233) 758251
F: (01233) 758054
I: www.ryetourism.co.uk

B&B per person per night:
S £40.00
D £30.00–£35.00

OPEN All Year except Christmas

An attractive, mature, bricked, quiet, 16thC farmhouse in unrivalled position. Mature rose garden/ herbacious border. Extensive views over Romney Marsh, en suite bedrooms including 4-poster bed. Inglenook fireplaces in guest living room with wine/sherry. Close Rye/ Great Dixter. Large, sunny terrace and gardens for guests.

Bedrooms: 5 double
Bathrooms: 3 en suite, 2 private

P €

STREATLEY, Berkshire Map ref 2C2

Silver Award

PENNYFIELD

The Coombe, Streatley, Reading
RG8 9QT
T: (01491) 872048
F: (01491) 872048
E: mandrvanstone@hotmail.com
I: www.pennyfield.co.uk

Bedrooms: 2 double, 1 twin
Bathrooms: 3 en suite

B&B per person per night:
S £55.00
D £55.00

Charming house in beautiful Thames-side village, situated on Thames path, Ridgeway Walk routes. Featuring 4-poster bed and heated spa pool. One mile to rail station.

P

STUDLAND, Dorset Map ref 2B3

THE BANKES ARMS HOTEL

Manor Road, Studland, Swanage
BH19 3AU
T: (01929) 450225
F: (01929) 450307

B&B per person per night:
S £31.00–£41.00
D £32.00–£43.00

OPEN All Year except Christmas

Award-winning lovely old inn with own brewery and large gardens, overlooking the sea. En suite accommodation. Eight real ales, log fires, extensive home-cooked menu (open all day for food during the season). Fresh fish a speciality. Sandy beaches, water sports, golf, riding and coastal walks to start of World Heritage site.

Bedrooms: 6 double, 1 twin, 1 single
Bathrooms: 6 en suite

Evening meal available
CC: Delta, Diners, Mastercard, Switch, Visa

4 P

SWANAGE, Dorset Map ref 2B3 *Tourist Information Centre Tel: (01929) 422885*

PERFICK PIECE

Springfield Road, Swanage
BH19 1HD
T: (01929) 423178
F: (01929) 423558
E: perfick-piece@supanet.com
I: www.perfick-piece.co.uk

Bedrooms: 1 double, 1 twin, 1 single, 1 family
Bathrooms: 1 en suite

Evening meal available

B&B per person per night:
S £16.00–£21.00
D £16.00–£21.00

HB per person per night:
DY £23.50–£28.50

OPEN All Year

Home from home guesthouse situated in quiet cul-de-sac close to sea, shops and steam railway.

P €

SWAY, Hampshire Map ref 2C3

♦♦♦♦♦ Gold Award

THE NURSE'S COTTAGE

Station Road, Sway, Lymington SO41 6BA
T: (01590) 683402
F: (01590) 683402
E: nurses.cottage@lineone.net
I: www.nursescottage.co.uk

HB per person per night:
DY £75.00

This popular New Forest restaurant and guest accommodation enjoys an enviable reputation for comfort and good food. Formerly home to Sway's successive District Nurses, the cottage has been lovingly refurbished and now boasts an impressive array of awards, from Best Breakfast in Britain to prize-winning wine list.

Bedrooms: 1 double, 1 twin, 1 single
Bathrooms: 3 en suite

CC: Amex, Delta, Mastercard, Switch, Visa

Reduced rates for short breaks, e.g. £195 (3 nights), £406 (7 nights). No single-room supplement.

10 P

TUNBRIDGE WELLS

See under Royal Tunbridge Wells

UCKFIELD, East Sussex Map ref 2D3

♦♦♦♦ Silver Award

OLD MILL FARM

Chillies Lane, High Hurstwood, Uckfield TN22 4AD
T: (01825) 732279
F: (01825) 732279

Bedrooms: 1 double, 1 single, 1 family
Bathrooms: 2 en suite, 1 private

B&B per person per night:
S £25.00–£30.00
D £25.00–£30.00

OPEN All Year

Sussex barn and buildings converted to a comfortable home, situated in the quiet village of High Hurstwood, off A26. Ashdown Forest nearby.

P

WALLINGFORD, Oxfordshire Map ref 2C2 *Tourist Information Centre Tel: (01491) 826972*

♦♦♦♦

LITTLE GABLES

166 Crowmarsh Hill, Crowmarsh Gifford, Wallingford OX10 8BG
T: (01491) 837834
F: (01491) 834426
E: jill@stayingaway.com
I: www.stayingaway.com

Bedrooms: 1 double, 1 single, 1 family
Bathrooms: 2 en suite, 1 private

B&B per person per night:
S £35.00–£45.00
D £25.00–£30.00

OPEN All Year

Detached house, close to Ridgeway and Wallingford. Includes single and family room (cot), or twin, double or triple en suite. Tea/coffee-making facilities, colour TV, fridge.

P €

WALMER, Kent Map ref 3C4

HARDICOT GUEST HOUSE

Kingsdown Road, Walmer, Deal CT14 8AW
T: (01304) 373867
F: (01304) 389234
E: guestboss@talk21.com
I: www.smoothhound.co.uk/hotels/hardicot.html

B&B per person per night:
S Min £25.00
D £23.00–£25.00

OPEN All Year except Christmas

Large, quiet, detached Victorian house with Channel views and secluded garden, situated 100 yards from the beach. Guests have unrestricted access to rooms. Close to three championship golf courses, ferries and the Channel Tunnel. Ideal centre for cliff walks and exploring Canterbury and the castles and gardens of East Kent.

Bedrooms: 1 double, 2 twin
Bathrooms: 1 en suite, 2 private

7 nights for the price of 6.

5 P €

WANTAGE, Oxfordshire Map ref 2C2 *Tourist Information Centre Tel: (01235) 760176*

◆◆◆◆

B & B IN WANTAGE

50 Foliat Drive, Wantage OX12 7AL
T: (01235) 760495
E: eleanor@eaturner.freeserve.co.uk

Bedrooms: 2 double, 1 twin

B&B per person per night:
S £20.00–£22.00
D £18.00–£19.00

OPEN All Year

A clean, comfortable and homely establishment within easy walking distance of the town centre and buses. Evening self-catering possible. Extra bed for a child available.

P

WEST CLANDON, Surrey Map ref 2D2

◆◆◆◆

WAYS COTTAGE

Lime Grove, West Clandon, Guildford GU4 7UT
T: (01483) 222454
F: (01483) 222454

Bedrooms: 2 twin
Bathrooms: 1 en suite

Evening meal available

B&B per person per night:
S £30.00–£32.00
D £21.00–£22.50

HB per person per night:
DY £42.50–£44.50

OPEN All Year

Rural detached house with delightful garden, in quiet location five miles from Guildford. Easy reach of A3 and M25. Close to station on Waterloo/Guildford line.

P

WEST DEAN, West Sussex Map ref 2C3

◆◆◆

LODGE HILL FARM

West Dean, Chichester PO18 0RT
T: (01243) 535245

Bedrooms: 1 double, 2 twin

B&B per person per night:
S £22.00–£25.00
D £22.00–£25.00

Flint farmhouse built in 1813 on the South Downs, superb views, near Goodwood, 15 minutes to Chichester, ideal for walkers.

5 P

WEST HORSLEY, Surrey Map ref 2D2

◆◆◆

BRINFORD

Windmill Hill, Off Shere Road, West Horsley, Leatherhead KT24 6EJ
T: (01483) 283636

Bedrooms: 1 double, 1 twin, 1 single
Bathrooms: 1 en suite

B&B per person per night:
S £28.00–£38.00
D £24.00–£28.00

OPEN All Year

Modern house in Surrey hills, peaceful location with panoramic views. Easy reach Guildford, A3, M25, London, Wisley gardens and four NT properties. Good walking area.

5 P

WHITWELL, Isle of Wight Map ref 2C3

◆◆◆◆
Gold Award

THE OLD RECTORY

Ashknowle Lane, Whitwell, Ventnor PO38 2PP
T: (01983) 731242
F: (01983) 731288
E: rectory@ukonline.co.uk
I: www.wightonline.co.uk/oldrectory

Bedrooms: 1 double, 1 twin
Bathrooms: 2 en suite

CC: Delta, Mastercard, Switch, Visa

B&B per person per night:
S £30.00–£35.00
D £30.00–£35.00

OPEN All Year except Christmas

Enjoy the comfort of spacious, en suite bedrooms, all with colour TV, fridge, hairdryer. Guests' sitting room. Secluded garden. Good centre for walking, cycling and touring. Ventnor three miles.

P €

USE YOUR *i*s

There are more than 550 Tourist Information Centres throughout England offering friendly help with accommodation and holiday ideas as well as suggestions of places to visit and things to do. You'll find TIC addresses in the local Phone Book.

WIMBORNE MINSTER, Dorset Map ref 2B3 *Tourist Information Centre Tel: (01202) 886116*

Silver Award

ASHTON LODGE

10 Oakley Hill, Wimborne Minster
BH21 1QH
T: (01202) 883423
F: (01202) 886180
E: ashtonlodge@ukgateway.net
I: www.ashtonlodge.ukgateway.net

Spacious, detached family house with ample off-street parking. Relaxed, friendly atmosphere with all the comforts of home on offer, including a full English breakfast served in the dining room overlooking the attractively laid garden. All bedrooms are centrally heated, tastefully decorated and furnished to a high standard.

Bedrooms: 2 double, 2 single, 2 family
Bathrooms: 4 en suite

Spring/autumn/winter savers: 10% discount for couples staying 3 nights or more Oct-Mar.

P

B&B per person per night:
S £26.00–£27.00
D £25.00–£28.00

OPEN All Year

♦♦♦♦

HEMSWORTH MANOR FARM

Witchampton, Wimborne Minster
BH21 5BN
T: (01258) 840216
F: (01258) 841278

Lovely old manor house and garden in outstanding, peaceful location. 800 acres, mainly arable, with sheep and three horses. Spacious rooms, colour TV, fully equipped. Guests' sitting room. Thirty minutes Bournemouth, Poole, Salisbury, Dorchester, New Forest. Excellent local pubs. Open all year except Christmas. Brochure available.

Bedrooms: 3 double, 1 family
Bathrooms: 4 en suite

10 P

B&B per person per night:
S £27.50–£35.00

OPEN All Year except Christmas

♦♦♦

HOMESTAY

22 West Borough, Wimborne Minster
BH21 1NF
T: (01202) 849015
F: (01202) 849819
E: julietridg@onetel.com

A warm welcome to our Grade II Listed Georgian townhouse, just one minute's walk from the town centre, with its many restaurants and pubs, and the Tivoli Theatre. Bedrooms are individually furnished to a high standard of comfort with tea/coffee facilities. All are en suite or have private facilities.

Bedrooms: 3 double
Bathrooms: 2 en suite, 1 private

B&B per person per night:
S £30.00
D £22.50–£27.50

OPEN All Year

♦♦♦

TWYNHAM

67 Poole Road, Wimborne Minster
BH21 1QB
T: (01202) 887310

Bedrooms: 3 double

Friendly family home. TV, clock-radio, hairdyer and beverages in all rooms. Level walking to town centre, pubs, restaurants and shops.

10 P

B&B per person per night:
S £20.00
D £18.00–£20.00

OPEN All Year except Christmas

WINCHELSEA, East Sussex Map ref 3B4

THE NEW INN

German Street, Winchelsea TN36 4EN
T: (01797) 226252
F: (01797) 226238
E: terry@newinnwinchelsea.co.uk
I: www.newinnwinchelsea.co.uk

B&B per person per night:
S £30.00–£50.00
D £25.00–£40.00

OPEN All Year

Lovely 18thC inn in the centre of ancient and historic town of Winchelsea. Very attractive bedrooms all en suite, including one 4-poster room. Fresh, local fish our speciality, excellent homemade dishes, succulent steaks and much more. Real log fire in winter. Beautiful, peaceful Winchelsea is a must for visitors.

Bedrooms: 4 double, 1 twin, 1 family
Bathrooms: 6 en suite

Evening meal available
CC: Amex, Delta, Mastercard, Switch, Visa

3 nights for the price of 2, Nov-Mar (excl Christmas and New Year).

WINCHESTER, Hampshire Map ref 2C3 *Tourist Information Centre Tel: (01962) 840500*

12 CHRISTCHURCH ROAD

Winchester SO23 9SR
T: (01962) 854272
E: pjspatton@yahoo.co.uk

Bedrooms: 1 double, 1 twin

B&B per person per night:
S £28.00–£32.00
D £19.00–£22.50

OPEN All Year except Christmas

Family house, with much old furniture, conservatory and garden. In tree-lined residential area, 10 minutes' walk from the cathedral and city centre.

♦♦♦

MANOR HOUSE

Place Lane, Compton, Winchester SO21 2BA
T: (01962) 712162

Bedrooms: 1 double

B&B per person per night:
S £17.50
D £17.50

OPEN All Year except Christmas

Comfortable country house in a large garden, eight minutes from Shawford railway station and two miles from city of Winchester. Non-smokers preferred.

♦♦♦♦

SHAWLANDS

46 Kilham Lane, Winchester SO22 5QD
T: (01962) 861166
F: (01962) 861166
E: kathy@pollshaw.u-net.com

B&B per person per night:
S £33.00–£40.00
D £22.00–£27.00

OPEN All Year except Christmas

Attractive modern house in a quiet, elevated position overlooking open countryside, 1.5 miles from city centre. Bedrooms are spotlessly clean, bright and attractively decorated. Extra comforts include colour TV, hairdryer and welcome tray with tea and coffee. The inviting breakfast includes homemade bread and preserves with fruit from the garden.

Bedrooms: 2 double, 2 twin, 1 family
Bathrooms: 1 private

CC: Delta, Mastercard, Switch, Visa

IMPORTANT NOTE Information on accommodation listed in this guide has been supplied by the proprietors. As changes may occur you are advised to check details at the time of booking.

WINDSOR, Berkshire Map ref 2D2 *Tourist Information Centre Tel: (01753) 743900*

◆◆◆

ALMA HOUSE

56 Alma Road, Windsor SL4 3HA
T: (01753) 862983
F: (01753) 862983
E: info@almahouse.co.uk
I: www.almahouse.co.uk

Bedrooms: 1 double, 2 single, 1 family
Bathrooms: 4 en suite

CC: Amex, Delta, Mastercard, Switch, Visa

B&B per person per night:
S £50.00–£65.00
D £32.50–£35.00

OPEN All Year

Elegant, family-run Victorian house, recently refurbished, within 5 minutes' walk of castle, town centre, river and parks. Just a short drive to Legoland. Continental breakfast included.

P €

◆◆◆

BARBARA'S BED & BREAKFAST

16 Maidenhead Road, Windsor
SL4 5EQ
T: (01753) 840273
E: bbandb@btinternet.com

Bedrooms: 1 double, 1 twin, 1 single
Bathrooms: 1 en suite, 1 private

B&B per person per night:
S £25.00–£30.00
D £27.50

OPEN All Year

Welcoming, friendly, family Victorian home, many original features. Situated close to the River Thames and leisure centre. Ten minutes' walk from Windsor Castle and town centre.

P €

◆◆

CLARENCE HOTEL

9 Clarence Road, Windsor SL4 5AE
T: (01753) 864436
F: (01753) 857060
I: www.clarence-hotel.co.uk

B&B per person per night:
S £45.00–£61.00
D £25.00–£36.00

OPEN All Year except Christmas

Comfortable hotel with licensed bar and steam-sauna. Located near town centre and short walk from Windsor Castle, Eton College and River Thames. All rooms with en suite bathroom, TV, tea/coffee-making facilities, hairdryer and radio alarm. Convenient for Legoland and Heathrow Airport.

Bedrooms: 4 double, 6 twin, 4 single, 6 family
Bathrooms: 20 en suite

CC: Amex, Delta, Diners, Mastercard, Switch, Visa

P

WINSLOW, Buckinghamshire Map ref 2C1

◆◆◆

'WITSEND'

9 Buckingham Road, Winslow, Buckingham MK18 3DT
T: (01296) 712503
F: (01296) 712503
E: sheila.spatcher@aol.com

Bedrooms: 1 double, 1 twin
Bathrooms: 2 en suite

Evening meal available

B&B per person per night:
S £22.50–£25.00
D £22.50–£25.00

OPEN All Year

Homely semi-detached chalet bungalow with en suite bedrooms. Close to town centre, colour TV, tea/coffee facilities. A warm welcome assured. Great breakfast!

V P

WITNEY, Oxfordshire Map ref 2C1 *Tourist Information Centre Tel: (01993) 775802*

◆◆◆

THE COURT INN

43 Bridge Street, Witney OX28 1DA
T: (01993) 703228
F: (01993) 700980
E: info@thecourt.co.uk

Bedrooms: 2 double, 5 twin, 2 single, 1 family
Bathrooms: 5 en suite

Evening meal available
CC: Delta, Mastercard, Switch, Visa

B&B per person per night:
S £30.00–£45.00
D £27.50–£35.00

HB per person per night:
DY £35.00–£50.00

OPEN All Year

Historic inn with dining room and two bars. TV and telephone in all bedrooms. Car park. Friendly service.

V P

WITNEY continued

Silver Award

FIELD VIEW

Wood Green, Witney OX28 1DE
T: (01993) 705485
E: bandb@fieldview-witney.co.uk
I: www.fieldview-witney.co.uk

Bedrooms: 1 double, 2 twin
Bathrooms: 3 en suite

A warm welcome and fine hospitality await you in our Cotswold home. Ideal for Oxford University, Blenheim Palace and Cotswolds. Peaceful location, restaurants and pubs nearby.

B&B per person per night:
S £35.00–£40.00
D £26.00–£27.00

OPEN All Year except Christmas

◆◆◆

GREYSTONES LODGE HOTEL

34 Tower Hill, Witney OX28 5ES
T: (01993) 771898
F: (01993) 702064
E: greystoneslodge@aol.com
I: www.greystoneslodge.co.uk

Bedrooms: 4 double, 5 single, 2 family
Bathrooms: 10 en suite, 1 private

Evening meal available
CC: Amex, Delta, Mastercard, Switch, Visa

Family-run hotel close to Cotswolds and Oxford. Ideal location to base yourself while exploring the surrounding area. A friendly welcome awaits your arrival.

B&B per person per night:
S £35.00–£45.00
D £25.00–£30.00

HB per person per night:
DY Min £50.00

OPEN All Year except Christmas

WOKING, Surrey Map ref 2D2

GRANTCHESTER

Boughton Hall Avenue, Send, Woking
GU23 7DF
T: (01483) 225383
F: (01483) 596490
E: gary@hotpotmail.com

Attractive family house with large, superbly kept garden. Situated four minutes from Guildford and Woking town centres. Close to M25 and A3 motorways. Parking available. Long stays welcome. Close to Heathrow and Gatwick airports, Wisley Gardens and Clandon Park.

Bedrooms: 2 double

B&B per person per night:
S £35.00
D £25.00

OPEN All Year except Christmas

WOODCOTE, Oxfordshire Map ref 2C2

HEDGES

South Stoke Road, Woodcote,
Reading RG8 0PL
T: (01491) 680461
E: howard-allen@hedgeswoodcote.freeserve.co.uk

Bedrooms: 2 twin, 2 single
Bathrooms: 1 private

Peaceful, rural situation on edge of village. Historic Area of Outstanding Natural Beauty. Good access Henley, Oxford, Reading (Heathrow link), M4, M40.

B&B per person per night:
S £19.00–£21.00
D £19.00–£21.00

OPEN All Year except Christmas

WOODSTOCK, Oxfordshire Map ref 2C1 *Tourist Information Centre Tel: (01993) 813276*

◆◆◆

BURLEIGH FARM

Bladon Road, Cassington, Oxford
OX29 4EA
T: (01865) 881352
E: j.cook@farmline.com

Bedrooms: 1 double, 1 family
Bathrooms: 2 en suite

360-acre farm on Blenheim Estate (home of Duke of Marlborough) at Woodstock. Six miles north-west of Oxford, halfway between Cassington (A40) and Bladon (A4095), south of Woodstock.

B&B per person per night:
S £25.00–£35.00
D £25.00–£27.50

OPEN All Year

CREDIT CARD BOOKINGS If you book by telephone and are asked for your credit card number it is advisable to check the proprietor's policy should you cancel your reservation.

WOODSTOCK continued

Silver Award

GORSELANDS HALL

Boddington Lane, North Leigh, Witney
OX29 6PU
T: (01993) 882292
F: (01993) 883629
E: hamilton@gorselandshall.com
I: www.gorselandshall.com

Old Cotswold-stone country house with oak beams and flagstone floors. All rooms en suite with colour TV. Large, secluded garden. Tennis court. Snooker. Quiet, rural location. Convenient for Oxford, Blenheim Palace and Cotswolds. Stratford 32 miles, Heathrow 1.25 hours by car and London (Paddington) 1.25 hours by train.

Bedrooms: 3 double, 1 twin, 1 single, 1 family
Bathrooms: 6 en suite

CC: Delta, Mastercard, Switch, Visa

10% reduction for stays of 4 nights or more. Winter discounts available.

P €

B&B per person per night:
S £36.00–£38.00
D £24.00–£27.00

OPEN All Year

♦♦♦♦
Silver Award

THE LAURELS
Hensington Road, Woodstock, Oxford OX20 1JL
T: (01993) 812583
F: (01993) 810041
E: stay@laurelsguesthouse.co.uk
I: www.smoothhound.co.uk/hotels/thelaur.html

Bedrooms: 1 double, 1 twin, 1 single
Bathrooms: 2 en suite, 1 private

CC: Delta, Mastercard, Switch, Visa

B&B per person per night:
S £40.00–£50.00
D £25.00–£30.00

Fine Victorian house, charmingly furnished with an emphasis on comfort and quality. Just off town centre and a short walk from Blenheim Palace.

7 P

THE LAWNS

2 Flemings Road, Woodstock, Oxford
OX20 1NA
T: (01993) 812599
F: (01993) 812599
E: thelawns2@amserve.com
I: www.thelawns.co.uk

Attractive, well-maintained property. Homely, comfortable and welcoming. Free local taxi service. Also chauffered service. Laundry, ironing service. Free collection from Oxford rail or bus stations. Flag of country upon reception table. Quiet and peaceful, first-class accommodation (but not en suite). Five minutes' walk to town centre and Blenheim Palace.

Bedrooms: 1 double, 1 twin, 1 single

CC: Amex, Delta, Mastercard, Switch, Visa

10% discount 2 days or more.

2 P €

B&B per person per night:
S £28.00–£30.00
D £20.00–£22.50

OPEN All Year

THE PUNCHBOWL INN

12 Oxford Street, Woodstock, Oxford
OX20 1TR
T: (01993) 811218
F: (01993) 811393
E: info@punchbowl-woodstock.co.uk
I: www.punchbowl-woodstock.co.uk

18thC Grade II Listed traditional inn situated in the centre of Woodstock serving bar meals and afternoon tea/coffee. Guest en suite bedrooms are available, residents' car park. Ideal base for visiting Blenheim Palace, Oxford, Stratford-upon-Avon and the Cotswolds.

Bedrooms: 7 double, 2 twin, 1 family
Bathrooms: 10 en suite

Evening meal available
CC: Delta, Mastercard, Switch, Visa

P

B&B per person per night:
S £50.00–£55.00
D £35.00–£40.00

OPEN All Year

WOODSTOCK continued

◆◆◆

SHEPHERDS HALL INN

Witney Road, Freeland, Oxford OX29 8HQ
T: (01993) 881256
F: (01993) 883455

Bedrooms: 2 double, 2 twin, 1 single
Bathrooms: 5 en suite

Evening meal available
CC: Delta, Mastercard, Switch, Visa

B&B per person per night:
S £28.50–£38.50
D £27.50–£30.00

OPEN All Year

Well-appointed inn offering good accommodation. All rooms en suite. Ideally situated for Oxford, Woodstock and the Cotswolds, on the A4095 Woodstock to Witney road.

P

WORTHING, West Sussex Map ref 2D3 *Tourist Information Centre Tel: (01903) 210022*

◆◆◆

HIGHDOWN HOTEL & RESTAURANT

Littlehampton Road, Goring-by-Sea, Worthing BN12 6PF
T: (01903) 700152
F: (01903) 507518
I: www.highdown-towers.com

Bedrooms: 7 double, 6 twin
Bathrooms: 13 en suite

Evening meal available
CC: Amex, Delta, Mastercard, Switch, Visa

B&B per person per night:
S £49.95
D £34.95–£44.95

HB per person per night:
DY £37.50–£58.90

OPEN All Year

Converted 18thC manor house on South Downs with panoramic views over coast and Downs. Next to famous Chalk Gardens. Ideal for walkers and garden enthusiasts.

P

◆◆◆◆

ROSEDALE HOUSE

12 Bath Road, Worthing BN11 3NU
T: (01903) 233181
E: rosedale@amserve.net

Bedrooms: 1 double, 1 twin, 2 single
Bathrooms: 2 en suite

B&B per person per night:
S £25.00–£29.50
D £27.50–£30.00

OPEN All Year

Delightful Victorian house run by the friendly Nightingale family. Quality, comfortable, en suite accommodation, ideally situated for enjoying coast and countryside. Full, grilled, English breakfast.

TOWN INDEX

This can be found at the back of the guide. If you know where you want to stay, the index will give you the page number listing accommodation in your chosen town, city or village.

A brief guide to the main Towns and Villages offering accommodation in the **South East**

A ABINGDON, OXFORDSHIRE - Attractive former county town on River Thames with many interesting buildings, including 17th C County Hall, now a museum, in the market-place and the remains of an abbey.

ABINGER COMMON, SURREY - Small hamlet 4 miles south-west of Dorking.

ALTON, HAMPSHIRE - Pleasant old market town standing on the Pilgrim's Way, with some attractive Georgian buildings. The parish church still bears the scars of bullet marks, evidence of a bitter struggle between the Roundheads and the Royalists.

AMERSHAM, BUCKINGHAMSHIRE - Old town with many fine buildings, particularly in the High Street. There are several interesting old inns.

ANDOVER, HAMPSHIRE - Town that achieved importance from the wool trade and now has much modern development. A good centre for visiting places of interest.

ASHFORD, KENT - Once a market centre, the town has a number of Tudor and Georgian houses and a museum. Eurostar trains stop at Ashford International station.

ASHURST, HAMPSHIRE - Small village on the A35, on the edge of the New Forest and 3 miles north-east of Lyndhurst. Easy access to beautiful forest lawns.

AYLESBURY, BUCKINGHAMSHIRE - Historic county town in the Vale of Aylesbury. The cobbled market square has a Victorian clock tower and the 15th C King's Head Inn (National Trust). Interesting county museum and 13th C parish church.

B BANBURY, OXFORDSHIRE - Famous for its cattle market, cakes, nursery rhyme and Cross. Founded in Saxon times, it has some fine houses and interesting old inns. A good centre for touring Warwickshire and the Cotswolds.

BASINGSTOKE, HAMPSHIRE - Rapidly developing commercial and industrial centre. The town is surrounded by charming villages and places to visit.

BATTLE, EAST SUSSEX - The Abbey at Battle was built on the site of the Battle of Hastings, when William defeated Harold II and so became the Conqueror in 1066. The museum has a fine collection relating to the Sussex iron industry, and there is a social history museum - Buckleys Yesterday's World.

BEACONSFIELD, BUCKINGHAMSHIRE - Former coaching town with several inns still surviving. The old town has many fine houses and an interesting church. Beautiful countryside and beech woods nearby.

BEAULIEU, HAMPSHIRE - Beautifully situated among woods and hills on the Beaulieu river, the village is both charming and unspoilt. The 13th C ruined Cistercian abbey and 14th C Palace House stand close to the National Motor Museum. There is a maritime museum at Bucklers Hard.

BEMBRIDGE, ISLE OF WIGHT - Village with harbour and bay below Bembridge Down - the most easterly village on the island. Bembridge Sailing Club is one of the most important in southern England.

BERE REGIS, DORSET - This watercress-growing village was, in the Middle Ages, famed for its fairs and being a resort of kings on their way to the south-west; its former splendour is well commemorated by the medieval church.

BETHERSDEN, KENT - Typical Wealden village with plenty of weatherboarded houses. Famous in the Middle Ages for its marble, used in Canterbury and Rochester Cathedrals.

BICESTER, OXFORDSHIRE - Market town with a large army depot and well-known hunting centre with hunt established in the late 18th C. The ancient parish church displays work of many periods. Nearby is the Jacobean mansion of Rousham House with gardens landscaped by William Kent.

BIDDENDEN, KENT - Perfect village with black and white houses, a tithe barn and a pond. Part of the village is grouped around a green with a village sign depicting the famous Biddenden Maids. It was an important centre of the Flemish weaving industry, hence the beautiful Old Cloth Hall. A vineyard is nearby.

BLANDFORD FORUM, DORSET - Almost completely destroyed by fire in 1731, the town was rebuilt in a handsome Georgian style. The church is large and grand and the town is the hub of a rich farming area.

BOGNOR REGIS, WEST SUSSEX - Five miles of firm, flat sand has made the town a popular family resort. Well supplied with gardens.

BONCHURCH, ISLE OF WIGHT - Sheltered suburb at the foot of St Boniface Down.

BOURNEMOUTH, DORSET - Seaside town set among the pines with a mild climate, sandy beaches and fine coastal views. The town has wide streets with excellent shops, a pier, a pavilion, museums and conference centre.

BRACKNELL, BERKSHIRE - Designated a New Town in 1949, the town has ancient origins. Set in heathlands, it is an excellent centre for golf and walking. South Hill Park, an 18th C mansion, houses an art centre.

BRIGHSTONE, ISLE OF WIGHT - Excellent centre for visitors who want somewhere quiet. Calbourne, nearby, is ideal for picnics, and the sea at Chilton Chie has safe bathing at high tide.

BRIGHTON & HOVE, EAST SUSSEX - Brighton's attractions include the Royal Pavilion, Volks Electric Railway, Sea Life Centre, Marina Village, Conference Centre, The Lanes and several theatres.

BRIZE NORTON, OXFORDSHIRE - Village closely associated with the American Air Force. The medieval church is the only church in England dedicated to St Brice, from whom the village takes its name.

BROADSTAIRS, KENT - Popular seaside resort with numerous sandy bays. Charles Dickens spent his summers at Bleak House where he wrote parts of "David Copperfield". The Dickens Festival is held in June, when many people wear Dickensian costume.

BROCKENHURST, HAMPSHIRE - Attractive village with thatched cottages and a ford in its main street. Well placed for visiting the New Forest.

BURFORD, OXFORDSHIRE - One of the most beautiful Cotswold wool towns with Georgian and Tudor houses, many antique shops and a picturesque high street sloping to the River Windrush.

C CANTERBURY, KENT - Place of pilgrimage since the martyrdom of Becket in 1170 and the site of Canterbury Cathedral. Visit St Augustine's Abbey, St Martin's (the oldest church in England), Royal Museum and Art Gallery and the Canterbury Tales. Nearby is Howletts Wild Animal Park. Good shopping centre.

CARISBROOKE, ISLE OF WIGHT - Situated at the heart of the Isle of Wight and an ideal base for touring. Boasts a Norman church, formerly a monastic church, and a castle built on the site of a Roman fortress.

CHALFONT ST GILES, BUCKINGHAMSHIRE - Pretty, old village in wooded Chiltern Hills yet only 20 miles from London and a good base for visiting the city. Excellent base for Windsor, Henley, the Thames Valley, Oxford and the Cotswolds.

CHICHESTER, WEST SUSSEX - The county town of West Sussex with a beautiful Norman cathedral. Noted for its Georgian architecture but also has modern buildings like the Festival Theatre. Surrounded by places of interest, including Fishbourne Roman Palace, Weald and Downland Open-Air Museum and West Dean Gardens.

CHIPPING NORTON, OXFORDSHIRE - Old market town set high in the Cotswolds and an ideal touring centre. The wide market-place contains many 16th C and 17th C stone houses and the Town Hall and Tudor Guildhall.

CRANBROOK, KENT - Old town, a centre for the weaving industry in the 15th C. The 72-ft-high Union Mill is a 3-storey windmill, still in working order. Sissinghurst Gardens (National Trust) are nearby.

D DEDDINGTON, OXFORDSHIRE - On the edge of the Cotswolds and settled since the Stone Age, this is the only village in England to have been granted a full Coat of Arms, displayed on the 16th C Town Hall in the picturesque market square. Many places of interest include the Church of St Peter and St Paul.

DORKING, SURREY - Ancient market town and a good centre for walking, delightfully set between Box Hill and the Downs. Denbies Wine Estate - England's largest vineyard - is situated here.

DOVER, KENT - A Cinque Port and busiest passenger port in the world. Still a historic town and seaside resort beside the famous White Cliffs. The White Cliffs Experience attraction traces the town's history through the Roman, Saxon, Norman and Victorian periods.

DYMCHURCH, KENT - For centuries the headquarters of the Lords of the Level, the local government of this area. Probably best known today because of the fame of its fictional parson, the notorious Dr Syn, who has inspired a regular festival.

E EAST GRINSTEAD, WEST SUSSEX - A number of fine old houses stand in the high street, one of which is Sackville College, founded in 1609.

EASTBOURNE, EAST SUSSEX - One of the finest, most elegant resorts on the south-east coast situated beside Beachy Head. Long promenade, well-known Carpet Gardens on the seafront, Devonshire Park tennis and indoor leisure complex, theatres, Towner Art Gallery, "How We Lived Then" Museum of Shops and Social History.

EDGCOTT, BUCKINGHAMSHIRE - Small village within easy reach of Aylesbury, Milton Keynes and Bicester.

EWHURST, SURREY - Once a prosperous centre of the woollen trade. Nearby is Elstead Moat, a national nature reserve.

F FAREHAM, HAMPSHIRE - Lies on a quiet backwater of Portsmouth Harbour. The high street is lined with fine Georgian buildings.

FARINGDON, OXFORDSHIRE - Ancient, stone-built market town in the Vale of the White Horse. The 17th C market hall stands on pillars and the 13th C church has some fine monuments. A great monastic tithe barn is nearby at Great Coxwell.

FARNBOROUGH, HAMPSHIRE - Home of the Royal Aircraft Establishment and the site of the biennial International Air Show. St Michael's Abbey was built by the Empress Eugenie, wife of Napoleon III of France, and they and their son are buried in the crypt.

FARNHAM, SURREY - Town noted for its Georgian houses. Willmer House (now a museum) has a facade of cut and moulded brick with fine carving and panelling in the interior. The 12th C castle has been occupied by Bishops of both Winchester and Guildford.

FAVERSHAM, KENT - Historic town, once a port, dating back to prehistoric times. Abbey Street has more than 50 listed buildings. Roman and Anglo-Saxon finds and other exhibits can be seen in a museum in the Maison Dieu at Ospringe. Fleur de Lys Heritage Centre.

FITTLEWORTH, WEST SUSSEX - Quiet village that attracts artists and anglers. Groups of cottages can be found beside the narrow lanes and paths in the woodlands near the River Rother.

FOLKESTONE, KENT - Popular resort. The town has a fine promenade, the Leas, from where orchestral concerts and other entertainments are presented. Horse-racing at Westenhanger Racecourse nearby.

FORDINGBRIDGE, HAMPSHIRE - On the north-west edge of the New Forest. A medieval bridge crosses the Avon at this point and gave the town its name. A good centre for walking, exploring and fishing.

G GODALMING, SURREY - Several old coaching inns are reminders that the town was once a staging point. The old Town Hall is now the local-history museum. Charterhouse School moved here in 1872 and is dominated by the 150-ft Founder's Tower.

GODSHILL, HAMPSHIRE - On the Shanklin road. Hill-top church and museum.

GORING, OXFORDSHIRE - Riverside town on the Oxfordshire/Berkshire border, linked by an attractive bridge to Streatley with views to the Goring Gap.

GUILDFORD, SURREY - Bustling town with Lewis Carroll connections and many historic monuments, one of which is the Guildhall clock jutting out over the old High Street. The modern cathedral occupies a commanding position on Stag Hill.

H HARTFIELD, EAST SUSSEX - Pleasant village in Ashdown Forest, the setting for A A Milne's "Winnie the Pooh" stories.

HASLEMERE, SURREY - Town set in hilly, wooded countryside, much of which is in the care of the National Trust. Its attractions include the educational museum and the annual music festival.

HASTINGS, EAST SUSSEX - Ancient town which became famous as the base from which William the Conqueror set out to fight the Battle of Hastings. It later became one of the Cinque Ports and is now a leading resort. Castle, Hastings Embroidery, inspired by the Bayeux Tapestry, and Sea Life Centre.

HEATHFIELD, EAST SUSSEX - Old Heathfield is a pretty village which was one of the major centres of the Sussex iron industry.

HENLEY-ON-THAMES, OXFORDSHIRE - The famous Thames Regatta is held in this prosperous and attractive town at the beginning of July each year. The town has many Georgian buildings and old coaching inns and the parish church has some fine monuments.

HERSTMONCEUX, EAST SUSSEX - Pleasant village noted for its woodcrafts and the beautiful 15th C moated Herstmonceux Castle with its Science Centre and gardens open to the public. The only village where traditional Sussex trug baskets are still made.

HORLEY, SURREY - Town on the London to Brighton road, just north of Gatwick Airport, with an ancient parish church and 15th C inn.

HYTHE, HAMPSHIRE - Waterside village with spectacular views over Southampton Water. Marina with distinctive "fishing village"-style development, 117-year-old pier, wide range of interesting shops.

L LEWES, EAST SUSSEX - Historic county town with Norman castle. The steep High Street has mainly Georgian buildings. There is a folk museum at Anne of Cleves House and the archaeological museum is in Barbican House.

LINGFIELD, SURREY - Wealden village with many buildings dating back to the 15th C. Nearby there is year-round horse-racing at Lingfield Park.

LYMINGTON, HAMPSHIRE - Small, pleasant town with bright cottages and attractive Georgian houses, lying on the edge of the New Forest with a ferry service to the Isle of Wight. A sheltered harbour makes it a busy yachting centre.

LYMINSTER, WEST SUSSEX - Links up with Littlehampton looking inland, and across the watermeadows to the churches and towers of Arundel. There is a vineyard here.

LYNDHURST, HAMPSHIRE - The "capital" of the New Forest, surrounded by attractive woodland scenery and delightful villages. The town is dominated by the Victorian Gothic-style church where the original Alice in Wonderland is buried.

M MAIDENHEAD, BERKSHIRE - Attractive town on the River Thames which is crossed by an elegant 18th C bridge and by Brunel's well-known railway bridge. It is a popular place for boating with delightful riverside walks. The Courage Shire Horse Centre is nearby.

MAIDSTONE, KENT - Busy county town of Kent on the River Medway which has many interesting features and is an excellent centre for excursions. Museum of Carriages, Museum and Art Gallery, Mote Park.

MARLOW, BUCKINGHAMSHIRE - Attractive Georgian town on the River Thames, famous for its 19th C suspension bridge. The high street contains many old houses, and there are connections with writers including Shelley and T S Eliot.

MIDHURST, WEST SUSSEX - Historic, picturesque town just north of the South Downs, with the ruins of Cowdray House, medieval castle and 15th C parish church. Polo at Cowdray Park. Excellent base for Chichester, Petworth, Glorious Goodwood and the South Downs Way.

MILFORD-ON-SEA, HAMPSHIRE - Victorian seaside resort with shingle beach and good bathing, set in pleasant countryside and looking out over the Isle of Wight. Nearby is Hurst Castle, built by Henry VIII. The school chapel, former abbey church, can be visited.

MILTON KEYNES, BUCKINGHAMSHIRE - Designated a New Town in 1967, Milton Keynes offers a wide range of housing, and is abundantly planted with trees. It has excellent shopping facilities and 3 centres for leisure and sporting activities. The Open University is based here.

N NEW MILTON, HAMPSHIRE - New Forest residential town on the mainline railway.

NEWBURY, BERKSHIRE - Ancient town surrounded by the Downs and on the Kennet and Avon Canal. It has many buildings of interest, including the 17th C Cloth Hall, which is now a museum. The famous racecourse is nearby.

O OXFORD, OXFORDSHIRE - Beautiful university town with many ancient colleges, some dating from the 13th C, and numerous buildings of historic and architectural interest. The Ashmolean Museum has outstanding collections. Lovely gardens and meadows with punting on the Cherwell.

OXTED, SURREY - Pleasant town on the edge of National Trust woodland and at the foot of the North Downs. Chartwell (National Trust), the former home of Sir Winston Churchill, is close by.

P PARTRIDGE GREEN, WEST SUSSEX - Small village between Henfield and Billingshurst.

PETERSFIELD, HAMPSHIRE - Grew prosperous from the wool trade and was famous as a coaching centre. Its attractive market square is dominated by a statue of William III. Close by are Petersfield Heath, with numerous ancient barrows, and Butser Hill with magnificent views.

POLEGATE, EAST SUSSEX - Polegate used to be an important junction for the London, Brighton and South Coast Railway. Polegate Windmill and Milling Museum can be visited.

POOLE, DORSET - Tremendous natural harbour makes Poole a superb boating centre. The harbour area is crowded with historic buildings including the 15th C Town Cellars, housing a maritime museum.

PORTSMOUTH & SOUTHSEA, HAMPSHIRE - There have been connections with the Navy since early times and the first dock was built in 1194. HMS Victory, Nelson's flagship, is here and Charles Dickens' former home is open to the public. Neighbouring Southsea has a promenade with magnificent views of Spithead.

R RAMSGATE, KENT - Popular holiday resort with good sandy beaches. At Pegwell Bay is a replica of a Viking longship.

READING, BERKSHIRE - Busy, modern county town with large shopping centre and many leisure and recreation facilities. There are several interesting museums, and the Duke of Wellington's Stratfield Saye is nearby.

ROCHESTER, KENT - Ancient cathedral city on the River Medway. Has many places of interest connected with Charles Dickens (who lived nearby) including the fascinating Dickens Centre. Also there is a massive castle overlooking the river and Guildhall Museum.

ROMSEY, HAMPSHIRE - Town which grew up around the important abbey and lies on the banks of the River Test, famous for trout and salmon. Broadlands House, home of the late Lord Mountbatten, is open to the public.

ROYAL TUNBRIDGE WELLS, KENT - This "Royal" town became famous as a spa in the 17th C and much of its charm is retained, as in the Pantiles, a shaded walk lined with elegant shops. Heritage attraction "A Day at the Wells". Excellent shopping centre.

RUSTINGTON, WEST SUSSEX - Village with thatched cottages and a medieval church.

RYDE, ISLE OF WIGHT - The island's chief entry port, connected to Portsmouth by ferries and hovercraft. Seven miles of sandy beaches with a half-mile pier, esplanade and gardens.

RYE, EAST SUSSEX - Cobbled, hilly streets and fine old buildings make Rye, once a Cinque Port, a most picturesque town. Noted for its church with ancient clock, potteries and antique shops. Town Model Sound and Light Show gives a good introduction to the town.

S SANDOWN, ISLE OF WIGHT - The 6-mile sweep of Sandown Bay is one of the island's finest stretches, with excellent sands. The pier has a pavilion and sun terrace; the esplanade has amusements, bars, eating places and gardens.

SEAFORD, EAST SUSSEX - The town was a bustling port until 1579 when the course of the River Ouse was diverted. The downlands around the town make good walking country, with fine views of the Seven Sisters cliffs.

SELBORNE, HAMPSHIRE - Village made famous by Gilbert White, who was a curate here and is remembered for his classic book "The Natural History of Selborne", published in 1788. His house is now a museum.

SELSEY, WEST SUSSEX - Almost surrounded by water, with the English Channel on 2 sides and an inland lake, once Pagham Harbour, and the Brook on the other 2. Ideal for yachting, swimming, fishing and wildlife.

SEVENOAKS, KENT - Set in pleasant wooded country, with a distinctive character and charm. Nearby is Knole (National Trust), home of the Sackville family and one of the largest houses in England, set in a vast deer park.

SHANKLIN, ISLE OF WIGHT - Set on a cliff with gentle slopes leading down to the beach, esplanade and marine gardens. The picturesque, old thatched village nestles at the end of the wooded chine.

SMARDEN, KENT - Pretty village with a number of old, well-presented buildings. The 14th C St Michael's Church is sometimes known as the "Barn of Kent" because of its 36-ft roof span.

SOUTHAMPTON, HAMPSHIRE - One of Britain's leading seaports with a long history, now a major container port. In the 18th C it became a fashionable resort with the assembly rooms and theatre. The old Guildhall and the Wool House are now museums. Sections of the medieval wall can still be seen.

STEYNING, WEST SUSSEX - An important market town and thriving port before the Norman Conquest, lying at the foot of the South Downs. Retains a picturesque charm with fascinating timber-framed and stone buildings.

STOCKBRIDGE, HAMPSHIRE - Set in the Test Valley which has some of the best fishing in England. The wide main street has houses of all styles, mainly Tudor and Georgian.

STUDLAND, DORSET - On a beautiful stretch of coast and good for walking, with a National Nature Reserve to the north. The Norman church is the finest in the country, with superb rounded arches and vaulting. Brownsea Island, where the first scout camp was held, lies in Poole Harbour.

SWANAGE, DORSET - Began life as an Anglo-Saxon port, then a quarrying centre of Purbeck marble. The safe, sandy beach is set in a sweeping bay and is flanked by downs, making it an ideal resort and good walking country.

SWAY, HAMPSHIRE - Small village on the south-western edge of the New Forest. It is noted for its 220-ft tower, Peterson's Folly, built in the 1870s by a retired Indian judge to demonstrate the value of concrete as a building material.

U UCKFIELD, EAST SUSSEX - Once a medieval market town and centre of the iron industry, Uckfield is now a busy country town on the edge of the Ashdown Forest.

W WALLINGFORD, OXFORDSHIRE - Site of an ancient ford over the River Thames, now crossed by a 900-ft-long bridge. The town has many timber-framed and Georgian buildings, Gainsborough portraits in the 17th C Town Hall and a few remains of a Norman castle.

WEST CLANDON, SURREY - Home of Clandon Park (National Trust), the Palladian mansion built in the early 1730s and home of the Queen's Royal Surrey Regiment Museum.

WHITWELL, ISLE OF WIGHT - West of Ventnor, with interesting church, thatched inn and youth hostel. Good walking area.

WIMBORNE MINSTER, DORSET - Market town centred on the twin-towered Minster Church of St Cuthberga which gave the town the second part of its name. Good touring base for the surrounding countryside, depicted in the writings of Thomas Hardy.

WINCHELSEA, EAST SUSSEX - Edward I laid out the present town on its hilltop site in the 13th C to replace the ancient Cinque Port which was eventually engulfed by the sea.

WINCHESTER, HAMPSHIRE - King Alfred the Great made Winchester the capital of Saxon England. A magnificent Norman cathedral, with one of the longest naves in Europe, dominates the city. Home of Winchester College, founded in 1382.

WINDSOR, BERKSHIRE - Town dominated by the spectacular castle, home of the Royal Family for over 900 years. Parts are open to the public. There are many attractions including the Great Park, Eton and trips on the river.

WINSLOW, BUCKINGHAMSHIRE - Small town with Georgian houses, a little market square and a fine church with 15th C wall paintings. Winslow Hall, built to the design of Sir Christopher Wren in 1700, is open to the public.

WITNEY, OXFORDSHIRE - Town famous for its blanket making and mentioned in the Domesday Book. The market-place contains the Butter Cross, a medieval meeting place, and there is a green with merchants' houses.

WOKING, SURREY - One of the largest towns in Surrey, which developed with the coming of the railway in the 1830s. Old Woking was a market town in the 17th C and still retains several interesting buildings. Large arts and entertainment centre.

WOODCOTE, OXFORDSHIRE - Town in the Chilterns close to Goring and Henley-on-Thames.

WOODSTOCK, OXFORDSHIRE - Small country town clustered around the park gates of Blenheim Palace, the superb 18th C home of the Duke of Marlborough. The town has well-known inns and an interesting museum. Sir Winston Churchill was born and buried nearby.

WORTHING, WEST SUSSEX - Town in the West Sussex countryside and by the south coast, with excellent shopping and many pavement cafes and restaurants. Attractions include the award-winning Museum and Art Gallery, beautiful gardens, pier, elegant town houses, Cissbury Ring hill fort and the South Downs.

GOLD & SILVER AWARDS

These exclusive VisitBritain awards are given to establishments achieving the highest levels of quality and service. Further information can be found at the front of the guide. An index to all accommodation achieving these awards are at the back of this guide.

Campus Accommodation

VisitBritain has a separate rating scheme of One to Five Stars for Campus Accommodation which includes educational establishments such as universities and colleges with sleeping accommodation in halls of residence or student village complexes available for individuals, families and groups. Availability is mainly during the academic vacation during the summer from June to September, Easter and some Christmas availability. Some universities provide accommodation throughout the year and there is often a wide choice of recreational facilities, with most venues providing TV rooms, bars and restaurants and a variety of sporting and special interest holidays.

Establishments meet a minimum requirement for both the provision of facilities and services, including fixtures, fittings, furnishings, décor. Progressively higher levels of quality and customer care are provided for each of the Star ratings. Quite simply, the more Stars, the higher the overall level of quality you can expect.

What standards to expect at each rating level:

*	Acceptable
**	Good
***	Very Good
****	Excellent
*****	Exceptional

A complete list of assessed campus accommodation is included in the listings section at the back of this guide.

In addition to the symbols shown inside the back cover flap, the following also appear:

Non smoking rooms available	Foodshop on site	Business facilities
Laundrette	Public telephone	Cooking facilities

CANTERBURY, Kent Map ref 3B3 *Tourist Information Centre Tel: (01227) 766567*

★★-★★★

KENT HOSPITALITY

Tanglewood, The University,
Canterbury CT2 7LX
T: (01227) 828000
F: (01227) 828019
E: hospitality-enquiry@kent.ac.uk
I: www.kent.ac.uk/hospitality/

Bedrooms: 2960 singles, 31 twins, 1521 triples
Total no. of beds: 3022

Lunch available
Evening meal available
Payment: Mastercard, Visa, Switch, Delta

Per person per night
B&B £22.00-£30.00
Self-Catering from £395 per week

The university is situated overlooking the famous Canterbury Cathedral and is set in 300 acres of grounds. Comfortable accommodation. A variety of restaurants and bars available.

CHICHESTER, West Sussex Map ref 2C3 *Tourist Information Centre Tel: (01243) 775888*

★★

UNIVERSITY COLLEGE CHICHESTER

Bishop Otter Campus, College Lane,
Chichester PO19 6PE
T: (01243) 816070
F: (01243) 816068
E: conference@ucc.ac.uk
I: www.ucc.ac.uk

Bedrooms: 218 singles
Totel no. of beds: 218

Payment: Mastercard, Visa, Switch, Delta

Per person per night
B&B £25.50-£33.00

University campus accommodation within easy walking distance of the city centre. Conference facilities available.

LONDON, Greater London

Rating Applied For

IES STUDENT RESIDENCE HALL

Manresa Road, Corner of King's Road & Manresa Road, London SW3 6NA
T: (020) 7808 9200
F: (020) 7376 5167
E: info@iesreshall.com
I: www.iesreshall.com

New student residence for the discerning guest on The King's Road in Chelsea with upmarket shops and restaurants at our doors. All en suite, self-catering, common lounges with TV, DVD and VCR. 24/7 security/CCTV. Laundry facilities. On bus and tube lines (S. Ken/Sloane Sq.) Lively entertainment and weekly activities. Friendly, multi-lingual staff.

Bedrooms: 23 singles, 138 doubles/twin,
Total no. of beds: 296

Payment: Mastercard, Diners, Visa, American Express, Switch, Delta, JCB, Solo

Special summer and Christmas breaks available. Open year round for academic stays. Holiday lets from May-Sept and Dec.

Per person per night
Bed only £20.00-£40.00
B&B £24.50-£44.50

OAKHAM, Rutland Map ref 4C3 *Tourist Information Centre Tel: (01572) 724329*

★★★★

BARLEYTHORPE TRAINING AND CONFERENCE CENTRE

Barleythorpe, Oakham, Rutland LE15 7ED
T: (01572) 723711
F: (01572) 757657
E: info@eef-eastmids.org.uk
I: www.barleythorpe.com

Modern purpose-built conference centre in delightful rural setting. 9 well-equipped conference rooms with restaurant connected to residential lodge with 22 en suite bedrooms (accommodating max. 42 guests), spacious comfortably furnished residents' lounge with bar and patio. Badminton, volleyball, petanque. Available at weekends for residential groups of 12 or more.

Bedrooms:
2 singles, 20 twin
Total no.of beds: 42

Lunch and evening meal available by prior arrangement
Payment: Visa, Delta

Exclusive hire available at weekends. Special rates available in August.

Per person per night
B&B £36.00-£50.75

OXFORD, Oxfordshire Map ref 2C1 *Tourist Information Centre Tel: (01865) 726871*

★★

ST HUGH'S COLLEGE
Rachel Trickett Building, St Margarets Road, Oxford OX2 6LE
T: (01865) 274900
F: (01865) 274912

Bedrooms: 60 singles
Total no. of beds: 60
Bathrooms: 60

Payment: Mastercard, Visa, Switch

Per person per night
B&B £50.00–£75.00

Erected in 1992, the building boasts full en suite accommodation with shower, toilet and wash-hand basin in 60 single study bedrooms.

(12)

SHEFFIELD, South Yorkshire Map ref 4B2 *Tourist Information Centre Tel: (0114) 221 1900/(0114) 273 4671*

★★

TAPTON HALL OF RESIDENCE
The University of Sheffield, Crookes Road, Sheffield S10 2AZ
T: (0114) 222 8862
E: b&b@sheffield.ac.uk
I: www.conferencesheffield.com

Bedrooms: 355 singles, 10 doubles/twin, 365 triples
Total no. of beds: 375

Payment: Mastercard, Visa, American Express, Switch, Delta

Per person per night
B&B £28.45–£42.65

Situated in a quiet, attractive location overlooking the university's botanical gardens. The licensed bar and conservatory opens onto a terrace with views across the gardens.

WINCHESTER, Hampshire Map ref 2C3 *Tourist Information Centre Tel: (01962) 840500*

Rating Applied For

KING ALFRED'S COLLEGE
Sparkford Road,
Winchester SO22 4NR
T: (01962) 827322
F: (01962) 827264
E: conferences@wkac.ac.uk
I: www.kingalfreds.ac.uk

Bedrooms: 65 singles
Total no. of beds: 65
Bathrooms: 65

Lunch available
Evening meal available
Payment: Mastercard, Visa, Switch

Per person per night
Bed only £27.50
B&B £33.50
HB £44.00

Groups only

Set on a hillside in a beautiful corner of historic Winchester, King Alfred's offers comfortable en suite bedrooms and full English breakfast.

(8)

The network of Regional Tourist Boards run a range of training recognition awards which demonstrate a commitment to improving customer service within all types of accommodation and other tourism organisations.

Wherever you find the Welcome to Excellence logo, you can be assured of a commitment to:

- achieving excellence in customer service
- exceeding guest needs and expectations
- providing an environment where courtesy, helpfulness and a warm welcome are standard
- a focus on developing individual skills.

Those displaying the logo have at least 50% of staff trained to the required standard.

VisitBritain's
assessed accommodation

On the following pages you will find an exclusive listing of all Guest Accommodation in England that has been assessed for quality by VisitBritain.

Campus Accommodation is listed separately at the end of this section.

The information includes brief contact details for each place to stay, together with its Diamond rating, and quality award if appropriate. The listing also shows if an establishment has a National Accessible rating (see the front of the guide for further information).

More detailed information on all the places shown in blue can be found in the regional sections (where establishments have paid to have their details included). To find these entries please refer to the appropriate regional section, or look in the town index at the back of this guide.

The list which follows was compiled slightly later than the regional sections. For this reason you may find that, in a few instances, a Diamond rating and quality award may differ between the two sections. This list contains the most up-to-date information and was correct at the time of going to press.

LONDON

E4

Aucklands
♦♦♦♦ SILVER AWARD
25 Eglington Road, London E4 7AN
T: (020) 8529 1140
F: (020) 8529 9288
E: drumandhelen@amserve.net

Ridgeway Hotel ♦♦♦
115-117 The Ridgeway, North Chingford, London E4 6QU
T: (020) 8529 1964
F: (020) 8542 9130

E7

Forest View Hotel ♦
227 Romford Road, Forest Gate, London E7 9HL
T: (020) 8534 4844
F: (020) 8534 8959
E: forestviewhotel@hotmail.com
I: www.forestviewhotel.net

E15

Park Hotel ♦♦
81 Portway, London E15 3QJ
T: (020) 8257 9034
F: (020) 8279 8094

N1

Kandara Guest House ♦♦♦
68 Ockendon Road, Islington, London N1 3NW
T: (020) 7226 5721
F: (020) 7226 3379
E: admin@kandara.co.uk
I: www.kandara.co.uk

N4

Costello Palace Hotel ♦♦
374 Seven Sisters Road, London N4 2PG
T: (020) 8802 6551
F: (020) 8802 9461
E: costellopalacehotel@ukonline.co.uk
I: www.costellopalacehotel.co.uk

Spring Park Hotel ♦♦
400 Seven Sisters Road, London N4 2LX
T: (020) 8800 6030
F: (020) 8802 5652
E: sphotel400@aol.com
I: www.springparkhotel.co.uk

N7

Europa Hotel ♦♦♦
60-62 Anson Road, London N7 0AA
T: (020) 7607 5935
F: (020) 7607 5909
E: info@europahotellondon.co.uk
I: www.europahotellondon.co.uk

Queens Hotel ♦♦
33 Anson Road, London N7 0RB
T: (020) 7607 4725
F: (020) 7697 9725
E: queens@stavrouhotels.co.uk

N8

White Lodge Hotel ♦♦♦
1 Church Lane, Hornsey, London N8 7BU
T: (020) 8348 9765
F: (020) 8340 7851

N10

The Muswell Hill Hotel ♦♦♦
73 Muswell Hill Road, Muswell Hill, London N10 3HT
T: (020) 8883 6447
F: (020) 8883 5158
E: reception@muswellhillhotel.co.uk
I: www.muswellhillhotel.co.uk

N20

The Corner Lodge ♦♦♦♦
9 Athenaeum Road, London N20 9AA
T: (020) 8446 3720
F: (020) 8446 3720
I: www.thecornerlodge.com

N22

Pane Residence ♦♦
154 Boundary Road, Wood Green, London N22 6AE
T: (020) 8889 3735

NW1

Americana Hotel ♦♦♦
172-174 Gloucester Place, London NW1 6DS
T: (020) 7723 1452
F: (020) 7723 4641
E: manager@americanahotel.demon.co.uk
I: www.americanahotel.activehotels.com

NW3

Dillons Hotel ♦♦
21 Belsize Park, Hampstead, London NW3 4DU
T: (020) 7794 3360
F: (020) 7431 7900
E: desk@dillonshotel.com
I: www.dillonshotel.com

NW6

Cavendish Guest House ♦♦♦♦
24 Cavendish Road, London NW6 7XP
T: (020) 8451 3249
F: (020) 8451 3249

Dawson House Hotel ♦♦♦♦
72 Canfield Gardens, London NW6 3ED
T: (020) 7624 0079
F: (020) 7644 6321
E: dawsonhtl@aol.com

NW10

Aran Guest House ♦♦
21 Holland Road, London NW10 5AH
T: (020) 8968 6402

NW11

Anchor-Nova Hotel ♦♦♦
Flat 2, London NW11 7QH
T: (020) 8458 8764
F: (020) 8455 3204
E: enquir@anchor-hotel.co.uk
I: www.anchor-hotel.co.uk

SE3

The Grovers ♦♦♦
96 Merriman Road, London SE3 8RZ
T: (020) 8488 7719
F: (020) 8488 7719
E: james.grover13@ntlworld.com

Hill Crest Guesthouse ♦♦
2 Hardy Road, London SE3 7NR
T: (020) 8305 0120
F: (020) 8305 0120
E: hillcrest@dial.pipex.com

59a Lee Road ♦♦♦
Blackheath, London SE3 9EN
T: (020) 8318 7244
E: angecall@blackheath318.freeserve.co.uk

59 Lee Terrace ♦♦
London SE3 9TA
T: (020) 8852 6334
E: susan.bedbreakfast@virgin.net

Mrs Dove's ♦♦
68 Wricklemarsh Road, London SE3 8DS
T: (020) 8856 1331
F: (020) 8480 6653
E: mrsdove@cwcom.net

Number Nine Blackheath ♦♦♦♦
9 Charlton Road, Blackheath, London SE3 7EU
T: (020) 8858 4175
F: (020) 8858 4175
E: derek@numbernineblackheath.com
I: www.numbernineblackheath.com

3 Tilbrook Road ♦♦
Kidbrooke, London SE3 9QD
T: (020) 8319 8843
E: m.hutson@ntlworld.com

SE4

Crofton Park Holdenby ♦
28 Holdenby Road, London SE4 2DA
T: (020) 8694 0011
E: savitri.gaines@totalise.co.uk
I: www.ukhomestay.net

66 Geoffrey Road ♦♦♦
London SE4 1NT
T: (020) 8691 3887
F: (020) 8691 3887
E: andrea.dechamps@btclick.com

SE6

The Heathers ♦♦♦
71 Verdant Lane, Catford, London SE6 1JD
T: (020) 8698 8340
F: (020) 8461 3980
E: berylheath@yahoo.co.uk
I: www.theheathersbb.com

Tulip Tree House ♦♦♦
41 Minard Road, Catford, London SE6 1NP
T: (020) 8697 2596
F: (020) 8698 2020

SE8

M B Guest House ♦♦
7 Bolden Street, London SE8 4JF
T: (020) 8692 7030
F: (020) 8691 6241
E: mbguesthouse@yahoo.co.uk

SE9

Abigail House ♦♦♦
68 Dunvegan Road, London SE9 1SB
T: (020) 8859 3924

Benvenuti ♦♦♦♦
217 Court Road, Eltham, London SE9 4TG
T: (020) 8857 4855
F: (020) 8265 5635
E: val-alan@benvenuti-guesthouse.co.uk
I: www.benvenuti-guesthouse.co.uk

Boru House ♦♦
70 Dunvegan Road, London SE9 1SB
T: (020) 8850 0584

Weston House ♦
8 Eltham Green, London SE9 5LB
T: (020) 8850 5191
F: (020) 8850 0030
E: reservation@westonhousehotel.co.uk

SE10

The Corner House ♦♦♦
28 Royal Hill, London SE10 8RT
T: (020) 8692 3023
F: (020) 8692 3023
E: joannacourtney@aol.com

Greenwich Parkhouse Hotel ♦♦
1 Nevada Street, London SE10 9JL
T: (020) 8305 1478
I: www.greenwich-parkhouse-hotel.co.uk

81 Greenwich South Street
♦♦♦♦ SILVER AWARD
London SE10 8NT
T: (020) 8293 3121
E: matilda.wade@btopenworld.com

Mitre Inn ♦♦♦
291 Greenwich High Road, London SE10 8NA
T: (020) 8355 6760
F: (020) 8355 6761

16 St Alfeges ♦♦
16 St Alfege Passage, Greenwich, London SE10 9JS
T: (020) 8853 4337
E: nicmesure@yahoo.co.uk
I: www.st-alfeges.co.uk

White Swan Hotel ♦♦
13 Blackheath Road, London SE10 8PE
T: (020) 8692 8855

SE13

Brooklands Bed & Breakfast
Rating Applied For
25 Morden Hill, Lewisham, London SE13 7NN
T: (020) 8691 1899
E: benefituk@amserve.net

Manna House ♦♦♦
320 Hither Green Lane, Lewisham, London SE13 6TS
T: (020) 8461 5984
F: (020) 8695 5316
E: mannahouse@aol.com
I: www.members.aol.com/mannahouse

13 Wellmeadow Road ♦♦♦
Hither Green, London SE13 6SY
T: (020) 8697 1398
F: (020) 8697 1398

8 Yeats Close ♦♦
London SE13 7ET
T: (020) 8318 3421
F: (020) 8318 3421
E: pathu@tesco.net

SE20

Melrose House ♦♦♦♦
89 Lennard Road, London
SE20 7LY
T: (020) 8776 8884
F: (020) 8325 7636
E: melrose.hotel@virgin.net
I: www.guesthouseaccommodation.co.uk

SE22

Shepherd's London ♦♦♦♦
39 Marmora Road, London
SE22 0RX
T: (020) 8693 4355
F: (020) 8693 7954
E: dulwichdragon@hotmail.com
I: www.shepherdslondon.co.uk

SW1

Airways Hotel, London ♦♦
29-31 St George's Drive,
Victoria, London SW1V 4DG
T: (020) 7834 0205
F: (020) 7932 0007
E: sales@airways-hotel.com
I: www.airways-hotel.com

Carlton Hotel ♦♦
90 Belgrave Road, Victoria,
London SW1V 2BJ
T: (020) 7976 6634
F: (020) 7821 8020
E: info@cityhotelcarlton.co.uk
I: www.cityhotelcarlton.co.uk

Caswell Hotel ♦♦
25 Gloucester Street, London
SW1V 2DB
T: (020) 7834 6345
E: manager@hotellondon.co.uk
I: www.hotellondon.co.uk

Central House Hotel ♦♦
39 Belgrave Road, London
SW1V 2BB
T: (020) 7834 8036
F: (020) 7834 1854
E: info@centralhousehotel.co.uk

Colliers Hotel ♦
97 Warwick Way, London
SW1V 1QL
T: (020) 7834 6931
F: (020) 7834 8439
E: cmahotel@aol.com
I: www.affordablehotel.com

Collin House ♦♦♦
104 Ebury Street, London
SW1W 9QD
T: (020) 7730 8031
F: (020) 7730 8031
E: booking@collinhouse.co.uk
I: www.collinhouse.co.uk

Dover Hotel ♦♦
44 Belgrave Road, London
SW1V 1RG
T: (020) 7821 9085
F: (020) 7834 6425
E: reception@dover-hotel.co.uk
I: www.dover-hotel.co.uk

Elizabeth Hotel ♦♦♦
37 Eccleston Square, London
SW1V 1PB
T: (020) 7828 6812
F: (020) 7828 6814
E: info@elizabethhotel.com
I: www.elizabethhotel.com

Georgian House Hotel ♦♦
35 St Georges Drive, London
SW1V 4DG
T: (020) 7834 1438
F: (020) 7976 6085
E: reception@georgianhousehotel.co.uk
I: www.georgianhousehotel.co.uk

Hanover Hotel ♦♦♦
30 St Georges Drive, London
SW1V 4BN
T: (020) 7834 0367
F: (020) 7976 5587
E: reservations@hanoverhotel.co.uk
I: www.hanoverhotel.co.uk

Huttons Hotel ♦
55 Belgrave Road, London
SW1V 2BB
T: (020) 7834 3726
F: (020) 7834 3389
E: reservations@huttons-hotel.co.uk
I: www.huttons-hotel.co.uk

Knightsbridge Green Hotel ♦♦♦♦
159 Knightsbridge, London
SW1X 7PD
T: (020) 7584 6274
F: (020) 7225 1635
E: thekghotel@aol.com
I: www.thekghotel.co.uk

Luna-Simone Hotel ♦♦♦
47 Belgrave Road, London
SW1V 2BB
T: (020) 7834 5897
F: (020) 7828 2474
E: lunasimone@talk21.com
I: www.lunasimone.com

Melita House Hotel ♦♦♦
35 Charlwood Street, Victoria,
London SW1V 2DU
T: (020) 7828 0471
F: (020) 7932 0988
E: reserve@melitahotel.com
I: www.melitahotel.com

Oxford House Hotel ♦♦
92 Cambridge Street, London
SW1V 4QG
T: (020) 7834 6467
F: (020) 7834 0225
E: oxfordhousehotel@hotmail.com

Stanley House Hotel ♦♦
19-21 Belgrave Road, Victoria,
London SW1V 1RB
T: (020) 7834 5042
F: (020) 7834 8439
E: cmahotel@aol.com
I: www.londonbudgethotels.co.uk

Vandon House Hotel ♦♦♦
1 Vandon Street, London
SW1H 0AH
T: (020) 7799 6780
F: (020) 7799 1464
E: info@vandonhouse.com
I: www.vandonhouse.com

Victor Hotel ♦♦♦
51 Belgrave Road, London
SW1V 2BB
T: (020) 7592 9853
F: (020) 7592 9854
I: www.victorhotel.co.uk

The Victoria Inn London ♦♦♦
65-67 Belgrave Road, London
SW1V 2BG
T: (020) 7834 6721
F: (020) 7931 0201
E: welcome@victoriainn.co.uk
I: www.victoriainn.co.uk

Windermere Hotel
♦♦♦♦ SILVER AWARD
142-144 Warwick Way, Victoria,
London SW1V 4JE
T: (020) 7834 5163
F: (020) 7630 8831
E: reservations@windermere-hotel.co.uk
I: www.windermere-hotel.co.uk

SW5

Beaver Hotel ♦♦♦
57-59 Philbeach Gardens,
London SW5 9ED
T: (020) 7373 4553
F: (020) 7373 4555
E: hotelbeaver@hotmail.com
I: www.beaverhotel.co.uk

Comfort Inn Earl's Court ♦♦
11-13 Penywern Road, London
SW5 9TT
T: (020) 7373 6514
F: (020) 7370 3639
E: info@comfortinnearlscourt.co.uk
I: www.comfortinnearlscourt.co.uk

Hotel Earls Court ♦♦
28 Warwick Road, London
SW5 9UD
T: (020) 7373 7079
F: (020) 7912 0582
E: res@hotelearlscourt.com
I: www.hotelearlscourt.com

Kensington International Inn ♦♦♦
4 Templeton Place, London
SW5 9LZ
T: (020) 7370 4333
F: (020) 7244 7873
E: hotel@kensingtoninternationalinn.com
I: www.kensingtoninternationalinn.com

London Town Hotel ♦♦♦
15 Penywern Road, London
SW5 9TY
T: (020) 7370 4356
F: (020) 7370 7923
E: londontownhotel@tiscali.co.uk
I: www.londontownhotel.com

Lord Jim Hotel ♦♦
23-25 Penywern Road, London
SW5 9TT
T: (020) 7370 6071
F: (020) 7373 8919
E: ljh@lgh-hotels.com
I: www.lgh-hotels.com

Lord Kensington Hotel ♦♦♦
38 Trebovir Road, Earls Court,
London SW5 9NJ
T: (020) 7373 7331
F: (020) 7460 3524
E: lkh@lgh-hotels.com
I: www.lgh-hotels.com

Maranton House Hotel ♦♦♦
14 Barkston Gardens, London
SW5 0EN
T: (020) 7373 5782
F: (020) 7244 9543
E: marantonhotel@hotmail.com

Merlyn Court Hotel ♦♦
2 Barkston Gardens, London
SW5 0EN
T: (020) 7370 1640
F: (020) 7370 4986
E: london@merlyncourthotel.com
I: www.merlyncourthotel.com

Mowbray Court Hotel ♦♦
28-32 Penywern Road, London
SW5 9SU
T: (020) 7370 2316
F: (020) 7370 5693
E: mowbraycrthot@hotmail.com
I: www.mowbraycourthotel.co.uk

Hotel Oliver ♦♦
198 Cromwell Road, London
SW5 0SN
T: (020) 7370 6881
F: (020) 7370 6556
E: reservations@hoteloliver.freeserve.co.uk
I: www.hoteloliver.co.uk

Oliver Plaza Hotel ♦♦♦
33 Trebovir Road, Earls Court,
London SW5 9NF
T: (020) 7373 7183
F: (020) 7244 6021
E: oliverplaza@capricornhotels.co.uk
I: www.capricornhotels.co.uk

Hotel Plaza Continental ♦♦♦
9 Knaresborough Place, London
SW5 0TP
T: (020) 7370 3246
F: (020) 7373 9571
E: hpc@lgh-hotels.com

Ramsees Hotel ♦♦
32-36 Hogarth Road, Earls
Court, London SW5 0PU
T: (020) 7370 1445
F: (020) 7244 6835
E: ramsees@rasool.demon.co.uk
I: www.ramseeshotel.com

Rasool Court Hotel ♦♦
19-21 Penywern Road, Earls
Court, London SW5 9TT
T: (020) 7373 8900
F: (020) 7244 6835
E: rasool@rasool.demon.co.uk
I: www.rasoolcourthotel.com

Swiss House Hotel ♦♦♦
171 Old Brompton Road, London
SW5 0AN
T: (020) 7373 2769
F: (020) 7373 4983
E: recep@swiss-hh.demon.co.uk
I: www.swiss-hh.demon.co.uk

SW7

Aster House
♦♦♦♦♦ SILVER AWARD
3 Sumner Place, London
SW7 3EE
T: (020) 7581 5888
F: (020) 7584 4925
E: AsterHouse@btinternet.com
I: www.asterhouse.com

Five Sumner Place Hotel ♦♦♦♦
5 Sumner Place, London
SW7 3EE
T: (020) 7584 7586
F: (020) 7823 9962
E: reservations@sumnerplace.com
I: www.sumnerplace.com

Establishments printed in blue have a detailed entry in this guide

SW8

Comfort Inn ♦♦♦♦
87 South Lambeth Road, London SW8 1RN
T: (020) 7735 9494
F: (020) 7735 1001
E: stay@comfortinnvx.co.uk
I: www.comfortinnvx.co.uk

SW11

Lavender Guest House ♦♦♦
18 Lavender Sweep, London SW11 1HA
T: (020) 7585 2767
F: (020) 7924 6274

SW13

Barnes Bed & Breakfast Rating Applied For
106 Elm Grove Road, Barnes, London SW13 0BS
T: (020) 8876 9033
F: (020) 8412 9402
E: mcleve@themail.co.uk
I: www.barnesbedandbreakfast.co.uk

SW14

106 East Sheen Avenue ♦♦♦
London SW14 8AU
T: (020) 8255 1900
F: (020) 8876 8084
E: rpratt@easynet.co.uk

The Plough Inn ♦♦♦
42 Christchurch Road, East Sheen, London SW14 7AF
T: (020) 8876 7833
F: (020) 8392 8801
E: ploughthe@hotmail.com
I: www.theplough.org

SW16

The Konyots ♦
95 Pollards Hill South, London SW16 4LS
T: (020) 8764 0075

SW18

The Brewers Inn ♦♦♦
147 East Hill, London SW18 2QB
T: (020) 8874 4128
F: (020) 8877 1953
E: brewersinn@youngs.co.uk

2 Melrose Road ♦♦♦
London SW18 1NE
T: (020) 8871 3259

W1

Bentinck House Hotel ♦♦
20 Bentinck Street, London W1U 2EU
T: (020) 7935 9141
F: (020) 7224 5903
E: b.hh@virgin.net

Blandford Hotel ♦♦♦
80 Chiltern Street, London W1U 5AF
T: (020) 7486 3103
F: (020) 7487 2786
E: blandfordhotel@dial.pipex.com
I: www.capricornhotels.co.uk

The Edward Lear Hotel ♦♦
28-30 Seymour Street, London W1H 7JB
T: (020) 7402 5401
F: (020) 7706 3766
E: edwardlear@aol.com
I: www.edlear.com

Hallam Hotel ♦♦♦
12 Hallam Street, Portland Place, London W1W 6JF
T: (020) 7580 1166
F: (020) 7323 4527
E: hallam_hotel@hotmail.com
I: www.hallamhotel.com

Lincoln House Hotel – Central London ♦♦
33 Gloucester Place, Marble Arch, London W1U 8HY
T: (020) 7486 7630
F: (020) 7486 0166
E: reservations@lincoln-house-hotel.co.uk
I: www.lincoln-house-hotel.co.uk

Marble Arch Inn ♦♦
49-50 Upper Berkeley Street, Marble Arch, London W1H 5QR
T: (020) 7723 7888
F: (020) 7723 6060
E: sales@marblearch-inn.co.uk
I: www.marblearch-inn.co.uk

Hotel La Place ♦♦♦♦
17 Nottingham Place, London W1U 5LG
T: (020) 7486 2323
F: (020) 7486 4335
E: reservations@hotellaplace.com
I: www.hotellaplace.com

St.George Hotel ♦♦♦♦
49 Gloucester Place, London W1U 8JE
T: (020) 7486 8586
F: (020) 7486 6567
E: reservations@stgeorge-hotel.net
I: www.stgeorge-hotel.net

Ten Manchester Street ♦♦♦♦
London W1U 4DG
T: (020) 7486 6669
F: (020) 7224 0348
E: stay@10manchesterstreet.fsnet.co.uk
I: www.10manchesterstreet.com

Wigmore Court Hotel ♦♦♦
23 Gloucester Place, London W1U 8HS
T: (020) 7935 0928
F: (020) 7487 4254
E: info@wigmore-court-hotel.co.uk
I: www.wigmore-court-hotel.co.uk

Wyndham Hotel ♦♦♦
30 Wyndham Street, London W1H 1EB
T: (020) 7723 7204
F: (020) 7724 2893
E: wyndhamhotel@talk21.com
I: www.lhghotels.co.uk

W2

Abbey Court & Westpoint Hotel ♦♦♦
174 Sussex Gardens, London W2 1TP
T: (020) 7402 0281
F: (020) 7224 9114
E: info@abbeycourt.com
I: www.abbeycourthotel.com

Admiral Hotel ♦♦
143 Sussex Gardens, London W2 2RY
T: (020) 7723 7309
F: (020) 7723 8731
E: frank@admiral143.demon.co.uk
I: www.admiral-hotel.com

Albro House Hotel ♦♦
155 Sussex Gardens, Hyde Park, London W2 2RY
T: (020) 7724 2931
F: (020) 7262 2278
E: joe@albrohotel.freeserve.co.uk
I: www.albrohousehotel.co.uk

Alexandra Hotel ♦♦♦
159-161 Sussex Gardens, London W2 2RY
T: (020) 7402 6471
F: (020) 7724 1049
E: hotels.leventis-group@virgin.net
I: www.hotels-leventisgroup.co.uk

Allandale Hotel ♦♦
3 Devonshire Terrace, London W2 3DN
T: (020) 7723 8311
F: (020) 7723 8311
E: info@allandalehotel.co.uk
I: www.allandalehotel.co.uk

Apollo Hotel ♦♦♦
62 Queensborough Terrace, London W2 3SH
T: (020) 7727 3066
F: (020) 7727 2800
E: apollohotel@btinternet.com
I: www.hotelapollo.com

Ashley Hotel ♦♦♦
13-17 Norfolk Square, London W2 1RU
T: (020) 7723 3375
F: (020) 7723 0173
E: ashhot@btinternet.com
I: www.ashleyhotels.com

Athena Hotel ♦♦♦
110-114 Sussex Gardens, London W2 1UA
T: (020) 7706 3866
F: (020) 7262 6143
E: athena@stavrouhotels.co.uk
I: www.stavrouhotels.co.uk

Barry House Hotel ♦♦♦
12 Sussex Place, London W2 2TP
T: (020) 7723 7340
F: (020) 7723 9775
E: hotel@barryhouse.co.uk
I: www.barryhouse.co.uk

Caring Hotel ♦♦
24 Craven Hill Gardens, London W2 3EA
T: (020) 7262 8708
F: (020) 7262 8590
E: caring@tiscali.co.uk
I: www.caringhotel.co.uk

Crownwall Hotel ♦♦
10/11 Craven Terrace, Hyde Park, London W2 3QD
T: (020) 7262 9977
F: (020) 7262 5542
E: info@crownwallhotel.com

Dylan Hotel ♦♦
14 Devonshire Terrace, Lancaster Gate, London W2 3DW
T: (020) 7723 3280
F: (020) 7402 2443
E: booking@dylan-hotel.com
I: www.dylan-hotel.com

Euro-UK Investments Ltd T/As Tria ♦♦
35-37 St Stephens Gardens, London W2 5NA
T: (020) 7221 0450
F: (020) 7229 6717
E: triahotel@hotmail.com
I: www.triahotellondon.com

Europa House Hotel ♦♦
151 Sussex Gardens, London W2 2RY
T: (020) 7723 7343
F: (020) 7224 9331
E: europahouse@enterprise.net
I: www.europahousehotel.com

Gower Hotel ♦♦
129 Sussex Gardens, London W2 2RX
T: (020) 7262 2262
F: (020) 7262 2006
E: gower@stavrouhotels.co.uk
I: www.stavrouhotels.co.uk

Hyde Park House ♦
48 St Petersburgh Place, London W2 4LD
T: (020) 7229 9652

Hyde Park Radnor Hotel ♦♦♦♦
7-9 Sussex Place, Paddington, London W2 2SX
T: (020) 7723 5969
F: (020) 7262 8955

Hyde Park Rooms Hotel ♦♦
137 Sussex Gardens, Hyde Park, London W2 2RX
T: (020) 7723 0225
I: www.hydeparkroomshotel.com

Kensington Gardens Hotel ♦♦♦
9 Kensington Gardens Square, London W2 4BH
T: (020) 7221 7790
F: (020) 7792 8612
E: info@kensingtongardenshotel.co.uk
I: www.kensingtongardenshotel.co.uk

Kingsway Hotel ♦♦
27 Norfolk Square, London W2 1RX
T: (020) 7723 5569
F: (020) 7723 7317
E: kingswayhotel@hotmail.com
I: www.kingswayhotel.net

Kingsway Park Hotel Hyde Park ♦♦♦
139 Sussex Gardens, London W2 2RX
T: (020) 7724 9346
F: (020) 7402 4352
E: info@kingswaypark.hotel.com
I: www.kingswaypark-hotel.com

Kyriad Princes Square Hotel ♦♦♦♦
23-25 Princes Square, London W2 4NJ
T: (020) 7229 9876
F: (020) 7229 4664
E: info@princessquarehotel.co.uk
I: www.princessquarehotel.co.uk

London Guards Hotel ♦♦♦
36-37 Lancaster Gate, London W2 3NA
T: (020) 7402 1101
F: (020) 7262 2551
E: info@londonguardshotel.co.uk
I: www.londonguardshotel.co.uk

Manor Court Hotel ♦
7 Clanricarde Gardens, London W2 4JJ
T: (020) 7727 5407
F: (020) 7229 2875

Nayland Hotel ♦♦♦
132-134 Sussex Gardens, London W2 1UB
T: (020) 7723 4615
F: (020) 7402 3292
E: info@naylandhotel.com
I: www.naylandhotel.com

Oxford Hotel ♦♦♦
13-14 Craven Terrace, London W2 3QD
T: (020) 7402 6860
F: (020) 7262 7574
E: info@oxfordhotellondon.co.uk
I: www.oxfordhotellondon.co.uk

Park Lodge Hotel ♦♦♦
73 Queensborough Terrace, London W2 3SU
T: (020) 7229 6424
F: (020) 7221 4772
E: info@hotelparklodge.com
I: www.hotelparklodge.com

Parkwood Hotel ♦♦
4 Stanhope Place, London W2 2HB
T: (020) 7402 2241
F: (020) 7402 1574
E: prkwd@aol.com
I: www.parkwoodhotel.com

Pembridge Palace Hotel ♦♦♦
52-57 Prince's Square, London W2 4PX
T: (020) 7229 6262
F: (020) 7792 3868
E: london@pembridgehotel.co.uk

The Piccolino Hotel ♦♦♦
14 Sussex Place, London W2 2TP
T: (020) 7402 4439
F: (020) 7402 4439
E: nick@piccolino.fsnet.co.uk

Prince William Hotel ♦♦♦
42-44 Gloucester Terrace, London W2 3DA
T: (020) 7724 7414
F: (020) 7706 2411
E: info@princewilliamhotel.co.uk
I: www.princewilliamhotel.co.uk

Rhodes House Hotel ♦♦♦
195 Sussex Gardens, London W2 2RJ
T: (020) 7262 5617
F: (020) 7723 4054
E: chris@rhodeshotel.com
I: www.rhodeshotel.com

Rose Court Hotel ♦♦♦
1-3 Talbot Square, London W2 1TR
T: (020) 7723 5128
F: (020) 7723 1855
E: rosehotel@aol.com
I: www.rosecourthotel.com

St David's and Norfolk Court Hotel ♦♦
16 Norfolk Square, London W2 1RS
T: (020) 7723 3856
F: (020) 7402 9061
E: info@stdavidshotels.com
I: www.stdavidshotels.com

Springfield Hotel ♦♦♦
154 Sussex Gardens, London W2 1UD
T: (020) 7723 9898
F: (020) 7723 0874
E: info@springfieldhotellondon.co.uk
I: www.springfieldhotellondon.co.uk

Westland Hotel ♦♦♦♦
154 Bayswater Road, London W2 4HP
T: (020) 7229 9191
F: (020) 7727 1054
E: reservations@westlandhotel.co.uk
I: www.westlandhotel.co.uk
♿

W4

Chiswick Guest House ♦♦♦
40 Spencer Road, London W4 3SP
T: (020) 8994 0876
E: rooms@chiswickguesthouse.co.uk
I: www.chiswickguesthouse.com

Foubert's Hotel ♦♦
162-166 Chiswick High Road, London W4 1PR
T: (020) 8994 5202

Ivy Gate House ♦♦
6 Temple Road, London W4 5NW
T: (020) 8994 8618
E: thejones@ivygatehouse.co.uk
I: www.ivygatehouse.co.uk

W5

Abbey Lodge Hotel ♦♦
51 Grange Park, Ealing, London W5 3PR
T: (020) 8567 7914
F: (020) 8579 5350
E: enquiries@londonlodgehotels.com
I: www.londonlodgehotels.com

Grange Lodge Hotel ♦♦♦
48-50 Grange Road, Ealing, London W5 5BX
T: (020) 8567 1049
F: (020) 8579 5350
E: enquiries@londonlodgehotels.com
I: www.londonlodgehotels.com

W6

New Century Inn ♦♦♦
112 Shepherds Bush Road, London W6 7PD
T: 0870 780 4872
F: (020) 7751 1002
E: reservations@newcenturyinn.co.uk
I: www.newcenturyinn.co.uk

Hotel Orlando ♦♦
83 Shepherds Bush Road, Hammersmith, London W6 7LR
T: (020) 7603 4890
F: (020) 7603 4890
E: hotelorlando@btconnect.com
I: www.hotelorlando.co.uk

W7

Boston Manor Hotel ♦♦♦
146-152 Boston Road, Hanwell, London W7 2HJ
T: (020) 8566 1534
F: (020) 8567 9510
E: bmh@bostonmanor.com
I: www.bostonmanor.com

W8

Hotel Atlas-Apollo ♦♦♦
18-30 Lexham Gardens, London W8 5JE
T: (020) 7835 1155
F: (020) 7370 4853
E: reservations@atlas-apollo.com
I: www.atlas-apollo.com

Clearlake Hotel ♦♦
18-19 Prince of Wales Terrace, Kensington, London W8 5PQ
T: (020) 7937 3274
F: (020) 7376 0604
E: clearlake@talk21.com

W11

Kensington Guest House ♦♦
72 Holland Park Avenue, London W11 3QZ
T: (020) 7229 9233
F: (020) 7221 1077
E: HoteLondon@aol.com
I: www.hotelondon.co.uk

W14

Avonmore Hotel ♦♦♦♦
66 Avonmore Road, London W14 8RS
T: (020) 7603 3121
F: (020) 7603 4035
E: reservations@avonmorehotel.co.uk
I: www.avonmorehotel.co.uk

Holland Court Hotel ♦♦♦
31-33 Holland Road, London W14 8HJ
T: (020) 7371 1133
F: (020) 7602 9114
E: reservations@hollandcourthotel.com
I: www.hollandcourthotel.com

WC1

Arran House Hotel ♦♦
77-79 Gower Street, London WC1E 6HJ
T: (020) 7636 2186
F: (020) 7436 5328
E: arran@dircon.co.uk
I: www.london-hotel.co.uk

Comfort Inn Kings Cross ♦♦♦
2/5 St Chads Street, Kings Cross, London WC1H 8BD
T: (020) 7837 1940
F: (020) 7278 5033
E: info@comfortinnkingscross.co.uk
I. www.comfortinnkingscross.co.uk

Crescent Hotel ♦♦♦
49-50 Cartwright Gardens, Bloomsbury, London WC1H 9EL
T: (020) 7387 1515
F: (020) 7383 2054
E: General.Enquiries@CrescentHotelofLondon.com
I: www.CrescentHotelofLondon.com

Euro Hotel ♦♦♦
53 Cartwright Gardens, London WC1H 9EL
T: (020) 7387 4321
F: (020) 7383 5044
E: Reception@eurohotel.co.uk
I: www.eurohotel.co.uk

George Hotel ♦♦♦
58-60 Cartwright Gardens, London WC1H 9EL
T: (020) 7387 8777
F: (020) 7387 8666
E: ghotel@aol.com
I: www.georgehotel.com

Gower House Hotel ♦♦
57 Gower Street, London WC1E 6HJ
T: (020) 7636 4685
F: (020) 7636 4685
E: info@gowerhousehotel.co.uk
I: www.gowerhousehotel.co.uk

St Athans Hotel ♦
20 Tavistock Place, Russell Square, London WC1H 9RE
T: (020) 7837 9140
F: (020) 7833 8352
E: stathans@ukonline.co.uk
I: www.stathanshotel.com

Staunton Hotel ♦♦♦♦
13-15 Gower Street, London WC1E 6HE
T: (020) 7580 2740
F: (020) 7580 3554
E: enquiries@stauntonhotel.com
I: www.stauntonhotel.com

WC2

Royal Adelphi Hotel ♦♦
21 Villiers Street, London WC2N 6ND
T: (020) 7930 8764
F: (020) 7930 8735
E: info@royaladelphi.co.uk
I: www.royaladelphi.co.uk

BEXLEY

66 Arcadian Avenue ♦♦♦
Bexley DA5 1JW
T: (020) 8303 5732

Buxted Lodge Bed and Breakfast ♦♦♦
40 Parkhurst Road, Bexley DA5 1AS
T: (01322) 554010
F: (01322) 550870
E: buxted.lodge@cwcom.net

Dee + Dees ♦♦♦♦
30 Blendon Road, Bexley DA5 1BW
T: (020) 8303 2571
F: (020) 8303 2571

BEXLEYHEATH

Vivenda House ♦♦♦♦
1 Ferndale Close, Bexleyheath DA7 4ES
T: (020) 8304 5486
E: francisvivenda@aol.com

BRENTFORD

Kings Arms ♦♦♦
19 Boston Manor Road, Brentford TW8 8EA
T: (020) 8560 5860
F: (020) 8847 4416

BROMLEY

Avondale House ♦♦♦♦
56 Avondale Road, Bromley BR1 4EP
T: (020) 8402 0844
E: fortis@ukonline.co.uk
I: www.avondale-house.co.uk

Glendevon House Hotel ♦♦♦
80 Southborough Road, Bromley BR1 2EN
T: (020) 8467 2183
F: (020) 8295 0701

CHEAM

St Margarets Guest House ♦♦♦
31 Devon Road, Cheam, Sutton SM2 7PE
T: (020) 8643 0164
F: (020) 8643 0717
E: margarettrotman@hotmail.com

CROYDON

Alpha Guest House ♦♦
99 Brigstock Road, Thornton Heath CR7 7JL
T: (020) 8684 4811
F: (020) 8405 0302

Bramley ♦♦♦
7 Greencourt Avenue, Croydon CR0 7LD
T: (020) 8654 6776
F: (020) 8654 6776

70 Chelsham Road ♦♦♦♦
Croydon CR2 6HY
T: (020) 8649 9116
E: mikeaf@lineone.net

Croydon Court Hotel ♦♦
597-603 London Road, Croydon CR7 6AY
T: (020) 8684 3947
F: (020) 8664 9293
E: bookings@croydoncourthotel.co.uk

Croydon Friendly Guesthouse ♦♦♦
16 St Peter's Road, Croydon CR0 1HD
T: (020) 8680 4428
E: admin@croydonhotel.com
I: www.croydonhotel.com

Croydon Hotel ♦♦♦
112 Lower Addiscombe Road, Croydon CR0 6AD
T: (020) 8656 7233
F: (020) 8655 0211
I: www.croydonhotel.co.uk

Foxley Mount ♦♦♦
44 Foxley Lane, Purley CR8 3EE
T: (020) 8660 9751
F: (020) 8645 9368
E: enquiries@foxleymount.co.uk
I: www.foxleymount.co.uk

Ginetta Guest House ♦♦♦
32 Rylandes Road, Selsdon, South Croydon CR2 8EA
T: (020) 8657 3132

Owlets ♦♦♦
112 Arundel Avenue, South Croydon CR2 8BH
T: (020) 8657 5213
F: (020) 8657 5213

The Park ♦♦♦
63 Addington Road, South Croydon CR2 8RD
T: (020) 8657 8776
F: (020) 8657 8776

Waldenbury ♦♦♦
33 Crossways, South Croydon CR2 8JQ
T: (020) 8657 7791
F: (020) 8657 7791
E: waldenbury@tesco.net

Woodstock Hotel ♦♦♦
30 Woodstock Road, Croydon CR0 1JR
T: (020) 8680 1489
F: (020) 8667 1229
E: woodstockhotel@croydon-surrey.fsworld.co.uk
I: www.woodstockhotel.co.uk

ENFIELD

1 Chinnery Close ♦♦♦
Enfield EN1 4AX
T: (020) 8363 3887
F: (020) 8366 5496

HAMPTON

Friars Cottage ♦♦♦
2B Priory Road, Hampton TW12 2WR
T: (020) 8287 4699

14 Nightingale Road ♦♦♦♦
Hampton TW12 3HX
T: (020) 8979 8074

Riverine ♦♦♦
Taggs Island, Hampton Court Road, Hampton TW12 2HA
T: (020) 8979 2266
E: malcolm@feedtheducks.com
I: www.feedtheducks.com

HARROW

Crescent Hotel ♦♦♦
58-62 Welldon Crescent, Harrow HA1 1QR
T: (020) 8863 5491
F: (020) 8427 5965
E: jivraj@crsnthtl.demon.co.uk
I: www.crsnthtl.demon.co.uk

Hindes and Central Hotels ♦♦♦
6-8 Hindes Road, Harrow HA1 1SJ
T: (020) 8427 7468
F: (020) 8424 0673
E: central@hindeshotel.com

McKees Bed & Breakfast ♦♦♦
4 Shaftesbury Avenue, South Harrow, HA2 0PH
T: (020) 8357 2548
E: mckeefourguests@bushinternet.com

HAYES

Shepiston Lodge ♦♦♦
31 Shepiston Lane, Hayes UB3 1LJ
T: (020) 8573 0266
F: (020) 8569 2536
E: shepistonlodge@aol.com
I: www.shepistonlodge.co.uk

HOUNSLOW

Abbeyglade Villa ♦♦♦
51 Heath Road, Hounslow TW3 2NJ
T: (020) 8737 2717
F: (020) 8737 0228
E: nilruparelia@hotmail.com

Civic Guest House ♦♦
87-93 Lampton Road, Hounslow TW3 4DP
T: (020) 8572 5107
F: (020) 8814 0203
E: enquiries@civicguesthouse.freeserve.co.uk
I: www.civicguesthouse.freeserve.co.uk

Lampton Park Guesthouse ♦♦♦
4 Lampton Park Road, Hounslow TW3 4HS
T: (020) 8572 8622
F: (020) 8570 1220
E: michael.duff1@virgin.net

Shalimar Hotel ♦♦
215-221 Staines Road, Hounslow TW3 3JJ
T: (020) 8577 7070
F: (020) 8569 6789
E: shalimarhotel@aol.com
I: www.shalimarhotel.co.uk

Skylark Bed & Breakfast ♦♦
297 Bath Road, Hounslow TW3 3DB
T: (020) 8577 8455
F: (020) 8577 8741
E: info@skylark-bb.com
I: www.skylark-bb.com

ILFORD

Cranbrook Hotel ♦♦
22-24 Coventry Road, Ilford IG1 4QR
T: (020) 8554 6544
F: (020) 8518 1463

Park Hotel ♦♦♦
327 Cranbrook Road, Ilford IG1 4UE
T: (020) 8554 9616
F: (020) 8518 2700
E: parkhotelilford@netscapeonline.co.uk

ISLEWORTH

80 Bassett Gardens ♦♦♦
Isleworth TW7 4QY
T: (020) 8570 8362

Harewood Lodge ♦♦♦
43 Harewood Road, Isleworth TW7 5HN
T: (020) 8560 3627
F: (020) 8758 2105
E: harewoodlodge@hotmail.com

The Swans Nest ♦♦♦
The Swan Inn, 1 Swan Street, Isleworth TW7 6RJ
T: (020) 8560 5457
F: (020) 8560 4835

KENLEY

Appledore ♦♦♦
6 Betula Close, Kenley CR8 5ET
T: (020) 8668 4631
F: (020) 8668 4631

KEW

35 Beechwood Avenue ♦♦♦♦
Kew, Richmond TW9 4DD
T: (020) 8878 0049
F: (020) 8878 0049

1 Chelwood Gardens ♦♦♦
Kew, Richmond TW9 4JG
T: (020) 8876 8733
F: (020) 8255 0171
E: MrsLJGray@aol.com

11 Leyborne Park ♦♦♦♦
Kew, Richmond TW9 3HB
T: (020) 8948 1615
F: (020) 8255 1141
E: mary@stay-in-kew.com
I: www.stay-in-kew.com

40 Marksbury Avenue ♦♦♦
Kew, Richmond TW9 4JF
T: (020) 8878 9572

Melbury ♦♦♦
33 Marksbury Avenue, Kew, Richmond TW9 4JE
T: (020) 8876 3930
F: (020) 8876 3930

West Lodge ♦♦♦
179 Mortlake Road, Kew, Richmond TW9 4AW
T: (020) 8876 0584
F: (020) 8876 0584
E: westlodge@thakria.demon.co.uk

29 West Park Road ♦♦♦♦
Kew, Richmond TW9 4DA
T: (020) 8878 0505
E: alanbrooklands@aol.uk

KINGSTON UPON THAMES

40 The Bittoms ♦♦
Kingston upon Thames KT1 2AP
T: (020) 8541 3171

The Foresters ♦♦♦
45 High Street, Hampton Wick, Kingston upon Thames KT1 4DG
T: (020) 8943 5379
E: foresterspub@yahoo.com

8 St Albans Road ♦♦♦
Kingston upon Thames KT2 5HQ
T: (020) 8549 5910

MORDEN

28 Monkleigh Road ♦♦
Morden SM4 4EW
T: (020) 8542 5595

NORTHOLT

Brenda & Bertie Woosters Guesthouse ♦♦♦
5 Doncaster Drive, Northolt UB5 4AS
T: (020) 8423 5072

PINNER

Delcon ♦♦
468 Pinner Road, Pinner HA5 5RR
T: (020) 8863 1054
F: (020) 8863 1054

PURLEY

Arcadia ♦♦♦
212 Brighton Road, Purley CR8 4HB
T: (020) 8668 2486

Guest House ♦♦
12 Grasmere Road, Purley CR8 1DU
T: (020) 8660 1742
F: (020) 8660 1742
E: agmandrews@callnet.uk.com

The Maple House ♦♦♦
174 Foxley Lane, Purley CR8 3NF
T: (020) 8407 5123
F: (020) 8405 3918
E: tobrugger@aol.com

Purley Cross Guest House ♦♦♦
50 Brighton Road, Purley CR8 2LG
T: (020) 8668 4964
F: (020) 8407 2133
E: bookings@purleycross.com

Woodlands ♦♦♦
2 Green Lane, Purley CR8 3PG
T: (020) 8660 3103

RICHMOND

Chalon House ♦♦♦♦♦ GOLD AWARD
8 Spring Terrace, Richmond TW9 1LW
T: (020) 8332 1121
F: (020) 8332 1131
E: chalonhouse@hotmail.com

Doughty Cottage ♦♦♦♦♦ GOLD AWARD
142 Richmond Hill, Richmond TW10 6RN
T: (020) 8332 9434
F: (020) 8948 3716
E: deniseoneill425@aol.com
I: www.doughtycottage.com

Dukes Head Inn ♦♦♦
42 The Vineyard, Richmond TW10 6AZ
T: (020) 8948 4557
F: (020) 8948 4557
E: thedukeshead@yahoo.com
I: www.dukeshead.com

Hobart Hall Hotel ♦♦♦
43-47 Petersham Road, Richmond TW10 6UL
T: (020) 8940 0435
F: (020) 8332 2996
E: hobarthall@aol.com
I: www.smoothhound.co.uk/hotels/hobarthall.html

Ivy Cottage ♦♦♦
Upper Ham Road, Ham Common, Richmond TW10 5LA
T: (020) 8940 8601
F: (020) 8940 3865
E: taylor@dbta.freeserve.co.uk
I: www.dbta.freeserve.co.uk

Larkfield Apartments Rating Applied For
19 Larkfield Road, Richmond TW9 2PG
T: (020) 8948 6620
E: shipplets@ukgateway.net
I: www.shipplets.com

195 Mortlake Road ♦♦♦
Kew Gardens, Richmond TW9 4EW
T: (020) 8878 7018
F: (020) 8487 2748
E: alees.home@virgin.net

147 Petersham Road ♦♦♦♦
Petersham, Richmond TW10 7AH
T: (020) 8940 3424
E: sylviapeile@peile.force9.co.uk

Pro Kew Gardens B & B ♦♦♦
15 Pensford Avenue, Richmond TW9 4HR
T: (020) 8876 3354
E: info@prokewbandb.demon.co.uk
I: www.prokewbandb.demon.co.uk

Quinns Hotel ♦♦♦
48 Sheen Road, Richmond TW9 1AW
T: (020) 8940 5444
F: (020) 8940 1828
E: quinnshotel@hotmail.com
I: www.quinnshotel.com

The Red Cow ♦♦♦
59 Sheen Road, Richmond TW9 1YJ
T: (020) 8940 2511
F: (020) 8940 2581
E: tom@redcowpub.com
I: www.redcowpub.com

Richmond Inn Hotel ♦♦♦♦
50-56 Sheen Road, Richmond TW9 1UG
T: (020) 8940 0171
F: (020) 8332 2596
I: www.richmondinnhotel.com

Riverside Hotel ♦♦♦
23 Petersham Road, Richmond TW10 6UH
T: (020) 8940 1339
F: (020) 8948 0967
E: riversidehotel@yahoo.com
I: www.riversiderichmond.co.uk

The Rose of York ♦♦♦
Petersham Road, Richmond TW10 6UY
T: (020) 8948 5867
F: (020) 8332 6986
E: roseofyork@compuserve.com

248 Sandycombe Road ♦♦♦
Kew, Richmond TW9 3NP
T: (020) 8940 5970

9 Selwyn Court ♦♦
Richmond TW10 6LR
T: (020) 8940 3309

454 Upper Richmond Road West ♦♦♦
Richmond TW10 5DY
T: (020) 8876 0327

West Park Gardens ♦♦♦
105 Mortlake Road, Kew, Richmond TW9 4AA
T: (020) 8876 6842
F: (020) 8876 6842
E: edwardsnjdr@aol.com

ROMFORD

The Orchard Guest House ♦♦♦
81 Eastern Road, Romford RM1 3PB
T: (01708) 744099
F: (01708) 768881
E: johnrt@gxn.co.uk

SIDCUP

Hilbert House ♦♦♦
Halfway Street, Sidcup DA15 8DE
T: (020) 8300 0549

SURBITON

6 Beechwood Close ♦♦♦
Surbiton KT6 6PF
T: (020) 8390 3597
E: maryshaw@fsmail.com

26 St Matthews Avenue ♦♦♦
Surbiton KT6 6JQ
T: (020) 8399 6603
E: jane-wood@blueyonder.co.uk

Villiers Lodge Bed and Breakfast ♦♦
1 Cranes Park, Surbiton KT5 8AB
T: (020) 8399 6000

TEDDINGTON

93 Clarence Road ♦♦♦♦
Teddington TW11 0BN
T: (020) 8977 3459
F: (020) 8943 1560
E: suto.noble@virgin.net

Glenhurst ♦♦♦
93 Langham Road, Teddington TW11 9HG
T: (020) 8977 6962
F: (020) 8977 6962
E: lesley@stayinteddington.com
I: www.stayinteddington.com

6 Grove Gardens ♦♦♦
Teddington TW11 8AP
T: (020) 8977 6066

Hazeldene ♦♦♦♦
58 Hampton Road, Teddington TW11 0JX
T: (020) 8286 8500
E: glasslisa58@hotmail.com

King Edwards Grove ♦♦♦
Teddington TW11 9LY
T: (020) 8977 7251

126 Kingston Road ♦♦♦
Teddington TW11 9JA
T: (020) 8943 9302

Polly's Bed and Breakfast ♦♦♦
166 High Street, Teddington TW11 8HU
T: (020) 8287 1188

THORNTON HEATH

The Lloyd's House ♦♦
41 Moffat Road, Thornton Heath CR7 8PY
T: (020) 8768 1827

TWICKENHAM

33 Arlington Road ♦♦♦♦
St Margarets, Twickenham TW1 2AZ
T: (020) 8287 7492
F: (020) 8287 7492
E: info@33arlingtonroad.co.uk
I: www.33arlingtonroad.co.uk

Avalon Cottage ♦♦♦
50 Moor Mead Road, Twickenham TW1 1JS
T: (020) 8744 2178
F: (020) 8891 2444
E: avalon@mead99.freeserve.co.uk
I: www.avalon-cottage.com

39 Grange Avenue ♦♦♦
Twickenham TW2 5TW
T: (020) 8894 1055
F: (020) 8893 3346
E: carole@fanfoliage.fsbusiness.co.uk

136 London Road ♦♦♦
Twickenham TW1 1HD
T: (020) 8892 3158
E: jenniferjfinnerty@hotmail.com

The Old Stables ♦♦♦♦
1 Bridle Lane, St Margarets, Twickenham TW1 3EG
T: (020) 8892 4507
F: (020) 8892 4503
E: nuttmail@btinternet.com
I: www.smoothhound.co.uk

11 Spencer Road ♦♦♦
Twickenham TW2 5TH
T: (020) 8894 5271
F: (020) 8994 4751
E: bruceduff@hotmail.com

3 Waldegrave Gardens ♦♦♦
Twickenham TW1 4PQ
T: (020) 8892 3523

UPMINSTER

Corner Farm ♦♦♦
Fen Lane, North Ockendon, Upminster RM14 3RB
T: (01708) 851310
F: (01708) 852025
E: info@corner-farm.co.uk
I: www.corner-farm.co.uk

WEMBLEY

Adelphi Hotel ♦♦
Flat 4, Wembley HA9 9EB
T: (020) 8904 5629
F: (020) 8908 5314
E: adel@dial.pipex.com
I: www.hoteladelphi.co.uk

Arena Hotel ♦♦♦
6 Forty Lane, Wembley HA9 9EB
T: (020) 8908 0670
F: (020) 8908 2007
E: enquiry@arenahotel.fsnet.co.uk
I: www.arena-hotel.co.uk

Elm Hotel ♦♦♦
1-7 Elm Road, Wembley HA9 7JA
T: (020) 8902 1764
F: (020) 8903 8365
E: elm.hotel@virgin.net
I: www.elmhotel.co.uk

WHITTON

113 Staines Road Rating Applied For
Twickenham TW2 5BD
T: (020) 8898 3514

WORCESTER PARK

The Graye House ♦♦♦
24 The Glebe, Worcester Park KT4 7PF
T: (020) 8330 1277
F: (020) 8255 7850
E: graye.house@virgin.net
I: www.s-h-systems.co.uk

CUMBRIA

AINSTABLE Cumbria

Bell House ♦♦♦♦
Ainstable, Carlisle CA4 9RE
T: (01768) 896255
F: (01768) 896255
E: mrobinson@bellhouse.fsbusiness.co.uk

ALLONBY Cumbria

Ship Hotel ♦♦♦
Main Street, Allonby, Maryport CA15 6QF
T: (01900) 881017
F: (01900) 881017
E: theshipallonby@aol.com

ALSTON Cumbria

Brownside House ♦♦♦
Leadgate, Alston CA9 3EL
T: (01434) 382169
F: (01434) 382100
E: brownside_hse@hotmail.com
I: www.cumbria1st.com/brown_side/index.htm

Greycroft ♦♦♦♦ SILVER AWARD
Middle Park, The Raise, Alston CA9 3AR
T: (01434) 381383
E: enquiry@greycroft.co.uk
I: www.greycroft.co.uk

AMBLESIDE
Cumbria

Ambleside Country Hotel – Grey Friar Lodge
◆◆◆◆◆ SILVER AWARD
Clappersgate, Ambleside
LA22 9NE
T: (015394) 33158
F: (015394) 33158
E: greyfriar@veen.freeserve.co.uk
I: www.cumbria-hotels.co.uk

Amboseli Lodge ◆◆◆◆
Rothay Road, Ambleside
LA22 0EE
T: (015394) 31110
F: (015394) 31110
E: enquiries@amboselilodge.co.uk
I: www.amboselilodge.co.uk

Barnes Fell Guest House
◆◆◆◆ SILVER AWARD
Low Gale, Ambleside LA22 0BB
T: (015394) 33311
F: (015394) 34693

Brantfell House ◆◆◆◆
Rothay Road, Ambleside
LA22 0EE
T: (015394) 32239
F: (015394) 32239
E: brantfell@kencomp.net
I: www.brantfell.co.uk

Broadview ◆◆◆
Low Fold, Lake Road, Ambleside
LA22 0DN
T: (015394) 32431
E: enquiries@broadviewguesthouse.co.uk
I: www.broadviewguesthouse.co.uk

3 Cambridge Villas ◆◆◆
Church Street, Ambleside
LA22 9DL
T: (015394) 32307
E: cambridgevillas3@aol.com

Claremont House ◆◆◆
Compston Road, Ambleside
LA22 9DJ
T: (015394) 33448
E: enquiries@claremontambleside.co.uk
I: www.claremontambleside.co.uk

Compston House American-Style B&B ◆◆◆◆
Compston Road, Ambleside
LA22 9DJ
T: (015394) 32305
E: compston@globalnet.co.uk
I: www.compstonhouse.co.uk

The Dower House ◆◆◆◆
Wray Castle, Ambleside
LA22 0JA
T: (015394) 33211
F: (015394) 33211

Easedale Lodge Guest House Rating Applied For
Compston Road, Ambleside
LA22 9DJ
T: (015394) 32112
F: (015394) 32112
E: enquiries@easedaleambleside.co.uk
I: www.easedaleambleside.co.uk

Elder Grove ◆◆◆◆
Lake Road, Ambleside LA22 0DB
T: (015394) 32504
F: (015394) 32251
E: info@eldergrove.co.uk
I: www.eldergrove.co.uk

Far Nook
◆◆◆◆◆ SILVER AWARD
Rydal Road, Ambleside
LA22 9BA
T: (015394) 31605
F: (015394) 31605
E: farnook@tiscali.co.uk
I: www.farnook.co.uk

Fern Cottage ◆◆◆
6 Waterhead Terrace, Ambleside
LA22 0HA
T: (015394) 33007

Ferndale Lodge ◆◆◆
Lake Road, Ambleside LA22 0DB
T: (015394) 32207
E: info@ferndalehotel.com
I: www.ferndalehotel.com

Fisherbeck Garden ◆◆◆
Old Lake Road, Ambleside
LA22 0DH
T: (015394) 33088
E: janice@fisherbeck.net1.co.uk

Foxghyll ◆◆◆◆
Under Loughrigg, Ambleside
LA22 9LL
T: (015394) 33292
E: foxghyll@hotmail.com
I: www.foxghyll.co.uk

Freshfields
◆◆◆◆ SILVER AWARD
Wansfell Road, Ambleside
LA22 0EG
T: (015394) 34469
F: (015394) 34469
E: info@freshfieldsguesthouse.co.uk
I: www.freshfieldsguesthouse.co.uk

Ghyll Head Hotel ◆◆◆◆
Waterhead, Ambleside
LA22 0HD
T: (015394) 32360
F: (015394) 34062
E: ghyllhead@btopenworld.com
I: www.hotelscumbria.com

Glenside ◆◆◆◆
Old Lake Road, Ambleside
LA22 0DP
T: (015394) 32635

High Wray Farm ◆◆◆◆
High Wray, Ambleside LA22 0JE
T: (015394) 32280
F: (015394) 32280
E: sheila@highwrayfarm.co.uk
I: www.highwrayfarm.co.uk

Highfield ◆◆◆
Lake Road, Ambleside LA22 0DB
T: (015394) 32671
E: norman.henderson1@btopenworld.com

Hillsdale ◆◆◆◆
Church Street, Ambleside
LA22 0BT
T: (015394) 33174
F: (015394) 31226
E: stay@hillsdaleguesthouse.co.uk
I: www.hillsdaleguesthouse.co.uk

Holmeshead Farm ◆◆◆◆
Skelwith Fold, Ambleside
LA22 0HU
T: (015394) 33048
E: info@holmesheadfarm.co.uk
I: www.amblesideonline.co.uk/adverts/holmeshead/main.html

Kent House
◆◆◆◆ SILVER AWARD
Lake Road, Ambleside LA22 0AD
T: (015394) 33279
F: (015394) 33279
E: mail@kent-house.com
I: www.kent-house.com

Lakes Lodge ◆◆◆
Lake Road, Ambleside LA22 0DB
T: (015394) 33240
F: (015394) 33240
E: u@lakeslodge.co.uk
I: www.lakeslodge.co.uk

Lattendales Guest House ◆◆◆
Compston Road, Ambleside
LA22 9DJ
T: (015394) 32368
E: info@lattendales.co.uk
I: www.lattendales.co.uk

Lyndale Guesthouse ◆◆◆
Low Fold, Lake Road, Ambleside
LA22 0DN
T: (015394) 34244
E: alison@lyndale-guesthouse.co.uk
I: www.lyndale-guesthouse.co.uk

Lyndhurst Hotel ◆◆◆
Wansfell Road, Ambleside
LA22 0EG
T: (015394) 32421
F: (015394) 32421
E: lyndhurst@amblesidehotels.co.uk
I: www.amblesidehotels.co.uk

Meadowbank ◆◆◆
Rydal Road, Ambleside
LA22 9BA
T: (015394) 32710
F: (015394) 32710
E: enquiries@meadowbank.org.uk
I: www.meadowbank.org.uk

Melrose ◆◆◆◆
Church Street, Ambleside
LA22 0BT
T: (015394) 32500
F: (015394) 31495
E: info@melrose-guesthouse.co.uk
I: www.melrose-guesthouse.co.uk

Norwood House ◆◆◆◆
Church Street, Ambleside
LA22 0BT
T: (015394) 33349
F: (015394) 34938
E: mail@norwoodhouse.net
I: www.norwoodhouse.net

The Old Vicarage ◆◆◆◆
Vicarage Road, Ambleside
LA22 9DH
T: (015394) 33364
F: (015394) 34734
E: the.old.vicarage@kencomp.net
I: www.oldvicarageambleside.co.uk

Red Bank
◆◆◆◆ SILVER AWARD
Wansfell Road, Ambleside
LA22 0EG
T: (015394) 34637
F: (015394) 34637
E: info@red-bank.co.uk
I: www.red-bank.co.uk

Riverside Hotel ◆◆◆◆
Under Loughrigg, Rothay Bridge, Ambleside LA22 9LJ
T: (015394) 32395
F: (015394) 32440
E: info@riverside-at-ambleside.co.uk
I: www.riverside-at-ambleside.co.uk

Rothay Garth Hotel ◆◆◆◆
Rothay Road, Ambleside
LA22 0EE
T: (015394) 32217
F: (015394) 34400
E: enquiries@rothay-garth.co.uk
I: www.rothay-garth.co.uk

The Rysdale Hotel ◆◆◆◆
Rothay Road, Ambleside
LA22 0EE
T: (015394) 32140
F: (015394) 33999
E: info@rysdalehotel.co.uk
I: www.rysdalehotel.co.uk

Stepping Stones Country House ◆◆◆◆
Under Loughrigg, Ambleside
LA22 9LN
T: (015394) 33552
F: (015394) 33552
E: info@steppingstonesambleside.com
I: www.steppingstonesambleside.com

Thorneyfield Guest House
◆◆◆◆
Compston Road, Ambleside
LA22 9DJ
T: (015394) 32464
F: (0870) 167 1968
E: info@thorneyfield.co.uk
I: www.thorneyfield.co.uk

Tock How Farm ◆◆◆◆
High Wray, Ambleside LA22 0JF
T: (015394) 36106
F: (015394) 36294
E: info@tock-how-farm.com
I: www.tock-how-farm.com

Walmar Hotel ◆◆◆
Lake Road, Ambleside LA22 0DB
T: (015394) 32454

Wanslea Guest House ◆◆◆◆
Low Fold, Lake Road, Ambleside
LA22 0DN
T: (015394) 33884
E: wanslea.guesthouse@virgin.net
I: www.wansleaguesthouse.co.uk

Wateredge Inn ◆◆◆◆
Waterhead, Ambleside LA22 0EP
T: (015394) 32332
F: (015394) 31878
E: contactus@wateredgeinn.co.uk
I: www.wateredgeinn.co.uk

APPLEBY-IN-WESTMORLAND
Cumbria

Broom House ♦♦♦
Long Marton, Appleby-in-Westmorland CA16 6JP
T: (017683) 61318
F: (017683) 61318
E: sandra@bland01.freeserve.co.uk
I: www.broomhouseappleby.co.uk

ARNSIDE
Cumbria

Willowfield Hotel ♦♦♦♦
Promenade, Arnside, Carnforth LA5 0AD
T: (01524) 761354
E: janet@willowfield.net1.co.uk
I: www.willowfield.uk.com

BAILEY
Cumbria

Cleughside Farm ♦♦♦
Bailey, Newcastleton TD9 0TR
T: (01697) 748634
F: (01697) 748634
E: alicewhy@aol.com
I: www.cleughside.freeserve.co.uk

BARROW-IN-FURNESS
Cumbria

King Alfred Hotel ♦♦♦♦
Ocean Road, Walney Island, Barrow-in-Furness LA14 3DU
T: (01229) 474717
F: (01229) 476181
E: kingalfred@walney4.fsnet.co.uk
I: www.thekingalfred.co.uk

BASSENTHWAITE
Cumbria

Dalton Cottage ♦♦♦♦
Bassenthwaite, Keswick CA12 4QG
T: (01768) 776952
F: (01768) 776952
E: deborah@daltoncottage.co.uk
I: www.daltoncottage.co.uk

Herdwick Croft Guest House ♦♦♦♦
Bassenthwaite, Keswick CA12 4RD
T: (01768) 776241
E: info@herdwick-croft.co.uk
I: www.herdwick-croft.co.uk

High Side Farmhouse ♦♦♦♦ SILVER AWARD
Embleton, Cockermouth CA13 9TN
T: (017687) 76893
F: (017687) 76893
E: enquiries@highsidefarmhouse.co.uk
I: www.highsidefarmhouse.co.uk

Link House ♦♦♦♦
Bassenthwaite Lake, Cockermouth CA13 9YD
T: (017687) 76291
F: (017687) 76670
E: info@link-house.co.uk
I: www.link-house.co.uk

Ravenstone Lodge ♦♦♦♦
Bassenthwaite, Keswick CA12 4QG
T: (01768) 776629
F: (01768) 776629
E: ravenstone.lodge@talk21.com
I: www.ravenstonelodge.co.uk

Robin Hood House ♦♦♦♦
Bassenthwaite, Keswick CA12 4RJ
T: (017687) 76296

BASSENTHWAITE LAKE
Cumbria

Lakeside Guesthouse ♦♦♦♦ SILVER AWARD
Dubwath, Bassenthwaite Lake, CA13 9YD
T: (017687) 76358
E: info@lakesidebassenthwaite.co.uk
I: www.lakesidebassenthwaite.co.uk

BEETHAM
Cumbria

Barn Close/North West Birds ♦♦♦
Barn Close, Beetham, Milnthorpe LA7 7AL
T: (015395) 63191
F: (015395) 63191
E: anne@nwbirds.co.uk
I: www.nwbirds.co.uk

BIRKBY
Cumbria

The Retreat Hotel and Restaurant ♦♦♦♦
Birkby, Maryport CA15 6RG
T: (01900) 814056
E: enquiries@retreathotel.co.uk
I: www.retreathotel.co.uk

BOLTON
Cumbria

Eden Grove Farm House ♦♦♦♦ SILVER AWARD
Bolton, Appleby-in-Westmorland CA16 6AX
T: (017683) 362321
E: edengrovecumbria@aol.com
I: www.ukworld.net/edengrove

Glebe House ♦♦♦♦
Bolton, Appleby-in-Westmorland CA16 6AW
T: (017683) 61125
E: derick.cotton@btinternet.com
I: www.glebeholidays.co.uk

Tarka House ♦♦♦
Bolton, Appleby-in-Westmorland CA16 6AW
T: (017683) 61422
F: (017683) 61422
E: neilson@tarka-house.fsnet.co.uk

BOOT
Cumbria

The Burnmoor Inn ♦♦♦
Boot, Holmrook CA19 1TG
T: 0845 130 6224
F: (019467) 23337
E: stay@burnmoor.co.uk
I: www.burnmoor.co.uk

BORROWDALE
Cumbria

Greenbank Country House Hotel ♦♦♦♦ SILVER AWARD
Borrowdale, Keswick CA12 5UY
T: (017687) 77215
E: jeanwwood@lineone.net
I: www.greenbankcountryhousehotel.co.uk

Hazel Bank Country House ♦♦♦♦♦ GOLD AWARD
Rosthwaite, Borrowdale, Keswick CA12 5XB
T: (017687) 77248
F: (017687) 77373
E: enquiries@hazelbankhotel.co.uk
I: www.hazelbankhotel.co.uk

Seatoller House ♦♦♦
Seatoller, Borrowdale, Keswick CA12 5XN
T: (017687) 77218
F: (017687) 77189
E: seatollerhouse@btconnect.com
I: www.seatollerhouse.co.uk

BOWNESS-ON-SOLWAY
Cumbria

Maia Lodge ♦♦♦
Bowness-on-Solway, Carlisle CA7 5BH
T: (016973) 51955
E: d.chettle@virgin.net

Wallsend House ♦♦♦♦
The Old Rectory, Church Lane, Bowness-on-Solway, Carlisle CA7 5AF
T: (016973) 51055
E: wallsend@btinternet.com
I: www.wallsend.net

BRAITHWAITE
Cumbria

Coledale Inn ♦♦♦
Braithwaite, Keswick CA12 5TN
T: (017687) 78272
F: (017687) 78416
E: info@coledale-inn.com
I: www.coledale-inn.co.uk

Maple Bank ♦♦♦♦
Braithwaite, Keswick CA12 5RY
T: (017687) 78229
F: (017687) 78000
E: maplebank@aol.com
I: www.maplebank.co.uk

Middle Ruddings Hotel ♦♦♦
Braithwaite, Keswick CA12 5RY
T: (017687) 78436
F: (017687) 78438
E: info@middle-ruddings.com
I: www.middle-ruddings.co.uk

BRAMPTON
Cumbria

Blacksmiths Arms Hotel ♦♦♦
Talkin, Brampton CA8 1LE
T: (01697) 73452
F: (01697) 73396
E: blacksmithsarmstalkin@yahoo.co.uk
I: www.blacksmithsarmstalkin.co.uk

Howard House Farm ♦♦♦♦ SILVER AWARD
Gilsland, Brampton CA8 7AJ
T: (01697) 747285
F: (01697) 747996
E: elizabeth@howardhousefarmfsnet.co.uk

Langthwaite ♦♦♦
Lanercost Road, Brampton CA8 1EN
T: (01697) 72883
E: anneharding@nicetoseeyou.co.uk

Low Rigg Farm ♦♦♦
Walton, Brampton CA8 2DX
T: (01697) 73233
E: lowrigg@tiscali.co.uk
I: www.smoothhound.co.uk/hotels/lowrigg.html

Nags Head ♦♦♦
Market Place, Brampton CA8 1RW
T: (01697) 72284

New Mills House ♦♦♦
Brampton CA8 2QS
T: (01697) 73376
F: (01697) 73457
E: newmills@btinternet.com
I: www.info@newmillshouse.co.uk

Oakwood Park Hotel ♦♦♦
Longtown Road, Brampton CA8 2AP
T: (01697) 72436
F: (01697) 72436
E: donald.collier@amserve.net

South View ♦♦♦♦
Banks, Brampton CA8 2JH
T: (01697) 72309
E: sandrahodgson@southviewbanks.f9.co.uk
I: www.southviewbanks.f9.co.uk

Vallum Barn ♦♦♦♦
Irthington, Carlisle CA6 4NN
T: (01697) 742478
E: vallumbarn@tinyworld.co.uk
I: www.vallumbarn.co.uk

Walton High Rigg ♦♦♦
Walton, Brampton CA8 2AZ
T: (01697) 72117
F: (01697) 741697
E: mounsey.highrigg@hotmail.com
I: www.waltonhighrigg.co.uk

BRISCO
Cumbria

Crossroads House ♦♦♦♦
Brisco, Carlisle CA4 0QZ
T: (01228) 528994
F: (01228) 528994
E: viv@crossroadshouse.co.uk
I: www.crossroadshouse.co.uk

BROUGH
Cumbria

River View ♦♦♦♦
Brough, Kirkby Stephen CA17 4BZ
T: (017683) 41894
F: (017683) 41894
E: riverviewbb@btinternet.com
I: riverviewbb.co.uk

BROUGHTON-IN-FURNESS
Cumbria

Broom Hill ♦♦♦♦
New Street, Broughton-in-Furness LA20 6JD
T: (01229) 716358
F: (01229) 716358

The Dower House ♦♦♦
High Duddon, Duddon Bridge, Broughton-in-Furness LA20 6ET
T: (01229) 716279
F: (01229) 716279
E: rozanne.nichols@ukgateway.net

Middlesyke
♦♦♦♦ SILVER AWARD
Church Street, Broughton-in-Furness LA20 6ER
T: (01229) 716549

Oak Bank ♦♦♦
Ulpha, Duddon Valley, Broughton-in-Furness LA20 6DZ
T: (01229) 716393
E: susan@soakbank.freeserve.co.uk
I: www.duddonvalley.co.uk

The Workshop Studios ♦♦♦♦
Church Street, Broughton-in-Furness LA20 6HJ
T: (01229) 716159
F: (01229) 716159
E: workshop.accom@virgin.net
I: www.theworkshopstudios.com

BURTON-IN-KENDAL
Cumbria

Kings Arms Hotel ♦♦♦♦
Main Street, Burton-in-Kendal, Kendal LA6 1LR
T: (01524) 781409
F: (01524) 782924
E: roger@kingsarmshotel.net
I: www.kingsarmshotel.net

Royal Hotel ♦♦♦
Main Street, Burton-in-Kendal, Kendal LA6 1LY
T: (01524) 781261
F: (01524) 781261

CALDBECK
Cumbria

The Briars ♦♦♦
Friar Row, Caldbeck, Wigton CA7 8DS
T: (01697) 478633

Gate House ♦♦♦
Caldbeck, Wigton CA7 8EL
T: (01697) 478092
E: ray@caldbeckgatehouse.co.uk
I: www.caldbeckgatehouse.co.uk

Swaledale Watch
♦♦♦♦ SILVER AWARD
Whelpo, Caldbeck, Wigton CA7 8HQ
T: (01697) 478409
F: (01697) 478409
E: nan.savage@talk21.com
I: www.swaledale-watch.co.uk

CARLETON
Cumbria

River Forge Bed and Breakfast ♦♦♦♦
Carleton, Carlisle CA4 0AA
T: (01228) 523569

CARLISLE
Cumbria

Abberley House ♦♦♦♦
33 Victoria Place, Carlisle CA1 1HP
T: (01228) 521645
E: stay@abberleyhouse.co.uk
I: www.abberleyhouse.co.uk

Abbey Court ♦♦♦♦
24 London Road, Carlisle CA1 2EL
T: (01228) 528696
F: (01228) 528696

Arkale Lodge Ltd ♦♦
59 London Road, Carlisle CA1 2LE
T: (01228) 532927
F: (01228) 532927

Ashleigh House ♦♦♦♦
46 Victoria Place, Carlisle CA1 1EX
T: (01228) 521631

Avar House
Rating Applied For
12 Scotland Road, Carlisle CA3 9DG
T: (01228) 540636
E: guesthouse@avarhouse.fslife.co.uk

Avondale ♦♦♦♦
3 St Aidans Road, Carlisle CA1 1LT
T: (01228) 523012
F: (01228) 523012
E: info@bed-breakfast-carlisle.co.uk
I: www.beeanbee.co.uk

Bessiestown Farm Country Guesthouse
♦♦♦♦♦ SILVER AWARD
Penton, Catlowdy, Longtown, Carlisle CA6 5QP
T: (01228) 577219
F: (01228) 577019
E: info@bessiestown.co.uk
I: bessiestown.co.uk

Brooklyn House ♦♦♦
42 Victoria Place, Carlisle CA1 1EX
T: (01228) 590002

Caldew View ♦♦♦
Metcalfe Street, Denton Holme, Carlisle CA2 5EU
T: (01228) 595837

Cartref Guest House ♦♦♦
44 Victoria Place, Carlisle CA1 1EX
T: (01228) 522077

Claremont Guest House ♦♦♦
30 London Road, Carlisle CA1 2EL
T: (01228) 524691
F: (01228) 524691
E: enquiries@claremontguesthouse.com
I: www.claremontguesthouse.com

Corner House ♦♦♦
4 Grey Street, Off London Road, Carlisle CA1 2JP
T: (01228) 533239
F: (01228) 546628
E: bcartner@aol.com

Cornerways Guest House ♦♦♦♦
107 Warwick Road, Carlisle CA1 1EA
T: (01228) 521733

Courtfield House
♦♦♦♦ SILVER AWARD
169 Warwick Road, Carlisle CA1 1LP
T: (01228) 522767
F: (01228) 522767
E: mdawes@courtfieldhouse.fsnet.co.uk

Croft End ♦♦♦
Hurst, Ivegill, Carlisle CA4 0NL
T: (017684) 84362

Dalroc ♦♦♦
411 Warwick Road, Carlisle CA1 2RZ
T: (01228) 542805
E: margaret@dalroc.fsnet.co.uk
I: www.dalroc.co.uk

East View Guest House ♦♦♦
110 Warwick Road, Carlisle CA1 1JU
T: (01228) 522112
F: (01228) 522112
I: www.guesthousecarlisle.co.uk

Fern Lee Guest House ♦♦♦♦
9 St Aidans Road, Carlisle CA1 1LT
T: (01228) 511930
F: (01228) 511930

Hazeldean Guest House ♦♦♦
Orton Grange, Wigton Road, Carlisle CA5 6LA
T: (01228) 711953

Howard Lodge Guesthouse ♦♦♦
90 Warwick Road, Carlisle CA1 1JU
T: (01228) 529842
E: pat90howardlodge@aol.com

Ivy House ♦♦♦♦
101 Warwick Road, Carlisle CA1 1EA
T: (01228) 530432
F: (01228) 530432

Kates Guest House ♦♦♦
6 Lazonby Terrace, London Road, Carlisle CA1 2PZ
T: (01228) 539577
E: katesguesthouse@hotmail.com

Langleigh Guest House ♦♦♦♦
6 Howard Place, Carlisle CA1 1HR
T: (01228) 530440
F: (01228) 530440
E: langleighouse@aol.com
I: www.langleighhouse.co.uk

Lynebank House ♦♦♦♦
Westlinton, Carlisle CA6 6AA
T: (01228) 792820
F: (01228) 792693
E: info@lynebank.co.uk
I: www.lynebank.co.uk

Marchmain House
♦♦♦♦ SILVER AWARD
151 Warwick Road, Carlisle CA1 1LU
T: (01228) 529551
F: (01228) 529551

New Pallyards ♦♦♦♦
Hethersgill, Carlisle CA6 6HZ
T: (01228) 577308
F: (01228) 577308
E: info@newpallyards.freeserve.co.uk
I: www.newpallyards.freeserve.co.uk

Newfield Grange Hotel ♦♦♦♦
Newfield Drive, Kingstown, Carlisle CA3 0AF
T: (01228) 819926
F: (01228) 546323
E: bb@newfield53.freeserve.co.uk
I: www.newfield53.freeserve.co.uk

Number Thirty One
♦♦♦♦♦ GOLD AWARD
Howard Place, Carlisle CA1 1HR
T: (01228) 597080
F: (01228) 597080
E: bestpep@aol.com
I: number31.freeservers.com

Townhouse Bed & Breakfast ♦♦♦
153 Warwick Road, Carlisle CA1 1LU
T: (01228) 598782
E: townhouse@christine60.freeserve.co.uk
I: www.townhouse-bandb.com

Vallum House Garden Hotel ♦♦♦
Burgh Road, Carlisle CA2 7NB
T: (01228) 521860

Warren Guesthouse ♦♦♦
368 Warwick Road, Carlisle CA1 2RU
T: (01228) 533663
F: (01228) 533663

White Lea Guest House ♦♦♦
191 Warwick Road, Carlisle CA1 1LP
T: (01228) 533139
F: (01228) 533139

CARTMEL
Cumbria

Bank Court Cottage ♦♦♦
The Square, Cartmel, Grange-over-Sands LA11 6QB
T: (015395) 36593
F: (015395) 36593

Hill Farm
♦♦♦♦♦ SILVER AWARD
Cartmel, Grange-over-Sands LA11 7SS
T: (015395) 36477
F: (015395) 36636
E: pafoulerton@talk21.com
I: www.hillfarmcartmel.co.uk

Newlands ♦♦♦♦
Aynsome Road, Cartmel, Grange-over-Sands LA11 6PR
T: (015395) 36562
E: info@newlandscartmel.co.uk
I: www.newlandscartmel.co.uk

Prior's Yeat ♦♦♦♦
Aynsome Road, Cartmel, Grange-over-Sands LA11 6PR
T: (015395) 35178
E: priorsyeat@hotmail.com

CARTMEL FELL
Cumbria

Lightwood Country Guesthouse ♦♦♦♦
Cartmel Fell, Grange-over-Sands LA11 6NP
T: (015395) 31454
F: (015395) 31454
E: enquiries@lightwoodguesthouse.com
I: www.lightwoodguesthouse.com

COCKERMOUTH
Cumbria

The Melbreak Hotel ♦♦♦♦
Winscales Road, Little Clifton, Workington CA14 1XS
T: (01900) 61443
F: (01900) 606589

Rose Cottage ♦♦♦♦
Lorton Road, Cockermouth CA13 9DX
T: (01900) 822189
F: (01900) 822189
E: bookings@rosecottageguest.co.uk
I: www.rosecottageguest.co.uk

° Establishments printed in blue have a detailed entry in this guide

CONISTON
Cumbria

Bank Ground ♦♦♦♦
East of Lake, Coniston LA21 8AA
T: (015394) 41264
F: (015394) 41900
E: info@bankground.com
I: www.bankground.com

Beech Tree Guest House ♦♦♦♦
Yewdale Road, Coniston LA21 8DX
T: (015394) 41717
F: (015394) 41717

Coniston Lodge ♦♦♦♦♦ GOLD AWARD
Station Road, Coniston LA21 8HH
T: (015394) 41201
F: (015394) 41201
E: info@coniston-lodge.com
I: www.coniston-lodge.com

Crown Hotel ♦♦♦♦
Tilberthwaite Avenue, Coniston LA21 8ED
T: (015394) 41243
F: (015394) 41804
E: info@crown-hotel-coniston.com
I: www.crown-hotel-coniston.com

Cruachan ♦♦♦♦
Collingwood Close, Coniston LA21 8DZ
T: (015394) 41628
F: (015394) 41628
E: cruachan21@lineone.net

How Head Cottage ♦♦♦
East of Lake, Coniston LA21 8AA
T: (015394) 41594
E: howhead@lineone.net
I: www.howheadcottages.co.uk

Lakeland House ♦♦♦
Tilberthwaite Avenue, Coniston LA21 8ED
T: (015394) 41303
E: reservations@lakelandhouse.com
I: www.lakelandhouse.com

Oaklands ♦♦♦♦
Yewdale Road, Coniston LA21 8DX
T: (015394) 41245
F: (015394) 41245
E: judithzeke@oaklandsguesthouse.fsnet.co.uk
I: www.geocities.com/oaklandsguesthouse

The Old Rectory Hotel ♦♦♦♦ SILVER AWARD
Torver, Coniston LA21 8AX
T: (015394) 41353
F: (015394) 41156
E: enquiries@theoldrectoryhotel.com
I: www.theoldrectoryhotel.com

Orchard Cottage ♦♦♦♦
18 Yewdale Road, Coniston LA21 8DU
T: (015394) 41319
F: (015394) 41373
E: jean.orchardcottage@virgin.net
I: www.conistonholidays.com

Shepherds Villa ♦♦♦
Tilberthwaite Avenue, Coniston LA21 8ED
T: (01539) 441337
F: (01539) 441337

Sunny Brae Cottage ♦♦♦
Haws Bank, Coniston LA21 8AR
T: (015394) 41654
F: (015394) 41532
E: sunnybraecottage@aol.com
I: www.sunnybraecottage.co.uk

Thwaite Cottage ♦♦♦♦
Waterhead, Coniston LA21 8AJ
T: (015394) 41367
E: m@thwaitcot.freeserve.co.uk
I: www.thwaitcot.freeserve.co.uk

Townson Ground ♦♦♦♦
East of Lake Road, Coniston LA21 8AA
T: (015394) 41272
E: info@conistoncottages.net
I: www.conistoncottages.net

Wheelgate Country Guesthouse ♦♦♦♦♦
Little Arrow, Coniston LA21 8AU
T: (015394) 41418
F: (015394) 41114
E: wheelgate@conistoncottages.co.uk
I: www.wheelgate.co.uk

Wilson Arms ♦♦♦
Torver, Coniston LA21 8BB
T: (015394) 41237
F: (015394) 41590

COWGILL
Cumbria

Hillfarm House ♦♦♦♦
Cowgill, Sedbergh LA10 5RF
T: (01539) 625144
I: homepage.ntlworld.com/r.metcalfe2

CROOK
Cumbria

Mitchelland House ♦♦♦♦
Steeles Lane, Crook, Kendal LA8 8LL
T: (01539) 448589
E: marie.mitchelland@talk21.com

CROSBY RAVENSWORTH
Cumbria

Crake Trees Manor Rating Applied For
Maulds Meaburn, Crosby Ravensworth, Penrith CA10 3JG
T: (01931) 715205
E: ruth@craketreesmanor.co.uk
I: craketreesmanor.co.uk

CROSTHWAITE
Cumbria

Crosthwaite House ♦♦♦♦
Crosthwaite, Kendal LA8 8BP
T: (01539) 568264
F: (01539) 568264
E: bookings@crosthwaitehouse.co.uk
I: www.crosthwaitehouse.co.uk

The Punch Bowl Inn ♦♦♦♦
Crosthwaite, Kendal LA8 8HR
T: (015395) 68237
F: (015395) 68875
E: enquiries@punchbowl.fsnet.co.uk
I: www.punchbowl.fsnet.co.uk

CULGAITH
Cumbria

The Black Swan Inn ♦♦♦♦
Culgaith, Penrith CA10 1QW
T: (01768) 88223
F: (01768) 88223
I: blackswanculgaith.co.uk

DALEMAIN
Cumbria

Park House Farm ♦♦♦♦
Dalemain, Penrith CA11 0HB
T: (017684) 86212
F: (017684) 86212
E: mail@parkhousedalemain.freeserve.co.uk
I: www.parkhousedalemain.co.uk

DALTON-IN-FURNESS
Cumbria

Black Dog Inn ♦♦
Holmes Green, Broughton Road, Dalton-in-Furness LA15 8JP
T: (01229) 462561
F: (01229) 468036
E: jack@blackdoginn.freeserve.co.uk
I: www.blackdoginn.freeserve.co.uk

Park Cottage ♦♦♦♦ SILVER AWARD
Dalton-in-Furness LA15 8JZ
T: (01229) 462850
E: nicholson.parkcottage@quista.net
I: www.parkcottagedalton.co.uk

DENT
Cumbria

George and Dragon Hotel ♦♦♦
Main Street, Dent, Sedbergh LA10 5QL
T: (01539) 625256

Smithy Fold ♦♦♦
Whernside, Dent, Sedbergh LA10 5RE
T: (015396) 25368
E: cheetham@smithyfold.co.uk
I: www.smithyfold.co.uk

Stone Close Tea Shop ♦♦♦
Main Street, Dent, Sedbergh LA10 5QL
T: (01539) 625231
F: (01539) 726567
E: accommodation@stoneclose.co.uk
I: www.stoneclose.co.uk

Sun Inn ♦♦♦
Main Street, Dent, Sedbergh LA10 5QL
T: (015396) 25208
E: thesun@dentbrewery.co.uk
I: www.dentbrewery.co.uk/

DUFTON
Cumbria

Brow Farm Bed & Breakfast ♦♦♦♦
Dufton, Appleby-in-Westmorland CA16 6DF
T: (017683) 52865
F: (017683) 52865
E: wmswinbank@farmersweekly.net

ELTERWATER
Cumbria

Elterwater Park ♦♦♦♦
Skelwith Bridge, Ambleside LA22 9NP
T: (015394) 32227
F: (015394) 31768
E: enquiries@elterwater.com
I: www.elterwater.com

ESKDALE
Cumbria

Brook House Inn ♦♦♦♦
Boot, Holmrook CA19 1TG
T: (01946) 723288
F: (01946) 723160
E: stay@brookhouseinn.co.uk
I: www.brookhouseinn.co.uk

Forest How ♦♦♦
Eskdale Green, Holmrook CA19 1TR
T: (01946) 723201
F: (01946) 723190
E: fcarter@easynet.co.uk
I: www.foresthow-eskdale-cumbria.co.uk/

The Gatehouse Outward Bound ♦♦♦
Eskdale, Holmrook CA19 1TE
T: (019467) 23281
F: (019467) 23393
E: professional@outwardbound-uk.org
I: www.outwardbound-uk.org

Woolpack Inn ♦♦♦
Boot, Eskdale, Holmrook CA19 1TH
T: (019467) 23230
F: (019467) 23230
E: woolpack@eskdale.dial.lakesnet.co.uk
I: www.insites.co.uk/guide//cumbria/accom/woolpack

GARRIGILL
Cumbria

High Windy Hall Hotel and Restaurant ♦♦♦♦
Middleton-in-Teesdale Road, Garrigill, Alston CA9 3EZ
T: (01434) 381547
F: (01434) 382477
E: sales@hwh.u-net.com
I: www.hwh.u-net.com

GILSLAND
Cumbria

Bush Nook ♦♦♦♦
Gilsland, Brampton CA8 7AF
T: (016977) 47194
F: (016977) 47790
E: info@bushnook.co.uk
I: www.bushnook.co.uk

The Hill ♦♦♦♦
Gilsland, Brampton CA8 7DA
T: (016977) 47214
F: (016977) 47214
E: info@hadrians-wallbedandbreakfast.com
I: www.hadrians-wallbedandbreakfast.com

Slack House Farm ♦♦♦
Gilsland, Brampton CA8 7DB
T: (016977) 47351
F: (016977) 21100
E: slackhousefarm@lineone.net
I: www.slackhousefarm.co.uk

GRANGE-OVER-SANDS
Cumbria

Birchleigh Guest House ♦♦♦♦
Kents Bank Road, Grange-over-Sands LA11 7EY
T: (015395) 32592
F: (015395) 32592

Corner Beech Guest House ♦♦♦♦
1 Methven Terrace, Kents Bank Road, Grange-over-Sands LA11 7DP
T: (015395) 33088
E: info@cornerbeech.co.uk
I: www.cornerbeech.co.uk

Elton Hotel ♦♦♦♦
Windermere Road, Grange-over-Sands LA11 6EQ
T: (015395) 32838
F: (015395) 32838
E: chris.crane@btclick.com

Greenacres Country Guesthouse
♦♦♦♦ SILVER AWARD
Lindale, Grange-over-Sands LA11 6LP
T: (015395) 34578
F: (015395) 34578
I: www.smoothhound.co.uk/hotels/greenacres.html

The Laurels Bed and Breakfast ♦♦♦♦
Berriedale Terrace, Lindale Road, Grange-over-Sands LA11 6ER
T: (015395) 35919
F: (015395) 35919
E: gml@thelaurels71.freeserve.co.uk

Lymehurst Hotel ♦♦♦
Kents Bank Road, Grange-over-Sands LA11 7EY
T: (015395) 33076
F: (015395) 33076
E: enquiries@lymehurst.co.uk
I: www.lymehurst.co.uk

Mayfields ♦♦♦♦
3 Mayfield Terrace, Kents Bank Road, Grange-over-Sands LA11 7DW
T: (015395) 34730
I: www.accommodata.co.uk/010699.htm

Methven Hotel ♦♦♦♦
Methven Road, Grange-over-Sands LA11 7DU
T: (015395) 32031
E: methvenhotel@btinternet.com

Somerset House ♦♦♦
Kents Bank Road, Grange-over-Sands LA11 7EY
T: (015395) 32631
F: (015395) 36986
E: info@somersethouse-cumbria.co.uk
I: www.somersethouse-cumbria.co.uk

GRASMERE
Cumbria

Ash Cottage Guest House ♦♦♦♦
Red Lion Square, Grasmere, Ambleside LA22 9SP
T: (015394) 35224
I: www.ashcottage.com

Beck Allans ♦♦♦♦
College Street, Grasmere, Ambleside LA22 9SZ
T: (015394) 35563
F: (015394) 35563
E: mail@beckallans.com
I: www.beckallans.com

Chestnut Villa ♦♦♦
Keswick Road, Grasmere, Ambleside LA22 9RE
T: (015394) 35218

Dunmail House ♦♦♦♦
Keswick Road, Grasmere, Ambleside LA22 9RE
T: (015394) 35256
E: enquiries@dunmailhouse.freeserve.co.uk
I: www.dunmailhouse.com

Forest Side Hotel ♦♦♦
Forest Side, Grasmere, Ambleside LA22 9RN
T: (015394) 35250
F: (015394) 35947
E: hotel@forestsidehotel.com
I: www.forestsidehotel.com

The Harwood ♦♦♦
Red Lion Square, Grasmere, Ambleside LA22 9SP
T: (015394) 35248
F: (015394) 35545
E: harwoodian@aol.com
I: www.harwoodhotel.co.uk

How Foot Lodge ♦♦♦
Town End, Grasmere, Ambleside LA22 9SQ
T: (015394) 35366
F: (015394) 35268
E: enquiries@howfoot.co.uk
I: www.howfoot.co.uk

Lake View Country House ♦♦♦♦
Lake View Drive, Grasmere, Ambleside LA22 9TD
T: (015394) 35384
F: (015394) 35384
E: michelleking@buryend.freeserve.co.uk
I: www.lakeview-grasmere.com

Redmayne Cottage ♦♦♦♦
Grasmere, Ambleside LA22 9QY
T: (015394) 35635
E: enquiries@redmayne-grasmere.co.uk
I: www.redmayne-grasmere.co.uk

Riversdale
♦♦♦♦ SILVER AWARD
White Bridge, Grasmere, Ambleside LA22 9RQ
T: (015394) 35619
E: riversdalegrasmere@nascr.net
I: www.riversdalegrasmere.co.uk

Silver Lea Guest House ♦♦♦♦
Easedale Road, Grasmere, Ambleside LA22 9QE
T: (015394) 35657
F: (015394) 35657
I: www.silverlea.com

Titteringdales ♦♦♦♦
Pye Lane, Grasmere, Ambleside LA22 9RQ
T: (015394) 35439
E: titteringdales@grasmere.net
I: www.grasmere.net

Travellers Rest ♦♦♦
Grasmere, Ambleside LA22 9RR
T: (015394) 35604
F: (017687) 72309
E: stay@lakedistrictinns.co.uk
I: www.lakedistrictinns.co.uk

Woodland Crag Country House
♦♦♦♦ SILVER AWARD
How Head Lane, Grasmere, Ambleside LA22 9SG
T: (015394) 35351
F: (015394) 35351
E: woodlandcrag@aol.com
I: www.woodlandcrag.com

GRAYRIGG
Cumbria

Grayrigg Hall Farm ♦♦♦
Grayrigg, Kendal LA8 9BU
T: (01539) 824689

Punchbowl House
♦♦♦♦ SILVER AWARD
Grayrigg, Kendal LA8 9BU
T: (01539) 824345
F: (01539) 824345
E: enquiries@punchbowlhouse.co.uk
I: www.punchbowlhouse.co.uk

HARRAS MOOR
Cumbria

The Georgian House Hotel
Rating Applied For
9-11 Church Street, Whitehaven CA28 7AY
T: (01946) 696611
F: (01946) 696611
E: georgianhotel@aol.com

HAWKSHEAD
Cumbria

Borwick Lodge
♦♦♦♦ SILVER AWARD
Outgate, Ambleside LA22 0PU
T: (015394) 36332
F: (015394) 36332
E: borwicklodge@talk21.com
I: www.borwicklodge.com

The Drunken Duck Inn
♦♦♦♦ SILVER AWARD
Barngates, Ambleside LA22 0NG
T: (015394) 36347
F: (015394) 36781
E: info@drunkenduckinn.co.uk
I: www.drunkenduckinn.co.uk

Grizedale Lodge Hotel
♦♦♦♦ SILVER AWARD
The Hotel in the Forest, Grizedale, Ambleside LA22 0QL
T: (015394) 36532
F: (015394) 36572
E: enquiries@grizedale-lodge.com
I: www.grizedale-lodge.com

High Grassings ♦♦♦♦
Sunny Brow, Outgate, Ambleside LA22 0PU
T: (015394) 36484
F: (015394) 36140
E: info@highgrassings.com
I: www.highgrassings.com

Walker Ground Manor ♦♦♦♦
Vicarage Lane, Hawkshead, Ambleside LA22 0PD
T: (015394) 36219
E: info@walkerground.co.uk
I: www.walkerground.co.uk

Yewfield Vegetarian B&B ♦♦♦♦
Hawkshead Hill, Hawkshead, Ambleside LA22 0PR
T: (015394) 36765
F: (015394) 36096
E: derek.yewfield@btinternet.com
I: www.yewfield.co.uk

HEADS NOOK
Cumbria

Sirelands ♦♦♦
Heads Nook, Carlisle CA8 9BT
T: (01228) 670389
F: (01228) 670389
E: carr_sirelands@btinternet.com

HESKET NEWMARKET
Cumbria

Denton House ♦♦♦
Hesket Newmarket, Wigton CA7 8JG
T: (016974) 78415
E: dentonhnm@aol.com

HIGH LORTON
Cumbria

Swinside End Farm ♦♦♦♦
Scales, High Lorton, Cockermouth CA13 9UA
T: (01900) 85134
F: (01900) 85410

Terrace Farm ♦♦♦♦
High Lorton, Cockermouth CA13 9TX
T: (01900) 85278
I: www.terracefarm.co.uk

HOLME
Cumbria

Marwin House ♦♦
Duke Street, Holme, Carnforth LA6 1PY
T: (01524) 781144
F: (01524) 781144

HOUGHTON
Cumbria

The Steadings ♦♦♦
Townhead Farm, Houghton, Carlisle CA6 4JB
T: (01228) 523019
I: www.thesteadings.co.uk

IREBY
Cumbria

Daleside Farm ♦♦♦♦
Ireby, Carlisle CA5 1EW
T: (016973) 71268
E: info@dalesidefarm.co.uk
I: www.dalesidefarm.co.uk

Woodlands Country House ♦♦♦♦
Ireby, Carlisle CA7 1EX
T: (016973) 71791
F: (016973) 71482
E: stay@woodlandsatireby.co.uk
I: www.woodlandsatireby.co.uk

KENDAL
Cumbria

Beech House Hotel ♦♦♦♦♦
40 Greenside, Kendal LA9 4LD
T: (01539) 720385
F: (01539) 724082
E: hilary.claxton@virgin.net
I: www.beechhouse-kendal.co.uk

Burrow Hall ♦♦♦♦
Plantation Bridge, Kendal LA8 9JR
T: (01539) 821711
F: (01539) 821711
E: info@burrowhall.fsnet.co.uk
I: www.burrowhall.co.uk

Cragg Farm ♦♦♦
New Hutton, Kendal LA8 0BA
T: (01539) 721760
F: (01539) 721760
E: knowles.cragg@ukgateway.net
I: www.craggfarm.com

Fairways Guest House ♦♦♦
102 Windermere Road, Kendal LA9 5EZ
T: (01539) 725564
E: mp@fairways1.fsnet.co.uk

The Glen ♦♦♦
Oxenholme, Kendal LA9 7RF
T: (01539) 726386
E: greenintheglen@btinternet.com
I: www.smoothhound.co.uk/hotels/glen2.html

Hillside Bed & Breakfast ♦♦♦
4 Beast Banks, Kendal LA9 4JW
T: (01539) 722836
E: info@hillside-kendal.co.uk
I: www.hillside-kendal.co.uk

Hollin Root Farm ♦♦♦♦
Garth Row, Kendal LA8 9AW
T: (01539) 823638
E: b-and-b@hollin-root-farm.freeserve.co.uk
I: www.hollinrootfarm.co.uk

Kendal Arms and Hotel ♦♦♦
72 Milnthorpe Road, Kendal LA9 5HG
T: (01539) 720956
F: (01539) 724851

Lakeland Natural Vegetarian Guesthouse ♦♦♦
Low Slack, Queens Road, Kendal LA9 4PH
T: (01539) 733011
F: (01539) 733011
E: relax@lakelandnatural.co.uk
I: www.lakelandnatural.co.uk

Newalls Country House ♦♦♦♦
Skelsmergh, Kendal LA9 6NU
T: (01539) 723202

Riversleigh ♦♦♦
49 Milnthorpe Road, Kendal LA9 5QG
T: (01539) 726392

Sonata ♦♦♦♦
19 Burneside Road, Kendal LA9 4RL
T: (01539) 732290
F: (01539) 732290
E: chris@sonataguesthouse.freeserve.co.uk
I: www.sonataguesthouse.co.uk

Union Tavern ♦♦♦
159 Stricklandgate, Kendal LA9 4RF
T: (01539) 724004
E: uniontavern@edirectory.co.uk
I: www.edirectory.co.uk/uniontavern

KESWICK
Cumbria

Abacourt House
♦♦♦♦ SILVER AWARD
26 Stanger Street, Keswick CA12 5JU
T: (017687) 72967
E: abacourt@btinternet.com
I: www.abacourt.co.uk

Acorn House Hotel
♦♦♦♦ SILVER AWARD
Ambleside Road, Keswick CA12 4DL
T: (017687) 72553
E: info@acornhousehotel.co.uk
I: www.acornhousehotel.co.uk

Amble House Guest House
♦♦♦♦
Eskin Street, Keswick CA12 4DQ
T: (017687) 73288
F: (017687) 80220
E: info@amblehouse.co.uk
I: www.amblehouse.co.uk

The Anchorage ♦♦♦♦
14 Ambleside Road, Keswick CA12 4DL
T: (017687) 72813
E: anchorage.keswick@btopenworld.com
I: www.anchorage-keswick.co.uk

Avondale Guest House ♦♦♦♦
20 Southey Street, Keswick CA12 4EF
T: (017687) 72735
F: (017687) 75431
E: enquiries@avondaleguesthouse.com
I: www.avondaleguesthouse.com

Badgers Wood ♦♦♦♦
30 Stanger Street, Keswick CA12 5JU
T: (017687) 72621
E: enquiries@badgers-wood.co.uk
I: www.badgers-wood.co.uk

Beckstones Farm Guest House ♦♦♦
Thornthwaite, Keswick CA12 5SQ
T: (017687) 78510
E: beckstones@lineone.net
I: website.lineone.net/~beckstones/

Berkeley Guest House ♦♦♦♦
The Heads, Keswick CA12 5ER
T: (017687) 74222
E: berkeley@tesco.net
I: www.berkeley-keswick.com

Birkrigg Farm ♦♦♦
Newlands, Keswick CA12 5TS
T: (017687) 78278

Bowfell House ♦♦♦
Chestnut Hill, Keswick CA12 4LR
T: (017687) 74859
E: bowfell.keswick@virgin.net
I: www.stayinkeswick.co.uk

Braemar
♦♦♦♦ SILVER AWARD
21 Eskin Street, Keswick CA12 4DQ
T: (017687) 73743
E: enquiries@braemar-guesthouse.co.uk
I: www.braemar-guesthouse.co.uk

Brierholme Guest House ♦♦♦
21 Bank Street, Keswick CA12 5JZ
T: (017687) 72938
E: enquiries@brierholme.co.uk
I: www.brierholme.co.uk

Burnside Bed & Breakfast
♦♦♦♦
Penrith Road, Keswick CA12 4LJ
T: (017687) 72639
F: (018687) 72639
E: burnsidebb@keswickthelakes.fsnet.co.uk

The Cartwheel ♦♦♦
5 Blencathra Street, Keswick CA12 4HW
T: (017687) 73182
E: info@thecartwheel.co.uk
I: www.thecartwheel.co.uk

Charnwood Guest House
♦♦♦♦
6 Eskin Street, Keswick CA12 4DH
T: (017687) 74111

Charnwood Lodge ♦♦♦
Thrushwood, Keswick CA12 4PG
T: (017687) 71318

Cherry Trees ♦♦♦♦
16 Eskin Street, Keswick CA12 4DQ
T: (017687) 71048
E: cherry.trees@virgin.net
I: www.cherrytrees-keswick.co.uk

Clarence House ♦♦♦♦
14 Eskin Street, Keswick CA12 4DQ
T: (017687) 73186
F: (017687) 72317
E: info@clarencehousekeswick.co.uk
I: www.clarencehousekeswick.co.uk

Crag Wood ♦♦♦♦
44 Blencathra Street, Keswick CA12 4HT
T: (017687) 73792
E: cragwood@btopenworld.com
I: www.cragwood-keswick.co.uk

Cumbria House ♦♦♦♦
1 Derwentwater Place, Keswick CA12 4DR
T: (017687) 73171
E: ctb@cumbriahouse.co.uk
I: www.cumbriahouse.co.uk

Dalegarth House Country Hotel ♦♦♦♦
Portinscale, Keswick CA12 5RQ
T: (017687) 72817
F: (017687) 72817
E: john@dalegarth-house.co.uk
I: www.dalegarth-house.co.uk

Derwentdale Guesthouse ♦♦♦
8 Blencathra Street, Keswick CA12 4HP
T: (017687) 74187
E: liz@derwentdale.co.uk
I: www.derwentdale.co.uk

Dolly Waggon ♦♦♦
17 Helvellyn Street, Keswick CA12 4EN
T: (017687) 73593
E: info@dollywaggon.co.uk
I: www.dollywaggon.co.uk

Dunsford Guest House ♦♦♦♦
16 Stanger Street, Keswick CA12 5JU
T: (017687) 75059
E: enquiries@dunsford.net
I: www.dunsford.net

The Easedale Hotel ♦♦♦
Southey Street, Keswick CA12 4HL
T: (017687) 72710
F: (017687) 71127
E: easedalehotel@aol.com
I: www.easedalehotel.com

Eden Green Guest House
♦♦♦♦
20 Blencathra Street, Keswick CA12 4HP
T: (017687) 72077
F: (017687) 80870
E: sue.plant@edengreen.co.uk
I: www.edengreenguesthouse.com

Ellas Crag ♦♦♦♦
Newlands, Keswick CA12 5TS
T: (017687) 78217
E: ellascrag@talk21.com
I: www.ellascrag.co.uk

Ellergill Guest House ♦♦♦♦
22 Stanger Street, Keswick CA12 5JU
T: (017687) 73347
E: stay@ellergill.uk.com
I: www.ellergill.uk.com

Fell House ♦♦♦♦
28 Stanger Street, Keswick CA12 5JU
T: (017687) 72669
F: (017687) 72669
E: info@fellhouse.co.uk
I: www.fellhouse.co.uk

Glencoe Guest House ♦♦♦♦
21 Helvellyn Street, Keswick CA12 4EN
T: (017687) 71016
E: enquiries@glencoeguesthouse.co.uk
I: www.glencoeguesthouse.co.uk

Glendale Guest House ♦♦♦
7 Eskin Street, Keswick CA12 4DH
T: (017687) 73562
F: (017687) 80668
E: info@glendalekeswick.co.uk
I: www.glendalekeswick.co.uk

The Grange Country House
♦♦♦♦♦ SILVER AWARD
Manor Brow, Ambleside Road, Keswick CA12 4BA
T: (017687) 72500
E: info@grangekeswick.com
I: www.grangekeswick.com

Grassmoor Guest House ♦♦♦
10 Blencathra Street, Keswick CA12 4HP
T: (017687) 74008
E: grassmoor.keswick@ukonline.co.uk
I: www.grassmoor-keswick.co.uk

Greystones Hotel ♦♦♦♦
Ambleside Road, Keswick CA12 4DP
T: (017687) 73108
E: greystones@keslakes.freeserve.co.uk
I: www.greystones.tv

Hazeldene Hotel ♦♦♦♦
The Heads, Keswick CA12 5ER
T: (017687) 72106
F: (017687) 75435
E: info@hazeldene-hotel.co.uk
I: www.hazeldene-hotel.co.uk

Hedgehog Hill Guesthouse
♦♦♦
18 Blencathra Street, Keswick CA12 4HP
T: (017687) 74386
F: (017687) 80622
E: etc@hedgehoghill.co.uk
I: www.hedgehoghill.co.uk

Howe Keld Ltd ♦♦♦♦
5-7 The Heads, Keswick CA12 5ES
T: (017687) 72417
F: (017687) 72417
E: david@howekeld.co.uk
I: www.howekeld.co.uk

Hunters Way Guest House
♦♦♦♦
4 Eskin Street, Keswick CA12 4DH
T: (017687) 72324
F: (017687) 75459

Kalgurli Guest House ♦♦♦
33 Helvellyn Street, Keswick
CA12 4EP
T: (017687) 72935
E: info@kalgurli.co.uk
I: www.kalgurli.co.uk

Keskadale Farm ♦♦♦♦
Newlands Valley, Keswick
CA12 5TS
T: (017687) 78544
F: (017687) 78150
E: keskadale.b.b@kencomp.net

Keswick Park Hotel ♦♦♦♦
33 Station Road, Keswick
CA12 4NA
T: (017687) 72072
F: (017687) 74816
E: reservations@keswickparkhotel.com
I: www.keswickparkhotel.co.uk

Langdale Guest House ♦♦♦
14 Leonard Street, Keswick
CA12 4EL
T: (017687) 73977

Latrigg House ♦♦♦♦
St Herbert Street, Keswick
CA12 4DF
T: (017687) 73068
F: (017687) 72801
E: info@latrigghouse.com
I: www.latrigghouse.com

Leonard's Field House ♦♦♦
3 Leonard Street, Keswick
CA12 4EJ
T: (01768) 774170
E: leonardsfieldhouse@talk21.com
I: www.leonardsfieldhouse.com

Lincoln Guest House ♦♦♦
23 Stanger Street, Keswick
CA12 5JX
T: (017687) 72597
F: (017687) 73014
E: joan@lincoln-guesthouse.fsnet.co.uk
I: www.lincoln-guesthouse.fsnet.co.uk

Lindisfarne ♦♦♦♦
21 Church Street, Keswick
CA12 4DX
T: (017687) 73218
E: burns1067@freeserve.co.uk
I: www.lindisfarnehouse.com

Littlebeck ♦♦♦♦
Chestnut Hill, Keswick CA12 4LT
T: (017687) 72972
E: littlebeck@btinternet.com

Littletown Farm ♦♦♦
Newlands, Keswick CA12 5TU
T: (017687) 78353
F: (017687) 78437
I: www.littletownfarm.co.uk

Loch Villa ♦♦♦
34 Blencathra Street, Keswick
CA12 4HP
T: (017687) 73226

Lynwood ♦♦♦♦
12 Ambleside Road, Keswick
CA12 4DL
T: (017687) 72081
E: info@lynwood-keswick.co.uk
I: www.lynwood-keswick.co.uk

Lynwood House ♦♦♦♦
35 Helvellyn Street, Keswick
CA12 4EP
T: (017687) 72398
E: info@lynwoodhouse.net
I: www.lynwoodhouse.net

Melbreak House ♦♦♦
29 Church Street, Keswick
CA12 4DX
T: (017687) 73398
E: melbreakhouse@btinternet.com
I: www.melbreakhouse.co.uk

The Paddock ♦♦♦♦
Wordsworth Street, Keswick
CA12 4HU
T: (017687) 72510
F: (017687) 72510
E: val@thepaddock.info
I: www.thepaddock.info

Parkfield Guesthouse
♦♦♦♦ SILVER AWARD
The Heads, Keswick CA12 5ES
T: (017687) 72328
F: (017687) 71396
E: enquiries@parkfieldkeswick.com
I: www.parkfieldkeswick.com

Ravensworth Hotel
♦♦♦♦ SILVER AWARD
29 Station Street, Keswick
CA12 5HH
T: (017687) 72476
F: (017687) 75287
E: info@ravensworth-hotel.co.uk
I: www.ravensworth-hotel.co.uk

Rickerby Grange Country House Hotel ♦♦♦♦
Portinscale, Keswick CA12 5RH
T: (017687) 72344
F: (017687) 75588
E: val@ricor.co.uk
I: www.ricor.co.uk

Sandon Guesthouse ♦♦♦♦
13 Southey Street, Keswick
CA12 4EG
T: (017687) 73648
E: enquiries@sandonguesthouse.com
I: www.sandonguesthouse.com

Seymour House ♦♦♦
36 Lake Road, Keswick
CA12 5DQ
T: (017687) 72764
F: (017687) 71289
E: andy042195@aol.com
I: www.seymour-house.com

Shemara Guest House ♦♦♦♦
27 Bank Street, Keswick
CA12 5JZ
T: (017687) 73936
F: (017687) 80785
E: info@shemara.uk.com
I: www.shemara.uk.com/

The Silverdale Hotel ♦♦♦
17-19 Blencathra Street,
Keswick CA12 4HT
T: (017687) 72294
E: mandy@mdowson.fsnet.co.uk
I: www.silverdalehotelkeswick.co.uk

Skiddaw Grove Country Guest House ♦♦♦♦
Vicarage Hill, Keswick CA12 5QB
T: (017687) 73324
F: (017687) 73324
E: skiddawgrove@hotmail.com

Squirrel Lodge Guest House
Rating Applied For
43 Eskin Street, Keswick
CA12 4DG
T: (017687) 71189
E: squirrels43@aol.com
I: www.squirrellodge.co.uk

Stonegarth ♦♦♦♦
2 Eskin Street, Keswick
CA12 4DH
T: (017687) 72436
E: info@stonegarth.com
I: www.stonegarth.com

Sunnyside Guest House ♦♦♦♦
25 Southey Street, Keswick
CA12 4EF
T: (017687) 72446
E: enquiries@sunnysideguesthouse.com
I: www.sunnysideguesthouse.com

Swinside Farmhouse ♦♦♦♦
Newlands Farmhouse, Keswick
CA12 5UE
T: (01768) 778363
E: swinside.farmhouse@btopenworld.com

Swinside Inn ♦♦♦
Newlands, Keswick CA12 5UE
T: (017687) 78253
E: info@theswinsideinn.com
I: www.theswinsideinn.com

Tarn Hows ♦♦♦♦
3-5 Eskin Street, Keswick
CA12 4DH
T: (017687) 73217
F: (017687) 73217
E: info@tarnhows.co.uk
I: www.tarnhows.co.uk

Watendlath Guest House ♦♦♦♦
15 Acorn Street, Keswick
CA12 4EA
T: (017687) 74165
F: (017687) 74165
E: linda@watendlathguesthouse.co.uk
I: www.watendlathguesthouse.co.uk

West View Guest House
♦♦♦♦ SILVER AWARD
The Heads, Keswick CA12 5ES
T: (017687) 73638

Whitehouse Guest House
♦♦♦♦ SILVER AWARD
15 Ambleside Road, Keswick
CA12 4DL
T: (017687) 73176
F: (017687) 73176
E: whitehousekeswick@hotmail.com
I: www.whitehousekeswick.co.uk

Winchester Guest House
Rating Applied For
58 Blencathra Street, Keswick
CA12 4HT
T: (017687) 73664
F: (017687) 75313
E: bobgill@winchesterguesthouse.co.uk
I: www.winchesterguesthouse.co.uk

KIRKBY LONSDALE
Cumbria

Capernwray House
♦♦♦♦ SILVER AWARD
Borrans Lane, Capernwray,
Carnforth LA6 1AE
T: (01524) 732363
F: (01524) 732363
E: thesmiths@capernwrayhouse.com
I: www.capernwrayhouse.com

The Copper Kettle ♦♦
3-5 Market Street, Kirkby
Lonsdale, Carnforth LA6 2AU
T: (015242) 71714
F: (015242) 71714

Tossbeck Farm ♦♦♦
Middleton, Kirkby Lonsdale,
Carnforth LA6 2LZ
T: (015242) 76214
E: postmaster@tossbeck.f9.co.uk
I: www.tossbeck.co.uk

KIRKBY STEPHEN
Cumbria

Ing Hill Lodge ♦♦♦♦
Mallerstang, Kirkby Stephen
CA17 4JT
T: (017683) 71153
F: (017683) 72710
E: inghill@fsbdial.co.uk
I: www.ing-hill-lodge.co.uk

Jolly Farmers Guest House ♦♦♦♦
63 High Street, Kirkby Stephen
CA17 4SH
T: (017683) 71063
F: (017683) 71063
E: jollyf@cumbria.com
I: www.cumbria.com/jollyf/

Riddlesay Farm ♦♦♦♦
Soulby, Kirkby Stephen
CA17 4PX
T: (017683) 71474
F: (017683) 71483
E: mrarmstrong@btinternet.com

West View ♦♦♦♦
Ravenstonedale, Kirkby Stephen
CA17 4NG
T: (015396) 23415
E: enquiries@westview-cumbria.co.uk
I: www.enquiries@westview-cumbria.co.uk

KIRKLINTON
Cumbria

Clift House Farm ♦♦♦
Kirklinton, Carlisle CA6 6DE
T: (01228) 675237
F: (01228) 675237
E: clifthousefarm@hotmail.com
I: www.clifthousefarm.co.uk

LAKESIDE
Cumbria

The Knoll Country House
♦♦♦♦♦ SILVER AWARD
Lakeside, Newby Bridge,
Ulverston LA12 8AU
T: (015395) 31347
F: (015395) 30850
E: info@theknoll-lakeside.co.uk
I: www.theknoll-lakeside.co.uk

LANERCOST
Cumbria

Abbey Bridge Inn ◆◆◆
Lanercost, Brampton CA8 2HG
T: (016977) 2224
F: (016977) 42184
E: tim@abbeybridge.co.uk
I: abbeybridge.co.uk

LAZONBY
Cumbria

Banktop House ◆◆◆
Lazonby, Penrith CA10 1AQ
T: (01768) 898268
F: (01768) 898851
E: hartsop@globalnet.co.uk

LONGTOWN
Cumbria

Briar Lea House ◆◆◆◆
Brampton Road, Longtown, Carlisle CA6 5TN
T: (01228) 791538
F: (01228) 791538
E: info@briarleahouse.co.uk
I: www.briarleahouse.co.uk

Craigburn ◆◆◆◆
Catlowdy, Longtown, Carlisle CA6 5QP
T: (01228) 577214
F: (01228) 577014
E: louiselawson@hotmail.com
I: www.craigburnfarmhouse.co.uk

LOWESWATER
Cumbria

Askhill Farm ◆◆◆
Loweswater, Cockermouth CA13 0SU
T: (01946) 861640

LOWICK
Cumbria

Garth Row ◆◆◆
Lowick Green, Ulverston LA12 8EB
T: (01229) 885633
E: jon@garthrow.freeserver.co.uk
I: www.garthrow.co.uk

LOWICK GREEN
Cumbria

The Farmers Arms Hotel ◆◆◆
Lowick Green, Ulverston LA12 8DT
T: (01229) 861277
F: (01229) 861853
E: bookings@farmersarms.co.uk
I: www.farmersarmslowick.co.uk

MAULDS MEABURN
Cumbria

Trainlands Bed & Breakfast ◆◆◆
Maulds Meaburn, Penrith CA10 3HX
T: (017683) 51249
F: (017683) 53983
E: bousfield@trainlands.u-net.com

MILBURN
Cumbria

Low Howgill Farm ◆◆◆◆
Milburn, Penrith CA10 1TL
T: (017683) 61595
F: (017683) 61598
E: holidays@low-howgill.co.uk
I: www.low-howgill.f9.co.uk

Slakes Farm ◆◆◆
Knock, Appleby-in-Westmorland CA16 6DP
T: (017683) 61385
E: oakleaves5491@aol.com

MILLOM
Cumbria

The Duddon Pilot Hotel ◆◆◆◆
Borwick Rails, Devonshire Road, Millom LA18 4JT
T: (01229) 774116
F: (01229) 774116

MILNTHORPE
Cumbria

The Cross Keys Hotel ◆◆◆◆
1 Park Road, Milnthorpe LA7 7AD
T: (015395) 62115
F: (015395) 62446
E: info@thecrosskeyshotel.co.uk
I: www.thecrosskeyshotel.co.uk

MOSEDALE
Cumbria

Mosedale House ◆◆◆◆
Mosedale, Mungrisdale, Penrith CA11 0XQ
T: (017687) 79371
E: mosedale@northlakes.co.uk
I: www.mosedalehouse.co.uk
♿

MUNGRISDALE
Cumbria

Mosedale End Farm ◆◆◆
Mungrisdale, Penrith CA11 0XQ
T: (017687) 79605
E: armstrong@awmcmanus.screaming.net
I: www.smoothhound.co.uk/hotels/mosedale.html

Near Howe Hotel ◆◆◆
Mungrisdale, Penrith CA11 0SH
T: (017687) 79678
F: (017687) 79462
E: nearhowe@btopenworld.com
I: www.nearhowe.co.uk

NATEBY
Cumbria

The Black Bull Inn ◆◆◆◆
Nateby, Kirkby Stephen CA17 4JP
T: (017683) 71588

NEWBIGGIN-ON-LUNE
Cumbria

Tranna Hill ◆◆◆◆
Newbiggin-on-Lune, Kirkby Stephen CA17 4NY
T: (015396) 23227
E: trannahill@hotmail.com

NEWBY BRIDGE
Cumbria

Old Barn Farm ◆◆◆◆
Fidler Hall, Newby Bridge, Ulverston LA12 8NQ
T: (015395) 31842

OXENHOLME
Cumbria

Station Inn ◆◆◆◆
Oxenholme, Kendal LA9 7RF
T: (01539) 724094
F: (01539) 724094

PATTERDALE
Cumbria

Deepdale Hall Farm House ◆◆◆◆
Patterdale, Penrith CA11 0NR
T: (017684) 82369
F: (017684) 82608
E: brown@deepdalehall.freeserve.co.uk
I: www.deepdalehall.co.uk

PENRITH
Cumbria

Albany House ◆◆◆
5 Portland Place, Penrith CA11 7QN
T: (01768) 863072
F: (01768) 895527
E: info@albany-house.org.uk
I: www.albany-house.org.uk

Glendale Guest House ◆◆◆◆
4 Portland Place, Penrith CA11 7QN
T: (01768) 862579
F: (01768) 867934
E: glendale@lineone.net
I: www.glendaleguesthouse.net

Hornby Hall Country Guest House ◆◆◆◆
Brougham, Penrith CA10 2AR
T: (01768) 891114
F: (01768) 891114
E: enquire@hornbyhall.co.uk
I: www.hornbyhall.co.uk

Limes Country Hotel ◆◆◆
Redhills Lane, Redhills, Penrith CA11 0DT
T: (01768) 863343
F: (01768) 867190
E: jdhanton@aol.com
I: www.members.aol.com/jdhanton/index.htm

Little Blencowe Farm ◆◆◆
Blencow, Penrith CA11 0DG
T: (017684) 83338
F: (017684) 83054
E: bart.fawcett@ukgateway.net

The Old School ◆◆◆◆◆ SILVER AWARD
Newbiggin, Stainton, Penrith CA11 0HT
T: (017684) 83709
F: (017684) 83709
E: info@theold-school.com
I: www.theold-school.com

Roundthorn Country House ◆◆◆◆◆
Beacon Edge, Penrith CA11 8SJ
T: (01768) 863952
F: (01768) 864100
E: enquiries@roundthorn.co.uk
I: www.roundthorn.co.uk

POOLEY BRIDGE
Cumbria

Sun Inn ◆◆◆
Pooley Bridge, Penrith CA10 2NN
T: (017684) 86205
F: (017684) 86913

PORTINSCALE
Cumbria

Derwent Cottage ◆◆◆◆◆ GOLD AWARD
Portinscale, Keswick CA12 5RF
T: (017687) 74838
E: enquiries@dercott.demon.co.uk
I: www.dercott.demon.co.uk

RAVENSTONEDALE
Cumbria

The Stables Bed & Breakfast ◆◆◆◆ SILVER AWARD
The Stables, Coldbeck, Ravenstonedale, Kirkby Stephen CA17 4LW
T: (015396) 23641
F: (015396) 23641
E: enquiries@coldbeckstables.com
I: www.coldbeckstables.com

RYDAL
Cumbria

Nab Cottage Guest House ◆◆◆
Rydal, Ambleside LA22 9SD
T: (015394) 35311
F: (015394) 35493
E: tim@nabcottage.com
I: www.rydalwater.com

ST BEES
Cumbria

Fairladies Barn Guest House ◆◆◆
Main Street, St Bees CA27 0AD
T: (01946) 822718
F: (01946) 825838
E: info@fairladiesbarn.co.uk
I: www.fairladiesbarn.co.uk

Fleatham House ◆◆◆◆ SILVER AWARD
High House Road, St Bees CA27 0BX
T: (019468) 22341
F: (019468) 20862
E: fleathamhouse@aol.com
I: www.fleathamhouse.com

Stone House Farm ◆◆◆
133 Main Street, St Bees CA27 0DE
T: (019468) 22224
F: (019468) 24933
E: csmith.stonehouse@btopenworld.com
I: www.stonehousefarm.net

SANDSIDE
Cumbria

Plantation Cottage ◆◆◆◆
Sandside, Milnthorpe LA7 7JU
T: (01524) 762069

SAWREY
Cumbria

Beechmount Country House ◆◆◆
Near Sawrey, Ambleside LA22 0JZ
T: (015394) 36356
E: beechmount@supanet.com
I: www.beechmountcountryhouse.co.uk

Buckle Yeat Guest House ◆◆◆◆
Sawrey, Ambleside LA22 0LF
T: (015394) 36446
E: info@buckle-yeat.co.uk
I: www.buckle-yeat.co.uk

High Green Gate Guest House ◆◆◆
Near Sawrey, Ambleside LA22 0LF
T: (015394) 36296
E: highgreengate@amserve.net

Lakefield ◆◆◆◆
Near Sawrey, Ambleside LA22 0JZ
T: (015394) 36635
F: (015394) 36635
E: lakefield@aol.com
I: lakefield.golakes.co.uk

Tower Bank Arms ◆◆◆
Near Sawrey, Ambleside LA22 0LF
T: (015394) 36334
F: (015394) 36448
E: sales@towerbankarms.fsnet.co.uk

West Vale Country House and Restaurant
◆◆◆◆◆ GOLD AWARD
Far Sawrey, Hawkshead, Ambleside LA22 0LQ
T: (015394) 42817
F: (015394) 45302
E: enquiries@westvalecountryhouse.co.uk
I: www.westvalecountryhouse.co.uk

SCOTBY
Cumbria

Windsover ◆◆◆◆
Lambley Bank, Scotby, Carlisle CA4 8BX
T: (01228) 513550
F: (01228) 513550
E: jimcallaghan@tinyworld.co.uk
I: www.windsover.co.uk

SEASCALE
Cumbria

Victoria Villa Hotel and Egloff's Eating House ◆◆◆◆
58 Gosforth Road, Seascale CA20 1JG
T: (01946) 727309
F: (01946) 727158
I: www.egloffeatinghouse.co.uk

SEDBERGH
Cumbria

Bridge House ◆◆◆◆
Brigflatts Lane, Sedbergh LA10 5HN
T: (015396) 21820
F: (015396) 21820

Dalesman Country Inn ◆◆◆◆
Main Street, Sedbergh LA10 5BN
T: (015396) 21183
F: (015396) 21311
E: info@thedalesman.co.uk
I: www.thedalesman.co.uk

St Mark's ◆◆◆◆
Cautley, Sedbergh LA10 5LZ
T: (015396) 20287
F: (015396) 21585
E: st.marks@talk21.com

STANWIX
Cumbria

Aldingham House Townhouse B&B ◆◆◆◆◆ SILVER AWARD
1 Eden Mount, Carlisle CA3 9LZ
T: (01228) 522554
F: (01228) 522554
E: enquiries@aldinghamhouse.co.uk
I: www.aldinghamhouse.co.uk

Marlborough House ◆◆◆
2 Marlborough Gardens, Stanwix, Carlisle CA3 9NW
T: (01228) 512174
F: (01228) 512174
E: ian.brown@marlborough-housebb.co.uk
I: www.marlboroughhousebb.co.uk

STAVELEY
Cumbria

Eagle and Child Hotel ◆◆◆
Kendal Road, Staveley, Kendal LA8 9LP
T: (01539) 821320
E: eaglechildinn@btinternet.com
I: www.eaglechildinn.co.uk

Tarn House ◆◆◆◆
18 Danes Road, Staveley, Kendal LA8 9PW
T: (01539) 821656

TALKIN
Cumbria

Hullerbank ◆◆◆◆
Talkin, Brampton CA8 1LB
T: (016977) 46668
F: (016977) 46668
E: info@hullerbank.freeserve.co.uk
I: www.smoothhound.co.uk/hotels/huller.html

TEBAY
Cumbria

Primrose Cottage ◆◆◆◆
Orton Road, Tebay, Penrith CA10 3TL
T: (015396) 24791
E: primrosecottebay@aol.com
I: www.primrosecottagecumbria.co.uk

THORNTHWAITE
Cumbria

Jenkin Hill Cottage
◆◆◆◆ SILVER AWARD
Thornthwaite, Keswick CA12 5SG
T: (017687) 78443
F: (017687) 78445
E: quality@jenkinhill.co.uk
I: www.jenkinhill.co.uk

Thornthwaite Grange ◆◆◆
Thornthwaite, Keswick CA12 5SA
T: (01768) 778205
E: joan_berwick@hotmail.com
I: www.thornthwaite-grange.co.uk

THRELKELD
Cumbria

Scales Farm Country Guesthouse ◆◆◆◆
Scales, Threlkeld, Keswick CA12 4SY
T: (017687) 79660
F: (017687) 79510
E: scales@scalesfarm.com
I: www.scalesfarm.com

TIRRIL
Cumbria

Heughscar ◆◆◆◆
Tirril, Penrith CA10 2JF
T: (01768) 840459
F: (01768) 840459
E: nigelgardham@heughscar.co.uk
I: www.heughscar.co.uk

TROUTBECK
Cumbria

Gill Head Farm ◆◆◆
Troutbeck, Penrith CA11 0ST
T: (017687) 79652
F: (017687) 79130
E: enquiries@gillheadfarm.co.uk
I: www.gillheadfarm.co.uk

High Fold Farm ◆◆◆◆
Troutbeck, Windermere LA23 1PG
T: (015394) 32200
E: enquiries@highfoldfarm.co.uk
I: www.highfoldfarm.co.uk

High Green Lodge ◆◆◆◆
High Green, Troutbeck, Windermere LA23 1PN
T: (015394) 33005

Lane Head Farm Guest House ◆◆◆◆
Troutbeck, Penrith CA11 0SY
T: (017687) 79220
F: (017687) 79220
E: info@laneheadfarm.freeserve.co.uk
I: www.laneheadfarm.co.uk

Troutbeck Inn ◆◆◆◆
Troutbeck, Penrith CA11 0SJ
T: (01768) 483635
F: (01768) 483928
E: enquiries@troutbeck-inn.com
I: www.troutbeck_inn.com

ULLSWATER
Cumbria

Bank House Farm
◆◆◆◆ SILVER AWARD
Matterdale End, Penrith CA11 0LF
T: (017684) 82040
E: tjnhargreaves@aol.com
I: www.bankhousefarm.net

Elm House
◆◆◆◆ SILVER AWARD
High Street, Pooley Bridge, Penrith CA10 2NH
T: (017684) 86334
F: (017684) 86851
E: b&b@elmhouse.demon.co.uk
I: www.elmhouse.demon.co.uk

Knotts Mill Country Lodge ◆◆◆
Watermillock, Penrith CA11 0JN
T: (017684) 86699
F: (017684) 86190
E: relax@knottsmill.com
I: www.knottsmill.com

Land Ends Country Lodge ◆◆◆
Watermillock, Ullswater, Penrith CA11 0NB
T: (017684) 86438
F: (017684) 86959
E: infolandends@btinternet.com
I: www.landends.co.uk

Moss Crag ◆◆◆
Eagle Road, Glenridding, Penrith CA11 0PA
T: (017684) 82500
F: (017684) 82500
E: info@mosscrag.co.uk
I: www.mosscrag.co.uk

Netherdene Guest House ◆◆◆
Troutbeck, Penrith CA11 0SJ
T: (01768) 483475
E: netherdene@aol.com
I: www.netherdene.co.uk

Tymparon Hall ◆◆◆◆
Newbiggin, Stainton, Penrith CA11 0HS
T: (01768) 483236
F: (01768) 483236
E: margaret@tymparon.freeserve.co.uk
I: www.tymparon.freeserve.co.uk

Whitbarrow Farm ◆◆◆◆
Berrier, Penrith CA11 0XB
T: (017684) 83366
F: (017684) 83179
E: mary@whitbarrowfarm.co.uk
I: www.whitbarrowfarm.co.uk

ULVERSTON
Cumbria

Trinity House Hotel ◆◆◆
Princes Street, Ulverston LA12 7NB
T: (01229) 588889
F: (01229) 588552
E: traininghotel@aol.com
I: www.traininghotel.co.uk

Virginia House Hotel ◆◆◆◆
24 Queen Street, Ulverston LA12 7AF
T: (01229) 584844
F: (01229) 588565
E: virginia@ulverstonhotels.co.uk
I: www.ulverstonhotels.com

'Lightburne' Georgian Town House
Rating Applied For
13 Prince's Street, Ulverston LA12 7NB
T: (01229) 581930
E: enquiries@lightburne.co.uk
I: www.lightburne.co.uk

UNDERBARROW
Cumbria

Tranthwaite Hall ◆◆◆◆
Underbarrow, Kendal LA8 8HG
T: (015395) 68285
E: tranthwaitehall@aol.com
I: www.tranthwaitehall.co.uk

Tullythwaite House
◆◆◆◆ SILVER AWARD
Underbarrow, Kendal LA8 8BB
T: (01539) 568397

WALTON
Cumbria

Town Head Farm ◆◆◆
Walton, Brampton CA8 2DJ
T: (01697) 72730
F: (01697) 72730
E: armstrong_townhead@hotmail.com
I: www.town-head-farm.co.uk

WARWICK BRIDGE
Cumbria

Brookside Bed and Breakfast ◆◆◆◆
Warwick Bridge, Carlisle CA4 8RE
T: (01228) 560250
E: debra.wearing@lycos.co.uk
I: www.brookside-online.co.uk

WARWICK-ON-EDEN
Cumbria

Queens Arms Inn ◆◆
Warwick-on-Eden, Carlisle CA4 8PA
T: (01228) 560699
F: (01228) 562239

WATERHEAD
Cumbria

Waterhead Country Guest House ◆◆◆
Waterhead, Coniston LA21 8AJ
T: (015394) 41442
F: (015394) 41476
E: waterheadsteve@aol.com
I: www.waterheadguesthouse.co.uk

WHITEHAVEN
Cumbria

Corkickle Guest House ◆◆◆◆
1 Corkickle, Whitehaven CA28 8AA
T: (019466) 92073
F: (019466) 92073
E: corkickle@tinyworld.co.uk

Establishments printed in blue have a detailed entry in this guide

Moresby Hall
♦♦♦♦ SILVER AWARD
Moresby, Whitehaven CA28 6PJ
T: (01946) 696317
F: (01946) 694385
E: etc@moresbyhall.co.uk
I: www.moresbyhall.co.uk

WINDERMERE
Cumbria

Alice Howe Guest House
Rating Applied For
The Terrace, Windermere
LA23 1AJ
T: (015394) 43325
E: info@alicehowe.co.uk
I: www.alicehowe.co.uk

Almaria House ♦♦♦
17 Broad Street, Windermere
LA23 2AB
T: (015394) 43026

Aphrodites Lodge ♦♦♦♦
Longtail Hill, Bowness-on-Windermere, Windermere
LA23 3JD
T: (015394) 45052
F: (015394) 46702
E: enquiries@aphroditeslodge.co.uk
I: www.aphroditeslodge.co.uk

Applegarth Hotel ♦♦♦
College Road, Windermere
LA23 1BU
T: (015394) 43206
F: (015394) 46636
E: info@lakesapplegarth.com
I: www.lakesapplegarth.com

Applethwaite House ♦♦♦
1 Upper Oak Street, Windermere
LA23 2LB
T: (015394) 44689
E: info@applethwaitehouse.co.uk
I: www.applethwaitehouse.co.uk

The Archway ♦♦♦♦
13 College Road, Windermere
LA23 1BU
T: (015394) 45613
F: (015394) 45613
E: archway@btinternet.com
I: www.communiken.com/archway

Ashleigh Guest House ♦♦♦♦
11 College Road, Windermere
LA23 1BU
T: (015394) 42292
F: (015394) 42292
E: enquiries@ashleighhouse.com
I: www.ashleighhouse.com

At the White Rose ♦♦♦
Broad Street, Windermere
LA23 2AB
T: (015394) 45180
E: whiteroselakes@lineone.net
I: www.whiteroselakes.co.uk

Autumn Leaves Guest House ♦♦♦
29 Broad Street, Windermere
LA23 2AB
T: (015394) 48410
E: autumnleaves@nascr.net
I: www.autumnleaves.gbr.cc

The Beaumont ♦♦♦♦♦
Holly Road, Windermere
LA23 2AF
T: (015394) 47075
F: (015394) 47075
E: thebeaumonthotel@btinternet.com
I: www.lakesbeaumont.co.uk

Beaumont ♦♦♦♦
Thornbarrow Road, Windermere
LA23 2DG
T: (015394) 45521
F: (015394) 46267
E: gocumbria@beaumont-holidays.co.uk
I: www.beaumont-holidays.co.uk

Beckmead House ♦♦♦
5 Park Avenue, Windermere
LA23 2AR
T: (015394) 42757
F: (015394) 42757
E: beckmead_house@yahoo.com

Beckside Cottage ♦♦♦
4 Park Road, Windermere
LA23 2AW
T: (015394) 42069
E: becksidecottage@hotmail.com

Beechwood Private Hotel
♦♦♦♦ SILVER AWARD
South Craig, Beresford Road, Bowness-on-Windermere, Windermere LA23 2JG
T: (015394) 43403
F: (015394) 43403

Belsfield House ♦♦♦♦
4 Belsfield Terrace, Bowness-on-Windermere, Windermere
LA23 3EQ
T: (015394) 45823
F: (015394) 45913
E: enquiries@BelsfieldHouse.co.uk
I: www.belsfieldhouse.co.uk

Boston House
♦♦♦♦ SILVER AWARD
4 The Terrace, Windermere
LA23 1AJ
T: (015394) 43654
E: stay@bostonhouse.co.uk
I: www.bostonhouse.co.uk

Bowfell Cottage ♦♦♦
Middle Entrance Drive, Storrs Park, Bowness-on-Windermere, Windermere LA23 3JY
T: (015394) 44835
F: (015394) 44835

Braemount House
♦♦♦♦ SILVER AWARD
Sunny Bank Road, Windermere
LA23 2EN
T: (015394) 45967
F: (015394) 45967
E: enquiries@braemount-house.co.uk
I: www.braemount-house.co.uk

Brook House ♦♦♦
30 Ellerthwaite Road, Windermere LA23 2AH
T: (015394) 44932
E: brookhouse@nascr.net

Brooklands ♦♦♦
Ferry View, Bowness-on-Windermere, Windermere
LA23 3JB
T: (015394) 42344
E: brooklandsferryview@btinternet.com
I: www.smoothhound.co.uk/hotels/brooklands

Cambridge House ♦♦♦
9 Oak Street, Windermere
LA23 1EN
T: (015394) 43846
F: (015394) 46662
E: reservations@cambridge-house.fsbusiness.co.uk
I: www.cambridge-house.net

Cedar Manor Country Lodge
♦♦♦♦♦ SILVER AWARD
Ambleside Road, Windermere
LA23 1AX
T: (015394) 43192
F: (015394) 45970
E: cedarmanor@fsbdial.co.uk
I: www.cedarmanor.co.uk

Clifton House ♦♦♦
28 Ellerthwaite Road, Windermere LA23 2AH
T: (015394) 44968
E: info@cliftonhse.co.uk
I: www.cliftonhse.co.uk

College House ♦♦♦♦
15 College Road, Windermere
LA23 1BU
T: (015394) 45767
E: clghse@aol.com
I: www.college-house.com

The Common Farm ♦♦♦
Windermere LA23 1JQ
T: (015394) 43433

The Cottage ♦♦♦
Elleray Road, Windermere
LA23 1AG
T: (015394) 44796
F: (015394) 44721
E: enquiries@thecottageguesthouse.com
I: www.thecottageguesthouse.com

Craig Wood Guest House ♦♦♦
119 Craig Walk, Bowness-on-Windermere, Windermere
LA23 3AX
T: (015394) 44914
F: (015394) 44914
E: fernix@globalnet.co.uk

Crompton House ♦♦♦
Lake Road, Windermere
LA23 2EQ
T: (015394) 43020
E: enquiries@cromptonhouse.com
I: www.cromptonhouse.com

Dene Crest ♦♦♦
Woodland Road, Windermere
LA23 2AE
T: (015394) 44979
E: denecrest@btinternet.com
I: www.denecrest.com

Denehurst Guest House ♦♦♦♦
40 Queens Drive, Windermere
LA23 2EL
T: (015394) 44710
E: denehurst@btconnect.com
I: www.denehurst-guesthouse.co.uk

Dunvegan Guest House ♦♦♦
Broad Street, Windermere
LA23 2AB
T: (015394) 43502
F: (015394) 47721
E: bryan.twaddle@btinternet.com
I: www.dunveganguesthouse.co.uk

Eastbourne ♦♦♦♦
Biskey Howe Road, Bowness-on-Windermere, Windermere
LA23 2JR
T: (015394) 43525
F: (015394) 43525
E: mail@eastbourne-guesthouse.co.uk
I: www.eastbourne-guesthouse.co.uk

Elim Lodge ♦♦♦
Biskey Howe Road, Bowness-on-Windermere, Windermere
LA23 2JP
T: (015394) 47299
E: enquiries@elimlodge.co.uk
I: www.elimlodge.co.uk

Fair Rigg
♦♦♦♦ SILVER AWARD
Ferry View, Bowness-on-Windermere, Windermere
LA23 3JB
T: (015394) 43941
E: rtodd51257@aol.com
I: www.fairrigg.co.uk

The Fairfield Garden Guest House ♦♦♦♦
Brantfell Road, Bowness-on-Windermere, Windermere
LA23 3AE
T: (015394) 46565
F: (015394) 46565
E: info@the-fairfield.co.uk
I: www.the-fairfield.co.uk

Fir Trees ♦♦♦♦
Lake Road, Windermere
LA23 2EQ
T: (015394) 42272
F: (015394) 42512
E: enquiries@fir-trees.com
I: www.fir-trees.com

Firgarth ♦♦♦
Ambleside Road, Windermere
LA23 1EU
T: (015394) 46974
F: (015394) 42384
E: thefirgarth@KTDinternet.com

Glenville House ♦♦♦♦
Lake Road, Windermere
LA23 2EQ
T: (015394) 43371
F: (015394) 48457
E: mail@glenvillehouse.co.uk
I: www.glenvillehouse.co.uk

Greenriggs Guest House ♦♦♦
8 Upper Oak Street, Windermere
LA23 2LB
T: (015394) 42265
E: greenriggs@talk21.com
I: www.greenriggs.co.uk

Haisthorpe Guest House ♦♦♦♦
Holly Road, Windermere
LA23 2AF
T: (015394) 43445
F: (015394) 46252
E: haisthorpe@clara.co.uk
I: www.haisthorpe-house.co.uk

Heather Cottage Guest House ♦♦♦
11 Broad Street, Windermere
LA23 2AB
T: (015394) 44616
F: (015394) 44616
E: bookings@heather-cottage.co.uk
I: www.heather-cottage.co.uk

Heatherbank Guest House ♦♦♦
13 Birch Street, Windermere
LA23 1EG
T: (015394) 46503
F: (015394) 46503
E: heatherbank@btinternet.com
I: www.heatherbank.com

High View ♦♦♦♦ SILVER AWARD
Sun Hill Lane, Troutbeck Bridge, Windermere LA23 1HJ
T: (015394) 44618
F: (015394) 42731
E: info@accommodationlakedistrict.com
I: www.accommodationlakedistrict.com

Hilton House ♦♦♦♦
New Road, Windermere
LA23 2EE
T: (015394) 43934
F: (015394) 43934
E: enquiries@hiltonhouse-guesthouse.co.uk
I: hiltonhouse-guesthouse.co.uk

Holly Lodge ♦♦♦
6 College Road, Windermere
LA23 1BX
T: (015394) 43873
F: (015394) 43873
E: anneandbarry@hollylodge6.fsnet.co.uk
I: www.hollylodge20.fsnet.co.uk

Holly-Wood ♦♦♦♦
Holly Road, Windermere
LA23 2AF
T: (015394) 42219
F: (015394) 42219
I: www.hollywoodguesthouse.co.uk

Holmlea ♦♦♦
Kendal Road, Bowness-on-Windermere, Windermere
LA23 3EW
T: (015394) 42597

Ivy Bank ♦♦♦♦
Holly Road, Windermere
LA23 2AF
T: (015394) 42601
E: ivybank@clara.co.uk
I: www.ivybank.clara.co.uk

Kays Cottage ♦♦♦♦
7 Broad Street, Windermere
LA23 2AB
T: (015394) 44146
E: kayscottage@freenetname.co.uk
I: www.kayscottage.co.uk

Kenilworth Guest House ♦♦♦
Holly Road, Windermere
LA23 2AF
T: (015394) 44004
E: busby@kenilworth-lake-district.co.uk

Kirkwood Guest House ♦♦♦♦
Princes Road, Windermere
LA23 2DD
T: (015394) 43907
F: (015394) 43907
E: info@kirkwood51.co.uk
I: www.kirkwood51.co.uk

21 The Lakes ♦♦♦♦
Lake Road, Windermere
LA23 2EQ
T: (015394) 45052
F: (015394) 46702
E: enquiries@21thelakes.co.uk
I: www.21thelakes.co.uk

Lakes Hotel ♦♦♦
1 High Street, Windermere
LA23 1AF
T: (015394) 42751
F: (015394) 46026
E: admin@lakes-hotel.com
I: www.lakes-hotel.com

Langdale View Guest House ♦♦♦
114 Craig Walk, Off Helm Road, Bowness-on-Windermere, Windermere LA23 3AX
T: (015394) 44076
E: enquiries@langdaleview.co.uk
I: www.langdaleview.co.uk

Latimer House ♦♦♦
Lake Road, Bowness-on-Windermere, Windermere
LA23 2JJ
T: (015394) 46888
F: (015394) 46888
E: latimerhouse@hotmail.com
I: www.latimerhouse.co.uk

Laurel Cottage ♦♦♦♦
St Martin's Square, Bowness-on-Windermere, Windermere
LA23 3EF
T: (015394) 45594
F: (015394) 45594
E: enquiries@laurelcottage-bnb.co.uk
I: www.laurelcottage-bnb.co.uk

Lindisfarne House ♦♦♦
Sunny Bank Road, Windermere
LA23 2EN
T: (015394) 46295
E: enquiries@lindisfarne-house.co.uk
I: www.lindisfarne-house.co.uk

Lingwood ♦♦♦♦
Birkett Hill, Bowness-on-Windermere, Windermere
LA23 3EZ
T: (015394) 44680
F: (015394) 48154
E: enquiries@lingwood-guesthouse.co.uk
I: www.lingwood-guesthouse.co.uk

Little Longtail ♦♦♦
Ferry View, Bowness-on-Windermere, Windermere
LA23 3JB
T: (015394) 43884

The Lonsdale ♦♦♦
Lake Road, Bowness-on-Windermere, Windermere
LA23 2JJ
T: (015394) 43348
F: (015394) 43348
E: lonsdale@fsbdial.co.uk
I: www.south-lakes.com

Lowfell ♦♦♦♦ SILVER AWARD
Ferney Green, Bowness-on-Windermere, Windermere
LA23 3ES
T: (01539) 445612
F: (01539) 448411
E: lowfell@talk21.com
I: www.low-fell.co.uk

Lynwood Guest House ♦♦♦♦
Broad Street, Windermere
LA23 2AB
T: (015394) 42550
F: (015394) 42550
E: enquiries@lynwood-guest-house.co.uk
I: www.lynwood-guest-house.co.uk

Meadfoot Guest House ♦♦♦♦
New Road, Windermere
LA23 2LA
T: (015394) 42610
F: (015394) 45280
E: enquiries@meadfoot-guesthouse.co.uk
I: www.meadfoot-guesthouse.co.uk

Melbourne Guest House Ltd. ♦♦♦
2 -3 Biskey Howe Road, Bowness-on-Windermere, Windermere LA23 2JP
T: (015394) 43475
F: (015394) 43475
E: info@melbournecottage.co.uk
I: www.melbournecottage.co.uk

Mount View Guest House ♦♦♦
New Road, Windermere
LA23 2LA
T: (015394) 45548

Mylne Bridge House ♦♦♦
Brookside, Lake Road, Windermere LA23 2BX
T: (015394) 43314
F: (015394) 48052
E: mylnebridgehouse@aol.com
I: www.mylnebridgehouse.co.uk

Oakbank House Hotel ♦♦♦♦♦
Helm Road, Bowness-on-Windermere, Windermere
LA23 3BU
T: (015394) 43386
F: (015394) 47965
E: enquiries@oakbankhousehotel.co.uk
I: www.oakbankhousehotel.co.uk

Oldfield House ♦♦♦♦
Oldfield Road, Windermere
LA23 2BY
T: (015394) 88445
E: ben.want@kencomp.net
I: www.oldfieldhouse.co.uk

Park Beck ♦♦♦
3 Park Road, Windermere
LA23 2AW
T: (015394) 44025
E: parkbeck@supanet.com
I: www.parkbeck.co.uk

1 Park Road ♦♦♦♦
Windermere LA23 2AW
T: (015394) 42107
F: (015394) 48997
E: enquiries@1parkroad.com
I: www.1parkroad.com

Ravensworth Hotel ♦♦♦♦
Ambleside Road, Windermere
LA23 1BA
T: (01539) 443747
F: (01539) 443670
E: ravenswth@aol.com
I: www.ravensworthhotel.co.uk

Rayrigg Villa Guest House ♦♦♦♦
Ellerthwaite Square, Windermere LA23 1DP
T: (015394) 88342
E: rayriggvilla@nascr.net
I: www.rayriggvilla.co.uk

Rocklea ♦♦♦♦
Brookside, Lake Road, Windermere LA23 2BX
T: (015394) 45326
F: (015394) 45326
E: info@rocklea.co.uk
I: www.rocklea.co.uk

St John's Lodge ♦♦♦
Lake Road, Windermere
LA23 2EQ
T: (015394) 43078
F: (015394) 88054
E: mail@st-johns-lodge.co.uk
I: www.st-johns-lodge.co.uk

Sandown ♦♦♦
Lake Road, Bowness-on-Windermere, Windermere
LA23 2JF
T: (01539) 445275
F: (01539) 445275

Squirrel Bank ♦♦♦♦ SILVER AWARD
Ferry View, Bowness-on-Windermere, Windermere
LA23 3JB
T: (015394) 43329
E: soar@squirrelbank.co.uk
I: www.squirrelbank.co.uk

Storrs Gate House ♦♦♦♦
Longtail Hill, Bowness-on-Windermere, Windermere
LA23 3JD
T: (015394) 43272
E: enquiries@storrsgatehouse.co.uk
I: www.storrsgatehouse.co.uk

Tarn Rigg ♦♦♦♦
Thornbarrow Road, Windermere
LA23 2DG
T: (015394) 88777
E: stay@tarnrigg-guesthouse.co.uk
I: www.tarnrigg-guesthouse.co.uk

Thornbank House ♦♦♦
4 Thornbarrow Road, Windermere LA23 2EW
T: (01539) 443724
F: (01539) 443724

Tudor House ♦♦
60 Main Street, Ellerthwaite Square, Windermere LA23 1DP
T: (01539) 442363

Villa Lodge ♦♦♦♦
25 Cross Street, Windermere
LA23 1AE
T: (015394) 43318
E: david@villa-lodge.co.uk
I: www.villa-lodge.co.uk

Watermill Inn ♦♦♦
Ings, Staveley, Kendal LA8 9PY
T: (01539) 821309
F: (01539) 822309
E: all@watermillinn.co.uk
I: www.watermill-inn.demon.co.uk

The Westbourne ♦♦♦♦
Biskey Howe Road, Bowness-on-Windermere, Windermere LA23 2JR
T: (015394) 43625
F: (015394) 43625
E: westbourne@btinternet.com
I: www.milford.co.uk

Westbury House ♦♦♦
27 Broad Street, Windermere LA23 2AB
T: (01539) 446839
F: (01539) 442784
E: tonybaker@aol.com

White Lodge Hotel ♦♦♦♦
Lake Road, Windermere LA23 2JJ
T: (015394) 43624
F: (015394) 44749
E: enquiries@whitelodgehotel.com
I: www.whitelodgehotel.com

The Windermere Hotel ♦♦♦
Kendal Road, Windermere LA23 1AL
T: (015394) 42251
F: (015394) 88903
E: gm.win@barbox.net
I: www.shearingsholidays.com

WORKINGTON Cumbria

Morven Guest House ♦♦♦
Siddick Road, Siddick, Workington CA14 1LE
T: (01900) 602118
F: (01900) 602118
E: cnelsonmorven@aol.com
I: www.smoothhound.co.uk/hotels/morvenguesthouse.html

The Old Ginn House ♦♦♦♦
Great Clifton, Workington CA14 1TS
T: (01900) 64616
F: (01900) 873384
E: enquiries@oldginnhouse.co.uk
I: www.oldginnhouse.co.uk

NORTHUMBRIA

ACOMB Northumberland

The Sun Inn ♦♦♦♦
Main Street, Acomb, Hexham NE46 4PW
T: (01434) 602934
F: (01434) 606635
E: alanmcjannet@aol.com
I: www.eclipseatthesun.co.uk

ALLENDALE Northumberland

Oakey Dene ♦♦♦♦
Allendale, Hexham NE47 9EL
T: (01434) 683572
F: (01434) 683572

Plane Trees ♦♦♦♦
Keenley, Allendale, Hexham NE47 9NT
T: (01434) 345236

Struthers Farm ♦♦♦
Catton, Allendale, Hexham NE47 9LP
T: (01434) 683580

Thornley House ♦♦♦♦
Allendale, Hexham NE47 9NH
T: (01434) 683255
E: e.finn@ukonline.co.uk

ALNMOUTH Northumberland

B&B with Beaches Restaurant ♦♦♦
57 Northumberland Street, Alnmouth, Alnwick NE66 2RS
T: (01665) 830443
F: (01665) 830443
E: le.chef@breathe.com
I: www.beaches6yo.co.uk

Beech Lodge ♦♦♦♦
8 Alnwood, Alnmouth, Alnwick NE66 3NN
T: (01665) 830709
I: www.alnmouth.com

Bilton Barns Farmhouse ♦♦♦♦ SILVER AWARD
Alnmouth, Alnwick NE66 2TB
T: (01665) 830427
F: (01665) 830063
E: dorothy@biltonbarns.co.uk
I: www.biltonbarns.co.uk

The Grange – Alnmouth Rating Applied For
Northumberland Street, Alnmouth, Alnwick NE66 2RJ
T: (01665) 830401
F: (01665) 830401
E: enquiries@thegrange-alnmouth.com
I: www.thegrange-alnmouth.com

Hipsburn Farm ♦♦♦♦
Hipsburn Farmhouse, Alnmouth, Alnwick NE66 3PY
T: (01665) 830206
F: (01665) 830206
E: star@hipsburnfarmhouse.com
I: www.hipsburnfarmhouse.com

Hope and Anchor Hotel ♦♦♦
44 Northumberland Street, Alnmouth, Alnwick NE66 2RA
T: (01665) 830363
F: (01665) 603082
E: debbiephilipson@hopeandanchorholidays.fsnet.co.uk
I: www.hopeandanchorholidays.co.uk

Red Lion Inn ♦♦♦
22 Northumberland Street, Alnmouth, Alnwick NE66 2RJ
T: (01665) 830584

ALNWICK Northumberland

Aln House ♦♦♦♦
South Road, Alnwick NE66 2NZ
T: (01665) 602265
E: bill@alnhousealnwick.worldonline.co.uk

Alndyke Farmhouse ♦♦♦
Alnmouth Road, Alnwick NE66 3PB
T: (01665) 510252

Aydon House ♦♦♦
South Road, Alnwick NE66 2NT
T: (01665) 602218
I: www.smoothhound.co.uk.aydonhouse

1 Bailiffgate Rating Applied For
Bailiffgate, Alnwick NE66 1LZ
T: (01665) 602078

Bondgate House ♦♦♦
20 Bondgate Without, Alnwick NE66 1PN
T: (01665) 602025
E: aclarvin@aol.com
I: www.bondgatehouse.ntb.org.uk

21 Boulmer Village ♦♦♦♦
Alnwick NE66 3BS
T: (01665) 577262

Bridge End Rating Applied For
1 Bridge End, Alnmouth, Alnwick NE66 3NF
T: (01665) 830614

Charlton House ♦♦♦♦
2 Aydon Gardens, South Road, Alnwick NE66 2NT
T: (01665) 605185
I: www.s-h-systems.co.uk/hotels/charlt2.html

Crosshills House ♦♦♦♦
40 Blakelaw Road, Alnwick NE66 1BA
T: (01665) 602518

East Cawledge Park Farm ♦♦♦
Alnwick NE66 2HB
T: (01665) 605705
F: (01665) 605963

The Georgian Guest House Rating Applied For
3 Hotspur Street, Alnwick NE66 1QE
T: (01665) 602398
F: (01665) 602398
E: enquiries@georgianguesthouse.co.uk
I: www.georgianguesthouse.co.uk

Hawkhill Farmhouse ♦♦♦♦ SILVER AWARD
Lesbury, Alnwick NE66 3PG
T: (01665) 830380
F: (01665) 830093
E: margery.vickers@care4free.net
I: www.hawkhillfarmhouse.co.uk

Lilburn Grange ♦♦♦
West Lilburn, Alnwick NE66 4PP
T: (01668) 217274

Limetree Cottage ♦♦♦♦
38 Eglingham Village, Alnwick NE66 2TX
T: (01665) 578322

Masons Arms ♦♦♦♦
Stamford, Rennington, Alnwick NE66 3RX
T: (01665) 577275
F: (01665) 577894
E: masonsarms@lineone.net
I: www.masonsarms.net

Norfolk ♦♦♦♦ SILVER AWARD
41 Blakelaw Road, Alnwick NE66 1BA
T: (01665) 602892
I: www.norfolk.ntb.org.uk

The Oaks Hotel ♦♦♦
South Road, Alnwick NE66 2PN
T: (01665) 510014
F: (01665) 603219
I: www.theoakshotel.co.uk

Reighamsyde ♦♦♦♦
The Moor, Alnwick NE66 2AJ
T: (01665) 602535
F: (01665) 603387
E: reighamsyde@aol.com

Rock Midstead Organic Farm House ♦♦♦
Rock Midstead Organic Farm, Rock, Alnwick NE66 2TH
T: (01665) 579225
F: (01665) 579326
E: ian@rockmidstead.freeserve.co.uk
I: www.rockmidstead.co.uk

Rooftops ♦♦♦♦ SILVER AWARD
14 Blakelaw Road, Alnwick NE66 1AZ
T: (01665) 604201
E: rooftops.alnwick@talk21.com
I: www.rooftops.ntb.org.uk

Ros View ♦♦♦
Chatton, Alnwick NE66 5PR
T: (01668) 215289
F: (01668) 215289
E: spearfish@btinternet.com

Roseworth ♦♦♦♦
Alnmouth Road, Alnwick NE66 2PR
T: (01665) 603911
E: bowden@roseworthann.freeserve.co.uk

Tower Restaurant and Accommodation ♦♦♦♦
10 Bondgate Within, Alnwick NE66 1TD
T: (01665) 603888
F: (01665) 603222
E: roylhardy@02.co.uk
I: www.tower-alnwick.co.uk

AMBLE
Northumberland

Coquetside ♦♦♦♦
16 Broomhill Street, Amble, Morpeth NE65 0AN
T: (01665) 710352

The Hollies ♦♦♦♦
3 Riverside Park, Amble, Morpeth NE65 0YR
T: (01665) 712323
E: terrihollies@clara.co.uk
I: www.the-hollies-amble.co.uk

Marine House ♦♦♦
20 Marine Road, Amble, Morpeth NE65 0BB
T: (01665) 711965

Togston Hall Farmhouse ♦♦♦
North Togston, Morpeth NE65 0HR
T: (01665) 712699
F: (01665) 712699

BAMBURGH
Northumberland

Broome ♦♦♦♦
22 Ingram Road, Bamburgh NE69 7BT
T: (01668) 214287
E: mdixon4394@aol.com

Glenander Bed & Breakfast ♦♦♦♦
27 Lucker Road, Bamburgh NE69 7BS
T: (01668) 214336
F: (01668) 214695
E: johntoland@tiscali.co.uk
I: www.glenander.com

Green Gates ♦♦♦
34 Front Street, Bamburgh NE69 7BJ
T: (01668) 214535
E: greengatesbamburgh@amserve.com
I: www.greengatesbamburgh.co.uk

Hillcrest House ♦♦♦♦ SILVER AWARD
29 Lucker Road, Bamburgh NE69 7BS
T: (01668) 214639
E: enquiries@hillcrest-bamburgh.co.uk
I: www.hillcrest-bamburgh.co.uk

Hillside Bed & Breakfast ♦♦♦♦ SILVER AWARD
25 Lucker Road, Bamburgh NE69 7BS
T: (01668) 214674
F: (01668) 214674
E: enquiries@hillside-bamburgh.com
I: www.hillside-bamburgh.com

Squirrel Cottage ♦♦♦♦
1 Friars Court, Bamburgh NE69 7AE
T: (01668) 214494
E: theturnbulls2k@btinternet.com
I: www.geocities.com/thetropics/bay/3021

BARDON MILL
Northumberland

The Bowes Hotel ♦♦♦
Bardon Mill, Hexham NE47 7HU
T: (01434) 344237
E: susanenright@boweshotel.fsnet.co.uk
I: www.boweshotel.co.uk

Gibbs Hill Farm ♦♦♦♦
Once Brewed, Bardon Mill, Hexham NE47 7AP
T: (01434) 344030
F: (01434) 344030
E: val@gibbshillfarm.co.uk
I: www.gibbshillfarm.co.uk

Montcoffer ♦♦♦♦♦ GOLD AWARD
Bardon Mill, Hexham NE47 7HZ
T: (01434) 344138
F: (01434) 344730
E: john-dehlia@talk21.com
I: www.montcoffer.co.uk

Strand Cottage Bed and Breakfast ♦♦♦♦
Main Road (A69), Bardon Mill, Hexham NE47 7BH
T: (01434) 344643
E: strandcottage@aol.com
I: www.strand-cottage.co.uk

Twice Brewed Inn ♦♦♦
Military Road, Bardon Mill, Hexham NE47 7AN
T: (01434) 344534
E: twicebrewed@hotmail.com
info@twicebrewed.co.uk
I: www.twicebrewedinn.co.uk

Vallum Lodge Hotel ♦♦♦♦
Military Road, Twice Brewed, Bardon Mill, Hexham NE47 7AN
T: (01434) 344248
F: (01434) 344488
E: vallum.lodge@ukonline.co.uk
I: www.vallumlodge.ntb.org.uk

BARNARD CASTLE
Durham

Bowes Moor Hotel ♦♦♦
Bowes Moor, Barnard Castle DL12 9RH
T: (01833) 628331
F: (01833) 628331
E: bowesmoorhotel@btopenworld.com
I: www.barnard-castle.co.uk/accommodation/bowes_moor_hotel.html

Bowfield Farm ♦♦
Scargill, Barnard Castle DL12 9SU
T: (01833) 638636

Cloud High ♦♦♦♦ GOLD AWARD
Eggleston, Barnard Castle DL12 0AU
T: (01833) 650644
F: (01833) 650644
E: cloudhigh@btinternet.com
I: www.cloud-high.co.uk

Demesnes Mill ♦♦♦♦♦ GOLD AWARD
Demesnes, Barnard Castle DL12 8PE
T: (01833) 637929
F: (01833) 637974
E: themillbarnardcastle@btopenworld.com
I: www.webproze.com/millbb

Greta House ♦♦♦♦ GOLD AWARD
89 Galgate, Barnard Castle DL12 8ES
T: (01833) 631193
F: (01833) 631193
E: gretahousebc@btclick.com

The Homelands ♦♦♦♦ SILVER AWARD
85 Galgate, Barnard Castle DL12 8ES
T: (01833) 638757
E: homelands@barnard-castle.fsnet.co.uk
I: www.barnard-castle.co.uk/accommodation

Marwood House ♦♦♦♦
98 Galgate, Barnard Castle DL12 8BJ
T: (01833) 637493
F: (01833) 637493
E: john&sheila@kilgarriff.demon.co.uk
I: www.kilgarriff.demon.co.uk

Montalbo Hotel ♦♦♦
Montalbo Road, Barnard Castle DL12 8BP
T: (01833) 637342
F: (01833) 637342
E: suzannethomas@montalbohotel.co.uk
I: www.montalbohotel.co.uk

Moorcock Inn ♦♦♦
Hill Top, Gordon Bank, Eggleston, Barnard Castle DL12 0AU
T: (01833) 650395
F: (01833) 650052
E: zach1@talk21.com
I: www.moorcock-Inn.co.uk

33 Newgate ♦♦♦
Barnard Castle DL12 8NJ
T: (01833) 690208
E: peter.whittaker@tinyworld.co.uk
I: www.barnard-castle.co.uk/accommodation/whittaker.html

Raygill Farm ♦♦♦
Lartington, Barnard Castle DL12 9DG
T: (01833) 690118
F: (01833) 690118
E: anne@raygillriding.co.uk
I: www.raygillriding.co.uk

Red Well Inn ♦♦♦♦
Harmire Road, Barnard Castle DL12 8QJ
T: (01833) 637002
F: (01833) 638023
E: reservations@redwellinn.info
I: www.redwellinn.info

Spring Lodge ♦♦♦
Newgate, Barnard Castle DL12 8NW
T: (01833) 638110
F: (01833) 630389
E: ormston@telinco.co.uk
I: www.smoothhound.co.uk/hotels/springlodge

Strathmore Lawn East ♦♦♦
81 Galgate, Barnard Castle DL12 8ES
T: (01833) 637061
E: strathmorelawn@bb81g.fsnet.co.uk

Wilson House ♦♦♦♦
Barningham, Richmond DL11 7EB
T: (01833) 621218
F: (01833) 621110

BARRASFORD
Northumberland

Barrasford Arms ♦♦♦
Barrasford, Hexham NE48 4AA
T: (01434) 681237
F: (01434) 681237
I: www.smoothhound.barrasfordarms.co.uk

BEADNELL
Northumberland

Beach Court ♦♦♦♦♦ SILVER AWARD
Harbour Road, Beadnell, Chathill NE67 5BJ
T: (01665) 720225
F: (01665) 721499
E: info@beachcourt.com
I: www.beachcourt.com

Beadnell House Hotel ♦♦♦♦
Beadnell, Chathill NE67 5AT
T: (01665) 721380
F: (01665) 720217
E: enquiries@beadnellhouse.co.uk
I: www.beadnellhouse.co.uk

Low Dover Beadnell Bay ♦♦♦♦ SILVER AWARD
Harbour Road, Beadnell, Chathill NE67 5BJ
T: (01665) 720291
F: (01665) 720291
E: kathandbob@lowdover.co.uk
I: www.lowdover.co.uk

The New Beadnell Towers Hotel ♦♦♦♦
Beadnell, Chathill NE67 5AU
T: (01665) 721211
F: (01665) 721070
E: thenewbeadnelltowers@hotel66.fsnet.co.uk
I: www.newbeadnelltowers.com

Shepherds Cottage ♦♦♦♦
Beadnell, Chathill NE67 5AD
T: (01665) 720497
F: (01665) 720497
I: www.shepherdscottage.ntb.org.uk

BEAL
Northumberland

Brock Mill Farmhouse ♦♦♦
Brock Mill, Beal, Berwick-upon-Tweed TD15 2PB
T: (01289) 381283
F: (01289) 381283
E: brockmillfarmhouse@btopenworld.com

West Mains House ♦♦♦
Beal, Berwick-upon-Tweed TD15 2PD
T: (01289) 381227

BEAMISH
Durham

The Beamish Mary Inn ♦♦♦
Beamish, Stanley DH9 0QH
T: (0191) 370 0237
F: (0191) 370 0091
E: beamishmary@hotmail.com
I: www.beamishmary.co.uk

The Coach House ♦♦♦♦
High Urpeth, Beamish, Stanley DH9 0SE
T: (0191) 370 0309
F: (0191) 370 0046
E: coachhouse@foreman25.freeserve.co.uk
I: www.coachhousebeamish.ntb.org.uk

Malling House ♦♦♦
1 Oakdale Terrace, Newfield, Chester-le-Street DH2 2SU
T: (0191) 370 2571
F: (0191) 370 2118
E: mallingguesthouse@freeserve.co.uk
I: www.mallinghouse.com

No Place House Bed & Breakfast ♦♦
Beamish, Stanley DH9 0QH
T: (0191) 370 0891
E: gaz@nobeam.fsnet.co.uk
I: www.noplace.co.uk

BELFORD
Northumberland

Detchant Farm ♦♦♦
Belford NE70 7PF
T: (01668) 213261
F: (01668) 219261
E: detchant@farming.co.uk

Easington Farm
♦♦♦♦ SILVER AWARD
Easington, Belford NE70 7EG
T: (01668) 213298

The Farmhouse Guest House ♦♦♦♦
24 West Street, Belford NE70 7QE
T: (01668) 213083

Fenham-le-Moor ♦♦♦♦
Fenham-Le-Moor, Belford NE70 7PN
T: (01668) 213247
F: (01668) 213247
E: katie@fenhamlemoor.com

Oakwood House
♦♦♦♦ GOLD AWARD
3 Cragside Avenue, Belford NE70 7NA
T: (01668) 213303
E: oakwood@ilz.com

BELLINGHAM
Northumberland

Bridgeford Farm ♦♦♦♦
Bridgeford, Bellingham, Hexham NE48 2HU
T: (01434) 220940

The Cheviot Hotel ♦♦♦
Main Street, Bellingham, Hexham NE48 2AU
T: (01434) 220696
F: (01434) 220696

Ivy Cottage ♦♦♦
Lanehead, Tarset, Hexham NE48 1NT
T: (01434) 240337
F: (01434) 240073

Lyndale Guest House ♦♦♦♦
Bellingham, Hexham NE48 2AW
T: (01434) 220361
F: (01434) 220361
E: ken&joy@lyndalegh.fsnet.co.uk
I: www.SmoothHound.co.uk/hotels/lyndale.html

Milburn House ♦♦♦♦
6 West View, Bellingham, Hexham NE48 2AH
T: (01434) 220318
F: (01434) 220318

BELMONT
Durham

Moor End House Bed and Breakfast ♦♦♦
7-8 Moor End Terrace, Belmont, Durham DH1 1BJ
T: (0191) 384 2796
F: (0191) 384 2796

BERWICK-UPON-TWEED
Northumberland

Alannah House
♦♦♦♦ SILVER AWARD
84 Church Street, Berwick-upon-Tweed TD15 1DU
T: (01289) 307252
I: www.alannahhouse.co.uk

Bridge View ♦♦♦♦
14 Tweed Street, Berwick-upon-Tweed TD15 1NG
T: (01289) 308098
E: lynda@lweatherley.freeserve.co.uk

Castlegate ♦♦♦
32 Castlegate, Berwick-upon-Tweed TD15 1JT
T: (01289) 306120

The Cat Inn ♦♦♦
Great North Road, Cheswick, Berwick-upon-Tweed TD15 2RL
T: (01289) 387251
F: (01289) 387251

Cear Urfa ♦♦♦♦
15 Springfield Park, East Ord, Berwick-upon-Tweed TD15 2FD
T: (01289) 303528

Clovelly House
♦♦♦♦ SILVER AWARD
58 West Street, Berwick-upon-Tweed TD15 1AS
T: (01289) 302337
F: (01289) 302052
E: vivroc@clovelly53.freeserve.co.uk
I: www.clovelly53.freeserve.co.uk

Cobbled Yard Hotel ♦♦♦
40 Walkergate, Berwick-upon-Tweed TD15 1DJ
T: (01289) 308407
F: (01289) 330623
E: cobbledyardhotel@berwick35.fsnet.co.uk
I: www.cobbledyardhotel.com

Dervaig Guest House
♦♦♦♦ SILVER AWARD
1 North Road, Berwick-upon-Tweed TD15 1PW
T: (01289) 307378
E: dervaig@talk21.com
I: www.dervaig-guesthouse.co.uk

Eastfield House ♦♦♦♦
6 North Road, Berwick-upon-Tweed TD15 1PL
T: (01289) 308949
E: info@eastfieldhouse-berwick.co.uk
I: www.eastfieldhouse-berwick.co.uk

Fairholm ♦♦♦♦
East Ord, Berwick-upon-Tweed TD15 2NS
T: (01289) 305370

Four North Road
♦♦♦♦ SILVER AWARD
4 North Road, Berwick-upon-Tweed TD15 1PL
T: (01289) 306146
F: (01289) 306146
E: sandra@thorntonfour.freeserve.co.uk
I: www.fournorthroad.co.uk

The Friendly Hound ♦♦♦♦
Ford Common, Berwick-upon-Tweed TD15 2QD
T: (01289) 388554
E: friendlyhound@aol.com
I: www.thefriendlyhound.co.uk

Heron's Lee
♦♦♦♦ SILVER AWARD
Thornton, Berwick-upon-Tweed TD15 2LP
T: (01289) 382000
F: (01289) 382000
E: john_burton@btconnect.com
I: www.northumbandb.co.uk

High Letham Farmhouse
♦♦♦♦♦ SILVER AWARD
High Letham, Berwick-upon-Tweed TD15 1UX
T: (01289) 306585
F: (01289) 304194
E: hlf-b@fantasyprints.co.uk
I: www.ntb.org.uk

Ladythorne House ♦♦♦♦
Cheswick, Berwick-upon-Tweed TD15 2RW
T: (01289) 387382
F: (01289) 387073
E: valparker@ladythorneguesthouse.freeserve.co.uk
I: www.ladythorneguesthouse.freeserve.co.uk

Meadow Hill Guest House ♦♦♦♦
Duns Road, Berwick-upon-Tweed TD15 1UB
T: (01289) 306325
F: (01289) 306325
E: barryandhazel@meadow-hill.co.uk
I: www.meadow-hill.co.uk

Middle Ord Manor
♦♦♦♦♦ GOLD AWARD
Middle Ord Farm, Berwick-upon-Tweed TD15 2XQ
T: (01289) 306323
F: (01289) 308423
E: joan@middleordmanor.co.uk
I: www.middleordmanor.co.uk

No 1 Sallyport
♦♦♦♦ SILVER AWARD
Off Bridge Street, Berwick-upon-Tweed TD15 1EZ
T: (01289) 308827
F: (01289) 308827
E: info@1sallyport-bedandbreakfast.com
I: www.1sallyport-bedandbreakfast.com

The Old Vicarage Guest House ♦♦♦♦
24 Church Road, Tweedmouth, Berwick-upon-Tweed TD15 2AN
T: (01289) 306909
F: (01289) 309052
E: stay@oldvicarageberwick.co.uk
I: www.oldvicarageberwick.co.uk

Orkney House ♦♦
37 Woolmarket, Berwick-upon-Tweed TD15 1DH
T: (01289) 331710

6 Parade ♦♦♦
Berwick-upon-Tweed TD15 1DF
T: (01289) 308454
F: (01289) 308454

40 Ravensdowne
♦♦♦♦ SILVER AWARD
Berwick-upon-Tweed TD15 1DQ
T: (01289) 306992
F: (01289) 301606
E: petedot@dmuckle.freeserve.co.uk
I: www.secretkingdom.com/40/ravensdowne.htm

Rob Roy ♦♦♦♦
Dock Road, Tweedmouth, Berwick-upon-Tweed TD15 2BE
T: (01289) 306428
F: (01289) 303629
E: therobroy@btinternet.com
I: www.therobroy.co.uk

Tweed View House ♦♦♦
16 Railway Street, Berwick-upon-Tweed TD15 1NF
T: (01289) 302864

West Coates ♦♦♦♦
30 Castle Terrace, Berwick-upon-Tweed TD15 1NZ
T: (01289) 309666
F: (01289) 309666
E: karenbrownwestcoates@yahoo.com
I: www.westcoates.ntb.org.uk

Whyteside House
♦♦♦♦ SILVER AWARD
46 Castlegate, Berwick-upon-Tweed TD15 1JT
T: (01289) 331019
F: (01289) 331419
E: albert@whyteside100.freeserve.co.uk
I: www.secretkingdom.com/whyte/side.htm

BISHOP AUCKLAND
Durham

Five Gables Guest House ♦♦♦♦
Binchester, Bishop Auckland DL14 8AT
T: (01388) 608204
F: (01388) 663092
E: book.in@fivegables.co.uk
I: www.fivegables.co.uk

The Old Farmhouse ♦♦♦♦
Grange Hill, Bishop Auckland DL14 8EG
T: (01388) 602123
F: (01388) 602123

BOWBURN
Durham

Prince Bishop Guest House ♦♦♦
1 Oxford Terrace, Bowburn, Durham DH6 5AX
T: (0191) 377 8703
E: enquiries@durhamguesthouse.co.uk
I: www.durhamguesthouse.co.uk

BRANCEPETH
Durham

Nafferton Farm ♦♦♦
Brancepeth, Durham DH7 8EF
T: (0191) 378 0538
F: (0191) 378 0538
E: sndfell@aol.com
I: www.nafferton-farm.co.uk

BRIGNALL
Durham

Lily Hill Farm ♦♦♦
Brignall, Barnard Castle
DL12 9SF
T: (01833) 627254
E: karonerrington@yahoo.co.uk

BROTTON
Tees Valley

The Arches ♦♦♦
Low Farm, Brotton, Saltburn-by-the-Sea TS12 2QX
T: (01287) 677512
F: (01287) 677150
I: www.gorally.co.uk

BYWELL
Northumberland

The Old Vicarage
♦♦♦♦ SILVER AWARD
Bywell, Stocksfield NE43 7AD
T: (01661) 842521
F: (01661) 844089
E: strachan@oldvicaragebywell.com
I: www.oldvicaragebywell.com

CARRSHIELD
Northumberland

Smallburns Farm
Rating Applied For
Carrshield, Hexham NE47 8AB
T: (01434) 345353
F: (01434) 345315
E: lisatomlin@softhome.net
I: www.smallburnsfarm.com

CASTLESIDE
Durham

Dene View ♦♦♦
15 Front Street, Castleside, Consett DH8 9AR
T: (01207) 502925
E: okeefe789@fsnet.co.uk

CHATHILL
Northumberland

North Charlton Farm
♦♦♦♦♦ GOLD AWARD
North Charlton, Chathill
NE67 5HP
T: (01665) 579443
F: (01665) 579407
E: ncharlton1@agricplus.net
I: www.northcharlton.com

Swinhoe South Farmhouse
Rating Applied For
Swinhoe, Chathill NE67 5AA
T: (01665) 589302
E: vlwrightssf@hotmail.com

CHATTON
Northumberland

South Hazelrigg Farmhouse
♦♦♦♦ SILVER AWARD
South Hazelrigg, Chatton, Alnwick NE66 5RZ
T: (01668) 215216
E: sdodds@farmhousebandb.co.uk
I: www.farmhousebandb.co.uk

CHESTER-LE-STREET
Durham

Hollycroft ♦♦♦♦
11 The Parade, Chester-le-Street
DH3 3LR
T: (0191) 388 7088
E: cutter@hollycroft11.freeserve.co.uk

Low Urpeth Farm House
♦♦♦♦
Ouston, Chester-le-Street
DH2 1BD
T: (0191) 410 2901
F: (0191) 410 0088
E: stay@lowurpeth.co.uk
I: www.lowurpeth.co.uk

CHOLLERFORD
Northumberland

Brunton Water Mill ♦♦♦♦
Chollerford, Hexham NE46 4EL
T: (01434) 681002
F: (01434) 681002
E: derekspqr@aol.com
I: www.bruntonwatermill.co.uk

CHOPPINGTON
Northumberland

The Anglers Arms ♦♦♦
Sheep Wash Bank, Choppington
NE62 5NB
T: (01670) 822300

The Swan Hotel ♦♦♦
Choppington NE62 5TG
T: (01670) 826060
F: (01670) 531143

CONSETT
Durham

Bee Cottage Farmhouse ♦♦♦
Castleside, Consett DH8 9HW
T: (01207) 508224
E: welcome@beecottagefarmhouse.freeserve.co.uk
I: www.smoothhound.co.uk/hotels/beecottage.html

Wharnley Burn Farm ♦♦♦
Castleside, Consett DH8 9AY
T: (01207) 508374
F: (01207) 503420

CORBRIDGE
Northumberland

Dilston Mill ♦♦♦♦
Corbridge NE45 5QZ
T: (01434) 633493
F: (01434) 633513
E: susan@dilstonmill.com
I: www.dilstonmill.com

Dilston Plains ♦♦♦
Dilston Plains, Corbridge
NE45 5RE
T: (01434) 602785
E: anderson.dilstonplains@btinternet.com
I: www.dilstonplains.co.uk

Fellcroft ♦♦♦♦
Station Road, Corbridge
NE45 5AY
T: (01434) 632384
F: (01434) 633918
E: tove.brown@ukonline.co.uk

The Hayes ♦♦♦
Newcastle Road, Corbridge
NE45 5LP
T: (01434) 632010
F: (01434) 632010
E: mjct@mmatthews.fsbusiness.co.uk
I: www.hayes-corbridge.co.uk

Holmlea ♦♦♦
Station Road, Corbridge
NE45 5AY
T: (01434) 632486

Low Fotherley Farmhouse Bed and Breakfast ♦♦♦♦
Riding Mill NE44 6BB
T: (01434) 682277
F: (01434) 682277
E: hugh@lowfotherley.fsnet.co.uk
I: www.westfarm.freeserve.co.uk

Priorfield
♦♦♦♦ SILVER AWARD
Hippingstones Lane, Corbridge
NE45 5JP
T: (01434) 633179
F: (01434) 633179
E: nsteenberg@btinternet.com

Riggsacre
♦♦♦♦ SILVER AWARD
Appletree Lane, Corbridge
NE45 5DN
T: (01434) 632617
E: atclive@supanet.com

Riverside Guest House ♦♦♦♦
Main Street, Corbridge NE45 5LE
T: (01434) 632942
F: (01434) 633883
E: david@theriversideguesthouse.co.uk
I: www.theriversideguesthouse.co.uk

Town Barns ♦♦♦♦
Off Trinity Terrace, Corbridge
NE45 5HP
T: (01434) 633345

CORNHILL-ON-TWEED
Northumberland

East Moneylaws ♦♦♦
Cornhill-on-Tweed TD12 4QD
T: (01890) 850265

COTHERSTONE
Durham

Glendale ♦♦♦
Cotherstone, Barnard Castle
DL12 9UH
T: (01833) 650384
I: www.barnard-castle.co.uk/accommodation/glendale.html

CRASTER
Northumberland

Cottage Inn ♦♦♦
Dunstan Village, Craster, Alnwick NE66 3SZ
T: (01665) 576658
F: (01665) 576788
E: enquiry@cottageinnhotel.co.uk
I: www.cottageinnhotel.co.uk

Howick Scar Farmhouse ♦♦♦
Craster, Alnwick NE66 3SU
T: (01665) 576665
F: (01665) 576665
E: howick.scar@virgin.net
I: www.howickscar.co.uk

Stonecroft
♦♦♦♦ SILVER AWARD
Dunstan, Craster, Alnwick
NE66 3SZ
T: (01665) 576433
F: (01665) 576311
E: sally@stonestaff.freeserve.co.uk
I: www.stonecroft.ntb.org.uk

CRESSWELL
Northumberland

Cresswell House ♦♦♦♦
Cresswell, Morpeth NE61 5LA
T: (01670) 861302

CROOK
Durham

Dowfold House ♦♦♦♦
Low Job's Hill, Crook DL15 9AB
T: (01388) 762473
E: hilarygill@dowfoldhouse.freeserve.co.uk
I: dowfoldhouse.mysite.freeserve.com

CROOKHAM
Northumberland

The Coach House at Crookham
♦♦♦♦
Crookham, Cornhill-on-Tweed
TD12 4TD
T: (01890) 820293
F: (01890) 820284
E: stay@coachhousecrookham.com
I: www.coachhousecrookham.com

CROXDALE
Durham

Croxdale Inn ♦♦♦
Front Street, Croxdale, Durham
DH6 5HX
T: (01388) 815727
F: (01388) 815368
E: croxdale@talk21.com

DARLINGTON
Tees Valley

Aberlady Guest House ♦
51 Corporation Road, Darlington
DL3 6AD
T: (01325) 461449

Boot & Shoe ♦♦♦
Church Row, Darlington
DL1 5QD
T: (01325) 287501
F: (01325) 287501
E: enquiries@bootandshoe.com
I: www.bootandshoe.com

The Chequers Inn ♦♦♦
Darlington DL2 2NT
T: (01325) 721213
F: (01325) 722357

Clow-Beck House
♦♦♦♦♦ GOLD AWARD
Monk End, Croft on Tees, Darlington DL2 2SW
T: (01325) 721075
F: (01325) 720419
E: david@clowbeckhouse.co.uk
I: www.clowbeckhouse.co.uk

Greenbank Guest House ♦♦♦
90 Greenbank Road, Darlington
DL3 6EL
T: (01325) 462624
F: (01325) 250233

Harewood Lodge ♦♦♦
40 Grange Road, Darlington
DL1 5NP
T: (01325) 358152
E: Harewood.Lodge@NTLWorld.com

DURHAM
Durham

The Anchorage ♦♦♦
25 Langley Road, Newton Hall, Durham DH1 5LR
T: (0191) 386 2323
F: (0191) 386 8315
E: anchorageb@aol.com
I: www.theanchorage.co.uk

The Autumn Leaves Guest House ♦♦♦
Dragonville, Durham DH1 2DX
T: (0191) 386 3394
E: irene@autumnleaves.freeserve.co.uk
I: www.autumnleavesguesthouse.co.uk

12 The Avenue ♦♦♦
Durham DH1 4ED
T: (0191) 384 1020
E: janhanim@aol.com

The Avenue Inn ♦♦
Avenue Street, High Shincliffe, Durham DH1 2PT
T: (0191) 386 5954
F: (0191) 375 7415
E: wenmah@aol.com

Belle Vue Guest House ♦♦♦
4 Belle Vue Terrace, Gilesgate Moor, Durham DH1 2HR
T: (0191) 386 4800

Broom Farm Guest House ♦♦♦♦
Broom Farm, Broom Park Village, Durham DH7 7QX
T: (0191) 386 4755

Castle View Guest House ♦♦♦♦
4 Crossgate, Durham DH1 4PS
T: (0191) 386 8852
F: (0191) 386 8852
E: castle_view@hotmail.com

Castledene ♦♦♦
37 Nevilledale Terrace, Durham DH1 4QG
T: (0191) 384 8386
F: (0191) 384 8386

Cathedral View Town House ♦♦♦♦ SILVER AWARD
212 Gilesgate, Durham DH1 1QN
T: (0191) 386 9566
E: cathedralview@hotmail.com
I: www.cathedralview.com

College of Saint Hild and Saint Bede Guest Rooms ♦
St Hild's Lane, Durham DH1 1SZ
T: (0191) 374 3069
F: (0191) 374 4740
E: l.c.hugill@durham.ac.uk
I: www.dur.ac.uk/HildBede

Collingwood College Cumbrian Wing ♦♦♦
South Road, Durham DH1 3LT
T: (0191) 334 5000
F: (0191) 334 5035
E: collingwood_college.conference@durham.ac.uk
I: www.collconf.co.uk

Durham University Conference & Tourism Ltd ♦♦♦
Trevelyan College (Macaulay Wing), Elvet Hill Road, Durham DH1 3LN
T: (0191) 334 7000
F: (0191) 334 5371
E: trev.coll@durham.ac.uk
I: www.dur.ac.uk/trev.coll

Farnley Tower ♦♦♦♦ SILVER AWARD
The Avenue, Durham DH1 4DX
T: (0191) 375 0011
F: (0191) 383 9694
E: enquiries@farnley-tower.co.uk
I: www.farnley-tower.co.uk

The Gables Hotel ♦♦
Front Street, Haswell Plough, Durham DH6 2EW
T: (0191) 526 2982
F: (0191) 526 2982
E: jmgables@aol.com
I: www.the-gables-durham.co.uk

The Georgian Town House ♦♦♦♦
10 Crossgate, Durham DH1 4PS
T: (0191) 386 8070
F: (0191) 386 8070
E: enquiries@georgian-townhouse.fsnet.co.uk

10 Gilesgate ♦♦
Gilesgate, Durham DH1 1QW
T: (0191) 386 2026
F: (0191) 386 2026

14 Gilesgate ♦♦
Top of Claypath, Durham DH1 1QW
T: (0191) 384 6485
F: (0191) 386 5173
E: bb@nimmins.co.uk
I: www.nimmins.co.uk

The Gilesgate Moor Hotel ♦♦♦
Teasdale Terrace, Gilesgate, Durham DH1 2RN
T: (0191) 386 6453
F: (0191) 386 6453

Green Grove ♦♦♦
99 Gilesgate, Durham DH1 1JA
T: (0191) 384 4361
E: green-grove@guesthouse.fsnet.co.uk
I: www.smoothhound.co.uk/hotels/greengro

Grey College ♦♦
South Road, Durham DH1 3LG
T: (0191) 334 5565
F: (0191) 334 5901
E: joyce.dover@durham.ac.uk
I: www.dur.ac.uk/GreyCollege

Hatfield College, Jevons ♦♦
North Bailey, Durham DH1 3RQ
T: (0191) 334 2614
F: (0191) 334 3101
E: a.m.ankers@durham.ac.uk
I: www.dur.ac.uk/Hatfield/college/confrnce.html

Hillrise Guest House ♦♦♦♦
13 Durham Road West, Bowburn, Durham DH6 5AU
T: (0191) 377 0302
F: (0191) 377 0898
E: hillrise.guesthouse@btinternet.com
I: www.hill-rise.com

Knights Rest ♦♦♦
1 Anchorage Terrace, Church Street, Durham DH1 3DL
T: (0191) 386 6229
F: (0191) 386 6229

O'Neills Inn ♦
91a Claypath, Durham DH1 1RG
T: (0191) 383 6951

St Aidan's College ♦♦♦
University of Durham, Windmill Hill, Durham DH1 3LJ
T: (0191) 334 5769
F: (0191) 334 5770
E: aidans.conf@durham.ac.uk
I: www.st-aidans.org.uk

St Chad's College ♦♦
18 North Bailey, Durham DH1 3RH
T: (0191) 334 3358
F: (0191) 334 3371
E: St-Chads.www@durham.ac.uk
I: www.dur.ac.uk/StChads/

Saint Cuthberts Society ♦♦
12 South Bailey, Durham DH1 3EE
T: (0191) 334 3379
F: (0191) 334 3401
E: i.d.barton@durham.ac.uk
I: www.dur.ac.uk/st-cuthberts.society

St Johns College ♦♦
3 South Bailey, Durham DH1 3RJ
T: (0191) 334 3877
F: (0191) 334 3501
E: s.i.hobson@durham.ac.uk
I: www.durham.ac.uk/st-johns.college

Seven Stars Inn ♦♦♦
Shincliffe Village, Durham DH1 2NU
T: (0191) 384 8454
F: (0191) 386 0640
I: www.sevenstarsinn.co.uk

Three Horse Shoes Inn ♦♦♦
Running Waters, Sherburn House, Durham DH1 2SR
T: (0191) 372 0286
F: (0191) 372 3386
E: m.s.parkinson@threehorseshoes.fsbusiness.co.uk
I: www.smoothhounds.co.uk

Triermayne ♦♦♦♦ SILVER AWARD
Nevilles Cross Bank, Durham DH1 4JP
T: (0191) 384 6036
E: annjim@tridur.freeserve.co.uk

Van Mildert College (Tunstall Stairs) ♦♦♦
Mill Hill Lane, Durham DH1 3LH
T: (0191) 334 7100
F: (0191) 334 7130
E: van-mildert.college@durham.ac.uk
I: www.dur.ac.uk/VanMildert/Conferences/together.htm

Victoria Inn ♦♦♦
86 Hallgarth Street, Durham DH1 3AS
T: (0191) 386 5269
F: (0191) 386 0465

Waterside ♦♦♦♦ SILVER AWARD
Elvet Waterside, Durham DH1 3BW
T: (0191) 384 6660
F: (0191) 384 6996

EAST ORD
Northumberland

Tweed View House ♦♦♦♦
East Ord, Berwick-upon-Tweed TD15 2NS
T: (01289) 332378
F: (01289) 332378
E: khdobson@aol.com
I: www.tweedview.8k.com

EASTGATE-IN-WEARDALE
Durham

Rose Hill Farm Bed and Breakfast ♦♦♦♦ SILVER AWARD
Rose Hill Farm, Eastgate-in-Weardale, Bishop Auckland DL13 2LB
T: (01388) 517209
E: june@rosehillfarm.fsnet.co.uk
I: www.rosehillfarmholidays.co.uk

EGLINGHAM
Northumberland

Ash Tree House ♦♦♦♦
The Terrace, Eglingham, Alnwick NE66 2UA
T: (01665) 578533
E: prudence@ukpc.net
I: www.ashtreehouse.com

EMBLETON
Northumberland

Blue Bell Inn ♦♦♦
Embleton, Alnwick NE66 3UP
T: (01665) 576573

The Sportsman ♦♦♦
6 Sea Lane, Embleton, Alnwick NE66 3XF
T: (01665) 576588
F: (01665) 576524
E: stay@sportsmanhotel.co.uk
I: www.sportsmanhotel.co.uk

ESCOMB
Durham

The Gables ♦♦♦
3 Lane Ends, Escomb, Bishop Auckland DL14 7SR
T: (01388) 604745

FALSTONE
Northumberland

The Blackcock Inn ♦♦♦
Falstone, Hexham NE48 1AA
T: (01434) 240200
E: blackcock@falstone.fsbusiness.co.uk
I: www.theblackcockinn.com

High Yarrow Farm ♦♦♦
Falstone, Hexham NE48 1BG
T: (01434) 240264

Woodside ♦♦♦♦
Yarrow, Falstone, Hexham NE48 1BG
T: (01434) 240443

FENHAM
Tyne and Wear

The Brighton ♦♦
47-49 Brighton Grove, Fenham, Newcastle upon Tyne NE4 5NS
T: (0191) 273 3600
F: (0191) 226 0563

FIR TREE
Durham

Duke of York Inn ♦♦♦♦ SILVER AWARD
Fir Tree, Crook DL15 8DG
T: (01388) 762848

FORD
Northumberland

The Estate House ♦♦♦♦ SILVER AWARD
Ford, Berwick-upon-Tweed TD15 2PX
T: (01890) 820668
F: (01890) 820672
E: theestatehouse@supanet.com
I: www.theestatehouse.co.uk

Hay Farm Farmhouse
◆◆◆◆ SILVER AWARD
Ford, Berwick-upon-Tweed
TD12 4TR
T: (01890) 820647
F: (01890) 820659
E: tinahayfarm@tiscali.co.uk
I: www.hayfarm.co.uk

The Old Post Office ◆◆◆
2 Old Post Office Cottages, Ford, Berwick-upon-Tweed TD15 2QA
T: (01890) 820286
E: jwait309139627@aol.com
I: www.secretkingdom.com

FOURSTONES
Northumberland

8 St Aidans Park ◆◆◆◆
Fourstones, Hexham NE47 5EB
T: (01434) 674073
F: (01434) 674073
E: info@8staidans.co.uk
I: www.8staidans.co.uk

FROSTERLEY
Durham

High Laithe ◆◆◆
10A Hill End, Frosterley, Bishop Auckland DL13 2SX
T: (01388) 526421

GATESHEAD
Tyne and Wear

The Bewick Hotel ◆◆◆
145 Prince Consort Road, Gateshead NE8 4DS
T: (0191) 477 1809
F: (0191) 477 6146
E: bewickhotel@hotmail.com
I: www.bewickhotel.co.uk

Shaftesbury Guest House
◆◆◆
245 Prince Consort Road, Gateshead NE8 4DT
T: (0191) 478 2544
F: (0191) 478 2544

GREAT TOSSON
Northumberland

Tosson Tower Farm
◆◆◆◆ GOLD AWARD
Great Tosson, Rothbury, Great Tosson, Morpeth NE65 7NW
T: (01669) 620228
F: (01669) 620228
E: stay@tossontowerfarm.com
I: www.tossontowerfarm.com

GREENHAUGH
Northumberland

Hollybush Inn
Rating Applied For
Greenhaugh, Hexham
NE48 1PW
T: (01434) 240391
E: timmorris.hollybush@virgin.net
I: www.vizual4U.co.uk/hollybush.htm

GREENHEAD
Northumberland

Four Wynds ◆◆◆
Longbyre, Greenhead, Brampton
CA8 7HN
T: (01697) 747330
F: (01697) 747330
E: rozhadrianswall@aol.com
I: www.bed-breakfast-hadrianswall.com

Holmhead Guest House
◆◆◆◆
Thirlwall Castle Farm, Hadrian's Wall, Greenhead, Brampton
CA8 7HY
T: (016977) 47402
F: (016977) 47402
E: Holmhead@hadrianswall.freeserve.co.uk
I: www.bandbhadrianswall.com

GRETA BRIDGE
Durham

The Coach House
◆◆◆◆◆ SILVER AWARD
Greta Bridge, Barnard Castle
DL12 9SD
T: (01833) 627201
E: info@coachhousegreta.co.uk
I: www.coachhousegreta.co.uk

GUISBOROUGH
Tees Valley

Fox and Hounds ◆◆◆
Slapewath, Guisborough
TS14 6PX
T: (01287) 632964
F: (01289) 610778
E: enquiries@fox-and-hounds.com
I: www.fox-and-hounds.com

Fox Inn ◆◆
10 Bow Street, Guisborough
TS14 6BP
T: (01287) 632958

Pinchinthorpe Hall ◆◆◆◆◆
Pinchinthorpe, Guisborough
TS14 8HG
T: (01287) 630200
F: (01287) 630200
E: nyb@pinchinthorpe.freeserve.co.uk
I: www.pinchinthorpehall.co.uk

Three Fiddles Hotel ◆◆
34 Westgate, Guisborough
TS14 6BA
T: (01287) 632417

HALTWHISTLE
Northumberland

Ashcroft
◆◆◆◆ SILVER AWARD
Lantys Lonnen, Haltwhistle
NE49 0DA
T: (01434) 320213
F: (01434) 321641
E: enquiries@ashcroftguesthouse.freeserve.co.uk
I: www.ashcroftguesthouse.co.uk

Broomshaw Hill Farm
◆◆◆◆◆ GOLD AWARD
Willia Road, Haltwhistle
NE49 9NP
T: (01434) 320866
F: (01434) 320866
E: stay@broomshaw.co.uk
I: www.broomshaw.co.uk

Doors Cottage Bed and Breakfast ◆◆◆
Shield Hill, Haltwhistle
NE49 9NW
T: (01434) 322556
E: doors-cottage@supanet.com

The Grey Bull Hotel ◆◆◆
Main Street, Haltwhistle
NE49 0DL
T: (01434) 321991
F: (01434) 320770
E: PamGreyB@aol.com
I: www.vizual4u.co.uk/greybull.htm

Hall Meadows ◆◆◆◆
Main Street, Haltwhistle
NE49 0AZ
T: (01434) 321021
F: (01434) 321021

Kirkholmedale B&B
Rating Applied For
Lantys Lonnen, Haltwhistle
NE49 0HQ
T: (01434) 322948

The Mount ◆◆◆
Comb Hill, Haltwhistle NE49 9NS
T: (01434) 321075
E: the-mount@talk21.com

Oaky Knowe Farm ◆◆◆
Haltwhistle NE49 0NB
T: (01434) 320648
F: (01434) 320648

Saughy Rigg Farm ◆◆◆
Twice Brewed, Haltwhistle
NE49 9PT
T: (01434) 344120
E: kathandbrad@aol.com
I: www.saughyrigg.co.uk

The Spotted Cow Inn ◆◆◆
Castle Hill, Haltwhistle
NE49 0EN
T: (01434) 320327
F: (01434) 320009

HAMSTERLEY
Durham

Dryderdale Hall ◆◆◆◆
Hamsterley, Bishop Auckland
DL13 3NR
T: (01388) 488494
F: (01388) 488494

HARBOTTLE
Northumberland

The Byre Vegetarian B&B
◆◆◆◆
Harbottle, Morpeth NE65 7DG
T: (01669) 650476
E: rosemary@the-byre.co.uk
I: www.the-byre.co.uk

HARTFORD BRIDGE
Northumberland

Woodside
◆◆◆◆ SILVER AWARD
Hartford Bridge Farm, Hartford Bridge, Bedlington NE22 6AL
T: (01670) 822035

HARTLEPOOL
Tees Valley

Brafferton Guest House ◆◆
161 Stockton Road, Hartlepool
TS25 1SL
T: (01429) 273875
E: braffertonguesthouse@yahoo.co.uk

Hillcarter Hotel ◆◆◆
31-32 Church Street, Hartlepool
TS24 7DH
T: (01429) 855800
F: (01429) 855829
E: hillcarter@btopenworld.com
I: www.hillcarterhotel.co.uk

The Oakroyd Hotel ◆◆◆
133 Park Road, Hartlepool
TS26 9HT
T: (01429) 864361
F: (01429) 890535
E: mandyoakroydhotel@hotmail.com

The York Hotel ◆◆◆
185 York Road, Hartlepool
TS26 9EE
T: (01429) 867373
F: (01429) 867220
E: info@theyorkhotel.co.uk
I: www.theyorkhotel.co.uk

HAYDON BRIDGE
Northumberland

Hadrian Lodge ◆◆◆
Hindshield Moss, North Road, Haydon Bridge, Hexham
NE47 6NF
T: (01434) 684867
F: (01434) 684867
E: hadrianlodge@hadrianswall.co.uk
I: www.hadrianswall.co.uk

Railway Hotel ◆◆◆
Church Street, Haydon Bridge, Hexham NE47 6JG
T: (01434) 684254

HEXHAM
Northumberland

Alcea House
Rating Applied For
8 Alexandra Terrace, Hexham
NE46 3JQ
T: (01434) 603370

10 Alexandra Terrace ◆◆◆
Hexham NE46 3JQ
T: (01434) 601954
E: davesue@onetel.net.uk
I: www.hexham.lookscool.com

Anick Grange ◆◆◆
Anick, Hexham NE46 4LP
T: (01434) 603807
F: (01434) 603807
E: julie@anickgrange.fsnet.co.uk

The Beeches ◆◆◆◆
40 Leazes Park, Hexham
NE46 3AY
T: (01434) 605900
E: peter@beeches1.demon.co.uk
I: www.bandbhexham.com

Black Hall
◆◆◆◆ SILVER AWARD
Black Hall, Juniper, Hexham
NE47 0LD
T: (01434) 673218
F: (01434) 673218
E: nblackhall@lineone.net
I: www.blackhall-hexham.co.uk

The County Hotel ◆◆◆
Priestpopple, Hexham NE46 1PS
T: (01434) 603601
F: (01434) 603616
E: the-county-hotel-hexham@supanet.com

Dene House
♦♦♦♦ SILVER AWARD
Juniper, Hexham NE46 1SJ
T: (01434) 673413
F: (01434) 673413
E: margaret@denehouse-hexham.co.uk
I: www.denehouse-hexham.co.uk

Dukesfield Hall Farm ♦♦♦♦
Steel, Hexham NE46 1SH
T: (01434) 673634
F: (01434) 673170
E: cath@dukesfield.supanet.com

Hetherington ♦♦♦♦
Hetherington Farm, Wark-on-Tyne, Wark, Hexham NE48 3DR
T: (01434) 230260
F: (01434) 230260
E: a_nichol@hotmail.com

High Reins ♦♦♦♦
Leazes Lane, Hexham NE46 3AT
T: (01434) 603590
E: walton45@hotmail.com
I: www.highreins.co.uk

Kitty Frisk House
♦♦♦♦ SILVER AWARD
Corbridge Road, Hexham NE46 1UN
T: (01434) 601533
F: (01434) 601533
E: alan@kittyfriskhouse.co.uk
I: www.kittyfriskhouse.co.uk

Laburnum House ♦♦♦♦
23 Leazes Crescent, Hexham NE46 3JZ
T: (01434) 601828
E: laburnum.house@virgin.net

Number 18 Hextol Terrace
♦♦♦
Hexham NE46 2DF
T: (01434) 602265

Peth Head Cottage
♦♦♦♦ SILVER AWARD
Juniper, Hexham NE47 0LA
T: (01434) 673286
F: (01434) 673038
E: tedliddle@compuserve.com
I: www.peth-head-cottage.co.uk

Queensgate House ♦♦♦
Cockshaw, Hexham NE46 3QU
T: (01434) 605592

The Rose and Crown Inn ♦♦♦
Main Street, Slaley, Hexham NE47 0AA
T: (01434) 673263

Rye Hill Farm ♦♦♦♦
Slaley, Hexham NE47 0AH
T: (01434) 673259
F: (01434) 673259
E: info@ryehillfarm.co.uk
I: www.ryehillfarm.co.uk

Thistlerigg Farm ♦♦♦
High Warden, Hexham NE46 4SR
T: (01434) 602041
F: (01434) 602041

Topsy Turvy ♦♦♦♦
9 Leazes Lane, Hexham NE46 3BA
T: (01434) 603152
E: topsy.turvy@ukonline.co.uk

West Close House
♦♦♦♦ GOLD AWARD
Hextol Terrace, Hexham NE46 2AD
T: (01434) 603307

West Wharmley ♦♦♦♦
West Wharmley Farm, Hexham NE46 2PL
T: (01434) 674227
F: (01434) 674227

Woodley Field ♦♦♦♦
Allendale Road, Hexham NE46 2NB
T: (01434) 601600
I: www.woodleyfield.co.uk

HOLY ISLAND
Northumberland

The Bungalow ♦♦♦♦
Chare Ends, Holy Island, Berwick-upon-Tweed TD15 2SE
T: (01289) 389308
E: bungalow@lindisfarne.org.uk
I: www.lindisfarne.org.uk/bungalow

Castlereigh ♦♦♦
Holy Island, Berwick-upon-Tweed TD15 2RX
T: (01289) 389218

Crown & Anchor Hotel ♦♦♦
Market Place, Holy Island, Berwick-upon-Tweed TD15 2RX
T: (01289) 389215
F: (01289) 389041

Lindisfarne Hotel ♦♦♦
Holy Island, Berwick-upon-Tweed TD15 2SQ
T: (01289) 389273
F: (01289) 389284

The Ship ♦♦♦
Marygate, Holy Island, Berwick-upon-Tweed TD15 2SJ
T: (01289) 389311
F: (01289) 389316
E: theship@lindisfarneaccommodate.com
I: www.lindisfarneaccommodate.com

HORSLEY
Northumberland

Belvedere ♦♦♦♦
Harlow Hill, Horsley, Newcastle upon Tyne NE15 0QD
T: (01661) 853689
E: pat.carr@btinternet.com
I: www.belvederehouse.co.uk

HOUSESTEADS
Northumberland

Beggar Bog ♦♦♦♦
Housesteads NE47 6NN
T: (01434) 344652
F: (01434) 344652

Moss Kennels Farm ♦♦♦♦
Haydon Bridge, Housesteads NE47 6NL
T: (01434) 344016
F: (01434) 344016
E: tim.mosskennels@virgin.net

HOWICK
Northumberland

The Old Rectory ♦♦♦♦
Howick, Alnwick NE66 3LE
T: (01665) 577139
F: (01665) 576004

HUMSHAUGH
Northumberland

Greencarts Farm ♦♦♦
Humshaugh, Hexham NE46 4BW
T: (01434) 681320
E: sandra.maughan2@zoom.co.uk

JARROW
Tyne and Wear

Bedeswell Guest House ♦♦♦
146 Bede Burn Road, Jarrow NE32 5AU
T: (0191) 428 4794
F: (0191) 483 7743
I: www.where2stay.co.uk

KIELDER
Northumberland

Deadwater Farm ♦♦♦♦
Deadwater, Kielder, Hexham NE48 1EW
T: (01434) 250216

KIELDER WATER
Northumberland

The Pheasant Inn (by Kielder Water) ♦♦♦♦
Stannersburn, Falstone, Hexham NE48 1DD
T: (01434) 240382
F: (01434) 240382
E: thepheasantinn@kielderwater.demon.co.uk
I: www.thepheasantinn.com

KIRKWHELPINGTON
Northumberland

Cornhills Farmhouse
♦♦♦♦ SILVER AWARD
Cornhills, Kirkwhelpington, Newcastle upon Tyne NE19 2RE
T: (01830) 540232
F: (01830) 540388
E: cornhills@northumberlandfarmhouse.co.uk
I: www.northumberlandfarmhouse.co.uk

LITTLETOWN
Durham

Littletown Lodge ♦♦♦
Front Street, Littletown, Durham DH6 1PZ
T: (0191) 372 3712
E: littletownlodge@aol.com
I: www.littletownlodge.co.uk

LONGFRAMLINGTON
Northumberland

The Angler's Arms ♦♦♦♦
Weldon Bridge, Longframlington, Morpeth NE65 8AX
T: (01665) 570655
F: (01665) 570041
I: www.anglersarms.com

Coquet Bed & Breakfast
♦♦♦♦
Elyhaugh Farm, Longframlington, Morpeth NE65 8BE
T: (01665) 570305
F: (01665) 570305
E: coquetbb@fsmail.net

Lee Farm ♦♦♦♦ GOLD AWARD
Rothbury, Morpeth NE65 8JQ
T: (01665) 570257
F: (01665) 570257
E: enqs@leefarm.co.uk
I: www.leefarm.co.uk

LONGHORSLEY
Northumberland

The Baronial ♦♦♦
Cross Cottage, Longhorsley, Morpeth NE65 8TD
T: (01670) 788378
F: (01670) 788378

Kington ♦♦♦
East Linden, Longhorsley, Morpeth NE65 8TH
T: (01670) 788554
F: (01670) 788747
E: clive@taylor-services.freeserve.co.uk

Thistleyhaugh Farm
♦♦♦♦♦ SILVER AWARD
Thistleyhaugh, Longhorsley, Morpeth NE65 8RG
T: (01665) 570629
F: (01665) 570629
E: stay@thistleyhaugh.com
I: www.thistleyhaugh.co.uk

LOWICK
Northumberland

Black Bull Inn ♦♦♦♦
Main Street, Lowick, Berwick-upon-Tweed TD15 2UA
T: (01289) 388228
E: tom@blackbullowick.freeserve.co.uk

Church Lane House ♦♦♦♦
Main Street, Lowick, Berwick-upon-Tweed TD15 2UD
T: (01289) 388591
E: churchlanehouse@yahoo.co.uk

MARSKE-BY-THE-SEA
Tees Valley

Ship Inn ♦♦♦
High Street, Marske-by-the-Sea TS11 7LL
T: (01642) 482640
F: (01642) 482640
E: shipmates@supanet.com

Zetland Hotel ♦♦♦
9 High Street, Marske-by-the-Sea TS11 6JQ
T: (01642) 483973

MIDDLESBROUGH
Tees Valley

Marton Hotel & Country Club Rating Applied For
Stokesley Road, Marton, Middlesbrough TS7 8DS
T: (01642) 317141
F: (01642) 325355
I: www.martonhotel.co.uk

Newlands Lodge Rating Applied For
62 Newlands Road, Middlesbrough TS1 3EJ
T: (01642) 245039

MIDDLETON-IN-TEESDALE
Durham

Belvedere House ♦♦♦♦
54 Market Place, Middleton-in-Teesdale, Barnard Castle DL12 0QH
T: (01833) 640884
E: belvedere@thecoachhouse.net
I: www.thecoachhouse.net

Brunswick House ♦♦♦♦
Market Place, Middleton-in-Teesdale, Barnard Castle DL12 0QH
T: (01833) 640393
F: (01833) 640393
E: enquiries@brunswickhouse.net
I: www.brunswickhouse.net

Cornforth & Cornforth ♦♦♦
16 Market Place, Middleton-in-Teesdale, Barnard Castle DL12 0QG
T: (01833) 640300
I: www.cornforthandcornforth.co.uk

Grove Lodge ♦♦♦♦
Hude, Middleton-in-Teesdale, Barnard Castle DL12 0QW
T: (01833) 640798

Ivy House ♦♦♦
Stanhope Road, Middleton-in-Teesdale, Barnard Castle DL12 0RT
T: (01833) 640603

Lonton South Farm ♦♦♦
Middleton-in-Teesdale, Barnard Castle DL12 0PL
T: (01833) 640409

Snaisgill Farm ♦♦♦
Snaisgill Road, Middleton-in-Teesdale, Barnard Castle DL12 0RP
T: (01833) 640343

Wemmergill Hall Farm ♦♦♦♦
Lunedale, Middleton-in-Teesdale, Barnard Castle DL12 0PA
T: (01833) 640379
E: wemmergill@freenet.co.uk
I: www.wemmergill-farm.co.uk

MOORSHOLM
Tees Valley

Green Ghyl ♦♦♦♦
10 Recreation View, Moorsholm, Saltburn-by-the-Sea TS12 3HZ
T: (01287) 669050
F: (01287) 669050
E: info@greenghyl.co.uk
I: www.greenghyl.co.uk

MORPETH
Northumberland

Cottage View Guest House ♦♦♦
6 Staithes Lane, Morpeth NE61 1TD
T: (01670) 518550
F: (01670) 510840
E: cottageview.morpeth@virgin.net
I: www.cottageview.co.uk

Cotting Burn House ♦♦♦
40 Bullers Green, Morpeth NE61 1DE
T: (01670) 503195
F: (01670) 503195
I: www.cottingburn.co.uk

Elder Cottage ♦♦♦♦ SILVER AWARD
High Church, Morpeth NE61 2QT
T: (01670) 517664
F: (01670) 517644
E: cook@eldercot.freeserve.co.uk
I: www.eldercottage.co.uk

Newminster Cottage ♦♦♦
High Stanners, Morpeth NE61 1QL
T: (01670) 503124

Northumberland Cottage ♦♦♦♦
3 Chevington Moor, Morpeth NE61 3BA
T: (01670) 783339
F: (01670) 783339
E: info@northumberland-cottage.co.uk
I: www.northumberland-cottage.co.uk

Riverside Guest House ♦♦♦
77 Newgate Street, Morpeth NE61 1BX
T: (01670) 515026
F: (01670) 514646
E: elaine.riverside@virgin.net
I: www.riverside-guesthouse.co.uk

NEW BRANCEPETH
Durham

Alum Waters Guest House ♦♦♦♦
Unthank Farmhouse, Alum Waters, New Brancepeth, Durham DH7 7JJ
T: (0191) 373 0628
F: (0191) 373 0628
E: tony@alumwaters.freeserve.co.uk

NEWBIGGIN-BY-THE-SEA
Northumberland

Seaton House ♦♦♦
20 Seaton Avenue, Newbiggin-by-the-Sea NE64 6UX
T: (01670) 816057

NEWBROUGH
Northumberland

Allerwash Farmhouse ♦♦♦♦♦ GOLD AWARD
Allerwash, Newbrough, Hexham NE47 5AB
T: (01434) 674574
F: (01434) 674574

Newbrough Park ♦♦♦♦ SILVER AWARD
Newbrough, Hexham NE47 5AR
T: (01434) 674545
F: (01434) 674544
E: newbroughpark@aol.com

NEWCASTLE UPON TYNE
Tyne and Wear

Avenue Hotel ♦♦♦
2 Manor House Road, Jesmond, Newcastle upon Tyne NE2 2LU
T: (0191) 281 1396
F: (0191) 281 6588

Chirton House Hotel ♦♦♦
46 Clifton Road, Off Grainger Park Road, Newcastle upon Tyne NE4 6XH
T: (0191) 273 0407
F: (0191) 273 0407

Elm Cottage ♦♦ SILVER AWARD
37 Sunniside Road, Sunnise, Newcastle upon Tyne NE16 5NA
T: (0191) 496 0156

Jesmond Park Hotel ♦♦♦
74-76 Queens Road, Jesmond, Newcastle upon Tyne NE2 2PR
T: (0191) 281 2821
F: (0191) 281 0515
E: vh@jespark.fsnet.co.uk
I: www.jesmondpark.com

The Keelman's Lodge ♦♦♦♦
Grange Road, Newburn, Newcastle upon Tyne NE15 8NL
T: (0191) 267 1689
F: (0191) 267 7387
E: admin@petersen-stainless.co.uk
I: www.biglamp.com

The Lynnwood ♦♦♦
1 Lynwood Terrace, Newcastle upon Tyne NE4 6UL
T: (0191) 273 3497
F: (0191) 226 0563

Westland Hotel ♦♦♦
27 Osborne Avenue, Jesmond, Newcastle upon Tyne NE2 1JR
T: (0191) 281 0412
F: (0191) 281 5005
I: www.westland-hotel.co.uk

NEWTON
Northumberland

Crookhill Farm ♦♦♦
Newton, Stocksfield NE43 7UX
T: (01661) 843117
F: (01661) 844702
E: catherineleech@amserve.com

NORHAM
Northumberland

Dromore House ♦♦♦
12 Pedwell Way, Norham, Berwick-upon-Tweed TD15 2LD
T: (01289) 382313

Threeways ♦♦♦♦
Norham, Berwick-upon-Tweed TD15 2JZ
T: (01289) 382795

NORTH HYLTON
Tyne and Wear

The Shipwrights Hotel ♦♦♦
Ferry Boat Lane, North Hylton, Sunderland SR5 3HW
T: (0191) 549 5139
F: (0191) 549 7464
E: tony@theshipwrights.freeserve.co.uk

NORTH SHIELDS
Tyne and Wear

No 61
Rating Applied For
61 Front Street, Tynemouth, North Shields NE30 4BT
T: (0191) 257 3687
E: no.61@btconnect.com
I: www.no61.co.uk

NORTH SUNDERLAND
Northumberland

The Old Manse ♦♦♦♦
9 North Lane, North Sunderland, Seahouses NE68 7UQ
T: (01665) 720521
F: (01665) 720574
E: carruthers@the-old-manse.freeserve.co.uk
I: www.the-old-manse.freeserve.co.uk

NORTON
Tees Valley

Grange Guest House ♦♦♦
33 Grange Road, Norton, Stockton-on-Tees TS20 2NS
T: (01642) 552541
I: www.shlwell.co.uk

OTTERBURN
Northumberland

Butterchurn Guest House ♦♦♦♦
Main Street, Otterburn, NE19 1NP
T: (01830) 520585
E: keith@butterchurnguesthouse.co.uk
I: www.butterchurnguesthouse.co.uk

Dunns Houses Farmhouse Bed and Breakfast ♦♦♦♦
Dunns Houses, Otterburn, Newcastle upon Tyne NE19 1LB
T: (01830) 520677
F: (01830) 520677
E: dunnshouses@hotmail.com
I: www.northumberlandfarmholidays.co.uk

Redesdale Arms Hotel ♦♦♦♦
Otterburn, Rochester, Newcastle upon Tyne NE19 1TA
T: (01830) 520668
F: (01830) 520063
E: redesdalehotel@hotmail.com
I: www.redesdale-hotel.co.uk

Woolaw Farm ♦♦♦
Rochester, Newcastle upon Tyne NE19 1TB
T: (01830) 520686
F: (01830) 520686
E: info@woolawfarm.co.uk
I: www.woolawfarm.co.uk

OVINGTON
Northumberland

Southcroft ♦♦♦♦
Ovington, Prudhoe NE42 6EE
T: (01661) 830651
F: (01661) 834312

PIERCEBRIDGE
Durham

The Bridge House ♦♦♦
Piercebridge, Darlington DL2 3SG
T: (01325) 374727
E: Elizabeth.formstone@virgin.net

Holme House ♦♦♦
Piercebridge, Darlington DL2 3SY
T: (01325) 374280
F: (01325) 374280
E: graham@holmehouse22.freeserve.co.uk

PITY ME
Durham

The Lambton Hounds Inn ♦♦♦
Front Street, Pity Me, Durham DH1 5DE
T: (0191) 386 4742
F: (0191) 375 0805
E: lambtonhounds@aol.com

PLAWSWORTH
Durham

Lilac Cottage ♦♦
Wheatley Well Lane, Plawsworth, Chester-le-Street DH2 3LD
T: (0191) 371 2969

PONTELAND
Northumberland

Hazel Cottage
♦♦♦♦ SILVER AWARD
Eachwick, Ponteland, Newcastle upon Tyne NE18 0BE
T: (01661) 852415
F: (01661) 854797
E: hazelcottage@eachwick.fsbusiness.co.uk
I: www.hazel-cottage.co.uk

Stone Cottage ♦♦♦
Prestwick Road End, Ponteland, Newcastle upon Tyne NE20 9BX
T: (01661) 823957
E: klee@euphony.net
I: www.stonecottageguesthouse.com

Stonehaven Lodge ♦♦♦
Prestwick Road End, Ponteland, Newcastle upon Tyne NE20 9BX
T: (01661) 872363
E: brenanderson@ncletw.freeserve.co.uk
I: www.stonehavenlodge.co.uk

POWBURN
Northumberland

Crawley Farmhouse ♦♦♦
Powburn, Alnwick NE66 4JA
T: (01665) 578413

QUEBEC
Durham

Hamsteels Hall ♦♦♦♦
Hamsteels Lane, Quebec, Durham DH7 9RS
T: (01207) 520388
F: (01207) 520388
E: June@hamsteelshall.co.uk
I: www.hamsteelshall.co.uk

RAMSHAW
Northumberland

The Bridge Inn ♦♦♦
1 Gordon Lane, Ramshaw, Bishop Auckland DL14 0NS
T: (01388) 832509
F: (01388) 832509
E: dcox59@aol.com
I: www.bridgeinn.ntb.org.uk

REDCAR
Tees Valley

A 2 Z Guest House ♦♦
71 Station Road, Redcar TS10 1RD
T: (01642) 775533

All Welcome In
Rating Applied For
81 Queen Street, Redcar TS10 1BG
T: (01642) 484790

Central Hotel ♦♦
44 Queen Street, Redcar TS10 1BD
T: (01642) 482309

Clarendon Hotel ♦♦
2 High Street, Redcar TS10 3DU
T: (01642) 484301
F: (01642) 775819
E: fitzyone44618340@:aol.com

Claxton Hotel ♦♦♦
196 High Street, Redcar TS10 3AW
T: (01642) 486745
F: (01642) 486522
E: enquiries@claxtonhotel.co.uk
I: www.claxtonhotel.co.uk

Falcon Hotel ♦♦♦
13 Station Road, Redcar TS10 1AH
T: (01642) 484300

The Kastle Hotel ♦♦
55 Newcomen Place, Redcar TS10 1DB
T: (01642) 489313

Ocean View Guest House
Rating Applied For
32 Arthur Street, Redcar TS10 1BW
T: (01642) 489536

Park Hotel
Rating Applied For
3-5 Granville Terrace, Redcar TS10 3AR
T: (01642) 490888
I: www.parkhotelredcar.co.uk

Red Barns Hotel
Rating Applied For
31 Kirkleatham Street, Redcar TS10 1QH
T: (01642) 477622
F: (01642) 493346

Regency Hotel
Rating Applied For
Coatham Road, Redcar TS10 1RP
T: (01642) 486221
I: www.regencyhotelredcar.co.uk

RIDING MILL
Northumberland

Broomley Fell Farm ♦♦♦
Riding Mill NE44 6AY
T: (01434) 682682
F: (01434) 682728
E: enquiries@broomleyfell.co.uk
I: www.broomleyfell.co.uk

Woodside House ♦♦♦♦
Sandy Bank, Riding Mill NE44 6HS
T: (01434) 682306

ROCK
Northumberland

Rock Farm House ♦♦♦
Rock, Alnwick NE66 3SD
T: (01665) 579471

ROMALDKIRK
Durham

Mill Riggs Cottage ♦♦♦
Romaldkirk, Barnard Castle DL12 9EW
T: (01833) 650392

ROOKHOPE
Durham

High Brandon ♦♦♦♦
Rookhope, Bishop Auckland DL13 2AF
T: (01388) 517673
E: highbrandonbb@aol.com
I: www.weardale-accommodation.co.uk

ROTHBURY
Northumberland

The Chirnells ♦♦♦♦
Thropton, Morpeth NE65 7JE
T: (01669) 621507
E: chirnells@aol.com

Farm Cottage Guest House
♦♦♦♦ SILVER AWARD
Thropton, Morpeth NE65 7NA
T: (01669) 620831
F: (01669) 620831
E: joan@farmcottageguesthouse.co.uk
I: www.farmcottageguesthouse.co.uk

The Haven ♦♦♦♦
Backcrofts, Rothbury, Morpeth NE65 7YA
T: (01669) 620577
F: (01669) 620766
E: the.haven.rothbury@talk21.com

Katerina's Guest House
♦♦♦♦ GOLD AWARD
Sun Buildings, High Street, Rothbury, Morpeth NE65 7TQ
T: (01669) 620691
F: (01669) 620691
E: cath@katerinasguesthouse.co.uk
I: www.katerinasguesthouse.co.uk

Lorbottle West Steads ♦♦♦
Thropton, Morpeth NE65 7JT
T: (01665) 574672
F: (01665) 574672
E: helen.farr@farming.co.uk
I: www.cottageguide.co.uk/lorbottle.html

Newcastle Hotel ♦♦♦
Rothbury, Morpeth NE65 7UT
T: (01669) 620334
F: (01669) 620334

Orchard Guest House ♦♦♦♦
High Street, Rothbury, Morpeth NE65 7TL
T: (01669) 620684
E: jpickard@orchardguesthouse.co.uk
I: www.orchardguesthouse.co.uk

The Queens Head ♦♦♦
Townfoot, Rothbury, Morpeth NE65 7SR
T: (01669) 620470
E: enqs@queensheadrothbury.com
I: www.queensheadrothbury.com

Silverton House ♦♦♦♦
Silverton Lane, Rothbury, Morpeth NE65 7RJ
T: (01669) 621395
E: silverton_house@lineone.net
I: www.silvertonhouse.co.uk

Silverton Lodge
♦♦♦♦♦ SILVER AWARD
Silverton Lane, Rothbury, Morpeth NE65 7RJ
T: (01669) 620144
E: info@silvertonlodge.co.uk
I: www.silvertonlodge.co.uk

Wagtail Farm ♦♦♦♦
Rothbury, Morpeth NE65 7PL
T: (01669) 620367
E: wagtail@tinyworld.co.uk
I: www.wagtailfarm.info

Whitton Farmhouse Hotel
♦♦♦♦
Whitton, Rothbury, Morpeth NE65 7RL
T: (01669) 620811
F: (01669) 620811
E: whittonfarmhotel@supanet.com
I: www.smoothhound.co.uk/hotels

RUSHYFORD
Durham

Garden House ♦♦♦♦
Windlestone Park, Windlestone, Rushyford, Ferryhill DL17 0LZ
T: (01388) 720217
E: info@gardenhousedurham.co.uk
I: www.gardenhousedurham.co.uk

RYTON
Tyne and Wear

Hedgefield House ♦♦♦
Stella Road, Ryton NE21 4LR
T: (0191) 413 7373
F: (0191) 413 7373

ST JOHN'S CHAPEL
Durham

Low Chesters Guesthouse ♦
Hood Street, St John's Chapel, Bishop Auckland DL13 1QP
T: (01388) 537406

SALTBURN-BY-THE-SEA
Tees Valley

Amble Guest House ♦♦♦
2 Bath Street, Saltburn-by-the-Sea TS12 1BJ
T: (01287) 622314

Diamond Quay ♦♦♦
9 Diamond Street, Saltburn-by-the-Sea TS12 1EB
T: (01287) 203149
F: (01287) 203149
E: diamondquay@aol.com

The Rose Garden ♦♦♦♦
20 Hilda Place, Saltburn-by-the-Sea TS12 1BP
T: (01287) 622947
F: (01287) 622947
E: enquiries@therosegarden.co.uk
I: www.therosegarden.co.uk

The Spa Hotel
Rating Applied For
Saltburn Bank, Saltburn-by-the-Sea TS12 1HH
T: (01287) 622544
F: (01287) 625870
E: saltburnreservations@spahotels.co.uk
I: www.spahotels.co.uk

'Merhba' Bed & Breakfast
♦♦♦
11 Dundas Street West, Saltburn-by-the-Sea TS12 1BL
T: (01287) 622566
E: pcookmerhba@ntlworld.co.uk

SEAHOUSES
Northumberland

Braidstone Lodge ♦♦♦
1 Braidstone Square, Seahouses NE68 7RP
T: (01665) 720055

Fairfield ♦♦♦
102 Main Street, Seahouses NE68 7TP
T: (01665) 721736
E: jen2col@fairfield1.fsnet.co.uk

Gun Rock ♦♦♦♦
15 St Aidans Road, Seahouses NE68 7SS
T: (01665) 721980
E: judy@gunrock.co.uk
I: www.gunrock.co.uk

Kingsway ◆◆◆◆
19 Kings Street, Seahouses
NE68 7XW
T: (01665) 720449
F: (01665) 720449
I: www.kingsway-guesthouse.co.uk

Leeholme ◆◆◆
93 Main Street, Seahouses
NE68 7TS
T: (01665) 720230
E: Lisaevans67@btinternet.com

Railston House
◆◆◆◆ SILVER AWARD
133 Main Street, North Sunderland, Seahouses
NE68 7TS
T: (01665) 720912
I: www.railstonhouse.net

Rowena ◆◆◆
99 Main Street, Seahouses
NE68 7TS
T: (01665) 721309

St Aidan Hotel ◆◆◆◆
1 St Aidans, Seafield Road, Seahouses NE68 7SR
T: (01665) 720355
F: (01665) 721989
E: enquiries@staidanhotel.co.uk
I: www.staidanhotel.co.uk

Sharrow
Rating Applied For
98 Main Street, Seahouses
NE68 7TP
T: (01665) 721794
E: enquiry@sharrow-seahouses.co.uk
I: www.sharrow-seahouses.co.uk

Springwood ◆◆◆◆
South Lane, Seahouses
NE68 7UL
T: (01665) 720320
F: (01665) 720146
E: ian@slatehall.freeserve.co.uk
I: www.slatehallridingcentre.com

Stoneridge ◆◆◆
15 Quarry Field, Seahouses
NE68 7TB
T: (01665) 720835

Union Cottage Guest House ◆◆◆◆
11 Union Street, Seahouses
NE68 7RT
T: (01665) 720169
E: info@unioncottage.com
I: www.unioncottage.com

Westfield Farmhouse ◆◆◆◆
North Sunderland, Seahouses
NE68 7UR
T: (01665) 720161
F: (01665) 720713
E: info@westfieldfarmhouse.co.uk
I: www.westfieldfarmhouse.co.uk

SEATON CAREW
Tees Valley

Aarondale Hotel ◆◆◆
46-48 Station Lane, Seaton Carew, Hartlepool TS25 1BG
T: (01429) 868868
F: (01429) 286250
E: aarondale@ntl.com

Altonlea Lodge Guest House ◆◆◆
19 The Green, Seaton Carew, Hartlepool TS25 1AT
T: (01429) 271289
E: enquiries@altonlea.co.uk
I: www.altonlea.co.uk

Durham Hotel ◆◆
38-39 The Front, Seaton Carew, Hartlepool TS25 1DA
T: (01429) 236502

Norton Hotel
Rating Applied For
The Green, Seaton Carew, Hartlepool TS25 1AR
T: (01429) 268317
F: (01429) 283777
E: susanrusson@hotmail.com

SEDGEFIELD
Durham

Forge Cottage ◆◆◆
2 West End, Sedgefield, Stockton-on-Tees TS21 2BS
T: (01740) 622831
F: (01740) 622831
E: forgecottage@tiscali.co.uk

Glower-Oer-Him Farm ◆◆
Sedgefield, Stockton-on-Tees TS21 3HO
T: (01740) 622737

Todds House Farm ◆◆◆
Butterwick Road, Sedgefield, Stockton-on-Tees TS21 3EL
T: (01740) 620244
F: (01740) 620244
E: edgoosej@aol.com
I: www.toddshousefarm.co.uk

SHINCLIFFE
Durham

The Bracken Hotel
◆◆◆◆ SILVER AWARD
Bank Foot, Shincliffe, Durham DH1 2PD
T: (0191) 386 2966
F: (0191) 384 5423
E: r.whitleybrackenhol@amserve.com
I: www.smoothhound.co.uk/hotels/bracken2.html

SHOTLEY BRIDGE
Durham

The Manor House Inn
◆◆◆◆ SILVER AWARD
Carterways Heads, Shotley Bridge, Consett DH8 9LX
T: (01207) 255268
F: (01207) 255268
I: www.scoot.co.uk/manor.house/

SIMONBURN
Northumberland

Simonburn Guest House ◆◆◆
The Mains, Simonburn, Hexham
NE48 3AW
T: (01434) 681321

SKELTON
Tees Valley

Westerland's Guest House ◆◆◆◆
27 East Parade, Skelton, Saltburn-by-the-Sea TS12 2BJ
T: (01287) 650690

The Wharton Arms ◆◆
133 High Street, Skelton-in-Cleveland, Saltburn-by-the-Sea
TS12 2DY
T: (01287) 650618

SLALEY
Northumberland

Flothers Farm ◆◆◆
Slaley, Hexham NE47 0BJ
T: (01434) 673240
F: (01434) 673240
E: dart@flothers.fsnet.co.uk
I: www.flothers.co.uk

Travellers Rest
◆◆◆◆ SILVER AWARD
Slaley, Hexham NE46 1TT
T: (01434) 673231
F: (01434) 673906
E: enq@travellersrest.sagehost.co.uk
I: www.travellersrest.sagesite.co.uk

SOUTH SHIELDS
Tyne and Wear

Ainsley Guest House ◆◆◆
59 Ocean Road, South Shields
NE33 2JJ
T: (0191) 454 3399
F: (0191) 454 3399
E: ainsleyguesthouse@hotmail.com

Aquarius Guest House ◆◆◆
61 Ocean Road, South Shields
NE33 2JJ
T: (0191) 422 3340
F: (0191) 422 3340
E: helen@aquariusguesthouse.fsnet.co.uk

Beaches Guest House ◆◆◆
81 Ocean Road, South Shields
NE33 2JJ
T: (0191) 456 3262
E: bill@beaches.fsworld.co.uk
I: www.smoothhound.com

Britannia Guesthouse ◆◆◆
54/56 Julian Avenue, South Shields NE33 2EW
T: (0191) 456 0896
F: (0191) 456 3203
E: cbgh56@hotmail.com
I: www.britanniaguesthouse.com

Forest Guest House ◆◆◆◆
117 Ocean Road, South Shields
NE33 2JL
T: (0191) 454 8160
F: (0191) 454 8160
E: enquiries@forestguesthouse.com
I: www.forestguesthouse.com

The Kingsmere ◆◆◆
9 Urfa Terrace, South Shields
NE33 2ES
T: (0191) 456 0234
F: (0191) 425 5026

The Magpies Nest ◆◆◆
75 Ocean Road, South Shields
NE33 2JJ
T: (0191) 455 2361
F: (0191) 455 1709
E: Christine.Taylor3@btinternet.com
I: www.magpies-nest.co.uk

Marina Guest House ◆◆◆
32 Seaview Terrace, South Shields NE33 2NW
T: (0191) 456 1998
F: (0191) 456 1998
E: austin@marina32.fsnet.co.uk

North View ◆◆◆
12 Urfa Terrace, South Shields
NE33 2ES
T: (0191) 454 4950
F: (0191) 454 4950

Ravensbourne Guest House ◆◆◆
106 Beach Road, South Shields
NE33 2NE
T: (0191) 456 5849
F: (0191) 427 7626
I: www.sanddancer.co.uk

River's End Guest House ◆◆◆
41 Lawe Road, South Shields
NE33 2EU
T: (0191) 456 4229
F: (0191) 456 4229
E: Brian@riversend.fsnet.co.uk
I: www.riversend.fsnet.co.uk

Saraville Guest House ◆◆◆
103 Ocean Road, South Shields
NE33 2JL
T: (0191) 454 1169
F: (0191) 454 1169
E: Emma@saraville.freeserve.co.uk
I: www.geocities.com/saravillehouse

Sir William Fox Hotel ◆◆◆
5 Westoe Village, South Shields
NE33 3DZ
T: (0191) 456 4554
F: (0191) 427 6312
I: www.sirwilliamfox.co.uk

South Shore ◆◆◆
115 Ocean Road, South Shields
NE33 2JL
T: (0191) 454 4049
F: (0191) 454 4049

SPENNYMOOR
Durham

The Gables ◆◆◆
10 South View, Middlestone Moor, Spennymoor DL16 7DF
T: (01388) 817544
F: (01388) 812533
E: thegablesghouse@aol.com
I: www.thegables.ntb.org.uk

Highview Country House ◆◆◆◆
Kirkmerrington, Spennymoor
DL16 7JT
T: (01388) 811006
F: (01388) 811006
E: highviewhouse@genie.co.uk
I: www.highviewcountryhouse.co.uk

Idsley House ◆◆◆◆
4 Green Lane, Spennymoor
DL16 6HD
T: (01388) 814237

SPITTAL
Northumberland

All Seasons ◆◆◆
46 Main Street, Spittal, Berwick-upon-Tweed TD15 1QY
T: (01289) 308452
E: r.horsburgh@btinternet.com

Caroline House ◆◆◆
110 Main Street, Spittal, Berwick-upon-Tweed TD15 1RD
T: (01289) 307595
E: carolinehouse@hotmail.com

The Roxburgh ◆◆
117 Main Street, Spittal, Berwick-upon-Tweed TD15 1RP
T: (01289) 306266

STAINDROP
Durham

Grove Farm ♦♦♦
Staindrop, Darlington DL2 3LN
T: (01833) 660327
F: (01833) 660886
E: info@grovefarmbreaks.fsnet.co.uk
I: www.grovefarmbreaks.co.uk

STANHOPE
Durham

Horsley Hall
♦♦♦♦♦ SILVER AWARD
Eastgate, Weardale, Stanhope, Bishop Auckland DL13 2LJ
T: (01388) 517239
F: (01388) 517608
E: hotel@horsleyhall.co.uk
I: www.horsleyhall.co.uk

STANLEY
Durham

Bushblades Farm ♦♦♦
Harperley, Stanley DH9 9UA
T: (01207) 232722

Harperley Hotel ♦♦♦
Harperley, Stanley DH9 9TY
T: (01207) 234011
F: (01207) 232325
E: harperley-hotel@supernet.com

STANNERSBURN
Northumberland

Spring Cottage ♦♦♦♦
Stannersburn, Hexham NE48 1DD
T: (01434) 240388
E: springcottage2000@yahoo.co.uk
I: www.ukgeocities.com/springcottageuk

STANNINGTON
Northumberland

Cheviot View Farmhouse Bed & Breakfast ♦♦♦♦
North Shotton Farm, Stannington, Morpeth NE61 6EU
T: (01670) 789231
E: julia.philipson1@btopenworld.com
I: www.cheviotviewfarmhouse.co.uk

STOCKSFIELD
Northumberland

Old Ridley Hall ♦♦♦
Stocksfield NE43 7RU
T: (01661) 842816
E: oldridleyhall@talk21.com

Wheelbirks Farm ♦♦♦♦
Stocksfield NE43 7HY
T: (01661) 843378
F: (01661) 842613
I: www.wheelbirks.ndo.co.uk

STOCKTON-ON-TEES
Tees Valley

Four Seasons Guest House ♦♦♦
314 Norton Road, Stockton-on-Tees TS20 2PU
T: (01642) 554826
F: (01642) 554826

The Parkwood Hotel ♦♦♦♦
64-66 Darlington Road, Stockton-on-Tees TS18 5ER
T: (01642) 587933
E: theparkwoodhotel@aol.co.uk
I: www.theparkwoodhotel.co.uk

SUNDERLAND
Tyne and Wear

Abingdon Guest House ♦♦♦
5 St George's Terrace, Roker, Sunderland SR6 9LX
T: (0191) 514 0689
E: karen@abingdonguesthouse.co.uk
I: www.abingdonguesthouse.co.uk

Acorn Guest House ♦♦
10 Mowbray Road, Hendon, Sunderland SR2 8EN
T: (0191) 514 2170
E: theacornguesthouse@hotmail.com

April Guest House ♦♦♦
12 Saint Georges Terrace, Roker, Sunderland SR6 9LX
T: (0191) 565 9550
F: (0191) 565 2415
E: ian@aprilguesthouse.fsnet.co.uk
I: www.aprilguesthouse.com

Areldee Guest House ♦♦♦
18 Roker Terrace, Sunderland SR6 9NB
T: (0191) 514 1971
F: (0191) 514 0678
E: peter@areldeeguesthouse.freeserve.co.uk
I: www.abbeyandareldeeguesthouses.co.uk

The Ashborne ♦♦♦
7 St George's Terrace, Roker, Sunderland SR6 9LX
T: (0191) 565 3997
F: (0191) 565 3997

The Balmoral Guest House ♦♦♦
3 Roker Terrace, Roker, Sunderland SR6 9NB
T: (0191) 565 9217
F: (0871) 433 4979
E: thebalmoral@supanet.com
I: www.thebalmoral.supanet.com

Beach View ♦♦♦♦
15 Roker Terrace, Sunderland SR6 9NB
T: (0191) 567 0719

Belmont Guest House
Rating Applied For
8 St Georges Terrace, Sunderland SR6 9LX
T: (0191) 567 2438
E: belmontguesthouse@freedomnames.co.uk

Braeside Holiday Guest House ♦♦
26 Western Hill, (Beside University), Sunderland SR2 7PH
T: (0191) 565 4801
F: (0191) 552 4198
E: george@the20thhole.co.uk
I: www.the20thhole.co.uk

Brendon Park Guest House ♦♦♦
49 Roker Park Road, Roker, Sunderland SR6 9PL
T: (0191) 548 9303
F: (0191) 548 9303
E: brendonpark@rokerguesthouse.fsnet.co.uk

Brookside Bed and Breakfast ♦♦♦
6 Brookside Terrace, Tunstall Road, Sunderland SR2 7RN
T: (0191) 565 6739
E: p.edgeworth@btopenworld.com

The Chaise Guest House ♦♦♦
5 Roker Terrace, Roker Seafront, Sunderland SR6 9NB
T: (0191) 565 9218
F: (0191) 565 9218
E: thechaise@aol.com

Felicitations ♦♦♦
94 Ewesley Road, High Barnes, Sunderland SR4 7RJ
T: (0191) 522 0960
F: (0191) 551 8915
E: felicitations_uk@talk21.com

Lemonfield Hotel ♦♦♦
Sea Lane, Seaburn, Sunderland SR6 8EE
T: (0191) 529 3018
F: (0191) 529 3018
E: gary@lemonfieldhotel.com
I: www.lemonfieldhotel.com

Mayfield Hotel ♦♦♦
Sea Lane, Seaburn, Sunderland SR6 8EE
T: (0191) 529 3345
F: (0191) 529 3345

Terrace Guest House ♦♦♦
2 Roker Terrace, Sunderland SR6 9NB
T: (0191) 565 0132
F: (08714) 334979
E: thebalmoral@supanet.com
I: www.thebalmoral.supanet.com

SWALWELL
Tyne and Wear

The Angel Guest House ♦♦♦
6 Front Street, Swalwell, Newcastle upon Tyne NE16 3DW
T: (0191) 496 0186
F: (0191) 496 0186
E: angel@swalwell.freeserve.com

SWARLAND
Northumberland

Swarland Hall Golf Club ♦♦♦
Coast View, Swarland, Morpeth NE65 9JG
T: (01670) 787940
I: www.swarlandgolf.co.uk

Swarland Old Hall
♦♦♦♦ GOLD AWARD
Swarland, Morpeth NE65 9HU
T: (01670) 787642
E: proctor@swarlandoldhall.fsnet.co.uk
I: www.swarlandoldhall.com

TANFIELD
Durham

Tanfield Garden Lodge ♦♦♦
Tanfield Lane, Tanfield, Stanley DH9 9QF
T: (01207) 282821
F: (01207) 282821

TANTOBIE
Durham

Oak Tree Inn ♦♦♦
Front Street, Tantobie, Stanley DH9 9RF
T: (01207) 235445
F: (01207) 235445
E: anne@dorbiere.co.uk

TARSET
Northumberland

Snabdough Farm
Rating Applied For
Tarset, Hexham NE48 1LB
T: (01434) 240239

THROPTON
Northumberland

Three Wheat Heads ♦♦♦
Main Street, Thropton, Morpeth NE65 7LR
T: (01669) 620262
F: (01669) 621281

TOW LAW
Durham

Bracken Hill Weardale
♦♦♦♦ SILVER AWARD
Thornley, Tow Law, Bishop Auckland DL13 4PQ
T: (01388) 731329
E: farrow@bracken-hill.com
I: www.bracken-hill.com

TWEEDMOUTH
Northumberland

Westsunnyside House ♦♦♦♦
Tweedmouth, Berwick-upon-Tweed TD15 2QH
T: (01289) 305387

TYNEMOUTH
Tyne and Wear

Martineau Guest House
♦♦♦♦ SILVER AWARD
57 Front Street, Tynemouth, North Shields NE30 4BX
T: (0191) 296 0746
F: (07946) 501863
E: martineau.house@ukgateway.net
I: www.martineau-house.co.uk

WALL
Northumberland

Blossom Hill Bed & Breakfast ♦♦♦♦
High Brunton, Wall, Hexham NE46 4EH
T: (01434) 681274
F: (01434) 681274
E: jproudlock@lineone.net
I: www.blossom-hill.co.uk

The Hadrian Hotel ♦♦♦
Wall, Hexham NE46 4EE
T: (01434) 681232
E: david.lindsay13@btinternet.com
I: www.hadrianhotel.com

St Oswalds Farm ♦♦
Wall, Hexham NE46 4HB
T: (01434) 681307
E: ereay@fish.co.uk

WALLSEND
Tyne and Wear

Imperial Guest House ♦♦♦♦
194 Station Road, Wallsend NE28 8RD
T: (0191) 236 9808
F: (0191) 236 9808
E: enquiries@imperialguesthouse.co.uk
I: www.imperialguesthouse.co.uk

WARK
Northumberland

Battlesteads Hotel ♦♦♦
Wark, Hexham NE48 3LS
T: (01434) 230209
F: (01434) 230730
E: info@battlesteads-hotel.co.uk
I: www.Battlesteads-Hotel.co.uk

WARKWORTH
Northumberland

Beck 'N' Call ♦♦♦♦
Birling West Cottage, Warkworth, Morpeth NE65 0XS
T: (01665) 711653
E: beck-n-call@lineone.net
I: www.beck-n-call.co.uk

The Old Manse ♦♦♦♦
20 The Butts, Warkworth, Morpeth NE65 0SS
T: (01665) 710850
F: (01665) 710850

Roxbro House ♦♦♦♦
5 Castle Terrace, Warkworth, Morpeth NE65 0UP
T: (01665) 711416
E: roxborohouse@aol.com

7 Woodlands
Rating Applied For
Warkworth, Morpeth NE65 0SY
T: (01665) 711263
E: edithandjohn@another.com
I: www.accta.co.uk/north

WASHINGTON
Tyne and Wear

Ye Olde Cop Shop ♦♦♦♦
6 The Green, Washington Village, Washington NE38 7AB
T: (0191) 416 5333
F: (0191) 416 5333
E: yeoldecopshop@btinternet.com

WATERHOUSES
Durham

Ivesley ♦♦♦♦
Waterhouses, Durham DH7 9HB
T: (0191) 373 4324
F: (0191) 373 4757
E: ivesley@msn.com
I: www.ridingholidays-ivesley.co.uk

WEST AUCKLAND
Durham

Wheatside Hotel ♦♦
Bildershaw Bank, West Auckland, Bishop Auckland DL14 9PL
T: (01388) 832725
F: (01388) 832485

WEST WOODBURN
Northumberland

Bay Horse Inn ♦♦♦♦
West Woodburn, Hexham NE48 2RX
T: (01434) 270218
F: (01434) 270118

Plevna House
♦♦♦♦ SILVER AWARD
West Woodburn, Hexham NE48 2RA
T: (01434) 270369
F: (01434) 270179
E: bookings@plevnahouse.fsnet.co.uk
I: www.plevnahouse.ntb.org.uk

Yellow House Farm
Rating Applied For
West Woodburn, Hexham NE48 2SB
T: (01434) 270070
F: (01434) 270070
E: avril@yellowhousebandb.co.uk
I: www.yellowhousebandb.co.uk

WESTGATE-IN-WEARDALE
Durham

Lands Farm
♦♦♦♦ SILVER AWARD
Westgate-in-Weardale, Bishop Auckland DL13 1SN
T: (01388) 517210
F: (01388) 517210
E: barbara@landsfarm.fsnet.co.uk

WHICKHAM
Tyne and Wear

East Byermoor Guest House
♦♦♦♦ SILVER AWARD
Fellside Road, Whickham, Newcastle upon Tyne NE16 5BD
T: (01207) 272687
F: (01207) 272145
E: eastbyermoor-gh.arbon@virgin.net
I: www.eastbyermoor.co.uk

WHITFIELD
Northumberland

The Elk's Head ♦♦♦♦
Whitfield, Hexham NE47 8HD
T: (01434) 345282
F: (01434) 345034
E: elkshead@amserve.com
I: www.elkshead.co.uk

WHITLEY BAY
Tyne and Wear

Caprice Hotel ♦♦♦
14-16 South Parade, Whitley Bay NE26 2RG
T: (0191) 253 0141
F: (0191) 252 3329
E: stay@caprice-hotel.co.uk
I: www.caprice-hotel.co.uk

The Cara ♦♦♦
9 The Links, Whitley Bay NE26 1PS
T: (0191) 253 0172
I: www.thecara.co.uk

Chedburgh Hotel ♦♦♦
12 The Esplanade, Whitley Bay NE26 1AH
T: (0191) 253 0415
F: (0191) 253 0415
E: chedburghhotel@aol.com
I: www.SmoothHound.co.uk

The Glen Esk Guest House
♦♦♦
8 South Parade, Whitley Bay NE26 2RG
T: (0191) 253 0103
F: (0191) 253 0103
E: the.glenesk@talk21.com

Lindsay Guest House ♦♦♦♦
50 Victoria Avenue, Whitley Bay NE26 2BA
T: (0191) 252 7341
F: (0191) 252 7505
E: info@lindsayguesthouse.co.uk
I: www.lindsayguesthouse.co.uk

Marlborough Hotel ♦♦♦♦
20-21 East Parade, The Promenade, Whitley Bay NE26 1AP
T: (0191) 251 3628
F: (0191) 252 5033
E: reception@marlborough-hotel.com
I: www.marlborough-hotel.com

Shan-Gri-La ♦
29 Esplanade, Whitley Bay NE26 2AL
T: (0191) 253 0230

York House Hotel & Apartments Ltd ♦♦♦♦
106-110 Park Avenue, Whitley Bay NE26 1Dn
T: (0191) 252 8313
F: (0191) 251 3953
E: reservations@yorkhousehotel.com
I: www.yorkhousehotel.com

WHITTINGHAM
Northumberland

Callaly Cottage Bed and Breakfast ♦♦♦♦
Callaly, Alnwick NE66 4TA
T: (01665) 574684
E: callaly@alnwick.org.uk
I: www.callaly.alnwick.org.uk

WITTON GILBERT
Durham

The Coach House ♦♦♦♦
Stobbilee House, Witton Gilbert, Durham DH7 6TW
T: (0191) 373 6132
F: (0191) 373 6711
E: suzanne.cronin@btinternet.com
I: www.stobbilee.com

WOLSINGHAM
Durham

Bradley Hall ♦♦♦♦♦
Wolsingham, Bishop Auckland DL13 3JH
T: (01388) 527280
F: (08701) 374975
E: cjs@bradleyhall.net
I: www.bradleyhall.net

Holywell Farm ♦♦♦♦
Holywell Lane, Wolsingham, Bishop Auckland DL13 3HB
T: (01388) 527249
F: (01388) 527249

WOOLER
Northumberland

The Black Bull Hotel ♦♦♦
1 The High Street, Wooler NE71 6BY
T: (01668) 281309
I: www.theblackbullhotel.co.uk

Kimmerston Farmhouse Bed and Breakfast ♦♦♦♦
Kimmerston, Wooler NE71 6JH
T: (01668) 216301
F: (01668) 216311
E: stay@kimmerstonfarmhouse.com
I: www.kimmerstonfarmhouse.co.uk

The Old Manse
♦♦♦♦♦ GOLD AWARD
New Road, Chatton, Alnwick NE66 5PU
T: (01668) 215343
F: (01668) 215343
E: chattonbb@aol.com
I: www.oldmansechatton.co.uk

Ryecroft Hotel ♦♦♦
28 Ryecroft Way, Wooler NE71 6AB
T: (01668) 281459
F: (01668) 282214
E: ryecrofthtl@aol.com
I: www.ryecroft-hotel.com

Saint Hilliers ♦♦♦
6 Church Street, Wooler NE71 6DA
T: (01668) 281340
E: mhugall@onetel.net.uk

Tilldale House ♦♦♦♦
34-40 High Street, Wooler NE71 6BG
T: (01668) 281450
E: tilldalehouse@freezone.co.uk

West Weetwood Farmhouse
♦♦♦♦
West Weetwood, Wooler NE71 6AQ
T: (01668) 281497
F: (01668) 281497

WYLAM
Northumberland

Wormald House ♦♦♦♦
Main Street, Wylam NE41 8DN
T: (01661) 852529
F: (01661) 852529
E: john.craven3@btinternet.com

NORTH WEST

ABBEYSTEAD
Lancashire

Greenbank Farmhouse ♦♦♦
Abbeystead, Lancaster LA2 9BA
T: (01524) 792063
F: (01524) 792063
E: tait@greenbankfarmhouse.freeserve.co.uk.
I: www.greenbankfarmhouse.co.uk

ACCRINGTON
Lancashire

Horizons Hotel and Restaurant Traders Brasserie ♦♦♦
The Globe Centre, St James Square, Accrington BB5 0RE
T: (01254) 602020
F: (01254) 602021
E: horizons@theglobe111.fsnet.co.uk

Maple Lodge Hotel ♦♦♦
70 Blackburn Road, Clayton-le-Moors, Accrington BB5 5JH
T: (01254) 301284
F: (01254) 388152
E: maplelod@aol.com
I: http://www.maplelodgehotel.co.uk

Norwood Guest House ♦♦♦♦
349 Whalley Road, Accrington BB5 5DF
T: (01254) 398132
F: (01254) 398132
E: stuart@norwoodguesthouse.co.uk
I: www.norwoodguesthouse.co.uk

ACTON BRIDGE
Cheshire

Manor Farm ♦♦♦♦
Cliff Road, Acton Bridge, Northwich CW8 3QP
T: (01606) 853181
F: (01606) 853181
E: terri.mac.manorfarm@care4free.net

AINTREE
Merseyside

A Church View Guest House ♦♦
7 Church Avenue, Aintree, Liverpool L9 4SG
T: (0151) 525 8166

ALDERLEY EDGE
Cheshire

Mayfield
Rating Applied For
Wilmslow Road, Alderley Edge SK9 7QW
T: (01625) 583991

ALPRAHAM
Cheshire

Tollemache Arms ♦♦♦
Chester Road, Alpraham, Tarporley CW6 9JE
T: (01829) 260030
F: (01829) 260030

ALVASTON
Cheshire

Alvaston Hall Hotel
Rating Applied For
Middlewich Road, Nantwich CW5 6PD
T: (01270) 624341
F: (01270) 623395
I: www.warnervacations.com

ANDERTON
Cheshire

Park Villa Guest House
Rating Applied For
9 Dyar Terrace, Northwich CW8 4DN
T: (01606) 74533
F: (01606) 74533
E: paul@parkvilla.co.uk

APPLETON
Cheshire

Birchdale Hotel ♦♦♦
Birchdale Road, Appleton, Warrington WA4 5AW
T: (01925) 263662
F: (01925) 860607
E: rfw@birchdalehotel.co.uk
I: www.birchdalehotel.co.uk

ARKHOLME
Lancashire

Redwell Inn ♦♦♦
Kirkby Lonsdale Road, Arkholme, Carnforth LA6 1BQ
T: (015242) 21240
E: julie@redwellinn.co.uk
I: www.redwellinn.co.uk

The Tithe Barn ♦♦♦♦
Main Street, Arkholme, Carnforth LA6 1AU
T: (015242) 22236
F: (015242) 22207
E: tithebarn@btopenworld.com
I: www.mailerassoc.co.uk

ASHLEY
Greater Manchester

Birtles Farm ♦♦♦♦
Ashley, Altrincham WA14 3QH
T: (0161) 928 0458

ASHTON-IN-MAKERFIELD
Greater Manchester

Cranberry Hotel ♦♦
Wigan Road, Ashton-in-Makerfield, Wigan WN4 0BZ
T: (01942) 243519
F: (01942) 820677
I: www.thecranberry.co.uk

ASHTON-UNDER-LYNE
Greater Manchester

Lynwood Hotel ♦♦♦
3, Richmond Street, Ashton-under-Lyne OL7 7TX
T: (0161) 330 5358
F: (0161) 330 5358

BACUP
Lancashire

Pasture Bottom Farm ♦♦♦
Todmordan Road, Bacup OL13 9UZ
T: (01706) 873790
E: ha.isherwood@zen.co.uk
I: www.smoothhound.co.uk/hotels/pasture.html

Rossbrook House
Rating Applied For
New Line, Stacksteads, Bacup OL13 0BY
T: (01706) 878187
F: (01706) 878099
E: rossbkhouse@aol.com
I: www.a1touristguide.com/rossbrookhouse

BARLEY
Lancashire

The Pendle Inn ♦♦♦
Barley, Burnley BB12 9JX
T: (01282) 614808
F: (01282) 695242
E: john@pendleinn.freeserve.co.uk
I: www.pendleinn.freeserve.co.uk

BASHALL EAVES
Lancashire

Hodder House B & B ♦♦♦
Hodder House Farm, Mitton Road, Bashall Eaves, Clitheroe BB7 3LZ
T: (01254) 826328
F: (0870) 135 7687
E: heather@hodderhousebb.freeserve.co.uk
I: www.hodderhousebb.freeserve.co.uk

BAY HORSE
Lancashire

Stanley Lodge Farmhouse ♦♦♦♦
Cockerham Road, Bay Horse, Lancaster LA2 0HE
T: (01524) 791863
F: (01524) 793115
E: stanleylodgefarmhouse@zoom.co.uk
I: www.stanleylodgefarmhouse.co.uk

BETCHTON
Cheshire

Yew Tree Farm ♦♦♦♦
Love Lane, Betchton, Sandbach CW11 4TD
T: (01477) 500626
F: (01477) 500626

BILLINGTON
Lancashire

Rosebury Guest House ♦♦♦
51 Pasturelands Drive, Billington, Clitheroe BB7 9LW
T: (01254) 822658
F: (01254) 823759
E: carole.hamer@btopenworld.com
I: www.rosebury-guest-house.co.uk

BIRKDALE
Merseyside

Belgravia Hotel ♦♦♦
11 Trafalgar Road, Birkdale, Southport PR8 2EA
T: (01704) 565298
F: (01704) 562728
E: belgravias@aol.com
I: www.hotelsouthport.com

BIRKENHEAD
Merseyside

Shrewsbury Lodge Hotel ♦♦♦
31 Shrewsbury Road, Birkenhead CH43 2JB
T: (0151) 653 4079
I: www.shrewsbury-hotel.com

Sleep Station Hotel ♦♦♦
24-28 Hamilton Street, Birkenhead CH41 1AL
T: (0151) 647 1047
F: (0151) 650 1155
E: s.laprugne@sleepstation.co.uk
I: www.sleepstation.co.uk

Victoria Guest House ♦♦
12 Shrewsbury Road, Oxton, Birkenhead CH43 1UX
T: (0151) 652 8379
F: (0151) 652 8379
E: mary.atherton@whsmith.co.uk

Villa Venezia ♦♦♦
14-16 Prenton Road West, Birkenhead CH42 9PN
T: (0151) 608 9212
F: (0151) 608 6671

BLACKBURN
Lancashire

Shalom ♦♦♦♦ SILVER AWARD
531b Livesey Branch Road, Blackburn BB2 5DF
T: (01254) 209032
F: (01254) 209032
E: paul@shalomblackburn.co.uk

BLACKPOOL
Lancashire

Abbey Hotel
Rating Applied For
31 Palatine Road, Blackpool FY1 4BX
T: (01253) 624721
F: (01253) 624721
E: abbeybpool@aol.com
I: abbeyhotel-blackpool.co.uk

Adelaide House Hotel ♦♦♦
66-68 Adelaide Street, Blackpool FY1 4LA
T: (01253) 625172
F: (01253) 625172

Ailsa Hotel ♦♦♦
12 Napier Avenue, Blackpool FY4 1PA
T: (01253) 342368

Alderley Hotel ♦♦♦
581 South Promenade, Blackpool FY4 1NG
T: (01253) 342173

Allendale Hotel ♦♦♦
104 Albert Road, Blackpool FY1 4PR
T: (01253) 623268
E: salexander@ukonline.co.uk
I: www.allendale-hotel.co.uk

Ardsley Hotel ♦♦
20 Woodfield Road, Blackpool FY1 6AX
T: (01253) 345419
F: (01253) 345419

Arncliffe Hotel ♦♦♦
24 Osborne Road, Blackpool FY4 1HJ
T: (01253) 345209
F: (01253) 345209
E: arncliffehotel@talk21.com
I: www.blackpool-internet.co.uk/HOMEarncliffe.html

Ashcroft Hotel ♦♦♦
42 King Edward Avenue, Blackpool FY2 9TA
T: (01253) 351538
E: kandlatashcroft@aol.com

Astoria Hotel ♦♦♦
118-120 Albert Road, Blackpool FY1 4PN
T: (01253) 621231
E: abnw15916@blueyonder.co.uk

Baricia Hotel ♦♦♦
40-42 Egerton Road, Blackpool FY1 2NW
T: (01253) 623130
E: tkbariciahotel@aol.com

Baron Hotel ♦♦♦♦
296 North Promenade, Blackpool FY1 2EY
T: (01253) 622729
F: (01253) 297165
E: baronhotel@btinternet.com

Beachcomber Hotel ♦♦♦
78 Reads Avenue, Blackpool FY1 4DE
T: (01253) 621622
F: (01253) 299254
E: info@beachcomberhotel.net
I: www.beachcomberhotel.net

Beauchief Hotel ♦♦♦
48 King Edward Avenue, Blackpool FY2 9TA
T: (01253) 353314
E: beauchief-hotel@amserve.com

Beaucliffe Hotel ♦♦♦
20-22 Holmfield Rjoad, Blackpool FY2 9TB
T: (01253) 351663
E: don.s(iddall@talk21.com
I: members.netscapeonline.co.uk/beaucliffe

Belvedere Hotel ♦♦♦
91 Albert Road, Blackpool FY1 4PW
T: (01253) 628029
F: (01253) 297069
E: belvedere91@btopenworld.com
I: www.blackpoolhotels.org.uk

Berwick Hotel ♦♦♦
23 King Edward Avenue, North Shore, Blackpool FY2 9TA
T: (01253) 351496
E: chris@berwickhotel.fsnet.co.uk
I: www.smoothhound.co.uk/hotels/berwickpriv.html

Berwyn Hotel ♦♦♦♦
1 Finchley Road, Gynn Square, Blackpool FY1 2LP
T: (01253) 352896
F: (01253) 594391
I: www.blackpool-holidays.com

Beverley Hotel ♦♦♦
25 Dean Street, Blackpool FY4 1AU
T: (01253) 344426
E: beverley.hotel@virgin.net
I: www.beverleyhotel-blackpool.co.uk

Boltonia Hotel ♦♦♦
124-126 Albert Road, Blackpool FY1 4PN
T: (01253) 620248
F: (01253) 299064
E: info@boltoniahotel.co.uk
I: www.boltoniahotel.co.uk

Bona Vista Hotel ♦♦♦
104-106 Queens Promenade, Blackpool FY2 9NX
T: (01253) 351396
F: (01253) 594985
E: bona.vista@talk21.com
I: www.bonavistahotel.com

Brabyns Hotel ♦♦♦♦
1-3 Shaftesbury Avenue, Blackpool FY2 9QQ
T: (01253) 354263
F: (01253) 352915
E: brabynshotel@netscapeonline.co.uk
I: www.brabynshotel.co.uk

Braeside Hotel ♦♦♦
6 Willshaw Road, Gynn Square, Blackpool FY2 9SH
T: (01253) 351363
I: www.blackpoolholidays-braeside.co.uk

Brayton Hotel ♦♦♦
7-8 Finchley Road, Blackpool FY1 2LP
T: (01253) 351645
F: (01253) 595500
E: brayton@supanet.com
I: www.brayton.btinternet.co.uk

Briny View ♦♦
2 Woodfield Road, Blackpool FY1 6AX
T: (01253) 346584
I: www.brinyviewhotel@aol.com

Brooklands Hotel ♦♦♦
28-30 King Edward Avenue, Blackpool FY2 9TA
T: (01253) 351479
F: (01253) 500311
E: brooklandhotel@btinternet.com
I: www.brooklands-hotel.com

Canasta Hotel ♦♦♦♦
288 North Promenade, Blackpool FY1 2EY
T: (01253) 290501
F: (01253) 290501
E: canasta@blackpool.com
I: www.ontheprom.com

Cardoh Lodge ♦♦♦
21 Hull Road, Blackpool FY1 4QB
T: (01253) 627755
F: (01253) 295634
E: info@cardohlodge.co.uk
I: www.cardohlodge.co.uk

The Cheslyn ♦♦♦
21 Moore Street, Blackpool FY4 1DA
T: (01253) 349672

Cliff Head Hotel ♦♦
174 Queens Promenade, Bispham, Blackpool, FY2 9JN
T: (01253) 591086
F: (01253) 590952

Clifton Court Hotel ♦♦♦
12 Clifton Drive, Blackpool FY4 1NX
T: (01253) 342385
F: (01253) 342358
E: enquiries@clifton-court-hotel.co.uk
I: www.clifton-court-hotel.co.uk

Collingwood Hotel ♦♦♦♦
8-10 Holmfield Road, Blackpool FY2 9SL
T: (01253) 352929
F: (01253) 352929
E: enquiries@collingwoodhotel.co.uk
I: www.collingwoodhotel.co.uk

Colris Hotel ♦♦♦
209 Central Promenade, Blackpool FY1 5DL
T: (01253) 625461
E: cheryl703@hotmail.com

Commodore Hotel ♦♦♦
246 Queens Promenade, Blackpool FY2 9HA
T: (01253) 351400
E: campbell.harris@virgin.net

Courtneys of Gynn Square ♦♦♦♦
1 Warbreck Hill Road, Blackpool FY2 9SP
T: (01253) 352179
F: (01253) 352179

Cresta Hotel ♦♦♦
85 Withnell Road, Blackpool FY4 1HE
T: (01253) 343866
E: john@snelly.co.uk
I: www.snelly.co.uk

Croydon Hotel ♦♦♦♦
12 Empress Drive, Blackpool FY2 9SE
T: (01253) 352497
E: croydon@aol.com

Denely Private Hotel ♦♦♦
15 King Edward Avenue, Blackpool FY2 9TA
T: (01253) 352757

Derwent Private Hotel ♦♦♦
42 Palatine Road, Blackpool FY1 4BY
T: (01253) 620004
F: (01253) 620004
E: tanyaderwent@msn.com

Dudley Hotel ♦♦♦
67 Dickson Road, Blackpool FY1 2BX
T: (01253) 620281

Elgin Hotel ♦♦♦
36-42 Queens Promenade, Blackpool FY2 9RW
T: (01253) 351433
F: (01253) 353535
E: info@elginhotel.com
I: www.elginhotel.com

The Fairmont Private Hotel Rating Applied For
40 King Edward Avenue, Blackpool FY2 9TA
T: (01253) 351050

Fairway Hotel ♦♦♦
34-36 Hull Road, Blackpool FY1 4QB
T: (01253) 623777
F: (01253) 753455
E: bookings@fairway.gb.com
I: www.fairway.gb.com

Fern Royd Hotel ♦♦♦
35 Holmfield Road, Blackpool FY2 9TE
T: (01253) 351066
E: info@fernroydhotel.co.uk
I: www.fernroydhotel.co.uk

Glen ♦♦
25 Barton Avenue, South Shore, Blackpool FY1 6AP
T: (01253) 346978

Gleneagles Hotel ♦♦♦
75 Albert Road, Blackpool FY1 4PW
T: (01253) 295266

Glenmere Hotel ♦♦♦
7 Gynn Avenue, Blackpool FY1 2LD
T: (01253) 351259
E: glenmerehotel@aol.com

Grand Hotel Holiday Flats ♦♦♦
Blackpool
T: (01253) 343741
E: info@grandholidayflats.co.uk
I: www.grandholidayflats.co.uk

Granville Hotel ♦♦♦
12 Station Road, Blackpool FY4 1BE
T: (01253) 343012
F: (01253) 408594
E: wilft@thegranvillehotel.fsnet.co.uk
I: www.thegranvillehotel.co.uk

Graydon Hotel ♦♦♦
33/37 Banks Street, Blackpool FY1 2AR
T: (01253) 625012
E: graydonhotel@yahoo.com
I: www.graydonhotel.com

The Grosvenor View Hotel ♦♦♦
7-9 King Edward Avenue, Blackpool FY2 9TD
T: (01253) 352851
E: grosvenor_view@yahoo.co.uk

Hartshead Private Hotel ♦♦♦
17 King Edward Avenue, Blackpool FY2 9TA
T: (01253) 353133
I: www.hartsheadhotel.gbr.cc

Hatton Hotel ♦♦♦
10 Banks Street, Blackpool FY1 1RN
T: (01253) 624944
E: hattonhotel@hotmail.com
I: www.hattonhotel.gbr.cc

Hertford Hotel ♦♦♦
18 Lord Street, Blackpool FY1 2BD
T: (01253) 292931
E: ceges@blueyonder.co.uk
I: www.hertfordhotel.homestead.com

Holmsdale Hotel ♦♦♦
6-8 Pleasant Street, North Shore, Blackpool FY1 2JA
T: (01253) 621008
F: (0870) 133 1487
E: holmsdale@talk21.com
I: www.blackpool-hotels.co.uk/holmsdale.html

Homecliffe Hotel ♦♦♦
5-6 Wilton Parade, Blackpool FY1 2HE
T: (01253) 625147
F: (01253) 292667
E: enquiry@homecliffehotel.com
I: www.homecliffehotel.com

Hornby Villa Hotel ♦♦♦
130 Hornby Road, Blackpool FY1 4QS
T: (01253) 624959
E: hornby.villa@virgin.net
I: www.hornbyvillahotel.com

Hurstmere Hotel ♦♦♦
5 Alexandra Road, Blackpool FY1 6BU
T: (01253) 345843
F: (01253) 347188

Inglewood Hotel ♦♦♦
18 Holmfield Road, Blackpool FY2 9TB
T: (01253) 351668
E: patandpaulwest@aol.com
I: www.blackpool-hotels.co.uk/inglewood.html

The Kimberley ♦♦♦
25 Gynn Avenue, Blackpool
FY1 2LD
T: (01253) 352264
E: thekimberleygynnavenue@hotmail.com
I: www.kimberleyguesthouse.co.uk

Kingscliff Hotel
Rating Applied For
78 Hornby Road, Blackpool
FY1 4QJ
T: (01253) 620200
I: www.kingscliffhotel.co.uk

Kirkstall Hotel
Rating Applied For
25 Hull Road, Blackpool FY1 4QB
T: (01253) 623077
F: (01253) 620279
E: jean.dobson1@virginnet.co.uk
I: www.kirkstallhotel.co.uk

Llanryan Guest House ♦♦♦
37 Reads Avenue, Blackpool
FY1 4DD
T: (01253) 628446
E: keith@llanryanguesthouse.co.uk
I: www.llanryanguesthouse.co.uk

Lochinvar Christian Guest House ♦♦♦
14 Chatsworth Avenue,
Norbreck, Blackpool FY2 9AN
T: (01253) 351761
E: lochinvar@cghblackpool.fsnet.co.uk
I: www.lochinvar-christianholidays.co.uk

Lynbar Hotel ♦♦♦
32 Vance Road, Blackpool
FY1 4QD
T: (01253) 294504
E: enquiries@lynbarhotel.co.uk

Manor Grove Hotel ♦♦
24 Leopold Grove, Blackpool
FY1 4LD
T: (01253) 625577
F: (01253) 625577
E: lyndon@evans2000.freeserve.co.uk
I: www.manorgrovehotel.co.uk

Manor Private Hotel ♦♦♦
32 Queens Promenade,
Blackpool FY2 9RN
T: (01253) 351446
F: (01253) 355449
E: holidays@manorblackpool.co.uk
I: manorblackpool.co.uk

Marlow Lodge Hotel ♦♦
76 Station Road, Blackpool
FY4 1EU
T: (01253) 341580
F: (01253) 408330
E: hotelreception@yahoo.co.uk
I: www.blackpoolmarlowhotel.com

May-Dene Licensed Hotel
10 Dean Street, Blackpool
FY4 1AU
T: (01253) 343464
F: (01253) 401424
E: may_dene_hotel@hotmail.com

Merecliff Hotel ♦♦
24 Holmfield Road, Blackpool
FY2 9TE
T: (01253) 356858
E: enquiries@merecliffhotel.co.uk
I: www.merecliffhotel.co.uk

Middleton Hotel ♦♦♦
55 Holmfield Road, North Shore,
Blackpool FY2 9RU
T: (01253) 354559
F: (01253) 353206
E: info@middletonhotel.com

Mimosa Motel
Rating Applied For
24A Lonsdale Road, Blackpool
FY1 6EE
T: (01253) 341906
F: (01253) 341906
E: bobjan@mimosamotel.freeserve.co.uk
I: www.mimosamotel.com

Hotel Montclair ♦♦♦
95 Albert Road, Blackpool
FY1 4PW
T: (01253) 625860

New Bond Hotel ♦♦♦
72 Lord Street, Blackpool
FY1 2DG
T: (01253) 628123
E: newbond@btinternet.com
I: www.newbondhotel.com

New Central Hotel ♦♦
64a Reads Avenue, Blackpool
FY1 4DE
T: (01253) 623637
F: (01253) 620857
E: gavin_lees@hotmail.com
I: www.newcentralhotel.co.uk

Newholme Private Hotel ♦♦♦
2 Wilton Parade, Blackpool
FY1 2HE
T: (01253) 624010
I: www.newholme.4t.com

The Old Coach House
♦♦♦♦♦ GOLD AWARD
50 Dean Street, Blackpool
FY4 1BP
T: (01253) 349195
F: (01253) 344330
E: blackpool@theoldcoachhouse.freeserve.co.uk
I: www.theoldcoachhouse.freeserve.co.uk

Peacocks Guest House ♦♦♦♦
59 Park Road, Blackpool FY1 4JQ
T: (01253) 622682
E: info@peacocksguesthouse.com

Pembroke Private Hotel ♦♦♦♦
11 King Edward Avenue,
Blackpool FY2 9TD
T: (01253) 351306
F: (01253) 351306
E: stay@pembrokehotel.com
I: www.pembrokehotel.com

Penrhyn Hotel ♦♦♦
38 King Edward Avenue,
Blackpool FY2 9TA
T: (01253) 352762
E: janetpenrhyn@aol.com

Pickwick Hotel ♦♦♦
93 Albert Road, Blackpool
FY1 4PW
T: (01253) 624229
F: (01253) 624229

Poldhu Hotel
Rating Applied For
330 Queens Promenade,
Blackpool FY2 9AB
T: (01253) 356918
F: (01253) 354911
E: info@poldhu-hotel.co.uk
I: www.poldhu.hotel.co.uk

Raffles Hotel ♦♦♦♦
73-75 Hornby Road, Blackpool
FY1 4QJ
T: (01253) 294713
F: (01253) 294240
E: enq@raffleshotelblackpool.fsworld.co.uk
I: www.raffleshotelblackpool.co.uk

Robin Hood Hotel ♦♦♦
100 Queens Promenade,
Blackpool FY2 9NS
T: (01253) 351599
E: rhhblackpool@hotmail.com

Rockcliffe Hotel ♦♦♦
248 North Promenade,
Blackpool FY1 1RZ
T: (01253) 623476
F: (01253) 473825
I: www.rockcliffehotel.co.uk

Rowan Hotel ♦♦♦♦
8 Empress Drive, Blackpool
FY2 9SE
T: (01253) 352218

The Royal Seabank Hotel ♦♦♦
219-221 Central Promenade,
Blackpool FY1 5DL
T: (01253) 622717
F: (01253) 295148
E: royalseabank@hotmail.com
I: www.blackpool.net/wwwroyalseabank

Rutland Hotel ♦♦♦
330 Promenade, Blackpool
FY1 2JG
T: (01253) 622791
F: (01253) 622791
E: tony-morgan@rutland-hotel.co.uk
I: www.rutland-hotel.co.uk

Rutlands Hotel ♦♦♦
13 Hornby Road, Blackpool
FY1 4QG
T: (01253) 623067

St Ives Hotel ♦♦
10 King George Avenue,
Blackpool FY2 9SN
T: (01253) 352122
F: (01253) 352122
E: enquiries@st iveshotel-blackpool.co.uk
I: www.stiveshotel-blackpool.co.uk

Seabreeze Guest House ♦♦♦♦
1 Gynn Avenue, Blackpool
FY1 2LD
T: (01253) 351427
E: info@vbreezey.co.uk
I: www.vbreezy.co.uk

Seaforth Hotel ♦♦♦
18 Lonsdale Road, Blackpool
FY1 6EE
T: (01253) 345820
F: (01253) 345820
E: enquiries@seaforthhotel.co.uk

Sheron House ♦♦♦♦
21 Gynn Avenue, North Shore,
Blackpool FY1 2LD
T: (01253) 354614
E: sheronhouse@amserve.net
I: www.sheronhouse.co.uk

Shirley House ♦♦
73 Adelaide Street, Blackpool
FY1 4LN
T: (01253) 628650
I: www.shirleyhouseblackpool.co.uk

Hotel Skye ♦♦
571-573 New South Promenade,
Blackpool FY4 1NG
T: (01253) 343220
F: (01253) 401244
E: office@blackpool-hotel.co.uk
I: www.blackpool-hotel.co.uk

Somerville Hotel ♦♦♦
72 Station Road, Blackpool
FY4 1EU
T: (01253) 341219

South Lea Hotel ♦♦♦
4 Willshaw Road, Blackpool
FY2 9SH
T: (01253) 351940
F: (01253) 595758
E: reservations@southleahotel.fsnet.co.uk
I: www.blackpool-holidays.com/southlea.htm

Hotel St Elmo ♦♦♦
20-22 Station Road, Blackpool
FY4 1BE
T: (01253) 341820
F: (01253) 347559
E: hotelst.elmo@btopenworld.com
I: www.blackpoolhotels.org.uk/stelmo.html

The Strathdon Hotel ♦♦♦
28 St Chads Road, South Shore,
Blackpool FY1 6BP
T: (01253) 343549
E: stay@strathdonhotel.com

Sunnymede Hotel ♦♦♦
50 King Edward Avenue,
Blackpool FY2 9TA
T: (01253) 352877
E: enquiries@sunnymedehotel.co.uk
I: www.sunnymedehotel.co.uk

Sunnyside Hotel ♦♦♦
36 King Edward Avenue, North
Shore, Blackpool FY2 9TA
T: (01253) 352031
F: (01253) 354255
E: stuart@sunnysidehotel.com
I: www.sunnysidehotel.com

Surrey House Hotel ♦♦♦
9 Northumberland Avenue,
Blackpool FY2 9SB
T: (01253) 351743
E: cpsurreyhouse@aol.com
I: www.surreyhousehotel.com

Thorncliffe Hotel ♦♦
63 Dickson Road, Blackpool
FY1 2BX
T: (01253) 622508

Trafalgar Hotel ♦♦♦
106 Albert Road, Blackpool
FY1 4PR
T: (01253) 625000
E: trafalgarhotel@msn.com

Tudor Rose Original ♦♦♦♦
5 Withnell Road, Blackpool
FY4 1HF
T: (01253) 343485
E: tudororiginal@aol.com

Vidella Hotel ♦♦♦
80-82 Dickson Road, North Shore, Blackpool FY1 2BU
T: (01253) 621201
F: (01253) 620319

Waverley Hotel ♦♦♦
95 Reads Avenue, Blackpool
FY1 4DG
T: (01253) 621633
F: (01253) 753581
E: wavehotel@aol.com
I: www.thewaverleyhotel.com

Westdean Hotel ♦♦♦
59 Dean Street, Blackpool
FY4 1BP
T: (01253) 342904
F: (01253) 342926
E: mikeball@westdeanhotel.freeserve.co.uk
I: www.westdeanhotel.com

Westfield Hotel ♦♦♦
14 Station Road, Blackpool
FY4 1BE
T: (01253) 342468
E: bookings@westfieldhotel.fsbusiness.co.uk

Wilton Hotel ♦♦♦
108-112 Dickson Road, Blackpool FY1 2HF
T: (01253) 627763
F: (01253) 296222
E: wiltonhotel@supanet.com
I: http://www.wiltonhotel.co.uk

Wimbourne Hotel Rating Applied For
10 Moore Street, Blackpool
FY4 1DB
T: (01253) 347272
F: (01253) 348563
E: dave@wimbournehotel.co.uk
I: www.wimbournehotel.co.uk

Windsor Carlton Hotel Rating Applied For
6 Warley Road, Blackpool
FY1 2JU
T: (01253) 354924
E: jasonandkevin@windsorcarlton.fsnet.co.uk
I: www.windsorcarlton.com

Windsor Hotel ♦♦♦♦
21 King Edward Avenue, Blackpool FY2 9TA
T: (01253) 353735
F: (01253) 353725

Windsor House Hotel ♦♦♦
28 Rawcliffe Street, Blackpool
FY4 1BZ
T: (01253) 341062
F: (01253) 298551
E: enquiries@windsorhousehotel.co.uk
I: www.windsorhousehotel.co.uk

Windsor Park Hotel ♦♦♦
96 Queens Promenade, North Shore, Blackpool FY2 9NS
T: (01253) 357025
F: (01253) 357076

Woodleigh Hotel ♦♦♦
32 King Edward Avenue, Blackpool FY2 9TA
T: (01253) 593624

BLUNDELLSANDS
Merseyside

Blundellsands Bed and Breakfast
♦♦♦♦ SILVER AWARD
9 Elton Avenue, Blundellsands, Liverpool L23 8UN
T: (0151) 924 6947
F: (0151) 287 4113
E: lizmarshall@bsbb.freeserve.co.uk
I: www.blundellsands.info

BOLTON
Greater Manchester

Archangelos ♦♦♦
82 Pennine Road, Horwich, Bolton BL6 7HW
T: (01204) 692303
E: enquiries@archangelos.co.uk.
I: www.archangelos.co.uk

Ash Woods ♦♦♦
6 Oakenclough Drive, Smithills, Bolton BL1 5QY
T: (01204) 492100
E: neilmags@cwcom.net
I: www.boltonbandb.co.uk

Cheetham Arms ♦♦♦
987 Blackburn Road, Sharples, Bolton BL1 7LG
T: (01204) 301372
F: (01204) 598209
E: mike@cheethamarms.freeserve.co.uk

Fourways Hotel ♦♦♦
13-15 Bolton Road, Moses Gate, Farnworth, Bolton BL4 7JN
T: (01204) 573661
F: (01204) 862488
E: fourwayshotel@pureasphalt.co.uk

The Grosvenor Guest House ♦♦♦
46 Bradford Street, Bolton
BL2 1JJ
T: (01204) 391616

Highgrove Guest House ♦♦♦
63 Manchester Road, Bolton
BL2 1ES
T: (01204) 384928
E: thehighgrove@btconnect.com

Morden Grange Guest House ♦♦♦
15 Chadwick Street, The Haulgh, Bolton BL2 1JN
T: (01204) 522000
E: enquiries@mordengrange.co.uk
I: www.mordengrange.co.uk

BOLTON-BY-BOWLAND
Lancashire

The Coach and Horses ♦♦♦
20 Main Street, Bolton-by-Bowland, Clitheroe BB7 4NW
T: (01200) 447202
F: (01200) 447202

Middle Flass Lodge ♦♦♦♦
Forest Becks Brow, Settle Road, Bolton-by-Bowland, Clitheroe
BB7 4NY
T: (01200) 447259
F: (01200) 447300
E: info@middleflasslodge.fsnet.co.uk
I: www.middleflasslodge.co.uk

BOOTLE
Merseyside

Regent Maritime Hotel ♦♦♦
58-62 Regent Road, Bootle, Liverpool L20 8DB
T: (0151) 922 4090
F: (0151) 922 6308
E: regmarhotel@btconnect.com
I: www.regentmaritimehotel.com

BROMBOROUGH
Merseyside

Dibbinsdale Inn ♦♦♦
Dibbinsdale Road, Bromborough, Wirral CH63 0HJ
T: (0151) 334 5171
F: (0151) 334 0097

Woodlands Guest House ♦♦♦♦
10 Haigh Road, Waterloo, Bromborough, Wirral L22 3XP
T: (0151) 920 5373

BROMLEY CROSS
Greater Manchester

The Poplars ♦♦♦♦
58, Horseshoe Lane, Bromley Cross, Bolton BL7 9RR
T: (01204) 308001
E: patricia@v-b-elec.u-net.com
I: www.v-b-elec.u-net.com

BURNLEY
Lancashire

Higher Cockden Farm ♦♦♦♦
Todmorden Road, Briercliffe, Burnley BB10 3QQ
T: (01282) 831324
F: (01282) 831324

BURNLEY
Lancashire

Ormerod Hotel ♦♦♦
121-123 Ormerod Road, Burnley
BB11 3QW
T: (01282) 423255

Thorneyholme Farm Cottage ♦♦♦♦
Barley New Road, Roughlee, Burnley BB12 9LH
T: (01282) 612452

BURSCOUGH
Lancashire

Martin Inn ♦♦♦
Martin Lane, Burscough, Ormskirk L40 0RT
T: (01704) 892302
F: (01704) 895735

BURY
Greater Manchester

The Rostrevor Hotel ♦♦♦
146/148 Manchester Road, Bury
BL9 0TL
T: (0161) 764 3944
F: (0161) 764 8622
E: michelle@Rostrevorhotel.co.uk
I: www.rostrevorhotel.co.uk

CALDY
Merseyside

Cheriton Bed and Breakfast ♦♦♦♦
151 Caldy Road, Caldy, West Kirby, Wirral CH48 1LP
T: (0151) 625 5271
F: (0151) 625 5271
E: cheriton151@hotmail.com
I: www.cheritonguesthouse.co.uk

CAPERNWRAY
Lancashire

New Capernwray Farm
♦♦♦♦♦ SILVER AWARD
Capernwray, Carnforth LA6 1AD
T: (01524) 734284
F: (01524) 734284
E: info@newcapfarm.co.uk

CARNFORTH
Lancashire

Dale Grove ♦♦♦
162 Lancaster Road, Carnforth
LA5 9EF
T: (01524) 733382
E: cal.craig@ntlworld.com
I: www.dalegrove.co.uk

Galley Hall Farm ♦♦♦♦
Shore Road, Carnforth LA5 9HZ
T: (01524) 732544

The George Washington ♦♦♦
Main Street, Warton, Carnforth
LA5 9PJ
T: (01524) 732865

Grisedale Farm ♦♦♦♦
Leighton, Carnforth LA5 9ST
T: (01524) 734360

High Bank ♦♦♦♦
Hawk Street, Carnforth LA5 9LA
T: (01524) 733827

Longlands Hotel ♦♦♦
Tewitfield, Carnforth LA6 1JH
T: (01524) 781256
F: (01524) 781004
E: info@thelonglandshotel.co.uk
I: www.thelonglandshotel.co.uk

CHAIGLEY
Lancashire

Moorhead House Farm ♦♦♦
Thornley Road, Chaigley, Clitheroe BB7 3LY
T: (01995) 61108

CHEADLE
Greater Manchester

Curzon House ♦♦♦
3, Curzon Road, Heald Green, Cheadle SK8 3LN
T: (0161) 436 2804
E: curzonhouse@aol.com
I: www.smoothhound.co.uk

CHEADLE HULME
Greater Manchester

Spring Cottage Guest House ♦♦♦
60 Hulme Hall Road, Cheadle Hulme, Cheadle SK8 6JZ
T: (0161) 485 1037
F: (0161) 485 1037

CHELFORD
Cheshire

Astle Farm East ♦♦♦
Chelford, Macclesfield SK10 4TA
T: (01625) 861270
F: (01625) 861270
E: gill.farmhouse@virgin.net

CHESTER
Cheshire

Abbotsford Court Hotel ♦♦♦
17 Victoria Road, Chester
CH2 2AX
T: (01244) 390898
F: (01244) 380805
E: abbotsfordcourt@hotmail.com

Bawn Lodge ♦♦♦
10 Hoole Road, Hoole, Chester
CH2 3NH
T: (01244) 324971
F: (01244) 310951
E: info@bawnlodge.co.uk
I: www.bawnlodge.co.uk

Belgrave Hotel ♦♦♦
61 City Road, Chester CH1 3AE
T: (01244) 312138
F: (01244) 324951

Bowman Lodge ♦♦♦
52 Hoole Road, Chester CH2 3NL
T: (01244) 342208
E: jaynebowman@hotmail.com
I: freespace.virgin.net/cig.davies/bowman.htm

Buckingham House ♦♦♦
38 Hough Green, Chester
CH4 8JQ
T: (01244) 678600
F: (01244) 671028
I: buckinghamhousechester.com

Castle House ♦♦♦
23 Castle Street, Chester
CH1 2DS
T: (01244) 350354
F: (01244) 350354

Chester Town House ♦♦♦
23 King Street, Chester CH1 2AH
T: (01244) 350021
F: (01244) 350021
E: davidbellis@chestertownhouse.co.uk
I: www.chestertownhouse.co.uk

Chippings ♦♦♦♦
Cranford Court, Chester
CH4 7LN
T: (01244) 679728
F: (01244) 659470
E: elaine@gotogifts.co.uk

Comfort Inn Chester ♦♦♦♦
74 Hoole Road, Chester CH2 3NL
T: (01244) 327542
F: (01244) 344889
E: info@comfortinnchester.com
I: www.choicehotelseurope.com

The Commercial Hotel ♦♦♦
St Peters Churchyard, Chester
CH1 2HG
T: (01244) 320749
F: (01244) 348318
I: www.stayhereuk.com

Dee Hills Lodge ♦♦♦♦
7 Dee Hills Park, Chester CH 5AR
T: (01244) 325719

Derry Raghan Lodge ♦♦♦
54 Hoole Road, Chester CH2 3NL
T: (01244) 318740
E: welcome@derryraghanlodge.co.uk
I: www.derryraghanlodge.co.uk

Eastern Guest House ♦♦♦
Eastern Pathway, Chester
CH4 7AQ
T: (01244) 680104

Edwards House ♦♦♦
61-63 Hoole Road, Hoole,
Chester CH2 3NJ
T: (01244) 318055
F: (01244) 310948
E: steanerob@supanet.com
I: www.smoothHound.co.uk/hotels/edwardhou.html

Golborne Manor ♦♦♦♦
Platts Lane, Hatton Heath,
Chester CH3 9AN
T: (01829) 770310
F: (01829) 770370
E: ann.ikin@golbornemanor.co.uk
I: www.golbornemanor.co.uk

The Golden Eagle Hotel ♦♦♦
18 Castle Street, Chester
CH1 2DS
T: (01244) 321098
F: (01244) 321098
E: goldeneaglehotel@btopenworld.com

Greenwalls Bed & Breakfast ♦♦♦♦
Whitchurch Road, Waverton,
Chester CH3 7PB
T: (01244) 336799
F: (01244) 332124
E: jmitchellgreenwalls@hotmail.com
I: www.bedandbreakfastnationwide.com

Grosvenor Place ♦♦♦
2 - 4 Grosvenor Place, Chester
CH1 2DE
T: (01244) 324455
F: (01244) 400225

Grove House B & B ♦♦♦♦
Holme Street, Tarvin, Chester
CH3 8EQ
T: (01829) 740893
F: (01829) 741769

Grove Villa ♦♦♦
18 The Groves, Chester CH1 1SD
T: (01244) 349713
E: Grove.Villa@tesco.net

Halcyon Guest House ♦♦♦
18 Eaton Road, Handbridge,
Chester CH4 7EN
T: (01244) 676159
E: halcyon_house@tiscali.co.uk

Hameldaeus ♦♦♦
9 Lorne Street, Chester CH1 4AE
T: (01244) 374913
E: joyce33@brunton81.freeserve.co.uk

Holly House ♦♦♦
41, Liverpool Road, Chester
CH2 1AB
T: (01244) 383484

Homeleigh Guest House ♦♦♦
14 Hough Green, Chester
CH4 8JG
T: (01244) 676761
F: (01244) 679977
I: www.scoot.co.uk/homeleigh_guest_house/

Kent House ♦♦
147 Boughton, Chester CH3 5BH
T: (01244) 324171
F: (01244) 319758
E: kent-house@turner10101.freeserve.co.uk

The Kings Guesthouse ♦♦♦
14 Eaton Road, Handbridge,
Chester CH4 7EN
T: (01244) 671249
E: king@kings.plus.com

Laburnum House ♦♦♦
2 St Anne Street, Chester
CH1 3HS
T: (01244) 380313
F: (01244) 380313
E: laburnumhouse@bushinternet.com

Latymer Hotel ♦♦♦
82 Hough Green, Chester
CH4 8JW
T: (01244) 675074
F: (01244) 683413
E: info@latymerhotel.com
I: www.latymerhotel.com

Laurels ♦♦♦♦
14 Selkirk Road, Curzon Park,
Chester CH4 8AH
T: (01244) 679682
F: (01244) 659158
E: howell@ellisroberts.freeserve.co.uk

The Laurels Guest House ♦♦♦
61 Tarvin Road, Boughton,
Chester CH3 5DY
T: (01244) 346292
E: carlton40@btinternet.com

The Limes
♦♦♦♦ SILVER AWARD
12 Hoole Road, Hoole, Chester
CH2 3NJ
T: (01244) 328239
F: (01244) 322874
E: thelimeschester@btconnect.com
I: www.the-limes.co.uk

Mitchell's of Chester Guest House ♦♦♦♦ SILVER AWARD
Green Gables, 28 Hough Green,
Chester CH4 8JQ
T: (01244) 679004
F: (01244) 659567
E: mitoches@dialstart.net
I: www.mitchellsofchester.com

Newton Hall ♦♦♦♦
Newton Lane, Tattenhall,
Chester CH3 9NE
T: (01829) 770153
F: (01829) 770655
E: newton.hall@farming.co.uk

Rowland House ♦♦♦
2 Chichester Street, Chester
CH1 4AD
T: (01244) 390967
F: (01244) 390967
E: rowlandhousechester@hotmail.com
I: www.rowlandhouse-chester.co.uk

Strathearn Guest House ♦♦♦
38 Hoole Road, Chester CH2 3NL
T: (01244) 321522
F: (01244) 321522
E: stratherguesthouse@btopenworld.com

Ten the Groves ♦♦♦
10 The Groves, Chester CH1 1SD
T: (01244) 317907
E: ten-the-groves@freeuk.com

Tentry Heys ♦♦
Queens Park Road, Chester
CH4 7AD
T: (01244) 677857
F: (01244) 659439
E: njarthur@btconnect.com

Tower House ♦♦♦♦
14 Dee Hills Park, Chester
CH3 5AR
T: (01244) 341936
E: sueheather62@hotmail.com

Walpole House ♦♦♦♦
26 Walpole Street, Chester
CH1 4HG
T: (01244) 373373
F: (01244) 373373
E: walphse@aol.com
I: www.walpolehouse.co.uk

CHILDWALL
Merseyside

Childwall Abbey Hotel ♦♦♦
Score Lane, Childwall, Liverpool
L16 5EY
T: (0151) 722 5293
F: (0151) 722 0438

CHOLMONDELEY
Cheshire

Manor Farm ♦♦♦♦
Egerton, Cholmondeley, Egerton,
Malpas SY14 8AW
T: (01829) 720261
F: (01606) 853181

CHORLEY
Lancashire

Parr Hall Farm ♦♦♦♦
Parr Lane, Eccleston, Chorley
PR7 5SL
T: (01257) 451917
F: (01257) 453749
E: parrhall@talk21.com

CLAUGHTON
Lancashire

Old Rectory ♦♦♦♦
Claughton, Hornby, Lancaster
LA2 9LA
T: (015242) 21150
E: info@rectorylancs.co.uk
I: www.rectorylancs.co.uk

CLEVELEYS
Lancashire

Briardene Hotel ♦♦♦♦
56 Kelso Avenue, Cleveleys,
Blackpool FY5 3JG
T: (01253) 852312
F: (01253) 851190

CLITHEROE
Lancashire

Lower Standen Farm ♦♦♦
Whalley Road, Clitheroe
BB7 1PP
T: (01200) 424176
F: (01200) 424176
E: lowerstanden@hancox.com

Rakefoot Farm ♦♦♦♦
Thornley Road, Chaigley, Near
Clitheroe BB7 3LY
T: (01995) 61332
F: (01995) 61296
E: info@rakefootfarm.co.uk
I: www.rakefootfarm.co.uk

Selborne House ♦♦♦♦
Back Commons, Kirkmoor Road,
Clitheroe BB7 2DX
T: (01200) 423571
F: (01200) 423571
E: selbornehouse@lineone.net
I: www.selbornehouse.co.uk

Station Hotel ♦♦
King Street, Clitheroe BB7 2EU
T: (01200) 443205

The Swan & Royal Hotel ♦♦♦
26 Castle Street, Clitheroe
BB7 2BX
T: (01200) 423130
F: (01200) 444351
I: www.jenningsbrewery.co.uk

Timothy Cottage ♦♦♦
Whalley Road, Hurst Green, Clitheroe BB7 9QJ
T: (01254) 826337
F: (01254) 826737
E: jgordon@dial.pipex.com

COLNE
Lancashire

Blakey Hall Farm ♦♦♦
Red Lane, Colne BB8 9TD
T: (01282) 863121
E: blakeyhall@hotmail.com

Higher Wanless Farm ♦♦♦♦
Red Lane, Colne BB8 7JP
T: (01282) 865301
F: (01282) 865823
E: wanlessfarm@bun.com
I: www.stayinlancs.co.uk

Middle Beardshaw Head Farm ♦♦♦
Burnley Road, Trawden, Colne BB8 8PP
T: (01282) 865257
F: (01282) 865257
E: ursula@mann1940.freeserve.co.uk
I: http://www.smoothhound.co.uk/a11504.html

Reedymoor Farm ♦♦♦♦
Reedymoor Lane, Foulridge, Colne BB8 7LJ
T: (01282) 865074

Wickets ♦♦♦♦
148 Keighley Road, Colne BB8 0PJ
T: (01282) 862002
F: (01282) 859675
E: wickets@colne148.fsnet.co.uk

CONGLETON
Cheshire

Cloud House Farm ♦♦♦♦
Toft Green, Congleton CW12 3QF
T: (01260) 226272

The Plough at Eaton ♦♦♦♦
Macclesfield Road, Eaton, Congleton CW12 2NR
T: (01260) 280207
F: (01260) 298377
E: trev@plough76.fsnet.co.uk

Sandhole Farm ♦♦♦♦
Hulme Walfield, Congleton CW12 2JH
T: (01260) 224419
F: (01260) 224766
E: veronica@sandholefarm.co.uk
I: http://www.sandholefarm.co.uk

The Woodlands ♦♦♦♦
Quarry Wood Farm, Wood Street, Congleton ST7 3PF
T: (01782) 518877
F: (01782) 518877
E: L.Mullinex@amserve.com

Yew Tree Farm ♦♦♦♦
North Rode, Congleton CW12 2PF
T: (01260) 223569
F: (01260) 223328
E: yewtreebb@hotmail.com

COPSTER GREEN
Lancashire

The Brown Leaves Country Hotel ♦♦♦
Copster Green, Blackburn
T: (01254) 249523
I: www.brownleavescountryhotel.co.uk

CREWE
Cheshire

Balterley Green Farm ♦♦♦♦
Deans Lane, Crewe CW2 5QJ
T: (01270) 820214
F: (01270) 820214
E: greenfarm@balterley.fsnet.co.uk
I: http://www.greenfarm.freeserve.co.uk

Coole Hall Farm ♦♦♦♦ SILVER AWARD
Hankelow, Crewe CW3 0JD
T: (01270) 811232
F: 1270811232
E: goodwin200@hotmail.com

CRUMPSALL
Greater Manchester

Wilton Grange Hotel ♦♦♦
2 Crumpsall Lane, Crumpsall, Manchester M8 5FB
T: 0800 0563 468
F: (0161) 795 4354
E: robfiddaman@fsmail.net
I: www.wiltongrange.com

CULCHETH
Cheshire

99 Hob Hey Lane ♦♦♦♦
Culcheth, Warrington WA3 4NS
T: (01925) 763448
F: (01925) 763448

DUKINFIELD
Greater Manchester

Barton Villa Guest House ♦♦♦
Crescent Road, Dukinfield SK16 4EY
T: (0161) 330 3952
F: (0161) 285 8488
E: enquiries@bartonvilla.co.uk
I: www.bartonvilla.co.uk

DUNSOP BRIDGE
Lancashire

Wood End Farm ♦♦♦♦
Dunsop Bridge, Clitheroe BB7 3BE
T: (01200) 448223
E: spencers@beatrix-freeserve.co.uk
I: www.members.tripod.co.uk/Woodend

ELSWICK
Lancashire

Thornton House ♦♦♦♦
High Street, Elswick, Preston PR4 3ZB
T: (01995) 671863
F: (01995) 671863
E: john@thorntonhouse.biz
I: www.thorntonhouse.biz

FARNWORTH
Greater Manchester

Fernbank Guest House ♦♦♦♦
61 Rawson Street, Farnworth, Bolton BL4 7RJ
T: (01204) 708 832
E: fernbank.bolton@btinternet.com
I: www.fernbankguesthouse.co.uk

FOULRIDGE
Lancashire

Bankfield Guest House ♦♦♦
Skipton Road, Foulridge, Colne BB8 7PY
T: (01282) 863870
F: (01282) 863870
E: estaatbankfield@aol.com

Hare & Hounds Inn ♦♦♦
Skipton Old Road, Foulridge, Colne BB8 7PD
T: (01282) 864235
F: (01282) 865966
E: hareandhounds1@hotmail.com

FRODSHAM
Cheshire

Old Hall Hotel ♦♦♦♦
Main Street, Frodsham WA6 7AB
T: (01928) 732052
F: (01928) 739046
E: theoldhall@lineone.net
I: www.cheshire-hotel.co.uk

FULWOOD
Lancashire

Kiwi House ♦♦♦♦
6 Sharoe Green Park, Fulwood, Preston PR2 8HW
T: (01772) 719873
F: (01772) 719873

GARSTANG
Lancashire

Ashdene ♦♦♦
Parkside Lane, Nateby, Garstang, Preston PR3 0JA
T: (01995) 602676
F: (01995) 602676
E: ashdene@supanet.com
I: www.ashdenebedandbreakfast.gbr.cc

Guys Thatched Hamlet ♦♦♦
Canalside, St Michael's Road, Bilsborrow, Garstang, Preston PR3 0RS
T: (01995) 640010
F: (01995) 640141
E: guyshamlet@aol.com
I: http://www.guysthachedhamlet.co.uk

GARSTON
Merseyside

Aplin Guest House ♦♦
35 Clarendon Road, Garston, Liverpool L19 6PJ
T: (0151) 427 5047
F: (0151) 280 9841

GOODSHAW
Lancashire

The Old White Horse ♦♦♦♦
211 Goodshaw Lane, Goodshaw, Rossendale BB4 8DD
T: (01706) 215474
E: johnandmaggie54@hotmail.com
I: www.211oldwhitehorse.freeserve.co.uk

GOOSNARGH
Lancashire

Isles Field Barn ♦♦♦
Syke, Goosnargh, Preston PR3 2EN
T: (01995) 640398
E: susanmchugh@tetinco.co.uk
I: www.islesfieldbarn.com

GREASBY
Merseyside

At Peel Hey ♦♦♦♦ SILVER AWARD
Frankby Road, Frankby, Wirral CH48 1PP
T: (0151) 677 9077
E: enquiries@peelhey.co.uk
I: www.peelhey.co.uk

GREAT ECCLESTON
Lancashire

Cartford Hotel ♦♦♦
Cartford Lane, Little Eccleston, Preston PR3 0YP
T: (01995) 670166
F: (01995) 671785

HALE
Greater Manchester

Clovelly Court ♦♦♦♦
224 Ashley Road, Hale, Altrincham WA15 9SR
T: (0161) 927 7027

HANDFORTH
Cheshire

The Grange ♦♦♦
Clay Lane, Handforth, Wilmslow SK9 3NR
T: (01625) 523653
F: (01625) 530140
E: alisongodlee@lineone.net

HEATH CHARNOCK
Lancashire

The Coach House ♦♦♦
Long Lane, Heath Charnock, Chorley PR6 9EB
T: (01257) 279981
F: (01257) 279984
E: barlow.r(idges@virgin.net
I: www.bedbreakfast_gardenvisits.com

HESKIN
Lancashire

Farmers Arms ♦♦♦
85 Wood Lane, Heskin, Chorley PR7 5NP
T: (01257) 451276
F: (01257) 453958
E: andy@farmersarms.co.uk
I: www.farmersarms.co.uk

HEYSHAM
Lancashire

Furness View Private Hotel ♦♦♦
23 Sandylands Promenade, Heysham LA3 1DN
T: (01524) 401294

It'l Do ♦♦♦
15 Oxcliffe Road, Heysham LA3 1PR
T: (01524) 850763

HIGHER BEBINGTON
Merseyside

Bebington Hotel ♦♦♦
24 Town Lane, Bebington, Wirral CH63 5JG
T: (0151) 645 0608
E: veghena@aol.com

HOLMES CHAPEL
Cheshire

Bridge Farm B&B ♦♦♦
Bridge Lane, Blackden, Holmes Chapel, Crewe CW4 8BX
T: (01477) 571202
E: stay@bridgefarm.com
I: www.bridgefarm.com

Padgate Guest House ♦♦♦♦
Twemlow Lane, Cranage, Middlewich CW4 8EX
T: (01477) 534291
F: (01477) 544726
E: lynda@padgate.freeserve.co.uk

HOOLE
Cheshire

Glann Hotel ♦♦♦
2 Stone Place, Hoole, Chester CH2 3NR
T: (01244) 344800
E: glannhot@supanet.com

Hamilton Court Hotel ♦♦♦♦
5-7 Hamilton Street, Hoole, Chester CH2 3JA
T: (01244) 345387
F: (01244) 317404
E: hamiltoncourth@aol.com
I: www.smoothhound.co.uk/hotels/hamilton.html

Holly House Guest House ♦♦♦
1 Stone Place, Hoole, Chester CH2 3NR
T: (01244) 328967
E: runcas@hotmail.com

Oaklea Guest House ♦♦
63 Oaklea Avenue, Hoole, Chester CH2 3RG
T: (01244) 340516

HORWICH
Greater Manchester

Highercroft ♦♦♦
1 Foxholes Road, Horwich, Bolton BL6 6AS
T: (01204) 691323
F: (07941) 989887
E: highercroft@linone.net
I: www.highercroft.8m.net

HOYLAKE
Merseyside

Crestwood ♦♦♦
25 Drummond Road, Hoylake, Wirral CH47 4AU
T: (0151) 632 2937
E: elainehowe@totalise.co.uk

HURST GREEN
Lancashire

The Fold ♦♦♦♦
15 Smith Row, Hurst Green, Clitheroe BB7 9QA
T: (01254) 826252
E: derek.harwood1@virgin.net

HUXLEY
Cheshire

Higher Huxley Hall ♦♦♦♦ SILVER AWARD
Red Lane, Huxley, Chester CH3 9BZ
T: (01829) 781484
F: (01829) 781142
E: info@huxleyhall.co.uk
I: www.huxleyhall.co.uk

KIRKBY
Merseyside

Greenbank Guest House ♦♦♦
193 Rowan Drive, West Vale, Kirkby, Liverpool L32 0SG
T: (0151) 546 9971
F: (0151) 546 9971

KNUTSFORD
Cheshire

The Dog Inn ♦♦♦♦
Well Bank Lane, Over Peover, Knutsford WA16 8UP
T: (01625) 861421
F: (01625) 864800

Moat Hall Hotel ♦♦♦
Chelford Road, Marthall, Knutsford WA16 8SU
T: (01625) 860367
F: (01625) 861136
E: val@moathall.fsnet.co.uk
I: www.moat-hall-motel.co.uk

Wash Lane Farm ♦♦♦
Wash Lane, Allostock, Knutsford WA16 9JP
T: (01565) 722215
F: (01565) 722215

LACH DENNIS
Cheshire

Melvin Holme Farm ♦♦♦
Pennys Lane, Lach Dennis, Northwich CW9 7SJ
T: (01606) 330008

LANCASTER
Lancashire

Castle Hill House ♦♦♦
27 St Mary's Parade, Castle Hill, Lancaster LA1 1YX
T: (01524) 849137
F: (01524) 849137
E: gsutclif@aol.com

Farmhouse Tavern ♦♦♦
Morecambe Road, Lancaster LA1 5JB
T: (01524) 69255
F: (01524) 69255

Lancaster Town House ♦♦♦
11-12 Newton Terrace, Caton Road, Lancaster LA1 3PB
T: (01524) 65527
F: (01524) 383148
E: hedge-holmes@talk21.com
I: www.lancastertownhouse.co.uk

Low House Farm ♦♦♦
Claughton, Lancaster LA2 9LA
T: (015242) 21260
E: shirley@lunevalley.freeserve.co.uk

Middle Holly Cottage ♦♦♦
Middle Holly, Forton, Preston PR3 1AH
T: (01524) 792399

Old Station House ♦♦♦
25 Meeting House Lane, Lancaster LA1 1TX
T: (01524) 381060
F: (01524) 61845
E: oldstationhouse@amserve.com

Railton Hotel ♦
2 Station Road, Lancaster LA1 5SJ
T: (01524) 388364
F: (01524) 388364

The Shakespeare (Bed & Breakfast) ♦♦♦♦
96 St Leonardgate, Lancaster LA1 1NN
T: (01524) 841041

Wagon and Horses ♦♦♦
27 St Georges Quay, Lancaster LA1 1RD
T: (01524) 846094
E: davehorner@42oxfordstreet.freeserve.co.uk

LANGHO
Lancashire

Petre Lodge Country Hotel ♦♦♦♦
Northcote Road, Langho, Blackburn BB6 8BG
T: (01254) 245506
F: (01254) 245506
E: aslambert@fsbdial.co.uk

LARBRECK
Lancashire

Larbreck House Farm ♦♦♦♦
Well Lane, Larbreck, Preston PR3 0XR
T: (01995) 670416
E: harrypatknowles@aol.com
I: www.larbreckhousefarm.co.uk

LEYLAND
Lancashire

Oxen House Farm ♦♦♦
204 Longmeanygate, Leyland, Preston PR26 7TB
T: (01772) 423749
E: mal@oxen.fslife.co.uk
I: www.oxenhousefarm.gbr.cc

LITHERLAND
Merseyside

Litherland Park Bed and Breakfast ♦♦♦
34 Litherland Park, Litherland, Bootle L21 9HP
T: (0151) 928 1085

LITTLE BUDWORTH
Cheshire

Akesmere Farm ♦♦♦
Chester Road, Little Budworth, Tarporley CW6 9ER
T: (01829) 760348

LITTLEBOROUGH
Greater Manchester

Hollingworth Lake B&B ♦♦♦♦♦ GOLD AWARD
164 Smithy Bridge Road, Littleborough OL15 0DB
T: (01706) 376583
E: hollingworthlake@hotmail.co.uk
I: www.visitbritain.com

Swing Cottage ♦♦♦♦
31 Lakebank, Hollingworth Lake, Littleborough OL15 0DQ
T: (01706) 379094
F: (01706) 379091
E: swingcottage@aol.com
I: www.hollingworthlake.com

LIVERPOOL
Merseyside

Aachen Hotel ♦♦♦
89-91 Mount Pleasant, Liverpool L3 5TB
T: (0151) 709 3477
F: (0151) 709 1126
E: fpwaachen@netscapeonline.co.uk
I: www.aachenhotel.co.uk

Dolby Hotel ♦♦♦
36-42 Chaloner Street, Queen's Dock, Liverpool L3 4DE
T: (0151) 708 7272
F: (0151) 708 7266
E: liverpool@dolbyhotels.co.uk
I: www.dolbyhotels.co.uk

Feathers Hotel ♦♦♦♦
113-125 Mount Pleasant, Liverpool L3 5TF
T: (0151) 709 9655
F: (0151) 709 4840
E: feathershotel@feathers.uk.com
I: www.feathers.uk.com

Feathers Inn ♦♦
1 Paul Street, Liverpool L3 6DX
T: 0870 120 2348
F: 0870 120 2347

Holme-Leigh Guest House ♦♦
93 Woodcroft Road, Wavertree, Liverpool L15 2HG
T: (0151) 734 2216
F: (0151) 728 9521
E: bridges01@blueyonder.com

The Kensington 189 Rating Applied For
189 Kensington, Liverpool L7 2RF
T: (0151) 263 6807
F: (0151) 263 8349

Parkland Bed and Breakfast ♦♦♦
38 Coachman's Drive, Croxteth Park, Liverpool L12 0XH
T: (0151) 259 1417

Somersby ♦♦♦
100 Green Lane, Calderstones, Liverpool L18 2ER
T: (0151) 722 7549
F: (0151) 722 7549

LONGRIDGE
Lancashire

Oak Lea ♦♦♦♦
Clitheroe Road, Knowle Green, Longridge, Preston PR3 2YS
T: (01254) 878486
F: (01254) 878486
E: tandm.mellor@amserve.com

LONGTON
Lancashire

Willow Cottage ♦♦♦♦ SILVER AWARD
Longton Bypass, Longton, Preston PR4 4RA
T: (01772) 617570
E: info@lancashirebedandbreakfast.co.uk
I: www.lancashirebedandbreakfast.co.uk

LOWER WHITLEY
Cheshire

Tall Trees Lodge ♦♦♦
Tarporley Road, Lower Whitley, Warrington WA4 4EZ
T: (01928) 790824
F: (01928) 791330
E: bookings@talltreeslodge.co.uk
I: www.talltreeslodge.co.uk

LOWER WITHINGTON
Cheshire

Chapel Cottage Rating Applied For
Dicklow Cob, Lower Withington, Macclesfield SK11 9EA
T: (01477) 571489
E: wilbar1@supanet.com

LOWTON
Greater Manchester

Holley House ♦♦♦♦
7 Barnton Close, Lowton, Warrington WA3 2RS
T: (01942) 724166
F: (01942) 270556
E: denis@holleyhouse.fsnet.co.uk

LYDIATE
Merseyside

Goose Meadow Country Farm Bed and Breakfast ♦♦♦♦
Gore House Farm, Acres Lane, Lydiate, Liverpool L31 4EX
T: (0151) 526 0519
F: (0151) 527 2040
E: edwards@goosemeadow.co.uk
I: www.goosemeadow.co.uk

LYTHAM ST ANNES
Lancashire

Clifton Park Hotel ♦♦♦♦
299-301 Clifton Drive South, Lytham St Annes FY8 1HN
T: (01253) 725801
F: (01253) 721135
E: info@cliftonpark.co.uk
I: http://www.cliftonpark.co.uk

Strathmore Hotel ♦♦♦
305 Clifton Drive South, Lytham St Annes FY8 1HN
T: (01253) 725478

MACCLESFIELD
Cheshire

Carr House Farm ♦♦♦
Mill Lane, Adlington, Macclesfield SK10 4LG
T: (01625) 828337
F: (01625) 828337
E: isobel@carrhousefarm.fsnet.co.uk

Moorhayes House Hotel ♦♦♦
27 Manchester Road, Tytherington, Macclesfield SK10 2JJ
T: (01625) 433228
F: (01625) 429878
E: helen@moorhayes.co.uk
I: http://www.smoothhound.co.uk/hotels/moorhayes

Penrose Guest House ♦♦♦♦
56 Birtles Road, Whirley, Macclesfield SK10 3JQ
T: (01625) 615323
F: (01625) 432284
E: info@penroseguesthouse.co.uk
I: www.penroseguesthouse.co.uk

Sandpit Farm ♦♦♦
Messuage Lane, Marton, Macclesfield SK11 9HS
T: (01260) 224254

13 Sherwood Road
Rating Applied For
Macclesfield SK11 7RR
T: (01625) 420208

MAGHULL
Merseyside

Rosedene ♦♦♦
175 Liverpool Road South, Maghull, Liverpool L31 8AA
T: (0151) 527 1897

MALPAS
Cheshire

Hamilton House Bed and Breakfast ♦♦♦
Station Road, Hampton Heath, Malpas SY14 8JF
T: (01948) 820421
E: kath&ted@hamiltonhouse5.com
I: www.smoothhound.co.uk

MANCHESTER
Greater Manchester

Commercial Hotel ♦♦
125 Liverpool Road, Castlefield, Manchester M3 4JN
T: (0161) 834 3504
F: (0161) 835 2725

Dolby Hotel – Manchester ♦♦♦
55 Blackfriars Road, Manchester M3 7DB
T: (0161) 907 2277
F: (0161) 907 2266
E: info@dolbyhotel.com
I: www.dolbyhotel.com

Kempton House Hotel ♦♦♦
400 Wilbraham Road, Chorlton-cum-Hardy, Manchester M21 0UH
T: (0161) 881 8766
E: kempton.house@virgin.net
I: www.TheKempton.co.uk

Lansdowne Hotel
Rating Applied For
346 Wilmslow Road, Fallowfield, Manchester M14 6AB
T: (0161) 224 6244
F: (0161) 257 2938
E: lansdownehotelmanchester@hotmail.com
I: www.lansdownehotelmanchester.co.uk

Luther King House ♦♦♦
Brighton Grove, Wilmslow Road, Manchester M14 5JP
T: (0161) 224 6404
F: (0161) 248 9201
E: reception@lkh.co.uk
I: www.lkh.co.uk

Monroes Hotel ♦
38 London Road, Manchester M1 1PE
T: (0161) 236 0564

New Central Hotel
Rating Applied For
144-146 Heywood Street, Manchester M8 0PD
T: (0161) 205 2169
F: (0161) 205 2169

The Ox Bar Restaurant Hotel ♦♦♦
71 Liverpool Road, Castlefield, Manchester M3 4NQ
T: (0161) 839 7740
F: (0161) 839 7760
E: david@theox.co.uk
I: www.theox.co.uk

Rembrandt Hotel ♦♦♦
33 Sackville Street, City Centre, Manchester M1 3LZ
T: (0161) 236 1311
F: (0161) 236 4257
E: rembrandthotel@aol.com
I: www.rembrandtmanchester.com

MIDDLEWICH
Cheshire

Hopley House ♦♦♦
Wimboldsley, Middlewich CW10 0LN
T: (01270) 526292
F: (01270) 526292
E: margery@mread.freeserve.co.uk
I: www.hopleyhouse.co.uk

MINSHULL VERNON
Cheshire

Higher Elms Farm ♦♦
Minshull Vernon, Crewe CW1 4RG
T: (01270) 522252
F: (01270) 522252

MOBBERLEY
Cheshire

The Hinton
♦♦♦♦ SILVER AWARD
Town Lane, Mobberley, Knutsford WA16 7HH
T: (01565) 873484
F: (01565) 873484
I: www.hinton.co.uk

MORECAMBE
Lancashire

Ashley Hotel ♦♦♦
371 Marine Road East, Morecambe LA4 5AH
T: (01524) 412034
F: (01524) 421390
E: info@ashleyhotel.co.uk
I: www.ashleyhotel.co.uk

Balmoral Hotel ♦♦♦
34 Marine Road West, Morecambe LA3 1BZ
T: (01524) 418526
F: (01524) 400502
E: info@balmoralhotelmorecambe.co.uk
I: www.balmoralhotelmorecambe.co.uk

Belle Vue Hotel ♦♦♦
330 Marine Road, Morecambe LA4 5AA
T: (01524) 411375
F: (01524) 411375

Berkeley Private Hotel ♦♦♦
39 Marine Road West, Promenade West, Morecambe LA3 1BZ
T: (01524) 418201

Broadwater Hotel ♦♦
356 Marine Road East, Morecambe LA4 5AQ
T: (01524) 411333
F: (01524) 411333

Caledonian Hotel ♦♦
60 Marine Road West, Morecambe LA4 4ET
T: (01524) 418503
F: (01524) 401710

Craigwell Hotel ♦♦♦
372 Marine Road East, Morecambe LA4 5AH
T: (01524) 410095
E: lizdaniell@tesco.net

The Devonia ♦♦
11 Skipton Street, Morecambe LA4 4AR
T: (01524) 418506
F: (01524) 418506
E: thedevoniah@netscapeonline.co.uk

Durham Guest House ♦♦♦
73 Albert Road, Morecambe LA4 4HY
T: (01524) 424790
E: durhamhouse.com@bushinternet.com

Eidsforth Hotel ♦♦♦
317-318 Marine Road Central, Morecambe LA4 5AA
T: (01524) 411691
F: (01524) 832334

Glenthorn Hotel ♦♦
24-26 West End Road, Morecambe LA4 4DL
T: (01524) 411640
F: (01524) 411640
E: bookings@glenthorn.co.uk

Lakeland View Guest House ♦♦
130 Clarendon Road, Morecambe LA3 1SD
T: (01524) 415873
I: www.morecambebehta.co.uk

Roxbury Private Hotel ♦♦
78 Thornton Road, Morecambe LA4 5PJ
T: (01524) 410561
F: (01524) 420286
E: ritall@bigfoot.com

Seacrest ♦♦♦
9-13 West End Road, Morecambe LA4 4DJ
T: (01524) 411006

Tern Bay Hotel ♦♦♦
43 Heysham Road, Morecambe LA3 1DA
T: (01524) 421209
F: (01524) 831925
E: info@ternbayhotel.co.uk
I: www.ternbayhotel.co.uk

Trevelyan Hotel ♦♦♦
27 Seaview Parade, West End Road, Morecambe LA4 4DJ
T: (01524) 412013
F: (01524) 417590
E: thetrevelyan@supanet.com
I: www.thetrevelyan.freeserve.co.uk

Westleigh Hotel ♦♦♦
9 Marine Road, Morecambe LA3 1BS
T: (01524) 418352
F: (01524) 418352

Yacht Bay View Hotel ♦♦♦
359 Marine Road East, Morecambe LA4 5AQ
T: (01524) 414481
E: yachtbayview@hotmail.com
I: www.yachtbay.co.uk

MOTTRAM ST ANDREW
Cheshire

Goose Green Farm ♦♦♦
Oak Road, Mottram St Andrew, Macclesfield SK10 4RA
T: (01625) 828814
F: (01625) 828814
E: goosegreenfarm@talk21.com

MUCH HOOLE
Lancashire

The Barn Guest House ♦♦♦
204 Liverpool Old Road, Much Hoole, Preston PR4 4QB
T: (01772) 612654

NANTWICH
Cheshire

Henhull Hall ♦♦♦♦
Welshmans Lane, Nantwich
CW5 6AD
T: (01270) 624158
F: (01270) 624158
E: philip.percival@virgin.net

Stoke Grange Farm ♦♦♦♦
Chester Road, Nantwich
CW5 6BT
T: (01270) 625525
F: (01270) 625525
E: stokegrange@freeuk.com
I: www.stokegrangefarm.co.uk

NATEBY
Lancashire

Bowers Hotel and Brasserie ♦♦♦
Bowers Lane, Nateby, Preston
PR3 0JD
T: (01995) 601500
F: (01995) 603770

NELSON
Lancashire

Admergill Hall Farm ♦♦♦♦
Gisburn Road, Blacko, Nelson
BB9 6LB
T: (01282) 692909
E: admergillhallfm@btopenworld.com

Lovett House Guest House ♦♦♦
6 Howard Street, Nelson
BB9 7SZ
T: (01282) 697352
F: (01282) 700186
E: lovetthouse@ntlworld.com
I: www.lovetthouse.co.uk

NETHER ALDERLEY
Cheshire

Millbrook Cottage Guest House ♦♦♦♦
Congleton Road, Nether Alderley, Macclesfield SK10 4TW
T: (01625) 583567
F: (01625) 599556
E: millbrookcottage@hotmail.com
I: www.millbrookcottage.co.uk

NEW BRIGHTON
Merseyside

Sea Level Hotel ♦♦
126 Victoria Road, New Brighton, Wirral CH45 9LD
T: (0151) 639 3408
F: (0151) 639 3408

Sherwood Guest House ♦♦♦
55 Wellington Road, New Brighton, Wirral CH45 2ND
T: (0151) 639 5198
F: (0151) 639 9079
E: sheila@sherwood-guest-house.co.uk

Wellington House Hotel ♦♦♦
65 Wellington Road, New Brighton, Wirral CH45 2NE
T: (0151) 639 6594
F: (0151) 639 6594
I: www.wellington-house-hotel.freeserve.co.uk

NEWTON-LE-WILLOWS
Merseyside

The Pied Bull Hotel and Restaurant ♦♦♦
54 High Street, Newton-le-Willows WA12 9SH
T: (01925) 224 549
F: (01925) 291 929
E: piedbull@btopenworld.com
I: www.piedbull.com

NORTHWICH
Cheshire

Ash House Farm ♦♦♦♦
Chapel Lane, Acton Bridge, Northwich CW8 3QS
T: (01606) 852717
F: (01606) 853752
E: sue_scofield40@hotmail.com

Park Dale Guest House ♦♦♦
140 Middlewich Road, Rudheath, Northwich CW9 7DS
T: (01606) 45228
F: (01606) 331770

The Poplars
Rating Applied For
Norley Lane, Crowton, Northwich CW8 2RR
T: (01928) 788083
E: thepoplarsbandb@aol.com

OAKMERE
Cheshire

Springfield ♦♦♦
Chester Road, Oakmere, Northwich CW8 2HB
T: (01606) 882538
E: springfield_uk@hotmail.com

OLDHAM
Greater Manchester

Boothstead Farm ♦♦♦♦
Rochdale Road, Denshaw, Oldham OL3 5UE
T: (01457) 878622
E: boothsteadfarm@bushinternet .com

Globe Farm Guest House ♦♦♦
Huddersfield Road, Standedge, Delph, Oldham OL3 5LU
T: (01457) 873040
F: (01457) 873040
E: bookings@globe-farm.com
I: www.globefarm.co.uk

Temple Bar Farm ♦♦♦♦
Wallhill Road, Dobcross, Oldham OL3 5BH
T: (01457) 870099
F: (01457) 872003
E: chris@templebarfarm.co.uk
I: www.templebarfarm.co.uk

OVER ALDERLEY
Cheshire

Lower Harebarrow Farm ♦♦
Over Alderley, Macclesfield SK10 4SW
T: (01625) 829882

OVERTON
Lancashire

Globe Hotel ♦♦♦
40 Main Street, Overton, Morecambe LA3 3HG
T: (01524) 858228
F: (01524) 858073

PADIHAM
Lancashire

Windsor House ♦♦♦
71 Church Street, Padiham, Burnley BB12 8JH
T: (01282) 773271
E: churchstreetfb@talk21.com

PARBOLD
Lancashire

Red Lion Hotel ♦♦♦
9 Newburgh Village, Parbold, Wigan WN8 7NF
T: (01257) 462336
F: (01257) 462827
I: www.burtonwoodhotels.co.uk

PECKFORTON
Cheshire

Peckforton Castle ♦♦♦
Stone House Lane, Peckforton, Tarporley CW6 9TN
T: (01829) 260930
F: (01829) 261230
E: peckfortoncastle@peckforton.fsnet.co.uk
I: www.peckfortoncastle.co.uk

PICTON
Cheshire

Fox Covert Guest House ♦♦♦♦
Fox Covert Lane, Picton Gorse, Picton, Chester CH2 4HB
T: (01244) 300363
F: (01244) 300363
E: george.derby@virgin.net
I: www.thefoxcovert.co.uk

PRESTBURY
Cheshire

Artizana Suite ♦♦♦♦
The Village, Prestbury, Macclesfield SK10 4DG
T: (01625) 827582
F: (01625) 827582
E: suite@artizana.co.uk
I: www.artizana.co.uk/suite

PRESTON
Lancashire

Ashwood Hotel ♦♦♦
11-13 Fishergate Hill, Preston PR1 8JB
T: (01772) 203302
F: (01772) 203302

Derby Court Hotel ♦♦
1 Pole Street, Preston PR1 1DX
T: (01772) 202077
F: (01772) 252277

Olde Duncombe House ♦♦♦
Garstang Road, Bilsborrow, Preston PR3 0RE
T: (01995) 640336
F: (01995) 640336
E: oldedunc@aol.com
I: www.geocities.com/oldduncombehouse

Ye Horns Inn ♦♦♦♦
Horns Lane, Goosnargh, Preston PR3 2FJ
T: (01772) 865230
F: (01772) 864299
E: enquiries@yehornsinn.co.uk
I: www.yehornsinn.co.uk

PRESTWICH
Greater Manchester

The Church Inn ♦♦♦
Church Lane, Prestwich, Manchester M25 1A5
T: (0161) 798 6727
F: (0161) 773 6281
E: tom.gribben@virgin.com

RAWTENSTALL
Lancashire

Lindau Private Guest House ♦♦
131 Haslingden Old Road, Rawtenstall, Rossendale BB4 8RR
T: (01706) 214592
E: humm@globalnet.co.uk
I: www.lindau-guest-house.co.uk

RIBCHESTER
Lancashire

Park Hey ♦♦♦♦
Stoneygate Lane, Ribchester, Preston PR3 3YN
T: (01254) 878120
I: www.parkheybandb.co.uk

ROCHDALE
Greater Manchester

Fernhillbarn Bed & Breakfast ♦♦♦♦
Fernhill Lane, Lanehead, Rochdale OL12 6BW
T: (01706) 355671
F: (01706) 868405
E: info@meralfernhillbarnbb.com

ROSSENDALE
Lancashire

Peers Clough Farm ♦♦♦
Peers Clough Road, Rossendale BB4 9NG
T: (01706) 210552
E: peerscloughfarm@hotmail.com
I: www.peerscloughfarm.co.uk

RUSHTON
Cheshire

Hill House Farm ♦♦♦♦
The Hall Lane, Rushton, Tarporley CW6 9AU
T: (01829) 732238
F: (01829) 733929
E: rayner@hillhousefarm.fsnet.co.uk
I: www.hillhousefarm.info

SADDLEWORTH
Greater Manchester

Farrars Arms ♦♦♦
56 Oldham Road, Grasscroft, Oldham OL4 4HL
T: (01457) 872124
F: (01457) 820351

ST MICHAEL'S ON WYRE
Lancashire

Compton House ♦♦♦♦
Garstang Road, St Michael's on Wyre, Preston PR3 0TE
T: (01995) 679378
F: (01995) 679378
E: dave@compton-hs.co.uk
I: www.compton-hs.co.uk

SALE
Greater Manchester

Belforte House Hotel ♦♦♦
7-9 Broad Road, Sale M33 2AE
T: (0161) 973 8779
F: (0161) 973 8779
E: belfortehotel@aol.com

SALFORD
Greater Manchester

Hazeldean Hotel ♦♦♦
467 Bury New Road, Kersal Bar, Salford M7 3NE
T: (0161) 792 6667
F: (0161) 792 6668

Lyndale Court ♦♦♦
1-2 The Drive, Bury New Road, Salford M7 3ND
T: (0161) 792 7270
F: (0161) 792 7270
E: ian@lyndalecourt.co.uk
I: www.lyndalecourt.co.uk

White Lodge Hotel ♦♦
89 Great Cheetham Street West, Salford M7 2JA
T: (0161) 792 3047
F: (0161) 792 3047
E: wlh.man@orbix.uk.net
I: www.smoothhound.co.uk/hotels/whitelodgehotel.html

SALTNEY
Cheshire

Garden Gate Guest House ♦♦♦
8 Chester Street, Near Saltney, Chester CH4 8BJ
T: (01244) 682306
F: (01244) 723128
E: dollywal@msn.com

SANDBACH
Cheshire

Bagmere Bank Farm ♦♦♦♦
Brereton Park, Sandbach CW11 1RX
T: (01477) 537503
F: (01477) 537503

Tudor Lodge
Rating Applied For
101 Park Lane, Sandbach CW11 1EJ
T: (01270) 761304
E: allaways101@btinternet.com

SEALAND
Cheshire

The Elms Farmhouse Hotel ♦♦
Sealand Road, Sealand, Chester CH1 6BS
T: (01244) 880747
F: (01244) 880920

SIDDINGTON
Cheshire

Golden Cross Farm ♦♦♦
Siddington, Macclesfield
T: (01260) 224358

SILVERDALE
Lancashire

Silverdale Hotel ♦♦♦
Shore Road, Silverdale, Carnforth LA5 0TP
T: (01524) 701206

SLAIDBURN
Lancashire

Hark to Bounty Inn ♦♦♦
Slaidburn, Clitheroe BB7 3EP
T: (01200) 446246
F: (01200) 446361
E: isobel@hark-to-bounty.co.uk
I: www.hark-to-bounty.co.uk

SLYNE
Lancashire

Slyne Lodge ♦♦♦
92 Main Road, Slyne, Lancaster LA2 6AZ
T: (01524) 825035
F: (01524) 823467
I: www.slynelodge.co.uk

SOUTHPORT
Merseyside

Aaron Hotel ♦♦♦
18 Bath Street, Southport PR9 0DA
T: (01704) 530283
F: (01704) 501055
E: info@aaronhotel.co.uk
I: www.aaronhotel.co.uk

Ambassador Private Hotel ♦♦♦♦
13 Bath Street, Southport PR9 0DP
T: (01704) 543998
E: ambassador.walton@virgin.net
I: www.ambassadorprivatehotel.co.uk

Brae Mar Hotel ♦♦♦♦
4 Bath Street, Southport PR9 0DA
T: (01704) 535838
F: (01704) 535838
E: Mbraemar@aol.com

Carleton House Hotel ♦♦♦
17 Alexandra Road, Southport PR9 0NB
T: (01704) 538035
F: (01704) 538035
E: bookings@carleton-house.co.uk
I: www.carleton-house.co.uk

Carlton Lodge Hotel ♦♦♦♦
43 Bath Street, Southport PR9 0DP
T: (01704) 542290
F: (01704) 542290
E: benvale@which.net
I: www.smoothhound.co.uk/hotels/carlton

Clifton Villa Hotel ♦♦♦
6 Bath Street, Southport PR9 0DA
T: (01704) 535780
F: (01704) 549111
E: sales@cliftonvilla.co.uk
I: www.cliftonvilla.co.uk

Fairfield Private Hotel ♦♦♦
83 Promenade, Southport PR9 0JN
T: (01704) 530137

Le Maitre Hotel ♦♦♦♦
69 Bath Street, Southport PR9 0DN
T: (01704) 530394
F: (01704) 548755
E: enquiries@hotel-lemaitre.co.uk
I: www.hotel-lemaitre.co.uk

Leicester Hotel ♦♦♦
24 Leicester Street, Southport PR9 0EZ
T: (01704) 530049
F: (01704) 545561
E: leicester.hotel@mail.cybase.co.uk
I: www.leicesterhotelsouthport.co.uk

Lynwood Private Hotel ♦♦♦♦
11a Leicester Street, Southport PR9 0ER
T: (01704) 540794
F: (01704) 500724
I: www.smoothhound.co.uk/lynwood.html

Rosedale Hotel ♦♦♦♦
11 Talbot Street, Southport PR8 1HP
T: (01704) 530604
F: (01704) 530604
E: info@rosedalehotelsouthport.co.uk
I: www.rosedalehotelsouthport.co.uk

Sandy Brook Farm ♦♦♦
52 Wyke Cop Road, Scarisbrick, Southport PR8 5LR
T: (01704) 880337
F: (01704) 880337
E: sandybrookfarm@lycos.co.uk

Sidbrook Hotel ♦♦♦
14 Talbot Street, Southport PR8 1HP
T: (01704) 530608
F: (01704) 530608
E: sidbrookhotel@tesco.net
I: www.sidbrookhotel.co.uk

Silverdale Hotel ♦♦♦
10 Victoria Street, Southport PR9 0DU
T: (01704) 536479
F: (01704) 536479
E: jwade@free.uk.com

Sunnyside Hotel ♦♦♦
47 Bath Street, Southport PR9 0DP
T: (01704) 536521
F: (01704) 539237
E: sunnysidehotel@rapid.co.uk
I: www.sunny-lisa.co.uk

Waterford ♦♦♦♦
37 Leicester Street, Southport PR9 0EX
T: (01704) 530559
F: (01704) 542630
E: reception@waterford-hotel.co.uk
I: www.waterford-hotel.co.uk

Whitworth Falls Hotel ♦♦♦♦
16 Lathom Road, Southport PR9 0JH
T: (01704) 530074
E: whitworthfalls@rapid.co.uk
I: www.whitworthfallshotel.co.uk

Windsor Lodge Hotel ♦♦♦
37 Saunders Street, Southport PR9 0HJ
T: (01704) 530070

STOCKPORT
Greater Manchester

Hallfield Guesthouse ♦♦♦♦
50 Hall Street, Stockport SK1 4DA
T: (0161) 429 8977
F: (0161) 429 9017
E: hallfieldhouse@btconnect.com
I: www.hallfieldguesthouse.co.uk

Henry's Guest House ♦♦♦♦
204-206, Buxton Rd, Davenport, Stockport SK2 7AE
T: (0161) 292 0202
F: (0161) 355 6585
E: enquiries@henryshotel.com
I: www.henryshotel.com

Moss Deeping ♦♦♦
7 Robins Lane, Bramhall, Stockport SK7 2PE
T: (0161) 439 1969
F: (0161) 439 9985
E: gbanks7872@aol.com
I: www.mossdeeping.co.uk

Needhams Farm ♦♦♦
Uplands Road, Werneth Low, Gee Cross, Hyde SK14 3AG
T: (0161) 368 4610
F: (0161) 367 9106
E: charlotte@needhamsfarm.co.uk
I: www.needhamsfarm.co.uk

STONYHURST
Lancashire

Alden Cottage
♦♦♦♦ GOLD AWARD
Kemple End, Birdy Brow, Stonyhurst, Clitheroe BB7 9QY
T: (01254) 826468
F: (01254) 826468
E: carpenter@aldencottage.f9.co.uk
I: http://fp.aldencottage.f9.co.uk

TARPORLEY
Cheshire

Foresters Arms ♦♦♦
92 High Street, Tarporley CW6 0AX
T: (01829) 733151
F: (01829) 730020
E: stuart@forestersarms.fsbusiness.co.uk

TATTENHALL
Cheshire

Broad Oak Farm ♦♦♦
Birds Lane, Tattenhall, Chester CH3 9NL
T: (01829) 770325
F: (01829) 771546

Ford Farm ♦♦♦
Newton Lane, Tattenhall, Chester CH3 9NE
T: (01829) 770307

THURNHAM
Lancashire

The Stork Inn ♦♦♦
Conder Green, Thurnham, Lancaster LA2 0AN
T: (01524) 751234
F: (01524) 752660
E: the.stork@virgin.net
I: www.mortal-man-inns.co.uk

TIMPERLEY
Greater Manchester

Acorn of Oakmere ♦♦♦
6 Wingate Drive, Timperley, Altrincham WA15 7PX
T: (0161) 980 8391
F: (0161) 980 8391
E: oakmere@handbag.com

TORSIDE
Greater Manchester

The Old House ♦♦♦
Woodhead Road, Torside, Glossop SK13 1HU
T: (01457) 857527
E: oldhouse@torside.co.uk
I: www.oldhouse.torside.co.uk

TOSSIDE
Lancashire

Dog & Partridge ♦♦♦
Tosside, Skipton BD23 4SQ
T: (01729) 840668

UTKINTON
Cheshire

Yew Tree Farm ♦♦♦
Fishers Green, Utkinton, Tarporley CW6 0JG
T: (01829) 732441

WADDINGTON
Lancashire

Peter Barn Country House
♦♦♦♦
Cross Lane, Waddington, Clitheroe BB7 3JH
T: (01200) 428585
E: jean@peterbarn.co.uk

WALLASEY
Merseyside

The Russell Hotel ♦♦
44 Church Street, Wallasey CH44 7BA
T: (0151) 639 5723
F: (0151) 639 5723
E: mail@russellhotel.fnet.co.uk

WATERLOO
Merseyside

Marlborough Hotel ♦♦
21 Crosby Road South, Waterloo, Liverpool L22 1RG
T: (0151) 928 7709
F: (0151) 928 7709

WEST DERBY
Merseyside

Blackmoor Bed & Breakfast
♦♦♦
160 Blackmoor Drive, West Derby, Liverpool L12 9EF
T: (0151) 291 1407
F: (0151) 291 1407

WEST KIRBY
Merseyside

Caldy Warren Cottage ♦♦♦♦
42 Caldy Road, West Kirby, Wirral CH48 2HQ
T: (0151) 625 8740
F: (0151) 625 4115
I: www.warrencott.demon.co.uk

WESTHOUGHTON
Greater Manchester

Daisy Hill Hotel ♦♦♦
3 Lower Leigh Road, Westhoughton, Bolton BL5 2JP
T: (01942) 812096
F: (01942) 797180
E: daisy.hill@cwcom.net
I: www.daisyhillhotel.co.uk

WESTON
Cheshire

Snape Farm ♦♦♦
Snape Lane, Weston, Crewe CW2 5NB
T: (01270) 820208
F: (01270) 820208
E: jean@snapefarm.fsnet.co.uk

WHALLEY
Lancashire

Bayley Arms Hotel ♦♦♦
Avenue Road, Hurst Green, Whalley, Clitheroe BB7 9QB
T: (01254) 826478
F: (01254) 826797

WHITEWELL
Lancashire

The Inn at Whitewell ♦♦♦♦
Forest of Bowland, Whitewell, Clitheroe BB7 3AT
T: (01200) 448222
F: (01200) 448298

WHITWORTH
Lancashire

Hindle Pastures ♦♦♦♦
Highgate Lane, Whitworth, Rochdale OL12 0TS
T: (01706) 643310
F: (01706) 653846
E: p-marshall@breathemail.net
I: www.smoothhound.co.uk/hotels/hindlepastures

WIGAN
Greater Manchester

Wilden ♦♦♦
11a Miles Lane, Shevington, Wigan WN6 8EB
T: (01257) 251516
F: (01257) 255622
E: wildenbandb@aol.com

WILMSLOW
Cheshire

Finney Green Cottage ♦♦♦♦
134 Manchester Road, Wilmslow SK9 2JW
T: (01625) 533343
F: (01625) 533100
I: www.finneygreencottage.co.uk

Heatherlea Guest House
♦♦♦♦
106 Lacey Green, Wilmslow SK9 4BN
T: (01625) 522872
F: (01625) 527872

Hollow Bridge Guest House
♦♦♦♦
90 Manchester Road, Wilmslow SK9 2JY
T: (01625) 537303
F: (01625) 528718
E: lynandjack@hollowbridge.com
I: www.hollowbridge.com

King William Hotel ♦♦♦
35 Manchester Road, Wilmslow SK9 1BQ
T: (01625) 524022
I: www.kingwilliam.20m.com

Marigold House ♦♦♦♦
132 Knutsford Road, Wilmslow SK9 6JH
T: (01625) 584414

WINCLE
Cheshire

Hill Top Farm ♦♦♦♦
Wincle, Macclesfield SK11 0QH
T: (01260) 227257
E: a.brocklehurst@talk21.com

WINSFORD
Cheshire

Elm Cottage ♦♦♦
Chester Lane, Winsford CW7 2QJ
T: (01829) 760544
F: (01829) 760544
E: chris@elmcottagecp.co.uk
I: www.elmcottagecp.co.uk

Hermitage House ♦♦♦♦
1 Hareswood Close, Littler Lane, Winsford CW7 2TP
T: (01606) 550544
F: (01606) 860002
E: lgordon@heatherproducts.fsnet.co.uk

The Winsford Lodge ♦♦♦
85-87 Station Road, Winsford CW7 3DE
T: (01606) 862008
F: (01606) 591822
E: winsfordlodge@aol.com
I: www.winsfordlodge.co.uk

WINTERLEY
Cheshire

Field Mews B&B ♦♦♦♦
The Fields, 36 Hassall Road, Winterley, Sandbach CW11 4RL
T: (01270) 761858
F: (01270) 761858

WISWELL
Lancashire

Pepper Hill
♦♦♦♦ SILVER AWARD
Pendleton Road, Wiswell, Clitheroe BB7 9BZ
T: (01254) 825098

WORSTON
Lancashire

Calf's Head ♦♦♦♦
Worston, Clitheroe BB7 1QA
T: (01200) 441218
F: (01200) 441510

WRIGHTINGTON
Lancashire

Kings
Rating Applied For
170 Mossy Lea Road, Wrightington, Wigan WN6 9RD
T: (01257) 425053
E: kingwrightington@aol.com

WYCOLLER
Lancashire

Parson Lee Farm ♦♦♦
Wycoller, Wycoller BB8 8SU
T: (01282) 864747
F: (01282) 864747
E: pathodgson@hotmail.com
I: www.parsonleefarm.co.uk

YORKSHIRE

ACKLAM
North Yorkshire

Trout Pond Barn ♦♦♦♦
Acklam, Malton YO17 9RG
T: (01653) 658468
F: (01653) 698688
E: margaret@troutpondbarn.co.uk
I: www.troutpondbarn.co.uk

ADDINGHAM
West Yorkshire

The Crown Inn ♦♦♦
Main Street, Addingham, Ilkley LS29 0NS
T: (01943) 830278
F: (01943) 831715
E: mariawells350@aol.com

Lumb Beck Farmhouse Bed and Breakfast
♦♦♦♦ SILVER AWARD
Moorside Lane, Addingham, Ilkley LS29 9JX
T: (01943) 830400

Walker Acre House B&B ♦♦♦
School Lane, Addingham, Ilkley LS29 0JL
T: (01943) 839950
E: miladymarim@aol.com

AIRTON
North Yorkshire

Lindon House ♦♦♦
Airton, Skipton BD23 4BE
T: (01729) 830418

AISLABY
North Yorkshire

Blacksmiths Arms Restaurant
♦♦♦
Aislaby, Pickering YO18 8PE
T: (01751) 472182
E: blacksmiths@mail.com

ALDBROUGH
East Riding of Yorkshire

Wentworth House Hotel
♦♦♦♦
12 Seaside Road, Aldbrough, Hull HU11 4RX
T: (01964) 527246
F: (01964) 527246
E: enquiry@wentworthhouse.fsnet.co.uk
I: www.wentworthhouse.fsnet.co.uk

West Carlton
♦♦♦♦ SILVER AWARD
Carlton Road, Aldbrough, Hull HU11 4RB
T: (01964) 527724
F: (01964) 527505
E: caroline_maltas@hotmail.com
I: www.west-carlton.co.uk

ALDFIELD
North Yorkshire

Bay Tree Farm
♦♦♦♦ SILVER AWARD
Aldfield, Ripon HG4 3BE
T: (01765) 620394
F: (01765) 620394
E: btfarm@ppcmail.co.uk
I: www.baytreefarm.co.uk

ALLERTON
West Yorkshire

Victoria Hotel ♦♦♦
10 Cottingley Road, Sandy Lane, Allerton, Bradford BD15 9JP
T: (01274) 823820
F: (01274) 823820

AMOTHERBY
North Yorkshire

Old Station Farm Country Guest House ♦♦♦♦ GOLD AWARD
High Street, Amotherby, Malton YO17 6TL
T: (01653) 693683
F: (01653) 693683
E: info@oldstationfarm.co.uk
I: www.oldstationfarm.co.uk

AMPLEFORTH
North Yorkshire

Carr House Farm ♦♦♦
West End, Ampleforth, York YO62 4ED
T: (01347) 868526
E: enquiries@carrhousefarm.co.uk
I: www.carrhousefarm.co.uk

Daleside ♦♦♦♦♦ SILVER AWARD
East End, Ampleforth, York YO62 4DA
T: (01439) 788266
E: dalesidepaul@hotmail.com

Shallowdale House ♦♦♦♦♦ GOLD AWARD
West End, Ampleforth, York YO62 4DY
T: (01439) 788325
F: (01439) 788885
E: phillip@shallowdalehouse.co.uk
I: www.shallowdalehouse.co.uk

APPLETREEWICK
North Yorkshire

Knowles Lodge ♦♦♦♦ SILVER AWARD
Appletreewick, Skipton BD23 6DQ
T: (01756) 720228
F: (01756) 720381
E: pam@knowleslodge.com
I: www.knowleslodge.com

ARKENGARTHDALE
North Yorkshire

Chapel Farmhouse ♦♦♦♦
Whaw, Arkengarthdale, Richmond DL11 6RT
T: (01748) 884062
F: (01748) 884062
E: chapelfarmbb@aol.com

The Charles Bathurst Inn ♦♦♦♦ SILVER AWARD
Arkengarthdale, Richmond DL11 6EN
T: (01748) 884567
F: (01748) 884599
E: info@cbinn.co.uk
I: www.cbinn.co.uk

The Ghyll ♦♦♦
Arkle Town, Arkengarthdale, Richmond DL11 6EU
T: (01748) 884353
F: (01748) 884015
E: bookings@theghyll.co.uk
I: www.theghyll.co.uk

ASKRIGG
North Yorkshire

The Apothecary's House ♦♦♦♦ SILVER AWARD
Main Street, Askrigg, Leyburn DL8 3HT
T: (01969) 650626

Bottom Chapel ♦♦♦♦
Main Street, Askrigg, Leyburn DL8 3HT
T: (01969) 650180

Helm ♦♦♦♦♦ GOLD AWARD
Askrigg, Leyburn DL8 3JF
T: (01969) 650443
F: (01969) 650443
E: holiday@helmyorkshire.com
I: www.helmyorkshire.com

Home Farm ♦♦♦
Stalling Busk, Askrigg, Leyburn DL8 3DH
T: (01969) 650360

Milton House ♦♦♦♦
Leyburn Road, Askrigg, Leyburn DL8 3HJ
T: (01969) 650217

Stoney End ♦♦♦♦ SILVER AWARD
Worton, Leyburn DL8 3ET
T: (01969) 650652
F: (01969) 650077
E: pmh@stoneyend.co.uk
I: www.stoneyend.co.uk

Thornsgill House ♦♦♦♦
Moor Road, Askrigg, Leyburn DL8 3HH
T: (01969) 650617
E: thornsgill.house@virgin.net
I: www.thornsgill.co.uk

AUSTWICK
North Yorkshire

Dalesbridge House ♦♦♦♦
Austwick, Lancaster LA2 8AZ
T: (01524) 251021
F: (01524) 251051
E: info@dalesbridge.co.uk
I: www.dalesbridge.co.uk

Pengarth ♦♦♦♦
Austwick, Lancaster LA2 8BD
T: (015242) 51073
E: pengarth@austwick-nyorks.fsnet.co.uk
I: www.pengarthaustwick.co.uk

Wood View ♦♦♦♦
The Green, Austwick, Lancaster LA2 8BB
T: (015242) 51268
F: (015242) 51268
E: jennifersuri@msn.com
I: www.yorkshiredales.com

AYSGARTH
North Yorkshire

Cornlee ♦♦♦
Aysgarth, Leyburn DL8 3AE
T: (01969) 663779
F: (01969) 663779
E: cornlee@tesco.net
I: www.cornlee.co.uk

Field House ♦♦♦♦
Aysgarth, Leyburn DL8 3AB
T: (01969) 663556
E: Ros.evans@voidalimage.com
I: www.wensleydale.org

Stow House Hotel ♦♦♦♦
Aysgarth Falls, Aysgarth, Leyburn DL8 3SR
T: (01969) 663635
E: info@stowhouse.co.uk
I: www.stowhouse.co.uk

Wensleydale Farmhouse ♦♦♦
Aysgarth, Leyburn DL8 3SR
T: (01969) 663534
F: (01969) 663534
E: wykesarego@aol.com

Wheatsheaf Hotel ♦♦♦
Carperby, Leyburn DL8 4DF
T: (01969) 663216
F: (01969) 663019
E: wheatsheaf@paulmit.globalnet.co.uk
I: www.wheatsheafinwensleydale.co.uk

BAILDON
West Yorkshire

Ford House Farm Bed and Breakfast ♦♦♦♦
Ford Houses, Buck Lane, Baildon, Shipley BD17 7RW
T: (01274) 584489
F: (01274) 584489

BAINBRIDGE
North Yorkshire

Hazel's Roost ♦♦♦
Bainbridge, Leyburn DL8 3EH
T: (01969) 650400

High Force Farm ♦♦♦
Raydaleside, Askrigg, Bainbridge, Leyburn DL8 3DL
T: (01969) 650379
F: (01969) 650826
E: highforce@uk4free.net

The Manor House ♦♦♦
Bainbridge, Leyburn DL8 3EN
T: (01969) 650140
F: (01969) 640140
E: paul@manorhousebainbridge.fsnet.co.uk

BAINTON
East Riding of Yorkshire

Bainton Burrows Farm ♦♦♦
Bainton, Driffield YO25 9BS
T: (01377) 217202

BARLOW
North Yorkshire

Berewick House ♦♦♦♦
Park Lane, Barlow, Selby YO8 8EW
T: (01757) 617051
E: Wilson.Guesthouse@Berewick.co.uk
I: www.selbynet.co.uk/berewick/house.html

BARNETBY
South Humberside

Reginald House ♦♦♦♦
27 Queens Road, Barnetby DN38 6JH
T: (01652) 688566
F: (01652) 688510

Whistle & Flute ♦♦♦
Railway Street, Barnetby DN38 6DG
T: (01652) 688238
F: (01652) 688238

BARTON-LE-STREET
North Yorkshire

Laurel Barn Cottage ♦♦♦
Barton-le-Street, Malton YO17 6QB
T: (01653) 628329

BARTON-UPON-HUMBER
North Lincolnshire

Elio's Restaurant ♦♦♦
11 Market Place, Barton-upon-Humber DN18 5DA
T: (01652) 635147
F: (01652) 635147
E: elio1948@aol.com

George Hotel ♦♦
George Street, Barton-upon-Humber DN18 5ES
T: (01652) 662001
F: (01652) 662002

BECK HOLE
North Yorkshire

Brookwood Farm ♦♦♦♦ SILVER AWARD
Beck Hole, Whitby YO22 5LE
T: (01947) 896402
E: bookings@brookwoodfarm.co.uk
I: www.brookwoodfarm.co.uk

BEDALE
North Yorkshire

The Castle Arms Inn ♦♦♦♦
Snape, Bedale DL8 2TB
T: (01677) 470270
F: (01677) 470837
E: castlearms@aol.com

Elmfield Country House ♦♦♦♦♦
Arrathorne, Bedale DL8 1NE
T: (01677) 450558
F: (01677) 450557
E: stay@elmfieldhouse.freeserve.co.uk
I: www.elmfieldhouse.co.uk

Georgian Bed and Breakfast ♦♦♦♦
16 North End, Bedale DL8 1AB
T: (01677) 424454
E: georgian@bedale-town.com
I: bedaletown.com

Mill Close Farm ♦♦♦♦♦ SILVER AWARD
Patrick Brompton, Bedale DL8 1JY
T: (01677) 450257
F: (01677) 450585
E: millclosefarm@btopenworld.com
I: www.smoothhound.co.uk/hotels/millclosefarm.html

BEEFORD
East Riding of Yorkshire

Pinderhill Farm Bed & Breakfast ♦♦♦♦
Beverley Road, Beeford, Driffield YO25 8AE
T: (01262) 488645

BEESTON
West Yorkshire

Crescent Hotel ♦♦
274 Dewsbury Road, Beeston, Leeds LS11 6JT
T: (0113) 270 1819
F: (0113) 270 1819
I: www.crescentprivatehotel.co.uk

BELL BUSK
North Yorkshire

Lowlands Guest House ♦♦♦♦
Coniston Cold, Skipton BD23 4EA
T: (01756) 749805
F: (01756) 749805
E: janet.gilbert@amserve.com

Newton Grange Rating Applied For
Bank Newton, Gargrave, Skipton BD23 3NT
T: (01756) 748140
E: bookings@banknewton.fsnet.co.uk

Tudor House ♦♦♦♦
Bell Busk, Skipton BD23 4DT
T: (01729) 830301
F: (01729) 830301
E: bellbusk.hitch@virgin.net
I: www.tudorbellbusk.co.uk

BEVERLEY
East Riding of Yorkshire

Apple Tree House ♦♦♦♦
31 Norwood, Beverley
HU17 9HN
T: (01482) 873615
F: (01482) 866666
E: enquiries@appletreehouse.co.uk
I: www.appletreehouse.co.uk

Beck View Guest House ♦♦♦♦
1a Blucher Lane, Beverley
HU17 0PT
T: (01482) 882332
E: BeckViewHouse@aol.com

Eastgate Guest House ♦♦♦
7 Eastgate, Beverley HU17 0DR
T: (01482) 868464
F: (01482) 871899

Market Cross Hotel ♦♦♦
14 Lairgate, Beverley HU17 8EE
T: (01482) 679029
F: (01482) 679024
E: xkeysbev@xkeysbev.karoo.co.uk

North Bar Lodge ♦♦♦
28 North Bar, Beverley
HU17 7AB
T: (01482) 881375
F: (01482) 861184

Number One ♦♦♦
Woodlands, Beverley HU17 8BT
T: (01482) 862752
F: (01482) 862752
E: neilandsarah@mansle.karoo.co.uk
I: www.beverley.net/accommodation/numberone

The Pipe and Glass Inn ♦♦♦
West End, South Dalton,
Beverley HU17 7PN
T: (01430) 810246
F: (01430) 810246

Rudstone Walk Country Accommodation ♦♦♦♦
South Cave, Near Beverley,
Brough HU15 2AH
T: (01430) 422230
F: (01430) 424552
E: office@rudstone-walk.co.uk
I: www.rudstone-walk.co.uk

Springdale Bed and Breakfast ♦♦♦
Long Lane, Beverley HU17 0RN
T: (01482) 888264

6 St Mary's Close ♦♦♦
St Mary's Close, Beverley
HU17 7AY
T: (01482) 868837

Trinity Guest House ♦♦♦
Trinity Lane, Beverley HU17 0AR
T: (01482) 869537
E: info@trinity-house.net
I: www.trinity-house.net

The Tudor Rose Hotel & Restaurant ♦♦♦
Wednesday Market, Beverley
HU17 0DG
T: (01482) 882028
F: (01482) 882028

13 Westfield Avenue ♦♦♦
Westfield Avenue, Beverley
HU17 7HA
T: (01482) 860212

Windmill Inn ♦♦
53 Lairgate, Beverley HU17 8ET
T: (01482) 862817
F: (01482) 870741

BINGLEY
West Yorkshire

Ashley End ♦♦♦
22 Ashley Road, Bingley
BD16 1DZ
T: (01274) 569679

Five Rise Locks Hotel & Restaurant
♦♦♦♦ SILVER AWARD
Beck Lane, Bingley BD16 4DD
T: (01274) 565296
F: (01274) 568828
E: info@five-rise-locks.co.uk
I: www.five-rise-locks.co.uk

March Cote Farm ♦♦♦♦
Lee Lane, Cottingley, Bingley
BD16 1UB
T: (01274) 487433
F: (01274) 561074
E: jean.warin@nevisuk.net
I: www.yorkshirenet.co.uk/accqde/marchcote

BISHOP THORNTON
North Yorkshire

Dukes Place ♦♦♦♦
Bishop Thornton, Harrogate
HG3 3JY
T: (01765) 620229
F: (01765) 620454
E: jakimoorhouse@onetel.net.uk

BISHOP WILTON
East Riding of Yorkshire

High Belthorpe ♦♦♦
Thorny Lane, Bishop Wilton,
York YO42 1SB
T: (01759) 368238
I: www.holidayswithdogs.com

BLAXTON
South Yorkshire

Station Hotel ♦♦
Station Road, Blaxton,
Doncaster DN9 3AA
T: (01302) 770218

BOLTBY
North Yorkshire

Willow Tree Cottage Bed and Breakfast ♦♦♦♦
Boltby, Thirsk YO7 2DY
T: (01845) 537406
F: (01845) 537073
E: townsend.sce@virgin.net

BOLTON PERCY
North Yorkshire

Glebe Farm ♦♦♦♦
Bolton Percy, York YO23 7AL
T: (01904) 744228

BOROUGHBRIDGE
North Yorkshire

Arncliffe ♦♦♦
Church Lane, Boroughbridge,
York YO51 9BA
T: (01423) 322048
F: (01423) 322048
E: mht@arncliffe63.freeserve.co.uk

Burton Grange ♦♦♦
Helperby, York YO61 2RY
T: (01423) 360825
E: burton_grange@hotmail.com

BOSTON SPA
West Yorkshire

Crown Hotel ♦♦♦
128 High Street, Boston Spa,
Wetherby LS23 6BW
T: (01937) 842608
F: (01937) 541373

Four Gables
♦♦♦♦ SILVER AWARD
Oaks Lane, Boston Spa,
Wetherby LS23 6DS
T: (01937) 845592
F: (01937) 845592
E: info@fourgables.co.uk
I: www.fourgables.co.uk

BRADFORD
West Yorkshire

Brow Top Farm
♦♦♦♦ SILVER AWARD
Brow Top, Clayton, Bradford
BD14 6PS
T: (01274) 882178
F: (01274) 882178
E: ruthpriestley@farmersweekly.co.uk
I: www.browtopfarm.co.uk

Carnoustie ♦♦♦
8 Park Grove, Bradford BD9 4JY
T: (01274) 490561
F: (01274) 490561
E: carnoustie1@activemail.co.uk

Castle Hotel ♦♦♦
20 Grattan Road, Bradford
BD1 2LU
T: (01274) 393166
F: (01274) 393200
E: rooms@castle-bfd.freeserve.co.uk
I: www.thecastlehotel.britain-uk.com

Hillside House ♦♦♦
10 Hazelhurst Road, Daisy Hill,
Bradford BD9 6BJ
T: (01274) 542621

Ivy Guest House ♦♦
3 Melbourne Place, Bradford
BD5 0HZ
T: (01274) 727060
F: (01274) 306347
E: nickbaggio@aol.com

New Beehive Inn ♦♦♦
171 Westgate, Bradford
BD1 3AA
T: (01274) 721784
F: (01274) 375092
I: www.s-h-systems.co.uk/hotels/beehive.html

Norland Guest House ♦♦♦
695 Great Horton Road,
Bradford BD7 4DU
T: (01274) 571698
F: (01274) 503290
E: pipin@ic24.net
I: www.norlandguesthouse.gbr.cc

Shaw House ♦♦♦
35 Bierley Lane, Bradford
BD4 6AD
T: (01274) 682929

Westleigh Hotel ♦♦♦
30 Easby Road, Bradford
BD7 1QX
T: (01274) 727089
F: (01274) 394658
E: info@thewestleighhotel.co.uk
I: www.thewestleighhotel.co.uk

Woodlands Guest House ♦♦♦♦
2 The Grove, Shelf, Halifax
HX3 7PD
T: (01274) 677533
I: www.yorkshirenet.com

BRAMHOPE
West Yorkshire

The Cottages
♦♦♦♦ SILVER AWARD
Moor Road, Bramhope, Leeds
LS16 9HH
T: (0113) 284 2754
F: (0113) 203 7496

BRIDGE HEWICK
North Yorkshire

The Black A Moor Hotel
Rating Applied For
Boroughbridge Road, Bridge
Hewick, Ripon HG4 5AA
T: (01765) 603511

BRIDLINGTON
East Riding of Yorkshire

Balmoral Private Hotel ♦♦♦
21 Marshall Avenue, Bridlington
YO15 2DT
T: (01262) 676678
F: (01262) 424672
E: hotel@balmoral-bridlington.co.uk
I: www.balmoral-hotel.net

Bay Court Hotel
♦♦♦♦ SILVER AWARD
35a Sands Lane, Bridlington
YO15 2JG
T: (01262) 676288
E: bay.court@virgin.net
I: www.baycourt.co.uk

The Bay Ridge Hotel ♦♦♦
11-13 Summerfield Road,
Bridlington YO15 3LF
T: (01262) 673425
F: (01262) 673425

Belmont ♦♦♦♦
27 Flamborough Road,
Bridlington YO15 2HU
T: (01262) 673808

Blantyre House Hotel ♦♦♦
21 Pembroke Terrace,
Bridlington YO15 3BX
T: (01262) 400660
E: baker@blantyre21.fsnet.co.uk

Bluebell Guest House ♦♦♦
3 St Annes Road, Bridlington
YO15 2JB
T: (01262) 675163
E: judith@mybluebell.com
I: www.mybluebell.com

Bon Accord ♦♦
64 Windsor Crescent,
Bridlington YO15 3JA
T: (01262) 675589

Bosville Arms Country Hotel ♦♦♦♦
Main Street, Rudston, Driffield
YO25 4UB
T: (01262) 420259
F: (01262) 420259
E: hogan@bosville.co.uk
I: www.bosville.co.uk

The Brockton Hotel ♦♦♦
4 Shaftesbury Road, Bridlington
YO15 3NP
T: (01262) 673967
F: (01262) 673967
E: grbrocktonhotel@aol.com

The Chimes ♦♦♦
9 Wellington Road, Bridlington
YO15 2BA
T: (01262) 401659
F: (01262) 401659
E: sandisbb@aol.com
I: www.smoothhound.co.uk/hotels/chimesgu.html

The Crescent Hotel ♦♦♦
12 The Crescent, Bridlington
YO15 2NX
T: (01262) 401015
F: (01262) 400465

Dulverton Court Hotel ♦♦♦
17 Victoria Road, Bridlington
YO15 2BW
T: (01262) 672600

Edelweiss ♦♦♦
86/88 Windsor Crescent,
Bridlington YO15 3JA
T: (01262) 673822
F: (01262) 673822

The Glen Alan Hotel ♦♦♦
21 Flamborough Road,
Bridlington YO15 2HU
T: (01262) 674650

The Grantlea Guest House ♦♦♦
2 South Street, Bridlington
YO15 3BY
T: (01262) 400190

The Jasmine Guest House ♦♦♦
27-29 Richmond Street,
Bridlington YO15 3DL
T: (01262) 676608
E: thejasmineguesthouse@fsmail.net
I: www.uk-yorkshireexplore.co.uk

London Hotel ♦♦♦
1 Royal Crescent, York Road,
Bridlington YO15 2PF
T: (01262) 675377

Longcroft Hotel ♦♦♦♦
100 Trinity Road, Bridlington
YO15 2HF
T: (01262) 672180
F: (01262) 608240
E: longcroft53@hotmail.com

Longleigh Guest House ♦♦♦♦
12 Swanland Avenue,
Bridlington YO15 2HH
T: (01262) 676234

Maryland Bed & Breakfast ♦♦♦♦
66 Wellington Road, Bridlington
YO15 2AZ
T: (01262) 671088
E: mills@marylandbandb.fsbusiness.co.uk

The Mayville Guest House ♦♦♦
74 Marshall Avenue, Bridlington
YO15 2DS
T: (01262) 674420
F: (01262) 674420

The Mount Hotel ♦♦♦♦
2 Roundhay Road, Bridlington
YO15 3JY
T: (01262) 672306
F: (01262) 672306

Newcliffe Hotel ♦♦♦
6 Belgrave Road, Bridlington
YO15 3JR
T: (01262) 674244

Queens Hotel ♦♦♦
75/77 High Street, Bridlington
YO16 4PN
T: (01262) 672051

Rags Restaurant & Dyl's Hotel ♦♦♦
Langdales Wharf, Bridlington
YO15 3AN
T: (01262) 400355
F: (01262) 674729
E: lesdylrags@freedomland.co.uk
I: bridlington.net/accommodation

Rivendell Hotel ♦♦♦
19 Sands Lane, Bridlington
YO15 2JG
T: (01262) 679189

Rosebery House ♦♦♦♦
1 Belle Vue, Tennyson Avenue,
Bridlington YO15 2ET
T: (01262) 670336
F: (01262) 608381
E: roseberyhouse@zexus.co.uk

St Aubyn's Hotel ♦♦♦
111-113 Cardigan Road,
Bridlington YO15 3LP
T: (01262) 673002

Sandringham House Hotel ♦♦
11 The Crescent, Bridlington
YO15 2NX
T: (01262) 672064
F: (01262) 424631
E: sandringham-hotel@talk21.com

Sandsend Hotel ♦♦
8 Sands Lane, Bridlington
YO15 2JE
T: (01262) 673265

Seacourt Hotel
♦♦♦♦ SILVER AWARD
76 South Marine Drive,
Bridlington YO15 3NS
T: (01262) 400872
F: (01262) 400411

Seawinds Guest House ♦♦♦
48 Horsforth Avenue,
Bridlington YO15 3DF
T: (01262) 676330
E: seawinds@btinternet.com

Shellbourne Hotel ♦♦♦
14-16 Summerfield Road,
Bridlington YO15 3LF
T: (01262) 674697

South Dene Hotel ♦♦
94-96 Horsforth Avenue,
Bridlington YO15 3DF
T: (01262) 674436
E: ray@eyetechsportsltd.fsbusiness.co.uk

Spinnaker House Hotel ♦♦♦♦
19 Pembroke Terrace,
Bridlington YO15 3BX
T: (01262) 678440
F: (01262) 678440

Springfield Private Hotel ♦♦♦
12 Trinity Road, Bridlington
YO15 2EY
T: (01262) 672896
E: springfieldbrid@aol.com

Stonmar Guest House ♦♦♦
15 Flamborough Road,
Bridlington YO15 2HU
T: (01262) 674580
F: (01262) 674580
E: linda@stonmar.fsnet.co.uk
I: stonmar.web1000.com

Strathaven Hotel
Rating Applied For
56 Marshall Avenue, Bridlington
YO15 2DS
T: (01262) 676661
F: (01262) 676661
I: www.bridlingtonhotelsandguesthouses.co.uk

Strathmore Hotel ♦♦♦
63-65 Horsforth Avenue,
Bridlington YO15 3DH
T: (01262) 602828
F: (01262) 602828
E: Strathmore_Hotel@Bridlington-ey.freeserve.co.uk
I: www.bridlington-ey.freeserve.co.uk

Sunflower Lodge ♦♦♦
24 Flamborough Road,
Bridlington YO15 2HX
T: (01262) 400447

The Tennyson Hotel ♦♦♦♦
19 Tennyson Avenue,
Bridlington YO15 2EU
T: (01262) 604382
I: www.bridlington.net/accommodation/hotels/tennyson

Three Gables Private Hotel ♦♦♦
37 Windsor Crescent,
Bridlington YO15 3HZ
T: (01262) 673826
E: 3gables@web.com

Trinity Hotel ♦♦♦
9 Trinity Road, Bridlington
YO15 2EZ
T: (01262) 670444
F: (01262) 670444
E: trinityhotel@btconnect.com
I: www.trinityhotel.co.uk

Vernon Villa Guesthouse ♦♦♦♦
2 Vernon Road, Bridlington
YO15 2HQ
T: (01262) 670661
E: villa@sdinardo.freeeserve.co.uk

Victoria Hotel ♦♦♦
25/27 Victoria Road, Bridlington
YO15 2AT
T: (01262) 673871
F: (01262) 609431
E: victoria.hotel@virgin.net
I: www.victoriahotelbridlington.co.uk

Waverley Hotel ♦♦♦
105 Cardigan Road, Bridlington
YO15 3LP
T: (01262) 671040

White Lodge Guest House ♦♦♦
9 Neptune Terrace, Neptune
Street, Bridlington YO15 3DE
T: (01262) 670903
F: (01262) 670903
E: caitlyn@whitelodgeguesthouse.fsnet.co.uk
I: www.whitelodgeguesthouse.co.uk

The White Rose ♦♦♦
123 Cardigan Road, Bridlington
YO15 3LP
T: (01262) 673245
F: (01262) 401362
E: c.a.young@tesco.net
I: www.smoothhound.co.uk/hotels/thewhiterose

Winston House Hotel ♦♦♦
5-6 South Street, Bridlington
YO15 3BY
T: (01262) 670216
F: (01262) 670216
E: bob.liz@winstonhouse.fsnet.co.uk
I: www.winston-house.co.uk

BRIGG
North Lincolnshire

Albert House ♦♦♦♦
23 Bigby Street, Brigg DN20 8ED
T: (01652) 658081

Holcombe Guest House ♦♦♦♦
34 Victoria Road, Barnetby
DN38 6JR
T: 07850 764002
F: (01652) 680841
E: holcombe.house@virgin.net
I: www.holcombeguesthouse.co.uk

Lord Nelson Hotel & Hardy's Cafe Bar ♦♦♦
Market Place, Brigg DN20 8LD
T: (01652) 652127
F: (01652) 658952

The Woolpack Hotel ♦♦
4 Market Place, Brigg DN20 8HA
T: (01652) 655649
F: (01652) 655649
E: harry@woolpack488.freeserve.co.uk
I: www.woolpack-hotel.co.uk

BRIGGSWATH
North Yorkshire

Carr House ♦♦♦♦
29 Carr Hill Lane, Briggswath,
Whitby YO21 1RS
T: (01947) 810246
F: (01947) 810246
E: cole@cole8721freeserve.co.uk

BRIGHOUSE
West Yorkshire

The Black Bull Hotel ♦♦♦
46 Briggate, Brighouse HD6 1EF
T: (01484) 714816
F: (01484) 721711

BROUGH
East Riding of Yorkshire

Woldway ♦♦♦
10 Elloughton Road, Brough
HU15 1AE
T: (01482) 667666
I: www.woldway.co.uk

BUCKDEN
North Yorkshire

Low Raisgill ♦♦♦♦
Buckden, Hubberholme, Skipton
BD23 5JQ
T: (01756) 760351

Redmire Farm
♦♦♦♦ GOLD AWARD
Upper Wharfedale, Buckden,
Skipton BD23 5JD
T: (01756) 760253

The White Lion Inn ♦♦♦
Cray, Buckden, Skipton
BD23 5JB
T: (01756) 760262
F: (01756) 761024
E: admin.whitelion@btinternet.com
I: www.whitelioncray.com

BULMER
North Yorkshire

Grange Farm ♦♦♦
Castle Howard, Bulmer, York
YO60 7BN
T: (01653) 618376
F: (01653) 618600
E: foster@grangefarm35.fsnet.co.uk
I: www.grangefarmbulmer.co.uk

Lower Barn ♦♦♦♦
Wandales Lane, Castle Howard, Bulmer, York YO60 7ES
T: (01653) 618575
F: (01653) 618575
E: isabelhall@lowerbarn.fsnet.co.uk
I: www.lowerbarn.fsnet.co.uk

BURLEY IN WHARFEDALE
West Yorkshire

Hillcrest ♦♦♦
24 Hill Crescent, Burley in Wharfedale, Ilkley LS29 7QG
T: (01943) 863258
E: angela@hillcrest-burley.co.uk
I: www.hillcrest-burley.co.uk

Upstairs, Downstairs ♦♦♦
3 Elm Grove, Burley in Wharfedale, Ilkley LS29 7PL
T: (01943) 862567

BURNSALL
North Yorkshire

Valley View ♦♦♦♦
Burnsall, Skipton BD23 6BN
T: (01756) 720314
F: (01756) 720314
E: fitton_valley_view@lineone.net

BURNT YATES
North Yorkshire

High Winsley Farm ♦♦♦♦
Brimham Rocks Road, Burnt Yates, Harrogate HG3 3EP
T: (01423) 770376
E: highwinsley@aol.com

The New Inn Hotel ♦♦♦♦
Pateley Bridge Road, Burnt Yates, Harrogate HG3 3EG
T: (01423) 771070
F: (01423) 772360
I: www.newinnburntyates.co.uk

BURTON AGNES
East Riding of Yorkshire

Park Farm House ♦♦
Main Road, Burton Agnes, Driffield YO25 4NA
T: (01262) 490394
F: (01262) 490394

CARLTON
North Yorkshire

Abbots Thorn ♦♦♦♦
Carlton, Ambleside DL8 4AY
T: (01969) 640620
F: (01969) 640304
E: abbots.thorn@virgin.net
I: www.abbotsthorn.co.uk

Foxwood ♦♦♦
Carr Lane, Carlton, Wakefield WF3 3RT
T: (0113) 282 4786
F: (0113) 282 4786

Middleham House ♦♦♦♦
Carlton, Leyburn DL8 4BB
T: (01969) 640645
E: info@middlehamhouse.co.uk
I: www.middlehamhouse.co.uk

CARLTON HUSTHWAITE
North Yorkshire

Crofts ♦♦♦♦
Carlton Husthwaite, Thirsk YO7 2BJ
T: (01845) 501325
F: (01845) 501325
E: corbett465@amserve.com

CASTLE HOWARD
North Yorkshire

Lowry's Restaurant and Guest House ♦♦♦
Malton Road, Slingsby, York YO62 4AF
T: (01653) 628417
E: dgwilliams@onetel.net.uk

CASTLEFORD
West Yorkshire

Broadleigh House ♦♦♦♦
14 Hillcrest Avenue, Castleford WF10 3QL
T: (01977) 550102
F: (01977) 550102
E: jeanadamsuk@yahoo.co.uk
I: www.smoothhound.co.uk/hotels/broadleigh

CASTLETON
North Yorkshire

Eskdale Inn ♦♦♦
Castleton, Whitby YO21 2EU
T: (01287) 660234
E: esk_dale.6-9@tiscali.co.uk

Greystones ♦♦♦
30 High Street, Castleton, Whitby YO21 2DA
T: (01287) 660744

CATTERICK
North Yorkshire

Rose Cottage Guest House ♦♦♦
26 High Street, Catterick, Richmond DL10 7LJ
T: (01748) 811164

CATTERICK BRIDGE
North Yorkshire

St Giles Farm ♦♦♦♦
Catterick Bridge, Richmond DL10 7PH
T: (01748) 811372
F: (01748) 818262
E: janethor@aol.co.uk

CHAPEL ALLERTON
West Yorkshire

Green House ♦♦♦
5 Bank View Terrace, Chapel Allerton, Leeds LS7 2EX
T: (0113) 268 1380

CHAPELTOWN
South Yorkshire

The Norfolk Arms ♦♦♦
White Lane, Chapeltown, Sheffield S35 2YG
T: (0114) 240 2016
F: (0114) 246 8414
E: norfharri@aol.com

CHERRY BURTON
East Riding of Yorkshire

Burton Mount ♦♦♦♦♦ SILVER AWARD
Malton Road, Cherry Burton, Beverley HU17 7RA
T: (01964) 550541
F: (01964) 551955
E: pg@burtonmount.co.uk
I: www.burtonmount.co.uk

CHOP GATE
North Yorkshire

Beacon Guest Farm ♦♦♦
Chop Gate, Middlesbrough TS9 7JS
T: (01439) 798320
F: (01439) 798320

CLAPHAM
North Yorkshire

Brook House ♦♦♦
Station Road, Clapham, Lancaster LA2 8ER
T: (01524) 251580
E: brookhousecafe@yahoo.co.uk

CLEASBY
North Yorkshire

Cleasby House ♦♦♦♦
Cleasby, Darlington DL2 2QY
T: (01325) 350160
E: junehirst@aol.com
I: www.cleasbyhouse.co.uk

CLEETHORPES
North East Lincolnshire

Hotel 77 ♦♦♦
77 Kingsway, Cleethorpes DN35 0AB
T: (01472) 692035
F: (01472) 692035
E: hotel77@knox24.fsbusiness.co.uk

Abbeydale Guest House ♦♦♦
39 Isaacs Hill, Cleethorpes DN35 8JT
T: (01472) 692248
F: (01472) 311088
E: info@abbeydaleguesthouse.com
I: www.abbeydaleguesthouse.com

Adelaide Hotel ♦♦♦♦
41 Isaacs Hill, Cleethorpes DN35 8JT
T: (01472) 693594
F: (01472) 329717
E: robertcallison@ntlworld.com
I: www.adelaide-hotel.com

Alpine House ♦♦♦
55 Clee Road, Cleethorpes DN35 8AD
T: (01472) 690804

The Anchorage ♦♦♦♦
16 The Kingsway, Cleethorpes DN35 8QU
T: (01472) 696757
F: (01472) 696757
E: hotel@anchorage.f9.co.uk
I: www.theanchorage.uk.com

Ascot Lodge Guest House ♦♦♦♦
11 Princes Road, Cleethorpes DN35 8AW
T: (01472) 290129
E: ascotclee@aol.com
I: www.ascotlodge.co.uk

Brentwood Guest House ♦♦♦
9 Princes Road, Cleethorpes DN35 8AW
T: (01472) 693982
E: brentwoodguesthouse69@hotmail.com
I: www.brentwoodguesthouse.org

Brier Parks Guest House ♦♦
27 Clee Road, Cleethorpes DN35 8AD
T: (01472) 237456
E: a.brierley1@ntlworld.com

Clee House ♦♦♦♦
31-33 Clee Road, Cleethorpes DN35 8AD
T: (01472) 200850
F: (01472) 200850
E: david@cleehouse.com
I: www.cleehouse.com

Comat Hotel ♦♦♦♦
26 Yarra Road, Cleethorpes DN35 8LS
T: (01472) 694791
F: (01472) 694791
E: comat-hotel@ntlworld.com
I: www.comat-hotel.co.uk

Ginnies ♦♦♦
27 Queens Parade, Cleethorpes DN35 0DF
T: (01472) 694997
F: (01472) 693971
E: kimkwood@aol.com
I: www.ginniesguesthousecleethorpes.co.uk

Gladson Guest House ♦♦♦
43 Isaacs Hill, Cleethorpes DN35 8JT
T: (01472) 694858
E: enquiries@gladsonguesthouse.co.uk
I: www.gladsonguesthouse.co.uk

The Saxon House Hotel ♦♦♦♦
70 St Peters Avenue, Cleethorpes DN35 8HP
T: (01472) 697427
F: (01472) 602696
E: reservations@saxonhouse-hotel.co.uk

Sherwood Guest House ♦♦♦
15 Kingsway, Cleethorpes DN35 8QU
T: (01472) 692020
F: (01472) 239177
E: sherwood.guesthouse@ntlworld.com
I: www.sherwoodguesthouse.co.uk

Tudor Terrace Guest House ♦♦♦♦
11 Bradford Avenue, Cleethorpes DN35 0BB
T: (01472) 600800
F: (01472) 501395
E: enquiries.tudorterrace@ntlworld.com
I: www.tudorterrace.co.uk

White Rose Guest House ♦♦♦
13 Princes Road, Cleethorpes DN35 8AW
T: (01472) 695060
E: faypook@aol.com

CLIFTON
North Yorkshire

Astley House ♦♦♦
123 Clifton, York YO30 6BL
T: (01904) 634745
F: (01904) 621327
E: astleyhousehotel@aol.com
I: www.astley123.co.uk

Avenue Guest House ♦♦♦
6 The Avenue, Clifton, York YO30 6AS
T: (01904) 620575
E: allen@avenuegh.fsnet.co.uk
I: www.avenuegh.fsnet.co.uk

CLOUGHTON
North Yorkshire

Cober Hill ♦♦♦
Newlands Road, Cloughton, Scarborough YO13 0AR
T: (01723) 870310
F: (01723) 870271
E: enquiries@coberhill.co.uk
I: www.coberhill.co.uk

COLLINGHAM
West Yorkshire

Langston ♦♦♦
Langwith Valley Road, Off Hillcrest, Harewood Road, Collingham, Wetherby LS22 5DW
T: (01937) 572476

CONISTON
East Riding of Yorkshire

Gardeners Country Inn ♦♦♦
Hull Road, Skirlaugh, Coniston, Hull HU11 5AE
T: (01964) 562625
F: (01964) 564079
E: gardeners@mgrleisure.com
I: www.mgrleisure.com/gardeners

COTTINGHAM
East Riding of Yorkshire

Kenwood House ♦♦♦
7 Newgate Street, Cottingham HU16 4DY
T: (01482) 847558

Newholme ♦♦♦
47 Thwaite Street, Cottingham HU16 4QX
T: (01482) 849879

COUNTERSETT
North Yorkshire

Carr End House ♦♦♦♦
Countersett, Askrigg, Leyburn DL8 3DE
T: (01969) 650346

COWLING
North Yorkshire

Woodland House ♦♦♦♦
2 Woodland Street, Cowling, Keighley BD22 0BS
T: (01535) 637886
E: susansandybb@hotmail.com
I: www.woodland-house.co.uk

COXWOLD
North Yorkshire

Newburgh House ♦♦♦♦♦
Coxwold, York YO61 4AS
T: (01347) 868177
F: (01347) 868177
E: info@newburghhouse.com
I: www.newburghhouse.com

CRAYKE
North Yorkshire

The Durham Ox ♦♦♦♦
West Way, Crayke, York YO61 4TE
T: (01347) 821506
F: (01347) 823326
E: enquiries@thedurhamox.com
I: www.thedurhamox.com

The Hermitage ♦♦♦
Mill Lane, Crayke, York YO31 7TE
T: (01347) 821635

CROFTON
West Yorkshire

Redbeck Motel ♦♦
Doncaster Road, Crofton, Wakefield WF4 1RR
T: (01924) 862730
F: (01924) 862937
I: www.redbeckmotel.co.uk

CROPTON
North Yorkshire

High Farm
♦♦♦♦ SILVER AWARD
Cropton, Pickering YO18 8HL
T: (01751) 417461
F: (01751) 417807
E: highfarmcropton@aol.com
I: www.hhml.com/bb/highfarmcropton.htm

New Inn and Cropton Brewery ♦♦♦
Cropton, Pickering YO18 8HH
T: (01751) 417330
F: (01751) 417582
E: info@croptonbrewery.co.uk
I: www.croptonbrewery.co.uk

CROWLE
North Lincolnshire

Seven Lakes Motel ♦♦♦
Seven Lakes Leisure Park, Ealand, Crowle, Scunthorpe DN17 4JS
T: (01724) 710245
F: (01724) 711814

CROXTON
North Lincolnshire

Croxton House ♦♦♦
Croxton, Ulceby DN39 6YD
T: (01652) 688306
F: (01652) 680577
E: croxtenhouse@mail2hotel.com

CUNDALL
North Yorkshire

Cundall Lodge Farm
♦♦♦♦ SILVER AWARD
Cundall, York YO61 2RN
T: (01423) 360203
F: (01423) 360805
E: info@lodgefarmbb.co.uk
I: www.lodgefarmbb.co.uk

DACRE BANKS
North Yorkshire

Dalriada ♦♦♦
Cabin Lane, Dacre Banks, Harrogate HG3 4EE
T: (01423) 780512

Gate Eel Farm ♦♦♦♦
Dacre Banks, Harrogate HG3 4ED
T: (01423) 781707

The Royal Oak Inn ♦♦♦♦
Oak Lane, Dacre Banks, Harrogate HG3 4EN
T: (01423) 780200
E: enquiries@the royaloak.uk.com
I: www.theroyaloak.uk.com

DALTON
North Yorkshire

Throstle Gill Farm ♦♦♦♦
Dalton, Richmond DL11 7HZ
T: (01833) 621363
F: (01833) 621363
E: enquiries@throstlegill.co.uk
I: www.throstlegill.co.uk

Ye Jolly Farmers of Olden Times ♦♦♦
Dalton, Thirsk YO7 3HY
T: (01845) 577359

DANBY
North Yorkshire

Botton Grove Farm ♦♦♦
Danby Head, Danby, Whitby YO21 2NH
T: (01287) 660284
E: judytait@bottongrove.freeserve.co.uk

Butterwitts Farm
Rating Applied For
Little Fryup, Danby, Whitby YO21 2NP
T: (01287) 669020
E: butterwitts@yahoo.co.uk

Crag Farm ♦♦♦♦
Danby, Whitby YO21 2LQ
T: (01287) 660279
F: (01287) 660279
E: sal.b.b.cragfarm.n.y.@ukgateway.net

Crossley Gate Farm House
♦♦♦♦ SILVER AWARD
Fryup, Danby, Whitby YO21 2NR
T: (01287) 660165
E: bottomley@crossleygatefarm.fsnet.co.uk

Duke of Wellington Inn ♦♦♦♦
West Lane, Danby, Whitby YO21 2LY
T: (01287) 660351
E: landlord@dukeofwellington.freeserve.co.uk
I: www.danby-dukeofwellington.co.uk

The Fox & Hounds Inn ♦♦♦♦
45 Brook Lane, Ainthorpe, Danby, Whitby YO21 2LD
T: (01287) 660218
F: (01287) 660030
E: ajbfox@globalnet.co.uk
I: www.foxandhounds-ainthorpe.com

Rowantree Farm ♦♦♦
Fryup Road, Ainthorpe, Whitby YO21 2LE
T: (01287) 660396
E: krbsatindall@aol.com

Stonebeck Gate Farm ♦♦♦
Little Fryup, Danby, Whitby YO21 2NS
T: (01287) 660363
F: (01287) 660363
I: www.stonebeckgatefarm.co.uk

Sycamore House ♦♦♦♦
Danby Head, Danby, Whitby YO21 2NN
T: (01287) 660125
F: (01287) 669122
E: sycamore.danby@btinternet.com
I: www.smoothhound.co.uk/hotels/sycamore1.html

DARLEY
North Yorkshire

Brimham Guest house ♦♦♦♦
Silverdale Close, Darley, Harrogate HG3 2PQ
T: (01423) 780948

Elsinglea Guest House ♦♦♦♦
Sheepcote Lane, Darley, Harrogate HG3 2RW
T: (01423) 781069
F: (01423) 780189
I: www.elsingleaguesthouse.co.uk

DEEPDALE
North Lincolnshire

West Wold Farmhouse ♦♦♦♦
Deepdale, Barton-upon-Humber DN18 6ED
T: (01652) 633293
F: (01652) 633293
E: westworldfarm@aol.com

DEIGHTON
North Yorkshire

Grimston House ♦♦♦
Deighton, York YO19 6HB
T: (01904) 728328
F: (01904) 720093
E: grimstonhouse@talk21.com
I: www.grimstonhouse.com

Rush Farm ♦♦♦
York Road, Deighton, York YO19 6HQ
T: (01904) 728459
E: david@rushfarm.fsnet.co.uk
I: www.rushfarm.fsnet.co.uk

DENBY DALE
West Yorkshire

Eastfield Cottage ♦♦♦♦
248 Wakefield Road, Denby Dale, Huddersfield HD8 8SU
T: (01484) 861562

DISHFORTH
North Yorkshire

Fern Bank Bed and Breakfast
Rating Applied For
Chapel Yard, Dishforth, Thirsk YO7 3JX
T: (01845) 577460
E: hilaryanddavid@fernbankbb.freeserve.co.uk

DONCASTER
South Yorkshire

Ashlea Hotel ♦♦
81 Thorne Road, Doncaster DN1 2ES
T: (01302) 363374
F: (01302) 760215
E: brigby@ashlea25.freeserve.co.uk

The Balmoral Hotel ♦♦♦
129 Thorne Road, Doncaster DN2 5BH
T: (01302) 364385
F: (01302) 364385
E: thebalmoralhotel@blueyonder.co.uk
I: www.thebalmoralhotel@blueyonder.co.uk

The Grange Guesthouse
Rating Applied For
Grange Road, Moorends Thorne, Doncaster DN8 4LS
T: (01405) 815028
F: (01405) 815028
E: cliftonproprerties@btinternet.com

Low Farm
♦♦♦♦♦ SILVER AWARD
Clayton, Doncaster DN5 7DB
T: (01977) 648433
F: (01977) 640472
E: bar@lowfarm.freeserve.co.uk
I: www.lowfarm.freeserve.co.uk

Lyntone Hotel ♦♦♦
24 Avenue Road, Wheatley, Doncaster DN2 4AQ
T: (01302) 361586
F: (01302) 361079

DOWNHOLME
North Yorkshire

Walburn Hall
◆◆◆◆ SILVER AWARD
Downholme, Richmond
DL11 6AF
T: (01748) 822152
F: (01748) 822152
E: walburnhall@farmersweekly.net

DRIFFIELD
East Riding of Yorkshire

Kelleythorpe Farm ◆◆◆
Driffield YO25 9DW
T: (01377) 252297
E: jhopper@kelleythorpe.fsbusiness.co.uk

The Red Lion Hotel ◆◆◆
57 Middle Street North, Driffield
YO25 6SS
T: (01377) 252289
E: jane_marwood@yahoo.co.uk

DUNFORD BRIDGE
South Yorkshire

Stanhope Arms Inn ◆◆◆
Windle Edge Road, Dunford Bridge, Sheffield S36 4TF
T: (01226) 763104
F: (01226) 765022
E: stanhopearms@tiscali.co.uk
I: www.stanhopearms.co.uk

DUNGWORTH
South Yorkshire

Rickett Field Guest Accommodation ◆◆◆
Dungworth, Bradfield, Sheffield
S6 6HA
T: (0114) 285 1218
E: shepherd@rickettlathe.freeserve.co.uk

The Royal Hotel ◆◆◆◆
Main Road, Dungworth, Bradfield, Sheffield S6 6HF
T: (0114) 285 1213
F: (0114) 285 1723
E: reception@royalhotel-dungworth.co.uk
I: www.royalhotel-dungworth.co.uk

EASINGWOLD
North Yorkshire

Greenfield Farm Cottages & B&B ◆◆◆
Greenfield Farm, Thirsk Road, Easingwold, York YO61 3NJ
T: (01347) 822656

The Old Vicarage
◆◆◆◆ GOLD AWARD
Market Place, Easingwold, York
YO61 3AL
T: (01347) 821015
F: (01347) 823465
E: kirman@oldvic-easingwold.freeserve.co.uk
I: www.oldvicarage.co.uk

Thornton Lodge Farm ◆◆◆◆
Thornton Hill, Easingwold, York
YO61 3QA
T: (01347) 821306
F: (01347) 821306
E: sue.raper@btopenworld.com
I: www.thorntonlodgefarm.co.uk

Yeoman's Course House ◆◆◆
Thornton Hill, Easingwold, York
YO61 3PY
T: (01347) 868126
F: (01347) 868129
E: chris@yeomanscourse.fsnet.co.uk
I: www.yeomanscourse.co.uk

EAST HESLERTON
North Yorkshire

Manor Farm ◆◆◆
East Heslerton, Malton
YO17 8RN
T: (01944) 728268
F: (01944) 728277
E: dclumley@scarborough.co.uk
I: www.manorfarmholidays.co.uk

The Snooty Fox ◆◆◆
East Heslerton, Malton
YO17 8EN
T: (01944) 710554
F: (01944) 711164
E: faldo@btconnect.co.uk

EAST MARTON
North Yorkshire

Drumlins ◆◆◆◆
Heber Drive, East Marton, Skipton BD23 3LS
T: (01282) 843521
I: www.yorkshiredales.net/stayat/drumlins

EASTBY
North Yorkshire

The Masons Arms Inn ◆◆◆
Barden Road, Eastby, Skipton
BD23 6SN
T: (01756) 792754
E: info@masonsarmseastby.co.uk
I: www.masonsarmseastby.co.uk

EBBERSTON
North Yorkshire

Foxholm Hotel ◆◆◆
Main Street, Ebberston, Scarborough YO13 9NJ
T: (01723) 859550
F: (01723) 859550
E: kay@foxholm.freeserve.co.uk
I: www.foxholm.freeserve.co.uk

Littlegarth
◆◆◆◆ SILVER AWARD
High Street, Ebberston, Scarborough YO13 9PA
T: (01723) 850045
F: (01723) 850151
I: www.littlegarth.co.uk

Studley House ◆◆◆◆
67 Main Street, Ebberston, Scarborough YO13 9NR
T: (01723) 859285
F: (01723) 859285
E: brenda@yorkshireancestors.com
I: www.studley-house.co.uk

EDENTHORPE
South Yorkshire

Beverley Inn ◆◆◆
117 Thorne Road, Edenthorpe, Doncaster DN3 2JE
T: (01302) 882724
F: (01302) 887456

EGTON
North Yorkshire

Flushing Meadow ◆◆◆
Egton, Whitby YO21 1UA
T: (01947) 895395
F: (01947) 895395
E: flushing_meadow_egton@yahoo.co.uk

EGTON BRIDGE
North Yorkshire

Broom House ◆◆◆◆
Egton Bridge, Whitby YO21 1XD
T: (01947) 895279
F: (01947) 895657
E: mw@broom-house.co.uk
I: www.egton-bridge.co.uk

ELLERTON ABBEY
North Yorkshire

Ellerton Abbey ◆◆◆
Richmond DL11 6AN
T: (01748) 884067
F: (01748) 884160
E: claudia@ellertonabbey.co.uk
I: www.ellertonabbey.co.uk

ELLINGSTRING
North Yorkshire

Holybreen ◆◆◆
Ellingstring, Ripon HG4 4PW
T: (01677) 460216
F: (01677) 460106
E: Dales.accommodation@virgin.net

EMBSAY
North Yorkshire

Bondcroft Farm ◆◆◆◆
Embsay, Skipton BD23 6SF
T: (01756) 793371
F: (01756) 793371
E: bondcroftfarm@bondcroftfarm.yorks.net
I: www.bondcroft.yorks.net

EPWORTH
North Lincolnshire

Wisteria Cottage
Rating Applied For
10 Belton Road, Epworth, Doncaster DN9 1JL
T: (01427) 873988
F: (01427) 873988
E: wisteriacottage@hotmail.com
I: www.wisteriacottage.org.uk

ESCRICK
North Yorkshire

Glade Farm
Rating Applied For
Riccall Road, Escrick, York
YO19 6ED
T: (01904) 728098
F: (01904) 728254
E: n.leaf@farmline.com

FACEBY
North Yorkshire

Four Wynds Bed and Breakfast ◆◆◆
Faceby, Stokesley, Middlesbrough TS9 7BZ
T: (01642) 701315
F: (01642) 701315

FADMOOR
North Yorkshire

Mount Pleasant ◆◆◆
Rudland, Fadmoor, York
YO62 7JJ
T: (01751) 431579
E: info@mountpleasantbedandbreakfast.co.uk
I: www.mountpleasantbedandbreakfast.co.uk

FEATHERSTONE
West Yorkshire

Rolands Croft Guest House ◆◆
Waldenhowe Close, Featherstone, Pontefract
WF7 6ED
T: (01977) 790802
F: (01977) 790802
E: sut3@ail.com
I: www.rolandscroft.co.uk

FILEY
North Yorkshire

Abbot's Leigh Hotel ◆◆◆
7 Rutland Street, Filey YO14 9JA
T: (01723) 513334
E: barbara_abbots@yahoo.com

Cherries ◆◆◆◆
59 West Avenue, Filey YO14 9AX
T: (01723) 513299
E: cherriesfiley@hotmail.com

The Edwardian Guest House ◆◆◆
2 Brooklands, Filey YO14 9BA
T: (01273) 514557

The Forge ◆◆◆
23 Rutland Street, Filey
YO14 9JA
T: (01723) 512379
E: mikeforgefiley@aol.com
I: www.smoothhound.co.uk

Gables Guest House ◆◆◆◆
Rutland Street, Filey YO14 9JB
T: (01723) 514750
E: thegablesfiley@aol.com

Seafield Hotel ◆◆◆
9-11 Rutland Street, Filey
YO14 9JA
T: (01723) 513715

'This'll do' Binton Guest House ◆◆◆
25 West Avenue, Filey YO14 9AX
T: (01723) 513753

FREMINGTON
North Yorkshire

Broadlands Bed & Breakfast ◆◆◆
Fremington, Richmond
DL11 6AW
T: (01748) 884297
F: (01748) 884297

FRIDAYTHORPE
East Riding of Yorkshire

Manor House Inn and Restaurant ◆◆◆◆
Fridaythorpe, Driffield YO25 9RT
T: (01377) 288221
F: (01377) 288402

FRYUP
North Yorkshire

Crossley Side Farm ◆◆◆◆
Fryup, Danby, Whitby YO21 2NR
T: (01287) 660313
E: ruth.sjsfarm@farmersweekly.net

Furnace Farm ♦♦♦
Fryup, Danby, Whitby YO21 2AP
T: (01947) 897271

FYLINGTHORPE
North Yorkshire

Croft Farm ♦♦♦♦
Fylingthorpe, Whitby YO22 4PW
T: (01947) 880231
F: (01947) 880231
E: croftfarmbb@aol.com

GANTON
North Yorkshire

Cherry Tree Cottage ♦♦♦
23 Main Street, Ganton, Scarborough YO12 4NR
T: (01944) 710507
E: iris@hallaways.freeserve.co.uk
I: www.gantonholidays.co.uk

GARFORTH
West Yorkshire

Myrtle House ♦♦♦
31 Wakefield Road, Garforth, Leeds LS25 1AN
T: (0113) 286 6445

GARGRAVE
North Yorkshire

The Old Swan Inn ♦♦♦
20 High Street, Gargrave, Skipton BD23 3RB
T: (01756) 749232
F: (01756) 749232

GAYLE
North Yorkshire

Blackburn Farm/Trout Fishery ♦♦♦
Blackburn Farm, Gayle, Hawes DL8 3NX
T: (01969) 667524
E: blackburnfarm@hotmail.com
I: www.dalesaccommodation.com/blackburnfarm

Hunters Hill Bed and Breakfast ♦♦♦♦
Gayle, Hawes DL8 3RZ
T: (01969) 667137
E: clive@firehunter.freeserve.co.uk

GIGGLESWICK
North Yorkshire

Black Horse Hotel ♦♦♦♦
Church Street, Giggleswick, Settle BD24 0BE
T: (01729) 822506

The Harts Head Hotel ♦♦♦♦
Belle Hill, Giggleswick, Settle BD24 0BA
T: (01729) 822086
F: (01729) 824992
E: hartshead@hotel52.freeserve.co.uk
I: www.hotel52.freeserve.co.uk

GILDERSOME
West Yorkshire

End Lea
Rating Applied For
39 Town Street, Gildersome, Morley, Leeds LS27 7AX
T: (0113) 252 1661

GILLAMOOR
North Yorkshire

Manor Farm ♦♦♦
Main Street, Gillamoor, York YO62 7HX
T: (01751) 432695
F: (01751) 432695
E: gibson.manorfarm@btopenworld.com
I: www.manorfarm2.co.uk

Royal Oak Inn ♦♦♦
Main Street, Gillamoor, York YO62 7HX
T: (01751) 431414
F: (01751) 431414

GILLING EAST
North Yorkshire

The Firs ♦♦♦♦
Station Road, Gilling East, York YO62 4JL
T: (01439) 788382
E: geopearson@tinyonline.co.uk

GLAISDALE
North Yorkshire

Egton Banks Farm ♦♦♦♦
Glaisdale, Whitby YO21 2QP
T: (01947) 897289
E: egtonbanksfarm@agriplus.net
I: www.egtonbanksfarm.agriplus.net

Hollins Farm ♦♦♦
Glaisdale, Whitby YO21 2PZ
T: (01947) 897516

London House Farm ♦♦♦♦
Dale Head, Glaisdale, Whitby YO21 2PZ
T: (01947) 897166
F: (01947) 897166
E: gdanaherg@aol.com
I: www.londonhousefarm.com

GOATHLAND
North Yorkshire

Barnet House Guest House ♦♦♦♦
Goathland, Whitby YO22 5NG
T: (01947) 896201
F: (01947) 896201
E: barnethouse@hotmail.com
I: www.barnethouse.co.uk

The Beacon Guest House ♦♦♦♦ SILVER AWARD
Goathland, Whitby YO22 5AN
T: (01947) 896409
F: (01947) 896431
E: stewartkatz@compuserve.com
I: www.touristnetuk.com/ne/beacon

Fairhaven Country Hotel ♦♦♦
The Common, Goathland, Whitby YO22 5AN
T: (01947) 896361
F: (01947) 896099
E: royellis@thefairhavenhotel.co.uk
I: www.thefairhavenhotel.co.uk

Heatherdene Hotel ♦♦♦♦
Goathland, Whitby YO22 5AN
T: (01947) 896334
F: (01947) 896334
E: info@heatherdenehotel.co.uk
I: www.heatherdenehotel.co.uk

Heatherlands ♦♦♦
Goathland, Whitby YO22 5LA
T: (01947) 896311
E: keiththompson@yorkcollege.ac.uk

Prudom Guest House ♦♦♦♦ SILVER AWARD
Goathland, Whitby YO22 5AN
T: (01947) 896368
F: (01947) 896030
E: info@prudomhouse.co.uk
I: www.prudomhouse.co.uk

GOLDSBOROUGH
North Yorkshire

Bay Horse Inn ♦♦♦♦
Main Street, Goldsborough, Knaresborough HG5 8NW
T: (01423) 862212
F: (01423) 862212
E: bayhorseinn@btinternet.com
I: www.edirectory.co.uk/bayhorseinn/

GOOLE
East Riding of Yorkshire

The Briarcroft Hotel ♦♦♦
49-51 Clifton Gardens, Goole DN14 6AR
T: (01405) 763024
F: (01405) 767317
E: briarcofthotel@aol.com
I: hometown.aol.co.uk/briarcrofthotel/brochure.html

GOXHILL
North Lincolnshire

King's Well ♦♦♦
Howe Lane, Goxhill, Barrow upon Humber DN19 7HU
T: (01469) 532471
F: (01469) 532471
E: rjkingswell@amserve.com
I: www.freewebs.com/kings-well/

GRASSINGTON
North Yorkshire

Craiglands Guest House ♦♦♦♦
1 Brooklyn, Threshfield, Grassington, Skipton BD23 5ER
T: (01756) 752093
E: craiglands@talk21.com
I: www.craiglands.com

Foresters Arms Hotel ♦♦♦
20 Main Street, Grassington, Skipton BD23 5AA
T: (01756) 752349
F: (01756) 753633
E: theforesters@totalise.co.uk

Grassington Lodge ♦♦♦♦♦ SILVER AWARD
8 Wood Lane, Grassington, Skipton BD23 5LU
T: (01756) 752518
F: (01756) 752518
E: relax@grassingtonlodge.co.uk
I: grassingtonlodge.co.uk

Grove House ♦♦♦♦
1 Moor Lane, Grassington, Skipton BD23 5BD
T: (01756) 753364
F: (01756) 753603
E: lynngrovehouse@hotmail.com
I: www.grovehousegrassington.net

Long Ashes Inn ♦♦♦
Long Ashes Park, Threshfield, Skipton BD23 5PN
T: (01756) 752434
F: (01756) 752937
E: info@longashesinn.co.uk
I: www.longashesinn.co.uk

New Laithe House ♦♦♦♦
Wood Lane, Grassington, Skipton BD23 5LU
T: (01756) 752764
E: enquiries@newlaithehouse.co.uk
I: www.newlaithehouse.co.uk

Springroyd House ♦♦♦
8A Station Road, Grassington, Skipton BD23 5NQ
T: (01756) 752473
F: (01756) 752473
E: springroydhouse@hotmail.com

Station House ♦♦♦
Station Road, Threshfield, Skipton BD23 5ES
T: (01756) 752667
E: peter@station-house.freeserve.co.uk
I: www.yorkshirenet.co.uk/stayat/stationhouse

GREAT AYTON
North Yorkshire

Eskdale Cottage ♦♦♦♦
31 Newton Road, Great Ayton, Middlesbrough TS9 6DT
T: (01642) 724306
E: mandm.49@btopenworld.com

Food For Thought ♦♦♦
Bridge Street, Great Ayton, Middlesbrough TS9 6NP
T: (01642) 725236
F: (01642) 725236

Royal Oak Hotel ♦♦♦
High Green, Great Ayton, Middlesbrough TS9 6BW
T: (01642) 722361
F: (01642) 724047

Susie D's B & B ♦♦♦♦
Crossways, 116 Newton Road, Great Ayton, Middlesbrough TS9 6DL
T: (01642) 724351
E: susieD's@crossways26.fsnet.co.uk

The Wheelhouse ♦♦♦♦
Great Ayton, Middlesbrough TS9 6QQ
T: (01642) 724523

GREAT BARUGH
North Yorkshire

Hill Brow ♦♦♦♦
Great Barugh, Malton YO17 6UZ
T: (01653) 668426

White House Farm ♦♦♦♦
Great Barugh, Malton YO17 6XB
T: (01653) 668317

GREAT BUSBY
North Yorkshire

Chestnut Farm ♦♦♦
Stokesley, Great Busby, Middlesbrough TS9 5LB
T: (01642) 710676

GREAT EDSTONE
North Yorkshire

Cowldyke Farm ♦♦♦
Salton Road, Great Edstone, York YO62 6PE
T: (01751) 431242
E: info@cowldyke-farm.co.uk
I: www.cowldyke-farm.co.uk

GRIMSBY
North East Lincolnshire

The Danish Lodge ♦♦♦♦
2-4 Cleethorpes Road, Grimsby DN31 3LQ
T: (01472) 342257
F: (01472) 344156
E: danishlodge@aol.com
I: www.danishlodge.co.uk

Sunnyview Guesthouse ♦♦♦♦
Carr Lane, Healing, Grimsby DN41 7QR
T: (01472) 885015
F: (01472) 885015
E: starian@btinternet.com

GRINTON North Yorkshire

The Bridge Inn ♦♦♦
Grinton, Richmond DL11 6HH
T: (01748) 884224
F: (01748) 884044
E: atkinbridge@aol.com
I: www.bridgeinn-grinton.co.uk

GROSMONT North Yorkshire

Eskdale ♦♦♦
Grosmont, Whitby YO22 5PT
T: (01947) 895385
E: counsell@supanet.com
I: members.lycos.co.uk/eskdale.bnb/

GUISELEY West Yorkshire

Bowood ♦♦♦
Carlton Lane, Guiseley, Leeds LS20 9NL
T: (01943) 874556

Lyndhurst ♦♦♦
Oxford Road, Guiseley, Leeds LS20 9AB
T: (01943) 879985
I: www.guisley.co.uk/lyndhurst

GUNNERSIDE North Yorkshire

Dalegarth House ♦♦♦
Gunnerside, Richmond DL11 6LD
T: (01748) 886275
F: (01748) 886275
E: dalegarth@btinternet.com

HABROUGH North East Lincolnshire

Church Farm ♦♦♦♦
Immingham Road, Habrough, Immingham DN40 3BD
T: (01469) 576190

The Old Vicarage ♦♦♦♦
Killingholme Road, Habrough, Immingham DN40 3BB
T: (01469) 575051
F: (01469) 577160
E: ken@theoldvicarage.freeserve.co.uk

HACKFORTH North Yorkshire

Ainderby Myers Farm ♦♦♦
Ainderby Myers, Hackforth, Bedale DL8 1PF
T: (01609) 748668
F: (01609) 748424

HALIFAX West Yorkshire

Beech Court ♦♦♦
40 Prescott Street, Halifax HX1 2QW
T: (01422) 366004

The Dene ♦♦♦♦
Triangle, Sowerby Bridge, Halifax HX6 3EA
T: (01422) 823562
E: knoble@uk2.net

Field House ♦♦♦♦
Staups Lane, Stump Cross, Halifax HX3 6XW
T: (01422) 355457
E: stayatfieldhouse@yahoo.co.uk
I: www.fieldhouse-bb.co.uk

Heathleigh ♦♦♦♦
124 Skircoat Road, Halifax HX1 2RE
T: (01422) 323957

Joan's Guest House ♦♦♦
13 Heath Park Avenue, Halifax HX1 2PP
T: (01422) 369290

Lower Causeway ♦♦♦♦
Raw End Road, Warley, Halifax HX2 7SS
T: (01422) 882022
F: (01422) 886882
E: sootymel@aol.com

Mozart House ♦♦♦
34 Prescott Street, Halifax HX1 2QW
T: (01422) 340319
F: (01422) 340319

Rose Cottage ♦♦♦♦ SILVER AWARD
Shibden Fold, Halifax HX3 6XP
T: (01422) 365437
E: reservations@shibden-fold.co.uk
I: www.shibden-fold.co.uk

Travis House ♦♦♦
8 West Parade, Halifax HX1 2TA
T: (01422) 365727
F: (01422) 365727

HAMPSTHWAITE North Yorkshire

Graystone View Farm ♦♦♦♦
Grayston Plain Lane, Fellisccliffe, Hampsthwaite, Harrogate HG3 2LY
T: (01423) 770324
F: (01423) 772536
E: graystoneviewfarm@btinternet.co.uk

Lonsdale House ♦♦♦
Hampsthwaite, Harrogate HG3 2ET
T: (01423) 771311
F: (01423) 772810

HARMBY North Yorkshire

Sunnyridge ♦♦♦
Harmby, Leyburn DL8 5HQ
T: (01969) 622478
E: richah@freenet.co.uk

HARPHAM East Riding of Yorkshire

St Quintin Arms Inn ♦♦♦♦
Main Street, Harpham, Driffield YO25 4QY
T: (01262) 490329
F: (01262) 490329

HARROGATE North Yorkshire

Acomb Lodge ♦♦♦
6 Franklin Road, Harrogate HG1 5EE
T: (01423) 563599

Acorn Lodge Hotel ♦♦♦
1 Studley Road, Harrogate HG1 5JU
T: (01423) 525630
F: (01423) 564413

Alamah Guest House ♦♦♦♦
88 Kings Road, Harrogate HG1 5JX
T: (01423) 502187
F: (01423) 566175

Alderside Guest House ♦♦♦
11 Belmont Road, Harrogate HG2 0LR
T: (01423) 529400
F: (01423) 527531

The Alexander ♦♦♦♦
88 Franklin Road, Harrogate HG1 5EN
T: (01423) 503348
F: (01423) 540230
E: thealexander@amserve.net

Alvera Court Hotel ♦♦♦♦
76 Kings Road, Harrogate HG1 5JX
T: (01423) 505735
F: (01423) 507996
E: reception@alvera.co.uk
I: www.alvera.co.uk

Amadeus Hotel ♦♦♦♦
115 Franklin Road, Harrogate HG1 5EN
T: (01423) 505151
F: (01423) 505151
E: amadeushotel@btinternet.com
I: www.acartha.com/amadeushotel

Arden House Hotel Rating Applied For
69-71 Franklin Road, Harrogate HG1 5EH
T: (01423) 509224
F: (01423) 561170
E: susan@ardenhousehotel.co.uk
I: www.ardenhousehotel.co.uk

Argyll House ♦♦♦
80 Kings Road, Harrogate HG1 5JX
T: (01423) 562408
F: (01423) 567166
E: argyllharrogate@btopenworld.com

Ashbrooke House Hotel ♦♦♦♦
140 Valley Drive, Harrogate HG2 0JS
T: (01423) 564478
F: (01423) 564458
E: ashbrooke@harrogate.com
I: www.harrogate.com/ashbrooke

Ashley House Hotel ♦♦♦♦
36-40 Franklin Road, Harrogate HG1 5EE
T: (01423) 507474
F: (01423) 560858
E: ron@ashleyhousehotel.com
I: www.ashleyhousehotel.com

Askern Guest House ♦♦♦
3 Dragon Parade, Harrogate HG1 5BZ
T: (01423) 523057
F: (01423) 523057
E: info@askernhouse.co.uk
I: www.askernhouse.co.uk

Balmoral Guesthouse ♦♦♦
49 Eastville Terrace, Harrogate HG1 3HJ
T: (01423) 503854

Barkers Guest House ♦♦♦
202-204 Kings Road, Harrogate HG1 5JG
T: (01423) 568494

Belmont Hotel ♦♦♦♦
86 Kings Road, Harrogate HG1 5JX
T: (01423) 528086
E: marilyn@thebelmont86.fsnet.co.uk
I: www.smoothhound.co.uk/hotels/belmonthotel.html

Britannia Lodge ♦♦♦♦ SILVER AWARD
16 Swan Road, Harrogate HG1 2SA
T: (01423) 508482
F: (01423) 526840
E: info@britlodge.co.uk
I: www.britlodge.co.uk

Brookfield House ♦♦♦♦ SILVER AWARD
5 Alexandra Road, Harrogate HG1 5JS
T: (01423) 506646
F: (01423) 850383
E: brookfieldhouse@hotmail.com
I: www.brookfield-house.co.uk

Brooklands ♦♦♦♦
5 Valley Drive, Harrogate HG2 0JJ
T: (01423) 564609
E: brooklandsbb@supanet.com

Cavendish Hotel ♦♦♦♦
3 Valley Drive, Harrogate HG2 0JJ
T: (01423) 509637
F: (01423) 504434

Central House Farm ♦♦♦♦ SILVER AWARD
Haverah Park, Harrogate HG3 1SQ
T: (01423) 566050
F: (01423) 709152
E: jayne-ryder@lineone.net
I: www.centralhousefarm.co.uk

Claremont House ♦♦♦
8 West Cliffe Grove, Harrogate HG2 0PL
T: (01423) 502738
E: dtoomey_claremont@msn.com

Conference View Guest House ♦♦♦♦
74 Kings Road, Harrogate HG1 5JR
T: (01423) 563075
F: (01423) 563075
E: admin@conferenceview.co.uk
I: www.conferenceview.co.uk

The Coppice ♦♦♦♦
9 Studley Road, Harrogate HG1 5JU
T: (01423) 569626
F: (01423) 569005
E: coppice@harrogate.com
I: www.harrogate.com/coppice

Craigmoor Manor Hotel ♦♦♦
10 Harlow Moor Drive, Harrogate HG2 0JX
T: (01423) 523562
F: (01423) 523562

Delaine Hotel ♦♦♦♦ SILVER AWARD
17 Ripon Road, Harrogate HG1 2JL
T: (01423) 567974
F: (01423) 561723
E: delainehotel@satnet.me.uk

Dragon House ♦♦♦
6 Dragon Parade, Harrogate
HG1 5DA
T: (01423) 569888

The Franklin ♦♦♦
25 Franklin Road, Harrogate
HG1 5ED
T: (01423) 569028
E: leighrichardson@ntlworld.com
I: www.thefranklin.co.uk

Franklin View
♦♦♦♦ SILVER AWARD
19 Grove Road, Harrogate
HG1 5EW
T: (01423) 541388
F: (01423) 547872
E: jennifer@franklinview.com
I: www.franklinview.com

The Gables Hotel ♦♦♦♦
2 West Grove Road, Harrogate
HG1 2AD
T: (01423) 505625
F: (01423) 561312
E: gableshotel@quista.net
I: www.harrogategables.co.uk

Garden House Hotel ♦♦♦♦
14 Harlow Moor Drive, Harrogate HG2 0JX
T: (01423) 503059
F: (01423) 503059
E: gardenhouse@harrogate.com
I: www.harrogate.com/gardenhouse

Geminian Guest House ♦♦♦
11-13 Franklin Road, Harrogate
HG1 5ED
T: (01423) 523347
F: (01423) 523347
E: geminian@talk21.com
I: www.geminian.org.uk

Glynhaven Guesthouse ♦♦♦
72 Kings Road, Harrogate
HG1 5JR
T: (01423) 569970
F: (01423) 569970
E: glynhaven@ntlworld.com

Grafton Hotel (Harrogate)
♦♦♦♦
1-3 Franklin Mount, Harrogate
HG1 5EJ
T: (01423) 508491
F: (01423) 523168
E: enquiries@graftonhotel.co.uk
I: www.graftonhotel.co.uk

Half Moon Inn ♦♦
Main Street, Pool in Wharfedale, Otley LS21 1LH
T: (0113) 284 2878
F: (0113) 203 7895

The Herbitage ♦♦♦♦
71 St Winifreds Avenue West, Harrogate HG2 8LS
T: (01423) 884830
E: theherbitage@btopenworld.com
I: www.theherbitage.co.uk

Hollins House ♦♦♦
17 Hollins Road, Harrogate
HG1 2JF
T: (01423) 503646
F: (01423) 503646
E: hollins_house@lineone.net
I: www.hollinshouse.co.uk

Imbercourt Hotel ♦♦
57 Valley Drive, Harrogate
HG2 0JW
T: (01423) 502513
F: (01423) 562696

Kimberley Hotel ♦♦♦♦
11-19 Kings Road, Harrogate
HG1 5JY
T: (01423) 505613
F: (01423) 530276
E: info@thekimberley.co.uk
I: www.thekimberley.co.uk

Kingsway Hotel ♦♦♦
36 Kings Road, Harrogate
HG1 5JW
T: (01423) 562179
F: (01423) 562179
E: andy.noble@btinternet.com
I: www.kingswayhotel.com

Knabbs Ash
♦♦♦♦ GOLD AWARD
Skipton Road, Felliscliffe, Harrogate HG3 2LT
T: (01423) 771040
F: (01423) 771515
E: colin&sheila@knabbsash.freeserve.co.uk
I: www.yorkshirenet.co.uk/stayat/knabbsash

Lamont House ♦♦♦♦
12 St Marys Walk, Harrogate
HG2 0LW
T: (01423) 567143
F: (01423) 567143
E: mike@lamonthouse.freeserve.co.uk

Murray House ♦♦♦
67 Franklin Road, Harrogate
HG1 5EH
T: (01423) 505857
F: (01423) 50037
E: murrayhouse@totalise.co.uk

Oak Beck Bungalow ♦♦♦♦
4 Oakdale Glen, Harrogate
HG1 2JZ
T: (01423) 507336

Oakbrae Guest House ♦♦♦♦
3 Springfield Avenue, Harrogate
HG1 2HR
T: (01423) 567682
F: (01423) 567682
E: oakbrae@nascr.net
I: accommodation.uk.net/oakbrae.htm

Orient Townhouse ♦♦♦♦
51 Valley Drive, Harrogate
HG2 0JH
T: (01423) 565818
F: (01423) 504518
E: rowena@orienttownhouse.com
I: www.orienttownhouse.com

Parnas Hotel ♦♦♦♦
98 Franklin Road, Harrogate
HG1 5EN
T: (01423) 564493
F: (01423) 563554
E: info@parnashotel.co.uk
I: www.parnashotel.co.uk

17 Peckfield Close ♦♦♦
Hampsthwaite, Harrogate
HG3 2ES
T: (01423) 770765

Royd Mount
♦♦♦♦ GOLD AWARD
4 Grove Road, Harrogate
HG1 5EW
T: (01423) 529525
E: roydmount@btinternet.com
I: www.roydmount.com

Ruskin Hotel
♦♦♦♦♦ SILVER AWARD
1 Swan Road, Harrogate
HG1 2SS
T: (01423) 502045
F: (01423) 506131
E: ruskin.hotel@virgin.net
I: www.ruskinhotel.co.uk

Scotia House Hotel ♦♦♦
66-68 Kings Road, Harrogate
HG1 5JR
T: (01423) 504361
F: (01423) 526578
E: info@scotiahotel.harrogate.net
I: www.scotiahotel.harrogate.net

Shannon Court Hotel ♦♦♦♦
65 Dragon Avenue, Harrogate
HG1 5DS
T: (01423) 509858
F: (01423) 530606
E: shannon@hotels.harrogate.com
I: www.shannon-court.com

Sherwood ♦♦♦♦
7 Studley Road, Harrogate
HG1 5JU
T: (01423) 503033
F: (01423) 564659
E: sherwood@harrogate.com
I: www.sherwood-hotel.com

Spring Lodge Guest House
♦♦♦
22 Spring Mount, Harrogate
HG1 2HX
T: (01423) 506036
F: (01423) 506036
E: dv22harrogate@aol.com
I: www.spring-lodge.co.uk

Staveleigh ♦♦♦♦
SILVER AWARD
20 Ripon Road, Harrogate
HG1 2JJ
T: (01423) 524175
F: (01423) 524178
E: enquiries@staveleigh.co.uk
I: www.staveleigh.co.uk

The Welford ♦♦♦
27 Franklin Road, Harrogate
HG1 5ED
T: (01423) 566041
F: (01423) 566041

Wharfedale House ♦♦♦
28 Harlow Moor Drive, Harrogate HG2 0JY
T: (01423) 522233

HARTLINGTON
North Yorkshire

Walker Fold ♦♦♦♦
Raikes, Hartlington, Skipton
BD23 6BX
T: (01756) 720383
E: info@walker-fold.co.uk
I: www.walker-fold.co.uk

HARTWITH
North Yorkshire

Brimham Lodge ♦♦♦♦
Brimham Rocks Road, Hartwith, Burnt Yates, Harrogate HG3 3HE
T: (01423) 771770
F: (01423) 770370
E: neil.clarke@virgin.net
I: www.farmhousesbedandbreakfast.com

HARWOOD DALE
North Yorkshire

The Grainary ♦♦♦♦
Harwood Dale, Scarborough
YO13 0DT
T: (01723) 870026
F: (01723) 870026
E: thesimpsons@grainary.co.uk
I: www.grainary.co.uk

HATCLIFFE
North East Lincolnshire

The Old Farmhouse
♦♦♦♦ SILVER AWARD
Low Road, Hatcliffe, Grimsby
DN37 0SH
T: (01472) 824455
E: nicola@hatcliffe.freeserve.co.uk

HAWES
North Yorkshire

Bulls Head Hotel ♦♦♦♦
Market Place, Hawes DL8 3RD
T: (01969) 667437
F: (01969) 667048
E: jeff@bullsheadhotel.com
I: www.bullsheadhotel.com

The Bungalow ♦♦♦
Spring Bank, Hawes DL8 3NW
T: (01969) 667209

Cocketts Hotel and Restaurant
♦♦♦♦
Market Place, Hawes DL8 3RD
T: (01969) 667312
F: (01969) 667162
E: enquiries@cocketts.co.uk
I: www.cocketts.co.uk

East House ♦♦♦♦
Gayle, Hawes DL8 3RZ
T: (01969) 667405
E: lornaward@lineone.net
I: www.dalesaccommodation.com/easthouse

Ebor Guest House ♦♦♦
Burtersett Road, Hawes DL8 3NT
T: (01969) 667337
F: (01969) 667337
E: gwen@eborhouse.freeserve.co.uk

Fairview House ♦♦♦♦
Burtersett Road, Hawes DL8 3NP
T: (01969) 667348
F: (01969) 667348
E: fairview.hawes@virgin.net
I: www.wensleydale.org

Herriots Hotel & Restaurant
♦♦♦♦
Main Street, Hawes DL8 3QW
T: (01969) 667536
F: (01969) 667810
E: herriotshotel@aol.com
I: www.herriotshotel.com

Laburnum House ♦♦♦
The Holme, Hawes DL8 3QR
T: (01969) 667717
F: (01969) 667041
E: info@stayatlaburnumhouse.co.uk
I: www.stayatlaburnumhouse.co.uk

Old Station House ♦♦♦♦
Town Foot, Hawes DL8 3NL
T: (01969) 667785
E: alan.watkinson@virgin.net

Pry House ♦♦♦
Hawes, Hawes DL8 3LP
T: (01969) 667241
E: B&B@pryhousefarm.co.uk
I: www.pryhousefarm.co.uk

Rookhurst Country House Hotel ♦♦♦♦♦ GOLD AWARD
West End, Gayle, Hawes DL8 3RT
T: (01969) 667454
F: (01969) 667128
E: rookhurst@lineone.net
I: www.rookhurst.co.uk

South View ♦♦♦
Gayle Lane, Hawes DL8 3RW
T: (01969) 667447

Springbank House ♦♦♦
Spring Bank, Hawes DL8 3NW
T: (01969) 667376
F: (01969) 667376

Thorney Mire House ♦♦♦♦
Hawes DL8 3LU
T: (01969) 667159
E: sylvia.turner2@virgin.net
I: www.thorneymire.yorks.net

White Hart Inn ♦♦♦
Main Street, Hawes DL8 3QL
T: (01969) 667259
F: (01969) 667259
E: whitehart@wensleydale.org
I: www.wensleydale.org

HAWNBY
North Yorkshire

Easterside Farm ♦♦♦♦
Hawnby, York YO62 5QT
T: (01439) 798277
F: (01439) 798277
E: sarah@eastersidefarm.co.uk
I: www.eastersidefarm.co.uk

HAWORTH
West Yorkshire

Aitches Guest House & Restaurant ♦♦♦♦
11 West Lane, Haworth, Keighley BD22 8DU
T: (01535) 642501
E: aitches@talk21.com
I: www.aitches.co.uk

The Apothecary Guest House ♦♦♦
86 Main Street, Haworth, Keighley BD22 8DP
T: (01535) 643642
F: (01535) 643642
E: Sisleyd@aol.com
I: theapothecaryguesthouse.co.uk

Ashmount ♦♦♦♦ SILVER AWARD
Mytholmes Lane, Haworth, Keighley BD22 8EZ
T: (01535) 645726
F: (01535) 645726
E: ashmounthaworth@aol.com
I: members.aol.com/ashmounthaworth

Blue Lantern Guest House & Restaurant ♦♦♦♦
81 Main Street, Haworth, Keighley BD22 8DA
T: (01535) 642809
F: (01535) 642809

Bronte Hotel ♦♦
Lees Lane, Haworth, Keighley BD22 8RA
T: (01535) 644112
F: (01535) 646725
E: Brontehotel@btinternet.com
I: www.bronte-hotel.co.uk

Haworth Tea Rooms and Guest House ♦♦♦
68 Main Street, Haworth, Keighley BD22 8DP
T: (01535) 644278

Hole Farm ♦♦♦♦
Dimples Lane, Hole, Haworth, Keighley BD22 8QT
T: (01535) 644755
F: (01535) 644755
E: janet@bronteholidays.co.uk
I: www.bronteholidays.co.uk

Kershaw House ♦♦♦♦
90 West Lane, Haworth, Keighley BD22 8EN
T: (01535) 642074
F: (01535) 642074
E: jenny@kershaw-house.co.uk
I: www.kershawhouse.co.uk

Moorfield Guest House ♦♦♦
80 West Lane, Haworth, Keighley BD22 8EN
T: (01535) 643689
E: daveandann@moorfieldgh.demon.co.uk
I: www.moorfieldgh.demon.co.uk

The Old Registry ♦♦♦♦
2-4 Main Street, Haworth, Keighley BD22 8DA
T: (01535) 646503
F: (01535) 646503
E: oldregistry.haworth@virgin.net
I: www.oldregistry.com

Park Top House ♦♦♦♦
1 Rawdon Road, Haworth, Keighley BD22 8DX
T: (01535) 646102
E: gmilnes@parktophouse.fsnet.co.uk

6 Penistone Mews ♦♦♦♦
Penistone Mews, Rawdon Road, Haworth, Keighley BD22 8DF
T: (01535) 647412
E: philip@haworth3.freeserve.co.uk

Rosebud Cottage Guest House ♦♦♦
1 Belle Isle Road, Haworth, Keighley BD22 8QQ
T: (01535) 640321
E: rosebudcottag24@hotmail.com
I: www.rosebudcottage.co.uk

Woodlands Grange Private Hotel ♦♦♦
Belle Isle, Haworth, Keighley BD22 8PB
T: (01535) 646814
F: (01535) 648282
E: woodlandsgrange@hotmail.com
I: www.smoothhound.co.uk/hotels/woodlandsgrange.html

HAXEY
North Lincolnshire

Duke William ♦♦♦
Church Street, Haxey, Doncaster DN9 2HY
T: (01427) 752210
F: (01427) 752210

HEADINGLEY
West Yorkshire

Boundary Hotel Express ♦♦♦
42 Cardigan Road, Headingley, Leeds LS6 3AG
T: (0113) 275 7700
F: (0113) 275 7700
E: info@boundaryhotel.co.uk
I: www.boundaryhotel.co.uk

Oak Villa Hotel ♦♦♦
55-57 Cardigan Road, Headingley, Leeds LS6 1DW
T: (0113) 275 8439
F: (0113) 275 8439

HEALAUGH
North Yorkshire

Riddings Farm ♦♦♦
Reeth, Richmond DL11 6UR
T: (01748) 884267

HEALEY
North Yorkshire

The Olive ♦♦♦♦
Healey Mill, Healey, Ripon HG4 4LH
T: (01765) 689774
E: theolive.healeymill@virgin.net

HEBDEN
North Yorkshire

Court Croft ♦♦♦
Church Lane, Hebden, Skipton BD23 5DX
T: (01756) 753406

HEBDEN BRIDGE
West Yorkshire

Angeldale Guest House ♦♦♦
Hangingroyd Lane, Hebden Bridge HX7 7DD
T: (01422) 847321
E: enq@angeldale.co.uk
I: www.angeldale.co.uk

Badger Fields Farm ♦♦♦♦
Badger Lane, Blackshaw Head, Hebden Bridge HX7 7JX
T: (01422) 845161
E: badgerfields@hotmail.com
I: www.badgerfields.com

The Grove Inn ♦♦♦
Burnley Road, Brearley, Luddendenfoot, Halifax HX2 6HS
T: (01422) 883235
F: (01422) 883905

Myrtle Grove ♦♦♦♦
Myrtle Grove, Hebden Bridge HX7 8HL
T: (01422) 846078
E: myrtlegrove@btinternet.com
I: www.myrtlegrove.btinternet.co.uk

1 Primrose Terrace ♦♦
Hebden Bridge HX7 6HN
T: (01422) 844747

Prospect End ♦♦♦
8 Prospect Terrace, Savile Road, Hebden Bridge HX7 6NA
T: (01422) 843586
F: (01422) 843586

Robin Hood Inn ♦♦♦
Pecket Well, Hebden Bridge HX7 8QR
T: (01422) 842593
F: (01422) 844938
E: info@robinhoodsinn.com
I: www.robinhoodsinn.com

White Lion Hotel ♦♦♦
Bridge Gate, Hebden Bridge HX7 8EX
T: (01422) 842197
F: (01422) 846619
E: enquiries@whitelionhotelhb.co.uk
I: www.whitelionhotelhb.co.uk

HELMSLEY
North Yorkshire

Argyle House ♦♦♦♦
Ashdale Road, Helmsley, York YO62 5DD
T: (01439) 770590

Carlton Grange ♦♦♦
Helmsley, York YO62 5HH
T: (01439) 770259
I: www.carltongrange.co.uk

Carlton Lodge ♦♦♦♦
Bondgate, Helmsley, York YO62 5EY
T: (01439) 770557
F: (01439) 770623
E: enquiries@carlton-lodge.com
I: www.carlton-lodge.com

Griff Farm Bed & Breakfast ♦♦♦♦
Griff Farm, Helmsley, York YO62 5EN
T: (01439) 771600
F: (01439) 770462
E: j.fairburn@farmline.com

The Hawnby Hotel ♦♦♦♦
Hill Top, Hawnby, York YO62 5QS
T: (01439) 798202
F: (01439) 798344
E: info@hawnbyhotel.co.uk
I: www.hawnbyhotel.co.uk

High House Farm ♦♦♦
Cold Kirby, Sutton Bank, Thirsk YO7 2HL
T: (01845) 597557

Laskill Grange ♦♦♦♦
Easterside, Helmsley, Hawnby, York YO62 5NB
T: (01439) 798268
F: (01439) 798498
E: suesmith@laskillfarm.fsnet.co.uk
I: www.laskillfarm.co.uk

Mount Grace Farm ♦♦♦♦
Cold Kirby, Thirsk YO7 2HL
T: (01845) 597389
F: (01845) 597872
E: joyce@mountgracefarm.com
I: www.mountgracefarm.com

Oldstead Grange ♦♦♦♦♦ GOLD AWARD
Oldstead, Coxwold, York YO61 4BJ
T: (01347) 868634
E: oldsteadgrange@yorkshireuk.com
I: www.yorkshireuk.com

Redroofs ♦♦♦
3 Carlton Road, Helmsley, York YO62 5HD
T: (01439) 770175
F: (01439) 771596
E: babenm@globalnet.co.uk

Sproxton Hall ♦♦♦♦
Sproxton, York YO62 5EQ
T: (01439) 770225
F: (01439) 771373
E: info@sproxtonhall.demon.co.uk
I: www.sproxtonhall.co.uk

Stilworth House ♦♦♦♦
1 Church Street, Helmsley, York YO62 5AD
T: (01439) 771072
E: carol@stilworth.co.uk
I: www.stilworth.co.uk

HEPTONSTALL
West Yorkshire

Poppyfields House ♦♦♦
29 Slack Top, Heptonstall, Hebden Bridge HX7 7HA
T: (01422) 843636
F: (01422) 845621

HESSLE
East Riding of Yorkshire

Redcliffe House Luxury B&B ♦♦♦♦
Redcliff Road, Hessle HU13 0HA
T: (01482) 648655
I: www.redcliffehouse.co.uk

Weir Lodge Guest House ♦♦♦♦
Tower Hill, Hessle HU13 0SG
T: (01482) 648564
I: www.weirlodge.co.uk

HEWORTH
Yorkshire

The Nags Head ♦♦♦
56 Heworth Road, Heworth, York YO31 0AD
T: (01904) 422989

HIGH BENTHAM
North Yorkshire

Fowgill Park ♦♦♦♦
Bentham, High Bentham, Lancaster LA2 7AH
T: (01524) 261630

HIGH STITTENHAM
North Yorkshire

Hall Farm ♦♦♦♦
High Stittenham, York YO60 7TW
T: (01347) 878461
F: (01347) 878461
E: hallfarm@btinternet.com
I: www.hallfarm.btinternet.co.uk

HOLMBRIDGE
West Yorkshire

Corn Loft House ♦♦♦
146 Woodhead Road, Holmbridge, Holmfirth, Huddersfield HD9 2NL
T: (01484) 683147

HOLMFIRTH
West Yorkshire

Crimes House ♦♦♦♦
Far Lane, Hepworth, Holmfirth, Huddersfield HD9 1RN
T: (01484) 682395
F: (01484) 682395

The Old Bridge Bakery ♦♦
15 Victoria Street, Holmfirth, Huddersfield HD9 7DF
T: (01484) 685807
F: (01484) 682721

Red Lion Inn ♦♦♦
Sheffield Road, Jackson Bridge, Holmfirth, Huddersfield HD7 7HS
T: (01484) 683499

Springfield House ♦♦♦♦
95 Huddersfield Road, Holmfirth, Huddersfield HD9 3JA
T: (01484) 683031
E: ann_brook@hotmail.com

Uppergate Farm ♦♦♦♦
Hepworth, Holmfirth, Huddersfield HD9 1TG
T: (01484) 681369
F: (01484) 687343
E: stevenal.booth@virgin.net
I: www.uppergatefarm.co.uk

HOLMPTON
East Riding of Yorkshire

Elmtree Farm ♦♦♦
Holmpton, Withernsea HU19 2QR
T: (01964) 630957
E: cft-mcox@supanet.com

HOOTON PAGNELL
South Yorkshire

Rock Farm ♦♦♦
Hooton Pagnell, Doncaster DN5 7BT
T: (01977) 642200
F: (01977) 642200
E: info@rock-farm.com
I: www.rock-farm.com

HORNSEA
East Riding of Yorkshire

Merlstead Private Hotel ♦♦♦
59 Eastgate, Hornsea HU18 1NB
T: (01964) 533068
F: (01964) 536975
E: doreen.lamb@btopenworld.com

Sandhurst Guest House ♦♦♦
3 Victoria Avenue, Hornsea HU18 1NH
T: (01964) 534653
F: (01964) 534653
E: rhodes@hornsea15.fsnet.co.uk
I: Sandhurstguesthouse.co.uk

HORTON-IN-RIBBLESDALE
North Yorkshire

Crown Hotel ♦♦♦♦
Horton-in-Ribblesdale, Settle BD24 0HF
T: (01729) 860209
F: (01729) 860444
E: minehost@crown-hotel.co.uk
I: www.crown-hotel.co.uk

Middle Studfold Farm ♦♦♦
Horton-in-Ribblesdale, Settle BD24 0ER
T: (01729) 860236

HOVINGHAM
North Yorkshire

Hovingham Country Guest House ♦♦♦
Park Street, Hovingham, York YO62 4JZ
T: (01653) 628740
E: mike.mcandrew@lineone.net
I: www.hovinghamguesthouse.fsnet.co.uk

HUDDERSFIELD
West Yorkshire

Cambridge Lodge ♦♦♦
4 Clare Hill, Huddersfield HD1 5BS
T: (01484) 519892
F: (01484) 534534
E: cambridgelodge@btconnect.com
I: www.cambridgelodge.co.uk

Croppers Arms ♦♦♦
136 Westbourne Road, Huddersfield HD1 4LF
T: (01484) 421522
F: (01484) 301300

Ellasley Guest House ♦♦
86 New North Road, Huddersfield HD1 5NE
T: (01484) 423995
F: (01484) 432995

Elm Crest ♦♦♦♦
2 Queens Road, Edgerton, Huddersfield HD2 2AG
T: (01484) 530990
F: (01484) 516227
E: gmitchell@elmcrest.biz
I: www.elmcrest.biz

Holmcliffe Guest House ♦♦♦
16 Mountjoy Road, Edgerton, Huddersfield HD1 5PZ
T: (01484) 429598
F: (01484) 429598
E: jwilco@mwfree.net

Laurel Cottage Guest House ♦♦♦
34 Far Dene, Kirkburton, Huddersfield HD8 0QU
T: (01484) 607907

Manor Mill Cottage ♦♦♦♦
21 Linfit Lane, Kirkburton, Huddersfield HD8 0TY
T: (01484) 604109
E: manormill@paskham.freeserve.co.uk

The White House ♦♦♦
Slaithwaite, Huddersfield HD7 5TY
T: (01484) 842245
F: (01484) 842245
E: whthouse@globalnet.co.uk
I: www.whitehouse-hotel.co.uk

Woods End Bed & Breakfast
Rating Applied For
46 Inglewood Avenue, Huddersfield HD2 2DS
T: (01484) 513580
F: (01484) 513580
E: jmsm2306@hotmail.com
I: www.pennineyorkshire.co.uk

HULL
East Riding of Yorkshire

Acorn Guest House ♦♦♦
719 Beverley Road, Hull HU6 7JN
T: (01482) 853248
F: (01482) 853148

The Admiral Guest House ♦♦
234 The Boulevard, Hull HU3 3ED
T: (01482) 329664
F: (01482) 329664

Allandra Hotel
Rating Applied For
5 Park Avenue, Princes Avenue, Hull HU5 3EN
T: (01482) 493349
F: (01482) 492680

The Arches ♦♦♦
38 Saner Street, Hull HU3 2TR
T: (01482) 211558

Clyde House Hotel ♦♦♦
13 John Street, Hull HU2 8DH
T: (01482) 214981
F: (01482) 214981
E: anthonysmith@cwcom.net
I: www.clydehousehotel.co.uk

The Earlsmere Hotel ♦♦♦
76-78 Sunny Bank, Hull HU3 1LQ
T: (01482) 341977
F: (01482) 473714
E: su@earlsmerehotel.karoo.co.uk
I: www.earlsmerehotel.karoo.net

The Ivy ♦♦♦♦
Station Road, Patrington, Hull HU12 0NF
T: (01964) 631586
E: theivy.bandb@vigin.net

Roseberry House ♦♦♦♦
86 Marlborough Avenue, Hull HU5 3JT
T: (01482) 445256
F: (01482) 343215
I: www.smoothhound.co.uk/hotels/conway.html

West Park Hotel ♦♦♦
405-411 Anlaby Road, Hull HU3 6AB
T: (01482) 571888
F: (01482) 351215
E: westparkhotel@mandp.karoo.co.uk

HUMBERSTON
North East Lincolnshire

South Sea Lane Farm B&B ♦♦♦
South Sea Lane, Humberston, Grimsby DN36 4JY
T: (01472) 812144
E: milner@tinyworld.co.uk

HUNMANBY
North Yorkshire

Sea Cabin ♦♦♦
16 Gap Road, Hunmanby Gap, Filey YO14 9QP
T: (01723) 891368

HUTTON CRANSWICK
East Riding of Yorkshire

Londesborough Lodge ♦♦♦
44 Southgate, Cranswick, Hutton Cranswick, Driffield YO25 9QX
T: (01377) 271170
E: kate_ollett@hotmail.com

HUTTON-LE-HOLE
North Yorkshire

Barn Hotel and Tea Room ♦♦♦
Hutton-le-Hole, York YO62 6UA
T: (01751) 417311
E: fairhurst@lineone.net

Moorlands of Hutton-le-Hole ♦♦♦♦ SILVER AWARD
Hutton-le-Hole, York YO62 6UA
T: (01751) 417548
F: (01751) 417760
E: stay@moorlandshouse.com
I: www.moorlandshouse.com

Westfield Lodge ♦♦♦
Hutton-le-Hole, York YO62 6UG
T: (01751) 417261
F: (01751) 417876
E: sticklandrw@farmersweekly.net

HUTTON SESSAY
North Yorkshire

Burtree Country House ♦♦♦♦
York Road, Hutton Sessay, Thirsk YO7 3AY
T: (01845) 501333
F: (01845) 501596
E: dawn@burtreecountryhouse.co.uk
I: www.burtreecountryhouse.co.uk

HUTTONS AMBO
North Yorkshire

High Gaterley Farm ♦♦♦♦
Castle Howard Estate, Huttons Ambo, York YO60 7HT
T: (01653) 694636
F: (01653) 694636
E: relax@highgaterley.com
I: www.highgaterley.com

IBURNDALE
North Yorkshire

Mill Race Cottage ♦♦♦
8 Mill Lane, Iburndale, Whitby YO22 5DU
T: (01947) 810009
F: (01947) 810009

ILKLEY
West Yorkshire

Grove Hotel ♦♦♦♦
66 The Grove, Ilkley LS29 9PA
T: (01943) 600298
F: (0870) 706 5587
E: info@grovehotel.org
I: www.grovehotel.org

Ilkley Riverside Hotel ♦♦♦
Riverside Gardens, Bridge Lane, Ilkley LS29 9EU
T: (01943) 607338
F: (01943) 607338

One Tivoli Place ♦♦♦♦
Tivoli Place, Ilkley LS29 8SU
T: (01943) 600328
F: (01943) 600320
E: tivolipl@aol.com
I: www.onetivoliplace.co.uk

Roberts Family Bed and Breakfast ♦♦♦
63 Skipton Road, Ilkley LS29 9HF
T: (01943) 817542
F: (01943) 817542
E: petraroberts1@activemail.co.uk

Star Hotel ♦♦
1 Leeds Road, Ilkley LS29 8DH
T: (01943) 605438

Summerhill Guest House ♦♦♦
24 Crossbeck Road, Ilkley LS29 9JN
T: (01943) 607067

Summerhouse ♦♦♦♦
Hangingstone Road, Ilkley LS29 8RS
T: (01943) 601612
F: (01943) 601612

ILLINGWORTH
West Yorkshire

Whitehill Lodge ♦♦♦
102 Keighley Road, Illingworth, Halifax HX2 8HF
T: (01422) 240813
F: (01422) 240813
E: kmcmahon@aol.com

INGBIRCHWORTH
South Yorkshire

The Fountain Inn & Rooms ♦♦♦♦
Wellthorne Lane, Ingbirchworth, Penistone, Sheffield S36 7GJ
T: (01226) 763125
F: (01226) 761336
E: reservations@fountain-inn.co.uk
I: www.fountain-inn.co.uk

INGLEBY CROSS
North Yorkshire

Blue Bell Inn ♦♦
Ingleby Cross, Northallerton DL6 3NF
T: (01609) 882272
E: david.kinsella1@tesco.net

INGLEBY GREENHOW
North Yorkshire

Manor House Farm ♦♦♦♦
Ingleby Greenhow, Great Ayton, Middlesbrough TS9 6RB
T: (01642) 722384
E: mbloom@globalnet.co.uk

INGLETON
North Yorkshire

The Dales Guest House ♦♦♦
Main Street, Ingleton, Carnforth LA6 3HH
T: (015242) 41401
E: dalesgh@hotmail.com

Gatehouse Farm ♦♦♦♦
Westhouse, Ingleton, Carnforth LA6 3NR
T: (01524) 241458

Ingleborough View Guest House ♦♦♦♦
Main Street, Ingleton, Carnforth LA6 3HH
T: (01524) 241523
E: anne@ingleboroughview.co.uk
I: www.ingleboroughview.co.uk

Inglenook Guest House ♦♦♦
20 Main Street, Ingleton, Carnforth LA6 3HJ
T: (01524) 241270
E: inglenook20@hotmail.com
I: www.nebsweb.co.uk/inglenook

Marton Arms Hotel ♦♦♦♦
Thornton in Lonsdale, Ingleton, Carnforth LA6 3PB
T: (015242) 41281
F: (015242) 42579
E: mail@globalnet.co.uk
I: www.martonarms.co.uk

New Butts Farm ♦♦♦
High Bentham, Lancaster LA2 7AN
T: (01524) 241238

Pines Country House ♦♦♦♦
New Road, Ingleton, Carnforth LA6 3HN
T: (01524) 241252
F: (01524) 241252
E: pineshotel@aol.com
I: www.yorkshirenet.co.uk/stayat/thepines

Riverside Lodge ♦♦♦♦
24 Main Street, Ingleton, Carnforth LA6 3HJ
T: (015242) 41359
E: info@riversideingleton.co.uk
I: www.riversideingleton.co.uk

Springfield Country House Hotel ♦♦♦
26 Main Street, Ingleton, Carnforth LA6 3HJ
T: (01524) 241280
F: (01524) 241280
I: www.destination-england.co.uk.springfield

Station Inn ♦♦♦
Ribblehead, Ingleton, Carnforth LA6 3AS
T: (01524) 241274
E: enquiries@thestationinn.net
I: www.thestationinn.net

Thorngarth Country Guest House ♦♦♦♦
New Road, Ingleton, Carnforth LA6 3HN
T: (015242) 41295
F: (015242) 41033
E: Thorngarthcountryguesthouse@btinternet.com
I: www.Thorngarth.co.uk

Wheatsheaf Inn & Hotel ♦♦♦♦
22 High Street, Ingleton, Carnforth LA6 3AD
T: (01524) 241275
F: (01524) 241275
E: randall.d@ingleton01.freeserve.co.uk
I: www.yorkshirenet.co.uk/stayat/thewheatsheaf

KEIGHLEY
West Yorkshire

The King's Arms ♦♦♦
2 Church Street, Haworth, Stanbury, Keighley BD22 8DR
T: (01535) 647302
F: (01535) 647302
E: ksmukltd@pubco205.freeserve.co.uk

Rookery Nook
Rating Applied For
6 Church Street, Keighley BD22 8DR
T: (01535) 640873
F: (01535) 643374
I: www.bronte-country.com/welcome.html

KETTLESING
North Yorkshire

Green Acres
♦♦♦♦ GOLD AWARD
Sleights Lane, Kettlesing, Harrogate HG3 2LE
T: (01423) 771524
E: christine@yorkshiredalesbb.com
I: www.yorkshiredalesbb.com

KETTLEWELL
North Yorkshire

Blue Bell Inn ♦♦♦
Kettlewell, Skipton BD23 5QX
T: (01756) 760230
F: (01756) 760230
E: info@bluebellinn.co.uk
I: www.bluebellinn.co.uk

Chestnut Cottage ♦♦♦
Kettlewell, Skipton BD23 5RL
T: (01756) 760804

Lynburn ♦♦♦
Langcliffe Garth, Kettlewell, Skipton BD23 5RF
T: (01756) 760803
E: lorna@lthornborrow.fsnet.co.uk

KILBURN
North Yorkshire

Church Farm ♦♦
Kilburn, York YO61 4AH
T: (01347) 868318

The Forresters Arms Hotel ♦♦♦
Kilburn, York YO61 4AH
T: (01347) 868550
F: (01347) 868386
E: paulcussons@forrestersarms.fsnet.co.uk
I: www.forrestersarms.fsnet.co.uk

KILNWICK PERCY
East Riding of Yorkshire

Paws-A-While
Rating Applied For
Kilnwick Percy, Pocklington, York YO42 1UF
T: (01759) 301168
E: paws-a-while@lineone.net

KIRBY HILL
North Yorkshire

Shoulder of Mutton ♦♦♦
Kirby Hill, Richmond DL11 7JH
T: (01748) 822772
F: (01325) 718936
E: info@shoulderofmutton.net
I: www.shoulderofmutton.net

KIRBY MISPERTON
North Yorkshire

Beansheaf Hotel ♦♦♦
Malton Road, Kirby Misperton, Malton YO17 6UE
T: (01653) 668614
F: (01653) 668370

KIRKBURTON
West Yorkshire

The Woodman Inn ♦♦♦♦
Thunderbridge, Kirkburton, Huddersfield HD8 0PX
T: (01484) 605778
F: (01484) 604110
E: thewoodman@connectfree.co.uk
I: www.woodman-inn.co.uk

KIRKBY
North Yorkshire

Dromonby Hall Farm ♦♦♦
Busby Lane, Kirkby, Stokesley, Middlesbrough TS9 7AP
T: (01642) 712312
F: (01642) 712312
E: b-b@dromonby.co.uk
I: www.dromonby.co.uk

KIRKBY-IN-CLEVELAND
North Yorkshire

Dromonby Grange Farm ♦♦
Busby Lane, Kirkby-in-Cleveland, Middlesbrough TS9 7AR
T: (01642) 712227
E: jehugill@aol.com

KIRKBY MALHAM
North Yorkshire

Yeoman's Barn ♦♦♦♦
Kirkby Malham, Skipton BD23 4BL
T: (01729) 830639
E: info@yeomansbarn.co.uk
I: www.yeomansbarn.co.uk

KIRKBYMOORSIDE
North Yorkshire

Brickfields Farm
♦♦♦♦ SILVER AWARD
Kirkby Mills, Kirkbymoorside, York YO62 6NS
T: (01751) 433074

Cartoft Lodge ♦♦♦♦
Cartoft, Kirkbymoorside, York YO62 6NU
T: (01751) 431566

The Cornmill
♦♦♦♦ SILVER AWARD
Kirkby Mills, Kirkbymoorside, York YO62 6NP
T: (01751) 432000
F: (01751) 432300
E: cornmill@kirbymills.demon.co.uk
I: www.kirbymills.demon.co.uk

Eller House ♦♦♦♦
Farndale, Kirkbymoorside, York YO62 7LA
T: (01751) 433223

Feversham Arms Inn ♦♦♦
Church Houses, Farndale, Kirkbymoorside, York YO62 7LF
T: (01751) 433206

High Blakey House ♦♦♦♦
High Blakey, Kirkbymoorside, York YO62 7LQ
T: (01751) 417186

The Lion Inn ♦♦♦
Blakey Ridge, Kirkbymoorside, York YO62 7LQ
T: (01751) 417320
F: (01751) 417717
E: info@lionblakey.co.uk
I: www.lionblakey.co.uk

Sinnington Common Farm ♦♦♦♦
Cartoft, Kirkbymoorside, York YO62 6NX
T: (01751) 431719
E: Felicity@scfarm.demon.co.uk
I: www.scfarm.demon.co.uk

White Horse Hotel ♦♦♦
5 Market Place, Kirkbymoorside, York YO62 6AB
T: (01751) 431296

KIRKSTALL
West Yorkshire

Abbey Guest House ♦♦♦♦
44 Vesper Road, Kirkstall, Leeds LS5 3NX
T: (0113) 278 5580
F: (0113) 278 7780
E: abbeyleeds@aol.com

KNARESBOROUGH
North Yorkshire

Bay Horse Inn ♦♦♦
York Road, Green Hammerton, York YO26 8BN
T: (01423) 330338
F: (01423) 331279
E: thebayhorseinn@aol.com
I: www.thebayhorse.com

Ebor Mount ♦♦♦
18 York Place, Knaresborough HG5 0AA
T: (01423) 863315
F: (01423) 863315

Hermitage Guest House & Tea Garden ♦♦♦
10 Waterside, Knaresborough HG5 9AZ
T: (01423) 863349
I: www.smoothhound.co.uk/hotels/hermitage1.html

Holly Corner ♦♦♦♦
3 Coverdale Drive, Knaresborough HG5 9BW
T: (01423) 864204
F: (01423) 864204
E: hollycorner3@aol.com
I: www.hotelmaster.co.uk

Kirkgate House ♦♦♦♦
17 Kirkgate, Knaresborough HG5 8AD
T: (01423) 862704
F: (01423) 862704
I: www.knaresborough.co.uk/guest-accom/

Moray House ♦♦♦
Harrogate Road, Knaresborough HG5 8DA
T: (01423) 862085
F: (01423) 862085
E: moray_house@hotmail.com
I: www.knaresborough.co.uk

Newton House ♦♦♦♦
5-7 York Place, Knaresborough HG5 0AD
T: (01423) 863539
F: (01423) 869748
E: newtonhouse@btinternet.com
I: www.newtonhousehotel.com

Rosedale ♦♦♦
11 Aspin Way, Knaresborough HG5 8HL
T: (01423) 867210
F: (01423) 860675
I: www.knaresborough.co.uk/guest-accommodation

11a Silver Street ♦♦♦
Knaresborough HG5 8AJ
T: (01423) 863246
F: (01423) 863246
E: john.prudames@btinternet.com

Watergate Lodge ♦♦♦♦
Watergate Haven, Ripley Road, Knaresborough HG5 9BU
T: (01423) 864627
F: (01423) 861087
E: info@watergatehaven.com
I: www.watergatehaven.com

Yorkshire Lass ♦♦♦
High Bridge, Harrogate Road, Knaresborough HG5 8DA
T: (01423) 862962
F: (01423) 869091
E: yorkshirelass@knaresborough.co.uk
I: www.knaresborough.co.uk/yorkshirelass

KNOTTINGLEY
West Yorkshire

Wentvale Court ♦♦♦♦
Great North Road, Knottingley WF11 8PF
T: (01977) 676714
F: (01977) 676714
E: wentvale@aol.com
I: www.wentvalecourt.co.uk

LANGSETT
South Yorkshire

Waggon and Horses ♦♦♦
Langsett, Stocksbridge, Sheffield S36 4GY
T: (01226) 763147
F: (01226) 763147
E: info@langsettinn.com
I: www.langsettinn.com

LANGTOFT
East Riding of Yorkshire

The Ship Inn ♦♦♦
Scarborough Road, Langtoft, Driffield YO25 3TH
T: (01377) 267243

LAYCOCK
West Yorkshire

Far Laithe Farm
♦♦♦♦♦ SILVER AWARD
Laycock, Keighley BD22 0PP
T: (01535) 661993

LEALHOLM
North Yorkshire

The Board Inn ♦♦♦
Village Green, Lealholm, Whitby YO21 2AJ
T: (01947) 897279
F: (01947) 897764
E: theboardinn@amserve.net

High Park Farm ♦♦♦
Lealholm, Whitby YO21 2AQ
T: (01947) 897416
E: jeremywelford@care4free.net

LEEDS
West Yorkshire

Adriatic Hotel ♦♦♦
87 Harehills Avenue, Leeds LS8 4ET
T: (0113) 262 0115
F: (0113) 262 6071
E: adriatichotel@tiscali.co.uk
I: www.theadriatichotel.co.uk

Aintree Hotel ♦♦
38 Cardigan Road, Headingley, Leeds LS6 3AG
T: (0113) 275 8290
F: (0113) 275 8290
I: www.leeds-headingleyhotels.com

Avalon Guest House ♦♦♦
132 Woodsley Road, Leeds LS2 9LZ
T: (0113) 243 2545
F: (0113) 242 0649

Beckett's Park Bed & Breakfast ♦♦♦
49 St Chads Drive, Leeds LS6 3PZ
T: (0113) 275 0703

Broomhurst Hotel ♦♦♦
12 Chapel Lane, Off Cardigan Road, Headingley, Leeds LS6 3BW
T: (0113) 278 6836
F: (0113) 230 7099
E: broomhursthotel@hotmail.com
I: www.leeds-headingleyhotels.com

Central Hotel ♦♦
35-47 New Briggate, Leeds LS2 8JD
T: (0113) 294 1456
F: (0113) 294 1551
E: reception@central-hotel.freeserve.com.uk

Cliff Lawn Hotel ♦♦♦♦
44/45 Cliff Road, Leeds LS6 2ET
T: (0113) 278 5442
F: (0113) 278 5422
E: liz@clifflawn.fsnet.co.uk
I: www.clifflawn-hotel.co.uk

17 Cottage Road ♦♦
Cottage Road, Headingley, Leeds LS6 4DD
T: (0113) 275 5575

Fairbairn House ♦♦♦
71-75 Clarendon Road, Leeds LS2 9PL
T: (0113) 343 6633
F: (0113) 343 6914
E: m.a.timm@leeds.ac.uk

7 Glebelands Drive ♦♦
Leeds LS6 4AG
T: (0113) 275 6621
E: jprudames@aol.com

Glengarth Hotel ♦♦
162 Woodsley Road, Leeds LS2 9LZ
T: (0113) 245 7940
F: (0113) 216 8033

Highbank Hotel & Restaurant ♦♦
83 Harehills Lane, Leeds LS7 4HA
T: 0870 7456744
F: 0870 7456734
E: info@highbankhotel.co.uk
I: www.leedshotel.com

Hilldene Hotel ♦♦
99 Harehills Lane, Leeds LS8 4DN
T: (0113) 262 1292
F: (0113) 262 1292

Hinsley Hall ♦♦♦
62 Headingley Lane, Leeds LS6 2BX
T: (0113) 261 8000
F: (0113) 224 2406
E: info@hinsley-hall.co.uk
I: www.hinsley-hall.co.uk

Kirkstall Hall, Trinity and All Saints College ♦♦♦
Brownberrie Lane, Horsforth, Leeds LS18 5HD
T: (0113) 283 7240
F: (0113) 283 7239
E: commercial_services@tasc.ac.uk
I: www.tasc.ac.uk/conf/index.htm

Manxdene Private Hotel ♦♦
154 Woodsley Road, Leeds LS2 9LZ
T: (0113) 243 2586
F: (0113) 243 2586
E: manxdene@dial.pipex.com

The Moorlea Hotel ♦♦♦
146 Woodsley Road, Leeds LS2 9LZ
T: (0113) 243 2653
F: (0113) 246 5393
E: TheMoorleaHotel@aol.com

Number 23 ♦♦♦
23 St Chads Rise, Leeds LS6 3QE
T: (0113) 275 7825

St Michael's Tower Hotel ♦♦♦
5 St Michael's Villas, Cardigan Road, Headingley, Leeds LS6 3AF
T: (0113) 275 5557
F: (0113) 230 7491
E: saint_michaels@ntlworld.com
I: www.leeds-headingleyhotels.com

Sandylands ♦♦♦
44 Lidgett Lane, Leeds LS8 1PQ
T: (0113) 266 1666
E: stanpackman@hotmail.com

Temple Manor ♦♦♦♦
2 Field End Garth, Leeds LS15 0QQ
T: (0113) 264 1384

Weetwood B&B
Rating Applied For
65 Weetwood Lane, Leeds
LS16 5NP
T: (0113) 294 0315

Wheelgate Guest House ♦♦♦
7 Kirkgate, Sherburn in Elmet, Leeds LS25 6BH
T: (01977) 682231
F: (01977) 685287

LEEMING
North Yorkshire

Black Ox House ♦♦♦
Leeming, Northallerton DL7 9SB
T: (01677) 425593
F: (01677) 422251
E: brian@blackox.fsnet.co.uk
I: www.blackoxguesthouse.com

LEEMING BAR
North Yorkshire

Little Holtby
♦♦♦♦ SILVER AWARD
Leeming Bar, Northallerton
DL7 9LH
T: (01609) 748762
F: (01609) 748822
E: littleholtby@yahoo.co.uk
I: www.littleholtby.co.uk

LEVISHAM
North Yorkshire

Horseshoe Inn ♦♦♦
Main Street, Levisham, Pickering
YO18 7NL
T: (01751) 460240
F: (01751) 460240
I: www.horseshoe-inn-levisham.co.uk

The Moorlands Country House Hotel ♦♦♦♦♦ GOLD AWARD
Main Street, Levisham, Pickering
YO18 7NL
T: (01751) 460229
F: (01751) 460470
E: ronaldoleonardo@aol.com
I: www.moorlandslevisham.co.uk

LEYBURN
North Yorkshire

Clyde House ♦♦♦
5 Railway Street, Leyburn
DL8 5AY
T: (01969) 623941
F: (01969) 623941
E: info@clydehouseleyburn.co.uk
I: www.clydehouseleyburn.co.uk

Craken House Farm ♦♦♦♦
Middleham Road, Leyburn
DL8 5HF
T: (01969) 622204
F: (01969) 622204
E: marjorie@miveson.fsnet.co.uk

Eastfield Lodge Private Hotel ♦♦♦
St Matthews Terrace, Leyburn
DL8 5EL
T: (01969) 623196
F: (01969) 624599

Grove Hotel ♦♦♦
8 Grove Square, Leyburn
DL8 5AE
T: (01969) 622569
E: info@grove-hotel.com
I: www.grove-hotel.com

The Haven ♦♦♦♦
Market Place, Leyburn DL8 5BJ
T: (01969) 623814
E: warmwelcome@havenguesthouse.co.uk
I: www.havenguesthouse.co.uk

Hayloft Suite ♦♦♦
Foal Barn, Spennithorne, Leyburn DL8 5PR
T: (01969) 622580

The Old Vicarage ♦♦♦
Main Street, West Witton, Leyburn DL8 4LX
T: (01969) 622108
E: info@dalesbreaks.co.uk
I: www.dalesbreaks.co.uk

Park Gate House
♦♦♦♦♦ SILVER AWARD
Constable Burton, Leyburn
DL8 5RG
T: (01677) 450466
E: parkgatehouse@freenet.co.uk
I: www.parkgatehouse.co.uk

LINTON
West Yorkshire

Glendales ♦♦♦
Muddy Lane, Linton, Wetherby
LS22 4HW
T: (01937) 585915

LITTLE RIBSTON
North Yorkshire

Beck House ♦♦♦♦
Wetherby Road, Little Ribston, Wetherby LS22 4EP
T: (01937) 583362
F: (01937) 583174

LOCKTON
North Yorkshire

Farfields Farmhouse ♦♦♦♦
Lockton, Pickering YO18 7NQ
T: (01751) 460239
E: farfieldsfarm@btinternet.com

LOFTHOUSE
West Yorkshire

Tall Trees Hotel ♦♦♦♦
188 Leeds Road, Lofthouse, Wakefield WF3 3LS
T: (01924) 827666
F: (01924) 827555
E: gordon304@aol.com
I: www.talltreeshotel.co.uk

LONDESBOROUGH
East Riding of Yorkshire

Towthorpe Grange ♦♦
Towthorpe Lane, Londesborough, York YO43 3LB
T: (01430) 873814
E: towthorpegrange@hotmail.com

LONDONDERRY
North Yorkshire

Tatton Lodge ♦♦♦
Londonderry, Northallerton
DL7 9NF
T: (01677) 422222
F: (01677) 422222
E: enquiries@tattonlodge.co.uk
I: www.tattonlodge.co.uk

LOW ROW
North Yorkshire

Summer Lodge Farm ♦♦♦
Low Row, Richmond DL11 6NP
T: (01748) 886504

LUDDENDENFOOT
West Yorkshire

Bankfield Bed and Breakfast
♦♦♦♦ SILVER AWARD
Danny Lane, Luddendenfoot, Halifax HX2 6AW
T: (01422) 883147
E: jenden@bankfieldbb.fsnet.co.uk

Hollin Top Farm
Rating Applied For
Clough Lane, Midgley, Luddendenfoot, Halifax HX2 6XB
T: (01422) 881625
E: s.knutton@sheffield.ac.uk

Rockcliffe West ♦♦♦♦
Burnley Road, Luddendenfoot, Halifax HX2 6HL
T: (01422) 882151
F: (01422) 882151
E: rockcliffe.b.b@virgin.net

MALHAM
North Yorkshire

Beck Hall ♦♦♦
Cove Road, Malham, Skipton
BD23 4DJ
T: (01729) 830332
E: alice@beckhallmalham.com
I: www.beckhallmalham.com

Miresfield Farm ♦♦♦
Malham, Skipton BD23 4DA
T: (01729) 830414
E: chris@miresfield.freeserve.co.uk
I: www.miresfield-farm.com

River House Hotel ♦♦♦♦
Malham, Skipton BD23 4DA
T: (01729) 830315
F: (01729) 830315
E: info@riverhousehotel.co.uk
I: www.riverhousehotel.co.uk

MALTBY
South Yorkshire

The Cottages Guest House ♦♦
1, 3 & 5 Blyth Road, Maltby, Rotherham S66 8HX
T: (01709) 813382

MALTON
North Yorkshire

Barugh House
♦♦♦♦ SILVER AWARD
Great Barugh, Malton YO17 6UZ
T: (01653) 668615
E: barughhouse@aol.com

Mill House Bed & Breakfast ♦♦♦
East Knapton, Malton YO17 8JA
T: (01944) 728026
E: carol@millhouse822.freeserve.co.uk

The Old Lodge Hotel ♦♦♦♦
Old Maltongate, Malton
YO17 7EG
T: (01653) 690570
F: (01653) 690652
E: info@oldlodgehotel.com
I: www.oldlodgehotel.com

The Old Rectory
♦♦♦♦ SILVER AWARD
West Heslerton, Malton
YO17 8RE
T: (01944) 728285
F: (01944) 728436
E: bhillas@supanet.com
I: www.theoldrectoryny.co.uk

The Wentworth Arms ♦♦♦♦
111 Town Street, Old Malton, Malton YO17 7HD
T: (01653) 692618
F: (01653) 600061
E: wentwortharms@btinternet.com

MANKINHOLES
West Yorkshire

Cross Farm ♦♦♦♦
Stock Hey Lane, Mankinholes, Todmorden OL14 6HB
T: (01706) 813481

MAPPLEWELL
South Yorkshire

The Grange ♦♦♦
29 Spark Lane, Mapplewell, Barnsley S75 6AA
T: (01226) 380078
E: the.grange@telinco.com

MARKET WEIGHTON
East Riding of Yorkshire

Arras Farmhouse ♦♦♦
Arras, Sancton, Market Weighton, York YO43 4RN
T: (01430) 872404
F: (01430) 872404

MARSDEN
West Yorkshire

Olive Branch Restaurant with Rooms and Bar
♦♦♦♦ SILVER AWARD
Olive Terrace, Manchester Road, Marsden, Huddersfield HD7 6LU
T: (01484) 844487
E: reservations@olivebranch.uk.com
I: www.olivebranch.uk.com

Throstle Nest Cottage B&B ♦♦♦♦
3 Old Mount Road, Marsden, Huddersfield HD7 6DU
T: (01484) 846371
F: (01484) 846371
E: throstlenest@btopenworld.com

MARTON
North Yorkshire

Orchard House
♦♦♦♦ SILVER AWARD
Marton, Sinnington, York
YO62 6RD
T: (01751) 432904
F: (01751) 430733
E: orchard.house1@btinternet.com
I: www.thebestbritishbedandbreakfast.com

MASHAM
North Yorkshire

Garden House ♦♦♦
1 Park Street, Masham, Ripon
HG4 4HN
T: (01765) 689989
E: S.Furby@freenet.co.uk
I: www.ukfreenet.co.uk

Haregill Lodge ♦♦♦♦
Ellingstring, Masham, Ripon
HG4 4PW
T: (01677) 460272
F: (01677) 460272
E: haregilllodge@freenet.co.uk

Establishments printed in blue have a detailed entry in this guide

Warren House Farm ♦♦♦♦
High Ellington, Masham, Ripon HG4 4PP
T: (01677) 460244
F: (01677) 460244
E: cath.e.broadley@btopenworld.com

MENSTON
West Yorkshire

Chevin End Guest House ♦♦♦
Menston, Ilkley LS29 6DU
T: (01943) 876845
E: chevinend.guesthouse@virgin.net
I: www.chevinendguesthouse.co.uk

MIDDLEHAM
North Yorkshire

The Black Bull Inn ♦♦♦♦
East Witton Road, Middleham, Leyburn DL8 4NX
T: (01969) 623669
E: blackbull.middleham@virgin.net

Chapelfields ♦♦♦
East Witton Road, Middleham, Leyburn DL8 4PY
T: (01969) 625075
F: (01765) 689991
E: chapelfieldsuk@aol.com
I: www.chapelfieldsuk.co.uk

Domus ♦♦♦♦
Market Place, Middleham, Leyburn DL8 4NR
T: (01969) 623497
E: domus_2000@yahoo.co.uk

Jasmine House
♦♦♦♦♦ GOLD AWARD
Market Place, Middleham, Leyburn DL8 4NU
T: (01969) 622858
E: enquiries@jasminehouse.net
I: jasminehouse.net

The Priory ♦♦♦
West End, Middleham, Leyburn DL8 4QG
T: (01969) 623279

Richard III Hotel ♦♦♦
Market Place, Middleham, Leyburn DL8 4NP
T: (01969) 623240

Yore View ♦♦♦♦
Leyburn Road, Middleham, Leyburn DL8 4PL
T: (01969) 622987

MIDGLEY
West Yorkshire

Midgley Lodge Motel ♦♦♦♦
Bar Lane, Midgley, Wakefield WF4 4JJ
T: (01924) 830069
F: (01924) 830087
I: www.midgleylodgemotel.co.uk

MIDHOPESTONES
South Yorkshire

Ye Olde Mustard Pot ♦♦♦♦
Mortimer Road, Midhopestones, Sheffield S36 4GW
T: (01226) 761155
F: (01226) 761161
E: reservations@yeoldemustardpot.co.uk
I: www.yeoldemustardpot.co.uk

MILLINGTON
East Riding of Yorkshire

Laburnum Cottage ♦♦♦
Millington, York YO42 1TX
T: (01759) 303055
E: Roger&Maureen@labcott.fslife.co.uk

MUKER
North Yorkshire

Bridge House ♦♦♦♦
Muker, Richmond DL11 6QG
T: (01748) 886461
E: alannichols88@hotmail.com

Hylands ♦♦♦♦
Muker, Richmond DL11 6QQ
T: (01748) 886003
E: jonesr3@btinternet.com

Muker Tea Shop
Rating Applied For
The Village Stores, Muker, Richmond DL11 6QG
T: (01748) 886409
F: (01748) 886409
E: rob@mukervillage.co.uk

NAWTON
North Yorkshire

Little Manor Farm ♦♦♦
Highfield Lane, Nawton, York YO62 7TH
T: (01439) 771672

Nawton Grange ♦♦♦♦
Gale Lane, Nawton, York YO62 7SD
T: (01439) 771146
E: chrisbaxter@themail.co.uk

NEW WALTHAM
North East Lincolnshire

Peaks Top Farm ♦♦♦
Hewitts Avenue, New Waltham, Grimsby DN36 4RS
T: (01472) 812941
F: (01472) 812941
E: lmclayton@tinyworld.co.uk

NEWBY WISKE
North Yorkshire

Well House ♦♦♦♦
Newby Wiske, Northallerton DL7 9EX
T: (01609) 772253
F: (01609) 772253

NEWTON-ON-RAWCLIFFE
North Yorkshire

Elm House Farm ♦♦♦♦
Newton-on-Rawcliffe, Pickering YO18 8QA
T: (01751) 473223

Swan Cottage ♦♦♦♦
Newton-on-Rawcliffe, Pickering YO18 8QA
T: (01751) 472502

NORTH CAVE
East Riding of Yorkshire

Albion House ♦♦
18 Westgate, North Cave, Brough HU15 2NJ
T: (01430) 422958
F: (01430) 470655
E: caroline@ccockin.freeserve.co.uk
I: www.hawleys.info

NORTH FERRIBY
East Riding of Yorkshire

B & B @103 ♦♦♦
103 Ferriby High Road, North Ferriby HU14 3LA
T: (01482) 633637
E: info@bnb103.co.uk
I: www.bnb103.co.uk

NORTHALLERTON
North Yorkshire

Alverton Guest House ♦♦♦
26 South Parade, Northallerton DL7 8SG
T: (01609) 776207
F: (01609) 776207
E: alvertonguesthse@btconnect.com

Elmscott
♦♦♦♦ SILVER AWARD
10 Hatfield Road, Northallerton DL7 8QX
T: (01609) 760575
E: elmscott@freenet.co.uk
I: www.elmscottbedandbreakfast.co.uk

Heyrose Farm ♦♦♦
Lovesome Hill, Northallerton DL6 2PS
T: (01609) 881554
F: (01609) 881554
E: heyrosefarm@hotmail.com

Ladyfield Grange Bed & Breakfast
Rating Applied For
Ainderby Steeple, Northallerton DL7 0PJ
T: (01609) 770494

Lovesome Hill Farm ♦♦♦♦
Lovesome Hill, Northallerton DL6 2PB
T: (01609) 772311
E: pearsonlhf@care4free.net

Masham House Bed And Breakfast ♦♦♦♦
18 South Parade, Northallerton DL7 8SG
T: (01609) 771541
E: jpbb@ukonline.co.uk

NORTON
North Yorkshire

Lynden ♦♦♦
165 Welham Road, Norton, Malton YO17 9DU
T: (01653) 694236

NUNNINGTON
North Yorkshire

Sunley Court ♦♦♦
Muscoates, Nunnington, York YO62 5XQ
T: (01439) 748233
F: (01439) 748233

OSMOTHERLEY
North Yorkshire

Oak Garth Farm ♦♦
North End, Osmotherley, Northallerton DL6 3BH
T: (01609) 883314

Osmotherley Walking Shop ♦♦♦
4 West End, Osmotherley, Northallerton DL6 3AA
T: (01609) 883818
E: walkingshop@osmotherley.fsbusiness.co.uk
I: www.coast2coast.co.uk/osmotherleywalkingshop

Vane House ♦♦♦
11A North End, Osmotherley, Northallerton DL6 3BA
T: (01609) 883448
F: (01609) 883448
E: allan@vanehouse.co.uk
I: www.coast2coast.co.uk/vanehouse

OSSETT
West Yorkshire

Heath House ♦♦♦
Chancery Road, Ossett WF5 9RZ
T: (01924) 260654
F: (01924) 260654
E: jo.holland@amserve.net
I: www.heath-house.co.uk

Mews Hotel ♦♦♦♦
Dale Street, Ossett WF5 9HN
T: (01924) 273982
F: (01924) 279389
E: enquiries@mews-hotel.co.uk
I: www.mews-hotel.co.uk

OTLEY
West Yorkshire

11 Newall Mount ♦♦♦
Otley LS21 2DY
T: (01943) 462898

Paddock Hill ♦♦♦
Norwood, Otley LS21 2QU
T: (01943) 465977
E: cheribeaumont@connectfree.co.uk

Scaife Hall Farm
♦♦♦♦ SILVER AWARD
Hardisty Hill, Blubberhouses, Otley LS21 2PL
T: (01943) 880354
F: (01943) 880374
E: christine.a.ryder@btinternet.com
I: www.scaifehallfarm.co.uk

Wood Top Farm ♦♦♦♦
Off Norwood Edge, Lindley, Otley LS21 2QS
T: (01943) 464010
F: (01943) 464010
E: mailwoodtop@aol.com

OTTRINGHAM
East Riding of Yorkshire

Highfield Farm ♦♦♦♦
Station Road, Ottringham, Hull HU12 0BJ
T: (01964) 622283
F: (01964) 624478
E: sylvia@highfieldfarm.ukf.net
I: www.highfieldfarm.ukf.net

PATELEY BRIDGE
North Yorkshire

Bewerley Hall Farm ♦♦♦
Bewerley, Harrogate HG3 5JA
T: (01423) 711636
E: chris@farmhouseholidays.freeserve.co.uk
I: www.bewerleyhallfarm.co.uk

Bruce House Farm ♦♦♦♦
Top Wath Road, Pateley Bridge, Harrogate HG3 5PG
T: (01423) 711813
F: (01423) 712843
E: brucehse@aol.com
I: members.aol.com/brucehse

Dale View ♦♦♦
Old Church Lane, Pateley Bridge, Harrogate HG3 5LY
T: (01423) 711506
F: (01423) 711506
E: bedandbreakfast@daleview.com
I: www.daleview.com

Greengarth ♦♦♦
Greenwood Road, Pateley Bridge, Harrogate HG3 5LR
T: (01423) 711688
E: greengarth.bb@btopenworld.com
I: www.bedandbreakfastexplorer.co.uk

Knottside Farm
♦♦♦♦♦ GOLD AWARD
The Knott, Pateley Bridge, Harrogate HG3 5DQ
T: (01423) 712927
F: (01423) 712927

Nidderdale Lodge Farm ♦♦♦
Fellbeck, Harrogate HG3 5DR
T: (01423) 711677

North Pasture Farm
♦♦♦♦ SILVER AWARD
Summerbridge, Harrogate HG3 4DW
T: (01423) 711470
F: (01423) 711470
I: www.yorkshirenet.co.uk/stayat/northpasturefarm

The Talbot ♦♦♦
27 High Street, Pateley Bridge, Harrogate HG3 5AL
T: (01423) 711597
F: (01423) 712119
E: enquiries@thetalbot.info
I: www.thetalbot.info

PATRICK BROMPTON
North Yorkshire

Neesham Cottage ♦♦♦
Patrick Brompton, Bedale DL8 1LN
T: (01677) 450271
E: info@neeshamcottage.co.uk
I: www.neeshamcottage.co.uk

PENISTONE
South Yorkshire

Cubley Hall Freehouse Pub-Restaurant-Hotel ♦♦♦♦
North Star Hotels Ltd, Mortimer Road, Penistone, Sheffield S36 9DF
T: (01226) 766086
F: (01226) 767335
E: cubley.hall@ukonline.co.uk

PICKERING
North Yorkshire

Banavie ♦♦♦♦
Roxby Road, Thornton Dale, Pickering YO18 7SX
T: (01751) 474616
E: info@banavie.uk.com/
I: www.banavie.uk.com

Barker Stakes Farm ♦♦♦♦
Lendales Lane, Pickering YO18 8EE
T: (01751) 476759
F: (01751) 476759
E: barkerstakes@virgin.net
I: www.barkerstakes.co.uk

Beech Cottage ♦♦♦
Newton-on-Rawcliffe, Pickering YO18 8QQ
T: (01751) 417625
E: www.bramspin@aol.com

Black Swan Hotel ♦♦♦
18 Birdgate, Pickering YO18 7AL
T: (01751) 472286
F: (01751) 472928

Bramwood Guest House
♦♦♦♦ SILVER AWARD
19 Hall Garth, Pickering YO18 7AW
T: (01751) 474066
F: (01751) 475849
E: bramwood19@aol.com
I: www.bramwoodguesthouse.co.uk

Burgate House Hotel & Restaurant ♦♦♦♦
Burgate, Pickering YO18 7AU
T: (01751) 473463
E: info@burgatehouse.co.uk
I: www.burgatehouse.co.uk

Burr Bank
♦♦♦♦♦ GOLD AWARD
Cropton, Pickering YO18 8HL
T: (01751) 417777
F: (01751) 417789
E: bandb@burrbank.com
I: www.burrbank.com

Cawthorne House
♦♦♦♦ SILVER AWARD
42 Eastgate, Pickering YO18 7DU
T: (01751) 477364
I: www.cawthornehouse.co.uk

Clent House ♦♦♦♦
15 Burgate, Pickering YO18 7AU
T: (01751) 477928
E: swiftlink/bb/1315@pb-design.com
I: www.pb-design.com/swiftlink/bb/1315.htm

Costa House
♦♦♦♦ SILVER AWARD
12 Westgate, Pickering YO18 8BA
T: (01751) 474291
E: rooms@costahouse.co.uk
I: www.costahouse.co.uk

Eden House
♦♦♦♦ SILVER AWARD
120 Eastgate, Pickering YO18 7DW
T: (01751) 472289
E: edenhouse@breathemail.net
I: www.edenhousebandb.co.uk

Fox and Hounds Country Inn ♦♦♦♦
Main Street, Sinnington, York YO62 6SQ
T: (01751) 431577
F: (01751) 432791
E: foxhoundsinn@easynet.co.uk
I: www.thefoxandhoundsinn.co.uk

Givendale Head Farm ♦♦♦
Ebberston, Scarborough YO13 9PU
T: (01723) 859383
F: (01723) 859383
E: sue.gwilliam@talk21.com
I: www.givendaleheadfarm.co.uk

Grindale House ♦♦♦♦
123 Eastgate, Pickering YO18 7DW
T: (01751) 476636
F: (01751) 476636
I: www.grindale-house.co.uk

Heathcote House ♦♦♦♦
100 Eastgate, Pickering YO18 7DW
T: (01751) 476991
F: (01751) 476991
E: joanlovejoy@lineone.net

Laurel Bank B&B
♦♦♦♦ SILVER AWARD
Middleton Road, Pickering YO18 8AP
T: (01751) 476399
E: laurelbank-pickering@fsmail.net
I: laurelbank-pickering.co.uk

Munda Wanga ♦
14 Garden Way, Pickering YO18 8BG
T: (01751) 473310
E: mundawanga@fish.co.uk

The Old Manse ♦♦♦♦
Middleton Road, Pickering YO18 8AL
T: (01751) 476484
F: (01751) 477124
E: the_old_manse@btopenworld.com
I: www.theoldmansepickering.co.uk

Rains Farm ♦♦♦♦
Allerston, Pickering YO18 7PQ
T: (01723) 859333
E: allan@rainsfarm.freeserve.co.uk
I: www.rains-farm-holidays.co.uk

Rectory Farm House ♦♦♦♦
Levisham, Pickering YO18 7NL
T: (01751) 460491
E: rectory@levisham.com
I: www.levisham.com

Rose Folly
♦♦♦♦ SILVER AWARD
112 Eastgate, Pickering YO18 7DW
T: (01751) 475057
E: gail@rosefolly.freeserve.co.uk
I: www.rosefolly.freeserve.co.uk

Rosebank Bed & Breakfast ♦♦♦♦
61 Ruffa Lane, Rosebank, Pickering YO18 7HN
T: (01751) 472531

Tangalwood ♦♦♦♦
Roxby Road, Thornton Dale, Pickering YO18 7SX
T: (01751) 474688

Vivers Mill ♦♦♦
Mill Lane, Pickering YO18 8DJ
T: (01751) 473640
E: viversmill@talk21.com
I: www.viversmill.com

Wildsmith House
♦♦♦♦ SILVER AWARD
Marton, Sinnington, Pickering, York YO62 6RD
T: (01751) 432702
E: wildsmithhouse@talk21.com
I: www.pb-design.com/swiftlink/bb/1102.htm

POCKLEY
North Yorkshire

West View Cottage
♦♦♦♦ SILVER AWARD
Pockley, York YO62 7TE
T: (01439) 770526
E: westviewcottage@bedbreakfast.freeserve.co.uk
I: www.s-h-systems.co.uk/hotels/westviewcottage

PRESTON
East Riding of Yorkshire

Little Weghill Farm ♦♦♦♦
Weghill Road, Preston, Hull HU12 8SX
T: (01482) 897650
F: (01482) 897650
I: www.littleweghillfarm.co.uk

PUDSEY
West Yorkshire

Heatherlea House ♦♦♦
105 Littlemoor Road, Pudsey LS28 8AP
T: (0113) 257 4397
E: heatherlea_pudsey.leeds@excite.co.uk

Lynnwood House ♦♦♦
18 Alexandra Road, Uppermoor, Pudsey LS28 8BY
T: (0113) 257 1117

RAMSGILL
North Yorkshire

Covill Barn ♦♦♦♦
Bouthwaite, Harrogate HG3 5RW
T: (01423) 755306
F: (01423) 755306
E: sales@jandsenterprises.co.uk
I: www.jandsenterprises.co.uk

RASKELF
North Yorkshire

Old Black Bull Inn ♦♦♦
Raskelf, York YO61 3LF
T: (01347) 821431
E: info@northyorkshotel.co.uk

RASTRICK
West Yorkshire

Elder Lea House
♦♦♦♦♦ SILVER AWARD
Clough Lane, Rastrick, Brighouse HD6 3QH
T: (01484) 717832
E: elder.lea.house@amserve.net

RATHMELL
North Yorkshire

The Stables ♦♦♦♦
Field House, Rathmell, Settle BD24 0LA
T: (01729) 840234
F: (01729) 840775
E: rosehyslop@layhead.co.uk
I: www.layhead.co.uk

RAVENSCAR
North Yorkshire

Cliff House
♦♦♦♦ SILVER AWARD
Station Road, Ravenscar, Scarborough YO13 0LX
T: (01723) 870889
E: hodgson@cliffhouse.fsbusiness.co.uk
I: www.clifftopstop.com

Smugglers Rock Country House ♦♦♦♦
Staintondale Road, Ravenscar, Scarborough YO13 0ER
T: (01723) 870044
E: info@smugglersrock.co.uk
I: www.smugglersrock.co.uk

RAVENSWORTH
North Yorkshire

The Bay Horse Inn ♦♦♦
Ravensworth, Richmond DL11 7ET
T: (01325) 718328
F: (01325) 718328

REETH
North Yorkshire

Arkle House ♦♦♦♦
Reeth, Richmond DL11 6SJ
T: (01748) 884815
F: (01748) 884942
E: andy@arklehouse.com
I: www.arklehouse.com

2 Bridge Terrace ♦♦♦
Reeth, Richmond DL11 6TP
T: (01748) 884572
E: davidsizer@freenetname.co.uk
I: coast2coast.co.uk/2bridgeterrace

Buck Hotel ♦♦♦
Reeth, Richmond DL11 6SW
T: (01748) 884210
F: (01748) 884802
E: enquiries@buckhotel.co.uk
I: www.buckhotel.co.uk

Elder Peak ♦♦♦
Arkengarthdale Road, Reeth, Richmond DL11 6QX
T: (01748) 884770

Hackney House ♦♦♦
Reeth, Richmond DL11 6TW
T: (01748) 884302
E: hackneyhse@tinyworld.co.uk

Springfield House ♦♦♦♦
Quaker Close, Reeth, Richmond DL11 6UY
T: (01748) 884634
E: springfield.house@breathemail.net

RICCALL
North Yorkshire

Park View Hotel ♦♦♦
20 Main Street, Riccall, York YO19 6PX
T: (01757) 248458
F: (01757) 249211
E: geoffandsue@hotel-park-view.co.uk

South Newlands Farm ♦♦♦
Selby Road, Riccall, York YO19 6QR
T: (01757) 248203
F: (01757) 249450
E: pswann3059@aol.com
I: www.yorkbandb.f9.co.uk

RICHMOND
North Yorkshire

Bridge House Hotel Rating Applied For
Catterick Bridge, Richmond DL10 7PE
T: (01748) 818331
F: (01748) 810910
E: bridgehousehotel@hotmail.com

The Buck Inn ♦♦
27-29 Newbiggin, Richmond DL10 4DX
T: (01748) 822259
F: (01748) 825770

Emmanuel Guest House ♦♦♦
41 Maison Dieu, Richmond DL10 7AU
T: (01748) 823584
F: (01748) 821554

Frenchgate Guest House ♦♦♦♦
66 Frenchgate, Richmond DL10 7AG
T: (01748) 823421
F: (01748) 823421

18 Gilling Road ♦♦♦
Richmond DL10 5AA
T: (01748) 825491
F: (01748) 821847

27 Hurgill Road ♦♦
Richmond DL10 4AR
T: (01748) 824092
F: (01748) 824092

Mount Pleasant Farm ♦♦♦♦
Whashton, Richmond DL11 7JP
T: (01748) 822784
F: (01748) 822784
E: info@mountpleasantfarmhouse.co.uk
I: www.mountpleasantfarmhouse.co.uk

Nuns Cottage ♦♦♦♦ SILVER AWARD
5 Hurgill Road, Richmond DL10 4AR
T: (01748) 822809
E: nunscottage@richmond.org.uk
I: www.richmond.org.uk/business/nunscottage

The Old Brewery Guest House ♦♦♦
29 The Green, Richmond DL10 4RG
T: (01748) 822460
F: (01748) 825561
E: info@oldbreweryguesthouse.com
I: www.oldbreweryguesthhouse.com

Pottergate Guest House ♦♦♦
4 Pottergate, Richmond DL10 4AB
T: (01748) 823826

The Restaurant on the Green ♦♦♦
5-7 Bridge Street, Richmond DL10 4RW
T: (01748) 826229
F: (01748) 826229
E: accom.bennett@talk21.com
I: www.coast2coast.co.uk/restaurantonthegreen

Victoria House ♦♦♦♦
49 Maison Dieu, Richmond DL10 7AU
T: (01748) 824830

West Cottage ♦♦♦
Victoria Road, Richmond DL10 4AS
T: (01748) 824046
E: kay.gibson@tesco.net

West End Guest House ♦♦♦♦
45 Reeth Road, Richmond DL10 4EX
T: (01748) 824783
E: westend@richmond.org
I: www.stayatwestend.com

Whashton Springs Farm ♦♦♦♦ SILVER AWARD
Whashton, Richmond DL11 7JS
T: (01748) 822884
F: (01748) 826285
E: whashton@turnbullg-f.freeserve.co.uk
I: www.whashtonsprings.co.uk

Willance House Guesthouse ♦♦♦
24 Frenchgate, Richmond DL10 7AG
T: (01748) 824467
F: (01748) 824467
E: willance@bun.com

RIEVAULX
North Yorkshire

Barn Close Farm Rating Applied For
Old Byland, Rievaulx, York YO62 5LH
T: (01439) 798321

RIPLEY
North Yorkshire

Slate Rigg Farm ♦♦♦
Birthwaite Lane, Ripley, Harrogate HG3 3JQ
T: (01423) 770135

RIPON
North Yorkshire

Bishopton Grove House ♦♦♦
Bishopton, Ripon HG4 2QL
T: (01765) 600888
E: wimpress@bronco.co.uk

Box Tree Cottages ♦♦♦♦
Coltsgate Hill, Ripon HG4 2AB
T: (01765) 698006

Cowscot House ♦♦♦
Kirkby Malzeard, Ripon HG4 3SE
T: (01765) 658266

Crescent Lodge ♦♦♦♦
42 North Street, Ripon HG4 1EN
T: (01765) 609589
F: (01765) 609594
E: simpgry@aol.com
I: www.crescent-lodge.com

Fremantle House ♦♦♦
35 North Road, Ripon HG4 1JR
T: (01765) 605819
F: (01765) 601313
E: jcar105462@aol.com
I: www.shopsinripon.co.uk

Mallard Grange ♦♦♦♦♦ SILVER AWARD
Aldfield, Ripon HG4 3BE
T: (01765) 620242
F: (01765) 620242
E: maggie@mallardgrange.co.uk
I: www.mallardgrange.co.uk

Middle Ridge ♦♦♦♦♦ GOLD AWARD
42 Mallorie Park Drive, Ripon HG4 2QF
T: (01765) 690558
F: (01765) 690558
E: john@midrig.demon.co.uk
I: www.middleridge.co.uk

Park Street B&B ♦♦♦♦
9 Park Street, Ripon HG4 2AX
T: (01765) 606781
F: (01765) 606781
E: enquiries@9parkstreet.com
I: www.9parkstreet.com

Ravencroft B&B ♦♦♦♦ GOLD AWARD
Moorside Avenue, Ripon HG4 1TA
T: (01765) 602543
F: (01765) 606058
E: guestmail@btopenworld.com
I: www.ravencroftbandb.com

River Side Guest House ♦♦♦
20-21 Iddesleigh Terrace, Ripon HG4 1QW
T: (01765) 603864
F: (01765) 602707
E: christopher-pearson3@virgin.net

The Royal Oak Rating Applied For
36 Kirkgate, Ripon HG4 1PB
T: (01765) 602284
F: (01765) 690031

St George's Court ♦♦♦♦ SILVER AWARD
Eavestone, Grantley, Ripon HG4 3EU
T: (01765) 620618
F: (01765) 620618
E: stgeorgescourt@bronco.co.uk
I: www.stgeorges-court.co.uk

Sharow Cross House ♦♦♦♦ SILVER AWARD
Dishforth Road, Sharow, Ripon HG4 5BQ
T: (01765) 609866
E: sharowcrosshouse@btinternet.com
I: www.sharowcrosshouse.com

The White Horse ♦♦♦
61 North Street, Ripon HG4 1EN
T: (01765) 603622
E: david.bate13@btopenworld.com

RISPLITH
North Yorkshire

Yeomans Well ♦♦♦♦ SILVER AWARD
Risplith, Ripon HG4 3EP
T: (01765) 620378
E: yeomanswell@hotmail.com
I: www.yorkshirebandb.co.uk

ROBIN HOOD'S BAY
North Yorkshire

Boathouse Bistro ♦♦♦
The Dock, Robin Hood's Bay, Whitby YO22 4SJ
T: (01947) 880099

Flask Inn and Flask Inn Travel Lodge ♦♦♦♦
Robin Hood's Bay, Fylingdales, Whitby YO22 4QH
T: (01947) 880692
F: (01947) 880592
E: flaskinn@aol.com
I: www.flaskinn.com

Lee-Side ♦♦♦♦
Mount Pleasant South, Robin Hood's Bay, Whitby YO22 4RQ
T: (01947) 881143

Ravenswood Bed and Breakfast ♦♦♦
Ravenswood, Mount Pleasant North, Robin Hood's Bay, Whitby YO22 4RE
T: (01947) 880690
F: (01947) 880690
E: ravenswood@mail.com
I: www.ravenswoodbb.co.uk

Victoria Hotel ♦♦♦♦
Station Road, Robin Hood's Bay, Whitby YO22 4RL
T: (01947) 880205
F: (01947) 881170

ROECLIFFE
North Yorkshire

The Crown at Roecliffe ♦♦♦
Roecliffe, York YO51 9LY
T: (01423) 322578
F: (01423) 324060
E: crownroecliffe@btopenworld.com
I: www.crowninnroecliffe.co.uk

ROMANBY
North Yorkshire

Bridge End ♦♦
159 Chantry Road, Romanby, Northallerton DL7 8JJ
T: (01609) 772655
F: (01609) 772655

ROSEDALE ABBEY
North Yorkshire

Sevenford House
♦♦♦♦ SILVER AWARD
Rosedale Abbey, Pickering
YO18 8SE
T: (01751) 417283
E: sevenford@aol.com
I: www.sevenford.com

ROTHERHAM
South Yorkshire

Fernlea Hotel ♦♦♦
74-76 Gerard Road, Rotherham
S60 2PW
T: (01709) 830884
F: (01709) 305951
E: timhayselden@aol.com

Fitzwilliam Arms Hotel ♦♦♦
Taylors Lane, Parkgate,
Rotherham S62 6EE
T: (01709) 522744
F: (01709) 710110

Phoenix Hotel ♦♦
1 College Road, Rotherham
S60 1EY
T: (01709) 364611
F: (01709) 511121

RUDSTON
East Riding of Yorkshire

Eastgate Farm Cottage ♦♦♦
Rudston, Driffield YO25 0UX
T: (01262) 420150
F: (01262) 420150
E: ebrudston@aol.com
I: www.eastgatefarmcottage.com

RUNSWICK BAY
North Yorkshire

Cockpit House ♦♦
Runswick, Runswick Bay,
Saltburn-by-the-Sea TS13 5HU
T: (01947) 840504

Ellerby Hotel
♦♦♦♦ SILVER AWARD
Ryeland Lane, Ellerby, Saltburn-by-the-Sea TS13 5LP
T: (01947) 840342
F: (01947) 841221
E: relax@ellerbyhotel.co.uk
I: www.ellerbyhotel.co.uk

The Firs ♦♦♦♦
26 Hinderwell Lane, Runswick,
Runswick Bay, Saltburn-by-the-Sea TS13 5HR
T: (01947) 840433
F: (01947) 841616
E: mandy.shackleton@talk21.com
I: www.the-firs.co.uk

Newholme ♦♦♦
8 Hinderwell Lane, Runswick
Bay, Saltburn-by-the-Sea
TS13 5HR
T: (01947) 840358
I: www.newholmeguesthouse.co.uk

The Runswick Bay Hotel ♦♦♦
Hinderwell Lane, Runswick Bay,
Saltburn-by-the-Sea TS13 5HR
T: (01947) 841010
F: (01947) 841337
I: www.therunswickbayhotel.co.uk

RUSWARP
North Yorkshire

Old Hall Hotel ♦♦♦
High Street, Ruswarp, Whitby
YO21 1NH
T: (01947) 602801
F: (01947) 602801
E: info@oldhallhotel.co.uk
I: www.oldhallhotel.co.uk

SALTERSGATE
North Yorkshire

Newgate Foot Farm ♦♦♦♦
Saltersgate, Pickering YO18 7NR
T: (01751) 460215
F: (01751) 460215
E: johnson@newgatefoot.co.uk

SANDSEND
North Yorkshire

The Haven Under The Hill
♦♦♦♦
Sandsend, Whitby YO21 3TG
T: (01947) 893202

Woodlands
Rating Applied For
Lythe Bank, Sandsend, Whitby
YO21 3TG
T: (01947) 893272
E: woodlandsinfo@aol.com
I: www.woodlandssandsend.co.uk

SCACKLETON
North Yorkshire

Church Farm ♦♦♦♦
Scackleton, York YO62 4NB
T: (01653) 628403
F: (01653) 628403
E: cynthiafirby@amserve.com

SCAGGLETHORPE
North Yorkshire

Scagglethorpe Manor
♦♦♦♦♦ GOLD AWARD
Main Street, Scagglethorpe,
Malton YO17 8DT
T: (01944) 758909
F: (01944) 758909
E: joyce@scagglethorpemanor.co.uk
I: www.scagglethorpemanor.co.uk

SCALBY
North Yorkshire

Holly Croft
♦♦♦♦♦ SILVER AWARD
28 Station Road, Scalby,
Scarborough YO13 0QA
T: (01723) 375376
F: (01723) 360563
I: www.holly-croft.co.uk

SCARBOROUGH
North Yorkshire

Abbey Court Hotel ♦♦♦
19 West Street, Scarborough
YO11 2QR
T: (01723) 360659

Aberdeen House Hotel ♦♦♦
34 Aberdeen Walk, Scarborough
YO11 1XW
T: (01723) 371158
F: (01723) 350959

Adene Hotel ♦♦♦
39 Esplanade Road,
Scarborough YO11 2AT
T: (01723) 373658

Admiral ♦♦♦
13 West Square, Scarborough
YO11 1TW
T: (01723) 375084

Airedale Guest House ♦♦♦
23 Trafalgar Square,
Scarborough YO12 7PZ
T: (01723) 366809
E: shaunatairedale@aol.com

Aldon Hotel ♦♦♦♦
120-122 Columbus Ravine,
Scarborough YO12 7QZ
T: (01723) 372198

The Alexander Hotel
♦♦♦♦ SILVER AWARD
33 Burniston Road, Scarborough
YO12 6PG
T: (01723) 363178
F: (01723) 354821
E: alex@atesto.freeserve.co.uk
I: www.alexanderhotelscarborough.co.uk

Hotel Almar ♦♦♦
116 Columbus Ravine,
Scarborough YO12 7QZ
T: (01723) 372887
E: karen@tulsiedass.fsnet.co.uk

Arlington Private Hotel
♦♦♦♦
42 West Street, South Cliff,
Scarborough YO11 2QP
T: (01723) 503600
F: (01723) 503600
E: alex@arlington-hotel.fsnet.co.uk
I: www.smoothhound.co.uk/hotels/arlingtonhotel.co.uk

Arran Licensed Hotel ♦♦♦
114 North Marine Road,
Scarborough YO12 7JA
T: (01723) 364692

Ashburton Hotel ♦♦♦
43 Valley Road, Scarborough
YO11 2LX
T: (01723) 374382
F: (01723) 374382
E: lindahindhaugh@ashburton43.freeserve.co.uk
I: www.yorkshirecoast.co.uk/ashburton

Atlanta Hotel ♦♦♦
62 Columbus Ravine,
Scarborough YO12 7QU
T: (01723) 360996
E: reservations@atlanta-hotel.co.uk
I: www.atlanta-hotel.co.uk

Boston Hotel ♦♦♦
1-2 Blenheim Terrace,
Scarborough YO12 7HF
T: (01723) 360296
F: (01723) 353838
E: suzannewhitton@bostonhotel.freeserve.co.uk
I: www.bostonhotelscarborough.co.uk

Brincliffe Edge Hotel ♦♦♦
105 Queens Parade,
Scarborough YO12 7HY
T: (01723) 364834
E: brincliffeedgehotel@yahoo.co.uk
I: www.brincliffeedgehotel.co.uk

Hotel Catania ♦♦
141 Queens Parade,
Scarborough YO12 7HU
T: (01723) 364516
F: (01723) 372640
E: hotelcatania@aol.com
I: www.catania.co.uk

Cavendish Private Hotel
♦♦♦♦
53 Esplanade Road,
Scarborough YO11 2AT
T: (01723) 362108

Chessington Hotel ♦♦♦
The Crescent, Scarborough
YO11 2PP
T: (01723) 365207
F: (01723) 375206
E: chessingtonhotel@btconnect.com
I: chessingtonhotel.co.uk

Cliffside Hotel ♦♦♦
79-81 North Marine Road,
Scarborough YO12 7HT
T: (01723) 361087
F: (01723) 366472
E: cliffside@fsmail.net
I: www.yorkshirecoast.co.uk/cliffside

Cordelia Hotel ♦♦♦
51 Esplanade Road,
Scarborough YO11 2AT
T: (01723) 363393
F: (01723) 363393

Donnington Hotel ♦♦♦
13 Givendale Road, Scarborough
YO12 6LE
T: (01723) 374394
E: bookings@donningtonhotel.co.uk
I: www.donningtonhotel.co.uk

Earlsmere Hotel ♦♦♦♦
5 Belvedere Road, Scarborough
YO11 2UU
T: (01723) 361340
E: peter@earlsmerehotel.fsnet.co.uk

Hotel Ellenby ♦♦♦
95-97 Queens Parade,
Scarborough YO12 7HY
T: (01723) 372916
F: (01723) 372916
E: thorn9523@aol.com

Empire Hotel ♦♦
39 Albemarle Crescent,
Scarborough YO11 1XX
T: (01723) 373564

Esplanade Gardens Hotel ♦♦♦
24 Esplanade Gardens,
Scarborough YO11 2AP
T: (01723) 360728
E: kerry@khubbard.fsnet.co.uk
I: www.yorkshirecoast.co.uk/martyns/index.htm

Falcon Inn ♦♦♦
Whitby Road, Cloughton,
Scarborough YO13 0DY
T: (01723) 870717
I: www.yorkshirecoast.co.uk/falcon

Gardens Hotel ♦♦♦
12 Esplanade Gardens,
Scarborough YO11 2AW
T: (01723) 361800
E: gardenshotel@beetl.com
I: www.gardenshotel.co.uk

Gordon Hotel ♦♦♦♦
Ryndleside, Scarborough
YO12 6AD
T: (01723) 362177
E: sales@gordonhotel.co.uk
I: www.gordonhotel.co.uk

The Grand Hotel ♦♦♦
St Nicholas Cliff, Scarborough
YO11 2ET
T: (01723) 375371
F: (01723) 378518
E: reservations@grandhotelscarborough.co.uk
I: www.grandhotelgroup.co.uk

Granville Lodge Hotel ♦♦♦♦
Belmont Road, Scarborough
YO11 2AA
T: (01723) 367668
F: (01723) 363089
E: granville@scarborough.co.uk
I: www.granville.scarborough.co.uk

Greno Seafront Hotel ♦♦
25 Blenheim Terrace, Queens Parade, Scarborough YO12 7HD
T: (01723) 375705
F: (01723) 355512

The Gresham Hotel ♦♦♦
18 Lowdale Avenue, Northstead, Scarborough YO12 6JW
T: (01723) 372117
F: (01723) 372117
E: karen.robinson3@tesco.net
I: www.thegreshamhotel.co.uk

Grosvenor Hotel ♦♦♦
51 Grosvenor Road, Scarborough YO11 2LZ
T: (01723) 363801
F: (01723) 366936
E: grosvenorhotelscarborough@msn.com

Harcourt Hotel ♦♦♦♦
45 Esplanade, Scarborough
YO11 2AY
T: (01723) 373930
E: harcourt@onetel.net.uk

Harmony Country Lodge ♦♦♦♦
80 Limestone Road, Burniston, Scarborough YO13 0DG
T: (01723) 870276
F: (01723) 870276
E: tony@harmonylodge.net
I: www.harmonylodge.net

Harmony Guest House ♦♦♦
13 Princess Royal Terrace, South Cliff, Scarborough YO11 2RP
T: (01723) 373562
E: harmonyguesthouse@hotmail.com
I: www.harmonyguesthouse.co.uk

Headlands Hotel ♦♦♦
Weydale Avenue, Scarborough
YO12 6AX
T: (01723) 373717
F: (01723) 373717

Hotel Helaina ♦♦♦
14 Blenheim Terrace, Scarborough YO12 7HF
T: (01723) 375191

Hillcrest Hotel ♦♦♦♦
2 Peasholm Avenue, Scarborough YO12 7NE
T: (01723) 361981

Howdale Hotel ♦♦♦♦
North Marine Road, 121 Queens Parade, Scarborough YO12 7HU
T: (01723) 372696
F: (01723) 372696
E: mail@howdalehotel.co.uk
I: www.howdalehotel.co.uk

Killerby Cottage Farm ♦♦♦♦
Killerby Lane, Cayton, Scarborough YO11 3TP
T: (01723) 581236
F: (01723) 585465
E: val@green-glass.demon.co.uk
I: www.killerbycottagefarm.fsnet.co.uk

La Baia Hotel ♦♦♦♦
24 Blenheim Terrace, Scarborough YO12 7HD
T: (01723) 370780

Londesborough Arms Hotel ♦♦♦
24 Main Street, Seamer, Scarborough YO12 4PS
T: (01723) 863230
F: (01723) 863230
E: londesborough@scarborough.co.uk
I: www.londesborough.scarborough.co.uk

Lonsdale Villa Hotel ♦♦♦♦
Lonsdale Road, Scarborough
YO11 2QY
T: (01723) 363383
E: lonsdalevilla@talk21.com

The Lyddon Hotel ♦♦♦
21 Albion Road, South Cliff, Scarborough YO11 2BT
T: (01723) 369265

Lyncris Manor Hotel ♦♦♦♦
45 Northstead Manor Drive, Scarborough YO12 6AF
T: (01723) 361052
E: lyncris@manorhotel.fsnet.co.uk
I: www.manorhotel.fsnet.co.uk

Lysander Hotel ♦♦♦
22 Weydale Avenue, Scarborough YO12 6AX
T: (01723) 373369
E: joy-harry@lysanderhotel.freeserve.co.uk
I: www.lysanderhotel.freeserve.co.uk

Maynard Hotel ♦♦♦
16 Esplanade Gardens, Scarborough YO11 2AW
T: (01723) 372289

Melita Hotel ♦♦
137 Queens Parade, Scarborough YO12 7HU
T: (01723) 362772

Moorings ♦♦♦♦
3 Burniston Road, Scarborough
YO12 6PG
T: (01723) 373786
F: (01723) 364276
I: www.s-h-a.dircon.co.uk/moorings

Moseley Lodge Private Hotel ♦♦♦♦
Avenue Victoria, Scarborough
YO11 2QT
T: (01723) 360564
F: (01723) 363088
I: www.yorkshirenet.co.uk/moseleylodge

Mount House Hotel
Rating Applied For
33 Trinity Road, Scarborough
YO11 2TD
T: (01723) 362967
E: bookings@mounthouse-hotel.co.uk
I: www.mounthouse-hotel.co.uk

Mountview Private Hotel (Non-Smoking) ♦♦♦♦
32 West Street, Scarborough
YO11 2QP
T: (01723) 500608
F: (01723) 501385
E: stay@mountview-hotel.co.uk
I: www.mountview-hotel.co.uk

Norbreck Hotel ♦♦♦
Castle Road, Scarborough
YO11 1HY
T: (01723) 366607
F: (01723) 500984
E: gm.nor@barbox.net
I: www.shearingsholidays.com

Norlands Hotel ♦♦♦
10 Weydale Avenue, Scarborough YO12 6BA
T: (01723) 362606
F: (01723) 372884
E: atkinsonhun@tinyworld.co.uk

The Old Mill Hotel ♦♦♦
Mill Street, Scarborough
YO11 1SZ
T: (01723) 372735
F: (01723) 377190
E: info@windmill-hotel.co.uk
I: www.windmill-hotel.co.uk

Outlook Hotel ♦♦♦
18 Ryndleside, Scarborough
YO12 6AD
T: (01723) 364900
E: info@outlookhotel.co.uk
I: www.outlookhotel.co.uk

Parmelia Hotel ♦♦♦
17 West Street, Scarborough
YO11 2QN
T: (01723) 361914
E: parmeliahotel@btinternet.com
I: parmeliahotel.co.uk

Peasholm Park ♦♦♦
21-23 Victoria Park, Scarborough YO12 7TS
T: (01723) 500954
E: peasholm.park.hote@amserve.net
I: www.yorkshirecoast.co.uk

Perry's Court ♦♦♦♦
1 & 2 Rutland Terrace, Queens Parade, Scarborough YO12 7JB
T: (01723) 373768
F: (01723) 353274
E: john@perryscourthotel.fsnet.co.uk
I: www.perryscourthotel.com

Philmore Hotel ♦♦♦♦
126 Columbus Ravine, Scarborough YO12 7QZ
T: (01723) 361516

Powy's Lodge Hotel ♦♦♦
2 Westbourne Road, Scarborough YO11 2SP
T: (01723) 374019
F: (01723) 374019
E: info@powslodge.co.uk
I: www.powyslodge.co.uk

Princess Court Guest House ♦♦♦
11 Princess Royal Terrace, Scarborough YO11 2RP
T: (01723) 501922
E: iruin@princesscourt.co.uk
I: www.princesscourt.co.uk

Raincliffe Hotel ♦♦♦♦
21 Valley Road, Scarborough
YO11 2LY
T: (01723) 373541
E: enquiries@raincliffehotel.co.uk
I: www.raincliffehotel.co.uk

Riviera Hotel ♦♦♦
St Nicholas Cliff, Scarborough
YO11 2ES
T: (01723) 372277
F: (01723) 372277
E: rivierahotel@scarborough.co.uk
I: www.rivierahotel.scarborough.co.uk

Rose Dene Hotel ♦♦♦
106 Columbus Ravine, Scarborough YO12 7QZ
T: (01723) 374252

The Russell Hotel ♦♦♦
22 Ryndleside, Scarborough
YO12 6AD
T: (01723) 365453
F: (01723) 369029
E: info@russellhotel.net
I: www.russellhotel.net

St Michael's Hotel ♦♦♦
27 Blenheim Terrace, Scarborough YO12 7HD
T: (01723) 374631
F: (01723) 374631
E: elstop@tiscali.co.uk

St Michael's Hotel
Rating Applied For
149 Columbus Ravine, Scarborough YO12 7QZ
T: (01723) 364658
F: (01723) 355779
E: stmichaelsscarb@aol.com
I: www.stmichaelshotel.scarborough.co.uk

Selbourne Hotel ♦♦♦
4 West Street, Scarborough
YO11 2QL
T: (01723) 372822
F: (01723) 372822

Selomar Hotel ♦♦♦♦
23 Blenheim Terrace, Scarborough YO12 7HD
T: (01723) 364964
F: (01723) 364964

Sheridan Hotel ♦♦♦
108 Columbus Ravine, Scarborough YO12 7QZ
T: (01723) 372094
F: (01723) 372094
I: www.s-h-a.dircon.co.uk

Sylvern Hotel ♦♦♦
25 New Queen Street, Scarborough YO12 7HJ
T: (01723) 360952
E: sylvernhotel@aol.com
I: www.smoothhound.co.uk/hotels/sylvern.html

The Terrace Hotel ♦♦
69 Westborough, Scarborough
YO11 1TS
T: (01723) 374937
E: theterracehotel@btinternet.com

Thoresby Hotel
Rating Applied For
53 North Marine Road, Scarborough YO12 7EY
T: (01723) 365715

Victoria Lodge Hotel ♦♦♦
19 Avenue Victoria, Southcliffe, Scarborough YO11 2QS
T: (01723) 370906

Victoria Seaview Hotel ♦♦♦♦
125 Queens Parade, Scarborough YO12 7HY
T: (01723) 362164
E: victoria-seaview-hotel@tinyworld.co.uk

Villa Marina ♦♦♦♦
59 Northstead Manor Drive, Scarborough YO12 6AF
T: (01723) 361088

Wharncliffe Hotel ♦♦♦♦
26 Blenheim Terrace, Scarborough YO12 7HD
T: (01723) 374635
E: dandawharncliffe@aol.com
I: www.s-h-a.dircon.co.uk/members/wharncliffehotel.htm

White Rails Hotel ♦♦♦♦
128 Columbus Ravine, Scarborough YO12 7QZ
T: (01723) 362800

The Whiteley Hotel
♦♦♦♦ SILVER AWARD
99-101 Queens Parade, Scarborough YO12 7HY
T: (01723) 373514
F: (01723) 373007
E: whiteleyhotel@bigfoot.com
I: www.yorkshirecoast.co.uk/whiteley

SCAWBY
North Lincolnshire

The Old School ♦♦♦♦
Church Street, Scawby, Brigg DN20 9AH
T: (01652) 654239

Olivers ♦♦♦
Church Street, Scawby, Brigg DN20 9AH
T: (01652) 650446
E: eileen_harrison@lineone.net

SCHOLES
West Yorkshire

The Willows ♦♦♦♦
Scholes Moor Road, Scholes, Holmfirth, Huddersfield HD9 1SJ
T: (01484) 684231

SCOTCH CORNER
North Yorkshire

Vintage Hotel ♦♦♦
Middleton Tyas, Scotch Corner, Richmond DL10 6NP
T: (01748) 824424
F: (01748) 826272
E: thevintagescotchcorner@btopenworld.com
I: www.vintagehotel.co.uk

SCUNTHORPE
North Lincolnshire

Beverley Hotel ♦♦♦
55 Old Brumby Street, Scunthorpe DN16 2AJ
T: (01724) 282212
F: (01724) 270422

Cosgrove Guest House ♦♦♦
33-35 Wells Street, Scunthorpe DN15 6HL
T: (01724) 279405
F: (01724) 863416

The Downs Guest House ♦♦♦
33 Deyne Avenue, Scunthorpe DN15 7PZ
T: (01724) 850710
F: (01724) 330928
I: www.thedownsguesthouse.co.uk

Elm Field ♦♦
22 Deyne Avenue, Scunthorpe DN15 7PZ
T: (01724) 869306

Kirks Korner ♦♦
12 Scotter Road, Scunthorpe DN15 8DR
T: (01724) 855344
E: paul.kirk1@ntlworld.com

Larchwood Hotel ♦♦♦
1-5 Shelford Street, Scunthorpe DN15 6NU
T: (01724) 864712
F: (01724) 864712
I: www.thelarchwoodhotel.co.uk

Normanby Hotel ♦♦♦
9-11 Normanby Road, Scunthorpe DN15 6AR
T: (01724) 289982

SELBY
North Yorkshire

Hazeldene Guest House ♦♦♦
34 Brook Street, Doncaster Road, Selby YO8 4AR
T: (01757) 704809
E: selbystay@breathe.com
I: www.hazeldene-selby.co.uk

SETTLE
North Yorkshire

Arbutus Guest House ♦♦♦♦
Riverside, Clapham, Near Settle LA2 8DS
T: (01524) 251240
F: (01524) 251197
E: info@arbutus.co.uk
I: www.arbutus.co.uk

Golden Lion Hotel ♦♦♦♦
Duke Street, Settle BD24 9DU
T: (01729) 822203
F: (01729) 824103
E: bookings@goldenlion.yorks.net
I: www.yorkshirenet.co.uk/stayat/goldenlion

Husbands Barn
♦♦♦♦ SILVER AWARD
Main Road, Stainforth, Settle BD24 9PB
T: (01729) 822240
F: (01729) 822240
E: kath@doukghyll.freeserve.co.uk
I: www.husbands.force9.co.uk

Mainsfield
♦♦♦♦ SILVER AWARD
Stackhouse Lane, Giggleswick, Settle BD24 0DL
T: (01729) 823549
E: mainsfield-bb@btopenworld.com

Maypole Inn ♦♦♦
Maypole Green, Main Street, Long Preston, Skipton BD23 4PH
T: (01729) 840219
E: landlord@maypole.co.uk
I: www.maypole.co.uk

Oast Guest House ♦♦♦
5 Penyghent View, Settle BD24 9JJ
T: (01729) 822989
E: stay@oastguesthouse.co.uk
I: www.oastguesthouse.co.uk

Ottawa ♦♦♦♦
Four Lane Ends, Giggleswick, Settle BD24 0AE
T: (01729) 822757

Penmar Court ♦♦♦♦
Duke Street, Settle BD24 9AS
T: (01729) 823258
F: (01729) 823258
E: stay@penmarcourt.freeserve.co.uk
I: www.settle.org.uk

Scar Close Farm ♦♦♦♦
Feizor, Austwick, Lancaster LA2 8DF
T: (01729) 823496

Station House ♦♦♦
Station Road, Settle BD24 9AA
T: (01729) 822533
E: stationhouse@btinternet.com
I: www.stationhouse.btinternet.co.uk

Whitefriars Country Guest House ♦♦♦
Church Street, Settle BD24 9JD
T: (01729) 823753
E: info@whitefriars-settle.co.uk
I: www.whitefriars-settle.co.uk

SEWERBY
East Riding of Yorkshire

The Poplars Motel ♦♦♦
45 Jewison Lane, Sewerby, Bridlington YO15 1DX
T: (01262) 677251
F: (01262) 677251

SHAROW
North Yorkshire

Half Moon Inn ♦♦♦
Sharow, Ripon HG4 5BP
T: (01765) 600291
E: info@halfmoonsharow.co.uk
I: www.halfmoonsharow.co.uk

SHEFFIELD
South Yorkshire

Abbey View House ♦♦♦
168 Prospect Road, Totley Rise, Sheffield S17 4HX
T: (0114) 235 1349

Beighton Bed & Breakfast ♦♦♦
48-50 High Street, Beighton, Sheffield S20 1EA
T: (01142) 692004
F: (01142) 692004
E: Beightonbandb@aol.com

Coniston Guest House ♦♦♦
90 Beechwood Road, Hillsborough, Sheffield S6 4LQ
T: (0114) 233 9680
F: (0114) 233 9680
E: coniston@freeuk.co.uk
I: www.conistonguest.freeuk.co.uk

Etruria House Hotel ♦♦♦
91 Crookes Road, Broomhill, Sheffield S10 5BD
T: (0114) 266 2241
F: (0114) 267 0853
E: etruria@waitrose.com

Gulliver's Bed And Breakfast ♦♦♦
167 Ecclesall Road South, Sheffield S11 9PN
T: (0114) 262 0729

Hardwick House ♦♦♦
18 Hardwick Crescent, Ecclesall, Sheffield S11 8WB
T: (0114) 266 1509
E: hardwickhouse@hardwickhouse.fsnet.co.uk
I: www.lennox01.freeserve.co.uk

Harvey House ♦♦♦♦
159 Dobcroft Road, Sheffield S7 2LT
T: (0114) 236 1018
F: (0114) 236 1018
I: www.harvey-house.co.uk

High Riggs Hall ♦♦♦♦
Riggs High Road, Stannington, Sheffield S6 6DA
T: (0114) 234 3114
F: (0114) 234 3114
E: triciatwlvtr@aol.com
I: www.highriggshall.co.uk

Hillside ♦♦♦
28 Sunningdale Mount, Sheffield S11 9HA
T: (0114) 262 0833

Ivory House Hotel ♦♦♦
34 Wostenholm Road, Sheffield S7 1LJ
T: (0114) 255 1853
F: (0114) 255 1578
E: ivoryhousehotel@amserve.com

Lindrick Hotel ♦♦♦
226-230 Chippinghouse Road, Sheffield S7 1DR
T: (0114) 258 5041
F: (0114) 255 4758
E: reception@thelindrick.co.uk
I: www.thelindrick.co.uk

Lindum Hotel ♦♦♦
91 Montgomery Road, Nether Edge, Sheffield S7 1LP
T: (0114) 255 2356
F: (0114) 249 4746
E: lindumhotel@freenetname.co.uk

Loadbrook Cottages
♦♦♦♦ SILVER AWARD
Loadbrook, Stannington, Sheffield S6 6GT
T: (0114) 233 1619
E: acolver@commontime.com
I: www.smoothhound.co.uk

The Martins Guest House ♦♦
397 Fulwood Road, Sheffield S10 3GE
T: (0114) 230 8588
F: (0114) 230 2281

Priory Lodge Hotel ♦♦
40 Wostenholm Road, Netheredge, Sheffield S7 1LJ
T: (0114) 258 4670
F: (0114) 255 6672
I: www.priorylodgehotel.co.uk

Psalter House ♦♦♦♦
17 Clifford Road, Sheffield S11 9AQ
T: (0114) 255 7758
F: (0114) 255 7758
E: psalterhouse@waitrose.com
I: www.smoothhound.co.uk/hotels/psalter.html

Tyndale ♦♦♦
164 Millhouses Lane, Sheffield S7 2HE
T: (0114) 236 1660
F: (0114) 236 1660

Whirlow Park Guest House ♦♦♦
20 Whirlow Park Road, Whirlow, Sheffield S11 9NP
T: (0114) 236 0909
F: (0114) 235 0214
E: julie.bradwell@virgin.net

SHELF
West Yorkshire

Rook Residence ♦♦♦
69 Shelf Hall Lane, Shelf, Halifax HX3 7LT
T: (01274) 601586
F: (01274) 670179
E: rookbnb@btinternet.com

SHERBURN
North Yorkshire

Cherry Tree Cottage ♦♦♦
37 St Hildas Street, Sherburn, Malton YO17 8PG
T: (01944) 710851
E: cherrybnb@ntlworld.com
I: www.Cherrybnb.co.uk

SHIBDEN
West Yorkshire

Ploughcroft Cottage ♦♦♦
53 Ploughcroft Lane, Shibden, Halifax HX3 6TX
T: (01422) 341205
E: ploughcroft.cottage@Care4free.net
I: www.ploughcroftcottage.com

Staups House ♦♦♦♦
36 Staups Lane, Shibden, Halifax HX3 7AB
T: (01422) 362866

SHIPLEY
West Yorkshire

Clifton Lodge Guest House ♦♦♦
75 Kirkgate, Shipley BD18 3LU
T: (01274) 580509
F: (01274) 580343
E: jaynefoster75@hotmail.com

SILSDEN
West Yorkshire

Dalesbank Holiday Park ♦♦♦
Low Lane, Silsden, Keighley BD20 9JH
T: (01535) 653321

SINNINGTON
North Yorkshire

Green Lea ♦♦♦
Main Street, Sinnington, York YO62 6SH
T: (01751) 432008

Sinnington Manor ♦♦♦♦
Sinnington, York YO62 6SN
T: (01751) 433296
F: (01751) 433296
E: charles.wilson@sinningtonmanor.fsnet.co.uk
I: www.sinningtonmanor.co.uk

SKEEBY
North Yorkshire

The Old Chapel ♦♦♦♦
Richmond Road, Skeeby, Richmond DL10 5DR
T: (01748) 824170
E: hazel@theoldchapel.fsnet.co.uk

SKIPSEA
East Riding of Yorkshire

The Grainary ♦♦♦
Skipsea Grange, Hornsea Road, Skipsea, Driffield YO25 8SY
T: (01262) 468745
F: (01262) 468840
E: francesdavies@btconnect.com
I: www.the-grainary.co.uk

SKIPTON
North Yorkshire

Bourne House ♦♦♦
22 Upper Sackville Street, Skipton BD23 2EB
T: (01756) 792633
F: (01756) 701609
E: bournehouse@totalise.co.uk
I: www.bournehouseguesthouse.co.uk

Carlton House ♦♦♦♦
46 Keighley Road, Skipton BD23 2NB
T: (01756) 700921
F: (01756) 700921
E: carltonhouse@rapidial.co.uk
I: www.carltonhouse.rapidial.co.uk

Craven Heifer Inn ♦♦♦
Grassington Road, Skipton BD23 3LA
T: (01756) 792521
F: (01756) 794442
E: philandlynn@cravenheifer.co.uk
I: www.cravenheifer.co.uk

Cravendale Guest House ♦♦♦
57 Keighley Road, Skipton BD23 2LX
T: (01756) 795129
F: (01756) 795129

Dalesgate Lodge ♦♦♦♦
69 Gargrave Road, Skipton BD23 1QN
T: (01756) 790672
E: dalesgatelodge@hotmail.com

Napier's Restaurant & Accommodation ♦♦♦♦
Chapel Hill, Skipton BD23 1NL
T: (01756) 799688
F: (01756) 798111
I: www.restaurant-skipton.co.uk

Skipton Park Guest'otel ♦♦♦
2 Salisbury Street, Skipton BD23 1NQ
T: (01756) 700640
F: (01756) 700641
E: derekchurch@skiptonpark.freeserve.co.uk
I: www.milford.co.uk/go/skiptonpark.html

Spring Gardens Cottage ♦♦♦
20 Queens Street, Skipton BD23 1HE
T: (01756) 790739

Unicorn Hotel ♦♦♦
Keighley Road, Skipton BD23 2LP
T: (01756) 794146
F: (01756) 793376
E: jean@btopenworld.com
I: www.unicornhotelskipton.co.uk

The Woolly Sheep ♦♦♦♦
28 Sheep Street, Skipton BD23 1HY
T: (01756) 700966
F: (01756) 794815
I: www.timothytaylor.co.uk

SLAITHWAITE
West Yorkshire

Hey Leys Farm ♦♦♦♦
Marsden Lane, Cop Hill End, Slaithwaite, Huddersfield HD7 5XA
T: (01484) 845404
F: (01484) 843188
I: www.yorkshireholidays.com

SLEDMERE
North Humberside

Life Hill Farm ♦♦♦♦ SILVER AWARD
Wetwang, Sledmere, Driffield YO25 3EY
T: (01377) 236224
F: (01377) 236685
E: info@lifehillfarm.co.uk
I: www.lifehillfarm.co.uk

The Triton Inn ♦♦♦
Sledmere, Driffield YO25 3XQ
T: (01377) 236644
E: thetritoninn@sledmere644.fsnet.co.uk
I: www.sledmere.fsbusiness.co.uk

SLEIGHTS
North Yorkshire

Hedgefield ♦♦♦♦
47 Coach Road, Sleights, Whitby YO22 5AA
T: (01947) 810647
E: hedgefield@ntlworld.com
I: www.hedgefieldguesthouse.co.uk

The Lawns ♦♦♦♦♦ GOLD AWARD
73 Carr Hill Lane, Briggswath, Sleights, Whitby YO21 1RS
T: (01947) 810310
F: (01947) 810310
E: lorton@onetel.net.uk

The Salmon Leap Hotel ♦♦
6 Coach Road, Sleights, Whitby YO22 5AA
T: (01947) 810233

SOWERBY
North Yorkshire

Long Acre Bed and Breakfast ♦♦♦
86A Topcliffe Road, Sowerby, Thirsk YO7 1RY
T: (01845) 522360
F: (01845) 527373
E: dawsonlongacre@aol.com

STAINFORTH
North Yorkshire

2 Bridge End Cottage ♦♦♦
Stainforth, Settle BD24 9PG
T: (01729) 822149

STAINTONDALE
North Yorkshire

Island House ♦♦♦♦
Staintondale, Scarborough YO13 0EB
T: (01723) 870249
E: roryc@tinyworld.co.uk
I: www.islandhousefarm.co.uk

Wellington Lodge ♦♦♦♦
Staintondale, Scarborough YO13 0EL
T: (01723) 871234
F: (01723) 871234
E: b&b@llamatreks.co.uk
I: www.llamatreks.co.uk

STAIRFOOT
South Yorkshire

The Old Coach House Guest House ♦♦♦
255 Doncaster Road, Stairfoot, Barnsley S70 3RH
T: (01226) 290612
F: (01226) 298967

STAITHES
North Yorkshire

Brooklyn ♦♦♦
Brown's Terrace, Staithes, Saltburn-by-the-Sea TS13 5BG
T: (01947) 841396

The Endeavour Restaurant ♦♦♦♦
1 High Street, Staithes, Saltburn-by-the-Sea TS13 5BH
T: (01947) 840825
E: theendeavour@ntlworld.com
I: www.endeavour-restaurant.co.uk

The Giardini Guest House ♦♦♦
Roxby Lane, Staithes, Saltburn-by-the-Sea TS13 5DZ
T: (01947) 840572
F: (01947) 841642

The Grapes ♦♦♦
Scaling Dam, Easington, Staithes, Saltburn-by-the-Sea TS13 4TP
T: (01287) 640461
E: mark79@kenny7997.freeserve.co.uk
I: www.touristnetwk.com/ne/grapes/

Grinkle Lodge ♦♦♦♦♦ GOLD AWARD
Snipe Lane, Easington, Staithes, Saltburn-by-the-Sea TS13 4UD
T: (01287) 644701
E: grinklelodge@yahoo.co.uk
I: www.yorkshirecoast.co.uk/grinklelodge

Springfields ♦♦♦♦
42 Staithes Lane, Staithes, Saltburn-by-the-Sea TS13 5AD
T: (01947) 841465

STAMFORD BRIDGE
East Riding of Yorkshire

High Catton Grange ♦♦♦♦
High Catton, Stamford Bridge, York YO41 1EP
T: (01759) 371374
F: (01759) 371374

STANBURY
West Yorkshire

Ponden House ♦♦♦♦
Stanbury, Keighley BD22 0HR
T: (01535) 644154
E: brenda.taylor@pondenhouse.co.uk
I: www.pondenhouse.co.uk

STAPE
North Yorkshire

Rawcliffe House Farm ♦♦♦♦
Stape, Pickering YO18 8JA
T: (01751) 473292
F: (01751) 473766
E: office@yorkshireaccommodation.com
I: www.yorkshireaccommodation.com

Seavy Slack ♦♦♦♦
Stape, Pickering YO18 8HZ
T: (01751) 473131

STARBOTTON
North Yorkshire

Bushey Lodge Farm
♦♦♦♦ SILVER AWARD
Starbotton, Skipton BD23 5HY
T: (01756) 760424
E: busheylodge@btopenworld.com
I: www.yorkshirenet.co.uk/stayat/busheylodgefarm

STAVELEY
North Yorkshire

Staveley Grange
Rating Applied For
Main Street, Staveley, Knaresborough HG5 9LD
T: (01423) 340265
F: (01423) 340539

STEARSBY
North Yorkshire

The Granary
♦♦♦♦ SILVER AWARD
Stearsby, York YO61 4SA
T: (01347) 888652
F: (01347) 888652
E: robertturl@thegranary.org.uk
I: www.thegranary-stearsby.com

STOKESLEY
North Yorkshire

The Buck Inn ♦♦♦
Chop Gate, Stokesley, Middlesbrough TS9 7JL
T: (01642) 778334
F: (01642) 778084
E: sarwilson5@aol.co.uk

STONEGRAVE
North Yorkshire

Manor Cottage Bed and Breakfast ♦♦♦♦
Stonegrave, York YO62 4LJ
T: (01653) 628599
E: gideon.v@virgin.net
I: business.virgin.net/gideon.v/index.html

STUDLEY ROGER
North Yorkshire

Downing House Farm ♦♦♦♦
Studley Roger, Ripon HG4 3AY
T: (01765) 601014
F: (01765) 601014
E: dickhelen@supanet.com
I: www.downinghousefarm.co.uk

SUTTON BANK
North Yorkshire

Cote Faw ♦♦
Hambleton, Sutton Bank, Thirsk YO7 2EZ
T: (01845) 597363

Greystones ♦♦♦
Sutton Bank, Thirsk YO7 2HB
T: (01845) 597580

SUTTON-ON-THE-FOREST
North Yorkshire

Goose Farm ♦♦♦
Goose Lane, Sutton-on-the-Forest, York YO61 1ET
T: (01347) 810577
F: (01347) 810577
E: stay@goosefarm.co.uk
I: www.goosefarm.co.uk

The Old Village Stores ♦♦♦♦
Main Street, Sutton-on-the-Forest, York YO61 1DP
T: (01347) 811376
E: oldvillagestores@talk21.com
I: www.oldyork.co.uk

SWAINBY
North Yorkshire

Churchview House
♦♦♦♦♦ GOLD AWARD
72 High Street, Swainby, Northallerton DL6 3DG
T: (01642) 706058
E: churchviewhouse@aol.com
I: www.churchviewhouse.co.uk

SWILLINGTON
West Yorkshire

Bridge Farm Hotel ♦♦♦
Wakefield Road, Swillington, Leeds LS26 8PZ
T: (0113) 282 3718
F: (0113) 282 5135

SWINTON
North Yorkshire

Low Farm Bed & Breakfast ♦♦♦♦
East Street, Swinton, Malton YO17 6SH
T: (01653) 693684
F: (01653) 693684
E: owen.fran@lowfarmswin.fsnet.co.uk
I: www.lowfarmswinton.co.uk

TERRINGTON
North Yorkshire

Gate Farm ♦♦♦
Ganthorpe, Terrington, York YO60 6QD
T: (01653) 648269
E: millgate001@aol.com
I: www.ganthorpegatefarm.co.uk

THIMBLEBY
North Yorkshire

Stonehaven ♦♦♦
Thimbleby, Northallerton DL6 3PY
T: (01609) 883689

THIRSK
North Yorkshire

The Gallery Bed And Breakfast ♦♦♦
18 Kirkgate, Thirsk YO7 1PQ
T: (01845) 523767
F: (01845) 523767
E: jenkin@tesco.net

Laburnum House
♦♦♦♦ SILVER AWARD
31 Topcliffe Road, Sowerby, Thirsk YO7 1RX
T: (01845) 524120
I: www.smoothhound.co.uk/hotels/laburnumhse.html

The Old Rectory
Rating Applied For
South Kilvington, Thirsk YO7 2NL
T: (01845) 526153
F: (01845) 523849
E: ocfenton@freenet.co.uk

The Poplars ♦♦♦♦
Carlton Miniott, Thirsk YO7 4LX
T: (01845) 522712
F: (01845) 522712
I: www.yorkshirebandb.co.uk

St James House ♦♦
36 St James Green, Thirsk YO7 1AQ
T: (01845) 526565

Station House ♦♦♦
Station Road, Thirsk YO7 4LS
T: (01845) 522063

Town Pasture Farm ♦♦♦
Boltby, Thirsk YO7 2DY
T: (01845) 537298

THIXENDALE
North Yorkshire

The Cross Keys ♦♦♦
Thixendale, Malton YO17 9TG
T: (01377) 288272

Manor Farm ♦♦♦♦
Thixendale, Malton YO17 9TG
T: (01377) 288315
F: (01377) 288315

THORALBY
North Yorkshire

Pen View ♦♦♦
Thoralby, Leyburn DL8 3SU
T: (01969) 663319
F: (01969) 663319
E: audrey@penview.yorks.net
I: www.penview.yorks.net

THORNTON
West Yorkshire

Ann's Farmhouse ♦♦♦
New Farm, Thornton Road, Thornton, Bradford BD13 3QE
T: (01274) 833214
E: ajdarby@aol.com

THORNTON DALE
North Yorkshire

Bridgefoot Guest House ♦♦♦
Thornton Dale, Pickering YO18 7RR
T: (01751) 474749

The Buck Hotel ♦♦♦
Chestnut Avenue, Thornton Dale, Pickering YO18 7RW
T: (01751) 474212
F: (01751) 474212
E: buckhotel.tld@btopenworld.com

Hall Farm ♦♦♦
Maltongate, Thornton Dale, Pickering YO18 7SA
T: (01751) 475526
E: hallfarmholidays@amserve.net

Nabgate ♦♦♦♦
Wilton Road, Thornton Dale, Pickering YO18 7QP
T: (01751) 474279

New Inn ♦♦♦♦
Maltongate, Thornton Dale, Pickering YO18 7LF
T: (01751) 474226
F: (01751) 477715
E: newinntld@aol.com

The Old Granary Bed and Breakfast
♦♦♦♦ SILVER AWARD
Top Bridge Farm, Thornton Dale, Pickering YO18 7RA
T: (01751) 477217

Warrington Guest House
Rating Applied For
Whitbygate, Thornton Dale, Pickering YO18 7RY
T: (01751) 475028
F: (01751) 475028
E: jonathan.rule1@btopenworld.com
I: www.warringtonhouse.co.uk

THORNTON IN CRAVEN
North Yorkshire

The Old Post Office ♦♦♦♦
Skipton Road, Thornton in Craven, Skipton BD23 3ST
T: (01282) 843482
E: crouch@totalise.co.uk

THORNTON RUST
North Yorkshire

Fellside ♦♦♦♦
Thornton Rust, Leyburn DL8 3AP
T: (01969) 663504
F: (01969) 663965
E: harvey@plwmp.freeserve.co.uk
I: www.wensleydale.org/accommodation/fellside

THORPE
North Yorkshire

Langerton House Farm ♦♦♦
Thorpe, Skipton BD23 5HN
T: (01756) 730260

THWAITES BROW
West Yorkshire

Golden View Guest House ♦♦♦♦
21 Golden View Drive, Thwaites Brow, Keighley BD21 4SN
T: (01535) 662138

TODMORDEN
West Yorkshire

Cherry Tree Cottage ♦♦♦♦
Woodhouse Road, Todmorden OL14 5RJ
T: (01706) 817492

Woodleigh Hall ♦♦♦♦
Ewood Lane, Todmorden OL14 7DF
T: (01706) 814664
F: (01706) 810673
E: woodleighhall@amserve.com

TOLLERTON
North Yorkshire

The Bungalow Farm ♦♦♦
Warehills Lane, Tollerton, York YO61 1RG
T: (01347) 838732
F: (01347) 838732

ULCEBY
North Lincolnshire

Gillingham Court ♦♦♦♦
Spruce Lane, Ulceby DN39 6UL
T: (01469) 588427

UPPER GREETLAND
West Yorkshire

Crawstone Knowl Farm ♦♦♦
Rochdale Road, Greetland, Upper Greetland, Halifax HX4 8PX
T: (01422) 370470

WAKEFIELD
West Yorkshire

Billy Budd ♦♦♦
10 Drury Lane, Wakefield WF1 2TE
T: (01924) 372069
F: (01924) 374787
E: Billybuddhotel@aol.com

WAKEFIELD
West Yorkshire

The Talbot and Falcon
Rating Applied For
58 Northgate, Wakefield
WF1 3AP
T: (01924) 201693
F: (01924) 201693
E: talbotandfalcon@hotmail.com

WALSDEN
West Yorkshire

Birks Clough ◆◆◆
Hollingworth Lane, Walsden, Todmorden OL14 6QX
T: (01706) 814438
F: (01706) 819002
E: mstorah@mwfree.net

Highstones Guest House ◆◆◆
Rochdale Road, Walsden, Todmorden OL14 6TY
T: (01706) 816534

WEAVERTHORPE
North Yorkshire

The Blue Bell Inn ◆◆◆
Main Street, Weaverthorpe, Malton YO17 8EX
T: (01944) 738204
F: (01944) 738204

The Star Country Inn ◆◆◆
Weaverthorpe, Malton YO17 8EY
T: (01944) 738273
E: info@starinn.net
I: www.starinn.net

WEETON
North Yorkshire

Arthington Lodge ◆◆◆◆
Wescoe Hill, Weeton, Leeds
LS17 0EZ
T: (01423) 734102
F: (01423) 734102

WELTON
East Riding of Yorkshire

Creyke Cottage ◆◆◆◆
Creyke Lane, Welton, Brough
HU15 1NQ
T: (01482) 668405

WENSLEYDALE
North Yorkshire

Ivy Dene Country Guesthouse ◆◆◆
Main Street, West Witton, Leyburn DL8 4LP
T: (01969) 622785
F: (01969) 622785
E: info@ivydeneguesthouse.co.uk
I: www.ivydeneguesthouse.co.uk

WEST BRETTON
West Yorkshire

The Old Manor House ◆◆◆
19 Sycamore Lane, Bretton, West Bretton, Wakefield
WF4 4JR
T: (01924) 830324
F: (01924) 830150

WEST BURTON
North Yorkshire

The Grange ◆◆◆◆◆
West Burton, Leyburn DL8 4JR
T: (01969) 663348
E: ashfordpaul5@aol.com
I: www.thegrange-yorkshiredales.co.uk

WEST WITTON
North Yorkshire

The Old Star ◆◆◆
Main Street, West Witton, Leyburn DL8 4LU
T: (01969) 622949
E: theoldstar@amserve.com

WESTOW
North Yorkshire

Blacksmiths Arms Inn ◆◆◆
Westow, York YO60 7NE
T: (01653) 618365
E: blacksmithsinn@hotmail.com

WETHERBY
West Yorkshire

Broadleys ◆◆◆
39 North Street, Wetherby
LS22 6NU
T: (01937) 585866

The Coach House Garden Studio ◆◆◆◆
North Grove Approach, Wetherby LS22 7GA
T: (01937) 586100

Lindum Fields ◆◆◆◆
48a Spofforth Hill, Wetherby
LS22 6SE
T: (01937) 520389
E: peter.stretton1@ntlworld.com

Linton Close
◆◆◆◆ SILVER AWARD
2 Wharfe Grove, Wetherby
LS22 6HA
T: (01937) 582711
F: (01937) 588499

Prospect House ◆◆
8 Caxton Street, Wetherby
LS22 6RU
T: (01937) 582428

Swan Guest House ◆◆
38 North Street, Wetherby
LS22 6NN
T: (01937) 582381
F: (01937) 584908
E: info@swanguesthouse.co.uk
I: www.swanguesthouse.co.uk

14 Woodhill View ◆◆◆
Wetherby LS22 6PP
T: (01937) 581200

WHENBY
North Yorkshire

Deerholme ◆◆◆◆
Main Street, Whenby, York
YO61 4SE
T: (01347) 878116
E: pufinny@aol.com
I: www.smoothhound.co.uk/hotels/deerholme.html

WHITBY
North Yorkshire

Abbotsleigh ◆◆◆◆
5 Argyle Road, Whitby YO21 3HS
T: (01947) 601142
F: (01947) 601142
E: kevinpeagam@tesco.net

Anchorage Non Smoking Hotel ◆◆◆
3 Crescent Terrace, Whitby
YO21 3EL
T: (01947) 821888

Arches Guesthouse ◆◆◆◆
8 Havelock Place, Hudson Street, Whitby YO21 3ER
T: (01947) 601880
E: archeswhitby@freeola.com
I: www.whitbyguesthouses.co.uk

Argyle House ◆◆◆◆
18 Hudson Street, Whitby
YO21 3EP
T: (01947) 602733
E: pat@argyle-house.co.uk
I: www.argyle-house.co.uk

Ashford Guest House ◆◆◆
8 Royal Crescent, Whitby
YO21 3EJ
T: (01947) 602138
E: info@ashfordguesthouse.co.uk
I: www.ashfordguesthouse.co.uk

Avalon Hotel ◆◆◆
13-14 Royal Crescent, Whitby
YO21 3EJ
T: (01947) 820313
F: (01947) 602349
I: www.avalonhotel.freeserve.co.uk

Boulmer ◆◆◆◆
23 Crescent Avenue, Whitby
YO21 3ED
T: (01947) 604284

Bramblewick Guest House ◆◆◆◆
3 Havelock Place, Whitby
YO21 3ER
T: (01947) 604504
E: bramblewick@nfieldhouse.freeserve.co.uk
I: www.bramblewick.co.uk

Bruncliffe Guest House ◆◆◆
9 North Promenade, Whitby
YO21 3JX
T: (01947) 602428
E: bruncliffewhitby@aol.com
I: www.bruncliffewhitby.co.uk

The Captain's Lodge ◆◆◆◆
3 Crescent Avenue, Whitby
YO21 3EF
T: (01947) 601178
E: enquiries@thecaptainslodge.co.uk
I: www.thecaptainslodge.co.uk

Chiltern Guest House ◆◆◆◆
13 Normanby Terrace, West Cliff, Whitby YO21 3ES
T: (01947) 604981
F: (01947) 604981
E: john@chilternguesthouse.fsnet.co.uk
I: www.chilternwhitby.co.uk

Corner Guest House ◆◆◆◆
3-4 Crescent Place, Whitby
YO21 3HE
T: (01947) 602444
I: www.thecornerguesthouse.co.uk

The Crescent Garden Hotel ◆◆◆◆
3 Royal Crescent, Whitby
YO21 3EJ
T: (01947) 603711

Crescent Lodge ◆◆◆◆
27 Crescent Avenue, Whitby
YO21 3EW
T: (01947) 820073

The Elders B&B ◆◆◆
3 Hanover Terrace, Whitby
YO21 1QQ
T: (01947) 602587

Elford House ◆◆◆
10 Prospect Hill, Whitby
YO21 1QE
T: (01947) 602135

Endeavour House ◆◆◆
11 Bridge Street, Whitby
YO22 4BG
T: (01947) 604153
F: (01947) 811797

Esklet Guest House ◆◆◆
22 Crescent Avenue, Whitby
YO21 3ED
T: (01947) 605663
I: www.eskletguesthouse.co.uk

The Esplanade Hotel ◆◆◆
2 Esplanade, Whitby YO21 3HH
T: (01947) 605053
F: (01947) 605053

The George Hotel ◆◆◆
Baxtergate, Whitby YO21 1BN
T: (01947) 602565
F: (01947) 820950

Glendale Guest House ◆◆◆◆
16 Crescent Avenue, Whitby
YO21 3ED
T: (01947) 604242

Glenora ◆◆◆
8 Upgang Lane, Whitby
YO21 3EA
T: (01947) 605363
I: http://glenora.users.btopenworld.com

Grantley House ◆◆◆◆
26 Hudson Street, Whitby
YO21 3EP
T: (01947) 600895
F: (01947) 600895
E: kevin@thegrantley.freeserve.co.uk
I: www.thegrantley.freeserve.co.uk

Grove Hotel ◆◆◆◆
36 Bagdale, Whitby YO21 1QL
T: (01947) 603551
I: www.smoothhound.co.uk/hotels/grove2.html

Havelock Guest House ◆◆◆
30 Hudson Street, Whitby
YO21 3EP
T: (01947) 602295
F: (01947) 602295

The Haven (Whitby) Ltd. ◆◆◆◆
4 East Crescent, Whitby
YO21 3HD
T: (01947) 603842
F: (01947) 605834
E: info@thehavenwhitby.co.uk
I: www.thehavenwhitby.co.uk

Haven Crest ◆◆◆◆
137 Upgang Lane, Whitby
YO21 3JW
T: (01947) 605187
F: (01947) 605189
E: enquiries@havencrest.co.uk
I: www.havencrest.co.uk

High Tor ◆◆◆
7 Normanby Terrace, Whitby
YO21 3ES
T: (01947) 602507
E: hightorguesthouse@hotmail.com
I: www.hightorguesthouse.co.uk

Jaydee Guest House ♦♦♦
15 John Street, Whitby YO21 3ET
T: (01947) 605422
F: (01947) 605422
E: info@whitbybnb.co.uk
I: www.whitbybnb.co.uk

The Langley Hotel ♦♦♦♦
Royal Crescent, West Cliff, Whitby YO21 3EJ
T: (01947) 604250
F: (01947) 604250
E: langleyhotel@hotmail.co.uk
I: www.langleyhotel.com

Lavender House
♦♦♦♦ SILVER AWARD
28 Love Lane, Whitby YO21 3LJ
T: (01947) 602917
F: (01947) 602917
E: dcrichmond@whitby28.freeserve.co.uk

Lavinia House ♦♦♦♦
3 East Crescent, Whitby YO21 3HD
T: (01947) 602945
F: (01947) 820656
E: tony@lavinia-whitby.freeserve.co.uk

Leeway Guest House ♦♦♦♦
1 Havelock Place, Whitby YO21 3ER
T: (01947) 602604
E: linda@leeway.co.uk
I: www.leeway.fsbusiness.co.uk

The Middleham ♦♦
3 Church Square, Whitby YO21 3EG
T: (01947) 603423
F: (01947) 603423

Morningside Hotel ♦♦♦♦
10 North Promenade, West Cliff, Whitby YO21 3JX
T: (01947) 602643

Netherby House
♦♦♦♦ SILVER AWARD
90 Coach Road, Sleights, Whitby YO22 5EQ
T: (01947) 810211
F: (01947) 810211
E: info@netherby-house.co.uk
I: www.netherby-house.co.uk

Number Five ♦♦♦
5 Havelock Place, Whitby YO21 3ER
T: (01947) 606361
F: (01947) 606361

Number Seven Guest House ♦♦♦♦
7 East Crescent, Whitby YO21 3HD
T: (01947) 606019
F: (01947) 606019
E: numberseven@whitbytown.freeserve.co.uk
I: www.1up.co.uk/whitby

The Olde Ford
♦♦♦♦ SILVER AWARD
1 Briggswath, Whitby YO21 1RU
T: (01947) 810704
E: gray@theoldeford.fsnet.co.uk

Pannett House ♦♦♦
14 Normanby Terrace, Whitby YO21 3ES
T: (01947) 603261

Parkholme Bed and Breakfast Rating Applied For
40 Upgang Lane, Whitby YO21 3EA
T: (01947) 603390

Partridge Nest Farm ♦♦♦
Eskdaleside, Sleights, Whitby YO22 5ES
T: (01947) 810450
F: (01947) 811413
E: barbara@partridgenestfarm.com
I: www.partridgenestfarm.com

The Pier ♦♦
4-6 Pier Road, Whitby YO21 2PU
T: (01947) 605284
F: (01947) 825646

Postgate Farm Holidays ♦♦♦♦
Postgate Farm, Glaisdale, Whitby YO21 2PZ
T: (01947) 897353
F: (01947) 897353
E: j-m.thompson.bandb@talk21.com
I: www.eskvalley.com/postgate/postgate.html

Prospect Villa Hotel ♦♦♦
13 Prospect Hill, Whitby YO21 1QE
T: (01947) 603118
F: (01947) 825445
E: chris@prospectvilla.freeserve.co.uk

The Resolution Hotel ♦♦♦♦
Skinner Street, Whitby YO21 3AH
T: (01947) 602085
F: (01947) 829187
E: resolutionhotel@aol.com
I: www.resolutionhotel.co.uk

Riviera Hotel ♦♦♦
4 Crescent Terrace, Whitby YO21 3EL
T: (01947) 602533
F: (01947) 606441
E: info@rivierawhitby.com
I: www.rivierawhitby.com

Rosslyn House ♦♦♦
11 Abbey Terrace, Whitby YO21 3HQ
T: (01947) 604086
E: rosslynhouse@bushinternet.com
I: www.guesthousewhitby.co.uk

Rothbury ♦♦♦♦
2 Ocean Road, Whitby YO21 3HY
T: (01947) 606282

The Royal Hotel ♦♦♦
East Terrace, West Cliff, Whitby YO21 3HA
T: (01947) 602234
F: (01947) 820355
E: gm.whi@barbox.net
I: www.shearingsholidays.com

Ryedale House ♦♦♦♦
156 Coach Road, Sleights, Whitby YO22 5EQ
T: (01947) 810534
F: (01947) 810534

Sandpiper Guest House ♦♦♦♦
4 Belle Vue Terrace, Whitby YO21 3EY
T: (01947) 600246
F: (01947) 600246
E: enquiries@sandpiperhouse.co.uk
I: www.sandpiperhouse.co.uk

Seacliffe Hotel ♦♦♦♦
12 North Promenade, West Cliff, Whitby YO21 3JX
T: (01947) 603139
F: (01947) 603139
E: julie@seacliffe.fsnet.co.uk
I: www.seacliffe.co.uk

Seaview ♦♦♦
5 East Crescent, Whitby YO21 3HD
T: (01947) 604462
I: www.seaviewguesthouse.co.uk

Serendipity ♦♦
17 Abbey Terrace, Whitby YO21 3HQ
T: (01947) 603868
F: (01947) 602025
E: enquiries@serendipityhotel.co.uk
I: www.serendipityhotel.co.uk

Sneaton Castle Centre ♦♦♦♦
Sneaton Castle, Whitby YO21 3QN
T: (01947) 600051
F: (01947) 603490
E: holden@connectfree.co.uk
I: www.sneatoncastle.co.uk

Storrbeck Guest House ♦♦♦♦
9 Crescent Avenue, Whitby YO21 3ED
T: (01947) 605468
E: storrbeck@bigfoot.com
I: www.storrbeck.fsnet.co.uk

Sunnyvale House ♦♦♦
12 Normanby Terrace, Whitby YO21 3ES
T: (01947) 820389
F: (01947) 821290
E: christinecroxton@hotmail.com
I: www.smoothhound.co.uk/hotels/sunnyvale.html

Wentworth House ♦♦♦
27 Hudson Street, Whitby YO21 3EP
T: (01947) 602433
E: info@whitbywentworth.co.uk
I: www.whitbywentworth.co.uk

Wheeldale Hotel ♦♦♦♦
11 North Promenade, Whitby YO21 3JX
T: (01947) 602365
E: wheeldale_hotel@lineone.net
I: www.wheeldale-hotel.co.uk

The White Linen Guest House ♦♦♦♦
24 Bagdale, Whitby YO21 1QS
T: (01947) 600265
F: (01947) 603635
E: mail@whitelinenguesthouse.co.uk
I: www.whitelinenguesthouse.co.uk

The Willows ♦♦♦
35 Bagdale, Whitby YO21 1QL
T: (01947) 600288

York House Hotel ♦♦♦♦
3 Back Lane, High Hawsker, Whitby YO22 4LW
T: (01947) 880314
F: (01947) 880314
E: yorkhtl@aol.com

WICKERSLEY
South Yorkshire

Millstone Farm ♦♦♦♦
Morthen Road, Wickersley, Rotherham S66 1EA
T: (01709) 542382

WIKE
West Yorkshire

Wike Ridge Farm ♦♦♦♦
Wike Ridge Lane, Wike, Leeds LS17 9JF
T: (0113) 266 1190

WILBERFOSS
East Riding of Yorkshire

Cuckoo Nest Farm ♦♦♦
York Road, Wilberfoss, York YO41 5NL
T: (01759) 380365

WILSDEN
West Yorkshire

Springhill Bed and Breakfast ♦♦
2 Spring Hill, Wilsden, Bradford BD15 0AW
T: (01535) 275211

WILSILL
North Yorkshire

The Birch Tree Inn ♦♦♦
Wilsill, Harrogate HG3 5EA
T: (01423) 711131
E: sandrathorpe@amserve.co.uk

WILTON
North Yorkshire

The Old Forge ♦♦♦♦
Wilton, Pickering YO18 7JY
T: (01751) 477399
F: (01751) 473122
E: theoldforge@themutual.net
I: www.forgecottages.themutual.net/fc.html

WOLD NEWTON
East Riding of Yorkshire

The Wold Cottage
♦♦♦♦♦ SILVER AWARD
Wold Newton, Driffield YO25 3HL
T: (01262) 470696
F: (01262) 470696
E: katrina@woldcottage.com
I: www.woldcottage.com

WOMBLETON
North Yorkshire

Rockery Cottage
♦♦♦♦ SILVER AWARD
Main Street, Wombleton, York YO62 7RX
T: (01751) 432257
E: angela@rockery-cottage.fsnet.co.uk

WORTLEY
South Yorkshire

Wortley Hall Ltd ♦♦
Wortley, Sheffield S35 7DB
T: (0114) 288 2100
F: (0114) 283 0695
E: info@wortleyhall.org.uk
I: www.wortleyhall.org.uk

WRAWBY
North Lincolnshire

Mowden House ♦♦♦♦
Barton Road, Wrawby, Brigg DN20 8SQ
T: (01652) 652145
E: dr@prabhakaran.fsnet.co.uk

Wish 'u' Well Guest House ♦♦♦
Brigg Road, Wrawby, Brigg DN20 8RH
T: (01652) 652301
F: (01652) 652301
E: wishuwell@talk21.com

WRELTON
North Yorkshire

Huntsman Licensed Guesthouse ♦♦♦
Main Street, Wrelton, Pickering YO18 8PG
T: (01751) 472530
E: info@theyorkshirehuntsman.co.uk
I: www.theyorkshirehuntsman.co.uk

WROOT
North Lincolnshire

Green Garth Country Guest House ♦♦♦♦
High Street, Wroot, Doncaster DN9 2BU
T: (01302) 770416
F: (07092) 006635
E: enquiries@greengarth.co.uk
I: www.greengarth.co.uk

YORK
North Yorkshire

Aaron Guest House ♦♦♦
42 Bootham Crescent, Bootham, York YO30 7AH
T: (01904) 625927

Abbey Guest House ♦♦♦
14 Earlsborough Terrace, York YO30 7BQ
T: (01904) 627782
F: (01904) 671743
E: abbey@rsummers.cix.co.uk
I: www.bedandbreakfastyork.co.uk

Abbeyfields ♦♦♦♦
19 Bootham Terrace, York YO30 7DH
T: (01904) 636471
F: (01904) 636471
E: info@abbeyfields.co.uk
I: www.abbeyfields.co.uk

The Abbingdon ♦♦
60 Bootham Crescent, York YO30 7AH
T: (01904) 621761
F: (01904) 621761
E: paula@abbingdon.co.uk
I: www.abbingdon.co.uk

The Acer Hotel ♦♦♦♦ SILVER AWARD
52 Scarcroft Hill, York YO24 1DE
T: (01904) 653839
F: (01904) 677017
E: info@acerhotel.co.uk
I: www.acerhotel.co.uk

Acres Dene Guesthouse ♦♦♦
87 Fulford Road, York YO10 4BD
T: (01904) 647482
F: (01904) 637330
E: acresdene@bigwig.net

Airden House ♦♦♦
1 St Marys, Bootham, York YO30 7DD
T: (01904) 638915
E: info@airdenhouse.co.uk
I: www.airdenhouse.co.uk

Alcuin Lodge ♦♦♦♦
15 Sycamore Place, Bootham, York YO30 7DW
T: (01904) 632222
F: (01904) 626630
E: alcuinlodg@aol.com

Aldwark Bridge House ♦♦♦
Boat Lane, Great Ouseburn, York YO26 9SJ
T: (01423) 331097
F: (01423) 331097
E: bbabh@netscapeonline.co.uk

Alexander House ♦♦♦♦♦ GOLD AWARD
94 Bishopthorpe Road, York YO23 1JS
T: (01904) 625016
E: info@alexanderhouseyork.co.uk
I: www.alexanderhouseyork.co.uk

Ambleside Guest House ♦♦♦
62 Bootham Crescent, Bootham, York YO30 7AH
T: (01904) 637165
F: (01904) 637165
E: ambles@globalnet.co.uk
I: www.ambleside-gh.co.uk

The Apple House ♦♦♦♦
74-76 Holgate Road, York YO24 4AB
T: (01904) 625081
F: (01904) 628918

Arndale Hotel ♦♦♦♦ SILVER AWARD
290 Tadcaster Road, York YO24 1ET
T: (01904) 702424
F: (01904) 709800

Arnot House ♦♦♦♦ SILVER AWARD
17 Grosvenor Terrace, York YO30 7AG
T: (01904) 641966
F: (01904) 641966
E: kim.robbins@virgin.net
I: www.arnothouseyork.co.uk

Ascot House ♦♦♦♦ SILVER AWARD
80 East Parade, York YO31 7YH
T: (01904) 426826
F: (01904) 431077
E: j&k@ascot-house-york.demon.co.uk
I: www.ascothouseyork.com

Ascot Lodge ♦♦♦
112 Acomb Road, York YO24 4EY
T: (01904) 798234
F: (01904) 786742
E: info@ascotlodge.com
I: www.ascotlodge.com

Ashbourne House ♦♦♦♦ SILVER AWARD
139 Fulford Road, York YO10 4HG
T: (01904) 639912
F: (01904) 631332
E: ashbourneh@aol.com
I: www.ashbourne-house.com

Ashbury Hotel ♦♦♦
103 The Mount, York YO24 1AX
T: (01904) 647339
F: (01904) 647339
E: ashbury@talk21.com
I: www.ashburyhotel.co.uk

Avondale Guest House ♦♦♦
61 Bishopthorpe Road, York YO23 1NX
T: (01904) 633989
E: kaleda@avondaleguesthouse.freeserve.co.uk
I: www.avondaleguesthouse.co.uk

The Bar Convent Enterprises Ltd ♦♦♦
17 Blossom Street, York YO24 1AQ
T: (01904) 643238
F: (01904) 631792
E: info@bar-convent.org.uk
I: www.bar-convent.org.uk

Barbican House ♦♦♦♦ SILVER AWARD
20 Barbican Road, York YO10 5AA
T: (01904) 627617
F: (01904) 647140
E: info@barbicanhouse.com
I: www.barbicanhouse.com

Barrington House ♦♦♦
15 Nunthorpe Avenue, York YO23 1PF
T: (01904) 634539
E: alan.bell@btinternet.com
I: barringtonhouseyork.com

Bay Tree Guest House ♦♦♦
92 Bishopthorpe Road, York YO23 1JS
T: (01904) 659462
F: (01904) 659462
E: info@baytree-york.co.uk
I: www.baytree-york.co.uk

Bedford Hotel ♦♦♦
108-110 Bootham, York YO30 7DG
T: (01904) 624412
F: (01904) 632851
E: info@bedfordhotelyork.co.uk
I: www.bedfordhotelyork.co.uk

The Beech House Hotel ♦♦♦
6-7 Longfield Terrace, Bootham, York YO30 7DJ
T: (01904) 634581
E: beechhouse@beeb.net
I: www.beech-house-york.co.uk

The Bentley Guest House ♦♦♦♦
25 Grosvenor Terrace, Bootham, York YO30 7AG
T: (01904) 644313
F: (01904) 644313
E: info@bentleyofyork.co.uk
I: www.bentleyofyork.co.uk

Bishopgarth Guest House ♦♦♦
3 Southlands Road, York YO23 1NP
T: (01904) 635220
F: (01904) 635220
E: megspreckley@aol.com
I: www.bishopgarth.co.uk

Bishops Hotel ♦♦♦♦ SILVER AWARD
135 Holgate Road, York YO24 4DF
T: (01904) 628000
F: (01904) 628181
E: bishops@ukonline.co.uk
I: www.bishopshotel.co.uk

Blakeney Hotel ♦♦♦
180 Stockton Lane, York YO31 1ES
T: (01904) 422786
F: (01904) 422786
E: reception@blakeneyhotel-york.co.uk
I: www.blakeneyhotel-york.co.uk

Blue Bridge Hotel ♦♦♦
Fishergate, York YO10 4AP
T: (01904) 621193
F: (01904) 671571
E: info@bluebridgehotel.co.uk
I: www.bluebridgehotel.co.uk

Bootham Guest House ♦♦♦
56 Bootham Crescent, York YO30 7AH
T: (01904) 672123
F: (01904) 672123
E: bgh@whsmithnet.co.uk
I: www.boothamguesthouse.co.uk

Bootham Park ♦♦♦♦
9 Grosvenor Terrace, York YO30 7AG
T: (01904) 644262
F: (01904) 645647
E: boothampark@aol.com
I: www.boothampark@aol.com

Brentwood Guest House ♦♦♦
54 Bootham Crescent, Bootham, York YO30 7AH
T: (01904) 636419
F: (01904) 636419
E: brentwood@aol.com
I: www.visitus.co.uk

Briar Lea Guest House ♦♦♦
8 Longfield Terrace, Bootham, York YO30 7DJ
T: (01904) 635061
F: (01904) 330356
E: briarleahouse@msn.com
I: www.briarlea.co.uk

Bronte Guesthouse ♦♦♦♦
22 Grosvenor Terrace, York YO30 7AG
T: (01904) 621066
F: (01904) 653434
E: enquiries@bronte-guesthouse.com
I: www.bronte-guesthouse.com/

Bull Lodge Guest House ♦♦♦
37 Bull Lane, York YO10 3EN
T: (01904) 415522
F: (01904) 415522
E: stay@bulllodge.co.uk
I: www.bulllodge.co.uk

Burton Villa Guest House ♦♦♦
24 Haxby Road, York YO31 8JX
T: (01904) 626364
E: burtonvilla@hotmail.com
I: www.burtonvilla.com

Carlton House Hotel ♦♦♦
134 The Mount, York YO24 1AS
T: (01904) 622265
F: (01904) 637157
E: etb@carltonhouse.co.uk
I: www.carltonhouse.co.uk

The Cavalier ♦♦♦
39 Monkgate, York YO31 7PB
T: (01904) 636615
F: (01904) 636615
E: julia@cavalierhotel.co.uk
I: www.cavalierhotel.co.uk

Chelmsford Place Guest House ♦♦♦
85 Fulford Road, York YO10 4BD
T: (01904) 624491
F: (01904) 624491
E: chelmsfordplace@btinternet.com
I: www.chelmsfordplace.co.uk

Chilton Guest House ♦♦♦
1 Claremont Terrace, Gillygate, York YO31 7EJ
T: (01904) 612465
F: (01904) 612465

City Guest House
♦♦♦♦ SILVER AWARD
68 Monkgate, York YO31 7PF
T: (01904) 622483
E: info@cityguesthouse.co.uk
I: www.cityguesthouse.co.uk

Clarence Gardens Hotel ♦♦♦
Haxby Road, York YO31 8JS
T: (01904) 624252
F: (01904) 671293
E: stay@clarencegardenshotel.com
I: www.clarencegardenshotel.com

Claxton Hall Cottage
♦♦♦♦ SILVER AWARD
Flaxton, York YO60 7RE
T: (01904) 468697
E: claxcott@aol.com
I: www.claxtonhallcottage.com

Cook's Guest House ♦♦♦
120 Bishopthorpe Road, York YO23 1JX
T: (01904) 652519
F: (01904) 652519
E: jslcook@hotmail.com

Cornmill Lodge Vegetarian Guest House ♦♦♦
120 Haxby Road, York YO31 8JP
T: (01904) 620566
F: (01904) 620566
E: cornmillyork@aol.com
I: www.cornmillyork.co.uk

Crescent Guest House ♦♦
77 Bootham, York YO30 7DQ
T: (01904) 623216
F: (01904) 623216
E: haroldwhitelegg@btconnect.com
I: www.guesthousesyork.net

Crook Lodge ♦♦♦♦
26 St Mary's, Bootham, York YO30 7DD
T: (01904) 655614
F: (01904) 655614
E: crooklodge@hotmail.com
I: www.crooklodge.co.uk

Crossways Guest House ♦♦♦
23 Wigginton Road, York YO31 8HJ
T: (01904) 637250
E: info@crosswaysguesthouse.freeserve.co.uk
I: www.crosswaysguesthouse.freeserve.co.uk

Cumbria House ♦♦♦
2 Vyner Street, Haxby Road, York YO31 8HS
T: (01904) 636817
E: candj@cumbriahouse.freeserve.co.uk
I: www.cumbriahouse.com

Curzon Lodge and Stable Cottages ♦♦♦♦
23 Tadcaster Road, Dringhouses, York YO24 1QG
T: (01904) 703157
F: (01904) 703157
I: www.smoothhound.co.uk/hotels/curzon.html

Dairy Guest House
Rating Applied For
3 Scarcroft Road, York YO23 1ND
T: (01904) 639367
E: stay@dairyguesthouse.co.uk
I: www.dairyguesthouse.co.uk

Dalescroft Guest House ♦♦♦
10 Southlands Road, York YO23 1NP
T: (01904) 626801
E: dalescroftg.h.@aol.com

Eastons ♦♦♦♦
90 Bishopthorpe Road, York YO23 1JS
T: (01904) 626646
F: (01904) 626165
E: eastonsbbyork@aol.com
I: members.aol.com/eastonsbbyork/home.htm

Elliotts ♦♦♦♦
Sycamore Place, York YO30 7DW
T: (01904) 623333
F: (01904) 654908
E: elliottshotel@aol.com
I: www.elliottshotel.co.uk

Fairthorne ♦♦♦
356 Strensall Road, Earswick, York YO32 9SW
T: (01904) 768609
F: (01904) 768609

Farthings Hotel ♦♦♦♦
5 Nunthorpe Avenue, York YO23 1PF
T: (01904) 653545
F: (01904) 628355
E: stay@farthingsyork.co.uk
I: www.farthingsyork.co.uk

Feversham Lodge International Guest House ♦♦♦
1 Feversham Crescent, York YO31 8HQ
T: (01904) 623882
F: (01904) 623882
E: bookings@fevershamlodge.co.uk
I: www.fevershamlodgeguesthouseyork.co.uk

Five Lions Hotel ♦♦♦
24 Walmgate, York YO1 9TJ
T: (01904) 625124

Foss Bank Guest House ♦♦♦
16 Huntington Road, York YO31 8RB
T: (01904) 635548
I: www.fossbank.co.uk

Four Seasons Hotel
♦♦♦♦ SILVER AWARD
7 St Peters Grove, York YO30 6AQ
T: (01904) 622621
F: (01904) 620976
E: roe@fourseasons.supanet.com
I: www.fourseasons-hotel.co.uk

Fourposter Lodge Hotel ♦♦♦
68-70 Heslington Road, Barbican Road, York YO10 5AU
T: (01904) 651170
F: (01904) 651170
E: fourposter.lodge@virgin.net
I: www.fourposterlodgehotel.co.uk

Friars Rest Guest House ♦♦♦
81 Fulford Road, York YO10 4BD
T: (01904) 629823
F: (01904) 629823
E: friarsrest@btinternet.com
I: www.friarsrest.co.uk

Gables Guest House ♦♦
50 Bootham Crescent, Bootham, York YO30 7AH
T: (01904) 624381
F: (01904) 624381
I: www.thegablesofyork.co.uk

George Hotel ♦♦♦
6 St Georges Place, Off Tadcaster Road, York YO24 1DR
T: (01904) 625056
F: (01904) 625009
E: sixstgeorg@aol.com
I: members.aol.com/sixstgeorg/

Goldsmiths Guest House ♦♦♦
18 Longfield Terrace, York YO30 7DJ
T: (01904) 655738
F: (01904) 675577
E: susan@goldsmith18.freeserve
I: www.goldsmithsguesthouse.co.uk

Grange Lodge ♦♦♦
52 Bootham Crescent, Bootham, York YO30 7AH
T: (01904) 621137
E: grangeldg@aol.com
I: grangelodge.co.uk

Greenside ♦♦♦
124 Clifton, York YO30 6BQ
T: (01904) 623631
F: (01904) 623631
E: greenside@amserve.com
I: www.greensideguesthouse.co.uk

The Hazelwood
♦♦♦♦ SILVER AWARD
24-25 Portland Street, York YO31 7EH
T: (01904) 626548
F: (01904) 628032
E: Reservations@thehazelwoodyork.com
I: www.thehazelwoodyork.com

Heworth Guest House ♦♦♦
126 East Parade, Heworth, York YO31 7YG
T: (01904) 426384
F: (01904) 426384
E: chris.thompson1@virgin.net
I: www.yorkcity.co.uk

Holgate Bridge Hotel ♦♦♦
106-108 Holgate Road, York YO24 4BB
T: (01904) 647288
F: (01904) 670049
E: info@holgatebridge.co.uk
I: www.holgatebridge.co.uk

The Hollies Guest House ♦♦♦
141 Fulford Road, York YO10 4HG
T: (01904) 634279
F: (01904) 625435
E: enquiries@hollies-guesthouse.co.uk
I: www.hollies-guesthouse.co.uk

Holly Lodge ♦♦♦♦
206 Fulford Road, York YO10 4DD
T: (01904) 646005
I: www.thehollylodge.co.uk

Holme Lea Manor Guest House ♦♦♦
18 St Peters Grove, York YO30 6AQ
T: (01904) 623529
F: (01904) 653584
E: holmelea@btclick.com
I: www.holmlea.co.uk

Holmwood House Hotel
♦♦♦♦ SILVER AWARD
114 Holgate Road, York YO24 4BB
T: (01904) 626183
F: (01904) 670899
E: holmwood.house@dial.pipex.com
I: www.holmwoodhousehotel.co.uk

Kirkham Coffee Shop & Guest House ♦♦♦
Station House, Kirkham Abbey, York YO60 7JS
T: (01653) 618658

The Limes ♦♦♦♦
135 Fulford Road, York YO10 4HE
T: (01904) 624548
F: (01904) 624944
E: queries@limeshotel.co.uk
I: www.limeshotel.co.uk

Linden Lodge ♦♦♦
6 Nunthorpe Avenue, Scarcroft Road, York YO23 1PF
T: (01904) 620107
F: (01904) 620985
E: bookings@lindenlodge.yorks.net
I: www.yorkshirenet.co.uk/stayat/lindenlodge

Meadowcroft Hotel ♦♦♦
84 Bootham, York YO30 7DF
T: (01904) 655194
F: (01904) 651384
E: mcroftyork@aol.com
I: www.scoot.co.uk/meadowcroft

Midway House Hotel ♦♦♦
145 Fulford Road, York YO10 4HG
T: (01904) 659272
E: midway.house@virgin.net
I: www.s-h-systems.co.uk/hotels/midway.html

Monkgate Guest House ♦♦♦
65 Monkgate, York YO31 7PA
T: (01904) 655947
E: 65monkgate@btconnect.com
I: www.monkgateguesthouse.com

Moorgarth Guest House ♦♦♦
158 Fulford Road, York YO10 4DA
T: (01904) 636768
F: (01904) 636768
E: moorgarth@fsbdial.co.uk
I: www.moorgarth-york.co.uk

Moorland House ♦♦♦
1A Moorland Road, York YO10 4HF
T: (01904) 629354
F: (01904) 629354

Mowbray House ♦♦♦
34 Haxby Road, York YO31 8JX
T: (01904) 637710
E: carol@mowbrayhouse.co.uk
I: www.mowbrayhouse.co.uk

Northolme Guest House ♦♦♦
114 Shipton Road, Rawcliffe, York YO30 5RN
T: (01904) 639132
E: g.liddle@tesco.net
I: www.northholmeguesthouse.co.uk

Nunmill House
♦♦♦♦ SILVER AWARD
85 Bishopthorpe Road, York YO23 1NX
T: (01904) 634047
F: (01904) 655879
E: info@nunmill.co.uk
I: www.nunmill.co.uk

Oaklands Guest House ♦♦♦♦
351 Strensall Road, Earswick, York YO32 9SW
T: (01904) 768443
E: mavmo@oaklands5.fsnet.co.uk
I: www.holidayguides.com

Olga's Licensed Guest House ♦♦
12 Wenlock Terrace, Fulford Road, York YO10 4DU
T: (01904) 641456
F: (01904) 641456
E: olgasguesthouseyork@talk21.com
I: www.olgas-guesthouse-york.co.uk

One3Two
♦♦♦♦♦ SILVER AWARD
132 The Mount, York YO24 1AS
T: (01904) 600060
F: (01904) 676132
E: enquiries@one3two.co.uk
I: www.one3two.co.uk

Orillia House ♦♦♦♦
89 The Village, Stockton on the Forest, Stockton-on-the-Forest, York YO32 9UP
T: (01904) 400600
F: (01904) 400101
E: orillia@globalnet.co.uk
I: www.orilliahouse.co.uk

Palm Court Hotel ♦♦♦♦
17 Huntington Road, York YO31 8RB
T: (01904) 639387
F: (01904) 639387

Papillon Hotel ♦♦
43 Gillygate, York YO31 7EA
T: (01904) 636505
F: (01904) 611968
E: papillonhotel@btinternet.com
I: www.btinternet.com/~papillonhotel

Park View Guest House ♦♦♦
34 Grosvenor Terrace, Bootham, York YO30 7AG
T: (01904) 620437
F: (01904) 620437
E: theparkviewyork@aol.com

The Priory Hotel ♦♦♦
126-128 Fulford Road, York YO10 4BE
T: (01904) 625280
F: (01904) 637330
E: reservations@priory-hotelyork.co.uk
I: www.priory-hotelyork.co.uk

Queen Anne's Guest House ♦♦♦
24 Queen Annes Road, York YO30 7AA
T: (01904) 629389
F: (01904) 619529
E: info@queenannes.fsnet.co.uk
I: www.s-h-systems.co.uk/hotels/queenann

Riverside Walk Guest House ♦♦♦
9 Earlsborough Terrace, York YO30 7BQ
T: (01904) 620769
F: (01904) 671743
E: riverside@rsummers.cix.co.uk
I: www.bedandbreakfastyork.co.uk

Romley Guest House ♦♦♦
2 Millfield Road, Scarcroft Road, York YO23 1NQ
T: (01904) 652822
E: info@romleyhouse.co.uk
I: www.romleyhouse.co.uk

St Deny's Hotel ♦♦♦
51 St Denys Road, York YO1 9QD
T: (01904) 622207
F: (01904) 624800
E: info@stdenyshotel.co.uk
I: www.stdenyshotel.co.uk

St Mary's Hotel ♦♦♦
17 Longfield Terrace, York YO30 7DJ
T: (01904) 626972
F: (01904) 626972
E: stmaryshotel@talk21.com
I: www.stmaryshotel.co.uk

St Paul's Hotel ♦♦♦
120 Holgate Road, York YO24 4BB
T: (01904) 611514
F: (01904) 623188
E: normfran@supanet.com

St Raphael Guest House ♦♦♦
44 Queen Annes Road, York YO30 7AF
T: (01904) 645028
F: (01904) 639735
E: straphael2000@yahoo.co.uk

Saxon House Hotel ♦♦♦
71-73 Fulford Road, Fishergate, York YO10 4BD
T: (01904) 622106
F: (01904) 633764
E: saxon@househotel.freeserve.co.uk
I: www.saxonhousehotel.co.uk

Shoulder of Mutton ♦♦
64 Heworth Green, York YO31 7TQ
T: (01904) 424793
F: (01904) 427945

Skelton Grange Farmhouse ♦♦♦♦
Orchard View, Skelton, York YO30 1YQ
T: (01904) 470780
F: (01904) 471229
E: info@skelton-farm.co.uk
I: www.skelton-farm.co.uk

Southlands Bed and Breakfast ♦♦♦♦
Huntington Road, Huntington, York YO32 9PX
T: (01904) 766796
F: (01904) 764536
E: southlandsbandb.york@btinternet.com
I: www.southlandsbandb.freeserve.co.uk

Southland's Guest House ♦♦♦
69 Nunmill Street, South Bank, York YO23 1NT
T: (01904) 675966
F: (01904) 675965
E: southlands.house@virgin.net
I: www.southlandsguesthouse.co.uk

23 St Marys
♦♦♦♦ SILVER AWARD
Bootham, York YO30 7DD
T: (01904) 622738
F: (01904) 628802
E: stmarys23@hotmail.com
I: www.23stmarys.co.uk

Staymor Guest House ♦♦♦♦
2 Southlands Road, York YO23 1NP
T: (01904) 626935
E: kathwilson@lineone.net
I: www.staymorguesthouse.com

The Steer Inn ♦♦♦
Hull Road, Wilberfoss, York YO41 5PF
T: (01759) 380600
F: (01759) 388904
E: kevin@steerinn.co.uk
I: www.steerinn.co.uk

Sycamore Guest House ♦♦♦
19 Sycamore Place, York YO30 7DW
T: (01904) 624712
F: (01904) 624712
E: thesycamore@talk21.com
I: www.guesthousesyork.co.uk

Tower Guest House ♦♦♦♦
2 Feversham Crescent, York YO31 8HQ
T: (01904) 655571
E: reservations@towerguesthouse.fsnet.co.uk
I: www.towerguesthouse.fsnet.co.uk

Tree Tops ♦♦♦
21 St Marys, York YO30 7DD
T: (01904) 658053
F: (01904) 658053
E: treetops.guesthouse@virgin.net
I: business.thisisyork.co.uk/treetops

Turnberry House ♦♦♦
143 Fulford Road, York YO10 4HG
T: (01904) 658435
F: (01904) 630263
E: turnberry.house@virgin.net

Tyburn House Hotel ♦♦♦
11 Albemarle Road, The Mount, York YO23 1EN
T: (01904) 655069
F: (01904) 655069
E: york@tyburnhotel.freeserve.co.uk

The Victoria Hotel ♦♦♦
1 Heslington Road, York YO10 5AR
T: (01904) 622295
F: (01904) 677860

Victoria Villa ♦♦
72 Heslington Road, York YO10 5AU
T: (01904) 631647
F: (01904) 651170
E: vicvilla@fsmail.net
I: www.smoothhound.co.uk/hotels/vicvilla.html

Warrens Guest House ♦♦♦
30-32 Scarcroft Road, York YO23 1NF
T: (01904) 643139
F: (01904) 658297
I: www.warrensgh.co.uk

Waters Edge ♦♦♦
5 Earlsborough Terrace, Marygate, York YO30 7BQ
T: (01904) 644625
F: (01904) 671325
E: julie@watersedgeyork.co.uk
I: www.watersedgeyork.co.uk

Wellgarth House ♦♦♦
Wetherby Road, Rufforth, York YO23 3QB
T: (01904) 738592
F: (01904) 738595

Wold View House Hotel ♦♦♦
173-175 Haxby Road, York YO31 8JL
T: (01904) 632061
F: (01904) 632061
E: enquiries@woldviewhousehotel.co.uk
I: www.woldviewhousehotel.co.uk

York House ♦♦♦♦
62 Heworth Green, York YO31 7TQ
T: (01904) 427070
F: (01904) 427070
E: yorkhouse.bandb@tiscali.co.uk
I: www.yorkhouseyork.com

York Lodge Guest House ♦♦♦
64 Bootham Crescent, York YO30 7AH
T: (01904) 654289
F: (01904) 628497
E: yorkldg@aol.com
I: www.york-lodge.com

HEART OF ENGLAND

AB KETTLEBY
Leicestershire

White Lodge Farm ♦♦♦♦
Nottingham Road, Ab Kettleby, Melton Mowbray LE14 3JB
T: (01664) 822286
I: www.farm-holidays.co.uk

ABBOTS BROMLEY
Staffordshire

Crown Inn ♦♦
Market Place, Abbots Bromley, Rugeley WS15 3BS
T: (01283) 840227
F: (01283) 840016

ABBOTS MORTON
Worcestershire

The Cottage Apartment ♦♦♦♦
The Cottage, Gooms Hill, Abbots Morton Manor, Abbots Morton, Worcester WR7 4LT
T: (01386) 792783
F: (01386) 792783
E: cottage@bedbrek.fsnet.co.uk
I: www.bedbrek.co.uk

ABTHORPE
Northamptonshire

Rignall Farm Barns ♦♦♦
Handley Park, Abthorpe, Towcester NN12 8PA
T: (01327) 350766
F: (01327) 350766

ACTON BURNELL
Shropshire

Acton Pigot
♦♦♦♦♦ SILVER AWARD
Acton Pigott, Acton Burnell, Shrewsbury SY5 7PH
T: (01694) 731209
E: acton@farmline.com
I: www.actonpigot.co.uk

ADSTONE
Northamptonshire

Manor Farm ♦♦♦♦
Adstone, Towcester NN12 8DT
T: (01327) 860284
F: (01327) 860685
I: www.manorfarmsports.co.uk

ALBRIGHTON
Shropshire

Boningale Manor ♦♦♦♦
Holyhead Road, Boningale, Albrighton, Wolverhampton WV7 3AT
T: (01902) 373376
E: boningalemanor@aol.com
I: www.boningalemanor.com

Parkside Farm
♦♦♦♦ SILVER AWARD
Holyhead Road, Albrighton, Wolverhampton WV7 3DA
T: (01902) 372310
F: (01902) 375013
E: jmshanks@farming.co.uk
I: www.parksidefarm.com

ALCESTER
Warwickshire

The Globe Hotel ♦♦♦♦
54 Birmingham Road, Alcester B49 5EG
T: (01789) 763287
F: (01789) 763287
I: www.theglobehotel.com

Orchard Lawns
♦♦♦♦ SILVER AWARD
Wixford, Alcester B49 6DA
T: (01789) 772668
E: margaret.orchardlawns@farmersweekly.net

Sambourne Hall Farm ♦♦♦♦
Wike Lane, Sambourne B96 6NZ
T: (01527) 852151

ALDERTON
Gloucestershire

Corner Cottage ♦♦♦♦
Stow Road, Alderton, Tewkesbury GL20 8NH
T: (01242) 620630
F: (01242) 621550
E: cornercottagebb@talk21.com

Gantier ♦♦♦♦
12 Church Road, Alderton, Tewkesbury GL20 8NR
T: (01242) 620343
F: (01242) 620343
E: johnandsueparry@yahoo.co.uk
I: www.gantier.co.uk

Moors Farm House
♦♦♦♦♦ GOLD AWARD
32 Beckford Road, Alderton, Tewkesbury GL20 8NL
T: (01242) 620523
E: moorsfarmhouse@ukworld.net
I: www.ukworld.net/moorsfarmhouse

ALDWARK
Derbyshire

Lydgate Farm ♦♦♦♦
Aldwark DE4 4HW
T: (01629) 540250
F: (01629) 540250
E: lomas.lydgate@lineone.net
I: www.peakdistrictfarmhols.co.uk

ALDWINCLE
Northamptonshire

Pear Tree Farm ♦♦♦♦
Main Street, Aldwincle, Kettering NN14 3EL
T: (01832) 720614
F: (01832) 720559
E: beverley@peartreefarm.net
I: www.peartreefarm.net

ALFORD
Lincolnshire

Half Moon Hotel and Restaurant ♦♦♦
25-28 West Street, Alford LN13 9DG
T: (01507) 463477
F: (01507) 462916
E: halfmoonalford25@aol.com
I: www.thehalfmoonalford.com

ALFRETON
Derbyshire

Crown Inn ♦♦
73 Sleetmoor Lane, Somercotes, Alfreton DE55 1RE
T: (01773) 602537

The Spinney Cottage ♦♦♦
Derby Road, Swanwick, Alfreton DE55 1BG
T: (01773) 609020

ALL STRETTON
Shropshire

Inwood Farm ♦♦♦♦
All Stretton, Church Stretton SY6 6LA
T: (01694) 724781
E: pauline.traill@btopenworld.com

ALMELEY
Herefordshire

Almeley House Bed and Breakfast ♦♦♦♦
Almeley House, Almeley, Hereford HR3 6LB
T: (01544) 327269
F: (01544) 328406
E: gwenda@hamesg.freeserve.co.uk

ALTON
Staffordshire

Admirals House Country Hotel and Restaurant ♦♦♦
Mill Road, Oakamoor, Stoke-on-Trent ST10 3AG
T: (01538) 702187
E: admiralshouse@btinternet.com
I: www.admiralshouse.co.uk

Alverton Motel ♦♦♦
Denstone Lane, Alton, Stoke-on-Trent ST10 4AX
T: (01538) 702265
F: (01538) 703284
I: www.alvertonmotel.co.uk

Bradley Elms Farm ♦♦♦♦
Alton Road, Threapwood, Cheadle ST10 4RB
T: (01538) 753135
F: (01538) 750202

Bramble Cottage ♦♦♦♦
Gallows Green, Alton, Stoke-on-Trent ST10 4BN
T: (01538) 703805

Bulls Head Inn ♦♦♦
High Street, Alton, Stoke-on-Trent ST10 4AQ
T: (01538) 702307
F: (01538) 702065
E: janet@alton.freeserve.co.uk
I: www.thebullsheadinn.freeserve.co.uk

Church Grange ♦♦♦♦
Bradley in the Moors, Alton, Stoke-on-Trent ST10 4DF
T: (01889) 507525
F: (01889) 507282
E: cdmasalt.chgrange@btinternet.com
I: www.chgrange.co.uk

The Cross Inn ♦♦♦
Cauldon Low, Stoke-on-Trent ST10 3EX
T: (01538) 308338
F: (01538) 308767
E: adrian_weaver@hotmail.com
I: www.crossinn.co.uk

Fernlea Guest House ♦♦♦
Cedar Hill, Alton, Stoke-on-Trent ST10 4BH
T: (01538) 702327

Fields Farm
♦♦♦♦ SILVER AWARD
Chapel Lane, Threapwood, Alton, Stoke-on-Trent ST10 4QZ
T: (01538) 752721
F: (01538) 757404
E: pat.massey@ukonline.co.uk
I: www.fieldsfarmbb.co.uk

Hansley Cross Cottage ♦♦♦
Cheadle Road, Alton, Stoke-on-Trent ST10 4DH
T: (01538) 702189
F: (01538) 702189
E: jeanhcross@aol.com
I: www.hansleycrosscottage.co.uk

Hillside Farm ♦♦♦
Alton Road, Denstone, Uttoxeter ST14 5HG
T: (01889) 590760
F: (01889) 590760
I: www.smoothhound.co.uk/hotels/hillside.html

The Lord Shrewsbury ♦♦♦
New Road, Alton, Stoke-on-Trent ST10 4AF
T: (01538) 702218
I: www.thewildduckinn.com

The Malthouse ♦♦♦♦
Malthouse Road, Alton, Stoke-on-Trent ST10 4AG
T: (01538) 703273
I: www.the-malthouse.gbr.fm/2001/contact.asp

The Old School House
♦♦♦♦♦ SILVER AWARD
Castle Hill Road, Alton, Stoke-on-Trent ST10 4AJ
T: (01538) 702151
E: old_school_house@talk21.com
I: www.geocities.com/denniseardley

The Peakstones Inn ♦♦
Cheadle Road, Alton, Stoke-on-Trent ST10 4DH
T: (01538) 755776

Royal Oak ♦♦
Horse Road, Alton, Stoke-on-Trent ST10 4BH
T: (01538) 702625
E: enq@royaloak-alton.co.uk
I: www.royaloak-alton.co.uk

Trough Ivy House ♦♦♦♦
1 Hay Lane, Farley, Alton, Stoke-on-Trent ST10 3BQ
T: (01538) 702683
F: (01538) 702013
E: bookings@trough-ivy-house.demon.co.uk
I: www.trough-ivy-house.demon.co.uk

Tythe Barn House ♦♦♦
Denstone Lane, Alton, Stoke-on-Trent ST10 4AX
T: (01538) 702852
I: www.tythebarnhouse.co.uk

The Warren ♦♦♦♦
The Dale, Battlesteads, Alton, Stoke-on-Trent ST10 4BG
T: (01538) 702493
F: (01538) 702493
I: www.staffordshire.gov.uk/thewarren

Yoxall Cottage ♦♦♦
Malthouse Road, Alton, Stoke-on-Trent ST10 4AG
T: (01538) 702537
F: (01538) 702537
E: bb_yoxallcottage@btopenworld.com

ALVASTON
Derbyshire

Grace Guesthouse ♦♦
1063 London Road, Alvaston, Derby DE24 8PZ
T: (01332) 571051
F: (01332) 341916

ALVECHURCH
Worcestershire

Alcott Farm ♦♦♦
Icknield Street, Alvechurch, Birmingham B48 7EH
T: (01564) 824051
F: (01564) 824051
E: janepoole@amserve.com

ALVELEY
Shropshire

Arnside Bed and Breakfast
♦♦♦♦ SILVER AWARD
Arnside, Kidderminster Road, Alveley, Bridgnorth WV15 6LL
T: (01746) 780007
F: (01746) 780007
E: terry@ptah.freeservce.co.uk
I: www.virtual-shropshire.co.uk/arnside

AMBERGATE
Derbyshire

Lord Nelson ♦♦♦
Bullbridge, Ambergate, Belper DE56 2EW
T: (01773) 852037
E: bob&sarah@thelordnelson.fsworld.co.uk
I: www.thelordnelson.fsworld.co.uk

AMBERLEY
Gloucestershire

High Tumps ♦♦♦♦
St Chloe Green, Amberley, Stroud GL5 5AR
T: (01453) 873584
F: (01453) 873587

AMPNEY CRUCIS
Gloucestershire

The Miller's House ♦♦♦
Ampney Crucis, Cirencester GL7 5RR
T: (01285) 850896
F: (01285) 850899

APPLEBY MAGNA
Leicestershire

Elms Farm
♦♦♦♦ SILVER AWARD
Swadlincote, Appleby Magna, Burton upon Trent DE12 7AP
T: (01530) 270450
F: (01530) 272718
E: geoffrisby@hotmail.com

ARLEY
Worcestershire

Tudor Barn
♦♦♦♦ SILVER AWARD
Nib Green, Arley, Bewdley DY12 3LY
T: (01299) 400129
E: tudorbarn@aol.com
I: www.tudor-barn.co.uk

ARMSCOTE
Warwickshire

Willow Corner
♦♦♦♦ SILVER AWARD
Armscote, Stratford-upon-Avon CV37 8DE
T: (01608) 682391
E: willowcorner@compuserve.com
I: www.willowcorner.co.uk

ARNOLD
Nottinghamshire

Rufford Guesthouse ♦♦♦♦
117 Redhill Road, Arnold, Nottingham NG5 8GZ
T: (0115) 926 1759
F: (0115) 926 1759
E: ruffordhouse@hotmail.com
I: www.ruffordhouse.co.uk

ASFORDBY VALLEY
Leicestershire

Valley End ♦♦♦♦
17 North Street, Asfordby Valley, Melton Mowbray LE14 3SQ
T: (01664) 812003

ASH MAGNA
Shropshire

Ash Hall ♦♦♦
Ash Magna, Whitchurch SY13 4DL
T: (01948) 663151

ASHBOURNE
Derbyshire

The Black Horse Inn ♦♦♦
Main Road, Hulland Ward, Ashbourne DE6 3EE
T: (01335) 370206
F: (01335) 370206

Cross Farm ♦♦♦♦
Main Road, Ellastone, Ashbourne DE6 2GZ
T: (01335) 324668
F: (01335) 324039
E: janecliffe@hotmail.com
I: www.cross-farm.co.uk

Cubley Common Farm ♦♦♦♦
Cubley, Ashbourne DE6 2EX
T: (01335) 330041

Green Gables ♦♦♦♦
107 The Green Road, Ashbourne DE6 1EE
T: (01335) 342431
I: www.cressbrook.co.uk/ashbourne/greengables

Holly Meadow Farm ♦♦♦♦
Bradley, Ashbourne DE6 1PN
T: (01335) 370261
F: (01335) 370261
I: www.hollymeadowbandb.freeserve.co.uk

Hurtswood ♦♦♦
Buxton Road, Sandybrook, Ashbourne DE6 2AQ
T: (01335) 342031
F: (01335) 347467
E: gl.hurtswood@virgin.net
I: www.hurtswood.co.uk

The Lilacs ♦♦♦♦
Mayfield Road, Ashbourne DE6 2BJ
T: (01335) 343749
F: (01335) 343749

Mona Villas Bed and Breakfast
♦♦♦
1 Mona Villas, Church Lane, Mayfield, Ashbourne DE6 2JS
T: (01335) 343773
F: (01335) 343773

Omnia Somnia
♦♦♦♦♦ GOLD AWARD
The Coach House, The Firs, Ashbourne DE6 1HF
T: (01335) 300145
F: (01335) 300958
E: alan@omniasomnia.co.uk
I: www.omniasomnia.co.uk

Overfield Farm ♦♦♦
Tissington, Ashbourne DE6 1RA
T: (01335) 390285
E: info@overfieldfarm.co.uk
I: www.overfieldfarm.co.uk

Shirley Hall Farm
♦♦♦♦ SILVER AWARD
Shirley, Ashbourne DE6 3AS
T: (01335) 360346
F: (01335) 360346
E: sylviafoster@shirleyhallfarm.com
I: www.shirleyhallfarm.com

Stanshope Hall ♦♦♦♦
Stanshope, Ashbourne DE6 2AD
T: (01335) 310278
F: (01335) 310127
E: naomi@stanshope.demon.co.uk
I: www.stanshope.demon.net

Tan Mill Farm ♦♦♦♦
Mappleton Road, Ashbourne DE6 2AA
T: (01335) 342387
F: (01335) 342387

Thorpe Cottage ♦♦♦♦
Thorpe, Ashbourne DE6 2AW
T: (01335) 350466
F: (01335) 350217
I: www.peakdistrict-bandb.com

The Wheelhouse ♦♦♦♦
Belper Road, Hulland Ward, Ashbourne DE6 3EE
T: (01335) 370953
E: samax@supanet.com

White Cottage ♦♦♦♦
Wyaston, Ashbourne DE6 2DR
T: (01335) 345503
E: jackie@previll.fsnet.co.uk

ASHBY-DE-LA-ZOUCH
Leicestershire

Church Lane Farm House
♦♦♦♦
Church Lane, Ravenstone, Coalville, Leicester LE67 2AE
T: (01530) 810536
F: (01530) 811299
E: annthorne@ravenstone-guesthouse.co.uk
I: www.ravenstone-guesthouse.co.uk

Holywell House Hotel ♦♦
58 Burton Road, Ashby-de-la-Zouch LE65 2LN
T: (01530) 412005

The Laurels Bed and Breakfast
♦♦♦♦
17 Ashby Road, Measham, Ashby-de-la-Zouch DE12 7JR
T: (01530) 272567
F: (01530) 272567
E: evanslaurels@onetel.net.uk
I: www.thelaurelsguesthouse.com

Measham House Farm ♦♦♦♦
Gallows Lane, Measham, Swadlincote DE12 7HD
T: (01530) 270465
F: (01530) 270465
E: jjlovett@meashamhouse.freeserve.co.uk
I: www.meashamhouse.co.uk

Queens Head Hotel ♦♦♦
79 Market Street, Ashby-de-la-Zouch LE65 1AH
T: (01530) 412780
F: (01530) 412134

White House Fields Farm
Rating Applied For
Worthington, Ashby-de-la-Zouch LE65 1RA
T: (01332) 862312
F: (01332) 865724
E: whitehousefields@aol.com

ASHBY ST LEDGERS
Northamptonshire

The Olde Coach House Inn
♦♦♦
Main Street, Ashby St Ledgers, Rugby CV23 8UN
T: (01788) 890349
F: (01788) 891922
E: oldecoachhouse@traditionalfreehouses.co.uk

ASHFORD IN THE WATER
Derbyshire

Chy-an-Dour
♦♦♦♦ SILVER AWARD
Vicarage Lane, Ashford in the Water, Bakewell DE45 1QN
T: (01629) 813162

Marble Cottage
Rating Applied For
The Dukes Drive, Ashford-in-the-Water, Bakewell DE45 1QP
T: (01629) 813624
F: (01629) 813624

Warlands ♦♦♦
Hill Cross, Ashford-in-the-Water, Bakewell DE45 1QL
T: (01629) 813736

Woodland View ♦♦♦
John Bank Lane, Ashford in the Water, Bakewell DE45 1PY
T: (01629) 813008
F: (01629) 813008
E: woodview@neilellis.free-online.co.uk
I: www.woodlandviewbandb.co.uk

ASHLEWORTH
Gloucestershire

Ashleworth Court ♦♦♦
Ashleworth, Gloucester GL19 4JA
T: (01452) 700241
F: (01452) 700411
E: chamberlayne@farmline.com
I: members.farmline.com/chamberlayne

ASHOVER
Derbyshire

Hardwick View ♦♦♦♦
Ashover Road, Littlemoor, Ashover, Chesterfield S45 0BL
T: (01246) 590876
E: sueworsey@talk21.com

Old School Farm ♦♦♦♦
Uppertown, Ashover, Chesterfield S45 0JF
T: (01246) 590813

Twitch Nook ♦♦♦♦
Hardwick Lane, Ashover, Chesterfield S45 0DE
T: (01246) 590153
F: (01246) 591641
E: valerieferrol@twitchnook.demon.co.uk
I: www.twitchnook.co.uk

ASHPERTON
Herefordshire

Pridewood ♦♦♦
Ashperton, Ledbury HR8 2SF
T: (01531) 670416
F: (01531) 670416

ASLACKBY
Lincolnshire

The Hayloft ♦♦♦♦
Martins, Temple Road, Aslackby, Sleaford NG34 0HJ
T: (01778) 440113
F: (01778) 440920
E: jacqueline.cole@talk21.com

ASTLEY
Worcestershire

Woodhampton House ♦♦♦
Weather Lane, Astley, Stourport-on-Severn DY13 0SF
T: (01299) 826510
F: (01299) 827059
E: pete-a@sally-a.freeserve.co.uk

ATHERSTONE
Warwickshire

Hall Farm ♦♦♦♦
The Green, Orton-on-the-Hill, Atherstone CV9 3NG
T: (01827) 880350
F: (01827) 881041
E: hallfm101@aol.com

Manor Farm Bed and Breakfast ♦♦♦
Manor Farm, Ratcliffe Culey, Atherstone CV9 3NY
T: (01827) 712269
F: (01827) 716947
E: jane@ausbeys.com

Vicki Garland's Bed & Breakfast ♦♦♦♦
Mythe Farm, Pinwall Lane, Sheepy Magna, Atherstone CV9 3PF
T: (01827) 712367
F: (01827) 715738
E: bosworth/advertising@connectfree.co.uk

AUDLEY
Staffordshire

The Domvilles Farm ♦♦♦♦
Barthomley Road, Audley, Stoke-on-Trent ST7 8HT
T: (01782) 720378
F: (01782) 720883

AVON DASSETT
Warwickshire

Crandon House
♦♦♦♦♦ SILVER AWARD
Avon Dassett, Leamington Spa CV47 2AA
T: (01295) 770652
F: (01295) 770632
E: crandonhouse@talk21.com
I: www.crandonhouse.co.uk

AWRE
Gloucestershire

Yew Trees ♦♦♦
Awre, Newnham-on-Severn GL14 1EW
T: (01594) 516687
F: (01594) 517209
E: b&b@yewtrees.uk.com
I: www.yewtrees.uk.com

AWSWORTH
Nottinghamshire

Hog's Head Hotel ♦♦♦
Main Street, Awsworth, Nottingham NG16 2RN
T: (0115) 938 4095
F: (0115) 945 9718

AYLBURTON
Gloucestershire

Bridge Cottage ♦♦♦
High Street, Aylburton, Gloucester GL15 6BX
T: (01594) 843527

AYMESTREY
Herefordshire

The Riverside Inn ♦♦♦♦
Aymestrey, Leominster HR6 9ST
T: (01568) 708440
F: (01568) 709058
E: richard.gresko@btinternet.com
I: www.fsvo.com/riversideinn/door

BADBY
Northamptonshire

Meadows Farm
♦♦♦♦♦ GOLD AWARD
Newnham Lane, Badby, Daventry NN11 3AA
T: (01327) 703302
F: (01327) 703085
I: www.northantsfarmholidays.co.uk www.farmstay.co.uk

BADSEY
Worcestershire

Orchard House ♦♦♦
99 Bretforton Road, Badsey, Evesham WR11 7XQ
T: (01386) 831245

BAKEWELL
Derbyshire

Castle Cliffe ♦♦♦
Monsal Head, Bakewell DE45 1NL
T: (01629) 640258
F: (01629) 640258
E: relax@castle-cliffe.com
I: www.castle-cliffe.com

Castle Inn ♦♦♦
Castle Street, Bakewell DE45 1DU
T: (01629) 812103
F: (01629) 814726

Easthorpe ♦♦♦♦
Buxton Road, Bakewell DE45 1DA
T: (01629) 814929
E: easthorpe@supanet.com

The Garden Room
♦♦♦♦ SILVER AWARD
1 Park Road, Bakewell DE45 1AX
T: (01629) 814299
E: the.garden.room@talk21.com
I: www.smoothhound.co.uk/hotels/thegarden.html

The Haven ♦♦♦♦
Haddon Road, Bakewell DE45 1AW
T: (01629) 812113
E: RoseArmstg@aol.com
I: members.aol.com/RoseArmstg

Housley Cottage ♦♦♦♦
Housley, Foolow S32 5QB
T: (01433) 631505
E: kevin@housley-cottage.freeserve.co.uk

Long Meadow House Bed and Breakfast
♦♦♦♦♦ SILVER AWARD
Coombs Road, Bakewell DE45 1AQ
T: (01629) 812500
E: amshowarth@aol.com
I: www.bakewellholidays.co.uk

Loughrigg
♦♦♦♦ SILVER AWARD
Burton Close Drive, Bakewell DE45 1BG
T: (01629) 813173
E: john@bakewell55.freeserve.co.uk
I: www.bakewell55.freeserve.co.uk

2 Lumford Cottages ♦♦♦
Off Holme Lane, Bakewell DE45 1GG
T: (01629) 813273
F: (01629) 813273
I: www.cressbrook.co.uk/bakewell/lumford

Mandale House
Rating Applied For
Haddon Grove, Bakewell DE45 1JF
T: (01629) 812416
F: (01629) 812416
E: julia.finney@virgin.net
I: www.mandalehouse.co.uk

Melbourne House ♦♦♦♦
Buxton Road, Bakewell DE45 1DA
T: (01629) 815357
E: melbournehouse@supanet.com

River Walk Bed and Breakfast ♦♦♦
River Walk, 3 New Lumford, Bakewell DE45 1GH
T: (01629) 812459

30 Riverside Crescent
♦♦♦♦♦ SILVER AWARD
Bakewell DE45 1HF
T: (01629) 815722
E: iain_mcbain@ibm.uk.com

Rushdale ♦♦♦
The Avenue, Bakewell DE45 1EQ
T: (01629) 814718
E: fjha@underhaddon.fsnet.co.uk

Tannery House
♦♦♦♦♦ GOLD AWARD
Matlock Street, Bakewell DE45 1EE
T: (01629) 815011
F: (01629) 815327
I: www.tanneryhouse.co.uk
National Accessible Scheme Rating Applied For

West Lawn Bed and Breakfast ♦♦♦♦
2 Aldern Way, Bakewell DE45 1AJ
T: (01629) 812243
I: www.westlawn.co.uk

Willow Croft ♦♦♦
Station Road, Great Longstone, Bakewell DE45 1TS
T:
E: willowcoftbandb@aol.com

BALSALL COMMON
West Midlands

Avonlea ♦♦
135 Kenilworth Road, Balsall Common, Coventry CV7 7EU
T: (01676) 533003
F: (01676) 533003
E: frank.welsh@ntl.com

Blythe Paddocks ♦♦♦
Barston Lane, Balsall Common, Coventry CV7 7BT
T: (01676) 533050
F: (01676) 533050

Camp Farm ♦♦♦
Hob Lane, Balsall Common, Coventry CV7 7GX
T: (01676) 533804
F: (01676) 533804

BALTERLEY
Staffordshire

Pear Tree Lake Farm ♦♦♦♦
Balterley, Crewe CW2 5QE
T: (01270) 820307
F: (01270) 820868

BAMFORD
Derbyshire

Pioneer House ♦♦♦♦
Station Road, Bamford, Hope Valley S33 0BN
T: (01433) 650638
E: pioneerhouse@yahoo.co.uk
I: www.pioneerhouse.co.uk

The Snake Pass Inn ♦♦
Ashopton Woodlands, Bamford, Hope Valley S33 0BJ
T: (01433) 651480
F: (01433) 651480

BARBER BOOTH
Derbyshire

Brookfield Guesthouse ♦♦♦
Brookfield, Edale, Barber Booth, Edale, Sheffield S33 7ZL
T: (01433) 670227

BARDNEY
Lincolnshire

The Black Horse ♦♦♦
16 Wragby Road, Bardney, Lincoln LN3 5XL
T: (01526) 398900
F: (01526) 399281
E: black-horse@lineone.net

Hawthorns Guesthouse
◆◆◆◆
53 Station Road, Bardney, Lincoln LN3 5UD
T: (01526) 398024
F: (01526) 398024
E: hawthornsguesthouse@btopenworld.com

BARKSTON
Lincolnshire

Kelling House
Rating Applied For
17 West Street, Barkston, Grantham NG32 2NL
T: (01400) 251440
E: sue.evans7@btopenworld.com
I: www.southwestlincs.com/skdc.com

BARLASTON
Staffordshire

Hurden Hall Farm ◆◆◆
Barlaston, Stoke-on-Trent ST12 9AZ
T: (01782) 372378
F: (01782) 372378

Wedgwood Memorial College
◆◆◆
Station Road, Barlaston, Stoke-on-Trent ST12 9DG
T: (01782) 372105
F: (01782) 372393
E: wedgwood.college@staffordshire.gov.uk
I: www.aredu.demon.co.uk/wedgwoodcollege

BARLBOROUGH
Derbyshire

Stone Croft Bed and Breakfast
◆◆◆
15 Church Street, Barlborough, Chesterfield S43 4ER
T: (01246) 810974
F: (01246) 810974

BARLOW
Derbyshire

Woodview Cottage ◆◆◆◆
Millcross Lane, Barlow, Dronfield S18 7TA
T: (0114) 289 0724
F: (0114) 289 0724

BARNBY MOOR
Nottinghamshire

White Horse Inn and Restaurant ◆◆◆
Great North Road, Barnby Moor, Retford DN22 8QS
T: (01777) 707721
F: (01777) 869445

BARROW-ON-TRENT
Derbyshire

5 Nook Cottages
◆◆◆◆ SILVER AWARD
The Nook, Barrow-on-Trent, Derby DE73 1NA
T: (01332) 702050
F: (01332) 705927
E: nookcottage@nookcottage.com
I: www.nookcottage.com

BARTESTREE
Herefordshire

Prospect Cottage Bed and Breakfast ◆◆◆
Bartestree, Hereford HR1 4BY
T: (01432) 851164
E: christine@prospectorganics.freeserve.co.uk

BARTON UNDER NEEDWOOD
Staffordshire

Fairfield Guest House
◆◆◆◆ SILVER AWARD
55 Main Street, Barton under Needwood, Burton upon Trent DE13 8AB
T: (01283) 716396
F: (01283) 716396
E: hotel@fairfield-uk.fsnet.co.uk
I: www.fairfield-hotel.com

Three Way Cottage ◆◆◆◆
2 Wales Lane, Barton under Needwood, Burton upon Trent DE13 8JF
T: (01283) 713572
E: marion@threewaycottage.fsnet.co.uk
I: http://communities.msn.co.uk/threewaycottagebedbreakfast

BASLOW
Derbyshire

Bubnell Cliff Farm ◆◆◆
Wheatlands Lane, Baslow, Bakewell DE45 1RF
T: (01246) 582454
E: c.k.mills@btinternet.com

Nether Croft ◆◆◆◆
Eaton Place, Baslow, Bakewell DE45 1RW
T: (01246) 583564
E: nethercroftB&B@aol.com

The Old School House
◆◆◆◆ SILVER AWARD
School Lane, Baslow, Bakewell DE45 1RZ
T: (01246) 582488
F: (01246) 583323
E: yvonnewright@talk21.com

BAUMBER
Lincolnshire

Baumber Park ◆◆◆◆
Baumber, Horncastle LN9 5NE
T: (01507) 578235
F: (01507) 578417

BAYSTON HILL
Shropshire

Lythwood Hall Bed and Breakfast ◆◆◆
2 Lythwood Hall, Lythwood, Bayston Hill, Shrewsbury SY3 0AD
T: 07074 874747
F: (07074) 874747
E: lythwoodhall@amserve.net
I: www.smoothhound.co.uk

BEESTON
Nottinghamshire

The Grove Guesthouse ◆◆◆
8 Grove Street, Beeston, Nottingham NG9 1JL
T: (0115) 925 9854
E: enquiries@groveguesthouse.co.uk
I: www.groveguesthouse.co.uk

Hylands Hotel ◆◆◆
Queens Road, Beeston, Nottingham NG9 1JB
T: (0115) 925 5472
F: (0115) 922 5574
E: hyland.hotel@btconnect.com
I: www.s-h-systems.co.uk/hotels/hylands.html

BELPER
Derbyshire

Amber Hills ◆◆◆◆
Belper Lane, Belper DE56 2UJ
T: (01773) 824080
F: (01773) 824080
E: amberhills@v21.me.uk

Broadhurst Bed and Breakfast
◆◆◆◆ SILVER AWARD
West Lodge, Bridge Hill, Belper DE56 2BY
T: (01773) 823596
F: (01773) 880810
E: stel.broadhurst@talk21.com

The Cedars ◆◆◆◆
Field Lane, Belper DE56 1DD
T: (01773) 824157
F: (01773) 825573
E: enquiries@derbyshire-holidays.com
I: www.derbyshire-holidays.com

Hill Top Farm ◆◆◆◆
80 Ashbourne Road, Cowers Lane, Belper DE56 2LF
T: (01773) 550338

The Old Shop ◆◆◆
10 Bakers Hill, Heage, Belper DE56 2BL
T: (01773) 856796

32 Spencer Road ◆◆◆◆
Belper DE56 1JY
T: (01773) 823877

BELTON IN RUTLAND
Rutland

The Old Rectory ◆◆◆
4 New Road, Belton in Rutland, Oakham LE15 9LE
T: (01572) 717279
F: (01572) 717343
E: bb@iepuk.com

BENNIWORTH
Lincolnshire

Glebe Farm
◆◆◆◆ SILVER AWARD
Benniworth, Market Rasen LN8 6JP
T: (01507) 313231
F: (01507) 313231
E: info@glebe-farm.com
I: www.glebe-farm.com

BENTHALL
Shropshire

Hilltop House ◆◆◆◆
Bridge Road, Benthall, Broseley TF12 5RB
T: (01952) 884821
E: hilltophouse@ukonline.co.uk
I: www.smoothhound.co.uk/hotels/hilltop.html

BEOLEY
Worcestershire

Windmill Hill ◆◆◆◆
Cherry Pit Lane, Beoley, Redditch B98 9DH
T: (01527) 62284
F: (01527) 64476
E: macotton@tinyworld.co.uk

BERKELEY
Gloucestershire

Pickwick Farm ◆◆◆
A38, Berkeley Heath, Berkeley GL13 9EU
T: (01453) 810241

BESTHORPE
Nottinghamshire

Lord Nelson Inn ◆◆◆
Main Road, Besthorpe, Newark NG23 7HR
T: (01636) 892265

BETLEY
Staffordshire

Adderley Green Farm
◆◆◆◆ SILVER AWARD
Heighley Lane, Betley, Crewe CW3 9BA
T: (01270) 820203
F: (01270) 820542
E: adderleygreenfarm@betley.fsbusiness.co.uk
I: www.adderleygreenfarm.freeserve.co.uk

BEWDLEY
Worcestershire

Kates Hill House
◆◆◆◆◆ GOLD AWARD
Red Hill, Bewdley DY12 2DR
T: (01299) 401563
F: (01299) 401563
E: kateshillhouse@aol.com

Lightmarsh Farm
◆◆◆◆ SILVER AWARD
Crundalls Lane, Bewdley DY12 1NE
T: (01299) 404027
I: www.farmstayworcs.co.uk

The Old Farmhouse ◆◆◆◆
Button Bridge, Bewdley DY12 3AW
T: (01299) 841277
F: (01299) 841277

Sydney Place ◆◆◆
7 Kidderminster Road, Bewdley DY12 1AQ
T: (01299) 404832

BIBURY
Gloucestershire

Cotteswold House
◆◆◆◆ GOLD AWARD
Arlington, Bibury, Cirencester GL7 5ND
T: (01285) 740609
F: (01285) 740609
E: cotteswold.house@btconnect.com
I: http://home.btconnect.com/cotteswold.house

The William Morris Bed & Breakfast
◆◆◆◆ GOLD AWARD
11 The Street, Bibury, Cirencester GL7 5NP
T: (01285) 740555
I: www.thewilliammorris.com

BICKENHILL
West Midlands

Church Farm Accommodation
◆◆
Church Farm, Church Lane, Bickenhill, Solihull B92 0DN
T: (01675) 442641
F: (01675) 442905

BIDDULPH
Staffordshire

Chapel Croft Bed and Breakfast ◆◆◆◆
Newtown Road, Biddulph Park, Biddulph, Stoke-on-Trent ST8 7SW
T: (01782) 511013
E: chapelcroft@biddulphpark.freeserve.co.uk
I: www.chapelcroft.com

BIDFORD-ON-AVON
Warwickshire

Avonview House ♦♦♦♦
Stratford Road, Bidford-on-Avon, Alcester B50 4LU
T: (01789) 778667
F: (01789) 778667
E: avonview@talk21.com

Brook Leys Bed and Breakfast ♦♦♦♦
Honeybourne Road, Bidford-on-Avon, Alcester B50 4PD
T: (01789) 772785
F: (01789) 774061
E: brookleys@amserve.net
I: www.brookleys.co.uk

Broom Hall Inn ♦♦♦
Bidford Road, Broom, Alcester B50 4HE
T: (01789) 773757
F: (01789) 778741

Fosbroke House ♦♦♦♦
4 High Street, Bidford-on-Avon, Warwick B50 4BU
T: (01789) 772327
F: (01789) 772327
E: mark@swiftvilla.fsnet.co.uk
I: www.smoothhound.co.uk/hotels/fosbroke

The Harbour ♦♦♦♦
Salford Road, Bidford-on-Avon, Alcester B50 4EN
T: (01789) 772975
E: pwarwick@theharbour-gh.co.uk
I: www.theharbour-gh.co.uk

BIGGIN-BY-HARTINGTON
Derbyshire

The Kings at Ivy House ♦♦♦♦ GOLD AWARD
Biggin-by-Hartington, Buxton SK17 0DT
T: (01298) 84709
F: (01298) 84710
E: kings.ivyhouse@lineone.net
I: www.SmoothHound.co.uk/hotels/kingsivy.html

BILLINGHAY
Lincolnshire

Old Mill Crafts ♦♦♦
8 Mill Lane, Billinghay, Lincoln LN4 4ES
T: (01526) 861996

BIRCH VALE
Derbyshire

Spinney Cottage ♦♦♦♦
Spinnerbottom, Birch Vale, High Peak SK22 1BL
T: (01663) 743230

BIRDLIP
Gloucestershire

Beechmount ♦♦♦
Birdlip, Gloucester GL4 8JH
T: (01452) 862262
F: (01452) 862262
E: thebeechmount@breathemail.net
I: www.thebeechmount.co.uk

BIRMINGHAM
West Midlands

Alden ♦♦♦
7 Elmdon Road, Marston Green, Birmingham B37 7BS
T: (0121) 779 2063
F: (0121) 788 0898

Atholl Lodge ♦♦♦
16 Elmdon Road, Acocks Green, Birmingham B27 6LH
T: (0121) 707 4417
F: (0121) 707 4417
E: davey@which.net

Central Guest House ♦♦♦
1637 Coventry Road, South Yardley, Birmingham B26 1DD
T: (0121) 706 7757
F: (0121) 706 7757
E: mmou826384@aol.com
I: www.centralguesthouse.com

Clay Towers ♦♦♦♦
51 Frankley Beeches Road, Northfield, Birmingham B31 5AB
T: (0121) 628 0053
F: (0121) 628 0053
I: www.claytowers.co.uk

Cook House Hotel ♦♦
425 Hagley Road, Edgbaston, Birmingham B17 8BL
T: (0121) 429 1916

Elmdon Guest House ♦♦♦
2369 Coventry Road, Sheldon, Birmingham B26 3PN
T: (0121) 742 1626
F: (0121) 742 1626
E: maurice66@blueyonder.co.uk

The Glades Guest House ♦♦♦
2469 Coventry Road, Sheldon, Birmingham B26 3PP
T: (0121) 742 1871
F: (0121) 742 1972

Greenway House Hotel ♦♦
978 Warwick Road, Acocks Green, Birmingham B27 6QG
T: (0121) 706 1361
F: (0121) 706 1361

Homelea ♦♦♦
2399 Coventry Road, Sheldon, Birmingham B26 3PN
T: (0121) 742 0017
F: (0121) 688 1879

Kensington Guest House Hotel ♦♦♦
785 Pershore Road, Selly Park, Birmingham B29 7LR
T: (0121) 472 7086
F: (0121) 472 5520
E: mail@kensingtonhotel.co.uk
I: www.kensingtonhotel.co.uk

Knowle Lodge Hotel ♦♦
423 Hagley Road, Edgbaston, Birmingham B17 8BL
T: (0121) 429 8366

Rollason Wood Hotel ♦♦
130 Wood End Road, Erdington, Birmingham B24 8BJ
T: (0121) 373 1230
F: (0121) 382 2578
E: rollwood@globalnet.co.uk

Woodville House ♦
39 Portland Road, Edgbaston, Birmingham B16 9HN
T: (0121) 454 0274
F: (0121) 454 5965

BISHOP'S CASTLE
Shropshire

Broughton Farm ♦♦♦
Bishop's Castle SY15 6SZ
T: (01588) 638393
F: (01588) 638393
E: broughtonfarm@micro-plus-web.net
I: www.virtual-shropshire.co.uk/lower-broughton-farm

The Castle Hotel ♦♦♦
The Square, Bishop's Castle SY9 5BN
T: (01588) 638403
F: (01588) 638403
I: www.bishops-castle.co.uk/castlehotel

Old Time ♦♦
29 High Street, Bishop's Castle SY9 5BE
T: (01588) 638467
F: (01588) 638467
E: jane@oldtime.co.uk
I: www.oldtime.co.uk

Shuttocks Wood ♦♦♦♦
Norbury, Bishop's Castle SY9 5EA
T: (01588) 650433
F: (01588) 650492
E: shuttockswood@btconnect.com
I: www.smoothhound.co.uk/hotels/shuttock.html

The Sun at Norbury ♦♦♦♦
Norbury, Bishop's Castle SY9 5DX
T: (01588) 650680
E: suninn.norbury@virgin.net
I: freespace.virgin.net/suninn.norbury

BISHOP'S CLEEVE
Gloucestershire

Manor Cottage ♦♦
41 Station Road, Bishop's Cleeve, Cheltenham GL52 8HH
T: (01242) 673537

BLACKMINSTER
Worcestershire

The Wheatsheaf Inn Rating Applied For
High Street, Badsey, Evesham WR11 7EW
T: (01386) 830380
F: (01386) 830380

BLEDINGTON
Gloucestershire

Kings Head Inn and Restaurant ♦♦♦♦ SILVER AWARD
The Green, Bledington, Oxford OX7 6XQ
T: (01608) 658365
F: (01608) 658902
E: kingshead@orr-ewing.com
I: www.kingsheadinn.net

BLOCKLEY
Gloucestershire

Arreton House ♦♦♦♦ SILVER AWARD
Station Road, Blockley, Moreton-in-Marsh GL56 9DT
T: (01386) 701077
F: (01386) 701077
E: bandb@arreton.demon.uk
I: www.arreton.demon.co.uk

Claremont Bed & Breakfast ♦♦♦♦
The Greenway, Blockley, Moreton-in-Marsh GL56 9BQ
T: (01386) 700744
F: (01386) 700412
E: enquiries@claremontbandb.co.uk
I: www.claremontbandb.co.uk

Mill Dene ♦♦♦♦ SILVER AWARD
Mill Dene, Blockley, Moreton-in-Marsh GL56 9HU
T: (01386) 700457
F: (01386) 700526
E: wendy@milldene.co.uk
I: www.milldene.co.uk

The Old Bakery ♦♦♦♦♦ GOLD AWARD
High Street, Blockley, Moreton-in-Marsh GL56 9EU
T: (01386) 700408
F: (01386) 700408

BOBBINGTON
Staffordshire

Blakelands Country Guest House and Restaurant ♦♦♦♦
Halfpenny Green, Bobbington, Stourbridge DY7 5DP
T: (01384) 221000
F: (01384) 221585
E: enquiries@blakelands.com
I: www.blakelands.com

BONSALL
Derbyshire

The Old School House ♦♦♦
The Dale, Bonsall, Matlock DE4 2AY
T: (01629) 826017

BOSTON
Lincolnshire

Bramley House ♦♦♦
267 Sleaford Road, Boston PE21 7PQ
T: (01205) 354538
F: (01205) 354538

The Chestnuts ♦♦♦♦
117 London Road, Boston PE21 7EZ
T: (01205) 354435
F: (01205) 366662
E: 113015.2032@compuserve.com

Dovedale ♦♦♦
90 Pilleys Lane, Boston PE21 9RB
T: (01205) 360723

Fairfield Guest House ♦♦♦
101 London Road, Boston PE21 7EN
T: (01205) 362869

Park Lea Guest House ♦♦♦
Norfolk Street, Boston PE21 6PE
T: (01205) 356309
E: park.lea@btopenworld.com

The Poachers Inn ♦♦♦
A52 Swineshead Road, Kirton Holme, Boston PE20 1SQ
T: (01205) 290310
E: info@poachers-inn.co.uk
I: www.poachers-inn-co.uk

107 Spilsby Road ♦♦♦♦
Boston PE21 9PE
T: (01205) 352145

Ye Olde Magnet Tavern ♦
South Square, Boston PE21 6HE
T: (01205) 369186

BOTTESFORD
Leicestershire

The Thatch Hotel & Restaurant ♦♦♦♦
26 High Street, Bottesford, Nottingham NG13 0AA
T: (01949) 842330
F: (01949) 844407
E: thatch.hotelrestaurant@btinternet.com
I: www.thatchhotel.co.uk

BOURNE
Lincolnshire

Mill House ♦♦♦♦
64 North Road, Bourne PE10 9BU
T: (01778) 422278
F: (01778) 422546
E: millhousebnb@fsbdial.co.uk

BOURTON-ON-THE-WATER
Gloucestershire

Alderley Guesthouse Rating Applied For
Rissington Road, Bourton-on-the-Water, Cheltenham GL54 2DX
T: (01451) 822788
F: (01451) 822788
E: alderleyguesthouse@hotmail.com
I: www.AlderleyGuestHouse.com

Bourton Lodge ♦♦♦♦
Whiteshoots Hill, Bourton-on-the-Water, Cheltenham GL54 2LE
T: (01451) 820387
F: (01451) 812821

Broadlands Guest House ♦♦♦♦
Clapton Row, Bourton-on-the-Water, Cheltenham GL54 2DN
T: (01451) 822002
F: (01451) 821776
E: marco@broadlands-guest-house.co.uk
I: www.broadlands-guest-house.co.uk

Chestnuts Bed & Breakfast ♦♦♦♦
The Chestnuts, High Street, Bourton-on-the-Water, Cheltenham GL54 2AN
T: (01451) 820244
F: (01451) 820558
E: chestnutsbb@aol.com
I: www.smoothhound.co.uk/hotels/chestnutsbb.html

Coach and Horses ♦♦♦♦
Fosseway, A429, Bourton-on-the-Water, Cheltenham GL54 2HN
T: (01451) 821064
F: (01451) 810570
E: info@coach-horses.co.uk
I: www.coach-horses.co.uk

Coombe House ♦♦♦♦ SILVER AWARD
Rissington Road, Bourton-on-the-Water, Cheltenham GL54 2DT
T: (01451) 821966
F: (01451) 810477
E: coombe.house@virgin.net
I: www.2staggs.com

Cotswold Bed and Breakfast Rooftrees ♦♦♦♦
Rissington Road, Bourton-on-the-Water, Cheltenham GL54 2DX
T: (01451) 821943
F: (01451) 810614

Cotswold Carp Farm ♦♦♦♦
Bury Barn Lane, Bourton-on-the-Water, Cheltenham GL54 2HB
T: (01451) 821795

The Cotswold House ♦♦♦
Lansdowne, Bourton-on-the-Water, Cheltenham GL54 2AR
T: (01451) 822373

Elvington Bed and Breakfast ♦♦♦♦
Elvington, Rissington Road, Bourton-on-the-Water, Cheltenham GL54 2DX
T: (01451) 822026
F: (01451) 822026
E: the@tuckwells.freeserve.co.uk
I: www.bandb.fsnet.co.uk

Fairlie ♦♦♦
Riverside, Bourton-on-the-Water, Cheltenham GL54 2DP
T: (01451) 821842
F: (01451) 821842

Farncombe ♦♦♦♦
Clapton, Bourton-on-the-Water, Cheltenham GL54 2LG
T: (01451) 820120
F: (01451) 820120
E: jwrightbb@aol.com
I: www.SmoothHound.co.uk/hotels/farncomb.html and www.farncombecotswolds.com

Kingsbridge and Chester House Hotel ♦♦♦
Victoria Street, Bourton-on-the-Water, Cheltenham GL54 2BU
T: (01451) 820286
F: (01451) 820471
E: kingsbridgeinn.bourtononthewater@eldridge.pope.co.uk
I: www.roomathteinn.info

Lamb Inn ♦♦♦♦
Great Rissington, Bourton-on-the-Water, Cheltenham GL54 2LP
T: (01451) 820388
F: (01451) 820724
I: www.thelamb-inn.com

Lansdowne House ♦♦♦♦
Lansdowne, Bourton-on-the-Water, Cheltenham GL54 2AT
T: (01451) 820812
F: (01451) 822484
E: heart@lansdownehouse.co.uk
I: www.lansdownehouse.co.uk

Lansdowne Villa Guest House ♦♦♦♦
Lansdown, Bourton-on-the-Water, Cheltenham GL54 2AR
T: (01451) 820673
F: (01451) 822099
E: lansdownevilla@aol.com
I: www.lansdownevilla.co.uk

Larch House ♦♦♦♦♦ GOLD AWARD
Station Road, Bourton-on-the-Water, Cheltenham GL54 2AA
T: (01451) 821172
F: (01451) 821172
I: www.s-n-systems.co.uk/hotels/larchhse

The Lawns ♦♦♦♦
Station Road, Bourton-on-the-Water, Cheltenham GL54 2ER
T: (01451) 821195
F: (01451) 821195

Manor Close ♦♦♦♦ SILVER AWARD
High Street, Bourton-on-the-Water, Cheltenham GL54 2AP
T: (01451) 820339

Mousetrap Inn ♦♦♦
Lansdowne, Bourton-on-the-Water, Cheltenham GL54 2AR
T: (01451) 820579
F: (01451) 822393
E: mtinn@waverider.co.uk
I: www.mousetrap-inn.co.uk

The Painted House ♦♦♦♦♦ SILVER AWARD
Rissington Road, Bourton-on-the-Water, Cheltenham GL54 2DZ
T: (01451) 822357
F: (01451) 822357
E: paintedhouse@bourton-cotswolds.fsnet.co.uk
I: http://mysite.freeserve.com/thepaintedhouse

The Ridge Guesthouse ♦♦♦♦ SILVER AWARD
Whiteshoots Hill, Bourton-on-the-Water, Cheltenham GL54 2LE
T: (01451) 820660
F: (01451) 822448
E: info@theridge-guesthouse.co.uk
I: www.theridge-guesthouse.co.uk

Station Villa ♦♦♦
2 Station Villa, Station Road, Bourton-on-the-Water, Cheltenham GL54 2ER
T: (01451) 810406
F: (01451) 821359
E: rooms@stationvilla.com
I: www.stationvilla.com

Strathspey ♦♦♦♦ SILVER AWARD
Lansdowne, Bourton-on-the-Water, Cheltenham GL54 2AR
T: (01451) 820694
F: (01451) 821466
E: mel@strathspey-bed.fsnet.co.uk

Sycamore House ♦♦♦
Lansdowne, Bourton-on-the-Water, Cheltenham GL54 2AR
T: (01451) 821647

Touchstone ♦♦♦♦ SILVER AWARD
Little Rissington, Bourton-on-the-Water, Cheltenham GL54 2ND
T: (01451) 822481
F: (01451) 822481
E: touchstone.bb@lineone.net
I: website.lineone.net/~touchstone.bb

Trevone Bed & Breakfast ♦♦♦
Moore Road, Bourton-on-the-Water, Cheltenham GL54 2AZ
T: (01451) 822852

Upper Farm ♦♦♦♦♦
Clapton on the Hill, Bourton-on-the-Water, Cheltenham GL54 2LG
T: (01451) 820453
F: (01451) 810185
I: www.tuckedup.com/upperfarm.html

Whiteshoots Cottage Bed and Breakfast ♦♦♦♦
Whiteshoots Hill, Fosseway, Bourton-on-the-Water, Cheltenham GL54 2LE
T: (01451) 822698
E: whiteshootscottage@talk21.com

Willow Crest ♦♦♦♦
Rissington Road, Bourton-on-the-Water, Cheltenham GL54 2DZ
T: (01451) 822073

BOYLESTONE
Derbyshire

Lees Hall Farm ♦♦♦
Boylestone, Ashbourne DE6 5AA
T: (01335) 330259
F: (01335) 330259

BRACKLEY
Northamptonshire

Astwell Mill ♦♦♦♦
Helmdon, Brackley NN13 5QU
T: (01295) 760507
F: (01295) 768602
E: astwell01@aol.com
I: www.astwellmill.co.uk

Brackley House Private Hotel ♦♦♦♦ SILVER AWARD
Brackley House, 4 High Street, Brackley NN13 7DT
T: (01280) 701550
F: (01280) 704965
E: sales@brackleyhouse.com
I: www.brackleyhouse.com

7 Cross Keys Court ♦♦♦
Brackley NN13 6PH
T: (01280) 705734

Floral Hall Guest House ♦♦
50 Valley Road, Brackley NN13 7DQ
T: (01280) 702950
E: floralhallguesthouse@talk21.com

Hill Farm ♦♦♦♦
Halse, Brackley NN13 6DY
T: (01280) 703300
F: (01280) 704999
E: jg.robinson@farmline.com

Sharal House ♦♦♦
17 Burwell Hill, Brackley NN13 7AS
T: (01280) 706365

The Thatches ♦♦♦
Whitfield, Brackley NN13 5TQ
T: (01280) 850358

Walltree House Farm ♦♦♦♦
Steane, Brackley NN13 5NS
T: (01295) 811235
F: (01295) 811147

Establishments printed in blue have a detailed entry in this guide

BRADNOP
Staffordshire

Middle Farm ♦♦♦
Apesford, Bradnop, Leek
ST13 7EX
T: (01538) 382839
F: (01538) 382839

BRADWELL
Derbyshire

Stoney Ridge
♦♦♦♦ SILVER AWARD
Granby Road, Bradwell, Hope Valley S33 9HU
T: (01433) 620538
F: (01433) 623154
E: toneyridge@aol.com
I: www.cressbrook.co.uk/hopev/stoneyridge

Travellers Rest
Rating Applied For
Brough Lane End, Brough, Bradwell, Hope Valley S33 9HG
T: (01433) 620363
F: (01433) 623338
E: elliottstephen@btconnect.com
I: www.travellers-rest.net

BRAILES
Warwickshire

Agdon Farm ♦♦♦
Brailes, Banbury OX15 5JJ
T: (01608) 685226
F: (01608) 685226
E: maggie_cripps@hotmail.com

BRAMPTON
Derbyshire

Brampton Guesthouse ♦♦
75 Old Road, Off Chatsworth Road, Brampton, Chesterfield
S40 2QU
T: (01246) 276533
F: (01246) 211636
E: guesthouse@oldroadbrampton.freeserve.co.uk

BRAMSHALL
Staffordshire

Bowmore House ♦♦♦♦
Stone Road, Bramshall, Uttoxeter ST14 8SH
T: (01889) 564452
F: (01889) 564452
E: glovatt@furoris.com

BRASSINGTON
Derbyshire

Ivy Bank House
♦♦♦♦ SILVER AWARD
Church Street, Brassington, Matlock DE4 4HJ
T: (01629) 540818
E: june@ivybankhouse.co.uk
I: www.ivybankhouse.co.uk

The Old Barn ♦♦♦♦
Middle Lane, Brassington, Matlock DE4 4HL
T: (01629) 540317
E: tyler.family@lineone.net

BREAM
Gloucestershire

Lindum House Bed and Breakfast ♦♦♦
Oakwood Road, Bream, Lydney
GL15 6HS
T: (01594) 562051
E: lynne@lindumhouse.fsworld.co.uk
I: www.geocities.com/lynch63uk

BREDON
Worcestershire

Round Bank House ♦♦♦♦
Lampitt Lane, Bredon's Norton, Tewkesbury GL20 7HB
T: (01684) 772983
F: (01684) 773035

Royal Oak Inn ♦♦♦♦
Main Road, Bredon, Tewkesbury
GL20 7LW
T: (01684) 772393
I: royal_oak@btopenworld.com

BREDWARDINE
Herefordshire

Old Court Farm ♦♦♦
Bredwardine, Hereford HR3 6BT
T: (01981) 500375
E: whittall@oldcourt74.co.uk

The Red Lion Hotel
Rating Applied For
Bredwardine, Hereford HR3 6BU
T: (01981) 500303
F: (01981) 500400
E: info@redlion-hotel.com
I: www.redlion-hotel.com

BREWOOD
Staffordshire

The Blackladies
♦♦♦♦♦ GOLD AWARD
Kiddemore Green Road, Brewood, Stafford ST19 9BH
T: (01902) 850210
F: (01902) 851782

BRIDGNORTH
Shropshire

Bassa Villa Bar and Grill ♦♦♦
48 Cartway, Bridgnorth
WV16 4BG
T: (01746) 763977
F: (01952) 691604
E: sugarloaf@globalnet.co.uk
I: www.smoothhound.co.uk/hotels/bassavilla.html

Bulls Head Inn ♦♦♦♦
Chelmarsh, Bridgnorth
WV16 6BA
T: (01746) 861469
F: (01746) 862646
E: dave@bullshead.fsnet.co.uk
I: www.virtual-shropshire.co.uk/bulls-head-inn

The Croft Hotel ♦♦♦
St Mary's Street, Bridgnorth
WV16 4DW
T: (01746) 762416
F: (01746) 767431
E: crofthotel@aol.com

Dinney Farm ♦♦
Chelmarsh, Bridgnorth
WV16 6AU
T: (01746) 861070
F: (01746) 861002
E: hedley.southport@virgin.net
I: www.smoothhound.co.uk/hotels/dinney.html

The Golden Lion Inn ♦♦♦
83 High Street, Bridgnorth
WV16 4DS
T: (01746) 762016
F: (01746) 762016
E: jeff@goldenlionbridgnorth.co.uk
I: www.goldenlionbridgnorth.co.uk

Haven Pasture ♦♦♦♦
Underton, Bridgnorth WV16 6TY
T: (01746) 789632
F: (01746) 789333
E: havenpasture@underton.co.uk
I: www.underton.co.uk

Linley Crest
♦♦♦♦ SILVER AWARD
Linley Brook, Bridgnorth
WV16 4SZ
T: (01746) 765527
F: (01746) 765527
E: linleycrest@easicom.com
I: www.linleycrest.co.uk

The Old House ♦♦♦
Hilton, Bridgnorth WV15 5PJ
T: (01746) 716560
F: (01746) 716280
E: oldhousehilton@hotmail.com
I: www.oldhousehilton.co.uk

Pen-y-Ghent ♦♦♦
7 Sabrina Road, Bridgnorth
WV15 6DQ
T: (01746) 762880
E: firman.margret@freeuk.com
I: pen-y-ghent.8m.com

Saint Leonards Gate ♦♦♦
6 Church Street, Bridgnorth
WV16 4EQ
T: (01746) 766647

Sandward Guesthouse ♦♦♦
47 Cartway, Bridgnorth
WV16 4BG
T: (01746) 765913
E: sandward@amserve.net
I: www.virtual-shropshire.co.uk/sandward

BRIGSTOCK
Northamptonshire

Park Holm B&B ♦♦♦
9 Sudborough Road, Brigstock, Kettering NN14 3HP
T: (01536) 373835
E: parkholm@northamptonshire.co.uk
I: www.northamptonshire.co.uk/hotels/parkholm.htm

BRIMPSFIELD
Gloucestershire

Highcroft
♦♦♦♦♦ GOLD AWARD
Brimpsfield, Gloucester GL4 8LF
T: (01452) 862405

BRINKLOW
Warwickshire

White Lion ♦♦♦
32 Broad Street, Brinklow, Rugby CV23 0LN
T: (01788) 832579
F: (01788) 833844
E: brinklowlion@aol.com
I: www.thewhitelion-inn.co.uk

BROAD CAMPDEN
Gloucestershire

Marnic House
♦♦♦♦ GOLD AWARD
Broad Campden, Chipping Campden GL55 6UR
T: (01386) 840014
F: (01386) 840441
E: marnic@zoom.co.uk

BROADWAY
Worcestershire

Barn House
♦♦♦♦ SILVER AWARD
152 High Street, Broadway
WR12 7AJ
T: (01386) 858633
F: (01386) 858633
E: barnhouse@btinternet.com
I: www.btinternet.com/~barnhouse/

The Bell at Willersey ♦♦♦♦
The Bell Inn, Willersey, Broadway
WR12 7PJ
T: (01386) 858405
F: (01386) 853563
E: reservations@bellatwillersey.fsnet.co.uk
I: www.the-bell-willersey.com

Bourne House ♦♦♦
Leamington Road, Broadway
WR12 7DZ
T: (01386) 853486
E: kate.zuill@virgin.net
I: www.broadwayguesthouse.co.uk

Burhill Farm
♦♦♦♦♦ GOLD AWARD
Buckland, Broadway WR12 7LY
T: (01386) 858171
F: (01386) 858171
E: burhillfarm@yahoo.co.uk
I: www.burhillfarm.co.uk

Crown and Trumpet Inn ♦♦♦
Church Street, Broadway
WR12 7AE
T: (01386) 853202
E: ascott@cotswoldholidays.co.uk
I: www.cotswoldholidays.co.uk

Dove Cottage ♦♦♦♦
Colletts Fields, Broadway
WR12 7AT
T: (01386) 859085
I: www.broadway-cotswolds.co.uk

The Driffold Guest House
♦♦♦
Murcot Turn, Broadway
WR12 7HT
T: (01386) 830825
F: (01386) 830825
E: cotswold.bb@ntlworld.com
I: www.cotswoldsguesthouse.co.uk

Highlands Country House Bed and Breakfast ♦♦♦♦
Highlands, Fish Hill, Broadway
WR12 7LD
T: (01386) 858015
F: (01386) 852584
E: sue@adames.demon.co.uk

Horse and Hound ♦♦♦♦
54 High Street, Broadway
WR12 7DT
T: (01386) 852287
I: info@horseandhoundinn.com

Leasow House
♦♦♦♦ SILVER AWARD
Laverton Meadow, Broadway
WR12 7NA
T: (01386) 584526
F: (01386) 584596
E: leasow@clara.net
I: www.leasow.co.uk

Lowerfield Farm
◆◆◆◆ SILVER AWARD
Willersey, Broadway WR11 7hf
T: (01386) 858273
F: (01386) 854608
E: info@lowerfield-farm.co.uk
I: www.lowerfield-farm.co.uk

Mount Pleasant Farm ◆◆◆◆
Childswickham, Broadway
WR12 7HZ
T: (01386) 853424
F: (01386) 853424
E: helen@mount-pleasant.fslife.co.uk
I: www.smoothhound.co.uk

Old Stationhouse ◆◆◆◆
Station Drive, Broadway
WR12 7DF
T: (01386) 852659
F: (01386) 852891
E: oldstationhouse@eastbank-broadway.fsnet.co.uk
I: www.broadway-cotswolds.co.uk/oldstationhouse.html

Olive Branch Guest House
◆◆◆◆ SILVER AWARD
78 High Street, Broadway
WR12 7AJ
T: (01386) 853440
F: (01386) 859070
E: broadway@theolive-branch.co.uk
I: www.theolivebranch-broadway.com

Pathlow House ◆◆◆
82 High Street, Broadway
WR12 7AJ
T: (01386) 853444
F: (01386) 853444
E: pathlow@aol.com
I: www.pathlowguesthouse.co.uk

Sheepscombe House
◆◆◆◆ SILVER AWARD
Snowshill, Broadway WR12 7JU
T: (01386) 853769
F: (01386) 853769
E: reservations@snowshill-broadway.co.uk
I: www.broadway-cotswolds.co.uk

Shenberrow Hill ◆◆◆◆
Stanton, Broadway WR12 7NE
T: (01386) 584468
F: (01386) 584468
E: michael.neilan@talk21.com
I: www.cotswold-way.co.uk

Small Talk Lodge ◆◆◆
2 Keil Close, 32 High Street,
Broadway WR12 7DP
T: (01386) 858953
E: kathybarnes@totalise.com
I: www.broadway-cotswolds.co.uk

Southwold Guest House
◆◆◆◆ SILVER AWARD
Station Road, Broadway
WR12 7DE
T: (01386) 853681
F: (01386) 854610
E: susan.smiles1@btopenworld.com
I: www.broadway-southwold.co.uk

Whiteacres
◆◆◆◆ SILVER AWARD
Station Road, Broadway
WR12 7DE
T: (01386) 852320
F: (01386) 852674
E: whiteacres@btinternet.com
I: www.whiteacres.btinternet.co.uk

Windrush House
◆◆◆◆ SILVER AWARD
Station Road, Broadway
WR12 7DE
T: (01386) 853577
F: (01386) 853790
E: richard@broadway-windrush.co.uk
I: www.broadway-windrush.co.uk

BROADWELL
Gloucestershire

The White House ◆◆◆
2 South Road, Broadwell,
Coleford GL16 7BH
T: (01594) 837069
F: (01594) 832325
E: info@whitehousebroadwell.co.uk
I: www.whitehousebroadwell.co.uk

BROMSGROVE
Worcestershire

Bea's Lodge ◆◆
245 Pennine Road, Bromsgrove
B61 0TN
T: (01527) 877613

The Durrance ◆◆◆◆
Berry Lane, Upton Warren,
Bromsgrove B61 9EL
T: (01562) 777533
F: (01562) 777533
E: helenhirons@thedurrance.co.uk
I: www.thedurrance.co.uk

Fox Hollies ◆◆◆
78 New Road, Bromsgrove
B60 2LA
T: (01527) 574870

Merrivale ◆◆◆◆
309 Old Birmingham Road,
Lickey, Bromsgrove B60 1HQ
T: (0121) 445 1694
F: (0121) 445 1694
E: smithmerrivale@amserve.net

Overwood Bed and Breakfast ◆◆◆◆
Woodcote Lane, Woodcote,
Bromsgrove B61 9EE
T: (01562) 777193
F: (01562) 777689
E: info@overwood.net
I: www.overwood.net

Sprite House ◆◆◆
58 Stratford Road, Bromsgrove
B60 1AU
T: (01527) 874565
F: (01527) 870935

BROMYARD
Herefordshire

The Falcon Hotel ◆◆◆
Broad Street, Bromyard HR7 4BT
T: (01885) 483034
F: (01885) 488818

Linton Brook Farm ◆◆◆◆
Malvern Road, Bringsty,
Worcester WR6 5TR
T: (01885) 488875
F: (01885) 488875

The Old Cowshed
◆◆◆◆ SILVER AWARD
Avenbury Court Farm, Bromyard
HR7 4LA
T: (01885) 482384
F: (01885) 482367
E: combes@cowshed.uk.com
I: www.cowshed.uk.com

BROSELEY
Shropshire

Broseley House ◆◆◆◆
1 The Square, Broseley TF12 5EW
T: (01952) 882043
E: info@broseleyhouse.co.uk
I: www.broseleyhouse.co.uk

The Cumberland Hotel ◆◆◆
Jackson Avenue, Broseley
TF12 5NB
T: (01952) 882301
F: (01952) 884438

The Lion Hotel ◆◆◆◆
High Street, Broseley TF12 5EZ
T: (01952) 881128
F: (01952) 881128

Rock Dell
◆◆◆◆ SILVER AWARD
30 Ironbridge Road, Broseley
TF12 5AJ
T: (01952) 883054
F: (01952) 883054
E: rockdell@ukgateway.net

BROXHOLME
Lincolnshire

Carrier's Farm ◆◆◆◆
Broxholme, Lincoln LN1 2NG
T: (01522) 702976
E: igilkison@aaugonline.net

BROXWOOD
Herefordshire

Broxwood Court
◆◆◆◆◆ GOLD AWARD
Broxwood, Leominster HR6 9JJ
T: (01544) 340245
F: (01544) 340573
E: mikeanne@broxwood.kc3.co.uk

BRYN
Shropshire

Birches Mill
◆◆◆◆ SILVER AWARD
Clun, Craven Arms SY7 8NL
T: (01588) 640409
F: (01588) 640409
E: gill@birchesmill.fsnet.co.uk
I: www.virtual-shropshire.co.uk/birchesmill

BUCKMINSTER
Leicestershire

The Tollemache Arms ◆◆◆◆
48 Main Street, Buckminster,
Grantham NG33 5SA
T: (01476) 860252
F: (01476) 860731
E: info@tollemachearms.co.uk
I: www.tollemachearms.co.uk

BUCKNELL
Shropshire

The Hall ◆◆◆
Bucknell SY7 0AA
T: (01547) 530249
F: (01547) 530249
E: thehallbucknell@hotmail.com
I: www.smoothhound.co.uk/hotels/thehall.html

The Willows ◆◆◆◆
Bucknell, Ludlow SY7 0AA
T: (01547) 530201
E: the_willows@btopenworld.com
I: www.willows-bucknell.co.uk

BUGBROOKE
Northamptonshire

The Byre
◆◆◆◆ SILVER AWARD
2 Church Lane, Bugbrooke,
Northampton NN7 3PB
T: (01604) 830319

BULLO PILL
Gloucestershire

Grove Farm ◆◆◆◆
Bullo Pill, Newnham-on-Severn
GL14 1DZ
T: (01594) 516304
F: (01594) 516304
E: davidandpennyhill@btopenworld.com

BURFORD
Shropshire

Greenway Head Farm ◆◆◆◆
Burford, Tenbury Wells
WR15 8HW
T: (01584) 819494
F: (01584) 819068
E: annabelamphlett@hotmail.com

BURLTON
Shropshire

Petton Hall Farm
◆◆◆◆ SILVER AWARD
Petton, Burlton, Shrewsbury
SY4 5TH
T: (01939) 270601
F: (01939) 270601
I: www.virtual-shropshire.co.uk/petton-hall-farm

BURTON DASSETT
Warwickshire

The White House Bed and Breakfast
◆◆◆◆ SILVER AWARD
Burton Dassett, Southam
CV47 2AB
T: (01295) 770143
F: (01295) 770143
E: lisa@whitehouse10.freeserve.co.uk
I: www.thewhitehousebandb.info

BURTON UPON TRENT
Staffordshire

Meadowview ◆◆◆
203 Newton Road, Winshill,
Burton upon Trent DE15 0TU
T: (01283) 564046

New Inn Farm ◆◆◆
Burton Road, Needwood, Burton
upon Trent DE13 9PB
T: (01283) 575435

Primrose Bank House ◆◆
194A Newton Road, Burton
upon Trent DE15 0TU
T: (01283) 532569

BUTTERTON
Staffordshire

Black Lion Inn ◆◆◆
Butterton, Leek ST13 7ST
T: (01538) 304232
E: theblacklion@clara.net
I: www.blacklioninn.co.uk

Butterton House ♦♦♦♦
Park Road, Butterton, Newcastle-under-Lyme ST5 4DZ
T: (01782) 619085
E: buttertonhouse@lineone.net
I: www.buttertonhouse.co.uk

Butterton Moor House ♦♦♦♦ SILVER AWARD
Parsons Lane, Butterton, Leek ST13 7PD
T: (01538) 304506
F: (01538) 304506

Coxon Green Farm ♦♦♦♦ SILVER AWARD
Butterton, Leek ST13 7TA
T: (01538) 304221

Heathy Roods Farm ♦♦♦♦
Butterton, Leek ST13 7SR
T: (01538) 304397
E: heathyroods@tiscali.co.uk

New Hayes Farm ♦♦♦♦
Trentham Road, Butterton, Newcastle-under-Lyme ST5 4DX
T: (01782) 680889
E: adamsjn5@aol.com
I: www.SmoothHound.co.uk/Hotels/newhayes.html

BUXTON
Derbyshire

Abbey Guest House ♦♦♦
43 South Avenue, Buxton SK17 6NQ
T: (01298) 26419
E: aghbuxton@aol.com

All Seasons Guest House ♦♦♦♦
4 Wye Grove, Buxton SK17 9AJ
T: (01298) 74628
E: chrisandruss@allseasonsguesthouse.fsnet.co.uk
I: www.allseasonsguesthouse.fsnet.co.uk

Avalon ♦♦
31 South Avenue, Buxton SK17 6NQ
T: (01298) 72667
E: AvalonBandB@aol.com

Braemar ♦♦♦♦
Compton Road, Buxton SK17 9DN
T: (01298) 78050
E: buxtonbraemar@supanet.com
I: www.cressbrook.co.uk/buxton/braemar

Buxton Hilbre Bed & Breakfast ♦♦♦
8 White Knowle Road, Buxton SK17 9NH
T: (01298) 22358
E: min@8whiteknowl.fsnet.co.uk

Buxton Lodge Guest House ♦♦♦
28 London Road, Buxton SK17 9NX
T: (01298) 23522

Buxton Wheelhouse Hotel ♦♦♦♦♦ SILVER AWARD
19 College Road, Buxton SK17 9DZ
T: (01298) 24869
F: (01298) 24869
E: lyndsie@buxton-wheelhouse.com
I: www.buxton-wheelhouse.com

Buxton's Victorian Guesthouse ♦♦♦♦♦ SILVER AWARD
3A Broad Walk, Buxton SK17 6JE
T: (01298) 78759
F: (01298) 74732
E: buxvic@tiscali.co.uk
I: www.buxtonvictorian.co.uk

Compton House Guesthouse ♦♦♦
4 Compton Road, Buxton SK17 9DN
T: (01298) 26926
F: (01298) 26926
E: comptonbuxton@aol.com
I: www.cressbrook.co.uk/buxton/compton

Cotesfield Farm ♦♦
Parsley Hay, Buxton SK17 0BD
T: (01298) 83256
F: (01298) 83256

Devonshire Arms ♦♦♦
Peak Forest, Buxton SK17 8EJ
T: (01298) 23875
F: (01298) 23598
E: fiona.clough@virgin.net
I: www.devarms.com

Devonshire Lodge Guesthouse ♦♦♦♦ SILVER AWARD
2 Manchester Road, Buxton SK17 6SB
T: (01298) 71487

Fairhaven ♦♦♦
1 Dale Terrace, Buxton SK17 6LU
T: (01298) 24481
F: (01298) 24481
E: paulandcatherine@fairhavenguesthouse.freeserve.co.uk
I: www.fairhavenbedandbreakfast.com

Grendon Guesthouse ♦♦♦♦♦ GOLD AWARD
Bishops Lane, Buxton SK17 6UN
T: (01298) 78831
F: (01298) 79257
E: parkerh1@talk21.com
I: www.grendonguesthouse.co.uk

Grosvenor House ♦♦♦♦
1 Broad Walk, Buxton SK17 6JE
T: (01298) 72439
F: (01298) 214185
E: grosvenor.buxton@btopenworld.com
I: www.grosvenorbuxton.co.uk

Harefield ♦♦♦♦ SILVER AWARD
15 Marlborough Road, Buxton SK17 6RD
T: (01298) 24029
F: (01298) 24029
E: hardie@harefield1.freeserve.co.uk
I: www.harefield1.freeserve.co.uk

Hawthorn Farm Guesthouse Rating Applied For
Fairfield Road, Buxton SK17 7ED
T: (01298) 23230
F: (01298) 71322

Kingscroft ♦♦♦♦ SILVER AWARD
10 Green Lane, Buxton SK17 9DP
T: (01298) 22757
F: (01298) 27858

Lakenham Guesthouse ♦♦♦♦
11 Burlington Road, Buxton SK17 9AL
T: (01298) 79209

Linden Lodge ♦♦♦♦
31 Temple Road, Buxton SK17 9BA
T: (01298) 27591
E: info@lindentreelodge.co.uk
I: www.lindentreelodge.co.uk

Lowther Guesthouse ♦♦♦♦
7 Hardwick Square West, Buxton SK17 6PX
T: (01298) 71479
E: enquiries@pritchardbuxton.fslife.co.uk
I: www.lowtherguesthouse.co.uk

Netherdale Guesthouse ♦♦♦♦
16 Green Lane, Buxton SK17 9DP
T: (01298) 23896
F: (01298) 73771

Nithen Cottage ♦♦♦♦ SILVER AWARD
123 Park Road, Buxton SK17 6SP
T: (01298) 24679
E: therogersons@freeuk.com

The Old Manse Private Hotel ♦♦♦
6 Clifton Road, Silverlands, Buxton SK17 6QL
T: (01298) 25638
F: (01298) 25638
E: old_manse@yahoo.co.uk
I: www.oldmanse.co.uk

The Queens Head Hotel ♦♦♦
High Street, Buxton SK17 6EU
T: (01298) 23841
F: (01298) 71238

Roseleigh Hotel ♦♦♦♦
19 Broad Walk, Buxton SK17 6JR
T: (01298) 24904
F: (01298) 24904
E: enquiries@roseleighhotel.co.uk
I: www.roseleighhotel.co.uk

Sevenways Guesthouse ♦♦♦
1 College Road, Buxton SK17 9DZ
T: (01298) 77809
F: (01298) 77809

Staden Grange Country House ♦♦♦
Staden Lane, Staden, Buxton SK17 9RZ
T: (01298) 24965
F: (01298) 72067
E: enquiries@stadengrange.co.uk
I: www.StadenGrange.co.uk

Stoneridge ♦♦♦♦ SILVER AWARD
9 Park Road, Buxton SK17 6SG
T: (01298) 26120
E: hoskin@stoneridge.co.uk
I: www.stoneridge.co.uk

Templeton Guesthouse ♦♦
Compton Road, Buxton SK17 9DN
T: (01298) 25275
F: (01298) 25275
E: tembux@lineone.net

Twelve Trees Guest House ♦♦♦♦
Twelve Trees, Burlington Road, Buxton SK17 9AL
T: (01298) 24371
E: info@buxtonlet.com
I: www.buxtonlet.com

BYFIELD
Northamptonshire

Glebe Farm Bed and Breakfast ♦♦♦
Glebe Farm, 61 Church Street, Byfield, Daventry NN11 6XN
T: (01327) 260512
F: (01327) 260512

CALDECOTE
Warwickshire

Hill House Country Guest House ♦♦♦♦
Off Mancetter Road, Caldecote, Nuneaton CV10 0RS
T: (024) 7639 6685
F: (024) 7639 6685

CALLOW
Herefordshire

Knockerhill Farm ♦♦♦♦
Callow, Hereford HR2 8BP
T: (01432) 268460
F: (01432) 268460
E: beroldavies@waitrose.com

CALLOW END
Worcestershire

Henwick House ♦♦♦♦
Jennett Tree Lane, Callow End, Worcester WR2 4UB
T: (01905) 831736
F: (01905) 831886
E: henwick@lineone.net
I: www.henwickhouse.net

CALMSDEN
Gloucestershire

The Old House ♦♦♦♦ SILVER AWARD
Calmsden, Cirencester GL7 5ET
T: (01285) 831240
F: (01285) 831240
E: baxter@calmsden.freeserve.co.uk

CALVER
Derbyshire

Valley View ♦♦♦♦
Smithy Knoll Road, Calver, Hope Valley S32 3XW
T: (01433) 631407
F: (01433) 631407
E: sue@a-place-2-stay.co.uk
I: www.a-place-2-stay.co.uk

CANON PYON
Herefordshire

Nags Head ♦♦♦
Canon Pyon, Hereford HR4 8NY
T: (01432) 830252

CARDINGTON
Shropshire

Woodside Farm ♦♦♦♦
Cardington, Church Stretton SY6 7LB
T: (01694) 771314

CARSINGTON
Derbyshire

Breach Farm ♦♦♦♦
Carsington, Matlock DE4 4DD
T: (01629) 540265
E: breachfarm@carsington.fsnet.co.uk

Carsington Cottages
Rating Applied For
Swiers Farm, Carsington, Matlock DE4 4DE
T: (01629) 540513
F: (01629) 540513
E: riachclan@btinternet.com
I: www.carsingtoncottages.co.uk

CASEWICK
Lincolnshire

Lindsey Cottage
Rating Applied For
Greatford Road, Uffington, Stamford PE9 4ST
T: (01780) 752975

CASTLE DONINGTON
Leicestershire

Castletown House
♦♦♦♦ SILVER AWARD
4 High Street, Castle Donington, Derby DE74 2PP
T: (01332) 812018
F: (01332) 814550
E: enquiry@castletownhouse.fsnet.co.uk
I: www.castletownhouse.com

Scot's Corner Guesthouse Bed and Breakfast ♦♦♦
82 Park Lane, Castle Donington, Derby DE74 2JG
T: (01332) 811226
E: linda.deary@ntlworld.com
I: www.scots-corner.com

CASTLEMORTON
Worcestershire

Hawthorne Cottage ♦♦♦
New Road, Castlemorton, Malvern WR13 6BT
T: (01684) 833266
F: (01684) 833857

CASTLETON
Derbyshire

Bargate Cottage ♦♦♦♦
Bargate, Market Place, Castleton, Hope Valley S33 8WG
T: (01433) 620201
F: (01433) 621739
E: fionasaxon@bargatecottage78.freeserve.co.uk
I: www.bargatecottage.co.uk

Cryer House ♦♦♦
Castle Street, Castleton, Hope Valley S33 8WG
T: (01433) 620244
E: FleeSkel@aol.com

Dunscar Farm Bed & Breakfast ♦♦♦♦
Castleton, Hope Valley S33 8WA
T: (01433) 620483
I: www.dunscarfarm.co.uk

Hillside House ♦♦♦♦
Pindale Road, Castleton, Hope Valley S33 8WU
T: (01433) 620312
F: (01433) 620312

Ramblers Rest ♦♦♦
Mill Bridge, Castleton, Hope Valley S33 8WR
T: (01433) 620125
F: (01433) 621677
E: peter.d.m.gillott@btinternet.com
I: www.peakland.com/ramblersrest

Swiss House Hotel and Nero's Italian Restaurant ♦♦♦
How Lane, Castleton, Hope Valley S33 8WJ
T: (01433) 621098
F: (01433) 623781
E: info@swisshousehotel.co.uk
I: www.swisshousehotel.co.uk

Ye Olde Cheshire Cheese Inn ♦♦♦♦
How Lane, Castleton, Hope Valley S33 8WJ
T: (01433) 620330
F: (01433) 621847
E: kslack@btconnect.com
I: www.peakland.com.cheshirecheese

Ye Olde Nags Head Hotel ♦♦♦
Cross Street, Castleton, Hope Valley S33 8WH
T: (01433) 620248

CATESBY
Northamptonshire

Long Furlong Farm
Rating Applied For
Catesby, Hellidon, Daventry NN11 6LW
T: (01327) 264770
E: haighfamily@waitrose.com

CAUNTON
Nottinghamshire

Knapthorpe Lodge ♦♦♦
Hockerton Road, Caunton, Newark NG23 6AZ
T: (01636) 636262
F: (01636) 636415

CHADDESDEN
Derbyshire

Green Gables ♦♦♦
19 Highfield Lane, Chaddesden, Derby DE21 6PG
T: (01332) 672298
E: us@sallyandtony.fsnet.co.uk
I: www.greengablesuk.com

CHAPEL BRAMPTON
Northamptonshire

Brampton Hill Farm ♦♦♦♦
Welford Road, Chapel Brampton, Northampton NN6 8AG
T: (01604) 842154
F: (01604) 842154
E: bramptonhill@btopenworld.com

CHAPEL-EN-LE-FRITH
Derbyshire

The Potting Shed ♦♦♦♦
Bank Hall, Chapel-en-le-Frith, High Peak SK23 9UB
T: (0161) 388 8134
I: www.thepottingshedhighpeak.com

Slack Hall Farm ♦♦♦
Castleton Road, Chapel-en-le-Frith, High Peak SK23 0QS
T: (01298) 812845
F: (01298) 812845

CHARLTON KINGS
Gloucestershire

Orion House ♦♦♦
220 London Road, Charlton Kings, Cheltenham GL52 6HW
T: (01242) 233309
F: (01242) 233309
E: ena@orionhouse.fsnet.co.uk

CHEADLE
Staffordshire

Caverswall Castle
♦♦♦♦♦ GOLD AWARD
Caverswall, Stoke-on-Trent ST11 9EA
T: (01782) 393239
F: (01782) 394590
E: yarsargent@hotmail.com
I: www.caverswallcastle.co.uk

The Church Farm ♦♦♦♦
Holt Lane, Kingsley, Stoke-on-Trent ST10 2BA
T: (01538) 754759
F: (01538) 754759

Ley Fields Farm
♦♦♦♦ SILVER AWARD
Leek Road, Cheadle ST10 2EF
T: (01538) 752875
F: (01583) 752875
E: kathryn@leyfieldsfarm.freeserve.co.uk

Park Lodge Guest House ♦♦♦
1 Tean Road, Cheadle ST10 1LG
T: (01538) 753562
E: margaret.mower@amserve.net

Park View Guest House ♦♦♦
15 Mill Road, Cheadle ST10 1NG
T: (01538) 755412
E: stewart@parkviewguesthouse.fsworld.co.uk
I: www.theparkviewguesthouse.com

CHEDDLETON
Staffordshire

Brook House Farm ♦♦♦
Brookhouse Lane, Cheddleton, Leek ST13 7DF
T: (01538) 360296

Choir Cottage and Choir House
♦♦♦♦♦ GOLD AWARD
Ostlers Lane, Cheddleton, Leek ST13 7HS
T: (01538) 360561
E: enquiries@choircottage.co.uk
I: www.choircottage.co.uk

CHEDWORTH
Gloucestershire

The Vicarage ♦♦♦
Chedworth, Cheltenham GL54 4AA
T: (01285) 720392

CHELLASTON
Derbyshire

The Lawns Hotel ♦♦♦
High Street, Chellaston, Derby DE73 1TB
T: (01332) 701553
F: (01332) 690198

CHELMARSH
Shropshire

Hampton House
Rating Applied For
Hampton Loade, Chelmarsh, Bridgnorth WV16 6BN
T: (01746) 861436

Unicorn Inn ♦♦
Hampton Loade, Chelmarsh, Bridgnorth WV16 6BN
T: (01746) 861515
F: (01746) 861515
E: unicorninn.bridgnorth@virginnet.co.uk
I: freespace.virginnet.co.uk/unicorninn.bridgnorth

CHELMORTON
Derbyshire

Ditch House ♦♦♦♦
Chelmorton, Buxton SK17 9SG
T: (01298) 85719
F: (01298) 85719
E: rsimmonds@whsmithnet.co.uk

CHELTENHAM
Gloucestershire

The Abbey Hotel ♦♦♦♦
14-16 Bath Parade, Cheltenham GL53 7HN
T: (01242) 516053
F: (01242) 513034
E: office@abbeyhotel-cheltenham.com
I: www.abbeyhotel-cheltenham.com

Barn End ♦♦♦♦
23 Cheltenham Road, Bishop's Cleeve, Cheltenham GL52 8LU
T: (01242) 672404
F: (01242) 678320
E: joymerrell@aol.com

The Battledown ♦♦♦
125 Hales Road, Cheltenham GL52 6ST
T: (01242) 233881
F: (01242) 524198
E: smurth@fsbdial.co.uk
I: www.smoothhound.co.uk/hotels/battledown

Beaumont House Hotel
♦♦♦♦ SILVER AWARD
56 Shurdington Road, Cheltenham GL53 0JE
T: (01242) 245986
F: (01242) 520044
E: beaumonthouse@aol.com
I: www.beaumonthousehotel.co.uk

Beechcroft B&B and Apartments ♦♦♦
295 Gloucester Road, Cheltenham GL51 7AD
T: (01242) 519564
F: (01242) 519564
E: beechcroft.cheltenham@dial.pipex.com
I: www.geocities.com/beechcroftuk

Beechwood Lodge
Rating Applied For
138 London Road, Cheltenham GL52 6HJ
T: (01242) 518520
F: (01242) 245944
E: julie@beechwoodonline.co.uk
I: www.beechwoodonline.co.uk

Beechworth Lawn Hotel ♦♦♦♦
133 Hales Road, Cheltenham GL52 6ST
T: (01242) 522583
F: (01242) 574800
E: beechworth.lawn@dial.pipex.com
I: www.beechworthlawnhotel.co.uk

The Bell Inn
Rating Applied For
70 Bath Road, Cheltenham GL53 7JT
T: (01242) 521977
F: (01242) 521977
E: bellinnchelt@hotmail.com

Bentleyville ♦♦♦
179 Gloucester Road, Cheltenham GL51 8NQ
T: (01242) 581476
F: (01242) 700595
E: bentleyville_179@hotmail.com
I: www.bentleyville.co.uk

Bentons ♦♦♦
71 Bath Road, Cheltenham GL53 7LH
T: (01242) 517417
F: (01242) 527772

Bibury House ♦♦♦
Priory Place, Cheltenham GL52 6HG
T: (01242) 525014

Brennan Guest House ♦♦♦
21 St Lukes Road, Cheltenham GL53 7JF
T: (01242) 525904
F: (01242) 525904

Briarfields Motel
Rating Applied For
Gloucester Road, Cheltenham GL51 0SX
T: (01242) 235324
F: (01242) 262216

Bridge House ♦♦♦♦
88 Lansdown Road, Cheltenham GL51 6QR
T: (01242) 583559
F: (01242) 255920
E: bridgehouse@freeuk.com

Butlers Hotel
Rating Applied For
Western Road, Cheltenham GL50 3RN
T: (01242) 570771
F: (01242) 528724
E: info@butlers-hotel.co.uk
I: www.butlers-hotel.co.uk

Crossways Guest House ♦♦♦
Oriel Place, 57 Bath Road, Cheltenham GL53 7LH
T: (01242) 527683
F: (01242) 577226
E: cross.ways@btinternet.com
I: www.crossways.btinternet.co.uk

Detmore House ♦♦♦
London Road, Charlton Kings, Cheltenham GL52 6UT
T: (01242) 582868

Elm Villa ♦♦
49 London Road, Cheltenham GL52 6HF
T: (01242) 231909

Evington Hill Farm
♦♦♦♦ GOLD AWARD
Tewkesbury Road, The Leigh, Gloucester GL19 4AQ
T: (01242) 680255

Ham Hill Farm
♦♦♦♦ SILVER AWARD
Whittington, Cheltenham GL54 4EZ
T: (01242) 584415
F: (01242) 222535
E: hamhillfarm@msn.com

Hannaford's ♦♦♦♦
20 Evesham Road, Cheltenham GL52 2AB
T: (01242) 524190
F: (01242) 580102
E: sue@hannafords.icom43.net
I: www.hannafords.icom43.net

Home Cottage ♦♦♦
1 Priors Road, Cheltenham GL52 5AB
T: (01242) 518144
F: (01242) 518144
E: barrycott@msn.com
I: www.homecottage.co.uk

Home Farm ♦♦♦♦
Stockwell Lane, Woodmancote, Cheltenham GL52 9QE
T: (01242) 675816
F: (01242) 701319
E: info@homefarmbb.co.uk
I: www.homefarmbb.co.uk

Hope Orchard ♦♦♦
Gloucester Road, Staverton, Cheltenham GL51 0TF
T: (01452) 855556
F: (01452) 530037
E: info@hopeorchard.com
I: www.hopeorchard.com

Ivydene Guest House ♦♦♦
145 Hewlett Road, Cheltenham GL52 6TS
T: (01242) 521726
F: (01242) 525694
E: info@ivydenehouse.co.uk
I: www.ivydenehouse.co.uk

Lawn Hotel ♦♦♦
5 Pittville Lawn, Cheltenham GL52 2BE
T: (01242) 526638
F: (01242) 526638

Leeswood ♦♦
14 Montpellier Drive, Cheltenham GL50 1TX
T: (01242) 524813
F: (01242) 524813
E: leeswood@hotmail.com
I: www.leeswood.org.uk

Lonsdale House ♦♦♦
Montpellier Drive, Cheltenham GL50 1TX
T: (01242) 232379
F: (01242) 232379
E: lonsdalehouse@hotmail.com

Milton House
♦♦♦♦♦ GOLD AWARD
12 Bayshill Road, Royal Parade, Cheltenham GL50 3AY
T: (01242) 582601
F: (01242) 222326
E: info@miltonhousehotel.co.uk
I: www.miltonhousehotel.co.uk

Montpellier Hotel ♦♦♦
33 Montpellier Terrace, Cheltenham GL50 1UX
T: (01242) 526009

Moorend Park Hotel
Rating Applied For
11 Moorend Park Road, Cheltenham GL53 0LA
T: (01242) 224441
F: (01242) 572413
E: moorendpark@freeuk.com
I: www.moorendpark.freeuk.com

The Old Station ♦♦♦♦
Westfield, Notgrove, Cheltenham GL5 3BU
T: (01451) 850305
E: trotter98@hotmail.com

Parkview ♦♦♦
4 Pittville Crescent, Cheltenham GL52 2QZ
T: (01242) 575567
E: jospa@tr250.freeserve.co.uk

Penhill Farm ♦♦♦
Penhill, Colesbourne, Cheltenham GL53 9NS
T: (01242) 870300
F: (01242) 870300
E: pwgilder@farmersweekly.net

Saint Cloud ♦♦♦
97 Leckhampton Road, Cheltenham GL53 0BZ
T: (01242) 575245

St Michaels
♦♦♦♦ SILVER AWARD
4 Montpellier Drive, Cheltenham GL50 1TX
T: (01242) 513587
E: st_michaels_guesthouse@yahoo.com

Steyne Cross Bed and Breakfast ♦♦♦
Steyne Cross, Malvern Road, Cheltenham GL50 2NU
T: (01242) 255289
F: (01242) 255289
E: sumiko@susumago.f9.co.uk

Stray Leaves ♦♦♦
282 Gloucester Road, Cheltenham GL51 7AG
T: (01242) 572303
F: (01242) 572303

Westal Court
♦♦♦♦ SILVER AWARD
2 Westal Court, 27 Hatherley Road, Cheltenham GL51 6EB
T: (01242) 696679
F: (01242) 696679
E: martinkw@onetel.net.uk
I: web.onetel.net.uk/~martinkw

Westcourt ♦♦♦♦
14 Old Bath Road, Cheltenham GL53 7QD
T: (01242) 241777
F: (01242) 228666
E: michael.seston@which.net

White Lodge ♦♦♦
Hatherley Lane, Cheltenham GL51 6SH
T: (01242) 242347
F: (01242) 242347

Whittington Lodge Farm
♦♦♦♦ SILVER AWARD
Whittington, Cheltenham GL54 4HB
T: (01242) 820603
F: (01242) 820603
E: cathy@whittlodgefarm.fslife.co.uk
I: www.whittlodgefarm.fslife.co.uk

Wishmoor Guest House
♦♦♦♦ SILVER AWARD
147 Hales Road, Cheltenham GL52 6TD
T: (01242) 238504
F: (01242) 226090
E: wishmoor@aol.com

The Wynyards ♦♦♦♦
Butts Lane, Woodmancote, Cheltenham GL52 9QH
T: (01242) 673876
I: www.SmoothHound.co.uk/hotels/wynyards

CHESTERFIELD
Derbyshire

Abigails ♦♦♦
62 Brockwell Lane, Chesterfield S40 4EE
T: (01246) 279391
F: (01246) 854468
E: gail@abigails.fsnet.co.uk
I: www.abigailsguesthouse.co.uk

Anis Louise Guesthouse ♦♦♦
34 Clarence Road, Chesterfield S40 1LN
T: (01246) 235412
E: enquiries@anislouise.co.uk
I: www.anislouise.co.uk

Batemans Mill
♦♦♦♦ SILVER AWARD
Mill Lane, Old Tupton, Chesterfield S42 6AE
T: (01246) 862296
F: (01246) 865672
E: info@batemansmill.co.uk
I: www.ukhotel.com/heart-of-england/batemans-mill-hotel.htm

Brook House
♦♦♦♦ SILVER AWARD
45 Westbrook Drive, Brookside, Chesterfield S40 3PQ
T: (01246) 568535

Clarendon Guesthouse ♦♦♦
32 Clarence Road, West Bars, Chesterfield S40 1LN
T: (01246) 235004

Fairfield House ♦♦♦
3 Fairfield Road, Chesterfield S40 4TR
T: (01246) 204905
F: (01246) 230155
E: sp8@talk21.com

Flags ♦♦♦
89 Newbold Road, Chesterfield S41 7PS
T: (01246) 203896
E: info@virtualflags.com
I: www.virtualflags.com

Locksley ♦♦♦
21 Tennyson Avenue, Chesterfield S40 4SN
T: (01246) 273332

The Maylands ♦♦♦
56 Sheffield Road, Chesterfield S41 7LS
T: (01246) 233602

Rose Cottage Guest House ♦♦♦
Derby Road, Old Tupton, Chesterfield S42 6LA
T: (01246) 864949
F: (01246) 864949
E: bookings@rosecottagetupton.freeserve.co.uk
I: www.rose-cottage-tupton.co.uk

The Shoulder at Hardstoft ♦♦♦
Hardstoft, Chesterfield S45 8AF
T: (01246) 850276
F: (01246) 854760

Springbank Guesthouse ♦♦
35 Springbank Road, Chesterfield S40 1NL
T: (01246) 279232
F: (01246) 235999

The Tullamore Inn ♦♦
32 Springbank Road, Chesterfield S40 1NL
T: (01246) 550542
F: (01246) 235999

CHETWYND ASTON
Shropshire

Woodcroft Bed and Breakfast ♦♦♦♦
Woodcroft, Pitchcroft Lane, Chetwynd Aston, Newport TF10 9AU
T: (01952) 812406
E: judith_woodcroft@hotmail.com
I: www.virtual-shropshire.co.uk/woodcroft

CHINLEY
Derbyshire

Mossley House Farm ♦♦♦♦
Maynestone Road, Chinley, High Peak SK23 6AH
T: (01663) 750240
E: moseleyhouse@supanet.com

CHIPPING CAMPDEN
Gloucestershire

The Bantam Tearooms ♦♦♦♦
High Street, Chipping Campden GL55 6HB
T: (01386) 840386
E: thebantam@hotmail.com
I: www.thebantam.co.uk

Brymbo ♦♦♦♦
Honeybourne Lane, Mickleton, Chipping Campden GL55 6PU
T: (01386) 438890
F: (01386) 438113
E: enquiries@brymbo.com
I: www.brymbo.com

Dragon House ♦♦♦♦
High Street, Chipping Campden GL55 6AG
T: (01386) 840734
F: (01386) 840734
E: valatdragonhouse@btinternet.com
I: www.dragonhouse-chipping-campden.com

The Eight Bells ♦♦♦
Church Street, Chipping Campden GL55 6JG
T: (01386) 840371
F: (01386) 841669
E: neilhargreaves@bellinn.fsnet.co.uk
I: www.eightbellsinn.co.uk

Home Farm House ♦♦♦♦
Ebrington, Chipping Campden GL55 6NL
T: (01386) 593309
F: (01386) 593309
E: willstanley@farmersweekly.net
I: www.homefarminthecotswolds.co.uk

The Malins ♦♦♦
21 Station Road, Blockley, Moreton-in-Marsh GL56 9ED
T: (01386) 700402
F: (01386) 700402
E: johnmalin@btinternet.com
I: www.chippingcampden.co.uk/themalins.htm

Manor Farm ♦♦♦♦
Weston Subedge, Chipping Campden GL55 6QH
T: (01386) 840390
F: (08701) 640638
E: lucy@manorfarmbnb.demon.co.uk
I: www.manorfarmbnb.demon.co.uk

M'Dina Courtyard
♦♦♦♦ GOLD AWARD
Park Road, Chipping Campden GL55 6EA
T: (01386) 841752
F: (01386) 840942
E: barbara@mdina-bandb.co.uk
I: www.mdina-bandb.co.uk

Nineveh Farm
♦♦♦♦♦ GOLD AWARD
Campden Road, Mickleton, Chipping Campden GL55 6PS
T: (01386) 438923
E: stay@ninevehfarm.co.uk
I: www.ninevehfarm.co.uk

The Red Lion ♦♦♦
Lower High Street, Chipping Campden GL55 6AS
T: (01386) 840760
F: (01386) 841089
E: info@theredlionchippingcampden.co.uk
I: www.theredlionchippingcampden.co.uk

Sandalwood House ♦♦♦♦
Back-Ends, Chipping Campden GL55 6AU
T: (01386) 840091
F: (01386) 840091

Weston Park Farm ♦♦♦
Dovers Hill, Chipping Campden GL55 6UW
T: (01386) 840835
E: jane_whitehouse@hotmail.com
I: www.cotswoldcottages.uk.com

CHURCH EATON
Staffordshire

Slab Bridge Cottage
♦♦♦♦ SILVER AWARD
Little Onn, Church Eaton, Stafford ST20 0AY
T: (01785) 840220
F: (01785) 840220

CHURCH STRETTON
Shropshire

Acton Scott Farm ♦♦♦
Acton Scott, Church Stretton SY6 6QN
T: (01694) 781260
E: edandm@clara.co.uk
I: www.actonscottfarm.co.uk

Belvedere Guest House ♦♦♦♦
Burway Road, Church Stretton SY6 6DP
T: (01694) 722232
F: (01694) 722232
E: belv@bigfoot.com
I: www.belvedereguesthouse.btinternet.co.uk

Brereton's Farm ♦♦♦♦
Church Stretton SY6 6QD
T: (01694) 781201
F: (01694) 781201

Brookfields Guesthouse ♦♦♦♦
Watling Street North, Church Stretton SY6 7AR
T: (01694) 722314
F: (01694) 722314
E: paulangie@brookfields51.fsnet.co.uk
I: www.smoothhound.co.uk/hotels/brookfieldsgh.html

Cwm Dale Farm Bed and Breakfast ♦♦♦
Cwm Dale Farm, Cwm Dale Valley, Church Stretton SY6 6JL
T: (01694) 722362
F: (01694) 724656
E: cwmdale@hotmail.com
I: www.churchstretton.co.uk

Field House ♦♦♦♦
Cardington Moor, Church Stretton SY6 7LL
T: (01694) 771485
E: fieldhouse@cardington.fsworld.co.uk

Gilberries Cottage ♦♦♦♦
Gilberries Lane, Wall-under-Heywood, Church Stretton SY6 7HZ
T: (01694) 771400
F: (01694) 771663

Gretton Court
Rating Applied For
Gretton, Church Stretton SY6 7HU
T: (01694) 771630

Highcliffe ♦♦♦
Madeira Walk, Church Stretton SY6 6JQ
T: (01694) 722908

Hill House
Rating Applied For
Madeira Walk, Church Stretton SY6 6JQ
T: (01694) 722817

Jinlye ♦♦♦♦♦ GOLD AWARD
Castle Hill, All Stretton, Church Stretton SY6 6JP
T: (01694) 723243
F: (01694) 723243
E: info@jinlye.co.uk
I: www.jinlye.co.uk

Juniper Cottage ♦♦♦♦
All Stretton, Church Stretton SY6 6HG
T: (01694) 723427
F: (01694) 722061
E: mcintyrejuniper@ukonline.co.uk

Oakbank
Rating Applied For
Cunnery Road, Church Stretton SY6 6AQ
T: (01694) 720181
F: (01694) 720171
I: www.churchstretton.co.uk

Old Rectory House ♦♦♦
Burway Road, Church Stretton SY6 6DW
T: (01694) 724462
F: (01694) 724799
E: smamos@btinternet.com
I: www.oldrectoryhouse.co.uk

Ragdon Manor ♦♦♦
Ragdon, Church Stretton SY6 7EZ
T: (01694) 781389

Rheingold ♦♦♦♦
9 The Bridleways, Church Stretton SY6 7AN
T: (01694) 723969

Sayang House ♦♦♦♦
Hope Bowdler, Church Stretton SY6 7DD
T: (01694) 723981
E: madegan@aol.com
I: www.sayanghouse.com

Travellers Rest Inn ♦♦♦
Upper Affcot, Church Stretton SY6 6RL
T: (01694) 781275
F: (01694) 781555
E: reception@travellersrestinn.co.uk
I: www.travellersrestinn.co.uk

Willowfield Country Guesthouse
♦♦♦♦♦ GOLD AWARD
Lower Wood, All Stretton, Church Stretton SY6 6LF
T: (01694) 751471
F: (01694) 751471
I: www.willowfieldguesthouse.co.uk

CHURCHAM
Gloucestershire

The Pinetum Lodge ♦♦♦
Pinetum, Churcham, Gloucester GL2 8AD
T: (01452) 750554
F: (01452) 750402
E: carol@igeek.co.uk
I: www.pinetumlodge.ik.com

CIRENCESTER
Gloucestershire

Abbeymead ♦♦♦♦
39a Victoria Road, Cirencester GL7 1ES
T: (01285) 653740
F: (01285) 652721
E: abbeymead@amserve.net
I: www.smoothhound.co.uk/shs.html

Apsley Villa ♦♦♦
16 Victoria Road, Cirencester GL7 1ES
T: (01285) 653489

The Black Horse ♦♦♦
17 Castle Street, Cirencester GL7 1QD
T: (01285) 653187
F: (01285) 659772

Brooklands Farm ♦♦♦
Ewen, Cirencester GL7 6BU
T: (01285) 770487
F: (01285) 770487
I: www.glosfarmhols.co.uk

The Bungalow ♦♦♦♦
93 Victoria Road, Cirencester GL7 1ES
T: (01285) 654179
E: bob-joan.lamb@virgin.net
I: www.bandbcirencester.co.uk

Catherine Wheel ♦♦♦
Arlington Bibury, Cirencester GL7 5ND
T: (01285) 740250
F: (01285) 740779

Chesil Rocks ♦♦♦
Baunton Lane, Stratton, Cirencester GL7 2LL
T: (01285) 655031

Claremont Villa Bed and Breakfast ♦♦♦
131 Cheltenham Road, Stratton, Cirencester GL7 2JF
T: (01285) 654759

The Corner House ♦♦♦♦
101A Victoria Road, Cirencester GL7 1EU
T: (01285) 641958
F: (01285) 640805
E: info@thecornerhouse.info
I: www.thecornerhouse.info

Cotswold Willow Pool ♦♦♦♦ SILVER AWARD
Oaksey Road, Poole Keynes, Cirencester GL7 6DZ
T: (01285) 861485
E: enquiries@willowpool.com
I: www.willowpool.com

Eliot Arms Hotel Free House ♦♦♦♦
Clarks Hay, South Cerney, Cirencester GL7 5UA
T: (01285) 860215
F: (01285) 861121
E: eliotarms.cirencester@eldridge.pope.co.uk

Greensleeves ♦♦♦♦ SILVER AWARD
Baunton Lane, Cirencester GL7 2LN
T: (01285) 642516
F: (01285) 642761
E: johnps@tesco.net
I: www.greensleeves4u.co.uk

The Ivy House ♦♦♦
2 Victoria Road, Cirencester GL7 1EN
T: (01285) 656626
E: info@ivyhousecotswolds.com
I: www.ivyhousecotswolds.com

King's Head Hotel ♦♦♦♦
Market Place, Cirencester GL7 2NR
T: (01285) 653322
F: (01285) 655103
E: gm.kin@barbox.net
I: www.shearingsholidays.com

Landage House ♦♦♦♦
Rendcomb, Cirencester GL7 7HB
T: (01285) 831250

The Leauses ♦♦♦♦
101 Victoria Road, Cirencester GL7 1EU
T: (01285) 653643
F: (01285) 640805
E: info@theleauses.co.uk
I: www.theleauses.co.uk

The Masons Arms ♦♦♦
High Street, Meysey Hampton, Cirencester GL7 5JT
T: (01285) 850164
F: (01285) 850164
E: jane@themasonsarms.freeserve.co.uk
I: www.smoothhound.co.uk/hotels/mason

Millstone ♦♦♦♦ SILVER AWARD
Down Ampney, Cirencester GL7 5QR
T: (01793) 750475

No 12 ♦♦♦♦♦ SILVER AWARD
12 Park Street, Cirencester GL7 2BW
T: (01285) 640232
E: no12cirencester@ukgateway.net
I: www.no12cirencester.co.uk

The Oddfellows Arms Inn ♦♦♦
12-14 Chester Street, Cirencester GL7 1HF
T: (01285) 641540
F: (01285) 640771
E: mike@oddfellows.fsnet.co.uk
I: www.oddfellowsarms.com

The Old Brew House ♦♦♦♦
7 London Road, Cirencester GL7 2PU
T: (01285) 656099
F: (01285) 656099

The Old Rectory ♦♦♦♦
Rodmarton, Cirencester GL7 6PE
T: (01285) 841246
F: (01285) 841246
E: jfitz@globalnet.co.uk
I: www.rodmarton.com

Raydon House Hotel ♦♦♦
3 The Avenue, Cirencester GL7 1EH
T: (01285) 653485
F: (01285) 653485

Riverside House ♦♦♦♦
Watermoor Road, Cirencester GL7 1LF
T: (01285) 647642
F: (01285) 647615
E: riversidehouse@mitsubishi-cars.co.uk

Smerrill Barns ♦♦♦♦ SILVER AWARD
Kemble, Cirencester GL7 6BW
T: (01285) 770907
F: (01285) 770706
E: gsopher@smerrillbarns.com
I: www.smerrillbarns.com

Sunset ♦♦♦
Baunton Lane, Cirencester GL7 2NQ
T: (01285) 654822

The Talbot Inn ♦♦♦♦
14 Victoria Road, Cirencester GL7 1EN
T: (01285) 653760
F: (01285) 658014
E: info@talbotinncotswolds.co.uk
I: www.talbotinncotswolds.co.uk

The White Lion Inn ♦♦
8 Gloucester Street, Cirencester GL7 2DG
T: (01285) 654053
F: (01285) 641316
E: roylion@aol.com.
I: www.white-lion-cirencester.co.uk

Willows ♦♦♦
2 Glebe Lane, Kemble, Cirencester GL7 6BD
T: (01285) 770667
E: Kamma@Tesco.net

CLAVERLEY Shropshire

Woodman Inn ♦♦♦
Danford, Claverley, Wolverhampton WV5 7DG
T: (01746) 710553
F: (01746) 710566

CLENT Worcestershire

The French Hen ♦♦♦
Bromsgrove Road, Clent, Stourbridge DY9 9PY
T: (01562) 883040
F: (01562) 888000
I: www.frenchhen.co.uk

CLEOBURY MORTIMER Shropshire

Clod Hall ♦♦♦
Milson, Kidderminster DY14 0BJ
T: (01584) 781421
I: www.farmstayworcs.co.uk

Cox's Barn ♦♦♦♦
Bagginswood, Cleobury Mortimer, Kidderminster DY14 8LS
T: (01746) 718415
I: www.southshropshire.org.uk

The Old Bake House ♦♦♦♦
46/47 High Street, Cleobury Mortimer, Kidderminster DY14 8DQ
T: (01299) 270193
E: old-bake-house@amserve.net
I: www.smoothhound.co.uk/hotels/oldbakehouse.hmtl

The Old Cider House ♦♦♦♦
1 Lion Lane, Cleobury Mortimer, Kidderminster DY14 8BT
T: (01299) 270304
F: (01299) 270304
E: lennox@old-cider-house.fsnet.co.uk

Woodview ♦♦♦♦ GOLD AWARD
Mawley Oak, Cleobury Mortimer, Kidderminster DY14 9BA
T: (01299) 271422

CLEOBURY NORTH Shropshire

Cleobury Court ♦♦♦♦♦ SILVER AWARD
Cleobury North, Bridgnorth WV16 6RW
T: (01746) 787005
F: (01746) 787005
E: cleoburycourt@aol.com

CLIFFORD Herefordshire

Cottage Farm ♦♦♦
Middlewood, Clifford, Hereford HR3 5SX
T: (01497) 831496
F: (01497) 831496
E: julie@hgjmjones.freeserve.co.uk
I: www.smoothhound.co.uk/hotels/cottagef.html

CLIFTON Derbyshire

Stone Cottage ♦♦♦
Green Lane, Clifton, Ashbourne DE6 2BL
T: (01335) 343377
F: (01335) 34117
E: info@stone-cottage.fsnet.co.uk
I: www.stone-cottage.fsnet.co.uk

CLUN Shropshire

Llanhedric Farm ♦♦♦♦
Clun, Craven Arms SY7 8NG
T: (01588) 640203
F: (01588) 640203
E: llanhedric@talk21.com

New House Farm ♦♦♦♦♦ GOLD AWARD
Clun, Craven Arms SY7 8NJ
T: (01588) 638314
E: sarah@bishopscastle.co.uk
I: www.new-house-clun.co.uk

The Old Farmhouse ♦♦♦
Woodside, Clun, Craven Arms SY7 0JB
T: (01588) 640695
F: (01588) 640501
E: helen@vuan1.freeserve.co.uk
I: www.theoldfarmhousebandb.co.uk

The Old Stables, Crown House and Saddlery ♦♦♦♦
Church Street, Clun, Craven Arms SY7 8JW
T: (01588) 640780
E: crownhouseclun@talk21.com

CLUNGUNFORD Shropshire

Knock Hundred Cottage ♦♦♦♦ GOLD AWARD
Abcott, Clungunford, Craven Arms SY7 0PX
T: (01588) 660594
F: (01588) 660594

COALBROOKDALE Shropshire

Fat Frog Restaurant ♦♦♦
10 Wellington Road, Coalbrookdale, Telford TF8 7DX
T: (01952) 433269
F: (01952) 433269
E: frog@fat-frog.co.uk
I: www.fat-frog.co.uk

The Old Vicarage ♦♦♦♦
28 Church Road, Coalbrookdale, Telford TF8 7NT
T: (01952) 432525
F: (01952) 433053
E: sonia.sharman@btopenworld.com
I: oldvicarage.net

COALEY Gloucestershire

Silver Street Farmhouse ♦♦♦♦
Silver Street, Coaley, Dursley GL11 5AX
T: (01453) 860514

COALPORT Shropshire

Thorpe House ♦♦♦
High Street, Coalport, Telford TF8 7HP
T: (01952) 586789
F: (01952) 586789
E: thorpehouse@tiscali.co.uk

COALVILLE Leicestershire

Broadlawns ♦♦♦
98 London Road, Coalville, Leicester LE67 3JD
T: (01530) 836724
F: (01530) 811608

St Joseph's ♦♦♦
Abbey Road, Oaks in Charnwood, Coalville, Leicester LE67 4UA
T: (01509) 503943
E: m.havers@virgin.net

COLD ASTON
Gloucestershire

Grove Farm House ♦♦♦♦♦
Cold Aston, Cheltenham
GL54 3BJ
T: (01451) 821801
F: (01451) 821108
E: angela@cotswoldbedandbreakfast.com
I: www.cotswoldbedandbreakfast.com

COLEFORD
Gloucestershire

Forest House Hotel ♦♦♦♦
Cinder Hill, Coleford GL16 8HQ
T: (01594) 832424
F: (01594) 838030
E: suesparkes@tumphouse.fsnet.co.uk
I: www.forest-house-hotel.co.uk

Millend House and Garden ♦♦♦♦
Newland, Coleford GL16 8NF
T: (01594) 832128
F: (01594) 832128
E: apriljohnt@aol.com

Symonds Yat Rock Lodge ♦♦♦
Hillersland, Coleford GL16 7NY
T: (01594) 836191
E: enquiries@rocklodge.co.uk
I: www.rocklodge.co.uk

COLEORTON
Leicestershire

Zion Cottage ♦♦♦♦
93 Zion Hill, Peggs Green, Coleorton, Leicester LE67 8JP
T: (01530) 223914
F: (01530) 222488
E: zionbnb@aol.com
I: members.aol.com/zionbnb

COLESHILL
Warwickshire

The Old Rectory ♦♦♦♦
Church Lane, Maxstoke, Coleshill, Birmingham B46 2QW
T: (01675) 462248
F: (01675) 481615
I: www.SmoothHound.co.uk/hotels/oldrect.html

Packington Lane Farm ♦♦♦♦
Packington Lane, Coleshill, Birmingham B46 3JJ
T: (01675) 462228
F: (01675) 462228

COLLINGHAM
Nottinghamshire

Lime Tree Farm ♦♦♦♦
Lunn Lane, Collingham, Nottingham NG23 7LP
T: (01636) 892044

COLN ST ALDWYNS
Gloucestershire

Deer Park Cottage ♦♦♦
Coln St Aldwyns, Cirencester GL7 5AR
T: (01285) 750692
F: (01285) 750129

COLSTERWORTH
Lincolnshire

The Fox (A1) Ltd ♦♦♦
Great North Road southbound, Colsterworth, Grantham NG33 5LN
T: (01572) 767697
F: (01572) 767977

The Stables ♦♦♦♦
Stainby Road, Colsterworth, Grantham NG33 5JB
T: (01476) 861057
I: www.stablesbandb.co.uk

COLWALL
Herefordshire

Brook House ♦♦♦♦♦ SILVER AWARD
Walwyn Road, Colwall, Malvern WR13 6QX
T: (01684) 540604
F: (01684) 540604
E: Maggie@brookhouse.fsnet.co.uk
I: www.brookhouse-colwall.co.uk

Oakley House ♦♦♦
Evendine Lane, Colwall Green, Malvern WR13 6DX
T: (01684) 540215

Old Library Lodge ♦♦♦
Stone Drive, Colwall, Malvern WR13 6QJ
T: (01684) 540077

CONINGSBY
Lincolnshire

The Lea Gate Inn ♦♦♦♦
Leagate Road, Coningsby, Lincoln LN4 4RS
T: (01526) 342370
F: (01526) 345468
E: theleagateinn@hotmail.com
I: www.theleagateinn.co.uk

CONISHOLME
Lincolnshire

Wickham House ♦♦♦♦♦ SILVER AWARD
Church Lane, Conisholme, Louth LN11 7LX
T: (01507) 358465
F: (01507) 358465
E: kenmor_wickham@hotmail.com
I: www.wickham-house.co.uk

CORBY
Northamptonshire

Moat Cottage ♦♦♦♦
18 Little Oakley, Little Oakley, Corby NN18 8HA
T: (01536) 745013
F: (01536) 745013
E: enquiries@moat-cottage.fsbusiness.co.uk
I: www.moat-cottage.fsbusiness.co.uk

White Swan ♦♦♦♦
Seaton Road, Harringworth, Corby NN17 3AF
T: (01572) 747543
F: (01572) 747323
E: thewhiteswan@fsmail.net
I: www.thewhite-swan.com

CORELEY
Shropshire

Brookfield House ♦♦♦♦
Coreley, Ludlow SY8 3AS
T: (01584) 890059

CORRINGHAM
Lincolnshire

The Old Hall ♦♦♦♦
Field Lane, Corringham, Gainsborough DN21 5QX
T: (01427) 838470
F: (01427) 839333
E: wayneturner@btconnect.com

COVENTRY
West Midlands

Abigail Guesthouse ♦♦♦
39 St Patrick's Road, Coventry CV1 2LP
T: (024) 7622 1378
F: (024) 7622 1378
E: ag002a@netgates.co.uk
I: www.abigailuk.com

Aburley ♦♦♦♦
23 St Patricks Road, Cheylesmore, Coventry CV1 2LP
T: (024) 7625 1348
F: (024) 7622 3243

Acacia Guest House ♦♦♦♦
11 Park Road, Coventry CV1 2LE
T: (02476) 633622
F: (02476) 633622
E: acaciaguesthouse@hotmail.com

Albany Guest House ♦♦♦
121 Holyhead Road, Coundon, Coventry CV1 3AD
T: (024) 7622 3601
F: (024) 7622 3601
I: www.smoothhound.com

Arlon Guest House ♦♦♦
25 St Patricks Road, Coventry CV1 2LP
T: (024) 7622 5942

Ashdowns Guest House ♦♦♦
12 Regent Street, Earlsdon, Coventry CV1 3EP
T: (024) 7622 9280

Ashleigh House ♦♦♦
17 Park Road, Coventry CV1 2LH
T: (024) 7622 3804
F: (024) 7622 3804

Barnacle Hall ♦♦♦♦♦ SILVER AWARD
Shilton Lane, Shilton, Coventry CV7 9LH
T: (024) 7661 2629
F: (024) 7661 2629

Bede Guest House ♦♦♦
250 Radford Road, Coventry CV6 3BU
T: (024) 7659 7837
F: (024) 7660 1413

Bourne Brook Lodge ♦♦♦♦
Mill Lane, Fillongley, Coventry CV7 8EE
T: (01676) 541898
F: (01676) 541898
E: bournebrooklodge@care4free.net
I: www.bournbrooklodge.co.uk

Brookfields ♦♦♦♦ SILVER AWARD
134 Butt Lane, Allesley, Coventry CV5 9FE
T: (024) 7640 4866
F: (024) 7640 2022

Chester House ♦♦♦
3 Chester Street, Coventry CV1 4DH
T: (024) 7622 3857

Fairlight Guest House ♦♦♦
14 Regent Street, Off Queens Road, Coventry CV1 3EP
T: (024) 7622 4215
F: (024) 7622 4215
E: fairlight@btopenworld.com

Highcroft Guest House ♦♦
65 Barras Lane, Coundon, Coventry CV1 4AQ
T: (024) 7622 8157
F: (024) 7663 1609
E: deepakcov@hotmail.com

Lodge Farm House Bed and Breakfast ♦♦♦♦
Westwood Heath Road, Coventry CV4 8AA
T: (024) 7646 6786
F: (024) 7646 6786
E: lodgefarmhouse@aol.com

Merlyn Guest House ♦♦♦
105 Holyhead Road, Coventry CV1 3AD
T: (02476) 222800
F: (02476) 222800
E: noel@complete.u-net.com

Mount Guest House ♦♦♦
9 Coundon Road, Coventry CV1 4AR
T: (024) 7622 5998
F: (024) 7622 5998
E: enquiries@guesthousecoventry.com
I: www.guesthousecoventry.com

The Old Vicarage Rating Applied For
Withybrook, Coventry CV7 9LP
T: (01788) 832252
F: (01788) 832083
E: stewarts@ovbb.co.uk
I: www.ovbb.co.uk

St Mary's Cottage ♦♦♦
107 Kingsbury Road, Coventry CV6 1PT
T: (024) 7659 1557
F: (024) 7659 1557
E: afoster543@aol.com

Spire View Guest House ♦♦♦♦
36 Park Road (Near Railway Station), Coventry CV1 2LD
T: (024) 7625 1602
F: (024) 7622 2779
E: j-m@spireviewcov.freeserve.co.uk

Westwood Cottage ♦♦♦
79 Westwood Heath Road, Westwood Heath, Coventry CV4 8GN
T: (024) 7647 1084
F: (024) 7647 1084

COWLEY
Gloucestershire

Butlers Hill Farm ♦♦♦
Cockleford, Cowley, Cheltenham GL53 9NW
T: (01242) 870455
F: (01242) 870455
E: butlershill@aol.com

CRADLEY
Herefordshire

Hollings Hill Farm ♦♦♦♦
Bosbury Road, Cradley, Malvern WR13 5LY
T: (01886) 880203
E: ajgkhollingshill@farmersweekly.net

CRANWELL
Lincolnshire

Byards Leap Cottage ♦♦♦
Cranwell, Sleaford NG34 8EY
T: (01400) 261537
F: (01400) 261537

CRAVEN ARMS
Shropshire

The Firs ◆◆◆◆
Norton, Craven Arms SY7 9LS
T: (01588) 672511
F: (01588) 672511
E: thefirs@go2.co.uk
I: www.go2.co.uk/firs

Glebelands ◆◆◆
25 Knighton Road, Clun, Craven Arms SY7 8JH
T: (01588) 640442
F: (01588) 640442
E: Tourism@clun25.freeserve.co.uk

CRESSBROOK
Derbyshire

Cressbrook Hall ◆◆◆◆
Cressbrook, Buxton SK17 8SY
T: (01298) 871289
F: (01298) 871845
E: stay@cressbrookhall.co.uk
I: www.cressbrookhall.co.uk

The Old Toll House ◆◆◆◆
Cressbrook, Buxton SK17 8SY
T: (01298) 872547
E: loy@oldtollhouse.freeserve.co.uk
I: www.oldtollhouse.freeserve.co.uk

CRICH
Derbyshire

Penrose Avista Property Partnership
◆◆◆◆ SILVER AWARD
Sandy Lane, Crich, Matlock DE4 5DE
T: (01773) 852625
E: keith@avista.freeserve.co.uk
I: www.s-h-systems.co.uk/hotels/avista.html

CROPTHORNE
Worcestershire

Cropvale Farm Bed and Breakfast
◆◆◆◆ GOLD AWARD
Cropvale Farm, Smokey Lane, Cropthorne, Pershore WR10 3NF
T: (01386) 860237
F: (01386) 860237
E: susan@hutchings22.freeserve.co.uk
I: www.smoothhound.co.uk/hotels/cropvale.html

Oaklands Farmhouse ◆◆◆◆
Bricklehampton, Pershore WR10 3JT
T: (01386) 861716
E: barbara-stewart@lineone.net
I: www.oaklandsfarmhouse.co.uk

CROXDEN
Staffordshire

Farriers Cottage and Mews ◆◆◆◆
Woodhouse Farm, Croxden, Uttoxeter ST14 5JB
T: (01889) 507507
E: ddeb@lineone.net
I: www.alton-towers.glo.cc

CROXTON KERRIAL
Leicestershire

Peacock at Croxton ◆◆◆◆
Peacock Inn, 1 School Lane, Croxton Kerrial, Grantham NG32 1QR
T: (01476) 870324
F: (01476) 870171
E: peacockcroxton@globalnet.co.uk
I: www.peakcockcroxton.co.uk

CUBBINGTON
Warwickshire

Bakers Cottage ◆◆◆◆
52/54 Queen Street, Cubbington, Leamington Spa CV32 7NA
T: (01926) 772146

Staddlestones Bed and Breakfast ◆◆◆
67 Rugby Road, Cubbington, Leamington Spa CV32 7HY
T: (01926) 740253

DAGLINGWORTH
Gloucestershire

Windrush Cottage ◆◆◆
Itlay, Daglingworth, Cirencester GL7 7HZ
T: (01285) 652917

DARLEY ABBEY
Derbyshire

The Coach House ◆◆◆
185A Duffield Road, Darley Abbey, Derby DE22 1JB
T: (01332) 551795

DARLEY BRIDGE
Derbyshire

Square and Compass ◆◆◆
Station Road, Darley Bridge, Matlock DE4 2EQ
T: (01629) 733255
F: (01629) 732400
E: jlees49@aol.com

DAVENTRY
Northamptonshire

Drayton Lodge ◆◆◆◆
Staverton Road, Daventry NN11 4NL
T: (01327) 702449
F: (01327) 872110
E: annspicer@farming.co.uk

Kingsthorpe Guesthouse ◆◆◆
Badby Road, Daventry NN11 4AW
T: (01327) 702752
F: (01327) 301854

The Old Coach House
◆◆◆◆ SILVER AWARD
Lower Catesby, Daventry NN11 6LF
T: (01327) 310390
F: (01327) 312220
E: coachhouse@lowercatesby.co.uk
I: www.lowercatesby.co.uk

Threeways House
◆◆◆◆ SILVER AWARD
Everdon, Daventry NN11 6BL
T: (01327) 361631
F: (01327) 361359
E: elizabethbarwood@hotmail.com
I: threewayshouse.com

DENSTONE
Staffordshire

Denstone Hall Farm ◆◆◆◆
Denstone, Uttoxeter ST14 5HF
T: (01889) 590253
F: (01889) 590930
E: denstonehallfarm@talk21.com
I: www.denstonehallfarm.com

Manor House Farm
◆◆◆◆ SILVER AWARD
Quixhill Lane, Prestwood, Denstone, Uttoxeter ST14 5DD
T: (01889) 590415
F: (01335) 342198
E: cm_ball@yahoo.co.uk
I: www.4posteraccom.com

Rowan Lodge ◆◆◆◆
Stubwood, Denstone, Uttoxeter ST14 5HU
T: (01889) 590913
E: rowanlodge@hotmail.com
I: www.smoothhound.co.uk/hotels/rowanlodge.html

DERBY
Derbyshire

Alambie ◆◆◆
189 Main Road, Morley, Derby DE7 6DG
T: (01332) 780349
F: (01332) 780349
E: alambie@beeb.net
I: www.alambieguesthouse.co.uk

Bonehill Farm ◆◆◆
Etwall Road, Mickleover, Derby DE3 0DN
T: (01332) 513553
E: bonehillfarm@hotmail.com

Chuckles Guesthouse ◆◆◆
48 Crompton Street, Derby DE1 1NX
T: (01332) 367193
E: ianfraser@chucklesguesthouse.freeserve.co.uk
I: www.chucklesguesthouse.gbr.cc

The Hill House Hotel ◆◆◆
294 Burton Road, Derby DE23 6AD
T: (01332) 361523
F: (01332) 361523
E: amandafearn@hillhousehotel.co.uk
I: www.hillhousehotel-derby.co.uk

Red Setters Guesthouse ◆◆◆
85 Curzon Street, Derby DE1 1LN
T: (01332) 362770
E: yvonne@derbycity.com
I: www.derbycity.com/michael/redset.html

Rose & Thistle Guesthouse ◆◆◆
21 Charnwood Street, Derby DE1 2GU
T: (01332) 344103
F: (01332) 291006

DIGBETH
West Midlands

The Works Guesthouse ◆◆◆
29-30 Warner Street, Digbeth, Birmingham B12 0JG
T: (0121) 772 3326
F: (0121) 772 3326

DIGBY
Lincolnshire

Digby Manor ◆◆◆◆
The Manor, North Street, Digby, Lincoln LN4 3LY
T: (01526) 322064
E: gill@digbymanor.com
I: www.digbymanor.com

Woodend Farm Bed and Breakfast ◆◆◆
Woodend Farm, Digby, Lincoln LN4 3NG
T: (01526) 860347

DONNINGTON
Gloucestershire

Holmleigh ◆◆
Donnington, Moreton-in-Marsh GL56 0XX
T: (01451) 830792

DORRINGTON
Shropshire

Meadowlands ◆◆◆
Lodge Lane, Frodesley, Dorrington, Shrewsbury SY5 7HD
T: (01694) 731350
F: (01694) 731350
E: Meadowlands@talk21.com
I: www.meadowlands.co.uk

DORSTONE
Herefordshire

Westbrook Manor Bed and Breakfast ◆◆◆
Westbrook, Dorstone, Hereford HR3 5SY
T: (01497) 831431
F: (01497) 831431
E: roddyandlibby@nextcall.net
I: www.golden-valley.co.uk/wmanor

DROITWICH
Worcestershire

Foxbrook ◆◆◆◆
238A Worcester Road, Droitwich WR9 8AY
T: (01905) 772414

Middleton Grange
◆◆◆◆ SILVER AWARD
Ladywood Road, Salwarpe, Droitwich WR9 0AH
T: (01905) 451678
F: (01905) 453978
E: salli@middletongrange.com
I: www.middletongrange.com

The Old Farmhouse
◆◆◆◆◆ SILVER AWARD
Hadley Heath, Droitwich WR9 0AR
T: (01905) 620837
F: (01905) 621722
E: judylambe@ombersley.demon.co.uk
I: www.the-old-farmhouse.com

Richmond Guest House ◆◆
3 Ombersley St. West, Droitwich WR9 8HZ
T: (01905) 775722
F: (01905) 794642
I: www.infotel.co.uk/hotels/36340.htm

Temple Broughton Farm
◆◆◆◆ GOLD AWARD
Broughton Green, Droitwich WR9 7EF
T: (01905) 391456
F: (01905) 391515
E: suemaccoll@ukonline.co.uk
I: www.templebroughtonfarm.co.uk

DRONFIELD
Derbyshire

Cassita ♦♦♦♦
Off Snape Hill Lane, Dronfield S18 2GL
T: (01246) 417303
F: (01246) 417303

Horsleygate Hall ♦♦♦♦
Horsleygate Lane, Holmesfield, Dronfield S18 7WD
T: (0114) 289 0333

DUDDINGTON
Northamptonshire

The Royal Oak
Rating Applied For
High Street, Duddington, Stamford PE9 3QE
T: (01780) 444267
F: (01780) 444369
E: royaloak@pe93qe.freeserve.co.uk
I: www.theroyaloakduddington.co.uk

DUNCHURCH
Warwickshire

The Old Thatched Cottage Hotel and Restaurant ♦♦♦♦
Southam Road, Dunchurch, Rugby CV22 6NG
T: (01788) 810417
F: (01788) 810417

Toft Hill ♦♦♦♦
Dunchurch, Rugby CV22 6NR
T: (01788) 810342

DUNTISBOURNE ABBOTS
Gloucestershire

Dixs Barn ♦♦♦
Duntisbourne Abbots, Cirencester GL7 7JN
T: (01285) 821249
E: wilcox@dixsbarn.freeserve.co.uk

DURSLEY
Gloucestershire

Foresters ♦♦♦♦
Chapel Street, Upper Cam Village, Dursley GL11 5NX
T: (01453) 549996
F: (01453) 548200
E: foresters@freeuk.com

DUSTON
Northamptonshire

Hopping Hare ♦♦♦♦
18 Hopping Hill Gardens, Duston, Northampton NN5 6PF
T: (01604) 683888
F: (01604) 683889
E: enquiries@mcmanuspub.co.uk
I: www.mcmanuspub.co.uk

DYMOCK
Gloucestershire

Granary ♦♦♦♦
Lower House Farm, Kempley, Dymock GL18 2BS
T: (01531) 890301
F: (01531) 890301

The White House ♦♦♦
Dymock GL18 2AQ
T: (01531) 890516

EARDISLAND
Herefordshire

The Manor House ♦♦♦♦
Eardisland, Leominster HR6 9BN
T: (01544) 388138

EARL STERNDALE
Derbyshire

Chrome Cottage ♦♦♦
Earl Sterndale, Buxton SK17 0BS
T: (01298) 83360
F: (01298) 83360
E: adgregg@bigwig.net

Fernydale Farm ♦♦♦♦
Earl Sterndale, Buxton SK17 0BS
T: (01298) 83236
F: (01298) 83605
E: william.nadin@virgin.net

EAST BARKWITH
Lincolnshire

Bodkin Lodge
♦♦♦♦♦ GOLD AWARD
Grange Farm, Torrington Lane, East Barkwith, Market Rasen LN8 5RY
T: (01673) 858249
F: (01673) 858249

The Grange
♦♦♦♦ SILVER AWARD
Torrington Lane, East Barkwith, Market Rasen LN8 5RY
T: (01673) 858670
E: sarahstamp@farmersweekly.net
I: www.thegrange-lincolnshire.co.uk

EAST HADDON
Northamptonshire

East Haddon Lodge ♦♦♦
East Haddon, Northampton NN6 8BU
T: (01604) 770240

EAST LANGTON
Leicestershire

The Bell Inn ♦♦♦♦
Main Street, East Langton, Market Harborough LE16 7TW
T: (01858) 545278
F: (01858) 545748
I: www.thebellinn.co.uk

EASTCOTE
Northamptonshire

West Farm
♦♦♦♦ SILVER AWARD
Gayton Road, Eastcote, Towcester NN12 8NS
T: (01327) 830310
F: (01327) 830310
E: west.farm@eastcote97.fsnet.co.uk

EASTNOR
Herefordshire

Hill Farmhouse Bed and Breakfast ♦♦
Eastnor, Ledbury HR8 1EF
T: (01531) 632827

EASTWOOD
Nottinghamshire

Horseshoe Cottage ♦♦♦♦
25 Babbington Village, N.r. Awsworth, Eastwood, Nottingham NG16 2SS
T: (0115) 930 4769
F: (0115) 930 4769
E: janet@horseshoe-cottage.co.uk

ECCLESHALL
Staffordshire

Cobblers Cottage ♦♦♦♦
Kerry Lane, Eccleshall, Stafford ST21 6EJ
T: (01785) 850116
F: (01785) 850116
E: cobblerscottage@tinyonline.co.uk

The George Inn ♦♦♦
Castle Street, Eccleshall, Stafford ST21 6DF
T: (01785) 850300
F: (01785) 851452
E: information@thegeorgeinn.freeserve.co.uk
I: www.thegeorgeinn.freeserve.co.uk

Slindon House Farm ♦♦♦♦
Slindon, Eccleshall, Stafford ST21 6LX
T: (01782) 791237
E: bonsallslindonhouse@supanet.com

ECKINGTON
Worcestershire

The Anchor Inn and Restaurant ♦♦♦
Cotheridge Lane, Eckington, Pershore WR10 3BA
T: (01386) 750356
F: (01386) 750356
E: anchoreck@aol.com
I: www.anchoreckington.co.uk

Lantern House ♦♦♦
Boon Street, Eckington, Pershore WR10 3BL
T: (01386) 750003
E: ann@parker14.freeserve.co.uk

Nafford House ♦♦♦♦
Eckington, Pershore WR10 3DJ
T: (01386) 750233

EDALE
Derbyshire

Mam Tor House ♦♦♦
Edale, Hope Valley S33 7ZA
T: (01433) 670253
E: mam.tor@tiscali.co.uk

Stonecroft
♦♦♦♦ GOLD AWARD
Grindsbrook, Edale, Hope Valley S33 7ZA
T: (01433) 670262
F: (01433) 670262
E: enquiries@stonecroftguesthouse.co.uk
I: http://accommodation.uk.net/hotels/stonecroftguesthouse

EDGBASTON
West Midlands

Swiss Cottage Hotel ♦♦
475 Gillott Road, Edgbaston, Birmingham B16 9LJ
T: (0121) 454 0371
F: (0121) 454 0371

ELLASTONE
Staffordshire

Chapel House ♦♦♦♦
Wootton, Ellastone, Wootton DE6 2GW
T: (01335) 324554
F: (01335) 324554
E: lizzy@weaverband.co.uk
I: www.weaverbandb.co.uk

ELLESMERE
Shropshire

Hordley Hall ♦♦♦
Hordley, Ellesmere SY12 9BB
T: (01691) 622772

Oakhill ♦♦♦♦
Dudleston, Ellesmere SY12 9LL
T: (01691) 690548

ELMESTHORPE
Leicestershire

Badgers Mount ♦♦♦♦
6 Station Road, Elmesthorpe, Leicester LE9 7SG
T: (01455) 848161
F: (01455) 848161
E: info@badgersmount.com
I: www.badgersmount.com

ELMLEY CASTLE
Worcestershire

The Old Mill Inn ♦♦♦♦
Mill Lane, Elmley Castle, Pershore WR10 3HP
T: (01386) 710407
F: (01386) 710066
E: oldmilin@dircon.co.uk
I: www.elmleymill.com

ELTON
Derbyshire

Hawthorn Cottage
♦♦♦♦ SILVER AWARD
Well Street, Elton, Bakewell DE4 2BY
T: (01629) 650372
I: www.hawthorncottage-elton.co.uk

Homestead Farm ♦♦♦
Main Street, Elton, Matlock DE4 2BW
T: (01629) 650359

ENDON
Staffordshire

Hollinhurst Farm ♦♦♦
Park Lane, Endon, Stoke-on-Trent ST9 9JB
T: (01782) 502633
E: hjball@ukf.net

ENGLISH BICKNOR
Gloucestershire

Dryslade Farm ♦♦♦♦
English Bicknor, Coleford GL16 7PA
T: (01594) 860259
F: (01594) 860259
E: dryslade@agriplus.net
I: www.drysladefarm.co.uk

EVERTON
Nottinghamshire

The Blacksmiths Arms ♦♦♦♦
Church Street, Everton, Doncaster DN10 5BQ
T: (01777) 817281

EVESHAM
Worcestershire

Bredon View Guest House
♦♦♦♦ SILVER AWARD
Village Street, Harvington, Evesham WR11 8NQ
T: (01386) 871484
F: (01386) 871484
E: b.v.circa1898@bushinternet.com
I: www.bredonview.net

EWYAS HAROLD
Herefordshire

The Old Rectory ♦♦♦♦
Ewyas Harold, Hereford HR2 0EY
T: (01981) 240498
F: (01981) 240498

EYAM
Derbyshire

Crown Cottage ♦♦♦♦
Main Road, Eyam, Hope Valley S32 5QW
T: (01433) 630858
E: crown-cottage@amserve.com
I: www.crown-cottage.co.uk

EYDON
Northamptonshire

Crockwell Farm
◆◆◆◆ SILVER AWARD
Eydon, Daventry NN11 3QA
T: (01327) 361358
F: (01327) 361573
E: info@crockwellfarm.co.uk
I: www.crockwellfarm.co.uk

FAIRFIELD
Derbyshire

Barms Farm
◆◆◆◆ SILVER AWARD
Fairfield Common, Fairfield, Buxton SK17 7HW
T: (01298) 77723
F: (01298) 78692
E: barmsfarm@highpeak.co.uk
I: www.highpeak.co.uk/barmsfarm

9 Green Lane
Rating Applied For
9 Green Lane, Fairfield, Buxton SK17 9DP
T: (01298) 73731
E: book@9greenlane.co.uk
I: www.9greenlane.co.uk

FAIRFORD
Gloucestershire

East End House
◆◆◆◆◆ GOLD AWARD
Fairford GL7 4AP
T: (01285) 713715
F: (01285) 713505
E: diana.ewart@virgin.net
I: www.eastendhouse.co.uk

Kempsford Manor ◆◆◆
High Street, Kempsford, Fairford GL7 4EQ
T: (01285) 810131
F: (01285) 810131
E: ipek@lineone.net
I: members.lycos.co.uk/kempsford_manor/

Milton Farm ◆◆◆◆
Fairford GL7 4HZ
T: (01285) 712205
F: (01285) 711349
E: milton@farmersweekly.net
I: www.milton-farm.co.uk

Waiten Hill Farm ◆◆
Fairford GL7 4JG
T: (01285) 712652
F: (01285) 712652

FARNSFIELD
Nottinghamshire

Lockwell House ◆◆◆
Lockwell Hill, Old Rufford Road, Farnsfield, Newark NG22 8JG
T: (01623) 883067
F: (01623) 883067

FARTHINGHOE
Northamptonshire

Greenfield
◆◆◆◆ SILVER AWARD
Baker Street, Farthinghoe, Brackley NN13 5PH
T: (01295) 712380
F: (01295) 712380
E: vivwebb@aol.com
I: http://members.aol.com/vivwebb/

FECKENHAM
Worcestershire

Orchard House
◆◆◆◆ SILVER AWARD
Berrowhill Lane, Feckenham, Redditch B96 6QJ
T: (01527) 821497
F: (01527) 821497

The Steps ◆◆◆
6 High Street, Feckenham, Redditch B96 6HS
T: (01527) 892678
E: jenny@thesteps.co.uk
I: www.thesteps.co.uk

FENNY BENTLEY
Derbyshire

Cairn Grove ◆◆◆◆
Ashes Lane, Fenny Bentley, Ashbourne DE6 1LD
T: (01335) 350538
E: keith.wheeldon@virgin.net
I: www.cairngrove.co.uk

FENNY COMPTON
Warwickshire

The Grange ◆◆◆
The Slade, Fenny Compton, Southam CV47 2YE
T: (01295) 770590

FENNY DRAYTON
Leicestershire

White Wings
◆◆◆◆◆ SILVER AWARD
Quaker Close, Fenny Drayton, Nuneaton CV13 6BS
T: (01827) 716100
F: (01827) 717191
E: lloyd@whitewings.freeserve.co.uk

FERNHILL HEATH
Worcestershire

Dilmore House Hotel ◆◆◆◆
254 Droitwich Road, Fernhill Heath, Worcester WR3 7UL
T: (01905) 451543
F: (01905) 452015
E: dilmorehouse@ukgateway.net
I: www.smoothhound.co.uk/hotels/dilmore.html

Heathside ◆◆◆◆
Droitwich Road, Fernhill Heath, Worcester WR3 7UA
T: (01905) 458245
F: (01905) 458245

FIDDINGTON
Gloucestershire

Hillview B and B ◆◆◆◆
Fiddington, N.r. Ashchurch, Fiddington, Tewkesbury GL20 7BJ
T: (01684) 293231
F: (01684) 293231
E: hillviewbandb@aol.com

FILLONGLEY
Warwickshire

Manor House Farm
◆◆◆◆ SILVER AWARD
Green End Road, Fillongley, Coventry CV7 8DS
T: (01676) 540256

FLAXLEY
Gloucestershire

Waldron Farm ◆◆◆◆
Flaxley, Newnham-on-Severn GL14 1JR
T: (01452) 760581
F: (01452) 760581
E: charlesworth@waldronfarm.fsbusiness.co.uk
I: www.waldronfarm.co.uk

FOWNHOPE
Herefordshire

The Tan House ◆◆◆
Fownhope, Hereford HR1 4NJ
T: (01432) 860549
F: (01432) 860466
E: vera@ukbu.co.uk

FRODESLEY
Shropshire

The Haven ◆◆◆◆
Frodesley, Dorrington, Shrewsbury SY5 7EY
T: (01694) 731672
E: the-haven@frodesley.fsnet.co.uk
I: www.welcomingyou.co.uk/the-haven

GAINSBOROUGH
Lincolnshire

The Beckett Arms ◆◆◆
25 High Street, Corringham, Gainsborough DN21 5QP
T: (01427) 838201

GAYTON LE MARSH
Lincolnshire

Westbrook House ◆◆◆◆
Main Street, Gayton le Marsh, Alford LN13 0NW
T: (01507) 450624
E: westbrook_house@hotmail.com
I: www.bestbookwestbrook.co.uk

GLOSSOP
Derbyshire

Avondale ◆◆◆◆
28 Woodhead Road, Glossop SK13 7RH
T: (01457) 853132
F: (0161) 494 6078
E: avondale.glossop@talk21.com
I: www.cressbrook.co.uk/glossop/avondale

Peels Arms ◆◆◆
6-12 Temple Street, Padfield, Hyde SK13 1EX
T: (01457) 852719
F: (01457) 860536

GLOUCESTER
Gloucestershire

Albert Hotel ◆◆◆
56-58 Worcester Street, Gloucester GL1 3AG
T: (01452) 502081
F: (01452) 311738
E: enquiries@alberthotel.com
I: www.alberthotel.com

Brookthorpe Lodge ◆◆◆
Stroud Road, Brookthorpe, Gloucester GL4 0UQ
T: (01452) 812645
F: (01452) 812645
E: enq@brookthorpelodge.demon.co.uk
I: www.brookthorpelodge.demon.co.uk

The Chestnuts ◆◆◆◆
9 Brunswick Square, Gloucester GL1 1UG
T: (01452) 330356
F: (01452) 539571
E: dchampion@blueyonder.co.uk

The Coppins ◆◆◆◆
11c Kenilworth Avenue, Gloucester GL2 0QN
T: (01452) 302777

Kilmorie Small Holding
◆◆◆◆
Gloucester Road, Corse, Snigs End, Staunton, Gloucester GL19 3RQ
T: (01452) 840224
F: (01452) 840224
E: sheila-barnfield@supanet.com
I: www.SmoothHound.co.uk/hotels/kilmorie.html

Lulworth ◆◆◆
12 Midland Road, Gloucester GL1 4UF
T: (01452) 521881
F: (01452) 386149
E: lulworth-guest@tiscali.co.uk
I: www.myweb.tiscali.co.uk/lulworth

The New Inn Hotel ◆◆◆
16 Northgate Street, Gloucester GL1 1SF
T: (01452) 522177
F: (01452) 301054
E: newinn@soft-data.net
I: www.new-inn-hotel.com

Nicki's Hotel & Taverna ◆◆
105-107 Westgate Street, Gloucester GL1 2PG
T: (01452) 301359

Notley House and The Coach House ◆◆◆
93 Hucclecote Road, Hucclecote, Gloucester GL3 3TR
T: (01452) 611584
F: (01452) 371229
E: notleyhouse@aol.com
I: www.notleyhouse.co.uk

Pembury Guest House ◆◆◆
9 Pembury Road, St Barnabas, Gloucester GL4 6UE
T: (01452) 521856
F: (01452) 303418

Spalite Hotel ◆◆◆
121 Southgate Street, Gloucester GL1 1XQ
T: (01452) 380828
E: marsh@spalitehotel.fsnet.co.uk
I: www.spalitehotel.co.uk

The Tailors House ◆◆◆
43-45 Westgate Street, Gloucester GL1 2NW
T: (01452) 521750
F: (01452) 521750

GNOSALL
Staffordshire

The Leys House ◆◆◆◆
Gnosall, Stafford ST20 0BZ
T: (01785) 822532
F: (01785) 822060
E: proffitt.gnosall@virgin.net

GOADBY
Leicestershire

The Hollies ♦♦♦
Goadby, Leicester LE7 9EE
T: (0116) 259 8301
F: (0116) 259 8491
E: j.parr@btinternet.com

GRANGEMILL
Derbyshire

Middle Hills Farm ♦♦♦♦
Grangemill, Derby DE4 4HY
T: (01629) 650368
F: (01629) 650368
E: I.lomas@btinernet.com
I: www.peakdistrictfarmhols.co.uk

GRANTHAM
Lincolnshire

Beechleigh Guesthouse ♦♦♦♦
55 North Parade, Grantham NG31 8AT
T: (01476) 572213
F: (01476) 566058
E: info@beechleigh.co.uk
I: www.beechleigh.co.uk

The Red House
Rating Applied For
74 North Parade, Grantham NG31 8AN
T: (01476) 579869
F: (01476) 401597
E: enquiry@red-house.com
I: www.red-house.com

GREAT DALBY
Leicestershire

Dairy Farm ♦♦♦
8 Burrough End, Great Dalby, Melton Mowbray LE14 2EW
T: (01664) 562783

GREAT HUCKLOW
Derbyshire

The Old Manse ♦♦♦♦
Great Hucklow, Buxton SK17 8RF
T: (01298) 871262
F: (01298) 872916
E: bedandbreakfast@angus.co.uk
I: www.angus.co.uk/bedandbreakfast/

GREAT RISSINGTON
Gloucestershire

Lower Farmhouse ♦♦♦
Great Rissington, Cheltenham GL54 2LH
T: (01451) 810163
F: (01451) 810187
E: B&B@lowerfarmhouse.co.uk
I: www.lowerfarmhouse.co.uk

Stepping Stone ♦♦♦♦
Rectory Lane, Great Rissington, Cheltenham GL54 2LL
T: (01451) 821385
E: stepping-stone-b-b@excite.com

GREAT WITLEY
Worcestershire

Home Farm
♦♦♦♦♦ SILVER AWARD
Great Witley, Worcester WR6 6JJ
T: (01299) 896825
F: (01299) 896176
E: homefarm@yescomputers.co.uk
I: www.homefarmbandb.com

GRETTON
Gloucestershire

Elms Farm ♦♦♦♦
Gretton Fields, Gretton, Cheltenham GL54 5HQ
T: (01242) 620150
E: rosequilter@hotmail.com
I: www.elmfarm.demon.co.uk

GRIMSTON
Leicestershire

Gorse House
♦♦♦♦ SILVER AWARD
33 Main Street, Grimston, Melton Mowbray LE14 3BZ
T: (01664) 813537
F: (01664) 813537
E: cowdell@gorsehouse.co.uk
I: www.gorsehouse.co.uk

GRINDLEFORD
Derbyshire

Sir William Hotel ♦♦♦♦
Sir William Hill, Grindleford, Hope Valley S32 2HS
T: (01433) 630303
F: (01433) 639753
E: sirwilliamhotel@btinternet.com
I: www.sirwilliamhotel.com

Woodlands ♦♦♦♦
Sir William Hill Road, Grindleford, Hope Valley S32 2HS
T: (01433) 631593

GRINDON
Staffordshire

Summerhill Farm ♦♦♦♦
Grindon, Leek ST13 7TT
T: (01538) 304264
E: patandbriansimpson@summerhills-farm.fsnet.co.uk

GUILSBOROUGH
Northamptonshire

Lodge Farm
♦♦♦♦ SILVER AWARD
West Haddon Road, Guilsborough, Northampton NN6 8QE
T: (01604) 740392
F: (01604) 740392
I: lodgefarmbedandbreakfast.co.uk

GUITING POWER
Gloucestershire

Castlett Bank ♦♦♦♦
Castlett Street, Guiting Power, Cheltenham GL54 5US
T: (01451) 850300
F: (01451) 850300
E: wilderspin.castlettbank@btinternet.com
I: www.SmoothHound.co.uk/hotels/castlett.html

Cobnutt Cottage ♦♦♦♦
Winchcombe Road, Guiting Power, Cheltenham GL54 5UX
T: (01451) 850658

The Guiting Guest House
♦♦♦♦♦ SILVER AWARD
Post Office Lane, Guiting Power, Cheltenham GL54 5TZ
T: (01451) 850470
F: (01451) 850034
E: info@guitingguesthouse.com
I: www.guitingguesthouse.com

Halfway House ♦♦♦
Kineton, Guiting Power, Cheltenham GL54 5UG
T: (01451) 850344

The Hollow Bottom ♦♦♦♦
Winchcombe Road, Guiting Power, Cheltenham GL54 5UX
T: (01451) 850392
F: (01451) 850945
E: hollow.bottom@virgin.net
I: www.hollowbottom.com

Tally Ho Guesthouse ♦♦♦♦
1 Tally Ho Lane, Guiting Power, Cheltenham GL54 5TY
T: (01451) 850186
E: tallyhobb@aol.com
I: www.cotswolds-bedandbreakfast.co.uk

GUNBY
Lincolnshire

Brook House ♦♦♦♦
Gunby, Grantham NG33 5LF
T: (01476) 860010
F: (01476) 860010

HACKTHORN
Lincolnshire

Honeyholes ♦♦♦♦
South Farm, Hackthorn, Lincoln LN2 3PW
T: (01673) 861868
F: (01673) 861868

HADNALL
Shropshire

Hall Farm House ♦♦♦
Hadnall, Shrewsbury SY4 4AG
T: (01939) 210269
E: hallfarmhouse1@whsmithnet.co.uk

HAGWORTHINGHAM
Lincolnshire

White Oak Grange
♦♦♦♦ SILVER AWARD
Hagworthingham, Spilsby PE23 4LX
T: (01507) 588376
F: (01507) 588377
E: whiteoakgrange@amserve.com
I: whiteoakgrange.com

HAMPTON IN ARDEN
West Midlands

The Cottage Guest House ♦♦♦
Kenilworth Road, On A452 to Balsall Common, Hampton in Arden, Solihull B92 0LW
T: (01675) 442323
F: (01675) 443323

The Hollies Bed and Breakfast ♦♦♦♦
Kenilworth Road, Hampton-in-Arden, Hampton in Arden, Solihull B92 0LW
T: (01675) 442681
F: (01675) 442941
E: thehollies@hotmail.com
I: www.theholliesguesthouse.co.uk

HANDSACRE
Staffordshire

The Olde Peculiar ♦♦♦♦
The Green, Handsacre, Rugeley WS15 4DP
T: (01543) 491891
F: (01543) 493733

HANLEY
Staffordshire

Northwood Hotel Limited ♦♦♦
146 Keelings Road, Northwood, Hanley, Stoke-on-Trent ST1 6QA
T: (01782) 279729
F: (01782) 207507

HANLEY CASTLE
Worcestershire

The Chestnuts ♦♦♦♦
Gilberts End, Hanley Castle, Worcester WR8 0AS
T: (01684) 311219
E: heather@hanleyswans.demon.co.uk
I: hev-thechestnuts.com

HANLEY SWAN
Worcestershire

Brook Farm ♦♦♦♦
Tyre Hill, Hanley Swan, Worcester WR8 0EQ
T: (01684) 310796
F: (01684) 310796
E: bandb@brookfarm.org.uk
I: www.brookfarm.org.uk

Cygnet Lodge
♦♦♦♦♦ GOLD AWARD
Worcester Road, Hanley Swan, Worcester WR8 0EA
T: (01684) 310716
F: (01684) 311402
E: wendy@cygnetlodge.co.uk
I: www.cygnetlodge.co.uk

Meadowbank
♦♦♦♦ SILVER AWARD
Picken End, Hanley Swan, Worcester WR8 0DQ
T: (01684) 310917
E: dave@meadowbank.freeserve.co.uk
I: mysite.freeserve.com/meadowbank

Yew Tree House Bed and Breakfast
♦♦♦♦♦ SILVER AWARD
Yew Tree House, Hanley Swan, Worcester WR8 0DN
T: (01684) 310736
F: (01684) 311709
E: yewtreehs@aol.com
I: www.yewtreehouse.co.uk

HANLEY WILLIAM
Worcestershire

Hanley Mill
Rating Applied For
Hanley William, Tenbury Wells WR15 8QT
T: (01584) 781602
F: (01584) 781217
E: suethemiller@hotmail.com

HARLASTON
Staffordshire

The Old Rectory ♦♦♦♦
Churchside, Harlaston, Tamworth B79 9HE
T: (01827) 383583
F: (01827) 383583

HARLEY
Shropshire

Rowley Farm Hospitality ♦♦♦
Harley, Shrewsbury SY5 6LX
T: (01952) 727348

HARTINGTON
Derbyshire

Bank Top Farm ♦♦♦
Pilsbury Road, Hartington, Buxton SK17 0AD
T: (01298) 84205
F: (01298) 84859
E: owenjane@farming.co.uk
I: www.banktophartington.freeserve.co.uk

Manifold Inn ♦♦♦
Hulme End, Hartington, Buxton SK17 0EX
T: (01298) 84537
I: www.themanifoldinn.co.uk

Wolfscote Grange ♦♦♦♦
Hartington, Buxton SK17 0AX
T: (01298) 84342
E: wolfscote@btinternet.com

HASELOR
Warwickshire

Walcote Farm ♦♦♦♦
Walcote, Haselor, Alcester B49 6LY
T: (01789) 488264
E: john@walcotefarm.co.uk
I: www.walcotefarm.co.uk

HATHERSAGE
Derbyshire

Cannon Croft
♦♦♦♦ GOLD AWARD
Cannonfields, Hathersage, Hope Valley S32 1AG
T: (01433) 650005
F: (01433) 650005
E: soates@cannoncroft.fsbusiness.co.uk
I: www.cannoncroft.fsbusiness.co.uk

The Plough Inn
♦♦♦♦ SILVER AWARD
Leadmill Bridge, Hathersage, Hope Valley S32 1BA
T: (01433) 650319
F: (01433) 651049

Sladen ♦♦♦
Jaggers Lane, Hathersage, Hope Valley S32 1AZ
T: (01433) 650706
F: (01433) 650315

HAY ON WYE
Herefordshire

Haie Barn ♦♦♦♦
The Bage, Dorstone, Hereford HR3 5SU
T: (01497) 831729
E: goodfood@haie-barn.co.uk
I: www.golden-valley.co.uk/haiebarn

HENLEY-IN-ARDEN
Warwickshire

Holland Park Farm ♦♦♦
Buckley Green, Henley-in-Arden, Solihull B95 5QF
T: (01564) 792625
F: (01564) 792625

HEREFORD
Herefordshire

Alberta ♦♦
7-13 Newtown Road, Hereford HR4 9LH
T: (01432) 270313
F: (01432) 270313

Ancroft ♦♦♦
10 Cheviot Close, Kings Acre, Hereford HR4 0TF
T: (01432) 274394

The Bowens Country House ♦♦♦♦
Fownhope, Hereford HR1 4PS
T: (01432) 860430
F: (01432) 860430
E: thebowenshotel@aol.com
I: www.thebowenshotel.co.uk

Brandon Lodge
♦♦♦♦ SILVER AWARD
Ross Road, Grafton, Hereford HR2 8BH
T: (01432) 355621
F: (01432) 355621
E: info@brandonlodge.co.uk
I: www.brandonlodge.co.uk

Cedar Guest House ♦♦♦
123 Whitecross Road, Whitecross, Hereford HR4 0LS
T: (01432) 267235
F: (01432) 267235
E: info@cedarguesthouse.com
I: www.cedarguesthouse.com

Charades ♦♦♦
34 Southbank Road, Hereford HR1 2TJ
T: (01432) 269444

Corner House
Rating Applied For
Newton St Margarets, Hereford HR2 0QP
T: (01981) 510283
E: timstart@yahoo.co.uk
I: www.cornerhousenewton.co.uk

Grafton Villa Farm House
♦♦♦♦ SILVER AWARD
Grafton, Hereford HR2 8ED
T: (01432) 268689
F: (01432) 268689
E: jennielayton@ereal.net
I: www.graftonvilla.co.uk

Hedley Lodge ♦♦♦♦
Belmont Abbey, Abergavenny Road, Hereford HR2 9RZ
T: (01432) 374747
F: (01432) 277318
E: hedleylodge@aol.com
I: www.hedleylodge.com

Heron House Bed & Breakfast ♦♦♦
Heron House, Canon Pyon Road, Portway, Burghill, Hereford HR4 8NG
T: (01432) 761111
F: (01432) 760603
E: info@theheronhouse.com
I: www.theheronhouse.com

Holly Tree Guest House ♦♦♦
21 Barton Road, Hereford HR4 0AY
T: (01432) 357845

Hopbine Hotel ♦♦
The Hopbine, Roman Road, Hereford HR1 1LE
T: (01432) 268722
F: (01432) 268722
E: info@hopbinehotel123.fsnet.co.uk

Lower Calver Hill Farm ♦♦♦♦
Norton Canon, Hereford HR4 7BW
T: (01544) 318252
E: oates.home@btopenworld.com

Montgomery House ♦♦♦♦
12 St Owen Street, Hereford HR1 2PL
T: (01432) 351454
F: (01432) 344463
E: lizforbes@lineone.net
I: www.montgomeryhousehereford.com

Old Rectory
♦♦♦♦ SILVER AWARD
Byford, Hereford HR4 7LD
T: (01981) 590218
F: (07970) 512515
E: info@cm-ltd.com
I: www.smoothhound.co.uk/hotels/oldrectory2.html

The Somerville ♦♦♦
12 Bodenham Road, Hereford HR1 2TS
T: (01432) 273991
F: (01432) 268719

HIGH PEAK
Derbyshire

Sycamore Inn ♦♦♦
Sycamore Road, Birch Vale, High Peak SK22 1AB
T: (01663) 747568
F: (01663) 747382
E: sycamoreinn@aol.com
I: www.sycamoreinn.co.uk

Twiggys ♦♦♦
86 Hague Bar, New Mills, High Peak SK22 3AR
T: (01663) 745036
F: (01663) 745036
E: enquiries@twiggys-bandb.co.uk
I: www.twiggys-bandb.co.uk

HILCOTE
Derbyshire

Hilcote Hall ♦♦
Hilcote Lane, Hilcote, Alfreton DE55 5HR
T: (01773) 812608
F: (01773) 812608
I: www.hilcotehall.co.uk

HIMBLETON
Worcestershire

Phepson Farm ♦♦♦♦
Himbleton, Droitwich WR9 7JZ
T: (01905) 391205
F: (01905) 391338
E: havard@globalnet.co.uk
I: www.phepsonfarm.co.uk

HINTON IN THE HEDGES
Northamptonshire

The Old Rectory ♦♦♦
Hinton-in-the-Hedges, Hinton in the Hedges, Brackley NN13 5NG
T: (01280) 706807
F: (01280) 706809
E: lavinia@lavinia.demon.co.uk
I: www.northamptonshire.co.uk/hotels/oldrectory.htm

HOARWITHY
Herefordshire

Old Mill
♦♦♦♦ SILVER AWARD
Hoarwithy, Hereford HR2 6QH
T: (01432) 840602
F: (01432) 840602
E: carol.probert@virgin.net
I: www.theoldmillhoarwithy.co.uk

HOCKLEY HEATH
West Midlands

Illshaw Heath Farm ♦♦♦♦
Kineton Lane, Hockley Heath, Solihull B94 6RX
T: (01564) 782214

HOLBEACH
Lincolnshire

The Bull Inn ♦♦
Old Main Road, Fleet Hargate, Holbeach, Spalding PE12 8LH
T: (01406) 426866

Cackle Hill House
♦♦♦♦ SILVER AWARD
Cackle Hill, Holbeach, Spalding PE12 8BS
T: (01406) 426721
F: (01406) 424659
E: cacklehillhouse@farming.co.uk

HOLBECK
Nottinghamshire

Browns
♦♦♦♦♦ GOLD AWARD
The Old Orchard Cottage, Holbeck, Worksop S80 3NF
T: (01909) 720659
F: (01909) 720659
E: Browns@holbeck.fsnet.co.uk
I: www.brownsholbeck.co.uk

HOLLINGTON
Staffordshire

The Raddle Inn ♦♦♦
Quarry Bank, Hollington, Stoke-on-Trent ST10 4HQ
T: (01889) 507278
F: (01889) 507520
E: peter@logcabin.co.uk
I: www.logcabin.co.uk

Reevsmoor ♦♦♦♦
Hoargate Lane, Hollington, Ashbourne DE6 3AG
T: (01335) 330318
F: (01335) 330978
E: hlivesey@aol.com

HOLMESFIELD
Derbyshire

Carpenter House ♦♦♦
Millthorpe, Holmesfield, Dronfield S18 7WH
T: (0114) 289 0307

HOLYMOORSIDE
Derbyshire

Burnell ♦♦♦♦
Baslow Road, Holymoorside, Chesterfield S42 7HJ
T: (01246) 567570
I: www.geocities.com/burnellbnb

HOPE
Derbyshire

Causeway House ♦♦♦
Back Street, Castleton, Hope Valley S33 8WE
T: (01433) 623291
F: (0114) 236 0675
E: susanbridget@aol.com
I: www.causewayhouse.co.uk

Underleigh House
♦♦♦♦♦ SILVER AWARD
Off Edale Road, Hope, Hope Valley S33 6RF
T: (01433) 621372
F: (01433) 621324
E: underleigh.house@btinternet.com
I: www.underleighhouse.co.uk

Establishments printed in blue have a detailed entry in this guide

HOPE BAGOT
Shropshire

Croft Cottage ♦♦♦♦
Cumberley Lane, Hope Bagot, Ludlow SY8 3LJ
T: (01584) 890664
F: (0870) 129 9897
E: croft.cottage@virgin.net
I: www.croftcottage.org.uk

HOPE VALLEY
Derbyshire

The Chequers Inn ♦♦♦♦
Froggatt Edge, Hope Valley S32 3ZJ
T: (01433) 630231
F: (01433) 631072
I: www.chequers-froggatt.com

The Rambler Country House Hotel ♦♦♦
Edale, Hope Valley S33 7ZA
T: (01433) 670268
F: (01433) 670106
E: therambler@dorbiere.co.uk
I: www.therambleinn.co.uk

The Rising Sun Hotel ♦♦♦♦
Thornhill Moor, Near Bamford, Hope Valley S33 0AL
T: (01433) 651323
F: (01433) 651601
E: info@the-rising-sun.org
I: www.the-rising-sun.org

HORSLEY
Derbyshire

Horsley Lodge
♦♦♦♦ SILVER AWARD
Smalley Mill Road, Horsley, Derby DE21 5BL
T: (01332) 780838
F: (01332) 781118
E: enquiries@horsleylodge.co.uk
I: www.horsleylodge.co.uk

HORTON
Staffordshire

Croft Meadows Farm ♦♦♦
Horton, Leek ST13 8QE
T: (01782) 513039

HOW CAPLE
Herefordshire

How Caple Grange ♦♦♦
How Caple, Hereford HR1 4TF
T: (01989) 740208
F: (01989) 740301

HULME END
Staffordshire

Raikes Farm ♦♦♦♦
Nr Hartington, Hulme End, Buxton SK17 0HJ
T: (01298) 84344
F: (01298) 84344
E: a.shipley@ntlworld.com

Riverside
Rating Applied For
Hulme End, Buxton SK17 0EZ
T: (01298) 84474
F: (01298) 84474
E: roger@riversidevilla.co.uk
I: www.riversidevilla.co.uk

HUMBERSTONE
Leicestershire

The Squirrels ♦♦♦
9 Widford Close, The Square, Humberstone, Leicester LE5 0AN
T: (0116) 220 2894
F: (0116) 276 8424

HUNTLEY
Gloucestershire

Birdwood Villa Farm ♦♦
Main Road, Birdwood, Huntley, Gloucester GL19 3EQ
T: (01452) 750451
E: mking@farmersweekly.net
I: www.birdwoodvillafarm.co.uk

Forest Gate ♦♦♦
Huntley, Gloucester GL19 3EU
T: (01452) 831192
F: (01452) 831192
E: forest.gate@huntley-glos.demon.co.uk
I: www.huntley-glos.demon.co.uk

The Kings Head Inn ♦♦♦
Birdwood, Huntley, Gloucester GL19 3EF
T: (01452) 750348
F: (01452) 750348

HUSBANDS BOSWORTH
Leicestershire

Mrs Armitage's ♦♦
31-33 High Street, Husbands Bosworth, Lutterworth LE17 6LJ
T: (01858) 880066

IDRIDGEHAY
Derbyshire

Millbank House Bed and Breakfast ♦♦♦♦
Idridgehay, Belper DE56 2SH
T: (01629) 823161

ILAM
Staffordshire

Beechenhill Farm
♦♦♦♦ SILVER AWARD
Ilam, Ashbourne DE6 2BD
T: (01335) 310274
F: (01335) 310467
E: beechenhill@btinternet.com
I: www.beechenhill.co.uk

Throwley Hall ♦♦♦♦
Ilam, Ashbourne DE6 2BB
T: (01538) 308202
F: (01538) 308243
E: throwleyhall@talk21.com
I: www.throwleyhallfarm.co.uk

INKBERROW
Worcestershire

Bulls Head Inn ♦♦♦
The Village Green, Inkberrow, Worcester WR7 4DY
T: (01386) 792233
F: (01386) 793090

IRONBRIDGE
Shropshire

Bird in Hand Inn ♦♦♦
Waterloo Street, Ironbridge, Telford TF8 7HG
T: (01952) 432226

Bridge House
♦♦♦♦♦ SILVER AWARD
Buildwas, Telford TF8 7BN
T: (01952) 432105
F: (01952) 432105
I: www.smoothhound.co.uk/hotels/bridgehs.html

Bridge View ♦♦♦
10 Tontine Hill, Ironbridge, Telford TF8 7AL
T: (01952) 432541
F: (01952) 433405
I: www.ironbridgeview.co.uk

The Calcutts House ♦♦♦
Jackfield, Ironbridge, Telford TF8 7LH
T: (01952) 882631
F: (01952) 882951
E: alan&linda@calcuttshouse.co.uk
I: www.calcuttshouse.co.uk

Coalbrookdale Villa
♦♦♦♦ SILVER AWARD
Paradise, Coalbrookdale, Ironbridge, Telford TF8 7NR
T: (01952) 433450
F: (01952) 433450
E: coalbrookdalevilla@currantbun.com
I: www.coalbrookdalevilla.co.uk

The Firs Guest House ♦♦♦
32 Buildwas Road, Ironbridge, Telford TF8 7BJ
T: (01952) 432121
F: (01952) 433010
E: thefirsironbridge@tiscali.co.uk
I: www.ironbridge.ws/search/accomodation/hotels.asp?VID=49

The Golden Ball Inn ♦♦♦♦
Newbridge Road, Ironbridge, Telford TF8 7BA
T: (01952) 432179
F: (01952) 433123
E: matrowland@hotmail.com
I: www.goldenballinn.com

Greenways Guest House ♦♦♦♦
57 High Street, Madeley, Telford TF7 5AT
T: (01952) 583118
F: (01952) 408777
E: greenwaysguesthouse@hotmail.com
I: www.greenwaysguesthouse.com

The Library House
♦♦♦♦♦ GOLD AWARD
11 Severn Bank, Ironbridge, Telford TF8 7AN
T: (01952) 432299
F: (01952) 433967
E: info@libraryhouse.com
I: www.libraryhouse.com

Lord Hill Guest House ♦♦
Duke Street, Broseley TF12 5LU
T: (01952) 884270

The Malthouse ♦♦♦♦
The Wharfage, Ironbridge, Telford TF8 7NH
T: (01952) 433712
F: (01952) 433298
E: enquiries@malthousepubs.co.uk
I: malthousepubs.co.uk

The Meadow Lodge ♦♦♦♦
29 Buildwas Road, Ironbridge, Telford TF8 7BJ
T: (01952) 432632
F: (01952) 433625

Orchard House ♦♦♦
40 King Street, Broseley TF12 5NA
T: (01952) 882684

Post Office House ♦♦♦
6 The Square, Ironbridge, Telford TF8 7AQ
T: (01952) 433201
F: (01952) 433582
E: Hunter@pohouse-ironbridge.fsnet.co.uk
I: www.pohouse-ironbridge.fsnet.co.uk

Severn Lodge
♦♦♦♦♦ SILVER AWARD
New Road, Ironbridge, Telford TF8 7AU
T: (01952) 432147
F: (01952) 432148
E: julia@severnlodge.com
I: www.severnlodge.com

The Swan ♦♦♦♦
The Wharfage, Ironbridge, Telford TF8 7NH
T: (01952) 432306
F: (01952) 432994
I: www.malthousepubs.co.uk

Tontine Hotel ♦♦
The Square, Ironbridge, Telford TF8 7AL
T: (01952) 432127
F: (01952) 432094
E: tontinehotel@netscapeonline.co.uk
I: www.tontine-ironbridge.co.uk

Wharfage Cottage ♦♦♦
17 The Wharfage, Ironbridge, Telford TF8 7AW
T: (01952) 432721
F: (01952) 432639

Ye Olde Robin Hood Inn ♦♦♦
33 Waterloo Street, Ironbridge, Telford TF8 7HQ
T: (01952) 433100

KEGWORTH
Leicestershire

The Coach House ♦♦
35 High Street, Kegworth, Derby DE74 2DA
T: (01509) 674131
I: www.kegworthvillage.com/coachhouse

The Kegworth Lantern Inn
Rating Applied For
1 Market Place, Kegworth, Derby DE74 2EE
T: (01509) 673989
F: (01509) 673989

KEMPSEY
Worcestershire

Anchor Inn ♦♦
69 Main Road, Kempsey, Worcester WR5 3NB
T: (01905) 820411
E: gwenrig@netscapeonline.co.uk

Malbre Hotel ♦♦♦
Baynhall, Kempsey, Worcester WR5 3PA
T: (01905) 820412

KENILWORTH
Warwickshire

Abbey Guest House ♦♦♦♦
41 Station Road, Kenilworth CV8 1JD
T: (01926) 512707
F: (01926) 859148
E: the-abbey@virgin.net
I: www.abbeyguesthouse.com

Avondale B & B ♦♦♦♦
18 Moseley Road, Kenilworth
CV8 2AQ
T: (01926) 859072

Castle Laurels Hotel
♦♦♦♦ SILVER AWARD
22 Castle Road, Kenilworth
CV8 1NG
T: (01926) 856179
F: (01926) 854954
E: moores22@aol.com
I: www.castlelaurelshotel.co.uk

Enderley Guest House ♦♦♦♦
20 Queens Road, Kenilworth
CV8 1JQ
T: (01926) 855388
F: (01926) 850450
E: enderleyguesthouse@supanet.com

Ferndale House ♦♦♦♦
45 Priory Road, Kenilworth
CV8 1LL
T: (01926) 853214
F: (01926) 858336
E: ferndalehouse@tiscali.co.uk

Howden House ♦♦
170 Warwick Road, Kenilworth
CV8 1HS
T: (01926) 850310

The Old Bakery Hotel ♦♦♦♦
12 High Street, Kenilworth
CV8 1LZ
T: (01926) 864111
F: (01926) 864127
E: info@theoldbakeryhotel.co.uk
I: www.theoldbakeryhotel.co.uk

The Quince House ♦♦♦♦
29 Moseley Road, Kenilworth
CV8 2AR
T: (01926) 858652
E: georgina.thomas@ntlworld.com
I: www.balldesi.demon.co.uk/b_b.html

Victoria Lodge Hotel ♦♦♦♦
180 Warwick Road, Kenilworth
CV8 1HU
T: (01926) 512020
F: (01926) 858703
E: info@victorialodgehotel.co.uk
I: www.victorialodgehotel.co.uk

KETTERING
Northamptonshire

Dairy Farm ♦♦♦♦
Cranford St Andrew, Kettering
NN14 4AQ
T: (01536) 330273

Hawthorn House (Private) Hotel ♦♦♦
2 Hawthorn Road, Kettering
NN15 7HS
T: (01536) 482513
F: (01536) 513121

2 Wilkie Close
♦♦♦♦ SILVER AWARD
Kettering NN15 7RD
T: (01536) 310270
F: (01536) 310270
E: roxmere@aol.com

KEXBY
Lincolnshire

The Grange ♦♦♦
Kexby, Gainsborough DN21 5PJ
T: (01427) 788265

KIDDERMINSTER
Worcestershire

Bewdley Hill House ♦♦♦♦
8 Bewdley Hill, Kidderminster
DY11 6BS
T: (01562) 60473
F: (01562) 60473
E: judy-john@bewdleyhillhouse.fsnet.co.uk

The Brook House ♦♦♦♦
Hemming Way, Chaddesley Corbett, Kidderminster DY10 4SF
T: (01562) 777453
F: (01562) 777453
E: kenbartlett@lineone.net
I: www.thebrookhouse.co.uk

Collingdale Private Hotel ♦♦♦
197 Comberton Road, Kidderminster DY10 1UE
T: (01562) 515460
E: collingdale@sharvell.fsnet.co.uk
I: mysite.freeserve.com/collingdalehotel

Garden Cottages
♦♦♦♦ GOLD AWARD
Crossway Green, Kidderminster, Hartlebury, Kidderminster
DY13 9SL
T: (01299) 250626
E: mamod@btinternet.com
I: www.gardencottages.co.uk

Hollies Farm Cottage ♦♦♦♦
Hollies Lane, Franche, Kidderminster DY11 5RW
T: (01562) 745677
F: (01562) 824580
E: pete@top-floor.fsbusiness.co.uk

Parkmore Farm ♦♦♦♦
Torton Lane, Hartlebury, Kidderminster DY10 4HX
T: (01299) 251827
E: info@parkmorefarm
I: www.parkmorefarm.co.uk

Victoria House ♦♦♦
15 Comberton Road, Kidderminster DY10 1UA
T: (01562) 67240
E: victoriakidderminster@yahoo.co.uk

KILCOT
Gloucestershire

Withyland Heights Bed and Breakfast ♦♦♦
Withyland Heights, Beavans Hill, Kilcot, Newent GL18 1PG
T: (01989) 720582
F: (01989) 720238
E: withyland@farming.co.uk
I: www.withylandheights.co.uk

KINETON
Warwickshire

The Castle Inn ♦♦♦
Edgehill, Nr Banbury, Warwick
OX15 6DJ
T: (01295) 670255
F: (01295) 670521
E: castleedgehill@btopenworld.com
I: www.thecastle-edgehill.co.uk

Swan Inn ♦♦♦
Banbury Street, Kineton, Warwick CV35 0JS
T: (01926) 642517

KING'S CLIFFE
Northamptonshire

19 West Street ♦♦♦♦
King's Cliffe, Peterborough
PE8 6XB
T: (01780) 470365
F: (01780) 470623
E: kjhl_dixon@hotmail.com
I: www.kingjohnhuntinglodge.com

KINGS CAPLE
Herefordshire

Ruxton Farm ♦♦♦♦
Kings Caple, Hereford HR1 4TX
T: (01432) 840493
F: (01432) 840493
E: milly@ruxton.co.uk
I: www.wye-valleycottages.com

KINGSLAND
Herefordshire

The Buzzards ♦♦♦
Kingsland, Leominster HR6 9QE
T: (01568) 708941
E: holiday@thebuzzards.co.uk
I: www.thebuzzards.co.uk

The Corners Inn ♦♦♦♦
Kingsland, Leominster HR6 9RY
T: (01568) 708385
F: (01568) 709033
E: enq@cornersinn.co.uk
I: www.cornersinn.co.uk

KINGSTONE
Herefordshire

Mill Orchard
♦♦♦♦ GOLD AWARD
Kingstone, Hereford HR2 9ES
T: (01981) 250326
E: cleveland@millorchard.co.uk
I: www.millorchard.co.uk

KINNERLEY
Shropshire

Meadowbank Lodge Bed and Breakfast ♦♦♦♦
Dovaston, Kinnerley, Oswestry
SY10 8DP
T: (01691) 682023
E: derekroach@fsmail.net
I: www.virtual-shropshire.co.uk/meadowbank

KINVER
Staffordshire

Anchor Hotel and Restaurant ♦♦♦
Dark Lane, Kinver, Stourbridge
DY7 6NR
T: (01384) 872085
F: (01384) 878824
E: anchorhotel@kinver2000.freeserve.co.uk
I: www.anchorhotel.com

KISLINGBURY
Northamptonshire

The Elms ♦♦♦
The Green, Kislingbury, Northampton NN7 4AH
T: (01604) 830326

KNOWLE
West Midlands

Ivy House Guest House ♦♦♦
Warwick Road, Heronfield, Knowle, Solihull B93 0EB
T: (01564) 770247
F: (01564) 778063
E: email@ivy-guest-house.freeserve.co.uk
I: www.smoothhound.co.uk/hotels/ivyguest.html

LAMBLEY
Nottinghamshire

Magnolia Guest House ♦♦♦♦
22 Spring Lane, Lambley, Nottingham NG4 4PH
T: (0115) 931 4404
F: (0115) 931 4582
E: magnoliahouse@lineone.net
I: www.smoothhound.co.uk/magnoliahouse.html

LAXTON
Nottinghamshire

Lilac Farm ♦♦♦
Laxton, Newark NG22 0NX
T: (01777) 870376
F: (01777) 870376

Manor Farm ♦♦♦
Moorhouse Road, Laxton, Newark NG22 0NU
T: (01777) 870417

Spanhoe Lodge
♦♦♦♦ GOLD AWARD
Haringworth Road, Laxton, Corby NN17 3AT
T: (01780) 450328
F: (01780) 450328
E: jennie.spanhoe@virgin.net
I: www.spanhoelodge.co.uk

LEA MARSTON
West Midlands

Reindeer Park Lodge ♦♦♦♦
Kingsbury Road, Lea Marston, Sutton Coldfield B76 0DE
T: (01675) 470811
F: (01675) 470710

LEADENHAM
Lincolnshire

George Hotel ♦♦♦
High Street, Leadenham, Lincoln
LN5 0PN
T: (01400) 272251
F: (01400) 272091
E: the-george-hotel@willgoose.freeserve.co.uk

LEAMINGTON SPA
Warwickshire

Adelaide ♦♦♦
15 Adelaide Road, Leamington Spa CV31 3PN
T: (01926) 450633
F: (01926) 450633

Almond House ♦♦♦♦
8 Parklands Avenue, Lillington, Leamington Spa CV32 7BA
T: (01926) 424052

Avenue Lodge Guest House ♦♦♦
61 Avenue Road, Leamington Spa CV31 3PF
T: (01926) 338555
F: (01926) 338555

Braeside ♦♦♦♦
26 Temple End, Harbury, Leamington Spa CV33 9NE
T: (01926) 613402
E: rosemary@braesidebb.co.uk
I: www.braesidebb.co.uk

Buckland Lodge Hotel ♦♦♦
35 Avenue Road, Leamington Spa CV31 3PG
T: (01926) 423843
F: (01926) 423843
E: buckland.lodge1@btinternet.com
I: www.Buckland-Lodge.co.uk.

Bungalow Farm ♦♦♦♦
Windmill Hill, Cubbington, Leamington Spa CV32 7LW
T: (01926) 423276
E: sheila@lewitt.freeserve.co.uk

Charnwood Guest House ♦♦♦
47 Avenue Road, Leamington Spa CV31 3PF
T: (01926) 831074
F: (01926) 831074

8 Clarendon Crescent
♦♦♦♦ SILVER AWARD
Leamington Spa CV32 5NR
T: (01926) 429840
F: (01926) 424641
E: lawson@lawson71.fsnet.co.uk
I: www.shakespeare-country.co.uk

The Coach House
♦♦♦♦ SILVER AWARD
Snowford Hall Farm, Hunningham, Leamington Spa CV33 9ES
T: (01926) 632297
F: (01926) 633599
E: the_coach_house@lineone.net
I: lineone.net/~the_coach_house

Corkill Bed and Breakfast ♦♦♦
27 Newbold Street, Leamington Spa CV32 4HN
T: (01926) 336303
F: (01926) 336303
E: mrscorkill@aol.com

The Dell Guesthouse ♦♦♦
8 Warwick Place, Leamington Spa CV32 5BJ
T: (01926) 422784
F: (01926) 422784
E: dellguesthouse@virgin.net
I: www.dellguesthouse.co.uk

Garden Cottage
♦♦♦♦ SILVER AWARD
Dove Villa, 99 Radford Road, Leamington Spa CV31 1JZ
T: (01926) 882494
E: cottage@transformation-uk.com

5 The Grange ♦♦♦
Cubbington, Leamington Spa CV32 7LE
T: (01926) 744762

Hedley Villa Guest House ♦♦♦
31 Russell Terrace, Leamington Spa CV31 1EZ
T: (01926) 424504
F: (01926) 886861
E: hedley-villa@hotmail.com

Hill Farm ♦♦♦♦
Lewis Road, Radford Semele, Leamington Spa CV31 1UX
T: (01926) 337571
E: rebecca@hillfarm3000.fsnet.co.uk

4 Lillington Road ♦♦♦
Lillington Road, Leamington Spa CV32 5YR
T: (01926) 429244
E: squirburton@aol.com

Milverton House Hotel ♦♦♦♦
1 Milverton Terrace, Leamington Spa CV32 5BE
T: (01926) 428335
F: (01926) 428335

Trendway Guest House ♦♦♦
45 Avenue Road, Leamington Spa CV31 3PF
T: (01926) 316644
F: (01926) 337506

Victoria Park Hotel ♦♦♦♦
12 Adelaide Road, Leamington Spa CV31 3PW
T: (01926) 424195
F: (01926) 421521
E: info@victoriaparkhotelleamingtonspa.co.uk
I: www.victoriaparkhotelleamingtonspa.co.uk

The Willis ♦♦♦
11 Eastnor Grove, Leamington Spa CV31 1LD
T: (01926) 425820

Wymondley Lodge
♦♦♦♦♦ SILVER AWARD
8 Adelaide Road, Leamington Spa CV31 3PW
T: (01926) 882669
F: (01926) 882669

York House Hotel ♦♦♦
9 York Road, Leamington Spa CV31 3PR
T: (01926) 424671
F: (01926) 832272
E: York1@mwfree.net

LECHLADE
Gloucestershire

Apple Tree Guest House ♦♦♦
Buscot, Faringdon SN7 8DA
T: (01367) 252592
E: emreay@aol.com

New Inn Hotel ♦♦♦
Market Square, Lechlade-on-Thames, Lechlade GL7 3AB
T: (01367) 252296
F: (01367) 252315
E: info@newinnhotel.com
I: www.newinnhotel.co.uk

LECHLADE ON THAMES
Gloucestershire

Cambrai Lodge
♦♦♦♦ SILVER AWARD
Oak Street, Lechlade on Thames GL7 3AY
T: (01367) 253173

LEDBURY
Herefordshire

Brook House ♦♦♦♦
Birtsmorton, Malvern WR13 6AF
T: (01531) 650664
F: (01531) 650664
E: maryd@lineone.net

The Hopton Arms ♦♦♦
Ashperton, Ledbury HR8 2SE
T: (01531) 670520
E: peter@hoptonarms.co.uk
I: www.hoptonarms.co.uk

Little Marcle Court ♦♦♦♦
Little Marcle, Ledbury HR8 2LB
T: (01531) 670936
I: www.visitledbury.co.uk

LEEK
Staffordshire

Beechfields ♦♦♦♦
Park Road, Leek ST13 8JS
T: (01538) 372825
E: judith@beech-fields.fsnet.co.uk
I: www.beech-fields.fsnet.co.uk

The Green Man ♦♦♦
38 Compton, Leek ST13 5NH
T: (01538) 388084
E: diane@greenman.fsworld.co.uk
I: www.greenman-guesthouse.co.uk

The Hatcheries ♦♦♦
Mount Pleasant, Leek ST13 5EX
T: (01538) 399552
F: (01538) 399552
I: www.thehatcheries.co.uk

Little Brookhouse Farm ♦♦♦♦
Cheddleton, Leek ST13 7DF
T: (01538) 360350

New House Farm ♦♦♦
Bottomhouse, Leek ST13 7PA
T: (01538) 304350
F: (01538) 304338
E: newhousefarm@btinternet.com
I: www.staffordshiremoorlandsfarmholidays.co.uk

Peak Weavers Hotel ♦♦♦♦
21 King Street, Leek ST13 5NW
T: (01538) 383729
F: (01538) 387475
E: peak.weavers@virgin.net
I: www.peakweavershotel.com

Prospect House ♦♦♦♦
334 Cheadle Road, Cheddleton, Leek ST13 7BW
T: 0870 7703063
F: 0870 7703063
E: prospect@talk21.com
I: www.prospecthouseleek.co.uk

LEICESTER
Leicestershire

Abinger Guest House ♦♦♦
175 Hinckley Road, Leicester LE3 0TF
T: (0116) 255 4674
F: (0116) 255 4674
E: bobwel1234@aol.com
I: www.openroads.com

Beaumaris Guesthouse ♦♦♦
18 Westcotes Drive, Leicester LE3 0QR
T: (0116) 254 0261
E: beaumarisgh@talk21.com

Burlington Hotel ♦♦♦
Elmfield Avenue, Stoneygate, Leicester LE2 1RB
T: (0116) 270 5112
F: (0116) 270 4207
E: welcome@burlingtonhotel.co.uk
I: www.burlingtonhotel.co.uk

Croft Hotel ♦♦♦
3 Stanley Road, Leicester LE2 1RF
T: (0116) 270 3220
F: (0116) 270 3220
E: crofthotel@hotmail.com

Glenfield Lodge Hotel ♦
4 Glenfield Road, Leicester LE3 6AP
T: (0116) 262 7554

Haynes Hotel ♦♦♦♦
185 Uppingham Road, Leicester LE5 4BQ
T: (0116) 276 8973
F: (0116) 276 8973
E: hayneshotel@yahoo.co.uk

Scotia Hotel ♦♦♦
10 Westcotes Drive, Leicester LE3 0QR
T: (0116) 254 9200
F: (0116) 254 9200
E: scotiahotel@hotmail.com

South Fork Guesthouse ♦♦♦
464-466 Narborough Road, Leicester LE3 2FT
T: (0116) 299 9960
F: (0116) 299 4332
E: southfork@ntlworld.com

Spindle Lodge Hotel ♦♦♦
2 West Walk, Leicester LE1 7NA
T: (0116) 233 8801
F: (0116) 233 8804
E: spindlelodgeleicester@orange.net
I: www.smoothhound.co.uk/hotels/spindle.html

LEIGH SINTON
Worcestershire

Chirkenhill ♦♦♦♦
Sherridge Road, Leigh Sinton, Malvern WR13 5DE
T: (01886) 832205
E: wenden@eidosnet.co.uk

LEINTWARDINE
Herefordshire

Lower Buckton ♦♦♦♦
Leintwardine, Craven Arms SY7 0JU
T: (01547) 540532
F: (01547) 540532
E: carolyn@lowerbuckton.co.uk
I: www.lowerbuckton.co.uk

Lower House
♦♦♦♦ SILVER AWARD
Adforton, Leintwardine, Craven Arms SY7 0NF
T: (01568) 770223
F: (01568) 770592
E: cutler@sy7.com
I: www.sy7.com/lowerhouse

The Wardens ♦♦♦♦
Watling Street, Leintwardine, Craven Arms SY7 0LL
T: (01547) 540498
F: (01547) 540500
E: janewells@supanet.com
I: www.shropshiretourism.com

LEOMINSTER
Herefordshire

Bedford House ♦♦♦
Dilwyn, Hereford HR4 8JJ
T: (01544) 388260

Bramlea ♦♦♦
Barons Cross Road, Leominster HR6 8RW
T: (01568) 613406
F: (01568) 613406
E: lesbramlea@netlineUK.net

Chesfield ♦♦♦
112 South Street, Leominster HR6 8JF
T: (01568) 613204

Church House
Rating Applied For
Millbrook Way, Orleton, Ludlow SY8 4HW
T: (01584) 831471

Copper Hall ♦♦♦♦
South Street, Leominster HR6 8JN
T: (01568) 611622
E: sccrick@copperhall.freeserve.co.uk

The Farmhouse ♦♦♦♦
Aymestrey, Leominster HR6 9ST
T: (01568) 708075

Ford Abbey
♦♦♦♦♦ GOLD AWARD
Pudleston, Leominster HR6 0RZ
T: (01568) 760700
F: (01568) 760264
E: info@fordabbey.co.uk
I: www.fordabbey.co.uk

Highfield ♦♦♦♦
Newtown, Ivington Road, Leominster HR6 8QD
T: (01568) 613216
E: info@stay-at-highfield.co.uk
I: www.stay-at-highfield.co.uk

Highgate House ♦♦♦♦
29 Hereford Road, Leominster HR6 8JS
T: (01568) 614562
F: (01568) 614562
E: highgatehouse@easicom.com

Home Farm ♦♦♦♦
Bircher, Leominster HR6 0AX
T: (01568) 780525

Little Bury Farm ♦♦♦
Luston, Leominster HR6 0EB
T: (01568) 611575

The Paddock
♦♦♦♦ GOLD AWARD
Shobdon, Leominster HR6 9NQ
T: (01568) 708176
F: (01568) 708829
E: thepaddock@talk21.com

Rossendale House ♦♦♦
46 Broad Street, Leominster HR6 8BS
T: 0845 1668831
F: (01568) 612464
E: enquiries@rossendalehouse.co.uk
I: www.rossendalehouse.co.uk

Tyn-Y-Coed ♦♦♦
Shobdon, Leominster HR6 9NY
T: (01568) 708277
F: (01568) 708277
E: jandrews@shobdondesign.kc3.co.uk

LICHFIELD
Staffordshire

Altair House ♦♦♦
21 Shakespeare Avenue, Lichfield WS14 9BE
T: (01543) 252900

32 Beacon Street ♦♦♦♦
Lichfield WS13 7AJ
T: (01543) 262378

Chimneys ♦♦♦♦
26 Friary Avenue, Lichfield WS13 6QQ
T: (01543) 263370

Coppers End Guest House ♦♦♦
Walsall Road, Muckley Corner, Lichfield WS14 0BG
T: (01543) 372910
F: (01543) 360423
E: info@coppersendguesthouse.co.uk
I: www.coppersendguesthouse.co.uk

Davolls Cottage ♦♦♦♦
156 Woodhouses Road, Burntwood, Lichfield WS7 9EL
T: (01543) 671250

16 Dimbles Lane ♦♦♦
Lichfield WS13 7HW
T: (01543) 251107

The Farmhouse
♦♦♦♦ GOLD AWARD
Lysway Lane, Longdon Green, Stafford WS15 4PZ
T: (0121) 378 4552
F: (0121) 311 2915
E: jaynetdrury@aol.com
I: www.smoothhound.co.uk/hotels/thefarmhouse.html

Freeford Farm ♦♦♦
Freeford, Lichfield WS14 9QL
T: (01543) 263330

Holly House Bed and Breakfast ♦♦♦
198 Upper St John Street, Lichfield WS14 9EF
T: (01543) 263078

Mrs H A Ogram ♦♦♦
4 Hayes View, Lichfield WS13 7BT
T: (01543) 253725

Pauline Duvals Bed and Breakfast ♦♦♦♦
21-23 Dam Street, The Bogey Hole, Lichfield WS13 6AE
T: (01543) 264303

Twenty Three The Close ♦♦♦♦
23 The Close, Lichfield WS13 7LD
T: (01543) 306142
E: charles.taylor@lichfield-cathedral.org

The White House
Market Lane, Wall, Lichfield WS14 0AS
T: (01543) 480384

LINCOLN
Lincolnshire

AA and M Guesthouse ♦♦♦
79 Carholme Road, Lincoln LN1 1RT
T: (01522) 543736
F: (01522) 543736

Aaron Whisby Guest House ♦♦♦
262 West Parade, Lincoln LN1 1LY
T: (01522) 526930
E: dianajones@aaronwhisby.fsnet.co.uk

Allwood Guesthouse ♦♦
258 West Parade, Lincoln LN1 1LY
T: (01522) 887868

Crown Lodge and Restaurant ♦♦♦
Chapel Hill, Tattershall, Lincoln LN4 4PX
T: (01526) 342262
F: (01526) 342262
E: barryharrington@hotmail.com
I: www.smoothhound.co.uk/hotels/crownlodge

Damon's Motel ♦♦♦♦
997 Doddington Road, Lincoln LN6 3SE
T: (01522) 887733
F: (01522) 887734

Hamilton Hotel ♦♦♦
2 Hamilton Road, Lincoln LN5 8ED
T: (01522) 528243
F: (01522) 528243

Honeysuckle House Rating Applied For
128 West Parade, Lincoln LN1 1LD
T: (01522) 534450
F: (01522) 526296
E: honeysucklebandb@aol.com

1 Limelands ♦♦♦♦
Greetwell Road, Lincoln LN2 4AR
T: (01522) 512061

Manor Farm Stables ♦♦♦♦
Broxholme, Lincoln LN1 2NG
T: (01522) 704220
E: pfieldson@lineone.net

Manor House
♦♦♦♦ SILVER AWARD
Bracebridge Heath, Lincoln LN4 2HW
T: (01522) 520825
F: (01522) 542418
E: mikescoley@farming.co.uk

Mayfield Guest House ♦♦♦
213 Yarborough Road, Lincoln LN1 3NQ
T: (01522) 533732
F: (01522) 533732
E: stay@mayfieldguesthouse.co.uk
I: www.mayfieldhguesthouse.co.uk

Newport Cottage ♦♦♦♦
Newport Cottage, 21 Newport, Lincoln LN1 3DQ
T: (01522) 534470

Newport Guest House ♦♦♦
26-28 Newport, Lincoln LN1 3DF
T: (01522) 528590
F: (01522) 542868
E: info@newportguesthouse.co.uk
I: www.newportguesthouse.co.uk

Old Bakery Guesthouse ♦♦♦
26-28 Burton Road, Lincoln LN1 3LB
T: (01522) 576057
E: oldbakery-guesthouse@ntlworld.com
I: www.theold-bakery.co.uk

Savill Guesthouse ♦♦♦♦
203 Yarborough Road, Lincoln LN1 3NQ
T: (01522) 523261
E: vvn@themail.co.uk
I: www.savillguesthouse.co.uk

73 Station Road ♦♦♦
Branston, Lincoln LN4 1LG
T: (01522) 828658

Tennyson Hotel ♦♦♦♦
7 South Park, Lincoln LN5 8EN
T: (01522) 521624
F: (01522) 521355
E: tennyson.hotel@virgin.net
I: www.tennysonhotel.com

Truro House ♦♦♦♦
421 Newark Road, North Hykeham, Lincoln LN6 9SP
T: (01522) 882073

Welbeck Cottage ♦♦♦♦
19 Meadow Lane, South Hykeham, Lincoln LN6 9PF
T: (01522) 692669
F: (01522) 692669
E: mad@wellbeck1.demon.co.uk

The Wren Guesthouse ♦♦♦
22 St Catherines, Lincoln LN5 8LY
T: (01522) 537949
F: (01522) 831156
E: kateatthewren@aol.com

LINTON
Derbyshire

The Manor
♦♦♦♦ SILVER AWARD
Hillside Road, Linton, Swadlincote DE12 6RA
T: (01283) 761177
E: themanor@ukonline.co.uk

LITTLE BRINGTON
Northamptonshire

The Saracens Head ♦♦♦♦
Main Street, Little Brington, Northampton NN7 4HS
T: (01604) 770640
F: (01604) 770640

LITTLE BYTHAM
Lincolnshire

The Willoughby Arms ♦♦♦♦
Station Road, Little Bytham, Grantham NG33 4RA
T: (01780) 410276
F: (01780) 410190
E: willo@willoughbyarms.co.uk
I: www.willoughbyarms.co.uk

LITTLE COWARNE
Herefordshire

Three Horseshoes Inn ♦♦♦♦
Little Cowarne, Bromyard HR7 4RQ
T: (01885) 400276
F: (01885) 400276
I: www.threehorseshoes.co.uk

LITTLE HAYFIELD
Derbyshire

Lantern Pike Inn ♦♦♦
Glossop Road, Little Hayfield, High Peak SK22 2NG
T: (01663) 747590
I: www.lanternpikeinn.co.uk

LITTLE INKBERROW
Worcestershire

Perrymill Farm ♦♦♦
Little Inkberrow, Worcester WR7 4JQ
T: (01386) 792177
F: (01386) 793449
E: alexander@perrymill.com

LITTLE STRETTON
Shropshire

Elmsdale B&B ♦♦♦
Ludlow Road, Little Stretton, Church Stretton SY6 6RB
T: (01694) 723696
F: (01694) 723696
E: info@elmsdalebandb.co.uk
I: www.elmsdalebandb.co.uk

LITTLE WENLOCK
Shropshire

Wenboro Cottage ♦♦♦
Church Lane, Little Wenlock, Telford TF6 5BB
T: (01952) 505573
E: rcarter@wenboro.freeserve.co.uk

LITTON
Derbyshire

Beacon House ♦♦♦♦
Litton, Buxton SK17 8QP
T: (01298) 871752

Hall Farm House ♦♦♦♦
Litton, Buxton SK17 8QP
T: (01298) 872172
E: jfscott@waitrose.com
I: www.users.waitrose.com/~jfscott

LLANGROVE
Herefordshire

Prospect Place ♦♦♦
Llangrove, Ross-on-Wye HR9 6ET
T: (01989) 770596
E: prospectplacehr96et@btinternet.com

LONG BUCKBY
Northamptonshire

Murcott Mill ♦♦♦
Murcott, Long Buckby, Northampton NN6 7QR
T: (01327) 842236
F: (01327) 844524
E: bhart6@compuserve.com

LONG CLAWSON
Leicestershire

Elms Farm ♦♦♦♦
52 East End, Long Clawson, Melton Mowbray LE14 4NG
T: (01664) 822395
F: (01664) 823399
E: elmsfarm@whittard.net
I: www.whittard.net

Old Manor House ♦♦♦
West End, Long Clawson, Melton Mowbray LE14 4PE
T: (01664) 822698
E: sshouler@oldmanorhouse.u-net.com

LONG COMPTON
Warwickshire

Butlers Road Farm ♦♦♦
Long Compton, Shipston-on-Stour CV36 5JZ
T: (01608) 684262
F: (01608) 684262
E: eileenwhittaker@easicom.com

LONG WHATTON
Leicestershire

The Falcon Inn ♦♦♦♦
Main Street, Long Whatton, Loughborough LE12 5DG
T: (01509) 842416
F: (01509) 646802

LONGBOROUGH
Gloucestershire

The Long House ♦♦♦
Old Rectory Gardens, Longborough, Moreton-in-Marsh GL56 0QF
T: (01451) 830577
E: thelonghouse@btopenworld.com

LONGDON
Staffordshire

Grand Lodge ♦♦♦♦
Horsey Lane, Longdon, Rugeley WS15 4LW
T: (01543) 686103
F: (01543) 676266
E: grandlodge@edbroemt.demon.co.uk

LONGHOPE
Gloucestershire

New House Farm
Rating Applied For
Barrel Lane, Aston Ingham, Longhope GL17 0LS
T: (01452) 830484
F: (01452) 830484
E: scaldbrain@aol.com
I: www.newhousefarm-accommodation.co.uk

The Old Farm ♦♦♦♦
Barrel Lane, Longhope GL17 0LR
T: (01452) 830252
F: (01452) 830255
E: lucy@the-old-farm.co.uk
I: www.the-old-farm.co.uk

Royal Spring Farm ♦♦♦♦
(A4136), Longhope GL17 0PY
T: (01452) 830550

LONGNOR
Staffordshire

Crewe and Harpur Arms Hotel ♦♦♦
Longnor, Buxton SK17 0NS
T: (01298) 83205

White Gables ♦♦♦♦
Back Lane, Longnor, Shrewsbury SY5 7PP
T: (01743) 718468
F: (01743) 718468

LONGTOWN
Herefordshire

Olchon Cottage Farm ♦♦♦
Longtown, Hereford HR2 0NS
T: (01873) 860233
F: (01873) 860233
I: www.golden-valley.co.uk/Olchon

LOUGHBOROUGH
Leicestershire

The Beauchief Hotel ♦♦♦
29 Pinfold Gate, Loughborough LE11 1BE
T: (01509) 268096
F: (01509) 268586
I: www.corushotels.co.uk/thebeauchief

Charnwood Lodge ♦♦♦♦
136 Leicester Road, Loughborough LE11 2AQ
T: (01509) 211120
F: (01509) 211121
E: charnwoodlodge@charwat.freeserve.co.uk
I: www.morningtonweb.com/charnwood

Demontfort Hotel
88 Leicester Road, Loughborough LE11 2AQ
T: (01509) 216061
F: (01509) 233667
E: thedemontforthotel@amserve.com
I: www.thedemontforthotel.co.uk

The Dower House
Rating Applied For
77 Brook Street, Wymeswold, Loughborough LE12 6TT
T: (01509) 881046
F: (01509) 881046
E: barney@kegb.fsnet.co.uk

Forest Rise Hotel ♦♦♦
55-57 Forest Road, Loughborough LE11 3NW
T: (01509) 215928
F: (01509) 210506

Garendon Park Hotel ♦♦♦
92 Leicester Road, Loughborough LE11 2AQ
T: (01509) 236557
F: (01509) 265559
E: info@garendonparkhotel.co.uk
I: www.garendonparkhotel.co.uk

The Highbury Guesthouse ♦♦♦
146 Leicester Road, Loughborough LE11 2AQ
T: (01509) 230545
F: (01509) 233086
E: emkhighbury@supanet.com
I: www.thehighburyguesthouse.co.uk

Holywell House ♦♦♦
40 Leicester Road, Loughborough LE11 2AG
T: (01509) 267891
F: (01509) 214075
E: holywell.house@virgin.net
I: www.holywell.here.co.uk

Lane End Cottage
♦♦♦♦ SILVER AWARD
45 School Lane, Old Woodhouse, Loughborough LE12 8UJ
T: (01509) 890706
F: (01509) 890246
E: mary.hudson@talk21.com

The Lindens ♦♦♦
22 Halstead Road, Mountsorrel, Loughborough LE12 7HF
T: (0116) 230 2163
F: (0116) 230 2163

Lubcloud Farm Bed & Breakfast
♦♦♦♦ SILVER AWARD
Oaks Road, Charley, Loughborough LE12 9YA
T: (01509) 503204
F: (01509) 651267
E: lubcloudfarm@aol.com

The Mountsorrel Hotel ♦♦♦♦
217 Loughborough Road, Mountsorrel, Loughborough LE12 7AR
T: (01509) 412627
F: (01509) 416105
E: info@mountsorrelhotel.co.uk
I: www.mountsorrelhotel.co.uk

New Life Guesthouse ♦♦♦
121 Ashby Road, Loughborough LE11 3AB
T: (01509) 216699
F: (01509) 210020
E: jean-of-newlife@assureweb.com

Peachnook Guest House ♦♦
154 Ashby Road, Loughborough LE11 3AG
T: (01509) 264390
I: www.SmoothHound.co.uk/hotels/peachnohtml

Sutton Fields House
Rating Applied For
Station Road, Sutton Bonington, Loughborough LE12 5NU
T: (01509) 673754
F: (01509) 673754
E: houston.suttonfields@virgin.net

LOUTH
Lincolnshire

Masons Arms ♦♦♦
Cornmarket, Louth LN11 9PY
T: (01507) 609525
F: (0870) 706 6450
E: justin@themasons.co.uk
I: www.themasons.co.uk

Olive House
Rating Applied For
34 St Michaels Road, Louth LN11 9DA
T: (01507) 602304

LOWER SLAUGHTER
Gloucestershire

Greenfingers ♦♦♦♦
Wyck Rissington Lane, Lower Slaughter, Cheltenham GL54 2EX
T: (01451) 821217
E: suepete@tesco.net

The Rectory ♦♦♦♦
Copse Hill Road, Lower Slaughter, Cheltenham GL54 2HY
T: (01451) 810812
F: (01451) 810157

LOXLEY
Warwickshire

Elm Cottage ♦♦♦♦
Stratford Road, Loxley, Warwick CV35 9JW
T: (01789) 840609

LUBENHAM
Leicestershire

The Old Bakehouse ♦♦♦♦
9 The Green, Lubenham, Market Harborough LE16 9TD
T: (01858) 463401

LUDLOW
Shropshire

The Brakes
♦♦♦♦ SILVER AWARD
Downton, Ludlow SY8 2LF
T: (01584) 856485
F: (01584) 856485
E: thebrakes@cwcom.net
I: www.ludlow.org.uk/brakes

Bromley Court B&B
♦♦♦♦♦ GOLD AWARD
73 Lower Broad Street, Ludlow SY8 1PH
T: 0845 0656 192
E: phil@ross-b-an-b-ludlow.co.uk
I: www.ross-b-and-b-ludlow.co.uk

Bull Hotel ♦♦♦
14 The Bull Ring, Ludlow SY8 1AD
T: (01584) 873611
F: (01584) 873666
E: info@bull-ludlow.co.uk
I: www.bull-ludlow.co.uk

Castle View ♦♦♦
7 Castle View Terrace, Ludlow SY8 2NG
T: (01584) 875592
F: (01584) 875592

Cecil Guest House ♦♦♦
Sheet Road, Ludlow SY8 1LR
T: (01584) 872442
F: (01584) 872442

The Crown Inn
◆◆◆◆ SILVER AWARD
Hopton Wafers, Cleobury Mortimer, Kidderminster DY14 0NB
T: (01299) 270372
F: (01299) 271127
E: desk@crownathopton.co.uk
I: www.go2.co.uk/crownathopton

Earnstrey Hill House ◆◆◆◆
Abdon, Craven Arms SY7 9HU
T: (01746) 712579
F: (01746) 712631

Eight Dinham ◆◆◆◆
Dinham, Ludlow SY8 1EJ
T: (01584) 875661

Elm Lodge B&B ◆◆◆
Fishmore, Ludlow SY8 3DP
T: (01584) 877394
F: (01584) 877397
E: apartments@sjweaver.fsnet.co.uk
I: www.ludlow.org.uk/elmlodge

Elsich Manor Cottage ◆◆◆
Seifton, Ludlow SY8 2DL
T: (01584) 861406
F: (01584) 861406

Hen and Chickens Guesthouse
◆◆◆◆
103 Old Street, Ludlow SY8 1NU
T: (01584) 874318
E: sally@hen-and-chickens.co.uk
I: www.hen-and-chickens.co.uk

Henwick House ◆◆◆
Gravel Hill, Ludlow SY8 1QU
T: (01584) 873338

Longlands ◆◆◆
Woodhouse Lane, Richards Castle, Ludlow SY8 4EU
T: (01584) 831636
E: iankemsley@aol.com
I: www.ludlow.org.uk/longlands

Lower House Farm
◆◆◆◆ GOLD AWARD
Clee Downton, Ludlow SY8 3EH
T: (01584) 823648
E: gsblack@talk21.com
I: www.ludlow.org.uk/lowerhousefarm

Manna Oak ◆◆◆◆
Mill Street, Ludlow SY8 1BE
T: (01584) 873204

Mill House ◆◆◆
Squirrel Lane, Lower Ledwyche, Ludlow SY8 4JX
T: (01584) 872837
E: millhousebnb@aol.com
I: www.virtual-shropshire.co.uk/mill

Mulberry House ◆◆◆◆
10 Corve Street, Ludlow SY8 1DA
T: (01584) 876765
F: (01584) 879871
E: bookings@tencorvestreet.co.uk
I: www.tencorvestreet.co.uk

Nelson Cottage ◆◆◆
Rocks Green, Ludlow SY8 2DS
T: (01584) 878108
F: (01584) 878108
E: info@ludlow.uk.com
I: www.ludlow.uk.com

55 Old Street and The Cottage Rating Applied For
55 Old Street, Ludlow SY8 1NW
T: (01584) 874481
E: julietjohn@diamond63.freeserve.co.uk

Palmers House Bed and Breakfast ◆◆◆
19 Mill Street, Ludlow SY8 1BE
T: (01584) 876009

Pengwern ◆◆◆◆
St Julians Avenue, Ludlow SY8 1ET
T: (01584) 874635
F: (01584) 872649
E: butterdev@aol.com
I: www.pengwern.org.uk

Ravenscourt Manor
◆◆◆◆ GOLD AWARD
Woofferton, Ludlow SY8 4AL
T: (01584) 711905
F: (01584) 711905
E: ravenscourtmanor@amserve.com
I: www.smoothhound.co.uk/hotels/ravenscourt

The Wheatsheaf Inn ◆◆◆◆
Lower Broad Street, Ludlow SY8 1PQ
T: (01584) 872980
F: (01584) 877990
E: karen.wheatsheaf@tinyworld.co.uk

LUSTON
Herefordshire

Knapp House ◆◆◆
Luston, Leominster HR6 0EB
T: (01568) 615705

Ladymeadow Farm ◆◆◆◆
Luston, Leominster HR6 0AS
T: (01568) 780262
E: ladymeadowfarm@agriplus.net

LUTTERWORTH
Leicestershire

The Greyhound Coaching Inn
◆◆◆
9 Market Street, Lutterworth LE17 4EJ
T: (01455) 553307
F: (01455) 554558
E: bookings@greyhoundinn.fsnet.co.uk
I: www.greyhoundinn.co.uk

Orchard House ◆◆◆◆
Church Drive, Gilmorton, Lutterworth LE17 5LR
T: (01455) 559487
F: (01455) 553047
E: diholman@hotmail.com

LYDDINGTON
Rutland

Lydbrooke ◆◆◆◆
2 Colley Rise, Lyddington, Oakham LE15 9LL
T: (01572) 821471
F: (01572) 821471
E: lydbrookebb@hotmail.com

LYONSHALL
Herefordshire

Penrhos Farm ◆◆◆◆
Lyonshall, Kington HR5 3LH
T: (01544) 231467
F: (01544) 340273
E: sallyw@totalise.co.uk
I: www.penrhosfarm.ukfarmers.com

MACKWORTH
Derbyshire

Thames House ◆◆◆◆
6 Thames Close, Mackworth, Derby DE22 4HT
T: (01332) 513526
F: (01332) 513526
E: jswarbrooke@aol.com

MADLEY
Herefordshire

Shenmore Cottage Bed and Breakfast ◆◆◆◆
Shenmore Cottage, Upper Shenmore, Madley, Hereford HR2 9NX
T: (01981) 250507
E: shenmorecottage@aol.com
I: www.smoothhound.co.uk/hotels/shenmore.html

MALTBY LE MARSH
Lincolnshire

Farmhouse Bed and Breakfast
◆◆◆
Grange Farm, Maltby le Marsh, Alford LN13 0JP
T: (01507) 450267
F: (01507) 450180
E: grangefarm@beeb.net
I: www.grange-farmhouse.co.uk

MALVERN
Worcestershire

Acorn Cottage ◆◆◆
17 St Ann's Road, Malvern WR14 4RG
T: (01684) 560152

Berewe Court ◆◆◆◆
Whiting Lane, Berrow, Malvern WR13 6AY
T: (01531) 650250
F: (01531) 650057
E: susanmaryprice@hotmail.com
I: www.ourworcester.net/berewecourt

Cannara ◆◆◆
147 Barnards Green Road, Malvern WR14 3LT
T: (01684) 564418
F: (01684) 564418
I: www.cannara.co.uk

Clevelands ◆◆◆
41 Alexandra Road, Malvern WR14 1HE
T: (01684) 572164
F: (01684) 576691
E: jonmargstocks@aol.com

Como House ◆◆◆
Como Road, Malvern WR14 2TH
T: (01684) 561486
E: kevin@como-house.freeserve.co.uk

Cowleigh Park Farm ◆◆◆◆
Cowleigh Road, Malvern WR13 5HJ
T: (01684) 566750
E: cowleighpark@ukonline.co.uk

Danemoor Farm ◆◆◆
Welland, Malvern WR13 6NL
T: (01684) 310905
F: (01684) 310905

Edgeworth ◆◆◆
4 Carlton Road, Malvern WR14 1HH
T: (01684) 572565

The Elms ◆◆◆
52 Guarlford Road, Malvern WR14 3QP
T: (01684) 573466
E: jili-holland@yahoo.co.uk

The Firs ◆◆◆
243 West Malvern Road, Malvern WR14 4BE
T: (01684) 564016
F: (01684) 564016
E: valshearerthefirs@hotmail.com
I: www.smoothhound.co.uk/hotels/firs.html

Guarlford Grange
◆◆◆◆ SILVER AWARD
11 Guarlford Road, Malvern WR14 3QW
T: (01684) 575996
F: (01684) 575996
E: guarlfordgrange@msn.com
I: www.malvern-hills.co.uk/gg

Harcourt Cottage ◆◆◆
252 West Malvern Road, West Malvern, Malvern WR14 4DQ
T: (01684) 574561
F: (01684) 574561
E: harcourtcottage@aol.com

Hidelow House
◆◆◆◆ SILVER AWARD
Acton Green, Acton Beauchamp, Malvern WR6 5AH
T: (01886) 884547
F: (01886) 884658
E: stay@hidelow.co.uk
I: www.hidelow.co.uk

Homestead Lodge ◆◆◆
25 Somers Park Avenue, Malvern WR14 1SE
T: (01684) 573094
F: (01684) 573094
E: trant@homesteadlodge.freeserve.co.uk
I: www.homesteadlodge.freeserve.co.uk

Mellor Heights ◆◆◆
46A West Malvern Road, Malvern WR14 4NA
T: (01684) 565105
F: (01684) 565105
E: mellorheights@onetel.net.uk

Montrose Hotel ◆◆◆
23 Graham Road, Malvern WR14 2HU
T: (01684) 572335
F: (01684) 575707

Priory Holme ◆◆◆◆
18 Avenue Road, Malvern WR14 3AR
T: (01684) 568455

Ramblers Roost Rating Applied For
52 Old Wyche Road, Malvern Wells, Malvern WR14 4EP
T: (01684) 562559

Rathlin ◆◆◆◆
1 Carlton Road, Malvern WR14 1HH
T: (01684) 572491
E: guiver@rathlin-malvern.fsnet.co.uk

The Red Gate
♦♦♦♦ SILVER AWARD
32 Avenue Road, Malvern
WR14 3BJ
T: (01684) 565013
F: (01684) 565013
E: enquiries@the-red-gate.co.uk
I: www.SmoothHound.co.uk/hotels/redgate.html

Sunnydale
♦♦♦♦ SILVER AWARD
69 Tanhouse Lane, Malvern
WR14 1LQ
T: (01886) 832066

Wyche Keep Country House
♦♦♦♦ SILVER AWARD
22 Wyche Road, Malvern
WR14 4EG
T: (01684) 567018
F: (01684) 892304
E: wychekeep@aol.com
I: www.jks.org/wychekeep

MANSFIELD
Nottinghamshire

Blue Barn Farm ♦♦♦
Nether Langwith, Mansfield
NG20 9JD
T: (01623) 742248
F: (01623) 742248
E: ibbotsonbluebarn@netscape-online.co.uk

MARCHINGTON
Staffordshire

Forest Hills ♦♦♦♦
Moisty Lane, Marchington,
Uttoxeter ST14 8JY
T: (01283) 820447
F: (01283) 820447

MARKET DRAYTON
Shropshire

Crofton ♦♦♦♦
80 Rowan Road, Market Drayton
TF9 1RR
T: (01630) 655484
F: (01630) 655484
E: eric.russell@ic24.net

Heath Farm Bed and Breakfast ♦♦♦
Heath Farm, Wellington Road,
Hodnet, Market Drayton TF9 3JJ
T: (01630) 685570
F: (01630) 685570
E: adrysdale@telco4u.net

Milford ♦♦♦♦
Adderley Road, Market Drayton
TF9 3SW
T: (01630) 655249

Millstone ♦♦♦♦
Adderley Road, Market Drayton
TF9 3SW
T: (01630) 657584

Red House Cottage ♦♦♦
31 Shropshire Street, Market
Drayton TF9 3DA
T: (01630) 655206

Stafford Court Hotel ♦♦♦
Stafford Street, Market Drayton
TF9 1HY
T: (01630) 652646
F: (01630) 658496
I: www.staffordcourthotel.co.uk

The Tudor House Hotel and Restaurant ♦♦♦
1 Cheshire Street, Market
Drayton TF9 1PD
T: (01630) 657523
F: (01630) 657806
E: sugarloaf@globalnet.co.uk

Willow House ♦♦♦♦
Shrewsbury Road, Tern Hill,
Market Drayton TF9 3PX
T: (01630) 638326
F: (01630) 638326
E: moira@willowhouse.free-online.co.uk

MARKET HARBOROUGH
Leicestershire

The George at Great Oxendon ♦♦♦♦
Great Oxendon, Market
Harborough LE16 8NA
T: (01858) 465205
F: (01858) 465205

Hunters Lodge ♦♦♦♦
By Foxton Locks, Gumley,
Market Harborough LE16 7RT
T: (0116) 279 3744
F: (0116) 279 3855
E: info@hunterslodgefoxton.co.uk
I: www.hunterslodgefoxton.co.uk

MARKET RASEN
Lincolnshire

Beechwood Guesthouse ♦♦♦♦
54 Willingham Road, Market
Rasen LN8 3DX
T: (01673) 844043
F: (01673) 844043
E: beechwoodgh@aol.com
I: www.beechwoodguesthouse.co.uk

The Dell Bed & Breakfast ♦♦♦♦
Private Lane, Normanby by
Spital, Market Rasen LN8 2HF
T: (01673) 878514

Sunnybrow ♦♦♦♦
Ludford Road, Binbrook, Market
Rasen LN8 6DR
T: (01472) 398181
E: sunnyseed@btinternet.com
I: www.smoothhound.co.uk

Waveney Cottage Guesthouse ♦♦♦♦
Willingham Road, Market Rasen
LN8 3DN
T: (01673) 843236
F: (01673) 843236
E: vacancies@waveneycottage.co.uk
I: www.waveneycottage.co.uk

MARSTON
Lincolnshire

Gelston Grange Farm ♦♦♦♦
Marston, Grantham NG32 2AQ
T: (01400) 250281
F: (01400) 250281

MARSTON MONTGOMERY
Derbyshire

The Old Barn ♦♦♦♦
Marston Montgomery,
Ashbourne DE6 2FF
T: (01889) 590848
F: (01889) 590698

MARTIN
Lincolnshire

The Stables Studio ♦♦♦♦
94 High Street, Martin, Lincoln
LN4 3QT
T: (01526) 378528
F: (01526) 378528
I: www.stable-studio.co.uk

MARTIN HUSSINGTREE
Worcestershire

Knoll Farm Bed and Breakfast ♦♦♦
Knoll Farm, Ladywood Road,
Martin Hussingtree, Worcester
WR3 7SX
T: (01905) 455565
E: aligriggs@hotmail.com

MARTLEY
Worcestershire

Admiral Rodney Inn ♦♦♦♦
Berrow Green, Martley,
Worcester WR6 6PL
T: (01886) 821375
F: (01886) 822048
E: rodney@admiral.fslife.co.uk
I: www.admiral-rodney.co.uk

The Chandlery ♦♦♦♦
Martley, Worcester WR6 6QA
T: (01886) 888318
F: (01886) 889047
E: john.nicklin@virgin.net
I: www.thechandlerybandb.co.uk

MATLOCK
Derbyshire

Bank House
♦♦♦♦ SILVER AWARD
12 Snitterton Road, Matlock
DE4 3LZ
T: (01629) 56101
E: jennyderbydales@hotmail.com

Derwent House ♦♦♦
Knowleston Place, Matlock
DE4 3BU
T: (01629) 584681
F: (01629) 55331
E: stay@derwenthouse.co.uk
I: www.derwenthouse.co.uk

Edgemount ♦♦
16 Edge Road, Matlock DE4 3NH
T: (01629) 584787

Ellen House ♦♦♦♦
37 Snitterton Road, Matlock
DE4 3LZ
T: (01629) 55584

Home Farm ♦♦♦
Ible, Grange Mill, Matlock
DE4 4HS
T: (01629) 650349

Jackson Tor House Hotel ♦♦♦
76 Jackson Road, Matlock
DE4 3JQ
T: (01629) 582348
F: (01629) 582348

Jug and Glass
Rating Applied For
Lea Main Road, Lea, Matlock
DE4 5GJ
T: (01629) 534232
F: (01629) 534232
E: roy.fretwell@btinternet.com

The Old English Hotel ♦♦
77 Dale Road, Matlock DE4 3LT
T: (01629) 55028
F: (01629) 55028

Riverbank House ♦♦♦♦
Derwent Avenue, (Off Old
English Road), Matlock DE4 3LX
T: (01629) 582593
E: bookings@riverbankhouse.co.uk
I: www.riverbankhouse.co.uk

Robertswood Country House
♦♦♦♦♦ GOLD AWARD
Farley Hill, Matlock DE4 3LL
T: (01629) 55642
F: (01629) 55642
E: robertswood@supanet.com
I: www.robertswood.com

Sheriff Lodge
♦♦♦♦ SILVER AWARD
51 Dimple Road, Matlock
DE4 3JX
T: (01629) 760760
F: (01629) 760860
E: info@sherifflodge.co.uk
I: www.sherifflodge.co.uk

Town Head Farmhouse ♦♦♦♦
70 High Street, Bonsall, Matlock
DE4 2AR
T: (01629) 823762

Warren Carr Barn
♦♦♦♦ SILVER AWARD
Warren Carr, Matlock DE4 2LN
T: (01629) 733856
E: cherry@warrencarrbarn.freeserve.co.uk
I: www.SmoothHound.co.uk/hotels/warrenca.html

White Thorns B&B
Rating Applied For
Warren Carr, South Darley,
Matlock DE4 2Ln
T: (01629) 733240
E: drawl@tiscali.co.uk

MATLOCK BATH
Derbyshire

Ashdale ♦♦♦
92 North Parade, Matlock Bath,
Matlock DE4 3NS
T: (01629) 57826
E: ashdale@matlockbath.fsnet.co.uk
I: www.ashdaleguesthouse.co.uk

The Firs ♦♦♦
180 Dale Road, Matlock Bath,
Matlock DE4 3PS
T: (01629) 582426
F: (01629) 582426
E: moira@thefirs180.demon.co.uk

Fountain Villa ♦♦♦♦
86 North Parade, Matlock Bath,
Matlock DE4 3NS
T: (01629) 56195
F: (01629) 581057
E: enquiries@fountainvilla.co.uk
I: www.fountainvilla.co.uk

Hodgkinsons Hotel ♦♦♦♦
150 South Parade, Matlock Bath,
Matlock DE4 3NR
T: (01629) 582170
F: (01629) 584891
E: enquiries@hodgkinsons-hotel.co.uk
I: www.hodgkinsons-hotel.co.uk

Old Museum Guesthouse ♦♦♦
170-172 South Parade, Matlock
Bath, Matlock DE4 3NR
T: (01629) 57783
E: lindsayandstewartbailey@tinyworld.co.uk

Sunnybank Guesthouse
◆◆◆◆ SILVER AWARD
37 Clifton Road, Matlock Bath, Matlock DE4 3PW
T: (01629) 584621
E: sunward@lineone.net
I: www.SmoothHound.co.uk/hotels/sunbankgh.html

MAVESYN RIDWARE
Staffordshire

The Old Rectory
◆◆◆◆ GOLD AWARD
Mavesyn Ridware, Rugeley WS15 3QE
T: (01543) 490792
E: sandraryder@waverider.co.uk

MEDBOURNE
Leicestershire

Homestead House
◆◆◆◆ SILVER AWARD
5 Ashley Road, Medbourne, Market Harborough LE16 8DL
T: (01858) 565724
F: (01858) 565324
E: june@homesteadhouse.co.uk
I: www.homesteadhouse.co.uk

MELBOURNE
Derbyshire

Burdett House ◆
Derby Road, Melbourne, Derby DE73 1DE
T: (01332) 862105
E: jjvglaze@btinternet.com

MELTON MOWBRAY
Leicestershire

Amberley Gardens B&B
◆◆◆◆
4 Church Lane, Asfordby, Melton Mowbray LE14 3RU
T: (01664) 812314
F: (01664) 813740
E: doris@amberleygardens.net
I: www.amberleygardens.net

Hall Farm ◆◆◆
1 Main Street, Holwell, Melton Mowbray LE14 4SZ
T: (01664) 444275
F: (01664) 444731

Hillside House ◆◆◆◆
27 Melton Road, Burton Lazars, Melton Mowbray LE14 2UR
T: (01664) 566312
F: (01664) 501819
E: peter@hillsidehouse.co.uk
I: www.hillside-house.co.uk

Tole Cottage ◆◆◆◆
10 Main Street, Kirby Bellars, Melton Mowbray LE14 2EA
T: (01664) 812932
E: enquiries@tolecottage-melton.co.uk
I: www.tolecottage-melton.co.uk

MELVERLEY
Shropshire

Church House ◆◆◆◆
Melverley, Oswestry SY10 8PJ
T: (01691) 682754
E: melverley@aol.com
I: members.aol.com/melverley

MEOLE BRACE
Shropshire

Meole Brace Hall
◆◆◆◆◆ SILVER AWARD
Church Road, Meole Brace, Shrewsbury SY3 9HF
T: (01743) 235566
F: (01743) 236886
E: hathaway@meolebracehall.co.uk
I: www.meolebracehall.co.uk

MERIDEN
West Midlands

Barnacle Farm ◆◆◆◆
Back Lane, Meriden, Coventry CV7 7LD
T: (024) 7646 8875
F: (024) 7646 8875

Bonnifinglas Guest House ◆◆
3 Berkswell Road, Meriden, Coventry CV7 7LB
T: (01676) 523193
F: (01676) 523193

Cooperage Farm Bed and Breakfast ◆◆
Old Road, Meriden, Coventry CV7 7JP
T: (01676) 523493
F: (01676) 523876
E: lucy@cooperagefarm.co.uk
I: www.copperagefarm.co.uk

Dumela B&B ◆◆◆◆
Berkswell Road, Meriden, Coventry CV7 7LB
T: (01676) 523118
F: (01676) 523118
E: wadejanice@hotmail.com

Innellan House ◆◆◆
Eaves Green Lane, Meriden, Coventry CV7 7JL
T: (01676) 523005
F: (01676) 523005
E: caroled@innellanhouse.fsnet.co.uk
I: www.smoothhound.co.uk/hotels/innellan.html

MICHAELCHURCH ESCLEY
Herefordshire

The Grove Farm ◆◆◆◆
Michaelchurch Escley, Hereford HR2 0PT
T: (01981) 510229
F: (01981) 510229

MICKLETON
Gloucestershire

Myrtle House
◆◆◆◆ SILVER AWARD
High Street, Mickleton, Chipping Campden GL55 6SA
T: (01386) 430032
E: kate@myrtlehouse.co.uk
I: www.myrtlehouse.co.uk

MIDDLE DUNTISBOURNE
Gloucestershire

Manor Farm ◆◆◆
Middle Duntisbourne, Cirencester GL7 7AR
T: (01285) 658145
F: (01285) 641504
E: duntisborne@aol.com
I: www.smoothhound.co.uk/hotels/manorfar.html

MIDDLETON
Derbyshire

Eastas Gate ◆◆◆◆
18 Main Street, Middleton, Matlock DE4 4LQ
T: (01629) 822790
E: eastasgate@hotmail.com
I: www.eastasgate.users.btopenworld.com

Middleton House Farm
◆◆◆◆ SILVER AWARD
Tamworth Road, Middleton, Tamworth B78 2BD
T: (01827) 873474
F: (01827) 872246
E: contact@middletonhousefarm.co.uk
I: www.middletonhousefarm.co.uk

Valley View ◆◆◆
3 Camsdale Walk, Middleton, Market Harborough LE16 8YR
T: (01536) 770874

MIDDLETON-BY-YOULGREAVE
Derbyshire

Castle Farm ◆◆◆◆
Middleton-by-Youlgrave, Middleton-by-Youlgreave, Bakewell DE45 1LS
T: (01629) 636746

Smerrill Grange ◆◆◆
Middleton-by-Youlgreave, Bakewell DE45 1LQ
T: (01629) 636232

MILLTHORPE
Derbyshire

Cordwell House ◆◆◆◆
Cordwell Lane, Millthorpe, Holmesfield, Dronfield S18 7WH
T: (0114) 289 0271

MILTON
Nottinghamshire

The Stables
◆◆◆◆ SILVER AWARD
The Avenue, Milton, Newark NG22 0PW
T: (01777) 871920
F: (01777) 871920
E: wellez@hotmail.com

MINSTERLEY
Shropshire

The Callow Inn ◆◆◆
Bromlow, Minsterley, Shrewsbury SY5 0EA
T: (01743) 891933
F: (01743) 891933
E: del@callowinn.freeserve.co.uk
I: www.callowinn.freeserve.co.uk

Cricklewood Cottage ◆◆◆◆
Plox Green, Minsterley, Shrewsbury SY5 0HT
T: (01743) 791229
E: paul.crickcott@bushinternet.com
I: www.smoothhound.co.uk/hotels/crickle

Holly House ◆◆
Bromlow, Minsterley, Shrewsbury SY5 0EA
T: (01743) 891435
E: paul.jaquesl@btinternet.com

Mandalay Bed and Breakfast
◆◆◆◆
The Grove, Minsterley, Shrewsbury SY5 0AG
T: (01743) 791758
E: mandalaybandb@freeuk.com
I: http://home.freeuk.com/mandalaybandb/index.htm

MITCHELDEAN
Gloucestershire

Gunn Mill House
◆◆◆◆ SILVER AWARD
Lower Spout Lane, Mitcheldean GL17 0EA
T: (01594) 827577
F: (01594) 827577
E: info@gunnmillhouse.co.uk
I: www.gunnmillhouse.co.uk

MONNINGTON-ON-WYE
Herefordshire

Dairy House Farm ◆◆◆
Monnington-on-Wye HR4 7NL
T: (01981) 500143
F: (01981) 500043
E: pearson-greg@clara.co.uk

MONSAL DALE
Derbyshire

Upperdale House ◆◆◆
Monsal Dale, Buxton SK17 8SZ
T: (01629) 640536
F: (01629) 640536
E: bookings@upperdale.fsnet.co.uk
I: www.monsaldale.com

MONYASH
Derbyshire

Chapel View Farm ◆◆◆◆
Chapel Street, Monyash, Bakewell DE45 1JJ
T: (01629) 814317
F: (01629)814317

High Rakes Farm
◆◆◆◆ SILVER AWARD
Rakes Road, Monyash, Bakewell DE45 1JL
T: (01298) 84692

MOORHOUSE
Nottinghamshire

Brecks Cottage Bed and Breakfast ◆◆◆◆
Green Lane, Moorhouse, Newark NG23 6LZ
T: (01636) 822445
F: (01636) 821384
E: BandB@breckscottage.co.uk
I: www.breckscottage.co.uk

MORETON-IN-MARSH
Gloucestershire

Acacia ◆◆◆
2 New Road, Moreton-in-Marsh GL56 0AS
T: (01608) 650130

The Bell Inn ◆◆◆
High Street, Moreton-in-Marsh GL56 0AF
T: (01608) 651688
F: (01608) 652195
E: keith.pendry@virgin.net
I: www.bellinncotswold.com

Blenheim Cottage ◆◆◆◆◆
Upper Oddington, Moreton-in-Marsh GL56 0XG
T: (01451) 831066
F: (01451) 831563
E: cotswoldsoddington@nicedayforit.com

Blue Cedar House ♦♦♦
Stow Road, Moreton-in-Marsh GL56 0DW
T: (01608) 650299
E: gandsib@dialstart.net

Bran Mill Cottage ♦♦♦
Aston Magna, Moreton-in-Marsh GL56 9QW
T: (01386) 593517
F: (01386) 593517
E: enquiries@branmillcottage.co.uk
I: www.branmillcottage.co.uk

Fosseway Farm B&B ♦♦♦♦
Stow Road, Moreton-in-Marsh GL56 0DS
T: (01608) 650503

Kymalton House ♦♦♦♦
Todenham Road, Moreton-in-Marsh GL56 9NJ
T: (01608) 650487

Neighbrook Manor ♦♦♦♦♦
Near Aston Magna, Moreton-in-Marsh GL56 9QP
T: (01386) 593232
F: (01386) 593500
E: info@neighbrookmanor.com
I: www.neighbrookmanor.com

New Farm ♦♦♦
Dorn, Moreton-in-Marsh GL56 9NS
T: (01608) 650782
F: (01608) 652704
E: cath.righton@amserve.net
I: www.smoothhound.co.uk/hotels/newfa.html

The Old Chequer
♦♦♦♦ SILVER AWARD
Draycott, Moreton-in-Marsh GL56 9LB
T: (01386) 700647
F: (01386) 700647
E: g.f.linley@tesco.net
I: www.smoothhound.co.uk/hotels/oldchequer.html

Old Farm ♦♦♦
Dorn, Moreton-in-Marsh GL56 9NS
T: (01608) 650394
F: (01608) 651700
E: info@oldfarmdorn.co.uk
I: www.oldfarm.co.uk

Staddle Stones Guest House ♦♦♦
Rowborough, Stretton-on-Fosse, Moreton-in-Marsh GL56 9RE
T: (01608) 662774

Townend Cottage and Coach House ♦♦♦♦
High Street, Moreton-in-Marsh GL56 0AD
T: (01608) 650846
E: markmarilyndaniel@hotmail.com
I: www.townend-cottage.co.uk

Treetops ♦♦♦♦
London Road, Moreton-in-Marsh GL56 0HE
T: (01608) 651036
F: (01608) 651036
E: treetops1@talk21.com

Warwick House ♦♦♦
London Road, Moreton-in-Marsh GL56 0HH
T: (01608) 650773
F: (01608) 650773
E: charlie@warwickhousebnb.demon.co.uk
I: www.snoozeandsizzle.com

MORETON PINKNEY
Northamptonshire

Englands Rose ♦♦♦
Upper Green, Moreton Pinkney, Daventry NN11 3SG
T: (01295) 760353
F: (01295) 760353
E: sheila@englandsrose.freeserve.co.uk

The Old Vicarage
♦♦♦♦ SILVER AWARD
Moreton Pinkney, Daventry NN11 3SQ
T: (01295) 760057
F: (01295) 760057
E: tim@tandjeastwood.fsnet.co.uk
I: www.tandjeastwood.fsnet.co.uk

MORVILLE
Shropshire

Hannigans Farm ♦♦♦♦
Morville, Bridgnorth WV16 4RN
T: (01746) 714332
E: Hannigansfarm@btinternet.com

Hurst Farm Cottages ♦♦♦♦
Hurst Farm, Morville, Bridgnorth WV16 4TF
T: (01746) 714375
F: (01746) 714133
E: hurstfarm@talk21.com
I: www.cottagefishingholidays.co.uk

MUCH BIRCH
Herefordshire

The Old School ♦♦♦
Much Birch, Hereford HR2 8HJ
T: (01981) 541317

MUCH MARCLE
Herefordshire

New House Farm ♦♦♦
Much Marcle, Ledbury HR8 2PH
T: (01531) 660604
F: (01531) 660674

MUCH WENLOCK
Shropshire

Broadstone Mill
♦♦♦♦♦ GOLD AWARD
Broadstone, Much Wenlock TF13 6LE
T: (01584) 841494
F: (01584) 841515
E: hargreaves@broadstones.fsnet.co.uk
I: www.broadstonemill.co.uk

Danywenallt ♦♦♦
Farley Road, Much Wenlock TF13 6NB
T: (01952) 727892

The Longville Arms ♦♦♦
Longville in the Dale, Much Wenlock TF13 6DT
T: (01694) 771206
F: (01694) 771742
E: longvillearms@aol.com

Old Quarry Cottage ♦♦♦
Brockton, Much Wenlock TF13 6JR
T: (01746) 785596
E: rod@brockton.fsbusiness.co.uk

Seraphique
Rating Applied For
16 Stretton Road, Much Wenlock TF13 6AS
T: (01952) 728588
F: (01952) 728329
E: malcolm.m-r@ukf.net

Talbot Inn ♦♦♦
Much Wenlock TF13 6AA
T: (01952) 727077
F: (01952) 728436

MUNSTONE
Herefordshire

Munstone House ♦♦♦♦
Munstone, Hereford HR1 3AH
T: (01432) 267122

MYDDLE
Shropshire

Oakfields ♦♦♦
Baschurch Road, Myddle, Shrewsbury SY4 3RX
T: (01939) 290823

NAILSWORTH
Gloucestershire

Hazelwood Bed & Breakfast ♦♦♦♦
Church Street, Nailsworth, Stroud GL6 0BP
T: (01453) 839304
E: alan@hazelwood.me.uk
I: www.hazelwood.me.uk

Highlands ♦♦♦♦
Shortwood, Nailsworth, Stroud GL6 0SJ
T: (01453) 832591
F: (01453) 833590

1 Orchard Mead ♦♦♦
Nailsworth, Stroud GL6 0RE
T: (01453) 833581

The Upper House ♦♦♦♦
Spring Hill, Nailsworth, Stroud GL6 0LX
T: (01453) 836606
F: (01453) 836769

NASSINGTON
Northamptonshire

Fairlands ♦♦♦
35 Church Street, Nassington, Peterborough PE8 6QG
T: (01780) 783603
E: marriottann@hotmail.com

Sunnyside ♦♦♦
62 Church Street, Nassington, Peterborough PE8 6QG
T: (01780) 782864

NAUNTON
Gloucestershire

The Black Horse Inn ♦♦♦
Naunton, Cheltenham GL54 3AD
T: (01451) 850565

Fox Hill ♦♦♦
Old Stow Road, Naunton, Cheltenham GL54 5RL
T: (01451) 850496
F: (01451) 850602

Naunton View Guesthouse ♦♦♦
Naunton, Cheltenham GL54 3AS
T: (01451) 850482
F: (01451) 850482

NAVENBY
Lincolnshire

Barn Bed and Breakfast
♦♦♦♦ SILVER AWARD
North Lane, Navenby, Lincoln LN5 0EH
T: (01522) 810318
F: (01522) 810318
E: gill@barnbb.fsnet.co.uk

NETHER HEYFORD
Northamptonshire

Heyford Bed and Breakfast ♦♦
27 Church Street, Nether Heyford, Northampton NN7 3LH
T: (01327) 340872

NETTLEHAM
Lincolnshire

The Old Vicarage ♦♦♦♦
East Street, Nettleham, Lincoln LN2 2SL
T: (01522) 750819
F: (01522) 750819
E: susan@oldvic.net

NEW DUSTON
Northamptonshire

Rowena ♦♦♦♦
569 Harlestone Road, New Dudston, New Duston, Northampton NN5 6NX
T: (01604) 755889
F: (0870) 137 6484
E: info@rowenaBB.co.uk
I: www.rowenaBB.co.uk

NEWARK
Nottinghamshire

The Boot and Shoe Inn ♦♦♦♦
Main Street, Flintham, Newark NG23 5LA
T: (01636) 525246
E: bootshoe@flintham1234.fsbusiness.co.uk
I: www.bootandshoe.net

Crosshill House Bed and Breakfast ♦♦♦♦
Crosshill House, Laxton, Newark NG22 0NT
T: (01777) 871953
E: roberta@crosshillhouse.freeserve.co.uk
I: www.crosshillhouse.com

NEWCASTLE-UNDER-LYME
Staffordshire

Graythwaite Guest House ♦♦♦♦
106 Lancaster Road, Newcastle-under-Lyme ST5 1DS
T: (01782) 612875
E: cooke.graythwaite@dsl.pipex.com
I: www.smoothhound.co.uk/hotels/grayth

NEWENT
Gloucestershire

George Hotel ♦♦♦
Church Street, Newent GL18 1PU
T: (01531) 820203
F: (01531) 822899
E: enquiries@georgehotel.uk.com
I: www.georgehotel.uk.com

Newent Golf and Lodges ♦♦♦
Newent Golf Course, Coldharbour Lane, Newent GL18 1DJ
T: (01531) 820478
E: tomnewentgolf@aol.com
I: www.short-golf-break.com

Sandyway Nurseries Countryside B & B ♦♦♦♦
Redmarley Road, Newent GL18 1DR
T: (01531) 820693
E: jean@sandy.f9.co.uk
I: www.visitheartofengland.com/wheretostay/index.htm

Three Ashes House ♦♦♦♦ GOLD AWARD
Ledbury Road, Newent GL18 1DE
T: (01531) 820226
F: (01531) 820226
E: jrichard.cockroft@tinyworld.co.uk

NEWNHAM-ON-SEVERN
Gloucestershire

Hayden Lea ♦♦♦
Dean Road, Newnham-on-Severn GL14 1AB
T: (01594) 516626

Swan House ♦♦♦♦
High Street, Newnham-on-Severn GL14 1BY
T: (01594) 516504
F: (01594) 516177
E: enquiries@swanhousenewnham.co.uk
I: www.swanhousenewnham.co.uk

The White House World ♦♦♦
Popes Hill, Newnham-on-Severn GL14 1LE
T: (01452) 760463
F: (01452) 760934
E: whitehouseworld@btopenworld.com
I: www.whitehouseworld.co.uk

NEWPORT
Shropshire

Church Aston Farmhouse ♦♦♦♦ SILVER AWARD
Church Aston, Newport TF10 9JJ
T: (01952) 825220

Lane End Farm ♦♦♦♦ SILVER AWARD
Chester Road, Chetwynd, Newport TF10 8BN
T: (01952) 550337
F: (01952) 550337
E: ian.park@bushinternet.com
I: www.virtual-shropshire.co.uk/lef

Norwood House Hotel and Restaurant ♦♦♦
Pave Lane, Newport TF10 9LQ
T: (01952) 825896
F: (01952) 825896

Pear Tree Farmhouse ♦♦♦♦
Farm Grove, Newport TF10 7PX
T: (01952) 811193
F: (01952) 812115
E: patgreen@peakfarmhouse.co.uk
I: www.peartreefarmhouse.co.uk

Sambrook Manor ♦♦♦
Sambrook, Newport TF10 8AL
T: (01952) 550256

NEWTON BURGOLAND
Leicestershire

Millview Cottage Rating Applied For
School Lane, Newton Burgoland, Leicester LE67 2SL
T: (01530) 272600
F: (01530) 274516
E: amanda@amandacooper.com
I: www.millviewcottage.co.uk

NEWTON-ON-TRENT
Lincolnshire

The Old Vicarage Guest Accommodation Rating Applied For
4 High Street, Newton-on-Trent, Lincoln LN1 2JS
T: (01777) 228772
F: (01777) 228772
E: jbeard@bmihs.co.uk

NEWTOWN LINFORD
Leicestershire

Wondai ♦♦♦
47-49 Main Street, Newtown Linford, Leicester LE6 0AE
T: (01530) 242728
E: j_weazel@eggconnect.net

NORBURY
Shropshire

Oulton House Farm ♦♦♦♦
Norbury, Stafford ST20 0PG
T: (01785) 284264
F: (01785) 284264
E: judy@oultonhousefarm.co.uk
I: www.oultonhousefarm.co.uk

NORMANTON-ON-TRENT
Nottinghamshire

Square and Compass Inn ♦♦♦♦
Eastgate, Normanton-on-Trent, Newark NG23 6RN
T: (01636) 821439
F: (01636) 822794
E: info@squareandcompass.co.uk
I: www.squareandcompass.co.uk

NORTH COTES
Lincolnshire

Fleece Inn ♦♦♦
Lock Road, North Cotes, Grimsby DN36 5UP
T: (01472) 388233
F: (01472) 388233

NORTH HYKEHAM
Lincolnshire

Lakeview Guesthouse ♦♦♦♦
50 Station Road, North Hykeham, Lincoln LN6 9AQ
T: (01522) 680455

NORTH KYME
Lincolnshire

Old Coach House Motel & Cafe ♦♦♦♦
Church Lane, North Kyme, Lincoln LN4 4DJ
T: (01526) 861465
F: (01526) 861658
E: Barbara@motel-plus.co.uk
I: www.Motel-Plus.co.uk

NORTH SOMERCOTES
Lincolnshire

Pigeon Cottage Bed & Breakfast & LLA Summer Camps ♦♦
Conisholme Road, North Somercotes, Louth LN11 7PS
T: (01507) 359063
F: (01507) 359063
E: lla.hill@ukgateway.net
I: www.llalincs.co.uk

NORTH WINGFIELD
Derbyshire

South View ♦♦♦
95 Church Lane, North Wingfield, Chesterfield S42 5HR
T: (01246) 850091
E: 95-southview@tiscali.co.uk

NORTHAMPTON
Northamptonshire

Aarandale Regent Hotel and Guesthouse ♦♦
6-8 Royal Terrace, Barrack Road (A508), Northampton NN1 3RF
T: (01604) 631096
F: (01604) 621035
E: info@aarandale.co.uk
I: www.aarandale.co.uk

The Gables Guest House ♦♦♦♦
74 Fulford Drive, Links View, Northampton NN2 7NR
T: (01604) 713858

Haselbech House Farm ♦♦♦♦
Haselbech Hill, Haselbech, Northampton NN6 9LL
T: (01604) 686266
F: (01604) 686266
E: lesueur@haselbech.freeserve.co.uk
I: www.haselbechhousefarm.co.uk

Poplars Hotel ♦♦♦♦
Cross Street, Moulton, Northampton NN3 7RZ
T: (01604) 643983
F: (01604) 790233
E: thepoplars@btopenworld.com
I: www.northamptonshire.co.uk/hotels/poplarshotel.htm

NORTHLEACH
Gloucestershire

Cotteswold House ♦♦♦♦ SILVER AWARD
Market Place, Northleach, Cheltenham GL54 3EG
T: (01451) 860493
F: (01451) 860493
E: cotteswoldhouse@aol.com
I: www.cotteswoldhouse.com

The Eastington Suite ♦♦♦♦♦ GOLD AWARD
Japonica, Upper End Eastington, Northleach, Cheltenham GL54 3PJ
T: (01451) 861117
F: (01451) 861117
I: members.tripod.co.uk/the2eastingtonsuite/

Long Barrow ♦♦♦♦
Farmington, Northleach, Cheltenham GL54 3NQ
T: (01451) 860428
F: (01451) 860166
E: ghowson@longbarrow.fsnet.co.uk

Northfield Bed and Breakfast ♦♦♦♦ SILVER AWARD
Cirencester Road (A429), Northleach, Cheltenham GL54 3JL
T: (01451) 860427
F: (01451) 860427
E: nrthfield0@aol.com
I: www.northfieldbandb.co.uk

Prospect Cottage ♦♦♦♦ SILVER AWARD
West End, Northleach, Cheltenham GL54 3HG
T: (01451) 860875
F: (01451) 860875
E: info@prospectcottage.co.uk
I: www.prospectcottage.co.uk

The Wheatsheaf Inn ♦♦♦
West End, Northleach, Cheltenham GL54 3EZ
T: (01451) 860244
F: (01451) 861037

NOTTINGHAM
Nottinghamshire

Acorn Hotel ♦♦♦
4 Radcliffe Road, West Bridgford, Nottingham NG2 5FW
T: (0115) 981 1297
F: (0115) 981 7654
E: reservations@acorn-hotel.co.uk
I: www.acorn-hotel.co.uk

Andrews Private Hotel ♦♦♦
310 Queens Road, Beeston, Nottingham NG9 1JA
T: (0115) 925 4902
F: (0115) 917 8839
E: andrews.hotel@ntlworld.com

Elm Bank Lodge ♦♦♦
9 Elm Bank, Mapperley Park, Nottingham NG3 5AJ
T: (0115) 962 5493
F: (0115) 962 5493
E: stewpot1a@aol.com
I: www.smoothhound.co.uk/hotels/elmbank

The Gallery Hotel ♦♦♦
8-10 Radcliffe Road, West Bridgford, Nottingham NG2 5FW
T: (0115) 981 3651
F: (0115) 981 3732
I: www.yell.co.uk/sites/galleryhotel/

Grantham Hotel ♦♦♦
24-26 Radcliffe Road, West Bridgford, Nottingham NG2 5FW
T: (0115) 981 1373
F: (0115) 981 8567
E: granthamhotel@netlineuk.net

Greenwood Lodge City Guesthouse ♦♦♦♦♦ GOLD AWARD
Third Avenue, Sherwood Rise, Nottingham NG7 6JH
T: (0115) 962 1206
F: (0115) 962 1206
E: pdouglas71@aol.com
I: www.greenwoodlodgecityguesthouse.co.uk

Nelson and Railway Inn ♦♦
Station Road, Kimberley, Nottingham NG16 2NR
T: (0115) 938 2177
I: www.nelsonandrailway.fsnet.co.uk

Orchard Cottage ♦♦♦♦
Moor Cottages, Nottingham Road, Trowell, Nottingham NG9 3PQ
T: (0115) 928 0933
F: (0115) 928 0933
E: orchardcottage.bandb@virgin.net
I: www.orchardcottages.com

Yew Tree Grange ♦♦♦♦
2 Nethergate, Clifton Village, Nottingham NG11 8NL
T: (0115) 984 7562
F: (0115) 984 7562
E: yewtree1@nascr.net
I: www.yewtreegrange.co.uk

NUNEATON
Warwickshire

La Tavola Calda ♦♦
70 Midland Road, Abbey Green, Nuneaton CV11 5DY
T: (024) 7638 3195
F: (024) 7638 1816
I: http://tavolacalda.bravepages.com

Leathermill Grange
♦♦♦♦♦ GOLD AWARD
Leathermill Lane, Caldecote, Nuneaton CV10 0RX
T: (01827) 714637
F: (01827) 716422
E: davidcodd@leathermillgrange.co.uk
I: www.leathermillgrange.co.uk

Royal Arms ♦♦♦♦
Main Street, Sutton Cheney, Nuneaton CV13 0AG
T: (01455) 290263
F: (01455) 290124
I: www.royalarms.co.uk

OAKAMOOR
Staffordshire

Bank House
♦♦♦♦♦ GOLD AWARD
Farley Road, Oakamoor, Stoke-on-Trent ST10 3BD
T: (01538) 702810
F: (01538) 702810
E: john.orme@dial.pipex.com
I: www.smoothhound.co.uk/hotels/bank.html

Beehive Guest House ♦♦♦♦
Churnet View Road, Oakamoor, Stoke-on-Trent ST10 3AE
T: (01538) 702420
F: (01538) 702420
E: thebeehiveoakamoor@btinternet.com
I: www.thebeehiveguesthouse.co.uk

Crowtrees Farm ♦♦♦♦
Crowtrees Farm, Oakmoor, Oakamoor, Stoke-on-Trent ST10 3DY
T: (01538) 702260
F: (01538) 702260
E: dianne@crowtreesfarm.co.uk
I: www.crowtreesfarm.co.uk

The Laurels ♦♦♦♦
Star Bank, Oakamoor, Stoke-on-Trent ST10 3BN
T: (01538) 702629
F: (01538) 702796
E: bbthelaurels@aol.com
I: www.thelaurels.co.uk

The Lord Nelson ♦♦♦
Carr Bank, Oakamoor, Stoke-on-Trent ST10 3DQ
T: (01538) 702242

Ribden Farm ♦♦♦♦
Oakamoor, Stoke-on-Trent ST10 3BW
T: (01538) 702830
F: (01538) 702830
E: ribdenfarm@aol.com
I: www.ribden.fsnet.co.uk

Tenement Farm ♦♦♦♦
Three Lows, Ribden, Oakamoor, Stoke-on-Trent ST10 3BW
T: (01538) 702333
F: (01538) 703603
E: stanleese@aol.com
I: www.tenementfarm.co.uk

OAKENGATES
Shropshire

Chellow Dene ♦♦♦
Park Road, Malinslee, Dawley, Telford TF3 2AY
T: (01952) 505917

OAKHAM
Rutland

The Grange at Whitwell
♦♦♦♦
Oakham LE15 8BW
T: (01780) 686555
F: (01780) 686549
E: enquiries@whitwell-learning.co.uk
I: www.whitwell-learning.co.uk

OASBY
Lincolnshire

The Houblon Inn ♦♦♦
Oasby, Grantham NG32 3NB
T: (01529) 455215

The Pinomar ♦♦♦♦
Mill Lane, Oasby, Grantham NG32 3ND
T: (01529) 455400
F: (01529) 455681

OLD
Northamptonshire

Wold Farm
♦♦♦♦ SILVER AWARD
Old, Daventry NN6 9RJ
T: (01604) 781258
F: (01604) 781258
I: www.woldfarm.co.uk

OMBERSLEY
Worcestershire

Greenlands
♦♦♦♦ SILVER AWARD
Uphampton, Ombersley, Droitwich WR9 0JP
T: (01905) 620873
E: xlandgreenlands@onetel.net.uk

ORLETON
Herefordshire

Hope Cottage Bed and Breakfast ♦♦♦
Hope Cottage, Orleton, Ludlow SY8 4JB
T: (01584) 831674
F: (01584) 831124
E: hopecott@aol.com

Line Farm
♦♦♦♦♦ GOLD AWARD
Tunnel Lane, Orleton, Ludlow SY8 4HY
T: (01568) 780400
F: (01568) 780995
E: linefarm@lineone.net
I: www.virtual-shropshire.co.uk/linefarm

Rosecroft
♦♦♦♦ SILVER AWARD
Orleton, Ludlow SY8 4HN
T: (01568) 780565
F: (01568) 780565
E: gailanddavid@rosecroftorleton.freeserve.co.uk
I: www.stmem.com/rosecroft

OSGATHORPE
Leicestershire

Royal Oak House ♦♦♦
20 Main Street, Osgathorpe, Loughborough LE12 9TA
T: (01530) 222443

OSWESTRY
Shropshire

Bridge House ♦♦♦♦
Llynclys, Oswestry SY10 8AE
T: (01691) 830496
F: (01691) 830496
E: jenny@llynclys.freeserve.co.uk

The Greyhound
Rating Applied For
Willow Street, Oswestry SY11 1AJ
T: (01691) 653392

Harthill ♦♦♦
80 Welsh Walls, Oswestry SY11 1RW
T: (01691) 679024
E: thecatmurs@lineone.net

5 Llanforda Close ♦♦♦
Oswestry SY11 1SZ
T: (01691) 655823

Llwyn Guesthouse ♦♦♦
5 Llwyn Terrace, Oswestry SY11 1HR
T: (01691) 670746
E: llwyn@virtual-shropshire.co.uk
I: www.virtual-shropshire.co.uk/llwyn

87 Llwyn Road ♦♦♦
Llwyn Road, Oswestry SY11 1EW
T: (01691) 650205
E: barbara@williams87.fsnet.co.uk

Montrose ♦♦♦
Weston Lane, Oswestry SY11 2BG
T: (01691) 652063
I: www.shropshiretourism.com/placestostay

35 Oak Drive ♦♦♦
Oswestry SY11 2RX
T: (01691) 655286

The Old Rectory ♦♦♦
Selattyn, Oswestry SY10 7DH
T: (01691) 659708

Railway Cottage ♦♦♦
51 Gobowen Road, Oswestry SY11 1HU
T: (01691) 654851
F: (01691) 654851
E: pmull36823@aol.com

Red Lion ♦♦♦♦
Bailey Head, Oswestry SY11 1PZ
T: (01691) 655459
F: (01691) 655459

OUNDLE
Northamptonshire

Ashworth House ♦♦♦♦
75 West Street, Oundle, Peterborough PE8 4EJ
T: (01832) 275312
F: (01832) 275312
E: sue@ashworthhouse.co.uk
I: www.ashworthhouse.co.uk

2 Benefield Road ♦♦♦♦
Oundle, Peterborough PE8 4ET
T: (01832) 273953
F: (01832) 273953

Castle Farm Guesthouse
♦♦♦♦
Castle Farm, Fotheringhay, Peterborough PE8 5HZ
T: (01832) 226200
F: (01832) 226200

Lilford Lodge Farm ♦♦♦♦
Barnwell, Oundle, Peterborough PE8 5SA
T: (01832) 272230
F: (01832) 272230
E: trudy@lilford-lodge.demon.co.uk
I: www.lilford-lodge.demon.co.uk

OXLYNCH
Gloucestershire

Tiled House Farm ♦♦♦♦
Oxlynch, Stonehouse GL10 3DF
T: (01453) 822363
F: (01453) 822363
E: dmj@ukgateway.net

OXTON
Nottinghamshire

Far Baulker Farm ♦♦♦♦
Oxton, Southwell NG25 0RQ
T: (01623) 882375
F: (01623) 882375
E: j.esam@virgin.net
I: www.farbaulkerfarm.info

PAINSWICK
Gloucestershire

Cardynham House ♦♦♦♦
The Cross, Painswick, Stroud GL6 6XX
T: (01452) 814006
F: (01452) 812321
E: info@cardynham.co.uk
I: www.cardynham.co.uk

Hambutts Mynd ♦♦♦
Edge Road, Painswick, Stroud GL6 6UP
T: (01452) 812352
F: (01452) 813862
E: ewarland@aol.com
I: www.accommodation.uk.net/hambutts.htm

Meadowcote ♦♦♦♦
Stroud Road, Painswick, Stroud GL6 6UT
T: (01452) 813565

St Annes
Rating Applied For
Gloucester Street, Painswick, Stroud GL6 6QN
T: (01452) 812879

Skyrack ♦♦♦
The Highlands, Painswick, Stroud GL6 6SL
T: (01452) 812029
F: (01452) 813846
E: wendyskyrack@hotmail.com
I: www.painswick.co.uk/skyrack

Thorne ♦♦♦
Friday Street, Painswick, Stroud GL6 6QJ
T: (01452) 812476
F: (01458) 10925
I: www.painswick.co.uk.forward/thorne.

Upper Doreys Mill ♦♦♦
Edge, Painswick, Stroud GL6 6NF
T: (01452) 812459
F: (01452) 814756
E: sylvia@doreys.co.uk
I: www.doreys.co.uk

Wheatleys
♦♦♦♦♦ GOLD AWARD
Cotswold Mead, Painswick, Stroud GL6 6XB
T: (01452) 812167
F: (01452) 814270
E: wheatleys@dial.pipex.com
I: www.wheatleys-b-and-b.co.uk

PANT Shropshire

The Palms ♦♦♦♦
Pant, Oswestry SY10 8JZ
T: (01691) 830813
F: (01691) 830813

PAPPLEWICK Nottinghamshire

Forest Farm ♦♦♦
Mansfield Road, Papplewick, Nottingham NG15 8FL
T: (0115) 963 2310

PARKEND Gloucestershire

Deanfield ♦♦♦
Folly Road, Parkend, Lydney GL15 4JF
T: (01594) 562256
F: (01594) 562524

Edale House ♦♦♦
Folly Road, Parkend, Lydney GL15 4JF
T: (01594) 562835
F: (01594) 564488
E: edale@lineone.net
I: www.edalehouse.co.uk

The Fountain Inn & Lodge ♦♦♦
Fountain Way, Parkend, Lydney GL15 4JD
T: (01594) 562189
F: (01594) 564438
E: thefountaininn@aol.com
I: www.thefoutaininnandlodge.com

PARWICH Derbyshire

Flaxdale House
♦♦♦♦ SILVER AWARD
Parwich, Ashbourne DE6 1QA
T: (01335) 390252
F: (01335) 390644
E: mike@flaxdale.demon.co.uk
I: www.flaxdale.demon.co.uk

PEMBRIDGE Herefordshire

Lowe Farm Bed and Breakfast
♦♦♦♦ GOLD AWARD
Lowe Farm, Pembridge, Leominster HR6 9JD
T: (01544) 388395
E: williams_family@lineone.net
I: www.lowe-farm.co.uk

PENTRICH Derbyshire

Coney Grey Farm ♦♦♦
Chesterfield, Pentrich, Ripley DE5 3RF
T: (01773) 833179

PERSHORE Worcestershire

Aldbury House
♦♦♦♦ SILVER AWARD
George Lane, Wyre Piddle, Pershore WR10 2HX
T: (01386) 553754
F: (01386) 553754
E: aldbury@onetel.net.uk

Arbour House
♦♦♦♦ SILVER AWARD
Main Road, Wyre Piddle, Pershore WR10 2HU
T: (01386) 555833
F: (01386) 555833
E: lizbrownsdon@hotmail.com
I: www.smoothhound.co.uk/arbourhouse.html

Byeways ♦♦♦♦
Pershore Road, Little Comberton, Pershore WR10 3EW
T: (01386) 710203
F: (01386) 710203
E: pwbyeways@aol.com

Tibbitts Farm ♦♦♦♦
Russell Street, Great Comberton, Pershore WR10 3DT
T: (01386) 710210
F: (01386) 710210
E: pixiefarr@aol.com

PILLERTON HERSEY Warwickshire

The Old Vicarage
♦♦♦♦♦ SILVER AWARD
Pillerton Hersey, Warwick CV35 0QJ
T: (01789) 740185
E: oldvicarage98@hotmail.com

PITCHCOMBE Gloucestershire

Gable End ♦♦♦
Pitchcombe, Stroud GL6 6LN
T: (01452) 812166
F: (01452) 812719

PITSFORD Northamptonshire

Ashley House ♦♦♦♦
19 Broadlands, Pitsford, Northampton NN6 9AZ
T: (01604) 880691
F: (01604) 880691

PONTESBURY Shropshire

Jasmine Cottage
♦♦♦♦ SILVER AWARD
Pontesford, Pontesbury, Shrewsbury SY5 0UA
T: (01743) 792771
I: www.jasminecottage.net

PONTRILAS Herefordshire

Station House ♦♦
Pontrilas, Hereford HR2 0EH
T: (01981) 240564
F: (01981) 240564
E: john.pring@tesco.net
I: www.golden-valley.co.uk/stationhouse

POULTON Gloucestershire

Sprucewood ♦♦♦♦
Elf Meadow, Poulton, Cirencester GL7 5HQ
T: (01285) 851351
F: (01285) 851351

PRIORS HARDWICK Warwickshire

Hill Farm ♦♦♦
Priors Hardwick, Southam CV47 7SP
T: (01327) 260338
E: simon.darbishire@farming.co.uk
I: www.stayathillfarm.co.uk

PULVERBATCH Shropshire

Lane Farm B&B and Stables ♦♦♦
Lane Farm, Wilderley, Pulverbatch, Shrewsbury SY5 8DF
T: (01743) 718935
E: sarahgreig2002@yahoo.com
I: www.lane.farm.users.btopenworld.com

QUENIBOROUGH Leicestershire

Three Ways Farm ♦♦♦
Melton Road, Queniborough, Leicester LE7 3FN
T: (0116) 260 0472

QUENINGTON Gloucestershire

Bank View B&B ♦♦♦♦
Quenington, Cirencester GL7 5BP
T: (01285) 750573

RAITHBY Lincolnshire

The Red Lion Inn ♦♦♦
Main Street, Raithby, Spilsby PE23 4DS
T: (01790) 753727
E: alcaprawn@aol.com

REDDITCH Worcestershire

Avonhill Lodge Guest House ♦♦♦
Alcester Road, Beoley, Redditch B98 9EP
T: (01564) 742413
F: (01564) 741873

Black Horse Cottage
♦♦♦♦♦ SILVER AWARD
Gorcott Hill, Redditch B98 9EU
T: (01527) 854124
E: jaynepotter@msn.com

REDMILE Leicestershire

Peacock Farm Guesthouse and The Feathers Restaurant ♦♦♦
Redmile, Nottingham NG13 0GQ
T: (01949) 842475
F: (01949) 43127
E: peacockfarm@primeuk.net
I: www.peacock-farm.co.uk

Peacock Inn ♦♦♦♦
Church Corner, Main Street, Redmile, Nottingham NG13 0GA
T: (01949) 842554
F: (01949) 843746
E: peacock@redmile.fsbusiness.co.uk

RETFORD Nottinghamshire

The Barns Country Guesthouse ♦♦♦♦
Morton Farm, Babworth, Retford DN22 8HA
T: (01777) 706336
F: (01777) 709773
E: peter@thebarns.co.uk
I: www.thebarns.co.uk

Bolham Manor
♦♦♦♦ SILVER AWARD
Retford DN22 9JG
T: (01777) 703528
E: pamandbutch@bolhammanor.com
I: www.bolham-manor.com

The Brick and Tile ♦♦♦
81 Moorgate, Retford DN22 6RR
T: (01777) 703681
E: elvira.foster@btinternet.com

RIPLEY Derbyshire

Hellinside ♦♦♦
1-3 Whitegates, Codnor, Ripley DE5 9QD
T: (01773) 742750
F: (07977) 556576
E: hellinside@aol.com

Spinney Lodge Guesthouse ♦♦♦
Coach Road, Butterley Park, Ripley DE5 3QU
T: (01773) 740168

RIPPLE Worcestershire

Green Gables ♦♦♦
Ripple, Tewkesbury GL20 6EX
T: (01684) 592740
F: (01684) 592740

ROADE Northamptonshire

Roade House Restaurant and Hotel ♦♦♦♦ SILVER AWARD
16 High Street, Roade, Northampton NN7 2NW
T: (01604) 863372
F: (01604) 862421
E: chris@roadehousehotel.demon.co.uk

RODBOROUGH Gloucestershire

Hillview ♦♦♦
104 Kingscourt Lane, Rodborough, Stroud GL5 3PX
T: (01453) 758234

ROSS-ON-WYE Herefordshire

The Arches ♦♦♦
Walford Road, Ross-on-Wye HR9 5PT
T: (01989) 563348
F: (01989) 563348
E: the.arches@which.net

Beechcroft Bed & Breakfast ♦♦♦♦
Gloucester Road, Ross-on-Wye HR9 5LR
T: (01989) 566685
E: re.wallis@ntlworld.com

Forest Edge
♦♦♦♦ GOLD AWARD
4 Noden Drive, Lea, Ross-on-Wye HR9 7NB
T: (01989) 750682
E: don@wood11.freeserve.co.uk
I: www.wood11.freeserve.co.uk

Four Seasons ♦♦♦♦
Coughton, Walford, Ross-on-Wye HR9 5SE
T: (01989) 567884

Haslemere
♦♦♦♦ SILVER AWARD
Ledbury Road, Ross-on-Wye HR9 7BE
T: (01989) 563046
F: (01989) 563046
E: bandb@rossonwye.fsnet.co.uk
I: www.smoothhound.co.uk/hotels/haslemere2.html

The Hill House ♦♦♦
Howle Hill, Ross-on-Wye HR9 5ST
T: (01989) 562033
E: thehillhouse2000@hotmail.com
I: www.thehowlinghillhouse.com

Lavender Cottage ♦♦♦
Bridstow, Ross-on-Wye HR9 6QB
T: (01989) 562836
F: (01989) 762129
E: barbara_lavender@yahoo.co.uk

Linden House ♦♦♦♦
14 Church Street, Ross-on-Wye HR9 5HN
T: (01989) 565373
F: (01989) 565575
I: www.lindenhouse.wyenet.co.uk

Lumleys
♦♦♦♦ SILVER AWARD
Kerne Bridge, Bishopswood, Ross-on-Wye HR9 5QT
T: (01600) 890040
E: helen@lumleys.force9.co.uk
I: www.lumleys.force9.co.uk

Lyndor Bed and Breakfast ♦♦♦
Lyndor, Hole-in-the-Wall, Ross-on-Wye HR9 7JW
T: (01989) 563833

Norton House
♦♦♦♦ GOLD AWARD
Whitchurch, Ross-on-Wye HR9 6DJ
T: (01600) 890046
F: (01600) 890045
E: sue@norton.wyenet.co.uk
I: www.Norton-House.com

The Old Court House ♦♦♦
53 High Street, Ross-on-Wye HR9 5HH
T: (01989) 762275
F: (01989) 762275
E: theoldcourthouse@hotmail.com

The Old Rectory ♦♦♦♦
Hope Mansell, Ross-on-Wye HR9 5TL
T: (01989) 750382
F: (01989) 750382
E: rectory@mansell.wyenet.co.uk

Radcliffe Guest House ♦♦♦
Wye Street, Ross-on-Wye HR9 7BS
T: (01989) 563895
E: Radcliffegh@btinternet.com

Sunnymount Hotel ♦♦♦♦
Ryefield Road, Ross-on-Wye HR9 5LU
T: (01989) 563880
F: (01989) 566251
E: sunnymount@tinyworld.co.uk

Thatch Close ♦♦♦♦
Llangrove, Ross-on-Wye HR9 6EL
T: (01989) 770300
E: thatch.close@virgin.net

Vaga House ♦♦♦
Wye Street, Ross-on-Wye HR9 7BS
T: (01989) 563024
F: (01989) 763260
E: vagahouse@yahoo.co.uk
I: www.vagahouse.co.uk

Walnut Tree Cottage Hotel
♦♦♦♦ SILVER AWARD
Symonds Yat West, Ross-on-Wye HR9 6BN
T: (01600) 890828
F: (01600) 890828
E: enquiries@walnuttreehotel.co.uk
I: www.walnuttreehotel.co.uk

Welland House ♦♦♦
Archenfield Road, Ross-on-Wye HR9 5BA
T: (01989) 566500
E: wellandhouse@hotmail.com

ROUGH CLOSE
Staffordshire

Chestnut Grange ♦♦♦♦
Windmill Hill, Rough Close, Stoke-on-Trent ST3 7PJ
T: (01782) 396084
F: (01782) 396084

ROWSLEY
Derbyshire

The Old Station House ♦♦♦♦
4 Chatsworth Road, Rowsley, Matlock DE4 2EJ
T: (01629) 732987
F: (01629) 735169
E: patches@proach.fsnet.co.uk

Vernon House ♦♦♦♦
Bakewell Road, Rowsley, Matlock DE4 2EB
T: (01629) 734294
E: vernon.houserowsley@btopenworld.com

1 Vicarage Croft ♦♦♦
Church Lane, Rowsley, Matlock DE4 2EA
T: (01629) 735429

ROWSTON
Lincolnshire

The Shepherd's Cottage
Rating Applied For
40 North Street, Digby, Lincoln LN4 3LY
T: (01526) 323151

RUDFORD
Gloucestershire

The Dark Barn Cottages ♦♦♦
Barbers Bridge, Rudford, Gloucester GL2 8DX
T: (01452) 790412
F: (01452) 790145
I: www.barbersbridge.co.uk

RUGBY
Warwickshire

Arnold Villas Bed & Breakfast ♦♦♦
4 Arnold Villas, Rugby CV21 3AX
T: (01788) 562626

Carlton Hotel ♦♦♦♦
130 Railway Terrace, Rugby CV21 3HE
T: (01788) 560211
F: (01788) 563939
I: www.thecarltonrugby.co.uk

The Croft Bed and Breakfast ♦♦♦
69 Rugby road, Dunchurch, Rugby CV22 6PQ
T: (01788) 816763
E: tlong79@hotmail.com

Diamond House Hotel ♦♦♦
28-30 Hillmorton Road, Rugby CV22 5AA
T: (01788) 572701
F: (01788) 572701
E: diamondhouse2830@aol.co.uk

Lawford Hill Farm
♦♦♦♦ SILVER AWARD
Lawford Heath Lane, Rugby CV23 9HG
T: (01788) 542001
F: (01788) 537880
E: lawford.hill@talk21.com
I: www.lawfordhill.co.uk

Marston House
♦♦♦♦ SILVER AWARD
Priors Marston, Southam CV47 7RP
T: (01327) 260297
F: (01327) 262846
E: kim@mahonand.co.uk
I: www.ivabestbandb.co.uk

The Old Rectory ♦♦♦
Main Street, Harborough Magna, Rugby CV23 0HS
T: (01788) 833151
F: (01788) 833151
E: parkinnen@btopenworld.com
I: www.theoldrectorywarwickshire.co.uk

Teapot Hall Guest House ♦♦♦
178 Murray Road, Rugby CV21 3JU
T: (01788) 578134
E: teapothall@aol.com
I: www.teapothall.co.uk

The Three Horseshoes ♦♦♦
Southam Road, Princethorpe, Rugby CV23 9PR
T: (01926) 632345

Village Green Hotel
♦♦♦♦ SILVER AWARD
The Green, Dunchurch, Rugby CV22 6NX
T: (01788) 813434
F: (01788) 814714
E: info@vghrugby.co.uk
I: www.vghrugby.co.uk

White Lion Inn ♦♦♦
Coventry Road, Pailton, Rugby CV23 0QD
T: (01788) 832359
F: (01788) 832359
I: ww.whitelionpailton.co.uk

RUGELEY
Staffordshire

Lea Hall Farm
♦♦♦♦ SILVER AWARD
Admaston, Rugeley WS15 3NN
T: (01889) 500662
E: parkosplace@aol.com

Park Farm ♦♦♦
Hawkesyard, Armitage Lane, Rugeley WS15 1ED
T: (01889) 583477
F: (01889) 583477

RUSHDEN
Northamptonshire

The Green House
Rating Applied For
32 Montague Street, Rushden NN10 9TS
T: (01933) 313706
I: www.greenhouse

RUSHTON SPENCER
Staffordshire

Heaton House Farm ♦♦♦♦
Rushton Spencer, Macclesfield SK11 0RD
T: (01260) 226203
F: (01260) 226562
E: mick@heatonhouse.fsnet.co.uk
I: www.heatonhousefarm.co.uk

RUSKINGTON
Lincolnshire

Sunnyside Farm ♦♦♦
Leasingham Lane, Ruskington, Sleaford NG34 9AH
T: (01526) 833010
E: sunnysidebb@tiscali.co.uk
I: www.sunnysidefarm.co.uk

ST OWENS CROSS
Herefordshire

Amberley
♦♦♦♦ SILVER AWARD
Aberhall Farm, St Owen's Cross, Hereford HR2 8LL
T: (01989) 730256
F: (01989) 730256
E: freda@ereal.net
I: www.SmoothHound.co.uk/hotels/amberley2.html

SANDHURST
Gloucestershire

Brawn Farm ♦♦♦♦
Sandhurst, Gloucester GL2 9NR
T: (01452) 731010
F: (01452) 731102
E: williams.sally@excite.com

SAXILBY
Lincolnshire

Orchard Cottage ♦♦♦♦
3 Orchard Lane, Saxilby, Lincoln LN1 2HT
T: (01522) 703192
F: (01522) 703192
E: margaretallen@orchardcottage.org.uk
I: www.smoothhound.co.uk/hotels/orchardcot.html

SCALDWELL
Northamptonshire

The Old House
♦♦♦♦ SILVER AWARD
East End, Scaldwell, Northampton NN6 9LB
T: (01604) 880359
F: (01604) 880359
E: mrsv@scaldwell43.fsnet.co.uk
I: www.the-oldhouse.co.uk

SCOTTER
Lincolnshire

Ivy Lodge Hotel ♦♦♦♦
Messingham Road, Scotter, Gainsborough DN21 3UQ
T: (01724) 763723
E: hotel@choxx.co.uk
I: www.SmoothHound.co.uk/hotels/ivylodge.html

SHAWBURY
Shropshire

Sowbath Farm ♦♦♦
Shawbury, Shrewsbury SY4 4ES
T: (01939) 250064
F: (01939) 250064
E: sowbath_farm@yahoo.co.uk

SHEEPSCOMBE
Gloucestershire

Sen Sook ♦♦♦
Far End Lane, Sheepscombe, Stroud GL6 7RL
T: (01452) 812047
E: AnneHawkins@sensook.freeserve.co.uk

SHEPSHED
Leicestershire

Croft Guesthouse ♦♦♦
21 Hall Croft, Shepshed, Loughborough LE12 9AN
T: (01509) 505657
F: (0870) 052 2266
E: ray@croftguesthouse.demon.co.uk
I: www.croftguesthouse.demon.co.uk

The Grange Courtyard
♦♦♦♦♦ SILVER AWARD
The Grange, Forest Street, Shepshed, Loughborough LE12 9DA
T: (01509) 600189
E: lindalawrence@thegrangecourtyard.co.uk
I: www.thegrangecourtyard.co.uk

SHIFNAL
Shropshire

Naughty Nell's Limited ♦♦♦
1 Park Street, Shifnal TF11 9BA
T: (01952) 411412
F: (01952) 463336
I: www.naughtynells.co.uk

Odfellows – The Wine Bar ♦♦♦
Market Place, Shifnal TF11 9AU
T: (01952) 461517
F: (01952) 463855
E: odfellows@odley.co.uk

SHIPSTON-ON-STOUR
Warwickshire

White Bear Hotel ♦♦
High Street, Shipston-on-Stour CV36 4AJ
T: (01608) 661558
F: (01608) 662612
E: whitebearhot@hotmail.com
I: www.whitebearhotel.co.uk

SHIREBROOK
Derbyshire

The Old School Guesthouse ♦♦♦
80 Main Street, Shirebrook, Mansfield NG20 8DL
T: (01623) 744610
F: (01623) 744610
E: pemiles@oldschoolguesthouse.fsnet.co.uk
I: www.oldschoolguesthouse.co.uk

SHIRLEY
Derbyshire

The Old Byre Guesthouse ♦♦♦♦
Hollington Lane, Shirley, Ashbourne DE6 3AS
T: (01335) 360054
F: (01335) 360054
E: alan@theoldbyre.fsbusiness.co.uk
I: www.theoldbyre.fsbusiness.co.uk

SHOBDON
Herefordshire

Four Oaks ♦♦♦♦
Uphampton, Shobdon, Leominster HR6 9PA
T: (01568) 708039
F: (01568) 708039
E: bandb@fouroaks.plus.com

SHOBY
Leicestershire

Shoby Lodge Farm
♦♦♦♦ SILVER AWARD
Shoby, Melton Mowbray LE14 3PF
T: (01664) 812156

SHORNCOTE
Gloucestershire

Glebe Farm ♦♦♦
Shorncote, Cirencester GL7 6DE
T: (01285) 860206
F: (01285) 860206
E: pip@knightfarm.demon.co.uk

SHREWSBURY
Shropshire

Abbey Court House ♦♦♦♦
134 Abbey Foregate, Shrewsbury SY2 6AU
T: (01743) 364416
F: (01743) 358559
E: info@abbeycourt.org
I: www.abbeycourt.org

Abbey Lodge Guest House ♦♦♦
68 Abbey Foregate, Shrewsbury SY2 6BG
T: (01743) 235832
F: (01743) 235832
E: lindsay.abbeylodge@virgin.net
I: www.abbeylodgeshrewsbury.co.uk

Anton Guest House ♦♦♦♦
1 Canon Street, Monkmoor, Shrewsbury SY2 5HG
T: (01743) 359275
F: (01743) 270168
E: clairealford@hotmail.com
I: www.antonhouse.supanet.com

Ashley House ♦♦♦♦
Crew Green, Shrewsbury SY5 9AS
T: (01743) 884936

Ashton Lees ♦♦♦♦
Dorrington, Shrewsbury SY5 7JW
T: (01743) 718378

Avonlea ♦♦
33 Coton Crescent, Coton Hill, Shrewsbury SY1 2NZ
T: (01743) 359398

164 Bed and Continental Breakfast ♦♦♦
164 Abbey Foregate, Shrewsbury SY2 6AL
T: (01743) 367750
F: (01743) 367750
E: chris@164bedandbreakfast.co.uk
I: www.164bedandbreakfast.co.uk

The Bell Inn ♦♦♦
Old Wenlock Road, Cross Houses, Shrewsbury SY5 6JJ
T: (01743) 761264

Brambleberry ♦♦♦♦
Halfway House, Shrewsbury SY5 9DD
T: (01743) 884762
E: bedandbreakfast@brambleberry.freeserve.co.uk

The Burlton Inn
♦♦♦♦ SILVER AWARD
Burlton, Shrewsbury SY4 5TB
T: (01939) 270284
F: (01939) 270204
E: bean@burltoninn.co.uk
I: www.burltoninn.co.uk

Castlecote ♦♦♦
77 Monkmoor Road, Shrewsbury SY2 5AT
T: (01743) 245473
F: (01743) 340274
E: btench@castlecote.fsbusiness.co.uk

College Hill Guest House ♦♦
11 College Hill, Shrewsbury SY1 1LZ
T: (01743) 365744
F: (01743) 365744

Eye Manor ♦♦♦♦
Leighton, Shrewsbury SY5 6SQ
T: (01952) 510066
F: (01952) 510967

Golden Cross Hotel ♦♦♦
14 Princess Street, Shrewsbury SY1 1LP
T: (01743) 362507

Lyth Hill House
♦♦♦♦ SILVER AWARD
28 Old Coppice, Lyth Hill, Shrewsbury SY3 0BP
T: (01743) 874660
E: bnb@lythhillhouse.com
I: www.lythhillhouse.com

Noneley Hall ♦♦♦♦
Noneley, Near Wem, Shrewsbury SY4 5SL
T: (01939) 233271
F: (01939) 233271
E: Noneley Hall@aol.com
I: www.noneleyhall.co.uk

The Old Post Office
Rating Applied For
1 Milk Street, Shrewsbury SY1 1SZ
T: (01743) 236019
F: (01743) 231305
E: psw@blueyonder.co.uk
I: www.oldpostofficepub.com

The Old Station
♦♦♦♦ SILVER AWARD
Leaton, Bomere Heath, Shrewsbury SY4 3AP
T: (01939) 290905

The Old Vicarage
♦♦♦♦ SILVER AWARD
Leaton, Shrewsbury SY4 3AP
T: (01939) 290989
F: (01939) 290989
E: m-j@oldvicleaton.com
I: www.oldvicleaton.com

Restawhile ♦♦♦
36 Coton Crescent, Coton Hill, Shrewsbury SY1 2NZ
T: (01743) 240969
F: (01743) 231841
E: restawhile@breathemail.net
I: www.virtual-shropshire.co.uk/restawhile

Severn Cottage ♦♦♦♦
4 Coton Hill, Shrewsbury SY1 2DZ
T: (01743) 358467
F: (01743) 289920
E: david.tudor1@virgin.net
I: www.shrewsburynet.com

Shenandoah ♦♦♦
Sparrow Lane, Abbey Forgate, Shrewsbury SY2 5EP
T: (01743) 363015
F: (01743) 244918

The Stiperstones Guest House ♦♦♦
18 Coton Crescent, Coton Hill, Shrewsbury SY1 2NZ
T: (01743) 246720
E: thestiperstones@aol.com
I: www.thestiperstones.com

Sydney House Hotel ♦♦♦
Coton Crescent, Coton Hill, Shrewsbury SY1 2LJ
T: (01743) 354681
F: (01743) 362122
I: www.sydneyhousehotel.co.uk

Trevellion House ♦♦♦
1 Bradford Street, Monkmoor, Shrewsbury SY2 5DP
T: (01743) 249582
F: (01743) 232096
E: soniataplin@yahoo.co.uk

Ye Olde Bucks Head Inn ♦♦♦
Frankwell, Shrewsbury SY3 8JR
T: (01743) 369392
E: jennyhodges@onetel.net.uk

SHURDINGTON
Gloucestershire

Allards Hotel ♦♦
Main Road, Shurdington, Cheltenham GL51 4XA
T: (01242) 862498
F: (01242) 863017

Sundown ♦♦♦
Whitelands Lane, Little Shurdington,Shurdington, Cheltenham GL51 5TX
T: (01242) 863353

SHUSTOKE
Warwickshire

Ye Olde Station Guest House ♦♦♦
Church Road, Shustoke, Coleshill, Birmingham B46 2AX
T: (01675) 481736
F: (01675) 481736
E: yeoldestationguestho@talk21.com
I: www.yeoldestationguesthouse.activehotels.com/EZS

SKEGNESS
Lincolnshire

Aberdale Hotel ♦♦
15-17 Prince Alfred Avenue, Skegness PE25 2UH
T: (01754) 764465
F: (01754) 764465
E: aberdalehotel@hotmail.com
I: www.aberdale.co.uk

Arlyn House
Rating Applied For
10 Prince Alfred Avenue, Grand Parade, Skegness PE25 2UH
T: (01754) 763122
E: info@arlyn-house.co.uk
I: www.arlyn-house.co.uk

Belmont Guesthouse ♦♦
30 Grosvenor Road, Skegness PE25 2DB
T: (01754) 765439
I: www.belmont-guesthouse.co.uk

Charnwood Hotel ♦♦♦
29 Scarbrough Ave, Skegness PE25 2TQ
T: (01754) 764759
F: (01754) 764759

Chatsworth Hotel ♦♦♦
North Parade, Skegness PE25 2UB
T: (01754) 764177
F: (01754) 761173
E: Altipper@aol.com
I: www.chatsworthskegness.co.uk

Clarence House Hotel ♦♦♦
32 South Parade, Skegness PE25 3HW
T: (01754) 765588
E: colin-rita@lineone.net
I: www.clarence-house-hotel.co.uk

Crawford Hotel ♦♦♦
104 South Parade, Skegness PE25 3HR
T: (01754) 764215
F: (01754) 764215

The Dovedale Hotel ♦♦
118 Drummond Road, Skegness PE25 3EH
T: (01754) 768676
I: www.dovedale.ccom.co.uk

Eastleigh ♦♦♦
60 Scarbrough Avenue, Skegness PE25 2TB
T: (01754) 764605
F: (01754) 764605
I: www.eastleigh-skegness.co.uk

Fountaindale Hotel ♦♦♦
69 Sandbeck Avenue, Skegness PE25 3JS
T: (01754) 762731
I: www.fountaindale.co.uk

Grosvenor House Hotel
Rating Applied For
North Parade, Skegness PE25 2TE
T: (01754) 763376
F: (01754) 764650

Halcyon Guest House ♦♦♦
29 Park Avenue, Skegness PE25 2TF
T: (01754) 763914
E: eric@egarwood.freeserve.co.uk
I: www.halcyon-guesthouse.co.uk

Ivydene Hotel ♦♦♦
39-41 Drummond Road, Skegness PE25 3EB
T: (01754) 763834
E: sandrahaywood@ivydene1.fsnet.co.uk
I: www.ivydenehotel.co.uk

Karema Private Hotel
Rating Applied For
17 Sunningdale Drive, Skegness PE25 1BB
T: (01754) 764440
E: tina.skegness@virgin.net
I: www.karema.co.uk

Kildare Hotel
Rating Applied For
80 Sandbeck Avenue, Skegness PE25 3JS
T: (01754) 762935

Mayfair Hotel
Rating Applied For
10 Saxby Avenue, Skegness PE25 3JZ
T: (01754) 764687
F: (01754) 764687
E: glynisjobes@aol.com
I: www.skegness-resort.co.uk/mayfair

Merton Hotel ♦♦♦
14 Firbeck Avenue, Skegness PE25 3JY
T: (01754) 764423
F: (01754) 766627
I: www.skegness-resort.co.uk/merton

Mickleton Guesthouse
Rating Applied For
North Parade Extension, Skegness PE25 1BX
T: (01754) 763862
F: (01754) 763862
I: www.mickleton-guesthouse.co.uk

Monsell Hotel ♦♦♦
2 Firbeck Avenue, Skegness PE25 3JY
T: (01754) 898374
F: (01754) 898375
E: enquiries@monsel-hotel.co.uk
I: www.monsel-hotel.co.uk

Newhaven Guesthouse ♦♦♦
21 Sunningdale Drive, Skegness PE25 1BB
T: (01754) 762618
E: info@newhaven-skegness.co.uk
I: www.newhaven-skegness.co.uk

North Parade Hotel ♦♦♦
20 North Parade, Skegness PE25 2UB
T: (01754) 762309
F: (01754) 610949
E: northparadehotel@btinternet.com

Palm Court Hotel ♦♦♦
74 South Parade, Skegness PE25 3HP
T: (01754) 767711
F: (01754) 767711
E: palmcourtskegness@yahoo.co.uk

Rufford Hotel ♦♦♦
5 Saxby Avenue, Skegness PE25 3JZ
T: (01754) 763428
F: (01754) 761223
E: a14jrw@aol.com
I: www.ruffordhotel-skegness.com

Savoy Hotel ♦♦♦
12 North Parade, Skegness PE25 2UB
T: (01754) 763371
F: (01754) 761256
E: info@savoy-skegness.co.uk
I: www.savoy-skegness.co.uk

Saxby Hotel ♦♦♦
12 Saxby Avenue, Skegness PE25 3LG
T: (01754) 763905

Stoneleigh Hotel
Rating Applied For
67 Sandbeck Avenue, Skegness PE25 3JS
T: (01754) 769138
I: www.stoneleigh-hotel.com

Sun Hotel ♦♦♦
19 North Parade, Skegness PE25 2UB
T: (01754) 762364
F: (01754) 762364

Sunnybank Hotel ♦♦♦
29 Ida Road, Skegness PE25 2AU
T: (01754) 762583
E: sunnybank.hotel@amserve.net

Woodlands Private Hotel ♦♦♦
Drummond Road, Skegness PE25 3EQ
T: (01754) 763188
E: juleebunce@aol.com

SKILLINGTON
Lincolnshire

Jackson's House ♦♦♦♦
Middle Street, Skillington, Grantham NG33 5EU
T: (01476) 861634

SLEAFORD
Lincolnshire

The Barn
Rating Applied For
Spring Lane, Folkingham, Sleaford NG34 0SJ
T: (01529) 497199
F: (01529) 497199
E: sjwright@farming.co.uk

CherryTree
Rating Applied For
22A Northgate, Sleaford NG34 7DA
T: (01529) 306601

Farthings Guest House ♦♦♦♦
35 Northgate, Sleaford NG34 7BS
T: (01529) 302354
F: (01529) 413312
E: farthingsguesthouse@btopenworld.com

The Tally Ho Inn ♦♦♦
Aswarby, Sleaford NG34 8SA
T: (01529) 455205
F: (01529) 309024
E: tallyhoaswarby@aol.com

SMALLDALE
Derbyshire

Ivy Cottage
Rating Applied For
Smalldale, Buxton SK17 8EA
T: (01298) 24496
E: pamelahadfield@onetel.net.uk

SMISBY
Derbyshire

Forest Court Accommodation ♦♦♦
Annwell Place, Smisby, Ashby-de-la-Zouch LE65 2TA
T: (01530) 411711
F: (01530) 411146
I: www.ashbyonline.com/forestcourt

Hillside Lodge ♦♦♦♦
Derby Road, Smisby, Ashby-de-la-Zouch LE65 2RG
T: (01530) 416411
E: barbaraball2000@yahoo.co.uk
I: www.hillsidelodge.co.uk

SOLIHULL
West Midlands

Acorn Guest House ♦♦♦♦ SILVER AWARD
29 Links Drive, Solihull B91 2DJ
T: (0121) 705 5241
E: acorn.wood@btinternet.com

Boxtrees Farm ♦♦♦♦
Stratford Road, Hockley Heath, Solihull B94 6EA
T: (01564) 782039
F: (01564) 784661
E: b&b@boxtrees.co.uk
I: www.boxtrees.co.uk

Cedarwood Guesthouse ♦♦♦
347 Lyndon Road, Solihull B92 7QT
T: (0121) 743 5844
F: (0121) 743 5844
E: mail@cedarwoodguesthouse.co.uk
I: www.cedarwoodguesthouse.co.uk

Chelsea Lodge ♦♦♦♦
48 Meriden Road, Hampton in Arden, Solihull B92 0BT
T: (01675) 442408
F: (01675) 442408
E: chelsealodgebnb@aol.com
I: www.chelsealodgebnb.co.uk

Clovelly Guest House ♦♦♦
Coleshill Heath Road, Marston Green, Solihull B37 7HY
T: (0121) 779 2886

The Oaks Bed & Breakfast ♦♦♦
92 Cheswick Way, Shirley, Solihull B90 4HG
T: (0121) 744 9200
F: (0121) 744 9295
E: oaks92ches@aol.com
I: www.theoaksguesthouse.co.uk

Establishments printed in blue have a detailed entry in this guide

Ravenhurst ♦♦♦
56 Lode Lane, Solihull B91 2AW
T: (0121) 705 5754
F: (0121) 704 0717
E: ravenhurstaccom@aol.com
I: www.ravenhurst-guesthouse.co.uk

Shirley Guest House ♦♦♦
967 Stratford Road, Shirley, Solihull B90 4BG
T: (0121) 744 2846
F: (0121) 624 0044
E: shirleyguesthouse@post.com
I: www.smoothhound.co.uk/hotels/chalegue.htm

SOUTH HYKEHAM
Lincolnshire

Hall Farm House ♦♦♦
Meadow Lane, South Hykeham, Lincoln LN6 9PF
T: (01522) 686432
F: (01522) 686432
E: carol@hallfarmhouse.fsworld.co.uk

SOUTH LUFFENHAM
Rutland

The Coach House Inn ♦♦♦♦
Stamford Road, South Luffenham, Oakham LE15 8NT
T: (01780) 720166
F: (01780) 720866
I: www.coachhouserutland.co.uk

SOUTH NORMANTON
Derbyshire

The Boundary Lodge
♦♦♦♦ SILVER AWARD
Lea Vale, Broadmeadows, South Normanton, Alfreton DE55 3NA
T: (01773) 819066
F: (01773) 819006
E: manager@boundarylodge.fsnet.co.uk
I: www.theboundary.co.uk

SOUTH WINGFIELD
Derbyshire

Platts Farm Guesthouse ♦♦♦
High Road, South Wingfield, Alfreton DE55 7LX
T: (01773) 832280

SOUTH WITHAM
Lincolnshire

Barn Owl House ♦♦♦♦
20 High Street, South Witham, Grantham NG33 5QB
T: (01572) 767688
F: (01572) 767688
E: barnowl.house@btinternet.com
I: www.barnowlhouse.co.uk

The Blue Cow Inn and Brewery ♦♦♦
29 High Street, South Witham, Grantham NG33 5QB
T: (01572) 768432
F: (01572) 768432
E: richard@thirlwell.fslife.co.uk
I: www.thebluecowinn.co.uk

Rose Cottage ♦♦♦♦
7 High Street, South Witham, Grantham NG33 5QB
T: (01572) 767757
F: (01572) 767199
E: veronica@maryvankimmenade.freeserve.co.uk

SOUTHAM
Warwickshire

The Old Bakery ♦♦♦
25 Oxford Street, Southam CV47 1NS
T: (01926) 813204
E: bb@oldbakery25.fsnet.co.uk

Wormleighton Hall
♦♦♦♦ SILVER AWARD
Wormleighton, Southam CV47 2XQ
T: (01295) 770234
F: (01295) 770234
E: wormleightonhall@farming.co.uk
I: www.smoothhound.co.uk/hotels/wormleighton.html

SOUTHWELL
Nottinghamshire

Ashdene ♦♦♦♦
Radley Road, Halam, Southwell NG22 8AH
T: (01636) 812335
E: david@herbert.newsurf.net

Church Street Bed and Breakfast ♦♦♦♦
56 Church Street, Southwell NG25 0HG
T: (01636) 812004
E: ian.wright5@btinternet.com

Cremorne ♦♦♦♦
51 Halloughton Road, Southwell NG25 0LP
T: (01636) 815145
E: berylandbarry@prentice37.freeserve.co.uk

SPALDING
Lincolnshire

Belvoir House ♦♦♦♦
13 London Road, Spalding PE11 2TA
T: (01775) 723901
E: belvoir@fsbdial.co.uk

The Escape ♦♦♦♦
The Cottage, Lutton Bank, Lutton, Spalding PE12 9LL
T: (01406) 363528
E: traceyneil@lineone.net
I: www.escapetothecottage.co.uk

Lavender Lodge ♦♦♦
81 Pinchbeck Road, Spalding PE11 1QF
T: (01775) 712800

The String of Horses and Bridles Restaurant Rating Applied For
3 Boston Road, Holbeach, Spalding PE12 7LR
T: (01406) 425426
F: (01406) 425426
I: www.stringofhorsesandbridlesrestaurant.com

STAFFORD
Staffordshire

Cedarwood
♦♦♦♦ SILVER AWARD
46 Weeping Cross, Stafford ST17 0DS
T: (01785) 662981

The Foxes ♦♦♦
2A Thorneyfields Lane, Stafford ST17 9YS
T: (01785) 602589
F: (01785) 602589
E: thefoxes.beech@ntlworld.com

Littywood House ♦♦♦♦
Bradley, Stafford ST18 9DW
T: (01785) 780234
E: suebusby@amserve.com
I: www.littywood.co.uk

The Old House Bed & Breakfast ♦♦♦♦
Main Road, Wolseley Bridge, Stafford ST17 0XJ
T: (01889) 881264
E: oldhousebb@zoom.co.uk

Park Farm ♦♦♦
Weston Road, Stafford ST18 0BD
T: (01785) 240257
F: (01785) 225464
E: parkfarm12@hotmail.com

Wyndale Guest House ♦♦
199 Corporation Street, Stafford ST16 3LQ
T: (01785) 223069

STAMFORD
Lincolnshire

Abbey House and Coach House ♦♦♦♦
West End Road, Maxey, Peterborough PE6 9EJ
T: (01778) 344642
F: (01778) 342706
E: sales@abbeyhouse.co.uk
I: www.abbeyhouse.co.uk

Birch House ♦♦♦
4 Lonsdale Road, Stamford PE9 2RW
T: (01780) 754876
F: (01780) 754876
E: Birchhouse@hotmail.com

4 Camphill Cottages ♦♦♦♦
Little Casterton, Stamford PE9 4BE
T: (01780) 763661
E: anna.martin@tesco.net

40 Casterton Road ♦♦♦
Stamford PE9 2YL
T: (01780) 762765
E: carolandbillniehorster@btopenworld.com

86 Casterton Road ♦♦♦
Stamford PE9 2UB
T: (01780) 754734

Dolphin Guesthouse ♦♦
12 East Street, Stamford PE9 1QD
T: (01780) 757515
F: (01780) 757515
E: mikdolphin@mikdolphin.demon.co.uk

Gwynne House ♦♦♦♦
13 Kings Road, Stamford PE9 1HD
T: (01780) 762210
E: john@johnng.demon.co.uk
I: www.gwynnehouse.pisem.net

Midstone Farmhouse
♦♦♦♦ SILVER AWARD
Southorpe, Stamford PE9 3BX
T: (01780) 740136
F: (01780) 749294
E: ahsmidstonehouse@amserve.net

The Oak Inn ♦♦♦
48 Stamford Road, Easton on the Hill, Stamford PE9 3PA
T: (01780) 752286
F: (01780) 756931
E: peter@klippon.demon.co.uk

Rock Lodge
♦♦♦♦♦ SILVER AWARD
1 Empingham Road, Stamford PE9 2RH
T: (01780) 481758
F: (01780) 481757
E: rocklodge@innpro.co.uk
I: www.rock-lodge.co.uk

5 Rock Terrace ♦♦♦♦
Scotgate, Stamford PE9 2YJ
T: (01780) 755475
E: averdieckguest@talk21.com

Spires View ♦♦♦
North Street, Stamford PE9 1AA
T: (01780) 764419

The Stamford Lodge Guesthouse ♦♦♦
24 Scotgate, Stamford PE9 2YQ
T: (01780) 482932
F: (01780) 482932
E: mail@stamfordlodge.co.uk
I: www.stamfordlodge.co.uk

Ufford Farm ♦♦♦
Main Street, Ufford, Stamford PE9 3BH
T: (01780) 740220
F: (01780) 740220
E: vergette@ufford1.freeserve.co.uk

STANDISH
Gloucestershire

Oaktree Farm ♦♦♦♦
Little Haresfield, Standish, Stonehouse GL10 3DS
T: (01452) 883323
E: Jackie@oaktreefarm.fsnet.co.uk

STANFORD BISHOP
Herefordshire

The Hawkins Farm ♦♦♦♦
Stanford Bishop, Worcester WR6 5TQ
T: (01886) 884250
F: (01886) 884250

STANTON-BY-BRIDGE
Derbyshire

Ivy House Farm
♦♦♦♦ SILVER AWARD
Ingleby Road, Stanton-by-Bridge, Derby DE73 1HT
T: (01332) 863152
F: (01332) 863152
E: mary@guesthouse.fsbusiness.co.uk
I: www.ivy-house-farm.com

STANTON IN PEAK
Derbyshire

Congreave Farm
♦♦♦♦ GOLD AWARD
Congreave, Stanton in Peak, Matlock DE4 2NF
T: (01629) 732063
E: deborahbettney@congreave.junglelink.co.uk
I: www.matsam16.freeserve.co.uk/congreave/

STANTON-ON-THE-WOLDS
Nottinghamshire

Laurel Farm ♦♦♦
Browns Lane, Stanton-on-the-Wolds, Keyworth, Nottingham NG12 5BL
T: (0115) 937 3488
F: (0115) 937 6490
E: laurelfarm@yahoo.com
I: www.s-h-systems.co.uk/laurelfa.html

STAPLETON
Shropshire

Stapleton Cottage ♦♦♦♦
Stapleton, Dorrington, Shrewsbury SY5 7EQ
T: (01743) 718314
F: (01743) 718314
E: wilkinson@ichthusltd.fsnet.co.uk
I: www.stapletoncottage.com

STOCKINGFORD
Warwickshire

Aberglynmarch Guest House ♦♦♦
198 Church Road, Stockingford, Nuneaton CV10 8LH
T: (02476) 342793
F: (02476) 342793

STOKE-ON-TRENT
Staffordshire

Cedar Tree Cottage ♦♦♦♦ SILVER AWARD
41 Longton Road, Trentham, Stoke-on-Trent ST4 8ND
T: (01782) 644751

The Hollies ♦♦♦
Clay Lake, Endon, Stoke-on-Trent ST9 9DD
T: (01782) 503252
F: (01782) 503252
E: theholliesendon@faxvia.net

Holly Trees ♦♦♦♦
Crewe Road, Alsager, Stoke-on-Trent ST7 2JL
T: (01270) 876847
F: (01270) 883301
E: hollytreeshotel@aol.com
I: www.hollytreeshotel.co.uk

The Limes ♦♦♦
Cheadle Road, Blythe Bridge, Stoke-on-Trent ST11 9PW
T: (01782) 393278

The Old Dairy House ♦♦♦♦♦ SILVER AWARD
Trentham Park, Stoke-on-Trent ST4 8AE
T: (01782) 641209
F: (01782) 712904
E: olddairyhouse@hotmail.com

Old Vicarage Guesthouse ♦♦♦♦
Birchenwood Road, Newchapel, Stoke-on-Trent ST7 4QT
T: (01782) 785270
E: peter.kent-baguley@birchenwood.freeserve.co.uk

The Olde House on the Green ♦♦♦♦
Fulford, Stoke-on-Trent ST11 9QS
T: (01782) 394555
F: (01782) 392030

Reynolds Hey ♦♦♦♦
Park Lane, Endon, Stoke-on-Trent ST9 9JB
T: (01782) 502717
E: reynoldshey@hotmail.com

Shaw Gate Farm ♦♦♦
Shay Lane, Foxt, Stoke-on-Trent ST10 2HN
T: (01538) 266590
F: (01538) 266590
E: ken@shawgatefarm.co.uk
I: www.shawgatefarm.co.uk

Sneyd Arms Hotel ♦♦
Tower Square, Tunstall, Stoke-on-Trent ST6 5AA
T: (01782) 826722
F: (01782) 826722
I: www.thesneydarms.co.uk

Verdon Guest House ♦♦♦
44 Charles Street, Hanley, Stoke-on-Trent ST1 3JY
T: (01782) 264244
F: (01782) 264244
E: debbie@howlett18.freeserve.co.uk
I: www.verdonguesthouse.co.uk

STONE
Staffordshire

Lock House ♦♦♦♦
74 Newcastle Road, Stone ST15 8LB
T: (01785) 811551
F: (01785) 286587
E: mbd@fsbdial.co.uk

Mayfield House ♦♦♦
112 Newcastle Road, Stone ST15 8LG
T: (01785) 811446

STONEHOUSE
Gloucestershire

The Grey Cottage ♦♦♦♦♦ GOLD AWARD
Bath Road, Leonard Stanley, Stonehouse GL10 3LU
T: (01453) 822515
F: (01453) 822515
I: www.greycottage.ik.com

Merton Lodge ♦♦
8 Ebley Road, Stonehouse GL10 2LQ
T: (01453) 822018

STOTTESDON
Worcestershire

Hardwicke Farm ♦♦♦♦ SILVER AWARD
Stottesdon, Kidderminster DY14 8TN
T: (01746) 718220
E: Hardwickefarm@hotmail.com
I: www.bridgnorthshropshire.com

STOURBRIDGE
West Midlands

St Elizabeth's Cottage ♦♦♦♦
Woodman Lane, Clent, Stourbridge DY9 9PX
T: (01562) 883883
F: (01562) 885034
E: st_elizabeth_cot@btconnect.com

STOURPORT-ON-SEVERN
Worcestershire

Baldwin House ♦♦♦
8 Lichfield Street, Stourport-on-Severn DY13 9EU
T: (01299) 877221
F: (01299) 877221
E: baldwinhousebb@aol.com

STOW
Lincolnshire

Belle Vue Farm Rating Applied For
21 Church Road, Stow, Lincoln LN1 2DE
T: (01427) 788981

STOW-ON-THE-WOLD
Gloucestershire

Aston House ♦♦♦♦ SILVER AWARD
Broadwell, Moreton-in-Marsh GL56 0TJ
T: (01451) 830475
E: fja@netcomuk.co.uk
I: www.netcomuk.co.uk/~nmfa/aston_house.html

The Beeches ♦♦♦
Fosse Lane, Stow-on-the-Wold, Cheltenham GL54 1EH
T: (01451) 870836

Corsham Field Farmhouse ♦♦♦
Bledington Road, Stow-on-the-Wold, Cheltenham GL54 1JH
T: (01451) 831750
F: (01451) 832247
E: farmhouse@corshamfield.co.uk
I: www.corshamfield.co.uk

The Cotswold Garden Tea Room & B&B. ♦♦♦
Wells Cottage, Digbeth Street, Stow-on-the-Wold, Cheltenham GL54 1BN
T: (01451) 870999

Crestow House ♦♦♦♦
Stow-on-the-Wold, Cheltenham GL54 1JX
T: (01451) 830969
F: (01451) 832129
E: fsimonetti@btinternet.com
I: www.crestow.co.uk

Cross Keys Cottage ♦♦♦
Park Street, Stow-on-the-Wold, Cheltenham GL54 1AQ
T: (01451) 831128
F: (01451) 831128

Fairview Farmhouse ♦♦♦♦ SILVER AWARD
Bledington Road, Stow-on-the-Wold, Cheltenham GL54 1JH
T: (01451) 830279
F: (01451) 830279
E: sdavis0145@aol.com
I: www.SmoothHound.co.uk/shs

The Gate Lodge ♦♦♦♦
Stow Hill, Stow-on-the-Wold, Cheltenham GL54 1JZ
T: (01451) 832103

Honeysuckle Cottage ♦♦♦♦ SILVER AWARD
Kings Arms Lane, The Square, Stow-on-the-Wold, Cheltenham GL54 1AF
T: (01451) 830973
E: hsucklecottage@aol.com

The Kings Arms ♦♦♦♦
The Square, Stow on the Wold, Stow-on-the-Wold, Cheltenham GL54 1AF
T: (01451) 830364
F: (01451) 830602
E: info@kingsarms-stowonthewold.co.uk
I: www.kingsarms-stowonthewold.co.uk

Littlebroom ♦♦♦♦
Maugersbury, Stow-on-the-Wold, Cheltenham GL54 1HP
T: (01451) 830510
F: (01457) 830313
E: davidandbrenda@talk21.com
I: www.completely-cotswold.com

Maugersbury Manor ♦♦♦
Stow-on-the-Wold, Cheltenham GL54 1HP
T: (01451) 830581
F: (01451) 870902
E: karen@manorholidays.co.uk
I: www.manorholidays.co.uk

Mount Pleasant Farm ♦♦♦♦
Oddington Road, Stow-on-the-Wold, Cheltenham GL54 1JJ
T: (01451) 832078
F: (01451) 832078
E: sgaden72@aol.com

Pear Tree Cottage ♦♦♦
High Street, Stow-on-the-Wold, Cheltenham GL54 1DL
T: (01451) 831210
E: peartreecottage@btinternet.com

South Hill Farmhouse ♦♦♦♦
Fosseway, Stow-on-the-Wold, Cheltenham GL54 1JU
T: (01451) 831888
F: (01451) 832255
E: info@southhill.co.uk
I: www.southhill.co.uk

South Hill Lodge ♦♦♦♦ SILVER AWARD
Fosseway, Stow-on-the-wold, Stow-on-the-Wold, Cheltenham GL54 1JU
T: (01451) 831083
E: digby@southilllodge.freeserve.co.uk
I: www.SmoothHound.co.uk/hotels/southhill

Tall Trees ♦♦♦♦
Oddington Road, Stow-on-the-Wold, Cheltenham GL54 1AL
T: (01451) 831296
F: (01451) 870049
E: talltreestow@aol.com

White Hart Inn ♦♦♦
The Square, Stow-on-the-Wold, Cheltenham GL54 1AF
T: (01451) 830674
F: (01451) 830090
I: www.whiteharthotel@tablesire.com

STOWE-BY-CHARTLEY
Staffordshire

The Plough Inn ♦♦♦
Amerton, Stowe-by-Chartley, Stafford ST18 0LA
T: (01889) 270308
F: (01889) 271131

STRAGGLETHORPE
Lincolnshire

Stragglethorpe Hall ♦♦♦♦ SILVER AWARD
Stragglethorpe, Lincoln LN5 0QZ
T: (01400) 272308
F: (01400) 273816
E: stragglethorpe@compuserve.com
I: www.stragglethorpe.com

STRATFORD-UPON-AVON
Warwickshire

Aidan Guest House ♦♦♦♦
11 Evesham Place, Stratford-upon-Avon CV37 6HT
T: (01789) 292824
F: (01789) 269072
E: john2aidan@aol.com
I: www.aidanhouse.co.uk

All Seasons ♦♦
51 Grove Road, Stratford-upon-Avon CV37 6PB
T: (01789) 293404
F: (01789) 293404

Amelia Linhill Guesthouse ♦♦♦
35 Evesham Place, Stratford-upon-Avon CV37 6HT
T: (01789) 292879
F: (01789) 299691
E: Linhill@bigwig.net
I: Linhillguesthouse.co.uk

The Applegarth ♦♦♦
Warwick Road, Stratford-upon-Avon CV37 6YW
T: (01789) 267388
F: (01789) 415422
E: applegarth21@tiscali.co.uk

Arden Park Non Smoking Hotel ♦♦♦
6 Arden Street, Stratford-upon-Avon CV37 6PA
T: (01789) 262126
F: (07092) 018007
E: enquiries@ardenparkhotel.co.uk
I: www.ardenparkhotel.co.uk

Arrandale Guesthouse ♦♦♦
208 Evesham Road, Stratford-upon-Avon CV37 9AS
T: (01789) 267112
I: www.arrandale.netfirms.co.uk

Avon View Hotel ♦♦♦♦
121 Shipston Road, Stratford-upon-Avon CV37 7LW
T: (01789) 297542
F: (01789) 292936
E: avon.view@lineone.net

Avonlea ♦♦♦♦
47 Shipston Road, Stratford-upon-Avon CV37 7LN
T: (01789) 205940
F: (01789) 209115
E: avonlea-stratford@lineone.net
I: www.avonlea-stratford.co.uk

Barbette ♦♦♦
165 Evesham Road, Stratford-upon-Avon CV37 9BP
T: (01789) 297822

The Blue Boar Inn ♦♦♦
Temple Grafton, Alcester B49 6NR
T: (01789) 750010
F: (01789) 750635
E: blueboar@covlink.co.uk
I: www.blueboarinn.co.uk

Bradbourne House ♦♦♦♦
44 Shipston Road, Stratford-upon-Avon CV37 7LP
T: (01789) 204178
F: (01789) 262335
E: ian@bradbourne-house.co.uk
I: www.bradbourne-house.co.uk

Brett House ♦♦♦
8 Broad Walk, Stratford-upon-Avon CV37 6HS
T: (01789) 266374
F: (01789) 414027
E: cyril21@btopenworld.com
I: www.bretthouse.co.uk

Broadlands Guest House ♦♦♦♦
23 Evesham Place, Stratford-upon-Avon CV37 6HT
T: (01789) 299181
F: (01789) 551382
E: broadlands.com@virgin.net
I: www.stratford-upon-avon.co.uk/broadlands.htm

Brook Lodge Guest House ♦♦♦♦ SILVER AWARD
192 Alcester Road, Stratford-upon-Avon CV37 9DR
T: (01789) 295988
F: (01789) 295988
E: brooklodgeguesthouse@btinternet.com
I: www.smoothhound.co.uk/hotels/brooklod.html

Burton Farm ♦♦♦♦
Bishopton, Stratford-upon-Avon CV37 0RW
T: (01789) 293338
F: (01789) 262877

Carlton Guest House ♦♦♦
22 Evesham Place, Stratford-upon-Avon CV37 6HT
T: (01789) 293548
F: (01789) 293548

Chadwyns Guest House ♦♦♦♦
6 Broad Walk, Stratford-upon-Avon CV37 6HS
T: (01789) 269077
F: (01789) 298855
E: stay@chadwyns.co.uk
I: www.chadwyns.co.uk

Church Farm ♦♦♦
Dorsington, Stratford-upon-Avon CV37 8AX
T: (01789) 720471
F: (01789) 720830
E: chfarmdorsington@aol.com
I: www.churchfarmstratford.co.uk

Church Farm ♦♦♦
Welford Road, Long Marston, Stratford-upon-Avon CV37 8RH
T: (01789) 720275
F: (01789) 720275
E: wiggychurchfarm@hotmail.com
I: www.churchfarmhouse.co.uk

Courtland Hotel ♦♦♦
12 Guild Street, Stratford-upon-Avon CV37 6RE
T: (01789) 292401
F: (01789) 292401
E: courtland.hotel@virgin.net
I: www.uk-vacation.com/courtland

Craig Cleeve House Hotel & Restaurant ♦♦♦♦
67-69 Shipston Road, Stratford-upon-Avon CV37 7LW
T: (01789) 296573
F: (01789) 299452
E: craigcleev@aol.com

Curtain Call ♦♦♦
142 Alcester Road, Stratford-upon-Avon CV37 9DR
T: (01789) 267734
E: curtaincall@btinternet.com
I: www.curtaincallguesthouse.co.uk

Cymbeline House ♦♦♦
24 Evesham Place, Stratford-upon-Avon CV37 6HT
T: (01789) 292958
F: (01789) 292958
E: cymbelinebb@btopenworld.com

Dylan Guesthouse ♦♦♦♦
10 Evesham Place, Stratford-upon-Avon CV37 6HT
T: (01789) 204819
E: dylanguesthouse@lineone.net
I: www.thedylan.co.uk

East Bank House ♦♦♦♦
19 Warwick Road, Stratford-upon-Avon CV37 6YW
T: (01789) 292758
F: (01789) 292758
E: eastbank.house@virgin.net
I: www.east-bank-house.co.uk

Eastnor House Hotel ♦♦♦♦
Shipston Road, Stratford-upon-Avon CV37 7LN
T: (01789) 268115
F: (01789) 551133
E: enquiries@eastnorhouse.com
I: www.eastnorhouse.com

The Emsley Guest House ♦♦♦♦
4 Arden Street, Stratford-upon-Avon CV37 6PA
T: (01789) 299557
F: (01789) 299023
E: val@theemsley.co.uk
I: www.theemsley.co.uk

Ettington Chase Conference Centre ♦♦♦♦♦ SILVER AWARD
Banbury Road, Ettington, Stratford-upon-Avon CV37 7NZ
T: (01789) 740000
F: (01789) 740909
E: ettington@hayleycc.co.uk
I: www.hayley-conf.co.uk

Faviere ♦♦♦♦
127 Shipston Road, Stratford-upon-Avon CV37 7LW
T: (01789) 293764
F: (01789) 269365
E: reservations@faviere.com
I: www.faviere.com

Folly Farm Cottage ♦♦♦♦ GOLD AWARD
Back Street, Ilmington, Shipston-on-Stour CV36 4LJ
T: (01608) 682425
F: (01608) 682425
E: slowe@follyfarm.co.uk
I: www.follyfarm.co.uk

Green Gables ♦♦♦
47 Banbury Road, Stratford-upon-Avon CV37 7HW
T: (01789) 205557
E: jeankerr@talk21.com
I: www.stratford-upon-avon.co.uk/greengables.htm

Green Haven ♦♦♦♦
217 Evesham Road, Stratford-upon-Avon CV37 9AS
T: (01789) 297874
F: (01789) 550487
E: information@green-haven.co.uk
I: www.green-haven.co.uk

Grosvenor Villa ♦♦♦
9 Evesham Place, Stratford-upon-Avon CV37 6HT
T: (01789) 266192
F: (01789) 297353
E: marion@grosvenorvilla.com
I: www.grosvenorvilla.co.uk

Heron Lodge ♦♦♦♦
260 Alcester Road, Stratford-upon-Avon CV37 9JQ
T: (01789) 299169
F: (01789) 204463
E: chrisandbob@heronlodge.com
I: www.heronlodge.com

Highcroft ♦♦♦
Banbury Road, Stratford-upon-Avon CV37 7NF
T: (01789) 296293
F: (01789) 415236
E: suedavies_highcroft@hotmail.com
I: www.Smoothhound.co.uk

Houndshill House ♦♦♦
Banbury Road, Ettington, Stratford-upon-Avon CV37 7NS
T: (01789) 740267
F: (01789) 740075

Howard Arms ♦♦♦♦♦ SILVER AWARD
Lower Green, Ilmington, Shipston-on-Stour CV36 4LT
T: (01608) 682226
F: (01608) 682226
E: info@howardarms.com
I: www.howardarms.com

Hunters Moon Guest House ♦♦♦
150 Alcester Road, Stratford-upon-Avon CV37 9DR
T: (01789) 292888
F: (01789) 204101
E: thehuntersmoon@ntlworld.com
I: www.huntersmoonguesthouse.com

Ingon Bank Farm ♦♦♦
Warwick Road, Stratford-upon-Avon CV37 0NY
T: (01789) 292642
F: (01789) 292642

Kawartha House ♦♦♦
39 Grove Road, Stratford-upon-Avon CV37 6PB
T: (01789) 204469
F: (01789) 292845
E: kawarthahouse@btopenworld.com
I: www.kawarthahouse.co.uk

Marlyn Hotel ♦♦♦
3 Chestnut Walk, Stratford-upon-Avon CV37 6HG
T: (01789) 293752
F: (01789) 293752
E: evansmarlynhotel@aol.com
I: www.marlynhotel.co.uk

Mary Arden Inn ♦♦♦♦
The Green, Wilmcote, Stratford-upon-Avon CV37 9XJ
T: (01789) 267030
F: (01789) 204875

Melita Private Hotel ♦♦♦♦
37 Shipston Road, Stratford-upon-Avon CV37 7LN
T: (01789) 292432
F: (01789) 204867
E: info@melitahotel.co.uk
I: www.melitahotel.co.uk

Meridian Guest House ♦♦♦
3 St Gregory's Road, Stratford-upon-Avon CV37 6UH
T: (01789) 292356
F: (01789) 292356
E: meridian.guesthouse@virgin.net
I: www.meridianguesthouse.co.uk

Midway ♦♦♦♦
Evesham Road, Stratford-upon-Avon CV37 9BS
T: (01789) 204154
E: mealing@midway182.fsnet.co.uk
I: www.stratford-upon-avon.co.uk/midway.htm

Mil-Mar ♦♦♦♦
96 Alcester Road, Stratford-upon-Avon CV37 9DP
T: (01789) 267095
F: (01789) 262205
E: milmar@btinternet.com
I: www.stratford-upon-avon.co.uk/milmar.htm

Minola Guest House ♦♦♦
25 Evesham Place, Stratford-upon-Avon CV37 6HT
T: (01789) 293573
F: (01789) 551625

Moonlight Bed & Breakfast ♦♦♦
144 Alcester Road, Stratford-upon-Avon CV37 9DR
T: (01789) 298213

Moss Cottage ♦♦♦♦
61 Evesham Road, Stratford-upon-Avon CV37 9BA
T: (01789) 294770
F: (01789) 294770

Nando's ♦♦
18-19 Evesham Place, Stratford-upon-Avon CV37 6HT
T: (01789) 204907
F: (01789) 204907
E: rooms@nandosguesthouse.co.uk

Newlands ♦♦♦♦
7 Broad Walk, Stratford-upon-Avon CV37 6HS
T: (01789) 298449
F: (01789) 267806
E: newlandslynwalter@hotmail.com
I: www.smoothhound.co.uk/hotels/newlands.html

Oxstalls Farm ♦♦♦
Warwick Road, Stratford-upon-Avon CV37 0NS
T: (01789) 205277
F: (01789) 205277

Parkfield ♦♦♦
3 Broad Walk, Stratford-upon-Avon CV37 6HS
T: (01789) 293313
F: (01789) 293313
E: parkfield@btinternet.com
I: www.parkfieldbandb.co.uk

Peartree Cottage
♦♦♦♦ SILVER AWARD
7 Church Road, Wilmcote, Stratford-upon-Avon CV37 9UX
T: (01789) 205889
F: (01789) 262862
E: mander@peartreecot.co.uk
I: www.peartreecot.co.uk

Penryn Guesthouse ♦♦♦♦
126 Alcester Road, Stratford-upon-Avon CV37 9DP
T: (01789) 293718
F: (01789) 266077
E: penrynhouse@btinternet.com
I: www.penrynguesthouse.co.uk

Penshurst Guesthouse ♦♦♦
34 Evesham Place, Stratford-upon-Avon CV37 6HT
T: (01789) 205259
F: (01789) 295322
E: karen@penshurst.net
I: www.penshurst.net

The Poplars ♦♦♦
Mansfield Farm, Newbold-on-Stour, Stratford-upon-Avon CV37 8BZ
T: (01789) 450540
F: (01789) 450540
E: judith@poplars-farmhouse.co.uk
I: www.SmoothHound.co.uk/hotels/poplars2.html

The Queens Head ♦♦♦♦
Ely Street, Stratford-upon-Avon CV37 6LN
T: (01789) 204914
F: (01789) 772983
E: richard@distinctivepubs.freeserve.co.uk
I: www.distinctivepubs.co.uk

Quilt and Croissants ♦♦♦
33 Evesham Place, Stratford-upon-Avon CV37 6HT
T: (01789) 267629
F: (01789) 551651
E: rooms@quilt-croissants.demon.co.uk
I: www.smoothhound.co.uk/hotels/quilt.html

Ravenhurst ♦♦♦
2 Broad Walk, Stratford-upon-Avon CV37 6HS
T: (01789) 292515
E: ravaccom@waverider.co.uk
I: www.stratford-ravenhurst.co.uk

Salamander Guest House ♦♦♦
40 Grove Road, Stratford-upon-Avon CV37 6PB
T: (01789) 205728
F: (01789) 205728
E: p.delin@btinternet.com
I: salamanderguesthouse.co.uk

Shakespeare's View
♦♦♦♦♦ GOLD AWARD
Kings Lane, Snitterfield, Stratford-upon-Avon CV37 0QB
T: (01789) 731824
F: (01789) 731824
E: shakespeares.view@btinternet.com
I: www.shakespeares.view.btinternet.co.uk

Stratheden Hotel ♦♦♦
5 Chapel Street, Stratford-upon-Avon CV37 6EP
T: (01789) 297119
F: (01789) 297119
E: richard@stratheden.fsnet.co.uk
I: www.stratheden.co.uk

Victoria Spa Lodge
♦♦♦♦ SILVER AWARD
Bishopton Lane, Bishopton, Stratford-upon-Avon CV37 9QY
T: (01789) 267985
F: (01789) 204728
E: ptozer@victoriaspalodge.demon.co.uk
I: www.stratford-upon-avon.co.uk/victoriaspa.htm

Virginia Lodge Guest House ♦♦♦♦
12 Evesham Place, Stratford-upon-Avon CV37 6HT
T: (01789) 292157
F: (01789) 292157
E: pamela83@btinternet.com
I: www.virginialodge.co.uk

The White House
♦♦♦♦ SILVER AWARD
Kings Lane, Bishopton, Stratford-upon-Avon CV37 0RD
T: (01789) 294296
F: (01789) 294411
E: enquiries@stratfordwhitehouse.co.uk
I: www.stratfordwhitehouse.co.uk

Woodstock Guest House
♦♦♦♦ SILVER AWARD
30 Grove Road, Stratford-upon-Avon CV37 6PB
T: (01789) 299881
F: (01789) 299881
E: woodstockhouse@compuserve.com
I: www.woodstock-house.co.uk

STRATTON
Gloucestershire

Columbrae ♦♦♦♦
3 School Hill, Stratton, Cirencester GL7 2LS
T: (01285) 653114

STRETTON
Staffordshire

Dovecliff Hall
♦♦♦♦♦ SILVER AWARD
Dovecliff Road, Stretton, Burton upon Trent DE13 0DJ
T: (01283) 531818
F: (01283) 516546
E: enquiry@dovecliffhallhotel.co.uk
I: www.dovecliffhallhotel.co.uk

STRETTON ON FOSSE
Warwickshire

Jasmine Cottage ♦♦♦
Stretton on Fosse, Moreton-in-Marsh GL56 9SA
T: (01608) 661972

STROUD
Gloucestershire

Ashleigh House ♦♦♦♦
Bussage, Stroud GL6 8AZ
T: (01453) 883944
F: (01453) 886931
E: etc@ashleighgh.co.uk
I: www.ashleighgh.co.uk

Beechcroft ♦♦♦
Brownshill, Stroud GL6 8AG
T: (01453) 883422
E: jenny@beechcroftbb.fsnet.co.uk

Burleigh Farm
♦♦♦♦ SILVER AWARD
Minchinhampton, Stroud GL5 2PF
T: (01453) 883112
F: (01453) 883112

The Clothier's Arms ♦♦♦
1 Bath Road, Stroud GL5 3JJ
T: (01453) 763801
F: (01453) 757161
E: luciano@clothiersarms.demon.co.uk
I: www.clothiersarms.co.uk

Downfield Hotel ♦♦♦
134 Cainscross Road, Stroud GL5 4HN
T: (01453) 764496
F: (01453) 753150
E: info@downfieldhotel.co.uk
I: www.downfieldhotel.co.uk

Hillenvale ♦♦♦♦
The Plain, Whiteshill, Stroud GL6 6AB
T: (01453) 753441
F: (01453) 753441
E: bobsue@hillenvale.co.uk
I: www.hillenvale.co.uk

Keallasay ♦♦♦
73 Barrowfield Road, Farmhill, Stroud GL5 4DG
T: (01453) 765995
E: bakj@waitrose.com

Pretoria Villa
♦♦♦♦ SILVER AWARD
Wells Road, Eastcombe, Stroud GL6 7EE
T: (01452) 770435
F: (01452) 770435
E: glynis@gsolomon.freeserve.co.uk

Threeways ♦♦♦
Lypiatt Hill, Bisley Road, Stroud GL6 7LQ
T: (01453) 756001
E: jennifer.bircher1@btopenworld.com

The Withyholt
Rating Applied For
Paul Mead, Edge, Stroud GL6 6PG
T: (01452) 813618
F: (01452) 812375

Woodstock Bed and Breakfast
Rating Applied For
Kites Nest Lane, Kingscourt, Stroud GL5 3PN
T: (01453) 766084

The Yew Tree Bed and Breakfast ♦♦♦♦
Walls Quarry, Brimscombe, Stroud GL5 2PA
T: (01453) 887594
F: (01453) 883428
E: elizabeth.peters@tesco.net
I: www.uk-bedandbreakfasts.com/town.php?town=Stroud&county=Gloucestershire

STURTON-BY-STOW
Lincolnshire

Ivy Cottage ♦♦♦
Stow Road, Sturton-by-Stow, Lincoln LN1 2BZ
T: (01427) 788023

SULGRAVE
Northamptonshire

Rectory Farm ♦♦♦
Little Street, Sulgrave, Banbury OX17 2SG
T: (01295) 760261
F: (01295) 760089
E: rectoryfarm@talk21.com

SUTTON-ON-SEA
Lincolnshire

Athelstone Lodge Hotel ♦♦♦
25 Trusthorpe Road, Sutton-on-Sea, Mablethorpe LN12 2LR
T: (01507) 441521
I: www.athelstonelodge.co.uk

Bacchus Hotel ♦♦♦
High Street, Sutton-on-Sea, Mablethorpe LN12 2EY
T: (01507) 441204
F: (01507) 441204
I: www.bacchus-hotel.co.uk

SUTTON-ON-TRENT
Nottinghamshire

Fiveways ♦♦♦♦
Barrel Hill Road, Sutton-on-Trent, Newark NG23 6PT
T: (01636) 822086

Woodbine Farmhouse ♦♦♦
1 Church Street, Sutton-on-Trent, Newark NG23 6PD
T: (01636) 822549
F: (01636) 821716
E: woodbinefmhouse@aol.com
I: www.woodbinefarmhouse.co.uk

SWABY
Lincolnshire

Jasmine Cottage ♦♦♦♦
Church Lane, Swaby, Alford LN13 0BQ
T: (01507) 480283
F: (01507) 480283
E: fieldsend@btinternet.com

SWADLINCOTE
Derbyshire

Ferne Cottage ♦♦♦
5 Blackhorse Hill, Appleby Magna, Swadlincote DE12 7AQ
T: (01530) 271772
F: (01503) 270652

Forest Lodge Bed and Breakfast ♦♦♦♦
2 Shortheath Road, Moira, Swadlincote DE12 6AS
T: (01283) 210162
F: (01283) 210162
E: forestlodgebandb@hotmail.com

Manor Farm ♦♦♦♦
Coton in the Elms, Swadlincote DE12 8EP
T: (01283) 760340
F: (01283) 760340

The Odd House ♦♦♦
Bosworth Road, Snarestone, Swadlincote DE12 7DQ
T: (01530) 270223
F: (01530) 271597
E: info@oddhouse.com
I: www.oddhouse.com

SWANNINGTON
Leicestershire

Hillfield House ♦♦♦♦
52 Station Hill, Swannington, Leicester LE67 8RH
T: (01530) 837414
F: (01530) 458233
E: molly@hillfieldhouse.co.uk
I: www.hillfieldhouse.co.uk

SWARKESTONE
Derbyshire

October House ♦♦♦♦
The Water Meadows, Swarkestone, Derby DE73 1JA
T: (01332) 705849
E: longsons@talk21.com

SWAYFIELD
Lincolnshire

The Royal Oak Inn ♦♦♦
High Street, Swayfield, Grantham NG33 4LL
T: (01476) 550247
F: (01476) 550996

SWINSCOE
Staffordshire

Common End Farm ♦♦♦♦
Swinscoe, Ashbourne DE6 2BW
T: (01335) 342342
E: info@commonendfarm.co.uk
I: www.commonendfarm.co.uk

SYMONDS YAT EAST
Herefordshire

Garth Cottage
♦♦♦♦ SILVER AWARD
Symonds Yat East, Ross-on-Wye HR9 6JL
T: (01600) 890364
F: (01600) 890364
E: bertie@yateast.fsnet.co.uk
I: www.smoothhound.co.uk/hotels/garthcottage.html

Rose Cottage Tea Gardens ♦♦♦
Symonds Yat East, Ross-on-Wye HR9 6JL
T: (01600) 890514
F: (01600) 890498
E: rose.cottage.s.yat@virgin.net
I: www.SmoothHound.co.uk/hotels/rose2.html

TACHBROOK MALLORY
Warwickshire

Tachbrook Mallory House ♦♦♦♦
Oakley Wood Road, Leamington Spa CV33 9QE
T: (01926) 451450
F: (01926) 831716
E: h.miremadi@btinternet.com

TADDINGTON
Derbyshire

The Old Bake and Brewhouse ♦♦♦
Blackwell, Blakewell in the Peak, Taddington, Buxton SK17 9TQ
T: (01298) 85271
F: (01298) 85271
E: christine.gregory@btinternet.com
I: www.peakdistrictfarmhols.co.uk

TAMWORTH
Staffordshire

Bonehill Farm House ♦♦♦♦
Bonehill Road, Tamworth B78 3HP
T: (01827) 310797

The Chestnuts Country Guest House ♦♦♦♦ SILVER AWARD
Watling Street, Grendon, Atherstone CV9 2PZ
T: (01827) 331355
F: (01827) 896951
E: cclLtd@aol.com
I: www.thechestnutshotel.com

Oak Tree Farm
♦♦♦♦♦ GOLD AWARD
Hints Road, Hopwas, Tamworth B78 3AA
T: (01827) 56807
F: (01827) 56807

The Peel Hotel ♦♦♦♦
14b Aldergate, Tamworth B79 7DL
T: (01827) 67676
F: (01827) 69812

TANSLEY
Derbyshire

Packhorse Farm ♦♦♦♦
Tansley, Matlock DE4 5LF
T: (01629) 580950
F: (01629) 580950

Packhorse Farm Bungalow ♦♦♦♦
Tansley, Matlock DE4 5LF
T: (01629) 582781

TANWORTH-IN-ARDEN
Warwickshire

Grange Farm ♦♦♦♦
Forde Hall Lane, Tanworth-in-Arden, Solihull B94 5AX
T: (01564) 742911
I: www.grange-farm.com

Mows Hill Farm ♦♦♦♦
Mows Hill Road, Kemps Green, Tanworth-in-Arden, Solihull B94 5PP
T: (01564) 784312
F: (01564) 783378
E: mowshill@farmline.com
I: www.b-and-bmowshill.co.uk

TEDDINGTON
Gloucestershire

Bengrove Farm ♦♦♦
Bengrove, Teddington, Tewkesbury GL20 8JB
T: (01242) 620332
F: (01242) 620851

TELFORD
Shropshire

Albion Inn ♦♦♦
West Street, St Georges, Telford TF2 9AD
T: (01952) 614193

Coppice Heights ♦♦♦
Spout Lane, Little Wenlock, Telford TF6 5BL
T: (01952) 505655

Falcon Hotel ♦♦♦
Holyhead Road, Wellington, Telford TF1 2DD
T: (01952) 255011
E: falconhotel@hotmail.com

Grove House Guesthouse ♦♦♦♦
Stafford Street, St Georges, Telford TF2 9JW
T: (01952) 616140
F: (01952) 616140

The Mill House ♦♦♦♦
Shrewsbury Road, High Ercall, Telford TF6 6BE
T: (01952) 770394
F: (01952) 770394
E: mill-house@talk21.com
I: www.virtual-shropshire.co.uk/millhouse

Old Rectory
♦♦♦♦ SILVER AWARD
Stirchley Village, Telford TF3 1DY
T: (01952) 596308
F: (01952) 596308
E: hazelmiller@waitrose.com
♿

The Old Vicarage Country House ♦♦♦♦
Church Street, St George's, Telford TF2 9LZ
T: (01952) 616437
F: (01952) 616952
E: skristian@aol.com
I: www.oldvicarage.uk.com

Stone House ♦♦♦♦
Shifnal Road, Priorslee, Telford TF2 9NN
T: (01952) 290119
F: (01952) 290119
E: d.s.lcock@blueyonder.co.uk
I: www.smoothhound.co.uk/hotels/stonehou.html

West Ridge Bed and Breakfast ♦♦♦♦ SILVER AWARD
West Ridge, Kemberton, Shifnal TF11 9LB
T: (01952) 580992
F: (01952) 580992
E: westridge@ntlworld.com
I: www.westridgebb.com

Westbrook House ♦♦
78a Holy Head Road, Ketly, Telford TF1 5DJ
T: (01952) 615535

Willow House ♦♦♦
137 Holyhead Road, Wellington, Telford TF1 2DH
T: (01952) 223817
F: (01952) 223817

TEMPLE GUITING
Gloucestershire

The Plough ♦♦♦♦
Ford, Temple Guiting, Cheltenham GL54 5RU
T: (01386) 584215
F: (01386) 584042

TENBURY WELLS
Worcestershire

Court Farm ♦♦♦♦
Hanley Childe, Tenbury Wells WR15 8QY
T: (01885) 410265
E: yarnold@courtfarmhanley.fsnet.co.uk

TETBURY
Gloucestershire

Folly Farm Cottages ♦♦
Long Newnton, Tetbury GL8 8XA
T: (01666) 502475
F: (01666) 502358
E: info@gtb.co.uk
I: www.gtb.co.uk

The Old Rectory
♦♦♦♦ GOLD AWARD
Didmarton, Badminton GL9 1DS
T: (01454) 238233
F: (01454) 238909
E: mt@febcentral.com

TEWKESBURY
Gloucestershire

Abbey Antiques Bed and Breakfast ♦♦♦
62 Church Street, Tewkesbury GL20 5RZ
T: (01684) 298145

Abbots Court Farm ♦♦♦
Church End, Twyning, Tewkesbury GL20 6DA
T: (01684) 292515
F: (01684) 292515
E: abbotscourt@hotmail.com

Alstone Fields Farm
♦♦♦♦♦ GOLD AWARD
Teddington Hands, Stow Road, Tewkesbury GL20 8NG
T: (01242) 620592
E: alstone.fields@freeuk.com
I: www.alstone.fields.freeuk.com

Carrant Brook House ♦♦♦
3 Rope Walk, Tewkesbury GL20 5DS
T: (01684) 290355
E: lorraine@carrantbrookhouse.co.uk

The Fleet Inn ♦♦♦♦
Twyning, Tewkesbury GL20 6DG
T: (01684) 274310
F: (01684) 291612
E: fleetinn@hotmail.com
I: www.fleetinn.co.uk

Jessop House Hotel ♦♦♦♦
65 Church Street, Tewkesbury GL20 5RZ
T: (01684) 292017
F: (01684) 273076
E: LesThurlow@aol.com
I: www.jessophousehotel.com

Malvern View Guest House ♦♦♦
1 St Mary's Road, Tewkesbury GL20 5SE
T: (01684) 292776

Town Street Farm ♦♦♦
Tirley, Gloucester GL19 4HG
T: (01452) 780442
F: (01452) 780890
E: townstreetfarm@hotmail.com
I: www.townstreetfarm.co.uk

Two Back of Avon ♦♦♦
2 Back of Avon, Riverside Walk, Tewkesbury GL20 5BA
T: (01684) 298935

THORPE
Derbyshire

Hillcrest House ♦♦♦♦
Dovedale, Thorpe, Ashbourne DE6 2AW
T: (01335) 350436
E: hillcresthouse@freenet.co.uk
I: www.ashbourne-town.com/accom/hilcrest

The Old Orchard ♦♦♦
Stoney Lane, Thorpe, Ashbourne DE6 2AW
T: (01335) 350410
F: (01335) 350410

THORPE CULVERT
Lincolnshire

Bridge Bungalow Bed and Breakfast ♦♦
Steeping Road, Thorpe Culvert, Skegness PE24 4QU
T: (01754) 881362
I: www.skegness-resort.co.uk/bridge-bungalow/index.php

THRAPSTON
Northamptonshire

The Poplars ♦♦♦♦
50 Oundle Road, Thrapston, Kettering NN14 4PD
T: (01832) 732499

THURLBY
Lincolnshire

6 The Pingles
♦♦♦♦ SILVER AWARD
Thurlby, Bourne PE10 0EX
T: (01778) 394517

TIBSHELF
Derbyshire

Rosvern House Bed and Breakfast ♦♦♦♦
High Street, Tibshelf, Alfreton DE55 5NY
T: (01773) 874800
F: (01773) 874800
E: sara.byard@orange.net

TINWELL
Rutland

The Old Village Hall ♦♦♦♦
Main Road, Tinwell, Stamford PE9 3UD
T: (01780) 763900

TISSINGTON
Derbyshire

Bassett Wood Farmhouse Bed and Breakfast ♦♦♦
Bassett Wood Farm, Tissington, Ashbourne DE6 1RD
T: (01335) 350254
E: janet@bassettwood.freeserve.co.uk
I: www.bassettwoodfarm.co.uk

TOTON
Nottinghamshire

Brookfield Cottage ♦♦♦
108 Carrfield Avenue, Toton, Beeston, Nottingham NG9 6FB
T: (0115) 917 8046
E: sheila.done@amserve.net

TOWCESTER
Northamptonshire

Brave Old Oak
Rating Applied For
Watling Street, Towcester NN12 6BT
T: (01327) 358255
F: (01327) 352168

Home Farm
Rating Applied For
Caldecote, Towcester NN12 8HG
T: (01327) 352651
F: (01327) 358467
E: jharris@auctben.freeserve.co.uk

The Leys ♦♦♦♦
Field Burcote, Towcester NN12 8AL
T: (01327) 350431
F: (01327) 350431

Monk and Tipster ♦♦♦
36 Watling Street, Towcester NN12 6AF
T: (01327) 350416

Potcote
♦♦♦♦♦ SILVER AWARD
Towcester NN12 8LP
T: (01327) 830224
F: (01327) 830911
E: timbeckbrown@aol.com
I: www.potcote.co.uk

Seawell Grounds ♦♦♦♦♦
Foxley, Towcester NN12 8HW
T: (01327) 860226
F: (01327) 860226
E: seawellcharolais@bt.com

Slapton Manor
♦♦♦♦ SILVER AWARD
Chapel Lane, Slapton, Towcester NN12 8PF
T: (01327) 860344
F: (01327) 860758

TRUSTHORPE
Lincolnshire

The Ramblers Hotel ♦♦♦
Sutton Road, Trusthorpe, Mablethorpe LN12 2PY
T: (01507) 441171

TUNSTALL
Staffordshire

Victoria Hotel ♦♦♦
4 Roundwell Street, Tunstall, Stoke-on-Trent ST6 5JJ
T: (01782) 835964
F: (01782) 835964
E: victoria-hotel@tunstall51.fsnet.co.uk

TURKDEAN
Gloucestershire

Yew Tree Cottage ♦♦♦♦♦
Turkdean, Cheltenham GL54 3NT
T: (01451) 860222
E: vivienburford@hotmail.com

TUTBURY
Staffordshire

Woodhouse Farm Bed and Breakfast ♦♦♦
Woodhouse Farm, Tutbury, Burton upon Trent DE13 9HR
T: (01283) 812185
F: (01283) 815743
E: enquiries@tutbury.co.uk
I: www.tutbury.co.uk/woodhouse

TUXFORD
Nottinghamshire

The Corner House
♦♦♦♦ SILVER AWARD
2 Ollerton Road, Tuxford, Newark NG22 0LF
T: (01777) 871132
E: trishjohnbartle@btinternet.com

TWO DALES
Derbyshire

Hazel House ♦♦♦♦
Chesterfield Road, Two Dales, Matlock DE4 2EZ
T: (01629) 734443
E: adrian.jenny@btopenworld.com
I: www.info@hazel-house.co.uk

Norden House ♦♦♦♦
Chesterfield Road, Two Dales, Matlock DE4 2EZ
T: (01629) 732074
F: (01629) 735805
E: david.a.pope@talk21.com
I: www.nordenhouse.co.uk

UCKINGTON
Gloucestershire

Linthwaite ♦♦♦
3 Homecroft Drive, Uckington, Cheltenham GL51 9SN
T: (01242) 680146

UFFINGTON
Lincolnshire

Ashville House
Rating Applied For
22 Greatford Road, Uffington, Stamford PE9 4SW
T: (01780) 756699
F: (01780) 767128
E: carjanio@yahoo.com

ULLINGSWICK
Herefordshire

The Steppes
♦♦♦♦♦ SILVER AWARD
Ullingswick, Hereford HR1 3JG
T: (01432) 820424
F: (01432) 820042
E: info@steppeshotel.co.uk
I: www.steppeshotel.co.uk

UPPER COBERLEY
Gloucestershire

Upper Coberley Farm
♦♦♦♦ SILVER AWARD
Upper Coberley, Cheltenham GL53 9RB
T: (01242) 870306
E: allen@uppercoberley.freeserve.co.uk

UPPER HULME
Staffordshire

Paddock Farm Bed and Breakfast ♦♦♦♦
Paddock Farm, Upper Hulme, Leek ST13 8TY
T: (01538) 300345

Roaches Hall
♦♦♦♦ SILVER AWARD
Upper Hulme, Leek ST13 8UB
T: (01538) 300115
E: roacheshall@aol.com
I: www.roacheshall.co.uk

UPPER QUINTON
Warwickshire

Winton House
♦♦♦♦ SILVER AWARD
The Green, Upper Quinton, Stratford-upon-Avon CV37 8SX
T: (01789) 720500
E: gail@wintonhouse.com
I: www.wintonhouse.com

UPPER SAPEY
Herefordshire

The Baiting House ♦♦♦
Stourport Road, Upper Sapey, Worcester WR6 6XT
T: (01886) 853201

UPPINGHAM
Rutland

Garden Hotel ♦♦♦♦
High Street West, Uppingham, Oakham LE15 9QD
T: (01572) 822352
F: (01572) 821156
E: gardenhotel@btinternet.com

Grange Farm Bed & Breakfast ♦♦♦♦
Seaton Grange, Uppingham, Seaton, Oakham LE15 9HT
T: (01572) 747664
E: david.reading@farmline.com
I: www.rutnet.co.uk/customers/grangefarm

The Vaults ♦♦♦
Market Place, Uppingham, Oakham LE15 9QH
T: (01572) 823259
F: (01572) 820019
I: www.Rutnet.co.uk/vaults

UPTON SNODSBURY
Worcestershire

The French House Inn ♦♦♦
Worcester Road, Upton Snodsbury, Worcester WR7 4NW
T: (01905) 381631
F: (01905) 381635
I: www.frenchhousepub.co.uk

UPTON ST LEONARDS
Gloucestershire

Bullens Manor Farm ♦♦♦♦
Portway, Upton St Leonards, Gloucester GL4 8DL
T: (01452) 616463

UPTON-UPON-SEVERN
Worcestershire

Ryall House Farm ♦♦♦♦
Ryall, Upton-upon-Severn, Worcester WR8 0PL
T: (01684) 592013
F: (01684) 592013

The Star Inn ♦♦♦
High Street, Upton-upon-Severn, Worcester WR8 0HQ
T: (01684) 592300
F: (01684) 592929
E: thestarinn@uptonuponsevern.fsnet.co.uk

Tiltridge Farm and Vineyard
♦♦♦♦ SILVER AWARD
Upper Hook Road, Upton-upon-Severn, Worcester WR8 0SA
T: (01684) 592906
F: (01684) 594142
E: sandy@tiltridge.com
I: www.tiltridge.com

Welland Court ♦♦♦♦
Welland Court Lane, Upton-upon-Severn, Worcester WR8 0ST
T: (01684) 594426
F: (01684) 594426
E: archer@wellandcourt.freeserve.co.uk
I: www.wellandcourt.co.uk

UTTOXETER
Staffordshire

Oldroyd Guest House & Motel ♦♦♦
18-22 Bridge Street, Uttoxeter ST14 8AP
T: (01889) 562763
F: (01889) 568916
E: jim@oldroyd-guesthouse.com
I: www.oldroyd-guesthouse.com

Troutsdale Bed & Breakfast ♦♦♦♦
Alton Road, Denstone, Uttoxeter ST14 5DH
T: (01889) 590220
F: (07790) 577015
E: cliff@troutsdale.co.uk
I: www.troutsdale.co.uk

VOWCHURCH
Herefordshire

New Barns Farm ♦♦♦♦
Vowchurch, Hereford HR2 0QA
T: (01981) 250250
F: (01981) 250250
E: lloydnewbarns@tesco.net
I: www.golden-valley.co.uk

The Old Vicarage
♦♦♦♦ SILVER AWARD
Vowchurch, Hereford HR2 0QD
T: (01981) 550357
F: (01981) 550357
I: www.golden-valley.co.uk/vicarage

Upper Gilvach Farm
♦♦♦♦ SILVER AWARD
St Margarets, Vowchurch, Hereford HR2 0QY
T: (01981) 510618
F: (01981) 510618
E: ruth@uppergilvach.freeserve.co.uk
I: www.golden-valley.co.uk/gilvach

WADDINGTON
Lincolnshire

Bees Cottage
Rating Applied For
82 Grantham Road, Waddington, Lincoln LN5 9NT
T: (01522) 720883

Horse and Jockey ♦♦♦♦
High Street, Waddington, Lincoln LN5 9RF
T: (01522) 720224
F: (01527) 722551
E: ltott@globelnet.com
I: www.vanguardpubs.com/horseandjockey

WADSHELF
Derbyshire

Temperance House Farm
♦♦♦♦ SILVER AWARD
Bradshaw Lane, Wadshelf, Chesterfield S42 7BT
T: (01246) 566416
E: james.dethick@btopenworld.com

WALTERSTONE
Herefordshire

Coed Y Grafel ♦♦
Coed Y Grafel, Walterstone, Hereford HR2 0DJ
T: (01873) 890675
F: (01873) 890600
E: dianapalmer@btinternet.com

Lodge Farm Cottage ♦♦♦
Walterstone Common, Walterstone, Hereford HR2 0DT
T: (01873) 890263

WARWICK
Warwickshire

Agincourt Lodge Hotel ♦♦♦♦
36 Coten End, Warwick CV34 4NP
T: (01926) 499399
F: (01926) 499399
E: enquires@agincourtlodge.co.uk
I: www.agincourtlodge.co.uk

Apothecary's ♦♦♦♦
The Old Dispensary, Stratford Road, Wellesbourne, Warwick CV35 9RN
T: (01789) 470060
E: apothband@aol.com

Ashburton Guest House ♦♦♦
74 Emscote Road, Warwick CV34 5QG
T: (01926) 401082
F: (01926) 774642
E: ashburtongh@ntworld.com
I: www.smoothhound.co.uk

Austin House ♦♦♦
96 Emscote Road, Warwick CV34 5QJ
T: (01926) 493583
F: (01926) 493679
E: mike.austinhouse96@ntlworld.com
I: www.austinhousewarwick.co.uk

Avon Guest House ♦♦♦♦
7 Emscote Road, Warwick CV34 4PH
T: (01926) 491367
E: sue@comphouse.demon.co.uk
I: www.comphouse.demon.co.uk

Avonside Cottage
♦♦♦♦♦ GOLD AWARD
1 High Street, Barford, Warwick CV35 8BU
T: (01926) 624779
E: avonsidecottage@yahoo.co.uk

Cambridge Villa Hotel ♦♦♦
20A Emscote Road, Warwick CV34 4PP
T: (01926) 491169
F: (01926) 491169

Charter House
♦♦♦♦♦ GOLD AWARD
87-91 West Street, Warwick CV34 6AH
T: (01926) 496965
F: (01926) 411910
E: penon@charterhouse8.freeserve.co.uk
I: www.smoothhound.co.uk/hotels/charter.html

Cliffe Hill House Bed and Breakfast
♦♦♦♦ SILVER AWARD
37 Coventry Road, Warwick CV34 5HN
T: (01926) 496431
F: (01926) 496431
E: quirke@cliffehillhouse.freeserve.co.uk
I: www.cliffehillhouse.freeserve.co.uk

The Coach House
♦♦♦♦ GOLD AWARD
Old Budbrooke Road, Budbrooke, Warwick CV35 7DU
T: (01926) 410893
F: (01926) 490453
E: falcosource@btclick.com

The Croft Guesthouse ♦♦♦♦
Haseley Knob, Warwick CV35 7NL
T: (01926) 484447
F: (01926) 484447
E: david@croftguesthouse.co.uk
I: www.croftguesthouse.co.uk

Crown and Castle Inn ♦♦♦
2-4 Coventry Road, Warwick CV34 4NT
T: (01926) 492087
F: (01926) 410638

Forth House
♦♦♦♦ SILVER AWARD
44 High Street, Warwick CV34 4AX
T: (01926) 401512
F: (01926) 490809
E: info@forthhouseuk.co.uk
I: www.forthhouseuk.co.uk

Hill House ♦♦♦♦
Hampton Lucy, Warwick CV35 8AU
T: (01789) 840329
E: eliz_hunter@hotmail.com
I: www.stratford-upon-avon.co.uk/hillhouse.htm

Jersey Villa Guest House ♦♦♦
69 Emscote Road, Warwick CV34 5QR
T: (01926) 774607
F: (01926) 774607
E: jerseyvillaguesthouse@emscote.freeserve.co.uk

Longbridge Farm ♦♦♦♦
Stratford Road, Warwick CV34 6RB
T: (01926) 401857

Lower Watchbury Farm ♦♦♦♦
Wasperton Lane, Barford, Warwick CV35 8DH
T: (01926) 624772
F: (01926) 624772
E: valeykyn@btconnect.com
I: www.farmaccommodation.com

Merchant's House ♦♦♦♦♦
Hampton Lucy, Warwick CV35 8BE
T: (01789) 842280
E: hpmbel@another.com
I: www.merchants-hamptonlucy.co.uk

Northleigh House
♦♦♦♦ SILVER AWARD
Five Ways Road, Hatton, Warwick CV35 7HZ
T: (01926) 484203
F: (01926) 484006
E: sylviafen@amserve.com
I: www.northleigh.co.uk

The Old Rectory Hotel ♦♦♦♦♦
Vicarage Lane, Sherbourne, Warwick CV35 8AB
T: (01926) 624562
F: (01926) 624995

Park Cottage
♦♦♦♦ SILVER AWARD
113 West Street, Warwick CV34 6AH
T: (01926) 410319
F: (01926) 497994
E: Janet@park-cottage.com
I: www.park-cottage.com

Park House Guest House ♦♦♦
17 Emscote Road, Warwick CV34 4PH
T: (01926) 494359
F: (01926) 494359
E: park.house@ntlworld.com
I: www.parkhousewarwick.co.uk

Peacock Lodge ♦♦♦
97 West Street, Warwick CV34 6AH
T: (01926) 419480
F: (01926) 411892

Rushbrook Farmhouse ♦♦♦♦
Rushbrook Lane, Tanworth-in-Arden, Solihull B94 5HW
T: (01564) 742281
E: enquiries@rushbrookfarmhouse.co.uk
I: www.rushbrookfarmhouse.co.uk

The Seven Stars Public House ♦♦♦♦
Friars Street, Warwick CV34 6HD
T: (01926) 492658
F: (01926) 411747
E: sevenstarswarwick@hotmail.com
I: www.smoothhound.co.uk

Shrewley Pools Farm
◆◆◆◆ SILVER AWARD
Haseley, Warwick CV35 7HB
T: (01926) 484315
E: cathydodd@hotmail.com
I: www.s-h-systems.co.uk/hotels/shrewley.html

The Tilted Wig ◆◆◆◆
11 Market Place, Warwick CV34 4SA
T: (01926) 410466
F: (01926) 495740
I: www.thetiltedwig.com

Warwick Lodge Guest House ◆◆◆
82 Emscote Road, Warwick CV34 5QJ
T: (01926) 492927

Westham Guest House ◆◆◆
76 Emscote Road, Warwick CV34 5QG
T: (01926) 491756
F: (01926) 491756
E: westham.house@aol.com
I: www.smoothhound.co.uk/hotels/westham.html

WATERHOUSES
Staffordshire

Lee House Farm
◆◆◆◆ SILVER AWARD
Leek Road, Waterhouses, Stoke-on-Trent ST10 3HW
T: (01538) 308439

WELDON
Northamptonshire

Thatches on the Green ◆◆◆◆
9 School Lane, Weldon, Corby NN17 3JN
T: (01536) 266681
F: (01536) 266659
E: tom@thatches-on-the-green.fsnet.co.uk
I: www.thatches-on-the-green.fsnet.co.uk

WELFORD
Northamptonshire

West End Farm ◆◆◆◆
West End, Welford, Northampton NN6 6HJ
T: (01858) 575226
E: westendfarm@welford.org

WELFORD-ON-AVON
Warwickshire

Bridgend ◆◆◆◆
Binton Road, Welford-on-Avon, Stratford-upon-Avon CV37 8PW
T: (01789) 750900
F: (01789) 750900
E: bridgend.g.house@amserve.net

Mullions
◆◆◆◆ SILVER AWARD
Greenhill, Church Bank, Binton Road, Welford-on-Avon, Stratford-upon-Avon CV37 8PP
T: (01789) 750413
F: (01789) 750413
E: bandbpmw@aol.com

WELLAND
Worcestershire

The Lovells
◆◆◆◆ SILVER AWARD
Garrett Bank, Welland, Malvern WR13 6NF
T: (01684) 310795

WELLESBOURNE
Warwickshire

Brook House ◆◆◆◆
9 Chestnut Square, Wellesbourne, Warwick CV35 9QS
T: (01789) 840922

Meadow Cottage Bed and Breakfast ◆◆◆
36 Church Walk, Wellesbourne, Warwick CV35 9QT
T: (01789) 840220
F: (01789) 841822
E: robertharland@lineone.net

WELLINGBOROUGH
Northamptonshire

The Manor House
◆◆◆◆◆ GOLD AWARD
1 Orlingbury Road, Great Harrowden, Wellingborough NN9 5AF
T: (01933) 678505
E: info@harrowdenmanor.com
I: www.harrowdenmanor.com

WELLINGTON
Shropshire

Barnfield House ◆◆◆
5 Barnfield Court, Wellington, Telford TF1 2ET
T: (01952) 223406

Clairmont ◆◆◆
54 Haygate Road, Wellington, Telford TF1 1QN
T: (01952) 414214
F: (01952) 414214

Potford House ◆◆◆
Little Bolas, Wellington, Telford TF6 6PS
T: (01952) 541362
E: dsadler@potford.fsnet.co.uk

WEM
Shropshire

Aston Lodge ◆◆◆
Souton Road, Wem, Shrewsbury SY4 5BG
T: (01939) 232577
F: (01939) 232577

Lowe Hall Farm
◆◆◆◆ SILVER AWARD
The Lowe, Wem, Shrewsbury SY4 5UE
T: (01939) 232236
F: (01939) 232236
E: bandb@lowehallfarm.demon.co.uk
I: www.lowehallfarm.demon.co.uk

WENTNOR
Shropshire

Adstone Farmhouse ◆◆◆◆
Wentnor, Bishop's Castle SY9 5EQ
T: (01588) 650540
E: adstone50@aol.com

Crown Inn ◆◆◆◆
Wentnor, Bishop's Castle SY9 5EE
T: (01588) 650613
F: (01588) 650436
E: crowninn@wentnor.com
I: www.wentnor.com

WEOBLEY
Herefordshire

Garnstone House ◆◆◆
Weobley, Hereford HR4 8QP
T: (01544) 318943
F: (01544) 318197

The Marshpools Country Inn ◆◆◆
Ledgemoor, Weobley, Hereford HR4 8RN
T: (01544) 318215
F: (01544) 318847
E: enquires@country-inn.co.uk
I: www.country-inn.co.uk

WESSINGTON
Derbyshire

Crich Lane Farm ◆◆◆◆
Moorwood Moor Lane, Wessington, Alfreton DE55 6DU
T: (01773) 835186

WEST BARKWITH
Lincolnshire

The Manor House
◆◆◆◆ SILVER AWARD
Louth Road, West Barkwith, Market Rasen LN8 5LF
T: (01673) 858253
F: (01673) 858253

WEST BRIDGFORD
Nottinghamshire

Firs Guesthouse ◆◆◆
96 Radcliffe Road, West Bridgford, Nottingham NG2 5HH
T: (0115) 981 0199
F: (0115) 981 0199

Number 56 ◆◆
56 Melton Road, West Bridgford, Nottingham NG2 7NF
T: (0115) 982 1965

WEST HADDON
Northamptonshire

Pear Trees ◆◆◆◆
31 Station Road, West Haddon, Northampton NN6 7AU
T: (01788) 510389
E: peartrees@lineone.net
I: www.pear-trees.co.uk

WESTBURY
Northamptonshire

Mill Farm House ◆◆◆
Westbury, Brackley NN13 5JS
T: (01280) 704843
F: (01280) 704843

WESTBURY-ON-SEVERN
Gloucestershire

Boxbush Barn
◆◆◆◆◆ GOLD AWARD
Rodley, Westbury-on-Severn GL14 1QZ
T: (01452) 760949
E: bedandbreakfast@boxbushbarn.fsnet.co.uk

WESTON
Lincolnshire

Buffers Guest Accomodation
Rating Applied For
9 The Sidings, Moulton, Spalding PE12 6QT
T: (01406) 371994
F: (01406) 371994
E: karin@buffers-moulton.co.uk
I: www.karin@buffers-moulton.co.uk

Canalside Bed and Breakfast ◆◆◆
Bridge Cottage, Green Road, Weston, Stafford ST18 0HZ
T: (01889) 271403
E: melgodridge@canalsidebbweston.fsnet.co.uk

WESTON UNDER PENYARD
Herefordshire

Wharton Farm Bed and Breakfast ◆◆◆◆
Wharton Farm, Weston under Penyard, Ross-on-Wye HR9 5SX
T: (01989) 750255
F: (01989) 750255
E: je.savage@breathemail.net

WESTON UNDER WETHERLEY
Warwickshire

Wethele Manor Farm
◆◆◆◆◆ SILVER AWARD
Rugby Road, Weston under Wetherley, Leamington Spa CV33 9BZ
T: (01926) 831772
F: (01926) 632749
E: simonmoreton@wethelemanor.com
I: www.wethelemanor.com

WESTONBIRT
Gloucestershire

Avenue Farm ◆◆◆
Knockdown, Westonbirt, Tetbury GL8 8QY
T: (01454) 238207
F: (01454) 238207
E: sonjames@breathemail.net
I: www.glosfarmhols.co.uk

WETTON
Staffordshire

The Old Chapel ◆◆◆◆
Wetton, Ashbourne DE6 2AF
T: (01335) 310450
F: (01335) 310089

WHALEY BRIDGE
Derbyshire

Cote Bank Farm
◆◆◆◆ SILVER AWARD
Buxworth, Whaley Bridge, High Peak SK23 7NP
T: (01663) 750566
F: (01663) 750566
E: cotebank@btinternet.com
I: www.cotebank.co.uk

Springbank Guesthouse
Rating Applied For
Reservoir Road, Whaley Bridge, High Peak SK23 7BL
T: (01663) 732819
E: margot@whaleyspringbank.co.uk
I: www.whaleyspringbank.co.uk

WHAPLODE
Lincolnshire

Westgate House & Barn
◆◆◆◆ SILVER AWARD
Little Lane, Whaplode, Spalding PE12 6RU
T: (01406) 370546
E: bandb@westgatehouse.f9.co.uk
I: www.westgatehouse.f9.co.uk

WHATSTANDWELL
Derbyshire

Riverdale ◆◆◆◆
Middle Lane, Whatstandwell, Matlock DE4 5EG
T: (01773) 853905
F: (01773) 853905

WHATTON
Nottinghamshire

The Dell ◆◆◆◆
Church Street, Whatton, Nottingham NG13 9EL
T: (01949) 850832
E: sandyfraser5@btopenworld.com

Establishments printed in blue have a detailed entry in this guide

WHISTON
Staffordshire

Heath House Farm ♦♦♦
Ross Road, Whiston, Stoke-on-Trent ST10 2JF
T: (01538) 266497
E: heathhousefarm@aol.com
I: www.heathhousefarm@aol.com

WHITCHURCH
Shropshire

Pheasant Walk ♦♦♦
Terrick Road, Whitchurch SY13 4JZ
T: (01948) 667118

Roden View ♦♦♦♦
Dobsons Bridge, Whixall, Whitchurch SY13 2QL
T: (01948) 710320
F: (01948) 710320
E: rodenview@hotmail.com

Wayside ♦♦♦
Whitchurch, Ross-on-Wye HR9 6DJ
T: (01600) 890442
F: (01600) 890442
E: info@waysideb-b.co.uk
I: www.waysideb-b.co.uk

Wood Farm
♦♦♦♦ SILVER AWARD
Old Woodhouses, Whitchurch SY13 4EJ
T: (01948) 871224

WHITFIELD
Northamptonshire

Chestnut View ♦♦
Mill Lane, Whitfield, Brackley NN13 5TQ
T: (01280) 850246
F: (01280) 850246

WHITTINGTON
Staffordshire

The Dog Inn ♦♦♦
Main Street, Whittington, Lichfield WS14 9JU
T: (01543) 432252
F: (01543) 433748
E: thedoginn@whittington.1122.freeserve.co.uk

WICKHAMFORD
Worcestershire

Avonwood
♦♦♦♦ GOLD AWARD
30 Pitchers Hill, Wickhamford, Evesham WR11 7RT
T: (01386) 834271
F: (01386) 834271
E: enquiries@avonwood-guesthouse.co.uk
I: www.avonwood-guesthouse.co.uk

WIGMORE
Herefordshire

Gotherment House ♦♦♦
Wigmore, Leominster HR6 9UF
T: (01568) 770547
E: blair@gotherment.co.uk
I: www.gotherment.co.uk

Pear Tree Farm
♦♦♦♦ SILVER AWARD
Leominster, Wigmore, Leominster HR6 9UR
T: (01568) 770140
F: (01568) 770140
E: steveandjill@ptf.me.uk
I: www.peartreefarmco.freeserve.co.uk

WILTON
Herefordshire

Benhall Farm ♦♦♦♦
Wilton, Ross-on-Wye HR9 6AG
T: (01989) 563900
F: (01989) 563900
E: carol_m_brewer@btopenworld.com

WINCHCOMBE
Gloucestershire

Blair House ♦♦♦♦
41 Gretton Road, Winchcombe, Cheltenham GL54 5EG
T: (01242) 603626
F: (01242) 604214
E: chissurv@aol.com

Cleevely ♦♦♦♦
Wadfield Farm, Corndean Lane, Winchcombe, Cheltenham GL54 5AL
T: (01242) 602059
F: (01242) 602059
E: cleevelybxb@hotmail.com
I: www.smoothhound.co.uk/cleevely

Gaia Cottage
Rating Applied For
50 Gloucester Street, Winchcombe, Cheltenham GL54 5LX
T: (01242) 603495
E: sally.simmonds@tiscali.co.uk

Gower House ♦♦♦♦
North Street, Winchcombe, Cheltenham GL54 5LH
T: (01242) 602616
E: gowerhouse16@aol.com.uk

Ireley Grounds ♦♦♦♦
Broadway Road, Winchcombe, Cheltenham GL54 5NY
T: (01242) 603736
F: (01242) 603736
E: mike@ireley.fsnet.co.uk
I: www.ireleygrounds.freeserve.co.uk/

Manor Farm ♦♦♦♦
Greet, Winchcombe, Cheltenham GL54 5BJ
T: (01242) 602423
F: (01242) 602423
E: janet@dickandjanet.fsnet.co.uk

Mercia ♦♦♦♦ SILVER AWARD
Hailes Street, Winchcombe, Cheltenham GL54 5HU
T: (01242) 602251
F: (01242) 609206
F: mercia@uk2.net
I: www.merciaguesthouse.co.uk

North Farmcote Bed and Breakfast ♦♦♦
North Farmcote, Winchcombe, Cheltenham GL54 5AU
T: (01242) 602304
F: (01242) 603860

The Old Bakehouse ♦♦♦♦
Castle Street, Winchcombe, Cheltenham GL54 5JA
T: (01242) 602441
F: (01242) 602441
E: deniseparker@onetel.net.uk

Old Station House ♦♦♦♦
Greet Road, Winchcombe, Cheltenham GL54 5LD
T: (01242) 602283
F: (01242) 602283
E: old_station_house@hotmail.com

Parks Farm ♦♦♦♦
Sudeley, Winchcombe, Cheltenham GL54 5JB
T: (01242) 603874
F: (01242) 603874
E: rosemaryawilson@hotmail.com

The Plaisterers Arms ♦♦♦
Abbey Terrace, Winchcombe, Cheltenham GL54 5LL
T: (01242) 602358
F: (01242) 602360
E: plaisterers.arms@btinternet.com

Postlip Hall Farm
♦♦♦♦ GOLD AWARD
Winchcombe, Cheltenham GL54 5AQ
T: (01242) 603351
F: (01242) 603351
E: postuphallfarm@tiscali.co.uk
I: www.smoothhound.co.uk/hotels/postlip.html

1 Silk Mill Lane ♦♦♦♦
Winchcombe, Cheltenham GL54 5HZ
T: (01242) 603952
E: jenny.cheshire@virgin.net

Sudeley Hill Farm ♦♦♦♦
Winchcombe, Cheltenham GL54 5JB
T: (01242) 602344
F: (01242) 602344
E: scudamore4@aol.com

The White Hart Inn and Restaurant ♦♦♦♦
High Street, Winchcombe, Cheltenham GL54 5LJ
T: (01242) 602359
F: (01242) 602703
E: enquiries@the-white-hart-inn.com
I: www.the-white-hart-inn.co.uk

WING
Rutland

The Kings Arms Inn ♦♦♦♦
Top Street, Wing, Oakham LE15 8SE
T: (01572) 737634
F: (01572) 737255
E: enquiries@thekingsarms-wing.co.uk
I: www.thekingsarms-wing.co.uk

WINKHILL
Staffordshire

Country Cottage ♦♦♦♦
Back Lane Farm, Winkhill, Leek ST13 7XZ
T: (01538) 308273
F: (01538) 308098
E: mjb6435@aol.com
I: www.biophysics.umn.edu/~bent/

WINSLOW
Worcestershire

Munderfield Harold ♦♦
Winslow, Bromyard HR7 4SZ
T: (01885) 483231

WINSTER
Derbyshire

Brae Cottage ♦♦♦♦
East Bank, Winster, Matlock DE4 2DT
T: (01629) 650375

The Dower House
♦♦♦♦♦ GOLD AWARD
Main Street, Winster, Matlock DE4 2DH
T: (01629) 650931
F: (01629) 650932
E: fosterbig@aol.com
I: www.SmoothHound.co.uk/hotels/dowerho

Old Shoulder of Mutton
♦♦♦♦
West Bank, Winster, Matlock DE4 2DQ
T: (01629) 650778
E: brianskyrme@btinternet.com

WIRKSWORTH
Derbyshire

Avondale Farm
♦♦♦♦ SILVER AWARD
Grangemill, Matlock DE4 4HT
T: (01629) 650820
F: (01629) 650233
E: avondale@tinyworld.co.uk

Old Lock Up
♦♦♦♦♦ GOLD AWARD
North End, Wirksworth, Derby DE4 4FG
T: (01629) 826272
F: (01629) 826272
E: wheeler@theoldlockup.co.uk
I: www.theoldlockup.co.uk

Red Lion ♦♦♦
Market Place, Wirksworth, Derby DE4 4ET
T: (01629) 822214
E: shfarrand@aol.com
I: www.redlionwirksworth.co.uk

WISHAW
Warwickshire

Ash House ♦♦♦
The Gravel, Wishaw, Sutton Coldfield B76 9QB
T: (01675) 475782
F: (01675) 475782
E: kate@rectory80.freeserve.co.uk

WITCOMBE
Gloucestershire

Crickley Court
♦♦♦♦ SILVER AWARD
Dog Lane, Witcombe, Gloucester GL3 4UF
T: (01452) 863634
F: (01452) 863634
E: Lispilgrimmorris@yahoo.com geoffpm@fsmail.net

Springfields Farm ♦♦♦
Little Witcombe, Gloucester GL3 4TU
T: (01452) 863532

WITHINGTON
Gloucestershire

Willowside Farm ♦♦♦
Withington, Cheltenham GL54 4DA
T: (01242) 890362
F: (01242) 890557

WOLLASTON
Northamptonshire

Duckmire ♦♦♦♦
1 Duck End, Wollaston, Northampton NN29 7SH
T: (01933) 664249
F: (01933) 664249
E: kerry@foreverengland.freeserve.co.uk

WOLSTANTON
Staffordshire

Whispering Pines
♦♦♦♦♦ GOLD AWARD
11A Milehouse Lane, Wolstanton, Newcastle-under-Lyme ST5 9JR
T: (01782) 639376
F: (01782) 639376
E: timpriestman@whisperingpinesbb45.freeserve.co.uk
I: www.smoothhound.co.uk/hotels/whisperingpines.ltml

WOLSTON
Warwickshire

The Byre
♦♦♦♦ SILVER AWARD
Lords Hill Farm, Coalpit Lane, Wolston, Coventry CV8 3GB
T: (024) 7654 2098

WOLVERHAMPTON
West Midlands

Fox Hotel (Wolverhampton)
♦♦♦
112 - 118 School Street, Wolverhampton WV3 0NR
T: (01902) 421680
F: (01902) 711654
E: sales@foxhotel.co.uk
I: www.foxhotel.co.uk

WOODHALL SPA
Lincolnshire

Claremont Guesthouse ♦♦
9-11 Witham Road, Woodhall Spa LN10 6RW
T: (01526) 352000

The Dower House Hotel
♦♦♦♦
Manor Estate, Woodhall Spa LN10 6PY
T: (01526) 352588
F: (01526) 352588
E: cplumb_dowerhouse@yahoo.co.uk
I: www.dowerhousehotel.co.uk

Newlands ♦♦♦♦
56 Woodland Drive, Woodhall Spa LN10 6YG
T: (01526) 352881

Pitchaway Guesthouse ♦♦♦
The Broadway, Woodhall Spa LN10 6SQ
T: (01526) 352969

The Vale ♦♦♦
50 Tor-O-Moor Road, Woodhall Spa LN10 6SB
T: (01526) 353022
F: (01526) 354949
E: thevale@amserve.net

WOODMANCOTE
Gloucestershire

Gambles Farm B&B ♦♦♦♦♦
Gambles Farm, Gambles Lane, Woodmancote, Cheltenham GL52 9PU
T: (01242) 677719
E: ndeackes@blueyonder.co.uk

WOONTON
Herefordshire

Rose Cottage
♦♦♦♦ SILVER AWARD
Woonton, Hereford HR3 6QW
T: (01544) 340459
F: (01544) 340459

WORCESTER
Worcestershire

Barbourne ♦♦♦
42 Barbourne Road, Worcester WR1 1HU
T: (01905) 27507
F: (01905) 27507

The Black Pear ♦♦♦
49 Ombersley Road, Worcester WR3 7BS
T: (01905) 619816
E: guesthouse@theblackpearfsnet.co.uk

The Boot Inn
♦♦♦♦ SILVER AWARD
Radford Road, Flyford Flavell, Worcester WR7 4BS
T: (01386) 462658
F: (01386) 462547
E: thebootinn@yahoo.com

City Guest House ♦♦♦
36 Barbourne Road, Worcester WR1 1HU
T: (01905) 24695
F: (01905) 24695

The Croft ♦♦♦♦
25 Station Road, Fernhill Heath, Worcester WR3 7UJ
T: (01905) 453482
E: janetandbrian.thecroft@tesco.net

Five Ways Hotel ♦♦
Angel Place, Worcester WR1 3QN
T: (01905) 616980
F: (01905) 616344

Foresters Guest House ♦♦♦
2 Chestnut Walk, Arboretum, Worcester WR1 1PP
T: (01905) 20348
F: (01905) 20348

Green Farm ♦♦♦♦
Crowle Green, Crowle, Worcester WR7 4AB
T: (01905) 381807
F: (01905) 381706
E: lupa@beeb.net
I: www.thegreenfarm.co.uk

Hill Farm House
♦♦♦♦ GOLD AWARD
Dormston Lane, Dormston, Worcester WR7 4JS
T: (01386) 793159
F: (01386) 793239
E: jim@hillfarmhouse.co.uk
I: www.hillfarmhouse.co.uk

Little Lightwood Farm ♦♦♦♦
Lightwood Lane, Cotheridge, Worcester WR6 5LT
T: (01905) 333236
F: (01905) 333236
E: lightwood.holidays@virgin.net

Oaklands ♦♦♦♦
Claines, Worcester WR3 7RR
T: (01905) 458871
F: (01905) 759362
E: barbara.gadd@zoom.co.uk
I: www.ukbed.com/heart-of-england/oaklands.htm

Oldbury Farm Bed and Breakfast
♦♦♦♦ SILVER AWARD
Oldbury Farm, Lower Broadheath, Worcester WR2 6RQ
T: (01905) 421357
E: janejordan@oldburyfarm.freeserve.co.uk

Osborne House ♦♦♦
17 Chestnut Walk, Worcester WR1 1PR
T: (01905) 22296
F: (01905) 22296
E: enquiries@osborne-house.freeserve.co.uk
I: www.osborne-housefreeserve.co.uk

Retreat Farm ♦♦♦♦
Camp Lane, Grimley, Worcester WR2 6LX
T: (01905) 640266
F: (01905) 641397

Shrubbery Guest House ♦♦♦
38 Barbourne Road, Worcester WR1 1HU
T: (01905) 24871
F: (01905) 23620

Sundown ♦♦♦
7 Albert Park Road, Malvern WR14 1HL
T: (01684) 893612
F: (01684) 562459
E: sundown@ntlworld.com
I: www.malvern-b-and-b.info

The White House
♦♦♦♦ SILVER AWARD
8 Green Hill, Bath Road, Worcester WR5 2AT
T: (01905) 356970
F: (01905) 767438
E: bandb@trade-events.co.uk

Yew Tree House
♦♦♦♦ SILVER AWARD
Norchard, Crossway Green, Stourport-on-Severn DY13 9SN
T: (01299) 250921
F: (01299) 253472
E: yewtreehouse1@btopenworld.com
I: www.yewtreeworcester.co.uk

WORKSOP
Nottinghamshire

Carlton Road Guesthouse
♦♦♦
67 Carlton Road, Worksop S80 1PP
T: (01909) 483084

Sherwood Guesthouse ♦♦♦
57 Carlton Road, Worksop S80 1PP
T: (01909) 474209
F: (01909) 476470
E: CHERWOULD@aol.com

WORMELOW
Herefordshire

Lyston Villa ♦♦♦
Wormelow, Hereford HR2 8EL
T: (01981) 540130
F: (01981) 540130

WOTTON-UNDER-EDGE
Gloucestershire

Falcon Cottage ♦♦♦♦
15 Station Road, Charfield, Wotton-under-Edge GL12 8SY
T: (01453) 843528

Hillesley Mill ♦♦♦
Alderley, Wotton-under-Edge GL12 7QT
T: (01453) 843258

WYCK RISSINGTON
Gloucestershire

Hope Lodge ♦♦♦♦♦
Wyck Rissington, Stow-on-the-Wold, Cheltenham GL54 2PN
T: (01451) 822466
F: (01451) 822466
E: hopelodge@btopenworld.com

WYTHALL
Worcestershire

Inkford Hotel ♦♦♦♦
Alcester Road, Wythall, Birmingham B47 6DJ
T: (01564) 824330
F: (01564) 829697
E: inkfordhotel@aol.com
I: www.inkfordhotel.com

YARDLEY
West Midlands

Olton Cottage Guest House
♦♦♦♦
School Lane, Old Yardley Village, Yardley, Birmingham B33 8PD
T: (0121) 783 9249
F: (0121) 789 6545
E: olton.cottage@virgin.net
I: www.olton-cottage.co.uk

Yardley Guesthouse ♦♦♦♦
330 Church Road, Yardley, Birmingham B25 8XT
T: (0121) 783 6634
F: (0121) 783 6634
E: dave@yardleyguesthouse.fsnet.co.uk
I: www.yardleyguesthouse.com

YARKHILL
Herefordshire

Chelwood ♦♦♦♦
Chelwood, Yarkhill, Hereford HR1 3SS
T: (01432) 890387
F: (01432) 890699

YORTON HEATH
Shropshire

Country Bed & Breakfast
♦♦♦♦ SILVER AWARD
Mayfield, Yorton Heath, Shrewsbury SY4 3EZ
T: (01939) 210860
F: (01939) 210860
E: macdonalds@mayfieldyortonheath.freeserve.co.uk
I: www.mayfieldyortonheath.freeserve.co.uk

YOULGREAVE
Derbyshire

Bankside Cottage ♦♦♦
Bankside, Youlgreave, Bakewell DE45 1WD
T: (01629) 636689

Fairview ♦♦♦
Bradford Road, Youlgreave, Bakewell DE45 1WG
T: (01629) 636043
F: (01629) 636043

The Farmyard Inn ♦♦♦
Main Street, Youlgrave, Youlgreave, Bakewell DE45 1UW
T: (01629) 636221

The Old Bakery ♦♦♦
Church Street, Youlgrave,
Youlgreave, Bakewell DE45 1UR
T: (01629) 636887
E: croasdell@oldbakeryyoulgrave.freeserve.co.uk
I: www.cressbrook.co.uk/youlgve/oldbakery

EAST OF ENGLAND

ACTON Suffolk

Barbie's ♦♦
25 Clayhall Place, Acton,
Sudbury CO10 0BT
T: (01787) 373702

ALBURGH Norfolk

The Dove – Restaurant with Rooms ♦♦♦♦
Holbrook Hill, Alburgh,
Harleston IP20 0EP
T: (01986) 788315
F: (01986) 788315
E: thedovenorfolk@freeola.com
I: thedovenorfolk.co.uk

ALBURY Hertfordshire

Tudor Cottage
♦♦♦♦ SILVER AWARD
Upwick Green, Albury, Ware
SG11 2JX
T: (01279) 771440
E: peterandelphine@onetel.net.uk

ALDBOROUGH Norfolk

Butterfly Cottage ♦♦♦
The Green, Aldborough, Norwich
NR11 7AA
T: (01263) 768198
F: (01263) 768198
E: butterflycottage@btopenworld.com
I: www.butterflycottage.com

ALDEBURGH Suffolk

Faraway ♦♦♦
28 Linden Close, Aldeburgh
IP15 5JL
T: (01728) 452571

Lime Tree House B&B ♦♦♦
Benhall Green, Saxmundham
IP17 1HU
T: (01728) 602149
E: linda.pebody@limetreehouse.demon.co.uk

Margaret's ♦♦♦
50 Victoria Road, Aldeburgh
IP15 5EJ
T: (01728) 453239

The Oak ♦♦♦
111 Saxmundham Road,
Aldeburgh IP15 5JF
T: (01728) 453503
F: (01728) 452099
E: ppask18371@aol.com
I: www.ppaskletting.co.uk

Saffron House ♦♦♦♦
2 Barley Lands, Aldeburgh
IP15 5LW
T: (01728) 454716
F: (01728) 454716

Sanviv ♦♦♦
59 Fairfield Road, Aldeburgh
IP1 5JN
T: (01728) 453107

ALDEBY Norfolk

The Old Vicarage ♦♦♦
Rectory Road, Aldeby, Beccles
NR34 0BJ
T: (01502) 678229
E: butler@beccles33.freeserve.co.uk

ALDRINGHAM Suffolk

Fern House ♦♦♦
6 The Follies, Aldringham,
Leiston IP16 4LU
T: (01728) 830759
F: (01728) 830334
E: gallowaymd@aol.com

ALPHETON Suffolk

Amicus ♦♦♦♦
Old Bury Road, Alpheton,
Sudbury CO10 9BT
T: (01284) 828579
F: (01284) 828579
E: stanleyburcham@aol.com

ARDLEIGH Essex

Malting Farm ♦♦♦♦
Malting Farm Lane, Ardleigh,
Colchester CO7 7QG
T: (01206) 230207

Old Shields Farm ♦♦♦♦
Waterhouse Lane, Ardleigh,
Colchester CO7 7NE
T: (01206) 230251
F: (01206) 231825
E: ruth.marshall@amserve.net

ARKESDEN Essex

Parsonage Farm ♦♦♦♦
Arkesden, Saffron Walden
CB11 4HB
T: (01799) 550306
E: danijaud@aol.com

ASHDON Essex

Cobblers
♦♦♦♦ SILVER AWARD
Bartlow Road, Ashdon, Saffron
Walden CB10 2HR
T: (01799) 584666
E: cobblers@ashdon2000.freeserve.co.uk

ASHILL Norfolk

Moat Farm G C Pickering and Son ♦♦♦♦
Cressingham Road, Ashill,
Thetford IP25 7BX
T: (01760) 440357
F: (01760) 441447

ASPLEY GUISE Bedfordshire

Chain Guest House
♦♦♦♦ SILVER AWARD
Church Street, Aspley Guise,
Milton Keynes MK17 8HQ
T: (01908) 586511
F: (01908) 586511
E: chainhouse@ukgateway.net
I: www.chainhouse.ukgateway.net

The Strawberry Farm ♦♦♦♦
Salford Road, Aspley Guise,
Milton Keynes MK17 8HZ
T: (01908) 587070
F: (01908) 587070
E: strawberryfarm@onetel.net.uk
I: www.smoothhound.co.uk/hotels/thestraw.html

ATTLEBOROUGH Norfolk

Home Farm ♦♦♦♦
Stow Bedon, Attleborough
NR17 1BZ
T: (01953) 483592
F: (01953) 488449
E: ejdoveandson@btconnect.com
I: www.homefarm-bandb.co.uk

Scales Farm ♦♦♦♦
Old Buckenham, Attleborough
NR17 1PE
T: (01953) 860324
F: (01953) 860324

AYLSHAM Norfolk

The Old Pump House ♦♦♦♦
Holman Road, Aylsham, Norwich
NR11 6BY
T: (01263) 733789
F: (01263) 733789
E: tonyandlynda@oldpumphouse.fsworld.co.uk

BACTON-ON-SEA Norfolk

Keswick Hotel ♦♦♦
Walcott Road, Bacton-on-Sea,
Norwich NR12 0LS
T: (01692) 650468
F: (01692) 650788
E: bookings@keswickhotelbacton.co.uk
I: www.keswickhotelbacton.co.uk

BADINGHAM Suffolk

Colston Hall
♦♦♦♦ SILVER AWARD
Badingham, Woodbridge
IP13 8LB
T: (01728) 638375
F: (01728) 638084
E: lizjohn@colstonhall.com
I: www.colstonhall.com

BARHAM Suffolk

Tamarisk House ♦♦♦♦
Sandy Lane, Barham, Ipswich
IP6 0PB
T: (01473) 831825
I: www.hotelmaster.co.uk

BARNSTON Essex

Pear Tree Cottage ♦♦♦♦
Chelmsford Road, Barnston,
Great Dunmow CM6 3PS
T: (01371) 820229
E: admin@peartreebandb.co.uk
I: www.peartreebandb.co.uk

BASILDON Essex

38 Kelly Road ♦♦♦♦
Bowers Gifford, Basildon
SS13 2HL
T: (01268) 726701
F: (01268) 726701
E: patricia.jenkinson@tesco.net
I: www.uk-visit.co.uk

BATTLESBRIDGE Essex

The Cottages Guest House ♦♦
Beeches Road, Rawreth,
Battlesbridge, Wickford SS11 8TJ
T: (01702) 232105
E: cottages2000@totalise.co.uk
I: www.smoothhound.com

Muggeridge Farm Guesthouse ♦♦♦♦
5 Maltings Road, Battlesbridge,
Wickford SS11 7RF
T: (01268) 561700
E: accommodation@battlesbridge.com
I: www.battlesbridge.com

BAWDSEY Suffolk

Bawdsey Manor
Rating Applied For
Bawdsey Quay, Bawdsey,
Woodbridge IP12 3AZ
T: (01394) 411633
F: (01394) 410417
E: info@bawdseymanor.co.uk
I: www.bawdseymanor.co.uk

BECCLES Suffolk

Ashtree Cottage ♦♦♦♦
School Lane, Worlingham,
Beccles NR34 7RH
T: (01502) 715206
F: (01502) 711745
E: helen@dhswilcock.freeserve.co.uk

Catherine House ♦♦♦♦
2 Ringsfield Road, Beccles
NR34 9PQ
T: (01502) 716428
F: (01502) 716428

Colville Arms Motel ♦♦♦
Lowestoft Road, Worlingham, Beccles NR34 7EF
T: (01502) 712571
F: (01502) 712571
E: pat@thecolvillearms.freeserve.co.uk

Plantation House
♦♦♦♦ GOLD AWARD
Rectory Road, Haddiscoe, Beccles NR14 6PG
T: (01502) 677778
F: (01502) 677778
E: plantationhouse@ukonline.co.uk
I: www.broadland.com/plantationhouse

Saltgate House ♦♦♦♦
5 Saltgate, Beccles NR34 9AN
T: (01502) 710889
F: (01502) 710591
E: cazjohns@aol.com

BEDFORD
Bedfordshire

Church Farm
♦♦♦♦ SILVER AWARD
41 High Street, Roxton, Bedford MK44 3EB
T: (01234) 870234
F: (01234) 870234
E: churchfarm@amserve.net

Cornfields Restaurant and Hotel ♦♦♦♦ SILVER AWARD
Wilden Road, Colmworth, Bedford MK44 2NJ
T: (01234) 378990
F: (01234) 376370
E: reservations@cornfieldsrestaurant.co.uk
I: www.cornfieldsrestaurant.co.uk

Grafton Hotel ♦♦
141 Midland Road, Bedford MK40 1DN
T: (01234) 359294
F: (01234) 305402

Robertson's Bed & Breakfast ♦♦♦
4 Winifred Road, Bedford MK40 4ES
T: (01234) 340803
F: (01234) 344517
E: fleashouse@freeuk.com
I: www.bandbbedford.com

BEESTON
Norfolk

Holmdene Farm ♦♦♦
Beeston, King's Lynn PE32 2NJ
T: (01328) 701284
E: holmdenefarm@farmersweekly.net
I: www.northnorfolk.co.uk/holmdenefarm

BEESTON REGIS
Norfolk

Cheriton
Rating Applied For
3 Salisbury Road, Sheringham NR26 8EA
T: (01263) 825071

Hilltop
Rating Applied For
Old Wood, Beeston Regis, Cromer NR26 8TS
T: (01263) 824514
F: (01263) 826001
E: hilltopdc@lineone.net
I: www.hilltopoutdoorcentre.uk

Sheringham View Cottage ♦♦♦♦
Cromer Road, Beeston Regis, Cromer NR26 8RX
T: (01263) 820300

BEETLEY
Norfolk

Peacock House
♦♦♦♦ GOLD AWARD
Peacock Lane, Beetley, East Dereham NR20 4DG
T: (01362) 860371
E: PeackH@aol.com
I: www.smoothhound.co.uk/hotels/peacockh.html/

Shilling Stone ♦♦♦
Church Road, Beetley, East Dereham NR20 4AB
T: (01362) 861099
F: (01362) 869153
E: jeannepartridge@tiscali.co.uk
I: www.norfolkshillingstone.co.uk

BELCHAMP ST PAUL
Essex

The Plough (Private Residence)
♦♦♦♦ SILVER AWARD
Gages Road, Belchamp St Paul, Sudbury CO10 7BT
T: (01787) 278882
E: info@theplough-belchamp.co.uk
I: www.theplough-belchamp.co.uk

BENHALL
Suffolk

Kiln Farm B&B ♦♦♦♦
Kiln Lane, Benhall, Saxmundham IP17 1HA
T: (01728) 603166

BERKHAMSTED
Hertfordshire

Broadway Farm
♦♦♦♦ SILVER AWARD
London Road, Berkhamsted HP4 2RR
T: (01442) 866541
F: (01442) 866541
E: a.knowles@broadway.nildram.co.uk

BIGGLESWADE
Bedfordshire

Old Warden Guesthouse ♦♦♦
Shop and Post Office, Old Warden, Biggleswade SG18 9HQ
T: (01767) 627201

BILDESTON
Suffolk

Silwood Barns ♦♦♦
Consent Lane, Bildeston, Ipswich IP7 7SB
T: (01449) 741370
F: (01449) 740819
E: neilashwell@aol.com
I: www.lalaproducts.com

BILLERICAY
Essex

Badgers Rest
♦♦♦♦ SILVER AWARD
2 Mount View, Billericay CM11 1HB
T: (01277) 625384
F: (01277) 633912

BINHAM
Norfolk

Field House
♦♦♦♦ GOLD AWARD
Walsingham Road, Binham, Fakenham NR21 0BU
T: (01328) 830639

BISHOP'S STORTFORD
Hertfordshire

Acer Cottage ♦♦♦
17 Windhill, Bishop's Stortford CM23 2NE
T: (01279) 834797
F: (01279) 834797
E: admill@ntlworld.com
I: www.acercottage.co.uk

Aldbury's Farm
Rating Applied For
Boxley Lane, Hatfield Broad Oak, Bishop's Stortford CM22 7JX
T: (01279) 718282
E: aldbury@supanet.com

5 Ascot Close ♦♦♦
Bishop's Stortford CM23 5BP
T: (01279) 652228

6 Ascot Close ♦♦♦
Bishop's Stortford CM23 5BP
T: (01279) 651027
E: 113714.2346@compuserve.com

9 Carters Leys ♦♦♦
'Fairfield', Bishop's Stortford CM23 2RH
T: (01279) 658148
F: (07796) 214477
E: FairfieldBandB@aol.com

Chippendales ♦♦♦
7 Stort Lodge, Off Hadham Road, Bishop's Stortford CM23 2QL
T: (01279) 656315
E: gorsim@aol.com

The Cottage
♦♦♦♦ GOLD AWARD
71 Birchanger Lane, Birchanger, Bishop's Stortford CM23 5QA
T: (01279) 812349
F: (01279) 815045
E: bookings@thecottagebirchanger.co.uk
I: www.thecottagebirchanger.co.uk

26 Heath Row ♦♦♦♦
Bishop's Stortford CM23 5DE
T: (01279) 833870
F: (01279) 833870

Homesdale ♦♦♦♦
Lower Road, Little Hallingbury, Bishop's Stortford CM22 7QZ
T: (01279) 600647
F: (01279) 600647
E: elfieandsteve@btinternet.com
I: www.homesdale.net

26 Kestrel Gardens ♦♦♦♦
Bishop's Stortford CM23 4LU
T: (01279) 506014

Lancasters ♦♦♦♦
Castle House, Market Square, Bishop's Stortford CM23 3UU
T: (01279) 501307
E: linda@lancasterguesthouse.com
I: www.lancastersguesthouse.com

The Lawns ♦
46 Windhill, Bishop's Stortford CM23 2NH
T: (01279) 654114

3 Lindsey Close ♦♦♦
Bishop's Stortford CM23 2TB
T: (01279) 653206

Marrianno ♦♦♦
104 Hadham Road, Bishop's Stortford CM23 2QF
T: (01279) 508568
E: cattolica55@hotmail.com

Park Lane Bed & Breakfast
Rating Applied For
30 Park Lane, Bishop's Stortford CM23 3NH
T: (01279) 501920
F: (01279) 501920
E: gillcordell@hotmail.com
I: www.parklanerooms.co.uk

Phoenix Lodge ♦♦♦
No. 91 Dunmow Road, Bishop's Stortford CM23 5HF
T: (01279) 659780
F: (01279) 323958
E: phoenixlodge@ntlworld.com
I: www.phoenixlodge.co.uk

Pleasant Cottage ♦♦♦♦
Woodend Green, Henham, Stansted CM22 6AZ
T: (01279) 850792
F: (01279) 850792
E: george@pleasantcott.fsnet.co.uk
I: www.henham.org/accommodation

Saint Vincent ♦♦♦
24 Elm Road, Bishop's Stortford CM23 2SS
T: (01279) 658884
E: hilarydave@lineone.net

Tap Hall ♦♦♦
15 The Street, Takeley, Bishop's Stortford CM22 6QS
T: (01279) 871035
F: (01279) 871035

52 Thorley Hill ♦♦♦♦
Bishop's Stortford CM23 3NA
T: (01279) 658311
F: (01279) 658311

1B Thornbera Road ♦♦♦
Bishop's Stortford CM23 3NJ
T: (01279) 507900
E: airportbnb@aol.com
I: www.stanstedairportbedandbreakfast.com

32 Wentworth Drive ♦♦♦
Bishop's Stortford CM23 2PB
T: (01279) 507133

52 Windhill ♦♦♦
Bishop's Stortford CM23 2NH
T: (01279) 651712
E: aspence@btinternet.com

Woodlands Lodge ♦♦♦♦
Dunmow Road, Bishop's Stortford CM23 5QX
T: (01279) 504784
F: (01279) 461474
E: lynn_kingsbury@yahoo.com
I: www.woodlandslodge.co.uk

BLACKMORE
Essex

Little Lampetts ♦♦♦
Hay Green Lane, Blackmore, Ingatestone CM4 0QE
T: (01277) 822030
E: Shelagh.Porter@btinternet.com

BLAKENEY
Norfolk

Navestock Bed & Breakfast ♦♦♦♦
Cley Road, Blakeney, Holt NR25 7NL
T: (01263) 740998
F: (01263) 740998

BLAXHALL
Suffolk

The Ship Inn ♦♦
Blaxhall, Snape, Saxmundham IP12 2DY
T: (01728) 688316
F: (01728) 688316
E: shipinnblaxhall@aol.com
I: www.shipinnblaxhall.co.uk

BLETSOE
Bedfordshire

North End Barns
♦♦♦♦ SILVER AWARD
North End Farm, Risley Road, Bletsoe, Bedford MK44 1QT
T: (01234) 781320
F: (01234) 781320

BLICKLING
Norfolk

The Buckinghamshire Arms ♦♦♦
Blickling, Norwich NR11 6NF
T: (01263) 732133

BOVINGDON
Hertfordshire

Rose Farm-Accommodation ♦♦♦
Water Lane, Bovingdon, Hemel Hempstead HP3 0NA
T: (01442) 831779
E: rosefarmstables@aol.com

BOXFORD
Suffolk

Hurrells Farmhouse
♦♦♦♦ SILVER AWARD
Boxford Lane, Boxford, Sudbury CO10 5JY
T: (01787) 210215
F: (01787) 211806
E: hurrellsf@aol.com
I: members.aol.com/hurrellsf/index.htm

BRADFIELD
Essex

Emsworth House ♦♦♦
Ship Hill, Bradfield, Manningtree CO11 2UP
T: (01255) 870860
E: emsworthhouse@hotmail.com
I: www.emsworthhouse.co.uk

BRADFIELD COMBUST
Suffolk

Church Farm ♦♦♦♦
Bradfield Combust, Bury St Edmunds IP30 0LW
T: (01284) 386333
F: (01284) 386155
E: paul@williamsonff.freeserve.co.uk

BRAINTREE
Essex

16 Acorn Avenue ♦♦
Braintree CM7 2LR
T: (01376) 320155

Brook Farm c/o Mrs A Butler ♦♦♦♦
Wethersfield, Braintree CM7 4BX
T: (01371) 850284
F: (01371) 850284

Greengages Bed & Breakfast ♦♦♦♦
268 Broad Road, Braintree CM7 5NJ
T: (01376) 345868
I: www.greengagesbandb.co.uk

70 High Garrett ♦♦
Braintree CM7 5NT
T: (01376) 345330

The Old House ♦♦♦
11 Bradford Street, Braintree CM7 9AS
T: (01376) 550457
F: (01376) 343863
E: old_house@talk21.com
I: theoldhousebraintree.co.uk

2 Sims Cottages
Rating Applied For
Braintree Road, Wethersfield, Braintree CM7 4BX
T: (01371) 850935
F: (01371) 850935

BRANCASTER
Norfolk

The Ship Inn ♦♦♦
Main Road, Brancaster, King's Lynn PE31 8AP
T: (01485) 210333
F: (01485) 210333

BRANDON
Suffolk

The Laurels ♦♦♦
162 London Road, Brandon IP27 0LP
T: (01842) 812005

BRENTWOOD
Essex

Brentwood Guesthouse ♦♦♦
75/77 Rose Valley, Brentwood CM14 4HJ
T: (01277) 262713
F: (01277) 211146
E: info@brentwoodguesthouse.com
I: www.brentwoodguesthouse.com

Chestnut Tree Cottage ♦♦♦
Great Warley Street, Great Warley Village Green, Brentwood CM13 3JF
T: (01277) 221727
F: (01277) 221727

The Old Rectory ♦♦♦♦
Lower Dunton Road, Dunton Wayletts, Brentwood CM13 3SW
T: (01268) 544417
F: (01268) 492452
E: info@oldrectoryvenue.com
I: www.theoldrectoryvenue.com

BRIGHTLINGSEA
Essex

Bay Trees B & B
Rating Applied For
3 Stanley Avenue, Brightlingsea, Colchester CO7 0ND
T: (01206) 305293
E: enquiries@bay-trees.com
I: www.bay-trees.com

Paxton Dene ♦♦♦♦
Church Road, Brightlingsea, Colchester CO7 0QT
T: (01206) 304560
F: (01206) 304809
E: holben@btinternet.com
I: www.brightlingsea-town.co.uk/business

BRISLEY
Norfolk

Pond Farm ♦♦♦♦
Brisley, East Dereham NR20 5LL
T: (01362) 668332
F: (01362) 668332

Tully Lodge Riding Stables ♦♦♦♦
School Road, Brisley, East Dereham NR20 5LH
T: (01362) 668493
F: (01362) 668493

BROCKDISH
Norfolk

Grove Thorpe
♦♦♦♦♦ GOLD AWARD
Grove Road, Brockdish, Diss IP21 4JR
T: (01379) 668305
F: (01379) 668305
E: b-b@grovethorpe.co.uk
I: www.grovethorpe.co.uk

BROOKE
Norfolk

Hillside Farm ♦♦♦♦
Welbeck Road, Brooke, Norwich NR15 1AU
T: (01508) 550260
F: (01508) 550260
E: carrieholl@tinyworld.co.uk
I: www.hillside-farm.com

The Old Vicarage
♦♦♦♦ SILVER AWARD
48 The Street, Brooke, Norwich NR15 1JU
T: (01508) 558329

BROXTED
Essex

The Granary ♦♦♦♦
Moor End Farm, Broxted, Great Dunmow CM6 2EL
T: (01371) 870821
F: (01371) 870821
E: cathy@moorendfarm.com
I: www.moorendfarm.com

BRUNDALL
Norfolk

Braydeston House ♦♦♦♦
9 The Street, Brundall, Norwich NR13 5JY
T: (01603) 713123
E: ann@braydeston.freeserve.co.uk

3 Oak Hill ♦♦♦
Brundall, Norwich NR13 5AQ
T: (01603) 717903

BUNGAY
Suffolk

Castles ♦♦♦♦
35 Earsham Street, Bungay NR35 1AF
T: (01986) 892283
E: castles@lineone.net

Earsham Park Farm
♦♦♦♦ GOLD AWARD
Harleston Road, Earsham, Bungay NR35 2AQ
T: (01986) 892180
F: (01986) 892180
E: etb@earsham-parkfarm.co.uk
I: www.earsham-parkfarm.co.uk

Manor Farm House ♦♦♦♦
St Margarets Road, Bungay NR35 1PQ
T: (01986) 896895
F: (01986) 896840

BUNTINGFORD
Hertfordshire

Buckland Bury Farm ♦♦♦♦
Buckland Bury, Buntingford SG9 0PY
T: (01763) 272958
F: (01763) 274722
E: buckbury@farmersweekly.net

Chipping Hall ♦♦♦♦
Chipping, Buntingford SG9 0PH
T: (01763) 271514
F: (01763) 272833
E: jacquelinenoy@aol.com

BURES
Suffolk

Queen's House ♦♦♦♦
Church Square, Bures, Sudbury CO8 5AB
T: (01787) 227760
F: (01787) 227082
E: rogerarnold2@aol.com
I: www.queens-house.com

BURGH ST PETER
Norfolk

Shrublands Farm
♦♦♦♦ SILVER AWARD
Burgh St Peter, Beccles NR34 0BB
T: (01502) 677241
F: (01502) 677241

BURNHAM MARKET
Norfolk

Holmesdale ♦♦♦
Church Walk, Burnham Market, King's Lynn PE31 8DH
T: (01328) 738699
E: veronicagroom@lineone.net

The Lord Nelson Public House ♦♦♦♦
Creake Road, Burnham Market, King's Lynn PE31 8EN
T: (01328) 738321

Wood Lodge
♦♦♦♦ SILVER AWARD
Millwood, Herring's Lane, Burnham Market, King's Lynn PE31 8DP
T: (01328) 730152
F: (01328) 730158

BURNHAM-ON-CROUCH
Essex

Burnt Mill Cottage ♦♦♦
21 Mill Road, Burnham-on-Crouch CM0 8PZ
T: (01621) 783712
E: ria.jen@ntlworld.com

Eves Corner ♦♦♦
Southminster Road, Burnham-on-Crouch CM0 8QE
T: (01621) 784721
F: (01621) 784721
E: evesbb@hotmail.com

Holyrood House ♦♦♦
46 Green Lane, Ostend, Burnham-on-Crouch CM0 8PU
T: (01621) 784759

The Oyster Smack ♦♦♦
112 Station Road, Burnham-on-Crouch CM0 8HR
T: (01621) 782141
E: info@theoystersmack.co.uk
I: www.theoystersmack.co.uk

The Railway Hotel ♦♦♦♦
Station Road, Burnham-on-Crouch CM0 8BQ
T: (01621) 786868
F: (01621) 783002
I: www.therailwayhotelburnham.co.uk

BURNHAM THORPE
Norfolk

Whitehall Farm ♦♦♦♦
Burnham Thorpe, King's Lynn PE31 8HN
T: (01328) 738416
F: (01328) 730937
E: barrysoutherland@aol.com
I: www.whitehallfarm-accommodation.com

BURY ST EDMUNDS
Suffolk

Brighthouse Farm ♦♦♦♦
Melford Road, Lawshall, Bury St Edmunds IP29 4PX
T: (01284) 830385
F: (01284) 830385
E: info@brighthousefarm.fsnet.co.uk
I: www.brighthousefarm.fsnet.co.uk

Clarice House
♦♦♦♦♦ SILVER AWARD
Horringer Court, Horringer Road, Bury St Edmunds IP29 5PH
T: (01284) 705550
F: (01284) 716120
E: enquiry@clarice-bury.fsnet.co.uk
I: www.clarice.co.uk

Dunston Guesthouse/Hotel ♦♦♦
8 Springfield Road, Bury St Edmunds IP33 3AN
T: (01284) 767981
F: (01284) 764574
I: www.dunstonguesthouse.co.uk

The Glen ♦♦♦♦
84 Eastgate Street, Bury St Edmunds IP33 1YR
T: (01284) 755490
E: rallov@aol.com

Hilltop ♦♦
22 Bronyon Close, Bury St Edmunds IP33 3XB
T: (01284) 767066
E: bandb@hilltop22br.freeserve.co.uk
I: www.hilltop22br.freeserve.co.uk

Kent House ♦♦♦
20 St Andrews Street North, Bury St Edmunds IP33 1TH
T: (01284) 769661
E: lizkent@supanet.com
I: www.lizkent.supanet.com

Manorhouse
♦♦♦♦♦ GOLD AWARD
The Green, Beyton, Bury St Edmunds IP30 9AF
T: (01359) 270960
E: manorhouse@beyton.com
I: www.beyton.com

Northgate House ♦♦♦♦♦
8 Northgate Street, Bury St Edmunds IP33 1HQ
T: (01284) 760469
F: (01284) 724008
E: northgate_hse@hotmail.com
I: www.northgatehouse.com

Ounce House ♦♦♦♦
Northgate Street, Bury St Edmunds IP33 1HP
T: (01284) 761779
F: (01284) 768315
E: pott@globalnet.co.uk

Park House ♦♦♦
22A Mustow Street, Bury St Edmunds IP33 1XL
T: (01284) 703432
F: (01284) 703432

Regency House Hotel ♦♦♦♦
3 Looms Lane, Bury St Edmunds IP33 1HE
T: (01284) 764676
F: (01284) 725444
I: www.regencyhousehotel.co.uk

Sycamore House ♦♦♦♦
23 Northgate Street, Bury St Edmunds IP33 1HP
T: (01284) 755828
E: m.chalkley@ntlworld.com
I: www.sycamorehouse.net

The Wallow ♦♦♦♦
Mount Road, East Barton, Bury St Edmunds IP31 2QU
T: (01284) 788055
I: www.geocities.com/wallowbb

Westbank House B&B ♦♦♦
116A Westley Road, Bury St Edmunds IP33 3SD
T: (01284) 753874
F: (01284) 725775
E: graham@paske.fs.business.co.uk

CAMBRIDGE
Cambridgeshire

Acer House ♦♦♦
3 Dean Drive, Holbrook Road, Cambridge CB1 7SW
T: (01223) 210404
E: acerhouse@btopenworld.com
I: www.acerhouse.co.uk

Acorn Guesthouse ♦♦♦♦
154 Chesterton Road, Cambridge CB4 1DA
T: (01223) 353888
F: (01223) 350527
E: info@acornguesthouse.co.uk
I: www.acornguesthouse.co.uk

Alpha Milton Guesthouse ♦♦♦
61-63 Milton Road, Cambridge CB4 1XA
T: (01223) 311625
F: (01223) 565100

Arbury Lodge Guesthouse ♦♦♦
82 Arbury Road, Cambridge CB4 2JE
T: (01223) 364319
F: (01223) 566988
E: arburylodge@ntlworld.com
I: www.guesthousecambridge.com

Archway House
Rating Applied For
52 Gilbert Road, Cambridge CB4 3PE
T: (01223) 575314
F: (01223) 502508

Ashley Hotel ♦♦♦
74 Chesterton Road, Cambridge CB4 1ER
T: (01223) 350059
F: (01223) 350900
E: info@arundelhousehotels.co.uk
I: www.arundelhousehotels.co.uk

Assisi Guesthouse ♦♦♦
193 Cherry Hinton Road, Cambridge CB1 7BX
T: (01223) 246648
F: (01223) 412900

Avondale
Rating Applied For
35 Highfields Road, Caldecote, Cambridge CB3 7NX
T: (01954) 210746
E: avondale@amserve.net

Aylesbray Lodge Guesthouse ♦♦♦♦
5 Mowbray Road, Cambridge CB1 7SR
T: (01223) 240089
F: (01223) 528678
E: stay@aylesbray.com
I: www.aylesbray.com

Brooklands Guesthouse ♦♦♦
95 Cherry Hinton Road, Cambridge CB1 7BS
T: (01223) 242035
F: (01223) 242035
E: info@brooklandsguesthouse.co.uk
I: www.brooklandsguesthouse.co.uk

Cam Guesthouse ♦♦♦
17 Elizabeth Way, Cambridge CB4 1DD
T: (01223) 354512
F: (01223) 353164
E: camguesthouse@btinternet.com
I: www.camguesthouse.co.uk

The Cambridge Guesthouse
Rating Applied For
201A Milton Road, Cambridge CB4 1XG
T: (01223) 423239

Cambridge Lodge Hotel ♦♦♦♦
139 Huntingdon Road, Cambridge CB3 0DQ
T: (01223) 352833
F: (01223) 355166
E: cambridge.lodge@btconnect.com

Cristinas ♦♦♦
47 St Andrews Road, Cambridge CB4 1DH
T: (01223) 365855
F: (01223) 365855
E: cristinas.guesthouse@ntlworld.com
I: www.cristinasguesthouse.com

Dresden Villa Guesthouse ♦♦♦
34 Cherry Hinton Road, Cambridge CB1 7AA
T: (01223) 247539
F: (01223) 410640

Dykelands Guesthouse ♦♦♦
157 Mowbray Road, Cambridge CB1 7SP
T: (01223) 244300
F: (01223) 566746
E: dykelands@fsbdial.co.uk
I: www.dykelands.com

Finches ♦♦♦♦
144 Thornton Road, Girton, Cambridge CB3 0ND
T: (01223) 276653
F: (01223) 276653
E: liz.green.b-b@talk21.com
I: www.smoothhound.co.uk/hotels/finches

Hamilton Hotel ♦♦♦
156 Chesterton Road, Cambridge CB4 1DA
T: (01223) 365664
F: (01223) 314866

Harry's Bed & Breakfast
Rating Applied For
39 Milton Road, Cambridge CB4 1XA
T: (01223) 503866
F: (01223) 503866
E: cjmadden@ntlworld.com
I: www.welcometoharrys.co.uk

Hills Guesthouse ♦♦♦♦
157 Hills Road, Cambridge CB2 2RJ
T: (01223) 214216
F: (01223) 214216

Home From Home ♦♦♦♦
78B Milton Road, Cambridge CB4 1LA
T: (01223) 323555
F: (01223) 236078
E: homefromhome@tesco.net
I: www.homefromhomecambridge.co.uk

King's Tithe ♦♦♦♦
13a Comberton Road, Barton, Cambridge CB3 7BA
T: (01223) 263610
F: (01223) 263610

Kirkwood Guesthouse ♦♦♦
172 Chesterton Road, Cambridge CB4 1DA
T: (01223) 306283
F: (01223) 711782
E: info@kirkwoodhouse.co.uk
I: www.kirkwoodhouse.co.uk

Lensfield Hotel
♦♦♦♦ SILVER AWARD
53 Lensfield Road, Cambridge CB2 1EN
T: (01223) 355017
F: (01223) 312022
E: reservations@lensfield.co.uk & enquiries@lensfieldhotel.co.uk
I: www.lensfieldhotel.co.uk

Lovell Lodge Hotel ♦♦♦
365 Milton Road, Cambridge CB4 1SR
T: (01223) 425478
F: (01223) 426581

The Poplars
Rating Applied For
12 East Drive, Highfields Caldecote, Cambridge CB3 7NZ
T: (01954) 210396
F: (01954) 210396
E: thepoplars@onetel.net.uk

Railway Lodge Guest House ♦♦♦
150 Tenison Road, Cambridge CB1 2DP
T: (01223) 467688
F: (01223) 461934

Segovia Lodge ♦♦♦
2 Barton Road, Newnham, Cambridge CB3 9JZ
T: (01223) 354105
F: (01223) 323011

Somerset House
Rating Applied For
107 Milton Road, Cambridge CB4 1XE
T: (01223) 505131
E: www.somersetbedandbreakfast@msn.com
I: homepage.ntlworld.com/kim/cupeck

Southampton Guest House ♦♦♦
7 Elizabeth Way, Cambridge CB4 1DE
T: (01223) 357780
F: (01223) 314297
E: southamptonhouse@telco4u.net
I: www.southamptonguesthouse.com

Sycamore House ♦♦♦♦
56 High Street, Great Wilbraham, Cambridge CB1 5JD
T: (01223) 880751
F: (01223) 880751
E: barry@thesycamorehouse.co.uk
I: www.thesycamorehouse.co.uk

Tudor Cottage ♦♦♦♦
292 Histon Road, Cambridge CB4 3HS
T: (01223) 565212
F: (01223) 508656
E: tudor.cottage@ntlworld.com

Upton House
Rating Applied For
11b Grange Road, Cambridge CB3 9AS
T: (01223) 323201
F: (01223) 362009
E: tom.challis@talk21.com

Victoria Guest House ♦♦♦
57 Arbury Road, Cambridge CB4 2JB
T: (01223) 350086
E: victoriahouse@ntlworld.com
I: www.smoothhound.co.uk/hotels/victoria.html

Woodfield House ♦♦♦♦
Madingley Road, Coton, Cambridge CB3 7PH
T: (01954) 210265
F: (01954) 212650
E: wendy-john@wsadler.freeserve.co.uk

Worth House
♦♦♦♦ SILVER AWARD
152 Chesterton Road, Cambridge CB4 1DA
T: (01223) 316074
F: (01223) 316074
E: enquiry@worth-house.co.uk
I: www.worth-house.co.uk

CAMPSEA ASHE
Suffolk

The Dog & Duck ♦♦♦
Station Road, Campsea Ashe, Woodbridge IP13 0PT
T: (01728) 748439

CARBROOKE
Norfolk

White Hall
♦♦♦♦ GOLD AWARD
Carbrooke, Thetford IP25 6SG
T: (01953) 885950
F: (01953) 884420
E: shirleycarr@whitehall.uk.net

CARLETON RODE
Norfolk

Upgate Farm ♦♦♦
Carleton Rode, Norwich NR16 1NJ
T: (01953) 860300
F: (01953) 860300
E: upgatefarm@btinternet.com

CASTLE ACRE
Norfolk

Willow Cottage Tea Rooms ♦♦♦♦
Stocks Green, Castle Acre, King's Lynn PE32 2AE
T: (01760) 755551
F: (01760) 755799
E: willowcottage@webwise.fm
I: www.broadland.com/willowcottage.html

CASTLE CAMPS
Cambridgeshire

The Willows
Rating Applied For
High Street, Castle Camps, Cambridge CB1 6SN
T: (01799) 584140
F: (01799) 584140
E: lizzieatthewillows@btopenworld.com

CASTLE HEDINGHAM
Essex

Fishers ♦♦♦♦
St James Street, Castle Hedingham, Halstead CO9 3EW
T: (01787) 460382
F: (01787) 460382
E: Fishers@hutchingsh.freeserve.co.uk

The Old School House ♦♦♦
St James Street, Castle Hedingham, Halstead CO9 3EW
T: (01787) 461629
E: ccdawson@aol.com

CASTOR
Cambridgeshire

Cobnut Cottage ♦♦♦♦
45 Peterborough Road, Castor, Peterborough PE5 7AX
T: (01733) 380745
F: (01733) 380745
E: huckle.cobnut@talk21.com
I: www.cobnut-cottage.co.uk

The Old Smithy
♦♦♦♦ SILVER AWARD
47 Peterborough Road, Castor, Peterborough PE5 7AX
T: (01733) 380186
F: (01733) 380186
E: julie.e.m.taylor@lineone.net

CAVENDISH
Suffolk

Embleton House
♦♦♦♦ SILVER AWARD
Melford Road, Cavendish, Sudbury CO10 8AA
T: (01787) 280447
F: (01787) 282396
E: silverned@aol.com
I: www.smoothhound.co.uk/hotels/embleton

George Inn
Rating Applied For
The Green, Cavendish, Sudbury CO10 8BA
T: (01787) 280248
F: (01787) 281703
E: reservations@georgecavendish.co.uk
I: www.georgecavendish.co.uk

The Red House Bed and Breakfast
♦♦♦♦ SILVER AWARD
Stour Street, Cavendish, Sudbury CO10 8BH
T: (01787) 280611
F: (01787) 280611
E: mtheaker@btinternet.com
I: www.SmoothHound.co.uk/hotels/theredh.html

CHEDBURGH
Suffolk

Flint Lodge ♦♦♦♦♦
2 Kings Park, Chedburgh, Bury St Edmunds IP29 4TY
T: (01284) 851000
F: (01284) 851000
E: jeffstonell@aol.com
I: www.flintlodge.co.uk

CHELMSFORD
Essex

Aarandale ♦♦♦
9 Roxwell Road, Chelmsford CM1 2LY
T: (01245) 251713
F: (01245) 251713
E: aarandaleuk@aol.com

Beechcroft Private Hotel ♦♦♦
211 New London Road, Chelmsford CM2 0AJ
T: (01245) 352462
F: (01245) 347833
E: enquiries@beechcrofthotel.com
I: www.beechcrofthotel.com

Boswell House Hotel ♦♦♦♦
118 Springfield Road, Chelmsford CM2 6LF
T: (01245) 287587
F: (01245) 287587
E: SteveBoorman@aol.com

The Chelmer Hotel ♦♦
2-4 Hamlet Road, Chelmsford CM2 0EU
T: (01245) 353360
F: (01245) 609055
E: collingsnick@hotmail.com

The Compasses Motel
Rating Applied For
141 Broomfield Road, Chelmsford CM1 1RY
T: (01245) 292051

Crouch Valley Motel ♦♦
Burnham Road, Latchingdon, Chelmsford CM3 6EX
T: (01621) 740770
E: crouchvalley@globalnet.co.uk
I: www. crouch-valley-motel.co.uk

Fitzjohns Farmhouse ♦♦♦
Mashbury Road, Great Waltham, Chelmsford CM3 1EJ
T: (01245) 360204
F: (01245) 361724
E: RosRenwick@aol.com

Pemajero ♦♦♦
Cedar Avenue West, Chelmsford CM1 2XA
T: (01245) 264679
F: (01245) 264679

Sherwood ♦♦♦
Cedar Avenue West, Chelmsford CM1 2XA
T: (01245) 257981
F: (01245) 257981
E: jeremy.salter@btclick.com

Stump Cross House
♦♦♦♦ SILVER AWARD
Moulsham Street, Chelmsford CM2 9AQ
T: (01245) 353804

Wards Farm ♦♦
Loves Green, Highwood Road, Highwood, Chelmsford CM1 3QJ
T: (01245) 248812
F: (01245) 248812
E: alsnbrtn@aol.com

CHERRY HINTON
Cambridgeshire

The Old Rosemary Branch
Rating Applied For
67 Church End, Cherry Hinton, Cambridge CB1 3LF
T: (01223) 247161
E: s.anderson@constructionplus.net

CHEVELEY
Cambridgeshire

Jasmine Cottage ♦♦♦
Star and Garter Lane, Cheveley, Newmarket CB8 9DG
T: (01638) 730206
E: ems.morgan@virgin.net
I: www.nicomorgan.com/b&b

Juniper ♦♦♦♦ SILVER AWARD
9 Church Lane, Cheveley, Newmarket CB8 9DJ
T: (01638) 731244

The Old Farmhouse ♦♦♦
165 High Street, Cheveley, Newmarket CB8 9DG
T: (01638) 730771
F: (01638) 730771
E: amrobinson@clara.co.uk

The Red Lion Inn ♦♦♦
218 High Street, Cheveley, Newmarket CB8 9RH
T: (01638) 730233
F: (01638) 731872
E: redlionpatchris@BTopenworld.com

CHIPPENHAM
Cambridgeshire

The Maltings Yard Cottage ♦♦♦♦
20 High Street, Chippenham, Ely CB7 5PP
T: (01638) 720110

CHORLEYWOOD
Hertfordshire

Ashburton House
♦♦♦♦ SILVER AWARD
48 Berks Hill, Chorleywood, Rickmansworth WD3 5AH
T: (01923) 285510
F: (01923) 285513
E: vales@onetel.net.uk
I: www.ashburtonhouse.co.uk

CLACTON-ON-SEA
Essex

Adelaide Guesthouse ♦♦♦
24 Wellesley Road, Clacton-on-Sea CO15 3PP
T: (01255) 435628
E: adelaide_guesthouse@yahoo.co.uk
I: www.corporateillusion.com/adelaide-guesthouse

Beam Guest House ♦♦♦♦
26 Nelson Road, Clacton-on-Sea CO15 1LU
T: (01255) 433992
E: beamguesthouse@talk21.com

Bedford Lodge
Rating Applied For
14 Carnarvon Road, Clacton-on-Sea CO15 6PH
T: (01255) 425000
F: (01255) 225079
E: keysusan1@aol.com

Brunton House
Rating Applied For
15 Carnarvon Road, Clacton-on-Sea CO15 6PH
T: (01255) 420431

The Cabana ♦♦♦
8 Collingwood Road, Clacton-on-Sea CO15 1UL
T: (01255) 431913
F: (01255) 428221
E: cabana-hotel@fsbdial.co.uk
I: www.cabanahotel.co.uk

Grosvenor House Hotel
Rating Applied For
23 Carnarvon Road, Clacton-on-Sea CO15 6PH
T: (01255) 433001
F: (01255) 225079
E: keysusan1@aol.com

Le'Vere House Hotel ♦♦♦
15 Agate Road, Clacton-on-Sea CO15 1RA
T: (01255) 423044
F: (01255) 423044

Lyndale Lodge Hotel ♦♦♦
2-4 Colne Road, Clacton-on-Sea CO15 1PX
T: (01255) 423340
F: (01255) 425545
E: lyndalelodge@aol.com
I: www.lyndalelodgehotel.com

Pond House Farmhouse Bed & Breakfast ♦♦♦♦
Pond House, Earls Hall Farm, Clacton-on-Sea CO16 8BP
T: (01255) 820458
F: (01255) 822370
E: brenda_lord@farming.co.uk
I: www.earlshallfarm.info

Sandrock Hotel ♦♦♦
1 Penfold Road, Marine Parade West, Clacton-on-Sea CO15 1JN
T: (01255) 428215
F: (01255) 428215

The Shannon Guest House
Rating Applied For
25 Agate Road, Clacton-on-Sea CO15 1RA
T: (01255) 434921
E: jeanette@msn.co.uk
I: www.theshannon.com

Stonar Hotel ♦♦♦
19 Agate Road, Clacton-on-Sea CO15 1RA
T: (01255) 221011
E: stonar.hotel@btconnect.com

CLAPHAM
Bedfordshire

Narly Oak Lodge ♦♦♦♦
The Baulk, Green Lane, Clapham, Bedford MK41 6AA
T: (01234) 350353
F: (01234) 350353
E: fostert@csd.bedfordshire.gov.uk

CLARE
Suffolk

The Clare Hotel ♦♦♦
19 Nethergate Street, Clare, Sudbury CO10 8NP
T: (01787) 277449
F: (01787) 277161
E: rhrng@netscapeonline.co.uk

Ship Stores ♦♦♦♦
22 Callis Street, Clare, Sudbury CO10 8PX
T: (01787) 277834
E: shipclare@aol.com
I: www.ship-stores.co.uk

CLEY NEXT THE SEA
Norfolk

Cooke's of Cley ♦♦♦
High Street, Cley next the Sea, Holt NR25 7RX
T: (01263) 740776
F: (01263) 740776
I: www.broadland.com

CLOPHILL
Bedfordshire

Shallmarose Bed & Breakfast ♦♦♦
32 Bedford Road, Clophill, Bedford MK45 4AE
T: (01525) 861565

COLCHESTER
Essex

Apple Blossom House ♦♦♦
8 Guildford Road, Colchester CO1 2YL
T: (01206) 512303
F: (01206) 870260

Athelstan House ♦♦♦♦
201 Maldon Road, Colchester CO3 3BQ
T: (01206) 548652
E: enquiries@athelstanhouse.co.uk

Four Sevens Guesthouse ♦♦♦
28 Inglis Road, Colchester CO3 3HU
T: (01206) 546093
F: (01206) 546093
E: calypso1@hotmail.com

Fridaywood Farm
♦♦♦♦ SILVER AWARD
Bounstead Road, Colchester CO2 0DF
T: (01206) 573595
F: (01206) 547011

Hampton House ♦♦♦
224 Maldon Road, Colchester CO3 3BD
T: (01206) 579291

11 Harvest End ♦♦♦
Stanway, Colchester CO3 0YX
T: (01206) 543202

Lemoine ♦♦♦♦
2 Whitefriars Way, Colchester CO3 4EL
T: (01206) 574710

11a Lincoln Way ♦♦♦
Colchester CO1 2RL
T: (01206) 867192
F: (01206) 799993
E: johnmargaret@edwards11a.fsnet.co.uk

Nutcrackers ♦♦♦
6 Mayberry Walk, Colchester CO2 8PS
T: (01206) 543085
E: jean@aflex.net

Old Courthouse Inn ♦♦♦♦
Harwich Road, Great Bromley, Colchester CO7 7JG
T: (01206) 250322
F: (01206) 251346
E: oldcourthouseinn@21.com
I: www.theoldcourthouseinn.co.uk

Pescara House ♦♦♦
88 Manor Road, Colchester CO3 3LY
T: (01206) 520055
F: (01206) 512127
E: dave@pescarahouse.co.uk
I: www.pescarahouse.co.uk

Peveril Hotel ♦♦
51 North Hill, Colchester CO1 1PY
T: (01206) 574001
F: (01206) 574001

The Red House
♦♦♦♦ SILVER AWARD
29 Wimpole Road, Colchester CO1 2DL
T: (01206) 509005
F: (01206) 500311
E: theredhousecolchester@hotmail.com
I: www.smoothhound.co.uk/hotels/theredhousebandb.html

76 Roman Road ♦♦♦
Colchester CO1 1UP
T: (01206) 514949

Rye Farm ♦♦♦
Rye Lane, Layer-de-la-Haye, Colchester CO2 0JL
T: (01206) 734350
F: (01206) 734370
E: peter@buntingp.fsbusiness.co.uk

Scheregate Hotel ♦♦
36 Osborne Street, via St John's Street, Colchester CO2 7DB
T: (01206) 573034
F: (01206) 541561

Seven Arches Farm ♦♦
Chitts Hill, Lexden, Colchester CO3 5SX
T: (01206) 574896
F: (01206) 574896

Tall Trees ♦♦♦♦
25 Irvine Road, Colchester CO3 3TP
T: (01206) 576650
E: whitehead.talltrees@ntlworld.com

Telstar ♦♦♦
Layer Breton, Colchester CO2 0PS
T: (01206) 331642
F: (01206) 330761
E: irene@telstar123.fsnet.co.uk

COLTISHALL
Norfolk

Bridge House ♦♦♦♦
1 High Street, Coltishall, Norwich NR12 7AA
T: (01603) 737323
F: (01603) 737323
I: www.bridge-house.com

The Hedges Guesthouse ♦♦♦♦
Tunstead Road, Coltishall, Norwich NR12 7AL
T: (01603) 738361
F: (01603) 738983
E: info@hedgesbandb.co.uk
I: www.hedgesbandb.co.uk

Kings Head ♦♦♦
26 Wroxham Road, Coltishall, Norwich NR12 7EA
T: (01603) 737426
F: (01603) 736542

The Old Railway Station ♦♦♦♦
The Old Railway Station, Station Road, Coltishall, Norwich NR12 7JG
T: (01603) 737069
F: (01603) 736320
E: info@theoldrailwaystation.co.uk
I: www.theoldrailwaystation.co.uk

Terra Nova Lodge ♦♦♦♦
14 Westbourne Road, Coltishall, Norwich NR12 7HT
T: (01603) 736264

CORTON
Suffolk

Barn Owl Lodge ♦♦♦♦
Yarmouth Road, Corton, Lowestoft NR32 5NH
T: (01502) 733105

COTTENHAM
Cambridgeshire

Denmark House ♦♦♦♦
58 Denmark Road, Cottenham, Cambridge CB4 8QS
T: (01954) 251060
F: (01954) 251629
E: denmark@house33.fsnet.co.uk
I: www.denmarkhouse.fsnet.co.uk

CRANFIELD
Bedfordshire

Church House ♦♦♦
38 High Street, Cranfield, Bedford MK43 0DF
T: (01234) 751108
E: francis.white@ntlworld.com

Croft End Bed & Breakfast ♦♦♦
10 Hotch Croft, Cranfield, Bedford MK43 0BN
T: (01234) 750753
E: chambers@xalt.co.uk

49 Mill Road ♦♦♦
Cranfield, Bedford MK43 0JG
T: (01234) 750715

CRETINGHAM
Suffolk

The Cretingham Bell
♦♦♦♦ SILVER AWARD
The Street, Cretingham, Woodbridge IP13 7BJ
T: (01728) 685419

Shrubbery Farmhouse
♦♦♦♦ SILVER AWARD
Chapel Hill, Cretingham, Woodbridge IP13 7DN
T: (01473) 737494
F: (01473) 737312
E: sm@marmar.co.uk
I: www.shrubberyfarmhouse.co.uk

CROMER
Norfolk

Birch House ♦♦♦
34 Cabbell Road, Cromer NR27 9HX
T: (01263) 512521

Cambridge House ♦♦♦♦
Sea Front, East Cliff, Cromer
NR27 9HD
T: (01263) 512085
I: www.norfolk-holidays.org.uk

Captains House ♦♦♦♦♦
5 The Crescent, Cromer
NR27 9EX
T: (01263) 515434
F: (01263) 517114
E: captainshouse@aol.com
I: www.captains-house.co.uk

The Grove Guesthouse ♦♦♦♦
95 Overstrand Road, Cromer
NR27 0DJ
T: (01263) 512412
E: thegrovecromer@btopenworld.com
I: www.thegrovecromer.co.uk

Knoll Guesthouse ♦♦♦
23 Alfred Road, Cromer
NR27 9AN
T: (01263) 512753
E: ian@knollguesthouse.co.uk
I: www.knollguesthouse.co.uk

Seaspray ♦♦♦♦
1 Cliff Drive, Cromer NR27 0AW
T: (01263) 512116

Shrublands Farm
♦♦♦♦ SILVER AWARD
Northrepps, Cromer NR27 0AA
T: (01263) 579297
F: (01263) 579297
E: youngman@farming.co.uk
I: www.broadland.com/shrublands

Stenson ♦♦♦♦
32 Overstrand Road, Cromer
NR27 0AJ
T: (01263) 511308

Whispering Trees ♦♦♦♦
106 Compit Hills, Cromer
NR27 9LP
T: (01263) 514490

CULFORD
Suffolk

47 Benyon Gardens ♦♦♦
Culford, Bury St Edmunds
IP28 6EA
T: (01284) 728763

DALLINGHOO
Suffolk

Old Rectory ♦♦♦
Dallinghoo, Woodbridge
IP13 0LA
T: (01473) 737700

DANBURY
Essex

Southways ♦♦♦
Copt Hill, Danbury, Chelmsford
CM3 4NN
T: (01245) 223428

Wych Elm ♦♦♦
Mayes Lane, Danbury,
Chelmsford CM3 4NJ
T: (01245) 222674
E: axonwychelm@tiscali.co.uk

DARSHAM
Suffolk

Priory Farm ♦♦♦
Darsham, Saxmundham
IP17 3QD
T: (01728) 668459

White House Farm ♦♦♦
Main Road, Darsham,
Saxmundham IP17 3PP
T: (01728) 668632
F: (01728) 668169
E: VNewm1@aol.com

DEBDEN
Essex

Redbrick House ♦♦♦♦
Deynes Road, Debden, Saffron
Walden CB11 3LG
T: (01799) 540221
F: (0870) 164 3639
E: emma@redbrick-house.co.uk
I: www.smoothhound.co.uk/hotels/redbrickhouse.html

DEDHAM
Essex

Good Hall
♦♦♦♦ SILVER AWARD
Coggeshall Road, Dedham,
Colchester CO7 7LR
T: (01206) 322100
F: (01206) 323902
E: goodhall@ic24.net

May's Barn Farm
♦♦♦♦ SILVER AWARD
May's Lane, Off Long Road West,
Dedham, Colchester CO7 6EW
T: (01206) 323191
E: maysbarn@talk21.com
I: www.mays.barn.btinternet.co.uk

DENHAM
Suffolk

Low Farm ♦♦♦♦
Denham, Eye IP21 5ET
T: (01379) 873068
F: (01379) 870062
E: nigel.carol@virgin.net

DENNINGTON
Suffolk

Grange Farm Bed & Breakfast
♦♦♦
Grange Farm, Dennington,
Woodbridge IP13 8BT
T: (01986) 798388
I: www.framlingham.com/grangefarm

DENVER
Norfolk

Westhall Cottages ♦♦♦
20-22 Sluice Road, Denver,
Downham Market PE38 0DY
T: (01366) 382987
F: (01366) 385553

DEREHAM
Norfolk

Greenbanks Country Hotel
♦♦♦♦
Swaffham Road, Wendling,
Dereham NR19 2AR
T: (01362) 687742
F: (01362) 687742
E: jenny@greenbankshotel.co.uk
I: www.greenbankshotel.co.uk

Hill House ♦♦♦♦
26 Market Place, Dereham
NR19 2AP
T: (01362) 699699
E: jvellam@aol.com

Park Farm ♦♦♦♦
Bylaugh, East Dereham
NR20 4QE
T: (01362) 688584
E: lakeparkfm@aol.com

DERSINGHAM
Norfolk

Ashdene House ♦♦♦
Dersingham, King's Lynn
PE31 6HQ
T: (01485) 540395
I: www3.mistral.co.uk/ashdene

Barn House Bed & Breakfast
Rating Applied For
14 Station Road, Dersingham,
King's Lynn PE31 6PP
T: (01485) 543086
E: tomchapman_uk@yahoo.co.uk

The Corner House
♦♦♦♦ SILVER AWARD
2 Sandringham Road,
Dersingham, King's Lynn
PE31 6LL
T: (01485) 543532

Dove Lodge ♦♦♦♦
21 Woodside Avenue,
Dersingham, King's Lynn
PE31 6QB
T: (01485) 540053
F: (01485) 540053
E: dovelodgebb@fsnet.co.uk
I: www.dovelodge.20m.com

Spring Cottage ♦♦♦
11 Fern Hill, Dersingham, King's
Lynn PE31 6HT
T: (01485) 541012
E: hillarytuttle@hotmail.com

The Willows
Rating Applied For
Post Office Road, Dersingham,
King's Lynn PE31 6HR
T: (01485) 543602
E: thewillowsbandb@hotmail.com

DISS
Norfolk

Abbey Farm ♦♦♦
Great Green, Thrandeston, Diss
IP21 4BN
T: (01379) 783422
E: jean.carlisle@virgin.net
I: www.diss.co.uk

Dickleburgh Hall
♦♦♦♦♦ GOLD AWARD
Semere Green Lane, Dickleburgh,
Diss IP21 4NT
T: (01379) 741259
I: www.dickhall.co.uk

Koliba ♦♦♦
8 Louie's Lane, Diss IP22 4LR
T: (01379) 650046
F: (01379) 650046
E: olgakoliba@aol.com

The Old Rectory Hopton
Rating Applied For
High Street, Hopton, Diss
IP22 2QX
T: (01953) 688135
F: (01953) 681686
E: llewellyn.hopton@btinternet.com
I: www.theoldrectoryhopton.com

Old Vine Barn ♦♦♦♦♦
The Heywood, Diss IP22 5TB
T: (01379) 641682
F: (01379) 641432
E: oldvinebarn@aol.com

Oxfootstone Granary ♦♦♦♦
Low Common, South Lopham,
Diss IP22 2JS
T: (01379) 687490
E: paddie@oxfoot.co.uk
I: www.oxfoot.co.uk

The Snailmakers Restaurant
♦♦♦♦♦
65 Lower Denmark Street, Fair
Green, Diss IP22 4BE
T: (01379) 641300
F: (01379) 643633
E: thesnailmakers@aol.com
I: www.thesnailmakers.co.uk

South View ♦♦♦
High Road, Roydon, Diss
IP22 5RU
T: (01379) 651620
E: southviewcarol@aol.com

Strenneth ♦♦♦♦
Airfield Road, Fersfield, Diss
IP22 2BP
T: (01379) 688182
F: (01379) 688260
E: pdavey@strenneth.co.uk
I: www.strenneth.co.uk

DOCKING
Norfolk

Jubilee Lodge ♦♦♦
Station Road, Docking, King's
Lynn PE31 8LS
T: (01485) 518473
F: (01485) 518473
E: eghoward62@hotmail.com
I: www.jubilee-lodge.com

DOVERCOURT
Essex

Dudley Guesthouse ♦♦
34 Cliff Road, Dovercourt,
Harwich CO12 3PP
T: (01255) 504927

Homebay ♦♦♦
9 Bay Road, Dovercourt,
Harwich CO12 3JZ
T: (01255) 504428
E: sydiej9@btinternet.com

Sun View ♦♦♦
42 Cliff Road, Dovercourt,
Harwich CO12 3PP
T: (01255) 507816
E: enquiries@sunview.fsworld.co.uk

Tudor Rose ♦♦♦
124 Fronks Road, Dovercourt,
Harwich CO12 4EQ
T: (01255) 552398
E: janet@morgan-co12.freeserve.co.uk

DOWNHAM MARKET
Norfolk

Chestnut Villa ♦♦♦
44 Railway Road, Downham
Market PE38 9EB
T: (01366) 384099
E: chestnutvilla@talk21.com

Lion House Licensed Restaurant and Guest House
♦♦♦
140 Lynn Road, Downham
Market PE38 9QF
T: (01366) 382017
E: lionhouse@supanet.com
I: www.lionhouse.supanet.com

DUNSTABLE
Bedfordshire

Cherish End B & B ♦♦♦♦
21 Barton Avenue, Dunstable LU5 4DF
T: (01582) 606266
F: (01582) 606266
E: dandg4bandb@tinyworld.co.uk
I: www.smoothhound.co.uk/hotels/cherishend.html

EARITH
Cambridgeshire

Riverview Hotel ♦♦♦
37 High Street, Earith, Huntingdon PE28 3PP
T: (01487) 841405
E: riverviewhotel@tinyworld.co.uk
I: www.riverviewhotel.co.uk

EARL SOHAM
Suffolk

Bridge House
♦♦♦♦ SILVER AWARD
Earl Soham, Framlingham, Woodbridge IP13 7RT
T: (01728) 685473
F: (01728) 685289
E: bridgehouse46@hotmail.com
I: www.jenniferbaker.co.uk

EARLS COLNE
Essex

Chalkney Wood Cottage
♦♦♦♦
Tey Road, Earls Colne, Colchester CO6 2LD
T: (01787) 223522
I: www.chalkneywoodcottage.com

Greenlands Farm ♦♦♦♦
Lamberts Lane, Earls Colne, Colchester CO6 2LE
T: (01787) 224895
E: david@greenlandsfarm.freeserve.co.uk

Riverside Lodge ♦♦♦
40 Lower Holt Street, Earls Colne, Colchester CO6 2PH
T: (01787) 223487
F: (01787) 223487
E: bandb@riversidelodge-uk.com
I: www.riversidelodge-uk.com

EAST BARSHAM
Norfolk

White Horse Inn ♦♦♦
Fakenham Road, East Barsham, Fakenham NR21 0LH
T: (01328) 820645
F: (01328) 820645

EAST BERGHOLT
Suffolk

Rosemary ♦♦♦
Rectory Hill, East Bergholt, Colchester CO7 6TH
T: (01206) 298241
E: s.finch@bcs.org.uk

EAST HARLING
Norfolk

Hill House
Rating Applied For
Hill House Farm, East Harling, Norwich NR16 2LL
T: (01953) 717670
F: (01953) 717228
E: kemp@fast-mail.net
I: www.hillhousefarm.net

EAST MERSEA
Essex

Bromans Farm ♦♦♦♦
Mersea Island, East Mersea, Colchester CO5 8UE
T: (01206) 383235
F: (01206) 383235

Mersea Island Vineyard
♦♦♦♦
Rewsalls Lane, East Mersea, Colchester CO5 8SX
T: (01206) 385900
F: (01206) 383600
E: jacqui.barber@merseawine.com
I: www.merseawine.com

EASTON
Suffolk

Atlantis Stud Farm
♦♦♦♦ SILVER AWARD
Framlingham Road, Easton, Woodbridge IP13 0EW
T: (01728) 621553
F: (01728) 621553
E: atlantisbandb@yahoo.co.uk
I: www.eastanglia-bandb.co.uk

ELMSWELL
Suffolk

Elmswell Hall Bed & Breakfast
♦♦♦♦
Elmswell, Bury St Edmunds IP30 9EN
T: (01359) 240215
F: (01359) 240215
E: kate@elmswellhall.freeserve.co.uk
I: www.elmswellhall.co.uk

Kiln Farm ♦♦♦
Kiln Lane, Elmswell, Bury St Edmunds IP30 9QR
T: (01359) 240442
E: paul-jacky@kilnfarm.fsnet.co.uk

Mulberry Farm
♦♦♦♦ SILVER AWARD
Ashfield Road, Elmswell, Bury St Edmunds IP30 9HG
T: (01359) 244244
F: (01359) 244244

ELSENHAM
Hertfordshire

Aspens ♦♦♦♦
Park Road, Elsenham, Bishop's Stortford CM22 6DF
T: (01279) 816281

ELY
Cambridgeshire

Bowmount House
Rating Applied For
254 Columbine Road, Ely CB6 3WP
T: (01353) 669943

Casa Nostra Guesthouse ♦♦♦
6 Black Bank Road, Little Downham, Ely CB6 2UA
T: (01353) 862495
F: (01353) 862495
E: casanostra@btinternet.com
I: www.casanostraguesthouse.co.uk

Cathedral House ♦♦♦♦
17 St Mary's Street, Ely CB7 4ER
T: (01353) 662124
F: (01353) 662124
E: farndale@cathedralhouse.co.uk
I: www.cathedralhouse.co.uk

23 Egremont Street ♦♦♦
Ely CB6 1AE
T: (01353) 664557
F: (01353) 614681
E: vivienlaird@aol.com

71 Fleetwood ♦♦♦♦
Northwold, Ely CB6 1BH
T: (01353) 662149

The Flyer Restaurant, Public House & Hotel ♦♦♦
69 Newnham Street, Ely CB7 4PQ
T: (01353) 669200
F: (01353) 669100
I: www.flyerhotel.co.uk

The Fountain ♦♦♦
1 Churchgate Street, Soham, Ely CB7 5DS
T: (01353) 720374
F: (01353) 722103
E: enquiries@thefountain.co.uk
I: www.thefountain.co.uk

The Grove
♦♦♦♦ SILVER AWARD
Bury Lane, Sutton Gault, Ely CB6 2BD
T: (01353) 777196
F: (01353) 777425

Hill House Farm
♦♦♦♦ GOLD AWARD
9 Main Street, Coveney, Ely CB6 2DJ
T: (01353) 778369
F: (01353) 778369
E: hill_house@madasafish.com

29 Longfields ♦♦♦♦
Ely CB6 3DN
T: (01353) 663020
E: davidrigley@onetel.net

57 Lynn Road ♦♦♦♦
Ely CB6 1DD
T: (01353) 663685
F: (01353) 663767
E: marting7vgh@aol.com

96 Lynn Road
♦♦♦♦ SILVER AWARD
Ely CB6 1DE
T: (01353) 665044

Nyton Hotel ♦♦♦
7 Barton Road, Ely CB7 4HZ
T: (01353) 662459
F: (01353) 666217
E: nytonhotel@yahoo.co.uk

Old School House ♦♦♦♦
54 Downham Road, Ely CB6 2SH
T: (01353) 668848

Post House ♦♦♦
12A Egremont Street, Ely CB6 1AE
T: (01353) 667184
E: nora@covell.fsbusiness.co.uk

Rosendale Lodge
♦♦♦♦♦ SILVER AWARD
223 Main Street, Witchford, Ely CB6 2HT
T: (01353) 667700
F: (01353) 667799
E: val.pickford@rosendalelodge.co.uk
I: www.rosendale.lodge.co.uk

Spinney Abbey ♦♦♦♦
Stretham Road, Wicken, Ely CB7 5XQ
T: (01353) 720971
E: spinney.abbey@tesco.net
I: www.spinneyabbey.co.uk

Springfields
♦♦♦♦♦ SILVER AWARD
Ely Road, Little Thetford, Ely CB6 3HJ
T: (01353) 663637
F: (01353) 663130
E: springfields@talk21.com
I: www.smoothhound.co.uk/hotels/springfields.html

90 St Mary's Street
Rating Applied For
Ely CB7 4HH
T: (01353) 615102

Sycamore House ♦♦♦♦
91 Cambridge Road, Ely CB7 4HX
T: (01353) 662139
F: (01353) 662795
E: sycamore_house@hotmail.com
I: www.sycamorehouse.gb.com

Walnut House ♦♦♦♦
1 Houghton Gardens, Ely CB7 4JN
T: (01353) 661793
F: (01353) 663519
E: walnuthouse1@aol.com
I: www.ely.org.uk/walnuthouse

9 Willow Walk ♦♦♦
Ely CB7 4AT
T: (01353) 664205

EPPING
Essex

Brooklands ♦♦♦
1 Chapel Road, Epping CM16 5DS
T: (01992) 575424
E: abrookland@aol.com

Country House Bed & Breakfast ♦♦♦♦
16 Beulah Road, Epping CM16 6RH
T: (01992) 576044
F: (01992) 570430
E: epping.accomm@btinternet.com

Garnon Limes ♦♦♦♦
Kendal Avenue, Epping CM16 4PW
T: (01992) 573930
F: (01992) 573930
E: robin.dobson@dial.pipex.com

ERPINGHAM
Norfolk

Saracens Head Inn ♦♦♦
Wolterton, Erpingham, Norwich NR11 7LX
T: (01263) 768909
F: (01263) 768993
I: www.saracenshead-norfolk.co.uk

EYE
Suffolk

The Bull Auberge
♦♦♦♦♦ SILVER AWARD
Ipswich Road, Yaxley, Eye IP23 8BZ
T: (01379) 783604
F: (01379) 788486
E: bullauberge@aol.com

The White Horse Inn ♦♦♦
Stoke Ash, Eye IP23 7ET
T: (01379) 678222
F: (01379) 678557
E: whitehorse@stokeash.fsbusiness.co.uk
I: www.whitehorseinn.fsnet.co.uk

EYKE
Suffolk

Marsh Cottage ♦♦♦
Low Road, Eyke, Woodbridge IP12 2QF
T: (01394) 460203

The Old House ♦♦♦♦
Eyke, Woodbridge IP12 2QW
T: (01394) 460213

FAKENHAM
Norfolk

Abbott Farm ♦♦♦
Walsingham Road, Binham, Fakenham NR21 0AW
T: (01328) 830519
F: (01328) 830519
E: abbot.farm@btinternet.com

Erika's Bed and Breakfast ♦♦♦
3 Gladstone Road, Fakenham NR21 9BZ
T: (01328) 863058

Highfield Farm ♦♦♦♦
Great Ryburgh, Fakenham NR21 7AL
T: (01328) 829249
F: (01328) 829422
E: jegshighfield@onet.co.uk
I: www.broadland.com/highfield

Holly Lodge
♦♦♦♦♦ GOLD AWARD
The Street, Thursford Green, Fakenham NR21 0AS
T: (01328) 878465
F: (01328) 878465
E: hollyguestlodge@btopenworld.com
I: www.hollylodgeguesthouse.co.uk

The Old Brick Kilns Guesthouse ♦♦♦♦
Little Barney Lane, Barney, Fakenham NR21 0NL
T: (01328) 878305
F: (01328) 878948
E: enquire@old-brick-kilns.co.uk
I: www.old-brick-kilns.co.uk

Rosemary Cottage ♦♦♦
13 The Street, West Raynham, Fakenham NR21 7AD
T: (01328) 838318
F: (01328) 838318
E: francoisew@supanet.com

Southview ♦♦♦♦
Lynn Road, Sculthorpe, Fakenham NR21 9QE
T: (01328) 851300

FARCET
Cambridgeshire

Red House Farm ♦♦♦
Broadway, Farcet, Peterborough PE7 3AZ
T: (01733) 243129
F: (01733) 243129
E: gill.emberson@totalise.co.uk

FEERING
Essex

The Old Anchor ♦♦♦♦
132 Feering Hill, Feering, Colchester CO5 9PY
T: (01376) 572855
F: (01376) 572855

Old Wills Farm ♦♦♦
Wittletey Road, Feering, Colchester CO5 9RP
T: (01376) 570259
F: (01376) 570259
E: janecrayston@btconnect.com

Prested Hall
Rating Applied For
Prested Hall Chase, Feering, Colchester CO5 9EE
T: (01376) 573399
F: (0870) 706 1196
E: hall@prested.com
I: www.prested.com

FELIXSTOWE
Suffolk

Burlington House ♦♦♦♦
7 Beach Road West, Felixstowe IP11 2BH
T: (01394) 282051

Dolphin Hotel ♦♦
41 Beach Station Road, Felixstowe IP11 2EY
T: (01394) 282261
F: (01394) 278319

Dorincourt Guesthouse ♦♦♦
41 Undercliff Road West, Felixstowe IP11 2AH
T: (01394) 270447
F: (01394) 270447

The Grafton Guesthouse ♦♦♦♦
13 Sea Road, Felixstowe IP11 2BB
T: (01394) 284881
F: (01394) 279101
E: info@grafton-house.com
I: www.grafton-house.com

Iddlesleigh Private Guest House ♦♦♦
11 Constable Road, Felixstowe IP11 7HL
T: (01394) 670546
E: iddlesleigh@aol.com

The Ordnance Hotel ♦♦
1 Undercliffe Road West, Felixstowe IP11 2AN
T: (01394) 273427
F: (01394) 282513
E: mail@ordnancehotel.com
I: www.ordnancehotel.com

Primrose Gate Bed & Breakfast ♦♦♦♦
263 Ferry Road, Felixstowe IP11 9RX
T: (01394) 271699
F: (01394) 283614
E: lesley_berry@hotmail.com

FELMINGHAM
Norfolk

Larks Rise ♦♦
North Walsham Road, Felmingham, North Walsham NR28 0JU
T: (01692) 403173
I: www.broadland.com/larksrise

FELSTED
Essex

Potash Farm
♦♦♦♦ SILVER AWARD
Cobblers Green, Causeway End Road, Felsted, Great Dunmow CM6 3LX
T: (01371) 820510
F: (01371) 820510
E: enquiries@potashfarm.co.uk or jill@potashfarm.co.uk
I: www.potashfarm.co.uk

FENSTANTON
Cambridgeshire

Orchard House ♦♦♦
6A Hilton Road, Fenstanton, Huntingdon PE28 9LH
T: (01480) 469208
F: (01480) 497487
E: ascarrow@aol.com

FINCHAM
Norfolk

Rose Cottage Bed and Breakfast ♦♦♦♦
Downham Road, Fincham, King's Lynn PE33 9HF
T: (01366) 347426
F: (01366) 347426

FINCHINGFIELD
Essex

The Red Lion Inn ♦♦♦
6 Church Hill, Finchingfield, Braintree CM7 4NN
T: (01371) 810400
F: (01371) 851062
I: www.red-lion-finchingfield.com

FLATFORD MILL
Suffolk

The Granary
Rating Applied For
Granary Museum, Flatford Mill, East Bergholt, Colchester CO7 6UL
T: (01206) 298111
E: flatfordmill@fsdial.co.uk

FLITTON
Bedfordshire

Brook House ♦♦♦♦
18 Brook Lane, Flitton, Bedford MK45 5EJ
T: (01525) 861098
F: (01525) 861098
E: jacquelinecatlin@aol.com

FORDHAM
Cambridgeshire

Anne's Bed & Breakfast ♦♦♦♦
158 Mildenhall Road, Fordham, Ely CB7 5NS
T: (01638) 720514
F: (01638) 720514
E: annesb.b@btinternet.com

FORNHAM ALL SAINTS
Suffolk

The Three Kings ♦♦♦♦
Hengrave Road, Fornham All Saints, Bury St Edmunds IP28 6LA
T: (01284) 766979
F: (01284) 723308
E: enquiries@the-three-kings.com
I: www.the-three-kings.com

FOULDEN
Norfolk

The White Hart Inn ♦♦♦
White Hart Street, Foulden, Thetford IP26 5AW
T: (01366) 328638
E: sylvia.chisholm@virgin.net

FRAMLINGHAM
Suffolk

Fieldway Bed & Breakfast ♦♦♦♦
Saxtead Road, Dennington, Woodbridge IP13 8AP
T: (01728) 638456
F: (01728) 638456
E: dianaturan@hotmail.com
I: www.framlingham.com/fieldway

High House Farm ♦♦♦
Cransford, Framlingham, Woodbridge IP13 9PD
T: (01728) 663461
F: (01728) 663409
E: bb@highhousefarm.co.uk
I: www.highhousefarm.co.uk

Shimmens Pightle ♦♦♦
Dennington Road, Framlingham, Woodbridge IP13 9JT
T: (01728) 724036

FRECKENHAM
Suffolk

The Golden Boar Inn
Rating Applied For
The Street, Freckenham, Bury St Edmunds IP28 8HZ
T: (01638) 723000
F: (01638) 721166
E: Thegoldenboarinn@aol.com

FRESSINGFIELD
Suffolk

Elm Lodge Farm ♦♦♦♦
Chippenhall Green, Fressingfield, Eye IP21 5SL
T: (01379) 586249
E: sheila-webster@elm-lodge.fsnet.co.uk
I: www.elm-lodge.fsnet.co.uk

FRINTON-ON-SEA
Essex

Russell Lodge ♦♦♦
47 Hadleigh Road, Frinton-on-Sea CO13 9HQ
T: (01255) 675935
E: stay@russell-lodge.fsnet.co.uk
I: www.russell-lodge.fsnet.co.uk

Uplands Guesthouse ♦♦♦
41 Hadleigh Road, Frinton-on-Sea CO13 9HQ
T: (01255) 674889
F: (01255) 674889
E: info@uplandsguesthouse.com
I: www.uplandsguesthouse.com

FRISTON
Suffolk

The Flint House ♦♦♦♦
Aldeburgh Road, Friston, Saxmundham IP17 1PD
T: (01728) 689123
F: (01728) 687406
E: handsel@eidosnet.co.uk
I: www.soi.city.ac.uk/~sunil/flinthouse

The Old School ♦♦♦♦
Aldeburgh Road, Friston, Saxmundham IP17 1NP
T: (01728) 688173
E: oldschool@fristonoldschool.freeserve.co.uk

GARBOLDISHAM Norfolk

Ingleneuk Lodge ♦♦♦♦
Hopton Road, Garboldisham, Diss IP22 2RQ
T: (01953) 681541
F: (01953) 681138
E: info@ingleneuklodge.co.uk
I: www.ingleneuklodge.co.uk

GLEMSFORD Suffolk

The Cock Inn Glemsford Rating Applied For
Egremont Street, Glemsford, Sudbury CO10 7SA
T: (01787) 280544
F: (01787) 282792
I: www.the-cock-inn.com

GOOD EASTER Essex

Treloyhan Bed & Breakfast ♦♦♦
Chelmsford Road, Good Easter, Chelmsford CM1 4PU
T: (01245) 231425
E: p.dellar@btopenworld.com

GOSFIELD Essex

Rare View ♦♦♦
Shardlones Farm, Gosfield, Halstead CO9 1PL
T: (01787) 474696

GREAT BADDOW Essex

Homecroft ♦♦♦
Southend Road, Great Baddow, Chelmsford CM2 7AD
T: (01245) 475070
F: (01245) 475070

Orchard House ♦♦♦
The Bringey, Church Street, Great Baddow, Chelmsford CM2 7JW
T: (01245) 474333

GREAT BARDFIELD Essex

Bucks House ♦♦♦♦
Vine Street, Great Bardfield, Braintree CM7 4SR
T: (01371) 810519
F: (01371) 810710
E: postonbuckshouse@aol.com
I: www.smoothhound.co.uk/hotels/bucks.html

GREAT BARTON Suffolk

40 Conyers Way ♦♦♦
Great Barton, Bury St Edmunds IP31 2SW
T: (01284) 787632

GREAT BRICETT Suffolk

Riverside Cottage ♦♦♦♦
The Street, Great Bricett, Ipswich IP7 7DH
T: (01473) 658266
E: chasmhorne@aol.com

GREAT CHESTERFORD Essex

White Gates ♦♦♦♦
School Street, Great Chesterford, Saffron Walden CB10 1NN
T: (01799) 530249
E: margaret-mortimer@lineone.net
I: www.welcometowhitegates.co.uk

GREAT CRESSINGHAM Norfolk

The Vines ♦♦♦♦
The Street, Great Cressingham, Thetford IP25 6NL
T: (01760) 756303
E: stay@thevines.fsbusiness.co.uk
I: www.thevines.fsbusiness.co.uk

GREAT DUNMOW Essex

Harwood Guest House ♦♦♦♦ SILVER AWARD
52 Stortford Road, Great Dunmow CM6 1DN
T: (01371) 874627
F: (01371) 874627

Homelye Farm ♦♦♦♦
Homelye Chase, Braintree Road, Great Dunmow CM6 3AW
T: (01371) 872127
F: (01371) 876428
E: homelye@supanet.com
I: www.homelyefarm.co.uk

3 Jubilee Court ♦♦♦♦
Great Dunmow CM6 1DY
T: (01371) 878403

Mallards ♦♦♦♦
Star Lane, Great Dunmow CM6 1AY
T: (01371) 872641
F: (01371) 872172
E: millersmallardsdunmow@tesco.net

Rose Cottage ♦♦♦♦
Pharisee Green, Great Dunmow CM6 1JN
T: (01371) 872254

GREAT ELLINGHAM Norfolk

Home Cottage Farm ♦♦♦
Penhill Road, Great Ellingham, Attleborough NR17 1LS
T: (01953) 483734
E: royandmaureen@mail.com

Manor Farm ♦♦♦♦ SILVER AWARD
Hingham Road, Great Ellingham, Attleborough NR17 1JE
T: (01953) 453388
F: (01953) 453388
E: rivett.and.son@farmline.com

GREAT EVERSDEN Cambridgeshire

Red House Farm ♦♦♦♦♦
44 High Street, Great Eversden, Cambridge CB3 7HW
T: (01223) 262154
F: (01223) 264875
E: pbgtebbit@farmersweekly.net
I: www.redhousefarmuk.com

GREAT HOCKHAM Norfolk

Manor Farm Bed & Breakfast ♦♦♦♦
Manor Farm, Vicarage Road, Great Hockham, Thetford IP24 1PE
T: (01953) 498204
F: (01953) 498204
E: manorfarm@ukf.net
I: www.bedandbreakfastsinnorfolk.co.uk

GREAT RYBURGH Norfolk

The Boar Inn ♦♦♦
Station Road, Great Ryburgh, Fakenham NR21 0DX
T: (01328) 829212
I: ourworld.compuserve.com/homepages/boar_inn

GREAT SAMPFORD Essex

Stow Farmhouse ♦♦♦♦ SILVER AWARD
High Street, Great Sampford, Saffron Walden CB10 2RG
T: (01799) 586060
F: (01799) 586060
E: joanne.barratt@lineone.net

GREAT SNORING Norfolk

Top Farm ♦♦♦♦
Thursford Road, Great Snoring, Fakenham NR21 0HW
T: (01328) 820351
F: (01328) 820140
E: davidperowne@aol.com

GREAT TEY Essex

The Old Shop ♦♦♦
Chappel Road, Great Tey, Colchester CO6 1JQ
T: (01206) 211556
F: (01206) 211556

GREAT WALDINGFIELD Suffolk

Jasmine Cottage ♦♦♦♦
The Heath, Lavenham Road, Great Waldingfield, Sudbury CO10 0RN
T: (01787) 374665
I: www.jasminecottage-b-and-b.co.uk

GREAT WALSINGHAM Norfolk

Eastgate Farm Rating Applied For
Great Walsingham NR22 6AB
T: (01328) 820028
F: (01328) 821100

Port Hole Cottage ♦♦♦♦
Hindringham Road, Great Walsingham NR22 6DR
T: (01328) 820157

GREAT WILBRAHAM Cambridgeshire

Kettles Cottage ♦♦♦
30 High Street, Great Wilbraham, Cambridge CB1 5JD
T: (01223) 880801
E: kettlecottage@btopenworld.com

GREAT YARMOUTH Norfolk

Barnard House ♦♦♦♦ SILVER AWARD
2 Barnard Crescent, Great Yarmouth NR30 4DR
T: (01493) 855139
F: (01493) 843143
E: barnardhouse@btinternet.com
I: www.barnardhouse.com

The Bromley Hotel ♦♦
63 Apsley Road, Great Yarmouth NR30 2HG
T: (01493) 842321
F: (01493) 842322
E: thebromleyhotel@tiscali.co.uk
I: www.smoothhound.co.uk/hotels/bromleyhotel

Carlton Hotel ♦♦♦
Marine Parade, Great Yarmouth NR30 3JE
T: (01493) 855234
F: (01493) 852220
I: www.shearingsholidays.com

Cleasewood Private Hotel ♦♦♦
55 Wellesley Road, Great Yarmouth NR30 1EX
T: (01493) 843960

Concorde Private Hotel ♦♦♦
84 North Denes Road, Great Yarmouth NR30 4LW
T: (01493) 843709
F: (01493) 843709
E: concordeyarmouth@hotmail.com
I: www.concorde-hotel.co.uk

The Dragons Rest ♦♦
25 St Georges Road, Great Yarmouth NR30 2JT
T: (01493) 850676
F: (01493) 850676

The Edwardian Hotel ♦♦♦
18-20 Crown Road, Great Yarmouth NR30 2JN
T: (01493) 856482
E: julienicol55@hotmail.com
I: www.theedwardianhotel.co.uk

Hadleigh Gables Hotel ♦♦♦
6-7 North Drive, Great Yarmouth NR30 1ED
T: (01493) 843078
F: (01493) 843078
E: mike@hadleigh-gables.co.uk
I: www.hadleigh-gables.co.uk

The Haven Hotel ♦♦♦♦
78 Marine Parade, Great Yarmouth NR30 2DH
T: (01493) 850001

Midland Hotel ♦♦♦
7-9 Wellesley Road, Great Yarmouth NR30 2AP
T: (01493) 330046
F: (01493) 330046

Royston House ♦♦
11 Euston Road, Great Yarmouth NR30 1DY
T: (01493) 844680
F: (01493) 844680
E: roystonhotel@greatyarmouth.freeserve.co.uk

The Ryecroft ◆◆◆
91 North Denes Road, Great Yarmouth NR30 4LW
T: (01493) 844015
F: (01493) 856096
E: TheRyecroft@aol.com
I: www.ryecroft-guesthouse.co.uk

Sandy Acres ◆◆◆
80-81 Salisbury Road, Great Yarmouth NR30 4LB
T: (01493) 856553
E: sandyacres@talk21.com
I: www.sandyacres.co.uk

Silverstone House ◆◆◆
29 Wellesley Road, Great Yarmouth NR30 1EU
T: (01493) 844862

Spindrift Hotel ◆◆◆
36 Wellesley Road, Great Yarmouth NR30 1EU
T: (01493) 843772
E: bradleys@bt.internet.com

Sunnydene Hotel ◆◆◆
83 North Denes Road, Great Yarmouth NR30 4LW
T: (01493) 843554
F: (01493) 332391
E: sunnydenehotel@btopenworld.com
I: www.sunnydenehotel.co.uk

Trotwood Private Hotel ◆◆◆
2 North Drive, Great Yarmouth NR30 1ED
T: (01493) 843971
E: richard@trotwood.fsbusiness.co.uk
I: www.trotwood.fsbusiness.co.uk

The Waverley Hotel ◆◆◆
32-37 Princes Road, Great Yarmouth NR30 2DG
T: (01493) 842508
F: (01493) 842508
E: malcolm@waverley-hotel.co.uk
I: www.waverley-hotel.co.uk

GRESSENHALL
Norfolk

Wood Hill
◆◆◆◆◆ SILVER AWARD
Gressenhall, East Dereham NR19 2NR
T: (01362) 699186
F: (01362) 699291
E: tania.bullard@btopenworld.com

GRIMSTON
Norfolk

The Bell Inn ◆◆◆◆
1 Gayton Road, Grimston, King's Lynn PE32 1BG
T: (01485) 601156

HADLEIGH
Suffolk

Edgehall Hotel ◆◆◆◆◆
2 High Street, Hadleigh, Ipswich IP7 5AP
T: (01473) 822458
F: (01473) 827751
E: r.rolfe@edgehall-hotel.co.uk
I: www.edgehall-hotel.co.uk

Odds and Ends House ◆◆◆◆
131 High Street, Hadleigh, Ipswich IP7 5EJ
T: (01473) 822032
F: (01473) 829816
E: oddsandends@fsmail.net
I: www.oddsandends.org.uk

Weavers Restaurant ◆◆◆◆
25 High Street, Hadleigh, Ipswich IP7 5AG
T: (01473) 827247
F: (01473) 822805
E: cyndymiles@aol.com
I: www.weaversrestaurant.co.uk

HALESWORTH
Suffolk

The Angel Hotel ◆◆◆
Thoroughfare, Halesworth IP19 8AH
T: (01986) 873365
F: (01986) 874891
E: hotel@angel-halesworth.co.uk
I: www.angel-halesworth.co.uk

Fen-Way Guest House ◆◆◆
Fen-Way, School Lane, Halesworth IP19 8BW
T: (01986) 873574

The Huntsman and Hounds ◆◆◆
Stone Street, Spexhall, Halesworth IP19 0RN
T: (01986) 781341

HALSTEAD
Essex

The Dog Inn ◆◆◆
37 Hedingham Road, Halstead CO9 2DB
T: (01787) 477774
F: (01787) 477774

Hedingham Antiques Bed & Breakfast ◆◆◆
100 Swan Street, Sible Hedingham, Halstead CO9 3HP
T: (01787) 460360
F: (01787) 469109
E: patriciapatterson@totalise.co.uk
I: www.sudburysuffolk.com/adverts/hedinghamantiques

The Victory Inn
Rating Applied For
The Green, Wickham St Paul, Halstead CO9 2PT
T: (01787) 269364
F: (01787) 269843
E: jwe4607264@aol.com
I: www.thevictoryinn.net

HALVERGATE
Norfolk

School Lodge Country Guesthouse ◆◆◆
Marsh Road, Halvergate, Norwich NR13 3QB
T: (01493) 700111
F: (01493) 700111
E: schoollodge@uk-guesthouse.com
I: www.uk-guesthouse.com

HAPPISBURGH
Norfolk

Cliff House Guesthouse Teashop and Restaurant ◆◆◆
Beach Road, Happisburgh, Norwich NR12 0PP
T: (01692) 650775

Manor Farmhouse & Manor Barn ◆◆◆◆
Happisburgh, Norwich NR12 0SA
T: (01692) 651262
I: www.northnorfolk.co.uk/manorbarn

HARDWICK
Cambridgeshire

Wallis Farm ◆◆◆◆
98 Main Street, Hardwick, Cambridge CB3 7QU
T: (01954) 210347
F: (01954) 210988
E: wallisfarm@mcmail.com
I: www.wallisfarmhouse.co.uk

HARLESTON
Norfolk

Weston House Farm ◆◆◆◆
Mendham, Harleston IP20 0PB
T: (01986) 782206
F: (01986) 783986
E: holden@farmline.com

HARPENDEN
Hertfordshire

Hall Barn ◆◆◆◆
20 Sun Lane, Harpenden AL5 4EU
T: (01582) 769700

Holly Dene ◆◆◆◆
Bower Heath, Harpenden AL5 5EE
T: (01582) 769095
E: harriet@maylin.co.uk
I: www.sleepinharpenden.co.uk

Milton ◆◆◆
25 Milton Road, Harpenden AL5 5LA
T: (01582) 762914

HARTEST
Suffolk

The Hatch
◆◆◆◆◆ GOLD AWARD
Pilgrims Lane, Cross Green, Hartest, Bury St Edmunds IP29 4ED
T: (01284) 830226
F: (01284) 830226

HARWICH
Essex

8 Main Road
Rating Applied For
Dovercourt, Harwich CO12 3LZ
T: (01255) 502355
F: (01255) 502355

Oceanview ◆◆
86 Main Road, Dovercourt, Harwich CO12 3LH
T: (01255) 554078
F: (01255) 554519
E: oceanview@dovercourt.org.uk
I: www.oceanview.fsbusiness.co.uk

Paston Lodge ◆◆◆
1 Una Road, Parkeston, Harwich CO12 4PP
T: (01255) 551390

St Christopher's Place ◆◆◆
62 Church Street, Harwich CO12 3DS
T: (01255) 507995
F: (01255) 507995

The Stingray Freehouse ◆◆◆
56 Church Street, Harwich CO12 3DS
T: (01255) 503507

Woodview Cottage
◆◆◆◆ SILVER AWARD
Wrabness Road, Ramsey, Harwich CO12 5ND
T: (01255) 886413
E: anne@woodview-cottage.co.uk
I: www.woodview-cottage.co.uk

HATFIELD BROAD OAK
Essex

The Cottage ◆◆◆
Dunmow Road, Hatfield Broad Oak, Bishop's Stortford CM22 7JJ
T: (01279) 718230
E: elizabeth.britton@virgin.net

HATFIELD HEATH
Essex

The Barn ◆◆◆
Great Heath Farm, Chelmsford Road, Hatfield Heath, Bishop's Stortford CM22 7BQ
T: (01279) 739093

Friars Farm ◆◆◆◆
Hatfield Heath, Bishop's Stortford CM22 7AP
T: (01279) 730244
F: (01279) 730244

Hunters' Meet Restaurant and Hotel ◆◆◆◆
Chelmsford Road, Hatfield Heath, Bishop's Stortford CM22 7BQ
T: (01279) 730549
F: (01279) 731587
E: info@huntersmeet.co.uk
I: www.huntersmeet.co.uk

Oaklands ◆◆◆◆
Hatfield Heath, Bishop's Stortford CM22 7AD
T: (01279) 730240

HATFIELD PEVEREL
Essex

The Swan Inn ◆◆◆
The Street, Hatfield Peverel, Chelmsford CM3 2DW
T: (01245) 380238
F: (01245) 380238

HAUGHLEY
Suffolk

Red House Farm ◆◆◆◆
Station Road, Haughley, Stowmarket IP14 3QP
T: (01449) 673323
F: (01449) 675413
E: mary@noy1.fsnet.co.uk
I: www.farmstayanglia.co.uk

HAUXTON
Cambridgeshire

Dorset House
Rating Applied For
35 Newton Road, Little Shelford, Cambridge CB2 5HL
T: (01223) 844440
F: (01223) 844440
E: dorsethouse@msn.com
I: www.smoothhound.co.uk/hotels/dorsethouse

HEACHAM
Norfolk

The Grove ◆◆◆◆
Collins Lane, Heacham, King's Lynn PE31 7DZ
T: (01485) 570513
E: tm.shannon@virgin.net
I: www.thegrovebedandbreakfast.com

Holly House ♦♦♦
3 Broadway, Heacham, King's Lynn PE31 7DF
T: (01485) 572935

Malthouse Farm ♦♦♦♦
Cheney Hill, Heacham, King's Lynn PE31 7EQ
T: (01485) 571213
F: (01485) 572028

Saint Annes Guesthouse ♦♦♦
53 Neville Road, Heacham, King's Lynn PE31 7HB
T: (01485) 570021
F: (01485) 570021
I: www.smoothhound.co.uk/

HELLESDON
Norfolk

Cairdean ♦♦♦♦
71 Middletons Lane, Hellesdon, Norwich NR6 5NS
T: (01603) 419041
F: (01603) 423643
E: cairdean-b.b@ukgateway.net
I: www.cairdean.co.uk

The Old Corner Shop Guesthouse ♦♦♦
26 Cromer Road, Hellesdon, Norwich NR6 6LZ
T: (01603) 419000
F: (01603) 419000
E: theoldcornershop@aol.com

HEMEL HEMPSTEAD
Hertfordshire

47 Crescent Road ♦♦
Hemel Hempstead HP2 4AJ
T: (01442) 255137

The Red House Bed & Breakfast ♦♦♦
34 Alexandra Road, Hemel Hempstead HP2 5BS
T: (01442) 246665

HETHEL
Norfolk

Old Thorn Barn
♦♦♦♦ SILVER AWARD
Corporation Farm, Wymondham Road, Hethel, Norwich NR14 8EU
T: (01953) 607785
F: (08707) 066409
E: enquiries@oldthornbarn.co.uk
I: www.oldthornbarn.co.uk

HETHERSETT
Norfolk

Magnolia House ♦♦♦
Cromwell Close, Hethersett, Norwich NR9 3HD
T: (01603) 810749
F: (01603) 810749

HEVINGHAM
Norfolk

Marsham Arms Inn ♦♦♦♦
Holt Road, Hevingham, Norwich NR10 5NP
T: (01603) 754268
F: (01603) 754839
E: nigelbradley@marshamarms.co.uk
I: www.marshamarms.co.uk

HEYDON
Cambridgeshire

The End Cottage
Rating Applied For
Fowlmere Road, Heydon, SG8 8PZ
T: (01763) 838212

HICKLING
Norfolk

Black Horse Cottage ♦♦♦♦
The Green, Hickling, Norwich NR12 0YA
T: (01692) 598691
F: (01692) 598691
E: yvonne.pugh@lullingstone.freeserve.co.uk

Hickling Broad Bed & Breakfast ♦♦♦♦
Paddock Cottage, Staithe Road, Hickling, Norwich NR12 0YJ
T: (01692) 598259

HIGH EASTER
Essex

Maidens Farm ♦♦♦
High Easter, Chelmsford CM3 1HU
T: (01245) 231515
F: (01245) 231075
E: katherine@maidensfarm.com
I: www.maidensfarm.com

HIGH KELLING
Norfolk

Olive Tree Breaks ♦♦♦♦
Lynton, Vale Road, High Kelling, Holt NR25 6RA
T: (01263) 712933
E: lynton@highkelling.fsnet.co.uk
I: www.olivetreebreaks.co.uk

HILGAY
Norfolk

Crosskeys Riverside House ♦♦♦
Bridge Street, Hilgay, Downham Market PE38 0LD
T: (01366) 387777
F: (01366) 387777

HINDRINGHAM
Norfolk

Field House
♦♦♦♦♦ GOLD AWARD
Moorgate Road, Hindringham, Fakenham NR21 0PT
T: (01328) 878726
F: (01328) 878955
E: stay@fieldhousehindringham.co.uk
I: www.fieldhousehindringham.co.uk

HINTLESHAM
Suffolk

College Farm
♦♦♦♦ SILVER AWARD
Back Road, Hintlesham, Ipswich IP8 3NT
T: (01473) 652253
F: (01473) 652253
E: bryce1@agripro.co.uk
I: www.smoothhound.co.uk/hotels/collegefarm

HITCHIN
Hertfordshire

The Greyhound ♦♦♦
London Road, St Ippolyts, Hitchin SG4 7NL
T: (01462) 440989

The Lord Lister Hotel ♦♦♦
1 Park Street, Hitchin SG4 9AH
T: (01462) 432712
F: (01462) 438506
E: info@lordlisterhotel.co.uk
I: www.lordlisterhotel.co.uk

HOLBROOK
Suffolk

Highfield
♦♦♦♦ GOLD AWARD
Harkstead Road, Holbrook, Ipswich IP9 2RA
T: (01473) 328250
F: (01473) 328250

HOLKHAM
Norfolk

Peterstone Cutting Bed & Breakfast ♦♦♦♦
Peterstone Cutting, Peterstone, Holkham, Wells-next-the-Sea NR23 1RR
T: (01328) 730171
F: (01328) 730171
E: thefreesiders@yahoo.co.uk

HOLME NEXT THE SEA
Norfolk

Meadow Springs ♦♦♦♦
15 Eastgate Road, Holme next the Sea, Hunstanton PE36 6LL
T: (01485) 525279

Seagate House ♦♦♦♦
60 Beach Road, Seagate House, Holme next the Sea, Hunstanton PE36 6LG
T: (01485) 525510

HOLT
Norfolk

Felbrigg Lodge
♦♦♦♦♦ GOLD AWARD
Aylmerton, Holt NR11 8RA
T: (01263) 837588
F: (01263) 838012
E: info@felbrigglodge.co.uk
I: www.felbrigglodge.co.uk

Hempstead Hall ♦♦♦♦
Holt NR25 6TN
T: (01263) 712224
F: (01263) 710137
I: www.broadland.com/hempsteadhall

Lawns Hotel ♦♦♦♦
Station Road, Holt NR25 6BS
T: (01263) 713390
F: (01263) 710642
E: info@lawnshotel.co.uk
I: www.lawnshotel.co.uk

Three Corners ♦♦♦
12 Kelling Close, Holt NR25 6RU
T: (01263) 713389
E: roncox@supanet.com

The White Cottage ♦♦♦
Norwich Road, Holt NR25 6SW
T: (01263) 713353

HOLTON
Suffolk

Blythwood House ♦♦♦♦
Beccles Road, Holton, Halesworth IP19 8NQ
T: (01986) 873379
F: (01986) 873379

HOLTON ST MARY
Suffolk

Stratford House ♦♦♦♦
Holton St Mary, Colchester CO7 6NT
T: (01206) 298246
F: (01206) 298246
E: fjs.stratho@brutus.go-plus.net

HONINGTON
Suffolk

North View Guesthouse ♦♦♦
North View, Malting Row, Honington, Bury St Edmunds IP31 1RE
T: (01359) 269423
F: (01359) 269423

The Willow Bed & Breakfast ♦♦♦
The Willow, Ixworth Road, Honington, Bury St Edmunds IP31 1QY
T: (01359) 269600
F: (01359) 269600
E: celialawrence@talk21.com

HORNING
Norfolk

Gable Cottage ♦♦♦♦
61 Lower Street, Horning, Norwich NR12 8AA
T: (01692) 631239
E: gablecottage61@aol.com

HORRINGER
Suffolk

12 The Elms ♦♦♦
Horringer, Bury St Edmunds IP29 5SE
T: (01284) 735400
E: neca56@onetel.net.uk

HORSEHEATH
Cambridgeshire

Chequer Cottage ♦♦♦♦
43 Streetly End, Horseheath, Cambridge CB1 6RP
T: (01223) 891522
F: (01223) 890266
E: debbie@dsills.freeserve.co.uk

HORSEY
Norfolk

The Old Chapel ♦♦♦♦
Horsey Corner, Horsey, Great Yarmouth NR29 4EH
T: (01493) 393498
F: (01493) 393498
E: enquiries@norfolkbedbreakfast.com
I: www.norfolkbedbreakfast.com

HORSTEAD
Norfolk

Beverley Farm ♦♦♦
Norwich Road, Horstead, Norwich NR12 7EH
T: (01603) 737279

HUNSTANTON
Norfolk

Burleigh Hotel ♦♦♦♦
7 Cliff Terrace, Hunstanton PE36 6DY
T: (01485) 533080

Cambridge House ♦♦♦♦
32 Westgate, Hunstanton PE36 5AL
T: (01485) 535014
F: (01485) 534313

Cobblers Cottage ♦♦♦
3 Wodehouse Road, Old Hunstanton, Hunstanton PE36 6JD
T: (01485) 534036
E: lesley.cobblerscottage@btinternet.com

The Gables ♦♦♦♦
28 Austin Street, Hunstanton
PE36 6AW
T: (01485) 532514
E: bbatthegables@aol.com
I: www.thegableshunstanton.co.uk

Garganey House ♦♦♦
46 Northgate, Hunstanton
PE36 6DR
T: (01485) 533269
E: Garganey1.@f.s.net.co.uk

Gate Lodge ♦♦♦♦
2 Westgate, Hunstanton
PE36 5AL
T: (01485) 533549
F: (01485) 533361
E: lynn@gatelodge-guesthouse.co.uk
I: www.gatelodge-guesthouse.co.uk

Glenberis Bed & Breakfast ♦♦♦♦
6 St Edmunds Avenue,
Hunstanton PE36 6AY
T: (01485) 533663
F: (01485) 533663
E: glenberis.hunstanton@ntlworld.com

Kiama Cottage Guesthouse ♦♦♦
23 Austin Street, Hunstanton
PE36 6AN
T: (01485) 533615
E: kiamacottage@btopenworld.com

Lakeside ♦♦♦
Waterworks Road, Old
Hunstanton, Hunstanton
PE36 6JE
T: (01485) 533763

The Linksway Country House Hotel ♦♦♦♦
Golf Course Road, Old
Hunstanton, Hunstanton
PE36 6JE
T: (01485) 532209
F: (01485) 532209
E: linksway-hotel@totalize.co.uk
I: www.linkswayhotel.com

Miramar Guesthouse ♦♦♦
7 Boston Square, Hunstanton
PE36 6DT
T: (01485) 532902
I: www.miramar.co.uk

Neptune Inn ♦♦♦
85 Old Hunstanton Road, Old
Hunstanton, Hunstanton
PE36 6HZ
T: (01485) 532122
E: neptune-inn@supanet.com

Peacock House ♦♦♦♦
28 Park Road, Hunstanton
PE36 5BY
T: (01485) 534551
F: (01485) 534551
E: peacockhouse@onetel.net.uk
I: web.onetel.net.uk/~peacockhouse

Queensbury House ♦♦♦
18 Glebe Avenue, Hunstanton
PE36 6BS
T: (01485) 534320

Rosamaly Guesthouse ♦♦♦
14 Glebe Avenue, Hunstanton
PE36 6BS
T: (01485) 534187
E: vacancies@rosamaly.co.uk
I: www.rosamaly.co.uk

The Shelbrooke Hotel ♦♦♦
9 Cliff Terrace, Hunstanton
PE36 6DY
T: (01485) 532289
F: (01485) 535385
I: www.shelbrooke.force9.co.uk

Sunningdale Hotel ♦♦♦♦
3-5 Avenue Road, Hunstanton
PE36 5BW
T: (01485) 532562
F: (01485) 534915
E: reception@sunningdalehotel.com
I: www.sunningdalehotel.com

Sunset View ♦♦♦♦
3 Alexandra Road, Hunstanton
PE36 5BT
T: (01485) 535246

HUNTINGDON
Cambridgeshire

Prince of Wales ♦♦♦♦
Potton Road, Hilton,
Huntingdon PE28 9NG
T: (01480) 830257
F: (01480) 830257
E: princeofwales.hilton@talk21.com

ICKLETON
Cambridgeshire

Hessett Grange
Rating Applied For
60 Frogge Street, Ickleton,
Saffron Walden CB10 1SH
T: (01799) 530300

Shepherds Cottage ♦♦♦♦
Grange Road, Ickleton, Saffron
Walden CB10 1TA
T: (01799) 531171
E: jcase@nascr.net
I: www.shepherds-cottage.co.uk

INGATESTONE
Essex

Handley Green Bed & Breakfast ♦♦♦
Handley Green House, Handley
Green, Ingatestone CM4 0QB
T: (01277) 356052
E: handleygreen@btinternet.com

INGOLDISTHORPE
Norfolk

Pencob House
♦♦♦♦ SILVER AWARD
56 Hill Road, Ingoldisthorpe,
King's Lynn PE31 6NZ
T: (01485) 543882
F: (01485) 543882
E: swans.norfolk@virgin.net
I: www.swanholidays.co.uk

IPSWICH
Suffolk

Carlton Hotel ♦♦♦
41-43 Berners Street, Ipswich
IP1 3LT
T: (01473) 254955
F: (01473) 429811
E: carltonhotel3@hotmail.com

The Gatehouse Hotel Ltd
♦♦♦♦♦ SILVER AWARD
799 Old Norwich Road, Ipswich
IP1 6LH
T: (01473) 741897
F: (01473) 744236
E: info@gatehousehotel.co.uk
I: www.gatehousehotel.co.uk

Lattice Lodge Guest House
♦♦♦♦ SILVER AWARD
499 Woodbridge Road, Ipswich
IP4 4EP
T: (01473) 712474
F: (01473) 272239
E: lattice.lodge@btinternet.com
I: www.latticelodge.co.uk

Redholme Guesthouse ♦♦♦♦
52 Ivry Street, Ipswich IP1 3QP
T: (01473) 250018
F: (01473) 238174
E: john@redholmeipswich.co.uk
I: www.redholmeipswich.co.uk

Sidegate Guesthouse
♦♦♦♦ SILVER AWARD
121 Sidegate Lane, Ipswich
IP4 4JB
T: (01473) 728714
F: (01473) 728714
E: sidegate.guesthouse@btinternet.com

Stebbings ♦♦♦♦
Back Lane, Washbrook, Ipswich
IP8 3JA
T: (01473) 730216
F: (07989) 061088
E: caroline@foxworld.fsnet.co.uk

KEDINGTON
Suffolk

The White House
♦♦♦♦♦ GOLD AWARD
Silver Street, Kedington,
Haverhill CB9 7QG
T: (01440) 707731
F: (01440) 707731
E: tobybarclay@natsparks.co.uk
I: www.thewhitehouse.ukf.net

KELVEDON
Essex

Highfields Farm ♦♦♦♦
Kelvedon, Colchester CO5 9BJ
T: (01376) 570334
F: (01376) 570334
E: HighfieldsFarm@farmersweekly.net
I: www.highfieldsfarm.co.uk

3 Swan Street ♦♦♦
Kelvedon, Colchester CO5 9NG
T: (01376) 572457
F: (01376) 573768
E: dnspiers@lineone.net

KERSEY
Suffolk

Red House Farm ♦♦♦
Wickerstreet Green, Kersey,
Ipswich IP7 6EY
T: (01787) 210245

KETTLEBASTON
Suffolk

Box Tree Farm ♦♦♦
Kettlebaston, Ipswich IP7 7PZ
T: (01449) 741318
F: (01449) 741318

KETTLEBURGH
Suffolk

Church Farm ♦♦♦
Kettleburgh, Woodbridge
IP13 7LF
T: (01728) 723532
E: jbater@suffolkonline.net

KING'S LYNN
Norfolk

The Beeches Guesthouse ♦♦♦
2 Guanock Terrace, King's Lynn
PE30 5QT
T: (01553) 766577
F: (01553) 776664

Fairlight Lodge ♦♦♦♦
79 Goodwins Road, King's Lynn
PE30 5PE
T: (01553) 762234
F: (01553) 770280
E: enquiries@fairlightlodge-online.co.uk
I: www.fairlightlodge-online.co.uk

Maranatha Guesthouse ♦♦♦
115-117 Gaywood Road, King's
Lynn PE30 2PU
T: (01553) 774596
F: (01553) 763747
E: maranthaguesthouse@yahoo.co.uk

Marsh Farm ♦♦♦♦
Wolferton, King's Lynn
PE31 6HB
T: (01485) 540265
F: (01485) 543143
E: info@marshfarmbedandbreakfast.co.uk
I: www.marshfarmbedandbreakfast.co.uk

The Old Rectory ♦♦♦♦
33 Goodwins Road, King's Lynn
PE30 5QX
T: (01553) 768544
E: clive@theoldrectory-kingslynn.com
I: www.theoldrectory-kingslynn.com

The Victory Inn ♦♦♦
Main Road, Clenchwarton,
King's Lynn PE34 4AQ
T: (01553) 660682
E: trevorswift8@btopenworld.com

KINGS LANGLEY
Hertfordshire

67 Hempstead Road ♦♦♦
Kings Langley WD4 8BS
T: (01923) 400453
F: (01923) 400453
E: macpherson1@ntlworld.com

Woodcote House ♦♦♦♦
7 The Grove, Whippendell,
Chipperfield, Kings Langley
WD4 9JF
T: (01923) 262077
F: (01923) 266198
E: leveridge@btinternet.com

KIRBY CANE
Norfolk

Butterley House ♦♦♦
Leet Hill Farm, Kirby Cane,
Bungay NR35 2HJ
T: (01508) 518301
F: (01508) 518301

KNAPTON
Norfolk

Cornerstone House ♦♦♦♦
The Street, Knapton, North Walsham NR28 0AD
T: (01263) 722884
E: evescornerstone@hotmail.com

KNEBWORTH
Hertfordshire

Goldhill
Rating Applied For
10 Deards End Lane, Knebworth SG3 6NL
T: (01438) 813230
F: (01438) 813230

LANDBEACH
Cambridgeshire

The Orchard ♦♦♦
67 High Sreet, Landbeach, Cambridge CB4 8DR
T: (01223) 860178

LANGHAM
Essex

Oak Apple Farm ♦♦♦♦
Greyhound Hill, Langham, Colchester CO4 5QF
T: (01206) 272234
E: rosie@oakapplefarm.fsnet.co.uk
I: www.smoothhound.co.uk/hotels/oak.html

LAVENHAM
Suffolk

Anchor House
♦♦♦♦ SILVER AWARD
27 Prentice Street, Lavenham, Sudbury CO10 9RD
T: (01787) 249018
E: suewade1@aol.com
I: www.anchorhouse.co.uk

Angel Gallery ♦♦♦♦
17 Market Place, Lavenham, Sudbury CO10 9QZ
T: (01787) 248417
F: (01787) 248417
E: angel-gallery@gofornet.co.uk
I: www.lavenham.co.uk/angelgallery

Brett Farm ♦♦♦♦
The Common, Lavenham, Sudbury CO10 9PG
T: (01787) 248533
E: brettfarm@aol.co.uk
I: www.brettfarm.com

Guinea House ♦♦♦♦
Lavenham, Sudbury CO10 9RH
T: (01787) 249046
F: (01787) 249619
E: gdelucy@aol.com
I: www.guineahouse.co.uk

Hill House Farm
♦♦♦♦ GOLD AWARD
Preston St Mary, Lavenham, Sudbury CO10 9LT
T: (01787) 247571
F: (01787) 247571

Lavenham Great House Hotel
♦♦♦♦ SILVER AWARD
Market Place, Lavenham, Sudbury CO10 9QZ
T: (01787) 247431
F: (01787) 248007
E: info@greathouse.co.uk
I: www.greathouse.co.uk

Lavenham Priory
♦♦♦♦♦ GOLD AWARD
Water Street, Lavenham, Sudbury CO10 9RW
T: (01787) 247404
F: (01787) 248472
E: mail@lavenhampriory.co.uk
I: www.lavenhampriory.co.uk

Mortimer's Barn
♦♦♦♦ SILVER AWARD
Preston St Mary, Lavenham, Sudbury CO10 9ND
T: (01787) 248231
F: (01787) 248075
E: mervyn@mortimers.freeserve.co.uk
I: www.diggins.co.uk/mortimers/

The Old Convent ♦♦♦♦
The Street, Kettlebaston, Ipswich IP7 7QA
T: (01449) 741557
E: holidays@kettlebaston.fsnet.co.uk
I: www.kettlebaston.fsnet.co.uk

The Red House ♦♦♦♦
29 Bolton Street, Lavenham, Sudbury CO10 9RG
T: (01787) 248074
I: www.lavenham.co.uk/redhouse

Sunrise Cottage ♦♦♦
32 The Glebe, Sudbury Road, Lavenham, Sudbury CO10 9SN
T: (01787) 248439
E: deallen@talk21.com or derekeallen@hotmail.com

LAXFIELD
Suffolk

The Villa Stables ♦♦♦♦
The Villa, High Street, Laxfield, Woodbridge IP13 8DU
T: (01986) 798019
F: (01986) 798155
E: laxfieldleisure@talk21.com

LEIGH-ON-SEA
Essex

Grand Hotel ♦♦♦
The Broadway, Leigh-on-Sea SS9 1PJ
T: (01702) 710768
F: (01702) 716709
E: roymainman@aol.com

Undercliff B & B ♦♦♦
52 Undercliff Gardens, Leigh-on-Sea SS9 1EA
T: (01702) 474984

LEISTON
Suffolk

Field End
♦♦♦♦ SILVER AWARD
1 Kings Road, Leiston IP16 4DA
T: (01728) 833527
F: (01728) 833527
E: pwright@fieldend-guesthouse.co.uk
I: www.fieldend-guesthouse.co.uk

LEVINGTON
Suffolk

Lilac Cottage ♦♦♦♦
Levington Green, Levington, Ipswich IP10 0LE
T: (01473) 659509

LINDSELL
Essex

The Old Vicarage ♦♦♦♦
Church End, Lindsell, Great Dunmow CM6 3QR
T: (01371) 870349
E: fletcher.oldvicarage@btopenworld.com

LITTLE BADDOW
Essex

Chestnuts ♦♦♦
Chestnut Walk, Little Baddow, Danbury, Chelmsford CM3 4SP
T: (01245) 223905

LITTLE BEALINGS
Suffolk

Timbers ♦♦♦
Martlesham Road, Little Bealings, Woodbridge IP13 6LY
T: (01473) 622713

LITTLE CANFIELD
Essex

Canfield Moat
♦♦♦♦♦ GOLD AWARD
High Cross Lane West, Little Canfield, Great Dunmow CM6 1TD
T: (01371) 872565
F: (01371) 876264
E: falk@canfieldmoat.co.uk
I: www.canfieldmoat.co.uk

LITTLE DOWNHAM
Cambridgeshire

Bury House Bed & Breakfast ♦♦♦
11 Main Street, Little Downham, Ely CB6 2ST
T: (01353) 698766

LITTLE LEIGHS
Essex

Little Leighs Hall ♦♦♦♦
Little Leighs, Chelmsford CM3 1PG
T: (01245) 361462
F: (01245) 361462

LITTLE SAMPFORD
Essex

Bush Farm ♦♦♦
Bush Lane, Little Sampford, Saffron Walden CB10 2RY
T: (01799) 586636
F: (01799) 586636
E: aimreso@aol.com

Woodlands
♦♦♦♦ SILVER AWARD
Hawkins Hill, Little Sampford, Saffron Walden CB10 2QW
T: (01371) 810862
E: lynne.jameson@amserve.net

LITTLE WALDINGFIELD
Suffolk

The Swan Inn ♦♦♦
The Street, Little Waldingfield, Sudbury CO10 0SQ
T: (01787) 248584

LITTLE WALSINGHAM
Norfolk

The Black Lion Hotel ♦♦♦♦
Friday Market Place, Little Walsingham, Walsingham NR22 6DB
T: (01328) 820235
F: (01328) 821406
E: blacklionwalsingham@btinternet.com
I: www.blacklionwalsingham.com

The Old Bakehouse
♦♦♦♦ SILVER AWARD
33 High Street, Little Walsingham, Walsingham NR22 6BZ
T: (01328) 820454
F: (01328) 820454
E: chris.padley@btopenworld.com

St David's House ♦♦
Friday Market, Little Walsingham, Walsingham NR22 6BY
T: (01328) 820633
E: stdavidshouse@amserve.net
I: www.stilwell.co.uk

LITTLE WALTHAM
Essex

Little Belsteads ♦♦♦♦
Back Lane, Little Waltham, Chelmsford CM3 3PP
T: (01245) 360249
F: (01245) 360996

Windmill Motor Inn ♦♦♦
Chatham Green, Little Waltham, Chelmsford CM3 3LE
T: (01245) 361188
F: (01245) 362992

LODDON
Norfolk

Hall Green Farm B&B ♦♦♦♦
Norton Road, Loddon, Norwich NR14 6DT
T: (01508) 522039
F: (01508) 522079
E: hallgreenfarm@hotmail.com
I: www.geocities.com/hallgreenfarm

Poplar Farm ♦♦♦♦
Sisland, Loddon, Norwich NR14 6EF
T: (01508) 520706
E: milly@hemmant.myhome.org.uk
I: www.hemmant.myhome.org.uk

LONDON COLNEY
Hertfordshire

The Conifers ♦♦♦
42 Thamesdale, London Colney, St Albans AL2 1TL
T: (01727) 823622

LONG MELFORD
Suffolk

The Crown Hotel ♦♦♦
Hall Street, Long Melford, Sudbury CO10 9JL
T: (01787) 377666
F: (01787) 379005
E: quincey@crownmelford.fsnet.co.uk

George & Dragon ♦♦♦
Hall Street, Long Melford, Sudbury CO10 9JB
T: (01787) 371285
F: (01787) 312428
E: geodrg@msn.com

LONG STRATTON
Norfolk

Greenacres Farm ♦♦♦♦
Woodgreen, Long Stratton, Norwich NR15 2RR
T: (01508) 530261
F: (01508) 530261
E: greenacresfarm@tinyworld.co.uk

LOUGHTON
Essex

Forest Edge ♦♦♦
61 York Hill, Loughton IG10 1HZ
T: (020) 8508 9834
F: (020) 8281 1894
E: arthur@catterallarthur.fsnet.co.uk

9 Garden Way ♦♦♦
Loughton IG10 2SF
T: (020) 8508 6134

LOWER LAYHAM
Suffolk

Badgers ♦♦♦♦
Rands Road, Lower Layham, Ipswich IP7 5RW
T: (01473) 823396
E: catbadgers@aol.com
I: www.badgersbed.co.uk

LOWESTOFT
Suffolk

Albany Hotel ♦♦♦♦
400 London Road South, Lowestoft NR33 0BQ
T: (01502) 574394
F: (01502) 581198
E: geoffrey.ward@btclick.com
I: www.albanyhotel-lowestoft.co.uk

Church Farm ♦♦♦♦♦
Corton, Lowestoft NR32 5HX
T: (01502) 730359
F: (01502) 733426
E: medw149227@aol.com
I: www.churchfarmcorton.co.uk

Elizabeth Denes Hotel ♦♦♦
Corton Road, Lowestoft NR32 4PL
T: (01502) 500679
F: (01502) 565774
E: elizabeth.denes@elizabethhotels.co.uk
I: www.elizabethhotels.co.uk

Homelea Guest House ♦♦♦
33 Marine Parade, Lowestoft NR33 0QN
T: (01502) 511640

Longshore Guesthouse ♦♦♦♦
7 Wellington Esplanade, Lowestoft NR33 0QQ
T: (01502) 565037
F: (01502) 582032
E: SandraNolan@btconnect.com

Oak Farm ♦♦♦
Market Lane, Blundeston, Lowestoft NR32 5AP
T: (01502) 731622

St Catherines House ♦♦♦
186 Denmark Road, Lowestoft NR32 2EN
T: (01502) 500951

The Sandcastle ♦♦♦
35 Marine Parade, Lowestoft NR33 0QN
T: (01502) 511799
F: (01502) 574720
E: susie@thesandcastle.co.uk
I: www.thesandcastle.co.uk

LUTON
Bedfordshire

Adara Lodge ♦♦♦
539 Hitchin Road, Luton LU2 7UL
T: (01582) 731361

The Pines Hotel
Rating Applied For
10 Marsh Road, Luton LU3 3NH
T: (01582) 651130
F: (01582) 615182
E: pineshotelluton@aol.com
I: www.pineshotel.com

44 Skelton Close ♦♦
Barton Hills, Luton LU3 4HF
T: (01582) 495205
F: (01582) 495205

MALDON
Essex

Anchor Guesthouse ♦♦♦
7 Church Street, Maldon CM9 5HW
T: (01621) 855706
F: (01621) 850405

Crystal Motel & Cafe/Restaurant ♦♦
154 High Street, Maldon CM9 5BX
T: (01621) 853667
F: (01621) 853667

Jolly Sailor ♦♦
Church Street, Maldon CM9 5HP
T: (01621) 853463
F: (01621) 840253

The Limes ♦♦♦♦
21 Market Hill, Maldon CM9 4PZ
T: (01621) 850350
F: (01621) 850350
E: thelimes@ukonline.co.uk
I: www.smoothhound.co.uk

Little Owls ♦♦♦
Post Office Road, Woodham Mortimer, Maldon CM9 6ST
T: (01245) 224355
F: (01245) 224355
E: the.bushes@virgin.net

4 Lodge Road ♦♦♦
Maldon CM9 6HW
T: (01621) 858736

Star House Bed & Breakfast ♦♦♦
72 Wantz Road, Maldon CM9 5DE
T: (01621) 853527
F: (01621) 850635
E: star.house@talk21.com

The Swan Hotel ♦♦♦
73 High Street, Maldon CM9 5EP
T: (01621) 853170
F: (01621) 854490
E: info@swanhotel-maldon.co.uk
I: www.swanhotel-maldon.co.uk

Tatoi Bed & Breakfast ♦♦♦♦
31 Acacia Drive, Maldon CM9 6AW
T: (01621) 853841
E: diana.rogers@tesco.net

MANNINGTREE
Essex

Dry Dock
Rating Applied For
4 Quay Street, Manningtree CO11 1AU
T: (01206) 392620

MARCH
Cambridgeshire

Causeway Guest House ♦♦♦
6 The Causeway, March PE15 9NT
T: (01354) 650823
F: (01354) 661068

MARGARET RODING
Essex

Garnish Hall
♦♦♦♦ SILVER AWARD
Margaret Roding, CM6 1QL
T: (01245) 231209
F: (01245) 231224

Greys ♦♦♦
Ongar Road, Margaret Roding, Great Dunmow CM6 1QR
T: (01245) 231509

MARKYATE
Hertfordshire

Beechwood Home Farm ♦♦♦
Markyate, St Albans AL3 8AJ
T: (01582) 840209

MARSHAM
Norfolk

Plough Inn ♦♦♦
Old Norwich Road, Marsham, Norwich NR10 5PS
T: (01263) 735000
F: (01263) 735407
E: enquiries@ploughinnmarsham.co.uk
I: www.ploughinnmarsham.co.uk

MARSTON MORETAINE
Bedfordshire

Aldermans Tanglewood B&B ♦♦♦
35 Upper Shelton Road, Upper Shelton, Marston Moretaine, Bedford MK43 0LT
T: (01234) 768584
F: (01234) 764373
E: alanalder@freenetname.co.uk

Twin Lodge ♦♦♦
177 Lower Shelton Road, Lower Shelton, Marston Moretaine, Bedford MK43 0LP
T: (01234) 767597
F: (01234) 767597
E: pwillsmore@waitrose.com
I: www.twinlodge.co.uk

The White Cottage
♦♦♦♦ SILVER AWARD
Marston Hill, Marston Moretaine, Cranfield, Bedford MK43 0QJ
T: (01234) 751766
F: (01234) 757823
E: stay@thewhitecottage.fsbusiness.co.uk
I: www.thewhitecottage.net

MARTHAM
Norfolk

3 Nursery Close ♦♦♦♦
Bell Meadow, Martham, Great Yarmouth NR29 4UB
T: (01493) 740307
E: davena@vk-bedandbreakfasts.com

MELTON CONSTABLE
Norfolk

Lowes Farm ♦♦♦♦
Edgefield, Melton Constable NR24 2EX
T: (01263) 712317

MESSING
Essex

Crispin's Restaurant ♦♦♦♦
The Street, Messing, Colchester CO5 9TR
T: (01621) 815868
E: dine@crispinsrestaurant.co.uk
I: www.crispinsrestaurant.co.uk

MILDENHALL
Suffolk

Oakland House ♦♦♦
9 Mill Street, Mildenhall, Bury St Edmunds IP28 7DP
T: (01638) 717099
E: lardnerjk@btinternet.com
I: www.oaklandhouse.co.uk

MILTON BRYAN
Bedfordshire

Town Farm ♦♦♦♦
Milton Bryan, Milton Keynes MK17 9HS
T: (01525) 210001
F: (01525) 210001

MOULTON
Suffolk

Flint End House ♦♦♦
6 The Street, Moulton, Newmarket CB8 8RZ
T: (01638) 750966
E: hugo.bolus@awgps.com

37 Newmarket Road ♦♦♦♦
Moulton, Newmarket CB8 8QP
T: (01638) 750362
E: dkbowes@waitrose.com

MUCH HADHAM
Hertfordshire

1 Hall Cottages ♦♦♦
High Street, Much Hadham SG10 6BZ
T: (01279) 842640
E: marcusian@aol.com

MUNDESLEY
Norfolk

The Grange ♦♦♦♦
High Street, Mundesley, Norwich NR11 8JL
T: (01263) 722977

Overcliff Lodge ♦♦♦
46 Cromer Road, Mundesley, Norwich NR11 8DB
T: (01263) 720016
E: overcliffIodge@btinternet.com
I: www.broadland.com/overcliffIodgeguesthouse.html

MUNDFORD
Norfolk

Colveston Manor ♦♦♦♦
Colveston, Mundford, Thetford IP26 5HU
T: (01842) 878218
F: (01842) 879218
E: mail@colveston-manor.co.uk
I: www.colveston-manor.co.uk

NARBOROUGH
Norfolk

Park Cottage ♦♦♦
Narford Road, Narborough, King's Lynn PE32 1HZ
T: (01760) 337220

NAYLAND
Suffolk

Gladwins Farm ♦♦♦♦
Harpers Hill, Nayland, Colchester CO6 4NU
T: (01206) 262261
F: (01206) 263001
E: gladwinsfarm@aol.com
I: www.gladwinsfarm.co.uk

The White Hart Inn
◆◆◆◆ GOLD AWARD
High Street, Nayland, Colchester CO6 4JF
T: (01206) 263382
F: (01206) 263638
E: nayhart@aol.com
I: www.whitehart-nayland.co.uk

NEATISHEAD Norfolk

Allens Farmhouse ◆◆◆◆
School Lane, Neatishead, Norwich NR12 8BU
T: (01692) 630080
E: allensfarmhouse@lineone.net

Regency Guesthouse ◆◆◆◆
The Street, Neatishead, Norwich NR12 8AD
T: (01692) 630233
F: (01692) 630233
E: regencywrigley@btopenworld.com
I: www.norfolkbroads.com/regency

NEW BUCKENHAM Norfolk

Pump Court Bed & Breakfast Rating Applied For
Church Street, New Buckenham, Norwich NR16 2BA
T: (01953) 861039
F: (01953) 861153
E: pumpcourt@lineone.net
I: www.pump-court.co.uk

NEWMARKET Suffolk

2 Birdcage Walk
◆◆◆◆ GOLD AWARD
Newmarket CB8 0NE
T: (01638) 669456
F: (01638) 669456

Hilldown House ◆◆◆
19 Duchess Drive, Newmarket CB8 8AG
T: (01638) 664250

The Meadow House ◆◆◆◆
2A High Street, Burwell, Cambridge CB5 0HB
T: (01638) 741926
F: (01638) 741861
E: hilary@themeadowhouse.co.uk
I: www.themeadowhouse.co.uk

Sandhurst ◆◆◆
14 Cardigan Street, Newmarket CB8 8HZ
T: (01638) 667483
E: crighton@rousnewmarket.freeserve.co.uk

Warren Hill Cottage ◆◆◆
27 Bury Road, Newmarket CB8 7BY
T: (01638) 661103
F: (01638) 661103

York Terrace ◆◆◆
74 Exeter Road, Newmarket CB8 8LR
T: (01638) 665473
F: (01638) 665473

NEWPORT Essex

The Toll House
◆◆◆◆ SILVER AWARD
Belmont Hill, Newport, Saffron Walden CB11 3RD
T: (01799) 540880
F: (01799) 540880
E: teampoole@rdplus.net
I: www.tollhousebedandbreakfast.co.uk

NORTH FAMBRIDGE Essex

Ferry Boat Inn ◆◆◆
North Fambridge, Chelmsford CM3 6LR
T: (01621) 740208
F: (01621) 740208
E: sylviaferryboat@aol.com
I: www.ferryboatinn.net

NORTH LOPHAM Norfolk

Church Farm House
◆◆◆◆◆ GOLD AWARD
North Lopham, Diss IP22 2LP
T: (01379) 687270
F: (01379) 687270
E: b&b@bassetts.demon.co.uk
I: www.churchfarmhouse.org

NORTH MYMMS Hertfordshire

Little Gables Guest House ◆◆◆◆
3 Swanland Road, North Mymms, Hatfield AL9 7TG
T: (01707) 660804
F: (020) 8449 3556

NORTH WALSHAM Norfolk

Dolphin Lodge ◆◆◆
Trunch, North Walsham NR18 0QE
T: (01263) 720961

Green Ridges ◆◆◆◆
104 Cromer Road, North Walsham NR28 0HE
T: (01692) 402448
F: (01692) 402448
E: admin@greenridges.com
I: www.greenridges.com

Kings Arms Hotel ◆◆◆
Kings Arms Street, North Walsham NR28 9JX
T: (01692) 403054
F: (01692) 500095
E: martin@kingsarmshotel.fsnet.co.uk

Pinetrees ◆◆◆◆
45 Happisburgh Road, North Walsham NR28 9HB
T: (01692) 404213

NORTH WOOTTON Norfolk

Red Cat Hotel ◆◆◆
Station Road, North Wootton, King's Lynn PE30 3QH
T: (01553) 631244
F: (01553) 631574
E: enquiries@redcathotel.com
I: www.redcathotel.com

NORWICH Norfolk

The Abbey Hotel ◆◆◆
16 Stracey Road, Thorpe Road, Norwich NR1 1EZ
T: (01603) 612915
F: (01603) 612915

Arbor Linden Lodge ◆◆◆◆
Linden House, 557 Earlham Road, Norwich NR4 7HW
T: (01603) 451303
F: (01603) 250641
E: info@arborlindenlodge.com
I: www.guesthousenorwich.com

Aylwyne House ◆◆◆
59 Aylsham Road, Norwich NR3 2HF
T: (01603) 665798

Beaufort Lodge
◆◆◆◆ SILVER AWARD
62 Earlham Road, Norwich NR2 3DF
T: (01603) 627928
F: (01603) 440712
E: beaufortlodge@aol.com
I: www.beaufortlodge.com

Becklands ◆◆◆◆
105 Holt Road, Horsford, Norwich NR10 3AB
T: (01603) 898582
F: (01603) 754223
E: becklands@aol.com

Hotel Belmonte and Belmonte Restaurant ◆◆◆
60-62 Prince of Wales Road, Norwich NR1 1LT
T: (01603) 622533
F: (01603) 760805
E: bar7seven@yahoo.com
I: www.geocities.com/bar7seven/

The Blue Boar Inn ◆◆◆◆
259 Wroxham Road, Sprowston, Norwich NR7 8RL
T: (01603) 426802
F: (01603) 487749
E: blueboar102@hotmail.com
I: www.blueboarnorwich.co.uk

Blue Cedar Lodge Guesthouse ◆◆◆
391 Earlham Road, Norwich NR2 3RQ
T: (01603) 458331
F: (01603) 458331

Cavell House ◆◆◆◆
The Common, Swardeston, Norwich NR14 8DZ
T: (01508) 578195
F: (01508) 578195
E: joljean.harris@virgin.net

Church Farm Guesthouse ◆◆◆◆
Church Street, Horsford, Norwich NR10 3DB
T: (01603) 898020
F: (01603) 891649
E: churchfarmguesthouse.@btopenworld.com

Conifers Hotel ◆◆◆
162 Dereham Road, Norwich NR2 3AH
T: (01603) 628737
E: the-conifers@btopenworld.com
I: www.the-conifers.com

The Cottage Rating Applied For
Rectory Lane, Bunwell, Norwich NR16 1QU
T: (01953) 789226

NORWICH Norfolk

Earlham Guesthouse ◆◆◆◆
147 Earlham Road, Norwich NR2 3RG
T: (01603) 454169
F: (01603) 454169
E: earlhamgh@hotmail.com

Eaton Bower
◆◆◆◆ SILVER AWARD
20 Mile End Road, Norwich NR4 7QY
T: (01603) 462204
E: eaton_bower@hotmail.com
I: www.eatonbower.co.uk

Edmar Lodge ◆◆◆
64 Earlham Road, Norwich NR2 3DF
T: (01603) 615599
F: (01603) 495599
E: mail@edmarlodge.co.uk
I: www.edmarlodge.co.uk

Elm Farm Country House ◆◆◆◆
55 Norwich Road, St Faiths NR10 3HH
T: (01603) 898366
F: (01603) 897129
E: Pmpbelmfarm@aol.com

309 Fakenham Road ◆◆◆
Taverham, Norwich NR8 6LF
T: (01603) 860103
F: (01603) 860103
E: jeanshepherd@lineone.net

The Gables Guesthouse ◆◆◆◆
527 Earlham Road, Norwich NR4 7HN
T: (01603) 456666
F: (01603) 250320

Garden House ◆◆◆
Salhouse Road, Rackheath, Norwich NR13 6AA
T: (01603) 720007
F: (01603) 720007
E: gardenhousebandb@aol.com
I: www.thegardenhousehotel.uk.com

Hanover House ◆◆◆◆
60 Earlham Road, Norwich NR2 3DF
T: (01603) 667402
E: aylmus@clara.com

Harvey House Guesthouse ◆◆◆
50 Harvey Lane, Norwich NR7 0AQ
T: (01603) 436575
F: (01603) 436575
E: harvey.house@which.net

The Limes ◆◆
188 Unthank Road, Norwich NR2 2AH
T: (01603) 454282

Manor Barn House ◆◆◆◆
Back Lane, Rackheath, Norwich NR13 6NN
T: (01603) 783543
E: jane.roger@manorbarnhouse.co.uk
I: www.manorbarnhouse.co.uk

Marlborough House Hotel ◆◆◆
22 Stracey Road, Norwich NR1 1EZ
T: (01603) 628005
F: (01603) 628005

Establishments printed in blue have a detailed entry in this guide

Mousehold Lodge Guesthouse ♦♦♦
53 Mousehold Lane, Norwich NR7 8HL
T: (01603) 426026
F: (01603) 424590
E: info@mousehold-lodge.co.uk
I: www.mousehold-lodge.co.uk

The Old Lodge ♦♦♦♦
New Road, Bawburgh, Norwich NR9 3LZ
T: (01603) 742798
E: peggy@theoldlodge.freeserve.co.uk

The Old Rectory
♦♦♦♦ SILVER AWARD
Hall Road, Framingham Earl, Norwich NR14 7SB
T: (01508) 493590
F: (01508) 495110
E: oldrectory@f-earl.fsnet.co.uk
I: www.f-earl.fsnet.co.uk

Rosedale ♦
145 Earlham Road, Norwich NR2 3RG
T: (01603) 453743
F: (01603) 259887
E: drcbac@aol.com
I: www.members@aol.com/drcbac

Wedgewood House ♦♦♦
42 St Stephens Road, Norwich NR1 3RE
T: (01603) 625730
F: (01603) 615035
E: stay@wedgewoodhouse.co.uk
I: www.wedgewoodhouse.co.uk

Witton Hall Farm ♦♦♦
Witton, North Walsham NR13 5DN
T: (01603) 714580
E: wittonhall@yahoo.com

OCCOLD
Suffolk

The Cedars Guesthouse ♦♦♦♦
Church Street, Occold, Eye IP23 7PS
T: (01379) 678439

OLD CATTON
Norfolk

Catton Old Hall
♦♦♦♦♦ SILVER AWARD
Lodge Lane, Old Catton, Norwich NR6 7HG
T: (01603) 419379
F: (01603) 400339
E: enquiries@catton-hall.co.uk
I: www.catton-hall.co.uk

ORFORD
Suffolk

Amazing Place ♦♦♦
3 Toller Close, Orford, Woodbridge IP12 2LR
T: (01394) 450430
E: tashahodge@tiscali.co.uk
I: www.amazingplace.supanet.com

ORTON LONGUEVILLE
Cambridgeshire

Orton Mere Guest House ♦♦♦♦
547 Oundle Road, Orton Longueville, Peterborough PE2 7DH
T: (01733) 708432
F: (01733) 708425

OULTON
Suffolk

Laurel Farm ♦♦♦♦
Hall Lane, Oulton, Lowestoft NR32 5DL
T: (01502) 568724
E: janethodgkin@laurelfarm.com
I: www.laurelfarm.com

OVERSTRAND
Norfolk

Cliff Cottage Bed & Breakfast ♦♦♦
18 High Street, Overstrand, Cromer NR27 0AB
T: (01263) 578179
E: roymin@btinternet.com
I: uk.geocities.com/cliffcottagebandb/

Danum House ♦♦♦
22 Pauls Lane, Overstrand, Cromer NR27 0PE
T: (01263) 579327
F: (01263) 579327

PAKEFIELD
Suffolk

Pipers Lodge Hotel & Motel ♦♦♦♦
41 London Road, Pakefield NR33 7AA
T: (01502) 569805
F: (01502) 565383
I: www.piperslodge.co.uk

PALGRAVE
Suffolk

Brambley House ♦♦♦
Lion Road, Palgrave, Diss IP22 1AL
T: (01379) 644403

PELDON
Essex

Sunnyside Bed & Breakfast Rating Applied For
Colchester Road, Peldon, Colchester CO5 7QP
T: (01206) 735945
E: yvonne@romain.co.uk
I: www.romain.co.uk

PETERBOROUGH
Cambridgeshire

The Anchor Lodge ♦♦♦
28 Percival Street, Peterborough PE3 6AU
T: (01733) 312724

Aragon House ♦♦♦
75-77 London Road, Peterborough PE2 9BS
T: (01733) 563718
F: (01733) 563718
E: mail@aragonhouse.co.uk
I: www.aragonhouse.co.uk

Arman Lodge House ♦♦
3 Scotney Street, Newengland, Peterborough PE1 3NG
T: (01733) 554232
E: rajna@talk21.com
I: www.armanlodgehouse.com

The Brandon ♦♦♦
161 Lincoln Road, Peterborough PE1 2PW
T: (01733) 568631
F: (01733) 568631
I: www.peterboroughaccommodation.co.uk

Clarks ♦♦♦♦
21 Oundle Road, Peterborough PE2 9PB
T: (01733) 342482
F: (01733) 553227
E: fiona@clarksguesthouse.fsnet.co.uk
I: www.clarksguesthouse.com

The Graham Guesthouse ♦♦♦
296 Oundle Road, Peterborough PE2 9QA
T: (01733) 567824
F: (01733) 567824

Longueville Guesthouse ♦♦♦♦
411 Oundle Road, Orton Longueville, Peterborough PE2 7DA
T: (01733) 233442
F: (01733) 233442

Montana ♦♦♦
15 Fletton Avenue, Peterborough PE2 8AX
T: (01733) 567917
F: (01733) 567917
E: montana160141@aol.com
I: www.peterboroughguestaccommodation.com

Park Road Guesthouse ♦♦
67 Park Road, Peterborough PE1 2TN
T: (01733) 562220
F: (01733) 344279

Wisteria House ♦♦♦
5 Church Lane, Helpston, Peterborough PE6 7DT
T: (01733) 252272

PETTISTREE
Suffolk

The Three Tuns Coaching Inn ♦♦♦
Main Road, Pettistree, Woodbridge IP13 0HW
T: (01728) 747979
F: (01728) 746244
E: jon@threetuns-coachinginn.co.uk
I: www.threetuns-coachinginn.co.uk

PLESHEY
Essex

Acreland Green ♦♦♦♦
Pleshey, Chelmsford CM3 1HP
T: (01245) 231277
F: (01245) 231277

POLSTEAD
Suffolk

Polstead Lodge ♦♦♦♦
Mill Street, Polstead, Colchester CO6 5AD
T: (01206) 262196
E: howards@polsteadlodge.freeserve.co.uk
I: www.polsteadlodge.com

POTTER HEIGHAM
Norfolk

Hazelden ♦♦♦♦
Bridge Road, Potter Heigham, Great Yarmouth NR29 5JB
T: (01692) 670511

POTTERS BAR
Hertfordshire

Bruggen Lodge ♦♦♦♦
13 The Drive, Potters Bar EN6 2AP
T: (01707) 655904
F: (01707) 857287
E: andreaseggie@lineone.net

PULHAM MARKET
Norfolk

The Old Bakery
♦♦♦♦♦ GOLD AWARD
Church Walk, Pulham Market, Diss IP21 4SJ
T: (01379) 676492
F: (01379) 676492
E: jean@theoldbakery.net
I: www.theoldbakery.net

QUEEN ADELAIDE
Cambridgeshire

Greenways ♦♦♦
Prickwillow Road, Queen Adelaide, Ely CB7 4TZ
T: (01353) 666706
F: (01954) 251629
E: greenways.ely@tesco.net

RACKHEATH
Norfolk

Barn Court ♦♦♦
6 Back Lane, Rackheath, Norwich NR13 6NN
T: (01603) 782536
F: (01603) 782536
E: barncourtbb@hotmail.com

RAMSHOLT
Suffolk

The Ramsholt Arms ♦♦♦
Dock Road, Ramsholt, Woodbridge IP12 3AB
T: (01394) 411229
F: (01394) 411818
E: ramsholtarms@tinyworld.co.uk
I: www.ramsholtarms.co.uk

RAVENSDEN
Bedfordshire

Tree Garth ♦♦♦♦
Church End, Ravensden, Bedford MK44 2RP
T: (01234) 771745
F: (01234) 771745
E: treegarth@ukonline.co.uk
I: treegarth.co.uk

RENDHAM
Suffolk

Rendham Hall ♦♦♦
Rendham, Saxmundham IP17 2AW
T: (01728) 663440
F: (01728) 663245
E: dc.strachan@talk21.com

REPPS WITH BASTWICK
Norfolk

Grove Farm Bed & Breakfast ♦♦♦
Grove Farm, Repps With Bastwick, Great Yarmouth NR29 5JN
T: (01692) 670205
E: jenny@grovefarmholidays.co.uk
I: www.grovefarmholidays.co.uk

REYDON
Suffolk

Newlands Country House ♦♦♦♦
72 Halesworth Road, Reydon, Southwold IP18 6NS
T: (01502) 722164
F: (01502) 725363
E: newlandssouthwold@lycos.co.uk
I: www.newlandssouthwold.com
♿

Establishments printed in blue have a detailed entry in this guide

Ridge Bed & Breakfast ♦♦♦♦
The Ridge, 14 Halesworth Road, Reydon, Southwold IP18 6NH
T: (01502) 724855
E: jules.heal@ntlworld.com
I: www.southwold.ws/ridge

RIDLINGTON
Norfolk

Mill Common House
♦♦♦♦ SILVER AWARD
Mill Common Road, Ridlington, North Walsham NR28 9TY
T: (01692) 650792
F: (01692) 651480
E: johnpugh@millcommon.freeserve.co.uk
I: www.broadland.com/millcommon

RIVENHALL
Essex

The Granary B & B Apartments Rating Applied For
Clarks Farm, Cranes Lane, Kelvedon, Colchester CO5 9AY
T: (01376) 570321
F: (01376) 570321
E: enquiries@thegranary.me.uk

North Ford Farm ♦♦♦♦
Church Road, Rivenhall, Witham CM8 3PG
T: (01376) 583321
F: (01376) 583321

Rickstones Farmhouse Bed & Breakfast ♦♦♦♦
Rickstones Farmhouse, Rickstones Road, Rivenhall, Witham CM8 3HQ
T: (01376) 514351
F: (01376) 514351
E: rickstonesfarmhouse@btinternet.com

ROUGHTON
Norfolk

Grove Farm
Rating Applied For
Back Lane, Roughton, Norwich NR11 8QR
T: (01263) 761594
F: (01263) 761605
E: grove-farm@homestay.co.uk

ROXWELL
Essex

Cross Keys Inn ♦♦♦
Boyton Cross, Roxwell, Chelmsford CM1 4LP
T: (01245) 248201
E: crossedkeysinn1@btopenworld.com
I: www.crosskeysroxwell.co.uk

ROYSTON
Hertfordshire

The Aris Inn Hotel ♦♦♦
Flint Cross, Newmarket Road, Royston, SG8 7PN
T: (01763) 208272
F: (01763) 208268
E: arisinn@hotmail.com
I: www.arisinn.co.uk

Hall Farm ♦♦♦♦
Great Chishill, Royston SG8 8SH
T: (01763) 838263
F: (01763) 838263
E: wisehall@farming.co.uk
I: www.hallfarmbb.co.uk

RUMBURGH
Suffolk

Rumburgh Farm ♦♦♦♦
Rumburgh, Halesworth IP19 0RU
T: (01986) 781351
F: (01986) 781351
E: binder@rumburghfarm.freeserve.co.uk
I: www.rumburghfarm.freeserve.co.uk

Valley Farm Vineyards
♦♦♦♦ SILVER AWARD
Rumburgh Road, Wissett, Halesworth IP19 0JJ
T: (01986) 785535

SAFFRON WALDEN
Essex

Archway Guesthouse ♦♦♦♦
Archway House, Church Street, Saffron Walden CB10 1JW
T: (01799) 501500
F: (01799) 506003
E: archwayguesthouse@ntlworld.com

Ashleigh House ♦♦♦
7 Farmadine Grove, Saffron Walden CB11 3DR
T: (01799) 513611
E: info@ashleighhouse.dabsol.co.uk
I: www.ashleighhouse.dabsol.co.uk

The Bell House ♦♦♦♦
53-55 Castle Street, Saffron Walden CB10 1BD
T: (01799) 527857

The Bonnet
♦♦♦♦♦ SILVER AWARD
Overhall Lane, Stevington End, Ashdon, Saffron Walden CB10 2JE
T: (01799) 584955
E: thebonnetuk@yahoo.co.uk
I: www.thebonnett.co.uk

Buriton House
Rating Applied For
Station Road, Newport, Saffron Walden CB11 3PL
T: (01799) 542237
E: Buriton_house@hotmail.com

The Cricketers ♦♦♦♦
Clavering, Saffron Walden CB11 4QT
T: (01799) 550442
F: (01799) 550882
E: cricketers@lineone.net
I: www.thecricketers.co.uk

11 Dawson Close ♦♦♦
Saffron Walden CB10 2AR
T: (01799) 528491

Grimalkins B & B ♦♦♦
49 Castle Street, Saffron Walden CB10 1BD
T: (01799) 521557
E: gertrud@hill-castle.freeserve.co.uk

1 Gunters Cottages ♦♦♦♦
Thaxted Road, Saffron Walden CB10 2UT
T: (01799) 522091

Hollingate
Rating Applied For
Radwinter End, Radwinter, Saffron Walden CB10 2UD
T: (01799) 599184
E: hollingate@btopenworld.com

30 Lambert Cross ♦♦
Saffron Walden CB10 2DP
T: (01799) 527287

Oak House ♦♦♦
40 Audley Road, Saffron Walden CB11 3HD
T: (01799) 523290
E: oakhouse@macunlimited.net

Pudding House ♦♦♦
9a Museum Street, Saffron Walden CB10 1JL
T: (01799) 522089

Redgates Farmhouse ♦♦♦♦
Redgate Lane, Sewards End, Saffron Walden CB10 2LP
T: (01799) 516166

Rockells Farm ♦♦♦♦
Duddenhoe End, Saffron Walden CB11 4UY
T: (01763) 838053
F: (01763) 837001
E: evert.westerhuis@tiscali.co.uk
I: www.rockellsfarm.co.uk

Rowley Hill Lodge
♦♦♦♦ SILVER AWARD
Little Walden, Saffron Walden CB10 1UZ
T: (01799) 525975
F: (01799) 516622
E: eh@clara.net

Victoria House ♦♦♦
10 Victoria Avenue, Saffron Walden CB11 3AE
T: (01799) 525923

Yardley's
♦♦♦♦ SILVER AWARD
Orchard Pightle, Hadstock, Cambridge CB1 6PQ
T: (01223) 891822
F: (01223) 891822
E: yardleys@waitrose.com
I: www.b-and-b-yardleys.co.uk

ST ALBANS
Hertfordshire

5 Approach Road ♦♦
St Albans AL1 1SP
T: (01727) 852471
F: (01727) 847408
E: nigelcocks@compuserve.com

22 Ardens Way ♦♦♦
St Albans AL4 9UJ
T: (01727) 861986

Ardmore House ♦♦♦
24 Lemsford Road, St Albans AL1 3PR
T: (01727) 859313
F: (01727) 859313
E: info@ardmorehousehotel.altodigital.co.uk
I: www.ardmorehousehotel.com

Avalon Hotel
Rating Applied For
260 London Road, St Albans AL1 1TJ
T: (01727) 856757
F: (01727) 856750
E: hotelavalon@aol.com
I: www.avalonhotel.net

Avona ♦♦♦
478 Hatfield Road, St Albans AL4 0SX
T: (01727) 842216
F: (01727) 857578
E: murchu@ntlworld.com

Black Lion Inn ♦♦♦
198 Fishpool Street, St Albans AL3 4SB
T: (01727) 851786
F: (01727) 859243
E: info@theblacklioninn.com
I: www.theblacklioninn.com

Braemar House ♦♦♦♦
89 Salisbury Avenue, St Albans AL1 4TY
T: (01727) 839641
F: (01727) 839641
E: slaters@braemar435.fsnet.co.uk

55 Charmouth Road ♦♦♦
St Albans AL1 4SE
T: (01727) 860002
E: charmouth@btopenworld.com

35 Chestnut Drive ♦♦♦
St Albans AL4 0ER
T: (01727) 833401

5 Cunningham Avenue ♦♦♦
St Albans AL1 1JJ
T: (01727) 857388

Fern Cottage ♦♦♦♦
116 Old London Road, St Albans AL1 1PU
T: (01727) 834200
E: dorotheabristow@ntlworld.com
I: www.ferncottage.uk.net

Fleuchary House
♦♦♦♦ SILVER AWARD
3 Upper Lattimore Road, St Albans AL1 3UD
T: (01727) 766764
E: linda@fleucharyhouse.freeserve.co.uk
I: www.fleucharyhouse.com

32 Gurney Court Road ♦♦♦
St Albans AL1 4RL
T: (01727) 760250
E: v.salisbury@ntlworld.com

8 Hall Place Gardens ♦♦♦
St Albans AL1 3SP
T: (01727) 858939

2 The Limes ♦♦♦
Spencer Gate, St Albans AL1 4AT
T: (01727) 831080
E: hunter.mitchell@virgin.net

178 London Road ♦♦♦♦
St Albans AL1 1PL
T: (01727) 846726
F: (01727) 831267
E: bookings_178londonroad@btconnect.com
I: www.178londonroad.co.uk

Margaret's B&B ♦♦♦
16 Broomleys, St Albans AL4 9UR
T: (01727) 862421

7 Marlborough Gate ♦♦♦
St Albans AL1 3TX
T: (01727) 865498
E: michael.jameson@btinternet.com

Park House ♦♦♦
30 The Park, St Albans AL1 4RY
T: (01727) 832054

36 Potters Field ♦♦♦
St Albans AL3 6LJ
T: (01727) 766840
F: (01727) 766840
E: manners_smith@ntlworld.com

Riverside
♦♦♦♦ SILVER AWARD
24 Minister Court, St Albans
AL2 2NF
T: (01727) 758780
F: (01727) 758760
E: Ellispatriciam@aol.com

56 Sandpit Lane ♦♦♦♦
St Albans AL1 4BW
T: (01727) 856799
F: (01727) 856799

Tresco ♦♦♦♦
76 Clarence Road, St Albans
AL1 4NG
T: (01727) 864880
F: (01727) 864880
E: pat.leggatt@talk21.com
I: www.twistedsilicon.co.uk/76/index.htm

33 Upper Heath Road ♦♦
St Albans AL1 4DN
T: (01727) 856098

The White House ♦♦
28 Salisbury Avenue, St Albans
AL1 4TU
T: (01727) 861017

Wren Lodge ♦♦♦♦
24 Beaconsfield Road, St Albans
AL1 3RB
T: (01727) 855540
F: (01727) 766674
E: wren.lodge@ntlworld.com
I: www.destination-england.co.uk/wrenlodge.html

16 York Road ♦♦♦
St Albans AL1 4PL
T: (01727) 853647

ST NEOTS
Cambridgeshire

The Nags Head Hotel ♦♦♦
2 Berkley Street, Eynesbury, St Neots, Huntingdon PE19 2NA
T: (01480) 476812
F: (01480) 391881

SALFORD
Bedfordshire

Rose Cottage Guest Accommodation ♦♦♦♦
44 Broughton Road, Salford, Milton Keynes MK17 8BQ
T: (01908) 282029
F: (01908) 282029
E: rosecottagemk@btinternet.com

SALHOUSE
Norfolk

The Lodge Inn ♦♦♦
Vicarage Road, Salhouse, Norwich NR13 6HD
T: (01603) 782828
E: thelodgeinn@salhouse.f.s.business.co.uk

Oldfield ♦♦♦♦
Vicarage Road, Salhouse, Norwich NR13 6HA
T: (01603) 781080
F: (01603) 781083

SANDY
Bedfordshire

Highfield Farm
♦♦♦♦♦ SILVER AWARD
Tempsford Road, Great North Road, Sandy SG19 2AQ
T: (01767) 682332
F: (01767) 692503
E: margaret@highfield-farm.co.uk

Village Farm ♦♦♦
Thorncote Green, Sandy
SG19 1PU
T: (01767) 627345

SAWBRIDGEWORTH
Hertfordshire

7 Church Walk ♦♦♦
Sawbridgeworth CM21 9BJ
T: (01279) 723233
E: kent@sawbridgeworth.co.uk
I: www.ourbedandbreakfast.co.uk

SAWTRY
Cambridgeshire

A1 Bed & Breakfast ♦♦
5 High Street, Sawtry, Huntingdon PE28 5SR
T: (01487) 830201
F: (01487) 830201

SAXLINGHAM
Norfolk

The Map House
♦♦♦♦♦ SILVER AWARD
The Map House, Smokers Hole, Saxlingham, Holt NR25 7JU
T: (01263) 741304
E: enquiries@maphouse.net
I: www.maphouse.net

SAXLINGHAM THORPE
Norfolk

Foxhole Farm ♦♦♦♦
Foxhole, Saxlingham Thorpe, Norwich NR15 1UG
T: (01508) 499226
F: (01508) 499226
E: foxholefarm@hotmail.com

SAXMUNDHAM
Suffolk

The Georgian House
♦♦♦♦♦ SILVER AWARD
6 North Entrance, Saxmundham IP17 1AY
T: (01728) 603337
E: enquiries@thegeorgian-house.com
I: www.thegeorgian-house.com

Honeypot Lodge ♦♦♦♦
Aldecar Lane, Benhall Green, Saxmundham IP17 1HN
T: (01728) 602449
F: (01728) 602449
E: honeypot@freeuk.com
I: www.smoothhound.co.uk/hotels/honeypotlodge.html

Moat House Farm ♦♦♦♦
Rendham Road, Carlton, Saxmundham IP17 2QN
T: (01728) 602228
F: (01728) 602228
E: sally@goodacres.com
I: www.goodacres.com

SCOTTOW
Norfolk

Holmwood House ♦♦♦♦
Tunstead Road, Scottow, Norwich NR10 5DA
T: (01692) 538386
F: (01692) 538386
E: holmwoodhouse@lineone.net
I: www.norfolkbroads.com/holmwood

SCULTHORPE
Norfolk

Manor Farm Bed & Breakfast
♦♦♦♦ SILVER AWARD
Manor Farm, Sculthorpe, Fakenham NR21 9NJ
T: (01328) 862185
F: (01328) 862033
E: mddwo2@dial.pipex.com
I: www.manorfarmbandb.com

SHENFIELD
Essex

The Mulberries ♦♦♦♦
30 Mulberry Hill, Shenfield, Brentwood CM15 8JS
T: (01277) 233096
E: bs@dsl.pipex.com
I: www.stanbridge.fslife.co.uk

31 Mulberry Hill ♦♦♦
Shenfield, Brentwood CM15 8JS
T: (01277) 849160
E: wendy@sscott87.freeserve.co.uk
I: www.shenfieldbandb.co.uk

SHERINGHAM
Norfolk

Achimota ♦♦♦♦
31 North Street, Sheringham
NR26 8LW
T: (01263) 822379
I: www.broadland.com/achimota

Alverstone ♦♦♦
33 The Avenue, Sheringham
NR26 8DG
T: (01263) 825527

Ashcroft House Bed & Breakfast ♦♦♦♦
15 Morris Street, Sheringham
NR26 8JY
T: (01263) 822225
E: ashcrofthouse@tiscali.co.uk

The Burlington Lodge ♦♦♦
5 St Nicholas Place, Sheringham
NR26 8LF
T: (01263) 820931
F: (01263) 820964
E: r.mcdermott@hemscott.net

Camberley Guesthouse ♦♦♦
62 Cliff Road, Sheringham
NR26 8BJ
T: (01263) 823101
F: (01263) 821433
E: graham@camberleyguesthouse.co.uk
I: www.camberleyguesthouse.co.uk

Holly Cottage ♦♦♦♦
14a The Rise, Sheringham
NR26 8QB
T: (01263) 822807
F: (01263) 822807
E: hollyperks@aol.com
I: www.sheringham-network.co.uk

Maison ♦♦♦♦
9 Cremers Drift, Sheringham
NR26 8HX
T: (01263) 821945

The Melrose ♦♦♦
9 Holway Road, Sheringham
NR26 8HN
T: (01263) 823299
E: jparsonage@btconnect.com
I: www.themelrsosesheringham.co.uk

Olivedale ♦♦♦♦
20 Augusta Street, Sheringham
NR26 8LA
T: (01263) 825871
F: (01263) 821104
E: info@olivedale.co.uk
I: www.olivedale.co.uk

Priestfields
♦♦♦♦ SILVER AWARD
6B North Street, Sheringham
NR26 8LW
T: (01263) 820305
F: (01263) 820125
E: david.phillips10@which.net

Sheringham Lodge ♦♦♦
Cromer Road, Sheringham
NR26 8RS
T: (01263) 821954
E: mikewalker19@hotmail.com
I: www.sheringhamlodge.co.uk

Squirrels Drey ♦♦♦
27 Holt Road, Sheringham
NR26 8NB
T: (01263) 822982
F: (01263) 822982
E: squirrels-drey@lyttelton.fsnet.co.uk

The Two Lifeboats Hotel ♦♦♦
2 The High Street, Sheringham
NR26 8JR
T: (01263) 822401
F: (01263) 823130
E: info@twolifeboats.co.uk
I: www.twolifeboats.co.uk

Westwater B&B Guest House ♦♦♦
28 Norfolk Road, Sheringham
NR26 8HJ
T: (01263) 822321
F: (01263) 825932
E: bookings@westwater.uk.net
I: www.westwater.uk.net

Willow Lodge ♦♦♦♦
6 Vicarage Road, Sheringham
NR26 8NH
T: (01263) 822204
F: (01263) 822204
I: www.willow-lodge.co.uk

SHINGLE STREET
Suffolk

Lark Cottage ♦♦♦♦
Shingle Street, Woodbridge
IP12 3BE
T: (01394) 411292

SHOTLEY
Suffolk

Hill House Farm
♦♦♦♦ SILVER AWARD
Wades Lane, Shotley, Ipswich
IP9 1EW
T: (01473) 787318
F: (01473) 787111
E: richard@rjwrinch.fsnet.co.uk

SHUDY CAMPS
Cambridgeshire

Old Well Cottage ♦♦♦♦
Main Street, Shudy Camps, Cambridge CB1 6RA
T: (01799) 584387
F: (01799) 584486
E: jackiesamvet@aol.com

SIBLE HEDINGHAM
Essex

Brickwall Farm ♦♦♦♦
Queen Street, Sible Hedingham, Halstead CO9 3RH
T: (01787) 460329
F: (01787) 460329
E: brickwallfarm@btinternet.com

Tocat House ♦♦♦♦
9 Potter Street, Sible Hedingham, Halstead CO9 3RG
T: (01787) 461942

SIBTON
Suffolk

Church Farm
♦♦♦♦♦ SILVER AWARD
Yoxford Road, Sibton, Saxmundham IP17 2LX
T: (01728) 660101
F: (01728) 660102
E: dixons@church-farmhouse.demon.co.uk
I: www.church-farmhouse.demon.co.uk

Park Farm
♦♦♦♦ SILVER AWARD
Yoxford Road, Sibton, Saxmundham IP17 2LZ
T: (01728) 668324
E: margaret.gray@btinternet.com
I: www.farmstayanglia.co.uk/parkfarm

SNAPE
Suffolk

Flemings Lodge ♦♦♦♦
Gromford Lane, Snape, Saxmundham IP17 1RG
T: (01728) 688502
F: (01728) 688502

SNETTISHAM
Norfolk

The Hollies
♦♦♦♦ SILVER AWARD
12 Lynn Road, Snettisham, King's Lynn PE31 7LS
T: (01485) 541294
F: (01485) 541294

The Rose & Crown ♦♦♦♦
Old Church Road, Snettisham, King's Lynn PE31 7LX
T: (01485) 541382
F: (01485) 543172
I: www.roseandcrownsnettisham.co.uk

The Round House ♦♦♦♦
131 Lynn Road, Snettisham, King's Lynn PE31 7QG
T: (01485) 540580
F: (01485) 543415
E: ziphac@aol.com

SOHAM
Cambridgeshire

Greenbank ♦♦♦
111 Brook Street, Soham, Ely CB7 5AE
T: (01353) 720929

SOUTH CREAKE
Norfolk

Valentine House ♦♦♦
62 Back Street, South Creake, Fakenham NR21 9PG
T: (01328) 823413
E: nickhaywood@classic-sheds.fsnet.co.uk

SOUTH WALSHAM
Norfolk

Old Hall Farm ♦♦♦♦
Newport Road, South Walsham, Norwich NR13 6DS
T: (01603) 270271
E: veronica@oldhallfarm.co.uk
I: www.oldhallfarm.co.uk

SOUTHEND-ON-SEA
Essex

Arosa Guest House ♦♦
184 Eastern Esplanade, Southend-on-Sea SS1 3AA
T: (01702) 585416
F: (01702) 580599
E: jonwilson@arosa184.freeserve.co.uk
I: www.smoothhound.co.uk

Atlantis Guest House ♦♦♦♦
63 Alexandra Road, Southend-on-Sea SS1 1EY
T: (01702) 332538
F: (01702) 392736
E: atlantisnicali@aol.com

The Bay Guesthouse ♦♦♦♦
187 Eastern Esplanade, Thorpe Bay, Southend-on-Sea SS1 3AA
T: (01702) 588415
E: thebayguesthouse@hotmail.com
I: http://www.smoothhound.co.uk/hotels/thebayguest

Lee Villas Guesthouse ♦
1 & 2 Hartington Place, Southend-on-Sea SS1 2HP
T: (01702) 317214
F: (01702) 329869
E: SMCK764100@aol.com
I: www.leevillas.co.uk

Pebbles Guesthouse ♦♦♦♦
190 Eastern Esplanade, Thorpe Bay, Southend-on-Sea SS1 3AA
T: (01702) 582329
F: (01702) 582329
E: pebbles.guesthouse@virgin.net
I: www.smoothhound.co.uk/a10590.html

Strand Guesthouse ♦♦
165 Eastern Esplanade, Thorpe Bay, Southend-on-Sea SS1 2YB
T: (01702) 586611

Tower Hotel ♦♦♦
146 Alexandra Road, Southend-on-Sea SS1 1HE
T: (01702) 348635
F: (01702) 433044
I: www.towerhotelsouthend.co.uk

The Waverley Guesthouse ♦♦♦
191 Eastern Esplanade, Thorpe Bay, Southend-on-Sea SS1 3AA
T: (01702) 585212
F: (01702) 586764
E: waverleyguesthouse@hotmail.com
I: www.waverleyguesthouse.co.uk

SOUTHMINSTER
Essex

New Moor Farm ♦♦♦♦
Tillingham Road, Burnham-on-Crouch, Southminster CM0 7DS
T: (01621) 772840
F: (01621) 774087

SOUTHREPPS
Norfolk

Avalon ♦♦♦♦
Lower Southrepps, Southrepps, Norwich NR11 8UJ
T: (01263) 834461
F: (01263) 834461
E: mokies@msn.com

SOUTHWOLD
Suffolk

Acton Lodge ♦♦♦♦
South Green, Southwold IP18 6HB
T: (01502) 723217

Amber House ♦♦♦
24 North Parade, Southwold IP18 6LT
T: (01502) 723303
E: spring@amberhouse.fsnet.co.uk
I: www.southwold.blythweb.co.uk/amber_house/index.htm

Avocet House ♦♦♦♦
1 Strickland Place, Southwold IP18 6HN
T: (01502) 724720
E: barnett@beeb.net
I: www.southwold.ws/avocet-house

Broadlands ♦♦♦♦
68 Halesworth Road, Reydon, Southwold IP18 6NS
T: (01502) 724384
F: (01502) 724384
I: www.southwold.info

Dunburgh Guesthouse ♦♦♦♦
28 North Parade, Southwold IP18 6LT
T: (01502) 723253
I: www.southwold.ws/dunburgh

No 21 ♦♦♦♦
North Parade, Southwold IP18 6LT
T: (01502) 722573
F: (01502) 724326
E: jackie_comrie@onetel.net.uk
I: www.southwold.blythweb.co.uk/north_parade/index.htm

Northcliffe Guesthouse ♦♦♦♦
20 North Parade, Southwold IP18 6LT
T: (01502) 724074
F: (01502) 722218
E: northcliffe.southwold@virgin.net
I: www.northcliffe-southwold.co.uk

Number Three ♦♦♦♦
3 Cautley Road, Southwold IP18 6DD
T: (01502) 723611

The Old Vicarage ♦♦♦♦
Wenhaston, Halesworth IP19 9EG
T: (01502) 478339
F: (01502) 478068
E: theycock@aol.com
I: www.southwold.blythweb.co.uk

Prospect Place ♦♦♦♦
33 Station Road, Southwold IP18 6AX
T: (01502) 722757
E: sally@prospect-place.demon.co.uk
I: www.prospect-place.demon.co.uk

Shanklin House ♦♦♦♦
6 Chester Road, Southwold IP18 6LN
T: (01502) 724748
E: ratcliffshanklin@aol.com

Ventnor Villas ♦♦♦
4 Hurn Crag Road, Reydon, Southwold IP18 6RG
T: (01502) 723619
F: (01502) 723619
E: sue@ventnorvillas.co.uk
I: www.ventnorvillas.co.uk

Victoria House ♦♦♦♦
9 Dunwich Road, Southwold IP18 6LJ
T: (01502) 722317
E: victoria@southwold.info
I: www.victoria.southwold.info

SPELLBROOK
Hertfordshire

Spellbrook Farm B&B ♦♦♦
London Road, Spellbrook, Bishop's Stortford CM23 4AX
T: (01279) 600191
F: (01279) 722758

SPORLE
Norfolk

Corfield House
♦♦♦♦ SILVER AWARD
Sporle, Swaffham PE32 2EA
T: (01760) 723636
E: corfield.house@virgin.net
I: www.corfieldhouse.co.uk

SPROUGHTON
Suffolk

Finjaro ♦♦♦♦
Valley Farm Drive, Hadleigh Road, Sproughton, Ipswich IP8 3EL
T: 0705 0065465
F: (01473) 652139
E: jan@finjaro.freeserve.co.uk
I: www.s-h-systems.co.uk/hotels/finjaro.html

SPROWSTON
Norfolk

Driftwood Lodge ♦♦♦♦
102 Wroxham Road, Sprowston, Norwich NR7 8EX
T: (01603) 444908
E: johnniekate@driftwood16.freeserve.co.uk & john.brown6080@ntlworld.com
I: www.driftwoodlodge.co.uk

STALHAM
Norfolk

Bramble House
♦♦♦♦ SILVER AWARD
Cat's Common, Norwich Road, Smallburgh, Norwich NR12 9NS
T: (01692) 535069
F: (01692) 535069
E: bramblehouse@tesco.net
I: www.norfolkbroads.com/bramblehouse

Chapelfield Cottage ♦♦♦♦
Chapelfield, Stalham, Norwich NR12 9EN
T: (01692) 582173
F: (01692) 583009
E: gary@cinqueportsmarine.freeserve.co.uk
I: www.whiteswan.u-net.com

STANSFIELD
Suffolk

Ivy House
Rating Applied For
Lower Street, Stansfield, Sudbury CO10 8LP
T: (01284) 789262
F: (01284) 789435
E: ivyhouse@roweuk.fsnet.co.uk

STANSTED
Essex

Bentfield House ♦♦♦♦
Bentfield Bower, Stansted CM24 8TJ
T: (01279) 816968
F: (01279) 816976

High Trees ♦♦♦
Parsonage Road, Takeley, Bishop's Stortford CM22 6QX
T: (01279) 871306
F: (01279) 870569

STANSTED MOUNTFITCHET
Essex

Chimneys
♦♦♦♦ SILVER AWARD
44 Lower Street, Stansted Mountfitchet, Stansted CM24 8LR
T: (01279) 813388
F: (01279) 813388
E: info@chimneysguesthouse.co.uk
I: www.chimneysguesthouse.co.uk

Larches
Rating Applied For
Grove Hill, Stansted CM24 8SR
T: (01279) 813957

STANWAY
Essex

The Loft ♦♦♦
Frederick House, New Road, Stanway, Colchester CO3 0HU
T: (01206) 516006
F: (01206) 516007
E: theloft@frederickhouse.co.uk
I: www.frederickhouse.co.uk

STEEPLE BUMPSTEAD
Essex

Yew Tree House ♦♦♦♦
15 Chapel Street, Steeple Bumpstead, Haverhill CB9 7DQ
T: (01440) 730364
E: yewtreehouse@btinternet.com
I: www.yewtreehouse.biz

STOKE-BY-NAYLAND
Suffolk

The Angel Inn
♦♦♦♦ SILVER AWARD
Polstead Street, Stoke-by-Nayland, Colchester CO6 4SA
T: (01206) 263245
F: (01206) 263373
E: the.angel@tiscali.com
I: www.4hotels.co.uk/uk/colchester14237.html

Ryegate House
♦♦♦♦ GOLD AWARD
Stoke-by-Nayland, Colchester CO6 4RA
T: (01206) 263679
E: bandb@ryegate.co.uk
I: www.ryegate.co.uk

Thorington Hall ♦♦♦
Stoke-by-Nayland, Colchester CO6 4SS
T: (01206) 337329

STOKE HOLY CROSS
Norfolk

Salamanca Farm ♦♦♦
116-118 Norwich Road, Stoke Holy Cross, Norwich NR14 8QJ
T: (01508) 492322
I: www.smoothhound.co.uk/hotels/salamanc.html

STOWMARKET
Suffolk

Gipping Heights Hotel ♦♦♦♦
Creeting Road, Stowmarket IP14 5BT
T: (01449) 675264

The Step House ♦♦♦♦
Hockey Hill, Wetheringsett, Stowmarket IP14 5PL
T: (01449) 766476
F: (01449) 766476
E: stephouse@talk21.com

Stricklands ♦♦♦
Stricklands Road, Stowmarket IP14 1AP
T: (01449) 612450
F: (01449) 614944
E: poppy@stricklandshouse.fsnet.co.uk

The Three Bears House Mulberrytree Farm ♦♦♦
Blacksmiths Lane, Middlewood Green, Stowmarket IP14 5EU
T: (01449) 711707
F: (01449) 711707

Verandah House ♦♦♦♦
29 Ipswich Road, Stowmarket IP14 1BD
T: (01449) 676104
F: (01449) 616127
E: verandah.house@virgin.net
I: www.verandahhouse.co.uk

STRETHAM
Cambridgeshire

Bridge House ♦♦♦
Green End, Stretham, Ely CB6 3LF
T: (01353) 649212
F: (01353) 649212

The Red Lion ♦♦♦
High Street, Stretham, Ely CB6 3JQ
T: (01353) 648132
F: (01353) 648327
E: frank.hayes@gateway.net

SUDBOURNE
Suffolk

Long Meadows ♦♦♦
Gorse Lane, Sudbourne, Woodbridge IP12 2BD
T: (01394) 450269

SUDBURY
Suffolk

Fiddlesticks ♦♦♦♦
Pinkuah Lane, Pentlow Ridge, Pentlow, Sudbury CO10 7JW
T: (01787) 280154
F: (01787) 280154
E: sarah@fiddlesticks.biz
I: www.fiddlesticks.biz

The Hall ♦♦♦♦
Milden, Lavenham, Sudbury CO10 9NY
T: (01787) 247235
F: (01787) 247235
E: gjb53@dial.pipex.com
I: www.thehall-milden.co.uk

Olde Bull Hotel and Restaurant ♦♦♦
Church Street, Ballingdon, Sudbury CO10 2BL
T: (01787) 374120
F: (01787) 379044
E: oldebullhotel@aol.com
I: www.theoldbullhotel.co.uk

West House ♦♦♦
59 Ballingdon Street, Sudbury CO10 2DA
T: (01787) 375033
E: aitken@westhousebb.fsnet.co.uk

SUTTON
Cambridgeshire

Anchor Inn ♦♦♦♦
Sutton Gault, Sutton, Ely CB6 2BD
T: (01353) 778537
F: (01353) 776180
E: achorinnsg@aol.com
I: www.anchor-inn-restaurant.co.uk

SWAFFHAM BULBECK
Cambridgeshire

Black Horse ♦♦♦
35 High Street, Swaffham Bulbeck, Cambridge CB5 0HP
T: (01223) 811366
F: (01223) 811695
E: blackhorsepubandmotel@hotmail.com
I: www.blackhorsepubandmotel.com

SWAFFHAM PRIOR
Cambridgeshire

Sterling Farm ♦♦♦
Heath Road, Swaffham Prior, Cambridge CB5 0LA
T: (01638) 741431
F: (01638) 741431

SWANTON MORLEY
Norfolk

Frogs Hall Farm
♦♦♦♦ SILVER AWARD
Frogs Hall Lane, Woodgate, Swanton Morley, East Dereham NR20 4NX
T: (01362) 638355
F: (01362) 638355
E: accommodation@frogs-hall.fsnet.co.uk
I: www.frogs-hall.fsnet.co.uk

SWEFFLING
Suffolk

Sweffling Hall Farm ♦♦♦
Sweffling, Saxmundham IP17 2BT
T: (01728) 663644
F: (01728) 663644
E: stephenmann@suffolkonline.net

Wayside Bed and Breakfast ♦♦♦♦
Glemham Road, Sweffling, Saxmundham IP17 2BQ
T: (01728) 663256
E: anthonywilkinson@suffolkonline.net
I: www.wayside-sweffling.co.uk

TAKELEY
Essex

Campey's Cottage ♦♦♦
Brewers End, Takeley, Bishop's Stortford CM22 6QJ
T: (01279) 873947
F: (01279) 873947
E: campeyscottage@stanstedairport.freeserve.co.uk

Crossroads B & B ♦♦
2 Hawthorn Close, Takeley, Bishop's Stortford CM22 6SD
T: (01279) 870619
E: ajcaiger884@aol.com

Jan Smiths B&B ♦♦♦
The Cottage, Jacks Lane, Takeley, Bishop's Stortford CM22 6NT
T: (01279) 870603
F: (01279) 870603

Joseph's Drive ♦♦
2 Joseph's Drive, The Street, Takeley, Bishop's Stortford CM22 6QT
T: (01279) 870652
F: (01279) 871969
E: ethlyn_king@hotmail.com

Joyners ♦♦♦
The Street, Takeley, Bishop's Stortford CM22 6QU
T: (01279) 870944
F: (01279) 870944
E: andersonsi@joyners99.freeserve.co.uk

Little Bullocks Farm ♦♦♦♦
Hope End, Takeley, Bishop's Stortford CM22 6TA
T: (01279) 870464
F: (01279) 871430
E: julie@waterman-farm.fsnet.co.uk

Oak Lodge Bed and Breakfast ♦♦♦♦
Oak Lodge, Jacks Lane, Takeley, Bishop's Stortford CM22 6NT
T: (01279) 871667
F: (01279) 871667
E: oaklodgebb@aol.com
I: www.oaklodgebb.com

Pippins ♦♦♦
Smiths Green, Takeley, Bishop's Stortford CM22 6NR
T: (01279) 870369
F: (01279) 871216
E: kevinmatthews@pippinsbandb.co.uk

San Michelle ♦♦♦♦
Jacks Lane, Takeley, Bishop's Stortford CM22 6NT
T: (01279) 870946

Warish Hall Farm ♦♦♦♦
Takeley, Bishop's Stortford CM22 6NZ
T: (01279) 870275
F: (01279) 870571
E: warishbb@hotmail.com

TERRINGTON ST JOHN
Norfolk

Kismet Bed and Breakfast ♦♦♦♦
Kismet, Main Road, Terrington St John, Wisbech PE14 7RR
T: (01945) 881364
E: francesg6@aol.com
I: www.kismet-guest-house.com

Somerville House
♦♦♦♦ SILVER AWARD
Church Road, Terrington St John, Wisbech PE14 7RY
T: (01945) 880952
F: (01945) 881150
E: somervillemc@hotmail.com
I: www.somervillehouse.co.uk

THAXTED
Essex

Crossways Guesthouse
♦♦♦♦ SILVER AWARD
32 Town Street, Thaxted, Great Dunmow CM6 2LA
T: (01371) 830348

The Farmhouse Inn ♦♦♦
Monk Street, Thaxted, Great Dunmow CM6 2NR
T: (01371) 830864
F: (01371) 831196

The Rose & Crown
Rating Applied For
31 Mill End, Thaxted, Great Dunmow CM6 2LT
T: (01371) 831152

THEBERTON
Suffolk

The Alders ♦♦♦
Potters Street, Theberton, Leiston IP16 4RL
T: (01728) 831790
F: (01728) 831790

The Granary ♦♦♦♦
Theberton, Leiston IP16 4RR
T: (01728) 831633
F: (01728) 831633
E: granary-theberton@uku.co.uk
I: www.granary-theberton.co.uk

THETFORD
Norfolk

East Farm ♦♦♦♦
Euston Road, Barnham, Thetford IP24 2PB
T: (01842) 890231
F: (01842) 890457

The Glebe Country House Bed and Breakfast ♦♦♦♦
34 London Road, Elveden, Thetford IP24 3TL
T: (01842) 890027
F: (01842) 890027
E: deirdre@jrudderham.freeserve.co.uk
I: www.glebecountryhouse.co.uk

The Wereham House Hotel ♦♦♦
24 White Hart Street, Thetford IP24 1AD
T: (01842) 761956
F: (01842) 765207
E: mail@werehamhouse.co.uk
I: www.werehamhousehotel.co.uk

THOMPSON
Norfolk

The Chequers Inn ♦♦♦♦
Griston Road, Thompson, Thetford IP24 1PX
T: (01953) 483360
F: (01953) 488092
E: themcdowalls@barbox.net
I: www.thompsonchequers.com

THORNDON
Suffolk

Moat Farm ♦♦♦♦
Thorndon, Eye IP23 7LX
T: (01379) 678437
F: (01379) 678023
E: geralde@clara.co.uk
I: www.moatfarm.co.uk

THORNHAM
Norfolk

Rushmeadow ♦♦♦♦
Main Road, Thornham, Hunstanton PE36 6LZ
T: (01485) 512372
F: (01485) 512372
E: rushmeadow@lineone.net
I: www.rushmeadow.com

THORPE BAY
Essex

Beaches
♦♦♦♦ SILVER AWARD
192 Eastern Esplanade, Thorpe Bay, Southend-on-Sea SS1 3AA
T: (01702) 586124
F: (01702) 587793
E: beaches@adriancw.demon.co.uk
I: www.smoothhound.co.uk/hotels/beaches

THORPE MARKET
Norfolk

Manorwood ♦♦♦
Church Road, Thorpe Market, Norwich NR11 8UA
T: (01263) 834938

THORPENESS
Suffolk

The Dolphin Inn ♦♦♦
Thorpeness, Leiston IP16 4NA
T: (01728) 454994
F: (01728) 453868
E: info@thorpeness.co.uk
I: www.thorpeness.co.uk

THURSTON
Suffolk

Chalk Pit Lodge ♦♦♦♦
27 Barton Road, Thurston, Bury St Edmunds IP31 3PA
T: (01359) 232741
F: (01359) 232741

TOFT
Cambridgeshire

Orchard Farmhouse ♦♦♦♦
56 Comberton Road, Toft, Cambridge CB3 7RY
T: (01223) 262309
F: (01223) 263979
E: tebbit.bxb.toft@talk21.com
I: www.smoothhound.co.uk/hotels/orchfarm.html

TOLLESBURY
Essex

Fernleigh ♦♦♦
16 Woodrolfe Farm Lane, Tollesbury, Maldon CM9 8SX
T: (01621) 868245
F: (01621) 868245
E: gill.willson@ntlworld.com

TOLLESHUNT MAJOR
Essex

Mill Lodge ♦♦♦
Mill Lane, Tolleshunt Major, Maldon CM9 8YF
T: (01621) 860311

Wicks Manor Farm ♦♦♦♦
Witham Road, Tolleshunt Major, Maldon CM9 8JU
T: (01621) 860629
F: (01621) 860629
E: rhowie@aspects.net

TOPPESFIELD
Essex

Harrow Hill Cottage ♦♦♦
Harrow Hill, Toppesfield, Halstead CO9 4LX
T: (01787) 237425

TOTTENHILL
Norfolk

Andel Lodge Hotel & Restaurant ♦♦♦♦
48 Lynn Road, Tottenhill, King's Lynn PE33 0RH
T: (01553) 810256
F: (01553) 811429
E: reception@andellodge.co.uk
I: www.andellodge.co.uk

TRING
Hertfordshire

Livingston's Bed & Breakfast ♦♦♦
Chimanimani, Toms Hill Road, Aldbury, Tring HP23 5SA
T: (01442) 851527

TRUNCH
Norfolk

North Barn ♦♦♦♦
Mundesley Road, Trunch, North Walsham NR28 0QB
T: (01263) 722256
F: (01263) 722256
E: richardjelliff@hotmail.com
I: www.north-barn.co.uk

UFFORD
Suffolk

Strawberry Hill ♦♦♦♦
Loudham Lane, Lower Ufford, Ufford, Woodbridge IP13 6ED
T: (01394) 460252
E: strawberryhilly@yahoo.co.uk
I: www.smoothhound.co.uk/hotels/strawber.html

UPPER SHERINGHAM
Norfolk

Lodge Cottage ♦♦♦♦
Lodge Hill, Upper Sheringham, Sheringham NR26 8TJ
T: (01263) 821445
E: stay@lodgecottage.co.uk
I: www.lodgecottage.co.uk

UPWELL
Cambridgeshire

The Olde Mill Hotel
♦♦♦♦ SILVER AWARD
Town Street, Upwell, Wisbech PE14 9AF
T: (01945) 772614
F: (01945) 772614
E: oldemill@lineone.net

WAKES COLNE
Essex

Rosebank Bed and Breakfast ♦♦♦♦
Rosebank Station Road, Wakes Colne, Colchester CO6 2DS
T: (01787) 223552
F: (01787) 220415

WALBERSWICK
Suffolk

The Anchor Inn ♦♦♦
Main Street, Walberswick, Southwold IP18 6UA
T: (01502) 722112
F: (01502) 724464

Dickon ♦♦
Main Street, Walberswick, Southwold IP18 6UX
T: (01502) 724046

WALSHAM-LE-WILLOWS
Suffolk

Wagner Cottage ♦♦
Walsham-le-Willows, Bury St Edmunds IP31 3AA
T: (01359) 259380
E: gill@wagner123.fsnet.co.uk

WALTHAM ABBEY
Essex

22 Elm Close ♦
Waltham Abbey EN9 1SQ
T: (01992) 764892

WALTON-ON-THE-NAZE
Essex

Bufo Villae Guest House ♦♦♦♦
31 Beatrice Road, Walton-on-the-Naze CO14 8HJ
T: (01255) 672644
E: bufo@ukgateway.net

Maple Leaf ♦♦♦
22 Saville Street, Walton-on-the-Naze CO14 8PJ
T: (01255) 679185
E: themapleleaf22@aol.com

Naze Beach Studio
Rating Applied For
18 Percival Road, Walton-on-the-Naze CO14 8HH
T: (01255) 677675
F: (01255) 851270
E: alisonspeller@ukonline.co.uk

WANGFORD
Suffolk

Poplar Hall ♦♦♦♦
Frostenden Corner, Frostenden, Wangford, Beccles NR34 7JA
T: (01502) 578549
I: www.southwold.co.uk/poplar-hall/

WANSFORD
Cambridgeshire

The Cross Keys ♦♦♦
21 Elton Road, Wansford, Peterborough PE8 6JD
T: (01780) 782266
F: (01780) 782266

Stoneacre Guest House ♦♦♦♦
Elton Road, Wansford, Peterborough PE8 6JT
T: (01780) 783283
F: (01780) 783283
E: peter.stoneacre@virgin.net
I: freespace@virgin.net/stoneacre.guesthouse/

WASHBROOK
Suffolk

High View ♦♦♦♦
Back Lane, Washbrook, Ipswich IP8 3JA
T: (01473) 730494
E: rosanna.steward@virgin.net

WATERDEN
Norfolk

The Old Rectory ♦♦♦♦
Waterden, Walsingham NR22 6AT
T: (01328) 823298

WATTON
Norfolk

Park Farm Bed & Breakfast
♦♦♦♦ SILVER AWARD
Park Farm, Caston Road, Griston, Thetford IP25 6QD
T: (01953) 483020
F: (01953) 483056
E: parkfarm@eidosnet.co.uk
I: www.parkfarmbreckland.co.uk

The Willow House ♦♦♦♦
2 High Street, Watton, Thetford IP25 6AE
T: (01953) 881181
F: (01953) 885885
E: willowhousewatton@barbox.net
I: www.willowhouse.net

WELLINGHAM
Norfolk

Manor House Farm
♦♦♦♦ SILVER AWARD
Wellingham, King's Lynn PE32 2TH
T: (01328) 838227
F: (01328) 838348
E: libbyellis@farming.co.uk

WELLS-NEXT-THE-SEA
Norfolk

Blenheim House ♦♦♦♦
Theatre Road, Wells-next-the-Sea NR23 1DJ
T: (01328) 711368
F: (01328) 711368
E: jmarjoram@blenheimhse.freeserve.co.uk

The Cobblers ♦♦♦♦
Standard Road, Wells-next-the-Sea NR23 1JU
T: (01328) 710155
E: ina@cobblers.co.uk
I: www.cobblers.co.uk

Corner House ♦♦
Staithe Street, Wells-next-the-Sea NR23 1AF
T: (01328) 710701
E: lmoney@ukonline.co.uk
I: www.cornerhouseatwells.com

Glebe Barn ♦♦♦♦
7a Glebe Road, Wells-next-the-Sea NR23 1AZ
T: (01328) 711809
E: glebebarn@supanet.com

Hideaway ♦♦♦
Red Lion Yard, Wells-next-the-Sea NR23 1AX
T: (01328) 710524
F: (01328) 710524
E: hideaway.wells@btinternet.com

Ilex House ♦♦♦
Bases Lane, Wells-next-the-Sea NR23 1DH
T: (01328) 710556
F: (01328) 710556
E: tommcjay@aol.com
I: www.broadland.com/ilexhouse

Machrimorc ♦♦♦♦
Burnt Street, Wells-next-the-Sea NR23 1HS
T: (01328) 711653
E: dorothy.maccallum@ntlworld.com
I: www.machrimore.co.uk

Meadow View Guest House ♦♦♦♦
53 High Street, Wighton, Wells-next-the-Sea NR23 1PF
T: (01328) 821527
E: bookings@meadowview.net
I: www.meadow-view.net

Mill House Guesthouse ♦♦♦
Mill House, Northfield Lane, Wells-next-the-Sea NR23 1JZ
T: (01328) 710739
I: www.broadland.com/millhouse

The Normans ♦♦♦♦
Invaders Court, Standard Road, Wells-next-the-Sea NR23 1JW
T: (01328) 710657
F: (01328) 710468

The Old Custom House ♦♦♦
East Quay, Wells-next-the-Sea NR23 1LD
T: (01328) 711463
F: (01328) 710277
E: bb@eastquay.co.uk
I: www.eastquay.co.uk

Old Police House ♦♦♦♦
Polka Road, Wells-next-the-Sea NR23 1ED
T: (01328) 710630
F: (01328) 710630
E: ophwells@yahoo.co.uk
I: www.northnorfolk.co.uk/oldpolicehouse

WELWYN
Hertfordshire

Catbells
Rating Applied For
40 Firs Walk, Tewin Wood, Welwyn AL6 0NZ
T: (01438) 798412
F: (01438) 798412

WENHASTON
Suffolk

Rowan House ♦♦♦♦
Hall Road, Wenhaston, Halesworth IP19 9HF
T: (01502) 478407
E: rowanhouse@freeuk.com

WENTWORTH
Cambridgeshire

Desiderata ♦♦♦
44 Main Street, Wentworth, Ely CB6 3QG
T: (01353) 776131
E: chips.1@virgin.net

WEST BERGHOLT
Essex

The Old Post House ♦♦♦
10 Colchester Road, West Bergholt, Colchester CO6 3JG
T: (01206) 240379
F: (01206) 243301

WEST DEREHAM
Norfolk

Bell Barn ♦♦♦♦
Lime Kiln Road, West Dereham, King's Lynn PE33 9RT
T: (01366) 500762
F: (01366) 500762
E: chris@woodbarn.freeserve.co.uk

WEST MERSEA
Essex

Hazel Oak ♦♦♦♦
28 Seaview Avenue, West Mersea, Colchester CO5 8HE
T: (01206) 383030
E: ann.blackmore@btinternet.com
I: www.btinternet.com/~dave.blackmore/

WEST RUDHAM
Norfolk

Oyster House
Rating Applied For
Lynn Road, West Rudham, King's Lynn PE31 8RW
T: (01485) 528327
F: (01485) 528327
E: oyster-house@tiscali.co.uk
I: www.oysterhouse.co.uk

WEST RUNTON
Norfolk

The Old Barn ♦♦♦♦
Cromer Road, West Runton, Cromer NR27 9QT
T: (01263) 838285

WESTCLIFF-ON-SEA
Essex

The Asgard Guesthouse ♦♦♦
25 Cobham Road, Westcliff-on-Sea SS0 8EG
T: (01702) 345466
F: (01702) 343813

Chilton House ♦♦♦
3 Trinity Avenue, Westcliff-on-Sea SS0 7PU
T: (01702) 342282
F: (01702) 342282
E: manager@thechilton.fsbusiness.co.uk

Malvern Lodge Guest House
Rating Applied For
29 Seaforth Road, Westcliff-on-Sea SS0 7SN
T: (01702) 431399
F: (01702) 431399
E: sandra@hawkins9805.freeserve.co.uk

Pavilion Hotel ♦♦
1 Trinity Avenue, Westcliff-on-Sea SS0 7PU
T: (01702) 332767

Retreat Guesthouse ♦♦♦
12 Canewdon Road, Westcliff-on-Sea SS0 7NE
T: (01702) 348217
F: (01702) 391179
E: retreatguesthouse.co.uk@tinyworld.co.uk
I: www.retreatguesthouse.co.uk

Welbeck Hotel ♦♦♦♦
27 Palmerston Road, Westcliff-on-Sea SS0 7TA
T: (01702) 347736
F: (01702) 339140
E: welbeck@tinyworld.co.uk
I: www.thewelbeckhotel.co.uk

WESTLETON
Suffolk

Netherside B & B ♦♦♦♦
Mill Street, Westleton, Saxmundham IP17 3BD
T: (01728) 648400
F: (01728) 648400

Pond House ♦♦♦♦
The Hill, Westleton, Saxmundham IP17 3AN
T: (01728) 648773

WHITE NOTLEY
Essex

Old Mill Barn
♦♦♦♦ SILVER AWARD
The Street, White Notley, Witham CM8 1RQ
T: (01376) 585021
F: (01376) 583617
E: martyncrump@compuserve.com

WHITE RODING
Essex

Marks Hall Farmhouse ♦♦♦♦
Marks Hall, White Roding, Great Dunmow CM6 1RT
T: (01279) 876438
F: (01279) 876236
E: jane@markshall.fsnet.co.uk
I: www.marks-hall.co.uk

WHITTLESEY
Cambridgeshire

Whitmore House ♦♦♦♦
31 Whitmore Street, Whittlesey, Peterborough PE7 1HE
T: (01733) 203088

WICKHAM MARKET
Suffolk

The Old Pharmacy ♦♦♦♦
72 High Street, Wickham Market, Woodbridge IP13 0QU
T: (01728) 745012
E: juliefiona@talk21.com

WIGHTON
Norfolk

Shrublands ♦♦♦♦
Wells Road, Wighton, Wells-next-the-Sea NR23 1PR
T: (01328) 820743
F: (01328) 820743
E: shrublands@shrub-lands.freeserve.co.uk
I: www.shrub-lands.freeserve.co.uk

WILBURTON
Cambridgeshire

Willowtree Lodge ♦♦♦
Willowtree Cottage, Twentypence Road, Wilburton, Ely CB6 3PX
T: (01353) 741742
F: (01353) 741742

WIMBISH
Essex

Blossom Cottage ♦♦♦♦
Rowney Corner, Thaxted road, Wimbish, Saffron Walden CB10 2UZ
T: (01799) 599430
E: cmacpherson@waitrose.com

Newdegate House
♦♦♦♦ SILVER AWARD
Howlett End, Wimbish, Saffron Walden CB10 2XW
T: (01799) 599748
F: (01799) 599748
E: jackyhaigh@talk21.com

WINGFIELD
Suffolk

Gables Farm ♦♦♦♦
Earsham Street, Wingfield, Diss IP21 5RH
T: (01379) 586355
F: (01379) 588058
E: gables-farm@ntlworld.com
I: www.gablesfarm.co.uk

WINTERTON-ON-SEA
Norfolk

Cleveland House ♦♦♦♦
The Lane, Winterton-on-Sea, Great Yarmouth NR29 4BN
T: 07884 117440
F: (01493) 393352
E: cleveland.house@virgin.net

WISBECH
Cambridgeshire

Marmion House Hotel ♦♦♦
11 Lynn Road, Wisbech PE13 3DD
T: (01945) 582822
F: (01945) 475889

WITCHFORD
Cambridgeshire

Harvest House ♦♦♦♦
2 The Warren, Witchford, Ely CB6 2HN
T: (01353) 663517

The Woodlands ♦♦♦♦
Grunty Fen Road, Witchford, Ely CB6 2JE
T: (01353) 663746
E: uptonheath@tinyworld.co.uk

WITHAM
Essex

Chestnuts ♦♦♦♦
8 Octavia Drive, Witham Lodge, Witham CM8 1HQ
T: (01376) 515990
F: (01376) 515990
E: KBMONEY2@aol.com

WIX
Essex

Dairy House Farm
♦♦♦♦♦ SILVER AWARD
Bradfield Road, Wix, Manningtree CO11 2SR
T: (01255) 870322
F: (01255) 870186
E: bridgetwhitworth@hotmail.com
I: www.dairyhousefarm.info

WOOD NORTON
Norfolk

Manor Farm Bed and Breakfast
♦♦♦♦ SILVER AWARD
Manor Farm, Hall Lane, Wood Norton, East Dereham NR20 5BE
T: (01362) 683231
F: (01362) 683231

WOODBRIDGE
Suffolk

Deben Lodge ♦♦
Melton Road, Woodbridge IP12 1NH
T: (01394) 382740
I: www.SmoothHound.co.uk/shs.html

Grove House Hotel ♦♦♦
39 Grove Road, Woodbridge IP12 4LG
T: (01394) 382202
F: (01394) 380652
E: reception@thegrovehousehotel.com
I: www.thegrovehousehotel.co.uk

Moat Barn ♦♦♦♦
Bredfield, Woodbridge IP13 6BD
T: (01473) 737520
F: (01473) 737520
I: www.moat-barn.co.uk

Moat Farmhouse ♦♦♦
Dallinghoo Road, Bredfield, Woodbridge IP13 6BD
T: (01473) 737475

The Old Rectory
♦♦♦♦ SILVER AWARD
Campsey Ashe, Woodbridge IP13 0PU
T: (01728) 746524
F: (01728) 746524
E: mail@theoldrectorysuffolk.com
I: www.theoldrectorysuffolk.com

The Old Warehouse ♦♦♦
Brook Street, Woodbridge IP12 1BE
T: (01394) 388497
E: christina@woodbridgewarehouse.fsnet.co.uk

Sandpit House ♦♦♦
Loudham, Wickham Market, Woodbridge IP13 0NW
T: (01728) 747435
E: gilbey@sandpithouse@fsnet.co.uk

WOODHAM MORTIMER
Essex

Chase Farm Bed & Breakfast ♦♦♦
Chase Farm, Hyde Chase, Woodham Mortimer, Maldon CM9 6TN
T: (01245) 223268

WOODSTON
Cambridgeshire

White House Guesthouse ♦♦♦
White House, 318 Oundle Road, Woodston, Peterborough PE2 9QP
T: (01733) 566650

WOOLPIT
Suffolk

The Bull Inn & Restaurant ♦♦♦
The Street, Woolpit, Bury St Edmunds IP30 9SA
T: (01359) 240393
F: (01359) 240393
E: trevor@howling.fsbusiness.co.uk
I: www.bullinnwoolpit.co.uk

Grange Farm ♦♦♦♦
Woolpit, Bury St Edmunds IP30 9RG
T: (01359) 241143
F: (01359) 244296
E: grangefarm@btinternet.com
I: www.farmstayanglia.co.uk/grangefarm/

Swan Inn ♦♦♦
The Street, Woolpit, Bury St Edmunds IP30 9QN
T: (01359) 240482

WOOTTON
Bedfordshire

Maple Tree Cottage ♦♦♦♦
Wootton Green, Wootton, Bedford MK43 9EE
T: (01234) 768631
F: (01234) 768631
E: francy.mtc@cwcom.net
I: frances.lovell@btopenworld.com

WORLINGTON
Suffolk

Worlington Hall Country House Hotel ♦♦♦♦
The Street, Worlington, Bury St Edmunds IP28 8RX
T: (01638) 712237
F: (01638) 712631

WORSTEAD
Norfolk

Hall Farm Guesthouse ♦♦♦♦
Hall Farm, Sloley Road, Worstead, North Walsham NR28 9RS
T: (01692) 536124
E: d.lowe4@tinyworld.co.uk OR hallfarm@tiscali.co.uk

Holly Grove House
♦♦♦♦ SILVER AWARD
Lyngate, Worstead, North Walsham NR28 9RQ
T: (01692) 535546
E: michaelhorwood@freenetname.co.uk
I: www.broadland.com/hollygrove

The Ollands ♦♦♦♦
Swanns Loke, Worstead, North Walsham NR28 9RP
T: (01692) 535150
F: (01692) 535150
E: ollands@worstead.freeserve.co.uk

WOTHORPE
Cambridgeshire

Firwood ♦♦♦♦
First Drift, Wothorpe, Stamford PE9 3JL
T: (01780) 765654
F: (01780) 765654

WRENTHAM
Suffolk

The Five Bells ♦♦♦
Southwold Road, Wrentham, Beccles NR34 7JF
T: (01502) 675249
F: (01502) 676127
E: vh@five-bells.fsnet.co.uk

The Garden Flat ♦♦♦
68 Southwold Road, Wrentham, Beccles NR34 7JF
T: (01502) 675692
F: (01502) 675692
E: r.ashton@ecosse.net

Number Seven, Mill Lane ♦♦♦
Wrentham, Beccles NR34 7JQ
T: (01502) 675489

Southwold Lodge ♦♦♦♦
67 Southwold Road, Wrentham, Beccles NR34 7JE
T: (01502) 676148
F: (01986) 784797
E: qhbfield@aol.com
I: www.queensheadbramfield.co.uk/accommodation.htm

WRESTLINGWORTH
Bedfordshire

Orchard Cottage ♦♦♦
1 High Street, Wrestlingworth, Sandy SG19 2EW
T: (01767) 631355
F: (01767) 631355
E: robert@owenstrong.freeserve.co.uk

WRITTLE
Essex

Moor Hall
♦♦♦♦ SILVER AWARD
Newney Green, Writtle, Chelmsford CM1 3SE
T: (01245) 420814
E: moorhall@talk21.com

WROXHAM
Norfolk

The Coach House ♦♦♦♦
96 Norwich Road, Wroxham, Norwich NR12 8RY
T: (01603) 784376
F: (01603) 783734
E: bishop@worldonline.co.uk
I: www.coachhousewroxham.co.uk

The Dragon Flies
♦♦♦♦ SILVER AWARD
5 The Avenue, Wroxham, Norwich NR12 8TN
T: (01603) 783822
F: (01603) 783822
E: geoff.g.kimberley@talk21.com

Ridge House ♦♦♦♦
7 The Avenue, Wroxham, Norwich NR12 8TN
T: (01603) 782130

Wroxham Park Lodge ♦♦♦♦
142 Norwich Road, Wroxham, Norwich NR12 8SA
T: (01603) 782991
E: prklodge@nascr.net
I: www.smoothhound.co.uk/hotels/wroxhamp.html

WYMONDHAM
Norfolk

Witch Hazel
♦♦♦♦ SILVER AWARD
Church Lane, Wicklewood, Wymondham NR18 9QH
T: (01953) 602247
F: (01953) 602247
I: www.witchhazel-norfolk.co.uk

YOXFORD
Suffolk

The Griffin ♦♦♦
High Street, Yoxford, Saxmundham IP17 3EP
T: (01728) 668229
E: i.terry@thegriffin.co.uk
I: www.thegriffin.co.uk

Mile Hill Barn
♦♦♦♦♦ GOLD AWARD
Main Road, Kelsale, Saxmundham IP17 2RG
T: (01728) 668519
E: mail@mile-hill-barn.co.uk
I: www.mile-hill-barn.co.uk

The Old Methodist Chapel ♦♦♦♦
High Street, Yoxford, Saxmundham IP17 3EU
T: (01728) 668333
F: (01728) 668333
E: browns@chapelsuffolk.co.uk
I: www.chapelsuffolk.co.uk

SOUTH WEST

ABBOTSBURY
Dorset

Corfe Gate House
◆◆◆◆◆ SILVER AWARD
Coryates, Abbotsbury,
Weymouth DT3 4HW
T: (01305) 871483
F: (01305) 264024
E: maureenadams@corfegatehouse.co.uk
I: www.corfegatehouse.co.uk

Linton Cottage
◆◆◆◆ SILVER AWARD
Abbotsbury, Weymouth DT3 4JL
T: (01305) 871339
F: (01305) 871339
E: queenbee@abbotsbury.co.uk
I: www.lintoncottage.co.uk

Swan Lodge ◆◆◆
Rodden Row, Abbotsbury,
Weymouth DT3 4JL
T: (01305) 871249
F: (01305) 871249

ADVENT
Cornwall

Higher Trezion ◆◆◆◆
Tresinney, Advent, Camelford
PL32 9QW
T: (01840) 213761
F: (01840) 212509
E: highertrezion@virgin.net

ALLERFORD
Somerset

Exmoor Falconry & Animal Farm ◆◆◆
West Lynch farm, Allerford,
Minehead TA24 8HJ
T: (01643) 862816
F: (01643) 862816
E: exmoorfalcon@freenet.co.uk
I: www.exmoorfalconry.co.uk

Fern Cottage ◆◆◆◆
Allerford, Minehead TA24 8HN
T: (01643) 862215
F: (01643) 862215
E: ferncottage@bushinternet.com
I: www.exmoor.com/ferncottage

AMESBURY
Wiltshire

Fairlawn Hotel ◆◆
42 High Street, Amesbury,
Salisbury SP4 7DL
T: (01980) 622103
F: (01980) 624888

Mandalay ◆◆◆◆
15 Stonehenge Road, Amesbury,
Salisbury SP4 7BA
T: (01980) 623733
F: (01980) 626642

The Old Bakery ◆◆◆
Netton, Salisbury SP4 6AW
T: (01722) 782351
E: valahen@aol.com
I: members.aol.com/valahen

Solstice Farmhouse ◆◆◆
39 Holders Road, Amesbury,
Salisbury SP4 7PH
T: (01980) 625052
E: williamsmc@btinternet.com

Vale House ◆◆◆
Figheldean, Salisbury SP4 8JJ
T: (01980) 670713
E: strefford@valehouse.fslife.co.uk

ANGARRACK
Cornwall

Byways ◆◆
Steamers Hill, Angarrack, Hayle
TR27 5JB
T: (01736) 753463
E: bywaysbb@lineone.net
I: www.bywaysbb.co.uk

ASHBRITTLE
Somerset

Lower Westcott Farm ◆◆◆
Ashbrittle, Wellington TA21 0HZ
T: (01398) 361296
E: lowerwestcott@aol.com

ASHBURTON
Devon

Gages Mill
◆◆◆◆ SILVER AWARD
Ashburton, Newton Abbot
TQ13 7JW
T: (01364) 652391
F: (01364) 652391
E: moore@gagesmill.co.uk
I: www.gagesmill.co.uk

Sladesdown Farm
◆◆◆◆ SILVER AWARD
Ashburton, Landscove,
Ashburton, Newton Abbot
TQ13 7ND
T: (01364) 653973
F: (01364) 653973
E: sue@sladesdownfarm.co.uk
I: www.sladesdownfarm.co.uk

Wellpritton Farm ◆◆◆◆
Holne, Newton Abbot TQ13 7RX
T: (01364) 631273
E: info@wellprittonfarm.com
I: www.wellprittonfarm.com

ASHTON
Somerset

Ashton Road Farm ◆◆◆
Ashton, Wedmore BS28 4QE
T: (01934) 713462
F: (01934) 713462

ASHTON KEYNES
Wiltshire

Corner Cottage ◆◆◆
Fore Street, Ashton Keynes,
Swindon SN6 6NP
T: (01285) 861454

Wheatleys Farm ◆◆◆◆
High Road, Ashton Keynes,
Swindon SN6 6NX
T: (01285) 861310
F: (01285) 861310
E: wheatleys.farm@lineone.net
I: www.smoothhound.co.uk/hotels/wheatleys.html

ASKERSWELL
Dorset

Hembury House ◆◆◆◆
Askerswell, Dorchester DT2 9EN
T: (01308) 485297
F: (01308) 485032
E: peter.richards17@btopenworld.com

ATWORTH
Wiltshire

Church Farm ◆◆◆◆
Church Street, Atworth,
Melksham SN12 8JA
T: (01225) 702215
F: (01225) 704774
E: churchfarm@tinyonline.co.uk
I: www.churchfarm-atworth.freeserve.co.uk

AVEBURY
Wiltshire

Manor Farm ◆◆◆◆
High Street, Avebury,
Marlborough SN8 1RF
T: (01672) 539294
F: (01672) 539294

The New Inn ◆◆◆
Winterbourne Monkton,
Swindon SN4 9NW
T: (01672) 539240
F: (01672) 539150
E: the_new_inn@hotmail.com
I: www.thenewinn.net

AVETON GIFFORD
Devon

Helliers Farm ◆◆◆◆
Ashford, Aveton Gifford,
Kingsbridge TQ7 4NB
T: (01548) 550689
F: (01548) 550689
E: helliersfarm@ukonline.co.uk
I: www.helliersfarm.co.uk

AWLISCOMBE
Devon

Birds Farm ◆◆
Awliscombe, Honiton EX14 3PU
T: (01404) 841620

Godford Farm ◆◆◆◆
Awliscombe, Honiton EX14 3PW
T: (01404) 42825
F: (01404) 42825
E: lawrencesally@hotmail.com
I: www.devon-farm-holidays.co.uk

AXBRIDGE
Somerset

Lamb Inn ◆◆◆
The Square, Axbridge BS26 2AP
T: (01934) 732253
F: (01934) 733821

Waterside ◆◆◆
Cheddar Road, Axbridge
BS26 2DP
T: (01934) 743182

AXMINSTER
Devon

Beckford Cottage ◆◆◆◆
Dalwood, Axminster EX13 7HQ
T: (01404) 881641
F: (01404) 881108
E: beckfordcottage@hotmail.com
I: www.beckford-cottage.co.uk

Chalfont House ◆◆◆◆
Crewkerne Road, Raymonds Hill,
Axminster EX13 5SX
T: (01297) 33852
E: chalfont.house@btopenworld.com

Chattan Hall ◆◆◆◆◆
Woodbury Lane, Axminster
EX13 5TL
T: (01297) 32365
F: (01297) 32365
E: boston@chattanhall.co.uk
I: www.chattanhall.co.uk

Coaxdon Farm ◆◆◆◆
Axminster EX13 7LP
T: (01297) 35540
F: (01297) 32596
E: coaxdon@fish.co.uk
I: www.eclipse.co.uk/coaxdon

Kerrington House Hotel
◆◆◆◆◆ GOLD AWARD
Musbury Road, Axminster
EX13 5JR
T: (01297) 35333
E: ja.reaney@kerringtonhouse.com
I: www.kerringtonhouse.com

BABBACOMBE
Devon

Astral Palms Hotel ◆◆◆
2 York Road, Babbacombe,
Torquay TQ1 3SG
T: (01803) 327087
F: (01803) 329446
E: enquiries@inter-docs.co.uk
I: www.astralpalms.co.uk

Birch Tor ◆◆◆◆
315 Babbacombe Road,
Babbacombe, Torquay TQ1 3TB
T: (01803) 292707
E: terry@birchtor.co.uk
I: www.birchtor.co.uk

Regency Hotel ◆◆◆◆
33,35 Babbacombe Downs Road,
Babbacombe, Torquay TQ1 3LN
T: (01803) 323509
F: (01803) 323509
E: theregency@hotmail.com
I: www.regencytorquay.co.uk

Seabury Hotel ◆◆◆◆
Manor Road, Babbacombe,
Torquay TQ1 3JX
T: (01803) 327255
F: (01803) 315321

BACKWELL
North Somerset

Moorlands ◆◆◆◆
Backwell Hill, Backwell, Bristol
BS48 3EJ
T: (01275) 462755
E: moorlandsguesthouse@yahoo.co.uk

BAMPTON
Devon

Bampton Gallery ◆◆◆◆
2 - 4 Brook Street, Bampton,
Tiverton EX16 9LY
T: (01398) 331354
F: (01398) 331119
E: bampgall@aol.com
I: www.exmoortourism.org/bamptongallery.htm

Lodfin Farm Bed & Breakfast
◆◆◆◆ SILVER AWARD
Morebath, Bampton, Tiverton
EX16 9DD
T: (01398) 331400
F: (01398) 331400
E: info@lodfinfarm.com
I: www.lodfinfarm.com

BARBROOK
Devon

West Lyn Farmhouse ◆◆◆◆
Barbrook, Lynton EX35 6LD
T: (01598) 753618
F: (01598) 753618
E: info@westlynfarm.co.uk
I: www.westlynfarm.co.uk

BARFORD ST MARTIN
Wiltshire

Briden House ♦♦♦♦
West Street, Barford St Martin, Salisbury SP3 4AH
T: (01722) 743471
F: (01722) 743471
E: bridenhouse@barford25.freeserve.co.uk
I: www.smoothhound.co.uk/hotels/bridenho.html

BARNSTAPLE
Devon

Bradiford Cottage ♦♦♦♦
Bradiford, Barnstaple EX31 4DP
T: (01271) 345039
F: (01271) 345039
E: holidays@humesfarm.co.uk
I: www.humesfarm.co.uk

BARNSTAPLE
Devon

Field House
Rating Applied For
Muddiford, Barnstaple EX31 4ET
T: (01271) 376205
F: (01271) 376205

BARNSTAPLE
Devon

Little Orchard ♦♦♦
Braunton Road, Barnstaple EX31 1GA
T: (01271) 371714
F: (01271) 342590
E: terrychaplin@accanet.com

The Red House ♦♦♦♦
Roundswell, Barnstaple EX31 3NP
T: (01271) 345966
F: (01271) 379966
E: booking@theredhousenorthdevon.co.uk
I: www.theredhousenorthdevon.co.uk

The Spinney
♦♦♦♦ SILVER AWARD
Shirwell, Barnstaple EX31 4JR
T: (01271) 850282
E: thespinney@shirwell.fsnet.co.uk
I: www.thespinneyshirwell.co.uk

Waytown Farm ♦♦♦♦
Shirwell, Barnstaple EX31 4JN
T: (01271) 850396
F: (01271) 850396
E: info@waytownholidays.co.uk
I: www.waytownholidays.co.uk

BARRINGTON
Somerset

Kent House
♦♦♦♦ SILVER AWARD
Barrington, Ilminster TA19 0JP
T: (01460) 52613
E: jrclushington@yahoo.co.uk

BASONBRIDGE
Somerset

Merry Farm ♦♦♦♦
Merry Lane, Basonbridge, Highbridge TA9 3PS
T: (01278) 783655
E: janetdearing@aol.com

BATCOMBE
Somerset

Valley View Farm ♦♦♦
Batcombe, Shepton Mallet BA4 6AJ
T: (01749) 850302
F: (01749) 850302
I: mysite.freeserve.com/valleyviewfarm

BATH
Bath and North East Somerset

Abbey Rise ♦♦♦♦
97 Wells Road, Bath BA2 3AN
T: (01225) 316177
F: (01225) 316177
E: b+b@abbeyrise.co.uk

Abbot House ♦♦♦
168 Newbridge Road, Bath BA1 3LE
T: (01225) 314151
E: sandra.ashley@btinternet.com
I: www.abbothouseguesthouse.co.uk

The Albany Guest House
♦♦♦♦ SILVER AWARD
24 Crescent Gardens, Upper Bristol Road, Bath BA1 2NB
T: (01225) 313339
E: the_albany@lineone.net
I: www.bath.org/hotel/albany.htm

Apartment 1 ♦♦♦♦
60 Great Pulteney Street, Bath BA2 4DN
T: (01225) 464134
F: (01225) 483663
E: chanloosmith@aptone.fsnet.co.uk

Aquae Sulis ♦♦♦♦
174/176 Newbridge Road, Bath BA1 3LE
T: (01225) 420061
F: (01225) 446077
E: enquiries@aquaesulishotel.com
I: www.aquaesulishotel.com

Ashley House ♦♦♦
8 Pulteney Gardens, Bath BA2 4HG
T: (01225) 425027

Ashley Villa Hotel ♦♦♦♦
Newbridge Road, Bath BA1 3JZ
T: (01225) 421683
F: (01225) 313604
E: ashleyvilla@clearface.co.uk
I: www.ashleyvilla.co.uk

Astor House ♦♦♦♦
14 Oldfield Road, Bath BA2 3ND
T: (01225) 429134
F: (01225) 429134
E: astorhouse.visitus@virgin.net

Athole Guest House
♦♦♦♦♦ GOLD AWARD
33 Upper Oldfield Park, Bath BA2 3JX
T: (01225) 334307
F: (01225) 320009
E: info@atholehouse.co.uk
I: www.atholehouse.co.uk

Avon Guest House ♦♦♦
1 Pulteney Gardens, Bath BA2 4HG
T: (01225) 313009
F: (01225) 313009

Ayrlington Hotel
♦♦♦♦♦ GOLD AWARD
24/25 Pulteney Road, Bath BA2 4EZ
T: (01225) 425495
F: (01225) 469029
E: mail@ayrlington.com
I: www.ayrlington.com

Badminton Villa
♦♦♦♦ SILVER AWARD
10 Upper Oldfield Park, Bath BA2 3JZ
T: (01225) 426347
F: (01225) 420393
E: badmintonvilla@blueyonder.co.uk
I: www.smoothhound.co.uk/hotels/badminton.html

Bailbrook Lodge Hotel ♦♦♦
35/37 London Road West, Bath BA1 7HZ
T: (01225) 859090
F: (01225) 852299
E: hotel@bailbrooklodge.co.uk
I: www.bailbrooklodge.co.uk

Bay Tree House ♦♦♦♦
12 Crescent Gardens, Bath BA1 2NA
T: (01225) 483699
F: (01225) 483699
E: enquires@bay-tree-house.fsnet.co.uk
I: www.wherenow.net/baytree

The Belmont ♦♦♦
7 Belmont, Lansdown Road, Bath BA1 5DZ
T: (01225) 423082
E: archie_watson@hotmail.com

Bloomfield House
♦♦♦♦♦ SILVER AWARD
146 Bloomfield Road, Bath BA2 2AS
T: (01225) 420105
E: bloomfieldhouse@compuserve.com
I: www.bloomfield-house.co.uk

16 Bloomfield Road ♦♦♦
Bear Flat, Bath BA2 2AB
T: (01225) 337804

Bridgnorth House ♦♦♦♦
2 Crescent Gardens, Bath BA1 2NA
T: (01225) 331186

Brompton House ♦♦♦♦
St John's Road, Bath BA2 6PT
T: (01225) 420972
F: (01225) 420505
E: bromptonhouse@btinternet.com
I: www.bromptonhouse.co.uk

Carfax Hotel ♦♦♦♦
Great Pulteney Street, Bath BA2 4BS
T: (01225) 462089
F: (01225) 443257
E: reservations@carfaxhotel.co.uk
I: www.carfaxhotel.co.uk

Cherry Tree Villa ♦♦♦
7 Newbridge Hill, Bath BA1 3PW
T: (01225) 331671

Church Farm ♦♦♦
Monkton Farleigh, Bradford-on-Avon BA15 2QJ
T: (01225) 858583
F: (01225) 852474
E: rebecca@tuckerb.fsnet.co.uk
I: www.tuckerb.fsnet.co.uk

Corston Fields Farm ♦♦♦♦
Corston, Bath BA2 9EZ
T: (01225) 873305
E: corston.fields@btinternet.com
I: www.corstonfields.com

County Hotel
♦♦♦♦♦ GOLD AWARD
18-19 Pulteney Road, Bath BA2 4EZ
T: (01225) 425003
F: (01225) 466493
E: reservations@county-hotel.co.uk
I: www.county-hotel.co.uk

Crescent Guest House ♦♦♦
21 Crescent Gardens, Upper Bristol Road, Bath BA1 2NA
T: (01225) 425945
E: info@crescentbath.co.uk
I: www.crescentbath.co.uk

Edgar Hotel ♦♦♦
64 Great Pulteney Street, Bath BA2 4DN
T: (01225) 420619
F: (01225) 466916
E: edgar-hotel@pgen.net
I: www.edgar-hotel.co.uk

Elgin Villa ♦♦♦♦
6 Marlborough Lane, Bath BA1 2NQ
T: (01225) 424557
F: (01225) 424557
E: stay@elginvilla.co.uk
I: www.elginvilla.co.uk

The Firs ♦♦♦♦
2 Newbridge Hill, Bath BA1 3PU
T: (01225) 334575

Flaxley Villa ♦♦♦
9 Newbridge Hill, Bath BA1 3PW
T: (01225) 313237

Forres House ♦♦♦♦
172 Newbridge Road, Bath BA1 3LE
T: (01225) 427698
F: (01225) 338350
E: Jj.forres@btinternet.co.uk
I: www.forreshouse.co.uk

Glan Y Dwr ♦♦♦
14 Newbridge Hill, Bath BA1 3PU
T: (01225) 317521
F: (01225) 317521
E: glanydwr@hotmail.com

Glen View ♦♦♦♦
162 Newbridge Road, Bath BA1 3LE
T: (01225) 421376
F: (01225) 310271
E: info@glenviewbath.co.uk
I: www.glenviewbath.co.uk

Glentworth
♦♦♦♦ SILVER AWARD
12 Marlborough Lane, Bath BA2 2NQ
T: (01225) 334554
F: (01225) 425239
E: stay@glentworth.co.uk
I: www.glentworthbath.co.uk

Grove Lodge ♦♦♦♦
11 Lambridge, Bath BA1 6BJ
T: (01225) 310860
F: (01225) 429630
E: grovelodge@bath24.fsnet.co.uk

Hatt Farm ♦♦♦♦
Old Jockey, Box, Corsham SN13 8DJ
T: (01225) 742989
F: (01225) 742779
E: hattfarm@netlineuk.net

Haydon House
♦♦♦♦♦ SILVER AWARD
9 Bloomfield Park, Bath BA2 2BY
T: (01225) 444919
F: (01225) 444919
E: stay@haydonhouse.co.uk
I: www.haydonhouse.co.uk

Henrietta Hotel ♦♦♦
32 Henrietta Street, Henrietta Mews, Bath BA2 6LR
T: (01225) 447779
F: (01225) 444150
I: www.henrietta-hotel.co.uk

Hermitage ♦♦♦
Bath Road, Box, Corsham SN13 8DT
T: (01225) 744187
F: (01225) 743447
E: hermitage@telecall.co.uk

Highfields ♦♦♦♦♦
207 Bailbrook Lane, Batheaston, Bath BA1 7AB
T: (01225) 859782
F: (01225) 852778
E: acham@supanet.com
I: www.highfieldsbath.co.uk

Highways House ♦♦♦♦
143 Wells Road, Bath BA2 3AL
T: (01225) 421238
F: (01225) 481169
E: stay@highwayshouse.co.uk
I: www.highwayshouse.co.uk

The Hollies
♦♦♦♦ SILVER AWARD
Hatfield Road, Bath BA2 2BD
T: (01225) 313366
F: (01225) 313366
E: davcartwright@lineone.net
I: www.visitus.co.uk/bath/hotel.hollies.html

Holly Lodge
♦♦♦♦♦ SILVER AWARD
8 Upper Oldfield Park, Bath BA2 3JZ
T: (01225) 424042
F: (01225) 481138
E: stay@hollylodge.co.uk
I: www.hollylodge.co.uk

Kennard Hotel
♦♦♦♦♦ SILVER AWARD
11 Henrietta Street, Bath BA2 6LL
T: (01225) 310472
F: (01225) 460054
E: reception@kennard.co.uk
I: www.kennard.co.uk

Kinlet Villa Guest House ♦♦♦♦
99 Wellsway, Bath BA2 4RX
T: (01225) 420268
F: (01225) 420268
E: kinlet@inbath.freeserve.co.uk
I: www.visitus.co.uk/bath/hotel/kinlet.htm

Lamp Post Villa ♦♦♦
3 Crescent Gardens, Upper Bristol Road, Bath BA1 2NA
T: (01225) 331221
F: (01225) 426783

Laura Place Hotel ♦♦♦♦
3 Laura Place, Great Pulteney Street, Bath BA2 4BH
T: (01225) 463815
F: (01225) 310222

Lavender House
♦♦♦♦♦ SILVER AWARD
Bloomfield Park, Bath BA2 2BY
T: (01225) 314500
F: (01225) 448564
E: lavenderhouse@btintenet.com
I: www.lavenderhouse-bath.com

Leighton House
♦♦♦♦♦ GOLD AWARD
139 Wells Road, Bath BA2 3AL
T: (01225) 314769
F: (01225) 443079
E: welcome@leighton-house.co.uk
I: www.leighton-house.co.uk

Lilac Cottage ♦♦♦
Gurney Slade, Bath BA3 4TT
T: (01749) 840469
E: lilaccotbandb@aol.com

Lindisfarne Guest House ♦♦♦♦
41a Warminster Road, Bathampton, Bath BA2 6XJ
T: (01225) 466342
E: lindisfarne-bath@talk21.com
I: www.bath.org/hotel/lindisfarne.htm

The Manor House ♦♦♦
Mill Lane, Monkton Combe, Bath BA2 7HD
T: (01225) 723128
F: (01225) 722972
E: beth@manorhousebath.co.uk
I: www.manorhousebath.co.uk

Marisha's Guest House ♦♦♦
68 Newbridge Hill, Bath BA1 3QA
T: (01225) 446881
F: (01225) 446881
E: marishasinbath@amserve.net

Meadowland
♦♦♦♦♦ GOLD AWARD
36 Bloomfield Park, Bath BA2 2BX
T: (01225) 311079
F: (01225) 311079
E: meadowland@bath92.freeserve.co.uk
I: www.meadowlandbath.co.uk

Membland Guest House ♦♦♦
7 Pulteney Terrace, Pulteney Road, Bath BA2 4HJ
T: 07958 599572
E: prmoore@wimpey.co.uk

Midway Cottage ♦♦♦♦
Farleigh Wick, Bradford-on-Avon BA15 2PU
T: (01225) 863932
F: (01225) 866836
E: midway_cottage@hotmail.com

Milton Guest House ♦♦♦♦
75 Wellsway, Bear Flat, Bath BA2 4RU
T: (01225) 335632
E: sue@milton-house.fsnet.co.uk
I: www.milton-house.fsnet.co.uk

Monkshill
♦♦♦♦♦ GOLD AWARD
Shaft Road, Monkton Combe, Bath BA2 7HL
T: (01225) 833028
F: (01225) 833028
E: monks.hill@virgin.net
I: www.monkshill.com

Number 30 Crescent Gardens
♦♦♦♦ SILVER AWARD
Bath BA1 2NB
T: (01225) 337393
F: (01225) 337393
E: david.greenwood12@btinternet.com
I: www.numberthirty.com

The Old Mill Hotel
♦♦♦♦ SILVER AWARD
Tollbridge Road, Batheaston, Bath BA1 7DE
T: (01225) 858476
F: (01225) 852600
E: info@oldmillbath.co.uk
I: www.oldmillbath.co.uk

Parkside ♦♦♦♦
11 Marlborough Lane, Bath BA1 2NQ
T: (01225) 429444
F: (01225) 429444
E: parkside@lynall.freeserve.co.uk
I: www.visitus.co.uk/bath/hotel/parkside.html

Poplar Farm ♦♦♦♦
Stanton Prior, Bath BA2 9HX
T: (01761) 470382
F: (01761) 470382
E: poplarfarm@talk21.com

Pulteney Hotel ♦♦♦
14 Pulteney Road, Bath BA2 4HA
T: (01225) 460991
F: (01225) 460991
E: pulteney@tinyworld.co.uk
I: www.pulteneyhotel.co.uk

14 Raby Place ♦♦♦♦
Raby Place, Bathwick, Bath BA2 4EH
T: (01225) 465120

Radnor Guesthouse ♦♦♦♦
9 Pulteney Terrace, Pultney Road, Bath BA2 4HJ
T: (01225) 316159
F: (01225) 319199
E: info@radnorguesthouse.co.uk
I: www radnorguesthouse.co.uk

Ravenscroft
♦♦♦♦ SILVER AWARD
Sydney Road, Bath BA2 6NT
T: (01225) 469267
F: (01225) 448722
E: chmbaker@gatewayuk.net

Roman City Guest House ♦♦♦♦
18 Raby Place, Bathwick, Bath BA2 4EH
T: (01225) 463668
E: enquire@romanticityguesthouse.co.uk
I: www.romancityguesthouse.co.uk

Royal Park Guest House ♦♦
16 Crescent Gardens, Bath BA1 2NA
T: (01225) 317651
F: (01225) 483950
E: royal@parkb-b.freeserve.co.uk

St Georges Cottage ♦♦♦♦
Bathampton Lane, Bathampton, Bath BA2 6SJ
T: (01225) 466801
F: (01225) 426073
E: stgeorgescottage@aol.com
I: www.stgeorgescottagebath.co.uk

St Leonards
♦♦♦♦ SILVER AWARD
Warminster Road, Bathampton, Bath BA2 6SQ
T: (01225) 465838
F: (01225) 442800
E: stleon@dircon.co.uk
I: www.smoothhound.co.uk/hotels/stleonar.html

Stoke Bottom Farm ♦♦
Stoke St Michael, Bath BA3 5HW
T: (01761) 232273

Toghill House Farm ♦♦♦♦
Wick, Bristol BS30 5RT
T: (01225) 891261
F: (01225) 892128
I: www.toghillhousefarm.co.uk

The Town House
Rating Applied For
7 Bennett Street, Bath BA1 2QJ
T: (01225) 422505
F: (01225) 422505
E: stay@thetownhousebath.co.uk
I: www.thetownhousebath.co.uk

Villa Magdala Hotel
♦♦♦♦♦ GOLD AWARD
Henrietta Road, Bath BA2 6LX
T: (01225) 466329
F: (01225) 483207
E: office@villamagdala.co.uk
I: www.villamagdala.co.uk

Walton Villa ♦♦♦♦
3 Newbridge Hill, Bath BA1 3PW
T: (01225) 482792
F: (01225) 313093
E: walton.villa@virgin.net
I: www.walton.izest.com

Wellsway Guest House ♦♦
51 Wellsway, Bath BA2 4RS
T: (01225) 423434

Weston Lawn ♦♦♦
Lucklands Road, Weston, Bath BA1 4AY
T: (01225) 421362
F: (01225) 319106
E: reservations@westonlawn.co.uk
I: www.westonlawn.co.uk

Wheelwrights Arms ♦♦
Monkton Combe, Bath BA2 7HB
T: (01225) 722287
F: (01225) 723029
E: debbie@gillespie.fslife.co.uk
I: www.yell.co.uk/sites/the-wheelwright-arms/

BATHEASTON
Bath and North East Somerset

Brook Lodge ♦♦♦♦
199 London Road East, Batheaston, Bath BA1 7NB
T: (01225) 851158
F: (01225) 851158
E: reservations@brook-lodge.com
I: www.brook-lodge.com

BATHFORD
Bath and North East Somerset

Bridge Cottage ♦♦♦
Ashley Road, Bathford, Bath BA1 7TT
T: (01225) 852399
E: daphne@bridge-cottages.co.uk
I: www.bridge-cottages.co.uk

Garston Cottage ♦♦♦
28 Ashley Road, Bathford, Bath BA1 7TT
T: (01225) 852510
F: (01225) 852793
E: garstoncot@aol.com
I: www.garstoncottage.freeservers.com

The Lodge Hotel ♦♦♦♦
Bathford Hill, Bathford, Bath BA1 7SL
T: (01225) 858467
F: (01225) 858172
E: lodgethe@aol.com
I: www.lodgehotelbath.co.uk

BATHWICK
Bath and North East Somerset

Greenways ♦♦♦
1 Forester Road, Bathwick, Bath BA2 6QF
T: (01225) 310132
F: (01225) 310132
E: greenways@supanet.com
I: www.greenwaysbath.co.uk

Ravenscroft
♦♦♦♦ GOLD AWARD
North Road, Bathwick, Bath BA2 6HZ
T: (01225) 461919
F: (01225) 461919
E: patrick@ravenscroftbandb.co.uk
I: www.ravenscroftbandb.co.uk

BEAMINSTER
Dorset

Beam Cottage ♦♦♦♦
16 North Street, Beaminster DT8 3DZ
T: (01308) 863639
E: margie@beam-cottage.fsnt.co.uk

Jenny Wrens ♦♦♦
1 Hogshill Street, Beaminster DT8 3AE
T: (01308) 862814
F: (01308) 861181

Kitwhistle Farm ♦♦♦
Beaminster Down, Beaminster DT8 3SG
T: (01308) 862458
F: (01308) 862458

North Buckham Farm ♦♦♦
Beaminster DT8 3SH
T: (01308) 863054
F: (01308) 863054
E: trish@northbuckham.fsnet.co.uk

Slape Hill Barn ♦♦♦♦
Waytown, Bridport DT6 5LQ
T: (01308) 488429

The Walnuts
♦♦♦♦ SILVER AWARD
2 Prout Bridge, Beaminster DT8 3AY
T: (01308) 862211
F: (01308) 862211
E: caroline@thewalnuts.co.uk
I: www.thewalnuts.co.uk

Water Meadow House
♦♦♦♦♦ SILVER AWARD
Hooke, Beaminster DT8 3PD
T: (01308) 862619
F: (01308) 862619
E: enquiries@watermeadowhouse.co.uk
I: www.watermeadowhouse.co.uk

BEANACRE
Wiltshire

Beechfield House
♦♦♦♦♦ SILVER AWARD
Beanacre, Melksham SN12 7PU
T: (01225) 703700
F: (01225) 790118
E: csm@beechfieldhouse.co.uk
I: www.beechfieldhouse.co.uk

BECKINGTON
Somerset

Eden Vale Farm ♦♦♦
Mill Lane, Beckington, Bath BA11 6SN
T: (01373) 830371
F: (01373) 831233

Priors Court
Rating Applied For
Goose Street, Beckington, Frome BA11 6TS
T: (01373) 831392
F: (01373) 831186
E: info@beaunosh.co.uk

BELSTONE
Devon

The Cleave House ♦♦♦♦
Belstone, Okehampton EX20 1QY
T: (01837) 840055
I: www.caterham.force9.co.uk/cleavehouse.htm

BERROW
Somerset

Berrow Links House
♦♦♦♦ SILVER AWARD
Coast Road, Berrow, Burnham-on-Sea TA8 2QS
T: (01278) 751422

BERRY POMEROY
Devon

Berry Farm ♦♦♦♦
Berry Pomeroy, Totnes TQ9 6LG
T: (01803) 863231

BERRYNARBOR
Devon

Langleigh House ♦♦♦♦
The Village, Berrynarbor, Ilfracombe EX34 9SG
T: (01271) 883410
F: (01271) 882396
E: langleigh@hotmail.com

The Lodge ♦♦♦♦
Pitt Hill, Berrynarbor, Ilfracombe EX34 9SG
T: (01271) 883246
E: philbridle@aol.com
I: www.thelodgeberrynarbor.co.uk

BIDDESTONE
Wiltshire

The Granary ♦♦♦
Cuttle Lane, Biddestone, Chippenham SN14 7DA
T: (01249) 715077
E: mail@pennylloyd.com
I: www.pennylloyd.com

Home Farm ♦♦♦♦
Harts Lane, Biddestone, Chippenham SN14 7DQ
T: (01249) 714475
F: (01249) 701488
E: audrey.smith@homefarmbandb.co.uk
I: www.homefarmbandb.co.uk

Home Place ♦♦
The Green, Biddestone, Chippenham SN14 7DG
T: (01249) 712928

BIDEFORD
Devon

Bulworthy Cottage ♦♦♦♦
Stony Cross, Bideford EX39 4PY
T: (01271) 858441
E: bulworthy@aol.com

The Mount ♦♦♦♦
Northdown Road, Bideford EX39 3LP
T: (01237) 473748
F: (01271) 342268
E: andrew@themountbideford.fsnet.co.uk
I: www.themount1.cjb.net

The Orchard Hill Hotel ♦♦♦
Orchard Hill, Bideford EX39 2QY
T: (01237) 472872
F: (01237) 423803
E: info@orchardhillhotel.co.uk
I: www.orchardhillhotel.co.uk

Sunset Hotel ♦♦♦
Landcross, Bideford EX39 5JA
T: (01237) 472962
F: (01237) 422520
E: hazellamb@hotmail.com

BILBROOK
Somerset

Steps Farmhouse ♦♦♦♦
Bilbrook, Minehead TA24 6HE
T: (01984) 640974
E: info@stepsfarmhouse.co.uk
I: www.stepsfarmhouse.co.uk

BINEGAR
Somerset

Mansefield House
♦♦♦♦ SILVER AWARD
Binegar, Shepton Mallet BA3 4UG
T: (01749) 840568
F: (01749) 840572
E: mansfieldhouse@aol.com

BISHOP SUTTON
Bath and North East Somerset

Centaur ♦♦♦
Ham Lane, Bishop Sutton, Bristol BS39 5TZ
T: (01275) 332321

Withymede ♦♦♦♦
The Street, Bishop Sutton, Bristol BS39 5UU
T: (01275) 332069

BISHOP'S LYDEARD
Somerset

The Lethbridge Arms ♦♦♦
Gore Square, Bishop's Lydeard, Taunton TA4 3BW
T: (01823) 432234
F: (01823) 433982
E: thelethbridge@aol.com

Piffins
Rating Applied For
Piffin Lane, Bishops Lydeard, Bishop's Lydeard, Taunton TA4 3AS
T: (01803) 432208
E: d.hinton@talk21.com

West View ♦♦♦♦
Minehead Road, Bishops Lydeard, Bishop's Lydeard, Taunton TA4 3BS
T: (01823) 432223
F: (01823) 432223
E: westview@pattemore.freeserve.co.uk
I: www.westviewbandb.co.uk

BISHOPS HULL
Somerset

The Old Mill
♦♦♦♦♦ SILVER AWARD
Roughmoor, Bishops Hull, Taunton TA1 5AB
T: (01823) 289732
F: (01823) 289732

BISHOPSTEIGNTON
Devon

Whidborne Manor ♦♦♦♦
Ash Hill, Bishopsteignton, Teignmouth TQ14 9PY
T: (01626) 870177
E: nicky.dykes@btinternet.com

BISHOPSTON
Bristol

Basca Guest House ♦♦♦
19 Broadway Road, Bishopston, Bristol BS7 8ES
T: (0117) 942 2182

BISHOPSTONE
Wiltshire

Cheney Thatch ♦♦♦
Oxon Place, Bishopstone, Swindon SN6 8PS
T: (01793) 790508

The Royal Oak ♦♦
Bishopstone, Swindon SN6 8PP
T: (01793) 790481
F: (01793) 790481
E: royaloak_bishopsone@lineone.net
I: www.royaloak-bishopstone.co.uk

BLACK DOG
Devon

Hele Barton Farm Guest House
♦♦♦
Black Dog, Crediton EX17 4QJ
T: (01884) 860278
F: (01884) 860278
E: gillbard@eclipse.co.uk
I: www.eclipse.co.uk/helebarton

BLUE ANCHOR
Somerset

The Langbury ♦♦♦
Blue Anchor, Minehead TA24 6LB
T: (01643) 821375
F: (01643) 822012
E: post@langbury.co.uk
I: www.langbury.co.uk

BLUNSDON
Wiltshire

The Cott ♦♦♦
24 High Street, Blunsdon, Swindon SN26 7AF
T: (01793) 721246

BODMIN
Cornwall

Agan Chy ♦♦♦
68 Castle Street, Bodmin PL31 2DY
T: (01208) 75339
F: (01208) 75339
E: agan.chy@btinternet.com

Bedknobs ♦♦♦♦
Castle Street, Bodmin PL31 2DX
T: (01208) 77553
F: (01208) 77885
E: gill@bedknobs.co.uk
I: www.bedknobs.co.uk

Bokiddick Farm
♦♦♦♦♦ SILVER AWARD
Lanivet, Bodmin PL30 5HP
T: (01208) 831481
F: (01208) 831481
E: gillhugo@bokiddickfarm.co.uk
I: www.bokiddickfarm.co.uk

Hotel Casi Casa
Rating Applied For
11 Higher Bore Street, Bodmin PL31 1JS
T: (01208) 77592
F: (01208) 269067
E: book@hotelcasicasa.co.uk
I: www.hotelcasicasa.co.uk

Castle Canyke Farmhouse
Rating Applied For
Priors Barn Road, Bodmin PL31 1HG
T: (01208) 79109
F: (01208) 79216
E: castlecanykefarm@fsmail.net
I: www.castlecanykefarmhouse.com

The Colliford Tavern ♦♦♦♦
Colliford Lake, St Neot, Liskeard PL14 6PZ
T: (01208) 821335
F: (01208) 821335
E: colliford@tiscalli.co.uk
I: www.colliford-tavern.co.uk

Elm Grove ♦♦♦
Elm Grove, Cardell Road, Bodmin PL31 2NJ
T: (01208) 74044

Gwel An Nans Farm ♦♦♦
Little Downs, Cardinham, Bodmin PL30 4EF
T: (01208) 821359
F: (01208) 821359

Gwel Myre
♦♦♦♦ SILVER AWARD
1 Halgavor Park, Bodmin PL31 1DL
T: (01208) 269292
E: john@gwelmyre.fsnet.co.uk
I: www.gwelmyre.co.uk

Higher Windsor Cottage
♦♦♦♦
Castle Street, Bodmin PL31 2DU
T: (01208) 76474
E: johntrishpencheon@tinyworld.co.uk
I: www.higherwindsorcottage.co.uk

Kemsing ♦♦♦
44 Crabtree Lane, Bodmin PL31 1BL
T: (01208) 73343

The Old School House ♦♦♦♦
Averys Green, Cardinham, Bodmin PL30 4EA
T: (01208) 821303
E: libby@pidcock18.freeserve.co.uk

BODMIN
Cornwall

Orchard House Bed and Breakfast
Rating Applied For
Love Lane, Bodmin PL31 2BL
T: (01208) 79594
E: vicki.bucknall@btconnect.com
I: orchardhouselovelane.co.uk

BODMIN
Cornwall

Penville ♦♦♦♦
2 St Nicholas Street, Bodmin PL31 1AD
T: (01208) 78936
E: penvillebandb@btconnect.com

Priory Cottage Bed & Breakfast
♦♦♦
34 Rhind Street, Bodmin PL31 2EL
T: (01208) 73064
F: (01208) 73064
E: jackiedingle@yahoo.com
I: www.stayanite.com

Scrumptious ♦♦♦
Berrycombe Hill, Bodmin PL31 2PW
T: (01208) 75939
E: rosmcnary@scrumptious.fsnet.co.uk
I: www.cornwall-online.co.uk/scrumptious

Trebray House ♦♦♦
8 Cross Lane, Bodmin PL31 2EJ
T: (01208) 73007
F: (01208) 73190
E: beelew@clara.net
I: www.beelew.clara.net/trebray.html

BOLVENTOR
Cornwall

Jamaica Inn ♦♦♦
Bolventor, Launceston PL15 7TS
T: (01566) 86250
F: (01566) 86177
E: enquiry@jamaicainn.co.uk
I: www.jamaicainn.co.uk

BOSCASTLE
Cornwall

Bridge House ♦♦♦
The Bridge, Boscastle PL35 0HE
T: (01840) 250011
F: (01840) 250860

The Harbour Restaurant
♦♦♦♦♦
The Harbour, Boscastle PL35 0HD
T: (01840) 250380

Lower Meadows ♦♦♦
Penally Hill, Boscastle PL35 0HF
T: (01840) 250570
E: stay@lowermeadows.co.uk
I: lowermeadows.co.uk

The Old Coach House ♦♦♦♦
Tintagel Road, Boscastle PL35 0AS
T: (01840) 250398
F: (01840) 250346
E: parsons@old-coach.co.uk
I: www.old-coach.co.uk

Reddivallen Farmhouse
♦♦♦♦
Trevalga, Boscastle PL35 0EE
T: (01840) 250854
F: (01840) 250854
E: cardew@lineone.net
I: www.reddivallenfarm.co.uk

The Riverside Hotel
Rating Applied For
The Bridge, Boscastle PL35 0HE
T: (01840) 250216
F: (01840) 250860
E: reception@hotelriverside.co.uk
I: www.hotelriverside.co.uk

St Christopher's Hotel ♦♦♦
High Street, Boscastle PL35 0BD
T: (01840) 250412
F: (01840) 250412
E: stchristophers@hotmail.com
I: www.stchristophershotel.co.uk

Tolcarne House Hotel and Restaurant ♦♦♦♦
Tintagel Road, Boscastle PL35 0AS
T: (01840) 250654
F: (01840) 250654
E: crowntolhouse@eclipse.co.uk
I: www.milford.co.uk/go/tolcarne

Trefoil Farm ♦♦♦
Camelford Road, Boscastle PL35 0AD
T: (01840) 250606
E: trefoil.farm@tiscali.co.uk

Tregatherall Farm ♦♦♦
Minster, Boscastle PL35 0EQ
T: (01840) 250277
E: ness7tregatherall@yahoo.co.uk

Tremorvah B&B ♦♦♦
Fore Street, Boscastle PL35 0AU
T: (01840) 250636
F: (01840) 250616
E: jdrawingboard@aol.com
I: www.cornwall-online.co.uk/tremorvah

Trerosewill Farmhouse
♦♦♦♦♦ SILVER AWARD
Paradise Road, Boscastle PL35 0BL
T: (01840) 250545
F: (01840) 250545
E: trerosewill@ipl.co.uk
I: www.trerosewill.co.uk

Valency ♦♦♦
Penally Hill, Boscastle PL35 0HF
T: (01840) 250397

BOSSINGTON
Somerset

Buckley Lodge ♦♦♦♦
Bossington, Minehead TA24 8HQ
T: (01643) 862521
E: bucklodgeuk@yahoo.co.uk

BOVEY TRACEY
Devon

Brookfield House
♦♦♦♦♦ GOLD AWARD
Challabrook Lane, Bovey Tracey, Newton Abbot TQ13 9DF
T: (01626) 836181
F: (01626) 836182
E: brookfieldh@tinyworld.co.uk
I: www.brookfield-house.com

Frost Farmhouse ♦♦♦
Frost Farm, Hennock Road, Bovey Tracey, Newton Abbot TQ13 9PP
T: (01626) 833266
F: (01626) 833266
E: linda@frostfarm.co.uk
I: www.frostfarm.co.uk

The Riverside Inn ♦♦♦
Fore Street, Bovey Tracey, Newton Abbot TQ13 9AF
T: (01626) 832293
F: (01626) 833880
E: riversideinn83@hotmail.com
I: activehotels.co.uk

BOX
Wiltshire

Lorne House ♦♦♦♦
London Road, Box, Corsham SN13 8NA
T: (01225) 742597
E: lornehousebandb@aol.com
I: www.lornehouse.net

Norbin Farmhouse ♦♦♦♦
Box, Corsham SN13 8JJ
T: (01225) 866907
E: gillhillier@yahoo.co.uk

BRADFORD
Devon

Langaton Farm ♦♦♦♦
Whitstone, Bradford, Holsworthy EX22 6TS
T: (01288) 341215
F: (01288) 341215

BRADFORD ABBAS
Dorset

Purbeck House ♦♦♦♦
North Street, Bradford Abbas, Sherborne DT9 6SA
T: (01935) 474817

BRADFORD-ON-AVON
Wiltshire

The Beeches Farmhouse
♦♦♦♦♦
Westdale Gardens, Holt Road, Bradford-on-Avon BA15 1TS
T: (01225) 863475
F: (01225) 863996
E: beeches-farmhouse@netgates.co.uk
I: www.beeches-farmhouse.co.uk

Great Ashley Farm
♦♦♦♦ SILVER AWARD
Great Ashley, Bradford-on-Avon BA15 2PP
T: (01225) 864563
F: (01225) 309117
E: greatashleyfarm@farmersweekly.net
I: www.greatashleyfarm.co.uk

The Great Barn Maplecroft Bed and Breakfast ♦♦♦
Leigh Road West, Maplecroft, Bradford-on-Avon BA15 2RB
T: (01225) 868790
F: (01225) 868858
E: dty271@aol.com

Springfields ♦♦♦♦
Great Ashley, Bradford-on-Avon BA15 2PP
T: (01225) 866125
E: christine.rawlings@farmersweekly.net
I: www.bed-and-breakfast.org

Widbrook Grange ♦♦♦♦♦
Trowbridge Road, Widbrook, Bradford-on-Avon BA15 1UH
T: (01225) 864750
F: (01225) 862890
E: stay@widbrookgrange.com
I: www.widbrookgrange.com

Woodpeckers ♦♦♦♦
Holt Road, Bradford-on-Avon BA15 1TR
T: (01225) 865616
F: (01225) 865615
E: b+b@wood-peckers.co.uk
I: www.wood-peckers.co.uk

BRADPOLE
Dorset

Spray Copse Farm
♦♦♦♦♦ SILVER AWARD
Lee Lane, Bradpole, Bridport DT6 4AP
T: (01308) 458510
F: (01308) 421015
E: spray.copse@virgin.net

BRATTON FLEMING
Devon

Bracken House Country Hotel
♦♦♦♦♦ GOLD AWARD
Bratton Fleming, Barnstaple EX31 4TG
T: (01598) 710320
E: holidays@brackenhousehotel.com
I: www.brackenhousehotel.com

Haxton Down Farm ♦♦♦♦
Bratton Fleming, Barnstaple EX32 7JL
T: (01598) 710275
F: (01598) 710275

BRAUNTON
Devon

Moorsands ♦♦♦
34 Moor Lane, Croyde Bay, Braunton EX33 1NP
T: (01271) 890781
I: www.croyde-bay.com/moorsands.htm

BRAYFORD
Devon

Kimbland Farm ♦♦♦
Brayford, Barnstaple EX32 7PS
T: (01598) 710352
F: (01598) 710352
I: www.kimblandfarmholidays.co.uk

Rockley Farmhouse
♦♦♦♦ SILVER AWARD
Brayford, Barnstaple EX32 7QR
T: (01598) 710429
F: (01598) 710429
E: info@rockley.co.uk
I: www.rockley.co.uk

BREAN
Somerset

The Old Rectory Motel ♦♦♦
Church Road, Brean, Burnham-on-Sea TA8 2SF
T: (01278) 751447
F: (01278) 751800
I: www.old-rectory.fsbusiness.co.uk

BRENDON
Devon

Brendon House ♦♦♦♦
Brendon, Lynton EX35 6PS
T: (01598) 741206
E: brendonhouse4u@aol.com
I: www.brendonvalley.co.uk/brendon_house.htm

BRENT KNOLL
Somerset

The Hawthorns ♦♦♦♦
Crooked Lane, Brent Knoll, Highbridge TA9 4BQ
T: (01278) 760181
E: sue@thehawthornsbandb.co.uk
I: www.thehawthornsbandb.co.uk

BRIDESTOWE
Devon

Way Barton Barn ♦♦♦
Bridestowe, Okehampton EX20 4QH
T: (01837) 861513
E: jo.catling@btopenworld.com

BRIDGWATER
Somerset

Admirals Rest ♦♦♦
Taunton Road, Bridgwater TA6 3LW
T: (01278) 458580
F: (01278) 458580
E: susanparker57@hotmail.com
I: www.admiralsrest.co.uk

Ash-Wembdon Farm
♦♦♦♦ SILVER AWARD
Hollow Lane, Wembdon, Bridgwater TA5 2BD
T: (01278) 453097
F: (01278) 445856
E: mary.rowe@btinternet.com
I: www.farmaccommodation.co.uk

Brookland Hotel ♦♦♦
56 North Street, Bridgwater TA6 3PN
T: (01278) 423263
F: (01278) 452988

Cokerhurst Farm ♦♦♦♦
87 Wembdon Hill, Wembdon, Bridgwater TA6 7QA
T: (01278) 422330
F: (01278) 422330
E: cokerhurst@clara.net
I: www.cokerhurst.clara.net

Cotlake ♦♦♦
21 Wembdon Rise, Bridgwater TA6 7PN
T: (01278) 425778
F: (01278) 434040

Headford ♦♦♦
High Street, Spaxton, Bridgwater TA5 1BT
T: (01278) 671250

Manor Farm ♦♦♦
Waterpits, Merridge, Bridgwater TA5 1AT
T: (01823) 451266
E: info@manorfm.demon.co.uk
I: www.manorfm.deomon.co.uk

Model Farm ♦♦♦♦
Perry Green, Wembdon, Bridgwater TA5 2BA
T: (01278) 433999
E: info@modelfarm
I: www.modelfarm.com

Quantock View Guest House
♦♦♦
Bridgwater Road, North Petherton, Bridgwater TA6 6PR
T: (01278) 663309
E: irene@quantockview.freeserve.co.uk
I: www.smoothhound.co.uk/hotels/quantock

BRIDPORT
Dorset

At Home ♦♦♦♦
134 West Bay Road, West Bay, Bridport DT6 4AZ
T: (01308) 458880

BRIDPORT
Dorset

Britmead House ♦♦♦♦
West Bay Road, Bridport DT6 4EG
T: (01308) 422941
F: (01308) 422516
E: britmead@talk21.com
I: www.britmeadhouse.co.uk

The Bull Hotel ♦♦
34 East Street, Bridport DT6 3LF
T: (01308) 422878
F: (01308) 422878

Candida House ♦♦♦♦
Whitchurch Canonicorum, Whitchurch Canonicorum DT6 6RQ
T: (01297) 489629
E: cbain@globalnet.co.uk
I: www.candidahouse.co.uk

Durbeyfield Guest House ♦♦♦
10 West Bay, West Bay, Bridport DT6 4EL
T: (01308) 423307
E: manager@durbeyfield.co.uk
I: www.durbeyfield.co.uk

Eypeleaze
♦♦♦♦ SILVER AWARD
West Bay Road, Bridport DT6 4EQ
T: (01308) 423363
F: (01308) 420228
E: enquiries@eypeleaze.co.uk
I: www.eypeleaze.co.uk

Highway Farm ♦♦♦♦
West Road, Bridport DT6 6AE
T: (01308) 424321
F: (01308) 424321
E: bale@highwayfarm.co.uk
I: www.highwayfarm.co.uk

New House Farm ♦♦♦
Mangerton Lane, Bradpole, Bridport DT6 3SF
T: (01308) 422884
F: (01308) 422884
E: jane@mangertonlake.freeserve.co.uk
I: www.mangertonlake.co.uk

Patchwork House ♦♦♦♦
47 Burton Road, Bridport DT6 4JE
T: (01308) 456515
E: loveridge1@netlineuk.net
I: loveridge1@netlineuk.net

Polly's ♦♦♦♦ SILVER AWARD
22 West Allington, Bridport DT6 5BG
T: (01308) 458095
F: (01308) 421834
E: mail@hime.org.uk

Southcroft
♦♦♦♦ GOLD AWARD
Park Road, Bridport DT6 5DA
T: (01308) 423335
F: (01308) 423335
E: info@southcroftguesthouse.com
I: www.southcroftguesthouse.com

Southfield
Rating Applied For
Marsh Gate, Burton Road, Bridport DT6 4JB
T: (01308) 458910

Southview ♦♦♦
Whitecross, Netherbury, Bridport DT6 5NH
T: (01308) 488471
E: southview@beeb.net
I: www.southviewbb.members.beeb.net

The Well ♦♦♦
St Andrews Well, Bridport DT6 3DL
T: (01308) 424156

BRISLINGTON
Bristol

The Beeches ♦♦♦♦
Broomhill Road, Brislington, Bristol BS4 5RG
T: (0117) 972 8778
F: (0117) 971 1968

Kingston House ♦♦
101 Hardenhuish Road, Brislington, Bristol BS4 3SR
T: (0117) 971 2456

Woodstock ♦♦♦
534 Bath Road, Brislington, Bristol BS4 3JZ
T: (0117) 987 1613
F: (0117) 987 1613
E: woodstock@blueyonder.co.uk
I: www.homestead.com/wstock/

BRISTOL

Hotel @ Walkabout - Bristol
♦♦♦
St Nicholas Court, St Nicholas Street, Bristol BS1 1UB
T: (0117) 945 9699
F: (0117) 945 1830
E: bristolhotel@walkabout..eu.com

Arches Hotel ♦♦♦
132 Cotham Brow, Cotham, Bristol BS6 6AE
T: (0117) 924 7398
F: (0117) 924 7398
E: ml@arches-hotel.co.uk
I: www.arches-hotel.co.uk

Cumberland Guest House
♦♦♦
Clift House Road, Ashton, Bristol BS3 1RY
T: (0117) 966 0810
F: (0117) 966 0810
E: cumberlandguesthouse@talk21.com

Naseby House Hotel ♦♦♦
Pembroke Road, Clifton, Bristol BS8 3EF
T: (0117) 973 7859
F: (0117) 973 7859
I: www.nasebyhousehotel.co.uk

Norfolk House ♦♦
577 Gloucester Road, Horfield, Bristol BS7 0BW
T: (0117) 951 3191
F: (0117) 951 3191

Oakfield Hotel ♦♦♦
52 Oakfield Road, Clifton, Bristol BS8 2BG
T: (0117) 973 5556
F: (0117) 974 4141

The Old Court
♦♦♦♦♦ SILVER AWARD
Main Road, Temple Cloud, Bristol BS39 5DA
T: (01761) 451101
F: (01761) 451224
E: oldcourt@gifford.co.uk
I: www.theoldcourt.com

The Paddock ♦♦♦
Hung Road, Shirehampton, Bristol BS11 9XJ
T: (0117) 923 5140

Sunderland Guest House ♦♦♦
4 Sunderland Place, Clifton, Bristol BS8 1NA
T: (0117) 973 7249
E: sunderland.gh@blueyonder.co.uk
I: www.sunderlandguesthouse.pwp.blueyonder.co.uk

Treborough ♦♦♦
3 Grove Road, Coombe Dingle, Bristol BS9 2RQ
T: (0117) 968 2712

Tricomo House B & B ♦♦♦
183 Cheltenham Road, Cotham, Bristol BS6 5RH
T: (0117) 924 8082
F: (0117) 373 5162
E: tricomohouse1@activemail.co.uk

Trowle Guest House ♦♦♦
7 Southover Close, Westbury-on-Trym, Bristol BS9 3NG
T: (0117) 950 3115
E: bbrowe@ukonline.co.uk

Washington Hotel ♦♦♦
11-15 St Paul's Road, Clifton, Bristol BS8 1LX
T: (0117) 973 3980
F: (0117) 973 4740
E: washington@cliftonhotels.com
I: www.cliftonhotels.com

Wellington Hotel ♦♦♦
Gloucester Road, Horfield Common, Bristol BS7 8UR
T: (0117) 951 3022
F: (0117) 951 3022
E: wellington@bathales.co.uk
I: www.bathales.com

Westfield House
Rating Applied For
37 Stoke Hill, Sneyd Park, Bristol BS9 1LQ
T: (0117) 962 6119
E: ann@mahood.demon.co.uk
I: www.bristolgallery.com/westfield/index.htm

BRIXHAM
Devon

Brioc Hotel ♦♦♦
11 Prospect Road, Brixham TQ5 8HS
T: (01803) 853540
E: bill@brioc-hotel.fsnet.co.uk
I: www.brioc-hotel.fsnet.co.uk

Brookside Guest House ♦♦♦♦
160 New Road, Brixham TQ5 8DA
T: (01803) 858858
E: joythompson@onetel.net.uk

Lamorna ♦♦♦
130 New Road, Brixham TQ5 8DA
T: (01803) 853954
E: pauljohn.miller@virgin.net

Melville Hotel ♦♦♦
45 New Road, Brixham TQ5 8NL
T: (01803) 852033
E: melvillehotel@brixham45.fsnet.co.uk
I: www.smoothhound.co.uk/hotels/melville2.html

Raddicombe Lodge
♦♦♦♦ SILVER AWARD
Kingswear Road, Brixham TQ5 0EX
T: (01803) 882125
F: (01803) 882125
E: val-trev@raddicombe-fsbusiness.co.uk

Ranscombe House Hotel
♦♦♦♦
Ranscombe Road, Brixham TQ5 9UP
T: (01803) 882337
F: (01803) 882337
E: ranscombe@lineone.net
I: www.RanscombeHouseHotel.co.uk

Redlands Hotel ♦♦♦
136 New Road, Brixham TQ5 8DA
T: (01803) 853813
F: (01803) 853813
E: redlandsbrixham@aol.com
I: www.members.aol.com/redlandsbrixham/index.html

Sampford House ♦♦♦
57-59 King Street, Brixham TQ5 9TH
T: (01803) 857761
E: sampfordhouse@supaworld.com

Sea Tang Guest House ♦♦♦
Berry Head Road, Brixham TQ5 9AA
T: (01803) 854651
F: (01803) 854651
E: seatangguesthouse@yahoo.co.uk
I: www.smoothhound.co.uk/hotels/seatang.html

The Shoalstone Hotel ♦♦♦
105 Berry Head Road, Brixham TQ5 9AG
T: (01803) 857919
F: (01803) 850540

Tor Haven Hotel ♦♦♦
97 King Street, Brixham TQ5 9TH
T: (01803) 882281

Westbury Guest House ♦♦♦
51 New Road, Brixham TQ5 8NL
T: (01803) 851684
E: ann.burt@lineone.net

Woodlands Guest House ♦♦♦
Parkham Road, Brixham TQ5 9BU
T: (01803) 852040
F: (01803) 852040
E: diparry@aol.com
I: www.dogfriendlyguesthouse.co.uk

BRIXTON
Devon

Venn Farm ♦♦♦♦
Brixton, Plymouth PL8 2AX
T: (01752) 880378
F: (01752) 880378

BROAD CHALKE
Wiltshire

The Queens Head Inn ♦♦♦♦
1 North Street, Broad Chalke, Salisbury SP5 5EN
T: (01722) 780344
F: (01722) 780344

BROADHEMBURY
Devon

Lane End Farm ♦♦♦
Broadhembury, Honiton EX14 3LU
T: (01404) 841563
F: (01404) 841563

Stafford Barton Farm
♦♦♦♦♦
Broadhembury, Honiton EX14 3LU
T: (01404) 841403
E: jeanwalters1@tesco.net

BROADOAK
Dorset

Dunster Farm ♦♦♦♦
Broadoak, Bridport DT6 5NR
T: (01308) 424626
F: (01308) 423544
E: dunsterfarm@ukonline.co.uk
I: www.dunsterfarm.co.uk

BROADWOODWIDGER
Devon

Rexon Cross Farm ♦♦♦
Broadwoodwidger, Lifton PL16 0JJ
T: (01566) 784295
F: (01566) 784295
E: john.worden@btclick.com
I: www.rexoncross.co.uk

BROMHAM
Wiltshire

Paddock House ♦♦♦
Devizes Road, Bromham, Chippenham SN15 2DZ
T: (01380) 850970
F: (01380) 850970
E: mikjan.argue.paddock@virgin.net

Yew Tree Cottage ♦♦♦♦♦
46 Chittoe Heath, Bromham, Chippenham SN15 2EJ
T: (01380) 850515
F: (01380) 850515
E: diclaudio7@aol.com

BROUGHTON GIFFORD
Wiltshire

Frying Pan Farm ♦♦♦
Melksham Lane, Broughton Gifford, Melksham SN12 8LL
T: (01225) 702343
F: (01225) 793652
E: fr65@dial.pipex.com
I: www.fryingpanfarm.dial.pipex.com

Honeysuckle Cottage ♦♦♦♦
95 The Common, Broughton Gifford, Melksham SN12 8ND
T: (01225) 782463
E: dmehta@globalnet.co.uk
I: www.honeysucklecottage.org.uk

BRUTON
Somerset

Gants Mill & Garden ♦♦♦♦
Gants Mill Lane, Bruton BA10 0DB
T: (01749) 812393
E: shingler@gantsmill.co.uk
I: www.gantsmill.co.uk

BRYHER
Cornwall

Bank Cottage Guest House
♦♦♦♦ SILVER AWARD
Bryher TR23 0PR
T: (01720) 422612
F: (01720) 422612
E: macmace@patrol.i-way.co.uk

Soleil D'or ♦♦♦♦
Bryher TR23 0PR
T: (01720) 422003

BUCKERELL
Devon

Broadlands ♦♦♦♦
Buckerell, Honiton EX14 3EP
T: (01404) 850894

BUCKFAST
Devon

Furzeleigh Mill Country Hotel
♦♦♦
Dartbridge, Buckfastleigh TQ11 0JP
T: (01364) 643476
F: (01364) 643476
E: enquiries@furzeleigh.co.uk
I: www.furzeleigh.co.uk

BUCKLAND NEWTON
Dorset

Holyleas House
♦♦♦♦ SILVER AWARD
Buckland Newton, Dorchester DT2 7DP
T: (01300) 345214
F: (01305) 264488
E: tiabunkall@holyleas.fsnet.co.uk
I: www.holyleashouse.co.uk

Rew Cottage ♦♦♦♦
Buckland Newton, Dorchester DT2 7DN
T: (01300) 345467
F: (01300) 345467

Whiteways Farmhouse Accommodation
♦♦♦♦ SILVER AWARD
Bookham, Buckland Newton, Dorchester DT2 7RP
T: (01300) 345511
F: (01300) 345511
E: andy.foot1@btopenworld.com
I: www.bookhamcourt.co.uk

BUDE
Cornwall

Atlantic Calm
♦♦♦♦ SILVER AWARD
30 Downs View, Bude EX23 8RG
T: (01288) 359165
E: atlanticcalm@btinternet.com
I: www.atlanticcalm.co.uk

Bentley House ♦♦♦
Killerton Road, Bude EX23 8EW
T: (01288) 353698

Brendon Arms ♦♦
Falcon Terrace, Bude EX23 8SD
T: (01288) 354542
F: (01288) 354542
E: enquiries@brendonarms.co.uk
I: www.brendonarms.co.uk

Cliff Hotel ♦♦♦♦
Maer Down, Bude EX23 8NG
T: (01288) 353110
F: (01288) 353110
I: www.cliffhotel.co.uk

Conna-Mara
Rating Applied For
Crooklets, Bude EX23 8NE
T: (01288) 356340
F: (01288) 356340
E: t.collins@v.net
I: www.visitwestcountry.com/connamara

Edgcumbe Hotel ♦♦♦♦
19 Summerleaze Crescent, Bude EX23 8HJ
T: (01288) 353846
F: (01288) 355256
E: info@edgcumbe-hotel.co.uk
I: www.edgcumbe-hotel.co.uk

The Elms ♦♦♦
Lynstone Road, Bude EX23 8LR
T: (01288) 353429

Grosvenor Hotel ♦♦♦
Summerleaze Cres, Bude EX23 8HH
T: (01288) 352062
E: bern@peppercombe.fsnet.co.uk
I: www.grosvenorhotel-bude.co.uk

Harefield Cottage
♦♦♦♦ SILVER AWARD
Upton, Bude EX23 0LY
T: (01288) 352350
F: (01288) 352712
E: sales@coast-countryside.co.uk
I: www.coast-countryside.co.uk

Haven Cottage ♦♦♦♦
35 Killerton Road, Bude EX23 8EL
T: (01288) 354995

Highbre Crest
♦♦♦♦ SILVER AWARD
Whitstone, Holsworthy EX22 6UF
T: (01288) 341002
E: lindacole@ukonline.co.uk

Hillbrook
Rating Applied For
37 Killerton Road, Bude EX23 8EL
T: (01288) 353153

Inn on the Green ♦♦
Crooklets Beach, Bude EX23 8NF
T: (01288) 356013
F: (01288) 356244
E: info@innonthegreen.info
I: www.innonthegreen.info

Link's Side ♦♦♦♦
7 Burn View, Bude EX23 8BY
T: (01288) 352410
E: linksidebude@hotmail.com
I: www.north-cornwall.co.uk/bude/client/linkside

Lower Tresmorn
♦♦♦♦ SILVER AWARD
Lower Tresmorn Farm, Crackington Haven, Bude EX23 0LQ
T: (01840) 230667
F: (01840) 230667

Meadow View ♦♦♦
6 Kings Hill Close, Bude EX23 8RR
T: (01288) 355095

Old Orchard ♦♦♦
Lynstone, Bude EX23 0LR
T: (01288) 355617

Penleaze Farm Bed and Breakfast
♦♦♦♦ SILVER AWARD
Marhamchurch, Bude EX23 0ET
T: (01288) 381226
F: (01288) 381226
E: liz@penleaze.co.uk
I: www.penleaze.co.uk

Riverview
Rating Applied For
Granville Terrace, Bude EX23 8JZ
T:
E: vennings@beeb.net

Stratton Gardens Hotel ♦♦♦♦
Cot Hill, Stratton, Bude EX23 9DN
T: (01288) 352500
F: (01288) 359153
E: strattongardens@aol.com
I: www.cornwall-online.co.uk/stratton-gardens

Sunrise Guest House ♦♦♦♦
6 Burn View, Bude EX23 8BY
T: (01288) 353214
E: kathyandken@sunriseguesthouse.freeserve.co.uk
I: www.sunrise-bude.co.uk

Surf Haven ♦♦♦♦
31 Downs View, Bude EX23 8RG
T: (01288) 353923
F: (01288) 353923
E: info@surfhaven.co.uk
I: www.surfhaven.co.uk

Tee-Side Guest House ♦♦♦♦
Burn View, Bude EX23 8BY
T: (01288) 352351
F: (01288) 352351
E: info@tee-side.co.uk
I: www.tee-side.co.uk

Tresillian ♦♦♦♦
10 Killerton Road, Bude EX23 8EL
T: (01288) 356199

Valley View
Rating Applied For
Dizzard, St Gennys, Bude EX23 0NX
T: (01840) 230049
E: jimrae@pugh90.fsnet.co.uk

Wyvern House ♦♦♦♦
7 Downs View, Bude EX23 8RF
T: (01288) 352205
F: (01288) 356802
E: eileen@wyvernhouse.co.uk
I: www.wyvernhouse.co.uk

BUDLEIGH SALTERTON
Devon

Hansard House Hotel ♦♦♦♦
3 Northview Road, Budleigh Salterton EX9 6BY
T: (01395) 442773
F: (01935) 442475
E: enquiries@hansardhotel.co.uk
I: www.hansardhousehotel.co.uk

Lufflands
♦♦♦♦ SILVER AWARD
Yettington, Budleigh Salterton EX9 7BP
T: (01395) 568422
F: (01395) 568810
E: stay@lufflands.co.uk
I: www.lufflands.co.uk

BUDOCK WATER
Cornwall

The Home Country House Hotel ♦♦♦
Penjerrick, Budock Water, Falmouth TR11 5EE
T: (01326) 250427
F: (01326) 250143

BULFORD
Wiltshire

The Dovecot ♦♦♦♦
Watergate Lane, Bulford, Salisbury SP4 9DY
T: (01980) 632625
E: hadfields@o2.co.uk
I: www.thedovecot.com

BURLAWN
Cornwall

Pengelly Farmhouse ♦♦♦♦
Burlawn, Wadebridge PL27 7LA
T: (01208) 814217
E: hodgepete@hotmail.com

BURNHAM-ON-SEA
Somerset

Ar Dhachaedh ♦♦♦
36 Abingdon Street, Burnham-on-Sea TA8 1PJ
T: (01278) 783652
E: ardhachaedh@aol.com

Boundary's Edge ♦♦♦
40 Charlestone Road, Burnham-on-Sea TA8 2AP
T: (01278) 783128
F: (01278) 783128

Knights Rest ♦♦♦
9 Dunstan Road, Burnham-on-Sea TA8 1ER
T: (01278) 782318

Prospect Farm Guest House ♦♦♦
Strowlands, East Brent, Highbridge TA9 4JH
T: (01278) 760507

Sandhills Guest House ♦♦♦
3 Poplar Road, Burnham-on-Sea TA8 2HD
T: (01278) 781208

Shalimar Guest House ♦♦♦
174 Berrow Road, Burnham-on-Sea TA8 2JE
T: (01278) 785898

Somewhere House ♦♦♦
68 Berrow Road, Burnham-on-Sea TA8 2EZ
T: (01278) 795236
E: di@somewherehouse.com
I: www.somewherehouse.com

Walton House
♦♦♦♦ SILVER AWARD
148 Berrow Road, Burnham-on-Sea TA8 2PN
T: (01278) 780034
E: waltonhousebnb@aol.com

The Warren Guest House ♦♦♦
Berrow Road, Burnham-on-Sea TA8 2EZ
T: (01278) 786726
F: (01278) 786726
E: TheWarren@compuserve.com
I: www.Thewarrenguesthouse.co.uk

BURTLE
Somerset

The Tom Mogg Inn ♦♦♦
Station Road, Burtle, Bridgwater TA7 8NU
T: (01278) 722399
F: (01278) 722724
E: tommogg@telinco.com

BURTON BRADSTOCK
Dorset

Burton Cliff Hotel ♦♦♦
Cliff Road, Burton Bradstock, Bridport DT6 4RB
T: (01308) 897205
F: (01308) 898111
♿

Pebble Beach Lodge ♦♦♦♦
Coast Road, Burton Bradstock, Bridport DT6 4RJ
T: (01308) 897428
E: pebblebeachlodge@supanet.com
I: www.burtonbradstock.org.uk/pebblebeachlodge

BUTCOMBE
North Somerset

Butcombe Farm ♦♦♦♦
Butcombe Farm, Aldwick Lane, Butcombe, Bristol BS40 7UW
T: (01761) 462380
F: (01761) 462300
E: info@butcombe-farm.demon.co.uk
I: www.butcombe-farm.demon.co.uk

CALLINGTON
Cornwall

Green Pastures ♦♦♦
Longhill, Callington PL17 8AU
T: (01579) 382566
E: greenpast@aol.com
I: www.tamarvalleyview.co.uk

Higher Manaton Farm ♦♦♦
Callington PL17 8PX
T: (01579) 370460
F: (01579) 370460
E: dtrewin@manaton.fsnet.co.uk
I: www.turning-wood.com

CALNE
Wiltshire

Calstone Bed and Breakfast
♦♦♦♦ SILVER AWARD
Calstone, Calstone Wellington, Calne SN11 8PY
T: (01249) 816804
F: (01249) 817966
E: calstonebandb@farmersweekly.net
I: www.calstone.co.uk

Chilvester Hill House
♦♦♦♦♦ SILVER AWARD
Calne SN11 0LP
T: (01249) 813981
F: (01249) 814217
E: gill.dilley@talk21.com
I: www.wolsey-lodges.co.uk

Maundrell House ♦♦♦♦
Horsebrook, The Green, Calne SN11 8DL
T: (01249) 821267
F: (01249) 821267
E: liz@maundrell.net
I: www.maundrell.net

Queenwood Golf Lodge
♦♦♦♦♦ GOLD AWARD
Bowood Golf & Country Club, Derry Hill, Calne SN11 9PQ
T: (01249) 822228
F: (01249) 822218
E: golfclub@bowood.org
I: www.bowood.org

CAMELFORD
Cornwall

The Countryman Hotel ♦♦♦
Victoria Road, Camelford PL32 9XA
T: (01840) 212250
F: (01840) 212250
I: www.cornwall-online.co.uk/countryman

Culloden Farmhouse ♦♦♦
16 Victoria Road, Camelford PL32 9XA
T: (01840) 211128

Old Manse ♦♦♦♦
11 Victoria Road, Camelford PL32 9XA
T: (01840) 211066
F: (01840) 211066
E: oldmanse@btinternet.com
I: www.cornwall-online.co.uk/old-manse

Penlea House ♦♦♦
Camelford PL32 9UR
T: (01840) 212194
F: (01840) 212194
E: j.andrews@ic24.net

CAMERTON
Bath and North East Somerset

Abbey Farm ♦♦♦
Camerton Hill, Camerton, Bath BA2 0PS
T: (01761) 471640
F: (01761) 471640

CANNINGTON
Somerset

Blackmore Farm
♦♦♦♦♦ SILVER AWARD
Blackmore Lane, Cannington, Bridgwater TA5 2NE
T: (01278) 653442
F: (01278) 653427
E: dyerfarm@aol.com
I: www.dyerfarm.co.uk
♿

The Friendly Spirit ♦♦♦
Brook Street, Cannington, Bridgwater TA5 2HP
T: (01278) 652215
F: (01278) 653636

Gurney Manor Mill ♦♦♦♦
Gurney Street, Cannington, Bridgwater TA5 2HW
T: (01278) 653582
F: (01278) 653993
E: gurneymill@yahoo.co.uk
I: www.gurneymill.freeserve.co.uk

CARDINHAM
Cornwall

The Stables ♦♦♦
Cardinham, Bodmin PL30 4EG
T: (01208) 821316
E: geraldmoseley@lineone.net

CASTLE CARY
Somerset

Clanville Manor
♦♦♦♦ SILVER AWARD
Clanville, Castle Cary BA7 7PJ
T: (01963) 350124
F: (01963) 350719
E: info@clanvillemanor.co.uk
I: www.clanvillemanor.co.uk

The Horse Pond Inn and Motel
♦♦♦
The Triangle, Castle Cary BA7 7BD
T: (01963) 350318
F: (01963) 351764
E: horsepondinn@aol.com
I: www.horsepondinn.co.uk

Orchard Farm ♦♦♦
Cockhill, Castle Cary BA7 7NY
T: (01963) 350418
F: (01963) 350418
E: boyeroj@talk21.com
I: www.orchardfm.freeuk.com

CASTLE COMBE
Wiltshire

Fosse Farmhouse ♦♦♦♦
Nettleton Shrub, Nettleton, Chippenham SN14 7NJ
T: (01249) 782286
F: (01249) 783066
E: caroncooper@compuserve.com
I: www.fossefarmhouse.8m.com

Goulters Mill Farm ♦♦♦
Nettleton, Chippenham SN14 7LL
T: (01249) 782555

Thorngrove Cottage ♦♦♦
Summer Lane, Littleton Drew, Castle Combe, Chippenham SN14 7NG
T: (01249) 782607
E: chrisdalene@sn147ng.fsnet.co.uk

CATTISTOCK
Dorset

Fullers Earth
Rating Applied For
Cattistock, Maiden Newton, Dorchester DT2 0JL
T: (01300) 320190
F: (01300) 321105
E: stay@fullersearth.co.uk
I: www.fullersearth.co.uk

CAWSAND
Cornwall

Penmillard Farm
♦♦♦♦ SILVER AWARD
Rame, Cawsand, Torpoint PL10 1LG
T: (01752) 822215

CERNE ABBAS
Dorset

Badger Hill ♦♦♦♦
11 Springfield, Cerne Abbas, Dorchester DT2 7JZ
T: (01300) 341698
F: (01300) 341698
E: badgerhill@amserve.com

CHAGFORD
Devon

Easton Court ♦♦♦♦
Easton Cross, Chagford, Newton Abbot TQ13 8JL
T: (01647) 433469
F: (01647) 433654
E: stay@easton.co.uk
I: www.easton.co.uk

CHALLACOMBE
Devon

Twitchen Farm ♦♦♦♦
Challacombe, Barnstaple EX31 4TT
T: (01598) 763568
F: (01598) 763310
E: holidays@twitchen.co.uk
I: www.twitchen.co.uk

CHARD
Somerset

Ammonite Lodge ♦♦♦♦
43 High Street, Chard TA20 1QL
T: (01460) 63839
E: info@ammonitelodge.co.uk
I: www.ammonitelodge.co.uk

Bath House Restaurant and Hotel ♦♦♦
28 Holyrood Street, Chard TA20 2AH
T: (01460) 67575
F: (01460) 64106

Bellplot House Hotel ♦♦♦♦♦
High Street, Chard TA20 1QB
T: (01460) 62600
F: (01460) 62600
E: info@bellplothouse.co.uk
I: www.bellplothouse.co.uk

Home Farm ♦♦♦♦
Hornsbury Hill, Chard TA20 3DB
T: (01460) 63731

Wambrook Farm ♦♦♦
Wambrook, Chard TA20 3DF
T: (01460) 62371
E: wambrookfarm@aol.com

Yew Tree Cottage
♦♦♦♦ SILVER AWARD
Hornsbury Hill, Chard TA20 3DB
T: (01460) 64735
F: (01460) 68029
E: ytcottage@aol.com
I: www.yewtreecottage.org.uk

CHARLTON HORETHORNE
Somerset

Longbar ♦♦♦
Level Lane, Charlton Horethorne, Sherborne DT9 4NN
T: (01963) 220266
E: longbar@tinyworld.co.uk
I: www.longbarfarm.co.uk

CHARMINSTER
Dorset

The Bungalow ♦♦♦
25 Herrison Road, Charminster, Dorchester DT2 9RJ
T: (01305) 261694
E: penny.suarez@talk21.com

Slades Farm ♦♦♦♦
North Street, Charminster, Dorchester DT2 9QZ
T: (01305) 265614
F: (01305) 265713
I: www.sladesfarm.co.uk

Three Compasses Inn ♦♦♦
Charminster, Dorchester DT2 9QT
T: (01305) 263618

CHARMOUTH
Dorset

Cardsmill Farm ♦♦♦
Whitchurch Canonicorum, Whitchurch Canonicorum DT6 6RP
T: (01297) 489375
F: (01297) 489375
E: cardsmill@aol.com
I: www.farmhousedorset.com

Fernhill Hotel ♦♦♦♦
Fernhill, Charmouth, Bridport DT6 6BX
T: (01297) 560492
F: (01297) 561159
E: fernhill@tiscali.co.uk
I: fernhill-hotel.co.uk

Queen's Armes Hotel ♦♦♦♦
The Street, Charmouth, Bridport DT6 6QF
T: (01297) 560339
F: (01297) 560339
E: peterm@netcomuk.co.uk

Spence Farm
♦♦♦♦♦ GOLD AWARD
Wootton Fitzpaine, Charmouth DT6 6DF
T: (01297) 560814
F: (01297) 560727
E: bookings@spence-farm.com
I: www.spence-farm.com

CHEDDAR
Somerset

Applebee South Barns B & B ♦♦
The Hayes, Cheddar BS27 3AN
T: (01934) 743146
F: (01934) 743146

Bay Rose House ♦♦♦
The Bays, Cheddar BS27 3QN
T: (01934) 741377
F: (01934) 741377
E: enquiries@bayrose.co.uk
I: www.bayrose.co.uk

Chedwell Cottage ♦♦♦♦
59 Redcliffe Street, Cheddar BS27 3PF
T: (01934) 743268
F: (01934) 743268
E: suecriddle@lineone.net
I: www.westcountrynow.com

Constantine ♦♦♦
Lower New Road, Cheddar BS27 3DY
T: (01934) 741339

Gordons Hotel ♦♦♦
Cliff Street, Cheddar BS27 3PT
T: (01934) 742497
F: (01934) 742511
E: gordons.hotel@virgin.net
I: www.gordonshotel.co.uk

Market Cross Hotel ♦♦♦
Church Street, Cheddar BS27 3RA
T: (01934) 742264
F: (01934) 741411
E: annfieldhouse@aol.com
I: www.marketcrosshotel.co.uk

Neuholme ♦♦♦♦
The Barrows, Cheddar BS27 3BG
T: (01934) 742841

Tor Farm ♦♦♦♦
Nyland, Cheddar BS27 3UD
T: (01934) 743710
F: (01934) 743710
E: bcjbkj@aol.com
I: www.torfarm.co.uk

Wassells House ♦♦♦♦
Upper New Road, Cheddar
BS27 3DN
T: (01934) 744317
E: aflinders@wassells99.freeserve.co.uk

CHEDZOY
Somerset

Apple View
♦♦♦♦ SILVER AWARD
Chedzoy Lane, Chedzoy, Bridgwater TA7 8QR
T: (01278) 423201
F: (01278) 423201
E: temple_farm@hotmail.com
I: www.apple-view.co.uk

CHELSTON
Devon

Colindale Hotel ♦♦♦♦♦
20 Rathmore Road, Chelston, Torquay TQ2 6NY
T: (01803) 293947
E: bronte@eurobell.co.uk
I: www.colindalehotel.co.uk

Elmdene Hotel ♦♦♦♦
Rathmore Road, Chelston, Torquay TQ2 6NZ
T: (01803) 294940
F: (01803) 294940
E: elmdenehoteltorq@amserve.net
I: www.s-h-systems.co.uk/hotels/elmdene.html

Millbrook House Hotel
♦♦♦♦♦ SILVER AWARD
Old Mill Road, Chelston, Torquay TQ2 6AP
T: (01803) 297394
F: (01803) 297394
E: millbrookhotel@virgin.net

Parks Hotel ♦♦♦♦
Rathmore Road, Chelston, Torquay TQ2 6NZ
T: (01803) 292420
F: (01803) 296006
E: enquiries@parks-hotel.co.uk
I: www.parks-hotel.co.uk

Tower Hall Hotel ♦♦♦
Solsbro Road, Chelston, Torquay TQ2 6PF
T: (01803) 605292
E: johnbutler@towerhallhotel.co.uk
I: www.towerhallhotel.co.uk

CHELYNCH
Somerset

The Old Stables ♦♦♦♦
Chelynch, Shepton Mallet BA4 4PY
T: (01749) 880098
E: maureen.keevil@amserve.net
I: www.the-oldstables.co.uk

CHEW MAGNA
Bath and North East Somerset

Valley Farm ♦♦♦♦
Sandy Lane, Stanton Drew, Bristol BS39 4EL
T: (01275) 332723
F: (01275) 332723
E: highmead.gardens@virgin.net
I: www.smoothhound.com

Woodbarn Farm ♦♦♦
Denny Lane, Chew Magna, Bristol BS40 8SZ
T: (01275) 332599
F: (01275) 332599
E: woodbarnfarm@hotmail.com
I: www.smoothhound.co.uk\hotels\woodbarn.html

CHEW STOKE
Bath and North East Somerset

Orchard House ♦♦♦
Bristol Road, Chew Stoke, Bristol BS40 8UB
T: (01275) 333143
F: (01275) 333754
E: orchardhse@ukgateway.net
I: www.orchardhse.ukgateway.net

CHEWTON MENDIP
Somerset

Copper Beeches ♦♦♦♦
Lower Street, Chewton Mendip, Bath BA3 4GP
T: (01761) 241496
E: copper.beeches@tiscali.co.uk

CHICKERELL
Dorset

Stonebank
♦♦♦♦♦ GOLD AWARD
14 West Street, Chickerell, Weymouth DT3 4DY
T: (01305) 760120
F: (01305) 760871
E: ContactUs@stonebank-chickerell.com
I: www.stonebank-chickerell.co.uk

CHILSWORTHY
Devon

Ugworthy Barton
♦♦♦♦ SILVER AWARD
Chilsworthy, Holsworthy EX22 7JH
T: (01409) 254435
F: (01409) 254435

CHILTON CANTELO
Somerset

Higher Farm ♦♦♦♦
Chilton Cantelo, Yeovil BA22 8BE
T: (01935) 850213
E: susankerton@tinyonline.co.uk

CHILTON TRINITY
Somerset

Chilton Farm ♦♦♦♦
Chilton Trinity, Bridgwater TA5 2BL
T: (01278) 421864
E: warmt@beeb.net

CHIPPENHAM
Wiltshire

Bleys House
Rating Applied For
Rowden Hill, Chippenham SN25 2AR
T: (01249) 446705
E: enquiries@bleyshouse.com
I: www.bleyshouse.com

The Bramleys ♦♦♦
73 Marshfield Road, Chippenham SN15 1JR
T: (01249) 653770

Church Farm ♦♦♦♦
Hartham, Corsham SN13 0PU
T: (01249) 715180
F: (01249) 715572
E: kmjbandb@aol.com
I: www.churchfarm.cjb.net

Fairfield Farm ♦♦♦♦
Upper North Wraxall, Chippenham SN14 7AG
T: (01225) 891750
F: (01225) 891050
E: mcdonoug@globalnet.co.uk

Glebe House ♦♦♦♦
Chittoe, Chippenham SN15 2EL
T: (01380) 850864
F: (01380) 850189
E: info@glebehouse-chittoe.co.uk
I: www.glebehouse-chittoe.co.uk

New Road Guest House ♦♦♦
31New Road, Chippenham SN15 1HP
T: (01249) 657259
E: mail@newroadyguesthouse.co.uk
I: www.newroadguesthouse.co.uk

Teresa Lodge (Glen Avon)
♦♦♦
43 Bristol Road, Chippenham SN15 1NT
T: (01249) 653350
F: (01249) 653350

CHIPPING SODBURY
South Gloucestershire

Rounceval House Hotel
♦♦♦♦ SILVER AWARD
Rounceval Street, Chipping Sodbury, Bristol BS37 6AR
T: (01454) 334410
F: (01454) 314944
E: rouncevalhousehotel@tiscali.co.uk
I: www.rouncevalhousehotel.co.uk

CHISELDON
Wiltshire

Norton House
♦♦♦♦ SILVER AWARD
46 Draycott Road, Chiseldon, Swindon SN4 0LS
T: (01793) 741210
F: (01793) 741020
E: sharian@clara.co.uk
I: www.nortonhouse.uk.com

CHITTLEHAMPTON
Devon

Higher Biddacott Farm ♦♦♦
Chittlehampton, Umberleigh EX37 9PY
T: (01769) 540222
F: (01769) 540222
E: waterers.@sosi.net
I: www.heavyhorses.net

CHRISTIAN MALFORD
Wiltshire

Beanhill Farm ♦♦♦
Main Road, Christian Malford, Chippenham SN15 4BS
T: (01249) 720672

The Ferns ♦♦♦
Church Road, Christian Malford, Chippenham SN15 4BW
T: (01249) 720371
E: susan.ault@btopenworld.com

CHUDLEIGH
Devon

Farmborough House
♦♦♦♦ SILVER AWARD
Chudleigh, Newton Abbot TQ13 0DR
T: (01626) 853258
F: (01626) 853258
E: holidays@farmborough-house.com
I: www.farmborough-house.com

The Old Coaching House ♦♦♦
25 Fore Street, Chudleigh, Newton Abbot TQ13 0HX
T: (01626) 853270
F: (01626) 852122
E: kelly_townsend@coachinghouse.freeserve.co.uk
I: www.oldcoachinghouse.co.uk

CHUDLEIGH KNIGHTON
Devon

Church House ♦♦♦♦
Chudleigh Knighton, Chudleigh, Chudleigh Knighton TQ13 0HE
T: (01626) 852123
F: (01626) 852123
E: brandon@churchhouse100.freeserve.co.uk
I: www.smoothhound.co.uk/hotels/churchho.html

CHURCHILL
North Somerset

Clumber Lodge ♦♦♦
New Road, Churchill, Winscombe BS25 5NW
T: (01934) 852078

Hillslee House ♦♦♦♦
New Road, Churchill, Winscombe BS25 5NP
T: (01934) 853035
F: (01934) 852470

CHURCHINFORD
Somerset

The York Inn ♦♦♦
Honiton Road, Churchinford, Taunton TA3 7RF
T: (01823) 601333
F: (01823) 601026
E: wdatheyorkinn@aol.com
I: www.the-york-inn.freeserve.co.uk

CLAPHAM
Devon

Yeo's Farm
Rating Applied For
Dunchideock, Kennford, Exeter EX2 9UJ
T: (01392) 883927
F: (01392) 832591
E: killinger.legg@tiscali.co.uk

CLATFORD
Wiltshire

Clatford Park Farm ♦♦♦
Clatford, Marlborough SN8 4DZ
T: (01672) 861646
I: www.clatfordparkfarm.co.uk

CLAWTON
Devon

The Hollies ♦♦♦
Clawton, Holsworthy EX22 6PN
T: (01409) 253770
E: the_hollies_2001@hotmail.com
I: www.TheHolliesFarm.co.uk

The Old Vicarage ♦♦♦♦
Clawton, Holsworthy EX22 6PS
T: (01409) 271100
E: enquiries@oldvicarageclawton.co.uk
I: www.oldvicarageclawton.co.uk/welcome/intro.asp

CLEVEDON
Somerset

Highcliffe Hotel ♦♦♦
Wellington Terrace, Clevedon BS21 7PU
T: (01275) 873250
F: (01275) 873572
E: highcliffehotel@aol.com
I: www.highcliffehotel.com

Maybank Guest House ♦♦
4 Jesmond Road, Clevedon BS21 7SA
T: (01275) 876387

CLIFTON
Bristol

Downs View Guest House ♦♦♦
38 Upper Belgrave Road, Clifton, Bristol BS8 2XN
T: (0117) 973 7046
F: (0117) 973 8169
E: bookings@downsviewguesthouse.co.uk

Number 31 ♦♦♦♦
31 Royal York Crescent, Clifton, Bristol BS8 4JU
T: (0117) 973 5330

Rosebery House ♦♦♦♦
14 Camden Terrace, Clifton, Bristol BS8 4PU
T: (0117) 914 9508
F: (0117) 914 9508
E: anne@amalindine.freeserve.co.uk
I: www.roseberyhouse.net

CLOVELLY
Devon

Dyke Green Farm ♦♦♦♦
Higher Clovelly, Clovelly, Bideford EX39 5RU
T: (01237) 431699
E: roy&jacquijohns@dykegreen.fsnet.co.uk

Fuchsia Cottage ♦♦♦♦
Burscott, Clovelly, Bideford EX39 5RR
T: (01237) 431398
E: curtis@fuchsiacottage.fslife.co.uk
I: www.clovelly-holidays.co.uk

COLLINGBOURNE KINGSTON
Wiltshire

Manor Farm B & B ♦♦♦
Collingbourne Kingston, Marlborough SN8 3SD
T: (01264) 850859
F: (01264) 850859
E: stay@manorfm.com
I: www.manorfm.com

Old School House ♦♦♦♦
High Street, Collingbourne Kingston, Marlborough SN8 3SD
T: (01264) 850799

COLYFORD
Devon

Hayes Holme ♦♦♦♦♦
2 Kingsholme, Colyford, Colyton EX24 6RJ
T: (01297) 553808
E: www.pathayes@youremail.co.uk

COLYTON
Devon

Smallicombe Farm
♦♦♦♦ SILVER AWARD
Northleigh, Colyton EX24 6BU
T: (01404) 831310
F: (01404) 831431
E: maggie_todd@yahoo.com
I: www.smallicombe.com
♿

COMBE DOWN
Bath and North East Somerset

Beech Wood ♦♦♦♦
Shaft Road, Combe Down, Bath BA2 7HP
T: (01225) 832242
E: info@beechwoodbath.co.uk
I: www.beechwoodbath.co.uk

Grey Lodge ♦♦♦♦
Summer Lane, Combe Down, Bath BA2 7EU
T: (01225) 832069
F: (01225) 830161
E: greylodge@freenet.co.uk
I: www.greylodge.co.uk

COMBE FLOREY
Somerset

Redlands ♦♦♦♦
Trebles Holford, Bishops Lydeard, Combe Florey, Taunton TA4 3HA
T: (01823) 433159
E: redlandshouse@hotmail.com
I: www.escapetothecountry.co.uk

COMBE MARTIN
Devon

Channel Vista ♦♦♦♦
Woodlands, Combe Martin, Ilfracombe EX34 0AT
T: (01271) 883514
F: (01271) 883963
E: channelvista@freeuk.com
I: www.channelvista.aonesites.co.uk

Mellstock House ♦♦♦♦
Woodlands, Combe Martin, Ilfracombe EX34 0AR
T: (01271) 882592
F: (01271) 889134
E: mary@mellstockhouse.co.uk
I: www.mellstockhouse.co.uk

Saffron House Hotel ♦♦♦
King Street, Combe Martin, Ilfracombe EX34 0BX
T: (01271) 883521
E: stay@saffronhousehotel.co.uk
I: www.saffronhousehotel.co.uk

COMBPYNE
Devon

1 Granary Cottage ♦♦♦♦
Combpyne, Axminster EX13 8SX
T: (01297) 442856

COMPTON BASSETT
Wiltshire

The White Horse
Rating Applied For
Compton Bassett, Calne SN11 8RG
T: (01249) 813118
F: (01249) 811595

COMPTON DANDO
Bath and North East Somerset

Cottage Garden ♦♦♦♦
Tynings Cottage, Fairy Hill, Compton Dando, Bristol BS39 4LH
T: (01761) 490421
F: (01761) 490030
E: vivsands@hotmail.com
I: www.cottage-garden.ukgateway.net/

The Old Chapel ♦♦♦♦
Court Hill, Compton Dando, Bristol BS39 4JZ
T: (01761) 490903
F: (01761) 490903
E: info@the-old-chapel.com
I: www.the-old-chapel.com

COMPTON DUNDON
Somerset

Rickham House ♦♦♦♦
Compton Dundon, Somerton TA11 6QA
T: (01458) 445056
F: (01458) 445056
E: rickham.house@talk21.com

COOMBE BISSETT
Wiltshire

Evening Hill ♦♦♦
Blandford Road, Coombe Bissett, Salisbury SP5 4LH
T: (01722) 718561
E: henrys@tesco.net
I: www.smoothhound.co.uk/hotels/eveninghillhtml

CORSHAM
Wiltshire

Ashley Wood Farm ♦♦♦♦
Kingsdown, Corsham SN13 8BG
T: (01225) 742288

Boyds Farm
♦♦♦♦♦ SILVER AWARD
Gastard, Corsham SN13 9PT
T: (01249) 713146
F: (01249) 713146
E: dorothyboydsfarm@aol.com
I: www.smoothhound.co.uk/hotels/boydsfarm.html

Heatherly Cottage
♦♦♦♦ SILVER AWARD
Ladbrook Lane, Gastard, Corsham SN13 9PE
T: (01249) 701402
F: (01249) 701412
E: ladbrook1@aol.com
I: www.smoothhound.co.uk/hotels/heather3.html

Pickwick Lodge Farm ♦♦♦♦
Guyers Lane, Pickwick, Corsham SN13 0PS
T: (01249) 712207
F: (01249) 701904
I: www.pickwickfarm.co.uk

Saltbox Farm ♦♦♦♦
Box, Corsham SN13 8PT
T: (01225) 742608
F: (01225) 742608

Thingley Court Farm ♦♦♦
Thingley, Corsham SN13 9QQ
T: (01249) 713617
F: (01249) 713617
E: thingleycourtfarmbandb@hotmail.com

CORTON
Wiltshire

The Dove Inn ♦♦♦♦
Corton, Warminster BA12 0SZ
T: (01985) 850109
F: (01985) 851041
E: info@thedove.co.uk
I: www.thedove.co.uk

COSSINGTON
Somerset

Brookhayes Farm ♦♦♦♦
Bell Lane, Cossington, Bridgwater TA7 8LR
T: (01278) 722559
F: (01278) 722559

COVERACK
Cornwall

The Paris Hotel ♦♦♦
Coverack, Helston TR12 6SX
T: (01326) 280258
F: (01326) 280372

CRACKINGTON HAVEN
Cornwall

Venn Park Farm ♦♦♦
Crackington Haven, Bude EX23 0LB
T: (01840) 230159
F: (01840) 230159

CRAFTHOLE
Cornwall

Finnygook Inn ♦♦♦
Crafthole, Torpoint PL11 3BQ
T: (01503) 230329
I: www.finnygook.co.uk

CRANTOCK
Cornwall

Highfield Lodge Hotel ♦♦♦♦
Halwyn Road, Crantock, Newquay TR8 5TR
T: (01637) 830744
F: (01637) 830568
E: info@highfieldlodge.co.uk
I: www.highfieldlodge.co.uk

CREECH ST MICHAEL
Somerset

Curvalion Villa ♦♦♦♦
Curvalion Road, Creech St Michael, Taunton TA3 5QQ
T: (01823) 444630
F: (01823) 444629
E: enquiries@curvalionvilla.co.uk
I: www.curvalionvilla.co.uk

CREWKERNE
Somerset

The George Hotel & Courtyard Restaurant ♦♦♦
Market Square, Crewkerne TA18 7LP
T: (01460) 73650
F: (01460) 72974
E: eddie@thegeorgehotel.sagehost.co.uk
I: www.thegeorgehotel.sagenet.co.uk

Honeydown Farm ♦♦♦♦
Seaborough Hill, Crewkerne
TA18 8PL
T: (01460) 72665
F: (01460) 72665
E: cb@honeydown.freeserve.co.uk
I: www.honeydown.freeserve.co.uk

The Manor Arms ♦♦♦
North Perrott, Crewkerne
TA18 7SG
T: (01460) 72901
F: (01460) 72901
E: info@manorarmshotel.co.uk
I: www.manorarmshotel.co.uk

CRICKLADE
Wiltshire

Waterhay Farm ♦♦♦♦
Waterhay, Leigh, Swindon
SN6 6QY
T: (01285) 861253
F: (01285) 861253

CROCKERTON
Wiltshire

Easter Cottage ♦♦♦♦
Easter Cottage, Foxholes, Crockerton, Warminster
BA12 7DB
T: (01985) 219367
E: askew.easter@btinternet.com

Stoneyside ♦♦♦♦
Potters Hill, Crockerton, Warminster BA12 8AS
T: (01985) 218149
F: (01985) 218149

CROYDE
Devon

Combas Farm ♦♦♦♦
Croyde, Braunton EX33 1PH
T: (01271) 890398
F: (01271) 890398

Denham House ♦♦♦♦
North Buckland, Braunton
EX33 1HY
T: (01271) 890297
E: info@denhamhouse.co.uk
I: www.denhamhouse.co.uk

CROYDE BAY
Devon

West Winds ♦♦♦♦
Moor Lane, Croyde, Croyde Bay, Braunton EX33 1PA
T: (01271) 890489
F: (01271) 890489
E: chris@croydewestwinds.freeserve.co.uk
I: www.westwindsguesthouse.co.uk

CULLOMPTON
Devon

Newcourt Barton ♦♦♦♦
Langford, Cullompton EX15 1SE
T: (01884) 277326
F: (01884) 277326
E: newcourtbarton@btinternet.com
I: www.newcourtbarton-devon.co.uk

Upton House
♦♦♦♦♦ GOLD AWARD
Cullompton EX15 1RA
T: (01884) 33097
F: (01884) 33097

Wishay ♦♦♦
Trinity, Cullompton EX15 1PE
T: (01884) 33223
F: (01884) 33223
E: wishaytrinity@hotmail.com
I: www.smoothhound.co.uk/hotels/wishay

CURRY RIVEL
Somerset

Orchard Cottage
♦♦♦♦ SILVER AWARD
Townsend, Curry Rivel, Langport
TA10 0HT
T: (01458) 251511
F: (01458) 251511

CURY
Cornwall

Nanplough Farm ♦♦♦
Cury Cross Lanes, Cury, Helston
TR12 7BQ
T: (01326) 241088
E: william.lepper@btopenworld.com
I: www.nanplough.co.uk

DARTMEET
Devon

Hunter's Lodge ♦♦♦♦
Dartmeet, Princetown, Dartmeet, Princetown, Yelverton
PL20 6SG
T: (01364) 631173
E: mail@dartmeet.com
I: www.dartmeet.com

DARTMOUTH
Devon

Barrington House
♦♦♦♦♦ SILVER AWARD
Mount Boone, Dartmouth
TQ6 9HZ
T: (01803) 835545
F: (01803) 835545
E: enquiries@barrington-house.com
I: www.barrington-house.com

DARTMOUTH
Devon

de Beer's Bed & Breakfast
♦♦♦♦♦
51 Victoria Road, Dartmouth
TQ6 9RT
T: (01803) 834694
E: enquiries@debeersdartmouth.com
I: www.debeersdartmouth.com

DARTMOUTH
Devon

Hill View House
♦♦♦♦ GOLD AWARD
76 Victoria Road, Dartmouth
TQ6 9DZ
T: (01803) 839372
F: (01803) 839372
E: enquiries@hillviewdartmouth.co.uk
I: www.hillviewdartmouth.co.uk

The Little Admiral Hotel
♦♦♦♦ SILVER AWARD
27-29 Victoria Road, Dartmouth
TQ6 9RT
T: (01803) 832572
F: (01803) 835815
E: info@little-admiral.co.uk
I: www.little-admiral.co.uk

Skerries Bed & Breakfast
♦♦♦♦ SILVER AWARD
Strete, Dartmouth TQ6 0RH
T: (01803) 770775
F: (01803) 770950
E: jam.skerries@rya-online.net
I: www.skerriesbandb.co.uk

Townstal Farmhouse
Rating Applied For
Townstal Road, Dartmouth
TQ6 9HY
T: (01803) 832300
F: (01803) 835428

Westbourne House
♦♦♦♦ SILVER AWARD
4 Vicarage Hill, Dartmouth
TQ6 9EW
T: (01803) 832213
F: (01803) 839209
E: peterwalton@westbourne-house.co.uk
I: www.westbourne-house.co.uk

Woodside Cottage
♦♦♦♦ SILVER AWARD
Blackawton, Totnes TQ9 7BL
T: (01803) 712375
F: (01803) 712761
E: stay@woodsidedartmouth.co.uk
I: www.woodsidedartmouth.co.uk

DAWLISH
Devon

Smallacombe Farm ♦♦♦
Aller Valley, Dawlish EX7 0PS
T: (01626) 862536

DAWLISH WARREN
Devon

Shutterton Farm ♦♦♦♦
Shutterton Lane, Dawlish Warren, Dawlish EX7 0PD
T: (01626) 863766
F: (01626) 863766
E: shuttertonfarm@aol.com
I: www.shuttertonfarm.co.uk

DELABOLE
Cornwall

Tolcarne ♦♦♦
Trebarwith Road, Delabole
PL33 9DB
T: (01840) 213558
E: susantheobald@tiscali.co.uk

DENBURY
Devon

Tornewton ♦♦♦♦
Denbury, Newton Abbot
TQ12 6EF
T: (01803) 812257
F: (01803) 812257

DEVIZES
Wiltshire

The Artichoke Inn ♦♦♦
The Nursery, Bath Road, Devizes
SN10 2AA
T: (01380) 723400
E: avocainns@freddieboxall.co.uk

Ashwood House ♦♦♦
Old Park, Devizes SN10 5JP
T: (01380) 723931
E: jan@ashwoodhousedevizez.co.uk
I: www.ashwoodhousedevizes.co.uk

Asta ♦♦
66 Downlands Road, Devizes
SN10 5EF
T: (01380) 722546

Blounts Court Farm
♦♦♦♦♦ GOLD AWARD
Coxhill Lane, Potterne, Devizes
SN10 5PH
T: (01380) 727180
E: caroline@blountscourtfarm.co.uk
I: www.blountscourtfarm.co.uk

Eastcott Manor ♦♦♦
Easterton, Devizes SN10 4PH
T: (01380) 813313

Eastleigh House ♦♦♦♦
3 Eastleigh Road, Devizes
SN10 3EE
T: (01380) 726918
F: (01380) 726918

The Gate House ♦♦♦
Wick Lane, Devizes SN10 5DW
T: (01380) 725283
F: (01380) 722382
E: laura@gatehouse-b-and-b.freeserve.co.uk

Littleton Lodge ♦♦♦♦
High Street, Littleton Panell (A360), West Lavington, Devizes
SN10 4ES
T: (01380) 813131
F: (01380) 816969
E: stay@littletonlodge.co.uk
I: www.littletonlodge.co.uk

Longwater ♦♦♦
Lower Road, Erlestoke, Devizes
SN10 5UE
T: (01380) 830095
F: (01380) 830095
E: pam.hampton@talk21.com

The Old Manor ♦♦♦♦
The Street, Chirton, Devizes
SN10 3QS
T: (01380) 840777
F: (01380) 840927
E: theoldmanor@talk21.com
I: www.visitwiltshire.co.uk/theoldmanorchirton

Roundway Farm House ♦♦♦♦
Roundway, Devizes SN10 2HZ
T: (01380) 723113
F: (01380) 723113
E: staying@roundwayfarm.com

DINTON
Wiltshire

Honeysuckle Homestead ♦♦♦
Dinton, Salisbury SP3 5HA
T: (01722) 717887
F: (01722) 716036
E: honeysuckle@dinton21.freeserve.co.uk

Marshwood Farm B&B ♦♦♦♦
Dinton, Salisbury SP3 5ET
T: (01722) 716334

Morris' Farm House ♦♦♦
Baverstock, Dinton, Salisbury
SP3 5EL
T: (01722) 716874
F: (01722) 716874
E: marriott@waitrose.com
I: www.kgp-publishing.co.uk

DITTISHAM
Devon

Red Lion Inn ♦♦♦♦
The Level, Dittisham, Dartmouth
TQ6 0ES
T: (01803) 722235

DIZZARD
Cornwall

Bears and Boxes ♦♦♦
Dizzard, Bude EX23 0NX
T: (01840) 230318
F: (01840) 230318
E: rwfrh@btinternet.com
I: www.bearsandboxes.com

Establishments printed in blue have a detailed entry in this guide

DODDISCOMBSLEIGH
Devon

Whitemoor Farm ♦
Doddiscombsleigh, Exeter
EX6 7PU
T: (01647) 252423
E: blaceystaffyrescue@easicom.com

DOLTON
Devon

Rams Head Inn
Rating Applied For
South Street, Dolton, Winkleigh
EX19 8QS
T: (01805) 804255
F: (01805) 804509
E: ramsheadinn@compuserve.com

DORCHESTER
Dorset

Aquila Heights ♦♦♦♦
44 Maiden Castle Road,
Dorchester DT1 2ES
T: (01305) 267145
F: (01305) 267145
E: aquila.heights@tiscali.co.uk

The Beagles ♦♦♦
37 London Road, Dorchester
DT1 1NF
T: (01305) 267338
E: joyce.graham@talk21.com

The Casterbridge Hotel ♦♦♦♦
49 High East Street, Dorchester
DT1 1HU
T: (01305) 264043
F: (01305) 260884
E: reception@casterbridgehotel.co.uk
I: www.casterbridgehotel.co.uk

Churchview Guest House ♦♦♦♦
Winterbourne Abbas, Dorchester
DT2 9LS
T: (01305) 889296
F: (01305) 889296
E: stay@churchview.co.uk
I: www.churchview.co.uk

Cornflowers ♦♦♦♦
4 Durngate Street, Dorchester
DT1 1JP
T: (01305) 751703
E: erichancock@onetel.net.uk
I: www.westcountrynow.com/main/accommodation/details.cfm?I_id=11043&mx=0

Higher Came Farmhouse
♦♦♦♦ SILVER AWARD
Higher Came, Dorchester
DT2 8NR
T: (01305) 268908
F: (01305) 268908
E: highercame@eurolink.ltd.net
I: www.highercame.co.uk

Hillfort View ♦♦
10 Hillfort Close, Dorchester
DT1 2QT
T: (01305) 268476
E: maurice_d55@hotmail.com

The King's Arms Hotel ♦♦♦
30 High East Street, Dorchester
DT1 1HF
T: (01305) 265353
F: (01305) 260269
I: www.kingsarmsdorchester.com

Maiden Castle Farm
♦♦♦♦ SILVER AWARD
Dorchester DT2 9PR
T: (01305) 262356
F: (01305) 251085
E: maidencastlefarm@euphony.net
I: www.maidencastlefarm.co.uk

The Old Manor
♦♦♦♦♦ GOLD AWARD
Kingston Maurward, Dorchester
DT2 8PX
T: (01305) 261110
F: (01305) 263734
E: thomson@kingston-maurward.co.uk
I: www.kingston-maurward.co.uk

The Old Rectory
♦♦♦♦ SILVER AWARD
Winterbourne Steepleton,
Dorchester DT2 9LG
T: (01305) 889468
F: (01305) 889737
E: trees@eurobell.co.uk
I: www.trees.eurobell.co.uk

Port Bredy
♦♦♦♦ SILVER AWARD
107 Bridport Road, Dorchester
DT1 2NH
T: (01305) 265778
F: (01305) 265778
E: B&Benquires@portbredy.fsnet.co.uk

Sunrise Guest House ♦♦♦♦
34 London Road, Dorchester
DT1 1NE
T: (01305) 262425

Tarkaville ♦♦♦♦
30 Shaston Crescent, Dorchester
DT1 2EB
T: (01305) 266253
E: tarkaville@lineone.net

Westwood House Hotel ♦♦♦♦
29 High West Street, Dorchester
DT1 1UP
T: (01305) 268018
E: reservations@westwoodhouse.co.uk
I: www.westwoodhouse.co.uk

The White House ♦♦♦
9 Queens Avenue, Dorchester
DT1 2EW
T: (01305) 266714
E: sandratwh@yahoo.co.uk
I: www.rynhorn.com/whitehouse/index.htm

Whitfield Farm Cottage
♦♦♦♦ SILVER AWARD
Poundbury Whitfield, Dorchester
DT2 9SL
T: (01305) 260233
F: (01305) 260233
E: dc.whitfield@clara.net
I: www.milford.co.uk&www.dc.whitfield.clara.net

Yalbury Park
♦♦♦♦ SILVER AWARD
Frome Whitfield Farm, Frome
Whitfield, Dorchester DT2 7SE
T: (01305) 250336
F: (01305) 260070
E: yalburypark@tesco.net

Yellowham Farm
♦♦♦♦ SILVER AWARD
Yellowham Wood, Dorchester
DT2 8RW
T: (01305) 262892
F: (01305) 848155
E: b&b@yellowham.freeserve.co.uk
I: www.yellowham.freeserve.co.uk

DOWNTON
Wiltshire

Barlings ♦♦♦♦
Gravel Close, Downton,
Salisbury SP5 3JQ
T: (01725) 510310

Witherington Farm
♦♦♦♦♦ GOLD AWARD
Witherington, Downton,
Salisbury SP5 3QT
T: (01722) 710222
E: bandb@witheringtonfarm.co.uk
I: www.witheringtonfarm.co.uk

DULOE
Cornwall

Carglonnon Farm ♦♦♦♦
Duloe, Liskeard PL14 4QA
T: (01579) 320210
F: (01579) 320210

DULVERTON
Somerset

Exton House Hotel
♦♦♦♦ SILVER AWARD
Exton, Dulverton TA22 9JT
T: (01643) 851365
F: (01643) 851213

Highercombe Farm
♦♦♦♦ SILVER AWARD
Dulverton TA22 9PT
T: (01398) 323616
F: (01398) 323616
E: abigail@highercombe.demon.co.uk
I: www.highercombe.demon.co.uk

Springfield Farm ♦♦♦♦
Ashwick Lane, Dulverton
TA22 9QD
T: (01398) 323722
F: (01398) 323722
E: info@springfieldfarms.co.uk
I: www.springfieldfarms.co.uk

Three Acres Country House
Rating Applied For
Brushford, Dulverton TA22 9AR
T: (01398) 323730
E: enquiries@threeacrescountryhouse.co.uk
I: www.threeacrescountryhouse.co.uk

Town Mills
♦♦♦♦ SILVER AWARD
High Street, Dulverton TA22 9HB
T: (01398) 323124
E: townmills@onetel.net.uk
I: www.townmillsdulverton.co.uk

Winsbere House ♦♦♦
64 Battleton, Dulverton
TA22 9HU
T: (01398) 323278
I: www.winsbere.co.uk

DUNSTER
Somerset

Cobbles Bed & Breakfast ♦♦♦♦
14-16 Church Street, Dunster,
Minehead TA24 6SH
T: (01643) 821305
F: (01643) 821305

Conygar House
♦♦♦♦ SILVER AWARD
2A The Ball, Dunster, Minehead
TA24 6SD
T: (01643) 821872
F: (01643) 821872
E: bale.dunster@virgin.net
I: homepage.virgin.net/bale.dunster

Dollons House
♦♦♦♦♦ SILVER AWARD
10 Church Street, Dunster,
Minehead TA24 6SH
T: (01643) 821880
E: jmott@onetel.net.uk

Exmoor House Hotel
♦♦♦♦ SILVER AWARD
12 West Street, Dunster,
Minehead TA24 6SN
T: (01643) 821268

Higher Orchard ♦♦♦♦
30 St Georges Street, Dunster,
Minehead TA24 6RS
T: (01643) 821915
E: lamacraft@higherorchard.fsnet.co.uk
I: www.higherorchard.fsnet.co.uk

The Old Bakery
♦♦♦♦ SILVER AWARD
14 West Street, Dunster,
Minehead TA24 6SN
T: (01643) 822123
F: (01643) 821139
I: www.dunsterbandb.co.uk

Spears Cross Hotel
♦♦♦♦ SILVER AWARD
1 West Street, Dunster,
TA24 6SN
T: (01643) 821439
E: mjcapel@aol.com
I: www.SmoothHound.co.uk/hotels/spearsx.html

EAST CHINNOCK
Somerset

Gables Guest House
Rating Applied For
East Chinnock, Yeovil BA22 9DR
T: (01935) 862237
E: tony.whitehead@genie.co.uk

EAST COKER
Somerset

Granary House
♦♦♦♦ SILVER AWARD
East Coker, Yeovil BA22 9LY
T: (01935) 862738
E: granary.house@virgin.net
I: www.granaryhouse.co.uk

EAST LOOE
Cornwall

Sea Breeze Guesthouse ♦♦♦
Lower Chapel Street, East Looe,
Looe PL13 1AT
T: (01503) 263131
E: JohnJenkin@sbgh.freeserve.co.uk
I: www.cornwallexplore.co.uk/seabreeze

EAST TYTHERTON
Wiltshire

Barnbridge ♦♦
East Tytherton, Chippenham
SN15 4LT
T: (01249) 740280
F: (01249) 447463
E: bgiffard@aol.com
I: www.smoothhound.co.uk/hotels/barnbrdg.html

EASTON ROYAL
Wiltshire

Follets B & B ♦♦♦♦
Easton Royal, Pewsey SN9 5LZ
T: (01672) 810619
F: (01672) 811268
E: margaretlandless@talk21.com
I: www.folletsbb.com

EDMONTON
Cornwall

The Paddock ♦♦♦
Edmonton, Wadebridge
PL27 7JA
T: (01208) 812832
F: (01208) 813704
E: srus14@aol.com
I: www.paddock-bedandbreakfast.co.uk

EGLOSHAYLE
Cornwall

Little Brook
Rating Applied For
Mill Close, Egloshayle, Wadebridge PL27 6HA
T: (01208) 814267

ENFORD
Wiltshire

Three Horseshoes Cottage ♦♦♦♦
Enford, Pewsey SN9 6AW
T: (01980) 670459

EVERCREECH
Somerset

The Bell Inn ♦♦♦
Bruton Road, Evercreech, Shepton Mallet BA4 6HY
T: (01749) 830287
E: richrewardsltd@ukonline.co.uk

EVERLEIGH
Wiltshire

The Crown Hotel ♦♦♦
Everleigh, Marlborough SN8 3EY
T: (01264) 850229
F: (01264) 850819
E: crowner@aol.com
I: www.thecrownhotel.info

EVERSHOT
Dorset

The Acorn Inn ♦♦♦♦
28 Fore Street, Evershot, Dorchester DT2 0JW
T: (01935) 83228
F: (01935) 83707
E: stay@acorn-inn.co.uk
I: www.acorn-inn.co.uk

EXETER
Devon

Culm Vale Country House ♦♦♦
Culm Vale, Stoke Canon, Exeter
EX5 4EG
T: (01392) 841615
F: (01392) 841615
E: culmvale@talk21.com
I: www.smoothhound.co.uk/hotels/culmvale

Fairwinds Village House Hotel ♦♦♦♦
Kennford, Exeter EX6 7UD
T: (01392) 832911
E: fairwindshotbun@aol.com

The Grange ♦♦♦♦
Stoke Hill, Exeter EX4 7JH
T: (01392) 259723
E: dudleythegrange@aol.com

Hayne Barton Milverton Country Holidays ♦♦♦
Whitestone, Exeter EX4 2JN
T: (01392) 811268
F: (01392) 811343
E: g_milverton@hotmail.com
I: www.milvertoncountryholidays.com

Hayne House ♦♦♦
Silverton, Exeter EX5 4HE
T: (01392) 860725
F: (01392) 860725
E: haynehouse@ukonline.co.uk
I: www.haynehouse-devon.co.uk

Park View Hotel ♦♦♦
8 Howell Road, Exeter EX4 4LG
T: (01392) 271772
F: (01392) 253047
E: enquiries@parkviewexeter.co.uk
I: www.parkviewexeter.co.uk

Raffles Hotel ♦♦♦♦
11 Blackall Road, Exeter
EX4 4HD
T: (01392) 270200
F: (01392) 270200
E: raffleshtl@btinternet.com
I: www.raffles-exeter.co.uk

Rydon Farm ♦♦♦♦
Woodbury, Exeter EX5 1LB
T: (01395) 232341
F: (01395) 232341
E: sallyglanvill@hotmail.com

St Andrews Hotel ♦♦♦♦
28 Alphington Road, Exeter
EX2 8HN
T: (01392) 276784
F: (01392) 250249

Silversprings
♦♦♦♦♦ SILVER AWARD
12 Richmond Road, St Davids, Exeter EX4 4JA
T: (01392) 494040
F: (01392) 494040
E: juliet@silversprings.co.uk
I: www.silversprings.co.uk

EXFORD
Somerset

Exmoor Lodge Guesthouse ♦♦♦
Exford, Minehead TA24 7PY
T: (01643) 831694
I: www.smoothhound.co.uk/hotels/exmoorlodge.html

Hunters Moon ♦♦♦
Exford, Minehead TA24 7PP
T: (01643) 831695
E: huntersmoon@bushinternet.com
I: www.exmooraccommodation.co.uk

Stockleigh Farm
Rating Applied For
Exford, Minehead TA24 7PZ
T: (01643) 831575
F: (01643) 831575
E: lyndsayann_smith@hotmail.com
I: www.stockleighfarm.co.uk

EXMOUTH
Devon

The Imperial ♦♦♦♦
The Esplanade, Exmouth
EX8 2SW
T: (01395) 274761
F: (01395) 265161
I: www.shearingsholidays.com

Knights Hotel & Restaurant
Rating Applied For
7 Stevenstone Road, Exmouth
EX8 2EP
T: (01395) 266349
E: info@knights-hotel.com
I: www.knights-hotel.com

The Swallows ♦♦♦♦
11 Carlton Hill, Exmouth
EX8 2AJ
T: (01395) 263937
F: (01395) 271040
E: swallows@amserve.net
I: www.exmouth-guide.co.uk/swallows.htm

FALMOUTH
Cornwall

Apple Tree Cottage ♦♦♦♦
Laity Moor, Ponsanooth, Truro
TR3 7HR
T: (01872) 865047
E: appletreecottage@talk21.com
I: www.cornwall-online.co.uk

Chelsea House Hotel
♦♦♦♦ SILVER AWARD
2 Emslie Road, Falmouth
TR11 4BG
T: (01326) 212230
E: info@chelseahousehotel.com
I: www.chelseahousehotel.com

Dolvean Hotel
♦♦♦♦♦ SILVER AWARD
50 Melvill Road, Falmouth
TR11 4DQ
T: (01326) 313658
F: (01326) 313995
E: reservations@dolvean.co.uk
I: www.dolvean.co.uk

Hawthorne Dene Hotel ♦♦♦
12 Pennance Road, Falmouth
TR11 4EA
T: (01326) 311427
F: (01326) 311994
E: enquiries@hawthornedenehotel.co.uk
I: www.hawthornedenehotel.com

Headlands Hotel ♦♦♦
4 Avenue Road, Falmouth
TR11 4AZ
T: (01326) 311141
F: (01356) 311141
E: acoddington@btconnect.com
I: www.cornwall-online.co.uk/headlands-falmouth

Ivanhoe Guest House ♦♦♦♦
7 Melvill Road, Falmouth
TR11 4AS
T: (01326) 319083
F: (01326) 319083
E: ivanhoe@enterprise.net
I: www.smoothhound.co.uk/hotels/ivanhoe

Poltair ♦♦♦
Emslie Road, Falmouth
TR11 4BG
T: (01326) 313158
I: www.poltair.co.uk

The Trevelyan ♦♦
6 Avenue Road, Falmouth
TR11 4AZ
T: (01326) 311545
F: (01326) 311545
E: gaunt@tre6.freeserve.co.uk
I: www.bedandbreakfastfalmouth.co.uk

Wickham Guest House ♦♦♦
21 Gyllyngvase Terrace, Falmouth TR11 4DL
T: (01326) 311140
E: enquiries@wickhamhotel.freeserve.co.uk
I: www.wickham-hotel.co.uk

FARMBOROUGH
Bath and North East Somerset

Barrow Vale Farm ♦♦♦♦
Farmborough, Bath BA2 0BL
T: (01761) 470300
F: (01761) 470300
E: cherilynlangley@hotmail.com
I: www.visitbath.co.uk

FAULKLAND
Somerset

Lime Kiln Farm ♦♦♦♦
Faulkland, Bath BA3 5XE
T: (01373) 834305
F: (01373) 834026
E: lime_kiln@hotmail.com
I: www.limekilnfarm.co.uk

FENNY BRIDGES
Devon

Skinners Ash Farm ♦♦♦
Fenny Bridges, Honiton
EX14 3BH
T: (01404) 850231
F: (01404) 850231
I: www.smoothhound.co.uk/skinnersash/b+b

FLEET
Dorset

Highfield
♦♦♦♦ SILVER AWARD
Fleet Road, Fleet, Weymouth
DT3 4EB
T: (01305) 776822
E: highfield.fleet@lineone.net

FOWEY
Cornwall

The Old Ferry Inn ♦♦♦♦
Bodinnick, Fowey PL23 1LX
T: (01726) 870237
F: (01726) 870116
E: ferryinn@bodinnick.fsnet.co.uk
I: www.oldferryinn.com

FREMINGTON
Devon

Lower Yelland Farm ♦♦♦♦
Yelland, Fremington, Barnstaple
EX31 3EN
T: (01271) 860101
F: (01271) 860101
E: pday@loweryellandfarm.co.uk
I: www.loweryellandfarm.co.uk

FRESHFORD
Bath and North East Somerset

Longacre ♦♦♦
17 Staples Hill, Freshford, Bath
BA3 6EL
T: (01225) 723254
F: (01225) 723254
E: fran.joe@talk21.com

FROME
Somerset

Abergele Guest House ♦♦♦♦
2 Fromefield, Frome BA11 2HA
T: (01373) 463998

The Full Moon at Rudge ♦♦♦♦
Rudge, Frome BA11 2QF
T: (01373) 830936
F: (01373) 831366
E: fullmoon@lineone.net
I: www.thefullmoon.co.uk

Kozy-Glen ♦♦♦♦ SILVER AWARD
Rooks Lane, Berkley Marsh, Frome BA11 5JD
T: (01373) 464767

The Lodge ♦♦♦♦
Monkley Lane, Rode, Nr Frome BA11 6QQ
T: (01373) 830071
E: mcdougal@nildram.co.uk

Lower Grange Farm ♦♦♦♦
Feltham, Frome BA11 5LL
T: (01373) 452938
F: (01373) 467124
E: bandb@thelowergrangefarm.com

Stonewall Manor ♦♦♦♦
Culver Hill, Frome BA11 4AS
T: (01373) 462131

The Sun Inn ♦♦♦
6 Catherine Street, Frome BA11 1DA
T: (01373) 471913

Wadbury House ♦♦♦
Mells, Frome BA11 3PA
T: (01373) 812359
E: sbrinkmann@btinternet.com

GALMPTON
Devon

Rose Cottage ♦♦♦♦
Galmpton, Hope Cove, Kingsbridge TQ7 3EU
T: (01548) 561953
F: (01548) 561953
I: www.rosecottagesalcombe.co.uk

GITTISHAM
Devon

Catshayes Farm ♦♦
Gittisham, Honiton EX14 3AE
T: (01404) 850302
F: (01404) 850302
E: catshayesfarm@aol.com
I: www.farmstay.co.uk

GLASTONBURY
Somerset

Appletree House ♦♦♦♦
27 Bere Lane, Glastonbury BA6 8BD
T: (01458) 830803
E: sue@appletreehouse.org.uk
I: www.appletreehouse.org.uk

ARP ♦♦♦♦
4 Chalice Way, Glastonbury BA6 8EX
T: (01458) 830794
E: ann@arp-b-and-b.freeserve.co.uk
I: www.arp-b-and-b.freeserve.co.uk

Avalon Barn ♦♦♦♦
Lower Godney, Wells BA5 1RZ
T: (01458) 835005
F: (01458) 835636
E: wigan@ukonline.co.uk

The Barn ♦♦♦
84b Bove Town, Glastonbury BA6 8JG
T: (01458) 832991

The Bolthole ♦♦♦
32 Chilkwell Street, Glastonbury BA6 8DA
T: (01458) 832800

46 Bove Town ♦♦♦
Bove Town, Glastonbury BA6 8JE
T: (01458) 833684

Coig Deug ♦♦
15 Helyar Close, Glastonbury BA6 9LQ
T: (01458) 835945
E: kath@coigdeug.freeserve.co.uk
I: www.coigdeug.freeserve.co.uk

Divine Light Bed and Breakfast ♦♦♦
16A Magdalene Street, Glastonbury BA6 9EH
T: (01458) 835909
E: glastonburyrose@lineone.net
I: www.divinelightcentre.co.uk

The Flying Dragon ♦♦♦♦
Hexton Road, Glastonbury BA6 8HL
T: (01458) 830321
E: rench.ness@virgin.net
I: www.flyingdragon.co.uk

Hawthorns Hotel and Brasserie ♦♦
8-12 Northload Street, Glastonbury BA6 9JJ
T: (01458) 831255
F: (01458) 831255
E: enquiries@hawthorneshotel.com
I: www.hawthornshotel.com

The Lightship ♦♦♦
82 Bove Town, Glastonbury BA6 8JG
T: (01458) 833698
E: roselightship2001@yahoo.co.uk
I: www.lightship.ukf.net

Little Orchard ♦♦♦
Ashwell Lane, Glastonbury BA6 8BG
T: (01458) 831620
E: the.littleorchard@lineone.net
I: www.smoothhound.co.uk/hotels/orchard.html

Meadow Barn ♦♦♦
Middlewick Holiday Cottages, Wick Lane, Glastonbury BA6 8JW
T: (01458) 832351
F: (01458) 832351
E: info@middlewickholidaycottages.co.uk
I: www.middlewickholidaycottages.co.uk

Melrose ♦♦♦
Coursingbatch, Glastonbury BA6 8BH
T: (01458) 834706
F: (01458) 833091
E: melrose@underthetor.freeserve.co.uk

Number Three ♦♦♦♦♦
3 Magdalene Street, Glastonbury BA6 9EW
T: (01458) 832129
F: (01458) 834227
E: info@numberthree.co.uk
I: www.numberthree.co.uk

The Old Bakery ♦♦♦
84A Bove Town, Glastonbury BA6 8JG
T: (01458) 833400
E: oldbakery@talk21.com

1 Park Terrace ♦♦♦
Street Road, Glastonbury BA6 9EA
T: (01458) 835845
F: (01458) 833296
E: info@no1parkterrace.co.uk
I: www.no1parkterrace.co.uk

Pilgrims ♦♦♦
12/13 Norbins Road, Glastonbury BA6 9JE
T: (01458) 834722
E: pilgrimsbb@hotmail.com
I: www.pigrimsbb.co.uk

Pippin ♦♦♦
4 Ridgeway Gardens, Glastonbury BA6 8ER
T: (01458) 834262
E: daphne.slater@ukonline.co.uk
I: www.smoothhound.co.uk/hotels/pippin.html

Shambhala Health & Healing Retreat ♦♦♦
Coursingbatch, Glastonbury BA6 8BH
T: (01458) 831797
E: findyourself@shambhala.co.uk
I: www.shambhala.co.uk

Tordown B & B and Healing Centre ♦♦♦♦
5 Ashwell Lane, Glastonbury BA6 8BG
T: (01458) 832287
F: (01458) 831100
E: torangel@aol.com
I: www.tordown.com

Wearyall Hill House ♦♦♦♦
78 The Roman Way, Glastonbury BA6 8AD
T: (01458) 835510
E: enquiries@wearyallhillhouse.co.uk
I: www.wearyallhillhouse.co.uk

GODNEY
Somerset

Double-Gate Farm ♦♦♦♦ GOLD AWARD
Godney, Wells BA5 1RX
T: (01458) 832217
F: (01458) 835612
E: doublegatefarm@aol.com
I: www.doublegatefarm.com
♿

GOLDSITHNEY
Cornwall

Penleen ♦♦♦
South Road, Goldsithney, Penzance TR20 9LF
T: (01736) 710633
F: (01736) 711171
E: jimblain@penleen.com
I: www.penleen.com

GRAMPOUND
Cornwall

Perran House ♦♦♦
Fore Street, Grampound, Truro TR2 4RS
T: (01726) 882066
F: (01726) 882936

GREAT DURNFORD
Wiltshire

Meadow Croft ♦♦♦♦
Great Durnford, Salisbury SP4 6AY
T: (01722) 782643
F: (07714) 158791

GREENHAM
Somerset

Greenham Hall ♦♦♦
Greenham, Wellington TA21 0JJ
T: (01823) 672603
F: (01823) 672307
E: greenhamhall@btopenworld.com
I: www.greenhamhall.co.uk

GRITTLETON
Wiltshire

The Neeld Arms Inn ♦♦♦
The Street, Grittleton, Chippenham SN14 6AP
T: (01249) 782470
F: (01249) 782470
E: neeldarms@genie.co.uk
I: www.neeldarms.co.uk

GULWORTHY
Devon

Colcharton Farm ♦♦♦♦ SILVER AWARD
Gulworthy, Tavistock PL19 8HU
T: (01822) 616435
F: (01822) 616435
E: colchartonfarm@agriplus.net
I: www.visit-dartmoor.co.uk

Hele Farm ♦♦♦♦
Gulworthy, Tavistock PL19 8PA
T: (01822) 833084
F: (01822) 833084

GURNEY SLADE
Somerset

The Old Mendip Coaching Inn ♦♦♦
Gurney Slade, Bath BA3 4UU
T: (01749) 841234
E: floella@tinyonline.co.uk

GWEEK
Cornwall

Little Australia ♦♦♦♦
Mawgan, Gweek, Helston TR12 6BG
T: (01326) 221245

HALLATROW
Bath and North East Somerset

Tennis Court House ♦♦♦♦
Wells Road, Hallatrow, Bristol BS39 6EJ
T: (01761) 451568

HALSTOCK
Dorset

Quiet Woman House ♦♦♦
Halstock, Yeovil BA22 9RX
T: (01935) 891218
E: quietwomanhouse@ukonline.co.uk

HALWELL
Devon

The Old Inn ♦♦♦♦
Halwell, Totnes TQ9 7JA
T: (01803) 712329

Orchard House
♦♦♦♦♦ SILVER AWARD
Horner, Hallwell, Halwell, Totnes TQ9 7LB
T: (01548) 821448
I: www.orchard-house-halwell.co.uk

HAMBRIDGE
Somerset

Manor Farmhouse ♦♦♦
Hambridge, Langport TA10 0AY
T: (01460) 281207
F: (01460) 281207
E: manorfm@yahoo.co.uk

HARBERTONFORD
Devon

Pound Court Cottage ♦♦♦♦
Old Road, Harbertonford, Totnes TQ9 7TA
T: (01803) 732441

HARLYN BAY
Cornwall

The Harlyn Inn ♦♦♦
Harlyn Bay, Padstow PL28 8SB
T: (01841) 520207
F: (01841) 520722
E: harlyninn@aol.com
I: harlyn-inn.com

St Cadoc Farm ♦♦♦
Harlyn Bay, Padstow PL28 8SA
T: (01841) 520487
F: (01841) 520487

HARTLAKE
Somerset

Hartlake Farm ♦♦♦♦
Hartlake, Glastonbury BA6 9AB
T: (01458) 835406
F: (01749) 670373
I: www.hartlake.co.uk

HARTLAND
Devon

Elmscott Farm ♦♦♦♦
Hartland, Bideford EX39 6ES
T: (01237) 441276
F: (01237) 441076

Gawlish Farm ♦♦♦
Hartland, Bideford EX39 6AT
T: (01237) 441320

Golden Park
♦♦♦♦♦ GOLD AWARD
Hartland, Bideford EX39 6EP
T: (01237) 441254
F: (01237) 441254
E: YEO@gopark.freeserve.co.uk
I: www.goldenpark.co.uk

Hartland Quay Hotel ♦♦♦
Stoke, Hartland, Bideford EX39 6DU
T: (01237) 441218
F: (01237) 441371
I: www.hartlandquayhotel.com

Trutrese ♦♦♦♦
Harton Cross, Hartland, Bideford EX39 6AE
T: (01237) 441274

HATHERLEIGH
Devon

The George ♦♦♦
Market Street, Hatherleigh, Okehampton EX20 3JN
T: (01837) 810454
F: (01837) 810901
E: jfpozzetto@yahoo.co.uk
I: www.georgehoteldevon.co.uk

Seldon Farm ♦♦♦
Monkokehampton, Winkleigh EX19 8RY
T: (01837) 810312

HAWKRIDGE
Somerset

Parsonage Farm Guesthouse ♦♦♦♦
Hawkridge, Dulverton TA22 9QP
T: (01643) 831503
F: (01643) 831197
E: guests@parsonagefarm.plus.com
I: www.parsonagefarm.info

HELSTON
Cornwall

Jentone Bed & Breakfast Rating Applied For
Jentone, Carnkie, Helston TR13 0DZ
T: (01209) 860883
F: (01209) 860883
E: johns@jentone.net

HELSTON
Cornwall

Longstone Farm ♦♦♦
Trenear, Helston TR13 0HG
T: (01326) 572483
F: (01326) 572483
E: jane@longstone-farm.freeserve.co.uk

Lyndale Guest House ♦♦♦
4 Green bank, Meneage Road, Helston TR13 8JA
T: (01326) 561082
F: (01326) 565813
E: enquiries@lyndale1.freeserve.co.uk
I: www.lyndale1.freeserve.co.uk

Mandeley Guest House ♦♦♦
Clodgey Lane, Helston TR13 8PJ
T: (01326) 572550

Strathallan Guest House ♦♦♦♦
6 Monument Road, Helston TR13 8HF
T: (01326) 573683
F: (01326) 565777
E: strathallangh@aol.com
I: www.connexions.co.uk/strathallan

HENLADE
Somerset

Barn Close Nurseries ♦♦♦
Henlade, Taunton TA3 5DH
T: (01823) 443507

HENSTRIDGE
Somerset

Fountain Inn ♦♦♦
High Street, Henstridge, Templecombe BA8 0RA
T: (01963) 362722
I: www.fountaininnmotel.com

Quiet Corner Farm ♦♦♦♦
High Street, Henstridge, Templecombe BA8 0RA
T: (01963) 363045
F: (01963) 363045
E: quietcorner.thompson@virgin.net
I: www.smoothhound.co.uk

HERMITAGE
Dorset

Almshouse Farm
♦♦♦♦ GOLD AWARD
Hermitage, Holnest, Sherborne DT9 6HA
T: (01963) 210296
F: (01963) 210296

HEXWORTHY
Devon

The Forest Inn ♦♦♦♦
Hexworthy, Yelverton PL20 6SD
T: (01364) 631211
F: (01364) 631515
E: jimbob@iglenister.freeserve.co.uk
I: www.theforestinn.co.uk

HIGHBRIDGE
Somerset

46 Church Street ♦♦
Church Street, Highbridge TA9 3AQ
T: (01278) 788365

Knoll Farm ♦♦♦
Jarvis Lane, East Brent, Highbridge TA9 4HS
T: (01278) 760227

Sandacre ♦♦♦
75 Burnham Road, Highbridge TA9 3JG
T: (01278) 781221

HIGHWORTH
Wiltshire

Roves Farm ♦♦♦
Sevenhampton, Highworth, Swindon SN6 7QG
T: (01793) 766846
F: (01793) 763939
E: jb@rovesfarm.freeserve.co.uk
I: www.rovesfarm.co.uk

HILMARTON
Wiltshire

Burfoots ♦♦♦♦
The Close, Hilmarton, Calne SN11 8TH
T: (01249) 760492
F: (01249) 760609
E: anncooke@burfoots.co.uk
I: www.burfoots.co.uk

HILPERTON
Wiltshire

Ring O' Bells ♦♦♦
321 Marsh Road, Hilperton Marsh, Hilperton, Trowbridge BA14 7PL
T: (01225) 754404
F: (01225) 340325
E: ringobells@blueyonder.co.uk

HOLBETON
Devon

Bugle Rocks
♦♦♦♦ SILVER AWARD
Battisborough Cross, Holbeton, Plymouth PL8 1JX
T: (01752) 830422
F: (01752) 830558
E: stay@buglerocks.co.uk
I: www.buglerocks.co.uk

HOLSWORTHY
Devon

Bason Farm ♦♦♦♦
Bradford, Holsworthy EX22 7AW
T: (01409) 281277
E: info@basonfarmholidays.co.uk
I: www.basonfarmholidays.co.uk

Leworthy Farmhouse Bed & Breakfast
♦♦♦♦ SILVER AWARD
Pyworthy, Holsworthy EX22 6SJ
T: (01409) 259469

HONITON
Devon

Barn Park Farm ♦♦♦
Stockland Hill, Honiton EX14 9JA
T: 0800 3282605
F: (01404) 861297
E: pab@barnparkfarm.fsnet.co.uk
I: www.lymeregis.com/barnparkfarm

Bidwell Farm and Haybarton Annexe ♦♦♦♦
Bidwell Farm, Upottery, Honiton EX14 9PP
T: (01404) 861122
F: (08700) 554960
E: pat@rbwells.demon.co.uk
I: www.bidwellfarm.co.uk

HONITON
Devon

The Cottage ♦♦♦♦
Marsh, Honiton EX14 9AJ
T: (01460) 234240

HONITON
Devon

Fairmile Inn ♦♦♦♦
On old A30, Fairmile, Ottery St Mary EX11 1LP
T: (01404) 812827
F: (01404) 815806
E: leon.courtney@thefairmileinn.co.uk
I: www.fairmileinn.co.uk

Feniton Court Bed and Breakfast ♦♦♦♦
Feniton Court, Honiton EX14 3BE
T: (01404) 850277
F: (01404) 850968
E: info@fenitoncourt.co.uk
I: www.fenitoncourt.co.uk

Lelamarie ♦♦♦
Awliscombe, Honiton EX14 3PP
T: (01404) 44646
F: (01404) 42131

The Old Vicarage ♦♦♦♦
Yarcombe, Honiton EX14 9BD
T: (01404) 861594
F: (01404) 861594
E: jonannstockwell@aol.com
I: members.aol.com/Jonannstockwell/

Wessington Farm
♦♦♦♦ SILVER AWARD
Awliscombe, Honiton EX14 3NU
T: (01404) 42280
F: (01404) 45271
I: www.eastdevon.com/bedandbreakfast

HORNINGSHAM
Wiltshire

Mill Farm ♦♦♦♦
Horningsham, Warminster BA12 7LL
T: (01985) 844333
E: millfarm_horningsham@yahoo.co.uk

HORRABRIDGE
Devon

Overcombe Hotel ♦♦♦♦
Old Station Road, Horrabridge, Yelverton PL20 7RA
T: (01822) 853501
F: (01822) 853501
E: enquiries@overcombehotel.co.uk
I: www.overcombehotel.co.uk

HORSINGTON
Somerset

Half Moon Inn ♦♦♦
Horsington, Templecombe
BA8 0EF
T: (01963) 370140
F: (01963) 371450
E: halfmoon@horsington.co.uk
I: www.horsington.co.uk

HORTON
Wiltshire

Partacre ♦♦
Horton, Devizes SN10 3NB
T: (01380) 860261

HUISH EPISCOPI
Somerset

Spring View ♦♦♦♦
Wagg Drove, Huish Episcopi, Langport TA10 9ER
T: (01458) 251215
E: ruddockspring@aol.com
I: www.spring-view.co.uk

Wagg Bridge Cottage ♦♦♦♦
Ducks Hill, Huish Episcopi, Langport TA10 9EN
T: (01458) 251488
F: (0820) 4055 2077
E: sandy@waggbridgecottage.freeserve.co.uk
I: www.waggbridgecottage.co.uk

HULLAVINGTON
Wiltshire

Bradfield Manor
♦♦♦♦♦ SILVER AWARD
Malmesbury SN14 6EU
T: (01666) 838000
F: (01666) 838200
E: enquiries@bradfieldmanor.co.uk
I: www.bradfieldmanor.co.uk

IDDESLEIGH
Devon

Parsonage Farm
♦♦♦♦ SILVER AWARD
Iddesleigh, Winkleigh EX19 8SN
T: (01837) 810318

IFORD
Wiltshire

Dog Kennel Farm Cottage ♦♦
Iford, Bradford-on-Avon
BA15 2BB
T: (01225) 723533

ILFRACOMBE
Devon

Burnaby Lodge
Rating Applied For
Chambercombe Park Road, Ilfracombe EX34 9QN
T: (01271) 866301
E: ted@burnabylodge.freeserve.co.uk
I: www.burnabylodge.freeserve.co.uk

ILFRACOMBE
Devon

Cairn House Hotel ♦♦♦
43 St Brannocks Road, Ilfracombe EX34 8EH
T: (01271) 863911
F: (07070) 800630
E: info@cairnhousehotel.co.uk
I: www.cairnhousehotel.co.uk

Capstone Hotel and Restaurant ♦♦♦
St James Place, Ilfracombe
EX34 9BJ
T: (01271) 863540
F: (01271) 862277
E: steve@capstone.freeserve.co.uk
I: www.ilfracombe2000.freeserve.co.uk

Combe Lodge Hotel ♦♦♦
Chambercombe Park Terrace, Ilfracombe EX34 9QW
T: (01271) 864518
F: (01271) 867628
E: combelodgehotel@tinyworld.co.uk
I: www.members.aol.com/combelodgehotel

Dedes Hotel ♦♦♦
1-4 The Promenade, Ilfracombe
EX34 9BD
T: (01271) 862545
F: (01271) 862234
E: jackie@dedes.fsbusiness.co.uk
I: www.clayshooting-dedes.co.uk

Dilkhusa Grand Hotel ♦♦♦
Wilder Road, Ilfracombe
EX34 9AH
T: (01271) 863505
F: (01271) 864739
I: www.shearingsholidays.com

Dorchester Hotel ♦♦
59 St Brannocks Road, Ilfracombe EX34 8EQ
T: (01271) 866949

The Epchris Hotel ♦♦♦
Torrs Park, Ilfracombe EX34 8AZ
T: (01271) 862751
F: (01271) 879077
E: epchris-hotel@ic24.net
I: www.epchrishotel.co.uk

Glen Tor Hotel ♦♦♦♦
Torrs Park, Ilfracombe EX34 8AZ
T: (01271) 862403
F: (01271) 862403
E: info@glentorhotel.co.uk
I: www.glentorhotel.co.uk

Greyven House ♦♦♦
4 St James Place, Ilfracombe
EX34 9BH
T: (01271) 862505
F: (01271) 862505
E: sandratrevor@greyvenhouse.fsnet.co.uk
I: www.ilfracombe-tourism.co.uk/greyvenhouse

Grosvenor Hotel ♦♦♦
Wilder Road, Ilfracombe
EX34 9AF
T: (01271) 863426
F: (01271) 863714
E: grosvenor.hotel@btopenworld.com
I: www.grosvenorhotelilfracombe.co.uk

Laston House Hotel ♦♦♦♦
Hillsborough Road, Ilfracombe
EX34 9NT
T: (01271) 866557
F: (01271) 867754
E: hilary@lastonhouse.com
I: www.lastonhouse.com

Rivendell Guest House ♦♦♦
28 St Brannocks Road, Ilfracombe EX34 8EQ
T: (01271) 866852
E: jackie@rivendellguesthouse.co.uk
I: www.rivendellguesthouse.co.uk

Seven Hills Hotel ♦♦♦♦
Torrs Park, Ilfracombe EX34 8AY
T: (01271) 862207
F: (01271) 865976
E: holidays@sevenhillshotel.co.uk
I: www.sevenhillshotel.co.uk

Strathmore Hotel
♦♦♦♦♦ SILVER AWARD
57 St Brannocks Road, Ilfracombe EX34 8EQ
T: (01271) 862248
F: (01271) 862243
E: strathmore@ukhotels.com
I: www.strathmore.ukhotels.com

Sunnymeade Country Hotel ♦♦♦
Dean Cross, West Down, Ilfracombe EX34 8NT
T: (01271) 863668
F: (01271) 863668
E: info@sunnymeade.co.uk
I: www.sunnymeade.co.uk

Swallow Barn Farmhouse ♦♦♦
Mullacott Farm, Mullacott Cross, Ilfracombe EX34 8NA
T: (01271) 866877
F: (01271) 866877
E: info@mullacottfarm.co.uk
I: www.mullacottfarm.co.uk

The Towers Hotel ♦♦♦♦
Chambercombe Park Road, Ilfracombe EX34 9QN
T: (01271) 862809
F: (01271) 879442
E: info@thetowers.co.uk
I: www.thetowers.co.uk

Varley House ♦♦♦♦
Chambercombe Park Terrace, Ilfracombe EX34 9QW
T: (01271) 863927
F: (01271) 879299
E: info@varleyhouse.co.uk
I: www.varleyhouse.co.uk

Westaway ♦♦♦♦
Torrs Park, Ilfracombe EX34 8AY
T: (01271) 864459
F: (01271) 863486
E: westaway55@btopenworld.com
I: www.westawayhotel.co.uk

Wildersmouth Hotel ♦
Sommers Crescent, Ilfracombe
EX34 9DP
T: (01271) 862002
F: (01271) 862803
E: booking@devoniahotel.co.uk
I: www.devoniahotels.co.uk

ILLOGAN
Cornwall

Aviary Court Hotel ♦♦♦♦
Mary's Well, Illogan, Redruth
TR16 4QZ
T: (01209) 842256
F: (01209) 843744
E: info@aviarycourthotel.co.uk
I: www.aviarycourthotel.co.uk

ILMINSTER
Somerset

Dillington House
♦♦♦♦ SILVER AWARD
Ilminster, Ilminster TA19 9DT
T: (01460) 52427
F: (01460) 52433
E: dillington@somerset.gov.uk
I: www.dillington.co.uk

Graden ♦♦♦
Peasmarsh, Ilminster TA19 0SG
T: (01460) 52371
F: (01460) 52371

Hermitage ♦♦♦
29 Station Road, Ilminster
TA19 9BE
T: (01460) 53028
I: www.home.freeuk.net/hermitage

Minster View ♦♦♦♦
8 Butts Road, Ilminster
TA19 0AX
T: (01460) 54619
E: trishlee@freenet.co.uk
I: www.minsterview.co.uk

ISLES OF SCILLY

Hotel Beachcomber ♦♦♦
Thorofare, St Mary's TR21 0LN
T: (01720) 422682
F: (01720) 422532

Nundeeps ♦♦♦
Rams Valley, St Mary's TR21 0JX
T: (01720) 422517
E: cook@nundeeps.freeserve.co.uk

Polreath Guest House ♦♦♦
Higher Town, St Martin's
TR25 0QL
T: (01720) 422046
F: (01720) 422046
E: sarah.poat@ntlworld.com

Seaview Moorings
♦♦♦♦♦ SILVER AWARD
Strand, St Mary's, TR21 0PT
T: (01720) 422327
F: (01720) 422211
E: enquiries@isleofscillyholidays.com
I: www.isleofscillyholidays.com

IVYBRIDGE
Devon

Hillhead Farm
♦♦♦♦ SILVER AWARD
Ugborough, Ivybridge PL21 0HQ
T: (01752) 892674
F: (01752) 690111
I: www.hillhead-farm.co.uk

Venn Farm ♦♦♦
Ugborough, Ivybridge PL21 0PE
T: (01364) 73240
F: (01364) 73240
I: www.smoothhound.co.uk/hotels/vennfarm

JACOBSTOW
Cornwall

The Old Rectory
♦♦♦♦♦ SILVER AWARD
Jacobstow, Bude EX23 0BR
T: (01840) 230380
F: (01840) 230380
E: johntodd50@hotmail.com
I: www.jacobstowoldrectory.com

KELSTON
Bath and North East Somerset

Old Crown ♦♦♦
Kelston, Bath BA1 9AQ
T: (01225) 423032
F: (01225) 480115

KENN
Devon

Lower Thornton Farm ♦♦♦♦
Kenn, Exeter EX6 7XH
T: (01392) 833434
F: (01392) 833434
E: will@willclark.plus.com

KENTISBURY
Devon

Beachborough Country House ♦♦♦♦
Kentisbury, Barnstaple EX31 4NH
T: (01271) 882487
F: (01271) 882487
E: viviane@beachborough.freeserve.co.uk
I: www.BeachboroughCountryHouse.co.uk

KILVE
Somerset

The Old Mill ♦♦♦♦
Kilve, Bridgwater TA5 1EB
T: (01278) 741571

KINGSAND
Cornwall

Halfway House Inn ♦♦♦
Fore Street, Kingsand PL10 1NA
T: (01752) 822279
F: (01752) 823146
E: info@halfwayinn.biz
I: www.halfwayinn.biz

KINGSBRIDGE
Devon

The Ashburton Arms ♦♦♦
West Charleton, Kingsbridge TQ7 2AH
T: (01548) 531242

Ashleigh House ♦♦♦♦
Ashleigh Road, Kingsbridge TQ7 1HB
T: (01548) 852893
F: (01548) 854648
E: reception@ashleigh-house.co.uk
I: www.ashleigh-house.co.uk

Combe Farm B & B
♦♦♦♦ SILVER AWARD
Loddiswell, Kingsbridge TQ7 4DT
T: (01548) 550560
F: (01548) 550560
E: combefarm@btinternet.com
I: www.combe-farm-holidays.co.uk

Coombe Farm ♦♦♦♦
Kingsbridge TQ7 4AB
T: (01548) 852038
F: (01548) 852038

Globe Inn ♦♦
Frogmore, Kingsbridge TQ7 2NR
T: (01548) 531351
F: (01548) 531351
E: enquiries@theglobeinn.co.uk
I: www.theglobeinn.co.uk

Shute Farm ♦♦♦
South Milton, Kingsbridge TQ7 3JL
T: (01548) 560680
E: luscombe@shutefarm.fsnet.co.uk

Sloop Inn ♦♦♦
Bantham, Kingsbridge TQ7 3AJ
T: (01548) 560489
F: (01548) 561940

South Allington House
♦♦♦♦ SILVER AWARD
South Allington, Chivelstone, Kingsbridge TQ7 2NB
T: (01548) 511272
F: (01548) 511421
E: barbara@sthallingtonbnb.demon.co.uk
I: www.sthallingtonbnb.demon.co.uk

KINGSBURY EPISCOPI
Somerset

The Retreat ♦♦♦♦
Kingsbury Episcopi, Martock TA12 6AZ
T: (01935) 823500

KINGSKERSWELL
Devon

Harewood Guesthouse ♦♦♦
17 Torquay Road, Kingskerswell, Newton Abbot TQ12 5HH
T: (01803) 872228

KINGSWEAR
Devon

Coleton Barton Farm ♦♦♦
Brownstone Road, Kingswear, Dartmouth TQ6 0EQ
T: (01803) 752795
F: (01803) 752241
E: carolinehaddock@btconnect.com

KINGTON LANGLEY
Wiltshire

The Moors ♦♦♦
Malmesbury Road, Kington Langley, Chippenham SN14 6HT
T: (01249) 750288
F: (01249) 750 8814

KINGWESTON
Somerset

Lower Farm ♦♦♦♦
Kingweston, Somerton TA11 6BA
T: (01458) 223237
F: (01458) 223276
E: lowerfarm@btconnect.com
I: www.lowerfarm.net

KNOWSTONE
Devon

West Bowden Farm ♦♦♦
Knowstone, South Molton EX36 4RP
T: (01398) 341224

LACOCK
Wiltshire

King John's Hunting Lodge
Rating Applied For
21 Church Street, Lacock, Chippenham SN15 2LB
T: (01249) 730313
F: (01249) 730725

Lacock Pottery Bed & Breakfast ♦♦♦♦
1 Church Street, Lacock, Chippenham SN15 2LB
T: (01249) 730266
F: (01249) 730946
E: simonemcdowell@lacockbedandbreakfast.com
I: www.lacockbedandbreakfast.com

Lower Lodge ♦♦♦
35 Bowden Hill, Lacock, Chippenham SN15 2PP
T: (01249) 730711
F: (01249) 730955
E: kay.du-boulay@amserv.net

The Old Rectory ♦♦♦♦
Cantax Hill, Lacock, Chippenham SN15 2JZ
T: (01249) 730335
F: (01249) 730166
E: sexton@oldrectorylacock.co.uk
I: www.oldrectorylacock.co.uk

Pen-Y-Brook House ♦♦♦
Notton, Lacock, Chippenham SN15 2NF
T: (01249) 730376

Videl ♦♦♦
Bewley Lane, Lacock, Chippenham SN15 2PG
T: (01249) 730279

LAMORNA
Cornwall

Castallack Farm ♦♦♦♦
Castallack, Lamorna, Penzance TR19 6NL
T: (01736) 731969
F: (01736) 731969
E: hood@castallackfarm.fsnet.co.uk
I: www.castallackfarm.co.uk

LANDSCOVE
Devon

Thornecroft
♦♦♦♦ SILVER AWARD
Landscove, Ashburton, Newton Abbot TQ13 7LX
T: (01803) 762500
E: tonymatthews@lineone.net
I: www.b&b@thornecroft.co.uk

LANEAST
Cornwall

Stitch Park ♦♦♦♦
Laneast, Launceston PL15 8PN
T: (01566) 86687
E: stitchpark@hotmail.com

LANESCOT
Cornwall

Great Pelean Farm
Rating Applied For
Tywardreath, Par Pl24 2rx
T: (01726) 812106
F: (01726) 812106
E: andyjones74@hotmail.com

LANGPORT
Somerset

Amberley ♦♦♦♦
Martock Road, Long Load, Langport TA10 9LD
T: (01458) 241542
E: jean.atamberley@talk21.com

Gothic House ♦♦♦♦
Thorney, Muchelney, Langport TA10 0DW
T: (01458) 250626
E: joy-thorne@totalserve.co.uk

Muchelney Ham Farm
♦♦♦♦♦ GOLD AWARD
Muchelney Ham, Muchelney, Langport TA10 0DJ
T: (01458) 250737
F: (01458) 250737
I: www.muchelneyhamfarm.co.uk

The Old Pound Inn ♦♦♦
Aller, Langport TA10 0RA
T: (01458) 250469
F: (01458) 250469

LANIVET
Cornwall

St Benet's Abbey ♦♦♦♦
Truro Road, Lanivet, Bodmin PL30 5HF
T: (01208) 831352
F: (01208) 832052

Tremeere Manor ♦♦♦
Lanivet, Bodmin PL30 5BG
T: (01208) 831513
F: (01208) 832417
E: oliver.tremeere.manor@fwi.co.uk

Willowbrook ♦♦♦♦
Lamorrick, Lanivet, Bodmin PL30 5HB
T: (01208) 831670
F: (01208) 831670
E: miles.willowbrook@btinternet.com
I: www.bnbirdex.com/willowbrook

LANSALLOS
Cornwall

Lesquite
♦♦♦♦ SILVER AWARD
Lansallos, Looe PL13 2QE
T: (01503) 220315
F: (01503) 220137
E: lesquite@farmersweekly.net
I: www.lesquite-polperro.fsnet.co.uk

West Kellow Farmhouse ♦♦♦
Lansallos, Looe PL13 2QL
T: (01503) 272089
F: (01503) 272089
E: westkellow@aol.com
I: www.westkellow.co.uk

LAUNCELLS
Cornwall

Hersham Carpentry ♦♦♦
Launcells, Bude EX23 9LZ
T: (01288) 321369
F: (01288) 321369
E: tillinghast@ndirect.co.uk

LAUNCESTON
Cornwall

Berrio Bridge House ♦♦♦♦
North Hill, Launceston PL15 7NL
T: (01566) 782714
F: (01566) 782714
E: Helen@berriobridge.freeserve.co.uk

11 Castle Street ♦♦♦♦
Launceston PL15 8BA
T: (01566) 773873
F: (01566) 773873

Glencoe Villa ♦♦♦
Race Hill, Launceston PL15 9BB
T: (01566) 773012

Hill Park ♦♦♦♦
St Thomas, Launceston PL15 8SH
T: (01566) 86937
E: barbara_penfold@hotmail.com

Lynher Farm ♦♦♦
North Hill, Launceston PL15 7NR
T: (01566) 782273
F: (01566) 782273
E: wegribble@farmersweekly.net
I: users.farmersweekly.net/wegribble

Middle Tremollett Farm
◆◆◆◆
Coad's Green, Launceston
PL15 7NA
T: (01566) 782416
F: (01566) 782416
E: btrewin@talk21.com
I: www.tremollett.com

The Old Granary ◆◆◆◆
North Petherwin, Launceston
PL15 8LR
T: (01566) 785593
E: ptrbrr@aol.com

Panson Mill Farm ◆◆◆◆
St Giles-on-the-Heath,
Launceston PL15 9SQ
T: (01409) 211306
F: (01409) 211107
E: lizzie.browning@care4free.net

Thornbank Guest House ◆◆◆
6 Highfield Park Road,
Launceston PL15 7DY
T: (01566) 776136
F: (01566) 776136
E: bkressinger@btopenworld.com

Tregood Farm
Rating Applied For
Congdon's Shop, Launceston
PL15 7PN
T: (01566) 782263

Trevadlock Farm
◆◆◆◆ SILVER AWARD
Trevadlock, Congdon Shop,
Launceston PL15 7PW
T: (01566) 782239
F: (01566) 782239
E: trevadlock@farming.co.uk
I: www.trevadlock.co.uk

Wheatley Farm
◆◆◆◆◆ GOLD AWARD
Maxworthy, Launceston
PL15 8LY
T: (01566) 781232
F: (01566) 781232
E: valerie@wheatleyfrm.com
I: www.wheatleyfrm.com

White Hart Hotel ◆◆◆
15 Broad Street, Launceston
PL15 8AL
T: (01566) 772013
F: (01566) 773668
E: reception@whitehartho tellaunceston.co.uk
I: www.whiteharthotel-launceston.co.uk

The White Horse Inn ◆◆◆
14 Newport Square, Launceston
PL15 8EL
T: (01566) 772084
F: (01566) 779592
E: m.howard@talk21.com

LAVERSTOCK
Wiltshire

20 Potters Way ◆◆◆
Potters Way, Laverstock,
Salisbury SP1 1PY
T: (01722) 335031
F: (01722) 335031

1 Riverside Close ◆◆◆◆
Laverstock, Salisbury SP1 1QW
T: (01722) 320287
F: (01722) 320287
E: marytucker2001@yahoo.com

The Twitterings ◆◆◆
73 Church Road, Laverstock,
Salisbury SP1 1QZ
T: (01722) 321760

LAVERTON
Somerset

Hollytree Cottage ◆◆◆◆
Laverton, Bath BA2 7QZ
T: (01373) 830786
F: (01373) 830786
E: julia@naismith.fsbusiness.co.uk

LELANT
Cornwall

Hindon Hall ◆◆◆◆
Fore Street, Lelant, St Ives
TR26 3EN
T: (01736) 753046
F: (01736) 753046
E: hindonhall@talk21.com
I: hindonhall.co.uk

LEWDOWN
Devon

Stowford Grange Farm ◆◆
Lewdown, Okehampton
EX20 4BZ
T: (01566) 783298

LISKEARD
Cornwall

Elnor Guest House ◆◆◆
1 Russell Street, Liskeard
PL14 4BP
T: (01579) 342472
F: (01579) 345673
E: Elnor@btopenworld.com

Hyvue House ◆◆◆
Endsleigh Terrace, Liskeard
PL14 6BN
T: (01579) 348175

Lampen Farm ◆◆◆◆
St Neot, Liskeard PL14 6PB
T: (01579) 320284
F: (01579) 320284

Pencubitt Country House Hotel
◆◆◆◆
Station Road, Lamellion Cross,
Liskeard PL14 4EB
T: (01579) 342694
F: (01579) 342694
E: bookings@pencubitt.com
I: www.pencubitt.com

Trecorme Barton ◆◆◆◆
Quethiock, Liskeard PL14 3SH
T: (01579) 342646
F: (01579) 342646
E: renfree@trecormebarton.fsnet.co.uk

Tregondale Farm
◆◆◆◆ SILVER AWARD
Menheniot, Liskeard PL14 3RG
T: (01579) 342407
F: (01579) 342407
E: tregondale@connectfree.co.uk
I: www.tregondalefarm.co.uk

Trewint Farm
◆◆◆◆ SILVER AWARD
Menheniot, Liskeard PL14 3RE
T: (01579) 347155
F: (01579) 347155
I: www.trewintfarm.co.uk

LITTLE BEDWYN
Wiltshire

Bridge Cottage ◆◆◆
Forebridge, Little Bedwyn,
Marlborough SN8 3JS
T: (01672) 870795
F: (01672) 870795
E: rwdaniel@bridgecott.fsnet.co.uk
I: www.bridgecott.co.uk

LITTLE LANGFORD
Wiltshire

Little Langford Farmhouse
◆◆◆◆◆ GOLD AWARD
Little Langford, Salisbury
SP3 4NR
T: (01722) 790205
F: (01722) 790086
E: bandb@littlelangford.co.uk
I: www.littlelangford.co.uk

LITTLE PETHERICK
Cornwall

Molesworth Manor ◆◆◆◆
Little Petherick, Padstow
PL27 7QT
T: (01841) 540292
E: molesworthmanor@aol.com
I: www.molesworthmanor.co.uk

LITTLE SOMERFORD
Wiltshire

Stac Polly ◆◆◆◆
Little Somerford, Chippenham
SN15 5JT
T: (01666) 824758
E: dinah.post@talk21.com
I: www.stacpollybb.co.uk

LITTLE TORRINGTON
Devon

Smytham Manor Leisure ◆◆◆
Smytham Manor, Little
Torrington, Torrington EX38 8PU
T: (01805) 622110
F: (01805) 625451
E: info@smytham.fsnet.co.uk

LITTLEHEMPSTON
Devon

Post Cottage ◆◆◆
Littlehempston, Totnes TQ9 6LU
T: (01803) 868192
E: hugh.gf@virgin.net
I: www.postcottage.co.uk

LONDON APPRENTICE
Cornwall

Spindrift
Rating Applied For
London Apprentice, St Austell
PL26 7AR
T: (01726) 69316
E: mcguffspindrift@hotmail.com

LONG BREDY
Dorset

Middle Farm ◆◆◆
Long Bredy, Dorchester
DT2 9HW
T: (01308) 482215
F: (01308) 482215
E: jonchrisscott@aol.com

LONGBRIDGE DEVERILL
Wiltshire

The George Inn ◆◆◆◆
Longbridge Deverill, Warminster
BA12 7DG
T: (01985) 840396
F: (01985) 841333
I: www.thegeorgeinnlongbridgedeveril.co.uk

LONGLEAT
Wiltshire

Post Office Farm ◆◆◆
Corsley Heath, Longleat,
Warminster BA12 7PR
T: (01373) 832734
F: (01373) 832734
E: kmyoudan@lineone.net

LOOE
Cornwall

Allhays Country Bed & Breakfast
◆◆◆◆ SILVER AWARD
Porthallow, Talland Bay, Looe
PL13 2JB
T: (01503) 273188
E: info@allhays.co.uk
I: www.allhays.co.uk

Barclay House
◆◆◆◆ SILVER AWARD
St Martins Road, East Looe, Looe
PL13 1LP
T: (01503) 262929
F: (01503) 262632
E: info@barclayhouse.co.uk
I: www.barclayhouse.co.uk

Bucklawren Farm
◆◆◆◆ SILVER AWARD
St Martin-by-Looe, Looe
PL13 1NZ
T: (01503) 240738
F: (01503) 240481
E: bucklawren@btopenworld.com
I: www.bucklawren.com

Coombe Farm ◆◆◆◆
Coombe Farm, Widegates, Looe
PL13 1QN
T: (01503) 240223
F: (01503) 240329
E: coombe_farm@hotmail.com
I: www.coombefarmhotel.co.uk

Down Ende Country House
◆◆◆
Widegates, Looe PL13 1QN
T: (01503) 240213
F: (01503) 240656
E: enquiries@downende.com
I: www.downende.com

Little Larnick Farm
◆◆◆◆ SILVER AWARD
Pelynt, Looe PL13 2NB
T: (01503) 262837
F: (01503) 262837
E: littlelarnick@btclick.com

The Panorama Hotel ◆◆◆◆
Hannafore Road, Looe PL13 2DE
T: (01503) 262123
F: (01503) 265654
E: stay@looe.co.uk
I: www.looe.co.uk

Stonerock Cottage ◆◆◆◆
Portuan Road, West Looe, Looe
PL13 2DN
T: (01503) 263651
F: (01503) 263414
E: stonerock@ic24.net
I: stonerockcottage.com

Talehay ◆◆◆◆ SILVER AWARD
Tremaine, Pelynt, Looe PL13 2LT
T: (01503) 220252
F: (01503) 220252
E: paul@talehay.co.uk
I: www.talehay.co.uk

Trevanion Hotel ◆◆◆
Hannafore Road, Looe PL13 2DE
T: (01503) 262003
E: hotel@looecornwall.co.uk
I: www.looecornwall.co.uk

LOSTWITHIEL
Cornwall

Atkinson's Accommodation
◆◆◆
Carnsews, Lostwithiel PL22 0LH
T: (01208) 872548

LOWER STICKER
Cornwall

Luney Barton House
♦♦♦♦♦ SILVER AWARD
Lower Sticker, St Austell
PL26 7JH
T: (01726) 882219
E: info@luneybarton.com
I: www.luneybarton.com

LUSTLEIGH
Devon

Eastwrey Barton ♦♦♦♦
Moretonhampstead Road,
Lustleigh, Newton Abbot
TQ13 9SN
T: (01647) 277338
F: (01647) 277133
E: jb@ewbarton.fsnet.co.uk
I: www.eastwreybarton.co.uk

LUXBOROUGH
Somerset

The Royal Oak of Luxborough ♦♦♦
Luxborough, Watchet TA23 0SH
T: (01984) 640319
F: (01984) 641561
E: royaloakof.luxborough@virgin.net
I: www.smoothhound.co.uk/hotels/royallux

LYDIARD TREGOZE
Wiltshire

Park Farm ♦♦♦
Hook Street, Lydiard Tregoze,
Swindon SN5 3NY
T: (01793) 853608

LYME REGIS
Dorset

Charnwood Guest House ♦♦♦♦
21 Woodmead Road, Lyme Regis
DT7 3AD
T: (01297) 445281
E: enqetc@lymeregisaccommodation.com
I: www.lymeregisaccommodation.com

Clappentail House
♦♦♦♦♦ SILVER AWARD
Uplyme Road, Lyme Regis
DT7 3LP
T: (01297) 445739
F: (01297) 444794
E: pountain@clappentail.freeserve.co.uk

Cliff Cottage ♦♦♦
Marine Parade, Lyme Regis
DT7 3JE
T: (01297) 443334
E: merry.bolton@btinternet.com

Clovelly Guest House
Rating Applied For
View Road, Lyme Regis DT7 3AA
T: (01297) 444052
E: clovelly@lymeregisbnb.com
I: www.lymeregisbnb.com

Coombe House ♦♦♦
Coombe Street, Lyme Regis
DT7 3PY
T: (01297) 443849
F: (01297) 443849
E: dunc@hughduncan.freeserve.co.uk
I: www.coombe-house.co.uk

Coombe Street B&B ♦♦♦
33 Coombe Street, Lyme Regis
DT7 3PP
T: (01297) 444817
F: (01297) 444817
E: B&B@coombestreet.co.uk

Devonia Guest House ♦♦♦♦
2 Woodmead Road, Lyme Regis
DT7 3AB
T: (01297) 442869
F: (01297) 442869
E: roysue@fsmail.net.co.uk
I: www.devoniaguest.co.uk

Higher Spence ♦♦♦
Wootton Fitzpaine, Charmouth,
Wootton Fitzpaine, Bridport
DT6 6DF
T: (01297) 560556
E: higherspence@eurolink.ltd.net

Kent House hotel ♦♦♦
Silver Street, Lyme Regis
DT7 3HT
T: (01297) 443442
F: (01297) 444626
E: thekenthouse@talk21.com
I: www.kenthousehotel.co.uk

The London Bed and Breakfast ♦♦♦
40 Church Street, Lyme Regis
DT7 3DA
T: (01297) 442083

Lucerne ♦♦♦♦
View Road, Lyme Regis DT7 3AA
T: (01297) 443752
E: lucerne@lineone.net

Manaton Guest House ♦♦♦♦
Hill Road, Lyme Regis DT7 3PE
T: (01297) 445138
E: mould@lymeregis.freeserve.co.uk

The New Haven Hotel ♦♦♦
1 Pound Street, Lyme Regis
DT7 3HZ
T: (01297) 442499
F: (01297) 442499
E: cherylnewhaven@hotmail.com
I: www.lymeregishotels.co.uk

Ocean View ♦♦♦♦
2 Hadleigh Villas, Silver Street,
Lyme Regis DT7 3HR
T: (01297) 442567
E: Jaybabe@supanet.com
I: www.lymeregis.com/ocean/view

Old Lyme Guest House
♦♦♦♦ GOLD AWARD
Coombe Street, Lyme Regis
DT7 3PP
T: (01297) 442929
E: oldlyme.guesthouse@virgin.net
I: www.oldlymeguesthouse.co.uk

The Red House ♦♦♦♦
Sidmouth Road, Lyme Regis
DT7 3ES
T: (01297) 442055
F: (01297) 442055
E: red.house@virgin.net
I: www.smoothhound.co.uk/hotels/redhous2.html

Rotherfield ♦♦♦♦
View Road, Lyme Regis DT7 3AA
T: (01297) 445585
E: rotherfield@lymeregis.com
I: www.lymeregis.com/rotherfield/

Southernhaye ♦♦♦♦
Pound Road, Lyme Regis
DT7 3HX
T: (01297) 443077
F: (01297) 443077

Springfield ♦♦♦♦
Woodmead Road, Lyme Regis
DT7 3LJ
T: (01297) 443409
F: (01297) 443685
E: springfield@lymeregis.com
I: www.lymeregis.com/springfield

Thatch ♦♦♦♦
Uplyme Road, Lyme Regis
DT7 3LP
T: (01297) 442212
F: (01297) 443485
E: thethatch@lineone.net
I: www.uk-bedandbreakfasts.co.uk

Tudor House Hotel ♦♦♦♦
Church Street, Lyme Regis
DT7 3BU
T: (01297) 442472
E: tudor@eclipse.co.uk
I: www.thetudorhouse.co.uk

Victoria Hotel ♦♦♦
Uplyme Road, Lyme Regis
DT7 3LP
T: (01297) 444801
F: (01297) 442949
E: info@vichotel.co.uk
I: www.vichotel.co.uk

Westwood Guest House ♦♦♦
Woodmead Road, Lyme Regis
DT7 3LJ
T: (01297) 442376

LYNMOUTH
Devon

Bonnicott House Hotel ♦♦♦♦♦
Watersmeet Road, Lynmouth
EX35 6EP
T: (01598) 753346
F: (01598) 753724
E: bonnicott@hotmail.com
I: www.bonnicott.com

Coombe Farm ♦♦♦
Countisbury, Lynton EX35 6NF
T: (01598) 741236
F: (01598) 741236
E: coombefarm@freeserve.co.uk
I: www.brendanvalley.co.uk/coombefarm

Tregonwell 'The Olde Sea-Captain's Guesthouse' ♦♦♦
1 Tors Road, Lynmouth EX35 6ET
T: (01598) 753369
I: www.smoothhound.co.uk/hotels/tregonwl.html

The Village Inn ♦♦♦
19 Lynmouth Street, Lynmouth
EX35 6EH
T: (01598) 752354

LYNTON
Devon

The Denes Guest House ♦♦♦
15 Longmead, Lynton EX35 6DQ
T: (01598) 753573
F: (01598) 753573
E: j.e.mcgowan@btinternet.com
I: www.thedenes.com

Fernleigh Guest House ♦♦♦♦
Park Street, Lynton EX35 6BY
T: (01598) 753575
F: (01598) 753575
E: bookings@fernleigh.net
I: www.fernleigh.net

Kingford House
♦♦♦♦ SILVER AWARD
Longmead, Lynton EX35 6DQ
T: (01598) 752361
E: tricia@kingfordhouse.co.uk
I: www.kingfordhouse.co.uk

Lee House ♦♦♦
Lee Road, Lynton EX35 6BP
T: (01598) 752364
F: (01598) 752364
E: leehouse@freeuk.com
I: www.smoothhound.co.uk/hotels/lee.html

Longmead House Hotel
♦♦♦♦ SILVER AWARD
9 Longmead, Lynton EX35 6DQ
T: (01598) 752523
F: (01598) 752523
E: info@longmeadhouse.co.uk
I: www.longmeadhouse.co.uk

Millslade Country House Hotel ♦♦♦♦
Brendon, Lynton EX35 6PS
T: (01598) 741322
F: (01598) 741355
E: bobcramp@millslade.freeserve.co.uk
I: www.millslade.co.uk

North Walk House ♦♦♦♦
North Walk, Lynton EX35 6HJ
T: (01598) 753372
E: murphynwh@tesco.net

Pine Lodge
♦♦♦♦ SILVER AWARD
Lynway, Lynton EX35 6AX
T: (01598) 753230
E: info@pinelodgehotel.com
I: www.pinelodgehotel.com

Rockvale Hotel ♦♦♦♦
Lee Road, Lynton EX35 6HW
T: (01598) 752279
E: JudithWoodland@rockvale.fsbusiness.co.uk
I: www.rockvalehotel.co.uk

Seawood Hotel
Rating Applied For
North Walk, Lynton EX35 6HJ
T: (01598) 752272
F: (01598) 752272
E: glljnk@aol.com

Sinai House ♦♦♦♦
Lynway, Lynton EX35 6AY
T: (01598) 753227
F: (01598) 752633
E: enquiries@sinaihouse.co.uk
I: www.sinaihouse.co.uk

South View Guest House ♦♦♦
Lee Road, Lynton EX35 6BP
T: (01598) 752289
F: (01598) 752289

Southcliffe ♦♦♦♦
34 Lee Road, Lynton EX35 6BS
T: (01598) 753328
E: info@southcliffe.co.uk
I: www.southcliffe.co.uk

The Turret ♦♦♦♦
33 Lee Road, Lynton EX35 6BS
T: (01598) 753284
F: (01598) 753284
I: www.turrethotel.co.uk

Valley of Rocks ♦♦♦♦
Lee Road, Lynton EX35 6HS
T: (01598) 752349
F: (01598) 753720
I: www.shearingsholidays.com/hotels/lynton.htm

MALMESBURY
Wiltshire

Bremilham House ◆◆◆
Bremilham Road, Malmesbury
SN16 0DQ
T: (01666) 822680

The Kings Arms Hotel ◆◆◆◆
High Street, Malmesbury
SN16 9AA
T: (01666) 823383
F: (01666) 825327
E: kingsarmshotel@malmesburywilts.freeserve.co.uk
I: www.kingsarmshotel.info

Lovett Farm ◆◆◆◆
Little Somerford, Chippenham
SN15 5BP
T: (01666) 823268
F: (01666) 823268
E: lovettfarm@btinternet
I: www.lovettfarm.co.uk

Manor Farm ◆◆◆◆
Corston, Malmesbury SN16 0HF
T: (01666) 822148
F: (01666) 826565
E: ross@manorfarmbandb.fsnet.co.uk
I: www.manorfarmbandb.co.uk

Marsh Farmhouse ◆◆◆
Crudwell Road, Malmesbury
SN16 9JL
T: (01666) 822208

Oakwood Farm ◆◆◆
Upper Minety, Malmesbury
SN16 9PY
T: (01666) 860286
F: (01666) 860286

Rothay ◆◆◆◆
Milbourne Lane, Malmesbury
SN16 9JQ
T: (01666) 823509

Whychurch Farm ◆◆◆◆
Whychurch Hill, Malmesbury
SN16 9JL
T: (01666) 822156
E: chriswhychurch@aol.com

MANNAMEAD
Devon

Devonshire Guest House ◆◆◆
22 Lockyer Road, Mannamead,
Plymouth PL3 4RL
T: (01752) 220726
F: (01752) 220766
E: devonshiregh@blueyonder.co.uk
I: www.devonshiregh.pwp.blueyonder.co.uk

MANNINGFORD ABBOTS
Wiltshire

Huntlys
Rating Applied For
Manningford Abbots, Pewsey
SN9 6HZ
T: (01672) 563663
F: (01672) 563663
E: meg@gimspike.fsnet.co.uk

MANTON
Wiltshire

Sunrise ◆◆◆
Manton Drove, Manton,
Marlborough SN8 4HL
T: (01672) 512878
F: (01672) 512878

MARAZION
Cornwall

Chymorvah Private Hotel ◆◆◆
Marazion TR17 0DQ
T: (01736) 710497
F: (01736) 710508
I: www.smoothhound.co.uk/hotels/chymorva.html

MARK
Somerset

Burnt House Farm ◆◆◆
Yarrow Road, Mark, Highbridge
TA9 4LR
T: (01278) 641280
F: (01278) 641280
E: carmen.burnthouse@amserve.net

Laurel Farm ◆◆◆
The Causeway, Mark, Highbridge
TA9 4PZ
T: (01278) 641216
F: (01278) 641447

MARLBOROUGH
Wiltshire

Ash Lodge ◆◆◆◆
Chopping Knife Lane,
Marlborough SN8 2AT
T: (01672) 516745
E: alanatashlodge.ehoppingknife@vergin.net
I: www.ashlodge.co.uk

Cartref ◆◆◆
63 George Lane, Marlborough
SN8 4BY
T: (01672) 512771

Fishermans House ◆◆◆◆
Mildenhall, Marlborough
SN8 2LZ
T: (01672) 515390
F: (01672) 519009

The Lamb Inn ◆◆◆
The Parade, Marlborough
SN8 1NE
T: (01672) 512668
F: (01672) 512668

Merlin Hotel ◆◆◆
36/39 High Street, Marlborough
SN8 1LW
T: (01672) 512151
F: (01672) 515310
E: info@merlinhouse.co.uk

Monks Rest Lodge ◆◆◆◆
Salisbury Road, Marlborough
SN8 4AE
T: (01672) 512169
F: (01672) 516360
E: andrew@monksrest.co.uk
I: www.monksrest.co.uk

Upper Westcourt ◆◆◆◆
Burbage, Marlborough SN8 3BW
T: (01672) 810307
F: (01672) 810307
E: prhill@onetel.net.uk

Wernham Farm ◆◆◆
Clench Common, Marlborough
SN8 4DR
T: (01672) 512236
F: (01672) 515001
E: margglvsf@aol.com

Westcourt Bottom ◆◆◆◆
165 Westcourt, Burbage,
Marlborough SN8 3BW
T: (01672) 810924
F: (01672) 810924
E: westcourt.b-and-b@virgin.net
I: www.westcourtbottom.co.uk

MARSHGATE
Cornwall

Melrose ◆◆◆
Marshgate, Camelford PL32 9YN
T: (01840) 261744

MARSTON
Wiltshire

Home Farm ◆◆◆◆
Close Lane, Marston, Devizes
SN10 5SN
T: (01380) 725484
E: mauricereardon@lineone.net

MARTOCK
Somerset

Bartletts Farm ◆◆◆◆
Isle Brewers, Taunton TA3 6QN
T: (01460) 281423
F: (01460) 281423
E: sandjpeach@tesco.net
I: www.pcmanyeovil.co.uk/bnb.htm

Madey Mills ◆◆
Martock TA12 6NN
T: (01935) 823268

The Nags Head ◆◆◆
East Street, Martock TA12 6NF
T: (01935) 823432
E: Thenagschef@aol.com

The White Hart Hotel ◆◆◆◆
East Street, Martock TA12 6JQ
T: (01935) 822005
F: (01935) 822056
E: enquiries@whitehartholtelmartock.co.uk
I: www.whitehartholtelmartock.co.uk

Wychwood ◆◆◆◆
7 Bearley Road, Wychwood,
Martock TA12 6PG
T: (01935) 825601
F: (01935) 825601
E: wychwoodmartock@yahoo.co.uk
I: www.theaa.co.uk/region8/76883.html

MAWGAN PORTH
Cornwall

Bre-Pen Farm ◆◆◆◆
Mawgan Porth, Newquay
TR8 4AL
T: (01637) 860420
E: jill.brake@virgin.net
I: www.bre-penfarm.co.uk

Trevarrian Lodge ◆◆
Trevarrian, Mawgan Porth,
Newquay TR8 4AQ
T: (01637) 860156
F: (01637) 860422
E: trevarrian@aol.com
I: www.trevarrianlodge.co.uk

MEAVY
Devon

Callisham Farm ◆◆◆
Meavy, Yelverton PL20 6PS
T: (01822) 853901
F: (01822) 853901
E: wills@callishamfarm.fsnet.co.uk
I: www.callishamfarm.fsnet.co.uk

MELDON
Devon

Kerslake Farm ◆◆◆◆
Meldon, Okehampton EX20 4LU
T: (01837) 54892
F: (01837) 54892
E: booking@kerslakemeldon.co.uk
I: www.kerslakemeldon.co.uk

MELKSHAM
Wiltshire

Bowden House
Rating Applied For
27 Beanacre Road, Melksham
SN12 8AQ
T: (01225) 709443
F: (01225) 709443

Longhope Guest House ◆◆◆
9 Beanacre Road, Melksham
SN12 8AG
T: (01225) 706737
F: (01225) 706737

The Spa Bed & Breakfast ◆◆◆
402 The Spa, Melksham
SN12 6QL
T: (01225) 707984
I: www.melksham.org.uk/thespa

Springfield B & B ◆◆◆◆
403 The Spa, Melksham
SN12 6QL
T: (01225) 703694
F: (01225) 705820
E: springfieldbandb@ukworld.net
I: www.ukworld.net/springfieldbandb

The Town House ◆◆◆
18 Spa Road, Melksham
SN12 7NS
T: (01225) 700125
E: 18townhouse@tiscali.com

MELLS
Somerset

Claveys Farm
Rating Applied For
Mells Green, Mells, Frome
BA11 3QP
T: (01373) 814651
F: (01373) 814651
I: www.fleurkelly.com/bandb

MELPLASH
Dorset

Mount Meadow Farm ◆◆◆
The Mount, Melplash, Bridport
DT6 3TV
I: (01308) 488524
E: rosiegroves@newmail.net
I: www.mountmeadow.co.uk

MEMBURY
Devon

Oxenways House
◆◆◆◆◆ GOLD AWARD
Chapelcroft Road, Membury,
Axminster EX13 7JR
T: (01404) 881785
F: (01404) 881778
E: info@oxenways.com
I: www.oxenways.com

MERE
Wiltshire

The Beeches ◆◆◆
Mere, Warminster BA12 6AU
T: (01747) 860687

Downleaze ◆◆◆
North Street, Mere, Warminster
BA12 6HH
T: (01747) 860876

Establishments printed in blue have a detailed entry in this guide

Latimer House B&B
Rating Applied For
Castle Street, Mere, Warminster BA12 6JE
T: (01747) 860630
E: latimer.house@virgin.net
I: www.latimerhouse.net

The Old Police House ♦♦♦
North Street, Mere, Warminster BA12 6HH
T: (01747) 861768
E: gilly.gristwood@btopenworld.com

MERRYMEET Cornwall

Higher Trevartha Farm ♦♦♦♦
Pengover, Merrymeet, Liskeard PL14 3NJ
T: (01579) 343382

MEVAGISSEY Cornwall

Kerryanna Country House ♦♦♦♦
Treleaven Farm, Mevagissey, St Austell PL26 6RZ
T: (01726) 843558
F: (01726) 843558
E: linda.hennah@btinternet.com
I: www.kerryanna.co.uk

Rising Sun Inn ♦♦♦
Portmellon Cove, Mevagissey, St Austell PL26 6PL
T: (01726) 843235
F: (01726) 843235
E: cliffnsheila@tiscali.co.uk
I: www.risingsunportmellon.co.uk

Seapoint House Hotel ♦♦♦
Battery Terrace, Mevagissey, St Austell PL26 6QS
T: (01726) 842684
F: (01726) 844476
I: www.seapointhousehotel.com

MIDDLEMARSH Dorset

The Hunters Moon ♦♦♦♦
Middlemarsh, Sherborne DT9 5QN
T: (01963) 210966
E: rooms@thehuntersmoon.co.uk
I: www.thehuntersmoon.co.uk

White Horse Farm ♦♦♦♦
Middlemarsh, Sherborne DT9 5QN
T: (01963) 210222
F: (01963) 210222
E: enquiries@whitehorsefarm.co.uk
I: www.whitehorsefarm.co.uk

MIDSOMER NORTON Bath and North East Somerset

The Old Priory ♦♦♦♦♦ SILVER AWARD
Church Square, Midsomer Norton, Bath BA3 2HX
T: (01761) 416784
F: (01761) 417851
E: reservations@theoldpriory.co.uk
I: www.theoldpriory.co.uk

MILLBROOK Cornwall

Stone Farm Bed and Breakfast ♦♦♦♦ SILVER AWARD
Millbrook, Torpoint PL10 1JJ
T: (01752) 822267
F: (01752) 822267

MILVERTON Somerset

Cullendown ♦♦
Spring Grove, Milverton, Taunton TA4 1NL
T: (01823) 400731
E: doreen.orton@btinternet.com

MINEHEAD Somerset

Alcombe Cote Guest House ♦♦♦
19 Manor Road, Alcombe, Minehead TA24 6EH
T: (01643) 703309
F: (01643) 709901
E: collopalcombecote@bushinternet.com

Avondale ♦♦♦♦
Martlet Road, Minehead TA24 5QD
T: (01643) 706931

Bactonleigh Hotel ♦♦♦
20 Tregonwell Road, Minehead TA24 5DU
T: (01643) 702147

Baytree ♦♦♦
29 Blenheim Road, Minehead TA24 5PZ
T: (01643) 703374
E: derekcole@onetel.net.uk

Bethany Guest House
Rating Applied For
10 Townsend Road, Minehead TA24 5RG
T: (01643) 704289
E: stay@bethanyjunction.co.uk
I: www.bethanyjunction.co.uk

Beverleigh ♦♦♦♦
Beacon Road, Minehead TA24 5SE
T: (01643) 708450
E: beverleigh@talk21.com

Court Farm
Rating Applied For
Exford, Minehead TA24 7LY
T: (01643) 831207
E: beth@courtfarm.co.uk
I: www.courtfarm.co.uk

Dorchester Hotel ♦♦♦
38 The Avenue, Minehead TA24 5AZ
T: (01643) 702052
F: (01643) 702052
E: rooms@dorchester-minehead.com
I: www.dorchester-minehead.com

Dunkery Lodge ♦♦♦♦
Townsend Road, Minehead TA24 5RQ
T: (01643) 706170
F: (0870) 902 9111
E: book@dunkery-lodge.co.uk
I: www.dunkery-lodge.co.uk

The Exford Bridge Restaurant
Rating Applied For
Exford, Minehead TA24 7PY
T: (01643) 831304
E: exfordbridge@btopenworld.com
I: www.exfordbridge.co.uk

Gascony Hotel ♦♦♦♦
The Avenue, Minehead TA24 5BB
T: (01643) 705939
F: (01643) 709926

Higher Rodhuish Farm ♦♦♦
Rodhuish, Minehead TA24 6QL
T: (01984) 640253
F: (01984) 640253

Kingsway Hotel
Rating Applied For
36 Ponsford Road, Minehead TA24 5DY
T: (01643) 702313
F: (01643) 702313
E: kingswayhotel@msn.com
I: www.kingswayhotelminehead.co.uk

Lorna Doone Guesthouse ♦♦♦
26 Tregonwell Road, Minehead TA24 5DU
T: (01643) 702540
E: lornadooneguesthouse@msn.com
I: www.lornadooneguest.co.uk

Lyn Valley Guest House ♦♦♦
3 Tregonwell Road, Minehead TA24 5DT
T: (01643) 703748
F: (01643) 703748

Marston Lodge Hotel ♦♦♦♦
St Michaels Road, Minehead TA24 5JP
T: (01643) 702510
F: (01643) 702510
E: enquiry@marstonlodgehotel.co.uk
I: www.marstonlodgehotel.co.uk

1 Moorlands ♦♦♦
Moor Road, Minehead TA24 5RT
T: (01643) 703453
E: moorlands@amserve.net

Oakfield Guest House
Rating Applied For
Northfield Road, Minehead TA24 5QH
T: (01643) 704911

Old Ship Aground ♦♦♦
Quay Street, Minehead TA24 5UL
T: (01643) 702087
F: (01643) 709066
E: enquiries@oldshipaground.co.uk
I: www.oldshipaground.co.uk

The Parks Guest House ♦♦♦
26 The Parks, Minehead TA24 8BT
T: (01643) 703547
F: (01643) 709843
E: parksgh@tiscali.co.uk
I: myweb.tiscali.co.uk/parksgh

Promenade Hotel ♦♦♦
The Esplanade, Minehead TA24 5QS
T: (01643) 702572
F: (01643) 702572
E: jgph@globalnet.co.uk
I: www.johngroons.org.uk

Sunfield Private Hotel ♦♦♦
83 Summerland Avenue, Minehead TA24 5BW
T: (01643) 703565
F: (01643) 705822
E: sunfield@primex.co.uk
I: www.hotelsminehead.com

Tranmere House ♦♦♦
24 Tregonwell Road, Minehead TA24 5DU
T: (01643) 702647

Whites Hotel & Restaurant
Rating Applied For
Church Road, North Hill, Minehead TA24 5SB
T: (01643) 702032
F: (01643) 702032
E: info@whites-hotel.co.uk
I: www.whites-hotel.co.uk

Wyndcott Hotel ♦♦♦
Martlett Road, Minehead TA24 5QE
T: (01643) 704522
F: (01643) 707577
E: march.corp@which.net
I: www.wyndcotthotel.co.uk

MINSTER Cornwall

Branarth ♦♦♦♦
Minster, Boscastle PL35 0BN
T: (01840) 250102
F: (01840) 250102
E: arthur.bradley1@lineone.net
I: www.cornwall-online.co.uk/branarth

Home Farm ♦♦♦♦ SILVER AWARD
Minster, Boscastle PL35 0BN
T: (01840) 250195
F: (01840) 250195
E: jackie.haddy@btclick.com

MODBURY Devon

Weeke Farm ♦♦♦
Modbury, Ivybridge PL21 0TT
T: (01548) 830219
F: (01548) 830219

MONKLEIGH Devon

Annery Barton ♦♦♦
Monkleigh, Bideford EX39 5JL
T: (01237) 473629
F: (01237) 424468

MONTACUTE Somerset

Carents House ♦♦♦♦
7A Middle Street, Montacute TA15 6UZ
T: (01935) 824914
E: carentshouse@amserve.net

Mad Hatters Tearooms ♦♦♦
1 South Street, Montacute TA15 6XD
T: (01935) 823024
E: montacutemuseum@aol.com
I: www.montacutemuseum.com

The Phelips Arms ♦♦♦
The Borough, Montacute TA15 6XB
T: (01935) 822557
E: thephelipsarms@aol.com
I: www.thephelipsarms.co.uk

Slipper Cottage ♦♦♦
41 Bishopston, Montacute TA15 6UX
T: (01935) 823073
F: (01935) 826868
E: sue.weir@totalise.co.uk
I: www.slippercottage.co.uk

MORCOMBELAKE Dorset

Bullenside Bed and Breakfast ♦♦♦♦
Sun Lane, Morcombelake, Bridport DT6 6DL
T: (01297) 489350
E: bullenside@hotmail.com
I: www.bullenside.co.uk

Wisteria Cottage ♦♦♦♦
Taylors Lane, Morcombelake, Bridport DT6 6ED
T: (01297) 489019
E: dave@dorsetcottage.org.uk
I: www.dorsetcottage.org.uk

MORETONHAMPSTEAD Devon

Cookshayes Country Guest House ♦♦♦
33 Court Street, Moretonhampstead, Newton Abbot TQ13 8LG
T: (01647) 440374
F: (01647) 440374
E: cookshayes@eurobell.co.uk
I: www.cookshayes.co.uk

Great Doccombe Farm ♦♦♦♦
Doccombe, Moretonhampstead, Newton Abbot TQ13 8SS
T: (01647) 440694
E: david.oakey3@btopenworld.com
I: www.greatdoccombefarm.co.uk

Great Sloncombe Farm
♦♦♦♦ SILVER AWARD
Moretonhampstead, Newton Abbot TQ13 8QF
T: (01647) 440595
F: (01647) 440595
E: hmerchant@sloncombe.freeserve.co.uk
I: www.greatsloncombefarm.co.uk

Great Wooston Farm Bed & Breakfast
♦♦♦♦ SILVER AWARD
Moretonhampstead, Newton Abbot TQ13 8QA
T: (01647) 440367
F: (01647) 440367
E: info@greatwoostonfarm.com
I: www.greatwoostonfarm.com

Little Wooston Farm ♦♦♦
Moretonhampstead, Newton Abbot TQ13 8QA
T: (01647) 440551
F: (01647) 440551

Midfields ♦♦♦♦
North Bovey Road, Moretonhampstead, Newton Abbot TQ13 8PB
T: (01647) 440462
F: (01647) 440039
E: sharon@ridgetor.freeserve.co.uk
I: www.midfields.co.uk

Moorcote Guest House ♦♦♦♦
Chagford Cross, Moretonhampstead, Newton Abbot TQ13 8LS
T: (01647) 440966
E: moorcote@smartone.co.uk
I: www.moorcotehouse.co.uk

The Old Sheiling ♦♦♦♦
Moretonhampstead, Newton Abbot TQ13 8SD
T: (01647) 440151
F: (01647) 440156
E: info@oldsheiling.co.uk
I: www.oldsheiling.co.uk

Yarningale ♦♦♦
Exeter Road, Moretonhampstead, Newton Abbot TQ13 8SW
T: (01647) 440560
F: (01647) 440560
E: sally-radcliffe@virgin.net

MORTEHOE Devon

Baycliffe Hotel ♦♦♦♦
Chapel Hill, Mortehoe, Woolacombe EX34 7DZ
T: (01271) 870393
F: (01271) 870393
E: jane@baycliffehotel.fsnet.co.uk
I: www.baycliffehotel.co.uk

The Cleeve House
♦♦♦♦ SILVER AWARD
North Morte Road, Mortehoe, Woolacombe EX34 7ED
T: (01271) 870719
F: (01271) 870719
E: info@cleevehouse.co.uk
I: www.cleevehouse.co.uk
National Accessible Scheme Rating Applied For

MORVAL Cornwall

The Snooty Fox Country Hotel ♦♦♦
Morval, Looe PL13 1PR
T: (01503) 240233
F: (01503) 240233
E: mollytudor@aol.com
I: www.thesnootyfox.com

MORWENSTOW Cornwall

Cornakey Farm ♦♦♦
Morwenstow, Bude EX23 9SS
T: (01288) 331260

Little Bryaton ♦♦♦♦
Morwenstow, Bude EX23 9SU
T: (01288) 331755
E: little.bryaton@dial.pipex.com
I: www.little.bryaton.dial.pipex.com

MOSTERTON Dorset

Yeabridge Farm ♦♦♦♦
Whetley Cross, Mosterton, Beaminster DT8 3HE
T: (01308) 868944
F: (01308) 868944

MOUNT HAWKE Cornwall

Trenerry Farm ♦♦♦
Mingoose, Mount Hawke, Truro TR4 8BX
T: (01872) 553755
F: (01872) 553755
E: babatrenerry@btopenworld.com

MOUSEHOLE Cornwall

Kerris Farmhouse ♦♦♦♦
Kerris, Paul, Penzance TR19 6UY
T: (01736) 731309
E: susangiles@btconnect.com
I: www.cornwall-online.co.uk/kerris-farm

MUCHELNEY Somerset

The Priest's House
Rating Applied For
Muchelney, Muchelney Ham, Langport TA10 0DQ
T: (01458) 253771

MUDFORD Somerset

Half Moon Inn and Country Lodge ♦♦♦♦
Main Street, Mudford, Yeovil BA21 5TF
T: (01935) 850289
F: (01935) 850842
E: thehalfmoon@dclonline.net
I: www.visitwestcountry.com/thehalfmoon

MULLION Cornwall

Cobblers Cottage
♦♦♦♦♦ SILVER AWARD
Nantithet, Cury, Helston TR12 7RB
T: (01326) 241342
F: (01326) 241342

Meaver Farm
♦♦♦♦ SILVER AWARD
Mullion, Helston TR12 7DN
T: (01326) 240128
F: (01326) 240011
E: meaverfarm@eclipse.co.uk
I: www.meaverfarm.co.uk

Polhormon Farm ♦♦♦
Polhormon Lane, Mullion, Helston TR12 7JE
T: (01326) 240304
F: (01326) 240304
E: polhormonfarm@farmersweekly.net

Tregaddra Farm
♦♦♦♦ SILVER AWARD
Cury Cross Lanes, Cury, Helston TR12 7BB
T: (01326) 240235
F: (01326) 240235
E: holidays@tregaddra.freeserve.co.uk
I: www.tregaddra.freeserve.co.uk

Trenance Farmhouse ♦♦♦♦
Mullion, Helston TR12 7HB
T: (01326) 240639
F: (01326) 240639
E: info@trenancefarmholidays.co.uk
I: www.trenancefarmholidays.co.uk

MUSBURY Devon

Kate's Farm Bed & Breakfast ♦♦♦
Lower Bruckland Farm, Musbury, Axminster EX13 8ST
T: (01297) 552861

MUTLEY Devon

The Dudley Hotel ♦♦♦♦
42 Sutherland Road, Mutley, Plymouth PL4 6BN
T: (01752) 668322
F: (01752) 673763
E: whittingdudleyhotel@btopenworld.com

NANCEGOLLAN Cornwall

Little Pengwedna Farm ♦♦♦♦
Nancegollan, Helston TR13 0AY
T: (01736) 850649
F: (01736) 850649
E: ray@good-holidays.demon.co.uk
I: www.good-holidays.demon.co.uk

NETHER STOWEY Somerset

Castle of Comfort Country House
♦♦♦♦♦ SILVER AWARD
Dodington, Nether Stowey, Bridgwater TA5 1LE
T: (01278) 741264
F: (01278) 741144
E: reception@castle-of-comfort.co.uk
I: www.castle-of-comfort.co.uk

The Old Cider House ♦♦♦♦
25 Castle Street, Nether Stowey, Bridgwater TA5 1LN
T: (01278) 732228
F: (01278) 732228
E: info@theoldciderhouse.co.uk
I: www.theoldciderhouse.co.uk

Rose and Crown ♦♦
St Mary Street, Nether Stowey, Bridgwater TA5 1LJ
T: (01278) 732265
E: rose_crown@netherstowey.freeserve.co.uk

NETHERAVON Wiltshire

Paddock House Bed and Breakfast
Rating Applied For
Paddock House, High Street, Netheravon, Salisbury SP4 9QP
T: (01980) 670401
F: (01980) 670401

NETHERBURY Dorset

Jasmine Cottage
♦♦♦♦ SILVER AWARD
St James Road, Netherbury, Bridport DT6 5LP
T: (01308) 488767

NEWBRIDGE Cornwall

Wheal Buller
♦♦♦♦ SILVER AWARD
Newbridge, Penzance TR20 8PS
T: (01736) 787999
E: rwrgibson@supanet.com

NEWMILL Cornwall

Laidback Trailblazers ♦♦♦♦
The Old Barn, Newmill, Penzance TR20 8XA
T: (01736) 367742
F: (01736) 361721
E: info@laidback-trails.co.uk
I: www.laidback-trails.co.uk

NEWQUAY Cornwall

Alicia Guest House ♦♦♦♦
136 Henver Road, Newquay TR7 3EQ
T: (01637) 874328
F: (01637) 874328
E: aliciaguesthouse@mlimer.fsnet.co.uk
I: www.alicia-guesthouse.co.uk

Beresford Hotel ♦♦♦♦
Narrowcliff, Newquay TR7 2PR
T: (01637) 873238
F: (01637) 851874
I: www.shearingsholidays.com

Chichester Interest Holidays and Accommodation ♦
14 Bay View Terrace, Newquay TR7 2LR
T: (01637) 874216
F: (01637) 874216
E: sheila.harper@virgin.net
I: http://freespace.virgin.net/sheila.harper

Degembris Farmhouse
♦♦♦♦ SILVER AWARD
St Newlyn East, Newquay TR8 5HY
T: (01872) 510555
F: (01872) 510230
E: kathy@degembris.co.uk
I: www.degembris.co.uk

Edwardian Hotel Island Crescent ♦♦♦
3-7 Island Crescent, Newquay TR7 1DZ
T: (01637) 874087
F: (01637) 877577
E: info@edwardian-hotel.com
I: www.edwardian-hotel.com

The Gannel View Lodge ♦♦♦
91 Pentire Avenue, Newquay TR7 1PE
T: (01637) 875013
E: ken_pyrah@compuserve.com
I: www.kenandann.co.uk

The Harbour Hotel
♦♦♦♦ SILVER AWARD
North Quay Hill, Newquay TR7 1HF
T: (01637) 873040
E: alan@harbourhotel.co.uk
I: www.harbourhotel.co.uk

Marina Hotel ♦♦♦♦
Narrowcliff, Newquay TR7 2PL
T: (01637) 873012
F: (01637) 851273
I: www.shearingsholidays.com

Rose Cottage ♦♦♦♦
Shepherds, St Newlyn East, Newquay TR8 5NW
T: (01872) 540502
F: (01872) 540340

St Andrews Hotel ♦♦♦♦
Island Crescent, Newquay TR7 1DZ
T: (01637) 873556
F: (01637) 873556
E: enquiries@standrewsnewquay.co.uk
I: www.standrewsnewquay.co.uk

Tir Chonaill Lodge Hotel ♦♦♦
106 Mount Wise, Newquay TR7 1QP
T: (01637) 876492
E: tirchonailhotel@talk21.com
I: www.tirchonaill.co.uk

Trevilla ♦♦♦
18 Berry Road, Newquay TR7 1AR
T: (01637) 871504
E: trevillaguesthouse@hotmail.com

Wenden Guest House ♦♦♦
11 Berry Road, Newquay TR7 1AU
T: (01637) 872604
F: (01637) 872604
E: wenden@newquay-holidays.co.uk
I: www.newquay-holidays.co.uk

NEWTON ABBOT
Devon

Fairways
♦♦♦♦ SILVER AWARD
Shaldon Road, Combeinteignhead, Newton Abbot TQ12 4RR
T: (01626) 871095
I: www.visitwestcountry.com/fairways

The Mount ♦♦♦♦
Combe Cross, Ideford Combe, Sandygate, Newton Abbot TQ12 3GR
T: (01626) 331418
F: (01626) 331418
E: tom@themountguesthouse.co.uk
I: www.themountguesthouse.co.uk

Travellers Rest
Rating Applied For
19 Torquay Road, Kingskerswell, Newton Abbot TQ12 5HH
T: (01803) 873143

NEWTON FERRERS
Devon

Broadmoor Farm ♦♦♦♦
Collaton Cross, Yealmpton, Newton Ferrers, Plymouth PL8 2NE
T: (01752) 880407
E: agfarms@hotmail.com

NEWTON ST LOE
Bath and North East Somerset

Pennsylvania Farm ♦♦♦♦
Newton St Loe, Bath BA2 9JD
T: (01225) 314912
F: (01225) 314912
E: info@pennsylvaniafarm.co.uk
I: www.pennsylvaniafarm.co.uk

NORTH BOVEY
Devon

Ring of Bells Inn ♦♦♦♦
The Village, North Bovey, Dartmoor TQ13 8RB
T: (01647) 440375
F: (01647) 440218
E: info@ringofbellsinn.com
I: www.ringofbellsinn.com

NORTH BRADLEY
Wiltshire

49a Church Lane ♦♦♦♦
Church Lane, North Bradley, Trowbridge BA14 0TA
T: (01225) 762558
E: m-wise@amserve.com

NORTH CADBURY
Somerset

Ashlea House
♦♦♦♦ SILVER AWARD
High Street, North Cadbury, Yeovil BA22 7DP
T: (01963) 440891
F: (01963) 440891
E: ashlea@ashleahouse.com
I: www.ashleahouse.co.uk

The Catash Inn ♦♦♦
North Cadbury, Yeovil BA22 7DH
T: (01963) 440248
F: (01963) 440248
E: clive&sandra@catash.com
I: www.catash.com

NORTH PETHERWIN
Cornwall

Stenhill Farm
♦♦♦♦♦ SILVER AWARD
North Petherwin, Launceston PL15 8NN
T: (01566) 785686
F: (01566) 785686
E: e.reddock@btinternet.com
I: www.stenhill.com

West Barton ♦♦♦♦
North Petherwin, Launceston PL15 8LR
T: (01566) 785710
F: (01566) 785710
E: enquiries@westbarton.co.uk
I: www.westbarton.co.uk

NORTH TAWTON
Devon

Kayden House Hotel
Rating Applied For
3-5 High Street, North Tawton EX20 2HF
T: (01837) 82242
F: (01837) 82242

Lower Nichols Nymet Farm
♦♦♦♦ SILVER AWARD
North Tawton EX20 2BW
T: (01363) 82510
F: (01363) 82510
E: pylefarm@btinternet.com
I: www.pyle-farm-holidays.co.uk

Oaklands Farm ♦♦♦♦
North Tawton EX20 2BQ
T: (01837) 82340

NORTH WOOTTON
Dorset

Stoneleigh Barn
♦♦♦♦ SILVER AWARD
North Wootton, Sherborne DT9 5JW
T: (01935) 815964
E: stoneleigh@ic24.net

OAKFORD
Devon

Harton Farm ♦♦♦
Oakford, Tiverton EX16 9HH
T: (01398) 351209
F: (01398) 351209
E: lindy@hartonfarm.co.uk

OAKHILL
Somerset

Blakes Farm ♦♦♦
Oakhill, Bath BA3 5HY
T: (01749) 840301

The Boltons ♦♦♦
Sumach House, Neighbourne, Oakhill, Bath BA3 5BQ
T: (01749) 840366
F: (01749) 840366
E: sumachhouse@aol.com
I: www.somersetbreak.co.uk

OBORNE
Dorset

The Grange Restaurant and Hotel ♦♦♦♦♦ SILVER AWARD
Oborne, Sherborne DT9 4LA
T: (01935) 813463
F: (01935) 817464

OGBOURNE ST GEORGE
Wiltshire

The Old Crown 'The Inn with the Well' ♦♦♦
Marlborough Road, Ogbourne St George, Marlborough SN8 1SQ
T: (01672) 841445
F: (01672) 841056
E: theinnwiththewell@compuserve.com
I: theinnwiththewell.com

The Sanctuary ♦♦♦
Ogbourne St George, Marlborough SN8 1SQ
T: (01672) 841473
F: (01672) 841102
E: rebecca.macdonald@core-support.co.uk

OKEHAMPTON
Devon

Charlecott Lodge ♦♦♦♦
38 Station Road, Okehampton EX20 1EA
T: (01837) 53998

Higher Cadham Farm ♦♦♦♦
Exbourne, Jacobstowe, Okehampton EX20 3RB
T: (01837) 851647
F: (01837) 851410
E: kingscadham@btopenworld.com
I: www.highercadham.co.uk

The Knole Farm
♦♦♦♦ SILVER AWARD
Bridestowe, Okehampton EX20 4HA
T: (01837) 861241
F: (01837) 861241
E: mavis.bickle@btconnect.com
I: knolefarm-dartmoor-holidays.co.uk

Lower Trecott Farm ♦♦♦♦
Wellsprings Lane, Sampford Courtenay, Okehampton EX20 2TD
T: (01837) 880118
E: craig@trecott.fsnet.co.uk

Week Farm Country Holidays
♦♦♦♦
Bridestowe, Okehampton EX20 4HZ
T: (01837) 861221
F: (01837) 861221
E: accom@weekfarmonline.com
I: www.weekfarmonline.com

OLD SODBURY
South Gloucestershire

Dornden Guest House ♦♦♦♦
Church Lane, Old Sodbury, Bristol BS37 6NB
T: (01454) 313325
F: (01454) 312263
E: dorndenguesthouse@tinyworld.co.uk
I: www.westcountrynow.com

OLD TOWN
Cornwall

Carn Ithen
♦♦♦♦ SILVER AWARD
Trench Lane, Old Town, St Mary's TR21 0PA
T: (01720) 422917
F: (01720) 422917
E: roz-alfred@carn-ithen.fsnet.co.uk
I: www.scilly-oldtown.com

The Greenlaws
Rating Applied For
Old Town, St Mary's TR21 0NH
T: (01720) 422045

ORCHESTON
Wiltshire

The Crown Inn ♦♦♦
Stonehenge Park, Orcheston, Salisbury SP3 4SH
T: (01980) 620304
F: (01980) 621121
E: stp@orcheston.freeserve.co.uk
I: www.orcheston.freeserve.co.uk

OSMINGTON
Dorset

The Briary ♦♦♦
Main Road, Osmington, Weymouth DT3 6EH
T: (01305) 835397
F: (01305) 835397

OTTERY ST MARY
Devon

Pitt Farm ♦♦♦♦
Fairmile, Ottery St Mary EX11 1NL
T: (01404) 812439
F: (01404) 812439
E: pittfarm@tiscali.co.uk
I: www.pitt-farm-devon.co.uk

PADSTOW
Cornwall

Althea House
♦♦♦♦♦ SILVER AWARD
64 Church Street, Padstow PL28 8BG
T: (01841) 532579

Althea Library Bed and Breakfast
♦♦♦♦♦ SILVER AWARD
High Street, Padstow PL28 8BB
T: (01841) 532717
F: (01841) 532717
E: enquiries@althealibrary.co.uk
I: www.althealibrary.co.uk

Armsyde B&B ♦♦♦
10 Cross Street, Padstow PL28 8AT
T: (01841) 532271
F: (01841) 532271
E: info@armsyde.co.uk
I: www.armsyde.co.uk

Cally Croft ♦♦♦♦
26 Raleigh Close, Padstow PL28 8BQ
T: (01841) 533726
E: john@cally26.freeserve.co.uk
I: www.padstow-callycroft.co.uk

1 Caswarth Terrace ♦♦♦
Caswarth Terrace, Padstow PL28 8EE
T: (01841) 532025

50 Church Street ♦♦♦♦
50 Church Street, Padstow PL28 8BG
T: (01841) 532121
F: (01841) 532121
E: churchstreet50@hotmail.com

Chy Veor ♦♦♦
24 Hawkins Road, Padstow PL28 8EU
T: (01841) 533545
F: (01841) 532630
E: jim@jwhull.fsnet.co.uk

Chyloweth ♦♦♦♦
Constantine Bay, Padstow PL28 8JQ
T: (01841) 521012
F: (01841) 521012
E: roger.vivian@ukgateway.net

Khandalla B & B
Rating Applied For
Sarahs Lane, Padstow PL28 8EL
T: (01841) 532961
F: (01841) 532663
E: info@khandalla.co.uk
I: www.khandalla.co.uk

Lamorva House ♦♦♦♦
3 Sarah's Meadow, Padstow PL28 8LX
T: (01841) 533841

Mena Gwins ♦♦♦♦
6 Raleigh Close, Padstow PL28 8BQ
T: (01841) 533896
E: jenifervivian@free.uk

The Old Mill House ♦♦♦♦
Little Petherick, Wadebridge PL27 7QT
T: (01841) 540388
F: (0870) 056 9360
E: dwalker@oldmillbandb.demon.co.uk
I: www.oldmillbandb.demon.co.uk

Petrocstowe ♦♦♦♦
30 Treverbyn Road, Padstow PL28 8DW
T: (01841) 532429

12 Raleigh Road ♦♦♦♦
Raleigh Road, Padstow PL28 8ET
T: (01841) 532701

Sable House ♦♦♦♦
76 Sarahs View, Padstow PL28 8LU
T: (01841) 533358
E: info@sablehouse.co.uk
I: www.sable-house.co.uk

St Ervan Manor and Country Cottages
♦♦♦♦♦ GOLD AWARD
The Old Rectory, St Ervan, Padstow PL27 7TA
T: (01841) 540255
F: (01841) 540255
E: mail@stervanmanor.freeserve.co.uk
I: www.stervanmanor.co.uk

Symply Padstow ♦♦♦♦
32 Dennis Road, Padstow PL28 8DE
T: (01841) 532814
F: (01841) 533480
E: buttfish@btinternet.com
I: www.symply-padstow.co.uk

Trealaw ♦♦♦
22 Duke Street, Padstow PL28 8AB
T: (01841) 533161
F: (01841) 533161

Tregea Hotel
Rating Applied For
16-18 High Street, Padstow PL28 8BB
T: (01841) 532455
F: (01841) 533542
E: reservations@tregea.co.uk
I: www.tregea.co.uk

Tregudda ♦♦♦♦
5 Grenville Road, Padstow PL28 8EX
T: (01841) 532089
E: janestone11@aol.com

Treravel House ♦♦
Padstow Road, Padstow PL28 8LB
T: (01841) 532931
I: www.uk-cornwallexplore.co.uk

Treverbyn House ♦♦♦♦
Station Road, Padstow PL28 8DA
T: (01841) 532855
F: (01841) 532855
I: www.trverbynhouse.com

Trevone Bay Hotel ♦♦♦♦
Dobbin Close, Trevone, Padstow PL28 8QS
T: (01841) 520243
F: (01841) 521195
E: webb@trevonebay.demon.co.uk
I: www.trevonebay.co.uk

Trevorrick Farm ♦♦♦
St Issey, Wadebridge PL27 7QH
T: (01841) 540574
F: (01841) 540574
E: info@trevorrick.co.uk
I: www.trevorrick.co.uk

Treyarnon Bay Hotel ♦♦♦
Treyarnon Bay, St Merryn, Padstow PL28 8JN
T: (01841) 520235
F: (01841) 520239
I: www.treyarnon-bay-hotel.co.uk

West House ♦♦♦♦
Grenville Road, Padstow PL28 8EX
T: (01841) 533479
E: willis@bun.com
I: westcountrynow.com

The White Hart
♦♦♦♦ SILVER AWARD
1 New Street, Padstow PL28 8EA
T: (01841) 532350
E: whthartpad@aol.com
I: www.padstow.uk.com/whitehart

PAIGNTON
Devon

Arcadia Hotel
Rating Applied For
Marine Gardens, Paignton TQ3 2NT
T: (01803) 551039
F: (01803) 551039
E: jackie@arcadia-hotel.fsnet.co.uk

Arden House Hotel ♦♦♦♦
10 Youngs Park Road, Paignton TQ4 6BU
T: (01803) 558443
E: stan@ardenhousepaignton.co.uk
I: www.ardenhousepaignton.co.uk

Arrandale ♦♦♦
34 Garfield Road, Paignton TQ4 6AX
T: (01803) 552211
I: www.paigntondevon.co.uk/arrandale.htm

Baildon Royd Hotel ♦♦♦♦
Marine Park, Paignton TQ3 2NW
T: (01803) 550347
E: baildonroydhotel@aol.com
I: www.westcountrynow.com

Bay Sands Hotel ♦♦♦♦
14 Colin Road, Paignton TQ3 2NR
T: (01803) 524877
E: enquiries@baysands.co.uk
I: www.baysands.co.uk

Beach House ♦♦♦
39 Garfield Road, Paignton TQ4 6AX
T: (01803) 525742
F: (01803) 525742
E: beachhouse@L2222.fsbusiness.co.uk

Beecroft Hotel ♦
10 St Andrews Road, Paignton TQ4 6HA
T: (01803) 558702
F: (01803) 558702
I: www.beecrofthotel.co.uk

Bella Vista Guest House ♦♦♦
Berry Square, Paignton TQ4 6AZ
T: (01803) 558122
E: bellavista@berrysquare.fsbusiness.co.uk
I: www.english-riviera.co.uk/accommodation/guest-houses/bella-vista/index.htm

Benbows Hotel ♦♦♦
1 Alta Vista Road, Roudham, Paignton TQ4 6DB
T: (01803) 558128
E: Benbowshotel@aol.com
I: www.benbowshotel.co.uk

Beresford Hotel
♦♦♦♦ SILVER AWARD
5 Adelphi Road, Paignton TQ4 6AW
T: (01803) 551560
F: (01803) 552776
E: info@beresfordhotel.co.uk
I: www.beresfordhotel.co.uk

Birchwood House Hotel
♦♦♦♦ SILVER AWARD
33 St Andrews Road, Paignton TQ4 6HA
T: (01803) 551323
F: (01803) 401301
E: birchwoodhouse@aol.com
I: www.birchwoodhouse.net

Birklands Guest House ♦♦♦
33 Garfield Road, Paignton TQ4 6AX
T: (01803) 556970
F: (01803) 556970
E: trevor@trevor27.freeserve.co.uk
I: www.birklands.co.uk

Blue Waters Hotel ♦♦♦
4 Leighon Road, Paignton TQ3 2BQ
T: (01803) 557749
E: m.freeman@whsmithnet.co.uk

Briars Hotel ♦♦♦♦
Sands Road, Paignton TQ4 6EJ
T: (01803) 557729
F: (01803) 557729
E: enquiries@briarshotel.com
I: www.briarshotel.com

Bronte Hotel ♦♦♦♦
7 Colin Road, Paignton TQ3 2NR
T: (01803) 550254
F: (01803) 391489

Bruce Lodge Guest House ♦♦♦
2 Elmsleigh Road, Paignton
TQ4 5AU
T: (01803) 550972
F: (01803) 550972
E: roger_kingdon@Pineone.net
I: www.paigntondevon.co.uk/brucelodge

Carrington Hotel ♦♦
10 Beach Road, Paignton
TQ4 6AY
T: (01803) 558785

Cherwood Hotel ♦♦♦♦ SILVER AWARD
26 Garfield Road, Paignton
TQ4 6AX
T: (01803) 556515
F: (01803) 555126
E: James-pauline@cherwood-hotel.co.uk
I: www.cherwood-hotel.co.uk

Cleve Court Hotel ♦♦♦♦ SILVER AWARD
3 Cleveland Road, Paignton
TQ4 6EN
T: (01803) 551444
F: (01803) 664617
I: www.clevecourthotel.co.uk

Cliveden ♦♦♦♦
27 Garfield Road, Paignton
TQ4 6AX
T: (01803) 557461
F: (01803) 557461
E: cliveden@lineone.net
I: www.clivedenguesthouse.co.uk

Craigmore Guest House ♦♦♦
54 Dartmouth Road, Paignton
TQ4 5AN
T: (01803) 557373
F: (01803) 665801
E: bookings@craigmore-guesthouse.fsnet.co.uk
I: www.craigmore-guesthouse.fsnet.co.uk

Dalmary Guest House ♦♦♦
20 Garfield Road, Paignton
TQ4 6AX
T: (01803) 528145

Danethorpe Hotel Rating Applied For
23 St Andrews Road, Roundham, Paignton TQ4 6HA
T: (01803) 551251
F: (01803) 557075

Devon House Hotel ♦♦♦
20 Garfield Road, Paignton
TQ4 6AX
T: (01803) 559371
E: info@devonhousehotel.com
I: www.devonhousehotel.com

Earlston House Hotel ♦♦♦♦
31 St Andrews Road, Paignton
TQ4 6HA
T: (01803) 558355
E: earlstonhouse@aol.com
I: www.earlstonhouse.co.uk

Esplanade Hotel ♦♦♦
Sands Road, Paignton TQ4 6EG
T: (01803) 556333
F: (01803) 666786
I: www.shearingsholidays.com

Hotel Fiesta ♦♦♦
2 Kernou Road, Paignton
TQ4 6BA
T: (01803) 521862
F: (01803) 392978
E: hotelfiesta@blueyonder.co.uk

Garfield Lodge ♦♦♦♦
30 Garfield Road, Paignton
TQ4 6AX
T: (01803) 557764
E: garfieldlodge@aol.com
I: www.garfieldlodge.co.uk

Harbour Lodge ♦♦♦
4 Cleveland Road, Paignton
TQ4 6EN
T: (01803) 556932

Kingswinford Hotel ♦♦♦♦
32 Garfield Road, Paignton
TQ4 6AX
T: (01803) 558358
E: kingswinford@garfieldroad.freeserve.co.uk
I: www.kingswinfordhotel.co.uk

The Linton Hotel ♦♦♦♦
7 Elmsleigh Road, Paignton
TQ4 5AX
T: (01803) 558745
F: (01803) 665489
E: ronandmarg.thompson@tiscali.co.uk
I: www.paigntondevon.co.uk/linton

Mayfield Hotel ♦♦♦♦
8 Queens Road, Paignton
TQ4 6AT
T: (01803) 556802
F: (01803) 556802
E: mayfieldhotel@supanet.com

Meadowfield Hotel ♦♦♦♦
Preston Down Road, Paignton
TQ3 2RW
T: (01803) 522987
F: (01803) 554605
E: rpitchell@aol.com
I: www.meadowfieldhotel.co.uk

Middlepark Hotel ♦♦♦
3 Marine Drive, Paignton
TQ3 2NJ
T: (01803) 559025
F: (01803) 559025

Norbreck ♦♦♦
New Street, Paignton TQ3 3HL
T: (01803) 558033
F: (01803) 665755
E: norbreckguesthouse@hotmail.com
I: www.//members.tripod.co.uk/Norbreck/Bandb.html

Ocean Villa ♦♦♦♦
8 Kernou Road, Paignton
TQ4 6BA
T: (01803) 664121
E: BWeston@tiscali.co.uk
I: www.oceanvilla.co.uk

Paignton Court Hotel ♦♦♦♦
17-19 Sands Road, Paignton
TQ4 6EG
T: (01803) 553111
E: paigntoncourt@aol.com
I: www.paignton-court-hotel.co.uk

Richmond Guest House Rating Applied For
19 Norman Road, Paignton
TQ3 2BE
T: (01803) 550978
F: (01803) 558792
E: info@richmondgh.co.uk
I: www.richmondgh.co.uk

Rockview Guest House ♦♦♦
13 Queens Road, Paignton
TQ4 6AT
T: (01803) 556702

The Roscrea Hotel ♦♦♦♦
2 Alta Vista Road, Paignton
TQ4 6BZ
T: (01803) 558706
F: (01803) 558706
E: roscrea@globalnet.co.uk
I: www.paigntonhotels.com

Rosemead Guest House ♦♦♦
22 Garfield Road, Paignton
TQ4 6AX
T: (01803) 557944
E: pauldgama@aol.com
I: www.rosemeadpaignton.co.uk

Rougemont Hotel ♦♦♦
23 Roundham Road, Paignton
TQ4 6DN
T: (01803) 556570
F: (01803) 556570
E: beds@rougemonthotel.co.uk
I: www.rougemonthotel.co.uk

Roundham Lodge ♦♦♦♦♦ SILVER AWARD
16 Roundham Road, Paignton
TQ4 6DN
T: (01803) 558485
F: (01803) 553090
E: enquiries@roundham-lodge.co.uk
I: www.roundham-lodge.co.uk

Rowcroft Hotel ♦♦♦♦
14 Youngs Park Road, Paignton
TQ4 6BU
T: (01803) 559420
E: enquiries@rowcroft-hotel.com
I: www.rowcroft-hotel.com

St Edmund's Hotel ♦♦♦
25 Sands Road, Paignton
TQ4 6EG
T: (01803) 558756
E: stedmunds@currantbun.com
I: www.stedmundshotel.com

St Weonards Private Hotel ♦♦♦
12 Kernou Road, Paignton
TQ4 6BA
T: (01803) 558842
F: (01803) 558842

Hotel San Brelade ♦♦♦
3 Alta Vista Road, Paignton
TQ4 6DB
T: (01803) 553725

The Sands Hotel ♦♦♦
32 Sands Road, Paignton
TQ4 6EJ
T: (01803) 551282
E: hotel.sands@virgin.net

Sea Spray Hotel ♦♦♦
1 Beach Road, Paignton TQ4 6AY
T: (01803) 553141
I: www.seasprayhotel.co.uk

Seacroft Guest House ♦♦♦♦
41 Sands Road, Paignton
TQ4 6EG
T: (01803) 523791

Seaford Sands Hotel ♦♦♦
Roundham Road, Paignton
TQ4 6DN
T: (01803) 557722
F: (01803) 526071

Sealawn Hotel ♦♦♦
20 Esplanade Road, Paignton
TQ4 6BE
T: (01803) 559031

Seaways Hotel ♦♦♦♦
30 Sands Road, Paignton
TQ4 6EJ
T: (01803) 551093
F: (01803) 551167
E: seawayshotel@aol.com
I: www.seawayshotel.com

Sefton Hotel Rating Applied For
30 Esplanade Road, Paignton
TQ4 6BL
T: (01803) 557242
I: www.theseftonhotel.co.uk

Sonachan House Hotel ♦♦♦♦
35 St Andrews Road, Paignton
TQ4 6HA
T: (01803) 558021
F: (01803) 559233
E: info@sonachan.co.uk
I: www.sonachan.co.uk

Sundale Hotel ♦♦♦
10 Queens Road, Paignton
TQ4 6AT
T: (01803) 557431
E: sundalehotel@tinyworld.co.uk

Three Palms Hotel ♦♦♦
21 Sands Road, Paignton
TQ4 6EG
T: (01803) 551340
F: (01803) 552002

Two Beaches Hotel ♦♦♦♦
27 St Andrews Road, Paignton
TQ4 6HA
T: (01803) 522164
E: 2beaches@Tiscali.co.uk
I: www.TWOBEACHES.co.uk

Wulfruna Hotel ♦♦♦♦ SILVER AWARD
8 Esplanade, Paignton TQ4 6EB
T: (01803) 555567
F: (01803) 555567
E: julieatwulf@aol.com

Wynncroft Hotel ♦♦♦♦
2 Elmsleigh Park, Paignton
TQ4 5AT
T: (01803) 525728
F: (01803) 526335
E: wynncrofthotel@aol.com
I: www.wynncroft.co.uk

PANBOROUGH
Somerset

Garden End Farm ♦♦♦
Panborough, Wells BA5 1PN
T: (01934) 712414
F: (01934) 710311
E: sheila@gardenendfarm.freeserve.co.uk
I: www.gardenendfarm.freeserve.co.uk

PARRACOMBE
Devon

Moorlands ♦♦♦♦
Woody Bay, Parracombe, Barnstaple EX31 4RA
T: (01598) 763224
I: www.moorlandshotel.co.uk

PATTERDOWN
Wiltshire

Bennett's ♦♦♦♦
Lacock Road, Patterdown, Chippenham SN15 2NT
T: (01249) 652922
E: holywell-house@btinternet.com
I: www.holywell-house.co.uk

PAYHEMBURY
Devon

Yellingham Farm
♦♦♦♦ SILVER AWARD
Payhembury, Honiton EX14 3HE
T: (01404) 850272
F: (01404) 850873
E: JanetEast@compuserve.com

PEDWELL
Somerset

Sunnyside
♦♦♦♦ SILVER AWARD
34 Taunton Road, Pedwell, Bridgwater TA7 9BG
T: (01458) 210097
E: sheila@caruso.org.uk

PELYNT
Cornwall

Bake Farm ♦♦♦♦
Pelynt, Looe PL13 2QQ
T: (01503) 220244
F: (01503) 220244
E: bakefarm@btopenworld.com

Cardwen Farm ♦♦♦♦
Pelynt, Looe PL13 2LU
T: (01503) 220213
F: (01503) 220213
E: cardwenfarm@freenet.co.uk

Penkelly Farm ♦♦♦
Pelynt, Looe PL13 2QH
T: (01503) 220348
I: www.penkellyfarm.co.uk

Trenderway Farm ♦♦♦♦♦
Pelynt, Polperro, Looe PL13 2LY
T: (01503) 272214
F: (01503) 272991
E: trenderwayfarm@hotmail.com
I: www.trenderwayfarm.co.uk

PENDEEN
Cornwall

Field House ♦♦♦♦
8 Trewellard Road, Pendeen, Penzance TR19 7ST
T: (01736) 788097
E: fieldhousetrewellard@talk21.com
I: www.cornwall-online.co.uk/field-house

PENSFORD
Bath and North East Somerset

Green Acres ♦♦♦
Stanton Wick, Pensford BS39 4BX
T: (01761) 490397
F: (01761) 490397

Leigh Farm ♦♦
Old Road, Pensford BS39 4BA
T: (01761) 490281
F: (01761) 490281

The Model Farm ♦♦♦
Norton Hawkfield, Pensford BS39 4HA
T: (01275) 832144
F: (01275) 832144
E: margarethasell@hotmail.com

PENSILVA
Cornwall

Penharget Farm Bed and Breakfast ♦♦♦
Pensilva, Liskeard PL14 5RJ
T: (01579) 362221
F: (01579) 363965
E: penhargetfarm@ukonline.co.uk

PENZANCE
Cornwall

Carnson House Hotel ♦♦
2 East Terrace, Penzance TR18 2TD
T: (01736) 365589
F: (01736) 365594
E: carnson@netcomuk.co.uk
I: www.chycor.co.uk/carnson-house

Con Amore ♦♦♦
38 Morrab Road, Penzance TR18 4EX
T: (01736) 363423
F: (01736) 363423
I: www.conamore.com

Cornerways Guest House ♦♦♦
Leskinnick Street, Penzance TR18 2HA
T: (01736) 364645
F: (01736) 364645
E: enquiries@cornerways-penzance.co.uk
I: www.penzance.co.uk/cornerways

Estoril Hotel ♦♦♦
46 Morrab Road, Penzance TR18 4EX
T: (01736) 362468
F: (01736) 367471
E: estorilhotel@aol.com
I: www.estorilhotel.co.uk

Halcyon Guest House ♦♦♦♦
6 Chyandour Square, Penzance TR18 3LW
T: (01736) 366302
F: (01736) 366302
E: pat@halcyon1.co.uk
I: www.halcyon1.co.uk

Lombard House
♦♦♦♦ SILVER AWARD
16 Regent Terrace, Penzance TR18 4DW
T: (01736) 364897
F: (01736) 364897
E: rita.kruge@talk21.com
I: www.cornwall-online.co.uk/lombard-house

Lowenna
Rating Applied For
Raginnis Hill, Mousehole, Penzance TR19 6SL
T: (01736) 731077
E: mm4lowenna@aol.com

Lynwood Guest House ♦♦♦
41 Morrab Road, Penzance TR18 4EX
T: (01736) 365871
F: (01736) 365871
E: lynwoodpz@aol.com
I: www.lynwood-guesthouse.co.uk

Menwidden Farm ♦♦♦
Ludgvan, Penzance TR20 8BN
T: (01736) 740415
E: coraquick@menwiddenludgvanfreeserve.co.uk

Richmond Lodge ♦♦♦
61 Morrab Road, Penzance TR18 4EP
T: (01736) 365560
E: ivor@richmondlodge.fsnet.co.uk
I: www.geocities.com/richmondlodge_uk

Rose Farm ♦♦♦♦
Chyanhal, Buryas Bridge, Penzance TR19 6AN
T: (01736) 731808
F: (01736) 731808
E: lally@rosefarmcornwall.co.uk
I: www.rosefarmcornwall.co.uk

Roseudian ♦♦♦♦
Crippas Hill, Kelynack, St Just, Penzance TR19 7RE
T: (01736) 788556
E: roseudian@ukgateway.net
I: www.roseudian.ukgateway.net

The Summer House
♦♦♦♦♦ GOLD AWARD
Cornwall Terrace, Penzance TR18 4HL
T: (01736) 363744
F: (01736) 360959
E: reception@summerhouse-cornwall.com
I: www.summerhouse-cornwall.com

Treventon Guest House ♦♦♦
Alexandra Place, Penzance TR18 4NE
T: (01736) 363521
F: (01736) 361873
I: www.ukholidayaccommodation.com/treventonguesthouse

Trevine Bed & Breakfast ♦♦
Blowing House Hill, Ludgvan, Penzance TR20 8AW
T: (01736) 740770
E: trevineuk@tiscali.co.uk
I: www.trevine.org.uk

Trewella Guest House ♦♦♦
18 Mennaye Road, Penzance TR18 4NG
T: (01736) 363818
F: (01736) 363818
E: shan.dave@lineone.net
I: www.trewella.co.uk

Warwick House Hotel ♦♦♦
17 Regent Terrace, Penzance TR18 4DW
T: (01736) 363881
F: (01736) 363881
E: jules@warwickhouse.fsworld.co.uk
I: www.warwickhousepenzance.co.uk

Woodstock Guest House ♦♦♦
29 Morrab Road, Penzance TR18 4EZ
T: (01736) 369049
F: (01736) 369049
E: info@woodstockguesthouse.co.uk
I: www.woodstockguesthouse.co.uk

Wymering Bed and Breakfast ♦♦♦
15 Regent Square, Penzance TR18 4BG
T: (01736) 362126
F: (01736) 362126
E: pam@wymering.com
I: www.wymering.com

PERRANPORTH
Cornwall

Chy an Kerensa Guest House ♦♦♦
Cliff Road, Perranporth TR6 0DR
T: (01872) 572470
F: (01872) 572470

Ponsmere Hotel ♦♦♦
Ponsmere Road, Perranporth TR6 0BW
T: (01872) 572225
F: (01872) 573075
E: info@ponsmere.co.uk
I: www.ponsmere.co.uk

St Georges Country Hotel ♦♦♦♦
St Georges Hill, Perranporth TR6 0ED
T: (01872) 572184
F: (01872) 572184
E: nikcn@aol.com
I: www.stgeorgescountryhotel.com

Trevie Guest House ♦♦♦♦
Mill Road, Bolingey, Perranporth TR6 0PE
T: (01872) 573475
F: (01872) 573475

PIDDLEHINTON
Dorset

Muston Manor
♦♦♦♦ SILVER AWARD
Piddlehinton, Dorchester DT2 7SY
T: (01305) 848242
F: (01305) 848242

Whites Dairy House
♦♦♦♦♦ SILVER AWARD
High Street, Piddlehinton, Dorchester DT2 7TD
T: (01300) 348386
F: (01300) 348368
E: robin.adeney@care4free.web
I: www.whitesdairyhouse.co.uk

PIDDLETRENTHIDE
Dorset

The Poachers Inn ♦♦♦♦
Piddletrenthide, Dorchester DT2 7QX
T: (01300) 348358
F: (01300) 348153
E: thepoachersinn@piddletrenthide.fsbusiness.co.uk
I: www.thepoachersinn.co.uk

PILLATON
Cornwall

The Weary Friar Inn ♦♦♦♦
Pillaton, Saltash PL12 6QS
T: (01579) 350238
F: (01579) 350238

PILTON
Somerset

Bowermead House ♦♦♦♦
Whitstone Hill, Pilton, Shepton Mallet BA4 4DT
T: (01749) 890744
F: (01749) 890744
E: w.southcombe@btopenworld.com

PLUSH
Dorset

Kingsmead
Rating Applied For
Piddletrenthide, Dorchester DT2 7QX
T: (01300) 348234
F: (01300) 348234
E: mikehtkingsmead@aol.com

The Old Barn House ♦♦♦
Plush, Dorchester DT2 7RQ
T: (01300) 348730

PLYMOUTH
Devon

Athenaeum Lodge ♦♦♦♦
4 Athenaeum Street, The Hoe, Plymouth PL1 2RQ
T: (01752) 665005
F: (01752) 665005
E: us@athenaeumlodge.com

Berkeleys of St James ♦♦♦♦
4 St James Place East, Plymouth PL1 3AS
T: (01752) 221654
F: (01752) 221654
I: www.smoothhound.co.uk/hotels/berkely2html.

Blackhall Lodge B&B ♦♦♦♦
Old Staddiscombe Road, Staddiscombe, Plymouth PL9 9NA
T: (01752) 482482
F: (01752) 482482
E: johnm@jboocock.freeserve.co.uk
I: www.jboocock.freeserve.co.uk

Bowling Green Hotel
♦♦♦♦♦ SILVER AWARD
9-10 Osborne Place, Lockyer Street, Plymouth PL1 2PU
T: (01752) 209090
F: (01752) 209092
E: dave@bowlinggreenhotel.freeserve.co.uk
I: www.smoothhound.co.uk/hotels/bowling.html

Gabber Farm ♦♦♦
Down Thomas, Plymouth PL9 0AW
T: (01752) 862269
F: (01752) 862269
E: gabberfarm@tiscali.co.uk

The George Guest House ♦♦♦
Citadel Road, Plymouth PL1 2HU
T: (01752) 661517
F: (01752) 661517
E: georgeguesthouse@btconnect.com
I: www.accommodationplymouth.co.uk

Hotspur Guest House ♦♦
108 North Road East, Plymouth PL4 6AW
T: (01752) 663928
E: info@hotspurguesthouse.co.uk
I: www.hotspurguesthouse.co.uk

Lamplighter Hotel ♦♦♦
103 Citadel Road, The Hoe, Plymouth PL1 2RN
T: (01752) 663855
F: (01752) 228139
E: lamplighterhotel@ukonline.co.uk

Mayflower Guest House ♦♦♦
209 Citadel Road East, Plymouth PL1 2JF
T: (01752) 297749
F: (01752) 202727
E: info@mayflowerguesthouse.co.uk
I: www.mayflowerguesthouse.co.uk

Mountbatten Hotel ♦♦♦♦
52 Exmouth Road, Stoke, Plymouth PL1 4QH
T: (01752) 563843
F: (01752) 606014
I: www.mbhs.co.uk

Old Pier Guest House ♦♦♦
20 Radford Road, West Hoe, Plymouth PL1 3BY
T: (01752) 268468
E: enquiries@oldpier.co.uk
I: www.oldpier.co.uk

Osmond Guest House ♦♦♦♦
42 Pier Street, Plymouth PL1 3BT
T: (01752) 229705
F: (01752) 269655
E: mike@osmondgh.freeserve.co.uk
I: plymouth-explore.co.uk

Rosaland Hotel ♦♦♦♦
32 Houndiscombe Road, Plymouth PL4 6HQ
T: (01752) 664749
F: (01752) 256984
E: manager@rosalandhotel.com
I: www.rosalandhotel.com

St Lawrence Guest House ♦♦♦
10 St Lawrence Road, Mutley, Plymouth PL4 6HN
T: (01752) 667046
F: (01752) 667046
E: StLawrenceGuestHouse@plymouthdevon.fsbusiness.co.uk
I: www.st.lawrenceguesthouse.co.uk

Squires Guest House ♦♦♦♦
7 St James Place East, Plymouth PL1 3AS
T: (01752) 261459
F: (01752) 261459
E: squiresguesthouse@yahoo.com
I: www.squiresguesthouse.20m.com

Westwinds Hotel ♦♦♦
99 Citadel Road, The Hoe, Plymouth PL1 2RN
T: (01752) 601777
F: (01752) 662158
E: paul.colman@btinternet.com
I: business.thisisplymouth.co.uk/westwindshotel

POLBATHIC
Cornwall

Hendra Farm ♦♦♦♦
Polbathic, Torpoint PL11 3DT
T: (01503) 250225
F: (01503) 250225
E: polbathic@ic24.net

POLRUAN
Cornwall

Quayside House ♦♦♦♦
The Quay, Polruan, Fowey PL23 1PA
T: (01726) 870377
E: quayhousepolruan@aol.com

POLSHAM
Somerset

Squareacre
Rating Applied For
Godney Road, Polsham, Wells BA5 1RR
T: (01749) 676792
F: (01749) 676876
E: bandb@squareacre.co.uk

POLZEATH
Cornwall

The White Heron ♦♦♦
Polzeath, Wadebridge PL27 6TJ
T: (01208) 863623
E: info@whiteheronhotel.co.uk
I: www.whiteheronhotel.co.uk

PORCUPINE
Cornwall

Woodmill Farm
Rating Applied For
Prideaux Road, St Blazey, Par PL24 2SR
T: (01726) 810171

PORLOCK
Somerset

Burley Cottage Guest House ♦♦♦♦
Parsons Street, Porlock, Minehead TA24 8QJ
T: (01643) 862563
F: (01643) 862563
E: burleycottage@aol.com
I: www.Burnleycottage.com

Castle Hotel ♦♦♦
High Street, Porlock, Minehead TA24 8PY
T: (01643) 862504
F: (01643) 862504
E: castlehotel@btconnect.com

Leys B & B
♦♦♦♦ SILVER AWARD
The Ridge, Porlock, Minehead TA24 8HA
T: (01643) 862477
F: (01643) 862477

The Lorna Doone Hotel ♦♦♦
High Street, Porlock, Minehead TA24 8PS
T: (01643) 862404
F: (01643) 863018
E: lorna@doone99.freeserve.co.uk

Myrtle Cottage ♦♦♦
High Street, Porlock, Minehead TA24 8PU
T: (01643) 862978
F: (01243) 862978
E: bob.steer@talk21.com
I: www.smoothhound.co.uk/hotels/myrtle.html

Nutkin House ♦♦♦
Toll Road, Porlock, Minehead TA24 8JH
T: (01643) 863228
E: nutkinhouse@hotmail.com

Seapoint ♦♦♦♦
Upway, Porlock, Minehead TA24 8QE
T: (01643) 862289
F: (01643) 862289

PORT ISAAC
Cornwall

Anchorage ♦♦♦♦
12 The Terrace, Port Isaac PL29 3SG
T: (01208) 880629

Hathaway ♦♦♦♦
Roscarrock Hill, Port Isaac PL29 3RG
T: (01208) 880416
E: marion.andrews1@btopenworld.com
I: www.cornwall-online.co.uk/hathaway

Oceans 11
Rating Applied For
The Terrace, Port Isaac PL29 3SG
T: (01208) 880267
F: (01208) 880267
E: mail@wavehunters.co.uk
I: www.wavehunters.co.uk

The Slipway Hotel & Restaurant ♦♦♦
Middle Street, Port Isaac PL29 3RH
T: (01208) 880264
F: (01208) 880408
E: slipwayhotel@portisaac.com
I: www.portisaac.com

PORTESHAM
Dorset

The Old Fountain ♦♦♦♦
36 Front Street, Portesham, Weymouth DT3 4ET
T: (01305) 871278
F: (01305) 871278

PORTH
Cornwall

Porth Cliff Hotel ♦♦♦
Watergate Road, Porth, Newquay TR7 3LX
T: (01637) 872503
F: (01637) 872503
E: enquiry@porthcliffhotel.co.uk
I: www.porthcliffhotel.co.uk

PORTLAND
Dorset

Brackenbury House ♦♦♦
Fortuneswell, Portland DT5 1LP
T: (01305) 826509
E: brackenburybt@btinternet.com

POULSHOT
Wiltshire

Higher Green Farm ♦♦
Poulshot Road, Poulshot, Devizes SN10 1RW
T: (01380) 828355
F: (01380) 828355

Poulshot Lodge Farm ♦♦♦
Poulshot, Devizes SN10 1RQ
T: (01380) 828255

POWERSTOCK
Dorset

Three Horseshoes Inn
Rating Applied For
Powerstock, Bridport DT6 3TF
T: (01308) 485328
F: (01308) 485229

POYNTINGTON
Dorset

Welgoer ♦♦♦
Poyntington, Sherborne DT9 4LF
T: (01963) 220737

PRESTON
Devon

Innisfree Hotel ♦♦♦♦
12 Colin Road, Preston, Paignton TQ3 2NR
T: (01803) 550692
F: (01803) 550692
E: rick@innisfree12.fslife.co.uk

QUEEN CAMEL
Somerset

Mildmay Arms ♦♦
High Street, Queen Camel, Yeovil BA22 7NJ
T: (01935) 850456
F: (01935) 851610
E: mike@mildmayarms.greatxscape.net
I: www.mildmayarms.greatxscape.net

RADSTOCK
Bath and North East Somerset

Radstock Hotel & Bar ♦♦♦
Market Place, Radstock BA3 3AD
T: (01761) 420776
F: (01761) 420520
I: www.chapmansgroup.com

The Rookery ♦♦♦♦
Wells Road, Radstock BA3 3RS
T: (01761) 432626
F: (01761) 432626
E: brandons@therookeryguesthouse.co.uk
I: www.therookeryguesthouse.co.uk

RAMSBURY
Wiltshire

Marridge Hill Cottage ♦♦♦
Marridge Hill, Ramsbury, Marlborough SN8 2HG
T: (01672) 520486

RATTERY
Devon

Knowle Farm
♦♦♦♦ SILVER AWARD
Rattery, South Brent TQ10 9JY
T: (01364) 73914
F: (01364) 73914
E: lynn@knowle-farm.co.uk
I: www.knowle-farm.co.uk/b&b

REDLYNCH
Wiltshire

Templeman's Old Farmhouse ♦♦♦♦
Langford Lane, Redlynch, Salisbury SP5 2JS
T: (01725) 510331
F: (01752) 510331

ROCK
Cornwall

Silvermead ♦♦♦
Rock, Wadebridge PL27 6LB
T: (01208) 862425
F: (01208) 862919

ROOKSBRIDGE
Somerset

Rooksbridge House ♦♦♦♦
Mendip Road, Rooksbridge, Axbridge BS26 2UL
T: (01934) 750630

ROWDE
Wiltshire

Lower Foxhangers Farm ♦♦♦
Rowde, Devizes SN10 1SS
T: (01380) 828254
F: (01380) 828254

The Manor House ♦♦♦
High Street, Rowde, Devizes SN10 2ND
T: (01380) 729319

RUSHALL
Wiltshire

Little Thatch ♦♦♦
Rushall, Pewsey SN9 6EN
T: (01980) 635282
F: (01980) 635282

ST AGNES
Cornwall

Covean Cottage ♦♦♦♦
St Agnes TR22 0PL
T: (01720) 422620
F: (01720) 422620
E: coveancottage@fsmail.net

Penkerris ♦♦
Penwinnick Road, St Agnes TR5 0PA
T: (01872) 552262
F: (01872) 552262
E: info@penkerris.co.uk
I: www.penkerris.co.uk

ST AUSTELL
Cornwall

The Elms ♦♦♦♦
14 Penwinnick Road, St Austell PL25 5DW
T: (01726) 74981
F: (01726) 74981
E: sue@edenbb.co.uk
I: www.edenbb.co.uk

Greenbank ♦♦♦♦
39 Southbourne Road, St Austell PL25 4RT
T: (01726) 73326
F: (01726) 73326
E: greenbank@cornish-riviera.co.uk

Polgreen Farm ♦♦♦♦
London Apprentice, St Austell PL26 7AP
T: (01726) 75151
F: (01726) 75151
E: polgreen.farm@btclick.com

Smugglers House
Rating Applied For
Rattle Street, Gorran Haven, St Austell PL26 6JQ
T: (01726) 844100

ST BREWARD
Cornwall

Tarny ♦♦♦
Row, St Breward, Bodmin PL30 4LW
T: (01208) 851304
E: tarnybandb@aol.com
I: www.tarny.co.uk

ST BURYAN
Cornwall

Boskenna Home Farm
♦♦♦♦ SILVER AWARD
St Buryan, Penzance TR19 6DQ
T: (01736) 810705
F: (01736) 810705
E: julia.hosking@btclick.com
I: www.boskenna.co.uk

Tregurnow Farm ♦♦♦♦
St Buryan, Penzance TR19 6BL
T: (01736) 810255
F: (01736) 810255
E: tregurno@eurobell.co.uk
I: www.tregurno.eurobell.co.uk

Trelew Farm ♦♦♦
St Buryan, Penzance TR19 6ED
T: (01736) 810308
F: (01736) 810308
E: info@trelew.co.uk
I: www.trelewf.co.uk

ST EWE
Cornwall

Higher Kestle Farm
♦♦♦♦ SILVER AWARD
St Ewe, Mevagissey, St Austell PL26 6EP
T: (01726) 842001
F: (01726) 842001
E: vicky@higherkestle.freeserve.co.uk
I: www.higherkestle.co.uk

ST ISSEY
Cornwall

Cannalidgey Villa Farm ♦♦♦♦
St Issey, Wadebridge PL27 7RB
T: (01208) 812276
F: (01208) 812276

Olde Tredore House ♦♦♦♦
St Issey, Wadebridge PL27 7QS
T: (01841) 540291

Ring O' Bell ♦♦♦
Churchtown, St Issey, Wadebridge PL27 7QB
T: (01841) 540251
F: (01841) 540301
E: sringobells@aol.com

Rose Park ♦♦♦
Penrose Farm, St Issey, Wadebridge PL27 7RJ
T: (01208) 812595

The White House
Rating Applied For
St Issey, Wadebridge PL27 7QE
T: (01841) 540884

ST IVES
Cornwall

The Anchorage Guest House ♦♦♦♦
5 Bunkers Hill, St Ives TR26 1LJ
T: (01736) 797135
F: (01736) 797135
E: james@theanchoragebb.fsnet.co.uk
I: www.theanchoragebb.fsnet.co.uk

Blue Hayes Private Hotel ♦♦♦♦
Trelyon Avenue, St Ives TR26 2AD
T: (01736) 797129
F: (01736) 797129
E: malcolm@bluehayes.fsbusiness.co.uk
I: www.bluehayes.co.uk

Chy-an-Creet ♦♦♦♦
Higher Stennack, St Ives TR26 2HA
T: (01736) 796559
F: (01736) 796559
E: relax@chy.co.uk
I: www.chy.co.uk

Chy An Gwedhen ♦♦♦♦
St Ives Road, Treloyan, St Ives TR26 2JN
T: (01736) 798684
F: (01736) 798684
E: info@chyangwedhen.com
I: www.chyangwedhen.com

The Countryman at Trink ♦♦♦♦
The Old Coach Road, Trink, St Ives TR26 3JQ
T: (01736) 797571
F: (01736) 797571
E: countrymanstives@bushinternet.com
I: www.the-countryman-hotel-stives.co.uk

The Grey Mullet Guest House ♦♦♦
2 Bunkers Hill, St Ives TR26 1LJ
T: (01736) 796635
E: greymulletguesthouse@lineone.net
I: www.touristnetuk.com/sw/greymullet

Longships Hotel ♦♦♦♦
Talland Road, St Ives TR26 2DF
T: (01736) 798180
F: (01736) 798180
E: enquiries@longships-hotel.co.uk
I: www.longships-hotel.co.uk

Pierview Guesthouse ♦♦♦♦
32-34 Back Road East, St Ives TR26 1PD
T: (01736) 794268
F: (01736) 794268
I: www.pierview-stives.co.uk

The Pondarosa ♦♦♦♦
10 Porthminster Terrace, St Ives TR26 2DQ
T: (01736) 795875
F: (01736) 797811
E: pondarosa.hotel@talk21.com
I: www.cornwall-online.co.uk

Porthmeor Hotel ♦♦♦
Godrevy Terrace, St Ives TR26 1JA
T: (01736) 796712
F: (01736) 796712
E: info@porthmeor.com
I: www.porthmeor.com

St Ives Bay Hotel ♦♦♦
The Terrace, St Ives TR26 2BP
T: (01736) 795106
F: (01736) 793216
I: www.shearingsholidays.com/hotels/stives.htm

Tregony Guest House ♦♦♦♦
1 Clodgy View, St Ives TR26 1JG
T: (01736) 795884
F: (01736) 798942
E: info@tregony.com
I: www.tregony.com

ST JULIOT
Cornwall

Higher Pennycrocker Farm ♦♦♦♦
St Juliot, Boscastle PL35 0BY
T: (01840) 250488
F: (01840) 250488
E: Jackiefarm@aol.com
I: www.highpennycrockerfarmbandb.co.uk

The Old Rectory
♦♦♦♦♦ GOLD AWARD
St Juliot, Boscastle PL35 0BT
T: (01840) 250225
F: (01840) 250225
F: sally@stjuliot.com
I: www.stjuliot.com

ST JUST-IN-PENWITH
Cornwall

Bosavern House ♦♦♦
Bosavern, St Just-in-Penwith TR19 7RD
T: (01736) 788301
F: (01736) 788301
E: info@bosavern.com
I: www.bosavern.com

Boscean Country Hotel ♦♦♦♦
Boswedden Road, St Just-in-Penwith TR19 7QP
T: (01736) 788748
F: (01736) 788748
E: boscean@aol.com
I: www.connexions.co.uk/boscean/index.htm

Boswedden House ♦♦♦
Boswedden, St Just, St Just-in-Penwith TR19 7NJ
T: (01736) 788733
F: (01736) 788733
E: relax@boswedden.org.uk
I: www.smoothhound.co.uk/hotels/boswedd.html

The Old Sunday School ♦♦♦
Cape Cornwall Street, St Just-in-Penwith TR19 7JZ
T: (01736) 788444
F: (01736) 788444
E: info@oldsundayschool.co.uk
I: www.oldsundayschool.co.uk

ST KEVERNE Cornwall

Eden House ♦♦♦♦
Lemon Street, St Keverne, Helston TR12 6NE
T: (01326) 280005
E: RobertBOBhughes@aol.com

Old Temperance House Rating Applied For
The Square, St Keverne, Helston TR12 6NA
T: (01326) 280986
F: (01326) 280986
I: www.cornwall-online.co.uk/ginentonic

ST KEW Cornwall

Lane End Farm Rating Applied For
Pendoggett, St Kew, Bodmin PL30 3HH
T: (01208) 880013

Tregellist Farm ♦♦♦♦
Tregellist, St Kew, Bodmin PL30 3HG
T: (01208) 880537
F: (01208) 881017
E: jillcleave@tregellist.fsbusiness.co.uk
I: www.tregellistfarm.co.uk

ST KEW HIGHWAY Cornwall

Porchester House ♦♦♦♦
St Kew Highway, Bodmin PL30 3ED
T: (01208) 841725
E: jenny.ashley@porchester.f9.co.uk
I: www.thisisnorthcornwall.co.uk

ST MABYN Cornwall

Chrismar ♦♦
Wadebridge Road, St Mabyn, Bodmin PL30 3BH
T: (01208) 841518

Cles Kernyk ♦♦♦
Wadebridge Road, St Mabyn, Bodmin PL30 3BH
T: (01208) 841258
E: sue@mabyn.freeserve.co.uk

Treglown House ♦♦♦♦
St Mabyn, Bodmin PL30 3BU
T: (01208) 841896
F: (01208) 841896
E: treglownhouse@stmabyn.fsnet.co.uk
I: www.treglownhouse.co.uk

ST MARY'S Isles of Scilly

Anjeric Guest House ♦♦♦
The Strand, St Mary's TR21 0PS
T: (01720) 422700
F: (01720) 422700
E: judyarcher@yahoo.co.uk
I: www.scillyonline.co.uk/accomm/anjeric.html

Annet ♦♦♦♦ SILVER AWARD
St Mary's TR21 0NF
T: (01720) 422441
F: (01720) 422553
E: annet-cottage@lineone.net
I: www.annet-cottage.co.uk

April Cottage ♦♦♦♦ SILVER AWARD
Church Road, St Mary's TR21 0NA
T: (01720) 422279
F: (01720) 423247

Armeria ♦♦♦
1 Porthloo Terrace, St Mary's TR21 0NF
T: (01720) 422961

Auriga Guest House ♦♦♦♦
7 Porthcressa Road, St Mary's TR21 0JL
T: (01720) 422637
E: aurigascilly@aol.com

Beachfield House ♦♦♦♦
Porthloo, St Mary's TR21 0NE
T: (01720) 422463
F: (01720) 422463
E: whomersley@supanet.com

Belmont ♦♦♦♦
Church Road, St Mary's TR21 0NA
T: (01720) 423154
E: enquiries@the-belmont.freeserve.co.uk
I: www.the-belmont.freeserve.co.uk

Blue Carn Cottage ♦♦♦
Old Town, St Mary's TR21 0NH
T: (01720) 422309

The Boathouse ♦♦♦
Thorofare Hugh Town, St Mary's TR21 0LN
T: (01720) 422688

Broomfields ♦♦♦
Church Road, St Mary's TR21 0NA
T: (01720) 422309

Buckingham House ♦♦♦
The Bank, St Mary's TR21 0HY
T: (01720) 422543

The Bylet ♦♦♦
Church Road, St Mary's, Isles of Scilly TR21 0NA
T: (01720) 422479
F: (01720) 422479
E: thebylet@bushinternet.com
I: www.byletholidays.com

Cornerways ♦♦♦♦
Jacksons Hill, St Mary's TR21 0JZ
T: (01720) 422757
F: (01720) 422797

Crebinick House ♦♦♦♦ SILVER AWARD
Church Street, St Mary's TR21 0JT
T: (01720) 422968
E: wct@crebinick.co.uk
I: www.crebinick.co.uk

Eastbank ♦♦♦♦
Porthloo, St Mary's TR21 0NE
T: (01720) 423695
E: linda@scilly-holidays.co.uk
I: scilly-holidays.co.uk

Evergreen Cottage Guest House ♦♦♦♦
The Parade, Hugh Town, St Mary's TR21 0LP
T: (01720) 422711

Freesia Guesthouse ♦♦♦♦
The Parade, St Mary's TR21 0LP
T: (01720) 423676
F: (01720) 422068
E: freesiaguesthouse@hotmail.com

Garrison House ♦♦♦♦ SILVER AWARD
Garrison, St Mary's TR21 0LS
T: (01720) 422972
F: (01720) 422972
E: garrisonhouse@aol.com
I: www.isles-of-scilly.co.uk/guesthouses

Gunners Rock ♦♦♦♦
Jackson's Hill, St Mary's TR21 0JZ
T: (01720) 422595

Hazeldene ♦♦♦♦
Church Street, St Mary's TR21 0JT
T: (01720) 422864
E: albawilliams@btopenworld.com

High Lanes Farm ♦♦♦
Atlantic View, St Mary's TR21 0NW
T: (01720) 422684

Higher Trenoweth ♦♦♦♦ SILVER AWARD
St Mary's TR21 0NS
T: (01720) 422419

Jedi ♦♦♦♦
St Mary's TR21 0NS
T: (01720) 422762
F: (01720) 422762
E: ca@jediios.freeserve.co.uk

Kistvaen ♦♦♦♦
Sally Port, St Mary's TR21 0JE
T: (01720) 422002
F: (01720) 422002
E: chivy002@aol.com

Lamorna ♦♦♦
Rams Valley, St Mary's TR21 0JX
T: (01720) 422333

Lynwood ♦♦♦♦
Church Street, St Mary's TR21 0JT
T: (01720) 423313
F: (01720) 423313

Lyonnesse Guest House ♦♦♦
The Strand, St Mary's TR21 0PS
T: (01720) 422458

Marine House ♦♦♦
Church Street, St Mary's TR21 0JT
T: (01720) 422966
E: peggy@rowe55.freeserve.co.uk

Men-a-Vaur ♦♦♦
Church Road, St Mary's TR21 0NA
T: (01720) 422245

Morgelyn ♦♦♦
McFarlands Down, St Mary's TR21 0NS
T: (01720) 422897
E: info@morgelyn.co.uk
I: www.morgelyn.co.uk

Pier House ♦♦♦♦
The Bank, St Mary's TR21 0HY
T: (01720) 423061
I: www.isles-of-scilly.co.uk/pier-house.html

Rose Cottage ♦♦♦♦ SILVER AWARD
Strand, St Mary's TR21 0PT
T: (01720) 422078
F: (01720) 423588
E: rosecottage@infinnet.co.uk

St Hellena ♦♦♦♦
13 Garrison Lane, St Mary's TR21 0JD
T: (01720) 423231

Santa Maria ♦♦♦♦
Sallyport, St Mary's TR21 0JE
T: (01720) 422687
F: (01720) 422687

Scillonia ♦♦
Bank, St Mary's TR21 0HY
T: (01720) 422101

Shamrock ♦♦♦♦
High Lanes, St Mary's TR21 0NW
T: (01720) 423269

Shearwater Guest House ♦♦♦
The Parade, Hugh Town, St Mary's TR21 0LP
T: (01720) 422402
F: (01720) 422351
E: ianhopkin@aol.com
I: www.shearwater-guest-house.co.uk

Strand House ♦♦♦
Lower Strand, St Mary's TR21 0PS
T: (01720) 422808
F: (01720) 423009

Sylina ♦♦♦♦
McFarlands Downs, St Mary's TR21 0NS
T: (01720) 422129
F: (01720) 422129

Trelawney Guest House ♦♦♦♦
Church Street, St Mary's TR21 0JT
T: (01720) 422377
F: (01720) 422377
E: dtownend@netcomuk.co.uk
I: www.trelawney-ios.co.uk

Veronica Lodge ♦♦♦♦
The Garrison, St Mary's TR21 0LS
T: (01720) 422585
E: veronicalodge@freenetname.co.uk

Westford House ♦♦♦♦
Church Street, St Mary's TR21 0JT
T: (01720) 422510
F: (01720) 422424

The Wheelhouse ♦♦♦♦
Porthcressa, St Mary's TR21 0JG
T: (01720) 422719
F: (01720) 422719

Wingletang Guest House ♦♦♦
The Parade, St Mary's TR21 0LP
T: (01720) 422381

The Withies
♦♦♦♦ SILVER AWARD
Trench Lane, Old Town, St Mary's TR21 0PA
T: (01720) 422986

ST MARYS
Devon

The Town House
♦♦♦♦ SILVER AWARD
Little Porth, St Mary's TR21 0JG
T: (01720) 422793
E: scillytownhouse@hotmail.com
I: www.isles-of-scilly.co.uk/the-town-house.html

ST MAWES
Cornwall

The Ship and Castle ♦♦♦
The Waterfront, St Mawes, Truro TR2 5DG
T: (01326) 270401
F: (01326) 270152
I: www.shearingsholidays.com

ST MAWGAN
Cornwall

The Falcon Inn ♦♦♦♦
St Mawgan, Newquay TR8 4EP
T: (01637) 860225
F: (01637) 860884
E: enquiries@falconinn.net
I: www.falconinn.net

ST MERRYN
Cornwall

Tregavone Farm ♦♦♦
St Merryn, Padstow PL28 8JZ
T: (01841) 520148

Trewithen Farmhouse ♦♦♦♦
St Merryn, Padstow PL28 8JZ
T: (01841) 520420

ST MINVER
Cornwall

Porteath Barn ♦♦♦♦
St Minver, Wadebridge PL27 6RA
T: (01208) 863605
F: (01208) 863954
E: mbloor@ukonline.co.uk

ST NEOT
Cornwall

Higher Searles Down ♦♦♦♦
St Neot, Liskeard PL14 6QA
T: (01208) 821412
E: glenforster@compuserve.com

Lampen Mill
♦♦♦♦ SILVER AWARD
St Neot, Liskeard PL14 6PB
T: (01579) 321119
F: (01579) 321733
E: heather@lampen.ndo.co.uk
I: www.lampen.ndo.co.uk

ST TEATH
Cornwall

Trehannick Farm ♦♦♦
St Teath, Bodmin PL30 3JW
T: (01208) 850312
F: (01208) 850312

ST TUDY
Cornwall

Polrode Mill Cottage
♦♦♦♦♦ SILVER AWARD
Allen Valley, St Tudy, Bodmin PL30 3NS
T: (01208) 850203
E: polrode@tesco.net
I: www.cornwall-online.co.uk/polrode-mill

SALCOMBE
Devon

Burton Farmhouse & Garden Restaurant
♦♦♦♦ SILVER AWARD
Galmpton, Kingsbridge TQ7 3EY
T: (01548) 561210
F: (01548) 562257
I: www.burtonfarm.co.uk

SALISBURY
Wiltshire

Alabare House ♦♦♦
15 Tollgate Road, Salisbury SP1 2JA
T: (01722) 340206
F: (01722) 501586
E: alabarehouse@fsmail.net
I: www.alabare.org

Avila ♦♦♦
130 Exeter Street, Salisbury SP1 2SG
T: (01722) 421093

The Barford Inn ♦♦♦♦
Barford St Martin, Salisbury SP3 4AB
T: (01722) 742242
F: (01722) 743606
E: ido@barfordinn.co.uk
I: www.barfordinn.co.uk

The Bell Inn ♦♦♦
Warminster Road, South Newton, Salisbury SP2 0QD
T: (01722) 743336
F: (01722) 744202

78 Belle Vue Road ♦♦♦
Belle Vue Road, Salisbury SP1 3YD
T: (01722) 329477

Bridge Farm
♦♦♦♦ GOLD AWARD
Lower Road, Britford, Salisbury SP5 4DY
T: (01722) 332376
F: (01722) 332376
E: mail@bridgefarmbb.co.uk
I: www.bridgefarmbb.co.uk

Burcombe Manor ♦♦♦♦
Burcombe, Salisbury SP2 0E3
T: (01722) 744288
E: nick@burcombemanor.fsnet.co.uk
I: www.burcombemanor.com

Byways House ♦♦♦
31 Fowlers Road, Salisbury SP1 2QP
T: (01722) 328364
F: (01722) 322146
E: byways@bed-breakfast-salisbury.co.uk
I: www.bed-breakfast-salisbury.co.uk

The Edwardian Lodge ♦♦♦♦
59 Castle Road, Salisbury SP1 3RH
T: (01722) 413329
F: (01722) 503105
E: richardwhite@edlodge.freeserve.co.uk
I: www.edwardianlodge.co.uk

Farthings ♦♦♦
9 Swaynes Close, Salisbury SP1 3AE
T: (01722) 330749
F: (01722) 330749
E: enquiries@farthingsbandb.co.uk
I: www.farthingsbandb.co.uk

Glenshee
♦♦♦♦ SILVER AWARD
3 Montague Road, Salisbury SP2 8NJ
T: (01722) 322620
E: glenshee@breathemail.net
I: www.smoothhound.co.uk/hotels/glenshee.html

Griffin Cottage ♦♦♦♦
10 St Edmunds Church Street, Salisbury SP1 1EF
T: (01722) 328259
F: (01722) 416928
E: mark@brandonasoc.demon.co.uk
I: www.smoothhound.co.uk/hotels/griffinc.html

Highveld ♦♦♦
Hulse Road, Salisbury SP1 3LY
T: (01722) 338172
E: icedawn@amserve.net
I: www.salisburybedandbreakfast.com

Holly Tree House ♦♦
53 Wyndham Road, Salisbury SP1 3AH
T: (01722) 322955

Holmhurst Guest House ♦♦
Downton Road, Salisbury SP2 8AR
T: (01722) 410407
F: (01722) 323164
E: holmhurst@talk21.com

Kinvara ♦♦♦♦
28 Castle Road, Salisbury SP1 3RJ
T: (01722) 325233
F: (01722) 325233
E: kinvarahouse@aol.com

Leena's Guest House ♦♦♦
50 Castle Road, Salisbury SP1 3RL
T: (01722) 335419
F: (01722) 335419

Malvern ♦♦♦♦ GOLD AWARD
Hulse Road, Salisbury SP1 3LU
T: (01722) 327995
F: (01722) 327995
E: malvern_gh@madasafish.com
I: www.malverguesthouse.com

Manor Farm ♦♦♦♦
Burcombe Lane, Burcombe, Salisbury SP2 0EJ
T: (01722) 742177
F: (01722) 744600
E: sacombes@talk21.com

94 Milford Hill ♦♦♦
Milford Hill, Salisbury SP1 2QL
T: (01722) 322454

Newton Farm House
♦♦♦♦♦ SILVER AWARD
Southampton Road, Whiteparish, Salisbury SP5 2QL
T: (01794) 884416
F: (01794) 884416
E: enquiries@newtonfarmhouse.co.uk
I: www.newtonfarmhouse.co.uk

Number Eighty Eight ♦♦♦♦
88 Exeter Street, Salisbury SP1 2SE
T: (01722) 330139
E: enquiries@no88.co.uk
I: www.no88.co.uk

The Old Rectory Bed & Breakfast ♦♦♦♦
75 Belle Vue Road, Salisbury SP1 3YE
T: (01722) 502702
F: (01722) 501135
E: stay@theoldrectory-bb.co.uk
I: www.theoldrectory-bb.co.uk

Pathways ♦♦
41 Shady Bower, Salisbury SP1 2RG
T: (01722) 324252

The Pelican Inn
Rating Applied For
Warminster Road, Stapleford, Salisbury SP3 4LT
T: (01722) 790241
F: (01722) 790241

The Rokeby Guest House
♦♦♦♦ SILVER AWARD
3 Wain-a-Long Road, Salisbury SP1 1LJ
T: (01722) 329800
F: (01722) 329800
I: www.rokebyguesthouse.co.uk

34 Salt Lane ♦♦
Salt Lane, Salisbury SP1 1EG
T: (01722) 326141

Stratford Lodge ♦♦♦♦
4 Park Lane, Salisbury SP1 3NP
T: (01722) 325177
F: (01722) 325177
E: enquiries@stratfordlodge.co.uk
I: www.stratfordlodge.co.uk

Swaynes Firs Farm ♦♦♦
Coombe Bissett, Salisbury SP5 5RF
T: (01725) 519240
E: swaynes.firs@virgin.net
I: www.swaynesfirs.co.uk

Tiffany ♦♦♦
2 Bourne Villas, Off College street, Salisbury SP1 3AW
T: (01722) 332367

Torrisholme ♦♦♦
Stratford Road, Stratford sub Castle, Stratford Sub Castle, Salisbury SP1 3LQ
T: (01722) 329089
F: (01722) 321363
E: torrisholme@hotmail.com
I: www.torrisholme.net

Victoria Lodge Guest House ♦♦
61 Castle Road, Salisbury SP1 3RH
T: (01722) 320586
F: (01722) 414507
E: mail@viclodge.co.uk
I: www.viclodge.co.uk

Websters
♦♦♦♦ GOLD AWARD
11 Hartington Road, Salisbury SP2 7LG
T: (01722) 339779
F: (01722) 421903
E: enquiries@websters-bed-breakfast
I: www.websters-bed-breakfast.com

Wyndham Park Lodge ♦♦♦♦
51 Wyndham Road, Salisbury SP1 3AB
T: (01722) 416517
F: (01722) 328851
E: enquiries@wyndhamparklodge.co.uk
I: www.wyndhamparklodge.co.uk

SALTASH
Cornwall

Haye Farm ♦♦♦♦
Landulph, Saltash PL12 6QQ
T: (01752) 842786
F: (01752) 842786
I: www.hayefarmcornwall.co.uk

SAMPFORD COURTENAY
Devon

Langdale ♦♦
Sampford Courtenay, Okehampton EX20 2SY
T: (01837) 82433
E: chrisclayton7@lineone.net

SAND
Somerset

Townsend Farm
♦♦♦♦ SILVER AWARD
Sand, Wedmore BS28 4XH
T: (01934) 712342
F: (01934) 712405
E: smewillcox0@farmersweekly.net

SEATON
Devon

The Baytree Bed and Breakfast ♦♦♦
11 Seafield Road, Seaton EX12 2QS
T: (01297) 24611

Beach End at Seaton
♦♦♦♦ SILVER AWARD
8 Trevelyan Road, Seaton EX12 2NL
T: (01297) 23388
F: (01297) 625604
E: beachendatseaton@aol.com
I: www.smoothhound.co.uk/hotels/beachend

Beaumont ♦♦♦♦
Castle Hill, Seaton EX12 2QW
T: (01297) 20832
F: (0870) 055 4708
E: tony@lymebay.demon.co.uk
I: www.smoothhound.co.uk/hotels/beaumon1.html

Blue Haven ♦♦♦♦
Looe Hill, Seaton, Torpoint PL11 3JQ
T: (01503) 250310
E: bluehaven@btinternet.com
I: www.smoothhound.co.uk/hotels/bluehave.html

Four Seasons ♦♦♦
3 Burrow Road, Seaton EX12 2NF
T: (01297) 20761
F: (01297) 20761

Gatcombe Farm ♦♦♦♦
Seaton EX12 3AA
T: (01297) 21235
F: (01297) 23010
E: gatcombefarm@tinyworld.co.uk
I: gatcombe-farm-devon.co.uk

Hill House
♦♦♦♦ SILVER AWARD
Highcliff Crescent, Seaton EX12 2PS
T: (01297) 20377
E: jphil.beard@lineone.net

Mariners Hotel ♦♦♦
East Walk, Seaton EX12 2NP
T: (01297) 20560
F: (01297) 20560

Pinehurst Bed & Breakfast ♦♦♦♦
189 Beer Road, Seaton EX12 2QB
T: (01297) 21878
I: www.pinehurst.co.uk

SEMINGTON
Wiltshire

Newhouse Farm ♦♦♦♦
Littleton, Semington, Trowbridge BA14 6LF
T: (01380) 870349
E: derek.newhousefarm@virgin.net

SENNEN
Cornwall

Homefields Guest House ♦♦♦♦
Sennen, Penzance TR19 7AD
T: (01736) 871418
F: (01736) 871666
E: homefields1bandb@aol.com
I: www.smoothhound.co.uk/hotels/homefields

Treeve Moor House
Rating Applied For
Sennen, Penzance TR19 7AE
T: (01736) 871284
F: (01736) 871284
E: info@firstandlastcottages.co.uk
I: www.firstandlastcottages.co.uk

SHALDON
Devon

Glenside House Hotel ♦♦♦
Ringmore Road, Shaldon, Teignmouth TQ14 0EP
T: (01626) 872448
F: (01626) 872448
E: glensidehouse@amserve.com
I: www.smoothhound.co.uk/hotels/glensideho.html

Potters Mooring ♦♦♦♦
30 The Green, Shaldon, Teignmouth TQ14 0DN
T: (01626) 873225
F: (01626) 872909
E: mail@pottersmooring.co.uk
I: www.pottersmooring.co.uk

SHARCOTT
Wiltshire

The Old Dairy House ♦♦♦♦
Sharcott, Pewsey SN9 5PA
T: (01672) 562287
E: old.dairy@virgin.net
I: business.virgin.net/neville.burrell/sharcott.htm

SHEPTON MALLET
Somerset

Belfield Guest House ♦♦♦
34 Charlton Road, Shepton Mallet BA4 5PA
T: (01749) 344353
F: (01749) 344353
E: andrea@belfield-house.co.uk
I: www.belfield-house.co.uk

The Bell Hotel ♦♦♦
2 High Street, Shepton Mallet BA4 5AN
T: (01749) 345393
F: (01749) 347480

Burnt House Farm
♦♦♦♦ GOLD AWARD
Waterlip, West Cranmore, Shepton Mallet BA4 4RN
T: (01749) 880280
F: (01749) 880004

Hillbury House ♦♦♦♦
65 Compton Road, Shepton Mallet BA4 5QT
T: (01749) 345473
F: (01749) 345473
E: patandjerry@ukonline.co.uk

Hurlingpot Farmhouse ♦♦♦♦
Chelynch, Shepton Mallet BA4 4PY
T: (01749) 880256
F: (01749) 880893
I: www.smoothhound.co.uk/hotels/hurling.html

Knapps Farm
♦♦♦♦♦ SILVER AWARD
Beacon, Doulting, Shepton Mallet BA4 4LA
T: (01749) 880471
F: (01749) 880024
E: avril_mattews@yahoo.com

Middleton House ♦♦♦♦
68 Compton Road, Shepton Mallet BA4 5QT
T: (01749) 343720
E: lynandbob@shepton.freeserve.co.uk

Pecking Mill Inn and Hotel ♦♦
A371 Evercreech, Evercreech, Shepton Mallet BA4 6PG
T: (01749) 830336
F: (01749) 831316
E: peckingmill@peckingmill.freeserve.co.uk

Temple House Farm ♦♦♦♦
Doulting, Shepton Mallet BA4 4RQ
T: (01749) 880294
F: (01749) 880688

The Thatched Cottage
Rating Applied For
63-67 Charlton Road, Shepton Mallet BA4 5QF
T: (01749) 342058
F: (01749) 343265
I: www.thatchedcottageinn.co.uk

SHERBORNE
Dorset

The Alders
♦♦♦♦ SILVER AWARD
Sandford Orcas, Sherborne DT9 4SB
T: (01963) 220666
F: (01963) 220106
E: jonsue@thealdersbb.com
I: www.thealdersbb.com

Bridleways ♦♦♦
Oborne Road, Sherborne DT9 3RX
T: (01935) 814716
F: (01935) 814716
E: bridleways@tiscali.co.uk

Clatcombe Grange ♦♦♦♦
Lower Clatcombe, Sherborne DT9 4RH
T: (01935) 814355
F: (01935) 814696

Cumberland House ♦♦♦♦
Green Hill, Sherborne DT9 4EP
T: (01935) 817554
F: (01935) 817398
E: cumberlandbandb@aol.com

Huntsbridge Farm
♦♦♦♦♦ GOLD AWARD
Batcombe Road, Leigh, Sherborne DT9 6JA
T: (01935) 872150
F: (01935) 872150
E: huntsbridge@lineone.net
I: www.ruraldorset.co.uk/bed/huntsbridgefarm.shtml

The Old Vicarage Hotel ♦♦♦♦♦
Sherborne Road, Milborne Port, Sherborne DT9 5AT
T: (01963) 251117
F: (01963) 251515
E: theoldvicarage@milborneport.freeserve.co.uk
I: www.milborneport.freeserve.co.uk

Tintagel ♦♦♦♦
South Street, Sherborne DT9 3LZ
T: (01935) 389159
F: (01935) 389285
E: savileplatt@hotmail.com

Village Vacations ♦♦♦
Brookmead, Rimpton, Yeovil BA22 8AQ
T: (01935) 850241
F: (01935) 850241
E: villagevac@aol.com
I: www.villagevacations.co.uk

SHERSTON
Wiltshire

Widleys Farm ♦♦♦
Sherston, Malmesbury SN16 0PY
T: (01666) 840213
F: (01666) 840156
E: mary@hibbard840.fsnet.co.uk

SHIPHAM
Somerset

Herongates ♦♦♦♦
Horseleaze Lane, Shipham, Winscombe BS25 1UQ
T: (01934) 843280
F: (01934) 843280
I: www.bizbrowsers.com/herongates

SHIPTON GORGE
Dorset

Cairnhill
♦♦♦♦♦ GOLD AWARD
Shipton Gorge, Bridport DT6 4LL
T: (01308) 898203
F: (01308) 898203
E: cairnhill@talk21.com

SHREWTON
Wiltshire

Maddington House ♦♦♦♦
Maddington Street, Shrewton, Salisbury SP3 4JD
T: (01980) 620406
F: (01980) 620406
E: rsrobathan@freenet.co.uk

SHUTTA
Cornwall

The Jolly Sailor Inn
Rating Applied For
Princes Square, Shutta, Looe
PL13 2EP
T: (01503) 263387
E: bartlamjolly@aol.com
I: www.looedirectory.co.uk/jolly-sailor.htm

SIDBURY
Devon

Rose Cottage Sidbury ♦♦♦♦
Greenhead, Sidbury, Sidmouth
EX10 0RH
T: (01395) 597357
F: (01395) 597357
E: lincoln@rosecottagesidbury.co.uk
I: www.rosecottagesidbury.co.uk

SIDMOUTH
Devon

The Barn And Pinn Cottage Guest House ♦♦♦♦
Bowd Cross, Sidmouth
EX10 0ND
T: (01395) 513613
E: thebarnandpinncott@amserve.net

Berwick Guest House ♦♦♦♦
Albert Terrace, Salcombe Road, Sidmouth EX10 8PX
T: (01395) 513621
E: reservations@berwick-house.co.uk
I: www.berwick-house.co.uk

Canterbury Guest House ♦♦♦
Salcombe Road, Sidmouth
EX10 8PR
T: (01395) 513373
E: cgh@eclipse.co.uk

Coombe Bank Guest House
♦♦♦♦ SILVER AWARD
Alexandria Road, Sidmouth
EX10 9HG
T: (01395) 514843
F: (01395) 513558
E: info@coombebank.com
I: www.coombebank.com

Higher Coombe Farm ♦♦♦
Tipton St John, Sidmouth
EX10 0AX
T: (01404) 813385
F: (01404) 813385
E: KerstinFarmer@farming.co.uk
I: www.smoothhound.co.uk/hotels/higherco.html

Kyneton Lodge
♦♦♦♦ SILVER AWARD
87 Alexandria Road, Sidmouth
EX10 9HG
T: (01395) 513213
F: (01395) 513213
E: suawright@lineone.net

Lower Pinn Farm ♦♦♦♦
Pinn, Sidmouth EX10 0NN
T: (01395) 513733
F: (01395) 513733
E: liz@lowerpinnfarm.co.uk
I: www.lowerpinnfarm.co.uk

Lynstead ♦♦♦♦
Vicarage Road, Sidmouth
EX10 8UQ
T: (01395) 514635
F: (01395) 578954
E: lynstead@aol.com
I: wwwsmoothhound.co.uk/hotels/lynstead.html

Pinn Barton Farm
♦♦♦♦ SILVER AWARD
Peak Hill, Pinn, Sidmouth
EX10 0NN
T: (01395) 514004
F: (01395) 514004
E: betty@pinnbartonfarm.co.uk

The Salty Monk
♦♦♦♦♦ GOLD AWARD
Church Street, Sidford, Sidmouth EX10 9QP
T: (01395) 513174
F: (01395) 577232
I: www.saltymonk.co.uk

Tyrone
Rating Applied For
Sid Road, Sidmouth EX10 9AL
T: (01395) 516753
E: tyronehouse@msn.com

Willow Bridge Private Hotel ♦♦♦♦
Millford Road, Sidmouth
EX10 8DR
T: (01395) 513599
E: willowframing@c.s.com

Wiscombe Linhaye Farm ♦♦♦♦
Southleigh, Colyton EX24 6JF
T: (01404) 871342
F: (01404) 871342
E: rabjohns@btinternet.com

SILVERTON
Devon

Three Tuns Inn ♦♦♦
14 Exeter Road, Silverton, Exeter
EX5 4HX
T: (01392) 860352
F: (01392) 860636
I: www.threetuninn.co.uk

SKILGATE
Somerset

Blindwell Farm
Rating Applied For
Blinwell Lane, Skilgate, Taunton
TA4 2DJ
T: (01398) 331170
I: www.smoothhound.co.uk/hotels/blindwellfarm

Chapple Farm ♦♦♦
Skilgate, Taunton TA4 2DP
T: (01398) 331364

SLAPTON
Devon

Little Pittaford
♦♦♦♦♦ SILVER AWARD
Slapton, Kingsbridge TQ7 2QG
T: (01548) 580418
F: (01548) 580406
E: LittlePittaford@compuserve.com
I: www.littlepittaford.co.uk

Start House ♦♦♦
Slapton, Kingsbridge TQ7 2QD
T: (01548) 580254

SLAUGHTERFORD
Wiltshire

Manor Farm
Rating Applied For
Slaughterford, Chippenham
SN14 8RE
T: (01249) 782243
F: (01249) 782243

SOMERTON
Somerset

Littleton House ♦♦♦
New Street, Somerton TA11 7NU
T: (01458) 273072

Mill House
♦♦♦♦♦ SILVER AWARD
Mill Road, Barton St David, Somerton TA11 6DF
T: (01458) 851215
F: (01458) 851372
I: www.MillHouseBarton.co.uk

SOUTH BRENT
Devon

Coombe House
Rating Applied For
North Huish, South Brent
TQ10 9NJ
T: (01548) 821277
F: (01548) 821277
E: coombehouse@hotmail.com
I: www.coombehouse.uk.com

SOUTH MOLTON
Devon

Huxtable Farm
♦♦♦♦ SILVER AWARD
West Buckland, Barnstaple
EX32 0SR
T: (01598) 760254
F: (01598) 760254
E: info@huxtablefarm.co.uk
I: www.huxtablefarm.co.uk

Kerscott Farm
♦♦♦♦♦ GOLD AWARD
Ash Mill, South Molton
EX36 4QG
T: (01769) 550262
F: (01769) 550910
E: kerscott.farm@virgin.net
I: www.devon-bandb.co.uk

Old Coaching Inn ♦♦♦
Queen Street, South Molton, South Molton EX36 3BJ
T: (01769) 572526

SOUTH NEWTON
Wiltshire

Salisbury Old Mill House
♦♦♦♦ SILVER AWARD
Warminster Road, South Newton, Salisbury SP2 0QD
T: (01722) 742458
F: (01722) 742458
E: salisburymill@yahoo.com
I: www.smoothhound.co.uk

SOUTH PERROTT
Dorset

Shepherds Farmhouse ♦♦♦♦
South Perrott, Beaminster
DT8 3HU
T: (01935) 891599
F: (01935) 891977
E: shepherds@eclipse.co.uk
I: www.shepherds.eclipse.co.uk

SOUTH PETHERWIN
Cornwall

Oakside Bed and Breakfast ♦♦♦
Oakside Bungalow, South Petherwin, Launceston PL15 7LJ
T: (01566) 86733

SOUTHVILLE
Bristol

The Greenhouse ♦♦♦♦
61 Greenbank Road, Southville, Bristol BS3 1RJ
T: (0117) 902 9166
F: (0117) 902 9007
E: the_greenhouse@btopenworld.com
I: www.btinternet/~the_greenhouse

Walmer House ♦♦♦
94 Stackpool Road, Southville, Bristol BS3 1NW
T: (0117) 966 8253
F: (0117) 966 8253

The White House Guest Rooms ♦♦♦
28 Dean Lane, Southville, Bristol
BS3 1DB
T: (0117) 953 7725
E: whitehousebristol@fsmail.net
I: www.thewhitehouseguestrooms.com

SOUTHWELL
Dorset

Lobster Farmhouse ♦♦♦
Portland Bill, Southwell, Portland DT5 2JT
T: (01305) 861253
F: (01305) 861253

SPREYTON
Devon

The Tom Cobley Tavern ♦♦♦
Spreyton, Crediton EX17 5AL
T: (01647) 231314
F: (01647) 231506

ST AUSTELL
Cornwall

Lowarth Gwyth ♦♦
80 Truro Road, St Austell
PL25 5JS
T:
E: ann@lowarthgwyth.co.uk
I: www.lowarthgwyth.co.uk

Mandalay
Rating Applied For
School Hill, Mevagissey, St Austell PL26 6TQ
T: (01726) 842435
E: jill@mandalayhotel.freeserve.co.uk
I: www.manfalayhotel.freeserve.co.uk

Portmellon Cove Guest House
Rating Applied For
Portmellon Park, Mevagissey, St Austell PL26 6XD
T: (01726) 843410
E: stay@portmellon-cove.co.uk

Sunnycroft ♦♦♦
Penwinnick Road, St Austell
PL25 5DS
T: (01726) 73351
F: (01726) 879409
E: info@sunnycroft.net
I: www.sunnycroft.net

Tregilgas Farm
Rating Applied For
Gorran, St Austell PL26 6ND
T: (01726) 842342

STANTON DREW
Bath and North East Somerset

Greenlands ♦♦♦♦
Stanton Drew, Bristol BS39 4ES
T: (01275) 333487
F: (01275) 331211

STANTON WICK
Bath and North East Somerset

The Carpenters Arms ♦♦♦♦
Stanton Wick, Pensford, Stanton Wick, Pensford, Bristol BS39 4BX
T: (01761) 490202
F: (01761) 490763
E: carpenters@buccaneer.co.uk
I: www.the-carpenters-arms.co.uk

STAPLEFORD
Wiltshire

The Parsonage ♦♦♦♦
Stapleford, Salisbury SP3 4LJ
T: (01722) 790334

STARCROSS
Devon

The Croft Guest House ♦♦♦
Cockwood Harbour, Starcross, Exeter EX6 8QY
T: (01626) 890282
F: (01626) 891768

STAVERTON
Devon

Kingston House ♦♦♦♦♦ SILVER AWARD
Staverton, Totnes TQ9 6AR
T: (01803) 762235
F: (01803) 762444
E: info@kingston-estate.co.uk
I: www.kingston-estate.co.uk

STEEPLE ASHTON
Wiltshire

Church Farm ♦♦♦♦
High Street, Steeple Ashton, Trowbridge BA14 6EL
T: (01380) 870518
E: church.farm@farmline.com

Longs Arms Inn ♦♦♦
High Street, Steeple Ashton, Trowbridge BA14 6EU
T: (01380) 870245
F: (01380) 870245
E: chantal@stayatthepub.freeserve.co.uk
I: www.stayatthepub.freeserve.co.uk

STERT
Wiltshire

Orchard Cottage ♦♦♦
Stert, Devizes SN10 3JD
T: (01380) 723103
F: (01380) 723103

STIBB
Cornwall

Strands ♦♦♦
Stibb, Bude EX23 9HW
T: (01288) 353514

STOGUMBER
Somerset

Hall Farm ♦♦♦
Stogumber, Taunton TA4 3TQ
T: (01984) 656321

Northam Mill ♦♦♦♦ SILVER AWARD
Water Lane, Stogumber, Taunton TA4 3TT
T: (01984) 656916
F: (01984) 656144
E: bmsspicer@aol.com
I: www.northam-mill.co.uk

The White Horse Inn Rating Applied For
High Street, Stogumber, Taunton TA4 3TA
T: (01984) 656277
F: (01984) 656277

Wick House ♦♦♦
2 Brook Street, Stogumber, Taunton TA4 3SZ
T: (01984) 656422
E: sheila@wickhouse.fsbusiness.co.uk
I: www.wickhouse.fsbusiness.co.uk

STOKE-IN-TEIGNHEAD
Devon

Deane Thatch Accommodation ♦♦♦
Deane Road, Stoke-in-Teignhead, Newton Abbot TQ12 4QU
T: (01626) 873724
F: (01626) 873724
E: deanethatch@hotmail.com
I: www.deanethatch.co.uk

STOKE ST GREGORY
Somerset

Meare Green Farm ♦♦♦♦
Meare Green, North Curry, Stoke St Gregory, Taunton TA3 6HT
T: (01823) 490759
F: (01823) 490759
E: jane.pine@kitesourcing.com

STOKE SUB HAMDON
Somerset

Castle Farm ♦♦♦♦
North Street, Stoke sub Hamdon TA14 6QS
T: (01935) 822231
F: (01935) 822057

STOKENHAM
Devon

Brookfield ♦♦♦
Stokenham, Kingsbridge TQ7 2SL
T: (01548) 580615
F: (01548) 580615
E: heath@brookfield37.freeserve.co.uk

STONEY STRATTON
Somerset

Stratton Farm ♦♦♦♦
Stoney Stratton, Shepton Mallet BA4 6DY
T: (01749) 830830
F: (01749) 080181
I: www.strattonfarm.co.uk

STRATFORD SUB CASTLE
Wiltshire

Carp Cottage ♦♦♦♦
Stratford Road, Stratford sub Castle, Stratford Sub Castle, Salisbury SP1 3LH
T: (01722) 327219

STRATTON
Cornwall

Cann Orchard ♦♦♦♦
Howard Lane, Stratton, Bude EX23 9TD
T: (01288) 352098
F: (01288) 352098

STRATTON-ON-THE-FOSSE
Somerset

Oval House ♦♦♦
Fosse Road, Stratton-on-the-Fosse, Nr Bath BA3 4RB
T: (01761) 232183
F: (01761) 232183
E: mellotte@clara.co.uk
I: www.mellotte.clara.co.uk

STREET
Somerset

Leigh Nook ♦♦♦♦
Marshalls Elm, Street BA16 0TZ
T: (01458) 443511
E: williamavril@leighnook.fsnet.co.uk

Marshalls Elm Farm ♦♦♦
Street BA16 0TZ
T: (01458) 442878

Mullions Hotel ♦♦♦
51 High Street, Street BA16 0EF
T: (01458) 445110
F: (01458) 442874
E: info@mullionshotelstld.co.uk
I: www.mullionshotelsltd.co.uk

Old Orchard House ♦♦♦♦
Middle Brooks, Street BA16 0TU
T: (01458) 442212
E: old.orchard.house@amserve.com
I: www.oldorchardhouse.co.uk

SWINDON
Wiltshire

Appletree House ♦♦♦
29 Kingsdown Road, Upper Stratton, Swindon SN2 7PE
T: (01793) 829218

Courtleigh House ♦♦♦♦
40 Draycott Road, Chiseldon, Swindon SN4 0LS
T: (01793) 740246

The Royston Hotel ♦♦♦♦
34 Victoria Road, Oldtown, Swindon SN1 3AS
T: (01793) 522990
F: (01793) 522991
E: info@roystonhotel.co.uk
I: www.roystonhotel.co.uk

Swandown Hotel ♦♦
36/37 Victoria Road, Swindon SN1 3AS
T: (01793) 536695
F: (01793) 432551
E: swandownhotel@aol.com
I: www.swandownhotel.co.uk

SYDLING ST NICHOLAS
Dorset

Magiston Farm ♦♦♦
Sydling St Nicholas, Dorchester DT2 9NR
T: (01300) 320295

SYMONDSBURY
Dorset

Quarr Lane farm ♦♦♦♦
Quarr Lane, Symondsbury, Bridport DT6 6AQ
T: (01308) 421477
F: (01308) 421477
E: colette@cmowatt.freeserve.co.uk
I: quarrlanefarm.co.uk

TALATON
Devon

Larkbeare Farmhouse ♦♦♦♦
Talaton, Exeter EX5 2RY
T: (01404) 822069
F: (01404) 823746
E: stay@larkbeare.net
I: www.larkbeare.net

TALSKIDDY
Cornwall

Pennatillie Farm ♦♦♦♦ SILVER AWARD
Talskiddy, St Columb TR9 6EF
T: (01637) 880280
F: (01637) 880280
E: angela@pennatillie.fsnet.co.uk
I: www.cornish-riviera.co.uk/pennatilliefarm.htm

TAUNTON
Somerset

Acorn Lodge ♦♦♦
22 Wellington Road, Taunton TA1 4EQ
T: (01823) 337613

The Black Horse Inn ♦♦
36 Bridge Street, Taunton TA1 1UD
T: (01823) 272151
F: (01823) 272471

Close House ♦♦♦
Hatch Beauchamp, Taunton TA3 6AE
T: (01823) 480424
F: (01823) 480424
E: close.house@talk21.co.uk

Eastcombe Farm Bed & Breakast ♦♦♦
Eastcombe Farm, Bishops Lydeard, Taunton TA4 3HU
T: (01823) 433425

Fursdon House ♦♦
89-90 Greenway Road, Taunton TA2 6LE
T: (01823) 331955

Gatchells ♦♦♦♦
Angersleigh, Taunton TA3 7SY
T: (01823) 421580
E: gatchells@somerweb.co.uk
I: www.somerweb.co.uk/gatchells

Heathercroft ♦♦♦
118 Wellington Road, Taunton TA1 5LA
T: (01823) 275516

Higher Yarde Farmhouse ♦♦♦♦
Staplegrove, Taunton TA2 6SW
T: (01823) 451553
E: anita.hyf@rya-online.net

Lowdens House ♦♦♦
26 Wellington Road, Taunton TA1 4EQ
T: (01823) 334500

Lowtrow Cross Inn ♦♦♦
Upton, Taunton TA4 2DB
T: (01398) 371220
F: (01398) 371452
E: lowtrowcross@aol.com
I: www.lowtrowcross.co.uk

North Down Farm Bed & Breakfast ♦♦♦♦ SILVER AWARD
Wiveliscombe, Taunton TA4 2BL
T: (01984) 623730
F: (01984) 623730
E: jennycope@tiscali.co.uk

Orchard House ♦♦♦♦
Fons George, Middleway, Taunton TA1 3JS
T: (01823) 351783
F: (01823) 351785
E: orch-hse@dircon.co.uk
I: www.smoothhound.co.uk/hotels/orchard2.html

Prockters Farm ♦♦♦
West Monkton, Taunton TA2 8QN
T: (01823) 412269
F: (01823) 412269

Pyrland Farm ♦♦♦♦
Cheddon Road, Taunton TA2 7QX
T: (01823) 334148

Rydon Farm ♦♦♦♦
West Newton, Taunton TA7 0BZ
T: (01278) 663472
F: (01278) 663472
E: rydon@onet.co.uk
I: www.rydonfarm.com

The Spinney ♦♦♦♦
Curland, Taunton TA3 5SE
T: (01460) 234362
F: (01460) 234362
E: bartlett.spinney@zetnet.co.uk
I: www.somerweb.co.uk/spinney-bb

Staplegrove Lodge ♦♦♦♦
Staplegrove, Taunton TA2 6PX
T: (01823) 331153
I: www.staplegrovelodge.co.uk

Thatched Country Cottage and Garden B&B ♦♦♦
Pear Tree Cottage, Stapley, Churchstanton, Taunton TA3 7QA
T: (01823) 601224
F: (01823) 601224
E: colvin.parry@virgin.net
I: www.best-hotel.com/peartreecottage

Yallands Farmhouse
♦♦♦♦ SILVER AWARD
Staplegrove, Taunton TA2 6PZ
T: (01823) 278979
F: (01823) 278983
E: mail@yallands.co.uk
I: www.yallands.co.uk

TAVISTOCK
Devon

Acorn Cottage ♦♦♦♦
Heathfield, Tavistock PL19 0LQ
T: (01822) 810038

April Cottage
♦♦♦♦ SILVER AWARD
Mount Tavy Road, Tavistock PL19 9JB
T: (01822) 613280
F: (01822) 613280

Beera Farmhouse
♦♦♦♦ GOLD AWARD
Milton Abbot, Tavistock PL19 8PL
T: (01822) 870216
F: (01822) 870216
E: hilary.tucker@farming.co.uk
I: www.beera-farm.co.uk

Harrabeer Country House Hotel ♦♦♦♦
Harrowbeer Lane, Yelverton PL20 6EA
T: (01822) 853302
E: reception@harrabeer.co.uk
I: www.harrabeer.co.uk

Mallards ♦♦♦♦
48 Plymouth Road, Tavistock PL19 8BU
T: (01822) 615171
E: mallardstavistock@tinyworld.co.uk
I: www.mallardsoftavistock.co.uk

New Court Farm ♦♦♦
Lamerton, Tavistock PL19 8RR
T: (01822) 614319
E: newcourtfarm@aol.com

Rubbytown Farm
♦♦♦♦ SILVER AWARD
Gulworthy, Tavistock PL19 8PA
T: (01822) 832493

Tor Cottage
♦♦♦♦♦ GOLD AWARD
Chillaton, Lifton PL16 0JE
T: (01822) 860248
F: (01822) 860126
E: info@torcottage.co.uk
I: www.torcottage.co.uk

TEIGNMOUTH
Devon

Belvedere Hotel ♦♦♦
Barn Park Road, Teignmouth TQ14 8PJ
T: (01626) 774561
E: belvedere.hotel@amserve.net

Britannia House B&B
♦♦♦♦♦ SILVER AWARD
26 Teign Street, Teignmouth TQ14 8EG
T: (01626) 770051
F: (01626) 776302
E: gillettbritannia@aol.com
I: www.britanniahouse.org

The Moorings ♦♦♦♦
33 Teignmouth Road, Teignmouth TQ14 8UR
T: (01626) 770400
F: (01626) 770400
E: mickywaters@aol.com

Thomas Luny House
♦♦♦♦♦ GOLD AWARD
Teign Street, Teignmouth TQ14 8EG
T: (01626) 772976
E: alisonandjohn@thomas-luny-house.co.uk
I: www.thomas-luny-house.co.uk

TELLISFORD
Somerset

Farleigh Wood Guest Lodges ♦♦♦♦
Wood Cottage, Tellisford, Bath BA2 7RN
T: (01373) 831495
F: (01373) 830289
E: bella@farleighwood.fsnet.co.uk

THE LIZARD
Cornwall

Trethvas Farmhouse ♦♦♦♦
The Lizard, Helston TR12 7AR
T: (01326) 290720
F: (01326) 290720

THEALE
Somerset

Yew Tree Farm ♦♦♦
Theale, Wedmore BS28 4SN
T: (01934) 712475
F: (01934) 712475
E: enquiries@yewtreefarmbandb.co.uk
I: www.yewtreefarmbandb.co.uk

THORNBURY
Devon

Forda Farm ♦♦♦♦
Thornbury, Holsworthy EX22 7BS
T: (01409) 261369

THORNE
Somerset

Thorne Cottage ♦♦♦♦
Thorne, Yeovil BA21 3PZ
T: (01935) 421735
E: william.grimster@tesco.net

THORNE ST MARGARET
Somerset

Thorne Manor ♦♦♦♦
Thorne St Margaret, Wellington TA21 0EQ
T: (01823) 672264
E: thorne.manor@euphony.net

TIMBERSCOMBE
Somerset

The Dell ♦♦♦
Cowbridge, Timberscombe, Minehead TA24 7TD
T: (01643) 841564
E: hcrawford@dellcow.f9.co.uk
I: www.thedellfarmhouse.co.uk

Knowle Manor and Riding Centre ♦♦♦
Timberscombe, Minehead TA24 6TZ
T: (01643) 841342
F: (01643) 841644
E: knowlemnr@aol.com
I: www.ridingholidaysuk.com

TINHAY
Devon

Tinhay Mill Restaurant ♦♦♦♦
Tinhay, Lifton PL16 0AJ
T: (01566) 784201
F: (01566) 784201

TINTAGEL
Cornwall

9 Atlantic Way ♦♦♦
Atlantic Way, Tintagel PL34 0DF
T: (01840) 770732
F: (01840) 770732

Bosayne Guest House
Rating Applied For
Atlantic Road, Tintagel PL34 0DE
T: (01840) 770514
E: clark@clarky100.freeserve.co.uk
I: www.bosayne.co.uk

Cottage Teashop ♦♦♦♦
Bossiney Road, Tintagel PL34 0AH
T: (01840) 770639
E: cotteashop@talk21.com

Four Winds
Rating Applied For
Knights Close, Tintagel PL34 0DR
T: (01840) 770300
E: kay4windsaccom@aol.com

The Mill House Inn ♦♦♦♦
Trebarwith, Tintagel PL34 0HD
T: (01840) 770200
F: (01840) 770647
E: management@themillhouseinn.co.uk
I: www.themillhouseinn.co.uk

Pendrin House ♦♦♦♦
Atlantic Road, Tintagel PL34 0DE
T: (01840) 770560
F: (01840) 770560
E: pendrin@tesco.co.uk
I: www.pendrinhouse.co.uk

Polkerr Guest House ♦♦♦♦
Trenamett, Tintagel PL34 0BY
T: (01840) 770382
E: polkerr@tiscali.co.uk

Port William Inn ♦♦♦♦
Trebarwith Strand, Tintagel PL34 0HB
T: (01840) 770230
F: (01840) 770936
E: william@eurobell.co.uk

The Trewarmett Inn ♦♦
Trewarmett, Tintagel PL34 0ET
T: (01840) 770460
F: (01840) 779011
E: edwina@trewarmettlodge.co.uk
I: www.trewarmettinn.co.uk

TIVERTON
Devon

Brambles Bed and Breakfast/ Guesthouse
♦♦♦♦ SILVER AWARD
Whitnage Cottage, Whitnage, Tiverton EX16 7DS
T: (01884) 829211
F: (01884) 829211
E: info@bramblesguesthouse.co.uk
I: www.bramblesguesthouse.co.uk

Bridge Guest House ♦♦♦
Angel Hill, Tiverton EX16 6PE
T: (01884) 252804
F: (01884) 252804
I: www.smoothhound.co.uk/hotels/bridgegh.html

Courtyard Bed and Breakfast ♦♦♦♦
19 Fore Street, Bampton, Tiverton EX16 9ND
T: (01398) 331842
E: doreen@stonehengeinn.freeserve.co.uk
I: www.bampton.org.uk

Great Bradley Farm
♦♦♦♦ SILVER AWARD
Withleigh, Tiverton EX16 8JL
T: (01884) 256946
F: (01884) 256946
E: hann@agriplus.net
I: www.SmoothHound.co.uk/hotels/grbard

Lodgehill Farm Hotel ♦♦♦
Ashley, Tiverton EX16 5PA
T: (01884) 251200
F: (01884) 242090
E: checkin@lodgehill.co.uk
I: www.lodgehill.co.uk

Lower Collipriest Farm
♦♦♦♦ SILVER AWARD
Collipriest, Tiverton EX16 4PT
T: (01884) 252321
F: (01884) 252321
E: linda@lowercollipriest.co.uk
I: www.lowercollipriest.co.uk

TOLLER PORCORUM
Dorset

Barrowlands ♦♦♦
Toller Porcorum, Dorchester DT2 0DW
T: (01300) 320281
E: jrdovey@ukgateway.net

Colesmoor Farm ♦♦♦♦
Toller Porcorum, Dorchester DT2 0DU
T: (01300) 320812
F: (01300) 321402
E: rachael@colesmoorfarm.co.uk
I: www.colesmoorfarm.co.uk

Grays Farmhouse ♦♦♦♦
Clift Lane, Toller Porcorum, Dorchester DT2 0EJ
T: (01308) 485574
E: rosie@farmhousebnb.co.uk
I: www.farmhousebnb.co.uk

The Kingcombe Centre ♦♦♦
Lower Kingcombe, Toller Porcorum, Dorchester DT2 0EQ
T: (01300) 320684
F: (01300) 321409
E: nspring@kingcombe-centre.demon.co.uk
I: www.kingcombe-centre.demon.co.uk

TOLPUDDLE
Dorset

Tolpuddle Hall ♦♦♦
Main Road, Tolpuddle,
Dorchester DT2 7EW
T: (01305) 848986
F: (01305) 849318

TOPSHAM
Devon

The Galley Restaurant with Cabins ♦♦♦♦
41 Fore Street, Topsham, Exeter
EX3 0HU
T: (01392) 876078
F: (01392) 876078
E: fish@galleyrestaurant.co.uk
I: www.galleyrestaurant.co.uk

TORCROSS
Devon

Cove Guest House ♦♦♦
Torcross, Kingsbridge TQ7 2TH
T: (01548) 580350
F: (01548) 580350

TORQUAY
Devon

Abbeyfield Hotel ♦♦♦♦
Bridge Road, Torquay TQ2 5AX
T: (01803) 294268
F: (01803) 296310
E: abbeyfieldhotel@amserve.com
I: www.abbeyfield-hotel.co.uk

Abingdon House ♦♦♦♦
104 Avenue Road, Torquay
TQ2 5LF
T: (01803) 201832
E: abingdonhouse@torquay-104.fsnet.co.uk
I: www.abingdonhouse.pwp.blueyonder.co.uk

Acorn Lodge
Rating Applied For
28 Bridge Road, Torquay
TQ2 5BA
T: (01803) 296939
F: (01803) 296939
E: daryal@tiscali.co.uk

Alstone Hotel ♦♦♦
22 Bridge Road, Torquay
TQ2 5BA
T: (01803) 293243
E: alstonehotel@hotmail.com
I: www.english-riviera.co.uk

Arden Court Hotel ♦♦
525 Babbacombe Road, Torquay
TQ1 1HG
T: (01803) 293498
E: info@ardencourthotel.com
I: www.ardencourthotel.com

Ashfield Guest House ♦♦♦
9 Scarborough Road, Torquay
TQ2 5UJ
T: (01803) 293537

Ashleigh House ♦♦♦
61 Meadfoot Lane, Torquay
TQ1 2BP
T: (01803) 294660

Ashurst Lodge Hotel ♦
St Efrides Road, Torquay
TQ2 5SG
T: (01803) 292132

Ashwood Grange Hotel ♦♦♦
18 Newton Road, Torquay
TQ2 5BZ
T: (01803) 212619
F: (01803) 212619
E: stay@ashwoodgrangehotel.co.uk
I: www.ashwoodgrangehotel.co.uk

Avenue Park Guest House ♦♦♦
3 Avenue Road, Torquay
TQ2 5LA
T: (01803) 293902
F: (01803) 293902
E: avenuepark@bushinternet.com
I: www.torbay.gov.uk/tourism/t-hotels/avepark.htm

Avron Hotel ♦♦♦
70 Windsor Road, Ellacombe,
Torquay TQ1 1SZ
T: (01803) 294182
F: (01803) 403112
E: avronhotel@amserve.net
I: www.avronhoteltorquay.co.uk

Bahamas Hotel ♦♦♦
17 Avenue Road, Torquay
TQ2 5LB
T: (01803) 296005
E: bahamashotel@yahoo.co.uk

Banksea Hotel ♦♦♦
51 Avenue Road, Torquay
TQ2 5LG
T: (01803) 213911
F: (01803) 213911
E: rsgreenland@jggames.com
I: bankseahotel.com

The Baytree Hotel ♦♦♦
14 Bridge Road, Torquay
TQ2 5BA
T: (01803) 293718
I: www.thebaytreehotel.co.uk

Beverley House Hotel ♦♦♦♦
9 Clifton Grove, Old Torwood
Road, Torquay TQ1 1PR
T: (01803) 294626
F: (01803) 294648
E: judy.sunnybay@ukgateway.net

Blue Haze Hotel
♦♦♦♦♦ SILVER AWARD
Seaway Lane, Torquay TQ2 6PS
T: (01803) 607186
F: (01803) 607186
E: mail@bluehazehotel.co.uk
I: www.bluehazehotel.co.uk

Braddon Hall Hotel ♦♦♦♦
70 Braddons Hill Road East,
Torquay TQ1 1HF
T: (01803) 293908
E: info@braddonhallhotel.co.uk
I: www.braddonhallhotel.co.uk

Brampton Court Hotel ♦♦♦♦
St Lukes Road South, Torquay
TQ2 5NZ
T: (01803) 294237
F: (01803) 211842
E: stay@bramptoncourt.co.uk
I: www.bramptoncourt.co.uk

Brandize Hotel ♦♦♦
19 Avenue Road, Torquay
TQ2 5LB
T: (01803) 297798
F: (01803) 297798

Brantwood Hotel
Rating Applied For
Rowdens Road, Torquay
TQ2 5AZ
T: (01803) 297241
I: www.brantwoodhotel.com

Brocklehurst Hotel ♦♦♦
Rathmore Road, Torquay
TQ2 6NZ
T: (01803) 292735
F: (01803) 403204
E: enquiries@brocklehursthotel.co.uk
I: www.brocklehursthotel.co.uk

Brooklands Guest House ♦♦♦
Scarborough Road, Torquay
TQ2 5UJ
T: (01803) 296696

Buckingham Lodge ♦♦♦♦
Falkland Road, Torquay TQ2 5JP
T: (01803) 293538
F: (01803) 290343
E: bookingbucklodge@aol.com
I: www.buckinghamlodge.co.uk

Capri Hotel ♦♦♦♦
12 Torbay Road, Torquay
TQ2 6RG
T: (01803) 293158
E: stay@caprihoteltorquay.co.uk

Carlton Court Hotel
Rating Applied For
18 Cleveland Road, Torquay
TQ2 5BE
T: (01803) 297318
F: (01803) 290069
E: carltoncourt@onetel.net.uk
I: www.carlton-court.co.uk

Carysfort Guest House ♦♦♦
13 Warren Road, Torquay
TQ2 5TQ
T: (01803) 294160

Cedar Court Hotel ♦♦♦♦
3 St Matthews Road, Torquay
TQ2 6JA
T: (01803) 607851
F: (01803) 607851
E: enquiries@cedarcourt-hotel.co.uk
I: www.cedarcourt-hotel.co.uk

Charterhouse Hotel ♦♦♦
Cockington Lane, Torquay
TQ2 6QT
T: (01803) 605804
F: (01803) 690741
E: relax@charterhouse-hotel.co.ui
I: www.charterhouse-hotel.co.uk

Chesterfield Hotel ♦♦♦♦
62 Belgrave Road, Torquay
TQ2 5HY
T: (01803) 292318
E: joannefoskett@tinyworld.co.uk
I: www.chesterfieldhoteltorquay.co.uk

Hotel Cimon ♦♦♦
82 Abbey Road, Torquay
TQ2 5NP
T: (01803) 294454
F: (01803) 201988
E: englishbrian434@aol.com

Clevedon Hotel ♦♦♦♦
Meadfoot Sea Road, Torquay
TQ1 2LQ
T: (01803) 294260
E: clevedonhotel@btconnect.com
I: www.smoothhound.co.uk/hotels/clevedon.html

Clovelly Guest House ♦♦♦
91 Avenue Road, Chelston,
Torquay TQ2 5LH
T: (01803) 292286
F: (01803) 242286
E: clovellytorquay@ntlworld.com
I: homepage.ntlworld.com/clovelly.guesthouse

Coombe Court Hotel ♦♦♦♦
67 Babbacombe Downs Road,
Torquay TQ1 3LP
T: (01803) 327097
F: (01803) 327097
E: enquiries@coombecourthotel.co.uk
I: www.coombecourthotel.co.uk

Cranborne Hotel
♦♦♦♦♦ SILVER AWARD
58 Belgrave Road, Torquay
TQ2 5HY
T: (01803) 298046
I: www.cranbornehotel.co.uk

The Cranmore ♦♦♦♦
89 Avenue Road, Torquay
TQ2 5LH
T: (01803) 298488
E: thecranmore@tesco.net
I: www.thecranmore.co.uk

The Crest Hotel ♦♦♦
28-30 Newton Road, Torquay
TQ2 5BZ
T: (01803) 293681
F: (01803) 293681

Crimdon Dene Hotel ♦♦♦
Falkland Road, Torquay TQ2 5JP
T: (01803) 294651
F: (01803) 294651
E: marjohn@crimdondenehotel.co.uk
I: www.crimdondenehotel.co.uk

Crown Lodge ♦♦♦♦
83 Avenue Road, Torquay
TQ2 5LH
T: (01803) 298772
F: (01803) 291155
E: crown.lodge@virgin.net

Crowndale Hotel ♦♦♦♦
18 Bridge Road, Torquay
TQ2 5BA
T: (01803) 293068
F: (01803) 293068
E: info@crowndalehotel.co.uk
I: www.crowndalehotel.co.uk

The Daylesford Hotel ♦♦♦♦
60 Bampfylde Road, Torquay
TQ2 5AY
T: (01803) 294435
F: (01803) 292635
E: info@daylesfordhotel.com
I: www.daylesfordhotel.com

The Downs Hotel ♦♦♦
43 Babbacombe Downs Road,
Babbacombe, Torquay TQ1 3LN
T: (01803) 328543
F: (01803) 328543
E: manager@downshotel.co.uk
I: www.downshotel.co.uk

Ellington Court Hotel ♦♦♦♦
St Lukes Road South, Torquay
TQ2 5NZ
T: (01803) 294957
F: (01803) 201383
E: stay@ellingtoncourthotel.co.uk
I: www.ellingtoncourthotel.co.uk

Fairmount House Hotel
♦♦♦♦ SILVER AWARD
Herbert Road, Chelston, Torquay
TQ2 6RW
T: (01803) 605446
F: (01803) 605446
E: fairmounthouse@aol.com

Fairways ♦♦♦♦
72 Avenue Road, Torquay
TQ2 5LF
T: (01803) 298471
F: (01803) 298471
E: lorraine@hardy116.net.co.uk
I: www.fairwaystorbay.co.uk

Ferndale Hotel
Rating Applied For
22 St Marychurch Road, Torquay
TQ1 3HY
T: (01803) 295311
E: info@ferndalehotel-torquay.co.uk
I: www.ferndalehotel-torquay.co.uk

Fleurie House
♦♦♦♦ SILVER AWARD
50 Bampfylde Road, Torquay
TQ2 5AY
T: (01803) 294869
E: fleurie.house@virgin.net
I: fleuriehouse.co.uk

Gainsboro Hotel ♦♦♦♦
22 Rathmore Road, Torquay
TQ2 6NY
T: (01803) 292032
F: (01803) 292032
E: gainsboro@freeuk.com

The Garlieston Hotel ♦♦♦
Bridge Road, Torquay TQ2 5BA
T: (01803) 294050
E: garliestonhotel@jridewood.fsnet.co.uk

Glendower Hotel ♦♦♦
Falkland Road, Torquay TQ2 5JP
T: (01803) 299988
F: (01803) 403222
E: peter@hoteltorquay.co.uk
I: www.hoteltorquay.co.uk

Glenross Hotel
♦♦♦♦ SILVER AWARD
25 Avenue Road, Torquay
TQ2 5LB
T: (01803) 297517
F: (01803) 297517
E: holiday@glenross-hotel.co.uk
I: www.glenross-hotel.co.uk

Glenroy Hotel ♦♦♦
10 Bampfylde Road, Torquay
TQ2 5AR
T: (01803) 299255
F: (01803) 299255
E: glenroyhotel@aol.com
I: www.glenroy-hotel.co.uk

Grosvenor House Hotel ♦♦♦♦
Falkland Road, Torquay TQ2 5JP
T: (01803) 294110
E: etc@grosvenorhousehotel.co.uk
I: www.grovenorhousehotel.co.uk

The Haven Hotel ♦♦♦♦
Scarborough Road, Torquay
TQ2 5UJ
T: (01803) 293390
E: enquiries@havenhotel.biz
I: www.havenhotel.biz

Heathcliff House Hotel ♦♦♦♦
16 Newton Road, Torquay
TQ2 5BZ
T: (01803) 211580
E: heathcliffhouse@aol.com

The Hotel Newburgh ♦♦
14 Scarborough Road, Torquay
TQ2 5UJ
T: (01803) 293270
E: scorpriov38@btopenworld.com
I: www.the-newburgh-torquay.activehotels.com

Howard Court Hotel ♦♦♦
31 St Efrides Road, Torquay
TQ2 5SG
T: (01803) 295494

Hylton Court Hotel
Rating Applied For
109 Abbey Road, Torquay
TQ2 5NP
T: (01803) 298643
F: (01803) 298643
E: wilson@hyltoncourthotel.co.uk
I: www.hyltoncourthotel.co.uk

Hotel Iona ♦♦♦
5 Cleveland Road, Torquay
TQ2 5BD
T: (01803) 294918
F: (01803) 294918
E: hoteliona@btopenworld.com
I: www.hoteliona

Jesmond Dene Hotel ♦♦♦
85 Abbey Road, Torquay
TQ2 5NN
T: (01803) 293062

Kelvin House Hotel ♦♦♦♦
46 Bampfylde Road, Torquay
TQ2 5AY
T: (01803) 209093
E: kelvinhousehotel@amserve.com

Kings Hotel ♦♦♦♦
44 Bampfylde Road, Torquay
TQ2 5AY
T: (01803) 293108
F: (01803) 201499
E: kingshotel@bigfoot.com
I: www.kingshoteltorquay.co.uk

Kingsholm Hotel ♦♦♦♦
539 Babbacombe Road, Torquay
TQ1 1HQ
T: (01803) 297794
F: (01803) 297791
E: kingsholm.torquay@virgin.net

Kingston House
♦♦♦♦♦ SILVER AWARD
75 Avenue Road, Torquay
TQ2 5LL
T: (01803) 212760
F: (01803) 201425
E: butto@kingstonhousehotel.co.uk

Kingsway Lodge ♦♦♦
95 Avenue Road, Torquay
TQ2 5LH
T: (01803) 295288

Lanscombe House Hotel ♦♦♦
Cockington Village, Torquay
TQ2 6XA
T: (01803) 606938
F: (01803) 607656
E: enquiries@lanscombehouse.co.uk

Lee Hotel ♦♦♦
Torbay Road, Livermead, Torquay
TQ2 6RG
T: (01803) 293946
F: (01803) 293946
E: info@leehotel.co.uk
I: www.leehotel.co.uk

Lindens Hotel
♦♦♦♦ SILVER AWARD
31 Bampfylde Road, Torquay
TQ2 5AY
T: (01803) 212281

Lindum Hotel ♦♦♦♦
105 Abbey Road, Torquay
TQ2 5NP
T: (01803) 292795
F: (01803) 299358
E: lindum@eurobell.co.uk
I: www.lindum-hotel.co.uk

Maple Lodge Guest House
♦♦♦♦
36 Ash Hill Road, Torquay
TQ1 3JD
T: (01803) 297391
E: TheMapleLodge@aol.com
I: www.themaplelodge.co.uk

The Marstan Hotel ♦♦♦♦♦
Meadfoot Sea Road, Torquay
TQ1 2LQ
T: (01803) 292837
F: (01803) 299202
E: enquiries@marstanhotel.co.uk
I: www.marstanhotel.co.uk

Melba House Hotel ♦♦♦
62 Bampfylde Road, Torquay
TQ2 5AY
T: (01803) 213167
F: (01803) 211953

Mount Edgcombe Hotel
♦♦♦♦
23 Avenue Road, Torquay
TQ2 5LB
T: (01803) 292310
F: (01803) 292310

Mount Nessing Hotel ♦♦♦
St Lukes Road North, Torquay
TQ2 5PD
T: (01803) 294259
E: mntnessing@hotmail.com
I: www.english-riviera.co.uk/mount-nessing

Newlyn Hotel ♦♦♦♦
62 Braddons Hill Road East,
Torquay TQ1 1HF
T: (01803) 295100
F: (01803) 380724
E: Barbara@newlyn-hotel.co.uk
I: www.newlyn-hotel.co.uk

Norwood Hotel ♦♦♦♦
60 Belgrave Road, Torquay
TQ2 5HY
T: (01803) 294236
F: (01803) 294224
E: enquiries@norwoodhoteltorquay.co.uk
I: www.norwoodhoteltorquay.co.uk

The Pines ♦♦♦
19 Newton Road, Torre, Torquay
TQ2 5DB
T: (01803) 292882

Richwood Hotel ♦♦♦♦
20 Newton Road, Torquay
TQ2 5BZ
T: (01803) 293729
F: (01803) 213632
E: enq@richwoodhotel.co.uk
I: www.richwood-hotel-torquay.co.uk

Robin Hill International Hotel
♦♦♦♦
74 Braddons Hill Road East,
Torquay TQ1 1HF
T: (01803) 214518
F: (01803) 291410
E: jo@robinhillhotel.co.uk
I: www.robinhillhotel.co.uk

Sandpiper Hotel ♦♦♦♦
Rowdens Road, Torquay
TQ2 5AZ
T: (01803) 292779
E: sandpiper57@home13859.fsnet.co.uk
I: www.sandpiper-hotel.co.uk

Sandpiper Lodge Hotel ♦♦♦
96 Avenue Road, Torquay
TQ2 5LF
T: (01803) 293293

Sandway Hotel
Rating Applied For
72 Belgrave Road, Torquay
TQ2 5HY
T: (01803) 298499
E: sandwayhotel@btopenworld.co.uk

Seapoint Hotel ♦♦♦
Clifton Grove, Old Torwood
Road, Torquay TQ1 1PR
T: (01803) 211808
F: (01803) 211808
E: seapointhotel@hotmail.com
I: www.seapointhotel.co.uk

Shirley Hotel ♦♦♦♦
Braddons Hill Road East,
Torquay TQ1 1HF
T: (01803) 293016
E: shirleyhotel@eurobell.co.uk

Silverlands ♦♦♦
27 Newton Road, Torquay
TQ2 5DB
T: (01803) 292013

Southbank Hotel ♦♦♦♦
Belgrave Road, Torquay
TQ2 5HU
T: (01803) 296701
F: (01803) 292026
E: stay@southbankhotcl.co.uk

Suite Dreams Hotel
♦♦♦♦ SILVER AWARD
Steep Hill, Maidencombe,
Torquay TQ1 4TS
T: (01803) 313900
F: (01803) 313841
E: suitedreams@suitedreams.co.uk
I: www.suitedreams.co.uk

Tor Dean Hotel ♦♦♦
27 Bampfylde Road, Torquay
TQ2 5AY
T: (01803) 294669
E: tordeanhotel@aol.com
I: www.tordeanhotel.com

Tor Park Hotel ♦♦♦
24 Vansittart Road, Torquay
TQ2 5BW
T: (01803) 295151
F: (01803) 200584
I: www.shearingsholidays.com

Torbay Hotel ♦♦♦♦
Torbay Road, Torquay TQ2 5EY
T: (01803) 295218
F: (01803) 291127
I: www.shearingsholidays.com

Torbay Star Guest House ♦♦♦♦
73 Avenue Road, Torquay
TQ2 5LL
T: (01803) 293998
F: (01803) 293998

Trafalgar House Hotel ♦♦♦
30 Bridge Road, Torquay
TQ2 5BA
T: (01803) 292486
E: info@torquayhotelsuk.com
I: www.torquayhotelsuk.com

Tree Tops Hotel ♦♦♦
St Albans Road, Torquay
TQ1 3NP
T: (01803) 325135

Trelawney Hotel ♦♦♦
48 Belgrave Road, Torquay
TQ2 5HS
T: (01803) 296049
F: (01803) 296049
E: trelawneyhotel@hotmail.com
I: www.trelawneyhotel.net

Trouville Hotel ♦♦♦
70 Belgrave Road, Torquay
TQ2 5HY
T: (01803) 294979
E: ginagary@bvtrust.freeserve.co.uk

Villa Marina ♦♦♦♦
Tor Park Road, Torquay TQ2 5BQ
T: (01803) 292187

Villa Oasis Guest House ♦♦♦
21 Newton Road, Torquay
TQ2 5DB
T: (01803) 297404
E: info@villa-oasis.co.uk
I: www.villa-oasis.co.uk

The Wayland Hotel & Belgravia Self-Catering Holiday Suites ♦♦♦
Belgrave Road, Torquay TQ2 5HX
T: (01803) 293417
F: (01803) 291911
I: www.waylandhotel.co.uk

West Bank Hotel ♦♦♦♦
54 Bampfylde Road, Torquay
TQ2 5AY
T: (01803) 295271

Westbourne Hotel ♦♦♦♦
106 Avenue Road, Torquay
TQ2 5LQ
T: (01803) 292927
F: (01803) 292927

Whitburn Guest House ♦♦♦
St Lukes Road North, Torquay
TQ2 5PD
T: (01803) 296719
E: joe@lazenby15.freeserve.co.uk

Wilsbrook Guest House ♦♦♦
77 Avenue Road, Torquay
TQ2 5LL
T: (01803) 298413
E: wilsbrook@amserve.net
I: www.wilsbrook.freeserve.co.uk

TORRINGTON
Devon

Beaford House Hotel ♦♦♦♦
Beaford, Winkleigh EX19 8AB
T: (01805) 603305
F: (01805) 603305
E: katie_squire@hotmail.com
I: www.beafordhousehotel.co.uk

Cavalier Inn ♦♦
Well Street, Torrington EX38 8EP
T: (01805) 623832

Locksbeam Farm ♦♦♦♦ SILVER AWARD
Torrington EX38 7EZ
T: (01805) 623213
F: (01805) 623213
I: www.tarka-country.co.uk/locksbeamfarm

West of England Inn ♦♦♦
18 South Street, Torrington
EX38 8AA
T: (01805) 624949

TOTNES
Devon

Buckyette Farm ♦♦♦
Buckyette, Totnes TQ9 6ND
T: (01803) 762638
F: (01803) 762638

The Elbow Room ♦♦♦♦♦ SILVER AWARD
North Street, Totnes TQ9 5NZ
T: (01803) 863480
E: elbowroomtotnes@AOL.COM

Four Seasons Guest House ♦♦♦♦
13 Bridgetown, Totnes TQ9 5AB
T: (01803) 862146
F: (01803) 867779
E: fourseasonsdevon@btopenworld.com
I: www.fourseasonsdevon.com

Great Court Farm ♦♦♦♦ SILVER AWARD
Berry Pomeroy, Totnes TQ9 6LB
T: (01803) 862326
F: (01803) 862326

Higher Torr Farm
Rating Applied For
East Allington, Totnes TQ9 7QH
T: (01548) 521248
F: (01548) 521248
E: richard@hrtorr.freeserve.co.uk

Old Follaton ♦♦♦♦♦ SILVER AWARD
Plymouth Road, Totnes TQ9 5NA
T: (01803) 865441
F: (01803) 863597
E: bandb@oldfollaton.co.uk
I: www.oldfollaton.co.uk

The Old Forge at Totnes ♦♦♦♦ SILVER AWARD
Seymour Place, Totnes TQ9 5AY
T: (01803) 862174
F: (01803) 865385
E: enq@oldforgetotnes.com
I: www.oldforgetotnes.com

Steam Packet Inn ♦♦♦♦
4 St Peters Quay, Totnes
TQ9 5EW
T: (01803) 863880
F: (01803) 862754
E: esther@thesteampacketinn.co.uk
I: www.thesteampacketinn-totnes.co.uk

TREATOR
Cornwall

Woodlands Close ♦♦♦
Treator, Padstow PL28 8RU
T: (01841) 533109
E: john@stock65.freeserve.co.uk
I: www.cornwall-online.co.uk/woodlands-close

Woodlands Country House ♦♦♦♦
Treator, Padstow PL28 8RU
T: (01841) 532426
F: (01841) 533353
E: woodlandsbandb@hotmail.com
I: www.padstow.uk.com/woodlands

TREBETHERICK
Cornwall

Daymer House ♦♦♦♦♦
Daymer Bay, Trebetherick,
Wadebridge PL27 6SA
T: (01208) 862639
F: (01208) 813781

Elm Cottage ♦♦♦
Trebetherick, Wadebridge
PL27 6SB
T: (01208) 863805
E: h.thwaites@euphony.net

TREGONY
Cornwall

Tregonan ♦♦♦♦
Tregony, Truro TR2 5SN
T: (01872) 530249
F: (01872) 530249
E: tregonan@fwi.co.uk

TREGREHAN MILLS
Cornwall

Wisteria Lodge Guest House ♦♦♦♦ SILVER AWARD
Boscundle, Tregrehan Mills, St Austell PL25 3RJ
T: (01726) 810800
E: sally@wisteria-lodge.co.uk
I: www.wisteria-lodge.co.uk

TREHUNIST
Cornwall

North Trewint
Rating Applied For
Menheniot, Liskeard PL14 3RE
T: (01579) 344313
F: (01579) 344313
E: nrlthom@aol.com

TRELIGHTS
Cornwall

Long Cross Hotel and Victorian Garden ♦♦♦
Trelights, Port Isaac PL29 3TF
T: (01208) 880243
F: (01208) 880560

TRELILL
Cornwall

Trelulla ♦♦♦
Trelill, Bodmin PL30 3HT
T: (01208) 850938
E: eileenroberts@trellula.freeserve.co.uk
I: www.trelulla.biz

TREMAINE
Cornwall

Tremaine Chapel ♦♦♦
Tremaine, Launceston PL15 8SA
T: (01566) 781590

TRENANCE
Cornwall

Merrymoor Inn
Rating Applied For
Mawgan Porth, Newquay
TR8 4BA
T: (01637) 860258
F: (01637) 860258
E: info@merrymoorinn.com
I: www.merrymoorinn.com

TRESILLIAN
Cornwall

Polsue Manor Farm ♦♦♦
Tresillian, Truro TR2 4BP
T: (01872) 520234
F: (01872) 520616
E: geraldineholliday@hotmail.com

TREVALGA
Cornwall

Trehane Farm ♦♦♦
Trevalga, Boscastle PL35 0EB
T: (01840) 250510

TREWARMETT
Cornwall

Melrosa ♦♦♦♦
Trewarmett, Tintagel PL34 0ES
T: (01840) 770360
E: valerie.stephens@btinternet.com

TROWBRIDGE
Wiltshire

Herons Knoll ♦♦
18 Middle Lane, Trowbridge
BA14 7LG
T: (01225) 752593
F: (01225) 752593

Lion and Fiddle ♦♦♦
Devizes Road, Hilperton,
Trowbridge BA14 7QS
T: (01225) 776392
F: (01225) 774501

Old Manor Hotel ♦♦♦♦♦
Trowle, Bradford-on-Avon
BA14 9BL
T: (01225) 777393
F: (01225) 765443
E: oldbeams@oldmanorhotel.com
I: www.oldmanorhotel.com

62b Paxcroft Cottages ♦♦♦♦
Devizes Road, Paxcroft,
Hilperton, Trowbridge BA14 6JB
T: (01225) 765838
E: paxcroftcottages@hotmail.com

Sue's B & B ♦♦♦
25 Blair Road, Trowbridge
BA14 9JZ
T: (01225) 764559
E: sue_b_n_b@yahoo.com
I: www.visitbritain.com

Welam House ♦♦♦
Bratton Road, West Ashton,
Trowbridge BA14 6AZ
T: (01225) 755908

TRUDOXHILL
Somerset

Lilac Cottage ♦♦♦
Foghamshire Lane, Trudoxhill,
Frome BA11 5DG
T: (01373) 836222
F: (01373) 836222
E: paul@pwacey.freeserve.co.uk

TRULL
Somerset

The Winchester Arms ♦♦♦
Church Road, Trull, Taunton
TA3 7LG
T: (01823) 284723
F: (01823) 284723

TRURO
Cornwall

Bissick Old Mill
♦♦♦♦♦ SILVER AWARD
Ladock, Truro TR2 4PG
T: (01726) 882557
F: (01726) 884057
E: sonia.v@bissickoldmill.ndo.co.uk

Great Hewas Farm ♦♦♦
Grampound Road, Truro TR2 4EP
T: (01726) 882218
F: (01726) 882218

Gwel-Tek-Lodge ♦♦
Treyew Road, Truro TR1 2BY
T: (01872) 276843

Nansavallan Farm ♦♦♦
Killiow, Truro TR3 6AD
T: (01872) 272350
F: (01872) 272350

Trevispian-Vean Farm Guest House ♦♦♦♦
St Erme, Truro TR4 9AT
T: (01872) 279514
F: (01872) 263730
I: www.guesthousestruro.com

TUNLEY
Somerset

King William IV Inn ♦♦♦
Bath Road, Tunley, Bath
BA2 0EB
T: (01761) 470408
F: (01761) 470408
E: welcome@kingwilliaminn.co.uk
I: www.kingwilliaminn.co.uk

UPAVON
Wiltshire

The Manor ♦♦♦♦
Andover Road, Upavon, Pewsey
SN9 6EB
T: (01980) 635115
E: isabelbgreen@hotmail.com

UPLODERS
Dorset

Uploders Farm ♦♦♦
Dorchester Road, Uploders,
Bridport DT6 4NZ
T: (01308) 423380

UPLYME
Devon

Elton ♦♦♦♦
Lyme Road, Uplyme, Lyme Regis
DT7 3TH
T: (01297) 445986
E: mikecawte@aol.com

Hill Barn
♦♦♦♦ SILVER AWARD
Gore Lane, Uplyme, Lyme Regis
DT7 3RJ
T: (01297) 445185
F: (01297) 445185
E: jwb@lymeregis-accommodation.com
I: www.lymeregis-accommodation.com

UPOTTERY
Devon

Robins Cottage
♦♦♦♦ SILVER AWARD
Upottery, Honiton EX14 9PL
T: (01404) 861281

UPPER CASTLE COMBE
Wiltshire

Palm Cottage ♦♦♦
Upper Castle Combe,
Chippenham SN14 7HD
T: (01249) 782706
F: (01249) 783003
E: palm-cottage@castle-combe.com
I: www.palm-cottage@castle-combe.com

UPTON
Cornwall

The Chough Hotel ♦♦♦♦
Marine Drive, Upton, Bude
EX23 0LZ
T: (01288) 352386
F: (01288) 352386
E: Jinkschoughhotel@aol.com
I: www.thechoughhotel.activehotels.com

Upton Cross ♦♦♦
Upton, Bude EX23 0LY
T: (01288) 355310

Upton Lodge
♦♦♦♦♦ SILVER AWARD
Upton, Bude EX23 0LY
T: (01288) 354126
E: edwardwhitehouse@onetel.net.uk

UPTON LOVELL
Wiltshire

Prince Leopold ♦♦♦
Upton Lovell, Warminster
BA12 0JP
T: (01985) 850460
F: (01985) 850737
E: princeleopold@lineone.net
I: www.princeleopoldinn.co.uk

UPTON NOBLE
Somerset

Kingston House
♦♦♦♦ SILVER AWARD
Upton Noble, Shepton Mallet
BA4 6BA
T: (01749) 850805
F: (01749) 850806
E: timrstroude@onetel.net.uk

VERYAN
Cornwall

Treverbyn House ♦♦♦♦
Pendower Road, Veryan, Truro
TR2 5QL
T: (01872) 501201
E: holiday@treverbyn.fsbusiness.co.uk
I: www.cornwall-online.co.uk/treverbyn

WADEBRIDGE
Cornwall

Brookfields B & B
♦♦♦♦ SILVER AWARD
Hendra Lane, St Kew Highway,
Wadebridge PL30 3EQ
T: (01208) 841698
F: (01208) 841174
E: robbie.caswell@btinternet.com
I: www.brookfields-stkew.co.uk

Gwynarth ♦♦♦
Gonvena Hill, Wadebridge
PL27 6DH
T: (01208) 813137
F: (01208) 813947
E: felicity@hawkey-wadebridge-fsnet.co.uk

Higher Bodieve Bed and Breakfast ♦♦♦
Higher Bodieve Farm, Nichols
Lane, Wadebridge PL27 6EG
T: (01208) 816443

Monte Gordo ♦♦♦
Tregonce Farm, St Issey,
Wadebridge PL27 7QJ
T: (01208) 812082

The Mowhay ♦♦♦♦
Bodieve, Wadebridge PL27 6EG
T: (01208) 814078

Riverside ♦♦♦
10 Eglos Hayle Road,
Wadebridge PL27 6AD
T: (01208) 816054
E: pdff@btopenworld.com

Spring Gardens ♦♦♦
Bradford Quay Road,
Wadebridge PL27 6DB
T: (01208) 813771
F: (01208) 813771
E: jijen@aol.com

Tor View ♦♦♦
Whitecross, Wadebridge
PL27 7JD
T: (01208) 812261

Tregolls Farm ♦♦♦♦
St Wenn, Bodmin PL30 5PG
T: (01208) 812154
F: (01208) 812154
E: tregollsfarm@btclick.com
I: www.tregollsfarm.co.uk

33 Westerlands Road ♦♦♦
Wadebridge PL27 7EU
T: (01208) 813408

1 Whiterock Terrace
Rating Applied For
Wadebridge PL27 7EG
T: (01208) 816722

WAMBROOK
Somerset

Woodview ♦♦♦
Wambrook, Chard TA20 3EH
T: (01460) 65368
F: (01460) 65368

WARMINSTER
Wiltshire

Bugley Barton
♦♦♦♦♦ SILVER AWARD
Victoria Road, Warminster
BA12 8HD
T: (01985) 213389
F: (01985) 300450
E: bugleybarton@aol.com

Sturford Mead Farm ♦♦♦♦
Corsley, Warminster BA12 7QU
T: (01373) 832213
F: (01373) 832213
E: lynn_sturford.bed@virgin.net

WARMLEY
Gloucestershire

Ferndale Guest House ♦♦♦
37 Deanery Road, Kingswood,
Warmley, Bristol BS15 9JB
T: (0117) 985 8247
F: (0117) 904 4855
E: alexandmikewake@yahoo.co.uk

WASHFORD
Somerset

Green Bay ♦♦♦
Washford, Watchet TA23 0NN
T: (01984) 640303
E: greenbay@tinyonline.co.uk

WATCHET
Somerset

Esplanade House ♦♦♦♦
The Esplanade, Watchet
TA23 0AJ
T: (01984) 633444

WATERGATE BAY
Cornwall

The White House ♦♦♦♦
Tregurrian, Watergate Bay,
Newquay TR8 4AD
T: (01637) 860119
F: (01637) 860449
E: jenny.vallance@virgin.net
I: www.cornwallwhitehouse.co.uk

WATERROW
Somerset

Handley Farm Accommodation
♦♦♦♦ GOLD AWARD
Waterrow, Taunton TA4 2BE
T: (01398) 361516
F: (01398) 361516
E: leigh-firbank.george@ntlworld.com
I: www.handleyfarm.co.uk

WEDMORE
Somerset

Cricklake Farm ♦♦♦
Cocklake, Wedmore BS28 4HH
T: (01934) 712736
E: cricklake.farm@tiscali.co.uk

WELLINGTON
Somerset

Backways Farmhouse ♦♦♦♦
Wellington TA21 9RN
T: (01823) 660712
E: info@backways.co.uk

WELLS
Somerset

Bay Tree House ♦♦♦♦
85 Portway, Wells BA5 2BJ
T: (01749) 677933
F: (01749) 678322
E: baytree.house@ukonline.co.uk
I: www.baytree-house.co.uk

Beryl ♦♦♦♦♦
Off Hawkers Lane, Wells BA5 3JP
T: (01749) 678738
F: (01749) 670508
E: stay@beryl.co.uk
I: www.beryl-wells.co.uk

Burcott Mill Historic Watermill and Guesthouse ♦♦♦
Wookey Road, Wookey, Wells
BA5 1NJ
T: (01749) 673118
F: (01749) 677376
E: theburts@burcottmill.com
I: www.burcottmill.com

Cadgwith ♦♦♦♦
Hawkers Lane, Wells BA5 3JH
T: (01749) 677799
E: rplettscadgwith@aol.com

Canon Grange ♦♦♦♦
Cathedral Green, Wells BA5 2UB
T: (01749) 671800
E: canongrange@email.com
I: www.canongrange.co.uk

Carmen B & B
♦♦♦♦ SILVER AWARD
Bath Road, Wells BA5 3LQ
T: (01749) 677331
E: linda@carmenbandb.fsnet.co.uk

Franklyns Farm ♦♦♦
Chewton Mendip, Bath BA3 4NB
T: (01761) 241372

Glencot House
♦♦♦♦♦ GOLD AWARD
Glencot Lane, Wookey Hole, Wells BA5 1BH
T: (01749) 677160
F: (01749) 670210
E: relax@glencothouse.co.uk
I: www.glencothouse.co.uk

Littlewell Farm Guest House ♦♦♦♦
Coxley, Wells BA5 1QP
T: (01749) 677914

30 Mary Road ♦♦♦
Mary Road, Wells BA5 2NF
T: (01749) 674031
F: (01749) 674031
E: triciabailey30@hotmail.com

The Old Stores ♦♦♦♦
Westbury sub Mendip, Westbury-sub-Mendip, Wells BA5 1HA
T: (01749) 870817
F: (01749) 870980
E: moglin980@aol.com

The Pound Inn ♦♦♦
Burcott Lane, Coxley, Wells BA5 1QZ
T: (01749) 672785
E: poundinnwells@aol.com

Southway Farm ♦♦♦♦
Polsham, Wells BA5 1RW
T: (01749) 673396
F: (01749) 670373
E: southwayfarm@ukonline.co.uk
I: www.southwayfarm.co.uk

Worth House Hotel ♦♦♦
Worth, Wookey, Wells BA5 1LW
T: (01749) 672041
F: (01749) 672041
E: mblomeley2001@yahoo.co.uk

WEMBURY
Devon

Bay Cottage ♦♦♦
150 Church Road, Wembury, Plymouth PL9 0HR
T: (01752) 862559
F: (01752) 862559
E: thefairies@aol.com
I: www.bay-cottage.com

WEMBWORTHY
Devon

Lymington Arms ♦♦♦♦
Lama Cross, Wembworthy, Chulmleigh EX18 7SA
T: (01837) 83572
F: (01837) 680074
E: tonypeel@dialFSB.com.uk

WEST ANSTEY
Devon

Greenhills Farm
Rating Applied For
West Anstey, South Molton EX36 3NU
T: (01398) 341300

WEST BAY
Dorset

The George Hotel ♦♦♦
West Bay, Bridport DT6 4EY
T: (01308) 423191

Heatherbell Cottage ♦♦♦
Hill Close, West Bay, Bridport DT6 4HW
T: (01308) 422998
E: heatherbell4bnb@onetel.net.uk

WEST BUCKLAND
Somerset

Causeway Cottage ♦♦♦♦
West Buckland, Wellington TA21 9JZ
T: (01823) 663458
F: (01823) 663458
E: orrs@westbuckland.freeserve.co.uk
I: www.comestaywithus.com/england-hotels/causewaycottage.html

WEST COKER
Somerset

Millbrook House ♦♦♦♦
High Street, West Coker, Yeovil BA22 9AU
T: (01935) 862840
F: (01935) 863846

WEST DOWN
Devon

The Long House ♦♦♦♦
The Square, West Down, Ilfracombe EX34 8NF
T: (01271) 863242

WEST HUNTSPILL
Somerset

Greenwood Lodge ♦♦♦♦
76 Main Road, West Huntspill, Highbridge TA9 3QU
T: (01278) 795886
F: (01278) 795886
I: www.greenwoodlodgehotel.com

Ilex House ♦♦♦♦
102 Main Road, West Huntspill, Highbridge TA9 3QZ
T: (01278) 783801
F: (01278) 794254
E: rogwyn@onetel.net.uk

WEST KNIGHTON
Dorset

Church Cottage
♦♦♦♦ SILVER AWARD
West Knighton, Dorchester DT2 8PF
T: (01305) 852243
E: info@church-cottage.com
I: www.church-cottage.com

WEST MONKTON
Somerset

Springfield House ♦♦♦♦
Walford Cross, West Monkton, Taunton TA2 8QW
T: (01823) 412116
E: tina.ridout@btopenworld.com
I: www.springfieldhse.co.uk

WEST OVERTON
Wiltshire

Cairncot ♦♦♦
West Overton, Marlborough SN8 4ER
T: (01672) 861617

WEST PENNARD
Somerset

The Lion At Pennard ♦♦♦
Glastonbury Road, West Pennard, Glastonbury BA6 8NH
T: (01458) 832941
F: (01458) 830660
E: thelion@pennard.fsbusiness.co.uk
I: thelionatpennard.com

Page Cottage
♦♦♦♦ SILVER AWARD
Newtown, West Pennard, Glastonbury BA6 8NN
T: (01458) 833651

WEST PORLOCK
Somerset

West Porlock House ♦♦♦♦
West Porlock, Minehead TA24 8NX
T: (01643) 862880

WEST STAFFORD
Dorset

Keepers Cottage ♦♦♦♦
West Stafford, Dorchester DT2 8AA
T: (01305) 264389
F: (01305) 264389
E: keeperscottage@tinyworld.co.uk
I: www.keeperscottage.net

WESTBURY
Wiltshire

Black Dog Farm ♦♦♦
Chapmanslade, Westbury BA13 4AE
T: (01373) 832858

Sherbourne House ♦♦♦
Station Road, Westbury BA13 3JW
T: (01373) 864865

WESTHAY
Somerset

New House Farm
♦♦♦♦ SILVER AWARD
Shapwick Road, Westhay, Glastonbury BA6 9TT
T: (01458) 860238
F: (01458) 860568
E: newhousefarm@farmersweekly.net

WESTON
Devon

Higher Weston Farm ♦♦♦♦
Weston, Honiton EX10 0PH
T: (01395) 513741

WESTON-SUPER-MARE
Somerset

Algarve Guest House ♦♦♦
24 Quantock Road, Weston-super-Mare BS23 4DT
T: (01934) 626128
E: brian@b.pyle.fsnet.co.uk

Ashcombe Court ♦♦♦♦
Milton Road, Weston-super-Mare BS23 2SH
T: (01934) 625104
F: (01934) 625104
E: ashcombecourt@tinyonline.co.uk

Braeside Hotel ♦♦♦♦
2 Victoria Park, Weston-super-Mare BS23 2HZ
T: (01934) 626642
F: (01934) 626642
E: braeside@tesco.net
I: www.braesidehotel.co.uk

Cornerways ♦♦♦
14 Whitecross Road, Weston-super-Mare BS23 1EW
T: (01934) 623708
E: cornerwaysgh@aol.com

The Grand Atlantic ♦♦♦♦
Beach Road, Weston-super-Mare BS23 1BA
T: (01934) 626543
F: (01934) 415048
I: www.shearingsholidays.com

Highlea Hotel ♦♦♦
15 Upper Church Road, Weston-super-Mare BS23 2DX
T: (01934) 621859
F: (01934) 615511
E: paula@highlea-hotel.co.uk
I: www.highlea-hotel.co.uk

Moorlands Country Guesthouse ♦♦♦
Hutton, Weston-super-Mare BS24 9QH
T: (01934) 812283
F: (01934) 812283
E: margaret_holt@email.com
I: www.guestaccom.co.uk/35.htm

Orchard House
♦♦♦♦ SILVER AWARD
West Wick, Weston-super-Mare BS24 7TF
T: (01934) 520948
F: (01934) 520948

Richmond Hotel ♦♦♦
14 Park Place, Weston-super-Mare BS23 2BA
T: (01934) 644722
F: (01934) 644722
E: richmondsomerset@aol.com

Saxonia ♦♦♦
95 Locking Road, Weston-super-Mare BS23 3EW
T: (01934) 633856
F: (01934) 623141
E: saxonia@lineone.net
I: www.smoothhound.co.uk/hotels/saxonia.html

Spreyton Guest House ♦♦♦
72 Locking Road, Weston-super-Mare BS23 3EN
T: (01934) 416887
F: (01934) 416887
E: info@spreytonguesthouse.fsnet.co.uk
I: www.somersetcoast.com

Welbeck Hotel ♦♦♦
Knightstone Road, Marine Parade, Weston-super-Mare BS23 2BB
T: (01934) 621258
F: (01934) 643585
E: info@weston-welbeck.co.uk
I: www.weston-welbeck.co.uk

WESTONZOYLAND
Somerset

Staddlestones Guest House
♦♦♦♦♦ SILVER AWARD
3 Standards Road, Westonzoyland, Bridgwater TA7 0EL
T: (01278) 691179
F: (01278) 691333
E: staddlestones@euphony.net
I: www.staddlestonesguesthouse.co.uk

WESTROP
Wiltshire

Park Farm Barn ♦♦♦♦
Westrop, Corsham SN13 9QF
T: (01249) 715911
F: (01249) 715911

WESTWARD HO!
Devon

Brockenhurst ♦♦♦
11 Atlantic Way, Westward Ho!, Bideford EX39 1HX
T: (01237) 423346
F: (01237) 423346
E: snowball@brockenhurst1.freeserve.co.uk

WEYMOUTH
Dorset

Aaran House ♦♦♦
2 The Esplanade, Weymouth DT4 8EA
T: (01305) 766669

The Bay Guest House ♦♦♦♦
10 Waterloo Place, Weymouth DT4 7PE
T: (01305) 786289

Bay View Hotel ♦♦♦♦
35 The Esplanade, Weymouth DT4 8DH
T: (01305) 782083
F: (01305) 782083

Beach Guest House ♦♦♦
34 Lennox Street, Weymouth DT4 7HD
T: (01305) 779212

Beachview Guest House ♦♦♦
3 The Esplanade, Weymouth DT4 8EA
T: (01305) 786528
E: rmalees@beachview-hotel.fsbusiness.co.uk
I: www.beachview-hotel.co.uk

Beaufort Hotel ♦♦
24 The Esplanade, Weymouth DT4 8DN
T: (01305) 782088
F: (01305) 782088

Berolina Hotel ♦♦♦
Weymouth DT4 8DN
T: (01305) 787573

Bridge House
Rating Applied For
13 Frys Close, Portesham, Weymouth DT3 4LQ
T: (01305) 871685
F: (01305) 871620
E: thea@warwick17.freeserve.co.uk
I: www.bridgehousebandb.co.uk

Brierley Guest House
Rating Applied For
6 Lennox Street, Weymouth DT4 7HD
T: (01305) 782050

Brunswick Guest House ♦♦♦
9 Brunswick Terrace, Weymouth DT4 7RW
T: (01305) 785408
F: (01305) 785408

Cavendale Hotel ♦♦♦
The Esplanade, Weymouth DT4 8EB
T: (01305) 786960
F: (01305) 786960
E: stay@cavendale.co.uk

The Chandlers Hotel ♦♦♦♦
Westerhall Road, Weymouth DT4 7SZ
T: (01305) 771341
F: (01305) 830122
E: debbiesare@chandlershotel.com
I: www.handlershotel.com

The Channel Hotel ♦♦♦
93 The Esplanade, Weymouth DT4 7AY
T: (01305) 785405
F: (01305) 785405
E: lee@thechannel.freeserve.co.uk
I: www.channelhotel.co.uk

The Chatsworth ♦♦♦♦
14 The Esplanade, Weymouth DT4 8EB
T: (01305) 785012
F: (01305) 766342
E: david@thechatsworth.co.uk
I: www.thechatsworth.co.uk

Crofton Guest House ♦♦♦
36 Lennox Street, Weymouth DT4 7HD
T: (01305) 785903
F: (01305) 750165
E: stevemerrill1@excite.com

Cumberland Hotel ♦♦♦♦
95 The Esplanade, Weymouth DT4 7BA
T: (01305) 785644
F: (01305) 785644
I: www.cumberlandhotelweymouth.co.uk

Double Three ♦♦♦♦
Rodwell Road, Weymouth DT4 8QP
T: (01305) 786259
E: doublethree16762@aol.com
I: www.doubethree.co.uk

Eastney ♦♦♦♦
15 Longfield Road, Weymouth DT4 8RQ
T: (01305) 771682
E: eastneyhotel@aol.com
I: www.eastneyhotel.co.uk

Elwell Manor Guest House ♦♦♦♦
70 Rodwell Road, Weymouth DT4 8QU
T: (01305) 782434
F: (01305) 782434
E: burville@ntlworld.com
I: www.weymouthbedandbreakfast.com

Fairlie House ♦♦♦
13 Holland Road, Weymouth DT4 0AL
T: (01305) 783951

Flintstones Guest House ♦♦♦
10 Carlton Road South, Weymouth DT4 7PJ
T: (01305) 784153

Florian Guest House ♦♦♦
59 Abbotsbury Road, Weymouth DT4 0AQ
T: (01305) 773836
E: clare@florian-guesthouse.co.uk
I: www.florian-guesthouse.co.uk

Fosters Guest House ♦♦♦
3 Lennox Street, Weymouth DT4 7HB
T: (01305) 771685

The Freshford Hotel ♦♦♦
3 Grange Road, Weymouth DT4 7PQ
T: (01305) 775862
F: (01305) 775862
E: info@freshfordhotel.co.uk
I: freshfordhotel.co.uk

Gleneagles of Weymouth ♦♦♦
8 Lennox Street, Weymouth DT4 7HD
T: (01305) 771238
E: gleneagles1@aol.com
I: www.gleneaglesofweymouth.com

Glenthorne ♦♦♦♦
15 Old Castle Road, Weymouth DT4 8QB
T: (01305) 777281
E: info@glenthorne-holidays.co.uk
I: www.glenthorne-holidays.co.uk

Gloucester House ♦♦♦
96 The Esplanade, Weymouth DT4 7AT
T: (01305) 785191
F: (01305) 785191
E: gloucesterwey@aol.com
I: www.gloucesterhouseweymouth.co.uk

Golden Bay Hotel ♦♦
54-55 Esplanade, Weymouth DT4 8DG
T: (01305) 760868

Green Gables ♦♦♦♦
14 Carlton Road South, Weymouth DT4 7PJ
T: (01305) 774808
E: greengables@w-a-g.co.uk
I: www.w-a-g.co.uk/greengables

Harbour Lights ♦♦♦
20 Buxton Road, Weymouth DT4 9PJ
T: (01305) 783273
F: (01305) 783273
E: harbourlights@btconnect.com

Harbour Walk Guest House ♦♦♦
94 Rodwell Avenue, Weymouth DT4 8SQ
T: (01305) 770410
F: (01305) 770410
E: reservations@harbourwalk.co.uk
I: www.harbourwalk.co.uk

Harlequin House Guest House ♦♦♦♦
9 Carlton Road South, Weymouth DT4 7PL
T: (01305) 785598

Hazeldene Guest House ♦♦
16 Abbotsbury Road, Weymouth DT4 0AE
T: (01305) 782579
F: (01305) 761022

Heathwick House
♦♦♦♦♦ SILVER AWARD
Chickerell, Weymouth DT3 4EA
T: (01305) 777272
E: enquiries@heathwickhouse.com
I: www.heathwickhouse.com

Horizon Guest House ♦♦♦
16 Brunswick Terrace, Weymouth DT4 7RW
T: (01305) 784916
E: info@horizonguesthouse.co.uk
I: www.horizonguesthouse.co.uk

Kenora Private Hotel ♦♦♦♦
5 Stavordale Road, Weymouth DT4 0AB
T: (01305) 771215
E: kenora.hotel@wdi.co.uk
I: www.kenorahotel.co.uk

Kimberley Guest House ♦♦♦
16 Kirtleton Avenue, Weymouth DT4 7PT
T: (01305) 783333
F: (01305) 839603
E: kenneth.jones@btconnect.com

The Kingsley Hotel ♦♦♦♦
10 Kirtleton Avenue, Weymouth DT4 7PT
T: (01305) 777888

Hotel Kinley ♦♦♦
98 The Esplanade, Weymouth DT4 7AT
T: (01305) 782264
E: hotelkinley@hotmail.com

Langham Hotel ♦♦♦
The Esplanade, Weymouth DT4 7EX
T: (01305) 782530

The Lantana ♦♦♦
13 The Esplanade, Weymouth DT4 8EB
T: (01305) 784651
F: (01305) 780092
E: lantana@dgeorge.freeserve.co.uk
I: www.lantanaweymouth.col.uk

Lichfield House Hotel ♦♦♦
8 Brunswick Terrace, Weymouth DT4 7RW
T: (01305) 784112
F: (01305) 784112
E: lich.house@virgin.net
I: www.lichfieldhouse.co.uk

Lilac Villa Guest House ♦♦♦
Dorchester Road, Weymouth DT4 7LG
T: (01305) 782670
F: (01305) 782670
E: lilacvilla@lineone.net

Mar June Guest House ♦♦♦
32 Lennox Street, Weymouth DT4 7HD
T: (01305) 761320

Marina Court Hotel ♦♦♦
142 The Esplanade, Weymouth DT4 7PB
T: (01305) 782146
F: (01305) 782146

Mayfair Hotel ♦♦♦
The Esplanade, Weymouth DT4 7BE
T: (01305) 782094
F: (01305) 782094

Morven House Hotel ♦♦♦
2 Westerhall Road, Weymouth DT4 7SZ
T: (01305) 785075

Oaklands Edwardian Guesthouse ♦♦♦♦
1 Glendinning Avenue, Weymouth DT4 7QF
T: (01305) 767081
F: (01305) 767379
E: vicki@oaklands-guesthouse.co.uk
I: www.oaklandsguesthouse.co.uk

Old Castle Hotel ♦♦♦
Sudan Road, Weymouth DT4 9LB
T: (01305) 784642

The Pebbles Guest House ♦♦♦
18 Kirtleton Avenue, Weymouth DT4 7PT
T: (01305) 784331
F: (01305) 784695
E: pebblesguesthouse@hotmail.com

Royal Hotel ♦♦♦♦
90-91 The Esplanade, Weymouth DT4 7AX
T: (01305) 782777
F: (01305) 761088
I: www.shearingsholidays.com

St John's Guest House ♦♦♦
7 Dorchester Road, Weymouth DT4 7JR
T: (01305) 775523
F: (01305) 775815

Seacrest Guest House ♦♦♦
4 Esplanade, Weymouth DT4 8EA
T: (01305) 784759

The Seaham
♦♦♦♦ GOLD AWARD
3 Waterloo Place, Weymouth DT4 7NU
T: (01305) 782010
E: stay@theseaham.co.uk
I: www.theseaham.co.uk

SeaScape ♦♦♦
11 The Esplanade, Weymouth DT4 8EB
T: (01305) 771267

Seaways Guesthouse ♦♦♦
5 Turton Street, Weymouth DT4 7DU
T: (01305) 771646
E: Seawaysguesthouse@Newsupanet.com

The Sherborne Hotel ♦♦♦♦
117 The Esplanade, Weymouth DT4 7EH
T: (01305) 777888
F: (01305) 759111

Shirley Hotel ♦♦♦
20 Dorchester Road, Weymouth DT4 7JU
T: (01305) 782123

Southville Guest House ♦♦♦
5 Dorchester Road, Weymouth DT4 7JR
T: (01305) 770382

Spindrift Guest House ♦♦♦
Brunswick Terrace, Weymouth DT4 7RW
T: (01305) 773625
E: stayatspindrift@aol.com
I: www.resort-guide.co.uk/spindrift

Sunbay ♦♦♦
12 Brunswick Terrace, Weymouth DT4 7RW
T: (01305) 785992
F: (01305) 785992

Suncroft Hotel ♦♦♦♦
7 The Esplanade, Weymouth DT4 8EB
T: (01305) 782542
F: (01305) 770071
E: suncresthotel@hotmail.com

Hotel Sunnywey ♦♦♦
21-25 Kirtleton Avenue, Weymouth DT4 7PS
T: (01305) 786911
F: (01305) 767084

Trelawney Hotel
Rating Applied For
1 Old Castle Road, Weymouth DT4 8QB
T: (01305) 783188
F: (01305) 783181
I: www.trelawneyhotel.com

Trevann Guest House ♦♦♦
Lennox Street, Weymouth DT4 7HE
T: (01305) 782604
F: (01305) 782604

Warwick Court ♦♦♦
20 Abbotsbury Road, Weymouth DT4 0AE
T: (01305) 783261
F: (01305) 783261
E: sharon@warwickcourt.co.uk

Weyside Guest House ♦♦♦
1a Abbotsbury Road, Weymouth DT4 0AD
T: (01305) 772685
E: weysideguesthouse@btinternet.com
I: www.weysideguesthouse.btinternet.co.uk

Whitecliff Guest House ♦♦♦
7 Brunswick Terrace, Weymouth DT4 7RW
T: (01305) 785554
F: (01305) 785554
E: whitecliff@guest-house.fsnet.co.uk
I: www.whitecliffguesthouse.co.uk

WHEDDON CROSS
Somerset

Cutthorne
♦♦♦♦ GOLD AWARD
Wheddon Cross, Minehead TA24 7EW
T: (01643) 831255
F: (01643) 831255
E: durbin@cutthorne.co.uk
I: www.cutthorne.co.uk

Exmoor House
♦♦♦♦♦ SILVER AWARD
Wheddon Cross, Minehead TA24 7DU
T: (01643) 841432
F: (01643) 841811
E: exmoorhouse@hotmail.com
I: www.exmoorhotel.co.uk

Little Brendon Hill Farm
♦♦♦♦♦ GOLD AWARD
Wheddon Cross, Minehead TA24 7BG
T: (01643) 841556
F: (01643) 841556
E: info@exmoorheaven.co.uk
I: www.exmoorheaven.co.uk

Little Quarme Farm
♦♦♦♦♦ SILVER AWARD
Wheddon Cross, Minehead TA24 7EA
T: (01643) 841249
F: (01643) 841249
E: info@littlequarme.co.uk
I: www.littlequarme.co.uk

The Rest And Be Thankful Inn
♦♦♦♦ SILVER AWARD
Wheddon Cross, Minehead TA24 7DR
T: (01643) 841222
F: (01643) 841222
E: enquiries@restandbethankful.co.uk
I: www.restandbethankful.co.uk

Sundial Guesthouse
♦♦♦♦ SILVER AWARD
Wheddon Cross, Minehead TA24 7DP
T: (01643) 841188
E: admin@sundialguesthouse.co.uk
I: www.sundialguesthouse.co.uk

WHIMPLE
Devon

Higher Southbrook Farm
♦♦♦♦
Southbrook Lane, Whimple, Exeter EX5 2PG
T: (01404) 823000
E: hsf@currantbun.com

WHITECROSS
Cornwall

Hycroft ♦♦♦
Whitecross, Wadebridge PL27 7JD
T: (01208) 816568
E: vipcurr@freeuk.com

The Old Post Office ♦♦♦
Whitecross, Wadebridge PL27 7JD
T: (01208) 812620
F: (01208) 812620
E: bywaysoldpostoffice@supanet.com
I: www.bywaysactivityholidays.co.uk

WICK
Gloucestershire

Bury Manor Castle ♦♦♦♦
High Street, Wick, Bristol BS30 5SH
T: (0117) 303 9106
F: (0117) 937 4882
E: info@burrymanorcastle.com
I: www.info@burymanorcastle.com

WIDECOMBE-IN-THE-MOOR
Devon

Higher Venton Farm ♦♦♦
Widecombe-in-the-Moor, Newton Abbot TQ13 7TF
T: (01364) 621235
F: (01364) 621382
E: hhicks@ventonfarm.fsnet.co.uk

Sheena Tower ♦♦♦
Widecombe-in-the-Moor, Newton Abbot TQ13 7TE
T: (01364) 621308
E: sheenatower@compuserve.com

WIDEMOUTH BAY
Cornwall

Bay View Inn ♦♦
Marine Drive, Widemouth Bay, Bude EX23 0AW
T: (01288) 361273
F: (01288) 361273
E: enquiries@bayviewinn.co.uk
I: www.bayviewinn.co.uk

Beach House B & B
Rating Applied For
Marine Drive, Widemouth Bay, Bude EX23 0AW
T: (01288) 361256

Brocksmoor Hotel ♦♦♦
Poundstock, Widemouth Bay, Bude EX23 0DF
T: (01288) 361207
F: (01288) 361589

WILCOT
Wiltshire

Wilcot Lodge ♦♦♦♦
Wilcot, Pewsey SN9 5NS
T: (01672) 563465
F: (01672) 569040
E: gmikegswindells@hotmail.com
I: www.bed-breakfast-uk.com/bb-uk-wilts.htm

WILLITON
Somerset

Hartnells Walking Breaks, Bed and Breakfast ♦♦♦
28 Long Street, Williton, Taunton TA4 4QU
T: (01984) 634777
E: ibarratt@waitrose.com

WILTON
Wiltshire

The Pembroke Arms Hotel
♦♦♦♦
Minster Street, Wilton, Salisbury SP2 0BH
T: (01722) 743328
F: (01722) 744886
E: fleur@pembrokearms.co.uk

WINKLEIGH
Devon

The Old Parsonage ♦♦♦♦
Court Walk, Winkleigh EX19 8JA
T: (01837) 83772
F: (01837) 680074
E: tonypeel@dialFSB.co.uk

WINSFORD
Somerset

Kemps Farm ♦♦♦
Winsford, Minehead TA24 7HT
T: (01643) 851312

Larcombe Foot ♦♦♦♦
Winsford, Minehead TA24 7HS
T: (01643) 851306

WINSLEY
Wiltshire

The Conifers ♦♦
4 King Alfred Way, Winsley, Bradford-on-Avon BA15 2NG
T: (01225) 722482

Stillmeadow ♦♦♦♦♦
18 Bradford Road, Winsley, Bradford-on-Avon BA15 2HW
T: (01225) 722119
F: (01225) 722633
E: sue.gilby@btinternet.com

WINTERBOURNE BASSETT
Wiltshire

The Grove
Rating Applied For
Winterbourne Bassett, Swindon SN4 9QB
T: (01793) 731614

WINTERBOURNE STOKE
Wiltshire

Scotland Lodge Farm ♦♦♦♦
Winterbourne Stoke, Salisbury SP3 4TF
T: (01980) 621199
F: (01980) 621188
E: william.lockwood@bigwig.net
I: www.smoothhound.co.uk/hotels/scotlandl.html

WINTERSLOW
Wiltshire

Shiralee Bed & Breakfast ♦♦
Tytherley Road, Winterslow, Salisbury SP5 1PY
T: (01980) 862004
F: (01980) 862004
E: anything@faisa.co.uk
I: www.faisa.co.uk

WITHAM FRIARY
Somerset

Higher West Barn Farm
♦♦♦♦ SILVER AWARD
Witham Friary, Frome BA11 5HH
T: (01749) 850819
E: ea.harrison@tesco.net

WITHERIDGE
Devon

South Coombe Farm ♦♦♦♦
Witheridge, Tiverton EX16 8QL
T: (01884) 860302
F: (01884) 861064
E: holidays@southcoombe.ukf.net
I: www.southcoombe.ukf.net

Thelbridge Cross Inn ♦♦♦♦
Thelbridge, Crediton EX17 4SQ
T: (01884) 860316
F: (01884) 861318
E: thelbridgexinn@cwcom.net
I: www.westcountry-hotels.co.uk/thelbridgexinn

WIVELISCOMBE
Somerset

Mill Barn ♦♦♦♦
Jews Farm, Maundown, Wiveliscombe, Taunton TA4 2HL
T: (01984) 624739
F: (01984) 624408
E: Tony&Marilyn@mill-barn.freeserve.co.uk
I: www.mill-barn.freeserve.co.uk

WOODBOROUGH
Wiltshire

Well Cottage ♦♦♦
Honeystreet, Woodborough, Pewsey SN9 5PS
T: (01672) 851577
E: booking@well-cottage.org.uk

WOOKEY HOLE
Somerset

Broadleys
♦♦♦♦ SILVER AWARD
21 Wells Road, Wookey Hole, Wells BA5 1DN
T: (01749) 674746
F: (01749) 674746
E: broadleys.wells@btopenworld.com

Whitegate Cottage ♦♦♦
Milton Lane, Wookey Hole, Wells BA5 1DE
T: (01749) 675326
F: (01749) 672105
E: sueandnic@whitegate.freeserve.co.uk
I: synergynet.co.uk/somerset/whitegate.htm

WOOLACOMBE
Devon

Camberley ♦♦♦
Beach Road, Woolacombe EX34 7AA
T: (01271) 870231
E: eng@cambeleybandb.co.uk
I: www.camberleybandb.co.uk

Castle Hotel ♦♦♦♦
The Esplanade, Woolacombe EX34 7DJ
T: (01271) 870788
F: (01271) 870788

Gull Rock Hotel ♦♦♦♦
Mortehoe, Woolacombe EX34 7EA
T: (01271) 870534
F: (01271) 870534
E: info@thegullrockhotel.co.uk
I: www.thegullrockhotel.co.uk

Ossaborough House ♦♦♦♦
Ossaborough Lane, Woolacombe EX34 7HJ
T: (01271) 870297
E: info@ossaboroughhouse.co.uk
I: www.ossaboroughhouse.co.uk

Sandunes Guest House ♦♦♦♦
Beach Road, Woolacombe EX34 7BT
T: (01271) 870661
E: beaconhts@u.genie.co.uk
I: www.sandwool.fsnet.co.uk

WOOLLEY
Cornwall

East Woolley Farm ♦♦♦♦
Woolley, Bude EX23 9PP
T: (01288) 331525
F: (01288) 331525
E: east.woolley@virgin.net

WOOLVERTON
Somerset

The Old School House ♦♦♦
Woolverton, Bath BA2 7RH
T: (01373) 830200
F: (01373) 830200

WOOTTON BASSETT
Wiltshire

The Hollies ♦♦♦
Greenhill, Wootton Bassett, Swindon SN4 8EH
T: (01793) 770795
F: (01793) 770795

WRAXALL
Somerset

Rose's Farm ♦♦♦♦
Wraxall, Shepton Mallet BA4 6RQ
T: (01749) 860261
F: (01749) 860261

YARCOMBE
Devon

Crawley Farm ♦♦♦
Yarcombe, Honiton EX14 9AY
T: (01460) 64760
F: (01460) 64760
E: info@crawleyfarm.com
I: www.crawleyfarm.com

Croakham Farm ♦♦♦♦
Yarcombe, Honiton EX14 9LY
T: (01404) 861206
F: (01404) 861206
E: isobel@isobelnorwell.freeserve.co.uk

Stockhouse Cottage ♦♦♦♦
Yarcombe, Honiton EX14 9AT
T: (01404) 861306
E: stockhouse.yarcombe@virgin.net

YELVERTON
Devon

Brook House
♦♦♦♦♦ SILVER AWARD
Horrabridge, Yelverton PL20 7QT
T: (01822) 859225
F: (01822) 859225
E: info@brook-house.com
I: www.brook-house.com

Eggworthy Farm ♦♦♦
Sampford Spiney, Yelverton PL20 6LJ
T: (01822) 852142
F: (01822) 852142

The Old Orchard
♦♦♦♦ SILVER AWARD
Harrowbeer Lane, Yelverton PL20 6DZ
T: (01822) 854310
F: (01822) 854310
E: babs@baross.demon.co.uk
I: www.baross.demon.co.uk/theoldorchard

The Rosemont ♦♦♦♦
Greenbank Terrace, Yelverton PL20 6DR
T: (01822) 852175
E: office@rosemontgh.fsnet.co.uk
I: www.therosemont.co.uk

Torrfields ♦♦♦♦
Sheepstor, Yelverton PL20 6PF
T: (01822) 852161

YEOVIL
Somerset

Globetrotters Cafe, Bar, Restaurant and Lodge ♦♦♦
73-74 South Street, Yeovil BA20 1QF
T: (01935) 423328
F: (01935) 411701
E: Reception@theglobetrotters.co.uk
I: www.theglobetrotters.co.uk

Greystones Court ♦♦♦♦
152 Hendford Hill, Yeovil BA20 2RG
T: (01935) 426124
F: (01935) 426124
I: www.greystones.freeserve.co.uk

Jessops ♦♦♦♦
Vagg Lane, Chilthorne Domer, Yeovil BA22 8RY
T: (01935) 841097
F: (01935) 841097

Pendomer House ♦♦♦
Pendomer, Yeovil BA22 9PB
T: (01935) 862785
E: armitstead@compuserve.com

Royal Oak Farm ♦♦♦
Moor Lane, Hardington Moor, Yeovil BA22 9NW
T: (01935) 862348
F: (01935) 862348
I: www.sommysroyaloak.co.uk

The Sparkford Inn ♦♦♦
High Street, Sparkford, Yeovil BA22 7JH
T: (01963) 440218
F: (01963) 440358
E: sparkfordinn@sparkford.fsbusiness.co.uk

Sunnymede
♦♦♦♦ SILVER AWARD
26 Lower Wraxhill Road, Yeovil BA20 2JU
T: (01935) 425786

YEOVILTON
Somerset

Cary Fitzpaine ♦♦♦♦
Yeovilton, Yeovil BA22 8JB
T: (01458) 223250
F: (01458) 223372
E: acrang@aol.com
I: www.caryfitzpaine.com

Courtry Farm ♦♦♦
Bridgehampton, Yeovil BA22 8HF
T: (01935) 840327
F: (01935) 840964
E: courtryfarm@hotmail.com

YETMINSTER
Dorset

Bingers Farm
♦♦♦♦ SILVER AWARD
Ryme Road, Yetminster, Sherborne DT9 6JY
T: (01935) 872555
F: (01935) 872555
E: bingersfarm@talk21.com

Old Mill House ♦♦♦♦
Mill Lane, Yetminster, Sherborne DT9 6ND
T: (01935) 873672
F: (01935) 873672
E: theparks@inyetminster.freeserve.co.uk

ZEALS
Wiltshire

Cornerways Cottage ♦♦♦♦
Longcross, Zeals, Warminster BA12 6LL
T: (01747) 840477
F: (01747) 840477
E: cornerways.cottage@btinternet.com
I: www.smoothhound.co.uk/hotels/cornerwa.html

SOUTH EAST

ABBOTTS ANN
Hampshire

Carinya Farm ♦♦♦
Cattle Lane, Abbotts Ann, Andover SP11 7DR
T: (01264) 710269
E: carinyafarm@virgin.net
I: www.carinyafarm.co.uk

East Manor House ♦♦♦♦♦ SILVER AWARD
Abbotts Ann, Andover SP11 7BH
T: (01264) 710031

Virginia Lodge ♦♦♦
Salisbury Road, Abbotts Ann, Andover SP11 7NX
T: (01264) 710713
E: b_stuart@talk21.com

ABINGDON
Oxfordshire

Barrows End ♦♦♦♦
3 The Copse, Barrows End, Abingdon OX14 3YW
T: (01235) 523541
F: (01235) 523541
E: dsharm@tesco.net

Dinckley Court ♦♦♦♦
Burcot, Abingdon OX14 3DP
T: (01865) 407763
F: (01865) 407010
E: annette@dinckleycourt.co.uk
I: www.dinckleycourt.co.uk

75 Northcourt Road ♦♦♦
Abingdon OX14 1NN
T: (01235) 521195

Rowen Guest House Rating Applied For
42A Oxford Road, Abingdon OX14 2DZ
T: (01235) 522066
F: (01235) 522066

85 Shelley Close Rating Applied For
Shelley Close, Abingdon OX14 1PR
T: (01235) 522573

ABINGER COMMON
Surrey

Leylands Farm ♦♦♦♦
Leylands Lane, Abinger Common, Dorking RH5 6JU
T: (01306) 730115
F: (01306) 731675
E: annieblf@btopenworld.com

Park House Farm ♦♦♦♦
Hollow Lane, Abinger Common, Dorking RH5 6LW
T: (01306) 730101
F: (01306) 730643
E: peterwallis@msn.com
I: www.smoothhound.co.uk/hotels/parkhous.html

ADDERBURY
Oxfordshire

The Bell Inn ♦♦♦
High Street, Adderbury, Banbury OX17 3LS
T: (01295) 810338
F: (01295) 812221
E: tim@thebell-adderbury.com
I: www.thebell@adderbury.com

Le Restaurant Francais at Morgans Orchard ♦♦♦
9 Twyford Gardens, Adderbury, Banbury OX17 3JA
T: (01295) 812047
F: (01295) 812341
E: morgansorchard@aol.com
I: www.banbury-cross.co.uk/morgans

ADISHAM
Kent

Bossington Bed & Breakfast ♦♦♦♦
Bossington, Adisham, Canterbury CT3 3LN
T: (01227) 720921
F: (01227) 720921
I: www.holidayshorseriding.co.uk

ADSTOCK
Buckinghamshire

The Folly Inn ♦♦
Buckingham Road, Adstock, Buckingham MK18 2HS
T: (01296) 712671
F: (01296) 712671

ALBURY
Surrey

Barn Cottage ♦♦♦♦
Brook Hill, Farley Green, Albury, Guildford GU5 9DN
T: (01483) 202571
E: bookings@barn-cottage.com
I: www.barn-cottage.com

Foxton ♦♦♦♦
Brook Lane, Albury, Guildford GU5 9DH
T: (01483) 203591
F: (01483) 203591

ALDERHOLT
Dorset

Blackwater House ♦♦♦♦
Blackwater Grove, Alderholt, Fordingbridge SP6 3AD
T: (01425) 653443
E: bandb@blackwater47.fsnet.co.uk
I: www.blackwater47.fsnet.co.uk

ALDERMASTON
Berkshire

Hinds Head ♦♦♦
Wasing Lane, Aldermaston, Reading RG7 4LX
T: (0118) 971 2194
F: (0118) 971 4511

ALDERSHOT
Hampshire

73 Cranmore Lane ♦♦♦♦ SILVER AWARD
Cranmore Lane, Aldershot GU11 3AP
T: (01252) 337560
F: (01252) 312296
E: hemans@btopenworld.com

ALDINGBOURNE
West Sussex

Limmer Pond House ♦♦♦
Church Road, Aldingbourne, Chichester PO20 3TU
T: (01243) 543210

ALDINGTON
Kent

Hogben Farm ♦♦♦♦
Church Lane, Aldington, Ashford TN25 7EH
T: (01233) 720219
F: (01233) 720285
E: ros.martin@talk21.com

ALDWORTH
West Berkshire

Fieldview Cottage ♦♦♦♦
Bell Lane, Aldworth, Reading RG8 9SB
T: (01635) 578964
E: hunt@fieldview.freeserve.co.uk

ALFRISTON
East Sussex

Meadowbank ♦♦♦♦
Sloe Lane, Alfriston, Polegate BN26 5UR
T: (01323) 870742

Riverdale House ♦♦♦♦
Seaford Road, Alfriston, Polegate BN26 5TR
T: (01323) 871038
F: (01323) 871038

Russets ♦♦♦♦ SILVER AWARD
14 Deans Road, Alfriston, Polegate BN26 5XJ
T: (01323) 870626
F: (01323) 870626
E: russets@yahoo.co.uk

ALKHAM
Kent

Alkham Court ♦♦♦♦
Meggett Hill, Alkham, Dover CT15 7DG
T: (01303) 892056
E: alkhamcourt@aol.com
I: www.alkhamcourt.co.uk

ALRESFORD
Hampshire

Haygarth ♦♦♦
82 Jacklyns Lane, Alresford SO24 9LJ
T: (01962) 732715

Heronbrook House ♦♦♦♦ SILVER AWARD
New Farm Road, Alresford SO24 9QH
T: (01962) 738726
F: (01962) 732602
E: jane@heronbrookhouse.co.uk
I: www.heronbrookhouse.co.uk

Tichborne Grange B & B ♦♦♦♦
Grange Farm, Tichborne, Alresford SO24 0NE
T: (01962) 732120
F: (01962) 732365
E: gussieraimes@hotmail.com
I: www.tichbornegrange.co.uk

The Woolpack Country Inn ♦♦♦
Totford, Alresford SO24 9TJ
T: (01962) 732101
F: (01962) 732889

ALTON
Hampshire

Boundary House B & B ♦♦♦♦ SILVER AWARD
Gosport Road, Lower Farringdon, Alton GU34 3DH
T: (01420) 587076
F: (01420) 587047
E: BoundaryS@messages.co.uk
I: www.boundaryhouse.co.uk

Farthings ♦♦♦♦
Powntley Copse, Alton GU34 4DL
T: (01256) 862427
F: (01256) 862602
E: susiehare@powntleycopse.net
I: www.powntleycopse.net/farthings

8 Princess Drive ♦♦♦♦
8 Princess Drive, Alton GU34 1QS
T: (01420) 85075
F: (01420) 549495

St Mary's Hall ♦♦♦♦
18 Albert Road, Alton GU34 1LP
T: (01420) 82235

The Vicarage ♦♦♦
East Worldham, Alton GU34 3AS
T: (01420) 82392
F: (01420) 82367
E: wenrose@bigfoot.com
I: www.altonbedandbreakfast.co.uk

West End Farm ♦♦♦♦
Froyle, Alton GU34 4JG
T: (01420) 22130
F: (01420) 22930

AMBERLEY
West Sussex

Amberley House ♦♦♦♦ SILVER AWARD
Church Street, Amberley, Arundel BN18 9NF
T: (01798) 839507
F: (01798) 839020
E: relax@waterspirit.co.uk
I: www.waterspirit.co.uk

The Sportsman ♦♦♦
Rackham Road, Amberley, Arundel B18 9NR
T: (01798) 831787
F: (01798) 831787
E: mob.club@virgin.net
I: www.thesportsmanamberley.co.uk

AMERSHAM
Buckinghamshire

Coldmoreham House ♦♦♦♦
172 High Street, Amersham HP7 0EG
T: (01494) 725245

127 High Street ♦♦♦♦
Amersham HP7 0DY
T: (01494) 725352

Morningside ♦♦♦
Piggotts Orchard, Amersham HP7 0JG
T: (01494) 721134

Nita Hurley's Bed & Breakfast ♦♦♦
63 Hundred Acres Lane,
Amersham HP7 9BX
T: (01494) 433095
F: (01494) 433095
E: nitahurleybb@hotmail.com
I: www.nitasbnb.co.uk

39 Quarrendon Road ♦♦♦♦ SILVER AWARD
Amersham HP7 9EF
T: (01494) 727959

Rocquaine House ♦♦♦♦♦ GOLD AWARD
36 Stanley Hill Avenue,
Amersham HP7 9BB
T: (01494) 726671

St Catherins ♦♦♦
9 Parkfield Avenue, Amersham
HP6 6BE
T: (01494) 728125
E: james.elliott8@btopenworld.com

Saracens Head Inn ♦♦♦
38 Whielden Street, Old Town,
Amersham HP7 0HU
T: (01494) 721958
F: (01494) 725208
E: eamonn@thesaracensheadinn.com
I: www.thesaracensheadinn.com

The Vicarage ♦♦♦
70 Sycamore Road, Amersham
HP6 5DR
T: (01494) 729993
F: (01494) 727553

The White House ♦♦♦♦
20 Church Street, Amersham
HP7 0DB
T: (01494) 433015
F: (01494) 433015

AMPFIELD
Hampshire

The Taj ♦♦♦♦
2 Hook Crescent, Ampfield,
Romsey SO51 9DE
T: (023) 8027 0810
E: christine@jeaves.freeserve.co.uk

AMPORT
Hampshire

Broadwater ♦♦♦♦
Amport, Andover SP11 8AY
T: (01264) 772240
F: (01264) 772240
E: broadwater@dmac.co.uk
I: www.dmac.co.uk/carolyn

ANDOVER
Hampshire

Amberley Hotel ♦♦♦
70 Weyhill Road, Andover
SP10 3NP
T: (01264) 352224
F: (01264) 392555
E: amberleyand@fsbdial.co.uk

Amport Inn ♦♦♦
Amport, Andover SP11 8AE
T: (01264) 710371
F: (01264) 710112

Anton Lodge
Rating Applied For
5 Junction Road, Andover
SP10 3QU
T: (01264) 324130

Fernihurst ♦♦♦♦
1 Strathfield Road, Andover
SP10 2HH
T: (01264) 361936

Forest Edge ♦♦♦♦ SILVER AWARD
Andover Down, Andover
SP11 6LJ
T: (01264) 364526
E: david@forest-edge.co.uk
I: www.forest-edge.co.uk

The Hatchet Inn ♦♦♦
Lower Chute, Andover SP11 9PX
T: (01264) 730229
F: (01264) 730212

Holmdene Guest House ♦♦♦
1 Winchester Road, Andover
SP10 2EG
T: (01264) 365414

May Cottage ♦♦♦♦ SILVER AWARD
Thruxton, Andover SP11 8LZ
T: (01264) 771241
F: (01264) 771770
E: info@maycottage-thruxton.co.uk
I: www.maycottage-thruxton.co.uk

Old Grange ♦♦♦♦
86 Winchester Road, Andover
SP10 2ER
T: (01264) 352784

Salisbury Road Bed & Breakfast ♦♦♦♦
99 Salisbury Road, Andover
SP10 2LN
T: (01264) 362638
F: (01264) 396597
E: jenny@mosaicevents.co.uk
I: www.exploretestvalley.com/salisr

Shangri-La Guest House ♦♦♦
Walworth Road, Picket Piece,
Andover SP11 6LU
T: (01264) 354399

Sutherland Guest House ♦♦♦♦
Micheldever Road, Andover
SP10 2BH
T: (01264) 365307
E: mikejkelly@talk21.com

ANSTY
West Sussex

Netherby ♦♦♦♦
Bolney Road, Ansty, Haywards
Heath RH17 5AW
T: (01444) 455888
F: (01444) 455888
E: susan@gilbert58.freeserve.co.uk

ARDINGLY
West Sussex

Stonelands West Lodge ♦♦♦
Ardingly Road, West Hoathly,
East Grinstead RH19 4RA
T: (01342) 715372

ARDLEY
Oxfordshire

The Old Post Office ♦♦♦
Church Road, Ardley, Bicester
OX27 7NP
T: (01869) 345958
F: (01869) 345958

ARPINGE
Kent

Pigeonwood House ♦♦♦♦
Grove Farm, Arpinge, Folkestone
CT18 8AQ
T: (01303) 891111
F: (01303) 891019
E: samandmary@aol.com
I: www.pigeonwood.com

ARUNDEL
West Sussex

Arun Valley Bed & Breakfast ♦♦♦♦
Houghton Farm, Amberley,
Arundel BN18 9LW
T: (01798) 831327
F: (01798) 831183
E: rosemarylock@ukonline.co.uk

Arundel House ♦♦♦
11 High Street, Arundel
BN18 9AD
T: (01903) 882136
E: arundelhouse@btinternet.com
I: www.btinternet.com/~arundelhouse/

Medlar Cottage ♦♦♦
Poling Street, Poling, Arundel
BN18 9PT
T: (01903) 883106
F: (01903) 883106
E: medlarcottage@hotmail.com
I: www.medlarcottage.co.uk

Mill Lane House ♦♦♦
Mill Lane House, Slindon,
Arundel BN18 0RP
T: (01243) 814440
F: (01243) 814436
E: jan.fuente@btopenworld.com
I: www.mill-lane-house.com

Pindars ♦♦♦♦ SILVER AWARD
Pindars, Lyminster,
Littlehampton BN17 7QF
T: (01903) 882628
F: (01903) 882628

Swan Hotel ♦♦♦
27-29 High Street, Arundel
BN18 9AG
T: (01903) 882314
F: (01903) 883759
E: info@swan-hotel.co.uk
I: www.swan-hotel.co.uk

Woodpeckers ♦♦♦♦
15 Dalloway Road, Arundel
BN18 9HJ
T: (01903) 883948

ASCOT
Berkshire

Ascot Corner ♦♦♦♦ SILVER AWARD
Wells Lane, Ascot SL5 7DY
T: (01344) 627722
F: (01344) 627722
E: sajpo@onetel.net.uk

Ennis Lodge Private Guest House ♦♦♦
Winkfield Road, Ascot SL5 7EX
T: (01344) 621009
F: (01344) 621009

Tanglewood ♦♦♦
Birch Lane, Chavey Down, Ascot
SL5 8RF
T: (01344) 882528
F: (01344) 882528
E: beer.tanglewood@btinternet.com

Thistledoo
Rating Applied For
92 New Road, Ascot SL5 8QQ
T: (01344) 885461

ASCOTT-UNDER-WYCHWOOD
Oxfordshire

College Farm ♦♦♦♦
Ascott-under-Wychwood,
Oxford OX7 6AL
T: (01993) 831900
F: (01993) 831900
E: walkers@collegefarmbandb.fsnet.co.uk

The Mill ♦♦♦
Ascott-under-Wychwood,
Oxford OX7 6AP
T: (01993) 831282
F: (01993) 831282
E: Mill@auwoxon32.freeserve.co.uk

ASH
Kent

Nine Acres Bed & Breakfast ♦♦♦
Billet Hill, Ash, Sevenoaks
TN15 7HG
T: (01474) 872253
F: (01474) 872253

ASHENDON
Buckinghamshire

The Gatehangers ♦♦♦
Lower End, Ashendon, Aylesbury
HP18 0HE
T: (01296) 651296
F: (01296) 651340

ASHFORD
Kent

Ashford Warren Cottage Hotel and Restaurant ♦♦♦
136 The Street, Willesborough,
Ashford TN24 0NB
T: (01233) 621905
F: (01233) 623400
E: general@warrencottage.co.uk
I: www.warrencottage.co.uk

Beaver Guest House ♦♦♦
100 Beaver Road, Ashford
TN23 7ST
T: (01233) 733569
F: (01233) 732193
E: eurotunnel.town@amserve.net

Croft Hotel ♦♦♦
Canterbury Road, Kennington,
Ashford TN25 4DU
T: (01233) 622140
F: (01233) 635271
E: crofthotel@btconnect.com
I: www.crofthotel.com

Dean Court Farm ♦♦♦
Challock Lane, Westwell,
Ashford TN25 4NH
T: (01233) 712924

Fontenaye ♦♦♦
23 Jemmett Road, Ashford
TN23 4QD
T: (01233) 733569
F: (01233) 732193

Glenmoor ♦♦♦
Maidstone Road, Ashford
TN25 4NP
T: (01233) 634767
E: glenmoor.bandb@btopenworld.com

New Flying Horse Inn ♦♦♦
Upper Bridge Street, Wye, Ashford TN25 5AN
T: (01233) 812297
F: (01233) 813487
E: newflyhorse@shepherd-neame.co.uk
I: www.shepherd-neame.co.uk

Quantock House ♦♦♦
Quantock Drive, Ashford TN24 8QH
T: (01233) 638921
E: tucker100@madasafish.com

ASHURST
Hampshire

Forest Gate Lodge ♦♦♦♦
161 Lyndhurst Road, Ashurst, Southampton SO40 7AW
T: (023) 8029 3026
F: (023) 8029 3026
I: www.ukworld.net/forestgatelodge

Kingswood Cottage
♦♦♦♦ SILVER AWARD
10 Woodlands Road, Ashurst, Southampton SO40 7AD
T: (023) 8029 2582
F: (023) 8029 3435
E: kingswoodcottage@yahoo.co.uk

ASTON ABBOTTS
Buckinghamshire

The Royal Oak Inn ♦♦
Wingrave Road, Aston Abbotts, Aylesbury HP22 4LT
T: (01296) 681262
E: moulty.towers@btinternet.com

Windmill Hill Barns ♦♦♦♦
Moat Lane, Aston Abbotts, Aylesbury HP22 4NF
T: (01296) 681714

ASTON UPTHORPE
Oxfordshire

Middle Fell ♦♦♦♦
Moreton Road, Aston Upthorpe, Didcot OX11 9ER
T: (01235) 850207
F: (01235) 850207
E: middlefell@ic24.net

AWBRIDGE
Hampshire

Crofton Country Bed & Breakfast
♦♦♦♦ SILVER AWARD
Kents Oak, Awbridge, Romsey SO51 0HH
T: (01794) 340333
F: (01794) 340333
E: pauline@crofton-ca.fsnet.co.uk
I: www.croftonbandb.com

AYLESBURY
Buckinghamshire

Amber Court
Rating Applied For
116 Bierton Road, Aylesbury HP20 1EN
T: (01296) 432184
F: (01296) 437360

Bay Lodge Guest House ♦♦
47 Tring Road, Aylesbury HP20 1LD
T: (01296) 331404
F: (01296) 331404
E: blodge47@hotmail.com
I: www.bay-lodge.co.uk

Belmore
Rating Applied For
23 Faithfull Close, Stone, Aylesbury HP17 8PW
T: (01296) 749009

74 Friarscroft Way ♦♦♦
Aylesbury HP20 2TF
T: (01296) 489439
E: b.rowley@amserve.com

Little Venice B&B ♦♦♦
129 Mandeville Road, Aylesbury HP21 8AJ
T: (01296) 339242
F: (01296) 339242
E: info@littleveniceuk.com
I: www.littleveniceuk.com

The Old Forge Barn ♦♦♦
Ridings Way, Cublington, Leighton Buzzard LU7 0LW
T: (01296) 681194
F: (01296) 681194
E: waples@ukonline.co.uk

Spindleberries ♦♦♦♦
331 Tring Road, Aylesbury HP20 1PJ
T: (01296) 424012

Tanamera
♦♦♦♦ SILVER AWARD
37 Bishopstone Village, Aylesbury HP17 8SH
T: (01296) 748551
E: tanamera@macunlimited.net

Wallace Farm ♦♦♦
Dinton, Aylesbury HP17 8UF
T: (01296) 748660
F: (01296) 748851
E: jackiecook@wallacefarm.freeserve.co.uk
I: www.wallacefarm.co.uk

AYLESFORD
Kent

Wickham Lodge ♦♦♦♦
The Quay, High Street, Aylesford ME20 7AY
T: (01622) 717267
F: (01622) 792855
E: wickhamlodge@aol.com
I: www.wickhamlodge.com

BALCOMBE
West Sussex

Rocks Lane Cottage ♦♦♦
Rowhill Lane, Balcombe, Haywards Heath RH17 6JG
T: (01444) 811245
E: kpa@fsbdial.co.uk

BAMPTON
Oxfordshire

Chimney Farm House ♦♦♦♦
Chimney, Bampton OX18 2EH
T: (01367) 870279
F: (01367) 870279
I: www.country-accom.co.uk/chimneyfarmhouse

The Granary ♦♦♦
Main Street, Clanfield, Bampton OX18 2SH
T: (01367) 810266

BANBURY
Oxfordshire

Amberley Guest House ♦♦
151 Middleton Road, Banbury OX16 8QS
T: (01295) 255797
F: (01295) 255797

Ark Guest House ♦♦♦
120 Warwick Road, Banbury OX16 2AN
T: (01295) 254498
F: (01295) 254498

Ashlea Guest House ♦♦
58 Oxford Road, Banbury OX16 9AN
T: (01295) 250539
F: (01295) 250539

Avonlea Guest House ♦♦♦
41 Southam Road, Banbury OX16 2EP
T: (01295) 267837
F: (01295) 271946
E: whitforddebbie@hotmail.com

Aynho Fields ♦♦♦
Aynho, Banbury OX17 3AU
T: (01869) 810288

Banbury Cross Bed & Breakfast ♦♦♦♦
1 Broughton Road, Banbury OX16 9QB
T: (01295) 266048
F: (01295) 266698

College Farmhouse ♦♦♦♦
Kings Sutton, Banbury OX17 3PS
T: (01295) 811473
F: (01295) 812505
E: sealldąy@aol.com
I: www.banburytown.co.uk/accom/collegefarm/

Cotefields Bed & Breakfast ♦♦
Opposite Bodicote Park, Banbury OX15 4AQ
T: (01295) 264977
F: (01295) 264977
E: tony.stockford@ic24.net

Easington House ♦♦♦
50 Oxford Road, Banbury OX16 9AN
T: (01295) 270181
F: (01295) 269527
E: enquiries@easingtonhouse.co.uk
I: www.easingtonhouse.co.uk

Fernleigh Guest House ♦♦♦
67 Oxford Road, Banbury OX16 9AJ
T: (01295) 250853
F: (01295) 269349
E: a.cumberlidge@btinternet.com

George & Dragon ♦♦♦
Silver Street, Chacombe, Banbury OX17 2JR
T: (01295) 711500
F: (01295) 758827

The Glebe House ♦♦♦♦
Village Road, Warmington, Banbury OX17 1BT
T: (01295) 690642

The Lodge ♦♦♦♦
Main Road, Middleton Cheney, Banbury OX17 2PP
T: (01295) 710355

Prospect House Guest House ♦♦♦
70 Oxford Road, Banbury OX16 9AN
T: (01295) 268749
F: (01295) 268749

St Martins House ♦♦♦♦
Warkworth, Banbury OX17 2AG
T: (01295) 712684
F: (01295) 712838

Treetops Guest House ♦♦
28 Dashwood Road, Banbury OX16 8HD
T: (01295) 254444

White Cross House
Rating Applied For
7 Broughton Road, Banbury OX16 9QB
T: (01295) 277932
E: marian@kedwards50.fsnet.co.uk

BARCOMBE
East Sussex

The Anchor Inn ♦♦♦
Anchor Lane, Barcombe Mills, Barcombe, Lewes BN8 5BS
T: (01273) 400414
F: (01273) 401029
I: www.anchorinnandboating.co.uk

BARNHAM
West Sussex

Downhills ♦♦♦
87 Barnham Road, Barnham, Bognor Regis PO22 0EQ
T: (01243) 553104

Todhurst Farm ♦♦♦
Lake Lane, Barnham, Bognor Regis PO22 0AL
T: (01243) 551959
E: nigelsedg@aol.com

BARTLEY
Hampshire

Bartley Farmhouse ♦♦♦♦
Ringwood Road, Bartley, Southampton SO40 7LD
T: (023) 8081 4194
F: (023) 8081 4117

BARTON ON SEA
Hampshire

Everglades ♦♦♦♦
81 Sea Road, Barton on Sea, New Milton BH25 7ND
T: (01425) 617350

Hotel Gainsborough ♦♦♦♦
Marine Drive East, Barton on Sea, New Milton BH25 7DX
T: (01425) 610541

Laurel Lodge ♦♦♦
48 Western Avenue, Barton on Sea, New Milton BH25 7PZ
T: (01425) 618309

BARTON STACEY
Hampshire

The Swan Inn ♦♦♦
High Street, Barton Stacey, Winchester SO21 3RL
T: (01962) 760470
F: (01962) 761236

BASINGSTOKE
Hampshire

Fernbank Hotel ♦♦♦♦
4 Fairfields Road, Basingstoke RG21 3DR
T: (01256) 321191
F: (01256) 461476
E: availability@fernbankhotel.co.uk
I: www.fernbankhotel.co.uk

Street Farm House ♦♦♦♦
The Street, South Warnborough, Hook RG29 1RS
T: (01256) 862225
F: (01256) 862225
E: streetfarmhouse@btinternet.com

BATTLE
East Sussex

The Abbey Hotel ♦♦♦
84 High Street, Battle TN33 0AQ
T: (01424) 772755
F: (01424) 773378

Acacia House ♦♦♦♦
Starrs Green Lane, Battle
TN33 0TD
T: (01424) 772416

The Gateway Restaurant ♦♦♦
78 High Street, Battle TN33 0AG
T: (01424) 772856

The George Hotel ♦♦♦♦
23 The High Street, Battle
TN33 0EA
T: (01424) 775512
F: (01424) 775427

High Hedges ♦♦♦♦
28 North Trade Road, Battle
TN33 0HB
T: (01424) 774140
E: gloria.jones@btinternet.com

Kelklands ♦♦♦♦
Chain Lane, Battle TN33 0HG
T: (01424) 773013

Little Hemingfold Hotel ♦♦♦
Hastings Road, Battle TN33 0TT
T: (01424) 774338
F: (01424) 775351

Moons Hill Farm ♦♦♦
The Green, Ninfield, Battle
TN33 9LH
T: (01424) 892645
F: (01424) 892645
E: june@ive13.fsnet.co.uk

Tollgate Farm House ♦♦♦♦
59 North Trade Road, Catsfield,
Battle TN33 0HS
T: (01424) 777436
F: (01424) 774725

BEACONSFIELD
Buckinghamshire

Beacon House ♦♦♦♦
113 Maxwell Road, Beaconsfield
HP9 1RF
T: (01494) 672923
F: (01494) 672923
E: Ben.Dickinson@Tesco.net
I: www.beaconhouse.org.uk

Highclere Farm ♦♦♦♦
Newbarn Lane, Seer Green,
Beaconsfield HP9 2QZ
T: (01494) 875665
F: (01494) 875238

BEAN
Kent

Black Horse Cottage ♦♦♦
High Street, Bean, Dartford
DA2 8AS
T: (01474) 704962

BEARSTED
Kent

88 Ashford Road ♦♦♦
Ashford Road, Bearsted,
Maidstone ME14 4LT
T: (01622) 738278
F: (01622) 738346

BEAULIEU
Hampshire

Dale Farm House ♦♦♦
Manor Road, Applemore Hill,
Dibden, Southampton SO45 5TJ
T: (023) 8084 9632
F: (023) 8084 0285
E: info@dalefarmhouse.co.uk
I: www.dalefarmhouse.co.uk

Leygreen Farm House ♦♦♦♦
Lyndhurst Road, Beaulieu,
Brockenhurst SO42 7YP
T: (01590) 612355
F: (01590) 612355
I: www.newforest.demon.co.uk/leygreen.htm

Old School House ♦♦♦♦
High Street, Beaulieu,
Brockenhurst SO42 7YD
T: (01590) 612062
F: (01590) 612062
E: jeanie@eurolink.ltd.net
I: www.newforestwheretostay.co.uk

BECKLEY
East Sussex

Woodlands ♦♦♦
Whitebread Lane, Beckley, Rye
TN31 6UA
T: (01797) 260486
E: ericrobson99@hotmail.com
I: www.woodlandsrye.co.uk
♿

BEDHAMPTON
Hampshire

Cherry Trees ♦♦♦♦
23 Parkside, Bedhampton,
Havant PO9 3PJ
T: (023) 9248 2480

BEMBRIDGE
Isle of Wight

The Crab and Lobster ♦♦♦♦
32 Forelands Field Road,
Bembridge PO35 5TR
T: (01983) 872244
F: (01983) 873495

Sea Change
♦♦♦♦ SILVER AWARD
22 Beachfield Road, Bembridge
PO35 5TN
T: (01983) 875558
F: (01983) 875667
E: seachangewight@aol.com
I: www.wightonline.co.uk/accommodation/bandb/seachange.html

BENENDEN
Kent

The Bull At Benenden ♦♦♦♦
The Street, Benenden, Cranbrook
TN17 4DE
T: (01580) 240054
E: thebull@thebullatbenenden.co.uk
I: www.thebullatbenenden.co.uk

The Holt
Rating Applied For
New Pond Road, Benenden,
Cranbrook TN17 4EL
T: (01580) 240414
E: kate@theholt.org
I: www.theholt.org

BENSON
Oxfordshire

Brookside ♦♦♦♦
Brook Street, Benson,
Wallingford OX10 6LJ
T: (01491) 838289
F: (01491) 838289

The Crown Inn ♦♦♦
52 High Street, Benson,
Wallingford OX10 6RP
T: (01491) 838247

Fyfield Manor
♦♦♦♦ SILVER AWARD
Benson, Wallingford OX10 6HA
T: (01491) 835184
F: (01491) 825635
E: chris@fifield-software.demon.co.uk
I: www.bedandbreakfastnationwide.com

BENTLEY
Hampshire

Pittersfield ♦♦♦
Bentley, Farnham GU10 5LT
T: (01420) 22414
F: (01420) 22414

BENTWORTH
Hampshire

Newmans Cottage ♦♦♦♦
Drury Lane, Bentworth, Alton
GU34 5RJ
T: (01420) 563707
E: AdmiralD@aol.com

BERE REGIS
Dorset

The Dorset Golf Hotel ♦♦♦♦
The Dorset Golf & Country Club,
Hyde, Bere Regis, Wareham
BH20 7NT
T: (01929) 472244
F: (01929) 471294
E: admin@dorsetgolfresort.coom
I: www.dorsetgolfresort.com

The Royal Oak
Rating Applied For
West Street, Bere Regis,
Wareham BH20 7HQ
T: (01929) 471203
F: (01929) 471203
E: lizjayne@saintives82.fsnet.co.uk
I: www.theroyaloakhotel.co.uk

BERWICK
East Sussex

Lower Claverham Farm ♦♦♦♦
Berwick, Polegate BN26 6TJ
T: (01323) 811267
F: (01323) 811267
E: paul.rossi@talk21.com

BETHERSDEN
Kent

Cloverlea ♦♦♦
Bethersden, Ashford TN26 3DU
T: (01233) 820353
F: (01233) 820353
E: pam.mills@amserve.net

The Coach House ♦♦♦
Oakmead Farm, Bethersden,
Ashford TN26 3DU
T: (01233) 820583
F: (01233) 820583

The Old Stables ♦♦♦♦
Wissenden, Bethersden, Ashford
TN26 3EL
T: (01233) 820597
F: (01233) 820199
E: pennygillespie@theoldstables.co.uk
I: www.theoldstables.co.uk

Potters Farm ♦♦♦
Bethersden, Ashford TN26 3JX
T: (01233) 820341
F: (01233) 820469
E: ianmcanderson@cs.com
I: www.smoothhound.co.uk/hotels/potters.html

BEXHILL
East Sussex

Barkers Bed and Breakfast
♦♦♦
16 Magdalen Road, Bexhill
TN40 1SB
T: (01424) 218969

Barrington B & B ♦♦♦♦
14 Wilton Road, Bexhill
TN40 1HY
T: (01424) 210250
E: barrington@supaworld.com
I: www.barrington14.freeserve.co.uk

Buenos Aires Guest House
♦♦♦♦
24 Albany Road, Bexhill
TN40 1BZ
T: (01424) 212269
F: (01424) 212269
E: buenosairesguesthouse@hotmail.com

Cobwebs ♦♦♦♦
26 Collington Avenue, Bexhill
TN39 3QA
T: (01424) 213464
F: (01424) 212500
E: kobwebs@waitrose.com

Collington Lodge Guest House
♦♦♦
41 Collington Avenue, Bexhill
TN39 3PX
T: (01424) 210024
F: (01424) 210024
E: info@collington.co.uk
I: www.collington.co.uk

Hotel Dunselma ♦♦♦♦
25 Marina, Bexhill TN40 1BP
T: (01424) 734144
F: (01424) 221007
E: stay@dunselma.com

Hartfield House
♦♦♦♦ SILVER AWARD
27 Hartfield Road, Bexhill
TN39 3EA
T: (01424) 845715
F: (01424) 846510
E: mansi@hartfieldhouse.free-online.co.uk
I: www.hartfield-house.co.uk

Little Marabou Mansions ♦♦
58-60 Devonshire Road, Bexhill
TN40 1AX
T: (01424) 215052
E: lex100uk@yahoo.co.uk

Manor Barn ♦♦♦
Ninfield Road, Bexhill TN39 5JJ
T: (01424) 893018
F: (01424) 893018

Mulberry
♦♦♦♦ SILVER AWARD
31 Warwick Road, Bexhill
TN39 4HG
T: (01424) 219204

Park Lodge Hotel ♦♦♦♦
16 Egerton Road, Bexhill
TN39 3HH
T: (01424) 216547
F: (01424) 217460

Sackville Hotel
♦♦♦♦ SILVER AWARD
The Sackville, De la Warr Parade,
Bexhill TN40 1LS
T: (01424) 224694
F: (01424) 734132
E: info@sackvillehotel.com
I: www.sackvillehotel.com

Westwood Farm ♦♦♦
Stonestile Lane, Hastings
TN35 4PG
T: (01424) 751038
F: (01424) 751038
E: york@westwood-farm.fsnet.co.uk

BICESTER
Oxfordshire

Bowshot Bed and Breakfast ♦♦♦
Bowshot Court, 7 Aldergate Road, Bicester OX26 2BJ
T: (01869) 252355
E: reservations@bowshotholidays.com
I: www.bowshotholidays.com

Home Farm ♦♦♦
Mansmore Lane, Charlton on Otmoor, Charlton-on-Otmoor, Kidlington OX5 2US
T: (01865) 331267
F: (01865) 331267
E: triciahomefarm@aol.com

Manor Farm Bed & Breakfast ♦♦♦
Poundon, Bicester OX27 9BB
T: (01869) 277212
E: jeannettecollett@aol.com
I: www.smoothhound.co.uk/hotels/manor3.html

Oxford Terrace B&B ♦♦
28 Kings End, Bicester OX26 2AA
T: (01869) 248739
E: rmorgans@ntlworld.com

Priory House ♦♦♦
86 Chapel Street, Bicester OX26 6BD
T: (01869) 325687
E: anderson@prioryhouse.fsnet.co.uk
I: mysite.freeserve.com/prioryhouse/

BIDDENDEN
Kent

Bishopsdale Oast ♦♦♦♦
Bishopsdale Oast, Biddenden, Ashford TN27 8DR
T: (01580) 291027
F: (01580) 292321
E: drysdale@bishopsdaleoast.co.uk
I: www.bishopsdaleoast.co.uk

Heron Cottage ♦♦♦♦
Biddenden, Ashford TN27 8HH
T: (01580) 291358

Kingsmead ♦♦♦♦
Fosten Green, Biddenden, Ashford TN27 8ER
T: (01580) 292220
F: (01580) 292120

BILLINGSHURST
West Sussex

Groom Cottage ♦♦♦
Station Road, Billingshurst RH14 9RF
T: (01403) 782285

BILSINGTON
Kent

Willow Farm ♦♦♦
Stone Cross, Bilsington, Ashford TN25 7JJ
T: (01233) 720484
F: (01233) 720484
E: renee@willow-farm.freeserve.co.uk

BINFIELD
Berkshire

Berkshire Rooms ♦♦♦♦
The Ridges, Murrell Hill Lane, Binfield, Bracknell RG42 4DA
T: (01344) 360077
F: (01344) 641715
E: info@berkshirerooms.com
I: www.berkshirerooms.com

BINSTEAD
Isle of Wight

Elm Close Cottage ♦♦♦♦ SILVER AWARD
Ladies Walk, Church Road, Binstead, Ryde PO33 3SY
T: (01983) 567161
E: elm_cottage@hotmail.com
I: www.elmclosecottage.com

Newnham Farm Bed & Breakfast ♦♦♦♦♦ SILVER AWARD
Newnham Lane, Binstead, Ryde PO33 4ED
T: (01983) 882423
F: (01983) 882423
E: newnhamfarm@talk21.com
I: www.newnhamfarm.co.uk

BIRCHINGTON
Kent

Greenview ♦♦♦♦
28 Canute Road, Birchington CT7 9QJ
T: (01843) 844737

BIRLING
Kent

The Stable Block ♦♦♦
25 Ryarsh Road, Birling, West Malling ME19 5JW
T: (01732) 873437
F: (01732) 849320
E: carolinemoorhead1@hotmail.com

BISHOP'S WALTHAM
Hampshire

Post Mead ♦♦♦♦ SILVER AWARD
Shore Lane, Bishop's Waltham, Southampton SO32 1DY
T: (01489) 895795
F: (01489) 895795

BISHOPSTOKE
Hampshire

The Prince of Wales ♦♦♦♦
65 Bishopstoke Road, Bishopstoke, Eastleigh SO50 6LA
T: (02380) 612544
F: (02380) 610136

BIX
Oxfordshire

Barn at Bix ♦♦♦♦
Bix, Henley-on-Thames RG9 4RS
T: (01491) 414062
E: tom@bedseide.com
I: www.bedseide.com

Meadow Corner ♦♦♦
Bix, Henley-on-Thames RG9 6BU
T: (01491) 578456

BLACKTHORN
Oxfordshire

Lime Trees Farm ♦♦♦♦
Lower Road, Blackthorn, Bicester OX25 1TG
T: (01869) 248435
F: (01869) 325843
E: keithcrampton@tiscali.co.uk
I: www.smoothhound.co.uk/hotels/limetrees.html

BLADBEAN
Kent

Molehills ♦♦♦♦
Bladbean, Canterbury CT4 6LU
T: (01303) 840051
E: molehills84@hotmail.com

BLANDFORD FORUM
Dorset

Farmhouse B & B ♦♦♦♦
Lower Bryanston Farm, Blandford Forum DT11 0LS
T: (01258) 452009
F: (01258) 452009
E: tony@brylow.co.uk
I: www.brylow.co.uk

Farnham Farm House ♦♦♦♦♦ SILVER AWARD
Farnham, Blandford Forum DT11 8DG
T: (01725) 516254
F: (01725) 516306
E: info@farnhamfarmhouse.co.uk
I: www.farnhamfarmhouse.co.uk

Kings Arms Hotel Rating Applied For
White Cliff Mill Street, Blandford Forum DT11 7BE
T: (01258) 452163
F: (01258) 454411
E: kingsarmshotel@aol.com
I: www.hotelblandford.com

Meadow House ♦♦♦♦ SILVER AWARD
Tarrant Hinton, Blandford Forum DT11 8JG
T: (01258) 830498
F: (01258) 830498

St Leonards Farmhouse ♦♦♦♦
Wimborne Road, Blandford Forum DT11 7SB
T: (01258) 456635
F: (01258) 455598
E: jodi@brittours.com
I: www.brittours.com/st.leonard/st.leonards.htm

BLEDLOW
Buckinghamshire

Cross Lanes Guest House ♦♦♦♦ SILVER AWARD
Cross Lanes Cottage, Bledlow, Aylesbury HP27 9PF
T: (01844) 345339
F: (01844) 274165
E: ronaldcoul@aol.com

BLEDLOW RIDGE
Buckinghamshire

Old Callow Down Farm ♦♦♦♦
Wigans Lane, Bledlow Ridge, High Wycombe HP14 4BH
T: (01844) 344416
F: (01844) 344703
E: oldcallow@aol.com
I: www.chilternscottage.co.uk

BLETCHINGDON
Oxfordshire

The Black's Head Inn ♦♦♦
The Green, Bletchingdon, Oxford OX5 3DA
T: (01869) 350315
F: (01869) 350315
E: theblackshead@tiscali.co.uk
I: www.theblackshead.com

BLEWBURY
Oxfordshire

The Barley Mow ♦♦♦
London Road, Blewbury, Didcot OX11 9NU
T: (01235) 850296
F: (01235) 850296

BLOXHAM
Oxfordshire

Rowan Court ♦♦♦♦
Milton Road, Bloxham, Banbury OX15 4HD
T: (01295) 722566
F: (01295) 722566
E: enquiries@rowancourt.co.uk
I: www.rowancourt.com

BOARS HILL
Oxfordshire

Broomhill ♦♦♦♦
Lincombe Lane, Boars Hill, Oxford OX1 5DZ
T: (01865) 735339
E: sara@rralden.force9.co.uk
I: www.rralden.force9.co.uk

BOGNOR REGIS
West Sussex

Alderwasley Cottage ♦♦♦♦
Off West Street, Bognor Regis PO21 1XH
T: (01243) 821339
E: alderwasley@btinternet.com

Homestead Guest House ♦♦♦
90 Aldwick Road, Bognor Regis PO21 2PD
T: (01243) 823443
F: (01243) 823443

Jubilee Guest House ♦♦♦
5 Gloucester Road, Bognor Regis PO21 1NU
T: (01243) 863016
F: (01243) 868017
E: jubileeguesthouse@breathemail.net
I: www.jubileeguesthouse.com

The Maltings ♦♦♦♦ SILVER AWARD
199 Pagahm Road, Nyetimber, Bognor Regis PO21 4NJ
T: (01243) 261168
F: (01243) 262382
E: info@themaltings.org.uk
I: www.themaltings.org.uk

Regis Lodge ♦♦♦
3 Gloucester Road, Bognor Regis PO21 1NU
T: (01243) 827110
F: (01243) 827110
E: frank@regislodge.fsbusiness.co.uk
I: www.regislodge.co.uk

Sea Crest Private Hotel ♦♦♦
19 Nyewood Lane, Bognor Regis PO21 2QB
T: (01243) 821438

Spring Cottage Bed & Breakfast
Rating Applied For
90 Felpham Road, Felpham, Bognor Regis PO22 7PD
T: (01243) 868500
E: springcottage.bb@virgin.net

Swan Guest House ♦♦♦♦
17 Nyewood Lane, Bognor Regis PO21 2QB
T: (01243) 826880
F: (01243) 826880
E: swanhse@globalnet.co.uk
I: www.users.globalnet.co.uk/~swanhse

Tudor Cottage Guest House ♦♦♦♦
194 Chichester Road, Bognor Regis PO21 5BJ
T: (01243) 821826
F: (01243) 862189
E: tudorcottage@supernet.com

White Horses Bed & Breakfast
Rating Applied For
Clyde Road, Felpham, Bognor Regis PO22 7AH
T: (01243) 824320
E: bellamy@btinternet.com
I: www.whitehorsesfelpham.co.uk

BOLDRE
Hampshire

Pinecroft ♦♦♦
Coxhill, Boldre, Lymington SO41 8PS
T: (01590) 624260
F: (01590) 624025
E: enquiries@pinecroftbandb.co.uk
I: www.pinecroftbandb.co.uk

BOLNEY
West Sussex

Broxmead Paddock ♦♦♦♦
Broxmead Lane, Bolney, Cuckfield, Haywards Heath RH17 5RG
T: (01444) 881458
F: (01444) 881491
E: broxmeadpaddock@hotmail.com

Colwood Manor West ♦♦♦♦
Spronketts Lane, Bolney, Haywards Heath RH17 5SA
T: (01444) 461331
E: dmartin@ricsonline.org

New Farm House ♦♦♦♦
Nyes Hill, Wineham Lane, Bolney, Haywards Heath RH17 5SD
T: (01444) 881617
F: (01444) 881850
E: newfarmhouse@btinternet.com
I: www.newfarmhouse.co.uk

BONCHURCH
Isle of Wight

The Lake Hotel ♦♦♦♦
Shore Road, Bonchurch, Ventnor PO38 1RF
T: (01983) 852613
F: (01983) 852613
E: enquiries@lakehotel.co.uk
I: www.lakehotel.co.uk

Under Rock Country House Bed & Breakfast ♦♦♦
Shore Road, Bonchurch, Ventnor PO38 1RF
T: (01983) 855274
E: enquiries@under-rock.co.uk
I: www.under-rock.co.uk

BOROUGH GREEN
Kent

Yew Tree Barn ♦♦♦♦
Long Mill Lane, Crouch, Borough Green, Sevenoaks TN15 8QB
T: (01732) 883107
F: (01732) 883107
E: yewtreebarnbb@hotmail.com

BOSCOMBE
Dorset

Aloha Wyvern Hotel ♦♦♦♦
24 Glen Road, Boscombe, Bournemouth BH5 1HR
T: (01202) 397543
F: (01202) 256175
E: mail@wyvernhotel.co.uk
I: www.wyvernhotel.co.uk

Au-Levant Hotel ♦♦♦
15 Westby Road, Boscombe, Bournemouth BH5 1HA
T: (01202) 394884

Hotel Sorrento ♦♦♦
16 Owls Road, Boscombe, Bournemouth BH5 1AG
T: (01202) 394019
F: (01202) 394019
E: mail@hotelsorrento.co.uk
I: www.hotelsorrento.co.uk

BOSHAM
West Sussex

Crede Farmhouse
♦♦♦♦ SILVER AWARD
Crede Lane, Bosham, Chichester PO18 8NX
T: (01243) 574929
E: lesley@credefarmhouse.fsnet.co.uk

Good Hope ♦♦♦♦
Delling Lane, Bosham, Chichester PO18 8NR
T: (01243) 572487
F: (01243) 530760

Govers ♦♦♦
Crede Lane, Bosham, Chichester PO18 8NX
T: (01243) 573163

Hatpins
♦♦♦♦♦ SILVER AWARD
Bosham Lane, Old Bosham, Chichester PO18 8HG
T: (01243) 572644
F: (01243) 572644
E: mary@hatpins.co.uk
I: www.hatpins.co.uk

Lane End
Rating Applied For
Shore Road, Bosham, Chichester PO18 8QL
T: (01243) 573542
F: (01243) 573542

BOTLEY
Hampshire

Steeple Court Farm ♦♦♦
Church Lane, Botley, Southampton SO30 2EQ
T: (01489) 798824
E: theblue.room@btinternet.com

BOTOLPH CLAYDON
Buckinghamshire

Botolph Farmhouse ♦♦♦♦
Botyl Road, Botolph Claydon, Buckingham MK18 2LR
T: (01296) 712640
F: (01296) 714806
E: clive@tcsgroup.co.uk
I: www.botolphfarm.co.uk

Hickwell House ♦♦♦♦
40 Botyl Road, Botolph Claydon, Buckingham MK18 2LR
T: (01296) 712217
F: (01296) 712217
I: www.hickwellhouse.co.uk

BOUGHTON
Kent

Brenley Farm House ♦♦♦
Brenley Lane, Boughton-under-Blean, Boughton, Faversham ME13 9LY
T: (01227) 751203
F: (01227) 751203
E: maggie@brenley.freeserve.co.uk
I: www.kent-esites.co.uk/brenleyfarmhouse

10 Horselees Road ♦♦♦
Boughton-under-Blean, Boughton, Faversham ME13 9TG
T: (01227) 751332
F: (01227) 751332
E: keith@theleesbb.co.uk

Wellbrook Farmhouse ♦♦♦♦
South Street, Boughton, Faversham ME13 9NA
T: (01227) 750941
F: (01227) 750807
E: reservations@wellbrookfarmhouse.co.uk
I: www.wellbrookfarmhouse.co.uk

BOUGHTON MONCHELSEA
Kent

Hideaway ♦♦♦
Heath Road, Boughton Monchelsea, Maidstone ME17 4JD
T: (01622) 747453
F: (01622) 747453

Wierton Hall Farm ♦♦♦
East Hall Hill, Boughton Monchelsea, Maidstone ME17 4JU
T: (01622) 743535
F: (01622) 743535
E: phipps@jackie.68383.fsnet.co.uk

BOURNE END
Buckinghamshire

Hollands Farm ♦♦♦♦
Hedsor Road, Bourne End SL8 5EE
T: (01628) 520423
F: (01628) 531602

Lower Martins Cottage ♦♦♦♦
Lower Martins, Coldmoorholme Lane, Bourne End SL8 5PS
T: (01628) 521730
F: (01628) 523988
E: marianiwills@supanet.com

BOURNEMOUTH
Dorset

Alexander Lodge Hotel
♦♦♦♦ SILVER AWARD
21 Southern Road, Southbourne, Bournemouth BH6 3SR
T: (01202) 421662
F: (01202) 421662
E: alexanderlodge@yahoo.com
I: www.s-h-systems.co.uk/a28852.html

Balincourt Hotel
♦♦♦♦♦ SILVER AWARD
58 Christchurch Road, Bournemouth BH1 3PF
T: (01202) 552962
F: (01202) 552962
E: rooms@balincourt.co.uk
I: www.balincourt.co.uk

Bonnington Hotel ♦♦♦
44 Tregonwell Road, Bournemouth BH2 5NT
T: (01202) 553621
F: (01202) 317797
E: bonnington.bournemouth@btinternet.com
I: www.bonnington-hotel.com

Carisbrooke Hotel ♦♦♦♦
42 Tregonwell Road, Bournemouth BH2 5NT
T: (01202) 290432
F: (01202) 310499
E: all@carisbrooke58.freeserve.co.uk
I: www.carisbrooke.co.uk

Cavendish ♦♦♦♦
20 Durley Chine Road, West Cliff, Bournemouth BH2 5LF
T: (01202) 290489

Chelsea Hotel ♦♦♦
32 St Swithuns Road, East Cliff, Bournemouth BH1 3RH
T: (01202) 290111
F: (01202) 290111
E: info@thechelseahotel.co.uk
I: www.thechelseahotel.co.uk

Coniston Hotel ♦♦♦
27 Studland Road, Alum Chine, Bournemouth BH4 8HZ
T: (01202) 765386
E: coniston.hotel@virgin.net

Cransley Hotel ♦♦♦♦
11 Knyveton Road, East Cliff, Bournemouth BH1 3QG
T: (01202) 290067
F: (07092) 381721
E: info@cransley.com
I: www.cransley.com

Crosbie Hall Hotel ♦♦♦
21 Florence Road, Boscombe, Bournemouth BH5 1HJ
T: (01202) 394714
F: (01202) 394714
E: david@crosbiehall.fsnet.co.uk
I: www.crosbiehall.fsnet.co.uk

Denewood Hotel ♦♦♦
1 Percy Road, Boscombe, Bournemouth BH5 1JE
T: (01202) 394493
F: (01202) 391155
E: peteer@denewood.co.uk
I: www.denewood.co.uk

Earlham Lodge ♦♦♦♦
91 Alumhurst Road, Alum Chine, Bournemouth BH4 8HR
T: (01202) 761943
F: (01202) 768223
E: info@earlhamlodge.com
I: www.earlhamlodge.com

East Cliff Cottage Hotel ♦♦♦
57 Grove Road, Bournemouth BH1 3AT
T: (01202) 552788
F: (01202) 556400
E: info@otel57.freeserve.co.uk
I: www.otel57.freeserve.co.uk

Fairmount Hotel ♦♦♦♦
15 Priory Road, West Cliff, Bournemouth BH2 5DF
T: (01202) 551105
F: (01202) 553210
E: stay@fairmounthotel.co.uk
I: www.fairmounthotel.co.uk

Gervis Court Hotel ♦♦♦
38 Gervis Road, Bournemouth BH1 3DH
T: (01202) 556871
F: (01202) 467066
E: enquiries@gerviscourthotel.co.uk
I: www.gerviscourthotel.co.uk

Glenbourne Hotel ♦♦♦♦
81 Alumhurst Road, Alum Chine, Bournemouth BH4 8HR
T: (01202) 761607
F: (01202) 762837
E: enquiries@theglenbournehotel.com
I: www.theglenbournehotel.com

The Inver House Hotel ♦♦♦♦
12 Priory Road, Bournemouth BH2 5DG
T: (01202) 553319
F: (01202) 553313
I: www.inverhousehotel.co.uk

Inverness Hotel ♦♦♦♦
26 Tregonwell Road, West Cliff, Bournemouth BH2 5NS
T: (01202) 554968
F: (01202) 294197
E: inverness.hotel@btinternet.com
I: www.invernesshotel.net

Kings Langley Hotel ♦♦♦
1 West Cliff Road, Bournemouth BH2 5ES
T: (01202) 557349
F: (01202) 789739
E: john@kingslangleyhotel.com
I: www.kingslangleyhotel.com

Lawnswood Hotel ♦♦♦
22A Studland Road, Alum Chine, Bournemouth BH4 8JA
T: (01202) 761170
E: lawnswood_hotel_uk@yahoo.com
I: www.lawnswoodhotel.co.uk

Lynton Guest House
Rating Applied For
5 Upper Terrace Road, Bournemouth BH2 5NW
T: (01202) 290875
F: (01202) 297558
E: lyntonguesthouse@hotmail.com
I: www.lyntonguesthouse.com

Majestic Hotel ♦♦♦♦
34 Derby Road, East Cliff, Bournemouth BH1 3QE
T: (01202) 294771
F: (01202) 310962
I: www.shearingsholidays.com

Mayfield Guest House
♦♦♦♦ SILVER AWARD
46 Frances Road, Knyveton Gardens, Bournemouth BH1 3SA
T: (01202) 551839
F: (01202) 551839
E: accom@mayfieldguesthouse.com
I: www.mayfieldguesthouse.com

Mount Lodge Hotel ♦♦♦
19 Beaulieu Road, Alum Chine, Bournemouth BH4 8HY
T: (01202) 761173
F: (01202) 752951
E: mountlodgehotel@yahoo.com

Oxford Hall Hotel ♦♦♦♦
6 Sandbourne Road, Bournemouth BH4 8JH
T: (01202) 761016
F: (01202) 540465
E: oxfordhall@eurolinkltd.net

Parklands Hotel ♦♦♦♦
Rushton Crescent, Bournemouth BH3 7AF
T: (01202) 552529
F: (01202) 552529
E: enquiries@parklandshotel.net
I: www.parklandshotel.net

Redlands Hotel ♦♦♦♦
79 St Michaels Road, West Cliff, Bournemouth BH2 5DR
T: (01202) 553714
E: enquiries@redlandshotel.co.uk
I: www.redlandshotel.co.uk

St Winifrides Hotel
♦♦♦♦ SILVER AWARD
1 Studland Road, Alum Chine, Bournemouth BH4 8HZ
T: (01202) 761829
E: infa@stwinifrideshotel.co.uk
I: www.stwinifrideshotel.co.uk

Shoreline Hotel ♦♦♦♦
7 Pinecliffe Avenue, Southbourne, Bournemouth BH6 3PY
T: (01202) 429654
F: (01202) 429654
E: tjshorelinebb@aol.com

Silver How Hotel ♦♦♦♦
5 West Cliff Gardens, Bournemouth BH2 5HL
T: (01202) 551537
F: (01202) 551456
E: reservations@silverhowhotel.co.uk
I: www.silverhowhotel.co.uk

Southernhay Hotel ♦♦♦
42 Alum Chine Road, Westbourne, Bournemouth BH4 8DX
T: (01202) 761251
F: (01202) 761251
E: enquiries@southernhayhotel.co.uk
I: www.southernhayhotel.co.uk

Trelawny Guest House ♦♦♦♦
34 Wellington Road, Bournemouth BH8 8JW
T: (01202) 554015
F: (01202) 554015
E: trelawny34@talk21.com
I: trelawnyguesthouse.co.uk

The Twin Tops
♦♦♦♦ SILVER AWARD
33 Wheelers Lane, Bournemouth BH11 9QQ
T: (01202) 570080
F: (01202) 570080
E: twintops@btinternet.com
I: www.thetwintops.com

The Ventura Hotel ♦♦♦♦
1 Herbert Road, Bournemouth BH4 8HD
T: (01202) 761265
F: (01202) 757673
E: enquiries@venturahotel.co.uk
I: www.venturahotel.co.uk

The Vine Hotel ♦♦♦
22 Southern Road, Southbourne, Bournemouth BH6 3SR
T: (01202) 428309
F: (01202) 428309
I: www.bournemouthlinks.com/thevinehotel

West Cliff Sands Hotel ♦♦
9 Priory Road, Bournemouth BH2 5DF
T: (01202) 557013
F: (01202) 557013
E: wst.clff-sds@virgin.net
I: www.westcliffsands.sageweb.co.uk

Whitley Court Hotel ♦♦♦
West Cliff Gardens, Bournemouth BH2 5HL
T: (01202) 551302
F: (01202) 551302

Willowdene Hotel
♦♦♦♦ SILVER AWARD
43 Grand Avenue, Southbourne, Bournemouth BH6 3SY
T: (01202) 425370
F: (01202) 425370
E: willowdenehotel@aol.com
I: www.willowdenehotel.co.uk

Winter Dene Hotel ♦♦♦♦
11 Durley Road South, West Cliff, Bournemouth BH2 5JH
T: (01202) 554150
F: (01202) 555426
E: info@winterdenehotel.com
I: www.winterdenehotel.com

Wood Lodge Hotel ♦♦♦♦
10 Manor Road, Bournemouth BH1 3EY
T: (01202) 290891
F: (01202) 290892
I: www.woodlodge.com

The Woodlands Hotel ♦♦♦♦
28 Percy Road, Boscombe Manor, Bournemouth BH5 1JG
T: (01202) 396499
F: (01202) 396499
E: thewoodlandshotel@tinyworld.co.uk
I: www.the-woodlands-hotel.co.uk

Woodside Private Hotel
♦♦♦♦
29 Southern Road, Southbourne, Bournemouth BH6 3SR
T: (01202) 427213
F: (01202) 417609
E: ann.jeff@btinternet.com
I: www.smoothhound.co.uk/hotels/woodsid3.html

Wrenwood Hotel ♦♦♦
11 Florence Road, Boscombe, Bournemouth BH5 1HH
T: (01202) 395086
F: (01202) 396511
E: bookings@wrenwood.co.uk
I: www.wrenwood.co.uk

BOXGROVE
West Sussex

The Brufords ♦♦♦♦
66 The Street, Boxgrove, Chichester PO18 0EE
T: (01243) 774085
F: (01243) 781235
E: room4me@brufords.org
I: www.sussexlive.com

BOXLEY
Kent

Barn Cottage ♦♦♦
Harbourland, Boxley, Maidstone ME14 3DN
T: (01622) 675891
F: (01622) 675891

BRACKNELL
Berkshire

Elizabeth House Hotel Ltd
♦♦♦
Rounds Hill, Wokingham Road, Bracknell RG42 1PB
T: (01344) 868480
F: (01344) 648453
E: rooms@elizabeth-house.freeserve.co.uk
I: www.elizabeth-house.freeserve.co.uk

22 Evedon ♦♦
Birch Hill, Bracknell RG12 7NF
T: (01344) 450637
I: evedonbb@aol.com

BRAMLEY
Surrey

Old Timbers ♦♦♦
Snowdenham Links Road, Bramley, Guildford GU5 0BX
T: (01483) 893258
E: jpold_timbers@hotmail.com

Orchard Paddocks ♦♦♦♦
Iron Lane, Bramley, Guildford GU5 0BY
T: (01483) 894563
F: (01483) 894111

BRANKSOME PARK
Dorset

Grovefield Manor Hotel
♦♦♦♦ SILVER AWARD
18 Pinewood Road, Branksome Park, Poole BH13 6JS
T: (01202) 766798

BRANSGORE
Hampshire

The Corner House ♦♦♦♦
Betsy Lane, Bransgore, Christchurch BH23 8AQ
T: (01425) 673201
E: aerominx35@aol.com

Wiltshire House
♦♦♦♦ SILVER AWARD
West Road, Bransgore, Christchurch BH23 8BD
T: (01425) 672450
F: (01425) 672450
E: hooper@wiltshirehouse.freeserve.co.uk
I: www.wiltshirehouse.freeserve.co.uk

BRASTED
Kent

Lodge House ♦♦♦
High Street, Brasted, Westerham TN16 1HS
T: (01959) 562195
F: (01959) 562195
E: lodgehouse@brastedbb.freeserve.co.uk

The Mount House ♦♦♦♦
The Mount House, Brasted, Westerham TN16 1JB
T: (01959) 563617
F: (01959) 561296
E: jpaulco@webspeed.net
I: www.themolehouse.com

The Orchard House ♦♦♦
Brasted Chart, Westerham TN16 1LR
T: (01959) 563702
E: david.godsal@tesco.net

BREDE
East Sussex

Brede Court Country House ♦♦♦♦
Brede Hill, Brede, Rye TN31 6EJ
T: (01424) 883105
F: (01424) 883104
E: bredecrt@globalnet.co.uk
I: www.english-training.com

2 Stonelink Cottages ♦♦♦
Stubb Lane, Brede, Rye TN31 6BL
T: (01424) 882943
F: (01424) 883052
E: stonelinkc@aol.com

BRENCHLEY
Kent

Woodlands Cottage ♦♦♦♦
Fairmans Road, Brenchley, Tonbridge TN12 7BB
T: (01892) 722707
F: (01892) 724946
E: chris.omalley@virgin.net

BRENZETT
Kent

Beba Farms Brenzett ♦♦♦
Brenzett Place, Ivychurch Road, Brenzett, Romney Marsh TN29 0EE
T: (01797) 344621
F: (01797) 344172
E: apabeba@lineone.net
I: www.kent-esites.co.uk/bebafarmsbrenzett

BRIDGE
Kent

Harrow Cottage ♦♦♦
2 Brewery Lane, Bridge, Canterbury CT4 5LD
T: (01227) 830218
F: (01227) 830218
E: pamela@phooker.fsbusiness.co.uk

BRIGHSTONE
Isle of Wight

Chilton Farm ♦♦♦♦
Chilton Lane, Brighstone, Newport PO30 4DS
T: (01983) 740338
F: (01983) 741370
E: info@chiltonfarm.co.uk
I: www.chiltonfarm.co.uk

Moortown Cottage ♦♦♦
Moortown Lane, Brighstone, Newport PO30 4AN
T: (01983) 741428
E: denise_moortown@beeb.net

BRIGHTLING
East Sussex

Orchard Barn ♦♦♦
3 Twelve Oaks Cottages, Brightling, Robertsbridge TN32 5HS
T: (01424) 838263

Swallowfield Farm ♦♦♦♦
Brightling, Battle TN32 5HB
T: (01424) 838225
F: (01424) 838885
E: jssp@swallowfieldfarm.freeserve.co.uk
I: www.swallowfieldfarm.com

BRIGHTON & HOVE
East Sussex

Adelaide Hotel ♦♦♦♦ SILVER AWARD
51 Regency Square, Brighton BN1 2FF
T: (01273) 205286
F: (01273) 220904
E: adelaide@pavilion.co.uk

Aegean Hotel ♦♦♦
5 New Steine, Brighton BN2 1PB
T: (01273) 686547
F: (01273) 625613

Ainsley House Hotel ♦♦♦♦
28 New Steine, Brighton BN2 1PD
T: (01273) 605310
F: (01273) 688604
E: ahhotel@fastnet.co.uk
I: www.ainsleyhotel.co.uk

Ambassador Hotel ♦♦♦♦
22 New Steine, Marine Parade, Brighton BN2 1PD
T: (01273) 676869
F: (01273) 689988
E: ambassadorhoteluk@hotmail.com
I: www.ambassadorhotelbrighton.com

Andorra Hotel ♦♦♦
15-16 Oriental Place, Brighton BN1 2LJ
T: (01273) 321787
F: (01273) 721418

Aquarium Guest House ♦♦♦
13 Madeira Place, Brighton BN2 1TN
T: (01273) 605761
E: therese-cahillzooo@yahoo.com

Atlantic Hotel ♦♦♦
16 Marine Parade, Brighton BN2 1TL
T: (01273) 695944
F: (01273) 694944

Aymer Guest House ♦♦♦♦
13 Aymer Road, Hove, Brighton BN3 4GB
T: (01273) 271165
F: (01273) 321653
I: www.aymerguesthouse.co.uk

The Beach Hotel ♦♦♦
2-4 Regency Square, Brighton BN1 2GP
T: (01273) 323776
F: (01273) 747028
E: beachhotelbrighton@hotmail.com
I: www.beachotel.co.uk

Beynon House ♦♦♦
24 St Georges Terrace, Brighton BN2 1JJ
T: (01273) 681014
F: (01273) 681014
E: beynonhouse@hotmail.com
I: www.beynonhouse.co.uk

Brighton House Hotel ♦♦♦♦
52 Regency Square, Brighton BN1 2FF
T: (01273) 323282
E: enquiries@brightonhousehotel.co.uk
I: www.brightonhousehotel.co.uk

Brighton Kingsway Hotel ♦♦♦♦ SILVER AWARD
2 St Aubyn's, Hove, Brighton BN3 2TB
T: (01273) 722068
F: (01273) 778409
E: admin@kingswayent.demon.co.uk
I: www.kingsway-hotel.co.uk

Brighton Marina House Hotel ♦♦♦
8 Charlotte Street, Marine Parade, Brighton BN2 1AG
T: (01273) 605349
F: (01273) 679484
E: rooms@jungs.co.uk
I: www.brighton-mh-hotel.co.uk

Brighton Twenty One Hotel ♦♦♦♦
21 Charlotte Street, Marine Parade, Brighton BN2 1AG
T: (01273) 686450
F: (01273) 695560
E: the21@pavilion.co.uk
I: www.s-h-systems.co.uk/hotels/21

Brightside ♦♦♦♦
4 Shirley Road, Hove, Brighton BN3 6NN
T: (01273) 552557
F: (01273) 552557
E: mary.nimmo1@btopenworld.com

Brunswick Square Hotel ♦♦♦
11 Brunswick Square, Hove, Brighton BN3 1EH
T: (01273) 205047
F: (01273) 205047
E: brunswick@brighton.co.uk
I: www.brighton.co.uk/hotels/brunswick

C Breeze Hotel ♦♦♦
12a Upper Rock Gardens, Brighton BN2 1QE
T: (01273) 602608
F: (01273) 607166
I: www.c-breezehotel.co.uk

Cavalaire Hotel ♦♦♦♦
34 Upper Rock Gardens, Brighton BN2 1QF
T: (01273) 696899
F: (01273) 600504
E: welcome@cavalaire.co.uk
I: www.cavalaire.co.uk

Chatsworth Hotel ♦♦
9 Salisbury Road, Hove, Brighton BN3 3AB
T: (01273) 737360
F: (01273) 737360

Churchill Guest House ♦♦♦♦
44 Russell Square, Brighton BN1 2EF
T: (01273) 700777
F: (01273) 700887
E: enquiries@churchillguesthouse.com
I: www.churchillguesthouse.com

Claremont House Hotel ♦♦♦♦
Second Avenue, Hove, Brighton BN3 2LL
T: (01273) 735161
F: (01273) 735161
E: claremonthove@aol.com
I: www.claremonthousehotel.co.uk

Cosmopolitan Hotel ♦♦♦
31 New Steine, Marine Parade, Brighton BN2 1PD
T: (01273) 682461
F: (01273) 622311
E: enquire@cosmopolitanhotel.co.uk
I: www.cosmopolitanhotel.co.uk

Diana House ♦♦
25 St Georges Terrace, Brighton BN2 1JJ
T: (01273) 605797
F: (01273) 600533
E: diana@enterprise.net
I: www.dianahouse.co.uk

Dove Hotel ♦♦♦♦
18 Regency Square, Brighton BN1 2FG
T: (01273) 779222
F: (01273) 746912
E: dovehotel@dovehotelfree-online.co.uk

Dudley House ♦♦♦
10 Madeira Place, Brighton BN2 1TN
T: (01273) 676794
E: office@dudleyhousebrighton.com

Funchal Guest House ♦♦♦
17 Madeira Place, Brighton BN2 1TN
T: (01273) 603975
F: (01273) 603975

Fyfield House ♦♦♦♦
26 New Steine, Brighton BN2 1PD
T: (01273) 602770
F: (01273) 602770
E: fyfield@aol.com
I: www.fyfieldhotelbrighton.com

Georjan Guest House ♦♦♦
27 Upper Rock Gardens, Brighton BN2 1QE
T: (01273) 694951
E: georjan.gh@virgin.net

Harveys ♦♦♦
1 Broad Street, Brighton BN2 1TJ
T: (01273) 699227
F: (01273) 699227

Hudsons Guest House ♦♦♦
22 Devonshire Place, Brighton BN2 1QA
T: (01273) 683642
F: (01273) 696088
E: info@hudsonshotel.com
I: www.hudsonshotel.com

The Kelvin Guest House ♦♦♦
9 Madeira Place, Brighton BN2 1TN
T: (01273) 603735
F: (01273) 603735

Leona House ♦♦♦
74 Middle Street, Brighton
BN1 1AL
T: (01273) 327309
F: (01273) 777624
E: hazel.eastman@btopenworld.com

Lichfield House ♦♦♦
30 Waterloo Street, Hove, Brighton BN3 1AN
T: (01273) 777740
E: feelgood@lichfieldhouse.freeserve.co.uk
I: www.lichfieldhouse.freeserve.co.uk

Madeira Guest House ♦♦♦
14 Madeira Place, Brighton
BN2 1TN
T: (01273) 681115
F: (01273) 681115
I: www.madeiraguesthouse.co.uk

Miami Hotel ♦♦♦
22 Bedford Square, Brighton
BN1 2PL
T: (01273) 730169
F: (01273) 730169
E: themiami@pavilion.co.uk
I: www.brighton.co.uk/hotels/miami

New Madeira Hotel ♦♦♦
19-23 Marine Parade, Brighton
BN2 1TL
T: (01273) 698331
F: (01273) 606193
E: info@newmadeirahotel.com
I: www.newmadeirahotel.com

Oriental Hotel ♦♦♦
9 Oriental Place, Brighton
BN1 2LJ
T: (01273) 205050
F: (01273) 821096
E: info@orientalhotel.co.uk
I: www.orientalhotel.co.uk

The Palace Hotel ♦♦♦
10-12 Grand Junction Road, Brighton BN1 1PN
T: (01273) 202035
F: (01273) 202034
E: palacehotel@connectfree.co.uk
I: www.palacebrighton.co.uk

Pavilion Guest House ♦♦♦
Madeira Place, Brighton
BN2 1TN
T: (01273) 683195

Russell Guest House ♦♦♦
19 Russell Square, Brighton
BN1 2EE
T: (01273) 327969
F: (01273) 821535
E: russell.brighton@btinternet.com
I: www.smoothhound.co.uk/hotels/russellgh

Sandpiper Guest House ♦♦
11 Russell Square, Brighton
BN1 2EE
T: (01273) 328202
F: (01273) 329974
E: sandpiper@brighton.co.uk

Sea Spray ♦♦♦♦
25 New Steine, Marine Parade, Brighton BN2 1PD
T: (01273) 680332
E: seaspray@brighton.co.uk
I: www.seaspraybrighton.co.uk

Hotel Seafield ♦♦♦
23 Seafield Road, Hove, Brighton
BN3 2TP
T: (01273) 735912
F: (01273) 323525
I: www.brighton.co.uk/hotels/seafield/

Strawberry Fields Hotel ♦♦♦
6-7 New Steine, Brighton
BN2 1PB
T: (01273) 681576
F: (01273) 693397
E: strawberryfields@pavilion.co.uk
I: www.brighton.co.uk/hotels/strawberryfields

Valentine House Hotel ♦♦♦
38 Russell Square, Brighton
BN1 2EF
T: (01273) 700800
F: (01273) 707606
E: stay@valentinehousehotel.com
I: www.valentinehousehotel.com

The White House ♦♦♦♦
6 Bedford Street, Brighton
BN2 1AN
T: (01273) 626266
E: info@whitehousebrighton.com
I: www.whitehousebrighton.com

BRILL
Buckinghamshire

Laplands Farm ♦♦♦♦
Ludgershall Road, Brill, Aylesbury HP18 9TZ
T: (01844) 237888
F: (01844) 238870
E: enquiries@intents-marquees.co.uk
I: www.intents-marquees.co.uk

BRIZE NORTON
Oxfordshire

The Long Barn ♦♦♦♦
26 Carterton Road, Brize Norton, Carterton OX18 3LY
T: (01993) 843309
F: (01993) 843309
E: kgillians@the-long-barn.co.uk
I: www.the-long-barn.co.uk

The Priory Manor Farm
Rating Applied For
Manor Road, Brize Norton, OX18 3NA
T: (01993) 843062
F: (01993) 843062
E: mail@thepriorymanor.co.uk
I: www.thepriorymanor.co.uk

The Willows ♦♦♦♦
Quarry Dene, Burford Road, Brize Norton, Carterton
OX18 3NN
T: (01993) 842437
E: willowsbbbrize@aol.com

BROADSTAIRS
Kent

Anchor House ♦♦♦♦
10 Chandos Road, Broadstairs
CT10 1QP
T: (01843) 863347
F: (0871) 242 1939
E: anchor-house@tiscali.co.uk
I: www.anchorhouse.net

Bay Tree Hotel ♦♦♦♦
12 Eastern Esplanade, Broadstairs CT10 1DR
T: (01843) 862502
F: (01843) 860589

The Chandos Hotel ♦♦♦
5 Chandos Square, Broadstairs
CT10 1QW
T: (01843) 863579
F: (01843) 863579

Cintra Hotel ♦♦♦
24 Victoria Parade, Broadstairs
CT10 1QL
T: (01843) 862253
F: (01434) 869503
E: cintrahotel@aol.com

Copperfields Vegetarian Guest House ♦♦♦
11 Queens Road, Broadstairs
CT10 1NU
T: (01843) 601247
E: jroger600@aol.com
I: www.copperfieldsbb.co.uk

Devonhurst Hotel ♦♦♦♦
Eastern Esplanade, Broadstairs
CT10 1DR
T: (01843) 863010
F: (01843) 868940
E: info@devonhurst.co.uk
I: www.devonhurst.co.uk

Dundonald House Hotel ♦♦♦
43 Belvedere Road, Broadstairs
CT10 1PF
T: (01843) 862236
E: info@dundonaldhousehotel.co.uk
I: www.dundonaldhousehotel.co.uk

East Horndon Hotel ♦♦♦
4 Eastern Esplanade, Broadstairs
CT10 1DP
T: (01843) 868306
E: easthorndon@hotmail.com
I: www.easthorndonhotel.com

Hanson Hotel ♦♦♦
41 Belvedere Road, Broadstairs
CT10 1PF
T: (01843) 868936
E: hotelhanson@aol.com

Merriland Hotel ♦♦♦♦
The Vale, Broadstairs CT10 1RB
T: (01843) 861064
F: (01843) 861064
E: merrilandhotel@adl.com

Number 68
Rating Applied For
68 West Cliff Road, Broadstairs
CT10 1PY
T: (01843) 609459

Oakfield Private Hotel ♦♦♦♦
11 The Vale, Broadstairs
CT10 1RB
T: (01843) 862506
F: (01843) 600659
E: oakfield.hotel@lineone.net
I: www.oakfield-hotel.com

Pierremont ♦♦♦
102 Pierremont Avenue, Broadstairs CT10 1NT
T: (01843) 600462
E: jenny.barrett@hcsconsulting.co.uk

The Queens Hotel ♦♦♦
31 Queens Road, Broadstairs
CT10 1PG
T: (01843) 861727
F: (01843) 600993
E: enquiries@queenshotel.org
I: www.queenshotel.org

Shorelands ♦♦♦♦
16 Eastern Esplanade, Broadstairs CT10 1DR
T: (01843) 861324
F: (01843) 861324

Velindre Hotel ♦♦♦
10 Western Esplanade, Broadstairs CT10 1TG
T: (01843) 601081

The Victoria
♦♦♦♦♦ SILVER AWARD
23 Victoria Parade, Broadstairs
CT10 1QL
T: (01843) 871010
F: (01843) 860888
E: mullin@thevictoriabroadstairs.co.uk
I: www.thevictoriabroadstairs.co.uk

BROADSTONE
Dorset

Honey Lodge
♦♦♦♦ SILVER AWARD
41 Dunyeats Road, Broadstone
BH18 8AB
T: (01202) 694247

Tarven ♦♦♦
Corfe Lodge Road, Broadstone
BH18 9NF
T: (01202) 694338
E: browning@tarvencorfe.fsnet.co.uk

Weston Cottage ♦♦♦♦
6 Macaulay Road, Broadstone
BH18 8AR
T: (01202) 699638
F: (01202) 699638
E: westoncot@aol.com

BROCKENHURST
Hampshire

Annerley ♦♦♦♦
Waters Green, Brockenhurst
SO42 7RG
T: (01590) 624536
F: (01590) 624536
E: colin.h.horner@talk21.com

Briardale ♦♦♦
11 Noel Close, Brockenhurst
SO42 7RP
T: (01590) 623946
F: (01590) 623946
E: briardale@brockenhurst.fsbusiness.co.uk
I: www.brockenhurst.fsbusiness.co.uk

The Filly Inn ♦♦♦
Lymington Road, Setley, Brockenhurst SO42 7UF
T: (01590) 623449
F: (01590) 623449
E: pub@fillyinn.co.uk
I: www.fillyinn.co.uk

Garlands Cottage ♦♦♦♦
2 Garlands Cottage, Lyndhurst Road, Brockenhurst SO42 7RH
T: (01590) 623250
E: garlandscottage@hotmail.com

Goldenhayes ♦♦
9 Chestnut Road, Brockenhurst SO42 7RF
T: (01590) 623743

Jacmar Cottage ♦♦♦
Mill Lane, Brockenhurst SO42 7UA
T: (01590) 622019
E: jacmarcottage@aol.com

Pine Cottage
Rating Applied For
Whitley Ridge, Beaulieu Road, Brockenhurst SO42 7QL
T: (01590) 622396
E: pinecottage@jacob2.fslife.co.uk

BROOKLAND
Kent

Walland Cottage ♦♦♦♦
Boarmans Lane, Brookland, Romney Marsh TN29 9QZ
T: (01797) 344703

BUCKINGHAM
Buckinghamshire

The Britannia Inn ♦♦
Gawcott Road, Buckingham MK18 1DR
T: (01280) 822338
F: (01280) 822338

Churchwell ♦♦♦
Church Street, Buckingham MK18 1BY
T: (01280) 815415
F: (01280) 822223
I: www.churchwell.co.uk

Folly Farm ♦♦♦♦
Padbury, Buckingham MK18 2HS
T: (01296) 712413
F: (01296) 714923

Huntsmill House B&B ♦♦♦♦
Huntsmill Farm, Shalstone, Buckingham MK18 5ND
T: (01280) 704852
F: (01280) 704852
E: fiona@huntsmill.com
I: www.huntsmill.com

Radclive Dairy Farm ♦♦♦♦
Radclive Road, Gawcott, Buckingham MK18 4AA
T: (01280) 813433
F: (01280) 813433

BUCKLAND
Oxfordshire

The Inn on the Green
Rating Applied For
Carswell Golf & Country Club, Faringdon SN7 8PU
T: (01367) 870472
F: (01367) 870592

BURFORD
Oxfordshire

Barley Park
♦♦♦♦ SILVER AWARD
Shilton Road, Burford, Oxford OX18 4PD
T: (01993) 823573
F: (01993) 824220
E: barley_park@hotmail.com
I: www.burford-bed-and-breakfast.co.uk

Burford House Hotel
♦♦♦♦♦ GOLD AWARD
99 High Street, Burford, Oxford OX18 4QA
T: (01993) 823151
F: (01993) 823240
E: stay@burfordhouse.co.uk
I: www.burfordhouse.co.uk

The Highway ♦♦♦
117 High Street, Burford, Oxford OX18 4RG
T: (01993) 822136
F: (01993) 824740
E: rbx20@dial.pipex.com
I: www.oxlink.co.uk/burford

Manor Lodge
♦♦♦♦ SILVER AWARD
Shilton, Burford, Oxford OX18 4AS
T: (01993) 841444
F: (01993) 841446
E: enquiries@manorlodgebnb.co.uk
I: www.manorlodgebnb.co.uk

Merryfield ♦♦♦
High Street, Fifield, Oxford OX7 6HL
T: (01993) 830517
E: jpmgtd@freeuk.com
I: www.merryfieldbandb.co.uk

The Old Bell Foundry ♦♦♦♦
45 Witney Street, Burford, Oxford OX18 4RX
T: (01993) 822234
E: barguss@ukgateway.net
I: www.oxtowns.co.uk/burford/oldbellfoundry/

Old Bull Hotel ♦♦♦♦
105 High Street, Burford, Oxford OX15 4RG
T: (01993) 822220
F: (01993) 823243

Potters Hill Farm ♦♦♦
Leafield, Burford, Oxford OX8 5QB
T: (01993) 878018
F: (01993) 878018
E: k.stanley@virgin.net
I: www.country-accom.co.uk/potters-hill-farm

St Winnow ♦♦♦
160 The Hill, Burford, Oxford OX18 4QY
T: (01993) 823843
E: b&b@stwinnow.com
I: www.stwinnow.com

Tudor Cottage ♦♦♦♦
40 Witney Street, Burford, Oxford OX18 4SN
T: (01993) 823251
F: (01993) 823251

Willow Cottage ♦♦♦♦
Shilton, Burford, Oxford OX18 4AB
T: (01993) 842456
F: (01993) 842456
I: www.smoothhound.co.uk/hotels/willowcot.html

BURGESS HILL
West Sussex

Daisy Lodge B&B ♦♦♦
26 Royal George Road, Burgess Hill RH15 9SE
T: (01444) 870570
F: (01444) 870571
E: daisylodge@btinternet.com

87 Meadow Lane ♦♦♦
Burgess Hill RH15 9JD
T: (01444) 248421
F: (01444) 248421
E: bsayers@onetel.net.uk

Roman Way ♦♦♦
262 Chanctonbury Road, Burgess Hill RH15 9HJ
T: (01444) 242836
F: (01444) 242836

Roselands ♦♦♦
3 Upper St Johns Road, Burgess Hill RH15 8HB
T: (01444) 870491

St Owens ♦♦♦♦
11 Silverdale Road, Burgess Hill RH15 0ED
T: (01444) 236435
E: n.j.baker@amserve.net

Wellhouse ♦♦♦♦
Wellhouse Lane, Burgess Hill RH15 0BN
T: (01444) 233231
F: (01444) 233231

BURLEY
Hampshire

Bay Tree House ♦♦♦
1 Clough Lane, Burley, Ringwood BH24 4AE
T: (01425) 403215
F: (01425) 403215
E: Baytreehousebandb@burleyhants.freeserve.co.uk
I: www.newforest.demon.co.uk/baytreehouse.htm

Forest Teahouse ♦♦♦
Forest Cottage, Pound Lane, Burley, Ringwood BH24 4ED
T: (01425) 402305

Great Wells House
♦♦♦♦♦ GOLD AWARD
Beechwood Lane, Burley, Ringwood BH24 4AS
T: (01425) 402302
F: (01425) 402302
E: chrisstewart@compuserve.com

Holmans
♦♦♦♦ SILVER AWARD
Bisterne Close, Burley, Ringwood BH24 4AZ
T: (01425) 402307
F: (01425) 402307

Little Deeracres ♦♦♦♦
Bisterne Close, Burley, Ringwood BH24 4BA
T: (01425) 402477
F: (01425) 402477

The White Buck Inn ♦♦♦♦
Bisterne Close, Burley, Ringwood BH24 4AT
T: (01425) 402264

BURMARSH
Kent

Stable Cottage ♦♦♦♦
The Sheiling, Donkey Street, Burmarsh, Romney Marsh TN29 0JN
T: (01303) 872335
E: janjohn@tiscali.co.uk
I: roomcheck.co.uk or southeastengland.uk.com

BURPHAM
Surrey

Anderton House ♦♦♦
51 Marlyns Drive, Guildford GU4 7LU
T: (01483) 826951
F: (01483) 826951
E: mrsdmkelly@yahoo.co.uk

BUSCOT WICK
Oxfordshire

Weston Farm
♦♦♦♦ SILVER AWARD
Buscot Wick, Faringdon SN7 8DJ
T: (01367) 252222
F: (01367) 252230
E: westonfarmjean@amserve.net
I: www.country-accom.co.uk/weston-farm

CADMORE END
Buckinghamshire

South Fields ♦♦♦
Cadmore End, High Wycombe HP14 3PJ
T: (01494) 881976
F: (01494) 883765
E: crichtons@crichtonville.freeserve.co.uk
I: www.crichtonville.freeserve.co.uk

CADNAM
Hampshire

Kingsbridge House ♦♦♦
Southampton Road, Cadnam, Southampton SO40 2NH
T: (023) 8081 1161
E: linda@kingbridgehouse.freeserve.co.uk

CAMBER
East Sussex

The Place Cambersands
♦♦♦♦
New Lydd Road, Camber Sands, Camber, Rye TN31 7RB
T: (01797) 225057
I: www.theplacecambersands.co.uk

CAMBERLEY
Surrey

Abacus ♦♦♦
Woodside, Blackwater, Camberley GU17 9JJ
T: (01276) 38339
E: abacus@amserve.net

CANTERBURY
Kent

Abberley House ♦♦♦
115 Whitstable Road, Canterbury CT2 8EF
T: (01227) 450265
F: (01227) 478626

Acacia Lodge & Tanglewood
♦♦♦♦
39-40 London Road, Canterbury CT2 8LF
T: (01227) 769955
F: (01227) 478960
E: michaelcain@lineone.net
I: www.acacialodge.com

Alexandra House ♦♦♦♦
1 Roper Road, Canterbury CT2 7EH
T: (01227) 767011
F: (01227) 786617
E: alexandrahouse@ic24.net
I: www.alexandrahouse.net

Alicante Guest House ♦♦♦
4 Roper Road, Canterbury
CT2 7EH
T: (01227) 766277
F: (01227) 766277

Anns House ♦♦♦
63 London Road, Canterbury
CT2 8JZ
T: (01227) 768767
F: (01227) 768172

Ashley Guest House ♦♦
9 London Road, Canterbury
CT2 8LR
T: (01227) 455863

Bluebells Guest House
Rating Applied For
248 Wincheap, CT1 3TY
T: (01227) 478842

Carena ♦♦♦
250 Wincheap, Canterbury
CT1 3TY
T: (01227) 765630
F: (01227) 765630

Castle Court Guest House ♦♦
8 Castle Street, Canterbury
CT1 2QF
T: (01227) 463441
F: (01227) 463441
E: guesthouse@castlecourt.fsnet.co.uk
I: www.SmoothHound.co.uk/hotels/castlecourt.html

Castle House ♦♦♦♦
28 Castle Street, Canterbury
CT1 2PT
T: (01227) 761897
E: enquries@castlehousehotel.co.uk
I: www.castlehousehotel.co.uk

Cathedral Gate Hotel ♦♦♦
36 Burgate, Canterbury CT1 2HA
T: (01227) 464381
F: (01227) 462800
E: cgate@cgate.demon.co.uk
I: www.cathgate.co.uk

Charnwood B & B ♦♦♦
64 New Dover Road, Canterbury
CT1 3DT
T: (01227) 451712
F: (01227) 478232
E: charnwood.bb@btinternet.com

Chaucer Lodge ♦♦♦♦
62 New Dover Road, Canterbury
CT1 3DT
T: (01227) 459141
F: (01227) 459141
E: wchaucerldg@aol.com
I: www.thechaucerlodge.co.uk

Clare-Ellen Guest House
♦♦♦♦ SILVER AWARD
9 Victoria Road, Wincheap,
Canterbury CT1 3SG
T: (01227) 760205
F: (01227) 784482
E: loraine.williams@clareellenguesthouse.co.uk
I: www.clareellenguesthouse.co.uk

The Coach House ♦♦♦
34 Watling Street, Canterbury
CT1 2UD
T: (01227) 784324
F: (01227) 784324
E: dunxnteen@tiscali.co.uk

The Dickens Inn at House of Agnes Hotel ♦♦
71 St Dunstan's Street,
Canterbury CT2 8BN
T: (01227) 472185
F: (01227) 464527
E: enq@dickens-inn.co.uk
I: www.dickens-inn.co.uk

Elmstone Court
♦♦♦♦♦ SILVER AWARD
Out Elmstead Lane, Barham,
Canterbury CT4 6PH
T: (01227) 830433
F: (01227) 832403

Four Seasons ♦♦♦
77 Sturry Road, Canterbury
CT1 1BU
T: (01227) 787078
E: fourseasonsbnb@aol.com
I: members.aol.com/fourseasonsbnb

Greyfriars House ♦♦♦
6 Stour Street, Canterbury
CT1 2NR
T: (01227) 456255
F: (01227) 455233
E: christine@greyfriars-house.co.uk
I: www.greyfriars-house.co.uk

Hornbeams ♦♦♦♦
Jesses Hill, Kingston, Canterbury
CT4 6JD
T: (01227) 830119
F: (01227) 830119
E: b&b@hornbeams.co.uk
I: www.hornbeams.co.uk

Iffin Farmhouse ♦♦♦♦
Iffin Lane, Canterbury CT4 7BE
T: 0870 3210565
F: (01227) 762660
E: iffin.farmhouse@care4free.net

The Kings Head ♦♦♦
204 Wincheap, Canterbury
CT1 3RY
T: (01227) 462885
F: (01227) 459627

Kingsbridge Villa ♦♦♦
15 Best Lane, Canterbury
CT1 2JB
T: (01227) 766415
F: (01227) 766415
E: info@canterburyguesthouse.com
I: www.canterburyguesthouse.com

Kingsmead House ♦♦♦
68 St Stephens Road,
Canterbury CT2 7JF
T: (01227) 760132
E: john.clark52@btopenworld.com

Magnolia House
♦♦♦♦♦ GOLD AWARD
36 St Dunstans Terrace,
Canterbury CT2 8AX
T: (01227) 765121
F: (01227) 765121
E: magnolia_house_canterbury@yahoo.com
I: http://freespace.virgin.net/magnolia.canterbury

The Millers Arms ♦♦♦
2 Mill Lane, Canterbury CT1 2AW
T: (01227) 456057
F: (01227) 452421

Oak Cottage ♦♦♦♦
Elmsted, Ashford TN25 5JT
T: (01233) 750272
F: (01233) 750543
E: nichols@oakcottage.invictanet.co.uk
I: www.kent-esites.co.uk/oakcottage

Peregrine House ♦♦♦
18 Hawks Lane, Canterbury
CT1 2NU
T: (01227) 472153
F: (01227) 455233
E: christine@greyfriars-house.co.uk
I: www.cantweb.co.uk/peregrine

The Plantation ♦♦♦♦
Iffin Lane, Canterbury CT4 7BD
T: (01227) 472104
E: plantation@lycos.co.uk
I: www.theplantation.biz

Raemore House ♦♦♦
33 New Dover Road, Canterbury
CT1 3AS
T: (01227) 769740
F: (01227) 769432
E: enquiries@raemorehouse.com
I: www.raemorehouse.com

Renville Oast ♦♦♦♦
Bridge, Canterbury CT4 5AD
T: (01227) 830215
F: (01227) 830215
E: renville.oast@virgin.net
I: www.renvilleoast.co.uk

St Lawrence Guest House
♦♦♦
183 Old Dover Road, Canterbury
CT1 3EP
T: (01227) 451336
F: (01227) 451148
E: stlawrence@ic24.net
I: www.stlawrenceguesthouse.co.uk

St Stephens Guest House
♦♦♦
100 St Stephens Road,
Canterbury CT2 7JL
T: (01227) 767644
F: (01227) 767644
E: info@st-stephens.fsnet.co.uk
I: www.come.to/st-stephens

Thanington Hotel
♦♦♦♦♦ GOLD AWARD
140 Wincheap, Canterbury
CT1 3RY
T: (01227) 453227
F: (01227) 453225
E: enquiries@thanington-hotel.co.uk
I: www.thanington-hotel.co.uk

Tudor House ♦♦♦
6 Best Lane, Canterbury CT1 2JB
T: (01227) 765650

Twin Mays
♦♦♦♦ GOLD AWARD
Plumpudding Lane, Dargate,
Faversham ME13 9EX
T: (01227) 751346
E: janetm@harper128.freeserve.co.uk
I: www.harper128.freeserve.co.uk

Waltham Court Hotel ♦♦♦♦
Kake Street, Waltham, Petham,
Canterbury CT4 5SB
T: (01227) 700413
F: (01227) 700127
E: enquiries@walthamcourthotel.co.uk
I: www.walthamcourthotel.co.uk

White Horse Inn ♦♦♦♦
The Street, Boughton,
Faversham ME13 9AX
T: (01227) 751700
F: (01227) 751090
E: whitehorse@shepherd-neame.co.uk
I: www.shepherd-neame.co.uk

The White House ♦♦♦♦
6 St Peters Lane, Canterbury
CT1 2BP
T: (01227) 761836
E: whwelcome@aol.com
I: www.smoothhound.co.uk/hotels/thewhitehouse/html

Wincheap Guest House ♦♦♦
94 Wincheap, Canterbury
CT1 3RS
T: (01227) 762309
F: (01227) 762309
E: joe@wincheapguesthouse.co.uk
I: www.wincheapguesthouse.co.uk

Woodlands Farm ♦♦♦
The Street, Adisham, Canterbury
CT3 3LA
T: (01304) 840401
F: (01304) 841985
E: woodlands.farm@btinternet.com
I: www.woodlands-farm-stay.co.uk

The Woolpack Inn ♦♦♦♦
High Street, Chilham,
Canterbury CT4 8DL
T: (01227) 730208
F: (01227) 731053
E: woolpack@shepherd-neame.co.uk
I: www.shepherd-neame.co.uk

Yorke Lodge Hotel
♦♦♦♦ SILVER AWARD
50 London Road, Canterbury
CT2 8LF
T: (01227) 451243
F: (01227) 462006
E: enquiries@yorkelodge.com
I: www.yorkelodge.com

CAPEL
Surrey

Nightless Copse ♦♦♦♦
Rusper Road, Capel, Dorking
RH5 5HE
T: (01306) 713247
F: (01306) 711765
E: bb@nightlesscopse.co.uk
I: www.nightlesscopse.co.uk

CARISBROOKE
Isle of Wight

Alvington Manor Farm ♦♦♦
Carisbrooke, Newport PO30 5SP
T: (01983) 523463
F: (01983) 523463

CASHMOOR
Dorset

Cashmoor House ♦♦♦♦
Cashmoor, Blandford Forum DT11 8DN
T: (01725) 552339
F: (01725) 552219
E: spencer.jones@ukonline.co.uk
I: www.cashmoorhouse.cjb.net

CASSINGTON
Oxfordshire

St Margaret's Lodge ♦♦♦
The Green, Cassington, Oxford OX8 1DN
T: (01865) 880361
F: (01865) 731314

CASTLETHORPE
Buckinghamshire

Balney Grounds
♦♦♦♦ SILVER AWARD
Home Farm, Hanslope Road, Castlethorpe, Milton Keynes MK19 7HD
T: (01908) 510208
F: (01908) 516119
E: mary.stacey@tesco.net
I: www.lets-stay-mk.co.uk

CATHERINGTON
Hampshire

Flowerdown ♦♦♦
82 Downhouse Road, Catherington, Waterlooville PO8 0TY
T: (023) 9259 8029
F: (023) 9259 8029
E: gloria-butler@made-in-gb.freeserve.co.uk

Lone Barn ♦♦♦♦
Catherington, Waterlooville PO8 0SF
T: (023) 9263 2911
F: (023) 9263 2288
E: marchburn@ukonline.co.uk

CHADDLEWORTH
West Berkshire

Peacock Cottage ♦♦♦
Main Street, Chaddleworth, Newbury RG20 7EH
T: (01488) 638144
F: (01488) 638515
E: mapeng@msn.com

CHADLINGTON
Oxfordshire

Stone Croft ♦♦♦
East End, Chadlington, Oxford OX7 3LX
T: (01608) 676551

CHALE
Isle of Wight

Little Atherfield Farm ♦♦♦♦
Chale, Ventnor PO38 2LQ
T: (01983) 551363
F: (01983) 551033
E: david's.farm@virgin.net

CHALFONT ST GILES
Buckinghamshire

Gorelands Corner ♦♦♦♦
Gorelands Lane, Chalfont St Giles HP8 4HQ
T: (01494) 872689
F: (01494) 872689
E: bickfordcsg@onetel.net.uk

The White Hart Inn ♦♦♦♦
Three Households, Chalfont St Giles HP8 4LP
T: (01494) 872441
F: (01494) 876375
E: whitehartinn@supanet.com

CHALFONT ST PETER
Buckinghamshire

Whitewebbs ♦♦♦♦
Lower Road, Chalfont St Peter, Gerrards Cross SL9 9AQ
T: (01753) 884105
F: (01753) 884105

CHALGROVE
Oxfordshire

Cornerstones ♦♦♦
1 Cromwell Close, Chalgrove, Oxford OX44 7SE
T: (01865) 890298
E: corner.stones@virgin.net

CHANDLERS FORD
Hampshire

Blackbird Hill ♦♦♦
24 Ashbridge Rise, Chandler's Ford, Chandlers Ford, Eastleigh SO53 1SA
T: (023) 8026 0398
E: dotsid@onetel.net.uk

Landfall ♦♦♦
133 Bournemouth Road, Chandler's Ford, Chandlers Ford, Eastleigh SO53 3HA
T: (023) 8025 4801
F: (023) 8025 4801

Monks House
♦♦♦♦♦ GOLD AWARD
111 Hocombe Road, Chandlers Ford, Eastleigh SO53 5QD
T: (023) 8027 5986
F: (023) 8027 1505
E: info@monkshouse.com
I: www.monkshouse.com

Thornbury ♦♦♦♦
243 Winchester Road, Chandlers Ford, Eastleigh SO53 2DX
T: (023) 8026 0703

CHARING
Kent

Royal Oak Inn ♦♦♦
5 High Street, Charing, Ashford TN27 0HU
T: (01233) 712612
F: (01233) 713355
E: royal-oak.charingtn27@barbox.net

CHARLBURY
Oxfordshire

Banbury Hill Farm ♦♦♦♦
Enstone Road, Charlbury, Oxford OX7 3JH
T: (01608) 810314
F: (01608) 811891
E: angelawiddows@gfwiddows.f9.co.uk
I: www.charlburyoxfordaccom.co.uk

The Bell at Charlbury ♦♦♦
Church Street, Charlbury, Oxford OX7 3PP
T: (01608) 810278
F: (01608) 811447

CHARLTON
Hampshire

Acer ♦♦♦
16 Foxcotte Close, Charlton, Andover SP10 4AS
T: (01264) 363286
E: bridget@cobhfox.fsnet.co.uk

CHARLTON MARSHALL
Dorset

Keston House
♦♦♦♦ SILVER AWARD
314 Bournemouth Road, Charlton Marshall, Blandford Forum DT11 9NQ
T: (01258) 451973
F: (01258) 451973
E: bandb@kestonhouse.co.uk
I: www.kestonhouse.co.uk

CHART SUTTON
Kent

White House Farm ♦♦♦♦
Green Lane, Chart Sutton, Maidstone ME17 3ES
T: (01622) 842490
F: (01622) 842490
E: sue.spain@totalise.co.uk
I: www.whitehousefarm-kent.co.uk

CHARTHAM
Kent

Stour Farm ♦♦♦♦
Riverside, Chartham, Canterbury CT4 7NX
T: (01227) 731977
F: (01227) 731977
E: info@stourfarm.co.uk
I: www.stourfarm.co.uk

CHARTHAM HATCH
Kent

Wisteria Lodge ♦♦♦
New Town Street, Chartham Hatch, Canterbury CT4 7LT
T: (01227) 738654
F: (01227) 738654
E: wisteriabandb@yahoo.co.uk

CHATHAM
Kent

Normandy House ♦♦♦
143 Maidstone Road, Chatham ME4 6JE
T: (01634) 843047

Officers Hill
♦♦♦♦ SILVER AWARD
College Road, The Historic Dockyard, Chatham ME4 4QX
T: (01634) 828436
F: (01634) 828735
E: carol.chambers@ukgateway.net

10 Officers Terrace
♦♦♦♦ SILVER AWARD
Historic Dockyard, Chatham ME4 4LJ
T: (01634) 847512
E: sandrawsparks@aol.com

St George Hotel ♦♦♦
7-8 New Road Avenue, Chatham ME4 6BB
T: (01634) 841012
F: (01634) 812019
E: enquiries@george-hotel.co.uk
I: www.george-hotel.co.uk

Ship & Trades ♦♦♦
Maritime Way, Chatham ME4 3ER
T: (01634) 895200
F: (01634) 895201
E: ship&trades@shepherd-neame.co.uk
I: shepherd-neame.co.uk

CHECKENDON
Oxfordshire

Larchdown Farm
♦♦♦♦ SILVER AWARD
Whitehall Lane, Checkendon, Reading RG8 0TT
T: (01491) 682282
F: (01491) 682282
E: larchdown@onetel.net.uk
I: www.larchdown.com

CHELWOOD GATE
East Sussex

Holly House ♦♦♦♦
Beaconsfield Road, Chelwood Gate, Haywards Heath RH17 7LF
T: (01825) 740484
F: (01825) 740172
E: deebirchell@hollyhousebnb.demon.co.uk
I: hollyhousebnb.demon.co.uk

Laurel Cottage ♦♦♦
Baxters Lane, Chelwood Gate, Haywards Heath RH17 7LU
T: (01825) 740547
F: (01825) 740057
E: smartin@chelwood.fsnet.co.uk

CHERITON
Hampshire

Brandy Lea ♦♦♦
Cheriton, Alresford SO24 0QQ
T: (01962) 771534

Old Kennetts Cottage ♦♦♦♦
Cheriton, Alresford SO24 0PX
T: (01962) 771863

CHESHAM
Buckinghamshire

Braziers Well ♦♦♦♦♦
Oak Lane, Braziers End, Chesham HP5 2UL
T: (01494) 758956
E: info@brazierswell.co.uk
I: www.brazierswell.co.uk

49 Lowndes Avenue ♦♦♦
0, Chesham HP5 2HH
T: (01494) 792647
E: bbormelowndes@tiscali.co.uk

May Tree House Bed and Breakfast ♦♦♦♦
32 Hampden Avenue, Chesham HP5 2HL
T: (01494) 784019
F: (01494) 776896

Rose Cottage ♦♦♦
176 Bois Moor Road, Chesham HP5 4SS
T: (01494) 794433
F: (01494) 794444

CHESTERTON
Oxfordshire

Larchmont ♦♦♦
Alchester Road, Chesterton, Bicester OX26 1UN
T: (01869) 245033
F: (01869) 245033

CHEVENING
Kent

Crossways House ♦♦♦♦
Chevening Cross Road, Chevening, Sevenoaks TN14 6HF
T: (01732) 456334
F: (01732) 452312
E: info@cheveningconferences.co.uk
I: www.cheveningconferences.co.uk

CHICHESTER
West Sussex

Abelands Barn ♦♦♦♦
Merston, Chichester PO20 1DY
T: (01243) 533826
F: (01243) 784474
I: www.accomodata.co.uk/170998.htm

Anna's ♦♦♦♦
27 Westhampnett Road, Chichester PO19 7HW
T: (01243) 788522
F: (01243) 788522
E: nick@annas.freeserve.co.uk
I: www.annasofchichester.co.uk

Apiary Cottage ♦♦♦
Compton, Chichester PO18 9EX
T: (023) 9263 1306

Bayleaf ♦♦♦
16 Whyke Road, Chichester PO12 7AN
T: (01243) 774330

21 Brandy Hole Lane ♦♦♦
Chichester PO19 5RL
T: (01243) 528201
E: anneparry@anneparry.screaming.net

3 Clydesdale Avenue ♦♦♦♦
Chichester PO19 7PW
T: (01243) 531397

The Coach House ♦♦♦♦
Binderton, Chichester PO18 0JS
T: (01243) 539624
F: (01243) 539624
E: spightling@aol.com
I: www.sussexlive.com

The Cottage ♦♦♦
22B Westhampnett Road, Chichester PO19 7HW
T: (01243) 774979
E: mbc.techincal@virgin.net

Draymans ♦♦♦
112 St Pancras, Chichester PO19 7LH
T: (01243) 789872
F: (01243) 785474
E: liz@jaegerl.freeserve.co.uk
I: www.jaegerl.freeserve.co.uk

Encore ♦♦♦♦
11 Clydesdale Avenue, Chichester PO19 7PW
T: (01243) 528271

Englewood ♦♦♦♦
East Ashling, Chichester PO18 9AS
T: (01243) 575407
F: (01243) 575407
E: sjenglewood@tinyworld.co.uk

Finisterre ♦♦♦♦
9 Albert Road, Chichester PO19 3JE
T: (01243) 532680
F: (01243) 532680
E: leonard9@tiscali.co.uk
I: www.sussexlive.com

Forge Hotel
♦♦♦♦♦ SILVER AWARD
High Street, Chilgrove, Chichester PO18 9HX
T: (01243) 535333
F: (01243) 535363
E: reservations@forgehotel.com
I: www.forgehotel.com

Friary Close
♦♦♦♦ SILVER AWARD
Friary Lane, Chichester PO19 1UF
T: (01243) 527294
F: (01243) 533876
E: friaryclose@btinternet.com

George and Dragon Inn ♦♦♦
51 North Street, Chichester PO19 1NQ
T: (01243) 785660

Home Farm House
♦♦♦♦ GOLD AWARD
Elms Lane, West Wittering, Chichester PO20 8LW
T: (01243) 514252
F: (01243) 512804

Kia-ora Nursery ♦♦♦
Main Road, Nutbourne, Chichester PO18 8RT
T: (01243) 572858
F: (01243) 572858
E: ruthiefp@aol.com

Litten House ♦♦♦♦
148 St Pancras, Chichester PO19 7SH
T: (01243) 774503
F: (01243) 539187
E: victoria@littenho.demon.co.uk
I: www.littenho.demon.co.uk

5A Little London ♦♦♦
Chichester PO19 1PH
T: (01243) 788405

Longmeadow Guest House ♦♦♦
Longmeadow, Pine Grove, Chichester PO19 3PN
T: (01243) 782063
E: bbeeching@lineone.net
I: www.longmeadowguesthouse.com

1 Maplehurst Road
♦♦♦♦ SILVER AWARD
1 Maplehurst Road, Chichester PO19 6QL
T: (01243) 528467
F: (01243) 538867
E: philandsuespooner@talk21.com

The Old Store Guest House ♦♦♦♦
Stane Street, Halnaker, Chichester PO18 0QL
T: (01243) 531977
E: theoldstore4@aol.com
I: www.smoothhound.co.uk/hotels/store.html

Palm Tree Cottage ♦♦♦♦
110 Fishbourne Road West, Fishbourne, Chichester PO19 3JR
T: (01243) 782110
F: (01243) 785285
E: palmtree@meritz.co.uk

Richmond Close
♦♦♦♦ SILVER AWARD
27 Hunters Way, Chichester PO19 5RB
T: (01243) 532470
E: cilla.johnson@tjassoc.freeserve.co.uk
I: www.chichesterweb.co.uk/richmond.htm

Riverside Lodge ♦♦♦
7 Market Avenue, Chichester PO19 1JU
T: (01243) 783164
E: tregeardavid@hotmail.com
I: www.riverside-lodge-chichester.co.uk

Sea Shells ♦♦♦♦
42 Kingsway, Selsey, Chichester PO20 0SY
T: (01243) 604231

Strudwick House
♦♦♦♦ SILVER AWARD
4 The Lane, Summersdale, Chichester PO19 5PY
T: (01243) 527293
E: polly.davenport@btinternet.com

White Barn
♦♦♦♦ SILVER AWARD
Crede Lane, Bosham, Chichester PO18 8NX
T: (01243) 573113
F: (01243) 573113
E: chrissie@whitebarn.biz
I: www.whitebarn.biz

Woodstock House Hotel ♦♦♦♦
Charlton, Chichester PO18 0HU
T: (01243) 811666
F: (01243) 811666
E: info@woodstockhousehotel.co.uk
I: www.woodstockhousehotel.co.uk

CHIDDINGFOLD
Surrey

Greenaway ♦♦♦♦
Pickhurst Road, Chiddingfold, Godalming GU8 4TS
T: (01428) 682920
F: (01428) 685078
E: jfmarsh@nildram.co.uk
I: www.greenaway.nildram.co.uk

CHIDDINGSTONE
Kent

Hoath House ♦♦♦
Chiddingstone Hoath, Edenbridge TN8 7DB
T: (01342) 850362
E: jstreatfield@hoath-house.freeserve.co.uk
I: www.hoath_house.freeserve.co.uk

CHIEVELEY
Berkshire

19 Heathfields ♦♦♦
Heathfields, Chieveley, Newbury RG20 8TW
T: (01635) 248179
F: (01635) 248799
E: ingandco@aol.com

CHILBOLTON
Hampshire

Sycamores ♦♦♦
Meadow View, Chilbolton, Stockbridge SO20 6AZ
T: (01264) 860380
E: maureen@sycamoresbb.freeserve.co.uk
I: www.sycamoresbb.freeserve.co.uk/sycamores2

Tefilah House ♦♦♦♦
10 Test Rise, Chilbolton, Stockbridge SO20 6AF
T: (01264) 860553
E: roland.burberry@lineone.net

CHILCOMB
Hampshire

Complyns ♦♦♦♦
Chilcomb, Winchester SO21 1HT
T: (01962) 861600

CHILGROVE
West Sussex

The White Horse Inn ♦♦♦♦
High Street, Chilgrove, Chichester PO18 9HX
T: (01243) 535219
F: (01243) 535301
E: info@whitehorsechilgrove.co.uk
I: www.whitehorsechilgrove.co.uk

CHILHAM
Kent

Folly House ♦♦♦♦
Chilham, Canterbury CT4 8DU
T: (01227) 738669
F: (01227) 730425

The Old Alma ♦♦♦
Canterbury Road, Chilham, Canterbury CT4 8DX
T: (01227) 731913
F: (01227) 731078
E: oldalma@aol.com

Woodchip House ♦♦♦
Maidstone Road, Chilham, Canterbury CT4 8DD
T: (01227) 730386
F: (01227) 730685
E: woodchip@talk21.com

CHINNOR
Oxfordshire

Manor Farm Cottage ♦♦♦
Henton, Chinnor, Oxford OX39 4AE
T: (01844) 353301
F: (01844) 351883
E: dixonhenton@aol.com
I: www.manorfarmcottage.info

CHIPPING NORTON
Oxfordshire

The Bell Inn
Rating Applied For
56 West Street, Chipping Norton OX7 5ER
T: (01608) 642521
F: (01608) 646145

Lower Park Farm
♦♦♦♦ SILVER AWARD
Great Tew, Oxford OX7 4DE
T: (01608) 683170
F: (01608) 683859
E: lowerparkfarm@talk21.com
I: members.lycos.co.uk/lowerparkfarm/

The Old Vicarage ♦♦♦
5 Church Street, Chipping Norton OX7 5NT
T: (01608) 641562
E: anthony.ross@virgin.net

Rectory Farm ♦♦♦♦♦
Rectory Farm, Salford, Chipping Norton OX7 5YZ
T: (01608) 643209
F: (01608) 643209
E: colston@rectoryfarm75.freeserve.co.uk
I: www.rectoryfarm.info

CHIPSTEAD
Kent

Chevers ♦♦♦♦
Moat Close, Chipstead,
Sevenoaks TN13 2HZ
T: (01732) 779144
E: japarish@supanet.com

Windmill Farm ♦♦♦♦
Chevening Road, Chipstead,
Sevenoaks TN13 2SA
T: (01732) 452054

CHOLDERTON
Hampshire

Parkhouse Motel ♦♦♦♦
Cholderton, Salisbury SP4 0EG
T: (01980) 629256
F: (01980) 629256

CHOLSEY
Oxfordshire

The Well Cottage ♦♦♦
Caps Lane, Cholsey, Wallingford
OX10 9HQ
T: (01491) 651959
F: (01491) 651675
E: joanna@thewellcottage.com
I: www.thewellcottage.com

CHRISTCHURCH
Dorset

The Beech Tree ♦♦♦♦
2 Stuart Road, Highcliffe
BH23 5JS
T: (01425) 272038

Beechcroft Place
Rating Applied For
106 Lymington Road, Highcliffe,
Christchurch BH23 4JX
T: (01425) 277171
E: b&b@unique-southcoast-uk.com
I: www.unique-southcoast-uk.com

Belvedere Guest House ♦♦
3 Twynham Avenue,
Christchurch BH23 1QU
T: (01202) 485978
F: (01202) 485978
E: belvedere@eurolink.ltd.net

Beverly Glen Guest House ♦♦♦♦
1 Stuart Road, Highcliffe
BH23 5JS
T: (01425) 273811

Cafe 39 – The Pines Hotel ♦♦♦
39 Mudeford, Christchurch
BH23 3NQ
T: (01202) 475121
F: (01202) 487666
E: pineshotelcafe39@ic24.net
I: www.mudeford.com

Druid House
♦♦♦♦♦ SILVER AWARD
26 Sopers Lane, Christchurch
BH23 1JE
T: (01202) 485615
F: (01202) 473484
E: reservations@druid-house.co.uk
I: www.druid-house.co.uk

Golfers Reach
Rating Applied For
88 Lymington Road, Highcliffe,
Christchurch BH23 4JU
T: (01425) 272903
F: (01425) 272903

Salmons Reach Guest House ♦♦♦
28 Stanpit, Christchurch
BH23 3LZ
T: (01202) 477315
F: (01202) 477315

Seawards ♦♦♦♦
13 Avon Run Close, Friars Cliff,
Christchurch BH23 4DT
T: (01425) 273188

Stour Lodge Guest House ♦♦♦
54 Stour Road, Christchurch
BH23 1LW
T: (01202) 486902
E: kcat@stourlodge.fsnet.co.uk

The White House ♦♦♦♦
428 Lymington Road, Highcliffe
BH23 5HF
T: (01425) 271279
F: (01425) 276900
E: thewhitehouse@themail.co.uk
I: www.thewhitehouse-christchurch.co.uk

Wisteria
Rating Applied For
32 Eastcliff Way, Friars Cliff,
Christchurch BH23 4EY
T: (01425) 279531

CHURCHILL
Oxfordshire

The Forge ♦♦♦♦
Church Road, Churchill, Oxford
OX7 6NJ
T: (01608) 658173
F: (01608) 658173
E: rushbrooke@madasafish.com
I: www.theforge.co.uk

CLANVILLE
Hampshire

Flinty Cottage ♦♦♦♦
Clanville, Andover SP11 9HZ
T: (01264) 773307

CLIFTONVILLE
Kent

The Carnforth Hotel ♦♦♦♦
103 Norfolk Road, Cliftonville,
Margate CT9 2HX
T: (01843) 292127
F: (01843) 280020

Lynton House Hotel ♦♦
24-26 Sweyn Road, Cliftonville,
Margate CT9 2DH
T: (01843) 292046

Marsdon Hotel ♦♦♦
7 Ethelbert Crescent, Cliftonville,
Margate CT9 2AY
T: (01843) 220175
F: (01843) 280920
E: enquiries@marsdon.freeserve.co.uk
I: www.marsdon.freeserve.co.uk

St Malo Hotel
Rating Applied For
54 Surrey Road, Cliftonville,
Margate CT9 2LA
T: (01843) 224931

COBHAM
Kent

Burleigh Farmhouse ♦♦♦♦
Sole Street Road, Cobham,
Gravesend DA12 3AR
T: (01474) 814321
F: (01474) 813843

Roxena ♦♦♦
34 Manor Road, Sole Street,
Cobham, Gravesend DA13 9BN
T: (01474) 814174

COLD ASH
Berkshire

2 Woodside ♦♦♦♦
Cold Ash, Thatcham RG18 9JF
T: (01635) 860028
E: anita.rhiggs@which.net

COLE HENLEY
Hampshire

Long Barrow House ♦♦♦♦
Cole Henley, Whitchurch
RG28 7QJ
T: (01256) 895980
E: info@longbarrowhouse.co.uk
I: www.longbarrowhouse.co.uk

COLEHILL
Dorset

Long Lane Farmhouse ♦♦♦♦
Long Lane, Colehill, Wimborne
Minster BH21 7AQ
T: (01202) 887829
F: (01202) 842528
E: patricksmyth@btinternet.com
I: www.eastdorsetdc.gov.uk/tourism

COLEMANS HATCH
East Sussex

Gospel Oak ♦♦♦
Sandy Lane, Colemans Hatch,
Hartfield TN7 4ER
T: (01342) 823840

COLWELL BAY
Isle of Wight

Rockstone Cottage
♦♦♦♦ SILVER AWARD
Colwell Chine Road, Colwell Bay
PO40 9NR
T: (01983) 753723
F: (01983) 753721
E: enquiries@rockstonecottage.co.uk
I: www.rockstonecottage.co.uk

Shorefield House
♦♦♦♦ SILVER AWARD
Madeira Lane, Colwell Bay
PO40 9SP
T: (01983) 752232
E: shorefield.house@btinternet.com

COMPTON
Surrey

Little Polsted ♦♦♦♦
Polsted Lane, Compton,
Guildford GU3 1JE
T: (01483) 810398
F: (01483) 810398
E: cwalkinshaw@lineone.net

COMPTON ABBAS
Dorset

The Old Forge ♦♦♦♦
Fanners Yard, Compton Abbas,
Shaftesbury SP7 0NQ
T: (01747) 811881
F: (01747) 811881
E: theoldforge@hotmail.com
I: www.smoothhound.co.uk/hotels/oldforge

COOKHAM
Berkshire

The Chartered Institute of Marketing ♦♦♦♦
The Moor, Cookham,
Maidenhead SL6 9QH
T: (01628) 427500
F: (01628) 427499
E: reception@cim.co.uk
I: www.cim.co.uk

Wylie Cottage ♦♦♦
School Lane, Cookham,
Maidenhead SL6 9QJ
T: (01628) 520106
F: (01628) 520106
E: crowegc@btopenworld.com

COOKSBRIDGE
East Sussex

Lower Tulleys Wells Farm ♦♦♦
Beechwood Lane/East
Chiltington Road, Cooksbridge,
Lewes BN7 3QG
T: (01273) 472622

COOMBE KEYNES
Dorset

Highfield ♦♦♦
Coombe Keynes, Wareham
BH20 5PS
T: (01929) 463208
F: (01929) 463208
E: jmitchell@coombekeynes.freeserve.co.uk
I: www.highfield-bb.co.uk

CORFE CASTLE
Dorset

Bankes Hotel Ltd. ♦♦♦
East Street, Corfe Castle,
Wareham BH20 5ED
T: (01929) 480206
F: (01929) 480186
E: bankescorfe@aol.com
I: www.dorset-hotel.co.uk

Bradle Farmhouse
♦♦♦♦ SILVER AWARD
Bradle Farm, Church Knowle,
Wareham BH20 5NU
T: (01929) 480712
F: (01929) 481144
E: bradlefarmhouse@farmersweekly.net
I: www.bradlefarmhouse.co.uk

Knitson Old Farmhouse ♦♦♦
Knitson, Corfe Castle, Wareham
BH20 5JB
T: (01929) 422836
E: mark@knitson.freeserve.co.uk

Townsend House ♦♦♦♦
123 East Street, Corfe Castle,
Wareham BH20 5EG
T: (01929) 480265
F: (01929) 480265

COUSLEY WOOD
East Sussex

Fir Trees
Rating Applied For
Firtree Cottage, Newbury Lane,
Wadhurst TN5 6EY
T: (01892) 782883
F: (01892) 782446
E: raymond.austin@btinternet.com

COVE
Hampshire

21 Tay Close
Rating Applied For
Cove, Cove GU14 9NB
T: (01252) 663214

COWBEECH
East Sussex

Batchelors ♦♦♦♦
Cowbeech Hill, Cowbeech, Hailsham BN27 4JB
T: (01323) 832215
I: www.batchelors-bb.co.uk

COWDEN
Kent

Becketts Bed & Breakfast ♦♦♦♦
Hartfield Road, Cowden, Edenbridge TN8 7HE
T: (01342) 850514
F: (01342) 851281
E: bed-breakfast.becketts@tinyworld.co.uk
I: www.becketts-bandb.co.uk

Southernwood House ♦♦♦♦
(The Old Rectory), Church Street, Cowden, Edenbridge TN8 7JE
T: (01342) 850880

COWES
Isle of Wight

Comforts Gate ♦♦
108 Pallance Road, Northwood, Cowes PO31 8LS
T: (01983) 290342
F: (01983) 297810

Halcyone Villa ♦♦♦
Grove Road, Cowes PO31 7JP
T: (01983) 291334
E: sandra@wight365.net
I: www.halcyonevilla.freeuk.com

COWFOLD
West Sussex

Stable Court ♦♦♦♦
Picts Lane, Cowfold, Horsham RH13 8AW
T: (01403) 864748
F: (01403) 864748
E: petertoynton@stable-court.freeserve.co.uk

CRANBORNE
Dorset

Chaseborough Farm ♦♦♦
Gotham, Cranborne, Wimborne Minster BH21 5QY
T: (01202) 813166
E: jim@ghinn.fsnet.co.uk
I: www.chaseboroughfarm.com

The Fleur de Lys ♦♦♦
5 Wimborne Street, Cranborne, Wimborne Minster BH21 5PP
T: (01725) 517282
F: (01725) 517945
E: fleurdelys@btinternet.com
I: www.fleurdelys-cranborne.co.uk

La Fosse at Cranborne ♦♦♦
London House, The Square, Cranborne, Wimborne Minster BH21 5PR
T: (01725) 517604
F: (01725) 517778
E: mac@la-fosse.com
I: www.la-fosse.com

CRANBROOK
Kent

Bargate House ♦♦♦♦
Angley Road, Cranbrook TN17 2PQ
T: (01580) 714254
E: pennylanebargate@aol.com
I: www.bargatehouse.co.uk

Bull Farm Oast ♦♦♦
Corner of Hawkhurst Road & Bishops Lan, Cranbrook TN17 2ST
T: (01580) 714140
F: (0870) 055 7698
E: b+b@mixx.demon.co.uk
I: www.mixx.demon.co.uk

Guernsey Cottage ♦♦♦
Wilsley Green, Cranbrook TN17 2LG
T: (01580) 712542

Hallwood Farm House ♦♦♦
Hallwood Farm, Cranbrook TN17 2SP
T: (01580) 713204
F: (01580) 713204

Sissinghurst Castle Farm ♦♦♦♦
Biddenden Road, Sissinghurst, Cranbrook TN17 2AB
T: (01580) 712885
F: (01580) 712601
I: www.kent-esites.co.uk/sissinghurstcastlefarm

Swattenden Ridge ♦♦♦♦
Swattenden Lane, Cranbrook TN17 3PR
T: (01580) 712327
F: (01580) 712327
I: www.swattendenridge.co.uk

Tolehurst Barn ♦♦♦♦
Cranbrook Road, Frittenden, Cranbrook TN17 2BP
T: (01580) 714385
F: (01580) 714385
E: info@tolehurstbarn.co.uk
I: www.tolehurstbarn.co.uk

CRANLEIGH
Surrey

Long Copse ♦♦♦
Pitch Hill, Ewhurst, Cranleigh GU6 7NN
T: (01483) 277458
F: (01483) 268195

Pathstruie ♦♦♦
Stovolds Hill, Cranleigh GU6 8LE
T: (01483) 273551

CRAWLEY
West Sussex

Little Foxes Hotel ♦♦♦♦
Charlwood Road, Ifield Wood, Crawley RH11 0JY
T: (01293) 529206
F: (01293) 551434
E: info@littlefoxeshotel.co.uk
I: www.littlefoxeshotel.co.uk

Three Bridges Lodge ♦♦♦
190 Three Bridges Road, Crawley RH10 1LN
T: (01293) 612190
F: (01293) 553078
E: nisangah@yahoo.com

CRAWLEY DOWN
West Sussex

Tiltwood House
♦♦♦♦♦ SILVER AWARD
Hophurst Lane, Crawley Down, Crawley RH10 4LL
T: (01342) 712942
E: vjohnstiltwood@aol.com

CROPREDY
Oxfordshire

Poplars Farm
♦♦♦♦ SILVER AWARD
Claydon Road, Cropredy, Banbury OX17 1JP
T: (01295) 750561
E: colkathpoplars@supanet.com

CROWBOROUGH
East Sussex

Arthur Family Bed & Breakfast ♦♦♦♦
2 The Grove, Southview Road, Crowborough TN6 1NY
T: (01892) 653328
F: (01892) 653328
E: arthur.family@virgin.net

Bathurst ♦♦♦♦
Fielden Road, Crowborough TN6 1TR
T: (01892) 665476
F: (01892) 654189
E: bathurst@aslender.freeserve.co.uk

Braemore
♦♦♦♦ SILVER AWARD
Eridge Road, Steel Cross, Crowborough TN6 2SS
T: (01892) 665700

Bryher Patch ♦♦♦
18 Hydehurst Close, Crowborough TN6 1EN
T: (01892) 663038

Hope Court ♦♦♦♦
Rannoch Road, Crowborough TN6 1RA
T: (01892) 654017

CULHAM
Oxfordshire

Kingfisher Barn ♦♦♦
Rye Farm, Culham, Abingdon OX14 3NN
T: (01235) 537538
F: (01235) 537538
E: info@kingfisherbarn.com
I: www.kingfisherbarn.com

CURRIDGE
West Berkshire

The Bunk Inn ♦♦♦♦
Curridge Village, Curridge, Thatcham RG18 9DS
T: (01635) 200400
F: (01635) 200336
I: www.thebunkinn.co.uk

CUXTON
Kent

27 James Road ♦♦♦
Cuxton, Rochester ME2 1DH
T: (01634) 715154

DAMERHAM
Hampshire

The Compasses Inn ♦♦♦♦
Damerham, Fordingbridge SP6 3HQ
T: (01725) 518231
F: (01725) 518880

DANEHILL
East Sussex

New Glenmore ♦♦♦♦
Sliders Lane, Furners Green, Uckfield TN22 3RU
T: (01825) 790783
E: alan.robinson@bigfoot.com

DARTFORD
Kent

Chashir ♦♦
3 Tynedale Close, Dartford DA2 6LL
T: (01322) 227886

DATCHET
Berkshire

Chaseside ♦♦♦
71 The Myrke, Datchet, Slough SL3 9AB
T: (01753) 574354

DEAL
Kent

Cannongate House ♦♦♦
Gilford Road, Deal CT14 7DJ
T: (01304) 375238

The Hole in the Roof Hotel ♦♦♦
42-44 Queen Street, Deal CT14 6EY
T: (01304) 374839
F: (01304) 373768

Ilex Cottage ♦♦♦♦
Temple Way, Worth, Deal CT14 0DA
T: (01304) 617026
F: (01304) 620890
E: info@ilexcottage.com
I: www.ilexcottage.com

Keep House ♦♦♦
1 Deal Castle Road, Deal CT14 7BB
T: (01304) 368162
F: (01304) 368162
E: keephouse@talk21.com
I: www.keephouse.co.uk

Kings Head Public House ♦♦♦
9 Beach Street, Deal CT14 7AH
T: (01304) 368194
F: (01304) 364182

The Malvern ♦♦♦
5-7 Ranelagh Road, Deal CT14 7BG
T: (01304) 372944
F: (01304) 372944

Richmond Villa Guest House ♦♦♦♦
1 Ranelagh Road, Deal CT14 7BG
T: (01304) 366211
F: (01304) 381706
E: richmondvilla@btopenworld.com
I: www.richmondvilla.co.uk

The Roast House Lodge ♦♦♦
224 London Road, Deal CT14 9PW
T: (01304) 380824

The Royal Hotel ♦♦♦
Beach Street, Deal CT14 6JD
T: (01304) 375555
F: (01304) 372270
I: www.shepherd-neame.co.uk

DEDDINGTON
Oxfordshire

Hill Barn ♦♦
Milton Gated Road, Deddington, Banbury OX15 0TS
T: (01869) 338631
F: (01869) 338631
E: hillbarn-bb@supanet.com

Stonecrop Guest House ◆◆
Hempton Road, Deddington, Banbury OX15 0QH
T: (01869) 338335
F: (01869) 338505
E: info@stonecropguesthouse.co.uk
I: www.stonecropguesthouse.co.uk

DENSOLE Kent

Garden Lodge ◆◆◆◆
324 Canterbury Road, Densole, Folkestone CT18 7BB
T: (01303) 893147
F: (01303) 894581
E: stay@garden-lodge.com
I: www.garden-lodge.com

DIBDEN PURLIEU Hampshire

Ashdene Guest House ◆◆◆
Beaulieu Road, Dibden Purlieu, Southampton SO45 4PT
T: (023) 8084 6073
I: www.ashdenehouse.co.uk

DINTON Buckinghamshire

Dinton Cottage ◆◆◆
Dinton Cottage, Biggs Lane, Dinton, Aylesbury HP17 8UH
T: (01296) 748270
F: (01296) 748585
E: scribe@blankpage.freeserve.co.uk
I: www.dintoncottage.co.uk

DODDINGTON Kent

Palace Farmhouse ◆◆◆
Doddington, Sittingbourne ME9 0AU
T: (01795) 886820

DORKING Surrey

Bulmer Farm ◆◆◆◆
Holmbury St Mary, Dorking RH5 6LG
T: (01306) 730210

Claremont Cottage ◆◆◆
Rose Hill, Dorking RH4 2ED
T: (01306) 885487
F: (01306) 885487

Denbies Farmhouse B&B ◆◆◆
Denbies Wine Estate, London Road, Dorking RH5 6AA
T: (01306) 876777
F: (01306) 888930
E: info@denbiesvineyard.co.uk
I: www.denbiesvineyard.co.uk

Fairdene Guest House ◆◆◆
Moores Road, Dorking RH4 2BG
T: (01306) 888337
E: zoe.richardson@ntlworld.com

Kerne Hus
◆◆◆◆ SILVER AWARD
Walliswood, Dorking RH5 5RD
T: (01306) 627548
E: kerne_hus@lineone.net

Torridon Guest House ◆◆◆
Longfield Road, Dorking RH4 3DF
T: (01306) 883724
F: (01306) 880759

DOVER Kent

Amanda Guest House ◆◆
4 Harold Street, Dover CT16 1SF
T: (01304) 201711
E: amandaguesthouse@hotmail.com
I: www.amandaguesthouse.homestead.com

Blakes of Dover ◆◆◆◆
52 Castle Street, Dover CT16 1PJ
T: (01304) 202194
F: (01304) 202194
E: blakes-of-dover@hotels.activebooking.com

Bleriot's ◆◆◆
47 Park Avenue, Dover CT16 1HE
T: (01304) 211394

Castle Guest House ◆◆◆
10 Castle Hill Road, Dover CT16 1QW
T: (01304) 201656
F: (01304) 210197
E: dimechr@aol.com
I: www.castle-guesthouse.co.uk

Chrislyn's Guest House ◆◆◆◆
104 Maison Dieu Road, Dover CT16 1RU
T: (01304) 203317
F: (01304) 212593

Clare Guest House ◆◆◆
167 Folkestone Road, Dover CT17 9SJ
T: (01304) 204553

Cleveland Guest House ◆◆◆
2 Laureston Place, off Castle Hill Road, Dover CT16 1QX
T: (01304) 204622
F: (01304) 211598
E: albetcleve@aol.com
I: www.albetcleve.homestead.com/clevehp.html

Colret House ◆◆◆◆
The Green, Coldred, Dover CT15 5AP
T: (01304) 830388
F: (01304) 830388
E: jackie.colret@evnet.co.uk
I: www.colrethouse.co.uk

The Dell Guest House ◆◆◆
233 Folkestone Road, Dover CT17 9SL
T: (01304) 202422
F: (01304) 204816
E: mail@delldover.co.uk
I: www.delldover.co.uk

Frith Lodge ◆◆◆
14 Frith Road, Dover CT16 2PY
T: (01304) 208139
E: frithlodge@yahoo.co.uk

Gladstone Guest House
◆◆◆◆
3 Laureston Place, Dover CT16 1QX
T: (01304) 208457
F: (01304) 208457
E: kkd3gladstone@aol.com
I: www.doveraccommodation.co.uk/gladstone.htm

Le Clermont ◆◆◆
15 Park Avenue, Dover CT16 1ES
T: (01304) 202302
F: (01304) 202302
E: sally@leclermont32.freeserve.co.uk
I: www.doverstopover.com

Lenox House ◆◆◆◆
Granville Road, St Margarets Bay, Dover CT15 6DS
T: (01304) 853253
F: (01304) 851862

Linden Guest House ◆◆◆
231 Folkestone Road, Dover CT17 9SL
T: (01304) 205449
F: (01304) 212499
E: Lindenrog@aol.com
I: www.smoothhound.co.uk/hotels/linden.html

Little Guest House ◆◆◆
134 Folkestone Road, Dover CT17 9SP
T: (01304) 213378

Loddington House Hotel
◆◆◆◆
14 East Cliff, (Seafront - Marine Parade), Dover CT16 1LX
T: (01304) 201947
F: (01304) 201947
E: sscupper@aol.com

Longfield Guest House ◆◆◆
203 Folkestone Road, Dover CT17 9SL
T: (01304) 204716
F: (01304) 204716
E: res@longfieldguesthouse.co.uk
I: www.longfieldguesthouse.co.uk

Maison Dieu Guest House
◆◆◆
89 Maison Dieu Road, Dover CT16 1RU
T: (01304) 204033
F: (01304) 242816
E: lawrie@brguest.co.uk
I: www.brguest.co.uk

The Norman Guest House
◆◆◆
Folkestone Road, Dover CT17 9RZ
T: (01304) 207803
E: thenorman@btopenworld.com
I: www.thenorman-guesthouse.co.uk

Number Twenty- Four Bed & Breakfast ◆◆◆
24 East Cliff, Marine Parade, Dover CT16 1LU
T: (01304) 330549

Owler Lodge
◆◆◆◆ SILVER AWARD
Alkham Valley Road, Alkham, Dover CT15 7DF
T: (01304) 826375
F: (01304) 829372
E: owlerlodge@aol.com
I: www.owlerlodge.co.uk

The Park Inn
◆◆◆◆ SILVER AWARD
1-2 Park Place, Ladywell, Dover CT16 1DQ
T: (01304) 203300
F: (01304) 203324
E: theparkinn@aol.com
I: www.theparkinnatdover.co.uk

St Margaret's Holiday Park Hotel ◆◆◆◆
Reach Road, St-Margarets-at-Cliffe, Dover CT15 6AE
T: (01304) 853262
F: (01304) 853434

Swingate Inn and Hotel ◆◆◆
Deal Road, Swingate, Dover CT15 5DP
T: (01304) 204043
F: (01304) 204043
E: terry@swingate.com
I: www.swingate.com

Talavera House ◆◆◆◆
275 Folkestone Road, Dover CT17 9LL
T: (01304) 206794
F: (01304) 207067
E: john-jan@talavera-house.freeserve.co.uk
I: www.smoothhound.co.uk/hotels/talavera

Toddies at Mead House
◆◆◆◆
9 East Cliff, Marine Parade, Dover CT16 1LX
T: (01304) 201872
E: mail@toddiesdover.com
I: www.toddiesdover.com

Victoria Guest House ◆◆◆◆
1 Laureston Place, Dover CT16 1QX
T: (01304) 205140
F: (01304) 205140
E: WHam101496@aol.com
I: www.dover-victoria-guest-house.co.uk

Westbank Guest House ◆◆◆◆
239-241 Folkestone Road, Dover CT17 9LL
T: (01304) 201061
E: thewestbank@aol.com
I: www.westbankguesthouse.co.uk

DUDDLESWELL East Sussex

Duddleswell Manor
◆◆◆◆ SILVER AWARD
Duddleswell, Uckfield TN22 3JL
T: (01825) 712701
F: (01825) 712701
E: davidsmith@crosscastle.fsnet.co.uk

DUMMER Hampshire

Oakdown Farm Bungalow
◆◆◆
Dummer, Basingstoke RG23 7LR
T: (01256) 397218

DUNTON GREEN Kent

Lilac Cottage ◆◆◆
15 Pounsley Road, Dunton Green, Sevenoaks TN13 2XP
T: (01732) 469898
E: lilac_cottage@msn.com

DYMCHURCH Kent

The Ship Inn ◆◆
118 High Street, Dymchurch, Romney Marsh TN29 0LD
T: (01303) 872122
F: (01303) 872311
E: bookings@theshipinn.co.uk
I: www.theshipinn.co.uk

Waterside Guest House
♦♦♦♦
15 Hythe Road, Dymchurch, Romney Marsh TN29 0LN
T: (01303) 872253
F: (01303) 872253
E: info@watersideguesthouse.co.uk
I: www.watersideguesthouse.co.uk

EARNLEY
West Sussex

Millstone
♦♦♦♦ GOLD AWARD
Clappers Lane, Earnley, Chichester PO20 7JJ
T: (01243) 670116
E: michaelharrington@btinternet.com
I: www.sussexlive.com

EAST ASHLING
West Sussex

Horse & Groom ♦♦♦♦
East Ashling, Chichester PO18 9AX
T: (01243) 575339
F: (01243) 575560
E: horseandgroomea@aol.com
I: www.horseandgroom.sageweb.co.uk

EAST COWES
Hampshire

Crossways House ♦♦♦
Crossways Road, East Cowes PO32 6LJ
T: (01983) 298282
F: (01983) 298282

The Doghouse ♦♦♦♦
Crossways Road, East Cowes PO32 6LJ
T: (01983) 293677
E: timindoghouse@beeb.net

EAST GRINSTEAD
West Sussex

Cranston House ♦♦♦
Cranston Road, East Grinstead RH19 3HW
T: (01342) 323609
F: (01342) 323609
E: stay@cranstonhouse.screaming.net
I: www.cranstonehouse.co.uk

Moat House ♦♦♦♦
Moat Road, East Grinstead RH19 3JZ
T: (01342) 326785
F: (01342) 303235

The Star Inn ♦♦♦
Church Road, Lingfield RH7 6AH
T: (01342) 832364
F: (01342) 832364
E: thestarinn@breathemail.net
I: www.starinnlingfield.co.uk

Town House ♦♦
6 De la Warr Road, East Grinstead RH19 3BN
T: (01342) 300310
F: (01342) 324200

EAST HANNEY
Oxfordshire

Hazelwood
Rating Applied For
Berry Lane, East Hanney, Wantage OX12 0JF
T: (01235) 868412
E: len.firth@virgin.net

EAST HENDRED
Oxfordshire

A Monks Court ♦♦♦
Newbury Road, East Hendred, Wantage OX12 8LG
T: (01235) 833797
F: (01235) 862554
E: udsl@udg.org.uk

Cowdrays ♦♦♦
Cat Street, East Hendred, Wantage OX12 8JT
T: (01235) 833313
E: cowdrays@virgin.net

EAST HOATHLY
East Sussex

Aberdeen House Bed & Breakfast ♦♦♦♦
5 High Street, East Hoathly, Lewes BN8 6DR
T: (01825) 840219

EAST ILSLEY
Berkshire

The Star Inn ♦♦♦♦
High Street, East Ilsley, Newbury RG20 7LE
T: (01635) 281215
E: kimrichstar@aol.com
I: www.starinnhotel.co.uk

EAST LAVANT
West Sussex

The Flint House
♦♦♦♦♦ SILVER AWARD
Pook Lane, East Lavant, Chichester PO18 0AS
T: (01243) 773482
E: theflinthouse@ukonline.co.uk

The Royal Oak Inn
♦♦♦♦♦ SILVER AWARD
Pook Lane, East Lavant, Chichester PO18 0AX
T: (01243) 527434
F: (01243) 776052
I: www.sussexlive.co.uk/royaloakinn

EAST MEON
Hampshire

Dunvegan Cottage ♦♦♦♦
Frogmore Lane, East Meon, Petersfield GU32 1QJ
T: (01730) 823213
F: (01730) 823858
E: dunvegan@btinternet.com
I: www.dunvegan.btinternet.com

EAST PECKHAM
Kent

Roydon Hall ♦♦♦
Roydon Hall Road, East Peckham, Tonbridge TN12 5NH
T: (01622) 812121
F: (01622) 813959
E: roydonhall@btinternet.com
I: www.tourismsoutheast.com/member/webpages/A5224.htm

EAST PRESTON
West Sussex

Roselea Cottage ♦♦♦
2 Elm Avenue, East Preston, Littlehampton BN16 1HJ
T: (01903) 786787
F: (01903) 770220
E: roselea.cottage@tesco.net

EAST STOUR
Dorset

The Glen B & B ♦♦♦♦
Fern Hill, East Stour, Gillingham SP8 5ND
T: (01747) 839819
F: (08701) 371170
E: b&b@theglen-dorset.co.uk
I: www.theglen-dorset.co.uk

EAST WELLOW
Hampshire

Country Views B & B ♦♦♦♦
Dunwood Hill, East Wellow, Shootash, Romsey SO51 6FD
T: (01794) 514735
F: (01794) 521867
E: sue@countryviewsbandb.freeserve.co.uk
I: www.countryviewsbandb.freeserve.co.uk

EAST WITTERING
West Sussex

Stubcroft Farmhouse ♦♦♦
Stubcroft Lane, East Wittering, Chichester PO20 8PJ
T: (01243) 671469

EAST WORLDHAM
Hampshire

The Three Horseshoes ♦♦♦
Cakers Lane, East Worldham, Alton GU34 3AE
T: (01420) 83211
F: (01420) 88851

EASTBOURNE
East Sussex

Albert & Victoria
Rating Applied For
19 St Aubyns Road, Eastbourne BN22 7AS
T: (01323) 730948
F: (01323) 730948

The Alfriston Hotel ♦♦♦
16 Lushington Road, Eastbourne BN21 4LL
T: (01323) 725640
F: (01323) 725640
E: alfristonhotel@yahoo.co.uk

Birling Gap Hotel ♦♦♦
Birling Gap, Seven Sisters Cliffs, East Dean, Eastbourne BN20 0AB
T: (01323) 423197
F: (01323) 423030
E: info@birlinggaphotel.co.uk
I: www.birlinggaphotel.co.uk

Boyne House ♦♦♦
12 St Aubyn's Road, Eastbourne BN22 7AS
T: (01323) 430245
F: (01323) 723227
E: boynehouse@hotmail.com

Brayscroft Hotel
♦♦♦♦ SILVER AWARD
13 South Cliff Avenue, Eastbourne BN20 7AH
T: (01323) 647005
F: (01323) 720705
E: brayscroft@hotmail.com
I: www.brayscrofthotel.co.uk

Cambridge House ♦♦♦
6 Cambridge Road, Eastbourne BN22 7BS
T: (01323) 721100

Cromwell Private Hotel
♦♦♦♦
23 Cavendish Place, Eastbourne BN21 3EJ
T: (01323) 725288
F: (01323) 725288
E: lan@cromwellhotel.co.uk
I: www.cromwellhotel.co.uk/hotels/cromwell

Edelweiss Guest House ♦♦♦
12 Elms Avenue, Eastbourne BN21 3DN
T: (01323) 732071
F: (01323) 732071
E: peterbutler@fsbdial.co.uk

Gladwyn Hotel ♦♦♦
16 Blackwater Road, Eastbourne BN21 4JD
T: (01323) 733142
E: gladwynhotel@aol.com
I: www.gladwynhotel.com

Hanburies Hotel ♦♦♦
Hardwick Road, Eastbourne BN21 4NY
T: (01323) 730698
F: (01323) 730698

Little Foxes ♦♦♦♦
24 Wannock Road, Eastbourne BN22 7JU
T: (01323) 640670
F: (01323) 640670
E: chris@foxholes55.freeserve.co.uk

The Lynwood Hotel ♦♦♦
31-33 Jevington Gardens, Eastbourne BN21 4HP
T: (01323) 638716
F: (01323) 412646
E: gm.@lyn.barbox.net
I: www.shearingsholidays.com

Majestic Hotel ♦♦♦♦
26-34 Royal Parade, Eastbourne BN22 7AN
T: (01323) 730311
I: www.shearingsholidays.com

Nirvana Private Hotel ♦♦♦
32 Redoubt Road, Eastbourne BN22 7DL
T: (01323) 722603

Pinnacle Point
♦♦♦♦♦ GOLD AWARD
Dukes Drive, Eastbourne BN20 7XL
T: (01323) 726666
F: (01323) 643946
E: info@pinnaclepoint.co.uk
I: www.pinnaclepoint.co.uk

St Omer Hotel ♦♦♦♦
13 Royal Parade, Eastbourne BN22 7AR
T: (01323) 722152
F: (01323) 723400
E: stomerhotel@hotmail.com
I: www.st-omer.co.uk

Sea Beach House Hotel ♦♦♦♦
39-40 Marine Parade, Eastbourne BN22 7AY
T: (01323) 410458
F: (01323) 410458
E: enquiries@seabeachhousehotel.com
I: www.seabeachhousehotel.com

Sherwood Hotel ♦♦♦
7 Lascelles Terrace, Eastbourne
BN21 4BJ
T: (01323) 724002
F: (01323) 439989
E: sherwood-hotel@supanet.com
I: www.sherwoodhotel.com

Southcroft Hotel
♦♦♦♦ SILVER AWARD
15 South Cliff Avenue, Eastbourne BN20 7AH
T: (01323) 729071
E: southcroft@eastbourne34.freeserve.co.uk
I: www.southcrofthotel.co.uk

Trevinhurst Lodge
♦♦♦♦ SILVER AWARD
10 Baslow Road, Meads, Eastbourne BN20 7UJ
T: (01323) 410023
F: (01323) 643238
E: enquiries@trevinhurstlodge.com
I: www.trevinhurstlodge.com

EASTCHURCH
Kent

Dunmow House ♦♦♦
9 Church Road, Eastchurch, Sheerness ME12 4DG
T: (01795) 880576
F: (01795) 880230
E: mepordage@msn.com

EASTERGATE
West Sussex

Eastmere House ♦♦♦
Eastergate Lane, Eastergate, Chichester PO20 3SJ
T: (01243) 544204
E: bernardlane@hotmail.com
I: www.eastmere.com

EASTLEIGH
Hampshire

Carinya B & B ♦♦♦
38 Sovereign Way, Eastleigh
SO50 4SA
T: (023) 8061 3128
F: (023) 8061 3128

Endeavour Guest House
♦♦♦♦
40 Allbrook Hill, Eastleigh
SO50 4LY
T: (023) 8061 3400
F: (023) 8061 4486
E: dcs@btconnect.com

EDENBRIDGE
Kent

Mowshurst Farm House
♦♦♦♦ SILVER AWARD
Swan Lane, Edenbridge TN8 6AH
T: (01732) 862064

Shoscombe ♦♦♦♦
Mill Hill, Edenbridge TN8 5DA
T: (01732) 866781
F: (01732) 867807
E: shoscombe@onetel.net.uk

Starborough Manor
♦♦♦♦ SILVER AWARD
Marsh Green Road, Marsh Green, Edenbridge TN8 5QY
T: (01732) 862152
F: (01732) 865571
E: starboroughmanor@aol.com

Ye Old Crown Inn ♦♦♦♦
74-76 The High Street, Edenbridge TN8 5AR
T: (01732) 867896
F: (01732) 868316
E: yeoldcrown@lionheartinns.co.uk
I: www.lionheartinns.co.uk

EDGCOTT
Buckinghamshire

Perry Manor Farm ♦♦
Buckingham Road, Edgcott, Aylesbury HP18 0TR
T: (01296) 770257

EFFINGHAM
Surrey

Sir Douglas Haig ♦♦♦
The Street, Effingham, Leatherhead KT24 5LU
T: (01372) 456886
F: (01372) 450987

EGHAM
Surrey

Bulkeley House ♦♦♦
Middlehill, Englefield Green, Egham TW20 0JU
T: (01784) 431287
F: (01784) 431287

ELHAM
Kent

Abbot's Fireside Hotel
♦♦♦♦ SILVER AWARD
High Street, Elham, Canterbury CT4 6TD
T: (01303) 840265
F: (01303) 840852
E: info@abbotsfireside.com
I: www.abbotsfireside.com

The Rose and Crown ♦♦♦
High Street, Elham, Canterbury CT4 6TD
T: (01303) 840226
F: (01303) 840141
E: info@roseandcrown.co.uk
I: www.roseandcrown.co.uk

ELMSTED
Kent

Elmsted Court Farm ♦♦♦♦
Elmsted, Ashford TN25 5JN
T: (01233) 750269
E: carol.jakeman@btinternet.com

ELMSTONE
Kent

The Frog & Orange
Rating Applied For
Shatterling, Wingham, Shatterling, Canterbury CT3 1JR
T: (01304) 812525
F: (01304) 813505

EMSWORTH
Hampshire

Apple Blossom ♦♦♦
19A Bosmere Gardens, Emsworth PO10 7NP
T: (01243) 372201
E: neilandann@lanchbury.co.uk

Bunbury Lodge ♦♦♦♦
10 West Road, Emsworth
PO10 7JT
T: (01243) 432030
F: (01243) 432030
E: Bunbury.Lodge@breathemail.net
I: www.guestaccom.co.uk

Hollybank House
Rating Applied For
Hollybank Lane, Emsworth
PO10 7UN
T: (01243) 378353

The Merry Hall Hotel ♦♦♦
73 Horndean Road, Emsworth
PO10 7PU
T: (01243) 431377
F: (01243) 431411

Quackers Cottage ♦♦♦♦
40 Bath Road, Emsworth
PO10 7ER
T: (01243) 377177
F: (01243) 377177
E: quackerscottage@talk21.com

ENGLEFIELD GREEN
Surrey

The Old Parsonage
Rating Applied For
2 Parsonage Road, Englefield Green, Egham TW20 0JW
T: (01784) 436706
F: (01784) 436706
E: the.old.parsonage@talk21.com
I: www.theoldparsonage.com

EPWELL
Oxfordshire

Yarnhill Farm ♦♦♦
Shenington Road, Epwell, Banbury OX15 6JA
T: (01295) 780250
F: (01295) 780250
E: bedandbreakfast@yarnhillfarm.freeserve.co.uk

ETON
Berkshire

The Crown & Cushion Inn ♦♦
84 High Street, Eton, Windsor
SL4 6AF
T: (01753) 861531
E: sylvieglinister@yahoo.com

EWELME
Oxfordshire

Mays Farm ♦♦♦♦
Ewelme, Oxford OX10 6QF
T: (01491) 641294
F: (01491) 641191
E: passmore@farmersweekly.net

EWHURST
Surrey

Malricks ♦♦♦
The Street, Ewhurst, Cranleigh
GU6 7RH
T: (01483) 277575

Sixpenny Buckle ♦♦♦♦
Gransden Close, Ewhurst, Cranleigh GU6 7RL
T: (01483) 273988
E: dandpmort@tiscali.co.uk

EWSHOT
Hampshire

Dares Farm House ♦♦♦♦
Farnham Road, Ewshot, Farnham GU10 5BB
T: (01252) 851631
F: (01252) 852367
E: kate_bristow@lineone.net

EYNSHAM
Oxfordshire

Grange House ♦♦♦
Station Road, Eynsham, Oxford
OX29 4HX
T: (01865) 880326
F: (01865) 880326
E: bookings@grangehouse.co.uk
I: www.grangehouse.co.uk

FAIRLIGHT
East Sussex

Fairlight Cottage ♦♦♦♦
Warren Road, (Via Coastguard Lane), Fairlight, Hastings
TN35 4AG
T: (01424) 812545
F: (01424) 812545
E: fairlightcottage@supanet.com
I: www.rye.org.uk

FAIRWARP
East Sussex

Broom Cottage ♦♦♦♦
Fairwarp, Uckfield TN22 3BY
T: (01825) 712942

FAREHAM
Hampshire

Avenue House Hotel ♦♦♦
22 The Avenue, Fareham
PO14 1NS
T: (01329) 232175
F: (01329) 232196
I: www.travelrest.co.uk

Bridge House ♦♦♦♦
1 Waterside Gardens, Wallington, Fareham PO16 8SD
T: (01329) 287775
F: (01329) 287775
E: maryhb@fish.co.uk

Catisfield Cottage Guest House
♦♦
1 Catisfield Lane, Fareham
PO15 5NW
T: (01329) 843301
F: (01329) 841652

Seven Sevens Guest House
♦♦♦
56 Hill Head Road, Hill Head
PO14 3JL
T: (01329) 662408

Springfield Hotel ♦♦♦♦
67 The Avenue, Fareham
PO14 1PE
T: (01329) 828325

FARINGDON
Oxfordshire

Ashen Copse Farm ♦♦♦
Coleshill, Highworth, Faringdon
SN6 7PU
T: (01367) 240175
F: (01367) 241418
E: pat@hodd.demon.co.uk
I: www.hodd.demon.co.uk

Camden House
Rating Applied For
28 Market Place, Faringdon
SN7 7HU
T: (01367) 241121
F: (01367) 241999

Portwell House Hotel ♦♦♦
Market Place, Faringdon
SN7 7HU
T: (01367) 240197
F: (01367) 244330
E: enquiries@portwellhouse.com
I: www.portwellhouse.com

The Trout At Tadpole Bridge
♦♦♦♦
Buckland Marsh, Faringdon
SN7 8RF
T: (01367) 870382
E: info@trout-inn.co.uk
I: www.trout-inn.co.uk

FARNBOROUGH
Hampshire

Colebrook Guest House ♦♦♦
56 Netley Street, Farnborough GU14 6AT
T: (01252) 542269
F: (01252) 542269
E: derekbclark@ukonline.co.uk

The Oak Tree Guest House ♦♦♦
112 Farnborough Road, Farnborough GU14 6TN
T: (01252) 545491
F: (01252) 545491
E: joanne.dickinson21@ntlworld.com
I: www.theoaktreeguesthouse.com

The White Residence Town House Hotel
♦♦♦♦ GOLD AWARD
Farnborough Park, 76 Avenue Road, Farnborough GU14 7BG
T: (01252) 375510
F: (01252) 655567
E: info@countyapartments.com
I: www.whiteresidence.co.uk

FARNHAM
Surrey

Anne's Cottage
♦♦♦♦ GOLD AWARD
Green Cross Lane, Churt, Farnham GU10 2ND
T: (01428) 714181

High Wray ♦♦♦
73 Lodge Hill Road, Farnham GU10 3RB
T: (01252) 715589
F: (01252) 715746
E: crawford@highwray73.co.uk

Mala Strana ♦♦♦♦
66 Boundstone Road, Farnham GU10 4TR
T: (01252) 793262
E: carolemalastrana@aol.com

14 Nutshell Lane ♦♦♦
Farnham GU9 0HG
T: (01252) 710147
F: (01252) 710147

St Gallen ♦♦♦♦
Old Frensham Road, Lower Bourne, Farnham GU10 3PT
T: (01252) 793412
F: (01252) 793412
E: cary_wilkins@cw1999.freeserve.co.uk

FAVERSHAM
Kent

Barnsfield ♦♦♦
Fostall, Hernhill, Faversham ME13 9JH
T: (01227) 750973
F: (01227) 273098
E: barnsfield@yahoo.com
I: www.barnsfield.co.uk

Coach House Cottages ♦♦♦
7 Gatefield Lane, Faversham ME13 8NX
T: (01795) 533343
E: michaelacy@hotmail.com
I: www.coachhousecottages.co.uk

Fairlea ♦♦♦♦
27 Preston Avenue, Faversham ME13 8NH
T: (01795) 539610

Heronsmere ♦♦♦
Nobel Court, Faversham ME13 7SD
T: (01795) 536767
E: griffithskeith@lineone.net
I: www.heronsmere.co.uk

March Cottage ♦♦♦
5 Preston Avenue, Faversham ME13 8NH
T: (01795) 536514
E: sarah_marcot@onetel.net.uk
I: web.onetel.net.uk/~sarah_marcot

Owens Court Farm ♦♦♦
Selling, Faversham ME13 9QN
T: (01227) 752247
F: (01227) 752247
E: enquiries@owenscourt.com
I: www.owenscourt.com

Preston Lea
♦♦♦♦ SILVER AWARD
Canterbury Road, Faversham ME13 8XA
T: (01795) 535266
F: (01795) 533388
E: preston.lea@which.net
I: homepages.which.net/~alan.turner10

The Railway Hotel
Rating Applied For
Preston Street, Faversham ME13 8PE
T: (01795) 533173
F: (01795) 534508

FAWLEY
Hampshire

Walcot House ♦♦♦
Blackfield Road, Fawley, Southampton SO45 1ED
T: (023) 8089 1344

FAYGATE
West Sussex

The Willows
♦♦♦♦ SILVER AWARD
Wimlands Lane, Faygate, Horsham RH12 4SP
T: (01293) 851030
F: (01293) 852466
E: stay@the-willows.co.uk
I: www.the-willows.co.uk

FELPHAM
West Sussex

The Old Poor House ♦♦♦♦
22 Flansham Lane, Felpham, Bognor Regis PO22 6AB
T: (01243) 587217

FERNDOWN
Dorset

Carey
Rating Applied For
11 Southern Avenue, West Moors, Ferndown BH22 0BJ
T: (01202) 861159

Woodridings ♦♦♦♦
73 Beaufoys Avenue, Ferndown BH22 9RN
T: (01202) 876729

FIFEHEAD ST QUINTON
Dorset

Lower Fifehead Farm ♦♦♦♦
Fifehead St Quinton, Sturminster Newton DT10 2AP
T: (01258) 817335
F: (01258) 817335

FIFIELD
Berkshire

Victoria Cottage
Rating Applied For
2 Victoria Cottages, Fifield Road, Fifield, Maidenhead SL6 2NZ
T: (01628) 623564
F: (01628) 623564
E: janross@amserve.com

FINDON
West Sussex

John Henry's at Marigold Cottage
Rating Applied For
The Forge, Nepcote Lane, Findon, Worthing BN14 0SE
T: (01903) 877277
F: (01903) 872168
E: findev@btopenworld.com
I: www.john-henrys.com

FINGLESHAM
Kent

Orchard Lodge ♦♦♦
The Street, Finglesham, Deal CT14 0NA
T: (01304) 620192
E: hutsonbob@aol.com

FIRLE
East Sussex

New House Farm ♦♦♦♦
Wick Street, Firle, Lewes BN8 6ND
T: (01273) 858242
F: (01273) 858242
E: hecks@farming.co.uk

FISHBOURNE
West Sussex

The Byre
♦♦♦♦ SILVER AWARD
Salthill Park, Salthill Road, Fishbourne, Chichester PO19 3PS
T: (01243) 537943
F: (01243) 537943

FITTLEWORTH
West Sussex

The Old Post Office ♦♦♦♦
Lower Street, Fittleworth, Pulborough RH20 1JE
T: (01798) 865315
E: sue.moseley@ukgateway.net

Swan Inn
♦♦♦♦ SILVER AWARD
Lower Street, Fittleworth, Pulborough RH20 1EN
T: (01798) 865429
F: (01798) 865721
E: hotel@swaninn.com
I: www.swaninn.com

FIVE ASHES
East Sussex

Hadlow House
Rating Applied For
Hadlow Down, Uckfield TN22 4EP
T: (01825) 830430
F: (01825) 830430

FIVE OAK GREEN
Kent

Ivy House ♦♦♦
Five Oak Green, Tonbridge TN12 6RB
T: (01892) 832041
F: (01892) 832041

FLEET
Hampshire

Copperfield ♦♦♦
16 Glen Road, Fleet GU51 3QR
T: (01252) 616140

FLETCHING
East Sussex

The Griffin Inn
♦♦♦♦ SILVER AWARD
High Street, Fletching, Uckfield TN22 3SS
T: (01825) 722890
F: (01825) 722810
E: nigelpullan@thegriffininn.co.uk
I: www.thegriffininn.co.uk

FOLKESTONE
Kent

Beachborough Park ♦♦♦
Newington, Folkestone CT18 8BW
T: (01303) 275432
F: (01843) 845131
I: www.kentaccess.org.uk

Chandos Guest House ♦♦♦
77 Cheriton Road, Folkestone CT20 1DG
T: (01303) 851202
F: (01303) 272073
E: don@chandosguesthouse.com
I: www.chandosguesthouse.com

Chilton House Hotel ♦♦♦
14-15 Marine Parade, Folkestone CT20 1PX
T: (01303) 249786
F: (01303) 247525
E: chiltonhousehotel@btinternet.com
I: www.chiltonhousehotel.co.uk

Cliffside ♦♦♦♦
Radnor Cliff Crescent, Folkestone CT20 2JH
T: (01303) 248328
F: (01303) 240115
E: hilary@cliffside303.fsnet.co.uk
I: www.cliff-side.co.uk

Granada Guest House ♦♦♦
51 Cheriton Road, Folkestone CT20 1DF
T: (01303) 254913

Harbourside Hotel
♦♦♦♦♦ GOLD AWARD
12-14 Wear Bay Road, Folkestone CT19 6AT
T: (01303) 256528
F: (01303) 241299
E: joy@harboursidehotel.com
I: www.harboursidehotel.com

Kentmere Guest House ♦♦♦
76 Cheriton Road, Folkestone CT20 1DG
T: (01303) 259661
F: (01303) 259661
E: enquiries@kentmere-guesthouse.co.uk
I: www.kentmere-guesthouse.co.uk

The Rob Roy Guest House ♦♦♦
227 Dover Road, Folkestone CT19 6NH
T: (01303) 253341
F: (01303) 770060
E: RobRoyFolkestone@aol.com
I: www.therobroyguesthouse.co.uk

Seacliffe ◆◆◆
3 Wear Bay Road, Folkestone
CT19 6AT
T: (01303) 254592

Sunny Lodge Guest House ◆◆◆
85 Cheriton Road, Folkestone
CT20 2QL
T: (01303) 251498
E: linda.dowsett@btclick.com
I: www.s-h-systems.co.uk/hotels/sunnyl.html

Windsor Hotel ◆
5-6 Langhorne Gardens, Folkestone CT20 2EA
T: (01303) 251348
E: windsorhotel_folkestone@hotmail.com

FONTWELL
West Sussex

Woodacre ◆◆◆◆
Arundel Road, Fontwell, Arundel BN18 0QP
T: (01243) 814301
F: (01243) 814344
E: wacrebb@aol.com
I: www.woodacre.co.uk

FORDINGBRIDGE
Hampshire

Broomy ◆◆◆◆
Broomy, Ogdens, Fordingbridge
SP6 2PY
T: (01425) 653264

3 Camel Green Road
Rating Applied For
Alderholt, Fordingbridge
SP6 3AN
T: (01425) 655725

Drummond House ◆◆◆◆
Bowerwood Road, Fordingbridge
SP6 1BL
T: (01425) 653165
E: drumbb@btinternet.com
I: www.newforest.demon.co.uk/drummond.htm

Hillbury ◆◆◆
2 Fir Tree Hill, Camel Green Road, Alderholt, Fordingbridge
SP6 3AY
T: (01425) 652582
F: (01425) 657587
E: hillburybb@talk21.com
I: www.newforest.demon.co.uk/hillbury.htm

Merrimead
◆◆◆◆ SILVER AWARD
12 Station Road, Alderholt, Fordingbridge SP6 3RR
T: (01425) 657544
F: (01425) 650400
E: merrimead@ic24.net
I: www.newforest.demon.co.uk/merrimead.htm

Primrose Cottage ◆◆◆◆
Newgrounds, Godshill, Fordingbridge SP6 2LJ
T: (01425) 650447
F: (01425) 650447
E: ann@blake98.freeserve.co.uk

The Three Lions
◆◆◆◆◆ GOLD AWARD
Stuckton, Fordingbridge
SP6 2HF
T: (01425) 652489
F: (01425) 656144
E: the3lions@btinternet.com
I: www.thethreelionsrestaurant.co.uk

FOREST GREEN
Surrey

Bridgham Cottage
Rating Applied For
Horsham Road, Forest Green, Dorking RH5 5PP
T: (01306) 621044
F: (01306) 621044
E: max@bridghamcottage.fsnet.co.uk
I: mysite.freeserve.com/bridcott

FOREST ROW
East Sussex

Brambletye Hotel ◆◆◆
The Square, Forest Row
RH18 5EZ
T: (01342) 824144
F: (01342) 824833

FOUR ELMS
Kent

Oak House Barn ◆◆◆◆◆
Mapleton Road, Four Elms, Edenbridge TN8 6PL
T: (01732) 700725

FOUR MARKS
Hampshire

137 Winchester Road ◆◆◆
Four Marks, Alton GU34 5HY
T: (01420) 564091

FRAMFIELD
East Sussex

Beggars Barn
◆◆◆◆ SILVER AWARD
Barn Lane, Framfield, Uckfield
TN22 5RX
T: (01825) 890869
F: (01825) 890868
E: caroline@beggarsbarn.co.uk
I: www.beggarsbarn.co.uk

The Old Farmhouse
◆◆◆◆ GOLD AWARD
Honey's Green, Framfield, Uckfield TN22 5RE
T: (01825) 841054
F: (0870) 122 9055
E: stay@honeysgreen.com
I: www.honeysgreen.com

FREELAND
Oxfordshire

Malvern Villas Bed & Breakfast ◆◆◆
1 Malvern Villas, Witney Road, Freeland, Oxford OX29 8HG
T: (01993) 880019
E: lburge@malvernvillas.fsnet.co.uk
I: www.malvernvillas.co.uk

FRENSHAM
Surrey

The Mariners Hotel ◆◆
Millbridge, Frensham, Farnham
GU10 3DJ
T: (01252) 792050
F: (01252) 792649
I: www.themarinershotel.co.uk

FRESHWATER
Isle of Wight

Brookside Forge Hotel ◆◆◆
Brookside Road, Freshwater
PO40 9ER
T: (01983) 754644

Cherry Trees ◆◆◆◆
29 School Green Road, Freshwater PO40 9AW
T: (01983) 756000
F: (01983) 752681
E: cherrytrees@cuemedianet.com
I: www.islandbreaks.co.uk/cherrytrees

Field House Bed & Breakfast
◆◆◆◆ GOLD AWARD
Pound Green, Freshwater
PO40 9HG
T: (01983) 754190
E: alisson.smith@virgin.net
I: www.fieldhouseiow.co.uk

Royal Standard Hotel ◆◆◆
School Green Road, Freshwater
PO40 9AJ
T: (01983) 753227
F: (01983) 756405
E: sue@stephenson84.freeserve.co.uk

Seahorses ◆◆◆◆
Victoria Road, Freshwater
PO40 9PP
T: (01983) 752574
F: (01983) 752574
E: lanterncom@aol.com

Traidcraft ◆◆
119 School Green Road, Freshwater PO40 9AZ
T: (01983) 752451

FRESHWATER BAY
Isle of Wight

Wighthaven ◆◆◆◆
Afton Road, Freshwater Bay
PO40 9TT
T: (01983) 753184
E: wighthaven@btinternet.com

FRISTON
East Sussex

Forest Lodge ◆◆◆◆
Friston, Eastbourne BN20 0AN
T: (01323) 423990
F: (01323) 423991
E: forest.lodgebb@aol.com
I: www.forestlodgebb.co.uk

FRITHAM
Hampshire

Fritham Farm ◆◆◆◆
Fritham, Lyndhurst SO43 7HH
T: (023) 8081 2333
F: (023) 8081 2333
E: frithamfarm@supanet.com

FROXFIELD GREEN
Hampshire

The Trooper Inn and Hotel ◆◆◆◆
Alton Road, Froxfield, Froxfield Green, Petersfield GU32 1BD
T: (01730) 827293
F: (01730) 827103
E: troopersec@aol.com
I: www.trooperinn.com

FUNTINGTON
West Sussex

High Walls ◆◆◆◆◆
5 Weston Lane, Funtington, Chichester PO18 9LT
T: (01243) 576823
F: (01243) 576823

GALLOWSTREE COMMON
West Berkshire

Cherry Garth
Rating Applied For
The Hamlet, Gallowstree Common, Reading RG4 9BU
T: (0118) 972 2921

GARSINGTON
Oxfordshire

Hill Copse Cottage ◆◆◆
Wheatley Road, Garsington, Oxford OX44 9DT
T: (01865) 361478
F: (01865) 361478

GATCOMBE
Isle of Wight

Freewaters
◆◆◆◆ SILVER AWARD
New Barn Lane, Gatcombe, Newport PO30 3EQ
T: (01983) 721439
F: (01983) 294173
E: john@pitstopmodels.demon.co.uk
I: www.colourpointdesign.co.uk/freewaters

Little Gatcombe Farm
◆◆◆◆ SILVER AWARD
New Barn Lane, Gatcombe, Newport PO30 3EQ
T: (01983) 721580
E: anita@littlegatcombefarm.co.uk
I: www.littlegatcombefarm.co.uk

GATWICK
West Sussex

Brooklyn Manor Hotel ◆◆◆
Bonnetts Lane, Ifield, Crawley
RH11 0NY
T: (01293) 546024
F: (01293) 510366

Collendean Barn ◆◆◆
Collendean Lane, Norwood Hill, Horley RH6 0HP
T: (01293) 862433
F: (01293) 863102
E: collendean.barn@amserve.net

The Corner House ◆◆◆◆
Massetts Road, Horley RH6 7ED
T: (01293) 784574
F: (01293) 784620
E: info@thecornerhouse.co.uk
I: www.thecornerhouse.co.uk

Gainsborough Lodge ◆◆◆
39 Massetts Road, Horley
RH6 7DT
T: (01293) 783982
F: (01293) 785365
E: enquiries@gainsborough-lodge.co.uk
I: www.gainsborough-lodge.co.uk

The Manor House ◆◆◆
Bonnetts Lane, Ifield, Crawley
RH11 0NY
T: (01293) 512298
F: (01293) 518046
E: info@manorhouse-gatwick.co.uk
I: www.manorhouse-gatwick.co.uk

Southbourne Guest House Gatwick ◆◆
34 Massetts Road, Horley
RH6 7DS
T: (01293) 771991
F: (01293) 820112
E: reservations@southbournegatwick.com
I: www.southbournegatwick.com

GERRARDS CROSS
Buckinghamshire

15 Howards Wood Drive ♦♦♦
Gerrards Cross SL9 7HR
T: (01753) 884911
E: j.crosby@ntlworld.com

GIFFARD PARK
Buckinghamshire

Giffard House ♦♦♦
10 Broadway Avenue, Giffard Park, Milton Keynes MK14 5QF
T: (01908) 618868
F: (01908) 618868
E: lizziemm@btinternet.com

GILLINGHAM
Dorset

Ansty Rose Cottage ♦♦
Wyke Road, Gillingham SP8 4NH
T: (01747) 825379
E: kazworks@pottery82.freeserve.co.uk

Bugley Court Farm ♦♦♦♦
Gillingham SP8 5RA
T: (01747) 823242

Mayfield Guest House ♦♦
34 Kingswood Road, Gillingham ME7 1DZ
T: (01634) 852606

Ramsey House ♦♦♦
228A Barnsole Road, Gillingham ME7 4JB
T: (01634) 854193

GODALMING
Surrey

Heath Hall Farm ♦♦♦
Bowlhead Green, Godalming GU8 6NW
T: (01428) 682808
F: (01428) 684025
E: heathhallfarm@btinternet.com
I: www.heathhallfarm.co.uk

GODMERSHAM
Kent

Waggoners Lodge ♦♦♦
Eggarton Lane, Godmersham, Canterbury CT4 7DY
T: (01227) 731118
F: (01227) 730292
E: maud@waggoners.freeserve.co.uk
I: www.angelfire.com/wy/Waggoners

GODSHILL
Hampshire

Croft Cottage ♦♦♦
Southampton Road, Godshill, Fordingbridge SP6 2LE
T: (01425) 657955
I: www.croftcottagenewforest.co.uk

The Fighting Cocks ♦♦♦
Godshill, Fordingbridge SP6 2LL
T: (01425) 652462
F: (01425) 625462

Vennards Cottage ♦♦♦
Newgrounds, Godshill, Fordingbridge SP6 2LJ
T: (01425) 652644
E: gillian.bridgeman@virgin.net

GODSTONE
Surrey

The Godstone Hotel ♦♦♦
The Green, Godstone RH9 8DT
T: (01883) 742461
F: (01883) 742461
I: www.godstonehotel.com

GOODWOOD
West Sussex

The Coach House ♦♦♦♦
1 Pilleygreen Lodge, Goodwood, Chichester PO18 0QE
T: (01243) 811467
F: (01243) 811408
E: coachouse@pilleygreen.demon.co.uk
I: www.sussexlive@enta.net

GORING
Oxfordshire

Miller of Mansfield ♦♦♦
High Street, Goring, Reading RG8 9AW
T: (01491) 872829
F: (01491) 874200
I: www.millerofmansfield.co.uk

GOSPORT
Hampshire

Spring Garden Guest House ♦♦
Spring Garden Lane, Gosport PO12 1LP
T: (023) 9251 0336
F: (023) 9251 0336

West Wind Guest House ♦♦♦♦
107 Portsmouth Road, Lee on the Solent PO13 9AA
T: (023) 9255 2550
F: (023) 9255 4657
E: maggie@west-wind.co.uk
I: www.west-wind.co.uk

GOUDHURST
Kent

Mill House ♦♦♦♦
Church Road, Goudhurst, Cranbrook TN17 1BN
T: (01580) 211703
E: therussellsuk@yahoo.com
I: www.goudhurst-online.freeserve.co.uk

GRAFFHAM
West Sussex

Brook Barn ♦♦♦♦♦ SILVER AWARD
Selham Road, Graffham, Petworth GU28 0PU
T: (01798) 867356

GRAFTY GREEN
Kent

Who'd A Thought It ♦♦♦
Headcorn Road, Grafty Green, Maidstone ME17 2AR
T: (01622) 858951
F: (01622) 858078

GRATELEY
Hampshire

Gunville House ♦♦♦♦ SILVER AWARD
Gunville, Grateley, Andover SP11 8JQ
T: (01264) 889206
F: (01264) 889060
E: pct@onetel.net.uk
I: www.gunvillehouse.co.uk

GRAVESEND
Kent

48 Clipper Crescent ♦♦♦
Riverview Park, Gravesend DA12 4NN
T: (01474) 365360

Dot's B & B ♦♦♦
23 St James's Road, Gravesend DA11 0HF
T: (01474) 332193
E: dotriley@agassiz.worldonline.co.uk

Eastcourt Oast ♦♦♦♦
14 Church Lane, Chalk, Gravesend DA12 2NL
T: (01474) 823937
F: (01474) 823937
E: mary.james@lineone.net
I: www.eastcourtoast.co.uk

The Jolly Drayman ♦♦♦
Wellington Street, Gravesend DA12 1JA
T: (01474) 352355
F: (01474) 364869

GREAT BOOKHAM
Surrey

Selworthy ♦♦♦
310 Lower Road, Great Bookham, Leatherhead KT23 4DW
T: (01372) 453952
F: (01372) 453952
E: bnb@selworthy.fslife.co.uk

GREAT KINGSHILL
Buckinghamshire

Hatches Farm ♦♦
Hatches Lane, Great Kingshill, High Wycombe HP15 6DS
T: (01494) 713125
F: (01494) 714666

GREAT MISSENDEN
Buckinghamshire

The George Inn ♦♦♦
High Street, Great Missenden HP16 0BG
T: (01494) 862084
F: (01494) 865622
E: george@online.magnolia.co.uk

GREATSTONE
Kent

White Horses Cottage ♦♦♦♦
180 The Parade, Greatstone, New Romney TN28 8RS
T: (01797) 366626

GUESTLING
East Sussex

Mount Pleasant Farm ♦♦♦♦
White Hart Hill, Guestling, Hastings TN35 4LR
T: (01424) 813108
F: (01424) 813818
E: angelajohn@mountpleasantfarm.fsbusiness.co.uk
I: www.mountpleasantfarm.fsbusiness.co.uk

GUILDFORD
Surrey

Abeille House ♦♦♦
119 Stoke Road, Guildford GU1 1ET
T: (01483) 532200
F: (01483) 821220
E: abeille.house119@ntlworld.com
I: www.abeillehouse.co.uk

Albany House B & B ♦♦♦
21 South Hill, Guildford GU1 3SY
T: (01483) 450732
F: (01483) 874641
E: albany.house@ntlworld.com

Amberley ♦♦♦
Maori Road, Guildford GU1 2EL
T: (01483) 573198
E: amberleyjoyners@connectfree.co.uk

Bed & Breakfast ♦♦♦
31 Weston Road, Guildford GU2 8AU
T: (01483) 546018
E: lindsay-herbert@onetel.net.uk

Bluebells ♦♦♦
21 Coltsfoot Drive, Burpham, Guildford GU1 1YH
T: (01483) 826124
E: hughes.a@ntlworld.com

9 Boxgrove Lane ♦♦♦
Boxgrove Lane, Guildford GU1 2TE
T: (01483) 565524

Chalklands ♦♦♦
Beech Avenue, Effingham, Leatherhead KT24 5PJ
T: (01372) 454936
F: (01372) 459569
E: rreilly@onetel.net.uk

The Clavadel Hotel ♦♦♦
Epsom Road, Guildford GU1 2JH
T: (01483) 569066
F: (01483) 579868

Field Villa ♦♦♦
Liddington New Road, Guildford GU3 3AH
T: (01483) 233961
F: (01483) 234045

Hampton ♦♦♦♦
38 Poltimore Road, Guildford GU2 7PN
T: (01483) 572012
F: (01483) 572012
E: vgmorris@aol.com
I: www.hampton-bedandbreakfast.co.uk

High Edser ♦♦♦
Shere Road, Ewhurst, Cranleigh GU6 7PQ
T: (01483) 278214
F: (01483) 278200
E: franklinadams@highedser.demon.co.uk

Holroyd Arms Pubotel ♦♦
36 Aldershot Road, Guildford GU2 8AF
T: (01483) 560215
F: (01483) 531912

The Laurels ♦♦♦
Dagden Road, Shalford, Guildford GU4 8DD
T: (01483) 565753

Littlefield Manor ♦♦♦
Littlefield Common, Guildford GU3 3HJ
T: (01483) 233068
F: (01483) 233686
E: john@littlefieldmanor.co.uk
I: www.littlefieldmanor.co.uk

The Mansion ♦♦♦♦
Albury Park, Albury, Guildford GU5 9BB
T: (01483) 202964
F: (01483) 205013

Matchams ♦♦♦
35 Boxgrove Avenue, Guildford GU1 1XQ
T: (01483) 567643
F: (01483) 567643

The Old Malt House ♦♦♦
Bagshot Road, Worplesdon, Guildford GU3 3PT
T: (01483) 232152

Establishments printed in blue have a detailed entry in this guide

4 Park Chase ♦♦♦♦
Guildford GU1 1ES
T: (01483) 566482
E: jill.nicolson@ntlworld.com

Patcham ♦♦♦
44 Farnham Road, Guildford
GU2 4LS
T: (01483) 570789
F: (01483) 570789

Plaegan House ♦♦♦♦
96 Wodeland Avenue, Guildford
GU2 4LD
T: (01483) 822181
E: roxanephillips@onetel.net.uk

Quietways ♦♦♦
29 Liddington Hall Drive,
Guildford GU3 3AE
T: (01483) 232347
E: bill.white@amserve.net

Stoke House ♦♦
113 Stoke Road, Guildford
GU1 1ET
T: (01483) 453025
F: (01483) 453023
E: stokehouse@supanet.com

Three Gates Bed & Breakfast ♦♦
26 Worplesdon Road, Guildford
GU2 9RS
T: (01483) 578961
F: (01483) 578961

Westbury Cottage ♦♦♦♦
1 Waterden Road, Guildford
GU1 2AN
T: (01483) 822602
F: (01483) 822602
E: smythe.smythe@ntlworld.com

Weyview ♦♦♦
Upper Guildown Road, Guildford
GU2 4EZ
T: (01483) 564724

GURNARD
Isle of Wight

Hillbrow Private Hotel ♦♦♦♦
Tuttons Hill, Gurnard, Cowes
PO31 8JA
T: (01983) 297240
F: (01983) 297240

The Woodvale Hotel ♦♦♦♦
1 Princes Esplanade, Gurnard,
Cowes PO31 8LE
T: (01983) 292037
F: (01983) 292037
E: woodvaleparkin@aol.com
I: www.the-woodvale.co.uk

HADDENHAM
Buckinghamshire

The Majors
♦♦♦♦♦ SILVER AWARD
19-21 Townside, Haddenham,
Aylesbury HP17 8BQ
T: (01844) 292654
F: (01844) 299050

HADLOW
Kent

Leavers Oast ♦♦♦♦
Stanford Lane, Hadlow,
Tonbridge TN11 0JN
T: (01732) 850924
F: (01732) 850924
E: denis@leavers-oast.freeserve.co.uk

HAILSHAM
East Sussex

Longleys Farm Cottage ♦♦♦
Harebeating Lane, Hailsham
BN27 1ER
T: (01323) 841227
F: (01323) 841227

Windesworth ♦♦♦♦
Carters Corner, Hailsham
BN27 4HT
T: (01323) 847178
F: (01323) 440696
E: windesworth.bed&breakfast@virgin.net

HALLAND
East Sussex

Halland Forge ♦♦♦
Halland, Lewes BN8 6PW
T: (01825) 840456
F: (01825) 840773

Shortgate Manor Farm
♦♦♦♦ SILVER AWARD
Halland, Lewes BN8 6PJ
T: (01825) 840320
F: (01825) 840320
E: ewalt@shortgate.co.uk
I: www.shortgate.co.uk

Tamberry Hall
♦♦♦♦♦ SILVER AWARD
Eastbourne Road, Halland,
Lewes BN8 6PS
T: (01825) 880090
F: (01825) 880090
E: bedandbreakfast@tamberryhall.fsbusiness.co.uk
I: tamberryhall.co.uk

HALNAKER
West Sussex

Veronica Cottage ♦♦♦♦
Halnaker, Chichester PO18 0NG
T: (01243) 774929

HAMBLE
Hampshire

Farthings Bed & Breakfast
♦♦♦♦ SILVER AWARD
School Lane, Hamble,
Southampton SO31 4JD
T: (023) 8045 2009
F: (023) 8045 2613
E: strakers@hamble2.fsnet.co.uk
I: www.farthingsinhamble.co.uk

HAMBLEDON
Hampshire

Cams ♦♦♦
Hill Lane, Hambledon,
Waterlooville PO7 4SP
T: (023) 9263 2865
F: (023) 9263 2691

Forestside
Rating Applied For
Martins Corner, Hambledon,
Waterlooville PO7 4RA
T: (02392) 632338

HAMBROOK
West Sussex

Ridge Farm ♦♦♦♦
Scant Road East, Hambrook,
Chichester PO18 8UB
T: (01243) 575567
F: (01243) 576798
E: philip@medlams.co.uk

Willowbrook Riding Centre ♦♦♦
Hambrook Hill South, Hambrook,
Chichester PO18 8UJ
T: (01243) 572683

HAMSTEAD MARSHALL
West Berkshire

Holtwood Gate
Rating Applied For
Hamstead Marshall, Newbury
RG20 0JH
T: (01635) 253454
F: (01635) 255502

HAMWORTHY
Dorset

Harbourside Guest House ♦♦♦
195 Blandford Road,
Hamworthy, Poole BH15 4AX
T: (01202) 673053
F: (01202) 673053
E: harboursideguest@amserve.com

Holes Bay B & B ♦♦♦
365 Blandford Road,
Hamworthy, Poole BH15 4JL
T: (01202) 672069
E: me.dixon@ntlworld.com

Individual Touristik Poole
♦♦♦♦♦ GOLD AWARD
53 Branksea Avenue,
Hamworthy, Poole BH15 4DP
T: (01202) 673419
F: (01202) 667260
E: johnrenate@lineone.net

Seashells ♦♦♦
4 Lake Road, Hamworthy, Poole
BH15 4LH
T: (01202) 671921
F: (01202) 671921

HANSLOPE
Buckinghamshire

Cuckoo Hill Farm ♦♦
Hanslope, Milton Keynes
MK19 7HQ
T: (01908) 510748
F: (01908) 511669

Woad Farm ♦♦♦
Tathall End, Hanslope, Milton
Keynes MK19 7NE
T: (01908) 510985
F: (01908) 510985
E: mail@sarahstacey.freeserve.co.uk

HARRIETSHAM
Kent

Homestay ♦♦♦♦
14 Chippendayle Drive,
Harrietsham, Maidstone
ME17 1AD
T: (01622) 858698
F: (01622) 858698
E: 4homestay@lineone.net
I: www.kent-homestay.info

HARTFIELD
East Sussex

Bolebroke Castle ♦♦♦♦
Edenbridge Road, Hartfield
TN7 4JJ
T: (01892) 770061
F: (01892) 771041
E: bolebroke@btclick.com
I: www.bolebrokecastle.co.uk

HASLEMERE
Surrey

Little Hoewyck ♦♦♦♦
Lickfold Road, Fernhurst,
Haslemere GU27 3JH
T: (01428) 653059
E: suehodge@hoewyck.freeserve.co.uk

Sheps Hollow ♦♦♦
Henley Common, Haslemere
GU27 3HB
T: (01428) 653120

Strathire ♦♦♦♦
Grayswood Road, Haslemere
GU27 2BW
T: (01428) 642466
F: (01428) 656708

HASSOCKS
West Sussex

New Close Farm ♦♦♦♦
London Road, Hassocks
BN6 9ND
T: (01273) 843144
E: sharon.ballard@newclosefarm.co.uk
I: www.newclosefarm.co.uk

HASTINGLEIGH
Kent

Crabtree Farm ♦♦♦
Tamley Lane, Hastingleigh,
Ashford TN25 5HW
T: (01233) 750327

HASTINGS
East Sussex

Apollo Guest House ♦♦♦
25 Cambridge Gardens, Hastings
TN34 1EH
T: (01424) 444394
F: (01424) 444394
E: jim@apollogh.freeserve.co.uk
I: www.apolloguesthouse.co.uk

The Astral Lodge
Rating Applied For
4 Carlisle Parade, St Leonards,
Hastings TN34 1JG
T: (01424) 445599
F: (01424) 460501

Beechwood Hotel ♦♦♦
59 Baldslow Road, Hastings
TN34 2EY
T: (01424) 420078
E: beechwoodhastings@talk21.com

Bell Cottage ♦♦♦♦
Vinehall Road, Robertsbridge,
Hastings TN32 5JN
T: (01580) 881164
F: (01580) 880519
E: patricia.lowe@tesco.net
I: www.bellcottage.co.uk

Bryn-Y-Mor
♦♦♦♦♦ GOLD AWARD
12 Godwin Road, Hastings
TN35 5JR
T: (01424) 722744
F: (01424) 445933
E: karen-alun@brynymor.ndirect.co.uk
I: www.smoothhound.co.uk

Churchills Hotel ♦♦♦
3 St Helens Crescent, Hastings
TN34 2EN
T: (01424) 439359
F: (01424) 447938
E: manager@churchillshotelhastings.co.uk
I: www.churchillshotelhastings.co.uk

Croft Place ♦♦♦♦
2 The Croft, Hastings TN34 3HH
T: (01424) 433004
E: lorraine@croftplace.co.uk
I: www.croftplace.co.uk

Eagle House Hotel ♦♦♦♦
12 Pevensey Road, St Leonards-on-Sea, Hastings TN38 0JZ
T: (01424) 430535
F: (01424) 437771
E: info@eaglehousehotel.com
I: www.eaglehousehotel.com

The Elms ♦♦♦
9 St Helens Park Road, Hastings TN34 2ER
T: (01424) 429979

Emerydale ♦♦♦♦
6 King Edward Avenue, Hastings TN34 2NQ
T: (01424) 437915
F: (01424) 444124
E: jan@emerydale.co.uk

Europa Hotel ♦♦♦♦
2 Carlisle Parade, Hastings TN34 1JG
T: (01424) 717329
F: (01424) 717329

The Gallery ♦♦♦♦
19 Fearon Road, Hastings TN34 2DL
T: (01424) 718110
E: info@thegallerybnb.freeserve.co.uk

Grand Hotel ♦♦♦
Grand Parade, St Leonards, Hastings TN38 0DD
T: (01424) 428510
F: (01424) 428510

64 High Street ♦♦♦
Hastings TN34 3EW
T: (01424) 712584

98 High Street
Rating Applied For
Old Town, Hastings TN34 3ES
T: (01424) 444206
F: (01424) 447708

Holyers ♦♦♦♦ SILVER AWARD
1 Hill Street, Old Town, Hastings TN34 3HU
T: (01424) 430014
E: max@holyers.co.uk
I: www.holyers.co.uk

Lavender & Lace Guest House ♦♦♦♦
106 All Saints Street, Old Town, Hastings TN34 3BE
T: (01424) 716290
F: (01424) 716290

Hotel Lindum ♦♦♦♦
1A Carlisle Parade, Hastings TN34 1JG
T: (01424) 434070
F: (01424) 718833
E: Hotellindum@aol.com
I: www.hotellindum.co.uk

Lionsdown House
♦♦♦♦ SILVER AWARD
116 High Street, Old Town, Hastings TN34 3ET
T: (01424) 420802
F: (01424) 420802
E: sharonlionsdown@aol.com
I: www.lionsdownhouse.co.uk

The Lookout ♦♦♦♦
Chick Hill, Pett Level, Pett, Hastings TN35 4EQ
T: (01424) 812070
I: www.lookoutbb.co.uk

Millifont Guest House ♦♦♦
8-9 Cambridge Gardens, Hastings TN34 1EH
T: (01424) 425645
F: (01424) 425645

The Pines ♦♦♦
50 Baldslow Road, Hastings TN34 2EY
T: (01424) 435838
F: (01424) 435838
E: robert-jean@beeb.net

Sea Spray Guest House ♦♦♦♦
54 Eversfield Place, St Leonards, Hastings TN37 6DB
T: (01424) 436583
F: (01424) 436583
E: seaspraybb@faxvia.net
I: www.seaspraybb.co.uk

South Riding Guest House ♦♦♦
96 Milward Road, Hastings TN34 3RT
T: (01424) 420805

Summerfields House ♦♦♦♦
Bohemia Road, Hastings TN34 1EX
T: (01424) 718142
F: (01424) 718142
E: liz.orourke@totalise.co.uk

Tower House
♦♦♦♦ GOLD AWARD
26-28 Tower Road West, St Leonards, Hastings TN38 0RG
T: (01424) 427217
F: (01424) 430165
E: reservations@towerhousehotel.com
I: www.towerhousehotel.com

HAVANT
Hampshire

High Towers ♦♦♦
14 Portsdown Hill Road, Bedhampton, Havant PO9 3JY
T: (023) 9247 1748
F: (023) 9245 2770
E: hightowers14@aol.com
I: www.hightowers.co.uk

HAWKHURST
Kent

Conghurst Farm
♦♦♦♦♦ SILVER AWARD
Conghurst Lane, Hawkhurst, Cranbrook TN18 4RW
T: (01580) 753331
F: (01580) 754579
E: rosa@conghurst.co.uk

The Wren's Nest
♦♦♦♦♦ GOLD AWARD
Hastings Road, Hawkhurst, Cranbrook TN18 4RT
T: (01580) 754919
F: (01580) 754919

HAWKINGE
Kent

Braeheid Bed & Breakfast ♦♦♦♦
2 Westland Way, Hawkinge, Folkestone CT18 7PW
T: (01303) 893928
E: bill@forrest68.fsnet.co.uk

Terlingham Manor Farm ♦♦♦♦
Gibraltar Lane, Hawkinge, Folkestone CT18 7AE
T: (01303) 894141
F: (01303) 894144
E: diana@terlinghammanor.co.uk
I: www.terlinghammanor.co.uk

HAYLING ISLAND
Hampshire

Ann's Cottage ♦♦♦
45 St Andrews Road, Hayling Island PO11 9JN
T: (023) 9246 7048
E: ann.jay@virgin.net

Broad Oak Country Hotel ♦♦♦
Copse Lane, Hayling Island PO11 0QB
T: (023) 9246 2333
F: (023) 9263 7409
E: tim@hay-isle.demon.co.uk
I: www.hay-isle.demon.co.uk

16 Charleston Close ♦♦♦
Hayling Island PO11 0JY
T: (023) 9246 2527

The Coach House ♦♦♦♦
Church Lane, Northney Village, Hayling Island PO11 0SB
T: (023) 9246 6266
E: auto1@btinternet.com
I: www.tbinternet.com/~AUTO1/bb.htm

Maidlings ♦♦♦
55 Staunton Avenue, Hayling Island PO11 0EW
T: (023) 9246 6357

The Shallows ♦♦♦♦
Woodgaston Lane, Hayling Island PO11 0RL
T: (023) 9246 3713

Tide Reach ♦♦♦
214 Southwood Road, Hayling Island PO11 9QQ
T: (023) 9246 7828
F: (023) 9246 7828
E: welcome@tidereach.fsnet.co.uk

White House ♦♦♦♦
250 Havant Road, Hayling Island PO11 0LN
T: (023) 9246 3464

HAYWARDS HEATH
West Sussex

Copyhold Hollow Bed & Breakfast
♦♦♦♦ SILVER AWARD
Copyhold Lane, Borde Hill, Haywards Heath RH16 1XU
T: (01444) 413265
E: 2@copyholdhollow.freeserve.co.uk
I: www.copyholdhollow.freeserve.co.uk

HEADBOURNE WORTHY
Hampshire

Upper Farm ♦♦♦
Down Farm Lane, Headbourne Worthy, Winchester SO23 7LA
T: (01962) 882240
F: (01962) 886144

HEADCORN
Kent

Curtis Farm
Rating Applied For
Waterman Quarters, Headcorn, Ashford TN27 9JJ
T: (01622) 890393
F: (01622) 890393
E: marion@curtis-farm-kent.com
I: www.curtis-farm-kent.co.uk

Four Oaks ♦♦♦
Four Oaks Road, Headcorn, Ashford TN27 9PB
T: (01622) 891224
F: (01622) 890630
E: info@fouroaks.uk.com
I: www.fouroaks.uk.com

HEADINGTON
Oxfordshire

Barton Lane ♦♦♦
3 Barton Lane, Headington, Oxford OX3 9JR
T: (01865) 762637
E: ellis@oxfree.com

Bell House
Rating Applied For
222 London Road, Headington, Oxford OX3 9EG
T: (01865) 764480

HEADLEY
Hampshire

Coolgreany ♦♦♦
Mill Lane, Headley, Bordon GU35 0PB
T: (01428) 717036
F: (01428) 717036

HEATHFIELD
East Sussex

The Cottage
♦♦♦♦ SILVER AWARD
Rushlake Green, Heathfield TN21 9QH
T: (01435) 830348
F: (01435) 830715
E: cottageonthegreen@btinternet.com
I: www.thecottagebandb.com

Iwood B & B
♦♦♦♦ SILVER AWARD
Mutton Hall Lane, Heathfield TN21 8NR
T: (01435) 863918
F: (01435) 868575
E: iwoodbb@aol.com
I: www.iwoodbb.co.uk

Spicers Bed & Breakfast ♦♦♦♦
21 Spicers Cottages, Cade Street, Heathfield TN21 9BS
T: (01435) 866363
F: (01435) 866363
E: beds@spicersbb.co.uk
I: www.spicersbb.co.uk

HEDGE END
Hampshire

Montana Guest House ♦♦♦
90 Lower Northam Road, Hedge End, Southampton SO30 4FT
T: (01489) 782797

Strawberry Cottage ♦♦♦♦
Shamblehurst Manor, Old Shamblehurst Lane, Hedge End, Southampton SO30 2RX
T: (01489) 795289
E: strawbcott@supanet.com

HEMPSTEAD
Kent

4 The Rise ♦♦♦
Hempstead, Gillingham ME7 3SF
T: (01634) 388156
F: (01634) 388156

HENFIELD
West Sussex

1 The Laurels ♦♦♦♦
Martyn Close, Henfield BN5 9RQ
T: (01273) 493518
E: malc.harrington@lineone.net
I: www.no1thelaurels.co.uk

HENLEY-ON-THAMES
Oxfordshire

Abbottsleigh ♦♦♦
107 St Marks Road, Henley-on-Thames RG9 1LP
T: (01491) 572982
F: (01491) 572982
E: abbottsleigh@hotmail.com

Adnama ♦♦♦♦
29 St Andrews Road, Henley-on-Thames RG9 1HY
T: (01491) 577534
F: (01491) 577534
E: mandyw@bucksnet.co.uk

Alftrudis ♦♦♦♦
8 Norman Avenue, Henley-on-Thames RG9 1SG
T: (01491) 573099
F: (01491) 411747
E: sue@alftrudis.co.uk
I: www.alftrudis.co.uk

Apple Ash ♦♦♦♦
Woodlands Road, Harpsden, Henley-on-Thames RG9 4AB
T: (01491) 574198
F: (01491) 578183
E: aiden@mill-thomas.freeserve.co.uk

Avalon ♦♦♦
36 Queen Street, Henley-on-Thames RG9 1AP
T: (01491) 577829
E: avalon@henleybb.fsnet.co.uk
I: www.henleybb.fsnet.co.uk

Azalea House ♦♦♦♦
55 Deanfield Road, Henley-on-Thames RG9 1UU
T: (01491) 576407
F: (01491) 576407
E: masseyp@globalnet.co.uk
I: www.azaleahouse.co.uk

Badgemore Park Golf Club ♦♦♦
Badgemore, Henley-on-Thames RG9 4NR
T: (01491) 637300
F: (01491) 637301
E: info@badgemorepark.com
I: www.badgemorepark.com

Bank Farm ♦♦
The Old Road, Pishill, Henley-on-Thames RG9 6HS
T: (01491) 638601
F: (01491) 638601
E: bankfarm@btinternet.com

16 Baronsmead ♦♦♦♦
Henley-on-Thames RG9 2DL
T: (01491) 578044

The Beeches ♦♦♦♦
3a Coldharbour Close, Henley-on-Thames RG9 1QF
T: (01491) 579344
F: (01491) 579344
E: brian.duddy@tiscali.co.uk

4 Coldharbour Close ♦♦♦♦
Henley-on-Thames RG9 1QF
T: (01491) 575297
F: (01491) 575297
E: jenny_bower@email.com
I: www.henley-bb.freeserve.co.uk

Coldharbour House ♦♦♦♦
3 Coldharbour Close, Henley-on-Thames RG9 1QF
T: (01491) 575229
F: (01491) 575229
E: coldharbourhouse@aol.com

Denmark House ♦♦♦♦
2 Northfield End, Henley-on-Thames RG9 2HN
T: (01491) 572028
F: (01491) 572458

Falaise House ♦♦♦♦
37 Market Place, St Marys Court, Henley-on-Thames RG9 2AA
T: (01491) 573388
E: sarah@falaisehouse.com
I: www.falaisehouse.com

Gablehurst ♦♦♦
34 Cromwell Road, Henley-on-Thames RG9 1JH
T: (01491) 575876
F: (01491) 575876
E: gablehurst@rg91jh.free-online.co.uk
I: www.rg91jh.free-online.co.uk

26 Hart Street ♦♦♦
Hart Street, Henley-on-Thames RG9 2AU
T: (01491) 579031
F: (01491) 579031
E: pkmckenna@aol.com
I: www.26hartst.co.uk

Henley House ♦♦♦
School Lane, Medmenham, Marlow SL7 2HJ
T: (01491) 576100
E: admin@henley-house.com

Holmwood ♦♦♦♦
Shiplake Row, Binfield Heath, Henley-on-Thames RG9 4DP
T: (0118) 947 8747
F: (0118) 947 8637
E: wendy.cook@freenet.co.uk

The Knoll
♦♦♦♦ SILVER AWARD
Crowsley Road, Shiplake, Henley-on-Thames RG9 3JT
T: (01189) 402705
F: (01189) 402705
E: theknollhenley@aol.com
I: www.theknollhenley.co.uk

Lenwade ♦♦♦♦♦
3 Western Road, Henley-on-Thames RG9 1JL
T: (01491) 573468
F: (01491) 411664
E: lenwadeuk@aol.com
I: www.w3b-ink.com/lenwade

Little Parmoor Farm ♦♦♦♦
Frieth, Henley-on-Thames RG9 6NL
T: (01494) 881600
F: (01494) 883634
E: francesemmett@waitrose.com
I: www.parmoor.co.uk

New Lodge ♦♦♦
Henley Park, Henley-on-Thames RG9 6HU
T: (01491) 576340
F: (01491) 576340
E: newlodge@mail.com

No 4 Riverside ♦♦♦
4 River Terrace, Henley-on-Thames RG9 1BG
T: (01491) 571133
F: (01491) 413651
I: www.angelonthebridge.co.uk

Old School House ♦♦♦♦
Off Hart Street, Henley-on-Thames RG9 2AU
T: (01491) 573929
F: (01491) 411148
E: adrian.lake@btinternet.com

The Old Wood ♦♦♦
197 Greys Road, Henley-on-Thames RG9 1QU
T: (01491) 573930
F: (01491) 576285
E: janice@janicejones.co.uk

Park View Farm ♦♦
Lower Assendon, Henley-on-Thames RG9 6AN
T: (01491) 414232
F: (01491) 577515
E: thomasmartin@globalnet.co.uk
I: www.thomasmartin.co.uk

Pennyford House ♦♦
Peppard Common, Henley-on-Thames RG9 5JE
T: (01491) 628272
F: (01491) 628779

Robhill ♦♦♦
267 Greys Road, Henley-on-Thames RG9 1QS
T: (01491) 577391
F: (01491) 577391
E: jilly.ford@talk21.com
I: www.impactwp.com/robhill

Silver Birches ♦♦♦
6 Elizabeth Road, Henley-on-Thames RG9 1RG
T: (01491) 575727
E: clarktandh@aol.com

Slaters Farm ♦♦♦
Peppard Common, Henley-on-Thames RG9 5JL
T: (01491) 628675
F: (01491) 628675

Stag Hall ♦♦♦
Peppard, Henley-on-Thames RG9 5NX
T: (01491) 680338
F: (01491) 680338

Thamesmead House Hotel
♦♦♦♦♦ SILVER AWARD
Remenham Lane, Remenham, Henley-on-Thames RG9 2LR
T: (01491) 574745
F: (01491) 579944
E: thamesmead@supanet.com
I: www.thamesmeadhousehotel.co.uk

Vine Cottage ♦♦♦
53 Northfield Road, Henley-on-Thames RG9 2JJ
T: (01491) 573545
F: (01491) 410707

Windy Brow ♦♦♦♦
204 Victoria Road, Wargrave, Reading RG10 8AJ
T: (0118) 940 3336
F: (0118) 940 1260
E: heather.carver@orange.com

Woodlands ♦♦♦♦♦
Colmore Lane, Kingwood, Henley-on-Thames RG9 5NA
T: (01491) 628386
F: (01491) 628102
E: robertcb@talk21.com

HERMITAGE
Berkshire

Eling Farm ♦♦♦♦
Eling Hermitage, Hermitage, Thatcham RG18 9XR
T: (01635) 200021
F: (01635) 201105

HERSHAM
Surrey

Bricklayers Arms ♦♦♦♦
6 Queens Road, Hersham, Walton-on-Thames KT12 5LS
T: (01932) 220936
F: (01932) 230400
E: ff@bricklayers-arms.fsworld.co.uk

HERSTMONCEUX
East Sussex

Conquerors
♦♦♦♦ SILVER AWARD
Stunts Green, Herstmonceux, Hailsham BN27 4PR
T: (01323) 832446
F: (01323) 831578
E: Conquerors@ukgateway.net

Sandhurst ♦♦♦♦
Church Road, Herstmonceux, Hailsham BN27 1RG
T: (01323) 833088
F: (01323) 833088
E: junealanruss@aol.com

The Stud Farm ♦♦♦
Bodle Street Green, Herstmonceux, Hailsham BN27 4RJ
T: (01323) 833201
F: (01323) 833201
E: philippa@miroted.freeserve.co.uk

Waldernheath Country House ♦♦♦♦
Amberstone, Herstmonceux, Hailsham BN27 1PJ
T: (01323) 442259
F: (01323) 440553
E: waldernheath@lineone.net

HETHE
Oxfordshire

Manor Farm ♦♦♦♦
Main Street, Hethe, Bicester OX27 8ES
T: (01869) 277602
F: (01869) 278376
E: chrmanor@aol.com
I: www.freewebs.com/manorfarm

HEYSHOTT
West Sussex

Little Hoyle ♦♦♦♦
Hoyle Lane, Heyshott, Midhurst GU29 0DX
T: (01798) 867359
F: (01798) 867359

HIGH HALDEN
Kent

Badgers ♦♦♦♦
Ashford Road, High Halden, Ashford TN26 3LY
T: (01233) 850158
E: wendy@badgers-bb.co.uk
I: www.badgers-bb.co.uk

Durrants Court
Rating Applied For
Ashford Road, High Halden, Ashford TN26 3BS
T: (01233) 850003
E: sgentle@globalnet.co.uk

HIGH HURSTWOOD
East Sussex

Chillies Granary ♦♦♦♦
Chillies Lane, High Hurstwood, Uckfield TN6 3TB
T: (01892) 655560
F: (01892) 655560

Huckleberry ♦♦♦♦
Perrymans Lane, High Hurstwood, Uckfield TN22 4AG
T: (01825) 733170

The Orchard ♦♦♦♦
Rocks Lane, High Hurstwood, Uckfield TN22 4BN
T: (01825) 732946
F: (01825) 732946
E: turtonorchard@aol.com
I: www.theorchardbandb.co.uk

HIGH WYCOMBE
Buckinghamshire

Ayam Manor ♦♦♦
Hammersley Lane, High Wycombe HP10 8HF
T: (01494) 816932
F: (01494) 816338
E: jeansenior@ayammanor.freeserve.co.uk
I: www.ayammanorguesthouse.co.uk

The Birches ♦♦
30 Lucas Road, High Wycombe HP13 6QG
T: (01494) 533547

Bird in Hand ♦♦♦
81 West Wycombe Road, High Wycombe HP11 2LR
T: (01494) 523502
F: (01494) 459449

31 Green Road ♦♦♦
High Wycombe HP13 5BD
T: (01494) 522625
F: (01494) 522625

P Smails Guest Accommodation ♦♦♦
106 Green Hill, High Wycombe HP13 5QE
T: (01494) 524310
F: (01494) 461693
E: pauline@smails.fsnet.co.uk

9 Sandford Gardens ♦♦♦
Daws Hill, High Wycombe HP11 1QT
T: (01494) 441723

Spring View
Rating Applied For
133 Heath End Road, Flackwell Heath, High Wycombe HP10 9ES
T: (01628) 528719

HIGHAM
Kent

Kinsale ♦♦♦♦
1A School Lane, Mid Higham, Higham, Rochester ME3 7AT
T: (01474) 822106
E: kinsale@btinternet.com

HIGHCLERE
Hampshire

Highclere Farm ♦♦♦
Highclere, Newbury RG20 9PY
T: (01635) 255013
E: walshhighclere@newburyweb.net

HIGHCLIFFE
Dorset

10 Brook Way ♦♦♦
Friars Cliff, Highcliffe BH23 4HA
T: (01425) 276738
E: midgefinn@hotmail.com

Castle Lodge ♦♦♦♦
173 Lymington Road, Highcliffe BH23 4JS
T: (01425) 275170
F: (01425) 275170
E: chard_family@hotmail.com
I: www.four-runner.com/castlelodge

The Close ♦♦♦
12 Shelley Close, Highcliffe BH23 4HW
T: (01425) 273559

Sea Corner Guest House & Angolo Del Mare Italian Restaurant ♦♦♦♦
397 Waterford Road, Highcliffe BH23 5JN
T: (01425) 272731
F: (01425) 272077
E: marlene@seacorner.fsnet.co.uk

White Gables ♦♦♦♦
Seaview Road, Highcliffe BH23 5QJ
T: (01425) 280007
E: gable-net@supanet.com

HILDENBOROUGH
Kent

148 Tonbridge Road ♦♦♦
Tonbridge Road, Hildenborough, Tonbridge TN11 9HW
T: (01732) 838894

HINTON ST MARY
Dorset

The Old Post Office Guest House ♦♦♦♦
Hinton St Mary, Sturminster Newton DT10 1NG
T: (01258) 472366
F: (01258) 472173
E: sofields@aol.com

HINTON ST MICHAEL
Hampshire

The East Close Country Hotel ♦♦
Lyndhurst Road, Hinton St Michael BH23 7EF
T: (01425) 672404
F: (01425) 674315
E: eastclosecountryhotel@yahoo.co.uk
I: www.eastclosecountryhotel.co.uk

HINTON WALDRIST
Oxfordshire

The Old Rectory ♦♦♦♦
Hinton Waldrist, Faringdon SN7 8SA
T: (01865) 821228
F: (01865) 821193
I: www.taylor-net.com

HOLLINGBOURNE
Kent

Woodhouses ♦♦♦♦
49 Eyhorne Street, Hollingbourne, Maidstone ME17 1TR
T: (01622) 880594
E: woodhouses@supanet.com
I: www.smoothhound.co.uk/hotels/woodhouses.html

HOLMBURY ST MARY
Surrey

Holmbury Farm ♦♦♦♦
Holmbury St Mary, Dorking RH5 6NB
T: (01306) 621443
F: (01306) 621498
E: randvlloyd@holmbury100.fsnet.co.uk

Woodhouse Copse ♦♦♦
Horsham Road, Holmbury St Mary, Dorking RH5 6NL
T: (01306) 730136
F: (01306) 730956
E: woodhousemusic@mistral.co.uk

Woodhouse Place ♦♦♦♦
Holmbury St Mary, Dorking RH5 6NL
T: (01306) 730496
F: (01306) 731495

HOLYBOURNE
Hampshire

Bonhams Farm ♦♦♦
Holybourne, Alton GU34 4JA
T: (01420) 87483
F: (01420) 549205
E: mcannon@lapac.co.uk

The Manor House ♦♦♦♦
Church Lane, Holybourne, Alton GU34 4HD
T: (01420) 541321
F: (01420) 541588
E: clare@whately.net

HOOK
Hampshire

Cherry Lodge Guest House ♦♦♦
Reading Road, Hook RG27 9DB
T: (01256) 762532
F: (01256) 766068
E: cherrylodge@btinternet.com

Oaklea Guest House ♦♦♦
London Road, Hook RG27 9LA
T: (01256) 762673
F: (01256) 762150
E: oakleaguesthouse@amserve.net

Tundry House Bed & Breakfast ♦♦♦♦
Tundry House, Dogmersfield, Hook RG27 8SZ
T: (01252) 614677
F: (01252) 812205
E: swalters02@02.co.uk

HOOK NORTON
Oxfordshire

Manor Farm ♦♦♦
Hook Norton, Banbury OX15 5LU
T: (01608) 737204
F: (01608) 737204
E: jdyhughes@aol.com

HORAM
East Sussex

Oak Mead Bed & Breakfast ♦♦♦
Vines Cross, Cowden Hall Lane, Horam, Heathfield TN21 9ED
T: (01435) 812962

Wimbles Farm ♦♦♦
Vines Cross, Horam, Heathfield TN21 9HA
T: (01435) 812342
F: (01435) 813603
E: susan_ramsay@madasafish.com
I: www.sussexcountry.com

HORLEY
Surrey

Berrens Guest House ♦♦♦
62 Massetts Road, Horley RH6 7DS
T: (01293) 786125
F: (01293) 786125

Gatwick House ♦♦♦
3 Brighton Road, Horley RH6 7HH
T: (01293) 782738
F: (01293) 776106
E: info@gatwickhouse.com
I: www.gatwickhouse.com

Glenalmond Guest House ♦♦♦
64 Massetts Road, Horley RH6 7DS
T: (01293) 773564
F: (01293) 421728
E: glenalmondguesthouse@hotmail.com
I: glenalmondguesthouse.co.uk

The Lawn Guest House ♦♦♦♦ SILVER AWARD
30 Massetts Road, Gatwick, Horley RH6 7DF
T: (01293) 775751
F: (01293) 821803
E: info@lawnguesthouse.co.uk
I: www.lawnguesthouse.co.uk

Masslink House ♦♦♦
70 Massetts Road, Horley RH6 7ED
T: (01293) 785798
F: (01293) 783279

Melville Lodge Guest House
Rating Applied For
15 Brighton Road, Horley, Gatwick RH6 7HH
T: (01293) 784951
F: (01293) 785669
E: melvillelodge.guesthouse@tesco.net

Prinsted Guest House ♦♦♦
Oldfield Road, Horley RH6 7EP
T: (01293) 785233
F: (01293) 820624
E: kendall@prinstedguesthouse.co.uk
I: www.prinstedguesthouse.co.uk

Rosemead Guest House ♦♦♦♦
19 Church Road, Horley RH6 7EY
T: (01293) 784965
F: (01293) 430547
E: info@rosemeadguesthouse.co.uk
I: www.rosemeadguesthouse.co.uk

Sor Brook House Farm ♦♦♦♦
Horley, Banbury OX15 6BL
T: (01295) 738121

Trumbles Guest House ♦♦♦♦
Stanhill, Charlwood, Horley RH6 0EP
T: (01293) 863418
F: (01293) 862925
E: info@trumbles.co.uk
I: www.trumbles.co.uk

The Turret Guest House ♦♦♦
48 Massetts Road, Horley RH6 7DS
T: (01293) 782490
F: (01293) 431492
E: info@theturret.com
I: www.theturret.com

HORNDEAN
Hampshire

Rosedene ♦♦♦♦
63 Rosemary Way, Horndean, Waterlooville PO8 9DQ
T: (023) 9261 5804
F: (023) 9242 3948
E: pbbatt@aol.com

The Ship & Bell Hotel ♦♦♦
6 London Road, Horndean, Waterlooville PO8 0BZ
T: (02392) 592107

HORNTON
Oxfordshire

The Yews ♦♦♦
Church Lane, Hornton, Banbury OX15 6BY
T: (01295) 670460

HORSHAM
West Sussex

49 Broadwood Close ♦♦♦
Horsham RH12 4JY
T: (01403) 263651

The Deans ♦♦♦♦
8 Wimblehurst Road, Horsham RH12 2ED
T: (01403) 268166
F: (01403) 268166
E: contact@thedeans.co.uk
I: www.thedeans.co.uk

The Larches ♦♦♦
28 Rusper Road, Horsham RH12 4BD
T: (01403) 263392
F: (01403) 249980

The Studio
Rating Applied For
The Hermitage, Tower Hill, Horsham RH13 7JS
T: (01403) 270808

The Wirrals ♦♦♦
1 Downsview Road, Horsham RH12 4PF
T: (01403) 269400
F: (01403) 269400
E: p.archibald@lineone.net
I: website.lineone.net/~p.archibald/webba.htm

HORTON
Dorset

The Horton Inn ♦♦
Cranborne Road, Horton, Wimborne Minster BH21 5AD
T: (01258) 840252
F: (01258) 841400
I: www.activehotels.com

HUNGERFORD
Berkshire

Alderborne House ♦♦♦♦
33 Bourne Vale, Hungerford RG17 0LL
T: (01488) 683228
E: mail@honeybone.co.uk
I: www.honeybone.co.uk

Anne's B & B ♦♦♦
59 Priory Avenue, Hungerford RG17 0AS
T: (01488) 682290
F: (01488) 686993
E: anne@hungerfordberks.co.uk
I: www.hungerfordberks.co.uk

Fishers Farm ♦♦♦♦
Ermin Street, Shefford Woodlands, Hungerford RG17 7AB
T: (01488) 648466
F: (01488) 648706
E: mail@fishersfarm.co.uk
I: www.fishersfarm.co.uk

The Garden House ♦♦♦♦
34 High Street, Hungerford RG17 0NF
T: (01488) 685369
E: bevjess@ukgateway.net

Marshgate Cottage Hotel ♦♦♦♦
Marsh Lane, Hungerford RG17 0QX
T: (01488) 682307
F: (01488) 685475
E: reservations@marshgate.co.uk
I: www.marshgate.co.uk

Wilton House
♦♦♦♦ SILVER AWARD
33 High Street, Hungerford RG17 0NF
T: (01488) 684228
F: (01488) 685037
E: welfares@hotmail.com
I: www.wiltonhouse.freeserve.com

HUNSTON
West Sussex

Spire Cottage ♦♦♦♦
Church Lane, Hunston, Chichester PO20 6AJ
T: (01243) 778937
E: spirecottage@aol.com
I: www.spirecottage.co.uk

HURN
Dorset

Avon Causeway Inn ♦♦♦
Hurn, Christchurch BH23 6AS
T: (01202) 482714
F: (01202) 477416
E: avoncauseway@wadworth.co.uk
I: www.avoncausewayhotel.co.uk

HURSTPIERPOINT
West Sussex

Wickham Place ♦♦♦♦
Wickham Drive, Hurstpierpoint, Hassocks BN6 9AP
T: (01273) 832172
F: (01273) 832172
E: stay@wickham-place.co.uk
I: smoothhound.co.uk/hotels/wickham

HYTHE
Hampshire

Changri-La ♦♦♦♦
12 Ashleigh Close, Hythe, Southampton SO45 3QP
T: (023) 8084 6664

Fern Lodge Bed & Breakfast ♦♦♦
87 Seabrook Road, Hythe CT21 5QP
T: (01303) 267315
F: (01303) 267315
E: francebbferns@hotmail.com

Moyle Cottage ♦♦♦
The Fairway, Hythe CT21 6AU
T: (01303) 262106
F: (01303) 262106
E: msmunge@globalnet.co.uk

Seabrook House ♦♦♦♦
81 Seabrook Road, Hythe CT21 5QW
T: (01303) 269282
F: (01303) 237822
E: info@seabrook-house.co.uk
I: www.smoothhound.co.uk/hotels/seabrook.html

The Shrubsoles B&B ♦♦♦
62 Brockhill Road, Hythe CT21 4AG
T: (01303) 238832
E: info@theshrubsoles.co.uk
I: www.theshrubsoles.co.uk

The Swan Hotel ♦♦♦
59 High Street, Hythe CT21 5AD
T: (01303) 266236
F: (01303) 262584
I: www.theswanhotelhythe.co.uk

Watersedge ♦♦♦
The Watersedge, Red Lion Square, Hythe CT21 5AU
T: (01303) 266686
F: (01303) 269877

IBTHORPE
Hampshire

Staggs Cottage ♦♦♦
Windmill Hill, Ibthorpe, Andover SP11 0BP
T: (01264) 736235
F: (01264) 736597
E: staggscottage@aol.com

INKPEN
Berkshire

The Swan Inn ♦♦♦♦
Inkpen, Hungerford RG17 9DX
T: (01488) 668326
F: (01488) 668306
E: enquiries@theswaninn-organics.co.uk
I: www.theswaninn-organics.co.uk

ISFIELD
East Sussex

Farm Place ♦♦♦♦
Lewes Road, Isfield, Uckfield TN22 5TY
T: (01825) 750485
F: (01825) 750411

ITCHEN ABBAS
Hampshire

Hatch End
♦♦♦♦ SILVER AWARD
Main Road, Itchen Abbas, Winchester SO21 1AT
T: (01962) 779279

The Trout ♦♦♦♦
Trout Inn, Itchen Abbas, Winchester SO21 1BQ
T: (01962) 779537
F: (01962) 791046
E: thetroutinn@freeuk.com
I: www.thetroutinn.com

IVINGHOE
Buckinghamshire

Bull Lake B&B ♦♦♦♦
Ford End, Ivinghoe, Leighton Buzzard LU7 9EA
T: (01296) 668834
F: (01296) 668175
E: sophie@bull-lake.co.uk
I: www.bull-lake.co.uk

KIDLINGTON
Oxfordshire

Breffni House ♦♦♦
9 Lovelace Drive, Kidlington OX5 2LY
T: (01865) 372569

Colliers B & B ♦♦♦
55 Nethercote Road, Tackley, Kidlington OX5 3AT
T: (01869) 331255
F: (01869) 331670

Warsborough House ♦♦♦
52 Mill Street, Kidlington OX5 2EF
T: (01865) 370316
F: (01865) 370316
E: elizabethmair@lycos.co.uk
I: www.warsboroughhouse.co.uk

Wise Alderman Inn ♦♦♦
249 Banbury Road, Kidlington OX5 1BF
T: (01865) 372281
F: (01865) 370153

KIMMERIDGE
Dorset

Kimmeridge Farmhouse
♦♦♦♦ GOLD AWARD
Kimmeridge, Wareham BH20 5PE
T: (01929) 480990
F: (01929) 481503
E: kimmeridgefarmhouse@hotmail.com

KINGHAM
Oxfordshire

The Tollgate Hotel and Restaurant ♦♦♦♦
Church Street, Kingham, Oxford OX7 6YA
T: (01608) 658389
F: (01608) 659467
E: info@the-tollgate.com
I: www.the-tollgate.com

KINGSDOWN
Kent

Blencathra Country Guest House ♦♦♦♦
Kingsdown Hill, Kingsdown, Deal CT14 8EA
T: (01304) 373725
E: blencathra2000@hotmail.com
I: ww.blencathra-guesthouse.info

Sparrow Court ♦♦♦
Chalk Hill Road, Kingsdown, Deal CT14 8DP
T: (01304) 389253
F: (01304) 389016
E: gmaude@waitrose.com
I: www.farmstaykent.com

KINGSLEY
Hampshire

The Cricketers Inn ♦♦♦
Main Road, Kingsley, Bordon GU35 9ND
T: (01420) 476730
F: (01420) 477871

Spring Cottage ♦♦♦
Main Road, Kingsley, Bordon GU35 9NA
T: (01420) 472703
F: (01420) 472703

KINGSTON
Dorset

Kingston Country Courtyard ♦♦♦♦
Greystone Court, Kingston, Corfe Castle, Wareham BH20 5LR
T: (01929) 481066
F: (01929) 481256
E: annfry@kingstoncountrycourtyard.co.uk
I: www.kingstoncountrycourtyard.co.uk

KINGTON MAGNA
Dorset

Kington Manor Farm ♦♦♦♦
Church Hill, Kington Magna, Gillingham SP8 5EG
T: (01747) 838371
F: (01747) 838371
E: gosneykm@aol.com
I: www.smoothhound.co.uk/kingtonmanor.html

KINTBURY
Berkshire

Holt Lodge ♦♦♦♦
Kintbury, Hungerford RG17 9SX
T: (01488) 668244
F: (01488) 668244
E: johnfreeland@holtlodge.freeserve.co.uk
I: www.holt-lodge.co.uk

KIRTLINGTON
Oxfordshire

Vicarage Farmhouse ♦♦♦♦
Kirtlington, Oxford OX5 3JY
T: (01869) 350254
F: (01869) 350254
E: jahunter1@talk21.co.uk
I: www.country-accom.co.uk/vicaragefarm

LADDINGFORD
Kent

The Chequers ♦♦♦♦
The Street, Laddingford, Maidstone ME18 6BP
T: (01622) 871266
F: (01622) 873115

LAKE
Isle of Wight

Ashleigh House Hotel ♦♦♦♦
81 Sandown Road, Lake, Sandown PO36 9LE
T: (01983) 402340

Haytor Lodge ♦♦♦♦
16 Cliff Path, Lake, Sandown PO36 8PL
T: (01983) 402969

Osterley Lodge ♦♦♦♦
62 Sandown Road, Lake, Sandown PO36 9JX
T: (01983) 402017
F: (01983) 402854
E: osterleylodgeiw@aol.com
I: www.netguides.co.uk/wight/basic/osterley.html

Piers View Guest House ♦♦♦
20 Cliff Path, Lake, Sandown PO36 8PL
T: (01983) 404646
E: piers-view@zoom.co.uk

LAMBERHURST
Kent

Chequers Oast ♦♦♦
The Broadway, Lamberhurst, Royal Tunbridge Wells TN3 8DB
T: (01892) 890579
F: (01892) 890579
E: avrilandterry@yahoo.co.uk

LANCING
West Sussex

Edelweiss Guest House ♦♦♦
17 Kings Road, Lancing BN15 8EB
T: (01903) 753412
F: (01903) 527424

LANGRISH
Hampshire

Upper Parsonage Farm
Rating Applied For
Harvesting Lane, East Meon, Langrish, Petersfield GU32 1QW
T: (01730) 823490
F: (01730) 823855

Yew Tree Farm House ♦♦♦
Langrish, Petersfield GU32 1RB
T: (01730) 264959

LAUGHTON
East Sussex

Holly Cottage ♦♦♦♦
Lewes Road, Laughton, Lewes BN8 6BL
T: (01323) 811309
F: (01323) 811106
E: hollycottage@tinyworld.co.uk

Spences Farm ♦♦♦
Laughton, Lewes BN8 6BX
T: (01825) 840489
F: (01825) 840760
E: spencesfarm@fsmail.net

LAVANT
West Sussex

Flint Cottages ♦♦♦♦
47 Mid Lavant, Lavant, Chichester PO18 0AA
T: (01243) 785883
F: (01243) 785883

LEAFIELD
Oxfordshire

Greenside Cottage ♦♦♦
The Ridings, Leafield, Oxford OX29 9NN
T: (01993) 878368
F: (01993) 878368

Langley Farm ♦♦♦
Langley, Oxford OX29 9QD
T: (01993) 878686

LECKHAMPSTEAD
Berkshire

Catslide Cottage ♦♦♦♦
Hill Green, Leckhampstead, Newbury RG20 8RB
T: (01635) 247098
F: (01635) 247098
E: alancis@compuserve.com

Weatherhead Farm ♦♦♦♦
Leckhampstead, Buckingham MK18 5NP
T: (01280) 860502
F: (01280) 860535
E: ed@cgurney.fsnet.co.uk

LEE ON THE SOLENT
Hampshire

Apple Tree Cottage ♦♦♦
159 Portsmouth Road, Lee on the Solent PO13 9AD
T: (023) 9255 1176
F: (023) 9235 2492
E: lmgell@aol.com

Avon Manor Guest House ♦♦♦
12 South Place, Lee on the Solent PO13 9AS
T: (023) 9255 2773
E: karen@avonmanor.co.uk
I: www.avonmanor.co.uk

Chester Lodge ♦♦♦
20 Chester Crescent, Lee on the Solent PO13 9BH
T: (023) 9255 0894
F: (023) 9255 6291

LEEDS
Kent

Further Fields ♦♦♦
Caring Lane, Leeds, Maidstone ME17 1TJ
T: (01622) 861288
E: furtherfields@aol.com

West Forge ♦♦♦
Back Street, Leeds, Maidstone ME17 1TF
T: (01622) 861428

LEIGH
Kent

Charcott Farmhouse B & B
♦♦♦♦ SILVER AWARD
Charcott, Leigh, Tonbridge TN11 8LG
T: (01892) 870024
F: (01892) 870158
E: nicholasmorris@charcott.freeserve.co.uk
I: www.smoothhound.co.uk/hotels/charcott

Herons Head Farm ♦♦♦♦
Mynthurst, Leigh, Reigate RH2 8QD
T: (01293) 862475
F: (01293) 863350
E: heronshead@clara.net
I: www.seetb.org.uk/heronshead

LENHAM
Kent

Bramley Knowle Farm ♦♦♦
Eastwood Road, Ulcombe, Maidstone ME17 1ET
T: (01622) 858878
F: (01622) 851121
E: diane@bramleyknowlefarm.co.uk
I: www.bramleyknowlefarm.co.uk

The Dog & Bear Hotel ♦♦♦
The Square, Lenham, Maidstone ME17 2PG
T: (01622) 858219
F: (01622) 859415
E: dogbear@shepherd-neame.co.uk
I: www.shepherd-neame.co.uk

East Lenham Farm
♦♦♦♦ SILVER AWARD
Lenham, Maidstone ME17 2DP
T: (01622) 858686
F: (01622) 859474
E: eastlenham@farmline.com
I: www.eastlenhamfarm.co.uk

LETCOMBE REGIS
Oxfordshire

The Old Vicarage
Rating Applied For
Letcombe Regis, Wantage OX12 9JP
T: (01235) 765827
E: hugh.barton@virgin.net

Regis Bed & Breakfast ♦♦♦♦
2 Court Road, Letcombe Regis, Wantage OX12 9JH
T: (01235) 762860
F: (01235) 769975
E: regisbandb@aol.com

LEWES
East Sussex

The Crown Inn ♦♦♦
High Street, Lewes BN7 2NA
T: (01273) 480670
F: (01273) 480679
E: sales@crowninn-lewes.co.uk
I: www.crowninn-lewes.co.uk

Downsview ♦♦♦
15 Montacute Road, Lewes BN7 1EW
T: (01273) 472719

Eckington House
♦♦♦♦ SILVER AWARD
Ripe Lane, Ripe, Lewes BN8 6AR
T: (01323) 811274
E: sue@eckingtonhouse.co.uk
I: www.eckingtonhouse.co.uk

Hale Farm House ♦♦♦♦
Chiddingly, Lewes BN8 6HQ
T: (01825) 872619
F: (01825) 872619
E: s.burrough@virgin.net
I: www.halefarmhouse.co.uk

13 Hill Road ♦♦♦
Lewes BN7 1DB
T: (01273) 477723
F: (01273) 477723
E: kmyles@btclick.com

Knowle View
Rating Applied For
24 Mill Road, Lewes BN7 2RU
T: (01273) 477477

Millers ♦♦♦♦
134 High Street, Lewes BN7 1XS
T: (01273) 475631
F: (01273) 486226
E: millers134@aol.com
I: www.hometown.aol.com/millers134

Number 6 ♦♦♦♦
6 Gundreda Road, Lewes BN7 1PX
T: (01273) 472106
F: (01273) 472106
E: jacquelinelucas@yahoo.co.uk
I: www.stayinlewes.co.uk

Number Seven ♦♦♦♦
7 Prince Edwards Road, Lewes BN7 1BJ
T: (01273) 487038
E: numberseven@lewesbedandbreakfast.com
I: www.lewesbedandbreakfast.com

Settlands ♦♦♦♦
Wellgreen Lane, Kingston, Lewes BN7 3NP
T: (01273) 472295
E: diana-a@solutions-inc.co.uk

Sussex Countryside Accommodation
♦♦♦♦ SILVER AWARD
Crink House, Barcombe Mills, Lewes BN8 5BJ
T: (01273) 400625
E: crinkhouse@hgaydon.fsnet.co.uk

Whitesmith Barn
♦♦♦♦ SILVER AWARD
Whitesmith, Lewes BN8 6HA
T: (01825) 872867
E: snellings@whitesmith.fsnet.co.uk

LEWKNOR
Oxfordshire

Moorcourt Cottage ♦♦♦♦
Weston Road, Lewknor, Oxford OX49 5RU
T: (01844) 351419
F: (01844) 351419
E: moorcourt2002@yahoo.co.uk

LINDFIELD
West Sussex

Little Lywood ♦♦♦
Ardingly Road, Lindfield, Haywards Heath RH16 2QX
T: (01444) 892571
E: nick@littlelywood.freeserve.co.uk

LINGFIELD
Surrey

Long Acres Farm ♦♦♦
Newchapel Road, Lingfield RH7 6LE
T: (01342) 833205
F: (01622) 735038

LIPHOOK
Hampshire

The Bailiff's Cottage ♦♦♦
Liphook GU30 7LR
T: (01428) 722171
E: jenner@bailiffs.fsnet.co.uk

Tylston Lodge ♦♦♦♦
Headley Road, Liphook GU30 7PT
T: (01428) 722782
F: (01428) 722782
I: www.tylstonlodge.com

Woolmer Mist ♦♦♦♦
Hazeldene Road, Liphook GU30 7PH
T: (01428) 725529

LITTLE CHESTERTON
Oxfordshire

Cover Point ♦♦♦♦
Little Chesterton, Bicester OX25 3PD
T: (01869) 252500
F: (01869) 252500
E: lamb@coverpoint100.freeserve.co.uk

LITTLE MARLOW
Buckinghamshire

The Crooked Cottage ♦♦♦
Sheepridge Lane, Little Marlow, Marlow SL7 3SG
T: (01628) 521130

LITTLEBOURNE
Kent

King William IV ♦♦♦
4 High Street, Littlebourne, Canterbury CT3 1UN
T: (01227) 721244
F: (01227) 721244
E: paulharvey@kingwilliam04.fsbusiness.co.uk
I: www.kingwilliam4th.co.uk

LITTLEHAMPTON
West Sussex

Amberley Court
Rating Applied For
Crookthorn Lane, Climping, Littlehampton BN17 5SN
T: (01903) 725131
F: (01903) 725131

Arun Sands ♦♦♦
84 South Terrace, Seafront, Littlehampton BN17 5LJ
T: (01903) 732489
F: (01903) 732489
E: info@arun-sands.co.uk
I: www.arun-sands.co.uk

Arun View Inn ♦♦
Wharf Road, Littlehampton BN17 5DD
T: (01903) 722335
F: (01903) 722335

Quayside Guest House ♦♦♦
36 Pier Road, Littlehampton BN17 5LW
T: (01903) 721958
F: (01903) 721958

Racing Greens ♦♦♦
70 South Terrace, Littlehampton BN17 5LQ
T: (01903) 732972
F: (01903) 732932
E: urban.surfer@easynet.co.uk

Sharoleen Guest House ♦♦♦
85 Bayford Road, Littlehampton BN17 5HW
T: (01903) 713464
F: (01903) 713464

Tudor Lodge Guest House ♦♦♦
2 Horsham Road, Littlehampton BN17 6BU
T: (01903) 716203
F: (01903) 716203

LITTLESTONE-ON-SEA
Kent

York Cottage
Rating Applied For
Blenheim Road, Littlestone-on-Sea, New Romney TN28 8RD
T: (01797) 362286
F: (01797) 364141
E: sm@windsor6735.freeserve.co.uk

LITTLETON
Hampshire

The Garden Flat ♦♦♦
7A Bercote Close, Littleton, Winchester SO22 6PX
T: (01962) 883660
E: d.elsmore@virgin.net
I: www.garden-flat.com

LOCKERLEY
Hampshire

St Brelade's House
Rating Applied For
Mill Lane, Sherfield English, Lockerley, Romsey SO51 6FN
T: (01794) 324766
F: (01794) 324766
E: B&B@st_brelades.freeserve.co.uk

LONG HANBOROUGH
Oxfordshire

The Close Guest House ♦♦♦
Witney Road, Long Hanborough, Oxford OX29 8HF
T: (01993) 882485
F: (01993) 883819

Old Farmhouse ♦♦♦♦
Station Hill, Long Hanborough, Oxford OX29 8JZ
T: (01993) 882097
F: (01993) 880008
E: old.farm@virgin.net
I: www.country-accom.co.uk/old-farmhouse

LONG WITTENHAM
Oxfordshire

The Grange
Rating Applied For
High Street, Long Wittenham, Abingdon OX14 4QH
T: (01865) 407808
F: (01865) 407939
E: grahamneil@talk21.com
I: www.smoothhound.co.uk/hotels/grange5.html

Witta's Ham Cottage ♦♦♦♦
High Street, Long Wittenham, Abingdon OX14 4QH
T: (01865) 407686
F: (01865) 407469
E: martin.meller@sjpp.co.uk

LONGFIELD
Kent

Kaye Cottage ♦♦♦♦
Old Downs, Hartley, Longfield DA3 7AA
T: (01474) 702384
F: (01474) 702384
E: b-b@kaye-cottage.freeserve.co.uk

The Rising Sun Inn ♦♦♦
Fawkham Green, Longfield DA3 8NL
T: (01474) 872291
F: (01474) 872291

LONGPARISH
Hampshire

Yew Cottage Bed & Breakfast ♦♦♦
Yew Cottage, Longparish, Andover SP11 6QE
T: (01264) 720325
E: yewcottage@ukgateway.net

LOOSE
Kent

Vale House ♦♦♦♦
Old Loose Hill, Loose, Maidstone ME15 0BH
T: (01622) 743339
F: (01622) 743103
E: vansegethin@hotmail.com

LOUDWATER
Buckinghamshire

Trevona ♦♦♦
7 Derehams Lane, Loudwater, High Wycombe HP10 9RH
T: (01494) 526715
E: ssmith4739@aol.com

LOWER ASSENDON
Oxfordshire

Orchard Dene Cottage ♦♦♦♦
Lower Assendon, Henley-on-Thames RG9 6AG
T: (01491) 575490
F: (01491) 575490
E: orcharddene@freeuk.com
I: www.orcharddene.freeuk.com

LOWER BEEDING
West Sussex

The Village Pantry ♦♦♦♦
Handcross Road, Plummers Plain, Lower Beeding, Horsham RH13 6NU
T: (01403) 891319
F: (01403) 891319
E: bill@rh136nu.sfnet.co.uk

LYMINGTON
Hampshire

Britannia House
♦♦♦♦♦ GOLD AWARD
Mill Lane, Lymington SO41 9AY
T: (01590) 672091
E: enquiries@britannia-house.com
I: www.britannia-house.com

Dolphins ♦♦♦
6 Emsworth Road, Lymington SO41 9BL
T: (01590) 676108
F: (01590) 676108
E: dolphins@easynet.co.uk
I: www.dolphinsnewforestbandb.co.uk

Durlston House ♦♦♦
Gosport Street, Lymington SO41 9EG
T: (01590) 677364
F: (01590) 689077
E: durlstonhouse@aol.com

Efford Cottage
♦♦♦♦♦ GOLD AWARD
Everton, Lymington SO41 0JD
T: (01590) 642315
F: (01590) 641030
E: effcottage@aol.com
I: www.effordcottage.co.uk

Gleneagles ♦♦♦♦
34 Belmore Road, Lymington SO41 3NT
T: (01590) 675958
F: (01590) 675958
E: gleneagles34@hotmail.com

Gorse Meadow Guest House ♦♦♦
Gorse Meadow, Sway Road, Lymington SO41 8LR
T: (01590) 673354
F: (01590) 673336
E: mrs.tee@newforestguesthouse.com
I: www.newforestguesthouse.com

The Hillsman House
♦♦♦♦♦ SILVER AWARD
74 Milford Road, Lymington SO41 8DP
T: (01590) 674737
E: caroline@hillsman-house.co.uk
I: www.newforest.demon.co.uk/hillsman.htm

Monks Pool ♦♦♦♦
Waterford Lane, Lymington SO41 3PS
T: (01590) 678850
F: (01590) 678850
E: camandjohn@onetel.net.uk
I: www.camandjohn.com

Moonraker Cottage ♦♦♦♦
62 Milford Road, Lymington SO41 8DU
T: (01590) 678677
F: (01590) 678677
E: moonraker@waitrose.com

Pennavon House
♦♦♦♦ SILVER AWARD
Lower Pennington Lane, Lymington SO41 8AL
T: (01590) 673984

The Pink House
Rating Applied For
8 Keyhaven Road, Milford on Sea, Milford-on-Sea, Lymington SO41 0QY
T: (01590) 641358

Tranmere House
♦♦♦♦ GOLD AWARD
Tranmere Close, Lymington
SO41 3QQ
T: (01590) 671983
E: tranmere.house@tesco.net
I: www.tranmere_house.com

LYMINSTER
West Sussex

Sandfield House ♦♦♦♦
Lyminster Road, Wick, Littlehampton BN17 7PG
T: (01903) 724129
F: (01903) 715041
E: thefbs@aol.com

LYNDHURST
Hampshire

Burwood Lodge
♦♦♦♦ SILVER AWARD
27 Romsey Road, Lyndhurst
SO43 7AA
T: (023) 8028 2445
F: (023) 8028 4104
E: burwood.1@ukonline.co.uk
I: www.burwoodlodge.co.uk

Clayhill House
Rating Applied For
Clay Hill, SO43 7DE
T: (023) 8028 2304
F: (023) 8028 2093
E: clayhillhouse@tinyworld.co.uk
I: www.newforest.demon.co.uk/clayhill.htm

Englefield ♦♦♦♦
Chapel Lane, Lyndhurst
SO43 7FG
T: (023) 8028 2685

Forest Cottage
♦♦♦♦ SILVER AWARD
High Street, Lyndhurst
SO43 7BH
T: (023) 8028 3461
I: www.forestcottage.co.uk

Hurst End ♦♦♦
Clayhill, Lyndhurst SO43 7DE
T: (023) 8028 2606
F: (023) 8028 2606

Little Hayes ♦♦♦♦
43 Romsey Road, Lyndhurst
SO43 7AR
T: (023) 8028 3816
E: info@little-hayes.co.uk
I: www.little-hayes.co.uk

Lyndhurst House
♦♦♦♦ SILVER AWARD
35 Romsey Road, Lyndhurst
SO43 7AR
T: (023) 8028 2230
F: (023) 8028 3190
E: lyndhursthouse@aol.com
I: www.lyndhursthousebandb.co.uk

Pen Cottage ♦♦♦
Bournemouth Road, Lyndhurst
SO43 7DP
T: (023) 8028 2075

The Penny Farthing Hotel
♦♦♦♦
Romsey Road, Lyndhurst
SO43 7AA
T: (023) 8028 4422
F: (023) 8028 4488
E: stay@pennyfarthinghotel.co.uk
I: www.pennyfarthinghotel.co.uk

Reepham House ♦♦♦
12 Romsey Road, Lyndhurst
SO43 7AA
T: (023) 8028 3091
F: (023) 8028 3091

Rose Cottage ♦♦♦♦
Chapel Lane, Lyndhurst
SO43 7FG
T: (023) 8028 3413
F: (023) 8028 3413
E: cindy@rosecottageb-b.freeserve.co.uk
I: www.rosecottageb-b.freeserve.co.uk/

Rosedale Bed & Breakfast
♦♦♦
24 Shaggs Meadow, Lyndhurst
SO43 7BN
T: (023) 8028 3793
E: jenny@theangels.freeserve.co.uk

Rufus House Hotel
♦♦♦♦ SILVER AWARD
Southampton Road, Lyndhurst
SO43 7BQ
T: (023) 8028 2930
F: (023) 8028 2930
E: rufushousehotel@btopenworld.com
I: www.rufushousehotel.co.uk

Temple Lodge Guest House
♦♦♦♦
Queens Road, Lyndhurst
SO43 7BR
T: (023) 8028 2392
F: (023) 8028 4590
E: templelodge@lineone.net

MAIDENHEAD
Berkshire

Braywick Grange ♦♦♦♦
100 Braywick Road, Maidenhead
SL6 1DJ
T: (01628) 625915
F: (01628) 626222

Cartlands Cottage ♦♦
Kings Lane, Cookham Dean, Cookham, Maidenhead SL6 9AY
T: (01628) 482196

Clifton Guest House ♦♦♦
21 Crauford Rise, Maidenhead
SL6 7LR
T: (01628) 620086
F: (01628) 623572
E: clifton@aroram.freeserve.co.uk
I: www.cliftonguesthouse.co.uk

Gables End ♦♦
4 Gables Close, Maidenhead
SL6 8QD
T: (01628) 639630

Moor Farm
♦♦♦♦ SILVER AWARD
Ascot Road, Holyport, Maidenhead SL6 2HY
T: (01628) 633761
F: (01628) 636167
E: moorfm@aol.com
I: www.windsor.gov.uk/moorfarm

Ray Corner Guest House ♦♦♦
141 Bridge Road, Maidenhead
SL6 8NQ
T: (01628) 632784
F: (01628) 789029
E: info@raycorner.fsnet.co.uk
I: www.raycorner.fsnet.co.uk

Red Roofs at Oldfield ♦♦♦♦
Guards Club Road, Maidenhead
SL6 8DN
T: (01628) 621910
F: (01628) 638815

Sheephouse Manor ♦♦♦
Sheephouse Road, Maidenhead
SL6 8HJ
T: (01628) 776902
F: (01628) 625138
E: info@sheephousemanor.co.uk
I: www.sheephousemanor.co.uk

MAIDSTONE
Kent

51 Bower Mount Road ♦♦♦
Maidstone ME16 8AX
T: (01622) 762948
F: (01622) 202753
E: sylviabnb@compuserve.com

Conway House ♦♦♦♦
12 Conway Road, Maidstone
ME16 0HD
T: (01622) 688287
F: (01622) 662589
E: conwayhouse@ukgateway.net
I: www.conwayhouse.ukgateway.net

Elm Trees ♦♦♦
55 Upper Fant Road, Maidstone
ME16 8BU
T: (01622) 693620

Grove House Bed & Breakfast
♦♦♦♦
Grove Green Road, Weavering Street, Maidstone ME14 5JT
T: (01622) 738441
F: (01622) 735927
E: gelco@supanet.com

The Hazels ♦♦♦♦
13 Yeoman Way, Bearsted, Maidstone ME15 8PQ
T: (01622) 737943
E: ianbuse@hotmail.com
I: www.redrival.com/thehazels

The Howard Hotel ♦♦♦
22 - 24 London Road, Maidstone
ME16 8QL
T: (01622) 758778
F: (01622) 609984
E: howardhotel@btopenworld.com
I: www.thehowardhotel.net

King Street Hotel ♦♦♦♦
74 King Street, Maidstone
ME14 1BH
T: (01622) 663266
F: (01622) 663123
E: reservations@kingstreethotelmaidstone.co.uk
I: www.kingstreethotelmaidstone.co.uk

The Limes ♦♦♦♦
118 Boxley Road, Maidstone
ME14 2BD
T: (01622) 750629
F: (01622) 691266

39 Marston Drive ♦♦♦
Vinters Park, Maidstone
ME14 5NE
T: (01622) 202196
E: steveandlesley@steleybrown.freeserve.co.uk

54 Mote Avenue ♦♦
Maidstone ME15 7ST
T: (01622) 754016

Raigersfeld House ♦♦
Mote Park, Ashford Road, Maidstone ME14 4AE
T: (01622) 685211
F: (01622) 691013
E: chipdbs@aol.com

The Ringlestone Inn & Farmhouse Hotel
♦♦♦♦♦ GOLD AWARD
Ringlestone Hamlet, Harrietsham, Maidstone
ME17 1NX
T: (01622) 859900
F: (01622) 859966
E: bookings@ringlestone.com
I: www.ringlestone.com

Rock House Hotel ♦♦♦
102 Tonbridge Road, Maidstone
ME16 8SL
T: (01622) 751616
F: (01622) 756119

Rose Cottage ♦♦♦
10 Fant Lane, Maidstone
ME16 8NL
T: (01622) 729883

Roslin Villa ♦♦♦
St Michaels Road, Maidstone
ME16 8BS
T: (01622) 758301
F: (01622) 761459

West Belringham ♦♦♦
Chart Road, Sutton Valence, Maidstone ME17 3AW
T: (01622) 843995
I: www.travelengland.org.uk

4 White Rock Court ♦♦♦
White Rock Place, Maidstone
ME16 8HX
T: (01622) 753566
F: (01622) 753566
E: catnap.farnham@amserve.net

Wits End Guest House ♦♦♦♦
78 Bower Mount Road, Maidstone ME16 8AT
T: (01622) 752684
F: (01622) 752684
E: mail@thewitsend.co.uk
I: www.thewitsend.co.uk

MARDEN
Kent

Martin's Farmhouse
♦♦♦♦ SILVER AWARD
Collier Street, Marden, Tonbridge
TN12 9SB
T: (01892) 730220
F: (01892) 730220
E: martins.farmhouse@virgin.net

Tanner House ♦♦♦♦
Tanner Farm, Goudhurst Road, Marden, Tonbridge TN12 9ND
T: (01622) 831214
F: (01622) 832472
E: enquiries@tannerfarmpark.co.uk
I: www.tannerfarmpark.co.uk

MARGATE
Kent

Burlington Hotel ♦♦
8 Buenos Ayres, Margate
CT9 5AE
T: (01843) 292817

The Dane Valley Inn
Rating Applied For
Dane Valley Road, CT9 3RZ
T: (01843) 227458

Innsbrook Hotel ◆◆◆
Dalby Square, Cliftonville, Margate CT9 2ER
T: (01843) 298946
E: info@innsbrookhotel.co.uk
I: www.innsbrookhotel.co.uk

Vienna Guest House ◆◆◆
28 Canterbury Road, Margate CT9 5BN
T: (01843) 224522

MARK CROSS
East Sussex

Houndsell Cottage ◆◆◆
Mark Cross, Crowborough TN6 3PF
T: (01892) 782292

Rose Cottage ◆◆◆◆
Mill Lane, Mark Cross, Crowborough TN6 3PJ
T: (01892) 852592
F: (01892) 853268

MARLOW
Buckinghamshire

Acha Pani ◆◆◆
Bovingdon Green, Marlow SL7 2JL
T: (01628) 483435
F: (01628) 483435
E: mary@achapani.freeserve.co.uk

Acorn Lodge ◆◆◆
79 Marlow Bottom Road, Marlow Bottom, Marlow SL7 3NA
T: (01628) 472197
F: (01628) 472197
E: acornlodge@btconnect.com
I: www.acornlodgemarlow.co.uk

32 Barnhill Road ◆◆◆◆
Marlow SL7 3EY
T: (01628) 484770
E: alisonsm32@postmanpat.org.uk

The Boundary ◆◆◆◆
Seymour Plain, Marlow SL7 3DA
T: (01628) 476674

The Country House ◆◆◆◆
Bisham, Marlow SL7 1RP
T: (01628) 890606
F: (01628) 890983
I: www.countryhousemarlow.com

Glade End ◆◆◆◆◆
2 Little Marlow Road, Marlow SL7 1HD
T: (01628) 471334
E: sue@gladeend.com
I: www.gladeend.com

Granny Anne's ◆◆◆
54 Seymour Park Road, Marlow SL7 3EP
T: (01628) 473086
F: (01628) 472721
E: retaylor@nildram.co.uk

Hazeldene ◆◆◆
53 Stapleton Close, Marlow SL7 1TZ
T: (01628) 482183

Holly Tree House ◆◆◆◆
Burford Close, Marlow Bottom, Marlow SL7 3NE
T: (01628) 891110
F: (01628) 481278
E: hollytreeaccommodation@yahoo.co.uk

The Inn on the Green ◆◆◆◆
The Old Cricket Common, Cookham Dean, Cookham, Maidenhead SL6 9NZ
T: (01628) 482638
F: (01628) 487474
E: enquiries@theinnonthegreen.com
I: www.theinnonthegreen.com

31 Institute Road ◆◆◆
Marlow SL7 1BJ
T: (01628) 485662

10 Lock Road ◆◆◆
Marlow SL7 1QP
T: (01628) 473875

Merrie Hollow ◆◆◆
Seymour Court Hill, Marlow Road, Marlow SL7 3DE
T: (01628) 485663
F: (01628) 485663

Nia Roo ◆◆◆◆
4 Pound Crescent, Marlow SL7 2BG
T: (01628) 486679
F: (01628) 486679

Oak Lodge ◆◆◆
29 Oaktree Road, Marlow SL7 3ED
T: (01628) 472145

Old Barn Cottage ◆◆◆◆
Church Road, Little Marlow, Marlow SL7 3RZ
T: (01628) 483817
F: (01628) 477197
E: qs.falk@btinternet.com

Old Kiln House ◆◆◆
Marlow Common, Marlow SL7 2QP
T: (01628) 475615
F: (01628) 475615

The Prince of Wales ◆◆◆
1 Mill Road, Marlow SL7 1PX
T: (01628) 482970
F: (01628) 482970

Red Barn Farm ◆◆◆
Marlow Road, Marlow SL7 3DQ
T: (01494) 882820
F: (01494) 883545

Riverdale ◆◆◆
Marlow Bridge Lane, Marlow SL7 1RH
T: (01628) 485206
E: chrisrawlings@onetel.net.uk

18 Rookery Court
◆◆◆◆ SILVER AWARD
Marlow SL7 3HR
T: (01628) 486451
F: (01628) 486451
E: gillbullen@rookerycourt.fsnet.co.uk

Rosemary Cottage Bed & Breakfast ◆◆◆◆
99 Heath End Road, Flackwell Heath, High Wycombe HP10 9ES
T: (01628) 520635
F: (01628) 520635
E: mike.1@virgin.net
I: www.reservation.co.uk/rosemarycottagebedandbreakfast.co.uk

MARLOW BOTTOM
Buckinghamshire

61 Hill Farm Road ◆◆◆
Hill Farm Road, Marlow Bottom, Marlow SL7 3LX
T: (01628) 475145
F: (01628) 475775
E: paul.simmons8@btinternet.com

63 Hill Farm Road ◆◆
Marlow Bottom, Marlow SL7 3LX
T: (01628) 472970

T J O'Reillys ◆◆◆
61 Marlow Bottom Road, Marlow Bottom, Marlow SL7 3NA
T: (01628) 891187
F: (01628) 484926

MARNHULL
Dorset

Moorcourt Farm ◆◆
Moorside, Marnhull, Sturminster Newton DT10 1HH
T: (01258) 820271
F: (01258) 820271

The Old Bank ◆◆◆
Burton Street, Marnhull, Sturminster Newton DT10 1PH
T: (01258) 821019
F: (01258) 821019

Yew House Farm
◆◆◆◆ SILVER AWARD
Husseys, Marnhull, Sturminster Newton DT10 1PD
T: (01258) 820412
E: yewfarmhouse@aol.com

MARSH GIBBON
Buckinghamshire

Judges Close ◆◆◆
West Edge, Marsh Gibbon, Bicester OX27 0HA
T: (01869) 278508
F: (01869) 277189
E: jennylambourne@farmersweekly.net
I: www.smoothhound.co.uk/hotels/judgesclose.html

MARSHBOROUGH
Kent

Honey Pot Cottage ◆◆◆◆
Marshborough Road, Marshborough, Sandwich CT13 0PQ
T: (01304) 813374
E: honeypotcottage@lycos.com
I: www.honeypotcottage.co.uk

MEDSTEAD
Hampshire

Woodfield Bed & Breakfast ◆◆◆◆
Windsor Road, Medstead, Alton GU34 5EF
T: (01420) 563308
F: (01420) 561495
E: tonydrake@compuserve.com
I: www.vinntec.co.uk/woodfield

MELCOMBE BINGHAM
Dorset

Badgers Sett ◆◆◆◆
Cross Lanes, Melcombe Bingham, Dorchester DT2 7NY
T: (01258) 880006
F: (01258) 880697
E: seasteeluk@btinternet.com
I: www.seasteeluk.com/badgers_sett

MENTMORE
Buckinghamshire

The Orchard ◆◆◆
Mentmore, Leighton Buzzard LU7 0QF
T: (01296) 668976
F: (01296) 662189
E: jan.hc@virgin.net

MEOPHAM
Kent

Lamplights ◆◆◆
Wrotham Road, Meopham, Gravesend DA13 0QW
T: (01474) 813869
F: (0208) 306 1189

Nurstead Court ◆◆
Nurstead Church Lane, Meopham, Gravesend DA13 9AD
T: (01474) 812121
F: (01474) 815133
E: info@nursteadcourt.co.uk
I: www.nursteadcourt.co.uk

MERSTONE
Isle of Wight

Redway Farm ◆◆◆◆
Budbridge Lane, Merstone, Newport PO30 3DJ
T: (01983) 865228
F: (01983) 865228
E: redway@wightfarmholidays.co.uk
I: www.redway-farm.co.uk

MICKLEHAM
Surrey

Old House Cottage ◆◆◆
London Road, Mickleham, Dorking RH5 6EH
T: (01372) 375050

MIDDLE ASTON
Oxfordshire

Home Farm House ◆◆◆
Middle Aston, Oxford OX25 5PX
T: (01869) 340666
F: (01869) 347789
E: carolineparsons@tiscali.co.uk
I: www.country-accom.co.uk/home-farm-house

MIDDLE WALLOP
Hampshire

The George Inn – Middle Wallop ◆◆◆◆ SILVER AWARD
The Crossroads, Middle Wallop, Stockbridge SO20 8EG
T: (01264) 781224
F: (01264) 782830

MIDDLETON-ON-SEA
West Sussex

Seaway ◆◆◆◆
33 Seaway, Middleton-on-Sea, Bognor Regis PO22 7RZ
T: (01243) 586626
F: (01243) 586626
E: micheleborg@intelynx.net

MIDHURST
West Sussex

10 Ashfield Close ◆◆◆◆
Midhurst GU29 9RP
T: (01730) 814858
E: jennifer_morley@lineone.net

Carron Dune ◆◆◆
Carron Lane, Midhurst GU29 9LD
T: (01730) 813558

20 Guillards Oak ◆◆◆◆
Midhurst GU29 9JZ
T: (01730) 812550
F: (01730) 816765
E: coljen@tinyworld.co.uk

Pear Tree Cottage ♦♦♦
Lamberts Lane, Midhurst
GU29 9EF
T: (01730) 817216

18 Pretoria Avenue ♦♦♦
Midhurst GU29 9PP
T: (01730) 814868
F: (01730) 814868
E: eric@estratford.freeserve.co.uk

Severals House ♦♦♦♦
Bepton, Midhurst GU29 0LX
T: (01730) 812771

Ye Olde Tea Shoppe ♦♦♦
North Street, Midhurst
GU29 9DY
T: (01730) 817081
F: (01730) 810228

MILBORNE ST ANDREW
Dorset

3 The Rings ♦♦♦
Milborne St Andrew, Blandford Forum DT11 0HY
T: (01258) 837639
F: (01258) 837639

MILFORD
Surrey

Holly Tree Cottage ♦♦♦
Mousehill Lane, Milford, Godalming GU8 5BH
T: (01483) 426578
F: (01483) 420677
E: rlidbury@btinternet.com

MILFORD-ON-SEA
Hampshire

Alma Mater ♦♦♦♦
4 Knowland Drive, Milford-on-Sea, Lymington SO41 0RH
T: (01590) 642811
F: (01590) 642811
E: bandbalmamater@aol.com
I: www.almamater.org.uk

Briantcroft
♦♦♦♦♦ GOLD AWARD
George Road, Milford-on-Sea, Lymington SO41 0RS
T: (01590) 644355
F: (01590) 644185
E: florence.iles@lineone.net
I: www.briantcroft.co.uk

Compton Hotel ♦♦♦
59 Keyhaven Road, Milford on Sea, Milford-on-Sea, Lymington SO41 0QX
T: (01590) 643117
F: (01590) 643117
E: dbembo@talk21.com

Ha'penny House
♦♦♦♦♦ SILVER AWARD
16 Whitby Road, Milford-on-Sea, Lymington SO41 0ND
T: (01590) 641210
F: (01590) 641227
E: info@hapennyhouse.co.uk
I: www.hapennyhouse.co.uk

Laburnum Cottage ♦♦♦
19 Carrington Lane, Milford on Sea, Lymington SO41 0RA
T: (01590) 644225
I: www.simplybedandbreakfast.co.uk/laburnum/index.htm

MILSTEAD
Kent

The Cottage ♦♦♦♦
Frinsted Road, Milstead, Sittingbourne ME9 0SA
T: (01795) 830367

MILTON ABBAS
Dorset

Dunbury Heights ♦♦♦♦
Milton Abbas, Blandford Forum DT11 0DH
T: (01258) 880445

MILTON COMMON
Oxfordshire

Byways ♦♦♦♦
Old London Road, Milton Common, Oxford OX9 2JR
T: (01844) 279386
F: (01844) 279386
I: www.byways-oxfordshire.co.uk

MILTON KEYNES
Buckinghamshire

A City Central B & B ♦♦♦♦
37 Mitcham Place, Bradwell Common, Milton Keynes MK13 8BX
T: (01908) 663750
E: smaxfield@aol.com
I: www.mkweb.co.uk

Chantry Farm ♦♦♦
Pindon End, Hanslope, Milton Keynes MK19 7HL
T: (01908) 510269
F: (01908) 510269
E: chuff.wake@tiscali.co.uk

Conifers Bed & Breakfast ♦♦
29 William Smith Close, Woolstone, Milton Keynes MK15 0AN
T: (01908) 674506
F: (01908) 550628
E: george.shaw4@virgin.net

Fairview Cottage Rating Applied For
1 Newport Road, Woughton on the Green, Milton Keynes MK6 3BS
T: (01908) 679999
F: (01908) 679999

Furtho Manor Farm ♦♦♦
Northampton Road, Old Stratford, Milton Keynes MK19 6NR
T: (01908) 542139
F: (01908) 542139
E: dsansome@farming.co.uk
I: www.members.farmline.com/furtho

Kingfishers ♦♦♦
9 Rylstone Close, Heelands, Milton Keynes MK13 7QT
T: (01908) 310231
F: (01908) 318601
E: kanjass@yahoo.com
I: www.kingfishersmk.co.uk

Milford Leys Farm ♦♦♦
Castlethorpe, Milton Keynes MK19 7HH
T: (01908) 510153

Mill Farm ♦♦♦
Gayhurst, Newport Pagnell MK16 8LT
T: (01908) 611489
F: (01908) 611489
E: adamsmillfarm@aol.com

New Cottage ♦♦♦
London Road, Broughton Village, Milton Keynes MK10 9AA
T: (01908) 665461

Spinney Lodge Farm ♦♦♦
Forest Road, Hanslope, Milton Keynes MK19 7DE
T: (01908) 510267

Vignoble ♦♦♦
2 Medland, Woughton Park, Milton Keynes MK6 3BH
T: (01908) 666804
F: (01908) 666626
E: vignoblegh@aol.com

The White Hart ♦♦♦♦
1 Gun Lane, Sherington, Newport Pagnell MK16 9PE
T: (01908) 611953
F: (01908) 618109
E: whitehartresort@aol.com
I: www.whitehartsherington.com

MINSTEAD
Hampshire

Grove House ♦♦
Newtown, Minstead, Lyndhurst SO43 7GG
T: (023) 8081 3211

MINSTER-IN-SHEPPEY
Kent

Glen Haven ♦♦♦
Lower Road, Minster on Sea, Sheerness ME12 3ST
T: (01795) 877064
F: (01795) 871746
E: johnstanford@btinternet.com

Mia Crieff ♦♦♦♦
Mill Hill, Chequers Road, Minster-in-Sheppey, Sheerness ME12 3QL
T: (01795) 870620

MINSTER LOVELL
Oxfordshire

Hill Grove Farm ♦♦♦♦
Crawley Dry Lane, Minster Lovell, Oxford OX29 0NA
T: (01993) 703120
F: (01993) 700528
E: kbrown@eggconnect.net
I: www.country-accom.co.uk/hill-grove-farm/

MONKS RISBOROUGH
Buckinghamshire

26 Little Ham Lane ♦
Monks Risborough, Aylesbury HP27 9JW
T: (01844) 345410

MORETON
Oxfordshire

Elm Tree Farmhouse ♦♦♦♦
Moreton, Thame OX9 2HR
T: (01844) 213692
F: (01844) 215369
E: wvb@ntlworld.com
I: www.elmtreefarmhouse.co.uk

MORTIMER WEST END
Hampshire

Lovegrove Farm ♦♦♦
Farm Lane, Mortimer West End, Reading RG7 2HS
T: (0118) 970 1144
F: (0118) 970 1144

MOTCOMBE
Dorset

The Coppleridge Inn ♦♦♦♦
Elm Hill, Motcombe, Shaftesbury SP7 9HW
T: (01747) 851980
F: (01747) 851858
E: thecoppleridgeinn@btinternet.com
I: www.coppleridge.com

MOULSFORD ON THAMES
Oxfordshire

White House
♦♦♦♦ SILVER AWARD
Moulsford on Thames, Wallingford OX10 9JD
T: (01491) 651397
F: (01491) 652560
E: mwatsham@hotmail.com

MOULSOE
Buckinghamshire

The Old Stables ♦♦♦♦
Hermitage Farm, Moulsoe, Newport Pagnell MK16 0HR
T: (01908) 217766
F: (01908) 614224
E: oldstbles@aol.com

MUDEFORD
Dorset

Seahaze
♦♦♦♦ SILVER AWARD
4 Rook Hill Road, Friars Cliff, Mudeford, Christchurch BH23 4DZ
T: (01425) 270866
F: (01425) 278285
E: seahaze@eggconnect.net

MURSLEY
Buckinghamshire

Fourpenny Cottage ♦♦♦♦
23 Main Street, Mursley, Milton Keynes MK17 0RT
T: (01296) 720544
F: (01296) 720906
E: fourpennycottage@tinyworld.co.uk
I: www.fourpennycottage.co.uk

The Old Forge ♦♦♦
8 Main Street, Mursley, Milton Keynes MK17 0RT
T: (01296) 720374

NAPHILL
Buckinghamshire

Woodpeckers ♦♦♦
244 Main Road, Naphill, High Wycombe HP14 4RX
T: (01494) 563728
E: angela.brand@virgin.net
I: www.woodpeckersbedandbreakfast.co.uk

NETHER WALLOP
Hampshire

Halcyon ♦♦♦
Church Hill, Nether Wallop, Stockbridge SO20 8EY
T: (01264) 781348

York Lodge ♦♦♦♦
Five Bells Lane, Nether Wallop, Stockbridge SO20 8HE
T: (01264) 781313
F: (01264) 781313
E: bradley@yorklodge.fslife.co.uk
I: www.york-lodge.co.uk

NETTLEBED
Oxfordshire

Parkcorner Farm House ♦♦♦
Park Corner, Nettlebed, Henley-on-Thames RG9 6DX
T: (01491) 641450
E: parkcorner_farmhouse@hotmail.com

NETTLESTEAD
Kent

Rock Farm House ♦♦♦♦
Gibbs Hill, Nettlestead, Maidstone ME18 5HT
T: (01622) 812244
F: (01622) 812244
I: www.rockfarmhousebandb.co.uk

NEW MILTON
Hampshire

Fairways ♦♦♦♦
Sway Road, Bashley, New Milton BH25 5QP
T: (01425) 619001
E: ann@lymington-uk.fsworld.co.uk

Jobz-A-Gudn ♦♦♦♦
169 Stem Lane, New Milton BH25 5ND
T: (01425) 615435
F: (01425) 615435
E: jobzagudn@aol.com
I: www.jobzagudn.com

Pebble Beach
Rating Applied For
Marine Drive, Barton on Sea, New Milton BH25 7DZ
T: (01425) 627777
F: (01425) 610689

St Ursula ♦♦♦
30 Hobart Road, New Milton BH25 6EG
T: (01425) 613515

Taverners Cottage ♦♦♦♦
Bashley Cross Road, Bashley, New Milton BH25 5SZ
T: (01425) 615403
F: (01425) 632177
E: jbaines@supanet.com
I: www.taverners.cottage.bandb.baines.com

Willy's Well ♦♦♦
Bashley Common Road, Wootton, New Milton BH25 5SF
T: (01425) 616834
E: moyramac2@hotmail.com

Woodlands
Rating Applied For
Ashley Lane, Ashley, New Milton BH25 5AQ
T: (01425) 616425
F: (01425) 616425
E: bealwoodlands@yahoo.co.uk

NEW ROMNEY
Kent

Martinfield Manor ♦♦♦♦
Lydd Road, New Romney TN28 8HB
T: (01797) 363802

Warren Lodge Motel ♦♦♦
Dymchurch Road, New Romney TN28 8UE
T: (01797) 362138
F: (01797) 367377
E: admin@warrenlodge.co.uk
I: www.warrenlodge.co.uk

NEWBRIDGE
Isle of Wight

Homestead Farmhouse ♦♦♦
Newbridge, Yarmouth PO41 0TZ
T: (01983) 531270
F: (01983) 531270

NEWBURY
Berkshire

19 Kimbers Drive ♦♦
Speen, Newbury RG14 1RQ
T: (01635) 521571

Livingstone House ♦♦♦
48 Queens Road, Newbury RG14 7PA
T: (01635) 45444

Manor Farm House
♦♦♦♦ SILVER AWARD
Church Street, Hampstead Norreys, Thatcham RG18 0TD
T: (01635) 201276
F: (01635) 201035
E: bettsbedandbreakfast@hotmail.com
I: www.bettsbedandbreakfast.co.uk

The Old Farmhouse
♦♦♦♦ SILVER AWARD
Downend Lane, Chieveley, Newbury RG20 8TN
T: (01635) 248361
E: palletts@aol.com
I: www.smoothhound.co.uk/hotels/oldfarmhouse

The Paddock ♦♦♦
Midgham Green, Midgham, Reading RG7 5TT
T: (0118) 971 3098
F: (0118) 971 2925
E: david.cantwell@virgin.net
I: freespace.virgin.net/david.cantwell

Rookwood Farmhouse ♦♦♦♦
Stockcross, Newbury RG20 8JX
T: (01488) 608676
F: (01488) 657961

St Ann's ♦♦
32 Craven Road, Newbury RG14 5NE
T: (01635) 41353

White Cottage ♦♦♦
Newtown, Newbury RG20 9AP
T: (01635) 43097
F: (01635) 43097
E: meiklejohn@onetel.net.uk

The White Hart Inn ♦♦♦♦
Kintbury Road, Hamstead Marshall, Newbury RG20 0HW
T: (01488) 658201
F: (01488) 657192
E: info@thewhitehart-inn.co.uk
I: www.thewhitehart-inn.co.uk

NEWHAVEN
East Sussex

Newhaven Lodge Guest House ♦
12 Brighton Road, Newhaven BN9 9NB
T: (01273) 513736
F: (01273) 734619
E: newhavenlodge@aol.com
I: www.newhavenlodge.com

NEWICK
East Sussex

Firle Cottage ♦♦♦
High Street, Newick, Lewes BN8 4LG
T: (01825) 722392

Holly Lodge ♦♦♦♦
Oxbottom Lane, Newick, Lewes BN8 4RA
T: (01825) 722738
F: (01825) 723624

NEWINGTON
Oxfordshire

Hill Farm ♦♦♦
Newington, Wallingford OX10 7AL
T: (01865) 891173

NEWPORT
Isle of Wight

Castle Lodge ♦♦♦
54 Castle Road, Newport PO30 1DP
T: (01983) 527862
F: (01983) 527862
E: wcastlelodge@aol.com

Litten Park Guest House ♦♦♦
48 Medina Avenue, Newport PO30 1EL
T: (01983) 526836

Newport Quay Hotel ♦♦♦
14 Quay Street, Newport PO30 5BA
T: (01983) 528544
F: (01983) 527143

Wheatsheaf Hotel ♦♦♦
St Thomas Square, Newport PO30 1SG
T: (01983) 523865
F: (01983) 528255
E: information@wheatsheaf-iow.co.uk
I: www.wheatsheaf-iow.co.uk

NEWPORT PAGNELL
Buckinghamshire

The Clitheroes ♦♦
5 Walnut Close, Newport Pagnell MK16 8JH
T: (01908) 611643
F: (01908) 611643
E: shirleyderek.clitheroe@btinternet.com

The Limes
♦♦♦♦♦ SILVER AWARD
North Square, Newport Pagnell MK16 8EP
T: (01908) 617041
F: (01908) 217292
E: royandruth@8thelimes.freeserve.co.uk

Rectory Farm ♦♦♦
Brook End, North Crawley, Newport Pagnell MK16 9HH
T: (01234) 391213
F: (01234) 391213

Rosemary House ♦♦♦
7 Hill View, Wolverton Road, Newport Pagnell MK16 8BE
T: (01908) 612198
F: (01908) 612198

NINFIELD
East Sussex

Hollybank House ♦♦♦
Lower Street, Ninfield, Battle TN33 9EA
T: (01424) 892052
F: (01424) 892052

London House ♦♦♦♦
Manchester Road, Ninfield, Battle TN33 9JX
T: (01424) 893532
F: (01424) 893595

NORTH BERSTED
West Sussex

Lorna Doone Bed & Breakfast ♦♦♦♦
58 Sandymount Avenue, North Bersted, Bognor Regis PO22 9EP
T: (01243) 822203
F: (01243) 822203
E: joan@lornadoone.freeserve.co.uk
I: www.lornadoone.freeserve.co.uk

Willow Rise ♦♦♦
131 North Bersted Street, North Bersted, Bognor Regis PO22 9AG
T: (01243) 829544
F: (01243) 829544

NORTH LEIGH
Oxfordshire

Elbie House
♦♦♦♦ SILVER AWARD
East End, North Leigh, Witney OX29 6PX
T: (01993) 880166
E: mandy@cotswoldbreak.co.uk
I: www.cotswoldbreak.co.uk

Forge Cottage ♦♦
East End, North Leigh, Woodstock, Oxford OX29 6PZ
T: (01993) 881120
E: jill.french@talk21.com
I: www.country-accom.co.uk/forge-cottage/

The Leather Bottel Guest House ♦♦♦
East End, North Leigh, Witney OX29 6PX
T: (01993) 882174
F: (01993) 882174

NORTH MORETON
Oxfordshire

Stapleton's Chantry
♦♦♦♦ SILVER AWARD
Long Wittenham Road, North Moreton, Didcot OX11 9AX
T: (01235) 818900
F: (01235) 818555
E: stapletonchantry@aol.com

NORTH MUNDHAM
West Sussex

The Cottage
♦♦♦♦ SILVER AWARD
Church Road, North Mundham, Chichester PO20 1JU
T: (01243) 784586
E: lambrinudi-bandb@supanet.com

NORTH NEWINGTON
Oxfordshire

The Blinking Owl Country Inn ♦♦♦
Main Street, North Newington, Banbury OX15 6AE
T: (01295) 730650

NORTHFLEET
Kent

The Nook ♦♦♦
3 Falcon Mews, Vale Road, Northfleet, Gravesend DA11 8BW
T: (01474) 350748
F: (01474) 350748

NORTHMOOR
Oxfordshire

The Ferryman Inn ♦♦♦
Bablock Hythe, Northmoor, Oxford OX8 1BL
T: (01865) 880028
F: (01865) 881033

NUTLEY
East Sussex

The Court House ♦♦♦♦
School Lane, Nutley, Uckfield TN22 3PG
T: (01825) 713129
F: (01825) 712650
E: execrelocation@compuserve.com

West Meadows ♦♦♦♦
Bell Lane, Nutley, Uckfield
TN22 3PD
T: (01825) 712434
F: (01825) 712434
E: west.meadows@virgin.net
I: www.westmeadows.co.uk

OAKDALE
Dorset

Heathwood Guest House ♦♦♦♦
266 Wimborne Road, Oakdale, Poole BH15 3EF
T: (01202) 679176
F: (01202) 679176
I: www.heathwoodhotel.co.uk

OAKLEY
Buckinghamshire

New Farm ♦♦♦
Oxford Road, Oakley, Aylesbury
HP18 9UR
T: (01844) 237360

OAKLEY GREEN
Berkshire

Rainworth Guest House
Rating Applied For
Oakley Green Road, Oakley Green, Windsor SL4 5UL
T: (01753) 856749
F: (01753) 859192

OARE
Kent

Mount House ♦♦♦
Mount Pleasant, Oare, Faversham ME13 0PZ
T: (01795) 534735

OCKLEY
Surrey

The Kings Arms Inn ♦♦♦♦
Stane Street, Ockley, Dorking
RH5 5TS
T: (01306) 711224
F: (01306) 711224

OLD ALRESFORD
Hampshire

The Rosery
♦♦♦♦ SILVER AWARD
Basingstoke Road, Old Alresford, Alresford SO24 9DL
T: (01962) 732207
F: (01962) 732207
E: therosery@bigfoot.com
I: www.therosery.co.uk

OLD WINDSOR
Berkshire

Union Inn ♦♦♦
17 Crimp Hill Road, Old Windsor, Windsor SL4 2QY
T: (01753) 861955
F: (01753) 831378
I: unioninn.windsor@btclick.com

OLNEY
Buckinghamshire

Colchester House ♦♦♦♦
26 High Street, Olney MK46 4BB
T: (01234) 712602
F: (01234) 240564
I: www.olneybucks.co.uk

The Lindens ♦♦♦♦
30A High Street, Olney
MK46 4BB
T: (01234) 712891
E: thelindens@amserve.net
I: www.thelindens.com

Tile Barn ♦♦♦♦
11 Spring Lane, Olney MK46 5HT
T: (01234) 713723
E: trevorcooper820@msn.com

OTFORD
Kent

Darenth Dene ♦♦♦♦
Shoreham Road, Otford, Sevenoaks TN14 5RP
T: (01959) 522293

The Garden Room ♦♦♦
3 Darnets Field, Otford, Sevenoaks TN14 5LB
T: (01959) 522521
E: gardenroom@otford.org
I: www.otford.org/gardenroom

9 Warham Road ♦♦
Otford, Sevenoaks TN14 5PF
T: (01959) 523596

OUTWOOD
Surrey

The Coach House
♦♦♦♦ SILVER AWARD
Millers Lane, Outwood, Redhill
RH1 5PZ
T: (01342) 843193
F: (01342) 842544
E: coachselgw@aol.com

OVER NORTON
Oxfordshire

Cleeves Farm ♦♦♦
Over Norton, Chipping Norton
OX7 5PH
T: (01608) 645019
F: (01608) 645021
E: tillylamb@hotmail.com

Woodhaven Cottage ♦♦♦
The Green, Over Norton, Chipping Norton OX7 5PT
T: (01608) 646265

OVING
Buckinghamshire

The Cottage Bed & Breakfast ♦♦♦
The Cottage, Pitchcott Road, Oving, Aylesbury HP22 4HR
T: (01296) 641891
F: (01296) 424022
E: thegeorges@btinternet.com

OWLSMOOR
Berkshire

De-Rosen
Rating Applied For
43 Cambridge Road, Owlsmoor, Sandhurst GU47 0TA
T: (01344) 776400
F: (01344) 776400

OXFORD
Oxfordshire

Acorn Guest House ♦♦♦
260-262 Iffley Road, Oxford
OX4 1SE
T: (01865) 247998
F: (01865) 247998
E: acorn_gh_oxford@freezone.co.uk

Adams Guest House ♦♦
302 Banbury Road, Oxford
OX2 7ED
T: (01865) 556118
F: (01865) 514066

Arden Lodge ♦♦♦
34 Sunderland Avenue, off Banbury Road, Oxford OX2 8DX
T: (01865) 552076

Beaumont Guest House ♦♦♦
234 Abingdon Road, Oxford
OX1 4SP
T: (01865) 241767
F: (01865) 241767
E: info@beaumont.sagehost.co.uk
I: www.oxfordcity.co.uk/accom/beaumont

Becket House ♦
5 Becket Street, Oxford OX1 7PP
T: (01865) 724675
F: (01865) 724675

Brenal Guest House ♦♦♦
307 Iffley Road, Oxford OX4 4AG
T: (01865) 721561
F: (01865) 435814
E: brenalguesthouse@yahoo.co.uk

Brown's Guest House ♦♦♦♦
281 Iffley Road, Oxford OX4 4AQ
T: (01865) 246822
F: (01865) 246822
E: brownsgh@hotmail.com

The Bungalow ♦♦♦
Mill Lane, Old Marston, Oxford
OX3 0QF
T: (01865) 557171

Casa Villa Guest House ♦♦
388 Banbury Road, Oxford
OX2 7PW
T: (01865) 512642
F: (01865) 512642
E: stoya@casavilla.fsnet.co.uk
I: www.casavilla.fsnet.co.uk

Chestnuts ♦♦♦
72 Cumnor Hill, Oxford OX2 9HU
T: (01865) 863602

Chestnuts Guest House
♦♦♦♦♦ SILVER AWARD
45 Davenant Road, Off Woodstock Road, Oxford
OX2 8BU
T: (01865) 553375
F: (01865) 553375
E: stay@chestnutsguesthouse.co.uk

The Coach & Horses Inn ♦♦♦
Watlington Road, Chiselhampton, Oxford
OX44 7UX
T: (01865) 890255
F: (01865) 891995
E: david-mcphillips@lineone.net
I: www.coachhorsesinn.co.uk

College Guest House ♦♦♦
103-105 Woodstock Road, Oxford OX2 6HL
T: (01865) 552579
F: (01865) 311244
E: r.pal@ukonline.co.uk

Conifer Lodge ♦♦♦
159 Eynsham Road, Botley, Oxford OX2 9NE
T: (01865) 862280
F: (01865) 865135

Cornerways Guest House ♦♦♦
282 Abingdon Road, Oxford
OX1 4TA
T: (01865) 240135
F: (01865) 247652
E: jeakings@btinternet.com

Cotswold House
♦♦♦♦♦ SILVER AWARD
363 Banbury Road, Oxford
OX2 7PL
T: (01865) 310558
F: (01865) 310558
E: d.r.walker@talk21.com
I: www.house363.freeserve.co.uk

Dial House ♦♦♦
25 London Road, Headington, Oxford OX3 7RE
T: (01865) 425100
F: (01865) 427388
E: dialhouse@ntlworld.com
I: www.dialhouseoxford.co.uk

Earlmont Guest House ♦♦♦
322-324 Cowley Road, Oxford
OX4 2AF
T: (01865) 240236
F: (01865) 434903
E: earlmontguesthouse@yahoo.co.uk
I: www.oxfordcity.co.uk/accom/earlmont.html

Euro Bar & Hotel Oxford ♦♦♦
48 George Street, Oxford
OX1 2AQ
T: (01865) 725087
F: (01865) 243367
E: eurobarox@aol.com
I: www.oxfordcity.co.uk/accom/eurobar/

Falcon Private Hotel ♦♦♦
88-90 Abingdon Road, Oxford
OX1 4PX
T: (01865) 511122
F: (01865) 246642
E: stay@falconoxford.co.uk
I: www.oxfordcity.co.uk/hotels/falcon

Five Mile View Guest House ♦♦♦
528 Banbury Road, Oxford
OX2 8EG
T: (01865) 558747
F: (01865) 723873
E: 5mile@demon.co.uk
I: www.oxfordcity.co.uk/accom/fivemileview

Gables ♦♦♦♦ SILVER AWARD
6 Cumnor Hill, Oxford OX2 9HA
T: (01865) 862153
F: (01865) 864054
E: stay@gables-oxford.co.uk
I: www.oxfordcity.co.uk/accom/gables/

Green Gables ♦♦♦
326 Abingdon Road, Oxford
OX1 4TE
T: (01865) 725870
F: (01865) 723115
E: green.gables@virgin.net
I: www.greengables.uk.com

Head of the River ♦♦♦♦
Folly Bridge, St Aldates, Oxford
OX1 4LB
T: (01865) 721600
F: (01865) 726158

Heyford Hill Gardens ♦♦♦♦
Heyford Hill Lane, Littlemore, Oxford OX4 4YH
T: (01865) 777403
F: (01865) 395334
E: heyfordhillgdns@aol.com
I: www.guestaccom.co.uk/879.htm

Highfield West ♦♦♦
188 Cumnor Hill, Oxford
OX2 9PJ
T: (01865) 863007
E: highfieldwest@msn.com
I: www.oxfordcity.co.uk/accom/highfield-west

Hollybush Guest House ♦♦♦
Banbury Road, Oxford OX2 8EG
T: (01865) 554886
F: (01865) 554886
E: heather@hollybush.fsbusiness.co.uk
I: www.angelfire.com/on/hollybush

Home Farm House
♦♦♦♦ SILVER AWARD
Holton, Nr Wheatley, Oxford
OX33 1QA
T: (01865) 872334
F: (01865) 876220
E: sonja.barter@tiscali.co.uk

Homelea Guest House ♦♦♦♦
356 Abingdon Road, Oxford
OX1 4TQ
T: (01865) 245150
F: (01865) 245150
E: homelea@talk21.com
I: www.guesthouseoxford.com

Isis Guest House ♦♦
45-53 Iffley Road, Oxford
OX4 1ED
T: (01865) 248894
F: (01865) 243492
E: isis@herald.ox.ac.uk

Lakeside Guest House ♦♦♦
118 Abingdon Road, Oxford
OX1 4PZ
T: (01865) 244725
F: (01865) 244725
E: danielashirley@btclick.com

21 Lincoln Road ♦♦♦♦
Oxford OX1 4TB
T: (01865) 246944
F: (01865) 246944
E: gbaleham@hotmail.com

The Lodge ♦♦♦♦
Horton Hill, Horton cum Studley,
Oxford OX33 1AY
T: (01865) 351235
F: (01865) 351721
E: res@studleylodge.com
I: www.studleylodge.com

Lonsdale Guest House ♦♦♦
312 Banbury Road, Oxford
OX2 7ED
T: (01865) 554872
F: (01865) 554872

Marlborough House Hotel ♦♦♦♦
321 Woodstock Road, Oxford
OX2 7NY
T: (01865) 311321
F: (01865) 515329
E: marlboroughhouse@btconnect.com
I: www.oxfordcity.co.uk/hotels/marlborough

Milka's Guest House ♦♦♦
379 Iffley Road, Oxford OX4 4DP
T: (01865) 778458
F: (01865) 776477
E: reservations@milkas.co.uk
I: www.milkas.co.uk

Mulberry Guest House ♦♦♦
265 London Road, Headington,
Oxford OX3 9EH
T: (01865) 767114
F: (01865) 767114
E: reservations@mulberryguesthouse.co.uk
I: www.mulberryguesthouse.co.uk

Newton House ♦♦♦
82-84 Abingdon Road, Oxford
OX1 4PL
T: (01865) 240561
F: (01865) 244647
E: newton.house@btinternet.com
I: www.oxfordcity.co.uk/accom/newton

The Old Black Horse Hotel ♦♦♦
102 St Clements, Oxford
OX4 1AR
T: (01865) 244691
F: (01865) 242771
E: info@theoldblackhorsehoteloxford.co.uk
I: www.theoldblackhorsehoteloxford.co.uk

Park House ♦♦♦
7 St Bernard's Road, Oxford
OX2 6EH
T: (01865) 310824

Parklands Hotel ♦♦♦♦
100 Banbury Road, Oxford
OX2 6JU
T: (01865) 554374
F: (01865) 559860
E: stay@parklandsoxford.co.uk
I: www.oxfordcity.co.uk/hotels/parklands

Pembroke House ♦♦♦♦♦
379 Woodstock Road, Oxford
OX2 8AA
T: (01865) 310782
F: (01865) 310649
E: gaynordean@aol.co.uk

Pickwicks Guest House ♦♦♦♦
15-17 London Road,
Headington, Oxford OX3 7SP
T: (01865) 750487
F: (01865) 742208
E: pickwicks@tiscali.co.uk
I: www.oxfordcity.co.uk/accom/pickwicks/

Red Mullions ♦♦♦
23 London Road, Headington,
Oxford OX3 7RE
T: (01865) 742741
F: (01865) 769944
E: redmullion@aol.com
I: www.oxfordcity.co.uk/accom/redmullions

The Ridings ♦♦♦
280 Abingdon Road, Oxford
OX1 4TA
T: (01865) 248364
F: (01865) 251348
E: stay@theridingsguesthouse.co.uk
I: www.theridingsguesthouse.co.uk

River Hotel ♦♦♦
17 Botley Road, Oxford OX2 0AA
T: (01865) 243475
F: (01865) 724306
E: reception@riverhotel.co.uk
I: www.riverhotel.co.uk

Royal Oxford Hotel
♦♦♦♦ SILVER AWARD
Park End Street, Oxford OX1 1HR
T: (01865) 248432
F: (01865) 250049
E: frontdesk@royaloxfordhotel.co.uk
I: www.royaloxfordhotel.co.uk

Ryan's Guest House ♦♦♦
164 Banbury Road,
Summertown, Oxford OX2 7BU
T: (01865) 558876
F: (01865) 558876
E: ryansguesthouse@yahoo.co.uk

Sportsview Guest House ♦♦♦
106-110 Abingdon Road, Oxford
OX1 4PX
T: (01865) 200089
F: (01865) 249270
E: stay@sportsview.guest-house.freeserve.co.uk
I: www.smoothhound.co.uk/hotels/sportsvi.html

Tilbury Lodge ♦♦♦
5 Tilbury Lane, Botley, Oxford
OX2 9NB
T: (01865) 862138
F: (01865) 863700
E: tilburylodge@yahoo.co.uk
I: www.oxfordcity.co.uk/hotels/tilbury/

The Tower House Hotel ♦♦♦♦
15 Ship Street, Oxford OX1 3DA
T: (01865) 246828
F: (01865) 247508
E: thetowerhouse@btconnect.com
I: www.towerhouseoxford.co.uk

West Farm ♦♦♦
Eaton, Appleton, Abingdon
OX13 5PR
T: (01865) 862908
F: (01865) 865512

The Westgate Hotel ♦♦
1 Botley Road, Oxford OX2 0AA
T: (01865) 726721
F: (01865) 722078
E: westgatehotel@btopenworld.com

Whitehouse View ♦♦
9 Whitehouse Road, Oxford
OX1 4PA
T: (01865) 721626

OXTED
Surrey

Arawa ♦♦♦
58 Granville Road, Oxted
RH8 0BZ
T: (01883) 714104
F: (01883) 714104
E: david@davidgibbs.co.uk

Meads ♦♦♦♦
23 Granville Road, Oxted
RH8 0BX
T: (01883) 730115
E: Holgate@meads9.fsnet.co.uk

The New Bungalow ♦♦♦
Old Hall Farm, Tandridge Lane,
Oxted RH8 9NS
T: (01342) 892508
F: (01342) 892508
E: don.nunn@tesco.net

PADWORTH COMMON
Berkshire

Lanteglos House ♦♦
Rectory Road, Padworth
Common, Reading RG7 4JD
T: (01189) 700333

PANGBOURNE
Berkshire

Weir View House Hotel ♦♦♦♦
9 Shooters Hill, Pangbourne,
Reading RG8 7DZ
T: (01189) 842120
F: (01189) 843777
E: info@weirview.co.uk
I: www.weirview.co.uk

PARK GATE
Hampshire

Four Winds Guest House ♦♦♦
17 Station Road, Park Gate,
Southampton SO31 7GJ
T: (01489) 584433
F: (01489) 584433
E: mags@fourwindsguesthouse.com
I: www.fourwindsguesthouse.com

Little Park Lodge ♦♦♦
5 Bridge Road, Park Gate,
Southampton SO31 7GD
T: (01489) 600500
F: (01489) 605231
E: julie@manicmike.com
I: www.manicmike.com

60 Southampton Road ♦♦♦
Park gate, Park Gate,
Southampton SO31 6AF
T: (01489) 573994

PARKSTONE
Dorset

Danecourt Lodge ♦♦♦♦
58 Danecourt Road, Parkstone,
Poole BH14 0PQ
T: (01202) 730957

Toad Hall ♦♦♦♦
30 Church Road, Parkstone,
Poole BH14 0NS
T: (01202) 733900
F: (01202) 746814
E: toadhallguesthouse@btinternet.com
I: www.smoothhound.co.uk/hotels/toadhall.html

Viewpoint Guest House
♦♦♦♦ SILVER AWARD
11 Constitution Hill Road,
Parkstone, Poole BH14 0QB
T: (01202) 733586
F: (01202) 733586
E: heather@viewpoint-gh.co.uk
I: www.viewpoint-gh.co.uk

PARTRIDGE GREEN
West Sussex

Pound Cottage Bed & Breakfast ♦♦♦
Mill Lane, Littleworth, Partridge
Green, Horsham RH13 8JU
T: (01403) 710218
F: (01403) 711337
E: poundcottagebb@amserve.net
I: www.horsham.co.uk/poundcottage.html

PEASEMORE
West Berkshire

Peasemore House
Rating Applied For
Peasemore, Leckhampstead,
Newbury RG20 7JH
T: (01635) 248505
F: (01635) 248505

PEASLAKE
Surrey

The Garden Room ♦♦♦♦
Crest Hill, Peaslake, Guildford GU5 9PE
T: (01306) 737088
E: brimar@coltsfoot0.freeserve.co.uk

PEMBURY
Kent

Gates House ♦♦♦
5 Lower Green Road, Pembury, Royal Tunbridge Wells TN2 4DZ
T: (01892) 822866
F: (01892) 824626
E: simon@s.galway.freeserve.co.uk
I: www.ukworld.net/gates

PENN
Buckinghamshire

Little Twyford ♦♦♦
Hammersley Lane, Penn, High Wycombe HP10 8HG
T: (01494) 816934
F: (01494) 816934
E: tandt@twyford.freeserve.co.uk

PETERSFIELD
Hampshire

Beaumont ♦♦♦♦
22 Stafford Road, Petersfield GU32 2JG
T: (01730) 264744
F: (01730) 264744
E: jenny.bewes@btinternet.com

Border Cottage ♦♦♦
4 Heath Road, Petersfield GU31 4DU
T: (01730) 263179
E: lawrence@bordercottage.co.uk
I: www.bordercottage.co.uk

Causeway Guest House ♦♦♦
64A The Causeway, Petersfield GU31 4JS
T: (01730) 262924
E: eileen.fell@talk21.com

The Corner House ♦♦♦
1A Sandringham Road, Petersfield GU32 2AA
T: (01730) 261028
F: (01730) 261028
E: pat.elborough@ukonline.co.uk

Downsview ♦♦♦♦
58 Heath Road, Petersfield GU31 4EJ
T: (01730) 264171
F: (01730) 264171
E: john.grenfell@btopenworld.com
I: www.downsview.netfilms.com

Greywalls House ♦♦♦♦
London Road, Hill Brow, Liss GU33 7QR
T: (01730) 894246
F: (01730) 894865
E: hillbrow.la@lineone.net
I: www.bidbury.co.uk

Heath Farmhouse ♦♦♦
Heath Road East, Petersfield GU31 4HU
T: (01730) 264709
E: info@heathfarmhouse.co.uk
I: www.heathfarmhouse.co.uk

Heathside ♦♦♦
36 Heath Road East, Petersfield GU31 4HR
T: (01730) 262337
F: (01730) 262337

The Holt ♦♦♦
60 Heath Road, Petersfield GU31 4EJ
T: (01730) 262836

Lynton Guest House ♦♦♦
42 Charles Street, Petersfield GU32 3EH
T: (01730) 262364
E: jeanneclark@cwctv.net

Pipers ♦♦♦
1 Oaklands Road, Petersfield GU32 2EY
T: (01730) 262131

Ridgefield ♦♦
Station Road, Petersfield GU32 3DE
T: (01730) 261402
E: john.west@hants.gov.uk
I: www.ridgefieldguesthouse.co.uk

Riverside Guest House ♦♦♦♦
4 The Causeway, Petersfield GU31 4JS
T: (01730) 261246

Rose Cottage ♦♦♦
1 The Mead, Liss GU33 7DU
T: (01730) 892378

80 Rushes Road ♦♦♦
Rushes Road, Petersfield GU32 3BP
T: (01730) 261638
E: collins.tudor@lineone.net

South Gardens Cottage ♦♦♦
South Harting, Petersfield GU31 5QJ
T: (01730) 825040
F: (01730) 825040
E: rogerandjulia@beeb.net

1 The Spain ♦♦♦♦
Sheep Street, Petersfield GU32 3JZ
T: (01730) 263261
F: (01730) 261084
E: allantarva@cw.com.net

PETHAM
Kent

South Wootton House ♦♦♦
Capel Road, Petham, Canterbury CT4 5RG
T: (01227) 700643
F: (01227) 700613
E: mountfrances@farming.co.uk

PETWORTH
West Sussex

Badgers Tavern ♦♦♦♦
Station Road, Coultershaw Bridge, Petworth GU28 0JF
T: (01798) 342651
F: (01798) 343649

Burton Park Farm ♦♦♦
Burton Park Road, Petworth GU28 0JT
T: (01798) 342431

Eedes Cottage ♦♦♦♦
Bignor Park Road, Bury Gate, Pulborough RH20 1EZ
T: (01798) 831438
F: (01798) 831942
E: eedes.bandb.hare@amserve.com
I: www.visitsussex.org/eedescottage

Halfway Bridge Inn ♦♦♦♦
Halfway Bridge, Lodsworth, Petworth GU28 9BP
T: (01798) 861281
F: (01798) 861878
I: www.thesussexpub.co.uk

The Old Railway Station
♦♦♦♦♦ SILVER AWARD
Coultershaw Bridge, Petworth GU28 0JF
T: (01798) 342346
F: (01798) 342346
E: mlr@old-station.co.uk
I: www.old-station.co.uk

Rectory Cottage ♦♦♦
Rectory Lane, Petworth GU28 0DB
T: (01798) 342380
E: dcradd@aol.com

PEVENSEY BAY
East Sussex

The Bay Hotel
Rating Applied For
2-4 Eastbourne Road, Pevensey Bay, Pevensey BN24 6EJ
T: (01323) 768645
F: (01323) 743344

The Sandcastle
♦♦♦♦ SILVER AWARD
46 Val Prinseps Road, Pevensey Bay, Pevensey BN24 6JG
T: (01323) 743706
F: (01323) 743706
E: sandcastlebay@aol.com
I: www.sandcastlebay.co.uk

PICKET PIECE
Hampshire

Cherry Trees ♦♦♦
Picket Piece, Andover SP11 6LY
T: (01264) 334891
F: (01264) 334891

PIDDINGTON
Oxfordshire

Hill Farm House ♦♦♦♦
Hill Farm, Thame Road Piddington, Piddington, Bicester OX25 1QB
T: (01844) 238311

PILLEY
Hampshire

Mistletoe Cottage
♦♦♦♦ SILVER AWARD
3 Jordans Lane, Pilley, Lymington SO41 5QW
T: (01590) 676361

PILTDOWN
East Sussex

The Piltdown Man Free House
♦♦♦
Isfield, Piltdown, Uckfield TN22 5XL
T: (01825) 723563
E: enquiries@thepiltdownman.com
I: www.thepiltdownman.com

PISHILL
Oxfordshire

Orchard House ♦♦♦
Pishill, Henley-on-Thames RG9 6HJ
T: (01491) 638351
F: (01491) 638351
E: joanatpashill@btopenworld.com

PITT
Hampshire

Enmill Barn ♦♦♦♦♦
Enmill Lane, Pitt, Winchester SO22 5QR
T: (01962) 856740
F: (01962) 854219
E: jennywas21@hotmail.com
I: www.enmill-barn.co.uk

PLAYDEN
East Sussex

The Corner House ♦♦♦
Playden, Rye TN31 7UL
T: (01797) 280439
E: yvonne@thecornerhouse-bed-breakfast.co.uk
I: www.thecornerhouse-bed-breakfast.co.uk

Houghton Farm ♦♦♦♦
Houghton Green Lane, Playden, Rye TN31 7PJ
T: (01797) 280175

PLUCKLEY
Kent

Glebelands Bed & Breakfast
♦♦♦♦
Glebelands, Station Road, Pluckley, Ashford TN27 0QU
T: (01233) 840089
F: (01233) 840089
E: enquiries@bed-breakfast-pluckley-kent.co.uk
I: www.bed-breakfast-pluckley-kent.co.uk

PLUMMERS PLAIN
West Sussex

Cinnamon Cottage ♦♦♦
Handcross Road, Plummers Plain, Horsham RH13 6NZ
T: (01444) 400539

POLEGATE
East Sussex

The Cottage ♦♦♦♦
Dittons Road, Polegate BN26 6HS
T: (01323) 482011
F: (01323) 482011
E: Dream@tinyworld.co.uk

POOLE
Dorset

Annelise ♦♦♦
41 Danecourt Road, Lower Parkstone, Poole BH14 0PG
T: (01202) 744833
F: (01202) 744833

Ashdell ♦♦
85 Dunyeats Road, Broadstone BH18 8AF
T: (01202) 692032
E: ian@ashdell.fsnet.co.uk
I: www.ashdell.co.uk

Charlton Lodge ♦♦♦
826 Ringwood Road, Bournemouth BH11 8NF
T: (01202) 249977
E: friggs@cwctv.net

Corkers ♦♦♦♦ SILVER AWARD
1 High Street, The Quay, Poole BH15 1AB
T: (01202) 681393
F: (01202) 667393
E: corkers@corkers.co.uk
I: www.corkers.co.uk/corkers

Fernway ♦♦♦
56 Fernside Road, Poole
BH15 2JJ
T: (01202) 252044
F: (01202) 666587
E: dave.way@sequencecontrols.co.uk
I: www.fernway.co.uk

Fleetwater Guest House ♦♦♦
161 Longfleet Road, Poole
BH15 2HS
T: (01202) 682509

The Golden Sovereign Hotel ♦♦♦♦
97 Alumhurst Road,
Bournemouth BH4 8HR
T: (01202) 762088
F: (01202) 762088
E: scott.p@talk21.com
I: www.goldensovereignhotel.com

The Grange Guest House ♦♦♦
1 Linthorpe Road, Poole
BH15 2JS
T: (01202) 671336

Harlequins B & B ♦♦♦♦ SILVER AWARD
134 Ringwood Road, Poole
BH14 0RP
T: (01202) 677624
F: (01202) 677624
E: harlequins@tinyworld.com
I: www.harlequins.freeuk.com

Highways ♦♦♦
29 Fernside Road, Poole
BH15 2QU
T: (01202) 677060

Laurel Cottages ♦♦♦♦
41 Foxholes Road, Poole
BH15 3NA
T: (01202) 730894
F: (01202) 730894
E: anne.howarth@cwcom.net
I: www.laurel-cottages.cwc.net

Lytchett Mere ♦♦♦♦ SILVER AWARD
191 Sandy Lane, Upton, Poole
BH16 5LU
T: (01202) 622854

The Mariners Guest House ♦♦♦
26 Sandbanks Road, Poole
BH14 8AQ
T: (01202) 247218

Quay House ♦♦♦
3A Thames Street, Poole
BH15 1JN
T: (01202) 686335
E: goodeypoolequay@cwctv.net
I: www.poole-bed-and-breakfast.com

The Saltings ♦♦♦♦
5 Salterns Way, Lilliput, Poole
BH14 8JR
T: (01202) 707349
F: (01202) 701435
E: saltings_poole@yahoo.co.uk
I: www.thesaltingsfsnet.co.uk

Sarnia Cherie ♦♦♦♦
375 Blandford Road,
Hamworthy, Poole BH15 4JL
T: (01202) 679470
F: (01202) 679470
E: criscollier@aol.com

The Shah of Persia ♦♦♦♦
173 Longfleet Road, Poole
BH15 2HS
T: (01202) 676587
F: (01202) 679327

Tatnam Farm ♦♦♦♦
82 Tatnam Road, Poole
BH15 2DS
T: (01202) 672969
F: (01202) 682732
E: helenbishop@jrb.netkonect.co.uk

Vernon ♦♦♦
96 Blandford Road North,
Beacon Hill, Poole BH16 6AD
T: (01202) 625185
E: f.a.rendell@amserve.net

Waterside Bed & Breakfast Rating Applied For
5 Lulworth Avenue, Hamworthy,
Poole BH15 4DQ
T: (01202) 682753

PORCHFIELD
Isle of Wight

Youngwoods Farm ♦♦♦
Whitehouse Road, Porchfield,
Newport PO30 4LJ
T: (01983) 522170
F: (01983) 522170
E: judith@youngwoods.com
I: www.youngwoods.com

PORTCHESTER
Hampshire

Harbour View ♦♦
85 Windmill Grove, Portchester,
Fareham PO16 9HH
T: (023) 9237 6740

PORTSMOUTH & SOUTHSEA
Hampshire

Abbey Lodge ♦♦♦
30 Waverley Road, Southsea
PO5 2PW
T: (023) 9282 8285
F: (023) 9287 2943
E: linda@abbeylodge.co.uk
I: www.abbeylodge.co.uk

The Albatross Guest House ♦♦♦♦
51 Waverley Road, Southsea
PO5 2PJ
T: (023) 9282 8325

Arden Guest House ♦♦♦
14 Herbert Road, Southsea
PO4 0QA
T: (023) 9282 6409
F: (023) 9282 6409

Avarest Guest House ♦♦
10 Waverley Grove, Southsea
PO4 0PZ
T: (023) 9282 9444

Bembell Court Hotel ♦♦♦
69 Festing Road, Southsea
PO4 0NQ
T: (023) 9273 5915
F: (023) 9275 6497
E: keith@bembell.co.uk
I: www.bembell.co.uk

Birchwood ♦♦♦♦
44 Waverley Road, Southsea,
Portsmouth PO5 2PP
T: (023) 9281 1337
E: ged@birchwood.uk.com
I: www.birchwood.uk.com

Esk Vale Guest House ♦♦♦
39 Granada Road, Southsea
PO4 0RD
T: (023) 9286 2639
F: (023) 9235 5589
E: enquires@eskvaleguesthouse.co.uk
I: www.eskvaleguesthouse.co.uk

Everley Guest House ♦♦♦
33 Festing Road, Southsea
PO4 0NG
T: (023) 9273 1001
F: (023) 9278 0995

Fortitude Cottage ♦♦♦♦
51 Broad Street, Spice Island,
Portsmouth PO1 2JD
T: (023) 9282 3748
F: (023) 9282 3748
E: fortcott@aol.com
I: www.fortitudecottage.co.uk

Gainsborough House ♦♦
9 Malvern Road, Southsea
PO5 2LZ
T: (023) 9282 2604

Granada House Hotel ♦♦♦
29 Granada Road, Southsea
PO4 0RD
T: (023) 9286 1575
F: (023) 9271 8343

Greenacres Guest House ♦♦♦
12 Marion Road, Southsea
PO4 0QX
T: (023) 9235 3137

Hamilton House ♦♦♦♦
95 Victoria Road North,
Portsmouth PO5 1PS
T: (023) 9282 3502
F: (023) 9282 3502
E: sandra@hamiltonhouse.co.uk
I: www.hamiltonhouse.co.uk

131 The High Street ♦♦♦♦ SILVER AWARD
Old Portsmouth, Portsmouth
PO1 2HW
T: (023) 9273 0903

Hillside Lodge ♦♦♦
1 Blake Road, Farlington,
Portsmouth PO6 1ET
T: (023) 9237 2687

Homestead Guest House ♦♦♦
11 Bembridge Crescent,
Southsea PO4 0QT
T: (023) 9273 2362
E: b.currie1@ntlworld.com

Lamorna Guest House ♦♦
23 Victoria Road South,
Southsea PO5 2BX
T: (023) 9281 1157
F: (023) 9281 1157

Langdale Guest House ♦♦♦
13 St Edwards Road, Southsea
PO5 3DH
T: (023) 9282 2146
F: (023) 9282 2152
E: langdalegh@btinternet.com
I: www.smoothhound.co.uk/hotels/langdal.html

Oakleigh Guest House ♦♦♦
48 Festing Grove, Southsea
PO4 9QD
T: (023) 9281 2276
E: dwillett@cwtv.net
I: www.oakleighguesthouse.co.uk

The Parade Hotel ♦♦♦
31 Clarence Parade, Southsea
PO5 2ET
T: (023) 9282 4838
F: (023) 9282 4838
E: mathew.parker@btopenworld.coom
I: www.theparadehotel.com

Portsmouth Foyer Rating Applied For
22 Edinburgh Road, Portsmouth
PO1 1DH
T: (023) 9236 0001
F: (023) 9236 0004

Rees Hall University of Portsmouth ♦♦♦
Southsea Terrace, Southsea
PO5 3AP
T: (023) 9284 3884
F: (023) 9284 3888
E: reservation@port.ac.uk
I: www.port.ac.uk

The Rowans Guest House ♦♦♦♦ SILVER AWARD
43 Festing Grove, Southsea
PO4 9QB
T: (023) 9273 6614
F: (023) 9282 3711
E: mikejsmart@yahoo.com

Sally Port Inn ♦♦♦
57-58 High Street, Portsmouth
PO1 2LU
T: (023) 9282 1860
F: (023) 9282 1293

Victoria Court ♦♦♦
29 Victoria Road North,
Southsea PO5 1PL
T: (023) 9282 0305
F: (023) 9283 8277
E: stay@victoriacourt.co.uk
I: www.victoriacourt.co.uk

Waverley Park Lodge Guest House ♦♦♦♦
99 Waverley Road, Southsea
PO5 2PL
T: (023) 9273 0402
I: www.waverleyparklodge.com

Woodville Hotel ♦♦♦
6 Florence Road, Southsea
PO5 2NE
T: (023) 9282 3409
F: (023) 9234 6089
E: woodvillehotel@cwcom.net

POSTCOMBE
Oxfordshire

Beech Farm ♦♦♦♦
Salt Lane, Postcombe, Oxford
OX9 7EE
T: (01844) 281240
F: (01844) 281632
E: beech.farm@btopenworld.com
I: www.beechfarm.co.uk

PRINCES RISBOROUGH
Buckinghamshire

Grove House Bed & Breakfast Rating Applied For
The Grove, Thame Road,
Longwick, Princes Risborough
HP27 9SG
T: (01844) 347254
F: (01844) 344102
E: john@grovehousebnb.co.uk
I: www.grovehousebnb.co.uk

The Old Station Bledlow ♦♦♦♦♦
Sandpit Lane, Bledlow, Princes Risborough, Aylesbury HP27 9QQ
T: (01844) 345086
F: (01844) 274732
E: ianmackinson@hotmail.com
I: www.theoldstation-bledlow.co.uk

Solis Ortu ♦♦♦
Aylesbury Road, Askett, Princes Risborough, Aylesbury HP27 9LY
T: (01844) 344175
F: (01844) 343509

PULBOROUGH
West Sussex

Barn House Lodge ♦♦♦♦
Barn House Lane, Pulborough RH20 2BS
T: (01798) 872682
F: (01798) 872682
E: suehj@aol.com

Hurston Warren ♦♦♦
Golf Club Lane, Wiggonholt, Pulborough RH20 2EN
T: (01798) 875831
F: (01798) 874989
E: kglazier@btinternet.com
I: www.sussexlive.com

Moseleys Barn
♦♦♦♦ SILVER AWARD
Hardham, Pulborough RH20 1LB
T: (01798) 872912
F: (01798) 872912
I: www.smoothhound.co.uk/hotels/moseleys

QUAINTON
Buckinghamshire

Woodlands Farmhouse Country Bed and Breakfast ♦♦♦♦
Doddershall, Quainton, Aylesbury HP22 4DE
T: (01296) 770225
F: (01296) 770519
E: helen.howard@virgin.net

RADNAGE
Buckinghamshire

Highlands ♦♦♦♦
26 Green Lane, Radnage, High Wycombe HP14 4DN
T: (01494) 484835
F: (01494) 482633
E: janekhighlands@aol.com
I: www.country-accom.co.uk

RAINHAM
Kent

Abigails ♦♦♦
17 The Maltings, Rainham, Gillingham ME8 8JL
T: (01634) 365427

Sans Souci ♦♦♦♦
Wakeley Road, Rainham, Gillingham ME8 8HD
T: (01634) 370847

RAMSDEN
Oxfordshire

Ann's Cottage ♦♦♦
Lower End, Ramsden, Oxford OX7 3AZ
T: (01993) 868592
E: foxwoodfamily@lineone.net

RAMSGATE
Kent

Abbeygail Guest House ♦♦♦♦
17 Penshurst Road, Ramsgate CT11 8EG
T: (01843) 594154
F: (01843) 594154
E: lindi.groom@ukf.net
I: www.abbeygail.co.uk

Creedons
Rating Applied For
58 Queen Street, Ramsgate CT11 9EE
T: (01843) 595558
F: (01843) 595558
E: smcrdo@aol.com
I: www.creedons.co.uk

The Crescent ♦♦♦
19 Wellington Crescent, Ramsgate CT11 8JD
T: (01843) 591419
F: (01843) 591419
E: thecrescent@onetel.net.uk
I: www.ramsgate-uk.com

Glendevon Guest House ♦♦♦♦
8 Truro Road, Ramsgate CT11 8DB
T: (01843) 570909
F: (01843) 570909
E: adrian.everix@btopenworld.com

Glenholme ♦♦♦
6 Crescent Road, Ramsgate CT11 9QU
T: (01843) 595149

The Jalna Hotel ♦♦♦
49 Vale Square, Ramsgate CT11 9DA
T: (01843) 593848
F: (01843) 593848

The Royale Guest House ♦♦♦
7 Royal Road, Ramsgate CT11 9LE
T: (01843) 594712
F: (01843) 594712
E: theroyaleguesthouse@talk21.com

Sealan Hotel ♦♦
6 Avenue Road, Ramsgate CT11 8ET
T: (01843) 593044
F: (01843) 593044

Spencer Court Hotel ♦♦♦
Spencer Square, Ramsgate CT11 9LD
T: (01843) 594582
F: (01843) 594582
E: glendaandken@hotmail.com

Sunnymede
♦♦♦♦ SILVER AWARD
10 Truro Road, Ramsgate CT11 8DP
T: (01843) 593974
F: (01843) 594327
E: sunnymede@tinyworld.co.uk
I: www.thesunnymede.co.uk

READING
Berkshire

Abadair House ♦♦
46 Redlands Road, Reading RG1 5HE
T: (0118) 986 3792
F: (0118) 986 3792
E: abadair@globalnet.co.uk
I: www.smoothhound.co.uk/hotels/abadair/.html

Bath Hotel ♦♦♦
54 Bath Road, Reading RG1 6PG
T: (0118) 957 2019
F: (0118) 950 3203

Caversham Lodge ♦♦
133a Caversham Road, Reading RG1 8AS
T: (01189) 573529

Crescent Hotel ♦♦♦
35 Coley Avenue, Reading RG1 6LL
T: (01189) 507980
F: (01189) 574299

Dittisham Guest House ♦♦♦
63 Tilehurst Road, Reading RG30 2JL
T: (0118) 956 9483
E: dittishamgh@aol.com

The Elms ♦♦
Gallowstree Road, Rotherfield Peppard, Henley-on-Thames RG9 5HT
T: (0118) 972 3164
F: (0118) 972 4594

Greystoke Guest House ♦♦♦♦
10 Greystoke Road, Caversham, Reading RG4 5EL
T: (01189) 475784

The Old Forge ♦♦♦
109 Grovelands Road, Reading RG30 2PB
T: (0118) 958 2928
F: (0118) 958 2408
E: rees.family@virgin.net

The Roebuck Hotel ♦
De Hillier Taverns plc, Oxford Road, Tilehurst, Reading RG31 6TG
T: (0118) 942 7517
F: (0118) 941 7629
I: WWW.ROEBUCK-HOTEL.CO.UK

The Six Bells ♦♦♦
Beenham Village, Beenham, Reading RG7 5NX
T: (0118) 971 3368

Warren Dene Hotel ♦♦♦
1017 Oxford Road, Tilehurst, Reading RG31 6TL
T: (0118) 942 2556
F: (0118) 945 1096
E: wdh@globalnet.co.uk

REDHILL
Surrey

Ashleigh House Hotel ♦♦♦♦
39 Redstone Hill, Redhill RH1 4BG
T: (01737) 764763
F: (01737) 780308

REIGATE
Surrey

Highview ♦♦♦
76 Woodcrest Walk, Reigate RH2 0JL
T: (01737) 768294
F: (01737) 760433
E: highview@creative-eye.fsnet.co.uk
I: www.creative-eye.fsnet.co.uk/highview.html

RHODES MINNIS
Kent

Monsoon Lodge ♦♦♦
Rhodes Minnis, Canterbury CT4 6XX
T: (01303) 863272
F: (01303) 863272
E: jm@farmersweekly.net
I: www.monsoonlodge.co.uk

RINGMER
East Sussex

Bethany ♦♦♦
25 Ballard Drive, Ringmer, Lewes BN8 5NU
T: (01273) 812025
F: (01273) 812025
E: dimeadows@rockuk.net

Bryn-Clai ♦♦♦♦
Uckfield Road, Ringmer, Lewes BN8 5RU
T: (01273) 814042
I: www.brynclai.co.uk

Gote Farm ♦♦♦♦
Gote Lane, Ringmer, Lewes BN8 5HX
T: (01273) 812303
F: (01273) 812303
E: janecraig@ukgateway.net

RINGWOOD
Hampshire

The Auld Kennels ♦♦♦
215 Christchurch Road, Moortown, Ringwood BH24 3AN
T: (01425) 475170
F: (01425) 461577
E: auldkennels@aol.com

Fraser House ♦♦♦♦
Salisbury Road, Blashford, Ringwood BH24 3PB
T: (01425) 473958
F: (01425) 473958
E: mail@fraserhouse.net
I: www.fraserhouse.net

Torre Avon
♦♦♦♦ SILVER AWARD
21 Salisbury Road, Ringwood BH24 1AS
T: (01425) 472769
F: (01425) 472769
E: b&b@torreavon.freeserve.co.uk
I: www.torreavon.freeserve.co.uk

RIVER
Kent

Woodlands ♦♦♦
29 London Road, River, Dover CT17 0SF
T: (01304) 823635

ROBERTSBRIDGE
East Sussex

Glenferness ♦♦♦♦
Brightling Road, Robertsbridge, Battle TN32 5DP
T: (01580) 881841
E: ktwright@ukonline.co.uk
I: www.ktwright.ukonline.co.uk

ROCHESTER
Kent

10 Abbotts Close ♦♦♦♦
Abbotts Close, Rochester ME1 3AZ
T: (01634) 811126

Ambleside Lodge ♦♦♦
12 Abbotts Close, Priestfields, Rochester ME1 3AZ
T: (01634) 815926
F: (01634) 815926
E: bryan@mills19.fsnet.co.uk

The Cottage ♦♦♦
66 Borstal Road, Rochester ME1 3BD
T: (01634) 403888

Edelweiss ♦♦♦
12 Nashenden Lane, Rochester ME1 3JQ
T: (01634) 840346
E: john.moore40@virgin.net

Greystones ♦♦♦♦
25 Watts Avenue, Rochester
ME1 1RX
T: (01634) 409565

King Charles Hotel ♦♦♦
Brompton Road, Gillingham
ME7 5QT
T: (01634) 830303
F: (01634) 829430
E: enquiries@kingcharleshotel.co.uk
I: www.kingcharleshotel.co.uk

The Kings Head Hotel ♦♦♦
58 High Street, Rochester
ME1 1LD
T: (01634) 831103

Riverview Lodge ♦
88 Borstal Road, Rochester
ME1 3BD
T: (01634) 842241
F: (01634) 843404
E: msheikh97@aol.com

St Martin ♦♦♦
104 Borstal Road, Rochester
ME1 3BD
T: (01634) 848192
E: icolvin@stmartin.freeserve.co.uk

Salisbury House
Rating Applied For
29 Watts Avenue, Rochester
ME1 1RX
T: (01634) 400182

Sunshine House ♦♦
14 Beech Road, Strood,
Rochester ME2 2LP
T: (01634) 724291
E: melzo@strood1950.freeserve.co.uk

ROLVENDEN
Kent

Duck & Drake Cottage ♦♦♦
Sandhurst Lane, Rolvenden,
Cranbrook TN17 4PQ
T: (01580) 241533
F: (01580) 241533
E: duckanddrake@supanet.com

ROMNEY MARSH
Kent

Coxell House ♦♦♦♦
9 Manor Road, Lydd, Romney
Marsh TN29 9HR
T: (01797) 322037
E: coxellhouse@btopenworld.com
I: www.coxellhouse.co.uk

ROMSEY
Hampshire

Abbey Hotel ♦♦♦
11 Church Street, Romsey
SO51 8BT
T: (01794) 513360
F: (01794) 524318
E: di@abbeyhotelromsey.co.uk
I: www.abbeyhotelromsey.co.uk

Aylwards Bottom ♦♦♦♦
Top Green, Lockerley, Romsey
SO51 0JP
T: (01794) 340864

The Chalet Guest House ♦♦♦
Botley Road, Whitenap, Romsey
SO51 5RQ
T: (01794) 517299
E: b-and-b@the-chalet.freeserve.co.uk
I: www.homepage.ntlworld.com/obrian

3 Cherville Mews
♦♦♦♦ SILVER AWARD
Romsey SO51 8FY
T: (01794) 830518
F: (01794) 830518
E: patricia.townson@ntlworld.com
I: www.patsbnb.tripod.com

79 Mercer Way ♦♦♦
Romsey SO51 7PH
T: (01794) 502009
F: (01794) 503009

Pauncefoot House ♦♦♦♦
Pauncefoot Hill, Romsey
SO51 6AA
T: (01794) 513139
F: (01794) 513139
E: lendupont@aol.com

Pillar Box Cottage ♦♦♦
Toothill, Romsey SO51 9LN
T: (023) 8073 2390

Pyesmead Farm ♦♦♦
Plaitford, Romsey SO51 6EE
T: (01794) 323386
F: (01794) 323386
E: pyesmead@talk21.com

Ranvilles Farm House ♦♦♦♦
Ower, Romsey SO51 6AA
T: (023) 8081 4481
F: (023) 8081 4481
E: info@ranvilles.com
I: www.ranvilles.com

Roselea ♦♦♦♦
Hamdown Crescent, East
Wellow, Romsey SO51 6BJ
T: (01794) 323262
F: (01794) 323262
E: beds@roselea.info
I: www.roselea.info

Stoneymarsh Bed & Breakfast ♦♦♦
Stoneymarsh, Michelmersh,
Romsey SO51 0LB
T: (01794) 368867
F: (01794) 367290
E: mmmoran@btinternet.com

Toad Hall ♦♦♦♦♦
66 Mill Lane, Romsey SO51 8EQ
T: (01794) 512350

Tregoyd House ♦♦♦
Crook Hill, Braishfield, Romsey
SO51 0QB
T: (01794) 368307
F: (01794) 368307
E: tregoyd@waitrose.com

ROWLEDGE
Surrey

Borderfield Farm ♦♦♦
Boundary Road, Rowledge,
Farnham GU10 4EP
T: (01252) 793985

ROYAL TUNBRIDGE WELLS
Kent

Ash Tree Cottage ♦♦♦♦
7 Eden Road, Royal Tunbridge
Wells TN1 1TS
T: (01892) 541317
F: (01892) 616770
E: rogersashtree@excite.com

Badgers End ♦♦♦
47 Thirlmere Road, Royal
Tunbridge Wells TN4 9SS
T: (01892) 533176

Bankside ♦♦♦
6 Scotts Way, Royal Tunbridge
Wells TN2 5RG
T: (01892) 531776
E: amkibi@yahoo.co.uk

4 Bedford Terrace ♦♦♦
Royal Tunbridge Wells TN1 1YJ
T: (01892) 532084

Blundeston ♦♦♦♦
Eden Road, Royal Tunbridge
Wells TN1 1TS
T: (01892) 513030
F: (01892) 540255
E: daysblundeston@excite.com

Braeside ♦♦♦
7 Rusthall Road, Royal
Tunbridge Wells TN4 8RA
T: (01892) 521786
F: (01892) 521786
E: itucker@eggconnect.net

Broadwater
Rating Applied For
24 Clarendon Way, Royal
Tunbridge Wells TN2 5LD
T: (01892) 528161

Burrswood Chapel House ♦♦♦♦
Burrswood, Bird in Hand Lane,
Groombridge, Royal Tunbridge
Wells TN3 9PY
T: (01892) 863637
F: (01892) 862597
E: admin@burrswood.org.uk
I: www.burrswood.org.uk

Cheviots ♦♦♦♦
Cousley Wood, Wadhurst
TN5 6HD
T: (01892) 782952
E: b&b@cheviots99.freeserve.co.uk
I: www.cheviots.info

Clarken Guest House ♦♦♦
61 Frant Road, Royal Tunbridge
Wells TN2 5LH
T: (01892) 533397
F: (01892) 617121
E: barrykench@virgin.net

Danehurst
♦♦♦♦♦ SILVER AWARD
41 Lower Green Road, Rusthall,
Royal Tunbridge Wells TN4 8TW
T: (01892) 527739
F: (01892) 514804
E: info@danehurst.net
I: www.smoothhound.co.uk/hotels/danehurst.html

Ephraim Lodge
♦♦♦♦♦ GOLD AWARD
The Common, Royal Tunbridge
Wells TN4 8BX
T: (01892) 523053
F: (01892) 543582

Ford Cottage ♦♦♦♦
Linden Park Road, Royal
Tunbridge Wells TN2 5QL
T: (01892) 531419
E: fordcottage@tinyworld.co.uk

Hadleigh ♦♦♦
69 Sandown Park, Royal
Tunbridge Wells TN2 4RT
T: (01892) 822760
F: (01892) 823170
E: gardiner@hadleightw.freeserve.co.uk

Hamsell Wood Farm ♦♦♦
The Forstal, Eridge, Royal
Tunbridge Wells TN3 9JY
T: (01892) 864326

Hawkenbury Farm ♦♦♦♦
Hawkenbury Road, Royal
Tunbridge Wells TN3 9AD
T: (01892) 536977
F: (01892) 536200
E: rhwright1@aol.com

Hazelwood House ♦♦♦
Bishops Down Park Road, Royal
Tunbridge Wells TN4 8XS
T: (01892) 545924
E: judith02@globalnet.co.uk

Manor Court Farm ♦♦♦
Ashurst, Royal Tunbridge Wells
TN3 9TB
T: (01892) 740279
F: (01892) 740919
E: jsoyke@jsoyke.freeserve.co.uk
I: www.manorcourtfarm.co.uk

Number Ten ♦♦♦
Modest Corner, Southborough,
Royal Tunbridge Wells TN4 0LS
T: (01892) 522450
F: (01892) 522450
E: modestanneke@lineone.net

Overwells
Rating Applied For
Shandon Close, Tunbridge Wells
TN2 3RE
T: (01892) 532430
E: gillsinclair@overwells.org.uk
I: www.overwells.org.uk

Rosnaree ♦♦♦
189 Upper Grosvenor Road,
Royal Tunbridge Wells TN1 2EF
T: (01892) 524017
E: david@rosnaree.freeserve.co.uk

Studley Cottage
♦♦♦♦ SILVER AWARD
Bishops Down Park Road, Royal
Tunbridge Wells TN4 8XX
T: (01892) 539854
E: cookhouse28@hotmail.com

191 Upper Grosvenor Road ♦♦♦
Royal Tunbridge Wells TN1 2EF
T: (01892) 537305

Vale Royal Hotel ♦♦♦
54-57 London Road, Royal
Tunbridge Wells TN1 1DS
T: (01892) 525580
F: (01892) 526022
E: reservations@valeroyalhotel.co.uk
I: www.valeroyalhotel.co.uk

40 York Road ♦♦♦
Royal Tunbridge Wells TN1 1JY
T: (01892) 531342
F: (01892) 531342
E: yorkroad@tiscali.co.uk
I: www.wolsey-lodge.co.uk

RUDGWICK
West Sussex

The Mucky Duck Inn ♦♦♦
Loxwood Road Tismans
Common, Rudgwick, Horsham
RH12 3BW
T: (01403) 822300
F: (01403) 822300
E: mucky_duck_pub@msn.com
I: www.mucky-duck-inn.co.uk

RUSTINGTON
West Sussex

Kenmore
♦♦♦♦ SILVER AWARD
Claigmar Road, Rustington, Littlehampton BN16 2NL
T: (01903) 784634
F: (01903) 784634
E: kenmoreguesthouse@amserve.net
I: www.kenmoreguesthouse.co.uk

RYDE
Isle of Wight

Claverton ♦♦♦♦
12 The Strand, Ryde PO33 1JE
T: (01983) 613015
F: (01983) 613015
E: clavertonhouse@aol.com

The Dorset Hotel ♦♦♦
31 Dover Street, Ryde PO33 2BW
T: (01983) 564327
F: (01983) 614635
E: hoteldorset@aol.com
I: www.thedorsethotel.co.uk

The Elmfield ♦♦♦
18 Marlborough Close, Elmfield, Ryde PO33 1AP
T: (01983) 614131
E: jeanlewis18@hotmail.com

Fern Cottage ♦♦♦♦
8 West Street, Ryde PO33 2NW
T: (01983) 565856
F: (01983) 565856
E: sandra@psdferguson.freeserve.co.uk

Kemphill Farm
♦♦♦♦ SILVER AWARD
Stroudwood Road, Upton, Ryde PO33 4BZ
T: (01983) 563880
F: (01983) 563880
E: ron.holland@farming.me.uk
I: www.kemphill.com

Royal Esplanade Hotel ♦♦♦
16 The Esplanade, Ryde PO33 2ED
T: (01983) 562549
F: (01983) 563918
I: www.shearingsholidays.com/hotels/islewight.htm

Sea View ♦♦♦
8 Dover Street, Ryde PO33 2AQ
T: (01983) 810976

Seahaven Hotel ♦♦♦
36 St Thomas Street, Ryde PO33 2DL
T: (01983) 563069
F: (01983) 563570
E: seahaven@netguides.co.uk

Seaward Guest House ♦♦♦
14-16 George Street, Ryde PO33 2EW
T: (01983) 563168
F: (01983) 563168
E: seaward@fsbdial.co.uk

Sillwood Acre ♦♦♦♦
Church Road, Binstead, Ryde PO33 3TB
T: (01983) 563553
E: debbie@sillwood-acre.co.uk
I: www.sillwood-acre.co.uk

Stonelands ♦♦♦♦
Binstead Road, Binstead, Ryde PO33 3NJ
T: (01983) 616947
F: (01983) 812857
E: stone.lands@tiscali.co.uk

Trentham Guest House ♦♦♦
38 The Strand, Ryde PO33 1JF
T: (01983) 563418
F: (01983) 563418

The Vine Guest House ♦♦♦
16 Castle Street, Ryde PO33 2EG
T: (01983) 566633
F: (01983) 566633
E: vine@guesthouse49.freeserve.co.uk
I: www.thevineguesthouse.co.uk

RYE
East Sussex

At Wisteria Corner ♦♦♦
47 Ferry Road (Sloane Terrace), Rye TN31 7DJ
T: (01797) 225011
E: mmpartridge@line.net
I: www.rye-tourism.co.uk/wisteria

Aviemore Guest House ♦♦♦
28-30 Fishmarket Road, Rye TN31 7LP
T: (01797) 223052
F: (01797) 223052
E: aviemore@lineone.net
I: www.SmoothHound.co.uk/hotels/aviemore.html

The Benson
♦♦♦♦♦ SILVER AWARD
15 East Street, Rye TN31 7JY
T: (01797) 225131
F: (01797) 225512
E: info@bensonhotel.co.uk
I: www.thebenson.co.uk

Culpeppers
♦♦♦♦ SILVER AWARD
15 Love Lane, Rye TN31 7NE
T: (01797) 224411
F: (01797) 223085
E: peppersrye@aol.com
I: www.culpeppers-rye.com

Durrant House Hotel
♦♦♦♦♦ SILVER AWARD
2 Market Street, Rye TN31 7LA
T: (01797) 223182
F: (01797) 226940
E: kingslands@compuserve.com
I: www.durranthouse.com

Four Seasons
♦♦♦♦ SILVER AWARD
96 Udimore Road, West Undercliff, Rye TN31 7DX
T: (01797) 224305
F: (01797) 229450
E: coxsam@btinternet.com

11 High Street ♦♦♦
Rye TN31 7JF
T: (01797) 223952

The Hope Anchor Hotel
♦♦♦♦
Watchbell Street, Rye TN31 7HA
T: (01797) 222216
F: (01897) 223796

Jeake's House
♦♦♦♦♦ SILVER AWARD
Mermaid Street, Rye TN31 7ET
T: (01797) 222828
F: (01797) 222623
E: jeakeshouse@btinternet.com
I: www.jeakeshouse.com

Kimbley Cottage ♦♦♦
Main Street, Peasmarsh, Rye TN31 6UL
T: (01797) 230514
F: (01797) 230850
E: kimbley@onetel.net.uk

Layces Bed & Breakfast
♦♦♦♦ SILVER AWARD
Chitcombe Road, Broad Oak, Rye TN31 6EU
T: (01424) 882836
F: (01424) 882281
E: stephens@layces.co.uk
I: www.layces.co.uk

Little Orchard House
♦♦♦♦♦ SILVER AWARD
West Street, Rye TN31 7ES
T: (01797) 223831
F: (01797) 223831
I: www.littleorchardhouse.com

Manor Farm Oast
♦♦♦♦♦ GOLD AWARD
Main Road, Icklesham, Winchelsea TN36 4AJ
T: (01424) 813787
F: (01424) 813787
E: manor.farm.oast@lineone.net
I: www.manorfarmoast.com

Mint Lodge ♦♦♦
37-38 The Mint, Rye TN31 7EN
T: (01797) 223268
F: (01424) 772878

The Old Vicarage ♦♦♦
Rye Harbour Road, Rye TN31 7TT
T: (01797) 222088
F: (01797) 229620
E: jonathan@oldvicarageryeharbour.fsnet.co.uk

Owlet ♦♦♦
37 New Road, Rye TN31 7LS
T: (01797) 222544
E: owlet-rye@amserve.net
I: www.owlet.@50megs.com

The Rise
♦♦♦♦ SILVER AWARD
82 Udimore Road, Rye TN31 7DY
T: (01797) 222285
E: therise@bb-rye.freeserve.co.uk

St Margarets ♦♦♦
Dumbwomans Lane, Udimore, Rye TN31 6AD
T: (01797) 222586

Ship Inn ♦♦♦
The Strand, Rye TN31 7DB
T: (01797) 222233
F: (01797) 222715
E: shipinn@zoom.co.uk

Simmons of the Mint ♦♦♦♦
68-69 The Mint, Rye TN31 7EW
T: (01797) 226862
F: (01797) 226862

The Strand House
♦♦♦♦ SILVER AWARD
Tanyard's Lane, Winchelsea TN36 4JT
T: (01797) 226276
F: (01797) 224806
E: strandhouse@winchelsea98.fsnet.co.uk
I: www.s-h-systems.co.uk/hotels/strand.html

Thacker House ♦♦♦
Old Brickyard, Rye TN31 7EE
T: (01797) 226850
F: (01797) 226850
E: abb25@supanet.com

Tidings ♦♦♦♦
26A Military Road, Tidings, Rye TN31 7NY
T: (01797) 223760

Top o'The Hill at Rye ♦♦♦
Rye Hill, Rye TN31 7NH
T: (01797) 223284
F: (01797) 227030

Tower House ♦♦♦♦
(The Old Dormy), Hilders Cliff, Rye TN31 7LD
T: (01797) 226865
F: (01797) 226865

Vine Cottage ♦♦♦
25a Udimore Road, Rye TN31 7DS
T: (01797) 222822

White Vine House
♦♦♦♦♦ SILVER AWARD
24 High Street, Rye TN31 7JF
T: (01797) 224748
F: (01797) 223599
E: irene@whitevinehouse.freeserve.co.uk

The Windmill Guest House
♦♦♦
Mill Lane, (off Ferry Road), Rye TN31 7DW
T: (01797) 224027
F: (01797) 227212
I: www.rye-tourism.co.uk/windmill

Wish House ♦♦♦
Wish Ward, Rye TN31 7DH
T: (01797) 223672
E: wishhouse@zoom.com

Woodpeckers ♦♦♦
West Undercliff, Rye TN31 7DX
T: (01797) 223013
F: (01797) 222264
E: shirley@caresigns.com

RYE FOREIGN
East Sussex

The Hare & Hounds ♦♦♦
Rye Road, Rye Foreign, Rye TN31 7ST
T: (01797) 230483

ST CROSS
Hampshire

Dolphin House Studios
♦♦♦♦ SILVER AWARD
3 Compton Road, St Cross, Winchester SO23 9SL
T: (01962) 853284
F: (01962) 853284

ST LAWRENCE
Isle of Wight

Lisle Combe ♦♦♦
Bank End Farm, Undercliff Drive, St Lawrence, Ventnor PO38 1UW
T: (01983) 852582
E: lislecombe@yahoo.com
I: www.lislecombe.co.uk

Little Orchard ♦♦♦♦
Undercliff Drive, St Lawrence, Ventnor PO38 1YA
T: (01983) 731106

ST LEONARDS
East Sussex

Ashton House ♦♦♦
381 Battle Road, St Leonards on Sea, St Leonards, Hastings TN37 7BE
T: (01424) 853624

Hollington Croft ♦♦♦
272 Battle Road, St Leonards-on-Sea, St Leonards, Hastings TN37 7BA
T: (01424) 851795

Marina Lodge ♦♦♦
123 Marina, St Leonards, Hastings TN38 0BN
T: (01424) 715067
E: marinalodge@lineone.net
I: www.marinalodge.co.uk

May Tree House ♦♦♦
41 Albany Road, St Leonards, Hastings TN38 0LJ
T: (01424) 421760
F: (01424) 421760
E: maytreehouse@hotmail.com

Melrose Guest House ♦♦♦♦
18 De Cham Road, St Leonards, Hastings TN37 6JP
T: (01424) 715163
F: (01424) 432773
E: melrose18@fsmail.net

Rutland Guest House ♦♦♦
17 Grosvenor Cres, St Leonards, Hastings TN38 0AA
T: (01424) 714720
F: (01424) 714720

Sherwood Guest House ♦♦♦
15 Grosvenor Crescent, St Leonards, Hastings TN38 0AA
T: (01424) 433331
F: (01424) 433331
E: wendy@sherwoodhastings.co.uk
I: www.sherwoodhastings.co.uk

The Windsor Hotel ♦♦♦
9 Warrior Square, St Leonards-on-Sea, St Leonards, Hastings TN37 6BA
T: (01424) 422709
F: (01424) 422709

ST MARY IN THE MARSH
Kent

Star Inn ♦♦♦
St Mary in the Marsh, Romney Marsh TN29 0BX
T: (01797) 362139
E: marc@star-inn-the-marsh.co.uk
I: www.star-inn-the-marsh.co.uk

ST MICHAELS
Kent

Whitelands Farm ♦♦♦♦
Grange Road, St Michaels, Tenterden TN30 6TJ
T: (01580) 765971
E: whitelandsfarm@tinyonline.co.uk

SALTDEAN
East Sussex

Grand Ocean Hotel ♦♦♦
Longridge Avenue, Saltdean, Brighton BN2 8RP
T: (01273) 302291
F: (01273) 304255
I: www.grandhotelgroup.co.uk

SANDFORD
Isle of Wight

The Barn ♦♦♦♦
Pound Farm, Shanklin Road, Sandford, Ventnor PO38 3AW
T: (01983) 840047
F: (01983) 840047
E: barnpoundfarm@barnpoundfarm.free-online.co.uk

SANDGATE
Kent

Number Three ♦♦♦
3 Wellington Terrace, The Esplanade, Sandgate, Folkestone CT20 3DY
T: (01303) 220543
F: (01303) 220543
E: coast@zoo.co.uk

Royal Norfolk Hotel ♦♦
7 Sandgate High Street, Sandgate, Folkestone CT20 3BD
T: (01303) 248262
F: (01303) 248262
E: coasthosts@cwctv.net
I: www.southcoastholiday.co.uk/hotel

SANDHURST
Kent

Hope Barn ♦♦♦♦
Crouch Lane, Sandhurst, Cranbrook TN18 5PD
T: (01580) 850689
F: (01580) 850689
I: www.hopebarn.co.uk

SANDLEHEATH
Hampshire

Sandleheath Post Office & Stores ♦♦♦
Sandleheath, Fordingbridge SP6 1PP
T: (01425) 652230
F: (01425) 652230
E: sue@sandleheath.com
I: www.sandleheath.com

SANDOWN
Isle of Wight

The Belgrave Hotel ♦♦
14-16 Beachfield Road, Sandown PO36 8NA
T: (01983) 404550
F: (01983) 407257

Belmore Private Hotel ♦♦♦
101 Station Avenue, Sandown PO36 8HD
T: (01983) 404189
F: (01983) 405942
E: lowbelmore@talk21.com
I: www.islandbreaks.co.uk/belmore

Cavalier Guest House ♦♦♦♦
9 Carter Street, Sandown PO36 8BL
T: (01983) 403269

Denewood Hotel ♦♦♦♦
7 Victoria Road, Sandown PO36 8AL
T: (01983) 402980
F: (01983) 402980
E: holidays@denewoodhotel.co.uk
I: www.denewood-hotel.co.uk

Heathfield House Hotel ♦♦♦
52 Melville Street, Sandown PO36 8LF
T: (01983) 400002
F: (01983) 400002
E: mail@heathfieldhousehotel.com
I: www.heathfieldhousehotel.com

Homeland Private Hotel ♦♦♦
38 Grove Road, Sandown PO36 8HH
T: (01983) 404305

Inglewood Guest House ♦♦♦
15 Avenue Road, Sandown PO36 8BN
T: (01983) 403485
E: inglewood@yahoo.co.uk

Lanowlee ♦♦♦
99 Station Avenue, Sandown PO36 8HD
T: (01983) 403577

Lyndhurst Hotel ♦♦♦
8 Royal Crescent, Sandown PO36 8LZ
T: (01983) 403663
F: (01983) 403663

The Montpelier ♦♦♦
Pier Street, Sandown PO36 8JR
T: (01983) 403964
F: (07092) 212734
E: enquiries@themontpelier.co.uk
I: www.themontpelier.co.uk

Rooftree Hotel ♦♦♦♦
26 Broadway, Sandown PO36 9BY
T: (01983) 403175
F: (01983) 407354
E: rooftree@netguides.co.uk
I: www.rooftree@netguides.co.uk

St Catherines Hotel ♦♦♦♦
1 Winchester Park Road, Sandown PO36 8HJ
T: (01983) 402392
F: (01983) 402392
E: stcathhotel@hotmail.com
I: www.isleofwight-holidays.co.uk

St Michaels Hotel ♦♦♦♦
33 Leed Street, Sandown PO36 8JE
T: (01983) 403636

Sandhill Hotel ♦♦♦
6 Hill Street, Sandown PO36 9DB
T: (01983) 403635
F: (01983) 403695
E: sandhill@btconnect.com
I: www.sandhill-hotel.com

Shachri ♦♦♦
31Avenue Road, Sandown PO36 8BN
T: (01983) 405718

Westfield Hotel ♦♦♦♦
17 Broadway, Sandown PO36 9BY
T: (01983) 403802
F: (01983) 406404

SANDWICH
Kent

Durlock Lodge ♦♦♦
Durlock, Minster-in-Thanet, Ramsgate CT12 4HD
T: (01843) 821219
E: david@durlocklodge.co.uk
I: www.durlocklodge.co.uk

Fleur De Lis Hotel Inn & Restaurant ♦♦♦
6-8 Delf Street, Sandwich CT13 9BZ
T: (01304) 611131
F: (01304) 611199
E: thefleur@verinitaverns.co.uk
I: www.verinitaverns.co.uk

SARRE
Kent

Crown Inn (The Famous Cherry Brandy House) ♦♦♦♦
Court Street, Sarre, Birchington ME13 7AX
T: (01843) 847808
F: (01843) 847914
E: crown@shepherd-neame.co.uk
I: www.shepherd-neame.co.uk

SAUNDERTON
Buckinghamshire

Hunters Gate ♦♦♦
Deanfield, Saunderton, High Wycombe HP14 4JR
T: (01494) 481718
E: dadykes@attglobal.net
I: www.huntersgatebandb.co.uk

SEAFORD
East Sussex

Copperfields ♦♦♦♦
12 Connaught Road, Seaford BN25 2PU
T: (01323) 492152
F: (01323) 872311
E: sally.green@btinternet.com

Cornerways ♦♦♦
10 The Covers, Seaford BN25 1DF
T: (01323) 492400

Holmes Lodge ♦♦♦
72 Claremont Road, Seaford BN25 2BJ
T: (01323) 898331
F: (01323) 491346
E: holmes.lodge@freemail.co.uk
I: www.seaford.co.uk/holmes/holmes.htm

Malvern House ♦♦♦
Alfriston Road, Seaford BN25 3QG
T: (01323) 492058
F: (01323) 492000
E: MalvernBandB@aol.com
I: www.seaford.co.uk/malvern/

The Silverdale ♦♦♦♦
21 Sutton Park Road, Seaford BN25 1RH
T: (01323) 491849
F: (01323) 891131
E: silverdale@mistral.co.uk
I: www.mistral.co.uk/silverdale/silver.htm

Tudor Manor Hotel ♦♦♦♦ SILVER AWARD
Eastbourne Road, Seaford BN25 4DB
T: (01323) 896006
F: (01323) 892477
E: tudormanortl@aol.com
I: www.tudormanor.co.uk

SEAVIEW
Isle of Wight

1 Cluniac Cottages ♦♦♦♦
Priory Road, Seaview PO34 5BU
T: (01983) 812119
E: bill.elfenjay@virgin.net

Maple Villa ♦♦♦
Oakhill Road, Seaview PO34 5AP
T: (01983) 614826
E: mail@maplevilla.co.uk
I: www.maplevilla.co.uk

SEDLESCOMBE
East Sussex

Lower Marley Farm ♦♦♦♦
New Road, Sedlescombe, Battle
TN33 0RG
T: (01424) 871416

SELBORNE
Hampshire

Coneycroft House ♦♦♦♦
Selborne, Alton GU34 3JF
T: (01420) 511296
F: (01420) 511184
E: derek.edwards@ukonline.co.uk

8 Goslings Croft ♦♦♦♦
Selborne, Alton GU34 3HZ
T: (01420) 511285
F: (01420) 587451
E: timothyrouse@hotmail.com

Ivanhoe ♦♦♦♦
Oakhanger, Selborne, Alton
GU35 9JG
T: (01420) 473464

The Queen's & The Limes ♦♦♦
High Street, Selborne, Alton
GU34 3JJ
T: (01420) 511454
F: (01420) 511272
E: enquiries@queens-selborne.co.uk
I: www.queens-selborne.co.uk

Seale Cottage ♦♦♦
Gracious Street, Selborne, Alton
GU34 3JE
T: (01420) 511396
E: cw.gibson@virgin.net

SELSEY
West Sussex

Compass House ♦♦♦♦
18 Beacon Drive, Selsey,
Chichester PO20 0TW
T: (01243) 601439
F: (01243) 601439
E: sue.trotman@amserve.net

The Cornerways ♦♦♦♦
73 Hillfield Road, Selsey,
Chichester PO20 0LF
T: (01243) 605859

Greenacre ♦♦♦♦
5 Manor Farm Court, Selsey,
Chichester PO20 0LY
T: (01243) 602912
E: greenacre@zoom.co.uk

Ivy House B & B ♦♦♦♦
71 Hillfield Road, Selsey,
Chichester PO20 0LF
T: (01243) 601444
F: (01243) 603806
E: ivyhousebb@hotmail.com
I: www.smoothhound.co.uk/hotels/ivyhousebandb.himl

The Lodge ♦♦♦♦
21a Clayton Road, Selsey,
Chichester PO20 9DB
T: (01243) 601217
F: (01243) 605282
E: m.valmas@freenet.co.uk

Norton Lea ♦♦♦
Chichester Road, Selsey,
Chichester PO20 9EA
T: (01243) 605454
F: (01243) 605456
E: 100013.3142@compuserve.com

St Andrews Lodge ♦♦♦♦
Chichester Road, Selsey,
Chichester PO20 0LX
T: (01243) 606899
F: (01243) 607826
E: info@standrewslodge.co.uk
I: www.standrewslodge.co.uk

SEND
Surrey

Sommerhay Barn ♦♦♦♦
Church Lane, Send, Woking
GU23 7JL
T: (01483) 210107
E: angey_watson@hotmail.com

SEVENOAKS
Kent

Beechcombe ♦♦♦♦
4 Vine Lodge Court, Holly Bush
Lane, Sevenoaks TN13 3XY
T: (01732) 741643
F: (01732) 741643
E: anthonytait@hotmail.com

Burley Lodge ♦♦♦
Rockdale Road, Sevenoaks
TN13 1JT
T: (01732) 455761
F: (01732) 458178
E: dilatter@aol.com

Crofters ♦♦♦♦
67 Oakhill Road, Sevenoaks
TN13 1NU
T: (01732) 460189
F: (01732) 460189
E: ritamarfry@talk21.com

Double Dance ♦♦♦♦
Bates Hill/Tonbridge Road,
Ightham, Sevenoaks TN15 9AT
T: (01732) 884198
F: (01732) 780363
E: pacracknell@talk21.com
I: www.doubledance.co.uk

56 The Drive ♦♦♦
Sevenoaks TN13 3AF
T: (01732) 453236
E: jwlloydsks@aol.com

Garden House ♦♦♦♦
Solefields Road, Sevenoaks
TN13 1PJ
T: (01732) 457225

Hornshaw House ♦♦♦♦
47 Mount Harry Road,
Sevenoaks TN13 3JN
T: (01732) 465262
E: embates@hornshaw47.freeserve.co.uk
I: www.hornshaw-house.co.uk

The Moorings Hotel ♦♦♦
97 Hitchen Hatch Lane,
Sevenoaks TN13 3BE
T: (01732) 452589
F: (01732) 456462
E: moorings-hotel@btconnect.com
I: www.mooringshotel.co.uk

The Old Police House ♦♦♦♦
18 Shenden Way, Sevenoaks
TN13 1SE
T: (01732) 457150
F: (01732) 457150

Old Timbertop Cottage ♦♦♦♦
Bethel Road, Sevenoaks
TN13 3UE
T: (01732) 460506
F: (01732) 464484
E: anthony@ruddassociates.ndo.co.uk

The Pightle ♦♦♦♦
21 White Hart Wood, Sevenoaks
TN13 1RS
T: (01732) 451678
F: (01732) 464905
E: miketessa@pightle21.fsnet.co.uk or emtess@ontel.net.uk
I: www.pightle21.fsnet.co.uk

Robann ♦♦♦
5 Vestry Cottages, Old Otford
Road, Sevenoaks TN14 5EH
T: (01732) 456272

40 Robyns Way ♦♦♦
Sevenoaks TN13 3EB
T: (01732) 452401
E: ingram7oaks@onetel.net.uk

Welford ♦♦♦
6 Crownfields, Sevenoaks
TN13 1EE
T: (01732) 452689
F: (01732) 452689
E: rcjollye@aol.com

Wendy Wood ♦♦♦♦
86 Childsbridge Lane, Seal,
Sevenoaks TN15 0BW
T: (01732) 763755
E: wendywood@freeuk.com
I: www.wendywood.co.uk

SHAFTESBURY
Dorset

Aysgarth
♦♦♦♦ SILVER AWARD
Back Street, East Stour,
Gillingham SP8 5JY
T: (01747) 838351
E: aysgarth@lineone.net
I: website.lineone.net/~aysgarth

Beechmead ♦♦
Stour Row, Shaftesbury SP7 0QF
T: (01747) 838405

Cliff House
♦♦♦♦♦ SILVER AWARD
Breach Lane, Shaftesbury
SP7 8LF
T: (01747) 852548
F: (01747) 852548
E: dianaepow@aol.com
I: www.cliff-house.co.uk

3 Ivy Cross ♦♦♦
Shaftesbury SP7 8DW
T: (01747) 853837
E: stiktone@aol.com
I: www.3ivycross.co.uk

Ivy Cross House ♦♦♦
1 Ivy Cross, Shaftesbury
SP7 8DW
T: (01747) 850005
E: ivycrosshouse@aol.com
I: www.ivycrosshouse.com

The Kings Arms Inn ♦♦♦♦
East Stour Common, East Stour,
Gillingham SP8 5NB
T: (01747) 838325
E: jenny@kings-arms.fsnet.co.uk

The Knoll
♦♦♦♦ SILVER AWARD
Bleke Street, Shaftesbury
SP7 8AH
T: (01747) 855243
E: pickshaftesbury@compuserve.com
I: www.pick-art.org.uk

Maple Lodge
Rating Applied For
Christy's Lane, Shaftesbury
SP7 8DL
T: (01747) 853945

The Retreat ♦♦♦♦
47 Bell Street, Shaftesbury
SP7 8AE
T: (01747) 850372
F: (01747) 850372
E: at.retreat@virgin.net
I: www.the-retreat.org.uk

St James B&B ♦♦♦
6 St James Street, Shaftesbury
SP7 8HA
T: (01747) 853830
E: celloyd@onetel.net.uk

SHALFLEET
Isle of Wight

Hebberdens ♦♦♦
Yarmouth Road, Shalfleet,
Newport PO30 4NB
T: (01983) 531364
F: (01983) 531364
I: www.hebberdens.com

The Old Malthouse ♦♦
1 Mill Road, Shalfleet, Newport
PO30 4NE
T: (01983) 531329
E: b&b@oldmalthouse.demon.co.uk

SHALFORD
Surrey

2 Northfield ♦♦♦
Off Summersbury Drive,
Shalford, Guildford GU4 8JN
T: (01483) 570431
E: tonymorden@freeuk.com

SHALSTONE
Buckinghamshire

Barnita ♦♦♦
Shalstone, Buckingham
MK18 5DZ
T: (01280) 850639

SHANKLIN
Isle of Wight

Appley Private Hotel ♦♦♦♦
13 Queens Road, Shanklin
PO37 6AW
T: (01983) 862666
F: (01983) 863895
E: appley.htl@lineone.net
I: www.appleyhotel.co.uk

Atholl Court ♦♦♦
1 Atherley Road, Shanklin
PO37 7AT
T: (01983) 862414
F: (01983) 868985
E: info@atholl-court.co.uk
I: www.atholl-court.co.uk

Birkdale Hotel ♦♦♦♦
5 Grange Road, Shanklin
PO37 6NN
T: (01983) 862949
E: katetuppen@hotel.com
I: www.birkdalehotel.com

Brooke House Hotel ♦♦♦
2 St Pauls Avenue, Shanklin
PO37 7AL
T: (01983) 863162
E: mike@brookehouse.fsnet.co.uk
I: www.brookehouse.fsnet.co.uk

Cedar Lodge Hotel ♦♦♦♦
28 Arthurs Hill, Shanklin
PO37 6EX
T: (01983) 863268
F: (01983) 863268

Chestnuts Hotel ♦♦♦
Hope Road, Shanklin PO37 6EA
T: (01983) 862162
F: (01983) 862162

Claremont Guest House ♦♦♦♦
4 East Mount Road, Shanklin
PO37 6DN
T: (01983) 862083

Clifton Hotel ♦♦♦
1 Queens Road, Shanklin
PO37 6AN
T: (01983) 863015
F: (01983) 865911
E: info@cliftonhotel-shanklin.co.uk
I: www.cliftonhotel-shanklin.co.uk

Cliftonville Hotel ♦♦♦
6 Hope Road, Shanklin
PO37 6EA
T: (01983) 862197
F: (01983) 862197
E: cliftonvillehotel@talk21.com

Courtlands Hotel ♦♦♦
15 Paddock Road, Shanklin
PO37 6PA
T: (01983) 862167
F: (01983) 863308
E: simon@courtlandshotel.co.uk
I: www.courtlandshotel.co.uk

Culham Lodge Hotel ♦♦♦♦
31 Landguard Manor Road, Shanklin PO37 7HZ
T: (01983) 862880
F: (01983) 862880
E: metcalf@culham99.freeserve.co.uk
I: www.isleofwight-hotel.biz

The Edgecliffe Hotel ♦♦♦♦
7 Clarence Gardens, Shanklin
PO37 6HA
T: (01983) 866199
F: (01983) 868841
E: edgecliffehtl@aol.com
I: www.wightonline.co.uk/edgecliffehotel

Esplanade Hotel ♦♦♦
33 The Esplanade, Shanklin
PO37 6BG
T: (01983) 863001
F: (01983) 863001

Farringford Hotel ♦♦♦♦
19 Hope Road, Shanklin
PO37 6EA
T: (01983) 862176
E: farringford@excite.com
I: www.farringfordhotel.com

Fawley Guest House ♦♦♦
12 Hope Road, Shanklin
PO37 6EA
T: (01983) 868898
E: enquiries@the-fawley.co.uk
I: www.the-fawley.co.uk

Foxhills
♦♦♦♦♦ GOLD AWARD
30 Victoria Avenue, Shanklin
PO37 6LS
T: (01983) 862329
F: (01983) 866666
E: info@foxhillshotel.co.uk
I: www.foxhillshotel.co.uk

The Glen Hotel ♦♦♦
4 Avenue Road, Shanklin
PO37 7BG
T: (01983) 862154
E: theglenshanklin@totalise.co.uk

Grange Bank Hotel ♦♦♦♦
Grange Road, Shanklin
PO37 6NN
T: (01983) 862337
F: (01983) 862737
E: Grangebankhotel@aol.com
I: www.grangebank.co.uk

The Havelock Hotel
♦♦♦♦ SILVER AWARD
2 Queens Road, Shanklin
PO37 6AN
T: (01983) 862747

Hazelwood Hotel ♦♦♦
14 Clarence Road, Shanklin
PO37 7BH
T: (01983) 862824
F: (01983) 862824
E: barbara.tubbs@thehazelwood.free-online.co.uk
I: www.thehazelwood.free-online.co.uk

Hope Lodge Hotel
♦♦♦♦ GOLD AWARD
21 Hope Road, Shanklin
PO37 6EA
T: (01983) 863140
F: (01983) 863140
E: janetwf@aol.com
I: www.wight365.com/dart/hopelodge/index.htm

Kenbury Hotel ♦♦♦♦
Clarence Road, Shanklin
PO37 7BH
T: (01983) 862085
E: kenbury@isleofwighthotel.co.uk
I: www.isleofwighthotel.co.uk

The Lincoln Hotel ♦♦♦♦
30 Littlestairs Road, Shanklin
PO37 6HS
T: (01983) 861171
F: (01983) 861171
E: enquiries@thelincolnhotel.org.uk
I: www.thelincolnhotel.org.uk

Miclaran Hotel ♦♦♦
37 Littlestairs Road, Shanklin
PO37 6HS
T: (01983) 862726
F: (01983) 862726

Mount House Hotel ♦♦♦
20 Arthurs Hill, Shanklin
PO37 6EE
T: (01983) 862556
F: (01983) 867551
E: graham.mounthouse@btinternet.com
I: www.netguides.co.uk/wight/mount.html

Overstrand Hotel ♦♦♦♦
5 Howard Road, Shanklin
PO37 6HD
T: (01983) 862100
F: (01983) 862100

Palmerston Hotel ♦♦♦
Palmerston Road, Shanklin
PO37 6AS
T: (01983) 865547
F: (01983) 868008
E: info@palmerston-hotel.co.uk
I: www.palmerston-hotel.co.uk

Parkway Hotel ♦♦♦
6 Park Road, Shanklin PO37 6AZ
T: (01983) 862740
E: malcolm@parkwayhotel.flyer.co.uk
I: www.parkwayhotel.flyer.co.uk

Pink Beach Hotel ♦♦♦
20 The Esplanade, Shanklin
PO37 6BN
T: (01983) 862501
E: pinkbeach@btopenworld.com
I: www.pink-beach-hotel.co.uk

The Roseglen Hotel ♦♦♦♦
12 Palmerston Road, Shanklin
PO37 6AS
T: (01983) 863164
F: (01983) 862271
E: david@roseglen.co.uk
I: www.roseglen.co.uk

The Royson ♦♦♦♦
26 Littlestairs Road, Shanklin
PO37 6HS
T: (01983) 862163
F: (01983) 865403
E: theroyson@lineone.net
I: www.theroyson.co.uk

Rozelle Hotel ♦♦♦
Atherley Road, Shanklin
PO37 7AT
T: (01983) 862745
F: (01983) 862745
E: rozelle@fsmail.net

Ryedale Private Hotel ♦♦♦
3 Atherley Road, Shanklin
PO37 7AT
T: (01983) 862375
E: hayley@ryedale-hotel.co.uk
I: www.ryedale-hotel.co.uk

St Leonards Hotel
♦♦♦♦ SILVER AWARD
22 Queens Road, Shanklin
PO37 6AW
T: (01983) 862121
F: (01983) 868895
E: info@wight-breaks.co.uk
I: www.wight-breaks.co.uk

Somerville ♦♦♦
14 St Georges Road, Shanklin
PO37 6BA
T: (01983) 862821
E: billyfiona@fsmail.net

The Steamer Inn ♦♦♦
18 The Esplanade, Shanklin
PO37 6BS
T: (01983) 862641
F: (01983) 862741

Suncliffe Hotel ♦♦♦
8 Hope Road, Shanklin
PO37 6EA
T: (01983) 863009
E: suncliffe@whsmithnet.co.uk
I: www.suncliffe.co.uk

Swiss Cottage Hotel ♦♦♦
St Georges Road, Shanklin
PO37 6BA
T: (01983) 862333
E: mail@swisscottagehotel.fsnet.co.uk

The Triton Hotel ♦♦♦
23 Atherley Road, Shanklin
PO37 7AU
T: (01983) 862494
F: (01983) 861281
E: jackie@tritonhotel.freeserve.co.uk
I: www.iow-accommodation.com

Westbury Lodge Hotel ♦♦♦
25 Queens Road, Shanklin
PO37 6AW
T: (01983) 864926
F: (01983) 864926
E: enq@westburylodge.co.uk

Willow Bank Hotel ♦♦♦♦
36 Atherley Road, Shanklin
PO37 7AU
T: (01983) 862482
F: (01983) 862486
E: willowbank.hotel@virgin.net
I: www.wightonline.co.uk/willowbank/index.html

SHARPTHORNE
West Sussex

Coach House ♦♦♦
Courtlands, Chilling Street, Sharpthorne, East Grinstead
RH19 4JF
T: (01342) 810512
F: (01342) 810512
E: tm@mmarshell.vispa.com
I: www.visitsussex.org/coachhousesharpthorne

Saxons ♦♦♦♦
Horsted Lane, Sharpthorne, East Grinstead RH19 4HY
T: (01342) 810821
E: aliexcol@aol.com

SHAWFORD
Hampshire

Greenmead Cottage
♦♦♦♦ SILVER AWARD
Fairfield Road, Shawford, Winchester SO21 2DA
T: (01962) 713172
F: (01962) 711903
E: junetice@amserve.net

Orchard House ♦♦♦
Manor Road, Twyford, Winchester SO21 1RJ
T: (01962) 712087
F: (01962) 712087
E: susan@smflemons.fsnet.co.uk

SHEERNESS
Kent

The Ferry House Inn
Rating Applied For
Harty Ferry Road, Harty, Sheerness ME12 4BQ
T: (01795) 510214
F: (01795) 511529

Kingsferry House Bed and Breakfast ♦♦
247 Queenborough Road, Halfway, Sheerness ME12 3EW
T: (01795) 663606

Sheppey Guest House ♦
214 Queenborough Road, Minster on Sea, Sheerness
ME12 3DF
T: (01795) 665950
F: (01795) 661200
E: sophie@allen3877.fsbusiness.co.uk

SHENINGTON
Oxfordshire

The Bell ♦♦
Shenington, Banbury OX15 6NQ
T: (01295) 670274
E: thebell@shenington.freeserve.co.uk

Sugarswell Farm ♦♦♦♦
Shenington, Banbury OX15 6HW
T: (01295) 680512
F: (01295) 688149

Top Farm House ♦♦♦
Shenington, Banbury OX15 6LZ
T: (01295) 670226
F: (01295) 678170
E: info@topfarmhouse.co.uk
I: www.topfarmhouse.co.uk

SHENLEY CHURCH END
Buckinghamshire

The Malt House
Rating Applied For
Oakhill Road, Shenley Church End, Milton Keynes MK5 6AE
T: (01908) 501619

3 Selby Grove ♦♦♦♦
Shenley Church End, Milton Keynes MK5 6BN
T: (01908) 504663
E: ceyesmk@aol.com

SHEPPERTON
Surrey

Splash Cottage ♦♦♦
91 Watersplash Road, Shepperton TW17 0EE
T: (01932) 229987
F: (01932) 229987
E: info@lazy-river.co.uk
I: www.lazy-river.co.uk

SHERBORNE ST JOHN
Hampshire

Fairfield ♦♦♦♦
16 Aldermaston Road, Sherborne St John, Basingstoke RG24 9JY
T: (01256) 850308
F: (01256) 889663
E: jackie_elsley@hotmail.com
I: www.fairfields.org.uk

Manor Farm Stables ♦♦♦♦
Vyne Road, Sherborne St John, Tadley RG24 9HX
T: (01256) 851324
F: (01256) 855006

SHERE
Surrey

Cherry Trees ♦♦♦♦
Gomshall Lane, Shere, Guildford GU5 9HE
T: (01483) 202288

SHILLINGFORD
Oxfordshire

The Kingfisher Inn ♦♦♦♦
27 Henley Road, Shillingford, Wallingford OX10 7EL
T: (01865) 858595
F: (01865) 858286
E: enquiries@kingfisher-inn.co.uk
I: www.kingfisher-inn.co.uk

Marsh House ♦♦♦
7 Court Drive, Shillingford, Wallingford OX10 7ER
T: (01865) 858496
F: (01865) 858496
E: marsh.house@talk21.com

SHILLINGSTONE
Dorset

September Cottage
Rating Applied For
Cookswell, Shillingstone, Blandford Forum DT11 0QZ
T: (01258) 861588

SHIPLEY
West Sussex

Goffsland Farm ♦♦♦♦
Shipley, Horsham RH13 9BQ
T: (01403) 730434
F: (01403) 730434

SHIPPON
Oxfordshire

The White House ♦♦
Faringdon Road, Shippon, Abingdon OX13 6LW
T: (01235) 521998
F: (01235) 554796

SHIPTON-UNDER-WYCHWOOD
Oxfordshire

Court Farm
♦♦♦♦ SILVER AWARD
Mawles Lane, Shipton-under-Wychwood, Oxford OX7 6DA
T: (01993) 831515
F: (01993) 831813
E: belinda@courtfarmbb.fsnet.co.uk

Courtlands B&B ♦♦♦♦
6 Courtlands Road, Shipton-under-Wychwood, Oxford OX7 6DF
T: (01993) 830551
E: j-jfletcher@which.net
I: www.cotswoldsbandb.com

Garden Cottage ♦♦♦
Fiddlers Hill, Shipton-under-Wychwood, Oxford OX7 6DR
T: (01993) 830640
E: charmian@ukgateway.net

Lodge Cottage ♦♦♦
Shipton-under-Wychwood, Oxford OX7 6DG
T: (01993) 830811
F: (01993) 830811
E: h.a.savill@btopenworld.com

SHIRRELL HEATH
Hampshire

Highdown ♦♦♦♦
Twynhams Hill, Shirrell Heath, Southampton SO32 2JL
T: (01329) 835876
F: (01329) 835876
E: highdown2000@hotmail.com
I: www.highdown.net

SHOLDEN
Kent

The Sportsman
♦♦♦♦ GOLD AWARD
23 The Street, Sholden, Deal CT14 0AL
T: (01304) 374973
F: (01304) 374973

SHOREHAM
Kent

Church House
♦♦♦♦ SILVER AWARD
Church Street, Shoreham, Sevenoaks TN14 7SB
T: (01959) 522241
F: (01959) 522241
E: katehowie@compuserve.com
I: www.intacom.co.uk/shore/churchouse.htm

Preston Farmhouse ♦♦♦♦
Preston Farm, Shoreham, Sevenoaks TN14 7UD
T: (01959) 522029

SHORWELL
Isle of Wight

Northcourt
♦♦♦♦ SILVER AWARD
Main Road, Shorwell, Newport PO30 3JG
T: (01983) 740415
F: (01983) 740409
E: john@northcourt.info
I: www.northcourt.info

Westcourt Farm ♦♦♦♦
Limerstone Road, Shorwell, Newport PO30 3LA
T: (01983) 740233
E: julie@westcourt-farm.co.uk
I: www.westcourt-farm.co.uk

SHROTON
Dorset

The Cricketers
♦♦♦♦♦ SILVER AWARD
Main Street, Shroton, Blandford Forum DT11 8QD
T: (01258) 860421
F: (01258) 861800
E: the_cricketers@hotmail.com

SISSINGHURST
Kent

1 Hillview Cottage ♦♦♦
Starvenden Lane, Sissinghurst, Cranbrook TN17 2AN
T: (01580) 712823

Kings Head House ♦♦♦♦
The Street, Sissinghurst, Cranbrook TN17 2JE
T: (01580) 712612
F: (01580) 715353
E: duriepj@aol.com

SITTINGBOURNE
Kent

Scuttington Manor Guest House ♦♦♦♦
Dully Road, Dully, Sittingbourne ME9 9PA
T: (01795) 521316
F: (01795) 521316

Woodstock Guest House ♦♦♦♦
25 Woodstock Road, Sittingbourne ME10 4HJ
T: (01795) 421516
F: (01795) 421516
E: woodstockbnb@blueyonder.co.uk

SKIRMETT
Buckinghamshire

The Old Bakery ♦♦♦♦
Skirmett, Henley-on-Thames RG9 6TD
T: (01491) 638309
F: (01491) 638086
E: lizroach@euphony.net

SLINFOLD
West Sussex

The Red Lyon ♦♦♦
The Street, Slinfold, Horsham RH13 0RR
T: (01403) 790339
F: (01403) 791863
E: enquiries@theredlyon.co.uk
I: www.theredlyon.co.uk

Wendy's Cottage ♦♦♦
Five Oaks Road, Slinfold, Horsham RH13 7RQ
T: (01403) 782326
F: (01403) 782326

SMARDEN
Kent

Chequers Inn ♦♦♦♦
The Street, Smarden, Ashford TN27 8QA
T: (01233) 770217
F: (01233) 770623
I: www.thechequerssmarden.activehotels.co.uk

Hereford Oast ♦♦♦♦
Smarden, Ashford TN27 8PA
T: (01233) 770541
F: (01233) 770045
E: suzy@herefordoast.fsnet.co.uk

SONNING
Oxfordshire

The Bull Inn ♦♦♦
High Street, Sonning on Thames, Sonning, Reading RG4 6UP
T: (01189) 693901
F: (01189) 691057

SONNING COMMON
Oxfordshire

21 Red House Drive ♦♦♦
Sonning Common, Reading RG4 9NT
T: (0118) 972 2312
F: (0118) 972 2312

SOULDERN
Oxfordshire

The Fox Inn ♦♦
Fox Lane, Souldern, Bicester OX27 7JW
T: (01869) 345284
F: (01869) 345667

Tower Fields ♦♦♦
Tusmore Road, Souldern, Bicester OX27 7HY
T: (01869) 346554
F: (01869) 345157
E: hgould@strayduck.com
I: www.towerfields.com

SOUTH GORLEY
Hampshire

Hucklesbrook Farm
♦♦♦♦ SILVER AWARD
Ringwood Road, South Gorley, Fordingbridge SP6 2PN
T: (01425) 653180
E: dh.sampson@btinternet.com

SOUTHAMPTON
Hampshire

Abbey Lodge Guest House ♦♦♦
37 The Polygon, Southampton SO15 2BP
T: (023) 8022 1466

Alcantara Guest House ♦♦♦♦
20 Howard Road, Southampton SO15 5BN
T: (023) 8033 2966
F: (023) 8049 6163
E: alcantara@supanet.com
I: www.alcantaraguesthouse.co.uk

Argyle Lodge ♦♦♦
13 Landguard Road, Shirley, Southampton SO15 5DL
T: (023) 8022 4063
F: (023) 8033 3688
I: www.argylelodge.com

Ashelee Lodge ♦♦♦
36 Atherley Road, Shirley, Southampton SO15 5DQ
T: (023) 8022 2095
F: (023) 8022 2095

Banister House Hotel ♦♦♦
Banister Road, Southampton SO15 2JJ
T: (023) 8022 1279
F: (023) 8022 6551
E: banisterhotel@btconnect.com
I: www.banisterhotel.co.uk

The Bosun's Locker ♦♦
Castle Square, Upper Bugle Street, Southampton SO14 2EE
T: (02380) 333364
F: (02380) 333364

Brunswick Lodge ♦♦♦
100-104 Anglesea Road, Shirley, Southampton SO15 5QS
T: (02380) 774777
I: www.brunswicklodge.co.uk

Carmel Guest House ♦♦♦
306 Winchester Road, Shirley, Southampton SO16 6TU
T: (023) 8077 3579

Dormy House Hotel ♦♦♦♦
21 Barnes Lane, Sarisbury Green, Southampton SO31 7DA
T: (01489) 572626
F: (01489) 573370
E: dormyhousehotel@warsash.globalnet.co.uk
I: www.dormyhousehotel.net

Eaton Court Hotel ♦♦♦
32 Hill Lane, Southampton SO15 5AY
T: (023) 8022 3081
F: (023) 8032 2006
E: ecourthot@aol.com
I: www.eatoncourtsouthampton.co.uk

Ellenborough House ♦♦♦
172 Hill Lane, Southampton SO15 5DB
T: (023) 8022 1716
F: (023) 8034 8486

Fenland Guest House ♦♦♦
79 Hill Lane, Southampton SO15 5AD
T: (023) 8022 0360
E: fenlandguesthouse@ntlworld.com

Linden Guest House ♦♦♦
51-53 The Polygon, Southampton SO15 2BP
T: (023) 8022 5653
F: (023) 8063 0808

The Lodge ♦♦♦
No 1 Winn Road, The Avenue, Southampton SO17 1EH
T: (023) 8055 7537
F: (023) 8055 3586
E: lodgehotel@faxvia.net
I: www.yell.co.uk/siteslodgeso17

Madison House ♦♦♦
137 Hill Lane, Southampton SO15 5AF
T: (023) 8033 3374
F: (023) 8033 1209
E: foley@madisonhouse.co.uk
I: www.madisonhouse.co.uk

The Mayfair Guest House ♦♦♦♦ SILVER AWARD
11 Landguard Road, Southampton SO15 5DL
T: (023) 8022 9861
F: (023) 8021 1552

Mayview Guest House ♦♦♦
30 The Polygon, Southampton SO15 2BN
T: (023) 8022 0907
F: (07977) 017921
E: mayview@yahoo.co.uk

Primrose Cottage ♦♦♦
Allington Lane, West End, Southampton SO30 3HQ
T: (023) 8046 6348
F: (023) 8046 6348

Rivendell ♦♦♦
19 Landguard Road, Shirley, Southampton SO15 5DL
T: (02380) 223240
E: rivendellbb@amserve.net

The Spinnaker ♦♦♦♦
Bridge Road, Lower Swanwick, Southampton SO31 7EB
T: (01489) 572123
F: (01489) 577394

SOUTHBOURNE
Dorset

Hawkesmore Hotel ♦♦♦
Pine Avenue, Southbourne, Bournemouth BH6 3ST
T: (01202) 426787

Newpoint Hotel ♦♦♦♦
25 Pinecliffe Avenue, Southbourne, Bournemouth BH6 3PY
T: (01202) 425047

Shearwater Hotel ♦♦♦
61 Grand Avenue, Southbourne, Bournemouth BH6 3TA
T: (01202) 423396
E: enquiry@theshearwater.freeserve.co.uk
I: www.theshearwater.freeserve.co.uk

Sherbourne House Hotel ♦♦♦♦
14 Southern Road, Southbourne, Bournemouth BH6 3SR
T: (01202) 425680
F: (01202) 257423
E: ian@sherbournehousehotel.co.uk
I: www.sherbournehousehotel.co.uk

Sun Haven Guest House ♦♦♦
39 Southern Road, Southbourne, Bournemouth BH6 3SS
T: (01202) 427560

SOUTHWATER
West Sussex

Meadow House ♦♦♦
Church Lane/Bonfire Hill, Southwater, Horsham RH13 9BT
T: (01403) 730324
F: (01403) 730324

ST-MARGARETS-AT-CLIFFE
Kent

Holm Oaks ♦♦♦♦
Dover Road, St-Margarets-at-Cliffe, Dover CT15 6EP
T: (01304) 852990
F: (01304) 853433
E: holmoaks@hotmail.com

Merzenich Guest House ♦♦♦
Station Road, St-Margarets-at-Cliffe, Dover CT15 6AY
T: (01304) 852260
F: (01304) 852167
E: robclaringbould@lineone.net
I: www.smoothhound.co.uk/hotels/merzen.html

STANDLAKE
Oxfordshire

Pinkhill Cottage ♦♦♦♦ SILVER AWARD
45 Rack End, Standlake, Witney OX29 7SA
T: (01865) 300544
E: pinkhill@madasafish.com

STANFORD DINGLEY
West Berkshire

The Bull Country Inn ♦♦♦♦
Stanford Dingley, Reading RG7 6LS
T: (0118) 974 4409
F: (0118) 974 5249
E: admin@thebullatstanforddingley.co.uk
I: www.thebullatstanforddingley.co.uk

STANFORD IN THE VALE
Oxfordshire

Stanford Park House ♦♦♦
Park Lane, Stanford in the Vale, Faringdon SN7 8PF
T: (01367) 710702
F: (01367) 710329
E: gjd34@dial.pipex.com
I: www.stanfordpark.co.uk

STANSTED
Kent

The Black Horse ♦♦♦♦
Tumblefield Road, Stansted, Sevenoaks TN15 7PR
T: (01732) 822355
F: (01732) 824415

STANTON ST JOHN
Oxfordshire

The Talkhouse ♦♦♦
Wheatley Road, Stanton St John, Oxford OX33 1EX
T: (01865) 351648
F: (01865) 351085

STAPLEHURST
Kent

Overbridge Barn ♦♦♦♦
Marden Road, Staplehurst, Tonbridge TN12 0JH
T: (01580) 890189
F: (01580) 893164
E: paula@overbridge.co.uk
I: www.overbridge.co.uk

The White Cottage ♦♦♦♦
Hawkenbury Road, Hawkenbury, Staplehurst, Tonbridge TN12 0DU
T: (01580) 892554
F: (01580) 891553
E: batten.j.@talk21.com

STEDHAM
West Sussex

Meadowhills ♦♦
Stedham, Midhurst GU29 0PT
T: (01730) 812609
I: www.meadowhills.co.uk

STEEP
Hampshire

Little Shackles Rating Applied For
Harrow Lane, Petersfield GU32 2BZ
T: (01730) 263464
F: (01730) 263464
E: martgriff@freenet.co.uk

STEEPLE
Dorset

Blackmanston Farm Rating Applied For
Steeple, Wareham BH20 5NZ
T: (01929) 480743
F: (01929) 480743

STEEPLE ASTON
Oxfordshire

Westfield Farm Motel ♦♦♦♦
Fenway, Steeple Aston, Oxford OX25 4SS
T: (01869) 340591
F: (01869) 347594
E: info@westfieldmotel.u-net.com
I: www.oxlink.co.uk/accom/westfield-farm/

STELLING MINNIS
Kent

Bower Farm House ♦♦♦♦ SILVER AWARD
Bossingham Road, Stelling Minnis, Canterbury CT4 6BB
T: (01227) 709430
E: anne@bowerbb.freeserve.co.uk
I: www.bowerfarmhouse.co.uk

Great Field Farm ♦♦♦♦ SILVER AWARD
Misling Lane, Stelling Minnis, Canterbury CT4 6DE
T: (01227) 709223
F: (01227) 709223
E: Greatfieldfarm@aol.com
I: www.great-field-farm.co.uk

STEVENTON
Oxfordshire

Bramble Grange ♦♦♦♦
Hanney Road, Steventon, Abingdon OX13 6AP
T: (01235) 834664
E: helen@mgmidgets.com

Home Farm House ♦♦♦
14-16 Milton Lane, Steventon, Abingdon OX13 6SA
T: (01235) 831333
F: (01235) 863035
E: melanie@miller-smithbandb.co.uk
I: www.miller-smithbandb.co.uk

Orchard House ♦♦♦
40 Castle Street, Steventon, Abingdon OX13 6SR
T: (01235) 821351
F: (01235) 863705
I: homepage.ntlworld.com/orchardhouse40

Tethers End ♦♦♦
Abingdon Road, Steventon, Abingdon OX13 6RW
T: (01235) 834015
F: (01235) 862990
E: peterdmiller@btinternet.com
I: www.millerbandb.co.uk

STEWKLEY
Buckinghamshire

Mount Pleasant Farm ♦♦♦
Stewkley, Leighton Buzzard LU7 0LU
T: (01525) 240451
F: (01525) 240163

Oak Tree Cottage ♦♦♦
6 Ivy Lane, Stewkley, Leighton Buzzard LU7 0EN
T: (01525) 242225
E: karalynsparkes@hotmail.com

STEYNING
West Sussex

Chequer Inn ♦♦♦
41 High Street, Steyning BN44 3RE
T: (01903) 814437
F: (01903) 879707
E: chequerinn@btinternet.com

STOCKBRIDGE
Hampshire

Carbery Guest House ♦♦♦
Salisbury Hill, Stockbridge
SO20 6EZ
T: (01264) 810771
F: (01264) 811022

The White Hart Inn ♦♦♦♦
High Street, Stockbridge
SO20 6HF
T: (01264) 810663
F: (01264) 810268

STOKENCHURCH
Buckinghamshire

Hallbottom Farm ♦♦♦♦
Park Lane, Stokenchurch, High Wycombe HP14 3TQ
T: (01494) 482520
E: deborah@hallbottomfarm.co.uk
I: www.hallbottomfarm.co.uk

STONE-IN-OXNEY
Kent

Tighe Farmhouse ♦♦♦♦
Stone-in-Oxney, Tenterden
TN30 7JU
T: (01233) 758251
F: (01233) 758054
I: www.ryetourism.co.uk

STONEGATE
East Sussex

Battenhurst Farm ♦♦♦
Stonegate, Wadhurst TN2 7DU
T: (01435) 882884
F: (01435) 883112

STONELEIGH
Surrey

Number Sixty Two ♦♦♦♦
62 Newbury Gardens,
Stoneleigh, Epsom KT19 0NX
T: (020) 8393 5227
F: (020) 8393 5885
E: info@number62.biz
I: www.number62.biz

STORRINGTON
West Sussex

Chardonnay ♦♦♦♦
Hampers Lane, Storrington,
Pulborough RH20 3HZ
T: (01903) 746688
E: annsearancke@bigfoot.com
I: www.sussexlive.co.uk

STOURTON CAUNDLE
Dorset

Golden Hill Cottage ♦♦♦♦
Stourton Caundle, Sturminster
Newton DT10 2JW
T: (01963) 362109
F: (01963) 364205
E: anna@goldenhillcottage.co.uk
I: www.goldenhillcottage.co.uk

STOWTING
Kent

Pine Hill ♦♦♦♦
Stowting, Ashford TN25 6BD
T: (01303) 863708
E: sarahjanem@msn.com

STRATTON AUDLEY
Oxfordshire

West Farm ♦♦♦♦
Launton Road, Stratton Audley,
Bicester OX27 9AS
T: (01869) 278344
F: (01869) 278344
E: richardsarahowson@hotmail.com
I: www.westfarmbb.co.uk

STREATLEY
Berkshire

Pennyfield
♦♦♦♦ SILVER AWARD
The Coombe, Streatley, Reading
RG8 9QT
T: (01491) 872048
F: (01491) 872048
E: mandrvanstone@hotmail.com
I: www.pennyfield.co.uk

STROOD
Kent

Redwood House ♦♦♦
84 Goddington Road, Strood,
Rochester ME2 3DE
T: (01634) 725880
F: (01034) 725880
E: junejmprior@aol.com

The Sundial ♦♦♦
18 Ranscombe Close, Strood,
Rochester ME2 2PB
T: (01634) 721831
E: sean@company8234.freeserve.co.uk

The White Cottage ♦♦♦
41 Rede Court Road, Strood,
Rochester ME2 3SP
T: (01634) 719988

STUDLAND
Dorset

The Bankes Arms Hotel ♦♦♦
Manor Road, Studland, Swanage
BH19 3AU
T: (01929) 450225
F: (01929) 450307

Fairfields Hotel ♦♦♦
Swanage Road, Studland,
Swanage BH19 3AE
T: (01929) 450224
F: (01929) 450571

Shell Bay Cottage ♦♦♦♦
Glebe Estate, Studland, Swanage
BH19 3AS
T: (01929) 450249
F: (01929) 450249

STURMINSTER NEWTON
Dorset

Hazeldean Bed & Breakfast ♦♦♦♦
Bath Road, Sturminster Newton
DT10 1DS
T: (01258) 472224
F: (01258) 472224
E: sarah_grounds@hotmail.com
I: www.hazeldeanbnb.co.uk

The Homestead ♦♦♦
Hole House Lane, off Glue Hill,
Sturminster Newton DT10 2AA
T: (01258) 471390
F: (01258) 471090
E: townsend@dircon.co.uk
I: www.townsend.dircon.co.uk

SULHAMSTEAD
Berkshire

The Old Manor
♦♦♦♦♦ SILVER AWARD
White House Green,
Sulhamstead, Reading RG7 4EA
T: (0118) 983 2423
F: (0118) 983 6262
E: rags-r@theoldmanor.fsbusiness.co.uk

SUNNINGDALE
Berkshire

Beaufort House ♦♦♦♦
Broomfield Park, Sunningdale,
Ascot SL5 0JT
T: (01344) 622991
F: (01344) 873705
E: beaufort.louse@btinternet.com

SUTTON AT HONE
Kent

Hamilton ♦♦♦
Arnolds Lane, Sutton at Hone,
Dartford DA4 9HE
T: (01322) 272535
F: (01322) 284856

SUTTON VALENCE
Kent

Sparks Oast Farm ♦♦♦
Forsham lane, Sutton Valence,
Maidstone ME17 3EW
T: (01622) 842213
E: smc@sparksoast-farm-kent.co.uk
I: www.kent-esite.co.uk/sparksoastfarm

SWANAGE
Dorset

Amberlea ♦♦♦♦
36 Victoria Avenue, Swanage
BH19 1AP
T: (01929) 426213
E: amberlea-swanage@yahoo.co.uk

Bella Vista Hotel ♦♦♦♦
Burlington Road, Swanage
BH19 1LS
T: (01929) 422873
E: mail@bellavista-hotel.com
I: www.bellavista-hotel.com

The Castleton Hotel ♦♦♦♦
1 Highcliffe Road, Swanage
BH19 1LW
T: (01929) 423972
F: (01929) 422901
E: castletonhotel@aol.com
I: www.swanagecastletonhotel.com

Caythorpe House ♦♦♦
7 Rempstone Road, Swanage
BH19 1DN
T: (01929) 422892

Clare House
Rating Applied For
1 Park Road, Swanage
BH19 2AA
T: (01929) 422855
F: (01929) 422855

Easter Cottage
♦♦♦♦ SILVER AWARD
9 Eldon Terrace, Swanage
BH19 1HA
T: (01929) 427782
F: (01929) 427782
E: daveanddiane@eastercottage.fsbusiness.co.uk
I: www.eastercottage.co.uk

Firswood ♦♦♦
29 Kings Road West, Swanage
BH19 1HF
T: (01929) 422306
E: firswood@aol.com
I: www.firswoodguesthouse.co.uk

Glenlee Hotel ♦♦♦♦
6 Cauldon Avenue, Swanage
BH19 1PQ
T: (01929) 425794
E: info@glenleehotel.co.uk
I: www.glenleehotel.co.uk

Goodwyns ♦♦♦♦
2 Walrond Road, Swanage
BH19 1PB
T: (01929) 421088

Heather Cottage ♦♦♦
1 Higher Gardens, Corfe Castle,
Wareham BH20 5ES
T: (01929) 480230

Horseshoe House Hotel ♦♦♦♦
9 Cliff Avenue, Swanage
BH19 1LX
T: (01929) 422194
E: horseshoehotel@aol.com

The Limes Hotel ♦♦♦♦
48 Park Road, Swanage
BH19 2AE
T: (01929) 422664
F: (0870) 054 8794
E: info@limeshotel.demon.co.uk
I: www.limeshotel.demon.co.uk

Millbrook Guest House ♦♦♦
56 Kings Road West, Swanage
BH19 1HR
T: (01929) 423443
E: b.b.@millbrookswanage.net
I: freespace.virgin.net/bob.millbrook

The Oxford Hotel ♦♦♦
3-5 Park Road, Swanage
BH19 2AA
T: (01929) 422247
F: (01929) 475707

Perfick Piece ♦♦♦
Springfield Road, Swanage
BH19 1HD
T: (01929) 423178
F: (01929) 423558
E: perfick-piece@supanet.com
I: www.perfick-piece.co.uk

St Michael ♦♦♦♦
31 Kings Road West, Swanage
BH19 1HF
T: (01929) 422064

Sandhaven Guest House
Rating Applied For
5 Ulwell Road, Swanage
BH19 1LE
T: (01929) 422322

White Lodge Hotel ♦♦♦♦
Grosvenor Road, Swanage
BH19 2DD
T: (01929) 422696
F: (01929) 425510
E: whitelodge.hotel@virgin.net
I: www.whitelodgehotel.co.uk

SWAY
Hampshire

Little Arnewood Cottage ♦♦♦
Linnies Lane, Sway, Lymington
SO41 6ES
T: (01590) 682920
E: davina@littlearnewoodcottage.co.uk

Little Purley Farm ♦♦♦
Chapel Lane, Sway, Lymington
SO41 6BS
T: (01590) 682707
F: (01590) 682707

Manor Farm ♦♦♦
Coombe Lane, Sway, Lymington
SO41 6BP
T: (01590) 683542

The Nurse's Cottage
♦♦♦♦♦ GOLD AWARD
Station Road, Sway, Lymington
SO41 6BA
T: (01590) 683402
F: (01590) 683402
E: nurses.cottage@lineone.net
I: www.nursescottage.co.uk

Tiverton ♦♦♦
9 Cruse Close, Sway, Lymington
SO41 6AY
T: (01590) 683092
F: (01590) 683092
E: ronrowe@talk21.com
I: www.tivertonnewforest.co.uk

TAPLOW
Buckinghamshire

Bridge Cottage Guest House ♦♦♦
Bath Road, Taplow, Maidenhead
SL6 0AR
T: (01628) 626805
F: (01628) 788785

TARRANT HINTON
Dorset

Old South Farmhouse ♦♦♦
Tarrant Hinton, Blandford Forum
DT11 8JA
T: (01258) 830659
F: (01258) 830692

TARRANT LAUNCESTON
Dorset

Ramblers Cottage ♦♦♦♦
Tarrant Launceston, Blandford
Forum DT11 8BY
T: (01258) 830528
E: sworrall@ramblerscottage.fsnet.co.uk
I: www.ramblerscottage.fsnet.co.uk

TENTERDEN
Kent

Collina House Hotel ♦♦♦♦
East Hill, Tenterden TN30 6RL
T: (01580) 764852
F: (01580) 762224
E: enquiries@collinahousehotel.co.uk
I: www.collinahousehotel.co.uk

11 East Hill ♦♦♦
Tenterden TN30 6RL
T: (01580) 766805

Little Dane Court
Rating Applied For
Ashford Road, Tenterden
TN30 6AB
T: (01580) 765066
E: jenny.seager@btopenworld.com
I: www.littledanecourt.co.uk

Old Burren ♦♦♦♦
25 Ashford Road, Tenterden
TN30 6LL
T: (01580) 764442
E: poo@burren.fsbusiness.co.uk
I: www.oldburren.co.uk

Signal Cottage Bed & Breakfast ♦♦♦♦
3 Rogersmead, Tenterden
TN30 6LF
T: (01580) 761806

The Tower House ♦♦♦♦
Ashford Road, Tenterden
TN30 6LL
T: (01580) 761920
F: (01580) 764664
E: pippa@towerhouse.biz

White Cottage ♦♦♦
Ashford Road, St Michaels,
Tenterden TN30 6SR
T: (01233) 850583
I: www.smoothhound.co.uk/shs.html

White Lion Hotel ♦♦♦♦
High Street, Tenterden
TN30 6BD
T: (01580) 765077
F: (01580) 764157
I: www.lionheartinn.co.uk

TETSWORTH
Oxfordshire

Little Acre ♦♦♦♦
4 High Street, Tetsworth, Oxford
OX9 7AT
T: (01844) 281423
F: (01844) 281423
E: julia@little-acre.co.uk
I: www.little-acre.co.uk

THAME
Oxfordshire

The Dairy
♦♦♦♦♦ GOLD AWARD
Moreton, Thame OX9 2HX
T: (01844) 214075
F: (01844) 214075
E: thedairy@freeuk.com
I: www.thedairy.freeuk.com

Field Farm ♦♦♦♦
Rycote Lane, Thame OX9 2HQ
T: (01844) 215428
I: www.fieldfarm.mybravenet.com

Langsmeade House
♦♦♦♦ SILVER AWARD
Milton Common, Thame OX9 2JY
T: (01844) 278727
F: (01844) 279256
E: CerberusandCo@aol.com
I: www.langsmeadehouse.co.uk

Oakfield
♦♦♦♦ SILVER AWARD
Thame Park Road, Thame
OX9 3PL
T: (01844) 213709

THATCHAM
Berkshire

33 Green Lane ♦♦♦
Thatcham RG19 3RG
T: (01635) 863116
F: (01635) 863116

THREE LEGGED CROSS
Dorset

Thatch Cottage ♦♦♦♦
Ringwood Road, Three Legged
Cross, Wimborne Minster
BH21 6QY
T: (01202) 822042
F: (01202) 821888
E: dthatchcottage@aol.com
I: www.thatch-cottage.co.uk

THURNHAM
Kent

Court Farm Farmhouse ♦♦♦♦
Thurnham Lane, Thurnham,
Maidstone ME14 3LH
T: (01622) 737305
F: (01622) 737305
E: monleggo1@agriplus.net
I: www.courtfarmfarmhouse.co.uk

TICEHURST
East Sussex

The Bull Inn ♦♦♦
Three Leg Cross, Ticehurst,
Wadhurst TN5 7HH
T: (01580) 200586
F: (01580) 201289
E: michael@thebullinn.co.uk
I: www.thebullinn.co.uk

Cherry Tree Inn ♦♦♦
Dale Hill, Ticehurst, Wadhurst
TN5 7DG
T: (01580) 201229
F: (01580) 201996
E: boffins@btinternet.com

TILMANSTONE
Kent

Plough and Harrow ♦♦
Dover Road, Tilmanstone, Deal
CT14 0HX
T: (01304) 617582

TITCHFIELD
Hampshire

Westcote Bed & Breakfast ♦♦♦♦
325 Southampton Road,
Titchfield, Fareham PO14 4AY
T: (01329) 846297
F: (01329) 846297
I: www.westcote-guesthouse.co.uk

TONBRIDGE
Kent

Brown Bear's Den ♦♦♦
95 Barden Road, Tonbridge
TN9 1UR
T: (01732) 351195
E: brownbearsden@aol.com

Fieldswood
Rating Applied For
Hadlow Park, Hadlow, Tonbridge
TN11 0HZ
T: (01732) 851433
F: (01732) 851840
E: info@fieldswood.co.uk
I: www.fieldswood.co.uk

Hogswell Bed and Breakfast ♦♦♦♦
Hogswell, Three Elm Lane,
Tonbridge TN11 0AD
T: (01732) 850283
F: (01732) 850283
E: richard.morley@dial.pipex.com
I: www.hogswell.dial.pipex.com

Lodge Oast
♦♦♦♦ SILVER AWARD
Horns Lodge Lane, Shipbourne
Road, Tonbridge TN11 9NJ
T: (01732) 833976
F: (01732) 838394
E: maryann@lodgeoast.freeserve.co.uk
I: www.lodgeoast.electricfence.co.uk

Marigolds ♦♦♦
19 Old Hadlow Road, Tonbridge
TN10 4EY
T: (01732) 356539
E: jmtn10@aol.com
I: www.tonbridge-kent.com

Masters ♦♦♦
Matfield Green, Tonbridge
TN12 7LA
T: (01892) 722126
F: (01892) 722126

70 The Ridgeway ♦♦♦
Tonbridge TN10 4NN
T: (01732) 366459
F: (01732) 366459

30 Stacey Road ♦♦♦
Tonbridge TN10 3AR
T: (01732) 358027

TOTLAND BAY
Isle of Wight

Chart House ♦♦♦♦
Madeira Road, Totland Bay
PO39 0BJ
T: (01983) 755091

Country Garden Hotel
♦♦♦♦ SILVER AWARD
Church Hill, Totland Bay
PO39 0ET
T: (01983) 754521
F: (01983) 754521
E: countrygardeniow@aol.com
I: www.thecountrygardenhotel.co.uk

Frenchman's Cove ♦♦♦
Alum Bay Old Road, Totland Bay
PO39 0HZ
T: (01983) 752227
F: (01983) 755125
E: boatfield@frenchmanscove.co.uk
I: www.frenchmanscove.co.uk

The Highdown Inn ♦♦♦
Highdown Lane, Totland Bay
PO39 0HY
T: (01983) 752450
F: (01983) 752450
E: highdowninn@hotmail.com
I: www.netguides.co.uk/wight/highdown.html

Sandy Lane Guest House ♦♦♦♦
Colwell Common Road, Totland
Bay PO39 0DD
T: (01983) 752240
F: (01983) 752240
E: jane@sandylaneguesthouse.fsnet.co.uk

TOTTON
Hampshire

Ivy Lawn ♦♦♦♦
Eling Hill, Totton, Southampton
SO40 9HE
T: (023) 8066 0925
E: suleonard@ukonline.co.uk
I: www.ivylawn.co.uk

TOYS HILL
Kent

Corner Cottage
♦♦♦♦ SILVER AWARD
Puddledock Lane, Toys Hill,
Westerham TN16 1PY
T: (01732) 750362
F: (01959) 561911
E: olszowskiathome@jshmanco.com

TWYFORD
Hampshire

Highfield Cottage ♦♦♦♦
Old Rectory Lane, Twyford,
Winchester SO21 1NS
T: (01962) 712921
F: (01962) 712921
E: cjrees@estatesgazette.net

TYRINGHAM
Buckinghamshire

Park Farm ◆◆◆
Tyringham, Newport Pagnell
MK16 9ES
T: (01908) 218886
E: thefamilyhill@btopenworld.com

UCKFIELD
East Sussex

Hooke Hall
◆◆◆◆◆ GOLD AWARD
250 High Street, Uckfield
TN22 1EN
T: (01825) 761578
F: (01825) 768025
E: a.percy@virgin.net
I: www.hookehall.co.uk

Old Mill Farm
◆◆◆◆ SILVER AWARD
Chillies Lane, High Hurstwood, Uckfield TN22 4AD
T: (01825) 732279
F: (01825) 732279

South Paddock
◆◆◆◆◆ SILVER AWARD
Maresfield Park, Uckfield
TN22 2HA
T: (01825) 762335

UFFINGTON
Oxfordshire

Norton House ◆◆◆
Broad Street, Uffington, Faringdon SN7 7RA
T: (01367) 820230
F: (01367) 820230
E: carloberman@aol.com

UFTON NERVET
Berkshire

Hill Cottage ◆◆◆◆
Church Lane, Ufton Nervet, Reading RG7 4HQ
T: (0118) 983 2248
F: (0118) 983 2248
E: barkerhillcottage@hotmail.com

UPCHURCH
Kent

Suffield House
◆◆◆◆ SILVER AWARD
The Street, Upchurch, Sittingbourne ME9 7EU
T: (01634) 230409

UPPER BUCKLEBURY
Berkshire

Brockley ◆◆◆
Little Lane, Upper Bucklebury, Reading RG7 6QX
T: (01635) 869742
E: prue.matchwick@ukonline.co.uk
I: www.stayatbrockley.co.uk

UPTON
Oxfordshire

Prospect House ◆◆◆◆
Upton, Didcot OX11 9HU
T: (01235) 850268
F: (01235) 850987
E: srjpowell@lineone.net

The White House ◆◆◆
Reading Road, Upton, Didcot
OX11 9HP
T: (01235) 850289

VENTNOR
Isle of Wight

Delamere Guest House ◆◆◆◆
Bellevue Road, Ventnor
PO38 1DB
T: (01983) 852322
F: (01983) 852322
E: kk@delamere1.co.uk
I: www.delamere1.co.uk

The Hermitage Country House
◆◆◆◆◆
St Catherines Down, Ventnor
PO38 2PD
T: (01983) 730010

VERNEY JUNCTION
Buckinghamshire

The White Cottage ◆◆◆
Verney Junction, Buckingham
MK18 2JZ
T: (01296) 714416

VERNHAM DEAN
Hampshire

Upton Cottage ◆◆◆
Vernham Dean, Andover
SP11 0JY
T: (01264) 737640
F: (01264) 737640

WADDESDON
Buckinghamshire

The Georgian Doll's Cottage
◆◆◆◆
High Street, Waddesdon, Aylesbury HP18 0NE
T: (01296) 655553

The Old Dairy ◆◆◆
4 High Street, Waddesdon, Aylesbury HP18 0JA
T: (01296) 658627
E: gconyard@btinternet.com

WADHURST
East Sussex

Best Beech Inn ◆◆◆◆
Best Beech, Mayfield Lane, Wadhurst TN5 6JH
T: (01892) 782046
F: (01892) 785092
I: www.bestbeechinn.com

Bryants House ◆◆◆◆
Wards Lane, Wadhurst TN5 6HP
T: (01892) 784898
F: (01892) 784898

Four Keys ◆◆
Station Road, Wadhurst
TN5 6RZ
T: (01892) 782252
F: (01892) 784113

Spring Cottage ◆◆◆
Best Beech Hill, Wadhurst
TN5 6JH
T: (01892) 783896
F: (01892) 784866
E: enquiries@southerncrosstravel.co.uk

WALBERTON
West Sussex

Longacre Bed & Breakfast
◆◆◆
The Street, Walberton, Arundel
BN18 0PY
T: (01243) 543542
F: (01243) 543342
E: rhpalmer@tinyworld.co.uk

WALKFORD
Dorset

Chewton Edge ◆◆◆
127 Ringwood Road, Walkford, Christchurch BH23 5RB
T: (01425) 271430
F: (01425) 271430

WALLINGFORD
Oxfordshire

Fords Farm
◆◆◆◆ SILVER AWARD
Ewelme, Wallingford OX10 6HU
T: (01491) 839272
E: fordsfarm@callnetuk.com
I: www.country-accom.co.uk

Little Gables ◆◆◆◆
166 Crowmarsh Hill, Crowmarsh Gifford, Wallingford OX10 8BG
T: (01491) 837834
F: (01491) 834426
E: jill@stayingaway.com
I: www.stayingaway.com

North Farm
◆◆◆◆ SILVER AWARD
Shillingford Hill, Wallingford
OX10 8NB
T: (01865) 858406
F: (01865) 858519
E: northfarm@compuserve.com
I: www.country-accom.co.uk/north-farm/

North Moreton House
◆◆◆◆◆ SILVER AWARD
North Moreton House, North Moreton, Didcot OX11 9AT
T: (01235) 813283
F: (01235) 511305
E: miles_katie@hotmail.com
I: www.northmortonhouse.co.uk

WALMER
Kent

Hardicot Guest House ◆◆◆◆
Kingsdown Road, Walmer, Deal
CT14 8AW
T: (01304) 373867
F: (01304) 389234
E: guestboss@talk21.com
I: www.smoothhound.co.uk/hotels/hardicot.html

WALTHAM
Kent

Beech Bank
Rating Applied For
Duckpit Lane, Waltham, Canterbury CT4 5QA
T: (01227) 700302
F: (01227) 700302

WALTON-ON-THAMES
Surrey

Beech Tree Lodge ◆◆◆
7 Rydens Avenue, Walton-on-Thames KT12 3JB
T: (01932) 886667
E: joanspiteri@aol.com

WANTAGE
Oxfordshire

B & B in Wantage ◆◆◆◆
50 Foliat Drive, Wantage
OX12 7AL
T: (01235) 760495
E: eleanor@eaturner.freeserve.co.uk

Old Yeomanry Guest House
Rating Applied For
27 Wallingford Street, Wantage
OX12 8AU
T: (01235) 772778
F: (01235) 772778

WAREHAM
Dorset

Anglbury House ◆◆◆
15/17 North Street, Wareham
BH20 4AB
T: (01929) 552988
F: (01929) 554665

Ashcroft ◆◆◆
64 Furzebrook Road, Wareham
BH20 5AX
T: (01929) 552392
F: (01929) 552422
E: cake@ashcroft-bb.co.uk
I: www.ashcroft-bb.co.uk

The Old Granary
◆◆◆◆ SILVER AWARD
West Holme Farm, Wareham
BH20 6AQ
T: (01929) 552972
F: (01929) 551616
E: venngoldsack@lineone.net
I: www.theoldgranarybandb.co.uk

Springbrook Cottage
Rating Applied For
Springbrook Close, Corfe Castle, Wareham BH20 5HS
T: (01929) 480509

WARGRAVE
Berkshire

Appletree Cottage
◆◆◆◆ SILVER AWARD
Backsideans, Wargrave, Reading
RG10 8JS
T: (0118) 940 4306
E: trishlangham@appletreecottage.co.uk
I: www.appletreecottage.co.uk

WARLINGHAM
Surrey

Glenmore ◆◆◆
Southview Road, Warlingham, Oxted CR6 9JE
T: (01883) 624530
F: (01883) 624199
E: thirzapayne@yahoo.co.uk

WARNHAM
West Sussex

Nowhere House ◆◆◆
Dorking Road, Warnham, Horsham RH12 3RZ
T: (01306) 627272
F: (01306) 627190

WATER STRATFORD
Buckinghamshire

The Rolling Acres ◆◆◆◆
Water Stratford, Buckingham
MK18 5DX
T: (01280) 847302
E: david.abbotts@talk21.com

WATERLOOVILLE
Hampshire

Holly Dale ◆◆◆
11 Lovedean Lane, Waterlooville
PO8 8HH
T: (023) 9259 2047

New Haven Bed & Breakfast
◆◆◆◆
193 London Road, Waterlooville
PO7 7RN
T: (023) 9226 8559
F: (023) 9226 8559

WATERSFIELD
West Sussex

Beacon Lodge B & B ♦♦♦♦
London Road, Watersfield, Arundel RH20 1NH
T: (01798) 831026
F: (01798) 831026
E: beaconlodge@hotmail.com
I: www.beaconlodge.co.uk

WATERSTOCK
Oxfordshire

Park Farm House ♦♦♦♦
Waterstock, Oxford OX33 1JT
T: (01844) 339469
F: (01844) 338890

WATLINGTON
Oxfordshire

Huttons ♦♦♦
Britwell Salome, Watlington, Oxford OX49 5LH
T: (01491) 614389
F: (01491) 614993
E: jbowater@etonwell.com

WENDOVER
Buckinghamshire

Dunsmore Edge ♦♦♦
Dunsmore Lane, London Road, Wendover, Aylesbury HP22 6PN
T: (01296) 623080
E: uron@lineone.net.uk

Field Cottage
♦♦♦♦ SILVER AWARD
St Leonards, Tring HP23 6NS
T: (01494) 837602
F: (01494) 837137
E: susan_jepson@hotmail.com
I: www.smoothhound.co.uk/hotels/field.html

17 Icknield Close
Rating Applied For
Wendover, Aylesbury HP22 6HG
T: (01296) 583285
E: grbr.samuels@ntlworld.com

46 Lionel Avenue ♦♦♦
Lionel Avenue, Wendover, Aylesbury HP22 6LP
T: (01296) 623426

WEST BRABOURNE
Kent

Bulltown Farmhouse Bed & Breakfast ♦♦♦
Bulltown Lane, West Brabourne, Ashford TN25 5NB
T: (01233) 813505
F: (01227) 709544
E: wiltons@bulltown.fsnet.co.uk

WEST CHALLOW
Oxfordshire

Manor Farm
Rating Applied For
Silver Lane, West Challow, Wantage OX12 9TJ
T: (01235) 763188

WEST CHILTINGTON
West Sussex

New Barn Cottage ♦♦♦♦
New Barn Lane, off Harborough Hill, West Chiltington, Pulborough RH20 2PP
T: (01798) 813231
F: (01798) 813231
I: www.sussexlive.com

WEST CLANDON
Surrey

The Oaks ♦♦♦
Highcotts Lane, West Clandon, Guildford GU4 7XA
T: (01483) 222531
F: (01483) 224454
E: catherinebroad@callnetuk.com

Ways Cottage ♦♦♦♦
Lime Grove, West Clandon, Guildford GU4 7UT
T: (01483) 222454
F: (01483) 222454

WEST DEAN
West Sussex

Lodge Hill Farm ♦♦♦
West Dean, Chichester PO18 0RT
T: (01243) 535245

WEST HARTING
West Sussex

Three Quebec ♦♦♦♦
West Harting, Petersfield GU31 5PG
T: (01730) 825386
F: (01730) 826652
E: stevens@threequebec.co.uk
I: www.threequebec.co.uk

WEST HORSLEY
Surrey

Brinford ♦♦♦
Windmill Hill, Off Shere Road, West Horsley, Leatherhead KT24 6EJ
T: (01483) 283636

Silkmore ♦♦♦♦
Silkmore Lane, West Horsley, Leatherhead KT24 6JQ
T: (01483) 282042
F: (01483) 284109
E: kimpton@leporello.free-online.co.uk

Woolgars House ♦♦♦♦
Blakes Lane, West Horsley, Leatherhead KT24 6EA
T: (01483) 222915
F: (01483) 222431
E: barry.lester@virgin.net

WEST LULWORTH
Dorset

Abbots Orchard ♦♦♦
West Road, West Lulworth, Wareham BH20 5RY
T: (01929) 400592
E: theorchard@ic24.net

Gatton House ♦♦♦♦
West Lulworth, Wareham BH20 5RL
T: (01929) 400252
F: (01929) 400252
E: avril@gattonhouse.co.uk
I: gattonhouse.co.uk

Graybank ♦♦♦
Main Road, West Lulworth, Wareham BH20 5RL
T: (01929) 400256

Lulworth Cove Hotel ♦♦♦
Main Road, West Lulworth, Wareham BH20 5RQ
T: (01929) 400333
F: (01929) 400534
E: hotel@lulworth-cove.com
I: www.lulworth-cove.com

The Old Barn ♦♦♦
Lulworth Cove, West Lulworth, Wareham BH20 5RL
T: (01929) 400305
F: (01929) 400516

West Down Farm ♦♦♦♦
West Lulworth, Wareham BH20 5PU
T: (01929) 400308
F: (01929) 400308
E: sarah@westdownfarm.f.snet.co.uk

WEST MALLING
Kent

Appledene ♦♦♦♦
164 Norman Road, West Malling ME19 6RW
T: (01732) 842071
F: (01732) 842071
E: appledene@westmalling.freeserve.co.uk

Westfields Farm ♦♦♦
St Vincents Lane, Addington, West Malling ME19 5BW
T: (01732) 843209

WEST STOKE
West Sussex

West Stoke House ♦♦♦♦
Downs Road, West Stoke, Chichester PO18 9BN
T: (01243) 575226
F: (01243) 574655
E: info@weststokehouse.co.uk
I: www.weststokehouse.co.uk

WEST WELLOW
Hampshire

Lukes Barn ♦♦♦
Maury's Lane, West Wellow, Romsey SO51 6DA
T: (01794) 324431
F: (01794) 324431

WEST WITTERING
West Sussex

The Beach House ♦♦♦
Rookwood Road, West Wittering, Chichester PO20 8LT
T: (01243) 514800
F: (01243) 514798
E: info@beachhse.co.uk
I: www.beachhse.co.uk

Thornton Cottage
♦♦♦♦ SILVER AWARD
Chichester Road, West Wittering, Chichester PO20 8QA
T: (01243) 512470
F: (01243) 512470
E: thornton@b-and-b.fsbusiness.co.uk

WESTCOTT
Surrey

Corner House Bed & Breakfast ♦♦
Guildford Road, Westcott, Dorking RH4 3QE
T: (01306) 888798

WESTERHAM
Kent

Worples Field
♦♦♦♦ SILVER AWARD
Farley Common, Westerham TN16 1UB
T: (01959) 562869
E: marr@worplesfield.com
I: www.worplesfield.com

WESTFIELD
East Sussex

Four Winds ♦♦♦♦
Parsonage Lane, Westfield, Hastings TN35 4SH
T: (01424) 752585
F: (01424) 762828
E: stewarts@4-winds.fsnet.co.uk
I: www.4-winds.org

WESTGATE ON SEA
Kent

Seacroft ♦♦♦
St Mildreds Road, Westgate on Sea, Margate CT8 8RL
T: (01843) 833334

White Lodge Guest House ♦♦♦
12 Domneva Road, Westgate on Sea, Margate CT8 8PE
T: (01843) 831828
E: whitelodge.thanet@btinternet.com
I: www.whitelodge.thanet.btinternet.co.uk

WESTMARSH
Kent

The Way Out Inn ♦♦♦
Westmarsh, Canterbury CT3 2LP
T: (01304) 812899
F: (01304) 813181
E: mail@thewayoutinn.com
I: www.thewayoutinn.com

WESTON-ON-THE-GREEN
Oxfordshire

Westfield Court House ♦♦♦♦
North Lane, Weston-on-the-Green, Bicester OX25 3RG
T: (01869) 350777
E: jbrownwest@aol.com

Weston Grounds Farm ♦♦♦
Weston-on-the-Green, Bicester OX25 3QX
T: (01869) 351168
F: (01869) 350887

WESTON TURVILLE
Buckinghamshire

Brickwall Farm Cottage ♦♦♦
Mill Lane, Weston Turville, Aylesbury HP22 5RG
T: (01296) 612656
F: (01296) 614017
E: enquiries@brickwallfarmcottage.co.uk
I: www.brickwallfarmcottage.co.uk

The Hideaway ♦♦♦
Main Street, Weston Turville, Aylesbury HP22 5RR
T: (01296) 612604
F: (01296) 615705

Loosley House ♦♦♦♦
87 New Road, Weston Turville, Aylesbury HP22 5QT
T: (01296) 484157
F: (01296) 428285

WEYHILL
Hampshire

Juglans ♦♦♦♦
Red Post Lane, Weyhill, Andover SP11 0PY
T: (01264) 772651

WHADDON
Buckinghamshire

Lowndes Arms
Rating Applied For
4 High Street, Whaddon, Milton Keynes MK17 0NA
T: (01908) 501706
F: (01908) 521815

WHATLINGTON
East Sussex

Woodmans ♦♦♦♦
Whatlington, Battle TN33 0NN
T: (01424) 870342

WHERWELL
Hampshire

May Cottage ♦♦♦♦
May Cottage, Fullerton Road, Wherwell, Andover SP11 7JS
T: (01264) 860412
F: (01264) 860791
E: wildgoose_projects@attglobal.net

New House Bed & Breakfast ♦♦♦♦
New House, Fullerton Road, Wherwell, Andover SP11 7JS
T: (01264) 860817
E: DiWoodWherwell@aol.com
I: www.newhousebnb.co.uk

WHITCHURCH
Hampshire

Peak House Farm ♦♦♦
Cole Henley, Whitchurch RG28 7QJ
T: (01256) 892052
F: (01256) 892052
E: peakhousefarm@tesco.net

White Hart Hotel ♦♦
Newbury Street, Whitchurch RG28 7DN
T: (01256) 892900
F: (01256) 896628
E: adrian@white-hart.fsnet.co.uk
I: www.whitehart-hotel.co.uk

WHITSTABLE
Kent

Alliston House ♦♦♦
1 Joy Lane, Whitstable CT5 4LS
T: (01227) 779066
F: (01227) 779066
E: bobgough57@aol.com

The Cherry Garden ♦♦♦
62 Joy Lane, Whitstable CT5 4LT
T: (01227) 266497

Hotel Continental ♦♦♦
29 Beach Walk, Whitstable CT5 2BP
T: (01227) 280280
F: (01227) 280257
I: www.oysterfishery.co.uk

Copeland House ♦♦♦
4 Island Wall, Whitstable CT5 1EP
T: (01227) 266207
F: (01227) 266207
E: mail@copelandhouse.com
I: www.copelandhouse.co.uk

Marine ♦♦♦♦
Marine Parade, Tankerton, Whitstable CT5 2BE
T: (01227) 272672
F: (01227) 264721
E: marine@shepherd-neame.co.uk
I: www.shepherd-neame.co.uk

Victoria Villa ♦♦♦♦ GOLD AWARD
Victoria Street, Whitstable CT5 1JB
T: (01227) 779191
E: victoria-villa@i12.com
I: www.victoria-villa.i12.com

Wavecrest B & B ♦♦♦
2 Seaway Cottages, Wavecrest, Whitstable CT5 1EQ
T: (01227) 770155

Windyridge Guest House ♦♦♦♦
Wraik Hill, Whitstable CT5 3BY
T: (01227) 263506
F: (01227) 771191

WHITWELL
Isle of Wight

The Old Rectory ♦♦♦♦ GOLD AWARD
Ashknowle Lane, Whitwell, Ventnor PO38 2PP
T: (01983) 731242
F: (01983) 731288
E: rectory@ukonline.co.uk
I: www.wightonline.co.uk/oldrectory

WICKHAM
Hampshire

Chiphall Acre ♦♦♦♦
Droxford Road, Wickham, Fareham PO17 5AY
T: (01329) 833188
F: (01329) 833188
E: mavis.stevens@zoom.co.uk
I: www.smoothhound.co.uk/hotels/chiphall.html

WIDLEY
Hampshire

Roughay ♦♦♦
96 The Brow, Widley, Waterlooville PO7 5DA
T: (023) 9237 9341
E: gillcross@lineone.net
I: www.roughay.co.uk

WIDMER END
Buckinghamshire

The White House ♦♦♦
North Road, Widmer End, High Wycombe HP15 6ND
T: (01494) 712221
F: (01494) 712221
E: vaughanjane@hotmail.com

WILLESBOROUGH
Kent

Rosemary House ♦♦♦
94 Church Road, Willesborough, Ashford TN24 0JG
T: (01233) 625215

WILMINGTON
Kent

66 Tredegar Road ♦♦♦
Wilmington, Dartford DA2 7AZ
T: (01322) 270659

WIMBORNE MINSTER
Dorset

The Albion Hotel ♦♦
19 High Street, Wimborne Minster BH21 1HR
T: (01202) 882492
F: (01202) 880860

Ashton Lodge ♦♦♦♦ SILVER AWARD
10 Oakley Hill, Wimborne Minster BH21 1QH
T: (01202) 883423
F: (01202) 886180
E: ashtonlodge@ukgateway.net
I: www.ashtonlodge.ukgateway.net

Hemsworth Manor Farm ♦♦♦♦
Witchampton, Wimborne Minster BH21 5BN
T: (01258) 840216
F: (01258) 841278

Homestay ♦♦♦
22 West Borough, Wimborne Minster BH21 1NF
T: (01202) 849015
F: (01202) 849819
E: julietridg@onetel.com

Hopewell ♦♦♦♦ SILVER AWARD
Little Lonnen, Colehill, Wimborne Minster BH21 7BB
T: (01202) 880311
E: hopewell.wimborne@ntlworld.com

Lantern Lodge ♦♦♦♦ GOLD AWARD
47 Gravel Hill, Merley, Wimborne Minster BH21 1RW
T: (01202) 884183

The Old George ♦♦♦♦
2 Corn Market, Wimborne Minster BH21 1JL
T: (01202) 888510
F: (01202) 888513

Silvertrees ♦♦♦
Merley House Lane, Wimborne Minster BH21 3AA
T: (01202) 880418
F: (01202) 881415
E: fionashammick@aol.com

Twynham ♦♦♦
67 Poole Road, Wimborne Minster BH21 1QB
T: (01202) 887310

96 West Borough ♦♦♦
Wimborne Minster BH21 1NH
T: (01202) 884039

38 Wimborne Road West ♦♦♦
Wimborne Minster BH21 2DP
T: (01202) 889357

Woodlands ♦♦♦♦ SILVER AWARD
29 Merley Ways, Wimborne Minster BH21 1QN
T: (01202) 887625
E: stevemaggietopliss.woodlands@virgin.net
I: www.woodlandsbedandbreak.co.uk

WINCHELSEA
East Sussex

The New Inn ♦♦♦
German Street, Winchelsea TN36 4EN
T: (01797) 226252
F: (01797) 226238
E: terry@newinnwinchelsea.co.uk
I: www.newinnwinchelsea.co.uk

St Anthonys ♦♦♦♦
Castle Street, Winchelsea TN36 4EL
T: (01797) 226255

Winchelsea Lodge Motel & Restaurant ♦♦♦♦
Hastings Road (A259), Winchelsea TN36 4AD
T: (01797) 226211
F: (01797) 226312
E: orlandoatwinchelsealodge@tinyworld.co.uk
I: winchelsea-lodge-motel.co.uk

WINCHESTER
Hampshire

Acacia ♦♦♦♦ SILVER AWARD
44 Kilham Lane, Winchester SO22 5PT
T: (01962) 852259
F: (01962) 852259
E: eric.buchanan@mcmail.com
I: www.btinternet.com/~eric.buchanan

15B Bereweeke Avenue ♦♦♦♦
., Winchester SO22 6BH
T: (01962) 877883
F: (01962) 841616

Brymer House ♦♦♦♦ SILVER AWARD
29-30 St Faiths Road, St Cross, Winchester SO23 9QD
T: (01962) 867428
F: (01962) 868624
E: brymerhouse@aol.com

Cheriton House ♦♦♦
61 Cheriton Road, Winchester SO22 5AY
T: (01962) 620374
E: rowen43313@aol.com

37 Chilbolton Avenue ♦♦♦
Chilbolton Avenue, Winchester SO22 5HE
T: (01962) 853369
F: (01962) 853369
E: rogerslade@currantbun.com
I: www.37chilboltonavenue.com

12 Christchurch Road ♦♦♦
Winchester SO23 9SR
T: (01962) 854272
E: pjspatton@yahoo.co.uk

85 Christchurch Road ♦♦♦♦ SILVER AWARD
Winchester SO23 9QY
T: (01962) 868661
F: (01962) 868661
E: dilke@waitrose.com

Church Cottage ♦♦♦
20 St Johns Street, Winchester SO23 0HF
T: (01962) 865058
E: junerowlands@petuchio.freeserve.co.uk

5 Clifton Terrace ♦♦♦♦
Winchester SO22 5BJ
T: (01962) 890053
F: (01962) 626566
E: chrissiejohnston@hotmail.com
I: www.smoothhound.co.uk/hotels/cliftonterrace.html

5 Compton Road ♦♦♦
Winchester SO23 9SL
T: (01962) 869199
E: vicb@csma-netlink.co.uk
I: www.winchester.gov.uk

38 Courtenay Road ♦♦♦
Winchester SO23 7ER
T: (01962) 855314
E: tom_belshaw@lineone.net

Dawn Cottage ♦♦♦♦ SILVER AWARD
Romsey Road, Winchester SO22 5PQ
T: (01962) 869956
F: (01962) 869956
E: dawncottage@hotmail.com

East View ♦♦♦♦
16 Clifton Hill, Winchester SO22 5BL
T: (01962) 862986

The Farrells ♦♦♦
5 Ranelagh Road, St Cross, Winchester SO23 9TA
T: (01962) 869555
F: (01962) 869555
E: thefarrells@easicom.com

Giffard House Hotel
♦♦♦♦ SILVER AWARD
50 Christchurch Road, Winchester SO23 9SU
T: (01962) 852628
F: (01962) 856722

Heybridge
Rating Applied For
Clifton Road, Winchester SO22 5BP
T: (01962) 865007

The Lilacs ♦♦♦♦
1 Harestock Close, Off Andover Road North, Winchester SO22 6NP
T: (01962) 884122
F: (01962) 884122
E: susan@rbpell.freeserve.co.uk
I: www.smoothhound.co.uk/hotels/lilacs.html

Mallard Cottage ♦♦♦♦
64 Chesil Street, Winchester SO23 0HX
T: (01962) 853002
F: (01962) 820430
E: mallardsimpkin@aol.com
I: www.geocities.com/mallardcottageuk

Manor House ♦♦♦
Place Lane, Compton, Winchester SO21 2BA
T: (01962) 712162

The Old Blue Boar ♦♦♦♦
25 St John's Street, Winchester SO23 0HF
T: (01962) 865942
E: julietsurridge@aol.com

53A Parchment Street ♦♦♦
Winchester SO23 8BA
T: (01962) 849962
E: saraby@onetel.net.uk
I: www.accom.finder.co.uk

21 Rosewarne Court ♦♦♦
Hyde Street, Winchester SO23 7HL
T: (01962) 863737

9 Rosewarne Court ♦♦♦
Hyde Street, Winchester SO23 7HL
T: (01962) 864077

Rowanhurst
♦♦♦♦ SILVER AWARD
Northbrook Avenue, Winchester SO23 0JW
T: (01962) 862433
E: joanne.kingswell@talk21.com

St John's Croft ♦♦♦
St John's Street, Winchester SO23 0HF
T: (01962) 859976
E: n_fraser@ntl.com

St Margaret's ♦♦♦
3 St Michael's Road, Winchester SO23 9JE
T: (01962) 861450
E: brigid.brett@amserve.net
I: www.winchesterbandb.com

8 Salters Acres ♦♦♦♦
Winchester SO22 5JW
T: (01962) 856112
E: accommodation@8salters.freeserve.co.uk

Shawlands ♦♦♦♦
46 Kilham Lane, Winchester SO22 5QD
T: (01962) 861166
F: (01962) 861166
E: kathy@pollshaw.u-net.com

Somerville
Rating Applied For
19 Bereweeke Way, Winchester SO22 6BJ
T: (01962) 850979

South Lodge ♦♦♦
17 Andover Road North, Winchester SO22 6NN
T: (01962) 880403
F: (01962) 880403
E: southlodge17@hotmail.com

54 St Cross Road ♦♦♦♦
Winchester SO23 9PS
T: (01962) 852073
F: (01962) 852073
E: mcblockley@tcp.co.uk

9 St Faith's Road ♦♦♦♦
St Cross, Winchester SO23 9QB
T: (01962) 877522
E: denisehentall@waitrose.com

Sullivan's ♦♦
29 Stockbridge Road, Winchester SO22 6RW
T: (01962) 862027
E: sullivans_bandb@amserve.net

Sycamores ♦♦♦♦
4 Bereweeke Close, Winchester SO22 6AR
T: (01962) 867242
F: (01962) 620300
E: sycamores.b-and-b@virgin.net

152 Teg Downs Meads ♦♦♦
Winchester SO22 5NS
T: (01962) 862628
F: (01962) 862628
E: alfred.chalk@talk21.com

63 Upper Brook Street ♦♦♦♦
Winchester SO23 8DG
T: (01962) 620367

Windy Ridge ♦♦♦♦
99 Andover Road, Winchester SO22 6AX
T: (01962) 882527
E: angela.westall@virgin.net

Wolvesey View B & B ♦♦♦♦
10 Colebrook Place, Winchester SO23 9LP
T: (01962) 852082
E: j.holder@btinternet.com
I: www.wintonian.com

The Wykeham Arms
♦♦♦♦ SILVER AWARD
75 Kingsgate Street, Winchester SO23 9PE
T: (01962) 853834
F: (01962) 854411

WINDRUSH
Oxfordshire

Dellwood ♦♦♦
Windrush, Oxford OX18 4TR
T: (01451) 844268

WINDSOR
Berkshire

9 Albany Road ♦♦♦
Windsor SL4 1HL
T: (01753) 865564

Alma House ♦♦♦
56 Alma Road, Windsor SL4 3HA
T: (01753) 862983
F: (01753) 862983
E: info@almahouse.co.uk
I: www.almahouse.co.uk

The Arches ♦♦♦
9 York Road, Windsor SL4 3NX
T: (01753) 869268
F: (01753) 869268

Barbara Clemens
Rating Applied For
49 Longmead, Windsor SL4 5PZ
T: (01753) 866019
E: BandB@windsor4.demon.co.uk

Barbara's Bed & Breakfast ♦♦♦
16 Maidenhead Road, Windsor SL4 5EQ
T: (01753) 840273
E: bbandb@btinternet.com

Beaumont Lodge ♦♦♦♦
1 Beaumont Road, Windsor SL4 1HY
T: (01753) 863436
F: (01753) 863436
E: bhamshere@beaumontlodge.demon.co.uk
I: www.beaumontlodgeguesthouse.co.uk

Belmont House ♦♦♦♦
64 Bolton Road, Windsor SL4 3JL
T: (01753) 860860
F: (01753) 830330

Clarence Hotel ♦♦
9 Clarence Road, Windsor SL4 5AE
T: (01753) 864436
F: (01753) 857060
I: www.clarence-hotel.co.uk

The Dorset Hotel ♦♦♦♦
4 Dorset Road, Windsor SL4 3BA
T: (01753) 852669
F: (01753) 852669

Elansey ♦♦♦
65 Clifton Rise, Windsor SL4 5SX
T: (01753) 864438

Halcyon House ♦♦♦
131 Clarence Road, Windsor SL4 5AR
T: (01753) 863262
F: (01753) 863262
E: halcyonhouse@hotmail.com

Honeysuckle Cottage ♦♦♦♦
61 Fairfield Approach, Wraysbury, Windsor TW19 5DR
T: (01784) 482519
F: (01784) 482305
E: rooms@hotelswindsor.com
I: www.hotelswindsor.com

Jeans ♦♦
1 Stovell Road, Windsor SL4 5JB
T: (01753) 852055
F: (01753) 842932

Langton House ♦♦♦♦
46 Alma Road, Windsor SL4 3HA
T: (01753) 858299
F: (01753) 858299
E: enquiries@langtonhouse.co.uk
I: www.langtonhouse.com

Melrose House ♦♦♦
53 Frances Road, Windsor SL4 3AQ
T: (01753) 865328
F: (01753) 865328
E: m-mellor@supanet.com

Morton Lodge ♦♦♦♦
135 Clarence Road, Windsor SL4 5AR
T: (01753) 840439
F: (01753) 620375

The Oast Barn ♦♦♦
Staines Road, Wraysbury, Staines TW19 5BS
T: (01784) 481598
F: (01784) 483022
E: bandb@oastfarm.com
I: www.oastbarn.com

Oscar Hotel ♦♦♦
65 Vansittart Road, Windsor SL4 5DB
T: (01753) 830613
F: (01753) 833744
E: info@oscarhotel.com
I: www.oscarhotel.com

62 Queens Road ♦♦♦
Windsor SL4 3BH
T: (01753) 866036
F: (01753) 866036
E: bronwens_tuis@hotmail.com

Riverview Accommodation ♦♦♦♦
Stovell Road, Windsor SL4 5JB
T: (01753) 863628
F: (01753) 863628
E: janetn.riverview@virgin.net
I: www.riverviewaccommodation.com

The Trooper ♦♦♦
97 St Leonards Road, Windsor SL4 3BZ
T: (01753) 670123
F: (01753) 670124

22 York Avenue ♦♦♦
Windsor SL4 3PD
T: (01753) 865775

3 York Road ♦♦♦
Windsor SL4 3NX
T: (01753) 861741
F: (01753) 861741
E: kerrin@tiscali.co.uk

WINFRITH NEWBURGH
Dorset

Wynards Farm ♦♦♦♦
Winfrith Newburgh, Dorchester DT2 8DQ
T: (01305) 852660
F: (01305) 854094
E: canaven@hotmail.com
I: www.dorset-info.co.uk/wynards-farm

WINGHAM
Kent

Dambridge Oast ♦♦♦♦
Staple Road, Wingham, Canterbury CT3 1LU
T: (01227) 720082
F: (01227) 720082
E: info@pagoast.co.uk
I: www.pagoast.co.uk

WINKFIELD
Berkshire

Bluebell House ♦♦♦♦
Lovel Lane, Winkfield, Windsor SL4 2DG
T: (01344) 886828
F: (01344) 893256
E: registrations@bluebellhousehotel.co.uk
I: www.bluebellhousehotel.co.uk

WINKTON
Dorset

Fisherman's Haunt Hotel ♦♦♦
Salisbury Road, Winkton, Christchurch BH23 7AS
T: (01202) 477283
F: (01202) 478883

WINSLOW
Buckinghamshire

The Congregational Church ♦♦♦
15 Horn Street, Winslow, Buckingham MK18 3AP
T: (01296) 715717
F: (01296) 715717
E: sarahhood@waitrose.com
I: www.specialplacestostay.com/places/bbb2459

The Old Manse ♦♦
9 Horn Street, Winslow, Buckingham MK18 3AP
T: (01296) 712048

Puzzletree ♦♦♦♦
3 Buckingham Road, Winslow, Buckingham MK18 3DT
T: (01296) 712437
F: (01296) 712437
E: puzzletree@hotmail.com
I: www.puzzletree.bandb.co.uk

'Witsend' ♦♦♦
9 Buckingham Road, Winslow, Buckingham MK18 3DT
T: (01296) 712503
F: (01296) 712503
E: sheila.spatcher@aol.com

WINTERBORNE STICKLAND
Dorset

Stickland Farmhouse
♦♦♦♦ SILVER AWARD
Stickland Farmhouse, Winterborne Stickland, Blandford Forum DT11 0NT
T: (01258) 880119
F: (01258) 880119
E: sticklandfarmhouse@sticklanddorset.fsnet.co.uk

WINTERBORNE ZELSTON
Dorset

Brook Farm ♦♦♦
Brook Farm, Winterborne Zelston, Blandford Forum DT11 9EU
T: (01929) 459267
F: (01929) 459267
E: kerleybrookfarmzelston@yahoo.co.uk

WITNEY
Oxfordshire

The Court Inn ♦♦♦
43 Bridge Street, Witney OX28 1DA
T: (01993) 703228
F: (01993) 700980
E: info@thecourt.co.uk

Crofters Guest House ♦♦♦♦
29 Oxford Hill, Witney OX28 3JU
T: (01993) 778165
F: (01993) 778165
E: crofers.ghouse@virgin.net

Ducklington Farm ♦♦♦
Coursehill Lane, Ducklington, Witney OX29 7YL
T: (01993) 772175
I: www.country-accom.co.uk

Field View
♦♦♦♦ SILVER AWARD
Wood Green, Witney OX28 1DE
T: (01993) 705485
E: bandb@fieldview-witney.co.uk
I: www.fieldview-witney.co.uk

Greystones Lodge Hotel ♦♦♦
34 Tower Hill, Witney OX28 5ES
T: (01993) 771898
F: (01993) 702064
E: greystoneslodge@aol.com
I: www.greystoneslodge.co.uk

Hawthorn House ♦♦♦
79 Burford Road, Witney OX28 6DR
T: (01993) 772768
F: (01993) 772768
E: jdonohoe33@aol.com
I: www.hawthornhouse.netfirms.com

The Laurels ♦♦♦
53 Burford Road, Witney OX28 6DR
T: (01993) 702193
E: bbb@laurelguesthouse.com
I: www.laurelguesthouse.com

North Leigh Guest House ♦♦♦♦
28 Common Road, North Leigh, Witney OX8 6RA
T: (01993) 881622

Quarrydene ♦♦♦
17 Dene Rise, Witney OX28 6LU
T: (01993) 772152
F: (01993) 772152

Springhill Farm Bed & Breakfast ♦♦♦
Cogges, Witney OX29 6UL
T: (01993) 704919

The Witney Hotel ♦♦♦
7 Church Green, Witney OX28 4AZ
T: (01993) 702137
F: (01993) 705337
E: bookings@thewitneyhotel.co.uk
I: www.thewitneyhotel.co.uk

WITTERSHAM
Kent

Bettysland ♦♦♦♦
39 Swan Street, Wittersham, Tenterden TN30 7PH
T: (01797) 270652

WIVELROD
Hampshire

Halketts
Rating Applied For
72 Kings Hill, Beech, Wivelrod, Alton GU34 4AN
T: (01420) 562258

WOBURN SANDS
Buckinghamshire

The Old Stables ♦♦♦♦
Bow Brickhill Road, Woburn Sands, Milton Keynes MK17 8DE
T: (01908) 281340
F: (08712) 772545
E: info@theoldstables.biz
I: www.theoldstables.biz

WOKING
Surrey

Amberhurst ♦♦♦
Holly Bank Road, Hook Heath, Woking GU22 0JN
T: (01483) 762748
F: (01483) 762748

Grantchester ♦♦♦
Boughton Hall Avenue, Send, Woking GU23 7DF
T: (01483) 225383
F: (01483) 596490
E: gary@hotpotmail.com

St Columba's House ♦♦
Maybury Hill, Woking GU22 8AB
T: (01483) 766498
F: (01483) 740441
E: retreats@st.columba.org.uk
I: www.stcolumbashouse.org.uk

Swallow Barn ♦♦♦
Milford Green, Chobham, Woking GU24 8AU
T: (01276) 856030
F: (01276) 856030
E: swallowbarn@compuserve.com
I: www.bestbandb.co.uk

WOODCHURCH
Kent

Shirkoak Farm
♦♦♦♦ SILVER AWARD
Woodchurch, Ashford TN26 3PZ
T: (01233) 860056
F: (01233) 861402
E: shirkoakfarm@aol.com
I: www.shirkoakfarm.com

WOODCOTE
Oxfordshire

Hedges ♦♦♦
South Stoke Road, Woodcote, Reading RG8 0PL
T: (01491) 680461
E: howard-allen@hedgeswoodcote.freeserve.co.uk

The Highwayman ♦♦♦
Exlade Street, Checkendon, Reading RG8 0UA
T: (01491) 682020
F: (01491) 682229
E: thehighwayman@skyeinnsfsnet.co.uk
I: www.thehighwaymancheckendon.co.uk

WOODFALLS
Hampshire

The Woodfalls Inn ♦♦♦♦
The Ridge, Woodfalls, Salisbury SP5 2LN
T: (01725) 513222
F: (01725) 513220
E: woodfallsi@aol.com
I: www.woodfallsinn.co.uk

WOODSTOCK
Oxfordshire

Blenheim Guest House & Tea Rooms ♦♦♦♦
17 Park Street, Woodstock, Oxford OX20 1SJ
T: (01993) 813814
F: (01993) 813810
E: Theblenheim@aol.com
I: www.theblenheim.com

Burleigh Farm ♦♦♦
Bladon Road, Cassington, Oxford OX29 4EA
T: (01865) 881352
E: j.cook@farmline.com

The Duke of Marlborough ♦♦♦♦
A44 Woodleys, Wootton, Woodstock, Oxford OX20 1HT
T: (01993) 811460
F: (01993) 810165

Gorselands Hall
♦♦♦♦ SILVER AWARD
Boddington Lane, North Leigh, Witney OX29 6PU
T: (01993) 882292
F: (01993) 883629
E: hamilton@gorselandshall.com
I: www.gorselandshall.com

The Kings Head Inn ♦♦♦♦
Chapel Hill, Wootton, Woodstock, Oxford OX20 1DX
T: (01993) 811340
E: t.fay@kings-head.co.uk
I: www.kings-head.co.uk

The Laurels
♦♦♦♦ SILVER AWARD
Hensington Road, Woodstock, Oxford OX20 1JL
T: (01993) 812583
F: (01993) 810041
E: stay@laurelsguesthouse.co.uk
I: www.smoothhound.co.uk/hotels/thelaur.html

The Lawns ♦♦
2 Flemings Road, Woodstock, Oxford OX20 1NA
T: (01993) 812599
F: (01993) 812599
E: thelawns2@amserve.com
I: www.thelawns.co.uk

Plane Tree House
♦♦♦♦ SILVER AWARD
48 Oxford Street, Woodstock, Oxford OX20 1TT
T: (01993) 813075

The Punchbowl Inn ♦♦♦
12 Oxford Street, Woodstock, Oxford OX20 1TR
T: (01993) 811218
F: (01993) 811393
E: info@punchbowl-woodstock.co.uk
I: www.punchbowl-woodstock.co.uk

Shepherds Hall Inn ♦♦♦
Witney Road, Freeland, Oxford OX29 8HQ
T: (01993) 881256
F: (01993) 883455

Shipton Glebe
♦♦♦♦♦ GOLD AWARD
Upper Campsfield Road, Woodstock, Oxford OX20 1QQ
T: (01993) 812688
F: (01993) 813142
E: stay@shipton-glebe.com
I: www.shipton-glebe.com

The Townhouse ♦♦♦♦
15 High Street, Woodstock, Oxford OX20 1TE
T: (01993) 810843
F: (01993) 810843
E: info@woodstock-townhouse.com
I: www.woodstock-townhouse.com

WOOL
Dorset

Fingle Bridge ♦♦♦
Duck Street, Wool, Wareham
BH20 6DE
T: (01929) 462739
E: enquiries@finglebridge.co.uk
I: www.finglebridge.co.uk

WOOLSTONE
Buckinghamshire

Ediths Cottage ♦♦♦♦
21 Newport Road, Woolstone, Milton Keynes MK15 0AB
T: (01908) 604916
E: edithcott@biinternet.com

WOOTTON
Oxfordshire

Killingworth Castle Inn ♦♦♦
Glympton Road, Wootton, Woodstock, Oxford OX20 1EJ
T: (01993) 811401
E: wwigiscastle@aol.com
I: www.killingworthcastle.tablesir.com

WOOTTON BRIDGE
Isle of Wight

Grange Farm ♦♦♦♦
Staplers Road, Wootton Bridge, Ryde PO33 4RW
T: (01983) 882147
F: (01983) 882147

WORMINGHALL
Buckinghamshire

Crabtree Barn ♦♦♦♦
Field Farm, Worminghall, Aylesbury HP18 9JY
T: (01844) 339719
F: (01844) 339544
E: issymcguinness@crabtreebarn.co.uk
I: www.crabtreebarn.co.uk

WORPLESDON
Surrey

Hillside ♦♦♦♦
Perry Hill, Worplesdon, Guildford GU3 3RF
T: (01483) 232051
F: (01483) 232051
E: info@thehillsidehotel.com
I: www.thehillsidehotel.com

Maytime ♦♦♦
43 Envis Way, Fairlands, Worplesdon, Guildford GU3 3NJ
T: (01483) 235025
E: e.m.warby@amserve.net

WORTH
Kent

St Crispin Inn ♦♦♦
The Street, Worth, Deal
CT14 0DF
T: (01304) 612081
F: (01304) 614838
E: job.tob@virgin.net

WORTHING
West Sussex

The Acacia ♦♦♦♦
5-7 Warwick Gardens, Worthing
BN11 1PE
T: 0870 7107313
F: (01903) 210068
E: enquiries@theacacia.com
I: www.theacacia.com

Angel Lodge ♦♦♦♦
19 Malvern Close, Worthing
BN11 2HE
T: (01903) 233002
F: (01903) 233002
E: angellodge19@aol.com
I: www.angellodge.co.uk

Blair House Hotel ♦♦♦♦
11 St Georges Road, Worthing
BN11 2DS
T: (01903) 234071
F: (01903) 234071
E: stay@blairhousehotel.freeserve.co.uk
I: www.blairhousehotel.co.uk

Bonchurch House ♦♦♦♦
1 Winchester Road, Worthing
BN11 4DJ
T: (01903) 202492
F: (01903) 202492
E: bonchurch@enta.net
I: www.smoothhound.co.uk/hotels/bonchurc.html

Brooke House
♦♦♦♦ SILVER AWARD
6 Westbrooke, Worthing
BN11 1RE
T: (01903) 600291
F: (01903) 600291
E: brooke.house@ntlworld.com
I: www.smoothhound.co.uk/hotels/brooke.html

The Brunswick ♦♦
Thorn Road, Worthing
BN11 3ND
T: (01903) 202141
E: b&b@brunswick.freeserve.co.uk
I: www.brunswick.fsnet.co.uk

Bute House ♦♦♦♦
325 Brighton Road, Worthing
BN11 2HP
T: (01903) 210247
F: (01903) 208109

Camelot House ♦♦♦♦
20 Gannon Road, Worthing
BN11 2DT
T: (01903) 204334
F: (01903) 207006
E: stay@camelotguesthouse.co.uk
I: www.camelotguesthouse.co.uk

Delmar Hotel ♦♦♦
1-2 New Parade, Worthing
BN11 2BQ
T: (01903) 211834
F: (01903) 219052
I: www.SmoothHound.co.uk/hotels/delmar.html

Edwardian Dreams
Rating Applied For
77 Manor Road, Worthing
BN11 4SL
T: (01903) 218565

Haytor Guest House ♦♦♦
Salisbury Road, Worthing
BN11 1RB
T: (01903) 235287
E: alashipley@aol.com

Heenefields Guest House
♦♦♦♦
98 Heene Road, Worthing
BN11 3RE
T: (01903) 538780
E: heenefields.guesthouse@virgin.net
I: www.heenefields.com

High Beach ♦♦♦♦
201 Brighton Road, Worthing
BN11 2EX
T: (01903) 236389
F: (01903) 213399
E: highbeach@hotmail.com

High Trees Guest House
♦♦♦♦
2 Warwick Gardens, Worthing
BN11 1PE
T: (01903) 236668
F: (01903) 601688
E: bill@hightreesguesthouse.co.uk
I: www.hightreesguesthouse.co.uk

Highdown Hotel & Restaurant
♦♦♦
Littlehampton Road, Goring-by-Sea, Worthing BN12 6PF
T: (01903) 700152
F: (01903) 507518
I: www.highdown-towers.com

Marine View Hotel ♦♦♦
111 Marine Parade, Worthing
BN11 3QG
T: (01903) 238413
F: (01903) 238630
E: marineviewhotel@talk21.com
I: sussexlive.co.uk

Merton House ♦♦♦♦
96 Broadwater Road, Worthing
BN14 8AW
T: (01903) 238222
F: (01903) 238222
E: stay@mertonhouse.freeserve.co.uk
I: www.mertonhouse.co.uk

The Moorings Hotel ♦♦♦♦
4 Selden Road, Worthing
BN11 2LL
T: (01903) 208882
F: (01903) 236878
E: annette@mooringshotel.fsnet.co.uk
I: www.mooringsworthing.co.uk

Oakville Guest House ♦♦♦♦
13 Wyke Avenue, Worthing
BN11 1PB
T: (01903) 205026
F: (01903) 205026
E: enquiries@oakville-worthing.co.uk
I: www.oakville-worthing.co.uk

134 Offington Park
Rating Applied For
Offington Drive, Worthing
BN14 9PT
T: (01903) 261044

Olinda Guest House ♦♦♦♦
199 Brighton Road, Worthing
BN11 2EX
T: (01903) 206114
F: (01903) 206114
E: info@olindaguesthouse.co.uk
I: www.olindaguesthouse.co.uk

Pebble Beach ♦♦♦
281 Brighton Road, Worthing
BN11 2HG
T: (01903) 210766
F: (01903) 210766
E: pebblebeach281@aol.com
I: www.pebblebeach281.com

Queens Lodge ♦♦♦♦
2 Queens Road, Worthing
BN11 3LX
T: (01903) 205519
E: david.leal@ntlworld.com
I: www.smoothhound.co.uk/hotelsqueenslodge.html

Rosedale House ♦♦♦♦
12 Bath Road, Worthing
BN11 3NU
T: (01903) 233181
E: rosedale@amserve.net

St Albans Guest House ♦♦♦♦
143 Brighton Road, Worthing
BN11 2EU
T: (01903) 206623
F: (01903) 525597
E: suemurraywha@aol.com

School House ♦♦♦♦
11 Ambrose Place, Worthing
BN11 1PZ
T: (01903) 206823
F: (01903) 821902

Sea Lodge ♦♦♦
183 Brighton Road, Worthing
BN11 2EX
T: (01903) 201214
F: (01903) 201214

Southdene Guest House ♦♦
41 Warwick Gardens, Worthing
BN11 1PF
T: (01903) 232909

Tamara Guest House ♦♦♦
19 Alexandra Road, Worthing
BN11 2DX
T: (01903) 520332

Woodlands Guest House ♦♦♦
20 Warwick Gardens, Worthing
BN11 1PF
T: (01903) 233557
F: (01903) 536925
E: woodlandsghse@boltblue.com
I: www.woodlands20-22.freeserve.co.uk

WROXALL
Isle of Wight

The Grange ♦♦♦♦
Wroxall, Ventnor PO38 3DA
T: (01983) 857424
E: thegrange@mcgeoch.com
I: www.mcgeoch.com/thegrange

Little Span Farm ♦♦♦
Rew Lane, Wroxall, Ventnor
PO38 3AU
T: (01983) 852419
F: (01983) 852419
E: info@spanfarm.co.uk
I: www.spanfarm.co.uk

WYE
Kent

Mistral ♦♦♦♦
3 Oxenturn Road, Wye, Ashford
TN25 5BH
T: (01233) 813011
F: (01233) 813011
E: geoff@chapman.invictanet.co.uk
I: www.wye.org

YARMOUTH
Isle of Wight

Medlars ♦♦♦
Halletts Shute, Yarmouth
PO41 0RH
T: (01983) 761541
F: (01983) 761541
E: grey@lineone.net
I: www.milford.co.uk/go/medlars.html

Rosemead ♦♦
Tennyson Road, Yarmouth
PO41 0PX
T: (01983) 761078
E: barbara_boon@hotmail.com

YARNTON
Oxfordshire

Kings Bridge Guest House
♦♦♦
Woodstock Road, Yarnton, Kidlington OX5 1PH
T: (01865) 841748
F: (01865) 849662

Welcome *to* Excellence

Look out for the Welcome to Excellence sign – a commitment to achieve excellence in customer care

Displaying this logo signifies that the business aims to exceed visitor needs and expectations, and provides an environment where courtesy, helpfulness and a warm welcome are standard.

Visitor Attraction Quality Assurance

VisitBritain operates a Visitor Attraction Quality Assurance Standard. Participating attractions are visited annually by trained, impartial assessors who look at all aspects of the visit, from initial telephone enquiries to departure, customer services to catering, as well as facilities and activities. Only those attractions which have been assessed by VisitBritain and meet the standard receive the quality marque, your sign of a 'Quality Assured Visitor Attraction'.

Look out for the quality marque and visit with confidence.

BOGNOR REGIS
West Sussex

Bognor Regis Campus University College Chichester ★★
St Michaels, Upper Bognor Road, Bognor Regis PO21 1HR
T: (01243) 816070
F: (01243) 816068

BRADFORD
West Yorkshire

Bradford College ★
Margaret McMillan Hall of Residence, Easby Road, Bradford BD7 1QZ
T: (01274) 733291
F: (01274) 741358
E: andrewa@bilk.ac.uk
I: www.bilk.ac.uk

University of Bradford
Rating applied for
Laiseridge Lane, Dennis Bellamy Hall, Bradford BD5 0NH
T: (01274) 234898
F: (01274) 234881
E: j.humphreys/x11905@bradford.ac.uk
I: bradford.ac.uk

BRIGHTON
East Sussex

University of Brighton ★★ - ★★★
Mithras House, Lewes Road, Brighton BN2 4AT
T: (01273) 643120
F: (01273) 643113
E: conferences@brighton.ac.uk
I: www.brighton.ac.uk

CANTERBURY
Kent

Christ Church University College ★ - ★★★
North Holmes Road, Canterbury CT1 1QU
T: (01227) 782225
F: (01227) 782528

Kent Hospitality ★★ - ★★★
Tanglewood, The University, Canterbury CT2 7LX
T: (01227) 828000
F: (01227) 828019
E: hospitality-enquiry@kent.ac.uk
I: www.kent.ac.uk/hospitality/

CHICHESTER
West Sussex

University College Chichester ★★
Bishop Otter Campus, College Lane, Chichester PO19 6PE
T: (01243) 816070
F: (01243) 816068
E: conference@ucc.ac.uk
I: www.ucc.ac.uk

EGHAM
Surrey

Royal Holloway University of London
Rating applied for
Egham Hill, Egham TW20 0EX
T: (01784) 443045
F: (01784) 443797
E: sales-office@rhul.ac.uk
I: www.rhul.ac.uk/fm

FALMER
East Sussex

University of Sussex ★★★
Conference Office, Bramber House, Falmer, Brighton BN1 9QU
T: (01273) 678678
F: (01273) 677880
E: conferences@sussex.ac.uk
I: www.sussex.ac.uk/Units/conference

GREAT OUSEBURN
North Yorkshire

Queen Ethelburga's College *Rating applied for*
Thorpe Underwood Hall, Great Ouseburn, York YO26 9SS
T: 0870 742 3330
F: 0870 742 3310
E: remember@compuserve.com
I: www.queenethelburgas.edu

HATFIELD
Hertfordshire

University of Hertfordshire ★★
de Havilland Campus, Hatfield Avenue, Hatfield AL10 9FL
T: (01707) 284841
F: (01707) 268407
E: sales@fieldercentre.co.uk
I: www.uhhospitality.co.uk

LONDON
Greater London

IES Student Residence Hall *Rating applied for*
Manresa Road, Corner of King's Road & Manresa Road, London SW3 6NA
T: (020) 7808 9200
F: (020) 7376 5167
E: info@iesreshall.com
I: www.iesreshall.com

NOTTINGHAM
Nottinghamshire

University of Nottingham ★ - ★★★
C52 Portland Building, University Park, Nottingham NG7 2RD
E: uncc@nottongham.au.uk
I: uncc.co.uk

OAKHAM
Rutland

Barleythorpe Training and Conference Centre ★★★★
Barleythorpe, Oakham, Rutland LE15 7ED
T: (01572) 723711
F: (01572) 757657
E: pennyollerenshaw@eef-eastmids.org.uk
I: www.barleythorpe.com

OXFORD
Oxfordshire

St Hugh's College ★★
Rachel Trickett Building, St Margarets Road, Oxford OX2 6LE
T: (01865) 274900
F: (01865) 274912

READING
Berkshire

Reading Student Village ★★★★
Sherfield Drive, Reading RG2 7EZ
T: 08707 125002
F: (02070) 178273

SHEFFIELD
South Yorkshire

Tapton Hall of Residence ★★
The University of Sheffield, Crookes Road, Sheffield S10 2AZ
T: (0114) 222 8862
E: b&b@sheffield.ac.uk
I: www.conferencesheffield.com

1 1

SOUTHBOROUGH
Kent

Salomons ★★★
David Salomons Estate, Broomhill Road, Southborough, Royal Tunbridge Wells TN3 0TG
T: (01892) 515152
F: (01892) 539102
E: m.salomonson@salomons.org.uk
I: www.salomonscentre.org.uk

WINCHESTER
Hampshire

King Alfred's College
Rating applied for
Sparkford Road, Winchester SO22 4NR
T: (01962) 827322
F: (01962) 827264
E: conferences@wkac.ac.uk
I: www.kingalfreds.ac.uk

Information

Contents

The National Quality Assurance Scheme

A rating you can trust

When you're looking for a place to stay, you need a rating system you can trust. VisitBritain's ratings are your clear guide to what to expect, in an easy-to-understand form. Properties are visited annually by our trained impartial assessors, so you can have confidence that your accommodation has been thoroughly checked and rated for quality before you make a booking.

Using a simple One to Five Diamond rating, the system puts a much greater emphasis on quality and is based on research which shows exactly what consumers are looking for when choosing accommodation.

'Guest Accommodation' covers a wide variety of serviced accommodation for which England is renowned, including guesthouses, bed and breakfasts, inns and farmhouses. Establishments are rated from one to five Diamonds. The same minimum requirement for facilities and services applies to all Guest Accommodation from One to Five Diamonds. Progressively higher levels of quality and customer care must be provided for each of the One to Five Diamond ratings. The rating reflects the unique character of Guest Accommodation, and covers areas such as cleanliness, service and hospitality, bedrooms, bathrooms and food quality.

Look out, too, for VisitBritain's Gold and Silver Awards, which are awarded to those establishments which not only achieve the overall quality required for their Diamond rating, but also reach the highest levels of quality in those specific areas which guests identify as being really important for them. They will reflect the quality of comfort and cleanliness you'll find in the bedrooms and bathrooms and the quality of service you'll enjoy throughout your stay.

Diamond ratings are your sign of quality assurance, giving you the confidence to book the accommodation that meets your expectations.

What to expect at each rating level

The Diamond ratings for Guest Accommodation reflect visitor expectations of this sector. The quality of what is provided is more important to visitors than a wide range of facilities and services. Therefore, the same minimum requirement for facilities and services applies to all Guest Accommodation from One to Five Diamonds, while progressively higher levels of quality and customer care must be provided for each of the One to Five Diamond ratings.

- **At ONE DIAMOND Guest Accommodation, you will find:**

An acceptable overall level of quality and helpful service. Accommodation offering, as a minimum, a full cooked or continental breakfast. Other meals, where provided, will be freshly prepared. You will have a comfortable bed, with clean bed linen and towels and fresh soap. Adequate heating and hot water available at reasonable times for baths or showers at no extra charge.

- **At TWO DIAMOND Guest Accommodation, you will find (in addition to what is provided at One Diamond):**

A good overall level of quality and comfort, with a greater emphasis on guest care in all areas.

- **At THREE DIAMOND GUEST Accommodation, you will find (in addition to what is provided at Two Diamond):**

A very good overall level of quality. For example, good quality, comfortable bedrooms; well maintained, practical décor; a good choice of quality items available for breakfast; other meals, where provided, will be freshly cooked from good quality ingredients. A greater degree of comfort provided for you, with good levels of customer care.

- **At FOUR DIAMOND Guest Accommodation, you will find (in addition to what is provided at Three Diamond):**

An excellent overall level of quality in all areas and customer care showing very good levels of attention to your needs.

- **At Five Diamond Guest Accommodation, you will find (in addition to what is provided at Four Diamond):**

An exceptional overall level of quality. For example, Breakfast offering a wide choice of high quality fresh ingredients; other meals, where provided, featuring fresh, seasonal, and often local ingredients. Excellent levels of customer care, anticipating your needs.

NB. En suite and private bathrooms contribute to the quality score at all Diamond levels. Please check when booking or see entry details.

AWAITING CONFIRMATION OF RATING

At the time of going to press some establishments featured in this guide had not yet been assessed for their rating for the year 2004 and so their new rating could not be included. For your information, the most up-to-date information regarding these establishments' ratings is in the listings pages at the back of this guide.

General **Advice** & **Infomation**

MAKING A BOOKING

When enquiring about accommodation, make sure you check prices and other important details. You will also need to state your requirements, clearly and precisely - for example:

- Arrival and departure dates, with acceptable alternatives if appropriate.
- The type of accommodation you need; for example, room with twin beds, private bathroom.
- The terms you want; for example, room only, bed and breakfast, half board, full board.
- If you have children with you; their ages, whether you want them to share your room or be next door, any other special requirements, such as a cot.
- Particular requirements you may have, such as a special diet.

Booking by letter

Misunderstandings can easily happen over the telephone, so we strongly advise you to confirm your booking in writing if there is time.

Please note that VisitBritain does not make reservations - you should write direct to the accommodation.

DEPOSITS

If you make your reservation weeks or months in advance, you will probably be asked for a deposit. The amount will vary according to the time of year, the number of people in your party and how long you plan to stay. The deposit will then be deducted from the final bill when you leave.

PAYMENT ON ARRIVAL

Some establishments, especially large hotels in big towns, ask you to pay for your room on arrival if you have not booked it in advance. This is especially likely to happen if you arrive late and have little or no luggage.

If you are asked to pay on arrival, it is a good idea to see your room first, to make sure it meets your requirements.

CANCELLATIONS

Legal contract

When you accept accommodation that is offered to you, by telephone or in writing, you enter a legally binding contract with the proprietor.

This means that if you cancel your booking, fail to take up the accommodation or leave early, the proprietor may be entitled to compensation if he cannot re-let for all or a good part of the booked period. You will probably forfeit any deposit you have paid, and may well be asked for an additional payment.

You should be advised at the time of your booking what charges would be made in the event of cancelling the accommodation or leaving early. If this does not happen you should ask, to avoid any future dispute.

The proprietor cannot make a claim until after the booked period, however, and during that time every effort should be made by the proprietor to re-let the accommodation.

If there is a dispute it is sensible for both sides to seek legal advice on the matter.

If you do have to change your travel plans, it is in your own interests to let the proprietor know in writing as soon as possible, to give them a chance to re-let your accommodation.

And remember, if you book by telephone and are asked for your credit card number, you should check whether the proprietor intends charging your credit card account should you later cancel your reservation. A proprietor should not be able to charge your credit card account with a cancellation fee unless he or she has made this clear at the time of your booking and you have agreed. However, to avoid later disputes, we suggest you check with the proprietor whether he or she intends to charge your credit card account if you cancel.

INSURANCE

A travel or holiday insurance policy will safeguard you if you have to cancel or change your holiday plans. You can arrange a policy quite cheaply through your insurance company or travel agent. Some hotels also offer their own insurance schemes.

ARRIVING LATE

If you know you will be arriving late in the evening, it is a good idea to say so when you book. If you are delayed on your way, a telephone call to say that you will be late will help prevent any problems when you arrive.

SERVICE CHARGES AND TIPPING

These days many places levy service charges automatically. If they do, they must clearly say so in their offer of accommodation, at the time of booking. Then the service charge becomes part of the legal contract when you accept the offer of accommodation.

If a service charge is levied automatically, there is no need to tip the staff, unless they provide some exceptional service. The usual tip for meals is 10% of the total bill.

TELEPHONE CHARGES

Guest Accommodation establishments can set their own charges for telephone calls made through their switchboard or from direct-dial telephones in bedrooms. These charges are often much higher than telephone companies' standard charges (to defray the cost of providing the service).

Comparing costs

It is a condition of the national quality assurance standard that a hotel's unit charges are on display, by the telephones or with the room information. But in practice it is not always easy to compare these charges with standard telephone rates. Before using the telephone for long-distance calls, you may decide to ask how the charges compare.

SECURITY OF VALUABLES

You can deposit your valuables with the proprietor or manager during your stay, and we recommend you do this as a sensible precaution. Make sure you obtain a receipt for them.

Some places do not accept articles for safe custody, and in that case it is wisest to keep your valuables with you.

Disclaimer

Some proprietors put up a notice which disclaims liability for property brought on to their premises by a guest. In fact, they can only restrict their liability to a minimum laid down by law (The Hotel Proprietors Act 1956).

Under that Act, a proprietor is liable for the value of the loss or damage to any property (except a motor car or its contents) of a guest who has engaged overnight accommodation, but if the proprietor has the notice on display as prescribed under that Act, liability is limited to £50 for one article and a total of £100 for any one guest. The notice must be prominently displayed in the reception area or main entrance. These limits do not apply to valuables you have deposited with the proprietor for safe-keeping, or to property lost through the default, neglect or wilful act or the proprietor or his staff.

BRINGING PETS TO ENGLAND

The quarantine laws have changed in England, and a Pet Travel Scheme (PETS) is currently in operation. Under this scheme pet dogs and cats are able to come into Britain from over 50 countries via certain sea, air and rail routes into England.

Dogs and cats that have been resident in these countries for more than six months may enter the UK under the Scheme, providing they are accompanied by the appropriate documentation. Pet dogs and cats from other countries will still have to undergo six months' quarantine.

For dogs and cats to be able to enter the UK without quarantine under the PETS Scheme they will have to meet certain conditions and travel with the following documents: the official PETS certificate, a certificate of treatment against tapeworm and ticks and a declaration of residence.

A European Regulation on the movement of pet animals will apply from 3 July 2004. Broadly, the rules of PETS will continue to apply to dogs and cats entering the UK but certain other pet animals will also be included.

For details of participating countries, routes, operators and further information about the PETS scheme and the new EU Regulations please contact the PETS Helpline, DEFRA (Department for Environment, Food and Rural Affairs),
1a Page Street, London SW1P 4PQ
Tel: +44 (0) 870 241 1710
Fax: +44 (0) 20 7904 6834
Email: pets.helpline@defra.gsi.gov.uk, or visit their website at www.defra.gov.uk/animalh/quarantine.

CODE OF CONDUCT AND CONDITIONS OF PARTICIPATION

The proprietor/management is required to undertake and observe the following Code of Conduct:

- To maintain standards of guest care, cleanliness, and service appropriate to the type of establishment;
- To describe accurately in any advertisement, brochure, or other printed or electronic media, the facilities and services provided;
- To make clear to visitors exactly what is included in all prices quoted for accommodation, including taxes, and any other surcharges. Details of charges for additional services/facilities should also be made clear;
- To give a clear statement of the policy on cancellations to guests at the time of booking i.e. by telephone, fax, email as well as information given in a printed format;

- To adhere to, and not to exceed prices quoted at the time of booking for accommodation and other services;
- To advise visitors at the time of booking, and subsequently of any change, if the accommodation offered is in an unconnected annexe or similar and to indicate the location of such accommodation and any difference in comfort and/or amenities from accommodation in the establishment;
- To give each visitor on request details of payments due and a receipt, if required;
- To deal promptly and courteously with all enquiries, requests, bookings and correspondence from visitors;
- Ensure complaint handling procedures are in place and that complaints received are investigated promptly and courteously and that the outcome is communicated to the visitor;
- To give due consideration to the requirements of visitors with disabilities and visitors with special needs, and to make suitable provision where applicable;
- To provide public liability insurance or comparable arrangements and to comply with all applicable planning, safety and other statutory requirements;
- To allow a VisitBritain representative reasonable access to the establishment, on request to confirm the Code of Conduct is being observed.

Conditions for Participation

All establishments participating in the National Quality Assurance Standards (NQAS) are required to:

- Meet or exceed the VisitBritain minimum entry requirements for a rating in the relevant accommodation sector;
- Observe the VisitBritain Code of Conduct;
- Be assessed annually, and in the event of complaints by authorised representatives of VisitBritain;
- Pay an annual participation fee;
- Complete an annual information collection questionnaire either online or by post as required.

Change of Ownership

When an establishment is sold, the existing rating cannot be transferred to the new owner, unless otherwise agreed by VisitBritain in writing. The new owner is required to make an application for participation in the VisitBritain National Quality Assurance Standard.

Signage

Where an establishment, for whatever reason, ceases to participate in the NQAS, all relevant display signs and print material must be removed.

Use of ratings should always be accompanied by the VisitBritain Quality Marque.

Any listing in a VisitBritain publication/web site and within the Tourist Information Centre network are conditional on continued participation in the NQAS.

Failure to observe these conditions may result in the establishment becoming ineligible to display or use the VisitBritain endorsement in any form whatsoever.

COMMENTS AND COMPLAINTS

Guest Accommodation and the law

Places that offer accommodation have legal and statutory responsibilities to their customers, such as providing information about prices, providing adequate fire precautions and safeguarding valuables. Like other businesses, they must also abide by the Trades Description Acts 1968 and 1972 when they describe their accommodation and facilities.

All the places featured in this guide have declared that they do fulfil all applicable statutory obligations.

Information

The proprietors themselves supply the descriptions of their establishments and other information for the entries, (except VisitBritain Ratings and Awards).

VisitBritain cannot guarantee the accuracy of information in this guide, and accepts no responsibility for any error or misrepresentation. All liability for loss, disappointment, negligence or other damage caused by reliance on the information contained in this guide, or in the event of bankruptcy or liquidation or cessation of trade of any company, individual or firm mentioned, is hereby excluded.

We strongly recommend that you carefully check prices and other details when you book your accommodation.

Problems

Of course, we hope you will not have cause for complaint, but problems do occur from time to time.

If you are dissatisfied with anything, make your complaint to the management immediately. Then the management can take action at once to investigate the matter and put things right. The longer you leave a complaint, the harder it is to deal with it effectively.

In certain circumstances, VisitBritain may look into complaints. However, VisitBritain has no statutory control over establishments or their methods of operating. VisitBritain cannot become involved in legal or contractual matters and cannot get involved in seeking financial recompense.

If you do have problems that have not been resolved by the proprietor and which you would like to bring to our attention, please write to: Quality Standards Department, VisitBritain, Thames Tower, Black's Road, Hammersmith, London W6 9EL.

About the Guide Entries

ENTRIES

All the acommodation featured in this guide has been assessed or has applied for assessment under VisitBritain's quality assurance standard. Assessment automatically entitles establishments to a listing in this guide. Additionally proprietors may pay to have their establishment featured in either a Standard Entry (includes description, facilities and prices) or Enhanced Entry (photographs and extended details).

LOCATIONS

Places to stay are listed under the town, city or village where they are located. If a place is out in the countryside, you may find it listed under a nearby village or town.

Town names are listed alphabetically within each regional section of the guide, along with the name of the county or unitary authority they are in (see note on page 699), and their map reference.

MAP REFERENCES

These refer to the colour location maps at the front of the guide. The first figure shown is the map number, the following letter and figure indicate the grid reference on the map.

Only place names under which Standard or Enhanced entries (see above) are included appear on the maps.

Some entries were included just before the guide went to press, so they do not appear on the maps.

ADDRESSES

County names, which appear in the town headings, are not repeated in the entries. When you are writing, you should of course make sure you use the full address and postcode.

TELEPHONE NUMBERS

Telephone numbers are listed below the accommodation address for each entry. Area codes are shown in brackets.

PRICES

The prices shown in Where to Stay 2004 are only a general guide; they were supplied to us by proprietors in summer 2003. Remember, changes may occur after the guide goes to press, so we strongly advise you to check prices when you book your accommodation.

Prices are shown in pounds sterling and include VAT where applicable. Some places also include a service charge in their standard tariff, so check this when you book.

There are many different ways of quoting prices for accommodation. We use a standardised method in the guide to allow you to compare prices.
For example, when we show:
Bed and breakfast, prices shown are per person per night for overnight accommodation with breakfast, for single and double rooms.
The per person per night price for a double room is based on 2 people sharing a double or twin room. If a double room is occupied by one person there is usually an increase in price.
Half board, prices shown are per person per night for breakfast and evening meal, and are usually based on two people sharing a room.

Some places provide only a continental breakfast in the set price, and you may have to pay extra if you want a full English breakfast.

Checking prices

According to the law, hotels with at least four bedrooms or eight beds must display their overnight accommodation charges in the reception area or entrance. In your own interests, do make sure you check prices and what they include.

Children's rates

You will find that many places charge a reduced rate for children, especially if they share a room with their parents.

Some places charge the full rate, however, when a child occupies a room which might otherwise have been let to an adult.

The upper age limit for reductions for children varies from one hotel to another, so check this when you book.

Seasonal packages and special promotions

Prices often vary through the year, and may be significantly lower outside peak holiday weeks. Many places offer special package rates - fully inclusive weekend breaks, for example - in the autumn, winter and spring. A number of establishments have included, in their Enhanced Entry information, any special offers, themed breaks etc that are available.

You can get details of other bargain packages that may be available from the establishments themselves, the Regional Tourist Boards or your local Tourist Information Centre (TIC).

Your local travel agent may also have information, and can help you make bookings.

BATHROOMS

Each accommodation entry shows you the number of en suite and private bathrooms available, the number of private showers and the number of public bathrooms.

'En suite bathroom' means the bath or shower and WC are contained behind the main door of the bedroom. 'Private bathroom' means a bath or shower and WC solely for the occupants of one bedroom, on the same floor, reasonably close and with a key provided. 'Private shower' means a shower en suite with the bedroom but no WC.

Public bathrooms normally have a bath, sometimes with a shower attachment. If the availability of a bath is important to you, remember to check when you book.

MEALS

It is advisable to check availability of meals and times when making your booking. Some smaller places may ask you at breakfast or midday whether you want an evening meal.

The prices shown in each entry are for bed and breakfast or half board, but many places also offer lunch, as you will see indicated in the entry.

OPENING PERIOD

If an entry does not state 'Open All Year', please check opening period with the establishment.

SYMBOLS

The at-a-glance symbols included at the end of each entry show many of the services and facilities available at each establishment. You will find the key to these symbols on the back-cover flap. Open out the flap and you can check the meanings of the symbols as you go.

SMOKING

Many places provide non-smoking areas - from no-smoking bedrooms and lounges to no-smoking sections of the restaurant. Some places prefer not to accommodate smokers, and in such cases the descriptions and symbols in each entry make this clear.

ALCOHOLIC DRINKS

Many places listed in the guide are licenced to serve alcohol. The licence may be restricted – to diners only, for example – so you may want to check this when you book. If they have a bar this is shown by the 🍷 symbol.

A NOTE ABOUT HOTELS

There is no restriction on any property that provides serviced accommodation using the word 'hotel' in the title. Hotels with a Star rating meet all the requirements for the 1 Star hotel standard and will usually have a drinks licence and offer meals in addition to breakfast. 'Hotel' establishments in VisitBritain's Guest Accommodation Guide meet the minimum entry requirements for the Guest Accommodation standard but do not automatically meet the Hotel 1 Star requirements.

PETS

Many places accept guests with dogs, but we do advise that you check this when you book, and ask if there are any extra charges or rules about exactly where your pet is allowed. The acceptance of dogs is not always extended to cats, and it is strongly advised that cat owners contact the establishment well in advance. Some establishments do not accept pets at all. Pets are welcome where you see this symbol 🐕.

The quarantine laws have changed in England, and pet dogs and cats are able to come into Britain from over 50 countries. For details of the Pet Travel Scheme (PETS) please turn to page 686.

CREDIT AND CHARGE CARDS

The credit and charge cards accepted by an establishment are listed in the entry following the letters CC.

If you do plan to pay by card, check that the establishment will take your card before you book.

Some proprietors will charge you a higher rate if you pay by credit card rather than cash or cheque. The difference is to cover the percentage paid by the proprietor to the credit card company.

If you are planning to pay by credit card, you may want to ask whether it would, in fact, be cheaper to pay by cheque or cash. When you book by telephone, you may be asked for your credit card number as 'confirmation'. But remember, the proprietor may then charge your credit card account if you cancel your booking. See under Cancellations on page 685.

CONFERENCES AND GROUPS

Places which cater for conferences and meetings are marked with the symbol 🍸. Rates are often negotiable, depending on the time of year, numbers of people involved and any special requirements you may have.

Distance Chart

The distances between towns on the chart below are given to the nearest mile, and are measured along routes based on the quickest travelling time, making maximum use of motorways or dual-carriageway roads. The chart is based upon information supplied by the Automobile Association.

To calculate the distance in kilometr[es] multiply the mileage by 1.6

For example: Brighton to Dover 82 miles x 1.6 =131.2 kilometres

	Aberdeen	Aberystwyth	Barnstaple	Birmingham	Brighton	Bristol	Cambridge	Cardiff	Carlisle	Carmarthen	Dorchester	Dover	Edinburgh	Exeter	Fort William	Glasgow	Gloucester	Guildford	Hereford	Holyhead	Hull	Inverness	Kendal	Leeds	Lincoln	Liverpool	Maidstone	Manchester	Middlesbrough	Newcastle	Northampton	Norwich	Nottingham	Oxford	Penzance	Perth	Peterborough	Plymouth	Portsmouth	Preston	Salisbury	Sheffield	Shrewsbury	Southampton	Stoke-on-Trent	Stranraer	Taunton	Wick	York
Aberystwyth	472
Barnstaple	608	214
Birmingham	436	124	180
Brighton	613	288	210	171
Bristol	518	130	100	90	169
Cambridge	463	215	267	97	120	170
Cardiff	537	111	128	109	202	44	203
Carlisle	236	236	371	199	376	281	256	300
Carmarthen	520	48	190	172	264	107	266	68	284
Dorchester	600	206	94	172	119	62	184	120	364	182
Dover	587	326	272	208	82	205	124	239	381	301	200
Edinburgh	126	336	471	299	476	381	333	400	100	386	463	458
Exeter	593	198	44	165	178	84	259	113	356	175	57	248	455
Fort William	156	435	570	398	576	480	456	499	199	485	562	580	137	554
Glasgow	150	332	467	295	472	377	353	396	96	382	459	477	47	451	102
Gloucester	484	113	126	56	155	36	150	63	248	125	118	192	346	110	445	343
Guildford	571	224	175	128	44	106	96	139	335	201	97	97	433	150	532	430	99
Hereford	487	79	144	59	189	54	153	59	250	85	136	225	349	129	448	346	34	133
Holyhead	464	102	339	167	345	249	259	202	228	150	331	369	326	323	425	323	215	302	156
Hull	376	227	320	139	258	230	138	250	170	311	312	262	247	304	367	266	196	239	198	218
Inverness	106	496	631	459	637	541	517	561	260	546	623	641	157	616	66	176	507	595	510	488	430
Kendal	283	189	324	153	330	234	251	254	47	240	316	354	145	309	245	143	200	288	203	181	164	307
Leeds	329	173	301	120	262	211	146	230	123	224	293	271	200	285	321	219	177	220	179	165	59	383	110
Lincoln	388	199	275	98	216	185	95	205	182	267	246	220	258	260	379	277	151	173	154	204	44	441	176	74
Liverpool	362	110	272	101	278	182	193	202	126	158	264	302	224	257	324	222	148	236	151	102	128	386	79	74	139
Maidstone	545	284	234	166	50	167	82	200	339	262	161	41	416	209	537	435	153	58	186	327	220	599	313	231	178	261
Manchester	357	134	261	89	266	171	160	190	120	184	253	290	219	245	318	216	136	224	139	125	97	380	74	44	85	34	248
Middlesbrough	276	244	357	176	318	267	197	286	95	294	349	322	146	341	283	190	232	276	235	235	89	308	84	64	122	145	280	114
Newcastle	235	275	388	207	349	298	229	317	60	325	380	353	106	372	242	153	264	307	266	266	142	267	102	95	154	176	311	145	39
Northampton	486	174	212	56	133	115	56	162	249	224	159	155	348	196	447	345	79	90	111	217	152	509	203	136	94	151	113	139	189	220
Norwich	488	278	329	160	168	233	63	266	282	328	241	172	359	313	480	378	212	160	215	321	147	542	276	174	103	240	130	185	223	254	118
Nottingham	395	162	232	51	193	142	86	161	189	223	224	210	266	216	387	285	107	151	110	178	93	449	164	77	39	112	168	71	130	161	64	119
Oxford	510	160	170	68	109	73	82	107	274	169	115	146	373	154	472	370	48	67	81	242	190	534	228	174	132	176	107	164	227	258	44	146	102
Penzance	702	308	108	274	287	193	368	222	466	284	167	357	564	109	663	562	220	259	238	434	415	726	419	403	370	367	318	356	451	482	326	433	326	265
Perth	86	388	523	351	529	433	378	453	152	438	515	503	42	507	102	64	399	486	401	379	291	114	199	245	303	278	461	275	192	150	400	404	310	426	617
Peterborough	435	204	263	86	158	173	37	193	229	255	204	162	306	248	427	325	139	115	142	225	110	489	223	121	51	159	120	132	170	201	45	78	58	86	357	351
Plymouth	633	239	62	205	218	124	299	153	397	215	98	288	495	44	594	493	151	190	169	365	346	657	350	334	301	298	249	287	382	413	257	364	257	196	78	544	288
Portsmouth	596	244	162	154	53	125	137	158	360	220	73	141	458	132	558	456	118	45	152	328	276	620	314	260	215	262	102	250	313	344	130	204	188	85	241	508	157	172
Preston	326	146	281	110	287	191	209	211	89	197	273	311	188	266	287	185	157	245	160	138	122	349	43	69	134	36	269	35	103	139	159	235	121	184	375	237	180	306	270
Salisbury	549	184	118	121	90	52	145	98	313	160	39	160	411	93	511	409	72	62	105	281	261	573	267	244	202	215	121	203	298	329	115	212	173	70	203	461	165	134	44	223
Sheffield	397	166	272	91	233	182	122	201	161	263	264	247	236	256	359	257	148	191	150	157	66	421	115	38	47	79	205	39	100	131	104	148	45	142	366	309	93	297	228	73	212
Shrewsbury	417	75	220	48	226	130	140	111	181	110	212	250	279	205	379	277	96	184	52	105	162	441	135	119	124	65	208	71	190	221	98	203	87	123	314	329	129	245	209	92	161	88
Southampton	578	225	142	135	66	106	136	140	342	201	53	152	440	111	539	437	100	49	133	309	258	601	295	241	199	243	113	232	294	325	111	204	169	67	221	489	157	152	20	252	23	209	191
Stoke-on-Trent	392	112	220	48	226	130	140	150	156	211	212	250	254	205	353	251	96	184	99	123	129	415	109	93	91	57	208	46	164	195	98	172	54	123	314	303	99	245	209	66	161	50	38	191
Stranraer	235	342	477	305	482	387	363	406	106	392	469	487	132	461	181	86	352	440	355	333	276	261	153	229	288	232	445	229	201	163	354	388	295	380	571	149	333	502	466	195	418	267	287	447	261
Taunton	560	165	50	132	160	51	226	80	323	142	45	224	422	34	521	419	77	126	96	291	272	583	277	261	228	225	185	213	309	340	183	291	184	123	144	471	215	75	114	234	70	224	172	94	172	429
Wick	207	597	732	560	738	642	618	662	361	647	724	742	258	716	166	277	608	695	610	588	531	104	408	484	543	487	700	484	409	367	609	644	550	635	826	215	589	757	721	451	673	523	542	702	516	362	684
York	323	201	314	133	275	224	154	243	116	251	306	279	193	298	314	212	189	233	192	192	38	376	91	24	79	102	237	71	51	89	146	180	87	184	408	239	125	339	269	96	254	57	146	251	120	223	265	477
LONDON	550	239	216	121	54	120	59	153	314	215	125	78	413	200	512	410	102	31	136	282	186	574	268	201	143	216	39	204	254	285	68	118	129	56	310	462	86	241	75	225	85	169	163	77	161	420	167	675	211

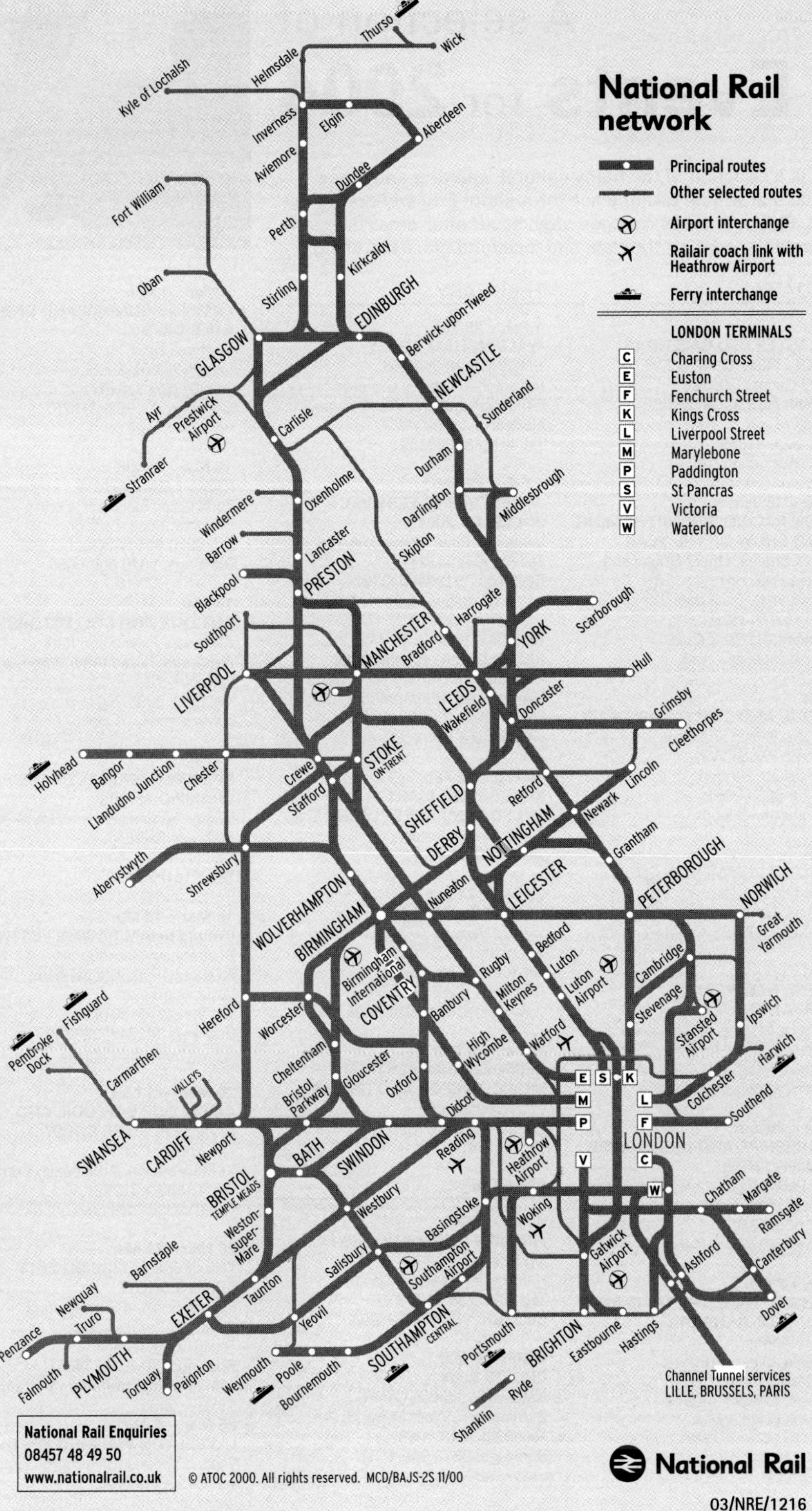

National Rail Enquiries
08457 48 49 50
www.nationalrail.co.uk

National Rail

03/NRE/1216

A selection of Events for 2004

This is a selection of the many cultural, sporting and other events that will be taking place throughout England during 2004. Please note, as changes often occur after press date, it is advisable to confirm the date and location before travelling.

JANUARY

11 Jan
LANCASTER OLD CALENDAR WALKS - NEW YEAR'S EVE
John O'Gaunt Gateway
Lancaster Castle, Lancaster, Lancashire
Tel: (01524) 32878
www.lancaster.gov.uk

17 Jan – 18 Jan
PIGEON RACING: BRITISH HOMING WORLD SHOW OF THE YEAR
Winter Gardens, Opera House and Empress Ballroom
Church Street, Blackpool, Lancashire
Tel: (01452) 713529
Bookings: (01253) 292029
www.pigeonracing.com

18 Jan
ANTIQUE AND COLLECTORS' FAIR
Alexandra Palace and Park
Alexandra Palace Way, Wood Green, London
Tel: (020) 8883 7061
www.allypally-uk.com

25 Jan
CHARLES I COMMEMORATION
Banqueting House
Whitehall, London
Tel: (01430) 430695

25 Jan
CHINESE NEW YEAR CELEBRATIONS
Gerrard Street, Leicester Square and Trafalgar Square
London
www.chinatownchinese.com

25 Jan – 26 Jan
THE CHESHIRE AND LANCASHIRE WEDDING SHOW
Tatton Park (NT)
Knutsford, Cheshire
Tel: (01625) 534400
Bookings: (01625) 534400

29 Jan – 8 Feb
WAKEFIELD RHUBARB TRAIL AND FESTIVAL OF RHUBARB
Various venues
Wakefield, West Yorkshire
Tel: (01924) 305911
Bookings: (01924) 305911
www.wakefield.gov.uk

FEBRUARY

1 Feb – 28 Feb
WALSINGHAM ABBEY SNOWDROP WALKS
Walsingham Abbey Grounds
Little Walsingham, Walsingham, Norfolk
Tel: (01328) 820259

1 Feb – 29 Feb*
JORVIK VIKING FESTIVAL – JOLABLOT 2004
Various venues throughout York
Tel: (01904) 643211
Bookings: (01904) 543402
www.vikingjorvik.com

6 Feb – 8 Feb
BIC WEDDING EXHIBITION
Bournemouth International Centre
Exeter Road, Bournemouth, Dorset
Tel: (01202) 456501
www.bic.co.uk

14 Feb – 28 Feb
KING'S LYNN MART TUESDAY MARKET PLACE
King's Lynn, Norfolk
Tel: (01508) 471772

20 Feb – 21 Feb
RALLYE SUNSEEKER
Various Venues
Bournemouth
Tel: (020) 8773 3404
Bookings: (020) 8773 3404
www.rallyesunseeker.co.uk

28 Feb – 6 Mar
BEDFORDSHIRE FESTIVAL OF MUSIC, SPEECH AND DRAMA
Corn Exchange
St Paul's Square, Bedford
Tel: (01234) 354211

MARCH

2 Mar – 7 Mar
FINE ART AND ANTIQUES FAIR
Olympia
Hammersmith Road, London
Tel: 0870 736 3105
Bookings: 0870 739 31054

4 Mar – 7 Mar
CRUFTS 2004
National Exhibition Centre
Birmingham, West Midlands
Tel: (020) 7518 1069
Bookings: 0870 909 4133
www.crufts.org.uk

7 Mar – 4 Apr
LAMBING SUNDAY AND SPRING BULB DAYS
Kentwell Hall
Long Melford, Sudbury
Tel: (01787) 310207
Bookings: (01787) 310207
www.kentwell.co.uk

10 Mar – 4 Apr
IDEAL HOME SHOW
Earls Court Exhibition Centre
Warwick Road, London
Tel: 0870 606 6080
Bookings: 0870 606 6080

14 Mar
ANTIQUE AND COLLECTORS' FAIR
Alexandra Palace and Park
Alexandra Palace Way, Wood Green, London
Tel: (020) 8883 7061
www.allypally-uk.com

14 Mar
BESSON NATIONAL BRASS BAND CHAMPIONSHIPS
Winter Gardens, Opera House and Empress Ballroom
Church Street, Blackpool, Lancashire
Tel: (0161) 707 3638

16 Mar – 18 Mar
CHELTENHAM RACING FESTIVAL
Cheltenham Racecourse
Prestbury Park, Cheltenham, Gloucestershire
Tel: (01242) 513014
Bookings: (01242) 226226
www.cheltenham.co.uk

20 Mar – 21 Mar
AMBLESIDE DAFFODIL AND SPRING FLOWER SHOW
The Kelsick Centre
St Mary's Lane, Ambleside, Cumbria
Tel: (015394) 32252
www.ambleside-show.org.uk

20 Mar – 21 Mar
THE SHIRE HORSE SOCIETY SPRING SHOW
East of England Showground
Alwalton, Peterborough,
Tel: (01733) 234451
Bookings: (01733) 234451
www.eastofengland.co.uk

26 Mar – 4 Apr*
ULVERSTON WALKING FESTIVAL
Various Venues, Ulverston, Cumbria
Tel: (01229) 580640
www.ulverston-festivals.fsnet.co.uk/walking.htm

27 Mar – 28 Mar
THRIPLOW DAFFODIL WEEKEND
Various Venues
Thriplow, Royston, Hertfordshire
Tel: (01763) 208538
www.thriplow.org.uk

28 Mar
OXFORD AND CAMBRIDGE BOAT RACE
River Thames
London
Tel: (020) 7611 3500
www.theboatrace.org

APRIL

9 Apr
MIDDLEHAM STABLES OPEN EVENT
Middleham Key Centre, Park Lane, Middleham, Leyburn, North Yorkshire
Tel: (01969) 624500
Bookings: (01969) 624502
www.middlehamstablesopenevent.co.u

9 Apr – 12 Apr
BLICKLING CRAFT SHOW
National Trust: Blickling Hall
Blickling, Norwich
Tel: (01263) 734711
www.paston.co.uk/easternevents

9 Apr – 12 Apr
GREAT EASTER EGG HUNT QUIZ AND RE-CREATION OF TUDOR LIFE
Kentwell Hall
Long Melford, Sudbury
Tel: (01787) 310207
Bookings: (01787) 310207
www.kentwell.co.uk

10 Apr – 11 Apr*
GATESHEAD SPRING FLOWER SHOW
Gateshead Central Nurseries
Whickham Highway, Lobley Hill, Gateshead, Tyne and Wear
Tel: (0191) 433 3838
Bookings: (0191) 433 3838

12 Apr
LONDON HARNESS HORSE PARADE
Battersea Park
London
Tel: (01737) 646132

12 Apr
MORRIS DANCING ON EASTER MONDAY
Various Venues
Norfolk
Tel: (01553) 768930
www.thekingsmorris.co.uk

15 Apr – 18 Apr
BRITISH OPEN SHOW JUMPING CHAMPIONSHIPS
Hallam FM Arena
Broughton Lane, Sheffield
Tel: (0114) 256 5656
Bookings: (0114) 256 5656
www.hallamfmarena.co.uk

18 Apr
FLORA LONDON MARATHON
Greenwich Park to The Mall
London
Tel: (020) 7902 0199
www.london-marathon.co.uk

22 Apr – 25 Apr
HARROGATE SPRING FLOWER SHOW
Great Yorkshire Showground
Harrogate, North Yorkshire
Tel: (01423) 561049
Bookings: (01423) 561049
www.flowershow.org.uk

29 Apr – 3 May*
CHELTENHAM INTERNATIONAL JAZZ FESTIVAL
Various venues throughout Cheltenham, Gloucestershire
Tel: (01242) 775888
Bookings: (01242) 227979
www.cheltenhamfestivals.co.uk

MAY

1 May – 3 May*
SWEEPS FESTIVAL
Various Venues
Rochester, Kent
Tel: (01634) 843666
www.medway.gov.uk/tourism

1 May – 23 May
BRIGHTON FESTIVAL
Various Venues
Brighton
Tel: (01273) 700747
Bookings: (01273) 709709
www.brighton-festival.org.uk

8 May
HELSTON FLORA DAY
Around Streets of Helston
Helston, Cornwall
Tel: (01326) 572082

9 May
ANTIQUE AND COLLECTORS' FAIR
Alexandra Palace and Park
Alexandra Palace Way, Wood Green, London
Tel: (020) 8883 7061
www.allypally-uk.com

16 May 2004
NORTHUMBRIAN WATER UNIVERSITY BOAT RACE
River Tyne
Quayside, Newcastle upon Tyne
Tel: (0191) 433 3820
www.gateshead.gov.uk

16 May – 17 May
INTERNATIONAL KITE FESTIVAL
Lower Promenade
Kingsway, Cleethorpes, North East Lincolnshire
Tel: (01472) 323352
www.nelincsevents.co.uk

20 May – 22 May
DEVON COUNTY SHOW
Westpoint Exhibition Centre
Devon County Showground, Clyst St Mary, Exeter, Devon
Tel: (01392) 446000
Bookings: (01392) 446000

25 May – 28 May
CHELSEA FLOWER SHOW
Royal Hospital Chelsea
Royal Hospital Road, Chelsea, London
Tel: (020) 7834 4333
Bookings: 0870 9063781
www.rhs.org.uk

27 May – 6 Jun*
BRITISH INTERNATIONAL MOTOR SHOW LIVE
National Exhibition Centre
Birmingham, West Midlands
Tel: (020) 7235 7000
www.motorshowlive.com

28 May – 13 Jun
BATH FRINGE FESTIVAL
Various Venues
Bath
Tel: (01225) 480079
www.bathfringe.co.uk

29 May – 31 May
CHATHAM NAVY DAYS
The Historic Dockyard Chatham
Chatham, Kent
Tel: (01634) 823800
Bookings: (01634) 403868
www.chdt.org.uk

31 May*
NORTHUMBERLAND COUNTY SHOW
Tynedale Park
Corbridge, Northumberland
Tel: (01697) 747848
Bookings: (01749) 813899
www.northcountyshow.co.uk

JUNE

Jun*
RACING AT ASCOT: THE ROYAL MEETING
Ascot Racecourse
Ascot, Berkshire
Tel: (01344) 876876
Bookings: (01344) 876876
www.ascot.co.uk

Jun*
THE MERSEY RIVER FESTIVAL
The Albert Dock
Suite 22, Edward Pavilion, Albert Dock, Liverpool, Merseyside
Tel: (0151) 233 3007

Jun*
TROOPING THE COLOUR – THE QUEEN'S BIRTHDAY PARADE
Horse Guards Parade
London
Tel: (020) 7414 2479
Bookings: (020) 7414 2479

* provisional/date not confirmed at time of going to press

2 Jun – 5 Jun
THE ROYAL BATH AND WEST SHOW
The Royal Bath and West Showground
Shepton Mallet, Somerset
Tel: (01749) 822200
Bookings: (01749) 822200
www.bathandwest.co.uk

4 Jun*
OAKS AND CORONATION CUP HORSE RACE MEETING
Epsom Downs Racecourse
Epsom Downs, Epsom, Surrey
Tel: (01372) 470047
Bookings: (01372) 470047
www.epsomderby.co.uk

4 Jun – 6 Jun
HOLKER GARDEN FESTIVAL
Holker Hall and Gardens
Cark in Cartmel, Grange-over-Sands, Cumbria
Tel: (015395) 58328
Bookings: (015395) 58328
www.holker-hall.co.uk

5 Jun*
D-DAY COMMEMORATIVE CHANNEL CROSSING
Portsmouth Harbour
Tel: (023) 9282 7261
www.portsmouthmuseums.co.uk

5 Jun*
DERBY HORSE RACE MEETING
Epsom Downs Racecourse
Epsom Downs, Epsom, Surrey
Tel: (01372) 470047
Bookings: (01372) 470047
www.epsomderby.co.uk

9 Jun – 10 Jun
CORPUS CHRISTI CARPET OF FLOWERS AND FLORAL FESTIVAL
Cathedral of Our Lady and St Philip Howard
London Road, Arundel, West Sussex
Tel: (01903) 882297
www.arundelcathedral.org

10 Jun – 12 Jun
ROYAL CORNWALL SHOW
Royal Cornwall Showground
Wadebridge, Cornwall
Tel: (01208) 812183
Bookings: (01208) 812183
www.royalcornwall.co.uk

10 Jun – 12 Jun
SOUTH OF ENGLAND AGRICULTURAL SHOW
South of England Showground
South of England Centre, Ardingly, Haywards Heath, West Sussex
Tel: (01444) 892700
Bookings: (01444) 892700
www.seas.org.uk

13 Jun
ROYAL AIR FORCE COSFORD 2004 AIR SHOW
Royal Air Force Museum, Cosford
Cosford, Shifnal, Shropshire
Tel: (01902) 376200
Bookings: (01902) 373520
www.cosfordairshow.co.uk

17 Jun – 20 Jun*
BLENHEIM PALACE FLOWER SHOW BLENHEIM PALACE
Woodstock, Oxfordshire
Tel: (01737) 379911
Bookings: (0115) 912 9188
www.bpfs2003.co.uk

17 Jun – 27 Jun
GOLOWAN FESTIVAL INCORPORATING MAZEY DAY
Various Venues
Theatre, Marquee, Street
Penzance, Cornwall
Tel: (01736) 332211
Bookings: (01736) 365520
www.golowan.com

18 Jun – 20 Jun
THE EAST OF ENGLAND COUNTRYSHOW 2004
East of England Showground
Alwalton, Peterborough,
Tel: (01733) 234451
Bookings: (01733) 234451

18 Jun – 26 Jun*
NEWCASTLE HOPPINGS
Town Moor
Grandstand Road,
Newcastle upon Tyne
Tel: (0191) 232 8520

19 Jun – 27 Jun
BROADSTAIRS DICKENS FESTIVAL
Various Venues
Broadstairs, Kent
Tel: (01843) 861827
Bookings: (01843) 861827
www.broadstairs.gov.uk/dickensfestival.html

21 Jun – 4 Jul
TENNIS: WIMBLEDON LAWN TENNIS CHAMPIONSHIPS
All England Lawn Tennis & Croquet Club
Church Road, London
Bookings: (020) 8946 2244

25 Jun – 27 Jun*
GLASTONBURY FESTIVAL
Worthy Farm
Pilton, Shepton Mallet, Somerset
Tel: (01458) 834596
Bookings: (01749) 890470
www.glastonburyfestivals.co.uk

27 Jun – 3 Jul
ALNWICK FAIR
Market Square
Alnwick, Northumberland
Tel: (01665) 711397
www.fair01.freeserve.co.uk/index.html

JULY

30 Jun – 1 Jul
ROYAL NORFOLK SHOW 2004
The Showground
New Costessey, Norwich
Tel: (01603) 748931
Bookings: (01603) 748931
www.royalnorfolkshow.co.uk

30 Jun – 4 Jul*
HENLEY ROYAL REGATTA
Henley Reach
Regatta Headquarters,
Henley-on-Thames, Oxfordshire
Tel: (01491) 572153
Bookings: (01491) 572153
www.hrr.co.uk

30 Jun – 11 Jul
WARWICK FESTIVAL
Various Venues throughout Warwick
Northgate, Warwick, Warwickshire
Tel: (01926) 410747
Bookings: (01926) 410747
www.warwickarts.org.uk

Jul*
AIRSHOW: FARNBOROUGH INTERNATIONAL 2004
Farnborough Airfield
PO Box 122, Farnborough, Hampshire
Tel: (020) 7227 1043
Bookings: (020) 7227 1043
www.farnborough.com

Jul*
FORMULA 1 BRITISH GRAND PRIX
Silverstone, Towcester, Northamptonshire
Bookings: (01327) 850260

Jul*
GOODWOOD FESTIVAL OF SPEED
Goodwood Park
Goodwood, Chichester, West Sussex
Tel: (01243) 755055
Bookings: (01243) 755055
www.goodwood.co.uk

Jul*
NETLEY MARSH STEAM AND CRAFT SHOW
Meadow Farm
Ringwood Road, Netley Marsh, Southampton
Tel: (023) 8086 7882

2 Jul – 11 Jul
YORK EARLY MUSIC FESTIVAL
Various venues, York
Tel: (01904) 645738
Bookings: (01904) 658338
www.ncem.co.uk

2 Jul – 25 Jul
GREENWICH AND DOCKLANDS INTERNATIONAL FESTIVAL
Various venues in Greenwich
Greenwich, London
Tel: (020) 8305 1818
Bookings: (020) 8305 1818
www.festival.org

3 Jul – 4 Jul
BEDFORD RIVER FESTIVAL
River Great Ouse
Ely, Cambridgeshire
Tel: (01234) 343992

3 Jul – 4 Jul
GRAND FIREWORKS CONCERT
Warwick Castle
Warwick, Warwickshire
Tel: 0870 4422000
Bookings: 0870 4422395
www.warwick-castle.co.uk

3 Jul – 4 Jul
HARTLEPOOL MARITIME FESTIVAL
Hartlepool Historic Quay
Maritime Avenue, Hartlepool, Cleveland
Tel: (01429) 523407
www.destinationhartlepool.com

3 Jul – 4 Jul*
SUNDERLAND INTERNATIONAL KITE FESTIVAL
Northern Area Playing Fields
Stephenson, Washington, Tyne and Wear
Tel: (0191) 514 1235
www.sunderland.gov.uk/kitefestival

3 Jul – 18 Jul
ROTHERHAM WALKING FESTIVAL
Various Venues throughout the Borough of Rotherham
Rotherham, South Yorkshire
Tel: (01709) 835904
www.rotherham.gov.uk

4 Jul – 7 Jul
ROYAL SHOW
National Agricultural Centre
Stoneleigh Park, Warwickshire
Tel: (024) 7685 8276
Bookings: 0870 3666544
www.royalshow.org.uk

6 Jul – 11 Jul
HAMPTON COURT PALACE FLOWER SHOW
Hampton Court Palace
Hampton Court, East Molesey, Surrey
Tel: (020) 7649 1885
Bookings: 0870 906 3791
www.rhs.org.uk

11 Jul
GRASMERE RUSHBEARING
Grasmere Parish Church
Grasmere, Ambleside, Cumbria
Tel: (015394) 35537

13 Jul – 15 Jul
GREAT YORKSHIRE SHOW
Great Yorkshire Showground
Harrogate, North Yorkshire
Tel: (01423) 541000
Bookings: (01423) 541000
www.yas.co.uk

16 Jul – 11 Sep
THE PROMS
Royal Albert Hall
Kensington Gore, London
Tel: (020) 7765 5575
Bookings: (020) 7589 8212
www.bbc.co.uk/proms

17 Jul – 6 Aug*
THE KESWICK CONVENTION
The Convention Centre
Skiddaw Street, Keswick, Cumbria
Tel: (01435) 866034
www.keswickconvention.org

23 Jul – 25 Jul
WEYMOUTH NATIONAL BEACH VOLLEYBALL
The Beach
Weymouth, Dorset
Tel: (01305) 785747
www.weymouth.gov.uk

24 Jul
CLEVELAND SHOW
Stewart Park
The Grove, Marton, Middlesbrough, Cleveland
Tel: (01642) 312231
Bookings: (01642) 312231

24 Jul – 25 Jul*
CUMBRIA STEAM GATHERING CARK AIRFIELD
Flookburgh, Grange-over-Sands, Cumbria
Tel: (015242) 71584
Bookings: (015242) 71584

24 Jul – 26 Jul*
POTFEST IN THE PARK
Hutton-in-the-Forest
Penrith, Cumbria
Tel: (017684) 83820
www.potfest.co.uk

27 Jul – 29 Jul
NEW FOREST AND HAMPSHIRE COUNTY SHOW
The Showground, New Park, Brockenhurst, Hampshire
Tel: (01590) 622400
Bookings: (023) 8071 1818
www.newforestshow.co.uk

30 Jul – 6 Aug
SIDMOUTH INTERNATIONAL FESTIVAL
Various venues
Sidmouth, Devon
Tel: (01296) 433669
Bookings: (01296) 433669
www.mrscasey.co.uk/sidmouth

31 Jul – 1 Aug*
GATESHEAD SUMMER FLOWER SHOW
Gateshead Central Nurseries
Whickham Highway, Lobley Hill, Gateshead, Tyne and Wear
Tel: (0191) 433 3838
Bookings: (0191) 433 3838

AUGUST

Aug*
INTERNATIONAL BEATLES FESTIVAL
Various venues
Liverpool
Tel: (0151) 236 9091
Bookings: (0151) 236 9091
www.cavern-liverpool.co.uk

Aug*
SKANDIA LIFE COWES WEEK 2004
The Solent
Cowes, Isle of Wight
Tel: (01983) 293303

6 Aug – 8 Aug*
LOWTHER HORSE DRIVING TRIALS AND COUNTRY FAIR
Lowther Castle
Lowther Estate, Lowther, Penrith, Cumbria
Tel: (01931) 712378
Bookings: (01931) 712378
www.lowther.co.uk

6 Aug – 8 Aug*
POTFEST IN THE PENS
Skirsgill Auction Market
Skirsgill, Penrith, Cumbria
Tel: (017684) 83820
www.potfest.co.uk

7 Aug
GARSTANG SHOW
Show Field
Wyre Lane, Garstang, Preston
Tel: (01995) 603180
Bookings: (01995) 603180
www.abarnett.co.uk

* provisional/date not confirmed at time of going to press

7 Aug – 14 Aug*
BILLINGHAM INTERNATIONAL FOLKLORE FESTIVAL
Forum Theatre
Town Centre, Billingham, Cleveland
Tel: (01642) 651060
Bookings: (01642) 552663
www.billinghamfestival.co.uk

12 Aug – 15 Aug
AIRBOURNE: EASTBOURNE'S INTERNATIONAL AIR SHOW
Seafront and Western Lawns
King Edwards Parade, Eastbourne, East Sussex
Tel: (01323) 411400
www.eastbourneairshow.com

21 Aug – 27 Aug
WHITBY FOLK WEEK
Various venues
Whitby, North Yorkshire
Tel: (01757) 708424
Bookings: (01757) 708424
www.folkwhitby.freeserve.co.uk

22 Aug*
GRASMERE LAKELAND SPORTS AND SHOW SPORTS FIELD
Stock Lane, Grasmere, Ambleside, Cumbria
Tel: (015394) 32127
Bookings: (015394) 32127

28 Aug – 30 Oct
MATLOCK BATH ILLUMINATIONS AND VENETIAN NIGHTS
Derwent Gardens
Matlock Bath, Matlock, Derbyshire
Tel: (01629) 761224

29 Aug – 30 Aug
NOTTING HILL CARNIVAL
Streets around Ladbroke Grove
London
Tel: (020) 8964 0544

30 Aug
LANCASTER GEORGIAN FESTIVAL FAIR & NATIONAL SEDAN CHAIR CARRYING
Lancaster Castle Green & Priory Churchyard
Lancaster, Lancashire
Tel: (01524) 32878
www.lancaster.gov.uk

SEPTEMBER

1 Sep – 5 Sep
THE GREAT DORSET STEAM FAIR
South Down
Tarrant Hinton, Blandford Forum, Dorset
Tel: (01258) 860361
Bookings: (01258) 488928
www.steam-fair.co.uk

Sep*
GOODWOOD REVIVAL MEETING
Goodwood Motor Circuit
Goodwood, Chichester, West Sussex
Tel: (01243) 755055
Bookings: (01243) 755055
www.goodwood.co.uk

Sep*
THE ROYAL COUNTY OF BERKSHIRE SHOW
Newbury Showground
Priors Court, Hermitage, Thatcham, Berkshire
Tel: (01635) 247111
Bookings: (01635) 247111
www.newburyshowground.co.uk

3 Sep – 7 Nov
BLACKPOOL ILLUMINATIONS
Blackpool Promenade
Blackpool
Tel: (01253) 478222
www.blackpooltourism.com

4 Sep – 6 Sep
WOLSINGHAM AND WEAR VALLEY AGRICULTURAL SHOW
Scotch Isle Park
Wolsingham, Bishop Auckland, County Durham
Tel: (01388) 527862
Bookings: (01388) 527862

6 Sep – 11 Sep
SCARBOROUGH OPEN GOLF WEEK
Various venues
Scarborough, North Yorkshire
Tel: (01723) 367579
Bookings: (01723) 367579

9 Sep*
WESTMORLAND COUNTY SHOW
Westmorland County Showfield
Lane Farm, Crooklands, Milnthorpe, Cumbria
Tel: (015395) 67804
www.westmorland-county-show.co.uk

10 Sep*
35TH ANNUAL KENDAL TORCHLIGHT CARNIVAL
Kendal, Cumbria
Tel: (015395) 63018
Bookings: (015395) 63018
www.lakesnet.co.uk/kendaltorchlight

11 Sep – 12 Sep
CARAVAN EXTRAVAGANZA
The Lawns
University of Hull, Harland Way, Cottingham, East Riding of Yorkshire
Tel: (01276) 686654
www.hercma.co.uk

11 Sep – 12 Sep
MAYOR'S THAMES FESTIVAL
River Thames
London
Tel: (020) 7928 0960
Bookings:
www.ThamesFestival.org

11 Sep – 12 Sep*
THE GREAT LEEDS CASTLE BALLOON AND VINTAGE CAR WEEKEND
Leeds Castle and Gardens
Maidstone, Kent
Tel: (01622) 765400
www.leeds-castle.com

18 Sep*
RNAS YEOVILTON: INTERNATIONAL AIR DAY
RNAS Yeovilton, Ilchester, Yeovil, Somerset
Tel: 0870 800 4030
Bookings: 0870 800 4030
www.yeoviltonairday.co.uk

18 Sep – 19 Sep
MIDLAND GAME & COUNTRY SPORTS FAIR
Weston Park
Weston-under-Lizard, Shifnal, Shropshire
Tel: (01952) 852100
www.weston-park.com

24 Sep – 26 Sep
NANTWICH LOCAL FOOD AND DRINK FESTIVAL 2004
Various Venues
Nantwich, Cheshire
Tel: (01270) 610983

26 Sep
ANTIQUE AND COLLECTORS' FAIR
Alexandra Palace and Park
Alexandra Palace Way, Wood Green, London
Tel: (020) 8883 7061
www.allypally-uk.com

OCTOBER

24 Oct
TRAFALGAR DAY PARADE
Trafalgar Square
London
Tel: (020) 7928 8978

NOVEMBER

3 Nov
PORTSMOUTH BONFIRE AND FIREWORK DISPLAY
King George V Playing Field
Northern Road, Cosham, Portsmouth
Tel: (023) 9282 6722
www.portsmouthcc.gov.uk/visitor

5 Nov
BRIDGWATER GUY FAWKES CARNIVAL TOWN CENTRE
Bridgwater, Somerset
Tel: (01278) 421795
www.bridgwatercarnival.org.uk

5 Nov
TAR BARRELS
Town Centre
Ottery St Mary, Devon
Tel: (01404) 813964
www.cosmic.org.uk

5 Nov
THE CITY OF LIVERPOOL FIREWORKS DISPLAY
Sefton Park, Liverpool
Tel: (0151) 233 3007

7 Nov
VETERAN CAR RUN
Madeira Drive
Brighton, East Sussex
Tel: (01753) 765100
www.msauk.org

13 Nov
LORD MAYOR'S SHOW
City of London
Tel: (020) 7606 3030

21 Nov
ANTIQUE AND COLLECTORS' FAIR
Alexandra Palace and Park
Alexandra Palace Way, Wood Green, London
Tel: (020) 8883 7061
www.allypally-uk.com

27 Nov – 28 Nov
THE BIRMINGHAM TATTOO
National Indoor Arena
King Edwards Road, Birmingham, West Midlands
Tel: (0118) 930 3239
Bookings: 0870 909 4144
www.telinco.co.uk/maestromusic

DECEMBER

16 Dec – 20 Dec 2004
OLYMPIA INTERNATIONAL SHOWJUMPING CHAMPIONSHIPS
Olympia
Hammersmith Road, London
Tel: (020) 7370 8206
Bookings: (020) 7370 8206
www.olympia-show-jumping.co.uk

* provisional/date not confirmed at time of going to press

VisitBritain's Where to Stay Bed & Breakfast Guest Accommodation 2004

Published by: VisitBritain, Thames Tower, Black's Road, Hammersmith, London W6 9EL
Publishing Manager: Michael Dewing
Production Manager: Iris Buckley
Compilation, Design & Production: Jackson Lowe Marketing, www.jacksonlowe.com
Typesetting: Tradespools Ltd, Somerset and Jackson Lowe Marketing, Lewes
Maps: © Maps in Minutes™ (1999)
Printing and Binding: Mozzon Giutina S.p.A, Florence and Officine Grafiche De Agostini S.p.A, Novara
Advertisement Sales: Jackson Lowe Marketing, 173 High Street, Lewes, East Sussex BN7 1YE. (01273) 487487

ISBN 0 7095 7754 0

IMPORTANT:
The information contained in this guide has been published in good faith on the basis of information submitted to VisitBritain by the proprietors of the premises listed, who have paid for their entries to appear. VisitBritain cannot guarantee the accuracy of the information in this guide and accepts no responsibility for any error or misrepresentation. All liability for loss, disappointment, negligence or other damage caused by reliance on the information contained in this guide, or in the event of bankruptcy, or liquidation, or cessation of trade of any company, individual or firm mentioned, is hereby excluded. Please check carefully all prices and other details before confirming a reservation.

PICTURE CREDITS:
Front Cover: The Knoll, Henley-on-Thames, South East **Back Cover: (Top)** Jeake's House, Rye, South East **(Bottom)** Bidwell Farm & Haybarton Annexe, Honiton, South West

Cumbria: Cumbria Tourist Board

Northumbria: Northumbria Tourist Board, Graeme Peacock, Mike Kippling, Colin Cuthbert and Michael Busselle

North West: North West Tourist Board, Chessire County Council, Lancashire County Council, Marketing Manchester

Yorkshire: Yorkshire Tourist Board

Heart of England: Heart of England Tourist Board

East of England: East of England Tourist Board

South West: South West Tourism

South East England: Tourism South East, Peter Titmuss, Chris Cove-Smith, Chris Parker and Iris Buckley

National Accessible Scheme Guest Accommodation Index

Establishments taking part in the National Accessible Scheme are listed below. For full details of accessible ratings please see pages 10 & 11. Listings in blue have an enhanced or standard entry. Use the Town Index at the back of the guide to find the page numbers for their full entries.

MOBILTY Level 1

Alford, Lincolnshire
- Half Moon Hotel and Restaurant

Arnside, Cumbria - Willowfield Hotel
Ashbourne, Derbyshire
- Mona Villas Bed and Breakfast

Basonbridge, Somerset - Merry Farm
Bath, Bath and North East Somerset - Carfax Hotel
Beverley, East Riding of Yorkshire
- Rudstone Walk Country Accommodation

Boscastle, Cornwall - The Old Coach House
Bournemouth, Dorset - Wood Lodge Hotel
Bourton-on-the-Water, Gloucestershire
- Kingsbridge and Chester House Hotel

Bratton Fleming, Devon
- Bracken House Country Hotel

Chelmsford, Essex - Boswell House Hotel
Chester, Cheshire - Comfort Inn Chester
Cleethorpes, North East Lincolnshire
- Tudor Terrace Guest House

Congleton, Cheshire - Sandhole Farm
Cressbrook, Derbyshire - Cressbrook Hall
Crookham, Northumberland
– The Coach House at Crookham

Dereham, Norfolk - Greenbanks Country Hotel
Devizes, Wiltshire - Longwater
Felixstowe, Suffolk - Dorincourt Guesthouse
Hadleigh, Suffolk - Odds and Ends House
Harbottle, Northumberland
- The Byre Vegetarian B&B

Holbeck, Nottinghamshire - Browns
Holmes Chapel, Cheshire - Padgate Guest House
Horrabridge, Devon - Overcombe Hotel
Ingleton, North Yorkshire - Riverside Lodge
Kirkbymoorside, North Yorkshire - The Cornmill
Leominster, Hereforshire - Bramlea
Lower Whitley, Cheshire - Tall Trees Lodge
Manchester, Greater Manchester
- Luther King House

Marlow, Buckinghamshire - Granny Anne's
Newnham-on-Severn, Gloucestershire
- Swan House

Northallerton, North Yorkshire - Lovesome Hill Farm
Otterburn, Northumberland - Redesdale Arms Hotel
Parkend, Gloucestershire
- The Fountain Inn & Lodge

Pateley Bridge, North Yorkshire - Greengarth
Petworth, West Sussex - The Old Railway Station
Preston, East Riding of Yorkshire
- Little Weghill Farm

Runswick Bay, North Yorkshire - Ellerby Hotel
Shawbury, Shropshire - Sowbath Farm
Sheffield, South Yorkshire
- Tapton Hall of Residence (see campus section)

Shrewsbury, Shropshire - Lyth Hill House
Sidmouth, Devon - Wiscombe Linhaye Farm
Skegness, Lincolnshire - Chatsworth Hotel
Skipton, North Yorkshire - Craven Heifer Inn
South Normanton, Derbyshire
- The Boundary Lodge

Stratford-upon-Avon, Warwickshire
- East Bank House

Sway, Hampshire - The Nurse's Cottage
Takeley, Essex - Warish Hall Farm
Taunton, Somerset - The Spinney
Threlkeld, Cumbria
- Scales Farm Country Guesthouse

Weston-super-Mare, Somerset
- Moorlands Country Guesthouse

Westow, North Yorkshire - Blacksmiths Arms Inn
Witney, Oxfordshire
- Ducklington Farm
- Springhill Farm Bed & Breakfast

MOBILTY Level 2

Chedzoy, Somerset - Apple View
Easingwold, North Yorkshire - Thornton Lodge Farm
Herstmonceux, East Sussex - Conquerors
Lincoln, Lincolnshire - Damon's Motel
Okehampton, Devon
- Higher Cadham Farm

Runswick Bay, North Yorkshire - The Firs
Salisbury, Wiltshire - Websters
Sudbury, Suffolk - Fiddlesticks

MOBILTY Level 3

Beckley, East Sussex - Woodlands
Burton Bradstock, Dorset - Burton Cliff Hotel
Cannington, Somerset - Blackmore Farm
Colyton, Devon - Smallicombe Farm
Godney, Somerset - Double-Gate Farm
Harwood Dale, North Yorkshire - The Grainary
Ilfracombe, Devon - Sunnymeade Country Hotel
W2, London - Westland Hotel
Mosedale, Cumbria - Mosedale House
Reydon, Suffolk - Newlands Country House
Skegness, Lincolnshire - Fountaindale Hotel
Telford, Shropshire - Old Rectory

HEARING IMPAIRMENT Level 1

Ilfracombe, Devon - Sunnymeade Country Hotel
Leominster, Herefordshire - Bramlea
Sheffield, South Yorkshire
- Tapton Hall of Residence (see campus section)

Sway, Hampshire - The Nurse's Cottage

VISUAL IMPAIRMENT Level 1

Leominster, Herefordshire - Bramlea
Sheffield, South Yorkshire
- Tapton Hall of Residence (see campus section)

In which **region** is the county I wish to visit?

COUNTY/UNITARY AUTHORITY	REGION
Bath & North East Somerset	South West
Bedfordshire	East of England
Berkshire	South East England
Bristol	South West
Buckinghamshire	South East England
Cambridgeshire	East of England
Cheshire	North West
Cornwall	South West
Cumbria	Cumbria
Derbyshire	Heart of England
Devon	South West
Dorset (Eastern)	South East England
Dorset (Western)	South West
Durham	Northumbria
East Riding of Yorkshire	Yorkshire
East Sussex	South East England
Essex	East of England
Gloucestershire	South West
Greater London	London
Greater Manchester	North West
Hampshire	South East England
Herefordshire	Heart of England
Hertfordshire	East of England
Isle of Wight	South East England
Isles of Scilly	South West
Kent	South East England
Lancashire	North West
Leicestershire	Heart of England
Lincolnshire	Heart of England
Merseyside	North West
Norfolk	East of England
North East Lincolnshire	Yorkshire
North Lincolnshire	Yorkshire
North Somerset	South West
North Yorkshire	Yorkshire
Northamptonshire	Heart of England
Northumberland	Northumbria
Nottinghamshire	Heart of England
Oxfordshire	South East England
Rutland	Heart of England
Shropshire	Heart of England
Somerset	South West
South Gloucestershire	South West
South Yorkshire	Yorkshire
Staffordshire	Heart of England
Suffolk	East of England
Surrey	South East England
Tees Valley	Northumbria
Tyne & Wear	Northumbria
Warwickshire	Heart of England
West Midlands	Heart of England
West Sussex	South East England
West Yorkshire	Yorkshire
Wiltshire	South West
Worcestershire	Heart of England
York	Yorkshire

UNITARY AUTHORITIES

Please note that many new unitary authorities have been formed - for example Brighton & Hove and Bristol - and are officially separate from the county in which they were previously located. To aid the reader we have only included the major unitary authorities in the list above and on the colour maps.

Gold and Silver Award Guest Accommodation Index

Establishments which have achieved a Gold or Silver Award are listed below. Listings in blue have an enhanced or standard entry. Use the Town Index on the following pages to find the page numbers for their full entries.

Bath	
- Athole Guest House	GOLD
- Ayrlington Hotel	GOLD
- County Hotel	GOLD
- Leighton House	GOLD
- Meadowland	GOLD
- Monkshill	GOLD
- Villa Magdala Hotel	GOLD
- The Albany Guest House	SILVER
- Badminton Villa	SILVER
- Bloomfield House	SILVER
- Glentworth	SILVER
- Haydon House	SILVER
- The Hollies	SILVER
- Holly Lodge	SILVER
- Kennard Hotel	SILVER
- Lavender House	SILVER
- No. 30 Crescent Gardens	SILVER
- The Old Mill Hotel	SILVER
- Ravenscroft	SILVER
- St Leonards	SILVER
Bathwick - Ravenscroft	GOLD
Beadnell	
- Beach Court	SILVER
- Low Dover Beadnell Bay	SILVER
Beaminster	
- The Walnuts	SILVER
- Water Meadow House	SILVER
Beanacre - Beechfield House	SILVER
Beccles - Plantation House	GOLD
Beck Hole - Brookwood Farm	SILVER
Bedale - Mill Close Farm	SILVER
Bedford	
- Church Farm	SILVER
- Cornfields Restaurant and Hotel	SILVER
Beetley - Peacock House	GOLD
Belchamp St Paul	
- The Plough (Private Residence)	SILVER
Belford	
- Oakwood House	GOLD
- Easington Farm	SILVER
Belper - Broadhurst Bed and Breakfast	SILVER
Bembridge - Sea Change	SILVER
Benniworth - Glebe Farm	SILVER
Benson - Fyfield Manor	SILVER
Berkhamsted - Broadway Farm	SILVER
Berrow - Berrow Links House	SILVER
Berwick-upon-Tweed	
- Middle Ord Manor	GOLD
- 40 Ravensdowne	SILVER
- Alannah House	SILVER
- Clovelly House	SILVER
- Dervaig Guest House	SILVER
- Four North Road	SILVER
- Heron's Lee	SILVER
- High Letham Farmhouse	SILVER
- No 1 Sallyport	SILVER
- Whyteside House	SILVER
Betley - Adderley Green Farm	SILVER
Bewdley	
- Kates Hill House	GOLD
- Lightmarsh Farm	SILVER
Bexhill	
- Hartfield House	SILVER
- Mulberry	SILVER
- Sackville Hotel	SILVER
Bibury	
- Cotteswold House	GOLD
- The William Morris Bed & Breakfast	GOLD
Biggin-by-Hartington	
- The Kings at Ivy House	GOLD
Billericay - Badgers Rest	SILVER
Binegar - Mansefield House	SILVER
Bingley	
- Five Rise Locks Hotel & Restaurant	SILVER
Binham - Field House	GOLD
Binstead	
- Elm Close Cottage	SILVER
- Newnham Farm Bed & Breakfast	SILVER
Bishops Hull - The Old Mill	SILVER
Bishop's Stortford - The Cottage	GOLD
Bishop's Waltham - Post Mead	SILVER
Blackburn - Shalom	SILVER
Blackpool - The Old Coach House	GOLD
Blandford Forum	
- Farnham Farm House	SILVER
- Meadow House	SILVER
Bledington	
- Kings Head Inn and Restaurant	SILVER
Bledlow - Cross Lanes Guest House	SILVER
Bletsoe - North End Barns	SILVER
Blockley	
- The Old Bakery	GOLD
- Arreton House	SILVER
- Mill Dene	SILVER
Blundellsands	
- Blundellsands Bed and Breakfast	SILVER
Bodmin	
- Bokiddick Farm	SILVER
- Gwel Myre	SILVER
Bognor Regis - The Maltings	SILVER
Bolton - Eden Grove Farm House	SILVER
Borrowdale	
- Hazel Bank Country House	GOLD
- Greenbank Country House Hotel	SILVER
Boscastle - Trerosewill Farmhouse	SILVER
Bosham	
- Crede Farmhouse	SILVER
- Hatpins	SILVER
Boston Spa - Four Gables	SILVER
Bournemouth	
- Alexander Lodge Hotel	SILVER
- Balincourt Hotel	SILVER
- Mayfield Guest House	SILVER
- St Winifrides Hotel	SILVER
- The Twin Tops	SILVER
- Willowdene Hotel	SILVER
Bourton-on-the-Water	
- Larch House	GOLD
- Coombe House	SILVER
- Manor Close	SILVER
- The Painted House	SILVER
- The Ridge Guesthouse	SILVER
- Strathspey	SILVER
- Touchstone	SILVER
Bovey Tracey - Brookfield House	GOLD
Boxford - Hurrells Farmhouse	SILVER
Brackley - Brackley House Private Hotel	SILVER
Bradford - Brow Top Farm	SILVER
Bradford-on-Avon - Great Ashley Farm	SILVER
Bradpole - Spray Copse Farm	SILVER
Bradwell - Stoney Ridge	SILVER
Bramhope - The Cottages	SILVER
Brampton - Howard House Farm	SILVER
Branksome Park - Grovefield Manor Hotel	SILVER
Bransgore - Wiltshire House	SILVER
Brassington - Ivy Bank House	SILVER
Bratton Fleming	
- Bracken House Country Hotel	GOLD
Brayford - Rockley Farmhouse	SILVER
Brewood - The Blackladies	GOLD

Bridgnorth - Linley Crest	SILVER
Bridgwater - Ash-Wembdon Farm	SILVER
Bridlington	
- Bay Court Hotel	SILVER
- Seacourt Hotel	SILVER
Bridport	
- Southcroft	GOLD
- Eypeleaze	SILVER
- Polly's	SILVER
Brighton & Hove	
- Adelaide Hotel	SILVER
- Brighton Kingsway Hotel	SILVER
Brimpsfield - Highcroft	GOLD
Bristol - The Old Court	SILVER
Brixham - Raddicombe Lodge	SILVER
Broad Campden - Marnic House	GOLD
Broadstairs - The Victoria	SILVER
Broadstone - Honey Lodge	SILVER
Broadway	
- Burhill Farm	GOLD
- Barn House	SILVER
- Leasow House	SILVER
- Lowerfield Farm	SILVER
- Olive Branch Guest House	SILVER
- Sheepscombe House	SILVER
- Southwold Guest House	SILVER
- Whiteacres	SILVER
- Windrush House	SILVER
Brockdish - Grove Thorpe	GOLD
Bromyard - The Old Cowshed	SILVER
Brooke - The Old Vicarage	SILVER
Broseley - Rock Dell	SILVER
Broughton-in-Furness - Middlesyke	SILVER
Broxwood - Broxwood Court	GOLD
Bryher - Bank Cottage Guest House	SILVER
Bryn - Birches Mill	SILVER
Buckden - Redmire Farm	GOLD
Buckland Newton	
- Holyleas House	SILVER
- Whiteways Farmhouse Accommodation	SILVER
Bude	
- Atlantic Calm	SILVER
- Harefield Cottage	SILVER
- Highbre Crest	SILVER
- Lower Tresmorn	SILVER
- Penleaze Farm Bed and Breakfast	SILVER
Budleigh Salterton - Lufflands	SILVER
Bugbrooke - The Byre	SILVER
Bungay - Earsham Park Farm	GOLD
Burford	
- Burford House Hotel	GOLD
- Barley Park	SILVER
- Manor Lodge	SILVER
Burgh St Peter - Shrublands Farm	SILVER
Burley	
- Great Wells House	GOLD
- Holmans	SILVER
Burlton - Petton Hall Farm	SILVER
Burnham Market - Wood Lodge	SILVER
Burnham-on-Sea - Walton House	SILVER
Burton Dassett	
- The White House Bed and Breakfast	SILVER
Bury St Edmunds	
- Manorhouse	GOLD
- Clarice House	SILVER
Buscot Wick - Weston Farm	SILVER
Butterton	
- Butterton Moor House	SILVER
- Coxon Green Farm	SILVER
Buxton	
- Grendon Guesthouse	GOLD
- Buxton Wheelhouse Hotel	SILVER
- Buxton's Victorian Guesthouse	SILVER
- Devonshire Lodge Guesthouse	SILVER
- Harefield	SILVER
- Kingscroft	SILVER
- Nithen Cottage	SILVER
- Stoneridge	SILVER
Bywell - The Old Vicarage	SILVER
Caldbeck - Swaledale Watch	SILVER
Calmsden - The Old House	SILVER
Calne	
- Queenwood Golf Lodge	GOLD
- Calstone Bed and Breakfast	SILVER
- Chilvester Hill House	SILVER
Cambridge	
- Lensfield Hotel	SILVER
- Worth House	SILVER
Cannington - Blackmore Farm	SILVER
Canterbury	
- Magnolia House	GOLD
- Thanington Hotel	GOLD
- Twin Mays	GOLD
- Clare-Ellen Guest House	SILVER
- Elmstone Court	SILVER
- Yorke Lodge Hotel	SILVER
Capernwray - New Capernwray Farm	SILVER
Carbrooke - White Hall	GOLD
Carlisle	
- Number Thirty One	GOLD
- Bessiestown Farm Country Guesthouse	SILVER
- Courtfield House	SILVER
- Marchmain House	SILVER
Cartmel - Hill Farm	SILVER
Castle Cary - Clanville Manor	SILVER
Castle Donington - Castletown House	SILVER
Castlethorpe - Balney Grounds	SILVER
Castor - The Old Smithy	SILVER
Cavendish	
- Embleton House	SILVER
- The Red House Bed and Breakfast	SILVER
Cawsand - Penmillard Farm	SILVER
Chandlers Ford - Monks House	GOLD
Chard - Yew Tree Cottage	SILVER
Charlton Marshall - Keston House	SILVER
Charmouth - Spence Farm	GOLD
Chatham	
- 10 Officers Terrace	SILVER
- Officers Hill	SILVER
Chathill - North Charlton Farm	GOLD
Chatton - South Hazelrigg Farmhouse	SILVER
Cheadle	
- Caverswall Castle	GOLD
- Ley Fields Farm	SILVER
Checkendon - Larchdown Farm	SILVER
Cheddleton	
- Choir Cottage and Choir House	GOLD
Chedzoy - Apple View	SILVER
Chelmsford - Stump Cross House	SILVER
Chelston - Millbrook House Hotel	SILVER
Cheltenham	
- Evington Hill Farm	GOLD
- Milton House	GOLD
- Beaumont House Hotel	SILVER
- Ham Hill Farm	SILVER
- St Michaels	SILVER
- Westal Court	SILVER
- Whittington Lodge Farm	SILVER
- Wishmoor Guest House	SILVER

Cherry Burton - Burton Mount	SILVER
Chesham - Braziers Well	SILVER
Chester	
- The Limes	SILVER
- Mitchell's of Chester Guest House	SILVER
Chesterfield	
- Batemans Mill	SILVER
- Brook House	SILVER
Cheveley - Juniper	SILVER
Chichester	
- Home Farm House	GOLD
- 1 Maplehurst Road	SILVER
- Forge Hotel	SILVER
- Friary Close	SILVER
- Richmond Close	SILVER
- Strudwick House	SILVER
- White Barn	SILVER
Chickerell - Stonebank	GOLD
Chilsworthy - Ugworthy Barton	SILVER
Chipping Campden	
- M'Dina Courtyard	GOLD
- Nineveh Farm	GOLD
Chipping Norton - Lower Park Farm	SILVER
Chipping Sodbury - Rounceval House Hotel	SILVER
Chiseldon - Norton House	SILVER
Chorleywood - Ashburton House	SILVER
Christchurch - Druid House	SILVER
Chudleigh - Farmborough House	SILVER
Church Eaton - Slab Bridge Cottage	SILVER
Church Stretton	
- Jinlye	GOLD
- Willowfield Country Guesthouse	GOLD
Cirencester	
- Cotswold Willow Pool	SILVER
- Greensleeves	SILVER
- Millstone	SILVER
- No 12	SILVER
- Smerrill Barns	SILVER
Cleobury Mortimer - Woodview	GOLD
Cleobury North - Cleobury Court	SILVER
Clun - New House Farm	GOLD
Clungunford - Knock Hundred Cottage	GOLD
Colchester	
- Fridaywood Farm	SILVER
- The Red House	SILVER
Colwall - Brook House	SILVER
Colwell Bay	
- Rockstone Cottage	SILVER
- Shorefield House	SILVER
Colyton - Smallicombe Farm	SILVER
Conisholme - Wickham House	SILVER
Coniston	
- Coniston Lodge	GOLD
- The Old Rectory Hotel	SILVER
Corbridge	
- Priorfield	SILVER
- Riggsacre	SILVER
Corfe Castle - Bradle Farmhouse	SILVER
Corsham	
- Boyds Farm	SILVER
- Heatherly Cottage	SILVER
Coventry	
- Barnacle Hall	SILVER
- Brookfields	SILVER
Craster - Stonecroft	SILVER
Crawley Down - Tiltwood House	SILVER
Cretingham	
- The Cretingham Bell	SILVER
- Shrubbery Farmhouse	SILVER
Crewe - Coole Hall Farm	SILVER
Crich	
- Penrose Avista Property Partnership	SILVER
Cromer - Shrublands Farm	SILVER
Cropredy - Poplars Farm	SILVER
Cropthorne	
- Cropvale Farm Bed and Breakfast	GOLD
Cropton - High Farm	SILVER
Crowborough - Braemore	SILVER
Cullompton - Upton House	GOLD
Cundall - Cundall Lodge Farm	SILVER
Curry Rivel - Orchard Cottage	SILVER
Dalton-in-Furness - Park Cottage	SILVER
Danby - Crossley Gate Farm House	SILVER
Darlington	
- Clow-Beck House	GOLD
Dartmouth	
- Hill View House	GOLD
- Barrington House	SILVER
- The Little Admiral Hotel	SILVER
- Skerries Bed & Breakfast	SILVER
- Westbourne House	SILVER
- Woodside Cottage	SILVER
Daventry	
- The Old Coach House	SILVER
- Threeways House	SILVER
Dedham	
- Good Hall	SILVER
- May's Barn Farm	SILVER
Denstone - Manor House Farm	SILVER
Dersingham - The Corner House	SILVER
Devizes - Blounts Court Farm	GOLD
Diss - Dickleburgh Hall	GOLD
Doncaster - Low Farm	SILVER
Dorchester	
- The Old Manor	GOLD
- Higher Came Farmhouse	SILVER
- Maiden Castle Farm	SILVER
- The Old Rectory	SILVER
- Port Bredy	SILVER
- Whitfield Farm Cottage	SILVER
- Yalbury Park	SILVER
- Yellowham Farm	SILVER
Dorking - Kerne Hus	SILVER
Dover	
- Owler Lodge	SILVER
- The Park Inn	SILVER
Downholme - Walburn Hall	SILVER
Downton - Witherington Farm	GOLD
Droitwich	
- Temple Broughton Farm	GOLD
- Middleton Grange	SILVER
- The Old Farmhouse	SILVER
Duddleswell - Duddleswell Manor	SILVER
Dulverton	
- Exton House Hotel	SILVER
- Highercombe Farm	SILVER
- Town Mills	SILVER
Dunster	
- Conygar House	SILVER
- Dollons House	SILVER
- Exmoor House Hotel	SILVER
- The Old Bakery	SILVER
- Spears Cross Hotel	SILVER
Durham	
- Cathedral View Town House	SILVER
- Farnley Tower	SILVER
- Triermayne	SILVER
- Waterside	SILVER
Earl Soham - Bridge House	SILVER
Earnley - Millstone	GOLD
Easingwold - The Old Vicarage	GOLD

East Barkwith	
- Bodkin Lodge	GOLD
- The Grange	SILVER
East Coker - Granary House	SILVER
East Lavant	
- The Flint House	SILVER
- The Royal Oak Inn	SILVER
Eastbourne	
- Pinnacle Point	GOLD
- Brayscroft Hotel	SILVER
- Southcroft Hotel	SILVER
- Trevinhurst Lodge	SILVER
Eastcote - West Farm	SILVER
Eastgate-in-Weardale	
- Rose Hill Farm Bed and Breakfast	SILVER
Easton - Atlantis Stud Farm	SILVER
Ebberston - Littlegarth	SILVER
Edale - Stonecroft	GOLD
Edenbridge	
- Mowshurst Farm House	SILVER
- Starborough Manor	SILVER
Elham - Abbot's Fireside Hotel	SILVER
Elmswell - Mulberry Farm	SILVER
Elton - Hawthorn Cottage	SILVER
Ely	
- Hill House Farm	GOLD
- 96 Lynn Road	SILVER
- The Grove	SILVER
- Rosendale Lodge	SILVER
- Springfields	SILVER
Evesham - Bredon View Guest House	SILVER
Exeter - Silversprings	SILVER
Eydon - Crockwell Farm	SILVER
Eye - The Bull Auberge	SILVER
Fairfield - Barms Farm	SILVER
Fairford - East End House	GOLD
Fakenham - Holly Lodge	GOLD
Falmouth	
- Chelsea House Hotel	SILVER
- Dolvean Hotel	SILVER
Farnborough	
- The White Residence Town House Hotel	GOLD
Farnham - Anne's Cottage	GOLD
Farthinghoe - Greenfield	SILVER
Faversham - Preston Lea	SILVER
Faygate - The Willows	SILVER
Feckenham - Orchard House	SILVER
Felsted - Potash Farm	SILVER
Fenny Drayton - White Wings	SILVER
Fillongley - Manor House Farm	SILVER
Fir Tree - Duke of York Inn	SILVER
Fishbourne - The Byre	SILVER
Fittleworth - Swan Inn	SILVER
Fleet - Highfield	SILVER
Fletching - The Griffin Inn	SILVER
Folkestone - Harbourside Hotel	GOLD
Ford	
- The Estate House	SILVER
- Hay Farm Farmhouse	SILVER
Fordingbridge	
- The Three Lions	GOLD
- Merrimead	SILVER
Framfield	
- The Old Farmhouse	GOLD
- Beggars Barn	SILVER
Freshwater - Field House Bed & Breakfast	GOLD
Frome - Kozy-Glen	SILVER
Gatcombe	
- Freewaters	SILVER
- Little Gatcombe Farm	SILVER
Goathland	
- The Beacon Guest House	SILVER
- Prudom Guest House	SILVER
Godney - Double-Gate Farm	GOLD
Graffham - Brook Barn	SILVER
Grange-over-Sands	
- Greenacres Country Guesthouse	SILVER
Grasmere	
- Riversdale	SILVER
- Woodland Crag Country House	SILVER
Grassington - Grassington Lodge	SILVER
Grateley - Gunville House	SILVER
Grayrigg - Punchbowl House	SILVER
Greasby - At Peel Hey	SILVER
Great Dunmow - Harwood Guest House	SILVER
Great Ellingham - Manor Farm	SILVER
Great Sampford - Stow Farmhouse	SILVER
Great Tosson - Tosson Tower Farm	GOLD
Great Witley - Home Farm	SILVER
Great Yarmouth - Barnard House	SILVER
Gressenhall - Wood Hill	SILVER
Greta Bridge - The Coach House	SILVER
Grimston - Gorse House	SILVER
Guilsborough - Lodge Farm	SILVER
Guiting Power - The Guiting Guest House	SILVER
Gulworthy - Colcharton Farm	SILVER
Haddenham - The Majors	SILVER
Hagworthingham - White Oak Grange	SILVER
Halifax - Rose Cottage	SILVER
Halland	
- Shortgate Manor Farm	SILVER
- Tamberry Hall	SILVER
Haltwhistle	
- Broomshaw Hill Farm	GOLD
- Ashcroft	SILVER
Halwell - Orchard House	SILVER
Hamble - Farthings Bed & Breakfast	SILVER
Hamworthy - Individual Touristik Poole	GOLD
Hanley Swan	
- Cygnet Lodge	GOLD
- Meadowbank	SILVER
- Yew Tree House Bed and Breakfast	SILVER
Harrogate	
- Knabbs Ash	GOLD
- Royd Mount	GOLD
- Britannia Lodge	SILVER
- Brookfield House	SILVER
- Central House Farm	SILVER
- Delaine Hotel	SILVER
- Franklin View	SILVER
- Ruskin Hotel	SILVER
- Staveleigh	SILVER
Hartest - The Hatch	GOLD
Hartford Bridge - Woodside	SILVER
Hartland - Golden Park	GOLD
Harwich - Woodview Cottage	SILVER
Hastings	
- Bryn-Y-Mor	GOLD
- Tower House	GOLD
- Holyers	SILVER
- Lionsdown House	SILVER
Hatcliffe - The Old Farmhouse	SILVER
Hathersage	
- Cannon Croft	GOLD
- The Plough Inn	SILVER
Hawes - Rookhurst Country House Hotel	GOLD

Hawkhurst
- The Wren's Nest GOLD
- Conghurst Farm SILVER

Hawkshead
- Borwick Lodge SILVER
- The Drunken Duck Inn SILVER
- Grizedale Lodge Hotel SILVER

Haworth - Ashmount SILVER

Haywards Heath
- Copyhold Hollow Bed & Breakfast SILVER

Heathfield
- The Cottage SILVER
- Iwood B & B SILVER

Helmsley - Oldstead Grange GOLD

Henley-on-Thames
- The Knoll SILVER
- Thamesmead House Hotel SILVER

Hereford
- Brandon Lodge SILVER
- Grafton Villa Farm House SILVER
- Old Rectory SILVER

Hermitage - Almshouse Farm GOLD

Herstmonceux - Conquerors SILVER

Hethel - Old Thorn Barn SILVER

Hexham
- West Close House GOLD
- Black Hall SILVER
- Dene House SILVER
- Kitty Frisk House SILVER
- Peth Head Cottage SILVER

Hindringham - Field House GOLD

Hintlesham - College Farm SILVER

Hoarwithy - Old Mill SILVER

Holbeach - Cackle Hill House SILVER

Holbeck - Browns GOLD

Holbeton - Bugle Rocks SILVER

Holbrook - Highfield GOLD

Holsworthy
- Leworthy Farmhouse Bed & Breakfast SILVER

Holt - Felbrigg Lodge GOLD

Honiton - Wessington Farm SILVER

Hope - Underleigh House SILVER

Horley - The Lawn Guest House SILVER

Horsley - Horsley Lodge SILVER

Hullavington - Bradfield Manor SILVER

Hungerford - Wilton House SILVER

Hutton-le-Hole
- Moorlands of Hutton-le-Hole SILVER

Huxley - Higher Huxley Hall SILVER

Iddesleigh - Parsonage Farm SILVER

Ilam - Beechenhill Farm SILVER

Ilfracombe - Strathmore Hotel SILVER

Ilminster - Dillington House SILVER

Ingoldisthorpe - Pencob House SILVER

Ipswich
- The Gatehouse Hotel Ltd SILVER
- Lattice Lodge Guest House SILVER
- Sidegate Guesthouse SILVER

Ironbridge
- The Library House GOLD
- Bridge House SILVER
- Coalbrookdale Villa SILVER
- Severn Lodge SILVER

Isles of Scilly - Seaview Moorings SILVER

Itchen Abbas - Hatch End SILVER

Ivybridge - Hillhead Farm SILVER

Jacobstow - The Old Rectory SILVER

Kedington - The White House GOLD

Kenilworth - Castle Laurels Hotel SILVER

Keswick
- Abacourt House SILVER
- Acorn House Hotel SILVER
- Braemar SILVER
- The Grange Country House SILVER
- Parkfield Guesthouse SILVER
- Ravensworth Hotel SILVER
- West View Guest House SILVER
- Whitehouse Guest House SILVER

Kettering - 2 Wilkie Close SILVER

Kettlesing - Green Acres GOLD

Kidderminster - Garden Cottages GOLD

Kimmeridge - Kimmeridge Farmhouse GOLD

Kingsbridge
- Combe Farm B & B SILVER
- South Allington House SILVER

Kingstone - Mill Orchard GOLD

Kirkby Lonsdale - Capernwray House SILVER

Kirkbymoorside
- Brickfields Farm SILVER
- The Cornmill SILVER

Kirkwhelpington - Cornhills Farmhouse SILVER

Lakeside - The Knoll Country House SILVER

Landscove - Thornecroft SILVER

Langport - Muchelney Ham Farm GOLD

Lansallos - Lesquite SILVER

Launceston
- Wheatley Farm GOLD
- Trevadlock Farm SILVER

Lavenham
- Hill House Farm GOLD
- Lavenham Priory GOLD
- Anchor House SILVER
- Lavenham Great House Hotel SILVER
- Mortimer's Barn SILVER

Laxton - Spanhoe Lodge GOLD

Laycock - Far Laithe Farm SILVER

Leamington Spa
- 8 Clarendon Crescent SILVER
- The Coach House SILVER
- Garden Cottage SILVER
- Wymondley Lodge SILVER

Lechlade on Thames - Cambrai Lodge SILVER

Leeming Bar - Little Holtby SILVER

Leigh - Charcott Farmhouse B & B SILVER

Leintwardine - Lower House SILVER

Leiston - Field End SILVER

Lenham - East Lenham Farm SILVER

Leominster
- Ford Abbey GOLD
- The Paddock GOLD

Levisham
- The Moorlands Country House Hotel GOLD

Lewes
- Eckington House SILVER
- Sussex Countryside Accommodation SILVER
- Whitesmith Barn SILVER

Leyburn - Park Gate House SILVER

Lichfield - The Farmhouse GOLD

Lincoln - Manor House SILVER

Linton - The Manor SILVER

Liskeard
- Tregondale Farm SILVER
- Trewint Farm SILVER

Little Canfield - Canfield Moat GOLD

Little Langford - Little Langford Farmhouse GOLD

Little Sampford - Woodlands SILVER

Little Walsingham - The Old Bakehouse SILVER

Littleborough - Hollingworth Lake B&B GOLD

London
- 81 Greenwich South Street SILVER
- Aster House SILVER
- Aucklands SILVER
- Windermere Hotel SILVER

Longframlington - Lee Farm GOLD
Longhorsley - Thistleyhaugh Farm SILVER
Longton - Willow Cottage SILVER
Looe
- Allhays Country Bed & Breakfast SILVER
- Barclay House SILVER
- Bucklawren Farm SILVER
- Little Larnick Farm SILVER
- Talehay SILVER

Loughborough
- Lane End Cottage SILVER
- Lubcloud Farm Bed & Breakfast SILVER

Lower Sticker - Luney Barton House SILVER
Luddendenfoot
- Bankfield Bed and Breakfast SILVER

Ludlow
- Bromley Court B&B GOLD
- Lower House Farm GOLD
- Ravenscourt Manor GOLD
- The Brakes SILVER
- The Crown Inn SILVER

Lyme Regis
- Old Lyme Guest House GOLD
- Clappentail House SILVER

Lymington
- Britannia House GOLD
- Efford Cottage GOLD
- Tranmere House GOLD
- The Hillsman House SILVER
- Pennavon House SILVER

Lyndhurst
- Burwood Lodge SILVER
- Forest Cottage SILVER
- Lyndhurst House SILVER
- Rufus House Hotel SILVER

Lynton
- Kingford House SILVER
- Longmead House Hotel SILVER
- Pine Lodge SILVER

Maidenhead - Moor Farm SILVER
Maidstone
- The Ringlestone Inn & Farmhouse Hotel GOLD

Malton
- Barugh House SILVER
- The Old Rectory SILVER

Malvern
- Guarlford Grange SILVER
- Hidelow House SILVER
- The Red Gate SILVER
- Sunnydale SILVER
- Wyche Keep Country House SILVER

Marden - Martin's Farmhouse SILVER
Margaret Roding - Garnish Hall SILVER
Marlow - 18 Rookery Court SILVER
Marnhull - Yew House Farm SILVER
Marsden
- Olive Branch Restaurant with Rooms and Bar SILVER

Marston Moretaine - The White Cottage SILVER
Marton - Orchard House SILVER
Matlock
- The Bank House SILVER
- Robertswood Country House GOLD
- Sheriff Lodge SILVER
- Warren Carr Barn SILVER

Matlock Bath - Sunnybank Guesthouse SILVER
Mavesyn Ridware - The Old Rectory GOLD
Medbourne - Homestead House SILVER
Membury - Oxenways House GOLD
Meole Brace - Meole Brace Hall SILVER
Mickleton - Myrtle House SILVER
Middle Wallop
- The George Inn - Middle Wallop SILVER

Middleham - Jasmine House GOLD
Middleton - Middleton House Farm SILVER
Midsomer Norton - The Old Priory SILVER
Milford-on-Sea
- Briantcroft GOLD
- Ha'penny House SILVER

Millbrook - Stone Farm Bed and Breakfast SILVER
Milton - The Stables SILVER
Minster - Home Farm SILVER
Mitcheldean - Gunn Mill House SILVER
Mobberley - The Hinton SILVER
Monyash - High Rakes Farm SILVER
Moreton Pinkney - The Old Vicarage SILVER
Moretonhampstead
- Great Sloncombe Farm SILVER
- Great Wooston Farm Bed & Breakfast SILVER

Moreton-in-Marsh - The Old Chequer SILVER
Morpeth - Elder Cottage SILVER
Mortehoe - The Cleeve House SILVER
Moulsford on Thames - White House SILVER
Much Wenlock - Broadstone Mill GOLD
Mudeford - Seahaze SILVER
Mullion
- Cobblers Cottage SILVER
- Meaver Farm SILVER
- Tregaddra Farm SILVER

Navenby - Barn Bed and Breakfast SILVER
Nayland - The White Hart Inn GOLD
Nether Stowey
- Castle of Comfort Country House SILVER

Netherbury - Jasmine Cottage SILVER
Newbridge - Wheal Buller SILVER
Newbrough
- Allerwash Farmhouse GOLD
- Newbrough Park SILVER

Newbury
- Manor Farm House SILVER
- The Old Farmhouse SILVER

Newcastle upon Tyne - Elm Cottage SILVER
Newent - Three Ashes House GOLD
Newmarket - 2 Birdcage Walk GOLD
Newport, Shropshire
- Church Aston Farmhouse SILVER
- Lane End Farm SILVER

Newport, Essex
- The Toll House SILVER

Newport Pagnell - The Limes SILVER
Newquay
- Degembris Farmhouse SILVER
- The Harbour Hotel SILVER

Newton Abbot - Fairways SILVER
North Cadbury - Ashlea House SILVER
North Leigh - Elbie House SILVER
North Lopham - Church Farm House GOLD
North Moreton - Stapleton's Chantry SILVER
North Mundham - The Cottage SILVER
North Petherwin - Stenhill Farm SILVER
North Tawton - Lower Nichols Nymet Farm SILVER
North Wootton - Stoneleigh Barn SILVER
Northallerton - Elmscott SILVER
Northleach
- The Eastington Suite GOLD
- Cotteswold House SILVER

- Northfield Bed and Breakfast	SILVER
- Prospect Cottage	SILVER
Norwich	
- Beaufort Lodge	SILVER
- Eaton Bower	SILVER
- The Old Rectory	SILVER
Nottingham	
- Greenwood Lodge City Guesthouse	GOLD
Nuneaton - Leathermill Grange	GOLD
Oakamoor - Bank House	GOLD
Oborne - The Grange Restaurant and Hotel	SILVER
Okehampton - The Knole Farm	SILVER
Old - Wold Farm	SILVER
Old Alresford - The Rosery	SILVER
Old Catton - Catton Old Hall	SILVER
Old Town - Carn Ithen	SILVER
Ombersley - Greenlands	SILVER
Orleton	
- Line Farm	GOLD
- Rosecroft	SILVER
Otley - Scaife Hall Farm	SILVER
Outwood - The Coach House	SILVER
Oxford	
- Chestnuts Guest House	SILVER
- Cotswold House	SILVER
- Gables	SILVER
- Home Farm House	SILVER
- Royal Oxford Hotel	SILVER
Padstow	
- St Ervan Manor & Country Cottages	GOLD
- Althea House	SILVER
- Althea Library Bed and Breakfast	SILVER
- The White Hart	SILVER
Paignton	
- Beresford Hotel	SILVER
- Birchwood House Hotel	SILVER
- Cherwood Hotel	SILVER
- Cleve Court Hotel	SILVER
- Roundham Lodge	SILVER
- Wulfruna Hotel	SILVER
Painswick - Wheatleys	GOLD
Parkstone - Viewpoint Guest House	SILVER
Parwich - Flaxdale House	SILVER
Pateley Bridge	
- Knottside Farm	GOLD
- North Pasture Farm	SILVER
Payhembury - Yellingham Farm	SILVER
Pedwell - Sunnyside	SILVER
Pembridge - Lowe Farm Bed and Breakfast	GOLD
Penrith - The Old School	SILVER
Penzance	
- The Summer House	GOLD
- Lombard House	SILVER
Pershore	
- Aldbury House	SILVER
- Arbour House	SILVER
Petworth - The Old Railway Station	SILVER
Pevensey Bay - The Sandcastle	SILVER
Pickering	
- Burr Bank	GOLD
- Bramwood Guest House	SILVER
- Cawthorne House	SILVER
- Costa House	SILVER
- Eden House	SILVER
- Laurel Bank B&B	SILVER
- Rose Folly	SILVER
- Wildsmith House	SILVER
Piddlehinton	
- Muston Manor	SILVER
- Whites Dairy House	SILVER
Pillerton Hersey - The Old Vicarage	SILVER

Pilley - Mistletoe Cottage	SILVER
Plymouth - Bowling Green Hotel	SILVER
Pockley - West View Cottage	SILVER
Ponteland - Hazel Cottage	SILVER
Pontesbury - Jasmine Cottage	SILVER
Poole	
- Corkers	SILVER
- Harlequins B & B	SILVER
- Lytchett Mere	SILVER
Porlock - Leys B & B	SILVER
Portinscale - Derwent Cottage	GOLD
Portsmouth & Southsea	
- 131 The High Street	SILVER
- The Rowans Guest House	SILVER
Pulborough - Moseleys Barn	SILVER
Pulham Market - The Old Bakery	GOLD
Ramsgate - Sunnymede	SILVER
Rastrick - Elder Lea House	SILVER
Rattery - Knowle Farm	SILVER
Ravenscar - Cliff House	SILVER
Ravenstonedale	
- The Stables Bed & Breakfast	SILVER
Redditch - Black Horse Cottage	SILVER
Retford - Bolham Manor	SILVER
Richmond, London	
- Chalon House	GOLD
- Doughty Cottage	GOLD
Richmond, Yorkshire	
- Nuns Cottage	SILVER
- Whashton Springs Farm	SILVER
Ridlington - Mill Common House	SILVER
Ringwood - Torre Avon	SILVER
Ripon	
- Middle Ridge	GOLD
- Ravencroft B&B	GOLD
- Mallard Grange	SILVER
- St George's Court	SILVER
- Sharow Cross House	SILVER
Risplith - Yeomans Well	SILVER
Roade	
- Roade House Restaurant and Hotel	SILVER
Romsey - 3 Cherville Mews	SILVER
Rosedale Abbey - Sevenford House	SILVER
Ross-on-Wye	
- Forest Edge	GOLD
- Norton House	GOLD
- Haslemere	SILVER
- Lumleys	SILVER
- Walnut Tree Cottage Hotel	SILVER
Rothbury	
- Katerina's Guest House	GOLD
- Farm Cottage Guest House	SILVER
- Silverton Lodge	SILVER
Royal Tunbridge Wells	
- Ephraim Lodge	GOLD
- Danehurst	SILVER
- Studley Cottage	SILVER
Rugby	
- Lawford Hill Farm	SILVER
- Marston House	SILVER
- Village Green Hotel	SILVER
Rugeley - Lea Hall Farm	SILVER
Rumburgh - Valley Farm Vineyards	SILVER
Runswick Bay - Ellerby Hotel	SILVER
Rustington - Kenmore	SILVER
Ryde - Kemphill Farm	SILVER
Rye	
- Manor Farm Oast	GOLD
- The Benson	SILVER
- Culpeppers	SILVER
- Durrant House Hotel	SILVER

- Four Seasons SILVER
- Jeake's House SILVER
- Layces Bed & Breakfast SILVER
- Little Orchard House SILVER
- The Rise SILVER
- The Strand House SILVER
- White Vine House SILVER

Saffron Walden
- The Bonnet SILVER
- Rowley Hill Lodge SILVER
- Yardley's SILVER

St Albans
- Fleuchary House SILVER
- Riverside SILVER

St Bees - Fleatham House SILVER
St Buryan - Boskenna Home Farm SILVER
St Cross - Dolphin House Studios SILVER
St Ewe - Higher Kestle Farm SILVER
St Juliot - The Old Rectory GOLD
St Mary's, Isles of Scilly
- Annet SILVER
- April Cottage SILVER
- Crebinick House SILVER
- Garrison House SILVER
- Higher Trenoweth SILVER
- Rose Cottage SILVER
- The Withies SILVER

St Mary's, Devon
- The Town House SILVER

St Neot - Lampen Mill SILVER
St Owens Cross - Amberley SILVER
St Tudy - Polrode Mill Cottage SILVER
Salcombe
- Burton Farmhouse & Garden Restaurant SILVER

Salisbury
- Bridge Farm GOLD
- Malvern GOLD
- Websters GOLD
- Glenshee SILVER
- Newton Farm House SILVER
- The Rokeby Guest House SILVER

Sand - Townsend Farm SILVER
Sandy - Highfield Farm SILVER
Sawrey
- West Vale Country House & Restaurant GOLD

Saxlingham - The Map House SILVER
Saxmundham - The Georgian House SILVER
Scagglethorpe - Scagglethorpe Manor GOLD
Scalby - Holly Croft SILVER
Scaldwell - The Old House SILVER
Scarborough
- The Alexander Hotel SILVER
- The Whiteley Hotel SILVER

Sculthorpe - Manor Farm Bed & Breakfast SILVER
Seaford - Tudor Manor Hotel SILVER
Seahouses - Railston House SILVER
Seaton
- Beach End at Seaton SILVER
- Hill House SILVER

Settle
- Husbands Barn SILVER
- Mainsfield SILVER

Shaftesbury
- Aysgarth SILVER
- Cliff House SILVER
- The Knoll SILVER

Shanklin
- Foxhills GOLD
- Hope Lodge Hotel GOLD
- The Havelock Hotel SILVER
- St Leonards Hotel SILVER

Shawford - Greenmead Cottage SILVER
Sheffield - Loadbrook Cottages SILVER
Shepshed - The Grange Courtyard SILVER
Shepton Mallet
- Burnt House Farm GOLD
- Knapps Farm SILVER

Sherborne
- Huntsbridge Farm GOLD
- The Alders SILVER

Sheringham - Priestfields SILVER
Shincliffe - The Bracken Hotel SILVER
Shipton Gorge - Cairnhill GOLD
Shipton-under-Wychwood - Court Farm SILVER
Shoby - Shoby Lodge Farm SILVER
Sholden - The Sportsman GOLD
Shoreham - Church House SILVER
Shorwell - Northcourt SILVER
Shotley - Hill House Farm SILVER
Shotley Bridge - The Manor House Inn SILVER
Shrewsbury
- The Burlton Inn SILVER
- Lyth Hill House SILVER
- The Old Station SILVER
- The Old Vicarage SILVER

Shroton - The Cricketers SILVER
Sibton
- Church Farm SILVER
- Park Farm SILVER

Sidmouth
- The Salty Monk GOLD
- Coombe Bank Guest House SILVER
- Kyneton Lodge SILVER
- Pinn Barton Farm SILVER

Slaley - Travellers Rest SILVER
Slapton - Little Pittaford SILVER
Sledmere - Life Hill Farm SILVER
Sleights - The Lawns GOLD
Snettisham - The Hollies SILVER
Solihull - Acorn Guest House SILVER
Somerton - Mill House SILVER
South Gorley - Hucklesbrook Farm SILVER
South Molton
- Kerscott Farm GOLD
- Huxtable Farm SILVER

South Newton - Salisbury Old Mill House SILVER
South Normanton - The Boundary Lodge SILVER
Southam - Wormleighton Hall SILVER
Southampton - The Mayfair Guest House SILVER
Sporle - Corfield House SILVER
Stafford - Cedarwood SILVER
Staithes - Grinkle Lodge GOLD
Stalham - Bramble House SILVER
Stamford
- Midstone Farmhouse SILVER
- Rock Lodge SILVER

Standlake - Pinkhill Cottage SILVER
Stanhope - Horsley Hall SILVER
Stansted Mountfitchet - Chimneys SILVER
Stanton in Peak - Congreave Farm GOLD
Stanton-by-Bridge - Ivy House Farm SILVER
Stanwix
- Aldingham House Townhouse B&B SILVER

Starbotton - Bushey Lodge Farm SILVER
Staverton - Kingston House SILVER
Stearsby - The Granary SILVER

Stelling Minnis
- Bower Farm House SILVER
- Great Field Farm SILVER

Stogumber - Northam Mill SILVER
Stoke-by-Nayland
- Ryegate House GOLD
- The Angel Inn SILVER

Stoke-on-Trent
- Cedar Tree Cottage SILVER
- The Old Dairy House SILVER

Stonehouse - The Grey Cottage GOLD
Stonyhurst - Alden Cottage GOLD
Stottesdon - Hardwicke Farm SILVER
Stow-on-the-Wold
- Aston House SILVER
- Fairview Farmhouse SILVER
- Honeysuckle Cottage SILVER
- South Hill Lodge SILVER

Stragglethorpe - Stragglethorpe Hall SILVER
Stratford-upon-Avon
- Folly Farm Cottage GOLD
- Shakespeare's View GOLD
- Brook Lodge Guest House SILVER
- Ettington Chase Conference Centre SILVER
- Howard Arms SILVER
- Peartree Cottage SILVER
- Victoria Spa Lodge SILVER
- The White House SILVER
- Woodstock Guest House SILVER

Streatley - Pennyfield SILVER
Stretton - Dovecliff Hall SILVER
Stroud
- Burleigh Farm SILVER
- Pretoria Villa SILVER

Sulhamstead - The Old Manor SILVER
Swainby - Churchview House GOLD
Swanage - Easter Cottage SILVER
Swanton Morley - Frogs Hall Farm SILVER
Swarland - Swarland Old Hall GOLD
Sway - The Nurse's Cottage GOLD
Symonds Yat East - Garth Cottage SILVER
Talskiddy - Pennatillie Farm SILVER
Tamworth
- Oak Tree Farm GOLD
- The Chestnuts Country Guest House SILVER

Taunton
- North Down Farm Bed & Breakfast SILVER
- Yallands Farmhouse SILVER

Tavistock
- Beera Farmhouse GOLD
- Tor Cottage GOLD
- April Cottage SILVER
- Rubbytown Farm SILVER

Teignmouth
- Thomas Luny House GOLD
- Britannia House B&B SILVER

Telford
- Old Rectory SILVER
- West Ridge Bed and Breakfast SILVER

Terrington St John - Somerville House SILVER
Tetbury - The Old Rectory GOLD
Tewkesbury - Alstone Fields Farm GOLD
Thame
- The Dairy GOLD
- Langsmeade House SILVER
- Oakfield SILVER

Thaxted - Crossways Guesthouse SILVER
Thirsk - Laburnum House SILVER
Thornthwaite - Jenkin Hill Cottage SILVER
Thornton Dale
- The Old Granary Bed and Breakfast SILVER

Thorpe Bay - Beaches SILVER
Thurlby - 6 The Pingles SILVER
Tiverton
- Brambles Bed and Breakfast/Guesthouse SILVER
- Great Bradley Farm SILVER
- Lower Collipriest Farm SILVER

Tonbridge - Lodge Oast SILVER
Torquay
- Blue Haze Hotel SILVER
- Cranborne Hotel SILVER
- Fairmount House Hotel SILVER
- Fleurie House SILVER
- Glenross Hotel SILVER
- Kingston House SILVER
- Lindens Hotel SILVER
- Suite Dreams Hotel SILVER

Torrington - Locksbeam Farm SILVER
Totland Bay - Country Garden Hotel SILVER
Totnes
- The Elbow Room SILVER
- Great Court Farm SILVER
- Old Follaton SILVER
- The Old Forge at Totnes SILVER

Tow Law - Bracken Hill Weardale SILVER
Towcester
- Potcote SILVER
- Slapton Manor SILVER

Toys Hill - Corner Cottage SILVER
Tregrehan Mills
- Wisteria Lodge Guest House SILVER

Truro - Bissick Old Mill SILVER
Tuxford - The Corner House SILVER
Tynemouth - Martineau Guest House SILVER
Uckfield
- Hooke Hall GOLD
- Old Mill Farm SILVER
- South Paddock SILVER

Ullingswick - The Steppes SILVER
Ullswater
- Bank House Farm SILVER
- Elm House SILVER

Underbarrow - Tullythwaite House SILVER
Upchurch - Suffield House SILVER
Uplyme - Hill Barn SILVER
Upottery - Robins Cottage SILVER
Upper Coberley - Upper Coberley Farm SILVER
Upper Hulme - Roaches Hall SILVER
Upper Quinton - Winton House SILVER
Upton - Upton Lodge SILVER
Upton Noble - Kingston House SILVER
Upton-upon-Severn
- Tiltridge Farm and Vineyard SILVER

Upwell - The Olde Mill Hotel SILVER
Vowchurch
- The Old Vicarage SILVER
- Upper Gilvach Farm SILVER

Wadebridge - Brookfields B & B SILVER
Wadshelf - Temperance House Farm SILVER
Wallingford
- Fords Farm SILVER
- North Farm SILVER
- North Moreton House SILVER

Wareham - The Old Granary SILVER
Wargrave - Appletree Cottage SILVER
Warminster - Bugley Barton SILVER
Warwick
- Avonside Cottage GOLD
- Charter House GOLD
- The Coach House GOLD
- Cliffe Hill House Bed and Breakfast SILVER

- Forth House SILVER
- Northleigh House SILVER
- Park Cottage SILVER
- Shrewley Pools Farm SILVER
Waterhouses - Lee House Farm SILVER
Waterrow - Handley Farm Accommodation GOLD
Watton - Park Farm Bed & Breakfast SILVER
Welford-on-Avon - Mullions SILVER
Welland - The Lovells SILVER
Wellingborough - The Manor House GOLD
Wellingham - Manor House Farm SILVER
Wells
- Glencot House GOLD
- Carmen B & B SILVER
Wem - Lowe Hall Farm SILVER
Wendover - Field Cottage SILVER
West Barkwith - The Manor House SILVER
West Knighton - Church Cottage SILVER
West Pennard - Page Cottage SILVER
West Wittering - Thornton Cottage SILVER
West Woodburn - Plevna House SILVER
Westbury-on-Severn - Boxbush Barn GOLD
Westerham - Worples Field SILVER
Westgate-in-Weardale - Lands Farm SILVER
Westhay - New House Farm SILVER
Weston under Wetherley
- Wethele Manor Farm SILVER
Weston-super-Mare - Orchard House SILVER
Westonzoyland
- Staddlestones Guest House SILVER
Wetherby - Linton Close SILVER
Weymouth
- The Seaham GOLD
- Heathwick House SILVER
Whaley Bridge - Cote Bank Farm SILVER
Whaplode - Westgate House & Barn SILVER
Wheddon Cross
- Cutthorne GOLD
- Little Brendon Hill Farm GOLD
- Exmoor House SILVER
- Little Quarme Farm SILVER
- The Rest And Be Thankful Inn SILVER
- Sundial Guesthouse SILVER
Whickham - East Byermoor Guest House SILVER
Whitby
- Lavender House SILVER
- Netherby House SILVER
- The Olde Ford SILVER
Whitchurch - Wood Farm SILVER
White Notley - Old Mill Barn SILVER
Whitehaven - Moresby Hall SILVER
Whitstable - Victoria Villa GOLD
Whitwell - The Old Rectory GOLD
Wickhamford - Avonwood GOLD
Wigmore - Pear Tree Farm SILVER
Wimbish - Newdegate House SILVER
Wimborne Minster
- Lantern Lodge GOLD
- Ashton Lodge SILVER
- Hopewell SILVER
- Woodlands SILVER
Winchcombe
- Postlip Hall Farm GOLD
- Mercia SILVER
Winchester
- 85 Christchurch Road SILVER
- Acacia SILVER
- Brymer House SILVER
- Dawn Cottage SILVER
- Giffard House Hotel SILVER
- Rowanhurst SILVER
- The Wykeham Arms SILVER

Windermere
- Beechwood Private Hotel SILVER
- Boston House SILVER
- Braemount House SILVER
- Cedar Manor Country Lodge SILVER
- Fair Rigg SILVER
- High View SILVER
- Lowfell SILVER
- Squirrel Bank SILVER
Winster - The Dower House GOLD
Winterborne Stickland
- Stickland Farmhouse SILVER
Wirksworth
- Old Lock Up GOLD
- Avondale Farm SILVER
Wiswell - Pepper Hill SILVER
Witcombe - Crickley Court SILVER
Witham Friary - Higher West Barn Farm SILVER
Witney - Field View SILVER
Wix - Dairy House Farm SILVER
Wold Newton - The Wold Cottage SILVER
Wolstanton - Whispering Pines GOLD
Wolston - The Byre SILVER
Wombleton - Rockery Cottage SILVER
Wood Norton
- Manor Farm Bed and Breakfast SILVER
Woodbridge - The Old Rectory SILVER
Woodchurch - Shirkoak Farm SILVER
Woodstock
- Shipton Glebe GOLD
- Gorselands Hall SILVER
- The Laurels SILVER
- Plane Tree House SILVER
Wookey Hole - Broadleys SILVER
Wooler - The Old Manse GOLD
Woonton - Rose Cottage SILVER
Worcester
- Hill Farm House GOLD
- Oldbury Farm Bed and Breakfast SILVER
- The Boot Inn SILVER
- The White House SILVER
- Yew Tree House SILVER
Worstead - Holly Grove House SILVER
Worthing - Brooke House SILVER
Writtle - Moor Hall SILVER
Wroxham - The Dragon Flies SILVER
Wymondham - Witch Hazel SILVER
Yelverton
- Brook House SILVER
- The Old Orchard SILVER
Yeovil - Sunnymede SILVER
Yetminster - Bingers Farm SILVER
York
- Alexander House GOLD
- 23 St Marys SILVER
- Arndale Hotel SILVER
- Arnot House SILVER
- Ascot House SILVER
- Ashbourne House SILVER
- Barbican House SILVER
- Bishops Hotel SILVER
- City Guest House SILVER
- Claxton Hall Cottage SILVER
- Four Seasons Hotel SILVER
- Holmwood House Hotel SILVER
- Nunmill House SILVER
- One3Two SILVER
- The Acer Hotel SILVER
- The Hazelwood SILVER
Yorton Heath - Country Bed & Breakfast SILVER
Yoxford - Mile Hill Barn GOLD

TOWN INDEX

The following cities, towns and villages all have accommodation listed in the full colour regional pages of this guide. If the place where you wish to stay is no shown, the location maps (starting on page 18) will help you to find somewhere to stay in the area.

A PAGE

B PAGE

C PAGE

S PAGE

T PAGE

U PAGE

W PAGE

Y PAGE

Finding **accommodation** is as easy as 1 2 3

Where to Stay makes it quick and easy to find a place to stay. There are several ways to use this guide.

1 TOWN INDEX

The town index at the back, lists all the places with accommodation featured in the regional sections. The index gives a page number where you can find full accommodation and contact details.

2 COLOUR MAPS

All the place names in black on the colour maps at the front have an entry in the regional sections. Refer to the town index for the page number where you will find one or more establishments offering accommodation in your chosen town or village.

3 ACCOMMODATION LISTING

Contact details for **all** VisitBritain assessed accommodation throughout England, together with their national Diamond rating are given in the listing section of this guide. Establishments with a full entry in the regional sections are shown in blue. Look in the town index for the page number on which their full entry appears.